ENCYCLOPEDIA OF COMPUTER SCIENCE AND ENGINEERING
SECOND EDITION

ENCYCLOPEDIA OF COMPUTER SCIENCE AND ENGINEERING

SECOND EDITION

ANTHONY RALSTON, EDITOR

EDWIN D. REILLY, JR., ASSOCIATE EDITOR

VNR VAN NOSTRAND REINHOLD COMPANY
New York

Manufactured in the United States of America

Published by Van Nostrand Reinhold Company Inc.
135 West 50th Street
New York, New York 10020

Van Nostrand Reinhold Company Limited
Molly Millars Lane
Wokingham, Berkshire RG11 2PY, England

Van Nostrand Reinhold
480 Latrobe Street
Melbourne, Victoria 3000, Australia

Macmillan of Canada
Division of Gage Publishing Limited
164 Commander Boulevard
Agincourt, Ontario M1S 3C7, Canada

15 14 13 12 11 10 9 8 7 6 5

Library of Congress Cataloging in Publication Data
Main entry under title

Encyclopedia of computer science and engineering.

  Includes index.
  1. Computers—Dictionaries. 2. Electronic data
processing—Dictionaries. 3. Information science—
Dictionaries. I. Ralston, Anthony. II. Reilly, Edwin D.
QA76.15.E48 1982   001.64′03′21   82-2700
ISBN 0-442-24496-7   AACR2

Contents

Editorial Board

Contributors

(Numbers after each name indicate the pages at which contributions by each author begin.)

John N. Ackley 1568
Ashok K. Agrawala, University of Maryland 1119
David H. Ahl, Creative Computing 317
Suad Alagic, University of Sarajevo, Yugoslavia 50
Jonathan Allen, Massachusetts Institute of Technology 1393
Saul Amarel, Rutgers University 364
J. K. Amsbaugh, Ocean Mining Associates 422
Paul Armer, Teknowledge 213
Malcolm P. Atkinson, University of Edinburgh 474
Isaac L. Auerbach, Auerbach Publishers, Inc. 59, 61, 132, 134, 135, 136, 185, 492, 771, 790, 793, 795, 797, 1343, 1344, 1345
Algirdas Avižienis, University of California at Los Angeles 11, 102, 1277
Henriette D. Avram, The Library of Congress 847

Charles W. Bachman, Cullinane Database Systems, Inc. 502
G. David Baer, Computer Task Group, Inc. 704, 1259
Jean-Loup Baer, University of Washington 401, 877, 1003, 1098
Mario R. Barbacci, Carnegie-Mellon University 674
Michael Barnard, Macmillan Production Ltd., U.K. 1250
John N. Barrer, The MITRE Corporation 918
David W. Barron, University of Southampton, U.K. 124, 851, 874
C. Gordon Bell, Digital Equipment Corporation 554
James R. Bell, Digital Equipment Corporation 554
John M. Bennett, University of Sydney 359
Robert P. Bigelow, Bigelow and Saltzberg 840
Gary G. Bitter, Arizona State University 198
William E. Boggs, Author 227
Andrew D. Booth, Autonetics Research, Inc., Canada 832
Kathleen H. V. Booth, Autonetics Research, Inc., Canada 832, 969
Fred Braddock, Delphi Communications Corporation 2, 1286
Fred M. Brasch, Jr., Bell Laboratories 772
Susan C. Brewer, Honeywell, Inc. 497, 1422, 1563
Peter J. Brown, University of Kent, U.K. 904, 906, 1156
William F. Brown, Ball State University 1308

G. Edward Bryan, Honeywell Corporation 1526
Janusz A. Brzozowski, University of Waterloo, Canada 1311
Werner Buchholz, IBM Corporation 1436
R. A. Buckingham, University of London 142

John Case, State University of New York at Buffalo 146
Yair Censor, University of Haifa 1089
Robert P. Cerveny, State University of New York at Buffalo 167, 668, 1127
Ned Chapin, Consultant 176, 514, 633, 641, 1348, 1474
B. G. Claybrook, The MITRE Corporation 629
W. J. Cody, Jr., Argonne National Laboratory 93
Sam D. Conte, Purdue University 1036, 1372
James W. Cooley, IBM Corporation 623
F. J. Corbató, Massachusetts Institute of Technology 1520
Joseph F. Cunningham, Boca Raton, FL 217

Charles H. Davidson, University of Wisconsin 1049, 1385
Gordon B. Davis, University of Minnesota 910
Dorothy E. Denning, Purdue University 817, 1091, 1246, 1474, 1486, 1518, 1519, 1574
Peter J. Denning, Purdue University 817, 996, 1060, 1091, 1246, 1253, 1466, 1474, 1486, 1518, 1519, 1560, 1574
George D. Detlefsen, Teknekron Controls, Inc. 166
David A. Dinneen, University of Kansas 116, 690
John K. Dixon, Naval Research Laboratory 852, 1291
T. A. Dolotta, Interactive Systems Corporation 232, 1489
Philip H. Dorn, Dorn Computer Consultants, Inc. 375
A. S. Douglas, London School of Economics and Political Science 1546
Phillippe L. Dreyfus, CAP Gemini Sogeti, Paris 1608

Patricia J. Eberlein, State University of New York at Buffalo 663
Richard H. Eckhouse, Jr., Digital Equipment Corporation 261, 985
Kurt Enslein, Health Designs, Inc. 1278, 1407
Philip H. Enslow, Georgia Institute of Technology 246, 563

Francis D. Federighi, State University of New York at Albany 1224

Jerome A. Feldman, University of Rochester 136

Domenico Ferrari, University of California at Berkeley 1362

Nicholas V. Findler, State University of New York at Buffalo 110, 682

Aaron Finerman, University of Michigan 585

Clive B. Finkelstein, Information Engineering Ltd., Australia 143, 467, 706, 1085

Patrick C. Fischer, Vanderbilt University 1539, 1568

Barry Flachsbart, McDonnell Douglas Automation Company 267

Ivan Flores, Baruch College, City University of New York 218, 579, 1375

Michael J. Flynn, Stanford University 413, 434, 687, 877, 977, 1220, 1264

Phyllis A. Fox, Bell Laboratories 1221

Dennis J. Frailey, Texas Instruments 275

Mark A. Franklin, Washington University 85

David N. Freeman, Ketron, Inc. 6, 174, 437, 439, 837, 955, 1052, 1090, 1217, 1272, 1307, 1544

Gideon Frieder, University of Michigan 428, 657, 712, 766, 899, 917, 1051, 1167, 1320

Daniel D. Gajski, University of Illinois 1143, 1458

Bernard A. Galler, University of Michigan 13, 1409, 1433

Susan L. Gerhart, University of Southern California 1243

Bruce Gilchrist, Columbia University 1136

Stanley Gill (deceased) 1434, 1570

George Glaser, Consultant 23

Jonathan Goldstine, Pennsylvania State University 642

Alan Greengrass, New York Times Information Service, Inc. 1018

Thomas S. Grier, Burroughs Corporation 429

Ralph E. Griswold, University of Arizona 1436, 1437

Fred Gruenberger, California State University, Northridge 188, 632, 658, 820, 1142

Stanley Habib, City College of New York 602

Patrick E. Hagerty, Sperry Corporation 1547

Mark Halpern, MDS Qantel 169, 184, 576, 884, 887

John W. Hamblen, University of Missouri, Rolla 225, 1136

Richard W. Hamming, Naval Postgraduate School 613

David R. Hanson, University of Arizona 1437

Louis W. Harm, International Computer Programs, Inc. 1364

Fred H. Harris, The University of Chicago 769

Thomas J. Harrison, IBM Corporation 1385

Marion J. Hart, Canadian Information Processing Society 200

Barry R. Hathaway, Hathaway Information Services, Inc. 779

David G. Hays, Medigram, Inc. 215

Robert V. Head, Company for the Analysis and Planning of Information Technology 1265

Jacques Hebenstreit, Ecole Superieure d'Electricite, Paris 598

Laurence B. Heilprin, University of Maryland 431

Herbert Hellerman 370, 801

Gabor T. Herman, University of Pennsylvania 57, 258, 513, 917, 1527

Lejaren A. Hiller, State University of New York at Buffalo 356

Richard C. Holt, University of Toronto 1053

John E. Hopcroft, Cornell University 54

David A. Huemer, VISA U.S.A., Inc. 599

J. N. P. Hume, University of Toronto 493

Horst Hünke, Commission of the European Communities, Brussels 1608

E. Gerald Hurst, Jr., University of Pennsylvania 1138, 1146

Harry D. Huskey, University of California at Santa Cruz 368, 599, 607, 807, 1217, 1465, 1571

Velma R. Huskey, Santa Cruz, CA 885

R. V. Jacobson, International Security Technology, Inc. 1308

M. Edward Jernigan, University of Waterloo, Canada 1110

Charles V. Jones, University of Toronto 846, 1109

John L. Jones, Southern Railway System 217

T. L. Jones, Systems and Applied Sciences Corporation 852

Laveen N. Kanal, University of Maryland 1119

Arthur I. Karshmer 646

R. H. Kay, IBM Corporation 1360

Tom W. Keller, University of Texas at Austin 410

Kenneth M. Kempner, National Institutes of Health 778

Brian W. Kernighan, Bell Laboratories 193, 1550

Robin H. Kerr, Schlumberger-Doll Research 166

Michael J. Kessler, Control Data Corporation 1108

Mark B. Ketchen, IBM Corporation 812

James C. King, IBM Corporation 1360

John L. King, University of California at Irvine 380

Peter T. Kirstein, University College, London 8, 161, 397, 450

Kenneth E. Knight, University of Texas 167, 668, 1127

Robert R. Korfhage, Southern Methodist University 51, 179, 1154

David J. Kuck, University of Illinois 1143, 1455

Shan S. Kuo, University of New Hampshire 603, 631

J. Paul Landauer, Electronic Associates, Inc. 694

Patience D. Landry, National CSS, Inc. 1316

Steve P. Landry, University of Southwestern Louisiana 471

Duncan H. Lawrie, University of Illinois 1455

Charles H. Lawson, California Institute of Technology 838

Burt Leavenworth, IBM Corporation 1022

Ruth Leavitt, Artist 288

John A. N. Lee, Virginia Polytechnic Institute and State University 106, 212, 254, 255, 658, 659, 709, 821, 824, 873, 969, 1105, 1178, 1218, 1232, 1276, 1398, 1452, 1454, 1473

Brian Lewis, Xerox Corporation 421

Cheryl Lickteig, Sales-Aid 520
Karl Lieberherr, Princeton University 800
Bennet P. Lientz, University of California at Los
Angeles 263
C. L. Liu, University of Illinois 228
Andrew Lloyd, Datamation 350
Keith R. London, Keith London Ltd., U.K. 565, 627
Ralph L. London, University of California at Irvine
1247
Harold Lorin, IBM Corporation 1100
William F. Luebbert, Computer Literacy Institute 684,
1019
Daniel H. Lufkin, Consultant 440

W. G. Madison, Consultant 1398
Leonard R. Marino, San Diego State University 990
George Marsaglia, Washington State University 997,
1260, 1409
Johannes J. Martin, Virginia Polytechnic Institute and
State University 621
Fred J. Maryanski, Digital Equipment Corporation 440
Francis P. Mathur, California State Polytechnic
University 907, 1021, 1276, 1280
David W. Matula, Southern Methodist University 1158,
1322, 1323
Michael M. Maynard, Sperry Corporation 581, 872,
1546. 1552
Davis B. McCarn, The H. W. Wilson Company 941
John McCarthy, Stanford University 1273
E. J. McCluskey, Stanford University 879
Daniel D. McCracken, Consultant 160, 619, 996, 1180
James L. McDonald, Productivity International, Inc.
267
William M. McKeeman, Wang Institute of Graduate
Studies 20, 189
John M. McKinney, University of Cincinnati 1255
John C. McPherson, Short Hills, NJ 1016, 1567
C. L. Meek, Calgary (Canada) Board of Education 204,
253, 387, 806, 811, 903, 906, 1285, 1543, 1552, 1553
Jeffrey A. Meldman, Massachusetts Institute of
Technology 1165
Norman Meyrowitz, Brown University 1495
Leslie Jill Miller, Xerox Corporation 1295
Richard G. Mills, Citibank, N.A. 161
Benjamin Mittman, Northwestern University 1168
Georgia G. Mollenhoff 141
Calvin N. Mooers, Rockford Research, Inc. 968
Bruce M. Moore, Louisiana State University 401
Howard L. Morgan, University of Pennsylvania 1049
Graham J. Morris, International Computers Ltd. 196,
205, 524, 562
Jack Moshman, Moshman Associates, Inc. 1154
Richard R. Muntz, University of California at Los
Angeles 1121
Jean E. Musinski, Comshare, Inc. 54

Richard E. Nance, Virginia Polytechnic Institute and
State University 1074
Jiri Necas, Prague, Czechoslovakia 201, 480, 674, 735,
818, 1078, 1095, 1104, 1142, 1152, 1159, 1486

Roger M. Needham, University of Cambridge, U.K. 377
Monroe M. Newborn, McGill University 303
Allen Newell, Carnegie-Mellon University 1324, 1466
Jerre D. Noe, University of Washington 679
Arthur C. Norman, University of Cambridge, U.K. 41
Susan H. Nycum, Gaston Snow and Ely Bartlett 844

Thomas F. O'Connell, Siena College 779
Thomas F. O'Leary, Jr., North American Philips 671
T. William Olle, T. William Olle Associates Ltd. 441
Holger Opderbeck, GTE Subscriber Network Products
456
Enrique I. Oviedo, Bell Aerospace 1608

Victor Ya. Pan, State University of New York at
Albany 1608
Donn B. Parker, SRI International 426
Azaria Paz, Technion, Israel 1167
Trevor Pearcey, Caulfield Institute of Technology,
Australia 206
C. Pearson, Georgia Institute of Technology 725
George J. Peters, McDonnell Douglas Automation
Company 267
James L. Peterson, University of Texas at Austin 1139
Montgomery Phister, Jr., Consultant 333
Milton Pine, Royal Melbourne Institute of Technology
206
Seymour V. Pollack, Washington University 185, 215,
395, 398, 519, 521, 619, 1194, 1404, 1530, 1534
Vaughn R. Pratt, Massachusetts Institute of Technology
882
C. E. Price, Union Carbide Corporation 224, 681, 817,
1479

Anthony Ralston, State University of New York at
Buffalo 96, 97, 106, 123, 158, 167, 212, 214, 255,
256, 412, 490, 615, 618, 658, 821, 1029, 1105, 1157,
1178, 1217, 1218, 1292, 1322, 1325, 1452, 1454
C. V. Ramamoorthy, University of California at
Berkeley 1349, 1370
Brian Randell, University of Newcastle upon Tyne 532
Bertram Raphael, Hewlett-Packard Laboratories 656,
858
H. K. Reghbati, University of Saskatchewan 463
Edwin D. Reilly, Jr., State University of New York at
Albany 124, 508, 520, 620, 966, 1297, 1444, 1549
Edward M. Reingold, University of Illinois 228
David A. Rennels, University of California at Los
Angeles 624
John R. Rice, Purdue University 925
Frederic N. Ris, IBM Corporation 804
Dennis M. Ritchie, Bell Laboratories 1550
Ronald L. Rivest, Massachusetts Institute of
Technology 470
Saul Rosen, Purdue University 13, 16, 17, 22, 92, 164,
519, 540, 657, 701, 967, 1053, 1092, 1346, 1359,
1464, 1476, 1572
Azriel Rosenfeld, University of Maryland 709
Daniel J. Rosenkrantz, State University of New York at
Albany 1026

Robert F. Rosin, Bell Laboratories 1565
Paul Roth, Department of Commerce 1327
Beverly C. Rowe, World Fertility Survey 1341
Arthur I. Rubin, Autodynamics, Inc. 63
Walter G. Rudd, Louisiana State University 401

Harry J. Saal, Nestar Systems Inc. 1005
Arto K. Salomaa, University of Turku, Finland 1279
David Salomon, California State University, Northridge 1384
Gerard Salton, Cornell University 429, 719, 819
Roy M. Salzman, Arthur D. Little, Inc. 151
Jean E. Sammet, IBM Corporation 1022, 1228, 1353, 1601
Jacob T. Schwartz, New York University 1318
M. H. Schwartz, Designtech Corporation 23
Sally Y. Sedelow, University of Kansas 116, 690
Adel S. Sedra, University of Toronto 139, 195, 433, 791, 792, 942, 1156
John A. Shangler, On-Line Business Systems, Inc. 1532
Eugene Shapiro, IBM Corporation 1413
Stuart C. Shapiro, State University of New York at Buffalo 1011
Alan C. Shaw, University of Washington 396
Mary Shaw, Carnegie-Mellon University 1, 8, 1311
Vincent Y. Shen, Purdue University 1372
Ben Shneiderman, University of Maryland 447, 507, 521, 615, 628, 688, 1290
Bruce D. Shriver, University of Southwestern Louisiana 471
Herbert A. Simon, Carnegie-Mellon University 716, 1466
K. Siyan, University of California at Berkeley 1349
James R. Slagle, Naval Research Laboratory 852, 1291, 1516
Vladimir Slamecka, Georgia Institute of Technology 725
Alvy Ray Smith, Lucasfilm Ltd. 204
Cecil L. Smith, Louisiana State University 401
I. A. Smith, Innovative Systems Science Concepts 370
Kenneth C. Smith, University of Toronto 139, 174, 195, 433, 791, 792, 1156, 1471
John S. Sobolewski, University of Washington 107, 165, 240, 434, 448, 672, 789, 942, 993, 998, 1487
Sargur N. Srihari, State University of New York at Buffalo 1110
V. P. Srini, University of Alabama 471
Richard E. Stearns, State University of New York at Albany 1026
Thomas B. Steel, Jr., American Telephone and Telegraph Company 1319
Theodor D. Sterling, Simon Fraser University 395, 1194, 1404, 1534
Adrian V. Stokes, St. Thomas' Hospital, London 1557
Elizabeth L. Stoll 916
Paul A. Strassmann, Xerox Corporation 582
K. Suzuki, Intel Corporation 1370

Andrew S. Tanenbaum, Vrije Universiteit of Amsterdam 224

Robert W. Taylor, IBM Corporation 187, 729, 878, 1051, 1396
Daniel Teichroew, University of Michigan 726
Walter M. Tichy, Purdue University 996
Anthony L. Torrance, Optical Sciences Group, Inc. 23, 618
Joseph F. Traub, Columbia University 258
Henry S. Tropp, Humboldt State University, California 40, 178, 581, 685, 933, 1564, 1569

Jayaram K. Udupa, University of Pennsylvania 169

Andries van Dam, Brown University 319, 431, 506, 815, 850, 1495
R. H. VanDenburg, Jr., Jefferson Data Services, Inc. 811

Jerrold L. Wagener, Amoco Production Research 413, 668
William M. Waite, University of Colorado 1352
Charles H. Warlick, University of Texas at Austin 1559
Jim C. Warren, Jr., Wireless Digital, Inc. 1131
Peter Wegner, Brown University 497, 822, 1151, 1219, 1225, 1397, 1535, 1555
A. H. Werkheiser, The MITRE Corporation 508
Eric A. Weiss, Sun Company 867
Barry D. Wessler, GTE Telenet Communications Corporation 479, 1093
Gio Wiederhold, Stanford University 686, 934
Maurice V. Wilkes, Digital Equipment Corporation and Emeritus Professor, Cambridge University 157, 522, 535, 584, 1545
James H. Wilkinson, Teddington, England 608, 927, 1538
Erich R. Willner, Citibank, N.A. 161
Theodore C. Willoughby, University of Evansville 1475
M. Wayne Wilson, IBM Corporation 1385
David S. Wise, Indiana University 647
Larry D. Wittie, State University of New York at Buffalo 969
Amy D. Wohl, Advanced Office Concepts Corporation 1573
David B. Wortman, University of Toronto 176, 216
Detlef Wotschke, Johann Wolfgang Goethe-Universität 1568
Marvin C. Wunderlich, Northern Illinois University 1035

Edward K. Yasaki, Datamation 353
Stephen S. Yau, Northwestern University 307, 772
David M. Young, University of Texas at Austin 1106
Marshall C. Yovits, Purdue School of Science 714

Heinz Zemanek, IBM Austria 1577
Karl L. Zinn, University of Michigan 144, 292, 294, 355, 1017
Stanley Zionts, State University of New York at Buffalo 918
Albert L. Zobrist, Jet Propulsion Laboratory 651

Preface to the Second Edition

The first edition of an encyclopedia is one of those tasks which must be undertaken so that it may be done right the next time. This is the next time.

Six years have elapsed since the publication of the first edition. In computer science and technology, this is a long time. While the pace of change in computing may be less breakneck than in the past, it is still more rapid than in any other scientific or technical discipline. Therefore, this "snapshot"—for a snapshot is all an encyclopedia can be—is markedly different from the one published six years ago.

How different?

The first edition of this encyclopedia contained 470 articles from 210 contributors. This edition has

- 550 articles from 301 contributors

of which over

- 90 are new articles
- 40 are rewritten articles on subjects covered in the first edition
- 100 are first edition articles which have been extensively modified and brought up to date.

In addition, almost all the other articles from the first edition have undergone at least minor modifications. Finally, four new appendices have been added—a glossary of computing terms in five languages and lists of programming languages, computer science and engineering departments in universities, and research journals in computer science and technology. The result is a second edition in which at least 40% of the material is either not contained in the first edition or is significantly modified from the first edition.

Furthermore, the title has been changed from *Encyclopedia of Computer Science* to *Encyclopedia of Computer Science and Engineering*. This change is both an attempt to describe the contents of this book more accurately and an explicit recognition of a greater emphasis in this edition than in the last on computer technology.

One feature of this edition, in contrast to its predecessor, which is perhaps worth noting is that the editors have tried to remove all instances of masculine pronouns which don't refer to specific people. Some, no doubt, slipped through our net, but not many.

The creation of a work of this size and scope is necessarily the work of many people—the editors, the editorial board, and the contributors, all of whom are listed in the preceding pages. Hidden in the list of contributors is one name which deserves special mention since the idea to produce the first edition of this encyclopedia was his. Since 1971 he has always been close to and supportive of this project and has been an enthusiastic contributor to both editions. But mainly because of his initial conception of such an encyclopedia, it is appropriate to recognize Isaac L. Auerbach.

Anthony Ralston
Edwin D. Reilly, Jr.

October 1981

NOTE: The editors and the publisher would appreciate comments from readers on how future editions of this encyclopedia could be improved. What additional subjects need to be covered? Which articles need improvement? And where are there errors of fact or typographical errors? All correspondence should be sent to Editor, *Encyclopedia of Computer Science and Technology,* Van Nostrand Reinhold, 135 West 50 Street, New York, NY 10020.

Editors' Foreword

The most important purpose of an encyclopedia in a particular disciplinary area is to be a basic reference work for non-specialists who need elaboration of subjects in which they are not expert. The implication of "basic" is that an encyclopedia, while it should attempt to be comprehensive in *breadth* of coverage, cannot be comprehensive in the *depth* with which it treats most topics. An encyclopedia should, however (and this one does), direct the reader to information at the next level of depth through cross-references to other articles and bibliographic references.

What constitutes breadth of coverage is always a difficult question, and it is especially so for computer science and technology. As a new discipline that has evolved over the past three decades, and that is still changing rather rapidly, its boundaries are blurred. This is complicated further because there is no general agreement among computer scientists or technologists about whether certain areas are or are not part of computer science and technology.

The choice of specific subject matter for this encyclopedia has been necessarily a personal one by the editors, modulated by the editorial board, and by the practical problems of finding authors to write particular articles. Our hope is that, while inevitably there will be quibbles about the inclusion of certain topics, little or nothing of major importance has been omitted.

Articles in this encyclopedia normally contain definitions of the article titles, but even the shortest articles also contain explanatory information to broaden and deepen the reader's understanding. Long articles contain historical and survey information in order to integrate the subject matter and put it into perspective. Overall, the encyclopedia is a basic reference to computer science and technology, as well as a broad picture of the discipline, its history, and its direction.

Organization. The organization of this volume is on an alphabetic basis according to the first word of each article title. Titles have been chosen in such a way that the first word is the one most likely to be selected by the reader searching for a given topic. In addition, main cross-references have been provided when more than one word in a title might reasonably be referenced. These cross-references are also used to refer to important subjects that are included in longer, more general articles rather than as separate articles.

Four additional aids to the reader have been provided. The first such aid is the CLASSIFICATION OF ARTICLES which follows this foreword. This classification is intended to guide the reader to clusters of related articles. It may also be useful in guiding curriculum development and to help readers to follow a self-study regime.

The second such aid is the CROSS-REFERENCE list at the beginning of each article, which lists titles of related articles.

The APPENDICES at the back of the book constitute the third aid. These include lists of abbreviations, acronyms, special notation, programming languages, academic departments of computer science and engineering, and research journals in computer science and technology, as well as some useful numerical tables and a five-language table of important computer terms.

The fourth aid is the INDEX. In a dictionary or glossary, all terms appear as entries, but in an encyclopedia only the most important terms are used as article titles or even main cross-references. Without an index, the location of much important information would be left to the ingenuity of the reader. In fact, the index contains all terms that should appear in a *dictionary* of computer science. In addition, it contains entries that would not normally appear in a dictionary, such as references to subcategories. The encyclopedia user who searches among the article titles unsuccessfully will find the index invaluable in locating specific information. In addition, the index will often provide pointers to unfamiliar terms.

Anthony Ralston
Edwin D. Reilly, Jr.

Classification of Articles

This classification of articles embodies a taxonomy that should be helpful to the reader in grasping the scope of material contained in this volume. Articles are classified under nine categories:

1. Hardware
2. Computer Systems
3. Information and Data
4. Software
5. Mathematics of Computing
6. Theory of Computing
7. Methodologies
8. Applications
9. Computing Milieux

Except for a minor variation in the name of category 3—"Information and Data" rather than just "Data"—these are the categories used in the *Taxonomy of Computer Science and Engineering* published by the AFIPS Press of Arlington, Virginia in 1980. Articles in this encyclopedia are listed in this classification in a way patterned after the *Taxonomy*.

Each encyclopedia article title appears at least once in the classification. Where appropriate, some titles appear more than once in order to eliminate cross-reference clutter. Most classification headings are themselves article titles, in which case they are followed by the relevant page reference. Headings preceded by an asterisk (*) are not actual article titles but rather were invented to provide coherence to the overall classification and, where possible, to increase parallelism to the *Taxonomy*.

1. *HARDWARE

*TYPES OF COMPUTERS

COMPUTER ARCHITECTURE   275

*EDUCATION IN COMPUTER SCIENCE AND TECHNOLOGY

*HISTORY

ENCYCLOPEDIA OF COMPUTER SCIENCE AND ENGINEERING

SECOND EDITION

ABSTRACT DATA TYPE

For articles on related subjects *see* ADA; CLASS; DATA STRUCTURES; DATA TYPE; MONITORS; PASCAL; PROGRAM VERIFICATION; and STRUCTURED PROGRAMMING.

A major issue for software development and maintenance is managing the complexity of the software system. Over the years, programming methodologies and languages have developed in response to new ideas about how to cope with this complexity. A dominant theme in the growth of methodologies and languages is the development of tools for dealing with abstractions. An *abstraction* is a simplified description, or *specification,* of a system that suppresses some of its details or properties. A *good* abstraction is one in which information that is significant to the reader (i.e., the user) is emphasized while details that are immaterial, at least for the moment, are suppressed. During the late 1970s, most research activity in abstraction techniques was focused on the language and specification issues raised by these considerations; much of the work is identified with the concept of *abstract data types.*

An *abstract data type* is a programming language facility for organizing programs into modules using criteria that are based on the data structures of the program. The specification of the module should provide all information required for using the type, including the allowable values of the data and the effects of the operations. However, details about the implementation, such as data representations and algorithms for implementing the operations, are hidden within the module. This separation of specification from implementation is a key idea of abstract data types.

Each module that defines an abstract data type may include both data declarations and subroutine definitions. The criteria for organizing the modules emphasize protecting the data structures from arbitrary manipulation—malicious or accidental—by arbitrary other parts of the program. Languages that support abstract data types include scope rules that guarantee this locality by hiding the names of local data from all parts of the program outside the module that defines the abstract data type. The objective of organizing a program using abstract data types is to expedite the program development process and to simplify the maintenance task by imposing a certain kind of predictable and useful structure on the program.

Like structured programming, the methodology of abstract data types emphasizes locality of related collections of information. In the case of abstract data types, attention is focused on data rather than on control, and the strategy is to form modules consisting of a data structure and its associated operations. The objective is to treat these modules in the same way as ordinary types, such as integers and reals, are treated; this requires support for declarations, infix operators, specification of parameters to subroutines, and so on. The resulting abstract data type effectively extends the set of types available to a program. It explains the properties of a new group of variables by specifying the values one of these variables may have, and it explains the operations that will be permitted on the variables of the new type by giving the effects the operations have on the values of the variables.

In designing a data type abstraction, we first specify

1

the functional properties of a data structure and its operations, then we implement them in terms of existing language constructs (and other data types) and show that the specification is accurate. When we subsequently use the abstraction, we deal with the new type solely in terms of its specification. This philosophy has been developed in several programming languages, including Ada, Alphard, CLU, Concurrent Pascal, Euclid, Gypsy, Mesa, Modula, and Simula. In these languages, the module-definition construct for abstract data types associates a specification with the implementation of a module and hides all information that is not explicitly included in the specification. This specification does not explain how the data structure is laid out; rather, it defines the effects of the various operations. As a result, the implementation of the abstract data type, including both the layout of the data structure and the algorithms for the operations, may be modified without requiring modification of user programs. When it has been verified that the implementation performs in accordance with its public specification, the specification may safely be used as the definitive source of information about how higher-level programs may correctly use the module. In one sense, we build up "bigger" definitions out of "smaller" ones; but because a specification alone suffices for understanding, the new definition is in another sense no bigger than the pre-existing components. It is this compression of detail that gives the technique its power.

For example, we might define a data type *Stack,* whose elements are of an arbitrary type *T* and for which operations *Push, Pop,* and *Top* are provided. The definition of the abstract data type would be

> **type** *Stack*(*T*:**type**);
> **specifications**
>> **procedure** *Push*(**var** *S*: *Stack*(*T*); *x*:*T*);
>>> [specification of *Push* in the formal notation of choice]
>> **procedure** *Pop*(**var** *S*: *Stack*(*T*));
>>> [specification of *Pop* in the formal notation of choice]
>> **function** *Top*(*S*: *Stack*(*T*)) **returns** *T*;
>>> [specification of *Top* in the formal notation of choice]
> **implementation**
>> [declarations of data structure used to represent *Stack*s]
>> [bodies of *Push, Pop,* and *Top*]
> **end type.**

A program might then declare stacks of integers, reals, or other data types, including types defined by the programmer. For example, after the definition above, the following program fragment would be legal.

> **declare**
>> *X*: *Stack*(*integer*);
>> *Y*: *Stack*(*real*);
>> *Z*: *Stack*(*MyType*);
>> *j*: *integer*;
>> *g*: *real*;
>> *p,q*: *MyType*;
>
>> . . . .
>
> *Push*(*X,j*); *Pop*(*Y*); *p* := *Top*(*Z*);
> *Pop*(*X*); *g* := *Top*(*Y*); *Push*(*Z,q*);

The specification techniques used for abstract data types evolved from the predicates used in simple sequential programs. The method for formally verifying that the specification of an abstract data type is consistent with its implementation was originally formulated by Hoare (1972). Additional expressive power was incorporated to deal with the way information is packaged into modules and with the problem of abstracting from an implementation to a data type (Guttag, 1980). One class of specification techniques defines the properties of a data type as a set of axioms; these techniques draw on the similarity between a data type and the mathematical structure called an algebra (Liskov and Zilles, 1975). Another class of techniques explicitly models a newly defined type by defining its properties in terms of the properties of common, well-understood types (Wulf *et al.,* 1976).

REFERENCES

1972. Hoare, C. A. R. "Proof of Correctness of Data Representations," *Acta Informatica* **1**, *No. 4.*
1980. Guttag, John V. "Notes on Type Abstraction (Version 2)," *IEEE Transactions on Software Engineering* **SE-6** (January).
1975. Liskov, Barbara H. and Zilles, Stephen N. "Specification Techniques for Data Abstractions," *IEEE Transactions on Software Engineering* **SE-1** (March).
1976. Wulf, Wm. A., London, Ralph L., and Shaw, Mary. "An Introduction to the Construction and Verification of Alphard Programs," *IEEE Transactions on Software Engineering* **SE-2** (December).

M. SHAW

ACCESS METHODS

For articles on related subjects *see* DATABASE MANAGEMENT; DIRECT ACCESS; FILES; HASHING; KEY; and RECORD.

An access method is a technique for accessing data that has been placed on some kind of mass storage device, most often a disk. While the term "access method" is used to describe the method used to retrieve the data, the process is frequently closely related to the structure of the data as it resides on the disk. As a result, the term is sometimes loosely used to describe the structure of the data itself and, often, "access method" is used as a synonym for the program or routine which implements the method.

All modern computer manufacturers provide service routines to implement access methods, generally as a component of the operating system. Instead of access method, terms such as data management, file control program, and I/O (input or output) supervisor are sometimes used, depending on the manufacturer. The terminology used in this discussion is common to several manufacturers, including IBM. However, the evolution and concepts of access methods apply to all manufacturers, although not all manufacturers support every variant described below.

Evolution of Access Methods. In the earliest days of computers and programming, each programmer had to program the flow of data to and from I/O devices, including auxiliary storage units such as disks, drums, and tapes. This required that the programmer be familiar with the characteristics of particular devices and write code for functions such as testing for available channels, testing for I/O errors, and programing error recovery. Many of these functions were time dependent. Programming I/O in this manner tended to bind the programs to a particular device. When the storage device changed, the programming had to be substantially modified.

Since I/O programming tended to be fairly similar from one program to the next, it was not long before utility service programs (or access methods) were developed. Such programs perform, in a generalized manner, all of the interactions with the storage device. The programmer need merely be concerned with requesting a record and providing a location in storage for it. The division of functions is depicted in Fig. 1. Note the assumption in this figure that the application program can continue processing while data is being transferred, a point to which we return below.

The interface between the application program and the access method tends to be fairly simple and standardized and is generally reducible to a set of parameters. The technique usually used is to place the input and/or output parameters in a table. This table may be called (among other names) the DTF (Define The File), DD (Data Definition), or FCT (File Control Table). The parameters include a pointer to an area of storage to and from which the data transfer is to be made (i.e., the record buffer), the size of the record, whether labels are to be written or exist at the front of the file, whether a tape is to be rewound at the end of the file, and pointers to special error-handling routines (provided by the application). The application program need only place the necessary data into the table. This is a far easier task than having the programmer write an I/O routine. The access method, when invoked by the application, uses the contents of the table to perform the task requested. This technique has the advantage that, when a new storage device becomes available, the access method rather than the application programs can be modified. Thus, all programs using the access method are able to use the new device without significant modification, and frequently without any modification. When access methods were first used, they rarely provided complete transparency (i.e., independence) from the device, because new devices provided new characteristics which required the addition of new variables to the parameter table. Today, most variables are known or have been anticipated. Thus, it is now commonplace for existing applications to utilize new devices without any change to the application. Applications thereby have achieved *physical device independence* and are transparent to the introduction of new devices.

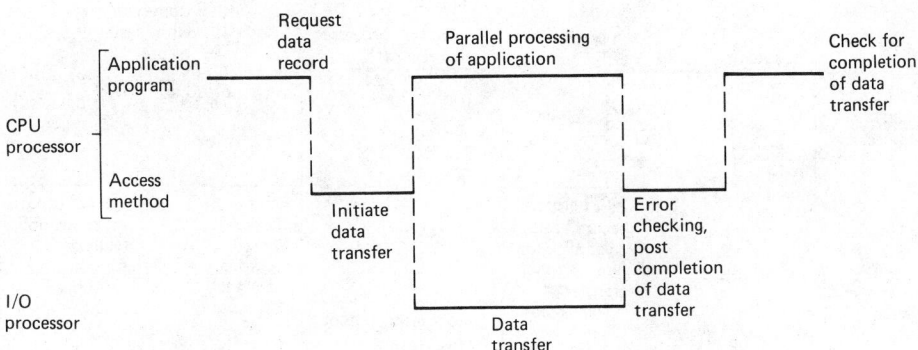

Fig. 1.   Division of functions.

On early computers without multiprogramming, it was important to use the central processing unit (CPU) as efficiently as possible. Fig. 1 illustrates an application that continues processing while data transfer takes place. This is achieved by having the access method return control to the application program after it starts the data transfer. When data transfer is complete, the interrupt mechanism gives control to the access method again. The access method performs checking for data transfer errors and, assuming no problem, "posts" or flags the file parameter table that the data transfer is complete. Control is then returned to the application program. The responsibility of ensuring that processing of data does not begin until the data transfer is complete is left to the application program, which must check the parameter table for completion of the data transfer.

The most popular auxiliary storage device on pre-multiprogrammed computers was magnetic tape. Because records are stored sequentially, one after the other, on magnetic tape, they must be processed sequentially for most efficient processing. The standard access method thus became known as SAM (Sequential Access Method). Using SAM, there was little processing that an application program could do on input while waiting for the next record (although, on output, it could start to generate the next record). A better method was needed to take advantage of the predictability that the next one of the sequentially stored records would be read. Thus, a new access method was designed to achieve what the application program generally could not—namely, to overlap processing with data transfer. When reading data, this is achieved by looking ahead and performing the access for the next record while the application program is processing the last (or current) record. This modification of the model of Fig. 1 is illustrated in Fig. 2.

As Fig. 2 illustrates, the data transmission proceeds in parallel with the application processing, with a brief time-out at the end of the transmission for the access method to handle the details of error checking. In this case, the access method does not have to post the completion of data transfer to the application, since the application is still working with the last record. Fig. 2 illustrates the normal situation, but clearly there are situations where the application finishes its work before the data transfer is complete. In this case, some waiting is necessary, but nevertheless some overlap of processing and data transfer has been achieved that otherwise would not have been. This access method is known as QSAM (Queued Sequential Access Method) and the sequential access method of Fig. 1 became known as BSAM (Basic Sequential Access Method). QSAM has been illustrated above for input, but applies equally well to output. On output, QSAM also absorbs the responsibility of blocking records—whereby several application program records are batched together to the same physical record on disk.

BSAM and QSAM were well suited to handling tape files which are inherently sequential. With the advent of direct (random) access storage devices, the need arose to support direct access of a record without passing (and inspecting) all previous records in the file. This need gave rise to two additional access methods.

In the first of these, it is assumed that the application program has the ability to compute the location of the data on the direct access device relative to the beginning of the file and to instruct the access method to retrieve (or replace) the data at that location. This access method is known as DAM (Direct Access Method) or BDAM (Basic Direct Access Method). As with BSAM, the application program is required to check that the input (or output) is complete before using the data. Since the location of the data is computed by the application program, there can be no "look ahead" by the access method. However, overall computer efficiency can still be maintained if BDAM is used in multiprogramming sys-

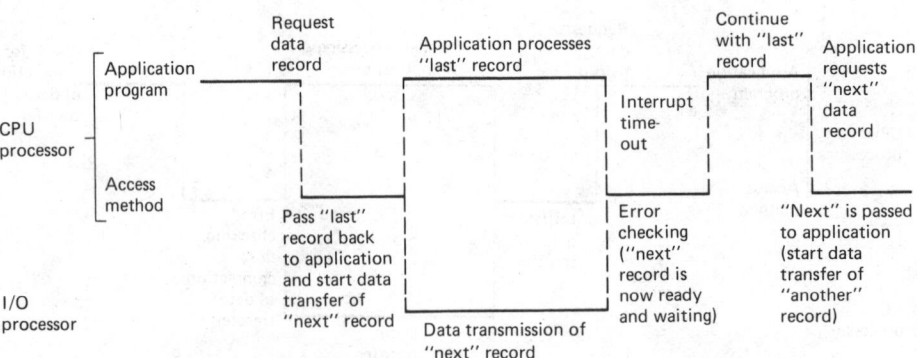

Fig. 2. Overlap of processing with data transfer.

tems so that while one application is waiting another is executing.

The second direct access method introduced combined the advantages of sequential and direct access. This access method is known as ISAM (Indexed Sequential Access Method). It combines the two modes of basic and queued access, depending upon whether the operation demands the application check for completion (Basic) or permits "look ahead" by the access method (Queued). Thus, when we speak generically of ISAM, we mean both BISAM (Basic ISAM) and QISAM (Queued ISAM). ISAM permits the application to process records sequentially, by the key within the record, or directly, by means of maintaining a separate index of keys (or list of pointers) to all records.

With ISAM, therefore, record keys become important. Typical examples of record keys are employee names in an alphabetized file or social security numbers in a file ordered numerically. QSAM always gets the next record and, thus, for QSAM (or BSAM), the key has no significance in accessing the record. In the case of ISAM, unlike QSAM, the records are not necessarily stored next to each other and the key becomes important as a means for locating the record. ISAM, in principle, keeps a list of keys and pointers to the appropriate records. In this manner, working from the index list, the records can be presented back to the application program in sequence by key (when all or a significant portion of the file is to be processed) or a unique record can be obtained directly without having to "pass over" any of the records logically preceding it. While ISAM doesn't always read the next record, because of the characteristics of disk storage devices, data transfer is most efficient when the records are adjacent. A great deal of effort goes into handling the organization of records on the device for optimum performance.

Since records in a file accessed by ISAM need not be stored in sequential order, the insertion of a new record in a large file is much more efficient than for files accessed by QSAM or BSAM, since a record can be placed anywhere and the index of the key list updated so that it may be found subsequently.

An example of how ISAM use indexes is shown in Table 1. Since use of a single index sometimes results in a search of a quite long list, it is common to use a hierarchy of indexes, as shown in the table. The table assumes that an exployee file with 10,000 records is stored in 100 blocks on a disk, with the first block starting at disk address 46217. Each block would store an average of 100 employee records, but would have the capacity to store more than 100 records so that change to, and growth of, the file would be possible before it is reorganized and the indexes updated. Table 1 also assumes that employee numbers are in the range 00000–99999. To re-

Table 1. A Hierarchical Block-Oriented Index

Index Level 1	Index Level 2	Block Number	Block Starting Address
	00000–00713	1	46217
	00718–01426	2	46337
	.	.	.
00000–08756	.	.	.
	.	.	.
	07823–08756	10	47395
.	41063–42217	41	50362
.	.	.	.
41063–52071	.	.	.
.	.	.	.
	49278–50593	49	51612
	50614–52071	50	51738
	.	.	
	.	.	

trieve the record for the employee whose number is 49731, the first level index would be searched until the fifth entry (41063–52071) was found; then the second level would be searched, starting at 41063–42217, until the ninth entry (49278–50593) was found; finally, address 51612 (the start of block 49) on the disk would be searched sequentially until the record with key 49731 was found. Note how much more efficient this is than searching the entire file sequentially. Note also how much more efficient a two-level index is than a single index search would be.

The next advance in access methods was the Virtual Storage Access Method (VSAM), which was introduced in conjunction with the introduction of Virtual Storage Operating Systems by IBM, although such operating systems were in use by Burroughs and several other manufacturers prior to IBM's adoption of the concept. VSAM combines many of the features of ISAM, QSAM, and BDAM into one comprehensive access method. It also incorporates improved techniques for the positioning of records on the disk and for increasing the degree of overlap of computation and I/O processing (buffering).

VSAM can operate like ISAM in that records can be accessed by keys, like QSAM in that records can be accessed by the order on the storage device, or like BDAM, where the record is accessed by a "relative" position in the file. However, the current state of the art only permits it to operate in one of these modes for any one file. Thus, if ISAM mode is chosen for a file, that file must always be accessed by VSAM in "ISAM mode."

A further step in the evolution of data organization is the advent of the concept of the Database Manager, a system software program which manages the data resources for a series of programs. An access method is concerned only with moving data back and forth from main storage to a peripheral storage device (generally disk or tape). A Database Manager has a wider spectrum of concerns, including maintaining relationships between different sets of data, converting the data format to fit that required by the application programs, and simultaneous use of the same data by different application programs. As organizations move towards a database environment, applications are using Database Managers where they formerly used access methods. Most Database Managers call upon the established access methods to perform input and output. The access methods used are generally based on BDAM or, occasionally, on VSAM.

Another aspect of access methods is related to the advent of on-line processing in which there is a need for the application program to interact with an on-line terminal. Many of the traditional problems solved by access methods are also apparent here: blocking, buffering, error recovery, protocols of communicating with the devices, etc. But there are differences, since there is no storage medium involved and the devices are intended for interacting with people. Communication with such devices is heavily influenced by communications (e.g., phone line) capabilities. Just as device access methods evolved in parallel with operating systems, so telecommunication access methods evolved in parallel with telecommunication monitors. Telecommunication access methods are, however, far less standard than mass storage device access methods.

Storage device access methods evolved to enable the application to process data stored on a variety of devices in a variety of ways in an efficient manner and to isolate the application from the physical characteristics of the device; telecommunication access methods evolved to allow the application to communicate with a variety of terminal devices and in a variety of ways in an efficient manner and to isolate it from the physical characteristics of the device. Thus, terminal access methods have evolved from BTAM (Basic Telecommunications Access Methods), whereby a terminal is locked to an application under a specific communications monitor, to VTAM (Virtual Telecommunications Access Method), where a terminal may be connected to any application under a variety of telecommunications monitors.

F. BRADDOCK

ACCESS TIME

For articles on related subjects *see* CYLINDER; DIRECT ACCESS: LATENCY; and MEMORY; AUXILIARY.

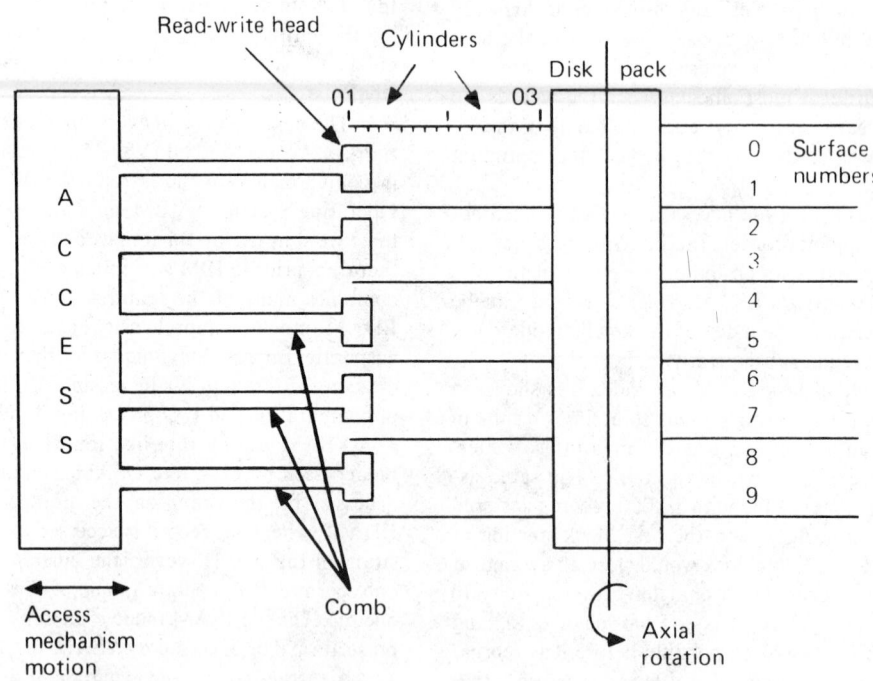

Fig. 1.   Side view of typical disk drive.

Direct access devices require varying times to position a read/write head over a particular record. In the case of a moving-head disk drive, this involves positioning the *comb* (head assembly, as in Fig. 1) to the designated cylinder, plus rotation of the selected track to the desired record. Comb-movement times for a typical medium-sized disk drive are shown in Fig. 2.

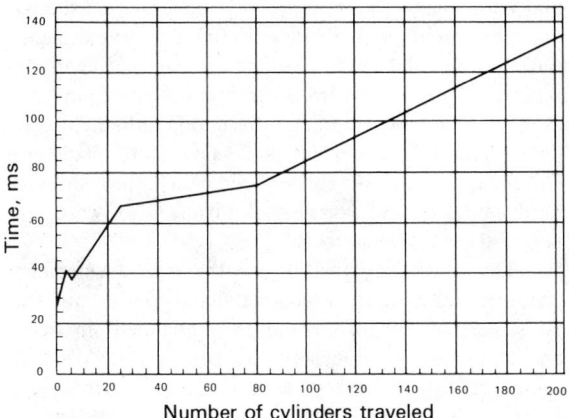

Fig. 2.   Comb-movement times for typical disk drive.

Access time is the sum of comb-movement and rotational times to reach a particular record (plus the time to switch from reading or writing one surface to another, but since this is done at electronic speeds, it contributes almost nothing to the access time). There is a different access time for each record retrieved at random from a disk drive, since it is necessary to move from cylinder C_1 to cylinder C_2 (Fig. 2), then await rotational positioning of record R. Suppose the disk drive, whose comb-movement time is shown in Fig. 2, rotates at 2400 rpm, which is equivalent to 25 ms per rotation. Then the *maximum access time* for this device is 160 ms (135 ms for the comb movement, plus 25 ms for the rotation), the *average access time* is about 82.5 ms (70 + 12.5) and the *minimum access time* is 25 ms. The latter time, which is the time required to move the comb to an adjacent cylinder is also called the *track-to-track access time.* Of course, if successive records are on the same cylinder, the access time can be zero.

Average access time is an important parameter for analytical planning of a real-time computer application, e.g., an on-line inquiry system. Minimum access time is more important for sequential usage of disk drives. The dominant component of delay for sequential retrieval of records from a disk drive is the average time for a half-rotation (12.5 ms for the drive described in Figs. 1 and 3).

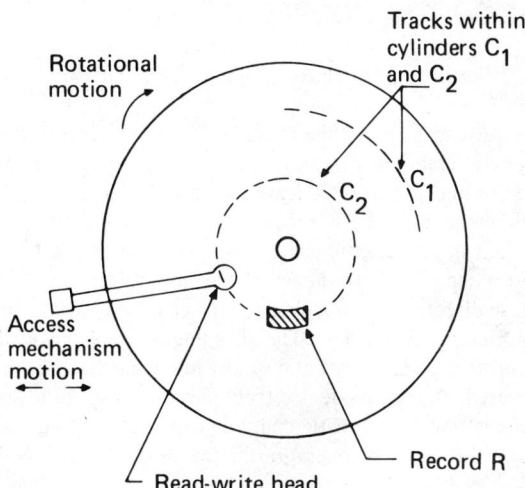

Fig. 3.   Top view of typical disk drive.

During the past 20 years, rotational speeds for disk drives have improved very little: 2400 rpm is typical. Bit densities per track have increased fivefold in this same period, so that average transfer speeds have increased even if track-to-track access times have not diminished. During this period, average access times have been halved, as a result of a widespread changeover from hydraulic actuators to "voice coil" actuators for moving the comb mechanism.

For a drum or fixed-head disk, average access time is a half-revolution and maximum access time is a full revolution, since both have heads which are fixed over the data areas. Average access times for drums are 5 to 10 ms.

For magnetic card and similar mass storage systems, average access times depend on movement of the medium to a read/write head. Typical average access times for magnetic card devices are 1 sec and maximum access times are 2 to 4 sec. For tape-cartridge mass storage systems, average access time is approximately 15 sec and minimum access time to a new cartridge is approximately 12 sec.

D. N. FREEMAN

ACCOUNTING, COMPUTER.
See COMPUTER ACCOUNTING AND RESOURCE CONTROL.

ACM.
See ASSOCIATION FOR COMPUTING MACHINERY.

ACOUSTIC COUPLER

For article on related subject *see* MODEM.

An acoustic coupler (see Fig. 1) is a modem in which the coupling between a computer processor or terminal device and the communications line (almost always the telephone network) is acoustic rather than electric. The output of an acoustic coupler is an audible sound which is applied directly to the telephone mouthpiece; in the reverse direction, the telephone earpiece is applied to a microphone in the modem. The advantage of an acoustically coupled modem is that almost any telephone handset can be used, and the modem is truly portable. The disadvantage is that the acoustic coupling can be noisy and may limit the speed of operation of the device; acoustically

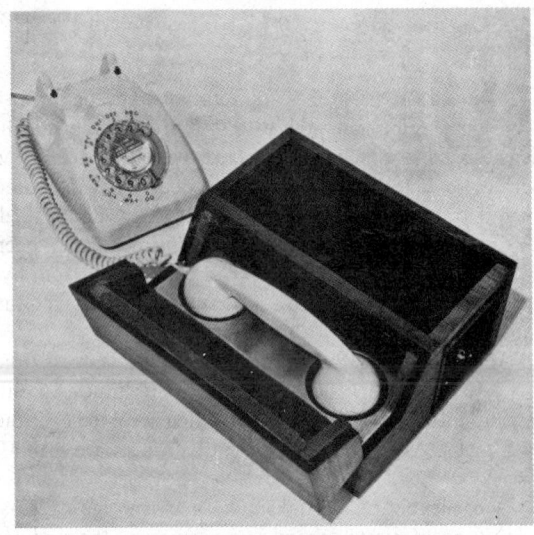

Fig. 1. Acoustic coupled modem with telephone handset. (Reproduced by kind permission of the manufacturers, K & N Electronics, Ltd., Maidenhead Berks, England.)

coupled modems are seldom used at data speeds above 300 bps (bits per second). With electric coupling, speeds of 1,200 bps or even 4,800 bps can be achieved with low error rates on switched telephone lines. The limiting component is usually the microphone in the telephone handset. If this is replaced by a better one, higher speeds can be obtained reliably.

P. T. KIRSTEIN

ADA

For articles on related subjects *see* PASCAL; PROGRAMMING LANGUAGES; and STRUCTURED PROGRAMMING

Ada is a programming language developed under the auspices of the United States Department of Defense (DOD) for the purpose of reducing software development and maintenance costs, especially for large, constantly-changing programs with long lifetimes. It was designed during the period 1975–1980, and it was specifically intended to support modern programming techniques such as structured programming, information hiding, abstract data types, and concurrent processing. DOD plans also call for a program support environment to provide standard interfaces and a variety of advanced software support and development tools.

The original motivation for the Ada development stemmed from military command-and-control applications, particularly for computers "embedded" in weapons, airplanes, or other military equipment. Although these applications have some special requirements, such as real-time processing, concurrency, and nonstandard I/O, the requirements that emerged are suitable for a general-purpose programming language. The design proceeded in that spirit, and as a result Ada may be widely used in industrial, business, and university facilities as well as in the military.

History. The impetus for the Ada development effort came in the early 1970s, when it became clear that DOD was supporting an enormous number of programming languages (estimates on the number range from a few hundred to a few thousand). In 1976, DOD issued a directive on the use of advanced computer technology in defense systems in order to halt the proliferation of similar languages. This directive required most new software to be developed in one of a small number of approved languages. The initial list of approved languages contained seven programming languages in which DOD had already made significant investment; these languages are CMS-2, SPL/1, TACPOL, Jovial J3, Jovial J73, Cobol, and Fortran.

At the same time, DOD initiated an effort to develop a modern language to add to this list. An initial draft of requirements for such a language, the "Strawman" proposal, was circulated in 1975. This was revised in response to the comments received, and a series of requirements proposals called "Woodenman," "Tinman," "Ironman," and "Steelman" resulted. The actual language design (DOD, 1980) was obtained through an international design competition, combined with extensive public review of the winning initial design, which was done by a Cii Honeywell Bull design team led by Jean Ichbiah.

The language was named Ada in honor of Lady Augusta Ada Byron, the Countess of Lovelace (*q.v.*). She programmed Babbage's analytical engine in the 1830s, and she is often named as the world's first computer programmer.

As of spring 1981, DOD agencies were contracting for compilers to be developed over about two years, and a number of other implementations were in progress. At least one of the DOD contracts included the programming environment as well as the compiler.

Language Characteristics.

Although the early Ada development was heavily influenced by the Pascal (*q.v.*) philosophy, extensive syntactic changes and semantic extensions make it a very different language from Pascal. The major additions include

- Module structures and interface specifications for large-program organizations and separate compilation.
- Encapsulation facilities and generic definitions to support abstract data types.
- Support for parallel processing.
- Control over low-level implementation issues related to the architecture of object machines.

There are three major abstraction tools in Ada. The *package* is used for encapsulating a set of related definitions and isolating them from the rest of the program. The *type* determines the values a variable (or data structure) may take on and how it can be manipulated. The *generic* definition allows many similar instances of a definition to be generated from a single template. Support for parallel processing includes concurrently-executable procedures called *tasks* and language facilities for synchronization. Support for low-level matters includes control over a type's storage layout and a loophole mechanism that provides access to machine-dependent features.

The following example, taken from Shaw (1980), illustrates some of the important features of Ada. The purpose of the example program is to produce the data needed to print an internal telephone list for a division of a small company. A database containing information about all employees, including their names, divisions, telephone numbers, and salaries, is assumed to be available. The program must produce a data structure containing a sorted list of the employees in a selected division and their telephone extensions.

An Ada program to solve this problem is organized in three components: 1) a definition of the record for each employee (Fig. 1); 2) declarations of the data needed by the program (Fig. 2); and 3) code for construction of the telephone list (Fig. 3).

```
package Employee is
   type PrivStuff is limited private;
   type EmpRec is
      record
         Name: string(1..24);
         Phone: integer;
         PrivPart: PrivStuff;
      end record;
   procedure SetSalary(Who: in out EmpRec; Sal: float);
   function GetSalary(Who: EmpRec) return float;
   procedure SetDiv(Who: in out EmpRec; Div: string(1..8));
   function GetDiv(Who: EmpRec) return string(1..8);
private
   type PrivStuff is
      record
         Salary: float;
         Division: string(1..8);
      end record;
end Employee;
```

Fig. 1. Ada package definition for employee records.

The **package** of information about employees whose specification is shown in Fig. 1 illustrates one of Ada's major additions to our tool kit of abstraction facilities. This definition establishes EmpRec as a data type with a small set of privileged operations. Only the specification of the package is presented here. Ada does not require the module body (i.e., the implementation of the procedures and functions) to accompany the specification (though it must be defined before the program can be executed); moreover, programmers should rely only on the specifications, not on the body of a package. This makes it possible to compile programs that use this package before the code of the package is actually compiled. The specification itself is divided into a visible part (everything from **package** to **private**) and a private part (from **private** to **end**). The private part is intended only to provide information needed by the compiler to generate code but not needed by the programmer.

Assume that the policy for using EmpRec's is that the Name and Phone fields are accessible to anyone, that it is permissible for anyone to read but not to write the Division field, and that access to the Salary field and modification of the Division field are supposed to be done only by authorized programs. The scope rules prevent any portion of the program outside a package from accessing any names except the ones listed in the visible part of the specification. In the particular case of the Employee package, this means that the Salary and Division fields of an EmpRec cannot be directly read or written outside the package but can only be accessed using the routines declared inside the package. Therefore, the integrity of the data can be controlled by verifying that the routines that are exported from the package are correct. Presumably the routines SetSalary, GetSalary, SetDiv, and GetDiv perform reads and writes as their names suggest; they might also keep records showing who made changes and when, or a password could be added as a parameter to the sensitive routines.

Although the field name PrivPart is exported from the Employee package along with Name and Phone, there is no danger in doing so. An auxiliary type was defined to protect the salary and division information; the declaration

type PrivStuff **is limited private**

indicates not only that the content and organization of the data structure are hidden from the user (private), but also that all operations on data of type PrivStuff are forbidden except for calls on the routines exported from the package. For limited private types, (i.e., if variables *p* and *q* are declared outside **package** Employee to be type PrivStuff, both "*p* := 1" and "**if** *p* = *q* **then** ..." are prohibited). Naturally, the code inside the body of the Employee package may manipulate these hidden fields; the purpose of the packaging is to guarantee that *only* the code inside the package body can do so.

The ability to force manipulation of a data structure to be carried out only through a known set of routines is central to the support of abstract data types. It is useful not only in examples such as the one given here, but also for cases in which the representation may change radically from time to time and for cases in which some kind of internal consistency among fields, such as checksums, must be maintained. Support for *secure* computation is not among Ada's goals. It can be achieved in this case, but only through a combination of an extra level of packaging and some management control. Even without guarantees about security, however, the packaging of information about how employee data is handled provides a useful structure for the development and maintenance of the program.

The declarations of Fig. 2 illustrate the use of abstract data types. One new type (PhoneRec) is defined; the type defined in Fig. 1 is used, and another non-primitive type, String, is used. The Employee package is used instead of a simple record. The clause

use Employee;

says that all the visible names of the Employee package are available in the current block.

The type definitions for EmpRec and PhoneRec ab-

```
declare
  use Employee;

  type PhoneRec is
    record
        Name: string(1..24);
        Phone: integer;
    end record;

  Staff: array (1..1000) of EmpRec;
  Phones: array (1..1000) of PhoneRec;
  StaffSize, DivSize, i, j: integer range 1..1000;
  WhichDiv: string(1..8);
  q: PhoneRec;
```

Fig. 2. Declarations for Ada version of telephone list program.

stract from specific data items to the notions "record of information about an employee" and "record of information for a telephone list." Both the employee database and the telephone list can thus be represented as vectors whose elements are records of the appropriate types.

The declarations of Staff and Phones have the effect of indicating that all the components are related to the same information structure. In addition, the definition is organized as a collection of records, one for each employee—so the primary organization of the data structure is by employee.

```
—Get data for division WhichDiv only

  DivSize := 0;
  for i in 1..StaffSize loop
    if GetDiv(Staff(i)) = WhichDiv then
      DivSize : = DivSize + 1;
      Phones(DivSize) : = (Staff(i).Name,
                           Staff(i).Phone);
    end if;
  end loop;

—Sort telephone list*

  for i in 1..DivSize loop
    for j in i+1..DivSize loop
      if Phones(i).Name > Phones(j).Name then
        q : = Phones(i);
        Phones(i) : = Phones(j);
        Phones(j) : = q;
      end if;
    end loop;
  end loop;
```

Fig. 3. Code for Ada version of telephone list program.

*This example uses a simple insertion sort, not as an endorsement of this method but because many readers will recognize it.

The telephone list is constructed in two stages (Fig.3). Note that Ada's ability to operate on strings and records as single units substantially simplifies the manipulation of names and the interchange step of the insertion sort used compared with a language such as Fortran where each element of the record would have to be processed separately. Ada also provides a way to create a complete record value and assign it with a single statement; thus the assignment Phones(DivSize) := (Staff(i).Name, Staff(i).Phone); sets both fields of the PhoneRec at once.

Programming Environment. DOD plans to support an integrated programming support environment for Ada programs. This environment will integrate conventional software tools into a framework that is sufficiently open-ended to accommodate a wide variety of programming methodologies and automated software tools. The current plans (DOD, February 1980) call for an environment with the following levels.

level 0. Hardware and host software as appropriate.

level 1. Kernel Ada Program Support Environment (KAPSE), which provides database, communication, and run-time support functions to enable the execution of an Ada program (including a MAPSE tool) and which presents a machine-independent portability interface.

level 2. Minimal Ada Program Support Environment (MAPSE), which provides a minimal set of tools, written in Ada and supported by the KAPSE, which are both necessary and sufficient for the development and continuing support of Ada programs.

level 3. Ada Program Support Environments (APSEs), which are constructed by extensions of the MAPSE to provide fuller support of particular applications or methodologies.

The development of this program support environment has followed a later schedule than the language. As with the language, a series of design requirements proposals, called "Sandman," "Pebbleman," and "Stoneman" (DOD, February 1980), were circulated for comment, and a competitive design process has been initiated.

REFERENCES

1980. United States Department of Defense. *Reference Manual for the Ada Programming Language.*
1980. United States Department of Defense. *"Stoneman" Requirements for Ada Programming Support Environments.*
1980. Shaw, M. "The Impact of Abstraction Concerns on Modern Programming Languages," *Proceedings of the IEEE* (Special issue on Software Engineering) **68**, *No. 9* (September) 1119–1130.
1981. *Computer* (contains six related articles on Ada). Los Alamitos, CA: IEEE Computer Society, June.

M. SHAW

ADDER

For articles on related subjects *see* ARITHMETIC, COMPUTER; ARITHMETIC-LOGIC UNIT; and LOGIC DESIGN.

An adder is a logic circuit that forms the sum of two or more numbers represented in digital form. The simplest adder is the binary one-position adder, also called a *full adder* (see Fig. 1), in which the ith bits of two summands and the carry from the previous $(i - 1)$ stage are added to form the ith sum bit and the carry to the next $(i + 1)$ stage. A *ripple-carry adder* for two n-bit binary numbers is formed by connecting n full adders in cascade (Fig. 2). The addition time of the ripple-carry adder corresponds to the worst-case delay, which is n times the time required to form the C_{i+1} (carry) output by one full adder, plus the time to form the S_i output, given the C_i input.

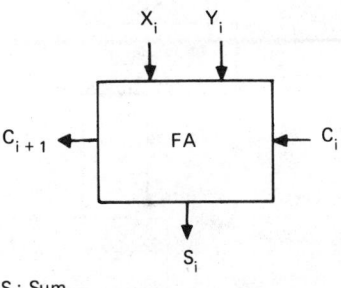

S : Sum
C : Carry   (a) Diagram

X_i	Y_i	C_i	S_i	C_{i+1}
0	0	0	0	0
0	0	1	1	0
0	1	0	1	0
0	1	1	0	1
1	0	0	1	0
1	0	1	0	1
1	1	0	0	1
1	1	1	1	1

(b) Truth table

Fig. 1.   The binary full adder (FA).

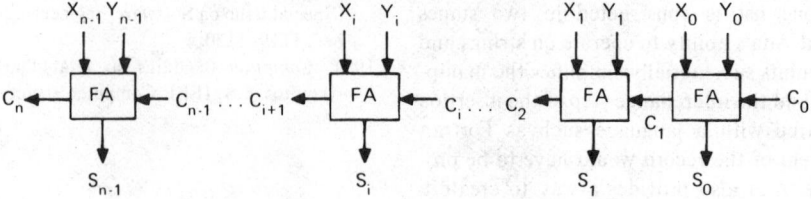

Fig. 2. Binary ripple-carry adder.

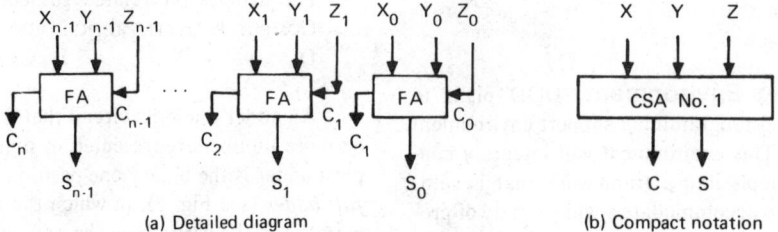

(a) Detailed diagram   (b) Compact notation

Fig. 3. Three-operand binary carry-save adder.

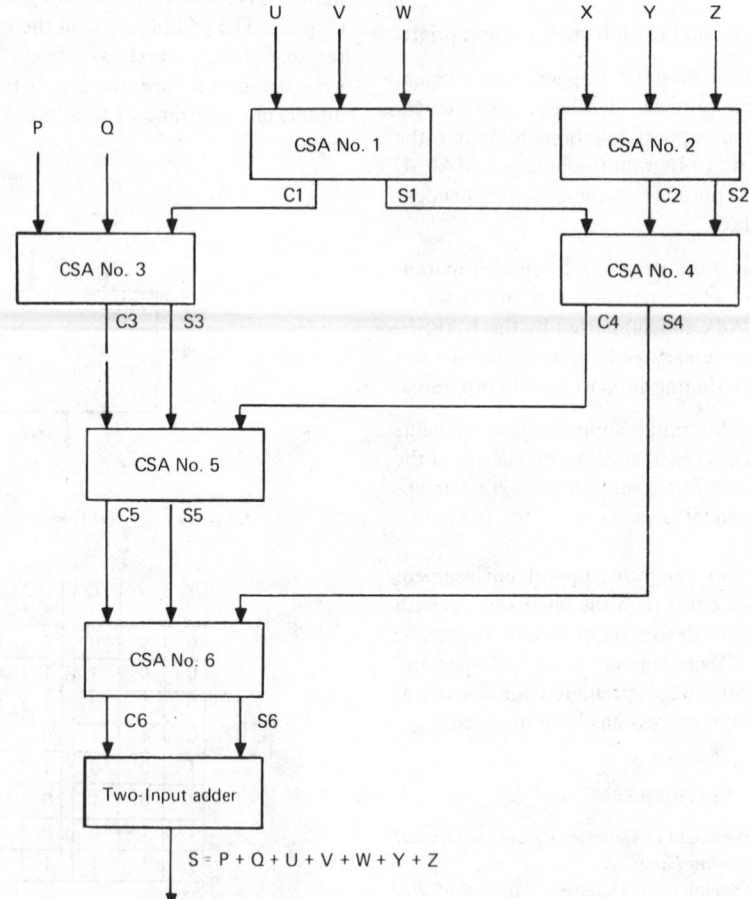

$$S = P + Q + U + V + W + Y + Z$$

Fig. 4. CSA summation of eight operands.

Higher speeds of two-operand addition can be attained by the use of *carry-completion sensing, carry-look-ahead,* and *conditional-sum* techniques (Garner, 1965). In these techniques, additional logic circuitry is employed to reduce the total delay in the adder circuits.

One-position adders for a higher radix r (for example, 4, 8, 10, or 16) are similar to the full adder of Fig. 1. The digits X_i and Y_i assume values 0 to $r - 1$, and they are represented by two or more binary variables. The values of the bits in S_i are easily described by a truth table; carry signals (C_i and C_{i+1}) remain two-valued (0 and 1). The adder speed-up techniques discussed for radix 2 also apply to two-operand addition of higher radix numbers.

Fast summation of three or more operands can be accomplished by the use of *carry-save* adders (CSA). A binary three-operand n-bit CSA is shown in Fig. 3. The third n-bit operand Z is entered on the C_i inputs of n binary full adders. The C_{i+1} outputs form a second output word $C = (C_n \cdots C_1)$ and the sum of the three input words X, Y, Z is represented by two output words C and $S = (S_{n-1} \cdots S_0)$. The time required to form C and S is equal to the time required by one binary full adder. The final sum, which is the sum of C and S, is then obtained in a two-operand adder, which may employ any of the speed-up techniques discussed above.

The summation of more than three operands uses CSAs in a similar manner to reduce the sum to two words. Fig. 4 illustrates the CSA configuration for eight operands P, Q, U, V, W, X, Y, Z. The abbreviated notation of Fig. 3(b) is employed. The time required to form the words $C6$ and $S6$ (representing the sum of the eight input operands) is equal to four full-adder operation times, regardless of the length of the operands.

Carry-save adders are frequently employed to implement fast multiplication by means of multiple-operand summation. The technique of *pipelining* (*q.v.*) may be employed to further improve the effective speed of CSA utilization.

REFERENCE

1965. Garner, H. L. "Number Systems and Arithmetic," in Alt, F. and Rubinoff, M. (Eds.), *Advances in Computers* **6**: 131-194. New York: Academic Press.

A. AVIŽIENIS

ADDRESS, INDIRECT.

see INDIRECT ADDRESS.

ADDRESSING

For articles on related subjects *see* ADDRESSLESS INSTRUCTION; BASE REGISTER; COMPUTERS, MULTIPLE ADDRESS; GENERAL REGISTER; INDEX REGISTER; INDIRECT ADDRESS; MACHINE INSTRUCTION SET; STORAGE ALLOCATION; and STORAGE ORGANIZATION.

BASIC TERMINOLOGY AND HARDWARE CONCEPTS

A typical computer instruction must indicate not only the operation to be performed but also the location of one or more operands, the location where the result of the computation is to be deposited, and, sometimes, the location where the next instruction is to be found. Of course, in certain kinds of instructions such as those involved in decision making, there may be no computational operands but only a determination of the next instruction to be executed. Normally, however, all parts of the instruction are either explicitly or implicitly given. We will first consider the hardware techniques by which an address (or location) in the computer may be specified. In what follows, we shall consider primarily storage in which each location has associated with it a sequentially assigned address. An alternative method of determining a desired storage location will be considered briefly in the later section "Content-Addressable Storage."

Historically and presently, computer hardware allows addresses to be specified in a variety of ways. The most straightforward approach would be to put the entire address directly into the instruction, representing a specific location of a word or part of a word in storage. Thus, on the IBM 650, an early decimal computer, the 2-digit operation code, and the two 4-digit addresses, representing the location of the data and the location of the next instruction, respectively, were represented in the instruction itself. (It should be noted that, on modern computers, except for the case of decision-making instructions, the address of the next instruction is virtually always taken implicitly to be the location after that of the instruction being executed.) The operation code in the 650 (as on modern computers) implied the location of one of the operands and the location of the result.

Op Code	Data Address	Next Inst. Address
2 digit	4 digit	4 digit

For example, the operation code AU (add to upper) implied that the upper half of the accumulator register was one of the operands, along with the explicitly named operand, and the result was to remain in the upper half of the accumulator.

As the amount of storage increases, however, and the number of digits (either binary or decimal) needed to represent an address becomes large relative to the size of the instruction, it becomes clear that it is no longer feasible to represent an entire address each time it occurs in an instruction. This is especially true when the address part of an instruction must be able to accommodate the largest possible storage that might be attached to a particular model of computer, even though an individual installation might only have a small part of that storage. In such cases the addresses actually occurring would use only a small portion of that part of the instruction set aside for addresses. The remaining portion must always contain zeros, representing a waste of a valuable resource.

Several hardware devices have been and are employed to obtain, from one of a small number of larger registers, most of the information needed to specify an address, with the instruction itself containing only the information needed to complete the address. A number of these methods were employed in the Control Data Corp. (CDC) 160 and 160A computers, early small machines that started out with 4,096 12-bit words of storage. In the CDC 160, which dates back to 1959, six bits were used for the operation code, while the other six bits (with only 64 possible values) were used in the determination of an address. By choosing an appropriate operation code, the address would be interpreted to be in one of five modes: direct address (d); indirect address (i); relative address forward (f), and backward (b); and no address (n).

The direct addressing mode (d-mode) corresponds to the IBM 650 situation discussed above in that the address referred to a 12-bit operand in one of the first 64 words of storage.

Relative addressing provided for operand addresses and jump addresses that were near the storage location containing the current instruction. In relative addressing forward (f), the six-bit address portion was added to the current contents of the program control register P. (This register held the full 12-bit address of the current instruction.) The new value was then used for obtaining the operand, or used to jump to one of the 63 addresses forward from the address holding the instruction that was being executed. For relative addressing backward (b), the operand or jump address was obtained by subtracting the six-bit address from the current contents of P.

In the no-address mode (n), which is usually now referred to as the "immediate" mode, the six-bit address part was not treated as an address, but as a constant to be used in the actual computation. Indirect addressing is considered below in a more general context.

In the CDC 160A, seven banks of 4,096 words each were added to the storage, thus complicating the specification of an address. The modes of addressing already available were retained, but several three-bit registers were added to contain the number of the bank (0–7) in which a designated address would be found, and different operations referred to different bank registers. Additional operations were provided so that the programmer could set the values of these registers as necessary. This later machine also provided for two-word instructions, in which the second word might be a 12-bit immediate operand as well.

Indirect Addressing. One way to address a memory larger than the address part of an instruction allows is to have the instruction address point to another address that stores the operand address. This facility, called *indirect addressing*, was available on the CDC 160 and is available on most contemporary computers. Fig. 1

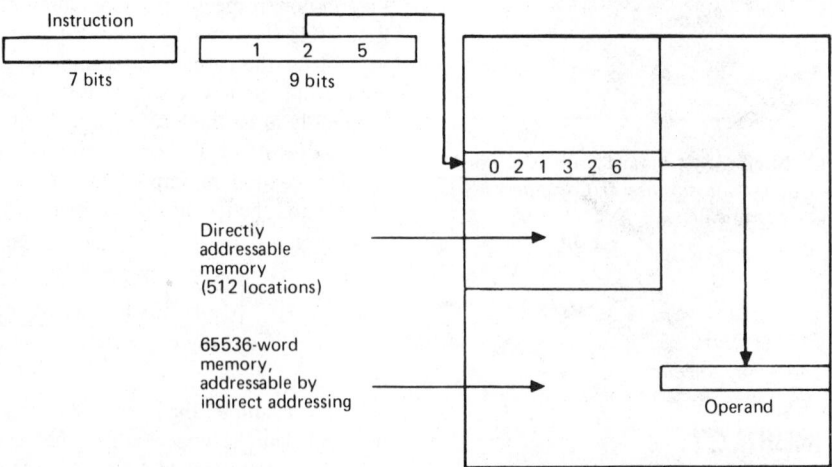

Fig. 1. Extension of addressing through indirect addressing.

illustrates this situation on a hypothetical 16-bit computer with a 7-bit instruction field and a 9-bit address field that permits the direct addressing of only 512 ($= 2^9$) memory locations.

Indirect addressing can be used to address a memory of up to 65,536 words. In the example in Fig. 1, the program has placed the operand address 021326 (where we express addresses in octal for convenience) at a specific address (125) in the first 512 words of memory. If the instruction is, for example, an "add indirect" instruction, the address 125 is interpreted as an indirect address or pointer to the actual operand at location 021326. The address stored at 125 (namely, 021326) becomes the *effective address*.

Some systems allow multilevel indirect addressing. Thus, the number stored at 021326 may have a bit set that indicates that it, itself, is an indirect address that points to another location which contains the operand address. Indirect addressing may be combined in various ways with the use of index registers to produce complex addressing chains.

Index Registers. The concept of an index register, sometimes called a "tally register" or "base register" (see below), grew out of the B-line or B-register introduced on some of the earliest computers developed in England at the University of Manchester. This represented a major advance in computer design. Index registers are hardware registers that can be set, incremented, tested, etc., by machine instructions. Each instruction contains an indication as to whether its address is to be added to (or subtracted from) the contents of a designated index register to form the effective address. One of the main purposes, as suggested by the name, was to allow the effective address to be used as an index into a set of contiguous storage registers, commonly referred to as a "vector." Without changing the part of the address which was in the instruction itself, one could refer to one after another of the contiguous registers, merely by changing the contents of the index register successively. This replaced the more time- and space-consuming sequence of instructions which would normally put an instruction containing an address into an arithmetic register, modify it by ordinary addition, and then store it back to replace its former value. (This modified instruction was then executed, and it would refer to a different storage location.)

The use of index registers eliminated the need for modification of the instruction itself by allowing the index register to be modified by special instructions added to the computer for that purpose. With the advent of newer systems in which more than one task may be executing the same instructions at the same time, it has become very important that instructions not be modified during execution, since the modification by one task might be inappropriate for another task executing the same set of instructions.

General Registers. The use of variable-length instructions has also become much more widespread in recent years. The IBM System/360 or 370, for example, uses instructions that may take one, two, or three half-words for their representation. In the System/360 or 370, 16 *general registers* are provided, each capable of acting as an arithmetic register, a base register for relative addressing, or as an index register. (The fact that one cannot tell by looking at one of these registers whether its contents represents an ordinary number or an address has sometimes led to other problems, but this degree of flexibility is very useful.) An instruction might refer only to one or two of these registers, in which case only four bits would be needed in the instruction for each one, and it could fit in a half-word (16 bits).

A full-word instruction could accommodate one reference to a general register (4 bits) and a reference to a storage address. The latter could be a combination of a base register (4 bits), an index register designation (4 bits), and a 12-bit displacement which could be used as a local offset from the contents of the base register. Fig. 2 illustrates the determination of an effective address from a System/360 or 370 instruction.

Relocation Registers. Many computers have one or more hardware relocation registers, which aid in the implementation and running of multiprogramming systems. An example is the CDC Cyber series. A number of different programs may be in the computer memory, each occupying a contiguous area. Thus, program A might occupy the area from 40,000 to 67,777, but this program (as well as all other programs in memory) is written and loaded into memory as if the area it occupies actually has the addresses 0 to 27,777. When program A is given control, the address 40,000 is stored in the hardware relocation register, and this constant is automatically added to all memory reference addresses while program A is running. The program could have been loaded anywhere else in memory, and can be loaded into different areas at different times. It will always produce the correct memory addresses, since all addressing is automatically made relative to the starting address of the area into which the program has been loaded.

In computers of this type, another hardware register will contain the *field length* or program size. Any attempt to reference beyond the area occupied by the program will be trapped, and an error condition will be signaled.

In a machine with two relocation registers, like the Univac 1108, a program may consist of two segments: for example, a program segment and a data segment, which can be placed independently anywhere in memory. The starting addresses of each of the two segments are placed

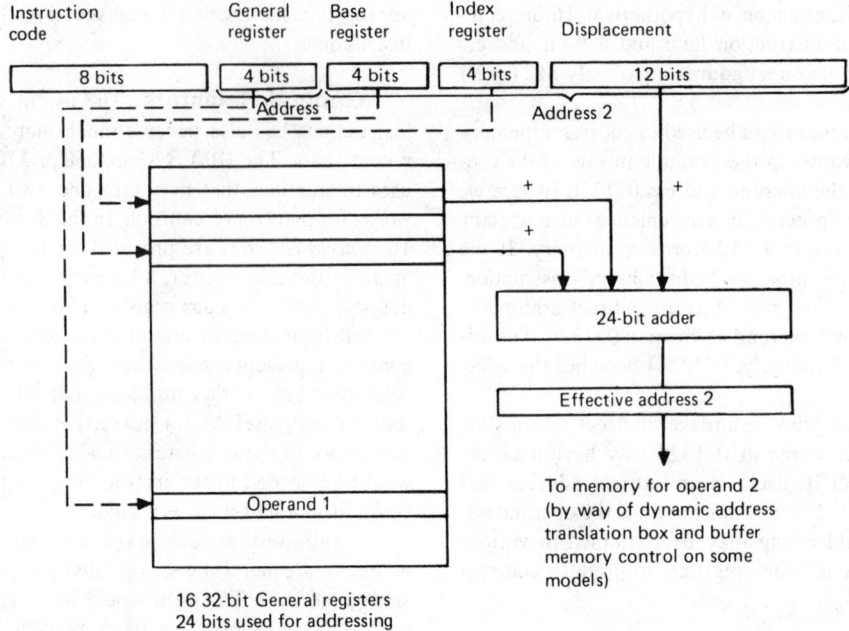

Fig. 2. Effective address calculation on IBM 360 and 370.

in the two relocation registers, and every effective address has an associated bit that specifies which relocation register is to be added.

A relocation register is quite different in nature from an index register or a register used as a base for relative addressing. The relocation register is a special hardware register whose contents can be accessed and changed only through the use of privileged instructions under control of the operating system.

Content-Addressable Storage. Content-addressable or associative memories are quite different in concept from the more conventionally addressed memories described above. In a content-addressable memory the data item itself contains a key, usually in a specified field. This key is, in effect, the address of the item. The key may be the whole data item itself. The desired data item is located by means of an examination of all relevant keys. This could be done by software in a computer system with conventional memory addressing, but it would be quite slow.

In an associative or content-addressable memory, comparison circuits are used to provide a hardware-assisted and presumably very fast search through all data items to find the one that matches the key. Small memories of this type have been used to speed up address translation in virtual memory systems. Larger systems in

which all addressing is associative have been proposed and some experimental models have been built.

The use of content-addressable memory was very expensive in terms of earlier technologies, but may prove practical with modern large-scale integration (LSI) technology. There are a number of important application areas in which associative memories would be very useful. The reader is referred to Hanlon (1966) for more information in this area.

B. A. GALLER AND S. ROSEN

SOFTWARE ASPECTS

Corresponding to each hardware aspect of addressing there must be one or more techniques by which the programmer specifies addresses in the program.

Absolute Addressing. In the earliest and most elementary programming systems a programmer would assign instructions and data to locations in memory, and instructions would refer to absolute locations in memory. Thus, using a decimal computer for convenience, a programmer might write and, as a result of the eventual loading process, the instruction ADD 3256 would appear in location 267. It was the responsibility of the programmer to make sure that the appropriate data word was in location 3256 at the time the program was to be run. These are absolute addresses in that 267 always represents the same physical location in memory and 3256 similarly represents a specific physical location.

Relative Addressing. Some of the first advances in programming involved permitting the programmer to write programs or parts of programs without having to be aware of the absolute physical locations in which the instructions and data were to be stored. One of the early approaches to this goal was by way of regional or relative programming. A programmer, or several programmers, might decide that the program would be divided into a number of regions, A, B, C, D, etc. Addresses would then be relative to the start of a region. A programmer might write

        A5   ADD   B15

to specify that an instruction located in the fifth location in region A is to add (to the accumulator) the data located in the fifteenth location in region B. A translator and loader would eventually take all regional addresses and convert them into absolute addresses.

There are a number of important advantages to this procedure. The programmer does not have to make arbitrary decisions about how large the regions are going to be. Separate sections of the program can be written independently, and unexpected or undesirable interactions can be avoided.

Symbolic Addressing. It was a relatively short step from regional addressing to free symbolic addressing. In the typical assembly system the programmer may write

        INCR   ADD   ALPHA

and leave it up to an assembler to decide where the instruction INCR is to be placed. Somewhere else in the program he/she would have a data item named ALPHA.

Indirect Addressing. In a computer that allows indirect addressing, the programmer typically indicates an indirect address by adding a character, such as *, to the absolute or symbolic address. Thus,

        INCR   ADD   ALPHA*

would indicate that the effective address is not ALPHA but is in the location specified by ALPHA.

Indexing. If an index register is to be used in calculating an effective address, this is normally specified following the instruction address. For example,

        ADD   A,4

indicates that the contents of index register 4 is to be added (subtracted on some computers) to A to determine the effective address. Indexing can be combined with indirect addressing so that

        ADD   A*,4

would specify the effective address as the sum of the contents of location A and index register 4.

Higher-Level Languages. The development of higher-level programming languages has relieved the programmer of the responsibility for many aspects of memory management. However, that responsibility must reside somewhere: Either the programmer or the language processor and operating system must take on the responsibility for allocating space for instructions and data and for producing the programs that make appropriate use of the addressing structure of the computer. The software features of addressing discussed in this article are therefore mainly of interest to the assembly language programmer. The programmer who writes in a higher-level language such as Fortran or Cobol usually does not have to be aware of the details of memory addressing in the computer on which a program will run, but may be sure that the Fortran or Cobol compiler is very much aware of these details, and usually expends a great deal of effort to take advantage of the memory-addressing hardware features provided on the computer.

S. ROSEN

VIRTUAL MEMORY

Overlays. Many programs are too long to fit into the space in main memory that can be allocated to them at run time. In a uniprogramming system this will be true when the amount of space required by the program is greater than the total memory available to problem programs. In a multiprogramming system it may be true because the amount of space that is needed is more than the operating system is willing to allocate to this particular program. In either case, it becomes necessary to break the program up into sections, segments, or overlays so that the entire program need not be in main memory at the same time. The term *folding* has sometimes been used for this process.

In many systems the programmer has the responsibility for breaking the program into overlays and for providing the loading instruction that bring necessary overlays into main memory as they are needed. Many software systems provide aids to overlay planning. The user can name the overlays so that all symbolic addresses in an overlay will be automatically tagged with a special identifier that indicates which overlay they belong to.

A loader or linkage editor creates an object program organized as a set of overlays and a root segment containing information about the overlay structure. The root segment is loaded into main memory along with the segments needed to get the program started. Any reference to a symbolic address in a segment that is not in main memory causes a call on the supervisor to load the required segment, overlaying other segments if necessary.

There have been a number of efforts to produce software systems that provide automatic folding of programs. In such systems a programmer would write a program as if there were enough main memory to contain the whole program, and the software system would organize the program into overlays to fit the actual amount of storage that would be available. Efforts to produce software systems of this type date back to the earliest computers, but none has been particularly successful.

Most workers in the field feel that hardware assistance of some kind is necessary. Such hardware assistance is provided in the so-called virtual memory systems that first made their appearance around 1959 and which became increasingly popular in the 1970s.

The Atlas System. The Atlas computer was probably the first virtual memory system. Its designers called it a single-level storage system. The idea was that a programmer would program as if all available memory were on a single level and directly addressable, whereas in fact memory was on two levels. In the Atlas the two levels were drum and core.

A program for the Atlas could be written as if it were to run in a homogeneous memory consisting of 2^{20} = 1,048,576 words. Memory was organized into *pages* of 2^9 = 512 words each. The physical core memory might consist only of 32 or 64 such pages. However, the "address space" (i.e., the addresses that a user could address) consisted of 2^{11} = 2,048 such pages. Thus, an address in the Atlas consisted of an 11-bit page number and a 9-bit number indicating the location within the page.

A hardware page-address register is associated with each physical page (or *page frame*, as it is sometimes called). A typical running program might consist of 50 pages, of which 20 pages at a particular time would be located in core memory and the other 30 located on the drum.

Each page of the program represents a set of 512 consecutive addresses with the same page number (i.e., the same 11 leftmost bits). The program page number is kept in the page address register of the physical page that is occupied by that program page. Thus, any program (or logical) page may occupy any physical page, and it may occupy different physical pages at different times during the running of the program.

Assume now (see Fig. 3) that the next instruction to be executed refers to an operand whose address (in octal) is 0231443. This is a reference to location 443 in page 231. Note that core memory of the machine contains nowhere near 231 pages, and there are only 50 pages in the program being executed. The programmer does not have to confine the program to the first 50 pages or to any contiguous block of 50 pages. He or she can use any areas in virtual memory that are convenient. Thus, the programmer does not have to know beforehand how long the code areas and data areas are going to be. The program can be broken-up into segments and placed far enough apart in virtual memory so their memory allocations will not overlap. There is no point at all to scattering a program at random over a large virtual memory; in fact, such programs will usually perform very inefficiently. One wants a very large virtual memory in order to be able to assign areas, whose ultimate size is not necessarily known in advance, to program and data modules that do not overlap and that form the structural units of a program. The segmented, two-dimensional virtual memories discussed below were introduced to make this type of modular programming more automatic and more convenient.

The page address registers form an associative or content-addressable memory. They are subject to a very rapid hardware scan to determine if one of them is page 231. If it is (say, if page 231 is in physical page 12, as in Fig. 3), then the operand sought is in physical location 12443, and the operand is fetched from that location. If, on the other hand, page 231 of this program is not in core memory, it must be fetched from the drum. An interrupt occurs, and the operating system initiates a transfer of that page from drum into core. Assume that physical page 16 is available. The supervisor will cause program page 231 to be loaded into physical page 16, and will place the number 231 in the corresponding page address register. It then returns control to the program, which tries again to access an operand in virtual location 231443. This time it finds logical page 231 in physical page 16 and translates the address 231443 to 16443.

Segments and Pages. The Atlas system is an example of a one-dimensional or single segment virtual memory system. The programmer or the language pro-

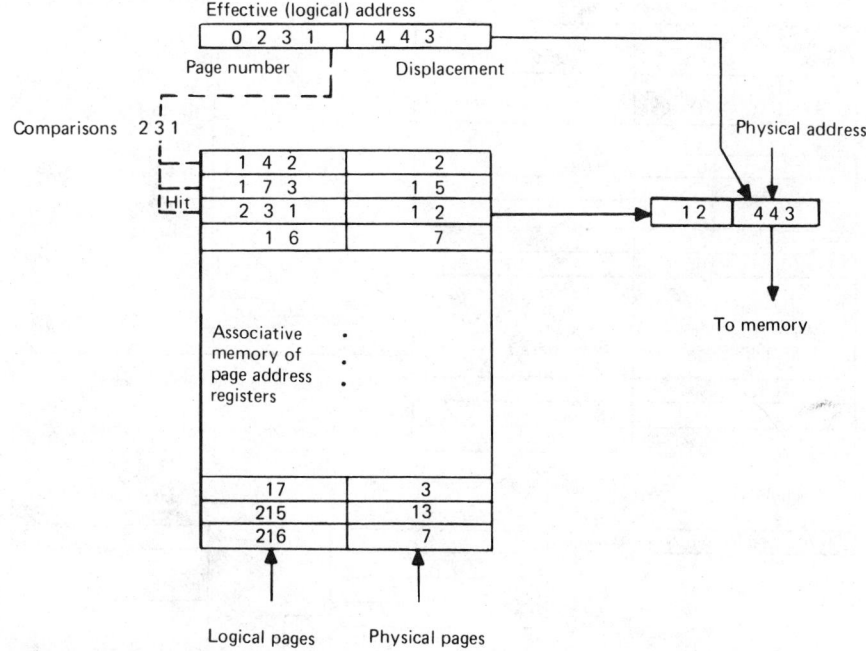

Fig. 3. Address translation on the Atlas computer.

cessor must provide symbolic or absolute addresses in the one-dimensional virtual memory. Many of the classical storage allocation problems remain, although they are helped considerably by the fact that the virtual memory is much larger than the actual central memory of the computer on which the program is run.

From the point of view of program organization there are a number of advantages to a two-dimensional organization of virtual memory. Although two-dimensional virtual memory systems usually are multiprogrammed systems, it is convenient to think of each program in the multiprogrammed environment as if it were running in its own virtual memory.

In such a system a program runs in a large virtual memory consisting of a number of segments. An address then consists of a segment name (or number) and a displacement relative to the beginning of the segment. This is somewhat analogous to the regional organization of programs in earlier computer generations and has some of the same advantages. The programmer or the language processor can assign programs and data to different segments without worrying about the relative position of the segments in the total addressing space. This is especially true if the segments are large enough so that possible segment overflow is not a problem. The segments themselves may be organized into pages.

A job (or process) is then represented in central memory by a segment table that provides a set of pointers to page tables corresponding to the active segments of the process. Each active segment will usually have one or more pages in memory. The actual address space or virtual memory is very large, and in most practical situations it consists mostly of unused space. Of the part of virtual memory that is actually used by a program, only a relatively few pages will be in central memory; the rest will reside on a paging drum (or disk) or in a backup mass storage system (usually disk storage). The segment may serve as a unit of sharing among programs. The same segment (i.e., a pointer to the same page table) may appear in several segment tables that correspond to several jobs that are simultaneously active. The possibility of sharing segments was one of the strong motivations for the development of the segmented virtual memory systems.

The first and perhaps the only complete implementation of this type of virtual memory system was attempted in the Multics system developed at M.I.T. on the General Electric (now Honeywell) 645 computer and its successors. The actual addressing and address translation scheme used is too complicated to be discussed here. The reader is referred to Organick (1972).

IBM Virtual Memory Systems. The IBM 360/67 introduced in 1965, and later the IBM 370 series introduced in 1972, helped to popularize some of the concepts of virtual memory. In the standard 370 systems, the virtual memory associated with a process consists of 16

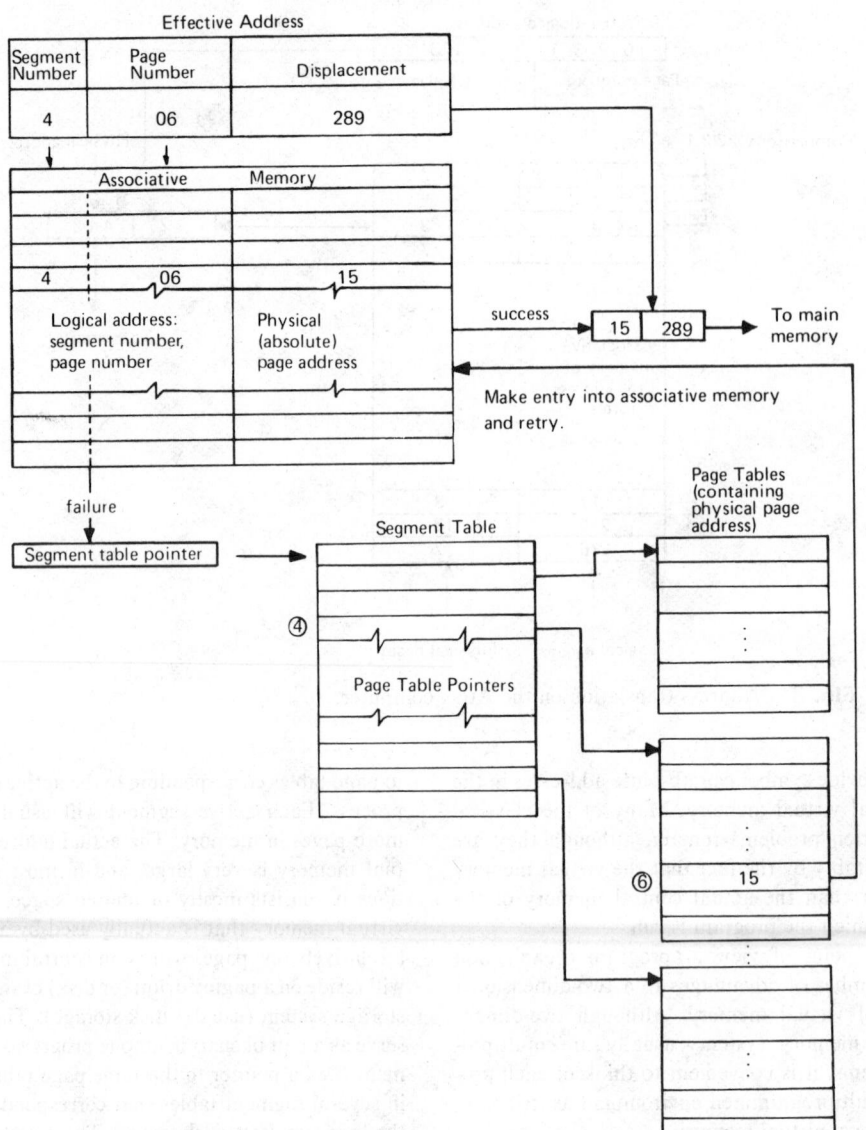

Fig. 4. Address translation of a virtual memory machine (IBM 370).

segments, and a segment consists of 256 pages, each of which has 4096 bytes. The relatively small size of the virtual memory loses some of the advantages associated with virtual memory systems, but it probably has the advantage of making memory addressing more manageable. In the standard 370, the 24-bit address field* contains a 4-

bit segment number, an 8-bit page number, and a 12-bit byte address within the page.

segment   page   displacement
  no.   no.

The operating system maintains a 16-(or 32-) word segment table for each process that contains the pointers to the page table for each segment. The page table con-

---

*An optional hardware modification on the 360/67 provided for the use of a 32-bit address field that made it possible to use a 12-bit segment system and thus address 4096 segments. Several software systems, including TSS (Time Shared System) 360, took advantage of this extended addressing capability.

tains the physical address of each page that is present in main memory. These tables are automatically searched when a memory reference is made. Thus, if page 4 of segment 6 is in main memory starting at physical byte location 15000 (hexadecimal), a reference to address location 406289 would cause the dynamic address translation hardware to search the segment table for segment 4 and retrieve the address of the page table for segment 4. It would search the page table for page 6 and retrieve absolute address 15. It would thus translate the segment/page address 406 into the physical address 15. (Actually 15000, but the three trailing zeros are understood.) The absolute address reference is thus 15289, and the operand is retrieved from that address.

Systems of this type usually have a small associative memory in which the most recent translations are stored (Fig. 4). Thus, the first reference to page 6 of segment 4 would proceed as discussed above, but the fact that 406 translates into 15 would be retained in the small associative memory. Then, so long as page 6 of segment 4 is one of the most recently referenced pages, its translation will be in the associative registers and the relatively slow address translation process does not have to be repeated.

Burroughs Computers. In the Burroughs B5000 series (*q.v.*) and its successors, a job is represented in memory by a program reference table (PRT). Along with some data and other information, the PRT contains "descriptors," which are pointers to data segments and to program segments. A descriptor for a data segment (an array) contains the address of the beginning of the array and the length of the array. Any reference to the array is automatically checked, and an interrupt occurs if it is attempting to reference beyond the array bounds.

In these systems, one bit of each data word is reserved as a marker bit that marks the word as a datum or as a descriptor. This has been generalized on some, *tagged memory* systems by allocating several bits of each data word to provide information about the data type and format along with each individual word or item of data.

The Burroughs systems are virtual memory systems based on the use of relatively small segments that are not broken into pages. A segment is moved as a unit between central memory and backing drum or disk storage. The operating system is a multiprograming system. Each active job has some of its segments in core memory and the rest on the drum. Each segment descriptor in the program reference table has a presence bit, which indicates whether or not that segment is present in central memory. Any attempt to refer to a segment that is not in central memory causes an interrupt to the supervisor, requesting that that segment be loaded. The supervisor can load the segment into any available contiguous area of memory

that is large enough to hold it. If necessary, it can move out other segments. When the segment has been loaded, its new starting address in central memory is placed in its descriptor, and the program that referred to the segment can be restarted.

S. Rosen

References

1966. Hanlon, A. G. "Content-Addressible and Associative Memory Systems—A Survey," *IEEE Transactions on Electronic Computers,* August.
1971. Bell, C. G. and A. Newell. *Computer Structures: Readings and Examples.* New York: McGraw-Hill.
1972. Organick, Elliott I. *The Multics Systems—An Examination of Its Structure.* Cambridge: M.I.T. Press.

ADDRESSLESS INSTRUCTIONS

For articles on related subjects *see* Addressing; Burroughs B5000 Series; Machine Instruction Set; and Stack.

Instructions in a von Neumann machine (*q.v.*) operate on information held in addressable memory. The location of information is indicated by address fields in the instruction. There have been computers using up to four in a single instruction. Because the number of addresses per instruction is a fairly uniform property of most computers, it is usual to name a machine for the number of such fields (e.g., a two-address computer). An *addressless,* or *zero-address, machine* operates on its operands in CPU registers, thereby requiring no memory addresses in its instructions. Transactions with memory are restricted to transfers to and from the registers. Memory addresses are either moved literally from the instruction stream into registers (where they are available to the *load* and *store* operations) or the load and store operations are in fact the only single-address instructions.

Addressless machines commonly have a stack for operands. Instructions operate on the top of the stack and return results there.

For example, suppose one wanted to compute $16 \times 3 \div (4 + 8)$. The corresponding sequence of actions is Load 16, Load 3, Multiply, Load 4, Load 8, Add, Divide, leaving the result, 4, on the stack. The sequence of actions and stack configurations is as shown in Fig. 1.

Addressless instructions have two principal advantages. First, the stack provides an elegant mechanism for the computation of high-level language expressions. Second, the absence of addresses allows the instructions to

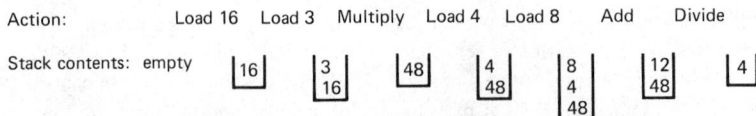

Fig. 1. An example of addressless instructions.

be encoded so that short encodings correspond to frequently used operations. This results in a high density (i.e., low number of bits/instruction) of code. The principal disadvantage is in preventing optimizations based on use of multiple registers to avoid repeated fetches of data from memory.

REFERENCES

1975. McKeeman, W. M. "Stack Computers," in Stone, H. S. (Ed.), *Introduction to Computer Architecture.* Chicago: Science Research Associates.

W. M. Mc KEEMAN

ADDRESS MODIFICATION

For article on related subject *see* ADDRESSING; INDEX REGISTER; ITERATION; LOOP; PURE PROCEDURE; and REENTRANT PROGRAM.

The idea that programs are data and can be stored just as data is stored in an electronic memory device was one of the most important ideas in the development of the stored program computer. When programs are stored as data, it is possible to bring instructions into the arithmetic unit of the computer and perform all arithmetic and logical operations of the computer on the instructions themselves.

This was of utmost importance on many of the early computers. A great deal of the power of the computer comes from its ability to execute loops in which the same program segment is applied to an array or sequence of data elements. In most of the early stored program computers, the only way of doing this was by successively changing the addresses of the instructions in the loop.

Fig. 1 is a program that adds 100 numbers stored in locations 2001 to 2100. The program itself is in locations 242 through 259 and the answer is placed in 241. This program is typical of the execution of loops through address modification on many early computers.

Even for this very simple calculation, the main loop requires the execution of nine instructions in order to add just one more number to the sum.

The use of index registers has eliminated much of

241		(Location of ultimate result)
242	FETCH 259	Initialize sum to zero (242 begins program)
243	STORE 241	
244	FETCH 256	Initialize location 250
245	STORE 250	
246	FETCH 250	Modify address in 250 to add next number
247	ADD 257	
248	STORE 250	
249	FETCH 241	Do the addition (Instruction in location 250 is the one modified; the
250	[ADD 2000 + n]	contents of this location before execution of the program are
251	STORE 241	irrelevant. It is initialized by the instruction in location 245.)
252	FETCH 250	Check if all numbers have been added
253	SUBTRACT 258	
254	BRANCH ON NEG 246	
255	JUMP OUT	
256	ADD 2000	Constants used by the program.
257	000 000 001	Note: some of the constants look
258	ADD 2100	like instructions.
259	000 000 000	

Main Loop (locations 246–254)

Fig. 1. Use of address modification in a simple program on an early computer.

this inefficiency, but address and instruction modification is still used in some programming situations.

Many recent computing systems use *reentrant code* for all or some of the programs executed. Reentrant code cannot be modified during the execution of a program, and, therefore, explicit address modification cannot be used in conjunction with it.

S. ROSEN

ADMINISTRATIVE APPLICATIONS

For articles on related subjects *see* APPLICATIONS, COMPUTER; BANKING APPLICATIONS; COMPUTER NETWORKS; COMPUTER SYSTEMS; CREDIT SYSTEM APPLICATIONS; DATA COMMUNICATION NETWORKS; DATA PROCESSING; MANAGEMENT INFORMATION SYSTEMS; OFFICE AUTOMATION; POINT-OF-SALE TERMINAL; PROCESSING MODES; SCIENTIFIC APPLICATIONS; SIMULATION; and TRANSACTION-BASED SYSTEMS.

The initial categories of computer applications in the very early years of electronic computing were simply "scientific" and "business." The essence of the distinction was that scientific applications involved substantial arithmetic operations on rather small volumes of data, whereas business applications involved modest arithmetic operations on substantial amounts of data. Internal speed was the crucial variable in scientific computing whereas input and output speed and versatility were the crucial variables in business data processing. Matrix inversion was "typical" of scientific applications, and insurance company premium transactions processing was "typical" of business applications. With the passage of time and with the pervasive evolution of computer applications, the original two-fold taxonomy no longer sufficed.

In the first place, government transactions processing grew no less rapidly than did business transactions processing as agencies like the Treasury Department and the Social Security Administration established pioneering large-scale government administrative applications that were strikingly similar to business applications. This led to the recognition that the term "administrative" applications was a more descriptive term than "business" applications. Both business and government *administered,* while only business conducted *business* in the usual commercial meaning of the word. In the second place, this simple taxonomy fell to the wayside with the establishment of other significant varieties of computer applications such as process control, information retrieval, voice and message switching, and advanced technical applications such as computer-aided design and computer-aided instruction.

Nowadays, administrative applications are widely considered to be those that involve the use of computers for processing information in support of the operational, logistical, and functional activities performed by all organizations—business and government, profit and not-for-profit. Some authorities categorize "management information systems" as similar to (but organizationally at a higher level than) administrative applications; other authorities feel that the two groupings of systems are quite distinct, the one serving day-to-day operations, the other serving decision support requirements; still other authorities argue that there is no real distinction between the two terms. The view taken here is that, as administrative applications become less transaction-oriented and less detailed, and more summary in nature, then such applications increasingly produce "management information."

Administrative applications may be classified from a number of vantage points. One major classification approach is by type of organization using computers—banking, insurance, government, manufacturing, mining, retail, wholesale, and other industry groups. Another major classification schema is by generic functional uses—accounting, budgeting, payroll, inventory, and numerous other industry-wide functional uses. Other classification bases are also useful, each for its purpose.

This article describes the evolution of administrative applications over the past 30 years, the uses of computers in three very different kinds of administrative organization, the manifold benefits of these uses that explain their existence, and specific applications that have been and are being computerized in each of the four major areas of administrative operations. Whereas the high cost of early computers limited their installation to large organizations, the extension of the minicomputer's capability—beyond its previously scientific or process control orientation—is making it possible for thousands of small organizations to computerize their operations. Finally, the References at the end of the article list sources of additional information about such systems.

Evolution of Administrative and Business Applications. In order to establish a frame of reference for reviewing specific systems, this section outlines briefly how such systems have evolved, and why, over the past 30 years.

Early Systems. When the first computers were installed in commercial and industrial organizations in the 1950s, they were most often used to automate office functions such as payroll, invoicing, and inventory accounting.

This was a logical step in the evolution of these activities, for several reasons:

1. These activities were well understood and reasonably well documented as a result of existing accounting and auditing requirements, both of which made computerization easy.
2. The precomputer step-by-step method of carrying out these activities suited the capabilities of early computers which could only process information serially from card files or magnetic tape. Moreover, in many cases these activities were already being processed on punched card equipment, making them easy to convert to a computer.
3. Computerization of these functions was readily justified by clerical staff reduction and by savings brought about by replacing more expensive punched card equipment.

These early computer systems processed data in batches; i.e., they executed one program at a time and handled transactions one by one after they had been sorted into numerical sequence. In general, they were simply more efficient electronic outgrowths of the punched card systems that were initially installed in the early 1930s. In spite of their greater speed and capability, they still retained many limitations of their predecessors: They required substantial manual intervention and their impact was confined to narrow functional areas of business. The applications they processed were similarly limited in scope.

Advances in Systems. Many of the administrative and business applications that are commonly processed on computers today differ greatly from the earlier accounting-oriented applications. Notably, they are *broader in scope:* Whereas early applications dealt with a single activity, current systems frequently consist of several integrated subsystems covering a broad segment of the business.

They are *more responsive:* Early systems performed simple calculations, printed out 100% of the transactions they processed, and were run usually at fixed intervals (weekly or monthly). Today's systems perform complex calculations, screen results so that only those that exceed a range of acceptable performance are printed out or displayed, and do so daily or even hourly, with the result that important information is made available in time for corrective action to be taken.

They *serve many more users:* Initially, an employee who wanted to run a computer program did so at a computer center, or sent the job to the center to be processed. Now, through easy-to-use terminals, computers can be accessed by large numbers of users who may be close by or thousands of miles away.

They *offer a variety of new benefits:* Traditionally, reduction of clerical costs was the primary benefit anticipated from automation of administrative or business functions. Today, computerized applications have the potential to provide information that can result in a wide range of benefits, from significantly improved customer service to tighter managerial control over major segments of the organization.

Some of the commercial systems in use today illustrate these advances. For example, by means of a Touch-Tone telephone or a small remote terminal, an airline reservation clerk can call upon a central computer to check a customer's credit rating; the computer can respond in a matter of seconds as to whether the credit card is stolen or the account is delinquent. Similarly, the sales clerk in a local store can be connected to a computer by telephone and can be told by computer-produced voice response whether a product requested by a customer is available, where it is located, and when it will be shipped. In a third example, manufacturers can install computers for conversational order entry. Instead of writing or typing out all detailed specifications about a machine to be ordered, the terminal operator merely enters an order for a specific model of machine. The computer then asks a series of questions about the order, which the operator answers in turn. When the dialog is completed, the full specifications are recorded in the computer ready for matching with production and shipping schedules. Exhibit 1 illustrates the type of dialog that takes place between terminal operator and computer in conversational order entry.

Benefits of Computer Applications for Administrative Information Processing. The remarkable growth in administrative applications of electronic computers has been nourished by the rapid improvements in both efficiency and effectiveness of organizational administration functions that are based upon those applications. No less nourishing have been underlying advances in: (1) computer performance per dollar—in terms of speed of circuitry, capacity of storage, human engineering, and other variables; (2) operating systems software; (3) application development facilities, notably programming languages and aids; (4) purchasable ready-to-run application packages; (5) communications technology; (6) terminals, both for human and machine interconnection; (7) data processing capabilities furnished by outside specialists such as service bureaus and remote computing services; and (8) education of developers, users, and managers, thanks mainly to the universities, but also to industry and professional associations, and to private business education vendors.

EXAMPLE: CONVERSATIONAL ORDER ENTRY

QUESTION: COMPUTER GENERATED DISPLAY	RESPONSE BY TERMINAL OPERATOR

ORDER ENTRY   OE
ORDER STATUS INQUIRY OS
PAYMENT POSTING   PP
  (etc.)

                        OE

CUSTOMER NAME OR NUMBER

                        SF5190 (or) SMITH DATA PROCESSING

SMITH DATA PROCESSING CO
ATTEN P.J. ANTHONY
635 JACKSON ST
LOS ANGELES CA 96402

SHIP VIA   CF
          IS THIS CORRECT?

                        C (correct)

ENTER MACHINE NUMBER, QUANTITY

                        129, 1

SPECIFY (1 AND 2 REQUIRED, 3 AND 4 OPTIONAL)
    1. VOLTAGE (AC, 1-PHASE, 60 CYCLE)
        A LOCKING PLUG, 115V   #9880
        B LOCKING PLUG, 208V   #9884
        C NON-LOCKING PLUG, 115V #9881
        D NON-LOCKING PLUG, 208V #9885

    2. CHARACTER ARRANGEMENT A11

    3. ACOUSTIC COVER FOR CARD TRANSPORT
        (FIELD INSTALLABLE)   #9014

    4. CARD I/O ATTACHMENT   #9619

                        9882, A11, 9014

9882 INVALID FEATURE NUMBER, REENTER
CORRECT VOLTAGE AND PLUG

                        9880

FEATURE 9014 - FACTORY OR FIELD INSTALLED?

                        FACTORY

SPECIAL FEATURES
NOTE: MAXIMUM COMBINATIONS ARE INDICATED
       BY X IN VERTICAL COLUMNS

ACCUMULATOR	#1020	XXXX
ACCUMULATE PROGRAM LEVELS	#1025	XXXX
AUXILIARY STORAGE	#1201	X
CARD I/O ATTACHMENT	#7503	X
INTERPRET	#4601	X
FEED, VARIABLE LENGTH	#3950	X
PRODUCTION STATISTICS	#4802	XXXX
SELF CHECK NUMBER MOD 10	#7061	X XX

                        1020, 1025, 4802, 7061

RPQ'S? (special engineering)

                        NO

DELIVERY REQUESTED

                        MAY 29, 1974

ADDITIONAL REMARKS?

                        CALL MR. ANTHONY BEFORE DELIVERY
                        TO RESERVE FREIGHT ELEVATOR

MORE ADDITIONAL REMARKS?

                        NO

END OF ORDER ENTRY PROCEDURE?

                        YES

ORDER ENTRY   OE
ORDER STATUS INQUIRY OS
PAYMENT POSTING   PP
  (etc.)

Exhibit 1

No similarly pervasive phenomenon, not even printing, has occurred with the speed and spread of computer application. The reasons are compelling. The interacting phenomena of increasing capability and facility at decreasing cost per unit are at the heart of the positive economics of administrative use of computers. Both efficiency and effectiveness of users are enhanced.

The efficiency impacts of computers in administration are mainly visible as reductions in transactions processing costs reflecting reductions in clerical costs, inventory costs, and other current costs, as well as better utilization of capital resource inputs such as factory, refinery, and other industrial plants and equipment. Recent advances in office systems (*office automation (q.v.)* or the *electronic office*) are the newest form of efficiency gains of administrative application.

The efficiencies of computer applications are more widely known and appreciated perhaps mainly because of their immediately visible dollar impact. Of no less significance over the longer run, however, is the effectivenss of computers. Increases in effectiveness mainly occur as value *added* to the information outputs of the administrative systems that are supported by computers rather than as cost *reductions*.

There are six specific sources of increased effectiveness. First, greater speed—the essence of the external character of computer hardware—increases effectiveness in two ways: (1) faster processing of *throughput*, and (2) faster response to *ad hoc* inquiry. The second factor, which is of rising significance, is increased accuracy. Computer applications are not infallible, but nearly 30 years of experience has demonstrated the greater accuracy of computer techniques over their manual forebears. Whether greater accuracy can, in fact, be designed into the extremely comprehensive electronic processes of the future, such as a fully electronic funds transfer system (*q.v.*), remains to be seen. The record, despite various well known and frequently joked-about aberrations, is extremely favorable. Without high accuracy, administrative systems could never have succeeded.

The third form of greater effectiveness of administrative applications lies in the more complete coverage of information computers can accept, process, retain, and provide. Greater completeness of the information set, however, is a two-edged sword with which users must be careful. Excessively complete detail can inundate users, with mischievous effects. Modern terminal-oriented presentation of information offers an appropriate compromise between complete detail and the capacity of humans to cope with information flows.

The fourth form of effectiveness impact lies in the growing precision in selectivity of a database management system supported by facile inquiry capabilities. In a sense, the need for great selectivity is generated by the completeness potential of modern systems; but that is only part of the story. The selectivity of present-day systems would have been appreciated with that first large-scale administrative data set organized by the Bureau of the Census only 30 years ago. The fifth effectiveness lies in the frequency with which reports can be furnished. For some time now, reports have been available upon demand from many systems. Increased facility in on-demand reporting is a major driver of increased use of computers in administrative applications.

The sixth and final aspect of value-added effectiveness lies in administrative uses of the analytical powers of computers, upon the growing body of proven uses of management science, econometrics, and other advanced methodologies of information analysis. Some administrative analytical applications are valuable at the lowest physical level in organizations, as in the daily scheduling of refinery output with the significant help of linear program models. Others, more recent, are becoming valuable at the strategic management level in an increasing number of organizations.

Four Stages of Evolution. The evolution of administrative and business systems to their current status has followed the expanding hardware and software capabilities of the computer. Exhibit 2 describes four broad stages of computer development and the application characteristics that correspond to those stages. Briefly:

1. *Basic batch* is the least complex level of computer processing. At this level, application systems are normally made up of small programs that are run through the computer one by one and which can process transactions only from sequential files.
2. *Expanded batch* programs perform complex computations and produce reports that analyze performance, not just report it as in basic batch systems. Larger programs, further automation of manual functions, and a small capability for processing transactions that occur in random sequence are characteristics that distinguish expanded batch from basic batch systems.
3. *On-line inquiry* application systems result from adding to expanded batch systems the capability to access immediately, by terminal, any record that is stored in the disk files attached to the computer. Processing of transactions that are not in numerical sequence is also possible at this higher level of systems complexity.
4. *Distributed computing* systems consist of combinations of large central computers, data communications networks, and remote terminals that enable terminal operators located remotely from the central computer to carry out complete opera-

EVOLUTION OF ADMINISTRATIVE AND BUSINESS SYSTEMS

Application Characteristics	Least Complex ————————————————————————————————————→ Most Complex			
Category of hardware system	Basic Batch - electronic unit record plus magnetic tape	Expanded Batch - electronic unit record, magnetic tape, small-capacity disk storage	On-Line Inquiry - electronic unit record, larger disks, typewriter, and CRT terminals	Distributed Computing - large disks, remote terminals (mini-computers, CRTs), data communications devices
Cost to develop an application system	Less than $50,000	—— increasing to ——		$000,000's to millions
Time required for development	Several man months	—— increasing to ——		Several man years (2-5 plus)
Degree of integration with other application systems	Low - normally 1 department served	More than 1 department served	Several departments served	High - many departments served
Degree of difficulty of development and implementation	Simple - mostly internal to data processing department	Relatively simple - some technical problems	Relatively difficult - operational problems in implementation	Difficult - often large operational as well as technical problems
Criticality of computerized system to departmental operation	Low - manual backup always possible	Medium - manual backup usually possible	Medium - manual backup difficult	High - manual backup almost impossible
Organization level at which commitment needed for development and implementation success	Manager of department requesting the system	Manager of department requesting the system	Vice president	President, top managing executive
Type of benefit	Clerical savings	Primarily clerical savings, some improvement in management control	Improved customer service, improved management control	Cost reductions, improved service, improved management control
Magnitude of benefit	Small, but demonstrable and immediate	—— increasing to ——		Large, difficult to quantify in advance, gained over time
Amount of user participation required in systems development	Limited, generally not critical	Needed in design phases	Needed in all phases	Extensive, critical to project success
Amount of user participation required in systems operation	None	Limited to coding of input data	Moderate - for inquiry operation	Extensive, user runs the system from terminals
Response time of system to user request for information	Week(s)-days	Days	Minutes - seconds	Minutes - seconds
Historical time frame of first systems	Early 1950s	Mid-1950s	Late 1950s	Late 1960s

Exhibit 2

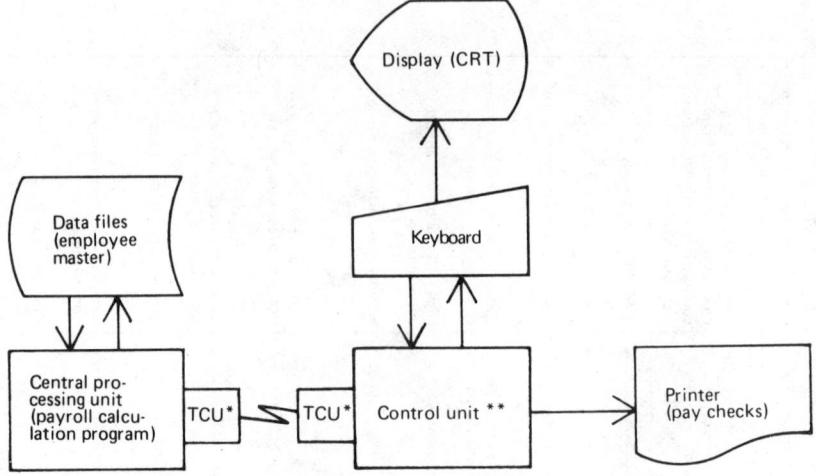

* — Transmission control unit.
** — Contains arithmetic, logic, and primary storage units. Auxiliary storage (e.g. disk unit)
would be attached to and controlled by this unit also.

CENTRAL (COMPUTER) SITE	REMOTE (TERMINAL) LOCATION
1. Receive data from remote location	1. Input payroll data (e.g. hours worked by job class) needed for central computer payroll calculation
2. Calculate payroll using programs and data files (e.g. employee master) located at central site	2. Control Unit edit of data, operator correction of invalid or incomplete data
3. Update payroll files	3. Transmit to central site computer
4. Transmit payroll data to remote location	4. Receive payroll data from central site computer, format and print pay checks

Exhibit 3

tions. For example, an employee's paycheck can be prepared while the operator is sitting at the terminal. Earlier, less sophisticated terminal systems would have required the operator to send the data (hours worked) to the central computer, where it would have been processed (in a batch mode) and the paycheck data later (hours or days) retransmitted to the remote terminal.

Distributed computer systems have the following characteristics.

- Processing is on-line, completed while the operator is at the terminal.
- They are hierarchical; at some point in the processing of a program, or under certain conditions, data is transmitted from the terminal to a central computer for processing that is not possible at the terminal.
- The remote location may, but need not, have either auxiliary storage or the capability to execute programs within the terminal.

Exhibit 3 illustrates a distributed computing system used in payroll processing. The mode of processing is on-line, with the terminal operator keying in the data required by the central site computer program, correcting errors caught by the terminal edit program, and transmitting the data to the central site computer. The central computer calculates the payroll and retransmits paycheck data to the remote terminal, where it is printed.

Exhibit 2 illustrates that as the computer's capabilities have progressed from basic batch processing to on-line inquiry and distributed computing, commercial applications have also advanced from relatively simple, low-cost, narrow-impact groups of programs to highly complex, expensive, and far-reaching systems.

The remainder of this article will discuss the four major types of administrative and business applications: customer service, manufacturing, accounting and finance, and payroll and personnel. To aid in reading the exhibit that accompanies each of these four sections, customer service will be reviewed in detail, while the remaining three categories will be discussed less extensively.

Customer Service Systems. Customer service systems relate to the interaction between an organization and its customers. Processing orders, keeping track of inventory available to meet customer demand, collecting accounts receivable, and analyzing sales transactions are representative of the functions that fall in the category of customer service.

Customer service is an area of vital concern in most industrial and commercial organizations both because of its great profit potential and because of the difficult management problems it poses (for example, how to provide a high level of service to customers without reducing profit margins). Increasingly, computerized customer service applications are helping managements resolve these problems and achieve better control over this area of operations. For example, customer service applications today can provide the information needed to answer important questions such as the following:

Is the amount of inventory on hand too much or too little?

Which products in the line are contributing to profitability?

Which customers are profit generators?

Are sales personnel merely selling as much business as they can, or are they selling profitable business?

Is the level of accounts receivable too high?

Are bad debt write-offs above industry norms? Are they increasing?

Although some of the earliest business computer applications were related to customer service, only very recently have computer capabilities advanced to the point where large-scale improvements in this area of business operations are possible. Today, many of the most sophisticated and expensive computer systems being installed in commercial and industrial organizations are in customer service. In addition, industry sources estimate that one-third of the computers installed throughout the world process customer service applications—another indication of their importance.

Exhibit 4 lists the applications that make up the customer service group and illustrates how sophistication and complexity increase as computer capabilities progress from basic batch to distributed computing.

Basic Batch. In most organizations, automation of customer service applications began at a relatively low level of complexity; i.e., in the form of basic batch systems. Despite their lack of sophistication, such systems were often able to produce important benefits.

The second column of Exhibit 4 describes the types of customer service applications typically executed in a basic batch mode. In this mode, the computer performs a number of calculating and record-keeping functions formerly performed manually. In order processing, for example, after the information about an order is entered into the computer (via key-punched cards or magnetic tapes or disks), the computer prepares shipping notices, warehousing packing lists, and later invoices showing items shipped and back ordered, price and discount amounts, and shipping, taxes, and other charges. After an order is processed, the same records that were used to prepare invoices can be sorted and rerun to generate weekly stock status reports showing beginning balance, amounts received, shipped, back ordered and on order, and balance on hand. The same records can be sorted again and processed to produce sales analysis reports listing sales volume by product, customer, and sales personnel; and finally, the records can be used to prepare aged trial balances and accounts receivable statements. Exhibit 5 illustrates examples of an aged statement and trial balance.

Despite their low level of complexity, basic batch customer service systems can be very successful. In many instances the introduction of such systems has permitted sizable reductions in clerical staffs. In almost all instances, organizations have benefited from faster processing and more accurate, up-to-date, and complete records about inventory levels, sales transactions, and accounts receivable status. With this information, managements have been better able to answer many of their basic questions about product movement, customer purchases, and sales force effectiveness.

Expanded Batch. The desires to perform more sophisticated analyses and to reduce further manual intervention in processing customer service functions were the forces that led many organizations to reprogram their basic batch systems into systems of greater complexity and capability. This second stage of customer service systems development is described in Exhibit 4 under the column headed Expanded Batch.

Many operations that were manual in the basic batch environment, such as credit checking, release of back orders, and handling of special billing instructions are automated in expanded batch customer service systems. Order entry, which was normally carried out by key-punching cards in the basic batch mode, is automated in numerous systems by the use of OMR (optical mark reading) and OCR (optical character recognition) order documents, which are filled out by the salesperson at the time the orders are taken and are then fed directly into the computer for processing. Rate and routing tables are frequently computerized, making calculation of freight charges and preparation of transportation documents possible. Computer printing of collection follow-up letters further reduces manual intervention.

CUSTOMER SERVICE SYSTEMS

Least Complex ──────────→ Most Complex

Application	Basic Batch	Expanded Batch	On-Line Inquiry	Distributed Computing

Order Processing	— Preparation of billing documents
	  • Warehouse picking lists
	  • Customer invoices
		— Automated order entry
		  • OCR (optical character recognition)
		  • OMR (optical mark recognition)
		— Order editing
		— Computation of freight charges
		— Handling of invoicing exceptions
			— Credit checking
			— Stock availability checking
			— Order status checking
				— Conversational order entry
				— Multiple location stock availability checking
				— Automatic order transmission to shipping warehouse
				— On-line invoicing

Inventory - Finished Goods	— Weekly stock status reporting	— Daily exception reporting — Sales forecasting — Simple EOQ calculations	— Stock status inquiry handling	— Continuous updating of inventory records — Multiple location balancing of stock — Complex EOQ calculations
Accounts Receivable	— Preparation of aged trial balances and monthly statements	— Preparation of follow-up letters	— Account status inquiry handling	— On-line cash posting and account maintenance — Automated scheduling of follow-up activities
Sales Analysis	— Breakdown of sales volume - by product, customer, and salesman	— Analysis of sales profitability by product, customer, and salesman		

Exhibit 4

Note: System component features listed in one column will be found where applicable (though not listed again) in all columns to the right   (e.g., order processing application feature "order editing" under "expanded batch" will be part of "on-line inquiry" and "distributed computing" systems)

The combination of an old receivable and no current payment indicates a problem requiring management attention.

Note: This type of trial balance—analyzed and listed by age of receivables—is very difficult to prepare by hand or bookkeeping machine.

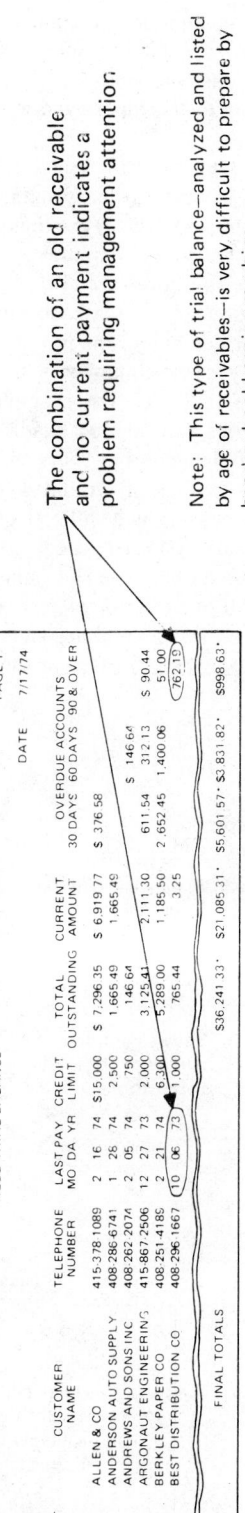

AGED TRIAL BALANCE DATE 7/17/74 PAGE 1

CUST NO	CUSTOMER NAME	TELEPHONE NUMBER	LAST PAY MO DA YR	CREDIT LIMIT	TOTAL OUTSTANDING	CURRENT AMOUNT	OVERDUE ACCOUNTS 30 DAYS	60 DAYS	90 & OVER
108	ALLEN & CO	415 378 1089	2 16 74	$15,000	$7,296.35	$6,919.77	$376.58		
165	ANDERSON AUTO SUPPLY	408 286 6741	1 26 74	2,500	1,665.49	1,665.49			
178	ANDREWS AND SONS INC	408 262 2074	2 05 74	750	146.64		$146.64		
189	ARGONAUT ENGINEERING	415 867 2506	12 27 73	2,000	3,125.41	2,111.30	611.54	312.13	$90.44
247	BERKLEY PAPER CO	408 251 4185	2 21 74	6,300	5,289.00	1,185.50	2,652.45	1,400.06	51.00
252	BEST DISTRIBUTION CO	408 296 1667	10 06 73	1,000	765.44	3.25			762.19
	FINAL TOTALS				$36,241.33*	$21,085.31*	$5,601.57*	$3,831.82*	$998.63*

In this accounts receivable system, payments are posted directly against a specific invoice, not just against an open balance

STATEMENT DATE 8 30 73

CUSTOMER NO 55438C

HITTON CORPORATION
136 MARSHALL DR
PO BOX 851
LONG PORT CALIF 94134

DATE MO DA YR	INVOICE NUMBER	REFERENCE NUMBER	DESCRIPTION	AMOUNT
09 08 73	185163		PRIOR BALANCE	$2,565.46
09 10 73	075126		INVOICE	1,685.91
09 16 73		091531	PAYMENT	1,856.00CR
09 30 73			LC ADJUSTMENT	13.00CR
			LATE CHARGES	6.96

CURRENT AMOUNT	30 DAYS	60 DAYS & OVER	BALANCE DUE
$1,693.91	$696.46		$2,390.37

PLEASE RETURN THIS PART WITH YOUR PAYMENT

STATEMENT DATE 8/30/73

CUSTOMER NO 55438E

HITTON CORPORATION
138 MARSHALL DR
PO BOX 851
LONG PORT CALIF 94134

DATE MO DA YR	INVOICE NUMBER	REFERENCE NUMBER	DESCRIPTION	AMOUNT
09 08 73	185163		PRIOR BALANCE	$2,565.46
09 10 73	075126		INVOICE	1,685.91
09 16 73		091531	PAYMENT	1,856.00CR
09 30 73			LC ADJUSTMENT	13.00CR
			LATE CHARGES	6.96

CURRENT AMOUNT	30 DAYS	60 DAYS & OVER	BALANCE DUE
$1,693.91	$696.46		$2,390.37

PLEASE RETURN THIS PART WITH YOUR PAYMENT

Computed automatically, based on overdue balance

Exhibit 5. Aged trial balance and statement.

In the basic batch mode, computerized sales analysis consisted merely of breakdowns of sales volume by customer, product, and salesperson. In expanded batch systems, as historical sales records and product cost information are made part of computer files, comparative analyses can be made of current versus historical sales volume and profitability by customer, product, and salesperson. Exhibit 6 shows examples of such reports. In addition, inventory systems are expanded to include programs for statistical sales forecasting and for the calculation and reporting of economic order quantities (EOQ) to aid inventory managers. Inventory levels are determined on the basis of current and historical sales records, price, and cost data, enabling many organizations to reduce investment in inventory without sacrificing customer service.

On-Line Inquiry. By the mid- to late 1960s, many organizations had developed comprehensive expanded batch customer service systems. The data files of these systems contained detailed information about many aspects of the customer service function; however, the information was not readily available because it was usually stored on a reel of magnetic tape located in a library away from the computer. Obtaining information from these data files to answer unscheduled requests (e.g., What is the balance on hand of a certain part in inventory?) took hours to accomplish and was a costly, disruptive operation.

On-line inquiry systems resolve the problem of inaccessibility by keeping primary data files (about customers, products, and orders) continuously mounted on disk drives attached to the computer. As a result, the data needed to answer questions are always available to operators of typewriter or CRT (cathode ray tube) terminals connected to the computer. The introduction of such systems has made possible a number of significant improvements in customer service. For example, in many cases customer inquiries can now be handled while the customer is on the telephone, not hours or days later.

The fourth column of Exhibit 4 lists the customer service applications in which on-line inquiry is most often used. These include systems to check the status of various items, such as credit in a given account or stock levels in a warehouse. All other customer service programs, such as preparation of invoices and accounts receivable statements, continue to be processed in the expanded batch mode.

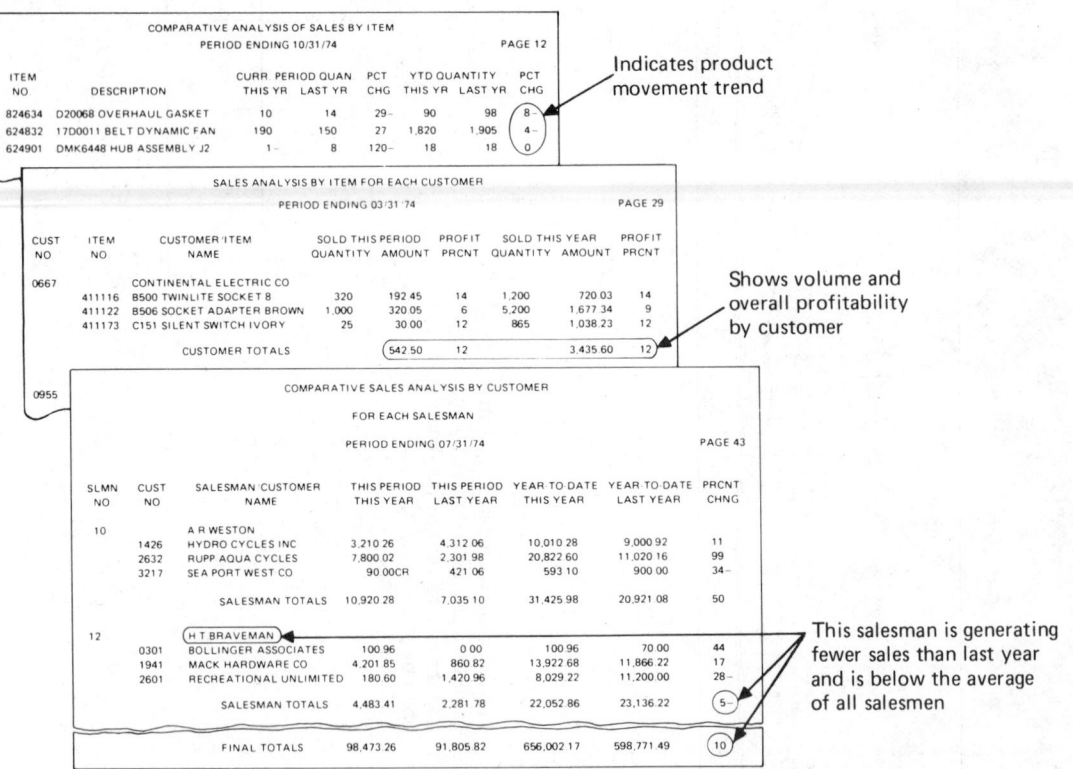

EXHIBIT 6. Sales analysis reports.

Distributed Computing. Today, computer systems are being installed in industrial and commercial organizations that extend the power of the computer to the user wherever located. Such systems—known as distributed computing systems—are complex and expensive. They can, however, offer benefits that outweigh their costs.

Being able to distribute the power of a large, central computer among many remote users is a relatively new capability in industrial and commercial applications processing, although it has existed for some time in the form of time sharing for mathematical and statistical problem solving. In customer service, in particular, such systems have permitted major improvements in management, control, and responsiveness.

The fifth column in Exhibit 4 outlines the customer service applications that can be processed in a distributed computing environment. Conversational order entry (the top item in the column) implies that the clerk enters an order by "talking" with the central computer via a terminal. The computer asks a number of questions about the order, and when all are answered the order is complete and ready for automatic transmission to the location from which the items will be manufactured or shipped. In this mode of processing, the central computer automatically checks all stock locations (not just the one at which an order is normally filled for a specific customer) before declaring an item out of stock. And when an order

is shipped, the computer notifies the order clerk, who completes the order-processing cycle by preparing the invoice at the remote terminal.

Distributed computing systems are complex. They may take years to design and may cost hundreds of thousands (and sometimes millions) of dollars to install. They require large central computers, complex software, and normally involve extensive communication and terminal networks. Nevertheless, they can be significantly less expensive than a number of decentralized stand-alone computers installed to do the same jobs.

In addition, distributed computing systems can help bring about major improvements in customer service. Such systems can significantly reduce order turnaround time. They can provide information that enables order clerks to locate items that are out of stock in their own locations. They can help inventory managers balance inventory levels across many warehouses, and they can make information instantly available for answering customer inquiries about the entire range of customer service activities. Exhibit 7 depicts a distributed computing orientation to processing customer service activities in a geographically dispersed organization.

Manufacturing Systems. Manufacturing applications (also known as production applications) include all computer systems used to assist in planning and

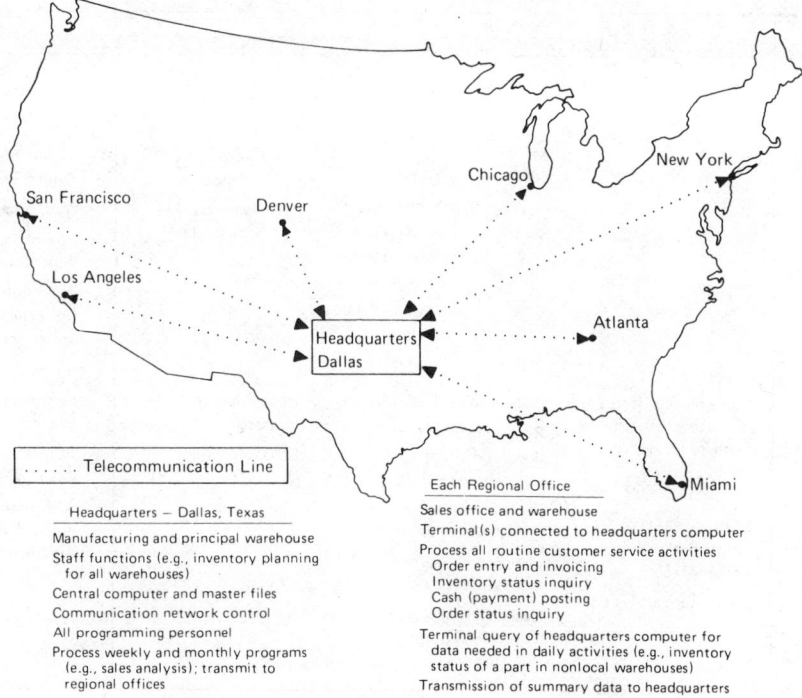

Exhibit 7.   Distributed computing—customer service.

controlling the manufacturing function of an organization. These include systems that determine raw material and work-in-process inventory requirements, help plan production schedules, aid dispatching operations, and monitor work-order status.

Because the manufacturing process in many organizations is highly complex, involving large numbers of people in many departments, manufacturing computer applications are also necessarily complex. In general, they are characterized by a high degree of subsystem integration, making the tasks of both developing and modifying such systems much more difficult than in other administrative and business areas. As a result, these systems are often very costly and may require years to develop.

In addition, there is normally a high degree of risk associated with manufacturing systems. Their success is dependent on their acceptance by the plant workers who must provide the data for the systems and use the system output. Problems can, and frequently do, arise from employees' lack of understanding of the system or lack of appreciation for the necessity of providing the computer with accurate, complete, timely information.

On the other hand, a very high potential benefit is generally associated with manufacturing systems. Since the manufacturing operation often accounts for the largest portion of product cost, even small improvements in its utilization of resources can generate large profits. Reduction of work-in-process inventory, elimination of duplicate parts, shortening of production-planning cycles, and order status information that permits the identification and expediting of behind-schedule orders are some of the benefits that are gained from computerized manufacturing systems.

Exhibit 8 describes the kinds of manufacturing applications used in systems environments of increasing complexity. A prerequisite for manufacturing application systems is an item-coding system that can be used for all subsystems of inventory, bills of materials, engineering changes, and purchasing records. At the simplest stage, inventory accounting systems are implemented, followed by requirements generation (bill of materials explosion) and physical inventory systems.

Up to this point, manufacturing applications are normally used to assist in staff planning and control op-

---

MANUFACTURING SYSTEMS

Application	Least Complex ————————————————————————→ Most Complex			
			On-Line Not Essential	On Line Essential
Production Planning and Control		— Work order preparation (manual dispatch) — Engineering specification file maintenance — Work order status reporting	— Work center analysis — Maintenance scheduling	— Infinite capacity machine loading — Work order scheduling — Automatic work order dispatching — Exception status reporting (for expediting of work orders, tooling)
Inventory	— Weekly stock status reporting with daily activity listings – Item catalog preparation — ABC analysis (distribution by value) — Net return analysis	— "Where used" reporting — Requirements reporting (low-level bill of materials explosion) — Time series requirements reporting — Listing of procurement requirements — Cycle count physical inventory accounting	— Requirements forecasting — EOQ calculation	— Continuous updating of inventory — Automatic item status reporting — Automatic replenishment initiation (purchase orders, work orders)

Exhibit 8

erations. The next state in the evolution of manufacturing systems, that of preparing work orders used to dispatch jobs, is the first time that the system directly affects the plant worker. Work center analysis helps identify bottlenecks in manufacturing by preparing reports for each work center that show production (actual versus standard), downtime, and backlog.

At the most complex level, the manufacturing computer system calculates work-order schedules and, via terminals located on the plant floor, records the completion of one job, dispatches the next, and notifies management of all behind-schedule orders.

Accounting and Finance Systems. Historically, operations such as accounts payable, cost accounting, and financial statement preparation were among the first to be automated, via punched-card systems in the 1930s and 1940s and on computers in the 1950s and 1960s. As in payroll procedures, these functions are largely routine, making them relatively easy to automate. The benefits offered by such applications traditionally have been in the form of clerical cost reduction, and although they have not normally led to dramatic increases in profitability, they have produced sufficiently large dollar savings to more than justify their computerization.

In spite of the traditional nature of accounting and finance applications, several sophisticated, high-benefit systems are being implemented in this administrative and business area. Cash management, financial modeling, and advanced purchasing systems are three examples of the new interest in accounting and finance applications.

In large, diversified, or widely dispersed organizations, the management of cash resources is a difficult job, yet one that has a large impact on profitability. Failure to invest temporarily available cash, premature payment of obligations, or shortsighted investment programs that force an organization to borrow at high rates, all result in less than optimal use of financial resources. In an attempt to avoid these problems, many large organizations are using their computers to help collect, analyze, and report data about cash requirements and reserves. The benefits of such systems include less frequent and smaller short-term loans (a result of being able to project needs over longer periods of time), lower rate loans (a result of being able to forecast needs and investigate multiple sources of debt financing), and higher returns on short-term investments (a result of being able to project how long funds should remain invested).

Financial analysis of proposals is a second area where computers are playing an increasingly important role. Relatively straightforward simulation models enable the financial manager or analyst to generate pro forma statements that show the financial impact of different proposals, such as adding a new product to a current line

or opening a new warehouse. The advantage of such models is that many possible outcomes can be evaluated in the time that one or two could be calculated by hand.

Advanced purchasing systems are a third area of current interest. Computer-based systems monitor data about price and quantity discounts, product quality (from product acceptance statistics) and reliability, and speed of delivery. On the basis of these data, computer programs calculate vendor rankings and economic-purchase quantities (EPQs) for individual items and store product information that helps buyers evaluate vendor performance and negotiate favorable contracts with suppliers.

Exhibit 9 lists many of the traditional accounting and finance applications as well as those of high current interest. In addition to those already described, make-or-buy analysis applications in manufacturing companies and computer-based systems for cost estimating are indicative of the trend toward more complex but also higher benefit applications in the accounting and finance area.

Payroll and Personnel Systems. Payroll and personnel systems constitute a fourth important category of administrative and business applications. This category includes all applications dealing in some way with the management and costs of an organization's human resources. The direct benefits of such systems are often less significant (in tangible dollar terms) than other categories of administrative and business systems.

Historically, the payroll function was often the first administrative operation to be computerized. The highly repetitive nature of the job, with its well-defined rules of computation, made it a logical target for automation, particularly since large numbers of clerical personnel— and hence high clerical costs—were required to perform the function manually. Moreover, by the early 1950s the payroll function in many instances had already been mechanized on punched-card equipment; thus, once an organization installed a computer, it was a relatively simple matter to convert the existing payroll system to the computer (with magnetic tape storage for data files rather than the trays of punched cards used with the former system).

In general, payroll applications have undergone no major changes over the past several years other than in the type of equipment used (e.g., from magnetic tape to disk files for storing data records). An example of one of the few relatively new applications is a computer-based system that simulates the effect of proposed changes in compensation packages. For example, such systems can make it much easier for an organization to evaluate the cost of proposed programs, such as granting a 6.5% across-the-board salary increase or giving an extra holiday to all employees.

In contrast to the relatively few advances in payroll

ACCOUNTING – FINANCE SYSTEMS			
Application	Least Complex —————————————————————————→ Most Complex		
General Accounting	– Cost record keeping	– Cost accounting · comparison to standards or projected amounts – Budgetary accounting – Daily exception reporting	– Cost estimating
Accounts Payable · A/P	– Preparation of A/P registers – Check processing – Check reconciliation – A/P distribution		
Purchasing		– Vendor analysis · volume of purchases – Purchase order preparation and follow-up	– Vendor analysis · quality, reliability, price, etc. – Derivation of economic purchase quantities (EPQs)	– Make-or-buy analysis
Finance		– Financial statements preparation	– Requirements planning · e.g., cash management system – Maintenance of stockholder records	– Analysis of financial proposals

Note: None of the application systems listed requires on-line or distributed computing capability.

Exhibit 9

applications, a number of new application systems have been developed in personnel management. In an attempt to cope with rising demands for various kinds of information about employees, many organizations have created computerized personnel systems. These systems are designed to answer requests for information from persons within the organization (e.g., how many employees have not taken their annual vacation this year?) and from outside agencies (e.g., what is the percentage of minority employees in clerical, supervisory, management, and executive positions?) Organizations are also using their personnel data files to monitor and evaluate the effectiveness of personnel management practices. For example, in cases where an organization has a "pay for performance" philosophy, computers help monitor the program by printing out correlations of performance rating and position within salary range. Other programs check to see if all employees are receiving their performance appraisals at the intervals prescribed by the organization.

In organizations with large numbers of employees or wide-ranging skill requirements, data banks containing information about employees' skills and experience have been computerized. When a specific skill mix is needed for an unfilled position, the computer performs a skills search to identify (and print out the names of) those who meet the qualifications. These systems are often very costly to establish and keep up to date, and some organizations have discontinued them after finding that their use frequency did not justify their expense.

Exhibit 10 describes the range of payroll and personnel applications systems that are found today in industrial, commercial, and governmental organizations.

Three Examples of Administrative Systems. *Point-of-Sale Retail Systems.* Modern retail stores operate across a broad range of rhythms from the rapid flow of the mass merchandising food supermarket to the leisurely pace of apparel specialty shops. The value of "point-of-sale" administrative systems is appropriately quite different across that range of rhythms. The contents of systems are correspondingly different. Yet the structural commonalities of retailing in its various forms permits surprisingly similar equipment configurations.

PAYROLL — PERSONNEL SYSTEMS

Application	Least Complex ──→ Most Complex		
Payroll	Calculation of net payroll from manually calculated gross — Preparation of payroll register — Check processing — Production of required reports (FICA, etc.)	— Attendance accounting — Calculation of net payroll from "hours worked" — Preparation of labor distribution reports	— Evaluation of proposed changes in compensation package	
Personnel		— Automation of basic personnel file — Preparation of scheduled reports, e.g., • Seniority • Vacation	— Salary analysis — Preparation of performance appraisal notices — High-potential employee tracking system — Preparation of unscheduled reports (using a generalized information retrieval system)	— Skills inventory accounting (skills search) — Manpower planning analyses * — On-line payroll/personnel record maintenance at location of employee (e.g., plant)

Note: Other than the system identified with the asterisk, none of the application systems requires on-line or distributed computing capability

Exhibit 10

The most substantial value of computer applications in mass merchandising lies in increased productivity of the salesperson at the checkout counter. Since the mass merchandising sales clerk spends very large amounts of time entering sales transactions, productivity increases are very significant. Labor costs of counter operations have risen steadily, along with clerical costs in general, in the past three decades, so that the productivity gains of recent automated systems have considerable impact upon operating expenses. Aside from internal computing capabilities, other major components of fast processing retail systems are the checkout scanner, which automatically "reads" the coded stock number of the contents of the merchandise, and the coded language, or symbol set, adopted by supermarket representatives. The scanner is a prerequisite for automated data entry, and the coded symbol set is a prerequisite for scanner feasibility.

The other major value to the mass merchandising retail business of administrative point-of-sale systems is the automatic capture of data on merchandise flows for improved inventory and other merchandise management functions (such as the use of space).

It is this secondary value of administrative systems in modern mass merchandising that is of primary value in traditional retailing. The capture of inventory control information for management of stock and replenishment quantities and schedules, for profitability analysis, and for merchandise planning in many dimensions is the great value of transactions-oriented systems in traditional retailing. Credit authorization and data capture for billing credit sales are among the further value of administrative systems to apparel, appliance, and many other traditional retail store types. The sales clerk in higher price, less rapidly moving environments, spends much less time entering transactions and much more time assisting the customer in many ways. The minute-by-minute transactions-handling productivity of the clerk is subordinated to the productivity of customer assistance, guidance, and persuasiveness. The merchandise planning and control feedback from the administrative systems are therefore of much greater relative significance than "cash register" manipulation productivity. Indeed, manual entry rather than machine scanning of individual transaction data continues to be quite satisfactory in traditional retailing in the early 1980s. The reader need only contemplate the logistics of a purchase of 20–50 food products at one time and compare that to the logistics of a purchase of a man's suit, or a lady's dress, or a refrigerator.

Of special significance in the consideration of the varieties of retailing operations and the varieties of roles played by administrative applications support is the phenomenon that quite different structures of objectives are fulfilled by essentially the same technology structured in quite similar logical and physical patterns. The real differences in technology are in the details, not in the broad sweep, and in the hierarchical network architecture rather than in the character of the processing. In all cases, terminals at various points in a store are connected to a local minicomputer. From that point, depending on the scale of the enterprise, differences in technological scale—not character—appear.

In a single store with its own local owner-manager or fully delegated manager, all administrative activities are performed right there and then. The minicomputer, whether on the store's premises or on the premises of a supplier of remote computing services, controls the terminals and executes all of the processing work of the store, whether point-of-sales transactions processing or end-of-month total profitability analysis. In the case of multiple, chain, or operational holding companies, only short-term management is performed by the store's immediate management. Management of inventory, purchasing, pricing, and other shared activities are performed at higher echelons of the enterprise—at a city, regional, or even national level. Implementations of administrative systems are hierarchically organized accordingly. A local minicomputer controls the terminal operations, but in turn communicates with a larger computer that coordinates the operation of minicomputers and terminals in other stores. The host computer performs the summary and analytic processing for management support. Hierarchies may extend several layers deep. Multiple store networks of terminals and computers was one of the pioneering successful applications of distributed data processing.

Manufacturing Inventories. More remote from our daily lives but of great commonality behind the scenes in manufacturing, or in retailing, are the administrative systems for inventory management. One of the inner problems of inventory management in most lines of business is the conflict between having inventory on hand when it is demanded and the enduring business objective of closely controlling expenses, including, importantly, expenses for carrying the very inventory whose absence precludes a sale or delays a manufacturing process. Moreover, there is more to inventory than goods in stock. One has to place inventory in manufacturing into the full con-

text of manufacturing planning and control. The context is now called "MRP" for "Materials Requirements Planning." The objective of MRP is to assure that raw materials and purchased or made semifabricated or fully fabricated parts, components, and assemblies are available as needed as production inputs and that, in providing enough, the firm avoids over-provision no less than under-provision.

The heart of modern inventory management—or MRP, as we should visualize it—is to compute material requirements as the balance among (1) what is now available, (2) what is or could be on order and when it will be available, and (3) manufacturing production schedule demands for the material (or parts, components, or assemblies).

Good accounting and other capabilities are required to fulfill this central computation and to perform other functional and logistical work of the organization. A full-fledged MRP administrative system depends upon four underlying administrative subsystems:

1. Incoming order entry subsystem.
2. Production planning and factory control subsystem.
3. Product bill of materials subsystem.
4. Inventory subsystem, consisting of
   a. Transactions and stock accounting subsystems.
   b. Purchasing subsystem.

The incoming order entry subsystem records order data furnished by the sales or some other equivalent business-gathering unit of the company. Order entry processing and record-keeping serves a number of purposes, including response to inquiry about the status of work and delivery expectation of particular work for a particular customer or order. Note that the incoming order in some version of order entry systems could include orders for stock of the company's finished product *to be held by the company.* Other versions of order entry handle only external customer orders and process internal orders elsewhere in the overall MRP system. The crucial MRP role of the order entry systems is to feed the production planning and factory control subsystem.

The production planning and factory control subsystem is used to predict production of the company's products on a tightly scheduled basis. This schedule draws upon the individual product bills of materials to determine, on a scheduled basis, the flow of materials required for the production process. These flows are the *raison d'etre* of inventory and thereby determine the minimum scheduled inventory of all materials if production schedules are to be met. Meanwhile, the subsystem keeps track of the performance of the work and the use of materials associated with the orders being fulfilled.

The inventory subsystem, supported by a traditional physical inventory accounting system and a fully detailed purchasing system, performs the computing and record-keeping required to match the production requirements to the stocks on hand and to what needs to be and has been ordered. In effect, it simulates the drawing down and replenishment of inventory. The purchasing subsystem provides vendor information and backlog information, and it keeps tabs on projected versus realized incoming materials flows.

The interplay of these four subsystems depends heavily upon highly integrated databases and processing sequences. The more varied the product structure of the company, the greater is the payoff of MRP. It is doubtful that complex manufacturing processes could be performed in anything like modern quantity-cost relationships without well-managed inventories in a materials requirements planning context.

Municipal Government. The government administrative systems that are closest to most people are those that support the governmental administration of the local jurisdiction in which they live. The municipality is the most common form of local jurisdiction in the U.S. The structure of computer administrative applications in support of municipal administration is very imposing. A modern municipality in the U.S. uses computers to varying degrees for budgeting, accounting, personnel, payroll, police and courts, accidents, inventory, tax appraisals and tax accounting, health services, sanitation, street maintenance, and numerous other purposes. Few people recognize the pervasive deployment of municipal computer applications.

The typical municipal accounting subsystems is a useful example because it lays bare the great similarity between commercial business systems and government systems for parallel management or administrative purposes, justifying the recognition of the single "administrative application" category of computer use. Like any full-fledged accounting system, a municipal system requires a codified body of policies, procedures, standards, and practices. The objectives of the municipal accounting system are to furnish the quantitative basis for control of budgeted municipal funds so as not to overcommit, to furnish reporting of financial experiences for management review, appraisal, and planning, and to furnish audit trails so that the transactions that give rise to all accounting results may be identified and "prove" the validity of the accounting results.

Among the subsystems into which a large, real municipal accounting system must be broken down if it is to be manageable are those for revenue, purchasing, pay-

ments, capital projects, and financial reporting. In larger municipalities, subsystems will be found for check reconciliation, grants and awards record-keeping, and other categories of accounting. The very largest municipalities could have subsystems for requisitions, orders, vouchers, and disbursements, compared to the purchasing subsystem of the smaller municipality. A similar hierarchy is found as one moves up the corporate scale: Individual accounting types are increasingly given independent visibility.

Study of the structure of personnel/payroll systems in industry and government reveals many more similarities than differences. The key components of a municipal system include employee status and history, position control, payroll processing, personnel reporting, and labor distribution by head count and by payroll charges. The role of the employee status and history subsystem is to assure highly accurate information about changes and events in the employment experience of each employee beginning with recruitment, continuing through employment and retirement, and terminating, as current information, only upon death of the employee. Basic payroll data, such as social security number and hourly wage or weekly salary, are kept current for ongoing payroll operations.

The position control subsystem furnishes information for planning and control of expenditures for personal services, a major category of municipal as well as business expense. Ceilings on personnel by organizational unit are monitored by the position control subsystem. Payroll processing for a municipality is no different in principle from that for a business enterprise.

REFERENCES

1966. Dearden, John. *Computers in Business Management.* Homewood, IL: Dow Jones-Irwin. (Hardware and software fundamentals, management problems of computer systems, mathematical programming, and future impact of computers in management.)

1968. Boutell, Wayne S. *Computer-Oriented Business Systems.* Englewood Cliffs, NJ: Prentice-Hall. (Basic forms of application systems—e.g., batch—data processing department organization, introduction to hardware and software.)

1968. Heany, D. F. *Development of Information Systems.* New York: Ronald Press. (History of computer use in business data processing; projections about future use; begin at p. 373.)

1969. Orlicky, Joseph. *The Successful Computer System.* New York: McGraw-Hill. (Application systems development.)

1970. Humphrey, Stuart and Yearsley, Ronald, *Computers for Management.* New York: American Elsevier. (Computer applications in business; e.g., marketing.)

1970. Krauss, Leonard I. *Computer-Based Management Information Systems.* New York: American Management Association. (Management-oriented treatment of concept, development, and implementation of management information system.)

1971. Smith, Leighton F. *An Executive Briefing on the Control of Computers*. Park Ridge, IL: Data Processing Management Association. (Development and management of computer systems—analogy to factory operation.)

G. GLASER, A. L. TORRANCE, AND M. H. SCHWARTZ

ADVANCED RESEARCH PROJECTS AGENCY.

See ARPA NETWORK.

AEDS.

See ASSOCIATION FOR EDUCATIONAL DATA SYSTEMS.

AFCET.

See ASSOCIATION FRANÇAISE POUR LA CYBERNETIQUE, ECONOMIQUE ET TECHNIQUE.

AFIPS.

See AMERICAN FEDERATION OF INFORMATION PROCESSING SOCIETIES.

AIKEN, HOWARD

For articles on related subjects *see* DIGITAL COMPUTERS, HISTORY: Early; HOPPER, GRACE MURRAY; MARK I; and WATSON. THOMAS. SR.

Howard Hathaway Aiken was born 8 March 1900, in Hoboken N.J., and died 14 March 1973, in St. Louis, Missouri. He grew up in Indianapolis, Indiana, where he attended Arsenal Technical High School while working 12 hours a night at the Indianapolis Light and Heat Company. Upon graduation he went to work for the Madison (Wisconsin) Gas Company, a position that allowed him to go to the University of Wisconsin. He received his B.A. degree in 1923 and was immediately promoted to chief engineer at Madison Gas.

In 1935 he returned to school, first at the University of Chicago and then at Harvard. His doctoral thesis at Harvard, resulting in a Ph.D. in 1939, was on the theory of space charge conduction. The research required laborious calculations of nonlinear differential equations. This experience led him to investigate the possibility of performing these types of calculations with machine assistance. His thoughts on this subject led him in 1937 to

Fig. 1. Howard Aiken.

circulate a memo entitled, "Proposed Automatic Calculating Machine" (reprinted in *Spectrum,* August 1964, pp. 62–69).

Harvard was not the most likely environment to get support for this type of research. Fortunately, Harvard professors Ted Brown (Business) and Harlow Shapley (Astronomy) were impressed with his work, and both knew of the interest of Thomas Watson Sr. in projects of this nature. With their encouragement, and the knowledge that IBM had the necessary technology, Aiken approached Watson. A contract was signed in 1939 whereby IBM would build the Automatic Sequence Controlled Calculator (Harvard Mark I). The machine was running in 1944, and Aiken and Grace Hopper described it in a paper in *Electrical Engineering* (Vol. 65, 1946, pp. 384–391, 449–454, 522–528).

The Mark I was followed by the Mark II (a relay machine built for the Naval Proving Ground at Dahlgren and completed in 1946), the Mark III (an electronic machine, also for Dahlgren, completed in 1950), and the Mark IV (an electronic machine built for and delivered to the Air Force in 1952). With the completion of Mark IV, Aiken got out of the business of building computers.

It is difficult to evaluate precisely the impact of Aiken's series of machines and the Harvard Computation Laboratory which he founded. Fortunately, the documents are available to anyone interested. One need only look at the log books of the computation lab for this period to see the worldwide range of people who visited the laboratory. Another source of Aiken's work is the many publications in the "Annals of the Harvard Computation Laboratory" series. The Harvard catalog also provides clear evidence of the existence of courses in "computer science" a decade before the emergence of this program at most universities.

In 1947 and again in 1949 Aiken organized symposia on large-scale digital devices at Harvard. Programs from both meetings strongly reflect his hand and his philosophy at that time. Perhaps his most profound impact was in the environment he created at Harvard, which enabled the University to become a vital training ground for many people who are outstanding in the field today. A perusal of those who did their doctoral dissertations under his direction is an excellent example of this impact.

Aiken retired from Harvard in 1961 and moved to Fort Lauderdale, Florida, where he formed Aiken Indusries. He also joined the faculty of the University of Miami as Distinguished Professor of Information Technology. In this latter position, he helped the University develop a computer science program and design a computing center.

His honors are much too numerous to mention in detail. They include honorary degrees (University of Wisconsin, Wayne State University, and Technische Hochschule, Darmstadt), prizes (Rochlitz Prize, Edison Medal of IEEE, the John Price Award of the Franklin Institute) as well as medals from both the United States (Air Force and Navy for distinguished service) and foreign governments (Sweden, Belgium, France, and Spain).

Howard Aiken felt that he had to be continuously involved in challenging endeavors in order to stay alive both physically and intellectually. His career is a document of that creed. Some of his detractors accused him of living in the past, but nothing could be further from the truth. He was a man of rare vision, whose insights have had a profound effect on the entire computing profession.

REFERENCES

1947. *Anon.* "Howard Hathaway Aiken," *Current Biography,* pp. 5–7.
1973. Oettinger. Anthony G. "Howard Aiken," *Communications of the ACM,* pp. 298–299, May.

H. S. TROPP

ALGEBRA, BOOLEAN. *See* BOOLEAN ALGEBRA.

ALGEBRAIC MANIPULATION

For articles on related subjects *see* ARTIFICIAL INTELLIGENCE; LIST PROCESSING LANGUAGES; NUMERICAL ANALYSIS; and SYMBOL MANIPULATION.

Algebraic manipulation by computers involves their use to create, combine, and simplify mathematical formulas. The systems that support algebra provide the user with facilities in which, for example, the "value" taken by a variable may be an expression (e.g., $4x^2 + 2x + 1$) rather than a number, and where, besides the usual arithmetic operators, there are facilities for analytic differentiation, for substituting values for some variables in an expression, and for decomposing complex expressions into their constituent parts.

The study of computer algebra has proceeded along three main lines—one driven by the needs of particular groups of users, one driven by the problems of algorithm analysis and design, and another driven by the challenge of creating coherent and generally useful algebra packages. Before considering the field of algebraic manipulation from these three viewpoints, it will be useful to present two sample problems to show how easy *and* how difficult computer algebra can be.

Many problems can be expressed simply as a sequence of additions, subtractions, multiplications, differentiations, and integrations of polynomials in one variable. One such problem is the use of a recurrence formula to obtain the first few Legendre or Chebyshev polynomials. Problems of this type can be solved using an "algebra system" consisting of only a few dozen lines of code! The polynomials may be represented by storing their coefficients in arrays, so that, for instance, $5x^3 - 2x + 3$ would be stored as

3	−2	0	5	0	0	0	$\cdots$
$[x^0]$	$[x^1]$	$[x^2]$	$[x^3]$	$[x^4]$	$[x^5]$	$\cdots$	

where the length of all arrays is greater than the highest degree of any polynomial expected in the calculation. It should be obvious that addition, subtraction, multiplication, differentiation, and integration of polynomials represented in this way are trivial operations.

The system described above can take pairs of polynomials with integer coefficients and form their product. Now consider the problem of extending it to provide the inverse operation; namely, the factorization of (possibly high-degree) polynomials into their irreducible factors. It turns out that such a facility can also be provided; however, current factorization packages run not to dozens but to thousands of lines of code. Furthermore, the worst case computing time for factorization grows as an exponential function of the degree of the polynomial being considered, and so even a sophisticated program will occasionally run for an unacceptably long time.

The sharp difference in algorithm and program complexity between these two classes of polynomial problems is characteristic of much of computer algebra. This can be seen also for polynomial division in which the reduction to lowest terms of polynomial quotients is hard. If, in addition to polynomials, expressions are allowed to involve transcendental functions, although differentiation remains simple, integration becomes nasty. If, to preserve the full algebraic structure of a computation, irrational numbers such as those defined by nested square and cube roots are to be kept in symbolic form (i.e., as roots rather than calculated out), even basic arithmetic becomes unexpectedly difficult: For instance, programs based on fairly elementary pure mathematics make it possible to compute symbolically even with numbers such as the roots of $x^5 + x + 1$, which cannot be expressed in radicals, but the representation they are forced to use involves polynomials with degrees of about 120!

It should be mentioned that various mathematical barriers impinge on algebraic manipulation, such as undecidability results and tasks that have been shown to be NP-complete *(q.v.)*.

Nevertheless, the range of problems that can be solved in predictable and reasonable amounts of time continues to grow, and the decreasing cost of machines with fairly large amounts of memory is making automated algebra available to an ever wider class of potential users.

Algebraic Systems and the User. The first of the three views of algebra to be presented here will be concerned with applications and the end user. Perhaps the most spectacular users of algebraic manipulation systems have been mathematicians from fields that have traditionally involved computing with large but fairly straightforward formulas—celestial mechanics, quantum electrodynamics, and general relativity. In each case, as soon as computers became large enough, special-purpose algebra packages started appearing to cope with the particular class of expressions generated by the problems. For celestial mechanics, this means a Poisson series (i.e., a series involving polynomial multiples of sine and cosine terms) such as

$$1 + e \sin t + (1 - e^2 f) \cos (2t - u) + \ldots$$

where e and f are polynomial variables and t and u represent angles. The main job of a Poisson series manipulator is the linearization of products of sines and cosines using such rules as

$$\sin a \cos b \rightarrow (\sin (a + b) + \sin (a - b))/2.$$

The successful application of computers to truly vast manipulative problems encouraged the belief that algebra packages could be used to do a great deal of the routine algebra needed by a working scientist or applied mathematician. This view, which presents the computer as a sort of automated mathematical assistant or as a semi-intelligent blackboard, has led to the bulk of today's applications. These span almost all the fields that can use mathematics, including algorithm design, biochemistry, combinatorial analysis, cosmology, economics, fluid dynamics, mechanics, numerical analysis, optics, and plasma physics. One of the ideas that has been found particularly profitable has been the use of computer algebra to derive exactly expressions that are subsequently evaluated numerically (say, by incorporating them into a Fortran program). This approach makes it possible to use exact calculation (i.e., precise algebraic manipulation) where this is relatively easy, or where ill-conditioning makes numerical work hazardous, while still using conventional floating-point arithmetic where that is adequate. For instance, it is known that symbolic differentiation and numerical quadrature are both usually well-behaved operations, whereas numerical differentiation and analytic integration can be troublesome. Given a problem requiring both sorts of transformation, a mixed numeric-symbolic solution may well combine the best of both worlds.

The new users' view of algebraic manipulation is that it is just another technique for solving problems. It complements numerical analysis and makes mathematical experiments more attractive than they would have been using paper and pencil algebra. For such a user, the utility of a system will rarely be limited by its performance when doing simple operations. The availability and efficiency of high-order packages (e.g., for computing Laplace transforms) is much more likely to be critical.

The startling way in which this efficiency depends on algorithm design rather than on detailed programming style leads naturally to the second view of algebraic manipulation—that of the theorist.

Algorithm Analysis and Design. It has already been indicated that apparently slight extensions to algebra systems may have dramatic effects on the complexity of the code needed in the system. This effect caused a great deal of concern when early "general-purpose" algebra systems started to be used to manipulate rational functions. It rapidly became apparent that unless common factors in rational forms were promptly cancelled, they accumulated very rapidly and led to vast unmanageable expressions. The obvious schemes for computing the common factors worked beautifully on small problems, but catastrophically badly on even moderately large ones. Analysis of the simple methods showed that their computing time usually grew as an exponential function of the degrees of their inputs. This confirmed that better compilers and larger computers would not solve the efficiency problem. Successions of new algorithms of increasing mathematical sophistication have been proposed, analyzed, and implemented, the aim always being to reduce the rate at which costs grew with problem size. Such algorithms are still being refined, as shown by the papers by Hearn and Zippel in Ng's book (1979).

Another line of theoretical work has grown out of a series of results used by Risch (1969) in his design for an algorithm to evaluate indefinite integrals. These ideas have also led to a better understanding of how and when "unexpected" cancellations may happen in calculations that involve many trigonometric, hyperbolic, and logarithmic functions. The most recent results indicate that it is possible to write programs that solve (algorithmically) a large range of algebraic integrals and important classes of ordinary differential equations.

Systems for Algebraic Manipulation. The third aspect of algebraic manipulation to be described here is concerned with systems. This heading covers implementation techniques, the selection of capabilities to be included, the design of user interfaces, and perhaps even documentation.

One decision that has to be taken early in the design of an algebra system is the language in which the system will be coded. Algebraic manipulation does not normally make much use of floating point arithmetic, but it does call for extensive storage management facilities and it will use the basic machine arithmetic to implement an arbitrary precision arithmetic package. In addition, many algebraic algorithms are naturally recursive. This, together with the historical links between computer algebra and artificial intelligence, have resulted in several of the more important algebra systems being based on Lisp. Often, the algebra work was a direct spur to extension or development of the Lisp system used: Macsyma is closely integrated with MACLisp and was one of the major packages for which the M.I.T. Lisp machines, Fateman's VAX-Lisp, and the M.I.T. NIL project were designed. Scratchpad was built on a special version of Lisp, and concern about the portability of Reduce led to the speci-

fication of a common core of Lisp and the adjustment, by workers at the University of Utah, of several Lisp systems to make them compatible with it.

A number of algebra systems have sought portability by using Fortran as a base. By adding a few arithmetic primitives provided as Fortran-callable assembly code routines, these systems have proved that the use of a language seemingly ill-suited to list processing and recursion need not hurt performance. Computer algebra systems have also been based on Algol-60 and 68, APL, C, Cobol, Pascal, PL/I, and so on, but none of these has yet grown to the status of well-distributed general-purpose codes.

Some systems, notably Reduce and SAC-II, have been written in specially designed languages, but with the implementation language coded in some existing portable language. Thus, although the cores of Reduce and SAC-II are influenced heavily by the underlying support they get from Lisp and Fortran, respectively, the bulk of their code is well isolated from the details of the computer systems that support them.

Even though the selection of an implementation language does not have a great theoretical impact on system design, in practice it has been closely related to various major policy decisions such as whether an algebra system should be tuned for batch or interactive use, how it should arrange its storage management, and what forms of data structure it should use. The immense range of possible sensible designs that result can best be appreciated by comparing some of the systems described below.

The package profiles that follow are intended to illustrate something of the range of capabilities of current algebra systems, and the gross differences between the input languages and output formats that have been adopted. For each language covered, there is a paragraph indicating particularly characteristic features of the system considered, and, for most, a figure giving some sample code or output. There is no intention that these figures be comprehensible in detail, and the problems being solved in them are not always very clearly defined: It is hoped, however, that inspection of them will help show the flavor of the systems.

Altran was developed at Bell Laboratories by W. S. Brown and A. D. Hall. Its data structure is a compact tabular one that supports polynomial and rational function work, and it also has a collection of procedures for the manipulation of truncated power series. Altran is implemented in Fortran and has an enviable reputation for portability. It was the host for some of the important research on greatest common divisor (gcd) algorithms and sparse polynomial arithmetic, and this, together with its restriction to rational calculations, can result in it performing large computations faster than most of its competitors. Fig. 1 shows an Altran program for producing using a recurrence formula, and gives the output produced by the program.

Camal started life as a collection of machine code subroutines for manipulating Poisson series used for celestial mechanics calculations. The system gradually grew, collected a user-level language based on the Autocode then commonly used in Cambridge, and eventually turned into a reasonably portable, general-purpose package. Camal's main aim throughout has been to support large computations on restrictive and limited hardware. It provides polynomial and Poisson series arithmetic using tightly packed data structures and carefully tuned code, and remains one of the smallest and fastest systems. An extended version of Camal supports the sort of general expressions commonly encountered in general relativity calculations. Part of the design philosophy of Camal was refusing to provide facilities that could not be supported efficiently; hence, Camal hardly attempts to

deal with rational functions. It does, however, provide a full set of facilities that the user can call on to inspect and dismantle expressions, and, in many cases, this means that Camal can be programmed to tackle tasks that would at first seem out of its range. Fig. 2 shows a Camal program that reverts a power series; i.e., it computes the series for the inverse of the function defined by the original series. Note that in the Camal output, exponentiation is represented using '^', whereas on input, '.' had to be used. Also observe how a fairly small calculation has led to the generation of rational numbers with quite long numerators and denominators.

Formac was produced by IBM as an extension to Fortran. A second version hosted by PL/I followed. In 1971, IBM ceased development of the system, and, in due course, the source code was released and maintenance and extension to it were performed by workers at a number of sites. The current version, distributed through the

```
# This Altran program computes Legendre polynomials
PROCEDURE MAIN

INTEGER ORD = 15 # Declare number of polynomials to be produced
INTEGER I

# Declare P to be an array of length ORD, whose
# entries are polynomials in X with highest degree ORD
LONG ALGEBRAIC (X:ORD) ARRAY (0:ORD) P

# Set up initial values so that Legendre polynomials can be
# computed using a recurrence formula.
P(0) = 1
P(1) = X

# Use recurrence to fill in further polynomials
DO I = 2, ORD
    P(I) = ((2*I - 1)*X*P(I - 1) - (I - 1)*P(I - 2))/I
    DOEND

# Now just write out the last result.
WRITE P(ORD)

# ... and stop
END
```

Fig. 1(a). An Altran program to compute Legendre polynomials.

```
# P(15)
    (9694845*X**15 - 35102025*X**13 + 50702925*X**11 -
    37182145*X**9 + 14549535*X**7 - 2909907*X**5 +
    255255*X**3 - 6435*X ) / 2048
```

Fig. 1(b). Output generated by the program of Fig. 1(a), showing the fifteenth Legendre polynomial literally in terms of a variable X.

‖ Power series reversion demonstration using series for arctan

$A = a − a.3/3 + a.5/5 − a.7/7 + a.9/9 − a.11/11 + @$
$a.13/13 − a.15/15 + a.17/17 − a.19/19 + a.21/21$
‖ On input Camal uses a '.' to indicate exponentiation,
‖ and the system distinguishes between upper case names
‖ (used for working variables) and lower case ones, which
‖ represent indeterminates.
‖ '@' is used to continue a statement from one line to the
‖ next.

‖ This program computes the power series expansion of
‖ the function $B(x)$ defined by $B(A) = a$ where A
‖ is the series defined above.
‖ Thus B is the inverse of the function A: here A is
‖ the arctan function, so B will turn out to be
‖ the series for tan (a).

$B = a$ ‖ An initial approximation to the result

‖ This loop refines the series B, each iteration
‖ makes it correct to one further power in a.
FOR $N = 3:2:21$
‖ The input series is odd, so we only need
‖ generate odd terms in the result.
‖ The SELECT statement arranges to discard all terms with
‖ degree greater than $N + 1$ in a.
SELECT $< a.(N + 1)$

‖ This iteration corrects the next term in B
$B = B + a − \text{SUB}(A,B,a)$
‖ SUB(A,B,a) substitutes B for a in A

REPEAT

‖ Now print answer
TEXT : The result is :
NEWLINE
LINEWIDTH $= 55$
PRINT(B)

STOP
END

The result is
$(a + (1/3) a\hat{\ }3 + (2/15) a\hat{\ }5 +$
$(17/315) a\hat{\ }7 + (62/2835) a\hat{\ }9 +$
$(1382/155925) a\hat{\ }11 + (21844/6081075) a\hat{\ }13 +$
$(929569/638512875) a\hat{\ }15 +$
$(6404582/10854718875) a\hat{\ }17 +$
$(443861162/1856156927625) a\hat{\ }19 +$
$(18888466084/194896477400625) a\hat{\ }21)$

Fig. 2.   A Camal program that derives the power series for
tan from that for arctan.

SHARE program library, is mainly the responsibility of K. Bahr. Formac stores expressions in parse-tree form, and so is able to manipulate quite general expressions. The most recent revisions are respectably fast. Fig. 3 shows the flavor of Formac by giving a program for computing successive derivatives of tan x. A preprocessor converts all the algebraic parts of the program (in particular, the LET statements) into calls to subroutines within Formac that perform the required algebra. Formac prints its results with exponents on the line above the body of expressions, and with the entire output underlined.

Macsyma is the largest and most powerful algebra system currently available. It is probably best thought of as a collection of packages and facilities, held together by its user-level language. Thus, Macsyma contains within itself modules for computation with polynomials, rational functions, and Poisson series, and each of these can use whatever special data structures and algorithms it needs to achieve high performance. When working in one of these restricted domains, Macsyma's speed and capabilities are very similar to those of other, simpler systems. As well as special-purpose packages, Macsyma has a general-purpose representation for expressions, and a collection of user-callable functions for making transformations on expressions kept in that format. Macsyma only rarely performs simplification of expressions automatically. If a polynomial is to be multiplied out, it is generally the user's responsibility to invoke the function EXPAND, while, if a rational form needs to be put over a common denominator, it will be necessary to call RATSIMP, and so on for all the other classes of expressions and standard representations that Macsyma supports.

The efforts of large numbers of students and post-doctoral researchers have been embedded in Macsyma in the form of expert packages for solving specific sets of mathematical problems. Probably the most famous of these is the package for indefinite integration, but the equation solving, factorization, tensor calculus, Taylor series expansion, definite integration, series summation, and gcd facilities are also worthy of note. Macsyma is sufficiently large that it can be hard for the casual user to keep track of all the capabilities that it provides. It has, however, demonstrated that this breadth of coverage of mathematical techniques is both possible and needed for the support of interactive algebraic problem solving. The main work of developing Macsyma has been done at the Laboratory for Computer Science (formerly project MAC) at M.I.T., and for some time support has come from a "Macsyma consortium" of interested users. Members of the consortium have used Macsyma on the computer at M.I.T. via the ARPA network *(q.v.)*, and the sys-

```
/* This program computes the first eight derivatives
of tan (x) and prints the eighth derivative */

TANS: PROCEDURE OPTIONS(MAIN);

FORMAC_OPTIONS; /* Initialization needed by Formac */
DCL I BIN FIXED (31); /*Formac is embedded, in PL/I,
                        and so shares PL/I's declarations */

OPTSET (LINELENGTH = 60); /* Limit length of lines printed */
OPTSET (EXPND); /* Expand all expressions fully */

LET (Y = TAN(X)); /* All algebraic operations are written
                      inside LET ( . . . ) statements */

DO I = 1 TO 8;
    LET (Y = DERIV (Y,X) ); /* Differentiate Y with respect to X */
    END;
PRINT-OUT( Y); /* Display the final result */

END;
```

$$Y = 40320 \, \text{SIN}^9(X) / \text{COS}^9(X) + 120960 \, \text{SIN}^7(X) /$$
$$\text{COS}^7(X) + 129024 \, \text{SIN}^5(X) / \text{COS}^5(X) + 56320 \, \text{SIN}^3(X) / \text{COS}^3(X) + 7936 \, \text{SIN}(X) / \text{COS}(X)$$

Fig. 3. A Formac program and its output, which is the eighth derivative of tan x.

Declare that y is a function of x, so dy/dx does not vanish identically

(C1) DEPENDS(Y,X)\$

Specify equation to be solved. Macsyma echoes
the input in displayed form.

(C2) EQ399:$(X + 1) * (X - 1)\hat{\ }2*(3*X + 5)\hat{\ }2*$DIFF $(Y,X,2) -$
$(3*X + 1) * (X - 1) * (3*X + 5)\hat{\ }2*$DIFF $(Y,X,1) +$
$36*(X + 1)\hat{\ }3*Y = 0;$

$$(D2)\ (X - 1)^2 (X + 1)(3X + 5)^2 \frac{d^2 Y}{dX^2}$$

$$- (X - 1)(3X + 1)(3X + 5)^2 \frac{dY}{dX} + 36 (X + 1)^3 Y = 0$$

Call on a package within Macsyma to solve
the equation, setting a flag (RADCAN) that controls
formatting and presentation of results involving radicals.

(C3) SOLFAC (EQ399,Y,X), RADCAN;

Solution as generated, with %K1 and %K2 representing
arbitrary constants

$(D3)\ Y = $ SQRT $(X - 1)$ SQRT $(3X + 5)$

$(X (\%K1 (\text{LOG } (3X + 5) + 3 \text{ LOG } (X - 1)) + 12 \%K2)$

$+ \%K1 (- \text{LOG } (3X + 5) - 3 \text{ LOG } (X - 1)) - 12 \%K2)/12$

Fig. 4. Macsyma solving an ordinary differential equation.

tem has not been widely distributed. With decreasing hardware costs, it seems probable that general export of the system might start soon: An experimental implementation of Macsyma now runs on a VAX-11, and there are plans to market computers patterned after the M.I.T. Lisp machine. Fig. 4 shows part of an interactive session with Macsyma, where a differential equation is solved.

muMATH is quite different from all the rest of the systems described here, because it does not pretend to be able to perform large calculations enormously fast. muMATH represents an experiment to find out how much serious algebra can be squeezed into a microcomputer; versions exist that run under the popular CP/M operating system and even for such small systems as the Radio Shack TRS-80. Its most important application area is in mathematical education. To make the best possible use of the limited address space available with eight-bit micros, muMath is provided as a collection of modules. The most basic of these provide a parser for a language loosely related to that employed by Reduce (see below), and a package for high-precision rational arithmetic. Higher-level packages provide a remarkable range of facilities, including various transformations on expressions involving trigonometric functions, logarithms and exponentials, differentiation, integration, and equation solving. The user can write and add extra packages fairly easily. The system is, of course, very much slower than the various mainframe-based systems, and the size of the

problem it can attack is definitely limited, but it has clearly grown to be more than just a toy, and gives some idea of how the field may respond to hardware developments.

Reduce is the most sophisticated algebra system that, in 1980, has been widely distributed. Its internal design is based on a hierarchy of languages, with a carefully documented dialect of Lisp in the middle, a portable optimizing Lisp compiler pushing downwards and an Algol-like source language that is used for almost all Reduce programming. Reduce performs most of its calculations using a canonical data structure for rational functions. In the last few years, there have been substantial changes made to both the algorithms used and the detailed coding of the rational function package, greatly improving generality and performance. Reduce has, or is about to have, packages for use in high-energy physics, for indefinite integration, for arbitrary precision floating point arithmetic, and for polynomial gcd and factorization. Because the system is written fairly cleanly and the source code has always been made freely available, it is easy for an experienced (or desperate!) user to make changes to Reduce or add arbitrary new facilities. The Reduce example given in Fig. 5 shows the user setting up a matrix with symbolic entries, evaluating its determinant exactly, and then substituting values for the parameters in the original matrix, leading eventually to a floating point result.

% This Reduce program computes the determinant of
% a matrix that has symbolic entries, it then evaluates
% the result by substituting a numeric value for
% the indeterminate used;

MATRIX A (4,4);

% The matrix used is a sort of Hilbert matrix,
% and working with it numerically might be unsafe;
FOR I = 1:4 DO
    FOR J: = 1:4 DO A(I,J): = 1/(I + J + X);

% Evaluate determinant using a procedure built into
% Reduce;

D := DET(A);

$$D := 144/(X^{16} + 80*X^{15} + 2980*X^{14} + 68600*X^{13} + 1092142$$
$$*X^{12} + 12748520*X^{11} + 112846340*X^{10} +$$
$$772507000*X^{9} + 4132320713*X^{8} + 17325828520*X^{7}$$
$$+ 56732436080*X^{6} + 143507100400*X^{5} +$$
$$274806780144*X^{4} + 384951602880*X^{3} +$$
$$37183052160031*X^{2} + 22113907200031*X +$$
$$60963840000)$$

% Now give X a numeric value;
$D1$:= SUB(X = 1,D); % Substitute x = 1 in D;

$D1$:= 1/10668672000

% So far all calculations have been exact: now
% that the bulk of the ill-conditioned calculations
% have been done, convert result to floating point;

% Set floating point option;
ON FLOAT;

% Re-display result;
$D1$;

9.37323783E-11

Fig. 5. Reduce evaluating a determinant.

SAC-I and SAC-II are both implemented in Fortran, and the most important aspect of each is the collection of advanced rational function algorithms implemented. SAC-I provided all these algorithms in the form of Fortran subroutines, and its users had to code direct calls to them, and had to do detailed storage management functions. Although various front-end languages for SAC-I were proposed, none came into general use, and the system remained a testbed for algorithm analysis, testing, and design, not making any particular concessions to people wanting to apply algebra. SAC-II, with its driver language, Aldes, continues to place heavy emphasis on the links between computer algebra and the mathematical development of algorithms. The Aldes language is based on a formalization of the notation used by Knuth for describing algorithms. The language has a publication form, which allows the use of Greek letters as well as Roman ones, and allows both kinds to be decorated with hats, bars, and primes. The machine-readable version of a program is obtained by applying simple transcription rules to the publication copy. SAC-II is being distributed, at least in a preliminary form, but has not been available for long enough yet to have collected a wide user base.

Schoonschip is capable of performing vast calculations and, in particular, ones where the size of expressions manipulated may exceed the amount of main store available. In its original form, Schoonschip was coded in assembly code for CDC machines in the 6000 series. It exploited the fast CDC hardware by using floating point coefficients in its expressions and by having the CDC peripheral processors (which manage input and output for the mainframe) do their full share of processing. Schoonschip is expected to be used when the magnitude of the algebra to be attempted means that all possible programming tricks and shortcuts must be applied. Its user language, therefore, while not enormously modern or flexible, allows for detailed editing of algebraic structures. As can be seen in Fig. 6, statements in the language are introduced by symbols such as Z, ID, and *, which identify the various classes of operation that can be performed. A version of Schoonschip has been converted from CDC assembly code via an intermediate PL/I-like stage into IBM assembly code, and is now available for distribution.

Scratchpad is not generally available, as it was developed as part of a research project within IBM and has not been released as a product. It is described here because, despite its narrow distribution, it is a large and powerful system and has influenced the rest of the field. Scratchpad takes the two-dimensional nature of conventional mathematical notation very seriously. At one time, the system hoped to be able to use a graphics tablet as an input device and a vector display for output. The present version accepts input from a conventional keyboard, but that input is always thought of as representing displayed expressions, and Scratchpad always echoes it in 2-D form. Scratchpad is driven by the specification of sets of rules, rather than by collections of assignments or procedure definitions. The main Scratchpad evaluator implements a Markov algorithm (*q.v.*), reducing expressions on the basis of both user-defined and system transformations. For many problems, this seems to provide a very concise and natural notation. Below the surface Scratchpad is a conglomeration of pieces of code, with large parts of Reduce and various other systems called on as required. New developments are being pursued in an attempt to bring the internal structure of an algebra system properly into line with the mathematical structure of the classes of formulas handled. Fig. 7 illustrates a Scratchpad conversation.

```
C In Schoonschip, the first symbol of each line
C indicates what form of statement is to follow: Z marks
C assignments . . .

Z FILE(1) = F1 (X,Y)*YXY
Z FILE(2) = F2 ((A + B) ,(C + E)) − (12.7)*2
Z FILE(3) = F1 (A,B) *YXY
Z FILE(4) = X*4Y*(F1(A,B)) *2+F1 (A,B) *X**2*F1 (A,B)

C Now introduce some patterns that will simplify the above
C expressions

ID,F1 (X,Y)*YXY = X**2 + Y**2
ID,F2 (A+,B+) = A + B
C The first rule will apply to F1 (X,Y), whereas the second
C will deal with any application of F2

C Start the computation
*BEGIN
FILE (1) = + X**2 + Y**2

FILE (2) =

    − 1.6129E2 + A + B + C + E

FILE (3) = + F1 (A,B)
    * ( YXY )
FILE (4) = + F1 (A,B) * F1 (A,B)

    * (4.*X*Y**3 + X**2 ) +0.
```

Fig. 6. A few simple examples of Schoonschip using patterns to transform the users' input.

"Binomial coefficients"
"the notation $c<r;;n>$ is a linearization of the $2D$ binomial
coefficient shown in Scratchpad's displayed echo.
Start by giving general rule"
$$c <r;;n> = c <r;;n-1> + c<r-1;;n-1>$$

$$\binom{a}{b}C = \binom{a-1}{b}C + \binom{a-1}{b-1}C$$

"Scratchpad's echo shows where sub- and superscripts went,
and has renamed dummy variables.
Now give special cases . . ."
$$c<0;;n> = 1$$

$$\binom{a}{0}C = 1$$

$$c<n;;n> = 1$$

$$\binom{a}{b}C = 1 \text{ WHEN } a = b$$

"Print out a sample value"
$$c<3;;5>$$

$$10$$

Fig. 7. A sample Scratchpad conversation. The lines shown
alternate between expressions typed in linear form
by the user and Scratchpad's 2-D echo.

REFERENCES

1969. Risch, R. H. "The Problem of Integration in Finite Terms," *Trans. A.M.S.* **139**.

1971. Petrick, S. (Ed.). *Proceedings of the Second Symposium on Symbolic and Algebraic Manipulation.* ACM.

1974. *Proceedings of EUROSAM '74,"* ACM SIGSAM Bulletin, No. 31.

1976. Jenks, R. D. (Ed.). *Proceedings of the 1976 ACM Symposium on Symbolic and Algebraic Computation.* ACM.

1977. *Proceedings of the First Macsyma Users Conference, NASA Report No. CP-2012.*

1979. Ng, E. (Ed.). *Symbolic and Algebraic Computation, Springer Lecture Notes in Computer Science 72* (Proceedings of EUROSAM-79).

1979. Lewis, V. E. *Proceedings of the 1979 Macsyma Users Conference.* Cambridge, MA: MIT. Press.

1981. *Proceedings of the 1981 ACM Symposium on Symbolic and Algebraic Computation.* ACM.

The SIGSAM Bulletin. Published quarterly by ACM.

A. C. NORMAN

ALGOL 68

For articles on related subjects *see* BLOCK STRUCTURE; EXTENSIBLE LANGUAGE; PASCAL; PROCEDURE-ORIENTED LANGUAGES; and PROGRAMMING LANGUAGES.

Algol 68 is a language designed by a working group (WG 2.1) of the International Federation for Information Processing (IFIP) in order to provide a general-purpose programming language that would be suitable for communicating algorithms, executing them efficiently on different computers, and teaching computer science. Even though Algol 68 is a successor of Algol 60, it is a completely new language, different from Algol 60 in many essential aspects. Its design reflects the 1968 understanding of a number of fundamental concepts of programming languages and computer science.

Algol 68 has great expressive power and yet a very elegant and interesting basic structure. It features five primitive types (called "modes") of values; **bool** (boolean), **char** (character), **int** (integer), **real** and **format**; and five rules for constructing new modes from the already defined ones. So, for example, values of mode [] **real** are one-dimensional arrays or *multiple values* of reals. Values of mode **struct** ([]**char** *name*, **bool** *sex*, **int** *age*) are personal records or *structured values*. Values of mode **union** (**real**, **int**) are either reals or integers, but no value of this mode can be both of mode **real** and **int**. *Ref-*

ALGORITHM   51

erences are values that refer (point) to other values. For example, values of mode **ref [] char** are references to one-dimensional arrays of characters. Values of mode **proc (int, real) bool** are *routines* (i.e., procedures) that take two arguments of respective modes **int** and **real** and return a value of mode **bool.**

Since references and routines are values, they can be manipulated like any other values. In particular, they can be passed as parameters in procedure calls. Because of this it is possible to achieve the effects of three types of procedure calls found in other programming languages: call by value, call by name, and call by reference. So, for example, values of mode **proc (ref [] char, int) int** are routines with the first formal parameter called by reference.

Different sorts of declarations (for example, array declarations and switch declarations) found in other programming languages are captured in the *identity declaration* of Algol 68. This concept is also the basis of the parameter-passing mechanism; it allows construction of an infinite number of new modes from the already defined ones and permits declaration of arithmetic and logical operators and their priorities.

The identity declaration and the concept of a reference clarify the distinction between a variable and a constant. An identity declaration in a program defines the value possessed by the identifier that appears in the declaration. This value may be a reference to another value, in which case the identifier is declared as a variable. An example of an initialized (i.e., one that includes assignment) declaration of that sort is **real** $x := 3.14$, which gives rise to the following scheme.

identifier $x \rightarrow$ reference to a real value $\rightarrow$ 3.14

The effect of a standard assignment statement is achieved by making the reference possessed by the identifier refer to the value specified in the statement. This is not possible if the value possessed by an identifier is not a reference, i.e., if this intermediate link is not present. In that case the identity declaration establishes the identifier as a constant, which can be changed only by redeclaring it. An example of a declaration that establishes *pi* as a constant 3.14 is **real** $pi = 3.14$, which gives rise to the following scheme.

identifier $pi \rightarrow$ 3.14

This careful distinction permits, in particular, the definition of constant and variable procedures. For example, the declaration **proc** $f = ($**real** $x,$ **real** $y)$ **real**: $(x + y)/2 - sqrt(x \times y)$ establishes f as a constant, as opposed to **proc** $f := ($**real** $x,$ **real** $y)$ **real**: $(x + y)/2 - sqrt(x \times y)$, which defines a variable procedure. In the latter case we can, at another point in the program, assign

some other value of mode **proc (real, real) real** to f; for example, we can write $f := ($**real** $x,$ **real** $y)$ **real**: $(x + y)/2.$

A number of standard statements are available in Algol 68: assignment, e.g., $x := (a + b)/2$; repetitive, e.g., (**for** i **from** 2 **to** n **do** $f := f \times i$; **go to**, e.g., **go to** *loop*; conditional, e.g., **if** $x \geq y$ **then go to** *label* **else go to** *end* **fi**, etc. In addition to the conventional serial statement execution, it is possible to specify parallel or *collateral* execution. In the latter case, execution of statements is merged in time in a way to be specified by the implementation. Parallel programming facilities in Algol 68 include elementary means of control or synchronization of collateral execution. These are language-defined values called "semaphores" (*q.v.*).

The Algol 60 concept of a *block* appears in a more general form in Algol 68 as a *range*. An example of a range is a sequence of declarations and statements placed between generalized parentheses. Examples of pairs of these parentheses are **begin** and **end, if** and **then, then** and **else, else** and **fi**, etc. References possessed by the identifiers declared in a range may be local to that range. Since the hardware representation of a reference is a memory location, storage is allocated dynamically to local variables; i.e., storage for local variables of a range is deallocated when leaving that range. In addition to these stack-controlled values, Algol 68 also has values whose lifetime does not fit into the last-in-first-out principle of a stack. Values of this sort are stored in a randomly organized memory region called the *heap*.

REFERENCES

1969. van Wijngaarden, A. *et al.* "Report on the Algorithmic Language ALGOL 68." Springer-Verlag *Numerische Mathematik,* **14.**
1971. Branquart, P., Lewi, J., Sintzoff, M., and Wodon, P. L. "The Composition of Semantics in Algol 68." *Communications of the ACM* **14,** No. 11.
1971. Lindsey, C. H. and van der Meulen, S. G. *Informal Introduction to Algol 68.* Amsterdam: North-Holland.
1975. van Wijngaarden, A., Mailloux, B. J., Peck, J. E. L., Koster, C. H. A., Sintzoff, M., Lindsey, C. H., Meertens, L. G. L. T., and Fisher, R. G. "Revised Report on the Algorithmic Language Algol 68," *Acta Informatica* **5**: 1–3. Springer-Verlag: Berlin, Heidelberg, New York.
1976. Tanenbaum, A. S. "A Tutorial on Algol 68," *Computing Surveys* **8**, No. 2.

S. ALAGIĆ

ALGORITHM

For articles on related subjects *see* ALGORITHMS, ANALYSIS OF; ALGORITHMS, THEORY OF; ERRORS;

Error Analysis; Markov Algorithm; Parallel Algorithm; Program Verification; Scheduling Algorithm; and Turing Machine.

In discussing problem solving, we presuppose both a problem and a device to be used in solving the problem. The problem may be mathematical or nonmathematical in nature, simple or complex. The basic requirements for a well-posed problem are that (1) the known information is clearly specified; (2) we can determine when the problem has been solved; and (3) the problem does not change during its attempted solution. The second requirement does not mean that the solution to the problem is known a priori, but only that we know when the solution has been attained. For example, in some numerical problems we obtain repeated approximations to the answer, terminating the solution process when two successive approximations are "sufficiently close" together. We can specify in the problem statement the exact meaning of "sufficiently close," without knowing the exact answer. The device to be used for problem solution may be human or machine, or a combination of the two.

Definition. Given both the problem and the device, an *algorithm* is the precise characterization of a method of solving the problem, presented in a language comprehensible to the device. In particular, an algorithm is characterized by these properties:

1. Application of the algorithm to a particular input set or problem description results in a finite sequence of actions.
2. The sequence of actions has a unique initial action.
3. Each action in the sequence has a unique successor.
4. The sequence terminates with either a solution to the problem, or a statement that the problem is unsolvable.

We illustrate these concepts with an example: "Find the square root of the real number x." As it is stated, this problem is algorithmically either trivial or unsolvable, owing to the irrationality of most square roots. If we accept "$\sqrt{2}$" as the square root of 2, for example, the solution is trivial: The answer is the square root sign ($\sqrt{}$) concatenated with the input. In Snobol, the entire algorithm is

```
OUTPUT = '√‾' INPUT
END
```

However, if we want a decimal expression, then the square root of 2 can never be exactly calculated. Hence, the requirement of a finite number of actions is violated.

A modified statement of the problem is more suited to our purposes. "Find the positive square root, to four decimal places, of the real number x." This statement has three useful properties:

1. It explicitly names the *positive* square root as the desired one, whereas the earlier statement left that quality ambiguous.
2. It eliminates the string "$\sqrt{x}$" as a problem solution.
3. By stating "four decimal places" (or any other fixed number of places), it provides a test for termination.

A possible method of solution is

(a) Choose a number y and compute y^2.
(b) If $|y^2 - x| < 5 \times 10^{-5}$, the solution is y; if not, return to step (a).

This method fails to be an algorithm, since no procedure is specified for choosing either the initial value y or subsequent values. Moreover, even if there is a solution, there is no guarantee that this method will find it.

Now consider another method:

1. Let $y = 1$.
2. Compute y^2.
3. If $|y^2 - x| < 5 \times 10^{-5}$, the solution is y, HALT; if not, go to step 4.
4. Replace y by $((x/y) + y)/2$; go to step 2. (This procedure is a special case of a general technique known as the Newton-Raphson technique.)

This method has the precise definition of each step required of an algorithm. Moreover, whenever applied to a nonnegative real number x, the method will produce the proper solution in a finite number of steps. However, whenever applied to a negative number, the method will endlessly recompute y without recognizing the futility of the task. This is typical of a class of methods called *semi-algorithms:* They will halt in a finite number of steps if the problem posed has a solution, but will not necessarily halt if there is no solution.

To transform the given method into an algorithm, two things must be done:

(a) Add a step, (0); if $x < 0$, there is no solution; HALT; and
(b) Rewrite the given method in a language suitable for the proposed device. (For English-speaking people, the given language is satisfactory; for a

ALGORITHM   53

computer, a programming language must be used. For example, the following algorithm in Basic is suitable for computers utilizing that language, with the data set {3, 107, 1, 0, −4}.)

```
10   READ X
20   IF X < 0 THEN 80
30   LET Y = 1
40   LET Z = Y ↑ 2
50   IF ABS (X − Z) < 0.00005 THEN 100
60   Y = ((X/Y) + Y) /2
70   GO TO 40
80   PRINT "THERE IS NO SOLUTION FOR", X,"."
90   GO TO 10
100  PRINT "THE SQUARE ROOT OF", X, "IS", Y,"."
105  GO TO 10
110  DATA 3, 107, 1, 0, −4
120  END
```

Note that statement 110 specifies the data set to be used with the algorithm and are not part of the algorithm itself. If the algorithm is applied to this particular data set, the result will be

```
THE SQUARE ROOT OF 3      IS 1.73205.
THE SQUARE ROOT OF 107    IS 10.3441.
THE SQUARE ROOT OF 1      IS 1.
THE SQUARE ROOT OF 0      IS 3.90625E−3.
THERE IS NO SOLUTION FOR −4.
```

Significance of Algorithms. While the concept of an algorithm is useful in crystallizing the informal notation of a "method of solution" for a problem, it has a much deeper significance. Whereas it was at one time assumed that any properly stated mathematical problem was solvable, mathematicians in the 1920s began to question this, asking what precisely it meant to say that we could "solve a problem" or "compute a function." Several important areas of mathematics have resulted from attempts to answer these questions, including the theory of Turing machines and the theory of algorithms. All the concepts proposed proved to be equivalent: Any problem that is solvable according to one concept is solvable according to all other concepts. Thus, while the algorithm, properly formalized, may not be the only way to solve problems, it appears to be essentially the only way that the human intellect in its present stage of development can comprehend.

Quality Judgments on Algorithms. Any computer program is at least a semi-algorithm, and any

program that always halts is an algorithm. (Of course it may not solve the problem for which the programmer intended it.) Given a solvable problem, there are many algorithms (programs) to solve it, not all of equal quality. The primary practical criteria by which the quality of an algorithm is judged are time and memory requirements, accuracy of solution, and generality. To cite an extreme example, since a properly defined game of chess has only a finite number of possible moves, there exists an algorithm to determine the "perfect" chess game. Simply examine all possible move sequences, in some specified order. Unfortunately, the time required to execute any algorithm based on this idea is measured in billions of years, even at today's computer speeds. The memory requirements for such an algorithm are similarly overbearing.

On a more practical plane, several numerical methods for solving problems fail to yield satisfactory algorithms because the rate of convergence is so slow that thousands or millions of iterations may be needed to determine the answer. For other numerical methods, rounding or truncation errors may accumulate so rapidly that they destroy the answer.

There is often a trade-off in time and memory requirements which must be settled pragmatically. The simplest case of this arises in the computation and repeated use of a complicated function. If the computation of each function value is sufficiently complex, then in repeated usage much time may be saved by precomputing a table of values and using table lookup (q.v.) techniques. However, such a table may require sufficient additional memory space that this becomes a critical factor. Thus, one may have to sacrifice some speed to stay within available memory bounds.

The accuracy of an algorithm is a characteristic often more closely related to time than to memory requirements. For example, the square root algorithm previously presented is not very accurate. (It yields 0.00390625 as the square root of zero). Its accuracy may be improved by changing the test constant in line 50, at the cost of a longer run time. Further improvement may be obtained from the corresponding algorithm in double-precision at a cost of both run time and additional memory space. In each case the basic algorithmic concept is unchanged.

Altering the basic algorithmic concept may provide an improved algorithm to accomplish a given task. For example, three multiplications and two additions are required to evaluate the quadratic expression $ax^2 + bx + c$ in the order $((ax^2) + (bx)) + c$. Changing the concept of the evaluation algorithm to $(((ax) + b)x) + c$ eliminates one multiplication, resulting in a more efficient process. This will improve the speed of solution of the problem, and probably also improve the accuracy of the result.

The remaining important characteristic of an algorithm is its generality. While there are occasions when an algorithm is needed to solve a single isolated problem, more often algorithms are designed to handle a range of input data. Generality, like accuracy, is often attained at the cost of speed and memory requirements. A general polynomial root finder is more costly in both time and storage than an algorithm for extracting the roots of a quadratic equation. But the increased generality may justify the cost. This is a pragmatic decision. In another example, an information retrieval system based on a free vocabulary is generally more expensive to design and operate than one based on a fixed or coded vocabulary. But the difference in utility may far outweigh the additional cost burden.

Questions of the minimal time and storage requirements posed by a given class of problems, and of the time and storage requirements of any proposed algorithm, have become increasingly important as we attempt to solve larger and more complex problems. In recent years, much of the work in algorithm theory has been focused on these questions of algorithmic complexity (*see also* COMPUTATIONAL COMPLEXITY).

R. R. KORFHAGE

ALGORITHM, MARKOV.

See MARKOV ALGORITHM.

ALGORITHM, PARALLEL.

See PARALLEL ALGORITHM.

ALGORITHM, SCHEDULING.

See SCHEDULING ALGORITHM.

ALGORITHMS, ANALYSIS OF

For articles on related subjects *see* ALGORITHM; ALGORITHMS, THEORY OF; COMBINATORICS; COMPUTATIONAL COMPLEXITY; ITERATION; NP-COMPLETE PROBLEMS; and RECURSION

The analysis of algorithms can be partitioned into two areas: algorithm complexity and problem complexity. The former is concerned with consideration of a specific algorithm for a problem and the analysis of its behavior with respect to the amount of memory space, time, or other resource used. The latter is concerned with the class of all algorithms for a particular problem and the determination of the minimum requirements of the problem with respect to space and time or other resources. Such analyses are second in importance only to the determination of the correctness of an algorithm. They provide the means to choose intelligently and improve algorithms.

Contrary to one's intuition, the advent of the electronic computer has made the efficiency of algorithms a topic of utmost concern. One might suspect that, as the speed of computers increases, the effects of the efficiency of the algorithms decrease. Actually, just the opposite is true. The reason for this is that the asymptotic behavior of the algorithm becomes more important, as we will now illustrate.

With a problem we associate an integer, which we call the size of the problem. For example, the size of a matrix multiplication problem is the dimension of the matrix, the size of a graph problem is the number of edges, etc. The growth rate of the execution time of the algorithm is determined as a function of the size of the problem. The limiting behavior of the growth rate is called the asymptotic growth rate. For example, the asymptotic behavior of the function $17 + 5n + 2n^2$ is $2n^2$, since, for sufficiently large n, $2n^2$ approximates $17 + 5n + 2n^2$ to arbitrary accuracy. For $n = 100$, the lower-order terms account for less than 3%.

In performing a hand computation, the size of the problem is small, and consequently the asymptotic growth rate is unimportant. On such small problems most algorithms perform reasonably well. However, on a high-speed computer, the problem size normally encountered is large and the asymptotic growth rate becomes important. Given two algorithms with growth rates n^2 and 2^n, for problems up to size 6, the difference in execution times is never more than a factor of 2. However, with a computer, a problem of size 100 might be encountered. In this case, the n^2 algorithm is easily executed, whereas the 2^n algorithm would require centuries to compute. This example illustrates why in the past ten years a tremendous effort has been devoted to analysis of algorithms.

Algorithm Complexity

Space and Time. Space and time are the most important considerations of algorithm complexity. Since both are limited, it is advisable to determine how much space and time an algorithm requires. An algorithm that requires relatively little memory space for execution may have a greater running time than another algorithm that requires more space, while both algorithms may provide a solution to the same problem. Thus, there is frequently a trade-off between space and time.

As an example of a space-time trade-off, consider an algorithm that requires the storage of an undirected graph. (An undirected graph is a set V of n vertices, $V = \{v_1, v_2, \ldots, v_n\}$, and a set E of edges, where an edge is an unordered pair of vertices.) The algorithm stores the graph as an $n \times n$ connection matrix A, where

$$a_{ij} = \begin{cases} 1 \text{ if } (v_i, v_j) \text{ is an edge in } E; \\ 0 \text{ otherwise.} \end{cases}$$

This requires n^2 bits of memory, regardless of the number of edges.

Assume that the algorithm is used only for planar graphs. (A planar graph is an undirected graph that can be drawn on a plane surface so that no edges intersect.) Let G be a planar graph with p vertices. Then G can be represented in the computer by a linked list of n vertices where the data structure for each vertex v_i is a linked list of all vertices adjacent of v_i. Since each edge (v_i, v_j) of G is stored twice (v_j is on the list of vertices adjacent to v_i, and v_i is on the list of vertices adjacent to v_j), the memory required to store the list representation of G is proportional to the number of edges. For planar graphs it can be shown that the number of edges is bounded by $3n - 6$, where n is the number of vertices. Thus, the memory required is bounded by $C \times n$, where C is a constant, rather than the n^2 that was required for the connection matrix representation. If the algorithm is required to determine if vertex v_i is connected to vertex v_j, then a trade-off between space and time occurs, since only one operation is needed with the connection matrix representation, whereas the list representation requires searching the entire list of vertices adjacent to v_i to see if v_j is on the list.

Frequency Analysis. A *frequency analysis* of an algorithm reveals the number of times certain parts of the algorithm are executed. Such an analysis indicates which parts of the algorithm consume large quantities of time and hence where efforts should be directed toward improving the algorithm. For example, the following section of Fortran-like code calculates

$$\sum_{i=1}^{N+1} a_i x^{i-1}$$

and stores the result in T.

```
      DIMENSION S(N), A(N + 1)
      DO 10 I = 1,N
1     Y = 1.0                    N
      DO 20 J = 1,I
2     Y = Y • X                  N(N − 1)/2
20    CONTINUE
3     S(I) = A(I + 1)•Y          N
10    CONTINUE
4     T = A(1)                   1
      DO 30 I = 1,N
5     T = T + S(I)               N
30    CONTINUE
```

The program is poorly written and just about every statement can be changed to decrease the amount of time required. To the right of each assignment statement is the number of times it is executed. As N increases, the program spends proportionally more and more time executing statement 2 than it does for statements 1, 3, 4, or 5. Thus, it is really futile to try to improve the program by decreasing the time spent executing the latter statements without first decreasing the time spent executing statement 2. The portion of the program containing statement 2 can be improved by using Horner's rule for polynomial evaluation. Again, the number of times each assignment statement is executed is given at its right.

```
      DIMENSION A(N + 1)
1     T = A(N + 1)               1
      DO 10 I = 1,N
2     T = T•X + A(N + 1 − I)     N
10    CONTINUE
```

Execution Time. To determine the actual execution time of an algorithm in seconds requires a knowledge of the operation times for each instruction of the computer on which the algorithm is to be executed and how the compiler generates code. In order to avoid becoming involved in the specific details of operation of a particular computer, it is customary to find upper and lower bounds c_1 and c_2, such that the execution time of every instruction is between c_1 and c_2. Then the execution time of an algorithm can be estimated from a count of the number of operations that are executed. This frees the analysis of the algorithm from peculiarities of individual computers.

Frequently the time required by an algorithm is data dependent. In this case one of the two types of analyses is possible. The first is called the "worst case analysis," in which that set of data of given size requiring the most work is determined and the behavior of the algorithm is analyzed for that specific set of data. The other alternative is to assume a probability distribution for the possible input data and compute the distribution of the execution time as a function of the input distribution. Usually, this computation is so difficult that only the expected or average execution time as a function of size is computed. This is called the "average case analysis."

Problem Complexity. In problem complexity we are concerned with analyzing a problem rather than an algorithm. The analysis provides us with lower bounds on the amount of time and space required for a solution to the problem, independent of the algorithm used. The lower bounds may be either "worst case" or "average case" bounds. These lower bounds can serve as an indication of how well an algorithm fits the problem and whether it can be improved. For example, such an analysis shows that any algorithm that evaluates an arbitrary n-degree polynomial represented by its coefficients requires at least n multiplications and n additions. Thus, Horner's rule (given above) cannot be improved upon.

On the other hand, an analysis of matrix multiplication gives a lower bound of order n^2 operations for multiplying two matrices of dimension n. The usual matrix multiplication algorithm has an asymptotic growth rate of order n^3. Thus, there is substantial interest in trying either to find a better lower bound or to improve on the current matrix multiplication algorithms. At the current state of knowledge the fastest algorithm has an asymptotic growth rate of order $n^{2.5}$, and thus there is a large gap between tne best known lower bound and the performance of the best known algorithm.

In problem analysis, it is often important to consider the frequency of occurrence of a specific operation. The reason for this is that reducing the number of occurrences of a specific operation can lead to a recursive algorithm with a lower asymptotic growth rate. Consider multiplying two n-digit numbers, where n is a power of 2. The usual algorithm learned in elementary school requires on the order of n^2 operations. A recursive method of multiplying two n-digit numbers x and y is to write $x = a10^{n/2} + b$ and $y = c10^{n/2} + d$, where a, b, c, and d are $n/2$-digit numbers. Compute ab, cd, and $ad + bc$. Then

$$xy = ab10^n + (ad + bc)10^{n/2} + cd.$$

The problem of computing xy is reduced to the problem of computing ab, cd, and $ad + bc$, which are computed by the three multiplications ab, cd, and $(a + c)(b + d)$. The formula $ad + bc$ is obtained by $(a + c)(b + d) - ad - cd$. Let $T(n)$ be the time to compute the product of two n-digit numbers. Then $T(n) \simeq 3T(n/2) + kn$, where the $3T(n/2)$ is the time to compute the three multiplications, k is a nonnegative constant, and kn is the time to compute the necessary sums. Successively applying the formula above to each product, we obtain

$$T(n) \simeq kn(1 + (3/2) + (3/2)^2 + \cdots + (3/2)^{\log_2 n})$$
$$\simeq 3kn^{\log_2 3} \simeq 3kn^{1.58}.$$

The asymptotic growth rate is of order $n^{1.58}$ rather than the n^2 of the more elementary method. The important observation is that in computing ab, cd, and $ad + bc$, the number of multiplications was reduced from four to three at the expense of increasing the number of additions from one to four. The reason for doing this is that the exponent in the asymptotic growth rate is affected by the number of multiplications, whereas the number of additions affects only the constant.

A major difficulty with problem analysis is that it is concerned with the class of all algorithms for a given problem. One no longer can postulate a computer with a given structure and operation set. Instead, one must envision an abstract computer that is sufficiently general to encompass any physically implementable algorithm. The difficulties involved are of such magnitude that one is forced to obtain bounds for certain limited classes of programs. For example, sorting n integers can be shown to require $n \log n$ operations if restricted to the class of algorithms that sorts by binary comparisons. This follows from the simple information theoretic argument that there are $n!$ possible permutations of n items, and each comparison can at best divide the set of possible permutations by a factor of 2. Since the asymptotic growth rate of $\log(n!)$ is $n \log n$, it takes at least $n \log n$ comparisons to determine uniquely the actual permutation. Of course, if one sorts by some method other than by comparisons (radix sort, for example), then the bound is no longer valid.

A typical assumption for a class of programs might be that the computation uses only the arithmetic operations of addition, subtraction, multiplication, and division. When this is done, it is necessary to specify the underlying algebraic structure. For example, the complexity of computing an algebraic expression may depend on whether the underlying structure is the rational, real, or complex number system.

One of the most powerful techniques for establishing results of this nature is due to Winograd, who showed that any algorithm for computing the product of an arbitrary vector X times a matrix A requires a number of multiplications at least as great as the number of nondependent columns of A. It immediately follows from this result that Horner's rule evaluates arbitrary n-degree polynomials with the minimum number of multiplications. Let $X = (x^n, x^{n-1}, \cdots, x, 1)$ and let $A = (a_{n+1}, a_n,$

$\cdots, a_1)^T$. Then

$$X A = \sum_{i=1}^{n+1} a_i x^{i-1}.$$

X has n nondependent columns, which implies that n multiplications are required. The result requires that the algorithm evaluate any polynomial, given its coefficients. Specific polynomials can often be evaluated with fewer multiplications. Similarly, if the polynomial is specified by parameters other than its coefficients, a saving in the number of multiplications is possible.

The one facet of problem complexity that is probably the most intriguing is the lack of nontrivial lower bounds for various problems. Almost all known lower bounds are either linear in the size of the problem or have been obtained by restricting the classes of algorithms. The notable exceptions are lower bounds obtained by the diagonalization techniques of recursive function theory. One of the major goals of computer scientists working in the analysis of algorithms is to close the gap in our knowledge of problem complexity. Hopefully, the next decade will provide powerful new tools in the area and startling improvements in the efficiency of algorithms.

References

1968, 1969, 1973. Knuth, D. E. *The Art of Computer Programming* 1, 2, 3. Reading, MA: Addison-Wesley.

1974. Aho, Alfred V., Hopcroft, John E., and Ullman, Jeffrey D. *The Design and Analysis of Computer Algorithms.* Reading, MA: Addison-Wesley.

1976. Wirth, Niklaus, *Algorithms + Data Structures = Programs.* Englewood Cliffs, NJ: Prentice-Hall.

J. E. HOPCROFT AND J. E. MUSINSKI

ALGORITHMS, THEORY OF

For articles on related subjects *see* ALGORITHM; ALGORITHMS, ANALYSIS OF; COMPUTABILITY; COMPUTATIONAL COMPLEXITY; DECIDABILITY; FORMAL LANGUAGES; NP-COMPLETE PROBLEMS; and TURING MACHINE.

The meaning of the word *algorithm,* like the meaning of most other words commonly used in the English language, is somewhat vague. In order to have a *theory of algorithms,* we need a mathematically precise definition of an algorithm. However, in giving such a precise definition, we run the risk of not reflecting exactly the intuitive notion behind the word. The finding of a mathematically precise replacement of the notion of algorithm was the earliest problem in the theory of algorithms. Many authors have tried to capture the essence of the intuitive notion of an algorithm. We give four examples.

Hermes (1965). "An algorithm is a general procedure such that for any appropriate question the answer can be obtained by the use of a simple computation according to a specified method.... [A] general procedure [is] a process the execution of which is clearly specified to the smallest details."

Minsky (1967). " ... an effective procedure is a set of rules which tells us, from moment to moment, precisely how to behave."

Rogers (1967). " ... an algorithm is a clerical (i.e., deterministic, bookkeeping) procedure which can be applied to any of a certain class of symbolic *inputs* and which will eventually yield, for each such input, a corresponding symbolic *output.*"

Hopcroft and Ullman (1969). "A *procedure* is a finite sequence of instructions that can be mechanically carried out, such as a computer program.... A procedure which always terminates is called an *algorithm.*"

Note that what Hermes calles "a general procedure" is what Minsky calls an "effective procedure" is what Hopcroft and Ullman call a "procedure." Other terms are also used in the literature, and some authors use the word "algorithm" to denote any procedure whatsoever. In the remainder of this article the Hopcroft and Ullman terminology will be used.

An important fact to note is that the notion of a procedure cannot be divorced from the environment in which it operates. What may be a procedure in certain situations, may not be considered a procedure in other situations. For example, the instructions of a computer program are not usually understood by most people. Alternatively, the description of a chess game that appears in a newspaper is a perfectly clear algorithm for a chess player who wants to reproduce the game, but it is quite meaningless to people who do not play chess. Thus, when we talk about a procedure as a finite sequence of instructions, we assume that whoever is supposed to carry out those instructions, be it human or machine, understands them in the same way as whoever gave those instructions.

Another sense in which the environment influences the notions of procedure and algorithm is indicated by the following examples. If the instruction requires us to take the integral part of the square root of a number, such an instruction can be carried out if we are dealing with positive integers only, but it cannot always be carried out if we are dealing with both positive and negative integers.

Thus, the same set of instructions may or may not be a procedure, depending on the subset of integers for which it is intended. Alternatively, we can easily give a procedure that, given an integer x, keeps subtracting 1 until 0 is reached and then stops. Such a procedure will be an algorithm if we intend to use it for positive integers only, but it will not be an algorithm if we also intend to apply it to negative integers.

The recognition of whether or not a sequence of instructions is a procedure or an algorithm is a subjective affair. No precise theory can be built on the vague definitions given above. In trying to build a precise theory, one must examine the situations in which the notion of algorithm is used. In the theory of computation, one is mainly concerned with algorithms that are used either for computing functions or for deciding predicates.

A *function f* with domain D and range R is a definite correspondence by which there is associated with each element x of the domain D (referred to as the "argument") a single element $f(x)$ of the range R (called the "value"). The function f is said to be "computable" (in the intuitive sense) if there exists an algorithm which, for any given x in D, provides us with the value $f(x)$.

A *predicate P* with domain D is a property of the elements of D which each particular element of D either has or does not have. If x in D has the property P, we say that $P(x)$ is true; otherwise, we say that $P(x)$ is false. The predicate P is said to be *decidable* (in the intuitive sense) if there exists an algorithm which, for any given x in D, provides us with a definite answer to the question of whether or not $P(x)$ is true.

The computability of functions and the decidability of predicates are very closely related notions because we can associate with each predicate P a function f with range $\{0,1\}$ such that, for all x in the common domain D of P and f, $f(x) = 0$ if $P(x)$ is true and $f(x) = 1$ if $P(x)$ is false. Clearly, P is decidable if and only if f is computable. For this reason we will hereafter restrict our attention to the computability of functions.

A further restriction customary in the theory of algorithms is to consider only functions whose domain and range are both the set of nonnegative integers. This is reasonable, since in those situations where the notion of a procedure makes any sense at all, it is usually possible to *represent* elements of the domain and the range by nonnegative integers. For example, if the domain comprises pairs of nonnegative integers, as in the case with an arithmetic function of two arguments, we can represent the pair (a,b) by the number $2^a 3^b$ in an effective one-to-one fashion. If the domain comprises strings of symbols over an alphabet of 15 letters, we can consider the letters to be nonzero hexadecimal digits, and assign that nonnegative integer to a string that is denoted by the string in the hexadecimal notation. The device of representing elements of a set D by nonnegative integers is referred to as "arithmetization" or "Gödel numbering," after the logician K. Gödel, who used it to prove the undecidability of certain predicates about formal logic. From now on we will be exclusively concerned with functions whose domain and range are subsets of the set of nonnegative integers.

In order to show that a certain function is computable, it is sufficient to give an algorithm that computes it. But without a precise definition of an algorithm, all such demonstrations are open to question. The situation is even more uncertain if we want to show that a given function is uncomputable, i.e., that no algorithm whatsoever computes it. In order to avoid such uncertainty, we need a mathematically precise definition of a computable function.

It is clear from the way in which algorithms are discussed above that for a proper algorithm we ought to be able to construct a machine that carries out the instructions of the algorithm. One possible way of making precise the concept of a computable function is to define an appropriate type of machine, and then define a function to be computable if and only if it can be computed by such a machine. This has indeed been done. The machine usually used for this purpose is the so-called Turing machine (*q.v.*). This simple device has a tape and a read-write head, together with a control that may be in one of finitely many states. The tape is used to represent numbers. A function f is called computable if there exists a Turing machine that, given a tape representing an argument x, eventually halts with the tape representing the value $f(x)$. Since a precise definition of a Turing machine can be given, the notion of a computable function has become a precise mathematical notion.

The question arises whether or not it is indeed the case that a function is computable in the intuitive sense if and only if it is computable by a Turing machine. The claim that this is true is usually referred to as *Church's thesis* (sometimes as *Turing's thesis*). Such a claim can never by "proved," since one of the two notions whose equivalence is claimed is mathematically imprecise. However, there are many convincing arguments in support of Church's thesis, and an overwhelming majority of workers in the theory of algorithms accept its validity. One of the strongest arguments in support of Church's thesis is the fact that all of the many diverse attempts at precisely defining the concept of computable function have ended up with defining exactly the same set of functions.

Given a precise definition of a computable function, it is now possible to show for particular functions that they are computable. Conversely, it becomes possible to prove that certain functions are not computable. We will give two examples.

Example 1. Consider the following problem. Give an algorithm that, for any Turing machine, decides whether or not the machine eventually stops if it is started on an empty tape. This problem is called the "blank-tape halting problem." The required algorithm would be considered a *solution* of the problem. A proof that there is no such algorithm would be said to show the (effective) *unsolvability* of the problem.

The blank-tape halting problem is in fact unsolvable. This is proved by rephrasing the problem into a problem about the computability of a function, as follows: Turing machines can be Gödel-numbered in an effective manner; i.e., there exists an algorithm which for any Turing machine will give its Gödel number. Furthermore, this can be done in such a way that every nonnegative integer is the Gödel number of some Turing machine. Let f be the function defined as follows.

$$f(x) = \begin{cases} 0 & \text{if } n \text{ is the Gödel number of a Turing} \\ & \text{machine that eventually stops if} \\ & \text{started on the blank tape;} \\ 1 & \text{otherwise.} \end{cases}$$

It is easy to see that f is computable if and only if the blank-tape halting problem is solvable. The unsolvability of the blank-tape halting problem is proved by showing that the assumption that f is computable leads to a contradiction.

Example 2. Our second example indicates that there are unsolvable problems in classical mathematics. The followings problem is known as "Hilbert's tenth problem" (after the German mathematician David Hilbert, 1862–1943):

Given a diophantine equation [an equation of the form $E = 0$, where E is a polynomial with integer coefficients; e.g., $xy^2 - 2x^2 + 3 = 0$] with any variables, give a procedure with which it is possible to decide after a finite number of operations whether or not the equation has a solution in integers.

Although this problem was stated by Hilbert in 1900 (long before there was such a thing as a theory of algorithms), it has only been recently that the Russian mathematician I. Matiajasevitch has shown it to be unsolvable.

That there are clearly defined problems, like the two given above, that cannot be solved by any computer-like device is probably the most striking aspect of the theory of algorithms. A whole superstructure has been built on such results, and there are methods to find out not only whether something is uncomputable, but also how badly it is uncomputable (see Rogers, 1967).

A typical question that one may ask is the following: Suppose we had a device which, for any given Turing machine, told us whether or not the Turing machine will eventually stop on the blank tape. Can we write an "algorithm" that makes use of this device and solves Hilbert's tenth problem? It has been known for some time that such an "algorithm" exists. In this sense, Hilbert's tenth problem is *reducible* to the blank-tape halting problem. It is the proof that the reverse is also true which gave us the unsolvability of Hilbert's tenth problem. Two problems that are both reducible to the other are said to be *equivalent*. Most of the theory of algorithms has, until recently, concerned itself with questions of the reducibility and equivalence of various unsolvable problems.

In recent years a new trend has developed. Much of the activity in the theory of algorithms began to concern itself with computable functions, decidable predicates, and solvable problems. Questions about the nature of the algorithms, the type of devices that can be used for the computation, and about the difficulty or complexity of the computation have been investigated and are discussed in other articles.

REFERENCES

1965. Hermes, H. *Enumerability, Decidability, Computability.* Berlin, Germany: Springer-Verlag.
1967. Minsky, M. *Computation: Finite and Infinite Machines.* Englewood Cliffs, NJ: Prentice-Hall.
1967. Rogers. H. *Theory of Recursive Functions and Effective Computability.* New York: McGraw-Hill.
1969. Hopcroft, J. E. and Ullman, J. D. *Formal Lanuages and Their Relation to Automata.* Reading, MA: Addison-Wesley.

G. T. HERMAN

ALLOCATION, STORAGE.

See STORAGE ALLOCATION.

AMERICAN FEDERATION OF INFORMATION PROCESSING SOCIETIES (AFIPS)

For articles on related terms *see* AMERICAN SOCIETY FOR INFORMATION SCIENCE; ASSOCIATION FOR COMPUTING MACHINERY; ASSOCIATION FOR EDUCATIONAL DATA SYSTEMS; INTERNATIONAL FEDERATION FOR INFORMATION PROCESSING; INSTITUTE OF ELECTRICAL AND ELECTRONIC ENGINEERS—COMPUTER SOCIETY; and SOCIETY FOR INDUSTRIAL AND APPLIED MATHEMATICS.

Purpose. The American Federation of Information Processing Societies is a national federation of professional societies established to represent the member societies on an international level and for the advancement and diffusion of knowledge of the information processing sciences. Toward the latter end it engages in appropriate literary and scientific activities. High on the list of its original goals was the provision of a complete, responsible, and effective public information program for the information processing community. AFIPS has performed this function primarily and most effectively through sponsorship of the Spring and Fall Joint Computer Conferences, which as of June 1973 were merged into an annual National Computer Conference. AFIPS represents the United States in a variety of international information processing activities, including IFIP (International Federation for Information Processing). AFIPS acts as national spokesman for the information processing community in matters dealing with or affected by computing, data processing, and related sciences.

AFIPS' Washington Office follows issues related to computers and information policy at the Federal level. At the request of the Federal Communications Commission, the Washington Office on two separate occasions provided briefings on computers and communications. AFIPS participates in activities sponsored by the National Academy of Sciences and the American Association for the Advancement of Science. It cooperates with such governmental groups as the National Commission on Library and Information Services.

How Established. AFIPS was organized as an unincorporated society on May 10, 1961. It was the outgrowth of the National Joint Computer Committee, which had been established ten years earlier to sponsor the Joint Computer Conferences. The AFIPS founding societies were the American Institute of Electrical Engineers and the Institute of Radio Engineers (which later merged into the Institute of Electrical and Electronic Engineers), and the Association for Computing Machinery.

The presidents who have held office in the National Joint Computer Committee and AFIPS are:

Morton M. Astrahan, 1956–1958
Harry H. Goode, 1959–1960
Willis Ware, 1961–1962
J. D. Madden, 1963
Edwin L. Harder, 1964–1965
Bruce Gilchrist, 1966–1967
Paul Armer, 1968
Richard I. Tanaka, 1969–1970
Keith W. Uncapher, 1971

Walter L. Anderson, 1972
George Glaser, 1973–1975
Anthony Ralston, 1975–1976
Theodore J. Williams, 1976–1978
Albert S. Hoagland, 1978–1980
J. Ralph Leatherman, 1980–

Organizational Structure. There are two classes of AFIPS participation: member societies, which have a principal interest in computers and information processing, and affiliated societies, which, although not principally concerned with computers and information processing, do have a major interest in this field. A minimum membership of 1,500 is required for admission to either class of membership. Each of the societies must publish a professional journal as well as hold an educational conference. The total membership of the 12 constituent societies exceeds 135,000.

In 1980, the 12 constituent societies of AFIPS were:

The Association for Computing Machinery, Inc. (ACM)
The Institute of Electrical & Electronics Engineers, Inc. (IEEE)
Data Processing Management Association (DPMA)
Society for Computer Simulation (SCS)—formerly Simulation Councils, Inc. (SCI)
The American Society for Information Science (ASIS)
Association for Computational Linguistics (ACL)
Society for Information Display (SID)
American Statistical Association (ASA)
Society for Industrial and Applied Mathematics (SIAM)
American Institute of Aeronautics and Astronautics (AIAA)
Instrument Society of America (ISA)
Association for Educational Data Systems (AEDS)

The Federation is managed by its Board of Directors. Each member society has one to three directors, depending on size; each affiliated society has one director. The President is the principal officer of the Federation and the Executive Director is the senior paid officer. Other AFIPS officers include a vice-president, secretary, and treasurer. Meetings of the Board of Directors are usually held twice a year to elect member and associate member societies, to act on constitutional amendments, and to conduct other pertinent business.

The headquarters of AFIPS is located at 1815 North Lynn Street, Suite 800, Arlington, Virginia 22209.

Technical Program. The chief contribution of AFIPS to the professional community has been made through its sponsorship each year of both Spring and Fall Joint Computer Conferences, which offered technical sessions in the widest possible spectrum of subjects, and an accompanying exhibit of the latest equipment and literature relevant to the computer sciences. In 1973, these conferences were replaced by an annual National Computer Conference, which continues to provide both the professional community and the interested public with the latest information regarding developments in the field of information technology. AFIPS also sponsors small meetings and workshops on specialized topics. Several of these have resulted in publications.

The Harry Goode Memorial Award was authorized in 1964, and since that time has been presented annually to an individual in recognition of outstanding achievement in the field of information processing. The recipients of this award are:

Howard Hathaway Aiken, 1964
George Robert Stibitz and Konrad Zuse, 1965
J. Presper Eckert and John William Mauchly, 1966
Samuel Nathan Alexander, 1967
Maurice Vincent Wilkes, 1968
Alston Scott Householder, 1969
Grace Murray Hopper, 1970
Allen Newell, 1971
Seymour R. Cray, 1972
(No award, 1973)
Edsger W. Dijkstra, 1974
Kenneth Iverson, 1975
Lawrence G. Roberts, 1976
Jay W. Forrester, 1977
Robert Noyce and Gordon Moore, 1978
Herman H. Goldstine, 1979
Fernando V. Corbató, 1980
C. A. R. Hoare, 1981

The AFIPS Press publishes proceedings of annual conferences and other publications of interest to its members and to the lay public, and is also the distributor of IFIP publications in the United States.

History-Related Activities. The AFIPS History of Computing Committee, composed of volunteers from all societies, published a guide to *Preserving Computer-Related Source Materials* which "indicates the types of source material that historians of science and technology will need to document the history of computing and explains how this material may be preserved."

Additionally, AFIPS has entered into an agreement with the Charles Babbage Institute (CBI), a not-for-profit private foundation, to establish a Center for the History of Computing. And AFIPS Press publishes a quarterly journal, the *Annals of the History of Computing,* an outgrowth of a study by the Federation's Publications Committee.

I. L. AUERBACH

AMERICAN SOCIETY FOR INFORMATION SCIENCE (ASIS)

For article on related subject *see* AMERICAN FEDERATION OF INFORMATION PROCESSING SOCIETIES.

Purpose. The American Society for Information Science is a not-for-profit professtional association organized for scientific, literary, and educational purposes, and dedicated to the creation, organization, dissemination, and application of knowledge concerning information and its transfer, with particular emphasis on the applications of modern technologies in these areas.

An auxiliary purpose of the Society is to provide its members with a variety of channels of communication within and outside the profession, including meetings and publications, and with a service organization to help them in their professional development and advancement.

How Established. ASIS was founded on 13 March 1937, as the American Documentation Institute (ADI) when Watson Davis, director of Science Service (which was operated out of the National Academy) and one of the first Americans to become interested in documentation as a separate field of endeavor, invited approximately 35 documentalist colleagues to meet with him at the National Academy of Sciences. ADI was made up of individuals nominated by and representing affiliated scientific and professional societies, foundations, and government agencies, of which there were 68 in 1937. In 1952, the bylaws were amended to admit individual as well as institutional members. By vote of the membership on 1 January 1968, the name was changed to American Society for Information Science, to indicate its concern with all aspects of the information-transfer process.

The following individuals have held the office of president.

Watson Davis, 1937–1943
Keyes D. Metcalf, 1944

Waldo G. Leland, 1945
Watson Davis, 1946
Waldo G. Leland, 1947
Vernon D. Tate, 1948–1949
Luther H. Evans, 1950–1952
E. Eugene Miller, 1953
Milton O. Lee, 1954
Scott Adams, 1955
Joseph Hilsenrath, 1956
James W. Perry, 1957
Herman H. Henkle, 1958
Karl F. Heumann, 1959
Cloyd Dake Gull, 1960
Gerald J. Sophar, 1961
Claire K. Schultz, 1962
Robert M. Hayes, 1963
Hans Peter Luhn, 1964
Laurence B. Heilprin, 1964–1965
Harold Borko, 1966
Bernard M. Fry, 1967
Robert S. Taylor, 1968
Joseph Becker, 1969
Charles P. Bourne, 1970
Pauline Atherton, 1971
Robert J. Kyle, 1972
John Sherrod, 1973
Herbert S. White, 1974
Dale Baker, 1975
Melvin S. Day, 1976
Margaret Fischer, 1977
Audrey Grosch, 1978
James Cretsos, 1979
Herbert Landau, 1980
Mary Berger, 1981

Organizational Structure. The ASIS Council, the governing body of the Society, is composed of 15 individuals: 13 hold office by election; the other two are ex officio.

The Council meets four times a year, in January, April, July, and during the Annual Meeting in the last quarter of the year. ASIS membership now totals nearly 4,000 individuals (including about 500 students) and more than 50 institutions.

ASIS has chartered 23 Special Interest Groups (SIGs) which provide those members with similar professional specialites the opportunity to exchange ideas and information about current and specialized developments. Special Interest Groups include the following areas.

Arts and Humanities (AH)
Automated Language Processing (ALP)
Behavioral and Social Sciences (BSS)
Biological and Chemical Information Systems (BC)

Classification Research (CR)
Community Information Services (CIS)
Computerized Retrieval Services (CRS)
Costs, Budgeting, and Economics (CBE)
Education for Information Science (ED)
Energy and Environment Information (EEI)
Foundations of Information Science (FIS)
Information Analysis and Evaluation (IAE)
Information Generation and Publishing (IGP)
Information Services to Education (ISE)
Law and Information Technology (LAW)
Library Automation and Networks (LAN)
Management of Information Activities (MGT)
Medical Information Systems (MED)
Non-Print Media (NPM)
Numeric Data Bases (NDB)
Public-Private Interface (PPI)
Technology, Information, and Society (TIS)
User On-Line Interaction (UOI)

The headquarters of ASIS are located at 1010 16th Street N.W., Washington, DC 20036 (telephone: 202-659-3644).

Technical Program. The technical and professional activities of ASIS extend from the work of the 23 Special Interest Groups and the 25 chapters to such activities on the national scale as operating the ERIC Clearinghouse on Library and Information Sciences, operating a Placement Service, and conducting a distinguished lecturer series.

Annual awards are presented for the Best Information Sciences Book, the Best Publication by an ASIS chapter or Special Interest Group, the Best Paper Published in the *Journal of the American Society for Information Science,* the Outstanding Information Sciences Movie, the Best ASIS Student Member Paper, and the Award of Merit, which is presented to a member of the profession who is deemed to have made a noteworthy contribution to the field of information science. Recipients of the Award of Merit are:

Hans Peter Luhn (posthumously), 1964
Charles P. Bourne, 1965
Mortimer Taube (posthumously), 1966
Robert A. Fairthorne, 1967
Carlos A. Cuadra, 1968
Cyril W. Cleverdon, 1970
Jerrold Orne, 1971
Phyllis Richmond, 1972
Jesse Shera, 1973
Manfred Kochen, 1974
Eugene Garfield, 1975
Lawrence Heilprin, 1976

Allen Kent, 1977
Calvin Mooers, 1978
Frederick G. Kilgour, 1979
Claire K. Shultz, 1980

ASIS publications include the following.

*Journal of the American Society for Information
    Science (JASIS)*
*Bulletin of the American Society for Information
    Science*
*Annual Review of Information Science and Tech-
    nology (ARIST)*
Proceedings of the ASIS Annual Meetings
*Computer-Readable Bibliographic Data Bases: A
    Directory and Data Sourcebook*
ASIS Handbook and Directory

I. L. AUERBACH

AMERICAN STANDARD CODE FOR INFORMATION INTERCHANGE.

See ASCII.

ANALOG COMPUTERS

For articles on related subjects *see* ANALOG-TO-DIG-
ITAL AND DIGITAL-TO-ANALOG CONVERTERS; DIF-
FERENTIAL ANALYZER; DIGITAL COMPUTERS; HYBRID
COMPUTERS; NUMERICAL ANALYSIS; SIMULATION;
and SPECIAL PURPOSE COMPUTERS.

BACKGROUND

The history of the analog computer goes back to an-
tiquity, when tax maps were first reported as being used
for assessments and surveying. However, this article is
confined to the analog computer as it evolved in the period from World War II to the present time. (For those
interested in the history of the analog computer from an-
tiquity to World War II, the reader is referred to an excellent article by J. Roedel, 1955.)

Between World Wars I and II, much work was done
in developing the mechanical differential analyzer, a
close relative of the modern analog computer. Simultaneous equation solvers and harmonic analyzers of many
types appeared in the 1920s and 1930s. Special computers in the form of network analyzers for the simulation of power networks appeared around 1925. The network
analyzer is a passive element analog. A scale model of the
particular network to be studied is made with resistors,
capacitors, and inductors. The early network analyzers
could be used only to investigate steady-state problems,
i.e., voltage drops along lines, possible current flow in
lines, etc. The more recent network analyzers can be used
to investigate transient conditions during faults or switching on networks. These may be considered true general-
purpose computers.

George H. Philbrick worked on an all-electronic analog computer in the mid-1930s and is credited by many
to have first used feedback amplifier theory to develop the
operational amplifier (see Holst, 1971). He envisioned
the analog computer as an electronic model of the system
to be studied. Independently of and shortly after Philbrick's first work, the Bell Telephone Laboratories developed the M-9 Gun Director under the impetus of the then
impending World War II. The M-9 computer was a
union of electronic analog computation and the mechanical differential analyzer. The first published work seems
to have been handbooks accompanying the M-9 Director.

Following World War II, J. B. Russell of Columbia
University brought the electronic circuitry used in the M-
9 Gun Director to the attention of J. Ragazzini and others. Basing their work on the operational amplifier used
in the M-9 Gun Director, Ragazzini, Randall, and Russell (1947) built an all-electronic d-c analog computer.

Immediately thereafter, several companies designed
and developed analog computers for their own use and for
sale to others. In 1948, Reeves Instrument Co., under a
Navy contract, built the forerunner of the first commercially available analog computer.

Many companies have entered and left the analog
computing field since its birth in 1948. The principal
manufacturers of general purpose analog computing
equipment today are Electronic Associates, Inc., Systron-
Donner, Inc., Applied Dynamics Corp., Telefunken, and
Hitachi.

TYPES OF ANALOG COMPUTERS

Fig. 1(a) shows the classification system used to
characterize analog computers. The two main branches
of analog computers are direct (special purpose) and indirect (general-purpose) computers, as shown in the
figure.

Direct Analog Computer. Direct analog computers are used in the solution of so-called field problems,
e.g., conductive and convective heat transfer, fluid flow,
and structures. The equations for these types of problems
are partial differential equations. A *thermal analyzer* is
an example of a direct analog computer that can be used

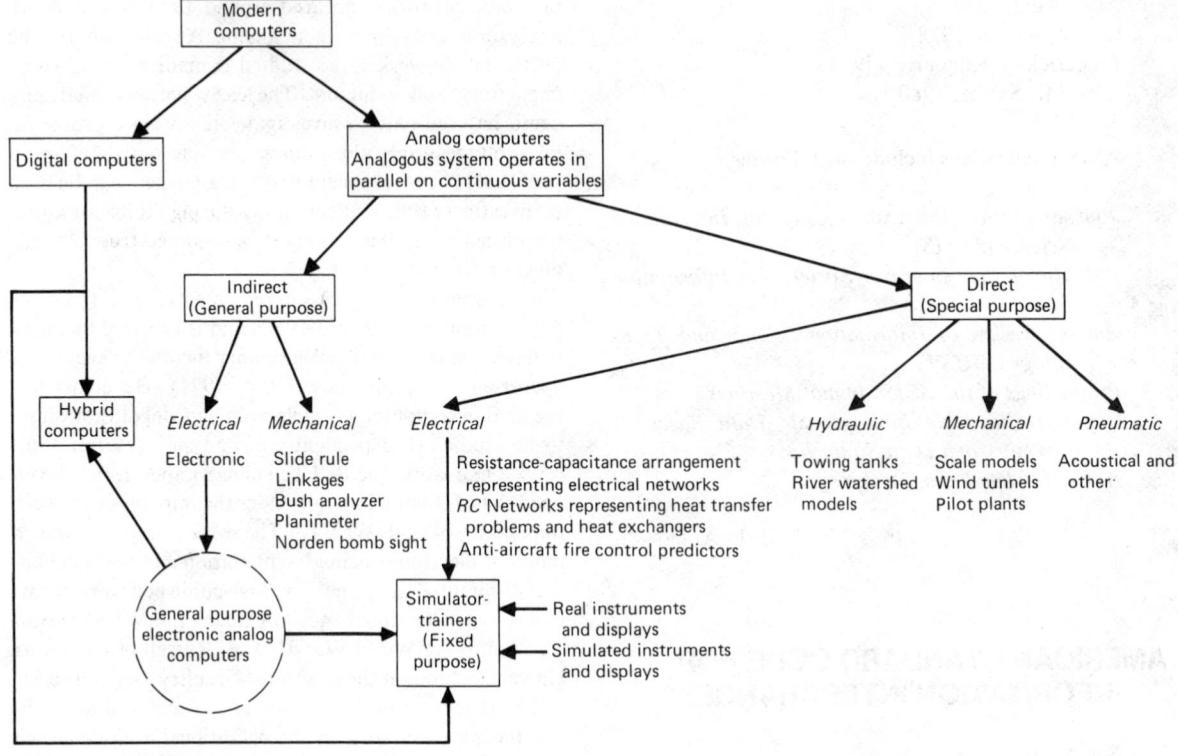

Fig. 1(a).   Types of analog computers.

in the solution of parabolic and elliptic type equations such as

$$\frac{\partial^2 \phi}{\partial x^2} = k\,\frac{\partial \phi}{\partial t}; \quad \frac{\partial^2 \phi}{\partial x^2} = 0$$

This type of computer has resistors and capacitors (and units that compute the fourth power of x for radiation studies). For the hyperbolic equation $\partial^2 \phi/\partial x^2 = k(\partial^2 \phi/\partial t^2)$, which describes structures, vibrating membranes, beams, etc., one might use a similar computer that has resistors, capacitors, inductors, and transformers. Both types are relatively special-purpose computers, and are usually referred to in the analog field as *passive analog computers*.

The programming techniques of the direct analog computer and its associated problems are a subject in themselves and will not be dealt with here, except to remark that the fundamental mathematical theory of programming these partial differential equations involves finite-difference techniques.

Indirect Analog Computer. The electronic differential analyzer, hereafter referred to as the *analog computer,* is best suited for the solution of systems of or-

dinary differential equations. In mathematical terms the analog computer gives particuar solutions to systems of linear or nonlinear differential equations of many variables.

Combined Direct and Indirect Analogs. One area of study in which the analog computer is particulary useful is the so-called real-time simulation problem. In such a problem there is a requirement that the solution proceed exactly in step with real time because a person and/or equipment may be part of the overall computing loop. Such simulations allow realistic hardware testing as well as training and evaluation of complex "human-machine" systems. In these instances there is a combination of the direct analog (a human is the direct analog of itself, and hardware is its own best direct analog) and the indirect analog (the general-purpose analog computer).

This combination of computers is also called *fixed purpose* when the computing system is designed to be dedicated to the real-time simulation. This is the largest and most rapidly growing application of analog computing. These systems are known as *simulator-trainers*, and are widely used in such fields as aircraft/spacecraft pilot training, naval ship operator training, nuclear reactor operator training, power plant operator training, and process plant operator training. Fig. 1(b) shows a typical process plant simulator-trainer.

The Modern Analog Computer. The modern analog computer consists of a large number of individual components, organized in such a manner that the inputs and outputs of these may be interconnected by a programmer-user. Fig. 2(a) shows a schematic representa-

tion of a computer as seen by a programmer. The main continuous components are integrators, represented in the figure by the symbol $\int$; summers, represented by Σ; multipliers/dividers, represented by $\times$; and arbitrary function generators, represented by F. The modern analog computer also contains a number of discrete components such as "and" gates, represented in the figure by A; flip-flops, FF; shift registers, SR; and counters, C. (All these components, and other elements, will be described

Fig. 1(b).   A Process Simulator-Trainer, Model 1501. (Courtesy Autodynamics, Inc., Neptune, NJ.)

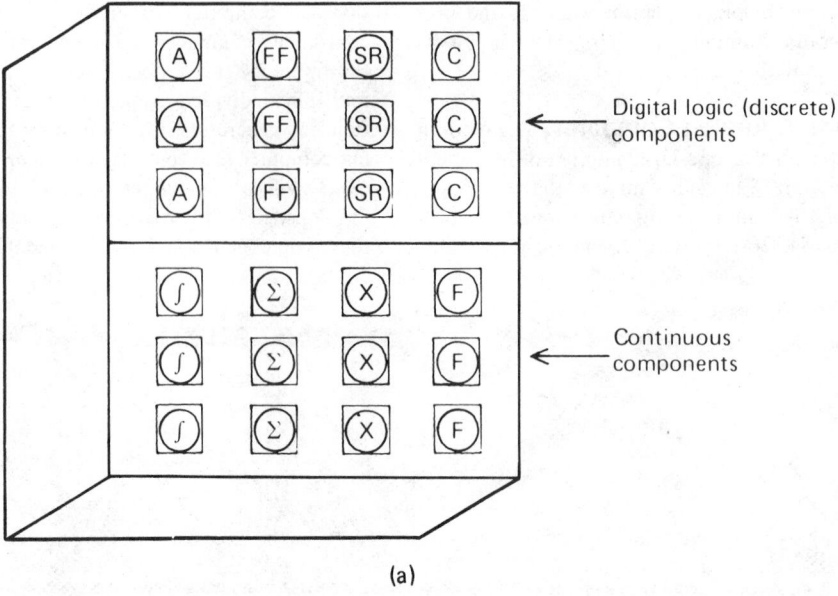

(a)

(b)

Fig. 2.   Analog computers (a) Analog computer with continuous and discrete components organized in parallel fashion. (b) Modern analog computing system, EAI Model 2000. (Courtesy Electronic Associates, Inc., W. Long Branch, NJ.)

later in more detail.) The inputs and outputs of all elements are brought to a central patch bay into which removable patch boards (or problem boards, prepatch panels) and outputs of these may be inserted. In turn, the patch boards are patched or plugged by the programmer, using patch cords (or plugs). These cords and plugs, when inserted, essentially specify the interconnections of the analog components to solve a particular problem. (For further information on patch boards and patch cords, see Korn, 1972.) A photograph of a modern medium-scale analog computer is shown in Fig. 2(b).

Voltage Range. Most large-scale, general-purpose analog computers in use today have a voltage range of ± 100 volts. However, the advent of the integrated circuit operational amplifier (op amp) has led to the development of many low-cost 10-volt systems, particularly for simulator-trainers. These systems far outnumber the ± 100-volt systems.

The high-voltage range has the advantage of good signal-to-noise ratio and relative insensitivity to small offsets and biases that are caused by components such as diodes (in multipliers). The low-voltage range has the advantages of generally greater bandwidth (higher frequency response), lower power requirements, and lower cost.

Accuracy. The accuracy of an analog computer is usually specified by its component accuracies. The linear components in high-quality computers have errors of less than 0.01% of value or full scale, as appropriate. For example, a resistor may have an error of 0.01% of its value, but a multiplier has a fixed minimum error, which is usually stated as a percent of its full-scale output. In the latter case the error changes with the output of the multiplier. The nonlinear components may have errors of 0.02% of full scale. Lower quality computers may have component errors as much as ten times larger than those given above.

Since a typical analog program requires the use of many computing components to obtain a solution, it is not easy to state what the overall accuracy of the solution will be. The overall accuracy depends not only on the quality (accuracy) of the components used, but also on the manner in which they are used (the program), as well as on the method of formulating the problem (analysis) for insertion in an analog computer. One can say, however, that if best practices are used throughout the programming process, the overall error of analog solutions to large problems is on the order of 0.1–0.5% for the best quality computers. Since most analog solution outputs consist of recordings on $X-Y$ plotters or strip-chart time-history recorders, the analog solution accuracy is of the same order as the accuracy of the usual output recording devices. The analog computer, however, is well matched for the job it is intended to perform, since it is used almost

exclusively for the solution of engineering and scientific problems or in simulator-trainers, in which much of the input data is empirically determined, generally to less accuracy than the analog computer solutions thereto. For a detailed discussion of error analysis of analog programs, see Hausner (1971).

Capacity. Modern self-contained analog computers may have any capacity, from the very smallest sold today (such as ten amplifiers and ten potentiometers) to the largest capacities currently being sold as single units, which have a capacity generally measured as 250–300 amplifiers, 200–300 potentiometers, 60 multipliers, 20–40 function generators, and significant quantities of digital logic devices such as comparators, flip-flops, "and" gates, "one-shots," shift registers, and counters. If a larger capacity than that available in a single unit is required in a single problem, then two or more units may be connected together to form a single, large, analog computing system. Analog computing systems containing more than 1,000 amplifiers have been successfully assembled.

A common use of analog computers occurs as a major portion of a hybrid computer. Hybrid computation generally enlarges the equivalent capacity of the analog part of the system by a factor of about 2. This is due to the mix of high-frequency and low-frequency parts of a problem. If a hybrid computer problem were put on an all-analog machine, it would usually require at least twice as much analog equipment as that required in the hybrid solution.

Multispeed Operaion. Most modern analog computers are equipped with controls to allow instantaneous change of the speed of solution. The solution time for a large set of simultaneous nonlinear differential algebraic equations may be as short as 1 ms or as long as 100 sec by appropriate manipulation of controls. With proper programming, analog solutions can be made to last for several hours.

BASIC OPERATIONS

In an analog computer circuit for investigating the behavior of a physical system, only a few of the operational amplifiers will be used as integrators; many others will be used as *summers, inverters,* or *high-gain amplifiers.*

BASIC CONCEPTS

The Operational Amplifier. 1. *General.* The operational amplifier is the basic component in the analog computer. It can be used in a "summing mode" to perform the operations of inversion, summation, and multiplication by a constant. It can also be used in an "integrating mode" to integrate a voltage or the sum of a number of voltages. The change from one mode of operation to another is determined by the feedback element around the amplifier.

2. *The Fundamental Relationship.* To understand the basic operations performed by the amplifier, consider the block diagram in Fig. 3. Associated with the high-gain amplifier are the input and feedback networks, having impedances of Z_i and Z_f, respectively. Now let the voltages at the input, the output, and the amplifier grid be V_i, V_0, and E, respectively. Using Kirchoff's and Ohm's laws, we may write

$$\frac{V_0 - E}{Z_f} + \frac{V_i - E}{Z_i} = i_s \qquad (1)$$

where i_s is the grid current. By definition

$$\frac{V_0}{E} = -A \qquad (2)$$

where $-A$ is the amplifier gain, and A is usually greater than 10^4.

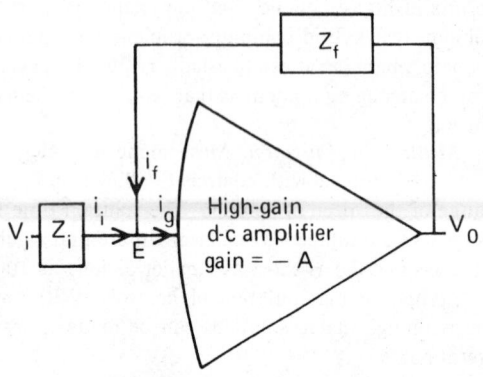

Fig. 3.   Block diagram of an operational amplifier.

A further property of the high-gain amplifier is that the current i_s is at least a factor of 10^4 smaller than i_i, so that i_s can be set equal to zero; consequently, E is a voltage that is much smaller (by at least a factor of 10^4) than either V_i or V_0 so that $E \simeq 0$. Then

$$\frac{V_0}{V_i} = -\frac{Z_f}{Z_i} \qquad (3)$$

This is the fundamental relationship in analog computation. The output voltage will not be affected by the internal characteristics of the amplifier; it will be governed by,

and its accuracy will be dependent upon, the accuracy of the input and feedback elements.

(a) *Inversion.* When both Z_i and Z_f are resistors, the amplifier output will be a constant times the input voltage. If both are equal, the constant is unity and we have an inverter, as shown in Fig. 4.

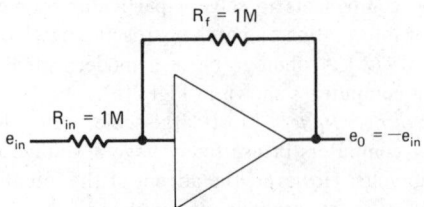

Fig. 4.   The inverting amplifier (M = megohm).

To represent an inverter on computer circuit diagrams, the symbol shown in Fig. 5 is used. Fig. 5 is the "shorthand notation" for Fig. 4. Note that the number 1 at the input to the amplifier signifies a gain of 1. The change in sign is inherent with the amplifier.

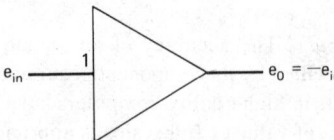

Fig. 5.   The symbol for the inverting amplifier.

(b) *Summation.* If several input resistors are connected to a summing point SJ at the grid of an amplifier and voltages are applied to them, as shown in Fig. 6, then (owing to the fact that the grid voltage of the amplifier is effectively at zero potential) no single input will interfere with any other input, and their effects on the output

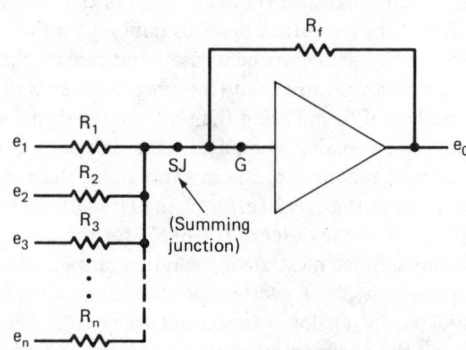

Fig. 6.   The summing amplifier.

will be independent of one another. It is easily derived, then, that

$$e_0 = -\left(\frac{R_f}{R_1} e_1 + \frac{R_f}{R_2} e_2 + \frac{R_f}{R_3} e_3 + \cdots + \frac{R_f}{R_n} e_n \right) \quad (4)$$

The resulting output is therefore minus the sum of the input voltages, each multiplied by a constant depending upon the ratio of the resistors involved.

From experience it was found that the most convenient values for the input resistors are 1M (1 megohm) and 0.1M for 100-volt computers. The resistors are correspondingly smaller on lower voltage computers. A typical summing amplifier with three 1 M and three 0.1 M resistors is shown in Fig. 7. These give gains of 1 and 10 as shown on the symbol for the summing amplifier in Fig. 8.

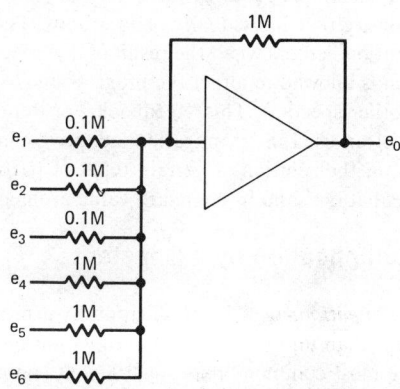

Fig. 7. Example of a summing amplifier.

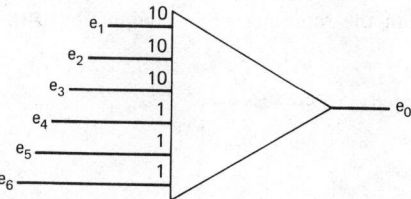

Fig. 8. Symbol for the summing amlifier.

(c) Integration with Respect to Time. Integration of an input voltage is obtained if a capacitor is substituted as the feedback component (Fig. 9).

Since the grid current i_g is zero, the current i through the input resistor R must pass through the feed-

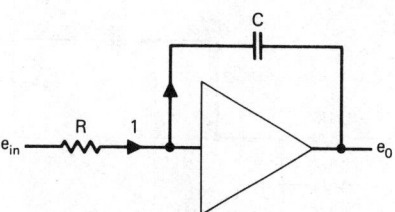

Fig. 9. Operational amplifier with capacitor feedback and resistor input.

back capacitor C, and will produce a potential difference between output and grid of the amplifier. Thus, in Fig. 9,

$$i = \frac{e_i}{R} \quad (5)$$

and

$$e_0 = \frac{q}{C} = - \int_0^t \frac{1}{C} i\, dt, \quad (6)$$

where q — charge on the capacitor and C = capacitance, usually expressed in micro-farads (uf). Thus,

$$e_0 = - \frac{1}{RC} \int_0^t e_i dt. \quad (7)$$

Alternatively, using operational notation for the impedances,

$$\frac{e_0}{e_i} = - \frac{Z_f}{Z_i} = - \frac{1}{RCp}$$

where $p = d/dt$. Therefore,

$$e_0 = - \frac{1}{RC} \int_0^t e_i dt.$$

Note that the proportionality factor RC is actually a time constant which, if we make $R = 1M$ and $C = 1\mu f$ (i.e., a time constant of 1 sec), will produce an integration rate of 1 volt/sec when e_i is equal to 1 volt.

Modern analog computers are equipped with integrators that have a variety of selectable time constants. The range of time constants normally encountered is from 10 sec (for very slow real-time solutions) to 100 μs (for very fast iterative and/or repetitive solutions).

Several inputs may be connected to produce the integral of the sum of a number of voltages. Figs. 10 and 11 show a typical integrating amplifier and its equivalent

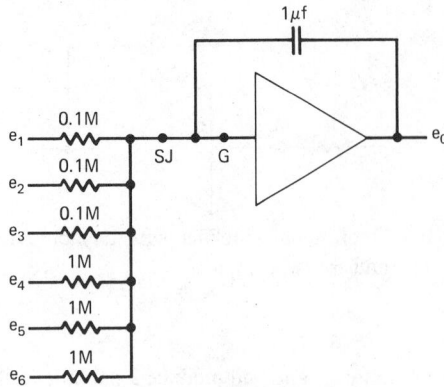

Fig. 10.   A typical integrating amplifier.

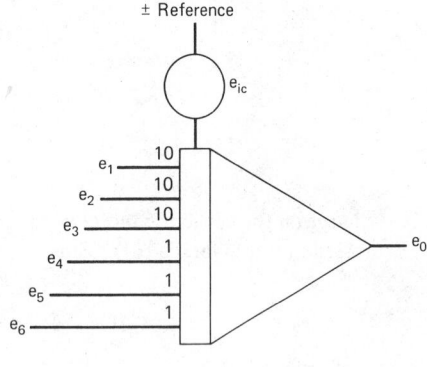

$$e_0 = \mp e_{ic} - \int_0^t (10e_1 + 10e_2 + 10e_3 + e_4 + e_5 + e_6)dt$$

Fig. 11.   The symbol for the integrating amplifier of Fig. 10, including the initial condition.

symbol. There is also an input terminal for inserting independent initial conditions on each integrator.

Control Modes

1. Ordinary Modes

(a) Reset. This mode produces a solution at $t = 0$. All derivative terms are disconnected from the grids of the integrating amplifiers, and initial condition networks are connected by control relays or electronic gates. (For a description of IC circuitry, see Korn and Korn, 1972.)

(b) Operate. This mode produces the time-variant solution. Derivative terms are connected to integrator grids, initial condition networks are disconnected, and capacitors associated with integrators are connected to the grids of integrator amplifiers.

(c) Hold. This mode provides a stationary solution at $t = T$ (HOLD may be selected manually by operator or selected by a computer for a previously defined value of t). Derivative terms and initial condition networks are

disconnected from the integrators, capacitors remaining associated with integrators.

2. Repetitive Operation. In this mode all integrators are switched or cycled automatically from reset-to-operate to reset-to-operate, etc. This mode is usually associated with high solution speeds, of the order of milliseconds in duration, and with the solution displayed on an oscilloscope. When such is the case, the user will obtain the impression that a solution is obtained "instantaneously." However, it is not necessary that high solution speeds be associated with repetitive operations. All that is required is the automatic cycling of the computer between the reset and operate modes for predetermined lengths of time.

3. Iterative Operation. This mode may appear to be similar to the repetitive mode, but it differs from it in several respects. In iterative operation there are usually at least two, sometimes more, speeds of operation. For example, one portion of the computer may be operating at a high speed while another portion is operating at low speed. This simply requires the ability to control the integrations, either individually or in groups. The concept of "iteration" enters when the result of one speed of computation is allowed to affect the progress and/or solution of the other speed(s). This "feedback," or iterative, concept is often used in optimization, adaptive control, prediction, in the solution of certain types of partial differential equations, and in boundary value problems.

Multiplication by a Constant

1. Potentiometers. Multiplication by a positive constant less than unity can be achieved with a potentiometer. The most common "pots" on 100-volt computers are ten-turn, 30,000-ohm, linear, wire-wound potentiometers with one end connected to ground, as shown diagrammatically in Fig. 12. They can be used either in conjunction with the reference to obtain a fixed accurate voltage less than the reference or in conjunction with a signal

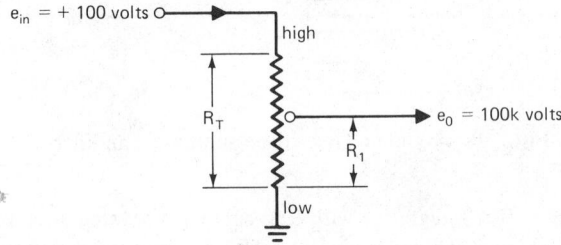

Fig. 12.   Schematic of a potentiometer shown with +100 volts connected to the input side to give an output at the wiper of $+100k$ volts, where $k = R_1/R_T$.

voltage to multiply that voltage by any constant less than unity. For example, if $+100$ volts is applied to the high end of the pot as shown in Fig. 12, the output at the wiper will be k times 100 volts, where $k = R_1 / R_T$ (neglecting the effect of external loading).

(a) The Potentiometer Symbol. Two forms of potentiometer or, as it is sometimes called, attenuator units are shown in Fig. 13; both electric circuits and analog programming symbols are shown.

(b) Pot-Set Mode. In order to set pots to their proper values under true load conditions, a special control mode called *pot set* is supplied in most analog computers. In this mode, the SJ (input resistors) are disconnected from the grid of the operating amplifier (see Figs. 6 and 10), and the SJ are grounded. Under these conditions, there will be no inputs to the amplifiers that could cause an amplifier overload while a pot is being set, for in order to set a pot a reference must be applied to its input terminal. Note that the load seen by the pot is the same as under normal operation, for in normal operation the grid voltage E is so small that it can be considered to be the same as if it were at ground potential, the potential at which the summing junction is held during *pot set*.

2. *Digital Coefficient Attenuators (DCA).* This component is a hybridized version of a potentiometer that permits very rapid setting of coefficient values, under digital computer control, in less than 10 μs. This unit is also known as a digital-to-analog multiplier (DAM) in some versions.

AMPLIFIER AND POTENTIOMETER CIRCUITS

Addition, Subtraction, and Sign Inversion

1. *Amplifiers Only.* Circuits are shown in Fig. 14.

2. *Arbitrary Gains (using pots), Including Multiplication and Division by a Constant.* Circuits providing these functions are shown in Fig. 15.

3. *Rule for High-Gain Amplifiers with Feedback.* High gain with feedback is expressed as

$$\Sigma \text{ input voltages multiplied by gains} = 0$$

This rule is true because of the high gain ($>10^4$) of the amplifier. Assume for the moment that there is a small net voltage at the grid (even 1 mv). The high-gain amplifier would amplify this small voltage to more than full scale of the amplifier output, which would cause the amplifier to saturate. However, in order to prevent this saturation, there must be a compensating or balancing negative feedback from the high-gain amplifier to its own input, so that for some output of the high-gain amplifier there will be an exact balance or "null" at the input, thus

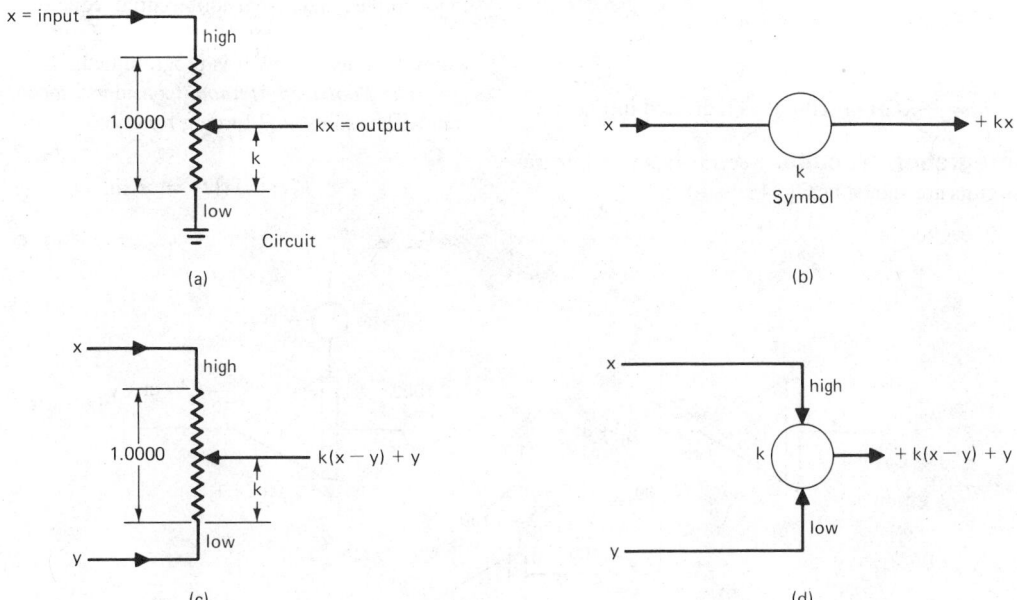

Fig. 13.   Here, (b) is the symbolic representation of the attentuator shown schematically in (a); (d) is the symbol used to represent the ungrounded attentuator shown schematically in (c).

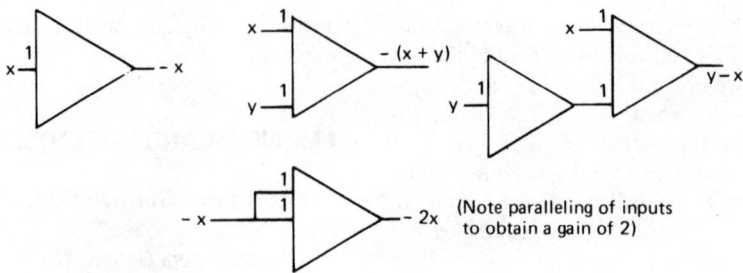

Fig. 14

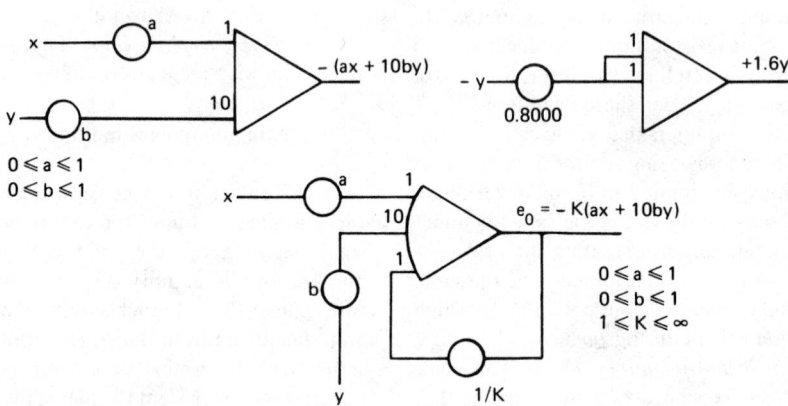

Fig. 15

leading to the rule given above. This rule is illustrated in Fig. 15, where, by invoking the rule above, we have

$$ax + 10by + \frac{e_0}{K} = 0 \qquad (8)$$

so that $e_0 = -K(ax + 10by)$, as indicated in Fig. 15.

Integration Circuits. Several types of integration circuits are shown in Fig. 16.

Application to Linear Differential Equations. While the analog computer is most useful in solving complex, nonlinear differential equations, it is instructive to consider a linear differential equation example to learn how it is programmed.

The Bootstrap Method. Consider a mechanical system with a sinusoidal forcing function

$$F(t) = y(t) = A \sin \omega t, \qquad (9)$$

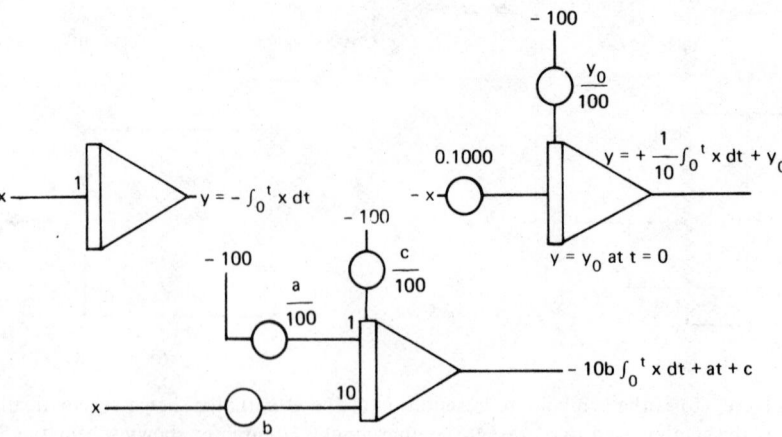

Fig. 16. Integration circuits.

where $F(t)$ is acting on a body of mass m which is restrained by a spring of stiffness k, and a "velocity type" damper with damping constant c. This system is shown in Fig. 17.

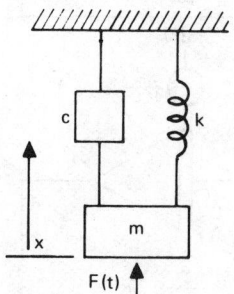

Fig. 17.

If x is the displacement of the body from its equilibrium position, the forces acting upon the body may be written as follows:

External force $= F(t) = y$,
Spring force $= -Kx$,
Damping force $= -c(\text{velocity}) = -c(dx/dt)$.

The equations to be solved are

$$m\frac{d^2x}{dt^2} + c\frac{dx}{dt} + kx = y(t) \qquad (10)$$

and

$$\frac{d^2y}{dt^2} + \omega^2 y = 0 \qquad (11)$$

The solution to Eq. 11 is the desired sinusoid.

The bootstrap method assumes that the terms for generating the highest-order derivatives of each variable are available. To execute the bootstrap method, the equations are rewritten in the form

$$\ddot{x} = -\frac{c}{m}\dot{x} - \frac{k}{m}x + \frac{y}{m} \qquad (12)$$

$$\frac{\ddot{y}}{\omega^2} = -y \qquad (13)$$

where

$$\ddot{x} = \frac{d^2x}{dt^2}; \; \ddot{y} = \frac{d^2y}{dt^2}; \; \dot{x} = \frac{dx}{dt}, \text{ etc.}$$

The symbolic analog computer diagram for Eqs. 12 and 13 is shown in Fig. 18.

Using the necessary summers, integrators, inverters, and pots, the inputs to the derivatives are generated and the diagram of Fig. 18 becomes that of Fig. 19.

The initial condition for $-y/\omega$ is obtained from

$$-\frac{1}{\omega}\frac{d}{dt}(A \sin \omega t) \text{ at } t = 0 \qquad (14)$$

An alternative method is to sum the acceleration terms for $\ddot{x}$ directly into the $\dot{x}$ integrator. This saves one summing amplifier, as shown in Fig. 20. The y circuit remains the same, since no saving of amplifiers would occur in that circuit.

NONLINEAR OPERATIONS

Multiplication and Division of Variables

The Quarter Square Multiplier. Consisting of a number of diode-resistor networks, coupled with op amps, this device can produce high-accuracy products of two variables, at frequencies up to 1 Khz. Its fundamental operation is derived from the relation

$$\tfrac{1}{4}(X + Y)^2 - \tfrac{1}{4}(X - Y)^2 = XY. \qquad (15)$$

For example, quarter-square multiplication could be mechanized as shown in Fig. 21. The boxes marked FG are function generators (described in the next section), which here have the property of producing the square of the input variable.

General-purpose analog computers have quarter-square multipliers with fixed squaring networks that can be used for either one product or two squares. Here we adopt the convention that the multiplier has all the necessary hardware and therefore can be regarded as a "black box." The symbol for multipliers is shown in Fig. 22.

The Transconductance Multiplier. Consisting basically of a number of transistor-resistor networks, this de-

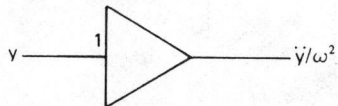

Fig. 18.

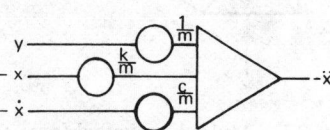

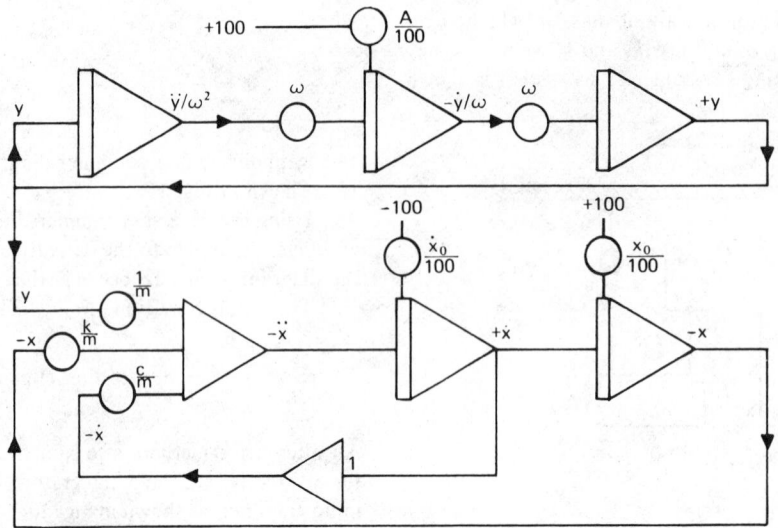

Fig. 19.

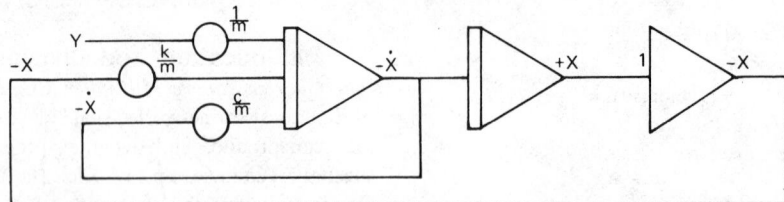

Fig. 20.

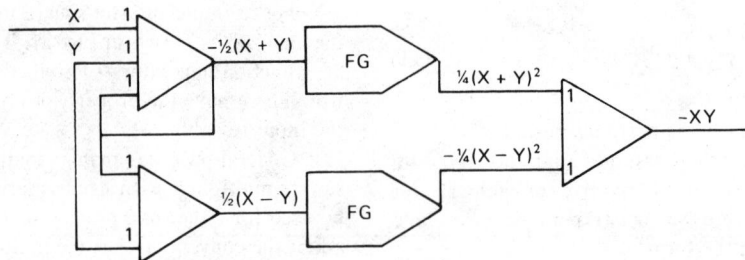

Fig. 21. Quarter-square multiplication.

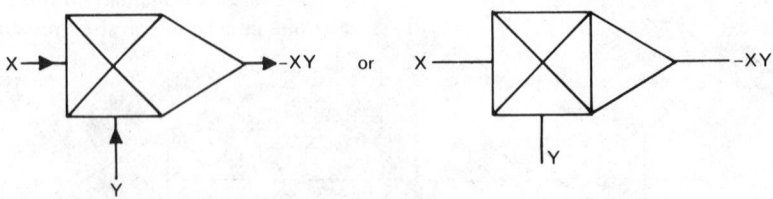

Fig. 22. Multiplier symbol (note the sign inversion).

vice can produce the best high-frequency-accuracy product available today. Manufactured in high volume, using integrated circuit and laser trimming techniques, it is also the lowest cost multiplier available (see Sheingold, 1978).

Squaring. Squaring is accomplished by connecting the same variable to both inputs of a multiplier, as shown in Fig. 23.

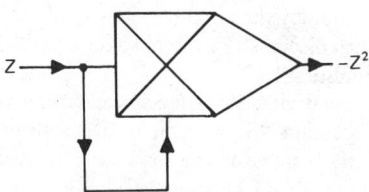

Fig. 23. Squaring circuit.

Division and Square Root by Use of Implicit Arithmetic. A nonlinear component may be used in the feedback loop around high-gain amplifiers to perform the inverse of the operation that the component performs in the forward loop configuration. The most frequent use of this technique is in division and square root circuits with multipliers.

1. *Square Root.* Refer to Fig. 24. Let

$$\epsilon = X - Z^2 \qquad (16)$$

and assume that, for a high-gain amplifier, the output is related to the input grid voltage

$$Z = A\epsilon \qquad (17)$$

where $A > 10^8$. Eliminating ϵ,

$$X - Z^2 = \frac{Z}{A} \simeq 0. \qquad (18)$$

Therefore,

$$Z = (X)^{1/2} \qquad (19)$$

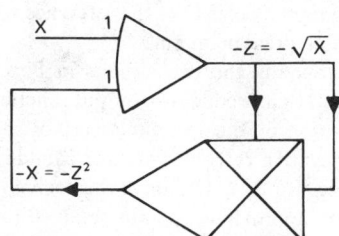

Fig. 24. Square root circuit ($X > 0$).

For stability, the feedback loop must have an odd number of inversions of the signal so that the sum of the currents through the input resistors to the amplifier grid is equal to zero (ϵ). It is this rule that allows the determination of the sign of the output, which would otherwise be indeterminate.

Note that a squaring device has the property of acting as a sign changer for only one sign of the input variable. In analog multipliers there is usually a built-in sign inversion, as described previously under "Amplifier and Potentiometer Circuits," so that analog squarers act as sign inverters for positive inputs only. Consequently, in the square root circuit the squarer counts for zero inversions, since when Z is negative the output $-Z^2$ is also negative. The one inversion in the circuit is the high-gain amplifier producing $-Z = -(X)^{1/2}$.

Note also that the circuit is stable only for $X > 0$. For values of $X < 0$, an additional inverter must be placed in the feedback loop, and the output of the high-gain amplifier becomes $+Z = (-X)^{1/2}$.

Since modern analog computers have provision for automatically converting a multiplier to a square root circuit, a convenient symbol to use is shown in Fig. 25.

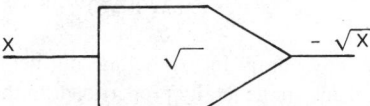

Fig. 25. Symbol for square root circuit.

2. *Division Circuit.* Similarly, for division (Fig. 26), let

$$\epsilon = Y - XZ, \quad Z = A\epsilon,$$
$$Y - XZ = Z/A \simeq 0, \quad Z = Y/X.$$

Note that X must be positive but that Y can be of either sign. Also note that the negative of X must be brought to the multiplier terminal in order to satisfy the stability rule described above for the square root circuit.

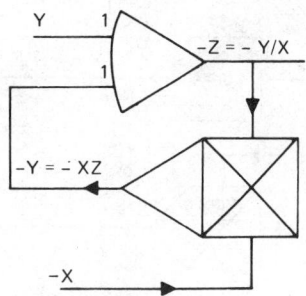

Fig. 26. Division circuit ($X > 0$).

Since some analog computers have provision for automatically converting a multiplier to a divider, a convenient symbol to use is shown in Fig. 27.

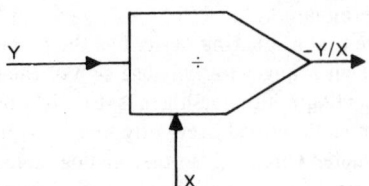

Fig. 27.   Symbol for divider.

Special Multiplier Hookups. Some multipliers have provisions for obtaining special sign-sensitive squares and square roots, which are important in fluid flow phenomena. As an example, take the case of the flow of fluid through an orifice, which is proportional to the square root of the pressure drop across the orifice. If the reverse flow is to take place, it is necessary to implement the equation.

$$Q = \text{sign}(\Delta P)(\Delta P)^{1/2} \qquad (20)$$

Similarly, drag forces acting on bodies moving through fluids are generally proportional to the square of the relative velocity between body and fluid, and are opposite in sign to the direction of motion. It is necessary to implement the equation

$$C_{\text{drag}} = -\text{sign}(V) \cdot V^2. \qquad (21)$$

By a simple patch change on modern analog computers, the two operations exemplified by Eqs. 20 and 21 are directly implemented without requiring any special logic-switching operations. Since these are direct analog outputs, convenient symbols may be used as shown in Fig. 28. Note that the two special multiplier hookups in Fig. 28 apply only to squaring and square rooting.

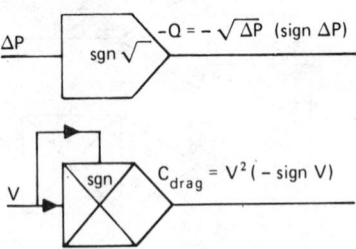

Fig. 28.   Other convenient nonlinear programming symbols.

Function Generators. There are two types of function generators commonly in use today, diode function generators (DFG), and digitally controlled function generators (DCFG). These are used to insert, or input, arbitrary functions of one variable, using a piecewise linear approximation on from 10 to 20 arbitrarily spaced points in the independent variable.

The Diode Function Generator. This component, which has been available since 1955, accomplishes the FG operation by the circuitry shown in Fig. 29, using the techniques discussed in the next section, "Simulation of Discontinuities."

By modifying the dead-space circuit (refer to the later discussion "Simulation of Discontinuities"), thus making both signs of the input and reference voltages available, one can choose "breakpoints and slopes" at will, as shown in Fig. 30.

The circuit works as follows: If X is positive, the lower diode is biased beyond cutoff (rendered nonconducting = open circuit) so that only the upper diode circuit can contribute. In the region $0 \leq X \leq$ b.p. (where b.p. is the breakpoint setting of the upper b.p. pot), the upper diode is also biased beyond cutoff so that there is no input to the Y amplifier (both input diodes are on open circuit). This is also shown in the characteristic graph of Y versus X in Fig. 30(b); i.e., there is no output Y between zero and the breakpoint. Now, when X is positive and greater than the upper breakpoint, the output of the upper b.p. pot will be positive, increasing linearly with X from a zero value when X is at the breakpoint value; see Fig. 13(d). The slope of the output characteristic will be determined by the slope pot. Note that the input to the Y amplifier is positive, thus creating the negative output Y as shown on the characteristic graph. In a similar manner, it can be shown that, when X is negative, the upper diode is always biased beyond cutoff, and that the lower diode will also be cut off for $-$b.p. $\leq X \leq 0$, where b.p. is the breakpoint setting of the lower b.p. pot. At this point the analysis of the lower circuit is identical to the upper circuit since $-X$, the input to the lower circuit, is now a positive voltage.

To obtain positive output values Y [in the upper two quadrants of Fig. 30(b)], it is only necessary to reverse the polarity of the diode connection while at the same time changing the polarity of the reference voltage on the corresponding breakpoint pot.

By combining the two circuits in Figs. 29–30, we have a circuit that produces an output function $Y(X)$; i.e., a superposition of the two functions. A coefficient pot from the negative reference voltage is added so that $Y_0 \neq 0$ (see Fig. 31). By extension of this technique, straight-line segment approximations are obtained for a wide variety of arbitrary functions. The symbol for an arbitrary function generator of one variable is shown in Fig. 32.

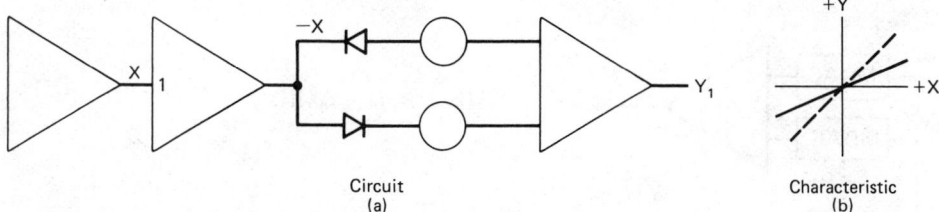

Circuit
(a)

Characteristic
(b)

Fig. 29. Diode circuit for output slope change at origin.

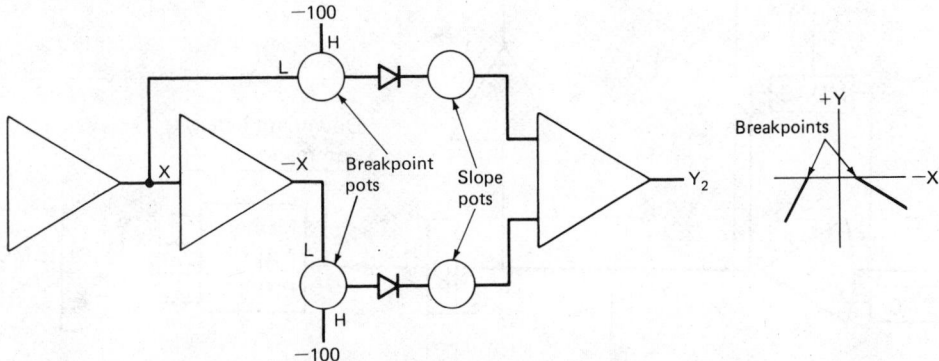

Fig. 30. Diode circuit for output slope changes away from the origin (see Fig. 13(d) for three-terminal pot).

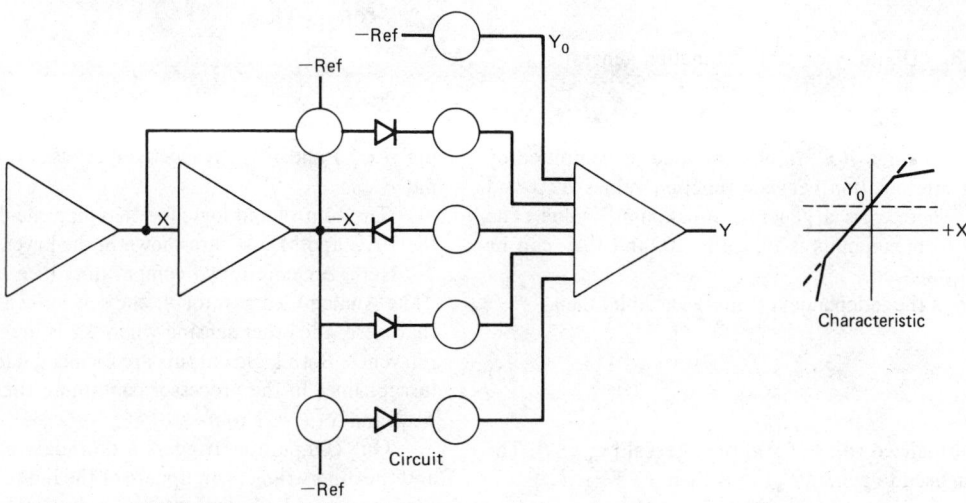

Fig. 31. Complete DFG circuits, including bias pot Y_0.

Fig. 32. Function generator symbol.

The Digitally Controlled Function Generator. The digitally controlled function generator (DCFG) is a hybrid computing device, now supplied as a fully self-contained unit in existing analog computers. It consists of a small, high-speed core memory (to contain the function data points) and multiplying digital-to-analog converters, organized as shown in Fig. 33.

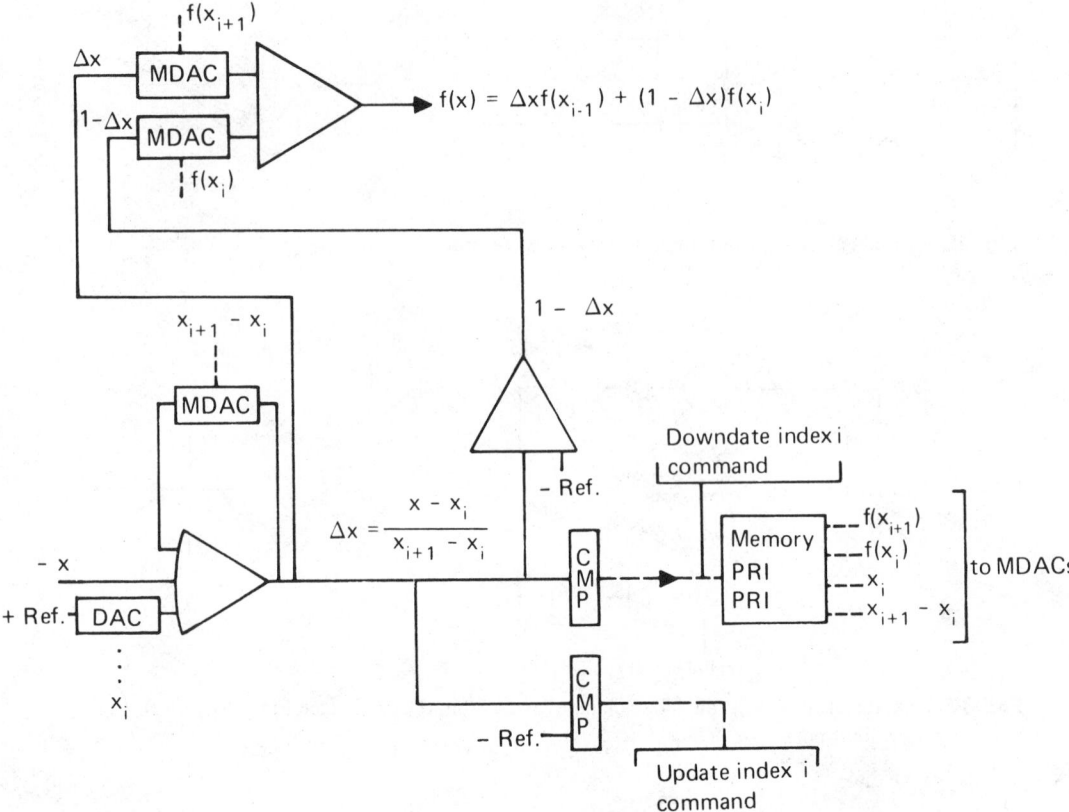

Fig. 33. Digitally controlled function generator.

The function $f(x)$, to be generated, is computed by a linear interpolation between function values $f(x_i)$ and $f(x_{i+1})$, where x_i is a general "breakpoint" value. The number of breakpoints is typically 20, and they can be unequally spaced.

If x is the independent (input) variable, then

$$\Delta x = \frac{x - x_i}{x_{i+1} - x_i} \tag{22}$$

is the normalized value of x in the interval $[x_i, x_{i+1}]$. The equation used to generate $f(x)$ is then

$$f(x) = \Delta x\, f(x_{i+1}) + (1 - \Delta x) f(x_i). \tag{23}$$

In Fig. 33, the independent variable $-x$ (at the lower left) is summed with a digital-to-analog converter (DAC) containing x_i, and is divided by a multiplying DAC (MDAC) containing $x_{i+1} - x_i$. The output of this circuit is Δx, defined in Eq. 22. The output Δx is subtracted from the reference, forming $1 - \Delta x$, and both Δx and $1 - \Delta x$ are fed to the MDAC (at top of figure) contain-

ing $f(x_{i+1})$ and $f(x_i)$, respectively, thus forming the output $f(x)$.

The control and logic for changing the digial data in the DAC and MDAC are shown in the lower right of Fig. 33. Here, Δx enters two comparators (see later section. "The Analog Comparator"), one sensing when Δx is less than zero, the other sensing when Δx is greater than the reference. Both logic outputs are connected to priority interrupt lines in the processor containing the digital data $f(x_i)$ and x_i, $i = 1$ to n.

One comparator triggers a downdate of the index i and the other triggers an update of the index i. Whenever a trigger occurs, the appropriate values of x_i, $x_{i+1} - x_i$, $f(x_i)$, and $f(x_{i+1})$ are transferred within a few memory-cycle times to the appropriate DAC and DMAC, thus allowing the circuit generating $f(x)$ to be correct in all intervals $x_{i+1} - x_i$.

Special Function Generators (Fixed-Function Generators). Certain functions such as exponentials, sines and cosines, squares, and cubes recur so often in engineering and scientific studies that it has been found useful to build fixed-function generators for these operations.

1. *Exponential Log Generator.* Perhaps the most flexible method for generating an exponential is to use a fixed-function generator from which any exponential can be generated. The symbol for such a device is shown in Fig. 34. Using this device, it is possible to generate any exponential by employing the logarithm generator in the feedback of a high-gain amplifier, thus obtaining the inverse operation (or antilog). (This is analogous to using a multiplier in the feedback of a high-gain amplifier to obtain division).

For example, to generate the exponential Ae^{cx}, where A and c are constants and x is a variable, let $y = Ae^{cx}$. Then

$$\log_e y = \log_e A + cx. \qquad (24)$$

The circuit for forming the $\log_e y$ from Eq. 24 is shown in Fig. 34(b). Inserting this sum into a high-gain amplifier, which has a $\log_e$ generator in its feedback path, will take the antilog of the input, thus producing the desired output y.

The DCFG can easily generate the fixed function just described by loading the appropriate function table in its memory. As the cost of the DCFG comes down, it will replace the diode function generator because of its ease of set-up, convenience in storing function tables for later use, and flexibility of use for math functions or arbitrary (empirical) functions.

2. *The Resolver (Sine-Cosine Generator).* A resolver is actually a combination of computing elements, including provisions for generating $\sin \theta$ and $\cos \theta$, given θ as an input, and also allowing for the multiplication of both $\sin \theta$ and $\cos \theta$ by any other variable V, thereby generating $V \cos \theta$. This device is an outgrowth of servomultiplying technology, wherein it was a relatively simple matter to change a linear pot to a sine or cosine pot (padded-pot technique) and (by applying $\pm V$ to the endpoints of the padded pot) to obtain $V \sin \theta$ and $V \cos \theta$. Modern computers, however, usually have a fixed (electronic) function generator or a DCFG to generate either the sine or the cosine function. This is shown symbolically in Fig. 35.

It is, of course, still possible to combine the preceding operation with electronic multipliers to obtain

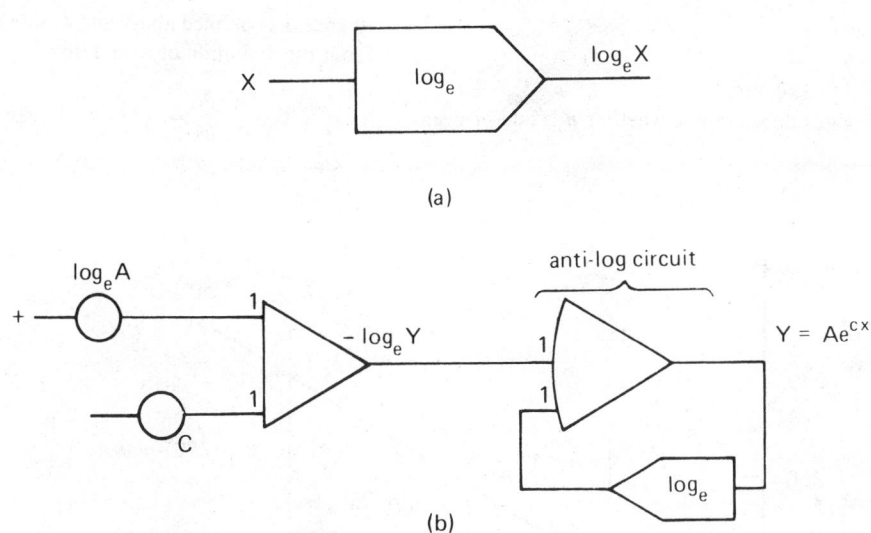

(a)

(b)

Fig. 34. Fixed function generator for generating the natural logarithm of a variable. (a) Symbol. (b) Circuit.

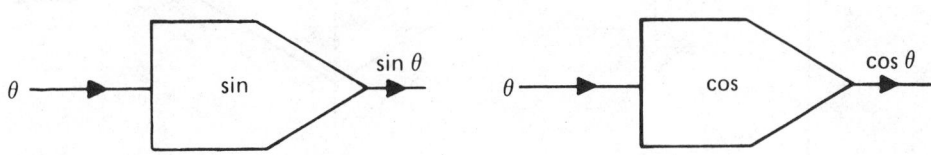

Fig. 35. The sin/cos generators.

$V \sin \theta$ and $V \cos \theta$. If one merely has a sine or cosine generator, then it is termed a "sinusoid" generator to include both functions (since it requires only a single patching change to obtain either function). If the sinusoid generators are intimately packaged with the multipliers to allow direct generation of $V \sin \theta$ and $V \cos \theta$, given V and θ as inputs, then the package is called a "resolver."

(a) Rate Resolver. A rate resolver allows the insertion of $\dot{\theta}$, instead of θ, into a resolver input terminal, and $\sin \theta$ and $\cos \theta$ will be automatically produced. This is simply accomplished by inclusion of an integrator within the resolver package, which will integrate θ and produce $\dot{\theta}$.

(b) Continuous Rate Resolver. The normal allowed range of input to the sinusoid generator (SG) is ± 180 deg. If θ should go larger than this—as, for example, in continuous rolling and/or tumbling—then a switch is incorporated on the rate input which changes the sign of the θ input to the resolver integrator whenever $|\theta_i|$ reaches 180 deg. At the same time, the sign of $\sin \theta$ is changed. This follows from the relations

$$\theta = n(360°) \pm \theta_i, \quad |\theta_i| < 180°,$$
$$\sin \theta = \pm \sin\theta_i, \quad \cos \theta = \cos \theta_i,$$

Input to SG = θ_i,

where $n = \pm 0, 1, 2$, etc.

The $\pm$ signs depend upon whether n is odd or even and whether θ is increasing or decreasing. A time history of θ and θ_i for increasing θ is shown in Fig. 36.

In particular, if $n = 1$ and $\theta = 360° - \theta_i$ and $\sin \theta = - \sin \theta_i$, then a sign change must occur at the output of the sine generator for odd n. Similarly, when $\theta = 360° - \theta_i$, then $\cos \theta = \cos \theta_i$, which is correct for all n. The circuit is shown in Fig. 37.

(c) Polar Resolution. The object here is, given the x and y components of a vector (or a complex variable), to find R, the magnitude of the vector, and θ, the angle that the vector makes with the X-axis. This is accomplished by forming the error equation $\epsilon = x \sin \theta - y \cos \theta$, which, as can be seen from the geometry of the relationships among x, y, and θ as shown in Fig. 38, is zero only when θ is the correct angle. In these circumstances—i.e., when an implicit algebraic relationship must be satisfied by a dependent variable θ—given the independent variables x and y, a mathematical method exists, called the "method of steepest descent" (see Hausner, 1971), which defines a stable formula for the generation of the time derivative of the dependent variable as follows:

$$\frac{d\theta}{dt} = -k\epsilon \frac{\partial \epsilon}{\partial \theta}, \tag{25}$$

where ϵ is as defined above and k is an arbitrary constant. From the definition of ϵ we derive

$$\frac{\partial \epsilon}{\partial \theta} = x \cos \theta + y \sin \theta. \tag{26}$$

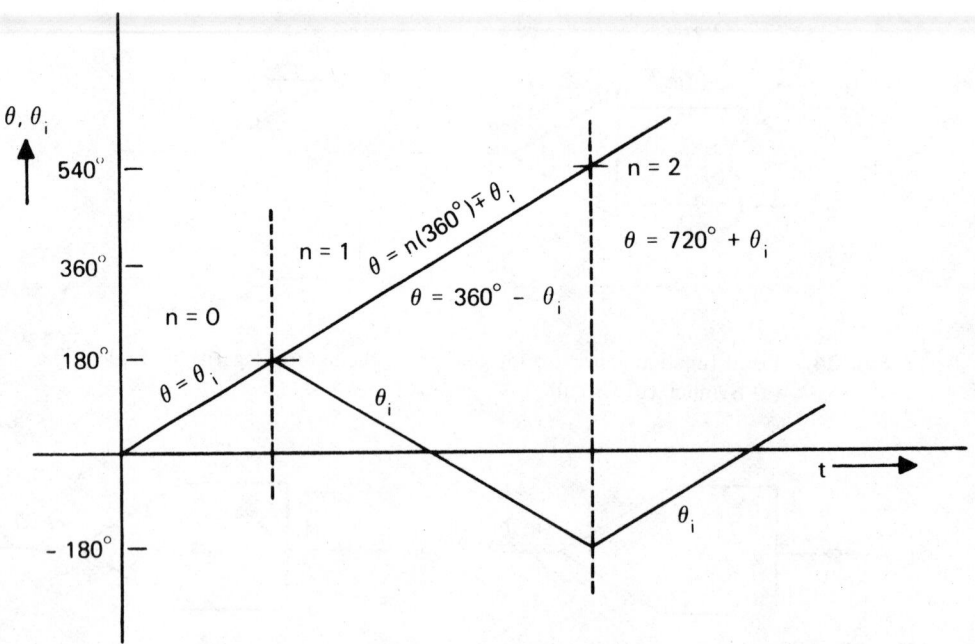

Fig. 36. Time history showing θ and θ_i with switching occurring at $\theta = 180°$ and $\theta = 540°$.

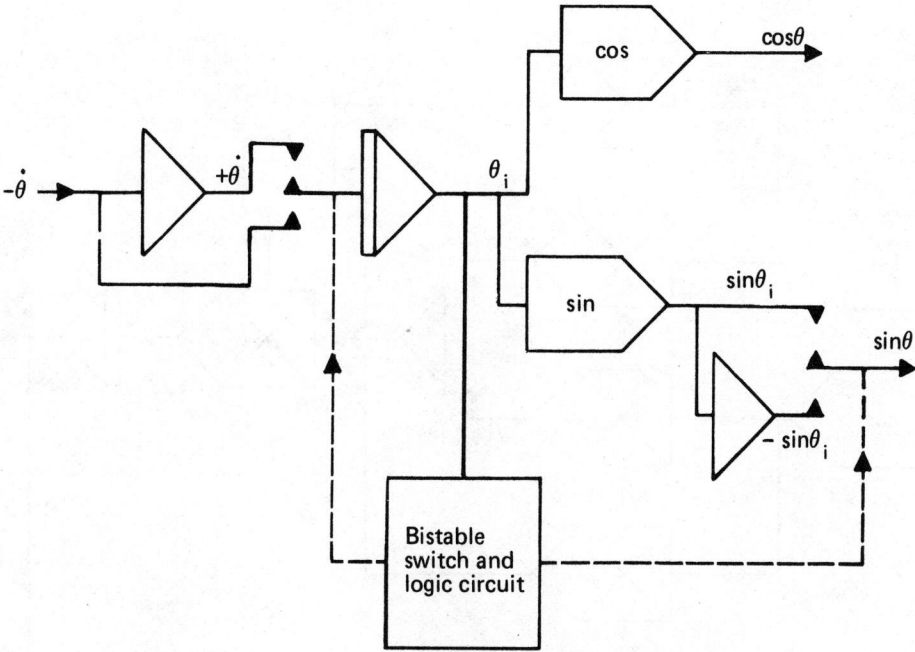

Fig. 37. Rate resolver and continuous resolver (multipliers not shown).

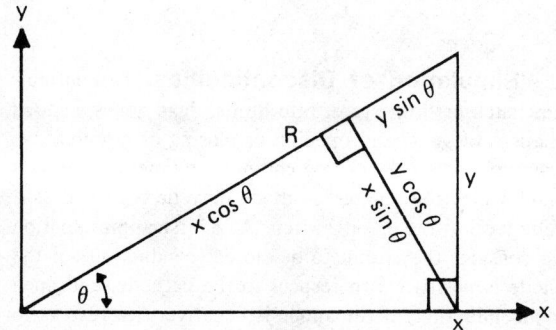

Fig. 38. Polar resolution geometry.

From the geometry of Fig. 38, we see that $x \cos \theta + y \sin \theta = R$, so that $\partial\epsilon/\partial\theta = R$. Substituting the last expression into the original equation for $d\theta/dt$, we obtain $d\theta/dt = -k\epsilon R$. Ihe circuit for obtaining R and θ from x and y is shown in Fig. 39.

(d) Polar Resolution Circuit. For fastest response in this circuit, k should be made as large as loop stability will permit. This is usually a value between 1,000 and 10,000. Such large gains are obtained by using small capacitors for the integrator feedback (0.01 μf or smaller).

Both the ordinary resolver and the polar resolution circuit can be readily replaced by a multivariable function generator (MVFG) (see Rubin, 1976), a new hybrid computing component that is similar in construction and

operation to the DCFG. It combines several DCFG's, plus other analog components, to allow the automatic generation of an arbitrary function of 2, 3 or, by a recent extension, 4 variables, at analog speeds. The symbols for the MVFG application to resolver functions are shown in Fig. 40.

3. *X^3 and X^4 Generators.* These are similar in operation to the previously discussed special generators, differing only in the output function. The programming symbols are shown in Fig. 41.

The X^4 generator is particularly useful in heat radiation studies.

Functions of More Than One Variable. In the past, most analog programmers resorted to some mathematical juggling or simplification of functions in order to be able to use multivariable functions in an analog computer. For example, a function $f(x,y)$, may sometimes be expressed as the sum or product of two functions of one varible, such as

$$f_1(x,y) = g_1(x) + h_1(y),$$

or

$$f_2(x,y) = g_2(x)h_2(y) + \text{similar terms.}$$

More details on purely analog techniques for multivariable function generation may be found in Hausner

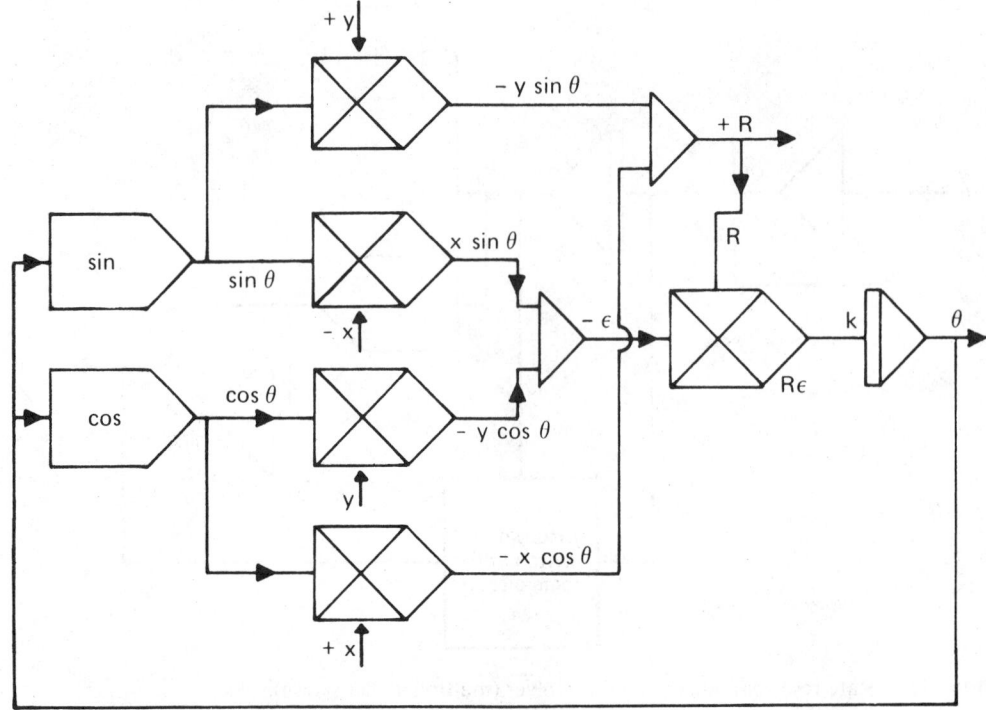

Fig. 39.   Polar resolution circuit.

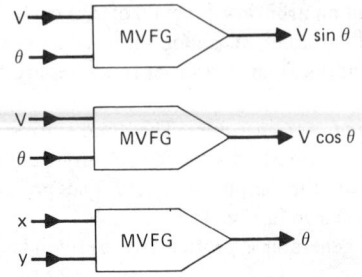

Fig. 40.   Resolver functions using MVFG.

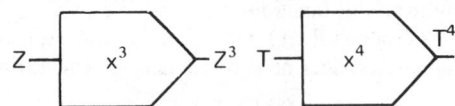

Fig. 41.   Programming symbols for X^3 and X^4 units.

(1971), and Korn and Korn (1972). There now exists a hybrid component for handling the generation of functions of up to four variables. This is an extension of the DCFG, and is described by Rubin (1976).

Simulation of Discontinuities. Discontinuities (such as limit stops, rate limits, dead zones, sudden changes of gain, and opening or closing of circuits) are programmed on the analog computer by means of diodes and/or electronic gates. A diode may be regarded as a voltage-sensitive on-off switch. As a first approximation we consider the circuit to be closed (conducting), if the anode is positive with respect to the cathode, and open (nonconducting) if the anode is negative with respect to the cathode. A simple circuit for introducing a discontinuity at the origin is shown in Fig. 42.

In the circuit shown in Fig. 42, $-X$ is connected to the cathode of the diode and the anode is connected to a pot. When $-X$ is negative, the cathode of the diode is negative with respect to the anode so the diode conducts and produces a positive output through the inversion of the Y-amplifier. When $-X$ is positive, the diode is rendered in the nonconducting state, and $Y = 0$. The circuit characteristic is shown to the right of the circuit diagram. This circuit is also called a nonnegative limiter (i.e., Y is constrained to positive values only). By reversing the diode, one can make a nonpositive limiter. The circuit in Fig. 42 can be considered to have a breakpoint at zero (a discontinuity in the derivative of the output occurs when $X = 0$). The discontinuity in the output can be

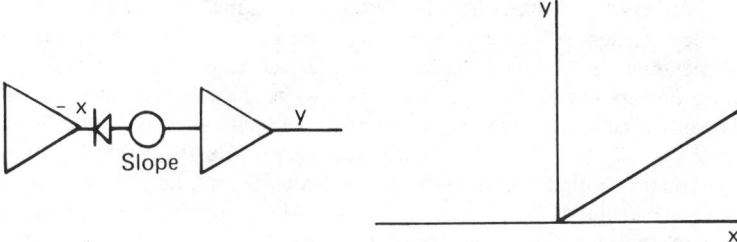

Fig. 42.   Origin discontinuity circuit.

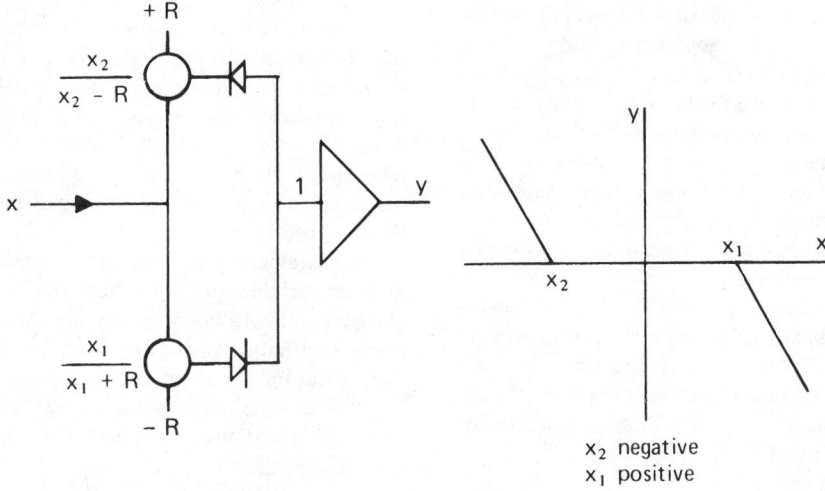

Fig. 43.   Dead-space circuit.

made to occur at any arbitrary value of X, as in the "dead-space" circuit shown in Fig. 43; see Fig. 13(d). Notice that the discontinuity occurs at other than $X = 0$.

For more details on the use of diode circuits to represent a variety of discontinuities, and for special time function generation, such as sine wave, triangular wave, and square wave generation, see Hausner, 1971.

DIGITAL LOGIC OPERATIONS

The Analog Comparator. The analog comparator has been a fundamental component of the analog computer from its inception. In the past it was intimately associated with a relay such that the comparator output drove the relay arm to one of two sets of contacts. Actually, the analog comparator is a true hybrid device, since it accepts analog inputs (usuaully two) and produces a digital logic level output (either a binary "1" or a binary "0"). The symbol is shown in Fig. 44.

If one of the two analog inputs is a constant voltage (as, for example, a reference voltage multiplied by a constant coefficient), then the output of the comparator shows when the other variable is greater than or less than the particular constant value.

The output of the comparator can be used to control the analog computer, to drive electronic gates, or as inputs to other digital logic components, to sense lines, control lines, interrupt lines, or priority interrupt lines of digital computers.

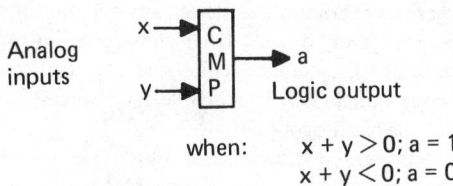

when: $x + y > 0$; $a = 1$
$x + y < 0$; $a = 0$

Fig. 44.   Analog comparator symbol.

General-Purpose Digital Logic Modules. It may seem strange to include a section on true general-purpose digital logic components with material on analog computers, but analog programmers have always made use of digital logic in the normal course of obtaining a solution to a problem.

Many years ago, general-purpose digital logic modules were not available, so the manufacturers of analog equipment did not supply such modules. The programmer, however, by using comparators, relays, diodes, limiters, and amplifiers, was usually able to simulate digital logic. This "logic" was asynchronous, and operated in parallel, so that outputs of all logic components were available to the programmer at all times. At present, analog manufacturers include a good supply of digital logic modules as part of the normal computing complement of the analog computer. These modules are patched one to another, just as analog components are, and operate in parallel and simultaneously, as analog components do. In view of the last statement, one may consider such logic modules to be discrete analog components.

The most common types of logic modules used with analog computers are flip-flops, "and" gates, "or" gates, "one shots" (or "pulsers," or "time delays," or "monostables"), and combinations of these elements to produce "exclusive or" circuits (or "modulo 2 adder," or "ring sum"), up-and-down counters, and shift registers. For details of the use of logic modules in programming analog computers, see Bennett (1974).

OUTPUT EQUIPMENT

The classical analog hard-copy output is a multichannel voltage-time recorder. The usual recorders associated with modern analog computers are eight channels wide, write rectangularly, and have adjustable voltage scales and chart speeds. As many variable outputs as desired may be recorded simultaneously, provided one has a sufficient number of recorders. The results produced are called *time histories*. The accuracy is good to about 0.25% of the voltage range at which one is recording, and the bandwidth is about 100 Hz.

For wider bandwidth recording, an optical recorder (oscillograph) or some form of magnetic tape recorder must be used.

To obtain $X-Y$ graphs (for example, pressure vs. flow), where any variable Y is plotted as a function of any other variable X (as distinct from plotting X and Y as functions of time), a storage oscilloscope is typically used. A hard-copy attachment is available for permanent recording of the oscilloscope output.

The classical instrument for observing static or slowly changing analog computer variables is the digital voltmeter (DVM). In the most modern analog computers, the DVM is incorporated into a sophisticated digital display terminal which displays the address and state, as well as the value of the variable. These terminals may also act as line printers, displaying lists of analog variable addresses and values in digital form. The terminal may also incorporate the storage oscilloscope function with hard-copy output, thus allowing all necessary I/O functions to be performed at a single terminal.

PROGRAMMING

Amplitude Scaling. Differential and/or algebraic equations, in order to be mechanized :n the analog computer, must first be converted to voltage equations. A scale factor, or volts per physical unit ratio, must be chosen for all the dependent variables. Scale factors are chosen from estimated ranges of the problem variables. These estimates are usually "educated guesses," derived from the engineer's personal experience. If the first estimates prove to be poor, scale factors can be changed at the computer.

Having determined the amplitude scale factors, the problem variables in the mathematical equations are replaced by the voltages or machine units representing them, and adjustments are made to the coefficients throughout the equations in order to maintain equality.

The equations are thus changed into voltage or machine unit equations from which a computer circuit diagram can be drawn.

Time Scaling. With the all-electronic, high-speed analog computers available today, extremely high solution speeds (as short as several milliseconds) as well as very slow solutions (lasting several hours) can be obtained with the same computer. The choice of the solution time is largely dependent on factors external to the computer, such as the method of recording or displaying the solution, the need for tying into real hardware (hence the necessity of operating in "real time"), or the desire to display results to a "human in the loop," etc. A time-scale change is defined by the equation $T = \beta t$, where T is machine time, t is original problem time, and β is the time scale factor and has the units of machine time/original problem time.

In order to slow down a problem (i.e., to cause machine time to be larger than original problem time), β is made greater than unity; to speed up a problem (i.e., to cause machine time to be smaller than original problem time), β is made less than unity.

An objective of time scaling is to change computer time with respect to original problem time, but without causing a change in the original equations, without giving rise to new definitions of derivatives, and without changing any amplitude scaling. For details on how to program an analog computer, see Bennett (1974).

MATHEMATICAL APPLICATIONS

Since the analog computer can solve nonlinear, ordinary differential equations, it is typically used in engineering design and real-time simulation. For up-to-date applications to the various engineering and science disciplines, the reader is referred to the publication *Simulation*. The analog computer can also be used effectively to solve a variety of other mathematical equations and to do analog data analysis. For example, algebraic equations, both linear and nonlinear, are readily solvable. Problems in complex variables are likewise amenable to solution by the analog computer (see Hausner, 1971) but such problems are not of major importance to analog computation. Partial differential equations (PDE), on the other hand, are of importance in the analog field.

REFERENCES

1947. Ragazzini, J., Randall, R. H., and Russell, F. A. "Analysis of Problems in Dynamics by Electronic Circuits," *Proc IRE* **35**:444–452.
1955. Rodel, J. In Paynter, H. M. (Ed.), *Palimpsest on the Electric Analog Art*. George H. Philbrick Researches, pp. 27–47.
Simulation, published since 1963 by Society for Computer Simulation, LaJolla, CA (Describes current analog, digital, and hybrid computer work.)
1971. Hausner, A. *Analog and Hybrid Computer Programming*. Englewood Cliffs, NJ: Prentice-Hall.
1971. Holst, P. A. "A Note of History," *Simulation* **17**, *No. 3:* 131–135, September.
1972. Korn, G. A. and Korn, T. M. *Electronic Analog and Hybrid Computers*, 2nd Edition. New York: McGraw-Hill.
1974. Bennett, A. W. *Introduction to Computer Simulation*. New York: West Publishing.
1976. Rubin, A. I. "Multi-Variable Function Generator," *Simulation* **27**, *No. 1:* 1–12 July.
1978. Sheingold, D. H. "Multiplier Application Guide." published by Analog Devices, Norwood, MA.

ARTHUR I. RUBIN

ANALOG-TO-DIGITAL AND DIGITAL-TO-ANALOG CONVERTERS

For articles on related subjects *see* ANALOG COMPUTERS; DATA COMMUNICATIONS; DIGITAL COMPUTERS; and HYBRID COMPUTERS.

Whenever it is necessary to communicate between analog and digital systems, analog-to-digital (A-D) and/ or digital-to-analog (D-A) converters are required. These converters form basic links between the world of "real" phenomena, where the variables are generally continuous analog quantities, and the "engineer designed" world of digital information processing and data communications, where the variables are discrete quantities.

The number of applications and types of converters available has grown significantly in recent years. In part, this has resulted from increased recognition of the capabilities of digital, as opposed to analog, signal processing and data transmission. The importance of these capabilities is application-dependent; however, in general, the advantages of digital processing and transmission lie in the increased accuracy, noise immunity, processing flexibility, and storage facilities afforded by the digital format. This increasing use of digital processing of analog signals has been aided by the rapid development of sophisticated, yet inexpensive, mini- and microcomputer systems. At the same time, the steady decline in price and the increase in the performance of A-D and D-A converters has allowed these computers to be coupled effectively to the analog world.

Some Applications. Successful and widespread use of digital processing has resulted in numerous examples of A-D and D-A converter use. A simple classification of application areas is given below (see also Hoeschele, 1968).

Digital Control Systems. Fig. 1 is a block diagram illustration of a digital control system. Variables originate within the plant or system. They are sensed by an analog sensor, digitized by an A-D converter, and then transmitted to a digital processor. If the processor merely manipulates and stores this information, the system is a simple data acquisition system. If, on the basis of the input information, control signals determined by the processor are returned to the plant, then a digital control system is present. A variation on this system requiring fewer converters can be designed if the signal frequencies and number of sensors and controllers are not excessive (Fig. 2).

Such control systems can be found in a wide variety of situations, from basic industrial processing to aerospace flight systems.

Communications Systems. The advantages of digital data transmission have resulted in extensive use of converters as parts of telemetering and voice communications systems. In telemetering systems, analog signals originating in remote locations are first converted into digital signals and then transmitted to the central station. Remote weather and defense-related monitoring systems fall in this category of applications.

Voice communications systems are also becoming increasingly oriented toward digital signal processing. In

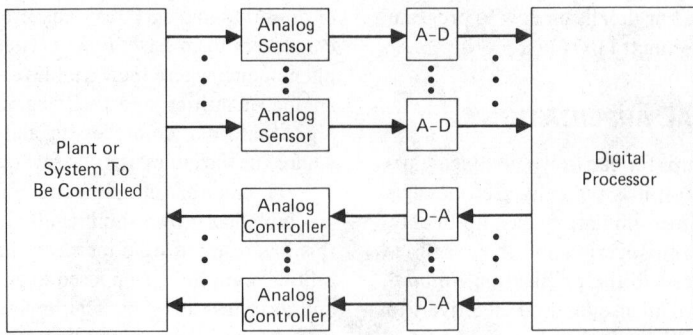

Fig. 1. Digital control system.

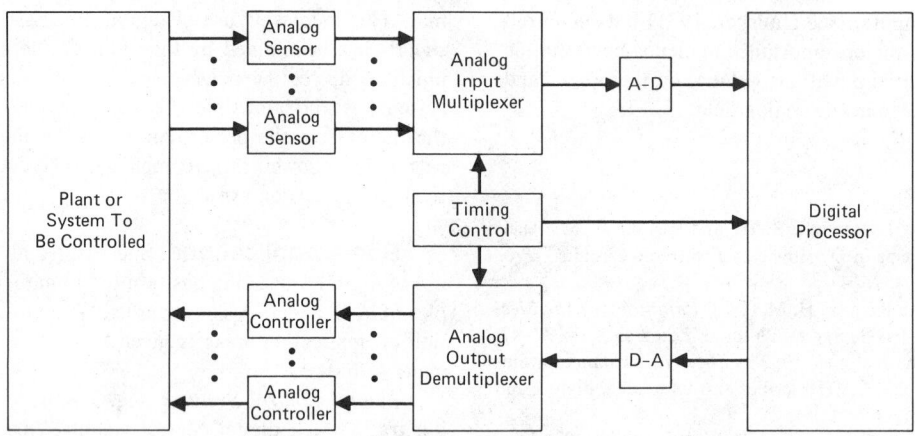

Fig. 2. Digital control system with multiplexers.

many situations, analog voice signals are digitized with A-D converters and subsequently transmitted over time-shared channels, with many conversations being "simultaneously" carried over the same channel. Such systems can be designed to be flexible and handle both speech and data at the same time while making nearly optimum use of the systems' bandwidth capabilities.

In the entertainment industry, digital recording schemes are being developed, and may become the next major movement in consumer-oriented high fidelity recording systems. Such systems will be extensive users of A-D and D-A converters.

Test, Measurement, and Monitoring. In contrast to monitoring systems which require extensive communications capabilities, many applications of A-D converters can be found in test and measurement equipment. Digital voltmeters, for example, are now commonplace, and the inclusion of digital readouts alongside analog displays on oscilloscopes has gained widespread acceptance. More complex measurement and monitoring applications, such

as on-line real-time patient monitoring, also have converters as key system elements.

Hybrid Computation Systems. Hybrid computers consist of an analog computer and a digital computer communicating with each other through an interface that normally includes several A-D and D-A converters. While the analog computer is a low-accuracy device, it does permit fast parallel solution of ordinary differential equations. The typical digital computer, on the other hand, is a high-accuracy serial machine with extensive logic and memory capabilities. Together, communicating through A-D and D-A converters, they permit efficient solution to certain classes of continuous system optimization and statistical problems.

The Basic Relationship. Analog variables such as position, temperature, and process rate are typically first converted during measurement into analog voltages and currents. Conversely, to control the analog variables, analog voltages and currents are usually supplied to the inputs of a controlling transducer. Rather than deal with the basic analog variable (e.g., temperature), it is therefore convenient to deal with the voltages or currents available at the output, or produced for the input, of the transducer. The analog variable considered here is thus a pure voltage or current, and questions concerning transducer operation, signal amplification, and signal conditioning are omitted. (Material on these important practical matters can be obtained from the references.)

Digital information is generally represented by the presence or absence of a fixed voltage or current level. Each unit of information or "bit" thus has two states, referred to as the *one* and *zero* states. On a single input line, information can be represented serially by periodically changing the voltage level or state of the line. A set of parallel lines or a grouping of serial bits can be used to represent a digital word where the meaning of this word depends on the number or symbol assigned to each possible combination of bits. This is referred to as the *code*. Different types of codes are used with A-D and D-A converters (e.g., offset binary, one's complement, two's complement). However, for simplicity, this article considers only *unipolar* or *natural binary* code. Table 1 presents this code for a three-bit word. In general, each word may have n bits, with the bit at left, the most significant bit (MSB), having a weight of 2^{-1}, the bit at right, the least significant bit (LSB), having a weight of 2^{-n}, and the ith bit ($1 \leq i \leq n$) having a weight of 2^{-i}.

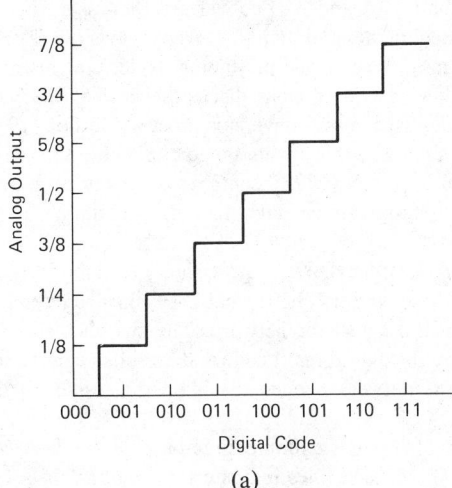

(a)

Transfer Function of a D-A Converter

Table 1.   Three-Bit Natural Binary Code

Decimal Value	Binary Value	BIT 1 MSB	BIT 2	BIT 3 LSB
0	0.000	0	0	0
⅛	0.001	0	0	1
²⁄₈	0.010	0	1	0
³⁄₈	0.011	0	1	1
⁴⁄₈	0.100	1	0	0
⁵⁄₈	0.101	1	0	1
⁶⁄₈	0.110	1	1	0
⁷⁄₈	0.111	1	1	1

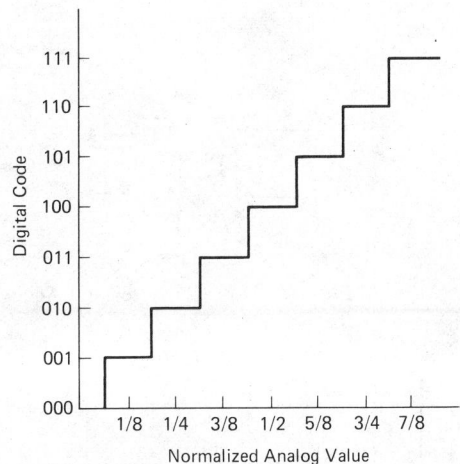

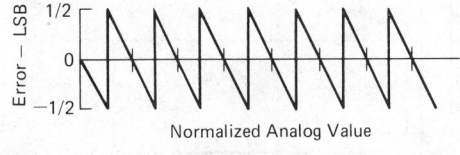

(b)

Transfer Function of an A-D Converter

Fig. 3.   The basic ideal relationships.

The basic conversion relationship for a three-bit binary code is given in Fig. 3(a) and (b). Any three-bit digital sequence entering into the D-A converter results in producing one of eight distinct voltage outputs, as seen in Fig. 3(a). Similarly, any voltage input into the A-D converter results in producing a distinct three-bit output code. The *ideal resolution* of these converters is equal to the value of the LSB or 2^{-n} for an n-bit converter. For A-D converters, associated with this resolution is an inherent *quantization error*, which reflects an uncertainty

in the results of A-D conversion due to quantification of the analog signal. For the system above, transitions occur in the middle of each voltage range, thus minimizing the *quantification error* to an optimum ±½ LSB. Other errors, such as noise and various nonlinearities, may increase this above ±½ LSB in real systems.

In both D-A and A-D converters, there is a wide variety of techniques and manufacturers. Davis (1972) provides a long list of firms producing devices in this area. The following two sections discuss several of the basic techniques used in the conversion process. Gordon (1978) reviews and compares a wide range of possible conversion techniques. Kurth (1978) contains a variety of articles related to design and specification of converters.

D-A Converters. Fig. 4 shows a block diagram for a D-A converter. The typical D-A converter contains switches and a resistor network. The switches are controlled by the digital input code and establish connections within the network needed to obtain the proper analog voltage.

Fig. 5(a) shows a simple three-bit plus sign D-A converter. The dashed lines indicate that the switch is controlled by the associated digital bit input. The switches themselves are generally integrated circuits which ideally would have no resistance when closed and infinite resis-

tance when open. For the 0100-input switch configuration shown, the output voltage V_0 is easily seen to be $V_R/2$. Similarly, the nth bit present can be shown to produce an output voltage increment equal to $2^{-n}V_R$; hence, the resulting output voltage is proportional to the binary input. A sign bit is present which controls a voltage reference switch. With certain codes, its absence indicates a positive digital input and results in switching in the positive reference voltage $+V_R$. Its presence indicates a negative input, and the negative reference voltage $-V_R$ is applied to the network.

Another simple D-A converter based on summing currents is shown in Fig. 5(b). This has the advantage of requiring only one resistor per bit; however, a large range of resistance values is necessary, making it impractical for monolithic and hybrid circuit manufacturing techniques.

A-D Converters. A simple form of A-D converter is shown in Fig. 6. A conversion begins after the reset sig-

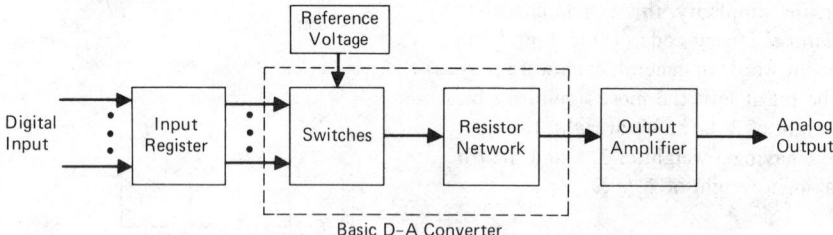

Fig. 4. D-A Converter and Accessories.

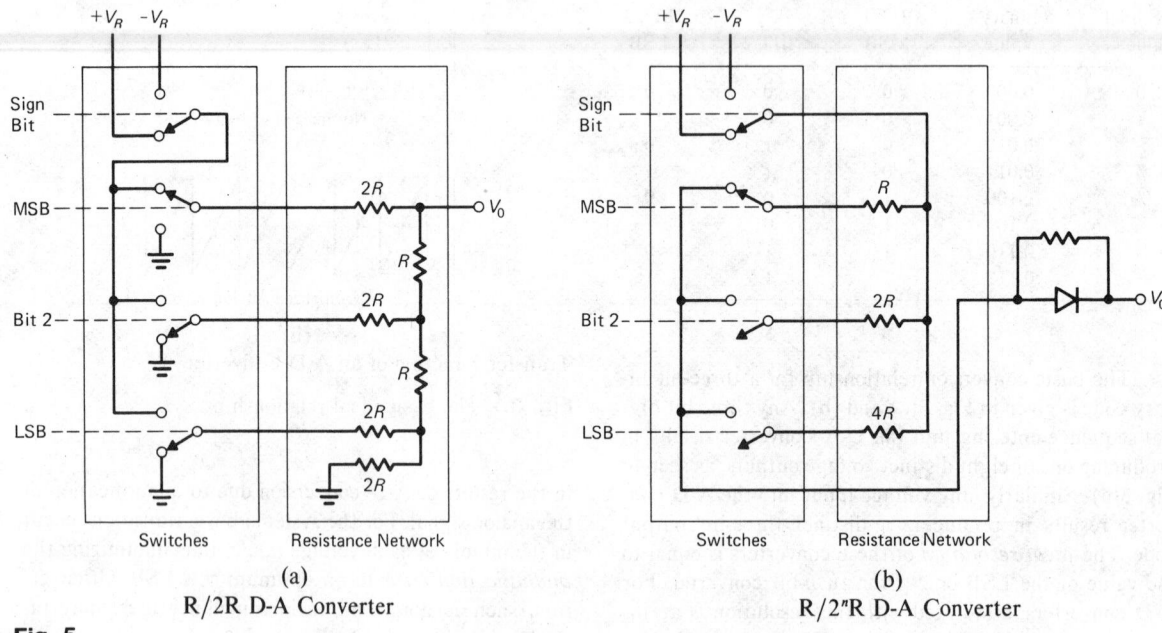

(a)

R/2R D-A Converter

(b)

R/2^nR D-A Converter

Fig. 5.

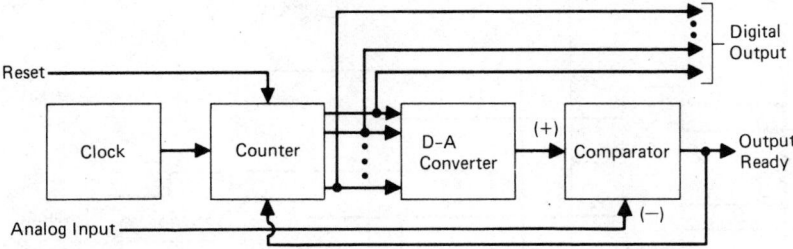

Fig. 6.   Counter A-D converter.

nal clears the counter. The counter now receives clock pulses and is incremented with each pulse. The counter output is a digital word representing a voltage level. This word, received by the D-A converter, results in an analog signal which is compared with the incoming analog signal. When the comparator signal becomes positive, the counter at that point holds the correct digital representation of the analog signal. An "output ready" signal indicates that this has occurred.

The method, though simple, requires a relatively long time for a complete A-D conversion due to the counting process. This time increases by a factor of two for each additional bit and makes the method unsuitable for certain applications. A modification to the above technique, which speeds up the converter, calls for the incrementing counter to be replaced with an "up-down" counter. Here, once a comparison has been made, the counter is designed to increment or decrement on each clock pulse, depending on the output of the comparator. The counter thus follows the analog signal and the full counting process is not necessary on each conversion if large changes in the analog input do not occur. To improve response to large input changes, additional comparators and logic may be included to allow the counter to increment and decrement by more than one unit.

A widely used and moderately high-speed A-D converter is the "Successive-Approximation" converter. Fig. 6 depicts such a converter if the counter box is assumed to contain a register and control logic. The converter operates by successively considering each bit position in the register and setting that bit to a one or a zero on the basis of the comparator output. The MSB is first set to a one with all other bit positions set to zero. This word then enters the D-A converter and the D-A output is compared with the analog input. If the result indicates the analog input is larger, then the one in the MSB is kept; otherwise it is set to zero. The remaining bit positions are considered successively in the same manner and a decision is made on each bit position. After the LSB is considered, the results of conversion are found in the register. Unlike the counting method, the conversion time with this method is constant for every possible analog input, and this approach is often used in high-speed converter design.

A somewhat lower-speed but high-accuracy A-D converter that is commonly used is the "Integrating" converter. A "dual slope" version is shown in Fig. 7. The converter operates by first integrating the unknown analog input voltage for a fixed period of time. During this time period, a voltage proportional to the input builds up on the integrating capacitor. After resetting the counter to zero, a fixed reference voltage of opposite polarity is now applied to the integrator and the counter started. When the null comparator recognizes that the integrator output has reached zero, the control logic is notified and the counter stopped. The output count is proportional to the ratio of the input voltage and referenced voltage. Since the reference voltage is known, the count is therefore a binary representation of the analog input. Triple and quad slope architectures which greatly increase the conversion speed at the cost of some added complexity are also possible (Gordon, 1978; Kurth, 1978; Sheingold, 1977).

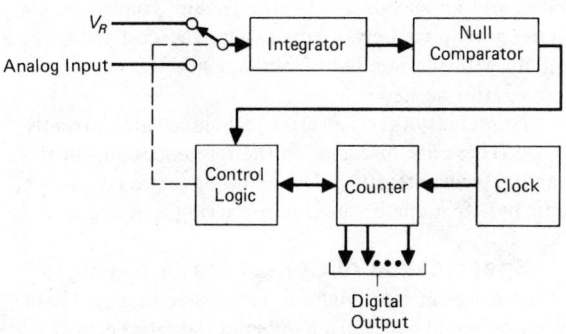

Fig. 7.   Dual slope integrating A-D converter.

While the previous A-D conversion methods considered are sequential in nature, all—or nearly all—parallel methods are available for very high speeds. The simplest method uses an analog comparator for each quantization

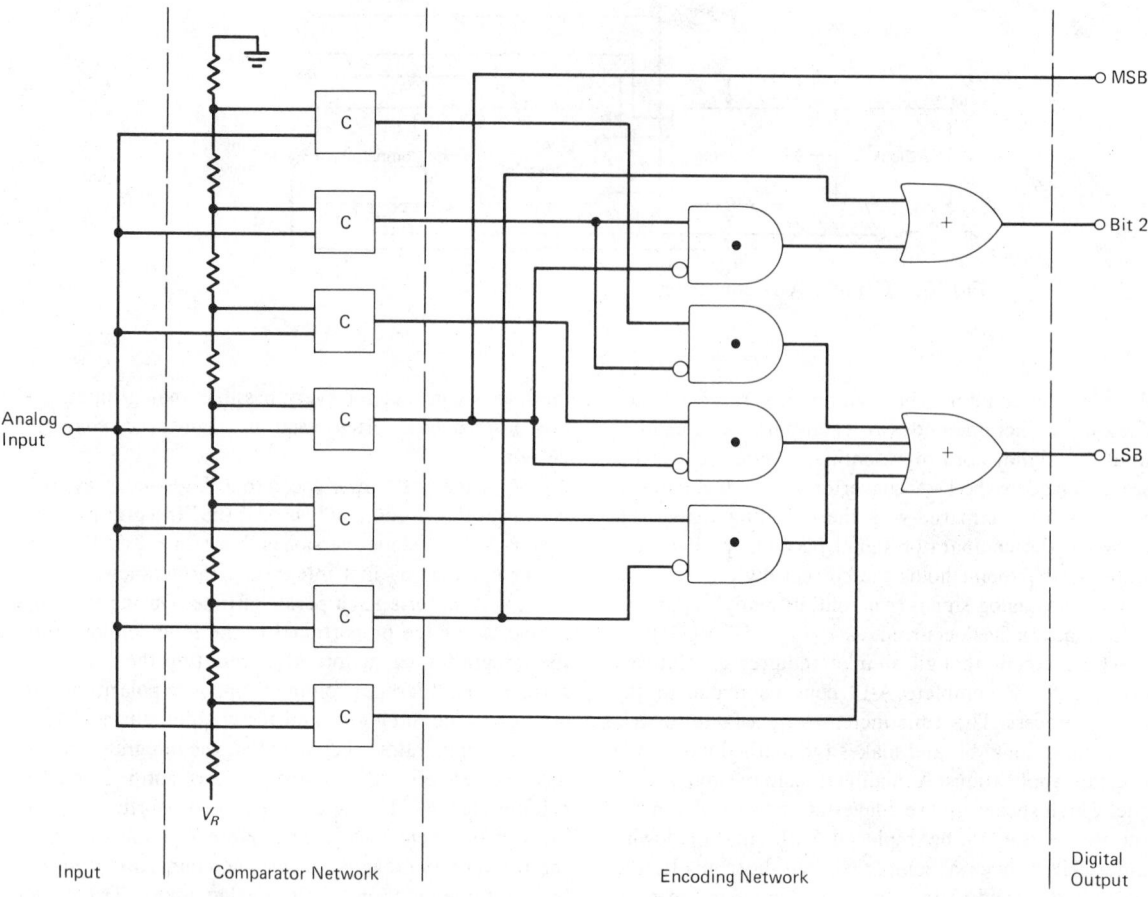

Fig. 8.   Three-bit parallel A-D converter.

(Fig. 8). Each comparator (C) represents a voltage level, and these levels are coded into the appropriate three-bit codes with an encoding network. Though conversion effectively requires only a single step, the cost increases rapidly with the number of bits n, since the number of comparators needed is $2^n - 1$.

Numerous other converter techniques are currently in use. These are discussed in the references and in the manufacturing literature. The following section considers some basic parameters used in specifying converters.

Specification of Converters. A host of measures are used in specifying converter performance. These are discussed in detail in a number of the references. The user should be cautious in evaluating manufacturer specifications and be clear on the meaning of the various terms used.

The application for which the converter is intended should be well understood, since this will determine which of the multitude of converters available offer the best

price performance tradeoffs. In addition to accuracy and speed requirements, questions regarding logic levels and codes, scale factors, reference voltages, impedance levels, power levels, temperature stability, and noise environment must be considered. These latter questions are not considered here and the reader should consult the references for detailed information.

A number of measures are normally used in specifying converter accuracy and speed. These measures in part isolate and indicate the various sources of error. With D-A converters, *accuracy* or *absolute accuracy* refers to the deviation of actual analog output from the output predicted by the ideal transfer function. Though this may vary over the range of the unit, specifications are normally given in terms of a single number representing the maximum error over the range. This may be stated as $\pm$ a percentage of full scale or $\pm$ a fraction of LSB. *Relative accuracy* measures the largest deviation of the analog output from a straight line drawn through the end points of a converter's transfer function.

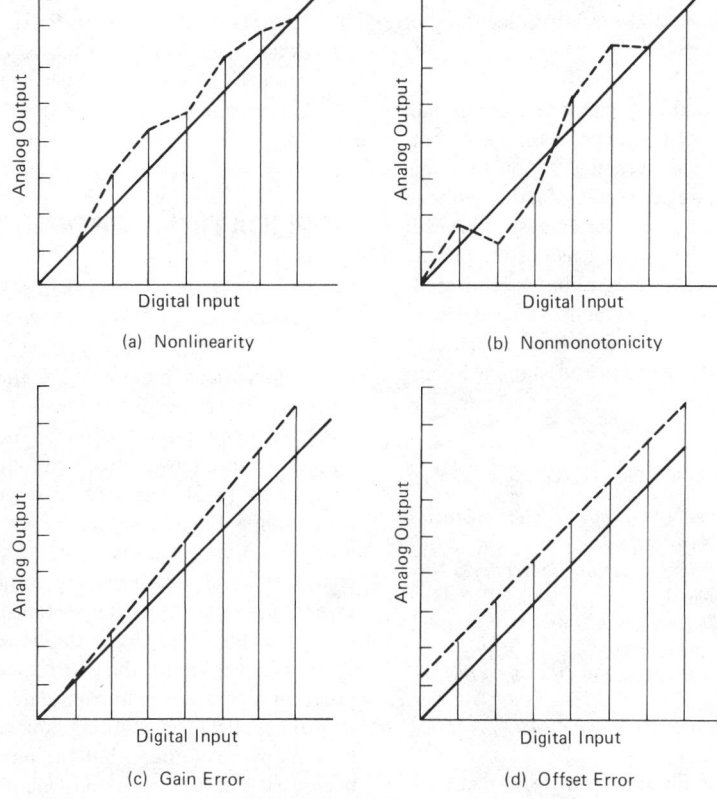

Fig. 9. D/A errors (Sheingold, 1977).

Several common error types which contribute to a loss of accuracy are illustrated in Fig. 9(a), (b), (c), and (d).

Fig. 9(a) shows *nonlinearity* in the conversion transfer function. The nonlinearity is, however, *monotonic* since increasing digital values produce increasing analog values. Fig. 9(b) shows a *nonmonotonic* nonlinearity. Such a nonlinearity could yield the same analog value for two different digital input codes, a result which might cause oscillations to occur in certain control applications. Figs. 9(c), and 9(d) illustrate *gain* and *offset* errors which respectively change the slope and zero crossing of the transfer function. The difference between the dotted line in the figures and the solid 45° angle line is the error associated with each digital input code.

Dynamic characteristics of D-A converters are normally specified in terms of a *settling time*. This is the time between arrival of the digital code, and settling of the analog output to within certain specified limits of accuracy. The shorter the settling time, the higher the conversion rate. For a typical high-speed converter, the full scale maximum settling time specification might read 2 μsec to settle within ± ½ LSB.

For A-D converters, accuracy refers to the deviation of the analog level represented by the digital output from the actual analog input. As with D-A converters, this is normally stated as either a percentage of full scale or a fraction of the LSB. The relative accuracy of an A-D converter measures the largest deviation of the converter's transfer function from a straight line drawn through its endpoints and is also expressed as a percentage of full scale or a fraction of the LSB. Errors here may be divided into two parts. The first, *quantization error*, was discussed earlier in this article. This results in an inherent error of ± ½ LSB, which can be reduced only by increasing the number of bits. All other errors are equipment errors, and error types directly corresponding to those found in D-A converters may be present. Offset, gain (scale factor) and nonlinearity errors have analogous definitions. The error corresponding to nonmonotonic nonlinearity is termed the *differential linearity error* and may result in entire digital outputs being missed.

The dynamic characteristics of A-D converters are normally specified in terms of the total conversion time. This is the time necessary for a complete measurement, its inverse being the *conversion rate* of the converter. A moderate speed 10-bit converter, for example, might have a conversion time of 40 μsec and a relative accuracy of ± ½ LSB.

Conclusion. A-D and D-A converters are finding increasing use as the scope of digital processing and communications widens. There is every indication that this trend will continue and be augmented by further gains in performance and decreases in converter cost. This will result in large part from the growing use of monolithic and VLSI (Very Large Scale Integration) circuit technologies. A proliferation of new products can be expected with increasing emphasis placed on ease of interfacing these products with microprocessors and standard communications systems and buses.

REFERENCES

1968. Hoeschele, D. F., Jr. *Analog-to-Digital/Digital-to-Analog Conversion Techniques.* New York: Wiley.
1970. Schmid, H. *Electronic Analog/Digital Conversions.* New York: Van Nostrand Reinhold.
1972. Davis, S. *"Selection Criteria for A-D and D-A Converters," Computer Design* (September).
1976. Hnatek, E. R. *A User's Handbook of D/A and A/D Converters.* New York: Wiley.
1977. Sheingold, D. H. (Ed.) *Analog-Digital Conversion Notes.* Norwood, MA: Analog Devices.
1978. Gordon, B. M. "Linear Electronic Analog/Digital Conversion Architectures, Their Origins, Parameters, Limitations, and Application," *IEEE Trans. on Ckts. and Sys.,* **CAS-25** (July).
1978. Kurth, C. F. (Ed.) "Special Isssue on Analog/Digital Conversion," *IEEE Trans. on Ckts. and Sys.* **CAS-25** (July).

M. A. FRANKLIN

ANALYST. *See* SYSTEMS ANALYST.

APL. *See* PROCEDURE-ORIENTED LANGUAGES.

APPLICATIONS OF COMPUTERS. *See* ADMINISTRATIVE APPLICATIONS; ARTS APPLICATIONS; BANKING APPLICATIONS; CONTROL APPLICATIONS; CREDIT SYSTEMS APPLICATIONS; ECONOMETRIC APPLICATIONS; ELECTRONIC FUNDS TRANSFER SYSTEMS; ENGINEERING APPLICATIONS; HUMANITIES APPLICATIONS; MEDICAL APPLICATIONS; NUMBER THEORETIC CALCULATIONS; PLANNING, COMPUTER APPLICATIONS IN; POLITICAL APPLICATIONS; PUBLISHING, COMPUTERS IN; REAL TIME APPLICATIONS; SCIENTIFIC APPLICATIONS; SOCIAL SCIENCE APPLICATIONS; STATISTICAL APPLICATIONS; TOMOGRAPHY, COMPUTED; and TRANSACTION-BASED SYSTEMS.

APPLICATIONS PROGRAMMING

For articles on related subjects *see* PROGRAMMING LANGUAGES; and SYSTEMS PROGRAMMING.

Applications programs are the programs that are written to solve specific problems, to produce specific reports, to update specific files. The programming languages that are mostly used in applications programming are Fortran for scientific applications and Cobol for data processing applications. Special Report Program Generator (RPG) languages are used on small data processing computers, and languages like Basic and APL are used extensively in time-sharing systems. The language PL/I was introduced by IBM in the hope that it would prove attractive over almost the entire spectrum of applications programming and might eventually supersede both Fortran and Cobol. The resulting language uniformity would have many advantages, but the impact of PL/I has not been very great. Fortran and Cobol remain the standard applications programming languages. However, the increasing use of Pascal *(q.v.)* on the one hand and the recent development of Ada *(q.v.)* on the other could change this situation by the end of the 1980s.

The ultimate aim of all software is to make it possible for the applications programmer to perform well and to write programs that produce results and make effective and efficient use of the computing system. Applications programs make use of subroutine libraries and special packages such as sort-merge *(q.v.)* systems and data access and data management systems. Most well-designed operating systems provide the applications programmer with special tools for analyzing and debugging programs.

There are very large applications systems such as airline reservations systems and on-line banking and merchandising systems in which many considerations of systems programming and of applications programming are intermixed.

S. ROSEN

APPROXIMATION. *See* CHEBYSHEV APPROXIMATION; and LEAST SQUARES APPROXIMATION.

APPROXIMATION THEORY

For articles on related subjects *see* CHEBYSHEV APPROXIMATION; LEAST SQUARES APPROXIMATION; and NUMERICAL ANALYSIS.

Approximation theory concerns the following problem: Given a function $f(x)$ defined for x in a prescribed set X, a family of functions G, and a metric $d(f,g)$ (a mathematical prescription for measuring the distance between two functions), determine a function $g(x)$ in G which is "close" to $f(x)$ for x in X. For computer applications, $f(x)$ is typically a continuous function of one real variable, X is a real interval, G is a family of polynomials or of rational functions (ratios of polynomials), and the metric is either a least squares metric

$$d_2(f,g,w) = \int_X [f(x) - g(x)]^2 w(x)\,dx,$$

or the Chebyshev metric

$$d_\infty(f,g,w) = \max_X |[f(x) - g(x)]\,w(x)|,$$

where $w(x)$ is a weight function. For the Chebyshev metric, the weight is usually either $w(x) = 1$ or $w(x) = 1/f(x)$, where $f(x)$ is assumed not to vanish for x in X. This latter weighting is most useful when $f(x)$ varies considerably in magnitude across the interval X. Basic theorems examine the existence, uniqueness, and characterization of $g(x)$, sometimes in very abstract settings. In this article we will concentrate on the Chebyshev metric, which is more important than the least squares metric in the generation of approximations to functions to be used on a computer.

Let $f(x)$ be defined and continuous over a finite real interval X. The theoretical justification for using the Chebyshev metric [with $w(x) = 1$] is the Weierstrass approximation theorem, which asserts the existence of real polynomials that are arbitrarily close to $f(x)$ over the entire interval X. These polynomials are often obtained by appropriately truncating an infinite power series expansion of the function,

$$f(x) = \sum_{k=0}^{\infty} a_k x^k,$$

provided the series converges to $f(x)$ over X, i.e., provided that for any fixed value of x in X and any $\epsilon > 0$, there is an integer N such that all partial sums

$$s_n(x) = \sum_{k=0}^{n} a_k x^k, \qquad n > N$$

differ from $f(x)$ by less than ϵ. Such expansions are unique whenever they exist.

Some of the more important methods for generating series expansions are based upon the analytic properties of the function. Let $f(x)$ be continuous and have continuous derivatives of all orders at some point x_0 in X. Then the *Taylor series* expansion of $f(x)$ about x_0 is given by

$$f(x) = \sum_{k=0}^{\infty} a_k(x - x_0)^k$$
$$a_k = f^{(k)}(x_0)/k! = \frac{1}{k!} \left. \frac{d^k f(x)}{dx^k} \right|_{x=x_0}$$

Since this expansion is based upon a detailed knowledge of the function of x_0, the Taylor polynomials $g_n(x)$ of degree n, obtained by truncating the series, approximate $f(x)$ well for small $|x - x_0|$, but the error $f(x) - g_n(x)$ typically grows monotonically in magnitude with increasing $|x - x_0|$. Frequently $\max_X |f(x) - g_n(x)|$ occurs at one of the boundaries of X. For example, Fig. 1 shows the error associated with the fourth-degree Taylor polynomial approximation of e^x over $[-1,1]$, where the Taylor series is

$$e^x = 1 + x + \frac{x^2}{2} + \frac{x^3}{6} + \frac{x^4}{24} + \cdots + \frac{x^n}{n!} + \cdots.$$

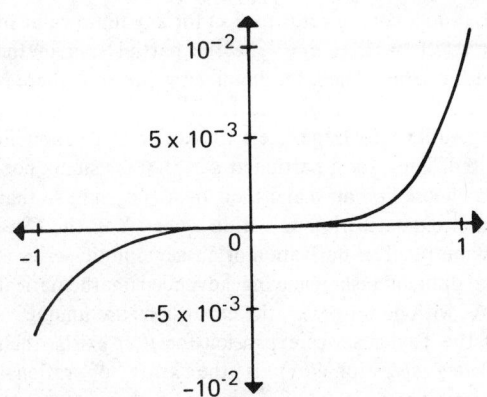

Fig. 1. Error $e^x - g_4(x) = 1 + x + (x^2/2!) + (x^3/3!) + (x^4/4!)$ for approximation over $[-1,1]$ by fourth degree Taylor polynomial.

A function $f(x)$ has a *pole* of finite integer order n at x_0 whenever the Taylor series for $(x - x_0)^m f(x)$ exists for $m = n$, but fails to exist for smaller integer values of m. The *Laurent series* is then given by $(x - x_0)^{-n}$ times the Taylor series for $(x - x_0)^n f(x)$. As an example, the

Laurent series for $\csc(x)$, which has an isolated pole of order 1 at $x = 0$, is

$$\csc(x) = \frac{1}{x} + \frac{x}{6} + \frac{7x^3}{360} + \frac{31x^5}{15,120} + \cdots,$$

which converges for $|x| < \pi$. When the function has an isolated pole of infinite order, the Laurent series takes the form

$$f(x) = \sum_{k=-\infty}^{\infty} a_k x^k,$$

where the derivation of the coefficients a_k generally involves methods from the theory of functions of a complex variable. The expansion

$$\arctan(x) = \frac{\pi}{2} - \frac{1}{x} + \frac{1}{3x^3} - \frac{1}{5x^5} + \cdots,$$

valid for $|x| > 1$, is of this type. Truncation of Laurent series leads to rational approximations for $f(x)$.

If the interval X is semi-infinite, $X = [b,\infty)$, $b > 0$, a divergent *asymptotic expansion* of $f(x)$,

$$f(x) \sim \sum_{k=0}^{\infty} a_k x^{-k},$$

may yield useful rational approximations to $f(x)$ even though it does not converge to $f(x)$ for any finite value of x. Let $s_n(x) = \sum_{k=0}^{n} a_k x^{-k}$ be the partial sum of the asymptotic series. Then, for any fixed value of x, there is an n which minimizes the error $|f(x) - s_n(x)|$. For fixed n, and x sufficiently large, the error can be made as small as desired. Thus, for a particular $\epsilon > 0$, it is usually possible to choose first an n and then an X (i.e., a,b) so that $s_n(x)$ approximates $f(x)$ to within ϵ over X in the Chebyshev metric. The derivation of an asymptotic series is often a difficult task involving advanced mathematical tools. As with power series, the expansions are unique.

If the Taylor series expansion for $f(x)$ exists, then the *Padé table* for $f(x)$ is the array of rational approximations

$$R_{mn}(x) = \frac{p_0 + p_1 x + \cdots + p_m x^m}{1 + q_1 x + \cdots + q_n x^n},$$

characterized by the property that the power series expansion of $R_{mn}(x)$ is identical to the Taylor series expansion through terms in x^{m+n}. The entries $R_{m0}(x)$ are the Taylor polynomials, and the entries $R_{00}(x)$, $R_{01}(x)$, $R_{11}(x)$, ... along and just above the main diagonal are the successive convergents of a Stieltjes continued fraction, or *S-fraction*, expansion of $f(x)$:

$$f(x) = \cfrac{a_0}{1 - \cfrac{a_1 x}{1 - a_2 x}}$$

Padé approximants $R_{mn}(x)$ are often better approximations to $f(x)$ than are the Taylor polynomials of degree $m + n$. All elements of the Padé table agree with $f(x)$ exactly at the point of expansion, but $f(x) - R_{mn}(x)$ tends to grow as x moves away from that point. As an example, the S-fraction expansion of e^x is

$$e^x = \cfrac{1}{1 - \cfrac{x}{1 + \cfrac{x/2}{1 - \cfrac{x/6}{1 + x/6}}}}$$

The corresponding Padé approximation $R_{22}(x)$ is obtained by truncating the S-fraction to just the terms given above, and is

$$R_{22}(x) = \frac{12 + 6x + x^2}{12 - 6x + x^2}$$

Fig. 2 shows the error $e^x - R_{22}(x)$ over the interval $[-1,1]$. Note that the maximum error is less than half of that associated with the fourth-degree Taylor polynomial.

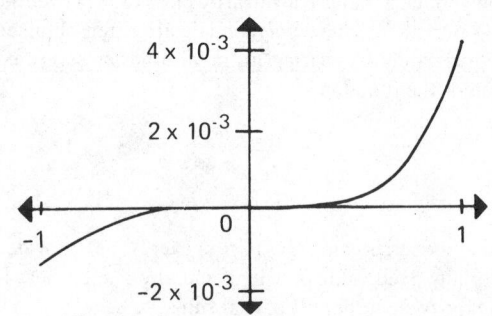

Fig. 2.   Error $e^x - R_{22}(x)$ for approximation over $[-1,1]$ by Padé element.

By sacrificing accuracy in the neighborhood of the point of expansion, it is possible to distribute the error over the interval of approximation and to obtain better approximations to $f(x)$ over X in the sense of the Chebyshev metric. The rational Chebyshev, or *minimax*, approximation to $f(x)$ of degree (m,n) is that rational function $R_{mn}^*(x)$, which minimizes $d(f,R_{mn},w)$. Basic theorems assert that such an $R_{mn}^*(x)$ exists, is unique, and is characterized by the error $[f(x) - R_{mn}^*(x)]w(x)$ achieving its maximum magnitude with alternating sign a prescribed number of times as x moves across the interval X. The determination of $R_{mn}^*(x)$ is not easy, but the characterization theorem leads to algorithms, such as the Remes algorithm, for computing approximations close to $R_{mn}^*(x)$.

The Chebyshev polynomials

$$T_n(x) = 2^{1-n} \cos(n \cos^{-1}x), \qquad -1 \le x \le 1,$$

are instrumental in the generation of near-minimax polynomial approximations. If $f(x)$ is continuous and sufficiently smooth, then

$$f(x) = \frac{1}{2} a_0 T_0(x) + \sum_{k=1}^{\infty} a_k T_k(x), \qquad -1 \le x \le 1,$$

where

$$a_k = \frac{2}{\pi} \int_{-1}^{1} \frac{f(x) T_k(x)}{(1 - x^2)^{1/2}} \, dx,$$

is the *Chebyshev polynomial expansion* of $f(x)$. (This is related to the *Fourier series* for $f(x)$ by the change of variable $w = \cos^{-1}x$). The partial sums of this expansion are the best polynomial approximations to $f(x)$ for the metric $d_2[f,g, 1/(1 - x^2)^{1/2}]$ and are very close to the minimax polynomial approximation to $f(x)$ in most cases. As an example, the coefficients in the Chebyshev series expansion for e^x are $a_k = 2I_k(1)$, where the I_k are modified Bessel functions. Truncation of this series after five terms leads to the approximation

$$\begin{aligned} g(x) = {} & 1.000045 + 0.997308x + 0.499197x^2 \\ & + 0.177347x^3 + 0.043794x^4 \end{aligned}$$

for the interval $[-1,1]$. The maximum error associated with this approximation is only about one-twentieth of that associated with the fourth-degree Taylor polynomial (see Fig. 3).

Legendre, Jacobi, Hermite, Laguerre, and Gegenbauer polynomials are other important families of polynomials similarly associated with particular choices of

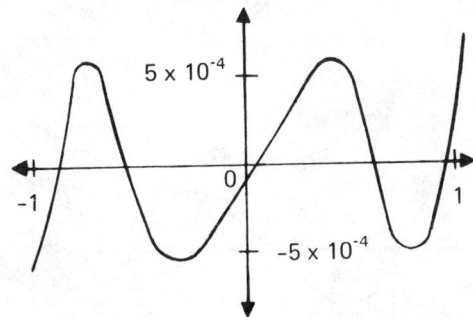

Fig. 3. Error $e^x - \Sigma_{k=0}^4 a_k T_k(x)$ for approximation over $[-1,1]$ by truncated Chebyshev series.

weights and intervals in least squares approximation. Since power series expansions are unique, the expansion of $f(x)$ in polynomials from any of these families can be formally obtained by replacing each x^k in the power series by its exact representation in polynomials of the family and then collecting terms. This "rearrangement" of the power series may alter the convergence of the series so that the new series converges for a larger (or smaller) interval than the original series.

Lanczos' telescoping, or economizing, process is similar to this rearrangement process. Starting from a truncated power series, such as a Taylor polynomial, over the interval $[-1,1]$ the degree of the polynomial is lowered by successively replacing the highest-order term x^n by the polynomial

$$P_{n-1}(x) = x^n - 2^{1-n} T_n(x),$$

which is the minimax approximation to x^n by a polynomial of degree less than n. The approximation error introduced at each step tends to distribute the cumulative error over the interval of approximation so that the polynomials in the resulting sequence tend to be better approximations to $f(x)$ than the corresponding truncations of the original power series, but they are not as good as those obtained by truncating the Chebyshev polynomial expansion. For example, the approximation

$$\begin{aligned} g(x) = {} & 1 + 0.997396x + 0.5x^2 + 0.177083x^3 \\ & + 0.041667x^4 \end{aligned}$$

to e^x is obtained by truncating the Taylor series after six terms and replacing x^5 by $P_4(x) = (20x^3 - 5x)/16$. The corresponding maximum error over $[-1,1]$ is more than four times that of the corresponding truncated Chebyshev series, but only one-fifth that of the fourth-degree Taylor polynomial (see Fig. 4).

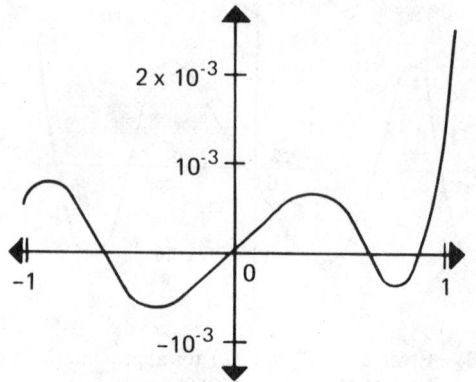

Fig. 4. Error $e^x - g(x)$ for approximation over $[-1,1]$ by fifth-degree Taylor polynomial telescoped to fourth degree.

An extensive theory of approximation exists for functions of a complex variable and for multivariate functions (functions of two or more real variables). The theory relies heavily upon convergent or asymptotic power series and continued fraction expansions. The Taylor and Laurent series and the Padé table extend to the complex case directly. While the theory of minimax approximation generalizes to these functions, the generalizations are not very useful (e.g., uniqueness is lost in the multivariate case) and reliable algorithms for generating the approximations do not exist. Except for certain elementary functions, direct approximations to complex or multivariate functions are not often used in computer applications. Instead, indirect evaluation methods based upon recurrence relations, differential equations, etc., are used.

REFERENCES

1967. Meinardus, G. *Approximation of Functions: Theory and Numerical Methods*, translated by L. Schumaker, New York: Springer-Verlag.
1968. Fike, C. T. *Computer Evaluation of Mathematical Functions*. Englewood Cliffs, NJ: Prentice-Hall.
1970. Cheney, E. W. *Introduction to Approximation Theory*, New York: McGraw-Hill.

W. J. CODY

APT. *See* PROBLEM-ORIENTED LANGUAGES.

ARCHITECTURE, COMPUTER. *See* COMPUTER ARCHITECTURE

ARGUMENT

For articles on related subjects *see* DATA TYPE; GLOBAL AND LOCAL VARIABLES; MACROINSTRUCTION; OPERAND; PROCEDURE; SUBPROGRAMS, CALLING; and SUBROUTINE.

In strict analogy to mathematics, where an argument of a function is the value of a variable used to evaluate the function, an argument in computing is a value supplied to a procedure, a subroutine, or a macroinstruction which is required in order to evaluate the procedure, subroutine, or macro. Another term used interchangeably with argument is *parameter*.

Two different kinds of arguments need to be distinguished: *dummy* or *formal* arguments, and *actual* or *calling* arguments. A dummy argument is an argument used in the definition of a procedure or macro; an actual argument is that which is substituted when the procedure or macro is invoked. For example, Fig. 1 displays a Fortran SUBROUTINE subprogram to compute the solution of a quadratic equation.

$$ax^2 + bx + c = 0.$$

The variables A, B, C, MODE, x1, and x2 in Fig. 1 are all dummy arguments. If this subroutine were to be used to

```
      SUBROUTINE QUAD (A,B,C,MODE,X1, X2)
      DISC = B*B − 4.0*A*C
      IF(DISC.LT.0.)GO TO 3
C PROGRAM IGNORES CASE A = 0
C   MODE PARAMETER SET TO 0 IF ROOTS ARE
C     REAL AND TO 1 IF THEY ARE COMPLEX
      MODE = 0
C TWO REAL ROOTS COMPUTED SO AS TO
C   AVOID DIFFERENCE OF TWO NEARLY
C     EQUAL QUANTITIES
      IF(B.LE.O) GO TO 5
         X1 = −B−SQRT (DISC)
         GO TO 7
5        X1 = −B + SQRT (DISC)
7     X2 = C/(X1*A)
      RETURN
3     MODE = 1
C FOR COMPLEX ROOTS COMPUTE REAL
C   AND IMAGINARY PARTS
      X1 = −B/(2.0*A)
      X2 = SQRT ( − DISC)/(2.0*A)
      RETURN
      END
```

Fig. 1. Quadratic equation subprogram.

compute the roots of

$$10.7X^2 + (R1 + 6.23)X + S \cdot S = 0 \qquad (1)$$

where R1 and s are variables appearing elsewhere in the program, the statement

CALL QUAD (10.7, R1 + 6.23, S·S, J, Y, Z)

might be given. Each argument in the CALL statement is an actual argument, i.e., the argument that will be associated with the dummy argument in the subroutine definition. Thus, when QUAD is executed in response to CALL,

- The values used for A, B, and C will be, respectively, 10.7, R1 + 6.23, and s*s, with the latter two being evaluated using the current main program values for R1 and S.
- The variable J in the main program will be set equal to the value of MODE in the subprogram.
- The main program variables Y and Z will contain the results of the solution of Eq. (1) after execution of QUAD.

Formal arguments are always required to be identifiers, but, as the example above indicates, actual arguments may be identifiers or numbers or arithmetic expressions. Most languages allow great generality in the form of the actual arguments, although there may be requirements that the calling arguments have the same *type* or *mode* as the formal arguments (i.e., a real calling argument if the formal argument denotes a real variable).

Subprogram arguments may also be classified as *input* or *output* arguments, with the former denoting arguments provided to the subprogram and the latter the arguments that convey results back to the main program. In the example given in Fig. 1, A, B, and C are input arguments and MODE, x1, and x2 are output arguments. Sometimes an argument may be both an input and output argument; for example, when a procedure to compute the next prime number receives as input the variable P denoting the current prime number and returns the value of the next prime number to P. Sometimes the arguments of a subprogram may be *implicit*; i.e., they are not stated explicitly in the statement heading the subprogram. This happens in block-structured languages when a procedure in a subblock uses variables global to that block. It happens in Fortran when arguments are held in so-called COMMON storage that is accessible and known by both the main program and the subprogram.

A. RALSTON

ARITHMETIC. *See* INTERVAL ARITHMETIC; and SIGNIFICANCE ARITHMETIC.

ARITHMETIC, COMPUTER

For articles on related subjects *see* COMPLEMENT; INTERVAL ARITHMETIC; NUMBERS and NUMBER SYSTEMS; PRECISION; ROUNDOFF ERROR; SIGNIFICANCE ARITHMETIC; and SIGNIFICANT DIGIT.

The earliest electronic computers were developed in the late 1940s to fill a need for fast arithmetic engines that could solve a variety of problems, many of them military. Although computers, as general symbol manipulators, now solve many problems that do not involve arithmetic computation, numerical calculations are still of vital importance in computer applications. Therefore, how computers perform arithmetic and, in particular, how computer arithmetic differs from ordinary hand computation are topics that should be understood by anyone who uses computers.

Storage of Numbers in Computers. In most computers, a single number occupies a single memory unit (in *word*-oriented memories) or a fixed number of memory units (in *character* or *byte*-oriented memories; e.g., four bytes in IBM 360-370 series computers), which is usually called a *word* or *full word*. Such numbers are sometimes called *single precision* numbers in contrast to *double precision* numbers, which are used when additional accuracy is required and which occupy twice the memory space of single precision numbers (e.g., eight bytes in IBM 360-370 computers). (Years ago, some computers—epitomized by the IBM 1400 series and the IBM 1620—had *variable* word lengths and therefore could handle variable length numbers. Almost no such computers are still in use).

A given number may be stored in one of two modes: *fixed point* or *floating point*. Fig. 1(a) illustrates the storage of .15625 as a fixed-point number in a word-oriented computer memory with 36 bits per word. (Throughout this article, numbers in the text will be decimal numbers and those illustrated in computer storage will be binary). Two points are worth noting about this example:

1. The left-hand bit (S) in Fig. 1 represents the sign of the number, 0 for + and 1 for −. (Hereafter in this article we will, for convenience, use only positive numbers in examples. Storage of negative numbers can be either in absolute value and sign form or in complement form.)
2. The binary point (i.e., the "decimal" or *radix* point) is assumed to be at the left end of the number;

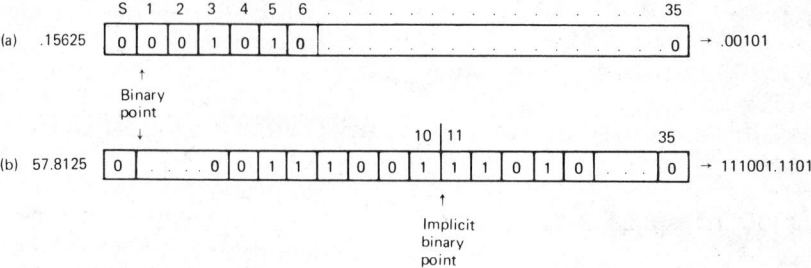

Fig. 1. Fixed-point numbers.

hence the name "fixed-point" numbers. All computers must embody an assumption on the invariant location of the binary point in fixed-point numbers. In many computers this assumption (used throughout this article) is the one shown in Fig. 1. However, other computers (e.g., CDC Cyber series) assume the binary point to be at the right-hand end of the number.

Hardware for storing and manipulating numbers in fixed-point form was the only kind available in early computers, but handling them and doing arithmetic with them created major problems:

1. How could numbers with magnitudes of 1 or greater be handled? The answer to this is that such numbers can be stored as fixed-point numbers but the programmer must be aware of and keep track of the implicit location of the radix point as such numbers are used in computations. Thus, 57.8125 could be stored as shown in Fig. 1(b).

2. More significant are the problems with numbers whose implicit radix points are in different positions. How could these be added, subtracted, multiplied, and divided? As a simple example, consider adding the numbers in Figs. 1(a) and 1(b). Before this can be done by adding the contents of the words, bit by bit, one of the numbers must be shifted relative to the other. The process of such shifting and the associated problem of choosing the location of the implicit binary point for numbers before they are stored is called *scaling*. The difficulty and tediousness of scaling for all but the simplest computations led to the introduction of floating-point hardware capabilities, which are now used for the vast majority of all numerical computation on computers.

Floating-point numbers are more than the solution to the above problems because they also allow computations where the range of the magnitude of the numbers is very large, larger than can be handled with fixed-point numbers except with great difficulty. Floating-point representation of numbers corresponds very closely to what is usually called *scientific notation*; that is, each number is represented as the product of a normal number with a radix point and an integral power of the radix. Thus, for example, the number of Fig. 1(b) might be expressed in scientific notation as

$$.578125 \times 10^2$$

with the .578125 being called the *fractional* part and the 2 the *exponent* part; or, borrowing from logarithmic terminology, the *mantissa* and *characteristic*, respectively. This notation is called "floating point" in computer arithmetic because the radix point of the entire number (57.8125 in Part (b) of Fig. 1) is not fixed but can "float," depending upon the value of the exponent.

In order to store such numbers in memory units of the same length as single-precision fixed-point numbers, separate portions of each unit must be assigned to the fractional part and the exponent part. Standard ways of

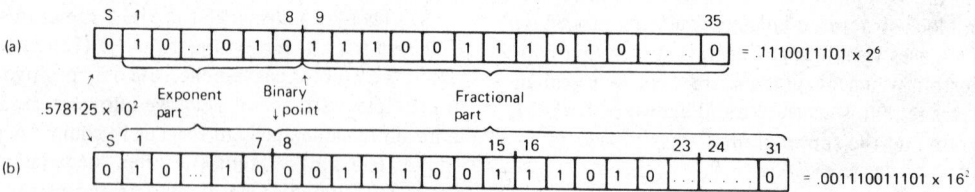

Fig. 2. Floating-point numbers.

doing this in computers having a 36-bit word memory or four 8-bit bytes to a word (like the **IBM 360-370** computers) are shown in Figs. 2(a) and 2(b) for the number $.578125 \times 10^2$. The following comments pertain to these figures.

1. A notation sometimes used for the number in Fig. 2(a) is (8,27), indicating 8 bits for the exponent part and 27 for the fractional part. Similarly, the number in Fig. 2(b) is a (7,24) number.

2. As with fixed-point numbers, the binary point of the fractional part is always assumed to be in the same place, usually at the left end, as in Fig. 2, but sometimes at the right-hand end (in which case the "fractional part" is an integer). The sign bit S always represents the sign of the fractional part.

3. Exponents may be positive or negative, but since the sign bit denotes the sign of the fractional part, the sign of the exponent must be handled by a special mechanism. One possibility would be to let bit 1 denote the sign of the exponent, but a much more common technique is to use "excess-n" notation. In Fig. 2(a) the 8 exponent bits can represent binary integers from 0 to $2^8 - 1 = 255$. If the desired exponent is X and the exponent part stored in bits 1 to 8 is Y, then $Y = X + 128$ is said to be an excess-128 exponent. Thus, true exponents X from -128 to $+127$ can be represented by values of Y from 0 to 255. Therefore it is necessary only for the arithmetic unit of the computer to interpret correctly the excess-128 exponent.

4. In IBM 360-370 computers the exponent is considered to be an excess-64 binary number, which is interpreted as a power of 16 because many of the internal operations of this series of computers are hexadecimally oriented. Thus, the exponent shown in Fig. 2(b) is interpreted as 16^2.

5. The range of exponents in the (8,27) case is from 2^{-128} to 2^{+127}, or from about 10^{-38} to 10^{+38}. In the (7,24) hexadecimal case, the range is from 16^{-64} to 16^{63}, or from about 10^{-77} to 10^{+76}. On CDC Cyber series computers, which use an (11,48) binary format with the mantissa radix point at the right, the range is from about 10^{-294} to 10^{322}. Even so, this range is not always adequate, as pointed out in the discussion on overflow in the next section.

The floating-point number in Fig. 2(a) is said to be *normalized* because the most significant bit in its fractional part (bit 9) is nonzero. Similarly, the floating-point number in Fig. 2(b) is normalized in a hexadecimal sense because the first hexadecimal digit in the fractional part (0011 = hexadecimal 3) is nonzero. Most computers automatically create normalized numbers as the result of floating-point arithmetic operations because in this way

the maximum number of significant bits is retained. Some computers allow the programmer to choose whether the result should be normalized or unnormalized. One school of thought believes that leaving results unnormalized gives a better picture of the true accuracy of the retained result.

Double precision floating-point numbers occupy two words, or twice the number of bytes, as single precision numbers. Two formats for these numbers are in use, with the first format below being more common today:

| S | EXP | FRACT. PART | | FRACTIONAL PART |

where the second fractional part is just an extension of the first and

| S | EXP1 | FRACT. PART | | S | EXP2 | FRACT. PART |

where the second fractional part is an extension of the first, but where EXP2 is less than EXP1 by the number of bits in each fractional part and both halves have the same sign.

Arithmetic, Fixed Point. The actual mechanics of fixed-point arithmetic are essentially those of ordinary binary arithmetic, given the restriction that negative numbers are generally stored and manipulated in some complement form. However, some aspects of fixed-point arithmetic on computers need to be considered explicitly. In the following examples we assume that fixed-point numbers are binary fractions of magnitude less than 1 (i.e., binary point at the left).

The only snare for the unwary in fixed-point addition and subtraction is the phenomenon known as *overflow*. Since not only the two operands but also the result in addition and subtraction must be less than 1 in magnitude, a result greater than this will not be handled correctly, as illustrated in Fig. 3. Overflow occurs when bit 1 has a carry-out. In some computers this carry-out is discarded; in others, as shown in Fig. 3, it replaces the sign bit, resulting in the example shown in a spurious negative number. In any case, the result is incorrect; normally this is indicated by setting an internal switch which the programmer can test, using a *branch on overflow* instruction.

Overflow cannot occur in fixed-point multiplication, since the product of two factors less than 1 in magnitude is also less than 1. But the multiplication of two n-bit factors results in a $2n$-bit product, which cannot be accommodated in an n-bit accumulator register in the arithmetic unit. Normally, the least significant n bits are placed in a second register, called the *multiplier-quotient (or MQ) register*, as shown in Fig. 4, in which for convenience we have assumed the word length to be only five

Fig. 3. Overflow in fixed-point numbers.

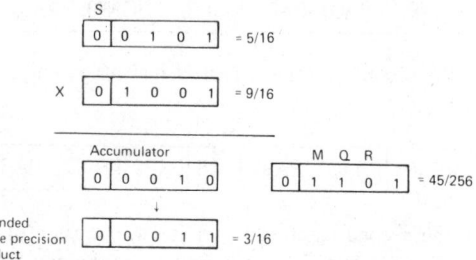

Fig. 4. Fixed-point multiplication.

bits. If the programmer wishes to retain the full $2n$-bit product, this may be done, but usually only the most significant n bits are retained after rounding, as shown in Fig. 4.

As with addition and subtraction, division can result in overflow if the dividend has magnitude greater than the divisor. Such an overflow, often called a *divide check*, is ordinarily tested by the programmer with an instruction separate from that used to test additive or subtractive overflow.

The dividend in fixed-point division can usually be double length (or precision), occupying both the accumulator and MQ registers. The single precision quotient is commonly placed in the MQ register and the remainder is placed in the accumulator, as illustrated in Fig. 5.

In actual practice the great majority of fixed-point arithmetic operations are normally performed on integer quantities in high-level language programs. Appropriate adjustments must be made when the computer assumes that the radix point is at the left-hand end of the number. However, the high-level language programmer need not be concerned about this, since the high-level language processor performs all the necessary manipulations. Fig. 6 illustrates what would actually happen in our hypothetical four-bit plus-sign computer in executing the Fortran statement

$$I = 14/5$$

to give the result 2, since remainders are discarded in Fortran integer division.

Arithmetic, Floating Point. The most difficult operations in floating-point arithmetic are addition and subtraction. A (simplified) algorithm for floating-point addition is the following: Let the two numbers to be added be A and B, and let C be the result. Let the exponent and fractional parts be denoted by E_a, E_b and E_c and F_a, F_b and F_c, respectively.

STEP 1. Set $E_c =$ the larger of E_a and E_b. Assume in what follows that $E_a \geq E_b$.

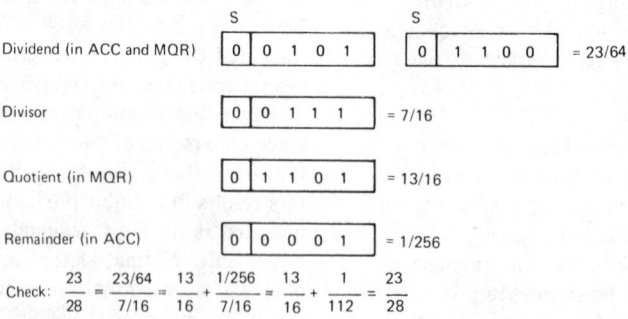

Fig. 5. Fixed-point division.

Dividend
l4 made least significant half of double-length dividend to avoid overflow
and give correct result directly.

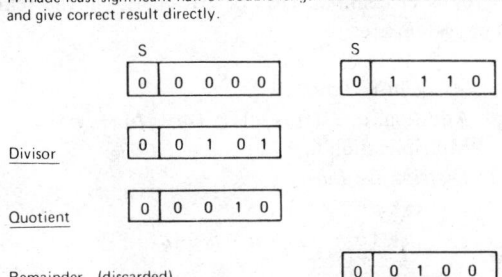

Divisor

Quotient

Remainder (discarded)

Fig. 6. Integer division in Fortran.

STEP 2. *Shift right.* Shift F_b to the right $E_a - E_b$ places (which has the effect of giving F_a and F_b the same exponent).

STEP 3. *Add.* Set $F_c = F_a + F_b$

STEP 4. *Normalize.* Shift F_c to make 1 its most significant digit and adjust E_c accordingly. This algorithm is illustrated in Fig. 7, assuming a hypothetical computer with a four-bit excess-8 exponent and a six-bit fractional part.

In proceeding through these four steps, several points should be considered:

1. Step 3 may result in a kind of overflow in that the two six-bit operands may produce a seven-bit result. But no error results because the "overflow" bit is always retained and shifted right in Step 4.

2. The final computer result is in error by 5/128 with respect to the true result. Some error is inevitable in general because the right shift in Step 2 may cause the loss of some significant bits of F_b. But if the final fractional part were 100001 instead of 100000, C would equal 2

+ 1/16, in which case the error would be 3/128 instead of 5/128. Many floating-point add algorithms would, in fact, achieve this result by *rounding F_c* after Step 3 (by adding 1 in the seventh position) before performing Step 4.

3. Many computers have machine instruction sets that allow the machine or assembly language programmer to choose either normalized or unnormalized floating-point operations (i.e., with or without Step 4, except that, when a right shift is required, it is always performed). The high-level language programmer has no such options. Normalized floating-point operations are almost always used in high-level language processors.

4. Floating-point subtraction or floating-point addition of numbers with different signs may result in a normalization that requires a left shift of F_c. In some computers the arithmetic unit will have retained the bits shifted right in Step 2, and these will now be shifted left to avoid the loss of precision that would be caused if zeros were inserted at the right. Other computers (e.g., the IBM 360–370 series) retain a single *guard digit* (a hexadecimal, not a binary digit, in IBM 360–370) on the right, which can be shifted left during normalization.

Overflow can occur in all floating-point operations when the magnitude of the result exceeds the capacity of the floating-point number system. Although, as noted previously, some computers can accommodate numbers as large as 10^{300} or more, overflow—particularly as the result of a programming error—is by no means unheard of. For our hypothetical floating-point number system, an example of overflow as a result of addition is shown in Fig. 8. The result of floating-point overflow is handled either by making the result the largest number possible ($\boxed{0\,|\,1111\,|\,111111}$) and setting an indicator that the programmer can test, or by stopping the computation with an appropriate error message.

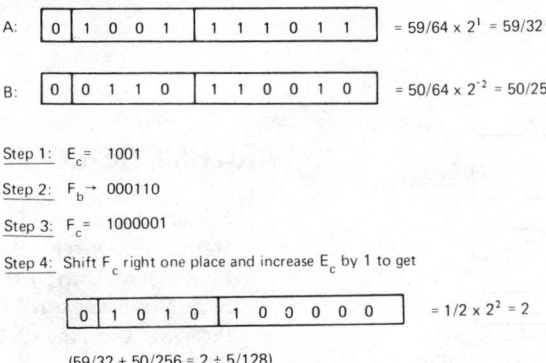

A: $\boxed{0\,|\,1\,0\,0\,1\,|\,1\,1\,1\,0\,1\,1}$ = 59/64 × 2^1 = 59/32

B: $\boxed{0\,|\,0\,1\,1\,0\,|\,1\,1\,0\,0\,1\,0}$ = 50/64 × 2^{-2} = 50/256

Step 1: E_c = 1001

Step 2: $F_b \rightarrow$ 000110

Step 3: F_c = 1000001

Step 4: Shift F_c right one place and increase E_c by 1 to get

$\boxed{0\,|\,1\,0\,1\,0\,|\,1\,0\,0\,0\,0\,0}$ = 1/2 × 2^2 = 2

(59/32 + 50/256 = 2 + 5/128)

Fig. 7. Floating-point addition.

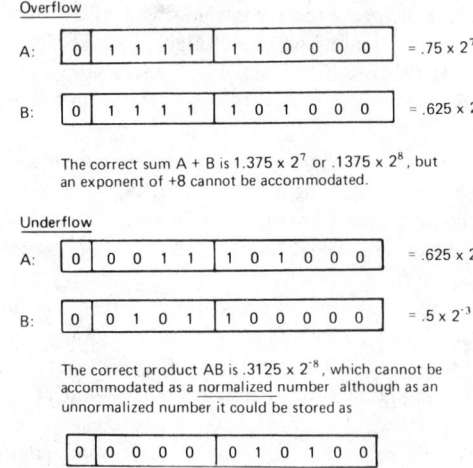

Overflow

A: = $.75 \times 2^7$

B: = $.625 \times 2^7$

The correct sum A + B is 1.375×2^7 or $.1375 \times 2^8$, but an exponent of +8 cannot be accommodated.

Underflow

A: = $.625 \times 2^{-5}$

B: = $.5 \times 2^{-3}$

The correct product AB is $.3125 \times 2^{-8}$, which cannot be accommodated as a <u>normalized</u> number although as an unnormalized number it could be stored as

Fig. 8. Floating-point overflow and underflow.

Underflow, which results from the attempt to produce a nonzero result too small (in magnitude) to be accommodated, can also result from any floating-point operation. The usual result is to generate a zero result; sometimes an indicator is also set, which the programmer can test. An example is given in Fig. 8.

Floating-point multiplication and division only require performing the appropriate action on the fractional parts, rounding the results, adding (for multiplication) or subtracting (for division) the exponents, and then normalizing if necessary. Examples are shown in Fig. 9.

Whereas computers do not normally provide hardware for double precision fixed-point arithmetic (which may, however, be programmed), hardware is often provided for double precision floating-point arithmetic. The details, however, do not differ sufficiently from those of single precision arithmetic to merit inclusion here. A comprehensive discussion of floating-point arithmetic is found in Sterbenz(1974).

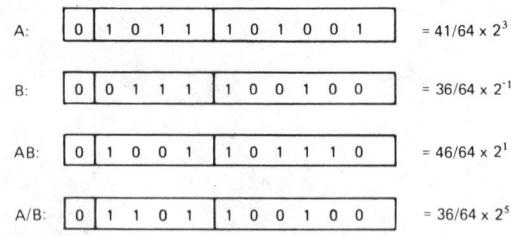

A: = $41/64 \times 2^3$

B: = $36/64 \times 2^{-1}$

AB: = $46/64 \times 2^1$

A/B: = $36/64 \times 2^5$

Fig. 9. Floating-point multiplication and division.

Computer Arithmetic and Real Arithmetic.

Two groups of common laws of arithmetic on the real-number system are:

1. *Associative Laws*
   Addition: $a + (b + c) = (a + b) + c$
   Multiplication: $a \cdot (b \cdot c) = (a \cdot b) \cdot c$
2. *Distributive Law*:

$$a \cdot (b + c) = a \cdot b + a \cdot c$$

The truth of these laws depends in part on the denseness of the real numbers on the number line or, equivalently, on the ability of numbers to have arbitrarily large numbers of digits. Due to the finiteness of computer arithmetic, these laws are not generally satisfied on computers, although the commutative laws for addition,

$$a + b = b + a$$

and for multiplication,

$$a \cdot b = b \cdot a$$

are generally satisfied. The failure of the associative and distributive laws to be satisfied affects relatively few computations, but on occasion such failure can be crucial. For a further discussion of this see Ralston (1971).

References

1963. Flores, I. *The Logic of Computer Arithmetic*. Englewood Cliffs, NJ: Prentice-Hall.
1969. Knuth, D. E. "Seminumerical Algorithms," in *The Art of Computer Programming*, **2**. Reading, MA: Addison-Wesley. (This book is *the* reference on the algorithms by which computer arithmetic is performed.)
1971. Ralston, A. *Introduction to Programming and Computer Science*. New York: McGraw-Hill.
1974. Sterbenz, P. H. *Floating-Point Computation*. Englewood Cliffs, NJ: Prentice-Hall.

A. Ralston

ARITHMETIC-LOGIC UNIT

For articles on related subjects *see* Adder; Arithmetic, Computer; Boolean Algebra; Central Processing Unit; Codes; Machine Instruction Set; Numbers and Number Systems; Operand; Pipeline and Array Processors; Register; and Shifting.

The arithmetic-logic unit (ALU) is a functional part of the digital computer which carries out arithmetic and logic operations on machine words that represent the operands. It is usually considered to be a part of the central processing unit (CPU). In some computer systems, separate units exist for arithmetic operations (the arithmetic unit, AU) and for logic operations (the logic unit, LU).

Many computers contain more than one AU. For example, a separate Index AU is frequently employed to perform additions or subtraction operations on address parts of instructions for the purpose of indexing, boundary tests for memory protection, etc. Large computer systems employ separate AUs for different classes of algorithms; for example, the IBM System 360, Model 91, contains a fixed-point AU and a floating-point AU. Multiprocessor systems contain several identical ALUs; for example, the ILLIAC IV contains 64 identical ALUs with associated memory modules.

A complete discussion of an ALU must describe its three fundamental attributes:

1. Operands and results.
2. Functional organization.
3. Algorithms.

Operands and Results. Two kinds of ALU organizations can be distinguished with respect to the length of machine words. In machines with *fixed* word length, all words consist of the same number of bits. In machines with *variable* word length, one byte is the shortest machine word; a typical length of one byte is eight bits. Longer machine words consist of some integral number of bytes.

The operands and results of the ALU are machine words of two kinds: *arithmetic words,* which represent numerical values in digital form, and *logic words,* which represent arbitrary sets of digitally encoded symbols.

Arithmetic words consist of strings of digits. Conventional radix r number representations allow r values for one digit: $0, 1, \ldots, r - 1$. Practical design considerations have limited the choice of radices to the values 2, 4, 8, 10, and 16. The value of every digit is represented by a set of bits. Radices 2, 4, 8, and 16 employ binary numbers having length of 1, 2, 3, and 4 bits, respectively, to represent the values of one digit. Radix-10 digit values are usually represented by four or five bits. Most commonly used are the four-bit BCD (binary-coded decimal) and excess-3, and the five-bit biquinary encodings (see CODES).

Two methods have been employed to represent negative numbers. In the sign-and-magnitude form, a separate *sign bit* is attached to the string of digits to represent the $+$ and $-$ signs. (Usually 0 represents the $+$, and 1 represents the $-$ sign.) In the true-and-complement form, the negative value $-x$ is represented as the complement (*q.v.*) with respect to A of the value x; i.e.,

$$-x \text{ is represented by } A - x$$

The value of A used in ALUs is either $A = r^{n+1}$ or $A = r^{n+1} - 1$, when x is represented by n digits in the sign-and-magnitude form. An illustration for radix 10 and radix 2 and $n = 4$ is given below.

Sign and Magnitude	$A = 10^5 - 1$ (9s complement)	$A = 10^5$ (10s complement)
$+4902$	04902	04902
-4902	95097	95098

	$A = 2^5 - 1$ (1s complement)	$A = 2^5$ (2s complement)
$+1010$	01010	01010
-1010	10101	10110

The use of complements to represent negative values makes it possible to replace the subtraction algorithm in an ALU by a complementation followed by an addition modulo A.

Other important properties of operands and results are (Avižienis, 1972):

1. Location of the radix point.
2. Use of multiple-precision representations.
3. Use of floating-point forms.
4. Explicit designation of the number of significant digits in a representation.
5. Encoding in error-detecting (or error-correcting) codes.

The use of nonconventional number representations in computers as a means to increase the speed of arithmetic has been proposed. Extensive studies have been made of *residue* number systems (Svoboda, 1962) and of *signed-digit* number systems (Avižienis and Tung, 1970); however, they have not reached practical application in ALU design.

Logic words that serve as operands represent alphanumeric information and are subject only to logic algorithms that are applied to individual bits of the operands. These algorithms are (1) negation for one operand, and (2) the 16 two-variable logic operations for corresponding bits of two operands.

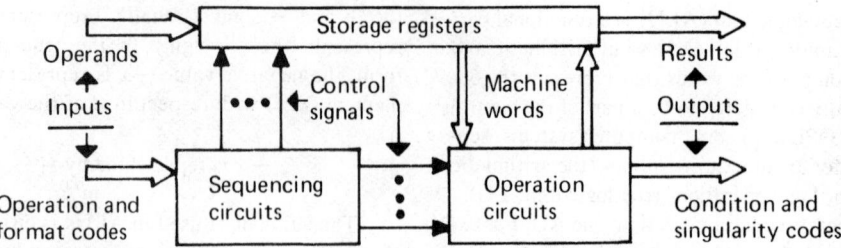

Fig. 1. Functions of an ALU.

Functional Organization and Algorithms of an ALU.

An ALU consists of three types of functional parts: storage registers, operations circuits, and sequencing circuits, as shown in Fig. 1. The inputs and outputs of the ALU are connected to other functional units of the computer, such as the main memory, the program execution control unit, and input/output devices. A *bus* is most frequently used as the means of connection. In some cases the ALU may be connected to two or more buses within the computer system.

The input information received by the ALU consists of operands, operation codes, and format codes. The operands are machine words that represent numeric or alphanumeric information in the form of a string of binary digits (bits). The operation code identifies one operation from the set of available arithmetic and logic operations, and also designates the location (within local storage) of the operands and of the results. The designation of operands is omitted in ALUs with limited local storage; for example, an ADD operation code in a single-accumulator ALU always means the addition of the incoming operand to the operand in the accumulator register and storage of the sum in the accumulator. The format code is used when the ALU can operate on more than one type of operand; for example, the ADD operation can be specified either for fixed-point or for floating-point operands. Often the operation code and the format code are represented by a single set of bits.

The output information delivered by the ALU consists of results, *condition codes,* and *singularity codes.* The results are machine words generated by the specified operations and stored in the local storage registers. The condition codes are bits or sets of bits that identify specific conditions associated with a result, such as that the value of the result is positive, negative, zero; that the result consists of all zeros, all ones, etc. The singularity codes indicate that the specified operation does not yield a representable result. Examples of singularities are *overflow,* i.e., the value of the result exceeds the allowed range; attempted division by zero; excessive loss of precision in floating-point operations; error caused by a logic

fault, etc. Singularity codes usually set a flip-flop in the machine status word.

Internally, the ALU is composed of storage registers, logic circuits that perform arithmetic and logic algorithms, and logic circuits that control the sequence of gating operations within the ALU. The diagram of a simple ALU is shown in Fig. 2.

The ALU contains three registers: the operand register, OPR; the accumulator register, ACC; and the multiplier-quotient register, MQR. Each register contains one machine word, i.e., for a machine word length of n bits, the register consists of n flip-flops.

The gating of words into the ALU registers and from the registers into the operation circuits or out of the ALU is controlled by the sequencing logic (SL), which applies a sequence of gate-enabling signals to the gates G_i of Fig. 2. Each sequence corresponds to one of the algorithms provided within the ALU. The sequencing logic is implemented either in "hard wired" form, using counters and decoding circuits, or by means of a microprogrammed control unit. The sequence of gating signals is initiated by the receipt of the operation and format codes in the ALU.

The operation circuits consist of the adder (AD), the shifter (SH), and the logic operator circuits (LO). The adder forms the sum of the numbers in OPR and ACC and returns it to the ACC. When the length of the sum exceeds the standard word length, the overflow detection (OD) circuit issues an overflow singularity code, and the excess digit of the sum is placed into an overflow digit position (AOD) which is located at the left end of the ACC. Subtraction is usually implemented as complementation of the subtrahend in OPR, followed by its addition to the minuend in ACC. A subtractor may be used instead of an adder in Fig. 2; in this case, subtraction is carried out directly, and addition is implemented as the complementation of the addend in OPR followed by its subtraction from the augend in ACC.

The SH circuits perform left-shift and right-shift operations on the words in ACC and MQR. A single-shift operation displaces every digit in the register to the adjacent position on the left or on the right. Shifts are spec-

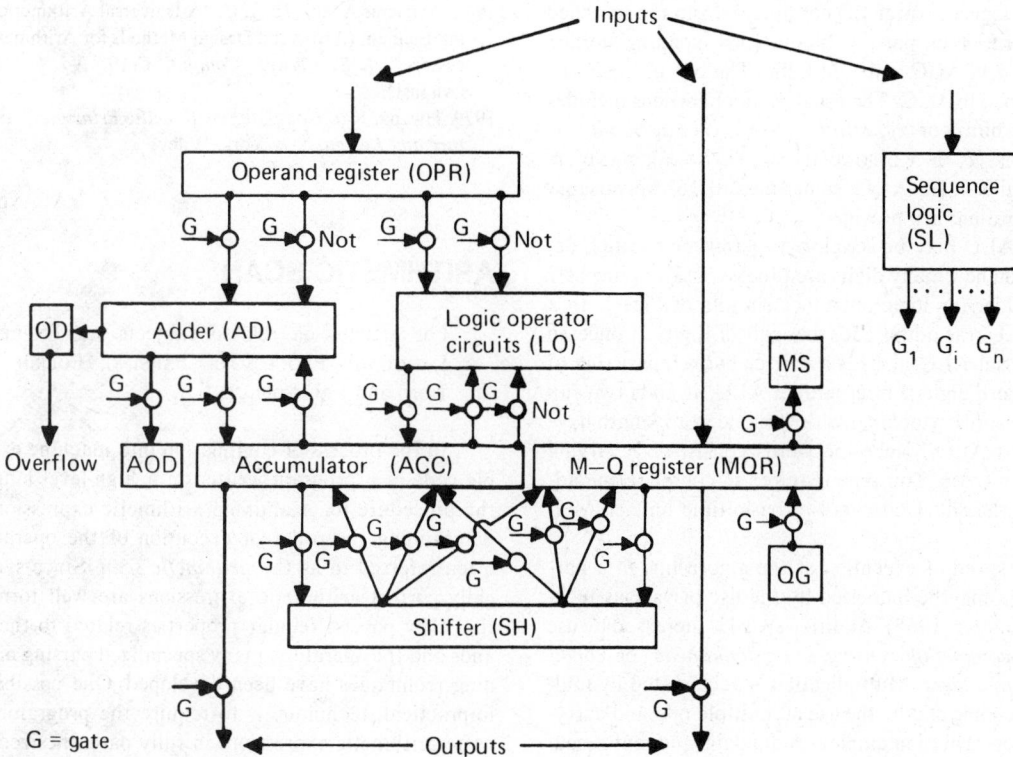

Fig. 2. Organization of an ALU.

ified either for one register or for both registers simultaneously, with the rightmost position of ACC adjoining the leftmost position of MQR. There are three classes of shifts:

1. *Circular Shifts.* The rightmost and the leftmost positions of a register are treated as adjacent during the shift.
2. *Logical Shifts.* Digits are discarded from end positions and zeros are inserted; e.g., during a single right shift, the rightmost digit is lost and the leftmost position is filled in with zero.
3. *Arithmetic Shifts.* The purpose of an arithmetic shift is to multiply (left) or to divide (right) the operand by the radix r. For negative numbers, the sign bit must be treated with special care (*see* SHIFTING.)

The shifter is frequently designed as an integral part of the ACC and MQ registers; they are then called *shift registers.*

Multiplication and division operations are carried out as a sequence of additions or subtractions and arithmetic shifts. The MQ register serves as the third register for these operations. In multiplication, the multiplicand x is placed into OPR register, the multiplier y into MQ register of Fig. 2, while ACC is cleared to zero. The least significant digit y_0 of the multiplier is sensed by the multiplier sensing (MS) circuit, and x is added y_0 times to the contents of ACC. Then ACC and MQ registers are arithmetically shifted one position to the right, and the next multiplier digit, y_1, is sensed by the MS circuit. After all n digits of y have been sensed, the double-length product xy is located in ACC and MQ registers. A roundoff operation is needed to reduce the product to single-word length.

To perform division, the dividend is placed into ACC. If the dividend is of double length, the MQ register receives its less significant half. The divisor is placed into OP register, and division is carried out as a sequence of trial subtractions and left arithmetic shifts. Quotient digits are generated one at a time in the quotient generation (QG) circuit and inserted at the right end of the MQ register after each shift, beginning with the most significant quotient digit, q_{n-1}. After n steps, the quotient is located in MQ register and the remainder in the ACC register.

The logic operator LO circuits perform the specified logic operation on pairs of bits in corresponding storage positions a_i of ACC and x_i of OPR. The bits of the result are returned to ACC. The usual set of operations includes NOT (one bit: $\bar{a}_i$ or $\bar{x}_i$), AND ($a_i \wedge x_i$), OR ($a_i \vee x_i$), EXCLUSIVE-OR ($a_i \oplus x_i$), EQUIVALENCE ($a_i \equiv x_i$), NAND ($\bar{a}_i \vee \bar{x}_i$) and NOR ($\bar{a}_i \wedge \bar{x}_i$); sometimes all 16 two-variable logic operations are provided.

An ALU may be serial, byte-serial, or parallel, depending on how many digits are processed simultaneously in the adder (or logic operator) circuits of Fig. 2. In a serial ALU, the adder adds one pair of digits at once; in a byte-serial ALU, it adds a pair of bytes (consisting of two or more digits); in a parallel ALU, it adds two full machine words. Machines with variable word length have byte-serial ALUs, since the words consist of a varying number of bytes. The time required to complete one addition in the adder circuits is a basic time unit of ALU operation.

The speed of execution of the algorithms in a parallel ALU may be increased by the use of various techniques (Garner, 1965). Addition speed is increased by use of *carry-completion sensing, carry-lookahead,* or *conditional-sum adders.* Multiplication is accelerated by multiplier recoding and by the use of multiple-operand carry-save adders. Division employs redundant quotient recoding techniques with approximate estimates, or quadratic convergence which uses fast multiplication to generate the quotient (Anderson et al., 1967). The technique of *pipelining* (*q.v.*) also has been employed to increase the effective throughput of an ALU (Anderson *et al.,* 1967).

The use of more storage registers within the ALU increases the speed of computing by reducing the number of memory accesses. Therefore, 8, 16, or more ALU registers are often used instead of the three registers shown in Fig. 2; each register may perform the function of ACC, OPR, or MQ registers. Several ALU registers may be used to hold a *stack* of ALU operands and results.

Some ALUs provide a more extensive set of algorithms, including square root, complex arithmetic, trigonometric functions, etc. Such ALUs are most often found in special-purpose computers.

REFERENCES

1962. Svoboda, A. "The Numerical System of Residual Classes," in *Digital Information Processors.* New York: Wiley Interscience, pp. 543–574.
1965. Garner, H. L. "Number Systems and Arithmetic," in Alt, F. L. (Ed.), *Advances in Computers* **6**: 131–194. New York Academic Press.
1967. Anderson, S. F., Earle, J. G., Goldschmidt, R. E., and Powers, D. M. "The IBM System/360 Model 91: Floating-Point Execution Unit," *IBM Journal of Research and Development* **11**, *No. 1:* 34–53 (January).
1970. Avižienis A. and Tung, C. "A Universal Arithmetic Building Element (ABE) and Design Methods for Arithmetic Processors," *IEEE Trans. Comput.* **C-19,** *No. 8:* 733–745 (August).
1979. Hwang, Kai. *Computer Arithmetic: Principles, Architecture and Design.* New York: Wiley.

A. AVIŽIENIS

ARITHMETIC SCAN

For articles on related subjects *see* EXPRESSION; LANGUAGE PROCESSORS; PARSING; POLISH NOTATION; and PRECEDENCE.

In the process of compilation into machine executable code of a program written in a high-level language, the procedure for examining arithmetic expressions and determining the order of execution of the operators is often referred to as the *arithmetic scan.* Since syntactically correct arithmetic expressions are well formed in that they possess regular properties related to the operands and the operators, many specialized parsing or scanning techniques have been developed. One possible, but impractical, technique is to require the programmer to write arithmetic expressions in fully parenthesized notation (i.e., parentheses must be placed around each pair of operands and its associated operator) so as to obviate the need for knowledge about the relationships between operators in determining the order in which the operations are to be performed.

Most commonly used are transformational systems, which convert the normal infix form (i.e., the form in which the operator is placed between its operands) to a Polish form in which there exists no parentheses and the order of execution of the operators is specified by their positioning. Such a system is needed because of the difficulty of associating operands with operators in infix notation. As an example, consider the Fortran expression

$$(A * X + B)/(C * X - D) \tag{1}$$

which, because of the *precedence* relations among Fortran arithmetic operators, is to be interpreted in fully parenthesized notation, as

$$(((A*X) + B)/((C*X) - D)) \tag{2}$$

By use of an algorithm (see Ralston, 1971), which scans across the string in expression (1) from left to right just once, this string can be converted to the Polish postfix string

$$AX*B + CX*D - / \tag{3}$$

which, without a need for parentheses or precedence relations, has uniquely the interpretation of expression (2). With one more single scan across the string, it can be compiled into machine code.

The arithmetic scan described above is a special case of a general syntactic analyzer that uses precedence *(q.v.)* relationships.

REFERENCE

1971, Ralston, A. *An Introduction to Programming and Computer Science.* New York: McGraw-Hill.

J. A. N. LEE AND A. RALSTON

ARPA NETWORK

For articles on related subjects *see* COMPUTER NETWORKS; DATA COMMUNICATIONS; DATA NETWORKS, PUBLIC; INTERFACE MESSAGE PROCESSOR; and TELEPROCESSING SYSTEMS.

In 1968, the Defense Advanced Research Projects Agency (DARPA) embarked on a project to implement a resource sharing network called the ARPA network, or ARPANET for short. The network was designated to provide effective and efficient communications between heterogeneous host computers so that hardware, software, and data resources could be shared conveniently and economically by a wide community of users.

Following the successful accomplishment of initial ARPANET design goals, it was considered appropriate to transfer operating responsibility for ARPANET from DARPA to the Defence Communications Agency in July 1975. In mid-1981, the network consisted of 94 nodes at 88 separate sites.

Network Properties. Each host is connected to the network via a small local computer called the Interface Message Processor (IMP). Each IMP, in turn, is connected to several other IMPs via wideband communications lines operating at bit rates between 50 and 1,000 kilobits/sec. Terminal IMPs (TIPs), shown in Fig. 1, with flexible terminal-handling capabilities, are also available to provide a wide variety of terminals direct access to the network. The early IMPs and TIPs were minicomputer based. The newer ones are based on PLURIBUS technology which is a multiprocessor, is expandable, and can service up to 18 hosts. The PLURIBUS IMP or TIP has higher throughput and can be configured redundantly for improved reliability.

Fig. 2 shows the geographic and logical maps of the network plus the computers at each node. Note that the

Fig. 1. A terminal interface message processor.

network is multiconnected; i.e., more than one path exists between any pair of nodes. The topology was selected to provide good response times and high reliability and to have good growth potential, while keeping costs to a minimum.

Message-switching rather than circuit-switching is used to establish communication between nodes. In a circuit-switched network, the source and destination are connected by a dedicated communication path established at the beginning of the connection and broken only at the end. In a message-switched system such as ARPANET, no dedicated path exists. Instead, a source host or terminal passes its message, including a destination address, to its local IMP or TIP. The message is then passed from IMP to IMP until it finally arrives at its destination. The choice of the path is determined dynamically. Each IMP forwards the message on the path it determines best to assure prompt delivery, taking into account the network loading and topology. The current design allows variable length messages of up to 8,095 bits. To improve transit times, the IMPs partition messages into 1,024-bit packets and send them one after the

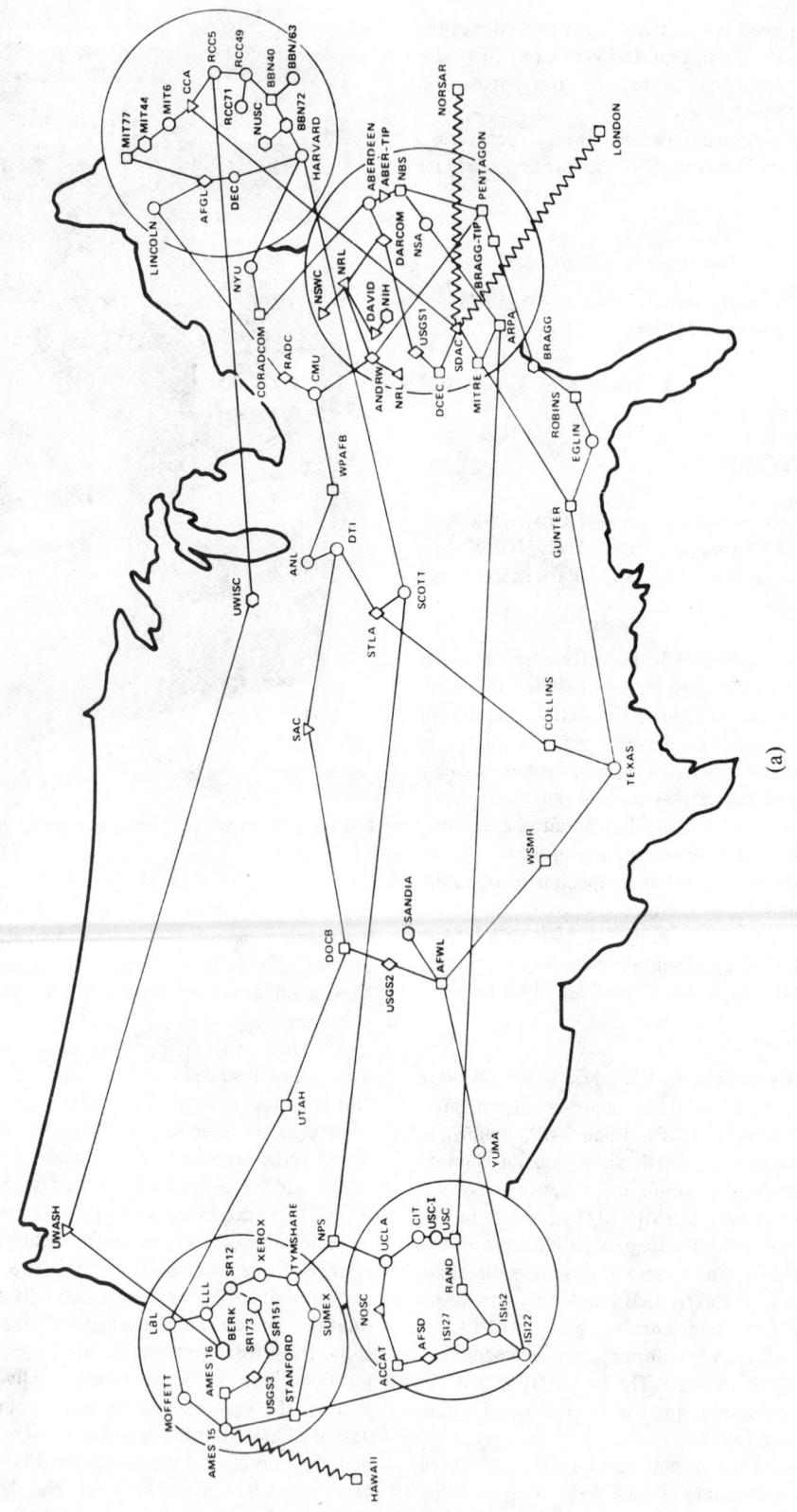

(a)

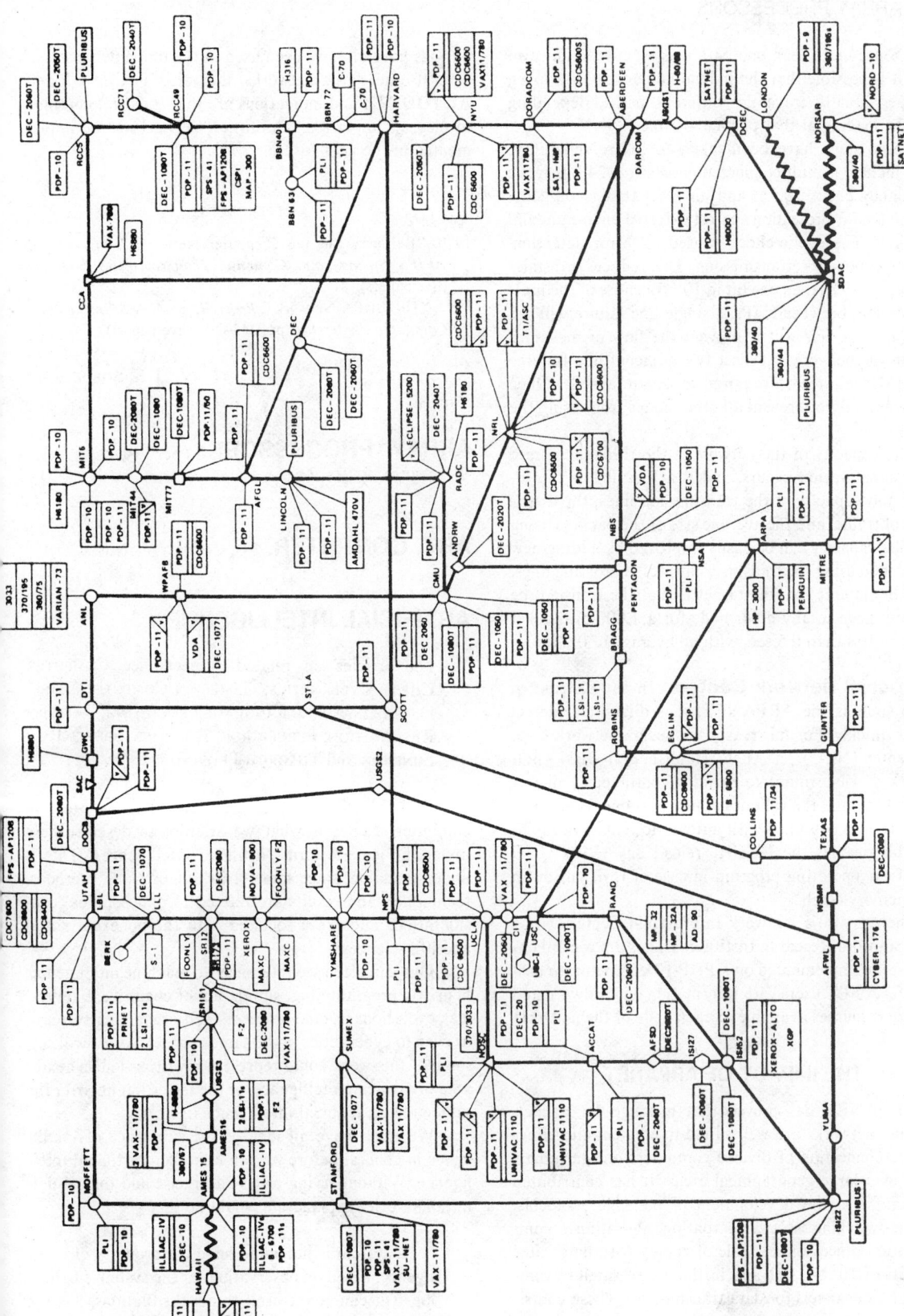

Fig. 2. Geographical (a) and logical (b) maps of the ARPA network issued by the ARPA Network Information Center (1981).

(b)

other. Since more than one path exists between any two hosts, it is possible that the individual packets of a given message actually travel by different paths, depending upon the loading at that particular time.

Three steps have been taken to insure reliability. These include a multiconnected network, a 24-bit cyclic redundancy check (*q.v.*), and an IMP that is ruggedly constructed for protection against external environmental conditions. The cyclic check is used for error detection, with correction by retransmission. This reduces transmission errors to less than one bit in 10^{12}. Because of the multiconnections between IMPs, a single line failure will not isolate a node, nor will it prevent the flow of messages through the network. At least two adjacent line failures or an IMP failure are required to isolate a node. Once again, this will not prevent all other nodes from using the net.

The capacity of the network is the throughput rate at which saturation occurs, and is a function of the topology and capacity of the transmission lines, the distribution of traffic, and the average size of the packets being sent. The capacity can be easily improved by adding new lines or increasing the transmission rates on existing lines. To enable interaction, the target is that the transit time from any node to any other node for a 1,000-bit packet should be less than 0.5 sec, with an average of 0.2 sec.

Special Network Centers. In any distributed system such as the ARPANET, it is difficult to detect failures quickly. For this reason, a special Network Control Center (NCC) has been established at BBN (Bolt Beranek and Newman) to monitor continuously line or IMP failures and the volumes of host and line traffic. The IMPs are also equipped with automatic reloading facilities. This enables the NCC to reload any IMP with a copy of the operating program in case of revisions or an IMP memory crash.

There is also a Network Information Center (NIC) at the Stanford Research Institute. This is a powerful online system, implemented on a PDP-10 computer, to provide ARPANET users with information on hardware and software resources available at each node of the network.

THE IMPACT OF ARPANET

ARPANET has proved that message- or packet-switching networks are well suited to efficient and effective interconnection of diverse computers and terminals spread over large geographical areas. It has contributed significantly in the development of message protocols, message-switching software, routing algorithms, communication processors capable of coping with data rates in excess of 10^6 bits/sec and in the use of satellite communication channels for data transmission. These contributions have already been used in the implementation of several other large networks, including TELENET and AUTODIN2, and indications are that they will continue to play an important role in new networks to be implemented in the near future.

REFERENCES

1970. "Resource Sharing Computer Networks," *Proceedings AFIPS Spring Joint Computer Conference,* pp. 543–597 (five papers).
1972. "The ARPA Network," *Proceedings AFIPS Spring Joint Computer Conference,* pp. 243–303 (five papers).

J. S. SOBOLEWSKI

ARRAY PROCESSORS. *See* PIPELINE AND ARRAY PROCESSORS.

ART, COMPUTER. *See* COMPUTER ART.

ARTIFICIAL INTELLIGENCE

For articles on related subjects see COMPUTER CHESS; CYBERNETICS; GAMES ON COMPUTERS; HEURISTICS; NATURAL LANGUAGE PROCESSING; PATTERN RECOGNITION; PERCEPTRON; ROBOTICS; SPEECH RECOGNITION and THEOREM PROVING.

Probably the most controversial area of study in computer science is what we attempt to describe here under the generic term "artificial intelligence." This is understandable, since some of its assumptions, methods, techniques, and results are related to philosophical considerations and are associated with the nonexact social and life sciences.

One can often see references to machine intelligence, heuristic programming, simulation of cognitive, biophysical, evolutionary, etc., processes, self-organizing systems, or even to cybernetics in the same context. As we will see, some of this work could represent investigation as a subarea of artificial intelligence, or the terms might cover the same area as artificial intelligence itself.

We must have an idea of the substance of intelligence in general before we can talk about artificial intelligence. Without trying to give a precise and formal definition, a brief explanation would be that

... a system is judged to have the property of intelligence, based on observations of the system's behavior, if it can adapt itself to novel situations, has the capacity to reason, to understand the relationships between facts, to discover meanings, and to recognize truth. Also, one often expects an intelligent system to learn; i.e., to improve its level of performance on the basis of past experiences.

This loose but suggestive definition might be applied to nonliving systems or artifacts as well as to humans and animals. In fact, it must be stated that there is no scientific evidence that would limit, in principle, the inherent intellectual capabilities attainable by nonliving systems. Within a remarkably short period of time, interesting and significant results have been obtained in a number of different areas of artificial intelligence. A brief description of these is given in the following sections.

Approaches to and Objectives of Artificial Intelligence. It is useful to subdivide the whole area of artificial intelligence into two branches of study. One of these may be somewhat simplistically called the "engineering approach"; the other, the "modeling approach." In the first case, the researcher wants to create a system that is able to deal with interesting and difficult intellectual tasks, regardless of whether the methods and techniques used are similar or identical to those used by humans. There is a job to accomplish inexpensively, efficiently, and reliably—that is all that matters. Examples of this approach are certain pattern recognition tasks (such as recognizing the characters printed in a special format on bank checks), translating text from one natural language into another, composing music by computer, locating warehouses across the country in an optimum manner, and so on.

The modeling approach has the basic research objective of trying to gain an understanding of the inside mechanisms of a real life system and to explain and predict its behavior. We can put in this category, for example, those projects that simulate human problem solving, decision making, or learning behavior by building models of neural networks.

There is, however, an area of transition between the two approaches, one that concerns certain intellectual tasks at which humans have been excellent over a long period of time. Chess, for example, has a written history of some 400 years and its rules have changed very little in many centuries. It has presented a challenge to researchers in artificial intelligence par excellence. About a dozen chess-playing programs have been reported in the literature and the more recent ones can play quite sophisticated games, at the master level and above (*see* COMPUTER CHESS). Because of the impossibility of reducing this game to a mathematical formalism (i.e., it is not amenable to an algorithmic solution) and because an exhaustive method of finding the optimum move is in general out of the question, a good chess-playing program has to incorporate so-called heuristics. These are based on loosely formulated rules of thumb that are occasionally referred to as "insight," "intuition," or simply "experience."

In other words, the knowledge of how humans perform certain tasks is indispensable to and must be incorporated into those programs whose main objective is to accomplish these intellectual tasks as well as possible.

We can now briefly enumerate the three basic motivations for research in artificial intelligence:

1. To replace human intelligence because it is expensive, scarce, and often less than reliable.
2. To establish theories of human intelligence in the form of simulation models.
3. To assess the capabilities for AI of presently available software and hardware, and to point to lines of development for future programming languages and computer systems.

Three Fundamental Problems. In the following discussion a large number of study areas will be outlined. Three problems are common among all these areas and it is therefore advisable to examine them briefly at this stage.

Problem of Representation. The selection and design of representation is a central issue in programming in general. How a particular task is translated into information structures and information processes inside the computer may render the solution of the task efficient and effective, or so cumbersome that it is prohibitively unwieldy.

One of the long-term objectives of artificial intelligence research is to automate the processes that make the decision on a particular representation after the specification of the task has been given, possibly in natural language. At present, however, the information structures and processes are chosen ad hoc and are assumed to be quasi-optimum for the task at hand. This task dependence in representation has obvious shortcomings.

Generality Versus Efficiency. Human intelligence is multipurpose by nature. The majority of projects in the study of artificial intelligence have, however, resulted in somewhat narrow and single-minded programs whose efficiency is reasonably high. As soon as the range of applicability of a program increases, its level of complexity rises, but its efficiency in solving individual problems drops.

Again, a long-term objective is to write highly efficient programs of "universal" applicability. A plausible avenue to this goal is via learning programs that can initially tackle simple problems and gradually acquire more and more power for a larger number of, and more difficult, problems. Also, a reasonable level of success has already been achieved with programs that subdivide a large and difficult task into smaller, possibly known ones. This technique has to be developed further.

Problem of Search. It is often the case that one can write a program that generates potential solutions to a problem, tests them, and, hopefully, sometimes discovers the right ones. With nontrivial problems, however, the "solution space" is very large, for practical purposes infinite, and there can be no exhaustive search performed. It has been, for example, estimated that in order to find the best possible starting move in chess, the machine would have to evaluate 10^{120} game positions. It has also been pointed out that if a computer consisting of all the elementary particles in the universe could be constructed and run with the speed of light, the current estimate of the age of the universe would not have been long enough to find the best first move according to the exhaustive search strategy.

It would therefore be a good idea to direct the search process by detecting relative improvements as the program moves around in the domain of all potential solutions. Heuristic rules should be built in or, in a more sophisticated manner, automatically generated by the program to recognize the structure of the search space and thereby cut down the computing time and memory requirements. Although many efficient search techniques have been developed in various studies in artificial intelligence, there is a great need for further work in this area.

Finally, it should be noted in a nonapologetic manner that the area discussed, like the majority of the branches of computer science, has a predominantly experimental flavor. Although more and more theoretical foundation is being developed in several directions, the basic motive of experimentation is likely to prevail in the foreseeable future.

Research Topics in Artificial Intelligence.

Mechanical and electromechanical toys have been built for a long time to demonstrate certain goal-oriented behavior. More recent ones (by Shannon, MacKay, Ashby, etc.) have shown certain *cybernetic* principles involving negative feedback concerning, for example, the recharge state of their batteries. The robotics projects currently pursued at Stanford University, Stanford Research Institute (see Fig.1), M.I.T., and various Japanese and British laboratories, go well beyond them in sophistication. The robots not only can perceive visual stimuli via television cameras but are also equipped with tactile receptors and some effectors to move, for example, wooden blocks around. The controlling computer may communicate with the robot via cables or radio signals, or the robot may carry the computer along its adventurous path.

These projects aim at integrating the many piece-

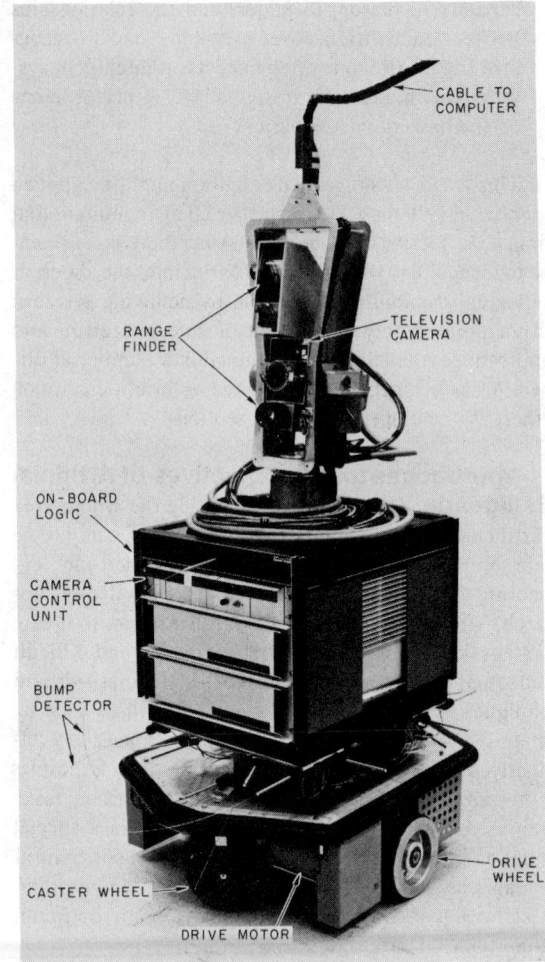

Fig. 1.   "Shakey," a robot project of the Artificial Intelligence Center of Stanford University.

meal results of artificial intelligence research, from theorem proving to pattern recognition and picture processing, from learning and problem-solving techniques to natural language processing and to question-answering systems. Beyond the interest in basic research, workers in this field hope to make use of their results in planetary or underwater exploration and in areas where human access is difficult or impossible.

Simulation of neurological and physiological phenomena often consists of building a computer model of a network of (idealized) nerve cells. These networks are self-adaptive; i.e., they can be trained to recognize audio and visual patterns by changing certain parametric values or the interconnections between them. One of the most remarkable of these experiments was made by Rochester, Holland, Haibt, and Duda to test Hebb's verbally described theory of neural cell assembly. They discovered some flaws in the assumptions, and after making some extensions of the model, they were able to show the learning capability of the network.

Rosenblatt and his coworkers investigated a class of random nets of neuron-like elements, called *perceptrons*. Their mathematical analysis was recently extended by Minsky and Papert. The EEG-like output of permanently connected nonlinear elements was demonstrated by Farley. Wooldridge and Broadbent tried in various studies to describe the activity of the brain in terms of electric circuitry.

Another idea of somewhat limited success by Fogel and others was to simulate the evolution of intelligence from its most primitive beginnings via mutations and natural selection.

Several projects have simulated robots in environments of varying complexity (Doran, Toda, Findler, and Allan). Planning and search behavior have been interesting aspects of these works. The problems of heuristic search have often formed the basis of some abstract investigations (Sandewall, Pohl, Nielsson), sometimes in connection with the special task of the Graph Traverser (Michie, Doran, Marsh, Ross). Techniques of tree search are of primary interest in game playing and theorem-proving programs.

The simulation of cognitive processes will now be discussed in some detail. (Affective processes involving motivation, ambition, etc., have been considered by Simon, Findler, and others.) The basic tenet here is that complex human behavior can be analyzed and broken down into elementary symbol manipulation processes. The computer can be programmed in terms of these elementary building blocks to perform the same information-processing tasks that humans do. The computer program, representing a psychological theory of various behavioral phenomena, becomes a convenient vehicle to determine objectively the implications of the model. The need for precise formulation in the program leaves no room for vagueness, ambiguity, and lack of rigor. A comparison with experimental data may lead to modifications in the model until the researcher is satisfied that a sufficient theory has been constructed. According to Newell and Simon, human thinking can be explained in information processing terms without waiting for a theory of the underlying neurological mechanisms.

An often used technique for finding out about the details of human thought processes is to make the experimental subject utter the reasons behind every step of his activity verbally into a tape recorder ("thinking aloud"). A detailed analysis of these "protocols" would lead to a flowchart of the subject's behavior. (Newell and his students have obtained promising results in trying to automate the process of analysis.) The flowchart is then trans-

lated into a program, several variants of which can be run to simulate different individuals.

Three classical pieces of work along these lines were produced by Newell, Shaw, and Simon. The first one, the *Logic Theorist,* is a heuristic theorem-proving program for the first-order predicate calculus. Its original version could prove 38 of the 52 theorems in Chapter 2 of Whitehead and Russell's *Principia Mathematica.*

The second work, the *General Problem Solver* (GPS), has been able to separate to a significant extent problem-solving techniques and task environments. The so-called means-ends analysis lies at the center of the program. It goes as follows: The present and the desired objects are given ("object" in the most general sense of the word). GPS discovers the difference between them and tries to find an operator (i.e., a transformation) relevant to this difference. If successful, the task is accomplished. Otherwise, it attempts to bridge over the much too large difference by creating objects in between the present and the desired objects. In this recursive manner, either it produces a sequence of operators that is the solution of the problem or it reports failure. The latter may also be due to the fact that the program has exceeded the prespecified time limit or has run out of memory. This basic paradigm of problem solving has penetrated many projects, including the Newell, Shaw, Simon chess program, which is the third piece of work referred to above.

Concept learning has been the target of several simulation models (Hunt, Holland, Johnson, Baker, and others). The behavior of these programs reflects the attribute and rule-learning characteristics of humans. The detection of temporal sequences implies an understanding of event generation in order to predict future members of the sequence. Simon and Kotovsky, Abrahams et al., D. S. Williams, and others have written programs to simulate humans in these tasks. The first of this kind of program was in fact Feldman's *Binary Choice Model,* which reproduced even the idiosyncratic behavior of several individuals.

The elementary perceiver and memorizer (EPAM) by Feigenbaum and Simon (1963) represents a theory of human memory and models the learning of associated nonsense syllables, a standard psychological test. It reproduces the increasing discriminative ability, retroactive inhibition, stimulus generalization, response oscillation, and other phenomena usually pinpointed and analyzed by psychologists conducting tests on experimental subjects.

Two other complex information-processing models also have an aspect of practical applicability. Tonge has written a heuristic program that balances factory assembly lines (to keep idle time of machines minimum or throughput maximum), and Clarkson's simulated financial advisor selects a quasi-optimum portfolio for investors.

In his study of human decision making under uncertainty and risk, Findler experimented with and simulated subjects that optimized certain state variables by selected control-variable values in a dynamic task environment. In a later work, Findler, Klein, and their students studied the generation and utilization of heuristic rules within the framework of the card game poker.

Evans' program is able to discover geometrical analogy between line drawings. Although formula-manipulating languages are outside the domain of this article, the heuristic formal integration programs of Slagle and Moses must be mentioned here.

Another program of great potential applicability is by Feigenbaum, Lederberg, and others, called the *heuristic dendral,* which discovers the most likely molecular configuration of certain chemical compounds on the basis of spectroscopic data and built-in chemical knowledge. F. A. Miller constructed a practical heuristic regression analysis program that improves with experience in a particular problem.

Individual belief systems have been simulated by Abelson and Carrol. Colby has worked on computer models of neurotic patients. Weizenbaum's ELIZA program can imitate a certain type of psychiatric interviewer.

McCarthy and his students proposed a system called *Advice Taker,* which is more formal than GPS but has similar objectives in making "common sense" deductions from facts. Interpersonal interactions were modeled by Gullahorn and Gullahorn, following Homan's sociological theory. McWhinney studied and simulated human communication network experiments.

Loehlin worked on a program that reproduced individuals' likes and dislikes, depending on a complex, interacting set of attributes. Findler and McKinzie wrote programs to simulate demographical processes, and to build and query complex kinship structures from primitive input information.

Research on intelligent question-answering programs has become very popular in the past few years. These programs not only retrieve information stored in the computer memory but also make logical inferences and (may) ask the user for more information in case of ambiguity. Bobrow's STUDENT, for example, solves high school algebra problems stated in much restricted English. Simmons and his coworkers have produced several question-answering systems of varying sophistication, from which the Protosynthex projects ought to be singled out for their very large database.

The basis of most of these projects is a *semantic network,* which consists of concept nodes connected by association links. Raphael's Semantic Information Retrieval program, Coles' Picture Language Machine, Black's Deductive Question-Answering System, and Quillian's Semantic Memory and Teachable Language Comprehender must be mentioned in this context. The problems of grammar of natural languages have been tackled by modern theories of syntax (by Chomsky and others) reasonably successfully, but *meaning* has eluded satisfactory treatment. Semantics has been shown to be the central problem in the study of language. One needs to think of the resolution of ambiguities only to appreciate the importance of it. Machine translation is unlikely to reach a significantly higher level of success until computer programs can exhibit understanding in the full sense of the word. Winograd's work in this area shows great promise. His system, which does not separate syntax and semantics, simulates a robot that follows instructions given in an interestingly rich subset of English that reasons, that asks questions of and provides answers to an interactive user about a small universe of wooden blocks of different colors and sizes. Information retrieval has become an endeavor in its own right. Many of its techniques, however, are closely related to those used in the area under discussion.

Interesting work is going on in automatic speech recognition (*q.v.*) and synthesis (Reddy, Hill, Vincens, and others). A task force comprising several university and research centers was set up to accomplish certain goals within five years. The goals were stated in terms of the number of recognizable words, the quality and number of different speakers, tolerable error rates, etc. Different approaches have led to complete or partial success after the five-year period of research and development. Work is going on to reach further objectives.

A new term has recently emerged in artificial intelligence efforts: *knowledge-based systems.* The idea is to store and utilize effectively large amounts of knowledge in pragmatically-oriented applications and to develop intelligent assistants for scientists and technologists. Mention was made above of the use of the heuristic dendral program as a chemist's assistant. MYCIN (Shortliffe) aids medical doctors in diagnosing blood and meningitis infections and in recommending antibiotic drug treatment. The PROSPECTOR (Duda, Hart, and others) is used by geologists in the exploration of ore deposits. Similar projects exist in the areas of electronic trouble-shooting and design processes (Sussman), mathematical discovery (Lenat), designing experiments in molecular genetics (Martin, Friedland, and others), etc.

Final Comments. We have given a necessarily cursory overview of the major research areas in artificial intelligence. Some topics were deliberately left out, such as game playing, pattern recognition, image and picture processing, computer assisted instructions, computer-aided design, management information systems, social science and humanities applications, language translation, arts and medical applications, each of which is closely related to and overlapping our interest and is discussed in other articles in this volume.

Two more issues should be discussed here briefly. First, one often hears the statement of the skeptic: "A computer can only do what it is told to do." If this is so— and no computer professional has ever doubted the plain truth of this saying—how can we expect intelligence to emerge from our machines if they simply follow our instructions? The answer lies in the interpretation of the statement. Admittedly, computers execute the orders in a program step by step. However, with every nontrivial program (and we are talking about extremely complex hierarchies of programs), its creator does not know what the intermediate or final results will turn out to be. There is no way of telling how a program will behave under any of a large, possibly infinite number of conditions it may be exposed to. The situation is not dissimilar to the case in which the parents and teachers of a child cannot, with any certitude, foretell how it will act later in life, given the hereditary, educational, and environmental information up to a certain point in time. Learning programs, although still somewhat in their infancy, often outperform the persons who wrote them.

The other side of the coin can be seen when a particular program that exhibits some high-level intellectual capability is described in terms of the elementary processes on which it has been built. Then our respect for the program suddenly drops because, as Minsky puts it, the problem is "explained away." Thus, many people will no longer consider that particular task to require intelligence. Human thinking may meet with this fate sometime, too.

The second issue is called the "superhuman fallacy." Many projects in artificial intelligence receive a paternalistic, deprecatory criticism: "Well, that computer-composed music is pretty awful"; or, "It is all right to prove those theorems in Euclidean geometry but the machine surely could not have *invented* Euclidean geometry"; and so on. Let us ask, however, how many Mozarts, Euclids, Einsteins, or Shakespeares have there been? We find only one of each, and each has been the descendant of the generation after generation development of human intelligence. We must compare this with only 25 years' progress in artificial intelligence research and development to obtain an approximate perspective.

SUGGESTED READINGS

The literature in artificial inteligence is naturally scattered over many books, conference proceedings, and journals. The following provides a first approximation to the most important subset of relevant literature and con-

tains discussions of or references to almost all the projects discussed in this article.

Books

1967–1979. Nine volumes of *Machine Intelligence* have so far been published with editors N. C. Collins and D. Michie; E. Dale and D. Michie; D. Michie; B. Meltzer and D. Michie; B. Meltzer and D. Michie; B. Meltzer and D. Michie; B. Meltzer and D. Michie; E. W. Elcock and D. Michie; and J. E. Hayes, D. Michie, and L. I. Mikulich (respectively) with Edinburgh University Press, Edinburgh, Great Britain. These are collections of important papers presented at one of a series of workshops.

1968. Minsky, M. (Ed.). *Semantic Information Processing.* Cambridge, MA.: M.I.T. Press. (This is a collection of Ph.D. theses plus contributions by Minsky and McCarthy.)

1971. Findler, N. V. and Meltzer, B. (Eds.). "Artificial Intelligence and Heuristic Programming." Edinburgh, Great Britain: Edinburgh University Press. (This is the *Proceedings of the First Advanced Study Institute on Artificial Intelligence and Heuristic Programming,* with 14 contributions.)

1971. Feigenbaum, E. A. and Feldman, J. *Computers and Thought.* New York: McGraw-Hill. (Contains some classical contributions to the area up to 1962.)

1971. Slagle, J. R. *Artificial Intelligence—The Heuristic Programming Approach.* New York: McGraw-Hill. (This is a more up-to-date introductory survey of the main research projects.)

1974. Jackson, P. C., Jr. *Introduction to Artificial Intelligence.* New York: Petrocelli/Charter. (This is a rather comprehensive description of research projects in artificial intelligence and in areas closely related to it.)

1979. Findler, N. V. (Ed.). *Associative Networks—The Representation and Use of Knowledge in Computers.* New York: Academic Press. (Fourteen contributors describe past, present, and future directions of research in knowledge representation.)

Conferences

As of 1981, there have been seven *International Joint Conferences on Artificial Intelligence;* the proceedings contain the most recent efforts in the field.

The Proceedings of the IFIP Congresses (Paris, 1959; Munich, 1962; New York, 1965; Edinburgh, 1968; Ljubljana, 1971; Stockholm, 1974; Toronto, 1977; Tokyo and Melbourne, 1980) contain several interesting contributions to the field. Similarly, the yearly *Spring* and *Fall Joint Computer Conferences* and the annual *ACM National Conferences* always publish papers in artificial intelligence in their respective proceedings. There are many other meetings in related areas every year; it is impossible to list them here.

Journals

International Journal of Man-Machine Studies, Information Sciences, International Journal of Computer and Information Sciences, Artificial Intelligence, Behavioral Science, ACM Communications and Journal, Computer Journal, Kybernetik, Cybernetica, IEEE Transactions on Computers, Systems Science and Cybernetics, Information and Control, Cognitive Science, Pattern Recognition and Machine Intelligence.

Surveys

Of the many survey papers of varying age, three are singled out.

1961. Minsky, M. "Steps toward Artificial Intelligence," *Proc. IRE* **49**: 8–30. (Reprinted in the book edited by Feigenbaum and Feldman, 1971.)

1963. Newell, A. and Simon, H. A. "Computers in Psychology," in Luce, Bush, and Galanter (Eds.), *Handbook of Mathematical Psychology* **I**. New York: Wiley.

1968. Hunt, E. B. "Computer Simulation: Artificial Intelligence Studies and Their Relevance to Psychology," *Annual Rev. of Psych.,* **19**: 135–168.

N. V. FINDLER

ARTS APPLICATIONS

For articles on related subjects *see* COMPUTER ART; COMPUTER GRAPHICS; COMPUTER MUSIC; DATA BANK; HUMANITIES APPLICATIONS; IMAGE PROCESSING; INFORMATION RETRIEVAL; and PATTERN RECOGNITION.

As is the case with computer applications in the humanities, computer applications in the arts (painting, sculpture, film making, music, and dance) include the use of data banks in pattern recognition (analysis) and pattern generation (synthesis).

Data Banks in the Arts. Just as libraries have traditionally served as data banks for the verbally oriented humanities, museums have traditionally served as data banks for the nonverbally oriented humanities. Efforts to use the computer to make museum collections more accessible to users have resulted in the development of a number of data bank projects for museums. Examples of such projects are GIPSY (General Information Processing System), used to record ethnographic museum specimens in Oklahoma, Missouri, and Arizona; GIS (General Information System), used in the FLORA N.A. program, a large-scale, centralized data bank designed to collect, analyze, maintain, and disseminate diverse kinds of information about the plants of North America; GRIPHOS (General Retrieval and Information Processing for Humanities Oriented Studies), used by the Museum Computer Network, an organization of several dozen museums and related organizations, primarily to record art objects and archeological data (see Eskind and Borsal, 1978); SELGEM (Self-Generating Master), used to record specimen inventories of mammals, conodont types, foraminifera, nematodes, crustacea, and other collections; and TAXIR (Taxonomic Information Retrieval), used primarily for the storage and retrieval of biological specimen data (see Chenhall *et al.,* 1972).

Other types of information banks necessary for pattern recognition and pattern generation in the arts include bibliographies, special-purpose catalogs, musical scores in computer-accessible form, and rules for combining elements and artifacts.

An example of a bibliographical project that includes abstracts as well as the standard author, title (etc.) reference information is the *Repertoire International de la Litterature Musicale,* known as RILM (see Brook, 1979). An example of a special-purpose catalog (in music) is that proposed for French chansons, which would include a listing of all manuscript and printed sources for chansons, musical incipits (notes at the beginning of the chansons), a melodic index, and other relevant information (see Hudson, 1970).

Information banks consisting of musical scores are requisite for pattern recognition studies focused on either a particular composer or a musical genre. No extensive data bank of musical scores has yet been provided, primarily because of the input problem. To date, almost all computer scores that have been put into computer-accessible form have been translated into Teletype keyboard characters using either the Ford-Columbia system of transcription (DARMS), developed by Stefan Bauer-Mengelberg of the State University of New York at Binghamton, or systems developed by various individual scholars for their own specific research needs. The Ford-Columbia system facilitated the development of one of the computerized systems for music printing (Gomberg, 1977; also see Byrd, 1974).

An alternative to transcribing musical scores into keyboard characters is the use of graphic input devices. One such experiment displays (on a cathode-ray tube) a musical staff as well as conventional notation for musical notes, pauses, and other standard music symbols. The scholar may then select the appropriate symbols and place them as desired on the musical staff. Although this system has been proposed for music editing, it is clear that such an approach could be used to input scores, once some of the limitations (e.g., the availability of upward stems only) of the experimental system are eliminated. The use of graphic input devices has also been advocated for data bank information necessary to computer generation of music.

An approach devised somewhat earlier than the one mentioned above considered the cathode-ray tube display as a grid across which the composer could draw graphlike lines to indicate amplitude, frequency, note duration, and so on (Mathews and Rosler, 1969). Because this particular graphic input system did not use common music notation, the user had to learn a notational system in order to input the data. Thus, the only presumed advantage of this system over transcription into keypunch characters would be the greater speed with which data could be input.

Another important type of data bank for both pattern recognition and generation in music is digitized sound. Breaking down musical acoustical signals into digitized form, as well as using the digitized form to generate acoustical signals, requires an analog-to-digital and digital-to-analog converter (*q.v.*) system with a speed sufficient for 20,000–50,000 samples/sec and a quantization accuracy of 10–13 bits. As is the case for speech, storage of digitized music poses space requirements that are sometimes a seriously limiting factor on the scope of the research being undertaken (Beauchamp, 1969).

Pattern Recognition. Pattern recognition projects focused on painting and sculpture are almost nonexistent. Thus far, fine arts museum information banks consist of listings of artists, works of art, dates when created, perhaps the date of acquisition by a given museum, and other comparable details. Although there is a strong interest in providing content information (e.g., physical objects represented in a painting, the medium, or the colors used, there is at present little effort to make such information available as part of computer-accessible information banks. Conceivably there will be some effort to hand-code such information, but any such encoding, albeit useful, will be prone to the subjective responses and lapses of any given encoder. It seems likely that in time (whether in years or in decades is not yet clear), pattern recognition efforts currently being pursued in other areas (e.g., aerial photography, artificial intelligence research on robots, character recognition) will be used to facilitate input of information concerning museum holdings.

Current work on image processing of two- and three-dimensional objects (Rosenfeld, 1979) and on the representation and recognition of visual information (Arbib and Riseman, 1976; Marr and Nishiharn, 1977; Winston and Brown, 1979) is obviously relevant to pattern recognition of paintings, sculpture, and other objects in museums.

Nonetheless, determination of characteristics sufficient to identify a few known artifacts is hardly comparable to digitizing and then describing the artifacts in even the smallest of museums. It may be that it will be many years, if ever, before it is feasible and practical to try to map categories such as "boat" or "vase" (let alone Etruscan vase as opposed to Grecian vase!) onto parameters indicating shape (such as eccentricity), or texture, or alignment of edges, or whatever indicators emerge from digitized representations of artifacts. However, we may expect the parameters that do emerge easily from such digitized representations will in themselves provide useful categories for the art historian or the student of style and content in painting and sculpture.

In contrast to painting and sculpture, pattern recognition in music is a very active research area. Pattern recognition involving digitized acoustical signals faces the storage problem mentioned earlier. For example, an early effort to analyze tones produced by a range of musical instruments used a hardware configuration that did not permit adequate continuous transfer of digitized analog samples to magnetic tape. As a result, only core storage was available in this particular configuration, and (using 29,952 samples/sec at a sample rate of 30 Kc) the maximum length of sound that could be digitized was 0.997 sec. This block of information could, of course, then be transferred to tape and a new 0.997 sec of acoustical signal could be stored and transferred. These blocks of data were characterized and graphed to show time-variant spectral information (Beauchamp, 1969).

In general, work on digitized music can deal with such parameters as frequency or pitch, amplitude, timbre, tone, and phase. When storage and processing speed problems are solved, there will probably be music information banks consisting of digitized music as performed, rather than (or in addition to) its appearance in a printed score. If and when such data banks are available, it may well be—analogously to possibilities for museum artifacts—that the parameters used for characterizing music will not all be mapped onto the traditional symbols of a printed score. In the case of music, as well as in spoken and written language, what could eventuate is a parallel development involving, on the one hand, graphic pattern recognition devices and, on the other hand, acoustic pattern recognition techniques.

Much pattern recognition in music has depended upon information banks consisting of musical scores. Representation systems, such as the Plaine and Easie

Code or DARMS, permit the scholar to encode in keypunch characters all the symbols in a written score. Written scores permit studies of styles of individual composers as well as groups of composers. Written scores cannot be used for studies of interpretations of a given work by conductors or performing artists; digitized acoustical recordings might have to be used for pattern recognition of this type.

Computer-accessible musical scores have been used for work on questions of harmony, composer identification, and particular themes or motives within the works of a particular composer, and for ethnomusicology. Many of these studies concentrate on pitch and combinations of pitches, although other information, such as duration of notes, amplitude of notes, and various frequency distributions of notes, is obviously available from musical scores. For example, studies concerned with harmony depend`upon chords and patterns of chords, which are described in terms of the pitches of the individual tones combined into chords (Jackson, 1970). A study of motif, or musical theme, again looks at the pitch of notes and the combination of pitches into chords, but it is also concerned with changes of dynamics and tempo. Studies of dynamics and tempo imply analyzing information concerning the amplitude (loudness-softness) with which the individual notes or chords are played and analyzing information about the duration of individual notes or chords. One project explicitly directed toward composer identification was concerned with root progression, which is a study of the way chords are connected—again, a study emphasizing pitch (Youngblood, 1970).

Work in ethnomusicology is directed toward describing the music of a particular culture or, sometimes, comparing the musical habits of a number of cultures (Suchoff, 1970). It should be noted that implicit in the pitch of any given tone is not only its location relative to any given octave, but also the octave in which it actually occurs (e.g., an A in the octave above middle C).

Pattern recognition in dance is of interest because, although notation systems do exist (see Eshkol and Wachmann, 1958), dances exist principally in the heads of choreographers and dancers, and often a particular dance vanishes when its originating dance company breaks up or a choreographer passes from the scene. It has been suggested that, by using techniques of pattern recognition and scene analysis, it might be possible to extract positions of a moving human body from successive frames of a film and to generate a symbolic representation of the movements (Badler, 1975), but this approach has not been used with "live" dancers. A recent approach is to use the dance notation system, Labanotation, as a means of representing human movement within a digital computer (Badler and Smoliar, 1979). For input of the dance movements, body movements observed on video or

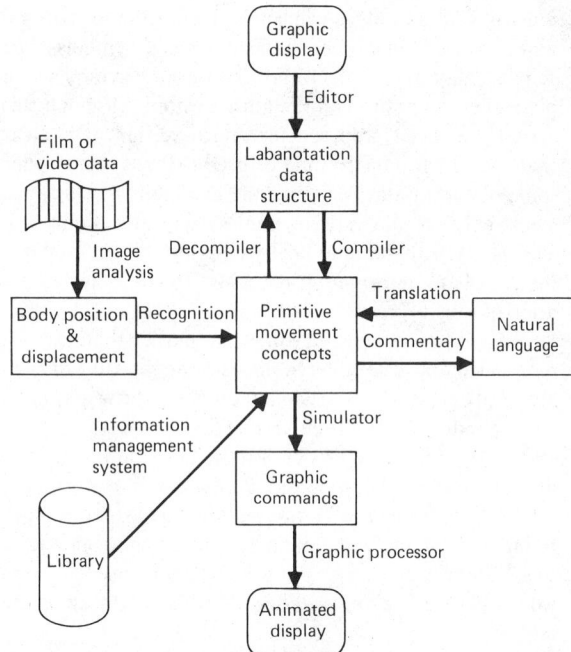

Fig. 1. Comprehensive computer system for notating, modeling, analyzing, and describing human movement.

film may be recognized and encoded as instances of the "primitive" movement concepts in the representation.

Pattern Generation. In contrast to computer-based pattern analysis, pattern generation in painting and sculpture and its allied field, film making, is firmly established. Computer-generated paintings and films in two, three, and even four dimensions have been produced. Output media have ranged from computer printers to cathode ray tubes, and input media from punched cards to lightpens. One early approach (Csuri and Shaffer, 1968) which resulted in a so-called "sine curve man" and a prize winning film, *Hummingbird,* used the following technique: (1) an artistic drawing was made with line segments of points of the subject matter to be used; (2) a drawing was digitized line by line, with the resulting coordinates punched into cards; (3) decisions were made about the type of form modification and the mathematical steps required to accomplish it; (4) the mathematical algorithm was programmed for a computer, which then generated the plotter commands; (5) at this point, another decision was made about the color and line width for the transformation; and (6) the transformed image was plotted on a Calcomp 563 plotter.

To produce a film from individual drawings, the figure of a hummingbird was transformed slightly in a succession of drawings, which were then filmed and projected in the conventional way to produce the illusion of movement.

Currently, graphics packages are available which permit an artist or film maker to sit down at a display console, specify the number of $x-y$ coordinates sufficient to define whatever figure he/she wishes to create, and then transform it according to the specifications made available in the graphics program. Three of the basic transformations are scaling, translating, and rotating. Scaling implies modifying the scale of all or some part of the figure that has been created; translating implies moving all or some part of the figure to another location on the output medium; and rotating implies altering the position of the object so as to make it seem to move around an axis as viewed from the perspective of the artist.

The art generated has ranged from very geometrical designs to highly random, apparently chaotic patterns (see Fig. 2). Some efforts have been made to approximate the painting styles of human artists (Canaday, 1970).

Two-dimensionality is achieved simply through specifying $x-y$ coordinates for a plane surface. According to Noll (1976b), a three-dimensional

> . . . perspective drawing is produced by choosing a point (representing the eye and formally called the station point) from which the object is viewed. The picture plane is then inserted between the object and station point. The points of intersection of these projection lines with the picture plane are joined together to produce the perspective drawing.

Four-dimensional objects can be specified mathematically and produced by mathematical formulas anal-

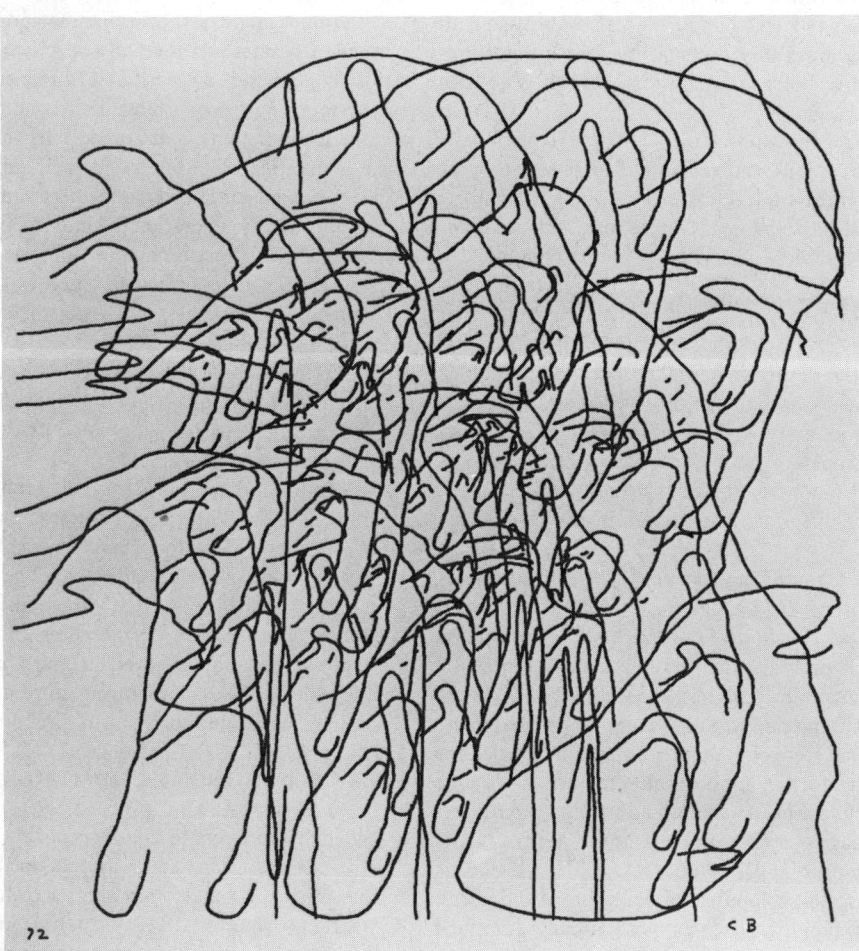

Fig. 2.   Contained contour II. Courtesy of Colette and Charles Bangert

ogous to those used for two-dimensional perspectives of three-dimensional objects. Although it is impossible to see a four-dimensional object, the three-dimensional (and, in turn, two-dimensional) projection of the four-dimensional object produces effects that differ from conventional two- and three-dimensional artifacts. It has been noted that "the programs and mathematical techniques for four-dimensional projection and rotations are quite general and can easily be extended to even higher dimensions" (Noll, 1976b).

A number of programming languages have been especially designed for the artist and film maker. Kenneth Knowlton and his associates at Bell Laboratories, Murray Hill, NJ, have developed two such languages: Beflix and Explor.

Beflix, a film-making language in Fortran IV, provides drafting operations that draw rectangles, straight lines, arcs, other curves, and alphanumeric characters, as well as operations concerning the content of rectangular areas, the specification of the projection grid, operations related to elements labeled bugs (not to be confused with the undesirable bugs that occur in many computer programs), and miscellaneous operations having to do with output, debugging, etc.

Explor—a generator of images from *explicit* *pat*terns, *local* *operations, and *random*ness—is a system for computer generation of still or moving images from explicitly defined patterns, local operations, and randomness. Explor produces output images comprising rectangular arrays (240 by 340) of black, white, and "twinkling" dots. Among its intended scientific and artistic applications are the "production of stimuli for visual experiments, the depiction of visual 'phosphors' such as moving checkerboards and stripes, and picture processing." This system may also be used to simulate a "variety of two-dimensional processes and mechanisms, such as crystal growth and etching, neural (e.g., retinal) nets, random walk, diffusion, and iterative arrays of logic modules."

Explor is a macrolanguage with sets of instructions for picture output, for changing the internal array, for defining patterns, for flow of control, and for instruction modification. It provides facilities for specifying periodic and/or random applications of its operations, and flexible means of specifying uniform or locality-dependent translation of internal symbols. Another approach to programming languages for the artist permits the artist to define his or her own vocabulary, built on an REL (rapidly extensible language) support system, as the work of art is created (Thompson *et al.,* 1969).

The use of the computer for sculpture is ordinarily to use graphic facilities, such as those already described for painting and film making, to display a range of design possibilities and perspectives for proposed sculpture. Pro-

grams that produce paper tapes, which in turn are used to drive milling machines that actually produce artifacts, have also been designed (Mallary, 1969).

Music. Computer-generated music produces either scores, which are then performed, or music for which the acoustic properties are specified and which is then synthesized by a digital-to-analog converter. (See Howe, 1975.)

Musicomp is a compositional programming language that provides techniques for generating original musical scores as well as for synthesizing music. An adaptable language that can be changed and expanded according to need, Musicomp consists of three basic parts: system regulatory routines, compositional and analytical subroutines, and sound synthesis routines. The latter "are not actual synthesis programs but rather routines that prepare and organize data that serve as input to sound-generating programs." Among Musicomp's compositional subroutines are a subroutine for choice of a rhythmic mode; a subroutine that provides choice of a range of pitches and then of a specific pitch from within this range; a subroutine that controls the melodic range rule (in a single line, a limit such as an octave is imposed on melodic motion); and others. The routines provide for the generation of phrases and their imitations and permutations; generation of all the permutations of the given role of *n* items; generation of similar rhythmic data from more than one instrument for any length of time; and generation of dynamics indications in playing styles according to serial processes. Musicomp can be used in conjunction with Fortran.

Output of musical scores either uses standard printer conventions that can then be translated onto regular music staffs, a cathode ray tube configuration such as that described earlier in terms of input of musical scores, or a plotter to draw a score. In one such program written for a Calcomp plotter, the notation makes use of a select set of symbols already available in the Calcomp library (triangles, circles, lines, and so on). The "language of the scores is given by the distribution, size, and position of symbols on each page of the scores; in effect, each page is a plot of dynamic level versus time. Once the performer is provided with a short introductory explanation of the notation, he is able to perform directly from the score" (Hiller, 1970).

Computer-generated scores have ranged from music that is highly random in character to music that is intended to approximate some aspects of the style of a given composer or musical genre. In fact, in the course of some experiments, a range from greater to less randomness is apparent (Moorer, 1972). Analysis of church hymns (Brooks *et al.,* 1957), using Markovian analysis, resulted in simulated hymns with considerable randomness when low-order probabilities (probabilities of orders 1 through 8 were assigned in this experiment) were used. The use of high-order probabilities produced parts of original hymns connected together. The *Illiac Suite,* one of the best known early computer compositions, was a string quartet comprising rhythms, chosen at random, and melodies constructed according to some rules of classical harmony and counterpoint. Another computer-generated composition, *Sonoriferous Loops,* written for instrumental ensemble and tape, used four parameters: pitch, register, rhythmic unit, and rhythmic mode. Rhythmic modes (basic metrical patterns) and rhythmic units within those modes were chosen in accord with assigned probability distributions; probability distributions that differed for each instrument and for different parts of the composition were also used to make choices between rest or play and for octave registers (Hiller, 1970). An effort to generate scores for western popular music (Moorer, 1972) proceeded according to the following sequence.

> . . . the overall form of the piece is chosen first, the chords are chosen second, and the melody, last . . . the choice of chords before melody is to avoid the problem of deciding what chords should go with a given melody. The problem is reversed and simplified to constraining some number of the prospective melody notes to lie in the chord. The overall structure is similarly chosen first, to prevent attempting to derive the structure from the melody. . . . The overall structure is decided upon by first choosing two numbers, the number of major groups and the number of minor groups. Each of these numbers is constrained to be a power of two times the number of beats per measure, a parameter supplied by the operation. The total piece length is then the product of the number of major groups times the number of minor groups times the number of beats per minor group.

Two parameters implicit in some of the choices made in experiments with computer-generated music are the periodicity of the melodic line and the consonance and/or dissonance implied by the structures of chords. Periodicity implies the repetition and transformation of melodic groups. Consonance and dissonance are subjective matters, but some combinations of notes, such as a perfect fifth or a major third, are considered to be more consonant than others (Moorer, 1972).

Composers who use the computer to synthesize sound rather than to produce musical scores are concerned with many of these same elements, although they are parameterized according to acoustic categories rather than graphic symbols. The composer using sound synthesis must be concerned with amplitudes, frequencies, am-

plitude modulation rate, and waveform specification. According to one set of specifications, the digital-analog converters used in music synthesis must be capable of converting 12–14-bit words at a rate of 40,000/sec. "The long word length ensures adequate dynamic range and the high rate, a sufficiently broad frequency response" (Freedman, 1969). Additionally, for pleasant sound, the computer equipment must have adequate block transfer rates between auxiliary storage and main memory so that there will be continuous reproduction of sound without breaks. Because electronically synthesized sound lacks some of the variability to which the human ear is accustomed, composers who are generating sound electronically have concerns with which those who are generating scores are not troubled. For example, electronically sustained tones seem to provide a constant stimulus that may fatigue the ear. To achieve a more pleasing timbre, it has been suggested (Roberts, 1969) that any one of the following techniques might be used: "(1) control of the amplitude envelope: crescendo, diminuendo, exponential decay, and so on; (2) variation of the pitch—vibrato or glissando; (3) variation of wave form." Roberts also notes that "another feature of electronic tone that the listener finds distressing, or at least unnatural, is that quality is independent of loudness. . . . It is, of course, easy to correct this feature by introducing deliberate nonlinearities into the computer-simulated oscillators."

As is the case with computer-generated art, the field of computer-generated music is very extensive and cannot be done full justice in an article of this length. For a useful survey of music composed with the computer, the reader is referred to Hiller (1970) and Howe (1975).

Dance. Computer-generated dance is in a much more embryonic state. One experiment used the computer to specify the number of dancers on the stage at any given time and to indicate the positions they would occupy on that stage throughout the period of time they were on stage (Sagasti and Page, 1970). Another early experiment (Noll, 1967a) used a computer display to delineate the spatial and arm movements of a group of dancers on stage. Recently, a system based on Labanotation for representing and simulating human body movement has been suggested. This research has defined movement "primitives" which can be used to translate movement notation onto an animated display of human figures performing the represented movement (Badler *et al,* 1978). In this system, the earlier stick figures have been replaced by a body model formed of overlapping spheres (310), articulated with 19 joints and 20 body segments. This model yields a more realistically formed and shaded body image on a master graphics display (Badler *et al.,* 1979). This research is promising, although specifying the intricacies of movements entailed by dance is

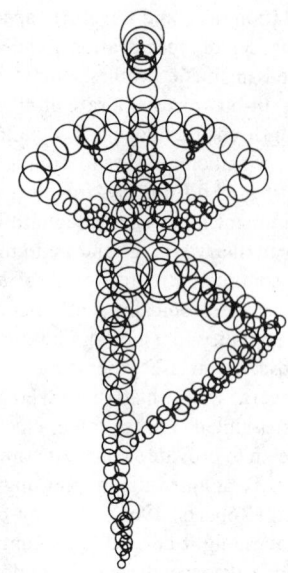

Fig. 3. Human body model drawn with spheres projected as circles. (Badler *et al.,* 1979.)

exceedingly complicated and, as yet, unachieved in any current experiment.

REFERENCES

1957. Brooks, F. P., Hopkins, A. L., Newmann, P. G., and Wright, W. V. "An Experiment in Musical Composition," *IRE Trans. Electronic Computers* **EC-6,** *No. 1:* 175–182, September.

1958. Eshkol, N. and Wachmann, A. *Movement Notation.* London: Weidenfeld and Nicolson.

1967a. Noll, Michael. "Choreography and Computers," *Dance Magazine,* January.

1967b. Noll, Michael. "Computers and the Visual Arts," *Design and Planning No. 2,* Hastings House Publications.

1968. Csuri, Charles and Shaffer, James. "Art, Computers and Mathematics," *AFIPS—Conference Proceedings* **33:** 1293–1298. Wayne, PA: MDI Publications.

1969. Beauchamp, James W. "A Computer System for Time-Variant Harmonic Analysis and Synthesis of Musical Tones," in von Foerster, Heinz and Beauchamp, James W. (Eds.), *Music by Computers.* New York: Wiley, pp. 19–62.

1969. Freedman, M. David. "On-Line Generation of Sound," von Foerster, Heinz and Beauchamp, James W. (Eds.), *Music by Computers.* New York: Wiley, pp. 13–18.

1969. Mallary, Robert. "Computer Sculpture: Six Levels of Cybernetics," *Art Forum,* pp. 29–35, May.

1969. Rosenfeld, Azriel. *Picture Processing by Computer.* New York: Academic Press.

1969. Thompson, F. B., Lockeman P. C., Dostert, B. H., and Deverill, R. S. "REL: A Rapidly Extensible Language System," *Proceedings 24th National ACM Conference* **24,** August.

1970. Canaday, John. "Less Art, More Computer, Please," *The New York Times,* 30 August, Section D, p. 19.

1970. Hiller, Lejaren. "Music Composed with Computers—A Historical Survey," in Lincoln, H. B. (Ed.), *The Computer and Music.* Ithaca, NY: Cornell University Press, pp. 49–96.

1970. Hudson, Barton. "Toward a Comprehensive French Chanson Catalogue," in Lincoln, H. B. (Ed.), *The Computer and Music.* Ithaca, NY: Cornell University Press, pp. 277–287.

1970. Jackson, Roland. "Harmony Before and After 1910: A Computer Comparison," in Lincoln, H. B. (Ed.), *The Computer and Music.* Ithaca, NY: Cornell University Press, pp. 132–146.

1970. Sagasti, Francisco and Page, William. "Computer Choreography: An Experiment on the Interaction Between Dance and the Computer," *Computer Studies in the Humanities and Verbal Behavior* **3,** *No. 1:* 46–69, January.

1970. Sedelow, Sally Yeates. "The Computer in the Humanities and Fine Arts," *Computing Surveys* **2,** *No. 2:* 89–110, June.

1970. Suchoff, Benjamin. "Computer-Oriented Comparative Musicology," in Lincoln, H. B. (Ed.), *The Computer and Music.* Ithaca, NY: Cornell University Press, pp. 193–206.

1970. Youngblood, Joseph. "Root Progressions and Composer Identification," in Lincoln, H. B. (Ed.), *The Computer and Music.* Ithaca, NY: Cornell University Press, pp. 172–180.

1972. Chenhall, Robert G. *et al. Report of Museum Data Bank Study Group.* Hershey, PA. (Available from Dr. Chenhall, Museum of Science, Buffalo, NY.)

1972. Moorer, James Anderson. "Music and Computer Composition," *Communications of the ACM* **15,** *No. 2:* 104–113, February.

1974. Byrd, Donald. "A System for Music Printing by Computer," *Computers and the Humanities* **8,** *No. 3:* 161–172, May.

1975. Badler, N. *Temporal Scene Analysis: Conceptual Descriptions of Object Movements.* Technical Report No. 80. Department of Computer Science, University of Toronto, February.

1975. Howe, Hubert S., Jr. *Electronic Music Synthesis: Concepts, Facilities, Techniques.* New York: W. W. Norton and Company.

1976. Arbib, Michael A. and Riseman, Edward M. *Computational Techniques in Visual Systems, Part I, The Overall Design.* COINS Technical Report 76–10, University of Massachusetts, Amherst, July.

1976. Leavitt, Ruth (Ed.). *The Artist and the Computer,* New York: Harmony Books.

1977. Gomberg, David A. "A Computer-Oriented System for Music Printing," *Computers and the Humanities* **11,** *No. 2:* 63–80, March/April.

1977. Marr, David and Nishihara, H. K. *Representation and Recognition of the Spatial Organization of Three Dimensional Shapes.* MIT Artificial Intelligence Laboratory, AIM 416, Cambridge, May.

1978. Badler, Norman; O'Rourke, Joseph; Smoliar, Stephen; and Weber, Lynne. *The Simulation of Human Movement by Computer.* Movement Project Report No. 14, Moore School of Electrical Engineering, University of Pennsylvania, Philadelphia, September.

1978. Del Molin, Armando. "A Terminal for Music Manuscript Input," *Computers and the Humanities* **12**, *No. 3:* 287–90.

1978. Eskind, Andrew and Barsel, Deborah. "Application of MCN Systems in International Museum of Photography," *Image* **21**, *No. 4,* December.

1979. Badler, Norman and Smoliar, Stephen. "Digital Representations of Human Movement," *Computing Surveys* **11**, *No. 1:* 19–38, March.

1979. Badler, Norman; O'Rourke, Joseph; and Toltzis, Hasida. "A Spherical Representation of a Human Body for Visualizing Movement," *Proceedings of the IEEE* **67**, *No. 10:* 1397–1403, October.

1979. Brook, Barry S. *Dialog Information Retrieval Service, RILM Abstracts,* PE 40. International RILM Center, City University of New York, September.

1979. Rosenfeld, Azriel. "Picture Processing: 1978," *Computer Graphics and Processing* **9**, 354–93.

1979. Winston, Patrick Henry and Brown, Richard Henry (Eds.). *Understanding Vision, Manipulation, Computer Design, Symbol Manipulation.* Cambridge: MIT Press.

D. A. DINNEEN AND S. A. SEDELOW

ARTSPEAK

For articles on related subjects *see* ARTS APPLICATIONS; and PROGRAMMING LANGUAGES.

Artspeak is a programming language whose essential ideas are due to Jacob T. Schwartz of New York University. Its intent is to provide a language of particular utility in university courses for non-mathematics or science students which would enable them to do interesting computer projects after learning only a quite small amount of programming language syntax.

The Artspeak language was designed to make use of the electro-mechanical plotters (*see* INPUT/OUTPUT DEVICES) which are so commonly a part of college and university computer installations. The language allows the user to define the following.

1. *Points.* LET P1 BE POINT (4,6)
   LET P2 BE POINT (8,9.5)
   on a 10 × 10 grid subdivided into any fraction of an inch.
2. *Lines.* LET C1 BE LINE P1, P2
   which defines the line between the points P1 and P2 defined above.
3. *Circles.* LET C1 BE CIRCLE, RADIUS 0.7, CENTER (2,3)
4. *Curves.* LET C2 BE CURVE P1, (2,3), P2, 0.5
   which defines a curve between points P1 and P2 in the direction of the external point (2,3) and with a curving factor of 0.5 [if the curving factor were 1.0, the curve would pass through (2,3)].

With these objects, the user then can:

1. Draw lines, circles and curves.
2. Rotate these about other points· by defined amounts.
3. Reflect curves about defined lines.
4. Translate curves from one portion of the grid to another.

Other, more complex manipulations can also be performed.

The following annotated program similar to one from Mullish (1974) gives the flavor of the kinds of things one can do with Artspeak.

```
      LET P1 BE POINT (5,5)           Define points
      LET P2 BE POINT (5,7)
      COPYPOINT P2 TO P3             P3 same point as P2
      ROTATE P2 ABOUT P1,ANGLE 45    Changes P2 but not P3
      LET C1 BE LINE P3,P2
L1    DRAW C1                        One side of octagon
L2    ROTATE C1 ABOUT P1,ANGLE 45
      REPEAT L1 TO L2,7 TIMES        Other 7 sides of octagon
L3    COPYPOINT P1 TO P4             P4 same point as P1
      EXPAND P1 FROM P2,FACTOR 0.8   Redefine P1, P2, P3 as
      EXPAND P2 FROM P3,FACTOR 0.8     8/10 of distance from
      EXPAND P3 FROM P4,FACTOR 0.8     P2, P3, P4
      LET C2 BE LINE P1,P2,P3.P1
L4    DRAW C2                        One of 8 triangles
L5    ROTATE C2 ABOUT (5,5),ANGLE 45
L6    REPEAT L4 TO L5,7 TIMES        Other 7 triangles
      REPEAT L3 TO L6, 25 TIMES      Define and draw new
      STOP                             triangles 25 times
```

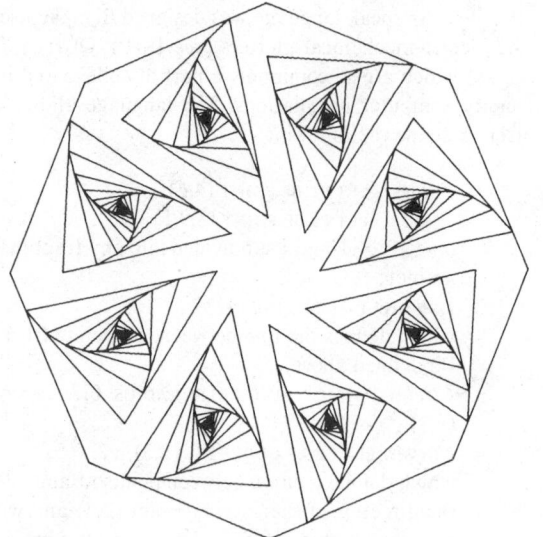

Fig. 1.

The result of this program is shown in Fig. 1 and illustrates how the rotation of quite simple figures can lead to interesting and pleasing drawings.

Artspeak has been used with considerable success in introductory computer courses for arts and humanities majors in a number of universities.

REFERENCE

1974. Mullish, H. *The Art of Programming Artspeak,* Courant Institute of Mathematical Sciences, New York University.

A. RALSTON

ASCII

For articles on related subjects *see* BINARY-CODED DECIMAL; CHARACTER SET; CODES; COLLATING SEQUENCE; and EBCDIC.

The American Standard Code for Information Interchange (ASCII) is a seven-bit code also known as the USA Standard Code for Information Interchange (USASCII).

Because eight-bit bytes are common on computers, ASCII is commonly embedded in an eight-bit field in which the high order (leftmost) bit is either used as a parity bit or is set to zero. An 8-bit version of ASCII using the latter option is shown as Exhibit 1. The leftmost four bits (or first hexadecimal digit) of the eight-bit code are shown as column heads across the top and the rightmost

four bits (or second hexadecimal digit) are listed on the side. Thus, for example, we have

Character	Code	
	Binary	Hexadecimal
4	00110100	34
Y	01011001	59
c	01100011	63
=	00111101	3D

The meanings of the control characters and special graphic characters are shown below the illustration.

E. D. REILLY, JR.

ASIS. *See* AMERICAN SOCIETY FOR INFORMATION SCIENCE.

ASM. *See* ASSOCIATION FOR SYSTEMS MANAGEMENT.

ASSEMBLERS

For articles on related subjects *see* ADDRESSING; BASE REGISTER; CROSS ASSEMBLERS AND COMPILERS; GENERAL REGISTER; INDEX REGISTER; INDIRECT ADDRESS; LANGUAGE PROCESSORS; LINKAGE EDITOR; LOADER; MACHINE AND ASSEMBLY LANGUAGE PROGRAMMING; MACHINE INSTRUCTION SET; MACROINSTRUCTION; OPERAND; OPERATION CODE; AND PROGRAM COUNTER.

An assembler (contraction for "assembly program") is a program that facilitates the preparation of programs at the machine language level by taking symbolic representations of individual (instruction or data) words and converting them into a form (binary or byte) suitable for input to a linker or loader. It permits the use of mnemonic operation codes, allows symbolic names to be assigned to memory locations, provides facilities for address calculations in terms of such symbolic names, and (usually) enables the user to introduce numerical and character constants in various forms. Assemblers are used for systems programming when the need to access all the facilities of the "raw" machine precludes the use of a high-level language. They are also used for programming microcomputers that are too small to support a high-level language. If the micro is too small to support an assembler, a cross-assembler (*q.v.*) is used. This is an assembler which runs

		0000	0001	0010	0011	0100	0101	0110	0111
		0	1	2	3	4	5	6	7
0000	0	NUL	DLE	SP	0	@	P	`	p
0001	1	SOH	DCI	!	1	A	Q	a	q
0010	2	STX	DC2	"	2	B	R	b	r
0011	3	ETX	DC3	#	3	C	S	c	s
0100	4	EOT	DC4	$	4	D	T	d	t
0101	5	ENQ	NAK	%	5	E	U	e	u
0110	6	ACK	SYN	&	6	F	V	f	v
0111	7	BEL	ETB	'	7	G	W	g	w
1000	8	BS	CAN	(	8	H	X	h	x
1001	9	HT	EM	)	9	I	Y	i	y
1010	A	LF	SUB	*	:	J	Z	j	z
1011	B	VT	ESC	+	;	K	[	k	{
1100	C	FF	FS	,	<	L	\	l	¦
1101	D	CR	GS	−	=	M	]	m	}
1110	E	SO	RS	.	>	N	ˆ	n	~
1111	F	SI	US	/	?	O	—	o	DEL

Exhibit 1 ASCII code values. (For explanation of symbols see next page.)

Control Character Representations

NUL	Null	DLE	Data Link Escape (CC)
SOH	Start of Heading(CC)	DC1	Device Control 1
STX	Start of Text (CC)	DC2	Device Control 2
ETX	End of Text (CC)	DC3	Device Control 3
EOT	End of Transmission (CC)	DC4	Device Control 4
ENQ	Enquiry (CC)	NAK	Negative Acknowledge (CC)
ACK	Acknowledge (CC)	SYN	Synchronous Idle (CC)
BEL	Bell	ETB	End of Transmission Block (CC)
BS	Backspace (FE)	CAN	Cancel
HT	Horizontal Tabulation (FE)	EM	End of Medium
LF	Line Feed (FE)	SUB	Substitute
VT	Vertical Tabulation (FE)	ESC	Escape
FF	Form Feed (FE)	FS	File Separator (IS)
CR	Carriage Return (FE)	GS	Group Separator (IS)
SO	Shift Out	RS	Record Separator (IS)
SI	Shift In	US	Unit Separator (IS)
		DEL	Delete

(CC)	Communication Control
(FE)	Format Effector
(IS)	Information Separator

Special Graphic Characters

SP	Space	<	Less Than
!	Exclamation Point	=	Equals
"	Quotation Marks	>	Greater Than
#	Number Sign	?	Question Mark
$	Dollar Sign	@	Commercial At
%	Percent	[	Opening Bracket
&	Ampersand	\	Reverse Slant
'	Apostrophe	]	Closing Bracket
(	Opening Parenthesis	^	Circumflex
)	Closing Parenthesis	—	Underline
*	Asterisk	`	Grave Accent
+	Plus	{	Opening Brace
,	Comma	¦	Vertical Line (This graphic is sometimes stylized to distinguish it from the unbroken Logical OR which is not an ASCII character)
—	Hyphen (Minus)		
.	Period (Decimal Point)		
/	Slant	}	Closing Brace
:	Colon	~	Tilde
;	Semicolon		

on one (usually larger) machine producing object code for another (usually smaller) machine.

Although the term "assembly subroutine" was used as long ago as 1951 for a routine that assembled a master routine and a number of subroutines into a single program (Wilkes, Wheeler, and Gill, 1951), this function is now typically called *linking*. The current established connotation of the term "assembler" probably derives from its function of assembling the internal binary form of the program from symbolic definitions.

History. Although the use of a symbolic representation of machine language programs now seems obviously desirable, this was not always so. Right from the start there was a dichotomy of view between the Cambridge group (EDSAC), which advocated a measure of symbolic programming, and the Manchester group, (MARK I) which believed that the programmer should write the program in a form as close as possible to the internal form (Wilkes, 1956). (A similar dichotomy can be found today amongst programmers of microcomputers.)

The EDSAC had a rudimentary assembler called Initial Orders, which allowed the user to write machine instructions consisting of a single alphabet letter operation code, a decimal address, and a terminating letter, which caused one of 12 constants preset by the programmer to be added to the address at assembly time. (The Initial Orders were implemented in a form of read-only memory consisting of a wired telephone uniselector.)

Probably the first assembler in the sense used in this article was SOAP (Symbolic Optimizer and Assembly Program) on the IBM 650 computer in the mid-1950s. However, the symbolic assembly features of SOAP were not its main feature (the 650 was a decimal computer anyway, which removed some of the difficulties of direct machine language coding). The 650 had a magnetic drum memory and an instruction code in which each instruction specified the address of its successor. For maximum efficiency, instructions had to be placed on the drum in positions such that the execution of each instruction overlapped as far as possible the time for the drum to rotate to the next instruction position, thus minimizing the latency time waiting for instructions. Such minimum-access coding involved a very difficult optimizing process, and it was this that SOAP achieved.

The most significant event in the history of assemblers was the Symbolic Assembly Program (SAP) for the IBM 704. The original SAP assembler (UASAP) was written by programmers at United Aircraft Corporation and was distributed by the SHARE organization. SAP set the external form of an assembly language that was to be a model for all its successors, and which persists almost unchanged to the present day. On later versions of the 700 series computers, SAP was replaced by FAP (Fortran Assembly Program).

Facilities. A typical machine instruction consists of an operation code, an address, and one or more register fields. The address may refer to a data area or to another instruction (e.g., the destination of a transfer of control). A SAP-like assembler provides a fixed set of mnemonic operation codes and an open-ended set of programmer-defined symbols for use in address parts. Such address symbols may be defined explicitly or implicitly by attaching them as labels to particular instructions or data words. Although a symbol stands for an address, the assembler cannot convert label symbols directly into addresses, since the address in storage into which a particular instruction will be loaded is not known at assembly time. (It is finally determined only when a number of routines are combined together to form a complete program.) The difficulty is resolved by recording as the value of the label symbol the displacement of the instruction in question from the beginning of the code for the subroutine, and marking it in the assembler output as a relative or relocatable value, to be adjusted later by the linker or loader.

Thus, SAP introduced the basic structure of a symbolic instruction as being made up of three fields:

1. *Location* (possibly blank). A symbol placed here takes as its value the address of the memory cell in which the corresponding instruction or data word will be stored: Thus it serves as a label by which it can be referenced by other instructions.

2. *Operation code.* The symbol here is one of a fixed repertoire of operation-code symbols

3. *Operand.* This field is usually made up of a number of subfields, reflecting the address/register structure of the computer. The subfields may be simple integer constants or may be expressions made up of symbols (representing addresses), constants, and simple arithmetic operations (usually plus and minus). Alternatively, a literal operand may be supplied: The assembler will store this and substitute the appropriate address in the instruction.

The following fragment of SAP coding illustrates this structure.

```
        TRA   ALPHA
        LOC   16385
ALPHA   CLA   BETA
        STO   DELTA
SYMB    FAD   = 3.14159
        SXO   STMB-2,4
        STO   SYMT
```

Each instruction in this example is made up of three fields: location (label), operation code, and address. The operation codes are nmemonic, e.g., TRA = transfer control, CLA = clear accumulator, FAD = floating add, etc. The address fields show the various possible constructions. In the first line the address is a symbol ALPHA, as yet undefined. (It appears as a label on a later instruction.) In line 2 the address is explicit, and in lines 3 and 4 symbols (presumably defined elsewhere in the program of which this fragment forms a part) are used. Line 5 illustrates the use of a literal operand: the "equals" indicates that the 3.14159 following is the actual value to be loaded by the FAD, not the address of the operand. The next line illustrates a more complex address: It is a two-field form in which the first component is a storage address and the second component identifies an index register to be used; in this example the storage address is specified as an expression.

The following excerpt of OS/370 assembler code for the IBM System/370 computers, whose purpose is to sum 13 numbers, shows how little things have changed.

```
        L    3,   = F'0'    CLEAR REGISTER
        L    5,   = F'0'    USING LITERAL
        LH   4,   = H'14'   LOAD REGISTER
        B    BCNT           ENTER LOOP
BNTER   AH   5,STZ(3)       INDEX STZ BY REG 3
        AH   3,   = H'2'    INCREMENT INDEX
BCNT    BCT  4,BNTER        BRANCH ON COUNT

        ST   5,BSUM
STZ     DC   H'15,225, 1,52,10,48,76,42,88,26,14,4,32'
BSUM    DC   F'0'
```

The three-field format is still used, though the mnemonics have changed. With the exception of the branch (B) order, which has a label as its address, the address field is made up of a register designator and a second field, which in these examples is either a symbolic store address or a literal. (For certain instructions it might be another register designator.)

Literals are introduced by "equals," but now include a type code (F = full word, H = half word). Indexing (modification) is illustrated in the line starting BNTER, and finally there are specifications of a number of constants introduced by the DC (Define Constant) pseudo-operation. The comments on the right are part of the programmer's documentation of the program.

Assembler Directives. Assembler directives serve two purposes. One is to provide information to control the assembly process; the other is to provide a way of defining data words in a program. Assembler directives are often called *pseudo-operations* (a terminology introduced by SAP) since they are commonly designated by special codes in the operation field. A SAP-like pseudo operation is

   symbol BSS *integer constant*

which sets the symbol equal to the location counter, and then advances the location counter by the amount designated by the constant. The effect is thus to reserve a block of memory and label it for future reference. Another typical pseudo-operation is

   symbol SET *expression*

which assigns an explicit value to a symbol. Other uses of directives to control the assembly include setting the origin, marking entry points, and defining external symbols.

We have seen an example of a data-generating pseudo-operation in the fragment of 370 coding given above. Here the pseudo-operation DC (define constants) is followed by a list of constants, each with a type code. A simpler facility provided in some assemblers requires all the constants to be of the same type; e.g., the pseudo-operation DEC introduces a list of decimal constants in the address field.

Conditional Assembly. A feature of many assemblers is the ability to assemble selectively pieces of program. This is particularly useful in package programs that have to provide a large number of options. In its simplest form this facility is provided by a pseudo-instruction that controls the assembly of the immediately following instruction, but usually a more elaborate facility of assembly-time jumps and labels is provided. Typically, assembly-time labels (or sequence symbols) are preceded by a period and appear in the label field. However, they are ignored by the assembler except in the context of two new pseudo-instructions AGO and AIF. (The mnemonics are derived from "assembler GOTO" and "assembler IF.") Let .ss be a sequence symbol; then

AGO   .SS

causes assembly to be continued from the line in which the symbol .ss appears in the label field (usually, this must be a forward jump), and

AIF   *(symbol-1 relation symbol-2)* .SS

causes assembly to be continued from the line labeled .ss if the condition is true; otherwise, assembly continues with the next line of code, as usual.

Listings. An assembler usually provides a variety of information about the program that it has assembled.

Besides details of any obvious errors such as incorrect syntax or multiple definition of symbols, the following may be provided.

1. Listing of symbolic instructions side by side with generated binary or binary-symbolic code.
2. Table of symbols defined in a routine, with or without their values.
3. Table of symbols used in a routine.
4. Cross-reference table: for each symbol defined, its name, value, and a list of all the instructions that reference it.

The form of the listing is generally controlled by one or more pseudo-operations; for example:

LIST FULL
LIST NONE
LIST SYMBOLS
etc.

Other common pseudo-operations are EJECT, which causes a page feed on the printer at the point in the listing where it occurs, and SPACE *n,* which causes a spacing of *n* blank lines in the listing. The listing corresponding to the program fragment for the IBM System/370 (given in the section "Facilities") is shown in Fig. 1.

Macro Assemblers. An important attribute of an assembler is the ability to define and use macros. It often happens that a certain pattern of orders occurs in several places in a program with only minor variations. This is particularly the case if there is a common operation that requires several machine orders for its execution; for example, the calling sequence for a call of another routine. Thus, to call the routine SUB with parameters A and B, it might be necessary to write

LDX 4, *
TFR SUB
NOP A
NOP B

(The first instruction loads into register 4 the address of itself; i.e., its location in storage. From this the subroutine can compute the return address to resume operation of the main program after the calling sequence. The parameters A and B are assumed to be addresses, and have been

LOC	OBJECT CODE	ADDR1	ADDR2	ST#	NAME	OP	OPERANDS	
.								
.								
.								
00000C	5830 2030		00038	8		L	3, = F'0'	CLEAR REGISTER
000010	5850 2030		00038	9		L	5, = F'0'	USING LITERAL
000014	4840 2034		00030	10		LH	4, = H'14''	LOAD REGISTER
000018	47F0 2010		00024	11		B	BCNT	ENTER LOOP
00001C	4A53 2038		00040	12	BNTER	AH	5,STZ(3)	INDEX STZ BY REG 3
000020	4A30 2036		0003B	13		AH	3, = H'2'	INCREMENT INDEX
000024	4640 2014		0001C	14	BCNT	BCT	4,BNTER	BRANCH ON COUNT
000028	5050 2054		0005C	15		ST	5,BSUM	STORE SUM
				16	*			
000040	000F00E100010034			17	STZ	DC	H'15,225,1,52,10,48,76,42,88,26,14,4,32'	
000048	000A00300046002A	(Hexadecimal equivalents						
000050	0058001A000E0004	of 13 numbers)						
000058	0020	←						
00005A	0000 ← (Filler needed to align next instruction properly)							
00005C	00000000			18	BSUM	DC	F'0'	

The LOC column shows the address of each instruction relative to the beginning of the program. The OBJECT CODE columns show the contents of the instructions as they will appear in memory. The ADDR1 (not used in this example) and ADDR2 columns give the effective addresses of the operands. Thus, assuming general register 2 holds the value 8, 2030 has the effective value 8 + 30 = 38. The ST# column is a sequential line number for the programmer's convenience. Note that columns to left of ST# are all given in hexadecimal.

Fig. 1. Example of Listing from System/370 assembler.

placed as the address parts of two no-operation [i.e., null] instructions) Evidently, it would be convenient for the programmer to be able to write

CALL SUB,A,B

and have the system generate the calling sequence. The advantages of this approach are threefold. The programmer writes less; the program is more readable: and if at some future stage the calling sequence is changed, a change at one place in the program will insure that all CALLS are changed without the need to alter each one individually.

(In SAP the CALL macro was built into the system, and was described as a pseudo-operation. This usage of the term "pseudo-operation" is no longer current.) A macro assembler allows the programmer to define macroinstructions as sequences of ordinary instructions, and provides a means of inserting variable information in the generated sequences.

The Working of the Assembler. The "classic" assembler takes a routine (or subprogram) and converts it into binary symbolic form for subsequent processing by a linkage editor. The conversion is accomplished in two passes (i.e., the source program is scanned twice). The basic strategy is very simple. The first pass through the source program collects all the symbol definitions into a symbol table, and the second pass converts the program to binary symbolic form, using the definitions collected in the first pass.

Although the program is scanned twice, only in the crudest systems is the physical source material read twice. If the assembler is reading directly from cards, then the source material can be copied onto magnetic tape or disk during the first pass, and so preserved for the second pass. In the environment of modern operating systems, the assembler will in any case read card images from disk on the first pass. A good assembler may encode the information read in the first pass into a form that allows a more efficient second pass.

During the second pass, the assembler will have to recognize three sorts of quantities: absolute quantities, relocatable quantities, and references to externally defined symbols. In the simplest case, all relocatable quantities are expressed relative to an origin at the beginning of the routine. The assembler therefore has to categorize the symbols as it builds up the symbol table, and then check for illegal combinations in expressions. (For example, it is meaningless to add two relocatable symbols, though their difference may be a respectable absolute quantity.) The exact form of the output from the assembler depends on the linkage editor. Typically, the assembler might produce the following output.

Header	Name of routine,
RLB	Relocatable binary section: Consists of binary symbolic code and relocation information,
Definition table	Definitions of global symbols defined in the routine (i.e., symbols that will be referenced in other routines).
Use table	Details of use of global and COMMON symbols in the routine (i.e., symbols used here but defined elsewhere).

The *definition table* carries information about symbols defined in this routine which are to have a global meaning. Since these may be absolute or relative, the table must carry this information as well as the value. In the case of a relative symbol the value is relative to the beginning of the routine.

The *use table* is more complex, since it records all occurrences of global symbols within the routine. Its exact form will depend on the facilities provided by the assembler—in particular the circumstances in which global symbols can be used.

If multiple location counters are used, an extra block must be output giving the amount of space used by the routine relative to each location counter. Each relocatable item will carry with it an indication of the relevant location counter.

Meta Assemblers. Assemblers for different machines have much in common. They organize symbol tables, evaluate expressions, and generate binary words from a number of symbolic fields. The idea of a meta assembler is to provide a system with these general capabilities, together with a means of describing (in machine-independent form) the assembly rules for a particular machine. The meta assembler accepts this description and then functions apparently as a normal assembler.

The idea of a meta assembler originated with Ferguson (1966). The idea had been utilized in the Utmost assembler for the Univac III, Sleuth 11 for the Univac 1107/8, and in Metasymbol for the SDS 900 series. An important feature of these systems (which is usually glossed over in their descriptions) is that the syntax of the input to a meta assembler is fixed. The meaning of the symbolic information can be defined by the user, but the user cannot change the syntax. Thus, although it is possible in using a meta assembler to write an assembler for most machines, it is not possible to mimic an existing assembler. (This is one of the many differences between a meta assembler and a compiler-compiler.)

The essentially new features of a meta assembler are (1) the provision of compile-time procedures and functions, and (2) a mechanism whereby the programmer can define binary output formats and cause such binary output to be generated.

Superficially, the input to a meta assembler looks like input to any assembler; each line has three fields—label, operation, and operand. The label is optional: If there is a symbol in this field, it is assigned a value equal to the current location-counter value. The operation may be the name of a built-in system operation, in which case it is no different from a pseudo-operation in a conventional assembler. If the operation is not the name of a built-in operation, it is assumed to be the name of a programmer-defined procedure, which will be obeyed, taking the operand field as an argument. This procedure may have the effect of generating some code, or may just perform housekeeping operations such as entering items in a table. It should be particularly noted that the procedure is obeyed during assembly. It is in many ways comparable to a macro, but instead of textual substitution we obey a piece of program written in *meta*-assembly language. This may itself contain calls to other procedures.

The operand field contains an expression, or group of expressions, made up of symbols and/or constants. These expressions are evaluated by the system in the same way that a normal assembler evaluates its address field. Unlike a normal assembler, the expressions may contain calls to user-defined functions.

Included in the built-in procedures are GEN and GENB, which output the values of the operand set as a sequence of words or bytes, respectively, and FORM, which allows the user to define a named template for binary output. Thus,

INSTR   FORM 6, 3, 15

defines (for a 24-bit word machine) a template made up of 3 fields consisting of 6, 3, and 15 bits, and attaches the name INSTR to this template FORM is a built-in operation. Suppose that subsequent to the definition of INSTR, we write

INSTR   LDA, 7, ALPHA + 1

(Here INSTR is in the operation field, and the operand field is a set of three expressions.) This will cause the three elements of the operand set to be evaluated, truncated, and concatenated to form a 24-bit binary output word. (Note that this technique would allow the operation code of an instruction to be written as an expression!)

The meta-assembler does not have any conventional built-in operations for machine instructions. The code emitted for what seems to be an assembly-language instruction is actually determined by a procedure having the name of the desired machine instruction. In this way,

and using procedures to produce the required effect for pseudo-instructions, a "conventional" assembler image can be built up.

"High-Level" Assemblers. An assembly language program is necessarily written at a fine level of detail, with each instruction representing a single primitive operation. An unfortunate effect of working at this level of detail is that programs are rarely as perspicuous as programs written in a high-level language can be.

Recently there has been a development in the direction of *high-level* or *Algol-like* assembly languages that attempt to combine fine control over machine registers and storage with a structure that reflects the overall structure of the program; for example, repetition loops, conditional statements, and functions and procedures. The facilities provided in such a language must correspond fairly closely to the actual hardware. For example, we cannot include anything that depends on dynamic storage allocation if the underlying hardware does not provide such facilities. (Put another way, the compiler for an Algol-like assembly language cannot assume the existence of a "run-time system." Every source statement except a procedure call must compile into open code.) The precise facilities provided in a system will depend on the particular machine, but will typically include the following.

1. Symbolic names (identifiers) with associated types. The types will correspond to the storage units manipulated by the machine instructions; for example, on the PDP II, they would include byte and word.
2. Reserved identifiers for machine registers. A synonym facility may also be provided to associate other names with registers.
3. Block structure, giving scopes to identifiers.
4. Conditional and compound statements.
5. One-dimensional arrays, but not multidimensional arrays (these canot be accessed by simple indexing on most machines).
6. Procedures and functions. (Usually only one parameter will be possible, called by passing the parameter as an address in an accumulator or general-purpose register.)
7. Simple expressions (but nothing involving temporary storage; all operators are of equal precedence and evaluation is by a simple left-to-right scan).
8. Provision for including basic assembly language (e.g., for input operations).

The first high-level assembler was the PL/360 system described by Wirth (1968) in a classic paper. As its name implies, it was designed for the IBM System 360 machines. An interesting development in this area is that the only assembler provided by the manufacturers of the GEC 4000 series machines is a high-level assembler (called BABBAGE).

REFERENCES

1951. Wilkes, M. V., Wheeler, D. J., and Gill, S. *The Preparation of Programs for an Electronic Digital Computer*. Cambridge, MA: Addison-Wesley.

1956. Wilkes, M. V. *Automatic Digital Computers*. London: Methuen & Co.

1965. Graham, Marvin Lowell and Ingerman, Peter Zilahy. "An Assembly Language for Reprogramming," *Communications of the ACM* **8**, *No.12:* 769–773, December.

1966. Ferguson, D. E. "The Evolution of the Meta-Assembly Program," *Communications of the ACM* **9**: 190.

1968. Wirth, N. "PL/360, A Programming Language for the 360 Computers," *Journal of the ACM* **15**: 37.

1968. Feldman, Jerome and Gries, David. "Translator Writing Systems," *Communications of the ACM* **11**, *No.2:* 77–113 (see Section C and references therein), February.

1978. Barron, D. W. *Assemblers and Loaders,* 3rd Ed. New York: American-Elsevier.

D. W. BARRON

ASSEMBLY LANGUAGE. *See* MACHINE AND ASSEMBLY LANGUAGE PROGRAMMING.

ASSOCIATION FOR COMPUTING MACHINERY (ACM)

For article on related subject *see* AMERICAN FEDERATION OF INFORMATION PROCESSING SOCIETIES.

Purpose. The Association for Computing Machinery is the largest scientific, educational, and technical society of the computing community. Founded in 1947, the Association is dedicated to the development of information processing as a discipline, and to the responsible use of computers in an increasing diversity of applications.

The purposes of the Association, quoting its constitution, are: (1) To advance the sciences and arts of information processing, including but not restricted to the study, design, development, construction, and application of modern machinery, computing techniques and appropriate languages for general information processing, storage, retrieval and processing of data of all kinds and the automatic control and simulation of processes. (2) To promote the free interchange of information about the sciences and arts of information processing, both among specialists and among the public in the best scientific and professional tradition. (3) To develop and maintain the integrity and competence of individuals engaged in the practices of the sciences and arts of information processing.

How Established. ACM was founded at Columbia University on 15 September 1947, as the Eastern Association for Computing Machinery. A constitution and bylaws were adopted in September 1949. ACM was incorporated in Delaware in December 1954. The following have held the office of ACM president.

J. H. Curtiss, 1947
John W. Mauchly, 1948–1950
Franz L. Alt, 1950–1952
Samuel B. Williams. 1952–1954
Alston S. Householder, 1954–1956
John W. Carr III, 1956–1958
Richard W. Hamming, 1958–1960
Harry D. Huskey, 1960–1962
Alan J. Perlis, 1962–1964
George E. Forsythe, 1964–1966
Anthony Oettinger, 1966–1968
Bernard A. Galler, 1968–1970
Walter M. Carlson, 1970–1972
Anthony Ralston, 1972–1974
Jean E. Sammet, 1974–1976
Herbert R. J. Grosch, 1976–1978
Daniel D. McCracken, 1978–1980
Peter J. Denning, 1980–

Organizational Structure. The Association is organized into 12 regions, 11 covering the United States and Canada, and one encompassing Europe. Each region is represented in the Council of the ACM (the elected governing body) by a regional representative. With an additional six members-at-large and the ex officio members (president, past-president, vice-president, secretary, treasurer, chairman of the Publications Board, and SIG Board Chairman), the full Council comprises 25 members.

Each region has local chapters and student chapters. Presently there are approximately 100 local chapters and 125 student chapters.

The four classes of ACM membership and their qualifications are:

Member—must subscribe to the purposes of the Association and have attained professional stature by demonstrating intellectual competence and ethical conduct in the arts and sciences of information processing.

Associate—must subscribe to the purposes of the Association, but need not be eligible for Member status.

Student—full-time registrant at an accreditied educational institution.

Institutional—institutions that subscribe to the purposes of the Association.

Total membership is about 55,000. The headquarters of ACM are at 1133 Avenue of the Americas, New York, NY 10036.

Technical Program. The major organizational units of ACM devoted to technical activities of its members are the Special Interest Groups (SIGs). The SIGs operate as semiautonomous bodies within ACM for the advancement of activities in the following subject areas: Automata and Computability Theory; Architecture of Computer Systems; Artificial Intelligence; Business Data Processing and Management; Biomedical Computing; Computers and the Physically Handicapped; Computers and Society; Data Communications; Computer Personnel Research; Computer Science Education; Computer Uses in Education; Design Automation; Systems Documentation; Computer Graphics; Information Retrieval; Language Analysis and Studies in the Humanities; Mathematical Programming; Measurement and Evaluation; Microprogramming; Management of Data; Numerical Mathematics; Office Automation; Operating Systems; Personal Computing; Programming Languages; Symbolic and Algebraic Manipulation; Simulation and Modeling; Small Computing Systems and Applications; Social and Behavioral Science Computing; Software Engineering; and University Computing Centers.

The ACM Lectureship Series was instituted in 1961 to enrich chapter activities by providing acknowledged specialists in various aspects of computing and its application as speakers.

In 1966, ACM established the Turing Award, honoring computing pioneer Alan M. Turing, and given annually to an individual selected for contributions of a technical nature made to the computing community. The award carries an honorarium of $2,000. The recipients to date have been: Alan J. Perlis, Maurice V. Wilkes, Richard W. Hamming, Marvin Minsky, J. H. Wilkinson, John McCarthy, Edsger W. Dijkstra, Charles W. Bachman, Donald E. Knuth, Allen Newell and Herbert A. Simon (jointly), Michael O. Rabin and Dana Scott, John Backus, Robert Floyd, Kenneth E. Iverson, C. A. R. Hoare, and Edgar F. Codd.

The ACM Distinguished Service Award was instituted in 1970. Its recipients have been Franz Alt, J. Donald Madden, George E. Forsythe, William Atchison, Saul Gorn, John W. Carr III, Richard J. Canning, Thomas B. Steel, Jr., Eric A. Weiss, Carl Hammer, Bernard A. Galler, and Aaron Finerman. A Programming systems and Language Paper Award was established in 1969. In 1971, in conjunction with the twenty-fifth anniversary of the invention of the modern digital computer, ACM established the Grace Murray Hopper Award, to be given annually to the outstanding young computer professional of the year as nominated by ACM. To qualify, candidates must have been 30 years or younger at the time the qualifying contribution was made. The first award was to Donald E. Knuth.

The ACM publishes nine major periodicals: *Journal of the Association for Computing Machinery* (established in 1954, published quarterly) is devoted to technical papers of lasting value reporting on research and advances in the computing sciences. *Communications of the ACM* (1958, monthly) publishes technical papers and timely articles on topics of interest to the computing profession. *Computing Reviews* (1960, monthly) comprehensively covers the literature on computing and its applications. *The Guide to Computing Literature,* keyed to *Computing Reviews,* but including additional materials, is published annually. *Computing Surveys* (1969, quarterly) presents comprehensive survey coverage of the state of the art in the various areas of computer science and business data processing. *Transactions on Mathematical Software* (1975, quarterly) publishes theoretical and applied articles on mathematical software as well as algorithms for computers. *Transactions on Database Systems* (1976, quarterly) publishes original papers on the theory and applications of all aspects of database systems and related subjects. *Transactions on Programming Languages and Systems* (1979, quarterly) contains original work on the development and use of programming languages, methods, and systems. *Transactions on Graphics* (1982, quarterly) contains papers on all aspects of computer graphics. *Collected Algorithms from ACM* is a looseleaf collection of all algorithms published in *Communications of the ACM* from 1960–1975, and in *Transactions on Mathematical Software* from 1975 on.

ACM holds an annual conference that stresses technical programs and publishes a proceedings of the papers presented. ACM sponsors the annual Computer Science Conference, which is devoted mainly to brief reports of current research. ACM is a founding member of the American Federation of Information Processing Societies (AFIPS) and participates in the annual (American) National Computer Conference. In addition, the Special Interest Groups and other subunits sponsor numerous technical symposia and meetings, primarily in North America, but also in various other parts of the world.

I. L. AUERBACH

ASSOCIATION FOR EDUCATIONAL DATA SYSTEMS (AEDS)

For article on related subject *see* AMERICAN FEDERATION OF INFORMATION PROCESSING SOCIETIES.

The Association for Educational Data Systems (AEDS) is a private, not-for-profit educational corporation founded and incorporated in Florida in 1962 by a group of professional educators and technical specialists interested in educational applications.

The purpose of AEDS is to provide a forum for the exchange of ideas and information about the relationship of modern technology to modern education. Its objectives are:

- To provide a national association for educational data systems and encourage and assist the establishment of associations for educational data systems.
- To provide for sharing and exchanging idea techniques, materials, and procedures for use in modern educational data processing.
- To promote general recognition of the vital professional role played by the educational data processing specialist in a modern school system and the high level of competence required for this role.
- To promote and encourage appropriate use of electronic data processing and computing equipment and techniques for the improvement of education.
- To cooperate with manufacturers, distributors, and operators of educational data processing equipment and supplies in establishing and maintaining proper technical standards, and in meeting new needs for specialized devices and systems.
- To encourage and advise concerning research relating to educational data processing.

The following have served as presidents of the Association.

Robert Gates, 1962–1963
John Caffrey, 1963–1964
Don D. Bushnell, 1964–1965
C. Taylor Whittier, 1965–1966
John W. Sullivan, 1966–1967
Ernest Anderson, 1967–1968
John W. Hamblen, 1968–1969
Ralph Van Dusseldorp, 1969–1970
L. Everett Yarbrough, 1970–1971
Sylvia Charp, 1971–1972
Russell E. Weitz, 1972–1973

James Augustine, Jr., 1973–1975
Thomas McConnell, 1975–1976
E. Ronald Corruth, 1976–1977
Judith Edwards, 1977–1978
Bradford Burris, 1978–1979
Donald Holznagel, 1979–1980
Winston C. Addis, 1980–1981

The headquarters of AEDS are located at 1201 Sixteenth Street, N. W., Washington, DC 20036.

AEDS conducts an annual meeting dedicated to general and technical sessions on educational data processing.

The following publications are included in the membership fee: *AEDS Monitor*—a quarterly publication giving current information about educational data processing; *AEDS Journal*—a quarterly publication containing technical information about the development and specific applications of educational data processing; and *AEDS Bulletin*, a quarterly newsletter.

I. L. AUERBACH

ASSOCIATION FOR SYSTEMS MANAGEMENT (ASM)

Purpose. The Association for Systems Management (ASM), founded in 1947, is dedicated to the proper use of information resource management, and to the creation of a broader understanding and acceptance of the systems function as a component of effective management.

The purposes of ASM are: (1) To encourage, establish, and maintain high standards of professional education, competence, and performance. (2) To further the exchange of professional knowledge and to conduct educational seminars and conferences. (3) To disseminate, by all appropriate means, accurate knowledge and information regarding systems operations.

How Established. ASM was chartered in Delaware in 1947 as the Systems and Procedures Association (SPA). Its name was changed in 1969 to reflect the broader scope of the systems field. The following have held the office of ASM president.

W. K. Wallace,* 1947–1948
Frank Hoffman, 1948–1949
R. B. Crean,* 1949–1950

---

*Deceased

J. G. Nagro,* 1950–1951
A. L. Mettler, 1951–1952
James Thomson,* 1952–1953
Harold R. Price, 1953–1954
Charles C. Chase, 1954–1955
Bruce L. Smyth, 1955–1956
Allen Y. Davis, 1956–1957
F. Walton Wanner, 1957–1958
Joseph A. MacQueen, Sr., 1958–1959
David D. Merriman, 1959–1960
Keith DeLashmutt, 1960–1961
William J. Bates, 1961–1962
James P. Mason, 1962–1963
Arthur Weiss, 1963–1964
N. L. Senensieb, 1964–1965
Allan L. Burns, 1965–1966
Michael Miskulin, 1966–1967
Colver Gordon, 1967–1968
Allen M. Motter, 1968–1969
Lorne T. Goat, 1969–1970
G. Oeter Ignasiak, 1970–1971
William J. Rost, 1971–1972
Harry L. Ritson, 1972–1973
Frank P. Congdon, Jr., 1973–1974
Kenton E. Ross, 1974–1975
James R. Gunderman, 1975–1976
Franklin E. Banks, 1976–1977
Larry S. Burr, 1977–1978
Benjamin Schauss, 1978–1979
Clarence H. King, Jr., 1979–1980
Bertha Kitover, 1980–1981
Fenwicke W. Holmes, 1981–1982

Organizational Structure. ASM is organized into 125 chapters in five regions covering North and South America, Europe, Africa, the Middle East, Asia, and the South Pacific. The 21-member International Board of Directors, which governs the Association, is comprised of three members elected from each of the five regions, five International Officers elected by all ASM Members, and the immediate Past International President. ASM chapters in the various regions are organized into 24 Division Councils, which meet regularly to conduct ASM activities.

The seven classes of ASM membership and their qualifications are:

Professional Member—must have baccalaureate or higher degree and three years of experience in systems work, or five years experience in systems work, or experience as an educator or consultant in activities related to systems.

Member—anyone engaged in or having an interest in systems work or teaching.

Student Member—any full-time student in a college or university not concurrently employed on a full-time basis in a remunerative vocation.

Organization Member—any recognized non-profit association which has an interest in systems management and technology.

Life and Honorary Member—Special Memberships conferred by the International Board.

Emeritus Member—any retired Professional Member no longer employed in a remunerative vocation.

Total membership is about 10,000. The headquarters of ASM are located at 24587 Bagley Road, Cleveland, OH 44138.

Technical Program. The major thrust of ASM is in education and publications. ASM has five Technical Departments, each of which publish six Technical Reports for the exchange of information and research activities. The five departments are:

Management Information Systems
Data Communications
Data Processing
Organization Planning
Written Communications

ASM also has Affiliated Sections, which are groups of 25 or more members involved in a particular industry. Currently, the Steel Industry Systems Association is an Affiliated Section of ASM. SISA has its own president, vice-president, secretary-treasurer, and Governing Board.

ASM sponsors a Distinguished Service Awards Program to honor members for service to the Association and profession at various levels. Top honor is the Distinguished Service Award, which also requires candidates to write books or articles for national publication and to give addresses on information resource management. One hundred members have received this award since its inception.

Publications. ASM publishes the *Journal of Systems Management,* a monthly dedicated to the advancement of information systems knowledge, and five *Technical Reports* every other month, plus a *Chapter Newsletter* monthly. There are more than 30 ASM publications, ranging from *Forms Design and Management* to *Information Resource Management.* Two are teaching texts with instructor's manuals.

Education. ASM offers more than 60 weeks of training each year. Four five-day courses are sponsored: Basic Systems Analysis, Computer Systems Analysis, Effective Systems Design, and Advanced Systems Analysis. There are also one- and three-day programs on more than 20 subjects offered at locations convenient to chapter members. Some selected subjects are: Systems Project Management, Developing Leadership Skills, and The Human Side of Systems.

ASM also conducts an Annual Conference each spring which presents more than 30 different seminars in two and one-half days. A wide variety of offerings assures registrants they can tailor their individual schedules to fit personal education needs. The schedule permits participation in as many as 10 seminars during the Conference. The 1979 Annual Conference, for example, explored the rapid technological changes in today's society and their impact on individuals, business, and the community.

I. L. AUERBACH

ASSOCIATION FRANÇAISE POUR LA CYBERNETIQUE ECONOMIQUE ET TECHNIQUE (AFCET)

For article on related subject *see* INTERNATIONAL FEDERATION OF INFORMATION PROCESSING.

Purpose. AFCET endeavors to bring together French scientists, engineers, users, and manufacturers working and interested in data processing, automation, and operational research, as well as in measurement and applied mathematics.

How Established. The organization was established in 1969 as a result of the amalgamation of: AFIRO (Association Française d'Informatique et de Recherche Operationnelle), AFRA (Association Française de Regulation et d'Automatisme), and AFIC (Association Française d'Instrumentation et de Controle). The merger was due to the relation between measurement and instrumentation as well as the relation of operational research to automation and data processing. The presidents of AFCET since 1969 have been

R. Mercier, 1969
J. Csech, 1970–1971
F. Genuys, 1972–1973
L. Guileysse, 1974–1975
B. Roy, 1976–1977
Y. Carteron, 1978–1979
A. Danzin, 1980–1981

Organizational Structure. AFCET had about 4,000 members in 1980. In addition, about 300 industrial companies are registered with AFCET and pay a much higher contribution than do members. The Association has various independent sections, each headed by a chairman. These include three divisions: ADSG—Aide a la Decision et Systemes de Gestion, AI—Automatisme et Instrumentation, and TTI—Theorie et Techniques de l'Informatique; three colleges: MA—Mathematiques Appliquées; COSTAM—College des Sciences et Techniques de l'Amenagement; and the College Bureautique.

AFCET's headquarters are at 156 Boulevard Pereire, 75017 Paris, France.

Technical Program. The sections organize seminars regularly (for 150 to 300 persons) on current subjects. Every year, AFCET holds a congress on data processing or on other subjects closely connected with its activities. It also participates in and organizes international symposia, such as the Fifth IMEKO Congress, Versailles 1970; the First IFAC/IFIP Symposium on Traffic Control, Versailles 1970; the Fifth IFAC World Congress on Automatic Control, Paris 1972; the International Conference IFIP Teleinformatics, Paris, 1979; and the IFIP Second World Conference on Computers in Education, Marseilles, 1975.

Publications. The Assoication issues four official publications:

Rairo (Revue Française d'Automatique, d'Informatique et de Recherche Operationnelle), published, in five series of four issues each, per year (publishes reports of a very high level on the work done in laboratories and research institutes, Ph.D. theses, etc.).

Automatisme, published in ten issues per year (covers industrial applications of automatic control and computer systems).

Informatique de Gestion, published in ten issues during the year (treats administrative data processing systems and computers).

Mesures, published in ten issues over the year (covers measurement, instrumentation, and components).

I. L. AUERBACH

ASSOCIATIVE LANGUAGES

For articles on related subjects *see* ARTIFICIAL INTELLIGENCE; ASSOCIATIVE MEMORY; INFORMATION AND DATA; INFORMATION RETRIEVAL; LIST PROCESSING LANGUAGES; LISTS AND LIST PROCESSING; PROGRAMMING LANGUAGES; AND STRING PROCESSING LANGUAGES.

Associative language research has been motivated by two considerations. The languages might be useful in associative computers or could simply be a better way of stating algorithms. Applications have been suggested or carried out in essentially all nonnumerical problems and in a few special numerical ones such as sparse matrix calculations.

The essential fact about an *associative memory* is that it does not rely on explicit addresses. A reference to information contained in a memory cell is specified by a partial description of its contents. All cells in the memory which meet the specification are referred to by the statement. A conventional coordinate-addressed memory can be thought of as a special case in the following way: Each cell of the associative memory will be a pair consisting of a conventional cell and its address:

Associative cell: | address | conventional cell |

To access a cell in this special associative memory, one specifies the contents of one particular part (the address field) of a cell. In the general associative memory, a cell can be accessed by specifying the contents of any part of the cell.

The following example may help point out the importance of this seemingly minor difference. Suppose one were to store the contents of a telephone directory in a computer memory. There are several ways in which the data could be organized so that the telephone number of a given person could be found fairly quickly. However, the problem of going from a telephone number to its owner is rather difficult. One could, of course, create an *inverted list,* namely, enter a second directory ordered by numbers rather than names, but this entails representing the same information twice in the memory. There are several other possibilities, but all lead to compromises between inefficiency in time and inefficiency in storage. In an associative memory either question could be answered in one memory access and without any redundant information being stored in the memory.

This example is so clear and striking that it should be suspect. First of all, it is often the case that one person has several telephone numbers or that several people are listed for the same number. This is the so-called multiple-hit situation and is at the root of many of the problems encountered in using associative memories. Many other difficulties arise in the design of hardware associative memories. There is even a theoretical basis for questioning the inherent practicality of a hardware associative memory. However, the idea of referring to information by a partial specification of its contents is intriguing and has found its way into a number of programming systems.

Let us consider the behavior of an associative memory each of whose cells contains an ordered 3-tuple:

3-element associative cell: | a | o | v |

written $a \cdot o \equiv v$. The symbols a, o, and v can be thought of as mnemonics for attribute, object and value.

The elements of the 3-tuple are drawn from a universe of items; a 3-tuple of items is an association. Typical associations might be

father·john doe $\equiv$ don doe
end·line $\equiv$ point.

If a universe of associations was stored in an associative memory, any partial specification should lead to retrieval. Letting x, z represent unspecified positions in an association, Table 1 enumerates the partial specifications (forms) possible in a 3-element associative memory.

Table 1

Form Name	Form	Example	Interpretation
F0	$a \cdot o \equiv v$	son · john $\equiv$ don	The association itself, if in memory
F1	$a \cdot o \equiv x$	son · john $\equiv x$	Sons of john
F2	$a \cdot x \equiv v$	son · x $\equiv$ don	Father of don
F3	$x \cdot o \equiv v$	x · john $\equiv$ don	Relation of john to don
F4	$a \cdot x \equiv z$	son · x $\equiv z$	All father-son pairs
F5	$x \cdot z \equiv v$	x · z $\equiv$ don	All associations with don as third component
F6	$x \cdot o \equiv z$	x · john $\equiv z$	All associations with john as second component

Alternatively, Table 1 can be viewed as a generalization of the property list features of languages such as Lisp and IPL-V, the associative TABLE feature of Snobol, and of the records (structures) features of languages such as Algol 68, Simula, Pascal, and PL/I. In all these systems there are provisions for directly treating forms F0 and F1 and handling F3 and F6 fairly efficiently. The associative languages treat the association symmetrically and attempt to process efficiently all the forms of Table 1.

The basic operations on the universe of associations are entry, removal, and retrieval. Typically,

MAKE father·tom $\equiv$ bill

will place the new association in the universe if it is not already there. Similarly,

ERASE father·ANY ≡ bill

will erase all associations that match the specification.

The heart of any associative system is its retrieval capability. One problem is that a retrieval statement is, in general, multiple-valued. This has led to the inclusion of *sets* in several systems and to statements like sons←son·john, which assigns to *sons* all the sons of john.

Another technique is to have iteration statements ranging over all values; e.g.:

foreach x **suchthat** son · x ≡ don **do**···

The situation becomes much more complicated when there are several unspecified elements in a retrieval request. For example, consider

$$\textbf{foreach}\ x,y,z\ \textbf{suchthat}$$
$$\text{father} \cdot x \equiv y\ \text{and father} \cdot y \equiv z\ \textbf{do} \qquad (1)$$
$$\textbf{make}\ \text{granddad} \cdot x \equiv z.$$

Statement 1 requires solving for three variables. It is clearly inadequate to solve for each variable independently; the system must form an assignment of items that satisfies the associative context. For example, if the associations of the universe were

father·tom ≡bill
father·pete ≡tom
father·bill ≡don
father·george ≡clyde,

statement 1 would yield assignments

(x,y,z) = (tom, bill, don)
(x,y,z) = (pete, tom, bill)

and, after the execution of statement (1), the universe would also contain the associations

granddad · tom ≡ don
granddad · pete ≡ bill.

Treating statements like this requires a system to make use of intermediate structures and a fairly sophisticated interpreter. It should be noted that *no associative processing hardware has been suggested which can directly solve the general case of the problem above.* Statement 1 also suggests yet another way to view associative languages—as a generalization of pattern matching sys-

tems (e.g., Snobol) to move complex structures. If we picture an association as a labeled arrow in a graph, e.g.,

john $\overset{son}{\Rightarrow}$ don,

the associative language is a graph-matching system.

Most associative languages incorporate the concepts described above, but differ in other ways. One natural extension is to drop the restriction to triples. Most of the research on *n*-ary relations has been done in work oriented toward information retrieval and database systems (Codd, 1970). Although there is no clear demarcation, the following points generally separate the two fields. Associative languages are designed to (1) be used by programmers, (2) respond in fractional seconds, (3) have their database fit in secondary storage. Information retrieval presupposes very large files, naive users and a somewhat slower response. There is currently no known mechanism for efficiently handling all the forms analogous to Table 1 for *n*-ary relations.

One problem that is common to information retrieval and associative languages is the question of how much deduction to incorporate. For example, one probably wants a system to use the fact that "bigger" is transitive in retrieval. Tramp (Ash and Sibley, 1968) incorporates a few simple deduction rules. The problem is where to stop; one could incorporate many such rules or even a general theorem prover. At this point, the associative retrieval problem becomes part of artificial intelligence. In fact, all the new AI languages (Sussman and McDermott, 1972) incorporate associative retrieval features, including mechanisms for retrieving implied relations.

There has been quite a bit of work on the problem of implementing efficiently associative languages. Most systems employ a combination of hash-coding (Feldman and Rovner, 1969) and list-processing techniques. This work overlaps similar studies in data structures and information retrieval. A related problem is to retrieve compound requests (like statement (1)) efficiently; one should not, for example, find all males and then select only those over 7 feet tall. Some work has been done along these lines, but much more could be done.

References

1968. Ash, W. L. and Sibley, E. H. "TRAMP: An Interpretive Associative Processor with Deductive Capabilities," in *Proc. ACM 23rd National Conference*, pp. 143–156.

1969. Feldman, J. A. and Rovner, P. D. "An ALGOL-Based Associative Language," *Communications of the ACM* **12**, No. 8: 439–449.

1970. Codd, E. F. "A Relational Model of Data for Large Shared Data Banks," *Communications of the ACM* **13**, No. 6: 377–387 (June).

1971. Findler, N. V. Pfaltz, J. L., and Bernstein, H. J. *Four High-Level Extensions of FORTRAN IV: SLIP, AMPPL II, TREETRAN, and SYMBOLANG, Part II.* New York: Spartan Books.

1972. Sussman, G. J. and McDermott, D. V. "From PLANNER to CONNIVER—A Genetic Approach," in *Proc. AFIPS Fall Joint Computer Conference,* **41,** *Part II:* 1171–1179

1976. Foster, C. C. *Content Addressable Parallel Processors.* New York: Van Nostrand Reinhold.

1980. Kohonon, T. *Content Addressable Memories.* Berlin: Springer.

J. FELDMAN

ASSOCIATIVE MEMORY

For articles on related subjects *see* ADDRESSING; ASSOCIATIVE LANGUAGES; CACHE MEMORY; and MEMORY: Main.

Data in an associative memory (Lewin, 1972) or content-addressable memory is not accessed by address as in conventional memory. Rather than being identified by the name of its location, it is identified from properties of its own value. To retrieve a word from associative store, a search key (*q.v.*) (or descriptor) must be presented which represents particular values of all or some of the bits of the word. This key is compared in parallel with the corresponding lock or tag bits of all stored words, and all words matching this key are signaled to be available. If the key is loose, with few attributes, it will access many words. The memory might indicate the number of such words and would in any case normally provide each of these in turn for examination. The order in which they are presented is usually related to their order in physical storage and tells nothing of their value. Once available, each word can be used or, if not wanted, flagged (by a change of a single search bit) so that succeeding words can be retrieved.

It is obvious that associative search can be fairly complex if the search key has few elements and the association is loose. A limiting case is that in which at most one occurrence of a search key match exists. This is the case in the use of associative stores between levels in a memory hierarchy where the associative store is a scratch pad denoting the existence of a copy of a record in the next higher-level store. Such is also the use of associative storage in cache memory (*q.v.*) management.

Various attempts have been made to build associative processors in which the main memory is partially or completely associative (Lewin, 1972). In this case each memory word, in addition to match or equality logic on each bit, has other facilities such as "greater than" detection.

Fig. 1 illustrates the logical structure of an associative store, showing the possibility of search inputs ("don't care") whose value results in a positive match independent of the bit stored in the associative memory. In practice, such a store will normally be implemented using integrated circuit technology. In addition to the associative search mechanism, the memory is usually equipped with conventional read/write facilities (not shown in Fig. 1).

A flip-flop is shown as the basic storage element and is shaded to indicate its current state. An equivalence circuit (denoted by $=$) is used to make the comparison with the search key. An additional OR circuit (denoted by $+$) per bit allows the use of a "don't care" search condition. The output from each bit is combined in an AND, represented by the horizontal line on the figure. A match output is 1 if and only if the stored data and key data bits match everywhere that "don't care" inputs are zero. Fig. 1 shows a match between a stored value of (1,0,0) and a search key of (1,0,X), where X indicates the "don't care" condition.

One important application of associative storage is in paging memory management. In such systems, of which the Atlas computer was an early major example, a relatively small, fast, main store is used in conjunction with a slow, large bulk or backup store. Each memory is divided into blocks or *pages* whose size may vary typically from 64 to 1,024 words. The small main memory will hold a small number of these, say 8 to 32, while the bulk store may have a capacity of thousands of pages. Data is transferred between main and backup store in page-size quantities. When the central processor requires a new word of information, high-order bits of its address are checked against appropriate bits of an associative page-address store in order to ascertain the existence in main memory of the word sought. If the page is already present and recorded in the associative store, the associative store provides additional bits, giving its location in main store. If not present, or, if present but not found in the associative store (which, because it is relatively expensive, may have fewer pages than there are pages in the main store) related central processing unit (CPU) activity is halted while the page-memory access mechanism establishes a main store page location whose contents are returned to backup storage, after which this area of main store is refilled with the required new page.

A paging organization utilizing an associative page lookup is shown in Fig. 2. In this example a backup store of 1,024 pages of 64 words each is illustrated. The main store has a capacity of 8 pages of 64 words. An associative page lookup table of 4 words of 15 bits each is used to maintain order. In use, the upper 10 bits or page address of the effective address (1023) from the CPU is compared associatively with ten-bit page numbers in the associative store. If a match occurs, 5 bits are provided (3, 1, 1), giving the page location in main store (2 = 010)

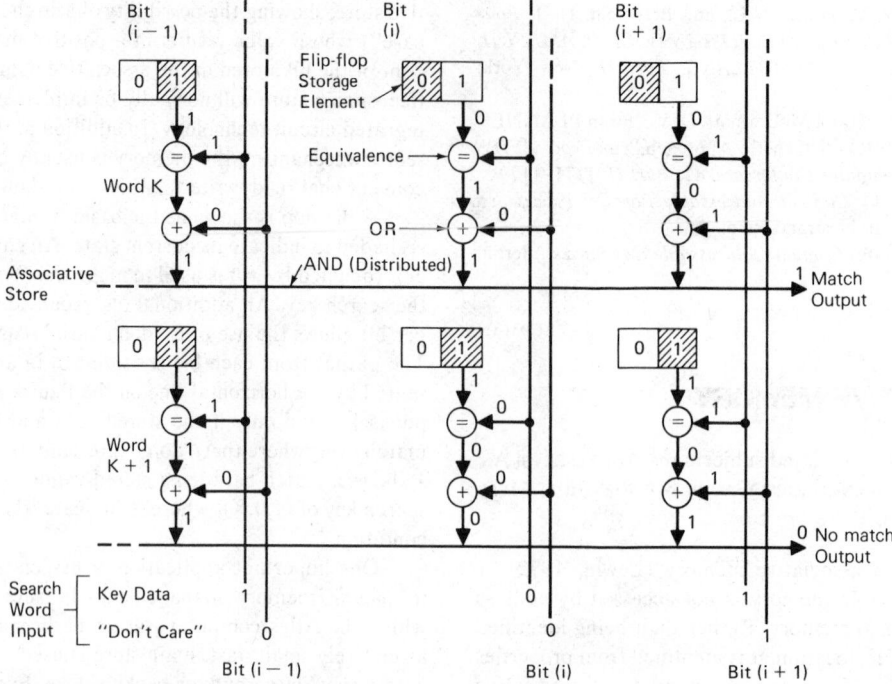

Fig. 1. Schematic of an associative store of two words of three bits each being accessed by match on two bits and by "don't care" on one.

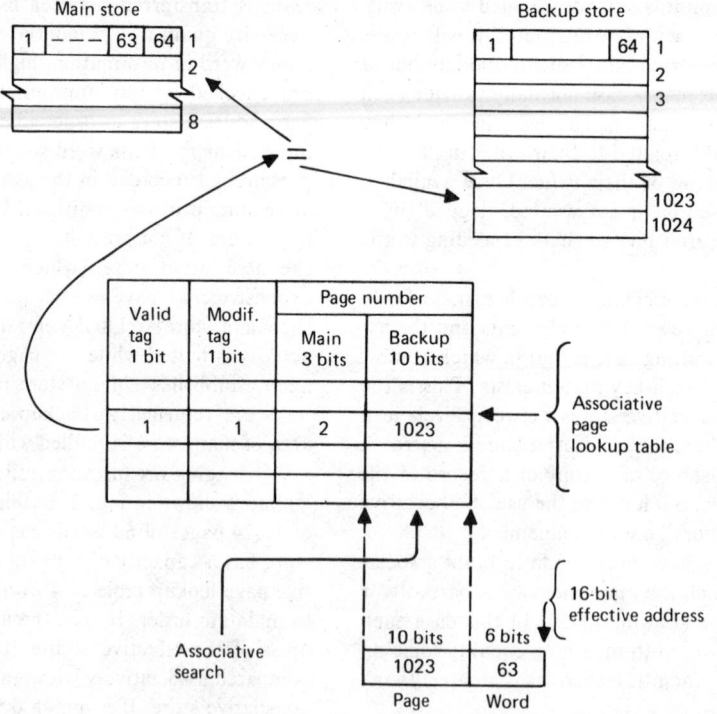

Fig. 2. A paging organization using an associative lookup table.

as well as two data integrity tags (1, 1). The valid tag indicates that the data in main store is a valid copy of that in backup store (i.e. that the backup store data has not been modified since the page was read into main store). The modified tag indicates that the data in main store has been modified by the CPU and is therefore not the same as in backup storage.

The result in the preceding example is that the word sought, number 63 from page 1023, is present at page 2, word 63 of the main store, that it is valid, and may differ from its image in backup store. Had the desired page not been in main store, one page of main store would have been selected for replacement, ideally one whose valid tag was zero, indicating it to be no longer needed. If all valid tags were 1, a page would be selected for replacement whose recent use is low (as established, for example, by automatic decrementing, at fixed time intervals, of a use counter associated with each page in the associative page-lookup table). This page, if its modified tag is 1, is stored in backup store and then replaced in main storage by the newly required page. The lookup table is modified accordingly to reflect a new backup page number for the corresponding main store page with validity tag 1, and modified tag 0.

REFERENCE

1972. Lewin, D. *Theory and Design of Digital Computers* . Camden, NJ: Thomas Nelson, Chapters 6 and 9.

K. C. SMITH AND A. S. SEDRA

ASYNCHRONOUS OPERATION. *see* SYN-CHRONOUS/ASYNCHRONOUS OPERATION.

ATANASOFF, JOHN VINCENT

For articles on related subjects *see* DIGITAL COM-PUTERS: Early; ECKERT, J. PRESPER; and MAUCHLY, JOHN W.

John Atanasoff (b. Hamilton, NY, 4 October 1903) received his B.S. at Florida State in 1925 and his M.S. at Iowa State in 1926.

Impeded by the cumbersome solving of large systems of equations and other complex calculations while working on his Ph.D. (Wisconsin, 1930, in math-physics), Atanasoff dismantled desk calculators in an attempt to adapt them and increase their computational capabilities. After receiving his doctorate, he returned to Iowa State

in 1930, where he remained until 1945 as a professor in mathematics and (later) in physics. During his tenure there, he revamped an IBM punched card machine in another attempt to speed tedious calculations for his graduate students.

Rejecting analog devices because they were too slow and not accurate enough, he concentrated on the digital approach. With the help of a graduate student, the late Clifford Berry, Atanasoff had built a prototype computer by December 1939. A working model of the Atanasoff-Berry computer was completed in 1942. It was a serial, binary, electromechanical machine, and employed various new techniques that Atanasoff had invented, including novel uses of logic circuitry and a regenerative memory.

Atanasoff did not understand completely the extent of the contribution he had made to the advancement of technology and did not anticipate the wide use of computers. IBM and Remington Rand rejected Atanasoff's overtures, and Iowa State—not fully realizing the poten-

Fig. 1.   John Vincent Atanasoff.

tial importance of his computer—failed to obtain patent rights. Discouraged by his own attempts to obtain a patent, Atanasoff gave up. He spent the rest of his professional career in various governmental and industrial jobs, including the presidency of two companies he founded, Ordnance Engineering Corporation and Cybernetics, Inc. For his work with the Naval Ordnance Laboratory during World War II, he received the U.S. Navy Distinguished Service Award in 1945.

Only very recently has Atanasoff achieved recognition as one of the fathers of the digital computer. In a patent infringement suit filed in 1973 by Sperry-Rand against Honeywell, there was testimony by Atanasoff and others concerning the development of the first electronic computer, the ENIAC (*q.v.*), by John Mauchly and J. Presper Eckert of the Moore School of Electrical Engineering at the University of Pennsylvania between 1942 and 1946. The decision in this case by Federal District Judge Earl R. Larson concluded that Eckert and Mauchly had derived some of their ideas from Atanasoff, partly as a result of a visit Mauchly made to Atanasoff at Iowa State in 1941.

G. G. MOLLENHOFF

ATLAS

For article on related subject *see* DIGITAL COMPUTERS: Contemporary and Future.

The Atlas computer was the third in a series of early computers designed in the United Kingdom by a team under T. M. Kilburn in the Department of Electrical Engineering, University of Manchester, in association with Ferranti Ltd. (later ICT Ltd.). Previous systems were the Ferranti Mark I and Ferranti Mark II (Mercury).

Design of Atlas began in 1958, and ultimately three systems, known as Atlas 1, were constructed and installed at the University of Manchester (1962), University of London (1963), and the Atlas Laboratory, Chilton (1963). All were operated until the early 1970s with the Chilton machine being the last to be switched off in March, 1973.

In many respects, Atlas led the way in design of an integrated computer system, combining many novel hardware features with an advanced software operating system. Among the new concepts that Atlas successfully introduced to the computer world were multiprogramming, one-level store, and paging. It was the first major system designed for multiprogramming and was provided with a composite memory, consisting of ferrite cores and mag-

netic drums linked by program to provide the user with a one-level store. This was achieved by a paging system in which page switching was controlled by a simple learning program, or swapping algorithm. There was also a wire-mesh/ferrite rod (hairbrush) memory of 8,000 words to hold the supervisor. The standard word length was 48 bits, equivalent to one single-adress instruction with two modifiers and allowing for up to 2^{20} addresses; 128 index registers were provided. Instructions were normally executed at an average rate of 0.5 ms, about a hundred times faster than the Mercury computer.

The magnetic tape system used 1-in. tapes, although standard 0.5-in. tapes could also be used. Magnetic disks were not standard, but were fitted later to the Manchester and Chilton machines. Multiple I/O channels provided for both paper-tape and punched-card peripherals as well as line printers.

Other features of the supervisor program, which was produced by a small team under D. J. Howarth (1961–1962) were the facilities for scheduling and streaming of jobs, automatic control of peripherals, detailed job accounting, and a sophisticated level of operator control. It was normal, wth some discretion in selecting the job mix, to obtain 60–80% effective use of the CPU.

A modified version of Atlas, known as Atlas 2, was produced with increased core memory and no magnetic drums (thereby dispensing with paging), the prototype being the Titan computer at the University of Cambridge, which was taken out of service at the end of 1973. Two others in this series were installed: one at the Atomic Weapons Research Establishment, Aldermaston, and one at the Computer-Aided Design Centre, Cambridge.

Although technical and economic reasons, partly due to advances in component manufacture, prevented the Atlas computers from achieving commercial success, they represent an important landmark in the development of advanced computer systems.

REFERENCES

1961–1962. Howarth, D. J., Payne, R. B., and Summer, F. H. "The Manchester University Atlas Operating System; Part II, Users' Description," *Computer J.* **4:** 226–229.

1962. Howarth, D. J., Jones, P. D., and Wyld, M. T. "The Atlas Scheduling System," *Computer J.* **5:** 238–244.

1961–1962. Kilburn, T., Howarth, D. J., Payne, R. B., and Summer, F. H. "The Manchester University Atlas Operating System; Part I, Internal Organisation," *Computer J.* **4:** 222–225.

1962. Kilburn, T. D., Edwards, B. G., Lanigan, M. J., and Summer, F. H. "One-Level Storage System," *IRE Trans.*, **EC-11, 2:** 223–235.

R. A. BUCKINGHAM

AUDIO TERMINALS

For articles on related subjects *see* DATA COMMUNICATIONS; INPUT/OUTPUT DEVICES; and TERMINALS.

Audio terminals are computer peripherals which accept voice input commands and/or respond in the form of a simulated or recorded spoken reply.

Audio Response Units. Basically, there are two techniques which allow a computer to generate a "spoken" reply. The first is to synthesize human speech by the generation of signals and frequencies similar to those produced in speech. This technique is used in the Voice Synthesizer for the Radio Shack TRS-80 microcomputer (see Fig. 1). The programming of spoken words is done by typing on the input keyboard of the TRS-80 representations of some 60 *phonemes* which, in turn, represent spoken sounds.

The other technique is based upon the storage in computer memory or on magnetic disk of words spoken

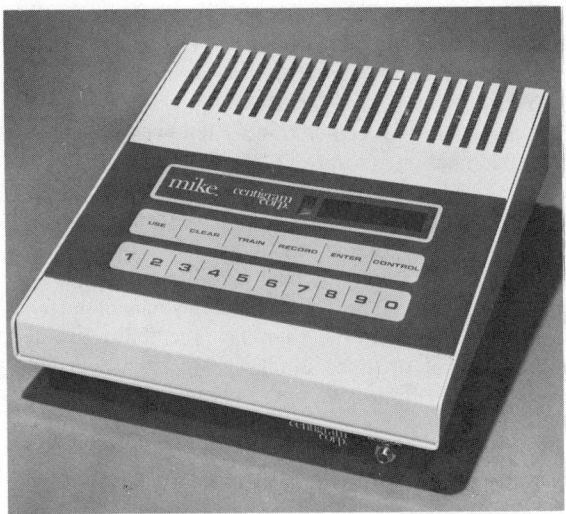

Fig. 2. Photo of MIKE, Centigram's voice recognition and response system.

by humans, similar to voice recording using home tape recorders. In this case, the audio response unit is able to select among a number of prerecorded words or phrases in order to construct a meaningful sentence or message. The MIKE Voice Recognition and Response System developed by Centigram Corp. (see Fig. 2) uses this technique. With this unit, groups of words (vocabularies) may be prerecorded as separate eight-second messages and then stored in an attached host computer. Under computer control, relevant vocabularies can be loaded into the MIKE as required. Thus, meaningful response vocabularies can be dynamically loaded by the computer for specific applications.

Voice Recognition. Voice recognition equipment is a recent development which can be expected to progress rapidly. An example of recently available commercial equipment is the MIKE (see Fig. 2), which is capable of recognizing individual words or short phrases. MIKE "learns" its recognition vocabulary by having each operator prerecord a vocabulary. Many recognition vocabularies can be learned, stored in the attached host computer, and then loaded into MIKE for recognition of the relevant user's spoken commands, which may be used to control the host computer or other on-line equipment.

A different recognition vocabulary can also be taught to MIKE for each application it serves. Typical vocabularies may consist of words such as *left, right, start, stop, open, close, raise, lower,* or *test* or the digits *zero* through *nine* and *cancel, erase, proceed, yes,* and *no.*

A voice recognition unit, the Voxbox, is also available with the TRS-80 microcomputer (see Fig. 1).

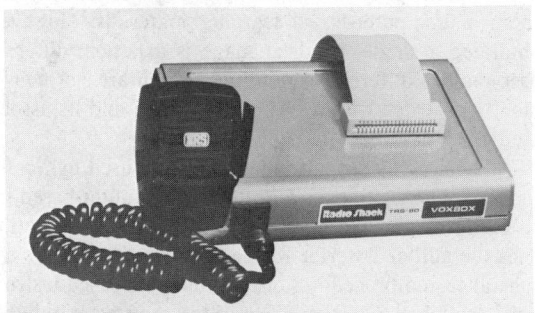

Fig. 1. Voice synthesizer (top) and Voxbox available with Radio Shack TRS-80 microcomputer. Courtesy of Radio Shack, a division of Tandy Corp.

The Touch Tone Telephone as an Audio Input Terminal. The Touch Tone telephone (Fig. 3), which uses buttons rather than a dial, is now in wide use. The depression of a particular button creates an audio frequency tone that can be transmitted over a telephone line. Each button generates a specific tone, so that each tone can be interpreted as a particular number.

As a computer input device, Touch Tone telephones are very economical and readily available, but they are generally limited only to numeric information, plus one or two other special keys or buttons; the general-purpose Touch Tone telephone does not have the ability to enter alphabetic information. Similarly, the only medium available for output is an audio response in the human speech frequency range.

Portable Audio Terminals. Portable Audio Terminals provide a full typewriter keyboard with alphabetic, numeric, and special character keys. These terminals are attached to a normal telephone handset, using an acoustic coupler, by placing the handset in a receptacle in the terminal. Thus, signals generated by the keyboard can be transmitted through the mouthpiece of the telephone to the computer, and a spoken reply from an audio response terminal can be received through the telephone receiver and amplified by the terminal if necessary.

Voice Recognition and Response Applications. The availability of voice recognition and voice response units, together with portable audio terminals, opens up a vast array of computer applications.

Fig. 3. Touch-Tone telephone, which may be used as an audio response terminal for numeric input.

With radio transmission, voice recognition and response systems can be used in emergency vehicles by police, ambulance, and fire brigade services for direct access to computer databases.

In manufacturing operations where a person's hands are required for other activities, voice recognition and response can be used for entry of specific data.

Using Touch Tone telephones and voice recognition, salespersons in the field can telephone a warehouse computer, place an order directly with a computer through spoken commands, and receive a spoken response indicating acceptance of that order by the computer. Within the warehouse, radio microphones and headsets allow warehouse personnel to enter inventory data orally while moving through the warehouse.

Voice commands will enable handicapped persons to control wheelchairs, or intensive care patients to control hospital beds, television sets and so on. Doctors and dentists whose hands are occupied can control automatic equipment, lights, and powered instruments. Nurses and technicians can query computer databases for records of prescriptions, past history, and so on.

C. B. FINKELSTEIN

AUTHORING LANGUAGES AND SYSTEMS

For articles on related subjects *see* COMPUTER-ASSISTED INSTRUCTION; COMPUTER-ASSISTED LEARNING AND TEACHING; COMPUTER-MANAGED INSTRUCTION; and PROGRAMMING LANGUAGES.

Considerable attention has been given to providing a convenient programming language for the use of authors of computer-based learning materials. However, obtaining a single, ideal language is a fiction; different uses require different capabilities, which are not conveniently provided within a single language and its associated processor.

The specific programming language used by an author is not so significant for effective computer-based instruction as are two other factors. With what notation does the author describe for personal use and others the substance and procedures of the computer-based instruction? By what means are these ideas and notes reliably transcribed into an executing computer program?

One concept of authoring languages and systems is represented in Fig. 1. The designer of material assembles information and opinion about what is needed, working with students and others who should know of the prob-

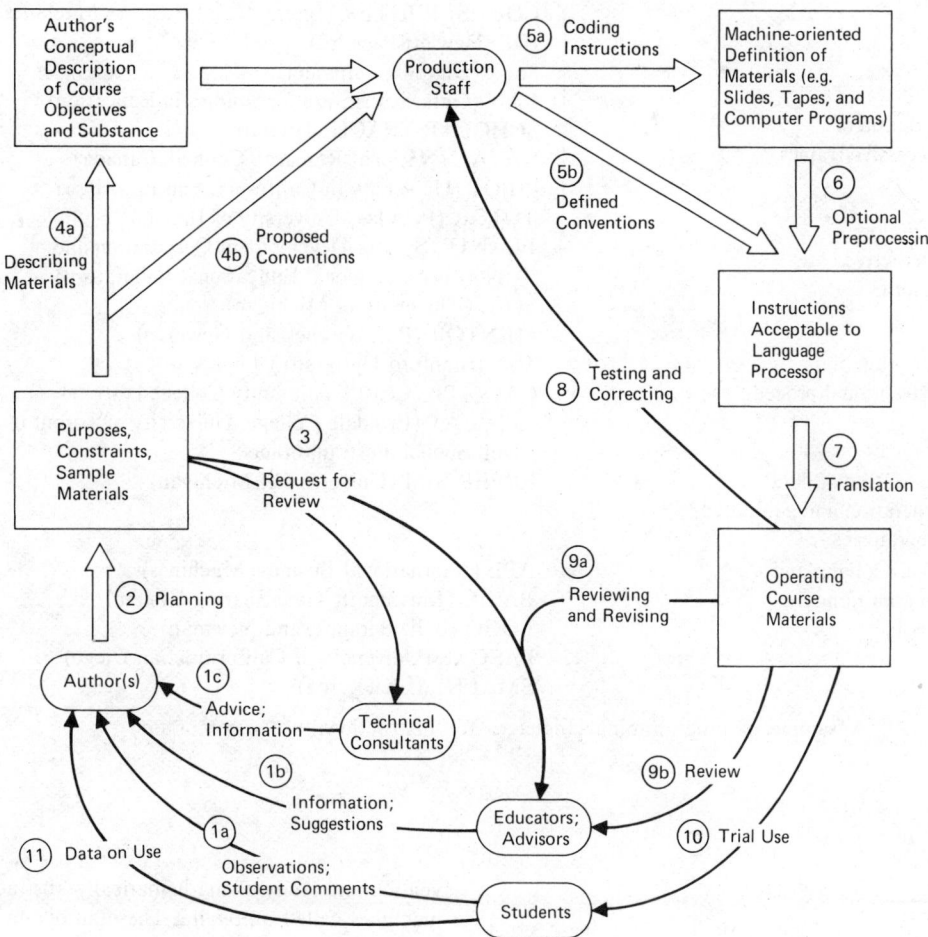

Fig. 1.   One representation of authoring activity.

lems and resources (steps 1 through 3). The designer may work with a language or notation devised especially for the topic and objectives (step 4), delegating to the machine or technical assistants the determination of minor details (step 5). Separation of the content of instruction from the description of program logic makes curriculum development less costly.

After a program is executing, the originator should receive complete and useful information about the performance and reaction of students (steps 9 through 11). Many developers continue to test and revise instruction-related computer programs over a long period of time.

Over 100 different languages and dialects have been put to use specifically for programming instructional use of computers. A select set are diagrammed in Fig. 2 to represent different approaches and uses: successive frames (computerization of programmed instruction); de-

scription of interactive case histories; description of instructional procedures; specification of data generation and simulated laboratories; problem solving and programming. Information about these and many other languages can be obtained from secondary sources (Bode and Dutting, 1974).

A sample of program code for an interactive "case history" is given in Fig. 3. The annotations in the right column point out the means by which the author specifies contingencies conveniently in the interaction between user and program. The example is adapted from a Mystery problem programmed in the Mentor language; both were developed at Bolt, Beranek, and Newman.

A language is efficient when it is used for the specific purpose for which it was designed to be convenient. The great diversity of instructional uses of computers requires a variety of languages.

Description of successive frames	⎧ COURSEWRITER (International Business Machines) IDF (Hewlett-Packard) Focal (Digital Equipment) CAN (Ontario Institute for Studies in Education) SCHOLAR-TEACH (Digital) NATAL (National Research Council, Canada)
Description of interactive case histories	PILOT (University of California, San Francisco) TUTOR (PLATO, University of Illinois) PLANIT (System Development Corporation and Northwest Regional Educational Laboratory) FOIL (University of Michigan) MENTOR (Bolt Beranek and Newman)
Description of instructional procedures	TSA (Stanford University) CAL/APL (Coast Community College District) APL/CAT (Erindale College, University of Toronto) Algol, Snobol, Fortran, others
Specification of data generation and simulated laboratories	EXPER SIM (University of Michigan)
Problem solving and programming (on-line)	APL (International Business Machines) BASIC (Dartmouth Time-Sharing System) LOGO (Bolt, Beranek, and Newman) PASCAL (University of California, San Diego) SMALLTALK (Xerox)

Fig. 2. A sample of programming languages for instructional use of computers.

REFERENCES

1974. Bode, Arndt, and Dutting, Martin. "Computer-Assisted Instruction: Problems, Languages, Systems, and Documentation" (translated from the German and edited by Karl L. Zinn). Ann Arbor: EXTEND Publications.

1978. Zinn, Karl L. and Bork, Alfred. "Aspects of Effective Authoring Systems and Assistance: Recommendations for Research and Development." Alexandria, VA: U.S. Army Research Institute for the Behavioral and Social Sciences.

K. L. ZINN

AUTOMATA. *See* CELLULAR AUTOMATA; and PROBABILISTIC AUTOMATA.

AUTOMATA THEORY

For articles on related subjects *see* ALGORITHM; CELLULAR AUTOMATA; FORMAL LANGUAGES; PERCEPTRON; PROBABILISTIC AUTOMATA; SEQUENTIAL MACHINES; and TURING MACHINE.

Introduction and Definitions. Automata theory is a mathematical discipline concerned with the invention and study of mathematically abstract, idealized machines called *automata*. These automata are usually abstractions of information processing devices, such as computers, rather than of devices that move about, such as mechanical toys or automobiles.

This article gives a short and informal survey of the major classes of automata that automata theorists have heretofore seen fit to study, and indicates the primary respective motivations (from the point of view of computer science) for the study of these classes of automata.

For the most part, the automata discussed here process strings of symbols from some finite alphabet of symbols. Let A be any alphabet (finite set of symbols). For example, A might be $\{a,b,c, \ldots ,z\}$ or $\{0,1\}$. We write A^* to mean the set of *all* finite strings of symbols chosen from A. If A is $\{a,b,c, \ldots ,z\}$, then A^* contains strings representing English words, such as "cat" and "mouse," along with nonsense strings such as "czzxyh". If A is $\{0,1\}$, then A^* contains the strings representing the nonnegative integers in binary notation $(0,1,10,11,100, \ldots)$ and also these same strings but with extra zeros on the left (e.g., 00010).

Automata generally perform one (or both) of two symbol-processing tasks. They compute partial functions

Program Statements	Description of Directive
GENERAL: "Proceed with investigation."	[type out message within quotation marks for the student to read: "GENERAL" labels this block of the program]
ACCEPT	[accept directive from student and execute statements which are indented below]
IF /suspects/ (REPORT 1)	[if the student mentioned "suspects" execute (1) or (2) indented below]
1) "Wife, brother and partner."	[first time, type message marked (1)]
2) "No new suspects."	[all other times, type message marked (2) and return to ACCEPT]
IF /lab, rifle, glass, pipe/	[if mentioned any of these, execute the following]
IF ALL REPORTS, GO TO LAB	[only if has requested all reports, defined elsewhere, process request for a laboratory test]
"I advise you to check reports first."	[if has not requested all reports, advise accordingly and return]
IF /interrogate/	
IF ALL LAB, GO TO INTERR	[if all lab tests have been requested, process request for interrogation]
"I advise you request lab tests first."	[otherwise, advise . . .]
. . .	[check for other requests]
. . .	
"I don't understand."	[if nothing is recognized in directive let student know and wait for another directive]
LAB "This is the lab."	
IF/glass/ (GLASS)	[if mentioned the "glass" set GLASS switch]
IF WIFE	[and if has already interrogated his wife]
"Glass contained arsenic."	[type damaging evidence]
1) "Prints belong to the wife."	[otherwise type (1) the first time]
2) "Nothing new."	[type (2) all other times]
. . .	[check for other lab tests requested]
. . .	
"What is it you want?"	[if no lab test request is recognized, type query]
ACCEPT	[accept directive]
TO LAB + 1	[go back to process a second directive relating to the lab]

Fig. 3. Sample of a notation suited for exercises in information gathering and diagnosis (interactive case histories). A sample conversation of this program is given on p. 293.

from X^* to Y^* for some finite alphabets X and Y or they *recognize* languages over some alphabet X.

A *partial function* from X^* to Y^* is a correspondence between some subset of X^* and the set Y^* that associates with each element of the subset of X^* a unique element in Y^*. For example, let $X = Y = \{0,1\}$ and let the subset of X^* be the elements x of X^* such that x begins with 1 or consists of a single 0. If f associates with x the string in Y^* that denotes the binary number rep-

resenting two times the binary number represented by x, then f is a partial function from X^* to Y^*.

We say roughly that an automaton α *computes* a partial function f from X^* to Y^* when, if α is given any input x in X^* such that $f(x)$ is defined, α eventually produces an output $y \in Y^*$ such that $f(x) = y$, and, otherwise, α produces no output. Automata usually receive their inputs on a linear or one-dimensional tape, which they are capable of reading one symbol at a time. The manner in which they read symbols on an input tape (left to right, back and forth, with or without changing symbols, etc.) depends on the particular class of automata under consideration. Automata for computing partial functions produce their output on a tape (perhaps the input tape, perhaps a different tape) in a manner also prescribed by the particular class of automata under consideration.

A *language* over an alphabet X is just a subset of X^*. For example, if $X = \{a,b,c, \ldots,z\}$, then $\{a,aa,aaa,..\}$ and $\{x \in X^* \mid x$ is a word in the English language$\}$ are both languages over X.

We say that an automaton α *recognizes* a language L over X when α reads an input $x \in X^*$ on its input tape in the manner of automata of its type; then, if $x \in L$, α eventually performs some particular act of recognition such as halting, emptying a particular auxiliary tape, or getting into some special internal state; whereas, if $x \notin L$, α never performs such an act of recognition. Exactly what constitutes an act of recognition depends on the particular class of automata under consideration.

It is presumably clear why it is of interest to computer scientists to study automata that compute (partial) functions, since computer science is the computation business. Among the interesting questions to ask are whether some function is or is not computable by some representative of a particular class of automata and, if it is computable, how efficiently (with respect to some mathematically precise measure of efficiency) can it be so computed.

We motivate the study of automata that recognize languages by some examples. Let X be the set of allowable symbols for some programming language P. Include in X the necessary punctuation symbols and the blank symbol. Let $L = \{x \in X^* \mid x$ is a valid program of $P\}$. In the process of compiling from P into some other language, it is useful to (among other things) *recognize* the valid programs of P as being valid. Automata theory gives some insight into the sort of computing ability that may be required to recognize valid programs. For example, *pushdown automata* (to be defined below) are capable of recognizing the valid syntactic classes of all (and only) Algol-like languages. Generally, there are many results of the form: The languages recognized by a particular class of automata are exactly those formal languages generated by a particular class of grammars.

Automatic theorem proving (*q.v.*), a subarea of artificial intelligence (*q.v.*), is also concerned with language recognition. The language to be recognized is the set of propositions derivable from some set of axioms. Automatic theorem proving has been applied to discover new mathematical theorems, to question-answering systems, and to robotics (*q.v.*).

Types of Automata.

Most (but not all) types of automata are special cases of the Turing machine (see Fig. 1). Turing machines may be operated either to recognize or to compute partial functions. Very roughly, a Turing machine is a finite-state deterministic device with read and/or write heads (which read and/or write one symbol at a time) attached to one or more tapes. *Finite state* means that the number of distinguishable internal configurations of the device is finite, and "deterministic" means that the next state of the device and its subsequent action (writing or motion) on the tapes is completely determined by its current state and the symbols it is currently reading on its tapes.

Turing machines were first introduced independently by Turing and Post in 1936 to give a precise mathematical definition of *effective procedure*. There is considerable evidence that the partial functions computed by (languages recognized by) Turing machines are exactly those computed (recognized) by informal effective procedures or algorithms. Any computation or recognition problem for which there is a known informal algorithm can be handled by a Turing machine. Turing machines with many (in general, *n*-dimensional) tapes and read/write heads can compute and recognize *no more* than can Turing machines with a single one-dimensional tape and single read/write head, although they may compute and recognize more efficiently.

Attempts to define effective procedures in terms of automata more closely resembling modern electronic stored-program digital computers have led to the unlimited register machines of Shepherdson and Sturgis and to

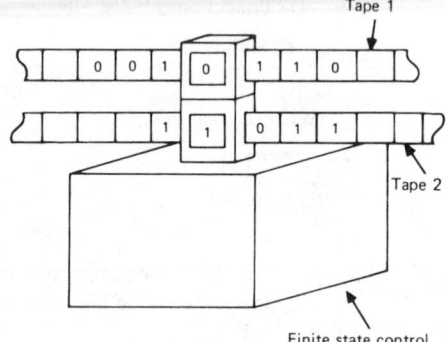

Fig. 1. A two-tape Turing machine. Each tape is scanned by a single read/white head. Tape 1 contains the string of nonblank symbols 0010110, with the underlined 0 currently being read. Tape 2 contains 11011, with the underlined 1 being currently read. If the tapes can move only in one direction, the same diagram would depict a two-tape automaton.

the *random-access* stored-program machines of Elgot and Robinson. These machines can be shown to compute the same partial functions (recognize the same languages) computed by Turing machines.

Turing machines model the most general sort of computation processes, in part by virtue of their ability to move about freely on their tapes without fear of running out of tape. In general no a priori bound can be set on the amount of tape a Turing machine computation will require. Some Turing machine computations may require more tape than is available in the universe! This, in part, motivates our consideration of the next class of automata, finite automata. We will limit our discussion to finite automata considered as recognizers of languages, and will leave their application as input/output devices to the article on Sequential Machines.

A *finite automaton* is a deterministic finite-state device equipped with a read (only) head attached to a single input tape. A special subset of the finite set of states of a finite automaton is designated as the set of *final*, or *recognition*, states. A finite automaton α processes a string of symbols thus: α begins in a special initial, or start, state and automatically reads the symbols of x (on its tape) from left to right, changing its states in a manner depending only on its previous state and the symbol just read. If, after the last (rightmost) symbol of x is read, α goes into a final state, α recognizes x; otherwise, α does not recognize x. Let $A = \{0,1\}$. It is possible, for example, to design a finite automaton α such that α recognizes $L = \{x \epsilon A^* | x$ ends in two consecutive 1s and does not contain two consecutive 0s$\}$. See Fig. 2. On the other hand, it can be shown that *no* finite automaton can recognize $L' = \{x \epsilon A^* | x$ consists of a consecutive string of n-squared 1s for some positive integer $n\}$. As might be expected, however, a Turing machine can be designated to recognize L'.

In Fig. 2 the circles represent the different states of α_0 and the number inside each circle is a name for the state that circle represents. Hence, 0 is the start state of α_0 and 4 is its only final state. An arrow (labeled with an alphabet symbol) from one state to another means that if α_0 is in the first state while scanning the alphabet symbol that labels the arrow, then it goes next into the second state. For example, if α_0 is in state 1 scanning a 0, it goes next into state 2; whereas, if it is in state 1 scanning a 1, it goes next into state 3. If α_0 is given the input string 010111, beginning in state 0, the successive states into which it is thereafter driven are (in order) 1,3,1,3,4,4. Since 4 is a final state, α_0 (correctly) recognizes the input string 010111. If α_0 is given 10011, beginning in state 0, the successive states into which it is thereafter driven are (in order) 3,1,2,2,2. Since 2 is *not* a final state, α_0 (correctly) fails to recognize 10011.

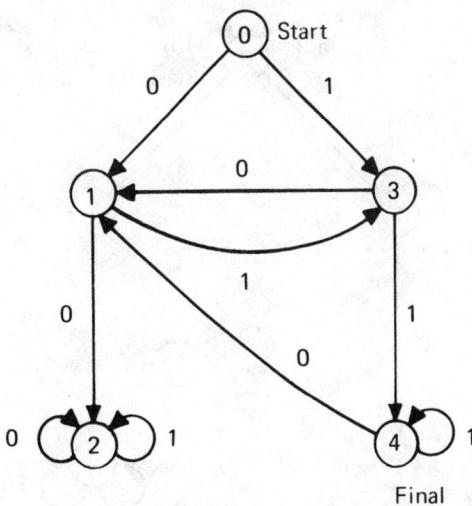

Fig. 2. The state diagram of a finite-state automaton for recognizing $\{\chi \epsilon \{0,1\} * | \chi$ ends in two consecutive 1s and does not contain two consecutive 0s$\}$.

A *nondeterministic finite automaton* is a device just like a finite automaton except that the next state is not completely determined by the current state and symbol read. Instead, a set of next *possible* states is so determined. A nondeterministic finite automaton α may be thought of as processing a string of symbols x, just like an ordinary finite automaton except that it has to be run over again several times so that each of the different possible state-change behaviors is eventually realized. One should imagine there being a separate, deterministic control device C which runs α and completely determines α's *actual* state-change behavior each time it is run. There are but finitely many different possible state-change behaviors for α processing x, and C simply systematically runs α first one way, then another, then another, etc., until all possibilities have been exhausted.

A nondeterministic finite automaton α *recognizes x* just in case at least one of the possible ways of running α on input x results in getting α into a final state after the last symbol of x has been read (see Fig. 3).

In Fig. 3, α_1 is nondeterministic because (for example, from state 0, if it is scanning a) it can go into either state 0 or state 1 next. From state 1, if it is scanning b, it "jams," since the set of next possible states is empty. If α_1 is given the input string *abababba*, beginning in state 0, one possible succession of states is (in order) 0,0,0,0,-0,0,0,1. Here, 1 is not one of the final states, so this way of running α_1 does not lead to recognition. Another possible succession of states is (in order) 0,0,0,1, jam. An-

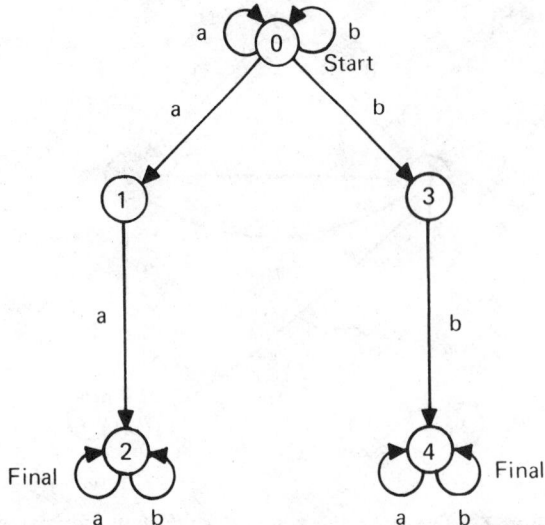

Fig. 3.   The state diagram of a nondeterministic finite-state automaton α_1 for recognizing $\{\chi \,\epsilon\, \{a,b\} * \mid \chi$ contains two consecutive a's or two consecutive b's (or both)$\}$.

other is 1, jam. However, 0,0,0,0,0,3,4,4 is still another possible succession of states. Since 4 *is* a final state, α_1 (correctly) recognizes *ababbaba*. It is easy to check that, if α_1 is given *babababab*, beginning in state 0, then *none* of the possible ways of running α_1 leads to a final state; hence, α_1 (correctly) does *not* recognize *babababab*.

Interestingly (and perhaps unexpectedly), it can be shown that nondeterministic finite automata recognize exactly tbe same class of languages as ordinary finite automata. Turing machine recognizers that operate nondeterministically can also be defined, but they cannot recognize more languages than can ordinary Turing machines. For nondeterministic Turing machine recognizers, as well as for some of the other nondeterministic devices to be discussed below, some of the different possible ways to process a given string x may take infinitely many steps. For such devices it is convenient to imagine the separate, deterministic control device C as operating in a parallel mode.

The point of nondeterminism is that it often is conceptually easier to program or design machines that operate nondeterministically. In fact, there are theoretical results to the effect that, for many types of automata, nondeterministic machines are significantly more compact than the corresponding deterministic ones. Furthermore, many practically important recognition tasks can be solved by easy-to-design nondeterministic Turing machines that run in time bounded by a polynomial in the size of their input strings. A famous open question in computer science asks if these tasks can be done at all in polynomial time by deterministic Turing machines.

In addition to ordinary and nondeterministic automata, a variety of automata called *probabilistic* automata have been studied. A probability of occurrence is assigned to each of the possible next states in a probabilistic automaton.

In 1943, McCulloch and Pitts introduced nets of formalized neurons and showed (in essence) that such neural nets could realize the state-change behavior of any finite automaton. These nets were composed of synchronized elements, each capable of realizing some boolean function such as *and, or,* or *not*. It has been suggested that von Neumann had these networks in mind when he established his logical design for digital computers. In 1948, von Neumann added to the computational and logical questions of automata theory by introducing new questions pertaining to construction and self-replication of automata. The iterated arrays of interconnected finite automata which he introduced have also been used to study pattern processing for patterns of symbols, including (but not restricted to) one-dimensional strings of symbols.

Automata theory, especially finite automata theory, impinges on both mathematical systems theory and modern algebra. In mathematical systems theory, one is interested in the problem of which, (if any) input sequences will drive an automaton to some desired internal state. In modern algebra one can study the relations between semigroups and automata. For example, certain decomposition theorems in group theory give information about decomposition of automata into particularly simple component automata.

A *linear-bounded automaton* is a nondeterministic, one-tape Turing machine whose read/write head is restricted to move only on the section of tape initially containing the input. Special end markers are placed on each side of an input string to prevent the tape head from leaving this restricted section of tape. A form of deterministic linear-bounded automaton was first studied by Myhill in an attempt to find models of computation more realistic than the completely general Turing machines, but less restricted than the finite automata. Later it was shown that linear-bounded automata recognize all (and only) the *context-sensitive* languages, an important and natural class of languages more restricted than the languages recognizable by Turing machines but more general than the *context-free* languages. It is an open question whether the linear-bounded automata can recognize more languages than the deterministic linear-bounded automata.

A *pushdown* automaton is a nondeterministic finite automaton with a special sort of auxiliary tape called a *pushdown store*. A pushdown store is a tape quite like the stack of plates found on a spring in cafeterias. It is a

"Last In-First Out" store. A special read/write head always scans the top symbol on the pushdown store. The pushdown store is initially loaded with a single special *start* symbol. The top symbol can be replaced by any finite string of symbols (stack of plates), including the empty string of symbols. Replacing the top symbol by the empty string has the effect of completely removing the top symbol and setting the read/write head to scan the next symbol down. The read (only) head on the input tape reads one symbol at a time from left to right, just as in a finite automaton, except that it is allowed (if desired) to stop scanning the input tape momentarily while only the pushdown store is operated.

Pushdown automata recognize a string x by one of two conventions. Either x is recognized by the device as it gets into one of its final states or by the pushdown store as it empties just after the rightmost symbol of x is read. The class of languages recognized by emptying the pushdown store is the same as that recognized by final states. Let $A = \{0,1\}$. For $x \epsilon A^*$, let x^R be x written backwards. For example, 001110^R is 011100. Then a language consisting of *palindromes* (strings which read the same forward and backward) $L = \{x \epsilon A^* | x$ is of the form w followed by w^R for some $w \epsilon A^*\}$ is recognizable by a suitable pushdown automaton; however, L is *not* recognizable by any finite automaton or even by any deterministic pushdown automaton. Pushdown automata recognize all (and only) the context-free (or equivalently, Algol-like) languages.

Many variations on a slight generalization of pushdown automata have been studied. A *stack* (*q.v.*) automaton is just like a pushdown automaton except that the read (only) head of the input tape is allowed to move both ways (but not off the section of tape containing the input) and the read/write head on the pushdown store is allowed to scan the entire pushdown list in a *read only* mode. The class of languages recognized by stack automata is intermediate between context-sensitive and Turing-machine recognizable.

Many other types of automata that have been and could be studied employ some other sort of limited data structure for their auxiliary storage or receive inputs in some form other than a string of symbols. For example, *tree* automata process inputs in the form of trees, usually trees associated with parsing expressions in context-free languages.

It should be remarked at the conclusion of this survey that automata theory is a growing, open-ended mathematical discipline. It readily admits of extensions of existing concepts and the introduction of totally new ideas. The motivations to make such extensions are esthetic on the one hand, and the need or desire to model some existing or proposed computational phenomenon on the other.

REFERENCES

1966. Von Neumann, J. *Theory of Self-Reproducing Automata* (edited and completed by A. W. Burks). Urbana: University of Illinois Press.

1967. Minsky, M. *Computation: Finite and Infinite Machines.* Englewood Cliffs, NJ: Prentice-Hall.

1969. Arbib, M. A. *Theories of Abstract Automata.* Englewood Cliffs, NJ: Prentice-Hall.

1969. Hopcroft, J. E. and Ullman, J. D. *Formal Languages and Their Relation to Automata.* Reading, MA: Addison-Wesley.

1969. Minsky, M. and Papert, S. *Perceptrons.* Cambridge, MA: M.I.T. Press.

1973. Bobrow, L. S. and Arbib, M. A. *Discrete Mathematics: Applied Algebra for Computer and Information Science.* Philadelphia: W. B. Saunders.

1973. Engeler, E. *Introduction to the Theory of Computation.* New York: Academic Press.

J. CASE

AUTOMATION

For articles on related subjects *see* COMMUNICATIONS AND COMPUTERS; COMPUTER-AIDED DESIGN; COMPUTER GRAPHICS; COMPUTER NETWORKS; COMPUTERS AND SOCIETY; CONTROL APPLICATIONS; DIGITAL COMPUTERS; ROBOTICS; and TIME SHARING.

Automation, in its strictest sense, implies the use of any technique to make a system or process more automatic—i.e., more self-acting and self-regulating and, hence, less dependent on human intervention for proper operation. Recently, however, the word has come to be associated with the use of computers to attain these functions. Thus, we tend to use the word "computerization" as a synonym for automation and to think in terms of the application of computers not only for the handling of information associated with a process, but also for the actual control and actuation of mechanisms that facilitate or completely accomplish that process with minimal human guidance.

It is this minimization of the human element that gives the concept of automation its negative overtones. People fear the image of factories, offices, wars—indeed, even whole societies—"run by computers." There is concern that the use of computers for management and operational functions will somehow get out of control and we will become victims of our own technological progress. (When one contemplates the use of sophisticated computer-aided design systems, computer-controlled robots, computer-driven testing equipment, etc. being used for the high-volume manufacture of yet more computers, this concern becomes more understandable.) Those involved with development of advanced automation techniques assure us that computers will always remain merely machines or tools for use by human beings, who always control their ultimate use. Certainly, the fact that work in artificial intelligence has not progressed as rapidly as anticipated by some (after the laboratory experiments in chess or other game-playing activities in the early 1960s) gives some credence to this assurance. Although optical character recognition, limited pattern recognition, and even voice or speech recognition is now feasible for certain classes of computer applications, we have really not seen the inclusion of computers into areas that are considered uniquely human, or which threaten the dominance of human control over automation techniques.

Elsewhere in this volume there are articles on various applications of computers to functions once carried out exclusively by humans, but now facilitated or augmented, to varying degrees, by intelligent electronic devices—i.e., computers.* In this article, we discuss the application of computers to the automation of the most directly productive of human activities—the planning, design, engineering, production, and testing of manufactured products. It is this usage of the term automation which is the most common.

Definition of Terms. The automation area, particularly as applied to design and manufacturing applications, has always suffered from a lack of clear definition, leading to considerable misunderstanding about what types of products and vendors are part of the business, what applications are included within its scope, what user industries are appropriate market segments, and, ultimately, what the size of the business and the state-of-the-art of various segments really are. While there can probably never be a perfectly clear line bounding the industry, this structural description of the field would be accepted by most people as characteristic of the bulk of it.

Computer-Aided Design/Computer-Aided Manufacturing (CAD/CAM) activities can be distinguished from the much broader universe of "technical computing" by limiting the definition to the following: *The direct application of specialized computer hardware or software to product and manufacturing engineering and manufacturing operations.* Excluded from this definition is the general application of general-purpose computers to research, analytic, and other technical problem-solving situations using Fortran, APL, or related scientifically-oriented programming languages. When specialized software packages are created using such general-purpose languages and computing power, however, they

---

*Office automation, library automation, computer art, computer music, etc.

would be included in this category of automation applications.

Further, CAD/CAM is distinguished from administrative data processing applications relating to manufacturing or engineering by emphasizing the engineering or technical computing orientation of the work over the sheer file-handling and record-processing orientation of the more conventional EDP universe. Normally excluded, for example, are manufacturing data processing applications such as production control, inventory control, labor distribution, cost accounting, and the like (even though some of these may be handled with applications packages, which somewhat confuses our definition).

To clarify this definition, listed below are a number of engineering functions and related specific examples of CAD/CAM systems.

FUNCTION	EXAMPLES
Design layout	Computer-aided drafting, printed circuit board layout.
Design analysis	Computer optimization, finite element analysis, piping interference checking.
Manufacturing engineering	Group technology, tool design, process planning.
Facilities engineering	Plant architecture and layout, equipment optimization.
Fabrication automation	Numerically controlled tools, process control systems.
Assembly automation	Robotics, computer-controlled transfer lines.
Materials handling	Stacker cranes, driverless tractor systems, automated storage and retrieval systems.
Industrial engineering	Shop floor data collection, labor standards calculations.
Quality assurance	Coordinate measuring machines, automated circuit test equipment.

More broadly, we could categorize engineering computing and manufacturing computing as each consisting of two main types.

- Engineering computing
  1. Design and analysis functions
  2. Engineering administration and information management functions

- Manufacturing computing
  1. Manufacturing operations functions (manufacturing engineering fabrication, assembly, inspection, etc.)
  2. Manufacturing control functions (scheduling, resource requirements planning, inventory control, etc.)

These broader classes of functions more accurately describe the total set of activities amenable to automation within the engineering/manufacturing environment, leading to the potential benefits of an integrated architecture of computing to be discussed later. Because of the potential organizational conflicts arising from the merging of engineering, manufacturing, and data processing responsibilities, however, they are frequently considered *too* broad and pervasive in their impact, hence the more narrowly defined term "CAD/CAM" is normally used.

Automation Concepts. Automation is based on computer technology which has made dramatic strides in the last two decades—both in application to virtually every segment of a modern industrialized culture and in cost/performance improvements enabling deep penetration into many of these application areas.

Over the years, engineering and manufacturing, no less than any other area of application, have been fertile fields for improvement through the application of computer technology. Design engineers, faced with problems requiring long iterative solutions and extensive data, have relied on computers to speed up solutions and analyze problems that could not have been solved before. Manufacturing engineers have used numerically controlled equipment to control machine tools, such as lathes and complex milling machines, in production of parts that heretofore required the advanced skills of machinists and toolmakers and were subject to annoying and expensive variations. Process manufacturing technology has benefited by minimizing the need for human surveillance and reaction in order to keep manufacturing processes within design tolerances and to correct for the inherent perturbations that occur. The use of data collection and accelerated data processing techniques in manufacturing have enabled tighter management control of the manufacturing enterprise and more rapid response to changes that inadvertently occur or may be required. Even plant design and facility layout have been optimized through computerized simulations and a variety of design aids. Virtually every segment of the production process, from product design and manufacturing, through sales, warehousing and distribution, has been touched by computer technology and rendered more efficient by its implementation.

Within each of the broad categories of design engineering, manufacturing engineering, and management systems, there is now a trend toward a growing interrelationship of systems. It has been noticed that programs and systems within any of those categories may have many common elements within their databases; may be related by similar input data and output data; or the output of one system may serve as a portion of the input to another system. The diminishing cost of computer power, the proliferation of software and the widespread introduction of affordable mini- and microcomputers has increased the number of sites within an organization for beneficial application of computers and data processing techniques. Thus, the pressure for an overall "architecture" of the computer systems within an organization has been increasing. The needs for commonality of language, compatibility of databases, and accessibility of information from "foreign" databases all become imperative for further progress. In short, the need for integration of the automation activities becomes more demanding with time.

Not only is an overall architecture required for the efficient automation of design engineering, manufacturing operations, and business management segments, but it is important to realize that such an integrated approach transcends the traditional boundaries within an industrial organization. For example, recent advances in the automation of the design phase of activity have enabled entire design layouts to be accomplished at a computer terminal, eliminating traditional distinctions between conceptual designers, detail designers, and draftsmen. Also, the boundaries are becoming indistinct between data processing, management information systems (MIS), and other such organizations devoted to business applications, and the engineering/manufacturing operations units which are employing computers for their functions.

Interactive graphic displays allow the designer to produce a "drawing" on a cathode ray tube (CRT) and store the design information in memory. Devices are available that can produce a quick hard copy of the displayed graphics and/or electromechanical pen and ink plotters can be used to produce accurate high-quality, full-scale layout. The development of a profusion of database software permits the storage and convenient access to information about standard components and subassemblies, in addition to the analytical and computation capability generally required in an engineering design. This entire approach to design, wherein an engineer/designer interacts with a computer using graphical input devices, various output systems, database information, and analytic computations, is the basis for *computer-aided design* (CAD).

In manufacturing, similar automation of data and control processes has occurred. Beyond the numerical control of individual machine tools and direct computer control of processes, there has been an explosion of available software which manipulates data on tool availability, materials requirements, flow of parts being manufactured, work-in-process inventory, finished goods inventory, etc. Different parts with similar geometric features and manufacturing characteristics have been classified and can be scheduled in manufacturing by software based on this categorization (group technology). The active control of processes and the timely collection and dissemination of production data have narrowed the response time required for the entire manufacturing operation to make decisions and cure production problems. The active involvement of the computer in the manufacturing processes and the control of production is the basis for *computer-aided manufacturing* (CAM).

Along with the consolidation of computer programs and systems within each of the design engineering, manufacturing, and management segments of an enterprise, integration is now occurring among these segments. Just as common database information is required internal to the various stages of manufacturing operation, there is a strong commonality in the data required by design, manufacturing, and management. For example, a bill of materials (or parts list), which is created in the design engineering phase of the production sequence, is a file of data that must be accessible to the manufacturing and management segments as well. The geometric dimensional and configurational data for a part that is created during the design stage is the essential information required by the programmer preparing the numerical control tapes that control the machine tools of the manufacturing operation.

This thrust toward integration is fostered by the efficient data storage and retrieval mechanisms made available by computer technology. The pressure to communicate and integrate has always been present, but until now communication has relied upon the active transfer of information by drawings, memoranda, or word of mouth. The avenue that has now been opened is the passive communication of any bit of information required by a particular segment immediately as it becomes available. Accessibility to a bill of materials can be as easy for management as for design engineering. Corrections to bills of materials suggested by manufacturing (or purchasing) can be immediately acted upon by design engineering and everyone in the organization has access to the updated information once the correction has been entered. The sharp line of demarcation between the design and manufacturing functions becomes diffuse and will gradually disappear. Computer-aided design can no longer be separated from computer-aided manufacturing; they are one and the same. Hence, the acronym, CAD/CAM.

Historical Background. Both CAD and CAM were born at about the same time—the early 1950s. The earliest electronic digital computers, developed in the mid- to late 1940s, were primarily used for scientific and mathematical applications—calculations of trajectories, weather forecasting, and the like. By the early 1950s, commercial versions of the early laboratory models—Univac 1s, IBM 701s and 702s, etc.—were emerging and finding their way into a few highly sophisticated business and engineering organizations such as G.E., G.M., Boeing, and other aerospace and automotive firms. By the late 1950s to the early 1960s, interactive graphical display devices were appearing and Ivan Sutherland was doing his pioneering work at M.I.T.'s Lincoln Laboratory on the SKETCHPAD system—the forerunner of modern CAD graphics systems. Unsuccessful attempts were made to commercialize this system (by CDC) and others like it (by IBM); and throughout the 1960s and into the mid-1970s, development work was performed primarily by the large engineering computing users—General Motors (with their famous DAC-1 system which provided a foundation for much future work), Lockheed, McDonnell Aircraft, Douglas, Pratt & Whitney, Caterpillar, etc.

The basic specialized hardward devices associated with CAD—interactive graphics terminals, digitizers, light pens, and plotters—became quite well developed by the mid-1960s and have not really changed significantly since (improved in cost performance, of course, but functionally essentially the same). The major changes that *have* taken place during the last 10–15 years have occurred in the areas of software and minicomputer development. Software for managing large amounts of complex and interrelated data (database management systems), for allowing communication of data and programs among computers and remote terminals (distributed processing systems), for representing the physical geometry of a part in terms that can be manipulated by a computer (geometric modeling systems), and for analyzing the effects of various external forces on complex parts (finite element analysis packages and the like) all matured significantly and were packaged in ways that made them easy to use. Minicomputer technology also made marked advances during this period, permitting economical, dedicated systems with considerable power to be placed at the disposal of designers and draftsmen; and, with the more recent advent of the minicomputer, permitting the specialized hardware devices mentioned earlier to have intelligence built into them to perform many functions locally that previously required the attention of a large, centralized computer.

Thus, beginning in the mid-1970s, a type of product became popular which incorporated many of the specialized hardware devices, software elements, and minicomputer capabilities referred to. These are known by various names but are most often called "turnkey CAD systems." About 2,500–3,000 of these systems were installed by 1980. Each such system is normally comprised of 4–5 work stations, on the average, each with a graphical visual display and often a supplementary alphanumeric display, a graphical digitizing or input device and a keyboard. Also, each system typically includes a large, high-quality plotter; smaller, more rapid but lower-quality hard copy devices; a more precise digitizer; and various forms of data storage; as well as, of course, the controlling minicomputer and its all-important software. In addition to such systems, which (at $250,000–$400,000 each) have popularized CAD technology, other offerings of packaged software or services have helped to make CAD more feasible for the average user who prefers to use a mainframe computer with specialized peripheral devices; e.g., interactive graphics terminals.

The CAM area has evolved with an initial spurt of development, then relatively slow gestation, and, in the last few years, maturing to the birth of a recognizable science with widespread interest. CAM is generally considered to have begun with the advent of numerically-controlled (NC) machine tools, pioneered at M.I.T. under Air Force sponsorship in the early 1950s. These early devices merely proved that it was possible to control the movements of metal-cutting milling machines (or lathes or drill presses or boring machines or whatever) by an electronic control mechanism actuated by punched tape. The real challenge was to create the punched tape quickly and accurately based on the geometry and physical characteristics of the part. The Air Force also helped solve that problem by sponsoring the initial development of the APT language at M.I.T. and Illinois Institute of Technology Research Institute in the late 1950s and early 1960s. This programming language allows a "part programmer" (a new occupation in the manufacturing engineering field) to describe the necessary cutting motions in a somewhat English-language-like notation which is then "compiled" (translated) into a standardized "cutter location file" (CLFILE) which, in turn, is processed by a special "post-processor" for each machine into explicit instructions for that machine on punched tape.

This development made widespread use of NC tools possible and they began to proliferate throughout industry in the 1960s and 1970s—more rapidly in Europe and Japan but also with considerable enthusiasm in the U. S. By the early 1970s (with the introduction of mini- and microcomputer technology), new control techniques were developed. Direct numerical control (DNC) and computerized numerical control (CNC) systems are being more widely accepted. These systems incorporate computers

directly into the machine controller to permit operator interaction with the programs and/or more of the machine functions to be controlled in real time. Also, parts programming in the batch-processing-oriented "blind" APT mode is gradually being replaced by direct creation of the APT language program or the CLFILE as a result of the geometric model of the part created on the graphical CAD system (one of the first instances of integration between CAD and CAM leading to CAD/CAM).

Other CAM developments have also been accelerating in the 1970s. Robot technology matured to the point where there are now about 3,200 installed in the U. S. (compared with about 1,800 in Western Europe and well over 4,000 in Japan, depending on one's definition of the term), performing all sorts of "pick and place" operations, welding, dipping, spray painting, and assembling functions. General purpose automated machining and assembly systems are also evolving for efficient production of small batches or products using techniques more like mass production assembly lines, except more readily reprogrammed. Many forms of automated materials handling devices and systems are finding acceptance—from computerized stacker cranes and conveyor systems to driverless tractors. Factory floor management systems (to the extent one considers them part of CAM or, at least, manufacturing computing) also had seen limited use in aerospace companies in the 1950s and 1960s, but gained respectability and widespread usage in the 1970s with development of materials requirements planning systems (MRP—sometimes interpreted as manufacturing resource planning) and related production and inventory control data processing systems. Even computer-controlled testing devices such as coordinate measuring machines and electronic test equipment have entered the manufacturing automation field.

Now, with the proliferation of such hardware and software components and the realization that both engineering and manufacturing are highly information-intensive activities, considerable interest is being shown in the integration of all these elements. The term *computer-integrated manufacturing* (CIM) is coming into vogue, as discussed in the concepts section, and many present and projected developments are taking place in that context. We project that the decade of the 1980s will see a "third generation" of CAD/CAM systems with common databases and electronic interfaces among these previously disparate subsystems.

Special Impact of Automation. As mentioned in the introductory paragraphs, there is some legitimate concern that automation represents a threat not only to employment through the replacement of human workers by machines, but also to human control over increasingly more comprehensive operations through computerized control systems. The employment threat issue is relatively easy to respond to by pointing out our steadily and dangerously decreasing labor productivity growth rate (even after the introduction of these technologies), indicating that more manual labor, not less, is being required in our automated society to produce our manufactured goods. Also, the phenomenal growth of the computer industry, and its associated excellent employment opportunities, suggests that increased automation will also provide job opportunities for people to design, program, produce, sell, support, maintain, apply, and operate these devices and systems. Finally, the growth of automation is being spurred by critical shortages of certain classes of labor—draftsmen, skilled machinists, manufacturing engineers, etc.—so for some considerable time, automation systems can hardly be considered a threat to these occupations.

Over the longer term, however, there is no question but that the ultimate forms of automation—"workerless factories"—such as those the Japanese are already striving for, will have a profound effect on our society. Kurt Vonnegut's book, *Player Piano,* depicting a futuristic society and the moral degradation that occurs when humans are almost totally replaced by machinery and electronics, suggests the kinds of problems that may occur—boredom, lethargy, class conflict, etc. While this extreme is unlikely, its potentiality suggests that the leaders of industrializing societies—statesmen, businessmen, technologists, academicians, and even philosophers and psychologists—would do well to monitor trends and attempt to find alternative ways of maintaining human dignity as automation advances. The concern over loss of human control of operations is likewise easy to respond to in the short term, but is more worrisome when viewed in the context of much longer-term potentials. The near-term need for human designers, programmers, operators *et al.* assures us that fundamental controls will be in human hands for a long time to come. The trend toward computers designing computers, robots producing robots, totally computerized factory control systems, etc., however, again suggests that things could conceivably go awry without responsible human beings being adequately aware of, or in control of, events. Careful attention toward integrating humans appropriately into control systems with good human-machine interaction should obviate these possibilities; but again, conscientious monitoring of trends is advisable.

REFERENCES

1952. Vonnegut, K., Jr. *Player Piano.* New York: Avon.
1973. Harrington, J., Jr. *Computer-Integrated Manufacturing.* New York: Industrial Press.
1979. Newman, W. M. and Sproull, R. F. *Principles of Interactive Computer Graphics.* New York: McGraw-Hill.

R. M. SALZMAN

AUXILIARY MEMORY. *See* MEMORY: Auxiliary.

B

BABBAGE, CHARLES

For articles on related subjects *see* DIGITAL COM-
PUTERS: HISTORY; LOVELACE, COUNTESS OF; and
STORED PROGRAM CONCEPT.

Charles Babbage was born in London on 26 December 1791. He was educated privately and went up to
Cambridge in 1810. At that time, Cambridge education
was strongly oriented toward mathematics and there was
intense competition for high honors in the Mathematical
Tripos. Babbage, however, soon discovered that Newton's
ideas still dominated the Cambridge curriculum, whereas
he had been exposed to, and was much drawn toward, the
type of mathematics then receiving attention on the Continent. He did not, therefore, compete for honors. Nevertheless, he acquired a high mathematical reputation
which increased with the years, so much so that in 1828
he was appointed Lucasian Professor, a position that
Newton himself had held many years before. The stipend
in Babbage's time was only £80 to £90 per annum. He
did not reside in Cambridge nor lecture there, though he
performed some of the other duties of the Professorship,
such as examining for the Smith's Prize.

It was while still a student that Babbage began to
work on the difference engine, a device intended to mechanize the production of the final values in a mathematical
table from the widely spaced pivotal values that are first
computed. It would also produce a stereotype mold, ready
for the printer, thus eliminating one source of error. Babbage's own attempt at implementing the difference engine failed, in spite of financial support from the British
government. The soundness of his ideas was, however,
demonstrated by the fact that an independent implementation by George and Edward Sheutz, who had read of
Babbage's ideas, was successful.

In a long life, Babbage turned his attention to many
subjects, including mathematics, railroads, lighthouses,

Fig. 1. Charles Babbage. *Courtesy of New York
Public Library.*

economics, the ophthalmoscope, politics, and public controversies of various kinds. But the dominating interest of his life was calculating machinery, and his claim to fame is through his work on the analytical engine, which was to have been an automatically sequenced, general-purpose calculating machine. Here he was profoundly original. He published some of his ideas and others have come down to us in his manuscript notebooks. The real breakthrough came in 1834 and the years immediately following, but Babbage continued to work on the subject for the remainder of his life.

Babbage's thoughts on the analytical engine were entirely in mechanical terms, with no suggestion, even in later years, that electricity might be called in aid. The analytical engine was to be decimal, although Babbage considered other scales of notation. Numbers were to be stored on wheels, with ten distinguishable positions, and transferred by a system of racks to a central *mill*, or processor, where all arithmetic would be performed. He had in mind a storage capacity for a thousand numbers of 50 decimal digits. He studied exhaustively a wide variety of schemes for performing the four operations of arithmetic and he invented the idea of anticipatory carry, which is much faster than carrying successively from one stage to another. He also knew about hoarding carry, by which a whole series of additions could be performed with one carrying operation at the end.

The sequencing of the analytical engine was to have been fully automatic, but not, of course, on what we would now call the stored-program principle. Punched cards of the type used in a Jacquard loom were to be adopted both for sequencing and for the input of numbers. Babbage proposed to have two sets of sequencing cards, one for controlling the mill and one for controlling the store; these would be separately stepped and would not necessarily move together.

Babbage never arrived at the idea of instructions containing both an operation part and an address part, nor at the formal concept of a program that we have today. Lady Lovelace, the daughter of Lord Byron, in notes to a translation that she made of a paper describing some of Babbage's ideas, published by Ménabréa in French in 1842, gives what at first sight appears to be a program along modern lines for computing Bernoulli numbers. This gives the arithmetic operations in detail, but does not contain anything corresponding to the conditional jump instructions in a modern program; after the main loop there is simply the sentence: "Here follows a repetition of operations 13 to 23."

Babbage's notebooks show him struggling with various ideas for handling the repetition of parts of a calculation, and although he sketched out many schemes that would have worked satisfactorily, one feels that he never arrived at one that entirely pleased him. For subsequencing within an operation he proposed to use drums with fixed studs, on the barrel-organ principle. It is odd that in his published writings there is no hint of the range and originality of his thoughts on the important matter of sequencing. Lady Lovelace has left us in her debt for the translation and notes referred to above, but there has been a tendency to exaggerate her importance in the Babbage saga.

Although he had workmen in his employ until the end of his life, Babbage failed to implement the analytical engine. We must conclude, as did some of his contemporaries, that he was temperamentally incapable of carrying a project through. Unfortunately, this time, there was no Sheutz to take up his ideas, and it may well be that the ultimate development of automatic calculating machinery was delayed by the aura of failure that surrounded Babbage's work. His detailed design studies lay buried in his unpublished notebooks and were forgotten. Of his genius, however, no one who has studied his work will have any doubt.

Babbage died in London on 18 October 1871. His youngest son, Henry, who had spent most of his life in various military and civil appointments in India, did what he could to carry on his father's work, and published a collection of papers relating to it. The eldest son, Herschel, migrated in 1851 to South Australia, where he became a prominent member of the colony.

REFERENCES

1889. Babbage, H. P. (Ed.). *Babbage's Calculating Engines.* London.

1961. Morrison, P., and Morrison, E. (Eds.). *Charles Babbage and His Calculating Engines.* New York: Dover.

1968. Babbage, C. *Passages from the Life of a Philosopher.* London, 1864; facsimile edition, London: Dawson's.

1971. Wilkes, M. V. "Babbage as a Computer Pioneer," Report of the Babbage Memorial Meeting, British Computer Society. Reprinted in *Historica Mathematica* **4**:415 (1977).

1975. Wilkes, M. V. "How Babbage's Dream Came True," *Nature* **257**:641.

M. V. WILKES

BACKTRACKING

For articles on related subjects *see* ALGORITHM; and HEURISTICS.

Often problems occur for which the only possible (or known) method of solution is by a search through the (perhaps very large) space of all possible solutions. In such cases it is important to attempt possible solutions systematically, eliminating potential solutions as quickly as possible, and never retrying a potential solution that has already been tried. The backtracking technique achieves these aims.

Three examples will suffice to explain backtracking. Fig. 1 shows a simple maze. One systematic technique to find a path through the maze is to always keep to the right until a dead end is reached, then *backtrack* until an alternate path is found, again keep to the right, etc. The dark line shows the path through the maze, the light lines show the other paths traversed in finding this path.

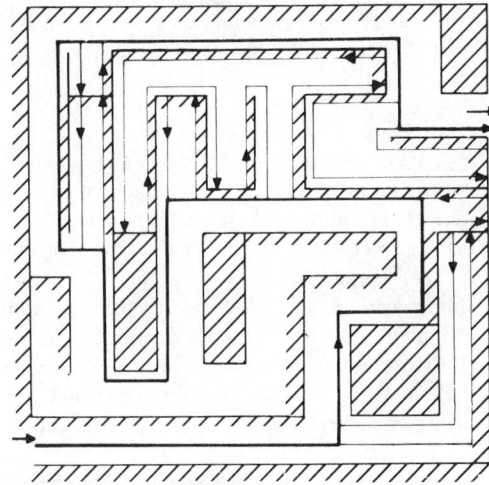

Fig. 1.

Fig. 2 shows a chessboard at a stage in an attempt to solve the 8-Queens problem in which eight queens are to be placed on a chessboard so that no two are in the same row or column or on the same diagonal. Our technique begins by placing a queen in the first column on the first row (1,1). The next queen is then placed in the second column on the first possible square, the third (3,2). Then subsequent queens are placed on (5,3), (2,4), and (4,5) as shown in Fig. 2. But with this arrangement no queen can be placed in column 6, so we *backtrack* to column 5 and move the queen to (5,8), again try but fail to place a queen in column 6, backtrack to column 5 but then, since we are already in row 8, backtrack again to column 4, move the queen on (2,4) to (7,4), etc. Eventually we find the first of 92 solutions, 12 of which are really distinct, that is, not related to others by some type of symmetry, at (1,1), (5,2), (8,3), (6,4), (3,5), (7,6), (2,7), (4,8). This method of solving the 8-Queens problem can be easily and efficiently programmed for a computer (see Wirth, 1971).

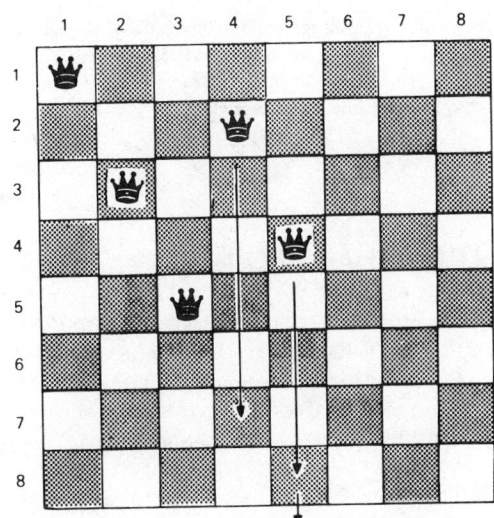

Fig. 2.

Our third example is also from Wirth (1973). We desire to generate a sequence of N characters, each of which is a 1, 2, or 3, such that no two immediately adjacent subsequences of any length are equal. For example, with $N = 6$, 131213 is acceptable, but neither 131212 (two adjacent 12s) nor 132132 (adjacent 132s) is. Our backtracking algorithm is quite straightforward:

1. Start with a 1.
2. If we have an acceptable sequence $s_1 s_2 \ldots s_n$, $n < N$, then set s_{n+1} equal to the smallest of 1, 2, or 3 which gives an acceptable sequence of length $n + 1$; if none is possible, backtrack and increase s_n until another acceptable sequence of length n is obtained; if none is possible, backtrack to a sequence of length $n - 1$, etc.

Applying this algorithm with $N = 9$ leads to the acceptable sequences 1,12,121,1213,12131,121312,1213121, 1213123,12131231, and 121312313. As the reader may verify, backtracking occurs only when passing from the first underlined sequence to the second underlined one.

Other areas in which backtracking is a commonly employed and useful technique are in the parsing process in the compilation of a high-level programming language, theorem-proving and game-playing programs, and generally those tasks whose search domain is "ill structured." A formal description of backtracking is found in Golomb and Baumert (1965).

REFERENCES

1965. Golomb, S. W. and Baumert, L. D. "Backtrack Programming," *Journal of the ACM* **12:**516–524.

1971. Wirth, N. "Program Development by Stepwise Refinement," *Communications of the ACM* **14**:221–227.

1973. Wirth, N. *Systematic Programming: An Introduction.* Englewood Cliffs, NJ: Prentice-Hall.

A. RALSTON

BACKUS-NAUR FORM

For articles on related subjects *see* METALANGUAGE; PROCEDURE-ORIENTED LANGUAGES, SURVEY OF; PROGRAMMING LANGUAGES; PROGRAMMING LINGUISTICS; SYNTAX, SEMANTICS, AND PRAGMATICS; and VIENNA DEFINITION LANGUAGE.

The Backus-Naur form, named after John W. Backus of the United States and Peter Naur of Denmark, and usually written BNF, is the best-known example of a *metalanguage;* i.e., one that syntactically describes a programming language. Using BNF it is possible to specify which sequences of symbols constitute a syntactically valid program in a given language. (The question of *semantics*—i.e., what such valid strings of symbols mean—must be specified separately.) A discussion of the basic concepts of BNF follows.

A *metalinguistic variable* (or *metavariable*), also called a *syntactic unit,* is one whose values are strings of symbols chosen from among the symbols permitted in the given language. In BNF metalinguistic variables are enclosed in brackets, ⟨ ⟩, for clarity and to distinguish them from symbols in the language itself, which are called terminal symbols or just *terminals.* The symbol : : = is used to indicate metalinguistic equivalence; a vertical bar (|) is used to indicate that a choice is to be made among the items so indicated; and concatenation (linking together in a series) is indicated simply by juxtaposing the elements to be concatenated.

For an example, here is how the definition of an Algol integer is built up: First, we have a definition of what a digit is, according to the usual meaning:

⟨digit⟩: : = 0 | 1 | 2 | 3 | 4 | 5 | 6 | 7 | 8 | 9.

Next we have a statement that an unsigned integer consists either of a single digit or an unsigned integer followed by another digit:

⟨unsigned integer⟩: : = ⟨digit⟩ |
⟨unsigned integer⟩⟨digit⟩

This definition may be applied *recursively* to build up unsigned integers of any length whatever. Since there must be a limit on the number of digits in any actual computer implementation, this would have to be stated separately in conjunction with each particular implementation or, as in some extensions to BNF, by an addition to the definition of *unsigned integer* (e.g., [10] above : : = could indicate a limit of 10 digits). Finally, the definition of an integer is completed by noting that it may be preceded by a plus sign, a minus sign, or neither:

⟨integer⟩: : = ⟨unsigned integer⟩ |
+ ⟨unsigned integer⟩ | − ⟨unsigned integer⟩.

For a second example, suppose that the metalinguistic variables ⟨unsigned number⟩, ⟨variable⟩, ⟨function designator⟩, and ⟨boolean expression⟩ have all been defined earlier, with usual meanings, and that the up-pointing arrow stands for exponentiation. Here, then, is the complete definition of an Algol arithmetic expression.

⟨adding operator⟩: : = + | −
⟨multiplying operator⟩: : = × | / | ÷
⟨primary⟩:: = ⟨unsigned number⟩ | ⟨variable⟩ |
⟨function designator⟩ | (⟨arithmetic expression⟩)
⟨factor⟩: : = ⟨primary⟩ | ⟨factor⟩↑⟨primary⟩
⟨term⟩: : = ⟨factor⟩ | ⟨term⟩⟨multiplying operator⟩⟨factor⟩
⟨simple arithmetic expression⟩: : = ⟨term⟩ | ⟨adding operator⟩⟨term⟩ | ⟨simple arithmetic expression⟩⟨adding operator⟩⟨term⟩
⟨if clause⟩: : = **if** ⟨boolean expression⟩**then**
⟨arithmetic expression⟩: : = ⟨simple arithmetic expression⟩ |
⟨if clause⟩⟨simple arithmetic expression⟩ **else** ⟨arithmetic expression⟩

It is no error that the third definition contains ⟨arithmetic expression⟩, enclosed in parentheses, even though it is an arithmetic expression that we are trying to define. This is another example of a recursive definition, and simply says in this case that one choice for a ⟨primary⟩ is just any ⟨arithmetic expression⟩ enclosed in parentheses.

The words **if, then,** and **else,** since they are not enclosed in the metalinguistic brackets, stand for themselves; they are like the character set (*q.v.*), basic elements of the Algol language which are not further defined.

Almost any programming language can be defined in BNF, but different metalanguages are sometimes used to define other procedure-oriented languages.

REFERENCE

1969. Sammet, Jean E. *Programming Languages: History and Fundamentals.* Englewood Cliffs, NJ: Prentice-Hall (Chap. 2, Sec. 6).

D. D. MCCRACKEN

BANDWIDTH

For articles on related subjects *see* COMMUNICA-TIONS AND COMPUTERS; and DATA COMMUNI-CATIONS.

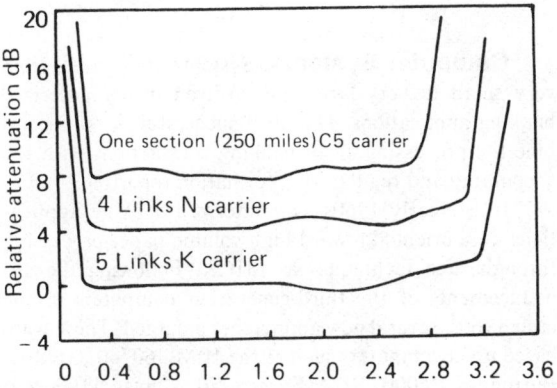

Fig. 1. Attentuation for frequency division multi-plexing (FDM) systems. (reproduced from *Communication-Networks for Computers* by D. W. Davies and D. L. A. Barber. New York: Wiley, 1973, Fig. 2.16.)

The bandwidth of a communication network is a measure of the range of frequencies it can transmit at or near maximum power levels. As an example, consider a normal telephone system, which is an analog communication network normally designed to carry voice traffic in the frequency range 300–3400 Hz. Thus, the equipment in the telephone exchange collects incoming data from the sound spectrum and arranges to attenuate sharply the signals outside that part of the spectrum. But even within that range there is further attenuation as the signals propagate through the telephone network, since the power of signals passing through the telephone transmission system is reduced. A typical measurement on the U.S. telephone network of attenuation is shown in Fig. 1, which indicates that somewhere below 300 Hz and above 3–4 KHz, the attenuation rises very rapidly. The range of frequencies in which the power level stays at above one-half its peak value (the so-called 3 *db* points) is the *nominal bandwidth* of the circuit. This is typically 3 KHz in a switched telephone line.

P. T. KIRSTEIN

BANKING APPLICATIONS

For articles on related subjects *see* ADMINISTRATIVE APPLICATIONS; CREDIT SYSTEM APPLICATIONS; DATA COMMUNICATION NETWORKS; ECONOMETRIC APPLI-CATIONS; ELECTRONIC FUNDS TRANSFER SYSTEMS; and TRANSACTION-BASED SYSTEMS.

Environment. The growth of the U.S. and world economies—particularly rapid since 1950—has resulted in extraordinary expansion of banking transactions in both number and dollar value. Banking "transactions," once mere bookkeeping records of movements of currency amounts, rapidly took on significance themselves. Because of this attribute of monetary value, these transactions came to be recorded on several pieces of paper and copied, microfilmed, etc., for control.

In the 1960s and 1970s, there was increased pressure on banks for more, new, and different financial services, inevitably including a growing requirement for information. At the same time, the government regulators, concerned with a large variety of national and international issues, increased their demands for information in the form of mandatory reports to be supplied frequently by the banks. As a result, computers have become a *sine qua non* for a wide variety of banking applications.

In broad terms, banking computer applications include processing the records of bank liabilities, bank assets, and processing fee-based financial services.

Traditionally, computers have only controlled banking transactions. The trend now is for computers to execute at least a part of the transactions. Additionally, reports must be produced for regulatory authorities and for bank management.

TYPICAL COMPUTERIZED BANKING APPLICATIONS

Bank Liability Applications. *Checking Accounts.* Bank customers make deposits in cash or checks in their accounts in one or several currencies. In exchange for the use of the funds, the bank provides check-collection and checking account services and renders periodic statements. All these processes heavily involve computers.

Savings Accounts. These are similar to checking accounts, but include the payment of interest and special conditions for withdrawal of funds.

Time Deposits. These are deposits for fixed periods of time, bearing negotiated interest.

Bank Asset Applications. *Personal Loans.* The bank makes loans to individual customers using a portion of its deposits. Computers are involved in executing the loan contracts, controlling payments, and determining the accruals for cost of deposits, earnings of interest/dividends, and taxes due.

Business Loans. Similar to personal loans, business

loans also have an enormous variety of disbursement and repayment options in one or multiple currencies.

Fee-Based Services. *Funds Transfer.* This is the principal payment process among corporations. A customer gives the bank instructions to move funds from the corporation's own checking account to a payee checking account at the same or at another bank. All parties involved require advice of such transactions. Timely execution and correct recording of the date of the transfers is critical, and different currencies may be required. Computers and computer communications are the essential elements in such transfers.

Letters of Credit. A letter of credit is a financial service: Banks guarantee that their customers will have funds when a payment becomes due.

Custodian Services. This is a banking service in which records are maintained for several categories of customers in return for service fees. The most frequent examples of these applications are investment accounts, securities funds, pension funds, and stock transfer registry.

Credit Cards. In this financial service, fees are collected from businesses and interest is received from cardholders. The high item volume could not be handled without computers.

Reports. *Accounting.* The content of reports results from government regulations and from banking traditions. The information in this application defines the financial condition of the bank. It is essential that the nature and situation of all bank assets and liabilities be represented accurately.

Management Reports. Also strongly affected by regulatory reporting requirements, these applications provide information on expenses and revenues to evaluate the effectiveness of managers and for planning the development of customer relationships.

DOMINANT BANKING TECHNOLOGIES

Paper. At least until the mid-1980s, paper will continue to be the primary information medium for banking applications. Paper is used almost exclusively in the transmittal of information between banks and their customers. The growth in transaction volume has been handled so far by faster paper-processing equipment. The physical signature, even today, plays a key role in authenticating high-value transactions, and signatures still imply paper in spite of efforts to decouple the two.

An early successful solution for the paper-handling problem was developed in the 1950s by the committee on banking of the American Bankers Association (ABA). A study, aided by federal authorities, culminated in the adoption of Magnetic Ink Character Recognition (MICR) for reading data from physical documents. Today's check-processing systems rely heavily on MICR.

Computer Systems. Systems of all sizes, from very small to very large, are utilized in computerized banking applications. The most successful systems combine the processing of all banking transactions with the accounting and regulatory information reporting.

In the early 1960s, computerized banking applications were oriented toward high-volume paper-processing through such techniques as MICR. Following the announcements of the third-generation computers in the later 1960s, several new approaches emerged. These were based upon computers such as the IBM 360/40, GE 400, Burroughs B5000, RCA Spectra 70, Univac 1100, and CDC 1600. Banking applications were implemented using on-line terminals. The pioneer on-line banking applications were savings accounts, on-line tellers (checking), overdraft accounts (loans), automated customer balance information, etc. Even though the data capture and validation and data inquiry were done on-line, the transactions were stored in the computer files for end-of-day batch processing.

This approach represented a compromise between satisfying immediate customer needs and maintaining secure controls. An example of the architecture of an on-line system with batch processing is shown in Fig. 1.

The minicomputer "revolution" became an impor-

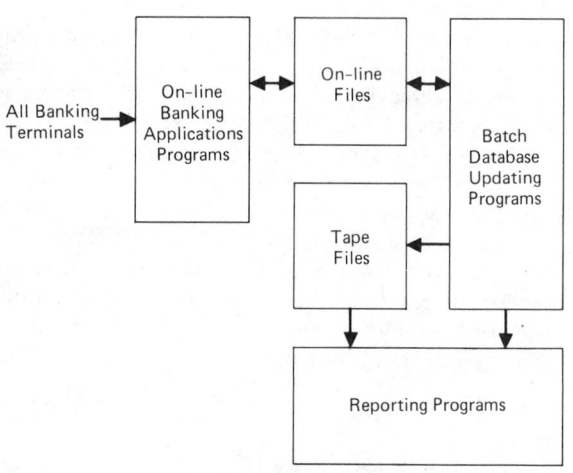

Fig. 1. General purpose integrated banking application.

tant part of banking applications in the mid-1970s. Minis provided the technology for computerized banking applications at the scale of a single department. For example, a single minicomputer was dedicated to handling the Letters of Credit Department or all the loans for one class of business customers. Success of this approach depended upon the fact that, with proper management, while computer hardware cost will actually go up, the net effect is to produce sufficient savings elsewhere to reduce the overall cost. Over time, technological progress further reduces hardware costs, thus yielding even greater total savings.

Telegraphy. For many decades, banks and customers have communicated using message services. "Advices" were delivered worldwide, by teleprinter, normally within one business day, and a paper record was produced. During the 1960s and 1970s, banking applications' use of wire services has increased to the point that justified establishing special funds-transfer networks. These techniques for moving money are encompassed within the rather sweeping term, "Electronic Funds Transfer" (EFT) (*see* ELECTRONIC FUNDS TRANSFER SYSTEMS).

TELECOMMUNICATIONS

An increasing variety of message and data-transmission options has begun to be used. The past two or three years have seen very rapid growth, particularly as circuits began to facilitate direct interaction between banking applications and bank customers acting through terminals of various types. Of a less "revolutionary" character is the role played by telecommunications in applications that call for interconnections among internal bank computers, as shown in Fig. 2.

The "live" interaction of customer-bank communication terminals (CBCTs) in supermarkets and other retail outlets with bank applications and bank databases

delivers vastly improved levels of customer service, while reducing operating costs and providing control of non-credit risks. It appears that their direct service delivery via computer/communications systems will drive the growth and development of computerized banking applications in the 1980s.

A needed collateral development is the technology of encryption. However strong or weak may be the Bureau of Standards' "DES" algorithm (*see* DATA ENCRYPTION), it is accepted as an industry standard, thus making possible the development of compatible encryptors that are off-the-shelf items, like modems. As a result, certain of the problems of customer-data privacy protection are, in effect, swept from the board, releasing resources to work on the multitude of remaining problems.

DATABASES

Optimum information management could be approached if it were possible to collect all the information from all of a bank's internal applications into logically-centralized but widely accessible files as shown in Fig. 3. This facilitates management of asset and liability aggregates and precise reporting of the bank's condition. Data-related activity, protection of customer privacy, file updating, and investigations would be greatly facilitated by a full database capability, but, at least for large banks, such a capability still eludes full realization. No database management system adequate for such a large-scale file is practical presently.

The banking applications developed in the 1970s and to be developed in the 1980s depend on database concepts. The principal difficulties are in the administration of thousands of information definitions, in establishing and maintaining the necessary structural relationships among data elements, and in coping with the current inefficiency and complexity of available database software. This indicates that the database administrator (*q.*

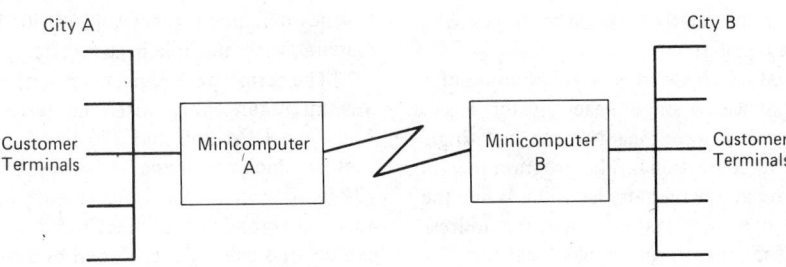

Fig. 2.   Dedicated banking application.

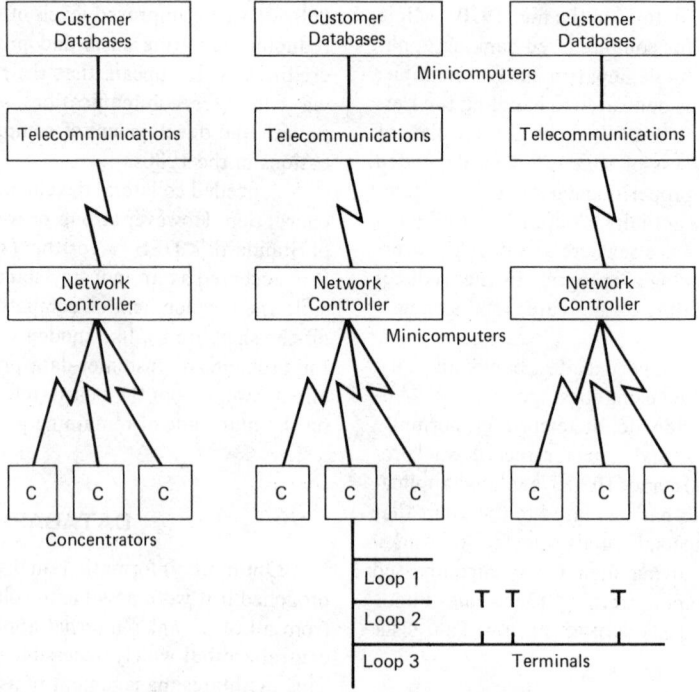

Fig. 3. Distributed banking application.

v.) function is clearly the key to future computerized banking applications.

R. G. MILLS AND E. R. WILLNER

BASE REGISTER

For articles on related subjects *see* ADDRESSING; and IBM 360-370 SERIES.

A base register is used in addressing a computer memory. In a computer that uses base registers, the effective address (i.e., the address field of the instruction, possibly modified by indexing and indirect addressing) is a relative address. The actual memory address used is determined by adding this relative address to the contents of one or more base registers.

The Control Data Cyber series is an example of a computer system that uses a single base register. Every program is written as if it were meant to run in a single memory area, starting at location 0. The program may in fact be loaded starting at any memory location. When the program is run, the operating system places the address of the first word of the program in the base register. The content of the base register is automatically added to every memory reference address, and thus every relative address is converted into an absolute address. This feature is useful in multiprogramming systems, since it permits programs to be loaded wherever space exists, and permits programs to be moved in memory, or to be removed from memory and then resumed in a different area of memory. Such base registers are thus often called *relocation registers*.

Some computers have several base registers. A relative address must then contain a field that indicates which register is selected, and the contents of that register are added to the relative address to form the absolute address. In such a machine a program may be constructed in parts or segments that can be independently loaded into available areas of memory. The Univac 1110 is an example of a machine with two base registers. The Multics machine (Honeywell 68/80) is an example of a machine with multiple base registers.

The term "base register" is sometimes used more or less interchangeably with the term "index register." Thus, the IBM 360 and 370 have 16 general registers, each of which provides a 24-bit base address to which the 12-bit address field (displacement) in an instruction is added to produce the effective address. These registers can be, and usually are, loaded by and stored in the programs that use them. It is conceptually better to think of them as index registers and to limit the use of the term "base register" to system registers that are not accessible to the programs whose addresses they modify.

S. ROSEN

BASIC. *See* PROCEDURE-ORIENTED LANGUAGES.

BATCH PROCESSING. *See* PROCESSING MODES.

BAUD

For articles on related subjects *see* BAUDOT CODE; and CHANNEL.

A baud is a unit of signaling speed and refers to the number of times the state (or condition) of a line changes per second. It is the reciprocal of the length (in seconds) of the shortest element in the signaling code. Historically, it is a contraction of the surname of the Frenchman J. M. E. Baudot, whose five-bit code was adopted by the French telegraph system in 1877. By contrast, a bit is the smallest unit of information in a binary system. The baud rate is therefore equal to the bit rate only if each signal element represents one bit of information.

The relationship between bauds and bits per second is illustrated in Fig. 1, where amplitude is used as a coding method. In this particular case, there are four line conditions, one for each of the four combinations of two bits. Each line change signal element is therefore represented by two bits and, if we can have one line change in 1 ms, the baud rate is 1,000, whereas the bit rate is actually 2,000 bits per second. Similarly, if the signals are coded into eight possible states, one line condition could represent three bits and one baud would then equal three bits per second and so on.

Unfortunately, in much of today's literature, the terms "baud" and "bits per second" are used synony-

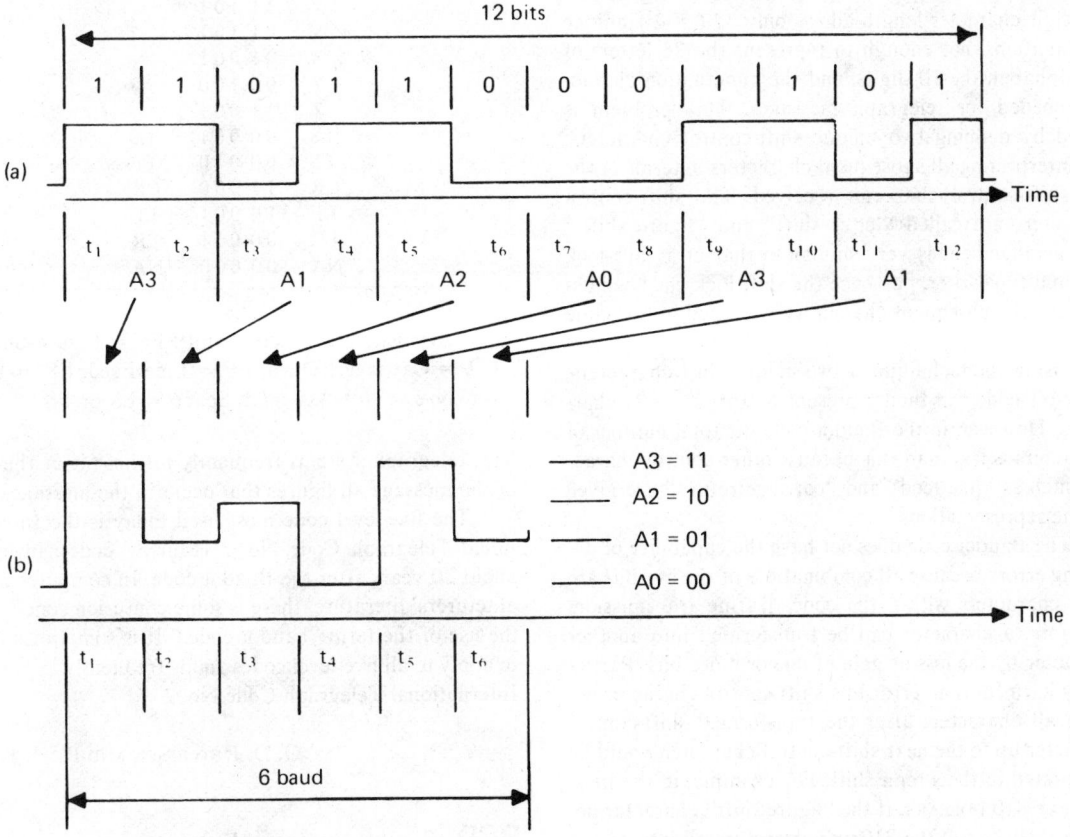

Fig. 1. Relationship between baud and bits per second. Each combination of two bits is encoded as one of four possible amplitudes; hence, one baud is equal to two bits per second.

mously. This is correct in cases where pure two-state signaling is used, as in Fig. 1(a), but is incorrect in general. For this reason, the term "baud" is gradually being replaced by "bits per second," since the latter is independent of the coding method and truly represents the information rate.

J. S. Sobolewski

BAUDOT CODE

For articles on related subjects *see* Baud; Codes; and Error Correcting Code.

The Baudot code, also known as the International Telegraph Code No. 1, is named after its inventor, J. M. E. Baudot (1845–1903). It was invented about 1880, and by the 1950s it had become one of the standards for international telegraph communication.

Baudot is a fixed character-length code in which each character is represented by five binary digits. The five-digit character length allows only 32 (= 2^5) unique combinations, not enough to represent the 26 letters of the alphabet, the 10 digits, and the punctuation characters needed for telegraph messages. This problem is solved by defining two unique shift-control characters, and interpreting all subsequent characters in terms of the last shift-control character received. The shift-control characters are called "letter shift" and "figure shift." This arrangement is very similar to that of a shift-lock key on a typewriter, i.e., once the shift lock has been depressed, all subsequent characters are typed in the same shift.

Using the technique of two unique shift characters, a five-bit code can then represent 62 (= $2^6 - 2$) characters. However, in the Baudot code the total number of characters is less than this because other control characters such as "line feed" and "carriage return" are given unique representations.

The Baudot code does not have the capability of detecting errors because all combinations of the five bits are valid characters within the code. During transmission, therefore, a character can be transformed into another character by the loss or gain of one or more bits. Particularly harmful is an error in a shift-control character because all characters after the transformed shift-control character up to the next shift-control character would be interpreted in the wrong shift. For example, in the message PAY 810 DOLLARS, if the "figure shift" character between the PAY and the 810 were transformed into, say, a J (i.e., 00010 to 10010), then the message would be received as PAYJBAD DOLLARS (see Table 1 for letter-shift, figure-shift equivalents). In order to alleviate this problem, telegraph systems frequently retransmit at the end of the message all figures that occur in the message.

The five-level code most used today is the International Telegraph Code No. 2 (Murray code), invented about 20 years after the Baudot code. In computer manufacturers' literature, there is some confusion concerning the use of the term "baudot code." It is sometimes used to apply to all five-level codes and is frequently applied to International Telegraph Code No. 2.

G. D. Detlefsen and R. H. Kerr

Table 1. Baudot Code Characters.

Letters		Figures
A	10 000	1
B	00 110	8
C	10 110	9
D	11 110	∅
E	01 000	2
F	01 110	NA
G	01 010	7
H	11 010	+
I	01 100	NA
J	10 010	6
K	10 011	(
L	11 011	=
M	01 011	)
N	01 111	NA
O	11 100	5
P	11 111	%
Q	10 111	/
R	00 111	–
S	00 101	
T	10 101	NA
U	10 100	4
V	11 101	'
W	01 101	?
X	01 001	,
Y	00 100	3
Z	11 001	:
LS	00 001	LS
FS	00 010	FS
CR	11 000	CR
LF	10 001	LF
ER	00 011	ER
NA	00 000	NA

Symbols: LS = Letter Shift, FS = Figure Shift, CR = Carriage Return, LF = Line Feed, ER = Error, NA = Not Assigned, Space = LS or FS.

BCD. *See* Binary-Coded Decimal.

BCS. *See* British Computer Society.

BENCHMARK

For articles on related subjects *see* GROSCH'S LAW; and PERFORMANCE OF COMPUTERS.

Benchmarks are standardized computer programs used to test the processing power of different computers. They specify the input data, the computations to be performed, and the output formats very rigidly while leaving the details as to how the calculation is to be performed flexible enough to allow the individual advantages of a particular computer being tested to be maximized.

Auerbach Information, Inc., who have been providing benchmark comparisons since 1962 in their "Standard EDP Reports," uses five general benchmark programs to compare computers: (1) a generalized file processing problem, (2) a random access file processing problem, (3) a sorting problem, (4) a matrix inversion problem, and (5) a generalized mathematical problem. This is probably the longest running series of benchmark programs and allows general comparison between machines over a considerable time frame.

If a specific type of problem will account for a large percentage of the use of a machine, more specific benchmark problems to evaluate various manufacturers' products can be run.

Benchmark programs are one way by which machine characteristics can be compared. Alternatively, a user may specify a set of instructions and compare machines on the basis of how well they perform this instruction mix. This allows comparison among machines regardless of programming language, hardware construction, etc.

Benchmark programs may either be actually run or their performance may be calculated from the manufacturer's published data on the characteristics of the computer. Either form of comparison may be useful in evaluating computers.

Benchmarks are used by computer purchasers to determine what machine is best for their particular use in terms of both speed and cost. However, benchmarks alone cannot be used for this purpose, since most large, general-purpose computers will be used to handle a wide class of problems whose frequency will be unpredictable before purchase. Thus, in addition to benchmarks, other evaluations, subjective and objective, will enter into the decision of what computer to obtain.

One example of another objective comparison is the computer power versus cost formula developed by Knight and Cerveny in the article Performance of Computers, which allows very general comparisons both by power/cost and by year.

REFERENCE

Auerbach Standard EDP Reports. Auerbach Publishers, Princeton, NJ.

R. P. CERVENY AND K. E. KNIGHT

BINARY-CODED DECIMAL (BCD)

For article on related subjects *see* ASCII; CHARACTER SET; CODES; and EBCDIC.

Codes which use binary digits to represent decimal digits are required to enable decimal information to be stored by the binary (two-state) devices that are the elements of which all computers are constructed. Many such codes have been constructed for various purposes, but the most common and natural one is called binary-coded decimal (BCD). In BCD, each decimal digit is represented by its four-bit binary equivalent, as shown in Table 1.

Table 1.   BCD.

Digit	BCD Combination
0	0000
1	0001
2	0010
3	0011
4	0100
5	0101
6	0110
7	0111
8	1000
9	1001

Four bits are required, since, with three, only eight different combinations can be represented. Since there are 16 possible combinations of four bits, six (1010, 1011, 1100, 1101, 1110, and 1111) are not used in BCD. BCD is called a weighted code, because, reading left to right in Table 1, the four bits in each BCD combination correspond to weights of 8, 4, 2, and 1. Thus, for example, 0110 has its two 1s weighted by 4 and 2 and corresponds to a decimal 6.

A. RALSTON

BINARY SEARCH

For articles on related subjects *see* COLLATING SEQUENCE; KEY; SORTING; and TABLE LOOKUP.

Binary search is a quick method for searching an ordered, dense list (i.e., every cell of the list contains a record) for a particular record by successively looking at that half of the remaining (or unexamined) portion of the list in which the record is known to be.

A record is recognized by a field, called its *key*. We assume that the list is ordered with respect to the collating sequence of its keys (e.g., in numerical order if the keys are numbers).

There are several ways to find a specific record identified only by its key. The simplest, but longest, is sequential search, in which cells of the list are searched in the physical order as they appear in the list. Binary search considerably reduces the time required to find a desired record.

Binary search is based on the plausible notion that it makes sense to examine first the cell in the (approximate) middle of the list. Then, either

1. The record sought is the one in the middle, in which case the search is over, or
2. The key of the middle record is greater than the one sought, in which case the record sought is in the *lower* half of the list, or
3. The key of the middle record is less than the one sought, so that the record sought is in the *upper* half of the list.

If either (2) or (3) above holds, then we repeat the process on the lower or upper half list. In this way, at each step we reduce by half the length of the list in which the record sought must lie.

To present the mathematical details of binary search, we shall use the following notation.

K = key of record sought.
N = number of records in the list.
$K_1, \ldots, K_N$ = keys of the records in the list.
F = index (subscript) of the first key in a sublist (initially, $F = 1$).
L = index of the last key in a sublist (initially, $L = N$).
M = index of the key in the middle of a sublist.

We begin by calculating

$$M = \lfloor (F + L)/2 \rfloor$$

where $\lfloor x \rfloor$ (the *floor* of x) is the largest integer less than or equal to x. (Thus, $\lfloor 5/2 \rfloor = 2$.) M is, therefore, the index of the middle key (if $F + L$ is even) or the smaller of the indices of the two middle keys (if $F + L$ is odd). Then we compare K_M with K:

If $K_M = K$, we have found the desired record.
If $K_M > K$, we set $L = M - 1$ and repeat on the sublist $K_1, \ldots, K_{M-1}$.
If $K_M < K$, we set $F = M + 1$ and repeat on the sublist $K_{M+1}, \ldots, K_N$.

Continuing in this way, we shall always find the i such that $K = K_i$ (if, indeed, such an i exists). The following algorithm expresses the entire procedure:

```
F ← 1; L ← N                    [Initialize F,L]
loop
    M ← ⌊(F + L)/2⌋
    if K_M = K then output 'record found: index ='
                        M
                        stop            [Success]
        K_M > K then L ← M − 1
        K_M < K then F ← M + 1
    endif
    if L < F then output 'failure'; stop    [Failure]
endloop
```

The reader may verify that when and only when L becomes less than F can it be ascertained that no K_i equals K.

For sequential search of a list of N items, a maximum of N comparisons of K with a key of a record is required for a successful search and the average number of comparisons is $(N + 1)/2$. For binary search, the maximum number of comparisons for a successful search is $\lceil \log_2 (N + 1) \rceil$, where $\lceil x \rceil$ (the *ceiling* of x) is the smallest integer greater than or equal to x, and the average number of comparisons is approximately $\log_2 N -$

i	1	2	3	4	5	6	7	8	9	10	11	12	13
K_i	−12	−8	2	5	11	20	21	30	44	46	50	60	72

```
         ↑
         F                 ↑              ↑  M                        ↑
                           M              L                          L
                              ↑  ↑
                              F  M
```

Fig. 1.   Binary search—$K = 11$.

1. When $N = 100$, the maximum and average number of comparisons is, respectively, 100 and 50 for sequential search but 7 and 5% for binary search. For larger values of N, the difference between the two methods is still greater.

Fig. 1 illustrates the binary search algorithm for a list of 13 items.

A. RALSTON

BINDING

For articles on related subjects *see* ASSEMBLERS; and LANGUAGE PROCESSORS.

Binding means translating an expression in a program into a form immediately interpretable by the machine on which the program is to run; *binding time* is the moment at which this translation is completed. Thus, an expression is completely bound when translated into absolute machine representation (*see* "Definition of ML" in MACHINE AND ASSEMBLY LANGUAGE PROGRAMMING) at a fixed location in a storage device. When the context so indicates, however, binding can refer to an intermediate point in this process, and binding time can mean the point at which a translator has gone as far in binding the expression as it can. For example, a compiler may, as a matter of course, leave the binding of some class of expressions to be completed by a linking loader, or even, as with PL/I, defer binding of some to run time. Similarly, a translator may partly bind a file specification by transforming it into a file descriptor block that needs further interpretation by an input/output (I/O) package or operating system before it can be used for actual I/O procedures.

In general, early binding means more efficient processing of a source program, but at some cost in flexibility and potentially useful information. The information sacrificed might have allowed the use of arrays whose dimensions could vary at run time, or the issuing of more informative error messages, or the ability to compile object programs for various configurations of the target machine or operating system. The rate at which binding is to take place, therefore, is an important design consideration in all kinds of language-processing software. Broadly speaking, the history of software development is the history of ever-later binding time, with user convenience and program adaptability given increasingly more emphasis, and processing speed obtained through use of faster hardware, and by relegation of optimization to special versions of the compiler that are used only when the source program concerned is thought to be debugged and stable.

This postponement of binding in the compilation of programs is analogous to the postponement of detailed decisions in the top-down design of programs; in both cases, the principle is that all options should be kept open until the last possible moment. But in addition to sharing this general principle (one that applies well beyond the designing and compiling of programs, in fact), each of the activities mentioned has its own peculiar reason for late binding. In the compiling process, binding involves the loss of information (e.g., the mnemonic name of a program variable) that can be helpful, even essential, in dealing with bugs or other problems requiring program modification. In the design process, earlier-than-necessary binding clutters the designer's vision with unnecessary detail (e.g., the mnemonic name of a program variable), distracting the designer from essentials.

Some translators have attempted to put the question of binding time, to some degree, in the user's hands. One, at least (Strachey, 1968), has for experimental purposes gone all the way, letting the user specify for each expression the time at which it is to be bound.

REFERENCES

1968. Strachey, C. "A General Purpose Macro Generator," *The Computer Journal*, **8:**225–241.
1968. Wegner, P. *Programming Languages, Information Structures and Machine Organization*. New York: McGraw-Hill.

M. HALPERN

BIOMEDICINE, COMPUTING IN

For articles on related subjects *see* COMPUTER GRAPHICS; MEDICAL APPLICATIONS; and TOMOGRAPHY, COMPUTED.

Because biomedical research often requires handling large amounts of data, computers have long been widely used in this area. However, although computers met the requirements for handling high data rates, automatic analysis of these data incorporating sophisticated pattern recognition techniques often did not produce satisfactory results. Therefore, attempts were made to incorporate an adaptive and learning system component in the analysis path embodying the knowledge of a medical expert. The advent of computer graphics made doing this practical by providing a communication link between the automatic processes and the medical personnel. Soon, this new tool, in addition to its natural use in the *analysis,* and the *visualization* of *complex anatomical structures,* found diverse applications as in *biomedical signal analysis, modeling physiological systems, therapy,* and *surgery.*

The present article highlights the important medical application areas of interactive graphics. Within each application area, only a glimpse of the various types of use of graphics is given. Further amplification may be found through the references.

Biomedical Image Analysis. Two-dimensional biomedical images are basically either microscopic images, such as images of cells and tissue cross-sections, or images of anatomic structures, such as radiographs, cineangiograms (a time sequence of radiographs obtained upon injecting a contrast medium into the heart chambers), nuclear medicine images, etc. The analysis of these

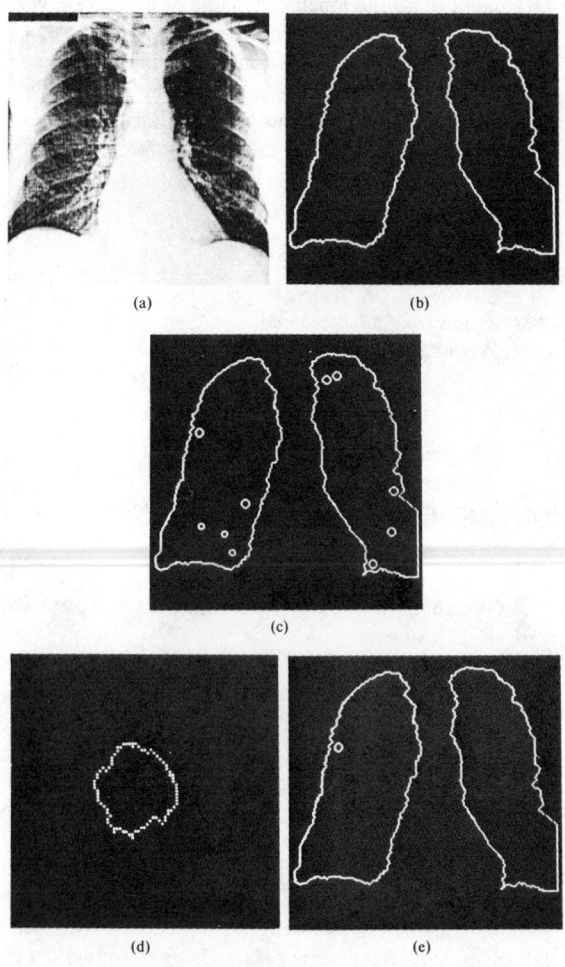

(a)

(b)

(c)

(d)

(e)

Fig. 1. Summary of a tumor detection process from chest radiographs: (a) a display of a digitized radiograph, (b) a display of lung boundaries, (c) a display showing candidate nodule sites, (d) a display of detailed nodule boundary, and (e) tumor selected by a pattern classifier.

images (see e.g., Bartels et al., 1977; Ballard et al., 1976) generally involves preprocessing (to reduce noise, to enhance images, etc.), segmentation (to identify the regions of interest), feature extraction (to determine certain properties of the identified regions) and recognition (to identify the objects represented by the regions). (See, for example, Fig. 1.) Optimal values for the various parameters used in these processing operations are best determined interactively by adjusting the parameter values and displaying the intermediate results. In particular, when input images are noisy or of low resolution, even the best automatic techniques are error-prone. Interaction provided by graphics is very effective in such situations.

Graphics represent an integral part of the "Bugsystem" of Greaves (1975), which determines the dynamics of a microorganism under different environmental stimulus conditions from video image data recorded over a period of time. Besides providing numerous dynamic display options, the system allows the user to specify interactively the desired transformations to determine the dynamic behavior of the organisms.

Biomedical Signal Analysis. Biomedical signals such as electrocardiograms (ECG), electroencephalograms (EEG—reflecting the electrical activity of the brain cells), electromyograms (EMG—reflecting the electrical activity of the cells in muscles), and vectorcardiograms (VCG—see below for explanation) reflect the health state of the physiological systems that generate them. Health care units monitor these signals during patient diagnosis, surgery, and recovery periods. Modern automatic monitoring systems have graphics as an integral part not only for conveniently displaying these signals but also for providing statistical summaries of the various signal parameters used for recognizing abnormal patterns—see *Proc. IEEE* (1977), special issue on biological signal analysis.

As an example, the electrical field distribution in the thorax at any instant during a cardiac cycle can be represented by a dipole whose strength and direction change from instant to instant. The loop traced by the tip of the vector representing the dipole forms the VCG and contains diagnostic information. True three-dimensional display afforded by interactive graphics permits visualization and manipulation of the VCG loops in three-space (Kalff et al., 1974), which is very important if the three-dimensional information on field distribution is to be effectively used (see Fig. 2).

Modeling Biomedical Phenomena. Interactive graphics plays a vital role in computer modeling of physiological systems as a basic research and teaching tool. Its flexibility permits the user to modify the model interactively, to incorporate defects for simulating var-

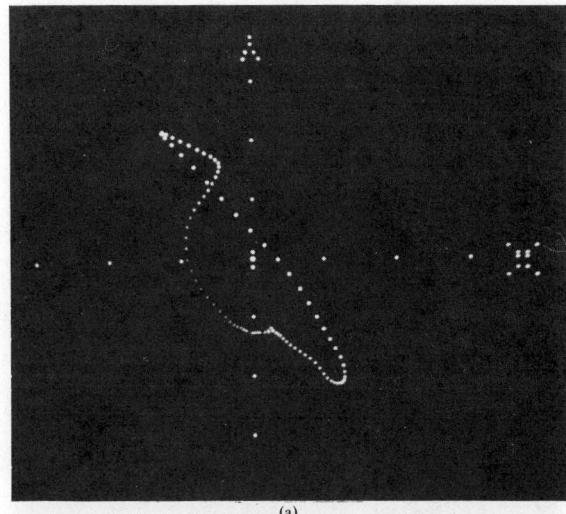

(a)

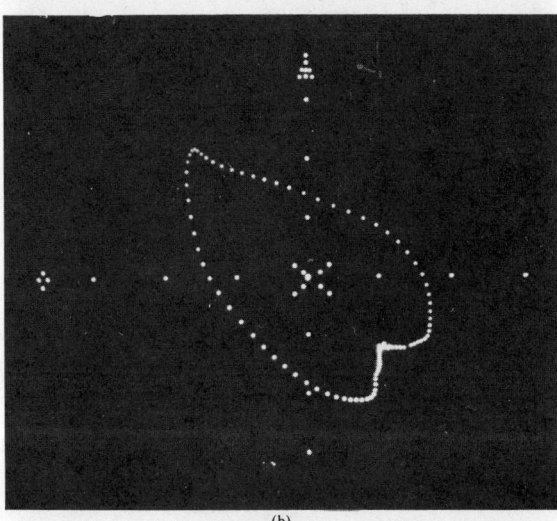

(b)

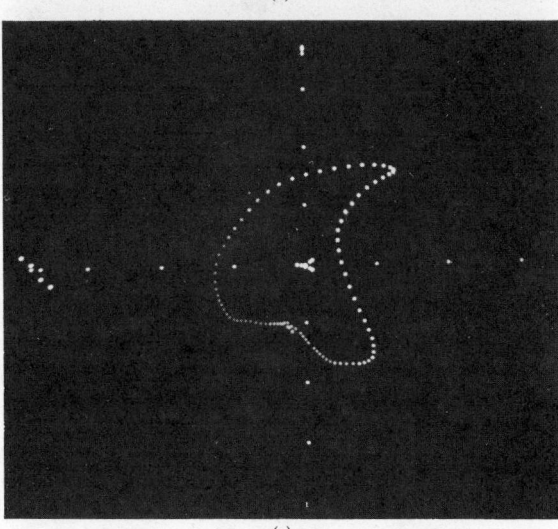

(c)

ious diseases, and to study the resulting functional responses. In his lumped parameter model of the heart and the circulatory system, Rupeiks (1972) used graphics to modify interactively the model to incorporate a user-specified congenital heart disease. The modified model and the various response functions were displayed on the screen upon request.

Display of Three-Dimensional Biomedical Structures. Imaging technologies, such as computed tomography (CT—*q.v.*), ultrasound, nuclear magnetic resonance (NMR), and electron microscopy, provide information about biological and anatomical structures in the form of three-dimensional images. Computer graphics finds its fullest utility in displaying the complex three-dimensional structures present in such images.

Another area where three-dimensional images are used is in the study of the conformation of biological molecules, which is important in molecular biology since conformation strongly influences molecular interactions and should, therefore, provide information about biological processes at a molecular level. A study of conformation requires construction and easy manipulability of molecular models, which is done very effectively by computer graphics techniques using the structural information provided by x-ray crystallography. Interactive manipulation involves display of the molecule on the screen, rotation to give a suitable view, and changing of the conformation by partial rotation about selected bonds until a structure that satisfies all available criteria is obtained. An example of a molecular display is illustrated in Fig. 3 (Perkins et al., 1976).

In the nervous system, information is conducted as voltage waveforms along dendrites and axons, which repeatedly branch into tree structures. In order to map the flow of information in the nervous system, it is necessary to understand the branching pattern of trees, to determine which trees interact with which other trees, to determine in which anatomical regions the trees branch, and to compare one tree with another. Interactive graphics makes possible effective achievement of these objectives through computer reconstruction and visualization of neuron models from tissue cross-sections (Capowski et al., 1979). Fig. 4 is an example of the display of computer-aided neuronal reconstruction.

It is difficult to perceive the three-dimensional structure of anatomical organs from a sequence of cross-sec-

Fig. 2. Three-dimensional displays of the VCG loops of a patient suffering from posterior infarct extending into the septum—standard orientations of the loops: (a) frontal plane, (b) sagittal plane, (c) horizontal plane.

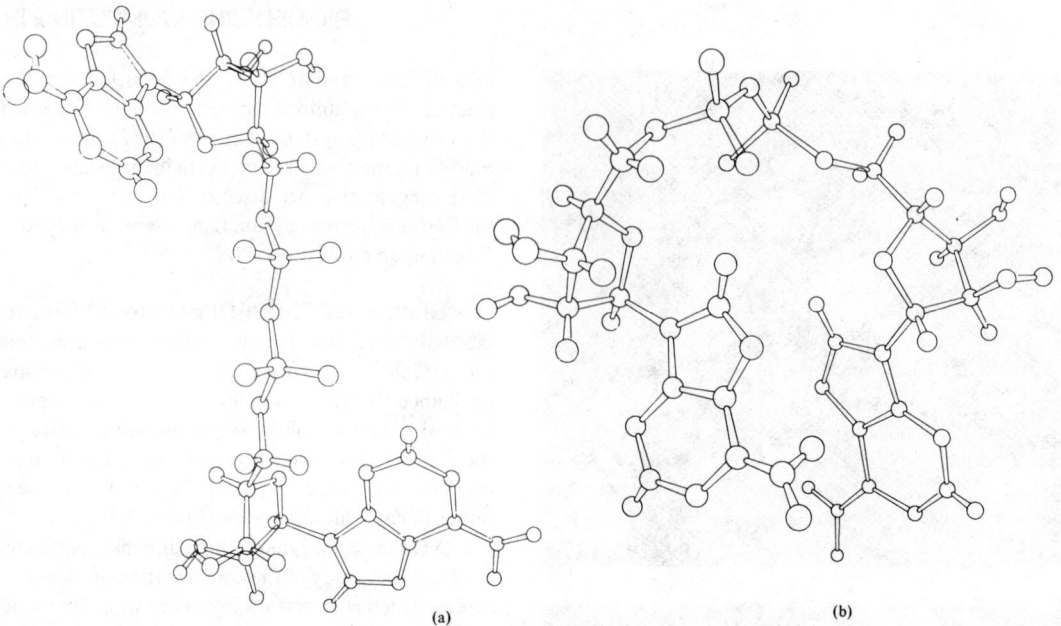

Fig. 3. A display of a molecular structure possessing 10 degrees of freedom: (a) initial state, (b) minimum energy state after adjustment of each torsional bond.

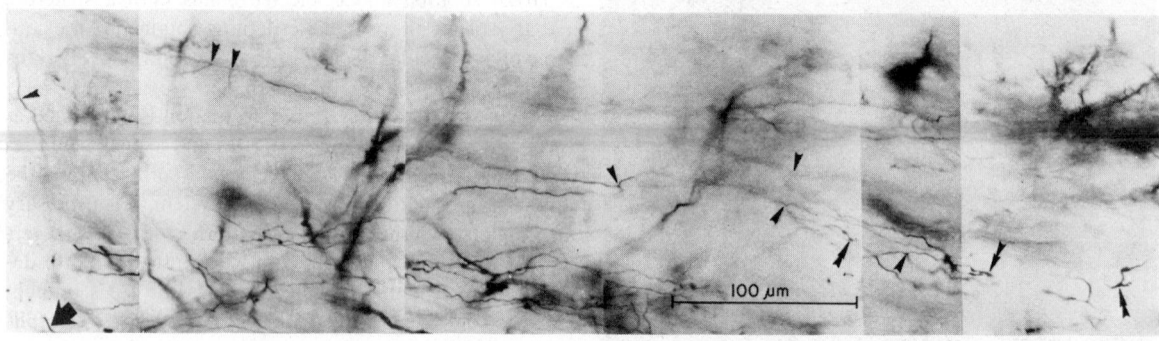

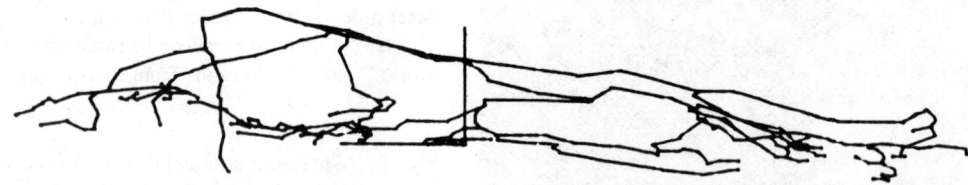

Fig. 4. Top: A low-power montage showing an axon tree in the substantia gelatinosa of an adult cat spinal cord. The axon was stained with Golgi-Kopsch stain, then the cord was sectioned sagittally. The thick arrowhead indicates the origin of the tree; slender arrowheads indicate branchpoints; double arrowheads indicate terminals. Bottom: The three-dimensional computer display of the same axon tree rotated into the same orientation.

172

tional images (such as those produced by CT, NMR, and ultrasound). Treating the stack of cross-sectional images as a three-dimensional array of numbers, effective computer algorithms have been developed recently for identifying the subregion of the three-dimensional array representing an organ of interest, for detecting a specified boundary surface of the subregion (Artzy et al., 1981), and for displaying the surface with hidden surface suppression and shading (Herman et al., 1979). Fig. 5 shows such a three-dimensional display of the part of the skull surface of a patient, produced from a sequence of

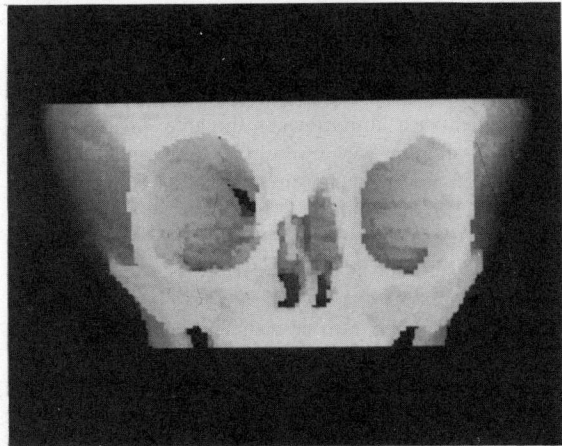

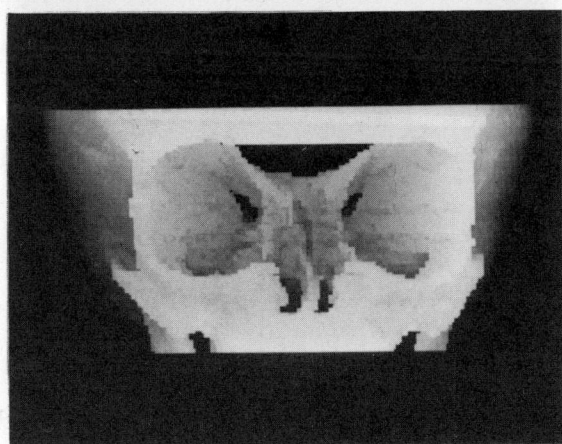

Fig. 5. Top: A display of a part of the skull surface of a patient suffering from nasal encephalocele (a disease in which cerebral tissue herniates into the nasal cavity, enlarging the nose and forcing the eyes to grow much farther apart than normal) produced from a series of CT slice images. Bottom: The display (same view as above) resulting after hypothetically performing a part of the corrective surgery (involving removal of bone and other tissues in the region of the nose) using the interactive graphics system.

CT slices. This system permits display of organs and organ systems and rotation in three-space about user-specified axes for visualization from arbitrary viewing angles. Such graphics techniques are sure to have an impact on future activities in diagnostic medicine.

Therapy and Surgery. One area in which the potential of computer graphics is still to be fully exploited is radiotherapy treatment planning—see *Comp. Prog. Biomed.* (1972). Treatment planning is the process of arriving at an effective plan for irradiating a specific body region such that the resulting distribution of absorbed dose meets the conditions set by a responsible radiotherapist. The dose distribution is usually presented as a set of isodose contours overlayed on a cross-sectional image display. Recent advances in the three-dimensional display of organs from CT images, combined with such features as multiple surface display, transparency, and color, are sure to be very useful in treatment planning leading to a better visualization of the planning strategy.

Stereotaxic neurosurgery involves the probing of deep subcortical structures by mechanically directed microelectrodes in an attempt to localize brain lesions. Since the structures in the path of the probing electrode cannot be seen, the various physiological responses of the patient to electrical stimulation are used as indicators of structures. A computer graphics display of a standard map in which descriptors of the evoked responses are overlayed on the anatomical image of the cross section being operated upon is very useful in correlating the response data with the structures. Also, the display system comes in very handy for efficient management of the massive patient response data generated during stereotaxic surgery (Hawrylyshyn et al., 1976).

Computer graphics holds great promise for preoperative surgical plans based on three-dimensional display of anatomical structures in CT images (Udupa, 1981). Using the graphics system, the surgeon interactively specifies the three-dimensional substructure to be removed surgically. The surgeon can subsequently visualize the operated anatomical structure (see Fig. 5). Risk and experimentation—both strictly unaffordable in the surgeon's patient world—are possible in the hypothetical world of graphics-generated anatomical organs, the graphics terminal forming the surgeon's scissors.

REFERENCES

1972. Rupeiks, I. "Computer-Aided Medical Instruction Using an Interactive Graphics Model of the Normal and Congenitally Defective Heart," *IEEE Trans. Bio Med. Eng.* **BME-19:**88–96.

1972. *Comp. Prog. Biomed.* (Special Issue on Radio Therapy Treatment Planning) **2** (April).

1974. Kalff, V. et al. "A Truly Three-Dimensional Vectorcardiographic Display," *Comp. Biol. Med.* **4:**137–144.

1975. Greaves, J. O. "The Bugsystem: The Software Structure for the Reduction of Quantized Video Data of Moving Organisms," *Proc. IEEE* **63**:1415–1425.

1976. Perkins, W. J. et al. "Computer Techniques for Conformational Studies of Biological Molecules," *Comp. Biol. Med.* **6**:23–31.

1976. Hawrylyshyn, P. et al. "A Computer System for Stereotaxic Neurosurgery," *Comp. Biol. Med.* **6**:87–97.

1976. Ballard, D. H. et al. "A Ladder-Structured Decision Tree for Recognizing Tumors in Chest Radiographs," *IEEE Trans. Comput.* **C-25**:503–513.

1977. *Proc. IEEE* (Special Issue on Biological Signal Analysis) **65** (May).

1977. Bartels, P. H. et al. "Computer Analysis and Biomedical Interpretation of Microscopic Images: Current Problems and Future Directions," *Proc. IEEE* **65**:252–261.

1979. Herman, G. T. et al. "Three-Dimensional Display of Human Organs from Computed Tomograms," *Comput. Graph. Im. Processing* **9**:1–21.

1979. Capowski, J. J. et al. "How to Configure a Computer-Aided Neuron Reconstruction and Graphics Display System," *Comp. Biomed. Res.* **12**:569–587.

1981. Artzy, E. et al. "The Theory, Design, Implementation and Evaluation of a Three-Dimensional Surface Detection Algorithm," *Comput. Graph. Im. Processing* **15**:1–24.

1981. Udupa, J. K. "Segmentation and Boundary Surface Formation for 3-D Digital Images," *Proc. SPIE,* **271** (Los Angeles Technical Symposium, Los Angeles, CA).

J. K. Udupa

BIT SLICING

For article on related subject *see* Integrated Circuitry.

Bit slicing refers to the technique of constructing an *m*-bit arithmetic-logic unit (ALU) by interconnecting a set of identical *n*-bit ($n < m$) LSI chips called *bit slices*. Bit slice chips—typically, one, two, or four bits wide—contain all of the circuits necessary to perform a large number of ALU functions, including arithmetic, logic, register storage, and even I/O, for their segment of a processor word. Then, for example, four four-bit slices may be combined to form the CPU of a 16-bit computer.

While the interconnection of functional components within each integrated circuit (IC) may be rigidly predefined, it is usual to include a degree of flexibility under the control of peripheral pin connections on which signals are established by an external microprogrammed controller (see Fig. 1). Such signals are usually connected in parallel to the corresponding peripheral pins of each slice. Accordingly, the complexity of the controller is to a degree independent of the length *m* of the ALU formed. Thus, the bit slice approach is most cost-effective for long word-length computer designs.

However, the major advantage of bit slicing is to provide a rational basis for packaging very high-speed, high-performance circuits in a reasonable number of IC chips, each with limitations on die area, pin count, and power dissipation. As a result of this approach, high-speed, high-power bipolar circuit technology can be used. For example, the Schottky TTL AMD 2900 series four-bit chip set operates with a 100-ns microcycle, while the ECL M10800 four-bit family performs typical micro-operations in tens of nanoseconds.

It is appropriate to note that the same motives for bit slicing extend as well to memory. Thus, a semiconductor memory system is normally sliced vertically, each *m* bit word being resident in several *n* bit ($n < m$) slices.

References

1978. Hamacher, V. C., Vranesic, Z. G., and Zaky, S. G. *Computer Organization.* New York: McGraw-Hill.

K. C. Smith

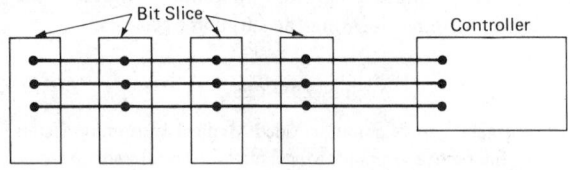

Fig. 1. Conceptual view of a (16-bit) ALU consisting of four (four-bit) slices operated in parallel by a (shared) controller. Only three of the many control lines are shown.

BLOCK and BLOCKING

For articles on related subjects *see* File; Memory: Auxiliary; Open and Close a File; Record; and Tape Label.

The term *block* is synonymous with *physical record:* A sequence of words or characters written contiguously by a computer on an external storage medium. Typically, one block is written each time a write command is executed by an I/O channel (or equivalent I/O facility). Analogously, one block is read from an external medium each time that a read command is executed by the channel.

The idea of a *block* is distinguished from that of a *logical record* as follows: A block is defined by the physical characteristics and constraints of the external storage medium, whereas a logical record is defined by a partic-

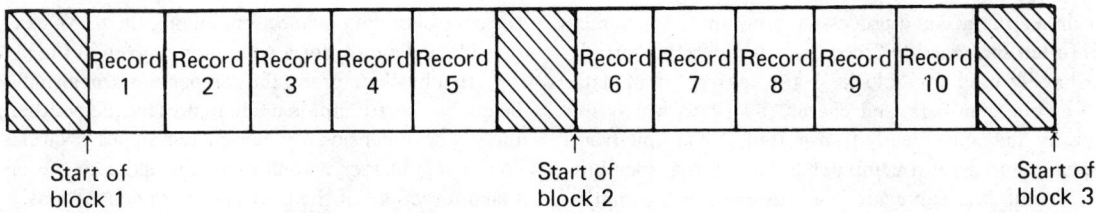

Fig. 1. Fixed length blocks: blocking factor = 5; all records have same length; block length = 5 × (record length).

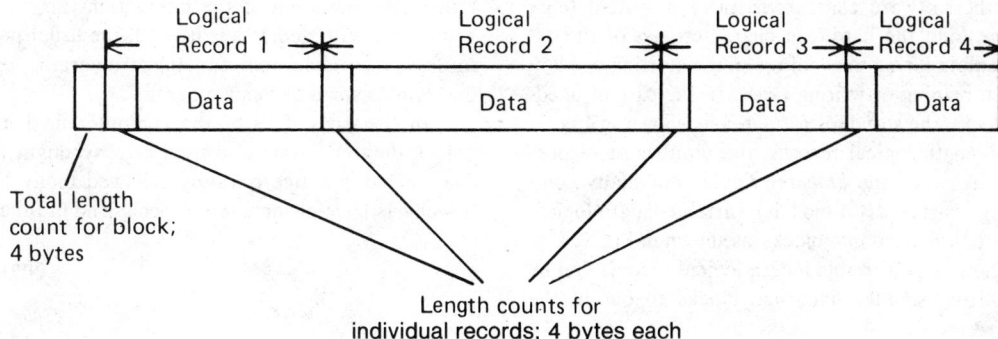

Fig. 2. Variable-block lengths (no logical record larger than one physical block): blocking factor, variable; block length = 4 + [(length of record-1) + 4] + [(length of record-2) + 4] + ...

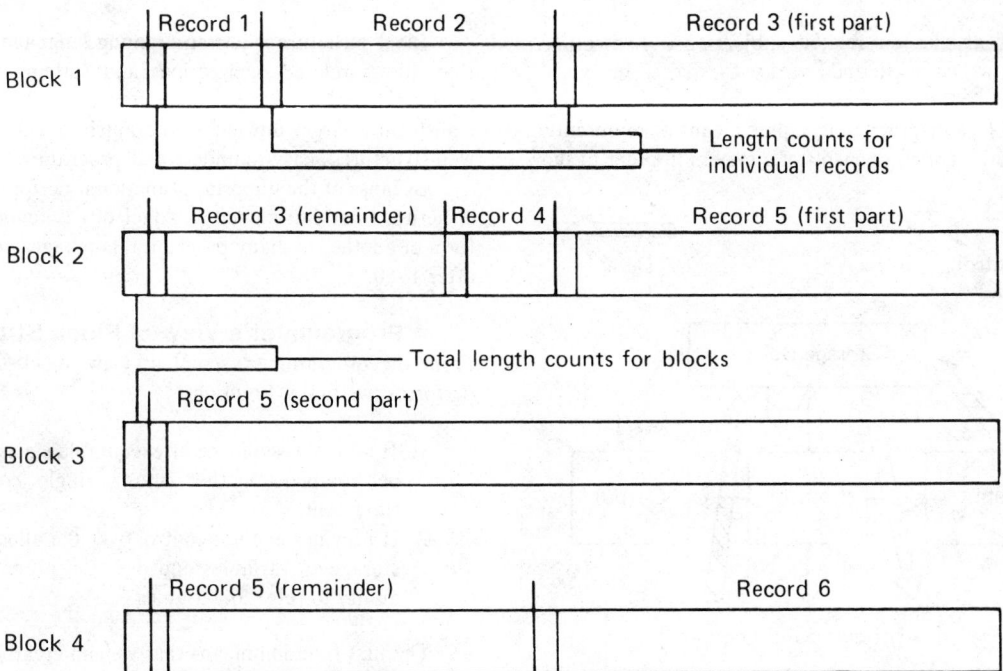

Fig. 3. Variable-length records (which may be larger than fixed-length physical blocks).

ular data structure in a processing program. Logical records (often shortened to "records," although this term is also loosely used for "blocks") are aggregates of data such as bits, numbers, and character strings, which are naturally and conveniently transmitted at one time from the main storage of a computer to an external medium. One type of data aggregate is a *master record*, comprising all attributes associated with a member of some population.

Blocks typically contain several logical records when written onto magnetic media such as drums, tape drives, and disk drives. The size of a block is chosen to take into account the software characteristics of a system (e.g., buffer size) and the hardware characteristics of the external medium (so as to avoid too much starting or stopping when reading or writing tape). In the case of fixed-length blocks, the standard format is as shown in Fig. 1. For fixed-length logical records, the number of records per block is called the *blocking factor*. For many computers (e.g., current IBM models), variable-length logical records are formatted into blocks, as shown in Fig. 2. Fig. 3 shows how large variable length logical records can be built up from smaller fixed-size blocks to obtain the *spanned record* format.

D. N. FREEMAN

BLOCK DIAGRAM

For articles on related subjects *see* FLOWCHART; FLOW DIAGRAM; and SYSTEM CHART.

A block diagram is a graphic means of representing the functions or components of a system in order to show

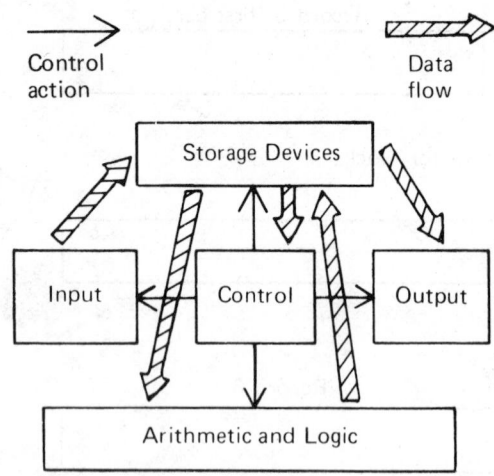

Fig. 1.   Block diagram of computer.

the control or data connections among them. An example of a block diagram for a computer is given in Fig. 1.

In a block diagram, the components are normally labeled, but no attempt is made to present them either pictorially or dimensionally. Simple rectangles or circles are common. Lines or arrows generally indicate the operational directions of the control or data connections.

Block diagrams may be drawn at any level of detail, but are most common at the grosser and more summary levels. Whatever the level of detail chosen, the usual focus of the block diagram is the control and data connections among the components identified. When a detailed representation of the interactions among components or circuit elements is needed, the usual practice is to draw logic diagrams, functional diagrams, or circuit diagrams instead of block diagrams.

In the early days of the computer field, the term "block diagram" was also used as a synonym for flowchart. That practice is rarely followed today now that flowcharts have become more specialized in function.

NED CHAPIN

BLOCK STRUCTURE

For articles on related subjects *see* PROCEDURE; PROCEDURE-ORIENTED LANGUAGES; PROGRAMMING LANGUAGES; and STRUCTURED PROGRAMMING.

Block structure is a programming language concept that allows related declarations and statements to be grouped together. When used judiciously, it can help transform a large, unwieldy program into a disciplined, well-structured, easy-to-understand program.

Because of the important function it performs, block structure (first introduced in Algol 60) is found in one form or another in many procedural languages developed after 1960.

A Programmer's View of Block Structure. From the programmer's point of view, block structure performs two major functions:

1. It allows a sequence of executable statements to be grouped together into a single *compound* statement.
2. It provides explicit control over the allocation of storage to variables and over the programmer's ability to refer to variables.

The first function means that we can create and use a compound statement anywhere that the programming language allows a single statement to be used (e.g., in either branch of an **if-then-else** statement). This allows us to think of a sequence of statements as a single entity and thus simplify the process of program construction. Since a block may contain other blocks as components, block structure can be used to decompose a large program into an orderly nest of blocks. This is perhaps the most important use of block structure from the programmer's point of view, since it allows programs to be constructed in a hierarchical fashion, which often results in increased program clarity and elegance.

Control over storage allocation and visibility of variables implies two things. First there is the ability to control dynamically the allocation and freeing of storage during program execution. The storage for variables declared within a block is allocated when the block is entered during program execution. Unless explicitly inhibited, this storage is freed automatically when the block is exited. Second, each block introduces a new scope (i.e., a domain of definition of variables). Variables declared within a block (i.e., local to the block) may only be used within that block (and any contained block). Thus variables declared within a block can have no effect on the program outside of the block. This provides a degree of data security, since a programmer can use a block to "hide" variables *(information hiding)* and thereby make them inaccessible outside of this block.

In order to appreciate the importance of block structure, let us consider the piece of Algol 60 code in Fig. 1.

```
begin
   comment first block - main program;
   integer sumx, sumxx;
   integer array x[1:100];
   real array y[1:50];
   . . .
   begin
      comment second block;
      integer p,y;
      integer array xx[1:100];
      sumx := sumxx := 0;
      for p := 1 step 1 until 100 do
         begin
            comment third block;
            sumx := sumx + x[p];
            xx[p] := x[p] * x[p];
            sumxx := sumxx + xx[p]
         end;
      for p := 1 step 1 until 100 do
         x[p] := xx[p] ÷ sumxx;
   end
end;
```

Fig 1.   A program using block structure.

In the program in Fig. 1, the first block is used to declare the global variables *sumx, sumxx, x* and *y*. The second block is used to introduce the new variables *p,y* and *xx*. Storage for these variables will exist only while execution is in the block. The third block is used to group three assignment statements so that they behave as one statement in the body of the first **for** loop.

Using Block Structure in Programs. The material in this section has been adopted from Wegner (1971).

Declarations. In most block-structured programming languages, a block has the form:

```
begin
   <block head>
   <block body>
end
```

A <block head> consists of a (possibly empty) list of variable, procedure and function declarations. A <block body> consists of a list of executable statements. The rules of Algol 60 state that all identifiers (e.g., names of variables) used within a block have to be declared in its block head or in the block head of some enclosing block. Identifiers can be used only within the block in which they are declared (including any contained blocks). This block is their *scope* and they are said to be *local* to it.

In addition to scalar variables, arrays may also be declared in the block head. In Algol 60, the expressions defining the lower and upper bounds for arrays are recalculated each time the block is activated. Thus, the bounds for a given array variable can be different for different activations of the same block.

Scope Rules. As mentioned above, a block body is a sequence of executable statements and a block is itself an executable statement. Therefore, blocks may be nested to any depth. This has several consequences:

1. Although an identifier may be used only once as the name of an object in a block, the same identifier may be used to name different objects in different blocks. A good programmer will use this facility sparingly (e.g., for utility variables like *i, j, k* used as counters and loop indices). Widespread reuse of identifiers can make a program difficult to understand.
2. If the same identifier is used to name objects in several nested blocks, the programming language's *scope rule* is used to disambiguate references to the identifier. The *Algol 60 scope rule* (used in most procedural languages) starts at the

point where the identifier is used and searches block heads starting with the block containing the use of the identifier and working outward toward the main program block until a declaration of the identifier is found. Note that with this rule, the redeclaration of an identifier in an inner block will make the object named by the same identifier in an outer block inaccessible. For example, in Fig 1., the declaration of an integer variable y in the second block makes the real array y declared in the main program inaccessible in the second block (and in all contained blocks).

3. Whenever a block is entered during program execution, fresh storage is allocated for all the variables declared in the block head. This storage, known as the *activation record* of the block, defines a particular instance of the block in time. When execution leaves the block, the storage occupied by the activation record is freed. In most procedural languages, the allocation and freeing of activation records follows a strict last-in-first-out discipline. This implies that a stack mechanism is ideally suited for the storage of activation records. This also facilitates the implementation of recursive procedures.

Fig. 2 illustrates these points. The identifier b is used to name variables in both the first and second blocks. In the block that is the body of the procedure P, the variable x declared in the first block is inaccessible because the identifier x was also used to name a formal parameter of P; the variable c declared in the first block is inaccessible in the body of P because another variable named c is declared there. In the assignment statement in the body of P, the identifier c refers to the variable c declared in P, the identifier x refers to a formal parameter of P, and the identifier b refers to the variable b declared in the first block.

Two Examples. Algol 60 and Pascal illustrate two approaches to providing block structure in a high-level programming language. In Algol 60, a block may be used anywhere that a statement can be used. Any block can contain declarations and thus introduce new variables. In Pascal, declarations may appear as a prefix to a block that is the body of a function or procedure. Other blocks can contain no declarations and therefore can only be used to group statements together.

REFERENCES

1964. Randell, B. and Russell, L. S. *Algol 60 Implementation,* New York: Academic Press.
1967. Eckman, T. and Froberg, C. E. *Introduction to Algol 60.* London: Oxford University Press. (This book contains the complete text of the revised Algol 60 report, as well as a good discussion of the control and data structures of Algol 60.)
1971. Wegner, P. "Structured Model Building in Computer Science." Department of Applied Mathematics, Brown University, Providence RI.
1975. Pratt, T. W. *Programming Languages: Design and Implementation.* Englewood Cliffs, NJ: Prentice-Hall.

D. B. WORTMAN

BNF. *See* BACKUS-NAUR FORM.

BOOLE, GEORGE

For article on related subject *see* BOOLEAN ALGEBRA.

George Boole (b. Lincoln, England, 1815; d. Cork, Ireland, 1864) was one of those rarities in an era of increasing specialization: The self-taught man who followed his own path to the penetration of territory untouched by his contemporaries. Due to the family's sparse financial resources, Boole's formal education was limited to elementary school and a short stint in a commercial school. Beyond this he was almost totally self-educated.

Boole's first scientific publication was an address on Newton to mark the presentation of a bust of Newton to the Mechanics Institution in Lincoln. In 1840 he wrote his first paper for the *Cambridge Mathematical Journal.*

```
begin
    comment first block;
    real c, b, x;
    procedure P(x,y);
        real x, y;
        begin
            comment body of P;
            real c;
            ...
            b := x + c;
            ...
            end P;
    begin
        comment second block;
        real b, d;
        ...
        P(d,b);
        ...
    end
end;
```

Fig 2. Block structure example.

In 1849, despite his lack of formal training, he was appointed to a professorship of mathematics in the newly established Queen's College, Cork, Ireland.

During his career he published approximately fifty scientific papers, two textbooks (on differential equations, 1859; and finite differences, 1860), and his two famous volumes on mathematical logic (see reference). In 1844, the Royal Society awarded him a medal for his papers on differential operators, and, in 1857, they elected him a Fellow. He was married in 1855 to Mary Everest, a niece of Sir George Everest after whom Mount Everest was named.

Although Boole made significant contributions in a number of areas of mathematics, his immortality stems from his two works that gave decisive impetus to the need to express logical concepts in mathematical form: "The Mathematical Analysis of Logic, Being an Essay Towards a Calculus of Deductive Reasoning" (1847) and "An Investigation of the Laws of Thought, on Which are Founded the Mathematical Theories of Logic and Probability" (1854). Through these works he truly became the founder of modern symbolic logic. He reduced logic to a propositional calculus, now called *boolean algebra,* which was extremely simple and perhaps too strongly based upon classical logic.

Under the influence of his work, a school of symbolic logic evolved, which made a determined effort to unify logic and mathematics. As is usual, the impact of this effort was not realized until much later in the latter part of the nineteenth century. Although de Morgan and Jevons expounded on his work during Boole's lifetime, it remained for Frege, Peano, and C. S. Peirce to relight the torch that finally led to the "Principia Mathematica" (1910–1913) of Russell and Whitehead.

Boole's discovery that the symbolism of algebra could be used in logic has had wide impact in the twentieth century. Today, boolean algebra is important not only in logic but also in the theory of probability, the theory of lattices, the geometry of sets, and information theory. It has also led to the design of electronic computers through the interpretation of boolean combinations of sets as switching circuits. For example, the logical sum of two sets corresponds to a circuit with two switches in parallel and the logical product corresponds to a pair of switches in series.

REFERENCE

1970. Broadbent, T. A. A., "George Boole," in *Dictionary of Scientific Biography* **II**:293–298. New York: Scribners. (This is an outstanding biography with an excellent bibliography of both primary and secondary sources.)

H. TROPP

BOOLEAN ALGEBRA

For articles on related subjects *see* ARITHMETIC, COMPUTER; and LOGIC DESIGN.

The concept of a boolean algebra was first proposed by the English mathematician George Boole in 1847. Since that time, Boole's original conception has been extensively developed and refined by algebraists and logicians. The relationships among boolean algebra, set algebra, logic, and binary arithmetic have given boolean algebras a central role in the development of electronic digital computers.

Set Algebras. The most intuitive development of boolean algebras arises from the concept of a set algebra. Let $S = \{a,b,c\}$ and $T = \{a,b,c,d,e\}$ be two sets consisting of three and five elements, respectively. We say that S is a *subset* of $T,$ since every element of S (namely, $a, b,$ and c) belongs to $T.$ Since T has five elements, there are 2^5 subsets of $T,$ for we may choose any individual element to be included or omitted from a subset. Note that these 32 subsets include T itself and the empty set, which contains no elements at all. If T contains all elements of concern, it is called the *universal set.* Given a subset of $T,$ such as $S,$ we may define the *complement* of S with respect to a universal set T to consist of precisely those elements of T which are not included in the given subset. Thus, S as above defined has as its complement (with respect to T) $\overline{S} = \{d,e\}.$ The *union* of any two sets (subsets of a given set) consists of those elements that are in one or the other or in both given sets; the *intersection* of two sets consists of those elements that are in both given sets. We use the symbol $\cup$ to denote the union, and $\cap$ to denote the intersection of two sets. For example, if $B = \{b,d,e\},$ then $B \cup S = \{a,b,c,d,e\},$ and $B \cap S = \{b\}.$

While other set operations may be defined, the operations of complementation, union, and intersection are of primary interest to us. A boolean algebra is a finite or infinite set of elements together with three operations—negation, addition, and multiplication—that correspond to the set operations of complementation, union, and intersection, respectively. Among the elements of a boolean algebra are two distinguished elements: 0, corresponding to the empty set; and 1, corresponding to the universal set. For any given element a of a boolean algebra, there is a unique complement a' with the property that $a + a' = 1$ and $aa' = 0.$ Boolean addition and multiplication are associative and commutative, as are ordinary addition and multiplication, but otherwise have somewhat different properties. The principal properties are given in Table 1, where $a, b,$ and c are any elements of a boolean algebra.

Table 1

Distributivity:	$a(b + c) = ab + ac$
	$a + (bc) = (a + b)(a + c)$
Idempotency:	$a + a = a$
	$aa = a$
Absorption laws:	$a + ab = a$
	$a(a + b) = a$
DeMorgan's laws:	$(a + b)' = a'b'$
	$(ab)' = a' + b'$

Since a finite set of n elements has exactly 2^n subsets, and it can be shown that the finite boolean algebras are precisely the finite set algebras, each finite boolean algebra consists of exactly 2^n elements for some integer n. For example, the set algebra for the set T defined above corresponds to a boolean algebra of 32 elements. Tables 2 and 3 define the boolean operations for boolean algebras of two and four elements, respectively.

Table 2.   Two elements.

$a + b$	0	1	$a \cdot b$	0	1	a	a'
0	0	1	0	0	0	0	1
1	1	1	1	0	1	1	0

Table 3.   Four elements.

$a + b$	0	p	p'	1	$a \cdot b$	0	p	p'	1	a	a'
0	0	p	p'	1	0	0	0	0	0	0	1
p	p	p	1	1	p	0	p	0	p	p	p'
p'	p'	1	p'	1	p'	0	0	p'	p'	p'	p
1	1	1	1	1	1	0	p	p'	1	1	0

While it is possible to use a different symbol to denote each element of a boolean algebra, it is often more useful to represent the 2^n elements of a finite boolean algebra by binary vectors having n components. With such a representation the operations of the boolean algebra are accomplished componentwise by considering each component as an independent two-element boolean algebra. This corresponds to representing subsets of a finite set by binary vectors. For example, since the set T has five elements, we may represent its subsets by five-component binary vectors, each component denoting an element of the set T. A numeral 1 in the ith component of the vector denotes the inclusion of the ith element of that particular subset; a 0 denotes its exclusion. Thus, the subset $S = \{a,b,c\}$ has the binary vector representation $\{1,1,1,0,0\}$. The set operations become boolean operations on the components of the vectors. This representation of sets, and the correspondence to boolean or logical operations, is very useful in information retrieval. Because of it, sets

of document and query characteristics may be easily and rapidly matched.

Elementary Logic. In information retrieval work, and in identifying boolean algebras as set algebras, we find that various logical connectives, such as "and," "or," and "not," recur frequently. Thus, it is not surprising to find that the two-element boolean algebra can be identified with elementary logic or propositional calculus. A *proposition* is a statement that can be said to be either true or false. We will denote propositions by letters such as p, q, and r.

The connectives or operators "and" and "or" combine two such propositions into a new one. If we consider two propositions, p and q, each may, independently of the other, assume the value true (T) or false (F). Hence, together the ordered pair $\langle p,q \rangle$ may assume $2 \cdot 2 = 4$ combinations of truth values: $\langle T,T \rangle$, $\langle T,F \rangle$, $\langle F,T \rangle$, and $\langle F,F \rangle$. If $\circ$ denotes a binary operator, then $p \circ q$ may assume either (T) or (F) independently for each of these four T-F combinations. Thus we can define $2^4 = 16$ distinct binary logical operators, as shown in Table 4. Of the 16 binary logical operators that can be defined, 5 are commonly used and are more than sufficient to define the remaining operators.

Table 4

p q	1	2	3	4	5	6	7	8	9	10	11	12	13	14	15	16
T T	T	T	T	T	T	T	T	T	F	F	F	F	F	F	F	F
T F	T	T	T	T	F	F	F	F	T	T	T	T	F	F	F	F
F T	T	T	F	F	T	T	F	F	T	T	F	F	T	T	F	F
F F	T	F	T	F	T	F	T	F	T	F	T	F	T	F	T	F

The "negation" or "not" operation, $\sim p$, is defined to form a proposition that is true precisely when the proposition p is false, and false whenever p is true. If we equate the truth values "true" and "false" with the boolean values 1 and 0, respectively, then we find that negation corresponds to boolean complementation. That is, $\sim p$ replaces the value "true" with "false," and vice versa, just as p' replaces the value "1" with "0," and vice versa. (In Table 4, column 13 is $\sim p$.)

The logical "conjunction" or "and," $p \wedge q$, forms a proposition that is true precisely when both p and q are true, and false otherwise. This corresponds to the boolean operation of multiplication, with the boolean expression pq having the value 1 if and only if both p and q have the value 1. (See Table 4, column 8.)

In ordinary usage the word "or" has two distinct meanings, referred to as the "inclusive or" and the "exclusive or." In the inclusive sense, the statement "p or q" is true if p or q or both are true; in the exclusive sense,

Table 5

p q r	(1) $p\equiv q$	(2) $p\vee\sim r$	(3) $\sim p\vee q$	(4) (2)$\wedge$(3)	(5) (4)$\supset r$	(6) $\sim$(5)	Expression (1)$\supset$(6)
T T T	T	T	T	T	T	F	F
T T F	T	T	T	T	F	T	T
T F T	F	T	F	F	T	F	T
T F F	F	T	F	F	T	F	T
F T T	F	F	T	F	T	F	T
F T F	F	T	T	T	F	T	T
F F T	T	F	T	F	T	F	F
F F F	T	T	T	T	F	T	T

the same statement is true if either p or q, but not both, is true. The logical "disjunction" or "or," $p \vee q$, is defined to be the inclusive "or." That is, $p \vee q$ is true precisely when at least one of the statements p and q is true. Thus, this operation corresponds to boolean addition as we have defined it. (See Table 4, column 2.)

The exclusive "or," $p \not\equiv q$, is commonly called *inequivalence,* since it defines a proposition that is true precisely when p and q have opposite or inequivalent truth values. This corresponds to any of several more complex boolean operations such as $pq' + p'q$, and $(p + q)(pq)'$. (See Table 4, column 10.)

The remaining conventional logical operator is the *conditional* or *implication,* $p \supset q$, corresponding to the statement "if p then q." The conditional proposition $p \supset q$ takes the value "false" if p is true and q is false, and takes the value "true" otherwise. Thus, it corresponds to the boolean operation $p' + q$. Note that if p is false, then $p \supset q$ is true, regardless of the value of q. This corresponds to the statement that one can prove anything (q, whether true or false) from a false hypothesis (p). (See Table 4, column 5.)

While the logical operators that we have defined suffice to define all logical operators, it is only necessary to use two of the above operators, namely, negation, and one of the operators conjunction, disjunction, or conditional. However, of importance to computer design is the fact that we can define all logical operators in terms of one basic operator, either the "nand" or the "nor" operator. These are the negation of the conjunction and disjunction operators, respectively. That is, the "nand" operator defines a statement, $p \mid q$, which has the value "false" precisely when both p and q are true, and the value "true" otherwise. The "nor" operator defines a statement, $p \downarrow q$, which has the value "true" precisely when both p and q are false, and the value "false" otherwise. (See Table 4, columns 9 and 15.)

Truth Tables. A truth table gives the truth values of a logical expression for each combination of the truth values of its variables. Thus, for a logical expression in n variables, the truth table contains 2^n lines, one for each combination of truth values of its variables. Since the truth value of an expression is determined from the truth values of various subexpressions, the truth table may be given in an extended form, which explicitly lists all subexpressions, a standard form in which the subexpressions are not separately listed and a condensed form in which the lines of the table are compressed by indicating the truth value of certain critical subexpressions. Tables 5 through 7 illustrate these three forms of truth table for the logical expression $(p \equiv q) \supset \sim (((p \vee \sim r) \wedge (\sim p \vee q)) \supset r)$.

In each of these three tables the truth values for the given expression are in the boxed column. In the condensed form, Table 7, each line of the table may represent one or more lines of the uncondensed table. For example, the first line of Table 7 represents the two lines TFT and TFF of the uncondensed table. In this particular example, the line FTF is represented three times,

Table 6

p q r	$(p\equiv q)$	$\supset$	$\sim$	$(((p\vee\sim r)\wedge(\sim p\vee q))\supset r)$			
T T T	T	F	F	T	T	T	T
T T F	T	T	T	T	T	T	F
T F T	F	T	F	T	F	F	T
T F F	F	T	F	T	F	F	T
F T T	F	T	F	F	F	T	T
F T F	F	T	T	T	T	T	F
F F T	T	F	F	F	F	T	T
F F F	T	T	T	T	T	T	F

Table 7

p q r	$(p\equiv q)$	$\supset$	$\sim$	$(((p\vee\sim r)\wedge(\sim p\vee q)\supset r$			
T F –	F	T	–	–	–	–	–
F T –	F	T	–	–	–	–	–
F – F	–	T	T	T	T	T	F
– T F	–	T	T	T	T	T	F
T T T	T	F	F	–	–	–	T
F F T	T	F	F	–	–	–	T

namely, in lines 2, 3, and 4 of the Table 7. Also in the condensed table, the dashes represent values that are immaterial and hence do not need to be calculated. For example, in the first line of Table 7, since $p \equiv q$ is false, we know that the entire expression has the value "true," regardless of the value of the remaining portion of the expression.

The truth table for an unknown logical function can be used to generate an expression for that function. The expression thus generated is called a *disjunctive normal form* or, in boolean algebra, a *sum of products form*. The development of this expression is illustrated in Table 8. For each line of the table wherein the unknown function has the value "true," an expression is formed by taking the conjunction of all variables that are true in that line and the negations of all variables that are false in that line. The expression for the function f is then the disjunction of all expressions formed for the single lines. In Table 8, f is given in this form, and in the corresponding boolean algebra form, as well as in a shorter form developed by direct inspection of the function values. (Equivalence, $\equiv$, is defined by column 7 of Table 4.)

The development of the disjunctive normal form shows that the logical operators conjunction, disjunction,

and negation are sufficient to develop an expression for any logical function. Furthermore, we may use DeMorgan's laws to transform conjunctions to disjunctions, or vice versa. Thus, as we previously asserted, any logical function can be developed from the operators negation and either conjunction or disjunction. Table 9 shows the development of the five common logical operators in terms of these two minimal combinations of operators. In turn, Table 10 shows the development of negation, conjunction, and disjunction in terms of both the "nand" and the "nor" operators, thus indicating that every logical operator can be defined in terms of either one of these latter two operators.

Computer Arithmetic. The identification of the logical constants T and F with the boolean constants 1 and 0, respectively, leads to the development of the arithmetic properties of the computer in terms of its logical or boolean operators. In binary arithmetic, the multiplication of bits is exactly the same as boolean multiplication: The product of two bits is 1 if and only if both bits are 1. However, the addition of two bits is quite different from boolean addition. This is apparent, since in boolean arithmetic $1 + 1 = 1$, while in binary arithmetic $1 + 1 = 10$.

We also observe that in binary arithmetic the sum bit is 1 if and only if one, but not both, summands have the value 1, while the carry bit is 1 if and only if both summands have the value 1. Thus, we can compute the sum bit by using the logical inequivalence (exclusive or) operation, and the carry bit by using the logical conjunction, or boolean multiplication operation. Finally, we observe that, since the negative of an integer is normally represented in the computer by a complementary bit pattern (1's complement), arithmetic negation can be accomplished by logical negation, or boolean complementation, with slight modification if 2's-complement arithmetic is used.

Logical Design. Logical design of a computer is the development of computer circuitry to perform the desired functions for the particular machine. It is necessary that the circuitry be accurate and reliable, and desirable that it be relatively simple so that it is inexpensive and easy to maintain. While logical design must include consideration of timing problems and the various electro-mechanical attachments to the computer, the heart of the problem resides in the development of logical circuitry to perform the desired functions.

Of the various devices designed to systematize study of this logic, the Venn diagram and Karnaugh map are particularly simple and highly effective for functions of 2, 3, 4, or 5 variables. However, the use of these devices becomes increasingly difficult as the number of variables increases beyond five. The classical Venn diagram con-

Table 8

p q r	$f(p,q,r)$	Generated expression
T T T	F	–
T T F	T	$p \wedge q \wedge \sim r$
T F T	T	$p \wedge \sim q \wedge r$
T F F	F	–
F T T	T	$\sim p \wedge q \wedge r$
F T F	F	–
F F T	F	–
F F F	T	$\sim p \wedge \sim q \wedge \sim r$

$$f(p,q,r) = (p \wedge q \wedge \sim r) \vee (p \wedge \sim q \wedge r) \vee (\sim p \wedge q \wedge r) \vee (\sim p \wedge \sim q \wedge \sim r)$$
$$f(p,q,r) = pqr' + pq'r + p'qr + p'q'r'$$
$$f(p,q,r) = p \equiv (q \not\equiv r)$$

Table 9

	$\wedge, \sim$	$\vee, \sim$
$\sim p$	$\sim p$	$\sim p$
$p \wedge q$	$p \wedge q$	$\sim(\sim p \vee \sim q)$
$p \vee q$	$\sim(\sim p \wedge \sim q)$	$p \vee q$
$p \supset q$	$\sim(p \wedge \sim q)$	$\sim p \vee q$
$p \equiv q$	$\sim(\sim(p \wedge q) \wedge \sim(\sim p \wedge \sim q))$	$(p \vee q) \vee \sim(\sim p \vee \sim q)$

Table 10

	$\mid$	$\downarrow$
$\sim p$	$p \mid p$	$p \downarrow p$
$p \wedge q$	$(p \mid q) \mid (p \mid q)$	$(p \downarrow p) \downarrow (q \downarrow q)$
$p \vee q$	$(p \mid p) \mid (q \mid q)$	$(p \downarrow q) \downarrow (p \downarrow q)$

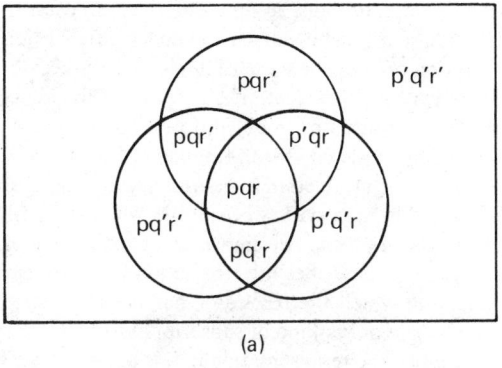

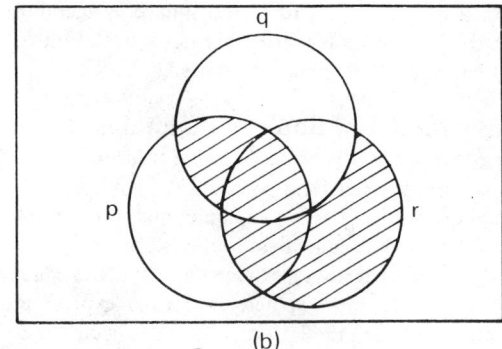

Fig. 1. Venn diagram.

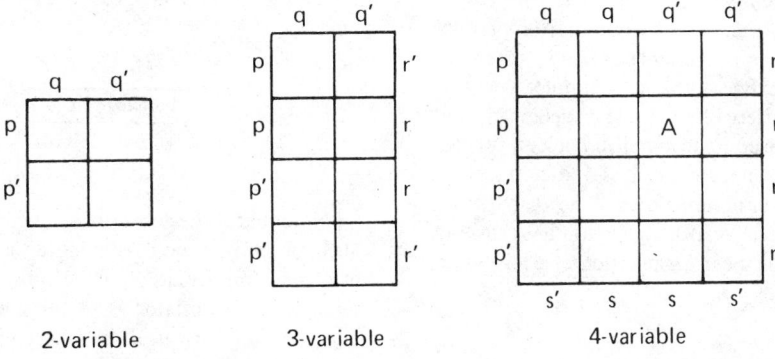

2-variable 3-variable 4-variable

Fig. 2. Karnaugh maps.

sists of a rectangle representing the universe, containing a circle or other simple closed curve for each variable represented. The interpretation is that within the circle the given variable has the value 1, while outside it has the value 0. These circles are arranged in such a way as to include all possible combination of 1's and 0's for the variables. The Venn diagram for a 3-variable problem is given in Fig. 1, with the various regions labeled in Fig. 1(a) and certain regions shaded to represent the boolean function $pq + pr + p'r$ in Fig. 1(b). In this form the Venn diagram is relatively ineffective for logical analysis. The varying shapes of the regions cause some difficulty in visualizing possible combinations of these regions, particularly if four or more variables are involved.

The Karnaugh map is a practical modification of the Venn diagram, with each region of the diagram represented by a square within a larger rectangle. The Karnaugh maps for 2-, 3-, and 4-variable problems are given in Fig. 2. The region represented by each square is determined by the product of the letters on the edges of the rectangle. For example, the square marked A in the 4-variable rectangle represents the region $pq'rs$. To represent a boolean function, say $pq + pr + q'r$, on a Karnaugh map, first expand each term of the functions to include all variables present:

$$pq + pr + q'r$$
$$= pq \cdot 1 + p \cdot 1 \cdot r + 1 \cdot q'r$$
$$= pq(r + r') + p(q + q')r + (p + p')q'r$$
$$= pqr + pqr' + pqr + pq'r + pq'r + p'q'r$$
$$= pqr + pqr' + pq'r + p'q'r.$$

Then mark each square corresponding to a term in the expanded expression.

Thus, the boolean function $pq + pr + q'r$ is represented by the squares marked "1" in Fig. 3, while 0's fill those squares not included in the representation. Note that $pq + q'r$ is also represented by the same four marked squares, and hence is equivalent to the given

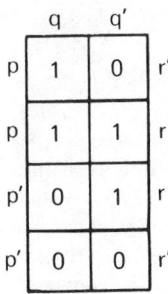

Fig. 3. Karnaugh map for pq plus pr plus $q'r$.

function. It is also possible to label a square *d,* denoting "don't care," if the value of that square is irrelevant to the particular function being represented.

Minimization of Boolean Functions. In the interest of economy it is often desirable to use the simplest possible expression for a boolean function in the design of computer circuitry. For example, since the expression $pq + pr + q'r$ is equivalent to the expression $pq + q'r$ in the sense that these expressions have the same value for given argument values, the former expression should be replaced by the latter whenever it occurs in a given circuit design. The determination of the simplest expression equivalent to a given one is. known as *minimization.* Minimization is understood to be with respect to a given function form, such as the sum of products form, since a change in permissible operators often permits one to find an expression that is simpler yet. Karnaugh maps and a variety of algebraic or geometrical algorithms have been used to accomplish boolean function minimization. The development of LSI and chip technology has made function minimization somewhat less important in hardware design, although it still has relevance both to this and to the clear formulation of decision criteria in programs.

REFERENCES

1965. McCluskey, E. J. *Introduction to the Theory of Switching Circuits.* New York: McGraw-Hill.
1966. Korfhage, R. R. *Logic and Algorithms.* New York: Wiley.
1970. Mendelson, E. "Theory and Problems of Boolean Algebra and Switching Circuits," in *Schaum's Outline Series.* New York: McGraw-Hill.
1972. Peatman, J. D. *The Design of Digital Systems.* New York: McGraw-Hill.

R. R. KORFHAGE

BOOTSTRAP

For articles on related subjects *see* LOADER; and MACHINE AND ASSEMBLY LANGUAGE PROGRAMMING.

Using some already running part of a language processor as a tool to get the rest of it running more easily (or using such a processor to get itself running on another machine without entirely rewriting it) is the programming counterpart of the apocryphal feat of lifting oneself by one's own bootstraps. These shortcuts are possible when the translator can be written using only a small but well-defined subset of the language it translates; when it

has this property, only so much of it as is necessary to translate that subset need be hand coded, after which the description of the whole translator can be processed by the handwritten fragment. The output of this procedure is the whole translator in object form, *bootstrapped* into existence by the handwritten fragment of itself.

The steps involved in bootstrapping can be usefully represented by schematic diagrams in which a translator is shown as an oblong, within which an expression of the form $'A \rightarrow B'$ describes the translation it performs. The language in which the translator has been , or is to be, written is noted as a kind of subscript outside the oblong. For example, the representation in this notation of a Fortran compiler producing machine language (ML) code for computer X, and itself existing as an ML program for X, is

$$\boxed{\text{Fortran} \rightarrow \text{ML'X'}} \qquad (1)$$
$$\text{ML'X'}$$

Note that if the subscript is a machine language, the translator in question is running on a real machine and can be used immediately; if the subscript is a high-level language, the translator is so far merely a source-language file that must itself be translated before it can be used to translate another source-language program. Given an immediately usable translator, the question of whether it can translate a given program is answered by matching the language in which the potential processee is written against part $'A'$ of the potential processor's $'A \rightarrow B'$ formula. If they are identical, or the former is a subset of the latter, the desired translation is feasible. In the notation (1) example, if the processee is a Fortran source program, it can be translated.

If we postulate that there exists some proper subset of the Fortran language in which a Fortran compiler can be written, the steps involved in bootstrapping into existence a Fortran compiler for and on machine X can be outlined in our notation. We must handwrite two programs:

$$\boxed{\text{Fortran} \rightarrow \text{ML'X'}} \qquad (2)$$
$$\text{Fortran Subset}$$

[This program written in the Fortran subset will translate any Fortran program to ML'X'.]

$$\boxed{\text{Fortran subset} \rightarrow \text{ML'X'}} \qquad (3)$$
$$\text{ML'X'}$$

[This program will translate any program written in the Fortran subset into ML'X'.]

Then we translate (2) by means of (3), yielding

$$\boxed{\text{Fortran} \rightarrow \text{ML}'\text{X}'}$$
$$\text{ML}'\text{X}'$$
$$(4)$$

which is the required product—a full Fortran-to-ML 'X' compiler running on machine X.

The question of when this approach is better than that of coding the desired product directly [as in notation (1)] is a complex one; some of the considerations involved are discussed in Halpern (1965).

"Bootstrapping" is used also to describe the process whereby a programmed loader, whose job it is to load other pieces of software into a machine, gets itself in. This task, which at first glance seems to threaten infinite regression, is made possible by a miniloader built into the hardware. In a typical example, the computer will offer the operator the ability to load into core and execute some small number of instructions—six, say—simply by pushing a console button. These six "free" instructions would be used by the programmer to load and transfer control to a full programmed loader, which, when thus "bootstrapped" in, could load any desired program with such niceties as check sums, relocation, and external symbol linking.

REFERENCE

1965. Halpern, M. "Machine Independence: Its Technology and Economics," *CACM* **8**, *No. 12:* 782–785 (December).

M. HALPERN

BREAKPOINT

For articles on related subjects *see* DEBUGGING; and DIAGNOSTICS.

A breakpoint is a position in a program at which the programmer has arranged for normal execution to be interrupted so that some type of external intervention can occur. This usually is associated with the debugging process in that the intervening activity is designed to provide status information and/or diagnostic data relative to the progress of the program up to that point. For example, the programmer may select one or more strategic places in the program at which to see a dump (i.e., a copy of the contents) of pertinent storage locations to assess the correctness of intermediate results.

In some systems the action at a breakpoint is performed automatically by a software component (an instruction inserted in the program for this purpose). For example, the programmer writing in PL/I for the IBM 360/370 series has direct access to a dump routine, with normal processing resuming after its completion. Accordingly, the breakpoint is set up like any other subroutine call:

$$\boxed{\text{PREVIOUS STATEMENT}}$$
$$\downarrow$$
$$\text{CALL THE DUMP;} \qquad (1)$$
$$\downarrow$$
$$\boxed{\text{FOLLOWING STATEMENT}}$$

In other types of breakpoints, the external action must be performed by an operator. Under these circumstances the action is independent of the user's program so that it is necessary for the operator to reactivate the program manually. An example of such a facility is seen in some dialects of Fortran, where one may write

PAUSE *message*   (2)

with the result that the program will halt and the message (e.g., to mount a disk pack) associated with the particular PAUSE statement will be displayed on the operator's console. Prior to the resumption of processing (which is done manually), the operator may interject the appropriate action. Whatever their form, the statements that create the breakpoint are retained until the programmer has identified and corrected the difficulties. Conversely, breakpoints may be created anew when unanticipated troubles develop in a seemingly operational program.

Additional types of breakpoints may be set up in conjunction with hardware. These facilities generally take the form of bistable switches, which may be set externally and tested by special statements within the program. Thus, the position of one of the switches may determine whether or not the program will halt at some point, to be restarted manually after some action is taken by the operator. Accordingly, that switch may be "on" during a debugging run; for normal execution, the switch is left in the "off" position, in which case the program will execute without interruption.

S. V. POLLACK

BRITISH COMPUTER SOCIETY (BCS)

For article on related subject *see* INTERNATIONAL FEDERATION OF INFORMATION PROCESSING.

The British Computer Society (BCS) was formed in September 1957 with the following main objectives:

1. To further the development and use of computational machinery, and the techniques related thereto.
2. To facilitate the exchange of information and views, and to inform public opinion on the subject.
3. To hold conferences and meetings for the reading of papers and delivery of lectures.
4. To publish information for the benefit of members.
5. To organize and conduct examinations, for members and others, in subjects requiring a knowledge of or otherwise in any way concerning the development and use of computational machinery and the techniques related thereto, and in any allied subjects.

A number of interested people, who foresaw the vital importance of computers to the community, met during the early 1950s to initiate lectures on different aspects of computing science and to discuss the problems of its application to industrial and commercial work. These conferees were, on the one hand, people with scientific and engineering interests, and on the other, members of the London Computer Group, which represented industry and commerce. As a result of these meetings, the British Computer Society, a company limited by guarantee, was formed on 14 October 1957.

At a special meeting in May 1968, the Society decided to become a fully professional body. To this end, the Society has introduced examinations (held annually in April each year since 1969); adopted a Code of Conduct (February 1971); and produced a Code of Good Practice (January 1973).

The following have held the office of BCS president:

Professor M. V. Wilkes, 1957–1960
Sir Frank Yates, 1960–1961
D. W. Hooper, Esq., 1961–1962
R. L. Michaelson, Esq., 1962–1963
Sir Edward Playfair, 1963–1965
Sir Maurice Banks, 1965–1966
Earl of Mountbatten of Burma, 1966–1967
Dr. S. Gill, M.A., Ph.D., 1967–1968
B. Z. de Ferranti, M.A., C.Eng., 1968–1969
The Earl of Halsbury, 1969–1970
A. d'Agapeyeff, Esq., 1970–1971
Professor A. S. Douglas, 1971–1972
G. J. Morris, Esq., 1972–1973
R. A. Barrington, Esq., 1973–1974
E. L. Willey, Esq., 1974–1975
C. P. Marks, Esq., 1975–1976

G. A. Fischer, Esq., 1976–1977
Prof. P. A. Samet, 1977–1978
Prof. F. H. Sumner, 1978–1979
J. L. Bogod, Esq., 1979–1980
Frank Hooper, Esq., 1980–1981
Peter Hall, Esq., 1981–1982

Organizational Structure. The British Computer Society is run by a Council which consists of 47 members: 18 elected; 12 from the branches of the BCS; and 17 others, including officers, students, and specialist group representatives. The Council, which meets quarterly, operates through boards and committees. The main boards are the Professional Board, the Technical Board, the Specialist Groups Board, the Finance Board, and the Branches Board.

Membership *Fellow.* Fellowship is by election from the Member grade. The minimum requirements are that Fellows must be over 30 and have eight years' experience in computing, five in a responsible position.

Member. Applicants must be over 25, have passed (or have been exempted from) BCS Parts I and II, and have five years' experience in computing, or have seven years' experience and be sponsored by reputable fellow computer users.

Associate Member. The minimum age requirement is 22 and applicants must have at least three years' experience and the correct qualifications and be sponsored by reputable people within the computing industry.

Affiliate. This grade is for those who do not wish to become fully professional members of the BCS.

Student. A student must be over 17 years of age. A student member becomes eligible to be an Associate member after passing Part I of the BCS examinations.

Education. The responsibility for the Society's educational activities lies with the Professional Board and its committees, assisted by a full-time education department. Education liaison officers appointed by each branch play a valuable role in communication between the Society and educational establishments throughout the country. Information is also provided on career prospects in the computer field, including presentations to schools and colleges.

The Society has played, and is sustaining, an important part in encouraging the spread of computer knowledge through its Schools Subcommittee, which consists of people from education administration, from the teaching profession and industry, and the Group for Computer Education, also affiliated with the Society. The Group, with a membership of 2,700—comprising secondary school teachers, college lecturers, and training officers from industry—has an international reputation through the publication of its quarterly bulletin, *Computer Education;* almost a quarter of its membership is drawn from abroad.

The Society plays a major role in setting and maintaining standards, at many levels of competence, by its representation on the advisory committees of national examining and educational bodies.

The work of the Society's members, individually or as government representatives, in international organizations concerned with education, places it at the international center of computer education circles.

The Society Examination. The Society's examination, set in two parts, is designed to assess the candidate's understanding of the underlying principles of the discipline, ability to reason and to evaluate information, and capacity for application of his/her knowledge to the solution of both practical and theoretical problems.

The Part I examination, set at the level of the Higher National Diploma, requires candidates to take two compulsory papers covering the general knowledge that all computer professionals should have, together with two papers from a number of widely defined areas of more specialized computer knowledge (computer technology, programming, data processing, analysis and design of systems, computational methods, and analog and hybrid computing). The Part II examination, set at the level of a university honors degree, requires candidates to take two papers in one area and one paper in a second, more specialized, area than those defined for Part I (digital computer technology, systems programming, data processing and information systems, advanced programming theory, data processing management, numerical analysis, and hybrid computing).

Branch Activities. There are 42 branches in the United Kingdom, one in Hong Kong, and one in Zambia. The branches, staffed entirely by volunteers, arrange programs of lectures and visits to installations.

Technical Activities. The Society is actively engaged in formulating and expressing professional viewpoints on a variety of subjects of importance. This is a primary responsibility of the Technical Board and its specialist committees.

In addition to its technical work in the United Kingdom, the Technical Board coordinates the work of its representatives on the IFIP technical committees and working groups and on the International Standards Organization. The Technical Board also coordinates the work of its 42 specialist groups, which study aspects of computer science ranging from advanced programming to urban planning.

Publications. In addition to the publications mentioned above, the Society has two other major publications. The *Computer Journal* is published quarterly. It contains articles and papers on scientific, business, and commercial subjects related to computers, together with reviews of the most important books and other publications in the field. The *Computer Bulletin* is also published quarterly and contains articles of a more general, tutorial nature than those in the *Journal.* The weekly *Computing* is published by Haymarket Publishing Group and contains a "BCS News Page," which is the main communication link between the Council and the members of the Society. It carries reports of branches and specialist groups, as well as advance notice of the Society's activities. Circulation is limited and a copy is sent to all BCS members.

Along with these publications are the reports of the proceedings of the Society's many specialized conferences, together with authoritative handbooks such as *Code of Practice, Code of Conduct, Job Control Languages,* and *Programming Techniques in CAD,* all published by the Society.

Conferences. The Society, in conjunction with its partners, presents a number of conferences of interest to the computing fraternity and conducts techniques workshops on a number of specialized subjects. It also provides a number of highly specialized conferences on such subjects as Word Processing, Security, Integrity, Reliability, and Microprocessors for DP staff.

I. L. Auerbach

BUFFER

For article on related subject *see* Input-Output Control Systems.

A buffer is an area of storage which temporarily holds data that will be subsequently delivered to a processor or input/output (I/O) transducer. Buffers exist as an integral part of many transducers; e.g., bits arriving serially over a telephone line are collected in a buffer before the appropriate teleprinter character is activated. Similarly, the bits representing a given keyboard stroke remain in a buffer while being serialized for transmission. Since the buffer is an integral part of the transducer, it is usually dedicated to the transducer and not shared with any other device.

Buffers are also used in conjunction with the input/output control system (IOCS) to hold the data which is the object of various I/O commands. In this case, the

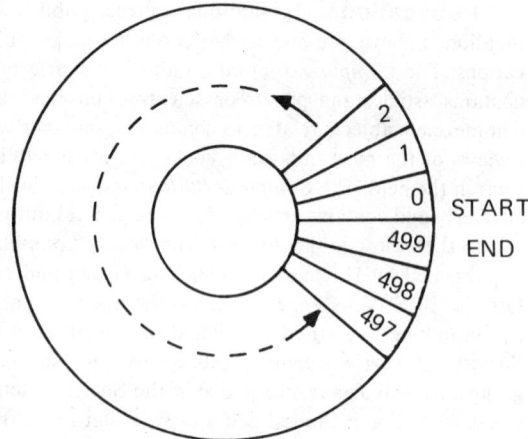 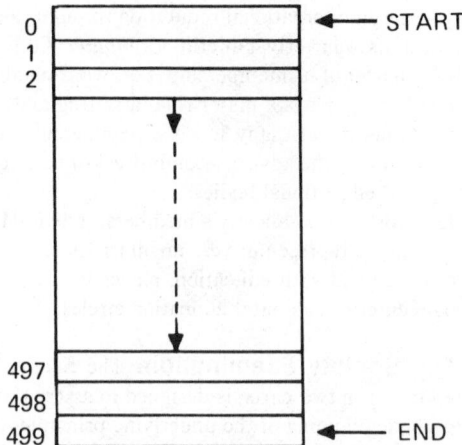

Fig. 1.   Circular buffer organization shown logically (left) and as it actually appears in memory (right).

buffer is usually a portion of main storage and is often dynamically allocated and freed by software. In either case, a buffer exists in order to accommodate the different rates at which data is produced or consumed by the processor or transducers involved.

In a typical situation, a processor will be capable of producing data three orders of magnitude faster than a transducer (e.g., a printer) can accept it. In order to make most efficient use of the processor, the data will be placed in a buffer and its location made known to the transducer. The transducer then proceeds to empty the buffer while the processor is freed for other work.

Various buffering techniques have evolved in IOCS. These techniques can be analyzed according to the policy used for (1) receiving data from the producer and (2) delivering data to the consumer.

When receiving data, two techniques are common: (1) a pool of buffers and (2) circular buffering. With the buffer-pooling technique a number of buffers are available to the IOCS. Usually, each buffer is large enough to hold the single physical record that is being transferred. When a record is produced, a buffer is taken from the pool and used to hold the data. Data is then consumed on a first-in, first-out basis, and when all data in a buffer has been transmitted, the buffer is returned to the pool.

Circular buffering, in contrast, typically uses a single buffer, usually larger than a single physical record. The basic strategy is to give the appearance that the buffer is organized in a circle, with data "wrapping around" as shown in Fig. 1. This appearance of circular organization is accomplished by using two pointers, IN and OUT, associated with the buffer; the starting and ending addresses of the buffer (START and END) are also known. Initially, START = IN = OUT. Data received from the producer fills the buffer, starting from START and incrementing the pointer IN. The consumer takes data from the buffer, in-

crementing the pointer OUT (and taking care not to go past IN − 1). When the last word of the buffer has been filled (IN = END), then IN is reset to START and subsequent data will wrap around to the start of the buffer.

Similarly, when OUT reaches END, it is reset to START and also wraps around. Clearly, the following restrictions hold:

1. If IN > OUT, then OUT must not become greater than IN − 1.
2. If OUT > IN, then IN must not become greater than OUT − 1.

If either of these two conditions is violated, then the consumer is trying to access data that has not been produced, *or* the producer is attempting to store over data that has not yet been consumed.

Data is delivered to the consumer either by moving it to a storage area provided by the consumer or by providing the consumer with a pointer to the data in the buffer. In the latter case, the consumer will frequently provide the IOCS with additional space, which becomes the new buffer. Such a technique is often called *exchange buffering.*

R. W. TAYLOR

BUG

For articles on related subjects *see* DEBUGGING; and GLITCH.

A bug is an error in either the syntax or the logic of a computer program. The term arose during World War II, in connection with electronic testing, as an outgrowth of "debug" which was a synonym for "troubleshoot." The earliest computer programmers, who were frequently the designers and builders of the computers, transferred the term to its present usage.

Most syntactical bugs can be detected during the translation from the symbolic languages that programmers use into the (binary) language which is eventually executed. For example, the proper symbolic code for addition on some machines is ADA ("add to accumulator"). If the programmer mistakenly writes ADD, this bug will be detected, an error message will be printed, and execution of the program will be halted, since the attempted operation code is illegal.

A bug is also created, and a more serious one, if the programmer writes the legal code SBA ("subtract from accumulator") when ADA was intended. This is a logical bug, and no coding system can catch such an error.

Properly speaking, the elimination of the first type of bug is the process of debugging, whereas the detection and elimination of the second type is the process of program testing. Program bugs can be so extremely subtle that they may resist great efforts to eliminate them. It is commonly accepted that all very large computer programs (such as compilers) have bugs remaining in them. The number of possible paths through a large computer program is enormous, and it is physically impossible to explore all of them. The single path containing a bug may not be followed in actual production runs for a long time (if ever) after the program has been certified as correct by its author or others.

F. GRUENBERGER

BURROUGHS B5000 SERIES

For articles on related subjects *see* ADDRESSLESS INSTRUCTIONS; COMPUTER INDUSTRY: United States; and STACK.

History. The Burroughs B5000 was designed in the early 1960s and first delivered in early 1963. It embodied a number of departures from the accepted models of computing. Although it was expected to serve best in research environments, the bulk of installations were commercial. It went out of production in 1973. Its successors, the B6700 and B7700, improved in both design and hardware technology, and not strictly upward compatible, are in production as of 1980.

Hardware. The internal logic was implemented with discrete components, packaged in small "cordwood" modules. The cycle time was 0.6 microseconds. Memory was 6 microsecond ferrite core, 6 bits per character, 8 characters plus parity per word, 4096 words per stack, and up to 8 stacks. The mainframe typically occupied nine 6-ft x 3-ft x 2½-ft bays, and could be connected to two lineprinters, two cardreaders, drums, disks, tapes, and other peripherals. The operator's console had only two controls, *Halt* and *Load,* with an option to load from cards or a fixed disk or drum location and a supervisory keyboard/printer. The internal state of the machine was accessible through a large maintenance panel which was not intended for normal use but was typically left exposed in day-to-day operation.

Instruction Set. The B5000 was designed for efficient implementation of Algol 60. It also provided operations for character processing and some operating system functions. The Algol instruction set was designed around a hardware stack. Operations were performed on data on the top of the stack. Storage for local variables, procedure parameters, and return addresses was also allocated in the stack. Access to storage was via automatically set base registers or indirectly through full-word pointers called *descriptors.* Later models in the family refined the initial capabilities and generalized them for the full generality of Algol 60, as well as Fortran, Cobol, and PL/I.

Parallelism. The B5000 had provision for up to two central processing units and up to four input/output (I/O) channels. All had direct access to main memory. Several programs could be run simultaneously. The eight memory modules were simultaneously accessible, increasing the effective memory bandwidth. Its successors increased the amount of memory and the number of processors that could be utilized.

Safety. Programs, including the operating system, were written in high-level languages, effectively screening out many potentially dangerous sequences of instructions. Memory for both procedures and data structures was accessed via descriptors containing information about the location and extent of the data. Requests out-of-range raised an exception that in turn terminated the offending process. The protection was nearly complete. Later models corrected the remaining loopholes and added even more elaborate protection mechanisms.

Memory Management. Program instructions and data were address-independent, facilitating relocation and roll-in/roll-out. The only information that needed updating after a memory management operation was the address and status bits contained in the descriptor. The segments of memory being managed were procedure bodies, array rows, I/O buffers, and similar structures with a median size of 60 words. Their small size and

Fig. 1. A Burroughs B5000 System.

close relation to program structures added to the efficiency of the system. Except for a few interrupt addresses, the operating system itself was also relocatable. Read-only data did not need to be written out. Roll-in/roll-out was sometimes deliberately defeated to avoid the swapping overhead for frequently accessed structures. Free, locked, read-only and read-write data were kept in separate chains. The memory manager used special-purpose instructions to search for available segments.

Evaluation. The B5000 was a major departure and, in many ways, a major advance in computer design. It developed a loyal user community which extended its use well beyond the viability of the raw hardware technology. It was difficult to quantify the basis for its success but it was clearly related to high-level attributes. Many of these attributes, described below, showed up later in competing systems. The operating system could accept additional jobs for immediate processing at any time. This freed the operating staff from many scheduling problems; a short, important job could be processed "right through" one or more simultaneously executing large tasks. Algol-60 was an important advance in computer languages; the Burroughs adaptation and implementation of it was very popular, and the only implementation to get serious commercial use in the U.S. Although not visible to the user, the Algol "Polish String" instruction set was very efficient for memory residence. Dense program code, together with the nearly transparent use of memory management, allowed very large systems to be built by users without incurring the very substantial costs of custom overlay schemes. Because the instruction set and programming languages were closely related, and particularly because of the automatic bounds checking of references through descriptors, diagnostics were generally at a high level and easily related to the specific faulty construct in the program. Neither assembly language nor memory dumps were needed or used. The ability of the B5000 to function with partial resources, such as memory modules, processors, or peripherals, gave it a fail-soft behavior. The operating system automatically compensated for reduced configurations, usually with no more operator intervention than switching off the defective hardware and pressing the load button. The result was an exceptionally cost/effective programming environment.

It is commonly believed that stack machines such as the B5000 are less computationally efficient than von Neumann machines. The traditional measures of performance are processor speed and memory use. The B5000 series required approximately ⅛ as much memory for program storage as von Neumann machines. Because of its descriptor logic, the B5000 occasionally required more memory references than other computers to get at its data, but compensated with more efficient procedure call mechanisms and arithmetic. For example, a comparison of carefully optimized linear equation solvers on the B5000 and IBM 7090 gave the following table of results:

Machine	Approximate Machine Cost	Multiply Time
IBM 7090	$3,000,000	22 μsec
B5000	$1,000,000	30 μsec

Memory Speed	Word Size	Relative Run Time
2.0 μsec	36 bits	1.0
6.0 μsec	48 bits	2.46

One can conclude that, relative to memory speed, and to machine cost, the B5000 was somewhat better than the 7090 for linear equations. Relative to arithmetic processor speed, it was somewhat slower.

REFERENCES

1961. Barton, R. S. "A New Approach to the Functional Design of a Digital Computer," *AFIPS Conference Proceedings* **19**:393, Western Joint Computer Conference.
1973. Organick, E. *Computer System Organization: The B5700/B6700 Series.* New York: Academic Press.
1975. Chu, Y. *High-Level Language Computer Architecture.* New York: Academic Press.
1980. McKeeman, W. M. *Stack Computers,* Chapter 7 in Stone, H. S., *Introduction to Computer Architecture,* 2nd Ed. Science Research Associates.

W. M. McKeeman

BUSINESS DATA PROCESSING. *See* Administrative Applications.

C

For articles on related subjects *see* PROCEDURE-ORI-ENTED LANGUAGES; PROGRAMMING LANGUAGES; STRUCTURED PROGRAMMING; and UNIX TIME-SHARING SYSTEM.

C is a general-purpose programming language featuring economy of expression, modern control flow and data structure capabilities, and a rich set of operators and data types.

C is best known as the primary language of the Unix* operating system, but is also used in several other environments. It has been used for a wide variety of programs, including the Unix operating system, the C compiler itself, and essentially all Unix applications software. In addition to "system" software, C has been used successfully for major numerical, text processing and database programs. Although C is a high-level language, it is sufficiently expressive and efficient to have completely displaced assembly language in many environments.

C was originally designed and implemented by Dennis Ritchie in 1972–1973 for the DEC PDP-11. C has its roots in BCPL** in much the same way that, for example, Pascal springs from Algol. (C is the successor to a short-lived BCPL-like language called B that was developed at Bell Labs; thus, the very name "C" derives from BCPL.) Like BCPL, C is relatively simple, notationally compact, and makes significant use of pointer arithmetic. One major distinction between them, however, is that, while BCPL is typeless, C supports a range of data types, thus better reflecting the architecture of most current computers.

The standard reference on C is Kernighan and Ritchie (1978); more information on the philosophy of the language may be found in Ritchie *et al.* (1978).

LANGUAGE COMPONENTS

Control Flow. Control flow in C is relatively conventional:

```
if (expr) stat1 else stat2
while (expr) stat
do stat while (expr)
for (expr1; expr2; expr3) stat
switch (expr) {
  case const1: stat1
  case const2: stat2
  ...
  default: stat
}
```

In each of these, *expr* is an expression, and *stat* is a statement, either simple or a group of statements enclosed in { . . . } (the equivalent of **begin . . . end**).

Within a loop, **break** causes an immediate exit and **continue** causes the next iteration to begin. There are also labels and a **goto**.

---

*Unix is a Trademark of Bell Laboratories.
**BCPL ("Basic Combined Programming Language") is a system programming language developed in 1969 by Martin Richards of Cambridge University. It has been transported to a variety of computers, and is still widely used.

Data Types. The basic data types in C are **char** (usually an eight-bit byte), **int, short,** and **long** (various sizes of integers), and **float** and **double** (floating point numbers).

In addition, there is a conceptually infinite hierarchy of derived types: if τ is a type, then there are pointers to objects of type τ, arrays of τ's, and structures and unions (records and variant records, in Pascal terminology) that may contain τ's. There are also pointers to functions, and an enumeration data type (i.e., one whose range of values is explicitly defined by the programmer).

C does not have a string data type; strings are represented as arrays of char's, usually with a null byte as terminator, and manipulated by library functions.

Pointer arithmetic is an integral part of C. If p is of type pointer to τ, and currently points to an element of an array of τ's, then $p+1$ is a pointer to the next element of the array. That is, arithmetic operations on pointers are scaled by the size of the object to which the pointer points. The programmer is (or should be) unconcerned with the actual size.

Operators and Expressions. In addition to the usual $+$, $-$, etc., C has a relatively rich set of operators (except compared to APL). Two classes are worth special mention. Any binary operator such as $+$ has a corresponding "assignment operator" (here $+=$) so that the statement

v = v + *expr*

can be more concisely written

v += *expr*

"$+=$" is analogous to "$:+=$" in Algol 68.

The unary operators $++$ and $--$ increment or decrement their operand:

++thing

is the preferred way to write

thing = thing + 1

An expression may be coerced to another type by preceding the expression with a type name, as in

x = sqrt((double) *integer expression*) ;

The coercion (*q.v.*) in this example converts the *integer expression* into double precision, the type required by the function sqrt.

Program Structure. A C program is a set of declarations of variables and functions in one or more source files that may be compiled separately. Function declarations may not be nested; C is otherwise block structured.

Objects—functions or external variables—at the top level are declared either global (i.e., available to all functions) or visible only within the source file where they are declared. Variables internal to a function are either automatic (that is, they appear when the function is entered and disappear when it is exited) or static (that is, they retain their values from one call of the function to the next). There is a **register** declaration to advise the compiler that a variable is likely to be heavily used. Normally, a compiler would attempt to store such a variable in a register for fast access, but the declaration is only a suggestion: compilers are free to ignore the advice.

All functions may be recursive. Arguments are passed by value, but passing a pointer provides call by reference when necessary. Function arguments and return values may be any basic type, pointers, structures, unions, and enumerations. Arrays are passed by passing a pointer to the first element.

A preprocessor provides source file inclusion, conditional compilation, and macro processing for symbolic names and short in-line functions.

Run-time Environment. C does not provide input/output (I/O) statements in the language. Nor does it supply storage management or string manipulation. Similarly, even though C was originally designed for system programming applications, it provides only single-thread control flow constructions—no multiprogramming, parallel operations, synchronization, or coroutines. All of these higher-level facilities must be provided by separate functions; a standard I/O library provides a uniform run-time environment for most C programs.

An Example. The following program computes the powers of 2 up to 2^{20}.

```
#define  LIMIT  20
main( )  /* test power function */
{
    int i;
    long power( ); /* power returns a long */
    for (i = 0; i <= LIMIT; ++i)
        printf("%d %ld\n", i, power(2,i));
}
long power(x, n) /*raise x to n-th power; n >= 0 */
    int x, n;
{
    int i;
    long p;
```

```
        p = 1;
        for (i = 1; i < = n; + +i)
            p = p * x;
        return(p);
}
```

Execution begins at main. The function printf does formatted output conversion according to the specification in its first argument. Here, %d signals an ordinary integer, and %ld a long integer; \n is a newline character.

The function power would normally be written more concisely by experienced C programmers as:

```
long power(x, n)   /* raise x to n-th power; n > = 0 */
    int x, n;
{
    long p = 1;
    while ( − −n > = 0)   /* decrement n before
                                    testing */
        p *= x;
}   return(p);
```

PORTABILITY

C is not tied to any particular hardware or operating system; C compilers run on a wide variety of machines, from micros to the largest mainframes. Most of these newer compilers are based on the "portable C compiler" developed by S. C. Johnson. The language and the standard library have been kept under strict enough control that they show little variation among machines. Accordingly, most C programs can be moved without change to any system that supports C and the run-time library. In particular, this has meant that the Unix operating system itself, which is largely written in C, can be transported to a variety of computers with relatively modest effort.

Moving the operating system overcomes the main obstacle to portability of applications programs—diversity of run-time environments on different machines.

REFERENCES

1978. Kernighan, B. W. and Ritchie, D. M. *The C Programming Language.* Englewood Cliffs, NJ: Prentice-Hall.
1978. Ritchie, D. M., Johnson, S. C., Lesk, M. E., and Kernighan, B. W. "UNIX Time-Sharing System: The C Programming Language," *Bell Sys. Tech. J.* **57**, *No. 6:* 1991–2019.
1978. Johnson, S. C. and Ritchie, D. M. "UNIX Time-Sharing System: Portability of C Programs and the UNIX System," *Bell Sys. Tech. J.* **57**, *No. 6:* 2021–2048.

B. W. KERNIGHAN

CACHE MEMORY

For articles on related subjects see ASSOCIATIVE MEMORY; MEMORY: Main; and STORAGE HIERARCHY.

A *cache memory* is a mechanism interposed in the memory hierarchy between main memory and the CPU to improve effective memory transfer rates and, accordingly, raise processor speeds. The name refers to the fact that the mechanism is essentially hidden and appears transparent to the user, who is aware only of an apparently higher-speed large main memory. The cache is usually implemented by semiconductor devices whose speeds are compatible with that of the processor, while the main memory utilizes a less costly, lower-speed technology. The cache concept anticipates the likely reuse by the CPU of data in main storage by organizing a copy of it in cache memory. The concept is further extended to include data that is adjacent to data that has been used. It is usual to transfer a block of several words from main store to the cache even though the immediate need is for only one word. If the required word is part of a stream of sequential instructions, it is likely that subsequent instructions will be retrieved with the required first word, making repeated access to main memory unnecessary.

When used in conjunction with a cache store, the main memory is equipped (by interleaving *(q. v.)*) to provide several words in address sequence at a high data rate. It remains for the cache memory organization to make adequate use of such multiword transfers.

When a request originates in the CPU for a new word, whether it be data or instruction, a check is made to see if it is already in the cache by accessing the tag directory (see Fig. 1). If present, the data is used directly; if not, a new access to main memory must be made. Since the cache is of limited size (32K bytes in the IBM 360/195, and only 2K bytes in the DEC 11/70), space must often be sought to accommodate the new information. An algorithm based on history of use is used to identify the least necessary block of data for overwriting. Since the data in main memory can be updated each time the CPU writes into the cache (a process called *store-through*), no data is lost in the overwriting process.

The search in the cache for the next word is made using an associative search in the address tag directory. In the search, the high-order bits of the target word address are compared with the corresponding bits in the tag directory. The result of a match provides the location in cache of the block in which the addressed word is found using the low-order bits of the address. No match initiates the main storage access process.

A general problem of updating of the cache and

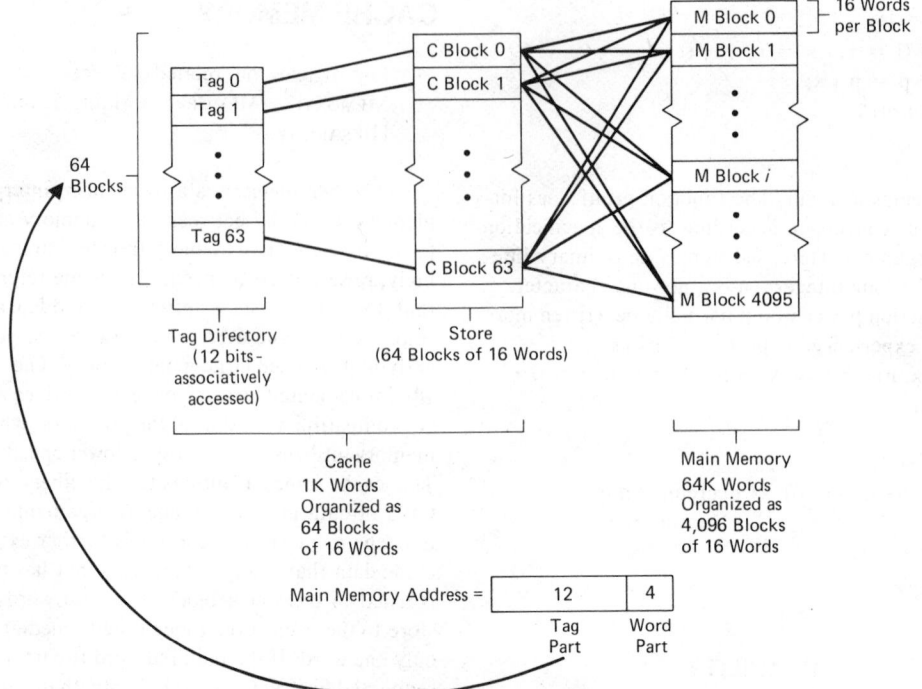

Fig. 1. A cache memory showing that the cache may contain any set of blocks from main memory and also showing how an associative tag directory is used to access the cache.

main store exists if, as is usual, the CPU and I/O do not both use the cache. This arises because, under these conditions, two versions of a variable might exist in two corresponding locations in cache and main store. Global and local solutions exist. The global solution usual in a memory hierarchy is to restrict processing to blocks of data that are static with respect to I/O transfers; this ensures that only consistent data is treated. This may be arranged by periodic programmed checking of flagged memory locations, modified by initiation and subsequent completion of I/O transfers. The local solution is to ensure that data modified by the CPU in cache is returned quickly and automatically to main store, as is done in the IBM 360/195.

K. C. SMITH AND A. S. SEDRA

CAD. *See* COMPUTER-AIDED DESIGN.

CAI. *See* COMPUTER-ASSISTED INSTRUCTION.

CALCULATOR, DESK

For articles on related subjects *see* CALCULATORS, ELECTRONIC AND PROGRAMMABLE; and DIGITAL COMPUTERS.

Human need for aids to calculation obviously began as counting became important, assuming that human memories in those days were as bad as they are today. Fingers were used, and perhaps toes (they were at least visible), and notches were cut in a stick when a permanent record was required.

It was a natural development to replace fingers by small pebbles that would slide in a groove carved in a piece of wood. Such an elementary abacus was simplified when the pebbles were replaced by beads sliding on a wire or slim rod. There is good evidence that the abacus was invented prior to 500 B.C.

The simplest abacus has either ten or nine beads on each wire, and the number system is obvious. In most modern forms of abacus (Chinese), the wire is divided into two parts and the coding system is essentially biquinary in that there are five beads below the division and two above. In the Japanese abacus, four beads are below and one above. The upper bead designates whether the rod represents more or less than 5; the lower one, whether 0 to 4 or 6 to 9.

Visitors to the Far East and the U.S.S.R. will know that the abacus is still a common form of desk calculator and is used with great dexterity and speed. It has been reported that a competition held in 1946 between users

Fig. 1. A Chinese abacus. (Courtesy Science Museum, London. British Crown copyright.)

of an abacus and an electric calculator was easily won by the operator of the abacus.

The invention of anything resembling today's desk calculator had to await the development of a system of decimal notation as we know it today, and this did not occur until as late as the sixteenth century. One of the earliest aids was Napier's "bones" (about 1620), which effectively had multiplication tables written out on strips of bone or wood. Napier also invented logarithms. These greatly assisted in arithmetic calculation, at the cost of some accuracy, and are the basis of slide rule operations.

The mechanical calculator was first invented by Pascal, about 1640, and depended on linking a toothed gear wheel to a shaft and an arrangement for a "carry" from one wheel to its left-hand neighbor when the original wheel passed from 9 to 0. The accumulation gear wheels were driven by other toothed wheels, set to represent a desired number and driven by a rotating hand crank. Such calculators, and they still exist today, were essentially adders and subtractors in which multiplication and division was performed by repeated additions and subtractions. In the 1670s Leibniz invented a much more complicated gearing arrangement by which a machine could multiply directly, but this found little common application.

The twentieth century saw a wide variety of desk calculators, all basically operating on a principle similar to that of Pascal's machine but with varying degrees of sophistication and aids to convenience. Input numbers were set by moving selector levers to designated positions or, in some cases, by a simple keyboard. Operation was either manual or electrical, and results were usually shown in plain figures on dials read through small windows (Fig. 2). There were also simple adding and listing machines that print results on a roll of tally tape (Fig. 3). Well-known manufacturers' names included Monroe, Marchant, Brunsviga, Facit, and Friden, among others. With the advent of the hand-held calculator, machines such as those shown in Figs. 2 and 3 have almost disappeared.

G. J. MORRIS

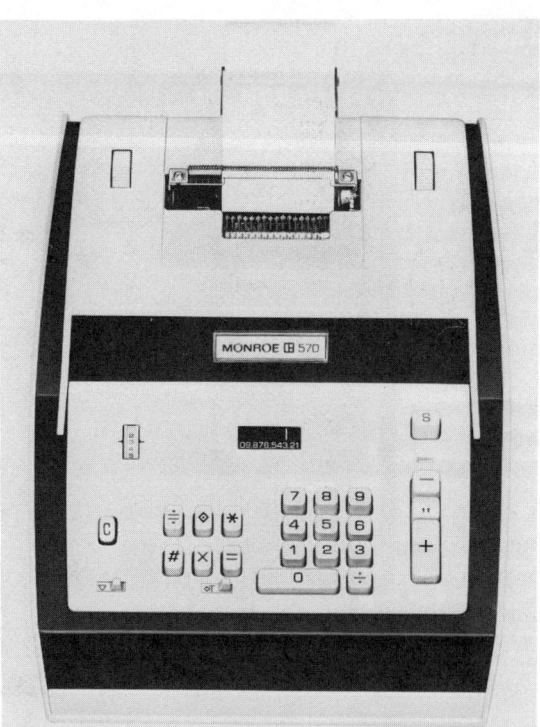

Fig. 3. The Monroe desk calculator with printed tally tape output.

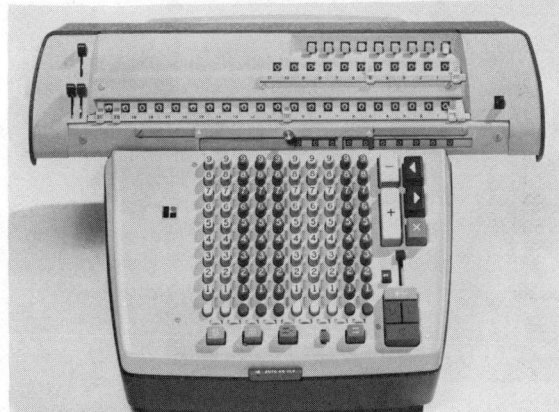

Fig. 2. The electromechanical Monroe 6F-212 calculator with output displayed but not printed.

CALCULATORS, ELECTRONIC AND PROGRAMMABLE

For articles on related subjects *see* CALCULATOR, DESK; INTEGRATED CIRCUITRY; PERSONAL COMPUTERS; and POLISH NOTATION.

Until the early 1960s, desk calculators, which performed only the basic arithmetic operations, were essentially mechanical in operation, driven by an electric motor. The invention of the transistor in 1948 and the integrated circuit in 1964 were the two events which formed the basis for the electronic calculator revolution. Using these inventions, the *calculator-on-a-chip* was first introduced in 1971 and was the basis for the electronic hand-held or pocket calculator. By 1974, calculators using such chips cost less than $50 and could out-perform a $1,500 mechanical calculator. Estimates indicated that 20 million Americans owned a hand-held calculator by 1974. From 1974 to 1977 (see Fig. 1), the number of electronic parts was reduced from 82 to 2 and the total number of parts from 119 to 17. Costs dropped accordingly, with the price stabilizing between $5 and $20 by 1981 for non-programmable, non-memory calculators capable of performing the basic arithmetic operations as well as some simple mathematical functions.

The late 1970s saw the introduction of many special features and functions into the hand-held calculator. At the same time, solar or other long-life batteries brought about calculators which can operate for thousands of hours without energy source replacement. Numerous functions and memory features became available. The size of the hand-held calculator was reduced to some which are wafer-thin and the size of business cards. The incorporation of time, music (Fig. 2), stopwatch, and specific functions became common by 1980. Calculators have been built into watches (Fig. 3), tie tacks, pocketbooks, and pens. All these approaches to merchandising the pocket calculator brought estimates that over 80 million Americans owned a pocket calculator by 1980. Numerous manufacturers (Table 1) market calculators with each specializing on specific consumer needs.

Electronic calculators are designed to perform their functions using either algebraic or Reverse Polish notation. Algebraic notation permits entry of calculations as normally written—e.g., (2 + 3)—with the arithmetic function between the two numbers. With RP notation, the operator is placed after the two numbers, (2 3 +), and, therefore, the operator is input after both numbers have been entered. The former requires parenthesizing for all but the simplest calculations, whereas RP notation allows any sequence of calculations to be entered

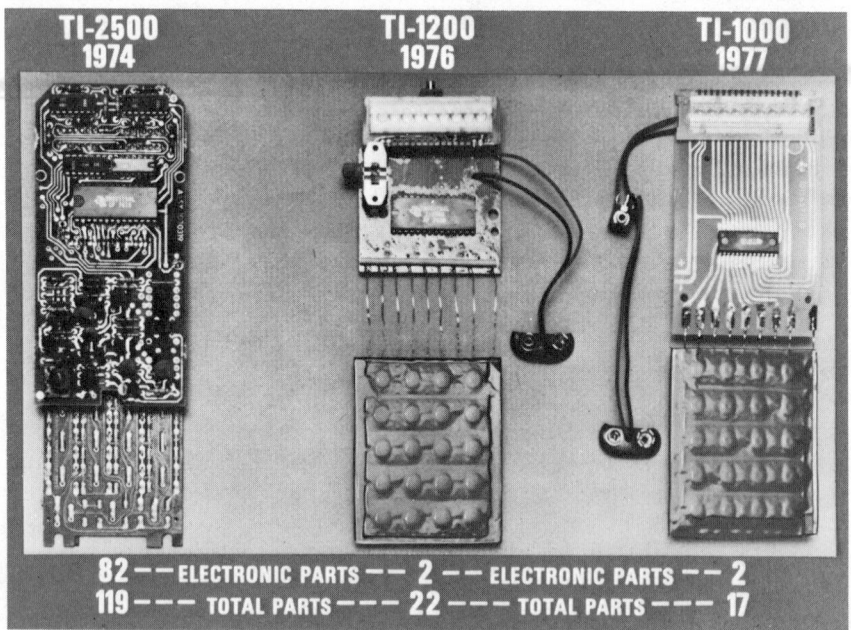

Fig. 1. Illustration showing the reduction in electronic and total parts in the electronic calculator from 1974–1977. Courtesy of Texas Instruments.

Fig. 2. The National Semiconductor thin pocket-sized calculator with audible entry keyboard. Courtesy of National Semiconductor Corporation.

Table 1   1978 Shares of Market for Electronic Calculators and Learning Aids

Brand	Market Share (% of Total Units)
Texas Instruments	41.3
Sharp	11.8
Unisonic	6.4
Novus (National Semiconductor)	5.8
Casio	5.2
APF	2.9
Lloyd's	2.5
Canon	1.6
Royal	0.8
Hewlett-Packard	0.7
All "Store Brands" combined	8.6
All other brands combined	12.4
Total	100.0

Source: Market facts, Inc. Consumer Mail Panel Survey, 1979.

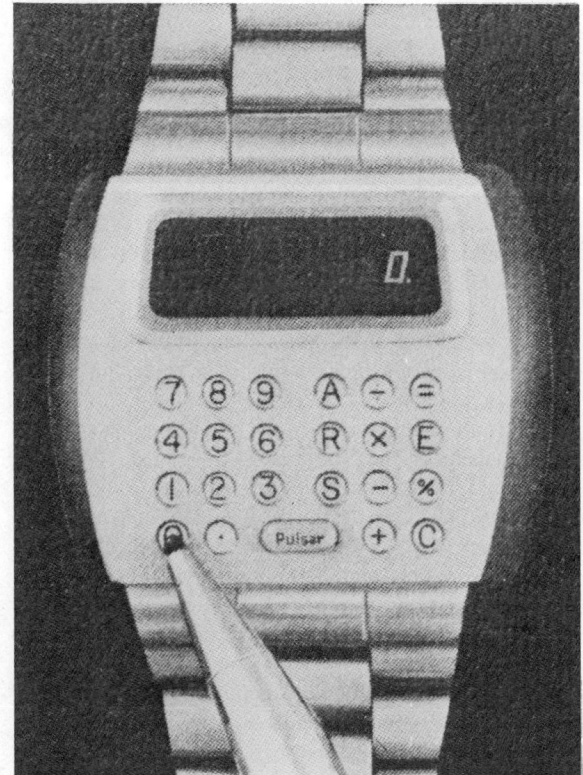

Fig. 3. The Pulsar watch with a built-in calculator.

without parentheses; however, it is unfamiliar and considerable learning is needed before it can be used easily.

Calculators typically compute non-zero numbers in a range from 10^{99} to 10^{-99} and print from 8 to 12 digits in the display, often using scientific notation. A typical advanced non-programmable electronic calculator would normally include the following scientific functions: x^2, $\sqrt{x}$, $1/x$, y^x, x-y interchange, normal and inverse trigonometric functions, logarithms to the bases 10 and e, e^x, 10^x, $x!$ and degrees-to-radians conversion. Statistical functions often included are summation, mean, and standard deviation. Other common calculator capabilities are to store a number in a memory, to add to memory, to subtract from memory, to multiply into memory, to divide into memory, and to exchange the display with memory.

The programmable calculator was first introduced in 1974 by Hewlett-Packard and has also developed rapidly. Many programmable calculators use magnetic strips and modules to store preprogrammed instructions. The programs are generally written in the specific language of the calculator. The Texas Instruments Programmable 59 calculator (Fig. 4) is an example of one of the sophisticated programmable machines of the late 1970s. It uses plug-in interchangeable solid state preprogrammed software modules with a capability of up to 5,000 program steps each. Modules are available for mathematics, applied statistics, electrical engineering, business decisions, aviation, leisure, etc. This calculator has added space for up to 960 program steps or 100 memory locations entered from two small magnetic cards. In addition, the TI-59 has alphabetic character printing and plotting capabilities through the use of a printer. In the 1980 Winter

Fig. 4. The TI-59 programmable calculator with printer. Courtesy of Texas Instruments.

Olympics, the TI-59 calculator was used by scorers to officially audit time and scores in many events.

Special-purpose calculators have been designed for many professions, including finance, statistics, business, mathematics, science, and real estate. Calculators of the future will be difficult to distinguish from computers because advancements in memory technology will provide storage and programming capabilities comparable to computers.

GARY BITTER

CAM. *See* AUTOMATION; and COMPUTER-AIDED DESIGN.

CANADIAN INFORMATION PROCESSING SOCIETY (CIPS)

Purpose. The essential objective of CIPS is the advancement of computer and information processing in Canada. To this end, it brings together scientists, business people, and others who make their careers in computing and information processing. The Society's activities include committees organized to pursue special interests, meetings, seminars, and conferences held at national and regional levels to exchange information, publications to disseminate information, and long-term commitments to promoting the use of computers in the best interests of society.

How Established. CIPS was born in 1958 as a result of the Canadian Conference on Computing and Data Processing held in Toronto, 9–10 June 1958. The Society, established originally as the Computing and Data Processing Society of Canada, shortened its name to the Computer Society of Canada in 1965, and in 1968 its name was again amended to the present title. The current membership is over 4,200.

Presidents of the society since its inception have been

Fred Thomas, 1958–1959
Hudson Stowe, 1959–1960
C. C. Gotlieb, 1960–1961
O. M. Mackey, 1961–1962
J. H. Aitchison, 1962–1963
J. C. Davidson, 1963–1964
Harvey S. Gellman, 1964–1965
J. W. Graham, 1965–1967
Bernard Hodson, 1967–1968
B. B. Goodfellow, 1968–1969
Mers Kutt, 1969–1970
George A. Fierheller, 1970–1971
James M. Kennedy, 1971–1972
James H. Finch, 1972–1973
Grant N. Boyd, 1973–1974
Robert T. Horwood, 1974–1975
Joseph B. Reid, 1975–1976
T. Ross Jewell, 1976–1977
Glenn McInnes, 1977–1978
Wayne A. Davis, 1978–1979
Larry R. Symes, 1979–1980
Chris G. K. Bishop, 1980–1981

Organizational Structure. The Management of the Society is vested in the National Board of Directors, consisting of six nationally elected Executive Committee members, eleven regionally-elected Directors, and one elected representative from each of the Society's Special Interest Groups. Members of the Executive Committee act as officers of the Society, and, together with the Regional Directors, they constitute the governing body of the Society.

The President normally holds office for one year and then remains on the Board as Past-President for an additional year. The First Vice-President (Al. G. Fowler for 1980–1981) automatically becomes the next president. The other three elected members of the Executive—the Second Vice-President, the Secretary, and the Treasurer—are elected as a group for a two-year period.

The various Standing Committees of the Society which report directly to the National Board of Directors include Publication, Constitution, Membership, Administration, Professional Standards, Government Liaison, Public Service/Public Relations, and Audit. Committee Chairmen are appointed by the President and normally serve two-year terms. The Committees are guided by

Terms of Reference which have been established by the National Board of Directors.

The 18 sections of CIPS across the country continue to be the focal point of Society activities. Local executives meet on an ongoing basis to plan programs and administer section affairs. Section activities include programs of invited speakers, panels, seminars, and tours.

To foster development in specialized areas, CIPS has a number of Special Interest Groups, including the *Computer Science Association,* the *Canadian Image Processing and Pattern Recognition Society,* and the *Canadian Society for the Computational Study of Intelligence.*

There are three classes of membership—Active, Student, and Honorary. Eligibility for active membership requires that the individual be engaged in the administration, practice, or teaching of computing and information processing. Student membership requires that the individual be registered full time in a recognized educational institution. Honorary membership is awarded to those who, in the opinion of the National Board, have made an outstanding contribution to computing and information processing.

The headquarters of CIPS are at 243 College Street, Toronto, Ontario, M5T 2Y1.

Technical Program. Conferences have remained a major activity of the Society. In addition to the National Conference held each year in the early summer, CIPS also organizes one-day national seminars. Important topics, such as *EDP Audit and Security* and *Distributed Data Processing,* have been covered by these seminars. CIPS also sponsors the annual *Canadian Computer Show and Conference* in Toronto and the *Salon de l'ordinateur* in Montreal. These two events, the largest of their kind in Canada, each attract upwards of 20,000 people.

The four main publications of CIPS are:

- *CIPS Review,* a bimonthly publication, which contains informative, useful, and controversial articles covering the broad spectrum of information processing. (Theme issues have included *Computers and Health, Manpower, Leasing,* and *Communications Policy.*)
- *The Canadian Computer Census,* the authoritative Canadian directory of computer installations in Canada, used by researchers, marketers, foreign companies, and government agencies, which has been published annually by the Society since the early 1960s.
- *The Canadian Salary Survey,* an annual publication which is a guide to Canadian salaries at all occupational levels in the data processing industry.

- *Infor Journal,* a quarterly publication, which is the leading scientific Canadian journal in the computing field, and contains refereed technical papers. *Infor* is published jointly by CIPS and the Canadian Operational Research Society.

Additionally, the Society publishes proceedings following each conference, and from time to time publishes special material such as *"CIPS Tips"—A Buyers Guide to Small Business Computers.*

M. J. HART

CARD. *See* IBM CARD; and NINETY-COLUMN CARD.

CARD READING AND PUNCHING TECHNIQUES

For articles on related subjects *see* IBM CARD; and INPUT/OUTPUT DEVICES.

Punched card reading used to be performed electromechanically by sensing pins or reading brushes. The need for higher speed, reliability in reading, and lower cost resulted in the introduction of the photoelectrical reading technique, which is widely applied now. High reliability of reading is usually secured by checking techniques, for example:

1. A dual read station.
2. Echo (in which the data transmitted is returned to the point from which it was sent and compared with original data).
3. Validity.
4. Parity.
5. Single-access clutch.
6. Column strobe count.
7. Light/dark probe.

Usually a combination of these types of checks is used. Cards with readings that do not match are generally sent to a secondary stacker. In present-day readers the scanning of a card is usually performed by columns (often referred to as *serial scanning*) as opposed to the previously used scanning by rows (also called *parallel scanning*).

Fig. 1 shows the principle of the photoelectrical reading technique. The reading of a card is performed at a dual read station consisting of two vertical columns of 12 photodiodes each and 2 gating diodes, located at each side of the read diode columns (these last two diodes are not shown in Fig. 1). Spacing between read diode columns is equal to that of one card column. Vertical spac-

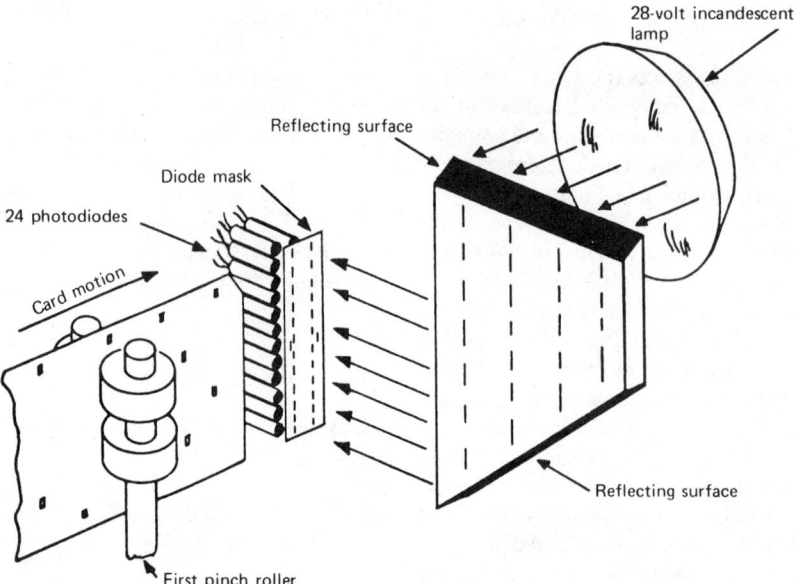

Fig. 1. The principle of a photoelectrical reading tecchnique as used by Control Data Corp. in its CDC 405 high-speed card reader.

ing between diodes is 0.25 in. and the diodes span the 12 information rows of the card.

The two gating diodes are located between the horizontal rows of read diodes in such a way that they always see the solid portions of the punched card. Hence, these diodes are triggered only by the leading or by the trailing edge of the card.

All read station photodiodes are covered by a mask that contains rectangular holes, which are slightly narrower than the width of the punched card holes. Masking slots covering gating diodes 1 and 2 are smaller than those used for read diodes. The smaller dimension allows for a minute card skew or the possibility of slight disorientation between the information holes contained in the punched card.

The photodiode exciter source is a 28-volt, incandescent lamp. Light rays from the lamp are directed toward a periscopic mirror element, where the reflective surface at the upper end directs light rays downward, through the optical glass, to strike the second reflective surface at the lower end. Parallel light rays are emitted from the edge of the glass and mirror element. The periscopic system distributes the light evenly over the 3-in. read station area.

When the punched card reaches the dual read station, parallel light rays pass through the information holes of the card and strike the corresponding read diodes. At the peak of the light transmission, timing circuits transmit a read gate probe, which permits information contained in the first card column to be recorded in the primary read register. Hence, each 12-bit column

of the punch card is read in character serial mode. Once read and recorded, the first card column is read again by the second group of read diodes. This operation is performed in sequence for each column of the card. If any two information groups do not correspond, in the automatic mode of operation, a compare error signal is transmitted to the computer, and the computer may return a gate command signal to channel the card into a secondary tray. In the manual mode of operation, the compare error signal acts as a gate command to channel the card into the secondary receiving tray.

Card punching is performed at the punch station of a card punch. The punch station consists of a punch matrix and punch dies with punch magnets. A punch matrix has 80 holes corresponding to the 80 punching positions in a punch row of an 80-column card (if the punching is performed by rows) or it has 12 holes corresponding to the 12 punching positions of a punch column in an 80-column card (if the punching is performed by columns). The 80- or 12-punch dies are positioned upright with respect to the holes in the punch matrix.

Each punch die has its assigned punch magnet. These are set by the electronic image of the output information to be punched in the card. When activated, the punch die moves against the hole in the punch matrix, thus causing the punching of all data relative to a row (or column) of a card that is being moved (by rows or by columns) between the punch dies and the punch matrix.

The check of correct punching is generally performed by a "read-after-punch" verification, echo, check on punching dies activated, and validity. Other error-

File Directory Listing

15 Owner	File Name	1 ED	2 C-Date	3 E-Date	4 L-Date	5 Use CT	6 F-Size	7 B-Size	8 BLK CT	9 SEG CT	10 SEG	11 DT	12 DN	13 LSL	14 SL
JOB	GATHER-FILE	00	7-19-80	12-31-99	7-19-80	3	20	256	1	1	1	854	8541	13792	20
MSOS	FILE 56	00	7-19-80	7-19-80	7-21-80	8665	80	960	277	1	1	854	8541	24640	80
MSOS	L-MSIO	00	12-22-78	12-31-99	7-21-80	14307	10	10240	4	1	1	854	8541	18640	10
NAD	NADSUB	21	6-03-80	6-03-80	7-19-80	217	3	960	9	1	1	854	8541	23520	3
NADS	SHORT CODES AND EXPANSION	00	7-18-80	7-18-80	7-19-80	8	6	504	43	1	1	854	8541	21568	6
RTS	ABSFILE	D6	6-07-80	12-31-99	6-07-80	1	92	4	1462	1	1	854	8541	30960	92
RTS	IDFILE	00	12-22-78	12-31-99	5-02-79	1	4	480	1	2	1	854	8541	240	2
RTS	LABELFILE	00	12-22-78	12-31-99	5-02-79	0	40	392	36	2	1	854	8541	32	13
TABLE	ORG CODES SORTED BY LEGAL ENT	01	7-06-80	7-06-80	7-11-80	6	2	256	6	1	1	854	8541	32432	2
TABLE	ORG CODES SORTED BY ORG CODE	01	7-06-80	7-06-80	7-11-80	3	2	256	6	1	1	854	8541	13712	2

Explanatory Notes

1 Edition number.
2 File creation date.
3 Expiration date.
4 Date file was last used.
5 Number of times file has been used since creation.
6 File size in disk segments.
7 Block size in characters.
8 Block count; number of blocks in file.
9 Segment count; number of segments into which file is divided.
10 Segment number stored at this location.
11 Type model of disk device on which file is stored.
12 Device number.
13 Lowest segment location is track number on disk where this segment of file starts.
14 Length of this segment.
15 Since two people may use the same file name, an additional name is attached, giving the owner's name. In these cases the owner is the name of a package of programs (or system) which uses that file.

Fig. 1. Example of an excerpt from a catalog. For purposes of finding a file, the file name consists of *owner, file name,* and *edition* for uniqueness.

checking capabilities generally built into the card punch include card synchronization and row-by-row hole-counting parity checking.

The rapidly increasing use of key-to-cassette or diskette encoders, key-to-disk systems, and direct input terminal devices has reduced the function of punched cards to little more than for program preparation and hardware maintenance. Hence, there is a decreasing demand for punched card machines as data preparation devices (with most requirements being met by refurbished machines). Consequently, there is little meaningful technological development of punched card input/output (I/O) devices.

J. NECAS

CATALOG

For articles on related subjects *see* FILES; and MEMORY: Auxiliary.

A catalog is a file, usually stored on some auxiliary storage medium, which contains an ordered list of names and other pertinent information on all files stored permanently in the computer system. In addition to the name of the file (e.g., "1980 EARNINGS-RECORDS"), the catalog record may contain the creation date, an edition (or version) number, and a proposed (or assumed) expiration date. Normally it must contain the size of the file, the location of the file in storage (where the file has been stored on what device), and it will often maintain some usage measures such as number of accesses since creation, date of last access, etc.

The catalog contains information on files stored on permanently mounted auxiliary storage units such as disks and drums. It also contains information on files stored on magnetic tape or on removable disk packs. When a tape or disk pack file is requested by a program, the information in the catalog together with other information is used by the operating system to determine if the file requested is available on line or if a tape or disk pack must be obtained and mounted. In the latter case, appropriate instructions for the operator are issued at the computer console.

Files are stored permanently and cataloged when it is anticipated that they will be used repeatedly. In addition to data files, both source programs and object programs are often cataloged, the former so that they can be easily modified and the latter to enable repeated use without recompiling the program from the source.

Fig. 1 contains an excerpt from a typical catalog of files showing the files stored on a particular disk pack.

The file catalog is also known by various other names among which the following are most common:

File Directory (as in Fig. 1)
File Name Table
Volume Table of Contents (for files on a particular pack)
Permanent File Directory

C. L. MEEK

CBI. *See* CHARLES BABBAGE INSTITUTE.

CELLULAR AUTOMATA

For article on related subject *see* AUTOMATA THEORY.

A cellular automaton or *polyautomaton* is a theoretical model of a parallel computer, subject to various restrictions to make formal investigation of its computing powers tractable. All versions of the model share these properties: Each is an interconnection of identical cells, where a cell is a model of a computer with finite memory—i.e., a finite-state machine. Each cell computes an output from inputs it receives from a finite set of cells, forming its neighborhood, and possibly from an external source.

All cells compute one output simultaneously and each cell computes an output at each tick of a clock, i.e., after each unit time step. The output of a cell is distributed to its neighborhood and possibly to an external receiver.

A version of the cellular automaton model exists for each set of choices in the following dichotomies: an infinite or a finite number of cells; a uniform interconnection scheme (all cells have neighborhoods of the same shape, e.g., that in Fig. 1) or a nonuniform scheme (Fig. 2); deterministic or nondeterministic cells (a choice of one output value at each unit time step or one of several values chosen randomly); the absence or presence of an external input (output), and in the case of an external input (output) the automaton is connected to all cells or to only a subset; Moore-type or Mealy-type cells (unit time steps allowed or not allowed, respectively, between inputs and

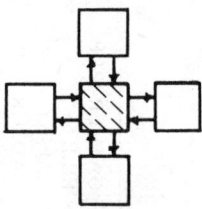

Fig. 1. A cell (hatched) and its neighborhood.

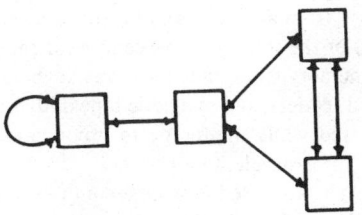

Fig. 2. A cellular automaton with nonuniform neighborhood.

the associated output); a static or dynamic interconnection scheme (neighborhood does or does not remain fixed in time). Some of the names associated with one or more of these versions are cellular automaton, tessellation automaton, modular computer, iterative automaton, intelligent graph, Lindenmayer system, and cellular network.

The first version of the cellular automaton, historically, was the cellular space obtained by selecting the first choice in each dichotomy above, but with no external input or output. It can be visualized in two dimensions as an infinite chessboard, each square representing a cell. It has been used to prove the existence of nontrivial self-reproducing machines, is capable of computing any computable function with only three states per cell and the four nearest cells as the neighborhood (Fig. 1), and can exhibit Garden of Eden configurations; i.e., patterns of cell states at one time, which can never arise in a given cellular space except at time zero. If an external input is assumed distributed to each cell, then the cellular space becomes what is usually called a "tessellation" space.

The cellular automaton is obtained from the cellular space by admitting only a finite, connected set of cells on the chessboard (Fig. 3). A cell with a neighbor missing has a special boundary signal substituted instead. The cellular automaton is particularly useful as a pattern recognizer, where the pattern comprises the states of the cells at time zero, especially if nondeterministic cells are allowed. A famous problem for the (deterministic) cellular automaton, the Firing Squad problem, calls each cell a soldier with one of them as the general—i.e., all

cells but one are "off" initially—and asks if all soldiers can begin firing simultaneously by going into the same state. The Firing Squad theorem, which solves this problem, guarantees an affirmative answer.

The Firing Squad theorem remains valid even when a nonuniform interconnection scheme is allowed. Thus, another version of the cellular sutomaton, the graphical cellular automaton (Fig. 2), requires only that the number of neighbors be fixed, not that they be in any fixed geometric relationship with a cell. They have been shown to be more powerful than the uniformly interconnected cellular automata.

The final type of cellular automaton to be mentioned, the dynamic cellular automaton, or Lindenmayer system, allows a cell to divide into children cells—regardless of the position of that cell in the initial array of cells—and allows the disappearance, or death, of cells. This version, with its dynamic interconnection scheme, is of interest to theoretical biologists as a model for the growth and development of living things.

If instantaneous communication is made possible between any two cells, by allowing Mealy-type cells, then each of the versions mentioned above gives rise to another. This class of cellular automata types is not well understood, although it is perhaps of the most interest in practical computing.

REFERENCES

1968. Codd, E. F. *Cellular Automata,* ACM Monograph Series. New York: Academic Press.
1970. Burks, A. W. (Ed.). *Essays on Cellular Automata.* Urbana: University of Illinois Press.
1971. Gardner, M. "On Cellular Automata, Self-Reproduction, the Garden of Eden, and the Game of Life." Mathematical Games Department, *Scientific American* **224**:112–117.
1976. Lindenmayer, A. and Rozenberg, G. (Eds.). *Automata, Languages, Development.* Amsterdam: North Holland.

ALVY RAY SMITH

CENTRAL PROCESSING UNIT (CPU)

For articles on related subjects *see* ARITHMETIC-LOGIC UNIT; DIGITAL COMPUTERS; MEMORY: Main; and STORED PROGRAM CONCEPT.

Although we still talk about "computers," some believe that the term "data processing system" or "computer system" is more descriptive of what is found in the normal computer room. The stress is on the term "system," implying that the modern computer consists of a selection of units of various types, all interconnected and functioning harmoniously with one another under central

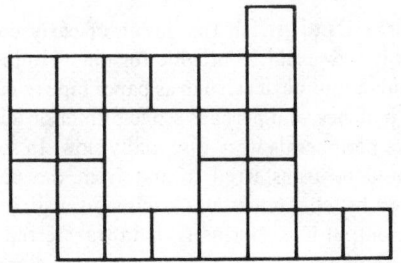

Fig. 3. A cellular automaton with uniform neighborhood of Fig. 1 assumed.

control. Most of the units in a system are called "peripheral" devices and serve either as the means of feeding raw data or file data into the system or of receiving results or updated files from the system.

The term "peripheral" conjures up a vision in which these units surround others which serve as the focal point or center of the system (although this is rarely true physically). The name "central processor," or *central processing unit* (CPU), is used to describe elements that carry out a variety of essential data manipulations and controlling tasks at the heart of the computer.

Probably the most obvious element is the one required to carry out arithmetic and other, mainly logical, operations on data, which is usually called the *arithmetic-logic unit* (ALU). It is designed to operate on a pair of numbers and carry out on them the processes of addition, subtraction, multiplication, and division. It can compare numbers and determine whether one is the greater or whether both are equal. These operations are carried out at very high speeds; even the slowest computers can do at least 10,000 such operations in a second, and the really fast "number crunchers" handle as many as 20 million.

Some computers can also be equipped with an *array processor* (*see* Pipelining and Array Processors), usually as an add-on facility. Such a device consists of many separate processing elements, each capable of carrying out basic arithmetic operations under the control of a master program, *in parallel*. The increased speed obtained through parallelism can be dramatic. For example, a minicomputer augmented with an array processor can outperform many large mainframes (*q.v.*) not so equipped on problems that require intensive floating point arithmetic.

The other obvious element is the *control unit* required to supervise the functioning of the machine as a whole, calling into operation the various units as required by the program. It receives the program instructions one by one in sequence, interprets them, and sends appropriate control signals to the various units. It acts in many ways as a very sophisticated telephone switchboard operator, making interconnections between various parts of the system. When the control unit recognizes special signals (for example, that the result of a subtraction is negative), it can depart from the strict sequence of program instructions and jump to a different part of the program which is designed to deal with those circumstances.

Both the arithmetic unit and control unit depend heavily on the third main part of the central processor, the main or central storage (or memory) unit. The arithmetic unit needs numbers on which to operate and needs to store intermediate results at some place until the end of the calculation. The control unit needs program instructions in rapid succession. Both data and instructions are held in memory. The program for a given job is read into memory from an input unit or auxiliary storage device as part of the setting-up procedure for the job. Data flows into memory from such devices as keyboards on terminals, card readers, and magnetic tape or disk units, and is manipulated while in storage to produce results that are output, for example, to a printer.

Memory is also used to store a complex of programs known as the *operating system (q.v.)*; this system is designed to supervise the total operation of the computer in as efficient a manner as possible. These programs function in some ways analogous to "traffic controllers" as they have to monitor the flow of data around the computer, giving some streams right of way over others, opening up clearways for top priority messages, looking out for emergency signals, and generally keeping things flowing smoothly.

The central processing unit thus consists of the control unit, the arithmetic-logic unit, and the main storage. It is aptly named since it is very much at the center of computer activity, and it completes a massive amount of processing work both directly to produce the desired results and generally to supervise the efficient operation of the computer system as a whole. With the advent of microprocessors *(q.v.)*, we now find entire CPUs contained on a single integrated circuit *(q.v.)* chip ("CPU on a chip"). These CPUs are as fast and as powerful as those that required entire cabinets of hardware only a few years ago.

G. J. MORRIS

CHAIN. *See* OVERLAY.

CHANNEL

For articles on related subjects *see* BUFFER; COMMUNICATION CONTROL UNIT; DATA COMMUNICATIONS; INTERRUPT; INPUT/OUTPUT DEVICES; MEMORY: Auxiliary; MULTIPLEXING; and SYNCHRONOUS/ASYNCHRONOUS OPERATION.

Early Design. In the design of early computing systems it was usual to provide for only a minimum of input and output devices, such as paper tape or card readers and punches, and perhaps a line printer or teleprinter. All these peripherals were essentially slow. In such cases data could be transferred to and from the peripheral, character by character, and each unit had its special input or output line. Normally, data transferred between an input/output (I/O) device and the store passed through the processor. Later it was found necessary to provide many I/O devices. With the advent of magnetic tape and disk units, faster devices with short crisis times (i.e., a need to be serviced very quickly if data was not to be lost), multicharacter block transfers became necessary.

In all cases, however, it was necessary to provide some indication of the status of the I/O device in use, such as "ready" or "busy." If a busy status of the device called upon was detected, the program usually had to stop and wait for the unit to become available again.

The need for block transfers to devices with short crisis times and the avoidance of delays due to unsuitable peripheral conditions led to the use of buffered peripherals and the development of continuously operating *channels* communicating directly with the store instead of through the processor. Additionally, the channel provides overlap of I/O processing with logical and arithmetic processing, thereby obtaining high throughput speed by performing different operations in parallel. The channel also provides a standard interface for a range of I/O devices. This gives a base architecture for device design and provides flexibility of configuration. Thus, a range of I/O devices may be connected to one processor in many combinations.

Autonomous Channel Operation. The eventual availability of fast buffered block peripherals such as magnetic tape and buffered peripherals such as card units and line printers called for the fast transfer of data to and from peripherals. If these transfers were controlled by the CPU, much time would be lost by the CPU, especially as character transfer was slow compared with other CPU operations. It follows that methods of autonomous transfer were needed. In these methods a whole block of data is transferred rapidly, word by word, to and from the main store, the cycles of the storage time taken for the word transfer being stolen from those available to the CPU. This usually causes only a slight hesitation of the CPU, whose storage cycle time of 200–1,000 ns should be compared with that of a high-speed disk drive which operates at about 10 μs per byte.

To facilitate block transfers directly between the store and the peripheral units, a controller called a *data channel* was introduced. There may be more than one channel. A data channel unit is essentially a small, special-purpose computer. I/O operations are initiated by the processor identifying a channel and a device. The channel then accesses a unique location in main memory where the processor has stored the address of the first instruction to the channel. Usually, a list of instructions (a *channel program*) is set up in storage. Each instruction is a particular operation which the channel must execute. The channel then fetches and executes successive instructions.

The CPU sends to the channel the length of the block of the continuous storage words to be transferred and the number of those words to be transferred. The channel initiates the transfer, if possible; i.e., if the channel is not already busy and the channel equipment is available and ready to operate.

Usually the transfer from store to channel unit is in words, but the channel usually divides the words into a number of fields (or bytes), each of between 6 and 12 bits, suitable for acceptance by the peripheral unit controller and the peripheral itself. Then each byte is sent in turn, usually starting at the leftmost or the most significant byte. As a word is transferred to and from the store, the word count (the number of words still to be transferred) is decremented and the address incremented until the word count becomes zero after all data has been transferred.

It is common for a read or write instruction relating to channel operations to be in two or more parts, since it is usually impossible to provide all data for the specification of the operation in one instruction word. Thus, the first part will specify and initiate the action of reading or writing, will give the address to which transfer will be made in the case of the rejection of the operation for any reason, and will contain the address of a *control word*. The control word contains the length and initial address of the block to be transferred and is that information which is actually passed to the channel unit. It is also possible to allow a sequence of data blocks to be transferred by providing a sequence or chain of control words that are sent one after another to the channel.

The control word also provides a function code that specifies and provides for certain types of variation of the normal mode of transfer of data such as skipping, reading, or writing zeros or terminating transfers, before or after the specified number of words indicated in the control word. However, the transfer of data is by no means the only function performed by a channel unit, for it may receive a variety of special orders from the processor, such as channel and equipment selection and channel and equipment status inquiry.

In the case in which there is more than one channel, the channels are connected at the processor end via a scanner circuit called a *director*. The director polls the various data channels in turn, and when data is ready it is transferred, the data channel providing the address to store it in, or from which data is to be provided, and then providing or receiving the word. This scanning is done sufficiently rapidly to avoid any crisis. The director has direct access to memory and activates the input to, and the output from, memory. It scans the channels in a defined order of priority. One director services as many as six channels.

The channels are connected to peripheral unit controllers. These break down the channel byte into units that can be handled by the actual I/O peripheral, e.g., a six- to eight-bit byte. The peripheral unit controller may not actually activate the output peripheral until its internal buffer has been filled by the channel, nor may it activate the input channel until its buffer has been filled by the peripheral device.

Channel Capacity. The rate at which a channel can transmit data to or from an I/O device, or to or from main storage, is the channel capacity. This is usually given in bytes or kilobytes per second. The channel capacity must, of course, be great enough to service the fastest I/O device connected to it.

Computer manuals and channel specifications usually give figures for data transfer rates under the assumption of ideal conditions. Actual data transmission rates are usually below these. If the channel hardware and the CPU hardware use the same registers, the channel may have to wait on the CPU for available registers (and vice versa), thus affecting transfer rates in a manner that cannot be determined a priori. The maximum rates given for discrete channels will also be lowered by the operation of other channels and by relative channel priorities.

Since *multiplexer* or *selector* channels are essentially independent computers controlling I/O, they will, of course, have their transfer rates affected by the way they are programmed. If the data is entered into a contiguous area of storage, the rate of data transmission will be greater than if it is entered into a noncontiguous set of areas, where all sorts of addresses must be computed and the CPU notified as to which storage area is being affected. This use of noncontiguous memory for a data set is known as *data chaining*. Of course, with data chaining, more areas of conflict with the CPU are possible, slowing either data transmission or processing.

Channel Command. A computer program is made up of a set of instructions that are decoded and executed by the CPU. Channel commands are instructions that are decoded and executed by the I/O channels. A series of commands in sequence constitute a channel program. Commands are stored in the main storage just as though they were instructions. They are fetched from main storage and are common to all I/O devices, but modifier bits are used to specify device-dependent conditions. The modifier bits of the command may also be used to order the I/O device to execute certain functions that are not involved in data transfer, such as tape rewinding.

During its execution of a program the CPU will initiate I/O operations. A command will specify a channel, a device, and an operation to be performed, and perhaps a storage area to be used, and perhaps also some memory protection information about the storage area involved. All this information may appear in the command word, or the command may tell the channel in which locations in memory to seek the necessary information. Upon receipt of this information, the multiplexer channel will attempt to select the desired device by sending the device address to all I/O units (including controllers) attached to the channel. A unit that recognizes its address connects itself logically to the channel. Once the connection is made, the channel will send the executable command to the I/O device. The device will respond to the channel, indicating if it can execute the command. The channel will then make this information available to the CPU.

An I/O operation involving data transfer to or from a series of noncontiguous memory locations may involve a series of channel commands. Termination of an I/O operation involves channel-end and device-end conditions. These conditions are brought to the attention of the CPU via interrupts or programmed interrogation of the I/O device. The channel-end condition occurs when the data transmission is completed. The channel is considered busy until this condition is accepted by the CPU. The device-end signal is given when the I/O device has terminated execution of the operation. The device remains unavailable until it is cleared by the CPU.

Lockout, Cycle Steal, Hesitation. The memory of a computer cannot be accessed continuously, but only at specific points in time. The time interval between two consecutive points in time when the memory may be accessed by the processor or an I/O channel is known as a *memory cycle*. The reason that the memory cannot be accessed continuously is that during a read/write operation, the information is not available, and some time must elapse before it is available again. Most memory cycle times are measured in microseconds or nanoseconds.

The CPU is essentially involved in processing the data that is in main memory while the channels are concerned with the flow of data between I/O devices and main memory. Main memory is a high-speed data store, whereas peripherals are comparatively low-speed data stores. The channels and the CPU are busy moving data into and out of main memory. A source of conflict arises if they both need access to data at the same time. Since memory behaves the same way, whether the source or destination of the data is the I/O channels or the CPU, some method is needed to resolve the conflict.

Suppose another request for memory access is initiated by another channel while a memory cycle is going on. Since all requests must eventually be granted, but some more quickly than others, a priority system must be set up. It is the comparatively slow I/O devices, rather than the high-speed CPU, that must have their requests answered first. A tape speeding under the read head must give up its data before the next data passes the read head; otherwise the data will be lost. The moving I/O devices

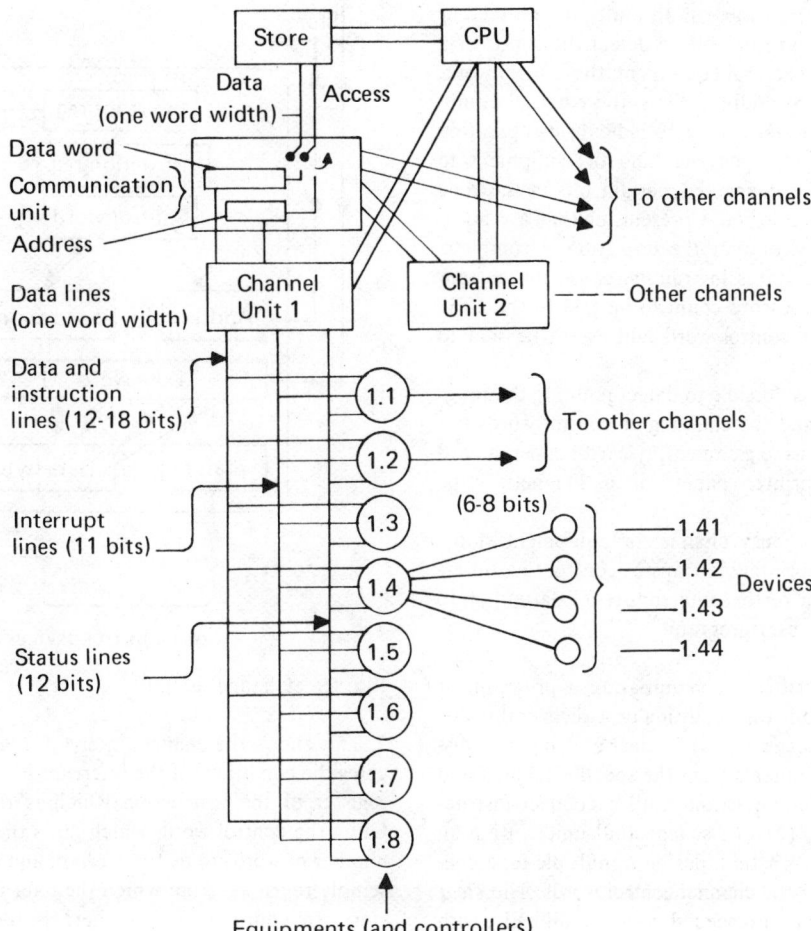

Fig. 1. Selector channel organization.

must always have open space to accept more data and cannot be concerned with memory access problems. The CPU, on the other hand, goes from one stable state to another. Once the information is in its registers, it can wait. This will slow the processing, but will not lose any information. Therefore, a priority lock up is set up whereby the CPU is locked out from access to memory at the instant that the channels want to access the memory.

The memory cycle during which the channels have access to memory and the CPU is locked out is known as a *cycle steal*, i.e., the channels have stolen the cycle from the CPU. For that cycle the CPU must stop and wait until it can access the memory again. This is known as *hesitation*.

Selecting a Peripheral. To select a particular peripheral unit, a special function code must initially be transferred to the channel, indicating the identity of the unit required. This is done by sending a *connect function*

via the data line that the selected unit uses to make connection to the channel. Usually, a channel unit with a variety of equipments attached is connected to these equipments in what a communications specialist might call *multidrop manner;* all are connected by the same communication path to the channel (see Fig. 1). It may also occur that a particular peripheral equipment may be connected to a number of peripheral devices (e.g., a magnetic tape controller and a number of tape units) and that it may also be connected to more than one channel in case the alternate channel is already busy.

Setting a Peripheral. A special function code sent to a selected peripheral by its connected channel may specify operating conditions within which the external equipment is to operate or a condition in which an interrupt may occur, such as stopping the channel activity, selecting an interrupt on detection of a parity error, or stopping the operation.

Status. It is necessary in all multiprogrammed or time-shared systems to be able to detect the status of a channel and of the external equipment, the control word, and the control word address. Thus, the external equipment will provide a status code to indicate its operating condition. Depending upon the kind of equipment to which the channel is connected, certain bits in the code indicate that a parity error is present, or that a read or write is in progress, or that the operation is complete. Other codes in the status instruction cause the current data address and the word count to be sent to the CPU and/or the current control word address to be sent to other CPU registers.

In this way it is possible to detect not only the progress of a transfer and the chaining of control words but also a complex status, e.g., an empty card hopper, a card jam, empty line-printer paper, or a magnetic tape condition.

Detection of a busy channel or equipment status may be used appropriately to transfer control to a different program until a further interrupt recalls attention to the channel and its user program.

Clear Channel. When initiating a program, or starting from a dead-stop condition or a recoverable difficulty, it may be necessary (1) to clear a channel by disconnecting all equipments from the specific channel and preventing any communication until a connect instruction is provided; or (2) to disconnect all units within an equipment (e.g., magnetic tapes on a multiple tape controller) and to clear the channel control words. The *clear channel* instruction is also needed in case of difficulty with a channel operation and may be initiated by the operator.

Interrupts. Selecting an interrupt condition is performed by a function instruction that can select occurrences of address, and data and channel transmission parity errors. Associated with each channel, there is usually a special register in a channel unit which indicates the occurrence of one or more of these conditions. There is usually one bit in the register for each equipment condition. Additional bits are reserved for the use of the channel itself, such as an interrupt from the channel, channel data parity error, or control-word parity errors, as shown in Fig. 1.

However, most systems will operate in a normal or *privileged* mode; in the latter all interrupts are held inactive when processing an interrupt. The activity state of an interrupt can be set by a special function instruction that sets interrupts active and returns the processor to the unprivileged state. The privileged status is automatically set on the detection of an interrupt when in normal state.

The structure of a channel unit is illustrated in Fig.

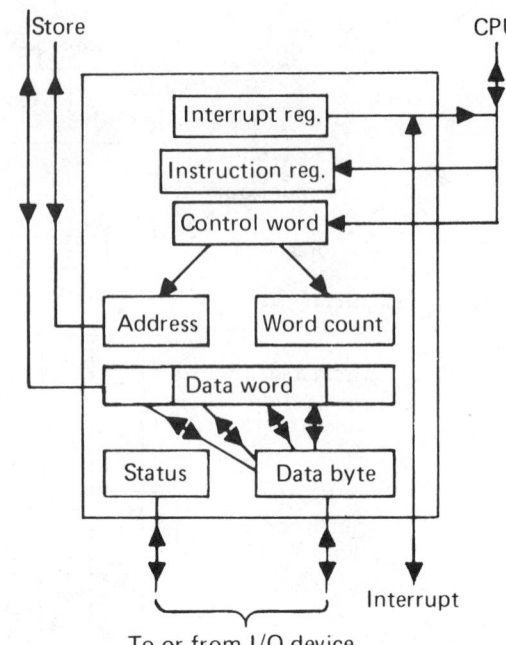

Fig. 2. Channel unit.

2. This shows the channel interrupt register, which indicates the conditions of the interrupt itself; the instruction register of the instruction which is received from the CPU; the control word, which gives the address and the number of words to be transferred; and the data word assembly registers, from which the data is to be sent from store. In addition to this, there is the status register, which is used to indicate the status of the connected unit of the channel.

Selector, Byte-Multiplexer and Block-Multiplexer Channels. Channels may be classified by the modes of operation they can perform. The channel facilities required for an I/O operation is called a *subchannel*. The capability of a channel to perform multiplexing requires more than one subchannel.

A selector channel has only one subchannel. Therefore, it forces the I/O device to transfer data in *burst* mode. The transmission of data continues uninterrupted until the whole block of data (or series of blocks of data) is transmitted. There can be only one data transfer operating at a time on a selector channel. Devices attached to the channel may be performing operations not requiring communication with the channel while data transfer is occurring in burst mode. When no data is being transferred, the selector channel monitors attached devices for status information.

The byte-multiplexer channel contains numerous

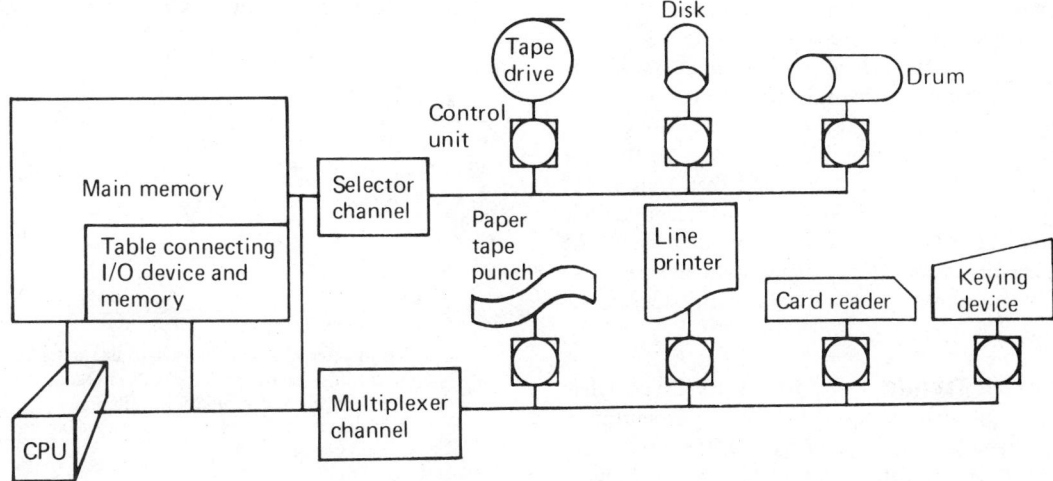

Fig. 3.   A selector and a multiplexer channel.

subchannels and may operate in burst or in byte-interleave mode. The mode of operation is determined by the device. In burst mode, only one device on the channel may transfer data. In byte-interleave mode, more than one device may operate simultaneously, each using a separate subchannel.

The block multiplexer channel also has multiple subchannels. It forces I/O devices to transfer data in burst mode, but the burst extends only over one block of data. Multiplexing or interleaving of blocks occurs between channel commands. Multiplexing between blocks may be inhibited by appropriate channel instructions. Byte-multiplexer and block-multiplexer channels can sustain more than one I/O operation per subchannel, with the proviso that the total load on the channel does not exceed its capacity. Each subchannel of a multiplexer channel appears to the program as an independent selector channel. When a multiplexer channel transfers data in burst mode, the subchannel it is using controls the data-transfer facilities of the channel. Other subchannels on the multiplexer channel cannot respond to device requests until the burst is completed.

A symbolic block diagram differentiating multiplexer and selector channels is shown in Fig. 3.

Communication Channels. Some channels may be devoted to communication between store or processor and a number of remote terminals. These terminals may be of the interactive type or of the batch type. In either case the channel makes connection via a multiplexer channel, and thence (usually) via public transmission lines of specified bandwidth prescribed by the data carrier organization. The communication outlets from the multiplexer are made via *data sets,* which pass the

data between the multiplexer and the transmission lines and convert signals to frequency modulation or otherwise adapt them to the communication line. Communication may be in one direction only (i.e., in *simplex* or *half-duplex* form, in which transmission may take place in either direction at any one time), or in *duplex* (needing four wires instead of two) in which transmission can pass in both directions at the same time.

Buffering. Buffering is used to gather information at a time when it is not needed so that the information will be available for processing when it is needed. An early use of buffering was to overlap I/O and CPU operations. For example, an I/O operation is initiated to read a block of data into memory. While the channels are controlling this operation, the CPU may go merrily on its way processing with available cycles. When the CPU needs the information from memory, it will be available and the CPU need not wait for the data.

Care must be taken during programming to see that the I/O is completed by the time the CPU needs the buffered information, and also that just enough information goes into each block of memory. Sometimes all I/O is directed toward a block of memory, a buffer, set aside just for I/O purposes by either the programmer or the supervisory program. The information is then moved to a working storage area for processing to take place; the I/O buffer area is then available for more I/O.

The concept of buffering has also found a significant application in peripherals. For example, in an on-line inventory control system, a salesperson may type out a message and check it on a display device for errors and then transmit it to a computer. The message is stored in a small buffer in the remote terminal and then transmitted as a whole message to the main computer, rather than transmitting character by character as typed. In this manner the communications lines may be more efficiently used. These buffered I/O devices are the heart of all keying systems such as key-to-tape and key-to-disk. A card reader will have some buffer memory so that the whole card may be read, stored, and then transmitted rather than read and transmitted one character at a time. Shrewd manipulation of buffers will greatly enhance the efficiency of its associated processing equipment by making necessary information available at the appropriate moment.

Current Trends. It is apparent that the complete function required of a channel allowing for multiprogramming and time sharing far exceeds those of simply reading and writing data. It is therefore becoming more common for channel units actually to be small programmed processors or minicomputers. This easily allows the extension of the channel functions; moreover, a greater variety of conditions can be specified by software design at a later stage of development. In this way a large CPU may be in charge of many small independent processors.

REFERENCES

1978. Kuck, D. J. *The Structure of Computers and Communications* **1.** New York: Wiley.

T. PEARCEY AND M. PINE.

CHARACTER SET

For articles on related subjects *see* ASCII; BINARY-CODED DECIMAL; COLLATING SEQUENCE; EBCDIC; and PROGRAMMING LANGUAGES.

A given set of symbols constitute the building blocks of any written language. For example, modern written English is composed of a character set that includes the so-called *alphabet* (A ... Z) in its two forms (upper and lower case, or small and capital letters), the digits (0 ... 9), some special punctuation marks such as comma (,), semicolon (;) etc., and the space character (). Using these elements, all written instances of the English language can be generated. However, the character set for English may not be sufficient for some other language such as (say) French in which additional characters must be added because of the use of accents.

Each computer language has its own character set which defines the set of characters that may be used in

Table 1. Character Sets of Fortran, PL/I, Cobol

Characters	Fortran	PL/I, 48-char. set	PL/I, 60-char. set	Cobol
A,B,C, . . .,Y,Z	X	X	X	X
0,1,2, . . .,8,9	X	X	X	X
= + − */)(,.$ blank	X	X	X	X
	Z	X	X	X
@ # % : & . − ? ¬			X	
; > <			X	Y

Notes:

X indicates character is part of character set.
Y indicates character is part of character set, but is not allowed at many installations.
Z indicates character is not part of character set, but often is allowed.

writing programs in that language. Table 1 gives the character sets of some common languages. PL/I has two possible character sets because it was designed at just the time when the IBM 026 keypunch (which had been the standard card-punching device and whose keyboard was limited to 48 characters) was being replaced by the IBM 029 keypunch, which allowed a larger character set, more convenient for writing programs in high-level languages (but which has no provision for lower-case letters). As indicated in Table 1, implementations of a language in a particular computer may not allow certain characters or may allow characters in addition to the officially defined ones.

Most of the characters in the character sets of high-level languages have their usual meanings. But this is not always the case for the *special characters*, those which are neither letters nor digits. For example:

   * usually denotes multiplication (e.g., in Fortran, Pascal)
   = often denotes *replacement* of the quantity on the left by the quantity on the right (e.g., Fortran, Snobol, Basic)

One language whose character set is markedly different from all other higher-level languages is APL *(A Programming Language)* developed by Kenneth Iverson. APL contains many special symbols which serve as special functional operations. Some of these are shown in Table 2. In addition, APL defines many functions as a combination of two symbols from the character set. These are produced in practice by striking one key of a typewriter (with a special keyboard), backspacing, and then striking a second key.

Various codes have been developed to enable the characters used in higher-level languages to be represented by combinations of bits in a single eight-bit byte. Of particular note are the ASCII and EBCDIC codes.

Table 2.   Some Special Characters in APL

Character	Name	Definition	Example (result of function given under it)
ι	Index	ιA generates indices in ascending order, starting from the defined origin to A	ι6 1 2 3 4 5 6 (origin = 1)
⌈	Ceiling	⌈B is the least integer greater than or equal to B	⌈14.7 15
⌊	Floor	⌊C is the greatest integer less than or equal to C	⌊−5.1 −6
○	Pi times	○D multiplies D by π	○3 9.424777962
!	Generalized factorial	!E is the factorial of E when E is a positive integer (and the gamma function of E+1 otherwise)	!7 5040

REFERENCES

1971. Ralston, A. *An Introduction to Programming and Computer Science*. New York: McGraw-Hill.
1972. Pakin, S. *APL/360 Reference Manual*. Chicago: Science Research Associates.

J. A. N. LEE AND A. RALSTON

CHARLES BABBAGE INSTITUTE (CBI)

For article on related subject *see* BABBAGE, CHARLES.

Purpose. The Charles Babbage Institute for the History of Information Processing was established in 1977 to support the study of the history of the "information revolution" and to be a clearinghouse for information about research resources related to this history and a repository for archival materials. CBI conducts research on the technical and socioeconomic aspects of the history of information processing and promotes awareness of its impact on society. CBI also encourages others engaged in this and related work activities, and promotes interchange among those interested in such activities.

CBI draws together the perspectives of business administrators, scholars, technicians, computer pioneers, and government officials. It is international in scope.

How Established. CBI was founded in 1977 by Erwin Tomash to fill the need for an organization that would develop a broad historical view of the entire computing industry. In 1978, Paul Armer accepted the position of Executive Secretary. On 21 June 1979, Tomash and Albert S. Hoagland, president of the American Federation of Information Processing Societies (AFIPS) signed an agreement whereby AFIPS would become a major supporter of the Charles Babbage Institute, thus bringing the resources of both organizations to bear on the development of the history of information processing (*see also* AFIPS).

Board of Trustees. Members of CBI's Board of Trustees have been vitally important to the successful launching and development of the organization. The Board, which meets annually, is composed of 25 members from academe and industry, including computer scientists, technologists, and industrial leaders, as well as historians of science. Erwin Tomash is chairman of CBI's board. The first meeting was held on 30 January 1979, at the Smithsonian Institution's Museum of History and Technology in Washington, DC.

Program. Temporary offices for CBI were established in Palo Alto, CA in April 1978. After a lengthy site selection process, CBI moved to a permanent home at the University of Minnesota in the fall of 1980. Prof. Roger H. Stuewer of the University of Minnesota is serving as Acting Director of CBI until a permanent director is chosen. When fully established in its new home, CBI will start to develop a full scale archival program.

From its beginning, CBI has offered an annual fellowship to graduate students working in the field of the history of information processing. The first CBI Fellow (1978–1980) was William F. Aspray, Jr.; the 1979–1980 fellowship was awarded to Paul Ceruzzi. In addition to its fellowship program, CBI has developed an extensive oral history program to record the experiences of pioneers in the field.

CBI publishes a newsletter which is available to anyone who requests it, and in other ways disseminates information through the data processing community. Publication of occasional papers and monographs is planned. CBI's address is University of Minnesota, 104 Walter Library, 117 Pleasant Street SE, Minneapolis, MN 55455, (612) 376-9336.

P. ARMER

CHEBYSHEV APPROXIMATION

For articles on related subjects *see* APPROXIMATION THEORY; LEAST-SQUARES APPROXIMATION; and NUMERICAL ANALYSIS.

Many computations on computers require the calculation of values of one or more functions such as square roots, sines, cosines, logarithms, exponentials, and other elementary functions or more complicated functions such as Bessel functions. Since computers can only perform the operations of arithmetic, these functions cannot be evaluated directly, but must be *approximated* by some other functions that can be evaluated arithmetically. For example, a common method for computing the square root of a number A is the following application of the Newton-Raphson method:

$$x_{i+1} = \frac{1}{2}\left(x_i + \frac{A}{x_i}\right) \quad i = 0,1,2,3,\ldots \quad x_0 = A$$

It can be shown that x_i gets arbitrarily close to A as $i \to \infty$. For example, let $A = 2$. Then

$$x_0 = 2$$
$$x_1 = 1.5$$
$$x_2 = 1.41666\cdots$$
$$x_3 = 1.414215\cdots$$

whereas $\sqrt{2} = 1.414213\ldots$.

The general problem we wish to consider here is: Given a function $f(x)$ and an interval $[a,b]$ on which we wish to approximate $f(x)$, find an approximation to $f(x)$ on this interval—which can be computed arithmetically—of minimum error. But what do we mean by minimum error? In many problems in mathematics this would mean minimum least squares error over the interval. But in approximating functions for computers we are more usually interested in minimizing the maximum error on the interval, for then the user of the approxi-

mation always knows that the worst possible case is as favorable as it can be. Rigorously stated, we wish to find an approximation $R(x)$ which has the property that

$$r = \max_{[a,b]} |f(x) - R(x)|$$

is smaller than for any other approximation. Such a *minimum-maximum error approximation, or minimax* approximation, is usually called a *Chebyshev approximation* after the great Russian mathematician P. L. Chebyshev (1821–1894), whose name is transliterated from the Russian in a variety of other ways (e.g., Tchebycheff).

The question remains of what form $R(x)$ should have. If it is to be evaluated arithmetically, then the most general function it can be is a *rational function,* i.e., the ratio of two polynomials. For example, the Chebyshev approximation to the exponential function e^x on the interval $[-1, 1]$, which is the ratio of two quadratic polynomials, is given by

$$R(x) = \frac{1.00007255 + 0.50863618X + 0.08582937x^2}{1.0 - 0.49109193x + 0.07770847x^2}$$

for which $r = 0.86899 \times 10^{-4}$. The error, $E(x) = e^x - R(x)$, is shown in Fig. 1. It exhibits the characteristic property of Chebyshev approximations of alternating between its greatest and least values twice more than the sum of the degrees of numerator and denominator of $R(x)$ or, in the example above, $2 + 2 + 2 = 6$ times.

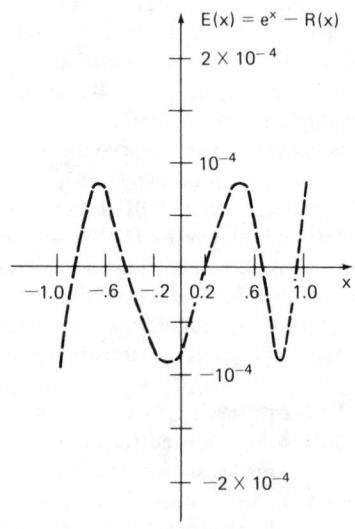

Fig. 1. Error in Chebyshev approximation to e^x on $[-1,1]$ as a ratio of two quadratics.

REFERENCE

1978. Ralston, A. and Rabinowitz, P. *A First Course in Numerical Analysis, 2nd ed.* New York: McGraw-Hill.

A. RALSTON

CHECKPOINT AND RESTART

For articles on related subjects *see* BREAKPOINT; and DEBUGGING.

A designated place in a program at which normal processing is interrupted specifically to preserve the status information necessary to allow resumption of processing at some arbitrary time in the future is called a *checkpoint*.

The primary purpose of a checkpoint is to avoid repeating the execution of a program from its beginning, should an error or malfunction occur somewhere in the middle of processing. This is especially effective in runs involving several hours of machine time. For such situations it is often appropriate to set up checkpoints at a number of strategic places in the program, either with all checkpoint information being saved, or by using a less conservative system in which the information captured at the most recent checkpoint replaces (overwrites) the previous set. Then, should difficulties arise, it is possible to take corrective action and resume processing from the last checkpoint, rather than starting over. Since the manipulations associated with checkpoint/restart procedures can consume substantial amounts of time and storage, it is possible to have situations in which it is more economical to avoid checkpoints.

A checkpoint capability is implemented by means of a procedure (often termed a *checkpoint routine*) that captures the status of the program at the particular instant when it stopped and copies it onto an auxiliary storage medium. This data includes the contents of the special registers, storage locations associated with the program, and other information relating to the status of input/output devices. Later on, another procedure (a *restart routine*) can reset the system to resume processing by reading in and restoring the checkpoint information.

In many systems the checkpoint and restart routines are prepackaged software components accessible to the high-level language programmer via ordinary CALL statements. These facilities usually include numerous options that allow the programmer to exercise some control over the type of information gathered, the form in which it is stored, and the circumstances under which the restart is to proceed.

The introduction of multiprogramming operating systems has prompted an expansion in the use of checkpoint-restart procedures beyond the context of insurance against malfunctions. Depending on the strategy implemented in a particular system, it may be decided to interrupt a particular run, releasing its storage for other purposes with the intent of resuming that run at some later (presumably more propitious) time. In order to handle that type of procedure without the user's involvement, the checkpoint/restart process must become completely automated.

S. V. POLLACK

CHESS. *See* COMPUTER CHESS.

CHOMSKY HIERARCHY

For articles on related subjects *see* AUTOMATA THEORY; FORMAL LANGUAGES; GRAMMARS; PROGRAMMING LINGUISTICS; LANGUAGE TRANSLATION; and TURING MACHINE.

For the mathematician, an *alphabet* is a set of symbols and a language is a set, finite or infinite, of strings formed from that alphabet. A *grammar* is a finite system that characterizes a language. Customarily, grammars work by substitution (production). Take the alphabet (or, as it is usually called, the *terminal* alphabet) of the language V_T; add a *nonterminal* alphabet V_N and a special symbol S that belongs to neither V_T nor V_N. A *production rule* or rule of substitution, R, is an ordered pair of strings, $R = T_1 \rightarrow T_2$. A grammar is a system, $G = <V_N, V_T, P, S>$, where P denotes the set of allowable productions. To use the grammar, start with S and find a rule (i.e., a production) $S \rightarrow T_1$ and substitute T_1, for S. Find another rule $S_1 \rightarrow T_2$, such that S_1 matches part or all of T_1, and substitute T_2 for the matched part of T_1. Continue with any member of P until the result is a string that contains only terminal symbols. This sequential process is called the *derivation* of the string, and the final string belongs to the language. The language consists of exactly the strings that can be so derived.

If, in a grammar, every rule has the form $n \rightarrow nt$ or $n \rightarrow t$, where n is a nonterminal symbol and t is a terminal symbol, the grammar is *regular* and characterizes a *regular language*.

If every rule has the form $n \rightarrow T$, where T is a string over the combined terminal and nonterminal alphabets, the grammar is *context-free* (the substitution $n \rightarrow T$ can be made wherever n occurs). A context-free grammar generates a context-free language.

If every rule has the form $S'nS'' \rightarrow S'TS''$, where S' and S'' are strings over the combined alphabet of termi-

Class of Grammar, G_i	Grammatical Characterization	Machine Characterization
Type 0	Unrestricted (or phrase structure)	Turing machine
Type 1	Context-sensitive	Linear bounded automaton
Type 2	Context-free	Pushdown automaton
Type 3	Regular (or right linear)	Finite state machine

Fig. 1. The Chomsky Hierarchy. Each class of grammars in the hierarchy contains all lower levels also. Thus $G_0 \supset G_1 \supset G_2 \supset G_3$

nal and nonterminal symbols, the grammar is *context sensitive* (the substitution $n \rightarrow T$ can be made only in the context $S' \ldots S''$). A context-sensitive grammar characterizes a context-sensitive language.

Changing the restrictions on the forms of rules changes the power of the grammar. Without restrictions on the form of rules, a grammar can characterize any *recursively enumerable* set of strings, that is, any language that can be characterized at all (call this class of languages type 0). Not every recursively enumerable set (i.e., type 0 language) is a context-sensitive language, but every context-sensitive language is a recursively enumerable set (call the context-sensitive systems type 1). Again, the context-sensitive systems characterize all context-free languages, but the context-free systems (type 2) cannot characterize some context-sensitive languages. Finally, a regular language can be characterized by a system of any type, but regular grammars (type 3) cannot characterize all context-free languages. The hierarchy of types 0, 1, 2, and 3 is due to Noam Chomsky (1946), and is commonly called the *Chomsky hierarchy* (see Fig. 1).

Many other classes of languages have been added to the hierarchy to form a partial order. To each type of grammar corresponds a kind of machine that *produces* or *accepts* a language of the given type: Turing machines (type 0), linear-bounded automata (type 1), nondeterministic pushdown automata (type 2), and finite-state machines (type 3).

REFERENCES

1946. Chomsky, Noam. "Three Models for the Description of Language," *IRE Trans. Information Theory* **IT-2**:113–124.
1969. Salomaa, Arto. *Theory of Automata*. Oxford: Pergamon Press.
1978. Denning, Peter J.; Dennis, Jack B.; and Qualitz, Joseph E. *Machines, Languages and Computation*. Englewood Cliffs, NJ: Prentice-Hall.

D. G. Hays

CIPS. *See* Canadian Information Processing Society.

CIRCUITRY. *See* Computer Circuitry; and Integrated Circuitry.

CLASS

For articles on related subjects *see* Abstract Data Types; Data Structures; and Data Type.

The class concept was introduced in the programming language Simula 67 as an extension to the block structure and procedure mechanisms of Algol 60. As a way of structuring programs, it is an alternative to the strict nesting of blocks in Algol 60.

Class Declaration. A class declaration resembles a procedure declaration in Algol 60. It was the inspiration for the abstract data type mechanism that is an important feature of several newer programming languages. A class may have formal parameters like a procedure. In general, a class declaration includes declarations for variables, functions, and procedures that are local to the class followed by the body of the class, which is usually a block. An example of class declaration is given in Fig. 1. Unlike an Algol 60 procedure declaration, a class declaration does not by itself cause storage to be allocated or executable code to be compiled. A class declaration is a template that can be used to create instances of the class. In Simula 67, these class instances are called *objects*. Simula 67 allows the declaration of variables that are references to objects. The built-in operation **new** is used to create objects (class instances). For example, if Z is a variable that is a reference to the class C declared in Fig. 1, then the statement

$$Z := \textbf{new } C(100)$$

would create an instance of the class C. The formal parameter n of the class is used to specify the characteristics of the object created from the class (e.g., the upper bound of the array A). In Simula 67, "dot notation" is used to reference variables within objects (e.g., $Z.A$ is a reference to the array A in the object Z and $Z.A[j]$ is a reference to the jth component of A in Z).

Note that there may be many objects of a given class: each with its own set of variables in existence at any given time. Thus, the strict Algol 60 nesting of block invocations has been replaced by a more flexible regime.

The class concept also involves a different rule for the execution of the statements in a class. When an object is created, control is transferred to the executable state-

```
class C(n);
   integer n;
   begin
     integer array A[1:n];
     integer k;
     procedure clear;
       begin
         integer i;
         for i: = 1 step 1 until n do
             A[i]: = 0
       end;
       ...
     comment end of declarations;
     comment execution of class object starts here;
     k: = 0;
     resume;
     k: = k + 1;
     ...
   end;
```

Fig. 1. Class declaration.

ments in the body of the class. Three situations are possible: (1) Control passes through the class definition to the end of the block; the object is terminated; execution cannot reenter the object, but its local storage remains allocated. (2) A **detach** statement is executed in the body of the object; in this case, the object becomes an independently executing entity; its lifetime may exceed that of the block in which it was created, which allows objects to be used to create processes in a multiprocessing system; for example, an operating system could be structured as a set of cooperating concurrently-executing class objects. (3) A **resume** statement is executed in the body of the object. Execution of the body is suspended at the point of the **resume** statement until it is reactivated by a **resume** statement from outside of the object. For example, if the class C in Fig. 1 is used to create the object named Z as shown above, then the statement

    resume (Z):

would cause execution to continue in the body of the object Z at the statement $k; = k + 1$. This allows coroutine structures to be built using objects.

Subclasses. The power and flexibility of the class concept is enhanced by the ability to declare subclasses. A subclass is formed by concatenating the formal parameters, local variables, procedures, and executable statements of an existing class with those of a class being declared. A subclass is created when the name of a class is used as a prefix to a class declaration. In the example in Fig. 2, the declaration of class D has class C as a prefix. The class D has formal parameters n and x, local vari-

```
C class D(x);
   real x;
   begin
     real y;
     real array B[1:100];
     ...
     comment note the use of variables from C and D;
     y: = x + A[k]
     ...
   end;
```

Fig. 2. Subclass declaration.

ables A, k, y, and B, and a body consisting of the body of C followed by the body of D.

REFERENCES

1972. Dahl, O. J. and Hoare, C. A. R. "Hierarchical Program Structures." in Dahl, O. J., Dijkstra, E. W., and Hoare, C. A. R. *Structured Programming*. London: Academic Press, pp. 175–220.
1973. Birtwistle, G. M.; Dahl, O. J.; Myhrhaug, B.; and Nygaard, K. *SIMULA Begin*, Philadelphia: Auerbach.

D. B. WORTMAN

CLOSE AND OPEN A FILE. *See* OPEN AND CLOSE A FILE.

CLOSED SHOP. *See* OPEN AND CLOSED SHOP.

CMI. *See* COMPUTER-MANAGED INSTRUCTION.

COBOL. *See* PROCEDURE-ORIENTED LANGUAGES; AND PROCEDURE-ORIENTED LANGUAGES, PROGRAMMING IN.

CODASYL

For articles on related subjects *see* DATABASE MANAGEMENT; PROCEDURE-ORIENTED LANGUAGES; and STANDARDS.

Codasyl (Conference on Data Systems Languages) is a volunteer organization consisting of professional computing personnel from the computing industry and from computing-systems user organizations. It was formed in 1959 to attempt to standardize the languages used in computer programs and thus to permit such programs to be "machine independent." Initially, it was the purpose of Codasyl to choose and standardize a common programming language from among the numerous common programming languages being promulgated at that time, mostly by computer hardware suppliers. A Codasyl task force, organized in 1959 to work on the technical aspects of this objective, found it impossible to achieve acceptance of any language as a standard and equally impossible to integrate features of one language with another. Therefore, this task force published a new common language in 1960, called Cobol (Common Business-Oriented Language). Initially, the only suppliers to implement Cobol were Univac and RCA. The U. S. Department of Defense, one of the original contributors to the standardization purpose and an organization with a candidate for the common language, Aimaco (*Air Material Command*), thereupon made Cobol mandatory for all suppliers of computing hardware and software who were bidding on defense procurements. This economic pressure resulted in persuading other suppliers to implement Cobol also.

Experience gained with the initial language resulted in the publication of an improved version of Cobol in 1961. Another version, called "Cobol 61 Extended," was published in 1962, and additional features and enhancements have been added to the language almost every year since then. Cobol compilers were generally provided with all computer equipment from 1962 on. Cobol was adopted as an American standard by ANSI in 1968. An updated standard was issued in 1974 and a new standard is currently (1981) under way.

The Codasyl organization consists of seven Standing Committees, namely: (1) Executive, (2) System, (3) Cobol, (4) Data Description Language, (5) Fortran Data Manipulation Language, (6) Operating System Language, and (7) End User Function.

The last five (3–7) are referred to as "development" committees since their task is to develop specifications for a common language in their area of assignment. These five committees have attendance and voting rules which are common to all and specified by the Executive Committee. The current Codasyl organization has evolved over the years from other organizational concepts that gave recognition to the separate interests of the hardware suppliers versus the users, as well as to short-range issues versus long-range developments. As the Cobol language achieved acceptance, the disparity between the interests of the manufacturers of computers and the users of computers, which had to be recognized in the early existence of Codasyl, began to disappear, and the current organization evolved.

The various development committees of CODASYL accept comments and proposals from any competent source, review these proposals, modify them, and publish the resultant actions in a *Journal of Development* (JOD) for each language in which it is currently interested. As of 1980, there are four *JOD*s for:

Cobol
Data Description Language
Operating System Control Language
Fortran Data Manipulation Language.

A fifth *JOD* to be initiated in 1981 will specify an End User Function Language. These *JOD*s are published at one- to two-year intervals, depending upon development activity.

Other Codasyl publications include *An Information Algebra, Decision Tables (D-Tab), Data Base Task Group Report, A Survey of Generalized Data Base Management Systems,* and *Feature Analysis of Generalized DBM Systems.*

All Codasyl effort continues to be totally voluntary and oriented towards data processing language specifications that are common to all types of computer systems. New committees are formed when a clear need exists that is not being addressed by another organization. All resultant effort, in the form of a *JOD*, is in the public domain and offered as a candidate for standardization.

J. F. CUNNINGHAM AND J. L. JONES

CODE, ERROR CORRECTING. *See* ERROR CORRECTING CODE.

CODER. *See* PROGRAMMER.

CODES

For articles on related subjects *see* ASCII; BAUDOT CODE; BINARY-CODED DECIMAL; EBCDIC; ERROR CORRECTING CODE; and UNIVERSAL PRODUCT CODE.

A code is a correspondence between a symbol of an alphabet (e.g., our alphabet of letters) and a number of digits of a number system (e.g., six bits for base 2). To be more precise, the mathematician would say that a code is a pair(Σ; Π) where Σ is the symbol space and the Π are numeric combinations. Suppose that S is some symbol in the symbol space Σ and P is one of the permutations of the digits in a numeric counting system Π. We might say "S is mapped into P" or that "S is represented by P," using the following symbols:

$$S \rightarrow P \text{ or } S \equiv P. \tag{1}$$

Each P in Π is called a *combination*. Since P consists of n digits, it can be written as

$$P = P_1 P_2 P_3 \cdots P_n \qquad (2)$$

where P_i is any digit of the counting system with radix r; i.e.,

$$P_i = 0, 1, 2, \ldots, \text{or } r - 1. \qquad (3)$$

To make this more concrete, let us examine the case where the symbol space Σ_A consists of letters of the alphabet. Let each combination P consist of two decimal digits; thus, $r = 10$ and $n = 2$. A very simple code might assign numbers consecutively to the letters so that we would have

$$A \equiv 01, B \equiv 02, C \equiv 03, \ldots, Z \equiv 26. \qquad (4)$$

It is convenient here to introduce the operator v, whose action is to find the number of elements in a set. For our example,

$$v\Sigma_A = 26 \text{ and } v\Pi = 100 \qquad (5)$$

Since there are many more permutations than there are symbols in the symbol space, many permutations are unassigned. These are sometimes called *forbidden combinations*.

Need. Data is an abstraction of information in the real world. People keep this information in the form of symbols. The computer stores information in the various hardware elements that constitute it. Elements have been designed which have two or more states. An element such as the Nixie tube has ten states. But by far the most common, least expensive, and most efficient element is the *bistable device*; it has only two stable states. For the computer to represent information, it must be structured so that the devices used in the computer can accommodate it. Since there are not enough states in a single bistable device to represent each symbol as a human being uses it, the symbols are represented by a combination of these settings, that is by a binary code.

It might seem initially that any representation of a symbol would do. This is not so. The design of a code usually must take into account the following requirements:

1. The original order relations (i.e., A before B, $1 < 2$) that apply to the symbols within the symbol space should apply to the relation between combinations in the code.
2. Operations applied to the symbols should have analogous operations, which—when defined upon the combinations—produce a corresponding result.
3. The representation should be efficient (to minimize the number of combinations that go to waste).

Decimal Codes. A decimal code provides a representation for the decimal numbers in binary. To summarize their characteristics:

$$v\Sigma_D = 10, r = 2, n \geq 4. \qquad (6)$$

Note that these codes can be four bits or more. There are many useful codes that consist of more than four bits, and it is an error to believe that decimal codes are *all* four bits; they are not.

There are two main means for associating the symbols with combinations:

1. *Weighted codes* assign different weights to each bit in the combination as discussed shortly.
2. *Transition rules* may be created to indicate how the code for the successor number is created from the code for any given number.

Four-Bit Codes. *Weighted Codes.* Let us label the bits of the combination that represents a decimal digit. Unlike (2), where the subscripts increase from left to right, we will now order the subscripts 1 through 4 in

Digits	Table 1 8 4 2 1 Code	Table 2 7 4 2 1 Code	Table 3 7 4 2-1 Code	Table 4 Excess-3 Code
0	0 0 0 0	0 0 0 0	0 0 0 0	0 0 1 1
1	0 0 0 1	0 0 0 1	0 0 1 1	0 1 0 0
2	0 0 1 0	0 0 1 0	0 0 1 0	0 1 0 1
3	0 0 1 1	0 0 1 1	0 1 0 1	0 1 1 0
4	0 1 0 0	0 1 0 0	0 1 0 0	0 1 1 1
5	0 1 0 1	0 1 0 1	0 1 1 1	1 0 0 0
6	0 1 1 0	0 1 1 0	1 0 0 1 (0110)	1 0 0 1
7	0 1 1 1	1 0 0 0 (0111)	1 0 0 0	1 0 1 0
8	1 0 0 0	1 0 0 1	1 0 1 1	1 0 1 1
9	1 0 0 1	1 0 1 0	1 0 1 0	1 1 0 0
*(A)	1 0 1 0	1 0 1 1	1 1 0 1	1 1 0 1
*(B)	1 0 1 1	1 1 0 0	1 1 0 0	1 1 1 0
*(C)	1 1 0 0	1 1 0 1	1 1 1 1	1 1 1 1
*(D)	1 1 0 1	1 1 1 0	-----	-----
*(E)	1 1 1 0	1 1 1 1	-----	-----
*(F)	1 1 1 1	----	-----	-----

*Forbidden combinations.

reverse, going from right to left. Thus, if D is a decimal digit, we have

$$D \equiv b_4 b_3 b_2 b_1. \tag{8}$$

A weighted code associates a weight W_i with each bit b_i and might be stated symbolically as

$$b_i \leftrightarrow W_i \qquad i = 1 \text{ to } 4. \tag{9}$$

The requirement of the weighted code is that, when each bit is multiplied by its weight and then these are totaled, the total must be equal in value to the digit. Stated symbolically, we have

$$D = \sum_1^4 b_i W_i = b_4 W_4 + b_3 W_3 + b_2 W_2 + b_1 W_1. \tag{10}$$

Some restrictions arise in setting up the weights:

1. For each digit to be encoded, there must be a combination of bits and their corresponding weights, whose total—using (10)—is equal to the value of the digit.
2. When two combinations exist which, when substituted into (10), yield the same digit, D, then another rule must be provided to decide which combination will be used.

8421 Code. The weighted 8421 code is illustrated in Table 1. From left to right, weights 8, 4, 2, and 1 are assigned to the bits that make up the combination. When the bits are set to 0 or 1, the resulting number is shown in the left column of the table.

The six entries at the bottom of the table provide values 10 through 15. Of course there are no digits to correspond to these values in the decimal system. Hence, these combinations are forbidden. If these occur, the computer should signal an error.

Note that these combinations would be legal if the base for our system were 16. Hence, we will return to this table when we discuss the hexadecimal (base 16) system.

Finally note that the sequence of combinations for the 8421 code is the same sequence in which these binary numbers occur in the binary counting system. Hence, the appellation *binary-coded decimal,* or simply BCD for the code of Table 1.

7421 Code. Table 2 presents the 7421 code. Again there are six forbidden combinations. The bits that constitute each combination are calculated so that (10) will yield the digit value.

A problem arises for encoding the digit 7. There are two combinations, 1000 and 0111, both of which yield the value 7. An auxiliary rule is required to settle this diffi-culty: Use the combination with the least number of 1s in it (i.e., 1000).

742−1 Code. The code for these weights is presented in Table 3. It illustrates that one or more of the weights may be negative as long as the weights fulfill the requirement that all digit values must be created. This time we find that there are two combinations that yield the digit value 6. Since both have the same number of 1's, we choose the combination with the 1 in the least significant place.

XS 3 Code. To show that not all codes require weights explicitly, we examine the XS 3 (excess-3) code presented in Table 4. The rule for generating this code requires that we use the BCD code for a digit, call it n_D, and add the binary number 0011 (i.e., 3 in decimal) to it:

$$D \equiv n_D + 0011 \tag{11}$$

What use would there be for this code? It has two advantages:

1. No proper combination consists of all zeros; therefore no combination will be mistaken for a null transmission or *vice versa.*
2. It is a self-complementing code.

A *self-complementing code* is very valuable because it possesses this quality: The combination for the complement of a digit is the complement of the combination for that digit. The complement of a number is needed when we do subtraction by addition and complementation. For decimal arithmetic this requires that we subtract the value of the digit from 9. In our binary code the complement of a combination b_D is taken with respect to the largest valued combination; for a four-bit code, this would be 1111. Then, our definition for a self-complementing code is one for which the following holds:

$$9 - D \equiv 1111 - b_D \tag{12}$$

As an example of how XS 3 fulfills this requirement, we have

$$2 \equiv 0101, \; 9 - 2 = 7, \tag{13}$$
$$1111 - 0101 = 1010, \; 7 \equiv 1010$$

Hexadecimal. Programmers often deal with data in units of a *byte,* which consists of eight bits or two halves, each consisting of four bits. If the combination for each half has a different symbol to represent it, then this simplifies the description. The binary values with decimal equivalents between 10 and 15 have been assigned the upper case letters A through F as shown in Table 1 in

Weights / Digits	Table 5 2-out-of-5 Code 74210	Table 6 Biquinary Code 50 43210	Table 7 MBQ Code 5421	Table 8 Gray Code
0	11000	01 00001	0000	0000
1	00011	01 00010	0001	0001
2	00101	01 00100	0010	1001
3	00110	01 01000	0011	1101
4	01001	01 10000	0100	0101
5	01010	10 00001	1000	0111
6	01100	10 00010	1001	1111
7	10001	10 00100	1010	1011
8	10010	10 01000	1011	0011
9	10100	10 10000	1100	0010
10	----	-------	----	1010
11	----	-------	----	1110
12	----	-------	----	0110
13	----	-------	----	0100
14	----	-------	----	1100
15	----	-------	----	1000

parentheses. Thus, the programmer can describe the byte consisting of 10110101 in hexadecimal as B5.

Other Decimal Codes. If we do not restrict ourselves to four-bit decimal codes, we can provide one or more of the following advantages:

1. Error detection.
2. Simplicity of combination construction.
3. Simplicity of implementation in hardware.

2-Out-of-5 Code. The 2-out-of-5 code provides the first advantage and is illustrated in Table 5. Every five-bit combination that represents a digit contains exactly two 1s. Since there are ten such combinations, this works out well. To assign each combination, we establish a set of five *pseudoweights.* One of these weights, W_1, is 0, and the bit corresponding to this weight, b_1, should be set to 1 when the value of the digit being encoded corresponds to precisely one of the nonzero weights; this is true for the digits 1, 2, 4, and 7. The weights work out for all digit values except 0; this digit uses bits with weights 7 and 4, which obviously do not sum to 0; hence, the term "pseudoweights."

Biquinary. The biquinary code is a seven-bit code using exactly two 1s; it is illustrated in Table 6. One of the 1s is chosen from the left two bits; the other is chosen from the right five bits. The weights are used as would be expected. This code provides error detection whenever more than one 1 appears in either half of a combination, and also provides a logical progression from one combination to the next, which is useful for implementing arithmetic.

MBQ Code. The modified biquinary code (MBQ). illustrated in Table 7, is derived from biquinary by replacing the first two bits by a single bit, and the last five bits (which represent 0, 1, 2, 3, or 4) by three bits, which represent them in BCD.

Gray Code. The Gray code, invented and patented by F. Gray, was developed to fill a particular requirement. At one time, many devices designed to convert analog (i.e., continuous) data depended on the mechanical position of a shaft. Attached to the shaft was an encoder that produced electromechanical or optical signals corresponding to the shaft rotation. This created a transition problem. From Table 1 it is clear that the combination for 7 is 0111 and that for 8 is 1000. As the shaft rotated, the apparatus for reading out the position could not be depended upon to change simultaneously in each bit position. Thus, totally erroneous readings occurred. If b_4 goes to 1 before the other bits change in going from 7 to 8, the output would be read as 15.

To overcome the transition difficulty, codes called *Gray codes* have been devised whereby successive combinations change in one-bit position only, as shown in Table 8. The length in bits of each combination L is a function of the number (N) of discrete shaft positions to be encoded, as given by the formula

$$2^{L-1} < N \le 2^L \text{ or } L = \lceil log_2 N \rceil \qquad (14)$$

Fig. 1 displays a code disk for the Gray code of Table 8, which indicates the change of one bit at a time.

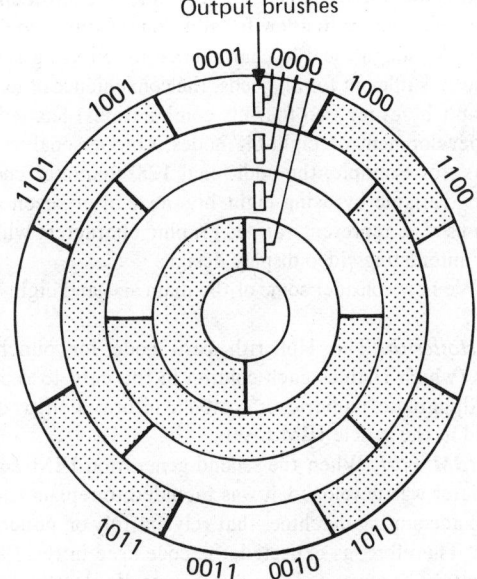

Fig. 1. The Gray code disk for Table 8. (Shading represents 1; no shading represents 0.)

Whereas the transition from one code value to the next in Table 8 cannot simply be described by a rule, there are Gray codes which can be so described. For example, if B_i is the binary equivalent of the integer i, $i = 0, 1, \ldots,$ $2^n - 1$ and if B_i' is the result of shifting B_i to the right one place (inserting a zero in the left), then $G_i = B_i \oplus B_i'$ where $\oplus$ represents the exclusive$-$OR operation is a Gray code. A three-bit code formed this way is 000, 001, 011, 010, 110, 111, 101, 100 where, for example, 101 (which corresponds to $i = 6$) is calculated as 110 $\oplus$ 011 = 101.

Full Alphabet. Thus far, we have restricted our symbol set Σ to decimal numerals. As computers went from infancy to early childhood, it was obvious they could be applied to many problems in which alphabetic output is mandatory, and where we encounter the following classes of symbols.

1. Letters: the alphabet from A to Z.
2. Numerals 0 through 9 (which we have already examined).
3. Punctuation.
4. Special symbols such as &, @, $.

The question arose of how large or how small the symbol space should be. With six bits, we can encode 64 symbols. Why should we want more than this? The most obvious reason is to accommodate the lower case as well as upper case alphabetic characters in order to allow printed (or displayed) output to look like normal printing. Additionally, there is a need for a variety of control characters and a desire to allow for additional future requirements. Although the 128 characters allowed using seven bits seem sufficient for all needs, the convenience of using eight-bit bytes (or two four-bit combinations) has led to the development of eight-bit codes. On personal computers, for example, the additional 128 character codes made available by using eight bits instead of seven are often used to represent various graphic characters which allow interesting video display designs.

We now consider some of the main six- and eight-bit codes.

Hollerith. The Hollerith card code for punched cards (which enables each column in the card to represent alphabetic, numeric, or symbolic information) is discussed in the article IBM CARD.

IBM 1401. When the second generation IBM 1401 computer was developed, it was intended to replace electronic accounting machines that rely entirely on punched cards. Therefore, as expected, the code used in the 1401 computers, as given in Table 9, corresponds closely to the Hollerith code. We note the following.

1. For digits 1 through 9, the 8421 columns are given by BCD, but 0 is represented by 1010.
2. The bits B and A represent the three zone punches 12, 11, and 0 on an IBM card as follows: BA = 11 for 12, = 10 for 11, = 01 for 0, and = 00 for no zone punch.
3. The C bit is the check bit (or *parity* bit, which is discussed in the following section, "Error Detection and Correction").

There are many other six-bit codes that are characteristic of the machine that employs them. They are generally listed in an appendix of the programmer's manual for the machine.

Numeric/Alphabetic	Table 9 IBM 1401 Code C	B	A	8	4	2	1	Table 10 EBCDIC in hex	Table 11 ASCII-8 in hex
A	0	1	1	0	0	0	1	C1	41
B	0	1	1	0	0	1	0	C2	42
C	1	1	1	0	0	1	1	C3	43
D	0	1	1	0	1	0	0	C4	44
E	1	1	1	0	1	0	1	C5	45
F	1	1	1	0	1	1	0	C6	46
G	0	1	1	0	1	1	1	C7	47
H	0	1	1	1	0	0	0	C8	48
I	1	1	1	1	0	0	1	C9	49
J	1	1	0	0	0	0	1	D1	4A
K	1	1	0	0	0	1	0	D2	4B
L	0	1	0	0	0	1	1	D3	4C
M	1	1	0	0	1	0	0	D4	4D
N	0	1	0	0	1	0	1	D5	4E
O	0	1	0	0	1	1	0	D6	4F
P	1	1	0	0	1	1	1	D7	50
Q	1	1	0	1	0	0	0	D8	51
R	0	1	0	1	0	0	1	D9	52
S	1	0	1	0	0	1	0	E2	53
T	0	0	1	0	0	1	1	E3	54
U	1	0	1	0	1	0	0	E4	55
V	0	0	1	0	1	0	1	E5	56
W	0	0	1	0	1	1	0	E6	57
X	1	0	1	0	1	1	1	E7	58
Y	1	0	1	1	0	0	0	E8	59
Z	0	0	1	1	0	0	1	E9	5A
0	1	0	0	1	0	1	0	F0	30
1	0	0	0	0	0	0	1	F1	31
2	0	0	0	0	0	1	0	F2	32
3	1	0	0	0	0	1	1	F3	33
4	0	0	0	0	1	0	0	F4	34
5	1	0	0	0	1	0	1	F5	35
6	1	0	0	0	1	1	0	F6	36
7	0	0	0	0	1	1	1	F7	37
8	0	0	0	1	0	0	0	F8	38
9	1	0	0	1	0	0	1	F9	39

EBCDIC. The Extended Binary Coded Decimal Interchange Code (EBCDIC) is an eight-bit code developed by IBM and is available on all IBM 360 and 370 computers. Hexadecimal may be used to convey each combination, as shown in Table 10. Thus, *A* is represented by *C*1, which in turn means 11000001. A more complete discussion of EBCDIC appears elsewhere in this encyclopedia.

ASCII. The American Standard Code for Information Interchange (ASCII) is actually a seven-bit code. To make it an eight-bit code, it is often embedded into a comparable eight-bit code (ASCII-8) in which the leftmost bit is either 0 (as in Table 11) or on some computers, a parity bit. Table 11 displays the encoding of the important characters—letters and numerals. A more complete discussion is found elsewhere in this book.

There is no clear superiority of either EBCDIC and ASCII-8, but there are two important differences. The collating sequence for EBCDIC has the numerals follow the letters; for ASCII-8, the reverse is true. Hence, documents coded and sorted under one system would be in a different order than if they were coded and sorted by the other. Secondly, the ASCII codes for the alphabet progress consecutively by $+1$, whereas EBCDIC has two gaps (between *I* and *J* and between *R* and *S*) which prove annoying in certain programming situations.

Error Detection and Correction. In the case of biquinary, we have seen how a code can be constructed with error detection properties. This is helpful, and even necessary, in many situations, such as when:

1. Information is transmitted from one site to another along lines where noise or other signal distortion might occur.
2. The data is recorded on a medium that is not impervious to noise so that 1s may get lost and be read as 0s, or 0s may be interpreted as 1s.
3. Devices within the computer may become faulty and create or destroy information.

Parity. The simplest means for detecting errors is to attach an extra bit to each combination of the code, called a *parity* bit. This bit is set to 0 or 1, according to the scheme used: For *odd* parity, the total number of 1s, including the parity bit, must be odd: for *even* parity, the total number of 1s, including the parity bit, must be 0 or even. An example of the use of an odd parity bit (also called a "check" bit), labeled *C*, is shown in Table 9. There are two phases in the use of the parity bit: creation and checking.

In the *creation phase,* the combination is examined and a parity bit is created so that the number of 1s in the total combination is proper. Now the combination can be transmitted from one place inside or outside the computer to another place. When it arrives there, the checking action follows. Circuitry similar to that for parity creation examines the combination exclusive of the parity bit as though it were creating that parity bit. If this developed bit and the accompanying parity bit coincide, a *single* bit error could not have occurred, and the information is accepted.

Other Codes. Many different kinds of computers have been built, and there are almost as many types of codes as there are computers. Further, some peripheral devices have their own codes. Magnetic tape usually uses the same code as that employed in the computer proper, but because magnetic tape is used for transmitting at densities and speeds approaching the limit of engineering capability, these devices are prone to error. A parity bit is added for each character of information. Thus, we find seven-track and nine-track tapes used with characters represented by six-bit and eight-bit codes, respectively, with the addition of a parity bit.

Punched paper tape devices that employ five-, six-, seven-, or eight-bit codes are available. The codes are usually peculiar to these devices.

Some typewriter consoles use a printing head that looks much like a golf ball. The head can tilt and rotate to get the proper character into position to strike the paper. To tell this golf ball at what angle to tilt and what angle to rotate, a *Tilt/Rotate code* (T/R) has been developed. Characters transmitted to the type mechanism in EBCDIC must be converted to the T/R code to activate the mechanism properly. It is interesting to note that when the operator presses a key on such a typewriter, a six-bit code is produced. This is normally converted into EBCDIC for transmission to the computer; this is then translated into the T/R code to energize the print ball. The operator can verify that both translations have occurred successfully, since the key struck produces only a code character; it prints the character wanted only if the code and two translations of the code are all correct.

REFERENCES

1961. Peterson, W. W. *Error Correcting Codes.* Cambridge, MA: M.I.T. Press.
1968. Berlekamp, E. R. *Algebraic Coding Theory.* New York: McGraw-Hill.
1977. McEliece, R. J. *The Theory of Information Coding,* Reading, MA: Addison-Wesley. (Vol. 3 of the *Encyclopedia of Mathematics and Its Applications.*)
1980. Mackenzie, C. E. *Coded Character Sets: History and Development* Reading, MA: Addison Wesley. (Part of the Systems Programming Series.)

I. FLORES

COERCION

For articles on related subjects *see* EXPRESSION; and PROCEDURE-ORIENTED LANGUAGES, PROGRAMMING IN.

As a matter of convenience to the programmer, many programming languages provide a mechanism for automatically converting from one data type to another in expressions. These automatic type conversions are called *coercions*.

A familiar example of coercion occurs in arithmetic expressions containing both integer and floating point operands, as in $K + 3.5$, where K is of type integer. The integer variable K is first automatically converted to floating point, and then the addition is performed in floating point mode. If the language does not have such a coercion, the programmer must make the conversion explicit, e.g. FLOAT $(K) + 3.5$. (For the sake of program readability, the conversion should be made explicit, if possible, even when coercion is allowed.)

The kind of coercion that must be applied to an operand depends on the type of that operand, as well as on the type of operand required by the context. As an illustration, consider the expression $X + K$, where K is again of type integer. If X is also of type integer, no coercion need be performed; if X is of type floating point or complex, K must be coerced to the same type as X before the addition can be performed. Note that a language may not simultaneously provide coercions from type A to type B and also from type B to type A, since expressions of the form $A + B$ would then be ambiguous.

Coercions are not restricted to converting between integer, floating point, and complex. In Snobol4, for example, an expression such as $K + {'}01.50{'}$ is permitted, since ${'}01.50{'}$ may be coerced from type string to type floating point. Other common coercions are from decimal base to binary base (PL/I), and scalar to array (APL).

The term coercion was first used in this context by Algol 68 (*q.v.*). In the revised Algol 68 report, there are six coercions—widening (e.g., integer to floating point), rowing (e.g., character to string), deproceduring (calling an argumentless function, for example, coercing a **proc real** to a **real**), dereferencing (converting a variable to its value), uniting (used to assign values to variables that accept several types), and voiding (used for discarding superfluous values).

Coercion is also used in other languages to describe the assignment of an expression of one mode to a variable of another. There is, of course, little difference between coercing as described above and then assigning or coercing *while* assigning.

A. S. TANENBAUM

COGO. *See* PROBLEM-ORIENTED LANGUAGES.

COLLATING SEQUENCE

For articles on related subjects *see* ASCII; EBCDIC; SORTING; and TABLE LOOKUP.

A collating sequence is an *ordering* assigned to a set of items. If two subsets of the set are both ordered as defined by the collating sequence, then they can easily be merged (i.e., collated) into a single ordered set. Collating, in the computer processing sense, derives from punched-card processing in which two decks of punched cards ordered in the same sequence on the same *key* are merged together, using a card collating machine. (The essence of the merging or collating methodology is explained elsewhere in this volume in the discussion of the merge search technique in the article on TABLE LOOKUP).

Collating is often necessary in data processing applications; a good example is the collating of a set of updated records into a master file (or set) of records. This requires that both sets of records be ordered or sorted on a key in the same sequence (ascending or descending). This is illustrated by the following example of collating two sets into one, using a person's social security number as a key.

| Set 1 (Updates) | |
Key	Action
408-44-6083	Add
414-22-3598	Delete
414-36-1776	Add

Set 2 (Master)
222-22-2222
333-33-3333
414-22-3598

Set 3 (New Master after Collating and Updating)
222-22-2222
333-33-3333
408-44-6083
414-36-1776

In the example given, a social security number (a supposedly unique identity number which is often used in the U.S. for identifying each person) is the key, and these numbers are collated in ascending numerical sequence.

In a general sense, a *collating sequence* must be considered when assigning codes to the various characters to be represented in a computing system in order that collating may also be done on non-numerical keys. For example, consider the ordering or sequence for this set of characters:

A, X, 2, 7, a, b, ?, /, #

It must be determined in what order the various graphic characters of the set are to be taken. The preceding characters would order as follows, using two common character representation schemes.

| ASCII (7 bit) | | EBCDIC (8 bit) | |
Character	Code	Character	Code
#	010 0011	/	0110 0001
/	010 1111	?	0110 1111
2	011 0010	#	0111 1011
7	011 0111	a	1000 0001
?	011 1111	b	1000 0010
A	100 0001	A	1100 0001
X	101 1000	X	1110 0111
a	110 0001	2	1111 0010
b	110 0010	7	1111 0111

Of course alphabetization is achieved by ordering the binary codes representing the alphabetic characters. Also, codes representing the numbers should order properly, but the decision as to whether alphabetic characters should collate before or after numbers is somewhat arbitrary. The collating sequence for special characters is also an arbitrary choice, and various schemes are found in practice. ASCII (American Standard Code for Information Interchange) and EBCDIC (Extended Binary Coded Decimal Interchange Code) are perhaps the codes most often encountered, and the characters they represent will have a collating sequence corresponding to the value of the binary number code assigned to each character, as may be inferred from the tables in the articles on ASCII and EBCDIC.

When multiple characters are used to constitute a key for an item, the keys will collate in accordance with the composite character codes. For example, the name JOHNSON collates before JONES because the key representing JOHNSON has a lower value then the key for JONES. When EBCDIC codes are used, the keys for JOHNSON and JONES appear as follows (using a ten-character maximum length, left-justified key):

Name	Key (in Hexadecimal)
JOHNSON	D1 D6 C8 D5 E2 D6 D5 40 40 40
JONES	D1 D6 D5 C5 E2 40 40 40 40 40

Note that hexadecimal 40 (binary 0100 0000) represents a blank—the character used to pad out the key.

C. E. PRICE

COLLEGES AND UNIVERSITIES, COMPUTERS IN

For articles on related subjects *see* DIGITAL COMPUTERS; and EDUCATION IN COMPUTER SCIENCE AND TECHNOLOGY.

Universities as Computer Builders. Much of the early research and development of calculators and (later) stored program digital computers was carried out by university personnel. A few examples are the "large systems of linear algebraic equations" solver at Iowa State College (1937–1942); the Mark I or IBM Automatic Sequence Controlled Calculator at Harvard (1939–1944); the ENIAC (Electronic Numerical Integrator and Computer) at the University of Pennsylvania (1942–1946); the EDVAC (Electronic Discrete Variable Computer) at the University of Pennsylvania (1945–1950); the ORDVAC (Ordnance Variable Automatic Computer) and the ILLIAC (Illinois Automatic Computer) at the University of Illinois (1948–1952); the MSUDC (Michigan State University Discrete Computer) at Michigan State; the Whirlwind I at the Massachusetts Institute of Technology (1947–1950); and the SWAC (Standards Western Automatic Conputer) at University of California at Los Angeles.

In recent years, very few computers have been built by universities. Even the ILLIAC IV developed at the University of Illinois was largely subcontracted to computer manufacturers. However, the University of Illinois continues to be active in computer design.

Universities as Computer Users. During the early 1950s universities began to acquire computers for general use in their research activities. Many were brought in to handle large-scale statistical and data processing tasks and were usually augmented by large punched-card processing machine installations. Early calculators included IBM's 602A, 604, and CPC (Card Programmed Calculator). The first stored-program digital computer to be utilized by universities in large numbers was the IBM 650, which was made available for several years (approximately 1955–1963) on a 60% educational allowance.

By early 1960 there were approximately 125 colleges and universities in the United States which had one or more stored-program digital computers. Sixty-five of these had the IBM 650, while the remaining 60 were

Table 1. Estimated Number of U.S. Institutions of Higher Education with Access to Computer Facilities

	Total No. of Institutions or Campuses	No. with Access to Computers
1960	2000 (Est.)	125
1965	2219	707
1967	2477	980
1970	2807	1681
1977*	3136	2163

*John W. Hamblen, 1979.

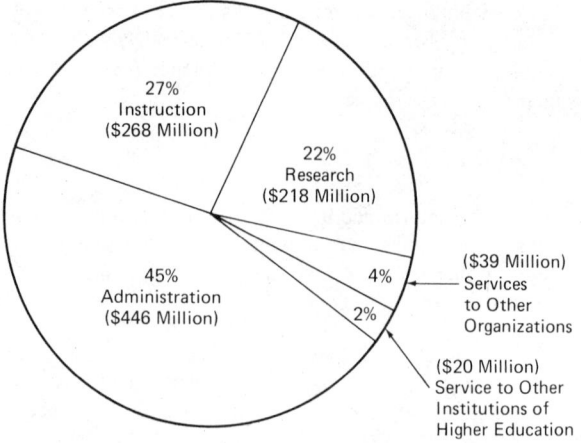

Fig. 1. Estimated distribution of expenditures for instruction, research, and administrative uses of computers in U.S. higher education, 1976–1977.

about equally split between smaller machines and those that were larger than the 650 (Keenan, 1959). Table 1 shows that the growth in the numbers of colleges and universities obtaining computers or acquiring access to computers was rapid. By 1975 practically every college and university campus had access to computer facilities for instruction, research, and/or administration.

The use of computers has permeated nearly every discipline. These widespread uses have pushed computer costs upward from 2% to 5% of the institutions' total budgets in most cases. Table 2 shows estimates of the total expenditures and expenditures per student for fiscal year 1979. Over three-fourths of computer funds for the 1977 fiscal year came from these institutions' own funds, with the remaining quarter coming from the federal government and other agencies.

By fiscal year 1978, the annual expenditures for computing by U.S. institutions of higher education was expected to have reached one billion dollars (Hamblen, 1979).

Distribution of Expenditures by Function. An estimated 27% of the reported expenditures were for on-campus instructional uses of the computing facilities. Approximately 22% was for research and 45% for institutional administration (see Fig. 1).

Studies on Computers in Higher Education. The

Table 2. Estimated Expenditures for Computing Total and per Student by Highest Level of Degree Offering 1976–1977*

Highest Degree Offered	Total Expenditure (Millions)	Expended per Pupil ($)
Associate	156	39
Bachelor's	50	56
Master's	146	61
Doctorate	639	164
Total (or average)	991	88

*John W. Hamblen, 1979.

first comprehensive study to be conducted on the status of computers in higher education was conducted by the National Research Council and published in 1966 (Keenan, 1966). This report is commonly known as the Rosser report, after the study committee chairman, Barkley J. Rosser. This was followed by a publication by the President's Science Advisory Committee (Pierce, 1967), commonly referred to as the Pierce report, and publications on four national surveys conducted by the Southern Regional Education Board and the University of Missouri, Rolla, for the National Science Foundation (Hamblen, 1979). Reports have also been published on studies sponsored by the American Council on Education (Caffrey and Mosmann, 1967), EDUCOM (Mosmann, 1973), and the Rand Corporation (Levien, 1971, 1972).

Associations, Groups, and Societies with Interests in Computers in Higher Education

ACM/SIGUCC, Special Interest Group on University Computer Centers and ACM/SIGCSE, Special Interest Group on Computer Science Education of the Association for Computing Machinery, 1133 Avenue of the Americas, New York, NY, 10036.

AACRAO, American Association of Collegiate Registrars and Admissions Officers, One Dupont Circle, Suite 330, Washington, DC, 20036.

AEDS, Association for Educational Data Systems, 1201 Sixteenth St. N.W., Washington, DC, 20036.

CUMREC, College and University Machine Record Conference, 42 Hannah Administration Bldg., Michigan State University, East Lansing, MI, 48823.

CAUSE, College and University System Exchange, 737 29th St. Boulder, CO, 80302.

EDUCOM, Interuniversity Communications Council, Box 364, Princeton, NJ, 08540.

REFERENCES

1966. Keenan, Thomas A. (Ed.). *Digital Computer Needs in Universities and Colleges.* Washington DC: National Research Council.

1967. Caffrey, John and Mosmann, Charles. *Computers on Campus.* Washington DC.: American Council on Education.

1967. Pierce, John R. (Chairman of Study Committee). *Computers in Higher Education.* Washington, DC: White House.

1971. Levien, R. *Computers in Instruction: Their Future for Higher Education.* Santa Monica, CA: Rand Corporation.

1972. Goldstine, Herman H. *The Computer: From Pascal to Von Neumann.* Princeton, NJ: Princeton University Press.

1972. Levien, R. *et al. The Emerging Technology, Instructional Uses of the Computer in Higher Education.* New York: McGraw-Hill.

1973. Mosmann, Charles. *Academic Computers in Service.* San Francisco: Jossey-Bass.

1979. Hamblen, John W. *Computer Manpower—Supply and Demand—By States.* St. James, MO: Information Systems Consultants.

1979. Hamblen, John W. and Baird, Thomas B. Fourth Inventory of Computers in U.S. Higher Education, 1976–1977. Princeton, NJ: EDUCOM.

J. W. HAMBLEN

COLOSSUS

For articles on related subjects *See* DATA ENCRYPTION; and DIGITAL COMPUTERS, HISTORY: Early.

Colossus was one of the earliest programmable electronic computers. It was developed in Britain during World War II to break top-level German machine ciphers, generated by the *Geheimfernschreiber,* a teletype machine manufactured by Siemens AG. The first tests with the ciphers were run successfully in December 1943. Several more Colossi were built before the end of the war. Because of engineering improvements, no two were identical. Many details about their design and performance, particularly their capacity for conditional branching, still remain secret.

As early as 1939, British cryptanalysts working at Bletchley Park, a country estate about halfway between London and Birmingham, invented an analog device to break the rotor ciphers of the German *Enigma* machine. Their success encouraged them to attack the much more difficult teletype ciphers. In 1942, when mathematics professor Max M. A. Newman arrived at Bletchley from Cambridge University, the cryptanalysts were trying to solve the *Geheimfernschreiber* ciphers with pencil and paper, using exhaustive techniques of Bayesian statistical analysis.

Newman set up a team of mathematical specialists to mechanize part of the task. Their early work led to the development of the "Heath Robinson" machines, which compared two punched paper tapes at rates of up to 2,000 characters per second. Mechanical problems with the Robinsons pushed Newman and his team toward a radical innovation. T. H. Flowers, an engineer from the Post Office Research Station at Dollis Hill, proposed to build a machine with 1,500 vacuum tubes, almost three times the number in any contemporary machine. It would execute the comparisons electronically rather than mechanically, a strategy that has guided the evolution of the computer ever since. The idea of automating the comparisons was probably influenced by Alan Turing's (*q.v.*) classic work on computability, and particularly by his notion of the Universal Automaton. Although Turing himself worked at Bletchley Park, his exact role in the development of Colossus remains obscure.

By redesigning the tape drive and the readers used in the Robinson machines, Flowers and his colleagues at Dollis Hill greatly increased the rate at which two ciphertexts could be compared. Colossus could read punched tape at 5,000 characters per second, a truly impressive speed even by postwar standards. Only one tape at a time was fed into the machine, and the results were stored in a memory consisting of gas-filled thyratron triodes. To eliminate cumulative timing errors, a clock pulse was generated by a photocell that read the sprocket holes in the tape. The necessary programming was done with plugboards. Although Flowers later noted that the prototype was probably less programmable than some contemporary IBM machines, Newman and his colleagues began to exploit the flexibility of the machine, making dynamically generated data dependent on the results of previous processing.

When installed at Bletchley, Colossus filled a large room in one of the temporary wartime huts. It operated in parallel arithmetic mode at 5,000 pulses per second and had electronic counting circuits, electronic storage resistors that were changeable by an automatically controlled sequence of operations, and typewriter output. The Mark II Colossus, completed in June 1944, had 2,400 tubes and was five times faster. The basic clock rate was the same, but five-stage shift registers increased the speed by providing access to five characters at a time. About ten of the Mark V machines were in successful operation in Bletchley Park by the end of the war in 1945.

Colossus went on-line two years before ENIAC. Colossus, though built as a special-purpose logical computer, proved flexible enough to be programmed to execute a variety of tasks, though it was not quite capable of decimal multiplication. ENIAC, a much larger and faster machine, programmed with patch cords, initially was intended for solving differential equations, but was used for a variety of numerical calculations.

Although it was the ENIAC group that made the final leap toward the modern general purpose digital computer with the design for EDVAC, Colossus stands as an impressive pioneering achievement in its own right, and was a powerful stimulus to postwar computer research in Britain.

REFERENCES

1974. Kahn, David. "The Ultra Secret," *New York Times Book Review,* December 29.
1977. Randell, Brian. "Colossus: Godfather of the Computer," *New Scientist,* February 10.
1980. Randell, Brian. "The Colossus," in *A History of Computing in the Twentieth Century.* New York: Academic Press.

W. E. BOGGS

COMBINATORICS

For articles on related subjects *See* ALGORITHMS, ANALYSIS OF; and GRAPH THEORY.

Combinatorics is the study of methods of counting how many objects there are of some type, or how many ways there are to do something. The items being counted are generally drawn from a finite system that has some structure, and the process of counting requires a detailed analysis of that structure. Such counting problems are ubiquitous in the sciences and especially in computer science; since the computer can aid in such analyses, combinatorics and computer science are developing a symbiotic relationship.

Most brain teasers, games, and puzzles are combinatorial in nature, and their solutions frequently become the basis for general theories in combinatorics. As brain teasers, certain combinatorial problems have attracted the attention of serious mathematicians since ancient times. For example, magic squares (square arrays of numbers with the property that the rows, columns, and diagonals add up to the same sum) were discovered by the Chinese as early as 2200 B.C. Other similar problems resulted in important contributions by such famous mathematicians as Blaise Pascal, Pierre de Fermat, Gottfried Wilhelm von Leibniz, Leonhard Euler, Arthur Cayley, and James Joseph Sylvester.

For many years, however, combinatorics was considered by some mathematicians as an area containing only fragments of clever ideas and tricks that could be em-

ployed to solve isolated problems, most of them recreational in nature. This situation has changed in the past few decades, with a significant increase in the intensity of activities in the area. Since the early 1960s, unifying principles and cross connections have appeared and have helped to make combinatorics a coherent body of concepts and techniques. Also, widely varied applications to problems in statistics, theoretical physics, chemistry, the social sciences, communication theory, and computer science have demonstrated the generality of the techniques and have enhanced the importance of combinatorics as a branch of applied mathematics.

Since it is not possible to cover in detail all the areas in combinatorics, we present as illustrations some of the problems and their solutions in three areas, namely, combinations and permutations, graph theory, and combinatorial designs. We note that many of the problems studied in combinatorics can be characterized as either (1) an existence problem, in which one determines whether a problem has a solution, (2) an enumerative problem, in which one determines the number of solutions a problem may have, and (3) a selection problem, in which one is to find, among all the solutions to a problem, one or more that have some special properties. Frequently, the selection problem is explicitly related to efficient procedures (algorithms) that produce the desired solutions.

As general references, books by Brualdi (1977), Hall (1967), Liu (1968), Riordan (1958), and Ryser (1969) are suggested.

Combinations and Permutations. One of the most important areas in combinatorics is the study of the various ways in which discrete objects are combined and permuted. A selection of r objects from a set of n objects is called a *combination.* An ordered arrangement of r objects chosen from n objects is called a *permutation.* The number of ways to select r distinct objects from n distinct objects is given by the formula $\dfrac{n!}{r!(n-r)!}$, where $i!$ stands for the product $i(i-1)(i-2)\ldots 3 \cdot 2 \cdot 1$ and is read i *factorial.* The quantity $\dfrac{n!}{r!(n-r)!}$ is usually denoted $\dbinom{n}{r}$ and is known as a *binomial coefficient* since it is the coefficient of the term x^r in the expansion of $(1 + x)^n$. The number of ways to arrange r distinct objects chosen from n distinct objects in order is given by the formula $n(n-1)(n-2)\ldots(n-r+1)$.

There are many possible variations on permutations and combinations. For example, one might wish to select r objects from n distinct objects allowing repetitive selections of the same object. One way to solve the problem is to note that the coefficient of x^r in the expansion of

$(1 - x)^{-n}$ is the answer. This example illustrates *generating functions*, a technique useful in enumeration problems. The generating function of a sequence of numbers $a_0, a_1, a_2, \ldots, a_r, \ldots, \ldots$ is defined to be the power series $a_0 + a_1 x + a_2 x^2 + \ldots + a_r x^r + \ldots$, where x is a formal variable (i.e., a variable without intrinsic meaning). In many enumeration problems, it is easier or more desirable to obtain the generating function of the solutions for a sequence of problems rather than to obtain an explicit closed-form expression of the solution for a particular problem. Thus, the generating function $(1 - x)^{-n}$ gives the number of ways to select, for all r, r objects from n distinct objects allowing unlimited repetitions. For example, when $n = 3$, $(1 - x)^{-3} = 1 + 3x + 6x^2 + \ldots$ and the six combinations of three objects, say a, b, and c, taken two at a time, are aa, ab, ac, bb, bc, and cc. Similarly, the number of ways to divide r distinct objects into n non-empty subsets is equal to $\dfrac{r!}{n!}$ times the coefficient of x^r in $(e^x - 1)^n$. Thus, for instance, when $n = 2$, $(e^x - 1)^2 = x^2 + (3!/2!)\, x^3 + \ldots$ and $3!/2!$ equals the three ways that three objects can be divided into two non-empty sets are (a, bc), (b, ac), and (c, ab).

Generating functions are also useful in determining the number of ways to arrange n open parentheses and n closed parentheses so that each open parenthesis is balanced by a corresponding closed parenthesis to its right. For example, $()(())$ is a well formed arrangement, while $())(()$ is not. If a_n denotes the number of such arrangements, we note that

$$a_n = a_{n-1} + a_1 a_{n-2} + a_2 a_{n-3} + \ldots + a_{n-2} a_1 + a_{n-1}$$

since all possible arrangements on n parentheses P_n are formed without repetition by $(P_j) P_{n-j-1}$ for $j = 0, 1, \ldots, n - 1$ with P_0 being the empty string of parentheses. This is an example of a *recurrence relation*, which, in general, is an equation relating a sequence of numbers $a_0, a_1, a_2, \ldots, a_n \ldots$. Often, a recurrence relation can be solved to obtain either a closed-form expression or the generating function for a_n. Indeed, many enumeration problems can be attacked by first setting up a recurrence relation and then solving it. In this case, the generating function can be found to be $(1 - \sqrt{1 - 4x})/2x$ and from this we can determine that $a_n = \dbinom{2n}{n}/(n + 1)$; these a_n are known as the *Catalan numbers*.

A derangement is a permutation of the integers $1, 2, \ldots, n$ so that the integer i does not occupy the ith position. The problem of counting the number of derangements of n distinct objects is a special case of the general problem of the permutation of objects with restrictions on the positions each object may occupy. The number of derangements of n objects can be determined by generating functions or by a formula known as the *principle of inclusion and exclusion* which states that for r sets $A_1, A_2, \ldots, A_r$,

$$
\begin{aligned}
|A_1 \cup A_2 \cup \ldots \cup A_r| &= |A_1| + |A_2| + \ldots + |A_r| \\
&\quad - |A_1 \cap A_2| - |A_1 \cap A_3| \\
&\quad - \ldots - |A_{r-1} \cap A_r| \\
&\quad + |A_1 \cap A_2 \cap A_3| + \\
&\quad |A_1 \cap A_2 \cap A_4| + \ldots \\
&\quad \ldots \\
&\quad + (-1)^{r-1} |A_1 \cap A_2 \cap \\
&\quad \ldots \cap A_r|
\end{aligned}
$$

where $|X|$ denotes the cardinality (number of members) of the set X. Thus, of the $n!$ permutations of the integers $1, 2, \ldots, n$, let A_i denote the set of those permutations in which the integer i is the ith position. It follows that the number of derangements is equal to

$$n! - |A_1 \cup A_2 \cup \ldots \cup A_n| = n! - \binom{n}{1}(n - 1)!$$

$$+ \binom{n}{2}(n - 2)! + \ldots + (-1)^n \binom{n}{n}$$

$$= n! \left(1 - \frac{1}{1!} + \frac{1}{2!} - \ldots + (-1)^n \frac{1}{n!} \right)$$

$$\approx n!/e.$$

Gian-Carlo Rota has observed that this principle of inclusion or exclusion and the well known Möbius inversion formula of number theory are special cases of a general inversion formula for partially ordered sets. Rota's work is an excellent example of unifying results that have emerged since the 1960s.

Permutation problems also arise from the study of molecular structures. We may ask, for example, how many ways there are to place molecules at the apexes of a regular polyhedron; two placements are considered equivalent if one can be obtained from another by a rotation of the polyhedron. If there are five kinds of molecules and the regular polyhedron is a tetrahedron (a pyramid with three sides and a base), then the number of placements is 75, a result which can be found using *Pólya's theory of counting* (see Liu, 1968).

Graph Theory. Graph theory is an area of significant importance in combinatorics, and it provides a good example of the study of the structural properties of discrete systems. A graph consists of a non-empty set of elements, called the *vertices* of the graph, and a set of two subsets of the vertices, called the *edges* of the graph. (More precisely, this is the definition of a linear undirected graph with no self-loops.) A graph can be used to model a discrete system containing a set of distinct objects (represented by the vertices) and a relation between these objects (represented by the edges). Thus, for example, the vertices of a graph might represent cities and the edges might represent highways connecting these cities. As another example, the vertices of a graph might represent books and the edges might represent the relationship that two books are cross-referenced. Berge (1962) and Harary (1969) provide general discussions of graph theory; Harary and Palmer's (1973) book covers the many enumeration problems arising naturally in the study of graphs (*see also* GRAPH THEORY).

Combinatorial Designs. Combinatorial designs constitute an area of combinatorics concerned with the arrangement of discrete objects. However, unlike the enumerative problems discussed above, its main emphasis is on proof of existence and nonexistence.

Typical of such arrangements are *Latin squares.* A Latin square of order n is an arrangement of n distinct symbols in an $n \times n$ square so that each symbol appears in each row and each column exactly once. Two Latin squares are said to be *orthogonal* if, when they are superimposed, the ordered pairs of entries are all distinct. A set of Latin squares is said to be *mutually orthogonal* if every two squares in the set are orthogonal. Latin squares were first studied by Euler when he posed the so-called "36 officers problem" in which six officers of different ranks from each of six regiments are to be arranged in a 6×6 square so that no two officers of the same rank or from the same regiment will stand in the same row or the same column. This problem is equivalent to the problem of the existence of a pair of orthogonal Latin squares of order 6. It is not difficult to discover that for $n \not\equiv 2 \pmod 4$ (i.e., when $n - 2$ is not divisible by 4), there always exists a pair of orthogonal Latin squares of order n. For example, Fig. 1 shows a pair of orthogonal Latin squares of order 10. Euler conjectured that for $n \equiv 2 \pmod 4$ (i.e., when $n - 2$ is divisible by 4) there is no pair of orthogonal Latin squares. Indeed, there do not exist orthogonal Latin squares of order 2 or 6, but in 1960 R. C. Bose, S. S. Shrikhande, and E. T. Parker proved the falsity of Euler's conjecture by discovering one pair of orthogonal Latin squares of all orders $n \geq 10$, $n \equiv 2$ (mod 4). Of related interest is the largest number of Latin squares in a mutually orthogonal set. A mutually orthogonal set of Latin squares of order n can contain at most $n - 1$ Latin squares; furthermore, for n equal to a

0	4	1	7	2	9	8	3	6	5
8	1	5	2	7	3	9	4	0	6
9	8	2	6	3	7	4	5	1	0
5	9	8	3	0	4	7	6	2	1
7	6	9	8	4	1	5	0	3	2
6	7	0	9	8	5	2	1	4	3
3	0	7	1	9	8	6	2	5	4
1	2	3	4	5	6	0	7	8	9
2	3	4	5	6	0	1	8	9	7
4	5	6	0	1	2	3	9	7	8

0	7	8	6	9	3	5	4	1	2
6	1	7	8	0	9	4	5	2	3
5	0	2	7	8	1	9	6	3	4
9	6	1	3	7	8	2	0	4	5
3	9	0	2	4	7	8	1	5	6
8	4	9	1	3	5	7	2	6	0
7	8	5	9	2	4	6	3	0	1
4	5	6	0	1	2	3	7	8	9
1	2	3	4	5	6	0	9	7	8
2	3	4	5	6	0	1	8	9	7

Fig. 1. A pair of orthogonal 10×10 Latin squares.

power of a prime, such a set exists. However, the question is still open for general n. In fact, the question is open even for $n = 10$. Various properties of Latin squares have been studied for the more restricted case in which entries in each *diagonal* or *superdiagonal* are distinct. The superdiagonals are the diagonals formed when the square is rolled into a cylinder with the first column adjacent to the last column.

The design of statistical experiments to test the effects and interrelations of various treatments (medications) leads to the area of combinatorial designs known as *block designs.* In fact, most of the terminology in this area is derived from such applications. Let $T = \{1, 2, \ldots, v\}$ be a set of distinct objects called *treatments.* Let $B_1, B_2, \ldots B_b$ be subsets of T called *blocks.* A collection of blocks is called a *design* on the treatments: A *balanced incomplete block design* is a design in which every block is of size k, every treatment appears in exactly r blocks, and every pair of treatments appears in exactly λ blocks. Since balanced incomplete block designs are characterized by the five parameters v, b, r, k, and λ, they are also referred to as (b, v, r, k, λ) designs. Most important is the question of the existence of a balanced incomplete block design for given values of v, b, r, k, and λ. This general problem is extremely difficult and has not been completely solved, although there are many results for specific sets of parameters. The special class of balanced incomplete block designs in which $v = b$ (and, consequently, $r = k$) is known as *symmetric balanced incomplete block designs.* Because of the additional constraints, more is known about such designs, although the general existence question remains a difficult one.

The construction of codes is closely related to that of block designs. Let $A = \{a_1, a_2, \ldots\}$ be a set of distinct symbols (letters). The set A is referred to as the *alphabet.* A *word* is an ordered sequence of letters from the alphabet; the *length* of a word is the number of letters in it. A *code* is a collection of words which are referred to as *codewords.* If no codeword is a prefix of another codeword, the code is a *prefix code.* If all codewords are the same length, the code is a *block code.* When A is the set of elements in a finite field, a block code is said to be linear if it forms a vector space over the finite field $(A, +, \cdot)$. An *error* is said to occur if one of the letters in a codeword is changed into another letter. Some codes are *t-error detecting;* that is, they can recognize when t or fewer errors occur in a codeword. A code is said to be *t-error correcting* if when t or fewer errors occur in a codeword, the original codeword can be reconstructed.

The three important parameters of a block code are the length of its words (short codewords yield low communication cost), its number of codewords (a large number of codewords gives the capability of representing a large number of messages), and its error-detecting and/ or error-correcting capability (detection or correction of errors means high reliability in communication.) The problem of code design is to select a set of codewords so that these parameters satisfy the needs of a particular communication problem. As expected, these parameters are interrelated in such a way that we cannot choose all of them freely. Furthermore, in designing a code it is also desirable to have efficient encoding algorithms for determining the codeword corresponding to a given message and efficient decoding algorithms for recovering (and perhaps correcting) a message from a codeword.

Asymptotics.

In enumerative combinatorial problems, it is necessary to count the number of occurrences of some configuration; the derangements mentioned above are typical examples. Frequently, it is fairly easy to express the number in which we are interested by means of a recurrence relation, a generating function, a sum of terms, or a product of terms. In addition to an exact answer of that type, we usually would like to know an approximation in more elementary terms. *Aysmptotics* is concerned with such approximations.

For example, the single most important asymptotic result of combinatorics is the answer to the question "How large is $n! = n(n - 1)(n - 2) \ldots 2 \cdot 1$?" The answer was found by James Stirling in the early eighteenth century. He showed that

$$n! \approx \sqrt{2\pi n} \left(\frac{n}{e} \right)^n,$$

where $\approx$ means "approximately equal to" and, as before, e is the base of the natural logarithms. Stirling's formula also gives us an approximation for the binomial coefficients since $\begin{pmatrix} n \\ r \end{pmatrix} = \frac{n!}{r!(n - r)!}$, and for many other similar functions.

The *harmonic numbers* $H_n = \sum_{i=1}^{n} \frac{1}{i}$ occur in many contexts in combinatorics and their approximation is also of interest:

$$H_n \approx \ln n + \gamma$$

where $\gamma \approx 0.5772$ (known as *Euler's constant*).

Both the approximation for $n!$ and H_n are derived by *Euler's summation formula,* which approximates a discrete summation, such as $\ln n! = \sum_{i=1}^{n} \ln i$ or $H_n = \sum_{i=1}^{n} \frac{1}{i}$ by the corresponding integral $\int_{1}^{n} \ln x \, dx$ or $\int_{1}^{n} \frac{dx}{x}$. The integral is then evaluated and the error is bounded by various analytical techniques.

Connections with Computer Science. The relation between combinatorics and computer science is twofold, and works to the advantage of both areas. Combinatorics gains in two quite distinct ways. First, the computer allows the large scale, exhaustive testing of conjectures and generation of data that would have been impossible or infeasible only a few decades ago. Before the age of the modern computers and programming techniques, results like Appel and Haken's proof of the four-color theorem could never have been found. Second, the application of techniques from combinatorics to problems in computer science infuses new vigor into the study of the techniques themselves and suggests new avenues for combinatorial investigation.

Computer science gains from combinatorics the tools necessary for the analysis of algorithms and data structures. The best example is found in algorithms for sorting elements according to some order. The analysis of the average, best, and worst case performance of most sorting algorithms hinges critically on the structure of permutations; the classical results in this area are just what are needed to understand the relative behavior of various sorting algorithms. Similarly, results on combinations, permutations, and trees (a special type of graph) facilitate the analysis of merging algorithms and search strategies. The techniques for the solution of recurrence relations and of asymptotic analysis are used in the analysis of almost all algorithms; without such techniques, we would never be able to answer questions about, for instance, the average number of interchanges in the bubble sort, the expected height of a search tree, or the average stack depth encountered in parsing arithmetic expressions.

Computer science also benefits from the computational problems suggested by the classical structures of combinatorics. How can we determine if a graph is planar? How do we find the shortest path between two nodes of a network? Is there an efficient way to determine whether two planar networks are isomorphic? These questions originated with combinatorics, but their algorithmic solutions came largely from computer science.

The books by Knuth (1968, 1969, 1973) and Reingold, Nievergelt, and Deo (1977) are recommended as references for the interface between combinatorics and computer science.

Concluding Remarks. The few subjects mentioned in this article certainly do not exhaust the subject of combinatorics. Rather, they should be considered as representative of the topic. We have not discussed many beautiful and deep topics, such as *Ramsey theory,* which is concerned with certain generalizations of the "pigeon hole principle" (if $n + 1$ pigeons are put into n holes, then one of the holes must contain two or more pigeons), partially ordered sets as exemplified by structural results such as Sperner's Lemma and Dilworth's Theorem, theory of matroids as generalizations of graphs, or the mathematical programming (*q.v.*) approach to optimization problems.

Finally, we note that techniques of combinatorics will undoubtedly continue to play a crucial role in computer science. The future design of computer hardware by VLSI is but one area in which deep combinatorial problems will emerge.

REFERENCES

1958. Riordan, J. *An Introduction to Combinatorial Analysis.* New York: Wiley.

1962. Berge, C. *The Theory of Graphs and Its Applications.* New York: Wiley.

1967. Hall, M., Jr. *Combinatorial Theory.* Waltham, MA: Blaisdell.

1968. Liu, C. L. *Introduction to Combinatorial Mathematics.* New York: McGraw-Hill.

1968, 1969, 1973. Knuth, D. E. *The Art of Computer Programming* **1, 2,** and **3**. Reading, MA: Addison-Wesley.

1969. Harary, F. *Graph Theory.* Reading MA: Addison-Wesley.

1969. Ryser, H. J. *Combinatorial Mathematics.* The Mathematical Association of America.

1973. Harary, F. and Palmer, E. M. *Graphical Enumeration.* New York: Academic Press.

1974. Denes, J. and Keedwell, A. D. *Latin Squares and Their Applications.* London: English University Press.

1977. Brualdi, R. A. *Introductory Combinatorics.* New York: North-Holland.

1977. Reingold, E. M.; Nievergelt, J.; and Deo, N. *Combinatorial Algorithms: Theory and Practice.* Englewood Cliffs, NJ: Prentice-Hall.

C. L. LIU AND E. M. REINGOLD

COMMAND AND JOB CONTROL LANGUAGES

For articles on related subjects *see* CATALOG; INTERACTIVE SYSTEMS, USING; JOB; LANGUAGE PROCESSORS; LINKAGE EDITOR; OPERATING SYSTEMS; TERMINALS; TIME-SHARING; and UNIX TIME-SHARING SYSTEM.

A *command language* (CL) or a *job control language* (JCL) is a language in which users of a computer (or data processing) system describe to that system the requirements of their *tasks* (or *jobs*—*q.v.*). Most computer systems operate under the control of an *operating system (q.v.).* (Operating systems are also referred to as *monitors, supervisors,* and *command systems.*) The users interact with a computer system via the command or job control language of its operating system; thus, this language is the primary interface between a computer system and its users. The term *command language* is most often used when speaking of *time-sharing (q.v.)* or interactive computers, while *job control language* is used primarily in relation to batch computers. Here, we will use the term *command language* to mean *both* CL and JCL.

More specifically, users of computer systems employ the command language to:

1. Identify themselves to the system for security and accounting purposes, and, in some instances, to inform the computer system about which data files and file *catalogs (q.v.)* are to be used in processing their respective tasks.
2. Inform the computer system about the particular resources required by their tasks [e.g., amount of storage needed, language translator(s) to be used, expected amount of *central processing unit (q.v.)* time].
3. Specify *input/output devices (q.v.)* required by their tasks (e.g., magnetic tapes, disks, line printer, plotter) and define the manner in which the information is or should be organized (or "formatted") on these devices.
4. Specify what action the computer system should take in exceptional cases (e.g., errors in programs, missing or incorrect input data, input-output device malfunctions).

Batch Command Languages. Early batch computers had no operating systems and were capable of executing only one task at a time. As a result, users of these systems controlled the execution of their tasks themselves; while the computer was executing their tasks, such users often acted as operators of the computer and controlled the operation of the entire system.

As computers grew in complexity (and, therefore, in cost), this mode of operation became no longer economically feasible. Primitive operating systems were developed to allow the computer system to sequence automatically the tasks of the various users through the system. These early, simple batch operating systems executed one task at a time, either to completion or until some error made it impossible to continue a task (Rosin, 1969; Jardine, 1975). In the latter case, the operating system would usually give the user (via a printed report) some rudimentary indication of what went wrong and would then immediately proceed to the next user's task. The user had only a very limited ability to affect the behavior of the operating system. The system simply sequenced the jobs through the computer, giving up on any task that did not behave exactly according to the user's (or, more accurately, the system's) expectations.

These systems utilized the computers more efficiently than the initial "hands-on" method, but at the price of increasing the overhead on the users' time; they also forced the users to work in a much more formal and regulated fashion, sometimes with large delays *(turnaround time—q.v.)* between the time a job was submitted by the user and the time when the user received the corresponding output.

Because of the large cost of computers, further attempts at making their use more efficient and at increasing their throughput resulted in the development of *multiprogramming (q.v.)* operating systems, which allow several independent tasks to use the computer simultaneously. Thus, one task might be performing calculations while a second task might be reading a magnetic tape, a third writing a disk, etc. In addition, all such concurrently executing tasks could, for instance, access the same disk (each task, of course, using only those portions of the disk that the operating system had assigned to it), or specify that their output was to be printed on the same printer (in which case each task's output was saved by the operating system on some secondary storage device—e.g., a disk—and then printed when the printer became available). This mode of operation required the users to inform the operating system about the specific resources needed by their tasks. This evolution had several effects:

1. The computer systems became used more efficiently.
2. The users became forced to state explicitly (and a priori) the resource requirements of their tasks in a formal way through the facilities of the CL, as opposed to remembering them, writing them on pieces of paper as "instructions to the operator," or coding them directly into their programs. The users could no longer assume that each of their tasks had total control of the computer system.
3. It became possible for the users to state their requirements in a more abstract fashion. Thus, the user could say, for instance, that a task required three tape drives, but the operating system would choose, each time that this task was executed, the actual tape drives to be used. This ability to state

one's resource requirements in such an abstract fashion tends to minimize the interference between the tasks belonging to different users and allows a computer system to continue operating even when some of its resources (e.g., a tape drive) are unavailable because of failures or other reasons. In this fashion, a certain amount of independence from the actual physical configuration of the computer system is achieved.

Thus, with the passage of time, it became necessary for the users to be able to state their requirements to the operating system in a more and more rigorous and detailed fashion. Simultaneously, the complexity of users' tasks grew. Increasingly often users want operating systems to take care of exceptional conditions (e.g., errors in input data) automatically without necessarily giving up on their tasks; to accomplish this, operating systems have to be able to make decisions based on what happens to a task while it is executing; therefore, CLs have to allow the user to state the rules and conditions for making these decisions.

As a result, the complexity of the user's interface (i.e., the CL) with the operating system has grown to accommodate these needs. As additional capabilities became needed in CLs, they were added, often in purely *ad hoc* ways, resulting in CLs that were very flexible and powerful, but also needlessly complex, difficult to learn, unnatural to use, and non-systematic (Barron and Jackson, 1972; IBM, 1979). This increase in complexity has had several results:

1. The need, in most big computer centers, for one or more (often full-time) "CL experts."
2. The development of *procedure* capabilities in CLs; these facilities allow a user to invoke, in a relatively simple fashion, a set of complex CL statements (i.e., a CL procedure) which that user, another user, or a "CL expert" has developed, "debugged," and which has been previously stored in the computer system under a specific name.
3. The emergence of research aimed at developing a theory of, and designs for, more general, systematic, simpler, and easier to use CLs (Dolotta and Irvine, 1969; Gram and Hertweck, 1975; Unger in Beech, 1980).
4. The emergence of attempts at standardizing CLs. The purpose of such standardization is to make CLs less machine-dependent, just as was done with several programming languages (e.g., Fortran, Cobol). We say more on this topic under *General Observations* below.
5. The increasing appeal, to many users, of time-sharing computers; this is due to the fact that, in

```
//SAMPLE    JOB 1234,JOHNDOE,CLASS=K                                  00000010
//JOBDECK   EXEC FORTCLG                                              00000020
//FORT.SYSIN DD *                                                     00000030
   ...
   ...
   ...  The Fortran source program to be compiled goes here.
   ...
   ...
//GO.SYSIN    DD *                                                    00001000
   ...
   ...
   ...  Data cards for the above Fortran program go here.
   ...
   ...
/*                                                                    00009000
//                                                                    00009999
```

Fig. 1. An IBM OS/MVS job deck.

```
//*        -------------------------------------------------------------- 00000010
//*        FORTCLG - FORTRAN COMPILE, LINK, AND EXECUTE.               00000020
//*        -------------------------------------------------------------- 00000030
//           PROC DECK=NODECK,SOURCE=,MAP=NOMAP,LOAD=LOAD,LIST=NOLIST  00000040
//FORT     EXEC PGM=IEYFORT,REGION=100K,                              00000050
//              PARM='&DECK,&SOURCE,&MAP,&LOAD,&LIST'                  00000060
//SYSPRINT   DD SYSOUT=A                                              00000070
//SYSPUNCH   DD SYSOUT=B                                              00000080
//SYSLIN     DD UNIT=SYSDA,SPACE=(CYL,(1,1)),DISP=(,PASS)             00000090
//LKED     EXEC PGM=IEWLF440,COND=(4,LT,FORT),REGION=96K,             00000100
//              PARM=(XREF,LIST,LET)                                  00000110
//SYSLIB     DD DSN=&&FORTLIB1,DISP=(SHR,PASS)                        00000120
//           DD DSN=&&FORTLIB2,DISP=(SHR,PASS)                        00000130
//SYSLMOD    DD DSN=&&GOSET(GO),DISP=(,PASS),UNIT=SYSDA,              00000140
//              SPACE=(CYL,(1,1,1))                                   00000150
//SYSPRINT   DD SYSOUT=A                                              00000160
//SYSUT1     DD DSN=&&SYSUT1,UNIT=SYSSQ,SPACE=(1024,(100,50),,,ROUND) 00000170
//SYSLIN     DD DSN=*.FORT.SYSLIN,DISP=(OLD,DELETE)                   00000180
//           DD DDNAME=SYSIN                                          00000190
//GO       EXEC PGM=*.LKED.SYSLMOD,COND=((4,LT,FORT),(4,LT,LKED))     00000200
//FT05F001   DD DDNAME=SYSIN                                          00000210
//FT06F001   DD SYSOUT=A                                              00000220
//FT07F001   DD SYSOUT=B                                              00000230
//*        -------------------------------------------------------------- 00000240
```

Fig. 2. An IBM OS/MVS catalogued procedure.

addition to some other important factors, these systems very often tend to have CLs that are easier to learn and to use than the more traditional batch computers. We return to this point under *Time-Sharing Command Languages* below.

The part of the operating system that interprets the user's CL statements is often referred to as a *command language interpreter*. In order to give the reader a better understanding of a contemporary batch CL, we show, in Fig. 1, a very simple "job deck," the purpose of which is to compile, link edit, and execute [under the operating system known as OS/MVS (IBM, 1979)], a Fortran *source program (q.v.)*.

The first (JOB) card of the deck gives the name of the job (SAMPLE), the user's account number (1234) and name (JOHNDOE), and the priority class (K) that the user is requesting for this job. The second card indicates that the "cataloged" (previously stored) CL procedure FORTCLG (for FORTran Compile, Link edit, and Go—i.e., execute) is to be invoked. (Fig. 2 is a listing of FORTCLG.) The third card in Fig. 1 is a Data Definition card (DD); it indicates that the Fortran source program is next in the deck. After the Fortran source program comes another DD card indicating that the data cards required by the program during the execution (GO) job step are next in the deck. After the data cards comes an end-of-data card (/*) and an end-of-job card (//). In large decks, all the cards are usually numbered so that a deck can be put back into proper order should it be dropped or otherwise shuffled. (The current practice is to store such decks on magnetic tapes and disks rather than as actual packets of cards; when certain cards need changing, they can be identified uniquely by their numbers.)

When the computer system (in this case, an IBM System/370 operating under OS/MVS) reads this deck, it verifies that the account number given on the first card is a valid one and then stores the job until a time when all the resources required for the first job step are available. At that time, the cataloged procedure FORTCLG (shown in Fig. 2) is executed. We will not explain this procedure in detail. We observe, however, that it consists of 20 cards (the first three cards and the last card are simply comments, which the operating system ignores). FORTCLG invokes two existing utility programs (IEYFORT for the FORT—Fortran compilation—step, and IEWLF440 for the LKED—link editing—step). For each job step, a number of additional files are specified by various, rather complex, Data Definition (DD) statements, and various *default parameters* are set. These parameters specify various choices that the user can override, such as, for instance, the amount of storage space allocated to a specific file. Three of the statements (those starting on cards 50, 100, and 140) have to be continued on additional cards because of their length.

The first job step (FORT) invokes the Fortran *language processor (q.v.)* to compile the source program (which follows card 30 in Fig. 1) into an *object program (q.v.)*. If no errors are detected by the compiler, the second job step (LKED) uses the *linkage editor (q.v.)* to link edit (i.e., combine) that object deck with other (already existing) programs needed by that object deck into a *load module*. If this operation is successful, the load module is "loaded" (i.e., read) into the computer's main memory by

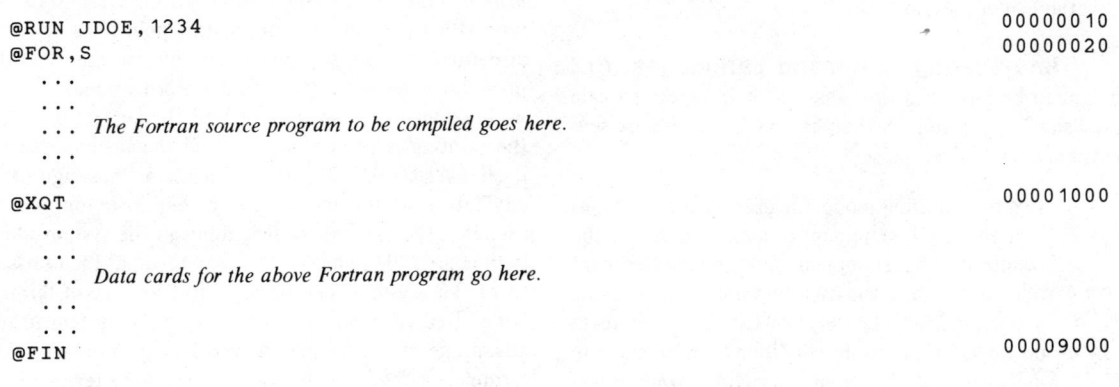

```
@RUN  JDOE,1234                                                    00000010
@FOR,S                                                             00000020
 . . .
 . . .
 . . .   The Fortran source program to be compiled goes here.
 . . .
 . . .
@XQT                                                               00001000
 . . .
 . . .
 . . .   Data cards for the above Fortran program go here.
 . . .
 . . .
@FIN                                                               00009000
```

Fig. 3. A UNIVAC EXEC-8 job deck.

the third job step (GO), and the user's program begins its execution, during which it presumably reads the data cards that follow card 1000 in Fig. 1.

Each job step produces output that is stored on magnetic tape or disk. Some of that output is of a temporary nature and is discarded at the end of the job step; other output (e.g., the object program) may be used by subsequent job steps; still other may be retained on disk or tape, as requested by the user, for use in other jobs at other times; finally, some output is usually returned to the user in the form of printouts, disks, tapes, and/or card decks.

Should any of the job steps run into some difficulty (e.g., errors in the source program), the printed output for that job step will so inform the user (occasionally in a rather cryptic fashion) and, at least in the example of Figs. 1 and 2, the job will be terminated at the end of that job step.

The reader should be warned that the OS/MVS command language is probably the most complex CL in general use today, and that it is very difficult to use. Barron and Jackson (1972) have said: "It is a language in which the articulate can speak powerful words of wisdom, but fluency is at the end of a long hard road." Many other batch CLs are significantly simpler, but, by the same token, also somewhat less flexible and versatile. The EXEC-8 CL, used on UNIVAC 1100 series of computers (UNIVAC, 1974) is an example of such a CL.

Fig. 3 shows an EXEC-8 job deck that is functionally quite analogous to the OS/MVS deck of Fig. 1. The first (@RUN) card identifies the user (JDOE) and account (1234). The second (@FOR) card requests the Fortran compilation of the immediately following Fortran source deck and a "short" (S) listing of that program. Card 1000 (@XQT) requests the execution of the just-compiled Fortran program (provided that that compilation is error-free); the data follow the @XQT card. The @FIN card signals the end of the job deck.

Time-Sharing Command Languages. CLs meant to be used in a time-sharing or interactive mode are usually much simpler than batch CLs. There are several reasons for this:

1. In a time-sharing mode, the user most often types in a *single* CL statement at a time, observes the result(s) of that statement, and then decides what to do next. Thus, the user does not have to decide and explicitly state a priori what the system is to do under *all* possible conditions; he or she can make these decisions, one at a time, while interacting with the computer system.
2. The user interacts *directly* and in real time with the computer, as opposed to having to use the

computer through operators who submit his or her tasks.
3. Users of a time-sharing computer are often geographically isolated from that computer (e.g., by working at home). Under such conditions, simplicity and ease of use of the CL is a very important factor (Dolotta and Irvine, 1969).
4. Because many, if not most, CL statements are typed every time they are executed, it is very important that they be simple and short.
5. The computer system can guide the user by printing prompting messages, thus making it less necessary for the user to remember all the details of the CL.

As a result, more attention has been paid to the human engineering of time-sharing CLs than to that of batch CLs. In addition, time-sharing CLs and computer systems have adapted the better features of batch systems. Thus, in many time-sharing CLs, it is possible to construct and save cataloged command procedures for repeated use. In time-sharing computers, all data files and programs are stored on-line. Editing programs are usually provided in a computer system to allow users to create, examine, and modify their on-line files of programs and data.

We will again use an example to give the flavor of a modern time-sharing CL (Ritchie and Thompson, 1978). Fig. 4 is a *verbatim* record of a short "terminal session" with such a system, except that, for ease of understanding, we have underlined everything that was typed by the user. The purpose of this session is, again, to compile and execute an already-existing Fortran program.

As soon as the user has dialed-up the computer from a *terminal (q.v.)*, the system asks for a "login" code, which the user types (janedoe). The system then asks for the user's secret password to make sure that the user is indeed the person who is authorized to log into the system with the code janedoe; at this point, the computer also turns off the terminal's printing mechanism, thus preserving the secrecy of the password by making it invisible. Once the user has entered the correct password, the printing is turned back on and the system identifies itself (WHITE-ONE); it then prints a "message of the day" about an impending system shut-down and tells the user that there are three new items in the system's "bulletin board" file (which can be examined at the user's leisure). The system then prompts for the type of terminal being used (this information enables the system to take advantage of the various features—e.g., tabs—that the terminal may have); the user identifies the terminal as a (Hewlett-Packard) 2621. The dollar sign ($) is a system prompting message, or "prompt," asking the user for the next command. The user asks for the **date** (knowing that

```
login: janedoe
Password: _____
System WHITE-ONE.
2/13/81: down at 19:00 for preventive maintenance.
3 news items.
terminal: 2621
$ date
Fri Feb 13 18:48:24 EST 1981
$ ed quad.f
1884
/Cong/
     54        format ('Congugate roots; real = ',1pg16.6,'  imag. = ',1pg16.6)
s/g/j
     54        format ('Conjugate roots; real = ',1pg16.6,'  imag. = ',1pg16.6)
w
1884
q
$ f77 -o quad quad.f
$ quad

Please enter the values of a, b, and c:
1, -2, 1
a =      1.000000       b =      -2.00000      c =      1.000000
Double real root:      1.000000

Please enter the values of a, b, and c:
1e4, 2e3, 3e2
a =      10000.00       b =       2000.00      c =      300.000
Conjugate roots: real =      -.100000      imag. =      .141421

Please enter the values of a, b, and c:
,,-6.25
a =      0.000000e+00  b =      0.000000e+00  c =      -6.25000
==> ERROR: input implies that      -6.25000      = 0

Please enter the values of a, b, and c:
1,,-6.25
a =      1.000000       b =      0.000000e+00  c =      -6.25000
Two real roots:      2.50000      and      -2.50000

Please enter the values of a, b, and c:
1.667e-3,6.375e+5
a =      1.667000e-03  b =       637500.      c =      0.000000e+00
Two real roots: 0 and      -3.824235e+08

Please enter the values of a, b, and c:
     (User hits the RETURN key without typing in any numbers.)
a =      0.000000e+00  b =      0.000000e+00  c =      0.000000e+00
All coefficients are zero.  Program stopped.

$ date
Fri Feb 13 18:51:07 EST 1981
$
```

Fig. 4. A terminal session with a time-sharing computer.

```
c quad.f - interactive Fortran program to solve quadratic equations of
c the form a*x**2 + b*x + c = 0; the following 5 cases are considered:
c      if a=0 & b=0 & c=0   ==>  stop program
c      if a=0 & b=0 & c≠0   ==>  input error          (200)
c      if a=0 & b≠0         ==>  only root is -c/b     (300)
c      if a≠0 & c=0         ==>  roots are 0 and -b/a  (400)
c      if a≠0 & c≠0         ==>  general case          (500)
c
c Get coefficients and echo them:
 100    write (6,10)
  10      format (/,'Please enter the values of a, b, and c:')
        read (5,12) a, b, c
  12      format (3g16.0)
        write (6,14) a, b, c
  14    format ('a = ',1pg16.6,'  b = ',1pg16.6,'   c = ',1pg16.6)
c Determine which of the 5 cases applies:
        if (a .ne. 0.0 .and. c .ne. 0.0) goto 500
          if (a .ne. 0.0) goto 400
            if (b .ne. 0.0) goto 300
              if (c .ne. 0.0) goto 200
c Stop program (a=0 & b=0 & c=0):
                write (6,18)
  18              format ('All coefficients are zero.  Program stopped.',/)
                stop
c Input error (a=0 & b=0 & c≠0):
 200            write (6,20) c
  20              format ('==> ERROR: input implies that ',1pg16.6,' = 0')
                goto 100
c Only root is -c/b (a=0 & b≠0):
 300        x = -c/b
            write (6,30) x
  30            format ('Single real root: ',1pg16.6)
            goto 100
c Roots are 0 and -b/a (a≠0 & c=0):
 400        x = -b/a
            write (6,40) x
  40          format ('Two real roots: 0 and ',1pg16.6)
            goto 100
c General case (a≠0 & c≠0):
 500    x = -b/(2.0*a)
        disc = b**2 - 4.0*a*c
        srdisc = sqrt(abs(disc))/(2.0*a)
        if (disc .gt. 0.0) goto 560
          if (disc .lt. 0.0) goto 540
            write (6,52) x
  52            format ('Double real root: ',1pg16.6)
            goto 100
 540        write (6,54) x, srdisc
  54          format ('Conjugate roots: real = ',1pg16.6,' imag. = ',1pg16.6)
            goto 100
 560    x1 = x + srdisc
        x2 = x - srdisc
        write (6,56) x1, x2
  56      format ('Two real roots: ',1pg16.6,' and ',1pg16.6)
        goto 100
        end
```

Fig. 5.   A Fortran source program. (Adapted from Kernighan and Plauger, 1978.)

this will cause the system to print both the date and the time). Observing that there is still in excess of 11 minutes before the system is to shut down, the user continues with the substance of the session.

The next command indicates that the user wishes to edit (ed) a Fortran source program that is stored in an on-line file called quad.f, the contents of which are shown in Fig. 5. The system reads this file and indicates it is ready for editing requests by printing the number of characters in that file (1884). (Note that, unlike most batch systems, most interactive systems accept both upper- and lower-case input; this is because most interactive terminals—unlike card punches—can type in both upper and lower case.) The user asks the editing program (the "editor") to find a source statement that contains the letters Cong; the system prints that line; the user corrects the typographical mistake by substituting (s) the first occurrence of the letter g by the letter j; the editor prints the corrected line. Satisfied with the result, the user writes out (w) the modified program onto on-line storage; the system reports that the length of the file is (still) 1884 characters. The user then quits (q) using the editor; the system prompts for the next command with $. The user asks that the just-modified quad.f file be compiled by the standard Fortran compiler called f77 (for Fortran 77), and indicates on the command line that the resulting output (-o) load module is to be called quad. The compiler, finding no errors in quad.f, does this and the user then executes quad by simply typing its name.

At this point, the compiled Fortran program begins interacting with the user. The purpose of this program is to solve quadratic equations of the form $ax^2 + bx + c = 0$, given the values of the coefficients a, b, and c. The program prompts the user for the first set of coefficients, which the user types in. The program "echoes" the values of the coefficients (a = 1.00000...), prints the type of the solution and the value of the root (Double real ...), and prompts for the next set of coefficients. The user solves three more equations, making a mistake on the second one of these, and thus having to do it over. Note that if the user does not supply the values of one or more coefficients, such missing coefficients are automatically set to zero; furthermore, the Fortran program assumes that it is to terminate itself if all three coefficients are zero (see the three lines bracketing statement 18 in Fig. 5). Therefore, the user terminates the Fortran program by simply typing an empty (blank) line, and the system prompts with a $ for the next command. The user asks again for the time, discovers that the session lasted a bit under three minutes, and, instead of entering another command, turns off the terminal, thus disconnecting it from the computer.

General Observations. Unlike programming languages (e.g., Fortran), different vendors' CLs have very little in common with each other (in fact, one often finds that the different CLs available from a *single* vendor are also incompatible); for example, as can be seen from Figs. 1, 2, and 3 above, there is no compatibility between the IBM's OS/MVS and UNIVAC's EXEC-8 CLs. In fact, even the terminology used to describe the various CL facilities is different between the two; so that, while it is relatively easy to convert a Fortran program from one of these systems to the other, the conversion of the corresponding CL statements is difficult. This situation leads to a great deal of inefficiency and is very unfortunate.

It is now common to provide both batch and time-sharing services on the same computer system. Users of some of these systems (IBM, 1978; IBM, 1979) are faced with the need to learn two CLs if they wish to use the system in both modes. Furthermore, since the two CLs in such a system must coexist (e.g., be able to access the same files), they both tend to be less than optimal for their respective tasks. For historical reasons, in such a situation the time-sharing CL usually "lives under" the batch CL, and must adjust to it, acquiring, in the process, many of the undesirable characteristics of its "parent" (IBM, 1978).

The large number of CLs in use today is, in itself, a serious problem for users of distributed computing facilities and of computer networks (see the paper by Hertweck in Beech, 1980, pp. 369–383). Users of such networks often have to use several CLs in a single session.

These various manifestations of the "Tower of Babel" effect provide a very strong impetus towards the development of a single, standard CL. On the other hand, because the state-of-the-art in CL design and implementation is still relatively rudimentary, it is not clear that such efforts (see the papers by Frampton et al., Harris, and Newman, pp. 101–113 in Beech, 1980) are desirable at this time; quite to the contrary, it is likely that progress in CLs will be slowed down significantly by such premature standardization.

A recent and very interesting trend has been toward CLs that have many, if not most, of the facilities that, until now, were available only in the traditional *programming* languages (see the paper by Dolotta and Mashey in Beech, 1980); such facilities, together with the ability to write and store CL procedures, allow one to perform, within a single CL procedure, tasks that previously required several separate programs to be written, compiled, debugged, etc. These new, "programming" CLs are rapidly gaining in popularity because they make the users' work simpler and, thereby, make the users more productive.

Another very interesting recent trend affecting CLs is the extremely rapid growth of microcomputers and home computers. These computers offer relatively limited resources (e.g., amount of random-access memory), while their users are often relatively unsophisticated. Therefore, it is very desirable that the CLs available on these computers be very simple (to use little of the available resources) and, at the same time, very natural and easy-to-use ("friendly"). These two sets of requirements are not compatible. Unless successful compromise CLs are developed, the growth of the home computer and, to a lesser extent, of the microcomputer market may suffer.

We expect future CLs to be more flexible, to possess more programming power and expressiveness, to be "subsetable," and to be designed and implemented in much more systematic ways and with much better human engineering factors.

REFERENCES

1969. Dolotta, T. A. and Irvine, C. A. "Proposal for a Time-Sharing Command Structure," *Information Processing 68.* Amsterdam: North-Holland; pp. 493–498.

1969. Rosin, R. F. "Supervisory and Monitor Systems," *Computing Surveys* **1,** *No. 1:*37–54.

1972. Barron, D. W. and Jackson, I. R. "The Evolution of Job Control Languages," *Software—Practice & Experience* **2,** *No. 2:*143–164.

1974. UNIVAC Division, Sperry Rand Corp. *UNIVAC 1100 Series Operating System Programmer Reference.* Form UP-4144, Rev. 3. Blue Bell, PA: UNIVAC.

1975. Gram, C. and Hertweck, F. R. "Command Languages: Design Considerations and Basic Concepts," in Unger, C. (Ed.), *Command Languages.* Amsterdam: North Holland; New York: American Elsevier; pp. 43–69.

1975. Jardine, D. A. "The Structure of Operating System Control Languages," in Unger, C. (Ed.), *Command Languages.* Amsterdam: North Holland; New York: American Elsevier, pp. 27–42.

1978. IBM Corp. *OS/VS2 TSO Command Language Reference.* Form GC28-0646. Poughkeepsie, NY: IBM.

1978. Kernighan, B. W. and Plauger, P. J. *The Elements of Programming Style,* Second Ed. New York: McGraw-Hill.

1978. Ritchie, D. M. and Thompson, K. "The UNIX Time-Sharing System," *The Bell System Technical Journal* **57,** *No. 6, Part 2:*1905–1929.

1979. IBM Corp. *OS/VS2 MVS JCL.* Form GC28-0692. Poughkeepsie, NY: IBM.

1980. Beech, D. (Ed.). *Command Language Directions.* Amsterdam: North Holland.

T. A. DOLOTTA

COMIT. *See* STRING PROCESSING LANGUAGES.

COMMUNICATION CONTROL UNIT

For articles on related subjects *see* CHANNEL; DATA COMMUNICATION NETWORKS; DATA COMMUNICATIONS; FRONT END PROCESSORS; MULTIPLEXING; PACKET SWITCHING; TELEPROCESSING SYSTEMS; and TERMINALS.

Modern large-scale computers generally have the capability of accepting data or jobs originating from many remote terminals or computers. This requires a data communication network for transmission of data. As shown in Fig. 1, such a network consists of a set of nodes

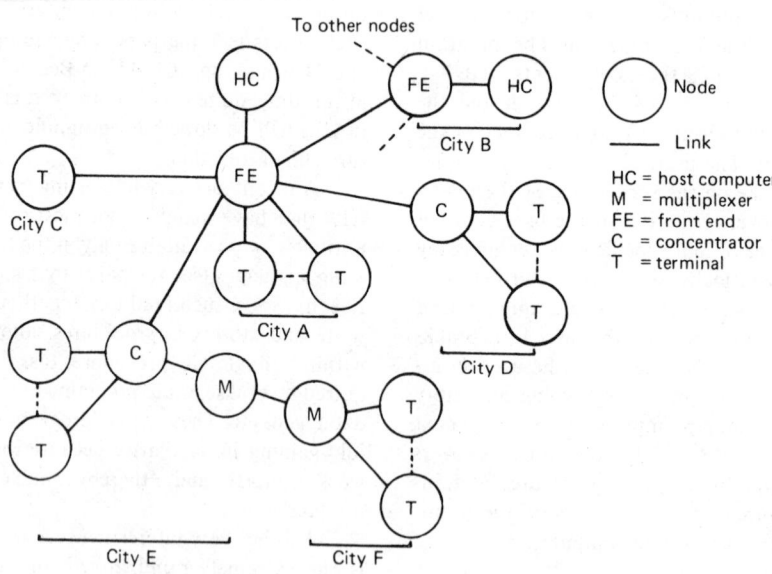

Fig. 1. Example of a data communication network.

(computers, terminals, and some type of communication control units) connected by a set of links which are usually lines leased from a common carrier and which provide the medium for transmission of data. Since transmission over such lines is usually analog, modems (*q.v*) are used to provide the interface between node and link.

The term *communication control unit* or *transmission control unit* is reserved for a wide variety of units which control the transmission and reception of data in computer communication networks and include front-end communication controllers, concentrators, message or data switchers, remote terminal controllers, and simple multiplexers. Until a few years ago, most of these units were hardwired but now most are based upon microprocessors or small computers programmed to perform the necessary transmission, reception, and control tasks. The term *communication processor* is sometimes used to describe such programmable units.

Function of Communication Control Units.

Almost all computer systems are logically organized to transmit data between CPU, memory, and peripheral devices in words or characters consisting of a variable number of bits in parallel. Remote terminals that are to communicate with host computers, on the other hand, must use serial transmission since only this type of channel is available from common carriers. Virtually all computer communications are, therefore, standardized around serial transmission of characters. Additional bits and characters may be added to the serial data stream for synchronization and control purposes much like a magnetic tape record which includes interrecord gaps, parity bits, and check characters. The data, together with these control bits and characters, are assembled into a serial bit string at the transmitting end. This serial bit string will end up at the receiving end where it will be reassembled to form the original data characters using the extra bits and control characters inserted. This is transparent to the end user who sees the serial link as a mechanism for transmitting parallel data.

Interconnection of computers and terminals over serial communication facilities requires, therefore, three basic functions:

1. Conversion of data from parallel to serial form at the transmitting end (serialization).
2. Conversion of data from serial to parallel form at the receiving end (deserialization).
3. Addition of control bits and characters for data synchronization and error control.

The above basic functions are performed by various types of communication control units. As the size and complexity of data communication networks has in-

creased over the last decade, more sophisticated units were required to perform additional tasks, including:

1. Line polling.
2. Auto-baud (automatic speed) detection.
3. Ability to handle many different line protocols.
4. Code conversion (e.g., ASCII to EBCDIC or vice versa).
5. Message assembly and simple editing.
6. Error correction.
7. Data compression.
8. Simple syntax checking.
9. Automatic loading and restart of remote computers and terminals.
10. Data buffering, multiplexing, and concentrating.
11. Automatic gathering of network statistics, including error logging.
12. Network diagnostics.

Communication Control Unit Hardware

Hardwired Controllers. Most early communication controllers were hardwired. Basically, such controllers consist of line interface units, character assembly and disassembly registers, some buffers (especially for high-speed synchronous lines), and a control unit. The complexity of the latter depends upon what functions are performed by software on the host and what functions are left to be performed by the hardware. They support relatively few low to medium speed terminals and perform only the basic functions of serialization, deserialization, and simple control. Other necessary communication related tasks must be handled as overhead by the host computer. This overhead can vary from tens to hundreds of host computer instructions per character transmitted or received. As the complexity and size of networks grew, not only did the hardwired control units become very costly, but the amount of overhead on the host became intolerable. This, together with decreasing costs of small computers, led to the development of programmable controllers.

Although hardwired controllers are still made today, they are predominantly used to control relatively small numbers of terminals on minicomputers. Large modern systems supporting large numbers of terminals use programmable controllers almost exclusively.

Programmable Controllers. These controllers consist of small computers to perform and control the various communication tasks. They tend to be cheaper, they help to reduce the overhead by handling many of the complex tasks which formerly were handled by the host, and they are more flexible in that they can be programmed to perform new functions or support new types of terminals.

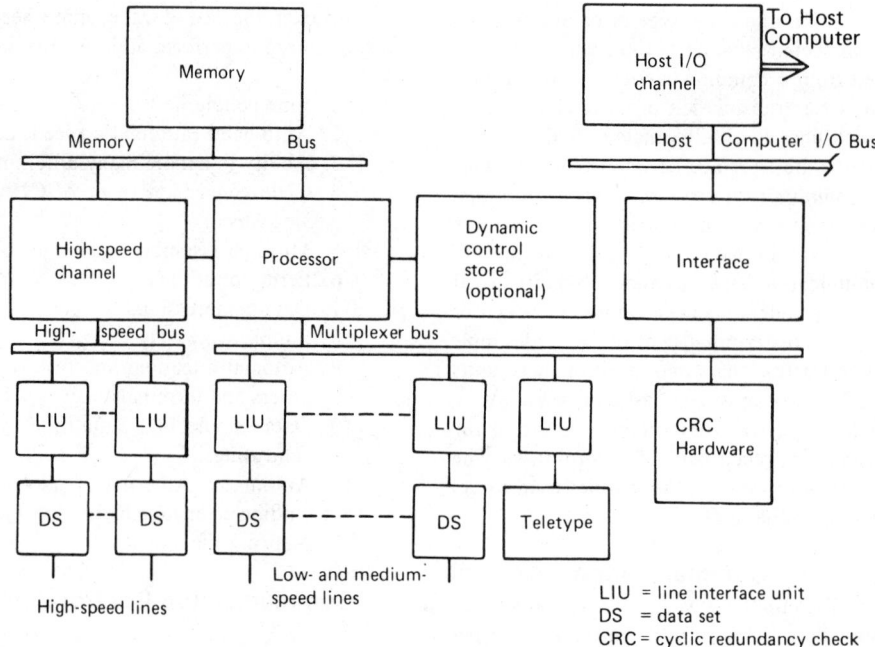

Fig. 2. Block diagram of a programmable front end.

Moreover, in many cases, programming of such units is much simpler than embedding the same functions into a complex operating system on the host.

The essential hardware components of a programmable communication control unit are as follows (see Fig. 2).

1. One or more processors.
2. Efficient input/output architecture.
3. A variety of line interface units.
4. An interface to the host computer in the case of front-end processors (*q.v.*).

The processor, which is a small stored program computer with data channels, should have a memory large enough to store the required program and provide adequate buffering for all lines. The instruction execution and memory cycle times should be small to allow many lines to be serviced without overruns; i.e., without loss of data. The instruction set should be oriented toward use in a communication environment where the main aim is the movement and manipulation of data. A powerful set of logical, bit-manipulation, character-moving, list-processing, and interrupt-handling instructions is necessary. Computers with dynamic control storage are desirable to enable "tailored instructions" to be written in microcode. Such instructions can improve the throughput significantly.

Communication processors must be easily interfaced to a large number of various terminals and data sets. The data rates on these may vary; they may be buffered or unbuffered, local or remote, and work in synchronous or asynchronous modes. To accommodate all of these interfaces, the input/output structure must be very flexible. For high-speed lines (above 40,000 bits per second, say), special channels with direct access to memory are desirable. Such channels can access memory on a cycle-stealing basis and provide no interference to the processor once a transfer is initiated. For the low- and medium-speed lines, a time division multiplexer channel with maskable multilevel interrupts and short interrupt service times is desirable. The address and status of the interrupt-causing device should be available quickly, and branching to the routine servicing the interrupt should be rapid. This may be accomplished by automatic swapping of current and new *program status words* that reflect the location of the interrupt routine to be executed, the condition code, and the state of the interrupt masks. Several such new program status words should be provided, one for each of the major types of interrupt. The handshaking (*q.v.*) on the high- and low-speed bus should be as simple as possible to ease the design of the various interfaces to terminals and data sets (modems).

The line interface units link the channels with the terminals or data sets terminating the communication lines. A general-purpose interface should be speed-independent and handle synchronous or asynchronous transmission. Because of the wide variety of speeds, this is not always possible. To simplify hardware, two or three different types of interface units are usually built, each optimized for a given speed range. Control of data sets and terminals is done by hardware or software, usually the latter. The hardware inputs data set status and outputs control signals. The software senses this status, interprets it, and outputs appropriate control signals. The amount of processing involved is small but the flexibility is high, since any changes in equipment may be accommodated by appropriate changes in software. This makes the line interface equipment independent and prolongs the usability of the system.

Since, as noted above, transmission between nodes is usually serial by bit, while on the bus it is parallel, the line interface must perform the necessary conversion (character assembly and disassembly). This conversion may be done by software or hardware, but the former method is rarely used in modern systems because of the high software overhead. The reduction in cost of integrated circuits over the past few years has made hardware assembly and disassembly practical and this method is now used almost exclusively since it reduces software overhead by generating interrupts only after an entire character or even an entire line of characters is assembled or disassembled. In systems using software conversion, an interrupt is generated after each bit of a character is received or transmitted.

Modems or data sets provide the interface between the line interface units and the communication lines. They change the digital signals into analog signals suitable for transmission over the network.

Error control, especially on higher speed synchronous lines, is usually handled by automatic retransmission of data. Errors are detected by appending cyclic redundancy check (CRC) characters to each data message on transmission. On reception, the CRC characters are recomputed and compared to the CRC characters received. If they do not agree, a transmission error has occurred and the transmitting station is requested to retransmit the message, otherwise the next sequential message is sent. CRC checking can be done by software, but since the overhead tends to be significant, special hardware is usually included for that task. This hardware may be separate, as shown in Fig. 2, or included within the line interface units.

Other hardware components that may be encountered in programmable communication control units include interfaces to mass storage devices (for message switching systems) and to host computers in the case of front-end processors. The latter allows transmission of data between host and front end. Single or multiple address host machine interfaces may be used. In a multiple address interface, each address corresponds to the front end and characters passed between the front end and the

Fig. 3. The Comten Model 3690 programmable communication controller can support up to 512 communication lines and up to eight channel attachments to the host computer.

host are accompanied by an "address field" specifying the terminal to or from which they came. A front-end processor is shown in Fig. 3.

Types of Communication Control Units.

Communication control units may be broadly classified as multiplexers, concentrators, remote terminal controllers, and front-end controllers, depending upon the primary function which they perform. Combinations of these functions within a single unit are possible and, in fact, many of the more recent programmable controllers perform several functions, such as concentration and message switching.

Multiplexers. Multiplexing permits the transmission of several lower speed data streams over a higher speed line for economy of transmission charges, as shown in Fig. 4. There are two basic techniques; frequency division multiplexing (FDM) and time division multiplexing (TDM). FDM divides the frequency spectrum of a line into several frequency bands and data is sent over these bands by frequency-shift keying. At the receiving end, band pass filters reconstruct the original data streams.

TDM is very similar to the action of a commutator. Each terminal is sampled one by one for one "bit time" in round-robin fashion, and the samples are assembled

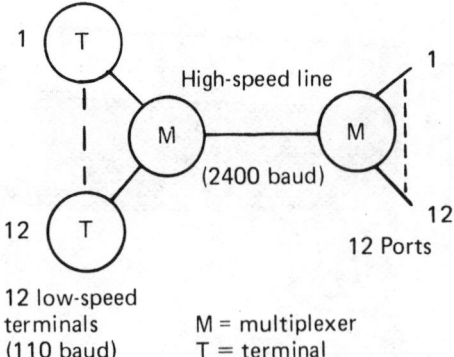

Fig. 4.   Example of the use of a multiplexer.

into a serial data stream. At the receiving end, the serial stream is disassembled and the data is routed to the correct terminal or computer port.

Multiplexers provide little or no buffering and require simple hardware. As shown in Fig. 4, they usually require demultiplexing at the other end and tend to be available from modem and communication system manufacturers rather than major computer system vendors.

Concentrators. The term *concentrator* is usually reserved for a small computer programmed to perform several communication control tasks, including buffered time division multiplexing. Concentrators can be character- or message-oriented. In a character-oriented concentrator, the "packets" of data sent or received over the main high-speed line consist of *single* characters from several different terminals with the necessary identifiers. In a message-oriented concentrator, a packet consists of a number of characters (a message) to or from *one* terminal.

Since, in practice, terminals do not transmit or receive data at their maximum rates over sustained periods of time, the buffering capability and stored program flexibility of concentrators allow them to multiplex data more efficiently than simple FDM or TDM multiplexers which have little or no buffering. The data buffers in a concentrator help absorb peak data loads, while occasional sustained loads can be accommodated by software which can temporarily inhibit transmission to some terminals or command some terminals to stop transmitting temporarily.

Concentrators can also be programmed to perform additional tasks such as code conversion, line polling, error control, data compression, data routing, and other control functions at little or no additional costs. Furthermore, interfaces may be built to enable them to accept

data from a wide range of local or remote units, including other concentrators using various line protocols.

Fig. 5 shows a concentrator accepting data from a number of terminals of various types and concentrating it onto three high-speed lines. The terminals are connected to the concentrator by dial-up, leased, or direct lines, as in the case of the local high-speed batch terminal. Notice the flexibility afforded by the remote TDM and FDM in supporting local and dial-up terminals. The FDM is also shown supporting several terminals on a *multidropped* line without the necessity of polling.

The Terminal Interface Processor (TIP) of the ARPA network (*q.v.*) is an example of a message-oriented concentrator. It accepts data from a large number of terminals, buffers it, and transmits it to various destinations in packets of several to several hundred characters.

Remote Terminal Controllers. Some remote terminals require sophisticated controllers. An example may be a cluster of several CRT terminals operating in block transmission mode or a remote batch processing station consisting of a card reader/punch, a line printer, and a control terminal, as shown in Fig. 6. Such remote terminal controllers can be hardwired or programmable, with the latter becoming increasingly popular because of their flexibility. Thus, the same programmable controller could be used, for example, to emulate IBM, CDC, or UNIVAC remote batch terminal stations with changes from one type to another requiring nothing besides a change in the emulation program used.

Front-End Communication Controllers. Front-end communication controllers or transmission control units, as they are sometimes called (Figs. 2 and 3), provide the interface between a large computer (a *host*) and the communication network. In the past, these were usually hardwired and, consequently, the mechanism of data transfer, error control, and modem control required substantial amounts of host CPU and memory resources. More recent units are programmable, in which case they are called front-end processors. Like concentrators, such systems perform many communication control tasks and accept data from a wide range of local and remote units including remote concentrators. The major difference between a concentrator and a front-end processor is that the latter includes an interface to an I/O channel of a host computer with the software necessary to transfer data to and from the host.

Message Switching Systems. The term *message switching system* refers to a special type of message-

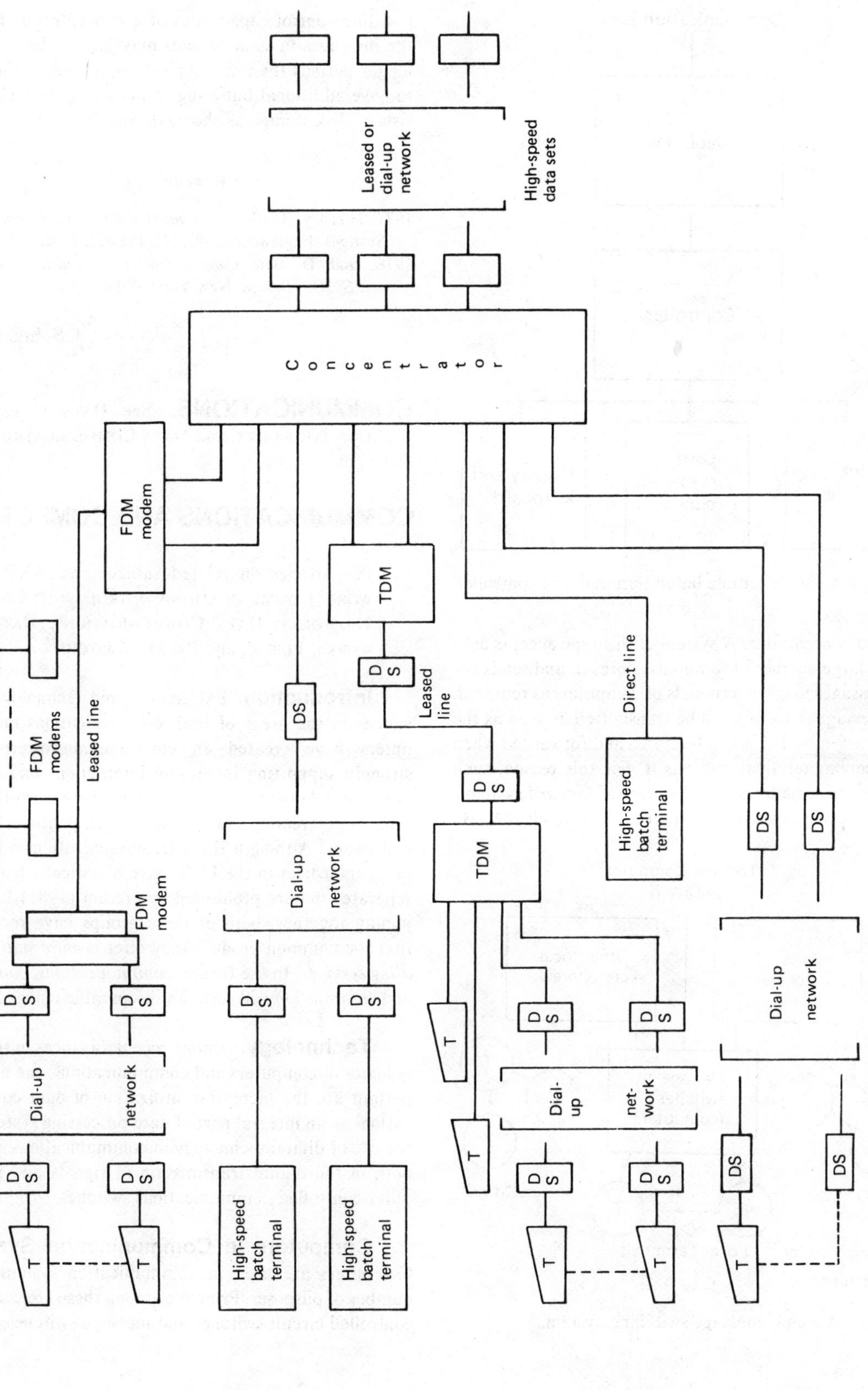

T = terminal
DS = data set

Fig. 5.   A concentrator supporting a large variety of local and remote terminals.

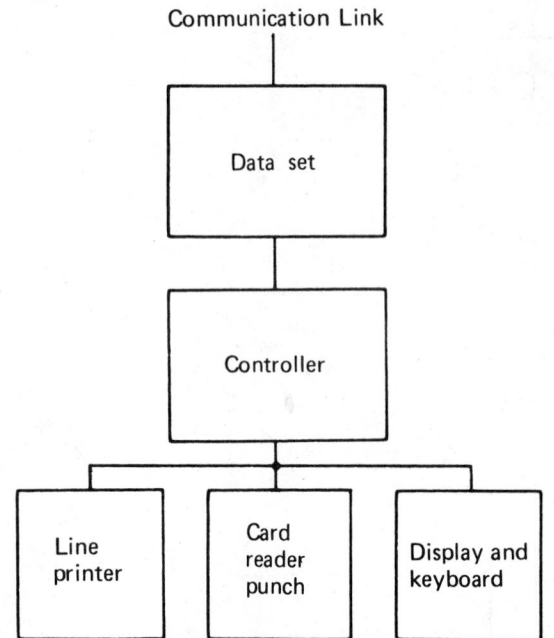

Fig. 6. A simple remote batch terminal and controller.

oriented concentrator. A system of this type accepts data from a large number of terminals, stores it, and sends entire messages to other terminals or computers as required. The message or packet can be transmitted as soon as the data is assembled or it can be stored and forwarded when the receiving terminal requests it. For this reason, such systems are sometimes called *store and forward* systems.

A message switching system must have all the I/O

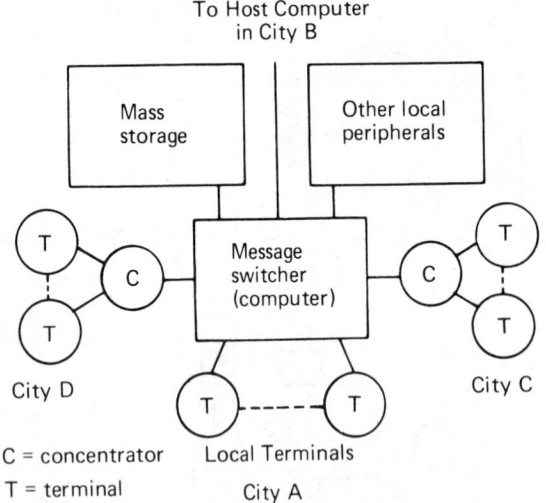

C = concentrator
T = terminal

Fig. 7. A simple message-switching system.

and line control capabilities of a concentrator. Because the messages in such systems may have to be stored for longer periods than in a typical concentrator, they have to have additional buffering, which, in many cases, consists of disk storage as shown in Fig. 7.

REFERENCES

1977. Housley, T. *Data Communications and Teleprocessing Systems.* Englewood Cliffs, NJ: Prentice-Hall.
1978. Doll, D. *Data Communications—Facilities, Networks and System Design.* New York: Wiley.

J. S. SOBOLEWSKI

COMMUNICATIONS.

See DATA COMMUNICATION NETWORKS; and DATA COMMUNICATIONS.

COMMUNICATIONS AND COMPUTERS

For articles on related subjects *see* ARPA NETWORK; COMMUNICATION CONTROL UNIT; COMPUTER NETWORKS; DATA COMMUNICATIONS; DATA NETWORKS, PUBLIC; and PACKET SWITCHING.

Introduction. Extremely rapid technological advances in the areas of both communications and computers have created an environment fostering and strongly supporting increasing interactions and interrelationships between these two technologies, while at the same time creating entirely new legal, political, and social issues. Although the telecommunications and computer industries in the U. S. have historically been quite separate, and are prohibited by present (1981) law from joining together, both of these groups have recognized that the common product they offer is *information handling services*. In the future, *communications, computers,* and *information* will form an inseparable trilogy.

Technology. Among recent advances in the technologies of computers and communications, the most important are the increasing utilization of data communications as an integral part of data processing systems and the use of digital technology in communications systems, both in the digital transmission of signals and in computer-controlled communications switches.

Computers in Communication Systems. Computers are used in communication systems for a number of purposes. Principle among these are computer-controlled circuit switches and message switches.

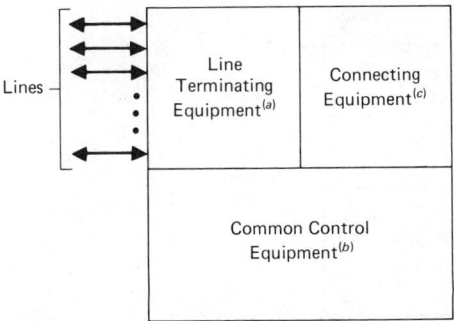

Fig. 1. Computer-controlled circuit switch.

(*a*) Provides the line-oriented services, such as detecting off-hook and sending dial tone, and receiving dialing signals. There is line-terminating equipment connected full-time (dedicated) to each line. Note that the lines are all bidirectional or *full-duplex.*

(*b*) Provides the control services which are common to all connection requests (e.g., determining if the called party is local or served by another switch or determining the connection path to be utilized). The common control equipment is shared by all lines since it is required only during call set-up (and, possibly, breakdown).

(*c*) Provides the physical path connecting the lines involved. This type of equipment is shared in the sense that there are usually not enough links provided to connect *all* lines *at the same time.*

Computer Controlled Switches. Circuit switching is used to establish a communication path between two users so that a conversation may be carried on. The most common examples of circuit switches are the numerous telephone exchanges installed throughout the country. Fig. 1 illustrates the basic components of a circuit switch. Once the communication path between two lines has been established by the connecting equipment, as directed by the control equipment, the connection remains in place and there is no further requirement for control functions until a signal is received to disconnect the circuit. Digital computers are being utilized to provide the control functions required in such switches.

Message Switches. Message switches operate in a mode known as *store and forward.* In a message-switch system, a dedicated path between the source and the destination of the message is not provided. A diagram of a simple message-switch system is shown in Fig. 2. Subscribers input their messages to the nearest node of the system, where the complete message is accepted and stored locally before further action is taken. After the complete message has been accepted by a node, the processor at that node determines to which node the message should be sent next so that it will eventually reach its destination. For example, in Fig. 2, if a subscriber of node B has a message to be delivered to a subscriber of node E,

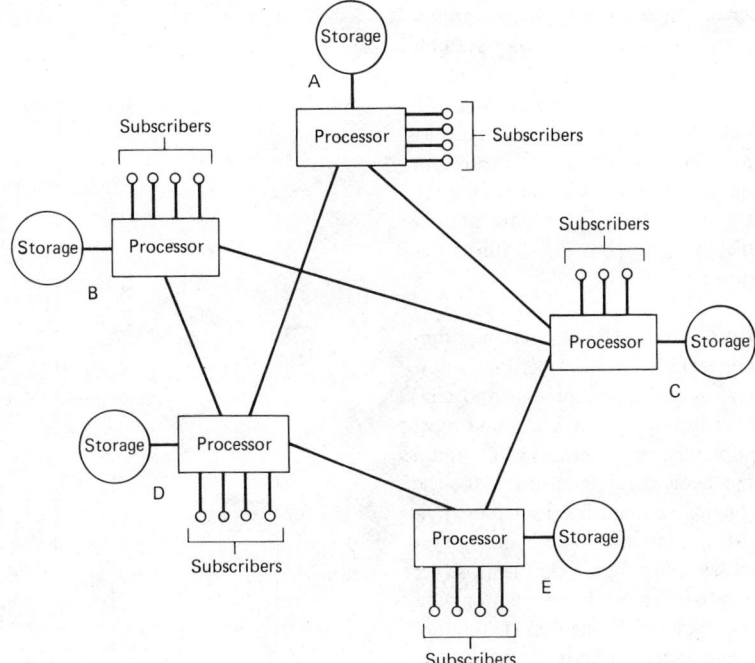

Fig. 2. Message-switching system.

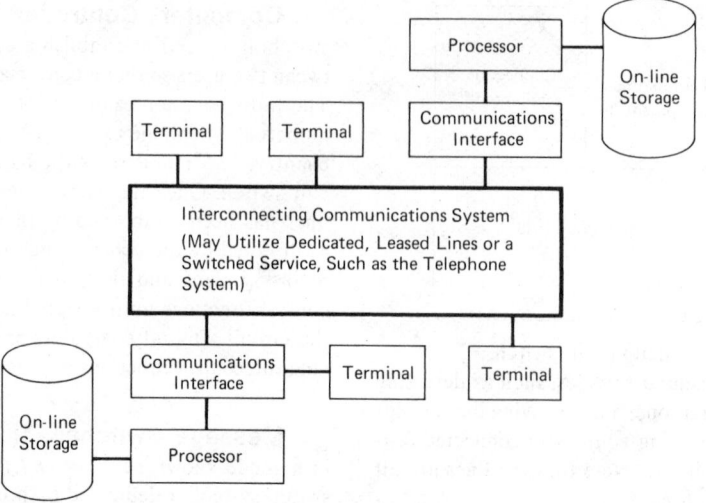

Fig. 3. A simple computer network.

the message would first be entered into the node B processor and temporarily stored at node B. Then, depending upon the current traffic on each link, the message is routed to node C or node D for further transmission to node E. A digital computer with good communications and storage capabilities may be used as a message switch.

Communications in Computer Systems.

Communications have become an integral and essential part of a large number of currently installed computer systems, and the proportion of data processing systems incorporating communications is expected to continue to increase in the future. Communications are used to provide terminal users access to computer systems that may be remotely located, as well as to provide a means for computers to communicate with other computers for the purpose of load sharing and accessing the data and/or programs stored at a distant computer. Fig. 3 illustrates a simple computer network.

Digital Communication.

The utilization of digital techniques to encode signals for transmission is now the standard technology for new developments and construction in the telephone systems of the U. S. and most other countries. A completely new hierarchy of digital transmission systems has been introduced to replace the previous one based on analog signals and frequency division multiplexing (see MULTIPLEXING). These analog systems require the transmission of a signal that is an *exact* replica of the waveform produced by the speaker or data device. The "standard voice channel" is 4,000 Hz, including appropriate guardbands to separate the different channels when they are each translated by an appropriate amount and "stacked" to produce the frequency division

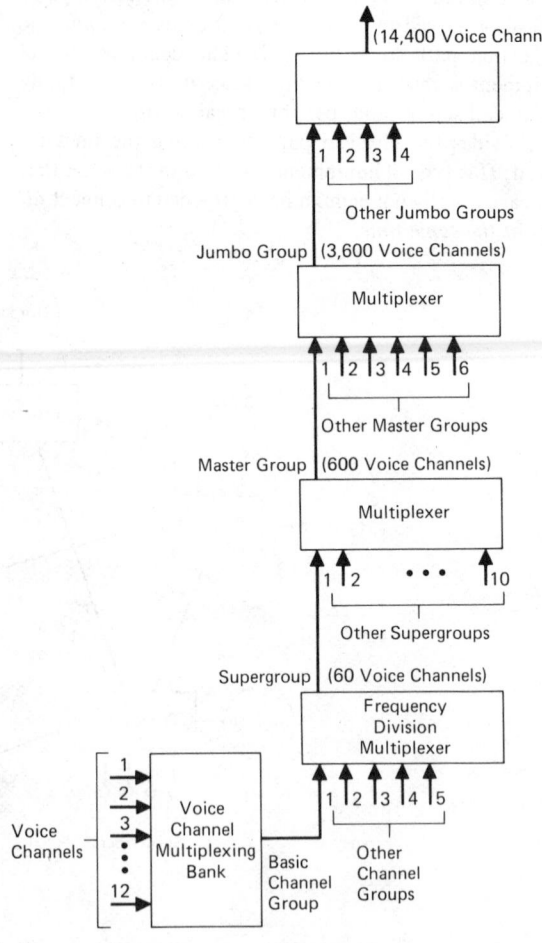

Fig. 4. The analog/frequency division transmission hierarchy.

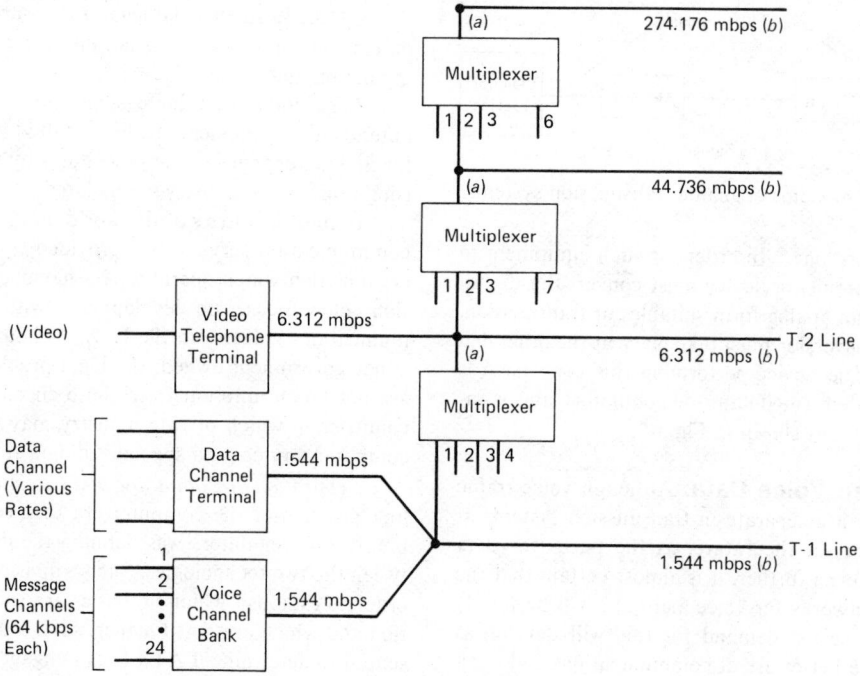

Fig. 5. The digital transmission hierarchy.
(*a*) These are cross-connection points or patch panels.
(*b*) These values are not exact multiples of the input line rates. The additional bits are required for control and timing.
(*c*) "DS-1" is a contraction of "digital signal number one."
(*d*) Representative transmission media that can be utilized to carry the digital signals; T-1 and T-2 refer to standard industry transmission systems.

multiplexed groupings shown in Fig. 4. There are both technical and economic advantages in transmitting a digital pulse stream (i.e., the signal takes on only a small set of fixed and discrete values) rather than analog signals. Although rapid progress is being made in "digitizing" the telephone transmission systems, the frequency hierarchy of analog signals shown in Fig. 4 remains the one most commonly found today because of the large amount of analog equipment already installed. Fig. 4 illustrates how individual analog voice channels are combined together into groups and then higher level groupings formed to make better use of the transmission capabilities of the intercity long-line facilities, such as microwave radio and buried coaxial cable, which provide the capability to carry extremely wide-band signals. The new digital multiplexing hierarchy adopted in the United States and being implemented in Canada as well is shown in Fig. 5. (The numbers for the "European" digital hierarchy are 64 Kbps per channel; 30 channels form a 2.048-Mbps primary signal (adopted); 4 primaries form a 120-channel, 8.448-Mbps secondary signed (adopted); 4 secondaries

give a 480-channel, 34.368-Mpbs signal (proposed); and 4 of these form an 1,820-channel, 139.264-Mbps signal (proposed).) Note that the basic message channel is now a 64,000 bit per second pulse stream. For normal telephone usage, the standard voice channel is converted to this digital stream, utilizing a technique known as pulse code modulation (*see* DATA COMMUNICATIONS). In pulse code modulation, the continuous (analog) waveform representing the voice signal to be transmitted is sampled at intervals, and the value of the sample is transmitted as a binary-coded number in which the transmitted signals take on only the discrete values "0" or "1." The transmission system required in this instance has the much simpler task of indicating only whether the signal is a "0" or a "1." The receiver detects these binary signals and reconstructs the original signal. From the point of view of computer users, the most important effect of this change in transmission is that *digital signals* may be brought directly to the user's installation. Computing devices, including both terminals and processors, communicate with one another using digital signals which take on only two

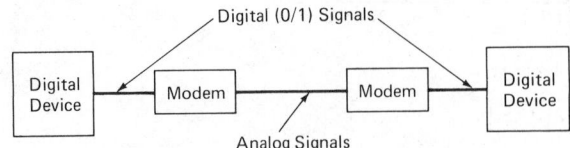

Fig. 6. Use of modems in analog transmission systems.

values, "zero" or "one." In order for such equipment to utilize analog circuits, a device must convert the digital 0/1 signal into an analog form suitable for transmission, and a reverse conversion must take place at the other end of the circuit. The device performing this conversion is known as a modem (modulator-demodulator) and is installed in a circuit as shown in Fig. 6.

Integrated Voice Data. Although voice traffic and data traffic are separate in transmission systems at the present time, in the future, as the needs for data traffic increase even further, it is almost certain that the transmission networks for voice and data will be totally integrated. Increasing demand for this will develop as businesses make better use of communications and computers to process and store all forms of data, not just numeric information. As this occurs, office communications systems handling both voice and data will need to be integrated, as shown in Fig. 7.

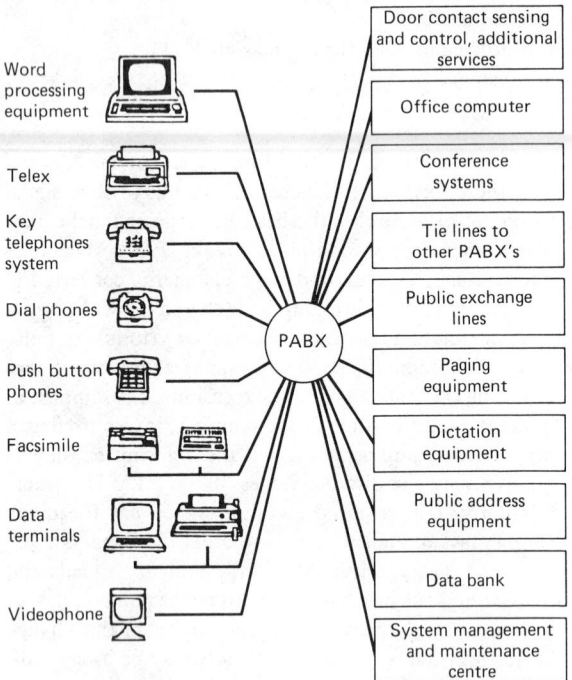

Fig. 7. The future business communication system (PABX-Private Automatic Branch Exchange). *(Courtesy Arthur D. Little.)*

Legal Issues. The legal issues surrounding computers and communications fall into two general areas—regulation and privacy.

Regulation. The increasing interrelation of computers and communications has resulted in strong forces for making changes in the procedures by which the telecommunications industry is regulated.

In most countries of the world other than the U. S., communication services are provided by a government organization which operates as a monopoly. The discussion below focuses on developments within the telecommunications industry in the U. S. Although the industry is not government owned, the legal problems it presents are not much different from those encountered in other countries in which private industry may provide remote computer services and specialized data transmission.

Separation of Computing and Communications. The first problem of the computer era that confronted communication regulators was defining the dividing line between the two technologies. Such a division is essential in order to establish which activities are subject to regulation and which are not. Further, such a distinction is essential to determine if AT&T can engage in a particular activity, since it is currently (1981) prohibited from engaging in any business other than regulated communications.* This question was first addressed by the Federal Communications Commission (FCC) in the late 1960s in its "Computer Inquiry." As a result of that inquiry, the Commission defined the two end points of the spectrum, *pure* communication and *pure* data processing; however, a large area of "hybrid services" was left without further appropriate definition or distinction. A significant comment in the final decision which resulted from that inquiry was that " . . . Data-processing cannot survive, much less develop further, except through reliance upon and use of communication facilities and services." This observation has certainly proven to be true, as has its converse, which was not stated: Digital computing technology has also become essential to the development of communications.

It was not very long after completion of the initial computer inquiry that the FCC recognized that there must be a better delineation of hybrid services. Important questions were being raised as to how much data processing could be considered as "incidental" to the primary function of communications. It has long been a function of some communications systems (e.g., teletype) to store a message at a switch before forwarding it to the next switch or to the final destination. Questions are raised when the switch is utilized to hold the message and then deliver it at some specific time in the future, to distribute it automatically to multiple addressees, or to pro-

*But a January 1982 consent decree would allow AT&T to enter the data processing business.

vide temporary storage and on-line editing capabilities for message preparation.

It was to address issues such as these that the FCC initiated "Computer Inquiry II" in 1976. In April 1980, the FCC released its decision on this inquiry. In this ruling, the FCC reversed its earlier decision to distinguish between enhanced voice and enhanced data services. The key points in this new decision on regulation of communications and computer services are as follows.

- There are only two categories of network services—*basic* (the simple transferral of voices or data) and *enhanced* (communication services combined with data processing).
- FCC regulation will apply only to basic services. Enhanced services will be unregulated.
- Terminal equipment of all types provided by common carriers will be unregulated.

Competition. For many years, competition within the communications industry in the U. S. was almost nonexistent. Rules and regulations of the FCC, as well as state and local regulatory bodies, established "regulated monopolies" within specific geographic areas. Although interconnection between the regulated common carriers was permitted, and even required to provide long-distance service, neither non-common carrier companies nor individuals were permitted to attach devices directly to the telephone system. The first change in this policy occurred in 1968 in the Carterfone Decision, in which the FCC ruled that customer-owned equipment could be connected to the telephone system as long as certain technical standards were met. Although the Carterfone case was precipitated by a desire to attach voice equipment to the telephone system, the implications to the data processing community, with its customer-owned terminals and modems, were enormous.

The next step in introducing competition into the U. S. telecommunications industry was the establishment of specialized common carriers (SCCs) in the early 1970s. These organizations were formed in response to the anticipated demand for large increases in the volume of data traffic. The SCCs were founded on the basis that they would build and operate long-haul communications facilities (primarily microwave) between major cities and utilize the facilities of the local telephone company to provide the interconnection to the customer's premises. Although the SCCs were originally formed to provide only data transmission services, they later expanded their operations to include long-distance voice as well.

The 1970s also saw the introduction of *value-added carriers* as another class of supplier of communication services. As contrasted to the "common carriers," the value-added carriers do not construct transmission facilities such as microwave and coaxial cable systems. They lease transmission services from the common carriers and utilize these to implement a value-added network (VAN) in which the "added value" may be features such as switching, shared usage, error control, enhanced reliability, and transmission speed and protocol conversions. Two of the largest VANs are GTE-Telenet and Tymnet.

More recently, Congress has become directly involved in the issue of competition in the telecommunications industry. The present basis for the regulation of the communications industries is the Communications Act of 1934, which covers all forms of communications (broadcast, in addition to common-carriers). It has become obvious that technological advances, as well as new economic factors, have rendered the 1934 Act almost unusable, especially with regard to telecommunications. As a result of this, legislation has been introduced in both houses of Congress to establish a new basis for the organization and regulation of the telecommunications industry. Such legislation will surely be passed in the early 1980s, although it is not yet possible to predict what form it will take.

Privacy. Privacy has become an important concern of the public from both a legal and a social point of view. It is a concern that encompasses individuals as well as organizations and companies. Although the interest in privacy far predates the computer era, the combined effects of computer and communications are raising the topic to a high level of sensitivity.

Governments and other agencies that deal with the public, such as credit bureaus, have long maintained extensive records and files on both individuals and companies. In the past, the sheer mass of those records and the difficulty in accessing them for anything other than the purpose for which they were collected and organized have been the primary protection against unauthorized use of that material. The development of the digital computer has provided the means with which to access quickly and inexpensively massive records, extracting both specific as well as summary data. Advances in communications have provided the means by which such information can be transferred from one record-keeping system to another so that information collected for one purpose can be utilized for a number of other purposes.

The 1970s saw a growing awareness of the problems of privacy, and a number of privacy laws were passed at the national and state levels, as well as in foreign countries.

Political Issues. The most significant political issue resulting from the wide utilization of computers and communications is that of *transborder data flow*. As the use of communications to transmit data to remote computer sites for processing and/or storage has become more and more prevalent, the "data exporting" countries are highly sensitized to the issues raised by data leaving

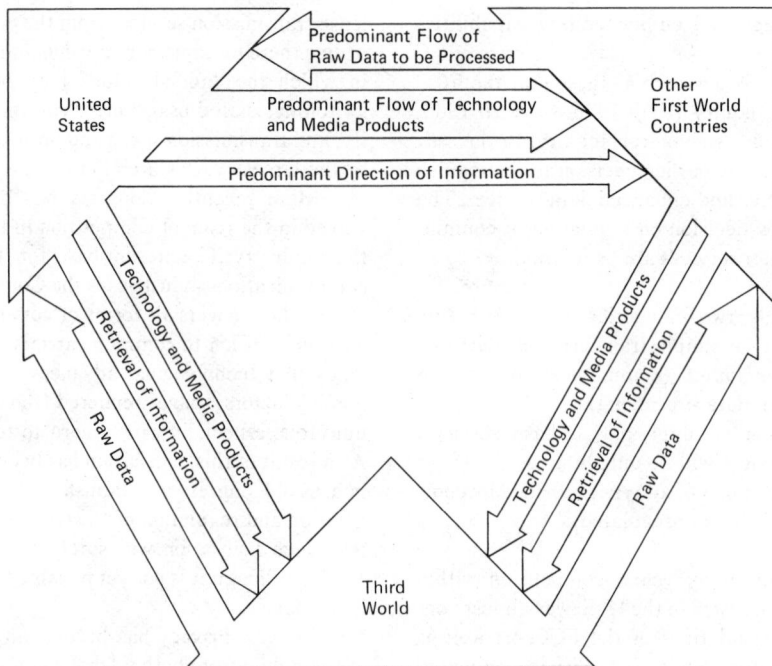

Fig. 8. The nature of transborder data flows (Turn, 1979; p. 5).

their country. These concerns fall into three general areas:

1. Concern that personal and corporate data that is exported from one country for processing on computers will be protected by privacy laws equivalent to those in the country of origin. Similarly, there is a concern that an "illegal" database (i.e., one not permitted in the country of origin) will be assembled in another country.
2. Concern by a lesser developed country that it become "data dependent" on another country that could hold private as well as government databases "hostage" in computer systems located in the more developed country.
3. Concern that the financial motivations for the development of a local computer or data processing industry will be curtailed by having such services and products provided external to the country.

The degree or level of concern about each of these three aspects of the problem is related to the level of development of the country in question. Nearly all countries have become involved with these issues to varying degrees (see Fig. 8). Although the "third world," or less developed countries, are most worried about becoming "informatics dependent" (see Fig. 9), they are not alone in their desire to insure against losing control of information vital to national sovereignty.

One result of the concerns over transborder data flow has been a number of stringent national regulations on the export of data, as well as discussions at the international level. The international discussions have been held primarily within the Organization for Economic Cooperation and Development (OECD), which is focusing on the protection and privacy of data crossing national borders. However, the Council of Europe is also very active in this area. The national laws that have been passed in some countries place such strong restrictions on the ex-

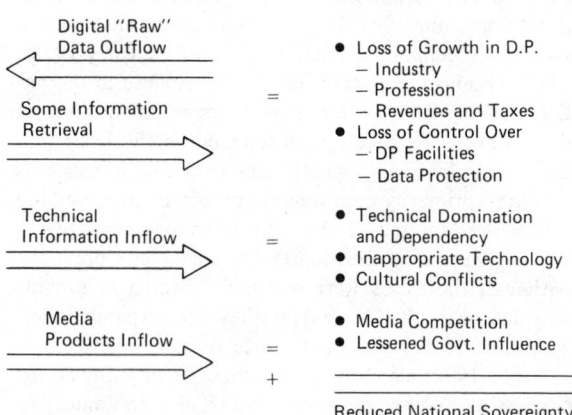

Fig. 9. The perspective of information dependent countries (Turn, 1979; p. 13).

port of data that an international data circuit may be almost useless.

Digital data is just one form of information flowing across borders today. Nationalistic concerns are also being focused on other media forms, such as television, radio, films, and newspapers, and it is difficult at this time to assess the total impact of all the changes being made in the rules governing international trade in information.

Social Awareness. The assessment of the current impact, much less the prediction of future impact, of a technology on society is extremely difficult. For two technologies that are becoming as pervasive as computing and communications, the task is almost impossible. However, there are some aspects of change, such as those discussed above, which are immediately obvious (e.g., privacy and transborder data flow). It is well recognized that there should be an awareness of the impact of computers and communications on our society; however, there is little concrete evidence of the extent of that impact, and there is very little guidance as to which impacts will be good or bad.

As the public becomes more and more familiar with computers and their utilization, and computers become more widely available, there will certainly be changes in the means by which the general public obtains and utilizes information. A significant example of such a change is a recent proposal by the French telephone authorities to abolish information operators in their system. To provide the directory assistance services that are presently the responsibility of such operators, all telephone subscribers would be provided with a data terminal that could directly access the directory database and obtain the desired information. Initial trials of this concept are already underway, and preliminary work on the development of a low-cost data terminal has already been undertaken. Economic studies clearly suggest that such a change would be economically justifiable.

In the U. S., the most recent computer phenomenon has been the "personal" or "home computer." At first, these devices were utilized in a stand-alone mode for limited applications. However, it soon became apparent that the availability of databases that could be searched by such computers would be economically important. Such information depositories and sources, as well as "personal computer networks," are beginning to appear. An isolated home computer is not going to be a very potent force, but when it is connected into a communications system, it will undoubtedly cause fundamental changes in public information habits.

Another example of coupling between computer databases and the general public are the viewdata (*q.v.*) systems, in which a portion of the television transmission time not presently required for picture transmission is utilized to transmit data to the home for display on the television screen. A large number of "pages" of data are available, and the local viewer can select a particular portion of the information for examination.

REFERENCES

1979. Lewin, L. (Ed.). *Telecommunications: An Interdisciplinary Survey.* Artech House.
1979. Turn, Rein (Ed.). *Transborder Data Flows* **1** and **2**. Arlington, VA: AFIPS.
1979. Uhlig, R. P., Farber, D. J., and Bair, J. H. *The Office of the Future—Communication and Computers.* Amsterdam: North-Holland.

P. H. ENSLOW

COMPATIBILITY

For articles on related subjects *see* CROSS ASSEMBLERS AND COMPILERS; EMULATION; PORTABILITY; SIMULATION: Principles; and SOFTWARE.

Two compilers or language translators (usually on different computers) are said to be *compatible* if source programs written for a compiler on one computer will compile and execute successfully on the other. Similarly, two versions of the same compiler (on the same computer) are said to be compatible if a source program written for one version of the compiler will successfully compile and execute using the other version. If the compatibility extends in only one direction, we speak of "upward" (older to newer) or "downward" (newer to older) compatibility. Occasionally, specific programs will be said to be compatible with specific computer systems when they can be compiled or assembled and executed correctly using that computer system; but the more common use of compatibility in computing is applied to two machines, two configurations, two operating systems, or two software packages with respect to the ease with which programs or data can be converted from one to the other. The term normally applied to a program to describe the ease with which it can be converted from one system to another is *portability*.

Since one-way acceptable compatibility is of more interest than exact intercompatibility, the terms "upward" and "downward" compatibility have come into common use. *Upward compatibility* refers to the amount of similarity of a newer, bigger, or better (hence, upward) computer compared to that of a smaller one, but this applies only to the transfer of programs *from* the older one *to* the newer one. Similarly, "downward" compatibility refers to the transfer from the newer one to the older one.

Upward compatibility refers not only to computers with respect to the programs that run on them, but also to the data that they accept and operate on. For example, a computer software system is said to be upward compatible if identical data will produce identical results on a more recent (hence, upward) version as on an older version, even though the newer version may also accept additional forms of data. The term "identical" in this context is somewhat utopian because it almost never is realized in practice.

Manufacturers have historically extolled upward compatibility as an improvement of their small machines extended to their own larger machines, while minimizing any compatibility (especially upward) between their machines and those of their competition. However, they have been quick to point out the upward compatibility of their equipment as compared with that of the competition. In fact, computing equipment and compilers of particular manufacturers have been deliberately designed so that programs running on competitive equipment can be easily converted to run on their systems. Conversely, equipment and systems have also been designed to maximize the difficulty of converting programs so that they cannot be run on competing equipment or systems. The result has been that true compatibility is almost never achieved between equipment from different manufacturers.

Hardware component compatibility is another area where competitive practices have been counterproductive. Since many peripheral devices are hooked to the computer by a relatively small number of cables (usually with a plug, in fact), so-called *plug-to-plug compatible* peripherals have been developed by some competitive firms. Their practice is to purchase, say, a tape drive, find out how it works (spending only a fraction of the original development costs), and build one that works exactly the same (and even has identical plugs on the ends of the cables) as the original, but which can be profitably marketed at a much lower price than the original. Thus, potential customers exist wherever the original equipment was installed.

Manufacturers have developed several defenses against these practices. Probably the most compelling deterrent is refusal to provide a maintenance contract on a system in which parts have been supplied by a competitor. The implication of this policy is, of course, that maintenance will be done by the hour (rather than on a flat-fee basis, as is usual with most contracts) and that sufficient service time will be spent to offset most of the user's savings earned by installing competitive equipment. This substitution practice has been declared illegal in several cases, and has been rendered less effective recently by the mass conversion (where price advantages show) to plug-to-plug compatible peripherals by the federal government (by far the largest owner and lessor of equipment in the computer world). It has also been countered by the original designers, who have designed peripheral equipment wherein the most expensive part (called the "controller")

is integrated (wired directly) into the central processor, leaving only the relatively less expensive mechanical part of the device to be a target for substitution by plug-to-plug compatible replacement.

Although integrated equipment serves to deter replication of parts by competitors, this approach has run into legal complication. In a landmark suit, IBM was held to be indulging in monopolistic practices by implementing this integration, despite the fact that the plaintiff in the case, Telex, was found guilty of stealing trade secrets when it built a plug-to-plug device (with controller) that made interchange possible. The verdict against IBM was later overturned on appeal, and was then settled by the litigants on terms favorable to IBM before reaching the U.S. Supreme Court. This result is having far-reaching effects throughout the computing industry.

C. L. MEEK

COMPILE AND RUN TIME

For articles on related subjects *see* BINDING; DIAGNOSTICS; LANGUAGE PROCESSORS; OBJECT PROGRAM; and PROCEDURE-ORIENTED LANGUAGES, PROGRAMMING IN.

The complete process of running a program that has been written in a high-level language such as Fortran or Cobol is accomplished in two steps:

1. Translation of the source program as written by the programmer into a machine executable form (a process commonly referred to as *compilation*).
2. Execution of the generated form; i.e., the *running* of the compiled or *object* program.

To distinguish between certain actions that may occur during one or another of these phases, the period of compilation is known as the *compile time* and the succeeding period as the *run time*. In the usual compile and execute system, these two phases are distinct and may be temporally separated. In fact, the running of a program may be accomplished many times without the need for the recompilation of the program, provided the compiled code is saved on, say, disk. In an interpretive system, however, the two phases are intertwined, since execution of each piece of source program follows immediately after its "compilation."

Typically, errors in a program are related to compile time or run time. Where the error is an error of language (i.e., incorrect syntax such as a missing parenthesis), then the system is capable of recognizing this at compilation time; on the other hand, errors in logic or arithmetic (i.e., semantic errors) are normally discovered (if at all) at run time. Some sophisticated language processor systems allow the programmer to use certain facilities called compile-time and run-time facilities. As an example of the latter, some systems allow the programmer to specify the format of the input data and output results at run time rather than in the source program.

J. A. N. LEE

COMPILER.

COMPILER. *See* COMPILER, INCREMENTAL; COMPILER, SYNTAX-DIRECTED; CROSS ASSEMBLERS AND COMPILERS; LANGUAGE PROCESSORS; and LOAD-AND-GO COMPILER.

COMPILER, INCREMENTAL

For articles on related subjects *see* COMPILER, SYNTAX-DIRECTED; and TIME SHARING.

The advent of conversational time-sharing systems, in which the problem-solving process invokes a dialog between the user at a terminal and a remote computer, has led to the development of various compiling techniques that can be of particular benefit to the time-sharing user. One of these is *incremental* compiling in which the compiler generates code for (or syntactically checks) a statement, or group of statements as received (i.e., "incrementally") independent of the code to be generated later for other statements. This is in contrast to the usual case in which the compiler only begins syntax checking or compilation after an "end" line is received.

Provided the language statements entered by the user are ordered in a standard fashion, the compilation process is closely related to that used in batch-processing operations. On the other hand, if the user is permitted to present the statements in any order, such as specifying array dimensions following the usage of an array element in a statement, then more sophisticated techniques of compilation are required. In any case, the advantage of incremental compiling to the user is that code may be compiled and tested for parts of the program as it is "composed" at the terminal rather than requiring the debugging process to be postponed until the entire program has been written.

J. A. N. LEE

COMPILER, SYNTAX-DIRECTED

For articles on related subjects *see* COMPILER, INCREMENTAL; GRAMMARS; and LANGUAGE PROCESSORS.

A *syntax-directed* compiler (sometimes called a *syntax-oriented* compiler) is a general-purpose compiler that will service a family of languages by providing the syntactic rules for language analysis in the form of data, typically in tabular form, rather than building the specific

Table 1.   Part of a Syntax Table

Language Construct		Index	Name*	Successor	Alternate
	Arithmetic	1.0	TE	1.1	Fail
expression (AE)		1.1	AO	1.2	Fail
		1.2	TE	OK	Fail
Term (TE)		2.0	FT	OK	2.1
		2.1	FT	2.2	Fail
		2.2	MO	2.3	Fail
		2.3	FT	OK	Fail
Factor (FT)		3.0	PR	OK	3.1
		3.1	PR	3.2	Fail
		3.2	EO	3.3	Fail
		3.3	PR	OK	Fail
Primary (PR)		4.0	CO	OK	Fail
		4.1	VA	OK	Fail
Exponentiation operator (EO)		5.0	**	OK	Fail
Add operator (AO)		6.0	+	OK	6.1
		6.1	−	OK	Fail
Multiply operator (MO)		7.0	*	OK	7.1
		7.1	/	OK	Fail

*CO = constant. VA = variable.

parsing algorithm for a particular language into the compiler. In this manner, a single processor can be used for the compilation of many differing languages, provided only that the syntactic rules of each language can be expressed in the required format of the data. Table 1 is an example (also discussed in GRAMMARS) of a part of a simplified syntax table that might be used by a syntax-directed compiler. To see how such a table is used, consider the entries 2.0–2.3. If the compiler is searching for the construct TERM, line 2.0 says that if it finds a factor (FT) without a following (successor) construct, this is acceptable (OK) but, if not, there is the alternate 2.1, which states that a factor followed by a multiply operator (2.2) followed by another factor (2.3) is OK, but that any other alternate fails. A syntax table, therefore, acts like a series of small programs. Note in particular that the syntax can be changed merely by changing entries in the table. For example, to allow a term to have the form FT ÷ FT where ÷ indicates division by integers, the "fail" in line 2.3 could be replaced by "2.4" and lines "2.4–2.6" would contain the entries for FT, ÷ and FT.

Syntax-directed compilers also form the basis for a *compiler-compiler,* which is a specialized processor that generates compilers (McKeeman, 1970).

REFERENCES

1966. Ingerman, P. Z. *A Syntax Oriented Translator.* New York: Academic Press.
1970. McKeeman, W. M. *A Compiler Generator.* Englewood Cliffs, NJ: Prentice-Hall.
1976. Lewis, P. M., II, Rosenkrantz, D. J., and Stearns, R. E. *Compiler Design Theory.* Reading, MA: Addison-Wesley.
1977. Aho, A. V. and Ullman, J. D. *Principles of Compiler Design.* Reading, MA: Addison-Wesley.

J. A. N. LEE AND A. RALSTON

COMPLEMENT

For articles on related subjects *see* ARITHMETIC, COMPUTER; and NUMBERS AND NUMBER SYSTEMS.

In ordinary arithmetic, we represent negative numbers by a minus sign followed by the absolute value (i.e., magnitude) of the number (e.g., -6.42). In computers, we can represent negative numbers this way also, and sometimes this is actually done, but more often a *complement* representation is used. Even when the sign-magnitude representation is used, the hardware of the computer normally will include a complementer to assist in carrying out the various arithmetic operations.

To motivate the need for complements or complementers, consider the addition of two numbers expressed in sign-magnitude form. Before the operation can be carried out, the signs of the numbers must be compared. If they are the same, the two numbers can be added; if they are different, the smaller in magnitude must be subtracted from the larger and the correct sign appended to the result. As we will see, the use of complements avoids much of this complication.

Definitions. There are two kinds of complements, *radix* complements and *diminished radix* complements, where *radix* refers to the base of the number system being used. Let x be a positive number in the decimal system. Then the diminished 10's complement of x, which we denote by $\bar{x}$ and which is generally called the *9's complement,* is formed by subtracting every digit of x from 9. Thus, if $x = 426.3091$, $\bar{x} = 573.6908$. The *10's complement* $\tilde{x}$ is defined as the result of adding 1 in the least significant place of $\bar{x}$ or, equivalently, as the result of subtracting x from 10^n, where n is such that the 1 in 10^n is one place to the left of the most significant digit of x. Using the above example, $\tilde{x} = 573.6909 = 1000.0000 - 426.3091$. Both the quantities $\bar{x}$ and $\tilde{x}$ are thus representations of the quantity $-x$.

The other complements of practical importance are those in the radix 2, or binary, system. If x is now a positive binary number, then its *1's complement* $\bar{x}$ is formed by changing all 0's in x to 1's and 1's to 0's (i.e., subtracting all bits of x from 1) and the *2's complement* $\tilde{x}$ is formed by adding 1 in the least significant place of $\bar{x}$ or, equivalently, subtracting x from 2^n with n chosen as above. Thus, if $x = 10.1101$, then $\bar{x} = 01.0010$ and $\tilde{x} = 01.0011 = 100.0000 - 10.1101$.

Properties of Complements. The useful properties of complements in computers are best illustrated using the binary system. For illustrative purposes consider a computer where the numbers on which arithmetic operations are to be performed each have eight bits, the first of which denotes the sign (0 for plus, 1 for minus) and the other seven bits are, for convenience, assumed to represent an integer. If the sign is negative, let us assume the integer is in the 2's complement form. Then, to add two such numbers, we need only treat them as eight-bit positive integers (i.e., treat the sign as another bit of the number), add them, and discard any carry to the left of the eighth position (see Fig. 1). Thus, we are able to ignore both the sign and relative magnitudes of the two numbers. With negative numbers in the 1's complement form, there is the slight additional complication that carries to the left of the eighth position must be added into the first (i.e., least significant) position (see Fig. 2).

Let $x = 00001000$ (decimal 8)
         $y = 00010101$ (decimal 21)
Then $\tilde{x} = 11111000$ (decimal -8)
         $\tilde{y} = 11101011$ (decimal -21)

Then $x + \tilde{y} =$ 00001000
                              $+ \underline{11101011}$
                              11110011

which is the 2's complement of 13 in decimal (00001101 in binary); and

         $\tilde{x} + \tilde{y} =$ 11111000
                              $+ \underline{11101011}$
                              11100011

which is the 2's complement of 29 in decimal (00011101 in binary).

Fig. 1.   Addition of numbers using 2's complements.

Both results given above are rather easily proved by writing complemented numbers as 2^n minus the corresponding positive number (minus 1 for 1's complements).

One interesting property of the 1's complement form is the existence, as in sign-magnitude representation, of two zeros, one with a positive sign and one with a negative sign. This follows because the 1's complement of 0000 0000 is 1111 1111. With 2's complements, however, there

Let $x = 00001000$
         $y = 00010101$
         $\bar{x} = 11110111$
         $\bar{y} = 11101010$

Then $x + \bar{y} =$ 00001000
                              $+ \underline{11101010}$
                              11110010

which is the 1's complement of 13 in decimal (00001101 in binary); and

         $\bar{x} + \bar{y} =$ 11110111
                              $+ \underline{11101010}$
                              111100001
                              $\underline{\quad\longrightarrow 1}$
                              11100010

which is the 1's complement of 29 in decimal (00011101 in binary).

Fig. 2.   Additions of numbers using 1's complements.

Let $x = 00001000$
         $y = 00010101$

Then $x - y$ is found by first forming

         $\bar{y} = 11101010$

and then adding $x + \bar{y}$, as in Fig. 2, to get 11110010, which is the 1's complement of 13 in decimal.

Fig. 3.   Subtraction using 1's complements.

is only one zero, since the 2's complement of 0000 0000 is 10000 0000, which has nine bits. In 2's complement representation, 1111 1111 is the complement of 0000 0001. The existence of two zeros can be used with advantage in some contexts, but requires a somewhat more difficult test to determine if a number is zero than would otherwise be the case.

Since 1's complements are generated merely by changing 0's to 1's, and vice versa, it is very easy to build a circuit to generate the 1's complement of a number. It is somewhat more difficult, but not very hard, to build a circuit to generate 2's complements. Therefore, it is easy to perform subtraction by first complementing the minuend and then adding (see Fig. 3). This means it is not necessary to have a hardware subtracter if there is a hardware adder and a complementer.

For performing multiplication and division, there are no direct advantages to the complement form and some disadvantages. However, the adjustments to algorithms for multiplying or dividing two positive numbers to allow them to handle operands in complement form are not major. Alternatively, negative operands in multiplication or division can first be complemented and then the appropriate sign can be appended at the end.

Most modern computers store negative numbers in either 1's or 2's complement form. Which of the two forms to choose depends upon some rather subtle and by no means conclusive considerations concerning the details of computer circuitry. Even in those rather rare cases when negative numbers are stored in sign-magnitude form, it is usual to have a complementer in the arithmetic unit for use in performing arithmetic operations involving negative numbers or subtraction.

A. RALSTON

COMPLEXITY.   *See* COMPUTATIONAL COMPLEXITY; NP-COMPLETE PROBLEMS; and SOFTWARE COMPLEXITY.

COMPUTABILITY

For articles on related subjects *see* ALGORITHMS, THEORY OF; and DECIDABILITY.

Computability is a property of *functions*. A function f with domain D and range R is a definite correspondence by which there is associated with each element x of the domain D (referred to as the *argument*) a single element $f(x)$ of the range R (called the *value*). The function f is said to be computable if there exists an algorithm that, for any given x in D, provides the value of $f(x)$.

For example, consider the function g, whose domain D is the set of all pairs of positive integers and whose range R is the set of positive integers, and which is defined as

$g(a,b)$ = the greatest common divisor of a and b.

This function is computable by the well-known Euclidean algorithm (Knuth, 1968).

The above definition is lacking rigor for the following reasons:

1. It is not explained in what form the argument x in D is "given." In particular, this part of the definition makes sense only if elements of D are in some way finitely describable. Thus, the notion of computability, as described above, makes no sense for a function f whose domain is the set of real numbers.
2. The notion of an algorithm is not precise.
3. It is not explained in what sense the algorithm provides us with the value of $f(x)$.

How the notion of computability of a function can be made mathematically rigorous is explained in the article, ALGORITHMS, THEORY OF.

REFERENCE

1968. Knuth, D. "The Art of Computer Programming," in *Fundamental Algorithms* **1**. Reading, MA: Addison-Wesley.

G. T. HERMAN

COMPUTATIONAL COMPLEXITY

For articles on related subjects *see* ALGORITHMS, THEORY OF; FAST FOURIER TRANSFORM; NP-COMPLETE PROBLEMS; and TURING MACHINE.

The subject matter of computational complexity is the determination of the intrinsic difficulty of mathematically posed problems arising in many disciplines. The study of complexity has led to more efficient algorithms than those previously known or suspected. We begin by illustrating some of the important ideas of computational complexity* with the example of matrix multiplication.

Computational Complexity of Matrix Multiplication. Consider the multiplication of 2×2 matrices. Let

$$A = \begin{bmatrix} a_{11} & a_{12} \\ a_{21} & a_{22} \end{bmatrix}, \quad B = \begin{bmatrix} b_{11} & b_{12} \\ b_{21} & b_{22} \end{bmatrix}, \quad C = \begin{bmatrix} c_{11} & c_{12} \\ c_{21} & c_{22} \end{bmatrix}$$

Given A and B, we seek $C = AB$.

The classical algorithm computes C by

$$c_{11} = a_{11}\,b_{11} + a_{12}\,b_{21}, \qquad c_{12} = a_{11}\,b_{12} + a_{12}\,b_{22},$$
$$c_{21} = a_{21}\,b_{11} + a_{22}\,b_{21}, \qquad c_{22} = a_{21}\,b_{12} + a_{22}\,b_{22},$$

at a cost of eight multiplications.

Until the late sixties, no one seems to have asked whether two matrices could be multiplied in fewer than eight scalar multiplications. Then Strassen showed that seven scalar multiplications are sufficient by introducing the following algorithm.

$$p_1 = [a_{11} + a_{22}]\,[b_{11} + b_{22}],$$
$$p_2 = [a_{21} + a_{22}]\,b_{11},$$
$$p_3 = a_{11}\,[b_{12} - b_{22}],$$
$$p_4 = a_{22}\,[-b_{11} + b_{21}],$$
$$p_5 = [a_{11} + a_{12}]\,b_{22},$$
$$p_6 = [-a_{11} + a_{21}]\,[b_{11} + b_{12}],$$
$$p_7 = [a_{12} - a_{22}]\,[b_{21} + b_{22}],$$
$$c_{11} = p_1 + p_4 - p_5 + p_7,$$
$$c_{12} = p_3 + p_5,$$
$$c_{21} = p_2 + p_4,$$
$$c_{22} = p_1 + p_3 - p_2 + p_6.$$

Consider next the multiplication of $N \times N$ matrices. The classical algorithm uses N^3 arithmetic operations. (Actually, this algorithm uses $2N^3 - N^2$ arithmetic operations -N^3 multiplications, and $N^3 - N^2$ additions. But in the study of computational complexity, we disregard multiplicative constants and all powers of the basic pa-

---

*In this article, we focus on *time complexity* (i.e., the speed with which algorithms can be implemented) rather than on the less important problem of *space complexity* (i.e., the amount of storage required by an algorithm).

rameter—N in this case—except the highest, since it is only the highest power of the parameter that determines the ultimate performance of the algorithm. Note, by the way, that, in the 2×2 example above, the number of multiplications is decreased by one, but the number of arithmetic operations is increased by 13.) By repeated partitioning of $N \times N$ matrices into 2×2 submatrices, two matrices can be multiplied in $N^{\log_2 7} \sim N^{2.81}$ arithmetic operations.

After a decade during which there was practically no progress on decreasing the number of arithmetic operations used in matrix multiplication, Schönhage and Pan in 1979 showed $N^{2.52}$ arithmetic operations are sufficient. More recently, Pan has shown that the exponent is less than 2.5.

We must emphasize that the above results are of theoretical rather than practical value. The value of N has to be enormous before the new algorithm would be faster than the classical one. On the other hand, there are some problems for which new algorithms have had profound influence. A good example is provided by the finite Fourier transform on N points. The fast Fourier transform uses only $N \log N$ arithmetic operations, compared to N^2 for the classical algorithms. Since $N \log N$ is much smaller than N^2 for even moderate values of N, and since the finite Fourier transform is often needed for a large number of points, the introduction of the fast Fourier transform (*q.v.*) has revolutionized computation in a number of scientific fields.

Using the matrix multiplication example, we can now introduce some basic terminology.

The minimal number of arithmetic operations is called the *computational complexity* (or *problem complexity*) of the matrix multiplication problem. We often write *complexity* for brevity.

The complexity of matrix multiplication is unknown. An *upper bound* is $N^{2.5}$. A *lower bound* is N^2. Since this lower bound is linear in the number of inputs and outputs, we say it is a *trivial* lower bound. No non-trivial lower bound is known.

Algorithm complexity is the cost of a particular algorithm. This should be contrasted with problem complexity, which is the minimal cost over all possible algorithms. People who do not work in complexity theory sometimes confuse these two terms.

Table 1.   Summary of Matrix Multiplication

Upper Bound	$N^{2.5}$
Lower Bound	N^2
Complexity	Unknown
Optimal Algorithm	Unknown

Fast algorithm is a qualitative term meaning faster than a classical algorithm or faster than previously known algorithms. An *optimal algorithm* is one whose complexity equals the problem complexity.

Table 1 summarizes the present state of our knowledge concerning matrix multiplication.

Computational Complexity in General. To study computational complexity requires a *model of computation* stating which "operations" or "steps" are permissible and how much they cost. Using the model, we can then ask the same questions as in the matrix multiplication example. For instance, we seek:

Problem complexity

Upper bounds

Lower bounds

Fast algorithms

Optimal algorithms.

Typically, an upper bound is the cost of the fastest known algorithm for solving the problem. A lower bound can only be established through a theorem that states there does not exist an algorithm whose cost is less than the lower bound. Not surprisingly, lower bounds are far harder to establish than upper bounds.

Numerous models of computation have been studied. In our matrix multiplication example, we counted arithmetic operations. In the study of combinatorial problems, we typically count comparisons. Very significant results have been obtained for space and time complexity in a Turing machine model. Another important model is a random access machine (RAM). Other models are appropriate for studying parallel, asynchronous, or VLSI computation.

Often, we assign a "size" N to a problem, such as the order of the matrix in the previous example or the number of records in a sorting problem. If the number of operations or steps required to solve a problem is an exponential function of N, we say the problem has *exponential time complexity*. If the problem requires a number of operations that constitute a polynomial function of N, we say the problem has *polynomial time complexity*.

Typical Applications of Computational Complexity. The complexity of numerous problems has been studied. To illustrate the variety of problems, we exhibit a dozen drawn from various areas.

1. Compute the finite Fourier transform at N points.

2. Determine if an N-digit integer is prime; if not, determine the factors.

3. Solve an elliptic partial differential equation to within an error ϵ.

4. Compute the Kendall rank correlation at N points.

5. Generate a function with error less than ϵ from values of a function at N points.

6. Multiply two polynomials of degree N.

7. Prove all theorems that can be stated in, at most, N symbols in a certain axiom system.

8. Solve the traveling salesman problem on N cities.

9. Solve to within ϵ a large sparse linear system of order N whose matrix is positive definite and has a condition number bounded by M.

10. Find the closest neighbor of P points in K dimensions.

11. Compute the first N terms of the Qth composite of a power series.

12. Compute the first N digits of π (for, say, $N = 20{,}000{,}000$).

Reducibility Among Problems. There are many problems for which the best algorithm known costs exponential time. Such problems occur in operations research, computer design, data manipulation, graph theory, and mathematical logic. Are there faster algorithms which solve these problems in polynomial time? We don't know. What we do know is that there is a large class of problems that are equivalent in that, if one of them can be solved in polynomial time, they all can.

For technical reasons, this class of problems is said to be *NP-complete* (*q.v.*). Because no one has succeeded in devising a polynomial time algorithm for any of these problems, many researchers believe that NP-complete problems are exponentially hard. There is no proof of this, and settling this question is one of the most important open problems in computational complexity.

Analytic Computational Complexity. For the matrix multiplication problem, we are interested in the minimum number of arithmetic operations to multiply two matrices exactly. This is a typical problem of *algebraic complexity*. However, many problems can be only approximately solved. Examples are optimal estimation, solution of nonlinear equations, optimization, and the solution of partial differential equations. Indeed, most problems occurring in mathematics, science, engineering, risk assessment, decision theory, and economics can be only approximately solved. Furthermore, to lower the cost, we may choose to solve approximately problems that could be solved exactly. Important examples are provided by the approximate solution of NP-complete problems and

the iterative solution of large sparse linear problems. *Analytic computational complexity* is the study of optimal algorithms for problems that are solved approximately.

Above, we illustrated some of the important ideas of computational complexity with the example of matrix multiplication. Here we will use integration as a simple prototypical example and use it to define basic terminology. Consider the computation of $\int_0^1 f(x)\,dx$ given the information $[f(x_1), f(x_2), \ldots, f(x_n)]$. This information is *partial* because there are many integrands that are indistinguishable using this information. If the information has errors (due, for example, to measurement), the information is *approximate*. It is clear that partial or approximate information causes *uncertainty* in the integral. This uncertainty is intrinsic and caused by the limited information. The *optimal information* is the choice of sample points that minimizes this intrinsic uncertainty.

An *algorithm* is any procedure for approximating the integral using the information. Any algorithm must have an error at least as large as the intrinsic uncertainty. An *optimal algorithm* is one whose error achieves the intrinsic uncertainty. The *computational complexity* of the integration problem is the minimal cost of computing the integral to within ϵ.

The information is *nonadaptive* if the sample points x_i are independently chosen. It is *adaptive* if we choose x_i only after we know $f(x_1), f(x_2), \ldots, f(x_{i-1})$. Nonadaptive information is desirable on a distributed computer system, since the information can then be computed independently on various processors.

We list some of the questions studied in analytic complexity. Although these questions are listed here in the context of integration, the same questions can be asked and have been answered in great generality. For integration, some of the answers depend on the nature of the integrand.

1. What is the minimal number of function samples for which the integral can be computed to within ϵ?

2. Is adaptive information "better" than nonadaptive information? (Surprisingly, the answer is no for integration and for many other problems.)

3. What is the optimal information?

4. What is the optimal algorithm?

5. What is the computational complexity of integration?

Axiomatic Complexity Theory. We discuss an abstract complexity model based on two axioms. Let $T_A(x)$ denote the cost of algorithm A applied to the input of integer x. Assume that $T_A(x)$ satisfies the following two axioms.

1. $T_A(x)$ is finite if and only if algorithm A applied to input x eventually halts and gives an output. (In other words, an algorithm halts if and only if it halts after a finite number of steps.)
2. There is an algorithm which, given as inputs any integers x and y and any algorithm A, will determine whether or not $T_A(x) = y$.

These straightforward axioms are enough to imply, for example, that there are computable functions that cannot be computed rapidly by any algorithm, and that more functions can be computed if more time is allowed. They also imply a much less obvious fact, known as the *Speed-up Theorem*: There is a computable function f with the property that given any algorithm A which computes f, there is another algorithm B which computes f "much faster" than A. "Much faster" is interpreted by choosing any rapidly growing computable function such as 2^w; then, according to the speed-up theorem, there is a function f such that, if A is any algorithm for f, there is always another algorithm B for f such that $2^{T_B(x)} \leq T_A(x)$ for all large integers x. Thus, algorithm B requires, at most, the logarithm of the time required by A.

Of course, since B is itself an algorithm for f, there must be another algorithm C for f which requires only the logarithm of the time for B, and so on. Clearly, there is no single most efficient way to compute such an f.

Also, notice that f must be hopelessly difficult to compute even though it has faster and faster programs. Each program for f must require more than 2^x, and more than 2^{2x}, and so on, steps for all large inputs x; otherwise, the program could only be exponentially "sped up" a fixed number of times before "hitting bottom," after which it could not be sped up further.

These conclusions may seem to violate intuition, but they follow from the two simple axioms given above. The speed-up theorem is proved using diagonal arguments similar to those used to establish the existence of undecidable problems (*see* DECIDABILITY).

Conclusions. Computational complexity deals with the fundamental issues of determining the intrinsic difficulty of mathematically posed problems. Through the study of complexity it has been established that certain problems are intrinsically hard. On the other hand, for some problem areas, new algorithms have been introduced which are far superior to any previously known. Problems occurring in a rich diversity of disciplines are being, and will be, subjected to complexity analysis.

REFERENCES

1968, 1969, 1973. Knuth, D. *The Art of Computer Programming* **I**, **II**, and **III**. Reading, MA: Addison-Wesley.

1974. Aho, A. V., Hopcroft, J. E., and Ullman, J. D. *The Design and Analysis of Computer Algorithms*. Reading, MA: Addison-Wesley.

1975. Borodin, A. and Munro, I. *The Computational Complexity of Algebraic and Numeric Problems*. New York: American Elsevier.

1979. Garey, M. R. and Johnson, D. S. *Computers and Intractability*. San Francisco, CA: W. H. Freeman.

1980. Arden, B. (Ed.). Chapter on Theory of Computation in *What Can be Automated? The Computer Science and Engineering Research Study (COSERS)*. Cambridge, MA: M.I.T. Press.

1980. Traub, J. F. and Woźniakowski, H. *A General Theory of Optimal Algorithms*. New York: Academic Press.

J. F. TRAUB

COMPUTATIONAL LINGUISTICS. *See* PROGRAMMING LINGUISTICS.

COMPUTER ACCOUNTING AND RESOURCE CONTROL

For articles on related subjects *see* BENCHMARK; COMPUTING CENTER; COMPUTING SYSTEMS; COMPUTING UTILITY; DATA SECURITY; FILES; OPERATING SYSTEMS: Contemporary Features of; and SOFTWARE MONITORS.

As computer/software systems have developed, there has been a corresponding need to develop an accounting system for the resources of the system. As with any accounting system, the goal of this capability must be to charge the user for the cost of services rendered in such a fashion that the user is motivated to evaluate the benefits of those services. Furthermore, the resources used by any one user must be limited in order to prevent that user from degrading the total effective services offered.

Accountability is important both to the computing center staff and to its users. In order to perform their duties as financial planners for the center, the administrators require some form of an accounting system. Such a system may be expected to yield statistics on hardware utilization and individual spending. These statistics can then be used to form the monthly and yearly reports submitted by the administrator(s) to their superiors.

A completely automated accounting and resource control system does the following.

- It provides minute details concerning both hardware and software utilization along with job statistics on account spending.

- It prevents unauthorized users from utilizing hardware and software facilities for which they have not received permission.
- It prevents users from exceeding their allocated funds or other account limits.
- It enforces job limitations on such things as page or line limits, computer time, memory size, and disk file space.
- It assists the operating system in providing more effective control of the resources (main memory, auxiliary memory, peripheral devices, etc.) of the system.

Development of Accounting and Resource Control Systems

Early Computer Systems. Since early computer systems consisted of hardware with little or no software support, automated accounting was almost nonexistent. The accounting that did exist was done by user sign-up sheets, time clocks, or a flat-rate charge per computer run.

The idea of basing charges on the value of resources used was not very important either. Because the entire computer was dedicated to the current user, there was little reason to charge less if the program used only half of the memory or no tape units, etc. Besides, the hardware could not usually support an accounting system because there was no hardware-readable clock and it was often not practical for the machine operator to type in the date and time for each job logged on the machine. (Interestingly, personal computer systems have put the user back into this mode of operation!).

Early Automated Accounting Systems. As Rosin (1969) points out, the first accounting systems were often nothing more than system logs produced by the "on-line" printing facility. Since the purpose of such a log was to record the use of major system components, the log was more useful for measuring system behavior than for actual user accounting.

Some systems were enhanced by a hardware-readable clock, which made it possible to log the time along with the system component in use. However, the content of each entry in the log was a function of the sophistication of the resident monitor and often provided only such information as log-on and log-off time. Thus, user accounting was still based on total machine time used, with the hardware clock now providing a more accurate method for recording that time.

Executive Systems and Automated Accounting. With the introduction of channels and interrupts, the establishment of resident monitors or supervisors became an accepted fact. These supervisors were complex routines that could process interrupts, software requests, and a new language called the *command language.* (*q.v.*) Thus, the computer user could communicate with the system via command language control cards that provided such information as name and account number, job limitations on time, pages, and cards to be used, and special resources (tapes, plotter, etc.) required.

Utilizing a hardware clock, most user interactions with the system were recorded, detailing what commands the system had received. The purpose of the accounting system was to monitor the individual user's interaction with the system and not simply the system performance.

Still, until the introduction of disk files, it was not feasible to verify each user's identification against some master file of valid users. Nor was it possible to determine user limits as to funds available, privileges, etc. Instead, accounting information was collected on magnetic tape or punched cards for later processing on an after-the-fact basis.

Disk Files. The introduction of disk files added another step in automated accounting. The disk file was sufficiently fast to provide for an on-line verification of valid user identification. The accounting information could be made resident within the system, available only to the supervisor and the accounting programs (i.e., privileged).

The accounting system could record each job transition or step, print out job charges at the completion of a job, and accumulate monthly statistics. By maintaining the accounting information in an on-line fashion, users could be prevented from using more than their current funds or exceeding their current account limits.

Multiprogramming and Time Sharing. The more recent advances in computer hardware/software—namely, multiprogramming and time sharing—have produced the greatest impact on automated accounting. Because these advantages have made it feasible to allocate and share the multiple resources of a computing system, it is possible to have multiple users on the system at the same time.

For each user of the system, the accounting system must know (1) who is responsible for the charges, (2) what type of service this user is entitled to (and with what constraints), (3) what resources have been allocated to the user, and (4) what price schedules apply. Further, the pricing structure must allow the user to estimate easily and predict costs, and should require only small amounts of system resources for the accounting.

Unbundling and Proprietary Software. With unbundling (*q.v.*) and time sharing have come new problems in automated accounting. Where it was previously possible to simply charge the proprietary system user for computer time used, more complex multiuser systems have made it possible to allow one user to provide service to another. The result is that users are billed by both the computing center (for hardware use, expendable supplies, etc.) and other users (for proprietary software use). Thus, the accounting system must be cognizant of the use of such proprietary software and should, in fact, allow some "higher-order" user to suballocate resources to another user. For instance, it should be possible for one user to develop and maintain a subsystem, fully consistent with the operating and accounting systems, which bills the individual users for actual resources used (both hardware and software).

Another example might be the course instructor who allocates fixed amounts of time or money to each student in a course in such a fashion that no student can use more than a fair share. Obviously, the person responsible for the account must be able to reallocate the resources without exceeding the total allotted. In addition, it should be possible to place limits, which may not be uniform, on each student account so that special projects may use extra memory or disk space, special hardware, etc.

Since some software can be charged only on a "value received" or transaction basis (such as ledger entries in an accounting system or students scheduled in an automated scheduling system), the accounting system must be flexible in terms of the algorithm used to calculate actual charges.

Costs of an Automated Accounting System and Charges Levied. The costs of an automated accounting system are directly a function of the resources used to gather and maintain the accounting information. In order that the overhead of collecting the information not interfere with normal system operation, the charges themselves must reflect the unique characteristics of the system. Normally, charges are based on such things as:

1. CPU time utilized.
2. Memory residence time (e.g., number of pages referenced or amount of memory occupied by a job).
3. Connect time and/or port cost.
4. I/O operations performed (e.g., disk reads and writes).
5. Physical I/O units used:
   (a) Cards read/punched
   (b) Lines printed
   (c) Magnetic tapes mounted
   (d) File space used.

However, these charges must relate to the characteristics of the operating system if they are to be easily collected. They should also relate to the allocation scheme for the

resources if they are to be fairly levied (i.e., disk space should not be charged on a bit or character basis if it is allocated on a track or sector basis).

An on-line system where each user has an active account, although costly in terms of disk space required, allows the accounting system to:

1. Encumber funds on a per-job basis so as to prevent negative spending.
2. Set dynamic limits on controlled privileges as a function of time, geographic entry point, and system load.
3. Maintain flexible and dynamic pricing with actual cost information available to users on demand.
4. Maintain up-to-the-minute accounting for each user and periodically inform users of their accumulated computer resource utilization.

As described, automated systems can be fairly costly. However, the benefits provided both to the computing center operations staff (e.g., current resource use, system load, operating difficulties, etc.) and to the users (e.g., current pricing structure, resources available, job flow, etc.) generally outweigh the costs. Indeed, by knowing the state of the computing system, both operators and users are able to optimize their interaction with it so as to increase its effective utilization.

REFERENCE

1969. Rosin, R. F. "Supervisory and Monitor Systems," *Computing Surveys* **1**:37–54.

R. H. ECKHOUSE

COMPUTER ACQUISITION

For articles on related subjects *see* BENCHMARK; COMPUTER ACCOUNTING AND RESOURCE CONTROL; COMPUTING CENTER; GROSCH'S LAW; HARDWARE MONITOR; PERFORMANCE MEASUREMENT AND EVALUATION; and SOFTWARE MONITORS.

For an organization wishing to use computers to support some of its functions, or for an organization already doing this but considering changes in its computer operations, there are many alternatives available today. Because of this, and because of the complexity of the problem, generally a multiple stage approach is useful.

Stage 1. Select the principal type of computer support and/or services most suited to the organization's needs and develop detailed specifications for the performance goals to be met. Alternatives include microcomputers, minicomputers, using a large mainframe computer in your organization, using an outside service bureau, or using an external time-sharing service. The costs and benefits of each of these varies, but the general factors shown in Fig. 1 apply.

Stage 2. Select the specific hardware, software, and communications equipment that most satisfactorily meet the specifications.

Stage 3. Acquire, install, and test the system under actual workload conditions until it performs according to expectation.

Which of the alternatives in Fig. 1 is appropriate depends on the nature of the applications to be processed. Additional specific factors to be considered include:

- Security and privacy protection needed.
- Requirement for sophisticated software tools.
- Frequency and volume of use.
- Sophistication and capabilities of users.
- Number of users that will be using the system at one time.
- Type of application—e.g., size of database, software, degree of interactive computing.

- Available budget for acquisition, installation, and operation.
- Physical space, power, and general office or work environment.

These remarks apply not only to general administrative data processing work, but also to such newer applications as those involved in office automation. Related to these issues is the relationship of the application system to other users and systems. This brings up the subject of distributed computing. The issues relating to distributed computing include:

- The distribution of functions to user areas including data entry, editing, inquiring, and report generation.
- The need for functions to be supported at remote locations and at central sites.
- The stability or growth potential of the application.
- The stability of the user organization and needs.
- Geographic dispersion of users.

Note that thus far we have ignored details relating, for example, to specific properties of communication

Alternative	Advantages	Disadvantages
Internal software development (microcomputer, minicomputer, or mainframe).	Customized solution, no legal negotiation, better development control, staff gains experience, moderate operation cost.	Longer development time, greater potential risk of failure, higher cost of development, ultimate costs can only be estimated, costs incurred even if effort ultimately fails.
Procurement of software packages for use on internal computer.	Low development cost, tested and demonstrated software, documentation available.	May not meet all user needs, legal negotiation (e.g., for right to modify package), dependence on external organization (lack of control).
Outside time-sharing and service bureaus using their packages, possibly augmented by internally developed applications.	Ease of use, access to flexible communication network, good software tools and specialized databases, potentially excellent service from vendor who is marketing-oriented.	Possible high operational unit cost, less control, lack of flexibility in moving software, dependence on external organization (lack of control).
Turnkey minicomputer or microcomputer system.	Faster development time, organization provided with a structure around the application, moderate initial cost, total cost more certain, potentially excellent service from vendor who is marketing-oriented.	May not meet all user needs, dependence on external support, some possible legal negotiation, need for operational staff, potential difficulty in integrating with other systems, dependence on external organization (lack of control), limited ability to increase power of system.

Fig. 1.   Some frequently encountered advantages and disadvantages of alternative types of computer support.

lines, hardware, and software. Since a full discussion of all the issues raised above is beyond the scope of this article, we shall focus here on the single most complex problem, namely acquiring a computer and its associated software.

Acquiring a Computer System. To acquire a computer, vendors must be contacted so that they may submit formal proposals. If a formal Request for Proposal (RFP) is published, you may be inundated with proposals. However, it is equally undesirable to deal with one vendor without at least a survey of the marketplace. A frequently employed approach by private business and industry is to prescreen the vendors and to solicit responses from, at most, three to five vendors. If, after a survey, only one vendor can satisfy the requirements, negotiating the contract can begin.

The information that should be given to the vendor so that a proposal can be submitted includes, at minimum, the following.

- User/system requirements (i.e., specification of the applications to be computerized).
- Schedule, budget restrictions.
- List of information needed for evaluation.
- Guidelines to make proposals uniform and complete (e.g., suggested outlines).
- Method of evaluation of proposals.

For larger systems, questionnaires would be developed for vendors to complete, including a list of all requirements. The list of information needed for evaluation of a vendor proposal includes the following.

- Relation between application requirements, as given in the request for the proposal, and system capabilities.
- Complete list of hardware, system software, and application software.
- Sample or proposed contract, including pricing and payment terms.
- List of current users who can be contacted, including some with similar requirements.
- Provision for growth/expansion/contraction.
- Estimated performance.
- The vendor's approach to maintenance of hardware and software and to new releases of the software.
- Correlation between the proposed system and user system requirements.
- Statement of vendor's financial condition.

Following receipt of proposals from vendors, the customer must (1) perform initial evaluation and elimination of vendors, thereby determining finalists; (2) conduct an in-depth analysis of the final proposals; and (3) negotiate a contract with the successful vendor.

The objective in the initial evaluation is to eliminate vendor proposals which clearly do not meet the stated requirements. Some examples of reasons for elimination are:

- Inability to meet specified deadlines.
- Lack of availability of function.
- Proposal does not satisfy a sufficient number of the user requirements.
- The financial or staff viability of the vendor is questionable.
- Lack of compatibility with standards/hardware/software.

The initial evaluation does not usually involve visits to other users or to the vendor sites. Vendors can be encouraged to make oral presentations of their proposals, but there are some reasons for avoiding this step, since it takes time, may add little information, and may increase vendor marketing pressure.

The initial evaluation should be tentative, since additional facts may emerge which disqualify finalists and make previous bidders more attractive. For this reason, no formal notification should be given to any vendor until the selection of the winning proposal is made.

To assist in the evaluation, checklists of user requirements are helpful (see Allen and Lientz, 1978). The same applies to system requirements, if they have been developed. Several people should read each proposal and evaluate it on the basis of the checklist.

If user requirements have been classified into those which are essential and those which are merely desirable, the finalists may satisfy all mandatory requirements, but may not meet all desirable ones. By this point, questions may have arisen on the specific capabilities of each finalist. Some examples might be: When will the vendor support word processing? What are the capabilities of the file management utilities? What are the vendor's plans for memory expansion? How is the processor network coupled? Will the vendor support the latest version of Cobol? Will the machine emulate some RJE terminal?

For each vendor, a list of questions and issues should be constructed on matters not covered explicitly or completely by the proposal.

After the issues and questions have been identified, the method and the forum for getting answers need to be defined. This can be a visit by the vendor, but (if possible) a visit to vendor facilities is preferable. This gives an opportunity to make many informal observations of the vendor's staff and facilities. The agenda for such a visit should be carefully reviewed to see that the appropriate topics are covered.

After an initial general presentation, the remainder of the visit should address specific issues. A brief summary of the requirements should be presented to provide a base for the discussion. Notes should be taken and a trip report prepared as soon after the visit as possible.

Visits to user sites or contacts with users can also be made. These visits or contacts should identify the length of time the equipment has been used; overall satisfaction; any problems in support, security, and maintenance; ease of use; reliability of vendor and products; efficiency and performance; and unexpected surprises.

After the visits to vendors and users, the evaluation of finalists can be done. Vendors can be eliminated individually, based on these visits, or a scoring system can be employed. With the latter approach, each proposal would score against a list of criteria, each with an associated weight. The proposal with the highest total weighted score is generally the preferred alternative. There are, however, several limitations to such a quantitative approach. For example, it assumes a certain level of commonality between alternatives beyond the criteria, despite the fact that the proposals may be very dissimilar. Therefore, the usual approach for a limited number of alternatives is to proceed by elimination.

Having selected a vendor, the legal negotiation begins. Internal legal groups can provide assistance in obtaining a suitable contract. However, it helps if potential users have knowledge of the issues that recur repeatedly in negotiations. This will facilitate working with the selected vendor as well as the attorneys involved. Contract terms need to be discussed from a user, as well as from a legal, point of view.

What can and must be negotiated? An obvious aspect is price, but even the price can be defined in terms of licenses (fixed term, perpetual), purchase, lease, lease with option to purchase, etc. How much will maintenance and new releases cost? All options must be spelled out in detail. The method of financing depends on a number of factors, including useful life of system, potential salvage value, and desire to use investment tax credit (ITC). A safe set of assumptions is two to three years of life with little or no salvage value. This, however, may be very conservative and so should be adjusted to the organization. After this period, users would then frequently move up to other equipment with more power.

In addition to price, below is a partial list of questions which must be answered for hardware, software, or services.

1. *Maintenance.* Who will fix it? When? What happens on weekends or after hours if the system fails?
2. *Warranty.* How long? What happens if the system is modified?
3. *Updates/later releases.* Are you assured of getting the latest releases of the system?
4. *Schedule.* What if schedules are not met? Who pays?
5. *Support.* How will the vendor support you during installation? How will the system be kept up to date?
6. *Rejection.* Do you have a trial period in which you can reject the system?
7. *Multiple sites.* Suppose you later wish to install the same system elsewhere—how much will it cost?
8. *Viability/fallback.* If the vendor goes bankrupt, what happens to you and your system?
9. *Disputes.* What procedures will be pursued to resolve problems?
10. *Payment.* Who gets paid? When? Under what conditions?
11. *Training.* Who will do the training? How much will be done?
12. *Performance.* How will the system performance be measured after installation?
13. *Compatibility.* What is the vendor's assurance that the vendor's product will remain compatible with the user's setting? What type of compatibility is needed?
14. *Acceptance.* Who is responsible for establishing these criteria, data collection, and evaluation? Under what conditions will the system be accepted?
15. *Failure.* How are the vendor performance and products likely to fail? What happens if they fail? Who decides when failure has occurred?
16. *Contract type.* What type of contract is most appropriate—a standard one from a vendor, a current contract in force, or a new contract?
17. *Tradeoffs/negotiable items.* What is your negotiating room on each requirement? What tradeoffs are you willing to make?

The above comments and questions are general. They apply to hardware, software, and services. There are additional, more specific questions which need to be asked individually for hardware and application software.

- *Hardware (including system software)*
  1. What do you get (e.g., hardware configuration, software attributes, and system performance)?
  2. What is the support for cabling, site preparation, physical installation, power support, air conditioning, water cooling, humidity and dust control, education, training materials, and test time)?

3. What will it cost? How long does the contract run? How much is paid? When? Under what conditions? Can funds be withheld pending evaluation of vendor performance? What are the taxes and transportation charges? Who gets the investment tax credit? Is credit issued if a failure occurs? What are the charges for spare parts, supplies, overtime and holiday work, training, and consulting? Is there protection against price increases?

4. What is the reliability? (This includes the estimated mean time to failure, mean time between failures, mean time to repair and percentage availability over a given period. Provisions are necessary for part replacement, back-up, and disaster. To make sure that these terms are met, acceptance testing must be done. The acceptance testing period ensures operation, performance, compatibility, and reliability. Of particular interest is stress testing, where a system is subjected to a high number of active terminals or other extreme loads.)

5. How, where, and how promptly will it be fixed? Also, what reporting and logging procedures are needed for malfunctions? Under what conditions will preventive maintenance be done?

6. When will the system be delivered (in its entirety)?

7. What are your rights? Can you add hardware to the system? What about equipment of other manufacturers? Can you upgrade it or trade it in? Can you move it around? Can you buy it? Under what terms?

- *Software (including services as well as packages)*
  1. What do you get? (The contract should specify the deliverable software items as to content, number of copies, software updates, and software enhancements, and it should also state the system software necessary to support each application.)
  2. What is the payment schedule? (If there is to be software development, payments should be based on the achievement of tangible events and milestones.)

Finally, we note that the following installation and maintenance issues can be addressed.

- How should the site for the computer be prepared? What steps are involved?
- What is the managerial and administrative structure necessary?

- How is the system accepted by users?
- What are the on-going requirements? What controls and reviews are needed?

REFERENCES

1973. Martin, J. *Security, Accuracy, and Privacy of Computer Systems.* Englewood Cliffs, NJ: Prentice-Hall. (Gives the control and security framework for information systems.)
1974. Nolan, R. L. *Managing the Data Resource Function.* St. Paul, MN: West Publishing. (Gives the administrative framework for information systems.)
1978. Allen, R. J. and Lientz, B. P. *Systems in Action.* Santa Monica, CA: Goodyear. (Gives the overall life cycle of systems and activities, including user and system requirements.)

B. P. Lientz

COMPUTER-AIDED DESIGN

For articles on related subjects *see* COMPUTER GRAPHICS; IMAGE PROCESSING; INPUT/OUTPUT DEVICES; LIGHTPEN: TERMINALS; and TIME SHARING.

Design. Design is primarily a creative activity in which a person takes an aesthetic or functional idea and incorporates it in some medium in a way which can be understood by someone else. The most common example of this activity is engineering design, where the ideas of the designer are generally put on paper as drawings which include both geometric descriptions and notes. The essence of computer-aided design (CAD) is the marriage created by applying the strengths and capabilities of computers to provide assistance for design needs.

Geometry is a vital factor in most design; description of the shape of an item and of its size is the essential element in most tangible representations of an item. Humans usually are able to visualize a geometric description of an item more easily than they can understand a word description of the same item. The old adage about a picture being worth a thousand words comes from this realization. Thus, a major portion of the time spent in design is often devoted to creating and modifying geometric "pictures" of the item being designed.

In most kinds of design work, a designer works with a number of previously defined elements that are selectively included in the design of an item. For example, the designer of an electrical circuit selects circuit elements and places them into the design. Even at the level of designing the elements, geometric entities such as circles are used to "build up" the element. This selection process is well suited to computer assistance, since computers can store large numbers of elements and allow designers rapid access to them for use in design. Another characteristic of the process of design is that it is highly iterative; designers frequently make multiple changes to various elements of the design as work proceeds. This also can be conveniently assisted by computers. Further, much of design is concerned with items for which some kind of analysis must be performed after the design is proposed. The results of the analysis often lead to additional changes in the design, such as to the selection of different elements in the item being designed.

Application Areas. The most obvious examples of CAD are connected with engineering design activities, which will be emphasized in this article. These include design of structures, highways, machine parts, printed circuit boards, plants, piping, assembly lines, airplanes, automobiles, etc. In addition, CAD often is thought of as including any use of computers to aid in a design and analysis process, such as structural analysis following the actual design work. Further, it is sometimes used to encompass design of computer programs themselves, patterns for clothing, architectural exterior and interior layouts, packaging containers, and management systems.

The main strengths of computers—speed, accuracy, and repeatability—are particularly well matched to these kinds of design activities. In addition, computers can store very large amounts of information (the database) that can be retrieved rapidly and used for additional calculations or for display. This database capability, by the very nature of design (geometric construction, selection, and iteration), plays an important role in CAD.

Computers—Only an Aid. It is important to note, however, that computers are used only as an *aid* to design. The process of design involves extensive decision-making and subjective evaluation, activities which are aided greatly by using computers, but which are generally carried out by computers under human direction.

This article will focus primarily on the area of interactive engineering design, primarily of machine parts. Especially in this area, as part of the design process, an engineer must be able to describe and communicate to others the geometric relationships of the design. The systems that assist in these needs are often called interactive computer graphics systems, and they are the foundation of most CAD systems. In fact, the terms are sometimes used interchangeably; however, the field of computer graphics includes many activities outside of design and CAD encompasses activities outside of computer graphics.

Until about 15 to 20 years ago, almost all engineering design was done on the drafting board. Selection of elements was implemented by tracing, drawing from templates, or pasting the elements onto the drawing of the design of each element. Iteration was obtained by se-

quential use of pencil, eraser, pencil, eraser, . . . The only way to improve the productivity of this process was to provide better templates or paste-ons, to use less iteration, or to speed up the human in some way. The recognition that significant gains in productivity could result from using computers to aid the process led to CAD systems. Early systems were very expensive and thus required large benefits from productivity gains in order to be worth their cost. As prices of CAD systems have come down relative to the cost of humans doing design work, the cost benefits from productivity gains have become more significant and the variety of CAD systems has grown greater. We will look at three types of systems.

Typical Minicomputer System. Most of the existing interactive CAD systems today are classified as minicomputer-based stand-alone systems. These systems were made possible a number of years ago by the development of relatively inexpensive graphics terminals (i.e., those based on a storage tube) and driven by small minicomputers. These have taken advantage of human-computer interaction to provide low-cost two-dimensional (2D) drafting and electrical component design as major applications. During the past few years, most such systems have been upgraded to encompass varying degrees of three-dimensional (3D) geometric design, along with ties to engineering analysis and manufacturing. These systems require only a small support staff (programmers, computer operators, etc.), usually have a limited number of work stations or terminals (normally a maximum of less than 8), and use a relatively small database. A typical minicomputer-based system is shown in Fig. 1.

Most minicomputer-based CAD systems are supplied by a vendor who purchases, manufactures, or develops the various hardware and software components and sells or leases the entire system as a total unit (a *turnkey* (*q.v.*) system) to the end user. Most such turnkey systems use the storage tube terminal; however, some vendors recently have begun to employ raster CRTs, and refresh CRTs are now also sometimes used on minicomputer-based CAD systems. Briefly, storage tube CRTs retain lines until they are erased and thus can display large amounts of data, while refresh CRTs must have lines continuously redrawn and provide maximum user interaction; raster CRTs are based on TV video technology and can provide brilliant colors, but with generally lower resolution. The choice of which CRT to use is a compromise among several factors, including cost, productivity of use, ease of interaction, amount of data to be displayed at any one time, and the required or desired data communication rates. The average CAD user, however, is not really concerned with the type of terminals used or with the other technical problems as long as the system can be conveniently used for the design functions.

As has been noted, the essence of these design func-

Fig. 1. MCAUTO's UNIGRAPHICS system, a typical minicomputer-based CAD system. The upper left shows the designer's work station with a function keyboard, and a CRT terminal. The upper right shows a plotter. The center shows the minicomputer system. The lower left and right show the printer and a typical part on the CRT.

tions is geometric construction. Geometric entities are typically built through repeated selection of "functions" or "tasks" to be performed from a "menu" of selection possibilities (see Fig. 2). Menus, function keyboards, data tablets, etc., are used not only for selection of geometric construction *functions* and tasks, but also for the selection of *elements* for insertion and for positioning them on the design. They are also used to select tasks which permit a designer to move elements or items from location to location (translations and rotations), to create a blown-up view of a portion of the drawing *(windowing)*, and to permit easy annotation or dimensioning of the drawings.

Using these and other functional capabilities, the user interactively builds the database (composed of both geometric and alphanumeric information). For a mechanical design, the present output often takes the format of a traditional drawing showing the classical orthographic principal views (front, top, and side), with a 3D view added. The general 3D view (see Fig. 3) is important because it helps to avoid misinterpretation and ambiguity and thus minimizes re-work later by engineering and manufacturing personnel. Note that even though the 3D

view is quite helpful, it could have been obtained by methods of projection from an existing 2D database. However, this would require considerably more time than would use of a 3D CAD system. As minicomputers and associated disk packs (used for storage of the database) have gotten larger, there has been a trend to the use of truly 3D geometric databases.

The productivity of CAD processes is magnified where there is a tie to computer aided manufacturing (CAM), and most systems which possess this tie are called CAD/CAM systems. The primary benefit of CAM is in the use of the computer description of the part(s), which permits use of this computer generated information to drive cutting, forming, and other operations in a manufacturing environment. When the same basic geometry from the database is used for both design and manufacturing, parts fit together with great precision. The creation, storage, and interface of 3D geometric data among various disciplines (e.g., engineering and manufacturing) provide communication which was sorely lacking until recently. The same geometric model—with mathematical integrity—is accessed and used by design-

CHOOSE LINE DEF MODE
1 TWO POINTS
2 TAN TO 2 CURVES
3 HORIZONTAL
4 VERTICAL
5 NORMAL
6 PT AND TAN CURVE
7 PT AND ABS ANGLE
8 PT - ANG FROM LINE
9 PT - PARALLEL LINE
10 PT - PERPEND LINE
11 PARALLEL AT DIST
12 PARLEL LN-TAN CURV
13 PERPTO LN-TAN CURV
14 ANGLE - TAN CURVE

Explanations of functions to be called

1. Create a line by indicating two points between which the line is to go.
2. Create a line tangent to two curves (user will indicate the curves).
3. Create a horizontal line in a construction plane (user will indicate where).
4. Create a vertical line in a construction plane (user will indicate where).
5. Create a line normal to the x-y plane through an indicated point.
6. Create a line through a point and tangent to a curve (user indicates point and curve).
7. Create a line through a point and at a given angle from horizontal.
8. Create a line through a point and at a given angle from an indicated line.
9. Create a line through a point and parallel to an indicated line.
10. Create a line through a point and perpendicular to an indicated line.
11. Create a line parallel to an indicated line, offset by a given distance (keyed in).
12. Create a line parallel to an indicated line and tangent to an indicated curve.
13. Create a line perpendicular to an indicated line and tangent to an indicated curve.
14. Create a line at a given angle to an indicated line and tangent to an indicated curve.

270

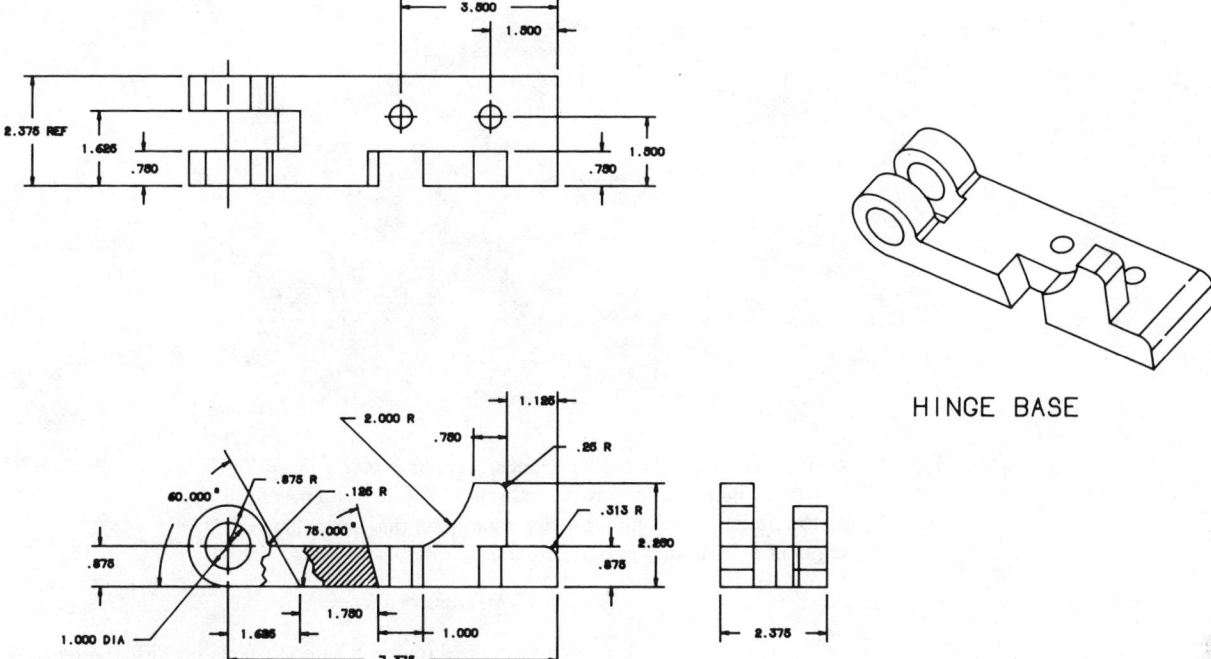

HINGE BASE

Fig. 3. A typical drawing format—three views plus a 3D view.

ers, part programmers (people who describe machine tool movements to create parts), structural analysts (engineers who calculate the structural strength of parts and assemblies), tool designers, and quality assurance personnel. CAD systems allow for this data to be captured during the construction phases of design.

Construction of the design is not the only way in which data can be captured, however. Fig. 4 shows an automatic laser scanner for 2D data capture. Here data is automatically entered into the database and is then available for further modification (or editing). In addition to this type of scanner, hand-held or movable scanning (or "digitizing") devices are available. These allow the locations of points to be input. They can be moved to various points on 2D or 3D models. At a desired point, the user causes the device to sense the location of the point and enter it into the database. After the points are entered into the database, CAD functions can be applied to create smooth lines, curves, or surfaces between the points. These lines, curves, or surfaces can then be used with the points for further design or for interfacing with CAM functions. Fig. 5 shows an interesting example of this technique. The key to this process is the functions available to the designer to carry out actions in creating

the design. These functions are, of course, not limited to minicomputer-based CAD systems, but are a characteristic of all CAD systems. Naturally, the functions are generally more powerful and more numerous in systems that operate on large computers.

Large Mainframe Systems. The aerospace and automotive industries have been the pioneers in the development of powerful interactive CAD systems using large mainframe (*q.v.*) computers. Their developmental activity, begun in the 1960s, was possible because they possessed the resources (size, technical personnel, and available money) to undertake them. Fig. 6 shows a typical product of these production-oriented companies. The basic shapes of many of the parts of this kind of product are designed with the use of effective CAD/CAM systems.

The mainframe systems are characterized by a large user environment, a centralized database (usually involving tens of thousands of computer drawings), work stations that are both local and remote to the computer, a large support staff, and computers shared by many disciplines.

The 3D databases and CAD/CAM interfaces were

←

Fig. 2. A typical "menu" of possible actions (functions) that the CAD user can request by pushing buttons on the function keyboard, by pointing a light-sensing device called a lightpen at the selected function, by positioning a sensing device on a data tablet, or by keying in the name or number of the function.

Fig. 4. A Broomall Industries laser scanner, which passes a laser-generated light over a drawing to "sense" the lines or curves on the drawing with high precision and pass this line or line segment information into a computer database.

first developed for mainframe systems because these systems had more computing power, more memory, and more disk capacity. Fig. 7 shows the spectrum of activities involved in one such system. Although the usual medium for transmitting engineering design data has been drawings on paper, systems like this show that the trend is definitely toward use of the computer model instead of

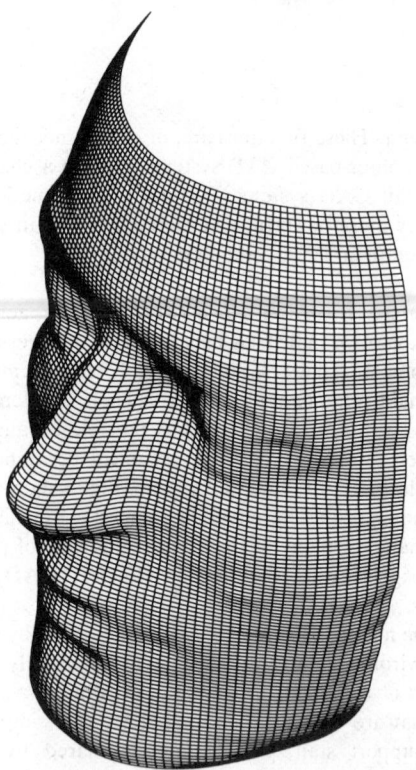

Fig. 5. A surface representation of a face, serving as the start of design of a fire protection mask. The physical sculpted model was digitized (scanned) to produce 3D data points, which were then used to create surfaces. The display shows the computer-generated surfaces.

Fig. 6. A product of the aerospace industry, designed in large part using CAD. Note the complicated 3D surfaces. The high cost of parts in this kind of product and the pressure to complete the design in as little time as possible all lead to high "payoffs" with the use of CAD.

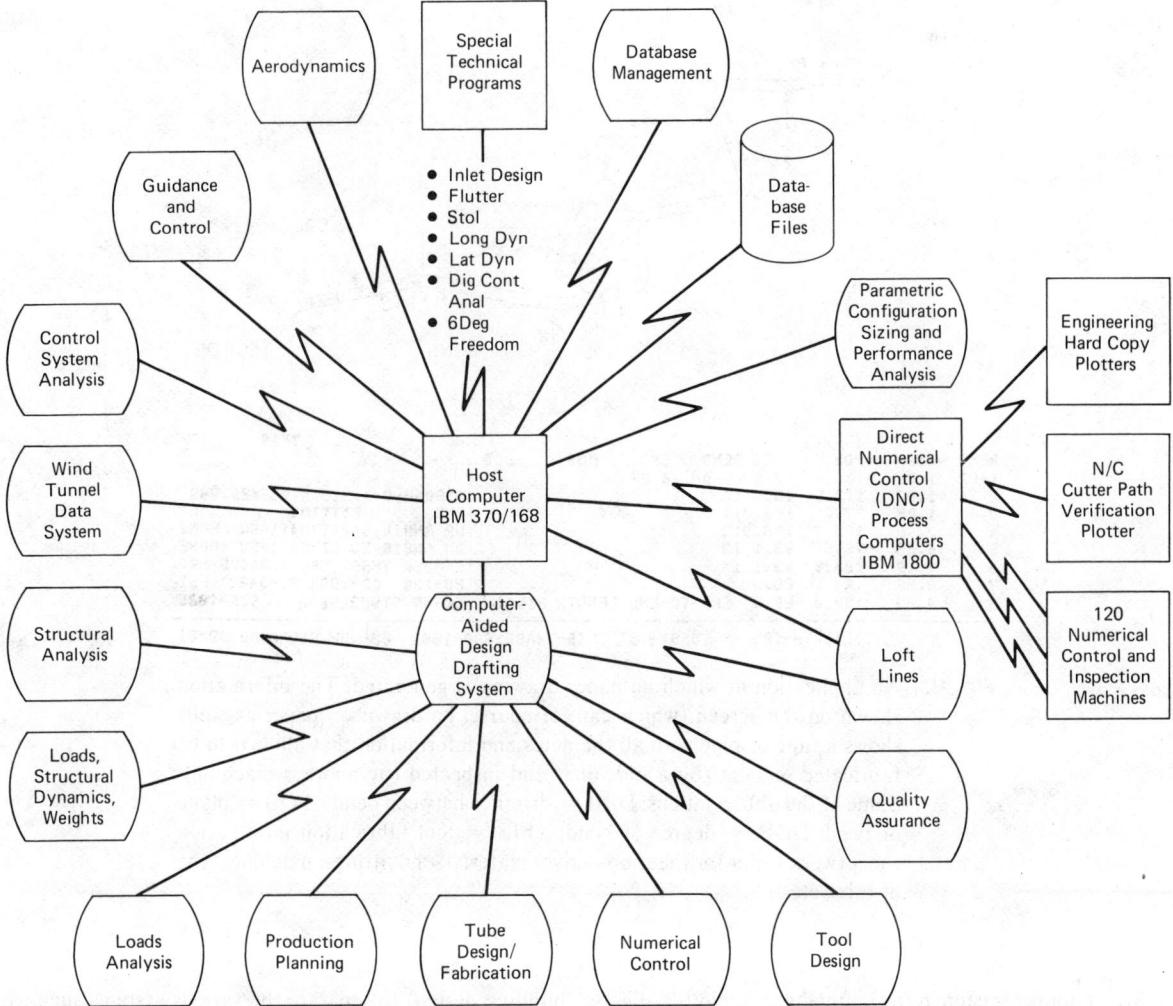

Fig. 7. A schematic of the various aspects of a large mainframe-based CAD system for an aerospace firm.

a drawing. This might be termed "pure CAD/CAM," or, as some have called it, "going paperless, cradle to grave." It already exists for certain applications. Fig. 8 shows one such application, in which the 3D design, fabrication, and inspection are accomplished without the generation of the usual engineering drawings.

Distributed Systems. During the past few years, CAD systems have evolved which combine some of the best features of both the minicomputer-based and the large mainframe systems. These *distributed systems* (*q.v.*) distribute the CAD tasks of a graphics environment between minicomputers and large mainframes. Their environment usually includes both a network of minicomputers and a generalized work station with "intelligent" or "smart" terminals (microprocessors included as part of the terminal).

The large mainframe (or host) performs those functions which are best suited for it; e.g., large sets of calculations, geometric modeling, and vector generation (mathematical calculation to determine the lines—or vectors—to display entities so they look "smooth" on the CRT). The minicomputer (at the user location—which may be remote by hundreds or even thousands of miles from the mainframe) serves to "offload" graphics functions from the host; e.g., display and operator interfaces. The microprocessor associated with the "intelligent" CRT usually performs clipping, scaling, and viewing functions. Hardware control dials at this terminal may be used for local graphics display manipulation independent of host operation.

Fig. 9 shows a state-of-the-art intelligent terminal used in CAD systems. The work station or cluster may provide the user with a myriad of features—vector ter-

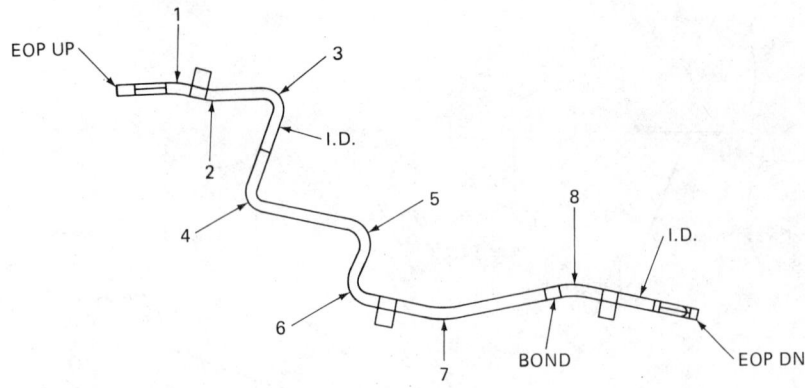

BEND	DBB	POB	DOB	BEND	DBB	POB	DOB
1-UP	1.95	.0	17.6	9-DN	4.22		
2	1.06	178.5	15.9	10			
3	1.08	77.6	105.011				
4	3.46	163.7	108.912				
5	2.26	-75.5	93.1	13			
6	1.19	-180.0	93.1	14			
7	2.26	.4	28.9				
8	4.29	180.0	28.9	END-TO-END LENGTH 21.41			

TFIS

```
AL5052-0   .313 X.035X29.999
END       FITTING        XMAT
UP AN818-5D/ST7M411-5W  NONE
DN AN818-5D/ST7M411-5W  NONE
BENDER TF55   BR-1.000WD-NR
PD-130  CB-.938 PT-340.  PSI
EC-NR ST9M389B0A     STF-1025
```

TOL:LGTH-.05   OFST-.07 TFIS-74A851600-1003 -00 WMP REV A 02/09/81

Fig. 8. An application in which no paper drawing is generated. The information shown on the screen (which can, of course, be drawn on paper as well) shows a tube or pipe with all the notes and information that allow it to be fabricated or bent (by a machine) and inspected (by another machine). Some of the abbreviations: DBB = distance between bends; POB = plane of bend; DOB = degree of bend; TFIS = tool fabrication information sheet (work order for the shop—gives material, end fittings, machine, type of tube, etc.).

minals (storage, raster, refresh, intelligent), plotter, digitizer, high-speed printer, time-sharing alphanumeric terminals, engineering word processing unit, etc. Distributed systems thus obviate the necessity for processing all functions on a host computer, while still providing the link to support a centralized database.

Trends. A number of significant trends are taking place in CAD. First, there is the development activity to provide color CRTs that will equal the storage tube CRT in sharpness and resolution. Color allows the designer to increase the visualization of the design, particularly in interpreting the results of analysis and in visualizing complex 3D relationships. In addition, color CRTs are used by manufacturing personnel to minimize misinterpretation of drawings and assist in assembly operations. Another trend in this area is its use in machining operations, where colors (and shading) can assist in visualizing material removal. Color is also used to separate fluid or solid flow in circuit schematics or paths, and (in the case of building design) to separate the various systems such as heating and ventilating, water, wiring, etc.

Second, more graphics operations previously done by software programming are now being performed by hardware. This is especially true of terminal hardware.

Third, there is increasing use of CAD in areas other than traditional engineering design. Design of medical equipment and improving the aesthetics of product containers are typical non-traditional CAD uses.

Fourth, the expanding use of computers in homes is leading toward use of at least primitive CAD in homes, in, for example, the design and planning of home woodworking projects. As another example, with 2D graphics, floor plan studies are possible, for remodeling, for storage planning, or just for trying various rearrangements of furniture. A 3D system would help even more with the aesthetics of such possible rearrangements.

Fifth, most CAD systems are now so firmly tied to or supplemented by CAM systems that almost all vendors refer to their products as CAD/CAM systems. The use

Fig. 9. An Evans and Sutherland "intelligent" terminal (containing a microprocessor), used in a distributed CAD system.

of robots and the expanding interface between CAD and the field of robotics (*q.v.*) is giving impetus to these ties, since robot movements are frequently described and "worked out" using CAD/CAM systems.

Sixth, CAD "standards" (especially for description of geometric entities) are now being developed and used. The field of CAD has long been characterized as fragmented, with very few systems able to "talk to" other systems. The implementation of CAD systems that use these "standards" will change this situation and bring more systems capabilities to users.

References

1974. Barnhill, Robert E. and Riesenfeld, Richard F. *Computer Aided Geometric Design.* New York: Academic Press.
1976. Adams, J. A. and Rogers, D. F. *Mathematical Elements for Computer Graphics.* New York: McGraw-Hill.
1978. Calma Corp. *Interactive CAD Considerations for AEC.* Hayward, CA: Suburban Press.
1979. Chasen, S. H. and Dow, J. W. *The Guide for the Evaluation and Implementation of CAD/CAM Systems.* Atlanta, GA: CAD/CAM Decisions.
1979. Newman, W. and Sproull, R. *Principles of Interactive Computer Graphics,* 2nd Ed. New York: McGraw-Hill.
1980. Machover, C. and Blauth, R. E. (Eds.). *The CAD/CAM Handbook.* Bedford, MA: Computervision Corporation.
1980. Taraman, K. (Ed.). *CAD/CAM: Meeting Today's Productivity Challenge.* Dearborn, MI: Computer and Automated Systems Association of SME.
Bimonthly journal. Pipes, A. (Ed.). *Computer-Aided Design.* Surrey, England: IPC Science and Technology Press, LTD.

BARRY FLACHSBART, G. PETERS, AND J. McDONALD

COMPUTER-AIDED MANUFACTURING.
See AUTOMATION; and COMPUTER-AIDED DESIGN.

COMPUTER ARCHITECTURE

For articles on related subjects *see* ADDRESSING; ARITHMETIC-LOGIC UNIT; CHANNEL; DATA COMMUNICATIONS: INPUT/OUTPUT DEVICES; INTERRUPT; MACHINE INSTRUCTION SET; MEMORY: Auxiliary; MEMORY: Main; MEMORY-MAPPED I/O; MICROPROCESSORS AND MICROCOMPUTERS; OPERATING SYSTEMS; SOFTWARE; SUPERCOMPUTERS; and VON NEUMANN MACHINE.

Introduction. Computer architecture is concerned with the physical or hardware structure of computer systems and the attributes of the various parts thereof, and with how these parts are interconnected. The field has evolved from that of computer design, originally viewed as an electrical engineering discipline, which dealt primarily with electrical and electronic circuits and their organization into a computer system. With the evolution of computer designs embodying software techniques, such as microprogramming and virtual machines, and as an increasing importance was attributed to operating systems and other software components in determining system behavior, it became evident that a computer system is an amalgam of both electronic and software elements, and that successful computer design requires an integrated view of these. More recently, with the development of large scale integration and microprocessors, fundamental device technology has begun to play an important role in computer design. Thus, computer architecture has become an interdisciplinary field, containing elements of computer science, operations research, electrical and electronic engineering, and even solid-state physics.

For our purposes in this article, two fundamental aspects of computer architecture will be identified: (1) *system architecture*—the functional behavior and conceptual structure of a hardware system as seen by the software developer (i.e., in terms of those characteristics which affect software design and development); and (2) *implementation architecture*—those characteristics which affect the relative cost and performance of a computer system and which are of concern to the semiconductor designer or electronic engineer, such as circuit technology and logic design. The significance of this distinction is illustrated by the IBM 360 and 370 series of computer systems (Fig. 1). The 360 series is a family of computer systems sharing a common system architecture—that is, software written for any model in the series

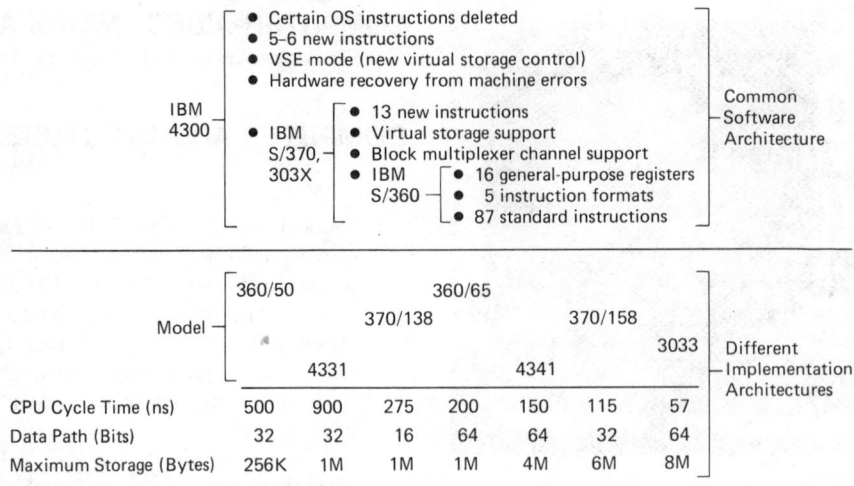

Fig. 1. IBM 360/370 architectures.

will operate correctly (although at different speeds) on any other model (with a few exceptions, mostly restricted to the operating system kernel). In order for this to happen, the various members of the 360 family share the same instruction set, arithmetic registers, I/O methods, channel structure, memory addressing mechanisms, and such. A single document, the *IBM System/360 Principles of Operation* (1966), is sufficient to allow one to write assembly language software, compilers, loaders, and most components of an operating system for any model in the series. (More recent IBM products in the 370, 3030, and 4300 families have extended the architecture of the 360 in an "upward compatible" way—that is, software written for the older series can run on the newer ones. This relationship is also illustrated in Fig. 1.)

From an implementation standpoint, the 360 series spans a variety of technologies and a performance range in excess of 100–1. At the low end, the 360 model 20 has an 8-bit data path, uses a common processor for both program execution and I/O channel operations, and utilizes microprogramming to "emulate" the complete 360 instruction set with a minimum of hardware support (the microcode is loaded into the main computer memory—a technique which yields low performance but broad capability). At the high end, the 360 model 195 features a 128-bit data path, separate I/O channel processors, and a "hard-wired," highly parallel implementation of the instruction set. (*See also* IBM 360/370 SYSTEM.) Other articles in this encyclopedia discuss similar families by other vendors, including the Control Data Cyber series and the Univac 1100 series.

Components. The three major components of a computer system are the storage system, the processor (i.e., the control and arithmetic/logic elements), and the I/O and communication system. These will be discussed from both the system and implementation architecture perspectives. The classic Von Neumann design is assumed, except where otherwise noted.

Storage. The *storage* or *memory* of a computer system contains both the data to be processed by the system and the instructions indicating what processing is to be performed. The fundamental unit of storage is the *bit,* conceptually containing one of two distinct values: 0 or 1. Aggregates of bits are combined into larger units such as *bytes* (usually eight bits), and *words* (anywhere from 8 to 64 bits or more). The "word size" of a computer has usually been treated as a distinguishing characteristic which serves as a basis for classification: 4–8 bits for a microcomputer, 12–24 bits for a minicomputer, and 32–64 bits for a "mainframe" computer. However, word length alone is no longer the sole basis for classification, as evidenced by the recent introduction of 32-bit "super-minicomputers" and 16-bit microprocessors.

More importantly, there are many different definitions of a machine's "word length." Early computer systems organized memory as follows: Bits were grouped into fixed-length "words," where each word was referenced as a unit by a single memory address and the individual bits of a word were transferred between a computer's main memory and its registers or secondary storage. Each word would contain a single instruction or datum. The arithmetic unit would operate on one word of data at a time.

In contrast, a typical modern computer might address data in groups of eight bits, transfer data to registers in groups of 16 bits, transfer data to secondary storage in groups of 64 bits, operate arithmetically on data "words" of 32 bits, have variable length instructions ranging from 16 to 48 bits, and use a 24-bit memory address. What is its word length? The most commonly accepted definition is the number of cells (the smallest addressable unit) to hold a single precision integer which is also usually the number of bits operated on in parallel by the arithmetic unit, but it should be clear that such a definition gives only a rough description of the memory system architecture.

A computer will generally have several different kinds of storage, each organized to hold one or more words of data. These types include *registers, main memory,* and *auxiliary* or *secondary storage.* The main differences between these types of storage are indicated in Table 1.

Registers. Registers are the fastest and most expensive memory units in a computer. Two fundamental categories can be distinguished: Registers that are directly accessible by application programs (part of the system architecture) and registers that are not directly accessible from software. The former generally hold data that are actively being processed by the computer's arithmetic and logical unit(s), the latter contain information describing the current state of the computation process, and may vary with different implementations of the same architecture family. The minimum complement of registers is essentially one: An arithmetic register or *accumulator.* This is a place where the results of computation or other data processing are accumulated. Although usually part of the system architecture, the accumulator may be hidden from the software in some designs (such as those using a stack for computation). Most computers today have multiple accumulators, so that several results may be maintained.

Most computer systems also have an *instruction register,* containing the instruction currently being executed; a *status register,* indicating the current condition of the various hardware components and computational results; and a *program counter* register, indicating the location in main memory of the next instruction to be executed.

(Certain designs have done without a program counter, typically by including the location of the "next" instruction as part of the "current" instruction.)

Other registers frequently encountered include *index registers,* for counting and for "pointing" into tables; *base* or *address* registers, containing addresses of blocks of main memory; a *stack pointer,* containing the address of a special block of memory which is treated like a push-down stack; and various special-purpose registers whose functions depend on the details of the particular computer.

A major architectural issue beyond the number, accessibility, and functions of registers is that of general-purpose versus special-purpose registers. In a special-purpose design, each register has a specific, narrow function whereas in a general purpose design, the registers may be used for a variety of purposes, as directed by the programmer. Real machines tend to have a mixture of special purpose and multi-purpose registers, but none that are totally general in purpose. The flexibility of general-purpose designs is attractive from a software viewpoint. Often, this flexibility will exact penalties in implementation efficiency because all parts of the processor require data paths to the general register set. On the other hand, in implementations where only a small number of registers can be accommodated, a general-purpose approach may be a necessity. The structure and discipline imposed by special-purpose registers may have software benefits as well, and recent computer designs aimed at supporting high-level languages tend to depend heavily on restricted use of registers. Fig. 2 illustrates the use of both general-purpose and special-purpose registers in the National 16032 microprocessor, which is designed to support block structured high-level languages.

Main Memory. The main memory contains programs and data that are ready for processing by the computer. It consists of a linear sequence of "words," each individually addressable, and each capable of being read or written to. In some implementations, different technologies will be used to implement different sections of a memory. For example, one section may have higher-

Table 1. Typical Storage Characteristics

Type	Access Time	Capacity, in Words	Use
Registers	10–750 ns	1–128	Data processing
Main memory	500 ns–2 μs	4,096–8,000,000	Instructions being executed; data needed for processing
Auxiliary memory	10–100 ms	1,000,000–1,000,000,000	Long-term storage; data and instructions not needed immediately

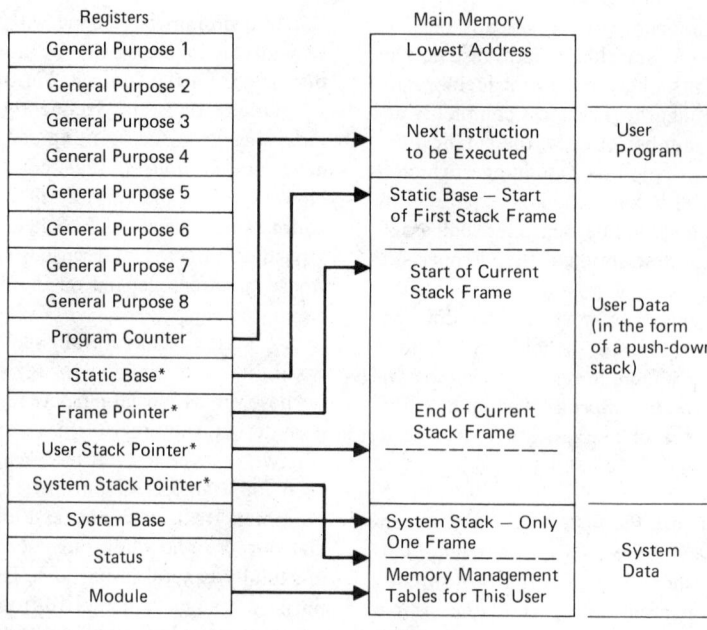

Fig. 2. Register and memory structure of National 16032 microprocessor.

speed memory than the others or one section may contain *read-only memory* (ROM), the contents of which may not be altered by running programs. The total number of words in a memory is typically a configuration decision, with upper and lower limits determined by the implementation architecture. Computer systems are often measured by how much main memory their architectures allow and how fast that memory may be accessed. Numerous techniques are used to increase the apparent speed of a memory system. *Cacheing* and *interleaving* are probably the two most popular.

Cacheing is a technique whereby a small, high-speed memory is used to contain the most frequently used words from a larger, lower-speed memory. If the "hit ratio" (percent of memory references found in the small, *cache memory—q.v.*) is high, the average speed of the entire memory is substantially increased.

With interleaving (*q.v.*), two or more independent memory systems are combined in such a way that they appear as one faster memory system. In one popular approach, two memory systems are organized so that all words with even addresses come from one system, and all words with odd addresses from the other. When an even-numbered word is fetched, the next-higher odd-numbered word may be fetched simultaneously from the other memory system, on the theory that it is likely to be the next word requested. If this guess is correct (as it often is), the next word's access time is essentially zero, thus nearly doubling the average memory access speed. Popular computer systems have employed 4-way, 8-way, and even 16-way interleaving, with a variety of organization strategies. The higher degrees of interleaving are used predominantly in systems requiring access to memory by multiple, parallel processors.

The system architecture characteristics of main memory will tend to differ somewhat from the implementation characteristics. The form in which memory is presented to the software is sometimes called the *logical address space* or the *virtual address space*. In the most straightforward designs, the logical address space is a linear sequence of words or bytes containing the programs being executed and the data not actively involved in a computation (active data are found in registers). It will differ from the physical memory mainly in size—in some cases smaller and in other cases larger.

In certain designs, the address space is perceived by software as a set of sequences of words, called *pages*. Each page has a distinct identification number and all have the same size. There may or may not be an implied spatial relationship between consecutively numbered pages. A more attractive model (from a software point of view) is the *segment* design in which there are several sequential blocks but with no requirement that they all be the same size. (Usually, in fact, the size is determined by software.) This permits each software module to be placed in whatever size segment is a close fit. Segment and page designs are often combined, so that each segment consists of one or more pages, and the size of a segment is a multiple of the page size. Other concepts of logical address space have often been discussed, but are only occasionally found in the architectures of commercially available systems (due to implementation costs). These concepts present memories whose "shapes" are closer in form to the actual patterns required by software, such as lists or trees. Content-addressable or associative memories (*q.v.*), in which data are accessed by content rather than address, have also seen limited use.

There are several other reasons for having a structured virtual memory rather than one large sequence. From a software viewpoint, a major objective is to provide a means of organizing programs and data according to common characteristics, such as type (instructions, characters, real numbers, integers), access rules (read only, execute only, read and write), or use (all data used during the same phase of a process may be grouped into one block). From a supervisory standpoint, memory structure enables efficient management of memory resources among multiple users. From an implementation perspective, structure may allow memory system design efficiencies, such as placement of frequently used data in one "high-speed" section of memory; convenient schemes for protection against unauthorized access, such as "access" keys for each segment or page; or (via memory mapping) may permit a small computer to support more memory than can be conveniently addressed with one word.

Memory Mapping. One of the most important aspects of computer architecture is *memory mapping:* the translation between the logical address space and the physical memory. The objectives of mapping are: (1) to translate from logical to physical addresses (where these are different); (2) to aid in memory protection; (3) to enable better management of memory resources. Mapping is important in determining the performance of a computer, both in a local sense (how long it takes to execute a given instruction) and in a global sense (how long it takes to run a given set of programs). In effect, each time a program presents a "logical" memory address and requests that the corresponding data be accessed, the mapping mechanism must translate that address into an appropriate physical memory location. The simpler this translation, the lower the cost of implementation and the higher the performance of the individual memory reference. However, more capable translation mechanisms permit protection of memory segments from unauthorized access and/or facilitate dynamic rearrangement of objects in physical memory. These enable efficiencies in

the programming, debugging, and supervisory phases of computing, which may far outweigh the cost of slower individual instruction execution times.

Although there are many techniques of memory mapping, there are two fundamental situations to be overcome: When the logical address space is smaller than the physical address space (common on many micro- and mini-computers, and certain older mainframe computers), mapping is needed to gain access to all of physical memory; and when the logical address space is larger than the physical address space, mapping is used to assure that each logical address actually used corresponds to a physical memory cell. The latter situation is discussed in more detail below, under "Virtual Memory."

The size of the logical address space is determined by the number of bits in a memory address. Typically, the size of an address is limited by the word length of the computer. On a typical minicomputer with a 16-bit word, only 2^{16} or about 65,000 words may be addressed. Technology now permits such systems to be attached physically to many times this much memory, but there is no direct way to address it without redesigning the instruction set. Thus, the primary purpose of a memory mapping mechanism on such a system is to enable the logical address space to be assigned to a desired portion of a larger physical address space. Three such methods are illustrated in Fig. 3: Relocation, paging, and segmentation. In the relocation scheme, the contents of a *bias* register are added to each logical memory address to produce a physical address. The effect is to offset the program by the biased amount in physical memory. Several different programs can coexist in the same physical memory without overlap by assigning different bias values to each of them.

In paging, the logical address space is divided into a set of equal-sized blocks called pages, and each is mapped onto a block of physical memory (called a page frame). The effect is similar to that of biasing, except that the program is broken into several separately-biased pieces (pages), and each page must begin at a page frame boundary in physical memory. The primary advantage of paging is that it allows a contiguous logical address space to be split into several noncontiguous physical frames. This makes memory management easier and also permits sharing of some of a program's pages among multiple processes without complete overlap of physical addresses. This scheme may be faster than the bias technique because it requires only a concatenation of two addresses instead of an addition to form the physical address. However, the page map file requires more register bits than the bias register.

Segmenting is somewhat like a combination of biasing and paging. It breaks the logical address space into several blocks, but does not require them to be of any particular size or to be mapped into any particular physical frames. Physical addresses are obtained by biasing the in-

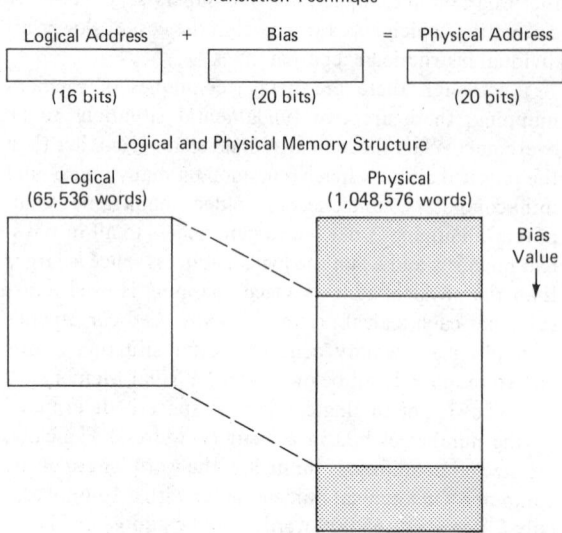

Fig. 3(a). Biased memory mapping (with sample values).

dividual segments. As might be expected, this approach is the most flexible and also the most costly, both in hardware and performance. It requires both a file of bias values (the segment table) and an extra addition operation per memory reference.

As noted above, mapping can enable protection against unauthorized access. A typical method, illustrated in Fig. 3(c), is to incorporate a set of access rights in the segment or page table. The access rights indicate a mode of access which is permitted to a segment (such as "read only" or "execute only"), and the memory mapping hardware can verify that each access to the segment fits this mode.

Auxiliary Memory (Secondary Storage). Auxiliary memory is the lowest-cost, highest-capacity, and slowest-access storage area in a computer system. It is where programs and data are kept for long-term storage, or when not in immediate use. Such memories tend to occur in two types—*sequential access* (data must be accessed in a linear sequence) and *direct access* (data may be accessed in any sequence). The most common sequential storage device is the magnetic tape, whereas direct access devices include rotating drums, disks, and certain low-speed semiconductor devices such as bubble memory.

Typically, a computer operates as follows. A program and its data are initially located on a secondary storage device. Program execution is achieved by copying the program and some of the data into main memory. Instructions are then executed, causing data to be copied into registers, operated on or tested, and results stored

back into main memory. Occasionally, an *input* operation is generated, causing more data to be copied from secondary storage, perhaps overwriting some that were previously read. As computation proceeds, results are sent back to secondary storage via *output* operations.

Many fundamental architectural issues are related to the means by which data and programs are transferred between main and secondary storage. The basic problem is that the storage and transfer characteristics of secondary devices do not match those of main storage. Typical access times for main and secondary storage were given in Table 1; but to understand this better, we must consider the structure of a secondary storage device. Data are stored in blocks whose size is determined by the characteristics of the device (anywhere from 64 to 512 words is typical). This leads to three distinct time periods related to data access (see Table 2 for some typical values of these times for various devices):

1. *Positioning time* is the amount of time required to move the read/write mechanism to the location of a block of data. In the case of a magnetic tape, this may involve moving to the next consecutive record or spinning all the way down to the other end of the tape. On a disk, it involves moving the read/write heads to the proper track. For a drum or a "fixed head" disk, positioning time is not a factor because there is always a read/write mechanism at every track.
2. *Latency* is the amount of time for a rotational storage device to attain the correct position for data access. For magnetic tape, this is essentially null, although one generally considers the tape "start-up" time as a latency time. For disks and drums, latency varies from 0 to the time of a complete rotation, depending on the location of the data.
3. *Transfer time* is the amount of time required to transfer a block of data to or from a storage device, once the positioning and latency have been completed. For tape, disk, and drum, the transfer time is reasonably small, but it is prudent to transfer an entire block at one time so as to avoid additional positioning and latency delays.

If a program is to access data sequentially, and the data are located on a secondary storage device, there is a delay for positioning and latency time, followed by a period when the data are transferred. Because the transfer rate of the secondary device is typically 5–50 times slower than that of the main storage, it is desirable to design a computer system so that the processor and main memory can carry out useful work both during the positioning and latency delays (when main storage is otherwise idle) and during the transfer period (when the main

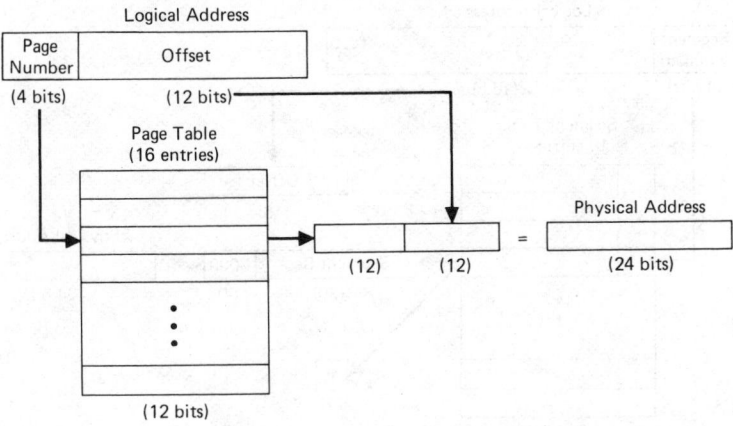

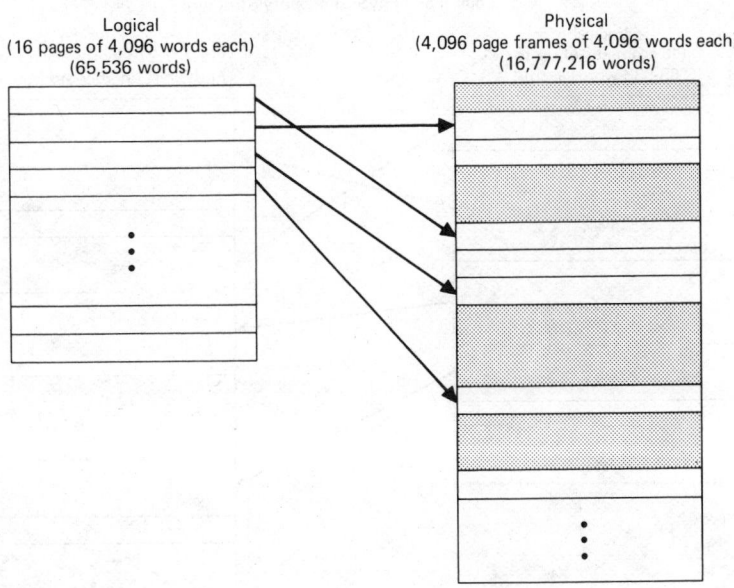

Fig. 3(b). Paged memory mapping (with sample values).

storage is only required 2–20% of the time). If a program is to access data in a nonsequential fashion, the latency and positioning delays become even more significant.

Architectural features such as interrupts and direct memory access I/O are designed to simplify the process of allowing the processor to do useful work while data are being transferred (see "Input/Output," below). Supervisory techniques such as multiprogramming (*q.v.*) have a similar objective; thus, architectural features which support multiprogramming are important to system performance.

An issue that is often overlooked in determining the initial configuration of a large system is achieving a balance between the system's complement of secondary storage devices and its main storage. For example, the path between main memory and a secondary device is usually called a *channel*. A channel will have a given transfer capacity, generally at least as high as the transfer speed of the secondary device to which it is connected. But a channel is largely idle during periods of positioning and latency, or when the storage device itself is not in active use. Thus, it is tempting to connect several secondary de-

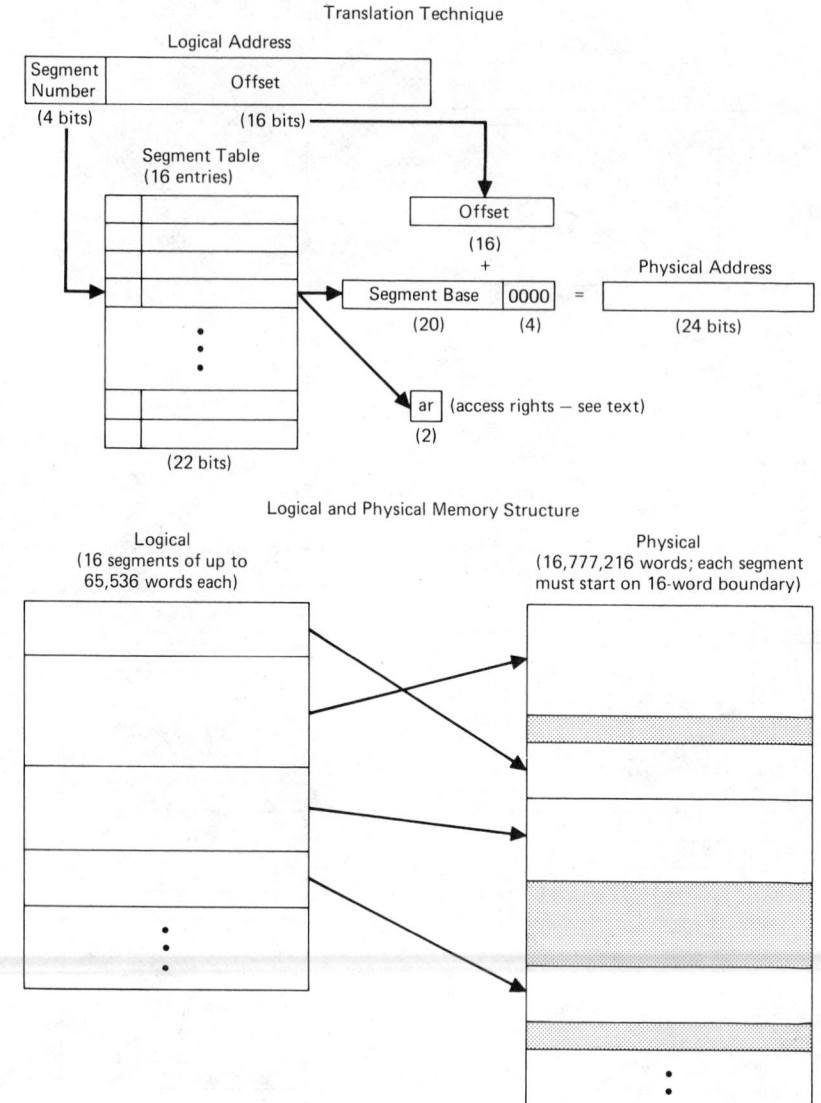

Fig. 3(c).   Segmented memory management (with sample values).

vices to the same channel on the theory that this will keep the channel busy. (This will also lower cost, since one need not provide a separate channel for each device.) Unfortunately, it also prevents transfer of data from two devices simultaneously. Consider, as a worst case, an attempt to copy data from one tape to another. If the tapes are on separate channels, they can each operate at maximum speed, one transferring data to main memory, the other transferring data out of main memory. If, however, the tape transports are located on the same channel, it is

necessary to read a block of data from one tape, then stop the tape while writing the block to the other. Due to the overhead of starting and stopping tapes, the net speed is less than half that of the two-channel case. (Similar, though more complex, situations arise when disks or drums are involved.)

Even in cases where assignment of channels to devices is well thought out, one can err by placement of the wrong data on the wrong secondary storage device. A typical mistake is to configure a system so that all pro-

Table 2. Data Access Comparison for Typical Devices

Storage Device	Positioning Time	Latency	Transfer Time
Main memory	0	0	0.5 μs
Magnetic drum or fixed head disk	0	5–50 ms	2–25 μs
Moving head disk	20–100 ms	10–50 ms	2–25 μs
Magnetic tape	0 sec–5 min	10 ms	2–25 μs

grams make frequent use of data located on the same secondary device. If one program is waiting for data from that device, and the others are simply waiting for their turn to request data from the same device, the benefits of multiprogramming are lost.

Virtual Memory and Memory Hierarchies. An increasingly popular concept in larger computer systems is that of *virtual memory* (*q.v.*). Fundamentally, the idea is to give the programmer the illusion of an infinite (or at least very large) main memory, even though only a modest amount of main memory is actually available. This is achieved by placing the contents of the large, virtual memory on an auxiliary memory device, and bringing parts of it into main memory, as required by the program, in a way that is transparent to the program. A minimal requirement for a virtual memory system is a large logical memory space; i.e., a large memory address size. Thus, virtual memory has been most prevalent on systems with word lengths (address sizes) larger than 16 bits.

Virtual memory is an excellent example of the subtle interplay between system and implementation architectures. Although the programmer with a virtual memory system can theoretically assume that a large amount of memory is available, seemingly minor changes in the data access pattern may have major ramifications on the amount of time required to execute programs. Thus, the programmer is driven to strive for *locality of reference,* in which consecutive references are made to objects that are physically adjacent, or nearly so; and to access multidimensional array data in a sequence corresponding to that used by the compiler for storing in memory. Conversely, the implementation of virtual memory calls for the architect to design hardware which "learns" (or makes good guesses at) the memory reference patterns of programs so that the data most frequently referenced will be kept in main memory. See Denning (1970) for more details.

A concept related to virtual memory is that of *hierarchical memory.* In its simplest form, this means that there is a hierarchy of memory types ranging from "large and slow" to "small and fast." The important idea, however, is to give the programmer access to only one type of logical memory (typically, "main" memory), with unseen implementation techniques making this memory appear both fast and plentiful. Caches (*q.v.*) and interleaving (see "Main Memory") are popular techniques for achieving a high apparent speed, and virtual memory techniques are used to achieve a large apparent size. In such an architecture, the registers may no longer be of concern to the programmer, who is given the view that all of main memory is fast. The real registers may be hidden from the system architecture or may be presented in the guise of distinguished, frequently used main memory locations for which there are special addressing modes.

The treatment of registers as though they were standard main memory cells has additional ramifications in terms of multiprogramming. One of the most significant overhead costs of sharing a processor among several activities is the "context switch" time—i.e., the time required to save the contents of the registers of one process and load up new values corresponding to another process. Although some designs have reduced this overhead by providing multiple sets of registers, the cost of registers and the potentially large number of active processes tend to make this a special case solution rather than a general approach.

Instead, the registers or "context" of a processor can be permanently assigned to a block of main memory associated with the program being executed. Early designs often used such a block for saving registers on a context switch, but the block was hidden from the program. Recent designs have taken an alternate approach: Hide the registers instead. To the software designer, there are no registers, just this "distinguished" block of main memory. Such an approach allows the implementor to consider a variety of cost-performance options, perhaps using different approaches in different models of a family. For example, a low-cost implementation can actually get by with few real registers, using main memory cells for functions traditionally associated with registers. This approach also yields a fast context switch and, as main memory technology permits faster and faster implementations, may have very reasonable performance characteristics. More expensive implementations can take successively more and more of these memory locations and copy them into real registers while a program is executing, saving them back in memory when a context switch is called for. The overhead of the context switch can be controlled by means of a "cache" form of register file which keeps track of register use between context switches and saves only those registers whose values have been modified. Studies have shown that, between context switches, many processes modify only a few registers.

Recent cost trends in computing have made it more economical to save programming effort at the expense of additional memory and circuitry. Hierarchical and virtual memory systems, with memory management hidden from the software designer, should therefore continue to be an architectural trend. For similar reasons, elimination of registers from the software architecture should be encountered in newer designs.

Processing. The processing unit of a computer system consists of two parts—the control unit, which governs the operation of the system, and the arithmetic-logic unit (ALU), which carries out the computational and processing functions. In addition to the register set, key issues in processing unit architecture are the instruction set and the extent of parallelism.

Instruction Set. An instruction tends to occupy one or more words of storage and its purpose is to specify an operation to be performed by the processor. An instruction (Fig. 4) consists of an operation code, which indicates the general nature of the function to be performed; possibly one or more flags, denoting special modes of operation; and possibly one or more addresses, which specify the operands or data to be operated upon. An instruction format is usually characterized by the number of such operand specifiers, and although a given processor will usually support several instruction formats, one will tend to predominate. Most common today are the "one-address" and "two-address" instruction formats.

By way of comparison, consider a typical instruction, "integer add," which requires three operands: Two integer numbers to be added, and one integer result. With a three-address format, all three operands would be specified directly. With a two-address format, one of the three would be implicit—typically, a register or the top of a stack. A one-address format would have two implicit operands, and so forth.

An issue of considerable debate among computer architects is which form of instruction has the highest "bit efficiency"—that is, which form allows "typical" programs to be written with the fewest bits. As a general rule, a format calling for more addresses requires more bits per instruction, but needs fewer instructions to perform a computation. An "ideal" instruction set would support several formats. (A frequently ignored aspect of this debate is that higher bit efficiency may yield higher implementation costs. The real debate should be over the net cost of various instruction formats.)

Operand addressing is usually more complex than is implied above. The field of an instruction that identifies an operand may contain several subfields, and may require a significant amount of computation just to determine the location of the operand. The various ways of identifying an operand are called *addressing modes*. A representative set of addressing modes is as follows.

Operand Specifier Format
(in address field of instruction)

type	designator

Type	Operand Class	Designator Interpretation
0	Immediate	Operand is designator itself
1	Direct	Designator is address of operand
2	Indirect	Designator is address of memory cell containing address of operand
3	Register	Designator indicates a register containing the operand

Many other operand formats have been used. The instruction set reference manual of any computer system will provide details on the specific approach used therein. (See also the articles in this encyclopedia on ADDRESSING and on specific systems such as the DEC PDP and the UNIVAC 1100 series.)

In addition to the format of a computer's instructions, the architect must consider their semantics—i.e., what functions they perform. Traditionally, instruction sets have been designed on the basis of the register set, word length, technology characteristics, and chance. The functions performed have been quite simple, such as controlling the sequence of instruction execution, shifting data, adding numbers, and comparing values. Among the first "higher-level" features found in instruction sets were instructions to perform floating point calculations. Recent trends have been based on empirical studies of what programs actually do. Such studies have led to direct instruction set support for such "high-level" functions as procedure calling and list searching, as well as focusing attention on the kinds of activities most frequently performed by programs, such as variable assignment.

Tagged Architectures. In the Von Neumann type of instruction set described above, there is no distinction made in storage between instructions and data, and between different types of data. That is, it would be possible to perform an addition on a bit pattern representing an

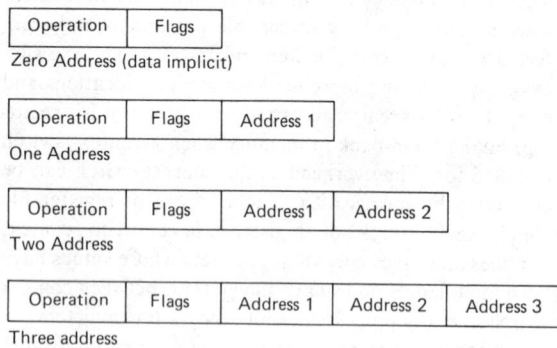

Fig. 4. Typical instruction formats.

instruction and, although the results might be meaningless, the computer would not detect any problem. Such cases are the cause of numerous programming errors; thus some have proposed *tagged architecture*—in which each memory word contains a tag field describing the nature of its contents. This would enable detection of such errors, and also has ramifications on instruction set design. Because the type of data is implied by the word containing the data, it is no longer necessary to have separate instructions for each data type supported by the machine. Instead of "integer add," "floating point add," and "decimal add," a tagged architecture permits use of a single, "generic" instruction: "add," with the tag fields indicating the specific type of addition to be performed.

Tagged architectures are a controversial subject in practice because of concerns about storage space efficiency, implementation cost, and the semantics of generic instructions when several different data types are used in the same instruction. See Feustel (1973) for a proponent's views on this subject.

Microprogramming and Writable Control Storage. One of the most popular techniques for implementation of processing units is *microprogramming* (*q.v.*). In this technique, each instruction can be thought of as a "subroutine call" to a program written in a lower-level language, whose domain includes the data paths and registers of the hardware. A major advantage of microprogramming is that hardware design errors can be corrected by simply revising the microprograms instead of changing the wiring. This becomes a particularly important advantage in today's world, where the entire processing function may be imbedded in a silicon chip, and a "wiring change" is a prohibitively expensive process. Moreover, the use of microprogramming allows the development of relatively complex instructions without a substantial increase in processing unit complexity; instead, the amount of storage for microprograms is increased. While such storage is expensive, it is composed of standard memory devices whose regular structure makes them relatively simple to design and build.

Normally, microprograms are stored in a "read-only" memory device (ROM), both to reduce cost and to avoid loss of information during a loss of power. With *writable control store* (WCS) a part of the microcode storage is composed of writable memory. This allows a general-purpose computer to be tailored to the requirements of a specific application by introduction of new instructions. The technique has achieved widespread use in research environments, but the complexities of software support (designing compilers which can make use of the new instructions, for example) have restricted commercial use to applications which can benefit significantly from the technique. The Burroughs B1800, for example, uses writable control store to permit tailoring of the instruction set to different application areas at different times.

Parallelism. The speed with which instructions can be processed is determined by two factors: How fast the circuitry can perform a single instruction and how many instructions can be performed in parallel. Fundamental circuit speed is largely determined by system cost, as limited by the available circuit technology (which, today, is often limited by the fundamental laws of physics). Thus, to achieve the speed of operation desired in high-performance systems, efforts are made to achieve high degrees of parallelism. Most of the techniques used to exploit parallelism belong to the implementation architecture realm, but certain of these have significant impact on software design. Flynn (1966) has categorized parallel architectures according to the scheme outlined in Table 3.

For each approach to parallelism, the programming techniques may be substantially different. In some architectures, such as that of the CDC Cyber (an MISD approach), the programmer may ignore the issues of parallelism, although the program will achieve higher performance if advantage is taken of it. In others, such as the ILLIAC IV (an SIMD design), the assembly language programmer or compiler designer must be aware of the parallelism in order for the program to operate correctly.

One highly popular technique of parallelism is known as *pipelining* (*q.v.*). Pipelining is an MISD approach in which instructions are executed in assembly line fashion: Consecutive instructions are operated upon in sequence, but with several being initiated before the first is complete. Many commercially available systems use this approach or some variation thereof.

A more dramatic impact on software architecture is exhibited by the *dataflow* (*q.v.*) approach. A major departure from the classical Von Neumann design, dataflow requires that the program take the form of a directed graph, with each instruction forming a node. The result of each instruction is distributed to all other instructions which require it on the theory that each of the recipients can be executed in parallel. The primary advantage of data flow is its high degree of potential parallelism, and its primary drawback is its low memory efficiency (because many copies are made of each result).

A higher-level form of parallelism is achieved by multiprocessor and multicomputer systems. Essentially, several activities are carried out simultaneously, with resources shared as required.

Input-Output and Communication

Fundamental Issues. The remaining major architectural aspects of a computer system are related to com-

Table 3.   Flynn's Categories of Parallelism

Symbol	Definition	Instruction Streams	Data Streams	Examples
SISD	Single-instruction stream, single-data stream (traditional computer design with little parallelism)	1	1	IBM 360/370 PDP 11
SIMD	Single-instruction stream, multiple-data stream (one instruction sequence, with each instruction affecting many data items simultaneously)	1	Many	ILLIAC IV
MISD	Multiple-instruction stream, single-data stream (several independent instruction sequences, all acting on the same data)	Many	1	CDC Cyber and STAR TI ASC Cray-1
MIMD	Multiple-instruction stream, multiple-data stream (several independent instruction sequences, each acting on a separate data stream)	Many	Many	Dataflow Univac 1108MP

municating between the computer and the "outside" world. A typical computer system will be surrounded by an array of devices such as terminals, printers, and plotters, which are collectively called its *input/output* (*I/O*) devices. The function of such devices is to transmit data between the computer and its users, with appropriate transformations along the way. For example, a printer will transform bits and bytes into control signals for a mechanical printing mechanism; a video terminal will translate keystrokes into bytes of data, and then back into dots on a cathode ray tube.

I/O devices share certain characteristics with auxiliary storage devices; thus, both tend to be handled in similar ways architecturally. These devices have relatively low access speed and are usually capable of operating more or less independently from the processing unit. Thus, a complex, "loosely coupled" connection to the processor and main memory is required. Because of their relatively low speed, it is desirable to keep these devices in continuous operation, so that their maximum performance potential can be realized. Low speed and independent operation make it attractive to allow several devices to operate simultaneously. The fundamental issues of I/O architecture relate to the means of transferring data between these devices and main memory, and to the process of coordinating and synchronizing multiple devices, with the goal of obtaining maximum performance from each.

Communication Paths. There are two common approaches for connecting a device to the processor and main memory—the *channel* and the *bus*. In its simplest form, a channel is a straightforward electronic path between a computer and one or more peripheral devices.

(Actually, the device is usually attached to a controller which, in turn, connects to a channel.) If more than one device is required, each may be connected to a different channel, although it is normal to share each channel among several devices. Simple shared channels permit only one device to transmit data at a time, whereas *multiplexer channels* allow interleaved data transfers from several devices. A *byte* multiplexer channel, used for slower I/O devices, transmits one byte of data at a time from a device. A *block* multiplexer channel, used for higher-performance devices (e.g., auxiliary storage), interleaves data in large blocks.

A *bus* is a sort of shared or multiplexed path which permits many (perhaps up to 256) devices to transmit data at the same time. The overhead of multiplexing the bus between devices tends to give it a lower "peak" performance than a channel with comparable implementation cost, but the ability to multiplex a large number of devices allows a lower net cost for systems with many peripherals.

Low-cost systems are often designed so that data goes from a peripheral to a register, and then to main memory (or vice versa). This simplifies the interface to main memory, as it need only connect directly to the processor and registers. A preferred approach from a performance standpoint is to connect the peripherals directly to memory, so that the overhead of going through registers can be eliminated. This is a classic tradeoff between performance and cost, but recent designs using advanced bus concepts have reduced the cost of the direct-to-memory approach.

There are many channel and bus designs, and there are fundamental architectural tradeoffs between cost, performance, and number of devices supported. The architect must have a thorough understanding of the system's application and its use of peripherals in order to design a suitable scheme.

Control. The most straightforward approach to controlling the transmission of data between computers and peripherals is *program controlled I/O.* Under such a scheme, the computer will have an instruction whereby it commands the device to accept a small amount of data (typically one word or byte) for display or storage (output), or to transmit a small unit of data to the processor (input). The instruction may wait for the data transmission to occur, or may simply initiate the activity, with subsequent "test" instructions required to determine when transmission is complete. Transmission usually occurs between the device and some processor register, although, in some designs, a main memory cell may be specified. Certain systems permit the processor to initiate activity on several devices, with subsequent testing to determine when each has finished. However, in the absence of further architectural support, it is difficult (or even impossible) for the processor to be programmed in such a way that it both performs useful work while the devices are busy, and keeps them in continuous operation.

The program controlled scheme tends to have limited value in cases where the peripheral device has a relatively high data transfer rate. This is due to the high overhead of having the processor execute a transmission command, a completion test, and perhaps a transfer between register and main memory for each word or byte of data transferred. *Direct memory access* (*DMA*) is a name used to describe a technique incorporating specific concepts of both control and communication. It not only allows transmission directly between peripherals and memory, as the name implies; but, as commonly defined, DMA eliminates the high processor control overhead described above. With the DMA technique, the processor will request transfer of a large block of data, with the "completion" notification coming only when the entire block has been moved. This requires more capability in the device controller and/or in the channel or bus interface to main memory. Essentially, the channel or device controller must have an independent capability to count the number of items transmitted and keep track of where they go in memory, and the interface must permit the device to send data directly to main memory rather than to the processor. But the advantage in lowering processor overhead is substantial with higher-speed devices.

Advanced DMA systems allow *chaining* and other approaches which permit multiple blocks of data to be transmitted to different areas of main memory with a single command from the processor.

Memory mapped I/O is a more recent concept in which the control between processor and peripheral is achieved, not by special instructions, but by having the processor write to certain reserved cells in its virtual memory space. These reserved cells are called *control words,* and are sometimes located within the device controller rather than physical memory. A control word may actually be a word of main physical memory, but need actually be nothing more than a set of signals used to direct the actions of a device controller. The act of writing into a control word causes the address of the given virtual memory word to be sent out across the memory bus. Each controller connected to this bus is designed to observe such memory addresses and to intercept those which correspond to its control words. The intercepting controller then reads the word of data being "written," treats it as a set of control signals, and acts accordingly. In some cases, the controller will contain a small memory in which it stores the values of these signals for later reference.

The memory mapped approach simplifies the control interface between processor and device: There are no special control lines or signals, only designated virtual addresses. The main drawbacks of the approach are: (1) it puts "holes" in the address space—i.e., sections of the address space cannot really be used as memory cells; (2) it complicates cacheing and virtualization. Thus, memory mapped I/O is most suitable in lower-cost systems having a "common" or "universal" bus connecting the processor to main memory as well as to the various peripherals. This approach was popularized on the DEC PDP-11 (Eckhouse, 1975) and is now found in many smaller systems.

Interrupts. An interrupt is a means of permitting a peripheral device to notify a processor that a data transfer has completed. This allows the processor to perform other work in the meantime, yet service the device immediately upon its completion. I/O interrupts can be used with any of the control or communication path schemes described above.

Fundamentally, the interrupt is a signal which notifies the processor that some external event has occurred. While interrupts are used in many contexts (*see* INTERRUPT), we focus here on their use in I/O applications. Typically, the interrupt signal is generated by an I/O device that has completed its most recent request or requires some other service. In response to the interrupt signal, a processor will usually stop its current activity and attend to the device. In the simplest schemes, all devices share the same interrupt and the processor must *poll* all devices to determine which has generated the interrupt. More elaborate schemes allow the processor to determine immediately which device caused the interrupt, and so-called *vectored* or *priority interrupt* schemes arrange it so that, if two devices interrupt at the same time, the "more important" device is the first attended to by the processor.

Interrupts are a valuable architectural feature, but they tend to cause numerous problems as well. A processor may inadvertently receive an interrupt from a device which the software is not prepared to handle, or at a time when it was not expected. A faulty device may send interrupts continuously, deluging the system with interrupt response activity and blocking other devices from service. Elaborate software may be required to handle such cases correctly, and in some systems such situations may result in uncorrectable hardware or software faults ("hangups"). As a result of many years of experience with interrupts, architects have begun to refine and "civilize" the interrupt systems of computers. For example, it is now usually possible for the software to mask or block interrupts, in cases where a software module requires higher priority than an external device, or where some particular device's interrupts are to be ignored. A very promising concept is to model interrupts after more general synchronization mechanisms, such as messages or semaphores (*q.v.*). This is an excellent example of how a technique developed to solve a software problem has impacted computer architecture in more fundamental ways.

Publications. Certain professional publications and organizations are concerned with the advancement of computer architecture. The Association for Computing Machinery has a special interest group on computer architecture (SIGARCH) which publishes a newsletter (*Computer Architecture News* or *CAN*) several times a year. Strongly related issues are covered in *Operating Systems Review,* the newsletter of the special interest group on operating systems (SIGOPS). Another special interest group focuses on microprogramming (SIGMICRO). The IEEE Computer Society has several publications relating to computer architecture and design. Most important are the monthly *Computer* and *IEEE Transactions on Computers.* The IEEE and SIGARCH sponsor an annual symposium on computer architecture, usually held in the spring, the proceedings of which are available from the IEEE Publications department, and as a special issue of *Computer Architecture News.* SIGMICRO sponsors an annual microprogramming symposium in the fall, the proceedings of which are available from ACM or as a special issue of the SIGMICRO newsletter.

REFERENCES

1962. Buchholz, Werner. *Planning a Computer System—Project Stretch.* New York: McGraw-Hill.

1966. Flynn, Michael J. "Very High-Speed Computing Systems," *Proc. IEEE* **54:** 1901–1909 (December).

1966. IBM. *System/360 Principles of Operation* (Form A22-6821-5). Poughkeepsie, NY: IBM Systems Development Division.

1970. Denning, Peter J. "Virtual Memory," *ACM Computing Surveys* **2,** *No. 3:* 153–190 (September).

1970. Foster, Caxton C. *Computer Architecture.* New York: Van Nostrand Reinhold.

1970. Thornton, J. E. *Design of a Computer—The Control Data 6600.* Glenview, IL: Scott, Forsman, and Co.

1971. Denning, Peter J. "Third Generation Computer Systems," *ACM Computing Surveys* **3,** *No. 4:* 175–216 (December).

1973. Feustel, E. A. "On the Advantages of Tagged Architecture," *IEEE Transactions on Computers* (July), pp. 644–656.

1975. Eckhouse, Richard H. *Minicomputer Systems: Organization and Programming (PDP-11).* Englewood Cliffs, NJ: Prentice-Hall.

1975. Patil, S. (Ed.). "Computer Systems Architecture," Special Issue: *ACM Computing Surveys* **7,** *No. 4* (December).

1976. Reddi, S. S. and Feustel, E. A. "A Conceptual Framework for Computer Architecture," *ACM Computing Surveys* **8,** *No. 2:* 277–300 (June).

1977. Feng, T. (Ed.). "Parallel Processors and Processing," Special issue: *ACM Computing Surveys* **9,** *No. 1* (March).

1978. Myers, Glenford J. *Advances in Computer Architecture.* New York: Wiley.

1980. Baer, J-L. *Computer Systems Architecture.* Potomac, MD: Computer Science Press.

1982. Siewiorek, D. P., Bell, C. G., and Newell, A. *Computer Structures: Principles and Examples.* New York: McGraw-Hill.

D. J. FRAILEY

COMPUTER ART

For articles on related subjects *see* ARTS APPLICATIONS; COMPUTER GRAPHICS; and IMAGE PROCESSING.

Efforts to create art with analog machines date back to the 1950s. However, it was not until January 1965 that the first exhibition of digital computer graphics was arranged by three mathematicians: Frieder Nake and George Nees, both Germans, and an American, A. Michael Noll. Their goal (Franke, 1971) was to create visually pleasing images, not merely graphics representing data. This exhibition was held at the Studio Gallery of the University of Stuttgart. Several shows followed the initial one in Germany, including one in New York City at the Howard Wise Gallery. Computer art became an international movement (Reichardt, 1971) practiced in Britain, Germany, Italy, Austria, Japan, Canada, and the U.S.

Non-utilitarian use of the machine was practiced in those countries which were technologically developed. An image reminiscent of this period is a graphic by Guenther Tetz (Fig. 1) created at the University of Illinois at Chi-

Fig. 1. Untitled image by Guenther Tetz, 1979.

cago Circle on the PDP-11/45-Vector General Graphic System. The event that made the world really take note of computer art was "Cybernetic Serendipity" (Reichardt, 1968), an exhibition held at the Institute of Contemporary Arts in London. The catalog for the show was a special issue of *Studio International* magazine and was subsequently published as the first book of art dealing with the computer and creativity. "Cybernetic Serendipity" brought together individuals who had been working in isolation and was a source of inspiration for others to begin working in this area. Artists from France, Spain, and Holland joined in making computer-aided art. They either learned to use the computer themselves or worked with computer experts. In 1970, works created with the aid of the computer were hung alongside traditionally made artworks at the Venice Biennial. Today, computer art hangs in permanent museum collections, corporate offices, and private homes. It is judged in competitions, along with traditional art, on its artistic merits, not on the tools that aided in its creation.

Developments in hardware have brought about changes in computer art. Towards the end of the 1960s, many artists began to use cathode ray tubes to visualize their work. This made it possible for the artist to work in a more traditional way, since artistic decisions are often made during the creation of a work. The interactive system allows the artist to see immediately his or her work and to modify it. With the development of color graphics terminals, the artist may now see images displayed in color. On one system, it is possible to choose from over a quarter-million different colors. Numerical values are assigned to each color in the spectrum and also to black and white. The consistency of the machine, moreover, makes it superior to mixing colors with the traditional artist's palette, since commercial artist's pigments sold under the same name can vary widely. With higher resolution terminals, the appearance of lines has changed as well. Today, the once jagged look is gone and it is difficult to differentiate between hand-drawn and machine-drawn lines.

Conventionally, the tools of the artist define the type of work that is produced. The painter, for example, uses brushes and paint, the photographer uses a camera, and so on. The computer artist, on the other hand, finds that the machine is multifaceted. Not only is it a high-powered design tool, but its output devices make it possible for the artist to express a particular idea in various media: Drawings may be produced with a vector or raster plotter; sculptures may be milled with computer-driven milling machines; paintings may be painted with computer-driven airbrushes; video, frames of film animations, and photographs may be taken directly off the cathode ray tube; graphics are made possible by a photo transfer process of computer images; and environmental art can be created where the computer senses and accordingly activates devices in a given space.

The advantages of using the computer in each medium differ. Drawings, for example, are made both as preliminary sketches for other work and as art objects themselves. Frequently, a random number generator is used at the drawing stage (Mezei, 1971). This yields two specific effects: (1) it is apt to produce variations that the artists would not ordinarily think of on their own, and (2) in a short amount of time, artists have a good many sketches from which they can choose to work or to use as finished pieces. The untitled lithograph (Fig. 2) by Roger Vilder, a Canadian artist, is a good example of producing multiple variations.

Paintings can be produced with computers starting from the preliminary drawings up to the final execution on canvas. The artist first utilizes the machine as a

Fig. 2. Untitled lithograph by Roger Vilder, 1976.

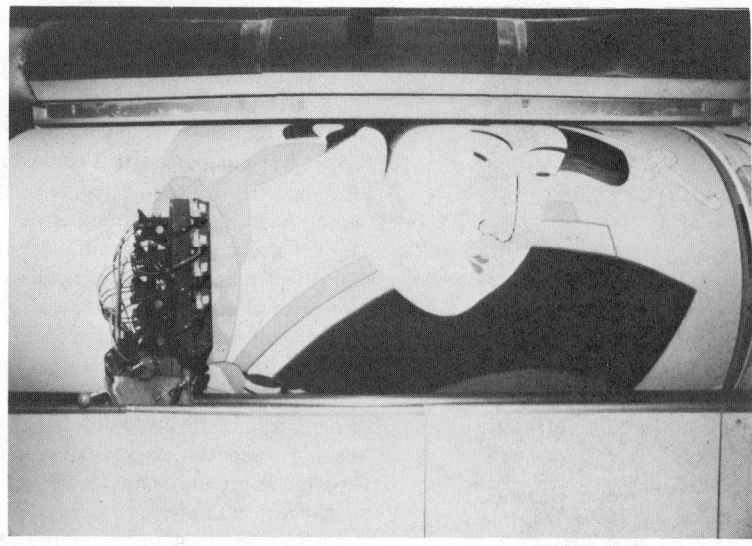

Fig. 3. Computer-controlled painting device. (Photograph courtesy of Minnesota Mining and Manufacturing Company.)

sketchpad, creating the design to be painted. This design may then, for example, be drawn by the machine onto 35 mm film by an electron beam gun through colored filters. The design on the slide is input by means of a scanning device to another computer which, in turn, controls airbrushes and paint to produce the final product. Wall-sized murals are being produced by the 3M Company of St. Paul, MN with just such a machine (Fig. 3).

Sculpture can also be a fully automated process. The use of the computer in this medium is especially impressive. The machine allows the sculptor to envision a piece of work at a given location from any perspective before it is completed and installed. This permits the artist to make changes before investing time, energy, and cost of materials on a project that might not succeed. The 6-ft-high wood and plaster sculpture in Fig. 4 would not have been produced without the aid of the computer. Not only was it designed on the machine, but also a plotter produced the template for its formation. The fact that the machine mills with exact precision extends the concept of what can be created as well as what materials can be employed. Highly detailed works can now be sculptured with computer-controlled milling machines having five degrees of freedom. On these output devices, the drill bit not only moves back and forth and up and down, but is able to make undercuts as well. The milling machine relieves artists of the physical demands of creation and allows them to concentrate on the exploration of ideas.

The production of film animation and graphics presents difficulties which the computer alleviates. Customarily, animation is extremely expensive to create, since each frame must be drawn by hand. The artist using the computer allows the machine to draw the intermediate pictures, thus saving both time and expense. Images can be produced on color displays and filmed directly off the scope. A major problem in creating graphics is the production of color separations. In serigraphy, for example, each color must be screened separately. An inherent quality of computers which display colored images is that they automatically color-separate each picture. To display each colored design, the computer must calculate what percentage of each of three colors plus black and white is used to create the desired picture. Thus, for the animator and the graphic artist the computer can save great amounts of time.

In creating environmental works, the computer is used to control devices which are part of the art object itself. The cybernetic sculpture, "Blue Wazoo" (1975–1976), by Jim Pallas, is an example of an environmental artwork. The "Blue Wazoo" (Fig. 5) is primarily a welded steel structure containing plastic shapes, circuitry, wires, light-emitting diodes (LED), solenoids, a motor, cloth, horsehair, a feather, and a bead. The sculpture is itself an information processing device which senses light and sound and responds with a behavior repertoire of various LED patterns, movements, inflations, deflations, whirrs, clicks, and jiggles. It is in the collection of the Allan Stone Gallery in New York.

The manner in which traditional artists employ their tools creates individual styles. We often recognize artists by their styles or the styles they imitate. There is, however, no unique style which typifies works of art as "com-

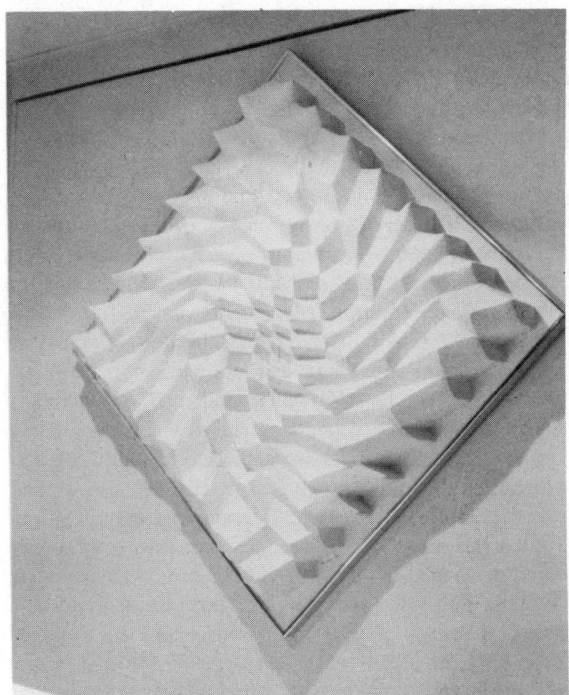

Fig. 4. Untitled sculpture by Ruth Leavitt. Wood and plaster, 6′ × 6′, 1980, private collection.

Fig. 5. "The Blue Wazoo" by Jim Pallas. (Photograph Courtesy of the Allan Stone Gallery, New York.)

puter art" (Leavitt, 1976). The statement an artist makes in his or her work is a function of the artist and the program, not the artist and the computer. Rather than identifying a style as having originated from a particular artist, in computer-aided art we can identify a style of work as having been created with a particular program. The program EXPLOR by Kenneth Knowlton exemplifies this. Artwork created with the EXPLOR program, although produced by different people at different locations, looks very similar because the uniqueness of the program causes it to define its own style. All computer art programs use one or more techniques such as rotation, scaling, windowing, zooming, transformations, and picture processing, but each uses these techniques in such a way as to be stylistically identifiable. Whether the artist approaches the work in a random or deterministic manner, the program still is the overriding factor regarding style.

An artist has the option of participating in the creation of the program to be used, as well as to explore the possibilities that exist within that particular program. This allows artists to determine their own styles. A unique feature of using the computer is that the artist can create an environment that does not exist in the real world. This permits the artist to explore ideas never before thought possible. In the past, artists created work

from the world around them. They translated the world in either figurative or abstract terms, but in either case, this was their sense of reality. Computer artists can create their own sense of reality, allowing them to transcend the role of the traditional artist.

REFERENCES

1968. Reichardt, Jasia. *"Cybernetic Serendipity"—The Computer and the Arts.* New York: Praeger.
1971. Franke, Herbert W. *Computer Graphics, Computer Art.* New York: Phaidon.
1971. Reichardt, Jasia. *The Computer in Art.* New York: Van Nostrand Reinhold.
1971. Mezei, Leslie. "Randomness in Computer Graphics," in Reichardt, Jasia (Ed.), *Cybernetics, Art and Ideas.* New York: New York Graphic Society.

1976. Leavitt, Ruth. *Artist and Computer*. New York: Harmony Books.

R. Leavitt

COMPUTER-ASSISTED INSTRUCTION (CAI)

For articles on related subjects *see* Computer-Assisted Learning and Teaching; and Computer-Managed Instruction.

Computer-assisted instruction (CAI) refers to the use of computers to present drills, practice exercises, and tutorial sequences to the student, and perhaps to engage the student in a dialog about the substance of the instruction. A CAI (tutorial) dialog is achieved between computer program and student when the responses derived from the program are highly responsive to the questions, answers, and directives given by the student, while at the same time the dialog advances the goals and means established by the author of the curriculum materials.

CAI is only one part of computer assistance in the processes of learning and teaching. It has proved successful where the goals of instruction are clearly defined, achievement of those goals is highly valued by the organization providing instruction, the substance of instruction is suited to automated delivery, and the student is lacking important skills, background, or motivation for self-instruction via less expensive media. Research studies tend to show advantages for CAI in terms of shorter learning times and improved performance. Inhibitors to operational use include high costs of delivery systems and curriculum development, conflicts between individualized instruction and current educational practices, and commitment of most of the computing resources available in schools to instructional use for education about computers. A comprehensive analysis of CAI effectiveness, along with other media for instruction, is given by Jamison, Suppes, and Wells (1974).

Major Demonstration Projects. A group of engineers and educators in the Computer-based Education Research Laboratory at the University of Illinois, Urbana, designed a computing system (PLATO) especially for effective and efficient teaching. It is a large system which provides instructional computing to about 1,000 simultaneous users throughout the University and also a number of other colleges and schools in Illinois. The design included notable advances in the technology for display and communications. The PLATO system is now marketed commercially by Control Data Corporation.

Stanford University operated a CAI system to distribute instructional computing to a number of centers throughout the country. A large-scale service operation using long-distance telephone communications, clusters of terminals, and some stand-alone computer systems, the remote centers were usually associated with elementary school demonstration projects and special education institutions. The service operation was conducted in parallel with an extensive program of research and development at the Institute for Mathematical Studies in the Social Sciences, Stanford University. Curriculum materials were prepared for young children (elementary school math and reading), learners with special difficulties (for example, the deaf), and certain university courses (especially second-language learning and logic). Some of these materials are marketed by the Computer Curriculum Corporation.

TICCIT (Time-shared, Interactive, Computer-Controlled Informational Television) is a name given to systems developed by the Mitre Corporation in McLean, Virginia and now marketed by Hazeltine Corporation. The first version of an instructional system was designed especially for use in a small college. It was a medium-sized computer system with video technology to obtain low-cost operation with about 100 simultaneous users. The hardware and software design was coordinated with the development of instructional materials, carefully prepared according to rules of effective instruction by instructional design teams at Brigham Young University in Utah, to provide basic remedial instruction in mathematical and language skills at small colleges.

The list of schools and colleges pursuing interesting development programs is very long. One of the long-standing operations combining development and applications is in the Philadelphia public schools. Activities there, under the direction of Sylvia Charp, include a wide range of CAI along with many other uses of computing in the instructional program.

Sample of Tutorial Dialog. Fig. 1 is an example of CAI taken from a student learning exercise in gathering information and making decisions. As a demonstration, it requires no specific content knowledge; the application of this computer teaching strategy is common in physics, chemistry, biology, and medical diagnosis where knowledge of the subject is essential to success in the exercise. The computer program guides the student in the exploration of a tree of possibilities, some of which lead to the solution of a simulated problem through reports, laboratory tests, and direct interrogation.

Areas of Application. CAI materials have been prepared for many subjects, from accounting to zoology, and from preschool through adult education. One representation of the available materials is provided by Wang

James Smith was found unconscious under suspicious circumstances. You are the Scotland Yard Inspector. Proceed with your investigation.

WHO ARE THE SUSPECTS?

The wife, brother and partner presently are considered the suspects.

WHAT IS THE MEDICAL REPORT?

The victim is in a coma. He has wounds on his head and symptoms of poisoning are evident.

GIVE ME THE CONSTABLE'S REPORT.

A glass was found next to the victim's bed, and a bottle labeled poison in the closet. The window has a bullet hole in it. A bloody pipe wrench was found in the shed.

I WANT TO INTERROGATE THE WIFE.

I advise you request the lab tests first.

LAB TESTS

This is the lab.
What is it you want?

WHAT DO YOU FIND ON THE GLASS?

This is the lab.
Fingerprints found which match those of the wife.

MEDICAL REPORT

No change in the condition of the victim.

ANY NEW SUSPECTS?

No new suspects.

The program recognizes "suspects" and provides the stored response.

"medical" is recognized.

"constable" is recognized.

The program recognizes "interrogate" but will not permit exploration of that branch until another one has been fully explored.

After the wife has been interrogated this branch of the program will release more incriminating information.

"medical" is recognized a second time.

The program includes a "stack" of replies for some directives so that on subsequent requests for information a fresh reply is given.

Fig. 1. Sample of CAI learning exercise (excerpted from a Bolt Beranek and Newman program).

(1979). Many more materials can be found in selected disciplinary areas by consulting teaching publications or professional committees associated with mathematics, physics, chemistry, biology, geography, political science, history, business, engineering, law, and medicine, among others.

Prospects for Wider Use. CAI has had many successes in military and industrial training, where the objectives are clear and a modest percentage advantage in delivery cost and trainee time adds up to considerable savings for the organization. Effective automation of training is essential in areas where new job requirements, employee turnover, and decreasing skills among those entering the workforce combine to force costs up.

Adoptions of CAI by educational institutions are not so common. Even where costs of instruction via computers have been shown to be lower, institutions have difficulty shifting dollars from people to machines, adjusting schedules and rules to realize the benefits of individualized instruction, and convincing students that technology can do the job on its own. Nevertheless, some schools and colleges regularly employ CAI for second language instruction, practice of basic skills in writing, remediation in mathematics and sciences, or preparation for laboratory exercises. That early and optimistic promises for CAI have not been realized does not surprise those who have labored on development of computer-based learning materials. Producing quality curriculum takes a long time and an expert support staff, at least as much as production of a textbook and film on the subject.

The prospects are good for broader use of CAI in education. Improving technologies are increasing the capabilities of computer systems for effective delivery of instruction (seen mostly in characteristics of the display) and bringing down the price of processors and memory. Videodiscs provide a low-cost, color, image storage medium under computer control, and animated graphics are practical on inexpensive color displays. Microprocessors and memory are packaged in personal computers which cost about the same as a fancy, portable, electric typewriter. Control of images and ease of access make qualitative differences in the use of computers in teaching and learning.

The locus of decisions about CAI in education is shifting from institutions to individuals. Parents are taking their children to CDC Learning Centers for automated tutoring to improve basic skills. Students and families are purchasing home computers to provide learning activities along with entertainment.

The installed base of popular microcomputers now provides a market for learning materials which is large enough to justify investments by educational publishers. However, the improvements in hardware technology aren't matched by computer software and learning materials. The application of artificial intelligence techniques to tutorial CAI (e.g., for training trouble shooting skills) holds some promise for considerable increase in flexibility and effectiveness of computer delivery with a wide range of learners. However, costs for curriculum development remain high. The field still is waiting for a breakthrough in software and materials development that may be a long time coming.

REFERENCES

1974. Jamison, Dean; Suppes, Patrick; and Wells, Stuart. "The Effectiveness of Alternative Instructional Media: A Survey." *Review of Educational Research* (AERA) **44,** *No. 1:* 1–67.
1979. Wang, Anastasia C. (Ed.). *Index to Computer Based Learning.* Instructional Media Center, University of Wisconsin, Milwaukee.

K. L. ZINN

COMPUTER-ASSISTED LEARNING AND TEACHING

For articles on related subjects *see* AUTHORING LANGUAGES AND SYSTEMS; COMPUTER-ASSISTED INSTRUCTION; COMPUTER-MANAGED INSTRUCTION; and NETWORKS FOR INSTRUCTION.

The impact of computers on teaching and learning activities at all levels of education is considerable and the extent of use is increasing rapidly. Current uses in postsecondary education are quite varied. A medical student practices diagnosis and prescription on a wide variety of hypothetical patients simulated by computer programs. A senior engineering student using computer assistance solves problems in road design which ten years ago were not approached until after two years of experience on the job. A sophomore in computer science develops a program to help a professor of chemistry evaluate the effectiveness of questions on a multiple-choice quiz. A freshman in general psychology directs a computer-based information system to assemble a complete bibliography on the relation between achievement motivation and college grades, which is as current as the journals received by his or her professor. A laboratory technician tests him/herself on newly acquired skills, using a terminal on a hospital information system.

Computing is also quite visible in education outside colleges and universities. A high school science student applies wildlife management practices to a computer simulation of the American bison herds that were slaughtered in the 1800s. An English literature student programs a computer to generate poetry. A child in the fifth grade explores mathematics by writing computer programs that draw spirals or solve mazes. A second grader practices spelling or addition problems "spoken" by a computer; the computer checks the answers that the student enters on the keyboard. In some experimental systems, the student simply speaks the answer to be "recognized" by the computer. A high school dropout improves language skills using a computer program made available on a community cable television system.

When the computer system is appropriate for educational uses and the programs are properly written, the learners should find the assistance to be: responsive to their needs; patient and not punitive while they learn; accurate in assessment of answers and problem solutions; individualized in a useful way; realistic in the presentation of training or testing situations; and helpful with many information processing tasks. Teachers find computer assistance valuable for keeping accurate records, summarizing data, projecting student-learning difficulties, assembling individualized tests, and retrieving information about films or other learning resources. Authors of textbooks and other learning materials use computers to draw figures, to animate motion picture sequences, or to keep track of the introduction and frequency of occurrence of concepts throughout a text. Researchers record and analyze data, build models of student learning and performance, and administer experiments on methods of instruction. Administrators use computers for keeping records, planning, scheduling, allocating resources, and processing data.

These applications and many others are described in the references at the end of this article.

Use of the computer as a tool for problem solving in education began in graduate schools about 1955, and a few years later moved into the classroom with the initiation of curriculum development projects in engineering and sciences. Computer use as a teaching machine dates from 1958; early developments took place at IBM's Watson Research Center, System Development Corporation, and the University of Illinois Coordinated Science Laboratory. The topic of computers in education became popular for meetings in 1965; separate conferences were held on computers in American education, higher education and physics teaching. In the following years of rapid growth, major conferences were organized for computers in mathematics teaching, chemistry education, computer science education, science education, undergraduate curriculum, and high school counseling. Instructional use of computers is a frequent topic at meetings of the contributing professions (computing, engineering, psychology, and educational research) and at meetings of teachers of most disciplines (ranging from engineering and physics to history, art, and modern languages). Various human components in effective computer use are related in Fig. 1.

Special interest groups on computers and learning have been formed by professional associations and other organizations. Newsletters, bulletins, and journals carry reports of use, development, and research (Zinn, 1978).

Kind of Use. Computer assistance with learning and teaching has been described by many different phrases. One could follow the word "computer" with two terms, one from each of the following lists.

-aided	
-assisted	
-augmented	training
-based	instruction
-extended	learning
-managed	teaching
-mediated	education
-monitored	
-related	
uses in	

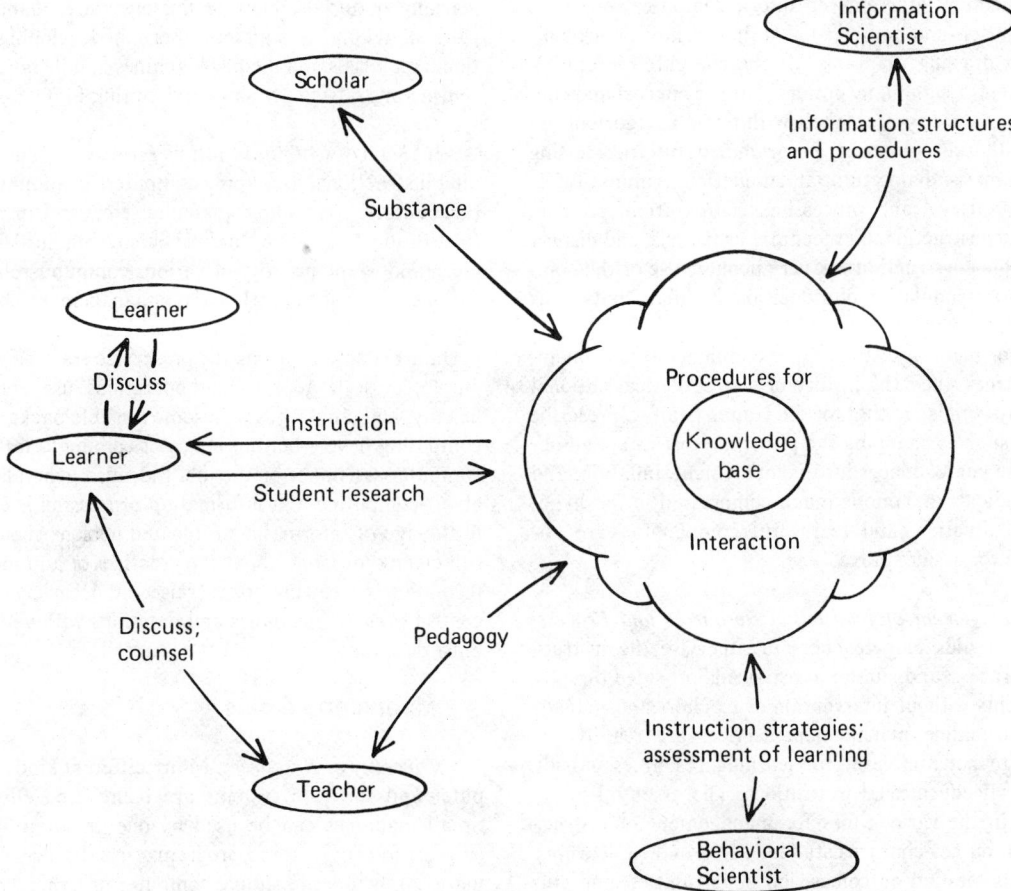

Fig. 1. Human components in effective computer use for learning and teaching.

The most common label has been CAI: computer-aided instruction. When "instruction" is replaced by "learning," as in CAL, the combination connotes greater emphasis on activities initiated by the learner than on the instructional materials created by a teacher-author. When "learning" is replaced by "education" to obtain CAE (or CBE, computer-based education), the implication is a greater variety of computer uses, including administrative data processing and materials production as well as student use of computers. If the role of the computer is to assist the teacher in managing instruction, for example, in retrieving and summarizing performance records and curriculum files, the label used is CMI: computer-managed instruction.

Instruction and the Learning Process. The most visible use of computers in instruction is to provide direct assistance to learners and to assist teachers, administrators, and educational technologists in helping learners. The users may work individually or in groups, using a device directly connected to a computer (on line) or using some medium later entered into a computer (off line), typing letters and numbers only (alphanumeric) or pointing and drawing diagrams for the computer (graphic), and so on through many options that vary in cost and convenience. Some typical labels within this category of use are: drill, skills practice, programmed tutorial, testing and diagnosis, dialog tutorial, simulation, gaming, information retrieval and processing, computation, problem solving, construction of procedures as models, and display of graphic constructions. A very popular use of the computer is for simulation of a decision-making situation, as in resource management, pollution control, business marketing, or medical testing. For example, college economics students study the history of a hypothetical national economy (similar to that for the United States), prescribe actions such as changing the prime interest rate, and observe the consequences for unemployment, inflation, and other indicators. Time is much compressed in the hypothetical situation, and real-world complexities are abstracted for easier study.

Management of Instruction Resources and Process. Computer aids help teachers to supervise the instructional process, and similar assistance is provided directly to students without intervention of teachers and managers. Information management services are readily extended to potential users of learning resources outside traditional educational institutions. The essential information in the various files for management of instructional resources concerns student performance, learning materials, desired outcomes, job opportunities, and student interests. For example, a student obtains information from the computer about achievement and then compares his/her own performance, interests, and goals with averages recorded for all similar students using the information system. After interpreting the information provided, the student uses the computer further to locate and retrieve suitable learning aids from a large file keyed to goals, learning difficulties, job opportunities, and interests.

Preparation and Display of Materials. Materials may be generated in "real time," i.e., as needed by a student in a seminar or by a teacher during a lecture. Text and problems also may be assembled by computer in advance of scheduled use so that individualized materials may be distributed at less expense than through on-line computing. Computers assist writers of materials in many ways—for example: procedures for generating films and graphs; on-line trial of materials under development; procedures for automatically editing and analyzing text materials for new uses, and information structures for representing new organizations of knowledge; hierarchies of instructional objectives; and libraries of learning materials. New technologies are changing the work of technicians and teachers in developing educational materials and media. Machines handle much of the routine in drafting graphics and editing film.

Other Uses of Information Processing. Those planning instructional uses apply computers in administration (accounting, scheduling, planning, etc.) and in research (institutional, sociological, psychological, instructional, etc.), and to the practice of various computer-related vocations in science, technology, management, banking, production, retailing, etc. The last area is especially important because of needs for preservice training. For example, most large retailing operations use computing heavily, and employees with some sensible background in computing have a better chance of coming to terms with computer assistance on the job. Indeed, a general literacy about computing and information processing is essential in the age of informatics. Educated persons should have sufficient knowledge about the practices of automated information processing to exercise on occasion effective control over the machines and data files with which they must deal.

Means and Goals

Diversity of Resources. Many different kinds of computer and software systems are being used effectively. Small machines can be used by one or a few students (Fig. 2) to access stored programs (usually drills or simulations) or to write simple computer programs. Slightly larger systems dedicated in a similar way to interactive instruction have been programmed for simultaneous use

Fig. 2. Small, inexpensive computers like that shown above are easy to use even by young children and open up new opportunities for learning in homes as well as schools.

by as few as 4 and as many as 100 students. Larger systems in operation now can handle up to 1,000 students accessing a variety of programs. The PLATO system at the University of Illinois was designed for up to 4,000 simultaneous users and diverse applications: self-instruction, self-testing, simulation, gaming, and problem solving. Many of the multipurpose computer systems serving general user communities at colleges and universities include instructional applications among other uses for research and administration. Examples at Dartmouth College, Massachusetts Institute of Technology, Carnegie-Mellon University, and the University of Michigan are often referenced.

Programming languages and systems (software) exhibit even more diversity than the computing equipment (hardware). More than 80 languages and dialects have been developed specifically for programming conversational instruction, although many programs have been written in general-purpose languages such as Fortran, PL/I, and Basic. Different kinds of users have distinguishable requirements: students, instructors, authors, instructional researchers, administrators, and computer programmers (who work on convenience programs for any of the other users). The characteristics of different subject areas also necessitate different language features. Authoring languages and systems are described in a separate article. Fig. 3 summarizes a perspective on software

and services for users; a set of concentric circles represents successive levels of access for users approaching the core of computing capability. Fig. 4 represents the perspective of the user at the center.

Instructional materials (sometimes called *courseware*) have been written in nearly all subject areas and for many age levels. While some of the materials use the computer as an information processing device, others use it as a presentation medium in competition with less expensive modes such as books, films, or video tapes.

Strategies of instruction associated with computer use (the name *teachware* has been proposed) are at an early stage of development. Guidelines for writing instruction-related computer programs have been derived from psychological and educational research, but most developers work from a "common sense" analysis and by trial and error. Some basis for a new science of instruction can be found in the research programs of Robert Glaser at the University of Pittsburgh, Robert Gagne at Florida State University, and M. David Merrill at Brigham Young University.

The costs of using various operational or experimental computer instruction systems and languages vary considerably. Figures reported by manufacturers and research projects range from $0.15 to $30.00 per student per hour. Some of the differences can be attributed to variations in assumptions about how many effective student hours can be scheduled in a month or a year; whether the equipment is rented, leased, or purchased; and how much time will be spent in utility jobs, preventive maintenance, or repair; and what accounting methods should be used. About $2.00 per hour was a typical charge for interactive use of computing within educational institutions in 1980.

Computer Contributions. The value of computer assistance for self-instruction depends on many factors: organization of the subject matter, the purposes of the author or institution, convenient means for interacting with the subject, and the characteristics of the student. Self-study material in text format has been adapted for computer presentation, with the following computer contributions proposed: First, the machine evaluates a response constructed by the student (the author must provide a key or standard); an automated procedure prints out discrepancies, tallies scores, and selects remedial or enrichment material. Second, the machine conceals and, to some extent, controls the teaching material so that the author can specify greater complexity in a strategy of instruction and assume more accuracy in its execution than is possible when the student is expected to find a way through the branching instructions in the pages of a large booklet (the scrambled text format for programmed instruction). Third, the computer carries out operations

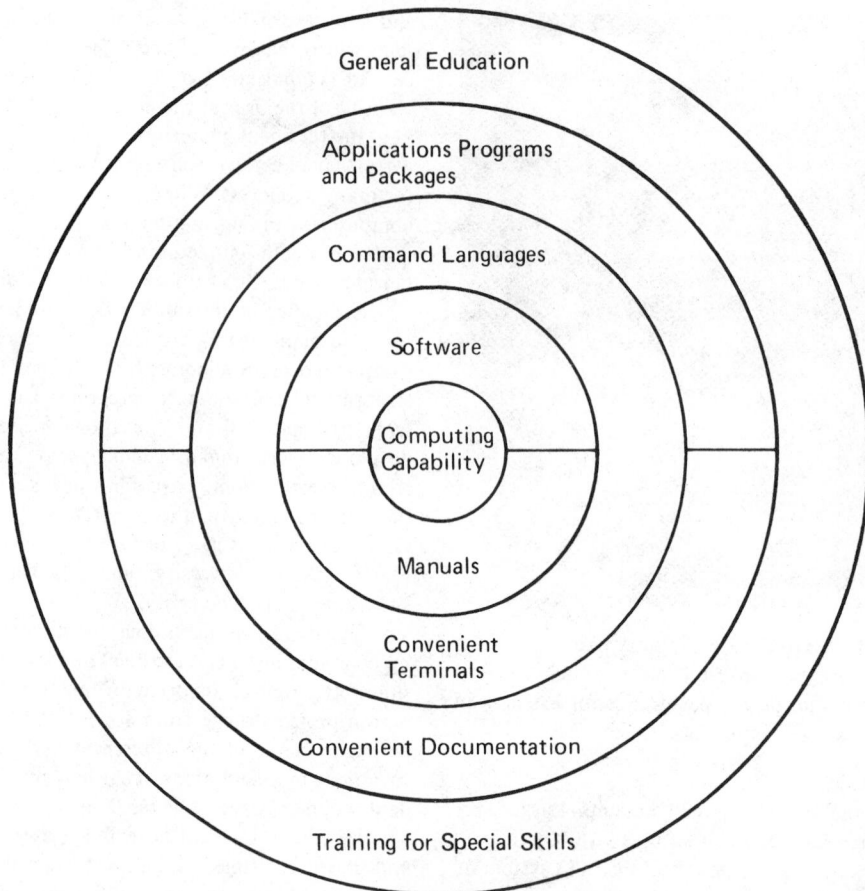

Fig. 3.   A perspective on software and services for users.

specified by the student, who uses a simple programming language or computer-aided design system. Fourth, the author or researcher obtains detailed data on student performance (and perhaps attitude) along with a convenient summarization of student accomplishment ready for interpretation. Fifth, the author is able to modify the text on the basis of student use and prepare alternative versions with relative ease.

The prepackaged self-instruction just described can be replaced by a dynamic information system that serves as a common working ground for a scholar and a learner; they share a computer-based, primary-source "textbook," continually updated by the scholar and occasionally annotated by each student who uses it (Fig. 5). Prototype systems have been demonstrated: HYPERTEXT was conceived by Theodor Nelson (then at Vassar College) and implemented by Andries van Dam and others at Brown University; and SPIRES was designed by Edwin Parker and others at Stanford. In a similar way, an automated information system helps a learner and

teacher share a common working environment for hypothesis testing. The environment is sometimes artificial, as in computer simulation of physical and social processes (e.g., a model of evolution), and sometimes real in the sense of actual data from experiments (e.g., election returns or radiation measures). Increased access to information processing tools is perhaps the most important contribution of computers to instruction and learning. Many such activities, perhaps not called computer-assisted instruction, demonstrate viable alternatives to strictly specified instructional strategies for computer use. For example, students in sociology retrieve and summarize information obtained from large-scale surveys and test hypotheses that might never have been conceived by those who executed and reported the survey. Students in physics test lens designs according to a detailed model of aberrations and corrections, perhaps finding variations on standard lens designs which better serve a particular photographic or instrumentation purpose.

Whatever the technique or philosophy of computer

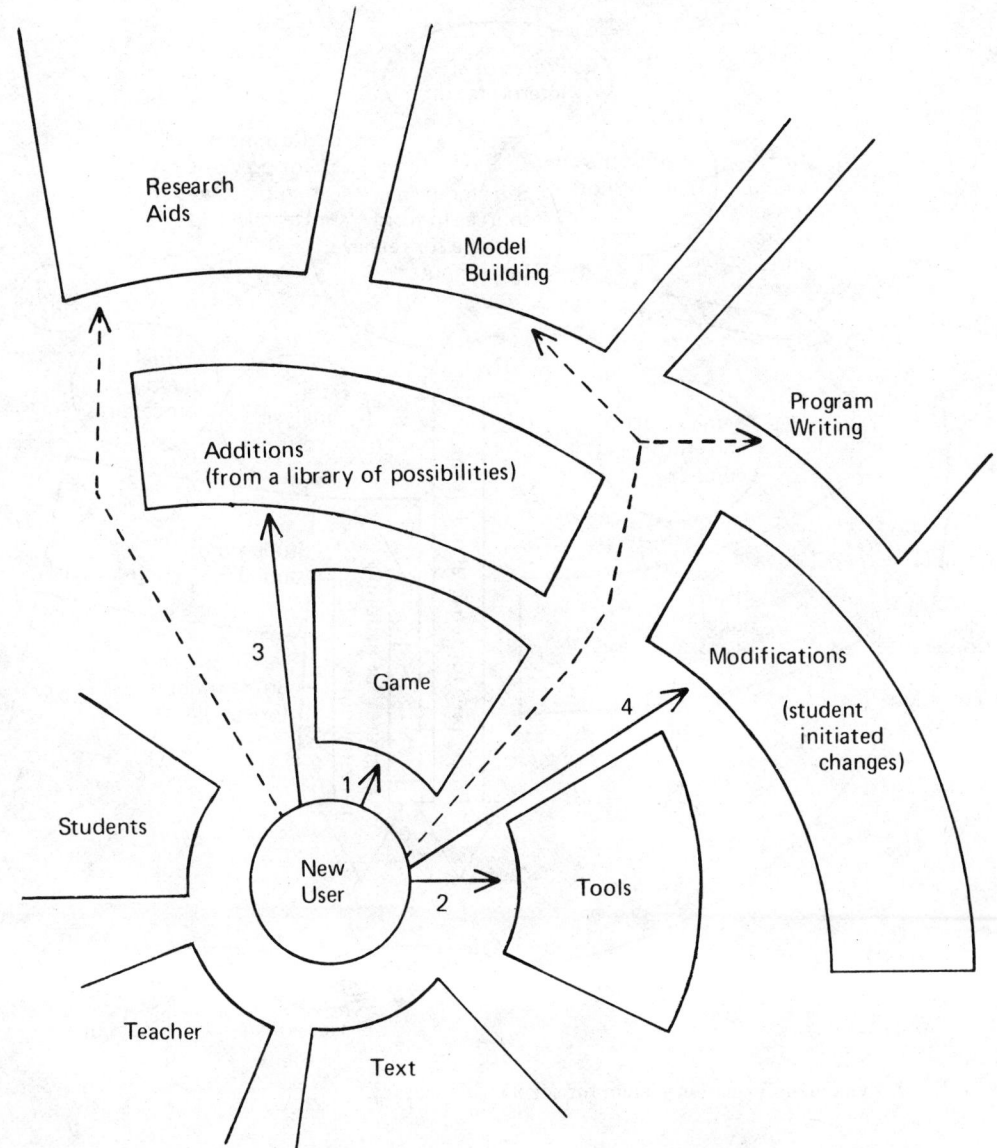

Fig. 4.   An open-ended approach to student involvement with computing activities.

use, the extent of use supported by educational institutions will ultimately be determined by judgments of appropriateness by subject experts, effectiveness observed from records of student performance, and costs that must be met by administrators of schools or training programs.

Some of the limitations imposed by present computer technology involve high cost and unreliability of processing lengthy verbal constructions, and inability to interpret bodily gestures or vocal intonations. Computing costs are decreasing even while capabilities are increasing, but one of the most difficult problems remaining is lack of organization of the subject matter. Somehow,

human teachers manage to be reasonably successful in spite of vague goals and material poorly organized for learning; instructional computing (and educational technology in general) seems to require specific text materials and clear guidelines (prepared by curriculum experts) for successful use.

Major Approaches

Educational Technology. Educational technology and instructional psychology have been the main sources of one kind of development activity. IBM's Coursewriter

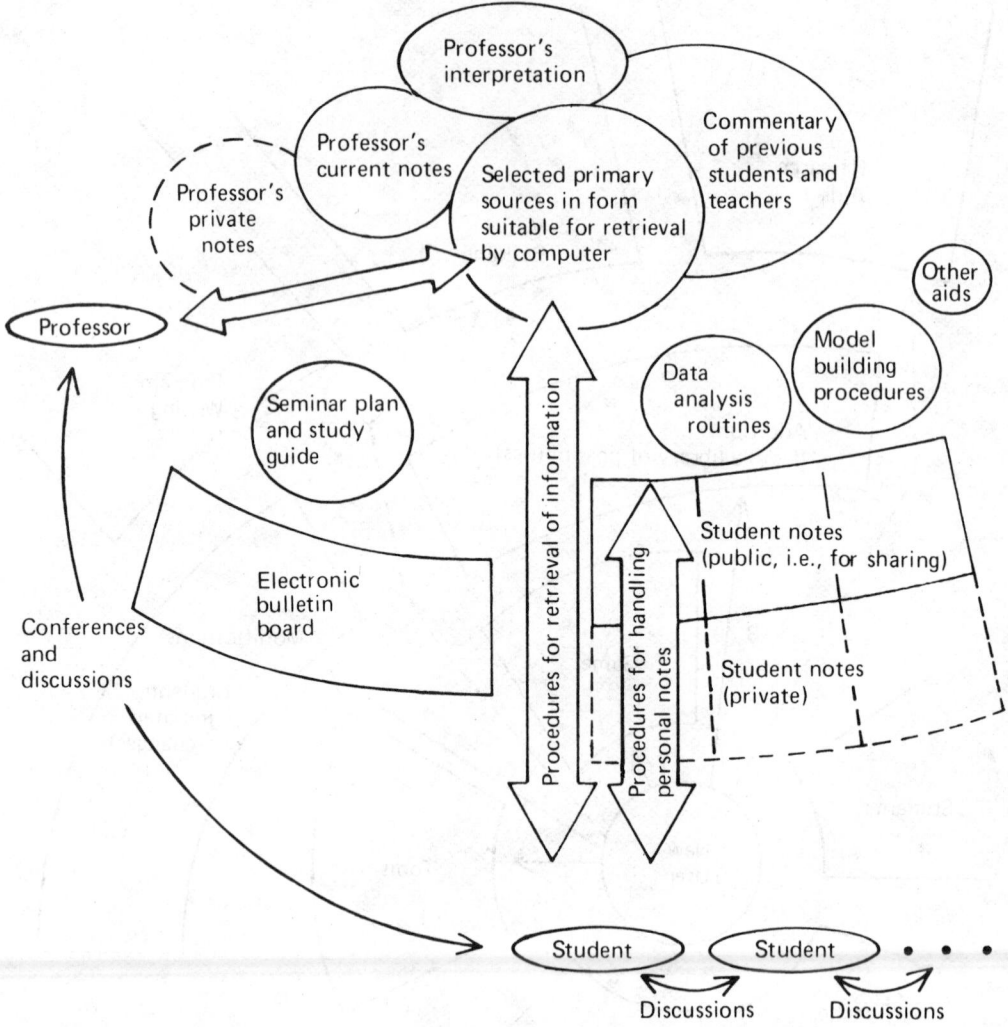

Fig. 5. A dynamic information system for scholar and learner.

programming language, one of the earliest languages for authors of computer-based lessons, characterizes this first approach to computer use. The software has built into it an implicit logic of instruction, requiring the author to fit text and key words into the following pattern: (1) the computer program presents information to the student; (2) the computer program then asks a question and waits for a response from the student; (3) the program scans a short textual response and classifies the response as right or wrong according to key words identified within it; and (4) if the student's response matches an anticipated wrong answer, the program displays a corrective hint, and if nothing was recognized, it offers a general hint. Many instances of this approach can be characterized as the computerization of programmed in-

struction. Careful development of a total curriculum for elementary school mathematics and reading was first carried out by teams of authors at Stanford University directed by Patrick Suppes and Richard Atkinson.

In some curriculum development projects the content has been assembled in files separate from the logic of the computer program (the strategy of instruction). Elements of the curriculum can thereby be varied without rewriting many lines of instructions to the computer, and different strategies can be tried on the same file of learning materials. This arrangement helps the instructional psychologist give full attention to the design of effective instructional strategies and helps the subject expert avoid the distraction of programming procedures. In fact, this approach is generally pursued by a team, with each member contributing different expertise. Authoring teams organized by C. Victor Bunderson at Brigham Young University developed materials for community college courses in mathematics and English for the TICCIT system developed by Mitre Corporation.

Problems faced by the educational technology approach to computer use result from the high cost of the computer as a primary medium for exposition of learning materials, the difficulties of accurately identifying unconstrained input (text, algebraic expressions, drawings, spoken expression, etc.), and the lack of a well-developed theory of instruction.

Disciplines and Curriculum. Discipline-oriented use of the computer was pursued by many institutions quite separately from the educational technology developments. Dartmouth College provides a prime instance of spreading computer uses throughout a college curriculum. The University of California at Irvine uses computing extensively in physics courses. Annual conferences were held on the topic of computers in the undergraduate curriculum from 1970 to 1978. Regional computing services, conferences, and newsletters have been established to serve the needs of colleges throughout a region. In contrast to the educational technology approach, the teacher as subject expert in the discipline approach assumes the central role in determining computer use, creating materials, and persuading colleagues to use them. Computing activity is likely to include more student initiative in solving problems and more problem-orienting program packages than does expository material. Student use of simulation and modeling tools is favored; one goal is to adapt the scholar's research tools to student use.

The discipline approach to computer use has many problems; among them are: sparse user documentation for instruction-related computing activities that are worthy of widespread use; lack of economic and professional incentives for the production and dissemination of programs and related materials; and difficult procedures for review and validation of programs. The purchase of thousands of microcomputers by students and teachers as well as institutions provides a market which now has the attention of publishers and authors in addition to professional societies.

Computing and Information Sciences. Some researchers suggest that major advances in instructional use of computers will occur through significant developments in artificial intelligence, natural language processing, speech recognition, and extensible programming languages. Although information scientists typically are more interested in their own disciplines and related research topics than in educational techniques and practice, the tools developed may be useful to others. The results

of computer science research may be an important source of suitable models for instruction strategies, information structures, and representations of knowledge. Projects giving particular attention to educational applications are located at the Massachusetts Institute of Technology, Bolt Beranek and Newman, Carnegie-Mellon University, the University of Texas, California Institute of Technology, and Stanford University. In addition to the tools to be borrowed from computing and information sciences, new models of human learning and information processing may be obtained.

The information science approach has not yet produced many operational systems. Development of techniques and materials is very costly and time consuming; the resulting applications are expensive in execution with students; skill in use of the specialized techniques is not easily acquired by persons outside computer science. Nevertheless, the projects based in computing and information sciences continue to provide important indicators of future resources which may be essential to success of computers in education. Furthermore, a project at the University of Illinois directed by Jurg Nievergelt has adapted ideas from computing and information sciences for economical execution so that the computer-based materials can be used by over 2,000 students per semester in a set of introductory courses. Because the courses are in computer science, the authors combine a detailed knowledge of the specialized techniques with considerable experience in teaching the subject.

Computing Technology, Engineering, and "Common Sense". A fourth category includes all other approaches, particularly those characterized by the engineering of a helpful technology, perhaps involving some combination of the first three approaches. Engineers at the Computer-Based Educational Research Laboratory, University of Illinois, designed and built a computer-based education system (PLATO, Fig. 6) which is intended to be convenient for: educational technologists presenting programmed instruction, instructional psychologists conducting research on teaching and learning, professors preparing a computer presentation of a lecture or laboratory, and computer specialists building information processing aids for learning and scholarly work. Specialists in computers and education at Bolt Beranek and Newman (led by Wallace Feurzeig) and the Massachusetts Institute of Technology (notably, Seymour Papert) have devised various programming languages (Mentor, Telcomp, Stringcomp, and Logo) and equipment (computer-controlled "turtle," music player, etc.) for computer-related learning activities.

Two other groups exhibit a similar philosophy but offer different approaches to creative student work: the Soloworks Project directed by Thomas Dwyer at the

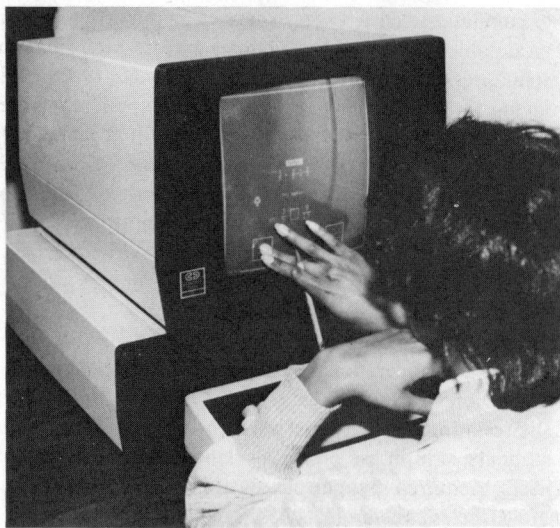

Fig. 6. Student terminal used with the PLATO computer-based education system which includes a high-resolution graphics display with a touch-sensitive panel. (Courtesy Center for Instructional Technology, Wayne State University.)

University of Pittsburgh and the Learning Research Group directed by Alan Kay at the Palo Alto Research Center of Xerox Corporation. In each case, children write simple programs for controlling robots, drawing and animating pictures, generating speech and music, and the like. Their interest in enhancing such capabilities motivates a new approach to mathematics and heuristics in which programming languages provide a powerful conceptual framework. The M.I.T. group has given particular attention to teaching children how to think, reason, and solve problems. These projects and others having an engineering approach are described in the proceedings of the World Conferences on Computer Education (Lecarme and Lewis, 1975; Lewis and Tagg, 1981).

Trends. A major trend in the design of computer-based exercises is a shift from programmer to learner control. The designer of the exercise invests less effort in a careful diagnosis and prescription accomplished by some automated instructional strategy, and instead provides information from which the student can derive a diagnosis from alternative interpretations and guidance. The student can assemble prescriptions specific to a particular situation.

Increased use of graphics is seen in many projects. Pictures are an important component of the learning process, and computer-drawn pictures can add to the responsive uses of computing. For many topics the picture is a valuable way of representing complex relationships derived by the computer.

Computer-based education systems and designers of materials are providing an increasing variety of functions for the user. More attention is being given to interaction between student and computer program, not simply to provide a quick reply to some question, but to increase the actual responsiveness of the system to the particular input. The SCHOLAR system designed by the late Jaime Carbonell at Bolt Beranek and Newman is a prime instance. Machine responses are increasingly dependent upon the commands and questions and answers constructed by the student, and the lessons are designed in a way that helps the student respond to information provided by the computer.

A very important trend concerns the role of the machine from the perspective of the individual using it. The teacher is now more likely to see computer-managed instruction as an aid to human management than as a replacement for it. Learners view the machine more as an aid to learning than as a drill master. All these developments are helped along by personal ownership of computers or other personalization of use.

Naturalness of communication between learner and system is being improved day by day. Computer-based learning exercises are achieving increased relevance for the subject being studied, and the nomenclature and conventions that have to be learned in order to use the system tend to be essential to the study of the topics rather than peculiar to the requirement of the computer as a medium of presentation.

REFERENCES

1974. Zinn, Karl L., Refice, Mario, and Romano, Aldo (Eds.). *Computers in the Instructional Process: Report of an International School.* Ann Arbor: Extend Publications.

1975. Lecarme, O. and Lewis, R. (Eds.). *IFIP Second World Conference on Computers in Education.* Amsterdam: North-Holland.

1975. Hunter, Beverly, Kastner, Carol S., Rubin, Martin L., and Seidel, Robert J. *Learning Alternatives in U.S. Education: Where Student and Computer Meet,* Englewood Cliffs, NJ: Educational Technology Publications.

1977. Seidel, Robert and Rubin, Martin (Eds.). *Computers and Communications: Implications for Education.* New York: Academic Press.

1978. DISPAC. House Science and Technology Subcommittee on Domestic and International Scientific Planning, Analysis and Cooperation. *Hearings on Computers and the Learning Society.* Washington, DC: U.S. Government Printing Office.

1978. Zinn, Karl L. "Sources of Information About Computing in Instruction," *Educational Technology* **18,** *No. 4:* 32–38 (April).

1979. Hamblen, John W. and Landis, Carolyn P. (Eds.). *The Fourth Inventory of Computers in Higher Education: An Interpretive Report.* Princeton, NJ: Educom.

1981. Lewis, R. and Tagg, E. D. (Eds.) *IFIP Third World Conference on Computers in Education.* Amsterdam: North-Holland.

K. L. ZINN

COMPUTER CHESS

For articles on related subjects *see* ARTIFICIAL INTELLIGENCE; GAMES ON COMPUTERS; and HEURISTICS.

Based on ideas outlined in the late 1940s by Claude Shannon and Alan Turing, chess programs have been developed and refined to the point where the best now play on giant computers at near Master level. Smaller programs written for microcomputers play well enough to have created a multimillion dollar industry in computer chess games for the home.

Shannon and Turing proposed that a computer be programmed to search a tree of all move continuations from a given position to some arbitrary depth, assign a score to the position at the end of each continuation, and then determine the expected or *principal continuation* by assuming each side will move toward the position with the best score for itself. Shannon specified that the score assigned to each end position be a function of material, piece mobility, and pawn structure; the more positive the score, the better for White. Conversely, the more negative, the better for Black. The first move on the principal continuation is the move to make in the given position. This algorithm, the *minimax algorithm,* is central to all chess programs (*see* COMPUTER GAMES).

Modifications have been made to the minimax algorithm to improve its efficiency. The *alpha-beta algorithm,* the most important, was first described by John McCarthy. It allows the minimax algorithm to skip searching large parts of the tree while still finding the same principal continuation. It is based on the reasoning that before concluding that a move by one side looks good, all replies by the opponent must be considered, but once a move is shown to be bad by a refutation, no further replies need be considered. The *killer heuristic* stores refutations on a list and tries to use them to refute other moves, thereby speeding up the search. *Iterative deepening* is the process of carrying out a sequence of increasingly deeper searches as long as time permits. Each successive iteration is sped up by using the results of the previous one. *Transposition tables* are used to store positions that have been scored along with the scores assigned. If one of these positions is reached later in the search by a transposition of moves, generally speaking no further continuations from it need be considered.

The good programs have opening libraries in the range of 10,000–300,000 positions. Moves made from the "book" require about one second. The better programs guess the opponent's reply and begin to calculate their own next move while the opponent considers his/her move. About 30–40% of the time, they guess correctly.

The first working programs of the 1950s played poorly. In 1956, at Los Alamos, John Kister, Paul Stein, Stanislaw Ulam, William Walden, and Mark Wells developed a program which played without bishops on a 6 × 6 board for the MANIAC I computer. In 1958, Alex Bernstein, Michael De V. Roberts, Tom Arbuckle, and Martin Belsky developed the first full-fledged programs for the IBM 704. Alan Newell, John Shaw, and Herbert Simon were the first to use a high-level language in developing their program which was modeled after the human thought process and developed at Carnegie-Mellon University in the late 1950s. Recent programs, however, make no attempt to mimic human thought processes.

Alan Kotok, working with McCarthy at MIT, developed a program which played a four-game match in 1966–1967 against a Soviet program developed by George Adelson-Velskiy, Vladimir Arlazarov, A. Ushkov, A. Bitman, and A. Zhivatovsky. The Soviet program won two and drew two. The Kotok-McCarthy program used forward pruning, i.e., weeded out moves at each position in the tree based on various heuristics, but the heuristics were unreliable and the program frequently made obviously weak moves. While many efforts have been made to use forward pruning, the best current programs avoid it. The Soviet program carried out three-ply exhaustive searches in the drawn games and five-ply exhaustive searches in its victories.

MAC HACK VI, developed at MIT by Richard Greenblatt, Steven Crocker, and Donald Eastlake, was the first program to compete successfully against humans. In 1967, it received a USCF rating in the 1400s for its performance in the Massachusetts State Championship.*

Chess tournaments exclusively for computers have been held since 1970 (see Table 1). Until 1978, these tournaments were dominated by David Slate and Larry Atkin's program, first called Chess 3.0 and now, after many revisions, called CHESS 4.9 ($\approx$2050 USCF rating). Developed at Northwestern University and cur-

---

*USCF ratings run as follows: Senior Master, over 2400 (85 players rated in this category by the USCF in January 1980; there are perhaps another 50–100 players in the U.S. who play at this level but were not rated because they didn't participate in tournaments in 1979); Master, 2200–2399 (307 rated at this level in January 1980); Expert, 2000–2199; Category I, 1800–1999; Category II, 1600–1799; Category III, 1400–1499 (this level is attained by most people who play seriously for three years); and Category IV, 1200–1399. The average USCF rating is between 1300 and 1400.

Table 1. Results of Major Computer Chess Tournaments

Year	Tournament	Location	Winning Program; Authors; Computer	Runner Up; Authors; Computer	Number of Entries
1970	1st Association for Computing Machinery's (ACM) United States Computer Chess Championship (USCCC)	New York	CHESS 3.0; Slate, Atkin, Gorlen; CDC 6400	Daly Chess Program; Daly; Varian 620/i	6
1971	2nd ACM's USCCC	Chicago	CHESS 3.5; Slate, Atkin, Gorlen; CDC 6400	TECH; Gillogy; PDP 10	8
1972	3rd ACM's USCCC	Boston	CHESS 3.6; Slate, Atkin, Gorlen; CDC 6400	OSTRICH; Arnold, Newborn; Nova 800	8
1973	4th ACM's USCCC	Atlanta	CHESS 4.0; Slate, Atkin, Gorlen; CDC 6400	TECH II; Baisley; PDP 10	12
1974	1st World Championship (IFIP Congress)	Stockholm	KAISSA; Donskoy, Arlazarov; ICL 4/70	CHESS 4.0; Slate, Atkin; CDC 6600	13
1974	5th ACM's USCCC	San Diego	RIBBIT; Hansen, Crook, Parry; Honeywell 6050	CHESS 4.0; Slate, Atkin; CDC 6400	12
1975	6th ACM's North American Computer Chess Championship (NACCC)	Minneapolis	CHESS 4.4; Slate, Atkin; CDC Cyber 175	TREEFROG; Hansen, Crook, Calnek, Parry; Honeywell 6080	12
1976	7th ACM's NACCC	Houston	CHESS 4.5; Slate, Atkin; CDC Cyber 176	CHAOS; Swartz, Rubin, Winograd, Berman, Toikka, Alexander; Amdahl 470	12
1977	2nd World Championship (IFIP Congress)	Toronto	CHESS 4.6; Slate, Atkin; CDC Cyber 176	DUCHESS; Truscott, Wright, Jensen; IBM 370/165	16
1977	8th ACM's NACCC	Seattle	CHESS 4.6; Slate, Atkin; CDC Cyber 176	DUCHESS; Truscott, Wright, Jensen; IBM 370/168	12
1978	Jerusalem Conference on Information Technology Invitational	Jerusalem	DUCHESS; Truscott, Wright, Jensen; IBM 370/168.	CHESS 4.6; Slate, Atkin; CDC Cyber 74	6
1978	9th ACM's NACCC	Washington	BELLE; Thompson, Condon; PDP 11/70, special hardware	CHESS 4.7; Slate, Atkin; CDC Cyber 176	12
1979	10th ACM's NACCC	Detroit	CHESS 4.9; Slate, Atkin; Cahlander; CDC Cyber 176	BELLE; Thompson, Condon; PDP 11/70, special hardware	12
1980	3rd World Championship	Linz	BELLE; Thompson, Condon; PDP 11/23, special hardware	CHAOS; Swartz, Alexander, O'Keefe, Berman; Amdahl 470	18

Table 1.   Results of Major Computer Chess Tournaments (_continued_)

Year	Tournament	Location	Winning Program; Authors; Computer	Runner Up; Authors; Computer	Number of Entries
1980	11th ACM's NACCC	Nashville	BELLE; Thompson, Condon; PDP 11/23, special hardware	CHAOS; Swartz, Alexander O'Keefe, Berman; Amdahl 470	10
1981	12th ACM's NACCC	Los Angeles	BELLE; Thompson, Condon; PDP 11/23, special hardware	NUCHESS; Slate, Blanchard; CDC Cyber 176	16

rently running on a CDC Cyber 176, CHESS 4.9 carries out a sequence of iteratively deeper exhaustive searches while examining 3,000–5,000 nodes per second (_see_ Fig. 1). At speed chess (games in which each side makes all its moves in five minutes), Slate and Atkin's program has managed victories over numerous Masters and several Grandmasters, including Robert Hübner of Germany.

BELLE (≈2100 USCF rating), developed at Bell Telephone Laboratories by Ken Thompson and Joe Condon, now (1980) seems to be the strongest program. Run-

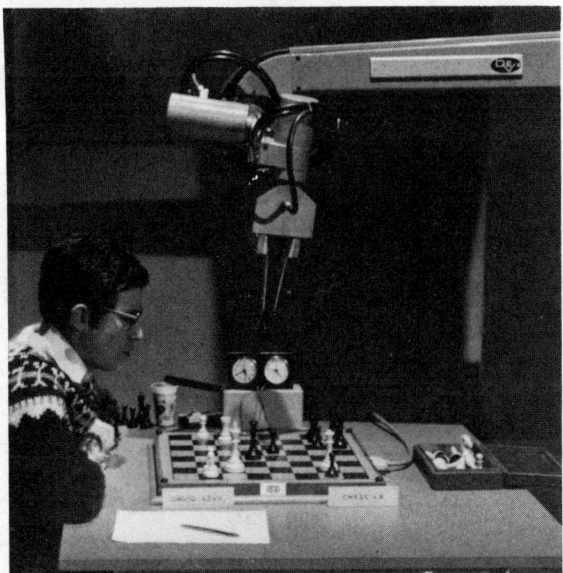

Fig. 1.   On 7 February 1979 in Hamburg, Germany, David Levy played—and beat—Chess 4.9 running on a CDC Cyber 176 computer in Minneapolis. The "robot" shown in the picture received signals directly from the computer via satellite communications and then moved the appropriate piece. Courtesy Lothar Alt.

ning on a PDP 11/23 system with special hardware for generating moves and scoring positions, BELLE examines as many as 30,000,000 nodes when computing a move in tournament play.

Other leading programs include DUCHESS, CHAOS, and KAISSA. DUCHESS, created at Duke University by Tom Truscott, Bruce Wright, and Eric Jensen, and CHAOS, the work of Fred Swartz, Mike Alexander, Jack O'Keefe, and Victor Berman at the University of Michigan, are playing at about the 1900 USCF level. CHAOS is the only successful selective search program, although it looks at trees with as many as 25,000 nodes when playing at tournament speeds on the powerful Amdahl 470 computer. KAISSA (≈1850 USCF rating) developed by Mikhail Donskoy and Vladimir Arlazarov at the U.S.S.R.'s Institute of Control Sciences, won the first world championship in 1974.

Most notable among programs developed for microcomputers are Dan and Kathe Spracklen's SARGON III (≈1600 USCF rating), Dave Kittinger's MYCHESS (≈1450 USCF rating), and Mike Johnson's MIKE (≈1450 USCF rating). These programs typically require 8–16K 8-bit words of read-only memory and 2–4K 8-bit words of random-access memory. They run on microcomputers which execute 2–4 million instructions per second. Commercially available chess machines are also on the market, selling for $100–500 (CHESS CHALLENGER, produced by Fidelity Electronics, Chicago, and BORIS, made by Chafitz of Rockville, Maryland, are the best and are playing 1200–1400 USCF level chess).

Special endgame programs have been developed in recent years. Thompson's King and Queen versus King and Rook endgame makes the best move possible on every play. It uses a database developed by starting with mating positions and then adding other positions that are one move removed from mate, then two, then three, and so on.

In August 1978, David Levy, International Master

White: CHESS 4.7   Black: David Levy

Latvian Gambit

1. P-K4	P-K4	20. R/B-K1	B-Q2	38. RxP+	K-B1
2. N-KB3	P-KB4	21. N-B3	PxP	39. R-Q7	R-Q6+
3. PxP	P-K5	22. PxP	R-R5	40. K-N2	B-B4
4. N-K5	N-KB3	23. P-B3	R/1-R1	41. RxP/5	R-Q7
5. N-N4	P-Q4	24. K-B1	B-N6	42. P-N4	BxP
6. NxN+	QxN	25. R-K2	B-B1	43. R-Q8+	K-B2
7. Q-R5+	Q-B2	26. K-N2	B-Q3	44. R-Q7+	K-B1
8. QxQ+	KxQ	27. B-N1	R-R6	45. RxP/4	R-N7
9. N-B3	P-B3	28. R/1-K1	R-N6+	46. K-B3	B-B4
10. P-Q3	PxP	29. K-B2	R/1-R6	47. R-Q8+	K-K2
11. BxP	N-Q2	30. R-K3	B-R3	48. B-R4+	K-B2
12. B-KB4	N-B4	31. N-K2	BxN	49. P-N5	P-N3
13. P-KN4	NxB+	32. R/1xB	P-B4	50. R-Q7+	K-B1
14. PxB	B-B4	33. P-B4!	RxR	51. PxP	RxP
15. 0-0	P-KR4	(turning the		52. P-B5	R-R6+
16. N-R4	B-Q5	game around)		53. K-N4	R-R5+
17. B-K3	B-K4	34. RxR	R-R5	54. K-R5	R-Q5
18. P-Q4	B-Q3	35. K-N3	R-R8	55. R-QB7	B-K2
19. P-KR3	P-QN3	36. B-B2	R-Q8	56. P-B6	Resigns
		37. R-R3!	PxP		

Fig. 2

from London, won a wager of several thousand dollars by defeating CHESS 4.7 in a match in Toronto. In 1968, he had wagered four computer scientists that no computer would defeat him in a match during the next ten years. He won three games, drew one, and lost one. His loss is presented in Fig. 2. It serves as a measure of the state of computer chess as the third decade of activity in this exciting field comes to an end.

In 1978, the Dutch Software House VOLMAC dwarfed Levy's wager by offering $50,000 to the team which first develops a program that beats former World Champion Dr. Max Euwe in a match of four games. Their offer remains open until 1 January 1984. Levy and *OMNI Magazine* have offered a prize of $5,000 to the programmer of the first program able to defeat Levy in a match; they give no time deadline. In 1980, the biggest prize of all was announced by Carnegie-Mellon University, which will award $100,000 to the programmers of the first program to defeat the world chess champion!

At the 1977 World Championship in Toronto, the International Computer Chess Association was formed to provide an international framework for activities in computer chess and to encourage advances in this field. There are currently about 300 members. For information on the ICCA, write to Professor Ben Mittman, Director, Vogelback Computer Center, Northwestern University, Evanston, IL, 60201.

REFERENCES

1950. Shannon, C. "Programming a Computer for Playing Chess," *Philosophy Magazine* **41**:256–275.

1953. Turing, A. M. "Digital Computers Applied to Games," in Bowden, B. V. (Ed.), *Faster than Thought*. London: Pitman, pp. 286–295.

1975. Newborn, M. *Computer Chess*. New York: Academic Press.

1976. Levy, D. N. L. *Chess and Computers*. Potomac, MD: Computer Science Press.

1977. Frey, P. (Ed.). *Chess Skill in Man and Machine*. New York: Springer-Verlag.

1979. Newborn, M. "Recent Progress in Computer Chess," *Advances in Computers* **18**:59–117.

1980. Levy, D. N. L. and Newborn, M. *More Chess and Computers*. Potomac, MD: Computer Science Press.

M. M. NEWBORN

COMPUTER CIRCUITRY

For articles on related subjects *see* BOOLEAN ALGEBRA GENERATIONS, COMPUTER; INTEGRATED CIRCUITRY; JOSEPHSON JUNCTION DEVICES; and MICROPROCESSORS AND MICROCOMPUTERS.

Although the development of digital computers can be traced back to Charles Babbage, who conceived a mechanical machine with toothed wheels to perform arithmetic processes, electrical principles first found application in digital computers in the form of electromechanical relays. The most prominent examples of this type were the Bell Telephone Laboratories' machines and the Harvard Mark I and Mark II. Even while these machines were under construction in the early and middle 1940s, it was recognized that an *electronic* computer would offer great advantages in terms of computational speed. This pattern of improving implementation technology has continued even to the present time. This article will survey the characteristics of circuits and circuit technology used in various generations of computers, present some commonly used computer circuits, and discuss the trend of future computer circuitry.

Boolean Algebra and Computer Circuitry.

Boolean algebra forms the theoretical cornerstone on which modern digital computers are built. Boolean algebra deals with functions and variables that take on only two values, commonly denoted by either T and F or 1 and 0. Using the axioms of Boolean algebra, it can be shown that any arithmetic or logic function, no matter how complex, can be composed from three primitive operations: *and, or,* and *not* (sometimes called *negate*). This set of logic operations is, therefore, said to be *functionally complete* (Kohavi, 1978). In fact, there are two primitive operations, widely used in the design of computer circuitry, that are functionally complete by themselves. These are *nand* (for *not and*), an *and* operation followed by a *not,* and *nor* (for *not or*), an *or* operation followed by a *not.* The implication of this is that one needs only design circuitry to implement a functionally complete set of Boolean operations in order to have the basic building blocks for a digital computer.

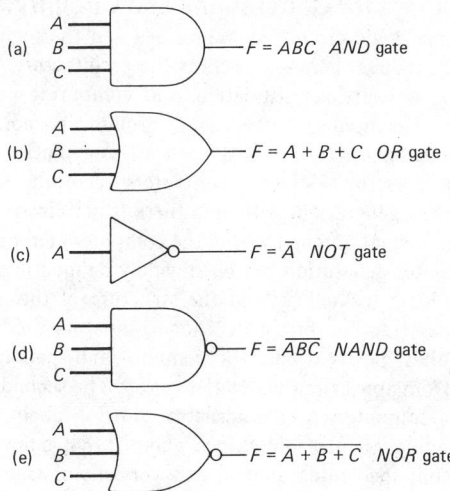

Fig. 1. Logic gate symbols.

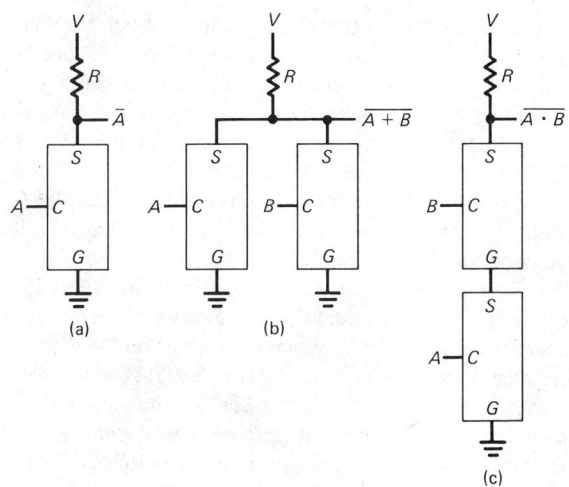

Fig. 2. Ideal gate implementation. a) *not;* b) *nor;* c) *nand.*

The association that is usually made between an abstract Boolean operation and circuitry that implements that operation is through voltage levels. That is, digital circuitry is designed to respond in terms of two voltage levels, designated high and low (e.g., +5 volts and 0 volts). Employing the *positive logic* convention, a Boolean value T (or 1) is associated with the high voltage level and an F (or 0) is associated with the low voltage level. In this manner, the operation of a circuit, as measured with a voltmeter, can be interpreted as implementing a Boolean function. Other correspondences between Boolean values and circuit quantities are possible. For example, it may be convenient to relate Boolean values to the direction of current flow. The *negative logic* convention (whereby T and the low voltage level are paired, as are F and the high voltage level) also finds application. In the remainder of this article, the positive logic convention will be used.

Circuits that implement the most primitive Boolean functions are called *gates* because they are the fundamental elements that direct the flow of logic signals. The symbols used to represent the commonly used gates are shown in Fig. 1. Notice that the small circle may appear in conjunction with any gate to denote negation of that gate's function. While many different circuits employing many different devices (relays, vacuum tubes, transistors) have been designed to perform the various logic functions, and while such designs require careful engineering to produce reliable operation in computers, the basic principles involved are not difficult to understand.

Essentially what is needed to build a gate is a *controlled switch.* Consider the three-terminal "black box" of Fig. 2. The three terminals are labeled C for control, S for switch, and G for ground. Suppose that inside the box is some circuitry that acts as follows: When the voltage between the C and G terminals is below some threshold value, L_T, there is an open circuit between the S and G leads, whereas, when the voltage between C and G exceeds L_T, there is effectively a short circuit between S and G. There is no internal current path between the S and C leads. Thus, depending on the voltage between the C and G terminals, an internal switch between S and G will be either opened or closed.

To make a *not* gate (Fig. 2a), all that is required is to connect the S terminal through a resistor to a voltage source of value, V volts. When the voltage on the control terminal is below threshold, L_T, (i.e., a zero) the internal switch is open and the voltage at the S terminal is V (i.e., a one). When the voltage at the control terminal is above the threshold (i.e., a one), the internal switch is closed and the voltage at the S terminal goes to ground (i.e., zero).

A pair of controlled switches can be used to make either a *nor* gate or a *nand* gate. (The required circuitry is shown in Figs. 2b and 2c.) The idea of the *nor* gate is that, should either or both of the control leads have a high voltage applied, the corresponding switch will close, allowing current flow through the resistor, and bringing the output voltage to ground. On the other hand, the output terminal of Fig. 2c will be low only when both control inputs are brought to a high voltage state. This is the *nand* function.

In modern digital computer circuitry, the function of the controlled switch is performed by either a bipolar or a MOS (metal-oxide semiconductor) transistor. (The symbols used for these devices are shown in Fig. 3.) In the past, vacuum tubes and relays have also been used. Of course none of these devices has all of the ideal characteristics postulated by the simple controlled switch, and hence practical circuitry is more complex than that of Fig. 2.

Logic circuits differ with respect to such things as their speed, the power required to operate, the voltage levels representing the logical 1 and 0, the logic threshold voltage, the power supply voltage or voltages required, the number of gates at the next logic stage that can be driven from a typical gate (also called fan-out), and noise immunity (a measure of the amount of interference that

can be tolerated before a gate incorrectly perceives a high voltage level as a low voltage level or vice versa). It is necessary for gate designers to make tradeoffs among the gate characteristics to achieve economical implementation of a computer. The most significant tradeoff that must be addressed is that between speed and power. A straightforward way to get a faster computer is to use faster gates. But faster switching circuitry dissipates more power and yields more heat, which must be disposed of in some manner. Power consumption can be reduced at the expense of decreased fan-out, if voltage levels are decreased, at the cost of decreased noise immunity.

When gates were constructed from discrete components, vacuum tubes or transistors, diodes, resistors, capacitors, etc., the circuit designer would optimize a basic gate design for a particular machine and literally thousands of copies of only a few circuits would be made. Designers frequently chose their circuitry from a reasonably small variety of circuit types known as logic families. Some of these families are described in the next section. The various logic families could be categorized according to their relative performance with respect to cost, speed of operation, power dissipation, and noise immunity. A gate designer, knowing generally what was expected of the computer, would then pick a logic family and optimize performance by selecting component values and types as well as voltage levels.

The concept of logic families carries over to integrated circuit implementation of circuitry. Thus, semiconductor manufacturers supply a variety of integrated logic circuitry in several logic families. Rather complete specifications are available for each family detailing power consumption, operating speed, logic levels, voltage levels, fan-out, and noise immunity. Some indication of the variety and types of circuitry is given in later sections.

Computer Generations and Circuitry. Over the years, logic circuit configurations and the technologies to produce them—as well as the architecture, complexity, software sophistication, and computing performance of computers—have gone through an enormous evolutionary process. So striking has this evolution been that it is useful to classify computers according to the concept of generation. Although there is not always general agreement among those in the computer community, a computer generation has been widely defined in terms of the logic technology and the structure of the active logic devices. The first-generation computers used vacuum tubes, mostly triodes and pentodes, and spanned the years from approximately 1945 to 1959. The second-generation computers used transistors, starting about 1959 and ending about 1964. Since about 1964, computers have contained integrated circuit versions of transistor circuits and have commonly been called third-generation

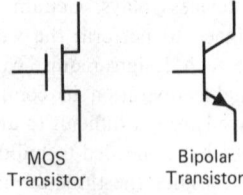

Fig. 3.   Transistor symbols.

computers. Computers in the 1980s, sometimes called fourth-generation computers, make extensive use of medium- or large-scale integrated circuits. Thus, several logic circuits will be described here according to the computer generations with which they are most closely associated.

First-Generation Computers. The first-generation electronic computers were primarily characterized by a

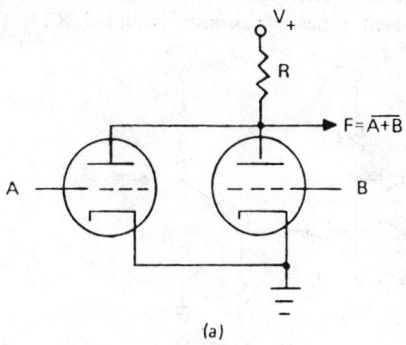

(a)

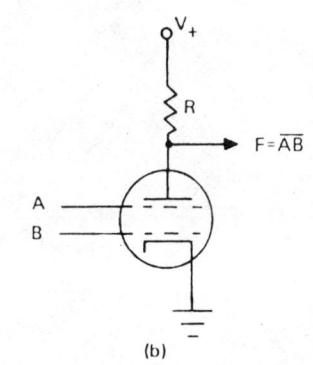

(b)

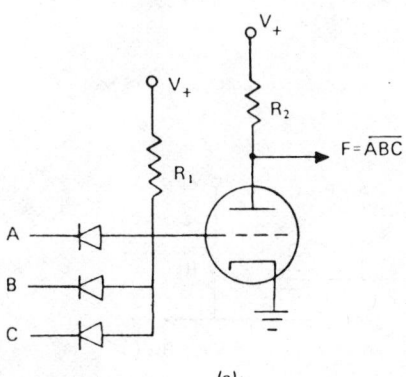

(c)

Fig. 4. First-generation circuits. (a) two-input *nor* gate; (b) two-input *nand* gate; (c) three-input *nand* gate.

logic technology utilizing vacuum tubes. A *nor* gate composed of two triodes is shown Fig. 4a. If one or two grid inputs (*A, B*) are at a logical 1 (i.e., high-voltage state), one or both triodes will conduct current, causing a potential drop across the load resistor *R* and an output of logical 0 (i.e., low-voltage state); otherwise, the triode will not conduct and the output will be a logical 1. With only one triode, the circuit performs a *not* function. The twin triodes performing *nor* functions were later put into one single vacuum chamber.

Another important vacuum tube for computer applications was the pentode. The high-impedance control and suppressor grids of a pentode were used as input grids, while the low-impedance screen grid was usually not used. A pentode circuit without the screen grid is shown in Fig. 4b and behaves as a *nand* gate. If either grid input is a logical 0, the pentode will not conduct and the output will be a logical 1. If both grid inputs are a logical 1, the pentode will conduct and the output will be a logical 0. A pentode *not* circuit is formed by setting one of the inputs constantly at a logical 1.

Since either the *nand* gate or the *nor* gate is sufficient to generate any Boolean function, either the twin-triode or pentode circuit is sufficient for realizing more complex circuits. However, the voltage levels for either circuit do not have compatible input and output requirements. Therefore, voltage-level restoring circuits have to be introduced for cascading either the twin triode or pentode logic circuits. A resistance-voltage divider circuit can be used for voltage-level restoring, but resistor tolerances may introduce imprecise logical levels.

Besides the high cost, computer circuits using vacuum tubes had other shortcomings. Vacuum tubes were limited by their large physical size, which introduced substantial transmission delays. Power consumption was high, so that cooling requirements were also high. Furthermore, they had a rather limited lifetime and a gradual deterioration property, which restricted the practical size of a system that could be seriously contemplated. Consequently, the complexity of the first-generation computers was quite limited. ENIAC—which was built in 1945 at the University of Pennsylvania for the U.S. Army, to solve ballistic problems—contained approximately 18,000 vacuum tubes and was the largest vacuum tube computer ever attempted. With so many vacuum tubes, reliability was quite poor.

A major advance in this technology was the practical application of germanium diodes as logic gates to reduce the required number of vacuum tubes. For example, a multi-input *nand* gate could be formed from a multi-input diode *and* gate followed by a triode or a pentode *not* circuit, as shown in Fig. 4c and thus replace an equivalent circuit requiring several vacuum tubes. The Whirlwind I computer (1951) built by Massachusetts Institute of Technology had a speed of 20,000 operations per second, the fastest computer of its time. This computer required only 5,000 vacuum tubes, mostly pentodes, but there were 11,000 diodes. The IBM 701 computer (1953) had 4,000 vacuum tubes, mostly twin triodes, and 13,000 germanium diodes.

Second-Generation Computers. The logic circuits used on second-generation computers were primarily discrete circuits using transistors. Although invented in 1948, the transistor required a decade of development ef-fort before it became a practical alternative to vacuum tubes. Transistors are faster, smaller, and more reliable, and dissipate less power than vacuum tubes.

There are many ways and configurations to implement logic circuits with semiconductor diodes, resistors, and transistors. The transistors in this second generation were primarily bipolar transistors, which means that carriers of both polarities, electrons and holes, are involved to form the total current. No single transistor configuration was superior to all others in all respects. The more widely-used types of circuits included RTL (resistor-

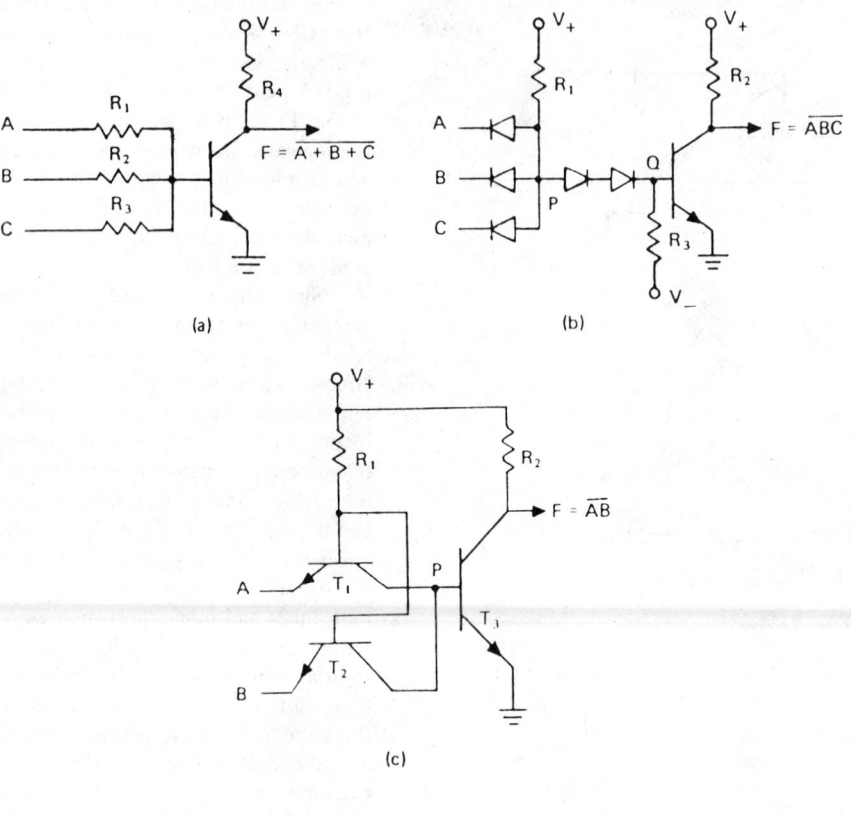

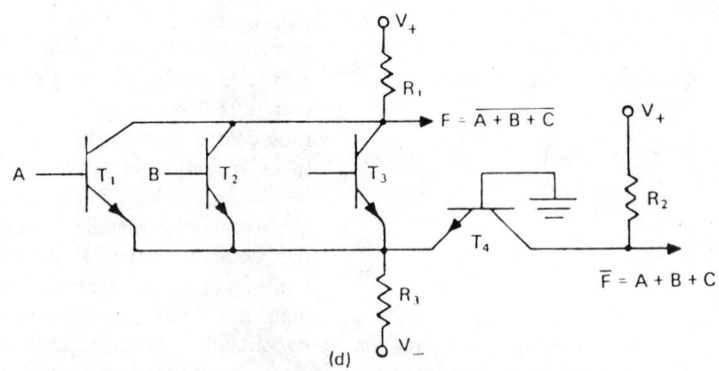

Fig. 5. Second-generation logic circuits. (a) RTL circuit; (b) DTL circuit; (c) TTL circuit; (d) ECL circuit.

transistor logic), DTL (diode-transistor logic), TTL (transistor-transistor logic), and ECL (emitter-coupled logic), which are shown in Fig. 5.

RTL (Resistor-Transistor Logic). The basic RTL circuit is shown in Fig. 5a. The RTL circuit is a simple and inexpensive logic circuit. Resistors R_1, R_2, and R_3 form an OR gate. The transistor T, along with its load resistor R_4, forms the amplifier-inverter section of the circuit in a manner similar to the controlled switch *not* gate of Fig. 2a. This RTL circuit is therefore a *nor* gate but it is relatively slow.

DTL (Diode-Transistor Logic). The basic DTL circuit is shown in Fig. 5b. Speed, fan-out capability, noise immunity, and power dissipation are good. When one or more of the inputs *(A, B, C)* are at logical 0, or the low-voltage state, current will flow from V_+ through resistor R_1 into the inputs. Point P as well as Q will be at a low voltage. The transistor will be off and the output F will assume a high-voltage, or logical 1, state. Only when all the inputs are at logical 1, the high-voltage state, will the current be directed to flow through R_1, two diodes in series, and R_3 into V_-. Point Q will now be at a high enough voltage level to turn on the transistor. Current will flow through the transistor, and the output F will assume a low-voltage, or logical 0, state. The two diodes in series are used in order to get the correct voltage level at point Q. The output can go to a logical 0 state only when all inputs are logical 1. The DTL circuit, therefore, performs a *nand* function.

TTL (Transistor-Transistor Logic). The basic TTL circuit is shown in Fig. 5c. The circuit is also a *nand* gate and is capable of significantly higher-speed operation than either RTL or DTL circuits. When either input A or input B, or both, are at logical 0 state, there will be sufficient base-to-emitter voltage difference so that either T_1 or T_2, or both, will be turned on. Point P, which connects to the collectors of both transistors, will assume a low-voltage state to turn off T_3. There will be little current flowing through R_2 and the output will be high, or at logical 1. When and only when both inputs A and B are high, both transistors T_1 and T_2 will be off and point P can return to a higher voltage level to turn on T_3. Output F will come to a low-voltage state when T_3 is on and current flows through R_2.

ECL (Emitter-Coupled Logic). The basic ECL circuit is shown in Fig. 5d and is potentially the fastest transistor logic circuit available, since all the transistors operate in a nonsaturating mode in order to attain high speeds. The emitter current passing through R_3 is essentially constant, with the current passing through R_1 when any of the inputs is a logical 1 or passing through R_2 when every input is a logical 0. Transistor T_4 establishes the reference voltage for the logical 0 and logical 1 states of the input transistors T_1, T_2, and T_3. The input transistors in combination with the reference transistor act as a dif-ferential amplifier having good common mode rejection of power-supply line noises. Also both a *nor* output F and an *or* output $\bar{F}$ are available, yielding complementary gating functions.

Typical second-generation computers using these circuits include the IBM 7000 series (first delivery 1960) and Burroughs B200 series (first delivery 1961).

Third-Generation Computers. A computer using vacuum tubes was considered a first-generation computer, and one using transistors was considered a second-generation computer. However, the distinction between second- and third-generation computers is not so clear-cut. Those manufacturers using integrated circuits tended to believe that the use of integrated circuit (IC) technology should be the criterion for distinguishing third- from second-generation computers. On the other hand, those manufacturers still using discrete component technology tended to believe that performance and architecture would be better measures. Thus, Control Data Corporation 6000 series computers, which were implemented by discrete component circuits, are usually classified as third-generation computers because of their performance. Furthermore, the IBM 360 family of computers is considered third-generation, although it utilizes hybrid circuit technology that is partially integrated circuit technology and partially discrete device technology. Nevertheless, from the computer circuitry point of view, integrated circuit technology will be used to define a third-generation computer whether the circuitry is fully or only partially integrated.

The logic circuits used in a third-generation computer have the same basic circuit configuration as those in second-generation computers. In integrated circuits, the transistors, diodes, and resistors are all fabricated simultaneously on a silicon wafer. Cost differentiation among these devices, which is of utmost importance in discrete components, is not significant in integrated circuits. TTL circuits and ECL circuits, which use more transistors, can be fabricated at about the same cost as RTL or DTL circuits, with the result that integrated RTL and DTL circuits have been supplanted by their TTL equivalents. In general, the integrated circuit versions of logic circuits have more transistors, are more complex, and have better performance at lower cost than their discrete counterparts.

Hybrid DTL. The IBM 360 family of computers (first delivery 1965) used hybrid circuits. One aspect of this design is that the transistors and diodes were encapsulated in a protective layer of glass so that a hermetic seal was unnecessary. Resistors are fabricated as thin-film devices and metallization patterns make the substrate interconnections. The logic substrate contains a DTL circuit, which is given in Fig. 6. Basically, the circuit is still a *nand* gate when A, B, and C are used. The

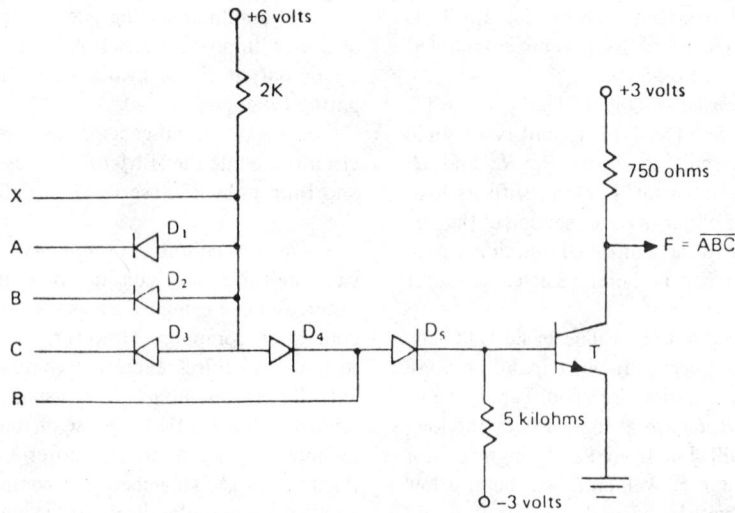

Fig. 6. The DTL circuit of the IBM 360 (SLT).

X input lead is called an "expander" and serves to connect additional diodes that may be added to increase fanin. The *R* input lead permits an *or* coupling circuit to be added to the logical operations of the circuit. Some of the advantages of this technology are better quality and reliability for both active and passive components, high component density, and high-speed performance.

Integrated TTL. The integrated version of TTL shown in Fig. 7a is quite different from the discrete component TTL shown in Fig. 5c. The input transistors T_1 and T_2 in Fig. 5c are combined into a single transistor with double emitters. The output circuit typically uses a so-called "totem pole" output stage consisting of active devices to pull up (T_3) and pull down (T_4) the output so that better and faster switching rates can be maintained even when the circuit is driving lines with considerable capacitance.

The IC versions of DTL and ECL have no significant differences from their counterparts in discrete components, and require no further discussion.

Integrated Field-Effect Transistor Circuits. Since the mid-1960s, the MOSFET (metal-oxide semiconductor field-effect transistor) has been a strong competitor of the bipolar transistor for logic applications. The MOSFET is a unipolar device whose current is transported by carriers of one polarity only. Integrated MOS logic circuits challenge bipolar circuits because of their lower cost, lower power consumption, and higher density. Typical MOSFET logic circuits are shown in Fig. 7b and 7c. A MOS device can be either an *N*-channel or a *P*-channel. In the former, the current is carried by electrons; in the latter, by holes.

LSI in Computers. The notion of computer classification according to generations based on underlying circuitry has become much less useful than previously as a means of differentiating third-generation machines from those appearing later. Nevertheless, the pace of technological innovation has continued unabated as more and more complex functions have been successfully implemented on integrated circuit chips. Simple 8-bit processors, implemented on a single integrated circuit, have been commercially available since the early 1970s. Recently, more advanced 8- and 16-bit processors have become available, with (as of 1980) 32-bit processors being promised in the near future. These so-called *microprocessors* require external memory and some support circuitry to form a working computer. Single-chip *microcomputers* incorporating processor, memory, and some I/O capabilities are also available. Peripheral controller chips greatly simplifying the amount of circuitry required to control disks, printers, CRT's, etc. are routinely in use. Fast arithmetic and logic units and microprogram sequencers are available in several logic families to assist the designers of more traditional mini- and large-scale computers.

The most dramatic improvements in integrated circuit technology have occurred using *N*-channel silicon gate devices. However, CMOS (complementary MOS) technology incorporating both *N*-channel and *P*-channel devices is very promising because of its low power dissipation. Bipolar technologies also remain very popular. In general, bipolar devices require more area to fabricate and dissipate more power than MOS devices and, hence, bipolar technology trails MOS with respect to complexity per chip. Standard TTL logic is being supplanted by a lower-power, higher-speed version known as LSTTL (low power Schottky TTL). In addition, a very promising bipolar technology known as I^2-L (integrated injection logic) is gaining favor because gates can be made quite

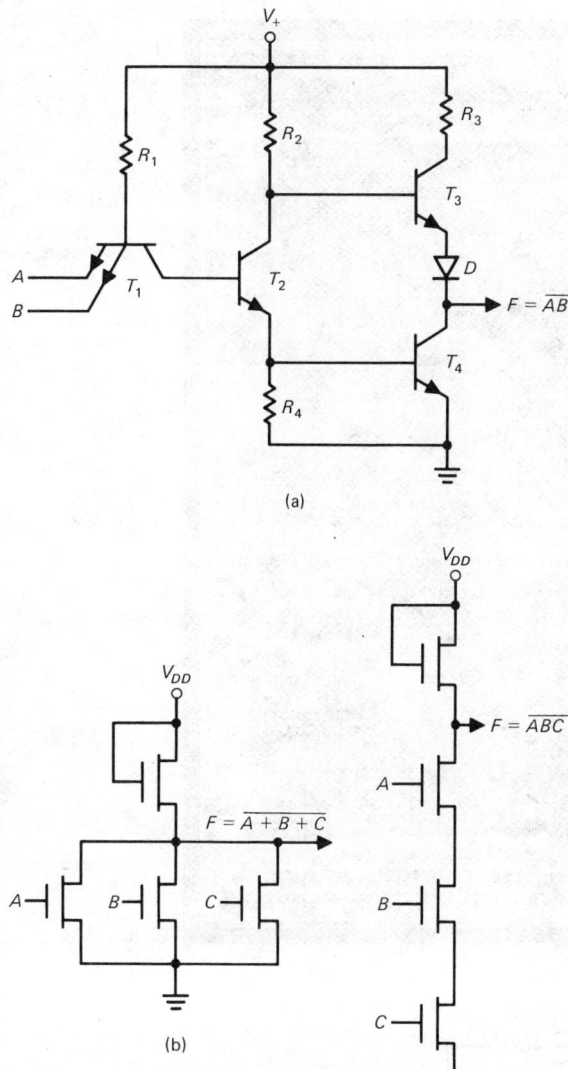

Fig. 7. (a) An integrated TTL circuit; (b) MOSFET *nor* circuit; (c) MOSFET *nand* circuit.

small, rivaling MOS gates in size and power dissipation and because the user can control the speed-power trade-off by choice of the power supply voltage. Fig. 8 shows a 16-bit microprocessor.

Some Commonly Used Computer Circuitry.
Computer circuitry can be divided into combinational circuits and sequential circuits.

Combinational Circuits. A combinational circuit is a logic circuit whose output is determined solely by the present state of inputs and is independent of the previous states of its inputs. Commonly used combinational circuits include multiplexers, comparators, adders, and decoders. They are built from the basic logic gates described previously. Most of them are available in either bipolar or MOS integrated circuit modules from semiconductor manufacturers. Some typical examples of combinational circuits are described below.

Full Adder. A binary full adder will add two binary bit inputs (A and B) and a previous carry bit (C_{in1}). The outputs will be a sum bit S_1 and a carry bit C_{out1}. The logic block diagram and the truth tables are shown in Fig. 9. Typically, four such adders are sold in one 16-pin package.

BCD-to-Decimal Decoder. This circuit decodes a four-bit BCD (binary-coded decimal) input to select one of ten outputs. The selected output is in the logical 0 state, and all the other outputs are in the logical 1 state. The logic layout and the truth table are shown in Fig. 10. Such circuits are also available in a 16-pin package.

Many other combinational circuits available commercially are implemented by various technologies. The reader is referred to the data sheets or catalogs of the numerous semiconductor manufacturers.

Sequential Circuits. Logic circuits that can store digital information are classified as sequential circuits. In contrast to that of a combinational circuit, the output of a sequential circuit depends not only on the present input state, but also on previous input states. From a topological point of view, a sequential circuit is different from a combinational circuit in that it has feedback paths that connect the outputs back to the inputs. The feedback loops enable the sequential circuit to have several stable states, which, in effect, record information about the past history of the inputs. Some of the more commonly used sequential circuits are described below.

Flipflop. A flipflop is a basic storage element used for computer arithmetic operations. The logic layout of a flipflop is shown in Fig. 11. To understand the principle of operation of a flipflop, assume that S and R are both 0, and note that there are two stable states. One occurs when Q is a 1, and $\overline{Q}$ is a 0, in which case the flipflop is said to be *set*. The other stable state is just the reverse, so that Q is a 0 and $\overline{Q}$ is a 1. Then the flipflop is said to be *reset* or *cleared*. The memory capabilities of such a flipflop can be illustrated by assuming that it is currently reset, the R line is a 0 and the S line is initially 0, brought to a 1 briefly, and then taken back to a zero. The 0 to 1 transition on the S line causes $\overline{Q}$ to go to a zero, which propagates to the bottom *nor* gate causing the $\overline{Q}$ output to become a 1. The flipflop remains set even when the S line goes back to 0. Similar reasoning shows that the flipflop can be cleared by applying a pulse on the R line. Pulsing the S line of a flipflop already set or the R line of one already reset does not change either the Q or $\overline{Q}$ out-

Fig. 8. The Z8000, a 16-bit microprocessor.

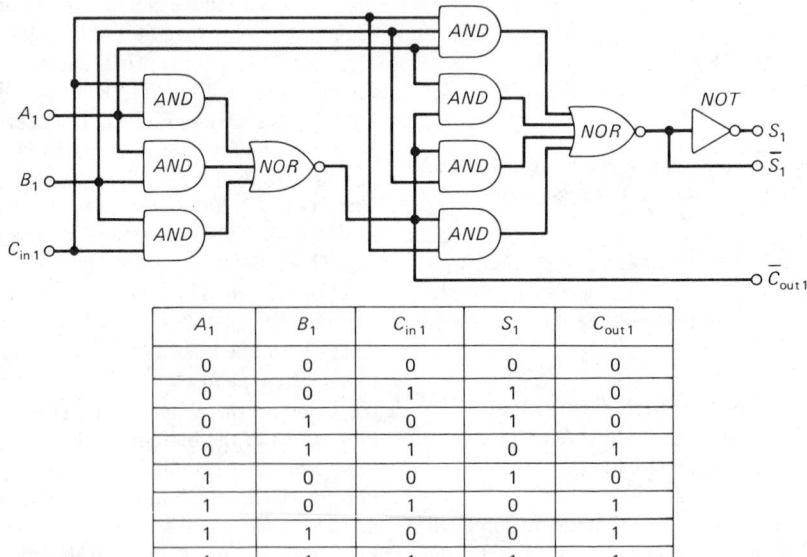

A_1	B_1	$C_{in\,1}$	S_1	$C_{out\,1}$
0	0	0	0	0
0	0	1	1	0
0	1	0	1	0
0	1	1	0	1
1	0	0	1	0
1	0	1	0	1
1	1	0	0	1
1	1	1	1	1

Fig. 9. Full adder.

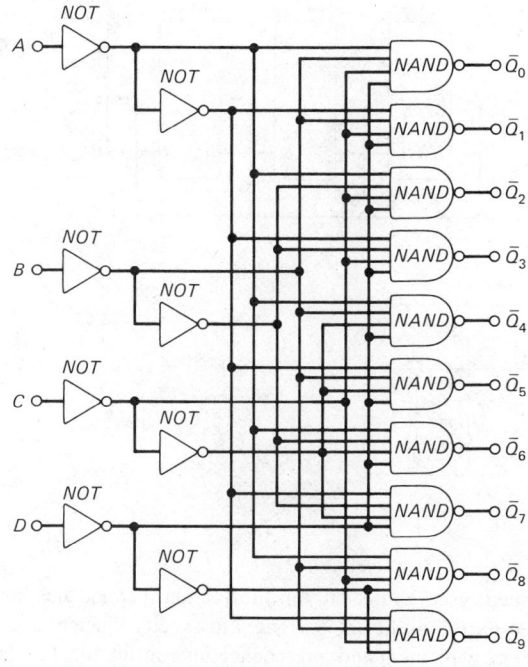

Inputs				Outputs									
D	C	B	A	$\bar{Q}_9$	$\bar{Q}_8$	$\bar{Q}_7$	$\bar{Q}_6$	$\bar{Q}_5$	$\bar{Q}_4$	$\bar{Q}_3$	$\bar{Q}_2$	$\bar{Q}_1$	$\bar{Q}_0$
0	0	0	0	1	1	1	1	1	1	1	1	1	0
0	0	0	1	1	1	1	1	1	1	1	1	0	1
0	0	1	0	1	1	1	1	1	1	1	0	1	1
0	0	1	1	1	1	1	1	1	1	0	1	1	1
0	1	0	0	1	1	1	1	1	0	1	1	1	1
0	1	0	1	1	1	1	1	0	1	1	1	1	1
0	1	1	0	1	1	1	0	1	1	1	1	1	1
0	1	1	1	1	1	0	1	1	1	1	1	1	1
1	0	0	0	1	0	1	1	1	1	1	1	1	1
1	0	0	1	0	1	1	1	1	1	1	1	1	1
1	0	1	0	1	1	1	1	1	1	1	1	1	1
1	0	1	1	1	1	1	1	1	1	1	1	1	1
1	1	0	0	1	1	1	1	1	1	1	1	1	1
1	1	0	1	1	1	1	1	1	1	1	1	1	1
1	1	1	0	1	1	1	1	1	1	1	1	1	1
1	1	1	1	1	1	1	1	1	1	1	1	1	1

Fig. 10.   BCD to decimal decoder.

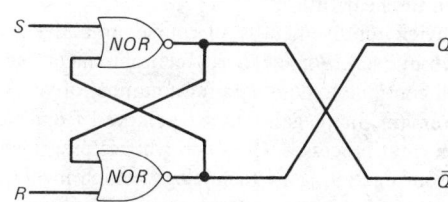

Fig. 11.   *S-R* flipflop logic diagram.

put. The flipflop, therefore, has the property of "remembering" which input line was pulsed last.

An important requirement for successful computer operation is the ability to transfer information from one storage cell to another at precisely defined times. One way to do this is with a *clock* signal. In its simplest form, a clock signal may be thought of as a train of pulses where the separation between pulses is constant. Transfer of information within the central processing unit is synchronized to the clock signal in modern computers. In modern computers, clock frequencies of 10 MHz and even higher are not unusual. Fig. 12 shows how a pair of *and* gates can be used with the *S-R* flipflop to produce a clocked *S-R* flipflop that will respond to requests to store information only if such requests are synchronized with a clock signal provided on the *C* lead. Fig. 12 also shows a MOSFET implementation of such a clocked *S-R* flipflop. Other forms of flipflops are also available. For example, notice that if both the *S* and *R* inputs are a 1 when the clock pulse arrives, the flipflop's state will be undefined. A *J-K* flipflop is similar to an *S-R* flipflop, but has the property that if *J* and *K* are active when the flipflop is clocked, then the output changes state. A *D* flipflop has only one input and its output assumes the state of the input upon arrival of a clock pulse.

Shift Registers. Shift registers may be formed from

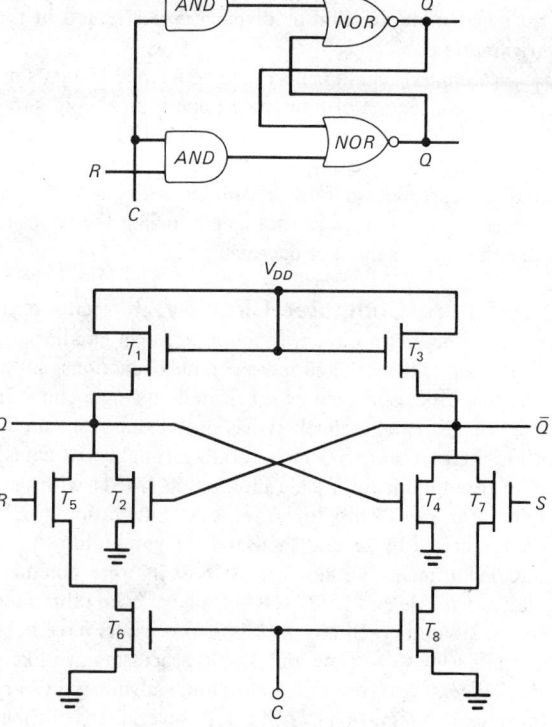

Fig. 12.   The logic layout and the MOSFET implementation of a clocked *S-R* flipflop.

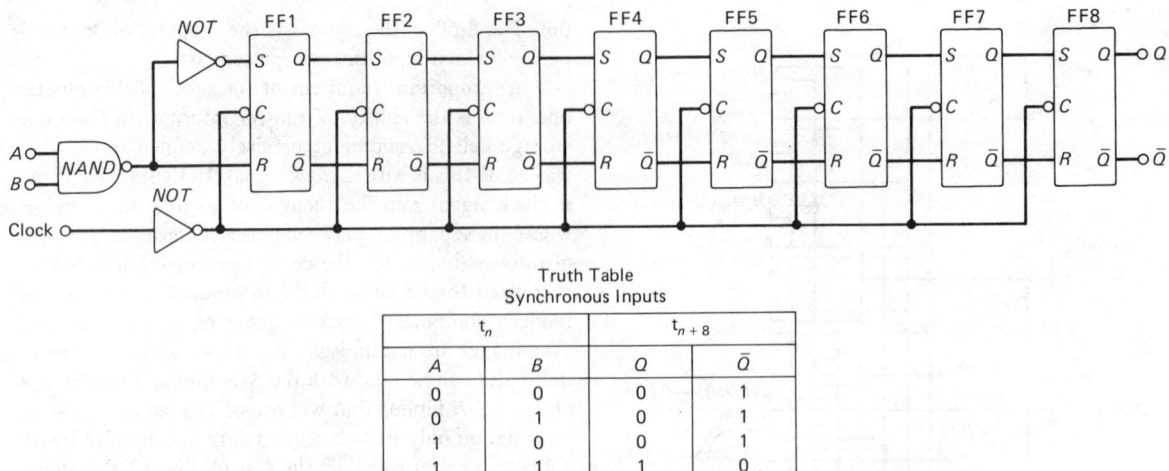

	t_n		t_{n+8}	
A	B	Q	$\bar{Q}$
---	---	---	---
0	0	0	1
0	1	0	1
1	0	0	1
1	1	1	0

Truth Table
Synchronous Inputs

Fig. 13. An eight-bit shift register.

a series of flipflop circuits. A typical shift register is shown in Fig. 13, where the clock signal is connected to all the flipflops. At each clock pulse, one bit of information will be written into the flipflop FF1 from inputs *A* and *B*. At the next clock pulse, this bit will move to the flipflop FF2 while a new bit is being written into FF1. Bidirectional shifting is possible when some additional control gates are added. Shift registers are especially useful when multiplication or division is performed in the arithmetic unit.

Counters. Counters may also be formed from a simple interconnection of flipflops. In one typical configuration, a 4-bit counter is packaged in a 16-pin package, with a high order carry provided so that several stages may be cascaded to form a counter with more stages. Some counters have a control lead allowing the count to be either incremented or decremented.

Future Computer Circuitry. It seems clear that computer circuitry will continue to get smaller and faster and that more and more complex functions, not to mention processors, will be fabricated on single chips. In the last 15 years, technology has progressed from small-scale integration (SSI) incorporating roughly 10 gates/chip through medium-scale integration (MSI) with perhaps 100 gates/chip to large scale integration (LSI) characterized by several thousands of gates/chip. As of late 1980, memory chips with 64K cells were commercially available and 256K cell chips have been fabricated in the laboratory. Similarly, 16-bit processors have been available for some time and 32-bit processors are likely in the next year or two. Continuing advances in very large-scale integration (VLSI), with several tens of thousands of gates/chip, are very much dependent upon con-

tinued research not only in fabrication technologies, but also on the ability of designers to specify efficiently the device placement and interconnection routing for the vast number of gates that are used in a modern computer.

Some impediments to progress are not directly related either to chip complexity or to the electrical properties of devices. One rather fundamental limitation is the difficulty in cooling chips adequately with large numbers of devices. Even with forced air cooling, conventional packages are capable of dissipating only a few watts. Since the ability of a package to dissipate heat is related to its bulk, and the desire is to package integrated circuits in smaller packages, it is imperative that the per gate power dissipation figure be decreased as circuit density increases.

Another impediment is the means of connecting integrated circuits. Current popular packages are limited to a maximum of 64 pins. This presents a definite constraint on the type, size, and speed of the circuitry which may be placed in a single package. For example, some current microprocessors share memory address and data information on a single set of pins. As larger processors are contemplated, this will become an even more significant limitation. New packaging techniques with more but smaller and more closely spaced pins are under development and may well replace the currently standard packaging in the near future.

Device improvement is, of course, an active area of research in itself. Some experts feel that silicon technology will continue to dominate for a number of years, and there remain many gains to be achieved from scaling down current processes. However, work is progressing in Josephson junction *(q.v.)* technology, which involves the use of a superconducting switch and which promises extremely fast operation. Another technology holding promise is based on gallium arsenide (GaAs) semiconductors. Once again, the promise is faster switching speed and lower power dissipation.

As denser, more efficient device technology becomes available, it seems likely that the approaches to circuit design will undergo some changes. With more devices on a chip, the problem of verifying the proper functioning of the chip becomes increasingly significant. In addition, current circuitry is fabricated with the premise that all gates will be fully functional. As more complex designs, encompassing larger chip area, are conceived, and as devices become smaller, the probability of every gate functioning perfectly is decreased. Future circuit designs will undoubtedly incorporate fault-tolerant techniques to enhance the reliability in the face of gate malfunction, as well as the testability of the circuitry.

The layout problem, mentioned earlier, is quite significant, and designers are being forced to use circuitry whose topology is very regular and repetitive in nature so that layout issues become tractable. Even so, the chip area taken by interconnections is equivalent to that occupied by active devices. Some experts feel that this problem can be alleviated by going to multi-valued logic circuitry. That is, instead of differentiating between two levels, circuitry can be used which has four or eight distinct states. Communicating with such signals allows more efficient use of the interconnections and should allow better use of the chip area. Another possible use of multi-valued logic is as an aid in overcoming the pinout limitation problems alluded to earlier.

The system advantages of dealing with circuitry that consists of one or a few LSI and MSI packages, as opposed to a large number of SSI packages, are overwhelming. These typically include lower cost, easier maintenance, reduced printed circuit board area, and reduced power consumption. Unfortunately, the effort and capital involved in developing and fabricating an LSI or VLSI part cannot normally be justified unless tens of thousands of copies of the part are required. For applications with less than this volume, and even for some high-volume parts, a gate array approach may be used. In this technique, the manufacturer provides a chip with a fixed number of independent unconnected gates. The logic designer specifies the interconnection pattern but has no control over gate placement. Since the forming of the interconnections is the last, and perhaps least critical, step in integrated circuit production, the incremental cost of customizing the final interconnection step is low enough to allow economical low volume production of integrated circuits.

Computer design aids have become necessities in the design of VLSI circuitry. These circuits may have hundreds of thousands of transistors and even more in-terconnections, all of which must be accurately positioned. It is clear that a computer is invaluable just in maintaining the data required to specify the design. But even more, if progress in new designs leading to more sophisticated integrated circuits is to continue at the rate it has in the past couple of decades, computer-based design tools are necessary. These include advanced graphics facilities, not only for the visual presentation of the design, but also to allow designs to be revised easily; programs to aid in transistor placement and interconnection routing; programs to perform design rule checking to insure manufacturability; and simulation programs to verify correct electrical as well as logical operation of the design without having actually to fabricate the part.

No one can predict with certainty what future computer circuitry will look like, but it seems safe to say that current trends toward smaller, faster devices will continue unabated, as will be trend towards building more complex systems on few chips.

REFERENCES

1976. Lee, S. C. *Digital Circuits and Logic Design.* Englewood Cliffs, N.J.: Prentice-Hall.
1978. Kohavi, Z. *Switching and Finite Automata Theory.* New York: McGraw-Hill.
1979. Millman, J. *Microelectronics.* New York: McGraw-Hill.
1980. Bartee, T. C. *Digital Computer Fundamentals* (5th Ed.). New York: McGraw-Hill.

S. S. YAU AND F. M. BRASCH, Jr.

COMPUTER GAMES

For articles on related subjects *see* GAMES ON COMPUTERS; MICROPROCESSORS AND MICROCOMPUTERS; and PERSONAL COMPUTERS.

The term "computer games" refers to a wide variety of recreational and educational uses of computers. The best known and least sophisticated are the hand-held, toy-like games, electronic chess, checker and backgammon games, and simple arcade and home games, in which balls and symbols bounce, dance, and splat on a TV screen. But computer simulations involving more flexible and advanced computers and used as games have already proved their value in a variety of settings but are only in their infancy. For recreation, they offer far more potential variety and sophistication than TV or handheld games. And for education, they provide an incomparable motivational tool.

As an example in the educational context, suppose it's 1847. Your team of oxen has been pulling your wagon across Kansas for the last two weeks and you reckon you've been covering a good 15 miles a day. Faced with the Republican River, you decide to ford it—but it's deeper than you thought! The wagon is swamped and you lose most of your food and clothes. Fortunately, you had secured your medical supplies and ammunition high in the wagon and you didn't lose those. But now you have to decide whether to make for the next fort, which is three days away, or to stop and hunt. Since you're in buffalo country, you decide to hunt and wait until later to stop at a fort.

And so it continues in the computer game "Oregon Trail." During your six-month journey, you face attacks from wild animals, Indians, and bandits. Your wagon can get swamped, break a wheel, or even have a fire. Your oxen can get injured or may wander off. In the mountains, heavy rains, snow, and impassable trails are constant hazards. Illness and injuries are always a threat.

Fewer than 30% of the pioneers that set off from Independence, MO from 1840 to 1870 ever made it to the west coast. Now it's your turn to see if you can be one of the survivors. But at least if *you* don't make it, you get another chance!

How would you like to learn about history by living through it vicariously via a computer game? Given the choice, millions of kids are choosing the computer game approach, and their teachers are finding the learning is frequently better than that provided by the traditional textbook.

These types of games, called simulations, are available in many subject areas for many grade levels. In social studies, young children can learn how a simple economic system works using the program "Hammurabi." Players decide how much land to plant with grain each year, how much to feed their people, and how much to trade with neighboring city-states. Harvests are good in some years, bad in others. Rats sometimes get in the grain bins. "King," a more complex simulation in the same vein, introduces the problems of industrial development, pollution, and tourism. Economics on a local scale can be experienced with the program "Lemonade Stand." In the simulation, players must decide how much lemonade to make, the price to charge, and how many signs to make. One outside variable is the weather; rainy days are obviously not good for lemonade sales. On the other hand, a circus parade is a big stimulant.

Science and ecology simulations allow players to experience situations and experiment with variables that are far beyond the reach of any normal classroom or textbook. For example, in "Malaria," students must try to control a malaria outbreak in a Central American country (see Fig. 1). Pesticides, treatment for the ill, preven-

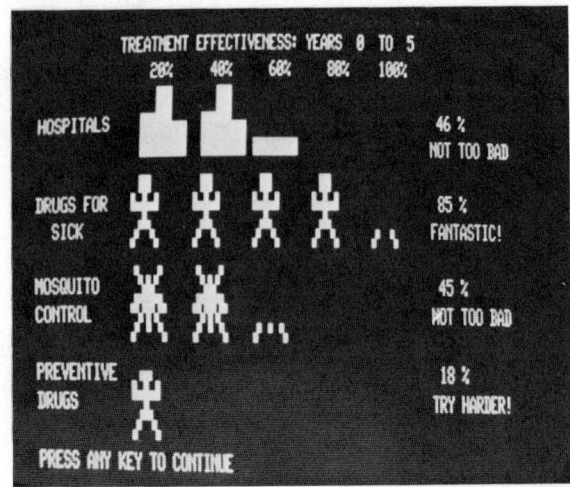

Fig. 1. In "Malaria," students try to control the disease using field hospitals, preventive drugs, and pesticide spraying.

tive inoculations, and field hospitals are the variables to be controlled. Students discover that the disease is easy to control if cost is no object, but, unfortunately, cost is a major barrier in most third world nations.

"Tag" lets students experiment with the tagging-and-recovery method of measuring wildlife populations. Users of "Sterl" try to eradicate the destructive screw worm fly with various types of pesticides, as well as with male sterilization.

In English, games such as "Hangman" and "Don't Fall" help teach children word skills in a highly motivational way. In "Madlibs" and "Red Riding," the program creates funny, often hilarious, stories. However, for them to be readable, the player must use various parts of speech correctly. "Spelling," "Haiku," "Bard," and other games provide practice in other aspects of language arts.

"Adventure" is a very popular computer game in which players explore a Tolkien-like environment complete with trolls, animals, and treasures in a landscape of hills, ravines, forests, and caves. You give the computer commands, such as "Go West," "Pick Up Lantern," or "Drink Water." Your object is to (1) discover how to play the game and (2) overcome the obstacles, find the treasure, and return to "civilization." Now imagine playing this fascinating and addictive game in French (or Spanish, or German). Language teachers have never before had such a powerful motivational tool to assist them in their teaching. Giving a child this game is like parachuting the student into the midst of a foreign country with the instructions, "Learn to speak the language and you will be able to survive, find some treasure, and escape."

Similarly fascinating games have been written in

many other subject areas: Mathematics, geometry, and logic (where it all started), physics, chemistry, biology, economics, business, medicine, geology, and many, many others.

Computer games know no age limits. For the new Sesame Street participatory play parks, Creative Computing Software has developed a series of games for players who cannot yet read. At the Lighthouse School in Wisconsin, first to third graders are writing their own games. Elementary and secondary schools, colleges, and graduate schools throughout the U.S. are using computer games. In Salt Lake City, a public education center is teaching adults English language skills via computer, while several museums have computer game exhibits oriented to visitors of all ages.

Of course, many of these "educational" games are being played just for sheer fun. The dividing line between education and recreation is a bit muddy: Is playing chess, for example, solely recreation, or is there learning taking place? There are, however, scores of computer games written specifically for fun. Computer programmers at many installations wrote games for their own enjoyment in the 1950s. The first of these to emerge on a widespread basis was "Space War", which surfaced at MIT's Department of Electrical Engineering around 1961. Also, some of the chess and checkers programs written as part of artificial intelligence research projects in the 1950s and 1960s started to become more widely available, too.

But the widespread availability of computer power in the late 1960s, and the mass availability with the advent of the microcomputer in 1975, saw hundreds of small companies and individuals rush to produce the "ultimate" computer game. "Star Trek" held the lead in popularity for about two years, but Paramount's unwillingness to license the name has precluded mass usage. As of late 1979, contenders for the leading computer game included "Breakout" (Atari) and its many derivatives, "Super Invader" (Creative Computing), "Adventure," and several chess and backgammon programs.

Where to from here? It's anybody's guess. Obviously, new games will use the newer technology now available—high resolution color graphics, multi-channel music and sound synthesizers, voice synthesis and recognition, light pens, and much more. The real-time "Air Traffic Controller" game/simulation today almost exactly duplicates the situation faced by an actual air traffic controller. Tomorrow, one will be able to eliminate the word "almost."

Computers weren't invented to play games. But computerists, right from the very beginning, found that these machines could be programmed to do so—and awfully well. The known motivation of games in general, and the fact that computer usage tends to increase personal interaction and peer tutoring, together make com-

puter games one of the most powerful educational tools and one of the most enjoyable recreational pastimes available today.

DAVID H. AHL

COMPUTER GENERATIONS. *See* GENERATIONS, COMPUTER.

COMPUTER GRAPHICS

For articles on related subjects *see* BIOMEDICINE, COMPUTER GRAPHICS IN; COMPUTER-AIDED DESIGN; CURSOR; DATA STRUCTURES; DATA TABLET; IMAGE PROCESSING; INPUT-OUTPUT DEVICES; JOYSTICK; LIGHTPEN; PICTURES, BASIC STRUCTURE; TERMINALS; and TIME SHARING.

Computer graphics may be defined as the input, construction, storage, retrieval, manipulation, alteration, and analysis of objects and their pictorial representation. Computer graphics in general include both off-line input of drawings or photographs of objects via scanners, digitizers, or pattern recognition devices, and output of drawings on paper or (micro) film via plotters and film recorders. Interactive graphics is a term used to emphasize user-computer dialogue, which takes place in real-time using an on-line display console with input (interaction) devices.

Among such input devices are the alphanumeric and function keyboards for typing text and activating preprogrammed subroutines, respectively, and the lightpen, data tablet, and joystick *(q.v.)* for identifying and entering graphic information by means of pointing and drawing.

The scope of this survey article is restricted to interactive graphics (called simply "graphics" in what follows), and therefore excludes scene analysis and pattern recognition, image processing and enhancement, computer animation, etc., which are covered elsewhere in this encyclopedia (*see* IMAGE PROCESSING). Newman and Sproull (1979) and Foley and van Dam (1982) discuss the technology and its applications in far greater detail.

The Advantages of Interactive Graphics.
Interactive computer graphics is the most important mechanized means for producing and reproducing pictures since such innovations as photography, xerography, and television, and has also the added advantage that, with the computer, we can make pictures of abstract, synthetic objects. Interactive graphics is a form of human-

machine interaction that combines the best features of the *interactiveness* of textual (alphanumeric) communication via on-line keyboard terminals with the *graphical communication* of two-dimensional plotting. With interactive graphics, we are largely liberated from the tedium and frustration of trying to look for patterns and trends by scanning many pages of linear text on line-printer listings or alphanumeric terminals.

While static pictures are often a good means of communicating information, dynamically varying pictures are frequently even better. This is especially true when one needs to visualize time-varying phenomena, both real (e.g., shock waves caused by a sharp object penetrating a soft one) and abstract (e.g., growth trends such as the use of nuclear energy or the population movement from cities to suburbs and back to the cities, as functions of time). Much of interactive graphics technology, therefore, deals with hardware and software techniques for user-controlled motion dynamics and update dynamics.

With *motion dynamics,* objects can be moved and tumbled with respect to a stationary observer. Equivalently, the objects can remain stationary and the viewer can move around them ("pan") to select the portion in view and "zoom" in or out for more or less detail, as if looking through the viewfinder of a rapidly moving camera. Flight simulators are used to train aircraft or ship pilots by letting them maneuver their simulated craft over a simulated three-dimensional landscape portrayed on one or more cockpit windows, which are actually large TV screens. Similarly, motion dynamics are used to let a user fly around and through buildings, molecules, two-, three-, or four-dimensional mathematical functions, or "clouds" (scatter diagrams) of data points in two- or three-dimensional space. In another form of motion dynamics, the "camera" is held fixed but the objects in the scene are moved relative to the camera. For example, a complex mechanical linkage, such as a gear train, may be animated on the screen by rotating all the individual gears appropriately.

Update dynamics refers to the actual change of the shape, color, or other properties of the objects being viewed. For instance, one can display the deformation of a metal frame by user-applied loads, or the state changes in a block diagram of a computer in response to data and control flows. The smoother the change, the more realistic and meaningful the result. Dynamic interactive graphics offers us a large number of user-controllable modes with which to encode and communicate information: The two- or three-dimensional shape of objects in a picture, their position and orientation, their *gray scale* (grayness value between white and black) or color, and the time variations of these properties. In the near future, this set will be extended by digitally encoded sound, so that objects and feedback from the program or the operating system can be heard as well as seen.

In summary, interactive computer graphics allows us to achieve much higher-bandwidth human-machine communication with a judicious combination of text and static and dynamic pictures than is possible with text alone. This higher bandwidth makes a significant difference in our ability to understand data, perceive trends, and visualize real or imaginary objects. By making communication more efficient, graphics makes possible greater productivity, higher-quality and more precise results or products, and lower design and analysis costs.

Some Representative Uses of Computer Graphics. Computer graphics is used today in many different areas of industry, business, government, education, entertainment, and, most recently, in the home. The list of applications is large and growing rapidly as simple display devices become routinely affordable. Below we list a representative sample of such areas.

(Interactive) Plotting in Business, Science, and Technology. Graphics today are probably still most frequently used to draw two- or three-dimensional graphs of mathematical, physical and economic functions, histograms, bar and pie charts, task scheduling charts, inventory and production charts, and a profusion of other plots. All are used to present trends and patterns in data in a meaningful and concise fashion in order to increase understanding of complex phenomena and to facilitate informed decision-making.

Cartography. Computer graphics are used for the production of highly accurate representations on paper or film of geographical and other natural phenomena. Examples include geographic maps, relief maps, exploration maps for drilling and mining, oceanographic charts, weather maps, contour maps, oil exploration maps, and population density maps.

Computer-Aided Drafting and Design. In computer-aided design (CAD—*q.v.*) interactive graphics are used to design components and systems of mechanical, electrical, electromechanical, and electronic devices (Prince, 1971). These systems include structures such as buildings, chemical and power plants, automobile bodies, airplane and ship hulls (and their contents), optical systems, and telephone and computer networks. The emphasis is sometimes on merely producing precise drawings of components and (sub)assemblies, as in on-line drafting or architectural rendering. More frequently, however, the emphasis is on interacting with a computer-based model of the component or system being designed in order to test, for example, its mechanical, electrical, or thermal properties. Often the model is interpreted by a simulator that feeds back the behavior of the system to the display console operator for further interactive design and test cycles. After objects have been designed, utility programs can *postprocess* the design database to make parts lists, do bill of materials processing, define numerical control tapes for cutting or drilling parts, etc. Computer-aided manufacturing (CAM) techniques also frequently make use of the database created with CAD; commercial CAD/CAM systems based on interactive graphics are proliferating.

Simulation and Animation. Computer-produced animated movies of the time-varying behavior of real or simulated objects are becoming increasingly popular. We can study mathematical models for such scientific phenomena as hydraulic flow, relativity, nuclear and chemical reactions, physiological systems and organs, and deformation of structures under load by seeing the effects of the transformations pictorially. A relatively new and also high-technology area is interactive two- and three-dimensional cartooning; this technique produces a very high visual quality and is becoming cost-effective through the use of modern computer graphics technology. Other sophisticated applications of animation are the flight simulators mentioned above. Simulators generate views not only of the fixed world in which the vehicle is moving, but also of special effects such as clouds, fog, smog, nighttime lights, and other craft of various sizes and shapes each on its own course. For the moon landings, astronauts piloting the lunar lander and its mother ship practiced docking maneuvers in a simulator.

As mentioned in the previous section, the execution and operation of hardware or software computer systems can also be nicely simulated and displayed graphically to show how components interact and change values. And finally, at the other end of the price-performance spectrum, penny-arcade games and home video games simulate primitive, artificial two- or three-dimensional worlds in real time, with limited animation, testing hand-eye coordination, and reaction time.

Process Control. While a flight simulator or penny-arcade game lets the user interact with a simulation of either a real or artificial world, many other applications enable the user to interact with some aspect of the real world itself. Status displays for refineries, power plants, and computer networks display data values from sensors attached to critical components in the system; the operator may then respond to exceptional conditions. Military commanders view field data (number and position of vehicles, weapons launched, troop movements, casualties) on *command and control* displays and revise their tactics as needed. Flight controllers at airports see computer-generated identification and status information along with the aircraft blips on their radar scopes and can thus control traffic more quickly and accurately than with the unannotated radar data alone. Spacecraft controllers

monitor telemetry data and initiate corrective procedures as needed.

Office Automation and Electronic Publication. The use of alphanumeric and graphic terminals which create and disseminate information in the office and even the home is increasing rapidly. Both traditional printed documents (hard-copy) and electronic documents (soft-copy) can be produced which contain not just text but also tables, graphs, and other two-dimensional information, as briefly disucssed in the next section.

Art and Commerce. Computer art and advertising have the common goal of expressing a "message" and attracting the attention of the public with aesthetically pleasing pictures. Very sophisticated mechanisms are available to the creator of the picture for modeling the objects and for the representation of light and shadows. Teletext and Videotex (discussed briefly in the next section; *see also* VIEWDATA) offer much simpler but still informative pictures. Finally, the production of slides for commercial, scientific, or educational presentations is also becoming a highly cost-effective use of graphics, given the steeply rising labor costs associated with tradiional means of processing such material.

Interactive Graphics in the Future: The Normal Mode of Interaction. Computer graphics today is still too often considered a special form of communication requiring special input/output hardware and software, to be used only where essential. Many of the applications cited above seem somewhat exotic to most people, and many require considerable hardware resources (both processing power and storage) and high-quality output devices. Pilot-controlled flight simulation, an extreme example, involves perhaps several million dollars' worth of special-purpose computer display equipment per installation.

Fortunately, primarily because of the rapidly decreasing cost of hardware (especially memory and microprocessors), interactive graphics is now feasible and practical for that large majority of applications that require only modest processor and display resources. Some of these applications are mentioned below to illustrate that graphics is coming of age as the normal means of user-computer communication (and even user-user communication).

As a first example, many introductory courses in computer science and other quantitative physical and social sciences now use interactive plotting and modeling or simulation on low-cost (TV-based) graphics terminals attached to time-sharing systems or personal computers. Simultaneously, a whole new generation of future college students is growing up with home computers which cost less than a thousand dollars and are given as presents or as a replacement for the traditional encyclopedia as "an investment in your child's future." Many of these home computers use low- to medium-resolution graphics terminals, increasingly with color. Their users are coming to view graphics as a natural, expected mode of communication rather than a unique mode requiring a special display device not easily available. The high cost of a convenient hard-copy output device on most home computers fortunately makes the old-fashioned habit of printing thick listings of output impossible and forces users to think in terms of simple but more compact graphical representations that typically fit on a single screen.

Another revolutionary development, now being imported to the U.S. from Europe and Canada, will vastly increase interactive graphics literacy. It involves the use of broadcast television and/or the telephone system, plus a simple keyboard, to let TV viewers select items from customized "electronic newspapers," browse through on-line encyclopedias and classified listings, and get stock quotations, entertainment listings, etc. (IEEE, 1974). Much of the information is transmitted in graphical form. These diagrams are still crude but are nonetheless effective in attracting the viewer's attention and communicating the necessary information. Once this medium becomes sufficiently reliable and cheap, using a computer-connected TV as an information resource for text and graphics will become as natural and commonplace as using the telephone.

On yet another front, the burgeoning fields of *word processing* and *office automation* are introducing large numbers of office workers and other producers and manipulators of documents to computer-based work stations for document preparation and electronic messaging and mail. More and more of these work stations will be based on high-quality display screens suitable for interactive graphics. While the emphasis until recently was on strictly alphanumeric interaction, the demand for charts and figures is sufficiently strong that systems sold in the near future can be expected to display them, along with surrounding high-quality "graphic arts" text, directly on the screen as they would appear on a hard-copy output device. This "what you see is what you get" design philosophy, in which the screen mirrors the printed page as much as possible, eliminates bothersome and unnatural formatting or typesetting codes whose effects are not seen on-line. Indeed, if one can see a page just as it will look when printed, much of the need to print will disappear, especially for documents without lasting value. Instead, most transient documents used in industry, commerce, government, and academia could be created, distributed, and responded to by electronic mail/publishing.

A Brief Historical Development of Graphics Technology.

Computer graphics started with plotting; crude plotting on hard-copy devices such as tele-

types and line printers dates from the early days of computing. M.I.T.'s 1950 Whirlwind Computer had computer-driven CRT displays for output (both for operators and for cameras to produce hard copy), while the Sage Air Defense System in the middle 1950s was the first to use "command and control" CRT (cathode ray tube) display consoles in which operators identified targets by pointing at them with lightpens. The CRT is the display device that also forms the basis of home TV sets. The beginnings of modern interactive graphics are found in Ivan Sutherland's seminal Sketchpad drawing system (Sutherland, 1963). He introduced data structures for storing symbol hierarchies that are built up via easy replication of standard components (a technique akin to the use of plastic templates for drawing flowchart or circuit symbols). He also developed interaction techniques for using the keyboard and lightpen for choice-making, pointing, and drawing, and formulated, in addition, many other fundamental ideas and techniques still in use today. The enormous potential for partially automating drafting and other drawing-intensive activities in computer-aided design (CAD) and computer-aided manufacturing (CAM) activities was not lost on manufacturers in the computer, automobile, and aerospace industries, and by the mid-1960s a number of research projects and commercial products began to appear. Prominent among these were General Motors' ambitious project for multiple time-shared graphics consoles for many phases of car design, the Digigraphic design system (first developed by Itek for lens design and later bought and marketed by CDC), and the IBM 2250 display system based on the General Motors prototype.

Despite this early promise, for many years interactive graphics remained beyond the resources of all but the most technology-intensive organizations. Among the reasons for this were:

- Underestimation of the *cost* of the graphics hardware (when produced without benefit of economics of scale).

- Significant *computing resources* required to support large databases, interactive picture manipulation, and the typically large set of postprocessing applications programs whose input came from the graphics design phase.

- The *difficulty of writing large, interactive programs* for a time-sharing environment at a time when both graphics and interaction were new to predominantly batch- (Fortran-) oriented programmers.

- *One-of-a-kind, nonportable software,* typically locked into a particular manufacturer's display device and produced without the benefit of modern software engineering principles for constructing modular, structured systems. When software is nonportable, moving to new display devices necessitates very expensive and time-consuming rewriting of working programs.

The significant developments in graphics hardware and software and in time-sharing technology which were required to make graphics both usable and affordable are discussed next.

Output Technology. The display devices developed in the middle 1960s and still in use today are called *vector,* stroke, or calligraphic displays. They consist of a display processor, a display buffer memory, and a CRT with its associated electronics. The buffer stores the computer-produced *display list* or *display program;* this contains point and line plotting commands with coordinates as endpoint data and character plotting commands (Fig. 1). These commands for plotting points, lines, and characters are interpreted by the display processor; it converts digital values to analog voltages that displace an electron beam writing on the phosphor coating of the CRT. Since the light output of the phosphor decays in hundreds of microseconds, the display processor must cycle through the list to *refresh* the phosphor at least 30 times per second to avoid flicker; hence the buffer holding the display list is usually called a *refresh buffer.* Note in Fig. 1 that the jump instruction loops back to the top of the display list to provide the cyclic refresh.

Both the buffer memory required for typical line

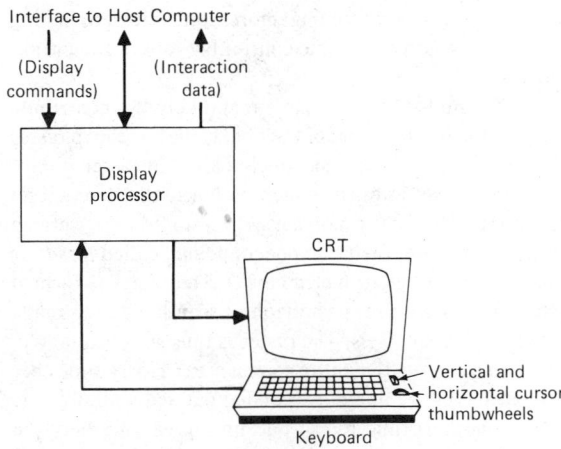

Interface to Host Computer

(Display commands)   (Interaction data)

Fig. 2.   Typical storage tube display.

drawings (8–32 kilobytes) and a processor fast enough to refresh at 30 cycles per second were very expensive in the 1960s. Thus, Tektronix's development in the late 1960s of the direct-view storage tube (DVST), which obviated both the buffer and the refresh process, was the vital step forward in making interactive graphics affordable (Fig. 2). In a DVST, the image is stored (until erased) by writing it once with a relatively slow-moving electron beam on a storage mesh in which the phosphor is embedded. This small, self-sufficient terminal-sized device was ideal for an inexpensive, low-speed (300–1,200 baud) telephone interface to a time-sharing system, and formed a most cost-effective alternative to the bulky, complex refresh systems attached via expensive, high-speed interfaces to input/output channels or peripheral controllers. DVSTs allowed interactive plotting for many simple applications at costs often an order of magnitude smaller than for refresh displays. Thus, they helped introduce many users and programmers not interested in complex CAD applications to interactive graphics. Storage tubes are still popular today for applications which demand large numbers (tens of thousands) of high-precision lines and characters but do not need dynamic picture manipulation.

The next major hardware advance was to relieve the central computer of the heavy demands of the refreshed display device (especially user-interaction handling and picture updating) by attaching it to a minicomputer. The minicomputer typically functions as a dedicated stand-alone computer for running applications programs as well as servicing the display and user interaction devices. Often it can also run as an "intelligent satellite" to the main computer, handling user interaction but leaving large computation or large-database jobs to the mainframe. At the same time, the hardware of the display pro-

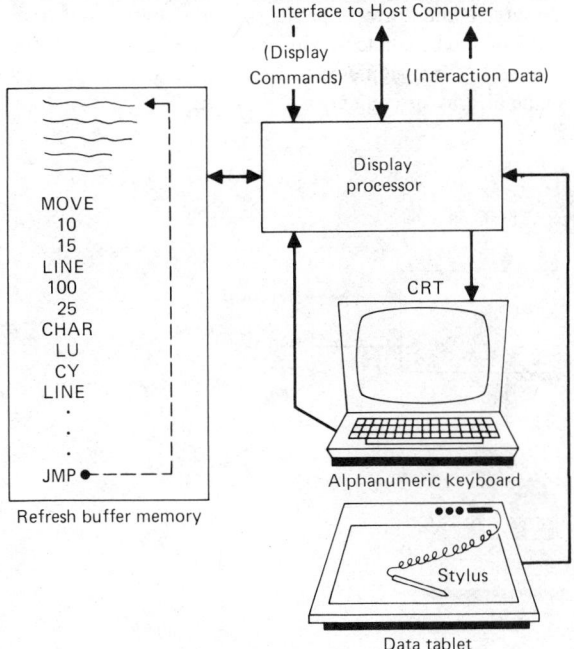

Fig. 1.   Typical refresh display device.

cessor itself was becoming more sophisticated, taking over many routine but time-consuming jobs of the graphics software.

The mid-1970s' development likely to contribute most to the development of the field is that of cheap raster graphics based on television technology. In raster graphics, the display primitives such as lines, characters, and solid areas (typically polygons) are stored in a refresh buffer in terms of their component points, called *pixels* or *pels* (short for "picture elements"). The image is formed from the *raster,* a set of horizontal scan lines each made up of individual pixels: The raster is thus simply a matrix of pixels covering the entire screen area. Thirty times per second the entire image is scanned out sequentially, one raster line at a time top to bottom, by varying only the intensity of the electron beam for each pixel on a line (Fig. 3). The storage needed is thus greatly increased in that the entire image of, say, 512 lines of 512 pixels each, must be stored explicitly in a *bit map* containing only points—which map one-for-one to points on the screen. On the other hand, the actual display of the simple image can now be handled by very cheap, absolutely standard television technology.

The development that made raster graphics possible was that of very cheap solid-state memory which can now provide refresh buffers considerably larger than those of a decade ago at a fraction of the price. Standard raster graphics systems do not (yet) have the resolution of a vector system (1,024 × 1,280 versus 4,096 × 4,096), nor do they have hardware fast enough to provide motion dynamics for high-resolution displays. This is because all pixels must be transformed in the buffer to their new coordinates, rather than just the endpoints of lines as in the vector case. For a 1,024 × 1,280 display, more than a million pixels would have to be altered in a fraction of a second, a demand on computational resources not yet affordable. However, Megetek's (1980) new display, costing less than $100,000, can display a dynamic 512 × 512 image created from many vectors spaced closely together to shade polygons in real time. Raster graphics does, however, make possible the display of solid areas, typically in color, which is an especially rich means for communicating information. Furthermore, the refresh process is independent of the complexity (number of lines, etc.) of the image, because the hardware is fast enough that each pixel in the buffer is read out on each refresh cycle, regardless of whether it represents information or background. Thus, there is no flicker. In contrast, refreshed vector displays often flicker when the number of primitives in the buffer grows so large that they cannot be read out and processed in a thirtieth of a second and the image is therefore not refreshed sufficiently often.

Input Technology. In a development parallel to that of better output technology, an improvement in input technology has also taken place. The clumsy, fragile lightpen has largely been replaced by a thin stylus moved on a data tablet or even a transparent, touch-sensitive panel mounted on the screen, and audio communication holds much exciting potential for the future. With these interaction devices, the user can either type or draw new information, or point to existing information on the screen in order to specify operations or picture components to be operated upon. These interactions require no knowledge of programming; the user simply makes choices, answers questions, places predefined symbols on the screen, and draws or paints (by indicating consecutive endpoints to be connected by lines, or (polygonal) regions defined by line segments to be filled in with a specified shade of gray or color).

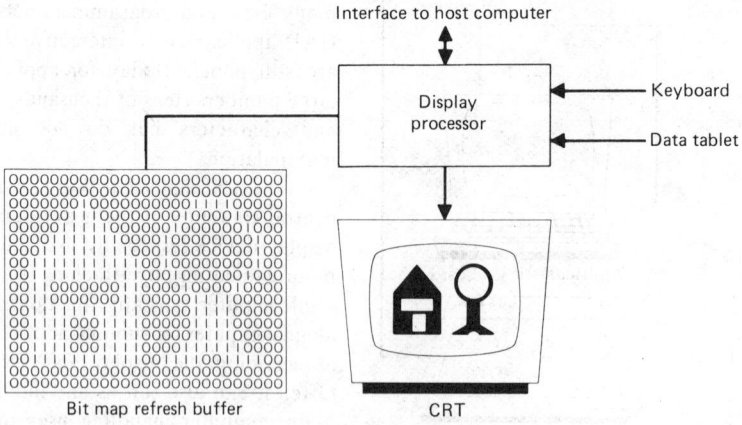

Fig. 3. Typical raster graphics display.

Software and Portability. While steady advances in hardware technology have thus made possible the evolution of graphics displays from a one-of-a-kind, special output device to a replacement for the ubiquitous alphanumeric display terminal as the standard human interface to the computer, one may well wonder whether software has kept pace. For example, what has happened to the early difficulties experienced with graphics systems and application software? Much of that difficulty lay in the primitive graphics software available to application programmers. By and large, there has been a long, slow process of maturation. We have moved from low-level, device-dependent subroutine packages supplied by manufacturers for their unique display devices to higher-level *device-independent* packages. These packages, typically supplied by independent developers, can drive a wide variety of display devices from plotters to high-performance vector and raster displays. The main purpose of a device-independent package used in conjunction with a high-level programming language is to induce application program (and programmer) portability. This portability is provided in much the same way that a "high-level" machine-independent language such as Fortran provides a large measure of portability by isolating the programmer from most machine peculiarities. The most well-known attempt to provide a standard for such device-independent graphics packages was produced by an ACM Siggraph Committee in 1977, refined in 1979, and then submitted to ANSI. It is called the "Core Graphics System" ("the Core" for short), and is serving as an important baseline definition for an evolving and maturing series of standards, much as Fortran has served in the field of programming languages.

Software. In order to understand graphics software, it is instructional to view the hardware system as seen by a graphics programmer (rather than a user). The conceptual framework on which the Core and many similar graphics packages are based is shown schematically in Fig. 4. The hardware component is a host computer that drives a display device (such as in Figs. 1 through 3). The display itself consists of an *output* component—the display screen or *view surface* on which pictures are displayed—and an *input* or interaction component. This input component typically consists of a set of devices such as an *alphanumeric keyboard* for entering text, a *function button keyboard* for invoking predefined options or functions, a *picking device* such as a lightpen or data tablet stylus for indicating picture components on the screen, *valuators* such as control dials and levers for entering scalar values, and an *X-Y* position indicator or *locator* such as a crosshair thumbwheel, lever, or joystick. Note that one physical device may be used to implement one or more of these logical input functions.

The software consists of three components. The first is the *application program;* it stores into and retrieves from the second component, the *application data structure/database.*

The data structure holds descriptions of real or abstract objects whose pictures are to appear on the screen. The data structure thus stores all of the pertinent information for such "objects" as circuits, flowcharts, buildings, mathematical or statistical functions, airplane fuselages, molecules, nuclear reactor models, and three-dimensional landscapes used for flight simulators.

The object's description typically contains *geometric* coordinate data that define the shape of components of

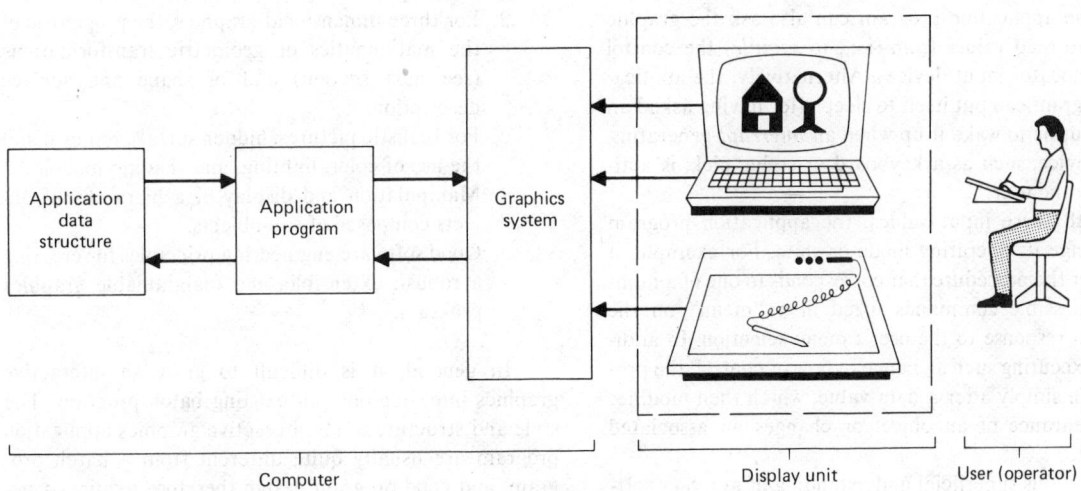

Fig. 4. The programmer's model of a graphics application program.

the object, object *attributes* such as line style, color, or even surface texture, and *connectivity* relationships and positioning data, which define how the components fit together. There often is also non-geometric textual or numeric "property" information useful to a post-processing program and/or the interactive user. Examples of such data for computer-aided applications include price and supplier data, thermal, mechanical, or electrical properties, and mechanical or electrical tolerances. Note that general-purpose database management systems are increasingly being used for the data structure function.

The application program describes the two- or three-dimensional geometry of the object whose picture is to be viewed on the view surface to the third component, the *graphics system,* which is typically a collection of output plotting subroutines compatible with a high-level language such as Fortran or Pascal. This subroutine package drives the specific output device(s) and causes the device to display the picture, usually from its display list representation in the refresh buffer that the package has just "compiled."

The application program uses the graphics system much as it uses the input/output subsystem of the operating system to read and write records in files. The input/output subsystem maintains a file directory, organizes records on disks and tapes, and shields the application programmer from having to know the many device-dependent parameters and conditions. Similarly, the graphics system shields the applications programmer from needing to know the specific low-level architecture of the display processor and the *X-Y* coordinate system of the physical screen.

While picture plotting is handled by the graphic system's output routines, input handling is controlled by the input routines, which pass user-supplied input data to the application program as part of an interaction sequence. Thus, the application program can also ask the graphic system to read values from (i.e., to *sample*) the control dials or locator input devices. Alternatively, the application program can put itself to sleep after having asked an input routine to wake it up when an *interrupt*-generating input device, such as a keyboard or stylus pick, is activated by the user.

With these input values, the application program can change its operating mode or state. For example, it can enter the procedure that corresponds to one of a number of possible commands listed in a "menu" on the screen in response to the user's menu selection. In addition to executing such a change in flow of control, the program can simply alter a data value, which then modifies the appearance of an object or changes an associated property.

With this superficial understanding of graphics software, we can now discuss how graphics application programs differ from conventional programs. First, the two- and three-dimensional geometry of graphical objects represents a different type of data, one with its own rapidly evolving body of mathematics and algorithms. This is especially true in the area of making realistic-looking pictures of three-dimensional objects. Second, interactive graphics programs are different from batch programs in that they tend to be *event-driven;* that is, they wait for the user to do something, react appropriately, and wait again. Essentially, the dialogue consists of a simple loop:

repeat
—provide a choice/pose a question
—**wait** for the user to respond with one of
 n allowed values
—**case**—branch to the appropriate procedure for
 the user's answer
until stop   {user responds with "stop"}

Note that this structure is nicely modeled by a state graph, with transitions and various forms of (output) actions caused by user input (Newman, 1968).

Third, use of a high-level device-independent graphics package makes interactive plotting and manipulation of simple charts, and drawings very straightforward. For more complex applications, however, good graphics programming practice requires some understanding of a number of areas not always mastered by application programmers.

1. Construction of dialogue and interaction "languages," with proper attention to expressive power, consistency, good "human factors" for the human interface for ease and speed of interaction, and graceful and informative error handling.
2. For three-dimensional graphics, the proper use of the mathematics of geometric transformations (see next section) and of shape and surface description.
3. For realistic pictures, hidden surface removal and the use of color, lighting, and shading models.
4. Manipulation and display of a hierarchy of objects composed of sub-objects.
5. Good software engineering principles for creating a robust, extensible, and maintainable graphics program.

In general, it is difficult to graft an interactive graphics interface onto an existing batch program: The style and structure of an interactive graphics application program are usually quite different from a batch program, and good program design therefore requires a before-the-fact, top-down analysis of all the required interaction sequences to lead to a properly structured design and implementation.

Scenario of a Typical Application.

The following scenario describes the interaction between user and computer as well as the underlying interaction between the various modules of the graphics program. Different organizations are possible for different application programs, or for different hardware, software, and data structure configurations; the scheme shown, however, is quite typical of a large class of interactive design applications.

As discussed in the previous section, objects are represented in an application data structure containing (1) pictorial data giving geometric and topological information that describes what the object looks like on the screen and (2) application data defining what the picture means. Notions of syntax and semantics of objects are sometimes used to distinguish these two types of information. Meaning is defined in terms of the application (analysis) programs that calculate the behavior of the object symbolized by the picture on the screen, which is accomplished by manipulating the application data structure. "Values" of components comprise the type of information usually stored in the application data structure. Naturally, some applications programs concentrate on geometry (e.g., mechanical structures), whereas others are virtually independent of geometry (e.g., topology, and not geometry, is important in network and circuit synthesis). In any case, object display and object analysis usually take place at different times and usually alternate, as described below.

Object Display. This involves reduction of the data structure to a viewable image. Assume the entire application program has been loaded and an initial prompting message has been displayed on the screen to orient the user. Some input device(s) have been provided for use and the program waits for the user to generate an action. Let us say a function key is pushed, generating an interrupt that is mapped by the graphics package into a request for service—say, retrieval of a previously stored drawing. The retrieval module of the application program tells the graphics system to add a prompting message (such as "please type in name of drawing") to the display.

When the user next transmits the typed-in name, the graphics system passes it to the retrieval program, which retrieves the named object from the disk library and puts it in main memory. The application program next reduces the device-independent data structure to a set of calls to the graphics package, using a *viewing specification* to determine which part of the object is to be viewed.

Object Modification. Let us assume that the user wants to delete a piece of the object on the screen. Again,

the appropriate module must be activated by pushing the appropriate function key or by menu selection (through (lightpen) picking a *light button*—the command name displayed as a character string or an easily recognized icon on the screen). The identification provided by the graphics system to the application program causes it to select the delete procedure. This procedure, which is part of the application's program data structure building and modification module, next enables the picking device and/or the typewriter keyboard to allow the user to identify the sub-object to be deleted. If the user points at (a line on) a resistor, the graphics package determines which displayed item has been identified and passes that information to the delete procedure. It deletes the data structure representation of that particular resistor, and calls the graphic package to update the screen.

In order to prevent the user from deleting the wrong part of the data structure inadvertently (in case of incorrect specification or a change of mind), a properly human-factored program would not go through the above procedure until a "soft-delete" had been tried out by the user. This process updates the screen, removing the item to be deleted; it then prompts the user to ask if that result was the one desired. If the user accepts (another pass through the graphics package and the delete procedure), the above data structure and screen update is done.

An additional feature of the delete process is that it tends to cause a "deletion ripple" in the data structure. For example, if an endpoint of a line is deleted, the user probably also expects the line to disappear, since it is no longer well defined. The line, in turn, might have been used as a part of other objects or it might be labeled, causing additional updating of the data structure and screen. If a node in a network were to be deleted, the user might similarly want to delete all components attached to that node. The utility of the "soft-delete" procedure with its option for allowing the effects of an operation to be undone ("reverted") should be obvious.

Object Analysis. As another typical scenario, assume that the user has finished construction of the object. To invoke an analysis program, an appropriate function key is pushed. The graphics package transfers control to the data structure scanning module of the application program that examines the part of the data structure that contains parameters such as physical dimensions and properties necessary for analysis. The data values are extracted and passed to the analysis program, which may call the graphics package to display feedback to the user in the form of graphed results; it may also use the graphics package to allow the user to identify elements of the displayed object with the picking device in order to get a display of appropriate parameters at the point indicated. At this time, a cycle of redesign usually takes place in which the user modifies the object in order to submit it for re-analysis.

Note the preponderance of data structure operations; very little output is displayed on the console without first involving data structure scanning, manipulation, and reduction to a viewable image. Much of the code in most graphics programs does not, in fact, deal with producing pictures or fielding interrupts. In common with most other (interactive) programs, the bulk of graphics application programs is concerned with interaction-syntax parsing and interpretation; data structure manipulation, computation, and analysis; space management for main and backing store; etc.* It is, therefore, fair to say that, in addition to the obvious differences, graphics programs require all the normal concerns required for any other nontrivial interactive program.

Role of Data Structure Modeling in Graphics.
Manipulating objects (as opposed to merely plotting their pictures) requires a conceptualization, or *modeling* of the object, which goes beyond a literal point-and-line representation. The totality of geometric and topological data, including the hierarchy of object parts and associations between them, constitute a model of the object referred to above as the data structure. The data structure should lend itself readily to displaying the picture, manipulating and transforming the object at the console.

---

*In interactive animation applications such as real-time flight simulators, there is no data structure modification, but the application data structure is traversed at refresh rates, with changing viewing specifications induced by pilot maneuvering. In the field of making realistic full-color pictures (e.g., movie animation, advertising) the calculations are dominated by those for simulating the physical laws of light—hidden surface elimination, refraction, reflection, shading, shadow calculation, etc.

and causing analysis routines to be applied to (parts of) the object.

Sutherland's interactive Sketchpad established full ring structures for "master/instance" definitions of object/sub-object hierarchies. Since that time (1963), hardware suppliers have for the most part ignored the data-structure aspect of graphics because the problems of implementing a data structure modeling package are more difficult than those of providing graphics packages. Moreover, the data structured aspects are, in general, application-dependent.

Classes of Data Structures.
The simplest type of storage structure required is that for displaying primitive objects made up of consecutive points and lines, say, for plotting purposes. In this case, a pair of arrays, one for points and one for lines, is all that is required. Most objects have more structure, requiring minimally some facility for collecting logically related atoms (points, lines, characters) in a group and naming this group so it can be manipulated as a unit (to be deleted, moved on the screen, made sensitive or insensitive to picking, etc.). Ordinary data graphs and many mechanical and structural drawings, for example, require only these facilities.

Sutherland handled a very common class of more complex objects that could be called "network graphs" (Fig. 5). These are two- or three-dimensional configurations in which discrete objects are connected to others in a network, and are typically decomposable into a hierarchy of lower-level sub-objects.

In the typical "bottom-up" interactive construction of a sub-object hierarchy (e.g., electric circuit design), components are gathered into subassemblies, which in turn are used in high-level assemblies; in the "top-down" method (e.g., flow charting), loose (macro) descriptions

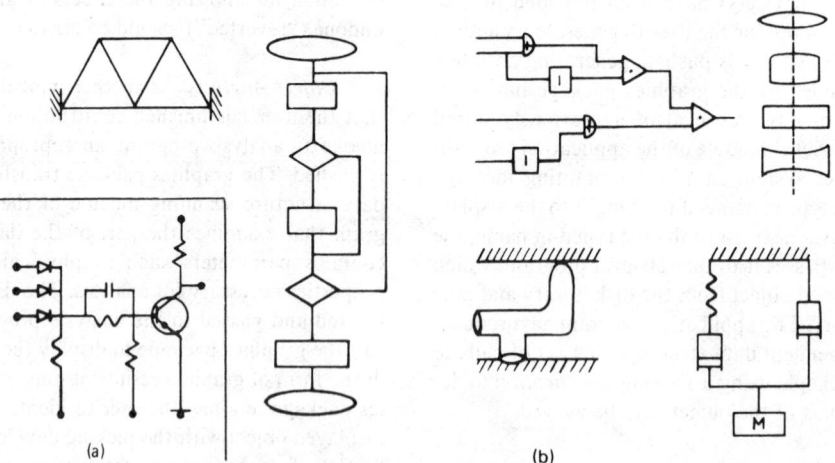

Fig. 5.   (a) NOR circuit; (b) other network graph examples.

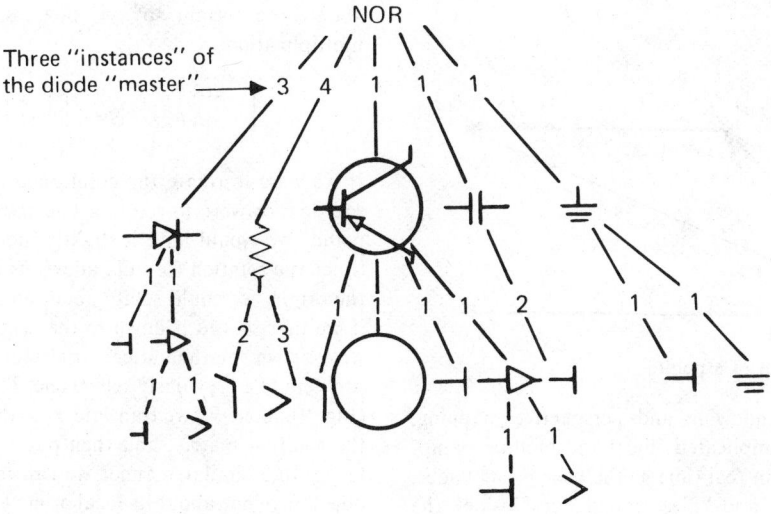

Three "instances" of the diode "master"

Fig. 6. Hierarchical representation of NOR.

are iteratively refined and expanded into subassemblies of more detailed (micro) boxes. The "NOR" circuit of Fig. 5(a), for example, can be constructed bottom-up as a hierarchy, as shown in the "parts explosion" of Fig. 6. Practically, one would not build up such an electric circuit starting at the low level shown here for illustration purposes; one would start instead at the level of primitive electrical components (such as resistors and transistors). Note that the tree form of the data structure is not strictly accurate in that some of the nodes are duplicated; in fact, the data structure is a directed graph (*see* GRAPH THEORY).

The data structure use of a sub-object in a given object closely parallels the programming use of a subroutine in a higher-level routine. The original data structure definition is called the "master," and its invocation is known as an "instance" of the master. The "subroutine" parameters, encoded with each instance portion of the data structure for the total calling object consist of the geometric parameters that determine position, orientation, and scale of the sub-object within the calling object (see next section). Often, such parameters are collected in a matrix called the "transformation" matrix. As with program subroutines, the advantage of using sub-objects with transformation matrices is the space saved by not duplicating their definitions.

Geometric and Windowing Transformations

Geometric Object Transformations and Real-Time Dynamics. Graphics become especially powerful through the ability to compose complicated objects from other previously drawn objects suitably transformed to fit into higher-level objects. Furthermore, these so-called object (or instancing) transformations are mathematically identical to those used to determine which portion of an object is in view and is to be displayed on (some portion of) the screen. While it is not feasible to discuss all possible geometric transformations in a survey such as this,* an indication can be given of their inherent simplicity by showing a two-dimensional example of the most used ones—translation, rotation, and scaling.

First, any object can be recursively defined in terms of its component primitives such as points, lines, polygons, character strings, and sub-objects, each suitably sized and positioned on the coordinate system of that object. We would like to find formulations that allow us to transform a point and, given that ability, transform the other types of components by simple extension. The transformations below allow just that: A line is transformed simply by transforming its endpoints, a polygon by its vertices; a character (string) is moved by moving the center or left bottom corner of the first character (rotating and scaling may be tricky without sophisticated hardware); and an instance of a sub-object is transformed by transforming it relative to the local origin with respect to which it was drawn and which serves as its "handle."

Many display manufacturers supply special hardware to carry out the transformations summarized below. Some even provide the ability to combine the basic trans-

---

*More complete formulations, using homogeneous coordinate matrix mathematics, may be found in Foley and van Dam (1982).

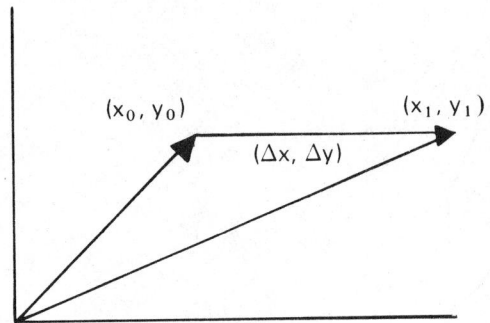

Fig. 7. Translation of a point.

formations with windowing and perspective mapping, thereby allowing complicated object and picture manipulations to proceed in real time as the user twists knobs, dials, and joysticks, and "flies around" or "inside" the picture world. If hardware is not available for real-time dynamics, software simulation may still provide useful and interesting effects.

First, to move a point, add x- and y-translation factors to the x- and y-components of the coordinate pair describing the point. To move a line, move both endpoints by the same factor. Thus, in Fig. 7, to move (x_0,y_0) by $(\Delta x,\Delta y)$:

$$\begin{bmatrix} x_0 \\ y_0 \end{bmatrix} + \begin{bmatrix} \Delta x \\ \Delta y \end{bmatrix} = \begin{bmatrix} x_1 \\ y_1 \end{bmatrix}$$

Second, to rotate a point about the center (origin) of the coordinate axes (the z-axis, in effect), rotate the vector with the beginning point at the origin and the endpoint at the desired point, Thus, in Fig. 8, to rotate (x_0,y_0)

about the origin by θ degrees, use the matrix multiplication:

$$\begin{bmatrix} \cos\theta & -\sin\theta \\ +\sin\theta & \cos\theta \end{bmatrix} \begin{bmatrix} x_0 \\ y_0 \end{bmatrix} = \begin{bmatrix} x_1 \\ y_1 \end{bmatrix}$$

If we were to rotate the point about any other center of rotation, or were to rotate a line about either of its endpoints, we would have a slightly more difficult problem. Since the rotation formula allows us to rotate only about the origin, we could rotate about an arbitrary point only if we first moved it down to the origin. This is simple a well-known mathematical trick for reducing a given problem to a previously solved one. Thus, to rotate line L_1 (Fig. 9) about P_1, we translate P_1 to the origin, then apply the rotation matrix, and then put P_1 back where it belongs. In a similar manner we can rotate an entire subobject instance about its local origin (rather than the picture origin) by translating, rotating, and "untranslating" all the individual object components. Naturally, all these calculations may be simplified by "solving" these matrix and vector operations beforehand, i.e., reducing them to simple equations for the endpoints. Thus, in Fig. 9, rotating L_1 about P_1 by θ degrees:

$$\begin{bmatrix} \cos\theta & -\sin\theta \\ \sin\theta & \cos\theta \end{bmatrix} \left(\begin{bmatrix} x_0 \\ y_0 \end{bmatrix} - \begin{bmatrix} c_x \\ c_y \end{bmatrix} \right) + \begin{bmatrix} c_x \\ c_y \end{bmatrix} = \begin{bmatrix} x_1 \\ y_1 \end{bmatrix}$$

To scale a line (scaling a point doesn't really make sense), we multiply the x- and y-components of its endpoints by x- and y-scale factors. Thus, in Fig. 10, scaling by different amounts in x and y (L_1 by (A, B)):

$$\begin{bmatrix} A & 0 \\ 0 & B \end{bmatrix} \begin{bmatrix} x_0 \\ y_0 \end{bmatrix} = \begin{bmatrix} x_1 \\ y_1 \end{bmatrix}$$

Fig. 8. Rotation of a point about origin.

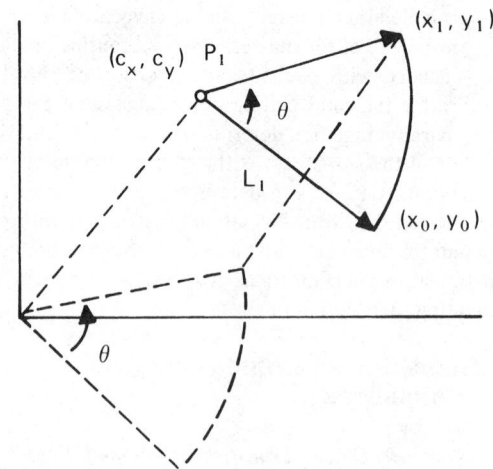

Fig. 9. Rotation about arbitrary centers.

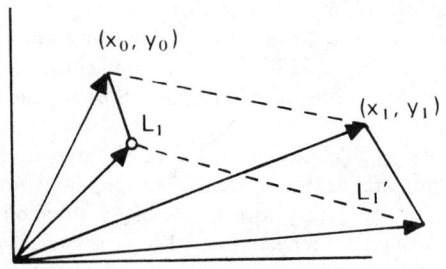

Fig. 10. Scaling.

Note that, in general, this will have the effect of moving the line as well. If we want a given point on the line to stay in place, a compensating translation must be applied. As with rotation, an entire sub-object instance (i.e., all its components) may be scaled about its local origin, by moving the local origin to the object origin, scaling as desired, and moving it back. If scaling about axes inclined with respect to the object axes is desired, the local axes should be translated down to the origin rotated to be parallel to the object axes, scaled, unrotated, and then untranslated (Fig. 11).

Windowing. Since large drawings of the type typically found in engineering applications cannot fit in their entirety on small display screens, we can either compress them to fit—and thereby obscure details and induce clutter—or we can display only a portion of the total drawing. The portion of a two-dimensional or three-dimensional object to be displayed is usually indicated by the user by placing a rectangular window on the compressed version of the drawing on the screen, and the hardware or software will then "clip" ("scissor") off any

primitives that fall outside the window. The operation may be performed repeatedly to achieve any desired degree of magnification.

A two-dimensional window is usually defined by a maximum and minimum value for *x* and *y*, or by a center of the window and maximum relative *x*- and *y*-values. Simple subtractions or comparisons suffice to find out whether or not a point is in view. For lines, the algorithm should allow any part of a line within the window to be displayed. If both endpoints lie in view, the line may be trivially accepted. If one of the endpoints lies in view, finding the other point is easy enough, and at least a portion of the line lies in the window. However, if both points are out of view, further tests must be made, since the line could be wholly outside or could cut the window. One method for deciding which case applies is to solve analytically for points of intersection of the line containing the line segment with the lines forming the edges of the window (Fig. 12).

Using notation from linear algebra, the equation of a line can be expressed in parametric form such that points of the form

$$X = tX[1] + (1 - t)X[2]$$

for real *t* are on the infinite line through the points $X[1]$ and $X[2]$. When *t* is restricted to the interval [0,1], the point is on the directed-line segment from $X[2]$ to $X[1]$. The problem can therefore be stated as finding parameters *t* and *s* such that

$$tP[1] + (1 - t)P[2] = sC[1] + (1 - s)C[2]$$

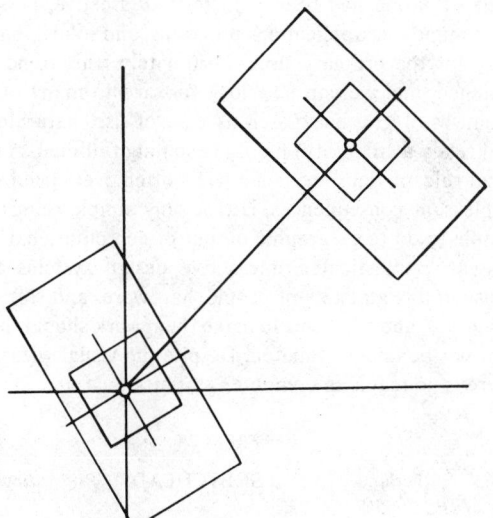

Fig. 11. Scaling about arbitrary axes.

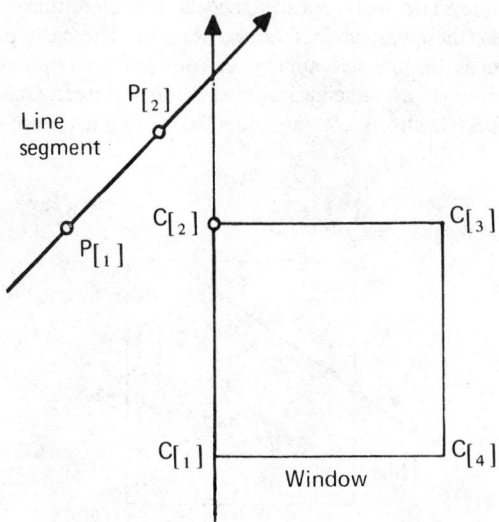

Fig. 12. Windowing.

If both t and s are between 0 and 1, then the point of intersection is both between $P[1]$ and $P[2]$ (so it actually lies on the line segment), and between $C[1]$ and $C[2]$ (so it is in view in the window).

As soon as one point to be displayed has been found, the line segment may be treated as two separate line segments, each of which has one endpoint in view. One of these segments may be rejected completely, as shown in Fig. 13.

To augment this straightforward analytical solution, special-purpose hardware has been built using various digital or analog methods for performing the window operation in real-time (Sproull and Sutherland, 1968). Both in hardware and software implementations, much effort is expended in accepting or rejecting the trivial cases (elements wholly inside or outside the window).

Enhancing the Illusion of Reality. The computer-generated scenes shown thus far in this article are not meant to be realistic; they are diagrammatic and symbolic in nature and are simple to draw. Presenting a realistic reproduction of a complex three-dimensional scene is several orders of magnitude more complex. First, line drawings themselves are often inadequate: We do not view real objects as sequences of lines but rather as various surfaces, some of which are connected one to another. Surfaces have color, texture, and light reflectance and transmittance properties. A solid surface close to the viewer can hide more distant surfaces (or portions thereof) from view. Objects of equal size appear to become smaller the farther they are from the viewer (perspective). Depending on where the source of illumination is, objects may cast shadows on other objects, making them appear darker than they are normally.

Considerable effort has been devoted to developing appropriate mathematical models and algorithms that take these various factors into account. The basic problem is the massive amount of computation required to transform a mathematical model into a picture. Current research efforts are thus directed as much toward improved algorithms as toward increased realism. A few of the faster algorithms to remove hidden lines and surfaces and do shading have been partially implemented in special-purpose hardware (Sutherland, Sproull, and Schumacker, 1974).

The applicability of this work to interactive computer graphics lies in the areas of design, simulation, and animation. It is easy to conceive of an automotive designer using pictures like Fig. 13 to view current efforts from many directions. In simulation, we want to achieve effects such as the presentation of a realistic road scene in a driving simulator, or a realistic airport scene in a flight trainer. The making of animated movies for entertainment or for scientific, mathematical, and medical modeling is another area needing realism.

A Sampling of Other Configurations and Technologies. The display system organizations shown in Figs. 1 to 3 are not the only ones in use, but are probably the most widespread. Another kind of organization is the satellite graphics system. The display processor is connected to a small micro- or minicomputer, which is in turn connected to a larger host computer. The graphics system and application programs may be distributed between the two computers, which may be separated by many miles. Motivations for such systems include placing the graphics terminal where the user is, not necessarily where the computer is, to provide fast response to simple user actions and to unburden the host CPU of some processing work (van Dam, 1974).

Graphics Progress. Graphics has suffered in the past decade from a preoccupation with its fascinating and still rapidly evolving technology and hardware; too little attention has been paid to cost-effective, possibly even mundane, applications programs, and to making life easy for the ordinary user. Fortunately, this trend has changed, and we can now look forward to many of the promises of graphics (such as ease of use, naturalness, and ready availability) finally becoming fullfilled. A cardinal rule, obvious but nonetheless often overlooked with unpleasant consequences, is that only simple things are simple to do (e.g., graphic output of computational processes). Sophisticated interactive design systems take considerable amounts of people, hardware, and software resources, and the effort to make them work should therefore not be underestimated. Despite the visual wizardry, there is no magic in computer graphics.

REFERENCES

1963. Sutherland, I. E. "SKETCHPAD," *Proceedings of AFIPS 1963 SJCC* **23**.

1963. Weizenbaum, J. "Symmetric List Processor," *Communications of the ACM* **6**, *No. 9*.

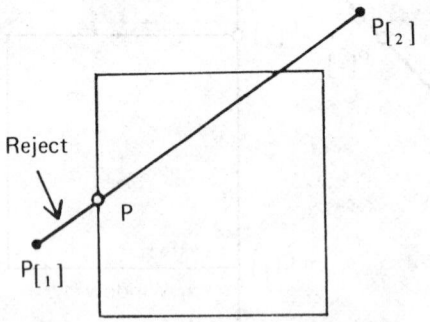

Fig. 13. Windowing: rejection of line segment.

1964. Knowlton, K. C. "A Programmer's Description of L⁶," *Communications of the ACM* **9**, No. 8.

1967. Gray, J. C. "Compound Data Structure for Computer-Aided Design—A Survey," *Proceedings 22nd ACM National Conference.*

1968. Newman, W. M. "A System for Interactive Graphical Programming." *Proceedings of AFIPS 1968 SJCC* **32.**

1968. Sproull, R. F. and Sutherland, I. E. "A Clipping Divider," *Proceedings of AFIPS 1968 FJCC* **33-1.**

1969. D'Imperior, M. "Data Structures and Their Representation in Storage," *Annual Review in Automatic Programming, No. 5.* New York: Pergamon.

1971. Prince, M. D. *Interactive Graphics for Computer-Aided Design.* Reading, MA: Addison-Wesley.

1972. van Dam, A. "Some Implementation Issues Relating to Data Structures for Interactive Graphics," *Journal of Computer and Information Sciences* (August).

1974. Institute of Electronic and Electrical Engineers. "Special Issue on Computer Graphics," *IEEE Proceedings* (April).

1974. Resch, R. D. "Portfolio of Shaded Computer Images," Special Issue on Computer Graphics, *IEEE Proceedings* (April).

1974. Sutherland, I. E., Sproull, R. F., and Schumacker, R. "A Characterization of Ten Hidden-Surface Algorithms," *ACM Computing Surveys* (March).

1974. van Dam. A., Stabler, G. M., and Harrington, R. J. "Intelligent Satellites for Interactive Graphics," Special Issue on Computer Graphics, *IEEE Proceedings* (April).

1979. Newman, W. M. and R. F. Sproull. *Principles of Interactive Computer Graphics, 2nd Ed.* New York: McGraw-Hill.

1982. Foley, James and van Dam, A. *Fundamentals of Interactive Graphics.* Reading, MA: Addison-Wesley.

A. VAN DAM

COMPUTER INDUSTRY

For articles on related subjects *see* BURROUGHS B5000 SERIES; CONTROL DATA CORPORATION CYBER SERIES; DIGITAL COMPUTERS: History; DIGITAL EQUIPMENT CORPORATION PDP SERIES; IBM 360-370 SERIES; IBM 1400 SERIES; RAMAC; SERVICE BUREAUS, DATA PROCESSING; UNBUNDLING; and UNIVAC 1100 SERIES.

UNITED STATES

Introduction. Organizations have recorded and processed data for centuries, and during that time trade and industry have supplied the necessary tools (pens and pencils and chalk, slide rules and abacuses, calculators and tabulating machines) and supplies (slates, paper, cards). The evolution of electronic technology and the invention, in the 1940s, of the stored program computer,

led to the development of what we now call the computer industry—a collection of business enterprises which supply computer equipment or computer-related services and supplies. The first commercial products were offered in the early 1950s by companies in the U.S. and in England. Today, many companies in Europe and in Japan manufacture and market computer equipment, and many others all over the world offer computer-related services and supplies. This article will discuss the U.S. computer industry.

Machlup (1962) and, more recently, Porat (1976) have drawn attention to the growing importance of "knowledge production and distribution" activities within the U. S. economy. Porat distinguishes two parts of what he calls the Information Sector: The primary sector contains those organizations whose functions it is to sell information services or to produce and distribute information machines, including research and development laboratories, law firms, schools and libraries, radio broadcasters, book publishers, advertising agencies, stock brokers, camera stores, and manufacturers of computers, paper, cameras, and printing machinery; the secondary sector is the public and private bureaucracy—the white collar workers who deal primarily with information. Fig. 1 shows Porat's estimate of how the U. S. workforce has changed during the past century as we have grown from an agricultural society to an industrial society to what is now an information-oriented society.

Computer equipment is potentially applicable wherever information is handled. The market is very elastic, in the economic sense, and more and more of the data in Porat's Information Sector will be handled by electronic equipment as computer costs fall. To distinguish between various actual and potential computer applications, it is helpful to distinguish two kinds of data. *Recorded data* is that which is recorded on media by organizations which expect to use it later. *Transient data* is data which is of momentary interest, and is not saved because the likelihood if its later use is low. Payroll records, engineering drawings, and customer correspondence are examples of recorded data. Seat availability requests (in an on-line reservation system), temperature measurements (in a thermostat), and telephone conversations (unless they are recorded) are examples of transient data. Obviously, recorded and transient data can coexist in a computer system. A process control computer deals mostly with transient data in its second-by-second measurements and control actions, but may record hourly averages or daily maxima and minima for later analysis.

In general, recorded data is more valuable to an organization than is transient data, and organizations are better able to justify spending money to process this data. However, the continuing drop in computer prices, and in particular the development of the microcomputer, has

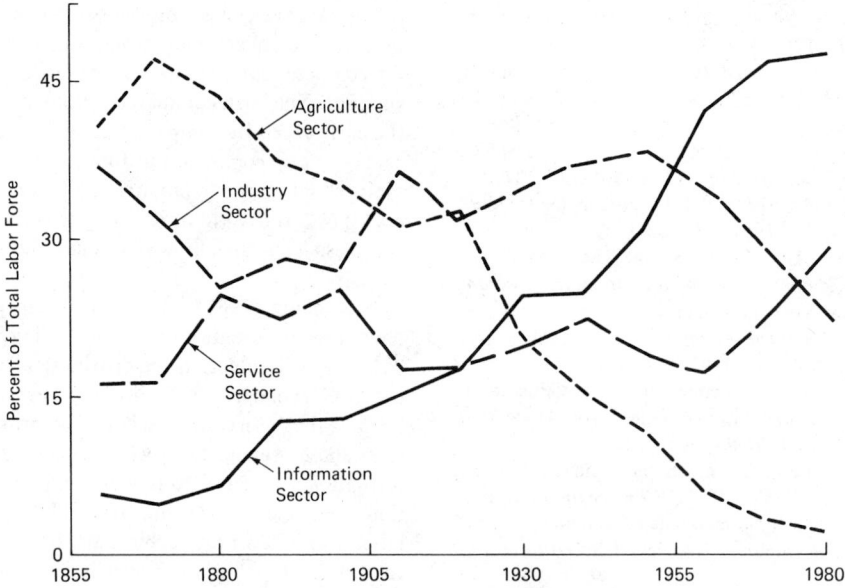

Fig. 1. Distribution of the U. S. workforce in various categories.

made it possible to apply computers in an enormous variety of transient applications—in games, automobiles, appliances, and tools, for example. In such applications, computers are basically used as electronic components, and for that reason we will not include them as part of the computer industry. Where microcomputers are used to process recorded data—in small business computers, word processors, personal computers, and "smart" terminals—we will, of course, include them.

To identify the potential market for computer systems (as opposed to computer components), we can simply count organizations, inasmuch as it is clear that every organization employs data in some form of record-keeping. Table 1 shows the number of proprietorships, partnerships, and corporations (PP&C's) in the U. S. in 1974–1975 by revenue-size class. It also shows the computer system each PP&C could afford to purchase, assuming (Phister, 1979) organizations can afford to purchase $14,000 of computer equipment for each $1,000,000 in annual revenue. However, even this long listing of potential computer system user locations is not complete. For example, many of these organizations have multiple offices at each plant, where small computers or word processors might be used. And PP&C's obviously don't include such potential locations as schools, government agencies, and homes.

Overview of the Industry. The computer industry includes companies which manufacture and distribute hardware, supply software or design and market

Table 1. Proprietorships, Partnerships, and Corporations (PP&C's), 1974–1975*

Revenue Range	Number of PP&C's	Estimated Price Each PP&C Could Pay for Computer Hardware
Over $1 billion	330	Over $14 million
$100 million to $1 billion	2,060	$1.4 million to $14 million
$10 million to $100 million	20,330	$140,000 to $1.4 million
$5 million to $10 million	27,780	$70,000 to $140,000
$1 million to $5 million	223,900	$14,000 to $70,000
$500,000 to $1 million	243,500	$7,000 to $14,000
$100,000 to $500,000	1,540,000	$1,400 to $7,000
$25,000 to $100,000	2,759,000	$350 to $1,400

*Source: Phister (1979), p. 652.

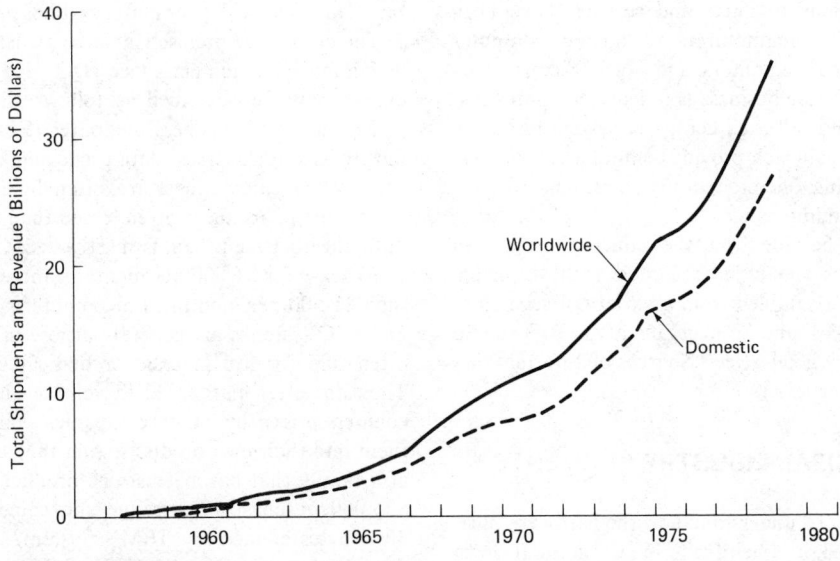

Fig. 2. Total data processing industry shipments and revenues by U. S. firms.

software products, furnish data processing services, provide data communications facilities, and manufacture and distribute data processing media. Fig. 2 shows how the industry has grown over the past 25 years, and Figs. 3 and 12 show the percent distribution of the various segments. The data in these figures represent shipments and revenues *by U. S. companies only*. The total "worldwide"

business would be much larger if foreign firms were included. Note that industry shipments and revenues were over $35 billion in 1978 and are still growing. Hardware shipments still account for over half the total of domestic shipments and revenues, though that percentage has declined over the years (see the solid line in Fig. 3).

The industry is, in fact, even bigger than the figures

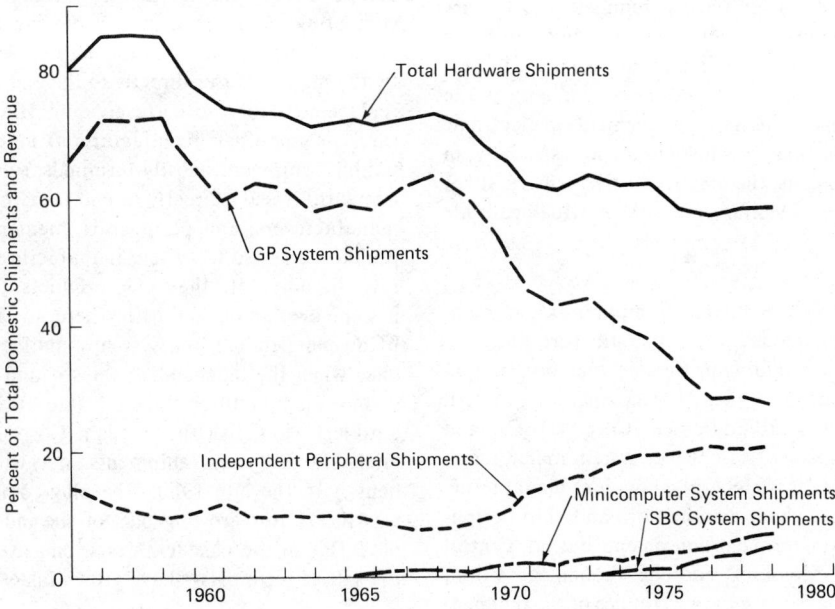

Fig. 3. Data processing industry domestic hardware revenues and shipments, percentage distribution versus time.

indicate, for various products and services have been omitted such as manufacturers of analog computer equipment, personal computers, and word processors; organizations whose sole business is to lease computer systems or to buy and sell used computer systems; and the many organizations which provide computer-related services—keypunching, operator training, personnel recruitment, or system maintenance.

It must also be noted that the data in these and in subsequent figures should be regarded with suspicion, since it has been assembled from a variety of secondary and tertiary sources, and an accuracy of $\pm$ 10% should be considered very good. (See "Sources of Information" at the end of the article.)

THE PRINCIPAL INDUSTRY SEGMENTS

Hardware. To understand how the hardware business has developed, it is helpful to break the total down in various ways. We will first examine shipments each year, broken down into shipments by system and peripheral equipment manufacturers. We will then look at equipment in use at the end of each year, broken down into processors, memories, individual peripheral types, terminals, and data entry equipment. In discussing the improvements that have taken place, we will mention the part played by various *technologies*, where a technology is defined as some combination of techniques, processes, materials, components, and assemblies whose specifications are well documented and which can realistically be employed in the non-scientific environment of a factory to produce reliable products, on schedule, meeting planned cost goals. The continuing improvement in performance per unit cost in the computer industry is the direct result of inventions and improvements in electronic and electromechanical technologies, and especially in solid state components, the magnetic core memory, magnetic recording engineering, and the moving-head file mechanism.

Hardware Shipments. Computer system manufacturers are companies which manufacture and ship complete systems, including processors, memory, peripherals, and software as well as the company's standard products. IBM, Digital Equipment Corp. (DEC), and Wang Laboratories are examples of system manufacturers. The independent peripheral equipment manufacturers are companies which manufacture and ship peripheral, data entry, or terminal equipment, but not central processing units. Memorex, Storage Technology Corp., and Mohawk Data Sciences are examples of the independents. Fig. 3 shows domestic hardware shipments, by system manufacturers and by the peripheral manufacturers, as a percentage of total domestic shipments and revenue.

Three classes of computer systems are shown in Fig. 3. The classes are precisely defined by listing the systems which fall into each class (see IDC 1979); but the three classes may be described as follows. General Purpose (GP) and small business computer (SBC) systems are mostly used for business data processing and scientific or engineering calculations, are often byte- or character-oriented, and are more often leased than purchased. The difference between them is mostly size: GP systems typically lease for $1,500 per month or more, SBC's for less than $1,500 per month. Minicomputer systems, like GP and SBC systems, are general-purpose in design, but are often sold for use in fixed or dedicated applications.* They are often purchased in volume quantities at discounted prices by other companies which incorporate them into their own products. And they are usually part of a family that has at least one product in the $2,000–$25,000 purchase price range and comes with at least 4096 bytes of memory. IBM's System/3s and 370s are all GP systems, as are DEC's PDP 10s, Burroughs' 1800s, and Sperry-Rand's 1100s. The IBM 32 and 34, the Burroughs 80, the DEC Datasystem 300, and the Wang Laboratories 2200 are all SBCs; and the IBM Series/1, the DEC PDP 11s and the Data General Novas are all minicomputers. Fig. 3 shows that the shipment value of GP systems has been declining as a percentage of the total, but is still more than twice the combined annual ship value of mini- and SBC systems.

The independent peripheral business grew at the remarkable (average) rate of 25% per year between 1968 and 1978. That business has three component parts: plug-compatible equipment, mostly moving head files, magnetic tape units, and main memory for IBM systems sold by the manufacturer directly to the end user as a plug-in replacement for the corresponding IBM (or, relatively rarely, some other manufacturer's) unit; non-plug-compatible equipment, mostly terminals, sold (like the plug-compatible gear) directly to end users by the peripheral manufacturers; and peripherals, memory, and terminal products shipped to system manufacturers who incorporate the units into their own products. (Note that there is some overlap or duplication here, for a peripheral sold by an independent to a system manufacturer is counted once when the independent ships it and again when the system manufacturer ships it. Note also that plug-compatible CPU's, like the Amdahl Corp. systems, are included with system shipments, not with the independents.) In the late 1960s, the plug-compatible business was the fastest growing part of the independents' business. But in the past few years, end user sales—mostly the sale of terminals—have grown fastest.

---

*For the purposes of this article, computers such as the LSI-11, which are single circuitboard replacements of minis, will be classified as minis.

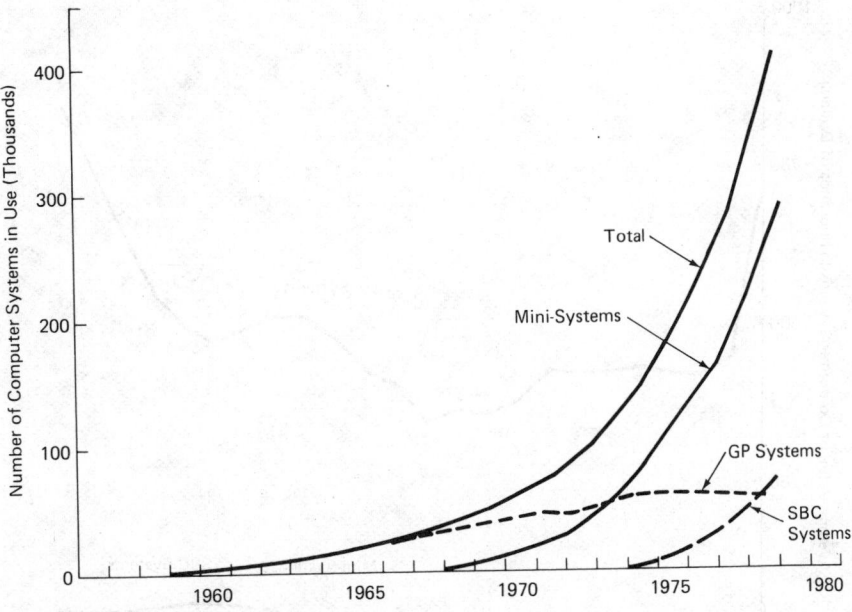

Fig. 4. Number of computer systems in use in the U. S.

Equipment in Use. Figs. 4 and 5 show the number and value of computers in use in the U. S. at the end of each year, and Fig. 6 shows their average values. The GP system has always been the principal contributor to the growth of the industry. However, since around 1974, the *number* of GP systems in use has remained fairly constant, while their average value has soared. Referring to Table 1, we infer that, for the most part, the 50,000 big organizations with annual revenues over $5,000,000 all operate GP systems, and have during the past few years been engaged in upgrading those systems—adding main memory, peripherals, and terminals. And the increasing availability of systems renting for $1,500 per month or less (selling for $60,000 or less) has led many of the 470,000 PP&C's with revenues of $500,000–$5,000,000 per year to acquire SBC's. Meanwhile, the population of mini-systems, used in applications such as process control, communications systems, data collection, laboratory instrumentation, factory test equipment, and as a component in SBC's, continues to grow.

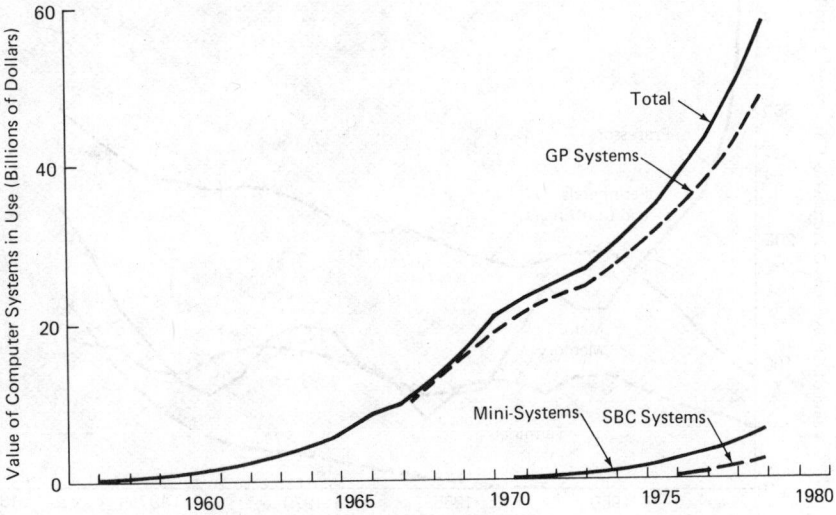

Fig. 5. Value of computer systems in use in the U. S.

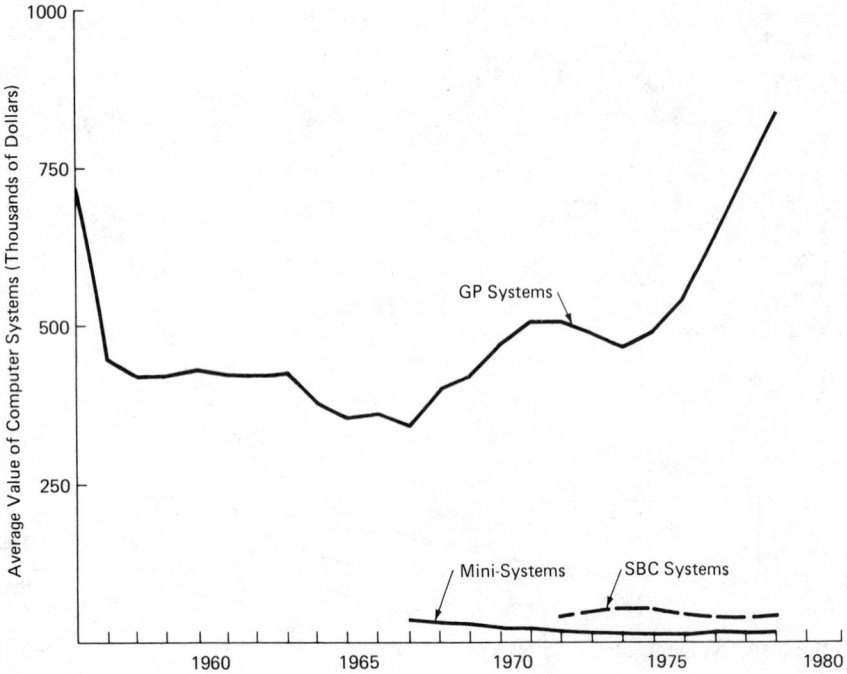

Fig. 6.   Average value of computer systems in use in the U. S.

Because GP systems are so important to the industry, it is instructive to examine them in more detail.

The recent increase in GP system average value can be understood by studying Fig. 7, which estimates the proportion of GP system value invested in peripherals and controllers, processors, main memory, and terminals, and shows how these proportions have changed with time. In the beginning, the processor was the costliest portion of the system, but since around 1960, peripherals and their controllers have contributed most to system value. The recent increase in average system value is a result of increases in all these components, especially terminals, and

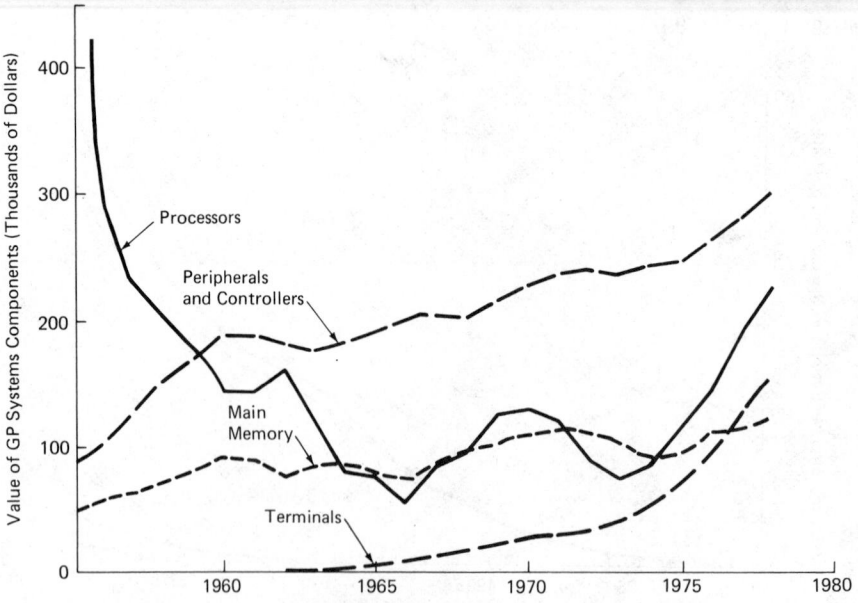

Fig. 7.   Components of an average GP system.

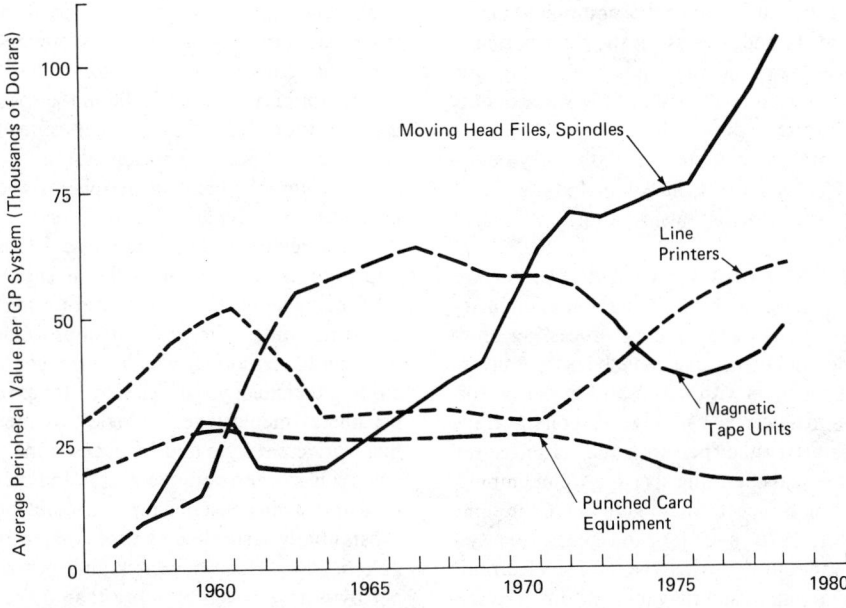

Fig. 8.   Value of peripheral equipment in use on an average GP system.

processors with main memory. (The apparent increase in processor value at the expense of main memory is misleading, being the result mostly of change in IBM pricing strategy, which resulted in an increase in processor prices accompanied by a decrease in incremental memory prices. Since 1974, the average number of bytes on a GP system has more than doubled.) Fig. 8 estimates how the per system value of peripherals has changed with time.

Printer costs dominated in the beginning, but by the early 1960s, the magnetic tape unit was the leading peripheral. Since around 1970, the moving head file has taken over and, in recent years, the line printer eclipsed the tape unit.

Data entry hardware, used off-line to record data on machine-readable media for later entry into the computer, is not included in Figs. 4–8. The solid line in Fig.

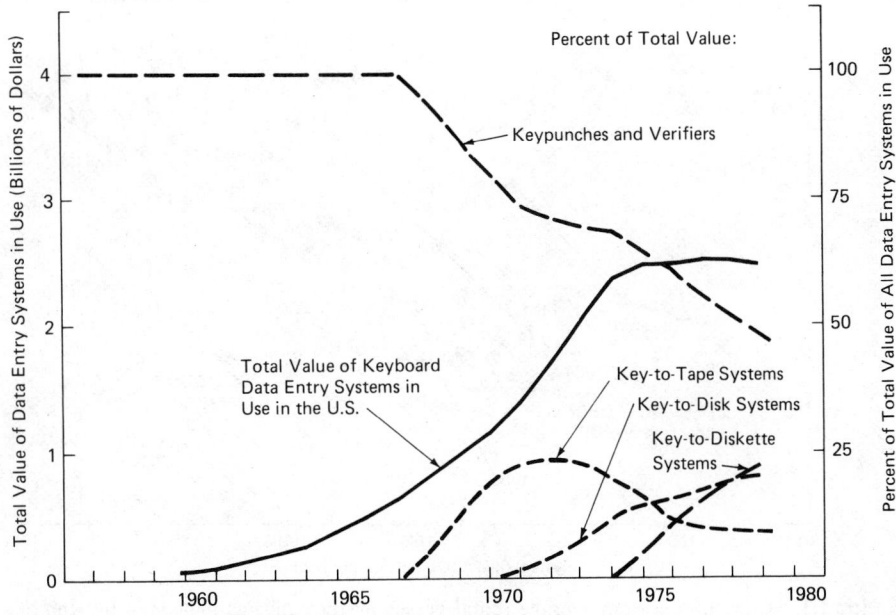

Fig. 9.   Total value of data entry equipment in use in the U. S. and its percent distribution.

9 estimates the total value of data entry equipment in use, and the dotted and dashed lines show the distribution of that value among keypunching and key-to-magnetic media devices. The recent leveling-off of the value of data entry equipment in use is the result of the increased use of terminals for data entry. Note that data entry equipment represents less than 5% of the value of all hardware in use, and that this proportion in shrinking.

Hardware Price and Performance. As was mentioned earlier, the growth of the computer industry is largely because the market for data processing products is very elastic, and companies have been very inventive in producing products with better and better performance at lower and lower prices. Fig. 10 plots average system rental against system performance, as measured by Knight's commercial operating speed. (A plot employing weighted arithmetic speed would give much the same result—see Phister, 1979, p. 541.) First-generation systems employed vacuum tubes as the active electronic components in logic, and used magnetic drums, electrostatic storage tubes, and mercury delay lines for main memory. The second generation replaced vacuum tubes with transistors, and the third and later generations have made use of the integrated circuit (IC). For main memory, second- and third-generation systems used the magnetic core but, more recently, the IC memory has become the most widely used. In general, the technology used in

each generation provided better performance (e.g., was faster or more flexible) than its predecessor *at a lower cost*. The result, as Fig. 10 indicates, has been an increase of a factor of more than 1,000 in the speed of a system at a given price, during the 25 years since the introduction of the earliest first-generation system.

The improvement in peripheral equipment has not been as spectacular. Punched card equipment has changed relatively little since the 1950s. Printers have improved much more, with the invention of a variety of new technologies for both line-at-a-time and character-at-a-time units. The greatest improvement has been in peripheral memories, which make use of magnetic recording technology. Fig. 11 shows the history of main and peripheral memory technologies, as measured by eqipment price per byte and by access time. Tape unit technology has improved the least, and yet representative tape units today cost one tenth as much per byte and have substantially faster access times than did the units available in 1955. Head per track and moving head file price per byte have fallen by more than a factor of 100. And the moving head file in particular, whose promise was first noted, and exploited, by IBM, has so improved that its on-line storage cost is today lower than that of the tape unit, while its access time approaches that of the head per track file. (Off-line data storage is still cheapest on magnetic tape, however.) Note that data cell technology was overtaken by the moving head file. The mass storage sys-

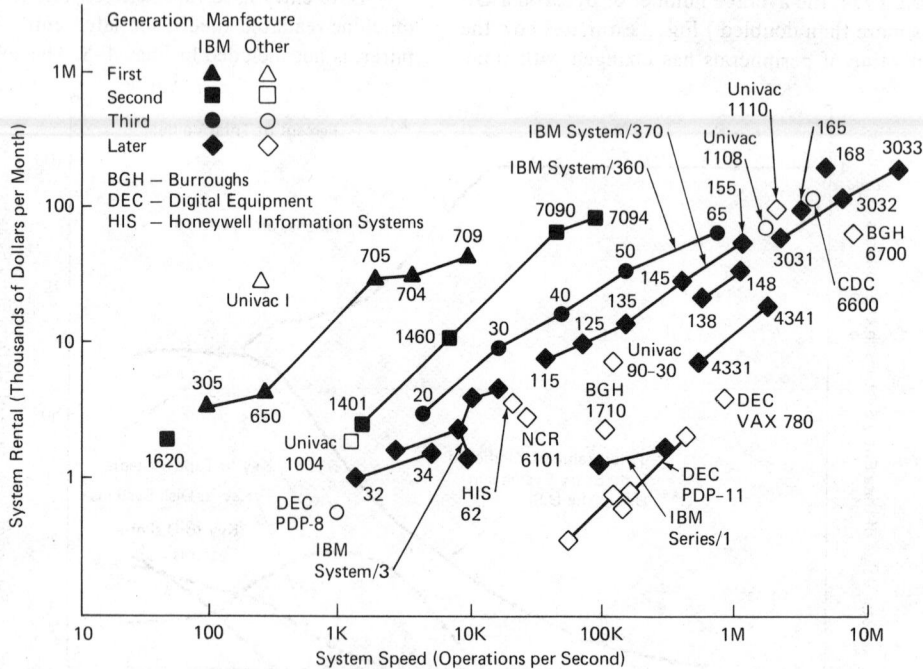

Fig. 10. Computer system average rental versus performance as measured by Knight's "commercial" speed.

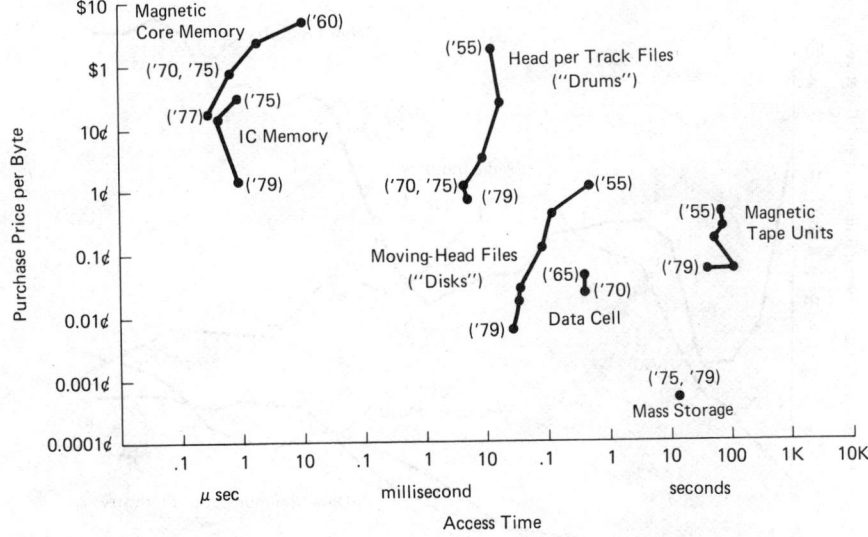

Fig. 11. Memory system price per byte versus access time, for representative products, at approximately five-year intervals.

tem (IBM 3850) is today cheaper per byte than the moving head file—but it has lost ground since its introduction in 1975.

The price/performance improvements shown in Figs. 10 and 11 are even more notable if we take into account the effects of inflation. The 1955 cent was equivalent to more than 2.5 cents in 1979, so the moving head file price per byte fell from 2.5 cents to 0.006 cents (using 1979 cents) between 1955 and 1979—by a factor of 417 to 1, instead of the 167 to 1 shown in Fig. 11.

OTHER INDUSTRY SEGMENTS

Fig. 3 showed the hardware components of the computer industry revenues and shipments given in Fig. 2. The remaining components are shown in Fig. 12, and are discussed below.

The Service Industry. Even before the invention of the stored program computer, there were firms which used tabulating equipment to provide data processing services. These firms were among the first to acquire computers and, by the end of 1976, over 1,500 companies, large and small, were in this business. In the early years, the service was typically provided in a periodic, batch form: Once a week, or once a month, the service company would collect input data from the customer, and would process it and return the contracted reports. The input data might be in the form of punched cards, or might be hand written; and pick-up and delivery of data and results would be by mail or messenger.

As time passed, the sophistication of these services grew. The introduction of data communications services by the communications common carriers, along with the development of the time-sharing concept, made it possible for companies to offer interactive computing services and permitted data to be transmitted by wire instead of by mail or messenger. And the continuing reductions in the cost of computation and storage have led firms to offer services based on the interactive access to common files (e.g., credit, ticket reservation, and stock market quotation services), or on the periodic use of proprietary programs written by the service company. Fig. 13 separates data processing service revenue into two component parts: Batch service implies that data pickup and delivery is by messenger or mail; on-line service implies that service is supplied by wire, either through the continuing action of an operator working interactively at a computer terminal, or via an unattended remote batch terminal. Table 2 shows how revenue from the batch, interactive, and remote batch access means were distributed in 1978 (the three columns), and also shows, for each one, how the revenues are distributed according to the use made by customers (the three rows). "Raw power" refers to the user providing his/her own programs, and simply making use of the service company's hardware. In the other two kinds of service, the customer makes use of the service firm's software as well, either to perform regular calculations, or to gain access to and make use of on-line data files maintained by the supplier.

Starting in the mid-1960s, some firms were successful in operating (and, usually, designing) data processing

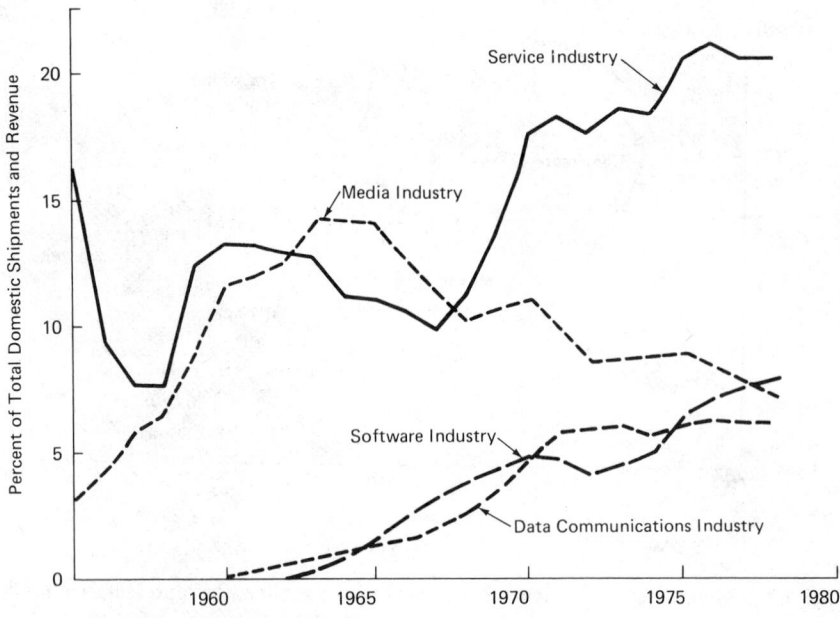

Fig. 12. Data processing industry domestic non-hardware revenues and shipments—precentage distribution versus time.

systems for customer companies. These "facilities management" service firms typically provide the same services to the customer that an in-house data processing group would provide, working on the customer's site with the customer's computer equipment. As is indicated in Fig. 13, this segment of the service industry appeared during the mid-1960s. It is the smallest of the service industry groups.

The Software Industry. Over 85% of the annual expenditures on programming in the U. S. is spent by users in paying the salaries of their own programmers and systems analysts. Part of the remaining 15% is spent by system manufacturers for software development and maintenance. But about 10% of the total represents payments, by computer users, to outside suppliers of software products or services. These outside suppliers constitute the software industry, whose revenues are shown in Fig. 14.

The first participants in this industry were independent companies which supplied custom software, on contract, to customers (users and system manufacturers)

Table 2.   Distribution of Data Processing Service Revenues in 1978 (Excludes Facilities Management Services)*

| | Computer Access Means | | | |
| | | Computer Terminal (On-Line) | | |
Computer Use	Messenger or Mail (Batch)	Remote Batch	Interactive Keyboard	Total
Purchase raw computer power	1.2%	10.3%	15.7%	27.2%
Perform regular calculations with vendor's software	40.5%	11.3%	10.8%	62.7%
Access common files with vendor's software	0.9%	0.3%	8.9%	10.1%
Total	42.7%	21.9%	35.4%	100.0%

*Source: IDC Briefing, 1979.

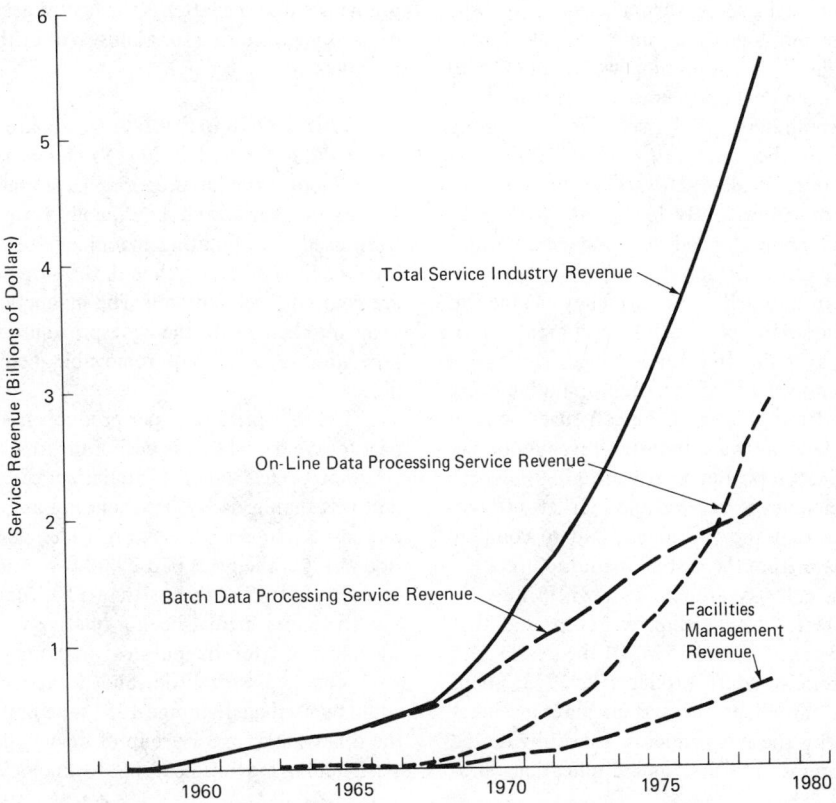

Fig. 13. Service industry revenue versus time.

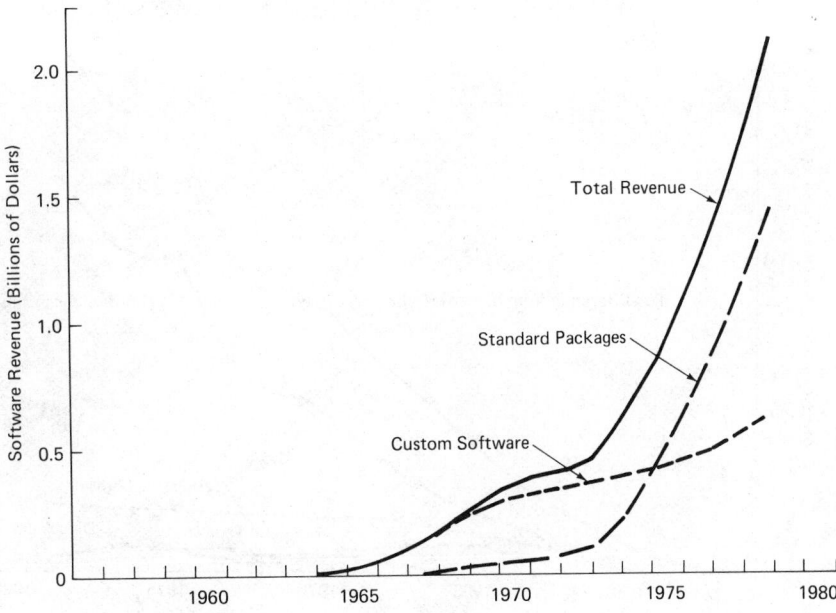

Fig. 14. Software industry revenue versus time.

who needed expertise in some particular area, or who didn't want to hire permanent programming staff to handle a short-term heavy programming workload. Meanwhile, users got a good deal of generalized, standard software (utilities, compilers, and assemblers, operating systems, etc.) from the system manufacturers at no cost—that is, the price of these software products was included in the hardware price. By 1968, IBM alone provided over five million lines of code as standard programming support for its System/360. In mid-1969, however, IBM announced an unbundling policy: They planned to offer certain services, and certain future computer programs, previously available free, for a charge. This policy change, adopted in part by other system manufacturers as well, stimulated the growth of the software industry both by creating new software industry revenue among the system manufacturers, and by encouraging independent software companies to develop and market software products, knowing that they no longer had to compete with "free" software from the system manufacturers.

The resulting industry growth is shown in Fig. 14. Note that revenue for standard packages passed that from custom software in around 1975. Of the nearly $1.5 billion revenue from standard products in 1978, about $800 million was earned by the system manufacturers and $700 million by the independents. If we divide the products into systems, utilities, and applications programs, we find the latter is the fastest growing segment—currently accounting for almost half of the independents' revenues.

The Media Industry. Media are the materials on which data is recorded. Fig. 15 shows how shipments of the principal media categories have changed with time. Tabulating cards and continuous form printing paper were used on tabulating machinery before the development of the computer, though the shipments shown here are computer-related only. The magnetic media industry came into being with the widespread use first of magnetic tape units and then of removable-media moving head files.

The unit price of paper products has soared over the past few years, while the cost of magnetic media has held constant or has fallen. Tabulating cards, for example, cost less than a dollar per thousand as recently as 1971, but cost $2.30 per thousand in 1978. Over that same period of time, the price of a 2,400-ft reel of ½-in. magnetic tape fell from $13 to less than $10. Magnetic tape has, like the paper media, been a relatively stable product—specifications for its physical and magnetic properties have changed very little, and a tape purchased today could be used on a vintage 1957 tape unit. Disk packs, on the other hand, are a group of devices each usable with a particular moving head file technology, and each new

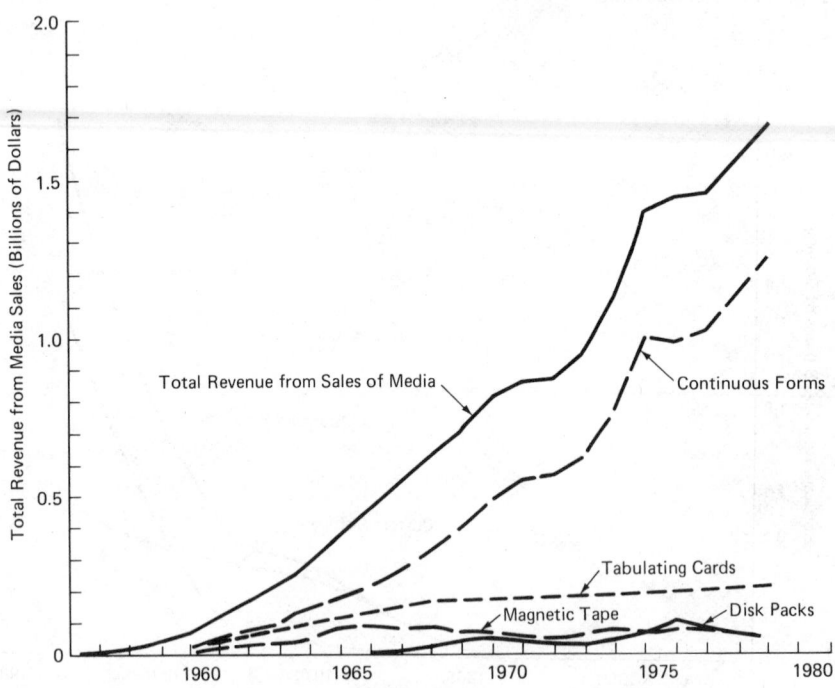

Fig. 15. Media industry revenues.

generation of files usually requires a new type of pack. When a new moving head file is first introduced, the price of its associated disk pack is typically quite high; but after the first year or so, several manufacturers will offer compatible packs, and competition will drive the price down. The disk pack for the IBM 3330, for example, cost $1,000 in 1971 but only $500 in 1978.

The Data Communications Industry. The communications industry used digital techniques to transmit coded information long before the invention of the computer. Telegrams, teletype service, and the stock market and wire service "tickers" all were based on primitive digital technology. In addition, all were limited, in transmission speed, to the output rate of a keyboard operator—60–100 words per minute or less.

The growing usefulness and acceptance of computers in the 1950s made it clear that data communications between computers, and between computers and people at sites remote from the computer, would be increasingly important as industry and government expanded computer applications. Accordingly, the communications common carriers in 1962 began offering a combination of communications lines and interface equipment which used the existing voice communication telephone network to transmit data at rates of 300–2,400 bits per second (the equivalent of 400–3,200 words per

minute). Subsequent offerings permitted even higher data rates. The interface devices, called data sets or modems, were required at each end of the line and converted data from its digital form at the terminal to an analog, voice-type signal on the telephone line, and *vice versa*. Thereafter, the transmission was treated just like any telephone signal.

Meanwhile, the Federal Communications Commission became convinced that competition in communications would benefit the end user, and in the late 1960s made it possible for "specialized common carriers" to compete with the Bell System and other common carriers in certain prescribed situations. By 1973, such carriers were offering services in which data was handled in digital form throughout the network, and, in 1974, the Bell System offered a comparable service, which it called Dataphone ® Digital Service, or DDS.

Fig. 16 estimates the growth of the data communications industry. The "data transmission" figures include only user costs of private lines used for data communications. However, many users make extensive use of the dial network to transmit data, and the telephone companies do not distinguish voice from data calls on that network. For this reason, and because we exclude revenues generated from the transport of computer data by mail or messenger, the graph underestimates data communications revenues by some unknown margin. The "data

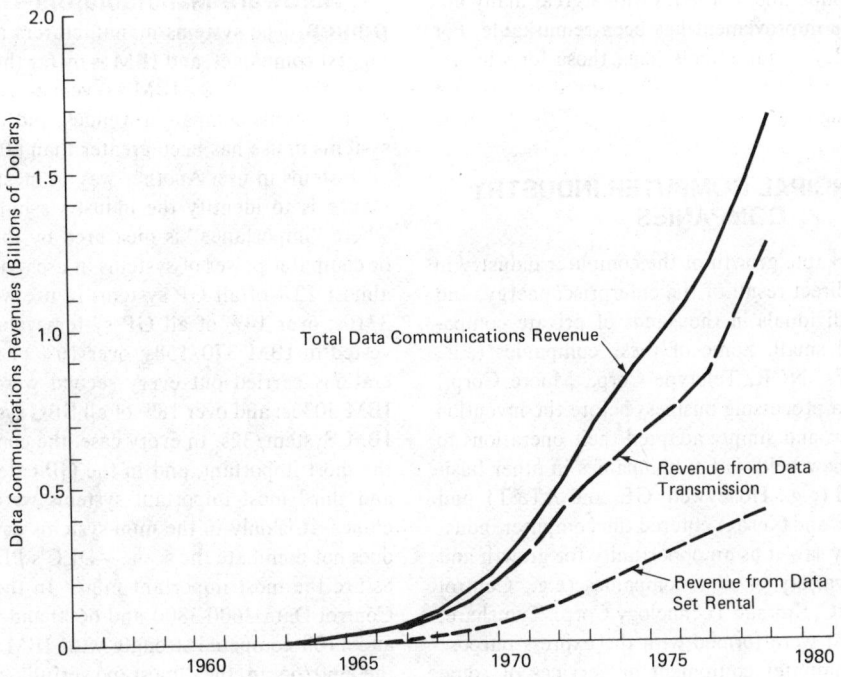

Fig. 16. Data communications industry revenues.

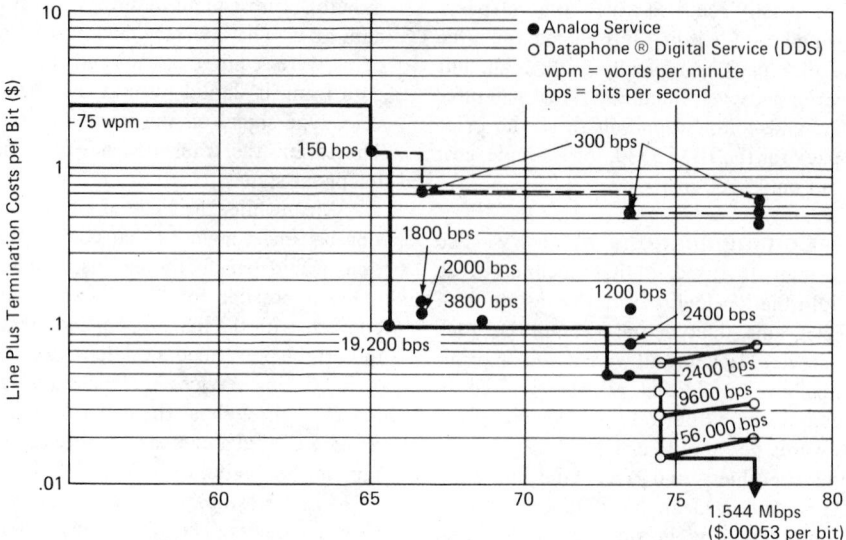

Fig. 17. Trends in data transmission costs. System costs (excluding terminals) for a 300-mile interstate line.

set" graph of Fig. 16 also requires special interpretation: It was derived assuming all modems are leased, though many independent manufacturers offer them for sale.

Fig. 17 shows how the cost of data transmission has fallen over the years. It plots cost per million bits transmitted, where costs include private line plus termination costs for a 300-mile line. For users with a great many bits to transmit, the improvement has been remarkable. For users with modest requirements (e.g., those for whom a 300-bit per second rate is adequate), cost reductions have been less striking.

THE PRINCIPAL COMPUTER INDUSTRY COMPANIES

The remarkable growth of the computer industry in the U. S. is a direct result of the enterprise, energy, and foresight of individuals in thousands of private companies, large and small. Some of these companies (e.g., IBM, Burroughs, NCR, Teletype Corp., Moore Corp.) were in the data processing business before the invention of the computer, and simply adapted their operations to grow with the new field. Other companies in other businesses, both old (e.g., Honeywell, GE, and AT&T) and new (e.g., TRW and Xerox) entered the computer industry because they saw it as an opportunity for growth and profit. And a variety of new companies (e.g., Control Data Corp., DEC, Storage Technology Corp., Tymshare, and Informatics) were formed with the express purpose of providing computer equipment or services of some kind.

Most companies in the industry participate in more than one of the segments discussed above. Table 3 lists the major companies in each segment, shows the other segments in which they operate, and sets forth total 1978 computer-related revenues.

Hardware Manufacturers—System Companies. The systems manufacturers are the industry's biggest companies, and IBM is by far the biggest of these. Since the mid-1950s, IBM's revenues have been over 60% of all systems company revenues, and the value of IBM systems in use has been greater than 60% of the value of all systems in use. Another way to measure IBM's dominance is to identify the industry's important products, where "importance" is measured by the number, value, or computer power of systems in use. At the end of 1978, almost 12% of all GP systems in use were IBM System 3/10s; over 14% of all GP system value in use was invested in IBM 370/158s; over 16% of all computer operations carried out every second were carried out by IBM 3033s; and over 18% of all SBC systems in use were IBM System/32s. In every case, the computer listed was the most important, and in the GP category, the second and third most important systems were also IBM machines. It is only in the mini-systems category that IBM does not dominate the scene—DEC's PDP-11s and PDP-8s are the most important minis. In the mid-1960s, the Control Data 3600-3800 and 6600 and the Univac 1107 and 1108 competed strongly with IBM's 7094 and then the 360/65 in the "most powerful" category and, at about the same time, the Univac 1004 briefly held second

Table 3. The Principal Companies in the Computing Industry and Their 1978 Revenues*

Industry Group	Company	Hardware Systems	Hardware Peripherals	Software	Services	Supplies	Data Communications	Total DP Revenues (Millions of Dollars)
System Manufacturers								
	IBM Corp.	x		x		x		17,072
	Burroughs Corp.	x		x		x		2,107
	NCR Corp.	x		x		x		1,932
	Control Data Corp. (CDC)	x	x	x	x	x		1,867
	Sperry Rand Corp.	x		x		x		1,807
	Digital Equipment Corp. (DEC)	x		x		x		1,437
	Honeywell, Inc.	x		x		x		1,294
	Hewlett-Packard Co.	x		x		x		657
	Data General Corp.	x		x				380
	Amdahl Corp.	x		x				321
Peripheral Equipment Suppliers								
	Memorex Corp.		x			x		570
	Storage Technology		x					300
	3M Company		x			x		280
	Northern Telecom Systems Corp.		x					275
	Xerox Corp.		x		x			236
	Mohawk Data Sciences Corp.		x					153
	Tektronix Inc.		x					126
	Dataproducts Corp.		x					125
	Teletype Corp.		x					124
	California Computer Products, Inc.		x					120
	Ampex Corp.		x			x		119
	Telex Corp.		x					107
Service Companies								
	TRW, Inc.	x	x	x				466
	Automatic Data Processing, Inc.				x			290
	Computer Sciences Corp.			x	x			255
	Electronic Data Systems				x			211
	General Electric Company (GE)	x			x			190
	Tymshare, Inc.				x		x	150
	System Development Corp. (SDC)				x			145
	McDonnell-Douglas Corp.				x			128
Software Companies								
	Informatics, Inc.			x	x			93
Supplies Manufacturers								
	Moore Corp.					x		1323
Data Communications Companies								
	American Telephone and Telegraph Co. (AT&T)	x					x	1845
	General Telephone and Electronics Corp.	x			x		x	207
	Western Union Corp.				x		x	172

*An "x" in a product category column opposite some company signifies that a portion of that company's revenues is included in the indicated category in Fig. 3 or 12. Thus, IBM and Burroughs supply peripherals and maintenance services to their customers—but revenue for those services is included with system manufacturers' revenues, not with peripheral manufacturers' or service companies' revenues. Control Data, on the other hand, supplies peripheral equipment to other system manufacturers, much as Memorex does, and in addition operates a network of computer centers from which it supplies computer services. Those revenues are included in the peripheral and service industry revenues, and therefore there are "x's" opposite CDC in those categories. (Source: *Datamation*, 1979)

place (to the IBM 1401) in the "most numerous" category. But, more recently, IBM systems have regained their dominant positions.

The first commercial computer product was the Univac I, first shipped in 1951 by the company which is now Sperry Rand. Two years later, IBM shipped its first computer, the 701, and, in the same year, Sperry Rand shipped a new model, the 1103. With such a lead, Sperry Rand was seemingly in an excellent position to seize and hold a strong position in the industry. However, the two Sperry machines were developed by two different companies, both of which had been purchased by Sperry to

get it started in the business. And these two groups operated independently until 1955 before being grouped under a common manager—by which time monolithic, well-organized IBM was shipping its very successful IBM 650.

Sperry Rand never regained its position of leadership and, in 1957, lost ground again when several key personnel left to form the Control Data Corp. Meanwhile, Burroughs and NCR had acquired small computer companies, and Honeywell, GE, and RCA had entered the field. The market grew and these companies grew, but IBM grew faster, and in addition was consistently profitable. The competitors found it very difficult to achieve profitability, for their development costs were high, their sales activities ineffective, and their costs of establishing maintenance organizations were large. Furthermore, they had to invest large amounts of cash, or had to borrow heavily, to build equipment for what cash-heavy IBM had established as a predominantly lease or rental market. In 1970, GE decided to leave the system marketplace, and a year later RCA made the same decision. Honeywell and Sperry Rand took over the GE and RCA machines and operations respectively.

IBM's success provided opportunities for some new firms. Starting in the mid-1960s, peripheral equipment manufacturers designed and marketed "plug-compatible" peripherals—mostly magnetic tape units and moving head files which were electrically and functionally interchangeable with their IBM counterparts, but which typically offered better performance at a lower price. And starting in the mid-1970s, some firms have offered plug-compatible CPU's—processors which are functionally and electrically interchangeable with IBM CPU's, operate under IBM's operating systems, and offer better performance at a lower price than the units they replace. Amdahl Corp., founded by one the chief architects of the IBM 360 system, was the first and most successful of these companies.

The rapid growth of the mini-system business since the mid-1960s and the more recent rapid growth of the SBC business (see Figs. 4 and 5) has led to the formation of a number of new companies. DEC has been by far the most successful of these, though Data General and other companies have also grown very rapidly.

Hardware Manufacturers—Peripheral Equipment Companies.

As soon as commercial computers began to be accepted as valuable tools for business and industry, some companies recognized the importance of peripheral and other related equipment, and began to offer appropriate products. The business might be classified according to the type of product offered (peripherals, main memory, terminals, or data entry equipment), and by the type of purchaser (end user, or system manufacturer). The years 1955 to 1965 were generally characterized by sales of peripherals and memory to systems manufacturers. That was inherently an unstable business, for new system companies would initially devote all their resources to developing processors and software, and would buy memory and peripherals from outside suppliers; but as soon as they became successful, they typically developed their own memories and peripherals, and the independent supplier lost the customer.

In the mid-1960s three things happened to change the picture: The plug-compatible peripheral market made its appearance, as mentioned above; the development of time sharing and the availability of data communications facilities led to the growth of the computer terminal business; and some manufacturers developed and marketed data entry systems—first key-to-tape, and later key-to-disk systems—to compete with keypunch equipment. All of these products were generally sold direct to end users. Teletype Corp., a subsidiary of AT&T, is a leading supplier of terminals. Memorex, California Computer Products, and Telex were early suppliers of plug-compatible equipment, and all three filed lawsuits (all unsuccessful) against IBM in response to the product and pricing strategies that company adopted when the plug-compatible manufacturers had achieved some success in selling their products. (The federal government's anti-trust lawsuit against IBM was filed in 1969 and was still in process in 1981.) Storage Technology Corp. is a new and very successful plug-compatible manufacturer. Mohawk Data Sciences was the company which first promoted the non-punched card-oriented data entry business.

Non-Hardware Companies.

There are over 1,500 companies in the U. S. which provide data processing services, and the great majority are quite small. The smallest 90% of the firms have an annual average revenue of less than $1 million. Of the bigger firms, some manufacture hardware (Control Data Corp., Xerox), and some supply software products or consulting services (TRW, Computer Sciences Corp.). Of the service companies listed in Table 3, TRW, GE, Tymshare, and McDonnell-Douglas specialize in providing remote computer services; Computer Science Corp. and Systems Development Corp. supply services to government agencies; Electronic Data Systems is the leading facilities management company; and Automatic Data Processing, Inc. is the largest of those service companies which provide a wide range of both batch and on-line services.

As was mentioned earlier, the systems manufacturers, led by IBM, account for more than half of the "standard package" software revenue shown in Fig. 15. The rest of the packaged software revenue comes from smaller companies, of which Informatics is the largest. TRW, Computer Sciences Corp., and Systems Development Corp. are suppliers of custom software.

The system manufacturers have always offered supplies to their customers, ranging from tabulating cards to magnetic tape and disk packs. Memorex and 3M sell magnetic media, and 3M also supplies microfilm—though that medium is not included in the data of Fig. 15. Moore Corp. is the largest media-only company. It is a manufacturer of paper products, including continuous forms for computer printers.

Finally, Table 3 lists the major data communication

companies. The biggest are the conventional communication carriers. Many of the service companies which provide remote computer services operate large data communication networks, making use of facilities provided by the common carriers. In a sense, they provide their customers with data communication services. But only one, Tymshare, offers a communication service to other customers—customers who do not buy Tymshare computing services.

The growth of the computer industry since the early 1950s has been extraordinary. But to keep that growth in perspective, we should compare it with that of other industries. In 1978, 27 years after shipment of the first Univac I, worldwide system shipments (of GP mini-, and SBC systems) by U. S. firms reached 0.9% of the U. S. Gross National Product (GNP). Early in this century, it took the automobile industry less than 15 years for factory sales to reach that level; starting in 1880, it took the telephone industry 44 years for telephone revenues to reach that level; and, starting in the late 1940s, it took the television industry less than 10 years for TV sales to reach a level of 0.5% of U. S. GNP. TV sales have never exceeded that 0.5% level, and have settled down in the range 0.2–0.3%. Automobile sales, which fluctuate widely from year to year, have for decades ranged between 1 and 3% of GNP. Meanwhile, telephone revenues have climbed, relatively smoothly, to about 2.3% of GNP in 1978. We have seen some evidence that most large-computer users already have GP systems, that their needs for increased data processing capacity can likely be met through price/performance improvements rather than through increases in their investment in hardware, and that the market for SBC's and minicomputers is far from saturated. We have also noted that low-cost digital technology has begun to enter the home and office with equipment such as word processors and personal computers. Table 4 shows the size of these two markets at the end of 1978, and we can expect them both to grow rapidly in the coming decade. But although all these low-priced prod-

ucts will add greatly to the number of systems in use, they will contribute much less, proportionally, to its total value, in comparison with the GP systems. And it therefore seems possible that computer industry system sales will not grow much beyond their present level, as a proportion of GNP.

Every new industry spawns a variety of subsidiary industries which depend upon it. The automobile stimulated the petroleum industry, and led to the development of drive-in movies, garage door openers, traffic lights, and interstate highways. Similarly, as we have seen, the computer stimulated the development of the peripheral equipment, service, software, media, and data communications industries, whose total revenues have grown faster than have system shipment values. The coming years, which will see the wide distribution of low-cost systems of all kinds, should see a corresponding growth in subsidiary industries. And the microcomputer, used as a component to process transient data in an increasing variety of products, from games and hi-fi equipment to dishwashers and automobiles, will help contribute to the growth of many other industries.

Sources of Information. International Data Corp. of Waltham, MA is generally recognized as the leading source of data about the computer industry. The "Annual Review and Forecast" in its *EDP/Industry Report*, along with its *Annual Briefing* publication, provide estimates of system shipments and company revenues, among other things. Though the graphs in the present article come from data in Phister (1979), much of that data is based on IDC reports. For information about the service and software industries, ADAPSO is a primary source, and has since 1966 sponsored an annual analysis of those industries. In recent years, *Datamation* magazine has annually published a survey of the top 50 and, more recently, the top 100 U. S. companies in the computer industry, though they did not include data communications companies until 1979, and still do not include the media companies (e.g., Moore Corp.)

Table 4. The Personal Computer and Word Processor Marketplace in 1978 in the U. S.*

	In Use at Year-End		Shipped during the Year	
	Number	Value	Number	Value
Personal computers	165,000	$ 550 million	115,000	$ 300 million
Word processors	300,000	$1200 million	55,000	$ 780 million
Total	465,000	$1750 million	170,000	$1080 million

*Sources: *EDP/Industry Report* (23, October 1979); International Data Corp. Report # 2026 (October 1979), "Word Processing Marketplace, 1979."

All sources of data about the industry acknowledge, however, that their figures are generally based on surveys, and on analyses of relatively small samples of large, disparate populations. Readers are warned that the data presented here is based on secondary and tertiary sources, and should be used with caution.

REFERENCES

1962. Machlup, F. *The Production and Distribution of Knowledge in the U. S.* Princeton, NJ: Princeton University Press.

1969. Sharpe, W. F. *The Economics of Computers.* Columbia University Press.

1976. Porat, M. U. "The Information Economy," Report No. 27. Palo Alto, CA: Institute for Communications Research, Stanford University.

1979. Phister, M., Jr. *Data Processing Technology and Economics,* 2nd Ed. Bedford, MA: Digital Press.

1979. International Data Corp. *EDP/Industry Report.* Waltham, MA. (Published 24 times per year. "Annual Review and Forecast" is generally available in June or July, covering the previous year. "IDC 79" in the text refers to the "1979 Annual Review and Forecast.")

1979. "Piecing Together the Datacom Industry," *Datamation* (July).

"The Top 50 U. S. Companies in the DP Industry," *Datamation* (June 1976; June 1977; June 1978; 25 May 1979).

"The Top 100 U. S. Companies in the DP Industry," *Datamation* (July 1980; June 1981).

International Data Corp. *(Annual) Computer Industry Briefing Session.* Waltham, MA. (A report published in conjunction with a meeting, held each February to review the past and appraise the coming year.)

International Data Corp. *(Annual) Computer Industry Briefing Session.* Waltham, MA. (A report published in conjunction with a meeting, held each February to review the past and appraise the coming year.)

ADAPSO. *Annual Industry Survey.* (From the Association of Data Processing Service Organizations.)

MONTGOMERY PHISTER, JR.

EUROPE

As in the U. S. and Japan, the European computer industry is made up of a number of different companies. But, in addition, 18 different governments in Western Europe alone—not including the handful of quasi-autonomous states like the Vatican, Monaco, and Liechtenstein—form pockets of political sovereignty which have a strong influence on industry and markets.

Many nations have specific national policies on information technology. These, together with noticeably varying cultures, management traditions, and regulatory environments, turn the European geographical entity into a number of relatively distinct markets. In 1980, these markets were still mainly the preserve of national firms,

especially in telecommunications. In data processing, IBM and other U. S. firms are the dominant forces, together with national suppliers if they exist in a particular country. The prevailing attitude in each country has been "us against IBM," though some of the stronger European firms are venturing more and more outside national boundaries (whether into other European countries or in the U. S.). National rivalry is still more important than corporate competition, to judge by politicians' and press pronouncements. Industry itself, and some governments, realize that the way to success will come with bigger and more open markets within Europe. But, except with the European Economic Community, it will be a long time before all protectionist barriers come down.

The German Federal Republic, France, and the U. K. have all heavily subsidized their computer industries, particularly during the 1970s, and particularly in the mainframe sector. The largest of the European vendors is currently ICL, the new appellation of International Computers, Ltd. ICL developed out of a series of mergers, the final one being between English Electric and International Computers and Tabulators, Ltd.

ICL itself was formed in 1968, and since then has received government aid in the form of around $12 million per year over the period 1968–1976. A government shareholding in ICL has recently been sold off. The company has also benefitted from preferential purchasing policies by the U. K. government. With its earlier 1900 range and the current 2900 series, the company has pursued a vigorous non-IBM-compatible policy, though English Electric left it a legacy of IBM-compatible systems. In the financial year to September 1979, it managed revenues of approximately $1.35 billion, with some $705 million from the home market.

The next largest mainframe firm is Cii-Honeywell Bull, the result of a 1976 merger. Cii-HB has a hybrid history like ICL and is the result of much maneuvering between the French government, major French industrial firms, Compagnie Générale d'Electricité, Thomson CSF, and Saint Gobain Pont à Mousson, as well as the U. S. firms, General Electric, and Honeywell Information Systems (HIS). En route to its present form, the company picked up a vast range of incompatible products which it only now has begun to sort out. Machines Bull had its own range, as did General Electric and Honeywell. But that was only one side of the family. French government-backed efforts to set up a purely French firm to rival Bull-GE (later to become Honeywell-Bull) produced the Compagnie Internationale pour l'Informatique (CII). CII embarked on a range of near-IBM-compatible systems in marked contrast to Honeywell architecture. To complete the product assortment, HIS also took over the Xerox user base. The present firm is basically a CII and Honeywell Bull mix, 53% controlled by French shareholders, with 47% remaining in HIS hands. The dominant share-holder is, however, a newcomer to the DP business, Saint Gobain, a $9 billion a year glass and construction conglomerate (which, as we shall see later, also has a substantial share of Italy's Olivetti). In 1979, Cii-HB posted revenues of $1.2 billion. Government funding for CII before the merger with HB was $350 million, while for Cii-HB it reached $1.4 billion between 1976 and 1980, if almost $1 billion guaranteed orders are included.

In Germany, Siemens data processing activities have been buried in the rest of the huge conglomerate's activities. Its data processing division, however, boasted a turnover of $1 billion in the year ending September 1979, including about $150 million within the group. Siemens sells the 7000 range, basically IBM-compatible, and has a marketing agreement to sell large Fujitsu computers. The huge German market will shortly see another mainframer competing against IBM, Siemens, and the rest. This is the aggressive Nixdorf Computer, which, in 1980, announced it was plunging into the IBM 4300-compatible field with an Israeli-designed machine from Elbit. Previously, Nixdorf had been exclusively involved in small computers though it had been placing heavy emphasis on software, too. Nixdorf had a 1979 turnover of $683 million and boasted a 40% increase in orders for the first five months of 1980.

Two large companies which dropped out of the mainframe market but which now appear set to come back with IBM-compatible systems are the Italian Olivetti and the Dutch Philips. Olivetti concluded a marketing agreement with Hitachi to sell the Japanese firm's computers in Europe, South America, and South Africa. By mid-1980, it had installed its first Hitachi system at a customer site and was planning to start selling operations in the U. K. and France by the turn of the year. Its French plans are under a mist of uncertainty, as Saint

Gobain now has a 20% share of the Italian company, and is clearly keen to make sure that Cii-HB and Olivetti product policies are as complementary as possible. To complicate the plot further, Saint Gobain has a close relationship with the U. S. firm National Semiconductor which has its own IBM-compatible offerings, including Hitachi products. Olivetti's 1979 DP revenues were $1.19 billion. These came, however, mainly from office systems and terminals.

Philips' venture, also IBM-compatible, is with Two-Pi, owned by U. S. Philips. The Dutch firm originally had its own mainframe range but dropped it when a mainframe collaboration project (Unidata) between Siemens, CII, and Philips broke down in 1975–1976. Philips, like Olivetti, has been mainly active in the office system and terminal business.

The European mainframe scene is, however, still dominated by IBM. Continual arguments range over just what constitutes a "European" firm. IBM computers sold in Europe contain as much, if not more, European-made hardware than the offerings of its European-owned rivals. However, its own pricing policies plus several vigorous government preferential purchasing policies and determined efforts from other manufacturers seem to have reduced IBM's revenue growth and, marginally, its market share over the last couple of years. Estimated dollar revenues for IBM and its four major competitors in domestic markets are shown in Table 1.

Apart from the bigger firms, there is a large number of companies involved in small business computers. These include Nixdorf (now entering the mainframe market), Kienzle, Triumph-Adler, Logabax, and a host of others. Europe has also generated quite a few minicomputer manufacturers. One reason for this has been a need for indigenous manufacturers of military minicomputers. The largest European mini firm is now SEMS (Société

Table 1.   Gross Revenues in the Major European Markets in 1979 (Source: Quantum Science Corp.)

Country	Firm	Total Revenues, $1B	Home Revenues, $1B	% Rise over 1978
German FR	IBM	3.6	2.4	10.2
	Siemens*	1.0	0.76	32
France	IBM	2.93	1.53	7.4
	Cii-HB	1.2	0.644	26.4
Italy	IBM	1.49	1.01	20.6
	Olivetti**	1.19	0.37	30.4
United Kingdom	IBM	1.87	0.95	16.8
	ICL*	1.34	0.705	31.4

NOTE: All figures converted from local currency using OECD supplied averages.

**Source figures are unofficial company estimates.

*Year ending 31 August.

Table 2.   Markets by Product Class as Percentage of Market (Source: Quantum Science Corp.)

Product Class	Western Europe 1979	Western Europe 1984 (Projected)	United States 1979	United States 1984 (Projected)
Communications equipment	6.7%	7.1%	7.1%	8.9%
Office equipment	22.1	24.1	21.9	32.4
Terminals	13.1	11.9	14.0	9.5
Small business systems	15.8	18.5	10.4	14.4
General purpose systems	42.1	38.4	46.4	34.8
Value ($1B)	$18	$32.8	$24.2	$40

Européan de Mini-informatique et de Systèmes), a subsidiary of the French electronics firm, Thomson CSF. A few years ago it was well into the top ten worldwide of mini manufacturers, but since then it has not achieved the growth rates of its U. S. rivals and has slipped down the rankings. It also owes most of its revenues to the 40% share it has of the French market. AEG-Telefunken and Dietz are major forces in the German market, while Ferranti, Plessey, and General Electric Company in the U. K. are representative of the mini sector. The Norwegian firm Norsk Data has carved out a niche for itself and is attacking other European markets, as is the Swedish firm DataSaab and the Israeli firm Elbit.

Europe has been particularly weak in the peripherals area, with few manufacturers of wide-ranging tape or disk systems. The chemical firms BASF and Rhone Poulenc have made some inroads into the magnetic media markets through their chemical know-how. BASF has a share in a joint disk manufacturing venture with Fujitsu and Hitachi. Cii-HB has had some success in specialized areas with its midi-disk family sold to OEM (q.v.) Siemens seems to have achieved a breakthrough with an advanced laser printer, for which it has concluded a number of OEM deals, while ICL is looking for commercial applications of its content-addressable file processor.

The terminal market in all its aspects is an area where many European firms are looking for future success. Hopes have been kindled by the tremendous upsurge of government and press interest in the advent of the information society.

Both German and French firms are driving hard to offer office automation-related products such as teletex (fast telex with display and editing capabilities), cheap telephone terminals which the French will use as a replacement for the standard handset and which will be able to access private or public databanks, plus electronic mail devices and the more banal communicating word processors. Governments are also beginning to spend money on voice processing.

The bug has bitten hardest in France, though this does not mean that that country's manufacturers will necessarily win the lion's share of the market. Still the world leader in digital telephone communications by lines installed, CIT-Alcatel is making a big push for office systems, while weapons firm Matra is a dark horse for the future. Siemens, Nixdorf, and Olivetti will also be fighting hard in this area. The U. K. has a government agency, Nexos, fighting the office systems battle.

There is also a special category of terminals pioneered in the U. K. These are what are now called *videotex* (the ITT standard term), but what has been known as Viewdata (q.v.). Videotex uses a domestic television receiver equipped with what should be (but isn't yet) a cheap decoder in conjunction with public telephone lines to provide easy access to databanks. Start-up has been slow, but the British have built up a lot of useful expertise in designing systems to interface with untrained operators. Again, the French are investing heavily to have a share of this market, and a number of other countries are running pilot schemes.

Much of the effort to set up systems like videotex comes from software firms. A recent Quantum Science

Table 3.   Value of Total General-Purpose Systems Shipped ($1B) (Source: Quantum Science Corp.)

Country	1979	1984 (Projected)
German FR	2.4	4.03
France	1.3	2.39
United Kingdom	1.4	1.77
Benelux	0.666	1.1
Italy	0.673	1.04
Scandinavia	0.506	0.811
Switzerland	0.351	0.59
Spain/Portugal	0.269	0.493
Austria	0.23	0.393

study says that the European software and services market will almost catch up with that in the U. S. by 1983, reaching nearly $12 billion compared with $5.7 billion in 1978.

The time-sharing industry in Europe has been relatively successful, though time-sharing services have tended to be provided by the U. S. giants. Whereas in the U. S. the industry is dominated by a handful of large firms, the European scene has been fragmented into much smaller entities. France has proved an exception to this after ten years of a government policy which encouraged software and service firms to acquire an "industrial size." The largest European firm, having grown mainly by acquisition is GSI (Générale de Service Informatique), another subsidiary of CIT-Alcatel. This services company was aiming for a $150 million turnover in 1981. Also giant-sized by Euro-standards is the French Atomic Energy Agency's CISI (Compagnie Internationale de Services en Informatique) services company and the software house, Cap-Gemini-Sogeti, which employs close to 3,000 people. French firms took four out of the top five places in the European Computing Services Association league table in 1978.

While governments play a huge role in Europe as users and by giving direct aid to national firms, there is one other major influence on the European computer industry which should not be forgotten. This is the influence of common carriers (i.e., the telecommunications networks or, as they are known in Europe, PTTs, for Postal-Telephone-Telegraph). Everywhere except in Finland, these are a state monopoly. Local regulations for voice and data transmission can make the market and hence the industry develop in a particular way. While the French PTT is encouraging low-cost communications to help its smaller firms use data communications and indirectly to create a bigger market for its data communication equipment companies, Germany's PTT has traditionally set high tariffs—a policy which has created a favorable environment for the development of discrete distributed processing systems.

Last, because European governments are much more conscious of societal issues than seems to be the case in either the U. S. or Japan, the industry has to pay much more attention to a range of issues varying from privacy/data protection to human engineering (which Europeans call ergonomics). Data protection forced IBM into bringing out special software and is pushing France's Cii-HB into developing a chip-in-card approach for point-of-sale systems. This, it is argued, will have fewer implications for privacy law as the holder of the card will carry the transaction details around instead of having them sent over telecommunication lines to a central data file. Another social phenomenon is concern for the vulnerability of data processing systems to terrorist attack. This is already causing firms to fortify their computer rooms—and will undoubtedly affect future systems design.

A. R. H. LLOYD

JAPAN

The computer community in Japan is an anomaly. In this crowded archipelago, one finds no less than six mainframe manufacturers, a large computer market second only to that of the U. S., and one of the few markets where IBM has less than a 50% share. None of this makes sense—until, that is, one understands the role played by the central government since 1957 to protect and promote the indigenous computer and electronics industry.

As with many other nations, Japan in the 1960s decided it wanted a domestic computer manufacturing industry and, accordingly, protected the fledgling ventures by imposing tariff and nontariff barriers on foreign competitors. Those barriers, for the most part, came down in the late 1970s. But by that time, the domestic manufacturers had begun eyeing foreign markets and preparing for an expansion abroad. As a result, Japanese manufacturers are deemed to be close to matching Western nations in hardware design and to be their equals, or even possibly superior, in manufacturing capabilities. In software, however, they are acknowledged to be behind the West but catching up fast.

No other nation in the Pacific Basin has developed a domestic industry, although many are users and are becoming significant markets for vendors of hardware, software, and services. Indeed, there are local software companies and service bureaus in Asian nations that cannot support their own mainframe or minicomputer manufacturing business.

Only South Korea has taken steps to develop a capability beyond that of a user. It encouraged Fujitsu, Ltd., a Japanese mainframe maker, to establish a programming group in Seoul, using Korean nationals trained by the Japanese. Not content with being merely an overseas electronics assembly point for foreign manufacturers, this nation has also begun to establish joint ventures with overseas firms to make electronic products there. Plans are to expand this from the assembly of semiconductors to the manufacture of microcomputers and minicomputer systems.

In Japan, the application of data processing has been traced back to the early 1920s with the use of Powers and Hollerith's punched card systems. A calculator using relays was constructed in 1941 by Fuji Electric, so the idea of harnessing electricity to the performance of digital calculation had occurred to the Japanese some time back.

But it was word of the development of the ENIAC at the Moore School that caught the fancy of the scientific and engineering community in Japan. As a result, the decade of the 1950s in Japan is peppered with new developments in digital technology. High hopes were held out for the parametron, which was invented in Japan in 1954. A number of computers were built in the late 1950s and early 1960s using this technology. The parametron was a device that had two stable states of oscillation, one at twice the frequency of the other, and was therefore capable of storing one binary digit.

At the first IFIP Congress in Paris in 1959, Hitachi sent its so-called HIPAC 101 (the acronym coming from Hitachi Parametron Automatic Computer). This scientific, fixed-point machine used some 4,500 parametrons as logic elements. At the same conference, Nippon Electric Co. exhibited its NEAC 2201, which has been described as Japan's first commercial transistorized computer.

But it did not take the Japanese long to realize they had much to learn from their Western counterparts. Accordingly, in the early 1960s, the mainframers signed technical licensing agreements with American companies. Hitachi came to an agreement with RCA, Nippon Electric with Honeywell, Toshiba (Tokyo Shibaura Electric Co.) with General Electric, and Oki Electric with Univac. Mitsubishi originally signed up with TRW, whose computer activities subsequently merged with General Electric's.

(Throughout all this, one company chose to go it alone. Fujitsu, the domestic manufacturer which today has the largest share of the Japanese market, had no technology exchange agreement until it established an equity position in Amdahl Corp., the first major manufacturer of mainframes that are software-compatible with the IBM System/370.)

In 1961, the six dominant mainframe manufacturers, with the encouragement and financial support of the government, got together and formed Japan Electronic Computer Co. This organization eases the financial burden on its six member companies in the renting and leasing of systems by paying the purchase price to the manufacturer for systems installed at a customer site, and then collecting monthly rental from the user. It thus serves to cushion the vendors from the enormous cash drain associated with financing leases.

By 1971, there were still six mainframe manufacturers vying not only for market share but also the meager profits. The domestic market obviously could not support six suppliers, and so the government took steps to reduce that number. It offered subsidies to pairings of companies, combinations that jointly would design, manufacture, and market families of computers.

Fujitsu and Hitachi got together to produce a family of IBM-compatible processors called the M Series. The M-160, the smallest of four processors in the family, had the approximate power of a 370/155, while the top-model M-190 had more power than a 168. Nippon Electric and Toshiba paired up to develop the ACOS series, which resembled the Honeywell line. And Mitsubishi and Oki cooperated in the development of the Cosmo Series.

The result was not exactly as planned. Work on the M Series, for example, was coordinated between the two companies, Fujitsu developing the top and bottom processors of the four-processor family, while Hitachi designed the middle two. But when it came to manufacturing, Fujitsu made and sold only the two it had designed, and Hitachi manufactured and sold only the two for which it was responsible. The two vendors developed separate and different operating systems for the M Series, which makes it difficult for users to migrate from one vendor's machine to the other's. And the family has since grown. Fujitsu added a top-of-the-line model, the M-200; Hitachi did likewise with what it calls the M-200H; and there are hardware differences between the two.

Among the domestic mainframe makers, Fujitsu is the most aggressive and chalks up the largest revenues from DP sales. This might be explained by the fact that Fujitsu is also the most heavily dependent on computer sales and service revenues (see Table 1). By way of contrast, Hitachi makes products ranging from home appliances to heavy industrial equipment, while Nippon Electric has been more of a communications-oriented manufacturer.

These companies, of course, must vie for sales not only among themselves but also with foreign vendors (see Table 2). Of them, IBM has the largest market share, in terms of the value of installed hardware. Based on the number of mainframes installed, however, Fujitsu is the leader. IBM's high installed value stems from its strength in large-scale machines, while Fujitsu's strength in small-scale machines gives it numerical prominence. Lately,

Table 1.   Computer Sales as Percentage of Corporate Sales (Source: _Computopia Magazine_, Tokyo)

Fujitsu	65%
Hitachi	13%
Nippon Electric	21%
Oki	38%
Mitsubishi	5%
Toshiba	4%

Table 2. Market Shares (Source: *Computopia Magazine*, Tokyo)

	Value	Units
IBM	28%	13%
Fujitsu	21%	32%
Hitachi	16%	15%
Nippon Electric	15%	17%
Univac	12%	7%
Burroughs	4%	6%
NCR	2%	4%
Mitsubishi	2%	5%

however, Fujitsu, Hitachi, and Nippon Electric have been successful in selling large machines, not only domestically but also in Europe, in the Peoples Republic of China, and in Australia.

Japanese companies tend to be heavily integrated, offering an extensive line of products, including peripherals and terminals, minicomputers, and, in more recent years, small business systems and personal computers. They can be expected to be participants in the market for office automation products, as well.

Many of them also rushed into developing an in-house semiconductor capability, producing chips not only for internal use but also becoming merchant suppliers. This capability, orchestrated and subsidized by the government, was so skillfully developed that Japanese vendors of RAM (random access memory) chips are acquiring ever larger shares of the world market, much to the dismay of the American companies that invented this technology. The Japanese have shown once again their ability to produce a quality product, but in this instance are also demonstrating an ability to advance the technology. This flies in the face of the widely held belief that the Japanese are skilled at copying but lacking in originality.

It has also been suggested that the Japanese may harness this new capability to overcome a weakness in software, implementing software functions in silicon. This possibility is attractive in the environment of systems architectures consisting of distributed, dedicated-function processors.

The software industry in Japan consists of perhaps a hundred major software companies, many of which are also service bureaus, along with hundreds of small, one-person and two-person software houses. Most of these companies are affiliated with one or another mainframe manufacturer, relying exclusively or in large part on that vendor for their business. We also see more than a hundred makers of peripheral equipment and upwards of 50 systems integration companies offering small business computers.

The Japanese market could not possibly support such an abundance of suppliers, which is one reason why the major vendors have begun establishing a foothold in markets abroad. Industry analysts view the success the Japanese have had in foreign markets with such products as electronic appliances and automobiles, and they reason that computer companies will do equally well.

But in order to succeed, it is thought, they will have to form joint marketing ventures with foreign companies—with American companies for the American market, European firms for the markets there. And should they do so, the Japanese will have come full circle, for their strength in large part can be traced back to the early technology licensing agreements they forged with American computer companies.

E. K. YASAKI

COMPUTER-MANAGED INSTRUCTION (CMI)

For articles on related subjects *see* COMPUTER-ASSISTED LEARNING AND TEACHING; and COMPUTER-ASSISTED INSTRUCTION.

Computer-managed instruction (CMI) refers to the use of computer assistance in testing, diagnosing, prescribing, grading, and record keeping. Some writers prefer "computer-aided management of instruction" in order to emphasize computer assistance *to* the human teacher or counselor, in contrast with management *by* the computer.

Computer assistance has been made available in many ways to those managing instruction, including aids for students managing their own instruction. The teacher of a large class finds assistance in scoring tests, keeping records, checking on which students need what kind of work, and computing grades. A manager of a self-instruction group uses the computer to obtain summary records showing where each student stands. A student or teacher may call upon the computer files and procedures to generate a test at random but according to set rules. The procedure may select from an item pool and plug in variations on standard question forms to obtain the specific test items so they appear fresh each time. Computer-based information systems are used by students and teachers to locate instructional materials in various media according to needs, interests, and the limitations of course time and instructional budget.

Major projects using the computer for assistance in the management of instruction are based on a large amount of curricular materials, probably in modular form, and a convenient testing and record-handling system. The arguments for CMI instead of CAI include: lower cost of operation, since students spend less time at computer terminals; more flexibility in learning formats, since students are referred to materials in a variety of media and learning settings apart from the computer; lower cost of development, since existing materials can be used for instruction. CMI and CAI may be used together; the management aids associated with CMI can refer the student to selected exercises that are presented by the computer (CAI) as well as to many others that do not benefit from presentation in the computer medium.

REFERENCE

1978. Baker, Frank B. *Computer-Based Management Systems*: *Theory and Practice*. Englewood Cliffs, NJ: Educational Technology Publications.

K. L. ZINN

COMPUTER MUSIC

For articles on related subjects *see* ARTIFICIAL INTELLIGENCE; ARTS APPLICATIONS; and HUMANITIES APPLICATIONS.

Historical. Musical applications of digital computers date from 1956 with the composition of the *Illiac Suite for String Quartet* by Lejaren Hiller and Leonard Isaacson using the ILLIAC I at the University of Illinois. Since then, many uses for computers have been found in music, not just in composition but also for sound synthesis and analysis, musicological research, music printing and development of library resources. Although emphasis will be given here on how computers aid composition and facilitate sound synthesis, briefer mention of the other applications will also be included for completenes.

Definitions. Computer music has come to denote two complementary types of computer output. The first (computer-composed music) involves composition, *per se* (i.e., note selection), while the second (computer-realized music) involves conversion into electronic sound of a score which may or may not have been composed with the aid of a computer. These two operations can be used in sequence so that a composer's score can be both "composed" and "realized" by means of a computer. This is sketched in Fig. 1. Depending upon the computer configuration and the programmer's objectives, the boundary between these two processes can vary from sharply defined to rather fuzzy.

Computer-Composed Music. Since composing the above mentioned *Illiac Suite*, Hiller has produced additional computer music compositions, including *Computer Cantata* (with Robert Baker), 1963; *Algorithms I*, 1968; *HPSCHD* (with John Cage), 1968; and *Persiflage*, 1977. Also active in the 1950s was the group at Bell Telephone Laboratories (John Pierce, Max Mathews *et al.*) who produced a number of experiments recorded in an album, *Music from Mathematics*. In France, Yannis Xenakis used a computer to compose "stochastic music" with titles such as *ST/10-01,080,262*, *Morsima-Amorsima*, and *Atrées*, and Pierre Barbaud has written what he terms *musique automatique*. Other composers who have produced significant computer music include Herbert Brun (U. S.), James Tenney (U. S.), and Gottfried-Michael Koenig (Holland).

In the work of all these composers, algorithms are used which express aspects of musical logic and syntax, such as pitches, durations, intensities, and other parameters defining musical notes and combinations thereof (phrases, sections of music, etc.). These are substantially chosen by the computer rather than by the composer/programmer. The idea is to delegate to the computer many of the step-by-step choices and the general bookkeeping; i.e., score assembly. For this reason, most computer-composed music has depended upon statistical and probabilistic operations in which random choices are accepted or rejected depending upon how they relate to the statistical ground plan of the composition being produced. Information theory (notions of disorder-order and entropy-redundancy) provides the theoretical background. This leads the composer/programmer to write algorithms that "impose order upon chaos" by restricting statistical distributions.

Computer-Realized Music. Electronic sound synthesis by computer is currently replacing electronic music synthesizers that depend on oscillators and adjunct audio equipment. Greater precision and versatility at less cost are the essential reasons for this.

The most important computer sound synthesis technique involves digital-to-analog conversion of 12–16-bit samples representing sound at a carrier frequency of up to 40 KHz. Because of the sampling theorem, made famous by Shannon's use of it in communication theory, the higher the rate, the higher the high-frequency cutoff can be, and 40 KHz is ideal because it is twice the upper limit of hearing of the normal ear. Sampling of sound for conversion is shown in Fig. 2. For sound analysis and/or other computer processing of real sounds, analog-to-digital conversion is an available option employed at similar rates and word size.

The first demonstration of practical digital/analog (D/A) sound synthesis was made at Bell Telephone Lab-

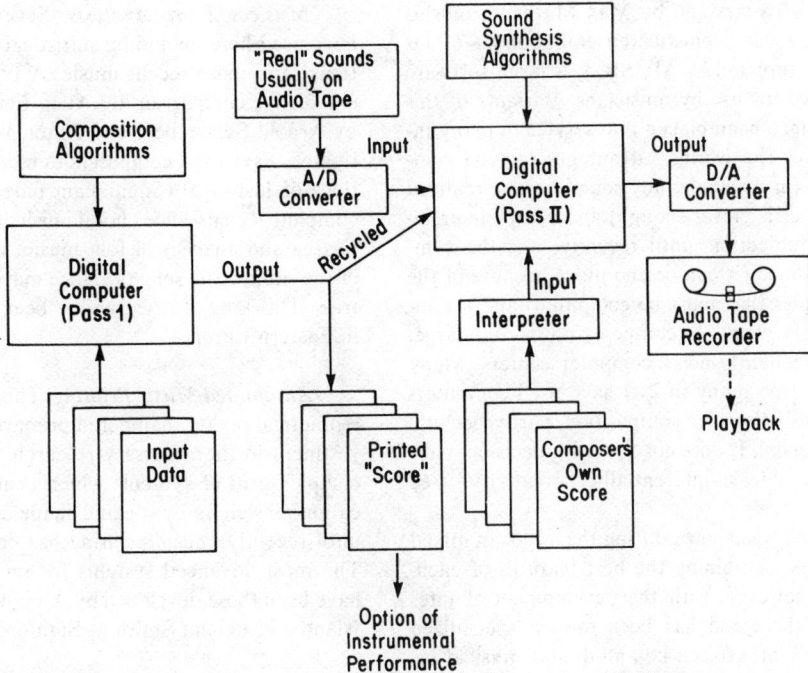

Fig. 1. The components of a computer music system.

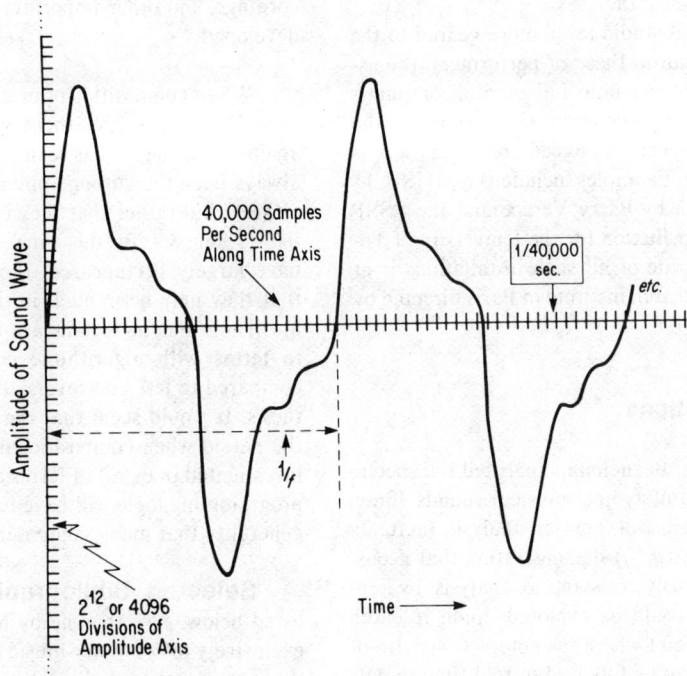

Fig. 2. Sound synthesis by digital-to-analog conversion of sound (or vice versa for sound analysis).

oratories about 20 years ago by Max Mathews and his colleagues. The most sophisticated embodiment of his technique was expressed by MUSIC5, a large software package designed for use by musicians. Variants of this compiler have since been placed into service in many institutions all over the world. Advantages include complete versatility (in principle, any sound can be realized if the programmer is clever enough) and complete precision. The main objection, until recently, was the computer time consumed (it can be enormous because of the millions of samples that must be computed) and the inconvenience of trying to compose music in large, crowded, and frequently noisy computer centers. Many more composers (too many to list) have used computers for sound synthesis than for composition, partly because it is less controversial. It does not deal with decision-making and, hence, at least inferentially, "creativity" (see below).

Some interest was shown during the 1960s in mixed D/A synthesizers, combining the best features of each. More recently, however, with the development of integrated circuits, the trend has been toward specialized computer music synthesizers; i.e., all-digital musical instruments with substantial memory. There is a commercial market for such instruments, particularly among performers. Typical of such instruments are the "Egg" synthesizer designed by Michael Manthey and the DMX-1000 "Signal Processing" computer manufactured by Digital Music Systems, Inc.

At the institutional studio level, more geared to the needs of composers than to those of performers, the assembly of a sophisticated studio full of minicomputers and auxiliary hardware (converters, plotters, audio equipment, etc.) specifically designed for composers is now a practical reality. Examples include the MUSIC11 system built for M.I.T. by Barry Vercoe and the SSSP studio built by William Buxton for the University of Toronto. The most elaborate of all such installations is at IRCAM, the music research institute in Paris directed by Pierre Boulez.

Other Applications

Acoustic Analysis. Beauchamp analyzed the spectra of the attack portions of typical musical sounds (flute, oboe, trumpet) by means of Fourier analysis (actually fast Fourier transform (*q.v.*)) demonstrating that acoustic phenomena previously resistant to analysis by precomputer technology could be explored. Such research has developed to the point where the complete spectra of instrumental sounds can be followed in real time in output displays, as has been demonstrated by Galler and Piszczalski.

Musical Score Analysis. Several approaches have been used here, including statistical ones, for both traditional and more recent music. A typical example is the exhaustive comparison by Allen Forte of 12 tone music by Arnold Schoenberg and Anton Webern. Other investigators have used computers to reconstruct missing portions of historically significant older music such as incomplete Renaissance choral music. Also important is the sorting and analysis of folk music, where many variants of the same basic song or dance may be collected on field trips. This kind of research has been especially promoted in Eastern Europe.

Automated Music Printing. This is rapidly becoming a practical reality, hampered primarily by inadequate investment in the necessary research. Music notation is a complex grid of symbols which acquire meaning by location as well as by specific shape and function. Hence, until recently, music printing has defied mechanization. The most advanced systems for music printing to date have been those developed by Armand dal Molin in Long Island and Leland Smith at Stanford University.

Library Resources and Archives. A worldwide computer bank of literature about music called RILM is now well established. This includes titles, abstracts, and other pertinent information as in similar archiving services in other fields. Similar storage plans for musical scores, recordings, and other important documents are now being developed.

When composition of music using computers was initiated 20 years ago, there was considerable agitation against it in that it was seen to threaten creativity. It has always been the author's opinion that computers are not a threat but rather that they enhance the composer's artistic resources. By this time, overtly negative responses have largely disappeared, though it must be admitted that they may be implicit in the fact that relatively few musicians and/or technicians have been willing to come to terms with algorithmic compositional processes as compared to less controversial topics such as sound synthesis. It would seem that the next decade or so will be the period when compositional processes will have to be investigated in detail in terms of programmability, and a programming logic will have to be developed of sufficient generality that many composers will find it useful.

Selected Bibliography. None of the books listed below, save the one by Mathews *et al.*, is devoted exclusively to computer music composition or sound synthesis, but each includes substantial material on the subject. Journals which frequently print articles on computer music include *Computer Music Journal, Perspectives of*

New Music, Journal of the Audio Engineering Society, Interface, and *Journal of Music Theory.*

1959. Hiller, L. A. and Isaacson, L. M. *Experimental Music.* New York: McGraw-Hill.

1969. Von Foerster, H. and Beauchamp, J. W. (Eds). *Music by Computers.* New York: Wiley.

1969. Mathews, M. V., with Miller, J. E., Moore, F. R., Pierce, J. R., and Risset, J. C. *The Technology of Computer Music.* Cambridge, MA: The M.I.T. Press.

1970. Lincoln, H. B. (Ed.) *The Computer and Music.* Ithaca, NY: Cornell University Press.

1971. Xenakis, Y. *Formalized Music.* Bloomington, IN: Indiana University Press.

1975. Howe, H. *Electronic Music Synthesis.* New York: W. W. Norton.

1975. Appleton, J. H. and Perera, R. C. (Eds). *The Development and Practice of Electronic Music.* Englewood Cliffs, NJ: Prentice-Hall.

Selected Recordings. The records below contain important examples of computer music, either composed or realized in sound.

CRISP310—L. Hiller and R. Baker, *Computer Cantata,* J. Melby, −91+5.

CRISP393—G. Winham, R. Hoffmann, B. Vercoe, and J. Gressel, *Computer Generations.*

Nonesuch, H71224—J. Cage and L. Hiller, *HPSCHD.*

Nonesuch, H71245—J. Randall, C. Dodge, and B. Vercoe, *Computer Compositions.*

Nonesuch, H71250—C. Dodge, *Earth's Magnetic Field.*

Decca DL9103—*Music from Mathematics* (experiments and compositions by Pierce, Mathews, Speeth, Lewin, Tenney, and Guttman).

Angel S36560/S36656—Y. Xenakis, *Atrées, ST/4, Achorripsis, ST/10* (plus other compositions).

L. A. HILLER

COMPUTER NETWORKS

For articles on related subjects *see* ARPA NETWORK; COMMUNICATIONS AND COMPUTERS; COMPUTER SYSTEMS; DATA COMMUNICATION NETWORKS; DATA COMMUNICATIONS; DATA NETWORKS, PUBLIC; DISTRIBUTED SYSTEMS; MULTIPLEXING; PACKET SWITCHING; TERMINALS; and TIME SHARING.

The term *computer networks* has been used to describe situations in which:

1. Geographically remote terminals and remote job entry (RJE) stations are connected to a central computer.

2. Geographically remote smaller computers are used for minor editing tasks and to transfer input to magnetic tape and from magnetic tape to output printers and plotters. Magnetic tapes are transferred by post or messenger between smaller machines and a central computer.

3. A central computing unit has connections to smaller machines with specialized functions, which provide it with services such as storage (and associated file management) and communication facilities (such as message concentration); in the case of small machines used for graphics, the central unit is used for major computing tasks.

4. Independent major computing systems ("hosts"), possibly in addition to the above, communicate with one another, and share resources such as hardware, programs or data (Fig. 1).

Computer networks should not be confused with information networks, a term usually applied to systems for the sharing of library resources. However, it is clear that, particularly with the growth of computerized printing (which provides text in machine-readable form—e.g., on magnetic tape—as a byproduct), a growing source of loading for computer networks will be their use as information networks.

The fourth definition of computer networks—resource-sharing networks of machines of comparable power—is coming to be the more widely accepted one. As an indication of the rate of growth of activity in this area, a bibliography published by the National Bureau of Standards in 1973 lists over 500 citations relating to resource-sharing networks, nearly all of which come from the previous decade. A more recent bibliography, five years later (Szentivanyi and Talloczy, 1978) includes over 1,800 citations.

The rate at which computer networks are now proliferating throughout the world indicates that they are becoming a powerful force in both the public and private sectors, both nationally and internationally. This upsurge of activity, which is of recent origin, may be ascribed to three main technological trends:

1. The greatly increased reliability of computers, which makes possible the implementation of complex systems that would have been unworkable a decade or so ago.

2. The availability of low-priced minicomputers suitable for carrying out most of the functions required to operate a network, with a minimum of change to the operating systems of the major connected computers (these operating systems are large, complex, and not designed to provide the

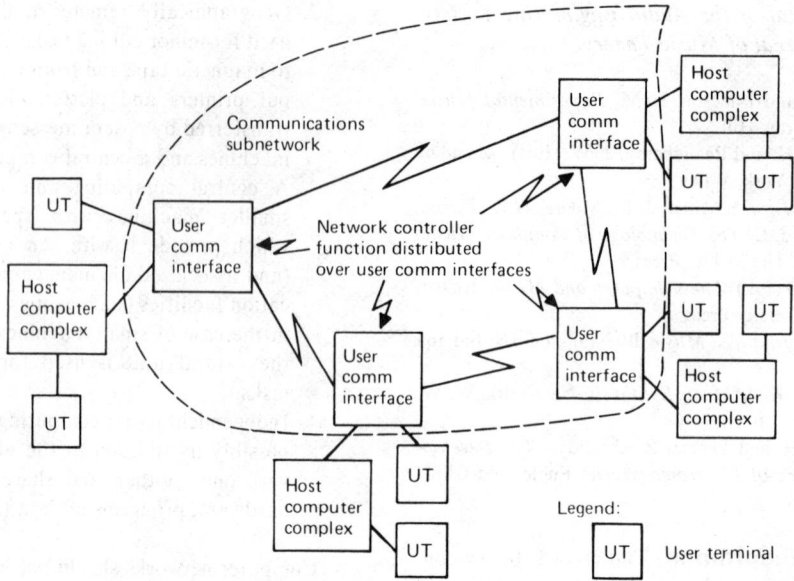

Fig. 1. Computer network. (Courtesy IEEE.)

quick interrupts needed for communications work).

3. Major changes in communications technology, which are reflected in a corresponding reduction of communication costs.

In terms of their broad end-use, computer networks, like some other branches of human activity, can be categorized as follows.

1. Monolithic empires, constructed for a single organization and an explicit purpose (such as an airline reservation system).
2. Alliances of several approximately equal partners (such as the North Carolina Triangle Universities Computing Center (TUCC) with three partners).
3. Free enterprise resource marketing facilities (such as Tymnet, a network operated since 1969 by Tymshare Inc.).
4. Facilities introduced by legislation (such as the state network in New Jersey) to consolidate state computing facilities.
5. Facilities constructed to acquire experience in a new experimental technique (ARPANET, sponsored by the U.S. Department of Defense Advanced Research Projects Agency (ARPA), was initially in this category).

Network Design Considerations. For a fuller description of various aspects of digital networks, the reader is referred to Davies and Barber (1973) or

Housley (1979). For an introduction to communications techniques, Martin (1969) should be consulted. An excellent "state-of-the-art" review is to be found in a special issue of *Proc. IEEE* (1978).

Computer networks may be viewed (Fig. 2) as being composed of nodes, with circuits, channels, or links connecting them. A node may vary from a small amount of fixed hardware logic to one of the major connected com-

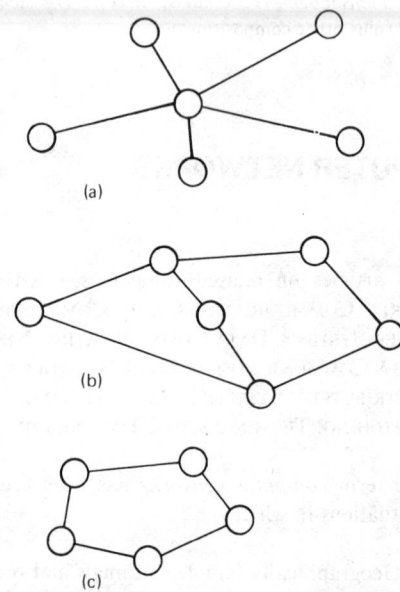

Fig. 2. Alternative network of configurations: (a) star; (b) distributed; (c) ring. (Courtesy IEEE.)

puters. Nodes may be used to support network connectivity as store-and-forward computers (i.e., to receive and store messages, and to dispatch them along one of several different routes), as concentrators (e.g., to take input characters from a number of slow terminals and assemble them into blocks), and as attachment points for major computer systems.

The extent of a network is to some extent arbitrary. A network may, for example, be considered to include the programs in a host computer which are needed to communicate with it, but not the attached terminals. The nodes and linking circuits of ARPANET are referred to as the *communications subnet*.

The details of physical channels (circuits or links)— which may be lines, microwave links, radio links, cable TV installations, or satellites—are of little consequence from the point of view of computer networks. The relevant parameters of a channel are its maximum data rate, its error characteristics, and its directional limitations. The setup characteristics are also important information if a point-to-point circuit is not always dedicated to a network. This information may include the signaling mechanism and delays for circuit setup and breaking.

Commonly available speeds vary from 60 to 300 bps (bits per second), suitable for supporting a slow-speed terminal, through voice-grade line speeds of 2,000 to 4,800 bps (or higher) to 5×10^4 bps, the speed currently used by ARPANET. Higher speeds are available if required—systems to carry several gigabits per second (a gigabit equals 10^9 bits, a volume equivalent to the Encyclopaedia Britannica)—are under development. For local area computer networks (in which the distances are limited to about 10,000 meters), high speeds (greater than 100 kilobits per second) are usual.

Requirements for data transmission arising in connection with computer networks are typically burst-oriented, with transmission from terminals or computers for a short period at a specified rate, and long time gaps with no transmission at all. Standard communications techniques (frequency division multiplexing, FDM; or time division multiplexing, TDM) make better use of available bandwidths by allocating smaller bandwidths or time slots to individual subchannels, but make no use of the burst characteristics of the data. If a channel is connected to one subchannel only when that subchannel is active, an address being added to indicate the source (available from timing considerations with FDM and TDM), more efficient use will be made of the channel; this approach is referred to as asynchronous time-division multiplexing (ATDM).

Since it would not be economic for every node (or its equivalent) to be connected to every other node with which communication may be desired, transmission is usually routed through a number of intermediate nodes. In a typical case, these nodes are minicomputers and the connecting links are leased lines. Messages with suitable header information and error checks are passed from one node to another on a store-and-forward basis, the route being chosen according to loading or fault conditions by the minicomputers or by separate machines with control and monitoring responsibilities. Because messages are variable in length, problems arise in selecting sizes for buffer storage, and so it is usual to break a message into fixed length segments called *packets*. These packets are transmitted on a store-and-forward basis and, with some networks, may go to their destination by different routes if changes occur in the loading of the links. Typical packet sizes are between 1,000 and 2,000 bits for text, with an additional 100 bits for header information.

Packets are checked after passage through each link (an acknowledgment being returned to the sending node if correct), are reassembled in correct order at the destination, and passed on to the relevant process in the host computer to which they are addressed.

When nodes are allowed to compete for a channel, there may be a clash; in this case the check sums will not tally, no acknowledgment will be sent, and retransmission may be arranged to occur after a delay, which is different for each node so that a second clash is unlikely. The ALOHA system developed by the University of Hawaii uses a single radio channel in this way. The efficiency of this method can be raised considerably by introducing a reservation system in which a number of time slots may be reserved, one of these being subdivided into smaller slots that convey information about reservation requests to all user stations so that each station will know the position of the next free time slot.

There is still considerable controversy as to the extent to which packet switching techniques should replace message switching techniques or the more conventional circuit switching techniques, in which a path is established from host to host by a dialing operation or its equivalent. The "best" solution depends on the mix of message lengths involved, and the trend appears to be towards a mixed system capable of adaptation to an optimum handling of independent packets ("datagrams") and "virtual calls" consisting of a sequence of packets with abbreviated headings, following a fixed routing that may be set up by the first packet in the sequence. The position is complicated by the trend toward digital transmission for general telecommunications usage.

Packet communications currently handle only a small proportion of the total amount of data transmitted over communications networks. In the U. S., for example, Tymnet and Telenet, the two major packet switching systems (PSSs), in 1977 jointly carried less than 3% of the data communications traffic. The ultimate PSS share of the data communications traffic is variously expected to be between 20% and 75% of the total data traffic (Logica, 1978, p. 117).

Network Configurations. With the simplest network [Fig. 2(a)], a star network, all communication between the points of the star must take place through a central node. If this node is inoperable, the network cannot function.

Networks with alternative routings between nodes are referred to as "distributed" networks [Fig. 2(b)]. The reliability of a network may be assessed (Abramson and Kuo, 1973) by determining the number of nodes or links that must be inoperative before the network becomes disconnected. i.e., before there ceases to be at least one path between any sender and any receiver (apart from the removed nodes).

A further design consideration is the maximum delay in a network. This delay (which is, for example, a half-second for individual packets in the case of the ARPA network) may vary according to the end-use of the data and the loading. However, once it has been specified, it is an important parameter: A network should be designed so as to achieve it for stated loadings at a minimum cost.

One structure [Fig. 2(c)] that has particular advantages is the loop or ring network structure. This structure lends itself to a TDM technique in which a node with a message for another node places packets in empty slots as they appear, and copies messages addressed to it as they are passed around the ring. When a message originating at a node is returned to it, it is checked to insure that it has been received and that it has not been corrupted, and is then replaced by a vacant slot.

Network Monitoring. A detailed knowledge of network traffic is essential for network planning and operation, and node computers should contain suitable monitoring programs to make this possible. Hardware monitors operating under computer control can supplement these software monitors.

Economics. It is difficult to make definite statements now about the relative economics of networks except for those constructed for special purposes (such as airline reservation systems). However, a number of commercial systems (e.g., Tymnet, Honeywell, and Cybernet) marketing facilities under a single management are clearly commercially viable.

Roberts (1974) has given some interesting figures concerning the economics of ARPANET. He advances arguments to show that work carried out through the network in 1973 would have cost about three times as much had equivalent local computing power been used, and that the difference more than offsets the annual cost of the network, even though at the time the network was only about 20% loaded.

Roberts draws some interesting conclusions about long-term trends. He points out that computing costs are being reduced by a factor of 10 every five years, as are satellite communication costs, whereas conventional land-line costs (which control the cost of transmission from ground stations to city centers) are reducing at the much lower rate of a factor of 10 every 22 years. These line costs would eventually dominate network costs were it not for the anticipated introduction of higher transmission frequencies, which are likely to eliminate the need for land lines by making possible direct satellite communication to rooftop aerials in city centers. Satellite Business Systems (with IBM and Comsat as principal shareholders) is constructing systems of this type. (This situation already applies with experimental stations that form part of the Pacific Educational Computer Network (PEACESAT) constructed under the aegis of the University of Hawaii. PEACESAT ground stations each cost as little as several thousands of dollars).

An excellent description of the economics of computer networks may be found in the Logica report (1978).

Management Problems. To make resources available through a computer network, a user must do the following.

1. Make arrangements for accounts at each host computer system.
2. Know the control language for each host.
3. Learn the peculiarities of network protocols (i.e., network management information provided in headers such as destinations and lengths of messages) as implemented by each host.
4. Determine what help facilities (if any) exist at each host and how to use them.
5. Determine who at each site can assist with systems problems and how to establish contact with that person.
6. Determine how to get data and/or programs to and from the serving site.
7. Learn how to use the resources of the remote site.

It is small wonder that the average user is deterred from making the best use of resources available. Clearly, there is a strong case for brokers who know what is available and will help the potential user, acting as retailers of computing power available to them through the network on a wholesale basis and as liaison links for strengthening help facilities obtainable through the network itself. REX, a resource location and acquisition service offered by the Mitre Corporation, was one of the first examples of this type of advisory service, offering information concerning the resources of ARPANET through the network itself and permitting terminal users to converse interactively with it. The problem with such services is ensuring that the information they provide is up-to-date.

In the U. S., the problem of funding network management has been facilitated by a decision made in November 1973 to approve the establishment of commercial "value added" communication networks. Operators of these networks obtain raw bandwidth from common carriers such as AT&T, and "repackage" it, using minicomputers, for leasing to the ultimate user.

Protocols and Standards. Protocols within a network must be standard so that nodes can function in a uniform manner; much of this information, because it is concerned only with the mechanics of packaging, will be supplied by the communications computers. Moreover, some additional information may be required by individual processes, and this may vary from one installation to another, particularly with a heterogeneous network (i.e., one that has as hosts different computers that are not compatible with one another).

Transmitting information from one network to another with a different protocol and packet length presents special problems, and the use of a special internetwork processor (a *gateway* machine) for the express purpose of reformatting messages and changing to new protocols has been proposed. An IFIP Technical Committee Working Group (WG6.1) is currently formulating guidelines for internetwork protocols on which future standards may be based.

The field of data transmission has been the subject of an extensive range of standards and international recommendations laid down by major U. S. and international standards organizations (ANSI, EIA, ECMA, CEPT, ISO, and CCITT) (Davies *et al.*, 1979; Logica, 1978). Of particular note is the CCITT standard X25, which defines an interface between host computers and intelligent data terminals.

Networks are no respecters of national frontiers, and will be required to conform to the laws of countries in which they operate. As many countries are introducing (or have introduced) privacy laws to control the use of data banks containing personal records, efforts are being made to ensure that these laws will be sufficiently harmonious to make international networking legally practicable. The two bodies which have provided a lead in this matter are the Organization for Economic Cooperation and Development (OECD) and the Council of Europe. OECD has recently agreed on a set of guidelines, which, it is expected, will be embodied in legislation by the member countries.

Some Typical Networks. The following examples of general-purpose networks are selected as illus-

trative rather than exhaustive. ARPANET is described elsewhere in this encyclopedia.

TELENET, a public packet-switched network, was first made available in the U. S. by the Telenet Communications Corporation in August 1975. The network architecture follows that of ARPANET. In mid-1978, it had over 200 connected organizations, of which over 40% were time-sharing bureaus. There were nine major switching stations interconnected by multiple high-speed lines (56 Kbps), and local nodes in 81 cities connected to major switching stations by leased lines (2.4 to 9.6 Kbps). Smaller nodes (160 at that time) with more restricted facilities providing access at line speeds up to 1,200 bps are available. Access is available from at least 18 countries, and over 200 databases and a wide variety of application programs are available through the network.

PRESTEL, the U. K. version of a viewdata (*q.v.*) system, is a network constructed by the British Post Office using domestic TV sets for display and the telephone outlet for communication with the network (at 75 bps input to and 1,200 bps output from the network). There is provision for any supplier of information (advertisers, news agencies, publishers, etc.) to connect a data bank to the network. In mid-1980, more than 500,000 pages of information from over 500 databases are available (a proportion of them on a paying basis) to over 4,000 users.

EURONET is a data network designed primarily to provide information retrieval services to ECC countries, using databases located initially at 16 host organizations. The network design, using 48 Kbps lines between nodes in a packet-switched mode, follows that of TRANSPAC, the French data network.

XEROX networks recently announced ETHERNET (using coaxial cables for interconnection in a single building) and XTEN (which will use its own satellites to transmit information between buildings using roof antennas).

The Source, a viewdata-type system, is a network aimed at the home terminal user. It began operations in mid-1979. It uses Telenet and Tymnet for transmission. It offers network mail facilities, access to, among other databases, the *New York Times* information bank and programs which analyze statistics from the Wall Street stock index.

The Cambridge Digital Communication Ring at the University of Cambridge is a local area ring transmitting bits from one station to another at a raw bit rate of 10 Mbps. A packet consists of a destination byte, a source byte, two information bytes, and a few control bits. A transmitted packet, when received, is marked as such by the destination, and marked as empty by the source on having completed the circuit of the ring. At an early stage, six computers have been connected together using twisted pairs and the system provides for servicing both high-speed and low-speed distribution computing needs of a number of users.

C.mmp (*Carnegie multi-mini*processor), using minicomputer processors (PDP11s), was initiated in 1971, and was intended to provide a multiprocessor system suitable for artificial intelligence research. The processors are loosely coupled to form a local network providing access from each processor to all primary memories (including memories local to each processor and a large central memory) and to all secondary memories and I/O devices. Address mapping is provided to convert processor-generated addresses to addresses for primary memory and for Unibusses.

MICRONET at SUNY/Buffalo is a recent example of a local network for distributed computing, constructed with loosely coupled microcomputers linked by packet-switching hardware with an initial configuration of 16 DEC LSI-11s.

Cm* at Carnegie-Mellon University is a tightly-coupled network of 50 DEC LSI-11s with references to distant memory modules in a shared address space being handled in a hardware-assisted manner which is transparent to the programmer. Configurations of this type might be viewed as a variant of a single multiprocessor installation, in which a number of processors share a common memory.

REFERENCES

1969. Martin, J. *Telecommunications and the Computer*. Englewood Cliffs, NJ: Prentice-Hall.
1973. Abramson, N. and Kuo, F. F. (Eds.). *Computer-Communications Networks*. Englewood Cliffs, NJ: Prentice-Hall.
1973. Davies, D. W. and Barber, D. L. A. *Communication Networks for Computers*. London: Wiley.
1974. Roberts, L. G. "Data by the Packet," *Spectrum* **11**, No. 2:46–51.
1978. Logica. *Packet Switching Report*. London.
1978. *Proc. of the IEEE* **66**, No.11 (November).
1978. Szentivanyi, T. and Talloczy, I. *Computer Networks (Bibliography)*. Budapest: Research Institute for Applied Sciences.
1979. Davies, D. W., Barber, D. L. A., Price, W. L., and Solomonides, C. M. *Computer Networks and their Protocols*. New York: Wiley.
1979. Housley, T. *Data Communication and Teleprocessing Systems*. Englewood Cliffs, NJ: Prentice-Hall.

J. M. BENNETT

COMPUTERS. See ANALOG COMPUTERS; COMMUNICATION AND COMPUTERS; DIGITAL COMPUTERS; HYBRID COMPUTERS; MINICOMPUTERS; MICROPROCESSORS AND MICROCOMPUTERS; PERSONAL COMPUTERS; SPECIAL-PURPOSE COMPUTERS; and SUPERCOMPUTERS.

COMPUTER SCIENCE

For articles on related subjects *see* ALGORITHMS, ANALYSIS OF; ARTIFICIAL INTELLIGENCE; AUTOMATA THEORY; COMPUTER ARCHITECTURE; COMPUTER GRAPHICS; COMPUTER SYSTEMS; DATABASE MANAGEMENT; DATA PROCESSING; EDUCATION IN COMPUTER SCIENCE AND TECHNOLOGY; FORMAL LANGUAGES; IMAGE PROCESSING; INFORMATION PROCESSING; INFORMATION RETRIEVAL; INFORMATION SCIENCE; NUMERICAL ANALYSIS; OPERATING SYSTEMS; PROGRAMMING LANGUAGES; SIMULATION; and SYMBOL MANIPULATION.

Computer science is concerned with information processes, with the information structures and procedures that enter into representation of such processes, and with their implementation in information processing systems. It is also concerned with relationships between information processes and classes of tasks that give rise to them.

The Domain of Computer Science. Even though the domain of discourse in computer science includes both human-made and natural information processes, the main effort in the discipline is now directed to *human-made* processes and to information processing systems that are designed to achieve desired goals (i.e., machines). The reason for this lies in the phenomenal growth of the computer field, its rapid penetration into almost all aspects of contemporary life, and the resulting pressure to bring some order into what is being done in the field, to educate the people behind the computing machines and to provide intellectual guidance for new developments in computer designs and applications. Thus, the bulk of empirical material currently available to computer science consists of systems, processes, and operational experience that grew in the computer field during the past quarter-century. Clearly, the empirical corpus in the science is not stationary. It is growing with new developments in the computer filed. Some of these developments are themselves stimulated by the ongoing activities in computer science.

The main objects of study in computer science today are the digital computer and the phenomena surrounding it. Work in the discipline is focused on the structure and operation of computer systems, on the principles that underlie their design and programming, on effective methods for their use in different classes of information processing tasks, and on theoretical characterizations of their properties and limitations. Also, a substantial effort is directed into explorations and experimentation with new computer systems and with new domains of intellectual activity where computers can be applied.

The central role of the digital computer in the discipline is due to its near universality as an information processing machine. With enough memory capacity, a digital computer provides the basis for modeling any information processing system, provided the task to be performed by the system can be specified in some rigorous manner. If its specification is possible, then the task can be represented in the form of a program that can be stored in the computer memory. Thus, the stored program digital computer enables us to represent conveniently and implement (run) any information process. It provides a methodologically adequate, as well as a realistic, basis for the exploration and study of a great variety of concepts, schemes, and techniques of information processing.

There exist in nature information processes that are of great interest to computer science (e.g., perceptual and cognitive processes in man, and cellular processes that are controlled by genetic information). An understanding of these processes is intrinsically important, and it promises to enrich the pool of basic concepts and schemes that are available to computer science. In turn, application of the current approaches and techniques of the discipline to cognitive psychology and to biosciences promises to result in important insights into natural information processes. To date, most of the work on these processes has proceeded either by modeling them on digital computers and studying these models experimentally, or by using existing theoretical models in computer science (e.g., in automata theory) for the analysis of certain properties of these processes. There is still little contribution from the study of natural information systems to the design and use of computing machines, or to the development of theoretical concepts in computer science.

Scope and Nature of Activities in Computer Science.

The subject matter of computer science can be broadly divided into two parts. The first part covers information processing tasks, procedures for handling them, and a variety of related representations. The second part is mainly concerned with a variety of structures, mechanisms, and schemes for processing information. From the point of view of the practitioner in the computer field, the first part corresponds to computer applications, and the second corresponds to computer systems. There are significant connections between the two parts. Indeed, it is a major goal of computer science to elucidate the relationships between application areas and computer systems.

Computer applications can be broadly subdivided into *numerical* applications and *nonnumerical* applications. Work in numerical applications is mainly oriented toward problems and procedures where numerical data are dominant, such as problems in the areas of numerical analysis, optimization, and simulation. These areas are important branches of computer science. Work in non-

numerical applications is primarily concerned with processes involving nonnumerical data such as representations of problems, programs, symbolic expressions, language, relational structures, and graphic objects. Branches of computer science with major activities in nonnumerical applications are artificial intelligence, information storage and retrieval, combinatorial processes, language processing, symbol manipulation, and graphics.

Computer systems can be partitioned into *software* systems and *hardware* systems. The emphasis of work in software systems is on machine-level representations of programs and associated data, on schemes for controlling program execution, and on programs for handling computer languages and for managing computer operations. Branches of computer science with major concern in software systems are programming languages and processors, operating systems, and utility programs and programming techniques. Computer architecture is concerned with software systems as well as with hardware systems. Other major branches of computer science with a main focus on hardware systems are machine organization and logical design.

Generally, applications-oriented activities in computer science are also concerned with related systems problems; e.g., with high-level languages and with their computer implementation. Similarly, systems-oriented activities are also concerned with the task environments (e.g., classes of applications and modes of human-machine interaction) in which the systems operate.

We can identify two major types of activities in computer science:

1. Building conceptual frameworks for understanding the available empirical material in the discipline via an active search for unifying principles, general methods, and theories.
2. Exploring new computer systems and applications in the light of new concepts and theories.

The first type of activity is analytic in nature; the second is oriented toward synthesis, experimentation, and probing for new empirical knowledge. A continuous interaction between these activities is essential for a vigorous rate of progress in the discipline. The situation is analogous to the interaction between theoretical and experimental work in any rapidly developing natural science.

At present, the theoretical underpinnings of computer science are at an early stage of development. In some areas, theoretical work is mainly oriented toward bringing elementary order into a rapidly accumulating mass of experience via the introduction of broad conceptual frameworks and analytic methodologies. In a few areas, theoretical work is concentrating on comprehensive analysis of specific classes of phenomena for which formal models exist. Branches of computer science involved in this type of work are theory of computation, automata theory, theory of formal languages, and switching theory. In general, theoretical work in computer science has been diffused over a large number of fairly narrow phenomena. Much of this work has not yet had an appreciable impact on the complex problems of systems and applications that are encountered in the computer field. There is a growing concern, however, with the development of unifying principles and models that are appropriate for understanding and guiding the major constructive and experimental activities in the field. The emerging work in the area of analysis of algorithms (which includes important approaches to the study of computational complexity) promises to contribute significant theoretical insights into problems that are in the mainstream of the computer field. As computer science continues to grow, theoretical work in the discipline is also likely to grow, not only in relative volume to the other activities in the discipline, but also in relevance to the significant problems in the domain of computer science.

Experimental work in computer science requires extensive use of computers, and it often stimulates new developments in computer design and utilization. Typical experimental activities may involve the development and evaluation of a new computer language or the testing of a procedure for a new class of problem. Theoretical work in the discipline relies on several branches of mathematics and logic. A typical theoretical problem may focus on the characterization of a class of computer procedures (e.g., procedures of sorting data), the analysis of their structure, and the establishment of bounds on the storage space and time that they require for execution. The objects of study in this example are computer procedures and their properties. The theoretical treatment of these objects is conducted within mathematical systems that provide the analytical framework needed to obtain the desired insights and specific results. Just as mathematics is used in chemistry (say, to develop theories of certain chemical processes), mathematics and logic are used in computer science to study information processes.

Relationships Between Computer Science and Other Disciplines.

The bond between computer science and mathematics is stronger than the normal bond between mathematics and the theoretical component of a science. Computer science and mathematics have a common concern with formalism, symbolic structures, and their properties. Both put emphasis on general methods and problem-solving tools that can be used in a great variety of situations. There are subjects, such as numerical analysis, that are being studied in both disciplines. These are some of the reasons why computer science is widely considered a *mathematical science.*

Computer science is also considered an *engineering science.* The structure of a computer system consists of physical components (the hardware) in the form of electronic or electromechanical building blocks for switching, storage and communication of information, and programs (the software) for managing the operation of the hardware. In the logical design and the system design of a computer system, the designer is concerned with the choice of hardware and software building blocks, and with their local and global organization in the light of given operational goals for the overall system. These design activities have strong points of contact with work in electrical engineering and in the emerging field of software engineering. They are also important subjects of study in computer science.

Every transition from the specification of an information processing task to a system for implementing the task involves a design process. In many cases, these processes are highly complex, and their effectiveness is strongly dependent on the availability of appropriate methodologies and techniques that may be used to guide and support them. This is one of the reasons why computer science is concerned with methodologies of systems analysis and synthesis and with general tools for design. This concern is shared not only with engineering, but also with other decision-oriented disciplines such as business administration and institutional planning. There is a more fundamental reason for a close coupling between computer science and a science of design. It comes from the concern of computer science with the information processes of problem solving and goal-directed decision making, which are at the core of design. Processes of this type are objects of study in artifical intelligence, a branch of computer science.

Several other disciplines are recognized as having domains of interest which overlap with computer science. One of these is library science. The problems of organizing and managing knowledge, and of designing systems for its storage and retrieval (in the form of documents or facts), are shared between computer science and library science. The activities at the interface between these two disciplines are often identified as part of information science. The main concern of information science is with processes of communication, storage, management, and utilization of information in large database systems. Thus, the domain of information science is included in the broader domain of computer science.

Another discipline whose domain of interest overlaps with computer science is linguistics, which shares with computer science a concern with language and communication. The study of linguistic processes, and of related phenomena of "understanding," establishes a special bond between computer science and psychology. Psychological research in information processing models of cognition, perception, and other mental functions has a substantial overlap with work in computer science.

The study of certain theoretical questions about processes of reasoning by computer (performing deductions, forming hypotheses, using knowledge effectively in problem-solving processes) is beginning to create points of contact between certain parts of philosophy (logic, epistemology, methodology) and computer science.

The development of computer science has been strongly stimulated by demands for the application of computers in a wide variety of new areas. The challenges created by new computer applications, and the constructive attempts to meet them, are important factors in the growth of computer science. The exploratory activity in the discipline, as it interacts with other disciplines in the development of computer applications, results both in a better understanding of the power and limitations of current knowledge in the computer field, and in the identification of new problems of information processing that require further study. At a more practical level, the exploratory work on computer applications is contributing to the solution of significant problems in various disciplines that could not be approached without the introduction of computer methods.

There is a large *surface of contact* between computer science and the disciplines where new computer applications are being developed. Virtually all disciplines are involved in this contact. The nature of the contact is similar to the relationship between mathematics and the physical sciences; this relationship involves the representation of scientific problems in mathematical systems wherein the problems can be studied and solved. In the case of computer science, the contact involves the representation of knowledge and problems of a discipline in forms that are acceptable to computers, and the development of computer methods for the effective handling of these problems. Since computers can be made to represent and manipulate problems of enormous variety and complexity, it is likely that the extent of fruitful contact between computer science and other disciplines will be much larger than the contact between mathematics and the "mathematics utilizing" disciplines. In particular, it is likely that the role played by computer science in behavioral and social sciences, the professions, and the humanities will be similar to that played by mathematics in the growth of the physical sciences.

An important application for computers, which is of special interest to computer science, is in the design of more powerful, efficient, and easy-to-use computer systems. The use of computers in the study of computers and in their improvement is a powerful means for gaining the knowledge and insights that computer science seeks, while at the same time the field is being bootstrapped.

From the previous discussion it can be seen that computer science has two types of interface with other disciplines: The first type is characterized by a *shared concern* with subjects of study that are of intrinsic interest to computer science. Here there is an area of overlap between work in computer science and work in other disciplines. Mathematics and electrical engineering have this type of interface with computer science. To a lesser extent, such an interface exists between computer science and the decision-oriented disciplines (e.g., business administration; institutional planning), library science, linguistics, psychology, and philosophy. The second type of interface includes disciplines in which new computer applications are being explored. The main role of computer science in these activities is *to support* and enhance work in a discipline. Practically all disciplines that involve some kind of intellectual activity have this type of interface with computer science.

The Internal Structure of Computer Science. The pattern of relationships between computer science and other disciplines is likely to change as the internal structure of activities in computer science continues to change. While the overall structure of the discipline is beginning to attain considerable stability, its detailed internal structure is less stable, and the relative emphasis that various subdisciplines are receiving is still far from stabilized.

The conception, formulation, computer implementation, analysis, and evaluation of procedures (algorithms) for a broad variety of problems constitute a major part of the activities in computer science. Closely associated with these activities are efforts to develop schemes, means, and tools for building and executing procedures—such as languages, major principles for structuring procedures, programming mechanisms, computer organizations, and design aids to facilitate these efforts. In addition, a significant amount of effort is directed to the design of advanced systems—software and hardware. All these activities have important connections with several theoretical efforts in the field, some in application areas and others in the analysis of algorithms, in formal languages, automata theory, switching theory, and systems analysis.

An outline of the major areas of study in computer science (and some of the major relationships among them) is presented next.

1. *Representations in Computer Language of Problems, Data, and Procedures in Various Application Areas.* The main problems in this area are to find solution methods for classes of problems in different domains of application, and to formulate them in a suitable computer language. As mentioned previously, the two major families

of applications in the discipline are numerical and non-numerical applications.

2. *Theory of Computation and Analysis of Algorithms.* Work in this area is concerned with computability, recursive functions and properties of classes of procedures (algorithms) such as complexity, validity, and equivalence. It is related to work in (1).

3. *High-Level Languages for Various Application Areas, Schemes for Structuring Data and Procedures, Language Descriptions, and Translation Schemes.* Work in this area is central to the facilitation of human-machine communication and it has a strong impact on computer applications. It is related to work in computer design and also to work in (1).

4. *Machine-Level Languages, Storage Schemes, and Programming Mechanisms.* This area is concerned with the art of programming computer hardware. It interfaces with (3) and to a lesser extent with (1), and also with (5).

5. *System Organization Schemes, Executive and Control Mechanisms, and Computer Design Processes.* Theoretical activities related to this area are system analysis and simulation (at the hardware/software configuration level), automata and switching theory (at the logical design level), and theory of digital circuits and devices (at the machine component level). This area is strongly related to professional activities in system design and computer architecture.

6. *Theory of Formal Languages, Automata Theory, and Switching Theory.* Theoretical activities in these areas are concerned with properties of computer languages, computer mechanisms and their realizations. They are related to work in (2), (3), and (5).

Computer science is a young and rapidly expanding discipline. In a period of less than 20 years, it has succeeded in establishing its distinct identity in universities and in laboratories throughout the world. One of its recognized roles is to provide the intellectual guidance needed for the understanding and development of the computer field. Another role, which is likely to grow in significance in the coming years, is to contribute to an understanding of the impact of computers on other disciplines and on society in general.

REFERENCES

1968. National Academy of Sciences. "The Mathematical Sciences: A Report," Publication 1681. Washington, DC.
1969. Hamming, R. W. "One Man's View of Computer Science," 1968 ACM Turing Lecture, *Journal of the ACM* **16**, *No. 1*: 5 (January).
1970. Wegner, P. "Three Computer Cultures-Computer Technology, Computer Mathematics, and Computer Science," in Freiberger, Walter (Ed.), *Advances in Computers* **10**. New York: Academic Press.
1971. Amarel, S. "Computer Science: A Conceptual Framework for Curriculum Planning," *Communications of the ACM* **14**, *No. 6* (June).
1980. Arden, B. W. (Ed.) *What Can Be Automated?—The Computer Science and Engineering Research Study.* Cambridge, MA: M.I.T. Press.
1980. *Taxonomy of Computer Science and Engineering.* Arlington, VA: AFIPS Press.

S. AMAREL

COMPUTER SCIENCE EDUCATION. *See* EDUCATION IN COMPUTER SCIENCE AND TECHNOLOGY.

COMPUTER SECURITY. *See* CRIME AND COMPUTER SECURITY; DATA ENCRYPTION; DATA SECURITY; and SECURITY OF COMPUTER INSTALLATIONS, PHYSICAL.

COMPUTERS, HISTORY OF. *See* DIGITAL COMPUTERS; History of; and MANUFACTURERS, COMPUTER.

COMPUTERS, MAINTENANCE. *See* MAINTENANCE OF COMPUTERS.

COMPUTERS, MULTIPLE ADDRESS

For articles on related subjects *see* ADDRESSING; INDEX REGISTER; INDIRECT ADDRESS; and MACHINE INSTRUCTION SET.

In addition to an operation (command) specification and other information (e.g., indexing), a computer instruction may contain from zero to four addresses. An address usually points either to a location in the memory which stores the value of the operand or to a location involved in the control process.

Computers may be classified according to the number of addresses in most or in common (e.g., arithmetic) instructions: zero, one, two, three, and four having been used. The number of addresses depends on both the register structure and central processor organization.

Zero-Address Instructions (*see also* ADDRESSLESS INSTRUCTIONS). Zero-address instructions do not require access to memory for operands. Examples include HALT and RESET OVERFLOW INDICATORS.

Arithmetic zero-address instructions occur in stack-type organizations in which arithmetic expressions are conveniently evaluated by conversion to Polish form. For example, ADD would cause the two top operands to be replaced by their sum, thereby shortening the stack by one item.

One-Address Instructions.

For many years, the high cost of hardware led to systems wherein the arithmetic operations were all associated with one particular register called an *accumulator*. Thus, the instructions to evaluate $C = A + B$ were LOAD A, ADD B, STORE C, with a natural instruction format of

[op code] [address]

where [address] points to a particular memory cell. Control instructions fitting this structure were JUMP, address; JUMP IF ACCUMULATOR POSITIVE, address; etc. In both zero-address and one-address structures, successive instructions came from sequential locations in memory as specified by a program counter which progressed in units of one until a jump occurred. The EDSAC (Cambridge, 1949) was an example of a one-address computer. The IBM 700-7000 series of computers were another example.

Two-Address Instructions.

Early computers can be divided into two groups according to memory organization—those with random access (Williams' tube (*q.v.*), and somewhat later, magnetic cores) and cyclic memory (mercury delay lines, and a little later, magnetic drum memories). In mercury delay line memories (*see* ULTRASONIC MEMORY), several words (8 to 32, say) circulate in a line and are sequentially available at the output. The time from the availability of the first to the availability of the last bit of a word might be 32 microseconds, and the time to the next appearance of this word might be 300 to 1000 microseconds. A similar relationship holds for drum memories. With this structure, faster programs could be written if each instruction had a second address specifying the location of the next instruction. This implied that instructions were no longer sequentially located but were scattered through memory so as to become available at the optimum time. This concept was used by the ACE computer at the National Physical Laboratories (England, 1946) and later in such computers as the Bendix G15 and the IBM 650. A more common use today of the two-address format, [opcode] [A] [B], has both addresses referring to memory locations for operands so that, for example, ADD [A] [B] means add the contents of A to the contents of B and place the result in A (or, occasionally, B).

Three-Address Instructions.

Motivated by the fact that arithmetic operations usually involve two operands and a result, a number of early computers used three addresses in arithmetic instructions. Examples include MIDAC (University of Michigan) and NORC (Naval Ordinance Research Computer). Thus, ADD [A] [B] [C] means add the contents of A to the contents of B and place the result in C.

Four-Address Instructions.

Some designers also specified the location of the next instruction, using three addresses for arithmetic purposes. The EDVAC, SEAC, and SWAC were examples of this structure. Thus, ADD [A] [B] [C] [D] means add the contents of A to the contents of B, place the result in C, and take the next instruction from D. Since every instruction is a potential jump, no unconditional jump instruction is needed on such computers.

In 1955, Weik reported on 65 computers giving the following distribution.

Address	Number of Systems
1	33
2	6
3	12
4	6
Combinations	8
Total	65

A similar compilation today would show a preponderance of one- and two-address systems, where often the addresses refer to *registers* rather than memory cells.

Multiple Address versus Multiple Instruction.

In early computers, memory was small (rarely more than 1,024 words) so addresses were ten bits or less. Ten decimal digit precision implied word lengths of 30 to 40 bits, so the designer's problem was to fit an op code-address structure into the desired word length. Many one-address systems stored two instructions per word, whereas three- and four-address systems could efficiently have one instruction per word.

Address Modification.

Only one of the first computers had index registers (the B box on the Manchester University Mark I), but designers soon realized their value, This forced designs toward one-address systems because of the word length compatibility and the pressure for simple control structures.

Since many operations in programs (particularly, operations related to control) involve operations with small integers, designers sometimes provide a modifier indicating that the "address" is the actual operand (saving a memory access). Such addressing is called *immediate*.

In the other direction, the address might point to a location in memory which contained a pointer to still another location, etc. (*indirect addressing*). Add to this the capability of indexing these various addresses and we see that the address has evolved from a simple explicit integer to a potentially quite complicated function. This complexity has also been a strong force toward one-address structures. However, the utility of source-destination structures has caused continued use of two-address instructions, although, as noted above, one or both of these may refer to registers.

Short Word Length Computers. The advent of 16-bit word minicomputers in the 1960s (the earlier Whirlwind I at MIT was also a 16-bit computer) and, more recently, the 8-bit microcomputer, and the decline in the cost of logic (so that multiple registers and much larger memories are prevalent) placed other pressures on designers. The PDP-11 structure represents one relatively successful approach to this problem using one- and two-address instructions.

The PDP11 has 8 registers (R0 to R7) with R6 being a stack pointer and R7 a program counter. Each instruction consists of an op code (4 or 10 bits), and one or two addresses. The address consists of a 2-bit MODE, a single bit specifying DIRECT/DEFERRED, and a 3-bit general register specification. In two-address instructions, the addresses specify source and destination.

REFERENCE

1955. Weik, M. H. "A Survey of Domestic Electronic Digital Computing Systems." Ballistic Research Laboratories, Aberdeen Proving Ground, Report No. 971.

H. D. HUSKEY

COMPUTERS, PERSONAL. *See* PERSONAL COMPUTERS.

COMPUTER SYSTEMS

For articles on related subjects *see* ARITHMETIC-LOGIC UNIT; CENTRAL PROCESSING UNIT; CHANNEL; COMMUNICATIONS AND COMPUTERS; COMPUTING CENTER; COMPUTER NETWORKS; INFORMATION SYSTEMS; INPUT/OUTPUT DEVICES; INTERRUPT; MEMORY: Main; MEMORY: Auxiliary; OPERATING SYSTEMS; PROCESSING MODES; SOFTWARE; and STORAGE HIERARCHY.

A modern computer system is one of the most complex and wonderful achievements of mankind. This is due to its incredible speed, very high reliability and almost limitless versatility. For example, a very large commercially available computer can (in 1980) execute about five to ten million instructions per second (MIPS). Furthermore, this raw processing potential can be programmed so that a single machine performs such diverse tasks as complex engineering computations, say in the design of high-speed aircraft, preparation of the payroll for thousands of employees, or keeping track of inventory for a whole chain of retail stores. The term "general purpose" is therefore a fair one to characterize the capabilities of a computer, although of course not every particular machine is actually used for such a wide variety of tasks.

As with any complex configuration, it is helpful to consider a computer system as composed of subsystems, each made up of various major components. Because it is more easily visualized, we will begin with a description of the equipment or *hardware* subsystem and then proceed to consider the programming, or *software,* subsystem. Finally, we will interpret how these appear first to computer users and then describe the programs created by the users.

The Hardware Subsystem. Fig. 1 shows the major hardware components. These can be classified into a number of categories:

Transducers. These are hardware devices that change information from one physical form to another and hence serve as communication links between the computer and its environment. Examples of transducers are video screen and keyboard terminals, typewriter and printer terminals, high-speed printers, punched card readers and punches, and graphics terminals and plotters. All these devices transform human-readable information into an electrical form suitable for computer processing (or *vice versa*).

Storage Devices. These computer system components store not only data but also instructions (programs). For economy and technology reasons, storage devices come in many sizes, speeds, and costs. They range from extremely inexpensive and slow (e.g., punched cards) to devices suitable for on-line use (e.g., magnetic disks and drums). The fastest access storage is supplied on semiconductor chips and is called the computer's main storage or *memory*. Because of its speed, this memory has the special "privilege" of being the storage type directly accessible by the processing unit (CPU).

Transformation Devices. These are the circuits that do most of the "work." They are typically concentrated in a structure called a central processing unit (CPU), which contains an adder circuit augmented by shift and other control features that together implement almost all of the system's arithmetic and processing operations. The CPU also contains the circuitry for program control

Fig. 1.   An IBM 4341 computer system.

which directs the machine from one of its instructions to the next with provisions for testing various conditions and *branching* (i.e., causing a change in the program sequence from strict progression in the written program). All these CPU functions require the use of extremely fast (but expensive, and hence small) storage, the CPU registers. The CPU uses the registers as a sort of scratch pad to jot down results that will be transferred later to primary storage.

Routing and Control Devices. Routing circuits include the networks or busses that direct the flow of information between the other functional parts of the hardware subsystem. For instance, the I/O channels control the flow of information between the transducers, auxiliary storage devices, and main storage. Other routing circuits control communication between main storage and the CPU. The control circuitry generates timing signals in various complex arrangements that specify at what times information is moved from place to place in the system.

Another classification scheme divides the hardware subsystem into internal components and external components. The internal components are the CPU, with its associated registers and routing circuits, and main storage and often the I/O channels. The "internal computer" is sometimes called the "processor complex." All other hardware devices are part of the *peripheral,* or I/O, *subsystem.*

Now that we have introduced the hardware components of a computer system, how do they work together? Let us trace the path of a program through the hardware.

The reader is advised to follow the description by tracing the events through the paths and facilities of Fig. 2. The program (say, as a deck of punched cards) must first be physically translated into electric-signal form, which is done by the card reader, a transducer device. To be executed, the program must be in the main storage, since this is usually the only store available to the CPU. Both the main store and CPU are very fast devices. To keep up with their speed, they should be fed program and data from a reasonably fast storage. Since the card reader is slow, its information is not moved directly to main storage for processing. Instead, it is first moved by an I/O channel to the intermediate-speed disk (briefly passing through main storage in the process), where it is held until the CPU is ready to work on it. At that time the program and its data is moved via an I/O channel from the disk store to main storage.

Once in main storage, the program is accessible to the CPU and can be executed. During execution, most of the storage accessing is to the main store. However, the program is capable of receiving/sending larger volumes of data from/to the auxiliary stores (disk or tape) via the I/O channels. When the program finishes executing, its results are moved (again by the channels) back to auxiliary storage, and finally they leave the computer system via a transducer such as a high-speed printer.

Because of the slow speed of I/O operations relative to central processing, it is best for efficiency if they can proceed concurrently (usually on different jobs) rather than in strict time sequence. A typical system has only one CPU, and its attention is required to service I/O op-

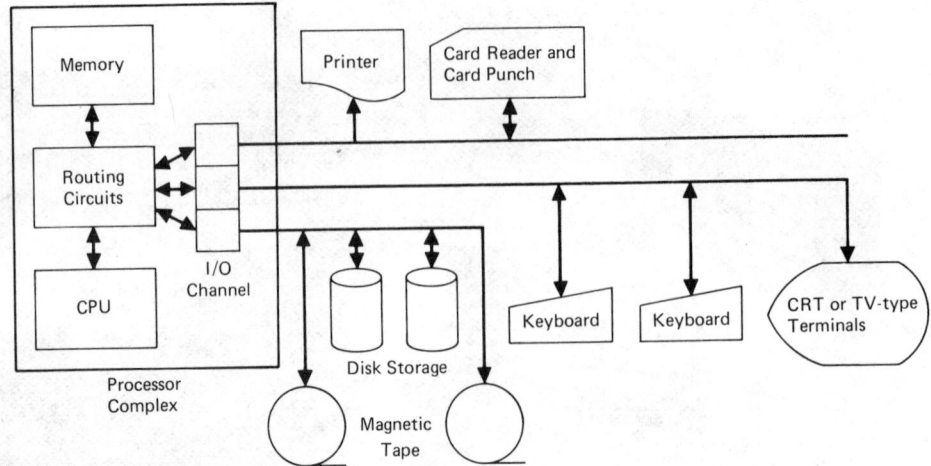

Fig. 2. General organization of the hardware subsystem of a typical digital computer.

erations rather frequently but briefly each time and at unpredictable times. The sharing of the single CPU between I/O and central processing is made possible by an *interrupt* scheme that permits channels to suspend ongoing CPU operations, give the required brief service to I/O or other external requests, and then return to what it was doing.

Until about 1968, most computers were very expensive and required considerable floor space, electric power, and air conditioning. However, due to rapid advances in the computer technologies, especially semiconductor circuitry, by the late 1960s, a genre of small-sized machines termed *minicomputers* started to be produced that only occupied the space of an office desk, and were inexpensive enough to be used for the solution of a single problem such as the control of a particular industrial process rather than a variety of shared uses.

By about 1973, further major advances in technology led to another class of even smaller, cheaper systems based on the *microprocessor,* a complete CPU contained on a single semiconductor chip. This method of manufacture eliminated all hand-wiring and separate-component manufacture of the CPU with substantial improvements not only in cost but also reliability. This great advance in technology was matched by corresponding advances in semiconductor memory that allowed compact, high-capacity memory to be offered at a price hundreds of times cheaper per unit of stored information than was available only a decade earlier. By 1980, many tens of thousands of microprocessor-based systems were already in use as personal computers in homes, and in small businesses. Each supplied computation power and high-speed memory only available from large, expensive processors a few years earlier. Furthermore, the progress in technology that has given us the microprocessor has also enhanced

the cost effectiveness of the larger minicomputer and general-purpose systems.

In this section, we have given only a very brief account of three main classes of computer system—general purpose, minicomputer, and microprocessor. It should be emphasized that these are not precise categories. For example, many minicomputers are shared by several users and applications in the same way as are general-purpose systems, and the rapid advance of semiconductor technology may soon see minicomputer and even general-purpose computer CPUs fabricated on a single semiconductor chip.

The Software Subsystem. Unlike the hardware components, we can't point to a specific physical object and say, "this is a part of the software subsystem." The software simply isn't composed of physical devices; it is composed of *programs* and certain *data structures.* The programs include those that the computer users write, which are generically called *application programs.* Another category of programs, of primary interest to us now, is called *system programs,* the purpose of which is to give all programmers convenient ways to manage and control the hardware, software, and stored data.

In the limited space available for the discussion of software, we cannot begin to do justice to all of the hardware classes discussed above. Instead we shall concentrate on certain fundamental properties common to all classes, with special emphasis on the most versatile class, the general-purpose computer system.

During the time that a user's program is being processed, it makes requests for stored data, executes instructions that process the data, and generally controls at least a portion of the computer system's hardware resources. Hence, while a user's program is being executed, it is a part of the active software subsystem.

The next portion of the software that we consider is the *operating system*. Unlike applications programs, it is a permanent part of the computer system. Its function is to control the execution of the other resources in the system. The operating system is a collection of interrelated system programs. These can be classified into three groups.

Control Programs. Typical examples are: a reader-interpreter program that reads input from a transducer, translates certain control and scheduling information, and stores the program on auxiliary storage (disk); and a scheduler program that determines which job the computer system should service next. Once the scheduler has selected the next job, its program is placed under the control of an initiator/terminator program, which obtains the resources (such as main storage) necessary for the execution of the program, starts it up, and "cleans up" after it has been completed. During execution, the job delivers its output to a disk. Later, a system "writer" program moves the output to a printer for delivery in human-readable form.

Installation (or manufacturer) Supplied Programs for User Convenience. These programs fall into various categories: first there are *translators,* like *compilers,* which are programs that translate user-written programs from the *source language* used by the programmer into a language the machine can execute. Second are *loader programs* that place the translated programs into main storage in a form that the computer system can execute. Third are *utilities,* which are programs that perform frequently required tasks such as sorting and merging two or more lists, moving large masses of data from one place to another within the system, etc.

System Data-Management Programs. These programs keep track of what is in the system and where it is located, and use various means to store and access the data efficiently. For instance, when a user's program calls for data, the data-management programs locate and fetch the data to the requesting program. For every data collection (file or data set), data-management programs record who is permitted to use the data, who is currently using it, what is being done with it, whether or not the data should be retained in the system after the job ends, etc.

The third part of the software subsystem comprises the *installation libraries.* These contain data and programs that are useful to a wide spectrum of users. What is specifically contained in the libraries will vary from installation to installation; a manufacturing company's library would probably contain an up-to-date inventory of its products, a list of recent orders, etc. An airline reservation system's library would probably contain a schedule of all flights with arrival and departure times, desinations, flight numbers, number of vacant seats on each flight, etc.

System software is designed in many sizes and complexities. A modern computer system that allows *multiprogramming* (more than a single program executing concurrently) or *time sharing* (several users interacting with the system at typewriter or TV-type terminals at human reaction times) would have a software subsystem that contained all the features previously discussed, and probably some others. However, in a less sophisticated computer system, a good deal of what we have described as software functions is done by human intervention (either by the operator or by the user).

We have described a computer system as a collection of two interrelating subsystems, hardware and software. There are, however, certain aspects of the system that do not fall into either subsystem: an example is a *microprogram,* which has been termed "firmware." Microprogramming, as the name implies, is a type of programming. Microprograms directly control the sequencing of computer circuits at the detailed level of the single instruction. Organizing the control hardware in a microprogrammed structure rather than as wired circuitry has several advantages. First is economy of circuitry if the machine must have complex instructions. A second advantage is that it is possible, by microprogramming, to produce an *emulator,* i.e., a set of microprograms that makes a given machine have the same appearance to a programmer as some other machine! This permits the same machine to run programs written for either itself or the machine it is emulating at reasonable efficiency. Yet another advantage is to produce faster operations for the special functions that are microprogrammed rather than programmed in the usual manner. There are, however, some negative aspects of microprogramming, such as the highly specialized knowledge needed and the great tedium of writing microprograms. Also, although microprograms are faster than doing the same functions with software, they are slower than using wired control circuitry.

The User's View of the Computer System.
Let us now imagine that we are the users of a large, modern computer system. How does this system appear to us? Our first problem is gaining access to the system. First, we must arrange with the computer personnel to issue an *account number* to us. This will be used in a number of ways: for example, to keep track of our use of computer time and resources so that we (or our employer) may be charged our fair share of the system's cost. Once we have an account number, we can attempt to interact with the

computer system. To do this, we write a program in one of the many languages available in our particular system.

Let us assume that we have written a Cobol program (for example, to compute a sales report), and that we now wish to enter this program into the computer system so that it can then be used to control the computer to process data and deliver the actual sales report. First, we find a terminal (a transducer) that connects to the computer system that has our account number. We then "log-on" by keying a certain message that includes our account number so that the system can verify that it is serving a valid customer. It will also then associate our terminal with our account number for convenient access to any data or programs previously stored for us. Once logged-on, we are given a menu of possible commands supplied by the systems program in control of our terminal. We then select one of these, by keying its name, typically **edit**, that provides an *editor facility,* itself a program, designed as a convenient means to permit input-keying of our Cobol program. Among the conveniences provided by the editor facility are easy ways to make corrections, and the ability to store our Cobol program into a named storage structure called a *file* so that it will be available (until specifically erased) in this or a later terminal session. (During the program-entry phase, the Cobol program is "data" to the system; i.e., its ultimate use to tell the system what to do is not significant, since the sole objective at this point is to store the program for later use). When we complete entering our program, we key a command requesting the system to process and then run our program using some appropriate data file (i.e., data entered and named previously using the editor facility).

But wait, you say, what happened to the CPU, main storage, I/O devices, etc., that you were talking about before? Amazingly, almost the entire computer system, with all its functional characteristics, can be ignored by the average computer user. (However, all this will reappear when we see how the computer system appears to our Cobol program.) To the average computer user, the entire physical computer system may be regarded as a "black box" into which input (a program) is submitted and from which results (output) are received.

The user, however, does perceive something extremely important about a computer system. The entire computer system (hardware and software) is itself but a subsystem of a much larger system that is the environment in which the user works. This includes the computer operator, the policies of the computer center in scheduling and billing of jobs, etc.

Program View of a Computer System.
When the system program in control of communicating with our terminal recognizes the command to process our Cobol program, it will store this request in a queue with other such requests for eventual processing. When the system scheduling program decides it is time to process our program, the following events take place.

1. The control of our program is passed to another operating system routine, the initiator-terminator. This program scans our command-request, determines from it that the program is written in Cobol, and hence must be translated into a language the computer can execute (machine language). The initiator-terminator calls for the Cobol compiler (the program that performs the translation) and then starts it executing. The Cobol compiler, using our program as input data, produces a machine-language translation. In the course of the translation process, the compiler will call on various other programs in the operating system for help in doing tasks such as allocating temporary auxiliary storage space. When the Cobol compiler finishes the translation, it stores the resulting machine-language program (often called an *object module*) on auxiliary storage, and then notifies the initiator-terminator that it is finished. The initiator-terminiator releases the space the Cobol compiler occupied in main storage, and then calls another operating system program, the loader.

2. The loader does some necessary processing on the object module and brings it into main storage so its execution can begin. As the program executes, it will interact with various operating system programs that fetch the data it requires, supply the program with any auxiliary storage it requires, etc. When the program finishes executing, it signals the initiator-terminator. The program's output is stored on auxiliary storage. The initiator-terminator "cleans up" after the program and supplies the operating system's "writer" program with the program's output. The writer moves the output (results) information to the user's terminal for display or else (at the user's option) to a high-speed printer.

Summary. A computer system is characterized by its high speed, high reliability, and great versatility. Since its commercial beginnings in 1950, there has been and continues to be remarkable improvement in the cost per computation. This has been due to rapid advances in the technologies of semiconductor circuits and memories. The 1970s saw the maturity of the minicomputer and the emergence of the microprocessor, a CPU (and sometimes other circuitry) on a single semiconductor chip. Systems built around them are available at such low cost that they are economically feasible in very small businesses and homes. Internally, a computer system is best considered as a collection of resources consisting of two broad classes, hardware, and software. Both are managed by a carefully designed collection of system programs called an *operating system* which controls the flow of work through the system, furnishes complex common services such as computer language translation, and provides various utilities.

A computer system, through its large-capacity storage, can serve as a repository for procedures (programs) that can be shared productively by members of an educational or industrial community.

REFERENCES

1973. Hellerman, H. *Digital Computer System Principles,* 2nd Ed. New York: McGraw-Hill.
1982. Siewiorek, D. P., Bell, C. G., and Newell, A. *Computer Structures: Principles and Examples.* New York: McGraw-Hill.

H. HELLERMAN AND I. A. SMITH

COMPUTER USER GROUPS

For article on related subject *see* COMPUTER INDUSTRY; CUBE; DECUS; GUIDE; JOINT USERS GROUP (JUG); SHARE: USE; and VIM.

The brief history of the rise, maturation, and old age of computer user groups represents a sociological textbook example of any volunteer organizational entity. Computer user groups began because the manufacturers only marginally understood how to support and enrich the hardware that they produced. The need for help was obvious and a forceful, activist community arose. However, as each manufacturer's products mature and the support infrastructure emerges, the need for a user group diminishes rapidly. The oldest and largest user groups have developed a bad case of stagnation while the newer groups still continue to grow and thrive. The newest of all, the computer clubs that are evolving with the spread of personal computers, have generated a lively and dynamic set of exchanges that are reminiscent of the early days of the older groups.

History. The precise origin, in 1955, of the first user group, SHARE, is obscure. Prior to 1955, users of the IBM 701 in the Los Angeles area had worked cooperatively on PACT-I, a primitive automatic programming system. While working on PACT-IA for the forthcoming IBM 704, the users felt an urgent need to create a united front against a proposed IBM assembler, since it was far short of being as useful as it should have been. A meeting was hastily called, and the first formal user group meeting was held in a basement room at the RAND Corporation's headquarters in Santa Monica, California, during the week of 22 August 1955 (see Armer, 1956).

Installations represented were a fitting cross section of the large-scale, scientifically oriented computer community of that era. There was one government agency, NSA (National Security Agency), three government-sponsored research establishments (RAND, Los Alamos, and Livermore), eight aerospace organizations (Boeing, Curtis-Wright, Hughes, North American, United Aircraft and three Lockheed divisions), three industrial giants (General Electric, General Motors, and Standard Oil of California), and IBM (Steel, 1956).

Just a few months after the founding of SHARE, a group of IBM users of commercial computers (the 702 and soon to appear 705) recognized that the user group idea had merit and founded GUIDE. Beginning in 1965 when IBM's System/360 was announced, the membership requirements for SHARE and GUIDE became virtually identical. GUIDE tends to be somewhat larger, since it appeals to the banks, insurance companies, retailers, and other very large commercial establishments while SHARE still retains the loyalties of many universities, engineering organizations, and research establishments.

Other SHARE spin-offs have included VIM for CDC 6600 and successors, and now defunct groups that supported the GE 600 series and the Philco Transac equipment.

The user group idea has spread beyond computers until today there are groups that support such widely diverse products and services as the Xerox 9700 copier, the MUMPS software system, and assorted hardware products.

While DECUS, with its 35,000 members, all users of DEC hardware, is probably the largest of all user groups, some of the most active groups are those in support of single software products, one piece of hardware on a regional basis, or local microcomputer clubs. The International Apple Core, IAC, made up of 20,000 Apple users in 105 clubs around the world may be a prototype for the new form of user group. Based on dealer training, hot-line support, and newsletters rather than formal meetings, the growth of IAC makes it clear that a need is being filled.

Purposes. In an era before software was sold, a fundamental purpose of a user group was the swapping of home-grown software. Before manufacturers supplied subroutines, users had little but their own ingenuity on which to rely for the countless routines necessary to keep a system running. Such routines as a memory dump from Phillips Petroleum, an internal sort from UCLA, an assembly program from United Aircraft, Bessel function subroutines from General Motors, all crossed and recrossed the country, spread by word of mouth and the SHARE library, founded and operated by Ben Faden of North American Rockwell Corporation.

It was not beyond the pale for a user group to generate the specifications and do most of the implementation for an entire operating system. One such example was SOS, the SHARE operating system, which was implemented for the IBM 7090. But the increasing complexity of today's systems has made it virtually impossible for a loosely organized, volunteer association to implement large projects successfully. To survive, user-group purposes had to be altered. The current SHARE purpose is stated in the group's by-laws as " . . . to foster the development, free exchange and public dissemination of research data pertaining to SHARE computers . . . in the best scientific tradition." It implies that the group now exists to generate a climate for the exchange of data rather than for the original creation of new data.

Despite this disclaimer of innovative objectives, the general view is that user groups have become little more than underpowered lobbying forces, attempting with only marginal success to translate user needs into product specifications. Instead of the aggressive developmental attitudes of the late 1950s and early 1960s, the groups now display reactive and defensive tendencies.

Membership. Membership in user groups is generally confined to those installations that have installed or have on order the specific hardware, program, or service which the group is organized around. However, groups such as CDC's VIM relax this requirement of eligibility to permit at least attendance at meetings by all who express interest in the "system." Although the relaxation of the rule is attractive, since it invites extended participation, this broader membership base may lead to more emphasis on sales prospects than on the interests of real customers for those groups under tight control by their vendor. This, then, is a sales device, a perversion of the reasons why users organize.

Membership counts vary widely. DECUS, as noted, claims 35,000. SHARE, the oldest, counts just over 1,500 installations. Local, regional, or one-product groups may be as small as 50 members. In most cases, acquiring and retaining membership requires little more than a declaration of interest or the installation of the particular products. However, some of the more formal groups may require meeting attendance on at least a biannual basis.

One still unsolved problem is that of the bona fide nature of an application for membership. With the industry's reluctance to release sales data, a user group has almost no way to verify that the statements on the application are genuine. It has not been unknown for a paper company, with no resources, to join a user group before its corporate certificate of incorporation was placed on file.

Legal Status. An often-used greeting at user-group meetings is: "Fellow Conspirators!" The legal status of user groups is vague; while no group intentionally frames a conspiracy to control the market, from time to time some of the groups have been on thin ice. The exact status of user-groups is questionable and will doubtless remain undefined, since nobody really is very interested in testing the matter in court.

A few user groups have incorporated to obtain the protections of corporate law for their offices. While accusations of secret societies and cabals have been made, no outsider has yet taken the matter seriously enough to use the courts to obtain entry, although in one case it was actually contemplated. From a tax viewpoint, a user group ought to be a not-for-profit, tax-exempt organization of a scientific and/or educational nature; unfortunately, the U.S. Internal Revenue Service (IRS) does not agree with this position. IRS rulings are rarely clear-cut, but the point of contention appears to be the restrictive nature of the membership rules. The IRS emphasized this point in taking action to withdraw the 501(c)(3) tax exemption from one user group, although this has not been generally applied to all user groups.

Practices. A first visit to a user-group meeting is equivalent to an introduction to a three-ring circus—exciting, stimulating, confusing, and almost overwhelming. Activity swirls from early in the morning to late at night; 20 meetings may be running in parallel; social events continue into the wee hours; and small knots of uptight people are seen huddling in corridors, engaging in apparently strategic planning. Actually, what is happening consists of small, face-to-face technical confrontations; limited-size working parties planning implementation and specification priorities; medium- to large-sized groups listening to technical presentations, with a minimum of interaction; and formal assemblies that are likely to be hearing sales pitches of the "you'll love it when you get it" variety, a term originated by Carl Reynolds of IBM at a SHARE meeting.

To be more than a listener, the attending representative should strive to match the installations needs to the information dispensed. This is not always an easy matter because meeting agendas are broad in scope and never include the most important sessions. It is the intimate, unlisted (but critical) meetings held at odd hours in private rooms that are the most important, and only the delegate who has meeting experience will know how to seek these out. These "non-meetings"—if you ask the vendor, you will discover they never happened—offer a convenient way for ideas to be explored while avoiding the commitment of a public disclosure. Too, it must be realized that there are vendor internal politics involved as several development teams seek out the favor and blessing of key members of the user group to back their position at a subsequent public session. At the 1970 CUBE (Burroughs equipment) meeting in St. Louis, certain key users did not meet with senior Burroughs development people in a hotel room that did not exist. Whatever effort Burroughs has given to developing PL/I compilers came from the now classic "non-meeting".

From a user's viewpoint, the happiest situation is the one in which the technical people meet quietly and engage in dialogue with the product development team. More often, however, users find themselves faced with a marketing representative who can speak technical jargon but who exhibits considerable skill at sidestepping issues, avoiding promises, and evading commitments. When users and developers are not subjected to such routines, the relationship is mutually satisfactory. However, manufacturers generally try to avoid this situation. Vendors have nightmares about permitting development teams to make implementation decisions based on technical issues. Current development costs are so high that even the smallest implementation decision may require lengthy examination from the marketing viewpoint. What needs to be answered is always the same question: "If this is implemented, do we either avoid the loss of some account or gain the sale of additional hardware?"

Accomplishments. What is actually accomplished by user groups? The record is erratic, and it appears that the group effectiveness curve is dipping sharply. What was once a viable entity that created new compiler languages, operating systems, and applications packages has today become a patch-and-fix and complaint exchange, with little creative activity. The vastness of today's systems, the size of the vendors, the difficulties of sustaining voluntary action against full-time workers, and the rising expenses involved have all combined to squeeze the user group's effectiveness.

As a result, a handful of dedicated people working part time are gradually being subordinated to paid professionals. Their user has almost no opportunity today to alter significantly the primary thrust of product developmental efforts; those lines are set by marketing requirements, competitive timings, and product life cycles. All the user group can do is perform minor cosmetic surgery on the specifications, detect and note the gross functional errors, and flag the basic implementation faults when the product is released to the field.

Does the user group have any lasting effect? Is there a positive return on the investment of time and money by the user community? Most outside observers doubt it. One critic has stated that all user groups ought to be dissolved six months after the first machine of its series has been installed; at that time its problems will either have been fixed or will never be fixed, no matter how long the system is out.

User groups will not fade away. As each grows too large to be effective, or as the manufacturer with whom it is dealing becomes too rigid and stratified, new groups form to deal more specifically with a single machine or product. The larger and more structured the group, the more likely it is that behind the facade of effectiveness, little is being accomplished. The manufacturers have recognized the value of even superficial cooperation as a marketing tool, and both sides enjoy the social amenities so the groups will not go away even when the original need is gone.

The newer small groups that pinpoint a single product or deal with a smaller manufacturer still carry considerable influence. There are documented cases on record of a user group demanding a change in even pricing policy and getting it. No vendor can stand still when a room packed with irate users representing 75% of annual revenue unanimously screams about a policy. In unity there is still strength, at least until the manufacturer involved gets so large that there is no penalty of significance if a few users grumble.

The bottom line to the installation is still fairly simple to measure. Getting one change or fix done properly and on time can save thousands of dollars of machine time and hundreds of programming and debugging hours. Therefore, the investment in user groups will probably continue to be justified so long as vendors maintain a reasonably responsive attitude to the collective body.

REFERENCES

1956. Armer, P. "SHARE—An Eulogy to Cooperative Effort," RAND Report P-969 (October).
1956. Steel, T. B. *SHARE Reference Manual*, p. 0.1–01.

P. DORN

COMPUTER UTILITY

For articles on related subjects *see* ARPA NETWORK; COMMUNICATIONS AND COMPUTERS; COMPUTER NETWORKS; COMPUTER SYSTEMS; DATA NETWORKS, PUBLIC; DISTRIBUTED SYSTEMS; TIME SHARING and VIEWDATA.

The expression *computer utility* has come into use by analogy with other public utilities such as those that supply water and electricity. These utilities provide, often for metered payment, a public service almost everywhere. Electricity is delivered to one's home and one may use it for general purposes, provided the bill is paid. The analogy is made between electric power and computing power; the intent is to make computing power or capacity available to all comers at their convenience and for their purposes, provided they pay for it. The usual means envisaged for providing this service is the use of terminals such as teletypewriters connected to a computer by telephone lines.

Early experiments that led to the idea of the computer utility emphasized the provision of scientific calculating power for people who were (more or less) skilled at computer use. The great value of the prepackaged program for the untrained customer was in a sense an accidental discovery, and it is this which leads to the vision of the computer utility as a provider of all kinds of services to all kinds of people. Household bookkeeping, personal records of all kinds, public inquiry services (even access to an encyclopedia such as this via a computer rather than a book on a shelf) are all among the facilities that have been suggested for computer utilities.

The analogy with other utility services must not be pushed too far. For physical reasons, many public utilities are provided on a local monopoly basis; insofar as a computer service can be considered a utility at all, its classification as such depends on its coordination with telecommunication facilities, which are themselves usually provided as a public utility. (For this reason, however, government regulation of computer utilities is an important subject of discussion, particularly in the United States.) Furthermore, for most public utilities, there is little difficulty in insuring that one customer's activities will not interfere with another customer's getting what is paid for. The electricity user, for example, needs no personal equipment located in the power station, and the power station contains no equipment dedicated solely to personal use. Moreover, the power channel from the user's equipment to the power station is very narrow and may readily be controlled (e.g., by a fuse). In the provision of computing power, by contrast, the computer is from time to time recognizably doing a particular customer's work, and there is a possibility of interference between one customer's work and another's. This interference may be caused either from sheer overloading of the machine (taking so much of its capacity that too little is left to give good service to others) or more indirectly as a result of accident or sabotage by altering another customer's data or programs.

These points lead to a number of requirements for a computer utility, each of which will be introduced briefly and then discussed in more detail. First is the requirement for very adequate and reliable *protection*. It is necessary that a computation done on behalf of one user will in no way alter another's material or have access to it illegitimately. Neither can one user's computation be allowed to affect noticeably the performance of the system as a whole, i.e., the rate at which it does work for others.

The second requirement is *reliability*. A computer utility as ordinarily conceived must be able to store a user's information and to give it up on request, as well as just being able to do computations. The system will not be used unless customers can trust it to retain information reliably and permanently, even if there are occasional failures of equipment. A customer will not pay to have computations wrongly executed or information mislaid. The customer is not interested in the mechanisms for insuring this, but is interested in their effectiveness.

The preceding two requirements may be regarded as basic. No computer utility will have the confidence of its users unless they are satisfied that these requirements have been adequately met. Equally, no computer utility will make money for its proprietor unless customers are prepared to use the system in sufficiently large volume. To insure that they will do so, it is necessary to meet several other requirements, which, although the economic motivation for meeting them may be just as strong, should be recognized as being in a different class.

The first of these is generally termed *programming generality*. This is a name for a means to an end, the end being that it should be easy to make successive or joint use of possibly a considerable number of pieces of program without getting into enormous difficulty over the process of connecting them together. At one level, it should be possible to put together without difficulty a package for maintaining a database about sewerage connections in a town, together with a package for drawing maps. At another level, it should be possible to plug together a subroutine for working out square roots with any mathematical program.

The second requirement in this class is for *predictability of performance*. A computer utility will be unattractive to its customers if the cost of a particular use is unclear, even if a similar use was made yesterday, or if elapsed time needed to perform the work is not definite. The utility must be predictable in both performance aspects.

A third requirement, which is worth mentioning at this point, although it is a requirement that bears more on the provider of the system than on the user, is that computing power of the system be readily enhanceable. It must be possible for the vendor of computing power via a computer utility to provide additional computing power when it is needed, without undue disturbance to existing customers. It must be possible to enhance the equipment used without either shutting the service down for a while or changing the way in which the computer has to be used.

All user and provider requirements present considerable challenge to a computer utility, and the remainder of this article will say a few words about each in turn.

Protection. If in a computer utility it were required to provide only brute computing power for service of a user, it would be sufficient to provide protection that insured that the work done for a particular user could not directly interfere with work being done for any other user or with the mechanisms that provide the entire service. However, it is usual to think of the user of a computer utility having available, possibly for a fee, a considerable number of programs. The proprietary nature of these programs must be protected if the owner of them is going to put them out for service.

Accordingly, protection systems must permit users to have access to programs without copying them, and programs must exist that will automatically and safely bill their users on every occasion. It must not be possible for a user to call a proprietary subsystem in such a way that it does the work without proper billing. It must also be possible for the owner of a program or subsystem to stipulate which other customers of the utility may use it. Similar remarks apply to stored databases.

Thus, it is evident that customer protection requires more than the simple encapsulation of the activities of a particular user. The imposition by the owner of a program or specific data of protection restrictions should be implementable by that owner directly, without the need to request the proprietors of the computer utility to do it. If this requirement is not met, the administrative burden is likely to impede effective exploitation of computer service. It would not be appropriate here to discuss at length the detailed techniques for effecting the protection required. The references give some pointers.

Reliability. Reliability of information storage poses very high technical requirements. If a system is to be trusted by users to retain their information indefinitely, it must be capable of providing a much higher degree of integrity than most users would ordinarily consider applying to data themselves in a more direct way. A user of an ordinary computer system will take steps to keep backup copies of information, in proportion to the value placed upon it and to the difficulty (which only the user knows) of recomputing it. The user may be prepared to take a risk sometimes, but will be most displeased if an automatic system assumes that prerogative. Keeping backup information of very diverse sorts for different people on a really large scale is a problem not yet solved. It is made more difficult by a reasonable desire on the part of the utility to provide the degree of safety that a user is prepared to pay for, no more and no less.

It is a question of policy whether the integrity system should protect users against their mistakes rather than against errors by the utility itself. This involves the relation between backup storage and performance failure—no matter how caused—and cheap archival storage for deliberate use. Although the two functions are logically quite distinct, the physical media used (usually magnetic tapes) are the same, and the required data organizations are at least similar. It is to some extent an open question how far the two functions can be given a common implementation.

Reliability is an area heavily dependent on the currently available storage technology, in which elaborate systems are very likely to become obsolete as technology progresses. Simple systems are, however, likely to be severely restrictive. For example, a very simple approach is to permit a user to request preservation of material on magnetic tape centrally, or to permit a request for its preservation locally on a (simpler) tape driven directly from the terminal. However, this works only if there is a solid distinction between the material belonging to the system (automatically preserved) and material belonging to users (their own responsibility). Since one of the most attractive attributes of computer utilities is the sharing of material, this distinction is not admissible. Reliability could be severely questioned if something went wrong with shared material and the utility had to appeal to the proprietor for a backup copy. Both the owner and the user of shared material must have confidence in the integrity of the central system. Current approaches to these problems depend on automatic means of recovering reserve copies when either the system or the user notices that there is something wrong, so that the worst experience of the user will be a slight delay. Ideally, recovering a data file should be as easy as redialing an abortive phone call.

Programming Generality. Programming generality places requirements on languages and system structure. It is commonplace to find that programs exist for doing the kind of calculation one wants, but that either they will not fit into the rest of one's program structure or will require an inconvenient (for the intended purpose) data organization. These problems lead to heavy and unnecessary programming costs. The avoidance or partial avoidance of such problems requires that there be discipline and convention in the entire structure of system and user programs. It is not clear to what exent this can be reconciled either with efficiency or with the possibility of progress. Programmers will have to be as disciplined as the installers of new telephone offices, and some way will have to be found to avoid a large investment in obsolete systems.

Predictability of Performance. Predictability of performance depends upon the existence of surplus capacity and a sufficient number of simultaneous users so that no single user's work will require a substantial portion of the capability of the system. Today, the number of users of multiple-access computer systems is so limited that even an isolated individual will have an effect; compare the few thousand customers of a computer system with the few million of a reasonably large electric company. Compare the minimal surplus capacity in most computer systems with the thousands of megawatts held in reserve in, say, the generating system of the United Kingdom—remembering that the comparative basis is not just one of proportionality but also one related to the demands of individuals. In this area there is hope, however, of progress. Prices of processing units are rapidly failing, and it should become possible to hold adequate reserves without incurring short-term economic problems. It is not yet so clear that this will also be possible for mechanical components such as disk stores for files, but the trends are favorable.

These points are clearly related to the matter of easy capacity enhancement. Only if components subject to capacity strain can be augmented will load reserve be maintained. To some extent this is possible with most current system designs. However, if we consider a computer to be an assemblage of processors, memories, channels, and peripherals, with as much mutual interconnection as required, then eventually a computer utility will come to consist of more than one CPU. Unless, as seems unlikely, the structure of computers becomes stable over longer periods than is now usual, the differences between early and late models will cause problems in the service given. Again, the analogy with other utilities is strained: The 1970 and 1980 electric generator models produce very similar 60-cycle alternating current, whereas 1970 and 1980 computer facilities are vastly different.

State-of-the-Art. Where are we in relation to the status of computer utilities as compared to other utilities? Early time-sharing systems, of a type intended to have a community of users rather than a mere collection (the M.I.T. Compatible Time-Sharing System (CTSS), the Cambridge Multple-Access System), made a good start in this direction. The more recent developments of Multics (M.I.T.—Honeywell) place it as near as any existing system actually being labeled a computer utility. Problems of scale still remain, however, and it is not quite clear when or whether market forces will promote the developments needed. There is, after all, competition: Minicomputers and microcomputers are becoming very cheap, and it may turn out that this low-cost computing power will seem more attractive than the higher cost of sharing programs, data, and power, the central theme of a computer utility. It would be contrary to experience in other developments in industrial society that the minicomputer would win out (rather like a cottage industry supplanting U.S. Steel), but it could happen. More likely, there will be a plurality of solutions involving large computers, minicomputers, microcomputers, and combinations of these.

REFERENCES

1969. Lampson, B. W. "Dynamic Protection Structures," *AFIPS Conf. Proc.* **35.**
1972. Organick, E. I. *The Multics System: An Examination of Its Structure.* Cambridge, MA: M.I.T. Press.
1972. Wilkes, M. V. *Time Sharing Computer Systems,* 2nd Ed., New York: American Elsevier.

R. M. NEEDHAM

COMPUTING AND SOCIETY

For articles on related subjects *see* AUTOMATION; CRIMEAND COMPUTER SECURITY; DATA BANK; DATA SECURITY; ELECTRONIC FUNDS TRANSFER SYSTEM; LEGAL ASPECTS OF COMPUTING; PERSONNEL IN COMPUTERS; and PRIVACY, COMPUTERS AND.

The phrase "computing and society" is often used as though there is a clearly identifiable and consistent "society" in question. In fact, the concept of society encompasses a complex array of concepts about individual and group behavior in the context of continually changing social and institutional settings. There is no "computing impact on society" *per se;* the impact of computing on society depends on what aspects of social life are looked at. This article discusses the role of computing in society in three sections, arranged in the order in which computing has had its greatest impacts: computing in organizations, computing and the individual, and computing in the broader social orders of modern life.

COMPUTING IN ORGANIZATIONS

Organizations—businesses, governments, educational institutions, etc.—were the first users of computers and they remain the major users. Service organizations use computing for administrative "housekeeping" (e.g., payroll or accounting), but they also make operational use of computing in three areas: to manage information related to specific "cases" such as policyholder records in insurance companies or criminal offender files in police information systems; for analytical applications related to the creation of the service organization's products, such as engineering calculations in engineering and construction firms or actuarial analysis in insurance companies;

and in direct service delivery such as the use of automated teller machines to provide 24-hour banking. Governments and educational institutions are basically service organizations, and use computers primarily for administrative housekeeping and "case" management.

Manufacturing industries have made use of computing primarily for administrative housekeeping, though recently more direct operational uses of computing have emerged. These are usually of three kinds: Product planning and design, which incorporates analytical use of computing for engineering and market analysis, as well as computer assisted drafting; manufacturing resource control, which includes materials requirements, planning systems, and finished product inventory management; and computer-assisted manufacturing itself that utilizes industrial robots either to control or perform actual manufacturing operations. It is important to understand the distinctions between service and manufacturing uses of computing in organizations because of their differing impacts on the organizations, and thereby on individuals and on society at large.

The first and most obvious impact of computing on organizations is *direct economic impact*. This kind of impact has been both desirable (as when computing reduces the cost of performing tasks resulting in efficiencies that allow avoidance of probable future costs, or brings improved service or products in a cost-beneficial manner) and undesirable, as when computing projects fail or result in costly organizational disruption while not returning economic benefit to the organization. Curiously, little is known about the true and specific economic impacts computing has had. Future work on the economics of computing might reveal a less positive picture of the economic impact of computing than commonly described, since many superficial economic analyses of computing have underestimated the costs of computing and imprecisely valued benefits.

A major positive but *indirect* economic impact of computing is a gradual and increasing sophistication in the way computing-using organizations plan for and adapt to changes in their operating environments. This is frequently noted in comments from managers who say that computing makes it possible to cope with complex and frequent changes in their environments such as product markets, financial markets, regulatory constraints, reporting requirements, or political conditions. Also, the advent of computer/telecommunications linkages is making it possible for organizations with decentralized operations (e.g., field offices) to provide local computing facilities for these operations connected to centralized organizational computing in order to provide managerial and policy information. This provides flexibility and central control, both of which are necessary.

The possible negative and indirect economic impacts of computing on organizations include increasing dependency on the technology and growing difficulties in managing the technology effectively. As computing becomes essential to organizational well-being, organizations become increasingly dependent on a technology that has proven to be difficult to keep ahead of managerially. Already, most organizations using computing have experienced the discomfort and often the chaos that occurs when a computing system essential to the organization fails and there is no reliable back-up.

The manageability of computing refers to continuing difficulties in bringing this rapidly changing technology, as well as the resulting organizational impacts it has, under consistent and effective managerial control. Computing not only is a volatile technology in terms of its own evolution (e.g., the move from first- to third-generation computers occurred in only two decades), but it also necessitates continual changes in organizational practices and even in managerial strategy. Many components of the "computing package," such as computer equipment vendors and educational institutions that train technical people for computing, are not under the organization's control. Thus, this larger "world of computing" can often dictate terms to organizational management instead of the other way around.

Neither the positive nor the negative indirect economic impacts of computing have been adequately researched to allow a reliable portrayal of the true impact of computing in this regard. Indeed, a comprehensive picture of the indirect economic impacts of computing probably cannot easily be drawn. As time goes on, understanding of these impacts will be built primarily from observations about the ways organizations *react* to the impacts.

The third impact of computing on organizations is on *organizational structure and behavior*. In a now classic article written in 1958, Leavitt and Whisler proposed that computing would have such drastic impact on management through automating the tasks of middle managers that by the 1980s middle management would largely cease to exist. A quick look at any large organization shows that this has not happened; indeed, it seems that the ranks of middle management have, if anything, grown in the past three decades (although this is probably not due to computing). The major debate about the impact of computing on organizational structure has been over whether computing has a fundamentally "centralizing" or "decentralizing" effect on organizations. Rationales for both impacts can be found in the literature, but to date no conclusive empirical work has demonstrated just what the centralizing and decentralizing impacts of computing are.

Impacts on organizational behavior from computing refer to the ways computing changes the routines and interactions among individual employees and among classes of employees (e.g., top management, middle management, technical staff). Again, there has been little detailed empirical work on this subject, but what there is indicates at least one interesting thing: Computing is a highly political activity within organizations in two senses. The first is that there is often high political value surrounding the information contained in computerized systems (i.e., "information is power"). Second, there are considerable "resource politics" surrounding the technology itself in that the organizational commitment to computing is often very large, and the individual or organizational unit that controls that resource has both direct resource power as well as indirect power through control over who utilizes the resource and with what priority. It is unclear at this point, however, whether the behavior of organizations with substantial computing operations differs systematically from analogous organizations that do not have such computing operations.

COMPUTING AND THE INDIVIDUAL

It is difficult to characterize accurately computing's impact on individuals because there are a great many ways individuals can come in contact with computing, and the reactions of individuals differ even in identical circumstances. The primary interaction individuals have had with computing has been through organizations that use computers, but the recent advent of smaller and less expensive computers has begun to make computing a more personal affair.

Computing Impacts as a Function of Organizational Computing Uses. The first impact to consider is the effect of computing on the workplace of employees, particularly in the context of job displacement and changes in the nature of jobs. An early prediction about computing's impact on workers was a massive job displacement (e.g., layoffs) in certain job sectors, such as the clerical and middle management ranks. This has not materialized in the manner predicted, in part because the change to computing is gradual and allows for natural attrition to make the necessary reductions in employees, and in part because computing often creates new demands that generate employment.

Nevertheless, computing has resulted in major reductions in the number of jobs available in certain service sectors (e.g., among telephone operators) over time, even though few individuals were laid off. Some workers who departed were simply not replaced. The growing application of computing directly to industrial operations will probably have a much more dramatic effect on employment than was the case with the introduction of administrative data processing. In industries such as newspaper printing, the move from manual typesetting to computer-assisted composing of camera-ready copy has already re-

sulted in major labor disputes because many jobs have been at stake. Similarly, secretarial and clerical jobs might be reduced by extensive adoption of word processing and office automation. Concern over job displacement is comparatively weak in the U.S. probably due to the very large size of the economy and the workforce, which can absorb even sizable dislocations, but it is a major and a growing issue in Western Europe, where it has become a central concern of trade unions. In both the U. S. and in other industrialized nations, perceptions about the severity of job displacement by computing impact will probably depend on the overall pace of the economy and, especially, the growth of new jobs.

Computing can change the nature of employee work environments in a number of ways, but, at least in administrative data processing environments in the U. S., it generally does not have a drastic positive or negative impact on employee work environments. Computing seems to be readily assimilated by most white collar workers. These employees tend to like working with computers and generally feel positive toward it in their jobs.

Yet computing affects different aspects of work environments in different ways, and it affects different kinds of users in different ways. More problematic impacts of computing for employees are in the areas of increased time pressure and routinization of job activity for certain kinds of workers, such as data entry clerks in some industries (banking, for example), and occasionally a sense of feeling more closely supervised by higher management due to the ability of the computer to report performance indicators to management (by key strokes per hour or the number of transactions executed). Available research indicates that computing's impacts are greater on lower level clerical staff and diminish as one moves toward top management; however, the research is inconclusive on whether computing's impacts are more negative among lower-level workers and more positive among higher-level workers.

The second major area of computing impact on individuals as a function of organizational computing uses is in the area of changes in customer/client interactions with organizations that utilize computers directly when they deal with individuals. There are three such situations. One is financial, where individuals purchase goods or services from organizations on credit (e.g., instead of cash on delivery), and the management of the customer's account is handled by computer. Another example of this is in collection of individual income and property taxes by government. The second category is when individuals receive services for a long period of time from organizations, and computing is used directly in helping the organization to manage the individual's "case." The most obvious example of such use is in the insurance industry, where policyholders' policies are managed by computer, but there is growing use of computing to manage client "cases" in the health care field (patient record management). The third category is when computerized records on individuals are used by third parties to make decisions about those individuals. Examples of this are when a store clerk checks a computerized check verification system before accepting a check, a prospective employer checks the computerized records of an employment investigation firm before hiring a person, or when a police officer checks a driver's license number or a license plate number against a computerized file to determine if an individual is wanted by the law or if a car is reported stolen.

The first significant impact is that, in many of these cases, computing creates new opportunities for the individual involved. For example, the computer has played an important part in the dramatic growth of consumer credit availability. Without computing capability, financial institutions could probably not afford to offer credit as widely as they do, and the charges to credit-using consumers would probably be higher. Similarly, on-line check verification systems make it possible for merchants to continue accepting checks for payment even in the face of rising bad-check rates.

Such systems can also result in financial or other advantage to the individual customers by making organizations more efficient and effective in their operations, since this makes them more competitive and thereby helps hold down costs and improve services. Also, when used deliberately to help a client or customer with a particular problem, computerized systems can expedite problem resolution by, for example, rapid tracing of records to clear up a dispute over an unpaid bill or an overcharge. Finally, systems that facilitate the direct performance of a service can work to the advantage of individuals who receive the service. Computerized stolen property files in law enforcement that result in confiscated property being returned to the rightful owners certainly help those owners.

However, computing can also have less positive impacts. Problems arise in customer/client situations when computing becomes an impediment to the successful resolution of a dispute. In the same way that computing can assist in the resolution of problems if the organization is willing to help the customer or client, it can also block effective efforts in several ways. Many systems, such as those that handle credit card accounts, are very complex. Unless these systems are designed with error-tracing capability, errors that arise in the course of preparing bills or recording payments can be difficult to trace. Even though by law organizations are obligated to resolve such disputes, and they usually do make a good effort, it is costly to do so. If the organization wishes to "stonewall" the customer or client, the computer becomes a useful tool in that process. At times, the customer is actually put in the position of having to "prove the computer is wrong" by producing a cancelled check or other evidence before the organization will act.

Consumer errors involving computerized systems are not very common. Sterling (1979) reports that about 20% of those sampled in his study of consumer problems with computing-using organizations did have such problems. The organizations involved usually resolved the disputes or "wrote off" the disputed amount and let the customer have his or her way. But in a significant number of cases, customers had to spend considerable time (e.g., 20 hours) trying to get the problem resolved, and in some cases gave up because it was too much of a hassle to get cooperation. In the same way that computing brings opportunity and advantage, it can bring new problems for customers and clients.

Another area of computing impact on individuals as a function of organizational uses of computing has to do with technology-driven changes in the control of so-called personal information on individuals. This area includes the subject of computers and privacy, which is probably the most extensively discussed aspect of computers and society and the one that is uppermost in the public mind. However, the issue of privacy is only a part of a larger set of concerns, and focusing too closely on it masks the importance of other issues. The most important aspect of the personal information and computing issue is that the ground rules that have traditionally governed the collection, sharing and use of personal information on individuals have been changed by the advent of computing and communications technologies. Social conventions, laws, and even public opinion on the issue have not kept up with these changes. The result is that there is now much concern over what all this change means, even though there is not much understanding about what actual changes have taken place and how they have affected individuals thus far.

The issue of how much control individuals have over information about themselves is not new. It has existed at least since the development of the press, and probably long before. It is rooted in a fundamental and persistent dilemma of social organization: Individuals rightly desire to withhold certain personal information from others to preserve their integrity or privacy; yet the state or other organizations representing social forces of the time need (or think they need) certain personal information on individuals in order to carry out the job of maintaining social order. The balance is struck between these two needs through social processes that take considerable time, and every society has its rules and protocols that govern what is legitimately private and personal information and what must be disclosed for non-personal use. The balance has always been built in large part around what is possible with respect to collecting, managing, and using information on individuals. Computing and communications technologies have altered the "what is possible" part of the equation in major ways, and this is the heart of the computers and personal information issue.

Prior to computing, it simply was impossible to manage effectively large numbers of detailed files of personal information on individuals because of high error rates, rapid obsolescence of the data, and the high costs of collecting, updating, and retrieving the data. As a result, both the collection of personal data and the use of that data were restricted. With computing, it has become possible to manage effectively vast numbers of individual data files with great accuracy. This ability, combined with needs and desires for personal data on the part of many public and private organizations, has resulted in a great increase in the collection and use of such data. The social and legal conventions for balancing such collection and use against legitimate concerns for personal withholding of information have not kept pace with each other.

The problem in understanding the issue of computing and privacy arises from a curious paradox. On one hand, recent surveys suggest that a large majority of adult citizens in the U. S. feel that there is a growing erosion of personal privacy, and that computer-using organizations such as government agencies are a major cause of such erosion. Yet there have been very few major privacy "disasters" to provide evidence that privacy is indeed in jeopardy. Most of the empirical research done on the subject has concluded that there has not been a widespread and drastic decline in personal privacy as a result of the use of computing *per se*. There has, however, been a large (and apparently growing) number of serious incidents in which individuals have been subjected to practices involving computing use that did constitute invasion of privacy. The impact of computing on privacy seems to be a slowly growing, incremental impact that is clouded by continually changing social values about what privacy means and how much of it is necessary. The privacy invasions that have come to light have resulted in some remedial legislation preventing the most odious information practices, and more such legislation will come in time.

However, these legislative patch-ups do not tackle the basic issue of striking a new balance between the right to withhold and/or control use of personal information, and the need to know about and use such information. Not one piece of legislation related to privacy and information passed thus far deals with the question of whether it is fair or just for certain personal information systems to be created at all, and certainly no legislation orders the dismantling of any such systems. The attitude, reinforced by governments and private organizations with an interest in such systems, seems to be "build and see what happens." Presumably, if problems arise, they can be dealt with on an as-needed basis.

This attitude has some sense to it; it asks whether it is reasonable to shut down systems unilaterally which *might* produce social or even individual benefits simply because they might cause problems of loss of privacy or personal integrity for individuals. Yet, the prevailing concerns of citizens over this issue of privacy indicates that there is a more basic problem that must be addressed. This problem is well articulated by James Rule (1974), who points out that the problems encountered so far with computerized information systems containing personal data are not nearly as critical as the *potential* problems that could arise if things do not go according to our expectations. Rule points out that the systems now being built containing personal information on millions of individuals are creating an enormous "surveillance potential" that could, and probably would, be turned against the subjects of these systems if political conditions changed in certain ways. The issue is not that such a thing *will* happen. Rather it centers on whether creation of systems with great surveillance potential will facilitate such changes, and how they will affect the outcome if such changes do take place.

It is not possible at this time to say whether computing's impact on individuals as a result of computing-using organizations is predominately positive or negative; most likely, it will never be possible to make such a comprehensive assessment. Moreover, to try to arrive at such an assessment misses a critical point—that the kinds of impacts computing has on individuals vary by the nature of the applications, the nature of the organization using computing, the prevailing social conditions, and the fact that individuals differ greatly in how they react to what happens to them.

Impacts on Individuals as a Result of Personal Computing Uses. Personal uses of computing refers to the uses individuals make of computing for their own purposes, and not as a result of their interaction with organizations. With the advent of new, small, and much less expensive computing hardware, systems now exist that can bring significant computing power into many people's homes. This phenomenon is so recent that very little is known about just what impact personal use of computing is having on individuals. Nevertheless, there is a great deal of speculation about the impacts that *will* occur.

Personal computing can take the form of direct personal use of a computing system belonging to oneself, another individual, or an organization that makes systems available for such use. Or it can take the form of computer-assisted communications, usually by way of a central computer system that has many remote computer terminals that individuals use to communicate with others who have terminals. This includes so-called "computer conferencing," in which a group of individuals holds either a time-bounded or on-going conference about a particular issue by individual participants typing in input to the other users and responding to messages received from other users. A related context, one that is hardly developed at all yet, is individual/organizational communications using computing, such as shopping from home using a home computer connected to a department store computer that takes orders, arranges delivery of the orders, and charges the customer's account. An actual use that approximates this is the current "Automated Teller Machine" used in banking, which is actually a small, special-purpose terminal mounted in a convenient place and connected to a bank computer that allows a depositor to make deposits, withdraw cash, and conduct other simple transactions at any time.

Very little is known about the impacts of these developments because they are so new; however, some observations can be made. One is that the reasons individuals obtain their own computing capability are only in part based on the practical utility of computing: the entertainment value computing can provide also is important, and this aspect of personal computing use will be promoted by manufacturers and developers of software for small computers. A further observation is that the use of such computing in classrooms will probably have a significant impact on education, partly on the substance of what students learn (e.g., mathematics, physics), and also with respect to students' familiarity with and competence in the use of computing itself. It seems likely that these new systems will initiate the training of whole new generations of computer-proficient individuals, with unpredictable effect.

Such predictions must be taken with great caution, however. The impact of general-purpose computing systems on organizations has been less dramatic than predicted, and many impacts have occurred that were not predicted at all. The number of variables that affect how a technology is assimilated into use and the impacts it has is so great that accurate prediction is almost impossible.

IMPACTS ON SOCIETY

The interaction of the impacts computing has on individuals can produce broader social impacts. Several such issues must be considered in this broader context. Since there has been very little empirical research on whether these impacts are in fact happening and, if so, in what ways, this discussion can only consider possible and perhaps predictable impacts of computing that have broad social significance.

Impact on Quality of Life. Under this heading are the broad concerns of how computing affects such aspects of life as social dependency on technology and social vulnerability as a result of dependence, complexity of large systems, and incomprehensibility as a consequence of complexity. The concept of social dependency on a technology is well illustrated in E. M. Forster's *The Machine Stops,* in which a large machine that supplies a utopian society with all its needs comes to a stop, with predictable consequences. Computing does not now represent such a machine, nor is society so dependent on it, but many socially important things are becoming dependent on computing—military communications, banking, social welfare programs, and the telephone system, for example. Concern about such dependency is not based on the assumption that all these computer-assisted activities will break down at once, but sizable failures in any one can cause major trouble.

Social dependency becomes vulnerability when the large technologies on which the society is dependent are in themselves dependent on conditions that cannot be easily controlled by the society. An example of potential vulnerability involving computers can be seen in large-scale electronic funds transfer involving automated debiting of accounts. Such systems might be very efficient compared to paper-based systems (checks) but they could be more vulnerable to a major failure such as a two-day-long "credit blackout" covering the Northeast that would be crippling. Some critics have pointed out such potential problems with EFT, but EFT development proceeds without a clear resolution of them.

The complexity of large systems and, more importantly, their incomprehensibility, is a major concern of Weizenbaum (1976). He argues that many such incomprehensible systems are now being used and depended on for important and sensitive tasks, and more are being built all the time. An incomprehensible system can be an unpredictable system, and unpredictable systems are unreliable. Moreover, through incomprehensibility, in a real sense, computing transcends human control. The systems are so complex, yet so crucial, it is often best simply to "let them alone" rather than disrupt them very much.

An illustrative and disturbing case in point can be found in a series of false alerts of Soviet missile attacks on the U. S. caused by "minor" malfunctions in Strategic Air Command computers in the winter of 1979 and the summer of 1980. While the specific problems with the computer systems were minor in themselves (e.g., a defective circuit), the magnitude of the trouble these malfunctions might have caused is staggering. The fact that the alerts were false was quickly discovered by Air Force personnel, but not before strategic bombers and other components of the U. S. defense arsenal had begun to act in response to the supposed Soviet attack. The seriousness of such incidents goes far beyond the mechanics of computer system reliability to the very core of the issue: To what extent is it reasonable and safe to rely on highly automated and complex systems for management and monitoring of critical tasks? This question has not been answered in a satisfactory way.

The crux of the problem of computing's impact on quality of life is ultimately the question of whether computing is really under human control. Some social critics and science fiction writers believe that a highly technical future, based in part on computers, will come to pass. Others, such as Weizenbaum, argue that society must begin now to prohibit building of the most "dangerous" of these large, incomprehensible, and dependency-creating technologies. Most observers apparently have not given the issue much thought, or are convinced both that the future includes computing and that the major problems will be taken care of one way or another.

Impact on Moral Behavior. If computing changes the social character of life in important ways, those changes could alter the nature of moral behavior in important ways also. This is a major concern of Mowshowitz (1976), who raises the question of whether computing will alter the work patterns and other social activities of people in ways that result in dysfunctional changes in moral behavior. As an example, he cites the characteristics of "computer criminals." He found that these individuals tend to have little in common with stereotyped criminal types; in fact, they are often described as model employees. Mowshowitz notes that their crimes are often perpetrated by committing acts that are only minor variations from work they normally do. These acts are viewed with challenge, and the perpetrators do not usually feel they are doing anything seriously wrong because it only hurts "big corporations that can afford it." Mowshowitz argues that there is something in the nature of computing-based changes in the workplace that precipitates such behavior. Computing, in a sense, can help create "criminogenic" work situations. Mowshowitz notes that such changes raise questions about the impact of computing on the self-direction society exercises for itself, and urges that society exercise firm moral authority over the development and use of computing.

Impact on Social Power. A common prediction in much of the predictive fiction and fantasy about the future is that future technological utopias will be built around huge, centralized computers that are either servants or masters of mankind. This is part of a frequently articulated but generally unproven conviction that computing tends to encourage centralization in organizations and in society. In fact, computing has not exercised—and probably will not exercise—a strongly centralizing influence on society because computing is used by many different political competitors, none of which wants to see centralization unless it is at the center.

A major finding of research that has looked at the political aspects of computing in the U. S. has shown that, by and large, computing tends to reinforce the power of those who already hold power, and does not generally result in shifts of power from one power bloc to another. For example, because computing is widely available, nearly all political candidates can afford to (and do) use computers in important ways, such as in maintaining donor files and printing mailings.

The most important question concerning computing's impact on social power centers on how computing can be used as a tool to further the ends of various vested interests. Even though computing is available to all who can afford it, there are many who cannot afford it. Moreover, there are many (e.g., elderly, uneducated, poor) who do not understand computing well enough to realize that computing can be used to tell lies and perpetrate falsehoods as easily as it can be used to enlighten decisions, and they are not well-equipped to confront financial institutions, government bureaucracies, and other computing-using organizations on computing issues. In this sense, computing does not necessarily bring new dilemmas of social power; rather, it calls attention to, and sometimes exacerbates, lingering and as yet unsolved ones.

Impact on Human Communication. Computing has already revolutionized telephone-switching systems and other aspects of the telecommunications field. Further major impacts are expected to result from the marriage of computers and telecommunications in such a way that computers will be able conveniently to "talk to one another." Already considerable experimentation has taken place in the U. S. through a large computerized network supported originally by the Advanced Research Projects Agency of the Department of Defense, and called the ARPANET. A major and, in some ways unexpected, use of the ARPANET has been personal and professional communications among participants in the network. A more recent and still on-going experiment is the Electronic Information Exchange System (EIES). Proponents of these systems maintain that they offer great social promise for changing the nature of human communication, even to the point of assisting in sensitive international diplomatic negotiation. The major problems with predicting the future based on experiences with systems such as ARPANET and EIES are that these systems are relatively small and involve a highly specialized and well-educated clientele compared to the general population. Whether the more ambitious predictions about such systems, such as the home computer attached by phone to the store to allow "shopping from home" actually occur remains to be seen. The social implications of such changes are even more difficult to predict. Nevertheless, it should be noted that these technological changes are of sufficient potency to have radical impacts on society.

There is a great shortage of careful and empirical research on exactly what is happening with the computing systems now in operation in the many organizations and households throughout our society as noted by Kling (1980). Without such data, it is impossible to state clearly the current case, much less predict the future with any confidence. Still, the stakes are high with a technology as potent as computing. Simply because there is as yet little empirical evidence that computing has serious negative impacts on society is no reason to conclude that there are or will be few negative impacts. Unfortunately, with computing, as with many technologies, the serious and intractable problems that do arise from a technology's use might not appear for decades. Computing use is a relatively recent phenomenon and its real and lasting social impacts are only now beginning to appear through the haze.

The observable social changes brought by computing might not yet be as spectacular as those brought by other technologies, such as nuclear power or modern chemistry or even the automobile. But the changes computing is bringing to basic aspects of social life, such as the way the economy operates or the manner in which a government communicates with its citizens, are very powerful indeed. The foregoing discussions of major issues in social impact from computing touch only on the most likely and most serious consequences as seen in 1980.

REFERENCES

1970. Whisler, Thomas. *The Impact of Computers on Organizations.* New York: Praeger.

1973. Gotlieb, C. C. and Borodin, A. *Social Issues in Computing.* New York: Academic Press.

1974. Laudon, Kenneth. *Computers and Bureaucratic Reform.* New York: Wiley.

1974. Rule, James. *Private Lives and Public Surveillance: Social Control in the Computer Age.* New York: Schocken Books.

1976. Weizenbaum, Joseph. *Computer Power and Human Reason: From Judgment to Calculation.* San Francisco: W. H. Freeman.

1977. Privacy Protection Study Commission. *Personal Privacy in an Information Society.* Washington, DC: Government Printing Office (July).

1977. Dorf, Richard. *Computers and Man,* 2nd Ed. San Francisco: Boyd and Fraser.

1979. Sterling, Theodore. "Consumer Difficulties with Computerized Transactions: An Empirical Analysis," *Communications of the ACM* **22**, No. 5: 283–289 (May).

1980. Hoffman, Lance (Ed.). *Computers and Privacy in the Next Decade.* New York: Academic Press.

1980. Kling, Rob. "Social Analyses of Computing: Theoretical Perspectives in Recent Empirical Research," *Computing Surveys* **12**, *No. 1* (March).

1980. Danziger, James; Dutton, William; Kling, Rob; and Kraemer, Kenneth L. *Computers and Politics: High Technology in American Local Governments.* New York: Columbia University Press.

J. L. KING

COMPUTING CENTER

For articles on related subjects *see* APPLICATIONS PROGRAMMING; DATA PROCESSING; DATA SECURITY; OPEN AND CLOSED SHOP; OPERATING SYSTEMS; PROCESSING MODES; PROGRAM LIBRARIES; SECURITY OF COMPUTER INSTALLATIONS, PHYSICAL; SERVICE BUREAUS, DATA PROCESSING; and SYSTEMS PROGRAMMING.

A computing center provides computer services to a variety of users through the operation of computer and auxiliary hardware, and through ancillary services provided by its staff. A not-for-profit service center usually provides such services *at cost* to its *users;* but a for-profit center does so with the intention, at least, of making a profit from providing services to its *customers.* Since there is little distinction between the two centers other than pricing and the label used for the consumers of their services, we will deal with the computing center as a service center with users.

Services. The extent to which the users participate in the operation of the center determines its staffing and organization. At one extreme is the completely *closed shop,* wherein the users supply only the initial specifications for the computations to be carried out or the reports to be provided. Thereafter, they supply only the new data and/or current information used to bring files up to date and satisfy requests to supply computed output or reports according to those specifications. This closed-shop organization requires that all skills and equipment required to provide its services be supplied by the computing center.

At the other extreme is the completely *open shop,* wherein the users supply the initial specifications, convert them into computer programs, supply the current information, convert it into machine-readable form, and operate the computer to obtain the desired results. This arrangement requires only that the computing center supply the computer, the manuals on how to use it, some supplies, and heat and light. Most centers today are nearer the former than the latter, but many maintain closed-shop machine operation while providing both open and closed-shop programming, as mentioned below.

Fundamentally, there are three services provided by a computing center, each usually offered with some degree of open-shop organization. The most obvious service is *machine operation*. This skill is not learned in a few minutes for any computer, and is acquired only after lengthy training on large sophisticated machines. For this and a variety of other reasons, as explained later, all but the smallest computing centers offer only closed-shop machine operation for the majority of their operating hours. Some provide open-shop (or partial open shop) operation during restricted hours or on weekends, but these are in the clear minority.

Perhaps the next most obvious service required is *programming and system analysis*. This service is most easily and conveniently provided on both an open- and closed-shop basis. Those users who wish to do their own analyses or write their own programs may do so, and those who wish to have them designed and written by the computing center staff (and can afford to pay for this service) may also be satisfied. Since (from the computing center's point of view) there are two kinds of programming, those services are usually divided into two departments: systems programming and applications programming.

The least obvious service provided is that of data control, scheduling, and quality control. This service deals with the inspection of the incoming information for completeness and timeliness, with scheduling the machine operation for applications whose current information and files are ready for processing, and with inspection and dispatching of output reports and updated files from applications that have been processed.

Machine Operation. In the smallest computing centers, or otherwise in those which provide the greatest degree of open-shop programming, open-shop machine operation is fairly common. Frequently, a machine operator is available to run the machine for some applications, to train prospective open-shop operators, and to assist with the machine operation of some aspects of other applications. Almost inevitably, however, as the workload of the center increases, open-shop machine operation is the first service to be restricted or eliminated.

One of the most compelling reasons for a restriction in open-shop operation is the security of the data files. As long as data files are small or easily replaced, little attention needs to be paid to their security. When files become large enough to be stored on some medium that must be kept at the computing center, however, the possibility that they could be destroyed or inspected (either inadvertently or deliberately) by another user arises. To the extent that either of the above is undesirable or costly, the cost of closed-shop operation can (and almost always does) become more attractive to the center owners.

As might be expected, open-shop operation frequently gives rise to inefficient use of the computer. In a new installation where there are not sufficient applications yet programmed, such inefficiency is of no particular moment. However, even if file security does not materialize as a problem, inefficient use of the computer may compel the introduction of closed-shop operation to escape the alternative requirement of a faster machine. In such cases the cost of operators is almost always the much more attractive alternative.

Machine operation varies in the amount of skill required, from nominal on small machines with simple or nonexistent operating systems to very substantial on large, fast machines with sophisticated operating systems. Since the operating system is supposed to speed up operation of the machine by providing a smooth transition from one application to the next (called *job-to-job transition),* operators must be trained in the language and procedures of the operating system.

The operating system and the operator must communicate about the running of some applications. This is accomplished via the operator's console, usually a display screen with a keyboard or a typewriter (most commonly the latter). The operating system sends messages to the computer, indicating that operator intervention is required. For example, if the card reader jams or tears a card, thus inhibiting its action, it usually indicates a "turned-off" state to the operating system when the system issues a request to read a card. Upon noting the card reader in a turned-off state (either due to a jam or a partial power failure, or whatever), the operating system would issue a message to the operator, indicating the condition. Once the problem had been cleared, the operator would need to know what characters should be keyed into the console to indicate the back-to-normal condition.

Of course, in very simple computers, the communication is much more simple-minded. The computer issues the request to read a card and then just waits until the information is transmitted. If the card reader is jammed or turned off, then everything comes to a standstill until the problem is rectified. The difficulty with this situation is that some training is required for the operator to notice that the machine is waiting longer than usual for some operation, and then to know where to look to find out what it is waiting for, and finally how to fix it. Since the largest and fastest machines can perform millions of operations per second, their operating systems will typically be designed to note the fault, issue a message to the operator, and carry on with whatever can be done without the use of the faulty component.

Systems Programming. Systems programming deals with the writing and maintenance of programs that are part of the computer operating system. The amount of systems programming skill required in a computing center is dependent probably as much on its management philosophy as on its size (an obvious factor). Most general-purpose computers are made available by their manufacturers complete with operating systems. The earliest machines had none or only very rudimentary operating systems, whereas modern machines have very sophisticated operating systems. These operating systems (or just systems) are designed for use by a typical installation and provide parameters which can be varied to meet that installation's needs.

For example, one parameter in most operating systems is the number of files that will be maintained on permanent mass-storage media (e.g., rotating magnetic disks). This parameter is important because space must be allocated to catalog all the attributes of each file (such as its name and number of records it contains). Since these are permanent files, these names must be stored somewhere for ready access by the operating system. It will not do, for instance, to store the catalog of file names on a tape that the operator must fetch and mount every time one of these files is referred to or altered. On the contrary, this catalog (often called the *file name table*) must be kept in main memory or on a mass-storage device. The point is that some large installations with very large numbers of files will have to allocate much space to store file-name tables, whereas a small installation will not wish to tie up a lot of valuable space for only a small file-name table.

Many such installation parameters are set to help tailor the operating system to fit a variety of needs. Often, however, the operating system, even with all of its parameters set, still falls short of the installation's needs. The usual case is that it can meet most needs, but meets some critical need only marginally or with low efficiency. For example, a computing center whose purpose is to run applications that simulate nuclear reactors will typically run a few very long jobs (on the order of hours of running time each) in a day. On the other hand, a programming school might run a very large number of very small jobs (each taking only a second or two to run). Even with a well-designed operating system, its machine accounting functions (to keep track of which jobs used what amounts of computer time) are unlikely to be adequate for both installations. In such a case the installation management must decide between the costs of inadequate or inefficient operating system performance in the accounting area, and the costs of systems programming talent to modify the operating system to meet its specific needs.

This decision is not nearly as simple to make as it seems on the surface. Since the computer manufacturer provides the operating system with the computer, and since such systems are made up of very sophisticated programs (even for relatively rudimentary systems), they are almost never fully debugged. Accordingly, the manufacturer provides software support (or operating system maintenance) to fix the bugs as they crop up.

Since the manufacturer has a support group of systems programmers, this group is the target of many requests for improvements and enhancements to parts of the system that perform their published tasks properly. These requests for improvements come from the installations using the equipment and from the manufacturer's own sales organization, which recognizes that it could sell more machines if the operating system had more or better capability in certain areas. Regardless, if an installation does not make any changes in the operating system it receives from the manufacturer, it can expect a much more sympathetic hearing if the system supposedly fails to perform in some area. Just as in manufactured goods, the manufacturer feels much less compelled to support a device that has been "tampered" with (even by competent people) than for one that is still in its delivery state.

Principally for this reason, systems programming tends to be an all-or-nothing proposition. Either a shop has no systems programming talent or it has enough to become completely familiar with and substantially provide overall support for its operating systems.

The argument for no systems programming talent is that the costs of inefficiency or incapacity in some areas are less than the costs of learning about and maintaining an operating system. The opposite point of view is that if the operating system needs work that the manufacturer is not inclined to supply, then work on many marginal areas may as well be done too. This is usually the policy of the larger shops with specialized work loads not encountered by most users of the equipment. Systems programming, because of the relatively high level of sophistication of the programs, is usually staffed with the more experienced programmers. For this reason the systems programming function often serves as a consulting function to the applications programming staff, as well as performing the functions mentioned above.

Applications Programming. Applications programming is concerned with the writing and maintenance of programs that accept as input the information supplied by the users and possibly combine it with information on file to produce output for the user. In that context, applications programming is at the heart of the purpose of a computing center: making machines do what people want. As mentioned above, this service is the one most likely to be a mixture of open and closed shop. In a bank, for example, it is very likely to be a closed-shop function. The people for whom reports will be written will not be expected to have much programming proficiency. In an engineering or research department or at a university, however, frequently the users will have had computer programming training. This, combined with the nature of the reports, often results in more open-shop programming in the latter than in the former.

Frequently, the nature of the output is all-important, however, and mandates a closed-shop approach. For example, a report to be prepared for reading by many users on the basis of data submitted by many users will not usually be a good candidate for open-shop programming. Such a report should probably be programmed by some central function (such as the computing center) with the needs and interests of all users in mind. On the other hand, a program to calculate some pump-flow rates for the only piping engineer in the department would probably be a good candidate to be written under open-shop programming conditions. In that case, since the engineer would likely be the only user, the instructions on how to prepare the input data might never be formalized (i.e., documented), a frequent result in open-shop programming environments.

Sometimes, the nature of the programming itself dictates the need for an open or closed-shop applications programming approach. Simple programs usually have still simpler specifications. Often, however, very complex experimental procedures, for example, can be specified only to the extent that they can be coded into programs. In such cases, especially when the procedures are not well defined, the trained user can code the programs about as easily as it is to specify exactly what must be done. In that case, one whole step—fraught with communications problems and potential errors—can be eliminated from the programming process by using an open-shop arrangement.

Data Control, Quality Control and Scheduling. Once again, the extent of this service is determined by the extent of open-shop practices at the installation. Clearly, in a fully open-shop (programming and operating) arrangement, users will provide their own data, validate and control it themselves, schedule their use of the machine to coincide with the availability of the latest data, and check their own reports. In that case, no service of this sort needs to be offered by the computing center. On the other hand, in a fully closed shop, a great deal of data handling prior to the production run will often be required. Thereafter, if the reporting system is complex, or if many reports are routed to several destinations, staff must be provided by the computing center to handle all those chores.

For example, in an application where hours worked are accumulated and posted for a department each week, somebody has to verify that each person submitted a time card. All the time cards must be checked to see that employee numbers are correct, that legitimate charge numbers were used, and that the hours charged are reasonable. Some of this checking can be done using computer programs that compare those numbers to sets of numbers on file. But that does not verify that the correct numbers were used, only that legitimate numbers were used— numbers that are permissible to use. Some parts of the checking are best done in the department. For instance, in a department with large fluctuations in personnel,

somebody familiar with everyone present might most efficiently check that a time card was collected from each person.

Keeping track of what has been received and processed by the computing center can be done only by the computing center staff. This service may be divided into two categories: checking that the center processes all the data it receives and checking that it receives all the data sent by the using department. Obviously, it will do little good to check that every person in a department submits a time card if the computing center cannot determine if it got all the time cards. Accordingly, much of the checking about amounts of data is handled by both the user and by the computing center. Then, before a production run is made, either on a special or periodic schedule, the user and computing center reconcile their separate control records to be sure there is agreement. Frequently, for example, in an application such as the time-card system, both the center and the user keep a written record with batch numbers, numbers of time cards, and total hours in each batch. The user counts the cards and totals the hours manually before sending the time cards to the computing center for processing. Upon receipt of the cards, the computing center punches the information into tab cards or some other machine-readable form. Such recording equipment sometimes accumulates card counts and total hours as the data is recorded. More commonly, a special computer program is used to read each batch of time cards, count the number of entries, total the hours, and verify that legitimate numbers are used, etc. Inspection of the counts and totals verifies (or contradicts) the manual counts and totals sent by the user. Once these are reconciled, the production run can be made.

Concern that all the information received is properly processed lies exclusively with the computing center. Typically, when each batch is added to the master file, a report is generated to display the total number of entries and total number of hours (using again the preceding example) on file at the start of the run, added as a result of the run, and on file at the end of the run. In addition to file-labeling and checking by the programs, a manual record is frequently kept to show counts and totals before and after every run made to add time cards to the file. In that way, in the case of reruns, when file-label checking sometimes needs to be bypassed, files can still be checked for completeness. Curiously, one of the biggest headaches in the data control area is not in making sure that all data has been added to the file, but that it has not been added more than once. This occurs most frequently when a file is updated with bad information, requiring a rerun.

Since the references in all the programs are to the latest file when one is updated, care must be taken in the case of a rerun to update the second-from-latest file. Further care must be taken to destroy the former latest file so it will not be confused with the one produced by the rerun. Every installation manager has aged visibly when, while walking through the machine room in such a situation involving novice operators, two files are seen, both labeled "latest." For these reasons, several generations of files are kept on hand at all times: the latest, the one before that (from which the latest was made), the one before that, and so on. Typically, four such copies are kept as backup to the latest file, but fewer are kept in applications not prone to error, and more are kept (up to six or eight) on applications subject to high error rates or many updates in a short time period. The shorter the period, the more backups are required. For example, three update runs, all in the same shift, all performed by the same operator may be handled incorrectly. If all the backups were created using the same bad technique, the file would be in danger of being wiped out (destroyed or rendered useless for purposes of making an update run).

Notice that each time a file is brought up to date (or *updated*), an entirely new copy of the file is made, to which the new information has been added. At the end of such an update run, the old file is intact, exactly as it was prior to the run, and the new copy contains everything from the preceding file plus all the new material. On the surface, this may seem extravagant, especially when compared to manual file maintenance. Imagine the cost to copy an entire file of letters everytime a new one was added to the file! But it would certainly insure that there would be adequate copies of the correspondence.

In computing, the cost of updating is nearly negligible by contrast. If the file is kept on tape, for example, a new copy can be made as each record is read, in substantially the same time as that required to simply read the file. Since there are always at least two tape drives available, the updated tape can contain a copy of the preceding generation of the file at substantially zero cost. This technique insures against operator, equipment, and program failure, since it allows for reproducibility of any update run. All that is needed to re-create any edition (or generation) of the file is the previous edition and the new material that was added. Contrast that with the case where the new edition is created by reading the old edition up to the end and then adding the new material to the end of the old file, thus making it the new one. Such a practice is not reproducible because the "end" of the old information is no longer identifiable. Accepted practice is to keep enough previous generations of files on hand so that any operator, equipment, or program error can be detected and corrected (by running the reproducible run that re-creates the faulty generation), all before either the backup or current information is discarded.

Occasionally, of course, errors are not detected in time, especially programming errors that introduce subtle errors into the files at each update. In such cases, files need to be regenerated from scratch. For this reason, current data is often stored for very long periods of times. Such a practice is called *archiving*, wherein either the cards themselves, microfilm images, or separate files on magnetic tape are stored in case it is necessary to go back to a version of the file beyond the usual backup period. To reduce the incidence of having to regenerate a file from scratch, sometimes year-end or quarter-end copies are stored separate from the usual backups. In addition, hard-copy reports are sometimes used as a starting point in the case where all file information is destroyed. At any rate, even though the data control function is supposed to keep these problems from occurring in the first place, it must be aware of how best to detect and recoup any foulups well before the last good copy of the file is retired.

Kinds of Computing Centers. Computing centers provide service to a variety of constituents, using a variety of equipment and personnel configurations. We have already seen that the degree to which open-shop practice is allowed determines to a large extent the amount and kinds of services supplied by a center. The character of the workload also determines what levels of which services must be provided, but to a relatively smaller extent than the degree of open-shop practice. Some workloads lend themselves much more easily to a high degree of open shop than do others. Principally, computing workload (and hence the installations that cater to them) can be classified into two categories: batch (including remote job entry) and time sharing. Historically, the first general-purpose computers were batch machines. In that kind of computing, jobs are processed in serial fashion, one after the other. Each job has exclusive use of the computer and all its peripheral devices (card reader, punch, magnetic-tape drives, disk drives, etc.) during the time it is being executed.

Until the mid-1960s, batch was by far the most common arrangement. But even the most casual observer will note that a batch arrangement makes very inefficient use of some resources most of the time. Consider, for example, the small job consisting of a program and some data on cards that produces a report on the printer, which is simply an exact listing of the information on the cards. Such a program is called a *card-to-print program,* and if it is generalized to provide headings and optional spacing and other information, it is called a *card-to-print utility.* At any rate, such a program does not use either tape or disk storage equipment. If the listing is short, of course, storage is not of much consequence, but if the listing is long, the tape and disk equipment are wasted for a long period of time. Similarly, the main memory of most machines is much larger and much faster than required for a card-to-print application, and presumably the arithmetic unit would be used only for counting line spacing, for page numbering, etc. Therefore, as faster computers were installed, ways had to be found to improve the efficiency of the computer use.

One fairly early solution was tape-oriented batch systems with two computers: The main computer and a smaller machine. All tape drives in such a system are wired to the main computer. At least one, and sometimes two, of them are also switchable to the smaller machine, to which the card reader, punch, and printer are also attached. Input jobs are loaded onto tape by the smaller machine from cards. The tape is then rewound and switched to the main computer, which is programmed to read that tape for all card input. Another tape drive is used by the main machine to write out all output destined for the printer and the card punch. After a batch of jobs has been run, that output tape is rewound and switched to the smaller machine to be read and listed and/or punched. Using this technique, processing times on the main computer are speeded up, because tape can be read faster than cards, but additional time is required to load a batch of jobs to tape. Of course, the first job cannot be started until the last job is loaded and the tape rewound and switched to the main computer.

This apparent paradox of a reduction in service (i.e., longer turnaround) with faster processing led to a search for a solution that allowed the latter without the penalty of the former. A number of schemes were developed, including the use of common disk files and two computers hooked together so that one could stoke the other's memory directly (called variously *direct-coupled systems* and *attached support processors*). These methods preserved the batch nature of a main machine and improved both efficiency and turnaround by providing faster transfer of information in and out of the main computer and by reducing the waiting time of information in the input and output streams. But the main computer efficiency was still low, and turnaround far from the instantaneous ideal. With a great deal of oversimplification, what was needed was a main computer that had a large enough memory to hold several jobs, and enough random access mass storage to hold files for all those jobs being processed, including one holding card input and printer output for each job.

Some overhead in switching from job to job is required, of course, and the operating system must be much more sophisticated if it is to keep track of what portions of memory are in use and by what jobs (especially since jobs are finishing and new ones starting all the time), and what files are in use in what positions and by what jobs. This arrangement might be referred to as a sort of si-

Fig. 1.   Computer room at Computer Center, State University of New York at Buffalo, showing parts of Control Data 6400 computer used for education and research computing, and also the Univac 1106 computer used for administrative data processing.

multaneous batch, but it is called *multiprogramming* (more than one program in execution at once), in fact. Although computer efficiency is greatly improved, turn-around is still far from instantaneous. Since there are only a few card readers and printers on such systems, and since it is desirable to have input and output on disk or tape whenever possible (so it can be read and written faster), a job cannot be a candidate to start until all of it is on disk, nor can its output be started on the printer until all of it has been written out to the output file (called the *output queue*). If there were many I/O devices, one could be associated with each job. Then the execution of that job could be carried out piecemeal as the input was available and as any output could be printed.

As noted above, the term *multiprogramming* originated to describe the situation in which the central memory is shared by many applications at the same time, with the central processor alternating attention among them. Thus, with careful scheduling, several applications are perceived as receiving attention from the central processor simultaneously. When two or more of the applications being given simultaneous attention are in communication with (usually remote) users at teletype-like or simple graphical display terminals, we say that the system is providing *time sharing*. Some early time-sharing applications followed the usual sequence previously employed in batch processing applications; namely, the reading of all the input, followed by the checking of the input, followed by the processing, and finally the preparation of reports. This sequence lent itself conveniently to the preparation of exhaustive error reports, for example, which allowed the user to correct all of the errors in the data at once. A more convenient arrangement quickly emerged, however, in which each line of input is accepted, checked for errors and sometimes partially processed, with error messages and preliminary output reported as soon as all of the necessary components are available. Using this arrangement, the user receives error messages following the input of the line in which the error occurs. The error may be in syntax (such as a spelling error or misplaced decimal point); or it may be an error in logic (such as the use of a number which results in an attempted division by zero).The former is referred to as line-by-line syntax checking; and the latter is referred to as *partial compilation*. In either of these arrangements, the user is said to be "interacting" with the computer (i.e., the computer is examining each line of data, testing, or doing some calculations using the input, and often providing a response); hence, this arrangement is referred to as *interactive* or *conversational* computing.

When batch jobs are submitted and reports are prepared on equipment which is located some distance from the computer, and connected to it via telephone lines, the arrangement is referred to as *remote batch*. When the program and/or the data for a job are stored locally to the computer, but the job is initiated from a terminal which is located remotely from the computer, the arrangement is referred to as *remote job entry*. In both of these cases, the equipment at the remote location usually has no processing capability, but only transmits information to the computer and receives information back. This remote equipment is referred to as *unintelligent* or, more commonly, *dumb*.

In other remote computing networks, the equipment which is located remotely from the computer also has some, perhaps quite substantial processing capability. This remote equipment is referred to as *intelligent* or *smart;* and, in some cases, the power of the remote devices rivals the power of the central or host computer. In these applications, some error checking, for example, or response to the user, can be undertaken by the processor at the remote location, and information which has been partially processed or summarized can then be transmitted to the central computer.

Since there is processing capability both at the remote locations and at the central location, this arrangement is referred to as *distributed processing (q.v.)*. With the advent of moderate- and low-priced, limited-processing computers, distributed processing systems will very likely become the dominant processing arrangement of the 1980s.

Kinds of Computing Center Applications. Early in the history of computing, and until about the mid-1960s, computers tended to be more specialized in the kinds of applications they could handle. Some of those machines were designed and built to meet the needs of commercial and industrial accounting and record keeping. These applications require fast, reliable input-output devices of large capacity but with relatively small main memory and unsophisticated arithmetic capability. Records are usually processed sequentially one at a time, as when writing paychecks for one person after another. In contrast, for engineering and scientific problem solving, machines were developed with an emphasis on their arithmetic units rather than on their input-output devices. In fact, since most scientific problems used relatively small amounts of data and produced limited amounts of output—but required extensive main memory space to store both the relatively large number of programmed instructions and all the intermediate numbers in the calculation—such machines were normally equipped with the slower (and therefore less expensive) input-output devices.

Until the mid-1960s, the two kinds of machines were much more distinct than today's machines. *Scientific machines* were characterized by slow peripheral equipment, large memories, and sophisticated arithmetic instruction sets. Their arithmetic instructions often included floating-point instructions, a feature almost never required in accounting and record keeping because answers need be computed only to the nearest cent. *Commercial machines,* on the other hand, were characterized by relatively limited arithmetic power, character rather than word addressability and substantial I/O capability.

Accordingly, computing centers tended to be divided along the same lines. Programming and operating staff who understood the need of commercial users for fast reliable access to large files of information were required for the commercial or data processing centers; and technically trained programming staff who could converse with and understand the requirements of engineers and scientists were required for the scientific and university centers. In recent years, however, an increasing need by scientists and engineers for exceptional amounts of very high speed calculations has coincided with the expansion by the commercial users into much more sophisticated record keeping (involving a greater need for better arithmetic performance) and an increasing requirement by the engineers and scientists in their applications for large amounts of data, particularly input data. Thus, the distinction between what was known as scientific computing and administrative data processing has become blurred. The result is that the machines of today need many fast, reliable peripheral devices with plenty of mass storage and main computers with large memory capacity and sophisticated instruction sets.

Floating-point instructions are available as an option on almost all machines, memory can be added in incremental banks of several thousand words, and peripheral devices with a wide range of speeds and capacities can be attached. Accordingly, computing centers are becoming more diversified, although many of the specialty shops still exist, especially for the commercial users. In a large firm, for example, where an early machine installed for record keeping in the early 1960s was found to be inadequate to meet the increasing computing needs of the engineering and research departments after about the mid-1960s, it was likely to be replaced with a machine suitable for both kinds of applications. Thus, new equipment can be configured to meet present and anticipated needs, through modular design and flexible financing, and configurations can be kept constantly in flux, changing to meet current needs. With this increasing flexibility in the equipment, many computing centers are also amply staffed to meet the needs of their users.

Physical Characteristics. Depending on the amounts and kinds of services provided, a typical computing center consists of a computer room (or machine room), a data preparation/dispatching area, a file-storage area, and offices for the personnel arranged in some logical manner. The machine room is about a third of the space (with wide variations between installations), and usually has a raised (or false) floor. This floor, usually tiled with 2 by 2 ft panels, rests on 8–14 inch pedestals above the main slab. Air conditioning and heating ducts force air under these panels, and power and control cables are also housed there. The (usually) cooled air and the cables come up through holes cut in the panels, often under the equipment modules, thus allowing each module to stand free of encumbrance by cabling or ductwork. In large systems, chilled-water piping is also housed under the panels and is hooked to the equipment through similar holes in the panels.

The machine room is usually heated and cooled, using equipment that is separated from all other areas of the center. This is done primarily because of the control nightmare that is generated by heat produced by the equipment, and also as a fire safety measure. Even in moderately cold climates, more heat is produced by the equipment in a computer room than is needed to keep the room at a comfortable temperature. Humidity also must be regulated much more rigidly for reliable operation of the machine than is required for human comfort. Usually, the absolute values of temperature and humidity are not nearly as important to regulate as are their fluctuations from one side of the machine to the other. Once set in the human comfort zone, tolerances are relatively narrow, and are typically narrower for larger machines than for smaller ones. As computers are made faster and their components become smaller, the heat-dissipation problem stays about the same. The faster equipment requires narrower tolerances because of the increasing importance of timing electronic speeds in conductors at certain temperatures; the smaller components produce less heat and require shorter wires to connect them, but this does not mitigate the problem.

The data preparation/dispatching area varies from a front counter in the input-output clerk's office, in a small installation, to several rooms in a large organization for input preparation of data, keypunching, file checking and scheduling of input; and for rows, bins, and counters for dispatching output, checking updated files, and preparing the files for storage. The file-storage area is usually separated from the machine room, for security and fire protection, but is close to the equipment with which it is used (tape storage near the tape drives; disk-pack storage near disk drives, etc.).

Pricing. Pricing of computing services in the early days of computing was a relatively easy task. Each job required exclusive use of the entire main processor and all peripheral equipment for a certain length of time. Virtually every job ran in exactly the same length of time if rerun with the same data. Managers simply divided total costs plus margin for a period by the number of production hours they could expect to run the machine during that period. This calculation produced a rate in dollars per hour of running time, one that appeared fair to the user because it was reproducible; running time could be controlled by varying the amount of data submitted and by specifying (or writing) programs that were more or less efficient in processing those amounts of data. Program and system development could also be fairly easily priced in dollars per person-hour for various levels of talent. Until the advent of time sharing and multiprogramming, pricing was one aspect of computing that was a fairly conventional procedure. Many other types of services were subject to the same pricing criteria. For example, printing is much like computing in that regard. Users can control the price of work by controlling the quality of paper used, the number of copies to be made, and by using or avoiding special ink colors, etc., but they cannot control the speed or width of the printing press. If a press runs at 100 copies per minute and is 10 inches wide, one may not expect a reduction in price for copy which is only 8½ inches wide.

When time sharing and multiprogramming became available, however, the user could expect that any memory not needed by the program might reasonably be sold to another customer. Hence, pricing in many centers has been subject to a great deal of controversy. The problem in multiprogramming arrangements is complicated by the fact that many measures of usage are not reproducible. For example, if a job writes a disk file, in some multiprogrammed systems the file may be written in either a large number of small blocks or a smaller number of large blocks, depending on how busy the system is (how much space is available for accumulation of large blocks, and how busy the disk storage device is). Therefore, as a result of the variability in the size of blocks that are accumulated before writing, the job can use a variable amount of computing time between writing each block. This, in turn, determines the amount of time the job spends taking up memory. The job may run in, say, 1 minute on an otherwise empty machine, and use 3 seconds of processor time during that minute (the rest being taken up by the writing out of the information on the disk file).

In a busy machine two effects are noticeable: There is less space for large blocks, so more time is spent writing a larger number of the smaller blocks; and the processor does not switch back to a particular job with any predictable regularity, since there is virtually no way to control whatever other jobs are running concurrently. The effect of both is to extend the amount of time that the job spends in main memory to perhaps 5 or 10 minutes. It still requires the same 3 seconds of processor time (because it still does exactly the steps it did before), but now

they are spread over, say, 5 minutes. That is five times as long as it would take on an otherwise idle machine. In the case of pricing based on usage, this job should cost more when run on a busy machine (because it ties up memory and disk-file space longer, requires more overhead to write more blocks, and uses more overhead because it uses the processor more often, due to the reduced block sizes). In the case of pricing based on service, this job should cost less because the turnaround time is worse.

Computing centers that are service centers (as opposed to profit centers) price their services on the basis of either service or cost. Few of the special arguments that apply to computing are not applicable to many other services within a corporate, university, or government environment. There is a paradoxical apparent simplicity but persistent overruns (with even the most competent staff) require extra attention, no matter what the pricing scheme, to insure that the processing that can be handled most profitably by the computer is what is processed. For example, if the service center that is newly installed must recover all costs from services rendered, it would have a high rate and an underutilized system. The well-heeled departments could use its services, but those not so well off (and who might be able to use the machine more profitably) could not afford the rates. The computer would be standing idle part of the time, and departments (which could use it to produce considerably more return than the incremental cost to have it running) would be doing without it. On the other hand, a computing center whose costs are fully absorbed into overhead, will be processing the unpopular chores for user departments (not necessarily the profitable ones). Since the users cannot control the costs of computing, they might as well have the computing center do whatever work the using department would like to farm out. As in any service, either pricing method has its drawbacks. The problem is further complicated by the difficulty in allocating costs in multiprogrammed and time-sharing systems. The services are a little easier to identify, but much harder to price. All things considered, computing center pricing presents about the same problem as that of any centralized service.

C. L. MEEK

CONCATENATION

For article on related subject *see* STRING PROCESSING LANGUAGES.

Concatenation (or, sometimes, *catenation*) is an operation wherein a number of conceptually related components are linked together to form a larger, organizationally similar entity.

In the context of string processing, concatenation refers specifically to the synthesis of longer character strings from shorter ones. In PL/I, for example, the string concatenation operation is indicated by a double vertical bar ($\|$) so that if W1 = 'CON', W2 = 'CAT', W3 = 'ION', then W4 = W1 $\|$ W2 $\|$ 'ENAT' $\|$ W3 is the title of this article. This kind of notation is generally used in high-level languages.

Though still within the same general context of string construction, concatenation also is used to refer to a specific technique in defining macroinstructions, where a particular type of symbol may be a character string consisting of fixed and variable segments. When such a macroinstruction is used in a program, an appropriate string constant, given in the specifications, is concatenated with the fixed portion of the symbol during the macroexpansion process to form a complete syntactic component.

Within the general framework of files and file processing, concatenation refers to the operation of creating a collection of data by linking together several smaller collections. The resulting concatenated data set then can be processed as a single collection without relinquishing the individual identities of its components.

S. V. POLLACK AND T. E. STERLING

CONCURRENT PROGRAMMING

For articles on related subjects *see* COROUTINE; LOCKOUT; MONITORS; PARALLEL PROCESSING; PETRI NETS; and SEMAPHORE.

Concurrent programming refers to the development of programs that specify the parallel execution of several tasks. Such programs are used in systems with multiple hardware processors that may be executing simultaneously; examples include multiprocessing systems, computer networks, and computer configurations with separate I/O processors. Concurrent programming is also convenient on single processors for applications where logical parallelism exists, such as in multi-user operating systems and some simulations. Many operating systems and database systems are written as concurrent programs that may run on and control several hardware processors and are composed of both physically and logically parallel sub-parts. Because of the availability of low-cost microprocessors and the continued development of distributed computing applications, it is expected that much future software will be written for large collections of connected processors, placing greater demands on techniques and tools for concurrent programming.

In order to program for real or logical parallelism,

there must be some means to *create* and *destroy* (i.e., establish and terminate) processes and a way for these processes to *communicate* and *synchronize* with one another. A number of systems and languages have provided such concurrent programming facilities. One operating system that explicitly offers such mechanisms is the UNIX (*q.v.*) system on the DEC PDP-11 and DEC VAX computers. Concurrent Pascal and Modula, which both run on the DEC PDP-11, the Mesa language developed at Xerox, and the Ada (*q.v.*) language designed for the U. S. Department of Defense, are examples of modern programming languages that contain constructs for parallel programming.

FORK and JOIN statements are one set that may be used for dynamically creating and destroying processes. A more static facility for specifying concurrency is the **cobegin/coend** construct. This has the form:

cobegin $S_1 // S_2 // \ldots // S_n$ **coend**

Indicating that the (possibly compound) statements S_1, $S_2, \ldots,$ and S_n may execute in parallel.

Synchronization mechanisms include machine language instructions such as TEST AND SET, which *indivisibly* performs the following sequence of operations: *tests* a storage cell for a 0 or a 1, stores the result of the test in a register, and *sets* the cell to 1; TEST AND SET is convenient for implementing locks or such low level synchronization primitives as the Dijkstra P and V operations on semaphores. At a higher level is the *monitor*. This facility is used to specify a shared data structure representing a resource and to define the procedures for acquiring, releasing, and accessing the resource; monitors permit the encapsulation and scheduling of resource objects that are usable by several processes.

Another common method for achieving synchronization is through message sending primitives. Simple examples are *send(p,m)*, which causes the transmission of message m to process p, and *receive (p,m)*, which waits for a message from process p, inserting the message into m. Since it does not rely on communication through shared variables in a common memory, message passing is useful for distributed computations where tasks are connected by communications lines.

The Ada language, which is still being refined and tested, has communications and synchronization statements that combine aspects of both procedure calls and message sending. Communication between two processes normally proceeds as follows.

One process calls the other with a *task entry call* containing input and output parameters, while the called process issues an **accept** statement that waits for such a call; the **accept** also includes an arbitrary sequence of statements that are executed as part of the *rendezvous* that occurs when the task entry call is accepted. After this interaction, both the caller and callee processes may again execute in parallel. Ada also provides a selective wait statement in which there is nondeterministic selection among those of a set of **accept** statements which are "open" (i.e., where a rendezvous is possible if a corresponding task entry call is issued).

As one example of concurrent programming, we present a solution to a common buffering problem. Suppose we wish to program a two-process system where one process, the producer, adds records to a storage area, while another process, the consumer, removes them. The producer might be a process associated with an input device, which is adding input records to a storage buffer, while the consumer is responsible for retrieving the records and processing them; alternatively, the producer may be producing output records for a consumer associated with an output device.

The common buffer area has storage for N records $(N \geq 1)$. The main problem is to synchronize the buffer manipulation so that:

1. The producer can only add a record to the buffer if there is space for it, and the consumer can only remove a record if one exists.
2. Only one process at a time can be manipulating the buffer area.

We assume that the producer and consumer are both cyclic processes that loop "forever." Using semaphores and **cobegin/coend,** the program outline is as follows.

```
semaphore empty(N),    {number of empty slots
                        in buffer, initially N}
         full(0),      {number of full records in
                        buffer, initially 0}
         lock(1);      {to ensure mutual exclusion
                        during buffer manipulation}
cobegin
  producer:
    loop
    begin  ProduceNextRecord;
           P(empty);   {proceed only if an empty
                        slot is available in buffer}
           P(lock);    {set lock to 0, preventing
                        buffer access by consumer}
           AddRecordToBuffer;
           V(lock);    {set lock to 1, enabling
                        access by either producer
                        or consumer}
           V(full)     {increase count of
                        full records in buffer]
    end
  consumer:
    loop
    begin  P(full);    {proceed only if a full
                        record is in buffer}
           P(lock);    {lock buffer for producer}
           TakeRecordFromBuffer;
           V(lock);    {unlock buffer}
           V(empty);   {increase count of
                        available slots in buffer}
           ProcessRecord
    end
coend
```

REFERENCES

1974. Shaw, A. *The Logical Design of Operating Systems.* Englewood Cliffs, NJ: Prentice-Hall.
1977. Brinch Hansen, P. *The Architecture of Concurrent Programs.* Englewood Cliffs, NJ: Prentice-Hall.
1978. Holt, R. C., Graham, G. S., Lazowska, E. D., and M. A. Scott. *Structured Concurrent Programming With Operating Systems Applications.* Reading, MA: Addison-Wesley.

A. C. SHAW

CONDITIONING

For article on related subject *see* DATA COMMUNICATIONS: General Principles.

Conditioning is the term used to describe the improvements made in the signaling characteristics of leased telephone lines over those in the normal switched telephone network.

When a telephone connection is leased between two points, restrictions on the frequencies that can be transmitted over the switched network because of attenuation and related problems no longer apply. Since a leased line uses the *same path* continually, it is possible to put in special *equalizing filters* to insure that its attenuations and related parameters have much squarer wave characteristics than can be guaranteed on switched connections. It is this equalization that is called *conditioning*. Standards are published of the characteristics the telephone company guarantees for lines to various degrees of conditioning (for which there is an extra charge). In such leased lines, it is also usual to have two pairs of connections to the nearest exchange (a so-called four-wire line) so that the full bandwidth can be used simultaneously in the two directions. Over the interexchange links, the conversations always go on different channels, but between the local exchange and the subscriber, the two directions of conversation share a normal switched telephone line.

Although the conditioning of a leased telephone line

will considerably improve its characteristics, there will be time variations in the characteristics of the line. For this reason, the modems in high-performance data transmission systems will themselves add a further (variable) amount to equalization by use of adaptive digital filters. These enable (currently) switched telephone lines to be used at up to 4.8K bits per second (bps) and leased telephone lines at up to 19.2K bps. When higher speeds of data transmission are desired, it is possible to put in special lines that connect straight to the primary group in the telephone exchange and use 12 or more telephone channels. By these means, 48 KHz or even wider bandwidth can be used with appropriately high data rates of 50 Kbps or even higher.

P. T. KIRSTEIN

CONFERENCE ON DATA SYSTEMS LANGUAGES. *See* CODASYL.

CONSTANTS

For articles on related subjects *see* ARITHMETIC, COMPUTER; EXPRESSION; IDENTIFIER; LABEL; NUMBERS AND NUMBER SYSTEMS; PROCEDURE-ORIENTED LANGUAGES; PROGRAMMING LANGUAGES; and STATEMENT.

In computing, a *constant* is a value which remains unchanged during a calculation. There are a variety of different types of constants discussed in this article—numerical, character, logical, location, and figurative constants. While it is fundamental to many aspects of a computer's internal operation that the basic reference to an item of information is by its location or address, it is more convenient to refer to constants by their values, since these are intrinsically meaningful in an algorithm. Consequently, all high-level languages and their translators are structured to allow the inclusion of actual values, specified directly in the program rather than being read by the program as data or produced by explicit computations. Whatever mechanisms may be required to reconcile these syntactic facilities with the processor's basic address orientation are embedded in the language translator, beyond the operating range of most users and therefore "invisible" to them.

The spectrum of items that may be expressed as direct literal values transcends the numerical quantities traditionally associated with the idea of a "constant." Depending on the scope and orientation of a particular language, a variety of nonnumeric constants also are rec-

ognized and handled. Some of these serve as data items, while others may provide operational information for the program.

Numerical Constants. In most instances the user need give little thought to the inclusion of numerical constants in high-level language statements. For many languages, their specification closely resembles conventional mathematical notation, with the compiler taking care of any necessary conversion to internal representation. Thus, the constants in the familiar distance formula

$$S = v_0 t + 0.5 a t^2$$

require no special form for specification in equivalent high-level language statements:

(Fortran) S = VO•T + 0.5•A•T••2

(Pascal) S := VO•T + 0.5•A•T•T;

(PL/I) S = VO•T + 0.5•A•T••2;

(Cobol) COMPUTE S = VO•T + 0.5•A•T••2.

A number of languages recognize an alternative representation for numerical constants. This form, similar to scientific notation, is particularly useful for expressing very large or very small values. Instead of writing long strings of zeros to establish a number's order of magnitude, the same value may be designated more concisely by showing only the significant digits in some convenient form, supplemented by an appropriate exponent value to adjust the scale. For instance, in languages like Basic, Fortran, and PL/I, the constant 0.00000513 can be expressed alternatively as 5.13E−06, 0.513E−5, or even 51.3E−7.

PL/I accepts numeric constants specified in binary form. The use of a B immediately after the rightmost digit of a string of 1's and 0's identifies that constant as being to the base 2. Thus, the constant in the assignment statement N = 11010.011B represents the binary value 11010.011_2 (whose decimal equivalent is 26.375).

In certain areas of application, the manipulation of complex numbers plays such an important role that several languages include directly appropriate computational capabilities. Accordingly, there are provisions for defining complex variables and specifying complex numerical constants. Strictly speaking, there is no specific form reserved for complex constants per se. Rather, those languages accepting such data deal with complex numbers as combinations of real and imaginary components. In Fortran, for example, the statement COMPLEX A, B defines variable names A and B as being associated with complex numbers and instigates appropriate storage allocation. Now, supposing one wished to assign a value of $2.7 + 3.6i$ to A. The required statement would have the form A = (2.7,3.6), thereby causing the compiler to treat the two arguments as the real and imaginary components, respectively, of complex variable A. Along the same lines, then, the statement B = 4.4 * A — (1.0,−0.8) would produce the calculations $4.4(2.7 + 3.6i) − (1 − 0.8i)$, with the final result (equivalent to $10.88 − 16.64i$) being placed in B. PL/I uses the specific form bI for imaginary constants (where b denotes an integer or real constant), so that the equivalent statements would be written as follows:

```
DECLARE (A, B) COMPLEX;
A = 2.7 + 3.6I;
B = 4.4*A − (1 − 0.8I);
```

Character String Constants. Growing insight into computers' capabilities, coupled with developing human ability to identify and describe a widening variety of "computable" algorithms, have produced numerous important applications involving the processing of non-numeric data. In response, special string-handling languages have been developed and more general high-level languages have been equipped with facilities to synthesize and decompose character strings, search them in response to arbitrarily complex criteria, and perform a variety of other manipulations. An elemental aspect of these facilities is the recognition of constant values consisting of arbitrary combinations of letters, digits, and other symbols completely analogous to the treatment of numerical constants.

The syntactic approach generally followed in many languages is to bracket a character string constant by special delimiters, thereby identifying that string as a data item and distinguishing it from other strings whose usage is fundamentally different (e.g., names of variables). For example, the PL/I statement DECLARE ESTRING CHARACTER (7); defines a variable named ESTRING, associating that name with a string capable of accommodating seven characters. Then, the assignment statement ESTRING = 'EEEEEEE'; fills the seven places with EEEEEEE (an E string if I ever saw one!). Note that the apostrophes are not part of the actual character string; they serve merely to define its extent. Distinction of an apostrophe that is an intrinsic part of a character string constant from one serving as a delimiter is handled by specifying a double apostrophe for each one to be shown. Thus, a constant consisting of the five characters CAN'T is indicated as 'CAN''T'. The languages Cobol, Snobol, and some dialects of Fortran and Algol also use the apostrophe as a character string delimiter, while other Algol implementations recognize strings bracketed by '(' and ')'.

Logical Constants. The construction and representation of decision mechanisms in high-level languages often are facilitated by the availability of vehicles for specifying logical conditions, i.e., expressions describing situations whose outcome is either "true" or "false." A number of languages offer such facilities in terms of logical variables supported by operations that allow the synthesis of arbitrarily complex boolean combinations. When embedded in a program, these expressions can form the basis for dynamically selecting one of two alternative actions. Accordingly, such variables are inherently bistable, limited by definition to one of two possible values. Hence, the standard repertoire of logical constants is similarly restricted.

Logical variables are accommodated in Fortran and Algol (where they are known as boolean variables). Both languages recognize the literal strings TRUE and FALSE as part of their respective vocabularies. Thus, in each of the examples listed here, the names V1 and V2 are declared to be associated with true-or-false types of variables. (Some versions of Fortran recognize the symbols .T. and .F.) Once this association has been defined, the assignment of one or the other alternative logical constant is straightforward. Conversion to the corresponding internal form used by the particular compiler is automatic so that evaluation of the expression proceeds without further intervention by the programmer.

Fortran	*Algol*
LOGICAL V1,V2	**boolean** V1,V2;
V1 = .TRUE.	V1 := **true**;

PL/I's analogous facility is part of a more general structure for handling multiplicities of such variables, each of which independently may assume a value of "true" or "false." Such variables, which may be of arbitrary length, are called *bit strings*. In this context a logical variable is a string having a length of one bit and the two logical constants have the forms '1'B and '0'B representing true and false, respectively. Then, the PL/I equivalent of the statements shown above for Fortran and Algol would be

```
DECLARE (V1,V2) BIT(1);
V1 = '1'B;.
```

Location Constants. When working in a high-level language, the programmer relinquishes direct knowledge and control of the storage locations from which the program is executed. Moreover, there is no reason to expect that those locations will be invariant from one run to the next. Yet, there are countless occasions requiring explicit references to specific statements, so that some vehicle must be provided through the language to give the programmer the opportunity to obtain unerring access to any part of the program. This is done by allowing a distinctive *label* to be attached to a statement, thereby establishing an identity that is fixed within the context of the program and is impervious to its eventual location in storage. In this sense, such labels are constants and references to them are direct. Fortran and Basic, for example, allow the use of labels that resemble numerical constants but which are distinguishable by their contextual position. Thus, the assignment statement

    22   X = 25.4 * Y ** 2

is equipped with the *label constant* 22 so that, at some other point in the procedure, one could write GO TO 22, thereby specifying a fixed directive to continue the processing from a particular point. Other languages differ with regard to the allowable construction of labels, but their use as constants still persists.

Extension of this idea of a location constant is seen in languages like PL/I and Algol, where label constants are constructed from alphanumeric characters, as are variable names. These languages allow components that act as location variables in that they may assume different "values" at various points during the execution of a program. For instance, the PL/I statement DECLARE PLACE LABEL; establishes a variable named PLACE whose "value" at any given time designates a particular statement in the program. This value is defined, conventionally, by an ordinary assignment statement. Thus, PLACE = THERE; defines a specific spot in the program, represented by the location constant THERE. Then, a reference to PLACE, e.g., GO TO PLACE; implies a reference to the statement with label THERE. Later on, it is possible to set PLACE to a different location constant, with the result that the same reference to PLACE now will lead to some other particular point in the program.

Figurative Constants. There are special types of constants that represent fixed and unambiguous values but which are unlike the other types discussed heretofore in that they are not designated by their literal values. Because their usage is particularly common, these fixed quantities are indicated by permanent parts of the language vocabulary. Such constants, known as *figurative constants,* are provided as conveniences to enhance the "naturalness" of high-level language statements. Cobol includes several such constants. For instance, a given variable may be set to a value of zero by any of the following statements,

MOVE ZERO TO X.
MOVE ZEROS TO X.
MOVE ZEROES TO X.

in which ZERO, ZEROS, and ZEROES are figurative constants. Similarly, the character string B may be filled with blanks by either of the Cobol statements MOVE BLANKS TO B. and MOVE SPACES TO B.

The convenience of figurative constants is recognized in several high-level languages containing generalized facilities for defining and using such values. In Fortran 77, for instance, the PARAMETER statement establishes an association between a programmer-defined name and a particular data value. To illustrate, the statement

PARAMETER (PI = 3.14159)

enables the programmer to use the name PI throughout the program containing the parameter statement, and the compiler will use the appropriate value. The Pascal language provides the same type of facility in the form of the *const* declaration, so that PI is defined by the statement

const PI = 3.14159.

The Snobol language has another type of figurative constant to provide apparent visibility for nothing. This constant, NULL, refers to the absence of any numbers, letters, or any other items. For example, a character string named Y can be emptied (depleted and, in an operational sense, reduced to a length of zero characters) by the statement Y = NULL. An alternative form to accomplish the same thing, namely Y =, is not much more mysterious in the overall context of the language. However, there are many more complex situations in which the explicit appearance of something for nothing is very helpful in clarifying the nature and intent of intricate string-processing constructions.

Arbitrary Constants. The figurative constants discussed in the previous section all operate under a common restriction: While the constants' symbolic names may be arbitrary, the values associated with them must conform to the predefined data types provided by the particular language. Pascal, however, provides an additional facility. Its fundamental concern with data structures is reflected in facilities which enable the programmer to define an arbitrary ("programmer-defined") data type and an associated spectrum of "allowable" values. For example, the declarations

type peach = (cling, stark, elberta, redhaven, mushchik);

const favorite = mushchik;
var dessert: peach;

define a data type named PEACH and equip it with the five assignable values shown in the parentheses. A symbolic constant FAVORITE is then defined and given the data value MUSHCHIK. Declaration of DESSERT, then, establishes that variable as being of the type PEACH, thereby enabling it to take on one of the five legitimate values associated with that data type. Accordingly, the symbolic constant can be used as expected. For example,

if dessert = favorite **then** (etc.).

Since the data type is defined arbitrarily, there is no explicit indication as to how the constant value is represented internally. Rather, the primary concern is to provide the programmer with a convenient way to use data values that are consistent and meaningful within the context of that particular program.

REFERENCES

1969. Sammet, J. *Programming Languages: History and Fundamentals*. Englewood Cliffs, NJ: Prentice-Hall (see especially Section III.4).
1974. Jensen, K. and Wirth, N. *Pascal User Manual and Report*. Berlin: Springer-Verlag.

S. V. POLLACK

CONTENTION

For articles on related subjects *see* COMMUNICATIONS AND COMPUTERS; LOCKOUT; MULTIPROCESSING; and MULTIPROGRAMMING.

Originally, the term *contention* was used to describe a communication system where the terminals, or lines, were competing for a circuit and the first one to find it free obtained it. This concept can be generalized to the case of multiple users (jobs, tasks, processes) competing for sharable resources (processors, channels, devices). For example, in a multiprogramming system, two jobs may simultaneously require the use of tape drives, thus possibly exceeding the capacity of the installation. This overflow situation would lead to contention delays, since one job would have to be put temporarily in a waiting state. Another example can be found in the case of a multiprocessing system where a process can be split into several tasks and the number of tasks ready to be processed

in parallel is larger than the number of available processors.

Contention is solved by using priority schemes; the simplest one is a first-come-first-serve strategy. However, all processes contending for a resource must be remembered so that they will, in turn, be able to use it. This implies the presence of queues, or buffers, associated with each sharable resource.

J-L. BAER

CONTROL APPLICATIONS

For articles on related subjects *see* ANALOG COMPUTERS; ANALOG-TO-DIGITAL AND DIGITAL-TO-ANALOG CONVERTERS; AUTOMATION; MINICOMPUTERS; REAL-TIME APPLICATIONS; and SPECIAL-PURPOSE COMPUTERS.

Modern automatic control is based upon a unified body of knowledge called *feedback control theory,* which can be used to analyze and control the performance of complex devices and processes. The development of the digital computer has provided a powerful new tool to use in applying the results of control theory to real-world applications.

As the term *control* implies, in every control problem there is a system (which may be a device, a process, or some phenomenon) with associated *output* or *controlled* variables that are to be forced to satisfy certain constraints. Typically, output variables cannot be adjusted freely; instead, they depend in an indirect way on another set of variables that can be adjusted. The variables in this second set are called *input* or *manipulated* variables.

The nature of the dependence of the output variables on the input variables is very often complex and cannot be determined precisely. However, the relationship that exists between the two sets of variables can often be approximated by a set of differential (or difference) equations, which is referred to as the *mathematical model* of the *system*. We will represent this model, with its input and output variables by a block diagram, illustrated in Fig. 1.

It may be that a given system performs very well as is. On the other hand, it may display unfavorable characteristics such as instability, sensitivity to parameter changes, slowness of response, or inefficient operation. Control theory embraces the problems of developing suitable mathematical models, determining system characteristics from the mathematical models and altering those characteristics when they are unacceptable.

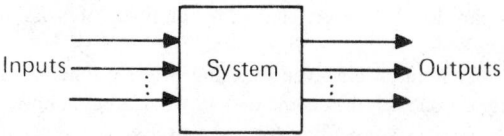

Fig. 1. Block diagram of model of system.

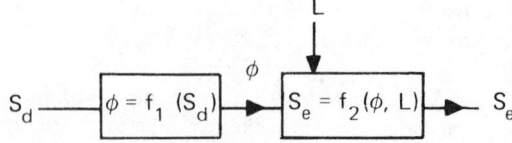

Fig. 2. Lawn mower model.

Consider, as an example of a practical control problem, a lawn mower with a small internal combustion engine and a speed-control lever connected to a butterfly valve in the carburetor. The butterfly valve regulates the flow of fuel into the cylinder.

In control terms (Fig. 2), the output of this system is the engine speed S_e. With a constant load applied to the engine, the engine speed is determined by the angle ϕ of the butterfly valve in the carburetor. The angle ϕ is a function of the desired speed S_d, which is considered to be the system input and is set by the operator with the speed-control lever.

The problem with this system is that the speed of the engine (S_e) in actual operation is determined by the angle ϕ and the load L on the engine. With ϕ held constant, an increase in the load will cause a decrease in engine speed. Consequently, if one attempts to use this machine to mow a lawn that is uneven and has thick patches of grass, it will be found that the speed-control lever must be frequently adjusted to keep the engine running at a constant speed.

An intuitively simple solution to this problem (Fig. 3) uses *feedback control* to control the system so that the operator need not make frequent manual changes of the engine speed. Here the angle ϕ is forced mechanically to be a function of S_d, the desired engine speed, and S_e, the actual engine speed. The control scheme works in the following manner.

The operator selects a desired speed S_d (a set point) by adjusting the speed control lever. With the use of springs, levers, and balanced weights, the engine speed S_e is continuously measured and used to change the angle ϕ in proportion to the engine speed error $S_d - S_e$. As a consequence, an increase in the desired speed (caused by the operator) or a decrease in actual speed (caused by an increase in the load on the engine) results in an increase in

fuel flow to the cylinder. This action tends to reduce the engine-speed error to zero. The mechanism that measures engine speed and makes the angle correction is called a *governor*.

Many other examples of automatic control problems, like the one discussed above, have simple solutions that can be implemented at a low cost. On the other hand, there are many complex automatic control problems requiring sophisticated control schemes that cannot be easily implemented with mechanical devices or with simple electronic feedback circuits. It is in the solution of these problems that the digital computer is most effective.

We will now discuss several applications of automatic control in which the computer plays an important role. In each of these areas the motivation or justification for computer control is one or more of the following: more flexible control, improved product quality, greater safety, greater precision, more efficient operation, or a savings in personnel or equipment. We begin with process control applications because the concepts involved apply directly to most other areas of computer control.

Process Control. Process control is the term given to the automatic control of industrial processes such as paper machines, blast furnaces, chemical plants, electric power generating stations, and sewage treatment plants. A digital process controller is normally expected to (1) make the necessary adjustments so that sudden disturbances in inputs do not seriously affect production and (2) regulate inputs and production sequences so that the controlled system behaves in an optimal manner. The latter objective is an *optimal control* problem. A prerequisite for optimal control is achievement of objective 1.

To illustrate the use of computers in control, we consider the simple hot-water heater in Fig. 4. As shown, the control system admits steam at the proper rate to main-

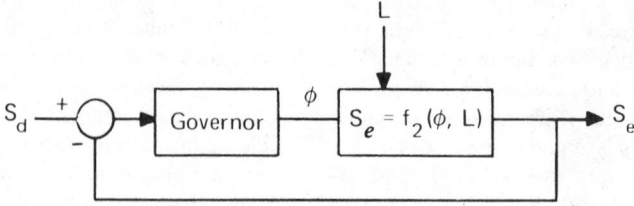

Fig. 3. Lawn mower model with feedback control.

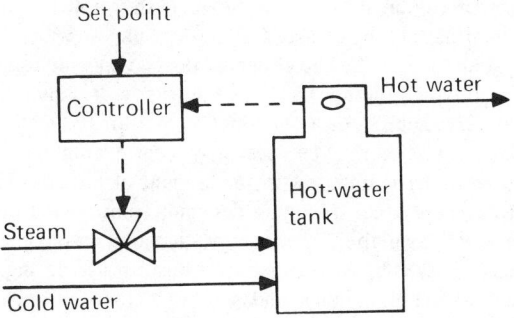

Fig. 4. Hot-water heater.

tain the outlet water at some desired value, the *set point*. The outlet water temperature is measured by the *sensor,* whose output is called the *feedback variable;* this outlet value is compared with the desired value to generate the error signal. In effect, the objective of the controller is to drive the error signal to zero. In so doing, the controller generates a signal, referred to as the *manipulated variable,* which in this example determines the opening of the steam valve and therefore the amount of steam flow.

The relationships between the elements in the system are best illustrated by the block diagram in Fig. 5. The process consists of the hot-water tank which is subject to two inputs. One input is the steam flow. The second input is the water flow through the tank, referred to as an "upset" or "disturbance," since changes in this flow affect the outlet temperature. These two inputs determine the flow of water from the tank and the temperature of the water; the latter is to be regulated by the control system, and is called the *controlled variable.* Its value is measured by the sensor and fed back to the comparator to generate the error signal. On receiving this signal, the control algorithm generates a signal to the actuator, which in this case is a steam valve. The valve then adjusts the flow of steam into the vessel. The elements in Fig. 5 are arranged in a loop, and the system is frequently referred to as a *control loop.*

In all loops in older industrial plants and in many loops in newer plants, the comparator and control algo-

rithm are implemented in a hardware unit known as a *controller.* In effect, this unit is a special-purpose analog computer, with the computing elements being either pneumatic, electronic, or occasionally hydraulic. This unit continuously monitors the feedback variable and set point, and generates adjustments to the steam valve in a continuous fashion. Analog control devices are often called *conventional* controllers.

With the appearance of digital computers, the possibility arose of replacing the collection of conventional controllers that comprised a control system with a digital computer; the first such installations appeared in the late 1950s. With the computer technology then available, a single general-purpose digital computer had to assume the responsibility of conventional controllers. Therefore, the computer's time was shared among many control loops. In effect, the computer services the loops in turn, i.e., computes the error signal, performs the algorithm computations, and proceeds to the next loop. The time between servicings for a given loop is referred to as the "sampling time," which is not necessarily the same for all loops. The use of digital computers in this fashion is called *direct digital control* (DDC).

In digital control, the output (the signal to the steam valve in Fig. 4) is usually computed from the error signal (e_n is the error at sampling time n) by an equation (the control algorithm) containing three terms:

1. A proportional term, $K_c e_n$, where K_c is a constant, the "proportional gain."
2. A summation or integral term, $(T/T_i)\sum_{i=0}^{n} e_i$, where T_i is a constant, the "reset time," and T is the sampling time.
3. A difference or derivative term $T_d(e_n - e_{n-1})/T$, where T_d is a constant, the derivative time.

The output of the controller is simply the sum of the values of these three terms. The proper values of K_c, T_i, and T_d depend upon the process being controlled, and the adjustment of these constants to their proper values is a procedure known as *tuning.* Although other control algorithms have been proposed, over 90% of the control

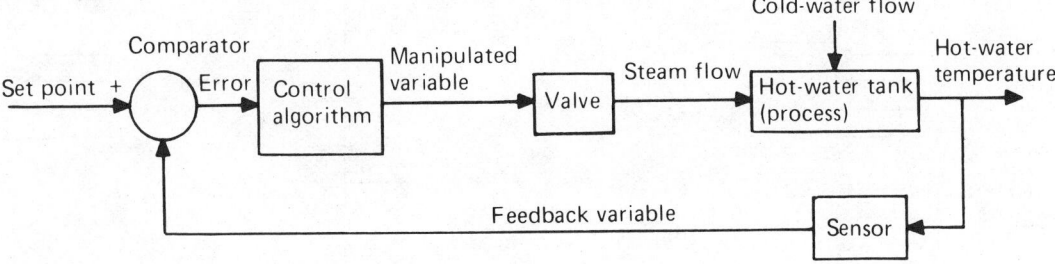

Fig. 5. Control loop.

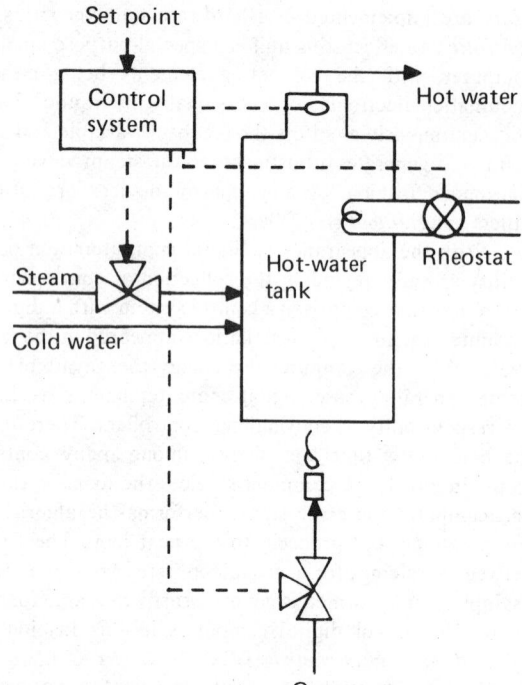

Fig. 6. Optimizing control problem.

loops in industry use this three-term, or proportional integral derivative (PID), algorithm. In some control loops the derivative term is omitted, leaving the two-term, or proportional integral (PI) algorithm.

To illustrate the optimizing control problem mentioned previously, suppose we have a hot-water heater in which the heat source may be either steam, electricity,

gas, or combinations of the three, as shown in Fig. 6. In this situation, the control system must choose which heat system to use. The choice should depend on which source can produce the hot water at the least cost. Any one of the three sources or a combination of all may be chosen. A combination may be necessary if, for example, a limit (constraint) is imposed on the amount of heat available from one source. Changing demands from night to day, changing availabilities of energy, changing cost of energy (electricity is often cheaper for industrial use during the hours after midnight), and similar factors require that the optimum requirements be recomputed on a frequent basis.

In many industrial systems, the output of the optimizing control system in Fig. 6 would not be set directly by the valves but would be determined by the values of the flows. In case of the steam flow, for example, a separate control loop must be installed to sense the volume or pressure of the steam flow and adjust the valve automatically to produce the flow specified by the optimizing control system. In this case, the optimizing control system is frequently referred to as a "supervisory control system."

Computer Systems for Control Applications. Fig. 7 shows a block diagram of a typical computer system for direct digital control. Such a system might be used, for example, to control one or more hot-water heaters as in Fig. 5, with some additional features such as perhaps the need to turn an electric pump on and off to refill the tank.

In general, a control computer includes the following hardware components.

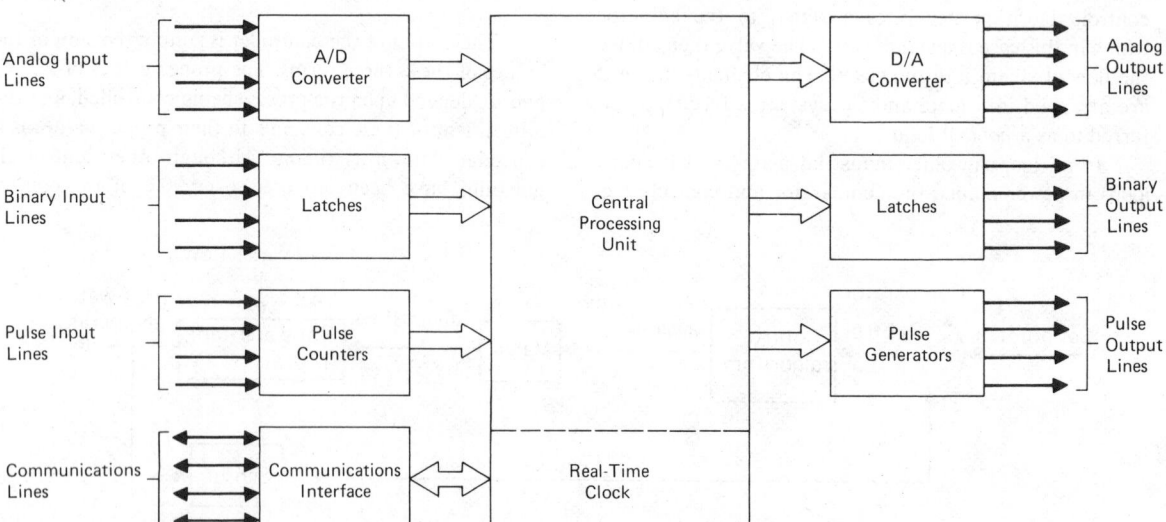

Fig. 7. Major components of a computer system for digital control.

1. Sensory inputs
2. Processor
3. Control outputs
4. Communications hardware
5. Real-time clock

Control inputs usually are one of three kinds—analog, binary, or pulse. Each kind requires different treatment by hardware and software. Analog inputs arise from signals whose values are represented by voltage levels. Such signals arise from devices like thermocouples for measuring temperatures and other devices which produce outputs on a continuous scale. Since all information processed in a digital computer must be represented in a digital format, analog input signals must be converted to their digital equivalent before they can be input into the computer. Special hardware devices called analog to digital or A/D converters (*q. v.*) carry out this process.

Binary (discrete) inputs arise from switches that can be either opened or closed. For example, a level sensor in a vat closes a switch when the fluid level rises above a fixed level. The control computer can test the 0–1 logic signal input into the computer to determine whether or not the fluid is above the prescribed level. Binary inputs also arise in systems in which it is necessary to determine the position of items on conveyor belts or whether or not items are above a given weight—in general, any physical quantity that can be represented by a yes or no value.

Pulse inputs arise from devices that can emit a pulse in response to an event, such as the arrival of an item on a conveyor belt or the passage of a cog on a rotating wheel beneath a detector. Most pulse detectors or counters on computers respond by adding one to a counter built into the pulse input device. The computer can determine the number of pulses that have arrived over a period of time by inputting the values in the pulse counter at the beginning and end of the period and computing the difference between these values. This is how computers determine the speed at which machinery, such as truck axles or electric motors, rotate.

Control outputs usually are either binary 0 or 1 signals or pulsed outputs. Binary outputs drive relays to turn motors off and on. Pulse outputs are used to control "stepper motors," which often are attached to valves to regulate the degree to which the valve is opened or closed. When a stepper motor receives a pulse of one polarity (or on one line) it opens the valve one "click." A pulse of the other polarity (or on another line) closes the valve one click.

Occasionally one needs analog output from a control computer, in which case a digital-to-analog or D/A converter is necessary to convert internal digital values to their external voltage-level equivalents. Some valves have continuous setting capabilities and require D/A converters to control them. D/A converters are also used in graphics applications, in which the analog x - y outputs are fed into an oscilloscope-like output device.

Communications hardware is often involved in control systems because, as described below, many of the modern systems require remote digital communications with other control or supervisory computers.

Process control software must provide for real-time execution of the fundamental input-process-output control cycle. In a typical system, the software must handle many control loops simultaneously, which requires sophisticated interrupt-handling, priority, and scheduling schemes. Such systems must not degrade when alarm conditions occur. These requirements make process control software especially difficult and expensive to develop.

Most control software is written in "extended" versions of Fortran or Basic, which provide special features for such needs as manipulation of boolean variables, scheduling of tasks and communications between tasks, timing of events, interrupt servicing, and I/O from "nonstandard" devices.

Distributed, Hierarchical Systems. We now consider computer process control systems as they have evolved in large-scale industrial applications. Before the advent of the microprocessor, these systems were based on rather large single or dual-processor hardware configurations. It is not unusual to find such systems responsible for well over 100 control loops simultaneously. These systems never have really displayed the full potential of computer control because of several factors, the most important of which is that the software for such a system is exceedingly complex, particularly in those portions which must respond to a virtually unlimited number of possible emergency conditions in real time. The problems of contention for computer response under alarm conditions in these systems are formidable. Hardware reliability is also a problem, since centralized control implies that the computer system must be in operation all the time in order to maintain control. In almost all such systems, complete conventional or manual systems are installed to back up the digital control system. Finally, signal wiring for sensory and control data in these systems is itself a source of possible loss of control in the event of an accident.

The availability of the microprocessor has radically altered the structure of a modern control system. Single-chip process control computers, including ROM and RAM memory, real-time clock, A/D converters, and binary inputs and outputs are now available off the shelf. The result is that it is now possible to divide the control computing formerly done by a large central computer among many small control computers physically located close to the plant facilities they control. In such *distributed* control systems, a typical processor controls five or ten loops. Many of the problems associated with centralized systems are eliminated as a result. Software problems and problems of contention are reduced because of the limited scope of responsibilities of each individual computer. Failure of an individual computer has a reduced effect on overall system performance, and many systems compensate for such failure by including back-up processors that can keep the system under control until the disabled processor is fixed. Finally, control computers communicate with each other using digital data communications techniques, which require less expensive wiring and permit redundant communications paths and sophisticated error-checking (and correcting) capabilities.

The net result is a more reliable and effective network of control computers. Each computer in the network has narrowly defined responsibilities. The computers communicate among themselves and with human operators at a central site when necessary, but are essentially independent in their normal operation.

This distributed network of small computers performing direct digital and set-point control is, in industries using the latest techniques, the lowest level in a *hierarchical* control system. While details may vary, Fig. 8 shows the structure of a typical hierarchical control system.

The lowest-level computers receive commands—set points and control sequences—from minicomputers at the next higher level, which perform a supervisory control function. Each production facility in a given plant has at least one computer functioning at this level. In principle, if a supervisory computer stops running, the production units for which it is responsible still can operate, although perhaps not at peak efficiency, under control of the lower-level network. The control data sent down by the supervisory computers to the lower-level computers are the results of optimization calculations done by the supervisory computers. The low-level computers transmit data back

indicating the current status of the production units they control. These data are fed back into the optimal control calculations and are also available for use by human operators, whose most direct link with the system is through the supervisory computers. The supervisory computers also transmit production summaries—raw materials used, products produced, inventories of each on hand, and projected production rates—to the plant-level computers which form the next higher level.

The plant-level computers are responsible for overall production scheduling, data processing, and reporting for the entire plant complex. These typically are large mainframe computers. They receive production quotas from the corporate-level systems and, based on these quotas, solve large optimization problems (typically linear programming problems) to determine the best production schedules to meet these quotas. The production schedules are then sent down to the supervisory computers for implementation.

The corporate-level computers are mainframes responsible for the overall accounting, data processing, management information, and planning functions for the corporation. Their contribution to the control efforts is the solution of very large optimization problems to select the optimal corporate production strategy over periods of up to a year or more. These calculations are based on world market and economic projections, availability of supplies and transportation, production capacities, and other global factors, including summaries of plant-level information received from computers lower in the hierarchy.

In summary, a complete hierarchical control system has computers at several levels. As we move down the tree, the control functions of the computers become more specific. The time periods over which they execute control operations become shorter as we get closer to the bottom

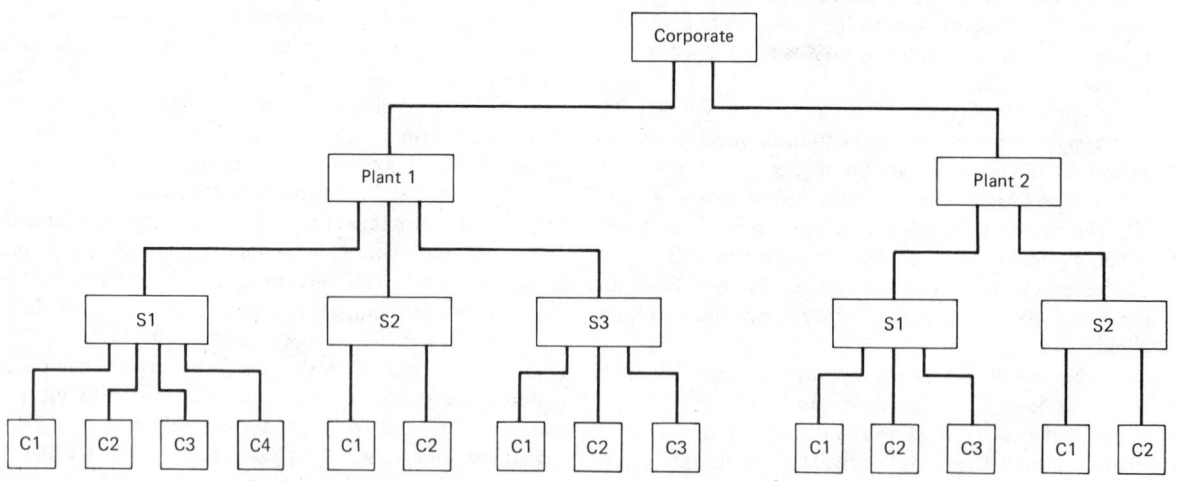

Fig. 8.   Structure of a hierarchical control system (S = supervisory computer; C = control computer).

of the tree, from the monthly projection cycle at the corporate level, to split-second direct digital control decisions at the lowest levels.

Batch Sequencing. Another kind of automatic control suitable for computer control is batch sequencing, in which the objective is to monitor and control a sequence of discrete steps in a production process. This is in contrast to continuous control as emphasized above, in which the objective ordinarily is to force a set of continuous controlled variables to fall between certain prescribed limits which ordinarily are fixed or slowly varying in time.

An example of batch sequencing is in the manufacture of semiconductor integrated circuit "chips." Here the final product is the result of a series of 50–100 discrete steps, from the original slicing of a silicon bar into wafers to the final testing and packaging of the circuit. These production steps include several separate sequences of depositing masks, depositing metallic components or etching through masks, removing masks, etc. Each step occurs at a different location in a different machine. The sequencing involves sensing when chips are in position for processing, sealing the container, turning on the depositing or etching device, timing the process, turning off the device, opening the container, and moving the chips to the next station. Such a highly complex operation is a natural candidate for computer control and, in fact, at least one minicomputer formerly on the market was designed specifically to control the batch sequences involved in manufacturing integrated circuits.

Another instance in which batch sequencing is common is the drug industry, in which a company uses the same equipment to produce hundreds of different compounds. In such settings, computers are often used to store "recipes"—sequences of mixing, heating, stirring, drying, and other physical activities, together with amounts of raw materials to be added at each step. In the production of a given compound, the computer controls the sequencing of events and addition of raw materials according to the recipe.

The sequencing of events in plant start-up and shutdown and emergency response in process control systems adds the need to include batch sequencing capabilities to most process control systems.

Another example of batch sequencing is in automatic warehouse control. In this application, the computer automatically maintains a complete inventory of all items in the warehouse, including their locations. In response to a request entered through a terminal, the computer controls machinery that automatically retrieves the desired items.

Traffic Control. Control of air traffic in and out of airports is now, as it has been in the past, the responsibility of air traffic controllers; these people from the air traffic control center monitor traffic data and give takeoff and landing instructions to aircraft pilots. The volume of controlled traffic through an airport is limited to the maximum number of aircraft that air traffic controllers can safely handle. This maximum number depends to a great degree on the form and extent of information available to the controller.

In the early years of air traffic control, the standard real-time information available to the controller consisted of a flight schedule, aircraft position and altitude communicated from each pilot by radio, and an overall view of close-range traffic movement shown on a radar screen.

As the volume of traffic increased over the years, the need for more sophisticated systems for gathering, processing, and displaying flight information grew accordingly. The past decade has seen a major effort to utilize the computer and other electronic devices to develop a data handling system capable of meeting the requirements of air traffic control today and in years to come.

Current airline traffic control systems store the locations, speeds, and altitudes of literally hundreds of airplanes simultaneously. They repeatedly cycle through this data, projecting future positions of the aircraft and generating alarm signals if it appears that two airplanes will come too close together or if an airplane is on a dangerous course. The systems suggest sequences in which to route aircraft into and out of airports so as to make optimal use of the facilities while preserving the safety of the planes.

These systems are exceedingly complex. A major problem that remains is the construction of adequate backup and fail-safe procedures and systems in the event of failure of the main systems.

Control of traffic on the freeways and surface roads of large cities is another problem that is receiving increased attention. Unlike air traffic control, the traffic routes are fixed, and the only means of control are traffic lights and possibly roadside messages to automobile drivers.

Many states now offer freeway-access control systems like that sketched in Fig. 9. In a typical system, sensor data input to the computer is used to detect the presence and speed of vehicles on the freeway as they approach an entrance ramp. Using anticipated future positions of the autos, the computer controls signal lights to regulate the entrance of vehicles waiting to enter the freeway.

In a similar fashion, computers are being used in several cities to synchronize traffic signals so that flow through the cities can proceed as efficiently as possible.

Defense Applications. The early development of the electronic digital computer was within a military framework. Computer control is still used extensively in

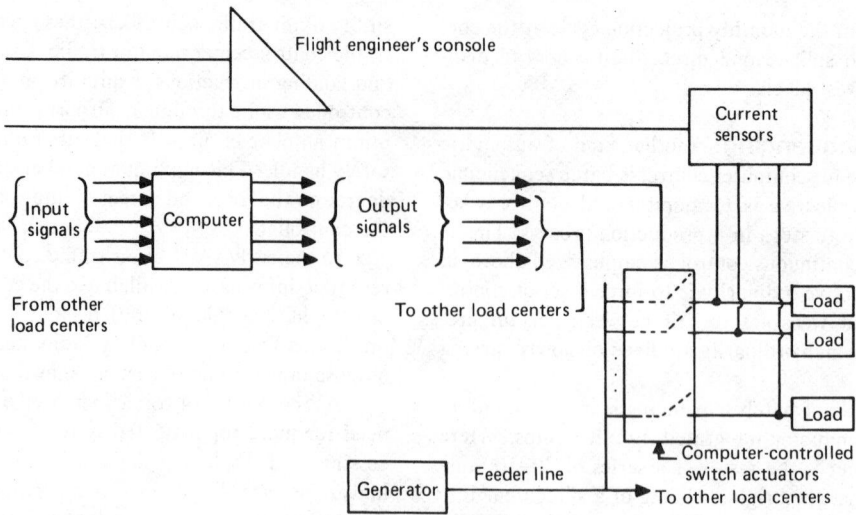

Fig. 9. Control of aircraft power distribution.

the armed services today but, compared to applications in industry and other commercial enterprises, the justification for its use is less dependent on economic considerations.

Although the details of most defense systems are classified, it is obviously true that the firing of many offensive and defensive weapons is performed under the control (either direct or supervisory) of a computer. Many applications that were initially developed within the defense department are now being used commercially. Automatic flight control with the use of inertial navigation, for example, was first developed to control the flight of ballistic missiles and is now being used for communications and weather satellite deployment, manned space flight, and control of commercial aircraft. This topic will be discussed in more detail in the next section of this article.

Applications in Air and Sea Transportation.

Computers are now being used for control purposes on board air and sea vessels. Although computer control on board merchant ships has lagged its use on shore, some vessels (such as Queen Elizabeth 2; see Phillips, 1971) utilize computers for direct as well as supervisory control.

Feedback control is used aboard the Queen Elizabeth 2 (*QE2*) to regulate scoop pumps that provide circulating water to the condensers in order to increase the efficiency of the engine and thereby decrease fuel consumption. The recommended relationship (provided by the turbine designer) between condenser vacuum and engine shaft-horsepower is stored in the computer. Computations are made periodically to determine the shaft horsepower of the engine and the corresponding recom-

mended condenser vacuum. The actual vacuum is compared with the recommended condenser vacuum, and the change in vane angle of the scoop pump necessary to give the recommended vacuum is computed. Finally, the computer sends a signal to an actuator to make the correct change in vane angle.

The computer on the *QE2* is also utilized for supervisory control to calculate the recommended power output, engine speed, and shaft speed of the ship over the route to be traveled. To accomplish this, the desired route is divided into as many as 20 sections. Over each section, wind speed and direction as well as ship's course are assumed constant. The calculations are based on weather reports and forecasts, the ship's load, and scheduled arrival time.

Plans are being made to have the computer control on a daily basis the generation of fresh water according to predicted usage. Scheduled stops would be considered to insure that fresh-water tanks are full when the ship stops and the evaporators are shut down.

In addition to its use on the ground for air traffic control, as discussed previously, the digital computer is being used on board commercial aircraft for control purposes, such as flight control and control of power distribution.

The Boeing 747 is equipped with an inertial navigation system, a compact version of systems used to control the flight of missiles and space vehicles. Gyroscopes are used to hold a platform in a fixed, level position with respect to true north. Two accelerometers placed on this platform continuously and accurately measure acceleration along a north-south axis and along an east-west axis. The output of each of these accelerometers is integrated with respect to time to determine aircraft velocity with respect to the two axes. Finally, the velocity along each axis is integrated with respect to time to determine the north-south and east-west components of the plane's position with respect to the point of departure. The integration is performed by a digital computer.

With the coordinates of the destination point stored in memory, the digital computer can easily compute correct headings and, with some additional information provided, calculate pilot control settings. Although closed-loop control is not presently being used, evidence indicates that computer control would be more accurate than pilot control for maintaining altitude during turns and for maintaining a correct heading during flight.

Numerical Control. In the manufacture of parts for such products as appliances, automobiles, airplanes, and the like, fabrication of the part is effected by such devices as milling and routing machines, rotary tables, lathe grinders, boring machines, flame cutters, drilling machines, and benders. When using any of these machines, some type of control mechanism is necessary to insure that the finished part meets specifications.

In the early manufacturing plants, such control was performed by a human operator. This mode of control was relatively expensive, and the consistency with which the resulting part met specifications was relatively low, especially for parts requiring extensive milling. With the development of the automotive industry, machines were designed with preset tool guides, automatic part holding and locating features, automatic feed systems, and the like. These machines, referred to as "fixed" or "Detroit automation," were designed to produce a specific part. Although part changes frequently required major mill modifications, this was no great obstacle because of the large quantities of each part produced in the automotive industry.

Many major industries, such as the aircraft industry, must fabricate parts in considerably smaller quantities. In these applications the mill should have the flexibility to produce a variety of parts with a relatively short changeover time. The milling machines generally have capabilities such as positioning the part in either the two- or three-dimensional coordinate system, rotating the part as in a lathe, positioning a cutter as in a drill, and the like. When the instructions that specify the positioning, movement, and other machine operations are in the form of numbers, the machine is a candidate for numerical control.

The control of the machines by numerical control can be classified in two types—point-to-point control and contouring control. In point-to-point control, the route by which the tool moves from point A to point B is immaterial except that, among other considerations, the movement must be sufficiently precise so that the tool does not strike the part. Drilling multiple holes in a part is an example of this type of control. In contouring control, milling is usually done along a path, which must be controlled at every point. This type of control is the more demanding.

Basically, an order for a part generally includes a drawing of the part and some additional explanatory information. From this data, the plant must produce the part. The steps are frequently as follows.

1. The dimensions and other pertinent data of the part are punched onto cards.
2. These cards constitute the input to computer programs that provide a generalized milling and positioning format.
3. The resulting data is then entered into a post-processor program, specific to the machine being used, to produce the numerical control instructions, usually in the form of a punched paper tape.
4. This paper tape is mounted on a paper-tape reader at the machine to provide direct instructions to the machine.

To convert from manufacturing one part to the next, the mill operator need change only the paper tape and make the usually minor modifications on the mill. To facilitate this changeover, many machines have selectable tools, e.g., multiple drill heads mounted on a turret.

In more modern numerical control systems, milling specifications are entered through computer terminals, and the control information for the machines is transmitted directly to them over communications lines.

There are now some prototype "robots" (*see* ROBOTICS) in use in the automobile industry, which have limited sensory capabilities, but which can, after careful "instruction," carry out some of the simpler assembly steps on automobile assembly lines.

Consumer Products. The advent of the microcomputer has opened up a new world for computer control applications. A host of consumer products, such as sewing machines, automobiles, microwave ovens, and television sets, now have built-in control computers. This trend is just beginning and will surely continue, although its precise directions cannot be predicted.

REFERENCES

1971. Phillips, H. "Computer Systems for Merchant Ships," *Electronics and Power* 17:35–39 (January).
1972. Smith, C. L. *Digital Computer Process Control.* Scranton, Pa: Intext.

1974. Weitzman, C. *Minicomputer Systems*. Englewood Cliffs, NJ: Prentice-Hall.

1977. Bibbero, R. J. *Microprocessors in Instruments and Control*. New York: Wiley.

1978. Auslander, D. M., Takahashi, Y., and Tomiyaka, M. "Direct Digital Process Control: Practice and Algorithms for Microprocessor Application," *Proceedings IEEE* **66**:199–208.

1978. Special Issue on Large-Scale Systems and Decentralized Control, *IEEE Transactions on Automatic Control* **AC-23**, No. 2.

1979. Eadie, D. *Minicomputers: Theory and Operation*. Reston, VA: Reston.

1979. Kahne, S., Lefkowitz, I., and Rose, C. "Automatic Control by Distributed Intelligence," *Scientific American* **240**:78–90.

1979. Sheldon, E. "Microcomputers and Control—The Critical Mass Has Been Reached," *Instruments and Control Systems* **52**:67–73.

1980. Sterling, M. and McLean, J. "Distributed System Increases Refinery Efficiency," *Instruments and Control Systems* **53**, No. 71.

C. L. SMITH, B. MOORE, AND W. G. RUDD

CONTROL DATA CORPORATION CYBER SERIES

For articles on related subjects *see* COMPUTER INDUSTRY: United States; and SUPERCOMPUTERS.

The Control Data Corporation (CDC) Cyber 170/700 series is a computer family ranging from the medium speed 170/720 to the powerful 170/760 and 176. The Cyber 170/700 family is a successor to the CDC 6000 series, a set of machines designed to provide high-speed arithmetic capability for large scientific applications. The innovative and highly successful 6000 series, which included the 6200, 6400, 6600, and their dual central processing versions, the 6500 and 6700, dominated the large-scale scientific market from 1964, when the 6600 was first delivered, until the introduction of the successor Cyber 70 series in 1970. The follow-on Cyber 170 family was announced in 1974. Current members of the 170/700 series are the 720, 730, 750, and 760. The functional architectures of all the models are very similar.

CDC's commitment to high-speed scientific processing resulted in the production of the 7600 in 1969, and its successor models, the Cyber 76 and then the Cyber 176, which sacrificed a small degree of implementation compatibility with the main-line 6000, 70, and 170 series machines in return for higher processing speeds. The 176 is nearly twice as fast as the 760, the most powerful 170/700 model, by employing faster memory and somewhat

faster central processing circuitry. The desire for continued dominance of the high-speed scientific market has also resulted in the architecturally dissimilar STAR vector processor and has carried forward into the present-day Cyber 205.

The Cyber 170/700 architecture has been described (Bell and Newell, 1982) as a *network computer;* it consists of a central memory, a central processing unit (CPU), a set of peripheral processing units (PPs), and peripheral equipment. A large *backing store,* termed Extended Core Storage (ECS) was designed for swapping and system libraries. The novel aspect of this architecture lies in the existence and interconnection of the PPs. Each PP is a functionally independent processor with its own arithmetic unit and private memory, in addition to access to central memory and the I/O channels. Thus, a CPU and 20 PP system is programmed as a 21-way multiprocessor system communicating via central memory. Since I/O functions and many system tasks are delegated to the PPs, I/O and operating systems functions may be performed concurrently with user programs running on the CPU.

The basis of the central processor architecture is "functional parallelism" (Thornton, 1970). It is achieved by the use of multiple, distinct, arithmetic functional units. In a typical central processor program at least two or three functional units will be in operation simultaneously. Instructions from memory are first loaded automatically into a high-speed, cache-like "instruction stack." Instructions are saved in the stack, which can often hold a complete program loop, thus allowing the program to loop within the stack at high speed without requiring central memory fetches for instructions. No such stack exists for data. The unit and register reservation control, or "scoreboard," schedules instructions and the functional units, taking an executable instruction from the stack whenever a unit is free.

The original 6600 employed eight functional units, as did the model 74. The first high-performance variant, the 7600, employed a slightly different set of nine functional units. It is the 7600's implementation that has carried through the Cyber 76, 175, and 176, and into the present-day 170/750 and 170/760. These CPUs are also implemented by discrete components, in contrast to the integrated circuits, which implement the CPUs of the slower members of the series. The more conventional and lower-cost, lower-performance alternative of a "unified" arithmetic unit was first employed in the 6400, introduced in 1967, and is continued in the 170/720 and 170/730. The "unified" CPUs have typically lacked an instruction stack, and have been augmented by a separate, additional compare-and-move functional unit, which allows for rapid character manipulation.

The 720 is able to add two 60-bit integer quantities

Fig. 1. A Control Data Cyber 170 System.

in 600 ns (the 760 in 100 ns), to add two 60-bit floating point quantities in 800 ns (the 760 in 100 ns), and to divide two 60-bit floating point quantities in 3200 ns (the 760 in 500 ns). The concurrency exploited by the nine functional units in the 750, 760, and 176 further increases the effective performance of these more powerful central processing units.

The maximum central memory available on the 6600 was 131,072 60-bit words of non-error detecting core storage. The maximum central memory of a 700 series machine is 262,144 words, with a single-bit error-correction, double-bit error-detection Hamming code provided by an additional 8 bits per word. Central memory is divided into 8 banks of MOS memory (16 banks of bipolar memory for the 176). Protection is by base-and-bounds registers not addressable by the programmer, which also allow programs to be moved about memory dynamically to help solve the storage-fragmentation problem of multiprogramming.

Extended Semiconductor Memory (ESM) was introduced in 1981 as an ECS replacement. This MOS memory offers speed and reliability advantages over the older, core, swapping storage. Up to 2,097,152 words of ESM backing store is available on the 700 series models. Although a single 68-bit word (60 data bits and 8 check bits) can be read or written by the CPU, the natural access mode is in units of 8-word records, which are transferred via the CPU between ESM and central memory. An 8-word ESM record can be read into central memory

in 800 ns over a 10 million words-per-second CPU port, or at a slower rate via a PP port.

A brief listing of some timing and mainframe architectural differences between the 6600, the fastest computer at the time of its introduction, and the present 170/760, illustrates how improvements have evolved by enhancement rather than redesign. Both machines are the most powerful single-CPU processors in their respective series. The inevitable improvements in circuitry implementation have resulted in increases in computing speed. The CPU cycle time has been decreased from 100 to 25 ns. The number of functional units have been increased by one, and all have been either partially or fully *pipelined* so that each can accept a new instruction before the previous instruction has completed. For example, the multiply unit can accept new instructions every other clock cycle, with each instruction taking five cycles to complete, and the integer add unit can accept a new instruction every clock cycle, with the instruction requiring two cycles to complete. The instruction stack of the 6600 employed only eight 60-bit words to the 760's 12. The memory cycle time has decreased by a factor of four. The maximum number of channels configurable has doubled from 12 to 24, as has the maximum number of PPs from 10 to 20, with a PP's cycle time being halved.

In spite of the undoubted early success of this architecture, some criticisms can be made. Floating point round is performed before rather than after normalization, contravening the principles of numerical analysis.

Fixed-point overflow is not detected. The storage into memory by the subroutine-jump instruction makes reentrant code difficult to implement. The addressing register length of 18 bits limits the size of central memory to a quarter-million words in an era where one-million word central memories are becoming commonplace, and virtual memory software systems are not easily supported by the implementation of the architecture.

The first operating system for the 6600 was developed by CDC's Chippewa Laboratory for the early 6600s and thus named the Chippewa Operating System, or Chippewa. Limitations in the batch processing, multiprogramming system, such as the lack of a time-sharing capability and a relocatable loader, prompted a number of early customers (in addition to CDC) into operating system development efforts. Chippewa formed the nucleus of its CDC successor, SCOPE 2, released in 1966. Many enhancements, including support of ECS and random disk accessing, were released as SCOPE 3 in 1967. A time-sharing subsystem for SCOPE 3, INTERCOM, was announced by CDC in 1969; its forerunner was the SHARER time-sharing system developed at New York University in 1966 as a Chippewa subsystem. The demand for a more robust time-sharing system that could support larger numbers of interactive users led to the introduction of the KRONOS operating system in 1970. KRONOS was a descendant of the MACE operating system developed in cooperation with McDonnell Automation in the late 1960s and enhanced at United Computing Systems and Purdue University.

With the introduction of the 170 series in 1974, the highly KRONOS-compatible Network Operating System (NOS) was announced as the replacement for both KRONOS and SCOPE. Slow acceptance of NOS by SCOPE users resulted in the release of the highly SCOPE-compatible NOS/BE (/Batch Environment) operating system in 1975.

NOS and NOS/BE support a number of high-level languages, including APL, Cobol, Algol60, Basic, Pascal, Lisp, Snobol4, and a very efficient Fortran, as well as the DMS-170 database management system.

A number of independently derived or SCOPE-derived operating systems are still in use on 6000 series machines and their descendants, including those at Purdue University, The University of Texas at Austin, the Livermore and Los Alamos National Laboratories, the Lawrence Radiation Laboratory, the European Center for Nuclear Research (CERN), the Institute for Defense Analysis, and the National Center for Atmospheric Research.

REFERENCES

1970. Thornton, J. E. *Design of a Computer: The Control Data 6000*. Glenview, IL: Scott, Foresman.

1982. Siewiorek, D. P., Bell, C. G. and Newell, A. *Computer Structures: Principles and Examples*. New York: McGraw-Hill.

T. W. KELLER

CONTROLLED VARIABLE

For articles on related subjects *see* ITERATION; PROCEDURE-ORIENTED LANGUAGES, Programming in; and STRUCTURED PROGRAMMING.

The term controlled variable is used for the variable that is controlled to take on a specific set of values in an iterative structure in a programming language. The number of values in this set determines or partially determines how many times the statements in the iteration are executed. For example, in the Algol statement

for i := 1 **step** 2 **until** j, j*j **while** $k < $ m, 6, v, x*y
do begin (iteration statements) **end**

i is the controlled variable. Its values—1,3,5 . . . as long as $i \leq j$, then j^2 as long as $k < m$, and then the three values $6,v,x*y$—are taken on successively each time the statements in the iteration are executed. Only the value j^2 may be taken on by i during more than one execution of the iteration statements; this value will be retained as long as $k < m$ (where k or m, or both, will be changed by the iteration statements). For this reason the sequence of values of i only partially determines the number of iterations. By contrast, in the Fortran structure

DO 212   I = 1, 13, 3
(iteration statements, with last one labeled 212),

The variable I takes on the values 1,4,7,10,13, once each, during the execution of the iteration statements, and thus the number of iterations is determined in advance.

Of course it must be noted that a statement in the set of iteration statements can itself terminate the iteration by (for example) transferring control to a statement outside the so-called **for**-loop in Algol or the DO-loop in Fortran. In this case the iteration terminates before the controlled variable has taken on all its values. Good programming practice, however, requires that such transfers be avoided if possible; usually, they can be in languages with a **while** structure, such as Algol and Pascal.

A. RALSTON

CONTROL POINT

For article on related subject *see* MICRO-PROGRAMMING.

The hardware locations at which the output of the instruction decoder of the processor activates the input to and output from specific registers as well as the operational resources of the system (adders, shifters, etc.) are called the *control points*. The control points basically determine intercycle register-to-register communications. For each register in the processor there are a fixed number of other registers to which data may be transmitted in one cycle. For each such possibility, a separate AND circuit is placed on the output of each bit of the source register, with the entry into the destination register being collected from all possible sources by an OR circuit.

Data may be communicated from one register to another directly or through some operational network (adder/shifter, etc.). Transmission to such a network must also be selected; the output of the network has a similar set of gates for each possible destination. In a typical system there must be control points corresponding to each bit of every register for each possible intercycle destination of that register and for each bit of each operational network that may be used in a cycle.

For example, consider a 32-bit computer with eight registers. Assume that each register can communicate with three other registers in one cycle. The number of control points required for register communication would therefore be $3 \times 8 \times 32$, or 768. In addition, assume the machine has three execution resources, each of whose 32-bit outputs can be gated to one of four registers. This would account for an additional $3 \times 4 \times 32$, or 384, control points. Of course there are additional control points for the selection of a particular function within a designated resource. This might account for 100 more control points. Thus, there is a total of somewhat over 1200 control points, which must be established for each cycle by the output of the instruction decoder (the control function). Fortunately, in most computer design situations, many of these control points are not independent. For example, one may not gate bit 7 of register 4 to another register, but one may gate the entire contents of register 7 to its destination register. Since only one line is required to control such multiple control points, the total number of outputs required can be significantly reduced. These outputs are then referred to as *independent control points*. For the hypothetical system described, there might be anywhere from 50 to 200 independent control points, depending upon the variety of instructions in the vocabulary of the system.

M. J. FLYNN

CONTROL STRUCTURES

DATA STRUCTURES; PROCEDURE-ORIENTED LANGUAGES; and STRUCTURED PROGRAMMING.

The term *control structures* refers to a programming language's facilities for specifying a departure from the normal sequential execution of statements. In its broadest sense, this includes calling a procedure, resuming a co-routine, and initiating tasks, all of which involve transferring the path of execution to another program unit (in the case of recursion, the "other" program unit is a "copy" of the calling program). It also includes, in its broadest sense, the "parallel" (simultaneous) performance of two or more operations within a given program unit. In its more common usage, however, *control structures* refers to the facilities for controlling the sequence of statement execution within a given program unit, and includes special facilities for selection control, repetition control, and exception handling. The description here is limited to this more common view. Usually, such facilities are in the form of "extended" statements, involving several parts in different lines—hence, the term *control structure*.

Arbitrary Control. The normal pattern of program execution is sequential control, in which statements are executed in the order they appear. If $\langle S1 \rangle$ and $\langle S2 \rangle$ are each a program statement (or self-contained sequence of statements) that performs some processing (e.g., assignment, I/O, or procedure call) then

$$\langle S1 \rangle; \langle S2 \rangle \quad \text{or} \quad \langle S1 \rangle \\ \langle S2 \rangle$$

represents the execution of $\langle S1 \rangle$ followed immediately by the execution of $\langle S2 \rangle$. A pictorial representation of sequential control is

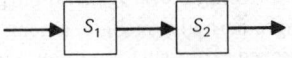

Virtually all useful programs (except those consisting only of procedure calls) involve intra-program execution path control different from sequential control, and therefore virtually all programming languages provide facilities for specifying such control. A simple and fundamental, yet powerful and "complete," set of execution control facilities consists of the ability to (1) insert a label $\langle L \rangle$ at any point in the program, for identification of that location:

$$\langle L \rangle:$$

and to (2) unconditionally or conditionally (depending upon the value of a boolean expression [*B*]) transfer execution control to such points, using **goto** (branching) statements.

$$\textbf{goto } \langle L \rangle$$
$$\textbf{if } \langle B \rangle \textbf{ goto } \langle L \rangle$$

The conditional **goto** involves two possible paths of execution, as shown, one of which continues sequential control (if $\langle B \rangle$ is **false**) and the other ($\langle B \rangle$ **true**) transferring control to the specified label.

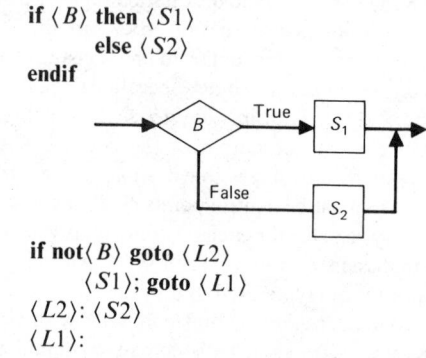

With conditional and unconditional **goto** statements, arbitrary execution control may be achieved. Typically, in programming languages, labels are either numbers (e.g., in Fortran: **goto** 210) or alphanumeric identifiers (e.g., in Ada: **goto** MATCH-FOUND).

While the **goto** is, in principle, sufficient for all conceivable intra-program sequence control, in practice it is not generally the most satisfactory in a high-level language environment. Most need for execution control is limited to a few highly systematic patterns. When implemented with **goto**s, such control patterns are not especially apparent to the reader of the program, which detracts from the understanding of the program. By the same token, primary reliance on **goto**s for specifying control when writing programs tends to be an error-prone way of programming. This was pointed out by Edsger Dijkstra in a now classic letter (1968). Bohm and Jacopini (1966) showed that essentially any control flow can be achieved without the **goto** by using appropriately chosen sequential, selection, and repetition control structures. Therefore, high-level general-purpose programming languages normally include, among their features, facilities designed expressly for optimum implementation of these and other commonly found control patterns. Software development (programming) tends to be significantly easier, and more reliable, if these control structures are used for most execution control, with **goto**s being used only in those occasional instances where the needed control has some unusual pattern.

Selection Control. A very common control pattern is that of selectively executing, or not executing, a sequence of statements $\langle S \rangle$, depending upon the current value (**true** or **false**) of a boolean expression $\langle B \rangle$. The control structure for such a control pattern is as follows,

with the equivalent control using **goto** shown below and a pictorial representation on the bottom.

$$\textbf{if } \langle B \rangle \textbf{ then } \langle S \rangle \textbf{ endif}$$

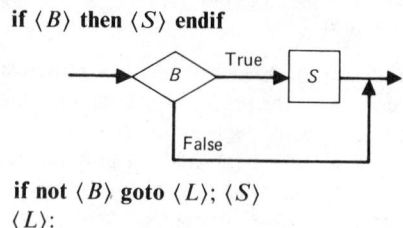

$$\textbf{if not } \langle B \rangle \textbf{ goto } \langle L \rangle; \langle S \rangle$$
$$\langle L \rangle:$$

Another common pattern has one group of statements, $\langle S1 \rangle$, being executed if $\langle B \rangle$ is true, and a different group, $\langle S2 \rangle$, if $\langle B \rangle$ is false.

$$\textbf{if } \langle B \rangle \textbf{ then } \langle S1 \rangle$$
$$\textbf{else } \langle S2 \rangle$$
$$\textbf{endif}$$

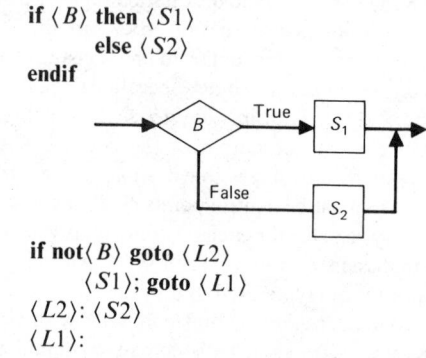

$$\textbf{if not} \langle B \rangle \textbf{ goto } \langle L2 \rangle$$
$$\langle S1 \rangle; \textbf{ goto } \langle L1 \rangle$$
$$\langle L2 \rangle: \langle S2 \rangle$$
$$\langle L1 \rangle:$$

This latter structure, which is simply an extension of the first one with the optional **else** $\langle S2 \rangle$ part, is known as the **if-then-else** selection control structure, and (with minor syntactic variations) is the most commonly found selection control structure in high-level languages.

Another common control pattern is that of selecting one group of statements to be executed, from among 3, 4, 5, or more different statement groups. In general one can think of *n* groups of statements ($n>0$), $\langle S1 \rangle$, $\langle S2 \rangle, \ldots, \langle Sn \rangle$, from which (at most) one group is to be selected for execution. The conditions governing the selection are formulated as a set of boolean expressions, $\langle B1 \rangle, \langle B2 \rangle, \ldots, \langle Bn \rangle$, as may be appropriate for the needed control, so that if $\langle B1 \rangle$ is true $\langle S1 \rangle$ is selected; otherwise if $\langle B2 \rangle$ is true $\langle S2 \rangle$ is selected and, in general, for the first $\langle Bi \rangle$ that is true, the corresponding $\langle Si \rangle$ is selected.

$$\textbf{if } \langle B1 \rangle \textbf{ then } \langle S1 \rangle$$
$$\langle B2 \rangle \textbf{ then } \langle S2 \rangle$$
$$\cdot$$
$$\cdot$$
$$\langle Bn \rangle \textbf{ then } \langle Sn \rangle$$
$$[\textbf{else } \langle Sn+1 \rangle]$$
$$\textbf{endif}$$

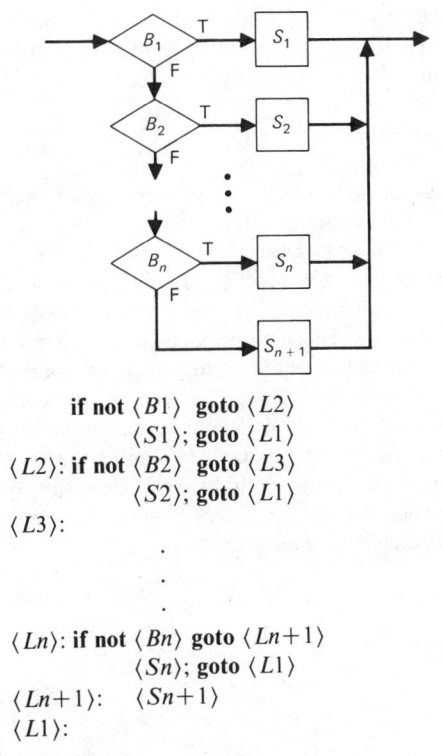

$$\textbf{if not } \langle B1 \rangle \textbf{ goto } \langle L2 \rangle$$
$$\langle S1 \rangle; \textbf{ goto } \langle L1 \rangle$$
$$\langle L2 \rangle: \textbf{if not } \langle B2 \rangle \textbf{ goto } \langle L3 \rangle$$
$$\langle S2 \rangle; \textbf{ goto } \langle L1 \rangle$$
$$\langle L3 \rangle:$$

.
.
.

$$\langle Ln \rangle: \textbf{if not } \langle Bn \rangle \textbf{ goto } \langle Ln+1 \rangle$$
$$\langle Sn \rangle; \textbf{ goto } \langle L1 \rangle$$
$$\langle Ln+1 \rangle: \quad \langle Sn+1 \rangle$$
$$\langle L1 \rangle:$$

Since there are no restrictions on the boolean expressions in this *n*-way selection control structure, more than one such expression may be true (**else** is always considered to be "true"). Still, at most, one statement group is executed—that one associated with the first true boolean expression—and none may be executed (if there are no true boolean expressions and the **else** option is absent). Square brackets, as around the **else** portion of the above structure, denote optionality.

In none of the selection control structures is there any restriction on the statements that any $\langle S \rangle$ may contain. And, in particular, any $\langle S \rangle$ may contain other (nested) selection control structures. *n*-way selection control may be achieved using nested **if-then-else** structures, for example. Therefore, the above *n*-way structure provides no additional functionality over the **if-then-else,** but highly nested structures detract enough from program readability that the arbitrary *n*-way selection structure is desirable. Note that **if-then-else** is simply a special case of *n*-way selection—i.e., for $n = 1$.

The *n*-way selection structure described above is a highly sequential selection mechanism, involving an ordered evaluation of a sequence of boolean expressions. Another common selection pattern involves, conceptually, "parallel" selection of one from among several statement groups. Here, the selection conditions are disjoint relations involving constant values, so that, in principle, selection may be "immediate" and not require the

evaluation of a sequence of boolean expressions. The **case** selection structure is often used to express such "parallel" selection. If $\langle X \rangle$ is an expression, and $\langle V \rangle$ is a constant value of the same data type as $\langle X \rangle$, the **case** structure has the form shown below.

$$\textbf{case } \langle X \rangle$$
$$\langle V1 \rangle \textbf{ then } \langle S1 \rangle$$
$$\langle V2 \rangle \textbf{ then } \langle S2 \rangle$$
.
.
$$\langle Vn \rangle \textbf{ then } \langle Sn \rangle$$
$$[\textbf{else } \langle Sn+1 \rangle]$$
$$\textbf{endcase}$$

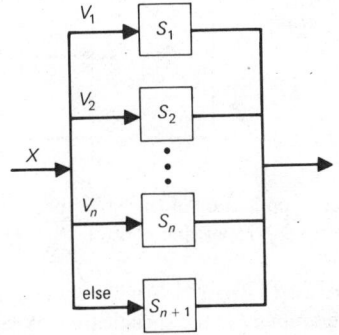

Since the $\langle V \rangle$s are disjoint, their order in the **case** structure is immaterial. Also, any $\langle V \rangle$ may consist of a set or range of values, rather than just a single value, as long as all of the $\langle V \rangle$s remain disjoint. As with the *n*-way **if**, there may be any number of cases in a **case** structure and the **else** part is optional. Unlike the **if** structure, however, if the value of $\langle X \rangle$ does not match any of the $\langle V \rangle$ values and the **else** part is omitted, then an error condition exists, from which recovery must be made (see exception handling below) or execution of the program is terminated. (In some languages, the above **case** syntax is used merely as a convenient alternative form of **if-endif** selection in which the boolean expressions involve comparisons with constant values. In this article such syntactic variations are not of major concern, and **case** is used here as the prototype structure for parallel selection.)

A significant variation of the **case** structure is the replacement of the expression $\langle X \rangle$ with an arbitrary program segment $\langle S \rangle$. At various points in this program segment, the case value groups are identified for subsequent execution (e.g., with a statement such as: **select** $\langle V \rangle$). Such a selection structure, generally known as a *Zahn structure,* provides for arbitrary selective execution based upon the results of an arbitrary algorithm, and has the general form given below.

case selection: $\langle V1 \rangle, \langle V2 \rangle, \ldots, \langle Vn \rangle$
    $\langle S \rangle$
    $\langle V1 \rangle$ **then** $\langle S1 \rangle$
    $\langle V2 \rangle$ **then** $\langle S2 \rangle$
    .
    .
    .
    $\langle Vn \rangle$ **then** $\langle Sn \rangle$
       [**else** $\langle Sn+1 \rangle$]
endcase

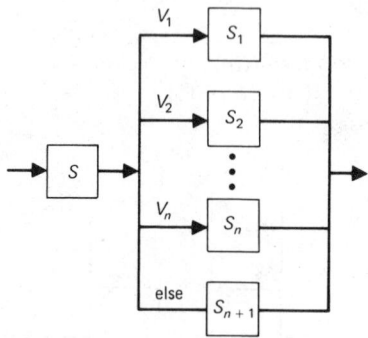

A special application of this structure is described in the next section on repetition control.

Repetition Control. An extremely important aspect of programming is the specification of repetitive execution of a statement group $\langle S \rangle$. The following structure, with its **goto** equivalent on the bottom, will repeat execution of $\langle S \rangle$ indefinitely.

loop
$\langle S \rangle$
endloop

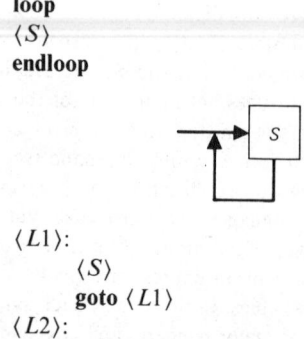

$\langle L1 \rangle$:
    $\langle S \rangle$
    goto $\langle L1 \rangle$
$\langle L2 \rangle$:

The above loop control results in an *infinite loop* unless execution of one of the statements in $\langle S \rangle$ causes either program termination (e.g., execution of a **stop** statement) or a branch out of the loop (e.g., **goto** $\langle L2 \rangle$). A **loop exit** statement is one whose purpose is to cause termination of loop execution, and is equivalent to **goto** $\langle L2 \rangle$. Loop exits are normally conditional, and may have a form equivalent to

    if $\langle Be \rangle$ **exit**

where $\langle Be \rangle$ is the loop exit condition. A common extension of this is to allow specification of some end-of-loop processing $\langle Se \rangle$ prior to exiting the loop:

    if $\langle Be \rangle$ **then** $\langle Se \rangle$ **exit**.

This is useful if the loop has different end-of-loop processing requirements at different exits.

Conditional **exit** statements can provide any kind of loop control; that is, whether or not $\langle S \rangle$ is executed again may be controlled completely by the use of **exit** statements. For often-encountered looping control patterns, however, it is convenient to be able to include, in the loop header, specification of the loop control. This usually makes writing the loop significantly easier, and makes the loop much more understandable in reading the program, both of which are highly desirable in the development and maintainance of reliable software. Therefore, loop structures often have the general form:

loop $\langle C \rangle$
    $\langle S \rangle$
endloop

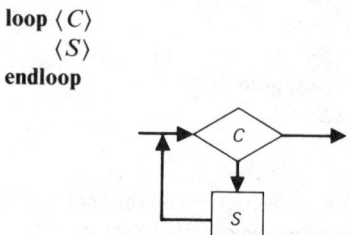

where $\langle C \rangle$ specifies the desired control of repetition. With loop control specified in this manner, the need for **exit** statements in $\langle S \rangle$ is typically much reduced (although **exit** statements may still be allowed in $\langle S \rangle$). Three of the more common types of control, $\langle C \rangle$, are:

1. Indexed: **for** $\langle I \rangle \leftarrow \langle X1 \rangle$ **to** $\langle X2 \rangle$ [**by** $\langle X3 \rangle$]
2. Bounded: $\langle X \rangle$ **times**
3. Conditional: **while** $\langle B \rangle$

where $\langle I \rangle$ is an integer variable, the $\langle X \rangle$s are integer expressions, and $\langle B \rangle$ is a boolean expression. The effect of each of these control options is as follows (Z and COUNT are "internal" integers "hidden" from the programmer).

loop for $\langle I \rangle \leftarrow \langle X1 \rangle$ **to** $\langle X2 \rangle$ **by** $\langle X3 \rangle$
    $\langle S \rangle$
endloop
(if $\langle X3 \rangle$ option is omitted, $+1$ is assumed)

    $Z \leftarrow \langle X3 \rangle / \mathbf{abs}\ (\langle X3 \rangle)$
    $\langle I \rangle \leftarrow \langle X1 \rangle - \langle X3 \rangle$
    loop
        $\langle I \rangle \leftarrow \langle I \rangle + \langle X3 \rangle$

if $Z*\langle I\rangle > Z*\langle X2\rangle$ **exit**
$\quad\langle S\rangle$
endloop

loop $\langle X\rangle$ **times**
$\quad\langle S\rangle$
endloop

loop for COUNT $\leftarrow$ 1 **to** $\langle X\rangle$
$\quad\langle S\rangle$
endloop

loop while $\langle B\rangle$
$\quad\langle S\rangle$
endloop

loop
$\quad$**if not** $\langle B\rangle$ **exit**
$\quad\langle S\rangle$
endloop

A number of variations of these loop control facilities are implemented in various computer languages, and occasionally an entirely different kind of control is defined and implemented for $\langle C\rangle$. One such class of variations is control at the bottom of the loop rather than at the top.

Loop structures may be nested, and occasionally it is necessary to exit more than one level of repetition. This may be done by using the **goto** statement, or by identifying loops with (the equivalent of) a label $\langle L\rangle$ and allowing "multi-level" **exit** statements of the form:

if $\langle B\rangle$ **exit** $\langle L\rangle$

A third way to achieve multi-level exits is to "cascade" the requisite number of single-level exits. This may be done by setting a boolean "flag" and exiting one level (e.g., **if** $\langle Be\rangle$ **then** MULTILEVEL $\leftarrow$ **true; exit**), then immediately (after **endloop**) exiting again (e.g., **if** MULTILEVEL **exit**).

Another facility occasionally provided in loop structures is that of proceeding directly to the next repetition cycle of a loop:

if $\langle B\rangle$ **cycle** $\langle L\rangle$

$\langle L\rangle$ refers to the desired loop identification; as with exits, the $\langle L\rangle$ may be omitted for single-level cycling. Since cycling is not needed often in practice, and may be achieved using **exit** and selection control, **cycle** is not as commonly implemented as is **exit**.

A reasonably common occurrence (some studies

have indicated for about 20% of all loops) is that of multiple (more than one) single-level exits in a given loop. Normally, one can expect the post-loop processing to be somewhat different for the different exits. For example, a search loop may contain two exits, one for when the search is successful and one when it is unsuccessful. The action taken after the search is normally dependent upon whether or not the search was successful, implying different processing at each of the two exits. Selection of the proper post-loop processing routine may be achieved by flagging each exit, just prior to departure from the loop, for use in ordinary selection control following the loop. Forms of the loop control specification $\langle C\rangle$ exist which facilitate such exit flagging.

A variation of the Zahn **case** selection structure, in which the pre-selection routine is the loop, integrates a loop and its various exit-processing routines into a single control structure. The form of such a structure is:

loop $\langle C\rangle$ **with exits** $(\langle E1\rangle, \langle E2\rangle, \ldots, \langle En\rangle)$
$\quad\langle S\rangle$
endloop
$\quad\langle E1\rangle$ **then** $\langle S1\rangle$
$\quad\langle E2\rangle$ **then** $\langle S2\rangle$
$\qquad\cdot$
$\qquad\cdot$
$\qquad\cdot$
$\quad\langle En\rangle$ **then** $\langle Sn\rangle$
endexits

where $\langle S1\rangle, \langle S2\rangle, \ldots, \langle Sn\rangle$ are the different post-loop exit-processing routines corresponding to exits $\langle E1\rangle$, $\langle E2\rangle, \ldots, \langle En\rangle$, respectively. Within the loop body $\langle S\rangle$, a certain exit may be specified with an exit statement of the form:

if $\langle Be\rangle$ **select exit** $\langle Ei\rangle$.

Exception Handling. A number of things can happen during program execution which can prevent execution from successfully continuing. These things include division by zero, subscript out of bounds, numeric overflow, **case** value missing, unavailable read-only file, wrong data type on input, insufficient storage available, and referencing an undefined value. Such exceptions, when detected, normally result in program termination without further processing unless provision is made for some other action, and possibly recovery. Such provision is called *exception handling* and, since execution control is the issue, constitutes a form of control structuring.

The structural nature of an exception handler is essentially that of a **case** selection control structure. One of a predefined set of exception values is presented to the handler, which then selects the routine that performs the action desired in the event that that particular exception occurs. If corrective action is possible, then that routine may include such action, followed by resumption of normal processing; otherwise program execution terminates after execution of the handling routine. The form of such an exception handler is as follows.

exception
  $\langle E1 \rangle$ **then** $\rangle S1 \rangle$
  $\langle E2 \rangle$ **then** $\langle S2 \rangle$
      .
      .
      .
  $\langle En \rangle$ **then** $\langle Sn \rangle$
endexception

When an exception occurs, execution control automatically is passed to the beginning of the exception handler, along with the identification $\langle E \rangle$ of the exception that has occurred. Selection is then made of the corresponding routine $\langle S \rangle$ to be executed. Program execution is terminated after execution of $\langle S \rangle$, unless $\langle S \rangle$ specifies recovery and resumption of program execution. For example, if the last statement in $\langle S \rangle$ is

recover

then, instead of terminating, program execution would resume from the point at which the exception occurred. Presumably, the statements in $\langle S \rangle$ preceding **recover** would provide suitable corrective action so that resumed program execution is sensible.

In addition to the intrinsic exception cases, some implementations allow the programmer to define additional exception values, and to specify explicitly that an exception has occurred. Such programmer defined and detected exceptions may be handled in the same manner, and with the same handler control structure as intrinsic exceptions. In terms of control structure considerations, the two main differences between **case** selection and exception handling are (1) that exception handling involves some intrinsic exception values in addition to programmer-defined ones, and (2) that the location in the program of an exception handler is immaterial, with the necessary branches to and from the handler taking place automatically (whereas a **case** structure must be placed in the program at the point the selection is to be performed). For this latter reason, the control involved with an exception handler is very much like that for a procedure, and therefore exception handlers may be implemented as procedures rather than occurring in-line in the program.

In most instances, the logic of a problem can be expressed in a relatively straightforward manner in terms of selection and repetition control structures, such as those described above. Arbitrary sequencing and nesting of selection and repetition structures is permitted, as is allowing any $\langle S \rangle$ to be empty. For example, loop bodies may contain other loops and/or any type of selection, without restriction; selection statement groups may contain additional selection structures and/or loops, without restriction. Although nesting can be carried to any level, after about three levels of nesting the control logic tends to become difficult for humans to read easily. The simple example program (for performing a bubble-sort on an array) in Fig 1. illustrates the use of control structures for expressing an algorithm.

Control structures are major aspects of high-level programming languages, and a language's control structuring facilities play a major role in its effectiveness in software development. The structures described above are commonly found in programming languages, but few individual languages contain all of these facilities. On the other hand, control structures not described above are occasionally found in programming languages—especially in special-purpose languages whose application areas commonly involve control patterns different from those described above as common. Table 1 shows the control structure features of several popular general-purpose programming languages. As mentioned at the outset, major

Bubble Sort an Array *EL* of *NE* Elements
```
      BP ← 0
      loop
          BP ← BP + 1; NS ← 0
          loop for I ← NE − 1 to BP by −1        [bubble next smallest element up into place BP]
              if EL(I) > EL (I + 1) then
                  EL(I) ↔ EL(I + 1)              [switch elements EL(I) and EL(I + 1)]
                  NS ← NS + 1                     [increment count of switches]
              endif
          endloop
          if NS = 0 exit                          [EL completely ordered if NS = 0]
      endloop
```

Fig. 1.

Table 1

Feature	ADA	BASIC	COBOL	FORTRAN 77	PASCAL	PL/I
1. Label example	⟨⟨LABEL⟩⟩	100	LABEL	100	100	LABEL
2. Branching	**goto** LABEL **if** ⟨B⟩ **then goto** LABEL **endif**	*goto* 100 *if* ⟨B⟩ *then* 100	*goto* LABEL *if* ⟨⟨B⟩⟩ *goto* LABEL	*goto* 100 *if* ⟨⟨B⟩⟩ *goto* 100	**goto** 100 **if** ⟨B⟩ **then goto** 100	*goto* LABEL *if* ⟨⟨B⟩⟩ *then goto* LABEL
3. If-then-else	**if** ⟨B⟩ **then** ⟨S_1⟩ [**else** ⟨S_2⟩] **endif**	N/A	*if* ⟨B⟩ ⟨S_1⟩ [*else* ⟨S_2⟩]	*if* ⟨⟨B⟩⟩ *then* ⟨S_1⟩ [*else* ⟨S_2⟩] *endif*	**if** ⟨B⟩ **then** ⟨S_1⟩ [**else** ⟨S_2⟩]	*if* ⟨⟨B⟩⟩ *then* ⟨S_1⟩ [*else* ⟨S_2⟩]
4. n-Way-branch	**if** ⟨B_1⟩ **then** ⟨S_1⟩ **elsif** ⟨B_2⟩ **then** ⟨S_2⟩ **elsif** ... [**else** ⟨S_{n+1}⟩] **endif**	N/A	nested if-then-else	*if* ⟨⟨B_1⟩⟩ *then* ⟨S_1⟩ *elseif* ⟨⟨B_2⟩⟩ *then* ⟨S_2⟩ *elseif* ... ⟨*else* ⟨S_{n+1}⟩⟩ *endif*	nested if-then-else	nested if-then-else
5. Case	**case** ⟨X⟩ **of:** **when** ⟨V_1⟩ → ⟨S_1⟩ **when** ⟨V_2⟩ → ⟨S_2⟩ **when** ... [**when others** → ⟨S_{n+1}⟩] **endcase**	N/A	*goto* ⟨L_1⟩, ⟨L_2⟩, ..., ⟨L_n⟩ *depending on* ⟨I⟩	"computed goto" *goto* ⟨⟨L_1⟩, ⟨L_2⟩, ..., ⟨L_n⟩⟩ ⟨I⟩	**case** ⟨X⟩ **of** ⟨V_1⟩:⟨S_1⟩ ⟨V_2⟩:⟨S_2⟩ ... ⟨V_n⟩:⟨S_n⟩ **end**	N/A
6. Looping	**loop** ⟨S⟩ **endloop** **while** ⟨B⟩ **loop** ⟨S⟩ **endloop** **for** ⟨I⟩ **in** ⟨X_1⟩..⟨X_2⟩ **loop** ⟨S⟩ **endloop**	*for* ⟨I⟩ → ⟨X_1⟩ *to* ⟨X_2⟩ [*step* ⟨X_3⟩] ⟨S⟩ *next* ⟨I⟩	*perform* ⟨L⟩ *until* ⟨B⟩ *perform* ⟨L⟩ *varying* ⟨I⟩ *from* ⟨X_1⟩ *by* ⟨X_2⟩ *until* ⟨B⟩ ⟨L⟩. ⟨S⟩	*do* ⟨L⟩ ⟨I⟩ = ⟨X_1⟩, ⟨X_2⟩, [⟨X_3⟩] ⟨S⟩ ⟨L⟩ *continue*	**while** ⟨B⟩ **do** ⟨S⟩ **repeat** ⟨S⟩ **until** ⟨B⟩ **for** ⟨I⟩ := ⟨X_1⟩ **to** ⟨X_2⟩ **do** ⟨S⟩	*do while* ⟨B⟩ ⟨S⟩ *end* *do* ⟨I⟩ = ⟨X_1⟩ *to* ⟨X_2⟩ [*by* ⟨X_3⟩] ⟨S⟩ *end*
7. Loop exits	**exit** [**when** ⟨B⟩]	*goto* ⟨L⟩	*goto* ⟨L⟩	*goto* ⟨L⟩	**goto** ⟨L⟩	*goto* ⟨L⟩

Table 1 (continued)

Feature	ADA	BASIC	COBOL	FORTRAN 77	PASCAL	PL/I
8. Exception handling	**begin** $\langle S_0 \rangle$ **exception** **when** $\langle E_1 \rangle \rightarrow \langle S_1 \rangle$ **when** $\langle E_2 \rangle \rightarrow \langle S_2 \rangle$ **when** . . . [**when others** $\rightarrow \langle S_{n+1} \rangle$] **end**	N/A	*on* $\langle E_1 \rangle \langle S_1 \rangle$. *on* $\langle E_2 \rangle \langle S_2 \rangle$. . . .	N/A	N/A	*on* $\langle E_1 \rangle \langle S_1 \rangle$ *on* $\langle E_2 \rangle \langle S_2 \rangle$ . . .

NOTES: Square brackets [ ] denote optional items.

N/A = not available in language.

$\langle B \rangle$ is a boolean (logical) expression.

$\langle S \rangle$ is a (compound) statement.

$\langle X \rangle$ is a (numeric) expression.

$\langle V \rangle$ is a variable identifier.

$\langle L \rangle$ is a label.

$\langle I \rangle$ is an integer variable identifier.

$\langle E \rangle$ is an exception condition (e.g., logical expression).

areas of execution control technology, such as procedure, coroutine, and task mechanisms have been omitted from the above presentation and from the table. Other articles are devoted to discussions of these topics.

A uniform style of syntax, chosen for its consistency and conciseness, was employed in the above descriptions in order that a complete and unified picture of control structure principles might be presented. This style was not drawn from any particular language, but, as is clear from Table 1, is similar to that found in many programming languages. In any given language, one might find a control structure functionally identical to one of those described above, but with totally different keywords and a somewhat different organization. Thus, functionally identical control structures may appear to be very different. Similarly, control structures which have the same appearance in two different languages may in fact behave quite differently because of different semantic interpretations of the same lexical construct. In other words, control structures have not yet acquired a standardized form for implementation, and many variations exist.

REFERENCES

1966. Bohm and Jacopini. "Flow Diagrams, Turing Machines, and Languages with Only Two Formation Rules," *Comm. ACM* (May).
1968. Dijksta, E. W. "**Goto** Statement Considered Harmful," *Comm. ACM* (March).
1974. Knuth, D. E. "Structured Programming with **goto** Statements," *Computing Surveys* (December).
1974. Kernighan and Plauger. *The Elements of Programming Style*. New York: McGraw-Hill.
1975. Goodenough, J. B. "Exception-Handling: Issues and a Proposed Notation," *Comm. ACM* (December).

J. L. WAGENER

COPYRIGHTS. See LEGAL PROTECTION OF SOFTWARE.

COROUTINE

For articles on related subjects *see* CONCURRENT PROGRAMMING; PROCEDURE; and SUBROUTINE.

A coroutine, like a subroutine, transforms a set of inputs to a set of outputs. Coroutines differ from subroutines, however, in that their lifetimes are not tied to the flow of control: When a subroutine is called, a new instance of its *activation record* (i.e., its control information and local variables) is created which is destroyed when

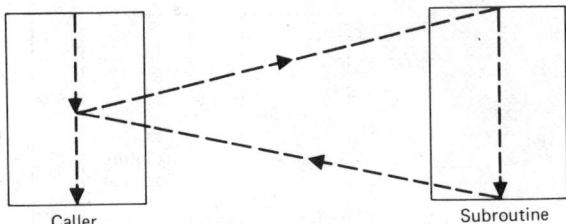

Fig. 1. A subroutine is finished when it returns.

control is returned to the calling program (see Fig. 1). On the other hand, when a coroutine returns, its execution is not finished and so its activation record is preserved. Each call of the coroutine begins where the previous call left off, and the coroutine's control and local data state is retained (Fig. 2).

For the simple reason that a new instance is not created on every call, coroutines are often more efficient than subroutines. Furthermore, because coroutines can be entered *directly* at the appropriate point to continue a computation, their use can simplify the implementation of some algorithms. This is especially true when the processing to be done on a call depends in a complex fashion upon previous calls. Finally, coroutines offer flexible control; a group of coroutines can freely transfer control among themselves.

Applications of coroutines include compilers, operating systems, and discrete event simulation programs. For example, the language Simula 67, which supports discrete event simulation, contains very flexible coroutine mechanisms (Dahl, 1972). Coroutines are also used in text manipulation, artificial intelligence, sorting, and numerical analysis programs.

Coroutines are often organized into *linear pipelines*. Linear pipelines are useful when the transformation implemented by a program can be decomposed into several simpler transformations that are applied one after the other. The coroutines of the pipeline can be envisaged as being arranged in a line: Information flows through the line in (essentially) one direction, with each coroutine implementing part of the overall transformation of the information. A coroutine obtains input items by transfer-

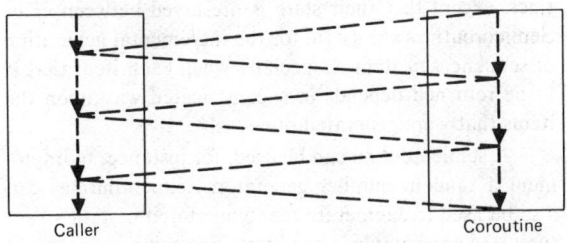

Fig. 2. A coroutine is reentered on a call where it left off.

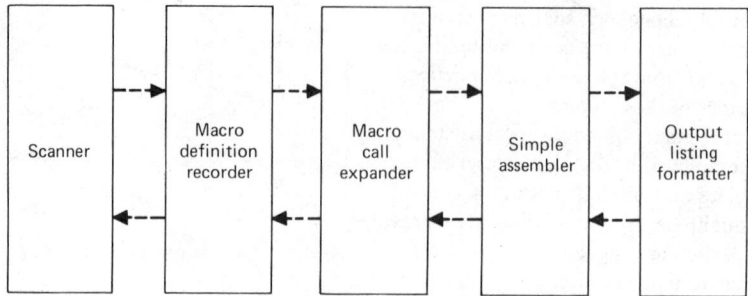

Fig. 3. A macro-assembler organized as a linear pipeline.

ring control to one neighbor, and outputs results by transferring control to the other. It treats its neighbors simply as input and output subprograms. Each coroutine is written as though it were the main program, and without any concern for the implementation of the other coroutines. These linear pipelines (with buffering) appear in the UNIX (*q. v.*) command language (Ritchie, 1974).

As an example, a macro-assembler can be organized as a linear pipeline (see Fig. 3). One coroutine collects input characters into tokens; another records macro-definitions and deletes them from the input stream; and a third expands macro-calls. A fourth coroutine is a simple assembler that assigns addresses and translates symbolic operation codes into machine instructions, while a fifth coroutine formats the output listing. The heart of the macro-assembler consists of the macro-expansion and simple assembler coroutines. The macro-expander recognizes macro-calls in its input stream, and outputs (by calling the assembler coroutine) the tokens that result from expanding the macro-definition. The assembler coroutine, in turn, inputs (by calling the expansion coroutine) a token stream in which all macro-calls have already been expanded. The macro-expander is written without concern for address assignment and machine code generation, while the assembler is coded as though macros did not even exist.

Another frequently used coroutine is the *semicoroutine*. Semicoroutines have the restriction that when they are called, they are obliged eventually to return control back to the caller. Thus, semicoroutines resemble subroutines, except that their state is preserved between calls. Semicoroutines are useful for the incremental generation of sequences of items, especially when each item that is to be returned depends in a complicated way upon the items that were generated previously.

A semicoroutine can be used, for instance, to implement a random number generator. Semicoroutines can also be used to enumerate the items stored in data structures. As an example, a semicoroutine can return, one at a time, the items recorded in a binary tree. The semicoroutine's local state can retain between calls the (consid-

erable) amount of information needed to locate the next tree element.

REFERENCES

1972. Dahl, O.-J. "Hierarchical Program Structures," in *Structured Programming*. New York: Academic Press, pp. 175–220.
1974. Ritchie, D. and Thompson, K. "The UNIX Time-Sharing System," *Comm. ACM* **17**, *No. 7*:365–375 (July).

B. LEWIS

COURSEWRITER. *See* AUTHORING LANGUAGES AND SYSTEMS.

CPM. *See* PERT/CPM.

CPU. *See* CENTRAL PROCESSING UNIT.

CREDIT SYSTEMS APPLICATIONS

For articles on related subjects *see* ADMINISTRATIVE APPLICATIONS; and POINT-OF-SALE TERMINAL.

In early Greece and Rome, and even up through the Industrial Revolution, a creditor did not need a computer to furnish information about a potential debtor. The creditor was already familiar with the applicant's character, ability to repay the debt, and the type of collateral available to secure the debt. Today, with over 500 million credit cards in existence in the U.S. and billions of credit transactions occurring annually, most credit systems require the use of a modern, high-speed computer.

Following the introduction of oil company credit cards in the late 1930s, their use soon became widespread, making personal knowledge of potential debtors virtually impossible. Any attempt to handle this large number of credit accounts without the use of large-storage, high-speed computers would certainly have met with economic failure. Other types of credit systems for bonds and mortgages have also been computerized, but their volumes are smaller than the number of transactions processed through credit cards. Today, in addition to providing credit cards for use in automated teller machines (ATM), most banks will process small consumer loans only through a bank credit card account. In general, a credit card can be used to purchase almost any retail good or service, to obtain cash and to establish identity.

Computers and Credit Systems. An effective credit system must be concerned with the entire spectrum of credit activities—credit approving, sale authorizing, imposing credit charges, billing, dunning, collecting, and responding to inquiries and complaints.

Credit Approval. The credit process usually begins when a person files a written application which includes name, address, telephone number, employment history and job statistics, bank references, and names of other creditors. An example of a credit card application is shown in Fig. 1. In evaluating the application, the creditor often uses a technique called "credit scoring," i.e., assigning a numeric value, depending upon the applicant's response to each item of information requested. The score or sum total of all points assigned to a particular application is then compared with predetermined values to decide whether to extend credit. Each credit-issuing company that uses a credit-scoring technique will use the categories, variables, and assigned scores it has found to be most significant to its own operation and consistent with existing legislation.

Sophisticated computer programs have been developed to analyze past experiences, to score applications and to recommend future changes in an attempt to reduce the loss from uncollectible accounts. It would be very difficult to process the large number of credit card applications today without such a technique.

In developing the unique account number to be assigned to a successful applicant, the use of a check digit is usually employed. The computer creates the check digit by using the first $N - 1$ digits of the account number as input to a check-digit generation routine. The resulting calculations produce a single, unique digit, which becomes the last digit of the account number. The oil company credit card displayed in Fig. 2 uses an 11-digit account number, with the first ten digits (123 456 789 0) being the actual account number and the eleventh digit (3) being the check digit. The use of a check digit helps reduce errors in the transcription of account numbers.

To generate a check digit using the "mod 10" tech-

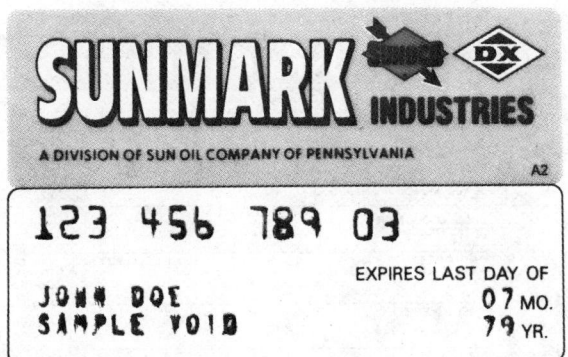

Fig. 1. Mod 10 method of generating credit card check digits.

nique, work from right to left. First, multiply the digits in the odd positions (0,8,6,4,2) by 2. If an individual result is greater than 10 ($2 \times 8 = 16$), add 1 to the units position ($6 + 1 = 7$) to obtain a single digit adjusted result. Sum these results ($0 + 7 + 3 + 8 + 4 = 22$) along with the even-positioned account digits ($22 + 1 + 3 + 5 + 7 + 9 = 47$). The number that must be added to make this result evenly divisible by 10 (3 in our example) is the check digit.

Sale Authorization. After credit has been approved and a credit limit has been established, each sale above the preset dollar amount must be authorized. The dollar limit is usually different for each card holder and is determined by factors such as payment history and credit rating. The authorization process determines whether the potential purchaser is actually allowed to make purchases on the account after considering whether the account has exceeded its credit limit, and the payment history for previous purchases.

Computers are playing an increasing role in the area of sales authorization, and several service bureaus now provide sales authorization services. When contacting a bureau, a merchant subscribing to such a service might communicate with a person who has access to the computer, or directly with the computer by means of a terminal or a push-button telephone. Increased sophistication in these terminals has eliminated the need for verbal exchange during this process. The merchant provides the customer's account number, the amount of the potential sale, and the location and identification number for service-billing purposes. The sales information is then evaluated according to information in the customer's file, and the sale is approved or rejected. Of course, the merchant has the final say and can override the computer's suggestion, but experience shows this is rarely done, since the credit card company guarantees payment only if prior approval is obtained.

SUNMARK CREDIT CARD APPLICATION

PLEASE CHECK THE "BOXES" THAT PROPERLY PERTAIN TO YOUR APPLICATION AND COMPLETE APPLICATION ACCORDINGLY.
IF YOU ARE APPLYING FOR AN ACCOUNT IN THE NAME OF A COMPANY PLEASE USE THE COMPANY NAME AS THE "APPLICANT" AND COMPLETE ONLY THE AREAS THAT CAN BE RELATED TO THE COMPANY.

Fill in only if SUNDINERS Account

IF YOU ARE PRESENTLY A SUNMARK, SUNOCO/DX OR SUNDINERS CARDHOLDER INDICATE ACCOUNT NUMBER IN THE BOXES

HAVE YOU APPLIED BEFORE? YES ☐ NO ☐
IF "YES" APPROX. WHEN? MO._____ YR._____

CHECK ONE:
☐ THIS ACCOUNT WILL BE USED FOR PERSONAL, FAMILY AND/OR HOUSEHOLD PURPOSES, EITHER WHOLLY OR PRIMARILY.
☐ THIS ACCOUNT WILL BE USED FOR BUSINESS, COMMERCIAL AND/OR AGRICULTURAL PURPOSES, EITHER WHOLLY OR PRIMARILY

CHECK AT LEAST ONE OF THE FOLLOWING:
☐ MY SPOUSE WILL BE PERMITTED TO USE THE ACCOUNT (COMPLETE ENTIRE APPLICATION INCLUDING SHADED PORTIONS)
☐ I RELY ON COMMUNITY PROPERTY AND/OR MY SPOUSE'S INCOME AS A BASIS FOR PAYMENT OF THE ACCOUNT (COMPLETE ENTIRE APPLICATION INCLUDING SHADED PORTIONS)
☐ NEITHER (DISREGARD SHADED PORTIONS)

FULL NAME OF APPLICANT FIRST, MIDDLE INITIAL, LAST | SOCIAL SECURITY NO. | NO. OF DEPENDENTS | NAME OF SPOUSE | DO NOT WRITE IN THIS AREA

NUMBER & STREET | TELEPHONE AREA CODE NUMBER

CR. CLASS CR. CODE COLL. CODE

CITY & STATE | ZIP CODE | HOW LONG AT THIS ADDRESS? YEARS MONTHS | NUMBER OF SUNMARK CREDIT CARDS DESIRED

PREVIOUS ADDRESS | HOW LONG AT PREV. ADDRESS? YEARS MONTHS

AGE | BUYING HOME ☐ OWN HOME ☐ RENT HOUSE ☐ RENT APT ☐ BOARD ☐ OTHER ☐ | NUMBER OWNED: CARS TRUCKS | HOW LONG AT PRESENT JOB? YEARS MONTHS

EMPLOYER | TYPE OF BUSINESS | POSITION

EMPLOYER'S ADDRESS | OTHER MONTHLY INCOME $

MONTHLY WAGES $ | INCOME FROM ALIMONY, CHILD SUPPORT OR SEPARATE MAINTENANCE PAYMENTS NEED NOT BE REVEALED IF YOU DO NOT CHOOSE TO HAVE IT CONSIDERED AS A BASIS FOR REPAYING THIS OBLIGATION

IF LESS THAN ONE YEAR AT PRESENT JOB OR RETIRED, GIVE PREVIOUS EMPLOYER & ADDRESS

IS SPOUSE EMPLOYED? YES ☐ NO ☐ | SPOUSE'S EMPLOYER | SPOUSE'S POSTION | HOW LONG EMPLOYED? | SPOUSE'S OTHER MONTHLY INCOME $

SPOUSE'S MONTHLY WAGES $ | INCOME FROM ALIMONY, CHILD SUPPORT OR SEPARATE MAINTENANCE PAYMENTS NEED NOT BE REVEALED IF YOU DO NOT CHOOSE TO HAVE IT CONSIDERED AS A BASIS FOR REPAYING THIS OBLIGATION

BANK (SHOW BRANCH OR ADDRESS) | SHOW TYPE OF ACCOUNT ☐ REGULAR CHECKING ☐ SPECIAL CHECKING ☐ SAVINGS ☐ LOAN

FINANCE COMPANY NAME & ADDRESS | ☐ ACCOUNT ACTIVE ☐ ACCOUNT CLOSED

NAME AND ADDRESS OF NEAREST RELATIVE (NOT LIVING WITH YOU)

OTHER OIL COMPANY CREDIT CARDS AND ACCOUNT NUMBERS | NAME & ADDRESS | ACCOUNT NUMBER
| NAME & ADDRESS | ACCOUNT NUMBER

OTHER CREDIT ACCOUNTS AND ACCOUNT NUMBERS | NAME & ADDRESS | ☐ 30 DAY ☐ INSTALL-MENT | ACCOUNT NUMBER
| NAME & ADDRESS | ☐ 30 DAY ☐ INSTALL-MENT | ACCOUNT NUMBER
| NAME & ADDRESS | ☐ 30 DAY ☐ INSTALL-MENT | ACCOUNT NUMBER

I AGREE THAT (1) SUNMARK INDUSTRIES A DIV. OF SUN OIL COMPANY OF PENNSYLVANIA HAS MY EXPRESS CONSENT TO CONDUCT AN INVESTIGATION AND (2) THE APPROVAL OF THIS APPLICATION IS SUBJECT TO RESULTS OF SUCH INVESTIGATION AND (3) I SHALL ACCEPT THE CREDIT CARD(S) SUBJECT TO THE TERMS DISCLOSED WHEN ISSUED

X
SIGNATURE OF APPLICANT—If account is to be in a company name, title and signature of authorized person.

DATE OF APPLICATION

SUN-SX-36 Rev. 22

Apply Today! Fill out, detach and enclose in attached envelope.

THE OHIO LAWS AGAINST DISCRIMINATION REQUIRE THAT ALL CREDITORS MAKE CREDIT EQUALLY AVAILABLE TO ALL CREDITWORTHY CUSTOMERS AND THAT CREDIT REPORTING AGENCIES MAINTAIN SEPARATE CREDIT HISTORIES ON EACH INDIVIDUAL UPON REQUEST. THE OHIO CIVIL RIGHTS COMMISSION ADMINISTERS COMPLIANCE WITH THIS LAW.

NEW YORK RESIDENTS: A CONSUMER CREDIT REPORT MAY BE ORDERED IN CONNECTION WITH THIS APPLICATION, OR SUBSEQUENTLY IN CONNECTION WITH THE UPDATE, RENEWAL OR EXTENSION OF CREDIT UPON YOUR REQUEST. YOU WILL BE INFORMED WHETHER OR NOT A CONSUMER CREDIT REPORT WAS ORDERED, AND IF IT WAS, YOU WILL BE GIVEN THE NAME AND ADDRESS OF THE CONSUMER REPORTING AGENCY THAT FURNISHED THE REPORT

Fig. 2. Typical credit card application form.

If a high-speed computer is used, the entire authorization process can be accomplished in less than a minute (often within a few seconds), depending on the technique used for communicating with the computer.

Most of the larger credit card-issuing companies are now applying a strip of magnetic recording material on the back of their credit cards. When the magnetic data strip is used in conjunction with point-of-sale terminals (i.e., a cash register type of terminal connected to the authorization computer), the credit-available field of the data strip can be modified each time the customer makes a purchase. Many banks now use this technique to make cash available to depositors after banking hours. Both the American Bankers Association (ABA) and the International Air Transportation Association (IATA) have developed standards for recording data on the strip.

Billing. The sales data may be captured automatically at the time of the transaction, such as when making a credit card telephone call or when purchasing merchandise at large department stores. These systems generally use the descriptive billing method, in which only an itemized list of charges is sent to the customer for billing purposes.

In systems where copies of the original sales slips are returned to the customer with the bill (country club billing), such as gasoline or food purchases on credit cards, the sales data is usually entered subsequent to the sale. Country club billing systems often use a special-purpose computer with optical character readers to read the sales data from the sales ticket and sort the tickets for return to the customer.

Dunning and Collection. This final phase of the credit process occurs only when a debtor is delinquent in payment. A computer-processed analysis of all active accounts will single out those accounts for which required payment was not received within the specified time period. Depending on the size of the balance due and the amount of time the account is past due, an appropriate dunning letter can be selected from those stored in the computer's memory, printed, and then sent to the customer. After the proper series of dunning letters has been sent, the account can be flagged for personal review or for collection procedures.

Federal Legislation. Federal legislation has had a significant impact upon the entire credit system. The primary purpose of this legislation was to protect all consumers by giving them equal access to credit and more information about the charges to be made in their particular contractual situation.

The Truth in Lending Act (the Consumer Credit Protection Act—effective in 1969), and subsequent amendments, compels every person granting consumer credit to disclose certain information before credit is extended, and in periodic billing statements. The law mandates disclosure of finance charges, including annual percentage interest rates, and also defines other consumer rights concerning rescission of contracts; settlement of disputes over billing; and protection from harassment, abuse, or other unfair practices by debt collectors.

The Equal Credit Opportunity Act prohibits creditors from discriminating against applicants for credit on the basis of race, color, religion, national origin, sex, marital status, or age or because of the source of their income. Applicants who are denied credit must be given the reason for denial.

The Federal Reserve Board and other federal enforcement agencies continue to promote compliance with the act and regulations. The act and its numerous amendments have made compliance increasingly difficult for creditors.

As a result of federal legislation, billing, dunning, and collecting procedures have become increasingly more complicated. Where a large number of accounts are involved, it would be impossible to determine appropriate interest charges and report to each customer without the capabilities of a modern computer.

The increasing centralization of credit data in large computers has caused increasing public concern about loss of privacy in financial transactions.

A Typical Computerized Credit Card System. A credit card system is a large database system, typified by millions of accounts, random access storage, and strictly specified formats for inputting data and generating output reports. Although real-time inquiry into the file is usually available, inputting of data, file updating, and printing of invoices and statistical reports are usually done in a batch mode on a scheduled basis.

The basic functions performed by different credit card systems are very similar; however, there has been little sharing or purchasing of existing credit management packages. Each company has tended to develop and write its own in-house credit system, most often using Cobol for transaction processing and machine language to handle the inquiry portion of the application.

As an example, we consider a typical credit card system, used by a petroleum company to process its credit card sales, which handles about five million accounts. At the service station level, it requires a dollar-amount imprinter capable of transferring the customer data from the credit card and printing the dollar amount of the sale on the basic multipart paper sales document. The sales tickets are processed in one location, where the data is captured and entered automatically into the computer system through magnetic tape. The tape is created by a computer with optical capabilities for reading the imprinted information from the paper sales ticket. At the initial reading, the customer's account number and the dollar amount of the sale is sprayed in ink, using a unique recording code consisting of vertical lines and spaces, onto the back of the ticket to assist later in sorting.

Since all accounts are not billed on the same day of the month, the sales tickets are stored in a vault until a customer's cycle is billed. "Cycle billing" is used to level the daily processing time required by the system and to provide a more favorable cash flow situation.

After being billed, a customer is requested to return a portion of the bill with his or her payment. The payment is sent to a post office lock box, where collections are gathered and processed by the credit card company itself or by a bank which charges a service fee.

In processing the payments, the amount of the check must be compared with the amount on the returned portion of the bill. Any discrepancy, either under- or overpayment, requires additional handling and processing time. The checks must be encoded with the magnetic ink characters representing the amount for which the customer's check is drawn. The sum of the checks deposited is compared with the sum of the returned portions of the bills, to keep the system in balance.

For a system of about five million gasoline credit card accounts, $4 million per day must be processed and applied to the appropriate customers' accounts in order to keep the master file current. A staff of 75 customer service representatives is needed to process customer inquiries concerning the bills, payments, and special charges, and to handle the collection of delinquent accounts. The work of the service representatives is supported by 25 CRT terminals capable of inquiring into the computer's customer file, 5 microfilm readers to examine past history files, 20 clerical and typing assistants, and 15 WATS telephone lines for sales verification use.

Name and address changes to the file, special handling of certain accounts, and entering data from sales tickets that could not be read automatically by the document reader require another 40 data entry operators. These operators use key-to-disk and key-to-tape machines to enter the data into the third-generation computer's 100 million bytes of mass storage.

REFERENCES

1971. Whiteside, Conon D. *EDP Systems for Credit Management*. New York: Wiley.
1972. Hendrickson, Robert A. *The Cashless Society*. New York: Dodd, Mead & Co.
1978. "Compare the Big-Name Credit Cards," *Changing Times* **32**, *No. 8*:37–40 (August).

J. K. AMSBAUGH

CRIME AND COMPUTER SECURITY

For articles on related subjects *see* COMPUTING AND SOCIETY; DATA SECURITY; and SECURITY OF COMPUTER INSTALLATIONS, PHYSICAL.

The need for security measures to protect computers and their contents was recognized from the beginnings of computer usage for classified government projects and data. This was easily accomplished for early batch-operated computers that were made to perform one job completely before going to the next. Security was merely adapted from techniques used in the protection of manual handling of assets.

Problems arose when technical advances allowed the sharing of resources by more than one job at a time, on-line storing of data from job to job, and on-line servicing of more than one user at a time. At the same time, computers were being used for more purposes where the possibilities for unauthorized or malicious acts could result in gain, and errors could result in serious losses. Money in electronic form and data records representing valuable property are being moved from vaults to computers at a rapid rate, resulting in computers becoming the new vaults.

Technical safeguards have been developed to protect computer facilities with electronic door locks, to permit on-line terminal access control by requiring passwords, to protect data files by access controls and encryption and to assure operating system and application program integrity by program design and hardware functions. Analytical methods of performing risk analysis and safeguard selection help in optimizing the allocation of limited funds for computer security. The new occupations of EDP auditor and computer security specialist have helped to formalize the new discipline of computer security. But the problems are mostly caused by people, and solutions still must be found to control people working in positions of trust.

The first computer-related act involving criminal prosecution occurred in 1964. A programmer in Texas stole his employer's computer programs, worth $5 million, and was convicted and served a five-year prison sentence *(Texas v. Hancock)*. The first federal crime involving the use of a computer occurred in 1966, when a programmer in a bank put a change in a program to ignore his checking account when checking for overdrafts *(U.S. v. Bennett)*. In 1968, an accountant was caught after embezzling $1 million over a six-year period, and was convicted and sentenced to ten years in prison *(California v. Mansfield)*. The first crime of stealing a program, held as a trade secret, from the memory of a computer through a remote terminal and telephone circuit occurred in 1971 *(California v. Ward)*. The first case of using a personal microcomputer to automate attacks on the telephone system occurred in 1977 *(Pennsylvania v. Draper)*. In 1978, a computer security consultant violated his position of trust to obtain banking codes from a computer terminal facility to transfer $10.2 million to his bank account in Zurich *(U.S. v. Rifkin)*.

Broadening the concept of computer crime to any kind of act associated with computers where the victims suffered or could have suffered losses, or where the perpetrator experienced or could have experienced gain, provides a more all-inclusive perspective on the computer security problem. The number of such recorded acts has increased dramatically as seen in Fig. 1.

A collection and study of 669 reported cases (Parker, 1976) produced valuable facts for developing more effective computer security. In the cases studied, it was found that computers play four roles:

1. *Subject*. Acts such as vandalism or unauthorized usage attack computers or their contents.
2. *Unique environment*. This refers to acts involving computer programs and data in computer-readable form.
3. *Tool*. The computer is used to plan or carry out a crime.
4. *Symbol*. Fraudulent acts, deceit, or intimidation are charged as due directly to the use of computers, such as in false advertising of computer dating services or abusive dunning of consumers for unpaid bills.

The offenders tend to be in computer-related occupations, for these are the people with the necessary skills, access, and knowledge to perform automated crimes. Perpetrators in other occupations usually need the help of computer people to accomplish their ends. In fact, one study comparing computer- and non-computer-related

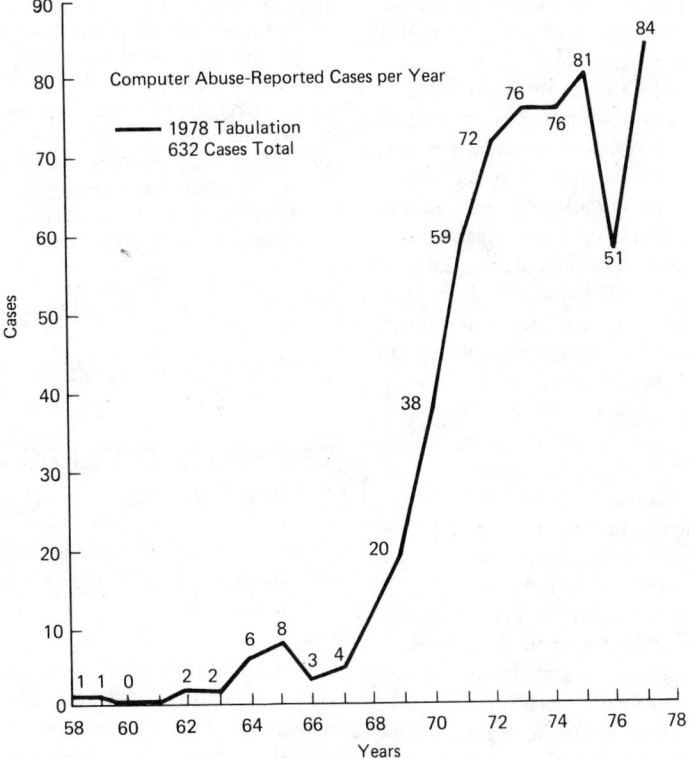

Fig. 1. Computer abuse case file history.

bank embezzlements bears this out. Collusion was present in one-third of the computer-related cases and in less than 4% of the other cases (Parker, 1976).

Perpetrators are generally young, energetic, highly motivated, intelligent people. In some cases, their acts deviate in only small ways from accepted practices of the perpetrators' associates, as in a case of program theft from the storage of a computer over a telephone circuit when it had become commonplace for programmers in computing service bureaus to obtain unauthorized access to one another's computers. One third of the perpetrators are managers. The "Robin Hood syndrome" is common—rationalizing acts against organizations, but believing acts against individuals to be immoral. This is combined with the "vending machine syndrome"—the challenge in the game of beating the machine and the absence of established ethical standards in the new computer-related occupations. A personal philosophy conducive to unauthorized acts and to criminal acts is created.

Assets subject to loss in computer-related acts are different enough from those in previous manual systems to confound the legal profession, the auditors, and traditional security people. Computer programs and data files represent entirely new types of assets—assets that are

being subjected to theft, fraud, unauthorized use, and use in extortion. Data stored magnetically and electronically is compact, volatile, only indirectly accessible, and highly time-dependent in value compared to paper-based data in previous manual systems. This produces a different environment for the criminal and offers real possibilities for effective protective measures because of the more structured and controlled environment in computers. It also appears that the stakes are high; losses noted among the reported computer-related crime cases are ten times higher than in comparable non-computer-related crime.

Computer security has several dimensions. It consists of physical, personnel, operational, data, program, and hardware protection. Security functions are avoidance, deterrence, prevention, detection, recovery, and correction. Expertise required includes industrial security, structural and electronic engineering, programming, computer operations, personnel management, and general management. Computer activities cover source data generation, data entry, software development, operations, system maintenance, and report distribution. Security can also be organized by application such as payroll, accounts payable, general ledger, inventory control, time-sharing, and so on. All of these dimensions show the wide scope of subjects and activities that come within computer security. However, the basic responsibility remains with each line manager for each particular area.

A computer system will be no more secure than its environment, the degree of trustworthiness of people in key positions or the procedures used in operation and maintenance. Adequate controls over physical access must be established, and sufficient administrative procedures and discipline in maintaining them must be imposed. Commonly accepted practices include manually or automatically guarded doors; coded badges to identify a wearer's authorized access area; separate performance and dual control of sensitive functions; pre-employment, in-depth screening of staff; posting appropriate warning signs; and control and labeling of valuable materials and media. Operational security audits should be made periodically, and backup copies of sensitive programs and data should be stored in safe places. Assignments of security responsibility should be made and a contingency plan drawn up and frequently tested. Error recovery and computer restart procedures should be formalized.

These security precautions should be present in any computer facility where possible threats that could result in losses, injuries, or damage are present. In the future, many security activities traditionally performed by people should be automated. However, technological methods are necessary, but not sufficient. Current computer systems cannot be sufficiently patched up—except in special cases and at high cost. No comprehensive technological solution is at hand (and none is expected for some years) so that new computer systems will have security included as a design criterion from the beginning. Even if such a solution is found, computers will still be vulnerable to a few systems maintenance people with sufficient skills, knowledge, and access. However, this limited accessibility would be a vast improvement over the present situation, in which large numbers of computer users have the capacity to subvert computers at both the system and application levels, as substantiated by actual experience.

The use of computers in data communication networks poses a new problem for security. Input and output functions are dispersed to remote terminals in relatively informal and isolated environments, making it especially difficult to identify the authorized terminals and terminal users, and to protect data transmission paths.

While theoretically an ideal protection of data paths is available with the use of data encryption techniques, the administration of encryption keys remains a problem. However, these problems should be solvable in the same time frame as other computer security problems.

References

1967. Ware, W. H. "Security and Privacy in Computer Systems," *AFIPS Proceedings,* Spring Joint Computer Conference.

1970. Smigel, E. and Ross, H. *Crimes Against Bureaucracy.* New York: Van Nostrand Reinhold.

1973. Anderson, J. P. *Computer Technology Planning Study* **1**. U. S. Air Force, ESD-TR-73-51.

1976. Parker, D. B. *Crime by Computer.* New York: Charles Scribner's Sons.

1979. Hsiao D., Kerr, D. S., and Madnick, S. *Computer Security.* New York: Academic Press.

1979. Krauss, L. I. and MacGahan, A. *Computer Fraud and Countermeasures.* Englewood Cliffs, NJ: Prentice-Hall.

D. B. PARKER

CRITICAL PATH METHOD. *See* PERT/CPM.

CROSS-ASSEMBLERS AND COMPILERS

For articles on related subjects *see* ASSEMBLERS; COMPATIBILITY; LANGUAGE PROCESSORS; and PORTABILITY.

A *cross-assembler (compiler)* is a program written to run on machine *A* and produce object code for another machine *B*. Thus, the cross-assembler (compiler) accepts as input a source program written for machine *B* and produces object code for that machine. For example, suppose machine *A* supports a language *L* which is particularly useful for writing compilers. Then a Fortran compiler for machine *B* can be written in *L*, to run on machine *A*. This compiler will accept Fortran statements in a form described in a Fortran manual for machine *B*, and it will produce object code in a form which can be run directly on machine *B*.

Cross-processors, a term including both cross-compilers and cross-assemblers, fulfill multiple needs. The major one is the ability to support software development for small or ill-equipped computers (i.e., machine *B*) on a machine (i.e., *A*) which has all the necessary tools for software development. Cross-processors also serve as a tool for production of software for hardware configurations that are not yet available, for the support of software for multiple diverse computers using only a single host for the cross-processors, for development of software for machines whose instruction set is such that compiler and assembler development is not feasible (e.g., floating point array processors, signal processors) and for support of development systems which are *down-loaded* from the host machine. Down-loading is a process in which a host computer transfers binary core images into another computer, so this second computer can then proceed with the program execution. The binary core images typically contain both programs and data, and can be a result of a program running on the host computer. A cross-processor together with a down-loader can be a powerful combination which accepts source language programs and data for them, creates the object program, and then loads the object computer with both programs and data.

G. FRIEDER

CRYPTOGRAPHY. *See* DATA ENCRYPTION.

CUBE

For article on related subject *see* COMPUTER USER GROUPS.

CUBE is the official organization of the users of Burroughs computers. The name CUBE is an acronym derived from *C*ooperating *U*sers of *B*urroughs *E*quipment.

CUBE was formed in 1962 through the merger of CUE (Burroughs B220 users' group) and DUO (B205, Datatron, users). The appearance in the early 1960s of the B200 and B5000 systems prompted the merger and ensured that a single association would serve the needs of all Burroughs computer users.

In 1972, CUBE was incorporated as a nonprofit association with the full name of CUBE, Incorporated. Membership is presently open to users of Burroughs B1000 through B7000 systems. At the beginning of 1980, CUBE members represented more than 1100 installations. CUBE membership is international in scope.

CUBE conferences are regularly held twice each year. These four-day conferences include technical workshops, user panels, and one-to-one clinics centered around hardware-oriented subgroups and industry-oriented common interest groups. The programs are planned and organized by the members in keeping with CUBE's purpose of providing a communications forum for the users of Burroughs equipment.

The communications emphasis within CUBE includes not only the sharing of ideas among users, but also the communicating to Burroughs of user sentiment on industry trends, future needs, and current products. Formal, two-way communication procedures have been established to facilitate this aspect of CUBE meetings.

Users of future Burroughs computers are assured of an opportunity to organize themselves into a CUBE subgroup by procedural mechanisms already present in the bylaws of CUBE.

More information about CUBE may be obtained by writing to the CUBE Secretary (Burroughs Corp., P. O. Box 418, Detroit, MI 48232).

The presidents of CUBE have been:

Vic Whittier, Dow Chemical Co., 1962–1963
Rusty Langenfeld, Northern Natural Gas Co., 1963–1964
John Lynn, NASA, 1964–1965
Bill Macomber, Harvard Trust Co., 1965–1966
Pete Jensen, Georgia Institute of Technology, 1966–1967
David Guest, Young & Rubicam, International, 1967–1968
Henry Bowlden, Westinghouse Electric Corp., 1968–1969
John Dorosk, Financial Computer Services, 1969–1970
Bill Eichelberger, University of Denver, 1970–1971
Bob Steffens, Michigan National Bank, 1971–1972
Henri Berce, Marathon Oil Co., 1972–1973
Henry Carter, United Data Centers, 1973–1974
Earl Betts, Michigan Bell Telephone Co., 1974–1975
Curtiss Berry, PPG Industries, 1975–1976
Wayne Jurgens, National Sharedata Corp., 1976–1977
Jerry Young, Livingston-Graham, Inc., 1977–1978
Milton Fredlund, Michigan Bell Telephone Co., 1978–1979
Thomas M. Locey, Electronic Processors, Ltd., 1979–1980

T. S. GRIER

CURRENT AWARENESS SYSTEMS

For articles on related subjects *see* INFORMATION RETRIEVAL; LIBRARY AUTOMATION; MEDLARS-MEDLINE; and NEW YORK TIMES INFORMATION BANK.

A current awareness system is a system for notifying users on a periodic basis of the acquisition of selected items of information (usually literature) by a central file or library. Such systems are designed to respond to the problems of search selectivity and timeliness by carrying out information searches, using only small files of selected documents. User queries, or *interest profiles,* are typically stored on a permanent basis, to be processed periodically against small files of documents that might be newly received at a given information center. Users are notified on a weekly or monthly basis of new acquisitions that match their interest profiles. Under ideal conditions, such systems for the *selective dissemination of information* (SDI) are able to retrieve information exactly tailored to meet the specific, possibly changing, needs of each user, while supplying the output directly on a periodic and dependable basis.

The rapid development of selective dissemination

services is due to two main factors: First, SDI services are much less expensive to implement than on-demand searches because there is no need to include in the document collections the backlog information covering many years in the past. Second, the existence of the many distribution services of magnetic tape databases—normally containing titles, citations, and sometimes index terms and abstracts of published articles and research—ensures the availability of the needed input data on a regular basis. Normally, the producers of the tape databases sell the SDI services directly on their own account, or they make the document tapes available to third parties, who in turn provide the dissemination service. SDI services are implemented in all areas of applied science and engineering, and in many of the natural and social sciences as well.

It has been conjectured that a flexible SDI service may be the answer to the inefficiencies now inherent in the normal publication system, in which each published item carries high publication costs and minimal readership. An improved, more economical system might then eliminate bound-volume journals entirely and restrict certain types of books to library use, while providing at the same time an efficient distribution of individual articles and citations that are tailored to specific user populations.

A flowchart outlining a typical SDI service is shown in Fig. 1. Specific SDI features are as follows.

1. *Universal features:* Utilization of user feedback; automatic or manual profile revision; option for hard copy of abstract and/or full text; and system evaluation.

2. *Optional features:* Use of free text (title or abstract) search; searching of multiple databases; incorporation of preprinted in addition to published information; incorporation of citation, author, or institution alert; and special distribution to designated recipients.

It should be noted that to improve services at a later time, nearly all SDI services include feedback provisions that utilize user opinions about the effectiveness of the search output. Specifically, response cards are often included with the output sent to the user population to enable the recipients to return information concerning the retrieved materials. Direct assessments of usefulness are sometimes wanted for each retrieved citation; alternatively, the return cards representing user requests for hard copies of certain retrieved documents are automatically taken by the system operators as an expression of approbation on the user's part.

In either case, the user profile statement may be updated, often manually, by reinforcing or increasing the weight of profile terms that match terms included in retrieved items designated as relevant by the users. Profile terms included in documents identified as nonrelevant

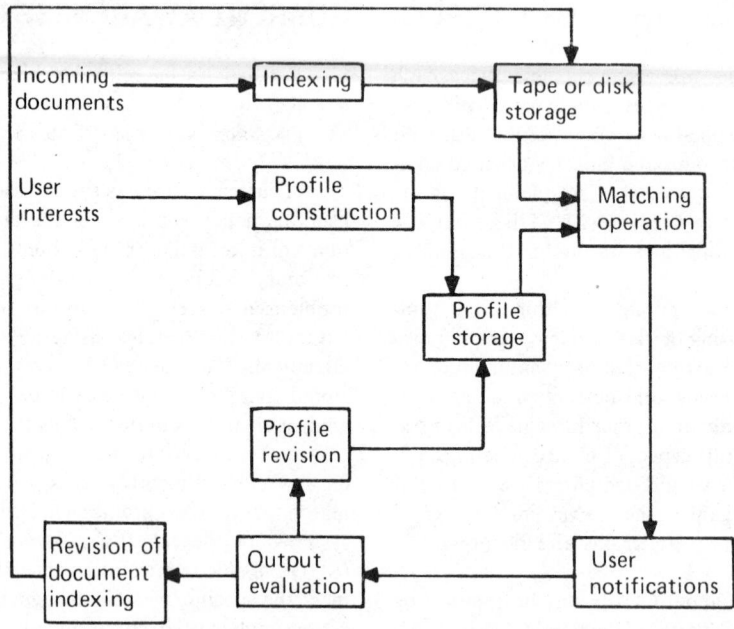

Fig. 1.   Typical simplified selective dissemination service.

may be similarly demoted or decreased in weight. Occasionally, the document indexing may also be changed as a function of user judgment. The corresponding feedback paths are indicated in Fig. 1.

The feedback feature is particularly useful in a research environment, where user interests may change fairly rapidly. The profiles can then be adjusted little by little as the users express satisfaction or dissatisfaction with the materials obtained from the retrieval service.

Among the useful optional SDI features is the possibility of including in the distribution service those documents in preprint form or other items that are not intended for eventual formal publication. This option provides the means for bypassing the normal publication process and for avoiding publication delays. Delays can also be avoided by having the authors of certain items provide a special distribution list of recipients to whom the corresponding documents are to be sent regardless of the profile-matching results. Finally, the participants in an SDI system can gain better service by extending their profiles to include not only subject terms, but also names of authors or of institutions whose documents they wish to receive automatically.

Another extension of optional service permits the inclusion of document citations in the user profiles so that new items citing the original profile documents will be automatically retrieved with other pertinent materials. In its simplest form, such a citation-monitoring system would alert a given participant whenever one of his or her own papers was being cited by some outside author, assuming that the users of the service include their own documents as part of their profiles. Alternatively, in many circumstances, a citation alert system can simplify normal subject searches by eliminating the problems of vocabulary know-how and control that affect document indexing and query formulations.

An evaluation of SDI services shows that a large proportion of the materials retrieved for the user population is indeed germane to user interests. However, complaints arise because of the large volume of output continually delivered by the services. Even if the proportion of relevant items is fairly high, users receiving 30 or 40 citations every week may eventually tire of the system and revert to on-demand searches that furnish output only when specific requests for service are made.

G. SALTON

CURSOR

For articles on related subjects *see* COMPUTER GRAPHICS; DATA TABLET; and JOYSTICK.

A cursor is a special character or symbol on a soft copy (display) terminal, which is used by an interactive program as a pointer or attention-focusing device to allow communication and interaction between the console operator and the program. On alphanumeric displays, for example, a (blinking) underscore or overscore character (or an inverted v, called a "caret") may be used by the program or the hardware to indicate where the next character to be typed by the operator will appear or where the program should start or stop reading the message prepared by the operator at the console. As the operator types, the cursor is automatically advanced, including automatic movement to successive lines. Additionally, many alphanumeric displays have several special keys to move the position of the cursor: left, right, up, down, home (upper left-hand corner of the display).

On a graphics console, the cursor symbol is typically used in conjunction with a manual input device such as a joystick or data tablet to provide the console operator with visual feedback as the joystick or the tablet stylus is moved. On a vector graphics display, the beam deflection applied to the cathode-ray tube to display the cursor is derived from the hardware registers that record the angular displacement or x-y position of the input device to which the cursor is coupled. On a raster graphics display, the cursor data is videomixed with the other data to be displayed in the analog voltages going to the guns. In effect, the operator can "drive" the cursor around the screen until it is placed at the exact x-y location desired. Once positioned, the operator can indicate to the system that this particular cursor position is to be transmitted to the program. The cursor x-y position can then be used by the program either to provide raw x-$\bar{y}$ *drawing* input data or to be compared against x-y positions of information already on the screen for identification purposes (thereby providing a substitute for identification by lightpen *picking*).

A. VAN DAM

CYBER. *See* CONTROL DATA CORPORATION CYBER SERIES.

CYBERNETICS

For articles on related subjects *see* AUTOMATION; CONTROL APPLICATIONS; and WIENER, NORBERT A.

Cybernetics is a science founded in the 1940s by a group of scientists and engineers led by N. Wiener and A. Rosenblueth, who coined the word "cybernetics" (from Greek: pilot, steersman, governor) to designate the science of "control and communication in the animal and the machine" (Wiener, 1948). This definition still expresses the substantial content of cybernetics, although there is a broad spectrum of current interpretations (Drozin *et al.*, 1973).

Cybernetic concepts cluster around three related component concepts: systems (animal or machine), communication between systems, and regulation or self-regulation of systems. Since the first two are common to nearly all fields of knowledge, it is the third component, regulation, that distinguishes the discipline. Cybernetics is the science of regulation and control—purposive regulation for adaptive system survival (Beer, 1966).

Cybernetics borrows ubiquitously from other sciences. Borrowing from mathematical concepts, cybernetics concerns all conceivable *sets* of systems (Ashby, 1970); and from physical and psychological concepts, it "deals with all forms of behaviour in so far as they are regular, or determinate, or reproducible" (Ashby, 1970, p. 1). However, to be of practical interest, cybernetic systems have two properties: (1) some aspect must provide observable data over a period of time (the *protocol*, Ashby, 1970, p. 88); (2) from the protocol it must be possible to infer some stable configuration or regularity in transformation of states. Without observable regularity in transformation, a system is said to be unconstrained. Without constraint, it is unpredictable; if it becomes unstable, it cannot be restored to stability or is uncontrollable. For regulation, a system must show some regularity.

Time is the principal cybernetic variable, while "variety" is the principal dependent variable. Variety is quantitatively measured by the logarithm (usually base 2) of the number of discriminations that an observer (or a sensing system) can make relative to a system (Ashby, 1968, p. 124). For example, in the phrase "take care" the variety is $\log_2 6 = 2.51$ bits if the system is the set of distinguishably different letters; $\log_2 2 = 1$ bit if the system is the set of words; and $\log_2 1 = 0$ if the system is the message considered as a unit. Because variety is based on discrimination of differences, it measures equally well all psychophysical or higher cognitive discriminations (Heilprin, 1973). For example the variety in five psychophysically discriminated shades of green is $\log_2 5 = 2.25$ bits, the same as the variety in a decision process from a choice of five abstract alternatives.

The real significance of variety lies not in its absolute amount, but in the possibility of its increase or decrease. We increase sensory variety when we gather data, decrease it when we summarize, compress, abstract. Both processes are necessary for cognition. However, "lower" cognitive processes are associated with data gathering or increase in concrete sensory variety, whereas "higher" cognitive processes are associated with data condensation, abstraction, or decrease in concrete variety.

When the variety shown by a system under one set of conditions is less than that shown by the system under another set of conditions, the relation between the two sets of variety is a *constraint* (Ashby, 1968, p. 127). For example, suppose two couples (A and B, or four voters) can each vote independently R or D. Then the number of distinguishably different outcomes is $2^4 = 16$ and the variety is $\log_2 16 = 4$ bits. If, however, Mr. A always defers to Mrs. A's judgment and votes the same as Mrs. A, the number of different outcomes is 8 and the variety shown $\log_2 8 = 3$ bits. If, further, Mr. and Mrs. B always vote R, then the variety in the outcomes is $\log_2 2 = 1$ bit. The progressive decrease in variety from 4 bits to 3 to 1 corresponds to increase in constraint on the system showing the variety. Returning to the requirement for regulation—that there must exist some constraint in order to predict the behavior of a system—it is apparent that to regulate a system is to impose a constraint on its variety.

The cybernetics of constrained and unconstrained sets was advanced by the insight of Wiener (1948) who said that "the transmission of information is impossible save as a transmission of alternatives," and by Shannon's observation that "the significant aspect is that the actual message is *selected from* a set of possible messages" (Shannon and Weaver, 1949). Thus, *regulation implies capability to prevent occurrence of unfavorable alternatives.* Therefore, it implies *transmission* of these alternatives to the regulator, which in turn must respond (with a command message directed toward preserving the stability of the regulated system).

Fig. 1 shows the basic elements of a regulatory system. The system whose essential variables (E) are to be kept within certain limits depends on communication of variety (information) between system disturbance (D), the regulator (R), and the environment (T). The most direct regulation is DR, shown in Fig. 1(a). The signal arrives from D in time for R to act on T before T affects E. Figs. 1(c) and 1(d) show paths DTR and DTER, progressively less effective. Perfect regulation [Fig. 1(b)] would leave E isolated from external disturbance—i.e., unaware because of noncommunication that a disturbance had occurred.

A system is said to be well regulated when, through the intervention of the regulator and the environment, a disturbance cannot permanently drive the system from a state in which it is stable (retains its structure and function—"survives"). Lack of regulation occurs when the system is transformed to a state from which it cannot return to a stable state; i.e., cannot survive.

The principal law of cybernetics (credited to Ashby, 1968, p. 206) is the *law of requisite variety*. This states that if $\log V_d$ is the variety in the possible ways in which a disturbance D can affect a system E (to be regulated by a regulator R), and $\log V_r$ is the variety in R's alternatives (optional ways of response to D), then the variety

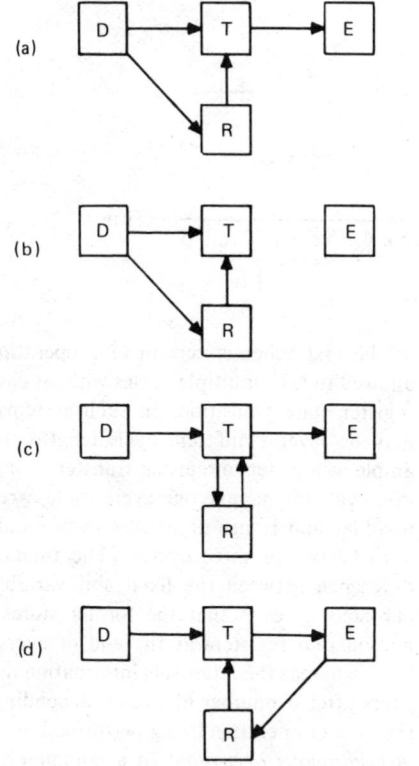

Fig. 1. Law of requisite variety. (a) One-step communication channel regulation: D → R. (b) Perfect (one step) regulaton: D → R. (c) Two-step regulation: D → T → R. (d) Three-step (error controlled) regulation: D → T → E → R.

and homomorphism, and epigenetic theory of regulation. See the references cited and a growing list of periodicals, among which are *Biological Cybernetics* (a continuation of *Kybernetik,* Vol. 1–16), *Cybernetica* (International Association of Cybernetics), *Cybernetics Forum* (American Society for Cybernetics), *Kybernetes, Transactions on Systems, Man and Cybernetics* (IEEE), and *Soviet Cybernetic Review.*

REFERENCES

1948. Wiener, N. *Cybernetics or Control and Communication in the Animal and the Machine.* Cambridge, MA: M.I.T. Press, New York: Wiley (2nd ed., 1965).

1949. Shannon, C. E. and Weaver, W. *The Mathematical Theory of Communication.* Urbana, IL: University of Illinois Press, p. 3.

1968, Ashby, W. R. *An Introduction to Cybernetics.* London: Methuen (University Paperbacks, 1956), Chap. 7.

1968. *Encyclopedia of Cybernetics* (translation of German *Lexicon der Kybernetik).* New York: Barnes and Noble.

1970. Beer, S. *Decision and Control.* New York: Wiley, Chap. 15.

1973. Drozin, V. G., Fisher, R., Kopstein, F. F., Pask, G., and Toda, M. "What is Cybernetics?," *FORUM, American Society for Cybernetics* V, *No. 4:*3–8 (December).

1973. Heilprin, L. B. *Impact of the Cybernetic Law of Requisite Variety on a Theory of Information Science.* College Park, MD: University of Maryland Computer Science Center, Report No. TR-236 (March), ERIC No. ED 073 777, pp. 9–10.

L. B. HEILPRIN

CYCLE STEALING

For article on related subject *see* MEMORY: Main.

Cycle stealing is a technique for memory sharing whereby a memory may serve two autonomous masters and in effect provide service to each simultaneously. One of the masters is commonly the central processing unit (CPU), and the other is usually an I/O channel or device controller. Fig. 1 illustrates two memory cycles (numbers 3 and 5) being stolen by an I/O channel (from the CPU) between two cycles of memory use by the CPU. This is possible and convenient, at least periodically, because the CPU is self-driven (except possibly between some substeps of a process it is conducting) and has no fixed time demands on memory. Furthermore, there are occasions, particularly in simpler CPU designs, where the instruction being obeyed (e.g., division) is processor-limited (i.e., uses all the processor's capabilities) and memory access is temporarily suspended.

The I/O equipment is, on the other hand, quite different. Its use of the memory, though generally less fre-

in the possible outcomes (log V_0) affecting E cannot be forced by R below (log V_d − log V_r), or log (V_d/V_r) ≥ log V_0.

This law applies to all forms of regulation, and is independent of field of science or technology or of specific mechanism. Loosely interpreted, it means that—assuming the disturbance, environment, and the system itself are fixed and cannot be altered—the only way to increase E's probability of survival is to increase R's variety (R's versatility, or the number of different modes of response which R can make in order to protect E's stability as affected by D). However, satisfying the law by increasing V_r does not guarantee perfect regulation, i.e., perfect shielding of E. Just as the existence of constraint is necessary but not sufficient for regulation, satisfying the law of requisite variety is necessary but not sufficient for successful regulation (Heilprin, 1973, p. 24).

Space prevents discussion of many prominent cybernetic features such as classification of cybernetic systems by intractability to control (determinate, complex, and "very large"), black-box theory, feedback, isomorphism

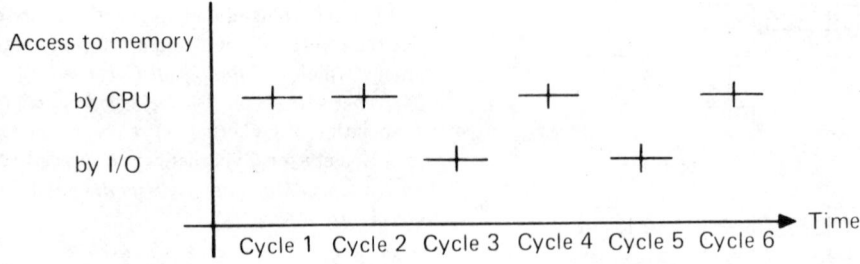

Fig. 1.   Cycle Stealing.

quent than that by the CPU, is much more time-constrained. For many I/O devices such as disks and tapes, data is produced or required at fixed intervals. The need for data transfer occurs relentlessly at fixed time intervals. In transferring data from a tape to memory, the previous byte or word must have been stored before the next arrives; otherwise data is lost. This problem is somewhat alleviated by the use of single or multiple buffers (*q.v.*) in the device controller and/or channel, but in any case there are important recurring time demands for memory access. These can be met by the technique of cycle stealing in those CPU designs in which processor activity can be suspended for a memory cycle while a memory access is made by the I/O system.

K. C. SMITH AND A. SEDRA

CYCLE TIME

For articles on related subjects *see* LOCAL STORE; REGISTER; and SYNCHRONOUS-ASYNCHRONOUS OPERATION.

The cycle time of a computer is the time required to change the information in a set of registers. This is also sometimes called the *state transition time*.

The register cycle time of a processor is sometimes referred to as the *internal cycle time, clock time,* or simply *cycle time;* occasionally, confusion develops between the internal cycle time (referenced to registers) and the main memory cycle time. The memory cycle time is usually several times the internal cycle time.

The internal cycle time may not be of constant value. There are basically three different types of cycle-timing organizations.

1. *Synchronous (fixed):* In this scheme all operations are composed of one or more cycles, with the fundamental time quantum being fixed by the design. Such systems are also referred to as *clocked,* since usually a master oscillator (or clock) is used to distribute and define these cycles.
2. *Synchronous (variable):* This is a slight variation

of the first scheme; certain long operations are allowed to take multiple cycles without causing a register state transition. In such systems there may be several different cycle lengths. For example, a register-to-register transfer of information cycle might take one cycle while a register-to-adder and return-to-register cycle would perhaps be two or three cycles. (The fundamental difference between the fixed and variable synchronous types is that the former stores information into registers at the end of every cycle time, whereas the latter sets information into registers after a number of cycles, depending upon the type of operation being performed.)

3. *Asynchronous operation:* In a completely asynchronous machine there is no clock or external mechanism that determines a state transition. Rather, the logic of the system is arranged in stages; when the output value of one stage has been stabilized, the logic signals the input at that stage to admit new operands. (Asynchronous operation is clearly advantageous when the variation in cycle time is significant, since a synchronous scheme must always wait for the worst possible delay in the definition of the time quantum required. On the other hand, when logic delays are predictable, synchronous approaches have an advantage because several additional stages of logic are required in the asynchronous scheme to signal completion of an operation.)

In actual practice, most systems are basically synchronous (either fixed or variable) with some asynchronous operations being used for particular parts of the machine, such as handling access to main memory.

M. J. FLYNN

CYCLIC REDUNDANCY CHECK

For articles on related subjects *see* CODES; ERROR CORRECTING CODES; and PARITY.

In modern computer systems, data is continuously transferred between the main processor and its peripherals, storage, or terminals. Errors may be introduced during the reading, writing, or actual transmission of this data. Consequently, error control has become an integral part in the design of modern computers and communication systems. The most commonly used methods for error detection involve the addition of one or more bits, called *redundancy* bits, to the information-carrying bits of a character or stream of characters. These redundancy bits do not carry any information; they are merely used to determine the correctness of the bits carrying the information.

Perhaps the most commonly used method for error detection is the simple parity check. Parity may be even or odd, meaning that the sum of the "one" bits of any character, including the parity bit itself, will always be even or odd, depending upon which arrangement is chosen.

Fig. 1 illustrates a form of two-dimensional parity checking used on some magnetic tapes that can detect and even correct some types of errors. The six-bit characters are arranged in columns with a seventh odd parity bit, called the *vertical redundancy check* (VRC), added to make the sum of the "one" bits in each column an odd number. Similarly, an odd parity-check bit, called the *longitudinal redundancy check* (LRC), is added at the end of the block for each row of bits. As the tape is read, the VRC and LRC are regenerated and checked with the

check characters read. If equal, the information is assumed correct. If not equal, the block is read again. Some types of errors, like the one shown in Fig. 1, may also be corrected by using this method.

Cyclic redundancy checking is a far more powerful error-detecting method. Here, all the characters in a message block are treated as a serial string of bits representing a binary number. This number is then divided modulo 2 by a predetermined binary number and the remainder of this division is appended to the block of characters as a cyclic redundancy check (CRC) character. The CRC is compared with the check character obtained in similar fashion at the receiving end. If they agree, the message is assumed correct. If they disagree, the receiving terminal will demand a retransmission. This is usually called the ARQ (automatic repeat request) method of error control and is very commonly used in data communication. The CRC character is also called the *cyclic check sum,* or simply the *check sum* character.

To show how the CRC is generated, let the message consist of k bits, $a_0 a_1 \cdots a_{k-1}$, $a_i = 0$ or 1. Then we form the $(k - 1)$-degree polynomial:

$$M(x) = a_0 + a_1 x + \cdots + a_{k-1} x^{k-1} = \sum_{i=0}^{k-1} a_i x^i. \quad (1)$$

If we wish to include r CRC bits, $r < k$, $M(x)$ is multiplied by x^r (this is equivalent to shifting the message bits r places to the right). Let $G(x)$ be another polynomial—

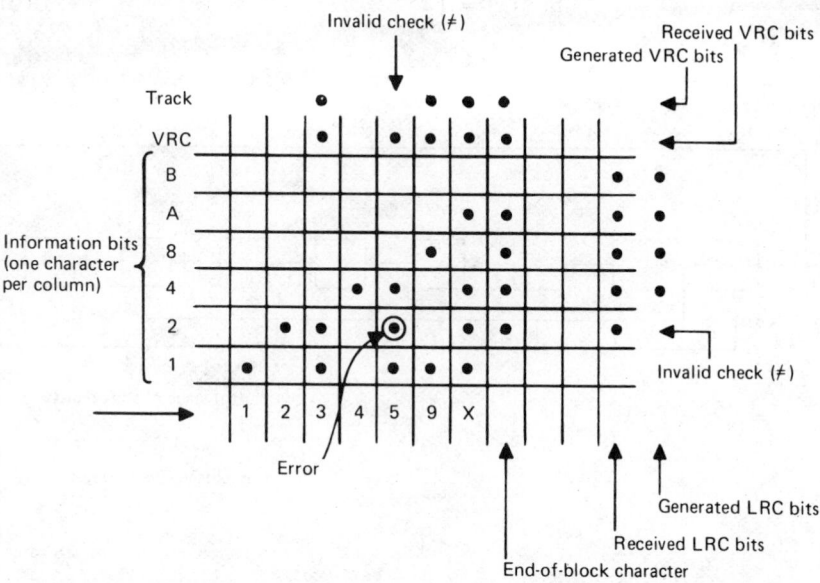

Fig. 1.   Error detection using LRC and VRC bits. An extra "1" bit has been introduced in the character "5." Assuming no errors in the received check bits, the error must occur at the intersection of the invalid check column and row. The error bit must be reversed. In this case, the "1" must be changed to "0."

called the "generator" or "checking" polynomial—of degree r, whose coefficients are also 0 or 1. We divide $x^r M(x)$ by $G(x)$, obtaining

$$\frac{x^r M(x)}{G(x)} = Q(x) + \frac{R(x)}{G(x)} \qquad \text{mod 2} \qquad (2)$$

where the "mod 2" indicates that all sums and differences of coefficients are taken as 0, if the result is 0 or even, and 1 if it is odd. Thus, from Eq. (2)

$$R(x) = x^r M(x) + Q(x) G(x) \qquad \text{mod 2} \qquad (3)$$

where $R(x)$ is the remainder and $Q(x)$ is the quotient. The code word $W(x)$ is

$$W(x) = Q(x) G(x) = x^r M(x) + R(x) \qquad \text{mod 2}, \qquad (4)$$

and what is transmitted are the coefficients of $W(x)$.

Note that $W(x)$, which is of degree $r + k - 1$, contains the original k message bits (the $x^r M(x)$ term) and r check bits (the $R(x)$ term). Furthermore, $W(x)$ is exactly divisible by $G(x)$. The division by $G(x)$ at the transmitting end is accomplished by an r stage-shift register with feedback paths represented by the coefficients of $G(x)$, as shown in Fig. 2. On the receiving end, $W(x)$ is also divided by $G(x)$, and the remainder in this case must be 0; otherwise, an error has occurred.

Consider the following example related to the shift register shown in Fig. 2. Let the message be 1010010001. Therefore, $M(x) = 1 + x^2 + x^5 + x^9$. With $G(x) = 1$ $+ x^2 + x^4 + x^5$, modulo 2 division of $x^5 M(x)$ by $G(x)$ yields

$$Q(x) = 1 + x + x^2 + x^3 + x^7 + x^8 + x^9$$

and $R(x) = 1 + x$. Thus

$$W(x) = 1 + x + x^5 + x^7 + x^{10} + x^{14},$$

and the transmitted message is

11000	1010010001
CRC	original
bits	message
	bits

The remainder, $R(x)$, is generated by the shift register (which is initially at 00000) as follows:

Message Bit	Shift Register Contents
	Stage 12345
1	10101
0	11111
0	11010
0	01101
1	00110
0	00011
0	10100
1	11111
0	11010
1	11000

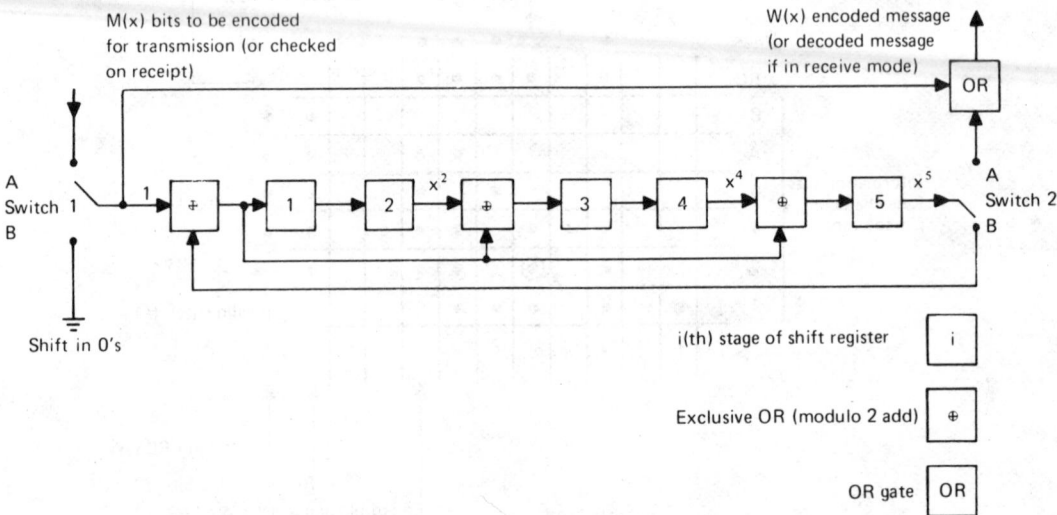

Fig. 2. Shift register for $G(x) = 1 + x^2 + x^4 + x^5$. Initially, the register contains 00000, switch 1 is in position A, and switch 2 is in position B. When all message bits have been transmitted, the register contains $R(x)$. Switch 1 now goes to B, and switch 2 goes to A to enable $R(x)$ to be shifted out. When data is being received, the resulting $R(x)$ must be zero; otherwise, the data is in error.

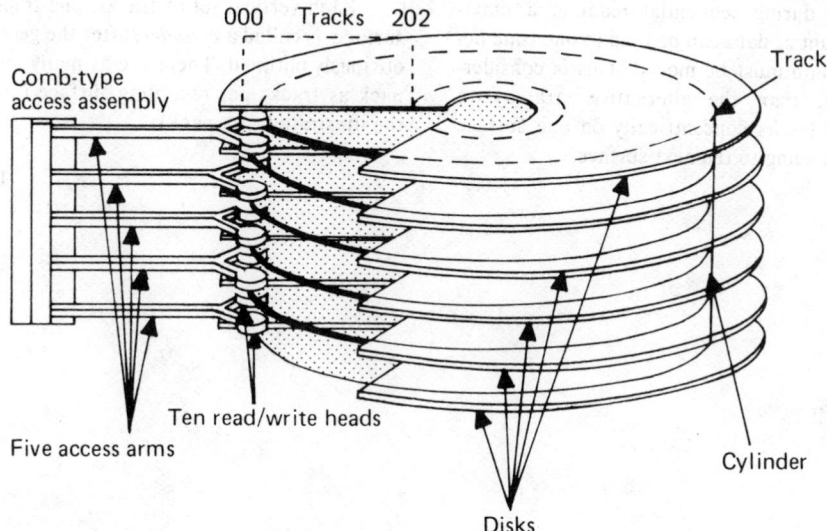

000   Tracks   202

Track

Comb-type
access assembly

Ten read/write heads

Five access arms

Cylinder

Disks

Fig. 1.   Typical moving-head disk drive and pack.

The final content is $R(x)$. Each successive shift register content represents a successive stage of the division of $x^5M(x)$ by $G(x)$, remembering that only the bits of $x^5M(x)$, which have been already transmitted at each stage, take part in the division. When all message bits have been transmitted, the contents of the shift register are shifted out by five successive right shifts to transmit $R(x)$. Note that during this operation, the zeros are shifted into stage 1 so that after $R(x)$ is transmitted, the contents are 00000; hence, the register is automatically cleared for more transmission.

Codes developed as described above are called *cyclic* codes. Such codes are used for error detection and correction for magnetic tape, disk, and data communication. The generator polynomial $x^{16} + x^{15} + x^2 + 1$, for example, is widely used in synchronous data communication systems. It can detect all odd numbers of error bits, all possible single-error bursts not exceeding 16 bits, 99.9969% of all possible single bursts 17 bits long, and 99.9984% of all possible longer bursts. This is much better than simple parity checking, for instance, which detects only all odd numbers of error bits and no others. Note that parity checking is equivalent to having a generator polynomial $G(x) = x + 1$.

The study of cyclic codes revolves principally upon determining the code characteristics resulting from various generator polynomials. Peterson and Weldon (1972) and Tang and Chien (1969) give some applications and a more thorough mathematical treatment of cyclic and other codes.

REFERENCES

1969. Tang, D. T. and Chien, R. T. "Coding for Error Control" *IBM Systems Journal* **8**, *No. 1*:48–86.

1972. Peterson, W. W. and Weldon, E. J. *Error-Correcting Codes,* 2nd Ed. Cambridge, MA: M.I.T. Press.
1977. MacWilliams, F. and Sloane, N. J. A. *The Theory of Error-Correcting Codes.* Amsterdam: Elsevier.

J. S. SOBOLEWSKI

CYLINDER

For articles on related subjects *see* ACCESS TIME; MEMORY; Auxiliary; and VOLUME.

Many rotating storage devices—drums, disks, data cells, and the like—have fewer read/write heads than recording tracks. Therefore, either the surfaces of these devices must move to position the desired information under a read/write head, or the read/write heads must move to hover above the appropriate tracks. The latter strategy is commonly used for large direct-access devices such as disks containing at least 20 million bytes.

For engineering convenience and efficient sequential processing of data, the following design has been adopted by most manufacturers of moving-head disk drives:

1. Disk surfaces are numbered from top to bottom for each horizontal position of the read/write comb (see Fig. 14 in MEMORY: Auxiliary).
2. During sequential writing operations, as the top track in each vertical plane becomes filled, control circuitry and system software allocate subsequent records to the beginning of the next vertical track. When this is filled, records are started on the third track, etc.

3. Therefore, during sequential reading, a maximum amount of data can be read at one time before the comb must be moved. This is considerably faster than the alternative strategy of writing all tracks concentrically on one surface before advancing to the next surface.

Each vertical set of tracks, one track per recording surface, is called a *cylinder*, after the geometrical surface obviously outlined. There are as many cylinders per disk pack as tracks per recording surface (203 cylinders for the illustrated disk pack).

D. N. FREEMAN

D

DATA ACQUISITION COMPUTER

For articles on related subjects *see* ANALOG-TO-DIG-
ITAL AND DIGITAL-TO-ANALOG CONVERTERS; POINT-
OF-SALE TERMINAL; and SPECIAL-PURPOSE
COMPUTERS.

Computers have been used for decades to acquire
and analyze data generated by instruments such as voltmeters, thermocouples, and electromechanical relays in
factories, refineries, missiles, or aircraft. Typical data acquisition (DA) computers have fast memory-cycle times
so that bursts of signals from real-time physical processes
such as video scan devices will not be lost. Although early
DA computers had relatively short word lengths (16–24
bits), many now have 32-bit words so as to utilize the
same architecture as general-purpose minicomputers,
permitting economies of scale in manufacturing and software support. Although most DA computers lack floating-point instructions (since measured data are inherently within predefined narrow ranges), the modest
incremental cost for FP hardware has encouraged its inclusion in large devices.

The main components of a data-acquisition computer are as follows.

1. Analog and digital input cables.
2. Analog to digital converter.
3. Disk or tape cassette for storage.
4. Central processor.
5. Main memory.
6. Operator console.

For low-volume data acquisition, a paper-tape punch or
floppy-disk drive may be substituted for the disk drive or
tape cassette.

Programs are loaded from punched paper tape, cassettes, floppy disks, or—in some newer models—a host
computer over a communications link.

Prices of data acquisition computers have decreased
considerably since 1965, improving their advantage over
manual methods for capturing and transcribing data in
many applications. Their inherent reliability—especially
central processor, main memory, and disk/tape components—has risen to such high levels that they may operate unattended for days at a time. To raise system reliability still higher, multiple (three to five) processors are
often packaged together, so that failure of one processor
leaves the DA computer functionally intact (albeit slowed
down).

Many data acquisition computers have been "rug-
gedized" to function in high-temperature environments
such as steel plants or high-acceleration environments
such as spacecraft.

During the 1980s, powerful, low-cost, miniaturized
DA computers are being installed increasingly close to
where the original data is generated: Factory floors, cash
registers, continuous-process plants, etc. They are connected by medium-speed (2,400 bits per second) telephone links to central computers, which periodically poll
them for data, display status reports on processing being
supervised, and print hardware-reliability reports on the
data acquisition computers themselves.

D. N. FREEMAN

DATA BANK

For articles on related subjects *see* COMPUTING AND SOCIETY; DATABASE MANAGEMENT; and FILES.

A data bank is a file of data derived from a variety of sources and stored for ready access by a number of users. The term first came into use in the 1960s for a data system in which, for example, a municipal government could combine school, tax, utility, welfare, health, police, and other files. All departments of government could then draw data from this bank in making operational and planning decisions. This term is often used synonymously with *database*.

Early versions of such systems triggered public protest as a threat to personal privacy on the grounds that people should be able to exercise reasonable control over the circulation of information about themselves. Although some authors (Miller, 1972, for example) saw the threat as serious, Westin and Baker (1972) studied the operation of actual data banks and concluded that computerization as such had had little effect on the content or use of files and had specifically not resulted in the creation of computer networks through which individual dossiers could be assembled. They warned, though, that technical developments might change the situation and recommended legal protection for the privacy of computerized personal data.

A committee of the Department of Health, Education, and Welfare recommended that the following principles be made the basis of a code of fair information practice, with statutory penalties to be provided for failure to observe the code in the operation of a data bank.

- There must be no personal data record-keeping systems the very existence of which is secret.
- There must be a way for an individual to find out what personal information is in a record and how it is used.
- There must be a way for an individual to prevent personal information, obtained for one purpose, from being used or made available for other purposes without consent.
- There must be a way for an individual to correct or amend a record of identifiable personal information.
- Any organization creating, maintaining, using, or disseminating records of identifiable personal data must ensure the reliability of the data for their intended use and must take reasonable precautions to prevent misuse of the data.

This code was incorporated, with some elaboration, into the Privacy Act of 1974 (88Stat. 1905[b][1]; PL93-579) and now applies to the majority of personal data records. The Act also created the Privacy Protection Study Commission, which issued a thorough analysis of the effects of the Act (PPSC, 1977) and made recommendations for future revisions.

Besides these statutory controls on possible misuse of data banks, recent developments in data encryption (*q.v.*) have improved security against unauthorized access to personal information.

REFERENCES

1972. Miller, Arthur R. *The Assault on Privacy: Computers, Data Banks, and Dossiers.* Ann Arbor: University of Michigan Press (New York: Signet Books).
1972. Westin, Alan F. and Baker, Michael A. *Data Banks in a Free Society.* New York: Quadrangle Books.
1973. U.S. Department of Health, Education, and Welfare, Secretary's Advisory Committee on Automated Data Systems. *Records, Computers, and the Rights of Citizens.* Cambridge, MA: MIT Press (Washington, DC: U.S. Government Printing Office).
1977. Privacy Protection Study Commission. *Personal Privacy in an Information Society.* Washington, DC: U.S. Government Printing Office.

D. H. LUFKIN

DATABASE ADMINISTRATOR

For articles on related subjects *see* DATABASE MANAGEMENT; DATABASE, ON-LINE; DATA DEFINITION LANGUAGES; and MANAGEMENT INFORMATION SYSTEMS.

Definition. A database administrator (DBA) is an individual or team performing the functions of planning, designing, maintaining, and monitoring the database of an organization at the operational level. The database administrator is responsible for all aspects of database usage, except for the details of the application programs.

Functions. The role of a database administrator varies among organization. The tasks listed below are common to most database administrators.

1. *Select database software.* The DBA must match the database requirements of the organization against the capabilities of available database packages.
2. *Development standards.* The successful use of a database system is dependent upon the establishment, within an organization, of standard practices for the definition and manipulation of data.

3. *Define database.* Using a data definition language, the DBA defines the *schema* which specifies the format and logical relationships of all data items in the database. Then a *subschema* for each application program is created in order to define the program's view of the database.

4. *Establish access policies.* For each application program, the DBA specifies the access restrictions (read, write, shared, exclusive) for the data in the subschema.

5. *Load the database.* This is a one-time task, the complexity of which is highly dependent upon the database package and the volume of data.

6. *Maintain the database.* The DBA must oversee all changes to the content, structure, and usage of the database.

7. *Forecast growth.* The DBA must be able to predict accurately the growth of the database in terms of both new and expanding applications.

Role. The role of the DBA within the corporate structure is still evolving. The generally accepted stance is that the DBA is primarily a technician, albeit a highly skilled one, who may have some managerial responsibilities. Although the database administration function is critical in any database installation, its practice is presently more an art form than a science.

REFERENCES

1976. Lyon, John K. *The Data Base Administrator.* New York: Wiley.
1979. Cardenas, Alfonso F. *Data Base Management Systems.* Boston: Allyn and Bacon.

F. MARYANSKI

DATABASE MANAGEMENT

For articles on relate subjects *see* ACCESS METHODS; DATA BANK; DATABASE ADMINISTRATOR; DATABASE, ON-LINE; DATA DEFINITION LANGUAGES; DATA SET; FILES; and PROGRAMMING LANGUAGES.

Database. The term *database* has yet to achieve a widely accepted standard meaning. However, it is to some extent accepted as conveying a more sophisticated concept than the older term *file,* which was carried over into data processing terminology from the precomputer era. Unfortunately, it is all too frequently used when all that is implied is a conventional file. The difference between a database and a file, in terms used prior to the advent of data processing, is perhaps analogous to the difference between a thoroughly cross-referenced set of files in cabinets in a library or in an office and a single file in one cabinet which is not cross-referenced to any other file.

The important difference is that the *database* must be stored in the computer on direct-access storage (such as disks) in order for the computer's central processing unit (CPU) to be able to utilize the cross-references within a reasonable time. By contrast, a set of cross-referenced *files* could be theoretically stored on magnetic tape. However, the computer would then spend unacceptable amounts of time searching the tapes because it is not possible to access a specific data record on tape without passing over all other data preceding it on the tape. However, despite this disadvantage, magnetic tape is likely to remain the principal storage medium for *archival* computer files for many years to come, in view of its relatively low cost and high retention qualities.

Another problem in practice with magnetic tapes as a principal working storage medium has proved to be the tendency to duplicate data on two or more files in order to achieve acceptable machine efficiency when processing the files. An important feature of a good database is that it is able to consolidate the data from several formerly sequential files and, in so doing, avoid redundancy and the consistency problems redundancy causes.

The term *cross-reference* is not usually used when talking about a database, the most usual term being *relationship.* One speaks of a relationship existing between types of records in a database. A record type is analogous to a color-coded folder in a filing cabinet where different record types are segregated by various colors. An individual folder may contain a reference to one or more other individual folders elsewhere in a set of cabinets. A referenced folder may have the same or a different color code as the folder that references it. In the database, these relationships are stored in such a way that searching for records can be done directly, without extensive cross-checking. Thus, the user has considerably more flexibility in the way in which the data is processed.

Record Types and Relationships. Conventional files as definable in Cobol since the early 1960s are regarded as consisting of a collection of records of the same type—or possibly of different types. A database must be regarded as a collection of records always of several different types. However, the difference between a multiple record type file (as permitted in Cobol) and a database is the following: In a database, relationships between different record types must be explicitly defined; in a multiple record type file, this is not the case, because relationships are necessarily implicit.

The term *relationship* needs careful explanation as it is very much at the heart of the database concept. Suppose a database containing data relevant to the purchasing activity has two record types, one for *suppliers* and the other for *purchase orders*. (In practice, a database would normally consist of considerably more than two record types.) Since each purchase order clearly has some kind of association with one supplier or other, there is a relationship between these two record types. The question remains: What is meant in concrete and formal terms by this relationship?

In the case of most commercially available database management systems (a concept to be discussed later in this article), a relationship between supplier and purchase order conveys *two* assertions, as follows.

1. Each supplier has zero, one, or more purchase order associated with it.
2. Each purchase order is associated with one and only one supplier.

A useful way of illustrating the situation implied in the relationship is by means of a cross-reference table, as follows.

Purchase Order \ Supplier	Smith	Jones	Brown	Black
PO 6	X			
PO 9		X		
PO 15		X		
PO 16				X
PO 17	X			
PO 21		X		

Looking along the rows, it is clear that each of the six purchase orders identified in the left-hand column has only one cross in it. In other words, each purchase order is associated with one and only one supplier. However, looking down the columns, each supplier has "zero, one, or more" crosses. No purchase orders have been sent to Brown; Black has one; Smith has two; and Jones has three.

Structure Diagrams. Diagrammatic techniques are widely used among database designers to present the overall picture of record types and relationships. This implies drawing a structure diagram. The above example of a relationship between supplier and purchase order could be illustrated in either of the following two ways (see Fig. 1).

Clearly, a relationship between any two record types is not a symmetric one, and there must be some way of indicating that it is the supplier who is associated with zero, one or more purchase orders and not the purchase

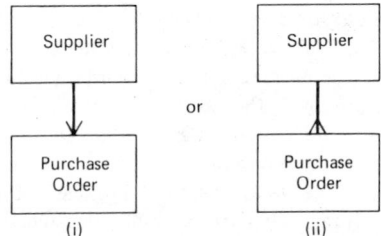

Fig. 1.   Representation of a relationship.

order which is associated with zero, one, or more suppliers.

Two alternative ways of indicating this asymmetry are in use. The older and probably more widely used way is with an arrow as illustrated in Fig. 1(i). A more recent approach using a "chicken foot" is shown on the right.

The problem with the use of arrows is psychological. Many people nowadays are accustomed to flow diagrams. A data structure diagram is an important step in any database design, but it is not a flow diagram. As database experts encounter this mental barrier in the discussion with users, there is a trend away from the use of the arrow in data structure diagrams.

Optional Relationships. In the above example, a relationship was illustrated in which each purchase order had to be associated with a supplier. Most of the relationships encountered in practice can be conveniently handled in this way, but a significant number call for a slightly varied approach.

An example is the relationship between purchase order and *price quotation*. It may be that the only basis on which the company, whose purchasing application is being designed, is willing to place purchase orders is on availability of a price quotation. If so, the relationship between purchase order and price quotation is exactly the same as between purchase order and supplier. It is more likely that the price quotation is optional. However, if indeed it exists, then information concerning it would be recorded in the database.

The relationship between price quotation and purchase order will then convey the following assertions.

1. Each price quotation has zero, one, or more purchase orders based on it.
2. Each purchase order is associated with zero or one price quotations.

Comparison of these assertions with those for the earlier example will show that the first assertion is similar and only the second of the two varies. In tabular form, the relationship would be depicted as follows.

Purchase Order \ Price Quotation	PQ 25	PQ 28	PQ 31	PQ 33	PQ 34
PO 6	X				
PO 9		X			
PO 15		X			
PO 16				X	
PO 17					
PO 21		X			

Purchase order PO 17 was placed independently of any price quotation. The other five purchase orders were each based on one of three price quotations.

Schematically, it is common practice to depict an optional relationship as shown in Fig. 2.

Database Management Systems.

The handling of relationships is the capability which distinguishes a database from a file. In order to build a database, it is the normal practice to use a piece of generalized software called a database management system (DBMS). A DBMS requires the database structure to be described in terms of record types, data items, and relationships. A typical commercial database might comprise some 30–50 record types with an approximately equivalent number of relationships. These are defined using a *data definition language* (*q.v.*). The resulting definition is often referred to as a *schema* or *database schema*.

The database schema is subsequently referred to when defining the processes to be performed on the data. Many such processes will be fairly simple and do not need to refer to all the record types and relationships of the schema. It is therefore possible to define a number of *subschemas* (i.e., parts of the schema), each of which contains some of the record types and some of the relationships in the schema.

The processes to be performed on the schema (or one of its subschemas) would often be defined using a conventional programming language such as Cobol or Fortran enhanced with several extra statements collectively referred to as *data manipulation language*.

Alternatively, most DBMS also have a *query language* facility which is a more self-contained nonprocedural language not forming part of a conventional programming language. A query language may be used by a person not skilled in programming in order to specify simple queries to a database.

There are variations in the capabilities provided by available DBMS, even on the level of the data definition language (i.e., the schema capabilities). Three widely recognized approaches will be reviewed here.

Network Database.

Some DBMS place essentially no restrictions on the number of relationships in which a record type may be involved. A record type might play a subordinate role in four relationships. This means that many records are associated with one record of each of the other four record types to which it is related in this way. At the same time, this record type might be related to three other record types as the superior partner in the relationship—as illustrated in Fig. 3.

It should be noted that there are two relationships between record type X and record type F.

When this kind of freedom is allowed, the DBMS can be said to allow the definition of network structures or *network databases*.

Hierarchical Database.

Other DBMS approaches impose constraints on the freedom to define unlimited relationships between each and every record type. One illustration of the kind of constraints encountered in practice is the *hierarchical database*. Compared with a network database, a hierarchical database is constrained in the following two ways.

1. Each record type may be involved in only one relationship as a subordinate.

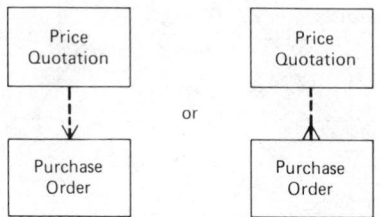

Fig. 2. Representation of optional relationship.

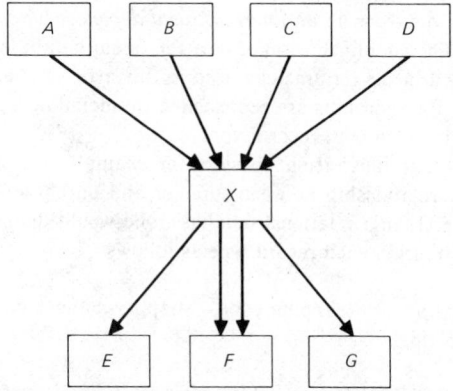

Fig. 3. Component of a network database.

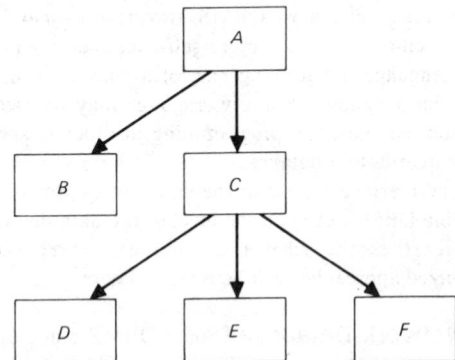

Fig. 4.   Illustration of a hierarchical database.

2. Only one relationship is allowed between any two record types.

Fig. 4 illustrates a hierarchical database.

When using a DBMS which imposes constraints on the freedom to define relationships between record types, the standard practice is to introduce extra artificial record types and relationships. Such additions can be thought of as "clutter" in that they make it harder to recognize the genuine application data.

Relational Databases.   The concept of a *relational database* has attracted considerable interest since it was first proposed in 1970. In effect, a relational database is a network database in which the relationships are handled in a very specific way. There is a body of terminology in use in connection with relational databases which is quite different from the terminology in everyday use by practitioners.

The term *relation,* in fact, is used to refer to what in this article has been called a *record type.* What has here been called a relationship would be referred to in a relational database an an *interrelational dependency.*

The simplified essence of a relational database (expressed in the terminology used in this article) is as follows. Relationships are represented by including certain data items in both record types.

As an illustration, consider the example of a one to many relationship between supplier and purchase order in Fig. 1. In a relational database, one would define the data items in each record type as follows.

Supplier (supplier-code, supplier-name, NYSE-rating,. . . .)

Purchase order (PO number, init-date, approval-date, supplier-ID, handling-clerk, ...)

The item supplier-code in *supplier* has here deliberately been assigned a different name from supplier-ID in *purchase order.* Nevertheless, if it is also clearly defined that any value which the item supplier-ID may assume must be the same as a value assumed by supplier-code, then purchase order has a functional dependency on *supplier.* (In relational terminology, one should assert that supplier-code and supplier-ID take their values from a common *domain.*)

This simple and sensible practice, which is the cornerstone of relational theory, hence requires that a relationship between two record types be expressed implicitly by means of having a data item in each record type (in relational terminology, an *attribute* in each relation) take its values from a common domain of values. The theory is actually rather more demanding in that, in one of the two record types, the item (or items) on which the relationship is based must serve as a unique primary key for that record type.

Some commercially available full network-oriented DBMS require that relationships be defined in exactly this way. Others permit the technique as one of a number of alternative options. Unfortunately, some of the network DBMS developed earlier did not allow the option and this led to the evolution of relational theory.

The reason for the item duplication (and for other facets of relational theory not explained here) is to facilitate the manipulation of a database by a higher-level (or less procedural) data manipulation language than those in use with the commercially available DBMS. Such a higher-level language is usually based on the use of a *relational algebra.*

As an example of a database, we consider the data processing for a warehouse (see Fig. 5). The warehouse needs to maintain data about each stock item. These are ordered in varying quantities by customers. If the stock of a particular item drops below a certain level, then new stocks are ordered from a supplier.

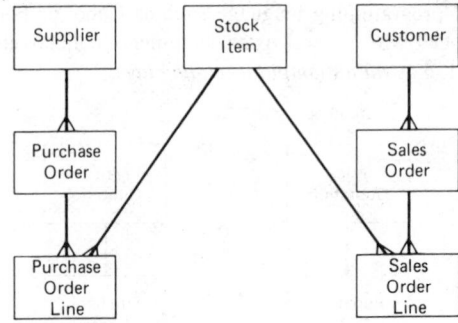

Fig. 5.   Example of simplified database structure for a warehouse application.

In the database, it is necessary to have three principal record types: stock item, supplier, and customer. Each time a customer places an order for one or more different kinds of stock item, a sales order is built up in the database. In data processing terms, this means that there is also a sales order record type. A single sales order may contain an order for several units of one stock item. More likely, a customer may order several different classes of stock items on the same sales order. To facilitate the processing of the database, sales order line is then regarded as a different record type; i.e., different from sales order, which contains data about the whole sales order, customer identification, date of issue, and so on. The other record type contains data about each line entry in the sales order, such as which stock item the line refers to and how many units are ordered.

The situation is similar for the purchase order that the warehouse issues to a supplier when the stock of a stock item is discovered to be low, but there is a slight difference. A sales order and all its lines enter the database together. A purchase order to a supplier is built up during the course of a day's or a week's processing. At a certain time, a program is run to issue the purchase orders. How many lines there are in a purchase order depends on the demands from customers for different stock items that a supplier provides and also on how many stock items the warehouse needs to replenish stock and restore it to its normal inventory level.

In summary, the database contains seven different *record types*—the three principal record types (stock item, supplier, customer) and the four subsidiary records (sales order, sales order line, purchase order, and purchase order line).

More important from a database point of view are the various *relationships* that are defined among these record types. In Fig. 5, six relationships are illustrated.

It is clear from this example that a record type can be involved in two or more relationships. For example, the purchase order record type is related both to supplier and to purchase order line.

Each purchase order line is related to both a purchase order and to a stock item. What this really means is that each purchase order may contain several stock items. Furthermore, a stock item may at the same time be included in several purchase orders. There is a clear relationship between purchase order and stock item, but *not* a one to many relationship of the kind described earlier in this article. The relationship between purchase order and stock item is usually called a many to many relationship.

DBMS Facilities. The DBMS available today provide many facilities over and above the basic and highly critical capability for defining a database in terms of record types, data items, and relationships.

A DBMS may be said to provide one or more techniques for representing the defined data in direct access storage. Representing relationships is one problem which invites many alternative solutions. Such solutions are used by programmers as they attempt to minimize processing time or storage space required, or sometimes to maximize flexibility. In earlier days, these techniques were used directly by the customer's application programmer.

A DBMS, as mentioned above, is a piece of software. Some vendors regard it as being part of the operating system; others build it in a way that it is very much an optional extra for which the customer must pay in order to use it.

A number of requirements are frequently stipulated for a DBMS in addition to the basic one of handling the data in the database. Integrity, privacy, and data independence are those most frequently cited.

Integrity refers to the ability of the DBMS to protect the database from hardware and software malfunctions. It should be possible to recognize a problem, report it, reconstruct the damaged part of the database, and restart the processing. Collectively, these processes are often referred to as a *recovery* system.

Privacy identifies a capability to protect the database against unauthorized access or modification. While the need for this kind of facility varies from one enterprise to another, it always becomes more critical if the database is to be accessed from on-line terminals.

Finally, *data independence* is a capability that many users regard as of paramount importance. It is defined as the independence of the application programs to structural changes in the database. In the example of the warehouse, it might be required to add one or two new record types and a new relationship. If the programs that act on the database do not need to be modified, and possibly not even recompiled after the changes to the database structure, then it can be said that there is a degree of independence. This capability serves to minimize the reprogramming problem, which has caused major expense when conventional programming methods have been used. Data independence is irrevocably associated with a DBMS. However, astute users have certainly been able to achieve some data independence without using a DBMS.

Role of a DBMS in Information Systems Design. A DBMS may be used as a tool when designing, implementing, and running an information system. One important aspect of information systems design on which database technology is having considerable impact is that of *integration.*

The term *integrated management information system* was quite popular in the late 1960s. The prefix *management* has fallen out of use to a certain extent because it is now widely recognized that a well conceived information system should serve all levels in the organization, including, of course, the various management levels.

The prefix *integrated* is one which calls for more discussion. In fact, an advanced DBMS, properly used, provides exactly the tool which enables a fairly complete integration within an information system and possibly among information systems which are separate entities.

Integration of Separate Applications. As with many other terms used in data processing terminology, *integration* is open to a number of interpretations. The purpose of the following paragraphs is to identify these and to emphasize the importance of deciding which of them is relevant in any given situation.

For the purpose of discussion, consider two application systems *A* and *B*. Whether *A* and *B* are major systems or merely components of larger systems is irrelevant to the present discussion. *A* and *B* may have some data that is common to both. This means that at least one item of data is updated and used by *A*, and is also required by *B* for inclusion in one of its reports or for use in one of its calculations. There are several says in which system *B* can get access to system *A* data.

System *A* generates reports. Those generated may include some that are specifically designed to meet the requirements of system *B;* in other words, these reports are requested by the people responsible for system *B*. If system *B* indeed requires some of *A*'s data for its own processing, then it may be necessary to copy the data off system *A* reports onto system *B* input forms for repunching because system *B* requires only part of the data generated by system *A* or because system *B* requires it in a rather different form. If reprocessing of the data is necessary for *any reason,* then it may be asserted that system *A* and system *B* are *not integrated in any sense;* in other words, they are totally uncoordinated.

Suppose, for example, that system *B* requires system *A* data, *but in a different form.* This normally means that some item of data that is common (at least in concept) to both systems has two sets of values, one for system *A,* one (maybe partially overlapping) for system *B.* On the other hand, the set of values may be the same for each system, but the way they are represented to the computerized system may differ. This introduces the topic of *data representation standards,* which is a problem that must always be addressed if a satisfactory degree of integration is to be achieved. It may happen that system *B* requires the data in exactly the same form as it is generated and processed in system *A.* This in itself represents a modicum of integration, by the very necessary standardization of data representation. No meaningful integration of any kind is conceivably unless there is this standardization of data representation.

The designers concerned with systems *A* and *B* may agree to pass data from *A* to *B* in mechanized form rather than by passing reports from which the system *B* people can then punch what they need. This level of integration can be thought of as *mechanized interaction.* In this case, system *A* would arrange to generate files (usually on tape) and system *B* would include input programs to read these files. This situation represents the first meaningful level of integration. Although magnetic tape files are suggested here, it is possible that the transmittal media could be some other device, such as movable discs. It is implied that system *A* and system *B* are separate systems and that they are run at separate times, possibly on separate machines at the same or separate geographic locations.

The most complete degree of integration possible would be achieved if system *A* and system *B* were to run concurrently on the same machine. The data they could process would be in one of the following three classes: Local to *A,* local to *B,* or common. Because the data common to both is the most important consideration, the designers responsible for the two systems must agree on record types to contain the common data. The programs of both systems may be written to access these record types, normally with agreement that only one system—for example, system *A*—is allowed to update any data in the record, while system *B* processing is limited to retrieval. It can then be said that systems *A* and *B* are *integrated.*

In summary, the following spectrum of potential situations can be identified when two application systems use data conceptually similar.

1. *Totally uncoordinated.* Each system has its own data collection.
2. *Partially interacting.* One system repunches data (and in so doing modifies the form) from reports generated by the other system.
3. *Mechanized interaction.* One system generates files, which can be used as direct input to programs in the other system. No modification of data representation is necessary.
4. *Integrated.* The two systems have agreed on record types to be used by both systems. Programs of both systems access the records as stored in direct-access storage. There is agreement on which system has authority to update the data contained in records of this type.

Concluding Remarks. The foregoing should substantiate that a discussion of database as a concept cannot be divorced from that of a database management system. Database technology has developed considerably since the early 1960s. It is now widely accepted as the key to the successful design of almost all fully integrated computer application systems.

REFERENCES

1978. Olle, T. William *The CODASYL Approach to Data Base Management.* New York: Wiley.
1979. Date, C. J. *An Introduction to Data Base Systems,* (2nd Ed.) Reading, MA: Addison-Wesley.

T. W. OLLE

DATABASE, ON-LINE

For articles on related subjects *see* DATABASE AD-MINISTRATOR; DATABASE MANAGEMENT; DATA NET-WORKS, PUBLIC; and DISTRIBUTED SYSTEMS.

An on-line database is one which can be directly accessed by a user from a terminal which is usually a visual display device but occasionally is a typewriter-like device. Searching a database on-line has the advantage that the response is prompt and queries can be modified quickly. Databases may contain bibliographic references to books or other documents, or (purportedly) factual information which is the object of the searcher's request, such as in databases used for credit searches.

The most popular databases for on-line searches are those containing psychological, biological, engineering, chemical, medical, or other scientific literature. Such databases may contain millions of abstracts and are updated regularly. Typically, by dialing a local telephone number, the user's terminal is connected to a retrieval system and the user then selects a database for searching. The user may examine a thesaurus containing keywords which are combined with ANDs, ORs, and NOTs to form a boolean expression describing the query—for example, ("liver" or "kidney") and ("viral infection" or "inflammation"). The retrieval system responds in seconds with an indication of how many documents satisfy the query. If the number is too large, the user may decide to add further keywords to qualify the query and reduce the number of documents referenced. If the number is too

```
#OPEN RESOURCE ABSTRACTS
resource file contains 634,971 entries
#BROWSE OCEAN POLLUTION

1:ocean platforms
2:ocean policy
3+ocean pollution
4:ocean resources
5:ocean ridges

#SELECT 3
set 1 contains 42 entries          (i.e., a file called set 1 contains
                                   42 entries on ocean pollution)


#BROWSE OIL POLLUTION

1:oil drilling
2:oil leaks
3+oil pollution
4:oil reserves
5:oil wells

#SELECT 2 or 3
set 2 contains 211 entries         (i.e., a file called set 2 contains
#COMBINE SET 1 AND SET 2           211 entries on oil leaks or oil pollution)
set 3 contains 23 entries          (i.e., a file called set 3 contains 23
#PRINT SET 3                       entries on the intersection of topics)
                                   (final statement is to print the abstracts
                                   in set 3)
```

Fig. 1. Sample interactive session with on-line bibliographic retrieval system.

small, the user may choose other keywords. Some systems permit qualification by author name, journal name, date, or other descriptors. The abstracts are available for on-line display or printing at the user terminal, but the full document must be obtained from traditional libraries or microfiche files.

Fig. 1 shows an example of the use of an on-line bibliographic system.

Bibliographic databases have been joined by a growing variety of information resources or fact retrieval systems, such as the New York Times Information Bank (*q.v.*), which produces references to newspaper and magazine articles, legal information systems that index court decisions, federal statutes or state laws, chemical information retrieval systems containing data about toxic substances, new drugs, or complex molecular structures, and economic, stock market, or trade data retrieval systems. A particularly interesting system is SCORPIO, maintained by the Library of Congress. In addition to offering on-line access to library information, it provides search capability for the reports of the Congressional Research Service, the status of current legislation, references to organizations which might be sources for further information, the *Congressional Record,* and other files.

B. SHNEIDERMAN

DATA COMMUNICATION NETWORKS

For articles on related subjects *see* ARPA NETWORK; COMPUTER NETWORKS; DATA COMMUNICATIONS; DATA NETWORKS, PUBLIC; DISTRIBUTED SYSTEMS; ELECTRONIC FUNDS TRANSFER SYSTEMS; MODEM; MULTIPLEXING; PACKET SWITCHING; and TELEPROCESSING SYSTEMS.

Teleprocessing systems provide a wide variety of data processing services to many locations simultaneously without the necessity of having a computer at each such location. With the rapid growth of such systems over the past decade, a need has arisen for efficient and effective data communication networks for transmission of digital data from one location to another. Such networks consist of sets of nodes connected by a set of links. The nodes may be computers, terminals, or some types of communication control units in various locations. The links are the communication channels between the nodes over which the data is transmitted.

Optimal transmission of digital data requires communication facilities and services quite different from those commonly used today for voice transmission. However, because of limited digital data transmission in previous years, most data communication networks today use private or switched lines which were originally designed for voice transmission and which are leased from a telephone company or other common carrier. Since the transmission over these lines is generally analog, while the data at the nodes is digital, modems are used to provide the interface between nodes and links.

A simple example of a data communication network is shown in Fig. 1, where the links between the modems are the communication lines leased from common carriers. The communication control unit in city E is used to multiplex or concentrate several lower-speed terminals over a higher-speed line. The single *multidrop* line also connects several terminals to the central host computer and is usually routed through several locations, providing service to terminals along the way.

In the past decade, the number, size, and complexity of teleprocessing systems has grown rapidly, and all indications are that this growth will continue. Since, in large systems of this kind, the costs directly related to data transmission are a very significant part of the overall cost, the planning and design of data communications networks is very important.

Network Planning. Planning and designing a data communication network can be very complex because of the wide variety of conflicting requirements and the large number of possible solutions. The objective is to satisfy all requirements at the lowest cost. Factors to consider in planning include:

1. The type of teleprocessing system used.
2. Volume and distribution of data to be transmitted.
3. Access and response times required.
4. Number and geographical location of nodes.
5. Type of terminal or equipment at each node and its transmission speed.
6. Error rate that may be tolerated.
7. Need for future expansion.
8. Availability, reliability, and maintenance of the network.

Network Design. Given the network objectives, the design process includes the choice of terminals, line control procedures, modems, communication processors or control units, common carrier facilities, and network configuration. The basic network configurations, shown in Fig. 2, include the point-to-point, multidrop, ring, and distributed connections, as well as the star connection, which consists of several point-to-point connections. In distributed connections, more than one path exists between nodes which can be used to improve the reliability. Most present networks are combinations of these basic configurations.

The cost of the various types of lines and common

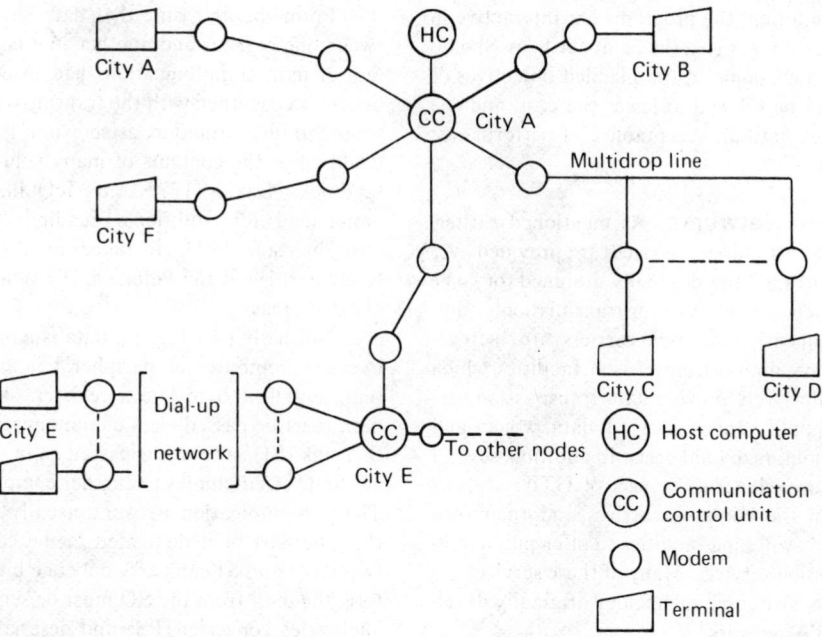

Fig. 1.   Example of a data communication network.

carrier facilities required are governed by very complex tariffs based upon location, circuit lengh, and type of line. Both the geometry and types of lines can in turn be greatly influenced by using appropriate communication control units, such as multiplexers or concentrators placed at strategic locations within the network. Such units can markedly improve the efficiency of the lines, reducing their number and hence the cost.

Based on the above considerations, a great deal of experience is necessary to design an effective network.

The design process is usually iterative in that the designer makes an initial guess at a possible network by deciding on the types of lines that should be used, the auxiliary equipment needed to improve line efficiency, and the network configuration. This initial design is tested to ensure that it meets the planned objectives; if it does, it is then evaluated for cost. For more complex networks, the design process is usually aided by computer programs to help evaluate the many possible alternatives for capacity, response time, and cost. Since computers cannot replace

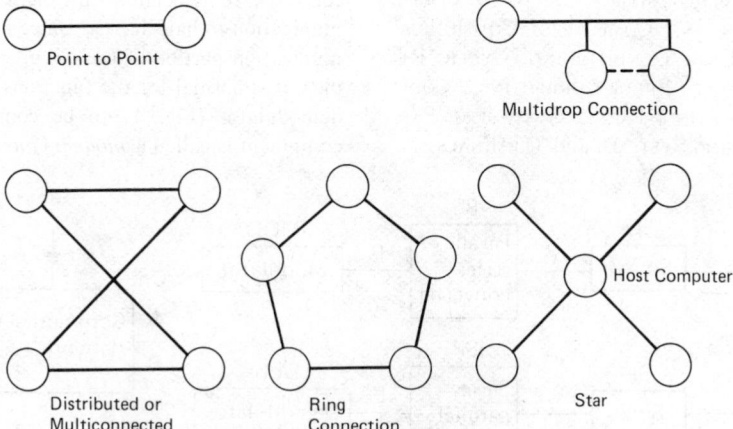

Fig. 2.   Three basic methods of interconnecting nodes in a data comunication network.

experience and intuition, the programs are interactive in the sense that the designer is in the feedback loop. Should the costs be too high, some of the planned objectives or specifications may be relaxed to lower the cost, and the process is repeated until an acceptable cost-performance network is found.

Digital Data Networks. As mentioned earlier, most present data transmission services are provided over telephone company facilities originally designed for voice transmission, which are not ideal for transmission of digital data. Consequently, common carriers are increasingly installing new digital transmission facilities which not only more effectively provide data transmission services but also simplify the mixing of data, voice, and video services to minimize total costs. In addition, several companies such as Telenet (now part of GTE) use circuits leased from the common carriers and their own store and forward switching facilities to offer public digital data transmission services. Many of these services are based upon packet-switching technology originally developed for the ARPA network.

REFERENCES

1978. Doll, D. *Data Communications--Facilities, Networks and System Design.* New York: Wiley.
1977. Housley, T. *Data Communications and Teleprocessing Systems.* Englewood Cliffs, NJ: Prentice-Hall.

J. SOBOLEWSKI

DATA COMMUNICATIONS

PRINCIPLES

For articles on related subjects *see* BAUD; CODES; COMMUNICATIONS AND COMPUTERS; COMMUNICATION CONTROL UNIT; CONDITIONING; CYCLIC REDUNDANCY CHECK; ERROR-CORRECTING CODE; MODEM; MULTIPLEXING; PACKET SWITCHING; PARITY; TELEPROCESSING SYSTEMS; and TERMINALS.

From the first time that data had to be passed between one register and another in a computer, the problem of data communications had to be addressed. This article is concerned with the transmission of data from its source to its destination, as shown in Fig. 1. This subject could cover the contents of many volumes. Two general textbooks (Davies, 1973, and McQuillan, 1978) are recommended for additional reading. Other references (Abrahamson 1973; Beauchamp, 1979; Kahn, 1978; Kretzmer, 1969; and Petersen, 1972) deal with more specialized areas.

Normally (see Fig. 1), data is passed in parallel between a computer or peripheral in finite-sized chunks (e.g., eight-bit bytes) to a register, shown as SO. This data must be passed via a communication network (CN) to a sink (SI), where it is passed on in the same or different finite-sized chunks to another computer or peripheral. The communication network usually has the property that the part of it dedicated to the communication between SO and SI can carry only one bit at a time. Therefore, the data from the SO must be serialized in the parallel-series converter (PS) and deserialized again in the series-parallel converter (SP). The data output of PS is usually a bistable binary signal that can be interpreted as one of two states: 0 or 1. To pass through the CN, it must usually be used to modulate an analog signal or to emit a short pulse. This is achieved in the modulator (MOD), and the digital level is recovered in the demodulator (DEM).

If information can flow only from SO to SI (Fig. 1), the communication is said to be *simplex*. If data can flow both from SO to SI and from SI to SO simultaneously, the communication is called *duplex*. If data transmission in these two directions does not proceed simultaneously, the communication is said to be *half-duplex*. In some cases, the communication channels themselves may be full-duplex, but either the hardware of the SO and SI or the software associated with them may restrict the communication to half-duplex. Since it is usual for the communication portion of the circuit to be at least half-duplex, it is normal for the functions of the modulator and demodulator (Fig. 1) to be combined. The resulting equipment is called a *modem* (*mo*dulator-*dem*odulator).

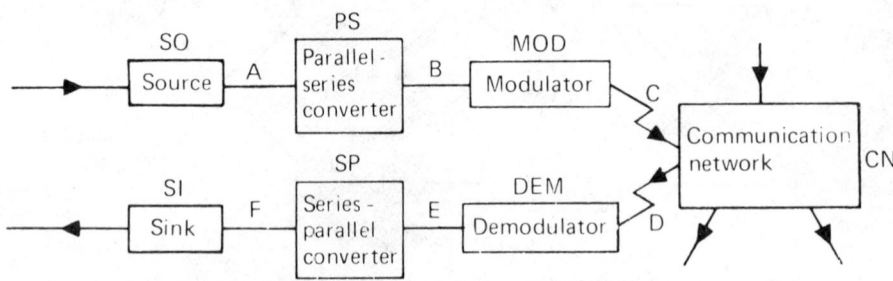

Fig. 1. Schematic of communications between source and destination.

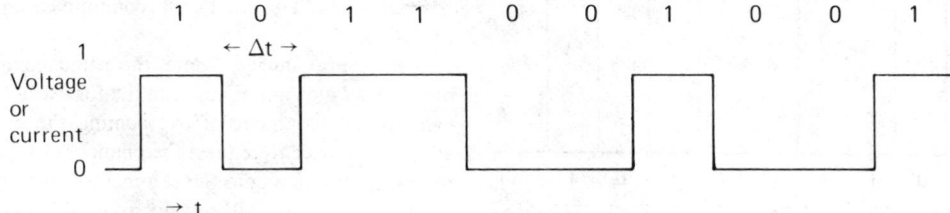

Fig. 2. Example of telegraph modulation.

Often a character input from a terminal to a computer will be echoed back onto the terminal's printer to show it was received correctly; this mode of working is called *echo-plex*. The devices SP and PS, and the interfaces A and F, are also often combined with additional buffers in each to permit duplex working.

It is beyond the scope of this article to say much about techniques of modulation (see Davies, 1973, and Kretzmer, 1968). The simplest way to modulate signals is to use telegraph techniques to ensure that the channel has one of two states—with current or without current. An example of this form of signaling is shown in Fig. 2.

The fastest signaling rate of a communication channel is called the *baud rate*. In the system shown in Fig. 2, the baud rate is $1/\Delta t$. When only two-level signaling is used, the baud is also equal to the rate of information transfer in bits per second (bps). If multiple-level signaling is used, as shown in Fig. 3 for four-level coding, then the bit rate is higher than the baud rate. To obtain the signals in Fig. 3, each pair of bits in Fig. 2 is taken together, and the four resulting combinations (00,01,10,11) are each coded to one level. Clearly, this approach can be extended to *n* levels, but the circuitry required to discriminate and decode the levels becomes increasingly complex.

The form of signaling described above has problems in long-distance transmission and it is more usual to use the pulsed signals shown in Fig. 2 or Fig. 3 to modulate the amplitude, frequency, or phase of the carrier sine wave. These forms of transmission are called *analog transmission,* and are well suited for use over the conven-

tional telephone system, which is designed for the transfer of analog signals.

When the analog facilities are used, each end-to-end channel has a certain *bandwidth* (*q.v.*) which limits the frequencies which can propagate. Typically, the signaling rate over normal telephone lines is limited by *noise* considerations to 2.4 Kbps. However, by the use of multi-level signaling and automatic line *conditioning* (*q.v.*), an effective data transmission rate of 19.2 Kbps can be achieved.

The theoretical limit to the information transfer rate or channel capacity, *C,* has been shown by Shannon to be

$$C = BW \log_2 (1 + S/N)$$

where *BW* is the bandwidth and *S/N* is the ratio of signal strength to noise level—the *signal to noise ratio.* If *S/N* is 15, this equation shows that the channel capacity is *BW* $\log_2 16 = 4BW,$ so that four-level coding (2 bits) can be used (see Fig. 3).

The mode of modulation may make it possible for the modems to generate timing pulses themselves; such a system is called *synchronous.* With these timing pulses, it is possible to synchronize the two modems and produce timing pulses in the modem to indicate when a bit is being sent or received.

A simpler modem is possible when such synchronization is not required. Moreover, certain human-oriented peripherals, such as keyboard terminals, need to send data only at irregular intervals. Such systems are termed *asynchronous:* In an asynchronous system, the signaling rate is predetermined, but it is necessary to indicate the start of each piece of information (usually, a byte or character) by sending a start-bit before, and one or more stop-bits (of opposite polarity) after transmission of the data. Thus, a byte 145 (in octal) would be sent as shown in Fig. 4. From the arrival time of the start-bit, the bit timings of the subsequent bits can be deduced. The stop-bit is required to ensure that, for at least a one-bit time, the signal has an appropriate value by which a subsequent start-bit can be recognized.

It is even possible for the data format to be asynchronous (i.e., start- and stop-bits are included) with synchronous modems so that the transmission system itself

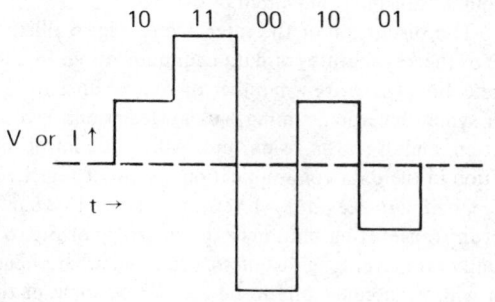

Fig. 3. Example of four-level coding.

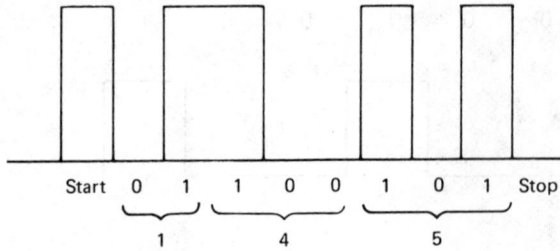

Fig. 4. Data sent for 145 in asynchronous system.

is synchronous. Although the start- and stop-bits are redundant in such a system, it is often convenient to include them when the same electronics in PS and SO of Fig. 1 is to be used with different modems. As described before, an asynchronous system has a fixed byte length, whereas a synchronous system may have a variable length (see below).

Recently, with the reduction in costs of digital circuitry, it is becoming possible to use pulse-code modulation for transmission. Here, each device is given a time slot, and during this period either a pulse is put on the channel or not. This is a modification of the original telegraph techniques, and is the basis of the digital transmission now being developed. This form of modulation is really two-level amplitude modulation in a synchronous system.

While the trunk portion of the telephone network is rapidly becoming based on digital transmission and switching, the local network is still mainly analog. It is for this reason that specialized data circuits are being introduced by the carriers, which are bringing digital facilities to the customer's premises.

The communication shown in Fig. 1, in which two parties, SO and SI, are connected, is called *point-to-point*. Alternate forms used in some applications are shown in Fig. 5. In the communication circuit depicted by Fig. 5, SO can send (or receive) data along the channel connecting it to SI_1, SI_2, and SI_3. By appropriate signaling, it is possible to ensure that the data is received at its correct destination, SI_1. This type of connection is called *multidrop* or *multipoint*. In some cases, it is desirable to have the same information received at all stations:

SI_1, SI_2, SI_3. This mode of communication is called *broadcast*.

If several devices share the same communication channel, as shown in Fig. 5, conflict for use of the channel can occur. One mode of overcoming the conflict is to allow any device to request the channel at will; its efforts to put information onto the channel will then be detected by the others, who will refrain from putting on their information until the message-sending transmitter has ceased. This mode of using a channel is called *contention;* it works well on a point-to-point basis, but reasonably complex strategies must be adopted for successful contention on multipoint channels because of the perceptible delay between information being placed on the channel and its receipt by the other parties.

Another way of resolving conflicts is particularly useful if one device, shown as SO in Fig. 5, can be used to control the others. This mode of control is called a *polling* philosophy; in this mode of communication, SO will ask each SI_i in turn whether it has anything to send, or will address an SI_i if it wishes to send data to that device. Clearly, the polling strategy can be carried further; SO can poll one device SI_i and address another one SI_j to ensure that the data is sent from SI_i to SI_j. Alternately, it can poll to see if any device has data to send. The whole question of address control is complex and depends on the nature of the communication channel. A normal telephone channel, for example, is usually point-to-point. A satellite communication channel is fundamentally broadcast, even if it is often used in a point-to-point manner.

To illustrate the problems of the control and synchronization required between SO and SI, we consider the interface inside a single computer system. Here, the data communication path usually has a fairly complex hardware interface with lines for passing data and control. The type of information passed is indicated in Fig. 6. This interface is for a synchronous autonomous simplex transfer, with eight-bit data lines and a parity line (PD). The AO and SO lines in Fig. 6 are to assure each device that the other is operational. The AC informs the source when new data is required, and SC then informs the acceptor when the data is ready. If an error (e.g., parity) is detected, AE informs the source, and completion of block transfer is indicated by ST.

The discussion of the interface of Fig. 6 illustrates one of the key features of data communication. In a local connection, there are a number of control lines to establish synchronization, timing, acknowledgment, error detection, end-of-transmission, etc. All such control information in the data communication system of Fig. 1 *must be carried with the data.* Moreover, in a local system, errors in transmitting data over the interface of Fig. 6 are usually rare; over long distances, noise and other phenomena will often cause bits to be lost. Since some of these

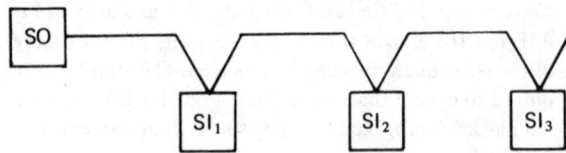

Fig. 5. Multipoint connection between SO and SI_1, SI_2, SI_3.

bits may contain control information, care must be taken in the communication environment to ensure that the correct action will be taken in all cases on *both sides of the link*. We will discuss below how some of this control information is passed.

In the communication of Fig. 6, the data is carried across the interface in parallel; in that of Fig. 1, it must first be serialized. We discussed previously that, in some systems, the modems of Fig. 1 established synchronization with each other, the so-called synchronous systems in which the bit timings are developed in the modems. It is merely necessary to establish this synchronization at the beginning of the transmission. Since this takes some time, it is usual to send data in a synchronous system in a block with some header information, followed by the data, and with some control and error detection data at the end. A synchronous system can be used only if the source SO of Fig. 5 has a buffer so that it can collect a whole block of information before transmission begins.

We mentioned earlier that the data format could be asynchronous with synchronous data transmission; redundant start- and stop-bits would be transmitted. In the same way, even an asynchronous communication system can be used to send block-oriented data, by prefacing it with an appropriate header and ending the block with appropriate end-of-block characters.

It is usual in a data communication system to send some bits additional to the actual useful data to identify the existence of, and possibly to correct, errors. The simplest error detection code is to add to each n bits of data an $(n + 1)$st bit, so chosen that the sum of the $(n + 1)$ bits is of a given parity (even or odd); such an extra bit is called a *parity* bit. In the asynchronous transmission system of Fig. 5, such a parity bit is often sent immediately before the stop-bit.

While this code is simple, it is not adequate if high information integrity is desired. Noise in transmission lines occurs fairly often; one incorrect bit in a thousand is a normal error rate on a switched line. Moreover, the nature of these errors is such that the noise that causes them often lasts more than one-bit time. For this reason, most data transmission systems, other than those involving the simplest keyboard terminals, send their information in blocks and use more sophisticated error-detection

codes that act on the whole block. One simple method considers the block as made up on n-bit bytes; it then does a parity check on the ith bits of each byte, and thus constructs the ith bit of a *block-parity check* byte. When this block-parity check is combined with a parity check on each byte, only errors that occur in rare combinations would remain undetected. A more sophisticated set of error-detection codes is based on *cyclic redundancy checks, (q.v.)* which require rather more logic, but are even safer. The subject of error-detection codes is discussed fully by Petersen (1972).

Just as a single byte in Fig. 4 of an asynchronous transmission system was framed by a start-bit (often a parity bit) and a stop-bit, so whole blocks are usually framed by some synchronizing bytes, a start-byte, error-detection bytes, and an end-of-block indication. This end-of-block indication used to be always a specific byte sequence, or an indication at the start of the block of its length. More recently, a structure has been standardized by the International Standards Organization (ISO, 1978). Here, the normal data bits have a "0" inserted into the data stream by its transmitting communication adaptor hardware after each consecutive five "1"-bits. The receiving hardware thus interprets six consecutive one-bits as signaling the end of a data block. For the case of *multiplexed* (*see* MULTIPLEXER), multipoint, or polling situations, the header may also contain polling or addressing information. Most synchronous communication systems are synchronous at the bit level, but are asynchronous at the block level. For this reason, the header and the end-of-block bear the same relation to the block as the start- and stop-bits do to the single byte shown in Fig. 4. Some special synchronizing bytes are sent in the header to obtain the bit synchronization achieved by the start-bit in an asynchronous system.

Just as the interface of Fig. 6 must have an error-return line, so it is usually necessary to acknowledge the correctness of each block sent. In some cases, this acknowledgment is made before any new block can be sent. In others, a header contains a block number, which is increased each time a block is sent. It is assumed that each block has been received correctly, unless a *negative acknowledgment* is sent subsequently. If that occurs, either only the faulty block or all subsequent blocks also are retransmitted. The philosophy is particularly important when there are significant delays in the communication network (e.g., when one or more satellite hops are involved) requiring a minimum of 0.5 sec for a round-trip signal. The standardized control procedure (HDLC) mentioned above prescribes variants at all these control functions. The control procedures for multiplexed communication over public data networks have been standardized further by the Consultative Committee on International Telephone and Telegraph (CCITT). Its

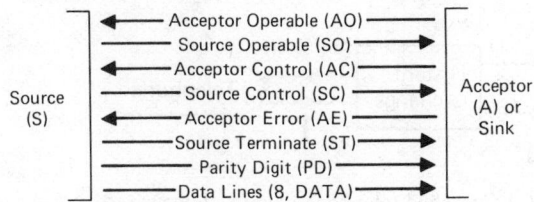

Fig. 6. Standard peripheral interface.

procedures (X25 to the customer, X75 between carriers, and X121 for international numbering) are the subject of another set of international recommendations (CCITT, 1978).

It is instructive to consider what speeds and modes of data communication are offered currently by the telecommunications authorities over the telephone networks. They usually offer facilities over both switched and leased lines. In the former, it is possible to dial up any other subscriber on the switched network and to communicate with him or her; in the latter, connection can be made along only one path (possible multidrop, as in Fig. 5). On a leased line, because only one path is used, it is possible for the telecommunications authorities to *condition* the line to improve its performance; such conditioning is called *line equalization.* Alternatively, both with switched and leased lines, it is possible to arrange for the modems to adjust to line conditions; this is called *equalizing* or *balancing* the modems. On a leased line, this balancing need not be done too often, unless very high performance is required, because the same path is always used. On switched lines, this balancing must be done on each call.

Fig. 7 illustrates the connection between two telephones and their local exchanges. Between the exchanges (C–D in Fig. 7.), there are separate channels in the two directions, ensuring duplex facilities. On a switched line, there is usually only one pair of lines, as shown in Fig. 7(a), between the telephone line and the local exchange; this is called a *two-wire circuit.* On a leased line, it is possible to order at comparatively low cost a second pair of lines to the local exchange, as illustrated in Fig. 7(b). In this case, one has a four-wire circuit, and is able to operate at maximum speed simultaneously in both directions. On a single pair, as in A–B of Fig. 7(a), it is possible to work at fairly low speeds in both directions simultaneously. It is also possible to work at a much higher speed in one direction with a lower-speed return path. Schematically, this situation is then as shown in

Fig. 7(b), but only one pair of physical connections need exist between A and B or E and F. This low-speed return path is called a "supervisory return," and varies in speed between 5 and 300 bps. It is used to turn around the line in the half-duplex situation or to signal acknowledgments or enter keyboard data in duplex. Thus, in the true four-wire case of Fig. 7(b), it is possible to have the high-speed data going simultaneously on each line, as shown in the figure, with additional reverse supervisory information. The range of facilities currently offered by the telecommunications authorities is illustrated in Fig. 8.

A new generation of specialized data circuits are being introduced by the telephone and other common carrier companies in the U.S. and by the government postal, telephone and telegraph companies (PTTs) in Western Europe. These use digital transmission at up to 64 Kbps to the nearest switch or concentration point (see below). From this point, the data is multiplexed digitally onto the standard digital data hierarchy becoming used by the PTTs for inter-exchange transmission. Over these circuits, the tariff is usually dependent on the speed of the access circuits. The interface standards have been defined by the CCITT (X21; CCITT, 1978). In totally leased facilities, the transmission circuits bypass any switches on PTT premises. However, in addition, a new set of *public data networks* provide digital switching. This switching can be of a *circuit-switched* type, as in the normal telephone system, or a *packet-switched* type. The choice of switching mode is quite separate from that of transmission mode.

Finally, a brief discussion of methods of data concentration and multiplexing is required. The situation is illustrated in Fig. 9. In Fig. 9, H represents a computer which may receive a multi-leaved stream. The multi-leaving may be in the form of a number of streams interleaved at transmission level by using a different frequency for each stream *(frequency division multiplexing-FDM)*, the bits of the different streams may be transmitted on a round robin basis by bit or byte *(time division*

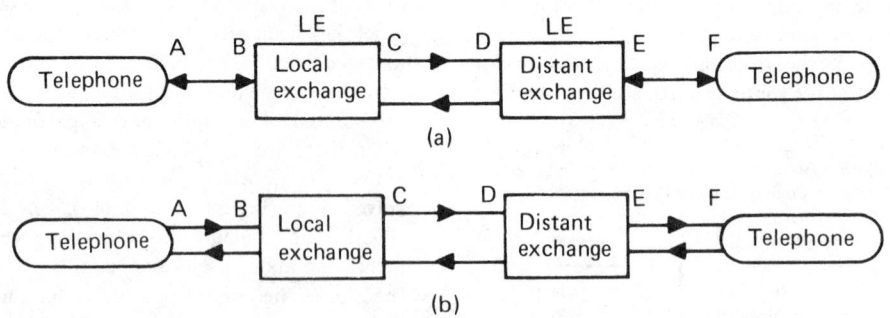

Fig. 7.   Schematics of telephone networks, (a) Switched telephone line. (b) Four-wire leased telephone line.

Speed Range (K bps)	Switched or Leased	Half- or Full Duplex	Line Equalization Required	Asynchronous or Synchronous	Levels of Coding	Note
Up to 0.2	S or L	H	No	A	2	Uses d-c telegraph techniques
Up to 0.3	S or L	F	No	A	2	Uses modems
Up to 1.2	S or L	H	No	A	2	May have low speed return
1.2 to 3.6	S or L	H	No	S	2–4	May have low speed return
Up to 4.8	L	F	No	S	4	Requires four-wire local connection for full duplex
Up to 9.6	L	F	Yes	S	4–8	Requires four-wire local connections for full duplex
Up to 72	L	F	Yes	S	2–4	Requires special treatment of the line and possibly repeaters
Above 72	L	F	Yes	S	2–4	Required special local lines and transmission facilities
1544 or 2048	L	F	Yes	S	2	Standard pcm digital transmission

Fig. 8. Typical telecommunications facilities available.

multiplexing TDM), or complete blocks may be sent (packet switching). Different forms of hardware and software are needed in the switch S in each case. Terminals T supporting only one duplex data stream may also be supported in one of two ways: Either a *concentrator* C may be used (in this case, the number of terminal ports to T is greater than the number which can be supported simultaneously; statistical averaging is used to reduce the number of terminals which would be refused service to acceptable proportions) or a *multiplexor* is used, wherein

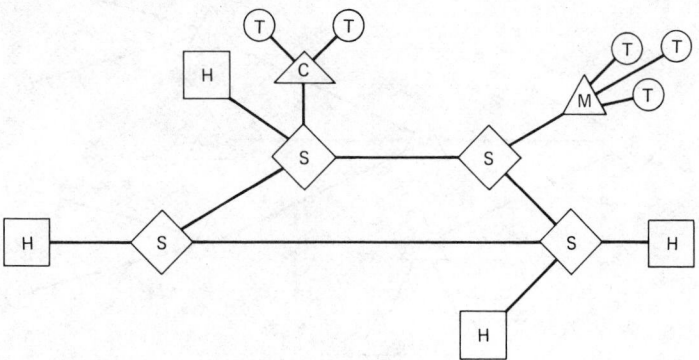

Fig. 9. Schematic of computer network.

each terminal can be serviced—albeit possibly at a reduced rate if all are active. The switches S in Fig. 9 will serve to demultiplex and then remultiplex the incoming streams to other switches S, concentrators C, and multiplexors M.

Note that there will usually be some limit to the number of simultaneous streams that can be handled by even a switch S. If *packet switching* is used, this limit may be fixed by the header address space (e.g., defined by HDLC or X25). If circuit switching (or even virtual call packet switching—*see* PACKET SWITCHING) is used, then the limit is set by the number of simultaneous buffers for each call that can be supported. Several levels of multiplexing and concentration may be supported. This is illustrated in Fig. 10.

Moreover, the type of multiplexing between different levels may be quite different. For example, between M_1 and M_2 a more powerful form of multiplexing such as packet switching would be used.

All these techniques take advantage of one or more of the following factors.

1. Normally not all terminals T operate simultaneously.
2. When in use, the data rate transmission between even an active terminal and a network may exhibit considerable variations.
3. The cost of a long distance communication channel increases much more slowly than its data capacity.
4. The communication channels installed often have greater capacity than the average traffic.

It is often cheaper to take advantage of the *transmission savings* by incorporating more complex *switching* or *multiplexing*. In *public data networks*, the savings are partially (or entirely) enjoyed by the carriers. In *leased networks,* the customers of the PTTs are the main beneficiaries. Partially to ease disparities of cost, and to encourage the use of public networks, some PTTs are starting to raise the cost of leased circuits, charge partly by volume of traffic on the leased facilities and restrict the switching permitted by the customer.

References

1968. Kretzmer, E. R. *Modern Techniques for Data Communication on Telephone Channels, IFIP 68.* Amsterdam: North-Holland, pp. 716–721.
1970. Martin, J. *Teleprocessing Network Organization.* Englewood Cliffs, NJ: Prentice-Hall.
1972. Petersen, W. W. *Error Correcting Codes.* Cambridge, MA: MIT Press.
1973. Abramson, N. *Computer Communications Networks,* Abramson, N. and Kuo, F. (Eds.). Englewood Cliffs, NJ: Prentice-Hall.
1973. Davies, D. W. and Barber, D. L. A. *Communication Networks for Computers.* London: Wiley.
1978. CCITT. "Provisional Recommendations X.3, X.21, X.25, X.29, X.75, X.121. Geneva: ITU.
1978. ISO. "High Level Data Link Control (HDLC), DIS 3309.2 and DIS 4335. Paris: International Standards Organization.
1978. McQuillan, J. M. *A Practical View of Computer Communications Protocols,* McQuillan, J. M. and Cerf, V. G. (Eds.). IEEE EHO 137-0, New York.
1979. Beauchamp, K. G. (Ed.). *Interlinking of Computer Networks.* Dordrecht: D. Reidel.

P. T. KIRSTEIN

SOFTWARE

The importance of (and the attention given to) data communications software has been increasing at a rapid pace over the last 10 years. This growing importance is

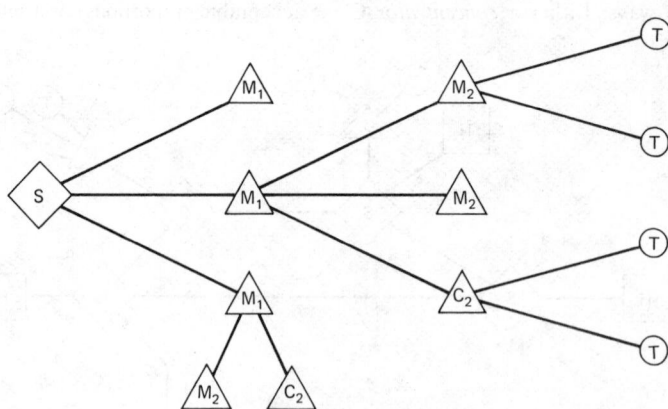

Fig. 10.   Example of multi-level multiplexing.

driven by an ever-increasing demand for low-cost, flexible, and powerful data communications systems.

The emergence of microprocessors has greatly accelerated the development of new data communications systems. Since these systems lend themselves easily to parallel processing organizations, a variety of multi-microprocessor systems for data communications applications have been built. The large number of existing and projected data communications devices has in turn created a wave of development of large-scale integration (LSI) in this field. Almost every month, a new, more powerful LSI chip is announced that performs functions that traditionally were performed by data communications software. Thus, the borderline between hardware and software is rapidly moving. Today's data communications engineer, therefore, has to be thoroughly familiar with both hardware and software problem-solving techniques.

The design of data communications software is heavily influenced by the real-time requirements associated with data communications applications. There is an endless variety in the sequence and timing in which messages and characters are to be processed. Therefore, even the most exhaustive test procedure will only test a small number of all possible interactions.

Various techniques have been developed to ensure the proper design of data communications software. The interactions between two communicating entities are normally defined by carefully specified *protocols*. The use of state-transition diagrams has proved to be a valuable tool for specifying protocols, as well as for the design of software to implement these protocols. (See as an example the state-transition diagram shown in Fig. 3).

Another technique to deal with the complexities of data communications that has proven highly successful is the hierarchical design or layering of protocols. The advantage of the layered approach is that changes in one layer do not affect the other layers. Thus, definition, implementation, and testing of the various layers can proceed in parallel. The International Standards Organization (ISO) identified seven functional layers in the ISO reference model for open systems interconnection (Fig. 1). The first level, or physical control layer, provides the physical, functional, and mechanical characteristics of the interface. The second, or link control layer, provides for the reliable exchange of messages. In particular, it specifies the rules for overcoming transmission errors. The third, or network control layer, provides the functions required for intra-network operation, such as addressing and routing. The fourth level, or transport end-to-end control layer, ensures the reliable transfer of data between end points across a communications network. The fifth level is concerned with the control of a session, which is the period of time during which a user

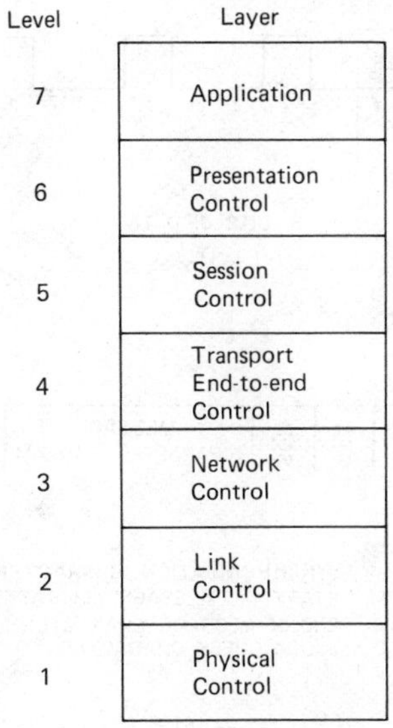

Fig. 1. ISO functional layers for open systems interconnection.

is connected to a computer system. In particular, this session control layer provides for identification and authentication of the user and for control of data flow during the session. The sixth level, or presentation control layer, formats the information as required by the interacting entities. The applications layer, which is concerned with applications software, is out of the scope of this article.

In the following sections, we will show what functions are typically performed by data communications software and discuss a possible software structure for implementing some of these functions.

Communication Line Characteristics. There are two main modes of transmission—asynchronous and synchronous. In asynchronous transmissions, the data is sent one character at a time [Fig. 2(a)]. Each character is framed by a start and stop bit. Bits within a character occur at well-defined intervals. The number of bits per character is fixed for a given communications line. The reading of this number of fixed bits is triggered by the reception of the start bit. In asynchronous transmission, characters do not recur at any predictable interval. This form of transmission is most commonly used for communication with slower-speed human-operated terminals.

In synchronous transmission, the bits of one character are followed immediately by those of the next [Fig. 2(b)]. The stream of characters is divided into blocks. Each block is surrounded by framing characters. The reading of the sequence of characters in a block is triggered by the reception of a start-of-block framing char-

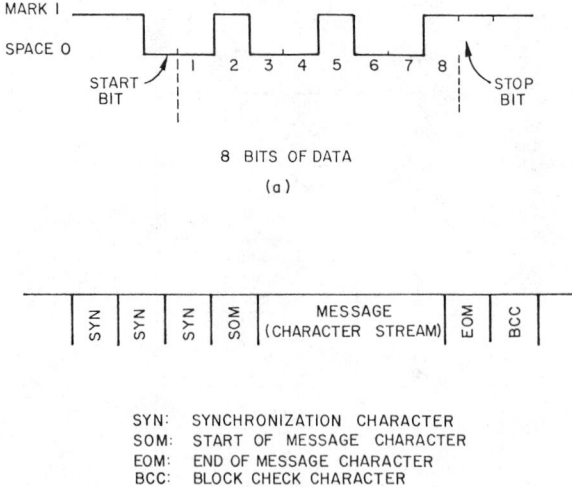

MARK I

SPACE 0

START
BIT

1 2 3 4 5 6 7 8

STOP
BIT

8 BITS OF DATA

(a)

SYN	SYN	SYN	SOM	MESSAGE (CHARACTER STREAM)	EOM	BCC

SYN: SYNCHRONIZATION CHARACTER
SOM: START OF MESSAGE CHARACTER
EOM: END OF MESSAGE CHARACTER
BCC: BLOCK CHECK CHARACTER

(b)

Fig. 2. Data transmission. a) asynchronous, b) synchronous

acter. Characters are received continuously until an end-of-block framing character is detected. Since there are no control bits for each character, synchronous transmissions generally result in a more efficient line utilization.

Communications lines are also distinguished with respect to their directionality. In simplex lines, data can be transmitted in only one direction. These are generally not used in data communications because they do not allow control signals to be sent back to the sender. Half-duplex lines can transmit in either direction, but only in one direction at once; i.e., the line has to be "turned around" before it can transmit in the opposite direction. To avoid conditions where both ends continue to send at the same time, a contention resolution strategy needs to be employed. For example, one station can be declared the master of the line. The master is then responsible for resolving possible conflicts among stations. Full-duplex lines transmit in both directions at the same time. One full-duplex line is equivalent to two half-duplex lines used in opposite directions. Since full-duplex lines often cost little more than half-duplex lines, they are rapidly becoming the dominant form of communication line.

Protocol Characteristics. Since data communications software is mainly concerned with data communications protocols, it is important to understand what protocol functions are typically implemented, at least partially, in software. Therefore, the following five protocol functions will be discussed in more detail: (1) call establishment and clearing; (2) error control; (3) flow control; (4) concentration; and (5) terminal-specific pro-

cedures. This, of course, is not an exhaustive list, but it highlights some of the main issues that need to be addressed in designing data communications software.

Call Establishment and Clearing. Before any data can be exchanged over data communications facilities, there needs to be a mechanism invoked by which one end can decide whether or not the other is operating at all (i.e., able and willing to establish a connection). In other words, both parties need to agree on a procedure by which one side can indicate to the other side that it either wants to establish or break a connection. Data set signals are used to convey this information at the physical communications level. Depending on the voltage of a particular pin of the interface, each side indicates that it is either operating or not available. In case a connection is established via the public telephone network, a more complex sequence of changes in the data set signals is required. At the link level, an exchange of special initialization commands and responses is normally required before data can be transmitted. The most sophisticated call establishment and clearing procedures are used at the network control level. In this case, highly structured call request and clear request messages are sent which carry information relating to the nature of the call. In particular, the call request message may indicate who intends to pay for the call, throughput requirements, what higher level protocol is to be used, etc. The clear message may carry information about the clearing cause, duration of the call, accounting data, etc.

Fig. 3 shows a state diagram for call establishment between two stations, A and B. Normally, a station sends out a call request and waits until it receives the matching call accept message. Call collision will occur when both stations try to establish a call at the same time. Note that, in the case presented, the call request from A to B takes precedence.

Error Control. One of the most important tasks of any data communications protocol is to deal with line errors. Various error detection and correction schemes have been studied and are in use today. They range from simple even or odd parity indication per character to powerful, usually hardware-generated, checksums per transmission block. All the more advanced procedures use positive acknowledgment schemes; i.e., the sender waits for an acknowledgment from the receiver. If an acknowledgment is not received within a given time period, the block is retransmitted. Since the acknowledgment may get lost on the line due to a line error, the receiver must be able to distinguish new incoming blocks from retransmissions of previously sent blocks. This can be accomplished through the use of sequence numbers. Whenever the receiver receives two blocks with the same sequence

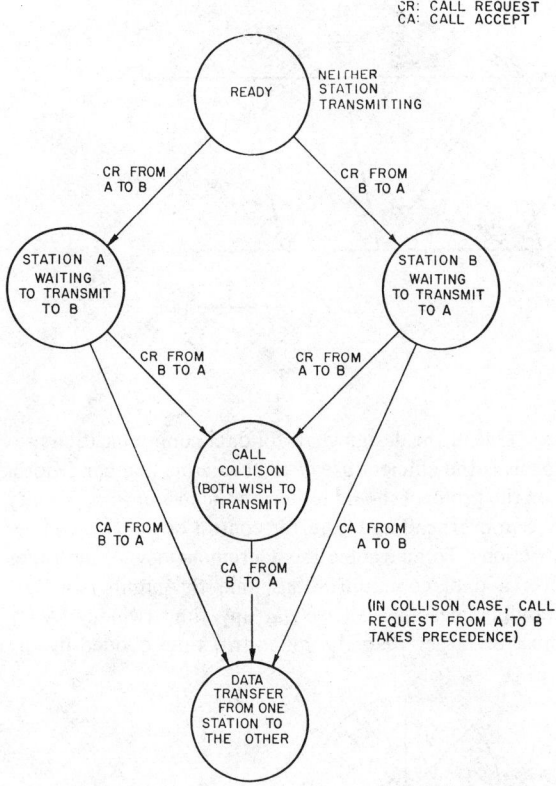

CR: CALL REQUEST
CA: CALL ACCEPT

Fig. 3. State transition diagram for call establishment.

next expected block, thereby acknowledging all blocks with sequence numbers N-1 or less. The range of sequence numbers is, of course, limited, since they occupy a finite space in each block. If K bits are reserved for the sequence number in the header of a block, then they are normally calculated modulo 2^K. In the simplest case, K is equal to 1; i.e., each block is labeled as block 0 or block 1. This requires only a single bit in the header for sequence control. This scheme has, however, the disadvantage that block 1 (or 0) can only be sent after block 0 (or 1) has been acknowledged. Therefore, the throughput is limited to one message per round-trip time (i.e., the time interval between sending a block and receiving its acknowledgment).

Sequence numbers are also used to detect blocks that reach the receiver out of sequence. In this case, two recovery actions are possible. The receiver discards all out-of-sequence blocks and asks the sender to retransmit all blocks from the point on where the first block was missed (reject scheme). The alternative possibility is that the receiver keeps the out-of-sequence blocks and asks the sender only for the retransmission of the missed blocks (selective retransmit scheme).

Figs. 4 and 5 demonstrate the use of the reject and the selective retransmit scheme. In both cases, message 2 is assumed to get lost on the line. The reject retransmit scheme causes messages 2, 3, and 4 to be retransmitted (Fig. 4). The selective retransmit scheme causes only message 2 to be retransmitted (Fig. 5). Messages 3 and 4 are only acknowledged after the successful retransmission of message 2.

Flow Control. To avoid loss of data, the average rate at which the receiver is able to accept data must be equal to or greater than the average rate at which the sender is sending it. Alternatively, there may be a mechanism by which the receiver can let the sender know that it should stop transmitting or at least slow down. This mechanism is called *flow control*.

number, it is known that the latter block is a retransmission of the first one and can be discarded as a duplicate if there was no error in the first one. The receiver will also send an acknowledgment for each duplicate to make sure that the sender eventually learns about the successful transmission.

A well-known technique for acknowledging blocks is to send back to the sender the sequence number N of the

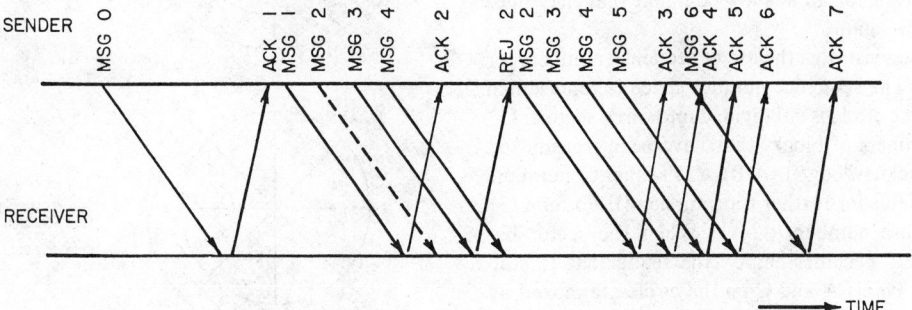

Fig. 4. Reject retransmit scheme (each acknowledgment carries the number of the next message expected).

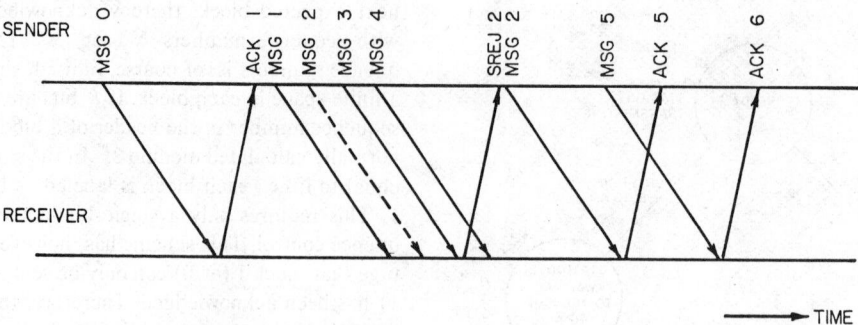

Fig. 5. Selective retransmit scheme.

In simple terminal protocols, flow control is provided by means of special characters. When the receiver is not willing to accept more characters, a so-called XOFF character will be transmitted. The receipt of this character causes the sender to stop transmitting. To restart the transmission of data, the receiver sends the so-called XON character. Since the XOFF and XON characters can be garbled or even generated by line errors, this simple scheme can lead to confusion. More sophisticated protocols, therefore, use checksum-protected commands to turn off and restart the flow of data from the sender.

All acknowledgment/retransmission protocols have a built-in natural flow control mechanism. Just by not acknowledging blocks (even though they were received with a good checksum), the receiver can stop the sender. More effective, however, is an extension of the sequence number scheme to cover flow control. In this scheme, the receiver returns with the acknowledgment not only of the sequence number of the next expected block, but also of an indication as to how many more blocks the receiver is willing to accept. This indication defines to the sender a window of legal sequence numbers it can use to send data. (Therefore, this scheme is called the *window technique*.) Once all sequence numbers in this window are used up (i.e., the window is closed), the sender must stop transmitting and wait for an acknowledgment that may open up the window again.

Fig. 6 demonstrates the use of sequence numbers for flow control. The sequence number space is represented as a circle. The circle is subdivided into three sectors: (1) sequence numbers of blocks that have been transmitted but not yet acknowledged (A-B); (2) sequence numbers that are available for further transmission (B-C); and (3) illegal sequence numbers (C-A). When the sector between B and C becomes empty, the sender has to stop transmitting. Points A and C on the circle are moved by the acknowledgments; point B is moved by the transmissions. The dashed areas represent the sequence number space used up by unacknowledged messages.

One of the design goals for data communication protocols is the efficient use of the available line bandwidth; i.e., the protocol should minimize the loss of line capacity due to overhead and/or error control or flow control restrictions. To guarantee the continuous flow of messages over a data communications link, the number of outstanding messages allowed at any time (window A-C) must be larger than the round-trip time divided by the

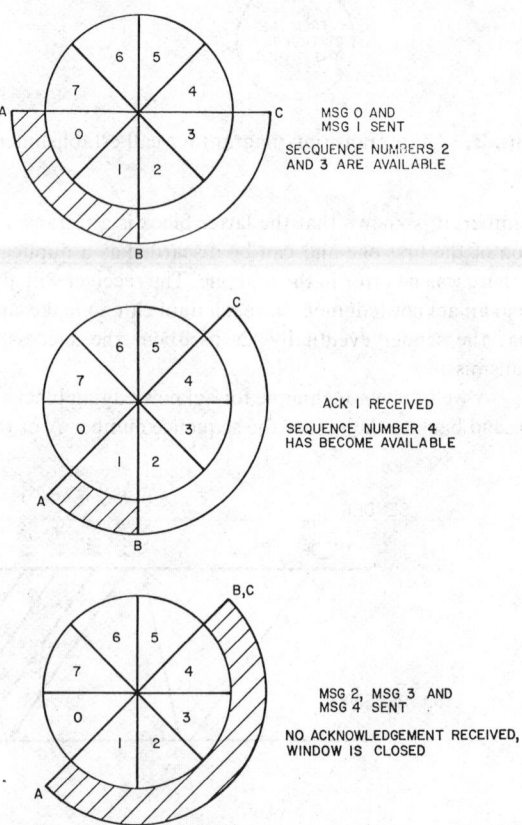

MSG 0 AND
MSG 1 SENT

SEQUENCE NUMBERS 2
AND 3 ARE AVAILABLE

ACK 1 RECEIVED

SEQUENCE NUMBER 4
HAS BECOME AVAILABLE

MSG 2, MSG 3 AND
MSG 4 SENT

NO ACKNOWLEDGEMENT RECEIVED,
WINDOW IS CLOSED

Fig. 6. Window technique.

time it takes to transmit one message. If this condition holds, the sender will never be blocked by a closed window B-C.

Concentration. The flow control condition of the previous paragraph can be relaxed if the protocol supports concentration. In this case, several data streams can be sent over the same physical channel. Each block carries an identifier signifying the data stream to which it belongs. Since each data stream is driven by an independent set of sequence numbers, the sender can keep on transmitting even though some of the data streams may be blocked. The use of independent sequence numbers for each data stream is also important in order to minimize the interference between them. In particular, a protocol must ensure that one data stream being blocked does not also block the users of the other data streams.

Terminal-Specific Procedures. A large variety of functions to be performed by the data communications software is common to many terminal types; others are only required for a given terminal type. Functions that are common to many asynchronous terminals are: (1) echo control; i.e., echoing of characters for full-duplex terminals and suppression of echo for half-duplex terminals; (2) padding; i.e., insertion of delay between characters to accommodate mechanical movement for characters like carriage return; (3) line folding; i.e., control of the maximum number of graphic characters that can be displayed on a single line; (4) code conversion; e.g., from EBCDIC (*q.v.*) to ASCII (*q.v.*); (5) editing; e.g., deletion of characters or lines of text; (6) keyboard control; i.e., locking and unlocking of the keyboard for certain half-duplex terminals; etc. Functions that are common to many display-type terminals are (1) cursor control (positioning of the cursor on the screen); (2) type and range checking on input data; (3) protection of read-only areas on the screen; (4) management of function keys; etc.

Network Operation. Communication protocols that are used in a network environment require additional functionality. In particular, the establishment of paths through the network to any desired destination needs to be specified in detail.

Computer communication networks are either *circuit-switched* or *packet-switched*. In a circuit-switched network, the source and destination are connected by a dedicated communication path that is established at the beginning of the connection and broken at the end. This type of connection is based on the traditional telephone technology, where subscribers require continuity in voice transmission and reception.

In packet-switching networks, short messages (called packets) are handled individually by the network. Packets are stored at intermediate nodes which switch them to the next transmission line on the path to the destination. Transmission capacity is shared among all connections. By avoiding the transmission of long data blocks, a packet-switching system is able to ensure that short blocks of high-priority data can be rapidly transmitted through the network. In a *message switching system,* complete messages are stored at intermediate nodes, sometimes for long periods, before they are forwarded to next node or the destination.

Software Structure. In the preceding section, we have shown what functions need to be performed by the data communications software. We will now turn to a discussion of software structures to implement these functions. In particular, we will present a simple communications software structure model to describe a software system for the handling of synchronous lines.

There are many ways by which data communications software can be organized. The model depicted in Fig. 7 represents a typical design that splits the entire task into functional units. Each of these functional units can be thought of as a process. The exchange of information between these processes can be done either on a shared memory basis or via a more formal message exchange procedure that is supported by the operating system.

Most of the handling of the hardware that interfaces

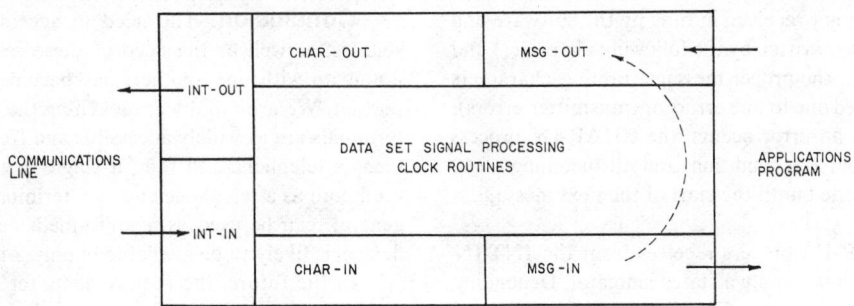

Fig. 7. Communications software structure.

the communications lines is normally implemented on interrupt level to satisfy the real time requirements of inflow and out-flow of data. The hardware interrupts occur either on a per character or on a per block basis. In the latter case, the hardware has the ability to deposit directly in memory and retrieve from memory a sequence of characters without software assistance. An interrupt is generated when this sequence has reached a predefined length or a special control character (or sequence of control characters) is encountered. Thus, if interrupts are only generated for a sequence of characters, the software is relieved of a great number of repetitive tasks. In the following discussion, we will, however, concentrate on the interrupt-per-character model, since it will allow us to describe more easily the various tasks involved in handling a communications line or terminal.

The interrupt level processes INT-IN and INT-OUT interact with the CHAR-IN and CHAR-OUT monitor level processes. The CHAR-IN process assembles characters into messages and passes the messages on to the MSG-IN process. In turn, the CHAR-OUT process receives messages from the MSG-OUT process, disassembles the messages, and passes individual characters on to the interrupt level process INT-OUT. The MSG-IN and MSG-OUT processes send messages to and receive messages from an applications program. We will now turn to a more detailed discussion of these processes for the handling of synchronous lines.

The main function of the INT-IN process is to store characters in a buffer in memory. This task involves the updating of an offset into the buffer, the detection of full buffers, and the switch-over to a new buffer. The start and end of message detection is also done by the INT-IN process. These events are either directly signaled by the hardware, or the software has to detect these conditions by searching through the stream of incoming characters for special control characters. The calculation of the checksum is almost always done by the hardware. The INT-IN process reads the result of that calculation from a control register and passes this information on to the CHAR-IN process. The INT-IN process also handles a large number of error conditions, such as underrun (i.e., a character was not received in time by the software and therefore was overwritten by the following character) and frame error (i.e., the proper message-framing characters were not detected due to line errors or transmitter errors). Whenever such an error occurs, the CHAR-IN process is informed about the condition, and all incoming characters are discarded until the start of the next message is found.

The CHAR-IN process receives from the INT-IN process buffers that contain a status indicator. Depending on this status indicator, the CHAR-IN process will build up chains of buffers if a message does not fit into a single buffer, pass these messages on to the MSG-IN process if the message was received with a correct checksum, or return the buffer to the operating system if any type of error was detected by the INT-IN process. The CHAR-IN process also has to supply the INT-IN process with buffers for the incoming messages.

The MSG-IN process ensures that messages are delivered to the applications program in correct order and without duplication. Messages that arrive out of order are either held until the missing messages are received or discarded and retransmitted later. All messages received in sequence, as well as all duplicate messages, are acknowledged. The acknowledgment information is passed on to the MSG-OUT process (dashed line in Fig. 7), which inserts it into the stream of outgoing messages. The MSG-IN process also informs the MSG-OUT process about any received acknowledgment information. This information allows the MSG-OUT process to free up buffer space that is occupied by messages that wait to be acknowledged. The main tasks of the MSG-OUT process is to accept messages from the applications program, provide them with the proper sequence number, if required, and pass them on to the CHAR-OUT process. A major part of the flow control procedure is implemented in the MSG-OUT process because it is this process that must, at any time, be aware of the ability of the receiver to receive more messages.

The CHAR-OUT process accepts messages from the MSG-OUT process. If the message is contained in a single buffer, this buffer is given to the INT-OUT process. In case the message consists of several buffers, each buffer is forwarded separately to the INT-OUT process. All buffers handed over to the interrupt level process carry a status indicator, which identifies them as either the head, middle section, or tail of a message. The INT-OUT process uses this status indicator to control proper framing of messages and the generation of the checksum. When the head of a message is received, the accumulation of the checksum is initialized. After the last buffer of the message has been emptied, the checksum is transmitted over the communications line.

Conclusion. The need to access computing resources, as well as the need of these resources to communicate with one another, has become ever-more important. We are rapidly approaching the days when data terminals are as widely accessible and frequently used as today's telephones. In fact, a single device that can be used both as a telephone and as a terminal and which, in general, can be used as a multi-media communications device, is likely to be available in only a few years.

In the future, the requirements for data communications system will be coupled more closely into the overall communications requirements. Today's data communications engineer will have to be more familiar with other means of communication. Complex software systems will be required to tie the existing means of communication together into one integrated system. The data communications software will, therefore, cease to exist as a separate subject but will be folded into software systems that satisfy a far greater range of communications requirements.

The design and implementation of these integrated communications systems represents a formidable challenge for the future. We have learned many valuable lessons in the course of designing data communications software systems over the last 10 years. This background and experience provides an important input to the design of software systems for a fully integrated communications environment.

REFERENCES

1979. Davies, D. W., Barber, D. L. A., Price, W. L., and Solomonides, C. M. *Computer Networks and Their Protocols.* New York: Wiley.
1979. Chu, Wesley W. *Advances in Computer Communications and Networking.* Artech House.
1979. Doll, Dixon R. *Data Communication Facilities, Networks, and Systems Design.* New York: Wiley.

H. OPDERBECK

DATA COMPRESSION AND COMPACTION

For articles on related subjects *see* CODES; DATA COMMUNICATIONS; DATA ENCRYPTION; and FILES.

Many data processing applications involve storage of large volumes of alphanumeric data such as names, addresses, inventory item descriptions, or a general ledger chart of accounts descriptions. Documents for text editors and for legal, medical, and library applications also require very high-capacity storage devices; and there is a rapid increase in the number of systems handling such material. At the same time, the proliferation of computer communication networks and teleprocessing applications involves massive transfer of data over long distance communication links.

To reduce the data storage requirements and/or the data communication costs, there is a need to reduce the redundancy in the data representation—i.e., to *compress* or *compact* the data. Data compression also reduces the load on I/O channels in a computer installation. Because of the reduced space requirements of compressed data, it may become feasible to store data at a higher, and thus faster, level of the storage hierarchy (*q.v.*).

It is also interesting to note that since data compression techniques remove some of the redundancy in a noncompressed text, they thereby automatically contribute to data security.

Data compression can be made transparent to the user and can be implemented in either hardware, firmware, or software. Note that the overhead involved in compression (followed later by expansion to recover the original data) is most severe in non-archival situations where the data is being actively processed rather than stored for later use.

The reason that data compression is not used in every situation is that it is not without its disadvantages. Assuming compression/expansion is done in software (which is often the case), the software complexity of the system is increased. This results directly in an increase in the processing load of the system mainly because of the CPU cycles needed for compression/expansion.

Another disadvantage of data compression is the decrease in portability. This is mainly caused by the absence of well defined standards in this area. Reliability is also reduced. This is because of the decrease in the redundancy, which is useful for error-detection purposes. In short, data compression techniques are most useful for large archival files, in I/O bound systems with spare CPU cycles, and in the transfer of voluminous amounts of data over long distance communication links. Sometimes data compression can achieve dramatic savings of total storage requirements. Savings of as much as 80% are not uncommon.

Data compression techniques can, in general, be divided into the *irreversible* and *reversible* categories. In the irreversible techniques (usually called *data compaction,* rather than data compression, although there are no standard definitions), the size of the physical representation of data is reduced, while that subset of the information deemed "relevant information" is preserved. For example, in some data sets, "leading zeros" or "trailing blanks" may be irrelevant information which may be discarded. Note that data compaction techniques are, by definition, dependent on the semantics of the data.

In data compression, all of the information is considered to be relevant, and the compression may be followed later by expansion which recovers the original data. The reversible procedures of data compression can be divided into two groups—*semantic independent* and *semantic dependent* techniques. The semantic independent techniques can be used on any data with varying degrees of effectiveness. They do not use any information regarding the information content of the data. On the other hand, the semantic dependent techniques depend on (and are optimized for) the context and semantics of the data to provide for redundancy reduction.

Below, we briefly discuss some of the more popular

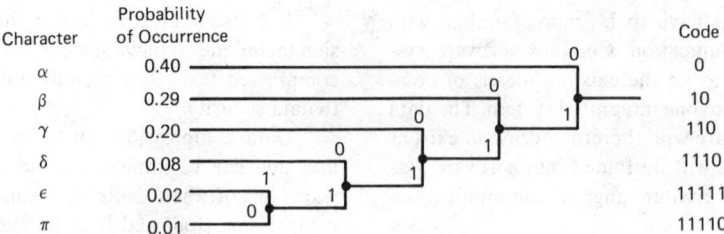

Fig. 1. An example showing a Huffman code for the given set of characters.

techniques used for data compression and then give an example of data compaction.

Adaptive Pattern Substitution. This method does not rely on the knowledge of any existing patterns; neither does it anticipate any specific ones (i.e., it is a semantic independent technique). It scans the entire text by looking for common patterns of two or more bytes occurring frequently and substitutes an unused byte pattern for the common long one. At the same time, the substitution dictionary is updated. Note that a new substitution dictionary is created specifically for a given text. For example, the text DAABFABC can be replaced with DAαFαC where α stands for AB. In this case, the substitution dictionary will have only the one entry, α = AB.

Variable-Length Character Encoding. Character-encoding schemes in normal use have a fixed number of bits per character. Tighter packing of data can be achieved with a code which employs a variable number of bits per character. With such a code, the most commonly occurring characters would be short, and the infrequently occurring characters would be long. The shortest character would be only one bit.

To provide a simple illustration, suppose that it were necessary to encode only six characters: α, β, γ, δ, ϵ, and π. To encode these in a conventional manner would require three bits per character. Suppose the relative frequency of the characters is as shown in Fig. 1. The figure also displays a coding of these six characters, called a *Huffman code,* which minimizes the total number of bits for characters appearing with the frequency shown, under the requirement that a message with this encoding can be decoded instantaneously as the bits arrive in the data stream (i.e., there must be no ambiguity when a bit arrives as to whether or not it is the end of a character).

As an example, the data string in the top portion of Fig. 2 can be decoded immediately by reading left to right, without waiting for the end of the string, since each 0 (or the fifth 1 in a sequence of 1s) must be the end of a character. Note that it is important to start at the beginning of a data stream in order to decode it properly.

Note that the Huffman encoding scheme pays off only with a skewed character distribution. For example, if all characters in Fig. 1 were used equally often, the mean number of bits per character would be 3.33—worse than with the fixed length character representation. For the probabilities given in Fig. 1, the average number of bits per character is 2.05.

Restricted Variability Codes. Because almost all computers are word-oriented, rather than bit-oriented, the variability in length of the Huffman code for different characters is usually considered to be a drawback. This shortcoming can be avoided with the use of the restricted variability codes. It should be noted that this advantage of the restricted variability codes usually comes at the price of less efficient use of bits in representing characters.

As an example, consider the so-called 5/10 code which can represent up to 63 characters. In this encoding scheme, the 31 most frequent characters are represented by the first 31 representations of the five-bit code. The thirty-second representation can be used as a temporary "switch character" to indicate that the actual character is encoded in the next five bits. In other words, the thirty-second representation of the first five bits plus the second five bits provide encodings for the less frequent 32 characters. Thus five bits are required to represent the 31 most frequent characters, while ten bits are used to denote the 32 less frequent ones. The similarity of this technique to the use of the SHIFT key on a typeqriter keyboard should be noted. Clearly for any n, there is an $n/$

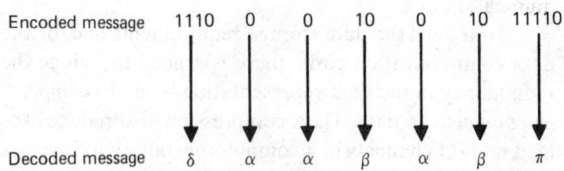

Fig. 2. Example of decoding a data stream encoded in the Huffman code of Fig. 1.

Character	Code
α	00
β	01
γ	10
δ	1100
ϵ	1101
π	1110
θ	1111

Fig. 3.   The 2/4 code for encoding seven characters.

$2n$ code. As an example, Fig. 3 demonstrates an encoding of seven characters in the 2/4 code with "11" the switch character. It is assumed that α, β, and γ are more frequent than δ, ϵ, π, and θ.

Compact Notation. When fields are stored in the form in which humans prefer to read them, they often contain more characters than are necessary. Dates are a common example. We may write 15 DEC 1979 or, in our most compact written form, 12.15.79, and so dates are often stored as six bytes in computer files. In the machine, however, the month needs no more than four bits, the day can be encoded in five bits, and the year needs no more than seven bits if the century (e.g., 19) is taken to be fixed—a total of 16 bits, or two eight-bit bytes.

Suppression of Repeated Characters. Numeric fields in some files contain a high proportion of leading zeros; other files contain repetitive blanks or other characters. A general scheme for suppressing repeated characters is called *run-length encoding*. One such method uses the fact that, in the conventional eight-bit EBCDIC (*q.v.*) character encoding, any character with a zero in the second position is not normally employed as a data character. Such a character is therefore employed to indicate repetition of other characters (see Fig. 4). The character in Fig. 4, therefore, indicates that the following character occurs $b_5b_4b_3b_2b_1b_0 + 3$ times ($+ 3$ because, if a character appears only twice, this method does not save any space).

Suppression of repeated characters is a highly desirable technique in most picture processing applications.

Avoidance of Null Fields. In some files, the fields in a record may be highly variable in length or even

missing. In the latter case, *presence bits* can show which fields there are, or, if only a few fields are usually present, *tags* can be used to denote the identity of the present fields. Fig. 5 shows a record format in which the presence bits field is used to indicate whether a data item is present or not.

Dictionary Substitution. Where a quantity can have only a limited set of attribute values, there is no need to spell the item out in full; instead, a code can be used. Examples are bank account type, insurance policy type, and sex. This technique is very similar to the compact notation technique.

Exploitation of Ordered Data. By examining the relationships between successive data items, one can sometimes derive an efficient coding scheme to achieve a high level of data compression. As an example, Fig. 6 displays the first column of a list of names taken from a telephone directory. Note that, in the encoded version of the names, only the changes from the previous name in the list appear. The number in front of the trailing end of the name represents the number of characters which are the same.

Differencing. This method is similar in philosophy to the previous one and is best for files of numerical data that have small variations in magnitude between entries. As an example, rather than storing the cumulative precipitation for each day (i.e., $c_1, c_2, \ldots, c_{365}$) we may store the difference between entries (i.e., $c_1, c_2\text{-}c_1, \ldots, c_{365}\text{-}c_{364}$). Note that c_1 is an absolute value and serves as the base. The saving in space which results is a consequence of the fact that the difference in the cumulative precipitation of two adjacent days is less than the absolute value of each of the former. In addition, we expect many of the differences to be zero. It should be noted that, usually, the differencing method is highly successful in compressing digitized pictures.

Decimal to Binary Conversion. Rather than storing numbers in (packed or unpacked) decimal notation (which take four and eight bits per decimal digit, respectively), binary representation acting as another form of compact notation can be used. As an example, numbers between 0 and 255 can be represented by using only

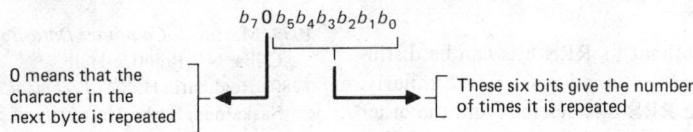

Fig. 4.

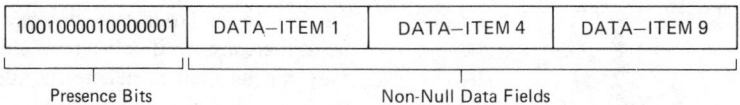

1001000010000001	DATA—ITEM 1	DATA—ITEM 4	DATA—ITEM 9

Presence Bits   Non-Null Data Fields

Fig. 5.   The use of the presence bits in a record which can have a maximum of 16 data items.

Name	Compressed Name
Aalbers	0 Aalbers
Aalderink	3 derink
Aamar	2 mar
Aamondt	3 ondt
Aaro	2 ro
Aarons	4 ns

Fig. 6.   The exploitation of ordered data for front compression.

an eight-bit byte. Note that the decimal to binary conversion procedure belongs to the semantic dependent group of data compression techniques.

Data Compaction. As an example of data compaction techniques, in addition to our previous example of removing leading zeros or trailing blanks, we consider a sequence of numerically ordered (i.e., sorted) keys in a directory of a file. In this example, we use *rear-compaction* to delete a rear redundant string (RRS) from a key. This string is composed of those rightmost bits of the key which are not necessary to distinguish uniquely the key from the set of all keys in the particular sequence to be rear-compacted. It can be shown that, given a set of sorted keys, in order to find the RRS of a key K, it is enough to look only at the previous key and the following key in the sorted sequence. Consider the following set of keys.

Key ($i-1$)   1 0 1 0 1 0 1 0 `[`1 0 1 0 1 0 1 0 1`]`   RRS

Key i 1 0 1 0 1 0 1 1 0 1 0 1 0 `[`1 0 1 0`]`   RRS

Key ($i+1$)   1 0 1 0 1 0 1 1 0 1 0 1 1 `[`1 0 1 1`]`   RRS

Note that key i without its RRS bits can be distinguished from both key ($i-1$) and key ($i+1$). Similarly, it is assumed that, with RRS bits deleted from the other two keys, one can still distinguish them from their adjacent keys.

In the above example, the removal of RRSs will result in compacted keys which are not of equal length. Since this is generally undesirable, the compacted keys can be forced to be of equal length by keeping a number of bits equal to the length of the longest compacted key. In the above example, this would result in:

Rear-compacted key ($i-1$)	1 0 1 0 1 0 1 0 1 0 1 0 1
Rear-compacted key i	1 0 1 0 1 0 1 1 0 1 0 1 0
Rear-compacted key ($i+1$)	1 0 1 0 1 0 1 1 0 1 0 1 1

More detailed information on data compaction is contained in Reghbati (1980).

Concluding Remarks. Although the methods described have been explained separately, it should be clear that it may be useful to use more than one procedure for the same data set. For example, it may be beneficial to suppress the repeated characters of a text file first and then Huffman encode the resulting text.

It is important to note that sometimes it may be possible to reduce the need for data compression by avoiding redundant storage of information. This is one of the major objectives of database management systems. For example, one should not store the part description in both the "parts file" and "inventory file." A somewhat related issue is that fields that are computable from others should not be stored. For example, store "monthly earnings" but not "tax withheld"—since the tax algorithm can be used to generate the tax withheld from the monthly earnings.

The comparison, analysis, and cost effectiveness issues of data compression and compaction techniques are beyond the scope of this article. For more information on data compression, the interested reader is referred to the references below.

REFERENCES

1977. Martin, J. *Computer Data-Base Organization.* Englewood Cliffs, NJ: Prentice-Hall.
1980. Reghbati, H. K. *Technical Aspects of Teleprocessing.* Saskatoon, Sask.: University of Saskatchewan.

H. K. REGHBATI

DATA DEFINITION LANGUAGES

For articles on related subjects *see* CODASYL; DATABASE MANAGEMENT; and DATA STRUCTURES, SET CONCEPTS FOR.

A data definition language (DDL) is used to specify the way in which data is to be stored and managed in a database environment by a database management system (DBMS). The defined data is subsequently referenced by data manipulation language (DML) commands as part of the programming language used by the DBMS user.

A database is an orderly, managed collection of different, but interrelated, data record types accessible concurrently by multiple users. The intrinsic relationships which exist between different data in an organization are mirrored in a database by relationships established between different data record types. For example, Fig. 1 shows the relationships which exist between a CUSTOMER data record and the ORDER records belonging to that customer. Fig. 1 illustrates that one customer may have many orders; similarly, each ORDER record and each PRODUCT record may have many ORDERED-PRODUCTS records associated with them.

One of the first DDLs was developed in the late 1960s by the CODASYL database task group (DBTG). This group specified a Cobol-like DDL and DML designed to be implemented by different manufacturers on various computers and intended as a database standard. However, the development of two other major database systems in the 1960s by IBM and Cincom resulted in three database "standards": Data Language/1 (IBM), TOTAL (Cincom), and the CODASYL "recommendation" standard.

Data definition languages differ from each other according to the characteristics of the particular DBMS being used. For example, in TOTAL or Data Language/1, a macro-type language is used as the DDL to

specify the data, its relationships, and the way it is to be stored. On the other hand, a procedural Cobol-like DDL is used for specification of CODASYL databases, as illustrated in Fig. 2 (which is discussed further below). Most DDLs used today provide for specification of three representations of data. These are the schema, the subschema, and the conceptual schema.

The *schema* specifies the physical ordering relationsips which exist between data record types (see Fig. 1). Each separate record type to be stored in the database is named, together with the data fields comprising that record, the way in which that record type is to be accessed (directly, through a randomizing algorithm, or through an identifying key) and where that record type is to be stored in the database relative to other record types. Thus, the CUSTOMER, ORDER, and ORDERED-PRODUCTS records in Fig. 1 would be specified as three different record types. The relationships which exist in Fig. 1 between these records are specified in the schema "set relationships." Fig. 2 illustrates part of the CODASYL schema data definition language specification for the data structure illustrated in Fig. 1.

The *subschema* data definition language defines only that subset of data in the database authorized for reference by a particular program. For example, an order entry program may need to reference the entire data structure in Fig. 1. On the other hand, a product enquiry program may only need to reference the PRODUCT record; this program's subschema would therefore only identify the PRODUCT record (and none other).

The *conceptual schema* specifies a transformation of data from that physically organized and stored in the database as specified by the schema, and that actually referenced in the program's subschema. For example, it may be necessary physically to organize the data structure in Fig. 1 for normal access first to the CUSTOMER record, then to the customer's related ORDER and ORDERED-PRODUCTS records. On the other hand, it may also be necessary to reference the PRODUCT record to identify all orders placed against a product and the customers who placed those orders,—for example, to notify them of a delay in delivery of that product. This indicates a need by a "product delivery" program to reference the database by product in the reverse (*inverted*) way from its physical organization by customer. Fig. 3 illustrates the inverted data structure as referenced by the product delivery program. The subschema specifies this program view of the database; the conceptual schema specifies the transformation of the data from its physical representation as specified in the schema to its logical representation as specified in the subschema, so that it appears to the product delivery program as if the database was *physically* structured as illustrated in Fig. 3.

Data definition languages therefore enable data to

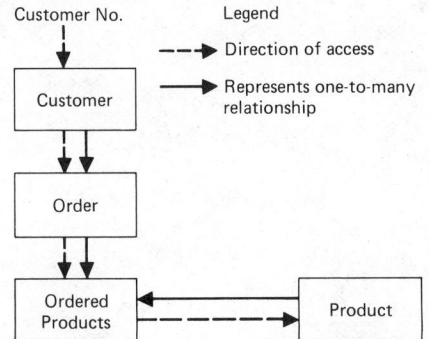

Fig. 1. A schematic representation of interrelated data records to be specified to a database using a data definition language.

SCHEMA DESCRIPTION.

SCHEMA NAME IS ORDERS.

FILE DESCRIPTION.

   FILE NAME IS ORDER-FILE   ASSIGN TO ORDENT.

   FILE NAME IS JOURNAL   ASSIGN TO IDMSJRNL.

AREA DESCRIPTION.

   AREA NAME IS ORDER-ENTRY
      RANGE IS 20001 THRU 20100
      WITHIN FILE ORDER-FILE FROM 1 THRU 100.

RECORD DESCRIPTION.   (Identifies CUSTOMER record—see Fig. 1)

RECORD NAME IS CUSTOMER.
RECORD ID IS 202.
LOCATION MODE CALC USING CUST-NO DUPLICATES NOT ALLOWED.
WITHIN ORDER-ENTRY.

03	CUST-NO	PIC X(8).	(CUSTOMER
03	CUST-NAM	PIC X(32).	record
03	CUST-ADD1	PIC X(32).	format)
03	CUST-ADD2	PIC X(32).	

RECORD NAME IS ORDER.   (Identifies ORDER record)
RECORD ID IS 302.
LOCATION MODE VIA CUST-ORDER-SET.
WITHIN ORDER-ENTRY.

03	ORDER-NO	PIC X (8).	(ORDER
03	ORDER-ENTRY-DATE	PIC X (8).	record
03	ORDER-DUE-DATE	PIC X (8).	format)

RECORD NAME IS ORDERED-PRODUCTS.   (ORDERED-PRODUCTS record)
RECORD ID IS 308.
LOCATION MODE VIA ORDER-ITEM-SET.
WITHIN ORDER-ENTRY.

03	ITEM-PROD-NO	PIC X (4).
03	ITEM-QTY	PIC X9(8).

RECORD NAME IS PRODUCT.   (PRODUCT record)
RECORD ID IS 402
LOCATION MODE CALC USING PRODUCT-NO
   DUPLICATES NOT ALLOWED.
WITHIN ORDER-ENTRY.

03	PRODUCT-NO	PIC X (4).
03	PRDUCT-NAME	PIC X (16).
03	PRODUCT-INFO	PIC X (24).
03	PRODUCT-QTY	PIC X9(8).

Fig. 2. An example of part of the schema data definition language used for Codasyl database management systems.

SET DESCRIPTION.

SET NAME CUST-ORDER-SET.
ORDER SORTED.
MODE CHAIN LINKED PRIOR.
OWNER CUSTOMER   NEXT POSITION 3   PRIOR POSITION 4
MEMBER ORDER   NEXT POSITION 1   PRIOR POSITION 2
                 LINKED OWNER   OWNER POSITION 3

(Identifies relationship
between CUSTOMER and
ORDER records—see Fig. 1)

     ASCENDING KEY IS ORDER-DUE-DATE DUPLICATES LAST
     MANDATORY AUTOMATIC.

SET NAME ORDER-ITEM-SET.
ORDER NEXT.

(Relationship between ORDER and
ORDERED-PRODUCTS records—see Fig. 1)

OWNER CHAIN LINKED PRIOR.
OWNER ORDER   NEXT POSITION 7   PRIOR POSITION 8
MEMBER ORDERED-PRODUCTS
                 NEXT POSITION 1   PRIOR POSITION 2
                 LINKED OWNER   OWNER POSITION 3

     MANDATORY AUTOMATIC

SET NAME PROD-ITEM-SET.
ORDER NEXT.
MODE CHAIN LINKED PRIOR.
OWNER PRODUCT   NEXT POSITION 1   PRIOR POSITION 2.
MEMBER ORDERED-PRODUCTS
                 NEXT POSITION 7   PRIOR POSITION 8
                 LINKED OWNER   OWNER POSITION 9

(Relationship between ORDERED-

     MANDATORY AUTOMATIC.

Fig. 2. (continued)

be specified to a DBMS so that it is physically organized in the database for most efficient access based on the expected most frequent means of referencing that data— while still enabling the data to be referenced in different ways to satisfy other programs' requirements.

Because the physical organization and referencing of data from the database is removed from the application program, and instead specified through a data definition language to a database management system, that data can be physically restructured and reorganized for most efficient use without requiring substantial modification of all programs which access the data. This is known as *data independence*. And because the same database can be used to satisfy different programs' views of that data, the need to maintain data redundantly in differently organized files for each different program view is removed. Thus *data redundancy* is reduced. Other database definition languages specify relationships between data through the use of separate indexes which are not an integral part of the database itself. These are referred to as inverted list database products.

The evolution of relational database systems will see database techniques extended further, with the DBMS eventually being implemented in hardware. The data definition language will then specify to these *database machines* the data to be managed and the relationships be-

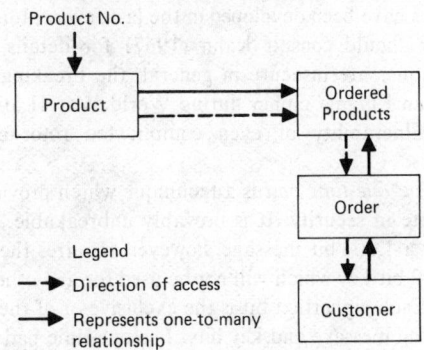

Fig. 3. An inverted data structure representing a different program view of the data physically organized as in Fig. 1.

tween data, based on concepts similar to those described above.

C. B. FINKELSTEIN

DATA ENCRYPTION

For articles on related subjects *see* CRIME AND COMPUTER SECURITY; DATA COMMUNICATIONS; DATA SECURITY; and KEY.

Cryptography is the science of transforming messages for the purpose of making the message unintelligible to all but the intended receiver of the message. The term *data encryption* refers to the use of cryptographic methods in computer communications for the same reason but also implies the additional goals of providing assurance to the receiver that the message is not a forgery, and/or allowing the receiver to prove to a third party that the message is not a forgery. These various aims are called, respectively, the goals of *communication security, authentication,* and *digital signatures.*

The transformation used to encipher a message typically involves both a general method, or algorithm, and a key. While the general method used by a pair of correspondents may be public knowledge, some or all of the key information must be kept secret. The process of transforming (enciphering) a message is to apply the enciphering algorithm to the message, where the key is used as an auxiliary input to control the enciphering. The reverse operation (deciphering) is performed similarly.

Classical encryption techniques involve such operations as substituting for each message letter a substitute letter; in this case, the key is the correspondence between message (plaintext) letters and the enciphered message (ciphertext) letters. Such *substitution ciphers* can also be based on substituting for two or more letters at a time. Another common technique is to permute the order of the message letters using an algorithm whose steps are determined by a *key.* Many complicated hand or mechanical ciphers have been developed in the last few centuries; the reader should consult Kahn (1967) for details. These techniques are insecure in general; the breaking of the German Enigma cipher during World War II attests to the vulnerability of even complicated rotor-machine ciphers.

The *one-time pad* is a technique which provides the ultimate in security: It is provably unbreakable. To encipher a 1,000-bit message, however, requires the use of a 1,000-bit key which will not be used for any other message. Each ciphertext bit is the exclusive-or of the corresponding message and key bits. The one-time pad is only used in very important applications (like the Moscow-Washington hot-line) because of the expense in creating and distributing the large amount of key information required.

Cryptosystems which, unlike the one-time pad, depend upon an amount of key information which is independent of message length are breakable in theory. What makes them usable in practice is that the person trying to break the cipher (the *cryptanalyst*) must use an impractical or infeasible amount of computational resources in order to break the cipher. These ciphers are constructed so that the "work-factor" in breaking them is high enough to prevent a successful attack.

The major application of cryptography today is for data transmitted between computers in computer communication networks and for computer data encrypted for storage.

The most widely used cipher in the U.S. for the encryption of stored or transmitted computer data is undoubtedly the Data Encryption Standard (DES), which was designed at IBM and approved as a standard by the National Bureau of Standards in 1976. The DES enciphers a 64-bit message block under control of a 56-bit key to produce a 64-bit ciphertext. The enciphering operation consists of roughly 16 iterations of the following two steps.

1. Exchange the left half of the 64-bit message with the right half.
2. Replace the right half of the message with the bit-wise exclusive-or of the right half and a 32-bit word which is a complicated function f of the left half, the key, and the iteration number. The function f involves in part a number of substitutions of short sub-blocks using specially constructed substitution tables (*S*-boxes) and permutations of the individual bit positions. The basic DES function has been implemented by a large number of manufacturers on special-purpose LSI chips, which can encipher at megabit per second rates.

Some applications (e.g., enciphering a line to a user's terminal) require that blocks shorter than 64 bits (e.g., a byte) be individually enciphered. The basic DES block can be used for this application in *cipher feedback mode:* each message byte is enciphered by an exclusive-or with the left-most byte of the result of taking the last eight ciphertext bytes and using them as input to the DES to obtain another 64-bit block of ciphertext.

Conventional cryptosystems (including DES) use the same key at both the enciphering and deciphering stations. In 1976, Diffie and Hellman proposed *public-key cryptosystems* in which the deciphering key was different from, and not computable from, the enciphering key (and vice versa). A person might create a matched pair of such keys and distribute copies of the enciphering key to all his/her friends, while keeping the deciphering key secret.

As a small example of the RSA method, the word "IT" can be encrypted as follows. Using the representation $A = 01, B = 02, \ldots, Z = 26$, we obtain the number 0920 for IT. Then with $n = 2773 = 47 \cdot 59$ and $e = 17$, we obtain the ciphertext:

$$C = 920^{17}(\text{modulo } 2773) = 948.$$

Using $p = 47$ and $q = 59$, a value of $d = 157$ can be derived, from which we can calculate 948^{157} (modulo 2773) $= 920$, the original message.

Fig. 1. Data encryption using the RSA method.

The friends can send to the creator of the enciphering key enciphered mail that only the creator can read. (Even if a cryptanalyst obtains a copy of the enciphering key, it does no good.) This demonstrates the flexibility of a public-key cryptosystem for *key distribution,* an area where conventional cryptosystems are awkward because all keys must be kept secret. Public-key cryptosystems can also be used to provide *digital signatures:* A user can create a signature for a message by enciphering it with a private key. (Here the enciphering/deciphering roles of the public/private keys are reversed.) Someone else can check the validity of the signature by checking that it deciphers to the message using the signer's public key. This capability of public-key cryptosystems promises to have important applications in electronic funds transfer systems (*q.v.*).

The first proposal for a function to implement public-key cryptosystems was by Rivest, Shamir and Adleman (1978). Their cryptosystem (the so-called *RSA cipher*) enciphers a message M (first coded into numeric form by, for example, setting $A = 01$, $B = 02$, etc.) using a public key *(e,n)* to obtain a ciphertext C as follows.

$$C = M^e(\text{mod } n).$$

That is, C is the remainder of M^e when divided by n. Here all quantities are large numbers (several hundred bits long), and n is the product of two very large prime numbers p and q. The security of the cipher rests mainly on the practical impossibility of factoring the number n into its parts p and q. The deciphering operation is similar, except that the exponent is different:

$$M = C^d(\text{mod } n).$$

Since d depends on p and q (in a way too complicated to explain here), it is provably as hard to compute d from e and n as it is to factor n. When n is more than roughly 400 bits long, this becomes a prohibitively time-consuming task. Although the enciphering operation itself is quite complicated, enciphering rates of 1–10 kilobits/second are possible with a special-purpose LSI chip.

An example of the RSA methods is shown in

Fig. 1. Another public-key cryptosystem has been proposed by Merkle and Hellman (1978). This technique is based on the difficulty of determining which subset of a given list of numbers adds up to a given target number (this is the NP-complete "knapsack" problem). A public key consists of a list, $a_1, a_2 \ldots a_{200}$, of two hundred 200-bit numbers. A 200-bit message, $m_1, \ldots, m_{200}$, is enciphered as follows.

$$c = \sum_{i=1}^{200} m_i \cdot a_i.$$

Deciphering is more complicated and depends on the special manner in which a_i is constructed. This technique does not easily lend itself to the creation of digital signatures (as does RSA) but it does permit substantially higher enciphering rates.

REFERENCES

1967. Kahn, D. *The Codebreakers.* New York: Macmillan.
1976. Diffie, W. and Hellman, M. "New Directions in Cryptography," *IEEE Trans. Information Theory* **IT-22,** pp. 644–654 (November).
1977. FIPS Publication 46. *Specifications for the Data Encryption Standard.*
1978. Rivest, R., Shamir, A., and Adleman, L. "A Method for Obtaining Digital Signatures and Public-Key Cryptosystems," *Comm. ACM,* pp. 120–126 (February).
1978. Merkle, R. and Hellman, M. "Hiding Information and Signatures in Trapdoor Knapsacks," *IEEE Trans. Information Theory* **IT-24,** pp. 535–530 (September).
1979. Diffie, W. and Hellman, M. "Privacy and Authentication: An Introduction to Cryptography," *Proc. IEEE* **67,** pp. 397–427 (March).

R. L. RIVEST

DATAFLOW

For articles on related subjects *see* COMPUTER ARCHITECTURE; FUNCTIONAL PROGRAMMING; GRAPH THEORY; and PARALLEL PROCESSING.

Dataflow is a generic term that pertains to algorithms or machines whose actions are determined by the availability of the data needed for these actions. Algorithms which are expressed and executed in dataflow terms are controlled by the arrival of data at operators (called *actors*). This is to be contrasted to control flow environments where the locus of execution is based on an instruction pointer that identifies the operation to be performed at any point in time. Dataflow algorithms can be represented as directed graphs in which the *arcs* are data paths and the *nodes* are operations to be performed on the data tokens arriving on the incoming arcs. The graph shown in Fig. 1 is a dataflow procedure.

The names within the nodes of the graph indicate the operation to be performed. The availability of the input tokens and the ability of the output arc(s) to receive data (which will be the case when the previous output has already been used as an input to another node) are the only conditions that must be satisfied for any operation to execute. The act of performing the operation is called *firing* the node and results in the consumption of the input tokens and production of output tokens.

The node labeled "OP1" in Fig. 1 has two input arcs associated with it; nodes "OP2" and "OP4" have one input arc and node "OP3" has three input arcs. If tokens arrive on both of OP1's input arcs and its output arc is empty, then the input tokens will be consumed, the transformation OP1 will be performed on the data, and an output token will be produced. If a token had arrived on the input arc to OP2, coincident with the arrival of input tokens to OP1, and OP2's output arcs were empty, then both nodes OP1 and OP2 can fire simultaneously.

Node OP4 must wait only until OP2 has finished executing in order to fire, whereas node OP3 must wait for both OP1 and OP2 to complete. Thus, the synchronization of asynchronous activities is accommodated very naturally in a dataflow graph. The graph of Fig. 1 is surrounded by a dashed line (called the *procedure boundary*) and given a name, PROCA, so that it may be used in other dataflow programs. Fig. 2 shows a convention flowchart for a sequential programming language and a corresponding dataflow program for determining the roots of a quadratic equation.

Although dataflow is a relatively new approach to computer systems organization, dataflow-related modeling techniques have been in use for quite some time (Karp and Miller, 1969). One of the first formal methods using a dataflow-like technique is PERT/CPM (*q.v.*), developed in the 1950s for project planning and control. Another major use of a dataflow-like technique is in the simulation language GPSS V (*see* SIMULATION), developed for modeling discrete stochastic systems. The designers of logic circuits and computer hardware have used dataflow-related techniques in describing, analyzing, and testing circuits in which data items are in the form of electrical signals. Dataflow, in this context, bears a strong resemblence to Petri nets (*q.v.*). Optimizing compilers analyze the flow of data in performing machine independent optimizations. Dataflow-related techniques have also been used in microcode optimization (Lanskov *et al.,* 1980), software specification, and reliability (Fosdick and Osterweil, 1976).

There are currently several different candidate architectures proposed for executing dataflow programs. The architecture first proposed by Dennis and Misunas (1975) consists (see Fig. 3) of a collection of addressable instruction cells (IC) connected by an arbitration network to a group of operation units (transformational devices). The operation units are, in turn, connected by a distribution network back to the instruction cells. The instruction cells correspond to nodes on the graph, while operation units are merely execution units. An enabled instruction cell transmits an *instruction packet* to an operation unit via the arbitration network. The arbitration network processes instruction packets on a round robin basis. The result of a node firing is a *data packet* which is sent to the destination instruction cells using the distribution network. A variation of Dennis' architecture was implemented by Texas Instruments, Inc. in their Distributed Data Processor (DDP). Each operation unit in the DDP has an arithmetic/logic unit and a memory for instruction cells. The operation units are called nodes and are connected by a shift register interconnection network. Both the operation units and instruction cells are addressable. The primitive operations correspond to those operations used in an intermediate language for compiling Fortran to TI's ASC computer. A front end processor accepts Fortran programs represented as dataflow graphs, identifies subgraphs having no data dependencies in the graphs and distributes the subgraphs to various nodes of the DDP execution.

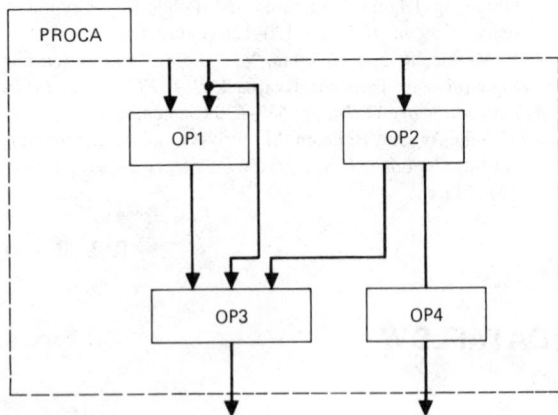

Fig. 1.   Sample dataflow program and graph.

Dataflow Program   Flowchart Program

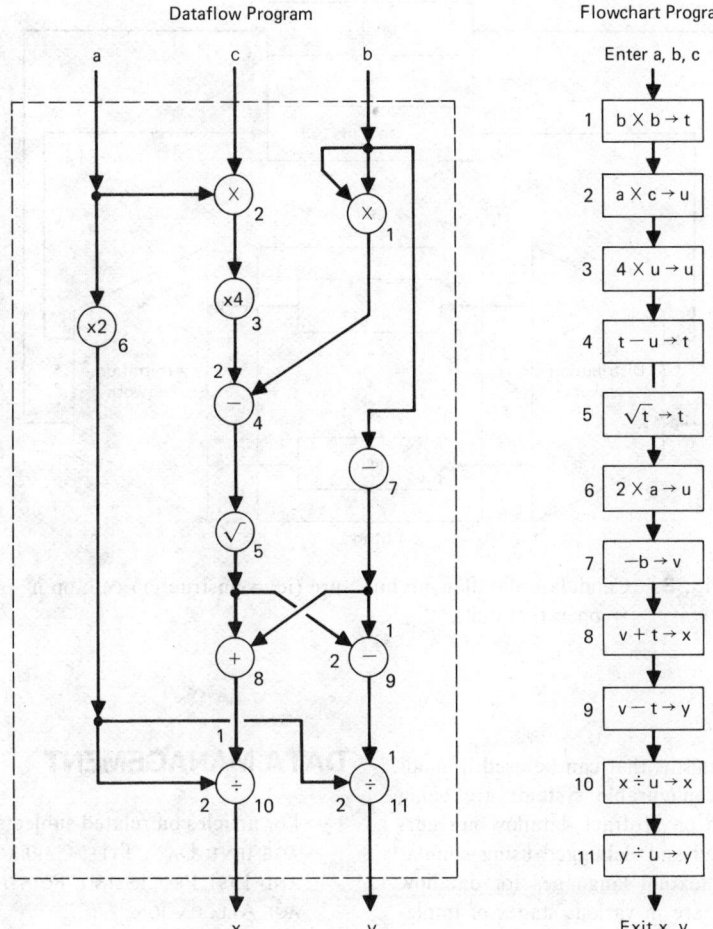

Fig. 2. Dataflow version of a sequential program to find the roots of a
quadratic equation ($ax^2 + bx + c = 0$) with real roots. The
labels on the lower right of the nodes of the dataflow program
correspond to the labels on the boxes on the left of the flowchart. The labels 1 and 2 on the incoming arrows to the dataflow nodes indicate the order of the operands for subtraction
and division.

Burroughs Corporation Data Driven Machine
(DDM1) executes dataflow programs using a tree structure for organizing the atomic units and a switch at each
node of the tree to distribute its output. Each atomic unit
consists of a processor with a number of microprogrammed functional units for manipulating data and
managing storage. Like TI's DDP, this dataflow architecture also requires a front end processor for identifying
and distributing subnets in dataflow graphs.

Toulouse's LAU (for Langageá Assignation
Unique) system also implements basic dataflow. The
LAU system consists of a collection of processors, a cen-
tral memory, and a control unit to detect all executable

instructions in memory. Architectures for basic dataflow
using conventional processors have also been proposed.

It is clear that dataflow languages can be used where
either parallelism or communication between asynchronous processes must be accommodated. The firing semantics associated with a node and the graphical nature of
dataflow enhance the overall understanding and control
of these complex activities. This is to be contrasted with
the traditional textual language solutions to these problems which often increase the overall complexity of the
algorithms involved. Architectures based on abstract dataflow are currently under development at various universities and industrial research laboratories. Extended

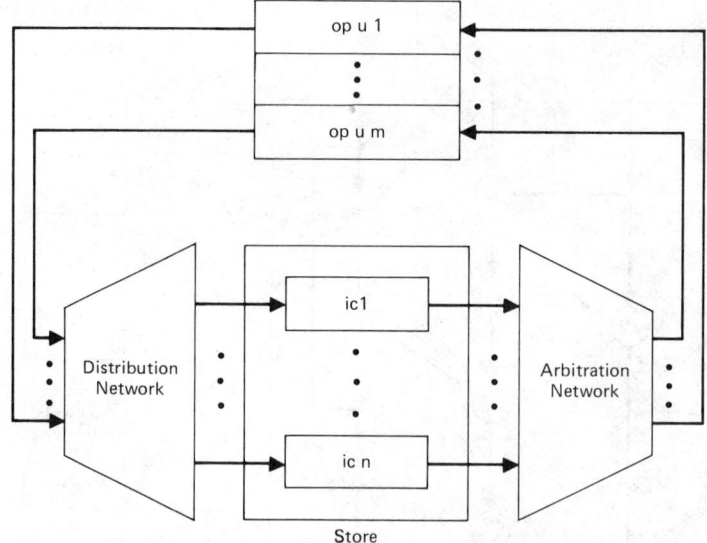

Fig. 3. Candidate dataflow architecture (ic = instruction cell; op u = operation unit).

abstract dataflow mechanisms that can be used in modeling and designing reconfigurable systems are being studied. Programs based on abstract dataflow are currently being implemented and debugged using simulators. Several high-level textual languages for dataflow have been proposed and are in various stages of implementation as of 1980. The languages are closely related to the functional (applicative) languages proposed by Backus (1978).

REFERENCES

1969. Karp, R. M. and Miller, R. E. "Parallel Program Schemata," *J. Comp. Syst. Sci.* **3**, *No. 2:* 147–195 (May).

1975. Dennis, J. B. and Misunas, D. P. "A Preliminary Architecture for a Basic Dataflow Processor," *Proceedings 2nd Symposium on Computer Architecture.* New York, pp. 126–132.

1976. Fosdick, L. D. and Osterweil, L. J. "Data Flow Analysis in Software Reliability," *ACM Comp. Surveys* **8**, *No. 3:* 305–330 (September).

1978. Backus, J. "Can Programming be Liberated from the Von Neumann Style? A Functional Style and its Algebra of Programs," *CACM* **21**, *No. 8:* 613–641 (August).

1980. Lanskov, D., Davidson, S., Shriver, B., and Mallet, P. W. "Local Microcode Compaction Techniques," *Comp. Surveys* (September).

B. D. SHRIVER, S. P. LANDRY, AND V. P. SRINI

DATA MANAGEMENT

For articles on related subjects *see* DATABASE MANAGEMENT; DATA TYPE; GARBAGE COLLECTION; LISTS AND LIST PROCESSING; POINTER; STACK; and STORAGE ALLOCATION.

Data management is concerned with the organization of the storage in which data is placed in a computer and with the identification and enforcement of the rules for interpreting and assigning meaning to the bits in the storage. Thus, it is closely related to database management. While there is no agreed division, the principle differences are that database management is concerned with data of longer persistence (that is, the data exists for more than the execution time of one program), shared data, and data design in the context of planning large scale systems, whereas data management is primarily concerned with the data used within a program for periods up to the duration of the program's execution. Since some of this data may have been obtained from sources outside the program, or may be left in a database, the two regimes interact closely, and the distinction may be unhelpful, though it is often enforced in current implementation environments.

Since data is not of use unless it can be manipulated, data management interacts strongly with programming languages. Most languages provide some space allocation facilities ("own" variables, local variables, and heap variables [Algol 68 and Pascal] for example). Programming languages have also developed the notion of *type* to identify the interpretation of the data bits, and of *strong typing* to ensure that operations on the data are consistent with its type declaration. Further development of this aspect of data management has occurred in providing facilities to define types (*modes* in Algol 68), leading to comprehensive definition facilities such as Simula classes and abstract data types.

Requirements for Storage Regimes

A Discipline of Interpretation. If one is working in a language which does not provide or enforce types, then it is necessary for the programmer to adopt some such discipline. But whether the discipline is adopted or enforced, it remains necessary for the programmer to manage the provision of storage space (i.e., to adopt a *storage regime*).

Programming languages have supported the provision of storage space using one of two policies. *Static allocation* is a policy in which the provision of space is determined at compilation time. Fortran is a language adopting this policy. If the programmer requires space to be allocated in ways which change as the computation progresses, then routines must be written which administer a policy within one of the statically allocated spaces. *Dynamic allocation* is a policy in which the provision of space is linked to the progress of a computation. The language Algol 68 and its derivations adopt this strategy. For example, they use a stack allocation scheme (see below) to provide local variables. More flexible dynamic allocation is provided in languages such as Pascal and Algol 60.

Dynamic storage regimes may be categorized by the demands made upon them, both by the objects stored, and by the sequences of operations by which space is claimed and freed. The space required by an object to be stored is called a *cell*. A cell is, therefore, a contiguous sequence of words or bytes in the computer memory. The cells may be of only one size, of a variety of sizes, or of varying size (i.e., an object once stored may change its size). The interaction of claims on and return of space gives rise to the following patterns of demand.

1. The space may be claimed by successive demands and then all relinquished.
2. The space may be claimed by successive demands and be explicitly returned in reverse order, or in blocks which are subsequences of the original claims in reverse order.
3. The space may be claimed by a sequence of demands and returned in random order.

4. The space may be claimed in sequence, and no space is explicitly returned, but the storage management algorithm is expected to discover (from time to time) which space is now unreachable and retrieve that space for reuse.

A Stack Regime for Heap Space Allocation. With a constant size or a variety of sizes, and with demand patterns (1) and (2) above, a space allocation strategy is straightforward. The total area of space available for allocation is viewed as a sequence of cells. A pointer records a position in this space indicating the start of the *next* place to allocate—the free cell. On making an allocation, the value of the pointer is returned as the address of the new cell, and the pointer is moved on, by the length of the space allocated, to the remaining cells. Such a scheme is shown in Fig. 1.

Such a regime is simple to implement and reasonably fast to operate. It is the basic strategy normally provided in Pascal, for example. This total area or allocatable space is called the *heap*. If space is relinquished in the reverse order from which it is claimed, noting the return of space is achieved merely by subtracting from *next* the size of the space returned. For safe operation, the correct size of the returned space must be available.

Blocked Return of Space to the Heap. Where the space is provided in blocks to be returned in the reverse order, the value of *next* may be recorded with the block. When the block is returned, *next* is reset to that recorded value. Such a strategy is used in many Pascal implementations, and is the normal way of allocating space for local variables in block structured languages.

Regimes for Handling Random Return of Space. When demand is interspersed with return in some random sequence—case (3) above—then different strategies are appropriate, depending on whether or not all the cells are of the same size. In either case, a list (or some more complex structure which is faster to search) is kept of all the cells available for issue. When a cell is returned, it is added to the list. This list is called the *free list* or, sometimes, the *list of available space*. If all cells are the same size, when a cell is requested, the first one on the list is allocated.

Strategies for Choosing the Best Cell to Allocate. When the cells vary in size, it is likely that the first cell in the list will not be large enough, or will not be the optimum one to allocate. Many algorithms are known for performing this allocation. In choosing one, it is necessary to choose a suitable compromise between the computational cost of finding the cell and the optimality of the cell found. The optimality depends on the rate of

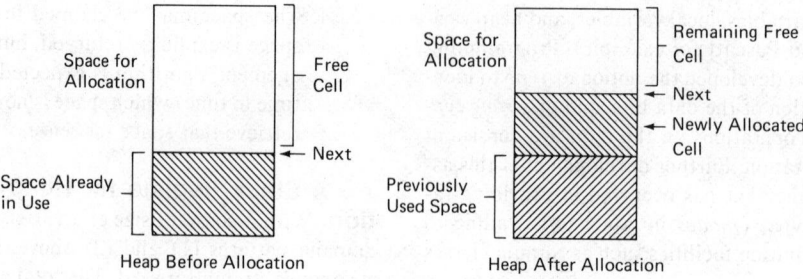

Fig. 1. The operation of a stack regime.

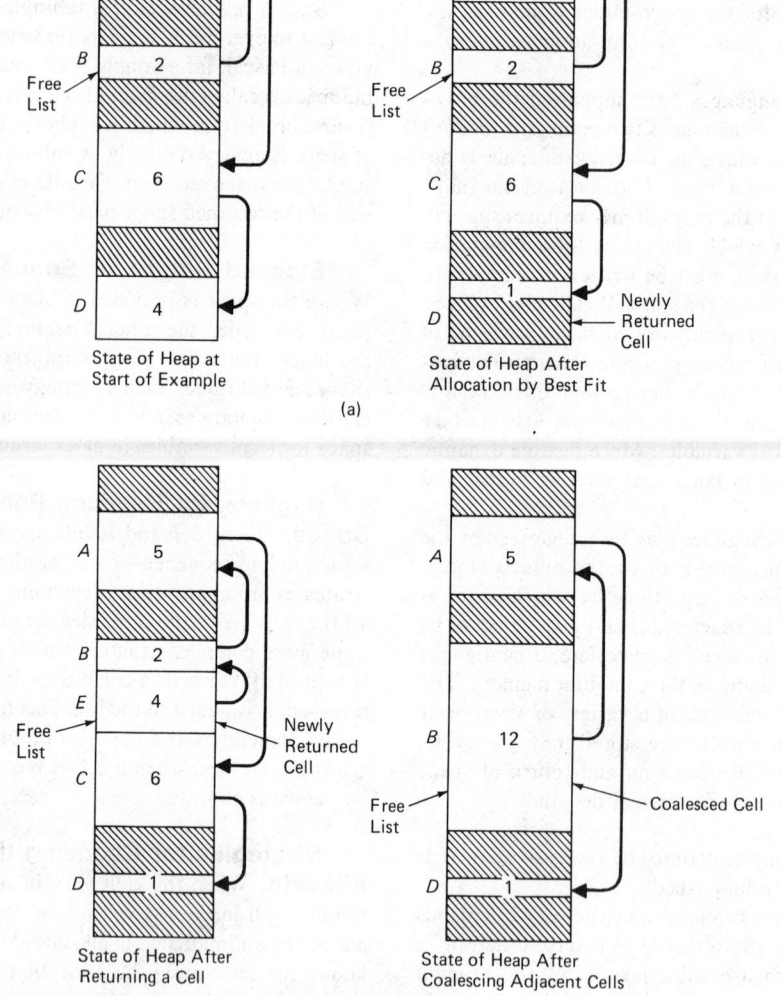

(a)

(b)

Fig. 2. The operation of a best fit strategy.

fragmentation; that is, on the proportion of small cells generated which are not contiguous and therefore cannot be amalgamated and which are too small to be useful. Three examples of this compromise are presented.

The Best Fit Strategy. The best fit algorithm requires a search of all cells available for allocation until one is found which is the correct size or is the smallest that is sufficiently large. When a cell is returned, it is placed at the start of the free list. These operations are shown in Fig. 2. It is possible to introduce more complex structures to hold the free list, such as a tree, a sorted list, or many lists corresponding to defined ranges of cell size. Such structures accelerate the search for the optimum cell, but increase the cost of returning a cell. In the example cells of Fig. 2(a), *A, B, C,* and *D* form the free list. If a cell of size 3 were requested, cell *D* would be allocated after a search of the entire free list.

Suppose that a cell is now returned consisting of the four words between *C* and *B.* Then the system could coalesce *B, E,* and *C,* as shown in Fig. 2(b), into a single cell. However, since the algorithm to coalesce cells is usually expensive to run, some systems do not implement it.

The First Fit Strategy. The first fit algorithm scans the list and allocates the first cell that is large enough, retaining the fragment left over. This takes minimal computation but may promote fragmentation (though the fragments produced may be large enough to be useful). Return of cells is similar to best fit. The operations involved in allocating a cell are shown in Fig. 3.

The Buddy System Strategy. The buddy system is based on the hypothesis that the sizes of cells requested are not random, but that, if a cell is requested, it is likely that other cells of that size will also be requested. It also takes advantage of the binary form of addresses to reduce the cost of coalescing returned cells with their neighbors. Separate lists are maintained for cells of each size (a power of two; i.e., 1, 2, 4, 8, etc.). When a request is made, the next larger power of two is the size of the space actually allocated. This results in some internal waste. If the list of cells of this size is empty, a cell from a list of double that size is split, and so on. Minimal searching is needed to allocate space. This allocation process is illustrated in Fig. 4.

On return of a cell, it may be coalesced with its neighbor, if that is also free, using an efficient algorithm. Only cells of the same size need be considered. It is possible to compute the address of the neighboring cell of the same size without a search, since the addresses of the two cells will differ only by one bit. If that cell is marked free, the list pointers in the cell can then be used to remove the cell and join it to the returned cell. (Using a doubly linked list for the free list makes this removal easier.) If a pair of cells are coalesced, the new cell formed is then considered for coalescing with the cells of its own size, and so on. Fig. 5 shows the return of a cell which causes buddy cells to coalesce twice.

Garbage Collection to Form the Free List.

When storage space is not explicitly returned, then, if the free list becomes empty (or does not contain a cell large enough to meet the current request), it is necessary to gather up the space which is no longer accessible to the program. To do this, all the accessible space is found and marked. The unmarked space can then be assembled into a new free list. This process is called *garbage collection* (*q.v.*). It is necessary to know all the places in the program which may refer to data, and to follow those references

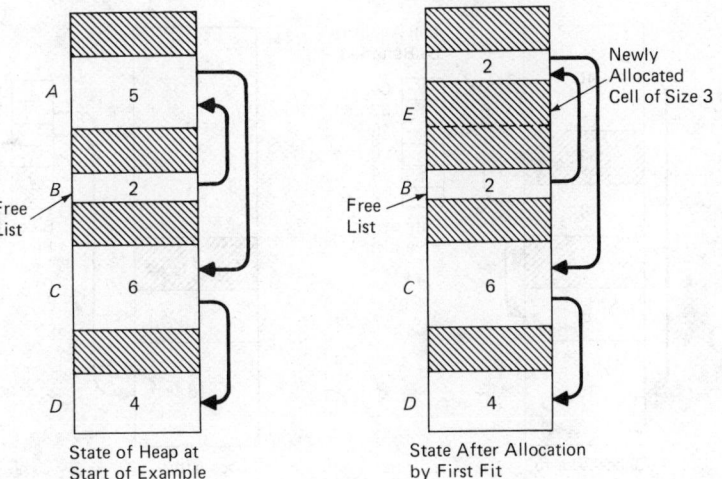

Fig. 3. The operation of a first fit strategy.

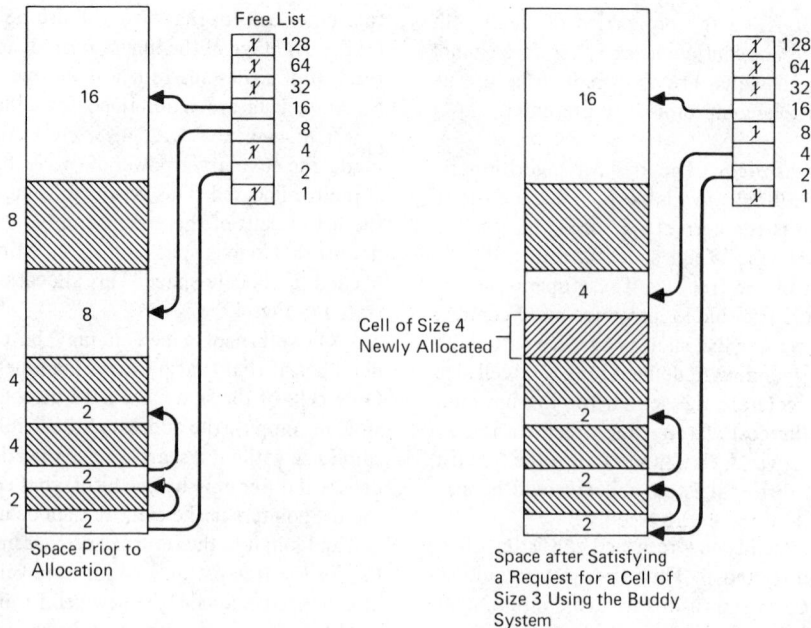

Fig. 4.   Space allocation using the buddy system.

to mark the accessible data. If the data itself may contain further references to other data, a scanning and searching algorithm is required. Such a search is only possible if there is a reliable type discipline so that the location of all references is known. Note that the criteria for invoking garbage collection may be different in a virtual memory system.

Compaction. When the new list has been formed, it may be used for allocation as before. However, it is possible that the space collected is large enough to satisfy a request, but not contiguous. It is then necessary to shuffle the data in use to make contiguous space. This process is known as *compaction,* and may be computationally expensive, as it is necessary to adjust all the references to refer to the new locations.

Storage for Varying Size Objects. The problem of providing for data cells which vary in size during use is more complex. One approach is to divide them into a linked list of fixed size fragments, since to allow them to change size *in situ* is expensive, as it involves similar

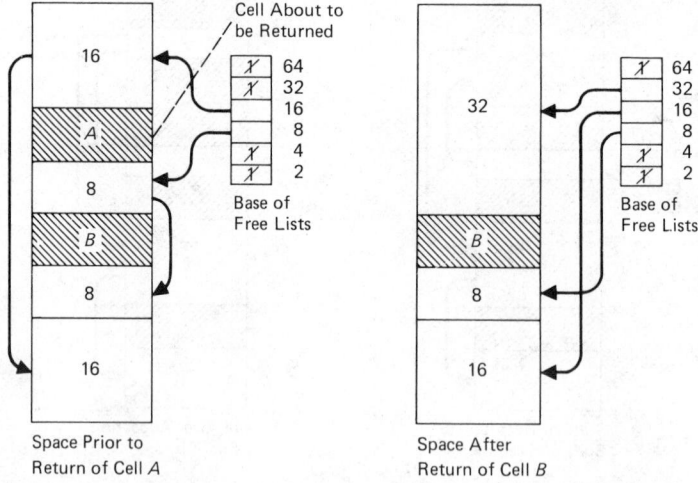

Fig. 5.   Return of a cell in the buddy system.

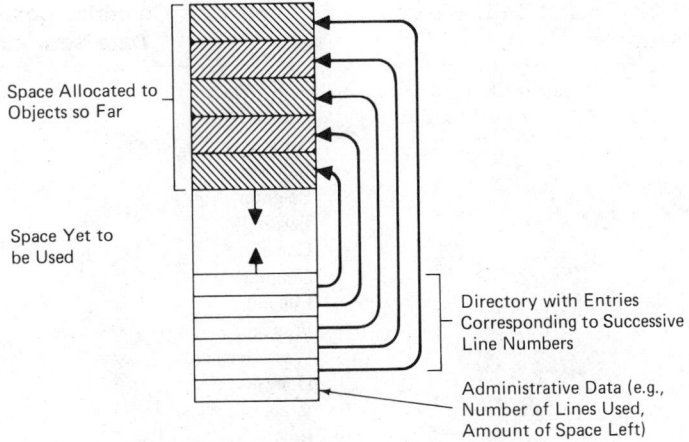

Space Allocated to
Objects so Far

Space Yet to
be Used

Directory with Entries
Corresponding to Successive
Line Numbers

Administrative Data (e.g.,
Number of Lines Used,
Amount of Space Left)

Fig. 6. Organization of a page to allow varying sized objects.

reference adjustment costs to compaction. An alternative is to arrange that all references to cells be indirect; for example, by a page and line number. The allocatable space is then divided into pages. At the beginning of each page is a set of "line pointers," which refer to the start of the data object corresponding to that line. As objects grow or shrink, the line parameters are adjusted accordingly. Thus, compaction within a page only involves adjusting the affected line pointers on that page and hence is of reasonable cost. The overheads are the space taken by line pointers, the cost of following them, and some extra fragmentation (the wastage left unused on each page). This technique, shown in Fig. 6, is used in many database systems.

Trends in Data Management. As the cost of memory is decreasing and the power of processors is increasing, the volume of data to be managed is increasing substantially, but the compromises which have to be made using the available algorithms remain fundamentally the same. With the increasing predominance of interactive computing, the unpredictable delays of garbage collection become less acceptable. This has led to experiments in concurrent garbage collection, and to an increased use of the page-based structures which permit incremental space management. Some language machines have been built which perform all the operations of space management using hardware.

REFERENCES

1972. Knuth, D. E. *The Art of Computer Programming* **1**: *Fundamental Algorithms*. Reading, MA: Addison-Wesley, Section 2.5.
1977. Wiederhold, G. *Database Design*. New York: McGraw-Hill.
1978. Gotlieb, C. C. and Gotlieb, L. R. *Data Types and Structures*. Englewood Cliffs, N.J.: Prentice-Hall.
1978. Coleman, D. *A Structured Programming Approach to Data*. New York: MacMillan.

M. P. ATKINSON

DATA NETWORKS, PUBLIC

For articles on related subjects *see* COMMUNICATIONS AND COMPUTERS; DATA COMMUNICATIONS; DISTRIBUTED SYSTEMS; and TELEPROCESSING SYSTEMS.

In an analogous fashion to the public telephone network, many domestic common carriers and foreign telecommunications administrations provide data communications service via a specialized network called a *public data network*.

The provision of telecommunications service in most countries throughout the world other than in the U.S. is accomplished through a government-owned or government-regulated monopoly corporation, usually referred to as a PTT (postal, telegraph, and telephone). As the name implies, this organization provides more than just telecommunications service.

In the United States, there is currently rapid movement away from monopoly services toward a competitive, regulated environment for the provision of basic telecommunications service. The regulation function is performed by the FCC (Federal Communications Commission) authorized by a federal law called the Communications Act of 1934. The FCC regulates common carriers providing public telecommunications service such as telephone and data services, determining what services are in the public interest, enforcing provision of uniform service to all customers, and publishing the service tariff.

Table 1.   National Public Packet Switched Data Networks

	Date (or Expected Date) of First Service
U.S.	
Telenet	1975
Tymnet	1976
ITT-DTS (COMPAK)	1980
AT&T (ACS)	1981–82
Canada	
Bell Canada (DATAPAC)	1977
CN/CPT (Infoswitch)	1978
Hawaii	
Hawaiian Telephone	1978
Mexico	
SCT	1981
Europe and Japan	
Spain (RETD)	1973
France (TRANSPAC)	1979
United Kingdom	1979
Japan (NTT)	1980
Japan (KDD-Venus)	1981
Switzerland	1981
West Germany	1981
Netherlands	1981
Belgium	1982
Denmark	1982
Norway	1982
Italy	1982
Sweden	1982

Table 2.   Countries Connected to U.S. Public Data Networks, 1980

Argentina	Japan
Australia	Luxembourg
Austria	Mexico
Bahrein	The Netherlands
Belgium	New Zealand
Bermuda	Norway
Canada	Philippines
Denmark	Portugal
Finland	Singapore
France	Spain
West Germany	Sweden
Hong Kong	Switzerland
Israel	Taiwan
Italy	United Kingdom

A public data network provides public service. It may provide circuit switching service and/or packet switching (*q.v.*) service and, in the future, may be expected to provide myriad other enhanced services. Examples of public data networks include GTE Telenet, Tymnet, Graphnet, and Faxpac in the U.S., as well as Datapac in Canada, PSS (Packet Switching Service) in the U.K., Transpac in France, DDX and Venus in Japan, and many others (see Table 1).

The public data networks are generally based on international standards set by the CCITT for governing the service features and providing the mechanism for interconnecting networks to one another. Standard protocols provide the specification to interface terminals to the network (X.21 for circuit switching and X.25 for packet switching) and to interface public data networks to one another (X.71 for circuit switching and X.75 for packet switching).

In 1980, public data networks in the U.S. such as GTE Telenet and Tymnet are interconnected to public data networks in more than 25 countries (see Table 2).

B. D. WESSLER

DATA PREPARATION DEVICES

For articles on related subjects *see* AUDIO RESPONSE TERMINAL; CARD READING AND PUNCHING; CODES; DATA ACQUISITION COMPUTER; DATA COMMUNICATIONS: General Principles; INPUT/OUTPUT DEVICES; MACHINE READABLE FORM; OPTICAL CHARACTER READERS; OPTICAL MARK READERS; and TERMINALS.

Data preparation devices permit *data capture* in which source data is collected and transformed into a medium or form capable of being read into a computer. These devices may either just prepare the data to be read later by a computer input device or they may perform not only the data capture but also the input to the computer. Since the latter devices are discussed in other articles (see cross-references above), this article focuses on devices used just for data preparation but not for computer input and discusses dual purpose devices only briefly. Furthermore, only devices for general application will be discussed here. More specialized devices designed specifically for source data entry applications, such as banking, retailing (point-of-sale systems), learning (CAL), word (text) processing, typesetting, and factory or laboratory data acquisition, as well as those requiring graphical input, are not discussed here; most are covered elsewhere is this encyclopedia.

The various data preparation devices and their associated data entry techniques can be separated into two main categories:

1. *Transcriptive data entry:* This term covers all data preparation devices where data, prepared on documents at their source or origin, is then transcribed to another medium that is capable of being read and interpreted by a computer. In this category are the following data prep-

aration devices: card punches, paper tape punches, magnetic tape encoders, cassette and diskette encoders, multistation key-to-tape systems, shared logic key-to-disk systems, on-line keypunch verify systems, sliding (setting) entry devices, and magnetic character readers.

2. *Source data entry:* For devices in this category, data is prepared at its source in a machine-readable form such that it can be directly read by a computer without the requirement for a separate intermediate data transcription step. Data entry techniques that fall into this category include optical character reading, optical mark reading, portable data capture devices, and the direct entry of information into a computer using terminals at the point of origin of the data.

We will first examine the advantages and shortcomings of these two categories of data entry.

Transcriptive Data Entry. Each extra step carried out on data before it finally enters the computer for processing introduces the possibility of the occurrence of errors. Studies have shown that of all of the errors detected in data by the computer, only about 15% of those errors occur in source data content, with the remaining 85% introduced through data transcription.

In order to reduce the number of errors occurring through data transcription, a number of techniques may be used. As data is transcribed into a machine-readable form, the data preparation device may carry out certain checks according to predefined conventions established for that particular data. Some of the editing that can be carried out (Trimble and Penta, 1970) includes:

1. Check digit validation.
2. Field-length check.
3. Check numeric-only fields.
4. Check alphabetic-only fields.
5. Develop batch control totals.

Data that cannot be validated by using check digits or control totals may be verified by keying it a second time, using a verifier unit to check that the second entry of the data agrees with the original entry.

The computer itself may carry out more extensive editing of the validity or reasonableness of information, applying various logical rules to the data, and possibly accessing other information held by the computer on disk or other files for confirmation purposes.

Errors that are detected must be corrected, using the original source document, rekeyed, verified again if necessary, and merged with the original data (Finklestein, 1970). The data is then edited by the computer once more, with errors recycled through the above steps until the data is error-free. Only then is the data ready for computer processing.

In addition to being involved, time consuming, and error prone, transcriptive data entry techniques require highly trained and highly paid personnel. Indeed, salaries of such personnel can represent as much as 80% of the total cost of data preparation (Finklestein, 1970). Moreover, these salaries are steadily increasing.

Source Data Entry. Studies of the cost of data entry show that while differences occur across companies and industries, approximately 75% of the cost of data entry occurs in non-data-processing personnel labor and delays in availability of data to the computer (see Fig. 1). Of the remaining 25% approximately 11% represents the cost of data processing and data entry equipment, approximately 11% represents the cost of data processing personnel, and approximately 3% represents other costs such as stationery and supplies.

The 75% cost of data entry contributed by non-data-processing personnel and time delays is expended in functions such as:

1. Retyping handwritten information for easier reading and faster operation by data preparation operators.
2. Validation, such as checking the availability of stock to fill an order before that order reaches the data preparation area.

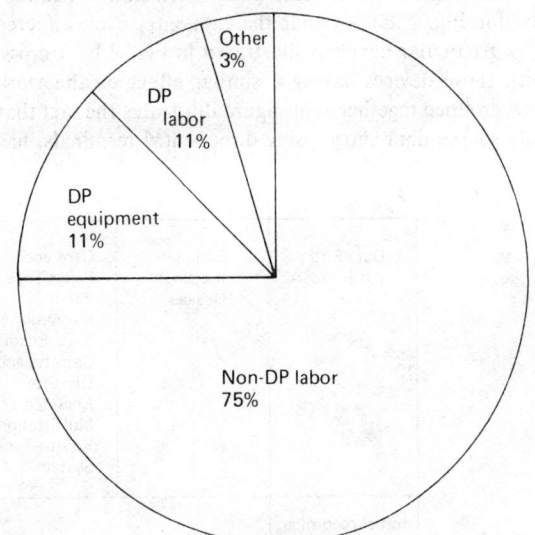

Fig. 1. Typical data entry cost breakdown. Item distribution: DP equipment—computers, peripherals, unit record, DE equipment; DP labor—KP operations, DP operations, DE programming; other—cards, magnetic tape, forms, contracted work, card storage; non-DP labor—initial recording, coding, batching, file reference, document handling.

3. Determining the price and discounts applicable for various products ordered in a preinvoicing environment.

These functions take time, with the result that before information reaches the computer, it may be several days old. Thus, the computer can produce results only as accurate and as timely as the input data. The computer in such an environment is being used only as a recording and high-speed printing machine. Its full potential cannot be realized until it is able to accept information as close as possible to the time of origination of that information.

Source data entry removes the need to retype hand-written information for easier reading by data preparation operators. In fact, the need for such data preparation is completely bypassed by entry of the data directly from its source. In addition, the computer itself can check the validity of the information.

In this way, instead of reflecting the status of information that may be several days old, the computer will maintain much more current information. Information, therefore, is available sooner, is more accurate, allows more meaningful decisions to be made, improves customer service, and reduces the amount of time before the organization will be paid for service performed.

The effect of each of the data preparation devices discussed above on the data entry work flow is summarized in Fig. 2. Each step in the data entry cycle affected by a particular device is illustrated in Fig. 2 by a cross, with those devices having a similar effect on the work flow grouped together. This figure illustrates the fact that only source data entry, using direct-entry terminals, has

an effect on every step in the entry of data into a computer.

We will now examine each of the various data preparation devices in more detail.

Transcriptive Data Entry Devices

Card Punch and Verifier. Until the 1960s, the capabilities of most card punches were limited. When the punch operator hit a key on the keyboard, the appropriate combination of holes was immediately punched into the card. In many cases, errors made by keypunch operators were detected by them immediately after the erroneous key had been depressed. However, corrections of such an error invariably required that the card be ejected, inserted into the read mechanism, and duplicated up to the point of the error. Then the error was corrected and punching continued. This procedure was time-consuming. Examples of these units are the IBM 24, 26, and 29 punches, and the IBM 56 and 59 verifiers (see Fig. 3).

The 1960s saw development of a buffer on the card punch so that an entire card of information could be keyed, and any error could be corrected by backspacing to the point of the error and re-keying. (This feature had, however, already been included earlier in many non-IBM electromechanical card punches.) Only after the operator was satisfied with the information keyed was that information released from the buffer for punching.

Other developments provided punches with capabilities of validating check digits and accumulating information for comparison against control totals. The 1960s also saw emergence of combined devices for both card

Data Entry Work Flow	Sliding (Setting) Devices	Card and Paper Tape Punch, Magnetic Tape Encoder, Cassette and Diskette Encoder, Multistation Key-to-Tape System	OCR, OMR, MICR (Partially), Portable Data Capture Devices	Shared Logic Key-to-Disk System, On-Line Keypunch/ Verify System	Direct-Entry Terminal System
Initial recording			X		X
Transport					X
File reference				X	X
Control				X	X
Transcribe	X	X	X	X	X
Verify		X	X	X	X
DP edit			X	X	X
System input				X	X
Error correction					X

Fig. 2.   Impact of data preparation devices on data entry work flow.

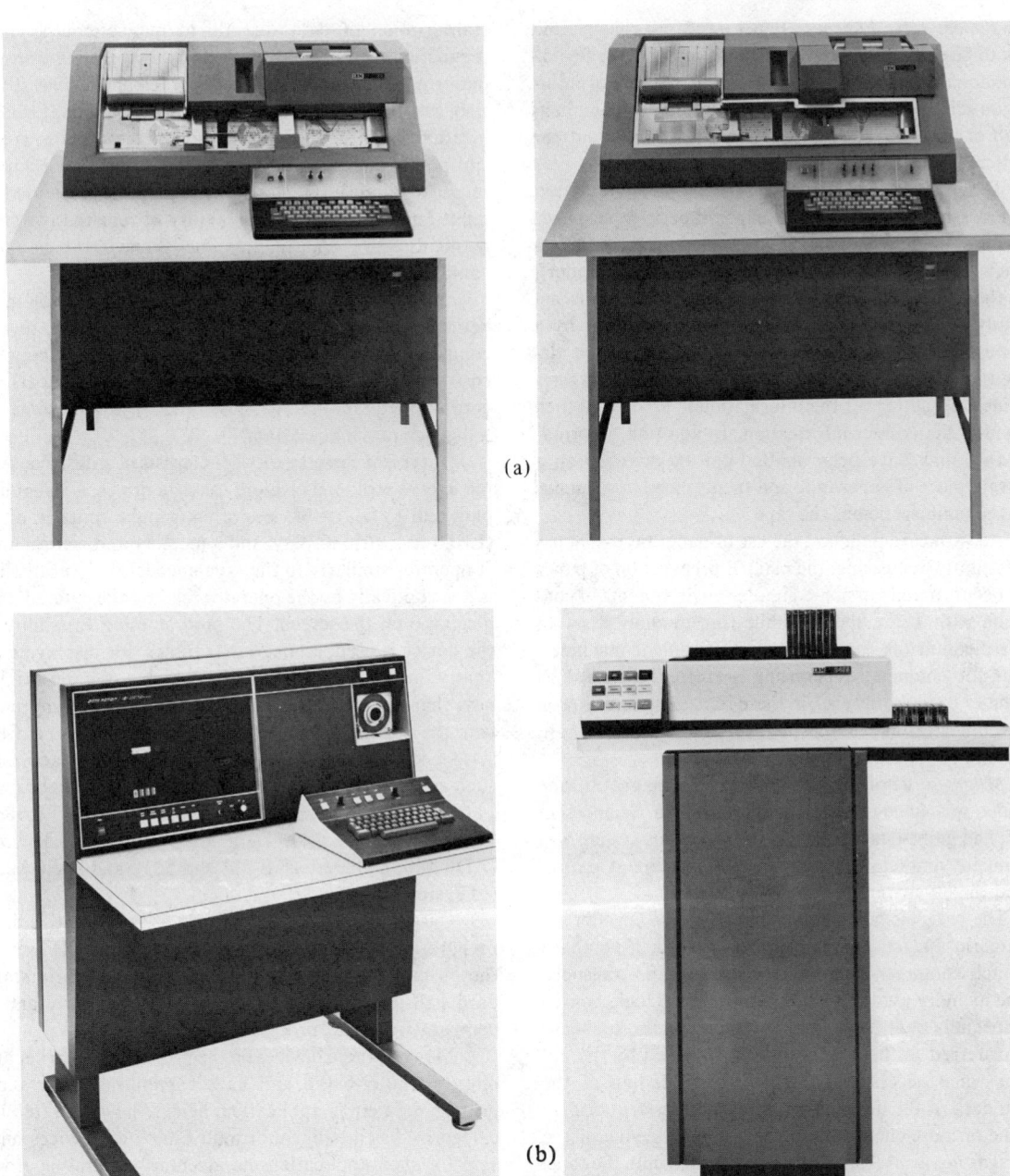

Fig. 3.   Data preparation devices. (a) IBM card punch and verifier. (b) Data Action 150 magnetic data inscriber and IBM 2495 tape cartridge reader used to transfer data entered on the Data Action 150 into a computer.

punching and verifying, thus enabling a keypunch operator to correct a punching error on the same device used for verification. Examples of such units were the Univac 1701 verifying punch, the Univac 1710 verifying interpreting punch, and the IBM 129 card punch.

The rapidly increasing use of more sophisticated transcriptive and source data entry devices caused a constantly decreasing demand for card punches as data preparation devices, leaving their use mainly to program preparation and hardware maintenance.

Paper Tape Punches. Paper tape punches permit data to be entered without the restriction of 80 or 96 columns for information on a card. Thus, records of information relating to a particular transaction can contain as much or as little information as necessary, without the physical limitations imposed by the card.

When errors are introduced by the punch operator, the error information on the paper tape is backspaced over, erased by punching a series of delete characters (which are ignored when read by a paper tape reader), and then re-keyed. In many cases, the correction is not directly verified; instead, the data is read directly by a computer and edited. In the event that errors are detected, corrections are generally keyed by punching a reversing transaction for the information in error, and then punching the correct information. In addition, information that may have been omitted can be punched on a separate piece of paper tape and then spliced in sequence into the main section of the tape.

As with card punches, the use of paper tape punches is constantly decreasing; the manual preparation of paper tape occurs mainly in non-computer environments in connection with Telex and facsimile transmission or as an input medium for control of numeric-control machines. Tapes for computer typesetting are often prepared as computer output. But even in these remaining application areas, other media, such as magnetic tape cassettes, are replacing paper tape.

Magnetic Tape Encoders. The first magnetic tape encoder was announced by Mohawk Data Sciences in 1965, and gained immediate acceptance. This system was specifically marketed as a keypunch replacement and retained the 80-character record.

The basic elements of the magnetic tape encoder are a numeric and/or alphanumeric keyboard, a standard half-inch computer-compatible magnetic tape transport, a core memory used as a buffer, and control logic housed in a specially built desk. Data entered from the keyboard is transferred to the core memory, corrected by the operator when necessary (either by proofreading of the keyed data, if the device is equipped with a strip display for one or more characters, or by a second keying, if the display is not available), and then recorded onto the tape.

Later devices of this category added a variety of programmable functions, such as check digit verification or generation, range check, key shifts, and other program functions identical to those of the card punch (such as, for example, automatic duplication). The record length was expanded to 200 characters. Almost all these encoders have the additional capability of serially pooling tapes produced by individual encoders into one consolidated large magnetic tape for more efficient input to the computer.

While the magnetic tape encoder can be used for the transcription of data directly to magnetic tape, most magnetic tape encoders also have the ability to transmit data from one point to another over telephone lines. Thus, they are well suited for the preparation of data at remote locations, and for the transmission of that data to a central point where it may be received by another encoder, recorded directly on magnetic tape, and then used as input into a computer. This ability of tape-to-tape communication over transmission lines is one of the main advantages of this device.

Cassette Encoders. Following the success of magnetic tape encoders as a keypunch replacement, several companies have explored the possibilities of reducing the cost per keystation by using another (and cheaper) recording medium—the cassette, and by adding some intelligence to the keystation.

A typical cassette encoder consists of a desk containing a keyboard; one or more cassette drives; a visual display unit (VDU)—or, less often, a light emitting diode (LED) as a strip display; and a memory and control unit. It operates similarly to the tape encoder, but verification is done optically by the operator reading the entered data displayed on the screen. The programming capability of the device is used, among other things, for displaying an "entry form" for the job in hand, which is of lower brightness than the displayed data on the VDU; cursors indicate the position on the form of the current entry. Cassette encoders are produced by many manufacturers, such as Texas Instruments (Silent 742), Burroughs (AE 111 and AE 501), NCR (7200/1 and 9761-3), ITT 3330 Dataprinter, Robotron Daro 1370 and 1372, Kienzle (ADP 1200), Olivetti (DE 521 and 523), and Facit-Addo (M-system).

Cassette encoders are suitable as transcriptive data preparation devices sited at dispersed locations. However, they usually require conversion from cassettes to standard half-inch magnetic tapes which is a costly and a comparatively slow process.

Many of these devices on the present-day market are microcomputer-based and have capabilities other than just the data entry application; hence, they will often be categorized as intelligent or multifunctional devices suitable for such applications as inventory control or order processing.

Diskette Encoders. Similar in concept to the cassette encoder is the diskette encoder, introduced in 1972 by IBM as the 3740 data entry system (and later as the 3741), which features a diskette memory. Weighing only an ounce, this diskette can store nearly 250,000 bytes, or 1,898 128-character records. To record data, an operator drops a diskette into a slot in a work station (see Fig. 4). Diskette data can be converted at the site to standard half-inch magnetic tape for computer processing, or the reusable diskette can be stored in an 8 × 8 in. (20 × 20

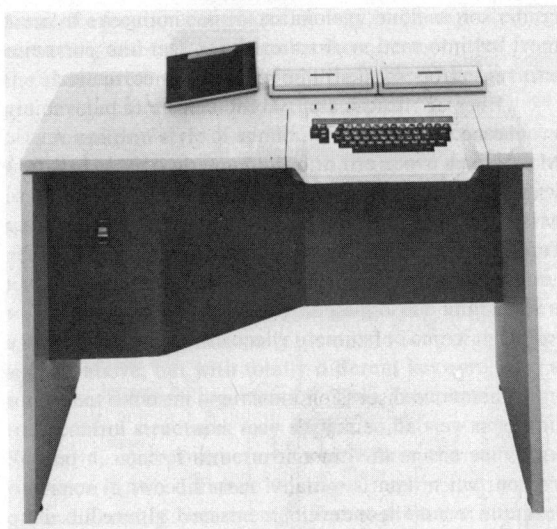

Fig. 4. To record data, an operator of the IBM 3741 data entry system drops a diskette into a slot in a work station.

cm) sleeve and sent to the central location for tape conversion. The use of a random access diskette as the storage medium allows the operator to search through the data stored in this memory. Diskette encoders are also produced by several other manufacturers, such as Univac (UDS), Honeywell (KDS 7255), Olivetti (DE 700), Juki (1840), Mael (1841), and BFI Electronics (Datamaster 11), as well as many others.

The reason for using diskettes and not disks in encoders is that the diskette capacity is large enough to store the shift work of one operator; a larger capacity would usually be redundant. However, diskettes with larger capacities than that described and devices with more than just one diskette drive are also available. Disks are sometimes used, but with word processing units, such as the Intype system, which puts information onto disk directly from a golf ball-type typewriter. The other advantages of diskette encoders are, in general, similar to those of tape cassette devices.

Multistation Keyboard-to-Tape Systems. This system is a central collection arrangement consisting of many keyboard work stations (often containing LED displays or VDUs) connected to a standard half-inch magnetic tape unit by means of a controller. This controller may be a special-purpose device or a minicomputer. In this way, several keystations can operate more economically than a comparable number of stand-alone units. In addition, the central collection arrangement provides sophisticated editing features, although microprocessor-based programmable stand-alone units may offer similar

capabilities. When compared with non-programmable stand-alone units, more errors can be detected earlier and correction of these errors is simpler.

The first such system, announced by Mohawk Data Sciences in 1969 (the 900 series key-to-tape system), grouped up to 16 stations around a control unit and pooled data from these stations onto magnetic tape. Shortly afterwards, Honeywell produced a similar unit, the Keytape, as did Singer-Friden, who introduced the 4300 Magnetic data recording system.

At present, systems of this category are rarely used, having been mainly replaced by intelligent cassette or diskette encoders, key-to-disk systems, or direct entry terminals.

Shared Logic Key-to-Disk Systems. These contain a cluster of up to 64 or even more keyboards with video displays performing as non-intelligent ("dumb") terminals plus one or more intelligent terminals attached and connected directly to a minicomputer, which can be programmed to perform various levels of checking of the input data, and stores the accepted data on a transient rotating memory file, usually a disk (or, sometimes, a magnetic drum). Having collected the whole batch of records or files, which is by then verified and reasonably clean, the transient batch is spooled to standard magnetic tape for later mainframe processing. This type of system has many advantages over the stand-alone non-intelligent encoder approach, in that much more pre-processing of data can be done, and operator performance can be much more accurately controlled.

On-Line Key Entry Systems. These systems provide a software capability similar to that of shared logic key-to-disk systems, but are controlled by a main computer rather than a minicomputer. Consequently, they offer the potential for validation against the full computer files, thus enabling complete editing of data without requiring a separate computer edit run. In this way, error correction is considerably simplified; however, correction of some errors would still require going back to the source.

Recently, several variations to this concept have appeared on the market, the most recent being aimed at distributed data processing systems in which the same sort of data entry capabilities as key-to-disk systems are provided, but, in addition, there are flexible communications and file handling capabilities, as, for example, in the Redifon R-Range systems. Such systems might be better called multifunction systems.

Sliding (Setting) Entry Devices. As opposed to keying, data entry in these devices is performed by setting pointers or switches. In the early days of punch card machines, a technique making use of the pantograph principle was used by Hollerith (IBM) to punch a hole in the card, its punching position being set by movement of

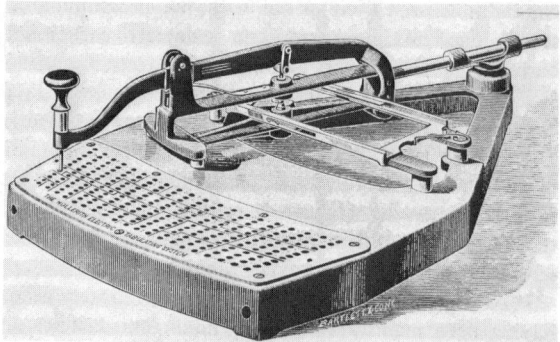

Fig. 5. One of the earliest models of the Hollerith punch which used the pantograph principle.

the handle (see Fig. 5). Later, Remington Rand (Univac) used pointer slides to set data to be punched for each of the 45 columns of the card; when all the data for the card was set, it was punched into the card in one stroke. At present, this technique is emerging again occasionally in devices developed for special purposes, such as a data entry device for entering Chinese characters (or, more generally, symbols) into computers and typesetting systems developed by scientists at Cambridge, England. Their machine will replace older, more cumbersome methods of input using keyboards, and promises to be cheaper, more reliable, and easier to use. Hitherto, the more than 10,000 ideographs in Chinese have been input using sequences of partial symbols, or special keyboards with up to 200 keys and 14 shifts.

The new machine uses a revolving drum on the surface of which are 4,356 of the most frequently used Chinese symbols. A pointer slides on a rail along the length of the cylinder. The operator turns the drum and slides the pointer to indicate each symbol in turn. The machine was developed at Cambridge University's Department of Oriental Studies to help in compiling a Chinese-English dictionary.

Magnetic Character Readers. Magnetic ink character recognition (MICR) of checks using the E-13B font in banking application is a transcriptive data entry technique. Information, such as the amount of the check is transcribed on an MICR encoder (such as the NCR 7740 Basic Encoder) and printed in magnetic ink on the surface of the check when it is accepted by the particular bank; this information is then added to the preprinted data identifying the check owner's band and account number. The encoded information may be verified by a second keying on a proof encoder, such as the NCR 7740 Proof Encoder.

Magnetic character readers are designed to be used off-line, away from a computer, for editing of information and physical sorting of checks using MICR document reader-sorters, and also on-line to a computer for direct entry of information from checks. After the computer edit run, errors must still be recycled for correction.

Other applications of MICR can be found, mainly in Europe, where the use of the CMC-7 alphanumeric MICR font is preferred to the numeric only E-13B font which is standard in the U.S. Furthermore, both of these MICR fonts can be read optically by many readers using OCR techniques, or by readers containing both MICR and OCR reading heads. Hence, applications not needing transcription (as opposed to those in banking which do) would make use of these devices in a source data entry mode.

The above discussion indicates that development in transcriptive data entry devices has been directed towards increasing the amount of editing that can be carried out when data is initially transcribed to a machine-readable form. These developments have also reduced the delays that occur in validating information and correction of errors, and have resulted in considerably greater throughput for shared logic key-to-disk systems and on-line key entry systems than for card punching. However, transcriptive data entry techniques affect only that small part of the total data entry cost that is represented by data entry equipment, data processing personnel labor cost, and supplies. Consequently, the net effect of newer devices on the total data entry cost is an effective increased throughput on the order of only some 10%.

SOURCE DATA ENTRY DEVICES

Optical (and Magnetic) Character, Mark, and Bar Code Readers. In this category are optical character readers, which use optical character recognition (OCR) techniques; mark readers, which use optical mark reading (OMR) techniques; and bar code readers, which use optical bar code reading (OBR) techniques. Similar categories of magnetic ink readers can be identified; but their use is still very restricted.

Table 1 summarizes the characteristics of the various kinds of optical readers. While the table should be generally self-explanatory, it is worth noting specifically that, whereas groups 1–6 describe devices in which the *data carrier* (generally paper or film) is drawn inside the machine in order to be read, groups 7–9 describe devices in which the data carrier remains outside the machine. For additional information on optical (and magnetic) character, mark, and bar code readers, *see* INPUT-OUTPUT DEVICES, OPTICAL CHARACTER READERS, OPTICAL MARK READERS, POINT-OF-SALE TERMINAL, and UNIVERSAL PRODUCT CODE.

Portable Data Capture Devices. A portable data capture device is one which can be carried by the

Table 1. Grouping of Optical Character, Mark, and Bar Code Readers as Source Data Entry Devices

Group Characteristics							Classes of Optical Readers*		
Reader		Data Carrier							
General or Special Purpose	Movement of Scanning Unit While Reading	Substance	Form	While Reading		Groups of Optical Readers	OCR	OMR	OBR
				Location	Movement				
G.P.	Stationary	Paper	Page	Inside scanner	Either moving or stationary	1. General-purpose page readers	0	0	0
			Document		(depending on reading-station design)	2. General-purpose document readers	0	0	0
			Journal tape			3. Journal tape readers	0	3	2
S.P.			Page			4. Special-purpose page readers	0	0	0
			Document or tag			5. Special-purpose document readers	0	0	0
G.P. or S.P.		Microfilm	Page image			6. Microfilm readers—computer input from microfilm (CIM)	0	0	0
G.P.	Moving	Generally paper	Generally labels	Outside scanner	Stationary	7. Miniature hand-held readers (optical wands)	0	3	0
	Stationary				Moving close to the slot	8. Stationary slot scanners	1	3	0
G.P. or S.P.		Any material	One or more short words inscribed		Moving at some distance from the slot	9. Stationary non-contact (long distance) scanners	1	3	0

*0 = existing device; 1 = the device either does not exist or is not commercially available, generally due to technical reasons (such devices would, however, be useful); 2 = the device does not exist or has ceased to exist, its usefulness is questionable, often due to the existence of some other, more suitable technique; 3 = the device does not exist, mainly because there is no known current application.

operator. It must have the capability to capture data on some computer-compatible storage medium. In many instances, such a device may act like a terminal to transmit data from a remote site to a central receiver located at the data center. The transmission is generally off-line, using either an acoustic coupler or other modem attached to the public telephone network.

Originally, portable data capture devices recorded data on punched cards and, sometimes, paper tapes. Present-day devices, however, consist of either tape cassette recorders incorporating a rechargeable battery pack, or magnetic bubble storage (see Fig. 6) which can record data into memory, and keyboards (mainly numeric, sometimes alphanumeric) for data entry, equipped with strip displays for data validation. Often, there is an optional capability to combine the keying facility with a miniature hand-held OBR or OCR reader to capture prerecorded information.

Portable terminals incorporate local validation checks on the data recorded, such as field length and check digit verification. As such terminals are intended to be used in a variety of environments by unskilled staff, the design concept is based on simplicity and ease of op-

Fig. 6. A Texas Instruments Model 765 portable bubble memory terminal with acoustic coupler shown at top.

eration. Key entry errors, such as double-key entry and entry of invalid code numbers, are signified by an audible tone, and the keyboard locks out until the condition is cleared by the operator.

Currently, the most common application for portable data entry terminals is in retail industry with a high volume of transactions involving orders, goods received, allocation to branches, inter-branch transfers, etc. The leading supplier of portable data entry terminals is MSI Data.

The market for portable data entry terminals is expanding, since distributed computing also requires the distribution of the data capture function, preferably to the source, where the transactions actually occur. Hence, the trend to hand-held, chip-based terminals, which claim the power of a small computer, such as the MSI Omega, a programmable version of the current MSI/88 range of portable terminals.

Direct-Entry Terminals. These terminals enable the computer not only to receive data immediately after it has been entered at its point of origin, but also to edit the data at its time of receipt, allowing computer files to be accessed to validate the information entered, and allowing the terminal operator to be notified immediately of any errors.

Information which cannot be checked against computer files may instead be verified by re-keying (or some other type of repetitive entry, such as by voice input), and the computer can check that the same information was entered each time. While verification may still be necessary in these cases, the amount of data to be verified is generally reduced. Thus, the correction process is simplified, and the time delays associated with the transport of data are almost eliminated.

A variety of devices can be attached to terminals for communication with a computer. Since most of these are discussed in separate articles, we shall consider them only briefly here.

Typewriter Terminals. These range from the normal office Telex machines used for telegraph communication (Fig. 7) to terminals that can be used as normal office typewriters when not required as terminals, such as the IBM 2741 (Fig. 8). Using typewriter terminals, a hard copy record of information entered via the keyboard and received from the computer via the printer can be recorded on paper for subsequent reference. Some of these terminals designed specifically for data entry may include a strip display of one or more characters keyed for ease of verification, the display being usually of the LED type.

In order to share the cost of communication among a number of terminals, typewriter terminals may often be attached to (or be *multidropped* off) the same communication line. In this instance, in order to avoid tie-up of

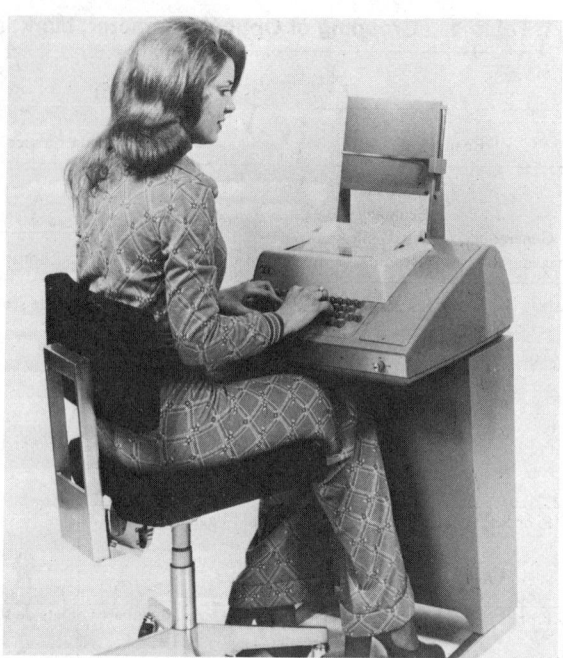

Fig. 7. A.T.&T. Teletypewriter #33 KSR (Keyboard Send-Receive).

Fig. 8. IBM 2741 typewriter communications terminal.

the line for relatively long periods of time while a terminal operator keys information, such terminals often feature buffers into which the data can be keyed. Once the data has been keyed, it can be input to a computer for transmission at line speed when the line is idle and available for use. The IBM 2740-2 communications terminal is an example of such a buffered terminal.

Visual Display Terminals. The two main categories of visual displays are the alphanumeric visual display units which display only textual information, and graphic displays which can display line drawings as well as alphanumeric data.

Visual display terminals generally use a keyboard for entry of information and a television-like screen for a display of that information, as well as for information received from the computer. An optional printer can usually be attached if hard copy is required. Data entry takes place by keying data into the display store, each key generating the appropriate alphanumeric code; the placement of data in the store is defined by a cursor which enables the operator to identify the information and to edit it before sending it to the computer.

Visual display terminals may be categorized as non-intelligent (or "dumb"), semi-intelligent, or intelligent. Non-intelligent terminals are generally intended as replacements for teletype (or typewriter) terminals; consequently, they are sometimes referred to as *glass teletypes*. Semi-intelligent VDUs have some local processing capability in that they can be programmed to supervise functions, such as entering, displaying (sometimes even in different colors), editing, printing, storing, transmitting, and receiving data. Intelligent terminals are discussed separately below.

Writing Tablet Terminals. These are on-line hand printing data entry systems, which, in principle, are analog-to-digital converters which make their own hard copy and produce machine-recognizable code at the same time. These writing systems use normal pens for writing and require special writing surfaces called tablets or pads.

An example of such a device is the Quest Automation Datapad, originally developed at the National Physical Laboratory in the United Kingdom under the name of Chit. To enter data, a standard form is placed over the pad, and the data is written using a ballpoint pen or a pencil. The sensitive pad recognizes the characters entered by detecting the movements and pressure of the pen as the character is formed. The pad has an associated strip display for character verification; when a character is not recognized, a question mark is displayed and the operator simply rewrites the character in the same box on the form. Similarly, when an incorrect character is entered, it can be changed simply by overwriting the correct character. Datapad will not accept data unless it is clearly written. The controlling minicomputer is the Data General Nova 3 which supports up to 16 Datapads. Datapad can also work on-line to the mainframe.

Several similar devices such as Micropad (Quest Automation, United Kingdom) or Quil terminal (Kurta Corp., U.S.) have been designed as intelligent writing terminals; however, they fall within the intelligent terminal data entry category. Furthermore, some of these on-line, hand-print data entry systems have reproduction capability; they can also be classified as graphic telecommunication systems (e.g., systems in which the layout and contents of the information at the transmitting end bear a close graphic relation to that at the receiving end). These systems usually incorporate the capability to transmit simple graphical images as well.

In the late 1970s, writing terminals were developed which make use of a specially instrumented ballpoint pen requiring no special writing surface. In these systems, the character recognition is based on real-time detection and analysis of the sequence of writing directions taken by the pen. Alternatively, writing terminals are also being used in special applications such as signature verification; examples of such systems are the Verisign system based on the Datapad tablet (NPL, United Kingdom) and those of IBM and the SRI International in the U.S.

Intelligent Terminals. An intelligent terminal has various programming capabilities, typically provided by a controlling processor with adequate storage space and software aids. This allows it to carry out extensive formatting and editing of information as data is entered and before it is transmitted to the computer. Thus, various edit checks may be carried out as data is entered, and errors may be corrected at that time. However, full editing by validating information against files is possible only after the data is transmitted to the computer. This can take place almost immediately when the terminal operates in on-line mode.

COMBINED DATA ENTRY DEVICES

Combined data entry devices are those which use more than one technique of data entry, often combining transcriptive and source data entry techniques. Examples would be a portable data entry terminal, which, in addition to a keyboard, also includes a miniature OCR or OBR hand-held scanner, or a point-of-sale terminal with an electronic cash register keyboard and an OCR or OBR hand-held or stationary scanner, or a word (text) processing device with OCR reading capabilities. These devices are delivered by several manufacturers specialized in portable data entry, point-of-sale or word processing systems.

An example of a larger combined data entry system is a shared logic key-to-disk system, generally called a multi-media system, with one or more page, document, or journal tape OCR or OMR readers in which one or more keying stations have the capability to enter corrected OCR or OMR rejects; examples of such systems are the Redifon R 550 mixed-media system and the Scan-Data 2250/3 multi-media system. Another similar example, but with a smaller configuration and with data transmission capabilities from remote sites, is the CDC Cyberdata with a CDC 939 OCR terminal page reader (the same as a Scan-Data 1150) or the Data 100 Corp. 77-107 disk-based data entry system. Still another example is an office information system such as the Wang OIS/145, which drives 32 peripherals, including up to 24 work stations, intelligent image printers, typesetters, OCR readers, card readers, telecommunications, and twin-head printers.

An advantage of combined data entry devices and systems is in elimination of redundant peripheral equipment, which means lower purchase or rental costs. Other advantages, depending on the device or system, may be:

- More flexible manipulation of source documents.
- Keyboard verification of data entered by an OCR or OMR device.
- Easier creation of data files, in which optical scanning and keyboard input operate concurrently, either in independent applications or by complementing each other in a single application.

References

1976. Benwell, N. S. (Ed.). *Data Preparation Techniques*. London: Advance Publications.
1977. Crane, H. D. and Savoie, R. E. "An On-Line Data Entry System for Hand-printed Characters," *Computer,* pp. 43–50, March.
1977. Gilb, T. and Weinberg, G. M. *Humanized Input: Techniques for Reliable Keyed Input.* Cambridge, MA: Winthrop.

J. NECAS

DATA PROCESSING

For articles on related subjects *see* ADMINISTRATIVE APPLICATIONS; INFORMATION AND DATA; INFORMATION PROCESSING; PROCEDURE-ORIENTED LANGUAGES; and SCIENTIFIC APPLICATIONS.

Data processing is a widely used term with a variety of meanings and interpretations ranging from one that makes it almost coextensive with all of computing (e.g., IBM's major marketing division is called the "Data Processing" Division) to much narrower connotations in the general area of computer applications to business and administrative problems.

In a broad sense, data processing may be said to be what computers *do*. In this context it should be compared to *information processing,* which some prefer to data processing because "information" does not carry the connotation of "number," as "data" sometimes does. Of course, the "data" in data processing is really intended to connote any kind of information in symbolic form. Thus, information may be viewed as "knowledge," while data are the physical symbols used to represent the information.

The term "data processing" is often used with various modifiers, the most common being:

1. Electronic data processing (EDP), a term widely used to describe *all* computing activity—or, at least, the part of computing that focuses on administrative or business applications—and particularly to distinguish computerized applications from manual methods.
2. Automatic data processing (ADP), closely analogous to EDP, since it is intended to distinguish computer data processing from data processing where significant human assistance or intervention is required.
3. Business data processing (BDP) refers specifically to administrative applications (e.g., personnel, payroll, accounting) and to broader business applications (e.g., inventory control, sales forecasting).
4. Scientific data processing, which is still a rather rarely used term and which is meant to imply the increasing recognition that business and scientific applications of computers have much more in common than was once realized or, indeed, than was actually the case in earlier days.

Until the 1960s it was common to divide the world of computer applications into two realms—business data processing and scientific computing—with the latter encompassing all engineering, scientific, or other technical applications of computers where the emphasis was on numerical calculations, usually extensive ones, rather than on the manipulation (sorting, organizing, etc.) of data (together with, at most, very simple arithmetic calculations), which was the province of business data processing.

Another distinct, although related contrast between the two areas was their relative dependence on the central processing unit facilities of the computer on the one hand and on the input-output facilities on the other hand. Most scientific calculations seemed to require little input data, produced relatively few numbers as results, but relied heavily on the arithmetic and logical capabilities of the CPU. Indeed, computers that handled mainly large scientific calculations were, and still are, often called "number crunchers." By contrast, business data processing tasks usually involved large amounts of input data (e.g., the entire employee file of a company)—hence the name "data" processing—performed relatively few calculations, and then produced large amounts of output (e.g., all payroll checks for the company).

To a degree, this dichotomy between scientific calculations and business data processing was always misleading. If the paradigm for business data processing— much input and output, little calculation—was, in fact, a rather good generalization, the paradigm for scientific calculation was much less so. Scientific calculations involving large volumes of input data and, more commonly, large quantities of results had been common since the earliest days of computing (e.g., the production of tables of mathematical functions such as the trigonometric or Bessel functions). Still, it has only been in recent years that the dichotomy has been seen to be less and less useful for any purpose.

Increasingly, scientific calculations (e.g., meteorological and high-energy physics applications) process large amounts of input data and produce copious results. Also increasingly, although less so, business applications involve sophisticated mathematical techniques involving large amounts of calculation (e.g., various statistical and related forecasting applications). Thus, while there remain many computer applications that conform to the original business data processing/scientific computing stereotype, it is increasingly common and, this author believes, more reasonable to use the terms "business data processing" and "scientific data processing" to distinguish between applications areas but not between the characteristics of the applications themselves.

The past distinction between business data processing and scientific calculations was reflected in the development of computers ostensibly designed for one application area but not the other. IBM's 700 series of computers of the 1950s illustrates this point. (The 700 series comprised first-generation computers, which utilized vacuum tube technology; with the advent of transistor technology and the second generation of computers, a zero was added, and this became the 7000 series. Thus, the 7040 and 7090 were transistorized and somewhat modified versions of the 704 and 709.) There were two pairs of computers in this series, first the 701 and 702, and later the 704 and 705. (There was also a 709, more powerful but quite similar to the 704.)

Both the 701 and 704 were designed for scientific computing. Their memories were binary and word-oriented and, on the 704, floating-point arithmetic was standard. By contrast, the 702 and 705 were specifically de-signed for "data processing" applications, meaning business data processing. Their memories were character- and digit-oriented and only fixed-point arithmetic was possible. By the time of the advent of the IBM 360 series of computers in the mid-1960s, the previous sharp distinction between scientific computing and business data processing was becoming blurred so that the existence of separate computers for the two areas was no longer considered necessary. Nevertheless the distinction still was considered important and, for example, one model of the 360 series, the 360/44, was specially designed for scientific computation.

In the 1970s some manufacturers still oriented their general-purpose computer line toward particular application areas, most notably Control Data with its 6000, 7000, Cyber 70, and Cyber 170 series of computers intended mainly for scientific applications, but the trend was clearly toward computers for data processing without a distinction between scientific and business applications.

As the 1980s begin, only the very largest and fastest computers, typically with only a few models of each produced, could be said to be strictly scientific computers. Examples are the Cray-1 and Texas Instruments' Advanced Scientific Computer.

The development of general-purpose high-level programming languages also parallels the history outlined in the preceding paragraph. The first such language in the mid-1950s, Fortran, was intended (and still is mainly used) for scientific calculations. Even the current version, Fortran 77, lacks the significant character manipulation and good data structure facilities needed for many data processing problems. The second such language in the late 1950s, Cobol, was intended (and still is virtually always used) for business data processing problems. Its arithmetic facilities, lacking as they do a floating-point arithmetic capability, virtually preclude its use for significant numerical calculations.

The development of PL/I in the mid-1960s had, among its motivations, the desire to develop a language that could be used for both scientific and business problems because of increasing cognizance about this time of common properties in these two applications areas. PL/I's failure, up to the early 1980s at least, to achieve wide popularity cannot be ascribed to any deficiency in this viewpoint. Rather, it is due to the very large inertia among Fortran and Cobol users which prevents them from switching to a new language because of their extensive investment in programs, libraries, and expertise in the older languages.

In the future we may expect the distinctions between the scientific and business applications areas to be further blurred as time-sharing, widespread use of data communications, and increasing use of large databases further pervade all applications areas. The name "data processing," therefore, will remain an inclusive term to describe computer applications of all kinds. It will continue to be one of a few terms (information processing and symbol manipulation are others) that may reasonably be used to denote what a computer does.

REFERENCE

1973. Davis, Gordon B. *Computer Data Processing* (2d ed.). New York: McGraw-Hill. One of the better books that focuses on business applications.
1980. Shelly, Gary B. and Cashman, Thomas J. Introduction to Computers and Data Processing. Fullerton, CA: Anaheim Publishing Co.

A. RALSTON

DATA PROCESSING MANAGEMENT ASSOCIATION (DPMA)

For articles on related subjects *see* AMERICAN FEDERATION OF INFORMATION PROCESSING SOCIETIES; and INSTITUTE FOR CERTIFICATION OF COMPUTER PROFESSIONALS.

Purpose. The Data Processing Management Association is one of the largest worldwide organizations serving the information processing and computer management community. It comprises all levels of management personnel and, through its educational and publication activities, seeks to encourage high standards of performance in the field of data processing and to promote a professional attitude among its members. Its specific purposes, as stated in its international bylaws, are as follows:

- To foster, promote and develop education and scientific inquiry in the field of data processing and data processing management.
- To inculcate among its members a better understanding of the nature and functions of data processing, and to engage in education and research in the technical methods pertaining thereto with a view to their improvement.
- To collect through research and to disseminate generally, by all appropriate means, all fundamentally sound data processing principles and methods.
- To study and develop improvements in equipment related to data processing.
- To supply to its members current information in the field of data processing management, and to cooperate with them and with educational institutions in the advancement of the science of data processing.
- To encourage and promote a professional attitude among its members in their approach to an understanding and application of the principles underlying the science of data processing and in their relations to others similarly engaged.
- To foster among executives, the public generally, and the members of the Association a better understanding of the vital business role of data processing, and the proper relationship of data processing to management.

How Established. Founded in Chicago as the National Machine Accountants Association, DPMA was chartered in Illinois on 26 December 1951. At this time the first electronic digital computer had yet to come into commercial use, and the name "machine accountant" was chosen to identify those associated with the operation and supervision of punched card accounting machines. Twenty-seven chapters were organized during the Association's first year. By 1955, the organization had taken on an international character with the admission of Montreal as the first Canadian chapter.

With the rapid advances in information processing techniques brought about by the introduction of computers, the nature of the Association further changed as membership swelled from the ranks of computer management. In step with this trend, the Association assumed its present name in 1962. The roster of past presidents includes the following:

Robert L. Jenal, 1952	Theodore Rich, 1967
Gordon C. Couch, 1953	Charles L. Davis, 1968
Richard L. Irwin, 1954	D. H. Warnke, 1969
Robert O. Cross, 1955	James D. Parker, Jr., 1970
Donald L. Gerighty, 1956	Edward O. Lineback, 1971
Willis L. Daniel, 1957	Herbert B. Safford, 1972
Lester E. Hill, 1958	James Sutton, 1973
D. B. Paquin, 1959	Edward J. Palmer, 1974
L. W. Montgomery, 1960	J. Ralph Leatherman, 1975–1976
Alfonso G. Pia, 1961	
Elmer F. Judge, 1962	Robert J. Marrigan, 1977
Robert S. Gilmore, 1963	Delbert W. Atwood, 1978
John K. Swearingen, 1964	George R. Eggert, 1979
Daniel A. Will, 1965	Robert A. Finke, 1980
Billy R. Field, 1966	P. Roger Fenwick, 1981

Organizational Structure. Individual chapters are organized geographically into 13 regions, each of which holds business meetings, conducts regional conferences and educational seminars, and carries on various types of interchapter educational activities. Governing authority is vested in the International Board of Directors, which consists of one representative from each chapter. An annual meeting of the Board is held in conjunction with the International Data Processing Conference & Business Exposition sponsored by the Association. International directors, appointed by chapters, also represent their chapters at regional meetings.

Implementation of policy established by the Board is carried out by an Executive Council consisting of 21 members: President, Executive Vice-President, Secretary-Treasurer, Immediate Past President, President DPMA Canada, three International Vice-Presidents (with the following areas of responsibility: Planning and Research Development, Education Activities, and Membership Liaison and Business Relations) and 12 regional Vice-Presidents. The Executive Council managing association affairs is the Corporate Operations Committee.

The local chapter is the heart of the Association. Every member must belong to a chapter except those applying for an individual international membership, which is granted to qualified individuals living outside North America upon approval by the International Executive Vice-President. Extensive educational programs are carried on by the local chapters through regular monthly meetings, seminars, and other activities.

Regular membership is granted by the individual chapter Board of Directors to persons engaged as (1) managerial or supervisory personnel in EDP installations; (2) systems and methods analysts, research specialists, and computer programmers employed in executive, administrative, or consulting capacities; (3) staff, managers, educators, and executive personnel with a direct interest in data processing; and (4) holders of the Certificate in Data Processing (CDP).

A computer-equipped international headquarters with modern facilities, located in Park Ridge, Illinois, serves as the administrative nucleus of the Association. It provides a wide range of programs and services to local chapters and contributes to regional educational programs. Major departments are Membership Programs and Services, Communications, and Financial and Administrative Services.

Programs and Services. DPMA members attend meetings, seminars, and conferences at the local chapter, and at regional and international levels. A major educational event is the Annual DPMA International Data Processing Conference & Business Exposition, attended by members and nonmembers from all parts of the United States, Canada, and other countries.

The Association was the first to introduce (in 1962) a certification program for computer management personnel. The Certificate in Data Processing (CDP) examination program is dedicated to the advancement of data processing and information management and to this end has established high standards based on a broad educational framework and practical knowledge. In 1970, DPMA also introduced the Registered Business Programmer examination, which seeks to identify those reaching the level of senior business programmers. Both examinations were developed by the DPMA Certification Council and are given annually in test centers at colleges and universities in the United States and in Canada. In 1974, DPMA transferred ownership of these examinations to the Institute for Certification of Computer Professionals (ICCP). Other programs offered to the membership include the Business and Management Principles one-day seminar, the video tape Management Development seminar, and Educator's Night for improving communications with the education community. DPMA encourages and provides assistance to student organizations interested in data processing in colleges and universities. It also offers the Future Data Processors Program for high school students, and provides counseling aid for Boy Scouts seeking the computer merit badge.

Other programs are being constantly developed to keep the membership abreast of changing developments in effective EDP management techniques and in technological advances.

Among DPMA publications are the monthly *Data Management* magazine (included in membership dues); *Guidelines to Data Processing Management; An Executive Briefing on the Control of Computers; Data Processing: Computers in Action;* and the Management Reference Series.

Its audiovisual program includes films and slide presentations ranging from technical to general management subjects. In 1969, DPMA originated the Computer-Science-Man-of-the-Year Citation (called, since 1980, the Distinguished Information Sciences Award) which in that year was presented to Commander Grace Murray Hopper, USNR. Subsequent recipients have been Dr. Frederick Phillips Brooks, Jr., 1970; Robert C. Cheek, 1972; Dr. Carl Hammer, 1973; Prof. Edward L. Glaser, 1974; Dr. Willis H. Ware and Dr. Donald L. Bitzer (Co-recipients), 1975; Dr. Gene M. Amdahl, 1976; Dr. J. Daniel Couger, 1977; Irwin J. Sitkin, 1978; Dr. Ruth M. Davis, 1979; John Diebold, 1980; and David Packard, 1981.

I. L. AUERBACH

DATA SECURITY

For articles on related subjects *see* COMPUTING AND SOCIETY; CRIME AND COMPUTER SECURITY; DATA ENCRYPTION; FAULT TOLERANT COMPUTING; RELIABILITY, HARDWARE; and SECURITY OF COMPUTER INSTALLATIONS, PHYSICAL.

The protection of data against the deliberate or accidental access by unauthorized persons is rapidly becoming a major problem. Ultimately, the security of data depends on some combination of *locks,* or access-control measures, for which certain users possess the *keys.* No such combination is completely secure. For the intruder, the effectiveness of security measures is really only a matter of the cost of breaking the combination of locks as compared to the value (to the intruder) of obtaining data in this way. Conversely, for someone wishing to maintain the security of data, the cost of devising and implementing a combination of locks on the data must be small relative to the cost of a breach of security.

In the case of, for example, military intelligence data banks, the information contained in them is considered to be of such value that almost no cost is spared to insure data security. Such systems, however, are clearly exceptional. This article deals instead with commercial or public data banks where there are clear limits to the number of high-cost security measures that can be justified.

It is to be noted that in a computer system, the protection of the data itself and of software search and retrieval programs are treated almost entirely in the same manner; thus, the safeguards that apply to program security also apply to data security.

Classification of Degree of Confidentiality.

In this section, the term *user* describes a single person or a group of persons, all of whom have equal rights with respect to accessing a particular body of data and who have a common identity to the system. Three classes of data are defined for an automated system: public, limited-access, and private.

Type 1. Public Data. Public data is open to all users, and no security measures are necessary as far as reading is concerned. When access is restricted to reading of the data, as it should be where data must remain unchanged, writing should be prevented. If it is not possible to prevent writing, check sums (a simple total of all data items) that should remain constant can be kept with the data, and the data can be refreshed from a secure copy whenever a test total of the data does not agree with the check sum. If users are permitted to alter data, a lock must be maintained on the system to ensure that while one user is making a change, no other user is permitted access to the data, since normally one user's alterations must be completed before another's may begin.

Type 2. Limited-Access Data. Only authorized users have access to data of this type. This means that an authorization table must be kept in the system, indicating for each body of data the identity of all users with access rights. When a user requests access: (1) identity should be authenticated, for example, by personal identification or password; (2) the authorization table should be checked to see that the user has appropriate access rights; (3) a record in a log should be made of the event. The purpose of the log is to provide an *audit trail* or record that can be consulted whenever any trouble is suspected. All unsuccessful attempts to access data should be logged in order to provide an indication of a possible security leak. If the frequency of unsuccessful entry is larger than normal error expectation warrants, an alarm should be generated.

Type 3. Private Data. This data is open to a single user only. When access to data is requested, the identity of the user should be authenticated to verify the fact that the user is the owner of the data. Here again, a record of all unsuccessful attempts at entry should be logged.

Access Rights to Data.

Data that is not a program is usually organized into discrete files. A *file* is composed of a number of records, or factual statements, each relating to a particular thing; or, in a file containing personal data, each is related to a particular individual. A *record,* in turn, is subdivided into fields. A *field* is a precisely defined location within a record where information may be recorded.

In a file of personal data, certain fields enable the reader of the record to identify the person. Access to a file of personal information is often permitted on the basis of "need to know," and access to a particular record in a file is allowed on the basis of an explicit or implicit consent of the individual to whom the record pertains. It would therefore follow that, if a person having access to a record needs to know only the information in certain fields of the record, that person should not have access to other fields in the same record. For example, persons who are preparing statistical summaries from files do not need to know the identity of the person to whom each record applies, and therefore should not have access to identifying fields.

In a data bank being used for statistical purposes, it is important that an enquirer be prevented from inferring information about an individual by a carefully chosen sequence of queries. Inference controls should be implemented so that the cost of compromising the system is adequately high. Snooping can sometimes be prevented if an audit trail is maintained and the trail is monitored for unusual patterns of enquiry.

Frequently, persons having access to a file have access to *all* fields of *all* records. In a manual file in which records are maintained in a manila folder, it is difficult to arrange to do otherwise. In a computerized system, however, access can be permitted to the entire file, or can be restricted to certain records or to certain fields of the file.

Access rights might be defined as follows: read an item (e.g., file, record, or field); write an item so as to produce a change, either by adding a new item or by changing an existing item; delete an item.

The access rights of a user must be explicitly denoted in any situation where partial rights exist, such as a limited access file, or where reading is permitted but changes and deletions are not. It is possible to have a table or matrix stored with the data (or separately) which lists authorized users of the data and their access rights. Access to this table must be strictly limited to persons authorized to modify the table, usually only the owner of the data. In many cases, access control is assigned to the system itself, since in most computer systems the operations pertaining to the read or write functions are already under system control.

Physical Storage of Data. Data in an automated system can exist in many physical forms. Storage media may be classified into five categories: Hard copy; display devices; magnetic tape and mountable disks; mounted magnetic tapes, disks, and drums; and magnetic core store.

Hard Copy. This is a term used for recording data that is more or less permanent and that can be stored, read, or written by humans independently of the computer hardware. Included in this category are printed pages, punched paper tape, punched cards, and microfilm. The security of hard copy is similar to the conventional security associated with manual files. The interpretation of the data by an intruder is usually very simple. Also, the destruction of the data requires the destruction of the medium. Machines for shredding hard copy are available.

Display Devices. These are devices on which data may be exhibited to a user but on which it has an evanescent form. As soon as it is no longer required, it will disappear. An example of this form of storage is a cathode-ray tube display. If such devices display sensitive data, they may have to be used in secure rooms where unwanted cameras or persons cannot observe them. When electric circuits are arranged to display images on one cathode-ray tube, stray electromagnetic radiation from these circuits might be amplified to produce a similar display on another such device that has no connection to the first.

Display devices like printers or card readers should also be appropriately shielded to guard against the possibility of electromagnetic eavesdropping. There is the possibility of telephone instruments acting as pickup devices for such radiations even when on the hook.

Magnetic Tape and Mountable Disks. These are media on which data can be recorded as variations in magnetization. They can be erased and used repeatedly, although—as with most erasing processes—small traces of previously recorded information may persist. When the tapes or disks are not mounted on a computer device to read them, they cannot be read, but they can be erased or destroyed, for example, by strong magnets or fire.

A careful banking system in secure rooms under strict control must be maintained to prevent loss of or violation of security during off-line storage. When tapes or disks are mounted on read/write devices, they become identical in nature to those integrated into the system (see below) of physical storage; when unmounted, they are similar in nature to hard copy.

Mounted Magnetic Tapes, Disks, and Drums. These mounted media are integral parts of the on-line storage system of a computer. They are usually classed as the secondary store, since the time to access information stored on them is long compared with the basic operation rate of the computer. Usually, the time for reading from or writing on them is overlapped by other operations. This means that the individual user does not direct the reading or writing, but has to go through the intermediary of the computer operating system. Access control almost always resides in the operating system.

Main Memory (Primary Storage). To operate, a program must be in the main memory; to be acted upon, data must be in the main memory. Thus, in the final analysis, on-line access to data must first be controlled by controlling access to the main memory. Since all users are permitted to use main memory one after another or even concurrently, it is important to erase any sensitive data that is there before allowing the next user's program to have control. Some operating systems do this clean-up job automatically; others do not.

Protection of Data in Main Memory. Each user in a multiprogrammed computer system is assigned, at a given instant of time, a region of the main memory as a private domain. The right to read from or write into this area of the memory is protected by a *key* (usually through a hardware device). A directory of keys is kept in a table in the main memory assigned to the operating system itself. This means that the user cannot alter the directory entry pertaining to the user's own memory area, for if this were possible, it might permit one user to access some other user's memory area. Each user memory area is thus private to an individual user.

Sharing data and programs can be achieved by having an area of memory that is common to the users concerned. If only specified users may share the data in this area, an authorization table must be maintained. Often, it is sufficient to declare the area as "public" in order to ensure that no access control is necessary.

Protection of Data in Secondary Storage.

In a secure system, all requests to read and write on secondary storage must pass through the input/output control of the operating system. In order to issue a READ or WRITE instruction to a file in secondary storage, it is necessary for a user to alert the operating system of the intention to perform operations on the file by issuing an instruction. At this time, the access rights to the file are examined.

Private files are usually labeled with the name and system identification number of the user, and may even contain in their labels a password that must be matched against one provided by the user at the time of issuing the access request. Only the owner of a limited-access file should be permitted to change the password. When a file has limited access, the access information is frequently stored separately from the data.

Protection of Data in Transmission.

Wiretapping or electromagnetic eavesdropping is a security threat whenever data travels through the air or over wires that are not in a secure area. Many systems use common carrier facilities, and this presents many problems. Sensitive data that is to be transmitted from one location to another should be transformed (i.e., encrypted) to make it private. Privacy transformations that involve static methods of coding require a certain amount of work to break, but can usually be decoded after some effort.

The best coding techniques involve keys that are as long as the data to be encrypted. The string of characters for the key is generated from a basic starting number, just as a sequence of pseudo-random numbers can be generated. The same starting value yields the same sequence every time. It is nearly impossible to determine the starting value and the generating algorithm from eavesdropping on the transmission. The work required to break the code is very extensive.

In 1977, the National Bureau of Standards, with IBM, developed an algorithm as a standard for data encryption (*q.v.*) based on a 56-bit key. The algorithm transforms each 64-bit block of data by substitutions and permutations through 16 levels, all controlled by the key. It can be implemented inexpensively using an LSI chip. Although whether this data encryption standard (DES) is an "unbreakable" method of encryption has been questioned, it has been suggested that the management of the security of the key poses a greater threat. Most encryption techniques involve the enciphering and deciphering of data by the same key. They are symmetric; the same key must be known at both ends of the transmission. An asymmetric method of encryption called *public key encryption* uses a published key, for each particular destination, to encipher the data and a private (secret) key, known only at the destination, to decipher the data. There is no need then to transmit secret keys. Signatures are simple on public key systems. A data source encrypts its signature using its secret key; on arrival, its public key can be used to decipher the signature. (The two keys applied successively in either order leave the text unchanged.)

Protection of Data Off-Line.

Stored data in the form of hard copy, or on magnetic tape or removable disks, must be kept in a strictly controlled environment. Protection against accidental or willful damage or theft must be insured. Access to the data will be basically through a manual system managed by a person charged with its security. There should be a record kept of all deposits and withdrawals from the data bank, after assuring that the person making the transaction has the appropriate access rights.

Frequently, data banks are located near the main computer installation where tapes are requested frequently, but it is common also for systems to have a separate repository of tapes containing data vital to regenerating the system. A remote storage vault in a protected location is essential for basic business or industrial data.

Integrity of Hardware.

The fashion of having computers prominently displayed to the public is dying out. The need for precise environmental control has always meant that hardware was housed in special rooms, but it is increasingly apparent that protection and control of access to the rooms is also critical to security. Without this isolation, not only could the equipment be destroyed, but data also could be compromised as it is being printed or displayed.

All persons having access to the rooms where hardware is kept should be properly identified and their "need to be present" should be verified. Systems of identification badges are common. Sometimes access is controlled by a security officer; sometimes by locks opened by badges or by combinations. The advantage of locks operated by badges or push-button combinations is that the combination can be more easily changed than can locks operated with ordinary keys. Thus, if there is any suspicion of a compromise of a lock, the combination should be altered. When the key is a badge, the rightful owner's picture may be displayed on it for further identification.

Where a piece of hardware is attached to the main computer hardware through a remote connection, the terminal equipment is often under minimal or no surveillance. As a result, at the present time, highly sensitive data is rarely handled in a computer system with remote terminals. It is important that remote users be properly identified and that the terminals be properly identified, not only at the time of beginning a "conversation," but also from time to time during any extended interaction. This is rarely the case except in military systems. No doubt the security of data in systems with remote terminals will be improved.

Integrity of Software. We have indicated that the security of data within the computer depends on the operating system. Many existing systems are complex; to some extent, their complexity protects them from invasion. However, accidental access routes (*trapdoors*) into the system have been found. When access routes via trapdoors are found, the usual result is that the system becomes inoperative; many of the breakdowns that occur daily in systems are the result of accidental entry into the operating system by an unsuspecting user.

To be secure, operating system structure should be cleanly designed and the documentation openly available. Secrecy should not be a requirement for a secure system. Perhaps only critical parts of operating systems need be under strict security control (e.g., tables of access rights and the programs that validate these rights) to insure data security.

REFERENCES

1969. Hoffman, Lance J. "Computers and Privacy: A Survey," *Computing Surveys* **1**, *No. 2* (June).
1970. Friedman, T. D. "The Authorization Problem in Shared Files," *IBM Systems Journal* **9**, *No. 4.*
1979. Hsiao, D. K., Kerr, D. S., and Madnick, S. E. *Computer Security.* New York: Academic Press.
1979. Denning, D. E. and Denning, P. J. "Data Security," *ACM Computing Surveys* (September), pp. 227–249.
1979. Special Issue: Cryptology, *ACM Computing Surveys* (December).

J. N. P. HUME

DATA SET

For articles on related subjects *see* ACCESS METHODS; and FILES.

This article deals with the software meaning of the term *data set*—a collection of related data items (Clarke, 1966)—and *not* the hardware meaning, which defines data set as a device used to couple a computer data link to a telephone line. Examples of data sets within our context are the collection of student records within a university, the collection of inventory items in a warehouse, the set of records describing books in a library, etc. The major objectives of grouping data items into data sets are efficient retrieval, searching, sorting, and recognition.

A data set may be described by a *data set label,* which might contain the name of the data set, its boundaries in physical storage, and certain characteristics of the data items within the set. Within a unit of physical storage (or *volume*), the set of all data set labels may be considered as a *table of contents* or *directory.* Searches, for example, may be expedited by searching the table of contents for data set labels exhibiting desired characteristics, and then searching for data items with more specific characteristics among only those data sets whose labels passed the first search.

To enhance the operating characteristics of the storage media used, data sets may be organized in various structures:

1. *Sequential,* as on magnetic tape.
2. *Indexed sequential,* where data items are stored sequentially on a key, but are also accessible via index tables maintained by the system.
3. *Direct,* without index tables; accessing of data items is up to the programmer.
4. *Partitioned,* where sequentially organized data sets are divided into *members,* and a directory is maintained of members' names and their storage locations.
5. *Telecommunication,* where the data items in the set are messages organized into queues (e.g., for communication between a computer and a remote terminal).

REFERENCE

1966. Clark, W. A. "Data Management," *IBM Systems Journal* **5**, *No. 1.*

S. C. BREWER

DATA STRUCTURES

For articles on related subjects *see* ABSTRACT DATA TYPE; DATA STRUCTURES, SET CONCEPTS FOR; FIFO-LIFO; LISTS AND LIST PROCESSING; STACK; STRING; and TREE.

The term *structure* is used in many different fields to denote objects that are constructed in a regular and characteristic way from their components. A data structure is a structure whose components are data objects.

Example. The arithmetic expression 3 + 4 * 5 is constructed in a systematic way from data components that are integers such as 3, 4, 5, and operators such as

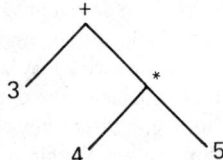

Fig. 1. A tree structure.

+ and ∗. The structure of this expression may be thought of as either a string or a tree structure in which each operator is the root of a subtree whose descendants are operands (Fig. 1).

When this data structure is stored in a computer, it must be stored so that components are readily accessible. This may be done by storing the expression 3 + 4 ∗ 5 as a character string A so that the ith character is retrieved by referring to the element $A[i]$ or $A(i)$, with the use of brackets or parentheses depending upon the programming language being used. Alternatively, the string may be stored as a list structure, in which the vertex associated with + has a left child 3 and a right child ∗, which in turn has left and right children 4 and 5 (Fig. 2).

Figs. 1 and 2 illustrate the relation between data structures, which specify *logical* relations between data components, and *storage structures*, which specify how such relations may be realized in a digital computer. The storage structure of Fig. 2 could be represented in a digital computer by five three-component storage cells, where each cell has one component containing an operator and two components respectively containing a pointer to the left and right children. The three cells that have no successors contain special markers in their pointer fields, here indicated by the word "nil."

In order to define a class of data objects having a common data structure, it is usual to start with a class of primitive data elements called *atoms*, or elementary objects, and to specify *construction operators* by means of which *composite objects* may be constructed from the atoms. In the preceding arithmetic-expression example, the atoms are operands (integers) and arithmetic operators. The construction operators specify how expressions are built up from operators and operands. The set of construction rules that specify how operators are built up from operands is sometimes referred to as a *grammar*.

In order to access and manipulate composite objects specified by a given set of atoms and construction rules, *selectors* must be defined which allow components of a data object to be accessed, and *creation* and *deletion* operators must be defined which allow components of data structures to be created and deleted. Data structures may be characterized by the nature of their accessing and their creation and deletion operators.

Some of the basic terminology relating to data structures will be mentioned by considering commonly occurring data structures such as arrays, records, sets, lists, trees, stacks, and queues.

An *array* is a data structure whose elements may be selected by integer selectors called "indexes." If A is a one-dimensional-array data structure, then $A[3]$ or $A(3)$ refers to the third element of A. If B is a three-dimensional array, then $B[I, J, K]$ or $B(I, J, K)$ refers to the I, J, K element (B_{ijk}) of the array B. The set of all elements of an array are generally created and deleted at the same time by means of *declarations,* as illustrated by the following examples:

REAL A (1,100)	Fortran array declaration
integer array A[1:N];	Algol 60 array declaration
[1:N] **int** A;	Algol 68 array declaration

In Fortran, the declaration "REAL A(100)" serves to reserve a block of cells for the array A at compile time. In Algol 60 or 68, declarations create an instance of the declared data structure when they are executed. Thus, execution of the declaration "**integer array** $A[1:N]$" causes allocation of a block of N storage cells large enough to hold integers using the current value assigned

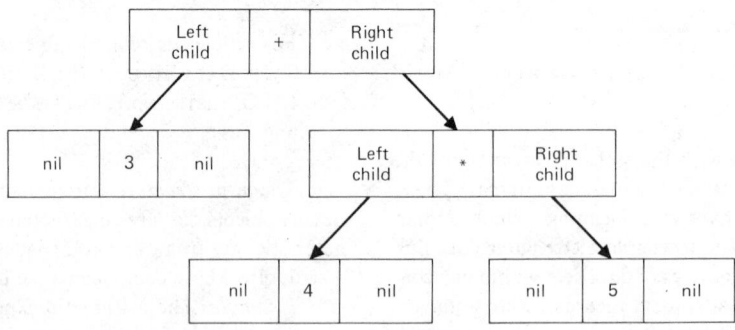

Fig. 2. Storage structure for the tree structure of Fig. 1.

to the variable N, and activates an accessing mechanism so that $A[i]$ will refer to the ith allocated cell.

The arrays introduced above are homogeneous because all elements of an array have the same data type, and are rectangular because all vectors in a given dimension have the same size. Programming languages such as Cobol and PL/I permit nonhomogeneous, nonrectangular arrays to be declared. The following is a PL/I declaration of a PAYROLL record with a 50-character name field, fields of the mode FIXED for the number of regular and overtime hours worked, and a field of the mode FLOAT for the rate of pay:

```
DECLARE 1  PAYROLL
           2  NAME CHARACTER(50),
           2  HOURS
              3  REGULAR FIXED,
              3  OVERTIME FIXED,
           2  RATE FLOAT;
```

If it is desired to refer to the number of overtime hours in the record PAYROLL, then this is given by PAYROLL.HOURS.OVERTIME. That is, component names rather than indexes are used to access a given element of the data structure.

Sets are a convenient form of data structure when the order of elements is irrelevant as in (**for** $x \in S$ **do** SUM:= SUM+x;). Sets and operations upon sets are supported in their full generality by the very high-level language SETL (*q.v.*), which allows the user to make mathematical assertions using mathematical set theoretic notations. Pascal also has a data type "set" which allows us to talk about subsets and test for set membership. However, Pascal sets have an implementation-dependent maximum size, and support only operations that can be simply defined in terms of the representation of finite sets as a binary string of zeroes and ones in a computer word.

The gap between abstract sets and their implementation is much greater than the corresponding gap for arrays or records. Sets are a "very high-level" data structure that can be completely implemented only by "very high-level languages."

List structures, just as array structures, may be characterized by their accessing creation and deletion operators. Elements of a list structure are generally accessed by "walking" along pointer chains, starting at the head of the list. In a linear list, each list element has a unique successor and the last element has an "empty" successor field, usually denoted by the symbol "nil." In general, list elements may have more than one successor, and lists may be circular in the sense that pointer chains may form cycles. Knuth (1968) introduces doubly linked lists that have forward and backward pointer chains passing through each element, and a number of other kinds of lists. Fig. 3 illustrates a doubly linked circular list named L whose head element H is linked both to the next element A and to the last element B.

If the forward pointer is referred to by RLINK (for right link) and the backward pointer is referred to by LLINK (left link), then the second list element (labeled A) may be accessed in either of the two following ways:

RLINK(L)	Forward chaining
LLINK(LLINK(L))	Backward chaining

Insertion and deletion of elements in a list is accomplished by creation of a new list cell and by updating pointers of existing list elements and the newly created list element. Fig. 4 illustrates that the insertion of the list element X between the list elements A and B requires updating of the RLINK of A, the LLINK of B, and initialization of the R and L links of X.

The instructions to perform this insertion might be as follows (assume that P points to node A):

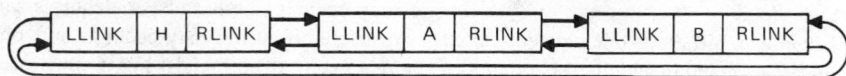

Fig. 3. Doubly linked circular list L.

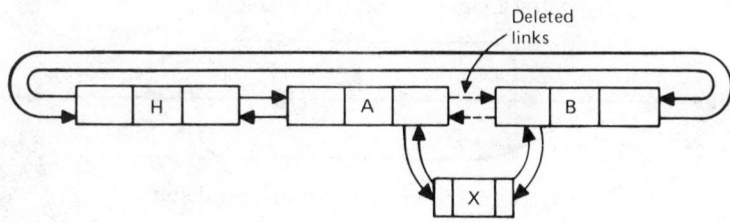

Fig. 4. Insertion of X in Fig. 3.

create X   pointed at by N
RLINK(N) = RLINK(P)
LLINK(N) = LLINK(RLINK(P))
RLINK(P) = N
LLINK(RLINK(N)) = N

The list processing language Lisp, which was developed by John McCarthy in the late 1950s, is probably the most important list processing language. The list format and instruction repertoire of Lisp will be briefly illustrated. For ease of presentation, however, we will use a notation different from that actually used in Lisp.

List elements in Lisp have two components selectable by the selectors *first* and *rest*. If L is a list then *first*(L) selects the first element of the list, which may be either an atom or a sublist, and *rest*(L) selects the rest of the list. The list $((A,B),C)$ is represented in Lisp by the list structure of Fig. 5.

For $L = ((A,B),C)$, *first*(L) = (A,B), *rest*(L) = (C), *first*(*first*(L)) = A and *rest*(*rest*(L)) = *NIL*.

Lisp also has a construction operator *cons*[$X;Y$] which constructs a list L such that *first*(L) = X and *rest*(L) = Y, and a predicate *atom*(X), which is true when X is an atom and false otherwise. In the above example, *atom*(*first*(L)) = *false* since *first*(L) = $(A;B)$, but *atom*(*first*(*first*(L))) = *true*.

In general, any language for the manipulation of data structures has not only *selectors* for selecting components of a data structure but also *constructors* for constructing data structures from their components, and *predicates* for testing whether a given data object has certain attributes. Lisp illustrates particularly clearly the role of selectors, constructors, and predicates in a programming language.

List structures are a flexible storage structure for objects of variable sizes or tables of fixed-size objects in which insertion and deletion is frequently required. A number of special classes of list structures will now be considered in greater detail.

A *tree* is a list in which there is one element called the *root* with no predecessor and in which every other element has a unique predecessor. That is, a tree is a list that contains no circular lists, and in which no two list

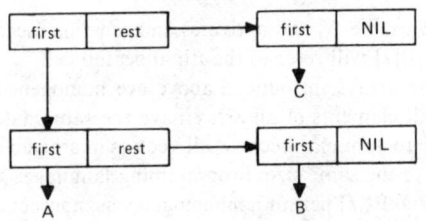

Fig. 5.   Representation of a list L.

elements may have a common sublist as a successor. Elements of a tree which have no successor are called *leaves* of the tree. Tree elements, just as list elements, are generally accessed by walking along a pointer chain. However, the guarantee that there are no cycles or common sublists makes it possible to define orderly procedures for insertion and deletion of subtrees.

A *stack* is a linear list in which elements are accessed, created, and deleted in a last-in-first-out (LIFO) order. In order to access an element in a stack, it is necessary to delete all more recently entered elements from the stack. Thus, only the top of the stack is accessible. The two principal stack operations are *popping* and *pushing*. If S is a stack, then *pop*(S) causes the top element of the stack to be deleted and *push*(S,x) causes x to be placed on top of the stack.

A *queue* is a linear list in which elements are created and deleted in a first-in-first-out order. A line of people waiting to be served in a cafeteria is a queue, since the person having waited longest is always the first to be served (deleted from the queue). In contrast, employees in a large organization generally form a stack with regard to being fired.

A generalization of queues and stacks in which elements may be added and deleted at both ends of a linear list is called a *deque*. A deque is said to be input-restricted if input is possible at only one end, but deletion may occur at both ends. A deque is said to be output-restricted if output may occur at only one end, but input may occur at both ends. Fig. 6 illustrates by means of a railway-switching network the notion of a deque with input and/or output restrictions (see Knuth, 1968, p.

Track closed in input-restricted deque

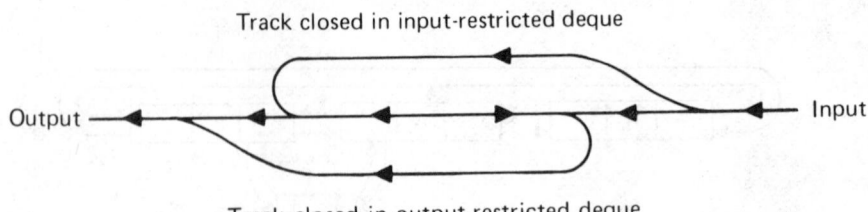

Track closed in output-restricted deque

Fig. 6.   A double-ended queue (deque).

236) ("Deque," a shortened form of "double-ended-queue", is pronounced "deck".)

Data structures include numerical structures such as integers that have arithmetic operations applicable to them, and nonnumerical structures such as arrays, lists, and trees whose primary purpose is to keep track of relations among data objects rather than to manipulate them.

Computational structures may be studied and analyzed at many different levels of abstraction. We have already remarked on the difference between logical data structures and the storage structures in terms of which they are realized. The characterization of structure by logical relations among components is clearly more abstract than the realization of the logical structure by particular configurations of cells and pointers. It is convenient to introduce an additional higher-level mathematical level of abstraction in which logical relations among components of a data structure are characterized even more abstractly by mathematical relations, and an additional lower-level "hardware" level of abstraction that specifies how storage structures are realized at the hardware level.

In programming languages, the choice of a data structure is made by selection of one of the available data types supported by the language. Usually, there are primitive data types for integers, real (floating point) numbers, and characters, composite data types for arrays and records, and data type definition mechanisms for defining new composite types in terms of primitive constituents.

One important programming language concept is that of an *abstract data type,* which has an interface of named operators accessible to the user and which operates on a hidden internal data representation. For example, an abstract "stack" data type would provide the user with "push," "pop," and "test empty" operators but hide from the user the stack data representation (as an array or list). The abstract data type mechanism is available in experimental languages like CLU but is not currently available in any major production language. The language Ada has a concept called *packages* which provide collections of resources with hidden implementation to the user, but are not actually data types.

Returning to the levels of abstraction listed above:

1. *Mathematical structure* is defined by specifying a set of objects and a set of operators (functions, relations) for transforming objects into other objects.
2. *Data structure* is defined by labeled, directed graphs that allow characteristic operators on data objects having the given structure to be naturally and simply defined by means of graph transformation rules. A given mathematical structure may, in general, be represented in many different ways by a data structure.
3. *Storage structure* is defined by storage cells with pointers between storage cells. Storage structures, like data structures, are chosen so that operators applicable to computational objects represented by a given storage structure may be simply and efficiently defined. There are, in general, many different storage structures that realize a given data structure.
4. *Hardware structure* specifies how storage structures and transformations of storage structures may be realized at the hardware level.

Example. In modeling databases, the mathematical level of abstraction models databases as mathematical relations, the data structure level considers databases to be directed labeled graphs, the storage structure level considers how the directed graphs representing particular data configurations can be efficiently realized by storage structures, and the hardware structure level considers hardware and microprograms for realizing particular storage structures.

Although these four levels of structure specification are somewhat arbitrary, they appear to be "robust" in the sense that attempts to quantify the notion of abstraction invariably result in something similar to the above characterization. For example, in considering abstraction for program structure, we generally distinguish between mathematical structure, program structure, implementation structure, and hardware realization. These distinctions are very similar to the previously discussed distinctions for the data structure case.

Data structures capture the notion of computational structure at a level that is sufficiently abstract to emphasize logical relations among components of a data object, independently of details of implementation but at the same time sufficiently concrete to preserve some relation between a structure and its computational realization. Data structures thus represent an appropriate and practicable level of abstraction for characterizing computational structure, and it is for this reason that the study of data structures is important in computer science.

REFERENCES

1973. Knuth, D. E. *The Art of Computer Programming* **1** (2nd ed.), Reading, MA: Addison-Wesley.

1978. Gotlieb, C. C. and Gotlieb, L. R. *Data Types and Structures.* Englewood Cliffs, NJ: Prentice-Hall.

1980. Standish, T. A. *Data Structure Techniques,* Reading, MA: Addison-Wesley.

P. WEGNER

DATA STRUCTURES, SET CONCEPTS FOR

For articles on related subjects *see* ACCESS METH-ODS; DATABASE MANAGEMENT; DATA STRUCTURES; FILES; and STORAGE MANAGEMENT STRUCTURES.

The database set concept unifies several programming techniques (table, list, chain, ring, file, and field array) that have been in common usage for most of the history of computers. (This concept is a specialization of the more general mathematical set concept from which the data structure set gets its name and many of its properties.) In this article, the word "set" will always be used in the data structure and not the mathematical sense.

Many software products support the set concept. The list-processing languages, such as IPL-V and Lisp, have used the set concept to support the organization of program structure. Simulation languages, such as Simscript and Simula, have used set concepts to assist in modeling the subject of study. In the database management area, the Honeywell integrated data store (IDS) system (Bachman and Williams, 1964) pioneered broad usage of the set concept to process complex manufacturing and banking problems. IDS uses the chain form of set implementation. General Motors Research (Dodd, 1966) produced a similar system, Associative Processing Language (APL) for graphic display purposes. After six years of study, the Codasyl Data Base Task Group (ACM, 1971) produced a specification that has been integrated into the Cobol language. The Cobol Data Description and Data Manipulation Language extensions make available the set description and manipulation capabilities of the IDS and APL systems. IBM's Information Management System (IMS II) and Informatic's MARK IV support hierarchical set structures with the multiple-level record array technique. Cobol and PL/I's recognition of the set concept is limited to constructing sets of member records with field arrays.

Record, Field, and Set Concepts. The set is one of three complementary concepts (record, field, and set) needed to build and store data structures that closely approximate their natural world counterparts. If the natural world is considered in terms of the entities that exist, the attributes that describe them, and the relationships that associate them, then the equivalent information system concepts are record, field, and set, respectively.

In a simple example taken from a school situation, the entities would be the teachers and the children. Some of the attributes of a teacher are "name," "grade level," and "classroom." Some of the attributes of a child would be "name," "age," and "parent name." A relationship exists between teachers and children. In an information system model of this natural world situation, two classes of records (one for teachers, one for children) would be created. In each teacher record there would be a field to store the teacher's name, another for the grade level, and another for the classroom number. Each child's record would have a field for the child's name, another for the age, and yet another for the parent's name. The information system could tie each child's record to the teacher's record in one of the several ways that have been invented to implement the set concept. This might be done by physically placing all the child records after their teacher's record array in the file. This is called a *table* or *record array*.

The data structure set concept thus described is a refinement of the mathematical set concept; i.e., in the data structure set, the set definition is embodied in the instance of the "owner" role. Set membership is embodied in the instance of the "member" role. Records may concurrently have many roles as owner and member of different sets. This property permits the creation and manipulation of complex structures that model the complexity of the real world. In this refinement of the mathematical set concept, one can go reversibly either from owner as definition to members or from any member to owner to reestablish the set definition.

For data structure sets, the set definition is normally based upon the value of some field or fields within the owner record, while the membership in the set is established by the matching value of an equivalent field or fields within a potential member record. Advantage is frequently taken of this phenomenon by removing the fields from the member records that carry the matching data and depending upon the owner record for reconstruction.

A data structure diagram (Bachman, 1969) would illustrate the teacher/child structure as shown in Fig. 1. It uses a box to represent the *entity* class concept and an arrow to represent the *simple relationship* class concept.

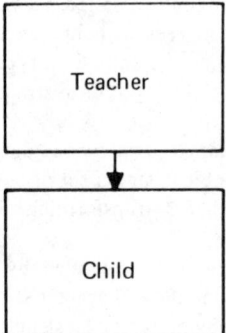

Fig. 1. Teacher to child relationship.

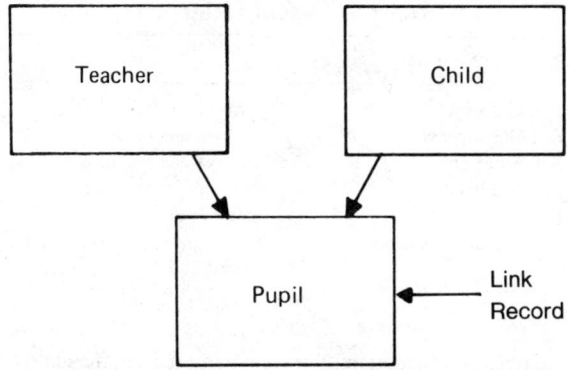

Fig. 2.   Teacher/pupil/child relationships.

(A simple relationship is a 1:*n* relationship between entities. Alternately, a complex relationship is an *m*:*n* relationship.) In this case there are two boxes, one for all the teacher entities and one for all the child entities. The arrow symbolizes the relationship that each teacher may have: zero, one, two, or more children. However, each child has only one teacher.

In the school example above, we said that a teacher has the role of "owner" of a teacher/children set. To extend this example, we will recognize that in most schools the relationship between teacher and child is not a simple relationship (1:*n*), but is rather a complex relationship (*m*:*n*), since the children have different teachers for different subjects. This complex *m*:*n* relationship of teacher:child may be transformed into a new relationship entity, "pupil," and two simple relationships, teacher:pupil and child:pupil. The teacher has many children as pupils and, as a pupil, the child has many teachers. This new view is illustrated in Fig. 2. The new "pupil" entity has the attributes "subject" and "hour," which serve to describe and differentiate one relationship entity from another. A diagram such as Fig. 2 is called a *schema*. A *link record* is one which jointly participates as a member of two different sets. From an *instance* of the schema, one may examine particular links (i.e., pupils) to ascertain, for example, which teachers teach any given pupil or which pupils are enrolled in a particular teacher's classes.

Set Formalisms. The data-structure set concept has four basic properties:

1. A set has one, only one, and always one record in the owner role (the teacher in Fig. 1 or Fig. 2).
2. A set has zero, one, or more records in the member role, and the number varies with time (the child in Fig. 1).
3. Any record may be the owner of zero, one, or more sets concurrently.

4. Any record may be a member in zero, one, or more sets concurrently, and thus be simultaneously owned by several owner records (the pupil in Fig. 2). Each record may appear only once as a member of a particular set. The member roles do not interfere with the owner roles.

Fig. 3 expresses the four basic properties of the set concept as a data structure diagram. The numbers used in the list above to enumerate the set properties are shown in order to point out their effect upon the structure. Only slight additions are necessary to complete the data structure concepts that govern data processing.

The fields of a record (p5 in Fig. 4) have been previously mentioned as the means of recording the attributes of an entity. All records must be stored in some container for safekeeping and reference. The file (p6) serves this function. Fig. 4 is an extension of Fig. 3, with the field concept and the file concept shown. The arrow from the box marked "file" to the box marked "record" symbolizes the fact that a file may hold zero, one, or more records, but a record may be in only one file. The arrow from "record" to "field" symbolizes the fact that a record may have zero, one, or more fields, but a particular field may appear in only one record.

Set Ordering. The notion of "next" and "prior" are important concepts to procedural algorithms that are basic to problem solving in a computer. In addition to the procedural limitation of handling one record at a time, there are important simplifying consequences to an algorithm if the member records within a set can be delivered to it in a predefined data-value ordered sequence or a time-of-insertion ordered sequence (FIFO or LIFO). The notions of "first" and "last" are vital to starting and stopping the iterative execution of these algorithms. Thus, the ordering of members in a set is a prerequisite to rational manipulation of the set.

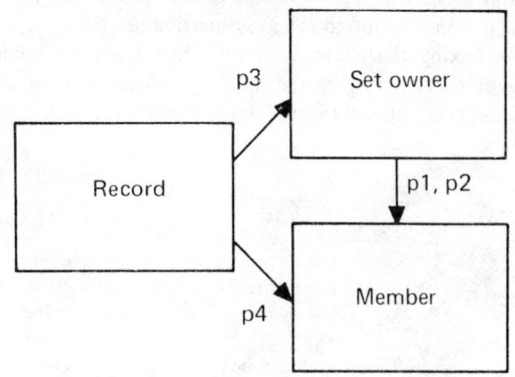

Fig. 3.   Record/owner/member entity relationships.

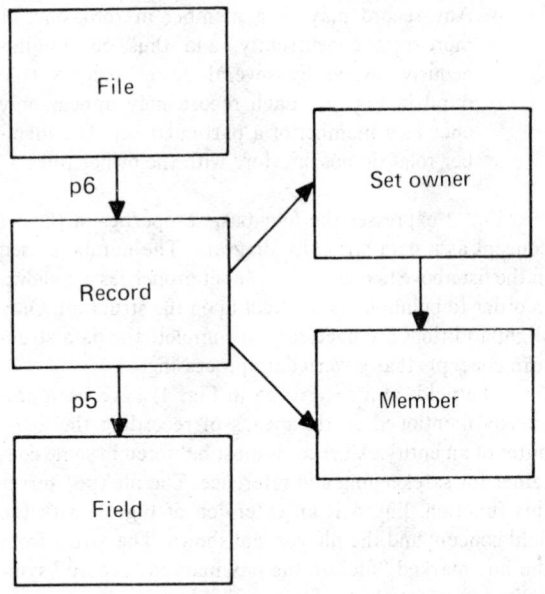

Fig. 4. Structure of file/record/field entity relationships

Table 1.   Access Methods

Method	Use
Direct access	Retrieves one record
Data-key access	Retrieves one record
Set-owner access	Retrieves one record
Set-member access	Used iteratively: retrieves each member of set
File-sequential access	Used iteratively; retrieves each record in file

Motivation for the Set Concept.

The primary motivation of associating records into sets within a file is to model natural world relationships and to assist in the accessing of selected records within the file that represents some particular relationship. The set access methods fall in between and complement the more traditional access methods. They are listed in Table 1.

The first four access methods in Table 1 are primarily used in transaction and inquiry processing, where there is a need to determine the recorded status of a particular entity or of a related group of entities, or to update their recorded status. The file-sequential access method is primarily used for periodic batch file updating and report generation. It is possible for the same record to be accessed by any of the five methods, as the occasion may require. Similarly, it is possible to use these access methods in combination to achieve a particular effect.

Taking the example of Fig. 2, a teacher's record might be retrieved by the data-key access method and then his/her pupils' records could be retrieved by the set-member access method. For each pupil record, the child's record may be retrieved with the set-owner access method. Alternately, retrieval might start with data-key access to the child's record and then proceed to access all pupil records of the child, and hence the teacher's records. The basic retrieval opportunities derived from a set are given in Table 2.

Operations on Sets.

There is a family of primitive operations that apply to sets. These are complementary to the primitive operations on records and fields, which are better known. Table 3 gives the primitive operations on all three for comparison.

The "insert" and "remove" operations on sets are the means by which a member record is procedurally introduced into a set and extracted. The insertion may be the first or last member, or logically between any two members, depending upon the set-ordering rules established for the set. The two set-access modes were described under "Motivation of Set Concept," and enumerated in Table 2. The two set-test operations relate to whether or not a particular set is currently empty (owner record, but no member records) and whether or not a record is currently inserted as a member of a particular set. More elaborate operations exist in higher-level languages (Bachman and Williams, 1964; Dodd, 1966; Codasyl Task Group, 1971), but they are based upon these primitives.

Set Descriptions, Set Classes, and Set Occurrences.

The sets described to this point have been completely free of any restrictions with regard to the

Table 2.   Retrieval Opportunities

Given	Access Method	Determine
The owner	Set member	First member, or get empty-set notice
The owner	Set member	ith member, or get out-of-set notice
The owner	Set member	Last member, or get empty-set notice
Any member	Set member	Next member, or get last-of-set notice
Any member	Set member	Prior member, or get first-of-set notice
Any member	Set owner	Owner of set

Table 3. Primitive Operations on Records, Field^, and Sets

Object	Operation
Record	Create
	Access
	Destroy
	Test for record class name
Field (content)	Initialize
	Reference
	Alter
	Test for null-value status
Set	Insert member
	Remove member
	Access set owner (record)
	Access set member (record)
	Test for set emptiness status
	Test for member insertion status

class of record that could appear in either the owner or member role, or both. In Cobol, PL/I, and most other data processing languages, there exist the concepts of record description, record occurrence, and record class.

The *record description* is the "01" entry that appears in the Data Division of a Cobol source program. It is concerned with providing a record name and other attributes of the record.

A *record occurrence* is an instance of a record created in accordance with a record description.

A *record class* consists of all the records that have been, or will be, created in accordance with a particular record description.

In parallel with these record concepts, there are equivalent concepts for sets. A set description defines a set class name, set-owner selection criteria, set-member eligibility rules, and set-member ordering rules. A set occurrence is an instance of a set created in accordance with a set description. It is owned by a particular record, and it holds specific record occurrences as members. A set class includes all the set occurrences that have been or may be created in accordance with a particular set description.

The main purpose of both the record class and set class concepts is to create a strong organizing force. For example, it changes a database with a million records from a million special situation into one where 40 or 50 situations exist: one situation for each record class and each set class. It changes the problem from something that could be chaos into something that is manageable.

The data structure diagram in Fig. 5 illustrates the integration of the description structure and occurrence structure for data as illustrated in Fig. 4. There is a corresponding element in the description structure for each occurrence element in the occurrence structure. An arrow points from the descriptive element to its equivalent occurrence element, symbolizing the fact that there may be zero, one, or more occurrence elements for each descrip-

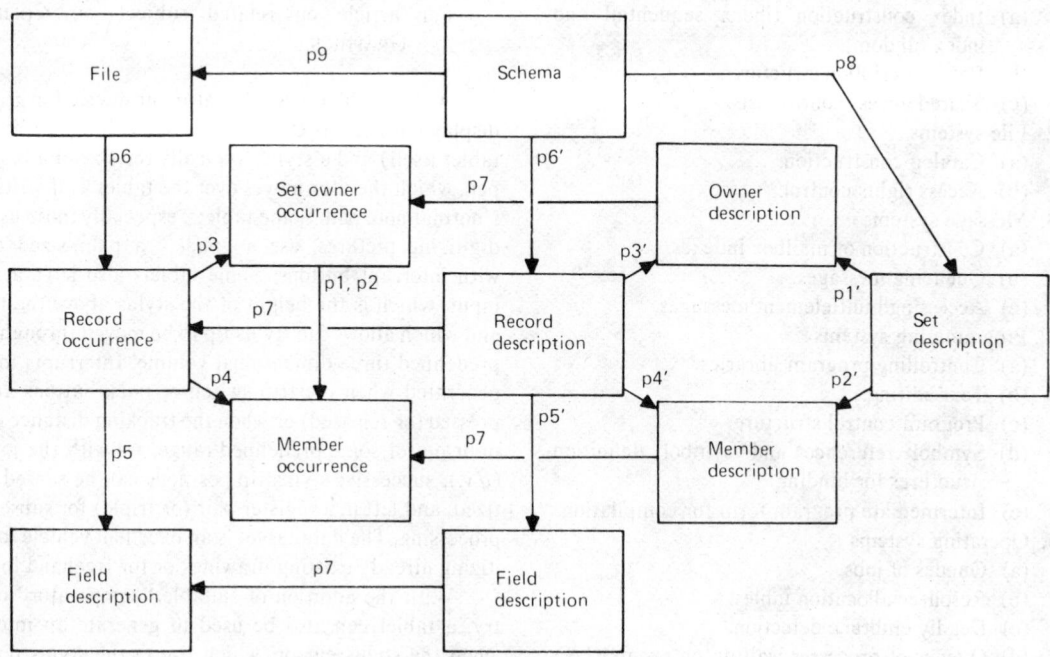

Fig. 5. Occurrence/description structures.

tive element. These occurrence elements are the embodiment of the class property and are all labeled "p7."

The properties p1 through p6, previously described in Figs. 3 and 4, are illustrated on the occurrence structure, and their descriptive counterparts (p1', p2', ··· p6') are mapped onto the description structure. It should be noted that the "set-owner occurrence" block in the occurrence structure is controlled by two description boxes in the description structure. The "owner description" block describes the eligibility of an occurrence of a record class to serve in the owner role, whereas the "set description" block describes the set class as a whole. This separation is necessary because several record classes at the description level may be eligible to serve as set owners while, at the occurrence level, one and only one record is the actual owner of a set occurrence. All the set descriptions in the schema are indicated by the arrow p8. All the files created in accordance with the schema are indicated by the arrow p9.

Auxiliary Uses of Sets. Assuming that the major usage of sets is to organize and provide access to records in an application database, then all other usages within an information system are auxiliary to the primary purpose. The tabulation below lists areas of system software and enumerates for each some usages in its respective area of the set concept. This list is intended to be illustrative of obvious usages and is in no way complete.

1. Database systems
   (a) Index construction (index sequential and index random).
   (b) Data description structures.
   (c) Shared access control lists.
2. File systems
   (a) Catalog construction.
   (b) Access rights control.
3. Message systems
   (a) Construction of mailbox indexes.
   (b) Queueing messages.
   (c) Accessing multielement messages.
4. Programming systems
   (a) Controlling program libraries.
   (b) Text editing.
   (c) Program control structure.
   (d) Symbol reference and symbol definition structures for binding.
   (e) Intermediate program form for compilation.
5. Operating systems
   (a) Queues of jobs.
   (b) Resource allocation tables.
   (c) Deadly embrace detection.
   (d) Queues of processes waiting on events (I/O completion timer).
   (e) Dispatching queues.

Summary. In summary, the set concept represents a new organizing force whose potential is now being realized. When fully recognized at the programming language level, in the training of programmers and system analysts, and in system software, it will substantially reduce some of today's problems, give clearer direction for file and application design, and improve the tenuous reliability normally associated with the development of new application systems.

REFERENCES

1964. Bachman, C. W. and Williams, S. B. "A General Purpose Programming System for Random Access Memories," Fall Joint Computer Conference.
1966. Dodd, G. G. "APL—A Language for Associative Data Handling in PL/I," Fall Joint Computer Conference.
1969. Bachman, C. W. "Data Structure Diagrams," *Data Base* (Quarterly News Letter of ACM-SIGBDP) **1**, *No. 2*.
1971. ACM. "Codasyl Cobol Data Base Task Group Report" (April).
1978. Olle, T. William. *The Codasyl Approach to Data Base Management*. New York: Wiley.
1979. Date, C. J. *An Introduction to Data Base Systems*. Reading, MA: Addison-Wesley.

C. W. BACHMAN

DATA TABLET

For article on related subject *see* COMPUTER GRAPHICS.

A data tablet is a manual input device for graphics display consoles. It consists of a flat writing surface (the tablet itself) and a stylus, typically the size of a ballpoint pen, which the user moves over the tablet as if writing on a normal note pad. Some tablets, especially those used for digitizing pictures, use a "puck," a palm-sized device with interrupt buttons. Some tablets also have a z-axis input, which is the height of the stylus above the tablet, and which allows the stylus tip to be moved through some predefined three dimensional volume. Interrupts may be generated when the trip switch or puck buttons are depressed (or released) or when the tracking distance moves in or out of some predefined range. As with the joystick ($q.v.$), successive stylus tip positions can be sensed, digitized, and left in a register pair (or triple) for subsequent processing. The data tablet is an excellent vehicle for digitizing already existing drawings or for freehand input.

With the addition of suitable "comparator" circuitry, a tablet can also be used to generate an interrupt when the stylus cursor, which tracks the stylus position on the screen, moves within a preset distance of some graphic element already on the screen. The tablet with comparator can therefore be used as a functional equivalent to the lightpen, but is found by most users to be superior to it from an ergonomic point of view.

Physically, tablets use either analog or digital techniques for locating the stylus. Analog tablets use electromagnetic or sonic pickups (detectors) to relate the strength of a received signal to the distance between the stylus tip and the boundaries of the tablet. Sonic, or spark tablets, for example, transmit an ultrasonic pulse train that is detected by receivers at the corners for triangulation on the stylus position. Digital tablets usually have transmission lines inscribed in the tablet along which pulse trains are transmitted. The stylus receives the pulse trains characteristic of the wires it is near, and these trains can be decoded by digital logic to determine the position of the stylus.

A. van Dam

DATA TYPE

For articles on related subjects *see* ABSTRACT DATA TYPE; ARITHMETIC, COMPUTER; COERCION; DATA STRUCTURES; and PROCEDURE-ORIENTED LANGUAGES.

A data type is an *interpretation* applied to a string of bits. Data types may be classified as structured or scalar. Scalar data types include real, integer, double precision, complex, logical (also called "boolean"), character, pointer, and label.

Structured data types are collections of individual data items of the same or different data types. An *array* is a data type that is a collection of data items of the same data type. *Records, structures,* or *files* are data types that are collections of data items of one or more data types.

Most programming languages provide a declaration statement or a standard convention to indicate the data type of the variable used. Thus, when the contents of the variable are accessed, they may be interpreted in the proper manner. This is necessary, since a string of bits may have several meanings, depending on the context in which it is used.

The *real* data type, which contains a normalized fraction (mantissa) and an exponent (characteristic), is used to represent floating-point data.

The *integer* data type is used to represent whole numbers, i.e., values without fractional parts.

Double precision is a generalization of the real data type, providing greater precision and sometimes a greater range of exponents.

Complex data contain two real fields representing the real and imaginary components of an imaginary number $a + bi$ (i is the square root of -1).

Logical data is of the true-false form; i.e., there are only two possible values, true or false.

Character data is the internal representation of printable characters. Some coding schemes (BCD) permit 64 characters and use six bits; others (EBCDIC and ASCII) permit up to 256 characters and use 8 bits.

Label data refers to locations in the program and *pointer* data refers to locations of other pieces of data.

The commonly used operators for addition $(+)$, subtraction $(-)$, multiplication $(*)$, division $(/)$, and exponentiation $(**$ or $\uparrow)$ may be applied to real, integer, double precision, or complex data in high-level language programs, with a few restrictions. The actual operation that takes place depends on the data type of the operands. Although some language processors permit "mixed mode" expressions (i.e., expressions involving operands of differing data types), this is accomplished by converting ("coercing") the operands to a common data type before the operation is performed.

For example, to execute

$$N = (\text{TEST} + 90)/3$$

the integer value 90 is converted to a real value, 90.0, so that it may be added to the value of TEST (assumed to be real-valued). Before the resultant real value can be divided, the integer value 3 must be converted to a real value, 3.0. Finally, the real result is truncated and converted to an integer so that it may be stored in the integer location N.

The logical operators *and* (.AND. or AND or &), *or* (.OR. or OR or |), *not* (.NOT. or ¬), *implies,* and *equivalence* may be applied to logical data having true or false values only. Character operations include concatenation and selection of substrings. For all data types, the assignment operator ($=$ or $\leftarrow$ or $:=$) may be used to copy the contents of one location into another, and relational operators may be used to compare values of data items.

Certain programming languages (Snobol or Algol 68) are extendable in the sense that users may define new data types to suit the needs of a particular problem. Such user-defined data types are becoming increasingly popular, and they are a major feature in new programming languages such as Pascal and Ada. User programs may contain declarations of new data types such as color, which might have a limited number of values such as *red, orange, yellow, green, blue,* and *violet.* Variable names could be declared to be of type color and could take on only the stated values. An example in Pascal would be:

type COLOR = (RED, ORANGE, YELLOW, GREEN, BLUE, VIOLET);
var CRAYON, PAINT: COLOR;

A user-defined data type might also be a subrange of a standard data type. For example, an age data type might be restricted to range from 1 to 120. An example in Pascal would be:

```
type AGE = 1..120;
var TREEAGE, CITIZENAGE: AGE;
```

The data type concept can also include sequential or random access files and complex structures such as records, arrays, or trees which are formed from basic data types such as integers, character data, ages, or colors.

REFERENCES

1976. Wirth, N. *Algorithms + Data Structures = Programs.* Englewood Cliffs, NJ: Prentice-Hall.
1978. Gotlieb, C. C. and Gotlieb, L. R. *Data Types and Structures.* Englewood Cliffs, NJ: Prentice-Hall.

B. SHNEIDERMAN

DATA TYPE, ABSTRACT. *See* ABSTRACT DATA TYPE.

DEADLOCK

For articles on related subjects *see* CONCURRENT PROGRAMMING; INTERRUPT; MULTIPROGRAMMING; PETRI NETS; SEMAPHORE; and TASK.

A task (process) in a multiprogramming system is *deadlocked* if it cannot proceed because it is waiting for an event that will never occur. A system deadlock or a deadlock situation exists if one or more tasks in a system are deadlocked.

The events awaited by deadlocked tasks are often resource assignments. Suppose tasks PETER and PAUL both require simultaneous use of resources CIRCLE and SQUARE (which might, for example, each be a tape drive) in order to proceed. Assume that PETER has been assigned CIRCLE and PAUL holds SQUARE. Say PETER requests SQUARE, but must wait until it is released by PAUL. However, PAUL will release SQUARE only at task completion time, and in order to proceed to completion it is necessary for PAUL to have CIRCLE, which is held by PETER. The two tasks have requested resources in opposite order and have become involved in a *mutual* deadlock, or *circular wait*. More than two tasks may be involved: A situation may exist in which PETER is waiting for PAUL who is waiting for FRED who is waiting for SAM who is waiting for PETER. Indeed, all tasks in a multiprogramming system may be involved, in which case there is a *total* deadlock. In spooling systems, total deadlock might occur because of competition for

spooling space on the disk. This would be the case if no task released disk space until it was completed and no task could complete without additional disk space. (Spooling space is not necessarily continually emptying in such a system; it empties only when tasks are complete.)

Another term for deadlock (due to E. W. Dijkstra) is *deadly embrace,* and still another is *knot.*

Various ad hoc and systematic methods have been suggested for prevention of deadlocks, or for detection and subsequent recovery. These methods are reviewed in Holt (1972) and Coffman et al. (1971). Included in the ad hoc methods are conventions for requesting resources in specified order, and constraints on the amount of time a task is permitted to wait for an event. That these ad hoc techniques work fairly well is evidenced by the fact that deadlocks are not a serious problem in current operating systems. Ad hoc prevention methods are routinely used and deadlocks occur infrequently. Those deadlocks that do occur are resolved mostly by the computer operator, who may abort a deadlocked task, preempt resources from one task in order to allow another task to continue, or restart the system.

It is possible, however, that the deadlock problem may be more pressing in the future as systems are developed with increased resource sharing and stronger concurrency. In this event, the systematic methods would appear more attractive, even through their cost might be relatively high. At present, most systematic methods confine themselves to those deadlocks attributable to contention for resources, as opposed to those caused by faulty synchronization of concurrent tasks, since the latter are more complex and less well understood.

REFERENCES

1971. Coffman, E. G., Elphick, M. J. and Shoshani, A. "System Deadlocks," *Computing Surveys* 3, *No. 2* (June).
1972. Holt, R. C. "Some Deadlock Properties of Computer Systems," *Computing Surveys* 4, *No. 3* (September).

A. H. WERKHEISER

DEBUGGING

For articles on related subjects *see* DIAGNOSTICS; DUMP; ERRORS; FLOWCHART; INTERACTIVE SYSTEMS, USING; LOOP; PATCH; PROCEDURE-ORIENTED LANGUAGES, Programming; PROGRAM; and TRACE.

In a 1966 article in *Scientific American,* the late English computer scientist, Christopher Strachey, wrote:

Although programming techniques have improved immensely since the early days, the process of finding and correcting errors in programming—known graphically if inelegantly as "debugging"—still remains a most difficult, confused and unsatisfactory operation. The chief impact of this state of affairs is psychological. Although we are happy to pay lip service to the adage that to err is human, most of us like to make a small private reservation about our own performance on special occasions when we really try. It is somewhat deflating to be shown publicly and incontrovertibly by a machine that even when we do try, we in fact make just as many mistakes as other people. If your pride cannot recover from this blow, you will never make a programmer.

Though almost two decades have now elapsed since those lines were written, they still capture the essence and mystique of *debugging*.

Types of Error. Mistakes *(bugs)* find their way into a computer program for many reasons, but they may generally be classified as follows.

1. An otherwise logically correct program contains one or more isolated statements or instructions that are syntactically (i.e. grammatically) incorrect in the programming language being used.
2. A potentially correct algorithm may be coded in a logically incorrect way.
3. The algorithm implemented may function correctly for some but not all data values, or, more insidiously, it may fail for just some few combinations of input values.

These three types of errors create debugging problems of increasing severity and typically require substantially different approaches to debugging.

Syntactic Errors. The more flexible the syntax of a programming language, the easier it is to make syntactic errors. Thus, the simplicity and rigidity of machine language makes syntactic errors (such as illegal operation codes) relatively rare. In assembly language up through high-level language, however, it becomes increasingly easy to write a statement that is not grammatically acceptable to the language processor. Whether such statements occur because of typographical errors, imperfect understanding of language syntax, or just plain lack of concentration, such statements will prove to be only a minor annoyance, since they will produce diagnostic messages *(diagnostics)* when the errant program is assembled, compiled, or interpreted.

Language processors vary greatly in the quality of their diagnostics. For example, consider the spectrum of possible responses to the statement:

$$C = 4A.$$

The message SYNTAX ERROR tells us nothing more than that the processor doesn't like it. The message ERROR 17 is annoying but at least raises the hope that if we look up ERROR 17 in some reference manual, we'll get to the root of the difficulty. Finally, the message IMPLIED MULTIPLICATION NOT ALLOWED attempts to be helpful, especially if given in conjunction with some such printout as

$$C = 4A,$$
$$\hat{}$$

which pinpoints the precise location of the alleged error. Note, however, that it makes the assumption that the programmer forgot to place a multiplication operator between the 4 and the A when, in fact, the error may have been the mistaken notion (for most computer languages) that $4A$ is a legal identifier.

The type of error cited above is generally called a *fatal error* because it prevents the compiler from generating the object program needed for execution. Other situations may generate only a warning message that potentially erroneous results might be obtained; it would then be up to the programmer's judgment as to whether the offending construction really need be modified. An example is the Fortran statement

IF (A .EQ. 4.3567) K=K+1,

which would cause many compilers to respond with:

THE TEST FOR EQUALITY BETWEEN REAL NUMBERS MAY NOT BE MEANINGFUL

(i.e., one cannot expect a computed value, A in the above, to be exactly equivalent to some other comparison value right down to the last bit of precision).

Designers of language translators intended for extensive student use try hard to make their diagnostics "friendly." However well they succeed, it is usually the case that students become unduly elated upon receipt of NO DIAGNOSTICS when, in fact, such a message is more likely to denote the real beginning of the debugging process rather than its conclusion.

Logical Errors. Logical errors are sometimes called *semantic errors* because they cause the program to have a meaning which, though syntactically valid, is other than what is needed for consistency with the algorithm being implemented. No translator will object to $C = A + B$ even if $C = A - B$ is what is needed, but such an error is virtually certain to cause incorrect results. Of course, most logical errors are more subtle. Typical errors cause programmed loops to run one time too few, one time too many, or to run indefinitely ("infinite" loops), or not at all; cause misallocation of memory relative to actual space needed; cause input data to be read with improper formats; or cause weird program behavior in any number of ways. Those errors that cause program termination with *run-time diagnostics* are easier to isolate than those that lead to infinite loops or to "normal" termination with incorrect answers. An example would be the very explicit message:

THE FOLLOWING INPUT RECORD DOES NOT CONFORM TO THE FORMAT SPECIFIED AT LINE 1023 (followed by a printout of the offending record)

but not all run-time diagnostics can be so precise.

When program execution does not lead to an easily localized error, the programmer has recourse to several debugging tools. One of the more efficient is to embed some temporary print statements at strategic places in the program flow in order to monitor the progress of intermediate results, the objective being to pinpoint the exact transition from successful progress to the point where the logic goes awry. (The information printed comprises what is sometimes called a *snapshot dump,* since, after capturing a record of conditions at a particular checkpoint, the computation continues. Of course, a prudent programmer would have had the foresight to include several such checkpoints in the program in anticipation of less than perfect initial operation, but it is almost inevitable that additional narrowing of focus will be needed. Interpretive languages can be easier vehicles for debugging in this sense, since the value of any desired variable can be solicited at the point of failure without prior inclusion of snapshot commands; this is more difficult with a compiler, since, by execution time, knowledge of the mapping between symbolic variable names and absolute memory cells has usually been lost.) At two other extremes, the programmer may ask for extensive printout only at (normal or abnormal) program termination—a so-called *post-mortem dump,*—or, a last resort because of its gross inefficiency, a printout of key registers or variables after every statement (or perhaps every nth statement) or instruction executed; i.e., a *trace* (*q.v.*) of program flow. Narrowing the source of the error to a small section of code by one of these means or another is the necessary prelude to final identification of the error being pursued.

Algorithmic Error. When all known syntactic and semantic errors have been removed from a program, there is still a question as to whether the implemented algorithm actually solves the desired problem for all legal combinations of input values. Because so few programs are genuinely new in the sense of testing untried algorithms, this type of error is rather rare among professionals but not among students who are prone to encode, even if "correctly," some rather bizarre "algorithms." In either case, such algorithmic error can be very difficult to detect. If a program has been running satisfactorily for a sustained period, its users may place undue confidence in its output to the point where they would not detect answers that are nearly, but not quite, correct. Extensively tested programs that compute reliable results for a wide range of input values and that carefully check and reject illegal input are said to be *robust.* Programs that lack robustness are far more likely to be deficient because of logical errors (usually unchecked pathways or unverified input) rather than algorithmic error. Consider the Pascal program statement:

if doubleletter **in** ['aa', 'ee', 'ii', 'oo', 'uv']
    then doublevowels := doublevowels + 1;

If the purpose of the program containing this statement is to isolate and count the number of occurrences of a double vowel in input textual material, the program may be thought to be correct for a long time until someone notices that it is not counting double u's (which occur only rarely, in such words as *vacuum*) because of the typographical error (*'uv'* rather than *'uu'*) in the cited Pascal statement.

A program that gives correct answers for some or even many input cases may nonetheless contain huge stretches of code that have never been executed. A significant component of programming talent is the ability to devise a sufficiently comprehensive set of test cases which, at a minimum, exercise all program branches not only serially but also in such sequential combinations as to give reasonable assurance that the program will indeed be robust.

Correction of Errors. The correction of a serious algorithmic error might necessitate the rewriting of all or a substantial portion of a program using essentially the same tools used to create it in the first place, but the correction of a syntactic or simple logical error is usually a trivial mechanical operation on a modern time-shared computer or even on a personal microcomputer. The principal tool is either a general text editor running under control of the computer's operating system or, in some cases, a special-purpose editor embedded in a specific language processor such as those that are typically part of

Basic and APL implementations. The programmer directs the editor to focus attention on the offending statement, which is located either by citing its line number, if known, or by asking for automatic search for the first statement that contains a particular character string, say, for example, *procedure*. After the statement that qualifies is located and displayed on the terminal by the editor, a decision is made to replace it, delete it, modify only a part of it, or add one or more new statements ahead of or after it. A still more powerful feature commonly provided is to be able to replace all occurrences of a given character string with a substitute string anywhere in the program, or in specifically delineated parts of a program; e.g., changing all occurrences of INTERGER to INTEGER can get a poor speller out of a bind pretty quickly, especially if the errant word occurs 57 times.

When all corrections are made, the programmer typically asks the operating system to save the updated text segment and to retranslate this source element into a machine language object element using a particular language processor. The debugging cycle then continues iteratively until the program is deemed to be "correct." Unfortunately, saying so doesn't make it so, and the program may still need considerable exercise before it become robust in the sense discussed earlier.

A Sample Debugging Session. As an example of a typical debugging session, consider the following Pascal program whose purpose is stated in its internal comments. The program contains three bugs, which are successively detected and corrected by a programmer (whose thoughts are given in [ ]s); all other material is a verbatim transcript of the interactive session in which lines following '>' (the *solicit character* in the Univac EXEC-8 operating system being used) are lines of input and all others are lines of output. Lines starting with @ request some service from EXEC-8.

REILLY*TPF   EDRHEXPRINT1   04/27/81 15:41:02

```
program hextest (input, output);
var n : integer;
    procedure printhex (n : integer);
    {will convert any 36-bit 1's complement number n}
    {to hexadecimal form and print as an (up to) 9 hex}
    {digit number. Algorithm used is successive divi-}
    {sion by 16 and subsequent conversion of remain-}
    {ders to legal ASCII characters via function}
    {chr(r)                                          }
    var q,r,i : integer; h : packed array[1. .9] of char;
    begin
        q:= n; i:= 10;
        if n<0 then h:='FFFFFFFFF'
               else h:='         ';
        repeat
            i:= i+1;
```

```
            r:= q MOD 16;
            q:= q DIV 16;
            if r<0 then r:= r+15;
            if r<9 then r:= r+48 else r:= r+55;
            h[i]:= chr(r)
        until q=0;
        writeln('decimal', n,' = hexadecimal ',h)
    end {printhex};
begin {main program};
    while not eof do
        begin
            readln( n); printhex (n)
        end
end.
```

> @PAS *LIB.PASLGO EDRHEXPRINT1
   University of Wisconsin Load and Go PASCAL
   (2:D:3) 04/27/81 15:42:42

```
   14   000027           r:= q M0D   16;
                              A   B
```

***(A) ERROR ***SYNTAX ERROR. ";" INSERTED BETWEEN MARKER AND "M0D"
***(B) ERROR *** SYNTAX ERROR. ":=" INSERTED BETWEEN MARKER AND "16"
***(B) ERROR *** M0D HAS NOT BEEN DECLARED

Compilation completed - 3 errors found. The last error is at line 14.
[Oh, oh! A syntax error at line 14, caused by one of the oldest mistakes in programming: spelling "MOD" with a zero in the middle rather than the letter "O." But look how the "smart" compiler tried to salvage the line; it thinks I intended to write the *two* statements

$$r := q; \text{M0D} := 16;$$

but of course that plausible (though mistaken) "repair" caused still another diagnostic; i.e., I didn't declare the "variable" M0D. Oh well, let's fix the actual error by calling the editor:]

```
>@ED,U EDRHEXPRINT1, EDRHEXPRINT2
0: > 14                    [Please display line 14]
    r:= q M0D 16;
14: > change/M0D/MOD/
    r:= q MOD 16;
> EXIT
```
[Now let's try again]
```
>@PAS*LIB.PASLGO EDRHEXPRINT2
   University of Wisconsin Load and Go PASCAL
```

(2:D:3) 04/27/81 15:44:53
Compilation completed-no errors found.
[Good! No more syntactic errors and the compu-
ter is asking for input. I'll give it a . . .]
>1
SUBSCRIPT OUT OF RANGE
ORD OF ERROR VALUE = 11
ERROR AT LINE 18 IN PRINTHEX
  N = 1; I = 11; R = 49; Q = 0
CALLED FROM LINE 25 IN HEXTEST

[Oops! Now there's a logical error. The subscript *i* has
reached 11 when I intended to count it *down* from 10.
Well of course, the *i* := *i* + 1 just after the repeat should
be *i* := *i* − 1. Let's fix it.]

> @ED,U EDRHEXPRINT2, EDRHEXPRINT3
0: > Locate *i*+1
     i:=*i*+1;
13:
> change /+/−/
     i:=*i*−1;
> EXIT

> @PAS∗LIB.PASLGO EDRHEXPRINT3
   University of Wisconsin Load and Go PASCAL
   (2:D:3) 04/27/81 15:45:10
Compilation completed—no errors found.

> 44
decimal 44 = hexadecimal 2C
> 1
decimal 1 = hexadecimal 1

[Now let's try some negative numbers]
> −1
decimal −1 = hexadecimal FFFFFFFE

> −0
decimal −0 = hexadecimal FFFFFFFF

[Good. Now how about a somewhat larger number]
> 2562
decimal 2562 = hexadecimal A02
[and its complement]
> −2562
decimal −2562 = hexadecimal FFFFF5FD

[So far so good; looks like we're done. But let's try one
more case for good measure]

> 12345
decimal 12345 = hexadecimal 303@

[What's that funny looking @? A misprint? Better keep
testing]

> 44444
decimal 44444 = hexadecimal AD@C

[There it is again! I wonder what the complement of
44444 is?]

> −44444
decimal −44444 = hexadecimal FFFFF5263

[Plausible. My arithmetic verifies this as being correct.
But each digit should be the 15's complement of its corresponding digit in +44444, implying that the complement of 6 (which should be 9) is printing out as @. Could
that be the case with 12345? Yes! If I evaluate hex 3039
(rather than the 303@ which printed), I indeed get
12345. There must be something wrong with the conversion of remainders to ASCII when they lie on the threshold of needing to be literal "digits" such as A through F
rather than conventional digits 0 to 9. Sure, note that in
the ASCII collating sequnce "@" has value decimal 64,
one below 65, the value of "A." Where do I deal with
this? In the statement:

   if *r* < 9 then *r* := *r* + 48 else *r*: = *r* + 55;

So there's the problem, right there. All digits less than
and including 9 should be incremented by 48. We'll need
r < = 9 or, say, *r* < 10 so . . .]

> @ED,U EDRHEXPRINT3, EDRHEXPRINT4
0: > Locate *r* < 9
   if *r* < 9 then *r*:=*r*+48 else *r*:=*r*+55;
17:
> change /10/9/
   if *r* < 10 then *r*:=*r*+48 else *r*:=*r*+55;
> EXIT
> @PAS∗LIB.PASLGO EDRHEXPRINT4
   University of Wisconsin Load and Go PASCAL
   (2:D:3) 04/27/81 15:45:10
Compilation completed—no errors found.
[Successive inputs to this version then yielded:]

decimal	1	=	hexadecimal	1
decimal	−0	=	hexadecimal	FFFFFFFF
decimal	−1	=	hexadecimal	FFFFFFFE
decimal	12345	=	hexadecimal	3039
decimal	44444	=	hexadecimal	AD9C
decimal	−44444	=	hexadecimal	FFFFF5263
decimal	34359738367	=	hexadecimal	7FFFFFFFF
decimal	− 34359738367	=	hexadecimal	800000000

[So the error has been corrected and the program works for up to the largest positive number representable in 36 bits, i.e. $2^{35} - 1 = 34359738367$, and for its complement. Now let's list the final version:]

```
REILLY*TPF  EDRHEXPRINT4   04/27/81 15:52:01
program hextest (input, output);
var n : integer;
    procedure printhex(n : integer);
    {will convert any 36-bit 1's complement number n}
    {to hexadecimal form and print as an (up to) 9 hex}
    {digit number. Algorithm used is successive divi-}
    {sion by 16 and subsequent conversion of remain-}
    {ders to legal ASCII characters via function}
    {chr(r)                                      }
    var q,r,i : integer; h : packed array[1..9] of char;
    begin
        q: = n; i: = 10;
        if n < 0 then h: = 'FFFFFFFFF'
                 else h: = '        ';
        repeat
            i:= i−1;
            r: = q MOD 16;
            q: = q DIV 16;
            if r < 0 then r:= r+15;
            if r < 10 then r:= r+48 else r:= r+55;
            h[i] := chr(r)
        until q = 0;
        writeln('decimal',n,' = hexadecimal ',h)
    end {printhex};
begin {main program};
    while not eof do
    begin
        readln(n); printhex (n)
    end
end.
```

Prevention of Errors. Clearly, better than finding and fixing errors would be to inhibit their introduction in the first place. In this sense, the subject of debugging is closely related to that of program design, documentation, and maintenance. Even when a program is deemed correct, it is seldom "finished"; i.e., it is almost inevitable that its sponsor will ultimately ask that it be modified. Often, the request will come well after the original programmer is still available. Experience has indicated that if certain good practices are followed during design and implementation, errors will be minimized to a degree well worth the extra original effort. Some of these are:

1. Program logic should be documented in the form of flowcharts or iteration diagrams.

2. Program variable names should be chosen mnemonically, e.g. RADIUS rather than simply R.
3. The symbolic program code should contain embedded comments that relate back to the flowchart.
4. As far as the structure of the host language permits, the principles of structured programming (q.v.) should be followed during program design.
5. All program input statements should be followed immediately by output statements that "echo" the input onto the output medium so that there can never be any confusion as to just which input case is being processed.
6. All output values should be carefully labeled. Two otherwise correct answers that are confused with each other might just as well have been incorrect.

Finally, it should also be mentioned that there is a growing school of adherents to a philosophy that program verification (q.v.) will allow programs to be "proved" correct to the point where bugs are never allowed to survive to the point where machine debugging in the sense discussed herein is needed at all. While there should be universal hope that such techniques succeed, the need for the more mundane advice cited in this article is likely to exist for some time to come.

REFERENCES

1978. Van Tassel, Dennie. *Program Style, Design, Efficiency, Debugging, and Testing.* Englewood Cliffs, NJ: Prentice-Hall.
1978. Hughes, C. E., Pfleeger, C. P., and Rose, L. L. *Advanced Programming Techniques.* New York: Wiley, Chapter 1.

E. D. REILLY, JR.

DEC. *See* DIGITAL EQUIPMENT CORPORATION

DECIDABILITY

For articles on related subjects *see* ALGORITHMS, THEORY OF; and COMPUTABILITY.

Decidability is a property of predicates. A *predicate* P with domain D is a property of the elements of D, which each particular element of D either has or does not have. If x in D has the property P, we say that "$P(x)$ is true;" otherwise, we say that "$P(x)$ is false." The predicate P is said to be *decidable* if there exists an algorithm which, for any given x in D, provides us with a definite answer to the question whether or not $P(x)$ is true.

For example, consider the predicate P whose domain D is the set of integers greater than 1, and which is defined as

$P(i)$ if and only if i is a prime number.

This predicate is decidable. An algorithm is described by Hopcroft and Ullman (1969).

The definition given above is lacking rigor for the following reasons:

1. It is not explained in what form the argument x in D is "given." In particular, this part of the definition makes sense only if elements of D are in some way finitely describable. Thus, the notion of decidability, as described above, makes no sense for a predicate P whose domain is the set of real numbers.
2. The notion of an algorithm is not precise.
3. It is not explained in what sense the algorithm provides us with an answer.

How the notion of decidability of a predicate can be made mathematically rigorous and how the decidability of predicates can be discussed in terms of the computability of functions are explained in the article ALGORITHMS, THEORY OF.

REFERENCES

1969. Hopcroft J. E. and Ullman, J. D. *Formal Languages and Their Relation to Automata*. Reading, MA: Addison-Wesley.
1979. Hofstadter, D. R. *Godel, Escher and Bach: An Eternal Golden Braid*. New York: Basic Books.

G. T. HERMAN

DECISION TABLES

PRINCIPLES

For articles on related subjects *see* DECISION TABLES; Languages; and FLOWCHART.

Decision tables are a tabular method of describing or specifying the various actions associated with combinations of conditions. The method is tabular in that it uses a special form of table to present the associations. The actions specified are transformations to be done to data or materials, usually by computers or people. The conditions are data variables that describe the characteristics of the environment and the events that happen in the environment. The relationship among the conditions specified in a decision table is usually the logical AND relationship. The history of the origin and development of decision tables is summarized in Chapin (1967).

Example. A simple example of a decision table is given in Fig. 1. This describes a procedure for ordering low-usage products under several conditions. By policy, a target inventory level has been set at 20 units of stock for items covered by this decision table. Consider, as an example of the procedure, the third column from the right in the decision table: If the weekly usage is low (less than 8 units) *and* the amount on order is not greater than 30 units, then a regular order should be placed if the stock on hand amounts to fewer than 20 units.

Terminology. As indicated in Fig. 2, decision tables are commonly regarded as consisting of four overlapping major parts. Each of these parts is a rectangle within the overall rectangle of the decision table. The propor-

On hand < 20	Y	Y	Y	Y	Y	Y	N	E
Weekly usage	>15	>15	8-15	8-15	8-15	<8	—	S
Local vendor available	—	—	N	N	Y	—	—	L
On order > 30	N	Y	N	Y	N	N	Y	E
Rush order	X		X					
Regular order		X		X	X	X		
Cancel order							X	
No action								X

Fig. 1.   Example of a decision table.

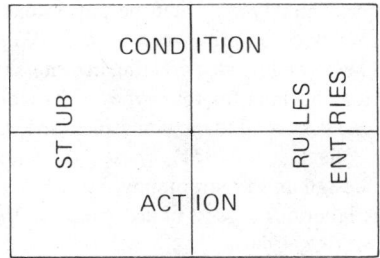

Fig. 2. Parts of a decision table.

tioning of the four-component rectangles varies from situation to situation.

The upper portion of a decision table is known as the *condition* portion. The lower portion of a decision table is known as the *action* portion. The left-hand portion of a decision table is known as the *stub*. The right-hand portion is known as the *entry* portion. Each column in it is known as a *decision rule*. Because of the overlap, the upper left-hand portion of a decision table is known as the *condition stub*. The upper right-hand portion is known as the *condition entries* in the decision rules. The lower left-hand portion is known as the *action stub*. The lower right-hand portion of a decision table is known as the *action entries* in the decision rules.

Decision rules are any of the columns in the rules or in the entry portion of the decision table. The rules in decision tables are meant to be read both horizontally and vertically. Thus, read vertically, each decision rule cites some combination of conditions and the associated actions to be taken when that combination of conditions is true (exists or is satisfied). Read horizontally, the rules list the alternative values of conditions and the presence or absence of the actions to be taken. The stub, read vertically, lists all conditions and actions. Taken together, the decision rules are exhaustive in that they must cover every possible combination of conditions. No such requirement is imposed on the actions, however. Conditions may be of three types: limited entry, extended entry, or mixed entry.

In *limited-entry decision tables,* the condition stub specifies exactly what the condition is, or what the value of the variable is. An example is, "Age is less than 18." Therefore, the condition portion of each decision rule may need only to identify if yes (Y), that condition is met; no (N), that condition is not met; or "don't care" (−), whether or not the condition is met. In the latter case, the rule is insensitive or indifferent to the particular values of that condition.

In *extended-entry decision tables,* the condition stub cites the identification of the condition, but not the particular values. Particular values are entered into the condition portion of the decision rules directly. An example

is "Age" in the stub, and "<18," "18," and ">18" in the rules.

In *mixed entry decision tables,* the condition stub includes one or more instances of both limited-entry conditions and extended-entry conditions. Fig. 1 is an example of a mixed-entry decision table.

Regardless of the form of the conditions, the action portion of the decision rules may be either unsequenced or sequenced. Unsequenced actions, the most common, are identified by any mark (such as X) in the rule, with the actions to be performed in the order in which they are listed from top to bottom in the action stub. If needed, actions may be cited more than once in the stub, to get them into the desired sequence for a decision rule. Actions not to be performed are left unmarked in the rule. For sequenced actions, the action entry is a sequence number instead of a mark, and the action stub may list the actions in any sequence.

Reading and Creating Decision Tables. The person who creates a decision table must give attention to completeness, accuracy, redundancy, inconsistency, endless loops, and size. For assistance on the first four matters, formal guides and check procedures are available [for examples, see London (1972) and Pollack *et al.* (1971)]. To avoid all endless loops, the person must require for every decision rule that at least one of the marked actions must change the value of at least one of the conditions cited in the condition stub.

In order to save space in the decision table, and to keep the decision table down to a workable size, rule consolidation is normally practiced as often as possible. This is usually accomplished in two ways. First, when the actions to be taken for different combinations of conditions are identical, and the patterns of conditions can be combined through the use of "don't care" condition entries, then one decision rule can replace two or more decision rules. Second, an "else rule" can be specified for all possible combinations of conditions not explicitly provided for in the other decision rules. Commonly, the else rule is the rightmost rule in a decision table (see, for example, Fig. 1). Large decision tables can be split into a connected group of much smaller decision tables by using decision table parsing techniques.

The user of decision tables commonly reads the decision rules individually from top to bottom, referring to the left of the stub as needed. Except for the "else" rule, the left-to-right sequence of the decision rules in the decision table is of no significance, but is commonly put into a logical order based upon the pattern of changes in the conditions. Having the most commonly used rules at the left is an aid to the user, but having the rules in an orderly progression of condition values is an aid to the creator of the decision table.

To use a decision table, the user first reads the condition stub and, for the situation at hand, notes the available values for each condition. Then these values of the conditions are matched against the condition portion of the decision rules, one rule at a time, from left to right. If the conditions do not match, the user rejects the decision rule and goes to the next decision rule to the right. If the table was correctly created, one and only one decision rule must fit the values of the conditions, be it only the "else" rule. When a rule is found that does match, the user goes next to its action portion to find out what actions are to be performed and in which sequence. When these actions are complete, the user applies the decision table afresh with a new set of input values for each condition.

Use. Decision tables have enjoyed their widest use in representing logically complex data-handling situations. These are situations where the actions to be taken depend upon the values of a large number of variables, taken in combination. Examples of such situations are commonly encountered in administrative and control applications of computers. Major users include insurance companies and other financial organizations, and manufacturing companies (McDaniel, 1970). Decision tables are rarely used in scientific or research organizations when the situations can be clearly described in mathematical terms. Having or using a computer is not a prerequisite to using decision tables.

Decision tables find use in many phases of computer work, including system analysis, system design, programming, debugging, and documentation. In systems analysis, decision tables help analysts in identifying the significant control variables for the operation being studied. In systems design, decision tables help link the desired action to the control variables. In programming, decision tables can be used as a programming language. In debugging, decision tables can help reduce the time to locate bugs because they force a sharp distinction between control logic in a program and the actual production of the output data. In documentation, decision tables can concisely summarize the system or program in written form.

Advantages. Decision tables can serve as a compact means of describing or specifying operations. How compact they are depends on the number of conditions being included, and on the number of possible different actions that need to be taken. In general, the compactness of decision tables decreases about in proportion to the sum of the number of variables included and the number of possible actions.

Because of its compactness, the decision table provides a convenient way of tersely stating logically complex processing. The practical size for a single decision

table is approximately what can be put on one page of paper. Larger decision tables can be parsed and linked together. The procedures for creating decision tables provide rules for checking for four types of possible errors: completeness, size, redundancy, and inconsistency (London, 1972; Pollack et al., 1971). These offer valuable aids in systems design and programming, but people must go through the laborious process of doing most of the checking work (Hurley, 1980).

Decision tables can be used to summarize much information in documentation, but in this case are sometimes regarded as being too concise. In programming, their precision and conciseness are major advantages, when supported with additional documentation.

Disadvantages. Decision tables have no theoretical size limit, but there are real practical limits imposed by people. Large decision tables become incomprehensible, and can be neither checked nor used well by people. Fortunately, the size can usually be reduced by rule consolidation and by parsing.

Decision tables do not reduce the human labor of thinking or discovery. Human beings still must do the work of defining, specifying, and following to its logical consequences each chain of conditions and actions. Decision tables take away from people none of this arduous work, but they can be used to pinpoint where that work can be best concentrated (Hurley, 1980).

Decision tables ignore the delicate interleaving of logic and action that seems so natural when people think about conditions and actions to be taken. Decision tables force the human user to consider conditions separately from actions.

The advantages of decision tables are drawing an increasing number of supporters, but their disadvantages are sufficiently major to keep this group of users fairly small. Typically, the experience of the first-time user is that the time and effort put in must be increased in order to prepare the decision table. This additional investment may pay off in less debugging and in more efficient operations, as is usually the case for the experienced user of decision tables, but the additional investment by the novice user is difficult to justify.

REFERENCES

1967. Chapin, Ned "An Introduction to Decision Tables," *DPMA Quarterly,* **3,** *No. 3:* 2–23 (April).
1970. McDaniel, Herman (Ed.). *Applications of Decision Tables.* Philadelphia: Auerbach Publishers.
1971. Pollack, Solomon L., Hicks, Harry T., and Harrison, William J. *Decision Tables: Theory and Practice.* New York: Wiley.
1980. Hurley, Richard B. *Decision Tables for Programmers.* New York: Van Nostrand Reinhold.

```
00050 000480 PROCEDURE DIVISION.                                                    FIXPOP
00051 000490 000-INITIALIZE-FILES.                                                  FIXPOP
00052 000500     OPEN INPUT PCP-FILE CARDS-IN-FILE                                   FIXPOP
00053 000510         OUTPUT CARDS-IN-FILE.                                           FIXPOP
00054 000520     PERFORM 030-READ-A-CARD THRU 030-END-READ-CARD                      FIXPOP
00055 000530     GO TO 040-READ-A-POP-RECORD.                                        FIXPOP
00056 000539 010-DECIDE-DTOO. NOTE              DETAP/IMI VA-0 06/01/70              FIXPOP
00057 000540     DETAP  010-DECIDE                        00001 03 05 05             OP
00058 000550     RL1                            0  0  0  0  0                        OP
00059 000560     RL2                            1  2  3  4  5 $                      OP
00060 000570     CONDITION SECTION                                                  OP
00061 000580     C POP REC-COLUMN-1 EQUAL TO 'T'  Y  Y  Y  N  N                     OP
00062 000590     C POP-REC-COLUMN-3-7                                               OP
00063 000600         CARDS-IN-REC-TEST-NO       <  =  >  –  –                       OP
00064 000610     C WS-SEARCH-OR-PUNCH EQUAL TO   –  –  –  'S' 'P'                    OP
00065 000620     ACTION SECTION                                                     OP
00066 000630     A MOVE 'S' TO WS-SEARCH-OR-PUNCH           X                       OP
00067 000640     A MOVE 'P' TO WS-SEARCH-OR-PUNCH        X                          OP
00068 000650     A PERFORM 015-NOT-FOUND        X                                   OP
00069 000660     A PERFORM 020-PUNCH-A-CARD              X        X                 OP
00070 000670     A PERFORM 030-READ-A-CARD THRU                                     OP
00071 000680             030-END-READ-CARD      X  X                                OP
00072 000690     A GO TO 040-READ-A-POP-RECORD        X  X  X  X                    OP
00073 000700     A GO TO 010-DECIDE             X                                   OP
00074 000710     TEND.                                                              OP
00075 000712 010-DECIDE SECTION.                                                    FIXPOP
00076 000714 DT0000-1000.                                                           FIXPOP
00077 000716     IF POP-REC-COLUMN-1 EQUAL TO 'T' GO TO DT00001001.                 FIXPOP
00078 000718     IF WS-SEARCH-OR-PUNCH EQUAL TO 'S' GO TO AT00001004.               FIXPOP
00079 000720     IF WS-SEARCH-OR-PUNCH EQUAL TO 'P' TO AT00001005                   FIXPOP
00080 000722         ELSE GO TO EL00001001.                                         FIXPOP
00081 000724 DT00001001.                                                            FIXPOP
00082 000726     IF POP-REC-COLUMN-3-7 CARDS-IN-REC-TEST-NO                         FIXPOP
00083 000728         GO TO AT00001001.                                              FIXPOP
00084 000730     IF POP-REC-COLUMN-3-7 CARDS-IN-REC-TEXT-NO                         FIXPOP
00085 000732         GO TO AT00001003 ELSE GO TO AT00001002.                        FIXPOP
00086 000734 AT00001001.                                                            FIXPOP
00087 000736     PERFORM 015-NOT-FOUND.                                             FIXPOP
00088 000738     PERFORM 030-READ-A-CARD THRU 030-END-READ-CARD.                    FIXPOP
00089 000740     GO TO 010-DECIDE.                                                  FIXPOP
00090 000742 AT00001002.                                                            FIXPOP
00091 000744     MOVE 'P' TO WS-SEARCH-OR-PUNCH.                                    FIXPOP
00092 000746     PERFORM 020-PUNCH-A-CARD.                                          FIXPOP
00093 000748     PERFORM 030-READ-A-CARD THRU 030-END-READ-CARD.                    FIXPOP
00094 000750     GO TO 040-READ-A-POP-RECORD.                                       FIXPOP
00095 000752 AT00001003.                                                            FIXPOP
00096 000754     MOVE 'S' TO WS-SEARCH-OR-PUNCH                                     FIXPOP
00097 000756     GO TO 040-READ-A-POP-RECORD.                                       FIXPOP
00098 000758 AT00001004.                                                            FIXPOP
00099 000760     GO TO 040-READ-A-POP-RECORD.                                       FIXPOP
00100 000762 AT00001005.                                                            FIXPOP
00101 000764     PERFORM 020-PUNCH-A-CARD.                                          FIXPOP
00102 000766     GO TO 040-READ-A-POP-RECORD.                                       FIXPOP
00103 000768 EL00001001.                                                            FIXPOP
00104 000770     DISPLAY 'ELSE RULE NONE SPECIFIED-TBL = 010-DECIDE'.               FIXPOP
00105 000772     STOP RUN.                                                          FIXPOP
```

Fig. 1. Decision table in the Detab programming language. The source language (OP) written by the programmer becomes a comment in the Cobol code (FIXPOP) generated by the Detab processor. *(Courtesy Information Management, Inc.)*

LANGUAGES

For articles on related subjects *see* DECISION TABLES: Principles; PROCEDURE-ORIENTED LANGUAGES; and PROGRAMMING LANGUAGES.

A decision table language is a high-level programming language whose source code has, in major part, the appearance of (and also serves as) a decision table. A decision table language is a part of a decision table programming system, with the decision table language supported by a translator or a processor (or a series of them) which produces an executable machine language code equivalent to the logic in the decision tables presented to it.

Description. Decision table languages differ from other high-level languages in several respects. First, portions of the source language look like a decision table. This permits the programmer to write a program in a decision table form in part, as illustrated by the "OP" part of Fig. 1. When the analysis or design work has resulted in a decision table, using a decision table language expedites the programming and reduces programmer-introduced logic bugs. Even when the analysis or design work has not resulted in a decision table, using a decision table language for the programming helps provide a check on the completeness and consistency of the design.

Second, usually the supporting translators or processors are effectively preprocessors yielding Cobol or Fortran programs which are then compiled and executed. Third, decision table languages show great diversity among themselves, enough so that what is acceptable syntax in one is commonly unacceptable in most of the others.

Historically, the first decision table language was TABSOL, produced in 1961 by the Computer Department of the General Electric Company (Chapin, 1967). In 1962 and 1963, a Codasyl committee proposed a decision table language extension or addition to Cobol, called Detab-X, and later Detab/65 (Codasyl, 1962). A 1969 summary of the major decision table languages available to that year listed 32 offerings (McDaniel, 1970). The number has declined greatly since then because of disuse.

Features. A comparison of a selection of decision table languages, based on their major features, helps indicate their general characteristics (see Fig. 2).

Source Language. The programmer writes a decision table as the source code. The syntax identifies the parts.

Target Language. Most translators produce as their output a high-level language (such as Cobol) translation of the table input (see Fig. 1, for example).

Output from Translator. The translator produces a network of comparisons with conditional and unconditional transfers of control to replace the decision rules (see Fig. 1). The translator usually uses the programmer-provided stub wording directly in the comparisons and to identify the actions.

Entry Form. All decision table languages accept limited-entry decision tables, and a few accept extended- or mixed-entry tables.

Number of Rules. The maximum number of rules permitted is usually between 25 and 50.

"Else" Rule. Usually the "else" rule is optional.

Number of Conditions. The maximum number of conditions permitted is usually between 25 and 100.

Number of Actions. The maximum number of actions permitted is usually between 25 and 100.

Sequencing of Actions. Most provide only for unsequenced actions.

Diagnostics. The variety of diagnostics available from the translators is extensive, covering not only syntax, but also logical errors in the table.

Size Reduction. Most attempt to consolidate rules by use of the "don't care" entry, but none provide for table parsing.

Other Aids. Some of the translators are restricted to just the translation work, while others can tie into more comprehensive software packages.

Configuration. The minimum computer configuration needed for translation is the same as that required for the translation of the usual target language, such as Fortran or Cobol.

Characteristics	DDT— U. S. Navy	Detab— Information Management, Inc.	SMP— Trilog Associates, Inc.	Tabtran— Westinghouse Tele-Computer Systems, Inc.
Number of rules	25	50	20	40
"Else" rule	Yes	Optional	Optional	Optional
Number of conditions	25	50	>1000	100
Number of actions	25	50	>1000	<150
Action sequencing	Unsequenced	Either	Sequenced	Unsequenced
Completeness diagnostics	No	Yes	Yes	No

Fig. 2. Highlights of four major decision table languages.

REFERENCES

1962. CODASYL Systems Group. *DETAB-X*. Santa Monica, CA: CODASYL Systems Group.

1967. Chapin, Ned. "An Introduction to Decision Tables," *DPMA Quarterly* **3**, *No. 3:* 2–23 (April).

1970. McDaniel, Herman. *Decision Table Software*. Philadelphia: Auerbach Publishers.

NED CHAPIN

DECLARATIVE STATEMENT

For articles on related subjects *see* EXECUTABLE STATEMENT; PROCEDURE-ORIENTED LANGUAGES; PROGRAMMING LANGUAGES; and STATEMENTS.

A *declarative statement* is one in a high-level programming language that provides descriptive information (contrasted with an *imperative statement* that specifies explicit processing operations).

Besides specifying the actual computations, decision rules, and input/output operations involved in the implementation of a particular algorithm, a high-level language program also must provide the compiler with descriptive information that allows it to perform a variety of organizational tasks directly connected with the production of an executable object program. For example, the description of a variable (its name, together with the type of data to be stored in it) enables the compiler to allocate the proper amount of storage, associate its location with the variable's name, and set up any necessary data conversion mechanisms prior to the assignment of a value to that variable. (This description also defines the set of operations that are applicable to the element.) Similarly, the definition and description of a data file makes it possible for the compiler to establish a relationship between references to that file and a particular collection of data transmitted to or from a specific input/output device.

In most languages, this type of information is supplied through a series of special statements, which often are characterized as being *non-executable* (or more properly, *declarative*). Once defined, simple variables, arrays, files, and other items can be used throughout the program simply by alluding to their properties by use of their names.

To illustrate the type of information conveyed by declarative statements, consider the following Fortran program, which reads a number N and uses it to compute

$$Y = \sum_{X=1}^{N} X(1 + \sqrt{X}).$$

N and Y are printed with appropriate identification:

```
    INTEGER N
    REAL X,Y
    READ (5,8) N
    Y=0.0
    DO 6 I=1,N
     X=I
     Y=Y+X*(1.0+SQRT(X))
  6 CONTINUE
    WRITE(6,16) N,Y
  8 FORMAT(I2)
 16 FORMAT(' N = ',I2,4X,'Y = ',E12.5)
    END
```

The first two declarative statements (underlined) define the three variables and instigate the necessary storage allocation; statement number 8 describes the form in which the input value will be found (a 2-digit integer punched in the first two columns of a card), and statement 16 provides formatting information for the output. Associations with the respective READ and WRITE statements are provided by appropriate statement number references.

Many other languages provide similar declarative facilities which may be interspersed throughout the program. A notable exception is Cobol, in which the declarative facilities are much more formally structured: Each program must consist of four organizational divisions in a fixed order, the first three of which consist entirely of declarative statements.

S. V. POLLACK

DECREMENT

For article on related subject *see* ADDRESSING; and INDEX REGISTER.

The dictionary defines a decrement as a negative increment; correspondingly, in a computing system, a decrement is a value that is subtracted from the contents of a register.

The term was used in the IBM 704 system and in successor IBM 700 and 7000 systems to denote a field that occurred in instructions to manipulate the index registers. Fig. 1 shows the format of these 36-bit instructions.

For example, if the first three bits were 010, the instruction was TIX (Transfer on Index). The tag field specified an index register, and this instruction compared the decrement (i.e., the contents of the decrement field) with the contents of the index register. If the decrement D was

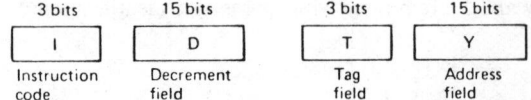

Fig. 1. Format of 36-bit instruction with decrement field.

smaller, the contents of the index register would be decreased (decremented) by the quantity D, and a transfer of control would occur to the address Y specified in the address field.

This class of computers, though very widely used, was almost unique in the use of subtracting rather than adding in connection with index registers. It was therefore appropriate to use decrements rather than increments in the index register with the modify-and-test instructions.

S. ROSEN

DECUS

For articles on related subjects *see* COMPUTER USER GROUPS; and DIGITAL EQUIPMENT CORPORATION PDP SERIES.

DECUS (The Digital Equipment Computer Users Society) is an organization of Digital Equipment Corporation (DEC) users whose objective is the exchange and dissemination of ideas and information pertinent to the use of DEC systems. DEC provides DECUS with administrative personnel and office space around the world.

Founded in 1961, DECUS is one of the largest computer user groups, with 35,000 members in 1980. In common with most such vendor-sponsored groups, membership is free—upon application—to owners of DEC computers and to their computer-interested employees.

DECUS maintains a program library with over 1,700 active programs. The library is available to members for the media fee and reproduction cost. Programs in the library range from enhanced editors and cross-compilers to statistical packages and games. Of particular interest to college and university customers, for example, might be a package of programs for registration, class scheduling, dormitory management, and annual giving records. A laboratory user could take advantage of various statistical packages, or programs that perform Fourier transforms or least squares fitting. There are programs for circuit analysis, resonance simulation, bloodcount evaluation, and stress testing, and scores of others which medical, scientific, or engineering customers could employ. Business people can find accounting packages,

case studies, and payroll programs among the library's offerings. In addition, of course, there is a wide range of data management, display graphics, and enhanced utility programs available.

DECUS has local, regional, and national organizations, as well as a number of Special Interest Groups. It sponsors a semi-annual national symposium which provides the stage for new product announcements and at which members give papers, participate in panel discussions, lead workshops, or conduct demonstrations for the benefit of other members.

DECUS also publishes newsletters focusing on special interests and proceedings of symposia presentations, as well as a society newsletter.

C. LICKTEIG

DEFAULT CONDITION

For articles on related subjects *see* EXPRESSION; PROCEDURE-ORIENTED LANGUAGES; and STATEMENTS.

A *default condition* or value is one set by software when a user elects not to make a choice that was available in a particular situation. Unlike its normal English usage, default carries no pejorative connotation; there is no suggestion that a person should have done something, merely that he or she *could* have. Some examples are:

1. The Fortran iteration statement DO 17 I = 1, 100 behaves as if the user had written DO 17 I = 1, 100, 1; i.e., the control variable (*q.v.*) I will be incremented by +1 by default since the step size is assumed to be +1 unless otherwise specified.

2. In Basic, subscripted variable references such as LET B (7) = 4 may be made without dimensioning B explicitly, provided the maximum subscript used does not exceed 10; i.e., Basic assumes an implicit DIM B (10) by default unless the programmer supplies a specific alternative.

3. In APL, the origin of all arrays is 1 by default, but the programmer may overrule this by inputting)ORIGIN *0.* (The only choices are 0 or 1.)

4. In Pascal, the heading **procedure** Zilch (*a,b* : integer); begins the definition of a procedure whose arguments a and b are called-by-value by default. The programmer could have elected call-by-reference by writing **procedure** Zilch (var *a, b* : integer);. Similarly, the default parameter passage in Algol 60 is call-by-name unless call-by-value is explicitly specified.

5. The Pascal statement **while** not eof **do**—acts like

while not eof(input) **do**—; i.e., the file whose end-of-file condition is being monitored is the "input" file by default though another file could have been specified.

Note that, in each of these situations, the language designers chose a default condition or value which, in their opinion, would be most commonly desired. Such a practice saves the user time by making it unnecessary to state the obvious. Not all default choices are benign, however, The language PL/I employs an unusually large number of default decisions and some of these can do insidious things to an inexperienced or careless user. A notorious example is the apparently innocuous expression 4EO*6EO, which could produce the strange result 2E1 (i.e., $4 \times 6 = 20$), since the default precision of the product, one significant digit, would be no more than the precision of the most precise number in the expression. Despite such occasional aberrations, the judicious use of default conditions facilitates rather than impedes programming productivity.

E. D. REILLY, JR.

DEFENSE ADVANCED RESEARCH PROJECTS AGENCY. *See* ARPA NETWORK.

DELAY-LINE MEMORY. *See* ULTRASONIC MEMORY.

DELIMITER

For article on related subject *see* PROCEDURE-ORIENTED LANGUAGES.

A delimiter is an item of lexical information whose form and/or position in a source program denotes the boundary between adjacent syntactic components of that program.

As is true with natural language, the *meaning* and clarity of statements in high-level programming languages often depend on the inclusion of explicit indicators that "punctuate" the statement; such signals are termed *delimiters*. Since high-level language statements must be processed by a compiler whose analytical and interpretive facilities must function without the equivalent of human cognition, it is necessary to equip programming languages with a fairly extensive variety of such delimiters, many of them highly specific. The most common of these, naturally, is the blank space, whose function as a separator is self-explanatory. Some languages, however, like

Fortran, ignore blanks; more common are languages which tolerate superfluous blanks between syntactic components.

Parentheses also represent a commonly used type of delimiter. One of their primary purposes in high-level languages parallels traditional mathematical usage; i.e., to define the extent of a component in a computational expression. For example, the use of parentheses in the ordinary arithmetic expression.

$$A + B(C - 2D) \qquad (1)$$

is clearly paralleled by the equivalent in many high-level languages. For example,

$$A + B * (C - 2 * D) \qquad (2)$$

Many programming languages provide a relatively free physical format where there is no intrinsic association with a specific input medium, such as the punched card or teletypewriter. Consequently, there is no implicit correspondence in such languages between the end of a statement and the physical boundary of the medium, thus necessitating the use of explicit delimiters. The semicolon serves that purpose in PL/I and Pascal, for example, so that a statement in those languages may be defined operationally as a string of characters between two semicolons (although, in Pascal, the semicolons are really *separators* not delimeters). Similarly, the period delimits certain types of Cobol statements.

In block-oriented languages such as PL/I and Pascal, special delimiters are provided to indicate the boundaries of major structural components. For instance, an arbitrarily long sequence of PL/I statements may be identified as a *compound* statement in certain contexts by using the delimiting statements DO and END at the beginning and end of the grouping, respectively. Similarly, a PL/I procedure is bracketed by PROCEDURE and END statements. **begin** and **end** provide the same function in Pascal.

S. V. POLLACK

DESIGN, LOGICAL. *See* LOGIC DESIGN.

DESK CALCULATOR. *See* CALCULATOR, DESK.

DIAGNOSTICS

For articles on related subjects *see* DEBUGGING; ERRORS; and MICROPROGRAMMING.

Diagnostics help determine whether there are hardware faults in a computer or errors in user programs.

Hardware diagnostics are programs designed to determine whether the components of a computer are operating properly. Circuit components are electronically exercised individually and in groups to try to induce failures. When a failure is detected, the location of the faulty element is printed and the maintenance staff can repair or replace the element. Diagnostics may test communication lines and controllers. Microcomputers may be constructed with diagnostics stored in the ROM.

Hardware diagnostic programs are run as part of a regular schedule of preventive maintenance and in the event of a failure. If a serious hardware failure has occurred, the diagnostic program may fail to operate properly, and may be useless in locating the difficulty.

Increasingly, hardware diagnostics take the form of *microdiagnostics*. A microdiagnostic program is a microprogram that tests a specific hardware component such as a bus or storage location. Microdiagnostics often provide more accurate location of a fault than hardware diagnostics written in machine language because of the addressability of individual components under microprogramming. Furthermore, these diagnostic programs are so fast that preventive maintenance testing may be interspersed transparently with other processing. Microdiagnostics, consequently, have furthered the development of self-diagnosing and self-repairing computers.

Diagnostic messages in software refer to the error messages produced by compilers, utilities, and operating system software. These messages are designed to give programmers an indication of where their programs are at fault. Diagnostic messages at compile time may only be warnings to the programmer, or they may indicate invalid syntax, which prohibits execution. A severity level indicator is often included in the diagnostic message.

Execution-time diagnostic messages are produced by the operating system or an execution-time monitor. These messages indicate attempts to perform illegal operations, such as dividing by zero, taking the square root of a negative number, illegal operation codes, illegal address references, and so on. The diagnostic message may be followed by program termination.

Finally, application programs may produce diagnostics when erroneous control cards or data cards are read. The creator of the application program has complete control over these diagnostic messages and the action taken.

Diagnostic messages should avoid negative tones and be non-threatening, specific, and constructive. Instead of just pointing out what is wrong, they should also tell the user what to do to set things right.

B. SHNEIDERMAN

DIFFERENTIAL ANALYZER

For articles on related subjects *see* ANALOG COMPUTERS; and DIGITAL COMPUTERS: Early.

In a paper published in the *Journal of the Franklin Institute* in 1931, Vannevar Bush described a machine (Fig. 1) that had been constructed under his direction at M.I.T. for the purpose of solving ordinary differential equations. He christened the machine a *differential analyzer*. This was what would now be called an "analog" computer, and was based on the use of mechanical integrators that could be interconnected in any desired manner. The integrator was in essence a variable-speed gear, and took the form of a rotating horizontal disk on which a small knife-edged wheel rested. The wheel was driven by friction, and the gear ratio was altered by varying the distance of the wheel from the axis of rotation of the disk. The principle is illustrated in Fig. 2.

The use of mechanical integrators for solving differential equations had been suggested by Kelvin, and various special-purpose integrating devices were constructed at various times. Bush's differential analyzer was, however, the first device of sufficiently general application to meet a genuine need, and in the period immediately before and during World War II quite a number of these devices were constructed. The one shown in Fig. 4 was installed at the Mathematical Laboratory in Cambridge, England.

In order to make a practical device, it is necessary to have some means of amplifying the small amount of torque available from the rotating wheel. Bush used a torque amplifier, working on the principle of the ship's capstan, but adapting it for continuous rotation. Fig. 3 is taken from his report (1931) and sufficiently indicates the principle. The friction drums are rotated in opposite directions by a continuously running motor of sufficient power. When the input shaft is turned, one of the cords

Fig. 1. Vannevar Bush shown with the M.I.T. differential analyzer.

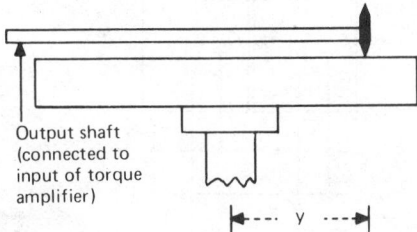

Fig. 2. Wheel and disk integrator. If the disk turns through an angle proportional of x, the output shaft turns through an angle proportional to $\int y\, dx$.

attached to the input arm begins to tighten on the friction drum round which it is wrapped. Which cord tightens depends on the direction of rotation of the input shaft. A very small tightening, and hence a very small tension in the end of the cord attached to the input arm, is sufficient, in view of the friction of the rotating drum, to produce a large tension in the end attached to the output arm. A small torque applied to the input shaft is thus ca-

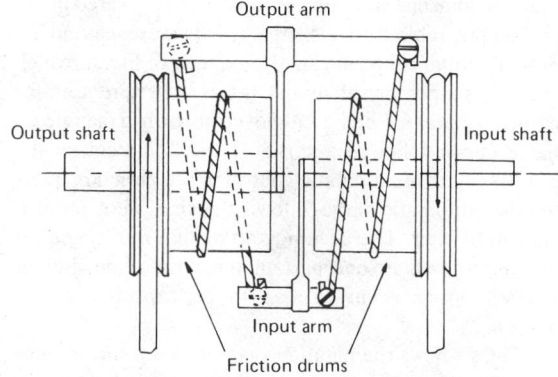

Fig. 3. Principle of torque amplifier. *(Courtesy of Journal of the Franklin Institute.)*

pable of producing a much larger torque in the output shaft.

The integrators and torque amplifiers can be clearly seen in Fig. 4, together with the system of shafting used for effecting the connections. Changing the problem was

1 Input table   3 Shafts and gears used   4 Torque amplifier
2 Output table   for interconnection   5 Integrator disk

Fig. 4. The differential analyzer system, showing integrators, torque amplifiers, and shafting.

a job for someone who did not mind hands covered in oil. The output table on which the results were plotted directly in graphical form can also be seen in Fig. 4, which also shows a number of similar tables that were used for input, an operator being employed to turn a handle so that a cursor followed a curve. It is a comment on the primitive state of automatic control in the period in question that automatic curve-following devices were not provided until later. The accuracy attainable in a single integrator was about one part in three thousand, but of course a lower accuracy was to be expected in the solution.

Fig. 5 shows the notation that was used for an integrator and Fig. 6 shows how two integrators could be interconnected to solve a simple differential equation. It was not difficult to arrive at a diagram such as Fig. 6, even for a complicated equation, but working out the gear ratios required was a distinctly tedious task calling for some experience, particularly as accuracy required that full use should be made of the available range of integrator motion.

In 1945, Bush and S. H. Caldwell described a new differential analyzer in which interconnection between the integrators was effected electrically instead of mechanically. However, during the decade that followed, competition from electronic analog computers and from digital computers began to build up, and although the new machine ran for a number of years at M.I.T., by 1955 the mechanical differential analyzer was already obsolete.

Digital Differential Analyzer. This device is based on the use of a *rate multiplier* as an integrator. In a rate multiplier a constant quantity y is held in a register and, on the receipt of an input pulse, is added to the number standing in an accumulator. If input pulses arrive at a rate R, overflow pulses will emerge from the most significant end of the accumulator at a rate proportional to yR. If y now varies and if input pulses arrive whenever a certain other variable x increases by δx, the number of output pulses emerging is proportional to $\Sigma y \, \delta x$ or, approximately, to $\int y \, dx$. Thus, the device serves as an integrator. Normally, δx is equal to one unit in the least

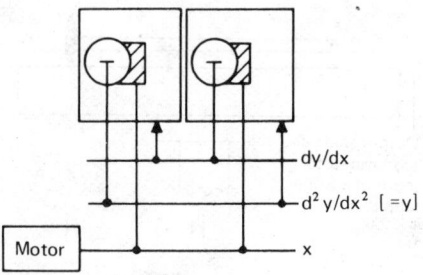

Fig 6.   Setup for solving the equation $d^2y/dx^2 = y$.

significant place, and continuously updated values of the variable x can be obtained by feeding the pulses into an accumulator.

The first digital differential analyzer was the MADDIDA developed in 1949 at the Northrop Aircraft Corporation. It had 44 integrators implemented using a magnetic drum for storage, the addition being done serially. There were six tracks in all on the drum, one being used for synchronizing purposes. The problem was specified by writing an appropriate pattern of bits onto one of the tracks. Compared with the digital computers then being built, the MADDIDA was on an impressively small scale. It lost some of its simplicity, however, when adequate input and output devices were added, and in the end competition from general-purpose digital computers proved too much for it. The MADDIDA and its descendants did not, therefore, have the bright future in scientific computation that was predicted for them. However, digital differential analyzers of a simple kind continue to have a place in certain control applications.

REFERENCES

1931. Bush, V. *J. Frank. Inst.* **212**: 447.
1945. Bush, V. and Caldwell, S. H. *J. Frank. Inst.* **240**: 255.
1947. Crank, J. *The Differential Analyser*. London: Longmans, Green and Co.
1962. Huskey, H. D., and Korn, G. A. *Computer Handbook*. New York: McGraw-Hill, pp.19–14.

M. V. WILKES

DIGITAL COMPUTERS

GENERAL PRINCIPLES

For articles on related subjects see ANALOG COMPUTERS; ARITHMETIC-LOGIC UNIT; CENTRAL PRO-

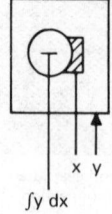

Fig. 5.   Schematic notation for an integrator.

CESSING UNIT; COMPUTER ARCHITECTURE; HYBRID COMPUTERS; MEMORY: Auxiliary; MEMORY: Main; MICROPROCESSORS AND MICROCOMPUTERS; MINICOMPUTERS; PERSONAL COMPUTING; SPECIAL-PURPOSE COMPUTERS; and SUPERCOMPUTERS.

The digital computer is a machine, a machine that will accept data and information presented to it in its required form; carry out arithmetic, transfer, and logical operations on this raw material; and then supply the required results in an acceptable form. The resulting information (output) produced by these operations is entirely dependent upon the accepted information (input). Thus, correct and complete answers cannot be obtained unless correct and sufficient input data has been provided.

The sequence of the operations required to produce the desired output must be accurately determined and specified by people known as system designers (or analysts) and programmers. The system designer produces a clear specification of the task to be undertaken, including elements such as clerical processing, which do not involve the computer directly. The programmer prepares the detailed set of instructions for the computer, and will follow it automatically and process the work from input to output.

Computer Characteristics. The main characteristics of the computer are identified as automatic, general purpose, electronic, and digital.

Automatic. We assume that a machine is automatic if it works by itself without human intervention. But this is not the whole story. Computers are machines and have no will of their own; they cannot start themselves; they cannot go out and find their own problems and solutions. They have to be instructed. They are, however, automatic, in that once started on a job, they will carry on until it is finished, normally without human assistance.

A computer works from a program of *coded* instructions that specify exactly how a particular job is to be done. While the job is in progress, the program is *stored* in the computer, and the parts of the instructions are obeyed. As soon as one instruction is completed, the next is obeyed automatically.

By contrast, a hand-held calculator can be described as semi-automatic. The user sets up the required numbers on a keyboard and has to press a key (for example, add or multiply) to initiate each individual arithmetic operation. Today's calculators can often carry out complex arithmetic operations at the touch of a single key, but the machine is still semi-automatic.

Because a computer does not need to stop between single operations, it can take full advantage of the high-speed components that enable it to add, subtract, and perform other individual operations in millionths of a second, or even faster.

An important corollary of the automaticity of the computer is that its program has to be complete. If there is no provision for intervention by the human operator, the program must be written to provide for all possible eventualities, however rare.

General Purpose. Computers (and hand-held calculators, though they are rarely described as such) are *general-purpose* machines. In other words, a computer can do any job that its programmer can break down into suitable basic operations. Put a payroll program into a computer and you make it, for the time being, a special-purpose payroll machine. Replace the program by one for inverting a matrix, and you make the computer temporarily a special-purpose mathematical machine.

Electronic. The word *electronic* refers, of course, to the components of the machine. It is the nature of the electronic components that make possible the very high speeds of individual operations in modern computers.

The history of electronic digital computers distinguishes a number of "generations" defined by the nature of the electronic components most prevalent in each. Thus, the first generation made extensive use of vacuum tubes, the second generation used discrete transistors, and the third used integrated circuits. There is little agreement about whether we are now on the fourth or fifth generation, or even at some midway point, as we have moved through progressively higher degrees of integration in our circuits.

Most computer users need no special knowledge of electronics, and the major practical distinctions between the generations—as far as they are concerned—are the reductions in size for a given power, the rapid increases in speed, and, above all, a substantial and continuous fall in the cost of computing.

Digital. A computer may be either *digital* or *analog.* The two types do have some principles in common, but they employ different types of data representations and are, in general, suited to different kinds of work. Digital computers are so called because they work with *numbers* in the form of separate discrete digits. More precisely, they work with information that is in digital or character form, including alphabetic and other symbols as well as numbers.

In a digital machine, the data, whether numbers, letters, or other symbols, is represented in digital form. An analog computer, on the other hand, may be said to deal with a "model" of the problem, in which the variables are represented by continuous physical quantities such as angular position and voltage. The decimal numbers 136 and

435, for instance, might be represented by 1.36 volts and 4.35 volts. Using familiar devices, we could say that a slide rule is an analog device, because numbers are represented by a linear length. The abacus, on the other hand, is a digital device, because movable counters are used for calculating.

Digital computers differ from analog computers much as counting differs in principle from measuring. Both types of machines employ electric currents, or signals, but in the analog system, a number is represented by the magnitude (e.g., voltage) of a signal, whereas, in a digital computer, it is not the magnitude of signals that is important, but rather the number of them, or their presence or absence in particular positions. Analog computers tend to be special-purpose machines designed for some specific scientific or technical application. They are frequently found useful in engineering design for such things as atomic power stations, chemical plants, and aircraft. In commercial and administrative data processing and for mathematical computation, we are concerned almost exclusively with digital computers.

Main Units. Only very rarely does a computer have a unique, fixed specification. Normally, it is better described as a computer system, consisting of a selection from a wide variety of units appropriate to meet a defined need. The principal groupings of these units commonly follow the pattern shown in Fig. 1 and are defined as follows.

1. *Input Units.* An input unit accepts the data, the raw material that a computer uses, communicated from outside. It is the actual means by which information is converted into electronic pulses, which are then fed into the machine's memory.
2. *Control Unit.* The directing force of the computer, the automatic operator, is the control unit. It provides the means of communication within the machine, by moving, advancing, or transferring information. It switches and integrates the various units into a whole system.
3. *Main Memory Unit.* All information is stored in

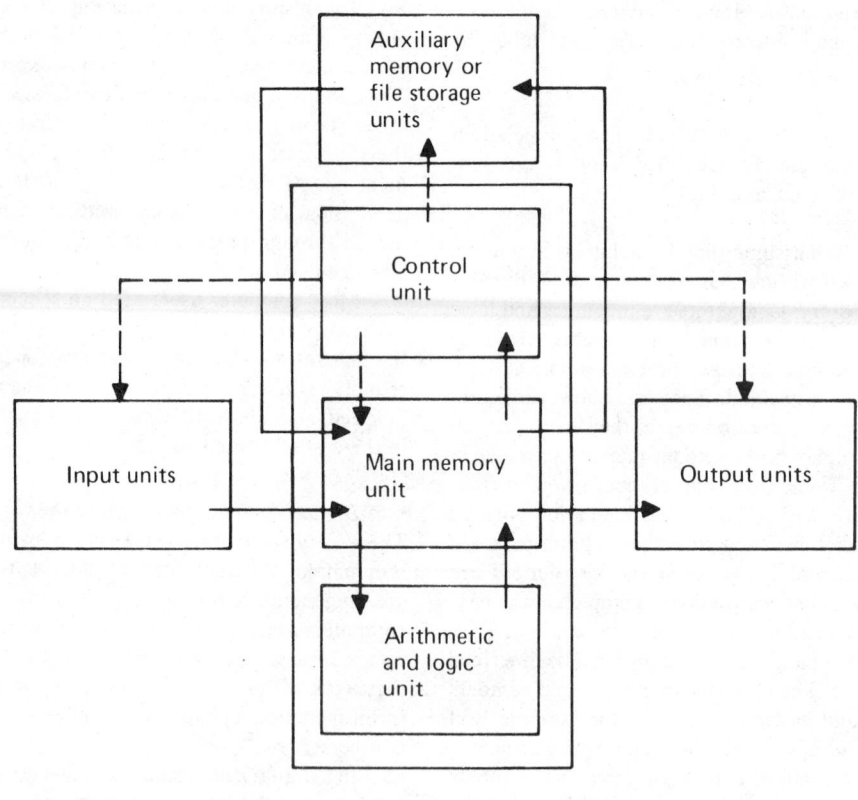

Legend:
⟶ Flow of information
--→ Control links

Fig. 1.   Central processing unit. Grouping of computer components.

the main memory unit and is "remembered" and made available to other units as required, under the direction of the control unit.

4. *Arithmetic-Logic Unit.* This unit performs the four arithmetic operations of add, subtract, multiply, and divide. By determining whether one number is larger than another, whether it is zero or whether it is positive or negative, it is said to have logical abilities; i.e., it can make logical decisions. In addition, it can sometimes perform other strictly logical operations.

5. *Output Units.* After information is processed, an output unit communicates it to the outside world. When needed, the results are recalled from memory under the direction of the control unit and presented by the output units in an appropriate form. A wide variety of output devices is available.

6. *File Storage Units.* These units store information required for reference.

We will now consider each of these main units in some detail.

Input. Input devices accept data from the world outside the computer and transfer it in suitably coded form into the memory, a process frequently described as *data capture.* A very high proportion of input data is prepared by the operation of a typewriter-like keyboard. This may be linked directly to the computer either from an adjacent room or remotely over a telephone line. Alternatively, there may be some intermediate carrier of the data, such as punched cards or magnetic tape or disks. In each case, the data preparation device produces a coded representation of the keyed data, which is recorded on the carrier medium in the form of punched holes or magnetized blips. These are subsequently scanned by an appropriate reading device and signals transferred at high speed into the computer's memory.

A data preparation process that depends on a manual typing operation is clearly expensive and error-prone. Since most original data appears as ink on paper, devices that can read such data automatically have a great attraction and *document readers* play an increasingly important part in the input process.

These readers are capable of feeding documents one by one and scanning numbers or letters printed in suitable type fonts. The first readers were developed for handling checks and read characters printed along the bottom of the check in a magnetized ink. When the characters pass the reading mechanism of the input unit, the shape of the magnetic field produced by each character is assessed by the reader and the character identified. Without such readers, the processing of today's

enormous volumes of checks would be quite impracticable.

Today, there are many "optical" readers capable of recognizing the shape of a character from its reflected light in much the same way as we humans do. They use type fonts that appear quite normal to us and, therefore, serve both the needs of people and computers. There are also readers that scan the bar codes increasingly found on packages in supermarkets and that, therefore, greatly speed up the check-out procedures.

Some progress has been made with voice recognition equipment that today's computers can recognize "their master's voice" in a limited repertoire of input messages.

Central Processing Unit (CPU). The central processing unit is the focal point of the computer system. It receives data from input units and file storage units, carries out a variety of arithmetic and logical operations on this data, and transmits results to output and file units. It is traditional, and still convenient, to consider the central processor as made up of three principal parts (not necessarily easily identifiable physically): (1) the memory; (2) the arithmetic-logic unit; and (3) the control unit.

The Memory. The *memory* (or *main memory,* as it is sometimes called to distinguish it from file storage or auxiliary memory) is able to hold, for as long as desired, coded representations of numbers and letters in convenient groupings; each group is held in a uniquely addressable part of the memory, from which it can be transferred on demand. The memory may be figuratively described as a large number of pigeonholes, each identifiable by a serial number that in effect is its address.

One purpose of the memory is to hold data. Numbers and letters flow into it from input, are sent for arithmetic processing to the arithmetic unit from which the results return to the memory, and the output information is stored in it before transfer to an output unit.

The access time to data in the internal memory is important. The memory is a vital crossroad in processing, and the very high-speed arithmetic facilities of the machine demand virtually instantaneous access to data. Typically, memories can supply requested data in an incredibly short time, measured in microseconds (millionths of a second) or nanoseconds (billionths of a second); in fact, their speed is usually from 8 μs down to 200 ns or less.

The second use of the memory is to hold all the instructions of the program required to carry out a job. These instructions are normally coded in numeric form and can be read into the memory from punched cards, magnetic tape, or any other input medium. They remain in memory indefinitely unless they are deliberately erased.

The Arithmetic-Logic Unit (ALU). This is obviously one of the simplest parts of the machine to understand. It is that part where actual arithmetic operations are carried out. It is quite common to find a machine that can add a pair of eight-digit numbers is about one millionth of a second, and there are models that can do the job in as little as one ten billionth of a second!

The term *logic* is used here to describe a non-arithmetic facility of the unit; e.g., an ability to differentiate between positive and negative numbers, and, as a result, to take alternative paths in the program. A simple example will illustrate its value.

In stock control, it is usual to compare a newly calculated stock balance with the preset minimum or danger level, to determine if reordering is necessary. If the "minimum" is subtracted from the "balance," then a positive (excess) result indicates that all is well; a negative result (a shortage) shows a need to reorder. In this latter case only, we can arrange for the machine to "jump to" (i.e., transfer operational control to) a part of the program that prints out reordering information on the printer for management action. If all is well, we need print nothing—one way in which the computer itself can reduce paperwork. This apparently simple facility is of fundamental significance, and a typical program of a few thousand instructions will contain many of the "test and jump to another phase of the program if negative" types of instruction.

The arithmetic and logic unit consists of one or a number of *registers* (each made up of electronic circuits), which may be termed *accumulators.* To add a number stored in address 113 of the memory to that stored in address 207, first the contents of address 113 are read into the accumulator and then the contents of address 207 are added to the accumulator. The answer is then copied to another address in memory, thereby leaving the accumulator free for the next operation.

The Control Unit. This part of the central processor functions so as to cause the whole machine to operate according to the instructions in the program. Instructions are normally transferred sequentially from the memory to the control unit, where each instruction is interpreted and the appropriate circuits are activated to "execute" the instruction. This strict sequence is broken, for example, when a "test and jump" type of instruction occurs and produces an exceptional result. There is then a transfer of control to a program step in a different part of the program, from which the sequential pattern continues until again broken.

The control unit of a computer contains special circuits known as *microprograms.* One of these corresponds to each type of elementary operation (and, therefore, to each type of instruction) in the computer repertoire. It is by the inclusion of a suitable microprogram that a given operation is "built" into the computer.

Output. The output devices of the computer enable it to communicate results to the outside world. Output devices fall into two main categories:

1. Those which produce output which is readily handled and understood by human beings (printers and display units).
2. Auxiliary storage devices, which hold data intended for further processing by machine (e.g., magnetic tapes, disks and drums).

The first group contains a number of types of device. The most obvious of these are printers, designed to produce results in the form of printing on paper.

Most printers in current use operate on the same basic principle as the typewriter, in which a character is printed through an impact of a typeface on an inked ribbon traversing the paper. There are, however, some printers that generate and print characters electronically.

Where the volume of printing is large, it is usual to use a *line printer,* one capable of producing a whole line of print at a time (usually from 120 to 160 characters). Such printers are capable of quite high speeds, typically up to 20 or more lines per second on a continuously fed roll of stationery. It is essential, or course, to have excellent paper-handling facilities to keep pace with such speeds. Such line printers (Fig. 2) are ideal for applications requiring voluminous end-results such as payrolls, invoices, or inventory listings, but are too often used to print more than necessary. Typewriter-like devices are extensively used for low-volume printed output, and their keyboards permit them to double as input units as well. These devices may be situated close to the computer or at

Fig. 2.   An IBM 3262 line printer.

Fig. 3. An IBM 3101 video display terminal.

a remote point, receiving the output messages over a telephone line.

A related device, which is quite commonplace, is the video display unit (Fig. 3). This has a keyboard like a typewriter, but the printing mechanism is replaced by a television-like tube on which letters or digits can be projected. Compared with the typewriter, VDUs have the advantage of displaying a large amount of information at once (often, several hundred characters), and a fresh display of additional information can be generated very rapidly. On the other hand, since they cannot produce "hard copy" (i.e., a permanent record), they are best used in circumstances where an operator needs to examine a small quantity of transient output information that does not have to be printed.

Video display units can also be used to display information in graphical form or in diagrams of moderate accuracy. Associated input techniques using a lightpen (a device that effectively draws lines electronically on the face of the tube) manipulate changes or additions to drawings and diagrams. Devices such as the lightpen are increasingly being used for computer-aided design in such fields as car body or electric-circuit design.

Where a permanent record of a graph or drawing is required, or where greater accuracy is needed, a graph-plotter can be attached to the computer and can produce intricate drawings on paper.

Results from one computer operation often need to be stored temporarily and then used as an input to a subsequent process. Magnetic tape (described in detail under *Storage Media*) is frequently used for this purpose. For

example, process A may produce payroll information that will subsequently be used as input to process B for a labor cost analysis. Magnetic tape may also be produced as an intermediary to carry data to other machines being operated "off-line" (i.e., not directly linked to the computer). These could include numerically controlled machine tools, printers, graph plotters, type-setting machines, etc.

File Storage (or Auxiliary Memory). There are relatively few applications of computers, particularly in the field of business data processing where the only input is fresh, raw data. For example, in inventory control, the new data consists of stock issues and receipts, but data in file storage indicates the number of items left in stock calculated at last inventory and the average value of that stock. These files also include more static information about each item, such as its name, dimensions, batch order quantity, and supplier.

Thus, the computer must also have its "filing cabinets" (albeit electronic ones) if it is to be used in business applications. It is obvious that such file storage units must act as input and output units to the computer, and as they are of special and fundamental importance in these applications, they are treated here separately.

The three most important factors relating to any filing system whether manual or electronic, are (1) its total capacity; (2) the speed of access to required information (i.e., how long it takes to find what is needed); and (3) the cost per unit of data. The two most commonly used media for holding computer files are magnetic tapes and magnetic disks. Each system has its advantages and disadvantages, and the choice depends on the particular circumstances; many installations indeed use both.

Magnetic tape holds records in a serial fashion in a way analogous to a domestic tape recorder. Thus, if the records are in no particular sequence, the user is forced to hunt backward and forward along the tape for any desired record. Although tape moves quite quickly on a computer tape unit (up to 12 feet or so per second), a reel of tape is usually 2,400 feet long and contains many thousands of records. (A 1-inch length of tape can accommodate up to 800 or more characters.) Thus, minutes could easily elapse between the location of succeeding required records. It is obvious, therefore, that the records in a magnetic tape file must be held in some predetermined sequence, such as employee number or customer number sequence, and that the new data being input in order to bring the file up to date (to "update" the file) must also be in the same sequence.

When used for file storage, magnetic tape units (Fig. 4) are generally operated in pairs—one carrying the brought-forward or current file, which is read by the machine; the other, a new carry-forward or updated file recorded or "written" by the machine, which, in turn, will become the brought-forward file when the job is next run. (Unaffected items on the brought-forward tape are obviously copied unchanged onto the carried-forward tape.)

Magnetic tape units (or *decks,* or *transports,* or *stations*) differ widely in performance (and price!), with reading and writing speeds varying from about 10,000 characters per second through a common speed of about 60,000 characters per second to a maximum speed of over 100,000 characters per second. Obviously, a tape system offers virtually unlimited file capacity at low cost per record, but it is not an acceptable medium when immediate random access is required to every item in the file.

There are two basic forms of the *disk* unit: In one the disks are usually large (over 3 feet in diameter) and are not removable from the unit; in the other, the "removable disk," or *disk pack,* system (Fig. 5) the disks are smaller (about 20 inches in diameter) and are demountable, usually in sets of 6 to 12. This is analogous to putting six phonograph records on a player that is equipped with one pickup for each of the surfaces of the set. (Computers can "play" their disks on both sides without inverting them!).

Unlike the phonograph record, which has one track

Fig. 4. ICL 1906A computer system at Oxford University.

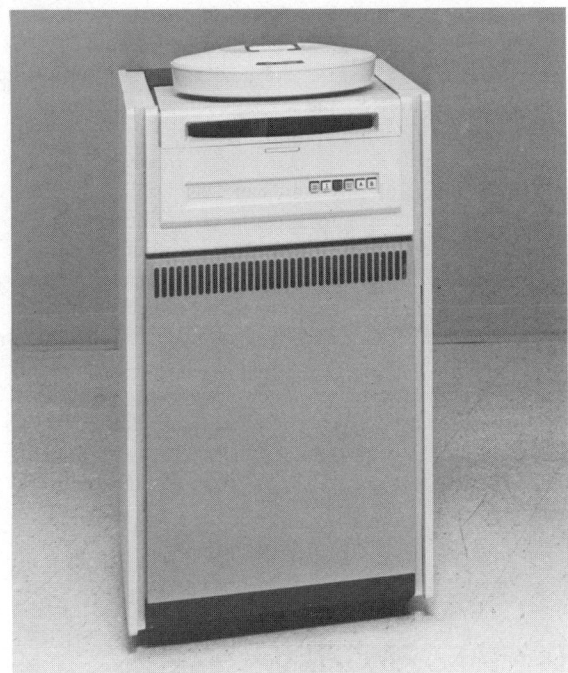

Fig. 5. A Digital Equipment Corporation RK06 disk pack drive.

spiraling from the periphery toward the center, the computer disk has a large number of concentric tracks on its surface, each capable of storing about 10,000 characters. The pick-up, or "recording head" can be moved radially across the disk surface to the desired track at very high speed. The total capacity of a set of six removable disks is usually about 60 million characters, and the recording head can move from one track to any other so quickly that direct access to any record at random can be obtained in about one-tenth of a second, or even less in some cases. For non-removable disk units, the capacity may be as large as 300 million characters.

Thus, disks offer the facility of processing data in random sequence without any undue delay in searching for a required item. However, their capacity is much more limited than magnetic tape and their cost is higher. In addition, the fact that essentially random access is possible means that, in contrast to magnetic tapes, data can be corrected or changed and the modified record can be put back on the disk in the same place that it originally occupied. One disadvantage is that the modified data could create an overflow problem, and then a way must be found to correct it.

A third type of disk is frequently used with small computers. This is the so-called "floppy" or "flexi" disk. It is roughly the same size as a 45 rpm phonograph record but is much thinner and very flexible. It doesn't operate to such fine tolerances as its bigger brothers and is much more robust—a floppy disk can easily be mailed in a stout envelope. A typical floppy disk has a storage capacity of about one million characters to which access can be made in about 100 milliseconds.

There are many facets to the problem of choosing between tape and disk for file storage. The simplest basis for choosing one over the other is that tape methods are in general cheaper, whereas disk systems offer greater speed and flexibility in the processing method, especially where the files must be frequently interrogated. Obviously, the choice depends on the application.

Another medium (although less important than tape or disk) used for file storage is the *magnetic drum*. Historically, it is interesting to note that, in early computers, a magnetic drum frequently provided the main memory. Its speed of access, however, was such that other processing units were frequently kept waiting for instructions and data, so it was replaced in favor by magnetic core or semiconductor stores.

However, this inherent limitation does not affect its use as a file store, now that drums of large capacity (up to twenty million characters and more) have been developed.

On a magnetic drum, the curved surface of a rapidly rotating cylinder is the recording medium. There are a large number of magnetic heads, each of which can read and write data on the drum. Each head is associated with a specific recording track that extends around the circumference of the drum. In many respects, the principles of operation and use of the magnetic drum are similar to those for the magnetic disk, but there are the following important differences.

1. Since there is usually a recording head for every track, no time is lost in the physical movement of heads to a required track.
2. A typical drum rotates about three or four times as fast as a magnetic disk system, which means that less time is lost waiting for the required data to come around to the recording head. Since each track has its own recording head, the fast rotation means that drums have a much shorter access time than disks.
3. Drums are more expensive per record stored than are disks. Moreover, they are permanently attached and are not exchangeable.

There are a variety of other file storage devices, in addition to the more common ones discussed above. The struggle in many business applications is always to accommodate larger and larger files with an acceptable access time without paying too high a price.

Distributed Computing, Computer Networks. In the earliest days of the computer, its power was confined to the computer room. Bundles of work had to be physically brought to it and results collected. A vital step in releasing the power of the computer occurred when terminal devices such as teletypes were connected to the computer over telephone lines. The problems to be solved were with the physical connection of the communications equipment and the writing of very sophisticated computer programs to control and manage an ever-increasing number of terminal devices.

The development first of minicomputers and today of the microprocessor and microcomputer have made it possible to build more "intelligence" (or local computing power) into the remote terminal devices so that they have become capable of carrying out more complex operations. For example, magnetic tape, card, or document readers may be used at a distant point for "remote job entry" and results fed back for local printing.

It is but a small step from this to the provision of computer facilities at the distant location so that many simple, routine tasks can be carried out locally and the communications facilities used either to feed results to the central installation or to make use of its greater power and wider facilities when necessary. It is then a further, relatively small step to conceive the idea of interconnecting a series of computers to form a network, passing work between themselves to be processed most economically where the most appropriate facilities are available. Again, the major obstacle was not just the physical interconnection but also the management and control of the entire system both within the computers themselves and over the telecommunications systems. Such networks now exist on both national and international scales, frequently using satellite communication facilities, and have reached the point where a user may not know, and need not know, on which computer the work is actually being processed.

Microprocessors and Microcomputers.
The foregoing applies in principle to all computer systems, however large or small. Under the heading *Electronic* in the section on *Computer Characteristics*, there is reference to the increasing scale of integration in computer circuits. This integration has now reached the stage where thousands of minute components and the printed wiring to interconnect them can be formed on the well-publicized "chip"—a thin slice of silicon about 0.5 cm square. The components include transistors, resistors, and capacitors, which are the raw material from which the computer's registers, arithmetic unit, control unit, and memory can be made.

The effect of achieving such a high packing density of components (or, as it is known, LSI, large-scale integration) is to make it possible to produce a complete processor or small memory unit on a single chip.

The implications of this are of quite fundamental importance since, with a cost per chip ranging from tens to a few hundred dollars, it enables computing power to be built into a wide variety of devices for use in offices, factories, laboratories, and even the home, and, indeed, to put a personal computer well within the range of purchase of many.

The effects of this increasing availability of cheap computing power are to cause a proliferation of more "intelligent" machines and to raise questions about the attendant social implications for both good and ill. In particular, there is great debate about the effects on employment. The word processor, for example, can greatly improve the productivity of a typist and, hence, theoretically reduce the number of available jobs. At the same time, the boring, routine aspects of many jobs such as typing can be eliminated and, indeed, new jobs created in the manufacture and use of new products hitherto undreamed of.

G. J. MORRIS

DIGITAL COMPUTERS: HISTORY

ORIGINS

For articles on related subjects *see* AIKEN, HOWARD; BABBAGE, CHARLES; DIGITAL COMPUTERS: Contemporary and Future, and Early; ECKERT, J. PRESPER; EDVAC; ENIAC; HOLLERITH, HERMAN; LEIBNIZ, GOTTFRIED WILHELM VON; MARK I; MAUCHLY, JOHN W.; PASCAL, BLAISE; STORED PROGRAM CONCEPT; TURING, ALAN; VON NEUMANN, JOHN; and ZUSE, KONRAD.

Mechanical aids to calculation and mechanical sequence-control devices were perhaps the earliest and most important achievements in the development of computer technology.

The first adding machines date from the early seventeenth century, the most famous of which was invented by the French scientist and philosopher Blaise Pascal, although it is now believed that his work was predated by that of William Schickard. A number of Pascal's machines, which he started to build in 1642, still exist. Even though he had intended them for practical use, their unreliability caused them to be treated mainly as objects of scientific curiosity. During the subsequent two centuries, numerous attempts to develop practical calculating machines were made by Morland, Leibniz, Mahon, Hahn, and Müller, among others. However, it was not until the mid-nineteenth century that a commercially successful machine was produced. This was the "arithmometer" of Thomas de Colmar, the first version of which was invented in 1820, and which used the stepped-wheel mechanism invented by Leibniz.

Mechanical devices for controlling the sequencing of a set of operations, such as the rotating pegged cylinders still seen in music boxes today, date back even earlier. For example, de Caus (1576–1626) used such a mechanism to control both the playing of an organ and the movements of model figures. One of the most famous designers of mechanical automata was Vaucanson. In 1736, he successfully demonstrated an automaton that simulated human lip and finger movements with sufficient accuracy to play a flute. Vaucanson was also involved in the development of what came to be known as the Jacquard loom, in which the woven pattern was specified and controlled by a sequence of perforated cards. The original idea can be traced back to Bouchon in 1725, but such automatic looms did not come into widespread use until early in the nineteenth century after the work by Jacquard.

In 1834, these two lines of development came together in the work of Charles Babbage, who had become dissatisfied with the accuracy of printed mathematical tables. Earlier, in 1822, Babbage had built a small machine, involving several linked adding mechanisms, which would automatically generate successive values of simple algebraic functions using the method of finite differences. His attempt at making a full-scale model with a printing mechanism was abandoned in 1834, and he then started to design a more versatile machine. In the space of a few years he had developed the concept of a program-controlled, mechanical, digital computer, incorporating a complete arithmetic unit, store, punched-card input and output, and printing mechanism. The machine, which he called an Analytical Engine, was to have been controlled by programs represented by sets of Jacquard cards, with conditional jumps and iteration loops being provided for by devices that skipped forward or backward over the required number of cards. Internally, the machine was essentially microprogrammed by rotating pegged cylinders that controlled the sequencing of subsidiary mechanisms.

Babbage's work inspired several other people, among whom were Ludgate, who designed an analytical engine in Ireland in 1909; Torres y Quevedo, who demonstrated the feasibility of an electromechanical analytical engine by successfully producing a typewriter-controlled calculating machine in 1920; and Couffignal, who started to design a binary analytical engine in France during the 1930s. However, Babbage's pioneering efforts were apparently unknown to most of the people who worked on the various computer projects during World War II and who were unaware that the problems they were tackling had been considered and often solved by Babbage more than a hundred years earlier.

The Jacquard loom was perhaps the source of Herman Hollerith's idea of using punched cards to represent logical and numerical data. Developed for use in the 1890 U. S. National Census, his system, incorporating hand-operated tabulating machines and sorters, was highly successful and spread rapidly to several other countries. Automatic card-feed mechanisms were soon provided, and the system began to be used for business accounting applications. Following a dispute with Hollerith, the Bureau of the Census developed in time for the 1910 Census a new tabulating system involving mechanical sensing of card perforations, as opposed to Hollerith's system of electrical sensing. James Powers, the engineer in charge of this work, eventually left the Bureau to form his own company, which eventually became part of Remington Rand. Hollerith's company merged with two others to become the Computing-Tabulating-Recording Company, which, in 1924, changed its name to the International Business Machines Corporation.

In 1937, Howard Aiken of Harvard University approached IBM with a proposal for a large-scale calculator, to be built from the mechanical and electromechanical devices that were used for punched-card machines. The resulting machine, the Automatic Sequence Controlled Calculator, or Harvard Mark I, was built at the IBM Development Laboratories at Endicott. The machine, which was completed in 1943, was a huge affair with 72 decimal accumulators, capable of multiplying two 23-digit numbers in 6 sec. It was controlled by a sequence of instructions specified by a perforated paper tape; somewhat surprisingly, in view of Aiken's knowledge of and respect for Babbage's efforts, it lacked general conditional jump facilities. After completion of the Mark I, Aiken and IBM pursued separate paths. Several more machines were designed at Harvard, the first being another tape-controlled calculator, built this time from electromagnetic relays. IBM produced various machines, including several plug-board-controlled relay calculators and the partly electronic Selective Sequence Electronic Calculator, which was very much in the tradition of the original Mark I.

Not until well after World War II was it found that in Germany there had been an operational program-controlled calculator built earlier than the Mark I, namely, Konrad Zuse's Z3 machine, which first worked in 1941. This machine, which had been preceded by two earlier but unsuccessful machines, had a mechanical store, but was otherwise built from telephone relays. It could store 64 floating-point binary numbers, and has been described as somewhat faster than the Harvard Mark I. The Z3, like several other machines built by Zuse, did not survive the war; the only one of Zuse's machines to do so was the

Z4 computer, which was later used successfully for several years at the Technische Hochschule in Zurich.

Various other electromechanical machines were built during and even after World War II, including an important series of relay calculators at the Bell Telephone Laboratories. The first of these, the Complex Computer, was demonstrated in September 1940 by being operated in its New York City location from a teletypewriter installed in Hanover, New Hampshire, on the occasion of a meeting of the American Mathematical Society. The Complex Computer, or Model 1, was capable of adding, subtracting, multiplying, and dividing two complex numbers, but lacked any sequence-control facilities. Later machines in the series incorporated successively more extensive sequencing facilities, so that the Model 5 relay calculator was a truly general-purpose (tape-controlled) computer that achieved very high reliability of operation.

The earliest known electronic digital calculating device was a machine for solving up to 30 simultaneous linear equations, initiated in 1938 at Iowa State College by John Atanasoff and Clifford Berry. Although the arithmetic unit had been successfully tested before the project

was abandoned in 1942, the input/output mechanism was still incomplete, so the machine never saw actual use. Other important work on the development of electronic calculating devices was done at IBM, starting in 1942 with the building of experimental versions of various punched-card machines, including a multiplier. This machine was the origin of the electronic multipliers and calculating machines, such as the Type 604 and the Card Programmed Calculator (CPC), which IBM produced in great quantities in the years immediately following World War II and which played an important role until stored program electronic computers became widely available.

The earliest known efforts at applying electronics to a general-purpose, program-controlled computer were those undertaken by Schreyer and Zuse in 1939, but their plans for a 1,500-valve (i.e., vacuum tube) machine were later rejected by the German government. In Britain, a series of large special-purpose electronic computers, intended for code-breaking purposes, was developed by a team at Bletchley Park, with which Alan Turing was associated (*see* COLOSSUS). The first of these machines, which incorporated about 2000 tubes, was operating in

Fig. 1.   Family tree of computers to mid-1950s. (Courtesy of the Smithsonian Institution.)

December 1943. It has been described as being, in a very limited fashion, a program-controlled device. Interestingly enough, several postwar British electronic computers were developed by people who had been involved with these secret machines.

However, by far the most influential line of development was that carried out at the Moore School of Electrical Engineering at the University of Pennsylvania by John Mauchly, J. Presper Eckert, and their colleagues, starting in 1943. This work, which derived at least as directly from Vannevar Bush's prewar mechanical differential analyzer as from any digital calculating device, first led to the development of the ENIAC, which was officially inaugurated in February 1946. This machine was intended primarily for ballistics calculations, but by the time it was completed, it was really a general-purpose device, programmed by means of pluggable interconnections. Its internal electronic memory consisted of 20 accumulators, each of 10 decimal digits, and it could perform 5,000 arithmetic operations per second—it was approximately a thousand times faster than the Harvard Mark I. The ENIAC was very much the most complex piece of electronic equipment that had ever been assembled, incorporating 19,000 tubes, and using nearly 200 KW of power. The machine was very successful, despite earlier fears regarding the reliability of electronic components.

However, even before the ENIAC was complete, the designers, who had been joined by John von Neumann, started to plan a radically different successor machine, the EDVAC. The EDVAC was a serial binary machine, far more economical on electronic tubes than ENIAC, which was a decimal machine in which each decimal digit was represented by a ring of ten flip-flops. A second major difference was that EDVAC was to have a very much larger internal memory than ENIAC, based on mercury delay lines. For these reaons, the initial design of EDVAC included only one-tenth of the equipment used in ENIAC, yet provided a hundred times the internal memory capacity.

It was apparently the discussions of the various ways in which the capabilities of ENIAC might be extended, together with the knowledge of the possibility of comparatively large internal memories, that led to realization that sequence-control information could be represented by words held in memory along with the numerical quantities entering into the computation, rather than by some external means such as perforated tape or pluggable interconnections. Thus, EDVAC could retain the great speed of operation that had been achieved by ENIAC, but could avoid the very lengthy setup time, often on the order of a day or more, that had made it impractical to use for other than very extensive calculations. The fact that a program could read and modify portions of itself

was heavily utilized, since ideas such as index registers and indirect addresses were still in the offing. Of more lasting significance was the practical and attractive proposition of using the computer to assist with the preparation of its own programs.

With EDVAC, therefore, the invention of the modern digital computer was basically complete. The plans for its design were widely published and extremely influential, so that even though it was not the first stored-program electronic digital computer to be put into operation, it undoubtedly was the major initial inspiration that started the vast number of computer projects during the late 1940s.

REFERENCES

1961. Morrison, P. and Morrison, E. (Eds.). *Charles Babbage and His Calculating Engines: Selected Writings by Charles Babbage and Others.* New York: Dover.
1968. de Beauclair, W. *Rechnen mit Maschinen: Eine Bildgeschichte der Rechentechnik.* Vieweg, Braunschweig.
1969. Rosenberg, J. M. *The Computer Prophets.* New York: Macmillan. (A popular account of the work of many of the computer pioneers.)
1972. Goldstine, H. H. *The Computer from Pascal to von Neumann.* Princeton: Princeton University Press.
1973. Randell, B. (Ed.). *The Origins of Digital Computers.* Berlin: Springer.
1973. Fleck, G. (Ed.). *A Computer Perspective.* By the Office of Charles and Ray Eames, Cambridge, MA: Harvard University Press. (A profusely illustrated book, containing a vast amount of information related directly or indirectly to the history of computing.)

B. RANDELL

EARLY

For articles on related subjects *see* AIKEN, HOWARD; COMPUTER INDUSTRY; DIGITAL COMPUTERS, Contemporary and Future, and Early; ECKERT, J. PRESPER; EDSAC; EDVAC; ENIAC; MARK I; MAUCHLY, JOHN W.; STORED PROGRAM CONCEPT; TURING, ALAN; ULTRASONIC MEMORY; UNIVAC I; VON NEUMANN, JOHN; WHIRLWIND; and ZUSE, KONRAD.

The digital computer age began when the Automatic Sequence Controlled Calculator (Harvard Mark I) started working in August 1944. This machine was based on the mechanical technology of rotating shafts, electromagnetic clutches, and counter wheels, developed over

Fig. 1.   The second Bell Model V relay calculator installed at Aberdeen Proving Ground. The first was installed at Langley Field, Virginia.

the years for punched card tabulating machinery. It was constructed by IBM, following the ideas of Howard Aiken, whose original proposals go back at least to 1937. The shaft rotation period, and hence the time required to transfer a number or perform an addition, was 0.3 sec, while multiplication and division took 6 and 11.4 sec, respectively.

No other large machines using rotating shafts were built, but there were a number of successful magnetic relay machines. Bell Telephone Laboratories had been working in this area since 1938. Their first fully automatic computer was the one now referred to as the Bell Model V (Fig. 1), of which two examples were constructed. The first of these began to work at the end of 1946. An addition took 0.3 sec and multiplication and division took up to 1.0 and 2.2 sec, respectively. The last of the series was the Model VI, commissioned in 1949. Harvard Mark II, a relay machine designed by Aiken and following a very different design philosophy, was run-

ning in September 1948. A relay computer constructed in Sweden (BARK) was operational early in 1950. Independent work on relay computers had also been done by K. Zuse in Germany, and a Zuse Z4 was running in Zurich in 1950. Relays lend themselves to complex circuit arrangements, and all the machines just mentioned had floating-point arithmetic operation, a feature that did not appear in electronic computers until well after the period now under review here. The Bell machines had elaborate checking arrangements, including a redundant representation for stored numbers. Model VI even had a re-try feature, designed to mitigate the effect of transient relay faults.

The concept of the large-scale electronic computer is due to J. Presper Eckert and John W. Mauchly. They were already building the ENIAC when the Harvard Mark I was commissioned. The ENIAC contained nearly 19,000 vacuum tubes, more than twice as many as any later vacuum-tube computer. Because it was by far the most complex machine constructed up to that time, its construction was a great act of technological courage, both on the part of the designers and of the Moore School of Electrical Engineering in Philadelphia where it was constructed. The ENIAC began to function in the summer of 1945. An addition took 200 μs and a multiplication took 2.8 ms.

The very early computers were extremely limited in the amount of internal storage that they had. Provision was usually made for tables to be held in read-only storage (banks of switches or punched paper tape) with arrangements for interpolation. It was frequently possible for the programmer to arrange that more than one arithmetic or transfer operation should take place at the same time. The ENIAC was programmed by setting up hundreds of plugs and sockets and switches, an operation that could take several hours. The other computers read their instructions from punched paper tape, endless loops being used for repeated sections of the program.

While the ENIAC was still under construction, Eckert and Mauchly began to realize that, by the application of logical principles, it would be possible to construct a machine not only much more powerful than the ENIAC but also much smaller. They were joined by John von Neumann on a part-time basis, and it was from the group so formed that the ideas of the modern *stored-program* computer emerged. They were summarized in a document entitled "First draft of a report on the EDVAC," prepared by von Neumann and dated 30 June 1945.

Eckert and Mauchly did not stay at the Moore School to work on the EDVAC, and it was not until January 1952 that a machine bearing that name was commissioned. Instead, they founded the Eckert-Mauchly Corporation, with the object of designing and marketing the UNIVAC. This company was finally absorbed into Remington Rand, but the name UNIVAC has happily survived.

From the beginning the UNIVAC was designed with an eye to business data processing, and the standards set for performance and reliability were very high. In March 1951, the first UNIVAC passed a rigorous acceptance test and was delivered to the U.S. Census Bureau. It was then a fully engineered machine, with magnetic tape and other peripherals required for large-scale business operations. The Eckert-Mauchly Corporation had demonstrated a smaller machine, the BINAC (Fig. 2), in August 1949, but this was not very successful and they decided to concentrate their efforts on the UNIVAC.

When the Moore School group broke up, von Neumann established a project for the construction of a computer at the Institute for Advanced Study, Princeton. Von Neumann himself, assisted by H. H. Goldstine, laid down the logical structure of this computer, and the en-

Fig. 2.   The BINAC computer.

Fig. 3.   The Ferranti Mark I computer at Manchester University, 1951.

Table 1.   Characteristics of Electronic Computers as of Early 1951

Computer	Serial or Parallel	Decimal or Binary	No. of Addresses	Word length	Clock frequency KH	Memory Type	Memory No. of Words
EDVAC[b]	S	B	3 + 1[d]	44 bits	1,000	U	1,024
UNIVAC	S	D	1	12 char.	2,250	U	1,000
IAS[b]	P	B	1	40 bits	Asynch.	W	1,024
EDSAC	S	B	1	35 bits	500	U	512
Ferranti I	S	B	1	40 bits	100	W	256
Pilot ACE	S	B	—[d]	32 bits	1,000	U	360
SEAC	S	B	3	45 bits	1,000	U	512
SWAC	P	B	4	36 bits	125	W	256
Whirlwind I	P	B	1	16 bits	1,000	E	256
Harvard Mark III	S/P	D	3	16 dec.	28	D	4,000[c]
Burroughs	S	D	1 or 1 + 1[d]	9 dec.	125	D	800
ERA 1101	P	B	1 + 1[d]	24 bits	400	D	16,384

Notes: (a) U = ultrasonic delay (mercury tank); W = Williams tube; D = magnetic drum; E = electrostatic (CRT)
(b) Not commissioned until 1952.
(c) Separate 200-word memory for instructions.
(d) Provision for minimum-access coding.

gineering development and design was in the hands of J. H. Bigelow. It was the first parallel computer to be designed, and it introduced techniques that are now commonplace, such as the register economizing device of putting the multiplier in the tail of the accumulator and shifting it out as the multiplication proceeds. Although the machine was not working until October 1952, the project had immense influence on the development of the digital computer field. The ultrasonic memory, which had been proposed for the EDVAC, was thought to be too slow for a parallel machine, and it was planned to use instead a memory based on the Selectron proposed by J. A. Rajchman. The Selectron did not fulfill its promise, but fortunately the Williams tube memory came along in time to save the situation.

The experimental computers that came into action first were those that were least ambitious, both in specification and in performance. One of these was the EDSAC, a computer directly inspired by the EDVAC, designed and constructed by myself and W. Renwick in Cambridge, England. This computer did its first calculation on 6 May 1949, and was used for much early work on the development of programming techniques. Activity at Manchester University arose out of work by F. C. Williams on what became known as the Williams tube memory. In order to test this system, Williams and T. Kilburn built a small model computer with a memory of 32 words and with 5 instructions in its instruction set. The only arithmetic instruction was for subtraction. Development work continued, and by the summer of 1949 a computer with a magnetic drum as a backing memory was demonstrated. The Ferranti Mark I computer (Fig. 3), of

which the first delivered model was inaugurated at Manchester University in July 1951, was based on this work.

A third center of activity in England was at the National Physical Laboratory, where the inspiration came from Alan Turing. Turing did not stay there long, leaving for Manchester University in 1948, but the Pilot ACE, which was running by December 1950, reflected very strongly his rather personal view of computer design. The Pilot ACE used an ultrasonic memory, and it was necessary for the programmer to know more of the structure of the machine and the timing of pulses within it than was required in the case of other machines.

The first of the American machines to be brought into use was the SEAC, dedicated on 20 June 1950. This was built under the direction of S. N. Alexander at the National Bureau of Standards in Washington and the success of that group is the more remarkable since the SEAC project started after many others. The SEAC was elegant in design and construction, and pioneered the use of small plug-in packages; each package contained a number of germanium diodes and a single vacuum tube. The SEAC used an ultrasonic memory, but a Williams tube memory was later added for evaluation purposes. Meanwhile, H. D. Huskey, who had formerly been a member of the team at the National Physical Laboratory in England and had worked on ENIAC, was completing the SWAC at the NBS Institute for Numerical Analysis at UCLA. This was a parallel machine with a Williams tube memory and was very fast by the standards of the day.

Whirlwind I was a computer with a short word length, aiming at very high speed and power, and in-

Max. Memory Access, (time ms)	Operation Time (incl. access)			Input Output	No. of Tubes	No. of Diodes (germanium)	Aux. Memory
	Add, ms	Mult., ms	Divide ms				
0.38	0.2–1.5	2.2–3.5	2.2–3.6	Paper tape	3,600	10,000	–
0.40	0.5 mean	2.15 mean	3.9 mean	Magn. tape	5,600	18,000	Magn. tape
0.025	0.062	0.44–1.0	1.1	Cards	2,300	0	–
1.1	1.5 mean	6 mean	–	Paper tape	3,800	0	–
0.64	1.2	3.36	–	Paper tape	3,800	0	Drum, 16K
1.0	–	2	–	Cards	800	–	–
0.38	1.5 max.	3.6 max.	3.6 max.	Paper tape	1,300	15,800	Magn. tape
–	0.064	0.38	–	Paper tape; cards	2,300	3,000	–
0.016	0.049	0.061	0.1	Paper tape	6,800	22,000	–
4.5	5	13	100	Magn. tape	5,000	1,300	–
32	0.6–17	30–50	–	Paper tape	3,271	6,773	–
17	0.1 min.	0.35 min.	0.42 min.	Paper tape	2,200	3,000	–

tended ultimately for air traffic control and similar applications. It was designed and built under the direction of J. W. Forrester at M.I.T. and was operating in December 1950. From its specification, one would take it to be the first of the minicomputers, but in fact it occupied the largest floor area of all the early computers, including the ENIAC. The memory was of the electrostatic type, but the cathode-ray tubes were of special design and operated on a different principle from that used by Williams.

Table 1 gives brief particulars of the computers mentioned above and also of several additional ones that became operational in the same period.

REFERENCES

1951. U.S. Navy, Office of Naval Research. *Digital Computer Newsletter* **1–3.**
1953. U.S. Navy, Office of Naval Research. *A Survey of Automatic Digital Computers.*
1972. Goldstine, H. H. *The Computer from Pascal to von Neumann.* Princeton: Princeton University Press.

M. V. Wilkes

CONTEMPORARY AND FUTURE

For articles on related subjects *see* BURROUGHS B5000 SERIES; COMPUTER INDUSTRY; CONTROL DATA CORPORATION CYBER SERIES. DIGITAL COMPUTERS: Origins of, and Early; DIGITAL EQUIPMENT CORPORATION PDP SERIES; GENERATIONS, COMPUTER; IBM 360–370 SERIES; MICROPROCESSORS AND MICROCOMPUTERS; MINICOMPUTERS; and UNIVAC 1100 SERIES.

The development of digital computers can be conveniently categorized as successive generations.

The First Generation. The modern history of computing starts with the invention of the stored program computer. The first generation of electronic computers is characterized by the use of vacuum tubes as active elements. In the first generation a number of storage media were tried for reasons of economy and reliability and the early computers can be classified according to the nature of their main memory system.

Mercury Delay Line Storage. Although mercury delay lines were important in a number of early research computers, UNIVAC I was the only computer delivered commercially that used this type of memory. The first UNIVAC I was delivered on 14 June 1951, several years ahead of the delivery of any competitive system. UNI-

VAC designers felt at that time that mercury-delay line memory was the only memory available that could provide adequate reliability at reasonably high speed. Average access time to the 1,000-word main memory was on the order of 500 μs. UNIVAC was a completely serial machine with duplicate arithmetic and control circuitry for detection of errors. The relatively low speed was partially compensated for by the use of minimum access-time coding and other sophisticated software devices. UNIVAC I had a number of features that did not become generally available on other computers until years later. These included a buffered tape system that could read tapes both forward and backward.

Electrostatic Storage. Most of the successful electrostatic storage systems were based on the Williams tube developed at Manchester University in England. Typical memories had from 1,000 to 4,000 words with random access times of from 10 to 50 μs. There is still some question as to whether these memories ever achieved adequate reliability. IBM's 701 (Fig. 1), of which 18 were delivered between 1953 and 1956, was the most important scientific computer that used this type of memory. Remington Rand offered the only competitive computer in this field, the 1103, which it obtained when it absorbed Engineering Research Associates.

IBM used electrostatic storage on its 702, which it started delivering for commercial data processing in 1955. The 702 was the prototype of many later character-oriented computers, but for a number of reasons, including memory problems, it was soon withdrawn from the market.

Magnetic Drum Storage. Prototype magnetic drum computers included the Harvard Mark III and the ERA 1101. The magnetic drum provided a large amount of slow memory at relatively low cost. The IBM 700 series and the UNIVAC 1103 series used drums as peripheral storage.

Typical drum-storage systems used a drum that rotated at about 3,600 rpm, providing average random access times of about 17 ms. This seems incredibly slow for a main memory by modern standards, but it was the only way to get moderately priced memory in any quantity in the early 1950s. The development of cheap, reliable magnetic drum systems made it possible for many companies to enter the computer field with a rather modest investment. There were literally dozens of magnetic drum computers of varying capacity that were the small-to-medium sized computers of the first generation. Only a few of those that are historically most important will be mentioned here.

Among the magnetic drum computers delivered as early as 1953 were the CADAC 100 series and the Con-

Fig. 1. An IBM 701 system.

solidated Engineering Corporation 200 series. The CADAC was produced by the Computer Research Corporation, which was absorbed by National Cash Register Corporation and became the forerunner of other computers in the NCR line. Consolidated Engineering spun off the ElectroData Corporation, which marketed such computers as the Datatron 203, 204, and 205. ElectroData was absorbed by the Burroughs Corporation and became an important part of Burroughs' computer activity.

IBM's 650 (Fig. 2) was introduced a bit later and soon became the most widely used of all first-generation computers. Many hundreds were delivered between 1955 and 1959. The 650 was somewhat faster than most other magnetic drum computers, but the chief reason for its great success was its well-integrated punched-card input and output and its adaptability to existing punched-card systems.

Remington Rand introduced a perhaps too ambitious UNIVAC file computer, a drum-and-tape based data processing system that was not a commercial success. Toward the end of the first generation, the company introduced the UNIVAC 80 and 90, which were reasonably effective competitors for the IBM 650 systems. The

use of solid-state components should perhaps place these computers in the second generation, but the solid-state components in the UNIVAC 80 and 90 were magnetic amplifiers, not transistors. At best, these computers belong in a transitional stage between generations.

Magnetic Core Memories. By 1953, both M.I.T. and RCA had developed working models of coincident-current magnetic core memories. Subsequent litigation awarded patent rights to the group at M.I.T., which made the memory design available to the computer industry. RCA developed the Bizmac, a very ambitious commercial data processing system that was unsuccessful for a number of reasons, of which the most obvious was its failure to exploit adequately the capabilities of the magnetic core memory.

IBM moved quickly to adapt the core memory technology to both its scientific and its commercial computer lines, and in 1956 started deliveries on the 704—a very powerful successor to the 701—and the 705, a viable successor to the faltering 702. Core memory was faster and more reliable than the cathode-ray tube memories that were replaced. The hardware floating-point arithmetic and index registers on the 704 and the logical changes

Fig. 2.   An IBM 650 system.

that permitted the 705 to work with groups of characters in multiple accumulators, coupled with the development of improved input/output and peripheral devices, made these computers orders of magnitude more powerful than their predecessors.

Remington Rand's UNIVAC division also quickly absorbed the new magnetic core memory technology and produced the UNIVAC II, which was a compatible extension of UNIVAC I, as an upgrade for its data processing customers. The 1103A was the magnetic core upgrade of the Univac Scientific Computer (the 1103), and optional floating-point and interrupt-handling hardware were soon added. The first UNIVAC I had been used to process the voluminous data collected in the 1950 Census. For the 1960 Census, UNIVAC added buffered input/output capacity to its scientific computer, which thus became the UNIVAC 1105. IBM added data channels to provide buffering capabilities to its 704 line, and introduced the 709 just as the first generation was coming to an end.

Other companies were quick to jump on the magnetic core bandwagon. Datamatic Corporation, which later became the computer division of Honeywell, produced a very large computer, the Datamatic 1000 (Figs. 3 and 4), which was used in a very few large data processing applications.

Burroughs produced its 220 system, a medium-size core memory machine that was much more powerful than competitive drum machines, but introduced it too late to

have much impact, since its major competition was to come from second-generation machines.

The Second Generation. The transistor was invented in 1948, and the advantages of transistors over vacuum tubes for computer applications were recognized almost immediately. There were many technological and production problems that had to be worked out, and it was 1959 before transistorized computers were delivered in any quantity. That year marks the beginning of the second computer generation, in which transistors completely replaced vacuum tubes as the active components of digital computers. All second-generation computers used magnetic core storage systems for main memory. Some of them used magnetic drums and disks in addition to magnetic tapes for auxiliary storage.

Large Scientific Computers. Philco Corporation engineers developed the first transistors suitable for really high speed computers. Philco decided to enter the computer field with its own large-scale Transac S-2000 systems, and had moderate success with its Model 211 and later the more powerful 212, but could not generate enough momentum to carry it into the third generation. Philco withdrew from the general-purpose computer field in 1964.

UNIVAC developed one of the first successful, large-scale transistorized computers for military applications, the UNIVAC M460. A group of UNIVAC em-

Fig. 3. Datamatic 1000 computer installed at Michigan Blue Cross–Blue Shield, Detroit.

Fig. 4. Vacuum tube racks of the central processor of the Datamatic 1000.

ployees left the company and set up Control Data Corporation, which used the new transistor technology in their 1604 (Fig. 5) computer. The 1604 was followed by a more powerful 3000 series, the 3600 and later the 3800. Control Data established itself as a major supplier of large computers and retained and expanded its position in the third generation.

The possibility of using transistors in very large numbers to produce large and powerful computers was attractive to the Atomic Energy Commission, which sponsored two of the early second-generation projects, Stretch (the IBM 7030) at IBM and Larc at UNIVAC. Both companies tried to market the resulting computers in the early 1960s, but both were unsuccessful because the rapid progress of technology made these early giant computers uneconomical.

IBM produced the 709TX system in 1959 in response to the demand for a transistorized computer for the Ballistic Missile Early Warning System. The 709TX became the 7090, a compatible extension of the first generation 709, designed to run at more than five times the speed of the 709. The 7090, later upgraded to the 7094, dominated the scientific computer market in the period 1960–1964. A similar but slightly less powerful series, the 7040 and 7044 were introduced in 1962–1963. Combinations of the 7040 and 7090 series machines with disk storage formed the direct-coupled systems that were popular from 1964 to 1966 and provided a partial hardware and software prototype of some IBM third-generation systems.

The UNIVAC 1107 appeared late in the second generation and served mainly as a prototype for the more successful 1108 model in the third generation.

Data Processing Computers. Some of the earliest second-generation computers were medium-scale data processing systems. National Cash Register was almost too early with its 304, a joint effort with General Electric. A more successful NCR 315 (Fig. 6) system was introduced in 1962. This system featured an interesting magnetic card cartridge auxiliary memory, CRAM.

The RCA 501 was another of the very early transistorized machines, but had limited performance. It featured one of the very first Cobol compilers. A much more powerful 601 introduced interesting microprogramming features. It was designed primarily for the scientific field, but was not competitive. RCA had most success with its small 301 computer, introduced somewhat later.

IBM introduced its 7070 series in 1960. The 7070 represented a major step up from the first-generation 650 but it did not satisfy the very large number of 705 users. IBM eventually produced the 7080, a large transistorized machine that was compatible with the 705.

Second-generation technology made it possible to build small character-oriented processors at low cost. IBM's 1401, first delivered late in 1960, was the first of a very successful series of such computers. They started out as programmed controllers of input/output devices and developed into full data processing systems, especially when the more powerful 1410 and eventually the 7010 processors were introduced.

Other manufacturers followed with the introduction of small computers in numbers of models too numerous to discuss here.

Transitional Computers. A number of second-generation computers were ahead of their time in introducing features usually associated with the third generation, even though they appeared early in the second generation. The Honeywell 800 introduced an ingenious hardware multiprogramming system along with a very interesting data processing software system, FACT.

The Atlas system, developed jointly by Ferranti and Manchester University in England, introduced the concept of virtual memory implemented through dynamic address translation.

The Burroughs B5000 system introduced a different implementation of virtual memory along with pushdown stacks and other features that help in compilation and in multiprogramming.

The Third Generation. Integrated circuits and large-scale integration (LSI) were the most striking technological developments of the third-generation of computers. However, some very important computers of the third generation made little or no use of integrated circuits. In this discussion, most computers introduced between 1964 and 1975 will be considered to be third-generation computers, along with several computers introduced earlier whose technology and system design were sufficiently advanced to permit most of their installations to survive into the 1970s.

The IBM 360 and 370. IBM announced its System 360 on 7 April 1964. The 360 was designed to replace all earlier IBM computers, and it represented a very major departure from IBM's second-generation systems. The 360 came in a number of compatible models. The Model 75 at the top of the line used conventional hardware sequencing techniques to implement a large instruction set. The other models (30, 40, 50, 65) used microprogramming in a variety of read-only memory systems to provide the same instruction set on computers with a wide range of memory and circuit speeds. The use of microprogramming in read-only storage also made it possible for these 360 models to run programs written for second-generation IBM computers by *emulation*; i.e., by hardware-assisted simulation.

Fig. 5. CDC 1604-A computer.

Fig. 6. NCR 315 system.

Many features of the 360 became standards in large segments of the computer industry. Among these are the use of eight-bit bytes for the representation of characters and the use of nine-track tapes. Multiple-spindle disk systems with removable disk packs were introduced on the 360 and were adopted on many other systems.

The 360 was tremendously successful, and there were many thousands of installations. New models were introduced at intervals after the initial announcement, including some like the Models 20 and 44 that were not quite compatible with the standard 360 systems

The 360 Model 67 followed shortly after the original 360 announcement, in response to the demand from universities and research laboratories for a large-scale *time-sharing* system. The Model 67 provided dynamic address translation that permitted the implementation of *virtual memory* operating systems.

In response to the delivery of the first Control Data 6600 in the fall of 1964, IBM announced a 90 series of very large and very fast 360s. Several of Model 91 and Model 95 were delivered before the series was withdrawn in favor of the Model 85. The 85 introduced the cache, or buffer memory, which provided an automatic multilevel memory system to help match memory speed to the very fast arithmetic speed. This type of buffer memory has since been incorporated into many different computers of all kinds and sizes. The 85 was at the top of the 360 line only very briefly. It was superseded in 1971 by the more powerful 195, which provided a 360 system that was competitive with the CDC 7600 in the scientific computer field.

During 1970, IBM announced its 370 line, which represented a relatively modest step up from the 360. All 360 programs, with a few exceptions, could run on the 370. An important feature of the 370 was held back until August 1972, at which time it was revealed that dynamic address translation already existed on the delivered Models 135 and 145 and would be standard on new 370 models.

At that time IBM also introduced two new large 370 systems, the 158 and 168, whose major difference from the earlier 155 and 165 was the replacement of core memory by faster and much cheaper metal oxide semiconductor (MOS) memories. The MOS large-scale integration technology has since been very widely used and has led to the rapid obsolescence of magnetic core memories.

RCA and Univac. RCA's strategy in the third generation was to accept most features of the IBM 360 as standards for the industry, and to attempt to become an alternate source of supply for users who found that type of equipment attractive. The company introduced the Spectra 70 series whose principal models, the 35 and 45,

were designed to fall, respectively, between the IBM 360/30 and 40 models and between the IBM 360/40 and 50. A virtual memory system, the Model 46, was also developed. RCA had only moderate success with the Spectra line, and a series of new virtual memory models introduced in advance of the IBM 370 series met with poor customer response. RCA abruptly departed from the general-purpose computer business in the fall of 1971, and shortly thereafter Sperry-Rand's Univac Division announced that it would purchase the remnants of RCA's computer division and would provide support for Spectra series installations.

Univac's own entry into the third generation was with the 1108, a compatible extension of its second-generation 1107. The 1108 and its successor in the 1970s, the 1110 (Fig. 7), made Univac an important factor in the large-scale computer field.

Another important Univac series was the 400, which was used in large real-time and control applications. In the very important small-to-medium scale data processing field, the Univac third-generation 9000 systems closely followed the pattern set by IBM 360 systems.

Control Data Corporation. The CDC 6000 series easily qualifies as belonging to the third generation, even though the first 6600 was delivered in 1964 and even though the discrete component technology used is more typical of the second generation. For several years after its introduction the 6600 was faster and more powerful than any other computer available, and CDC established a strong position in the large scientific computer field. The speed of the 6600 (estimated by the manufacturer at three million instructions per second) was enhanced by the use of an instruction stack along with multiple arithmetic and logical units. The same system without these features was offered as a lower-priced 6400 system and a multiprocessor 6500 system. All these systems could use a very high-speed extended core storage (ECS), a peripheral storage system with transfer rates up to ten million 60-bit words per second.

By 1969, Control Data had delivered its first 7600 system (Fig. 8). The 7000 series provided a good deal of compatibility with the 6000 series at three to seven times the speed of the 6600. Typical Atomic Energy Commission installations used the 6600 as a front-end computer for the faster 7600. Slight upgrades of these machines were marketed in the early 1970s as the CDC Cyber 70 Series.

Another very large computer, the CDC STAR (String Array) 100, was built for Livermore and offered to other customers. The STAR is based on a concept of streaming arrays of data through pipelined arithmetic units at very high rates of speed. Texas Instruments developed the Advanced Scientific Computer (ASC), whose

Fig. 7. Console and CPU of UNIVAC 1110 system.

Fig. 8. CDC 7600 system.

(a)

(b)

Fig. 9. The Burroughs Corporation B5500(a) and B6700(b) systems.

size and speed were comparable to the STAR 100 for similar classes of problems.

Control Data also had reasonable success with the third-generation versions of its 3000 series computers in the small- and medium-size computer field.

Burroughs. The Burroughs 5000 system was upgraded to the 5500 in 1962. Burroughs introduced a fixed-head disk for system residence and for use in its virtual memory system. Fixed-head disks became an IBM 370 component many years later. During the 1960s Burroughs used the slogan, "Burroughs dares to be different," and its stack organization and use of descriptors for memory addressing were indeed unique in the industry. The 6500 system, announced in 1965, was slow in delivery and in performance, and the very ambitious 8500 never reached completion, but the 6500 was soon replaced by a more capable 6700 and 7700 series. Fig. 9 shows the Burroughs B5500 and B6700 systems.

Meanwhile Burroughs made great progress with smaller series of computers, the 2500 and 3500, later upgraded to 2700 and 3700. These and the even smaller 1700 series systems made Burroughs a major factor in the third-generation computer field.

Burroughs also built the ILLIAC IV, a parallel system based on the use of a large number of synchronized, high-speed arithmetic units. For appropriate problems, the ILLIAC IV is potentially orders of magnitude faster than other computers.

Honeywell and General Electric. Honeywell entered the third generation with its 200 computer, which provided upward compatibility with the IBM 1400 series. The 200 grew into a whole series of computers that were very successful in the data processing field.

General Electric's third-generation entry was the 600 series, which provided limited upward compatibility with the IBM 7000 series. GE tried to make a spectacular entry into the large time-sharing computer field with the 645, a computer designed in cooperation with the M.I.T. Multics project, but the IBM 360 Model 67 took away most of that market. GE introduced a 200 and 400 series whose major success was in the time-sharing field. By 1970, it was clear that GE was not making much progress in the computer field, and it sold its computer division to Honeywell. The 600 series was upgraded to a 6000 series of more modern and more powerful computers, and this helped Honeywell become a leading contender in the computer industry.

Minicomputers. The most spectacular growth area in the latter part of the third-generation period was in the minicomputer field. The largest company in this field is Digital Equipment Corporation, which is famous for its PDP series (Fig. 10). These started in the second gener-

ation, but achieved major success with the third-generation PDP-8, which was first delivered in 1968 and which was installed in thousands of laboratories. The PDP-11 minicomputers, introduced in 1970, have been even more successful, and many PDP-11 features have become standards in the minicomputer field. These and other minicomputers have impinged on the medium-scale computer field, since large-scale integration technology has been applied to good effect to increase the power and speed of computers that are physically quite small. DEC also has had considerable success with its PDP-10, which is in the medium-to-large-scale class. There were many other successful manufacturers of minicomputers in the third generation, including Data General with their Nova and Super-Nova series, Hewlett-Packard, Varian, Interdata, and Microdata. Many minicomputer manufacturers use microprogramming techniques to increase the versatility of their products.

Table 1 summarizes the three generations of computers discussed in this article.

Modern Computers. It is not useful to carry the concept of computer generations beyond the third generation. There is no generally accepted definition of a fourth-generation computer. For the purposes of this article we shall consider that the third computer generation lasted into the mid-1970s. We consider computers introduced since then as modern computers, and refer to the third generation in the past tense.

Mainframe Manufacturers. All of the major mainframe manufacturers discussed above introduced new versions of their computers in the late 1970s. These were typically characterized by the increased use of large-scale integration technology, especially for central memory.

It is an indication of the maturity of the mainframe computer industry that the new computers introduced few if any changes in logical organization. They were mostly faster and cheaper versions of the earlier third-generation series. Thus, in 1977, IBM introduced its 30 series of large computers, the 3031, 3032, and 3033 which provided a compatible extension to and replacement for the high end of the 370 series. Similarly, the IBM 4300 series introduced in 1979 replaced the small and intermediate 370 systems with compatible equipment that provided more computing at a lower price.

Other mainframe manufacturers introduced their own compatible successor equipment. Univac produced a new 1100 series of successors to the 1108 and 1110, Honeywell introduced a 60 series of successors to its 6000 series, Control Data has a Cyber 170 series that replaced the Cyber 70 series and a Cyber 200 series to replace the Star 100, and Burroughs has a 6800 and 7800 series to replace its 6700 and 7700 machines.

Fig. 10.   DEC PDP-8/E minicomputer system.

IBM-Compatible Mainframes. Gene M. Amdahl, one of the designers of IBM's 360 series, left IBM in the fall of 1970 and started a new computer company, Amdahl Corporation. Major financial backing was obtained from Japanese sources. Amdahl's goal was to produce a computer compatible with the IBM 370 series, that would sell at roughly the same price as the Model 168, but would be considerably faster than the 168. The Amdahl computer used existing IBM 370 software and peripherals. The first Amdahl 470 V/6 system was installed at the University of Michigan in 1975.

Amdahl Corporation was quite successful and established itself as a serious competitor to IBM in the large computer field. The IBM 30 series was at least partially motivated by competitive pressure provided by Amdahl. Amdahl corporation in turn introduced more powerful computers, the V/7 and V/8 (see Fig. 11), in order to compete with IBM's newer offerings. Following the lead of Amdahl, a number of other companies introduced IBM-compatible computers. There is now a good deal of competition in this field. An organization that wishes to buy or rent a computer that runs IBM-compatible software can choose from among at least a half dozen different manufacturers including Control Data, IPL, Magnusson and National Advanced Systems along with IBM and Amdahl.

Cray Research. Seymour Cray, who was the principal architect of the CDC 6000 and 7000 series computers, left Control Data in 1972 and started a new computer company, Cray Research, Inc. Their first CRAY-I computer was delivered to Los Alamos late in 1975. Since then, a number of these very large, very powerful computers have been delivered, mostly to laboratories involved in research in areas like nuclear energy and weather prediction in which very large mathematical models need to be solved. The CRAY-I (see Fig. 12) is a vector machine; i. e., it has special register arrays and special instructions that facilitate operations with vectors. It is a very powerful computer estimated to be from 3–7 times the speed of the CDC 7600, the actual factor depending on the extent to which vector operations can be used. Other and even more powerful CRAY computers have been announced for future delivery.

Minicomputers and Intermediate Computers. The late 1970s were a period of tremendous growth and innovation in the area of small and intermediate computers. In addition to companies like Digital Equipment Corporation and Data General, which were important factors in the third generation, there are many other companies that have grown in importance in this area since 1975. These include Hewlett Packard, Prime, Wang, Tandem,

Table 1. Electronic Computer Generations

Development	Early First Generation, 1946–1953	Late First Generation, 1953–1959	Second Generation, 1959–1964	Early Third Generation, 1964–1969	Late Third Generation, 1969–1975
Component technology					
Vacuum tubes	————	————			
Transistors		————	————		
Hybrid circuits				————	—
Monolithic integrated circuits				————	————
Medium- and large-scale integration					————
Main memory technology					
Delay lines	————	————			
Electrostatic tubes	————	————			
Magnetic drums	————	————	————		
Magnetic cores		————	————	————	————
Large-scale integration					————
Main memory cycle time					
40–40,000 μs	————	————			
10–20 μs		————	————		
2–10 μs			————	————	
0.5–2 μs				————	————
0.020–1 μs					————
Peripheral storage					
Magnetic tapes	————	————	————	————	————
Magnetic drums	————	————	————	————	————
Magnetic disks		————	————	————	————
Laser and magnetic bubbles					————
Software systems					
Subroutine libraries	————	————	————	————	————
Intepreters	————	————	————	————	————
Assemblers		————	————	————	————
Compilers		————	————	————	————
Operating systems			————	————	————
Multiprogramming and time-sharing communications systems (networks)			————	————	————
Special features					
Interrupt systems				————	————
Virtual memory			————	————	————
Microprogramming			————	————	————
Typical examples	ENIAC, EDVAC SEAC,SWAC Harvard Mark III,IV IAS machine UNIVAC I,1103 Whirlwind IBM 701,702	IBM 650,704,705, 709 UNIVAC II, 1103A,SS80 Burroughs 205, 220 NCR 120,200 series Datamatic 1000 RCA Bizmac Many magnetic drum computers	Philco 2000 CDC 1604,3600 IBM 7000,1400 series Ferranti Atlas RCA 301,501 Honeywell 800 UNIVAC III, 1107	Burroughs B5500 CDC 6000 series, 3300 IBM 360 series UNIVAC 1108 Honeywell 200 series RCA Spectra 70 NCR Century G.E. 400,600	IBM 370 series, System 3 CDC Cyber 70 series DEC PDP-10,11 Honeywell 2000, 6000 UNIVAC 1110, 9400 Burroughs B6700, 1700 Many minicomputers

Fig. 11.   An Amdahl 470 V/8 system.

Datapoint, Perkin-Elmer, Gould Computer Systems, Modular Computer Systems, and others. The major mainframe manufacturers all have one or more series of minicomputers to augment their mainframe systems. Thus, IBM has a Series 1 of conventional minicomputers, an 8100 series, and a completely new series 38. Honeywell has a series 6, Univac has a 90 series, Burroughs has an 1800 series, and Control Data has a Cyber 18 and 19.

The traditional third-generation minicomputer was a 16-bit machine. A number of minicomputer manufacturers introduced 32-bit intermediate computers in the late 1970s. The best known of these is the DEC VAX 11/780. Others include the Data General MV/8000, the Perkin-Elmer 3240, and the SEL 32/77.

Microprocessors and Microcomputers. Large-scale integration technology made it possible to put a great number of logic circuits on a single chip, but the cost of designing and producing custom chips is very high. The economics of very large-scale integration calls for the design of relatively few chips of great versatility, and production of these chips in very large quantities. Intel Corporation seems to have been the first to realize that the full versatility of a general-purpose digital computer processor could be implemented on a single chip. In 1970, they introduced the first microprocessor, a four-bit computer on a chip, and a few years later they introduced their 8000 series of eight-bit microprocessors. A number of other companies have built microprocessors that have also been sold in very large quantities. These include Zilog, which was originally formed by former Intel employees, and Motorola with a very popular 6800 series.

Fig. 12.   The CPU of a CRAY-I.

Other companies that produce large numbers of microprocessors, either for their own use or for general sale, include IBM, Bell Laboratories, and Rockwell International. By 1979, several companies had started to deliver 16-bit microprocessors. These include the Intel 8069, the Zilog 8000 and the Motorola 68000. The processing power in one of these chips is equivalent to that of the processor in a large minicomputer.

A large number of microcomputers were introduced in the late 1970s. A typical microcomputer uses a microprocessor as its CPU and a number of associated interface and memory chips. Special peripheral devices in large numbers are available for such microcomputers. The best-known microcomputers are personal (i.e., single user) computers. These include the Commodore Pet, the Apple computer, and the TRS 80 that is sold by the Radio Shack chain of stores.

There is not very much distinction between microcomputers and small minicomputers. There are microcomputer versions of some of the popular minicomputers; e.g., the LSI-11 which is at the low end of the DEC PDP-11 line (see Fig. 13).

Communications and Networks. Communication with and among computers has increased in importance from one computer generation to the next. Many modern computers are connected to or are part of the computer networks. The line of demarcation between communication technology and computer technology is not very clear, and it may disappear completely. Major communications companies like AT&T and GTE are providing or planning to provide computer network services, and computer and computer equipment builders including IBM and Xerox are moving into the communications area.

The major large-scale computer network project in the third generation was Arpanet, a U.S. Defense Department project that created a major packet switching network connecting many university and research center computer systems. Telenet and other commercial packet switching networks are direct descendants of the Arpanet effort. New technologies, including Xerox Corporation's Ethernet, are spurring the development of local computer networks. The availability of satellite communication links will have a major accelerating effect on the development of national and international networks. Many software and hardware systems have been and continue to be developed to provide the necessary protocols to insure efficiency, reliability, and security of computer communication systems. Examples of such systems are IBM's SNA (System Network Architecture) and Digital Equipment Corporation's DECNET.

Fig. 13.   LSI-11/23 CPU board.

Future Prospects. In 1980 IBM announced the 3081 computer, which is the precursor of a new family of large computers, compatible with but an extension of 370 series computers. Thus, the huge investment that has been made in software development in the past 15 years will be protected. The cost per instruction executed will almost certainly be significantly less than on the IBM 30 series or on its compatible competitors. The other mainframe manufacturers will almost certainly counter with new models in their large-scale computer series. Little if any innovation in logical organization of either hardware or software is expected. There will be increased use of large-scale integration that will permit the construction of very compact, very powerful processors with very large, high-speed memories. There will be increased emphasis on multiprocessor systems, possibly incorporating smaller processors with special functions. Such special processors will almost certainly include powerful "backend" processors that will control the huge storage systems which will be available, and will perform searching and indexing and updating functions for the database management systems of the future.

Integrated circuit performance and economy will continue to improve at a very rapid rate through the further development and exploitation of the technologies that were developed in the 1970s. The industry has only just begun to use electron beam lithography, which promises to permit a major increase in the number of circuits on a chip. The 64K-bit memory chips will soon replace the widely used 16K-bit chips, and they themselves will be replaced by 256K-bit chips in a few years. There will be 32-bit microprocessors along with the 16-bit microprocessors that have recently been introduced. There will also be major advances that will result from the introduction of new and exotic technologies. For example, the Josephson Junction (*q.v.*) may eventually make it possible to provide computing power equivalent to that of today's largest computers in a volume of less than one cubic foot. Prototype computers using Josephson Junction technology are already being built, and large-scale computers using that technology may be available before the end of the century.

Magnetic disk storage has improved in capacity and in capacity per dollar much more rapidly than any replacement and will probably retain its place as the standard medium-speed peripheral storage system at least until the end of the century. Disk systems with over a billion bytes per spindle and with a 16-ms average access time became available in 1980. Even more storage per disk will be available in the future. There are other promising storage technologies under development, mostly for special areas in which large disks are not appropriate. Magnetic bubbles may provide large cheap storage for small computers. Videodisks with laser read-write systems may be able to provide huge amounts of storage measured in many trillions of bytes.

The most interesting developments in the computer field in the next 10 years will almost certainly be in the area of small computers. There will be microcomputers and intelligent terminals with the power of the intermediate computers that were introduced in 1979 and 1980. Some very interesting and powerful logical organizations will be possible using, for example, multiple 32-bit microprocessor chips associated with large numbers of 256K-bit or even denser memory chips. There will be a tremendous increase in the amount of processing power directly available to the individual user at a terminal. There will also be a tremendous increase in the information and in the processing power indirectly available to the user through the data communication systems and computer networks of the future.

REFERENCES

1969. Rosen, S. "Electronic Computers: A Historical Survey," *Computing Surveys* **1**:7–36.
1979. *Annals of the History of Computing* (A quarterly journal published by the American Federation of Information Processing Societies since July 1979).

S. ROSEN

DIGITAL EQUIPMENT CORPORATION PDP SERIES

For articles on related subjects *see* COMPUTER INDUSTRY; and MINICOMPUTERS.

PDP is a trademark (originally inspired by the phrase Programmed Data Processor) of Digital Equipment Corporation (DEC) for its various models of computers. These computers can be classified into four major families which can be distinguished by their respective word lengths. The genealogies of these four families may be seen in Fig. 1.

Each family has evolved along a slightly different dimension. The 12-bit family (consisting of the PDP-5, 8, and 12) has emphasized decreasing cost over time. The 18-bit machines (the PDP-1, 4, 7, 9, and 15) have generally targeted increased performance at a constant price. The 16-bit family, consisting of a variety of models of the PDP-11, has emphasized growth of range; this family spans a factor of 500 in price and in memory size from the largest model to the smallest. The 36-bit machines, the PDP-6 and PDP-10, are not generally classed as minicomputers. Their basic design strategy has been to use improved technology to provide compatible vehicles for executing sophisticated, relatively stable software. The individual PDP machines are discussed below.

PDP-1. DEC's first computer, the PDP-1, was built out of the modules which had previously been DEC's major product. At the time of PDP-1's first delivery in December 1959, most computer systems sold for over a million dollars. Thus, the typical PDP-1 configuration's price of $120,000 attracted widespread attention.

PDP-3. The PDP-3 was a 36-bit design which DEC elected not to build. However, a customer (Scientific Engineering Institute, Waltham, MA) did build a PDP-3 in 1960, and the machine was still operating in the 1970s.

PDP-4. The PDP-4 preserved the 18-bit word length of its predecessor, the PDP-1, but simplified the architecture somewhat. These changes, together with slower memory and different packaging, allowed the price to be lowered to $65,000.

PDP-5. The PDP-5 was designed to fill the gap between applications which could be solved efficiently by special-purpose systems built from logic modules and those needing the full power of a computer, such as the PDP-4. It was the first of the series of 12-bit computers which provided DEC's main product offering for the next decade. The PDP-5 is generally considered to be the world's first commercially produced minicomputer.

PDP-6. DEC's first large computer, the PDP-6, was released in late 1964. It was a 36-bit, register-oriented machine with about a megabyte of address space. The instruction set was notably easy to use, with a regular, complete operator set and a simple, uniform algorithm for effective address computation. However, the most noteworthy aspect of the PDP-6 was its general-purpose time-sharing software. This was the first such operating system to be offered by a computer manufacturer.

PDP-7. The PDP-7 was a physically smaller successor to the PDP-4. It appeared in 1964, and a second version, called the PDP-7A, followed it a year later.

PDP-8 Series. The PDP-8 was introduced in 1965 (see Fig. 2) and achieved a widespread acceptance based in part on its under-$20,000 price for minimum configurations. The initial model of PDP-8 was succeeded over the years by implementations emphasizing steadily decreasing prices. This trend started the following year with a serial version called the PDP-8/S, the first computer with 4K of memory to sell for under $10,000. The PDP-8/I and the PDP-8/L were beginning third-generation (integrated circuit) designs. The PDP-8 machines

up to this point had separate buses for memory, program controlled I/O, and direct memory access (channel-type) I/O. However, from this point on, these were combined into a single, simpler physical structure called an Omnibus, first seen in the PDP-8/E and its lower cost OEM version, the PDP-8/M. The PDP-8/A reduced costs further through a higher-density design including semiconductor memory.

By mid-1977, the PDP-8 processor had been reduced to a single CMOS chip; this CMOS-8 was offered as a separate component by semiconductor manufacturers, as well as embedded in DEC products such as the VT78 video terminal. Fig. 3 depicts the steadily declining prices which were a major factor in the PDP-8 family's market acceptance.

The hardware architecture of the PDP-8 is extremely simple, yet potentially completely general. The software has run the gamut between these extremes. On the one hand, the PDP-8 is an attractive choice for dedicated systems, especially where cost is a key constraint. Customers use it in this way, as has DEC itself in the case of such products as word-processing terminals. At the other end of the spectrum are full-function operating systems such as the OS/8 and the time-sharing system TSS-8. Using such operating systems together with high-level languages (both industry standard ones and proprietary languages, such as the scientific FOCAL and the commercial DIBOL), the virtual machine seen by the user is surprisingly similar to that seen on large computers.

PDP-9. The PDP-9 and its cost-reduced successor, the PDP-9/L, made their most notable advance over their predecessor, the PDP-7, in the area of memory. The memory cost was lowered in the PDP-9 by using three wires instead of four through each core, and moving from a 4K to an 8K word organization. The 9/L lowered memory costs still further by using memory planes developed for the PDP-8 line. The PDP-9 also contained a 64-bit-wide braided memory ROM used as a microcontrol store. This marked the first DEC use of the microprogrammed style of implementation, which would later become dominant over a widespread range of architectures and machine sizes.

PDP-10 Series. The PDP-10, which succeeded the PDP-6, consisted of four hardware-compatible basic designs, the KA10, KI10, KL10, and KL20. The general design goal of the family has been to let the price increase only slightly, while raising the performance significantly over time.

The PDP-10's major operating system over most of its life has been TOPS-10, which evolved from the PDP-6 operating system. In 1976, an alternate operating system, TOPS-20, was introduced, drawing heavily on the

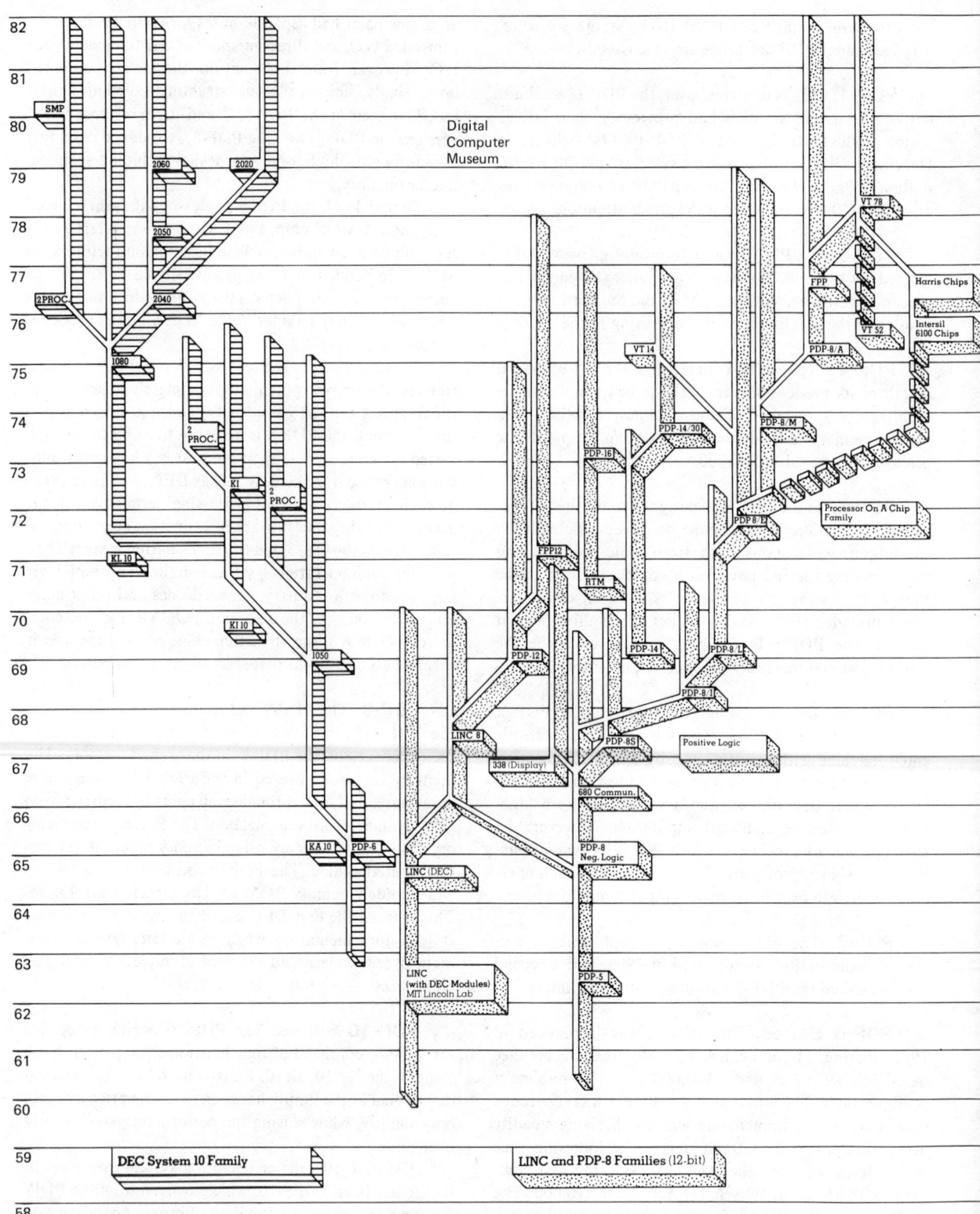

Fig. 1. DEC PDP family tree.

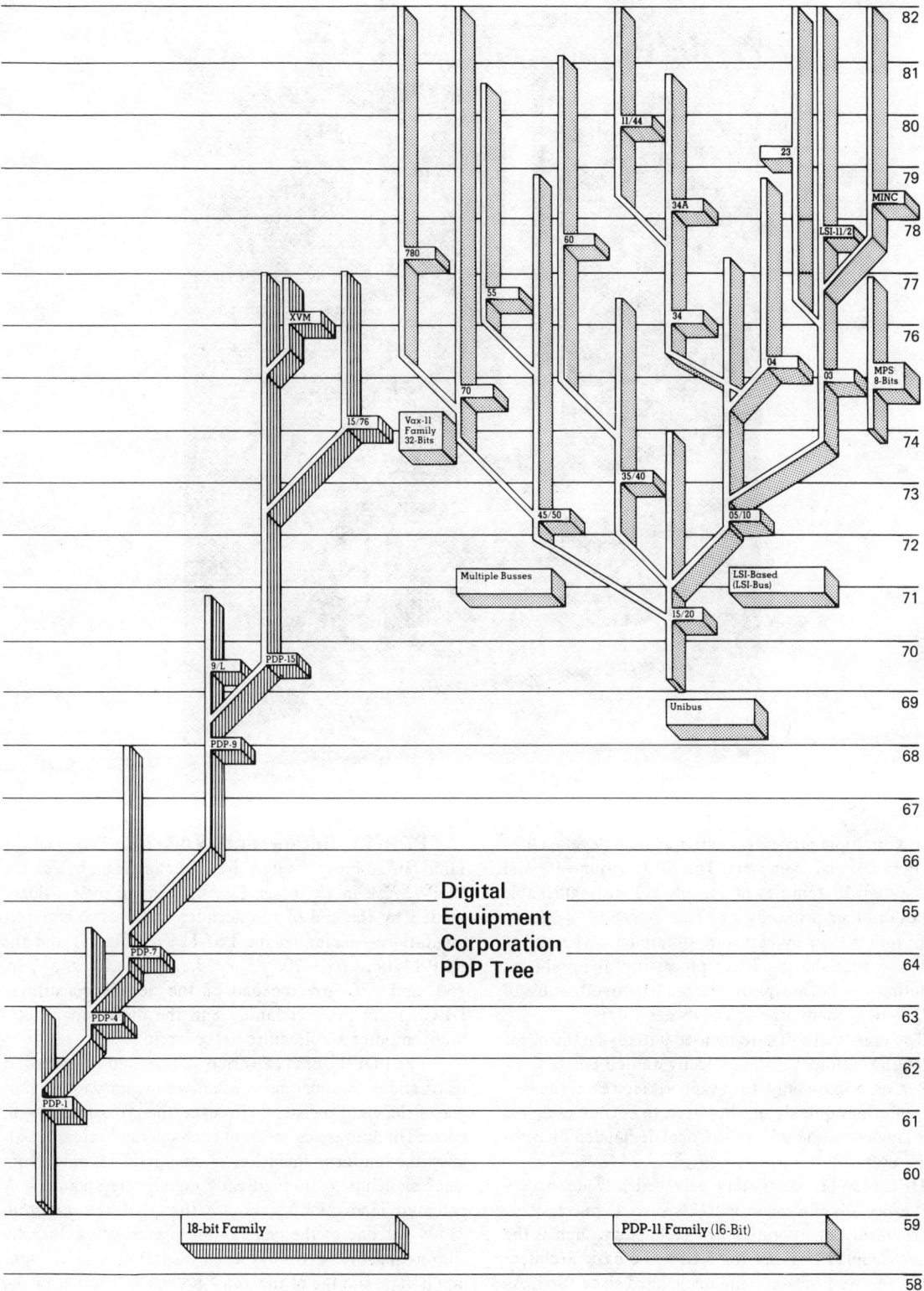

Digital Equipment Corporation PDP Tree

Fig. 2. PDP-8 introduced in 1965.

TENEX multiple process operating system developed by Bolt Beranek and Newman. The DEC system-10 and DEC system-20 families of models are distinguishable from each other primarily by their choice of operating system rather than by hardware differences. The ability to intermix time sharing, batch processing, and real-time computing has been a particularly attractive feature of the PDP-10 to many users since its early days.

The user-level software focused initially on the needs of scientific customers, who typically wanted Fortran, assembler, or, occasionally, Lisp support. However, the language offerings quickly mushroomed to encompass most major languages, including the Cobol demanded by commercial users.

DEC's 36-bit computers achieved a wide acceptance, especially in certain markets such as universities. By periodically incorporating new technology, such as the Emitter Coupled Logic of the KL10, the basic architecture has survived substantially unchanged since 1963. As of 1982, about fifteen hundred of these computers had been sold.

PDP-11 Series and VAX-11. The PDP-11 family of 16-bit computers grew from a single model, the PDP-11/20, in 1970 (see Fig. 4) to more than a dozen models by the end of the decade. These various implementations—including the LSI-11 (see Fig. 5) and the PDP-11/04, /05, /20, /23, /34, /34C, /40, /45, /55, /60, and /70—by the end of the decade constituted DEC's main product family and the most widely used minicomputer architecture in the world.

The PDP-11 offers a variety of one- and two-operand instructions. An operand is usually a memory location or one of the eight registers. However, the provision of eight choices of addressing mode in each operand reference allows the uniform inclusion of operands ranging from stack elements to automatically incremented pointers. A patented innovation is the treatment of the *program counter* as one of the general-purpose registers, thereby eliminating the need for special instructions to manipulate it. The storage of the *stack pointer* in another of the general-purpose registers and the mapping of the I/O data and control registers onto the memory address space

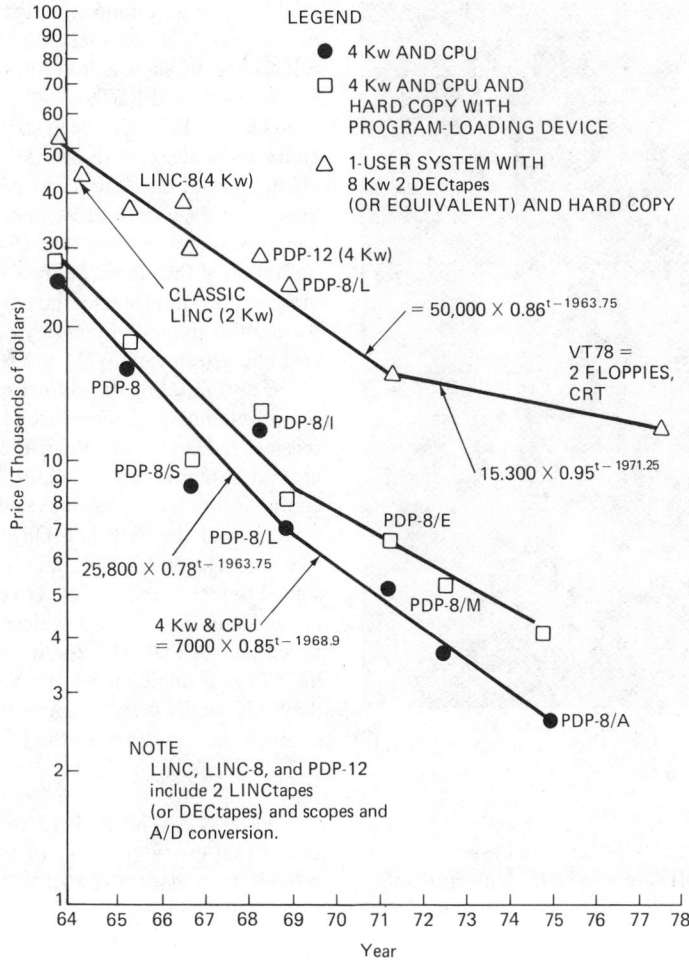

LEGEND

● 4 Kw AND CPU

□ 4 Kw AND CPU AND HARD COPY WITH PROGRAM-LOADING DEVICE

△ 1-USER SYSTEM WITH 8 Kw 2 DECtapes (OR EQUIVALENT) AND HARD COPY

LINC-8(4 Kw)

△ PDP-12 (4 Kw)

△ PDP-8/L

CLASSIC LINC (2 Kw)

$= 50{,}000 \times 0.86^{t-1963.75}$

VT78 = 2 FLOPPIES, CRT

PDP-8

PDP-8/I

PDP-8/S

$15.300 \times 0.95^{t-1971.25}$

PDP-8/E

PDP-8/L

$25{,}800 \times 0.78^{t-1963.75}$

PDP-8/M

4 Kw & CPU $= 7000 \times 0.85^{t-1968.9}$

PDP-8/A

NOTE
LINC, LINC-8, and PDP-12 include 2 LINCtapes (or DECtapes) and scopes and A/D conversion.

Price (Thousands of dollars)

Year

Fig. 3. Price of DEC's 12-bit computers versus time.

serve a similar role in simplifying the instruction set. Other architectural advances over previous DEC computers include the universal system bus (called the Unibus), the support of eight-bit bytes as a basic data type (previous DEC computers were all multiples of six bits in word lengths), and ease of reentrant coding, which facilitates ROM-based minicomputer applications.

From the users' perspective, one of the most valuable features of the PDP-11 was the simultaneous availability of models of varying sizes. As shown in Fig. 6, three different styles of design focusing on maximum performance, maximum cost/performance, and minimum cost, respectively, were all being pursued simultaneously. The various models of the PDP-11 were relatively compatible, but a steady stream of incremental features did occur in succeeding models as illustrated in Fig. 7.

As in the case of its hardware, the PDP-11 software expanded over time from the relatively unsophisticated

Fig.4. Original PDP-11 introduced in 1970.

Fig. 5. LSI-11/23 is the newest LSI-11 microcomputer.

could not be accommodated through a purely evolutionary approach. Thus, there evolved several distinct operating systems, such as Bell Labs' UNIX and DEC's RT-11, RSX-11, and RSTS.

The PDP-11 has been extremely successful in the commercial sense, with over 50,000 units sold in its first eight years of existence, and production volumes which have steadily increased as lower-cost versions have become available. By the late 1970s, however, the 16-bit limitation of the virtual address space became an increasingly important obstacle, since both application complexity and the amount of memory purchasable at reasonable cost had grown rapidly.

This limitation on address space was the impetus for the development of the VAX-11 ("Virtual Address Extension"). On the one hand, the VAX architecture is a natural extension of the PDP-11 (in fact, it includes a compatibility mode which executes the nonprivileged instructions of the PDP-11). On the other hand, in its native mode, the VAX is a 32-bit machine architecture designed to feel friendly to experienced PDP-11 users while at the same time making widespread improvements to it based on the PDP-11 experience. Originally introduced in 1978 as a single model, the VAX-11/780 (see Fig. 8), the VAX family is evolving to a broad range of computers in much the same way as the PDP-11 family has done.

paper tape and disk operating systems and assemblers to a broad spectrum of software products. Unfortunately, compatibility across the spectrum proved more elusive in the case of software than of hardware. The diversity of applications and of machine sizes created stresses which

PDP-12. The PDP-12 was a single physical processor that executed either PDP-8 or LINC instructions by switching modes. The LINC (Laboratory Instrument Computer) had been built at the M.I.T. Lincoln Laboratory in 1962. In addition to its use in the PDP-12, the LINC also influenced the design of the PDP-4, the PDP-

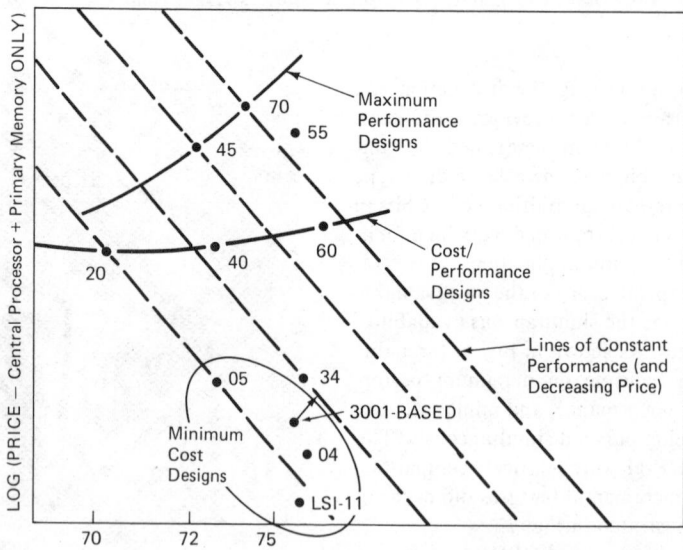

Fig. 6.   PDP-11 models price versus time with lines of constant performance.

Model(s)	Evolution
11/20	Base ISP (16-bit virtual address) and PMS (16-bit processor physical memory address) Unibus with 18-bit addressing
11/20	Extended Arithmetic Element (hardware multiply/divide)
11/45(11/55,11/70,11/60,11/34)	Floating-point instruction set with 6 additional registers (46 instructions) in the Floating-Point Process
11/45(11/55,11/70)	Memory management (KT11C), 3 modes of protection (Kernel, Supervisor, User); 18-bit processor physical addressing; 16-bit virtual addressing in 8 segments for both instruction and data spaces
11/45(11/66,11/70)	Extensions for second set of general registers and program interrupt request
11/40(11/03)	Extended Instruction Set for multiply/divide; floating-point instruction set (4 instructions)
11/40(11/34,11/60)	Memory Management (KT11D), 2 modes of protection (Kernel, User); 18-bit processor physical addressing; 16-bit virtual addressing in 8 segments
11/70	22-bit processor physical addressing; Unibus map for peripheral controller 22-bit addressing
11/70 (11/60)	Error register accessibility for on-line diagnosis and retry (e.g., cache parity error)
11/03 (11/04, 11/34)	Program access to processor status register via explicit instruction (versus Unibur address)
11/03	One level program interrupt
11/60	Extended Function Code for invocation of user-written microcode
VAX-11/780	VAX architectural extensions for 32-bit virtual addressing; VAX ISP
11/03	Commercial Instruction Set (CIS)
11/0mP	Interprocessor Interrupt and System Timers for multiprocessor

Fig. 7. Chronology of PDP-11 Instruction Set Processor (ISP) Evolution.

5, and the DECtape (DEC's unique small-reel magnetic tape), as well as being a forerunner of the highly integrated personal computer. The PDP-12 was first shipped in 1969 and sold about 1,000 units.

PDP-14. The PDP-14, together with its successors, the PDP-14/30 and the PDP-14/35, was designed for the replacement of dedicated relay logic controlling industrial processes. This application required the repeated evaluation of Boolean equations representing the logic network together with packaging suitable for industrial environments.

PDP-15. First shipped in 1970, the PDP-15 was the successor to the PDP-9. It added new features, such as an index register and an I/O processor. Yet, aided by its extensive introduction of integrated circuitry, it was able to offer these improved capabilities at decreased cost and in a package only one-third the size of its predecessor.

PDP-16. The PDP-16 was a series of printed circuit modules which could be connected together with or without programs in configurations specific to an individual application. This product was aimed at applications for which even the simplest general-purpose computer could not be cost-justified, a segment of the marketplace that shrank steadily as computer prices continued to drop. First delivered in 1971, PDP-16s were subsequently renamed RTMs (Register Transfer Modules).

Because of their widespread market acceptance (over 250,000 computers by 1982), the PDP computers have had broad influences on other computers, especially on other minicomputers and microcomputers. The 12-bit, 16-bit, 32-bit, and 36-bit families of computers are still being actively marketed as of 1982 in models using the latest technologies. There is every reason to expect that several such families will continue to co-exist indefinitely since smaller, simpler computers are economically advantageous for simpler applications and larger, more sophisticated machines are more attractive for complex applications. Additionally, the overriding importance of software costs encourages existing users to protect their software investment by preferring family extensions until inescapable limits are encountered.

REFERENCE

1978. Bell, C. G., Mudge, J. C., and McNamara, J. E. *Computer Engineering—A DEC View of Hardware Systems Design.* Digital Press, September. (This book is the major source for this article, and provides a comprehensive bibliography for further reference.)
1980. Levy, H. M. and Eckhouse, R. H., Jr. *Computer Programming and Architecture: The VAX-11.* Bedford, MA: Digital Press

C. G. BELL
J. R. BELL

DIGITAL-TO-ANALOG CONVERTERS.

See ANALOG-TO-DIGITAL AND DIGITAL-TO-ANALOG CONVERTERS.

Fig. 8. VAX-11/780 is the 32-bit extension of the PDP-11 family.

DIRECT ACCESS

For articles on related subjects *see* FILES; and MEM-
ORY: Auxiliary.

Early hardware, developed for the storage of large
files in a data processing system, depended on two
media—punched cards (in the very early days) and magnetic tapes on the early computers. Although widely different in physical characteristics, they had something in
common—they forced the user to store file records in
some predetermined sequence and to process them in that
same order.

Punched-card users had had no option but to accept
the limitations of their equipment, but there seemed to be
something quite out of balance between the short time a
computer took to update a file record and all the sorting,
collating, etc., necessary to find the record in the first
place. Worse, although users often could learn to live
with these limitations, there were certain types of commercial and industrial operations where they were quite
unacceptable. In processing banking transactions, for example, it is often very desirable to be able to update each
record as and when each transaction is made. In any system that calls for the interrogation of a file, such as airline seat reservations, it is obviously imperative to be able

to handle each separate transaction as and when it occurs
in a random sequence.

Records in magnetic tape files are stored in the sequence of some key identifier, and access to them is therefore "serial", i.e., item by item in that sequence. The
terms *sequential access* and *serial access* are therefore
used. What is required is a system for access directly to
any desired record; the term usually given to this is *direct
access*.

Not until the late 1950s was suitable hardware developed to permit files to be stored in such a way that
access to any desired record could be obtained in the
same time as to any other, and in an acceptably short
time. The machine that first accomplished this was the
IBM 305 RAMAC (*q.v.*—Random Access Method for
Accounting and Control), and the storage device was the
magnetic disk file.

The magnetic tape unit is in many ways like the domestic tape recorder, where we often have to run through
many feet of tape to find the recording we want. The
magnetic disk file is in many ways like the phonograph,
where the recording head can be moved very quickly
(given a steady hand) to any desired position on the surface of the disk to select the desired piece of recording.
In practice, the computer disk file is usually equipped
with a number of disks, with a separate recording head

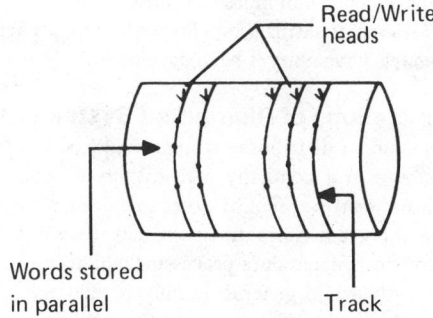

Fig. 1. Magnetic drum.

for every disk surface. In this way, the selection of a desired record at random can usually be made in a fraction of a second, and the computer system can therefore respond in an acceptable time scale to the input item, usually in about one-third of a second.

Where higher speeds are required (measured, say, in hundredths of a second), magnetic drums (Fig. 1) are used. These are fast, rotating cylinders with file information stored on tracks along the surface and with a recording head for every track. There is no need, therefore, to move the heads (as with disk files), and the time for access to required information depends only on the speed of rotation of the drum.

The need for speed in accessing file records is clear. What is even more obvious is the requirement for ultra-rapid access to program instructions and data held in the computer's main memory. These are required with an access time measured in millionths of a second or less so that the speed of the arithmetic unit is not wasted.

It is an interesting paradox that one of the fastest devices currently used for random access to files, the magnetic drum, was used in some of the earliest computers for the main memory and was rejected because it was too slow for random access to instructions and data!

It was replaced by magnetic core or semiconductor memory units which form the majority of main memories in today's computers. These are capable of providing required data or instructions in times ranging from a few microseconds (millionths of a second) down to a few nanoseconds (billionths of a second), speeds compatible with those of arithmetic and control units. Main memories are therefore also classifiable as *random* or *direct* access.

G. J. MORRIS

DISTRIBUTED SYSTEMS

For articles on related subjects *see* ARPA NETWORK: COMMUNICATIONS AND COMPUTERS; COMPUTER NETWORKS; and DATA COMMUNICATIONS.

Distributed systems are a natural outgrowth of the development of computer networks. Computer networking focused on having a number of processors communicate with one another, as well as on the utilization of such systems by remote users, whether the "user" was a terminal or another computer. With distributed data processing systems, we apply the results of the work in networking to the design of applications systems. A distributed data processing system is characterized by having both the processor and storage facilities physically dispersed and interconnected by data communications facilities, as shown in Fig. 1. Distributed processing systems have been proposed as a means to provide a large number of highly desirable user and operational benefits. Some of these benefits are listed in Table 1.

What Is Distributed. There are three activities of a data processing system that may be distributed: (1) processing functions; (2) storage of the database(s); and (3) system control. In order to achieve an appreciable portion of the benefits of distributed systems listed in

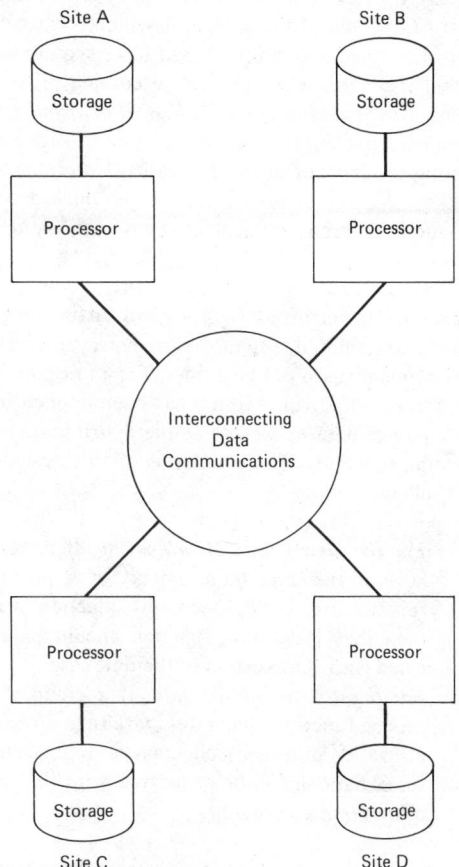

Fig. 1. Physical components of a distributed processing system.

Table 1. Benefits of Distributed Systems

High system performance—fast response
High throughput
High system reliability/high system availability
Graceful degradation (fail-soft capability)
Reduced network transmission costs
Ease of modular and incremental growth
Configuration flexibility
Automatic resource sharing
Automatic load distribution
High adaptability to changes in workload
Incremental replacement and/or upgrading of components
  (hardware and software)
Easy expansion in both capacity and function
Easy adaptation to new functions
Good response to temporary overloads

Table 1, it is essential that the system exhibit a high degree of distribution for all three of these activities.

Distributed and Decentralized Systems.

Although the term *centralized* has a very clear meaning, almost irrespective of the context in which it is used, the terms *distributed* and *decentralized* have acquired quite different meanings when used in discussing distributed systems. *Distributed* means the *physical distribution* of a component (or components) of the system, such as the operating system code or the database. *Decentralized,* on the other hand, describes an activity in which decisions are made at different physical locations in the system.

Distributed Systems Design.

Tools are not yet available to perform a rigorous cost justification of a particular distributed system design; however, there are some commonly used design guides. The most popular of these is the "80-20 rule" which has been applied to the distribution of data as well as to the distribution of the processing functions. The two forms of this design rule are as follows.

1. *For the distribution of processing.* If more than 80% of the data requirements of a processing function are met by one (sub)collection of data, then that processing function should be co-located with that portion of the database.
2. *For the distribution of data.* If a group of processing functions generates more than 80% of the utilization of a (sub)collection of data, then that set of data should be co-located with that group of processing functions.

Although these two rules are clearly related, they do provide two different design criteria. A complete design

must be based on much more than just the data requirements or the data utilization; however, comprehensive design models have not yet been developed.

Applications of Distributed Systems.

A situation in which a distributed system might be especially appropriate is in a company with dispersed operations, such as a national warehouse system or branch sales offices. The important characteristic is that there be a combination of storage and data processing which can be performed locally while generating only a relatively small amount of external activity that must be sent to other locations for further processing. It should be noted, however, that decisions on the distribution of both processing and data are more often than not based on management or organizational factors, rather than on the technical characteristics of the operation. Fig. 2 illustrates a simple example of what might be a portion of a complete distributed system. Branch office computers handle all local activities, while the headquarters' system processes aggregated data at the corporate level.

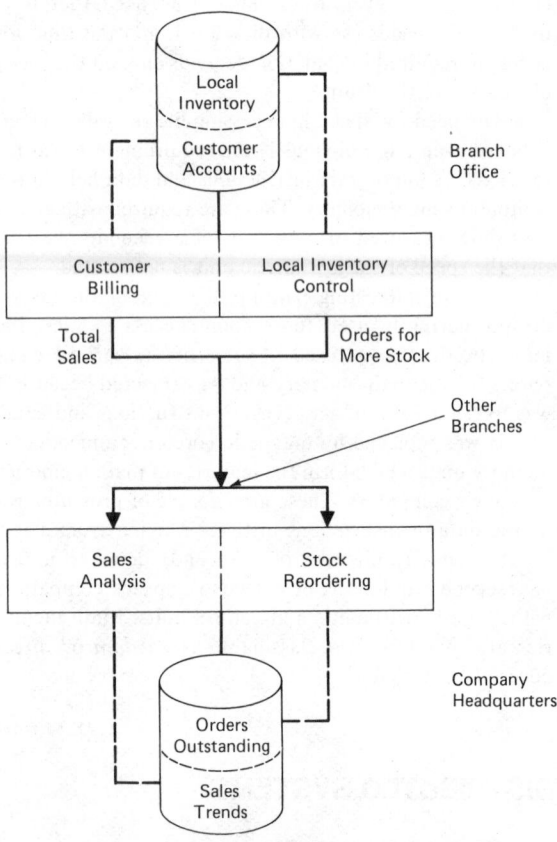

Fig. 2. An example of a distributed application.

Capabilities of Distributed Systems. A good distributed system should provide at least the following capabilities.

- The user should view the system in the same manner as a centralized or uniprocessor system.
- The selection of the specific resources to be utilized in servicing a user's request should be transparent to the users (i.e., occur without his or her knowledge), unless a specific designation of the resources to be used is desired.
- The distributed operating system should automatically distribute and balance the load over the resources available.
- The distributed database manager should control concurrent access to data files by different processors and should ensure that the contents of redundant copies of the database are at all times consistent.
- The system should be able to continue in operation despite the failure of individual components.

State-of-the-Art. The hardware required to implement a distributed system is already available or is within the current state-of-the-art with respect to both cost and performance. However, the situation with respect to system software is not as well advanced. There are unsolved problems in the design of the control algorithms, as well as in their performance. The algorithms necessary to control distributed and decentralized system resources are still under development. In addition, current solutions to distributed database management tend to execute very slowly when compared to centralized systems. The achievement of a large proportion of the system benefits listed above rests on the solution of these control software problems.

REFERENCES

1979. Katzan, Harry. *Distributed Information Systems.* New York: Petrocelli Books.
1980. Patrick, Robert L. *Application Design Handbook for Distributed Systems.* CBI Publishing Co.

P. H. ENSLOW

DOCUMENTATION

For articles on related subjects *see* ADMINISTRATIVE APPLICATIONS; BLOCK DIAGRAM; FEASIBILITY STUDY; FLOWCHART; FLOW DIAGRAM; PROGRAM SPECIFICATION; STANDARDS; and SYSTEM CHART.

Documentation is a vital part of developing and using a computer-based system. In some commercial organizations, 20% or even more of the total development effort goes into the documentation of the new system, recording how the new system is to work and how it was developed. Documentation of a computer project falls into two broad categories—development documentation and control documentation. Development documentation records how a computer-based system is structured and what it is supposed to do and gives the background information upon which the design is founded. Control documentation, on the other hand, serves an administrative function: It records the resources used in developing and implementing the system, and includes such documents as project plans, schedules, resource allocation details, and progress reports.

Functions of Documentation. Documentation serves four main functions:

1. Intertask/interphase communication.
2. Historical reference for modification and correction.
3. Quality and quantity control.
4. Instructional reference.

The relative importance of each of these depends on many factors. For example, one of the most important is the scope and type of the project; it may be a large-scale commercial system, or a scientific problem-solving program used by one or two technicians on a limited amount of data. Within each category, there are the variations in project size, problem complexity, organization of staff, and the time scale for development and use. Each function of documentation is described below.

Intertask/Interphase Communication. This operation records what has been done at each stage of the project so that instructions can be issued for the next phase of work, or so that all people involved in the project can agree what has been done before work proceeds to the next step. The amount of time and effort that must be devoted to documentation for this reason is a function of the scope of the system and the number of people involved.

In the development of a major commercial system, which requires procedures such as invoicing, inventory control, payroll, or production control, many people will be involved. In a production control system, for example, the business functions involved could include, among others:

1. Sales forecasting (linking with sales accounts).
2. Parts explosion and production batching/netting (linked with engineering design).
3. Plant resource allocation and scheduling.

4. Materials ordering/tooling and allocation.
5. Monitoring job progress.
6. Scrap and bonus reporting (linking with payroll).
7. Job costing (linking all systems).

Most of these functions are closely related to one another and with other systems in the company. Some 20 or 30 separate job functions or organizational units may be involved with the development, implementation, and running of the computer system. In addition to job functions such as those described above, different levels of user staff will involve senior or executive management, line management, and supervisors and operators. Similarly, a number of job functions will be performed by personnel in the data processing or management services department; for example:

1. Business analysts, internal business consultants who advise management on business methods and who identify areas for improvement.
2. Systems analysts, who investigate, analyze, and specify a new system.
3. Systems designers, who design the new system (computer and manual procedures) in detail.
4. Programmers, who design, code, and test the computer programs for the system.
5. Operators, who are responsible for the day-to-day running of the system.

There may also be general support or service staff within data processing, such as maintenance programmers, software support people, forward planners, and standards analysts. In a small installation, many of the job functions listed above may be performed by one person or a small group; in a large installation, each job function may be performed by a specialist group. It can be seen that keeping people informed, passing on information and ideas for approval, and giving instructions involves a complex communications network in which formal documentation plays a vital role.

A failure of communication through poor documentation (or a lack of it) can prove very expensive indeed. The documentation will also help to insure project continuity should staff changes occur.

The use of documentation for intertask/interphase communication is equally important in large technical or scientific projects. Where the development of a program or group of programs can be done by only a limited number of technicians, who are quite often both problem proponents and solution programmers, the importance of documentation during the project diminishes. However, the documentation of what has been done and how the programs work will be important for historical or instructional reference, as described below.

Historical Reference. The reference function is relevant to both commercial and scientific work. It is the documentation of how the system works that makes it easily changed after it is implemented. All systems are subject to change, with the sole exception of one-time problem-solving applications with limited amounts of data; these are usually scientific. (One-time applications should be treated with care. Many so-called one-time applications can become repetitive, routine jobs.) Maintenance of business systems and programs will be required because the nature of a business and its methods change, or because the organization is restructured, new types of products are developed, management reporting requirements change, and so on.

In scientific work, programs may have to be altered because the nature of the problem to be solved changes, possibly as a result of further research. A system may have to be changed because of new software or hardware. It may be desirable to change the processing methods because new techniques become available. The reason for the change may lie outside the organization altogether, as is the case with legal requirements and statutory changes. The changes may be made to the system as long as five or six years after implementation.

A system can be maintained efficiently only if the existing operation of all procedures and programs is clearly known and understood. The documentation of the system provides this knowledge. For example, a program written a year ago is to be changed today; the program consists of 2,000 instructions with many branches and nested loops. The programmer who originally wrote it is no longer available. The modifications require that logic of the program be understood; the new programmer must insure that errors are not introduced by overlooking the impact of some of the changes.

The documentation of a system may also be reviewed for performance purposes. Many installations develop performance standards based on records of time and resources budgeted and used in developing a system, as compared with system type, scope, and complexity. The control documentation is used for details of resources, and the development documentation for a description of the system. By formally capturing details of all projects, estimates of resources for future projects can be improved.

Quality/Quantity Control. As a system develops, various elements of documentation are completed as each step is finished. Management can use this documentation to evaluate project progress and individual performance.

Instructional Reference. The development documentation can be reviewed during and after development for many general purposes. For example, documentation will enable trainees to study a system developed by experienced technicians. This is particularly important for instructional reference to generalized systems or general-purpose software. Another benefit of documentation is that an outside party can evaluate the system and its method of operation to determine if the package is suitable for use in another environment. In this case, sufficient information must be given to enable the user to apply the software to other problems and requirements.

Instructional reference thus includes all literature provided by a software supplier, such as the reference manuals for all languages, utilities, operating systems, subroutines, and application packages. It also includes the documentation and library facilities in a large organization (such as a large decentralized company or a university) that produces its own generalized software or participates in a general interchange or pooling of programs.

Types of Documentation. Thus far, the functions of documentation have been discussed and the importance of providing it has been emphasized. In the development of a system, whether it is a large-scale commercial system or a group of scientific programs for analyzing data, certain categories of documentation must be considered. These are:

1. Analytical documentation.
2. Systems documentation.
3. Program documetation.
4. Operations documentation.
5. User/management aids.

Each of these categories is described below, and the major factors that influence the form of the documentation in any particular organization are then discussed.

Analytical documentation consists of all the records and reports produced when a project is initiated. For all projects except those that require a single, one-time, problem-solving program, some form of initial briefing is required. In most organizations, the technicians who design, program, and test a system are grouped into a computing or data processing department, and the users who commission work from the data processing department must define the nature and objectives of the project. In some technical or scientific environments, the user is capable of specifying in very exact terms what is required in the way of processing and outputs. Generally, for any type of project, however (including many business applications), the initial briefing should consist of a *user request,* stating the problem (i.e., what the user needs to achieve); a *feasibility study* that evaluates possible solutions (in outline); and a *project plan* that estimates the time and resources required to develop and implement

the system. Failure to produce and agree upon these three statements in the briefing will result in much wasted effort later in the project. They are vital whenever a user commissions work from computer technicians, and must be provided before money is actually committed to the more time-consuming tasks of system design and programming.

Systems documentation encompasses all information needed to define the proposed computer-based system to a level where it can be programmed, tested, and implemented. The major document is some form of *system specification,* which acts as a permanent record of the structure, its functions and work flow, and the controls on the system. It is the basic means of communication between the systems design, programming, and user functions. In a major project, the system specification comprises a number of documents. A sample outline of specification documentation for a major project is shown in Fig. 1. If the project will result in the development of only one or two programs for restricted use, then only the *program (processing) specification* would be produced. Fig. 2 is an example of part of a system flowchart taken from a system specification (Section 1.2).

Program documentation comprises the records of the detailed logic and coding of the constituent programs of a system. These records, prepared by the programmer, aid program development and acceptance, troubleshooting, general maintenance, machine/software conversion at a later date, and programmer changeover.

Program documentation covers both specific applications programs and general-purpose or in-house developed software. In addition to documenting *how* a program works (information not always released in the case of general software), instructions for *using* the program must be written for packaged software (this is described in "User/management aids" below).

Operations documentation specifies those procedures required for running the system by operations personnel. It gives the general sequence of events for performing the job and defines precise procedures for data control and security, data preparation, program running, output dispersal, and ancillary operations.

User/management aids consist of all the descriptive and instructive material necessary for the user to participate in the running of the operational system, including notes on the interpretation of the output results. Where a software package is produced, this category includes all the material necessary to evaluate the programs and all the instructions for use.

Every installation should establish documentation standards (i.e., rules for the completion of certain documents at certain times) that define the content, format, and distribution of the documents. Many factors influ-

SYSTEMS SPECIFICATION

Title and Administrative Material

1.0 Systems Summary
  1.1 User Summary
    1. Purpose and Function
    2. Files Maintained and Affected
    3. Input and Input Sources
    4. Output and Output Uses
  1.2 System Flowchart
    1. Flowchart
    2. Reference Lists
  1.3 Narrative Description
    1. Definitions
    2. System Flow
    3. General Timing and Size Estimates

2.0 File Specifications
  2.1 File Identification and Characteristics
    1. General Description
    2. File Abstract
  2.2 Record Format
  2.3 Data Element Descriptions
  2.4 Appendices
    1. Layouts
    2. Edit Lists
    3. Cross-Reference Lists
                cont./

3.0 Input Specifications
  3.1 Identification and Purpose
  3.2 Transaction Listing (media purpose, programs affected, frequency, volume and source)
  3.3 Input Layouts and Samples

4.0 Output Specifications
  4.1 Identification and Purpose
  4.2 Output Listing (program no., media, frequency, volume, no. of copies, and destination)
  4.3 Output Description
  4.4 Output Formats

5.0 Program (Processing) Specifications
  5.1 Program Specification 1
  5.2 Program Specification 2
      .
  5.n Program Specification n

6.0 Systems Test Plan
  6.1 Identification
  6.2 Test Organization
  6.3 Validity Criteria (control, processing, and output)
  6.4 Test Schedule
  6.5 Test Cases

7.0 Implementation Plan (timing, resources, responsibilities, and method)

Fig. 1. Sample outline of specification documentation. Note that items 2.0, 3.0, and 4.0 are repeated for each file. Data common to a number of programs may be defined in a Data Specification section (not shown). An added section might include a final cost-benefit analysis.

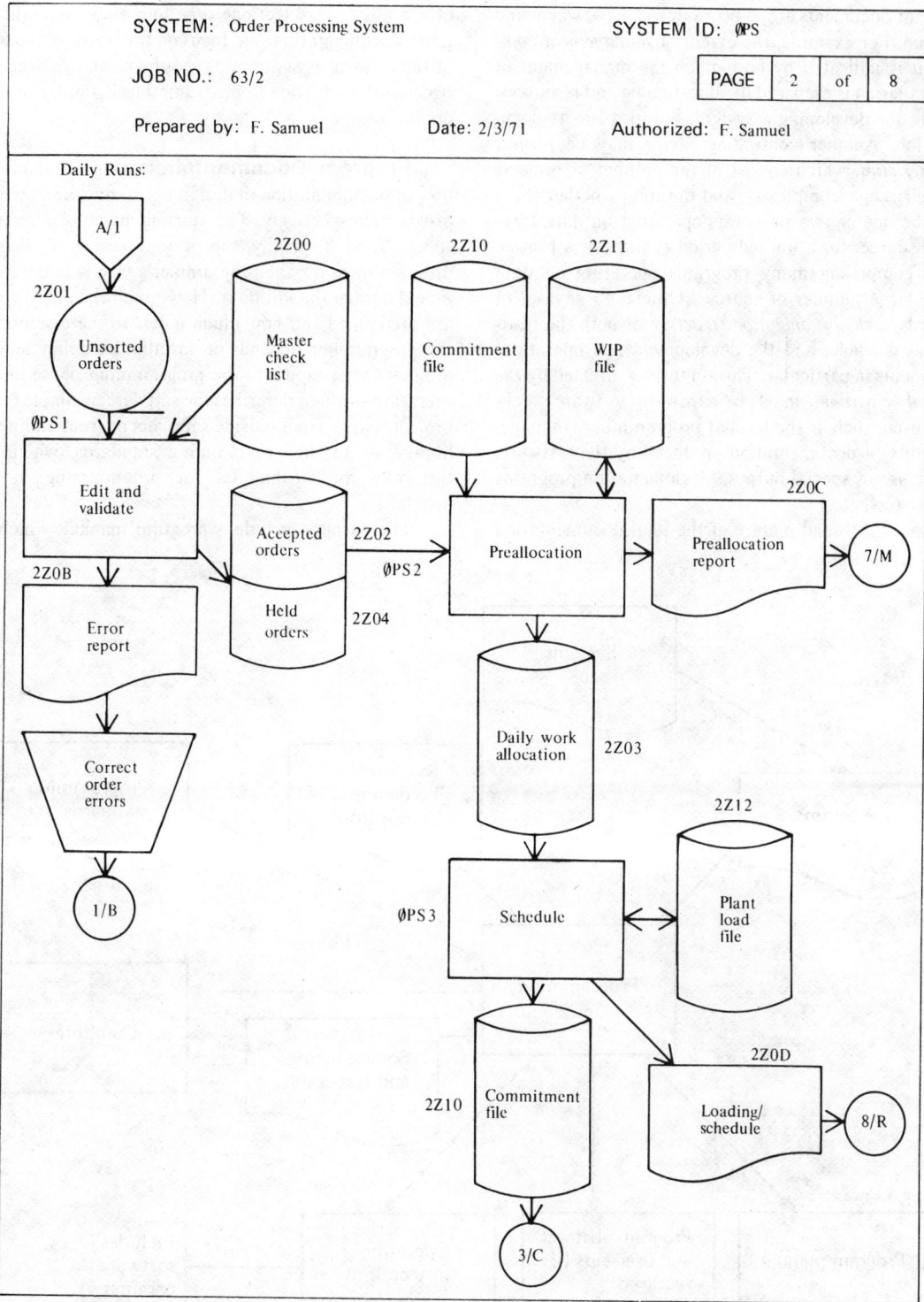

Fig. 2. Part of a system flowchart, showing the sequence of manual procedures and computer programs with their inputs and outputs. For each program box a Program Specification will be prepared. Data specifications will be prepared for all inputs, outputs, and files. See also Fig. 5.

ence what documents are to be produced, how, when, and by whom. For example, the extent of *management commitment* is indicated by how much the management of the installation is prepared to allocate time and resources, not only for developing a system, but also for its documentation. Another controlling factor may be *project characteristics,* which consist of the number of projects and their scope, complexity, and duration whether there are to be one or two programs operating on data from limited sources for a limited period of time, or a routine system comprising many programs operating on data from a large number of sources. Crucial to any set of standards is *the organization structure* of both the institution as a whole, and the development and operations departments in particular. This, in turn, is affected by *the technical environment:* The hardware/software techniques used, such as the level of programming language, the quality of documentation produced by the software, and the use of special-purpose documentation programs (flowcharters, etc.).

From this broad picture of the total documentation of a project, we select one type to review in detail: program documentation. We focus on this because the limits of the tasks of programming can be clearly defined, and because this function in programming is similar in many organizations.

Program Documentation. Fig. 3 shows the flow of documentation in designing, coding, and testing a program, respectively. The starting point is a program specification. Typically, this is a statement of *what* the program must do; the programmer's task is to determine *how* the program will do it. How much the data formats are predefined and how much is left to the discretion of the programmer depends on installation policy and the project. Other inputs to the programming phase include literature—which describes the software available for the project (either from outside suppliers or from an internal library)—and the programming standards, which give the rules and techniques for programming in that installation.

The outputs include a program manual, which de-

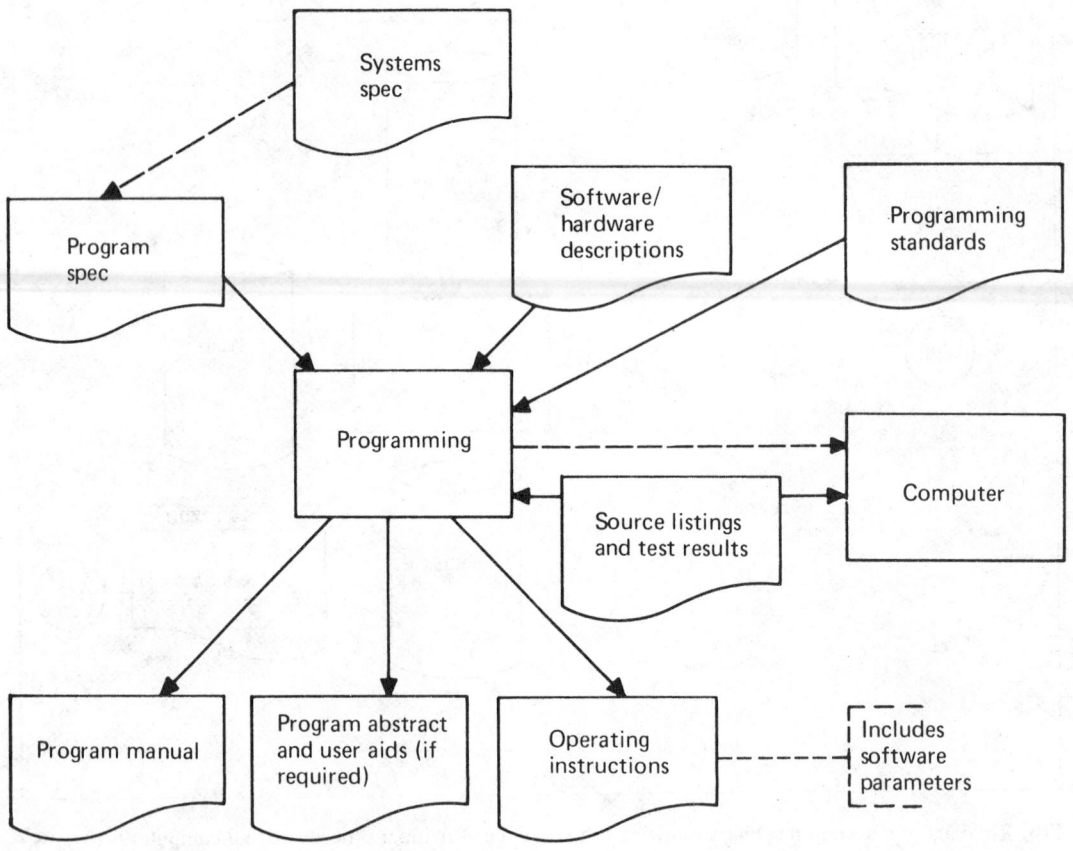

Fig. 3. Documentation flow.

scribes the programs in detail (construction, coding, and testing), instructions for use (for a generalized program), and computer operating instructions for day-to-day running. In many cases the task of documenting a program is one of adding to the initial program specification in order to build up the program manual (see Fig. 4). The various elements of program documentation are discussed below.

Program Specification. This is a statement of the data available for processing, the required outputs, and the details of the necessary processing. The specification can be prepared by the problem proponent, a specialist systems analyst/designer, or the programmer. It must be complete, accurate, and unambiguous; changes to the specification after programming begins can be very expensive. The specification usually contains the following information.

1. Input.
2. Output.
3. Major functions performed.
4. The means of communication between this program and previous and following programs.

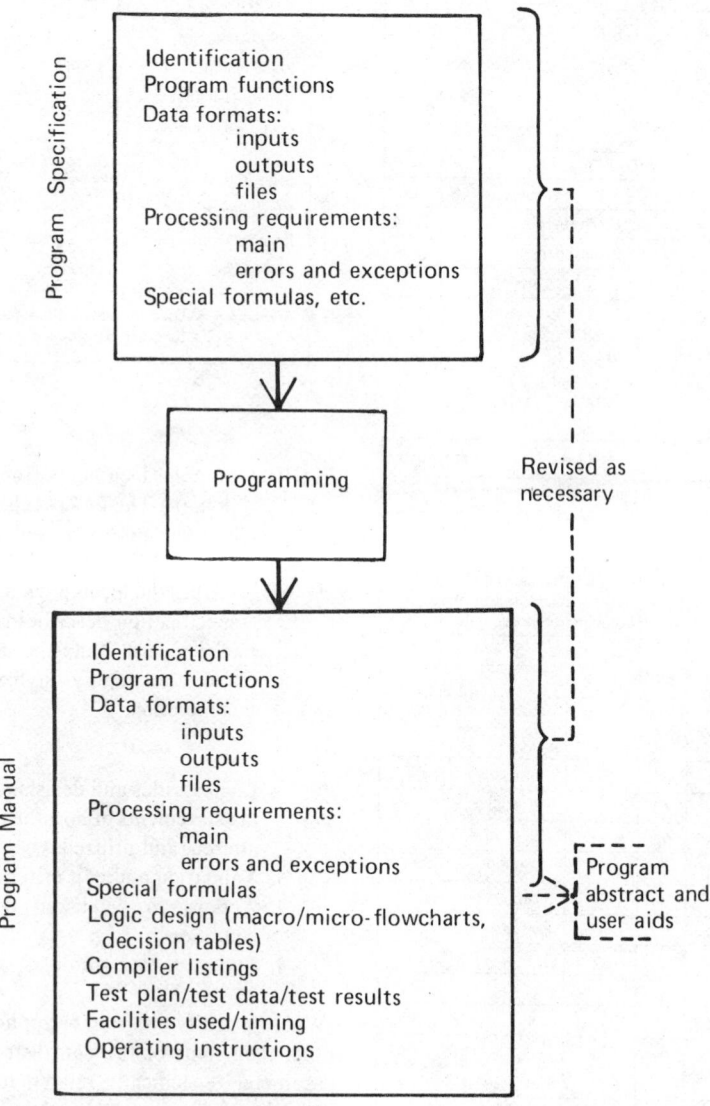

Fig. 4. Program specification and program manual.

SYSTEM: Order Processing System   SYSTEM ID: ϕPS

PROGRAM: Order Edit and Validate   PROGRAM ID: ϕPS1

Prepared by: J. Roberts   Date: 4/5/71   Authorized: I. Samuel

PROCESS CHART

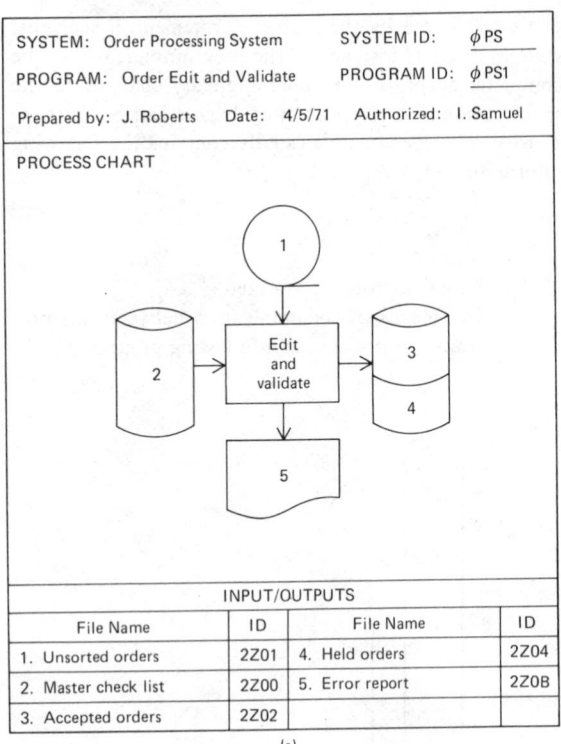

INPUT/OUTPUTS

File Name	ID	File Name	ID
1. Unsorted orders	2Z01	4. Held orders	2Z04
2. Master check list	2Z00	5. Error report	2Z0B
3. Accepted orders	2Z02		

(a)

File Specification   FILE ID: 2Z00

File Name: Master check list

Prepared by: J. Roberts   Date: 4/5/71   Authorized: I. Samuel

Medium:	Disk
Contents (record names):	Order Identity, Part Request, End Record
Sequence (if any):	Key field within record type
Retention and Protection:	Master
Used On (program ID's):	

File Description

Type of record   Organization

Blocked	√	Sequential	
Unblocked		Direct Access	
Fixed length	√	Index Sequential	√
Variable length			
Undefined length			

Sizes (bytes)	Average	Maximum	Minimum
Block length:	–	1232+4	–
Record length:	–	52+4	–
File length:	2,300	4,000	1,400

Remarks: Used to validate all input order requests by order identity and part characteristics.

(b)

File Name: Master check list   Record Name: Part request

Format codes: A = characters (alpha/mixed alpha-numeric)
                 N = zoned decimal
                 P = packed decimal
                 B = binary

Data Description			From Byte No.	No. of Bytes or Columns	Range: value (e.g., 1–5), blank (b̸), or master reference table
Field Name	Mnemonic	Format			
Record type		N	1	6	1
KEY FIELD					
Part number		A	7	30	Any character
DATA					
Dimension		A	37	6	Any character or b̸
Issue code		A	43	1	A, C, L, P, or S
Status		A	44	1	U, N, or b̸
Units		N	45	5	0–99999
Authority		A	50	3	Alpha
				52	

(c)

Fig. 5. Sample documents from a program specification. (a) The process chart identifies the system and the program, and shows inputs and outputs. (b) Sheet 1 of the file specification describes the file as a whole. (c) Sheet 2 of the file specification describes the content and format of a record. Note the use of preprinted forms and the highly stylized, rigid method of completion.

5. Logical rules and decisions to be followed, including statements of how the input is to be examined, altered, and utilized.

6. Validation and edit criteria.

7. Actions to be taken on error or exception conditions.

8. Special tables, formulas, and algorithms.

(Where a utility program or application package is being used, then some of the data listed will be omitted, and parameters specifically related to the program will be listed instead.) The description of the processing rules (item 5 in the list), can be given in narrative, flowchart,

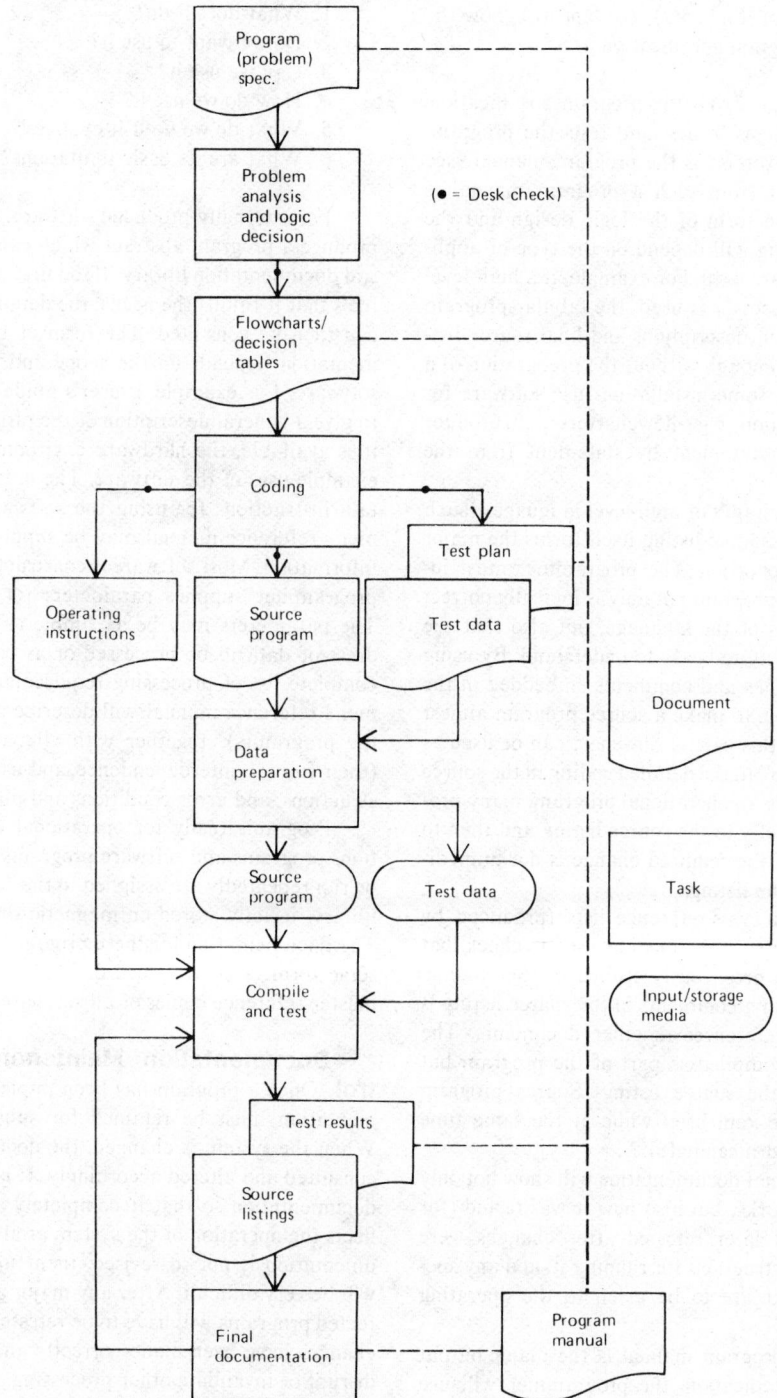

Fig. 6. A flowchart from a program manual.

or decision-table form. Figs. 5(a), (b), and (c) show the components of a program specification.

Program Manual. From the program specification, the programmer designs, codes, and tests the program. The output of this exercise is the program manual (see Fig. 4). A flowchart from such a program manual is shown in Fig. 6. The form of the logic design and the source program listing will depend on the type of application and the software used. For example, if a high-level decision-table preprocessor is used, the tabular program together with the data descriptions and final source listing will be complete enough without the preparation of a flowchart. Similarly, some installations use software for the final documentation; e.g., flowcharters that produce detailed flowcharts, statement by statement from the source program.

One of the advantages of high-level languages (such as Cobol) is that the source listing itself forms the major part of final documentation. The programmer must insure that the source program not only is logically correct and follows the rules of the language, but also that the program coding is neat and easy to understand. By using meaningful data names and comments embedded in the program, it is possible to make a source program almost self-explanatory. In this case, a flowchart can be used as a general "route map" to the detailed coding in the source listing. When altering an operational program, many programmers refer directly to the source listing and then to the flowchart only if the required change is not immediately obvious from the listing.

Flowcharts and cross-reference lists (produced by the compiler or other software) can be used to check that an alteration has not erroneously disturbed other coding. The advantage of using comments in the source listing is that it minimizes references to other documents. The comments are not compiled as part of the program but merely appear on the source listing. Source program comments should be kept brief while at the same time being descriptive and meaningful.

Note that the final documentation will show not only how the program works, but also how it was tested (for quality control and later retested after changes were made), operating instructions for running it, and any special parameters that are to be given to the operating system.

Although the program manual is the major output of the program specification, the programmer will use (and can produce) other types of documentation. If the program(s) being developed are for general use, either within or outside the organization, then additional user instructions will be needed. They should enable the prospective user to answer the following questions.

1. What does it do?
2. Do we want to use it?
3. Can we use it?
4. How do we use it?
5. What do we do if it changes?
6. What are its basic limitations?

For internally produced software, one approach is to produce a program abstract which can be held in a central documentation library. If, on first inspection, the user feels that it fulfills the needs, the detailed documentation can then be consulted. The form of this detailed documentation depends on the scope and complexity of the software. For example, a user's guide may be produced to give a general description of the program(s), the facilities available, the hardware environment required, and example uses of the software. The user's guide may contain instructions for using the software, or a programmer's reference manual may be supplied giving detailed information. Most software is constructed so that the user programmer supplies parameters for a particular job. The parameters may be as simple as specifying an address of data to be processed or as comprehensive as a complete list of processing requirements. The programmer's reference manual will describe the construction of the program(s), together with all parameters required (their format, interdependence, and usage), operating instructions, and error conditions and diagnostics.

Programs ready for operational use (both applications programs and software programs) and which are to be run repeatedly are assigned to the automated program library, usually stored on magnetic drum, disk, or tape. The documentation for these programs is usually held in some form of central records library, together with the master reference copies of all software descriptions.

Documentation Maintenance and Control. Once a program has been implemented, the documentation must be retained for subsequent reference. When the system is changed, the documentation will be consulted and altered accordingly. It is vital to revise the documentation so that it completely and accurately reflects the operation of the system at all times. If the documentation is not so revised, then further maintenance will be very difficult. After any major amendment, all affected programs will have to be retested to prove that the changes have been made correctly and that they do not disrupt or invalidate other processing.

It is necessary, therefore, to insure that the appropriate control procedures are used. All changes should be properly recorded and all copies of the documentation updated. There is a strong case here for restricting the number of copies of the documentation to reduce the time

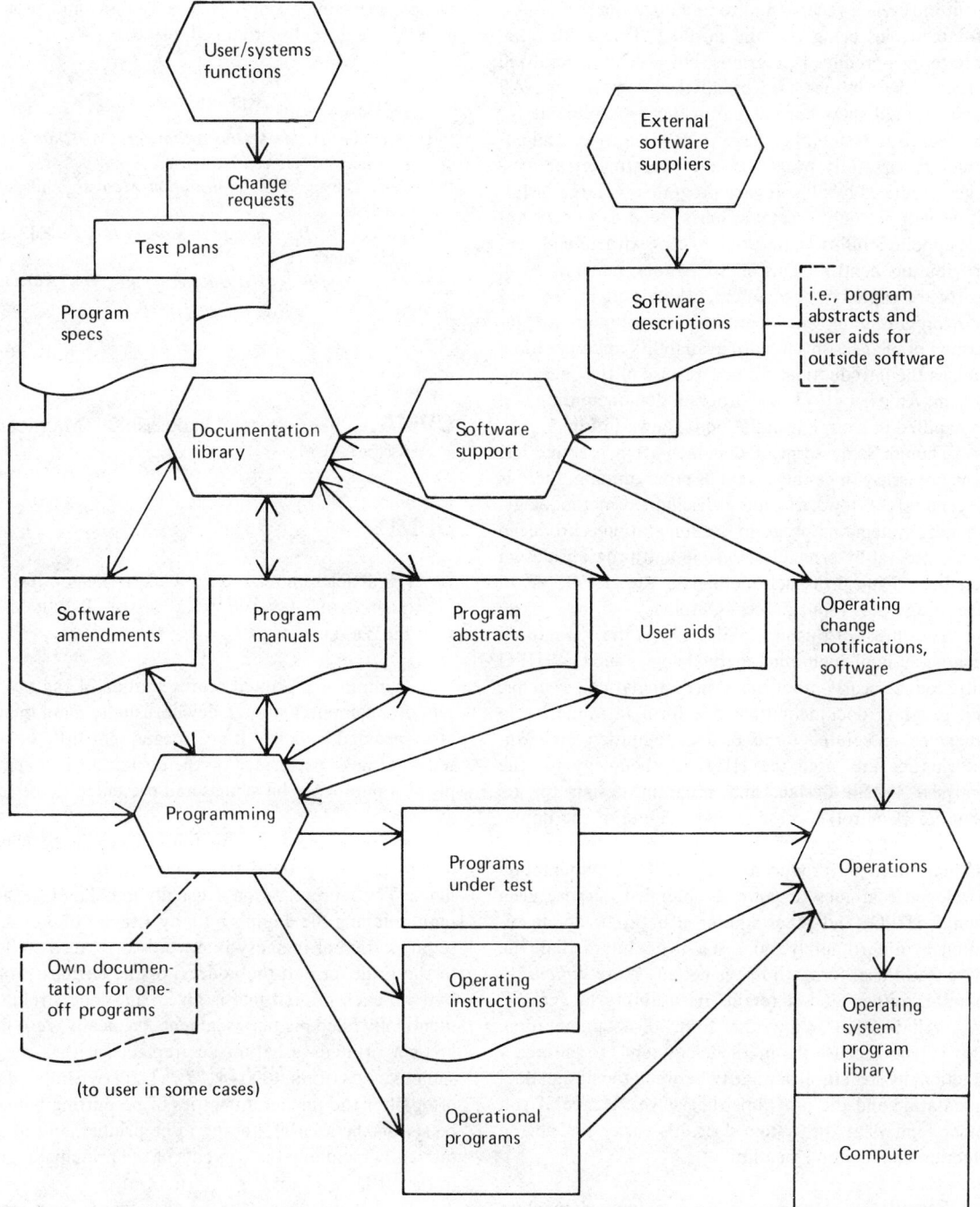

Fig. 7. Library and control program documentation. In addition, a documentation library may also accept and control systems documentation.

spent in revising records and to minimize the risk of out-of-date copies being used by mistake. This applies not only to own-produced programs, but also to generalized software descriptions used by all the programmers. All copies should show current parameter requirements for the operating system, language rules, limitations and parameters for utility programs, and operating error messages produced by all software programs. A large installation will not only create a central records library but also appoint a full-time librarian to cope with amendment distribution control. This is sometimes handled by a "software support" department, which will insure that both programming and operations departments are informed of changes in software availability and operation, such as the introduction of a new release of the operating system. An example of how program documentation will be handled in a large installation is shown in Fig. 7.

Though some form of documentation practice has been necessary since the advent of programming, there is a recent trend toward a more disciplined methodology, whereby system and program documentation is produced as an integral by-product of system and program design activities. Typical of such methods is the HIPO system (Hierarchy plus Input-Process-Output).

The thrust of this new philosophy is that structured design and implementation methodologies such as HIPO will produce nearly all of the desired analytical, systems, and program documentation in a form far superior to other, less integrated forms of documentation. In 1976, Informatics Inc. used the HIPO methodology for the analysis, system design, and program design for its ShopFloorControl/80 product. At the end of the implementation, it was concluded that only operations and user manuals need be produced. The HIPO documentation developed continues to serve its intended purpose even though HIPO (and other similar structured) documentation is, unfortunately, no easier to maintain than the more traditional forms. But it is not any more *difficult* to maintain either, and it retains its usability longer and more reliably than many other forms of documentation. This is true because the methodology tends to enforce a functionally structural similarity between the design documentation and the programs themselves. Hence, if you understand what the system does, it's easier to find the function and its implementation.

Summary. Documentation is a vital element in developing and running any computer project, whether in a government, business, academic, or military installation. It must not be handled in a haphazard fashion; formal documentation standards must be laid down and enforced. These standards must cover all areas—users, systems, and programming and operations. In a modern computer installation the flow of documentation can be complex, encompassing in-house systems and programs as well as externally produced software.

REFERENCES

1963. Brandon, D. *Management Standards for Data Processing.* Princeton, NJ: Van Nostrand.
1972. Van Duyan, J. *Documentation Manual.* Philadelphia: Auerbach.
1973. London, K. *Documentation Standards* (Rev. Ed.). Philadelphia: Auerbach.
1980. *Basic Concepts of HIPO Programming.* DATAPRO. Delpan, NJ.

K. R. LONDON

DPMA. *See* DATA PROCESSING MANAGEMENT ASSOCIATION.

DUMP

For articles on related subjects *see* DEBUGGING; MACHINE AND ASSEMBLY LANGUAGE PROGRAMMING; and TRACE.

A dump is a printed representation of the raw content of a computer storage device, usually main memory, at a specified instant. "Raw" means that little or no interpretation is performed on the content; it is taken simply as a number of bit strings and presented to the reader as such.

A few refinements are found in even the simplest dumps that keep them from being mere one-to-one bit maps: The representation is usually in octal or hexadecimal, reducing the dump's bulk by a factor of 3 or 4. The segmentation of memory into words or bytes is reflected in the print format; the address of the leftmost word or byte on each printed line is given; and long stretches of identically filled memory segments (typically, zero-filled) are not printed verbatim, but replaced with a message such as LOCATIONS 4000–4177 ALL ZERO. Simple dumps often offer the further amenities of permitting bounds to be set on the area of storage to be printed, and of automatically including the contents of the principal registers in the CPU.

Dumps may generally be classified as *post-mortem dumps* or *snapshot dumps*. The post-mortem dump, which occurs only when a program terminates (usually abnormally or prematurely), is the most primitive of debugging devices. It corresponds in vintage and sophistication to machine-language programming, and its use in debugging high-level language programs should be nil, but unfortunately is not. While it is far more commonly employed in debugging assembly-language programs than those written in high-level languages, it is still the last resort for programs of all descriptions, including those in high-level languages. Its total replacement by tools of greater power and convenience has long been expected, but accomplished—if at all—only where debugging is routinely done on line. Even there, it can be argued that the post-mortem dump is often not so much eliminated as disguised.

On-line debugging sessions do not involve extensive dumps, nor are the snapshot dumps that are involved so bit-oriented, but the representations of memory contents that are produced share the dump's essential characteristic of being instantaneous descriptions of a moving object, and of requiring the programmer to shift into another language, almost into another discipline, when debugging. (Another major family of debugging aids, known collectively as the *trace* escapes one of these shortcomings, that of being a static observer of a moving object, but not the other.)

The crudeness of debugging with the sole aid of dumps, program listings, and mother wit is due not merely to the dump's being a record of a single instant only, but to its being, usually, a record of the *wrong* instant. By the time an observer, human or programmed, has detected something wrong with a running program and ordered a dump taken, it is probable that some or all of the evidence that would enable the programmer to find the underlying bug has been erased or changed.

The total replacement of the dump—or, what is equivalent, the realization of "source-language debugging"—has proved to be more difficult to achieve than had initially been expected, and may still be a long time in coming. It may require the abandonment of the notion of "debugging"—i.e., curative, after-the-fact treatment of faulty programs—in favor of preventive or prophylactic approaches such as those suggested in the references given below.

REFERENCES

1965. Halpern, M. I. "Computer Programming: The Debugging Epoch Opens," *Computers and Automation* (November).
1971. Worley, W. S. "Toward Automatic Debugging of Low Level Code," IBM Technical Report TR 00.2211.

M. HALPERN

E

EBCDIC

For articles on related subjects *see* ASCII; BINARY-CODED DECIMAL; CHARACTER SET; CODES; COLLATING SEQUENCE; and IBM CARD.

The Extended Binary Coded Decimal Interchange Code (EBCDIC) was developed by IBM for use on the IBM System/360; it is also used on the IBM System/370. In order to remain compatible with IBM equipment, many other computers also use EBCDIC. The only eight-bit code that is a competitor to EBCDIC for use on computers is the eight-bit version of ASCII (*q.v.*).

Fig. 1 shows the 256 ($= 2^8$) combinations for EBCDIC, many of which are currently unassigned but may be assigned later as new developments in computer technology occur. The leftmost four bits (or first hexadecimal digit) of the eight-bit code are shown across the top of the Fig. 1 and the rightmost four bits (or second hexadecimal digit) in the first two columns on the side. Table 1 gives an example.

Also shown in Fig. 1 are the punches on an IBM card corresponding to each of the characters of the code. Zone punches (12, 11, 0, and occasionally 9) for characters above (below) the heavy black lines are shown at the top (bottom). Digit punches (1 to 9) for characters to the left (right) of the heavy black line are shown on the left (right). Table 2 gives an example.

Table 1

| Symbol | Code | |
	Binary	Hexadecimal
4	11110100	F4
Y	11101000	E8
c	10000011	83
=	01111110	7E

Table 2

Character	Card Punches
4	4
Y	0-8
c	12-0-3
=	8-6
IL	11-9-7

The meanings of the control characters and special graphics, and the card-punch patterns of characters that do not conform to the rules above are shown in Fig. 1.

I. FLORES

579

			00				01				10				11				Bit Positions 0,1
			00	01	10	11	00	01	10	11	00	01	10	11	00	01	10	11	Bit Positions 2,3
Bit Positions 4, 5, 6, 7	Second Hexadecimal Digit	Digit Punches	0	1	2	3	4	5	6	7	8	9	A	B	C	D	E	F	First Hexadecimal Digit
			12				12	12		12	12	12		12	12				
				11				11	11	11		11	11	11		11			Zone Punches
					0		0		0	0	0		0	0			0		Digit Punches
			9	9	9	9	9	9	9	9					9	9	9	9	
0000	0	8-1	NUL ①	DLE ②	DS ③	④	SP ⑤	& ⑥	- ⑦	⑧					⑨	⑩	⑪	0 ⑫	8-1
0001	1	1	SOH	DC1	SOS		/ ⑬				a	j		A	J	⑭	1	1
0010	2	2	STX	DC2	FS	SYN					b	k	s	B	K	S	2	2
0011	3	3	ETX	TM							c	l	t	C	L	T	3	3
0100	4	4	PF	RES	BYP	PN					d	m	u	D	M	U	4	4
0101	5	5	HT	NL	LF	RS					e	n	v	E	N	V	5	5
0110	6	6	LC	BS	ETB	UC					f	o	w	F	O	W	6	6
0111	7	7	DEL	IL	ESC	EOT					g	p	x	G	P	X	7	7
1000	8	8		CAN							h	q	y	H	Q	Y	8	8
1001	9	8-1		EM							i	r	z	I	R	Z	9	9
1010	A	8-2	SMM	CC	SM	⑮	¢	!	:									8-2
1011	B	8-3	VT	CU1	CU2	CU3	.	$	,	#								8-3
1100	C	8-4	FF	IFS		DC4	<	*	%	@								8-4
1101	D	8-5	CR	IGS	ENQ	NAK	(	)	_	'								8-5
1110	E	8-6	SO	IRS	ACK		+	;	>	=								8-6
1111	F	8-7	SI	IUS	BEL	SUB	|	¬	?	"								8-7
			12				12			12	12	12	12	12	12			12	
				11				11			11	11	11		11	11	11		Zone Punches
					0		0		0	0	0	0	0		0		0		
			9	9	9	9								9	9	9	9		

Card Hole Patterns

①	12-0-9-8-1	⑤	No Punches	⑨	12-0	⑬	0-1
②	12-11-9-8-1	⑥	12	⑩	11-0	⑭	11-0-9-1
③	11-0-9-8-1	⑦	11	⑪	0-8-2	⑮	12-11
④	12-11-0-9-8-1	⑧	12-11-0	⑫	0		

Control Character Representations

ACK	Acknowledge	EOT	End of Transmission	PF	Punch Off
BEL	Bell	ESC	Escape	PN	Punch On
BS	Backspace	ETB	End of Transmission Block	RES	Restore
BYP	Bypass	ETX	End of Text	RS	Reader Stop
CAN	Cancel	FF	Form Feed	SI	Shift In
CC	Cursor Control	FS	Field Separator	SM	Set Mode
CR	Carriage Return	HT	Horizontal Tab	SMM	Start of Manual Message
CU1	Customer Use 1	IFS	Interchange File Separator	SO	Shift Out
CU2	Customer Use 2	IGS	Interchange Group Separator	SOH	Start of Heading
CU3	Customer Use 3	IL	Idle	SOS	Start of Significance
DC1	Device Control 1	IRS	Interchange Record Separator	SP	Space
DC2	Device Control 2	IUS	Interchange Unit Separator	STX	Start of Text
DC4	Device Control 4	LC	Lower Case	SUB	Substitute
DEL	Delete	LF	Line Feed	SYN	Synchronous Idle
DLE	Data Link Escape	NAK	Negative Acknowledge	TM	Tape Mark
DS	Digit Select	NL	New Line	UC	Upper Case
EM	End of Medium	NUL	Null	VT	Vertical Tab
ENQ	Enquiry				

Special Graphic Characters

¢	Cent Sign	-	Minus Sign, Hyphen
.	Period, Decimal Point	/	Slash
<	Less-than Sign	,	Comma
(	Left Parenthesis	%	Percent
+	Plus Sign	_	Underscore
|	Logical OR	>	Greater-than Sign
&	Ampersand	?	Question Mark
!	Exclamation Point	:	Colon
$	Dollar Sign	#	Number Sign
*	Asterisk	@	At Sign
)	Right Parenthesis	'	Prime, Apostrophe
;	Semicolon	=	Equal Sign
¬	Logical NOT	"	Quotation Mark

Fig. 1. EBCDIC code combinations.

ECKERT, J. PRESPER

For articles on related subjects *see* ENIAC; MAUCHLY, JOHN W.; and UNIVAC I.

J. Presper Eckert, co-inventor of ENIAC, was born in 1919 in Philadelphia. He received a Bachelor of Science degree in electrical engineering from the University of Pennsylvania's Moore School of Electrical Engineering in 1941, and his Master's degree under a graduate fellowship from the Moore School in 1943.

Fig. 1.   J. Presper Eckert.

Dr. Eckert collaborated with Dr. John W. Mauchly, of the Moore School's staff, on developing ENIAC (Electrical Numerical Integrator and Computer) for Army Ordnance between 1943 and 1946. This was the world's first all-electronic digital computer, and could perform 5,000 additions or subtractions per second. Its development launched the computer industry as we know it today.

In 1947, Dr. Eckert and Dr. Mauchly incorporated their venture as the Eckert-Mauchly Computer Corporation. They developed BINAC, the first electronic and fully self-checking computer, in 1949. Their next project, UNIVAC (Universal Automatic Computer), was well under way when Remington Rand acquired the Eckert-Mauchly firm in 1950.

Dr. Eckert became director of engineering for Remington Rand's Eckert-Mauchly Division, which completed UNIVAC I. He became vice-president and director of research in 1955, vice-president and director of commercial engineering in 1957, vice-president and executive assistant to the general manager in 1959, and vice-president and technical advisor to the president of Sperry-Rand, Univac division, in 1963.

Dr. Eckert received an honorary degree of Doctor of Science in Engineering from the University of Pennsylvania in 1964.

In 1969, Dr. Eckert was awarded the National Medal of Science, the nation's highest award for distinguished achievement in science, mathematics, and engineering.

A Fellow of the Institute of Electrical and Electronics Engineers, and a member of the National Academy of Engineering, Dr. Eckert is listed as the inventor or co-inventor on 87 patents.

M. M. MAYNARD

ECKERT, WALLACE J.

For article on related subject *see* DIGITAL COMPUTERS: Early.

Wallace John Eckert, was born in Pittsburgh, PA, 19 June 1902 (d. Englewood, N.J., 24 Aug. 1971). Much of the credit for the introduction of machine computation into astronomy belongs to him. The significance of the computer impact on astronomy is comparable to that of the introduction and use of the telescope and photography.

Eckert was raised on a farm in Albion, PA, the second of four boys born to John and Anna (Heil) Eckert. He received his A.B. degree from Oberlin College in 1925 and his M.A. from Amherst in 1926. In 1931, he was awarded his Ph.D. in astronomy by Yale University. He joined the Columbia University Department of Astronomy as an assistant instructor in 1926.

In 1928, Professor Ben Wood formed the Columbia University Statistical Bureau using punched-card equipment donated by Thomas Watson, Sr., of IBM. It was here that Eckert was first exposed to the possibility of using machines to facilitate computation. From 1929 to 1933, he used the machines in Prof. Wood's laboratory for the interpolation of astronomical data, the reduction of observational data, and the numerical solution of planetary equations. In 1933, with the encouragement of Ben Wood, he convinced Watson to install punched-card equipment and a control unit for astronomical calculations. This led to the formation of the T. J. Watson Astronomical Computing Bureau, jointly operated by Columbia, IBM, and the American Astronomical Society

(1937–1945). During this period he published his landmark work (1940), "Punched Card Methods in Scientific Computation."

He was director of the U.S. Nautical Almanac Office in Washington, D.C., from 1940 to 1945. He introduced machine methods to data handling in the Naval Observatory as well as the Almanac Office. During the war he designed the "American Air Almanac," a great navigational influence that is still in use with only minor modifications.

In 1945 he was appointed head of IBM's Pure Science Department and became director of the Watson Scientific Computing Laboratory. The Laboratory not only performed needed computations, but also provided a training ground in machine computation for more than a thousand scientists in crystallography, geology, chemistry, statistics, optics, and solid-state physics, as well as astronomy.

Eckert was instrumental in the construction of IBM's Selective Sequence Electronic Calculator (SSEC, 1949) and the Naval Ordnance Research Calculator [NORC, 1954 (*q.v.*)]. Using the SSEC, Eckert, Dirk Brouwer of Yale, and G. M. Clemence (1951) of the U.S. Naval Observatory computed the precise positions of Jupiter, Saturn, Uranus, Neptune, and Pluto for the period 1652–2060. This work still serves as the Ephemeris predictions for these planets.

Eckert's most important purely astronomical contributions were in relation to the moon's orbital motion. This and later work in the area of lunar coordinates and orbital parameters (1966) provided the operational basis for NASA's Surveyor, Lunar Orbiter, and Apollo projects.

He retired from IBM in 1967 and as Professor of Celestial Mechanics at Columbia in 1970.

REFERENCES

Anon. "Dr. Wallace J. Eckert" (publications by W. J. Eckert, 38 items), and "Outstanding Contribution Award Report" (n.d.), IBM Archives.

1940. Eckert W. J. *Punched-Card Methods in Scientific Computation.* New York: Columbia University Press.

1951. Eckert, W. J., Brouwer, D., and Clemence, G. M. "Coordinates of the Five Outer Planets, 1653–2060," *Astronomical Papers*, NORC **12**. Washington, D.C.: U.S. Government Printing Office.

1966. Eckert, W. J. "Transformations of the Lunar Coordinates and Orbital Parameters," *Astronomical Journal* (June).

1971. J. A. "A Great American Astronomer," *Sky and Telescope* (October).

H. S. TROPP

ECONOMETRIC APPLICATIONS

For articles on related subjects *see* BANKING APPLICATIONS; ELECTRONIC FUNDS TRANSFER SYSTEMS; MODELS; OPERATIONS RESEARCH; and SIMULATION.

To better assess the economic environment within which countries or firms operate, planners are making increasing use of macroeconomic forecasts generated by econometric models. The main reason is that the models perform the forecasting task more efficiently by providing a consistent framework for the analysis of a large number of external variables.

Both the initial estimation procedure for defining model coefficients and the problem of choosing the appropriate variables require very great amounts of computation. Consequently, computers are essential for all econometric modeling. The most important recent development in this area is the establishment of modeling firms or institutes that maintain the logical structure as well as databases for use by private firms and government agencies. The number of permanent subscribers for the output of these models has now grown so that one can speak about an "econometric modeling consulting business." Economic models have also been constructed by special interest groups or projects to support conclusions about the projected outcome of new developments.

The first major macroeconomic model building effort was carried out in the early 1930s by Jan Tinbergen of the Netherlands, Ragnar Frisch of Norway, and Wassily Leontieff of the U.S. Lawrence Klein, who was awarded the Nobel Prize in Economics in 1980, built the first macroeconomic model of the U.S. shortly after World War II, but little actual use was made of these developments because the computational problems did not allow constructing models of sufficient detail to be of interest to users. Since the 1960s, there has been a vast increase in the number, scope, and complexity of econometric models. The widespread availability of computers and software, as well as the publication of national income and product accounts, has allowed the simulation of very short run changes of the economy.

An econometric model is the expression of an economic theory in mathematical terms (see Fig. 1). The models reflect the estimated impact of one economic variable on others. For example, a simple economic model may express the relationship between per capita income and personal consumption expenditures, or it may show how interest rates, capital investment, and unemployment are interdependent. A model reflecting the above relationships may be useful in setting government fiscal policy or might be useful to a corporation whose sales de-

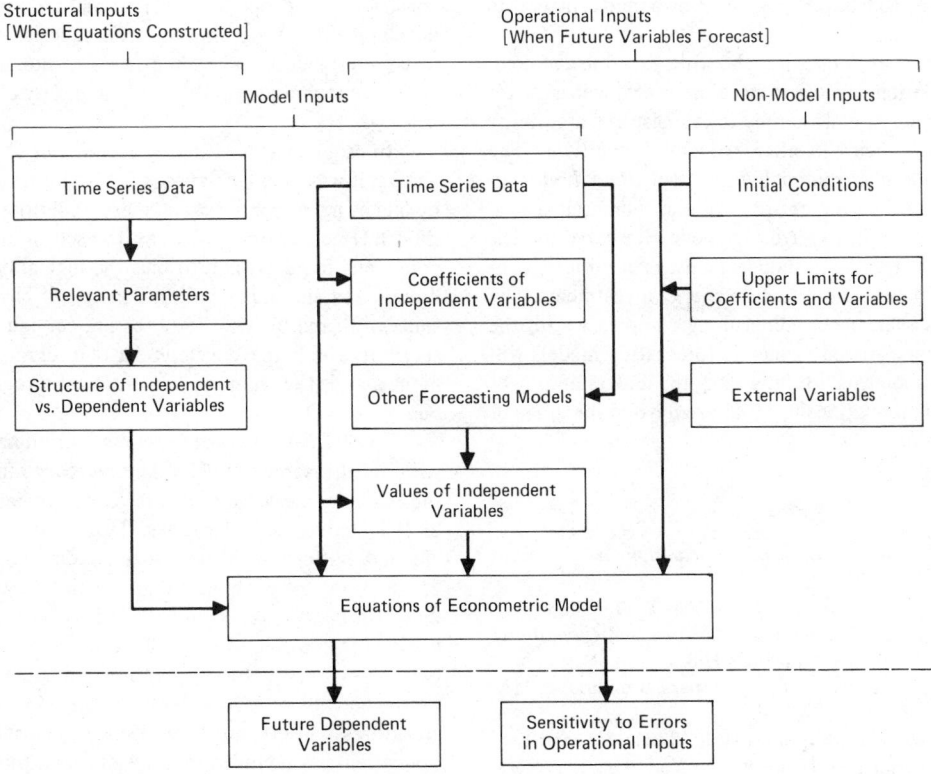

Fig. 1. The structure of econometric models.

pend on consumer spending patterns. Most modern models are nonlinear in structure, incorporating considerable detail on many different sectors. For example, the current version of the quarterly econometric model of the U.S. maintained at the Wharton School of Finance of the University of Pennsylvania has more than 200 variables.

In setting up a model, computational requirements arise in four separate stages. First, the parameters of the equations must be estimated from time series data. Second, calculations must be made to arrive at statistically valid relationships between dependent and independent variables. Third, in order to make the model function in a forecasting mode, projections of the independent variables must be made over the time span of the forecast. Only then is it actually possible to generate forecasted dependent variables.

All forecasting methods have weaknesses which can contribute to errors in both short-term and long-term forecasts. When the general public or a user receives the output from an econometric model, it may be difficult to evaluate the validity of the model simply on the basis of comparing actual against predicted results. A model may contain external variables which, although not part of the

econometric equations, have been inserted within the model as initial conditions, upper limits, or an approximation of factors that are excluded from the scope of the simulation. Insofar as these inputs affect the ultimate results, the model itself may give an insufficient accounting of events. In addition, errors arise from: (1) important limitations of economic theory in explaining the behavior of a firm, of consumers, or of national policies, (2) misjudgments in estimating independent variables, (3) inadequate definitions or inconsistencies in input data measurements, and (4) structural changes in the relationships between variables due to technology or change in behavioral patterns which invalidate projections made on the basis of prior assumptions.

Selected examples of computerized econometric models and services are Chase Econometrics of Bala Cynwyd, PA; Data Resources of Lexington, MA; General Electric's MAPCAST System; and the Wharton School of Finance model of the U.S. economy. Quarterly national economic models are also available for most advanced industrial countries and I/O analyses are available on a special study basis for most less-developed countries. Major corporations have also constructed econometric models relating their own performance to external changes.

A recent development is the widespread use of computer simulation models to predict future scenarios for economic systems and thereby to increase the credibility of proposed policies to alter economic conditions. The global attention attracted by the book *The Limits of Growth* in 1972 is an example of the increased use of computer models in an advocacy mode. Similarly, models are being constructed to support analyses of military conflict, urban policy, and alternate energy investments. The prognosis is that, in an increasingly complex world, the use of computer-based economic forecasting models will be applied as a means for improving the understanding of interdependent relationships that are beyond the grasp of simple insights.

REFERENCES

1950. Klein, Lawrence. *Economic Fluctuations in the United States*. New York: Wiley.
1957. Beach, E. F. *Economic Models*. New York: Wiley.
1965. Theil, H. *et al. Operations Research and Quantitative Economics*. New York: McGraw-Hill.
1969. Forrester, Jay W. *Urban Dynamics*. Cambridge, MA: M.I.T. Press.
1972. Meadows, D. H., Meadows, D. L., Randers, J., and Behrens, W. *The Limits to Growth*. New York: Universe Books.
1973. Meadows, D. *et al. Dynamics of Growth in a Finite World*. Cambridge, MA: Wright-Allen.
1975. Montroll, E. W. and Badger, L. W. *Introduction to Quantitative Aspects of Social Phenomena*. New York: Gordon and Breach.

P. A. STRASSMANN

EDITOR. *See* LINKAGE EDITOR; and TEXT EDITING SYSTEMS.

EDSAC

For articles on related subjects *see* DIGITAL COMPUTERS: Early, and Origins; EDVAC; ENIAC; ULTRASONIC MEMORY; and WILKES, MAURICE V.

The EDSAC (Electronic Delay Storage Automatic Calculator) was designed according to the principles expounded by J. Presper Eckert, John W. Mauchly, and others at the summer school held in 1946 at the Moore School of Electrical Engineering in Philadelphia, and which the author of this article was privileged to attend. The objectives in mind from the beginning were (1) to show that a binary stored-program computer could be constructed and operated; (2) to make a start with the development of programming techniques, even then seen to be a subject of more than trivial content; and (3) to apply the techniques developed in a variety of application fields.

In order to accelerate the attainment of the first objective, it was decided to ease the circuit design problems by choosing a conservative pulse repetition frequency (500 KHz compared with 1 MHz used in most contemporaneous projects) and to bias the logical design in the direction of simplicity rather than speed. This policy was successful, and by May 1949 the project had reached the stage at which the development of programming techniques and the running of practical programs could begin.

The EDSAC (Fig. 1) was a serial binary computer with an ultrasonic memory. The mercury tanks used for the main memory were about 1½ meters long and were built in batteries of 16 tanks. Two batteries were provided. A battery, with the associated circuits, could store 256 numbers of 35 binary digits each, one being a sign digit. An instruction occupied a half-word of 17 bits and it was also possible to use half-words for short numbers. Numbering of the storage locations was in terms of half-words, not full words. The instruction set was of the single-address variety, and there were 17 instructions. Multiplication was included, but not division. Input and output were by means of five-channel punched-paper tape. The input and output orders provided for the transfer of five binary digits from the tape to the memory, and vice versa.

Operation of the machine could not start until a short standard sequence of orders, known as the *initial orders*, had been transferred into the ultrasonic memory from a mechanical read-only memory formed from a set of rotary telephone switches. The space that the initial orders occupied in the memory could be re-used when they were no longer required for reading the input tape. The initial orders determined the way in which the instructions were punched on the paper tape, and this was quite an advancement for the period.

One row of holes, interpreted as a letter, indicated the function; this was followed by the address in decimal form, with leading zeros omitted and terminated by a code letter. In the first set of initial orders to be used, this code letter merely determined whether the address referred to a short or a long location; before the end of 1950, however, these initial orders had been replaced by a more elaborate set in which the terminating characters were used to provide relocation facilities for blocks of instructions or data punched on the tape.

The EDSAC did its first calculation on 6 May 1949, and ran until 1958, when it was finally switched off.

Fig. 1. The EDSAC.

REFERENCES

1950. Wilkes, M. V. "The EDSAC (Electronic Delay Storage Automatic Calculator)," *MTAC* **4**: p. 61.
1956. ———. *Automatic Digital Computers*. London: Methuen; New York: Wiley.

M. V. WILKES

EDUCATION, COMPUTERS IN HIGHER.

See COLLEGES AND UNIVERSITIES, COMPUTERS IN.

EDUCATION IN COMPUTER SCIENCE AND TECHNOLOGY

For articles on related subjects *see* ARTIFICIAL INTELLIGENCE; COLLEGES AND UNIVERSITIES, COMPUTERS IN; COMPUTER-ASSISTED INSTRUCTION; COMPUTER-ASSISTED LEARNING AND TEACHING; COMPUTER GRAPHICS; COMPUTER-MANAGED INSTRUCTION; COMPUTER SCIENCE; FORMAL LANGUAGES; NUMERICAL ANALYSIS; and PROGRAMMING LANGUAGES.

UNITED STATES

The forerunners of the modern electronic stored-program computer were first developed at U.S. universities in the 1940s, mainly in response to military needs during World War II. However, a lengthy gap then ensued between the conception of computers at universities and their attendant application to the host of educational, research, and administrative processes at these universities. The beginnings of the university computing center date only to the mid-1950s; in fact, it was only during the period from 1960 to 1965 that the "computer revolution" really took hold at U.S. institutions of higher education. In some cases, the computing center began as a separate organization, but more generally, the computing center evolved from a computer facility initially installed in a department of mathematics or school of engineering to support the research projects of the departmental faculty. Today's computer science and technology curricula often reflect these origins of the computing center by emphasizing the mathematical or engineering content of computing.

Higher Education Programs. The academic programs in computing at institutions of higher education began in the mid-1950s under pressure from early users of computing equipment, or from the computing center staff deluged with questions about the use of these new devices. Initially, the "educational program" might have consisted only of a short, noncredit course given by the computing center staff. Such a course mainly emphasized hardware characteristics, binary arithmetic, and how to program a problem for computer solution (usually in machine or assembly language). At times, some of the instructional material was absorbed into an existing course in mathematics or engineering, generally in three or four lectures. However, with the rapid growth of broadly-based university computing installations during the 1960–1965 period, and with the growth of an organized body of knowledge, it became necessary to establish more formal educational programs in computing.

Usually, these programs started as a collaborative effort between the computing center and the department of mathematics or school of engineering, depending upon the organizational origin of the computing center. One of the most influential of these early efforts took place at the University of Michigan, and subsequently at the University of Houston, during the period 1959–1962. These efforts, conducted jointly by the Computing Center and the College of Engineering, were aimed less at establishing computer science as a distinct academic discipline than at the "Use of Computers in Engineering Education" (University of Michigan Study, 1960 and 1961, and University of Houston Study, 1962). At approximately the same time, Stanford University, through the joint efforts of its computing center and the department of mathematics, was establishing the discipline of computer science as an optional field of study in the department of mathematics.

These early efforts were capped by the creation of separate departments of computer science. In 1962, Stanford University established a Department of Computer Science in the School of Humanities and Sciences; in the same year, Purdue University created a Department of Computer Science in the Division of Mathematical Sciences. In each case, the bond between the service and academic functions of computing was made evident by the fact that one person was both director of the computing center and chairman of the department; this pattern was followed subsequently by other universities. Another pattern established by Stanford and Purdue was that of initially offering only graduate programs in computer science, at the master's and doctorate levels. This reflected the thinking at the time that there could be no well-defined undergraduate program in computer science, and that specialization in computing should start only at the graduate level. (It also reflected the fact that there were few professors qualified to teach computing at the time.)

The arguments for and against a highly concentrated program in computing at the undergraduate level continue even today, and we will return to this point later in this article.

By the mid-1960s, events in computer science education were proceeding at a dynamic pace. Government and quasi-government reports made recommendations that spurred the growth of computer science academic programs. Two were of particular importance. The National Academy of Sciences report on "Digital Computer Needs in Universities and Colleges" (Rosser *et al.,* 1966) recommended, among other things, that campuses should "increase as rapidly as possible the number of specialists trained annually as computer specialists and the support of pioneering research into computer systems, computer languages, and specialized equipment." The President's Science Advisory Committee report on "Computers in Higher Education" (Pierce *et al.,* 1967) recommended that "the Federal Government expand its support of both research and education in computer sciences." These reports helped obtain government and university support for the new discipline.

During the same time period, university-sponsored conferences produced reports and books, such as "University Education in Computing Science" (Finerman, 1968), indicating that computer science was truly an emerging academic discipline and not a short-lived curiosity item. Indeed, the "intellectual respectability" of computer science was a controversial issue in the 1960s. Many educators argued that the computer was just a tool, and that a body of study based upon a tool was not a proper academic discipline; others took the position that computer science was not a coherent discipline but rather a collection of bits and pieces from other disciplines; still others felt that computers were not that important and were not proper objects of academic interest. However, by and large, this skepticism was itself short-lived, at times delaying but not preventing the eventual start of academic programs in computing.

At the same time, computing, mathematics, and engineering professional societies sponsored studies of the curricular effects of the new discipline. Reports of the Mathematical Association of America (Committee on the Undergraduate Program in Mathematics) and the Commission on Engineering Education (Cosine Committee) recommended changes in existing academic programs to assure that students in mathematics and engineering received adequate preparation in computing. This preparation was necessitated by the fact that a growing number of mathematics and engineering majors found themselves working in the computing field soon after graduation. The studies of the Association for Computing Machinery (ACM) had the most widespread effect. ACM chartered a Curriculum Committee on Computer Science to recommend necessary academic programs. The subsequent report of the Committee, "Curriculum 68" (Atchison *et al.*, 1968), for the first time defined the scope and content of a recommended undergraduate program in computer science. More recently, the Committee considerably revised and updated the recommended undergraduate program in its report, "Curriculum 78" (Austing *et al.*, 1979). ACM also chartered a Curriculum Committee on Computer Education for Management. This Committee issued two principal reports, one on undergraduate and the other on graduate programs in information systems. Separately, the Computer Society of the Institute of Electrical and Electronic Engineering (IEEE) chartered a Model Curricula Subcommittee of the Education Committee which published a report on undergraduate curricula in 1977. We will return to the recommendations of these committees later in this article.

The effect of all these studies, conferences, and reports was a proliferating and seemingly endless number of academic programs in computer science and technology. From the early graduate programs have come myriad graduate and undergraduate programs which abound at two-year colleges (Associate's degree), four-year colleges (Bachelor's), five-year colleges (Bachelor's and Master's), and universities (Bachelor's, Master's, and Doctorate); these programs are in addition to the numerous computing service courses available to students majoring in other disciplines. Furthermore, there are a multitude of vocational courses given by manufacturers of computing equipment and by technical schools. Indeed, during the past decade, computing courses have been introduced into the educational programs of many secondary schools.

Higher education programs in computing go by different names, such as computer science, computer technology, computer science and technology, information science, data processing, and information systems. Each name also has come to denote a particular emphasis and origin. For example, *computer science* usually indicates a mathematical and scientific emphasis generally found at universities; *information systems* usually indicates computing applied to organizational systems generally related to the business administration programs at universities; and *data processing* usually indicates computing applied to administrative and commercial applications generally taught at two-year colleges. The programs may be housed in a department of computer science, computer technology, or data processing, or given as an option in mathematics, engineering, or business administration. In any event, the academic program is now almost always housed in a department, separate from the computing center, and rarely is the same person in immediate charge of both activities.

Computer science (or whatever the actual name used) in higher education pervades almost all academic disciplines besides being a discipline in its own right; computing facilities and services are fundamental to most instructional, research, and administrative activities. Some of the data contained in the "Fourth Inventory of Computing in U.S. Higher Education" (Hamblen and Baird, 1979) serve to give quantitative meaning to these qualitative descriptions. The data following apply to the 3,136 institutions of higher education in the U.S. (from two-year colleges to university centers) for the 1976–1977 academic year; corresponding data for the 1966–1967 academic year where available are given in parentheses. On the service side, the almost 70% (40%) of these institutions that had access to computers spent 991 (221) million dollars on computing facilities and services, which amounted to more than 2% of the total expenditures of all 3,136 (2,477) institutions of higher education. On the academic side, there were 1,454 (414) degree-granting programs in the computer discipline—with 16 different program names and 20 different department names listed; of these, 570 (192) offered the Associate's degree, 541 (83) the Bachelor's, 224 (87) the Master's, and 119 (52) the Doctorate. Approximately 130,000 (27,000) students majored in the computer discipline, with 80% (82%) of these at the undergraduate level and the remaining graduate. As for actual degrees, 8,271 (1,281) Associate's degrees, 9,589 (594) Bachelor's, 3,161 (747) Master's, and 345 (174) Doctorate degrees were awarded. (Note that Taulbee and Conte, 1979, because they survey a narrower population, estimate that approximately 227 Doctorate degrees were awarded in 1976–1977.)

The changes in the corresponding data above for the ten-year time span, especially in degrees awarded, are indicative of the explosive growth in both academic and service programs in computing. This growth at institutions of higher education generally parallels corresponding growth in industry. Consequently, students graduating with a Bachelor's, Master's, or Doctorate degree in computer science (or in some other discipline with a strong background in computing) have little difficulty in finding employment. There is a more limited demand for graduates of a two-year college and even less demand for vocational school and high school graduates to fill professional positions, although many technician positions are available, especially for graduates with Associate's degrees. The Bachelor's (and, increasingly, the Master's) degree has rapidly become the entry-level degree for suitable professional positions in industry. This observation is reflected in the figures given above. Bachelor's degrees grew by 150% from the 1966–1967 to the 1976–1977 academic years (and Master's degrees were up by 320%). In recent years, the Doctoral graduate, especially, has been actively recruited by universities, research organizations, and manufacturers of computing equipment.

Non-University Educational Programs. We have noted that computer science educational programs originated at universities and spread downward, from graduate to undergraduate to two-year colleges and then to high schools. Although subsequent sections of this article deal almost exclusively with university and college programs (undergraduate and graduate), in this section, we discuss briefly other educational programs in computing, specifically those offered by high schools, manufacturers of computing equipment, and private technical schools or institutes. We also discuss the educational programs at two-year colleges, in some ways similar to those at technical schools and in other ways offering a preparation for four-year undergraduate work.

High School Programs. As yet, there is no identifiable high school educational program in the computer discipline itself. However, a growing number of high schools offer courses in computing as a tool for mathematical and scientific problems, and a growing number of high school graduates receive exposure to computer concepts. There are several reasons to account for the slow progress in an education program in the discipline of computer science. First, relatively few high school teachers have taken computing courses and still fewer understand the subject well enough to teach it. Second, until recently, computing equipment was relatively expensive, and not many high schools were affluent enough to install their own computers or even terminals to nearby computing centers. Third, there is some doubt, at least in the minds of many high school educators, as to whether the discipline of computing is fundamental enough—as, for example, are English, mathematics, or physics—to teach at the high school level. Indeed, there is no consensus opinion on the part of computer scientists themselves on the nature of an appropriate high school educational program in the computer discipline.

However, some changes are beginning to take place rapidly. A growing number of teachers are being exposed to computing, and attitudes about computing are being modified as the subject becomes better understood. But the most visible and striking change is that small computers have become much more affordable and have taken on the general-purpose characteristics of larger computers. As a result, microcomputers, in particular, are being installed in a large number of high schools, making them available to a higher proportion of the student population than previously. (A related result is that high school students are acquiring low-cost "home" (or "personal") microcomputers and thereby receiving some of their computing education on their own, away from the formal classroom environment.) In general, however, the computing educational program at the high school level, where it exists at all, generally consists of a cursory introduction to programming—given either as part of a mathematics course or as a separate course—with little emphasis on (and, in some cases, little understanding of) formulation of algorithms, analytical techniques, or program or data structure. Although high schools certainly will acquire more and more microcomputers as prices continue to decrease, and more and more students will be exposed to the use of computers and programming, it is problematical whether the intellectual content of high school computing courses will be upgraded significantly in the immediate future and whether these courses will delve into aspects of computing other than programming. This will occur only as high school teachers themselves gain a better understanding of the computing discipline and as computer scientists reach a consensus opinion on a meaningful educational program in computing.

Manufacturers' Programs. Manufacturers have been offering courses in computing for years. Indeed, this informal educational activity predates the formal university educational program; several years ago it was estimated that the greatest number of people entering the computing field had been exposed only to manufacturer-offered courses. Most such courses are intended only for customers of the manufacturers, and most are concerned only with the equipment offered by those manufacturers. In some cases, courses are as much an exercise in marketing as they are in education; the object is to sell the doubtful customer on the need for bigger and better computers, especially those offered by the manufacturer giving the course. However, some manufacturers have attempted to maintain high standards; some have separated the educational program from the marketing activity. Yet, on the whole, performance has been rather spotty. For years, these courses were given free to customers. Most recently, manufacturers have begun to offer certain courses for a fee. In these cases, the manufacturer-offered educational program may rival that of the private "computing institute" or technical school.

Technical School Programs. Private schools for training technicians have been operating for years. In many fields, they serve a worthwhile function by preparing people for jobs as secretaries, dental technicians, draftsmen, and the like. When the computing industry started expanding rapidly, a large number of private schools began offering educational programs in computing. There are many jobs in industry for which technician training is worthwhile, and the technical school graduate should be qualified to assume such jobs.

Unfortunately, at times the computing institute may intimate that its training will prepare students for well-paying professional jobs in the computing industry. The technical school graduate often discovers too late that most such positions are filled by college graduates, that the professional career path in computing, as in most other fields, requires a college education. People trained as secretaries are well aware that they will not be hired for, or can rarely advance to, executive positions; draftsmen know that they will seldom become professional engineers—at least not with technical school training alone. Perhaps because of the newness of the field and the attendant absence of uniform standards and professional certification, this same fact is not as yet well recognized in computing. Currently, efforts are under way by computing societies to develop certification examinations for computing practitioners, and a number of states have given serious attention to the need for certification. These efforts may, in time, lead to a sharper and more accepted distinction between technicians and professionals.

Community College Programs. Two-year community (or junior) colleges have grown phenomenally in recent years, both in quantity and in scope of offerings. Twenty years ago, the community college was rather rare, usually specializing in such areas as agriculture, forestry, and mining. Today, the community college has become as broadly based and diversified as its university cousin.

The community college serves a twofold purpose. One is to train the student for a position as a technician. For these graduates, the two-year Associate's degree is proof of better standards than those usually maintained by the technical school; the degree is also proof of a more well-rounded education. The second purpose of the community college is to serve as a bridge between the high school and the four-year college or university, especially for those students uncertain of their desire or ability to continue with higher education. For these students, the Associate's degree may be an intermediate step on the way towards a Bachelor's degree.

Two-year colleges have rapidly expanded their educational programs in computing to fill these two needs. As shown in the (Hamblen and Baird) figures cited earlier, 570 institutions awarded 8271 Associate's degrees in the 1976–1977 academic year, an increase of approximately 200% and 550%, respectively, over corresponding figures ten years prior. For those students wishing to terminate at the technician level, the community college education is a more satisfying alternative than the private computing institute. For others, the community college is a valuable stepping stone to the university computing science

program. But there are some problems associated with this educational background.

Students terminating after two years and entering industry suffer the same identity problem as do the technical school graduates. Indeed, they are more than technicians, but not the same as college graduates. More often than not, the career paths open to them are technician-oriented. On the other hand, graduates wishing to continue toward the Bachelor's degree sometimes find the transition quite difficult. Community college standards are not always the same as university standards; community college courses are not always identical or even similar to corresponding courses at the university.

Some of these difficulties are being addressed; for example, community colleges and universities have been cooperating in facilitating the transfer process by making courses more compatible. However, transfer still remains a problem, as does the technician versus professional issue. Increasingly, as the "computer profession" evolves and becomes better defined, the broader educational scope of a bachelor's degree becomes a prerequisite for a professional career.

We will not separately detail the usual curricula at two-year colleges. In some cases, these are similar to freshman and sophomore level computing courses at universities. In other cases, the differences are more visible. By and large, university programs are more theoretically oriented, emphasizing both the theoretical underpinnings of computing and the scientific or engineering applications. Two-year college programs tend to emphasize the practical aspects and the business applications (for example, accounting) of computing. The four-year university program allows more time to take unrelated courses outside those in computing, mathematics, and associated technical disciplines. (This is not always so, as we will discuss later.) Community college programs, because of the shorter time span, are more intensely oriented to courses in computing, business mathematics, accounting, and other technical areas. Accordingly, graduates of community colleges do not possess the broader educational background of graduates of four-year programs.

Trends in Undergraduate Education. Let us now consider some general trends in undergraduate education, particularly in the science, technology, and professional fields, and the relation of these trends to academic programs in computer science. At the present time, the general practice in the U.S. is that technology-oriented students receive an undergraduate education that is highly specialized in their particular fields. For example, engineering students take most of their courses in engineering and related science (mathematics, physics, and chemistry) fields. (This practice is followed even more in other countries, where students may take all courses in their particular faculty.) In the past few years, various institutions have begun to question whether or not this practice of intense specialization at the undergraduate level of study denies the student the benefits of a more general or liberal education. For example, the Massachusetts Institute of Technology several years ago established a Commission on Undergraduate Education to study the academic program and recommend necessary changes. The Commission identified three basic aspects of undergraduate education and some shortcomings of excessive specialization (The M.I.T. Commission, 1970).

The first aspect concerns integration of knowledge. Modern problems require that students develop the ability to synthesize as well as analyze. These problems point to the need for interdisciplinary curricula. The second deals with facts and values. The most difficult problems we face are those that relate facts and values; these require that intellectual tools from the humanities be included in the academic programs of engineers and scientists. The third concerns education for citizenship in a democracy. To some people these days, this may sound somewhat old-fashioned, but it has never been more important for students to understand the nature of a democracy and their roles as individuals in it.

Subsequently, the Commission on M.I.T. Education recommended: "It is time for us to recognize and revise our approach to undergraduate education, especially in its first two years . . ." (Report of Commission on M.I.T. Education, 1970). Accordingly, M.I.T. established a First Division for general education for the first two years of undergraduate education. The Division is the responsibility of the M.I.T. faculty as a whole rather than the faculty from the various departments. Program topics include such subjects as the social consequences of science and technology, the different approaches to knowledge in the humanities and sciences, and the nature of design from a variety of perspectives. Students begin their departmental affiliation in the third year.

Somewhat later, Harvard University underwent much the same type of introspective study and also concluded that extensive changes, resulting in less undergraduate specialization, were necessary. To achieve this, Harvard established a core curriculum: All undergraduate students, regardless of major, must choose a certain number of courses selected from an extensive core. The aim is for students to achieve a better understanding of subject matter in such fields as literature and the arts, foreign languages and cultures, history, social and philosophical analysis, and mathematics and science—including computer science.

More recently, Stanford University announced a sweeping revision of its undergraduate program. In the Stanford model, all entering students are now required to take a one-year course in Western culture to be taught by faculty members from a wide variety of departments. In addition, somewhat similar to the Harvard model, Stanford undergraduates are now required to take at least one course in each of seven broad subject areas—literature and fine arts; philosophical, social, and religious thought; human development, behavior, and language; social processes and institutions; mathematical science; natural sciences; and technology and applied sciences.

The M.I.T., Harvard, and Stanford revisions reflect a growing recognition of the need for all college-educated people to share "some common background." It has been said that if the student upon graduation "does not know something of philosophy and history; if he has not developed the critical skills that enable him to distinguish the moral from the immoral, flatulent language from genuine, art from artifact—then he is not educated."

This growing concern of the need for a more general education versus the need for increased specialization at the undergraduate level (breadth versus depth) is also a controversial issue in computer science education. There are those who believe that the computer science program must be highly specialized, and must emphasize computing, mathematics, and related technical subjects. Otherwise, it is argued, computer science majors will not be prepared to take a job in industry or continue with their graduate education. But there are others who believe that a more liberal undergraduate program is especially necessary in computing. Computing pervades many disciplines, and the computing student should have a background in those disciplines. Furthermore, if computing technology is to contribute to the meaningful development of society, the computer scientist must be a well educated and informed citizen. This observer comes down strongly on the side of a more liberal undergraduate education with greater specialization coming at the graduate level. (See Finerman and Ralston, 1970, for an elaboration of this viewpoint.) However, the controversy continues unabated and without resolution to this day. In fact, at the present time, many university curricula in computer science are highly specialized, following the general practice in undergraduate scientific education.

The Undergraduate Curriculum. Because computer science and technology are so new, there is as yet no well established standard curriculum in this discipline. The undergraduate program varies from university to university, depending upon such factors as the resources available, the amount of specialization deemed useful, and the interests of the faculty. Even the content of specific courses is, in some cases, quite variable. As noted earlier, the most comprehensive attempts made to date in defining the scope and content of an undergraduate program in computer science have been the works of the ACM Curriculum Committee, "Curriculum 68" and

"Curriculum 78." In particular, the 1968 report had a profound effect on shaping the direction of computer education in the then still emerging discipline. Many institutions continue to view its recommendations as the definitive yardstick by which to measure the adequacy of their programs.

Curriculum 68 contains detailed information on four beginning courses (prefixed by the letter B), nine intermediate courses (I), and nine advanced courses (A)—a total of 22 undergraduate courses, as outlined below.

B1. Introduction to Computing
   The basic knowledge of algorithms, languages, programming, and program structure necessary to use computers effectively.

B2. Computers and Programming
   The basic structure, language, and internal behavior of computers and the relation among these elements.

B3. Introduction to Discrete Structures
   Fundamental algebraic, logical, and combinatoric concepts from mathematics and their application to computer science.

B4. Numerical Calculus
   Fundamental numerical algorithms, in such areas as linear and nonlinear equations, used in scientific work.

I1. Data Structures
   Elements of data involved in problems, structure of storage media, methods of representing, and techniques for operating on structured data.

I2. Programming Languages
   Specification of syntax and semantics as applied to algorithms, list processing, string manipulation, and simulation languages.

I3. Computer Organization
   A continuation of concepts introduced in course B2, the organization, logic design, and components of digital computers.

I4. Systems Programming
   Software organization and the role of data structures and programming languages in the design and organization of computing systems.

I5. Compiler Construction
   The organization of compilers, including symbol tables, lexical scan, syntax scan, and object code generation.

I6. Switching Theory
   Theoretical principles and mathematical techniques involved in the design of digital systems logic.

I7. Sequential Machines
   Definition and representation of finite state automata and sequential machines, and decision problems of finite automata.

I8. Numerical Analysis 1 and

I9. Numerical Analysis 2
   Mathematically rigorous and computer-oriented methods in the solution of equations, linear systems, and differential equations.

A1. Formal Languages and Syntactic Analysis
   Theory of context-free grammars and formal languages, and syntactic recognition techniques.

A2. Advanced Computer Organization
   System design problems and comparison of specific examples of solutions for various computer organizations.

A3. Analog and Hybrid Computing
   Analog, hybrid, and related digital techniques, operational characteristics of analog components, and conversion methods.

A4. Systems Simulation
   Simulation and modeling of discrete systems, simulation methodology, and design of simulation experiments.

A5. Information Organization and Retrieval
   Natural language processing, particularly as applied to the design and operation of automatic information systems.

A6. Computer Graphics
   Problems and techniques for handling graphic information, such as line drawings, block diagrams, and handwriting.

A7. Theory of Computability
   Use of abstract machines and models in the study of computability and computational complexity.

A8. Large-Scale Information Processing Systems
   The design, organization, and integration of hardware, software, procedures, and techniques.

A9. Artificial Intelligence and Heuristic Programming
   Application of computing systems to problems that attempt to achieve goals normally considered to require human mental capabilities.

Curriculum 68 recommends that the major in computer science should consist of ten required computer courses (B1 to B4, I1 to I4, and two from I5 to I9), plus perhaps three elective computer courses. In addition, the report lists eight supporting courses in mathematics, covering such areas as calculus, linear algebra, algebraic structures, and probability and statistics. The report notes that an academic program in computer science must be well based in mathematics, since computer science draws so heavily upon mathematical concepts and methods. Consequently, at least six of the mathematical courses listed are recommended as required, and additional electives in mathematics are encouraged.

The program prescribed in Curriculum 68 reflects the viewpoint of those advocating a strong specialization in computing at the undergraduate level; as such, it follows the traditional pattern of most scientific and engineering undergraduate programs. The large component of computer and mathematics courses recommended (between one-half and two-thirds of the total undergraduate course load) plus technical electives in computer-related disciplines, leaves little room for non-technical subjects in the humanities and the social sciences within the normal four-year program.

As noted earlier, the recently published report, "Curriculum 78," revised the recommendations for the undergraduate program. The revision reflects the significant developments that have occurred within computer science education during the intervening decade. Curriculum 78 provides somewhat greater flexibility than Curriculum 68 in the content of courses, emphasizing the objectives of such a program and the subject matter to be covered. Aside from the proposed curriculum, the report discusses such topics as service courses, continuing education, computing facilities, and staff.

Briefly stated, Curriculum 78 proposes a core of eight computer courses required for all majors:

CS 1. Computer Programming I
CS 2. Computer Programming II
CS 3. Introduction to Computer Systems
CS 4. Introduction to Computer Organization
CS 5. Introduction to File Processing
CS 6. Operating Systems and Computer Architecture I
CS 7. Data Structures and Algorithm Analysis
CS 8. Organization of Programming Languages

Students select four courses from ten advanced electives:

CS 9. Computers and Society
CS 10. Operating Systems and Computer Architecture II
CS 11. Database Management Systems Design
CS 12. Artificial Intelligence
CS 13. Algorithms
CS 14. Software Design and Development
CS 15. Theory of Programming Languages
CS 16. Automata, Computability, and Formal Languages

CS 17. Numerical Mathematics: Analysis
CS 18. Numerical Mathematics: Linear Algebra

Students are required to take at least the first five of the following mathematics courses.

MA 1. Introductory Calculus
MA 2. Mathematical Analysis I
MA 2A. Probability
MA 3. Linear Algebra
MA 4. Discrete Structures
MA 5. Mathematical Analysis II
MA 6. Probability and Statistics

As noted in the report, "An understanding of and the capability to use a number of mathematical concepts and techniques are vitally important for a computer scientist. . . . For example, probability and statistics develop the required tools for measurement and evaluation of systems, two important aspects of computer science. Analysis . . . gives the mathematical bases for important concepts such as sets, relations, functions, limits and convergence. . . . Thus, mathematical requirements are integral to a computer science curriculum even though specific courses are not cited as prerequisites for most computer science courses."

All told, required computer science courses total 36 semester hours (credits) plus another 15 from mathematics. This is somewhat less than half the total hours of a typical undergraduate degree program, a relaxation of Curriculum 68 recommendations for required computer and mathematics courses.

To this observer, the reduction both in required computer and mathematics courses is a step in the right direction. Even more desirable, a liberal undergraduate program in computing would limit the recommended number of computer and mathematics courses to one-third of the total course load, and would require that another one-third be taken in the humanities and the social sciences. By allowing some flexibility in the remaining one-third, such a program would permit students to take a double major—in computing and in some other discipline such as physics, psychology, or economics—a freedom which would serve many students well.

However, some have criticized Curriculum 78 because of the reduced number of mathematics courses (from Curriculum 68) and the fact that those mathematics courses required are not prerequisite to the computer courses—and therefore are not as integral a part of the prerequisite structure as in Curriculum 68 (see, for example, Ralston and Shaw, 1980). A deficiency of both Curriculum 68 and 78 to most observers is the emphasis on traditional (continuous) mathematics rather than discrete mathematics. In fairness to Curriculum 78, however, the report notes: "Unfortunately the kind and amount of [mathematics] material needed for these areas for computer science can only be obtained, if at all, from the regular courses offered by departments of mathematics for their own majors. . . . If more appropriate courses are provided as a result of interaction between computer science and mathematics departments, then the specifications of required mathematics courses and the prerequisite structure should be reconsidered."

In any event, because the report has been published only recently, it is hard to predict whether it will have the same impact in revising existing curricula (and in establishing new programs) as its predecessor had in establishing curricula in the then emerging discipline.

Computer Engineering. As noted earlier, computing had its university origins both in mathematics and (electrical) engineering. While there are now numerous separate departments of computer science, the computer discipline still resides at times in departments of mathematics and more often in departments of electrical engineering (now commonly known as electrical engineering and computer science or, at times, electrical and computer engineering). Indeed, some universities have more than one department engaged in the computer discipline—in some cases, a separate department of computer science, a department of electrical (and computer) engineering, and perhaps a department of, or a group in, information systems (in the school of business administration, as noted below). At many universities, the distinction between computer engineering and computer science is fuzzy, but most often computer engineering emphasizes the hardware and engineering aspects, while computer science emphasizes the software and scientific aspects. To many, the ACM curricula fall into the latter category.

As already indicated, the IEEE Computer Society published a report on undergraduate curricula through the Model Curricula Subcommittee of its Education Committee. This report, "A Curriculum in Computer Science and Engineering" (Cain, 1977), provides model curricula for four-year bachelor's degree programs, detailed course descriptions, and a core curriculum. The emphasis is on the hardware and engineering aspects, although the proposed curricula attempt to bridge the gap between hardware and software mainly through laboratory courses.

The report identifies four major areas or subdisciplines of computer science and engineering (CSE): Digital Logic (designated as DL in the list of associated courses below), Computer Organization and Architecture (CO), Software Engineering (SE), Theory of Computing (TC), and an associated set of laboratories (L). It also provides a core curriculum ("the minimal set needed in a curriculum to provide a background for a career" in CSE). Although it does not fully identify specific courses as belonging to the core, it does point to certain courses as containing the concepts necessary to form the core. The full set of courses identified (an asterisk indicates that the course, in whole or in part, fits into the core) is listed below.

DL 1. Switching Theory and Digital Logic I *
DL 2. Switching Theory and Digital Logic II *
DL 3. Microprocessor Systems *
DL 4. Digital Logic Devices
DL 5. Digital Design Automation
CO 1. Introduction to Computer Organization *
CO 2. I/O and Memory Systems *
CO 3. Computer Architecture
CO 4. Microprogramming
CO 5. Distributed Processing and Networks
SE 1. Introduction to Computing and Programming Laboratory*
SE 2. Data Structures I *
SE 3. Data Structures II
SE 4. Programming Languages *
SE 5. Data Base Systems
SE 6. Operating Systems and Computer Architecture I *
SE 7. Operating Systems and Computer Architecture II
SE 8. Translators and Translator Writing Systems
TC 1. Discrete Structures *
TC 2. Design and Analysis of Algorithms *
TC 3. Automata and Formal Languages
TC 4. Theory of Computing
L1. Logic Laboratory *
L2. Minicomputer Laboratory *
L3. Microprocessors, Memory and I/O Laboratory *
L4. Digital Devices and Components Laboratory
L5. Systems Design Laboratory I
L6. Systems Design Laboratory II

The report does not identify complete curricula for these four major areas, nor does it discuss the role of mathematics in the curricula. It does note that the program is sufficiently flexible "to allow each institution to implement a CSE program after considering departmental facilities, faculty interests, regional needs, and accreditation requirements. The Regional Help Subcommittee of the Computer Society is charged with assisting implementation." A one-page appendix contains a "Suggested Outline for Electrical and Computer Engineering Curriculum to meet ECPD [Engineers' Council for Professional Development] Guidelines for Accreditation"; except for approximately 22–25 semester hours in the humanities and social sciences, communications, and accounting (optional), the curriculum consists entirely of courses from the natural and engineering sciences, mathematics, and electrical and computer engineering. Thus, the curriculum, in common with many engineering disciplines, contains breadth, but only in the sciences and engineering. It provides little ability for students to explore the wealth of knowledge outside these technical areas, to share "some common background" (in the broad sense of the term).

In any event, as already noted, most departments of computer science are generally oriented more toward "software" than "hardware." Students interested in the hardware aspects of computing normally major in departments of electrical (and computer) engineering. (Indeed, graduates of such programs generally are referred to as hardware "engineers" rather than computer "scientists," although the distinction often is not meaningful.) Courses at the interface (e.g., switching theory and microprogramming) may be given in computer science or electrical engineering or both.

Business Data Processing. While Curricula 68 and 78 emphasize the mathematical and scientific content of computer science education, and the Computer Society report emphasizes the engineering aspects, the reports pay little attention to the business-oriented computer student. Although computers were originally developed for scientific and engineering applications, somewhat later, the use of computer systems for commercial applications began to exceed the scientific applications. Today, more computers by far are applied to (and more computing practitioners are engaged in) administrative and business data processing than scientific computing. Yet students interested in business data processing find few academic programs meeting their needs, except for the host of "data processing" programs at community colleges or, sometimes, in the undergraduate and graduate programs in schools of business.

Perhaps a more subtle shortcoming of the scientifically-oriented computer program is that it does little to prepare students adequately for the more recent applications of computer technology. As users have gained experience and computing capabilities have become more general-purpose, the distinction between "scientific" and "business" applications has become increasingly blurred. Many modern applications require the successful integration of the systems analysis approach associated with data processing and the more rigorous mathematical analysis approach associated with scientific processing. Applications in space technology, library information retrieval, airline reservations, and corporate administration are but a few examples of these "large-scale" systems.

Large systems bring together many organizational units, technical disciplines, and people-oriented procedures; information flows through and across organizations, and causes problems at the interfaces; computer programs written by different people and organizations must be tested, accepted, and integrated into one operational system. Computer science academic programs may produce students expert in computer technology but not in management organization, human and organizational behavior, systems analysis and design, economics, and the like. Yet it is just this type of knowledge, as much as the mastery of computer technology, that is required to implement properly many large-scale applications. While there continue to be few defined curricula in business data processing at universities, the programs in information systems, described below, are intended more for the business-oriented students.

Information Systems. As indicated earlier, the ACM, several years ago, chartered a Curriculum Committee on Computer Education for Management. The approach of this committee has been to design curricula in the field of "information systems," systems in which computer technology is applied to the information needs of the organization. This concept is evident in the two major reports published by the Committee, "Curriculum Recommendations for Graduate Professional Programs in Information Systems" (Ashenhurst, 1972) and "Curriculum Recommendations for Undergraduate Programs in Information Systems" (Couger, 1973). Couger's report on the undergraduate program recommends a curriculum that gives students knowledge of the organization, its information needs, and its behavior, as well as of computer technology. Students enrolled in this program are required to take certain prerequisite and corequisite introductory courses in economics, psychology, mathematics, statistics, and computing. (The computing prerequisite may be quite similar to the "Introduction to Computing" course detailed in Curriculum 68.)

The courses in information systems are in four groups: Background (prefixed by UB), Computing (UC), Analysis of Organizations (UA), and Development of Systems (UD).

UB1. Operational Analysis and Modeling
Analytical and simulation modeling techniques useful in decision-making in the system design environment.

UB2. Human and Organizational Behavior
Principles governing human behavior, particularly in organizations, and use of computer-based information systems in organizations.

UC1. Information Structures

Structures for representing the logical relationship between elements of information, and techniques for operating on such structures.

UC2. Computer Systems

A working view of hardware and software configurations considered as integrated systems.

UC3. File and Communication Systems

Basic functions of file and communications systems, current realization of these systems, and analysis of these realizations.

UC4. Software Designs

Complex programming tasks; and subdividing such programs for maximum clarity, efficiency, and ease of maintenance and modification.

UA8. Systems Concepts and Implications

The basic concepts involved in the systems point of view, the organization as a system, information flows, and information systems.

UD8. Information Systems Analysis

Analysis of the design of an information system intended to facilitate decision-making and planning and control.

UD9. System Design and Implementation

The knowledge and tools necessary to develop a physical design and an operational system from the logical design.

Not all courses are required for all students. For example, students may decide to take an organizational or a technological concentration. For the former, there are two courses, UC8 and UC9, in place of the four courses UC1 to UC4; for the latter, course UB2 may be eliminated. The report also stresses the concept of a double major in information systems and (for example) accounting or engineering. It gives illustrations of sample programs for these two double majors. It is still uncertain whether such programs would be housed in a school of business, a school of engineering, or a department of computer science—or indeed whether universities would give such programs the priority given in the past to the scientifically-oriented programs in computing. It may be that, in future years, the effects of this report on undergraduate programs in information systems will be as widespread as those of Curriculum 68 in computer science.

As a final note on undergraduate programs in computing, it should be pointed out that many undergraduate courses in computer attract not only the major in computing science (or information systems) but also students majoring in other disciplines. The President's Science Advisory Committee report (Pierce *et al.,* 1967) esti-

mated that about three of every four college undergraduates have need for some educational exposure to computing. The extent of such exposure obviously depends upon the fields in which students are majoring. Those in the liberal arts might benefit only from some introductory knowledge of computer technology (although a more complete knowledge is becoming increasingly important for many such students). Students majoring in the natural and physical sciences, engineering, or business administration require more—in some cases extending to a "minor" or a double major in computing. Generally, there are few pure "service" courses in computing intended mainly for the non-computer science majors; these students usually enroll in selected courses together with the computer science majors. Nevertheless, the computer science program performs a necessary service function for these students.

The Graduate Program. Although graduate programs in computing predate the undergraduate programs, there are few descriptions of graduate curricula in the formal literature. Curriculum 68 contains a brief description of the master's and doctoral program. The book by Finerman (1968) is more explicit, since it derived from a conference on graduate academic programs.

A master's program in computer science may be terminal or non-terminal. In the first case, the goal is to develop programming and applied problem-solving capabilities so that the graduate can qualify for a responsible position in industrial or research organizations. The goal of the non-terminal program is to develop the intellectual capabilities so that the graduate can continue to the doctoral program (although some students go directly from the bachelor's degree to the doctorate). This dichotomous approach is in the pattern of more traditional master's programs in scientific and in professional disciplines. In the sciences, the master's program has been viewed as the testing ground for the doctorate. Students who prove they have the necessary capabilities can continue for the doctorate; those who cannot will receive the master's degree as compensation. However, in professional disciplines, the terminal master's degree is itself an honorable goal, since most people have no need for the doctorate. In business administration, for example, several excellent universities offer highly sought after terminal master's programs. Computer science, which is both a scientific and a professional discipline, increasingly offers both choices, depending upon the inclination of the student.

The master's program generally has three areas of specialization. The first encompasses information structures and processes. This is quite abstract and theoretical, involving advanced mathematical concepts; it includes such topics as computability, complexity, formal languages, analysis of algorithms, and switching and automata theory. The second category covers information processing systems. This deals with practical techniques in such areas as computer organization and design, programming languages, operating systems, and assemblers and compilers. The third category comprises methodologies. This deals with a broad spectrum of techniques appropriate to various computer applications, such as numerical analysis, text processing, graphics, symbol manipulation, simulation, database management, information retrieval, and artificial intelligence.

The master's program in the last two categories—information processing systems and methodologies—might be terminal or not; at many institutions it is assumed that students in these categories will not continue. These students take one or more courses in the theoretical aspects of computer science, but most courses are in their particular field of specialization, drawn from the intermediate and advanced courses in Curriculum 68 or from graduate versions of these courses. The theoretically inclined student is usually interested in continuing toward the doctorate. Therefore, the first category—information structures and processing—is generally a non-terminal program; again, students in this category are required to take some courses in the other areas.

At many institutions, the terminal master's student may elect to perform thesis work, or not. If not, two more courses or a major project may be substituted for the thesis. Non-terminal students are often expected or required to submit a thesis as further proof of their qualification to pursue the doctorate. Many students enter the master's program with undergraduate degrees that are not in computer science but in the sciences or engineering. Within the past few years, a Graduate Record Examination (GRE) has been offered for students seeking admission to graduate programs in computer science; increasingly, universities are requiring the GRE for students applying to graduate programs in computer science.

In contrast to this approach to computer science, Ashenhurst (1972) considers the professionally-oriented master's program in information systems. The philosophy expressed in the undergraduate curriculum carries forward to the graduate level (actually *vice versa,* since the graduate report came first). The program in information systems deals with computer technology as applied to the organization and its systems, and again there are four groups of courses. The first involves two background courses: One in operations research and the other in behavior in organizations. The second group, dealing with the environment in which systems function, involves four courses in the organization and systems requirements. The third group contains four courses dealing with computer and information technology. Finally, the fourth group integrates the previous two groups with three additional courses in the analysis and development of sys-

tems. The courses are more advanced versions of those at the undergraduate level.

Students can enter this program with a background in computing, economics, or other business areas, or even engineering. As we discussed previously, computer technology is applied to large engineering or scientific systems as well as to business or commercial systems; in many applications, the "scientific" or "business" distinction is meaningless. In any event, the entering student is required to have prerequisite undergraduate courses in mathematics, statistics, computing, economics, and psychology.

Doctoral programs in computer science are intended for students with theoretical or research interests, and most such programs especially reflect the research interests of the faculty members. In general, courses are similar to those in the master's degree programs and encompass the following areas: Logical design, switching theory, and computer circuits and devices; computer organization, programming languages, and compiler and operating systems; computability, computational complexity, formal languages, and automata; numerical mathematics and operations research; and methodologies such as artificial intelligence, simulation, and modeling. Of course, the doctoral thesis, drawn from one or more of these areas, lies at the heart of the doctoral program. It is the means by which the student demonstrates the capability for original contribution to knowledge. This demonstrated capability is the fundamental requirement for the doctorate.

Some universities are re-examining academic programs at the graduate as well as at the undergraduate level. In certain cases, this examination may lead to broader (and longer) interdisciplinary master's degree programs; in others, predoctoral intermediate degree programs may be established which do not require original contribution to knowledge but recognize a dimension of excellence in another area. In general, however, the traditional master's and doctorate programs still are regarded as the accepted models, and this is not likely to change in the near future.

Summary. Formal education in computer science and technology is quite new, dating back only to the early to mid-1960s. Educational programs originated at universities, resulting from the increasing use of computers by students, faculty, and administrators. Today, most colleges and universities offer academic programs in computing, either as a separate discipline or as an option in a related discipline. As can be expected in such a new field, the educational program still has fuzzy edges; at times, it overlaps applied mathematics, electrical engineering, business administration, and other disciplines. Yet, in just a few short years, it has become a visible and influential area of study. Computer science undergraduate programs also provide a service function by offering courses to the student majoring in other disciplines. Usually, these students require some computer courses so that they can better apply computing methods to their fields. Often, however, these students become computing practitioners after graduation.

In earlier days, entry into the computer field was always through some other discipline; there simply were no academic programs in computing. People learned by doing—by using computers, by programming, and by absorbing knowledge in this more informal manner. Today, many enter with a degree in computer science, information systems, or related programs. Because demand for qualified people continues to exceed supply, many people still enter from other disciplines. However, even these graduates generally have been exposed to computer courses. Furthermore, in earlier days, a university or college degree was not required for many professional positions in the computing organization (especially administrative data processing). Increasingly, prospective employers today require at least a bachelor's degree (in computing or some other field with concentration in computing) to qualify for the professional position. In many cases, a master's degree in computing is preferable. Even with the rapid increase in bachelor's and master's degree programs in the past decade, the demand for graduates with these degrees exceeds the supply. The graduate with a doctorate in computer science is in especially short supply both at universities and at industrial research organizations; this shortage is expected to continue at least for the near future.

Although the discussions in this article apply primarily to computing education in the U.S. and Canada, experiences in other countries are quite similar. The major difference is that computer science educational programs in other countries were introduced later than those in North America. For example, with some exceptions, universities in Western Europe and Israel initiated such programs around the late 1960s, in South America around the early 1970s, and in Southeast Asia around the mid-1970s. In Europe, especially, the title of the academic program usually is a variation of the term *informatics,* derived from the French "informatique."

One result of these educational programs is a recognition that computer science involves more than the study of a tool. The computer has given entirely new scope to the whole spectrum of computation applications. People who work with computers have found new approaches to problem-solving, even in areas to which the computer may never be applied as a tool. Too often, our early educational programs emphasized the study of the computer as a tool. Many programs, especially those below the college level, still do. But there is now an increasing awareness that the use of the computer stimulates and modifies intellectual processes, and as a result makes it possible for people to expand their intellectual capabilities. This added dimension—the extension of human intellect—must be part of any program in computer science or information systems.

REFERENCES

Early efforts to bring computing methods into engineering education are described in three related volumes:

1960. University of Michigan Study. "Electronic Computers in Engineering Education." Ann Arbor: University of Michigan.

1961. University of Michigan Study. "Use of Computers in Engineering Education, Second Annual Report." Ann Arbor: University of Michigan.

1962. University of Houston Study. "Use of Computers in Engineering Education—A Report of the Advanced Science Seminar." Houston: University of Houston.

There were two principal government-sponsored studies on computing in universities during the mid-1960s. Both gave background information on the use of computers in universities and recommended government financial support for computer education:

1966. Rosser, J. B. *et al.* "Digital Computer Needs in Universities and Colleges." Washington, DC: National Academy of Sciences/National Research Council.

1967. Pierce, J. *et al.* "Computers in Higher Education," The President's Science Advisory Committee, The White House. Washington, DC: U.S. Government Printing Office.

There are six principal references for undergraduate and graduate programs in computing. The first four shown below have been published in the monthly periodical, *Communications of the Association for Computing Machinery (CACM);* the fifth is a report of the IEEE Computer Society; and the sixth is a monograph of the ACM:

1968. Atchison, W. *et al.* "Curriculum '68," A Report of the ACM Curriculum Committee on Computer Science, *CACM* **11**:151–197 (March).

1972. Ashenhurst, R. (Ed.). "Curriculum Recommendations for Graduate Professional Programs in Information Systems," A Report of the ACM Curriculum Committee on Computer Education for Management, *CACM* **15**:363–398 (May).

1973. Couger, J. D. (Ed.). "Curriculum Recommendations for Undergraduate Programs in Information Systems," A Report of the ACM Curriculum Committee on Computer Education for Management, *CACM* **16**:727–749 (December).

1979. Austing, R. *et al.* "Curriculum '78," A Report of the ACM Curriculum Committee on Computer Science, *CACM* **22**:147–165 (March).

1977. Cain, J. T. (Ed.). "A Curriculum in Computer Science and Engineering," A Report of the IEEE Computer Society Education Committee Model Curricula Subcommittee, *IEEE Publication EH0119-8* (January).

1968. Finerman, A. (Ed.). "University Education in Computing Science," ACM Monograph. New York: Academic Press.

For a more complete bibliography on the subject, see "A Survey of the Literature in Computer Science Education since Curriculum 68" by Austing, Barnes, and Engel, *CACM* **20**:13–21

(January 1977). In addition, the quarterly *SIGCSE Bulletin* of the ACM Special Interest Group on Computer Science Education contains articles of interest on a continuing basis.

The case for less specialized undergraduate programs in computer is presented in the article:

1970. The MIT Commission. "A New Plan for Undergraduate Education," *Technology Review* **72**:85 (July/August).

1970. Report of the Commission on MIT Education. "Creative Renewal in a Time of Crisis" (November).

The case for less specialized undergraduate programs in computing is presented in the article:

1970. Finerman, A. and Ralston, A. "Undergraduate Programs in Computing Science in the Tradition of Liberal Education," *IFIP World Conference on Computer Education* **2**:195–199.

The mathematical background of the undergraduate student in computer science (and a critique of the approach taken by Curriculum 78) is examined in a *CACM* article:

1980. Ralston, A. and Shaw, Mary. "Curriculum '78—Is Computer Science Really That Unmathematical?" *Comm. ACM* **23**:67–70 (February).

There have been four national surveys on computers in higher education, conducted by Hamblen with support from the National Science Foundation. These report on computing facilities and related expenditures, and computer science and related degree programs. The latest of these (which references the preceding three) was published in 1979:

1979. Hamblen, J. and Baird, T. "Fourth Inventory of Computers in Higher Education 1976–77." New Jersey: Educom.

In recent years, there have been three articles by Taulbee and Conte giving data on Ph.D. academic programs. The latest of these (which references the preceding two) appeared in *CACM* in 1979:

1979. Taulbee, O. and Conte, S. "Production and Employment of Ph.D.'s in Computer Science—1977 and 1978," *Comm. ACM* **22**:75–76 (February).

A. Finerman

EUROPE

The teaching of computer science and technology has developed in Europe along more or less the same lines as in the U.S. and for the same reasons.

Some of the first computers in Europe were installed or built in universities: Cambridge and Manchester in the U.K.; Göttingen, Munich, and Darmstadt in West Germany and Paris, Grenoble and Toulouse in France. They were used mainly for research purposes in departments of applied mathematics and sometimes in electrical engineering, but these research projects led to the development of academic programs.

By the mid-1950s, optional courses had started at the universities which had their own computers or could afford to rent a computer mainly for students in mathematics or physics. At that time, a curriculum in computer science was usually divided into three parts—numerical analysis, hardware, and programming.

In England, in 1965, there was only one university offering a B.Sc. degree in computer science, but there were no degrees in computer science in Germany before 1970, despite a rather extensive teaching program at a number of Hochschulen (schools of engineering). In France, degrees in computer science were given by the Institut de Programmation starting in 1964, although the teaching of computer science started much earlier at the University of Grenoble (1956), Toulouse (1957), and Paris (1957). It was also in France that computer science and technology was very early given the status of an autonomous scientific discipline because of the definition of the word "informatique" by the Académie Française in 1966.

Except in English-speaking countries where computer science is still the normal designation, *informatique* or its variants in other languages is the standard name for the discipline.

In 1980, the teaching of informatics in Europe is not very different from what it is in the U.S. The curricula are more or less the same and the differences come mainly from the differences in the administrative organization of education in each country.

In the U.K., a number of universities offer traditional degrees in computer science (undergraduate, masters, and Ph.D.). Degrees in computer science are also offered at the Colleges of Technology and at the Polytechnics.

In West Germany, education is under the responsibility of the different "Länder" (i.e., states) but, in January 1976, a law was passed under which the federal government has been able to unify education at the university level. All post-secondary institutions are now called "Hochschulen." The scientific Hochschulen are the former universities and the "technische Hochschulen" are schools of engineering with the "Fach hochschulen" being for vocational education. There are 19 scientific and technical Hochschulen delivering degrees in computer science, but in most Hochschulen there are optional credits in informatics for degrees in electrical engineering, law, economics, medicine, etc.

In the schools of engineering, which, in France, are completely separate from Universities, optional credits in informatics started in the early 1960s and are today the rule in every school of engineering. In 1969, the first department of informatics was created at the Instituts Universitaires de Technologie with a degree for analysts and programmers at the vocational level. Today there are 19 of these departments, with an output of about 2,000 per year. In 1972, an M.Sc. in applications of data processing to management was created; this degree is now offered at 10 universities and the M.Sc. in informatics is offered at 20 universities. About 10 universities award Ph.D. degrees, which require three to four years after the M.Sc. degree.

There are, of course, also computer science programs in the other countries of Western Europe. But those in France, West Germany, and the U.K. are the largest and best developed and generally serve as models for the programs elsewhere.

J. HEBENSTREIT

EDVAC

For articles on related subjects *see* DIGITAL COMPUTERS: Early; ECKERT, J. PRESPER; ENIAC; MAUCHLY, JOHN W., STORED-PROGRAM CONCEPT; VON NEUMANN, JOHN; and VON NEUMANN MACHINE.

The EDVAC (Electronic Discrete Variable Automatic Computer) was a direct outgrowth of the work on the ENIAC. During the design and construction of the ENIAC in 1944 and 1945, the need for more storage (only twenty 10-decimal digit numbers in the ENIAC) was realized. The experience with acoustic delay lines for radar range measurement led to the concept of recirculating storage of digital information. The group at the Moore School of Electrical Engineering at the University of Pennsylvania started developmental work on mercury delay lines for such storage, and initiated the design of the EDVAC.

This was the first stored-program computer; the instructions controlling the computational process are stored in the same way that data is stored. The basic logical ideas were described by von Neumann (1945), and computers based on such designs have come to be known as *von Neumann computers*. The principles involved in the EDVAC design exerted a strong influence on the computers that followed it.

The EDVAC had about 4,000 tubes and 10,000 crystal diodes. It used a 1,024-word recirculating mercury-delay line memory, consisting of 23 lines, each 384 μs long. The words were 44 bits long. Instructions were of the four-address type (4-bit operation code and four 10-bit addresses). The arithmetic unit did both fixed and floating-point operations. Input and output were via punched paper tape and IBM cards. Information was all handled as series pulse trains and the clock frequency was 1 MHz.

Although the conceptual design of the EDVAC was complete in 1946, and it was delivered in 1949 to the Ballistic Research Laboratories at Aberdeen, Maryland, by 1950 the entire calculator had not yet worked as a unit and was still undergoing extensive tests (Stifler, 1950, pp. 200–201). The delay in completion of the EDVAC was primarily due to the efflux of computer people from the Moore School in 1946. Eckert and Mauchly resigned and launched a commercial venture (UNIVAC). Herman Goldstine and Arthur Burks went to Princeton to work with von Neumann, and the author left to work with Turing in England. T. K. Sharpless was put in charge, but he, too, left later to go into business for himself.

The EDVAC finally became operational as a unit in 1951. An Aberdeen Proving Ground report states that during 1952, the EDVAC "began to operate on a production basis." For nine months of 1952 the average available time per week was 47.4 hours (23.3 for code checking and 24.1 for production), and the average "engineering" time was 104.8 hours. Approximately 70.4 hours of this was unscheduled maintenance; 10,000 defective tubes (over twice the complement) and about 3,000 (of 10,000) germanium diodes had been replaced. In a later Aberdeen report, Weik notes that during 1956, the average error-free running period was approximately 8 hours, and that out of a run time of 8,728 hours, 6,752 were good (78%). This gave approximately 130 hours of "good time" per week. The EDVAC was used until December 1962 (Knuth, 1970, p. 259).

REFERENCES

1945. von Neumann, John, "First Draft of a Report on the EDVAC," Contract No. W-670-ORD-4926, U.S. Army Ordnance Department. Philadelphia: University of Pennsylvania, Moore School of Electrical Engineering (June 30).
1950. Stifler, W. W., Jr. (Ed.). *High Speed Computing Devices*. New York: McGraw-Hill.
1970. Knuth, Donald E. "Von Neumann's First Computer Program," *Computing Surveys* 2, *No. 4:* 247–260 (December).

H. D. HUSKEY

EFTS. *See* ELECTRONIC FUNDS TRANSFER SYSTEMS.

ELECTRONIC CALCULATOR. *See* CALCULATORS, ELECTRONIC AND PROGRAMMABLE.

ELECTRONIC FUNDS TRANSFER SYSTEMS

For articles on related subjects *see* BANKING APPLICATIONS; COMMUNICATIONS AND COMPUTERS; COMPUTER NETWORKS; CREDIT SYSTEMS APPLICATIONS; DATA COMMUNICATIONS; DATA ENCRYPTION; and PRIVACY, COMPUTERS AND.

EFTS (electronic funds transfer systems) can broadly be described as computer data collection and telecommunications techniques that electronically transport information about the movement of funds between accounts managed by financial institutions.

The Impetus for EFT Services. With the adoption of the MICR (magnetic ink character recognition) standard in 1956, the banking industry took the first step toward facilitating computerized handling of the growing number of checks used in America. By the mid-1970s paper check processing had reached a level where more than 33.5 billion individual pieces of paper moved through the banking system annually. In 1983, at the present rate of growth, it is anticipated that this number will reach 52.4 billion.

Two general approaches are being followed in an effort to reduce the burden of check processing: The elimination of or supplanting of check transactions by electronic messages and the reduction of the physical transport of paper.

Replacement of Check Transactions by Electronic Messages. Examples are the installation of automated teller machines (ATMs) by financial institutions to provide on-line computerized banking services, the development of automated clearinghouse services (such as checkless payroll deposits) and telephone bill-paying services which allow customers to enter bill-paying information directly in electronic form to a bank's computer through Touchtone telephones.

Automated teller machines are unattended computer terminal-type devices that offer most of the services available from a teller. They are activated by a customer through the combined use of (1) a plastic card with a magnetic strip bearing machine-readable account information, and (2) a special secret number known only by the customer (termed a PIN or personal identification number). Among the services offered through these machines are cash withdrawals, transfer of funds between accounts, and account balance inquiry. Although early development of these machines was restricted to providing off-line cash dispensing, almost all new ATM installations are on-line to the financial institution's account database.

Automated clearinghouses (ACHs) are regional computer centers (see Fig. 1) run for the most part by the Federal Reserve System and concentrating their activities on the processing of pre-authorized electronic deposits or withdrawals from checking accounts maintained by financial institutions.

Typical volume in early 1979 was over 11 million electronic items per month submitted to the ACHs primarily on magnetic tape for sorting and redistribution. The predominant types of electronic items processed by the 32 ACHs were military payroll and Social Security electronic deposits (representing 80% of the total volume). Other types of transactions include withdrawal of funds to pay bills pre-authorized by the customer for payment. Electronic deposits or withdrawals destined for a financial institution not served by a specific regional ACH are transmitted via telecommunications links to the appropriate regional ACH for local redistribution.

Bill-paying by telephone is another popular EFT service designed to eliminate paper check mailing and processing. In its most basic form, the service involves customer-direct input by a Touchtone telephone to a computer (operated by the customer's bank) of the data necessary to generate electronic withdrawals from an account maintained by the customer and an electronic deposit to an account maintained by the billing company. Deposits destined for a company that does not maintain an account with the customer's bank can be routed through the local ACH for delivery to an appropriate bank.

Reduction of Paper Flow. Truncation of the physical transport of paper bearing instructions for the movement of funds between accounts is another EFT application. For example, efforts to truncate the flow of checks through the use of image processing techniques are under development. The thrust of this effort is to create electronic images of checks at the point of first deposit and to transmit only these images to the customer or customer's banks.

The national credit card clearing and settlement systems are other examples of such truncation systems. When a customer uses Visa or MasterCard to make a purchase, he or she normally is not dealing with a merchant who has an account with the financial institution that has issued the card. As a result, the evidence of the completed sale (a copy of the sales receipt completed by the merchant and cardholder) in the past was physically forwarded to the merchant's contracting bank for credit to the merchant's account and then on to the card-issuing bank for posting to the customer's statement. In 1975, national systems were installed by the two competing bankcard organizations which truncated the flow of this paper at the merchant's bank of deposit and forwarded only an electronic message to the card issuer for posting to the cardholder's statement. These systems were later expanded to include worldwide bankcard sales. The system that supports this electronic transmission for Visa cards processed about 60 million customer purchases per month during the latter part of 1980, or approximately 60% of all Visa card sales worldwide. The Visa system transmits this sales data overnight in a form which can be directly posted to a customer's descriptive billing statement through a network linking together 250 Visa bank processing centers in Europe, Canada, and the United States. Magnetic tapes are sent to the balance of

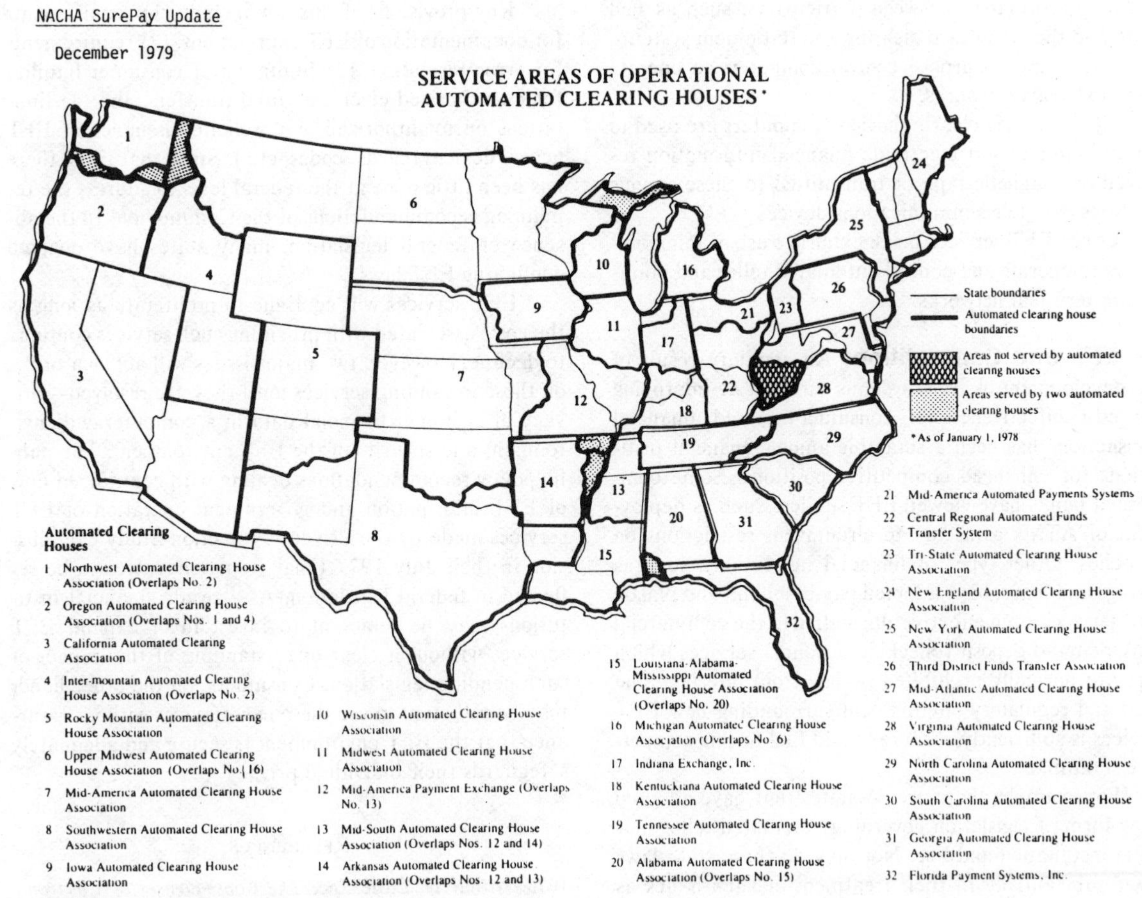

NACHA SurePay Update

December 1979

SERVICE AREAS OF OPERATIONAL AUTOMATED CLEARING HOUSES *

State boundaries

Automated clearing house boundaries

Areas not served by automated clearing houses

Areas served by two automated clearing houses

* As of January 1, 1978

Automated Clearing Houses

1 Northwest Automated Clearing House Association (Overlaps No. 2)

2 Oregon Automated Clearing House Association (Overlaps Nos. 1 and 4)

3 California Automated Clearing Association

4 Inter-mountain Automated Clearing House Association (Overlaps No. 2)

5 Rocky Mountain Automated Clearing House Association

6 Upper Midwest Automated Clearing House Association (Overlaps No. 16)

7 Mid-America Automated Clearing House Association

8 Southwestern Automated Clearing House Association

9 Iowa Automated Clearing House Association

10 Wisconsin Automated Clearing House Association

11 Midwest Automated Clearing House Association

12 Mid-America Payment Exchange (Overlaps No. 13)

13 Mid-South Automated Clearing House Association (Overlaps Nos. 12 and 14)

14 Arkansas Automated Clearing House Association (Overlaps Nos. 12 and 13)

15 Louisiana-Alabama-Mississippi Automated Clearing House Association (Overlaps No. 20)

16 Michigan Automated Clearing House Association (Overlaps No. 6)

17 Indiana Exchange, Inc.

18 Kentuckiana Automated Clearing House Association

19 Tennessee Automated Clearing House Association

20 Alabama Automated Clearing House Association (Overlaps No. 15)

21 Mid-America Automated Payments Systems

22 Central Regional Automated Funds Transfer System

23 Tri-State Automated Clearing House Association

24 New England Automated Clearing House Association

25 New York Automated Clearing House Association

26 Third District Funds Transfer Association

27 Mid-Atlantic Automated Clearing House Association

28 Virginia Automated Clearing House Association

29 North Carolina Automated Clearing House Association

30 South Carolina Automated Clearing House Association

31 Georgia Automated Clearing House Association

32 Florida Payment Systems, Inc.

Fig. 1

Visa banks operating in more than 125 countries throughout the rest of the world.

As a result of the implementation of these two systems, both national systems have uniformly adopted cardholder billing statements which simply list a description of the sale without including a copy of the sales receipt.

Further opportunities to truncate the flow of paper at the merchant point of sale are demonstrated by the JCPenney/Visa network system interface that occurred in late 1979. Through this connection, Visa card transaction data is collected electronically from over 20,000 electronic point-of-sale cash registers at JCPenney stores and nightly transmitted through the Visa network to the card issuer for preparation of the customer's statement.

Other EFT Systems. Although much of the impetus for the development of EFT systems focuses on the reduction of paper check processing, EFT techniques apply equally well to other paper transmission of financial information.

Thus, within the United States, the *Fed Wire* electronic network links together all 12 regional Federal Reserve Banks and their branches for the transmission of large dollar value transactions electronically between participants of the Federal Reserve. *Bank Wire* is another similar system, privately owned by 270 banks.

S.W.I.F.T. (Society for Worldwide Interbank Financial Telecommunications—a non-profit cooperative venture with over 500 active participants in more than 15 countries) has operated a private international banking network since 1977. Operating out of Belgium and providing service through terminals or direct computer interface to banks primarily in Europe and North America, the S.W.I.F.T. network transmits bank-to-bank funds transfer, customer funds transfer, and other international financial transaction information.

EFTS and the Computer. All of the previously mentioned EFT services rely on computers as an essential ingredient in providing the service. For example, telecommunications networks for transmitting electronic funds transfer information between participants, such as Fed Wire and the credit card clearing and settlement systems, use large general-purpose central computers to operate these extensive networks.

In automated clearinghouses, computers are used to consolidate and sort electronic financial information received on magnetic tape or transmitted to these service facilities over telecommunications devices.

Other EFT services make extensive use of minicomputers to operate and control automated teller and point-of-sale terminal networks.

EFT and Competition. An ancillary result of the development of EFT systems directed at improving the cost effectiveness of consumer-oriented financial transactions has been a scramble among financial institutions for enhanced competitive positions. Some commercial banks have viewed EFT services such as deployment of ATMs as a way to circumvent restrictions on branches. Other types of financial institutions, such as savings and loans, have adopted pay-by-phone and plastic card services as an effective alternative to the commercial bank demand deposit (checking account) services which they are normally prohibited by law from offering. The legal and regulatory environment surrounding new EFT services is sufficiently obscure to add fuel to this competitive scramble.

For example, there are 35 states that have adopted some form of legislation governing automated teller machine installation and use. Not only do these state laws differ substantially in their treatment of such issues as whether or not to mandate ATM sharing among all financial institutions in the state and whether or not to allow access to ATMs by out-of-state financial institutions, but they are also often at odds with regulations issued by the Comptroller of the Currency to national banks, the Federal Home Loan Bank Board to Federal savings and loans, and the National Credit Union Association to federally chartered credit unions on these same issues.

Experts on the Uniform Commercial Code that governs check processing law are uniform only in their agreement that the Code leaves many EFT questions unanswered.

The National Commission on Electronic Funds Transfers was established in 1974 to assess the impact of emerging EFT systems and services on future United States legislative and administrative policy goals. In their final report (October 1977), findings and recommendations were made in five areas—consumer interests, competitive and other developmental issues, technology, the federal government role, and international EFT developments. In 1978, a federal law was passed which addressed many of the consumer concerns expressed in the final report of the NCEFT.

Key provisions of this law include (1) requirements for documentation of EFT transactions, (2) requirements for error resolution, (3) limitation of consumer liability for unauthorized electronic fund transfers, and (4) limitations on unauthorized or unsolicited issuance of EFT access devices (cards, codes, etc.). Since that time, there has been little done at the federal level to address the remaining recommendations of the Commission. In the absence of federal legislation, many states have enacted conflicting EFT laws.

EFT services will continue to proliferate as long as the costs associated with providing such services continue to decline. However, two major issues will act as a brake on these expanding services until they are resolved—privacy of customer financial data in a computerized environment and security of the EFT environment. The public policy recommendations dealing with centralized flow of EFT information and government operation of EFT services made by the Privacy Protection Study Commission in their July 1977 Final Report have yet to be reflected in federal legislation. As a result, financial institutions may be reluctant to invest in or expand EFT services without a clear understanding of the impact of such pending legislation. Consumers, on the other hand, may be reluctant to use these new services without assurance that the EFT environment is secure and adequately safeguards their individual privacy.

REFERENCES

1975. Arthur D. Little, Inc. *The Consequences of Electronic Funds Transfer,* National Science Foundation.
1977. Peat, Marwick and Mitchell and Co. *EFT: A Strategy Perspective.*
1977. NCEFT. *EFT in the United States, Policy Recommendations and the Public Interest.*
1978. American Bankers Association. *Proceedings—1978 National Operations and Automation Conference.*

D. A. HUEMER

EMULATION

For articles on related subjects *see* HOST SYSTEM; MICROPROGRAMMING; and SIMULATION.

The most common meaning of *emulation* is the ability of one digital computer to interpret and execute the instruction set of another computer. To see how this can be done, it is necessary first to note that the control unit of a computer contains the necessary information for the sequence of operations (*microoperations*) that are to be performed when a particular operation code (op-code) is to be executed. The op-codes may be referred to as *macroinstructions* (not to be confused with the more common usage of macroinstruction—*q.v.*).

The control unit can consist of either *hard-wired logic* (that is, special-purpose digital logic circuitry for each op-code) or *microprogrammed* (*q.v.*) control. With microprogrammed control, the control unit contains a sequence of instructions *(microinstructions)* which, when decoded, control the gate operations in the central processing unit (*q.v.*) that will cause the op-code to be executed. This *microprogram* is stored in read-only memory (ROM—*q.v.*).

The microprogram in the control unit may simply be the sequence of microinstructions that will instruct the CPU to perform operations according to an instruction set which a computer designer wishes. For instance, if a computer designer desires an ADD Register-to-Register macroinstruction, the microinstruction sequence will consist of gating operations which gate each of the registers to the arithmetic-logic unit (ALU—*q.v.*) (and then the output of the ALU back to the appropriate register). Another possibility, however—and this is the essence of emulation—is to place a set of macroinstructions of another computer into the hardware of the given computer. That is, one encodes the macroinstruction set of the first computer by microprogramming those instructions on the hardware of the second computer. What we have then is an implementation of the macroinstruction set of one computer on hardware which differs from the originally intended hardware.

Another use of the term emulation concerns the possibility that one may wish to allow the replacement of one circuit board in the control unit by another in order to change the macroinstruction set. In fact, such approaches have been used to design, say, a Cobol machine or a Fortran machine. This is done because certain macroinstructions are more useful in some languages than in others.

Lately there has been a great deal of interest in moving certain portions of software systems into the microprogrammed control portion of the machine to effect increased speed. This has created the opportunity to experiment on tradeoffs between software and hardware and between software and microcode. Such implementation of software in hardware is called *firmware* and is still another type of emulation.

REFERENCES

1976. Salisbury, A. *Microprogrammable Computer Architectures.* New York: American Elsevier.
1976. Tanenbaum, A. S. *Structured Computer Organization.* Englewood Cliffs, NJ: Prentice-Hall.

S. HABIB

ENGINEERING APPLICATIONS

For articles on related subjects *see* COMPUTER-AIDED DESIGN; COMPUTER GRAPHICS; CONTROL APPLICATIONS; DATABASE MANAGEMENT; FINITE ELEMENT METHOD; NUMERICAL ANALYSIS; OPTIMIZATION METHODS; PERT/CPM; PROBLEM-ORIENTED LANGUAGES; SCIENTIFIC APPLICATIONS; and SIMULATION.

The engineering applications of large-scale computers, minicomputers, and microcomputers cover so wide a field that it seems impossible to deal here with their full extent. We will, however, attempt to discuss the following categories.

1. Numerical and process control.
2. Engineering analysis.
3. Simulation.
4. Optimization.
5. Engineering design.

Potential microprocessor applications such as data acquisition, peripheral control, and bioengineering instrumentation are discussed in other articles.

Numerical Control. One of the computer applications in production is in numerical control for machining metal parts. These parts are produced by either milling or routing. Essentially, the cutting tool is moved in a predetermined path so that a part is machined from sheet metal or other heavier metal stock.

If, for example, we wish to cut the two-dimensional contoured shape shown in Fig. 1, the basic operation involved is a movement of the cutting tool in the x and y directions. The cutting tool is advanced in, say, the x direction when the x-direction control receives a pulse. These pulses direct the *center* of the cutter, but the cutting is actually performed by the edge of the cutter. Therefore, the offset of the cutter must be determined first.

As far as a production engineer is concerned, cutting a contoured shape involves the following typical steps.

1. Translate the required part on the blueprint into a set of instructions in a user-oriented language such as APT (Automatically Programmed Tools).
2. Describe the offset path for the cutter.
3. Produce a punched tape by the computer. The tape, containing the information for detailed motions of the cutting tools, is used to control the milling machine.

In the three-dimensional case, the surfaces used to define the end product are of two types. One is the classic type, such as planes, spheres, and cylinders; and the other is commonly known as a "sculptured surface"—complex doubly curved surfaces. The art of machining these com-

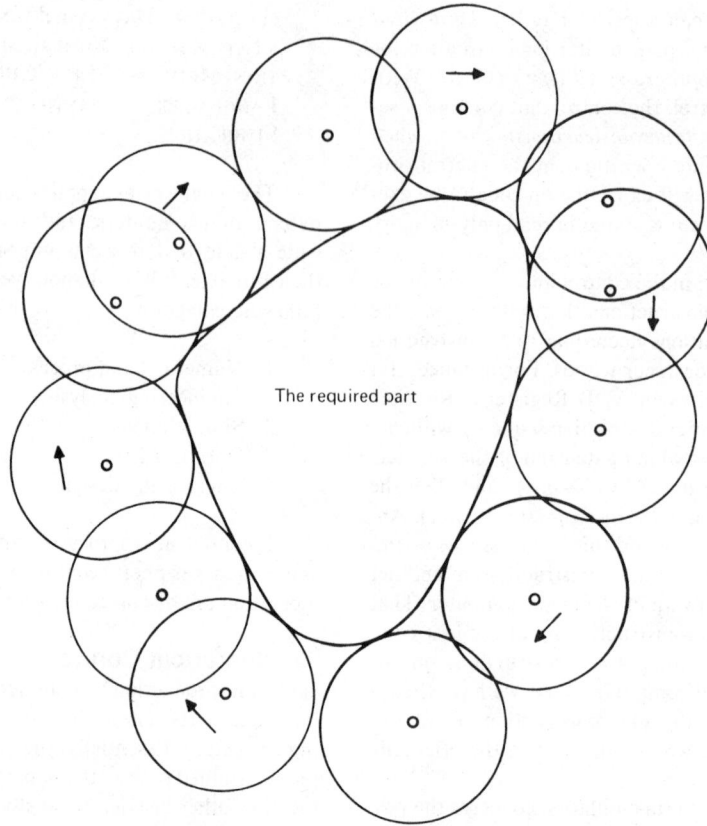

The required part

Fig. 1. Offset path for the cutter tool in numerical control. The circles indicate some of the successive positions of the cutter. The center of each circle represents the cutter center, which is directed by the control pulses.

plex surfaces has been recently enhanced by extensions to the APT language and its numerical control program.

Process Control. The numerical control described above provides automation of the discrete operations. By contrast, computers may be used to provide automation of continuous operations, known as "process control." A typical example is that of a chemical plant where a definitive sequence of decisions is required to process raw materials. Once all alternative possibilities are predetermined, computers can readily be used to control the entire processing.

The purpose of automatic control of chemical plants is twofold: to achieve optimum production and to obtain the highest possible quality of product. One unique feature of a typical chemical process is the large number of parameters involved, such as flow rate, viscosity, pressure, and temperature. Nonlinear relationships are used as a rule. Typically, information from various measuring

stations is transmitted to a computer, which will make decisions for the control mechanisms so that an optimum operation is maintained.

Computer control is also extensively used in many other fields of engineering. Applications include functional and faulty isolation testing of circuit board assemblies and complex shipboard control systems.

Engineering Analysis. Many analytical problems in engineering frequently reduce to one or two standard mathematical problems. Sometimes the explicit solutions may be found, and these are easily programmed for a digital computer. More frequently, they require approximate numerical treatment.

The two most common classes of mathematical problems seem to occur in matrix manipulations and ordinary differential equations. Matrix problems may arise in structural or network analysis, vibrations, and buckling. Usually a continuous system is idealized as a discrete system, a process known as "physical discretization." Matrix problems may also arise from a large class of partial differential equations through the use of finite differences, a process often known as "mathematical discretization." The advent of computer technology has enabled engineers to deal with matrices of very large size. Problems involving matrices on the order 100,000 have been handled successfully.

Ordinary differential equations occur in chemical reaction systems, spring-mass systems, temperature distribution, and many-body systems.

Other standard problems include the solutions of polynomial and transcendental equations, interpolation, curve fitting, and quadrature.

The popular mathematical software packages include SSP (Scientific Subroutine Package) and IMSL (International Mathematics and Statistics Libraries).

Since the advent of computers, the *finite element method* has gained popularity in various fields of engineering, including structural mechanics, heat transfer, fluid mechanics, and soil mechanics. In this method, the two- or three-dimensional domain of interest is first divided into small geometrical elements—a physical discretization. The elements may be of triangular, quadrilateral, tetrahedral, hexahedral, or other well-defined forms. The accuracy of the results is readily increased when the region is divided into smaller elements. The effect of the geometrical form of the elements on the behavior of the associated matrices has been extensively studied.

Simulation. An engineering system or device may be simulated on a computer. Such simulation is often used to aid in the engineering design. One chief advantage of simulation is the possible elimination of the actual building of expensive engineering systems before testing. A typical example is chemical process and control simulation. By means of modeling, the process equipment and controllers are in essence built within the computer. (The equipment may be a heat exchanger or a chemical reactor, while the controller may include valves and feed devices.) Once the information enters the computer to represent the factors for the real process, the process itself is dynamically simulated. During this simulated process, various revisions may be made and disturbances introduced. A new control element, say, may be inserted, or the setting of a control element may be changed.

A large number of simulation software packages are available in each engineering discipline. In chemical process simulation alone, there are more than 100 such packages available.

Optimization. This type of application is concerned mainly with the operational and system aspects of engineering problems. For example, we deal with how to obtain the largest possible number of gusset plates from a sheet of rolled plates, rather than how to design gussets. In a large system, the field data and measurements are usually integrated with some mathematical models and are processed on a large-scale computer. Important techniques include linear and dynamic programming and network analysis. PERT (Program Evaluation and Review Technique) and CPM (Critical Path Method) are also used to assist engineering decision making.

Engineering Design. Without computers, for most design problems the engineer would either make a "guestimate" from experience or, at best, estimate only one or two alternatives in the design. When a digital computer is used, a complete comparative study can be readily obtained to show the effect of numerous parameters. This is a typical situation where a computer is used to perform bulky and repetitive calculations.

An example is the structural design of orthotropic steel highway bridges. This type of bridge is found to require less steel than a bridge of the conventional type (plate girders) for medium or long spans. For a long time the design of orthotropic bridges was not popular, probably because it is complicated and time consuming. Now it seems almost routine to accomplish several types of bridge design by a computer. The weight computation, cost estimate, and many other items can be automatically tabulated.

In various engineering fields, many application packages (subsystems) are often assembled together. A typical user writes in a problem-oriented language to call one of the subsystems. Typical examples include ICES (Integrated Civil Engineering System), TIES (Total Integrated Engineering System), and ECAP (Electrical Circuit Analysis Program).

The most common subsystems used in ICES are:

1. COGO (COordinate GeOmetry), which solves geometric problems in civil engineering.
2. STRUDL (STRUctural Design Language), which performs structural analysis for two- or three-dimensional frames.
3. TABLE-1, which may be used to create or edit the data sets of tabular information. The data may then be used in connection with any other subsystem.

Continuous advances in software and hardware have made possible many new innovations in computer-aided design in engineering and also have permitted a more direct partnership between computers and their human users.

Time sharing, which brings the engineer closer to the

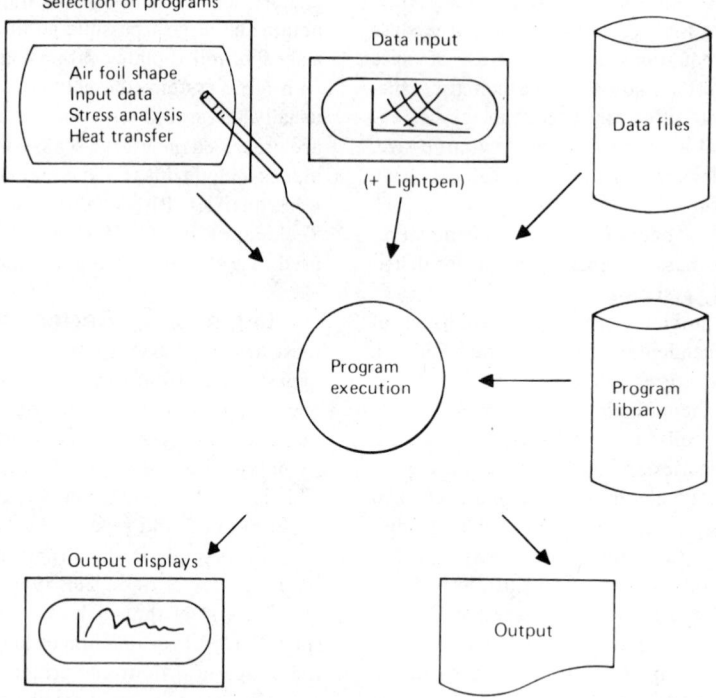

Fig. 2. Engineering design using a virtual machine time-sharing system.

computer, is often used in practice. At a local computer terminal, each engineer executes programs in an *interactive* manner.

Another interesting development is in the area of engineering graphics. By using a lightpen on a display scope, as shown in Fig. 2, one can draw two projections of a given object, ask the computer to straighten out lines, or rectify angles, or replace one part of the object with a new one. A sequence of perspective views can be produced by the computer. Similarly, modifications of a surface can be made on a display scope.

Several time-sharing systems are supplemented by virtual memory facilities. Virtual memory is a technique that makes a computer appear to have considerably more main storage capacity than it actually has. This makes possible the concurrent processing of programs that in total size would exceed main storage capacity.

The development of virtual machine time-sharing systems with color display consoles has been useful in CAD (computer-aided design). It allows an engineer to make the computer an integral part of an engineering design sequence through the interactive usage of display consoles. A typical example is the design of jet engine turbine blades. The following steps might be involved.

1. Sitting at a display console, the design engineer calls for a program for airfoil shape. Initial geo-

metric coordinates may be read in through a card reader. The points or lines of the resulting picture on a display scope may then be added, changed, or deleted.

2. The engineer calls for a program such as one to perform static or dynamic stress analysis. The result is graphically shown on the display console. At this point, it is possible to go back to step 1 or on to step 3.

3. The design engineer calls for another program, such as a heat transfer program, and so on.

These steps can be followed in Fig. 2. Other interactive CAD examples include tracking systems, framed dome structures, and architectural engineering designs.

Development Problems. We conclude our discussion by pointing out some development problems associated with engineering applications.

Application packages in some engineering disciplines have been developed with relatively little consideration given to language, hardware and software environment, documentation, and maintenance. The growth of these packages is extensive, but it is unmonitored and uncontrolled. As a result, problems of availability and usability of some packages do exist. Concentrated efforts, however, to distribute packages in various fields have been made. They include the following groups in the United States.

APEC (Automated Procedures for Engineering Consultants)

CEPA (Civil Engineering Programming Applications)

COSMIC (COmputer Software Management and Information Center)

STORE (STructures ORiented Exchange).

Computer-oriented standards and procedures are also being developed in the United Kingdom for engineering software; these are known as GENESYS (GENeral Engineering SYStem).

The usability of engineering software packages is measured by the three related factors: (1) portability; (2) adaptability; and (3) maintenance.

The quality of implementation involves: (1) documentation; (2) modular structure; (3) source language; (4) self-checking mechanisms in the programs, and (5) test data provided with the programs.

How to effectively increase the usability of application packages represents a constant challenge to the engineering profession.

REFERENCES

1967 Kuo, S. S. *Computer Analysis of Orthotropic Steel Plate Superstructures for Highway Bridges,* (4 vol., PB-173 355 through PB-173 358). Springfield, VA: U.S. Department of Commerce, National Technical Information Service.

1972. Kuo, S. S. *Computer Applications of Numerical Methods.* Reading, MA: Addison-Wesley.

1975. Chua, L. and Lin, P. *Computer Aided Analysis of Electronic Circuits.* Englewood Cliffs, NJ: Prentice-Hall.

1978. Clark, D. *Computer Aided Structural Design.* New York: Wiley.

S. S. KUO

ENIAC

For articles on related subjects *see* DIGITAL COMPUTERS: Early; ECKERT, J. PRESPER; and MAUCHLY, JOHN W.

The ENIAC (Electronic Numerical Integrator and Computer) was developed at the Moore School of the University of Pennsylvania in Philadelphia between 1943 and 1946. It was the first electronic automatic computer, and it was certainly a landmark leading to the development of many automatic computer designs. The logical design of the system was based on the ideas of John Mauchly, and credit for the engineering goes to J. Presper Eckert, Jr.

The ENIAC was literally a giant. It contained more than 18,000 vacuum tubes, weighed 30 tons, and occupied a room 30 by 50 ft.

The computer consisted of 20 electronic accumulators, multiplier control, divider and square root control, input, output, two function tables, and a master program control. Each accumulator could store, add, and subtract 10-decimal digit numbers. Two accumulators could be interconnected to perform 20 digit operations. Addition and subtraction took 200 μs. Multiplication involved six accumulators and took 2,600 μs.

Decimal digits were stored in ten-stage ring counters, and signed decimal numbers were transmitted in parallel over 11 lines. Each digit was represented during transmission by a train of 0–9 pulses. Clock rates were 100 KHz and pulse widths about 2 μs. All logic was accomplished with direct-coupled vacuum tube circuitry.

As initially designed, programming was by patch panel interconnection, with a wire being required for each event at each unit. Data paths were programmable, using 11 wire cables. The data paths were like a party-line telephone—many units could listen, but only one could transmit. Various units could operate in parallel, being initiated from the same program signal and perhaps using distinct data paths. Interlocks were provided so that independent actions of indeterminate length (e.g., card reading) could complete before follow-on actions were initiated. Signs of results could change the flow of control.

The ENIAC was converted later to a card-programmed computer. In this scheme, certain standard operations were set up in the patch panel wiring, and sequences of these macro operations were initiated from the card reader.

The ENIAC was designed to integrate ballistic equations, and a significant accomplishment at its dedication in February 1946 was the computation of the trajectory of a 16-in. naval shell in less than real time. It was formally accepted a few months after its dedication by the U.S. Army Ordnance Corps, but was still operated at the Moore School until late 1946, when it was dismantled and shipped to Aberdeen Proving Ground in Maryland. It became operational again in 1947, and was operated until 2 Oct 1955 (Weik, 1961, p. 575).

The first significant computation on the ENIAC involved atomic energy. Since World War II had ended, there was no longer urgent need for the firing tables that had motivated its design and the support of the Army Ordnance Corps. Among the problems first computed on it, in addition to those involving atomic energy, were random number studies, roundoff errors, cosmic ray studies, thermal ignition, wind tunnel design, and weather prediction. It was the major instrument for the computation of all ballistic tables for the U.S. Army and Air Force (Weik, 1961).

Aberdeen Proving Ground reported that during

Fig. 1. ENIAC. (Courtesy of Smithsonian Institution.)

1952 the "total machine time" for the ENIAC was 7,247 hr, divided as follows: production, 3,491 hr; problem setup and code-checking, 1,061 hr; idle, 195.3 hr; scheduled engineering, 651 hr; and unscheduled "engineering," 1,847.8 hr. The major portion of the scheduled engineering was preventive servicing, the remainder being for improvements and additions; 90% of the unscheduled engineering was devoted to locating and replacing defective tubes. During 1952 approximately 19,000 tubes were replaced (more than 100% of the tube complement).

The ENIAC proved that, with careful engineering, it was possible to build extremely complex logical devices that would perform at electronic speed, without error, for significant periods of time. This was the landmark leading to the development of many automatic computer designs, and paving the way for the "computer revolution." As modestly noted by the Ordnance Corps in *Army Ordnance* (1946), the ENIAC "established the fact that the basic principles of electronic engineering are sound." It was indeed "inevitable that future computing machines of this type would be improved through the knowledge and experience gained on this first one."

Portions of the ENIAC are now in the Smithsonian Institution at Washington, DC. Other ENIAC materials are in the custody of the Historical Services Division of the Department of the Army in Washington.

REFERENCES

1946. U.S. Army Ordnance Corps. "Mathematics by Robot," *Army Ordnance* **XXX**, *No. 156:* 329–331 (May–June).
1950. Stifler, W. W., Jr. (Ed.). *High Speed Computing Devices.* New York: McGraw-Hill.
1961. Weik, Martin H. "The ENIAC Story," *Army Ordnance* **XLV**, *No. 244:* 571–575 (January–February).

H. D. HUSKEY

EQUATIONS. *See* PARTIAL DIFFERENTIAL EQUATIONS, NUMERICAL SOLUTION OF; and NUMERICAL ANALYSIS.

ERROR ANALYSIS

For articles on related subjects *see* ARITHMETIC, COMPUTER; ERRORS; ERRORS, ABSOLUTE AND RELATIVE; INTERVAL ARITHMETIC; MATRIX COMPUTATIONS; NUMERICAL ANALYSIS; ROUNDOFF ERROR; and SIGNIFICANCE ARITHMETIC.

In general the basic arithmetic operations on digital computers are not exact but are subject to rounding or truncation errors. This article is concerned with the cumulative effect of these errors. It will be assumed that the reader has read the article on MATRIX COMPUTATIONS since the results will be illustrated by examples from that area.

Definitions. There are two main methods of error analysis, known as *forward analysis* and *backward analysis,* respectively. They may be illustrated by considering the solution of an $n \times n$ system of linear equations by Gaussian elimination. In this algorithm, the original system is reduced successively to equivalent systems $A^{(r)}\mathbf{x} = \mathbf{b}^{(r)}, r = 1, 2, \ldots, n - 1$. In the final system the matrix of coefficients, $A^{(n-1)}$ is upper-triangular, and the solution is found by back substitution.

In a forward analysis, one adopts the following strategy: Because of rounding errors the computed derived system $\overline{A}^{(r)}\mathbf{x} = \overline{\mathbf{b}}^{(r)}$ differs from that which would be obtained by exact arithmetic. It seems reasonable to assume that, if the algorithm is stable, $\overline{A}^{(r)} - A^{(r)}$ and $\overline{\mathbf{b}}^{(r)} - \mathbf{b}^{(r)}$ will be small, and with sufficient ingenuity bounds would be found for these "errors." This is perhaps the most natural approach.

Alternatively, one could adopt the following strategy: If the algorithm is stable, presumably the computed solution $\overline{\mathbf{x}}$ is the *exact* solution of some system $(A + E)\overline{\mathbf{x}} = \mathbf{b} + \mathbf{e}$, where E and $\mathbf{e}$ are relatively small. Of course there will be an infinite number of sets of which $\overline{\mathbf{x}}$ is the exact solution. A successful error analysis will obtain satisfactory bounds for the elements of E and $\mathbf{e}$. Such an approach is known as *backward* error analysis, since it seeks to replace all errors made in the course of the solution by an *equivalent* perturbation of the original problem. It has one immediate advantage. It puts the errors made during the computation on the same footing as those arising from the data. Hence, when the initial data is itself inexact, no additional problem is posed.

Early Error Analysis of Elimination Processes. In the 1940s, the imminent arrival of electronic computers stimulated an interest in error analysis, and one of the first algorithms to be studied was Gaussian elimination. Early analyses were all of the forward type, and typical of the results obtained was that of Hotelling, who showed that errors in solving an $n \times n$ system might build up by a factor 4^{n-1}. The relevance of this result was widely accepted at the time. Writing in 1946, Bargmann, Montgomery, and von Neumann said of Gaussian elimination: "An error at any stage affects all succeeding results and may become greatly magnified; this explains why instability should be expected." The mood of pessimism was very infectious, and the tendency to become enmeshed in the formal complexity of the algebra of the analysis seems to have precluded a sound assessment of

the nature of the problem. Before giving any error analyses, we discuss fundamental limitations on the attainable accuracy.

Norms and Floating-Point Arithmetic. We will need some way of assessing the "size" of a vector or a matrix. Such a measure is provided by vector and matrix *norms*. A norm of a vector $\mathbf{x}$, denoted by $\|\mathbf{x}\|$, is a nonnegative quantity satisfying the relations

$$\|\mathbf{x}\| \geq 0 \quad \text{and} \quad \|\mathbf{x}\| = 0 \quad \text{iff } \mathbf{x} = \mathbf{0},$$
$$\|\alpha\mathbf{x}\| = |\alpha| \, \|\mathbf{x}\|,$$
$$\|\mathbf{x} + \mathbf{y}\| \leq \|\mathbf{x}\| + \|\mathbf{y}\|.$$

We will use only two norms, denoted by $\|\mathbf{x}\|_2$ and $\|\mathbf{x}\|_\infty$ and defined by

$$\|\mathbf{x}\|_2 = (\Sigma |x_i|^2)^{1/2}, \quad \|\mathbf{x}\|_\infty = \max |x_i|.$$

Similarly, a norm of a matrix A, denoted by $\|A\|$, is a nonnegative quantity satisfying the relations

$$\|A\| \geq 0 \quad \text{and} \quad \|A\| = 0 \quad \text{iff } A = 0,$$
$$\|\alpha A\| = |\alpha| \, \|A\|,$$
$$\|A + B\| \leq \|A\| + \|B\|,$$
$$\|AB\| \leq \|A\| \, \|B\|.$$

We will use only two norms, denoted by $\|A\|_2$ and $\|A\|_\infty$ and defined by

$$\|A\|_2 = (\text{max eigenvalue of } AA^H)^{1/2}, \text{ where } A^H \text{ represents the conjugate transpose of } A$$
$$\|A\|_\infty = \max_i (\Sigma_j |a_{ij}|).$$

It may be verified that

$$\|A\mathbf{x}\|_2 \leq \|A\|_2 \|\mathbf{x}\|_2$$
$$\|A\mathbf{x}\|_\infty \leq \|A\|_\infty \|\mathbf{x}\|_\infty.$$

Most of the early error analyses were for fixed-point computation, but since virtually all scientific computation is now done in floating point, we restrict discussion to this case. We use the notation $\text{fl}(x \times y)$ to denote the product of two standard floating-point (fl) numbers as given by the computer under examination, with an analogous notation for the other arithmetic operations. We have the following results for each of the basic operations, using a mantissa of t digits in the base β:

$$\text{fl}(x \times y) = xy(1 + \epsilon), \quad |\epsilon| \leq m\beta^{-t},$$
$$\text{fl}(x \div y) = (x/y)(1 + \epsilon), \quad |\epsilon| \leq d\beta^{-t},$$
$$\text{fl}(x \pm y) = x(1 + \epsilon_1) \pm y(1 + \epsilon_2),$$
$$|\epsilon_1|, |\epsilon_2| \leq s\beta^{-t},$$

where m, d, and s are constants on the order of unity, depending on the details of the rounding or chopping procedure. Described in the language of backward error analysis, we might say, for example, that the *computed* sum of two numbers x and y is the *exact* sum of two numbers $x(1 + \epsilon_1)$ and $y(1 + \epsilon_2)$, each having a low relative error. On well-designed computers,

$$\text{fl}(x \pm y) = (x \pm y)(1 + \epsilon), \quad |\epsilon| \leq s\beta^{-t}.$$

For convenience from now on we assume that all ϵ in the above satisfy the bound $|\epsilon| \leq k \cdot \beta^{-t}$, where k is of the order of unity.

By repeated application we have, with an obvious notation,

$$\text{fl}(a_1 + a_2 + \cdots + a_n)$$
$$= a_1(1 + E_1) + a_2(1 + E_2) + \cdots + a_n(1 + E_n),$$
$$(1 - k\beta^{-t})^{n-1} \leq 1 + E_1 \leq (1 + k\beta^{-t})^{n-1},$$
$$(1 - k\beta^{-t})^{n+1-r} \leq 1 + E_r \leq (1 + k\beta^{-t})^{n+1-r}$$
$$r = 2, 3, \ldots, n.$$

The bounds on the errors are reasonably realistic and examples can be constructed in which they are almost attained. Naturally, when n is large, the statistical distribution can be expected, in general, to result in some cancellation of errors and, thus, in actual errors substantially less than the bounds.

One of the most important elements in elimination methods is the computation of expressions of the form

$$p = \text{fl}(a - x_1 \times y_1 - \cdots - x_n \times y_n).$$

The computed p and the error bounds are dependent on the order in which operations are performed. If the operations are performed in the order written above, we obtain

$$p = a(1 + E) - x_1 y_1(1 + F_1) - \cdots - x_n y_n(1 + F_n),$$

where

$$(1 - k\beta^{-t})^n \leq 1 + E \leq (1 + k\beta^{-t})^n,$$
$$(1 - k\beta^{-t})^{n+2-i} \leq 1 + F_i \leq (1 + k\beta^{-t})^{n+2-i}.$$

If one computes

$$p = \text{fl}(- x_1 \times y_1 - x_2 \times y_2 - \cdots - x_n \times y_n + a),$$

then

$$p = -x_1 y_1(1 + E_1) - \cdots - x_n y_n(1 + E_n) + a(1 + F),$$
$$(1 - k\beta^{-t})^{n+3-i} \leq (1 + E_i) \leq (1 + k\beta^{-t})^{n+3-i},$$
$$|F| \leq k\beta^{-t}.$$

In describing the last result in terms of backward error analysis, we might say, for example, that it is exact for data $x_i(1 + E_i)$, y_i, and $a(1 + F)$, putting all the perturbations in the x_i, and a. Alternatively, we could say it is exact for data x_i, $y_i(1 + E_i)$, and $a(1 + F)$.

Note that although the errors made can be equated with the effect of small relative perturbations in the data, the relative error in the computed p may be arbitrarily high, depending on the degree of cancellation that takes place. Indeed, if the true p is zero, one may have an infinite relative error. One would not think of attributing this to some malignant instability in this simple arithmetic process; it is the natural loss to be expected.

Inherent Sensitivity of the Solution of a Linear System.

For any computational problem the inherent sensitivity of the solution to changes in the data is of fundamental importance; yet oddly enough the early analyses of Gaussian elimination paid little attention to it. We consider in a very elementary way the effect of perturbations δA in the matrix A. We have

$$\bar{x} = (A + \delta A)^{-1}b = (A^{-1} - A^{-1}\delta A A^{-1} + \cdots)b$$
$$= x - A^{-1}\delta A x + (A^{-1}\delta A)^2 x - \cdots,$$

giving

$$\|\bar{x} - x\|/\|x\| \leq \|A^{-1}\delta A\|/(1 - \|A^{-1}\delta A\|),$$

provided $\|A^{-1}\delta A\| < 1$. The relative error in $\bar{x}$ will not be low unless $\|A^{-1}\delta A\|$ is small. Writing,

$$\|\delta A\| = \eta\|A\|,$$

we see that

$$\|\bar{x} - x\|/\|x\|$$
$$\leq \eta\|A\| \|A^{-1}\|/(1 - \eta\|A\| \|A^{-1}\|).$$

The inherent sensitivity is therefore dependent on $\|A\| \|A^{-1}\|$, and this is usually known as the *condition number* of A (for the given norm) with respect to inversion or to the solution of linear systems.

We might now ask ourselves what sort of limitation we should expect on the accuracy of Gaussian elimination even if it had no menacing instability. The solution of $Ax = b$ requires $n^3/3$ multiplications and additions, an average of $\frac{1}{3}n$ per element. From the elementary discussion given so far, we might risk the following prophecy: Even if Gaussian elimination is a stable process, then we can scarcely expect to obtain a bound for the resulting error, which is less than that resulting from a perturbation δA in A satisfying, say,

$$\|\delta A\| \leq \frac{1}{3}kn\beta^{-t}\|A\|.$$

In fact, this bound for the effect is usually reasonably realistic, provided pivoting is used. Indeed, the advantages conferred by the statistical distribution of rounding errors is such that the error is usually less than the maximum error that could be caused by such a perturbation.

Backward Error Analysis of Gaussian Elimination.

Gaussian elimination provides a very good illustration of the power and simplicity of backward error analysis. The elimination process may be described as the production of a unit lower triangular matrix L and an upper triangular matrix U such that $LU = A$. The solution of the system $A\mathbf{x} = \mathbf{b}$ is then carried out in the two steps:

$$L\mathbf{y} = \mathbf{b}, \quad U\mathbf{x} = \mathbf{y}$$

In the backward error analysis one shows that the computed L and U satisfy the relation $LU = A + E$ and obtains bounds for the elements of E. One then shows that the computed solution $\mathbf{y}$ and $\mathbf{x}$ of the triangular systems satisfies the equations

$$(L + \delta L)\mathbf{y} = \mathbf{b}, \quad (U + \delta U)\mathbf{x} = \mathbf{y}$$

and obtains bounds for the elements of δL and δU. The computed $\mathbf{x}$ therefore solves *exactly* the system

$$(L + \delta L)(U + \delta U)\mathbf{x} = \mathbf{b}$$

or

$$(A + E + \delta LU + L\,\delta U + \delta L\,\delta U)\mathbf{x} = \mathbf{b}.$$

Hence, it is the exact solution of $(A + F)\mathbf{x} = \mathbf{b}$, where

$$
\begin{aligned}
\|F\| &= \|E + \delta LU + L\,\delta U + \delta L\,\delta U\| \\
&\leq \|E\| + \|L\|\,\|\delta U\| \\
&\quad + \|U\|\,\|\delta L\| + \|\delta L\|\,\|\delta U\|,
\end{aligned}
$$

and from the bounds for E, δL, and δU, one obtains a bound for F.

The simplicity of the technique may be illustrated by presenting the analysis of the solution of the system $L\mathbf{y} = \mathbf{b}$. We first make the following observations:

1. The relevant system to be analyzed is that with the computed matrix L, *not* the L that would have resulted from exact computation.
2. Since during the course of the analysis we do not attempt a direct comparison between computed and exact values, there is no need to denote computed quantities by bars. It is to be understood that all symbols refer to computed quantities.
3. It is only at the final stage when we have ex-

pressed the computed solution as the exact solution of $(A + F)\mathbf{x} = \mathbf{b}$ and have obtained a bound for $\|F\|$ that we attempt to compare the computed $\mathbf{x}$ with the true $\mathbf{x}$, and at this stage we can use the result of the previous section.

At a typical stage in the triangular solution, y_1, y_2, $\ldots$, y_{r-1} have been computed and y_r is determined from the relation

$$y_r = \text{fl}(-l_{r1}y_1 - l_{r2}y_2 - \cdots - l_{r,r-1}y_{r-1} + b_r),$$

using, of course, the computed values of the y_i. Hence,

$$
\begin{aligned}
y_r = {} & -l_{r1}y_1(1 + E_{r1}) - l_{r2}y_2(1 + E_{r2}) \\
& - \cdots - l_{r,r-1}y_{r-1}(1 + E_{r,r-1}) + b_r(1 + F_r),
\end{aligned}
$$

where the factors $1 + E_{ri}$ and $1 + F_r$ are of the type discussed in connection with the computation of p above. Hence, the computed y_i satisfy exactly the relation

$$
\begin{aligned}
l_{r1}y_1(1 + G_{r1}) + l_{r2}y_2(1 + G_{r2}) & \\
+ \cdots + l_{r,r-1}y_{r-1}(1 + G_{r,r-1}) & \\
+ y_r(1 + G_{rr}) & = b_r,
\end{aligned}
$$

where

$$
\begin{aligned}
(1 + G_{ri}) &= (1 + E_{ri})/(1 + F_r), \\
& \qquad\qquad i = 1, \cdots, r - 1, \\
1 + G_{rr} &= 1/(1 + F_r).
\end{aligned}
$$

Notice that by dividing through by $1 + F_r$, we are able to restrict ourselves to perturbations in L. The computed $\mathbf{y}$ therefore satisfies exactly the relation $(L + \delta L)\mathbf{y} = \mathbf{b}$, where $\delta L_{ij} = L_{ij}G_{ij}$.

We certainly have

$$(1 - k\beta^{-t})^n \leq (1 + G_{ij}) \leq (1 + k\beta^{-t})^n,$$

most of the factors, of course, satisfying much better bounds. Bounds of the above type are cumbersome to use, and we observe that, if $kn\beta^{-t} < 0.1$, as will usually be the case, then, using the binomial theorem,

$$
\begin{aligned}
(1 + k\beta^{-t})^n &\leq 1 + (1.06)\,kn\beta^{-t}, \\
(1 - k\beta^{-t})^n &\geq 1 - (1.06)\,kn\beta^{-t}.
\end{aligned}
$$

Hence, we have

$$|\delta L_{ij}| \leq (1.06)\,kn\beta^{-t}|L_{ij}|,$$

giving, for example,

$$\|\delta L\|_\infty \leq (1.06)\,kn\beta^{-t}\|L\|_\infty.$$

The analysis is almost trivial, though earlier error analyses of the solution of triangular systems were extremely complicated.

If the computation of y_r had been expressed in the form

$$y_r = \text{fl}(b_r - l_{r1}y_1 - \cdots - l_{r,r-1}y_{r-1}),$$

then we could still obtain a relation of the form $(L + \delta L)\mathbf{y} = \mathbf{b}$, but in this case the bounds on the elements of δL would be appreciably larger.

On many computers it is possible to accumulate either of the expressions for y_r in double precision, rounding to single precision only on completion. If this is done, then we again obtain a relation of the form

$$l_{r1}y_1(1 + G_{r1}) + l_{r2}y_2(1 + G_{r2})$$
$$+ \cdots + l_{r,r-1}y_{r-1}(1 + G_{r,r-1})$$
$$+ y_r(1 + G_{rr}) = b_r,$$

but now the quantities $|G_{ri}|(i < r)$ have bounds of order β^{-2t} and can therefore virtually be neglected, while $|G_{rr}|$ has the bound $k\beta^{-t}$. We therefore have a result that might well be described as best possible, having regard to the precision of computation. Indeed, the residual vector $\mathbf{b} - L\mathbf{y}$ corresponding to the computed $\mathbf{y}$ will almost certainly be smaller than that corresponding to the correctly rounded solution!

The analysis of the solution of $U\mathbf{x} = \mathbf{y}$ is almost identical to that of $L\mathbf{y} = \mathbf{b}$, while the analysis of the factorization process is only marginally more complicated. If the L and U are produced as in classical Gaussian elimination, then one can show that $LU = A + E$, where, denoting the maximum modulus of any element arising during the decomposition by g, we certainly have

$$|e_{ij}| \leq (3.02)\, igk\beta^{-t} \qquad (i \leq j),$$
$$|e_{ij}| \leq (3.02)\, jgk\beta^{-t} \qquad (i > j).$$

If the factors L and U are determined directly, using the relations

$$l_{ij}u_{jj} = a_{ij} - l_{i1}u_{1j} - \cdots - l_{i,j-1}u_{j-1,j}$$
$$j = 1, \ldots, i - 1$$

and

$$u_{ij} = a_{ij} - l_{i1}u_{1j} - \cdots - l_{i,i-1}u_{i-1,j}$$
$$j = i, \ldots, n,$$

and the expressions on the right are accumulated in double precision, an even more satisfactory bound may be determined for E. Indeed, ignoring quantities of the order of magnitude of β^{-2t}, we certainly have $|e_{ij}| \leq gk\beta^{-t}$,

where g is now the element of maximum modulus in the computed U. Again, we have what may be regarded as a "best possible" result.

The reader may be surprised that no reference has been made to pivoting or to the size of the l_{pq}. The importance of pivoting is concealed. If any of the multipliers is large, g will usually be much larger than $\max|a_{ij}|$. When pivoting is used $|l_{pq}| \leq 1$, and there will not usually be much growth in the size of the elements of the reduced matrices or of U relative to the initial set of a_{ij}. When A is positive definite or diagonally dominant, no growth can take place, and we have a guaranteed a priori bound for $\|E\|$ in terms of A.

In 1947, von Neumann and Goldstine considered the special case of the inversion of a positive definite matrix with pivoting, and obtained a result for fixed point computation which is only marginally weaker than can be obtained by arguments of the above type, though the analysis was far more complicated. Their analysis is often described as a forward error analysis, but it is in fact of the backward type, although at no stage are results expressed in a form such as to emphasize this. The final result of an analysis of the above type for the solution of a positive definite system is to guarantee that it is the exact solution of $(A + E)\mathbf{x} = \mathbf{b}$ and to give a bound for E of the type

$$\|E\| \leq f(n)k\beta^{-t}\|A\|,$$

where $f(n)$ is a modest function of n, depending a little on the details of the arithmetic. When backward error analysis is applied to matrix inversion, one cannot show that X is the exact solution of $(A + E)X = I$, with a similar bound for E, because it is not true. However, the rth column, x_r, of X is the exact solution of some $(A + E_r)\mathbf{x}_r = \mathbf{e}_r$, where $\mathbf{e}_r$ is the rth column of I; the E_r are all different, but have the same satisfactory uniform bound. This result is implicit in that of von Neumann and Goldstine, but it is well concealed!

Orthogonal Transformations. Experience with error analyses of matrix processes gradually exposed the fact that control of *growth* in derived matrices is the key to stability. If orthogonal transformations Q are used, then—since $\|QA\|_2 = \|AQ\|_2 = \|A\|$—no general growth *can* take place. Although the algebra is a little complicated, a fairly general analysis can be given of whole classes of algorithms based on orthogonal transformations, both for the solution of equations and the eigenvalue problem. One can show, for example, that for a sequence of r orthogonal similarity transformations, the final computed transform $A^{(r)}$ satisfies *exactly* a relation of the form

$$A^{(r)} = Q^T(A + E)Q,$$

where Q is *exactly* orthogonal and

$$\|E\| \leq rf(n)\|A\|k\beta^{-t},$$

where $f(n)$ is some quite innocuous function of n. Hence, the eigenvalues of $A^{(r)}$ are exactly those of $A + E$, and we are back with perturbation theory.

A Posteriori Error Bounds. The bounds discussed so far are of the a priori type. The main function of such an analysis is to show whether or not an algorithm is stable and, if not, to pinpoint the reasons for its instability.

When a solution has been determined, one can usually obtain much sharper backward error bounds. For example, from a computed eigenvalue λ and an eigenvector $\mathbf{u}$, such that $\|\mathbf{u}\|_2 = 1$, one can compute the residual defined by $\mathbf{r} = A\mathbf{u} - \lambda\mathbf{u}$. This may be written in the form $(A - \mathbf{r}\mathbf{u}^H)\mathbf{u} = \lambda\mathbf{u}$, showing that λ *and* $\mathbf{u}$ are exact for the matrix $A - \mathbf{r}\mathbf{u}^H$. When A is Hermitian, this implies that A has an eigenvalue in the interval $\lambda - \|\mathbf{r}\|_2, \lambda + \|\mathbf{r}\|_2$. Similarly, when solving linear equations one can compute $\mathbf{r} = \mathbf{b} - A\mathbf{x}$. If $\mathbf{r}$ is computed accurately, it can then be used to obtain an improved solution by solving $A\delta = \mathbf{r}$. This process is called *iterative refinement*.

Iterative Methods. It was at one time thought that iterative methods for solving linear equations or the eigenvalue problem would give far greater accuracy than direct methods, since one works with the initial A throughout. In fact this advantage is largely illusory. In Jacobi's method for linear equations, one derives an improved $x_i^{(r+1)}$ from the relation

$$a_{ii}x_i^{(r+1)} = b_i - \sum_{j \neq i} a_{ij}x_i^{(r)},$$

but the right-hand side cannot be computed exactly. From the above analysis it is clear that one is really working with a matrix with elements $a_{ij}(1 + e_{ij})$, where the e_{ij} are different in each iteration. When iterative methods are used in practice, iteration is usually terminated before attaining the accuracy given immediately by a direct method, *even without iterative refinement*. Since, as we mentioned earlier, the results obtained with good direct methods are almost "best possible," this is to be expected.

Interval Arithmetic and Significant Digit Arithmetic. Attempts have been made to obtain error bounds for computed quantities on the computer itself. In *interval* arithmetic, an ordered pair $[a_l, a_u]$ of floating-point numbers is stored at each stage in the computation,

and it is guaranteed that the true number a lies in the interval $a_l \leq a \leq a_u$. Used in a direct manner, the results achieved are very pessimistic; in fact, the computer merely performs numerically the analog of what was done algebraically in the early forward error analysis of the Hotelling type. The intervals become very large. The apparently reasonable assumption that in stable algorithms the computed quantities will be close to those arising in exact computation is frequently quite false. This is particularly true of algorithms for the eigenvalue problem.

In *significant digit* arithmetic, one does not work with normalized floating-point numbers, on the grounds that when cancellation takes place, the zeros introduced are nonsignificant. The possibilities of significant digit arithmetic have been well exploited by Metropolis and Ashenhurst.

The realization that neither interval arithmetic nor significant digit arithmetic provides an automatic answer to error analysis led to an overreaction against them. The provision of the relevant hardware facilities should make them economic, and when combined with a more general appreciation of theoretical error analysis, they have an important role to play.

REFERENCES

1963. Wilkinson, J. H. *Rounding Errors in Algebraic Processes.* London: Her Majesty's Stationery Office.
1965. Wilkinson, J. H. *The Algebraic Eigenvalue Problem.* Oxford: Clarendon Press.
1966. Moore, R. E. *Interval Analysis.* Englewood Cliffs, NJ: Prentice-Hall.
1967. Forsythe, G. E. and Moler, C. B. *Computer Solution of Linear Algebraic Systems.* Englewood Cliffs, NJ: Prentice-Hall.
1973. Shampine, L. F. and Allen, R. C., Jr. *Numerical Computing: An Introduction.* Philadelphia: W. B. Saunders Company.

J. H. WILKINSON

ERROR-CORRECTING CODE

For articles on related subjects *see* CODES; ERRORS; and PARITY.

Error-detecting and error-correcting codes arose from the well-known phenomenon that if anything can go wrong, it will. Rather than try to do everything perfectly the first time, error-detecting and error-correcting methods use some form of redundancy to handle the inevitable errors.

Error detection has a long history. For example, suppose we have a block of n binary digits and add an $(n + 1)$st digit, chosen so that the whole message has an even (or odd) number of 1s in it. This is called an even (odd) parity check. At the receiving end, the complete block is checked. If there are not the proper number of 1s in the message, then there must be an odd number of errors in the message. If the block is chosen to be reasonably short (with respect to the probability p of an isolated error), so that we may ignore factors of $1 - p$, and if we assume that errors are independent, then to a close approximation there is a probability $(n + 1)p$ of a single error, and a probability $[n(n + 1)/2]p^2$ of two errors.

Upon the detection of an error, the message can be retransmitted, and generally this will produce an error-free message. In some circumstances, especially where it is suspected that the source is slightly defective (say, a magnetic recording), several retrials may be used before giving up. The retrial system is not entirely satisfactory because it takes extra time when errors occur and also requires two-way signaling to call for message repetition. However, if the error is in the original recorded form of the message before encoding, then nothing can be done about the error.

To overcome these difficulties, error-correcting codes are often used. They are based on the use of a high level of redundancy, i.e., repeated parity checks.

There are various ways of explaining how an error-correcting code works. In the algebraic approach, a parity check is assigned to those positions in the code that have a 1 in the rightmost position of their binary representation, a second parity check for those positions that have a 1 in their second to right position, etc. Thus, when a single error does occur, exactly those parity checks will fail for which the binary expansion of the position of the error has 1s. Thus, the pattern of the parity-check failures points directly to the position of the error; in a binary system of signaling, it is easy to change that bit to its opposite value and thus correct the error, with 000 meaning "no error."

As an example, consider the binary encoding of the decimal digits into an error-correcting code. In Table 1, positions 1, 2, and 4 are used for the check positions, leaving positions 3, 5, 6, 7 for the message (where we find the binary coding of the corresponding decimal digit).

The check positions are calculated by even parity checks as follows.

Parity check column 1
Columns 1, 3, 5, 7 (columns with a 1 in the rightmost position of their binary representation).
Parity check column 2
Columns 2, 3, 6, 7 (1 in second rightmost position).
Parity check column 4
Columns 4, 5, 6, 7 (1 in leftmost position).

Table 1

Decimal	Position						
	1	2	3	4	5	6	7
0	0	0	0	0	0	0	0
1	1	1	0	1	0	0	1
2	0	1	0	1	0	1	0
3	1	0	0	0	0	1	1
4	1	0	0	1	1	0	0
5	0	1	0	0	1	0	1
6	1	1	0	0	1	1	0
7	0	0	0	1	1	1	1
8	1	1	1	0	0	0	0
9	0	0	1	1	0	0	1

Let any line be copied and a single error inserted as a simulation of an error in message transmission. When the three parity checks are applied, we will find that if we write a 0 for successful parity check and a 1 for a failure (writing from right to left), the three digits we get will be *exactly* the position of the inserted error.

A second way of looking at the codes is a geometric approach. If an error is to be detected, then the distance between two messages (which we define to be the number of positions for which they differ) must be at least two for every pair of messages. Otherwise, there would be a message that a single error would carry over into another acceptable message, and that error could not be detected. For error correction, the minimum distance must be at least three (as in Table 1); for double error detection, the minimum distance must be at least four; etc.

The encoding process can thus be extended further in protecting against errors. As an example of double-error detection, consider the code in Table 1 with an additional bit added to each message, so chosen that the entire message will have an even number of 1s. If there were a *single* error, the original set of checks would indicate the position, but the last check would fail. If there were a *pair* of errors, the last check would not fail, but some of the original checks would, indicating a double error. The minimum-distance argument can be applied to show that the additional check made each minimal distance one greater, namely, now four.

The preceding examples are the simplest cases. The theory has been highly developed and now makes use of much of abstract algebra, including Galois theory.

REFERENCES

1968. Berlekamp, E., Jr. *Algebraic Coding Theory*. New York: McGraw-Hill.
1977. MacWilliams, F. and Sloane, N. J. A. *The Theory of Error Correcting Codes*. Amsterdam: Elsevier.
1977. McEliece, R. J. *The Theory of Information and Coding*. Reading, MA: Addison-Wesley.

R. W. HAMMING

ERRORS

For articles on related subjects *see* DEBUGGING; DI-AGNOSTICS; ERRORS, ABSOLUTE AND RELATIVE; ERROR ANALYSIS; ROUNDOFF ERROR; STRUCTURED PROGRAMMING; and SYNTAX, SEMANTICS, AND PRAGMATICS.

The indignant customer who receives an incorrect bill from a department store probably does not care what the source of the error was or even that, almost certainly, the fault was not the computer's but rather that of its data entry personnel or programmers. Neither is the astronaut descending toward the surface of the moon very concerned about the precise source of the error that caused the on-board computer to fail. But an understanding of the sources of errors in computers is important to anyone who wishes to use or even to comprehend digital computers.

Taxonomy of Computer Errors. When a computer produces an incorrect result, the error may come from one or more of a number of sources. These sources can be fairly readily grouped under four headings:

1. *Hardware errors,* which result from a malfunction of some physical component of the computer.
2. *Software errors,* which result from a coding error in *some* program, but not necessarily in the program that seemed to produce the wrong results (see below).
3. *Algorithm errors,* which result when the algorithm or method used to solve a problem does not produce correct results, perhaps only under certain conditions and/or for certain input data.
4. *Data entry errors,* probably the most common of all, which occur when the operator of some type of data entry terminal (e.g., a terminal for direct entry into the computer, a key-to-disk terminal, or a card punch) makes an error, usually by pressing the wrong key.

Data entry errors can be reduced by using good equipment, by careful training of personnel, and by verification techniques such as repetition of the data entry by another operator and then a comparison between the two. Because the other three types of errors are more subtle and, therefore, more difficult to recognize and/or correct, we shall focus on them in this article. However, before proceeding to discuss these three types of errors in some detail, we should stress that, whereas in the early days of computing it was usually rather easy to determine which of the three categories above was the source of an error, it is sometimes very difficult indeed to do this today. To give one example, the increasing use of micro-programming in contemporary computer systems makes it possible for hardware errors to manifest themselves in ways that look like software errors, and vice versa. The difficulty of determining the source of a computer error has heightened the need for good diagnostic techniques, a subject we consider in the last section of this article.

Hardware Errors. Considering the staggering complexity of modern computer systems, it is amazing that they work at all. The fact that they are designed to, and often do, operate for hundreds or thousands of hours without failure is even more startling. Modern computers contain literally millions of circuit elements, the failure of any one of which might cause failure of the entire system. This high level of reliability is a tribute to the careful work of circuit designers and the meticulous attention to detail and to testing on the part of the manufacturers. Still, computers are not perfect and the hardware occasionally does fail. The source of a failure may be difficult to determine, since the number of possible faulty components is so large.

A frequent source of errors is in the electromechanical peripheral devices that provide input or output for the central processing unit. The mechanical components of these peripheral devices are likely to wear out as a result of the stresses of frequent use. The staccato motion of movable disk arms, the rapid rotation of disk packs, drums, or tape drives, the stop-and-go movements in card readers and punches, all are possible sources of failures.

The recording medium associated with each of these devices is fragile and consequently a potential source of errors. The delicate magnetic coating of magnetic tapes, disks, or drums can be easily scratched, rendering the information incorrect or inaccessible. A speck of dust or dirt can mar these coatings easily, or tension can stretch a piece of magnetic tape. Punched cards may be folded, spindled, or mutilated, and paper tape reels may easily be torn. The failure of these media may not be fatal to the entire computer, but individual peripheral units may be disabled or data items may be entered incorrectly or lost. Telecommunication devices attached to a computer may also be faulty. Since the quality of the voice-grade telephone lines often used for communication with computers is low, special leased lines are sometimes used to reduce the frequency of errors.

The central processing unit, arithmetic and logical unit, and the high-speed memory are built entirely from electronic components, thereby reducing the chance of failure inherent in mechanical devices. The technology for creating the circuit elements involved in these components is extremely complex. Early computers used vacuum tubes (first generation) as the primary circuit element. These large devices were relatively slow, generated a large amount of heat, required a large amount of power, and wore out easily. The invention of the transistor (second generation) in 1948 made it possible to construct smaller, faster, and much more reliable computers. Combining several transistors and other electronic elements into a single component, called an *integrated circuit* (third generation), enabled designers to create still faster and more reliable computers.

At present, computers are built from a smaller number of very large-scale integrated circuits (VLSI). These highly reliable circuits contain thousands of discrete circuit elements built into a single replaceable component. These devices are carefully tested during the many stages of a sophisticated fabrication process. Still, they may fail as a result of temperature changes, humidity, shock, or electrical surges. When failure occurs, the faulty circuit component must be located and replaced. This sounds simple enough, but the problem may be hard to locate, since the failure may be intermittent, occurring only when a complex combination of conditions exists. To minimize the deterioration of circuit elements, computer center rooms are air conditioned to keep the temperature and humidity within acceptable ranges. The failure of the air conditioning would lead to overheating of circuit elements and to an increased chance of failure.

Modern computers are designed to monitor their own performance and constantly test themselves to assure that each operation has been performed properly. When a fault occurs, a machine interrrupt is issued, and the hardware and software attempt to identify and locate the error. Depending on the severity of the error, the control programs may shut down the entire machine, avoid use of the faulty component or simply record the fact that an error has occurred.

Software Errors. Anyone who has written a computer program knows that debugging can be difficult and tedious. Professionals writing even short programs (say, fewer than 100 lines of code) expect some difficulties and accept the fact that long programs, requiring many person-years of effort, may never be completely debugged. When writing programs in a high-level language, which requires the services of a compiler, utility programs, and an operating system, the number of software modules that come into play is large. Great effort is applied to debug the system software, but it is not currently possible to insure the correctness of such sophisticated programs. If an application program does not operate correctly, the most likely source of the error is in the application program itself. Only after a thorough and careful analysis of the situation can we begin to consider the possibility that the compiler, system utilities, or operating system are at fault. Locating the bug in the system software requires a deep understanding of the code and the expertise of a systems programmer.

Application program errors fall into two basic categories: syntactic and semantic. The syntactic errors include typographic errors, incorrectly spelled keywords and variable names, incorrect punctuation and improper statement formation, all of which result from violations of the programming language syntax. These errors are normally recognized by the language processor, and diagnostic messages are printed to assist the programmer in making corrections. Although some processors will attempt to fix improper syntax, programs with syntactic errors will generally not be permitted to execute.

Assuming all the syntactic errors have been fixed, the program will execute, but there is no guarantee that it will perform as the programmer intended. Semantic errors are a result of an improper understanding of the function of certain operators or mistakes in coding of an algorithm. Typical programming mistakes include exceeding the bounds of an array; failure to initialize variables; overflow or underflow; failure to account for special cases; attempted division by zero; illegal mixing of data types; and incorrect transfers of control. Isolating and locating the error can be a long tedious process and is a skill learned mainly through much experience.

Current research is being directed at reducing the possibility of semantic errors. Improved programming language design and sophisticated compilers are one possible answer. Educating programmers to proper program design techniques such as modularity, top-down structuring, and "goto-free" programming does, indeed, simplify the debugging process. Finally, attempts are being made to prove the correctness of programs through the use of formal mathematical techniques.

Algorithm Errors. Computer programs can be viewed as models or representations of real-world situations. Unfortunately, not all aspects of the real-world situation can be represented accurately inside a computer. Decimal quantities such as 1.2 or 6783846.678492104 may have to be approximated when stored in the memory of a binary computer. Since the initial representation is not precise, subsequent operations performed on these values may produce invalid results. The difficulty in locating such faults is that the error will manifest itself only for some sets of data. Thus, the program will produce reasonable results in most cases, but may produce erroneous results erratically.

The heart of this problem is the machine representation of values. While a 60-bit word length may provide a more accurate representation than a 36-bit word or a 32-bit word, a longer word length is not a guarantee of correctness. Since we are limited to the finite length of a computer word, the representation must be rounded off to the closest approximation possible. With each addition or multiplication the result must also be rounded off to fit the representation scheme; hence the name *roundoff error*.

Another flaw in the representation of the real world occurs when an infinite process must be approximated by a finite series of steps. In summing an infinite series, repeating an iterative process (e.g., the Newton-Raphson or secant methods), or approximating derivatives by differences, the result may become increasingly exact, but is never precisely correct. Since in all these cases an infinite process is cut short and represented by a finite process, this error is called *truncation* or *discretization error*.

One of the central concerns of numerical analysis is to estimate the roundoff and truncation errors for various algorithms. This analysis can then be used to select and design the optimum strategy for a given problem. A major goal of numerical analysis is to avoid *unstable* algorithms that operate erratically and to identify *ill-conditioned* data sets that are difficult to deal with. The use of double or multiple precision representations and operations may reduce the error, but not eliminate it.

Algorithms that fail sometimes because of roundoff or truncation problems are not the only type of algorithm failure. Another not uncommon one is the attempted use of an algorithm to solve a problem other than that for which it is intended. An example of this would be the use of an algorithm designed for the solution of a system of linear simultaneous equations with a symmetric coefficient matrix to solve a system with a nonsymmetric coefficient matrix resulting in an inevitably wrong result.

All too common is the development and use of an algorithm that just will not solve the problem at hand for any set of data, due to a design error, for example, or a failure to understand the underlying mathematics. A vital aspect of the avoidance of such errors is the careful debugging of all newly developed programs using data sets for which the results are known.

Coping with Errors. Since errors are a fact of life in computing, much has been done to assist programmers in locating errors. Syntactic errors are dealt with by the compiler and are not the source of serious difficulty. Although work remains to be done in the area of improving compile-time diagnostics, most compilers provide a reasonably lucid explanation of what has gone wrong. The programmer must then fix the mistake.

Execution-time errors that result from semantic errors are more difficult to deal with. If the program runs to completion, but does not produce the output that is expected, the programmer must carefully examine the output and attempt to locate the fault. The input data should be checked for validity, and then a careful step-by-step analysis of the program must be performed. If the output does not contain sufficient information to determine what the program was doing, then an additional run with detailed print-outs must be made. Special *trace* (*q.v.*) packages that print out the execution of the program on an instruction-by-instruction basis can be used. Alternatively, only the transfers of control or subprogram references can be printed. If desired, a particular location can be monitored to indicate when the value was set or referenced. Since the amount of output may be voluminous, the programmer must carefully select which features to use. Armed with this material and a thorough understanding of the program, the programmer must perform a careful analysis to locate the flaw.

If the program does not run to completion but is interrupted as a result of an attempt to perform an illegal instruction, the operating system will (or, at least, should) print a meaningful message. However, since the operating system has no knowledge of what the application program was attempting to do, these messages can be difficult to interpret. Some programming language systems contain an execution-time monitor to produce more meaningful diagnostic messages when an abnormal termination occurs.

If a program successfully executes for a given set of data, there is no guarantee that the program will always perform properly. To verify the correctness of a program, multiple sets of test data should be constructed to exercise the program as much as possible. As many as possible of the reasonable sets of input data should be run to validate the program. Unfortunately, there are many well-documented cases of programs that have run correctly for many years until a particular set of input data was run and resulted in failure. There is no way to guarantee the correctness of large programs, and programmers must accept the possibility of *bugs* in their programs. Large programs such as operating systems are continuously being modified as faults are located. Perfection in programming is illusory.

The diagnosis of hardware errors has become more complex with the advent of sophisticated hardware architecture constructs such as virtual memory and microprogramming. When it is suggested that a particular error may be a result of malfunctioning hardware, a set of hardware diagnostic programs may be run to assist the maintenance engineer in locating the fault. These programs exercise each of the circuit components and print out the location of the faulty element. This technique is not always successful, since the diagnostic program may not run properly because of the fault. Individual components may have to be removed and tested electrically, or components may be replaced until the machine operates properly.

REFERENCES

1963. Wilkinson, J. H. *Rounding Errors in Algebraic Processes.* Englewood Cliffs, NJ.: Prentice-Hall.

1977. Gilb, Tom and Weinberg, Gerald M. *Humanizing Input.* Cambridge, MA: Winthrop.

1978. Van Tassel, Dennie. *Program Style, Design, Efficiency, Debugging and Testing* (2nd Ed.). Englewood Cliffs, NJ: Prentice-Hall.

A. RALSTON AND B. SHNEIDERMAN

ERRORS, ABSOLUTE AND RELATIVE

For articles on related subjects *see* ERRORS; ERROR ANALYSIS; and NUMERICAL ANALYSIS.

Numerical calculations normally result in an approximation to the true value that is being sought. The *error* in this approximation is a measure of the discrepancy between the true value and the computed result. Estimates of, or bounds on, the error are usually expressed in either *absolute* or *relative* form. Let

TV be the true value of a quantity.
APP be its approximate value.
E be the absolute error.
RE be the relative error.

Then we define

$$E = TV - APP$$
$$RE = (TV - APP)/TV = E/TV$$

For example, if ⅓ is approximated by 0.333, then

$$E = \frac{1}{3} - 0.333 = \frac{1}{3} \times 10^{-3}$$

and $RE = 10^{-3}$.

More often than not it is *E* rather than *RE* that is of interest. For example, if we are calculating the stress on a strut in a bridge, then clearly the absolute error in the calculation is what counts. But in many numerical calculations where the result is very large or very small, relative error is a more meaningful quantity. Thus, if the true value of a quantity is 10^{12}, an error of 10^4 is probably not very serious, but this is more meaningfully expressed by noting that $RE = 10^{-8}$.

Much of numerical analysis is concerned with the estimation of *E* or *RE*, or the calculation of bounds on *E* or *RE*.

A. RALSTON

EXCEPTION REPORTING

For article on a related subject *see* ADMINISTRATIVE APPLICATIONS.

Exception reporting is a technique for screening large amounts of computerized data in order to print reports containing only that information requiring action. It differs from the traditional method of reporting, which entails printing the full contents of files and all activity against those files during some period of time. For example, monthly reports analyzing sales data might show the purchases of all regular customers during the month, for this year to date, during the same month last year, and also the year-to-date sales to this point last year. If an organization has 3,000 customers, the report will have 3,000 lines—one for each customer—plus appropriate totals. The manager who receives such a report must review all entries to determine what situations require action. In many organizations, managers are inundated with reams of computer paper presenting too much data to be assimilated and acted upon. This phenomenon is sometimes called *information overload*.

By contrast, exception reports present a user with concise information needed for specific actions. These reports are produced by screening large amounts of information, usually according to predetermined criteria, but sometimes nowadays using parameters which may be changed dynamically. Exception reports are briefer than conventional reports because they contain only exception data, not all the data in the file. They may, therefore, sometimes be presented on visual display devices instead of being printed. (Fig. 1 illustrates the basic differences between traditional and exception reporting.)

Exception reports generally fall into one of two types, depending on the need they are to meet. Each type is processed according to a different time schedule and uses a different character of screening device. The primary type of exception report is used to isolate exceptions to satisfactory performance. It is produced on a regular, repetitive schedule, and uses a predetermined screening mechanism. Examples of this type of exception reports are monthly inventory reports of all items with balance-on-hand quantities lower than calculated minimums, and monthly and year-to-date sales analyses showing only those customers whose purchases are less than 90% of last year's amounts. (Fig. 1 illustrates this type of report.)

The second type of exception report provides answers to specific inquiries. It is produced only when required, and uses a specially selected screening mechanism. For example, in order to respond to a one-time government request, a personnel manager may ask for the names of all employees who are eligible for veteran's benefits. The screening mechanism—in this case, all employees eligible for veteran's benefits—is developed just prior to processing, which occurs once in response to this single external request.

Exception reporting appears to offer clear and significant benefits. Why, then, are the vast majority of reports still printed in traditional mode—in lengthy, complete reports?

Both types of exception reports (those produced on a regular schedule and those produced to answer specific inquiries) require screening capability that is available with modern data processing equipment. Yet, many users who have modern equipment are still using systems designed for older machines that did not have the necessary screening capability. Generating exception reports for these application systems requires redesign and reprogramming.

The most common type of exception reports—those produced on a regular schedule—requires the user to have a certain level of knowledge and sophistication. First, a user must be able to determine in advance exactly what information will be needed in order to develop the appropriate screening mechanism. Many users have a real or perceived inability to predetermine their data needs. Second, a user must thoroughly understand the report's intended use and the limitations of the report's usefulness. For example, a credit follow-up report designed to list only those customers with account balances more than 90 days outstanding will not provide information about accounts that are overdue but have not reached the 90-day level.

Exception reports can fill a definite need for decision makers who want to make optimal use of the large and growing data files in today's computers. Out of the wealth of data available, only a small amount may be needed for any one decision. Traditional reporting methods provide full data printouts that are useful for general reference, but which contain too much data for timely decision making. Through either regularly scheduled or inquiry reports, exception reporting can provide the concise, focused information a decision maker needs for action.

A. L. TORRANCE

EXECUTABLE STATEMENT

For articles on related subjects *see* DECLARATIVE STATEMENT; and PROCEDURE-ORIENTED LANGUAGES: Programming.

An executable statement is a procedural step in a high-level programming language which calls for processing action by the computer, such as performing arithmetic, reading data from an external medium, making a decision, etc. In describing the structure and features of high-level languages, it is convenient to distinguish between executable statements and nonexecutable or *declarative* statements that provide information about the nature of the data or about the way the processing is to

be done without themselves causing any processing action.

Executable statements are sometimes called *imperative* statements because their form often closely resembles that of an imperative sentence in a natural language. For example, the formula

$$Y = a + bx + cx^2$$

follows an imperative form that persists in corresponding structures in programming statements:

[Pascal]   Y := A + B * X + C * X * X;

[Fortran]   Y = A + B * X + C * X ** 2

[PL/I]   Y = A + B * X + C * X ** 2;

This correspondence is emphasized more explicitly in some languages, namely,

[Basic]   LET Y = A + B * X + C * X ↑ 2

[Cobol]   COMPUTE Y = A + B * X + C * X ** 2.

Specifications for data transmission between internal storage and an external medium are constructed along similar lines:

[Fortran]   READ (5,12) HERE
WRITE (6,21) HERE
[Cobol]   READ INFILE INTO HERE.
WRITE OUTFILE FROM HERE.
[PL/I]   READ FILE (INFILE) INTO (HERE);
WRITE FILE (OUTFILE) FROM (HERE);

[The numerical specifications in the Fortran example are coded references to additional information about the source (for input), destination (for output), and form of the data to be transmitted.]

Sometimes executable statements are subdivided into imperative and conditional statements because the latter, such as the IF statement in Fortran, specify alternate imperative actions linked through a decision mechanism.

A language implementation may have rules about the relative placement of executable and nonexecutable statements. Sometimes it is required that all declarations about data appear before the first executable statement of a program; in other cases it is required only that declarations appear before any information in them is required by an executable statement. One of the distinguishing features of Cobol is its total separation of executable statements (in the *Procedure* division) from nonexecutable statements (in the *Environment* and *Data* divisions).

D. D. McCracken and S. V. Pollack

EXECUTIVE SYSTEM. *See* Operating Systems.

EXPRESSION

For articles on related subjects *see* Coercion; Constants; Parsing; Procedure-Oriented Languages, Programming in; and Statement.

An *expression,* one of the fundamental constituents of high-level language syntax, is a character sequence that specifies a rule for calculating a value. That value may be either numeric, as in the Pascal expression $a +$ 6, or alphanumeric, as in the Basic expression LEFT\$(A\$, 5) (whose value is the leftmost 5 characters of string A\$). An expression may appear to the right of the replacement symbol (usually = or := or ←) in statement-oriented languages such as Pascal or Fortran, or may stand alone and be evaluated immediately to yield a particular value in expression-oriented languages such as Lisp or APL.

A *statement-oriented language* is one in which sentence-like statements calculate and save intermediate values but (except for specific I/O statements) do not print them. In Pascal, for example, the statement $p := a * b + c$ is composed of an identifier (variable name) p, a replacement symbol, $:=$, and the expression $a * b + c$. Such an expression makes sense to the Pascal compiler if all of its identifiers have been previously declared as to type (real, integer, etc.) and if it is *well-formed* according to the grammatical rules of the language. The expression will make sense at execution time if, by the time it is reached during program flow, all of its identifiers have been assigned specific values that enable evaluation of the expression and storage of the result at the identifier specified to the left of the replacement symbol.

An *expression-oriented language* is one in which expressions may stand alone such that, when encountered during program flow, their value is calculated and printed immediately. Thus, if the expression $3 + 4$ is presented to APL at an interactive terminal session, APL will respond immediately by outputting 7.

An expression that is valid in one high-level language might be invalid in another or, even if valid, produce a different result. Thus, $a**b$ is a valid Fortran expression but is not valid in Pascal, which does not have an exponentiation operator. The upper-case equivalent of the expression used earlier, $A*B + C$, would be acceptable to APL but would have an entirely different meaning because of different interpretations of the $*$ operator (multiplication in Pascal, exponentiation in APL) and different operator precedence (*q.v.*). To obtain the same meaning, the APL programmer would write $(A \times B) + C$ or $C + A \times B$ and the Lisp programmer would write (PLUS (TIMES A B) C) because that language uses a fully-parenthesized notation in which operators precede their operands (prefix form).

Most high-level languages allow use of expressions in contexts other than replacement statements. A typical use is for subscript selection. For example, the Pascal statement

$$k := 3 * a + b[round(j + sqrt(x))]$$

will calculate and use the integer closest to the value of the expression $j + sqrt(x)$ to select a particular member of the one-dimensional array b. The sum of the selected value and the value of $3 * a$ is then assigned to k. In Algol and Pascal, a subscript may be any valid expression; other languages are more restrictive.

Expressions may also be classified as being either *homogeneous* (all constituents of the same type) or *mixed-mode*. An example of the latter is $A + J * Z$ where, perhaps, A has been declared as being real (floating-point), J as being integer, and Z as complex. What should be done? Early dialects of Fortran declared such expressions syntactically illegal and refused to process them. Almost all current languages accept mixed mode expressions whenever reasonable type conversions can be inferred (e.g., automatic conversion of A and J to complex prior to evaluation of the cited expression), which allow calculation to proceed.

An expression may be very simple as well as complicated. In most languages the single digit 7 or the single-letter variable Q are valid expressions. Thus, the Pascal statement cited earlier, $k := 3 * a + b[round(j + sqrt(x))]$, contains nine recognizable expressions:

1–4. 3, a, j, and x are expressions.
5. $3 * a$ is an expression.
6. The function $sqrt(x)$ is an expression.
7. The subscript $round(j + sqrt(x))$ is an expression.
8. The subscripted variable $b[round(j + sqrt(x))]$ is an expression.
9. The entire right-hand side is an expression.

The rules for recognizing a well-formed (syntactically valid) expression in any given language may be stated quite rigorously in a notation such as Backus-Naur

Definitions | Remarks

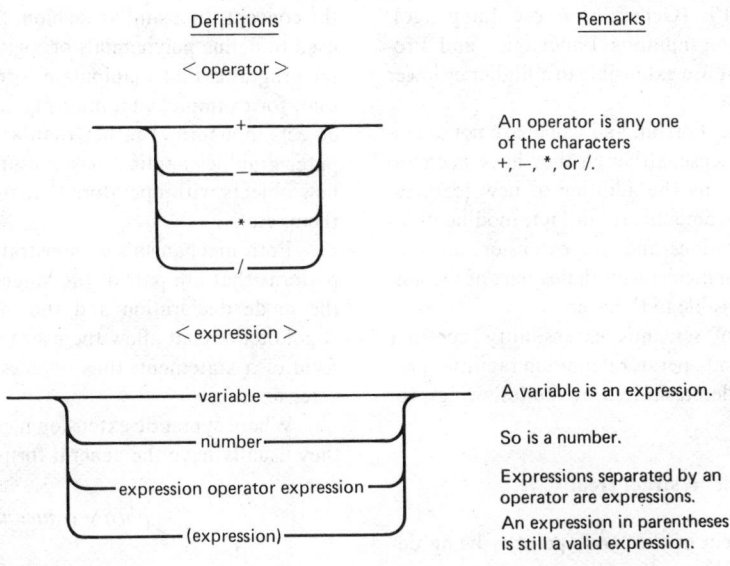

< operator >

An operator is any one of the characters +, −, *, or /.

< expression >

A variable is an expression.

So is a number.

Expressions separated by an operator are expressions. An expression in parentheses is still a valid expression.

Fig. 1.

Form (BNF—*q.v.*) or perhaps in the increasingly popular equivalent *syntax diagram* form commonly used to define Pascal. Consider the following example of the use of such diagrams (Fig. 1) to define first <operator> and then <expression> in a very simple hypothetical language (where we assume that the intuitive concepts of <variable> and <number> were defined earlier).

Using such diagrams, one can readily ascertain that such character sequences as

$(a + b) * (c − d)$
$(5 * 9/(h + 7))$ and
$r * s − t/u$

are valid expressions, but that others, such as $a*(b$ and $*a + b$ are not well-formed.

REFERENCES

1975. Pratt, T. W. *Programming Languages: Design and Implementation.* Englewood Cliffs, NJ: Prentice-Hall, pp. 123–136.
1973. Wirth, N. *Systematic Programming: An Introduction.* Englewood Cliffs, NJ: Prentice-Hall.

E. D. REILLY, JR.

EXTENDED BINARY CODED DECIMAL INTERCHANGE CODE. *See* EBCDIC.

EXTENSIBLE LANGUAGE

For articles on related subjects *see* ADA; ALGOL 68; PROCEDURE-ORIENTED LANGUAGES; and PROGRAMMING LANGUAGES.

The concept of extensible languages was evolved to permit the user to modify a programming language by adding new features to it or by modifying existing ones. One of the goals was to let the user mold the language to the requirements of the particular area of application, and thus improve the efficiency of the programmer and the clarity of the product.

Extensible languages consist of two basic components:

1. A base language, which provides a complete but minimal set of primitive facilities such as elementary data types, and simple operations and control constructs.
2. Extension mechanisms, which allow the definition of new language features in terms of the base language primitives.

The extension mechanisms can be further subdivided into *semantic extension* facilities and *syntactic extension* facilities.

Semantic extensions introduce new kinds of objects to the languages such as additional data types or operations, whereas syntactic extensions create new notations for existing or user defined mechanisms.

Among others, Ada, Algol 68, Basel, EL1 (Extensible Language 1), GPL (General Purpose Language), PPL (Polymorphic Programming Language), and Proteus are languages that are extensible to a higher or lower degree.

Languages such as Fortran and Cobol are not extensible in the technical sense, although they have been enhanced over the years by the addition of new features. However, these enhancements are, in fact, modifications of the language definitions and not extensions accomplished by an extension mechanism that is part of the language and, thus, accessible to the user.

As an example of semantic extensibility, consider the mode (i.e., type) and operator definition facilities provided by Algol 68 as demonstrated by the following program segment:

mode point = struct (real x, y);

Comment: A new object of the mode **point** is being defined as a structure of two real components. The components are accessed by the selectors *x* and *y*. ¢

priority - - = 6;

Comment: The symbol - - is declared to be an infix operator symbol of the priority level 6, i.e., the level of addition. ¢

op - - = **(point** pl, p2) **real:**
sqrt ((x **of** p1 — x **of** p2) ↑ 2 + (y **of** pl — y **of** p2) ↑ 2);

Comment: The symbol - -, if applied to operands of the mode *point,* is defined to denote the Euclidean distance between the two points p1 and p2.

The following segment demonstrates how the newly defined objects may be used. ¢

begin real a, **point** u, v;
u: = (.0,.0), v: = (3.0,4.0); a: = u - - v **end**

Comment: *a* is set to 5.0 ¢

It should be noted that all operators so defined are generic, i.e., the same operator symbol may be defined for and used with different operand modes evoking different computations. This is accomplished by checking and matching modes during the compilation.

The above example gives a glimpse of the power of the concept. In a similar fashion, these facilities could be used to define polynomials or logical formulas as objects for programs that manipulate formulas, with operations that, for example, add, multiply, intersect, or unite these objects in a formal rather than a numeric way. In computer graphics applications, pictures could be defined as new objects with operators that overlay, scale, or rotate them, etc.

Both mechanisms demonstrated use only notational patterns that are part of the language Algol 68, namely, the mode declaration and the infix operator notation. Algol 68 does not allow the user to redefine the *syntactic form* of a statement; thus, it does not provide syntactic extensions.

Where syntactic extension mechanisms are available they usually have the general form

phrase α means β

Here, α is a new syntactic pattern defined to invoke the program segment β. For more detail, see Schuman and Jorrand (1970) and *SIGPLAN Notices* (1971).

Extensible languages are mainly of historical importance. Together with the work in structured programming in the late 1960s and early 1970s, they furthered efforts to reexamine and generalize programming language primitives which have led to the more recent research in the area of abstraction mechanisms. As one result, for example, the importance of devices for the specification of what are now called abstract data types (*q.v.*) has been widely recognized. These devices, pioneered by Simula 67 (1967) with its *class* (*q.v.*) concept, have hence become central features of such later languages as CLU, Alphard, Euclid, and Modula.

REFERENCES

1970. Schuman, S. A. and Jorrand, P. "Definition Mechanisms in Extensible Programming Languages." *AFIPS Conference Proceedings* **37**. AFIPS Press, pp. 9–20.

1971. "Proceedings of the International Symposium on Extensible Languages" (September 1971, Grenoble, France), *SIGPLAN Notices* **6**, *No. 12* (December).

1976. Melkanoff, M. A. "Extensible Languages," in *Formal Languages and Programming,* R. Aguilar (Ed.). Amsterdam: North-Holland.

J. J. MARTIN

F

FAST FOURIER TRANSFORM

For articles on related subjects *see* ALGORITHMS, ANALYSIS OF; and NUMERICAL ANALYSIS.

The fast Fourier transform (FFT) refers to a family of numerical algorithms for computing the discrete Fourier transform (DFT). In complex notation, the DFT is defined by

$$a(n) = \sum_{j=0}^{N-1} x(j) W_N^{-nj} \quad n = 0, 1, \ldots, N-1 \quad (1)$$

where $x(j)$, $j = 0, 1, \ldots, N-1$ is a given sequence of complex numbers and

$$W_N = \exp(2\pi i/N) \quad (2)$$

is the principal Nth root of unity. This can be written as a series of sines and cosines by making the substitution

$$W_N^{-nj} = \cos(2\pi nj/N) - i \sin(2\pi nj/N). \quad (3)$$

Most of the important applications of the FFT involve the inversion theorem and the convolution theorem.

The inversion theorem states that Eq. (1) is a solution of the system of equations

$$x(j) = \frac{1}{N} \sum_{n=0}^{N-1} a(n) W_N^{nj} \quad (4)$$

This is referred to as the "inverse discrete Fourier transform (IDFT) of $a(n)$."

One important application of a program for computing Eq. (1) is in spectral analysis. Here, one wishes to obtain estimates (with perhaps some smoothing) of the amplitudes and phases given by the $a(n)$ of the sinusoidal components of a signal $x(j)$. Other applications involve the solution of systems of equations by substituting Eq. (4) for the solution and expressing the equations in terms of the $a(n)$. The latter are usually easily solvable and the computation consists mostly of the calculation of the DFT given in Eq. (4).

In some cases, it is expedient to process data by performing operations in the frequency domain, i.e., on the $a(n)$ instead of the $x(j)$. Such applications are usually based upon the convolution theorem, which may be expressed as follows:

Given two periodic sequences $x(j)$, $y(j)$, $j = 0, 1, \ldots, N-1$, with DFTs $a(n)$ and $b(n)$, $n = 0, 1, \ldots, N-1$, respectively, let the convolution sequence

$$z(j) = \sum_{k=0}^{N-1} x(k) y(j-k), \quad j = 0, 1, \ldots, N-1 \quad (5)$$

have the DFT $c(n)$, $n = 0, 1, \ldots, N-1$. The convolution theorem states that

$$c(n) = a(n) b(n). \quad (6)$$

Therefore, one may obtain $z(j)$ by computing $a(n)$ and $b(n)$ and then computing the IDFT of their product.

While the direct computation of Eq. (5) by accumulating products may take a number of operations (multiplications and additions) proportional to N^2, the use of Eq. (6) will require a number of operations proportional to the time required to compute the DFTs, which is proportional to $N\log N$. Since it is fairly typical to process long records of data in slices having a length of approximately $N = 1,000$, the computation is reduced by a factor of roughly $N/\log_2 N = 100$.

The FFT algorithms use the fact that if N is composite, i.e.,

$$N = r_1 \cdot r_2 \cdot \ldots \cdot r_m, \tag{7}$$

the series (1) can be expressed as a nested sequence of series of subseries which requires a number of operations proportional to

$$N_{op} = N(r_1 + r_2 + \cdots + r_m). \tag{8}$$

For $N > 4$, this is less than the N^2 operations that would be required by a direct accumulation of products for each value of j according to the defining formula (1). The number N_{op} is minimized by using as many factors as possible. If all factors are equal to r, then

$$N_{op} = Nr\log_r N = \frac{r}{\log_2 r} N\log_2 N. \tag{9}$$

A frequent choice, for programming efficiency, is to select N to be a power of 2 so that

$$N_{op} = 2 \cdot N\log_2 N. \tag{10}$$

The algorithm is easily derived when N is a product of two factors, r_1 and r_2. The indices n and j in Eqs. (1) and (4) are, in this case, replaced by index pairs (n_1,n_2) and (j_1,j_2), respectively, defined as

$$n = n_1 + r_1 n_2, \qquad j = j_2 + j_1 r_2, \tag{11}$$

where

$$\begin{aligned} n_1 &= 0, 1, \ldots, r_1 - 1, \\ n_2 &= 0, 1, \ldots, r_2 - 1, \\ j_1 &= 0, 1, \ldots, r_1 - 1, \\ j_2 &= 0, 1, \ldots, r_2 - 1. \end{aligned} \tag{12}$$

Using Eq. (11), one can perform the factorization

$$W_N^{-nj} = W_N^{-n_2 j_1 r_1 r_2}\, W_N^{-n_1 j_1 r_2}\, W_N^{-n_2 j_2 r_1}\, W_N^{-n_1 j_2}, \tag{13}$$

which is easily simplified by using the relations

$$W_N^{r_1 r_2} = 1, \quad W_N^{r_1} = W_{r_2}, \quad W_N^{r_2} = W_{r_1}. \tag{14}$$

The summation may then be taken over j_1 and j_2 instead of j to give

$$a(n_1 + r_1 n_2) = \sum_{j_2=0}^{r_2-1} \left\{ \sum_{j_1=0}^{r_1-1} x(j_2 + j_1 r_2) W_{r_1}^{-n_1 j_1} \right\} \times W_N^{-n_1 j_2} W_{r_2}^{-n_2 j_2} \tag{15}$$

The inner sum is, for each of the r_2 values of j_2, a DFT of an r_1-point sequence which, for all r_1 values of n_1, can be computed in r_1^2 operations. After multiplication of this result by the phase factor $W_N^{-n_1 j_2}$, or "twiddle factor," the outer sum may be calculated as a DFT of an r_2-point sequence, which for each of the r_1 values of n_1 takes r_2^2 operations. If the phase factor $W_N^{-n_1 j_2}$ is absorbed in either of the W_{r1} or W_{r2} factors, this will take a total of

$$N_{op} = r_2 r_1^2 + r_1 r_2^2 = N(r_1 + r_2) \tag{16}$$

operations. If r_2 can be factored into $r_2' \cdot r_3'$ and the process repeated on the r_2-point DFT, it is easily seen that the number of operations will be

$$N_{op} = N(r_1 + r_2' + r_3'). \tag{17}$$

By an inductive argument, one arrives at Eq. (8).

The algorithm described by Eq. (15) may be written so that the data is overwritten by the results, with practically no other storage required except, perhaps, that used for a table of sines.

REFERENCES

1977. Cooley, J. W., Lewis, P. A. W., and Welch, P. D. "The Fast Fourier Transform and Its Application to Time Series Analysis," in Enslein, Ralston, and Wilf (Eds.), *Mathematical Methods for Digital Computers* 3. New York: Wiley.

J. W. COOLEY

FAULT-TOLERANT COMPUTING

For articles on related subjects *see* ARPA NETWORK; DATA SECURITY; REDUNDANCY; and RELIABILITY, HARDWARE.

Fault-tolerant computing is the art of building computing systems that continue to operate satisfactorily in the presence of faults (i.e., hardware failures). An extensive methodology has been developed in this field over the past two decades. Several fault-tolerant machines have been developed and a large amount of supporting research has been reported.

The majority of past work has been directed toward building computers that automatically recover from faults occurring in internal hardware components and that continue to execute correct computations. The techniques employed to do this generally involve partitioning a computing system into modules. Each module is backed up with protective redundancy so that if the module fails, others can assume its function.

Two general approaches to fault recovery have been used: (1) fault masking, and (2) dynamic recovery. *Fault masking* is a structural redundancy technique that completely masks faults within a set of redundant modules. Triple modular redundancy (TMR) is the most commonly used form of fault masking. In a TMR configuration, each module is replaced by three identical modules and their outputs are compared (*voted*) to derive a correct majority result should one of the modules fail. The voting circuitry is also triplicated so that individual voter failures can also be corrected by the voting process. A TMR system fails whenever two modules in a redundant triplet fail so that the vote is no longer valid. Hybrid redundancy is an extension of TMR in which triplicated modules are backed up with additional spare modules, which can be used to replace faulty modules. When a module disagrees within a triplet, the two remaining good machines command its replacement with a spare. A triplet, backed up with N spares, can tolerate $N + 1$ module failures. Voted systems require greater than three times as much hardware as nonredundant systems due to triplication of modules and the further addition of voters—which is the price of automatic fault recovery.

Dynamic recovery involves automated self-repair. As in fault masking, the computing system is partitioned into modules backed up by protective redundancy. In the case of dynamic recovery, a special mechanism detects faults in the modules, switches out a faulty module, switches in a spare, and instigates those software actions (rollback, initialization, retry, restart) necessary to continue the ongoing computation. The few existing uniprocessors of this type depend upon special hardware to carry out this function of automated recovery. This special hardware is made as simple as possible and is protected by TMR or hybrid redundancy. In multiprocessors and distributed systems, the special recovery function is usually implemented by one of the other nonfaulty machines in the system.

History. The SAPO computer built in Prague, Czechoslovakia was probably the first fault-tolerant computer. It was built in 1950–1954 under the supervision of A. Svoboda, using relays and a magnetic drum memory. The processor used triplication and voting (TMR), and the memory implemented error detection with automatic retries when an error was detected. A second machine developed by the same group (EPOS) also contained comprehensive fault-tolerance features. The fault-tolerant features of these machines were motivated by the local unavailability of reliable components and the probability of reprisals by the ruling authorities should the machine not work properly.

Early fault-tolerant computers in the United States were developed in the 1960s for the Space Program and the telephone companies. Due to the unusually high reliability requirements of spacecraft and launch systems for manned flight, NASA was a primary sponsor of fault-tolerant computing. The first fault-tolerant machine to be developed and flown was the on-board computer for the Orbiting Astronomical Observatory (OAO), which used fault masking at the component (transistor) level. The second fault-tolerant machine to be flown was used as the Saturn V guidance computer and contained a TMR processor and duplicated memories (each using internal error detection).

A third fault-tolerant computer sponsored by NASA was the JPL Self-Testing-and-Repairing (STAR) computer. It was developed for spacecraft missions to the outer planets and was required to provide very long (10-year) life. The STAR computer, designed under the leadership of A. Aviżienis, was the first computer to employ dynamic recovery throughout its design. Various modules of the computer were instrumented to detect internal faults and signal fault conditions to a special Test and Repair Processor which effected reconfiguration and recovery. An experimental version of the STAR was implemented in the laboratory and its fault-tolerance properties were verified by extensive testing. Due to cancellation of its planned space mission, it was never flown. The United States Air Force sponsored the development of an on-board satellite computer, designated the Fault-Tolerant Spaceborne Computer (FTSC), which employed many of the techniques developed in the earlier STAR computer. It was designed to have a much higher computing capacity than the earlier on-board machines and was implemented and tested in the laboratory. This program was halted due to the unavailability of specialized components.

The most widely used fault-tolerant computer systems developed during the 1960s were the Electronic Switching Systems (ESS), which are used in telephone switching offices throughout the country. Duplication is used throughout these computers, which have since evolved over several generations.

Current Fault-Tolerant Computers.

A number of fault-tolerant machines developed in the 1970s are currently implemented as experimental systems and are expected to be used in the next decade.

Two fault-tolerant computers have been developed by NASA for fuel-efficient aircraft which require continuous computer control in flight. Since these machines are intended for life-critical applications, they are designed to meet the most stringent reliability requirements of any computer to date. Both machines employ hybrid redundancy. The first, designated Software Implemented Fault Tolerance (SIFT), uses off-the-shelf computers and achieves voting and reconfiguration through software. The second machine, the Fault-Tolerant Multiprocessor (FTMP) uses specialized hardware for these functions.

Although they are not designed to the stringent requirements of aerospace machines, a number of current commercial computers employ extensive fault-tolerance features. Among these are the Pluribus computer, which serves as a highly reliable second-generation interface message processor for ARPANET and the Tandem computer used in a variety of commercial applications. In large computers, the trend is to include additional circuitry to aid fault detection and diagnosis and to employ an external minicomputer or special-purpose machine as a maintenance processor.

Supporting Research.

Since it is impossible to cover the field of fault-tolerance research in a short article, this discussion is limited to two of the most critical areas that support computer development—design methodology and reliability modeling and verification.

Among the most influential work in design methodology has been the development of (1) coding techniques for concurrent detection of specific faults, (2) self-checking circuits, (3) software-implemented fault tolerance, (4) memory systems tolerating multiple faults, (5) reliable clocking and communications networks, and (6) design for provable correctness.

A number of probabilistic models have been developed to predict the reliability of fault-tolerant machines as a function of time. These models are based on component reliability, system architecture, and the effectiveness of the fault-tolerance mechanisms of a computer. One of the earliest models was Computer Aided Reliability Estimation (CARE) developed as part of the STAR computer project. A very important advance in modeling was provided by a group at IBM, who introduced the concept of *coverage*, and created a model that included its effects. Coverage (the conditional probability that a system recovers, given that a fault occurs) is a measure of the effectiveness of fault-tolerance mechanisms in a computer. A recent reliability modeling system is designated the UCLA Automated Reliability Estimation Program (ARIES). It subsumes most previous models and provides new models for degradable systems with or without off-line repair.

Future Development.

Future developments in fault-tolerant computing are expected to be heavily influenced by VLSI technology. Using VLSI, the cost of logic, and specifically the cost of protective redundancy, will be greatly reduced. This reduction in cost should greatly expand the range of applications in which fault-tolerant computers can be economically employed. It has already been shown that a completely self-checking computer can be built at only a small increase in cost using this advanced technology.

New problems in fault tolerance arise directly from VLSI devices and from VLSI systems. Testability is a critical issue in chips that contain tens of thousands of gates but only a few dozen pins for access. Device yields and reliability may be greatly improved by using on-chip redundancy. VLSI makes possible extremely complex, high-performance systems. Several such systems are already being investigated. Due to their high degree of complexity, it is expected that transient errors will be a common occurrence, and permanent failures will occur often enough to be a problem. Thus, fault-tolerant design will be required in a variety of new architectures.

Finally, a new and difficult area of research into fault-tolerant software has been undertaken by several groups. Two approaches that have been taken are recovery blocks and *N*-version programming. These are roughly equivalent to dynamic recovery and fault-masking techniques employed in fault-tolerance approaches to hardware faults. This is a relatively new field, which may have considerable influence on future systems.

REFERENCES

1971. Avižienis, A. et al. "The STAR (*Self-Testing And Repairing*) Computer: An Investigation of the Theory and Practice of Fault-Tolerant Computer Design," *IEEE Trans. Computers* C-20, *No. 11:* 1312–1321 (November).

1972. Carter, W. C. et al. "Computer Error Control by Testable Morphic Boolean Functions—A Way of Removing Hardware," *Digest of Papers—1972 Int. Symp. Fault-Tolerant Computing* (Newton, MA), pp. 154–159 (June).

1978. *Proceedings of the IEEE (Special Issue on Fault-Tolerant Computing) 66, No. 10* (October).

1980. *Computer (Special Issue on Fault-Tolerant Computing) 13, No. 13* (March).

1980. Ng, Y.-W. and Avižienis, A. "A Unified Reliability Model for Fault-Tolerant Computers, *"IEEE Trans. Computers* **C-29**, *No. 11:* 1002–1011 (November).

D. A. Rennels

FEASIBILITY STUDY

For articles on related subjects *see* Computer Acquisition; Documentation.

The feasibility study takes place at the beginning of a computer systems development project and leads to a *feasibility report*. It is a broad-brush study which seeks to determine two things: the exact nature of the problem to be solved and an outline of one or more solutions to the problem. It seeks to answer three questions: technical—will it work?; economic—will it pay?; operational/political—will it be used? The feasibility report is submitted to the problem proponent (user) who, after review, may authorize the detailed development work on a selected solution, modify the design, or possibly abandon the whole project.

The basis of the feasibility study is that it enables fundamental decisions to be made before time and money are committed to the systems and programming work. Provided the feasibility study is conducted carefully by experienced personnel, the outline solution(s) and cost/timing estimates will be confirmed in the detailed systems work. But, in practice, the findings of the study and the decisions based upon it may be reviewed in the light of the detailed investigation and analysis, and the project modified (or even abandoned) any time up to the beginning of programming. Revisions to the scope of the project or the design approach *after* programming has begun will be very expensive indeed. An example of the contents of a feasibility study report is given in Fig. 1.

As Fig. 1 shows, the study is based on an investigation of the proponent's (user's) problem area. The scope of the investigation and the resources required will depend on the type of project. The feasibility study for the development of a major accounting or production control system in a large company may take several systems analysts a number of months to complete. A study of a small subsystem to produce an additional report from an existing system, on the other hand, may take only a few days.

The statement of the user's requirements generally includes the following categories:

.1. *Objectives.* States what the user wants the new system to achieve. This should be quantified wherever possible. For example, rather than a general statement of "increase factory throughput," a quantified statement of requirements is preferable, such as "to reduce work in progress by 15% and to increase machine utilization by 5%."
2. *Boundaries and Constraints.* Stipulates what the user does not want changed or sets forth any restriction on the design approach or the facilities used. These may be imposed for various technical and business reasons. Examples: "The job docket currently being used should not be changed." "The system must not be justified on staff displacement." "No more clerks in Grades A and B can be used." "Existing computer facilities must be used."
3. *Time Scale.* Sets the date when the new system is required. There may be many good business reasons for requiring a new system to be operational by a certain date. For example, the new system must be available by the end of the financial year, or before research begins on a new project, or to coincide with the next annual stock inventory.
4. *Mandatory Reports.* Lists mandatory output reports, identified by the user, which must be produced in the new system.

This problem definition is the design brief for a systems analyst whose task is to produce and outline one or more solutions that meet the user's needs as described above. A range of solutions is generally preferable because this will give the user an objective choice (rather than "forcing" one solution upon the user). For example, if there is an existing system, one alternative solution is "do nothing—do not change method of working"; this will serve as a basis for comparison with new system designs. For each solution there must be sufficient information given to enable the user to answer the following questions:

"Does the system meet my requirements?"
"How much will it cost and how long will it take?"
"Is it worthwhile to proceed?" (a cost benefit analysis of expenditure against savings)

This means that a description of the proposed new system must be given, together with a statement of the objectives that are met by the design. The benefits can be estimated from the latter. Some benefits will be tangible and quantified, others will be intangible and qualified benefits on which no precise monetary value can be placed. From the outline design, estimates can be made of the resources and time necessary to develop the system; the operational costs of running the system can also be assessed. The

FEASIBILITY STUDY REPORT

Title
Contents
Administrative Information

1.   INTRODUCTION
     1.1   Terms of Reference
     1.2   Method
     1.3   Summary

2.   FINDINGS
     2.1   Description of Existing System
     2.2   Identified Problems
     2.3   User Request
           —Objectives
           —Boundaries and Constraints
           —Timescale
           —Mandatory Reports
           —Assumptions and Limitations

3.   SYSTEM SOLUTION   (repeated for each solution)
     3.1   System Outline
     3.2   Benefits Realized
     3.3   Development Schedule, Resources and
           Costs
     3.4   Operating Schedule, Resources and
           Costs
     3.5   Advantages and Disadvantages
           —Cost/Benefit Analysis
           —Impact on Existing Organization/
             System
           —General Comments and Summary

4.   RECOMMENDATIONS AND CONCLUSIONS
     4.1   Conclusions (these may include a comparison
           of solutions)
     4.2   Recommendations
     4.3   Further Actions

APPENDICES
(Detailed timing and cost figures, document
  samples, etc.)

Fig. 1.   Sample feasibility study table of contents.

cost/benefit analysis, using the appropriate costing methods, can then be drawn up.

K. R. LONDON

FFT. *See* FAST FOURIER TRANSFORM.

FIFO-LIFO

For articles on related subjects *see* DATA STRUCTURES; LISTS AND LIST PROCESSING; and STACK.

The terms FIFO and LIFO refer to two techniques for dealing with collection of items to which additions and deletions are to be made. The acronym FIFO stands for *first-in-first-out* and LIFO represents *last-in-first-out.* Derived from business accounting and inventory management notions, these techniques have found widespread application in computer science.

The FIFO concept is based on the simple idea of people waiting on line to be serviced at a bank teller's window, a supermarket checkout counter, or a bus stop. The first person to arrive is serviced, and if there is a line of customers the order of entry to the rear of the line is the order of service given at the front of the line. The same concept can be applied to ships waiting to unload at a dock, to jobs waiting to be run in a computer system, or to airplanes waiting to be serviced by a repair shop. The line of people or items waiting to be serviced is called the *queue* (Fig. 1).

There are a great number of variations to the basic theme of FIFO arrangement. Multiple-server queues have a single queue but several facilities that provide service. Many banks and airline ticket counters have adopted this technique by having a single line that feeds to a group of teller windows. Priority queueing permits persons with high priority to move up to the front of the queue. Bounded-length queueing puts an upper limit to the number of persons in the queue.

The LIFO concept is based on the notion that the most recently arrived item is dispatched first. Thus, the freshest vegetables in the grocery are sold first and the inventory items most recently put on the shelf are the first to be sold. This idea is familiar to card players in some games (gin rummy, for example), who may take a card from the top of the pile or place another card face up on the pile. The stack of plates on the spring-loaded dispenser found in cafeterias is another common example of the LIFO principle. The usual definition of this principle includes the specification that only the top element of the collection may be removed and that new items may be placed only on the top of the collection. A collection that has these rules for addition and deletion is called a *stack* or a *pushdown list* (Fig. 2). Automata theorists distinguish between these two terms: In a stack, the interior items may be examined; in a pushdown list, the interior items may not be examined.

The LIFO technique has widespread application in

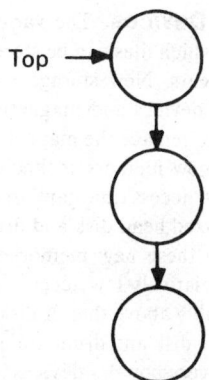

Fig. 2. LIFO stack; additions and deletions at top.

computer science, particularly in the parsing techniques employed by compilers and in the searching of data structures.

B. Shneiderman

FILES

For articles on related subjects *see* Catalog; Database Management; Open and Close A File; Record; Scratch Files; and Storage Management Structures.

The term *file* was used even before the advent of computers and was one of the first to be incorporated into data processing terminology. There are various definitions of the term in use today and those given below are typical. In general, a *file* is a collection of data representing a set of entities with certain aspects in common and organized for some specific purpose. An *entity* is any data object, such as *employee* or *part,* and is represented in a file by a record occurrence. A punched card deck containing information on automobile parts and a cabinet drawer filled with manila folders containing data sheets on employees are examples of (non-computer) files.

Definitions. In computer terminology, the word *file* can be defined in various ways and the definition depends on the level at which the file is being viewed. From an abstract viewpoint, a file can be considered to be a data object, with certain attributes and a set of operations for creating and manipulating it. A file has also been defined as a data structure stored in external memory. Perhaps the most common definition of file is the following: A file is an organized collection of data records, possibly of different types, stored on some external storage device such as magnetic tape, disk, drum, charge-coupled device, magnetic bubble memory, etc.

Fig. 1. FIFO queue; additions at back; deletions at front.

Storage Devices. The variety of external storage devices on which files can be stored has been increasing in recent years. New storage technologies, such as charge-coupled devices and magnetic bubble memories, are being used to replace the magnetic disk in certain situations. These new memory technologies have begun to fill the so-called "access time gap" that existed for several years between fixed head disk and drum devices and core memory. While these new memories are appealing because of their relatively low access time, the cost per bit is still considerably above that of disk and drum. For this reason, magnetic disk and drum are now, and will remain for some years, very popular devices for storing large files on line. In fact, the performance capabilities that can be derived from disk and drum devices have not yet been fully realized. Magnetic tape, because of its high access time, its portability and compactness characteristics, and its relatively low cost, has been relegated in many computer installations to serving as a storage medium for archival files and for backup copies of files.

File Structure. A file has structure that determines how the records in the file are organized. Structure can be subdivided into logical structure and physical structure. The *logical structure* of a file is essentially the application program's (i.e., the user's) view of the file (see Fig. 1). A file declaration that appears in a high-level language such as Cobol or PL/I is basically a logical structure specification and usually involves defining the attribute(s) of the record type(s) and possibly specifying a relationship (e.g., an ordering relationship) on the record occurrences. *Physical structure* is associated with how a file is actually organized on the storage medium on which

it resides. This normally involves pointers, indexes, etc., and how the records are "laid out" on the external storage device (see Fig. 1). The application program should have to be aware of only the logical structure of the file, whereas the access methods must know about the physical structure. *Access methods* (*q.v.*) are embodied in programs that satisfy user requests against a file; they provide the interface between a user program and a file.

Files can be structured and accessed in various ways. The earliest and most common type of file organization was sequential because computer files were first stored on inherently sequential storage media, such as magnetic tape. To access a record in a sequential file, the preceding records must be passed over. The appearance of random access storage devices such as magnetic disk and drum provided the capability not only for sequential accessing but also for random (or direct) accessing of records. With direct accessing, any record in a file can be retrieved without looking first at the records preceding it. Techniques for implementing direct access usually involve some method for translating a *key* (or a composite of several keys) that identify the record sought into the address (absolute or relative) of the corresponding record on the device on which it is stored. This translation is normally done via an index (or indexes) or a key-to-address transformation function (sometimes called a *hashing* function) that computes the address of the record from the key (or keys). Among the various access methods which have been developed are the sequential, indexed sequential, and direct access methods.

Files and Databases. The popularity of database management systems and the rather loose use of the

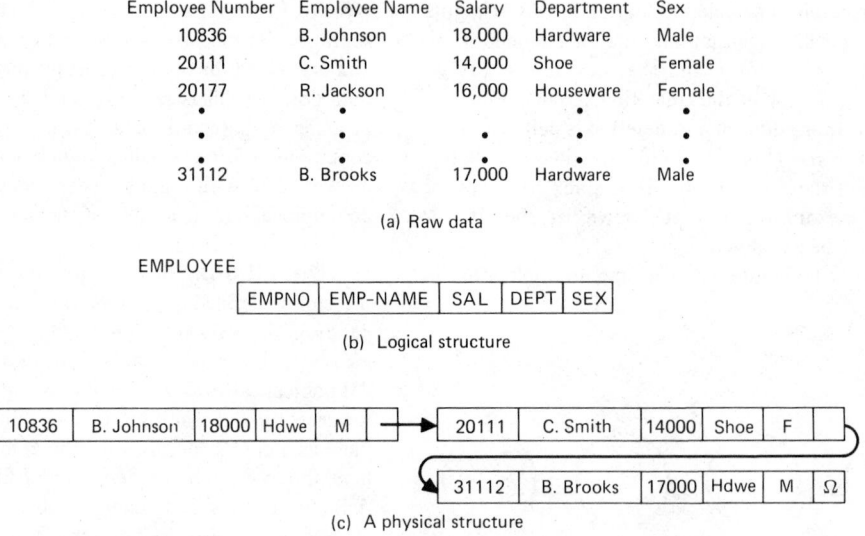

Employee Number	Employee Name	Salary	Department	Sex
10836	B. Johnson	18,000	Hardware	Male
20111	C. Smith	14,000	Shoe	Female
20177	R. Jackson	16,000	Houseware	Female
•	•		•	•
•	•	•	•	•
31112	B. Brooks	17,000	Hardware	Male

(a) Raw data

EMPLOYEE

| EMPNO | EMP-NAME | SAL | DEPT | SEX |

(b) Logical structure

| 10836 | B. Johnson | 18000 | Hdwe | M | → | 20111 | C. Smith | 14000 | Shoe | F |

| 31112 | B. Brooks | 17000 | Hdwe | M | Ω |

(c) A physical structure

Fig. 1. Raw data to logical file structure to physical file structure.

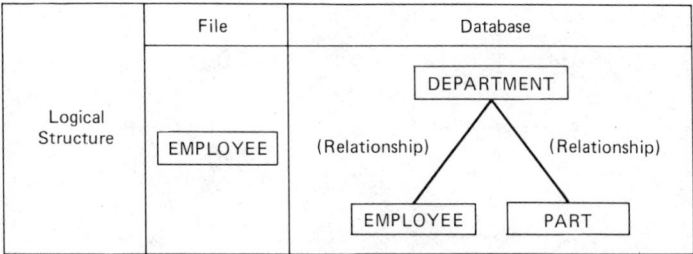

Fig. 2.   Logical structure.

term *database* has led to some confusion between a file and a database. One basic difference is their usage pattern. The use of a file is usually limited to one user or a few users and there is only one logical view of the file which is shared by the (usually small number of) application programs which access the file. On the other hand, a database brings together a variety of data and integrates it in such a way that it is available for a variety of users, with each user possibly having a different logical view of the database. In trying to make a clear distinction between a file and a database, some define a file as a collection of occurrences of records of one type and a database as a collection of occurrences of records of several types with specific relationships among the record types. Fig. 2 illustrates this distinction.

Kinds of Files. The word *file* is used in many ways in data processing. Examples are input file, output file, master file, scratch file, temporary file, card file, job file, and program file. Although the unmodified use of the term *file* usually means a data file holding data on "real-world" entities, some files are specifically called *program files* since they contain programs stored in source or object form. The availability of such program files or external storage devices is rapidly making obsolete the maintenance of extensive card-oriented program files.

B. G. CLAYBROOK

FINITE ELEMENT METHOD

For articles on related subjects *see* ENGINEERING APPLICATIONS; MATRIX COMPUTATIONS; NUMERICAL ANALYSIS; PARTIAL DIFFERENTIAL EQUATIONS, NUMERICAL SOLUTION OF; and SCIENTIFIC APPLICATIONS.

The finite element method is a relatively recent and very powerful approximate technique used to solve field problems in various engineering fields. Its development follows closely the increasing usage and availability of large-scale digital computers. Some areas of practical application are:

1. Static and dynamic analysis of complex structures such as airplanes, bridges, buildings, dams, ships, and cars.
2. Fluid flow, diffusion, and consolidation problems.
3. Liquid sloshing in an elastic container.
4. Lubrication problems.
5. Heat conduction and thermal stresses.

In the past decade, through applications of the technique, many engineers, mathematicians, and computer scientists have gained a large amount of direct experience with this new concept. We will briefly discuss this method as seen from the viewpoints of each of these three professional groups.

The Practicing Engineer. Practically on the basis of physical intuition alone, this method was initially used for aerospace structural analysis. Essentially, a continuous system is idealized as an assembly of discrete elements (Kuo, 1961). For example, an automobile may be idealized as a set of triangular elements as shown in Fig. 1. The common shape of a discrete element, known as the "shape" function, is the triangle for a two-dimensional structure and the tetrahedron for a three-dimensional one. However, other shape functions have also been used (see Fig. 2). Once this decision is made, the remaining

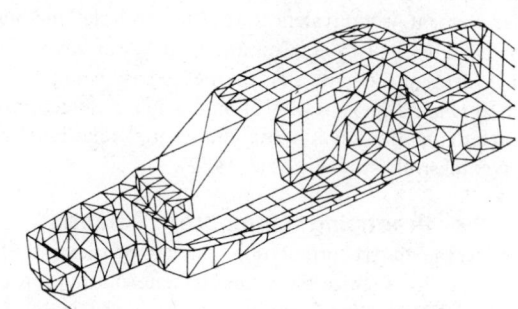

Fig. 1.   Idealization of a car body using finite elements.

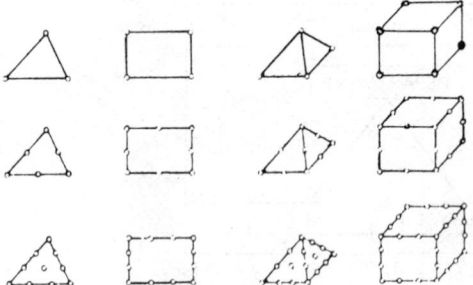

Fig. 2. Some common two-dimensional and three-dimensional finite elements.

steps follow a standard procedure. For example, in a structural problem using a stiffness matrix (Desai and Abel, 1972; Zienkiewicz, 1967), they are:

1. Choice of the displacement function for each element, assumed to be a polynomial usually, in terms of displacements at the nodes.
2. Selection of the stress-strain relationship.
3. Development of the stiffness matrix k for an element.
4. Consolidation of internal degrees of freedom.
5. Formation of k for the assemblage.
6. Computation of the displacements, strains, and stresses at various nodal points.

The Applied Mathematician. Many applied mathematicians view the finite element method as the approximation of a continuum by elements, each with multiple connecting points. It is similar to the Rayleigh-Ritz method with the following differences: (1) The piecewise continuous field definitions used in the finite element method are used to take care of irregular boundaries; and, (2) the resultant equations from the finite element method normally consist of banded or sparse matrices.

Mathematicians are also quick to point out that, while the finite difference method involves mathematical lumping, the finite element method uses physical lumping. Moreover, the finite element method, using a triangular element, is equivalent to the "hypercircle" method developed in 1943 by R. Courant. Today, various variational forms of the finite element method are being investigated (Pian and Tong, 1972), and a finite element approach to the solution of partial differential equations has been extensively studied (Aziz, 1972).

The Practicing Computer Scientist. In practice, the matrix formulation seems to be the most efficient way to organize the finite element solution for an idealized discrete model, but in adopting it, the computer scientist faces various new and challenging problems. They include (Oden *et al.*, 1972):

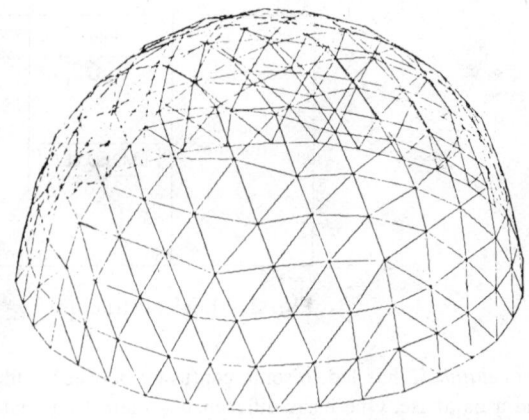

Fig. 3. Computer-generated mesh pattern.

1. Large-scale matrix problems involving banded or sparse matrices. The associated error bounds and convergence must be studied. Overlay techniques are often used.
2. Automatic mesh generation to avoid the error-prone input of large amounts of data. A typical mesh pattern (automatically generated) is shown in Fig. 3.
3. Computer-oriented interpolation techniques for two-dimensional and three-dimensional problems.
4. Hidden-line computer graphics for output.
5. Design of a general-purpose computer program versus some specially designed programs.

REFERENCES

1961. Kuo, S. S. "On Jacobi's Method for Real Symmetric Matrices," *Journal of the Aerospace Sciences* **28**, *No. 3:* 255 (March).

1972. Aziz, A. K. *The Mathematical Foundations of the Finite Element Method with Applications to Partial Differential Equations.* New York: Academic Press.

1976. Bathe, K. and Wilson, E. L. *Numerical Methods in Finite Element Analysis.* Englewood Cliffs, NJ: Prentice-Hall.

1976. Oden, J. T. and Reddy, J. N. *An Introduction to the Mathematical Theory of Finite Elements.* New York: Wiley.

1976. Tong, P. and Rossettos, J. N. *Finite Element Method: Basic Technique and Implementation.* Cambridge, MA: M.I.T. Press.

1978. Zienkiewicz, O. C. *Introductory Lectures on the Finite Element Method.* New York: Springer-Verlag.

S. S. KUO

FIX

For article on a related subject *see* PATCH.

As a verb, the word *fix* means to patch a program in an attempt to correct a bug (an error). More often it is used in computing as a noun. The *fix* can be made at the machine language level, but commonly, in assembly language or higher-level language coding, the source code is corrected and the entire program is reassembled or recompiled.

F. GRUENBERGER

FLOWCHART

For articles on related subjects *see* ALGORITHM; BLOCK DIAGRAM; DOCUMENTATION; FLOW DIAGRAM; PROGRAM; and SYSTEM CHART.

Definition. Flowcharts are graphic means of describing a sequence of operations done on data. They serve as a means of communication from one person to another about transformations on data. Flowcharts are graphic because they commonly use a two-dimensional pictorial format. The placement of the identifications of the operations in the pictorial format shows the sequence of the operations. The pictorial format typically incorporates wording to identify the data and the operations. The pictorial format is the subject of both an International and an American National Standard (ANSI, 1970).

Flowcharts get their name from their chart (graphic) representation of the flow (orderly passing of control) from one operation to the next in an explicit sequence. Flowcharts go by many other names, including block diagram, flow diagram, logic diagram, system chart, run diagram, process chart, procedure chart, and logic chart (Chapin, 1971). These different names reflect in part a lack of uniformity of nomenclature and in part the particular interests of specialized users. For example, prior to the advent of computers the name "flowchart" was used by systems analysts to designate a means of describing the flow of documents carrying data in an organization.

The two major varieties of flowchart in present day practice are the system chart and the flow diagram. As indicated in Fig. 1, the flow diagram concentrates on part of what a system chart shows. The unit of data transformation for the two is thus very different. For a flow diagram, the unit of data transformation is usually an operation or short sequence of operations that a computer can perform (such as an instruction or a series of instruc-

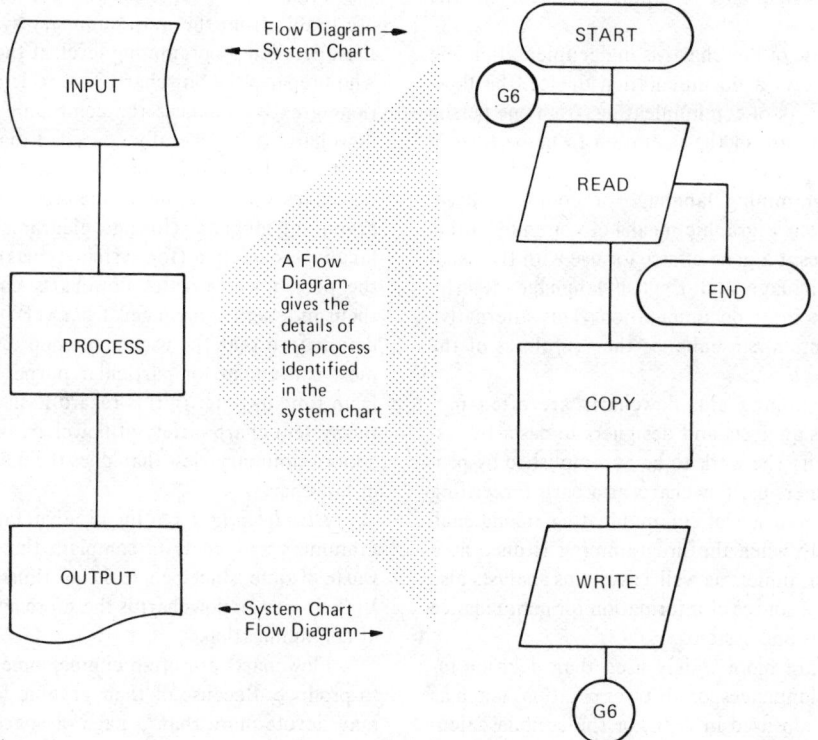

Fig. 1. Two types of flowcharts: the system chart and the flow diagram. (From N. Chapin, *Flowcharts*, Petrocelli Books, New York, 1971.)

tions that comprise a subroutine). An example is testing for the presence of leading zeros in a number.

By contrast, in a system chart the unit of data transformation is usually the work done by an entire computer program. Examples are: sorting a file of data, inverting a matrix, or producing a report. Flow diagrams commonly have an algorithmic orientation, stressing how data is transformed, whereas system charts primarily identify inputs and outputs to algorithms, stressing what data is used or produced at various points in a sequence of operations. System charts and flow diagrams are described in more detail later in this article.

The major varieties of flowcharts are alike in that they describe operations in sequence on data. They stress "what" and "how." Flowcharts are weak on "when," "why," and "what does the action." The only usual indication of "when" is the relative position in a sequence of operations. Usually, the doer of the action is the computer arithmetic and logic unit for a flow diagram, and the computer itself for a system chart, with exceptions possible.

Use. Flowcharts are the most widely used graphic method for describing computer operations. They are adaptable to a wide variety of different applications and circumstances and have enjoyed use from the early days of the computer field (see Chapin, 1971, for a brief history).

The major use of flowcharts is in documentation and in programming. As a documentation device, the flowchart provides a way of communicating, from one person to another, the nature of the operation to be performed and of the data upon which it is to be performed, regardless of the programming language or computer used. Since a flowchart is a graphic means of communication, this feature makes it a good choice for use with the usual programming language and English language descriptions included in most documentation. This alternative means of description can enhance the usefulness of the other means.

As a programming aid, flowcharts are often prepared by systems analysts and designers to describe systems and to specify the work to be accomplished by programs. Programmers use flowcharts as a basis for writing programs and as a means of communicating among each other, particularly when the programming is done as a team effort. Programmers as well as systems analysts also use flowcharts as a source of information for maintenance work on programs and systems.

Flowcharts are more widely used than decision tables, publication languages, or abstract notations (such as the Iverson notation used in APL, or the lambda calculus). This popularity appears to be due to the balance of advantages and disadvantages.

Advantages. Flowcharts have few features limiting their use. Hence, they are broadly applicable across a wide range of industries, computer applications, and types of work. For example, they are as convenient in administrative file handling as in scientific or engineering computation. This popularity, bred of wide applicability, generates further use as a lingua franca among persons working with computers.

Flowcharts are also largely language independent. Knowledge of a programming language is not normally necessary to be able to use them or to create them. This is always true for the pictorial part of flowcharts, and ideally should be true for the wording or symbols incorporated in a flowchart.

Flowcharts are constraining and precise in ways that are useful to programmers and analysts. They are a limited means of description that force the user to give attention to many significant matters while suppressing attention to a host of less important matters.

Flowcharts are a visual representation, and hence provide a convenient alternative to the usual narrative description for a program or system. This enables a more rapid scan or search of a flowchart than of a narrative description when particular items of information are sought. The graphic format enables a user to comprehend much at a glance.

Flowcharts offer a controllable level of detail. They are usable from the most summary systems level to the most detailed programming level, at the option of the one who prepares the flowchart. This wide range of detail options greatly enhances the communication value of the flowchart. It is generally conceded that the flowchart is most valuable to the user when the level of detail in the flowchart is more summary than that provided in the programming language (for flow diagrams) or in the English language narrative (for system charts). For this reason, the person who creates flowcharts commonly prepares them in a series, arranged from very summary to quite detailed, so that the user may choose the level of detail most convenient for particular purposes as they change from time to time. In this regard it should be noted that the system chart variety of flowchart inherently provides a more summary view than does the flow-diagram variety of flowchart.

Disadvantages. On the disadvantage side, some programmers and analysts complain that flowcharts are a waste of time, since people do not think in graphic terms. In their view, a flowchart is therefore an unnatural means of communication.

Flowcharts are often cumbersome to use and costly to produce. Because of their graphic format, flowcharts may devote more than a page of space to present what may require from a few lines to less than a half-page of equally detailed description in some other form. Manual preparation of flowcharts is slow, although detailed flow diagrams can be prepared by computer if the program to be flowcharted exists in source language form.

Flowcharts do not constitute a programming language. They are person-to-person means of communication, not person-to-computer. No translators exist for accepting programs or systems described in flowchart form.

The flow diagram variety of flowchart does not fit well with all programming languages. Although flow diagrams go well with Cobol, Fortran, Algol, PL/I, and Basic, for example, they seem ponderous or incongruent with Snobol, Comit, Lisp, or IPL-V.

Flowcharts may not highlight what is important. Each operation commonly receives as much attention in a flowchart as any other, given the level of detail at which the flowchart is prepared. Yet, intuitively, people feel that some operations are more significant than others.

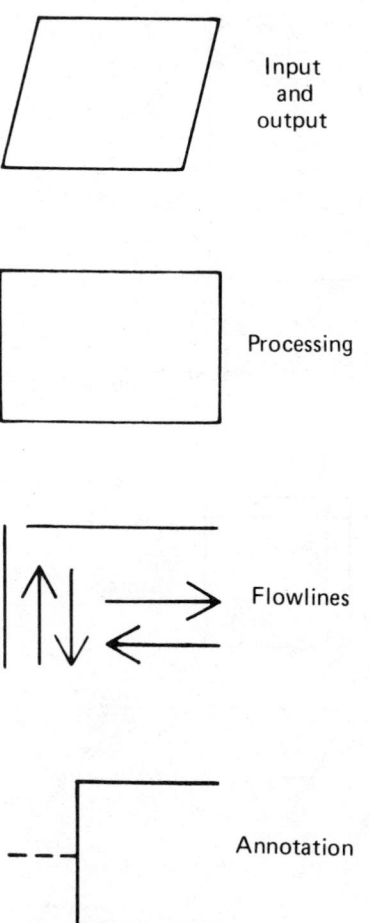

Fig. 2. Basic outlines. (From N. Chapin, *Flowcharts*, Petrocelli Books, New York, 1971.)

The flowchart does not provide any convenient, automatic way to highlight these.

Flowcharts are difficult to produce at a summary level. No consistent logical rules have yet been developed to aid the process of producing meaningful summary flowcharts at a consistent level of detail. When many operations are to be condensed and summarized into one operation, serious problems arise. What should be the summary operation? What details are to be suppressed?

Elements. Wide agreement exists on the major elements of flowcharts. They are the outlines, flow representation (sequence), and the symbols specifying the operation and identifying the data. Each interacts with and augments the work of the others, to provide the graphic presentation.

The outlines, sometimes called *symbols,* but called *boxes* in common speech, are in three groups: the basic, the specialized, and the additional. Complete flowcharts can be drawn using only the basic outlines. These outlines, as shown in Fig. 2, are a parallelogram for input or output, a rectangle for processing, and a line or lines with open arrowheads to represent the direction of flow, as commented upon later. When only the basic outlines are used, the rectangle serves for all operations except input and output. To provide explanatory data, the annotation outline (a partial rectangle attached by a dashed line) can be used, with the comment written within the rectangular part.

Specialized outlines are numerous, as shown in Fig. 3. These offer a way of visually identifying for the user of the flowchart the media used to carry data [Fig. 3(a)]; the equipment used for input, output, or storage of data [Fig. 3(b)]; and the general character of a processing operation, such as data transformation [Fig. 3(c)].

In system charts, the most commonly used of these specialized outlines are usually the document, magnetic tape, on-line storage (for data on magnetic disk, commonly), and punched card outlines. In flow diagrams, the most commonly used are the preparation, the decision, and the predefined process outlines. A predefined process is considered to be a sequence of operations not described in the flowchart but incorporated in the program, as by a call to a subroutine in a library. The manual operation outline is for representing operations done by people, such as "review data for conformance to policy." The auxiliary operation outline is for representing operations done by noncomputer machines, such as "interpret punched cards."

The additional outlines, as shown in Fig. 4, are connectors of three types, and serve to indicate that two or more sequences are to be performed simultaneously (parallel mode). The in-connector and the out-connector are distinguished by the direction of the flowlines leading to

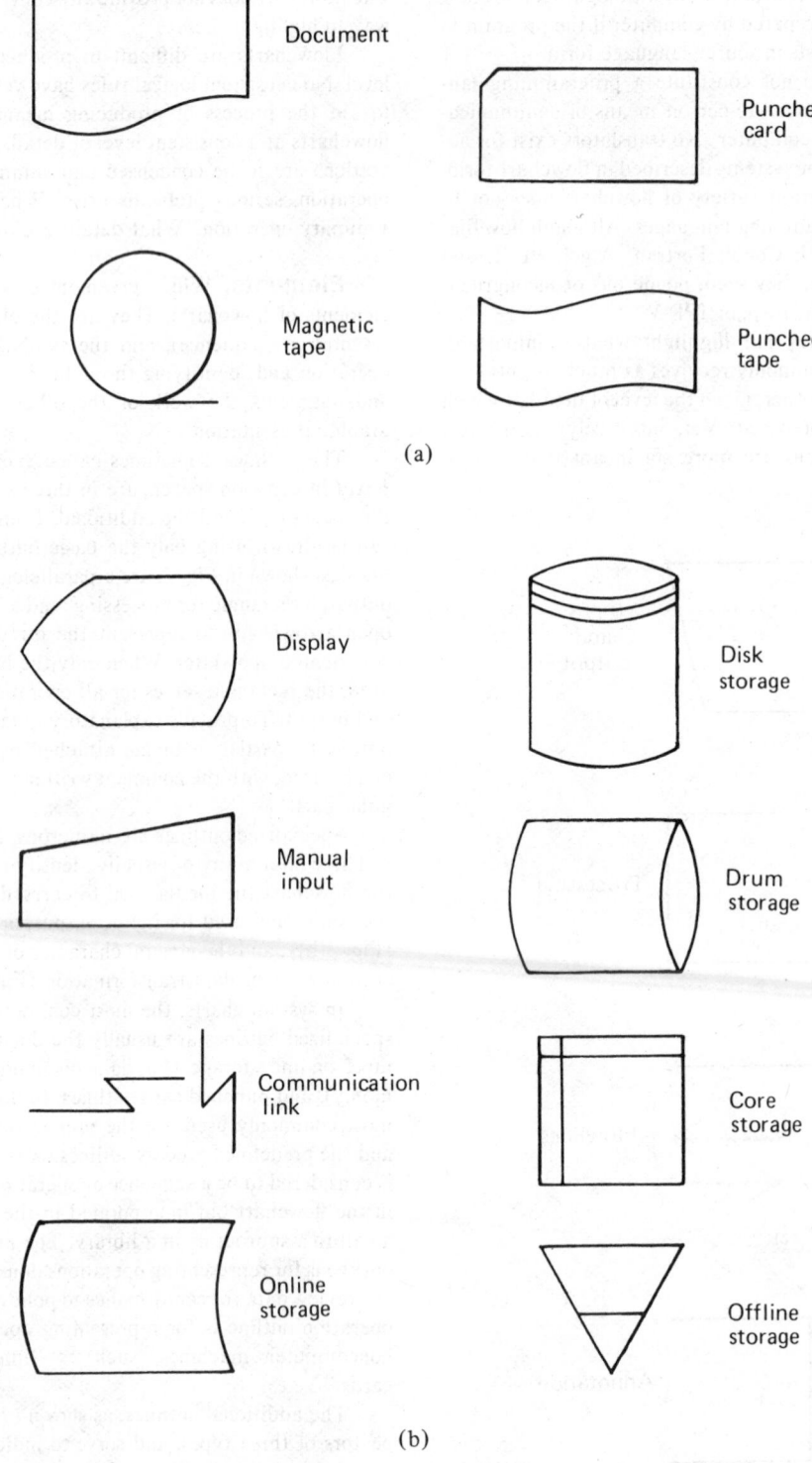

Fig. 3. Specialized oulines. (a) Media. (b) Equipment. (c) Processes. (From N. Chapin, *Flowcharts*, Petrocelli Books, New York, 1971.)

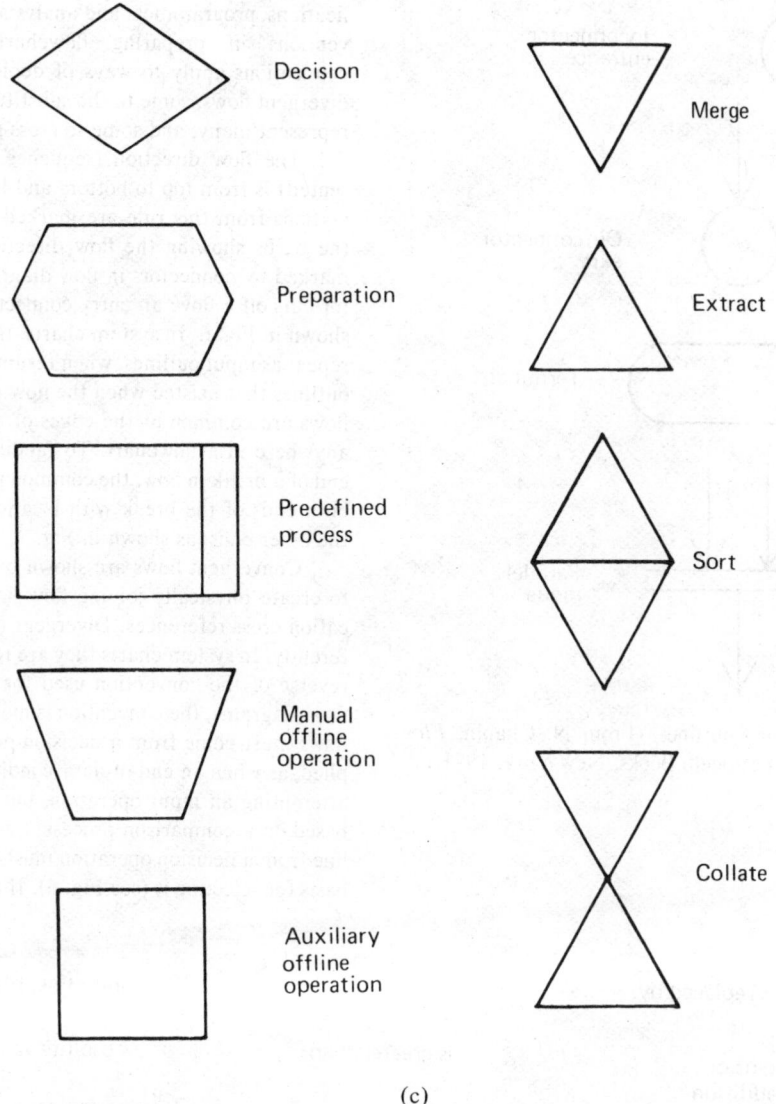

(c)

Fig. 3. (Continued)

and from them. An in-connector, or entrance connector, has a flowline leading from it, and is placed to the left or above the main line of flow or sequence. The out-connector, or exit connector, has a flowline leading into it, and is placed to the right or below the main line of flow or sequence. A terminal connector may also be used in an entrance or exit position as a marker to indicate the beginning or ending of a sequence of operations.

The wording within process outlines identifies the operation and (in flow diagrams) the data involved. The wording within the input or output outlines identifies the data and (in flow diagrams) whether the data is input or output. The wording used within and with the outlines in a flowchart has not been standardized, although the prob-

lem has been studied (ANSI, 1965). Common practice depends in major part upon the level of detail to be depicted. In summary flowcharts, English language phrases are the most common. Detailed system charts often include only the names of the inputs, outputs, and programs. Very detailed flow diagrams often use programming language instructions within the outlines; less detailed ones use symbols for operations, borrowed largely from logic and mathematics (shown in Fig. 5) or English language words.

Conventions. To preserve the graphic format and to improve the usefulness of the flowchart in conjunction with program listings and written system speci-

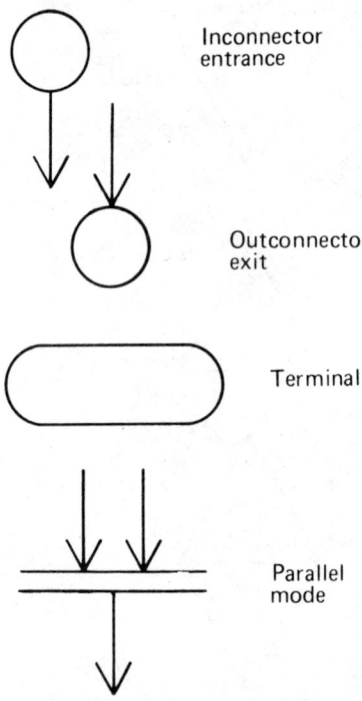

Fig. 4.   Additional outlines. (From N. Chapin, *Flowcharts*, Petrocelli Books, New York, 1971.)

fications, programmers and analysts use a number of conventions in preparing flowcharts. Some of these conventions apply to ways of depicting convergent and divergent flows, some to the substitution of one outline to represent many, and some to cross-references.

The flow direction (sequence of operations represented) is from top to bottom and left to right. Most deviations from this rule are marked by arrowheads, with the barbs showing the flow direction. Broken flows are marked by connectors in flow diagrams. An exit connector cuts off a flow; an entry connector resumes a flow, as shown in Fig. 6. In system charts, the usual practice is to repeat as input outlines, when resuming a flow, the output outlines that existed when the flow was cut off. Breaks in flows are common at the edges of pages, but may occur anywhere in a flowchart. To facilitate finding the other end of a break in flow, the common practice is to annotate both ends of the break with location cross-references to the other ends, as shown in Fig. 7.

Convergent flows are shown by entrance connectors to create physically joining flow lines, together with location cross-references. Divergent flows are handled differently. In system charts they are represented by just the reverse of the convention used for convergent flows. In flow diagrams, the convention is more complex; divergent flows must come from a decision process. It may be implied, as when an end-of-data condition is encountered in attempting an input operation, but usually it is explicit, based on a comparison process. Each multiple exit flowline from a decision operation must be identified as to the basis for selecting it (see Fig. 6). If a break in flow is also

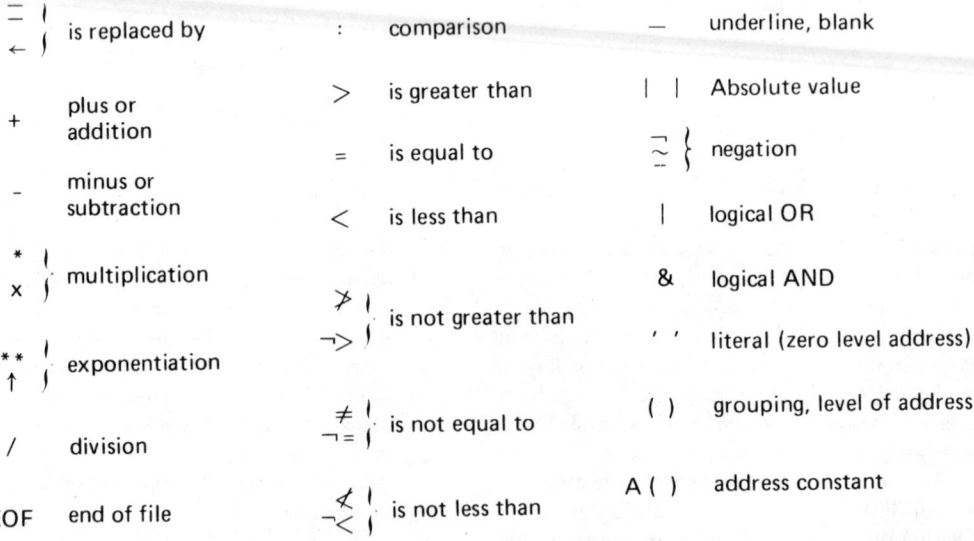

Fig. 5.   Symbols for use in flow diagrams. (From N. Chapin, *Flowcharts*, Petrocelli Books, New York, 1971.)

name the top area thus created in the outline. Then, within terminal connectors in flow diagrams or annotation outlines in system charts, this name is used to identify the full sequence of operations cited elsewhere in the flowchart. Adding location cross-references completes the substitution representation.

System Charts. The system chart variety of the flowchart identifies major sets or files of input and output data handled by the programs, people, and machines involved in a system. An example of a system chart is shown in Fig. 9. It is commonly prepared from the specialized outlines used to indicate the media or the equipment employed in the system to handle the data. Outlines for data that serve as inputs have flowlines drawn from them to a process outline. Outlines for data that are produced as outputs have flowlines drawn from the process outline to them. An outline that represents output from one process may represent input to another process.

Each process identified in a system chart has at least one input and produces at least one output. Some processes, because of their complexity, require many inputs and produce many outputs. An output that serves as an input later for the same process is usually shown twice (once on each side of the process) with a connecting flowline (see Fig. 9). In general, the structure of a system chart is of alternating layers or process outlines and input/output outlines. An input outline starts the system chart; an output outline ends the system chart.

Flow Diagrams. The flow diagram variety of the flowchart describes algorithms, usually as they are implemented in a computer program. Fig. 7 provides an example of a flow diagram for a simple statistical calculation. It is not necessary to identify the media or the equipment used for input or output because, under modern operating conditions, most of the input or output media and equipment typically can be changed from time to time without changing the program, and because computers can operate on data only within their internal storage units. Hence, the specialized media and equipment outlines find little use in flow diagrams. The basic input and output outline is normally the outline of choice.

Conventionally, a flow diagram begins with a terminal outline and ends with a terminal outline. Usually the first part of a flow diagram is concerned with initialization—operations to prepare the storage unit and the arithmetic and logic unit for the main operations.

The main operations and usually the middle part of a flow diagram involve reading in input data, performing some type of transformation action on the data, and producing some output data. Many decision or branching operations with divergent and later convergent flows are common.

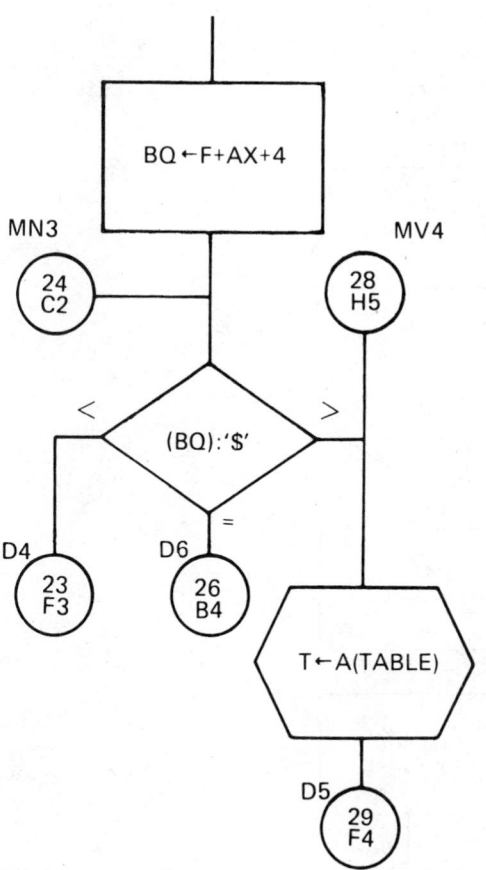

Fig. 6. Entry and exit flowlines in a flow diagram. (From N. Chapin, *Flowcharts*, Petrocelli Books, New York, 1971.)

involved, then a location cross-reference is also commonly added, as illustrated in Fig. 7.

At any point in the flowchart, the person who prepares it may add cross-references to other materials, such as system descriptions or program listings. This is usually done by writing in identifying names *(entry points* or *labels)* adjacent to a process or connector outline, as shown in Figs. 6 and 7. These names are taken from the corresponding points in the materials referenced. Additional or more extended cross-referencing can be done by using the annotation outline.

To save space in parts of flowcharts in order to provide for a more meaningful presentation of the operations, the horizontal striping convention is an aid. This allows one outline, suitably identified, to represent a sequence of outlines presented elsewhere in the flowchart, as shown in Fig. 8. Most commonly, it applies to process outlines. The person who prepares the flowchart draws a horizontal line through the outline, and identifies by a

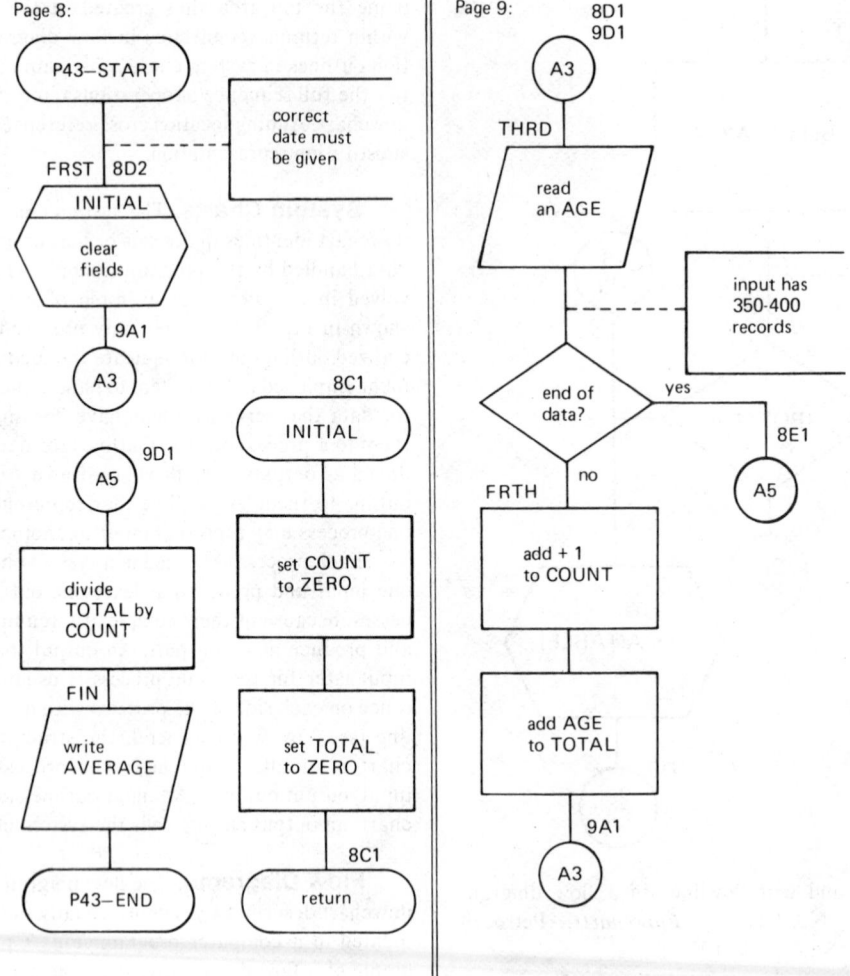

Fig. 7. Example of cross referencing in a flow diagram. (From N. Chapin, *Flowcharts*, Petrocelli Books, New York, 1971.)

The cleanup or final portion of most flow diagrams consists of completing the output data, terminating the use of the input and output equipment, and outputting any summary statistics. This structure is typically more complex than is the structure typical of the system chart, and is far less regular.

The specialized process outlines most used in flow diagrams are the decision, preparation, and predefined process outlines. The decision outline serves as the basis for selecting alternative flow paths, usually based upon comparison or test operations. The preparation outline is reserved for operations upon the program itself, such as setting the starting values of iteration controls, program switches, and the like. The role of the predefined process outline was noted previously.

In a flow diagram, cross-references are especially helpful to the user. This applies both to location cross-references within the flow diagram itself and to cross-references between the flow diagram and other descriptions or materials, such as the program listing.

Preparing and Using Flowcharts. Preparing flowcharts is usually a heuristic process of trying to set down a sequence of operations that might get the job done, given the data involved. Commonly, this is done in parts and in stages of increasing precision. Often it is done by elaborating and correcting a former flowchart, and then using it as the basis for a new flowchart. The person preparing a flowchart normally continues this process until, given the level of detail desired, the program or system data transformation has been completely described, step by step.

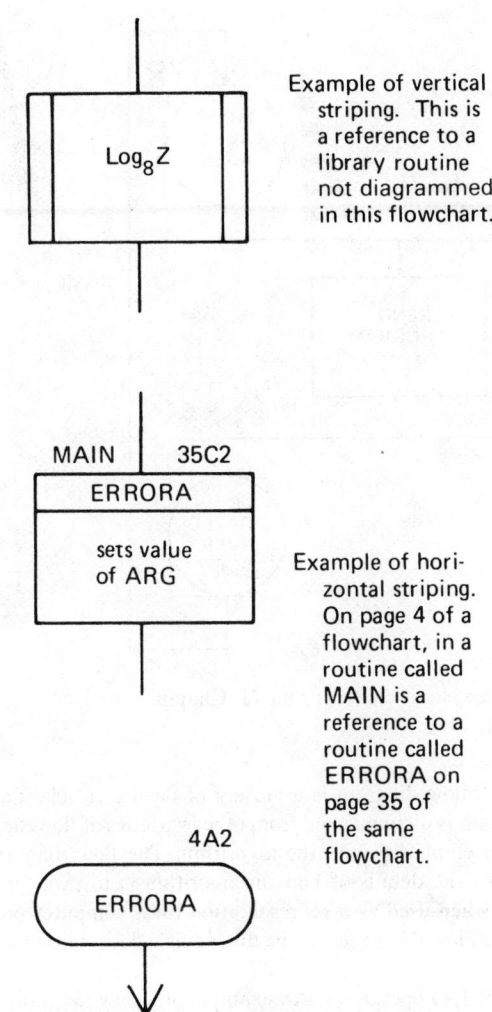

Example of vertical striping. This is a reference to a library routine not diagrammed in this flowchart.

Example of horizontal striping. On page 4 of a flowchart, in a routine called MAIN is a reference to a routine called ERRORA on page 35 of the same flowchart.

Fig. 8. Conventions for striping and references. (From N. Chapin, *Flowcharts*, Petrocelli Books, New York, 1971.)

Most people draw flowcharts initially by hand, typically roughing them out in freehand form. When more neatly prepared flowcharts are desired, plastic templates are available to add a regularity and symmetry to the outlines. Flowcharts produced as documentation after a program or system is completely implemented are typically prepared more neatly than are flowcharts produced as working documents for use by programmers and analysts in implementing programs and systems. Detailed flow diagrams can be produced from source-coded programs, whether partial or complete, by the computer.

Using flowcharts is greatly aided by taking full advantage of the graphic character of the flow representation and of the shapes of the outlines. If the user knows what to look for, the graphic features can be used to scan even a lengthy flowchart very rapidly. Basic to such a scan, of course, is first identifying the type, either system chart or flow diagram. Sometimes location cross-references and annotation will have to be read to follow a flow. Once the portion of interest has been located, the user can focus on the specific sequence shown, on the operations specified, and on the data acted upon, used in, or produced by the operations. For greater detail or for alternative descriptions, the user can follow the cross-references to related materials. In general, flowcharts are regarded as working documents upon which users freely enter comments, notations of difficulties encountered, changes made, and improvements possible in the program or system.

In the 1970s, the use of the flow diagram variety of the standard flowchart came under criticism as obstructing improvements in the structure of programs and systems (e.g., Hoare, 1975). Some new forms of flowcharts and related tools, such as Chapin charts (Chapin, 1974) and the Nassi-Shneiderman language of computation (Nassi, 1973), encourage improved structure in part via *structured flowcharts* (*see* STRUCTURED PROGRAMMING). In Europe, an attempt was started to establish a new form of flowchart as a new international standard aimed at aiding the design of programs and systems.

REFERENCES

1965. ANSI. "Graphic Symbols for Problem Definition and Analysis," *Communications of the ACM, 8, No. 6:* 363–365 (June).

1970. ANSI. *American National Standard Flowchart Symbols and Their Usage in Information Processing, X3.5-1970.* New York: American National Standards Institute.

1971. Chapin, Ned. *Flowcharts.* New York: Petrocelli.

1973. Nassi, Isaac and Shneiderman, Ben. "Flowchart Techniques for Structured Programming," *SIGPLAN Notices 8, No. 8:* 12–26 (August).

1974. Chapin, Ned. "New Format for Flowcharts," *Software Practice and Experience 4, No. 4:* 341–357 (October–December).

1975. Hoare, C. A. R. "Data Reliability," *Proceedings of the International Conference on Reliable Software.* Long Beach, CA: IEEE, pp. 528–533.

1979. Chapin, Ned. *et al.* "Full Report of the Flowchart Committee on ANS Standard X-3, 5-1970," *SIGPLAN Notices 14, No. 3:* 16–27 (March).

NED CHAPIN

FLOW DIAGRAM

For articles on related subjects *see* BLOCK DIAGRAM; DOCUMENTATION; FLOWCHART; and SYSTEM CHART.

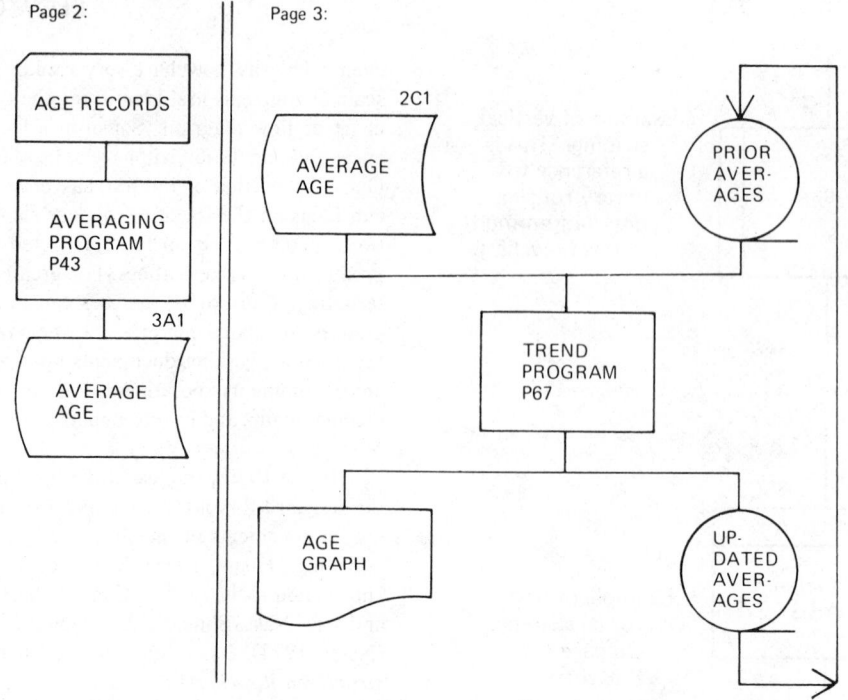

Fig. 9. Example of good practice in breaking a system chart. (From N. Chapin, *Flowchart*, Petrocelli Books, New York, 1971.)

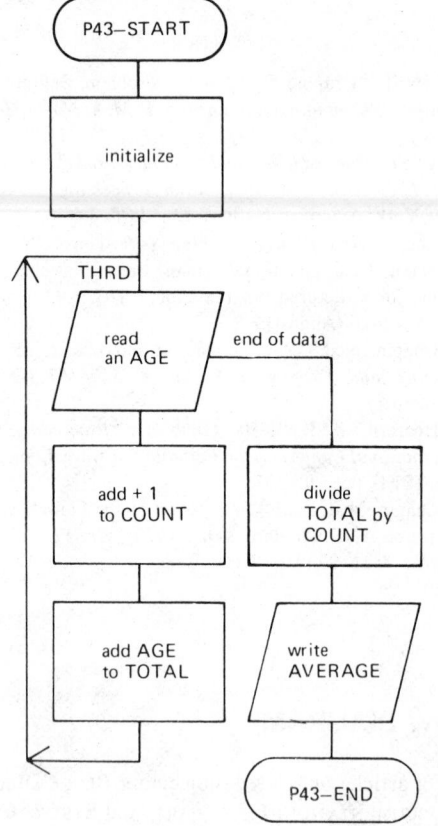

A flow diagram is a variety of flowchart. The flow diagram is distinguished from other varieties of flowchart by its emphasis upon the algorithm. The flow diagram depicts the details of how an algorithm is to transform data when used as a representation for a computer program. Flow diagrams can be distinguished from other varieties of flowchart by the relatively infrequent presentation of I/O operations. An example of a flow diagram is given in Fig. 1.

NED CHAPIN

FORMAL LANGUAGES

For articles on related subjects *see* AUTOMATA THEORY; BACKUS-NAUR FORM; CHOMSKY HIERARCHY; DECIDABILITY; GRAMMARS; LANGUAGE PROCESSORS; LANGUAGE TRANSLATION; REGULAR EXPRESSION; TURING MACHINE; and WELL-FORMED FORMULA.

Languages and Grammars. Formal languages are abstract mathematical objects used to model the syn-

Fig. 1. Example of a flow diagram for finding an average. (From Ned Chapin, *Flowcharts*, Petrocelli Books, New York, 1971.)

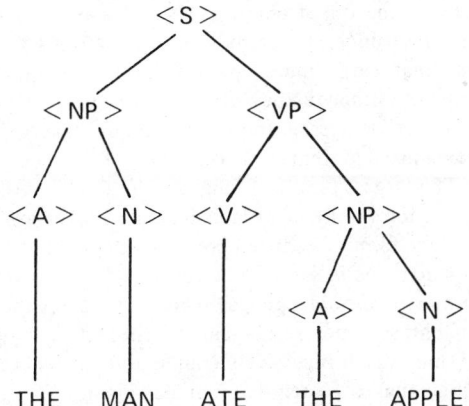

Fig. 1. Tree for parsing sentence.

The sample sentence given earlier can be parsed by the treelike diagram in Fig. 1, where $\langle S \rangle$, $\langle NP \rangle$, $\langle VP \rangle$, $\langle A \rangle$, $\langle N \rangle$, and $\langle V \rangle$ are six variables ranging over all *sentences, noun phrases, verb phrases, articles, nouns,* and *verbs,* respectively. Using the *rewriting* rules in Fig. 2, it is possible to generate our sample sentence from the variable $\langle S \rangle$. The generation proceeds as follows:

$$\langle S \rangle \Rrightarrow \langle NP \rangle \langle VP \rangle \Rrightarrow \langle A \rangle \langle N \rangle \langle VP \rangle$$
$$\Rrightarrow \langle A \rangle \langle N \rangle \langle V \rangle \langle NP \rangle \Rrightarrow \langle A \rangle \langle N \rangle \langle V \rangle \langle A \rangle \langle N \rangle$$
$$\Rrightarrow \text{THE } \langle N \rangle \langle V \rangle \langle A \rangle \langle N \rangle$$
$$\Rrightarrow \text{THE MAN } \langle V \rangle \langle A \rangle \langle N \rangle$$
$$\Rrightarrow \text{THE MAN ATE } \langle A \rangle \langle N \rangle$$
$$\Rrightarrow \text{THE MAN ATE THE } \langle N \rangle$$
$$\Rrightarrow \text{THE MAN ATE THE APPLE}$$

With these rules we can also generate various improbable but grammatically correct sentences such as THE APPLE ATE THE MAN, and with more rules we could generate more sentences. Rewriting schemes of this sort were introduced by the linguist Noam Chomsky, who called them *context-free grammars.* Chomsky observed that these grammars are not good models for the syntax of natural languages, but it was soon discovered that they do closely model the syntax of programming languages, and for this reason they have been studied in great detail.

To see a simple example of context-free rewriting rules that give rise to an infinite language, suppose that the vocabulary consists of two abstract symbols a and b, and let S be a variable. Then, using the rules $S \rightarrow aSb$ and $S \rightarrow ab$, we can generate the infinite language

$$L = \{a^n b^n \,|\, n \geq 1\} = \{ab, aabb, aaabbb, \ldots\}.$$

Rewriting rules of this type are called "context free" because they permit any occurrence of a variable within a string to be rewritten without regard to the context in which that variable occurs. By contrast, a rewriting rule like $aXab \rightarrow aYZcab$ is not context-free. It is called *context sensitive,* since it allows X to be rewritten as YZc only when X occurs in the context $s_1 a\_\_abs_2$, where s_1 and s_2 are arbitrary strings.

To describe different kinds of grammars more precisely, let us define a *phrase-structure* grammar to be a quadruple $G = (V_N, V_T, P, S)$, where

tax of programming languages or (less successfully) of natural languages such as English. For example, consider a simple English sentence, such as

THE MAN ATE THE APPLE.

Let us assume that individual English words are indecomposable objects. Then the study of English syntax attempts to answer the question: When is a string of words a grammatically correct English sentence? And when it is a sentence, how can it be parsed into its grammatical components?

To model this situation, we let V be a finite set of symbols, called a *vocabulary.* In the previous example, V contains the four indecomposable words (in this context, called *symbols* or *letters*): APPLE, ATE, MAN, THE. More generally, V might contain all English words and punctuation marks. Let V^* denote all finite-length strings of symbols from V. (It is mathematically convenient to include in V^* the *empty string* of length zero.) Then a *formal language* L is simply a set of strings from V^*. For example, if V^* is the set of all finite sequences of English words, then L could be the subset of V^* consisting of all grammatically correct sentences. Although V is always finite, in most cases of interest L will be infinite, and we will wish to have a finitely specified way of generating, or recognizing, or parsing the strings in L.

$$
\begin{aligned}
\langle S \rangle &\rightarrow \langle NP \rangle \langle VP \rangle \\
\langle NP \rangle &\rightarrow \langle A \rangle \langle N \rangle \\
\langle VP \rangle &\rightarrow \langle V \rangle \langle NP \rangle \\
\langle A \rangle &\rightarrow \text{THE} \\
\langle V \rangle &\rightarrow \text{ATE} \\
\langle N \rangle &\rightarrow \text{MAN} \\
\langle N \rangle &\rightarrow \text{APPLE}
\end{aligned}
$$

Fig. 2. Rewriting rules.

1. V_N is a finite vocabulary of nonterminal symbols or variables.
2. V_T is a finite vocabulary of terminal symbols.
3. P is a finite set of rewriting rules (also called *productions*) of the form $\alpha \rightarrow \beta$, where α is a nonempty string of variables and β is an arbitrary string of variables and terminal symbols.

4. S is a particular variable, called the *start variable*.

For all strings s_1 and s_2 we may write $s_1 \alpha s_2 \rightarrow s_1 \beta s_2$ if $\alpha \rightarrow \beta$ is a production of the grammar G. Then the language generated by G is the set of all strings t of *terminal symbols* such that

$$S \Rrightarrow s_1 \Rrightarrow s_2 \Rrightarrow \cdots \Rrightarrow s_n \Rrightarrow t$$

for some choice of intermediate strings $s_1, s_2, \ldots s_n$. The intermediate strings may consist of both variables and terminal symbols.

Let α, α_1, and α_2 denote arbitrary strings of variables and terminal symbols, and let A and B denote variables. If the productions in G have the specialized form $\alpha_1 A \alpha_2 \rightarrow \alpha_1 \beta \alpha_2$, where β represents any nonempty string, then G is a *context-sensitive* grammar. (Frequently, a grammar is called context-sensitive if the productions merely have the form $\alpha \rightarrow \beta$, with β at least as long as α. These two definitions are in fact equivalent in the sense that the same collection of languages is generated.) If the productions in the grammar G have the form $A \rightarrow \alpha$, then G is context-free. If the productions have the form $A \rightarrow w_1 B$ or $A \rightarrow w_2$, where w_1 and w_2 are strings of terminal symbols, then G is right-linear. A language is called a "phrase-structure" language, or a "context-sensitive," "context-free," or "right-linear" language, if it can be generated by a phrase-structure grammar, or a context-sensitive, context-free, or right-linear grammar, respectively.

The four types of grammars (phrase-structure, context-sensitive, context-free, and right-linear) are also known as type 0, type 1, type 2, and type 3 grammars, respectively. They form a grammatical hierarchy, called the *Chomsky hierarchy*. Among the four corresponding families of languages, the smallest family, the right-linear languages, is important because it turns out to consist precisely of those languages that can be recognized by finite-state automata. These languages arise in many different contexts, and they have the advantage of being very easy to parse.

The next family in the hierarchy, the family of context-free languages, is important because context-free languages are good approximations to the syntax of programming languages, even though this syntax is usually a little too complicated to be completely captured by context-free grammars. Context-sensitive languages are powerful enough to encompass any complications in syntax that may have been missed by the context-free model, but they are so general that they are difficult to work with. As a result, they have been studied less than the other models, and various attempts have been made to add to the power of context-free grammars without re-sorting to the full strength of context-sensitive productions. These efforts have produced various kinds of grammars that are more powerful than context-free grammars, although they are unfortunately more complicated as well: programmed grammars, macro grammars, indexed grammars, and others.

The largest family of languages in the Chomsky hierarchy, the family of phrase-structure languages, is an important family because it represents the largest class with which one is likely to be concerned when modeling natural or artificial languages. This is so because the family of phrase-structure languages is in fact the same as the family of all recursively enumerable languages, i.e., of all languages L such that membership of a string w in L can be verified by some algorithm (or, more precisely, by some Turing machine).

Languages and Equations. We have noted that context-free languages are good approximations to the syntax of many programming languages. Consider the following very simple example of syntax specifications in *Backus-Naur form*, or *BNF*:

$$\langle \text{digit} \rangle ::= 0 \mid 1 \mid 2 \mid 3 \mid 4 \mid 5 \mid 6 \mid 7 \mid 8 \mid 9$$
$$\langle \text{unsigned integer} \rangle ::= \langle \text{digit} \rangle \mid \langle \text{unsigned integer} \rangle \langle \text{digit} \rangle$$

This means that $\langle \text{digit} \rangle$ and $\langle \text{unsigned integer} \rangle$ are the smallest sets of strings satisfying the following conditions: 0, 1, . . . , 9 are digits (i.e., they are in the set $\langle \text{digit} \rangle$); any digit is an unsigned integer; and any unsigned integer followed by a digit is an unsigned integer. Rewriting these equations in a more algebraic form, we obtain:

$$D = \text{“0”} + \text{“1”} + \cdots + \text{“9”}$$
$$U = D + U \cdot D$$

Consider these as abstract equations. What is their meaning? The unknowns U and D are variables whose values are languages; $X + Y$ denotes the union of the languages X and Y; $X \cdot Y$ denotes the product of the languages X and Y, obtained by concatenating the strings in X with those in Y: $X \cdot Y = \{xy \mid x \epsilon X, y \epsilon Y\}$; and "0," "1," etc., are constants denoting the languages consisting of just the single symbol 0, 1, etc. In general, the equations corresponding to BNF syntax descriptions can be more complicated than in our example. A typical equation might have the form

$$A = abBAAaAb + BaC + ba.$$

(The letters a and b are terminal symbols; A, B, and C are variables; and we have omitted the dot in products.) The operations $+$ and $\cdot$ are roughly analogous to addition and multiplication of numbers; only $\cdot$ is not commutative. (If X and Y are languages, $X \cdot Y$ is not generally the same as $Y \cdot X$.) If the product of languages were commutative, then we could write the term $ab\text{-}BAAaAb$ as $aabbA^3B$. This would be similar to a fourth-degree term in a polynomial expression, except that the variables range over languages rather than numbers and the coefficient $aabb$ is a string of symbols instead of a number. Since the product of languages is not commutative, we cannot rearrange terms in this way, but we can still regard these equations as polynomial equations in noncommuting variables. In general, the right-hand side of each equation will be a finite sum of terms, and each term will be a string of variables and terminal symbols. A set of such equations always has a unique smallest solution, so it always makes sense to speak of the "smallest sets of strings" U and D satisfying equations like those in our original example. The languages definable in this way by polynomial equations turn out to be precisely the context-free languages.

As a simple example, the language $\{a^n b^n \mid n \geq 1\}$ can be specified either as the language generated by the context-free productions $S \to aSb$ and $S \to ab$ or as the smallest solution of the equation $S = aSb + ab$. Incidentally, note that this equation is a first-degree or "linear" equation, since each summand contains at most one occurrence of a variable. Languages defined by such equations are called "linear" context-free languages. They can also be characterized as the languages generated by linear context-free grammars; i.e., by context-free grammars having productions of the form $A \to \alpha$, where the string α contains at most one occurrence of a variable. It should now be clear why right-linear grammars are so named.

In view of the preceding discussion, any programming language whose syntax can be specified in BNF is context-free. Generally, most but not all of the syntax of a programming language can be specified in BNF. So languages such as Pascal and Fortran are not quite context-free, but they are close to being so, and context-free languages are useful approximations to their syntax.

Languages and Automata. The four families of languages in the Chomsky hierarchy can be obtained from automata as well as from grammars. (*See* AUTOMATA THEORY.) The phrase-structure languages are the languages accepted by Turing machines; the context-sensitive languages are the languages accepted by linear-bounded automata or *lba's;* the context-free languages are the languages accepted by pushdown automata; and the right-linear languages are the languages accepted by finite-state automata. For this reason, right-linear languages are sometimes called *finite-state* languages. Usually, however, right-linear languages are known as regular languages or regular sets. This terminology comes from Kleene's theorem, which states that a language is a finite-state language if and only if it can be represented by a *regular* expression. A regular expression is an expression that can be built up from individual strings by using the three operations $+$, $\cdot$, and $*$. The operations $+$ and $\cdot$ are the operations of union and product introduced earlier. (The symbol U is sometimes used instead of $+$, and the $\cdot$ may be omitted.) The operation $*$ is called the *Kleene closure* operation. If L is any set of strings, then $L*$ is defined to be the set of all strings that can be formed by concatenating together sequences of strings from $L : L* = \{s_1 s_2 \cdots s_n \mid n \geq 0, \text{each } s_i \in L\}$. (By convention, the empty string is always in $L*$) For example, $(a + b)* \cdot aaa \cdot (a + b)*$ is a regular expression representing the set of all strings of a's and b's containing at least three consecutive a's.

Let us consider the relation between context-free languages and pushdown automata a little more closely. A pushdown automaton is a non-deterministic device having a memory consisting of a finite-state control and a pushdown stack. It receives its input one symbol at a time on request. Every context-free language L is the set of input strings accepted by some pushdown automaton P. In fact, we can always find a pushdown automaton P for L that operates in real time; i.e., one that uses up one input letter on every move. This means that P recognizes strings in L very quickly—in fact, in an amount of time proportional to the length of the input string. The catch is that P is a nondeterministic device. It is credited with accepting an input string w if there is *any* sequence of choices of moves (i.e., any sequence of "guesses") it can make while processing w that will lead it to an accepting mode, even though there may be other choices which do not lead to an accepting mode. But if we want to simulate P in the real world, we would systematically have to test every sequence of choices that P could make.

Since P might have several choices available to it on each move, this simulation could take exponentially more time than P does. This might suggest that the task of parsing a context-free language can be prohibitively time consuming, but in fact it is not. General-purpose, context-free, parsing algorithms can be designed to require only time n^3, where n is the length of the input. One of the most popular such algorithms is Earley's algorithm. It takes time n^3 in the worst case, but for many context-free grammars it takes only a linear amount of time. The n^3 bound for an all-purpose, context-free parser can be improved slightly, but it is not yet known how much improvement is possible.

A nondeterministic pushdown automaton is a theoretical construct that is time consuming to simulate in the real world. So, in searching for classes of context-free languages that are easy to parse, it is reasonable to consider *deterministic* context-free languages—those languages that can be recognized by a deterministic pushdown automaton. As one might expect, all deterministic context-free languages can be parsed rapidly; in fact, in a linear amount of time. But not all context-free languages are deterministic. For example, the set of all binary strings (strings of 0's and 1's) which are palindromes is context-free but not deterministic because a pushdown automaton for this language must of necessity operate something like this: Store the first half of the input string on the stack, *guess* when half the input has been read, and use the stack to verify that the second half of the input agrees symbol by symbol, in reverse order, with the first half.

So, nondeterministic pushdown acceptors are more powerful than deterministic ones. Are the corresponding statements true for the other kinds of automata used to characterize the families of languages in the Chomsky hierarchy? For finite-state automata and for Turing machines, the answer is no. It is easy to show that the nondeterministic versions of these devices are no more powerful than the deterministic versions. In other words, the ability to make guesses may enable these devices to do their jobs more quickly, but it will not let them do anything that they could not have done without guessing. But for linear-bounded automata, it is still not known whether the nondeterministic version (which corresponds to the context-sensitive languages) is more powerful than the deterministic version.

This question, called the *lba* problem, can be recast in the following form: Can a Turing machine that performs a computation with the aid of guessing (i.e., of nondeterminism), using just a linear amount of storage space, always be simulated by a comparably efficient Turing machine that does not need to guess? The analogous question for Turing machines that use a polynomially-bounded amount of computation time rather than a linear amount of storage space is the very important P = NP problem (*see* COMPUTATIONAL COMPLEXITY; NP-COMPLETE PROBLEMS). In both cases, the answer is thought to be no, but such questions are notoriously difficult and have so far resisted all efforts at solution.

REFERENCES

1966. Ginsburg, S. *The Mathematical Theory of Context-Free Languages.* New York: McGraw-Hill.

1969. Hopcroft, J. E. and Ullman, J. D. *Formal Languages and Their Relation to Automata.* Reading, MA: Addison-Wesley.

1972. Aho, A. V. and Ulmann, J. D. *The Theory of Parsing, Translation and Compiling.* Englewood Cliffs, NJ: Prentice-Hall.

1972. Kain, R. Y. *Automata Theory: Machines and Languages.* New York: McGraw-Hill.

1973. Salomaa, A. *Formal Languages.* New York: Academic Press.

1978. Harrison, M. A. *Introduction to Formal Language Theory.* Reading, MA: Addison-Wesley.

J. GOLDSTINE

FORTRAN. *See* PROCEDURE-ORIENTED LANGUAGES: Survey of.

FRONT-END PROCESSORS

For articles on related subjects *see* CHANNEL; COMMUNICATIONS AND COMPUTERS; COMMUNICATION CONTROL UNIT; HOST SYSTEM; INTERRUPT; MODEM; MULTIPLEXING; and PROCESSING MODES.

A front-end processor is a small, limited capability, digital computer that is programmed to replace the hardwired input and output functions of a central computing system (e.g., for the control of remote terminals in a time-sharing system). The front-end processor thereby permits the host computer to perform its primary functions with little regard for the slower input/output activities associated with large-scale multiprogrammed or time-shared computing systems.

In addition to receiving and transmitting all data passing through a computing system, front-end processors may also support a wide variety of functions, such as:

1. *Data and/or format conversion*—the conversion of one or more incoming data codes and formats to that of the host system.
2. *Polling*—the determination by a front-end processor of a terminal's readiness to send or receive data.
3. *Assembly of characters and messages*—the assembly and disassembly of all data, which may be input at varying line speeds and in synchronous or asynchronous formats, to insure that the host system receives only complete messages.
4. *Error control and editing*—the detection and possible correction of transmission errors as well as corrections initiated at the terminals, prior to reception by the host system.
5. *Fail-soft functions*—the ability of the front-end processor to keep parts of the system operating (such as terminals) when a major element of the host system has failed.
6. *Queueing*—placing incoming messages in transmission order for processing by the host system, or in some cases queueing messages on auxiliary storage devices (*spooling*).
7. *Message switching*—a function of front-end pro-

cessors that service more than one central processing unit.

8. *Direct response*—the front-end processor may have the ability to respond to simple inquiries directly without contact with the host system.

The basic components of a typical front-end processor system are:

1. *Processor*—a stored program digital computer that has main memory which may vary in size from several hundred words to many thousand words, depending on the complexities of the specific application. Two important qualities required of a front-end processor are good facilities for bit manipulation and interrupt handling. The processor may or may not have its own on-line peripheral devices depending on the particular application.

2. *Central processor interface*—the hardware interface that allows the front-end processor to connect directly to the input/output channel of the host system. The host system is then able to communicate with the front-end processor as if it were a standard peripheral device controller.

3. *Communication multiplexer*—a device with programmable or hard-wired logic which produces logically independent data channels into the front-end processor's main memory from each transmission line serviced. The coordination of the data flow between the multiplexer, and processor is handled by the front-end processor's interrupt system.

4. *Line interface units*—the hardware devices that link the communication multiplexer with the modems that terminate each of the communication lines.

5. *Software*—the programs that integrate the functions of the various hardware components of the front-end processor. Included in the software package are such functions as terminal, line and message control, system interface procedures, and whatever other functions are required by a particular installation.

The front-end processor can be a powerful and economical means of relieving a central processor of its time-consuming overhead activities by placing these activities under the control of an independent and parallel processing unit. Fig. 1 shows such a unit, the Microdata 1600.

A. I. KARSHMER

Fig. 1. A Microdata 1600 in use as a front-end processor to a Univac 1100/80 at the State University of New York at Albany.

FUNCTIONAL PROGRAMMING

For articles on related subjects *see* LAMBDA CALCULUS; LIST PROCESSING LANGUAGES; PROCEDURE-ORIENTED LANGUAGES; and RECURSION.

Functional programming, sometimes also called *applicative programming,* is a style of programming that uses function application as the *only* control structure. Rather than conditional statements, one uses conditional expressions to yield alternative results; rather than an assignment statement, one uses binding of parameter to argument to place a name on a value; rather than explicit sequencing or looping of control flow, one uses patterns of nested function invocations to direct the generation of an answer.

There are various approaches to a pure applicative style. Some are restricted to functions that can only receive and return elementary data objects, respectively, as arguments and as results. Examples of this class include pure expressions in Iverson's APL (allowing its infamous "one-liners") and Backus' FP. APL is rich in primitive operators and naming conventions; FP is quite spartan in both respects.

Others allow functions themselves to be data objects and to be passed throughout the system. Examples include very pure versions of John McCarthy's Lisp (Henderson, 1980) and Backus' Formal Functional Programming (FFP). This category is far closer to the theoretical foundations of functional programming, since the domain of data objects includes the very function a user desires; all that is needed is to identify it.

The lambda calculus is one such theoretical scheme that ties functional programming to several other topics in computer science. It forms the foundation for pure Lisp, for much work in proving program correctness, and for the *denotational semantics* work by Dana Scott and Christopher Strachey; under their approach a program *must* be expressible as a function, since the only way the program takes on meaning is through the mathematical concept of a function's fixed points (Stoy, 1977).

For this reason, Lisp is chosen as the first language for an example here. The description of Lisp and the DIF example in the article on LIST PROCESSING LANGUAGES are useful starting points for understanding this code, especially CAR and CDR. Consider then the Fortran example in Figs. 1 and 3 in PROCEDURE-ORIENTED LANGUAGES. That program reads a list of triples and returns a list of pairs; a triple contains the coefficients of a quadratic equation and the pair is its computed roots.

Using a Lisp notation akin to lambda calculus, we would define

```
SOLVEQUAD = (LAMBDA (LISTOF3S) (COND
        ((NULL LISTOF3S) () )
        (T    (CONS (QUAD (CAR LISTOF3S))
                (SOLVEQUAD (CDR LISTOF3S)) )) )));
```

If the list of triples is empty, then so is the answer. Otherwise, build up a new list whose first element is the roots of the first triple, and whose remainder solves the remaining triples.

```
NULL = (LAMBDA (LIS) (EQ () LIS));
```

Predicate which is true when its argument equals the empty list.

```
QUAD = (LAMBDA (TRIPLE)
        (ROOTS (A TRIPLE) (B TRIPLE) (C TRIPLE)));
```

Applies ROOTS to the three elements of a triple.

```
A = (LAMBDA (X) (CAR X));
B = (LAMBDA (X) (CAR (CDR X)));
```

```
C = (LAMBDA (X) (CAR (CDR (CDR X))));
```

By default, A, B, and C will be functions that return, respectively, the first, second, and third elements of a list.

```
ROOTS = (LAMBDA (A B C)
        (TWORTS (MINUS B)
          (SQRT (DIFFERENCE
              (PRODUCT B B)
              (PRODUCT 4 A C)))
        (SUM A A)));
```

Here, A, B, and C are local parameters. From them, three terms are assembled and passed to TWORTS, which computes the two roots.

```
TWORTS = (LAMBDA (TERM1 TERM2 DENOMINATOR)
  (CONS (QUOTIENT (SUM TERM1 TERM2) DENOMINATOR)
  (CONS (QUOTIENT (DIFFERENCE TERM1 TERM2)
                        DENOMINATOR)
    () ))).
```

Forms a list of the two roots.

The arithmetic functions SUM, DIFFERENCE, PRODUCT, QUOTIENT, MINUS, and SQRT are primitive and have their obvious meaning. A similar solution, an APL expression, is more concise but uses the far richer primitives of that language.

```
∇ Q ← SOLVEQUAD M
Q ← 1 2 1 1 ⌽ ((−M[;2]) ∘ . + 1 ¯1 ∘ . x
      ((M[;2]*2) − 4 x M[;1] x M[;3]) *.5)
              ∘ . ÷ 2 x M[;1]
∇
```

Declare SOLVEQUAD as a function of one argument on an $n \times 3$ array. M[;i] extracts the ith column of M as a vector—either all values of A, of B, or of C. The operator $\circ . \otimes$ is an outer product in which $\otimes$ is applied pairwise to all components of each operand for any dyadic operator $\otimes$; in this example $\circ.+$, $\circ.\times$, and $\circ.\div$ are used, each operating on a vector and an array of dimension d, yielding an array of dimension $d + 1$. One may identify the outer products on the vectors composed of all values, respectively, of $-b$, of $(b^2 - 4ac)^{0.5}$, and of $2a$. The two-element vector $(+1 - 1)$ is used with an outer product to effect the alternative sum or difference of TWORTS, above. The apparent, intermediate result is a four-dimensional $n \times 2 \times n \times n$ matrix of which only one diagonal plane, that with equal first, third, and fourth indices, selected by the prefixed 1 2 1 1, is the desired answer.

In Backus' FP, the same solution appears as follows.

Def SOLVEQUAD $\equiv \propto$ QUAD

Def QUAD $\equiv$ TWORTS $\circ$ [$- \circ$ [$\overline{0}$,2] ,
      $\sqrt{} \circ - \circ$ [x$\circ$ [2,2], x$\circ$ [$\overline{4}$,x$\circ$ [1,3]] , $+ \circ$ [1,1]]

Def TWORTS $\equiv$ [$\div \circ$ [$+ \circ$ [1,2] , 3] ,
                         $\div \circ$ [$- \circ$ [1,2] , 3]]

Although FP can express SOLVEQUAD in one line, merely by expanding QUAD and TWORTS in place, these names are used here to mimic the Lisp code. These two have the same functionality here as they have there. The functional α applies QUAD to all triples in the input vector. Here 2 and $\overline{2}$ are both functions; the former returns the second item in its vector argument, and the latter is a constant function that always returns two. Composition is denoted $\circ$ and parallel application is directed by brackets. Thus, x$\circ$ [2,2] is a function that squares the second element in its argument, and x$\circ$ [$\overline{4}$, x$\circ$ [1,3]] computes the product of four, the first, and the third element in its vector argument. Thus, QUAD is a composition of TWORTS and a function which generates a triple of terms $-b$ ($= 0 - b$), $\sqrt{b^2 - 4ac}$, $2a$ ($= a + a$) and TWORTS computes the two roots extracting the terms with 1, 2, 3.

One important operational perspective is necessary to reconcile the equivalence between these solutions and the iterative Fortran code for the quadratic equation problem. It is possible to represent a data structure—in this case, the list of pairs or matrix of results—without it being explicitly in main memory. Landin (Burge, 1975) specified a *stream* to be a (perhaps infinite) list of which only the first element need be explicit. The rest of the list becomes explicit only as it is accessed. Each result of the functions above may be perceived as a stream, which will only become explicit *as* it is traversed. A typical use of such a stream is to print it, and the traversal during printing forces more pairs to be generated. Moreover, since an already-printed pair is immediately abandoned by such a traversal, its explicit representation may be erased after it is printed. Under that operational philosophy, only one pair at a time is generated, made explicit, printed, and

abandoned. In Lisp or FP the traversal can be done without using a recursion stack; no stacking need be done in this example. In APL, the large intermediate result is not necessarily generated—only the diagonal plane, a pair at a time.

The analogs of input values to a program are files passed as multiple arguments to a function; the analog of output is the (multiple) results returned from such an application. Just as each output file is implemented as a stream, so also may the input files be streams (above, a stream of triples) so that only a finite prefix of (perhaps infinite) input need be an explicit internal structure, and much of that may have already been abandoned. Thus, the code above can run using constant space and time proportional to the length of the input file—just as the original Fortran code does.

The preceding example was selected for comparison with a procedure-oriented language. It is a poor example for applicative programming because the code generates a very simple stream of involved but algebraically trivial results. A problem that better exhibits the facility of functional programming and its use of *recursion* is testing the equality of two arbitrarily complex structures. Within the constraints of the data domain of each language, the solutions follow.

In Lisp:

```
EQUALS = (LAMBDA (X Y) (COND
           ((ATOM X) (EQ X Y))
           ((ATOM Y) NIL)
           ((EQUALS (CAR X) (CAR Y))
                 (EQUALS (CDR X) (CDR Y)) )
           (T NIL));
```

If the first argument is atomic, see if it *eq*uals the second in a primitive sense; otherwise, if the second argument is atomic, then equality fails. (The empty list, for some strange reason, is atomic in Lisp and so, failure of both ATOM X and ATOM Y assures that the arguments of EQUALS are non-null.) Since the only remaining possibility is that both are non-empty lists, equality of their first elements implies that the structures will be equal exactly if their remainders are, using the EQUALS predicate recursively.

In APL (where X and Y are formal parameters), the solution is:

∇ E $\leftarrow$ X EQUALS Y
E $\leftarrow$ ((, X) $\wedge$. $=$ (ρ, X) $\uparrow$, Y) $\wedge$
        ((ρX) $\wedge$. $=$ ($\rho\rho$X) $\uparrow$ ρY) $\wedge$ (($\rho\rho$X) $= \rho\rho$Y)
∇

APL has only homogeneous arrays as data types. Thus equality is determined if the content of the two arrays is equal, and if their shapes are the same, and if they have the same dimension. Because APL evaluates all conjuncts and because operands must be conformable, the "simpler" expression

$$E \leftarrow (,X = ,Y) \wedge (\rho X = \rho Y) \wedge (\rho\rho X = \rho\rho Y)$$

cannot be used. Parsing of the more complicated expression requires APL's conventions on binary operators: All are of uniform precedence and associate to the right.

In FP (without formal parameters we have):

Def equals $\equiv$ atom∘1 → eq ;
         atom∘2 → $\overline{0}$;
         null∘1 → null∘2 ;
         null∘2 → $\overline{0}$;
         equals∘[1∘1, 1∘2] →
                equals∘[tl∘1, tl∘2] ;
         0.

This FP code reads very much the same as the Lisp code. The exception is that empty vectors must be tested explicitly, once we know that the two elements of the argument vector are both non-atomic.

The primitives l and tl are analogous to CAR and CDR of Lisp.

Functional programming offers much promise for machine architectures beyond the model used by typical procedure-oriented languages. Since results are defined without sequential imperatives, much in the program can be adapted to use available parallelism (e.g., multiple or pipelined processors) without rewriting it. Moreover, much of the material on *program verification* (*q.v.*) has a functional foundation, so this carries over quite well. Finally, the natural modularity of function definitions allows for facile, piecewise testing and maintenance of large programs.

REFERENCES

1975. Burge, W. H. *Recursive Programming Techniques*. Reading, MA: Addison-Wesley.

1977. Stoy, J. *Denotational Semantics*. Cambridge, MA: M.I.T. Press.

1977, 1978, 1980. ACM Turing Lectures: Scott, D. *Comm. ACM 20*, *No. 9*: 634–641; Backus, J. *Comm. ACM 21*, *No. 8*: 613–641; and Iverson, K. *Comm. ACM 23*, *No. 8*: 444–465.

1980. Henderson, P. *Functional Programming, Application and Implementation*. Englewood Cliffs, NJ: Prentice-Hall.

1982. Darlington, J., Henderson, P. and Turner, D. (Eds.). *Functional Programming and Its Applications*. Cambridge, England: Cambridge University Press.

D. S. WISE

G

GAMES, COMPUTER. *See* COMPUTER GAMES.

GAMES ON COMPUTERS

For articles on related subjects *see* ARTIFICIAL IN-
TELLIGENCE; COMPUTER CHESS; COMPUTER GAMES;
HEURISTICS; PERSONAL COMPUTING; and SYMBOL
MANIPULATION.

When the earliest digital computers were built, scientists immediately became fascinated with the possibility of having them play such games as chess, checkers,
and tic-tac-toe. Although this sort of activity proved to be
a great deal of fun, the scientists were not just playing
around; as it turns out, there are several good reasons to
study game playing by computers.

The first reason relates to the popular conception of
computers as "giant brains." Even the earliest digital
computers could do arithmetic and make decisions at a
rate thousands of times faster than humans could. Thus,
it was felt that computers could be set up to perform intelligent activities such as to translate French to English,
recognize sloppy handwriting, and play chess. At the
same time, it was realized that, if computers could not
perform these tasks, then they could not be considered
intelligent by human standards. A new scientific discipline arose from these considerations and became known
as *artificial intelligence.*

A second reason involves the understanding by humans of their own intelligence. It is conjectured that computer mechanisms for game playing will bear a resemblance to human thought processes. If this is true, then
game-playing computers can help us understand how
human minds work.

Another reason for studying games is that they are
well-defined activities. Most games use very simple
equipment and have a simple set of rules that must be
followed. Usually, the ultimate goal (winning) can be
very simply defined. Thus, a computer can be easily set
up to know the rules of any board game or card game.
This allows the computer scientists to devote more effort
to the problem of getting the computer to play an intelligent game.

There is also a practical payoff from computer
game-playing studies. Specific techniques developed in
programming a computer to play games have been applied to other more practical problems. To cite a few,
methods of search, which are used to consider alternative
moves in chess, have been adapted to find the correct path
through a switching network or the correct sequence of
steps for an assembly line. Learning methods developed
for a checker-playing program have been used to recognize elementary parts of spoken speech. It is felt that the
mechanisms of intelligence are general purpose, and
therefore the borrowing of techniques from one application to another will continue in the field of artificial
intelligence.

Basic Techniques. The fundamental reason for
the ability of computers to play a variety of games is that
computers have the ability to represent arbitrary situations and processes through the use of symbols and logic
operations. For example, one can set up a chess position

 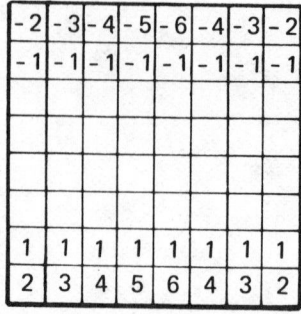 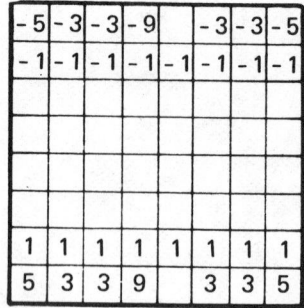

Fig. 1. Computer representation of a chess position. In the second array, numbers are used to represent the various pieces. The third array represents the values of the pieces for use by the computer in evaluating trades.

inside a computer by means of an 8 by 8 array of integers, and tentative moves can be made by computer instructions that change the positions of the numbers in the array (Fig. 1). This capability is extremely general. That is, the symbols could represent checker pieces, or with a slight rearrangement, they could be playing cards for poker or bridge.

Fig. 1 also shows the representation of derived information. The values of the pieces are stored in another 8 by 8 array for use by the computer. In effect, they are part of the computer's "knowledge" of the values of chess pieces. (The king may be considered to have an infinitely large value.)

Since symbols can be used to represent the objects of a particular game, computer instructions can be written by a programmer to specify the procedures for playing the game according to the rules and also for playing the game according to a strategy. In order for a set of procedures to be programmable, it is usually sufficient that they be defined in enough detail so that they can be translated into a computer language such as Fortran. For the purposes of this exposition, several game playing algorithms will be stated using English words in place of computer language. The game of tic-tac-toe, for example, can be played perfectly by the following algorithm, in which the word "row" refers to a row, column, or diagonal.

ALGORITHM A (THE COMPUTER PLAYS X)

A1. Perform the first applicable step which follows.

A2. Search for two X's in a row. If found, then make three X's in a row.

A3. Search for two O's in a row. If found, then block them with an X.

A4. Search for two rows that intersect with an empty square, each of which contains one X and no O's. If found, then place an X on the intersection.

A5. Search for two rows that intersect at an empty square, each of which contains one O and no X's. If found, then place an X on the intersection.

A6. Search for a vacant corner square. If found, then place an X on the vacancy.

A7. Search for a vacant square. If found, then place an X on the vacancy.

The algorithm is perfect in the sense that it will find a forced win if it exists and it will never lose. This algorithm may be called a rejection scheme because the first applicable step (following A1) is to be performed and all other steps are rejected or ignored (Fig. 2). A computer can be easily programmed to execute such an algorithm.

For another example, consider the following game, a special case of Nim. It is played with 13 matches; two players remove matches in turn until one player is forced to take the last match. A player may remove only one to three matches in a single turn, and the player who removes the last match is the loser. This is an algorithm for perfect play.

X	O	X
	O	2
O	1	X

Fig. 2. In the position shown here, algorithm A would choose a move at square 2 for a win rather than at square 1, to block the opponent win. This is done because step A2 precedes step A3.

ALGORITHM B (THE COMPUTER PLAYS SECOND)

B1. Let *n* be the number of matches taken by the opponent.

B2. Remove $(4 - n)$ matches.

B3. If the game is not over, go to Step B1.

Both tic-tac-toe and Nim are simple examples of a large number of games classed as two-person games of skill. An essential feature of these games is that both players have perfect information about the current state of the game. Chess, checkers, and GO are well-known games of pure skill. It can be shown mathematically that there is, in principle, an optimal strategy for each player and that its application always gives the same result. In the case of tic-tac-toe, the result is a draw. In the case of the match game, the second player always wins. The possibility of playing a perfect game of chess, checkers, or GO will now be examined.

In order to show that an optimal strategy exists for two-person games of skill, the principle of *minimax* must be explained. If the state of a game is represented by a circle and the moves from that state are represented by lines (Fig. 3), then a tree can be obtained which represents the set of all possible games. The end nodes of this tree (Fig. 4) can all be labeled with the terms *win, loss,* or *draw* for the first player. Now consider any node that is followed only by labeled nodes. If that node corresponds to the first player's move and it is connected to a node labeled, *win,* then it may be labeled with the term

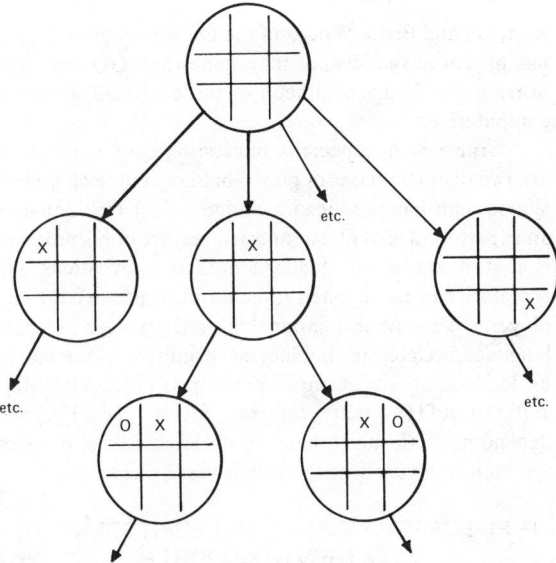

Fig. 3. Part of the lookahead tree for tic-tac-toe. Circles represent game positions and arrows represent moves by X or O.

win. It may be labeled with a *draw,* if it is connected to a draw. Otherwise, it is labeled with a *loss.* If it is the second player's move from a position, then a loss is most preferred. This procedure can be repeated to back up the values W, L, and D to the top of the lookahead tree. Optimal stragegy consists of following the path taken by the letter W, L, or D, which is backed up to the top. In other words, a player makes the best move, based on the assumption that the opponent will make the best reply, and the opponent's reply assumes that the player will make the best counter-reply, etc. (The best outcome is guaranteed, of course, even if the opponent makes less than optimum moves.)

Thus, since all possible chess games can be expressed in a tree like that in Fig. 3, it is known that there is a perfect strategy for chess, which guarantees a win or a draw for one player. Of course the strategy has never been found. It is the combinatorics of game playing which prevent the discovery of perfect strategies. In chess, when it is a player's turn to move, that player has on the average 30 legal moves resulting in 30 different positions. If the opponent also has 30 replies to each of those moves, then 900 positions result. This sort of calculation gives an estimate of 10^{125} as the size of the lookahead tree for chess (the number of paths from the top of the tree to the terminal positions). If a computer could examine a billion positions per second, it would still take 10^{108} years to examine the entire lookahead tree to determine the optimal strategy. It should be mentioned that the number of board positions is far smaller, approximately 10^{42}, so it is theoretically possible to store all positions together with their optimal moves in a large table. Storing one board position on an element the size of an atom would necessitate a memory of about the size of the earth. This gives a rather extreme example of the storage versus computational tradeoff that is so common to computer science.

A second class of game involves no skill at all, and a player's success depends only on chance. Examples are craps and roulette, in which the roll of dice or drop of a ball determines whether a bet is won or lost. A third and most important class of game involves a mixture of skill and chance of varying degrees. This includes games such as poker, bridge, backgammon, and Monopoly, which are affected by the distribution of cards or the roll of dice, although these randomizing features are generally overcome in the long run by the skill of a player. Computers can be set up to play these games of chance, but it is usually more difficult to represent the state of the game when probabilistic factors are present.

Games are also categorized according to whether players have incomplete or complete knowledge of the current state. Games of pure skill, such as chess and checkers, and some games involving chance, such as backgammon and parcheesi, have no elements that are

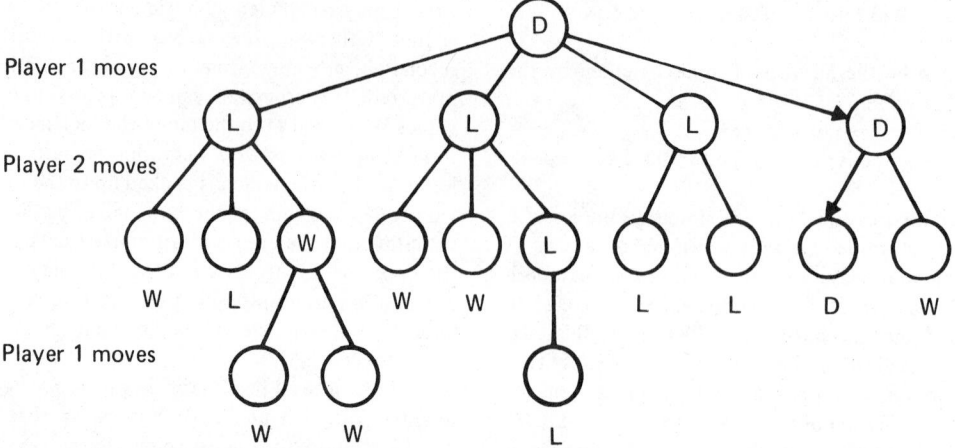

Player 1 moves

Player 2 moves

Player 1 moves

Fig. 4. Illustration of the minimax procedure. The values at the bottom are calculated by an evaluation function. The backed-up values in circles reflect the result of optimal play. The arrows show the path of optimal play.

hidden from the players. But in many games, such as poker, bridge, and salvo (battleship), each player can have information that is hidden from the other players. The presence of unknown factors poses additional problems for computerization. Methods developed here may be very useful, however, since real-world problems often involve unknown and probabilistic factors.

Game-Playing Programs. An early and very successful game-playing program is Arthur Samuel's (1967) checker player. Though checkers is a fairly difficult game (the game tree for checkers has an estimated 10^{40} paths), the checker program plays at a sound master level, having played a world champion to a draw. What is more amazing is that much of the program's skill is due to automatic learning procedures. In one experiment, the program was played against a copy of itself in which the copy was not allowed to "learn." As a result, the program improved itself enough to win consistently over the non-learning copy. Although the program uses a predetermined set of evaluation criteria, it learns the best means of combining these criteria to arrive at an overall evaluation of a board position. A more modern program has been written by Eric Jensen and Tom Truscott of Duke University. This program recently defeated the Samuel program and has exhibited strong play against highly rated players.

Go-Moku has become an extremely popular subject for computerization. It is essentially a game of the tic-tac-toe type, with each player trying to achieve five in a row on a 19 by 19 board. Since 1975, a North American Go-Moku tournament has been held, and, since 1977, there has also been a European tournament (see Table 1).

GO, an extremely difficult game played principally in the Orient, has been programmed by Zobrist. The main interest here was the difficult problem of representing the derived information that humans use to play the game. GO is played by placing white and black stones on a 19 by 19 grid. The most important feature of play is the emergence of groups or armies of similarly colored stones. Zobrist describes a method that allows the computer to "see" these armies and to represent them internally. The program was able to beat a human novice player, but was far short of expert play. A recent program by Walter Reitman and Bruce Wilcox of the University of Michigan has improved the level of play somewhat. GO may well prove to be the most difficult of the pure skill games to computerize.

Bridge is an especially interesting case, since there are two distinct phases of play—bidding and trick taking. Wasserman has produced a bridge bidder that achieves an expert level of skill. An unusual feature of his program is that it knows all standard bidding conventions and therefore can be adjusted to be an ideal partner for any player. Wasserman's approach was to use a base language, Algol, to implement primitive elements of bridge bidding; for example, a routine FIVECARDMA-JOR[NORTH] that returns TRUE or FALSE, depending on the north hand cards. Higher-level routines are built in layers over the primitives; for example:

IF FIVECARDMAJOR[*H*] AND POINTCOUNT[*H*]
> 12 THEN BIDMAJOR[*H*]

where *H* is a variable that can take on the values NORTH, SOUTH, EAST, or WEST.

A research project by Findler at the State University

Table 1.   Results of Computer Go-Moku Tournaments[1]

Year[2]	Tournament	No. of Entries	Winning Program, Author, Computer, Language	Runner-Up, Author, Computer, Language
1975	First North American	4	Arthur M. Compton, Canada IBM 370/158, PL/I	Plunc E. Johnson/A. Coston, U.S.A. PDP 8, 8-Tran
1976	Second North American	11	Plunc PDP 11, 11-Tran	Arthur
1977	Third North American	13	Arthur	Plunc
1977	First European	4	Zahle[2] T. U. Zahle, Denmark RC 4000, Algol 6	Darwin J. Janos/F. Brody, Hungary TPA-70, Assembler
1979	Fourth North American	10	Arthur Plunc Mogo J. Smith, U.S.A. IBM 370/165, Fortran/Assembler (3-Way Tie)	Shifty J. Day, U.S.A. PDP 11/70, Fortran
1979	Second European	11	Caesar G. Pedersen, Denmark RC 4000, Algol 60	Gomoku T. Bille, Denmark Burroughs B6700, Algol
1980	Fifth North American	10	Plunc	Arthur Shifty (2-Way Tie)
1980	Third European	10	Gomoku (Bille)	OX J. Janos, Hungary TPA-70, Assembler
1981	Sixth North American	8	Plunc Mogo (2-Way Tie)	Gomoku S. Wang/E. Slodysko, U.S.A. Vax 11/780, Fortran
1981	Fourth European	12	Caesar	Amoeba L. Merö, Hungary
1982	Seventh North American	8	Plunc	Gomoku (Wang/Slodysko) Mogo (tie)
	Fifth European	11	Gomoku (Bille)	Amoeba
1983	Eighth North American	4	Mogo	Plunc

[1]All games were played via telephone. [2]Zahle beat Compton 3-1 in a playoff for the world championship in 1977. [3]No tournament in 1978 due to a reorganization; Pederson beat Compton 3-1 for the world championship in 1979. [4]Bille beat Johnson/Coston 2-0 for the 1980 world championship.

of New York at Buffalo uses poker as a model for decision-making in the real world. Instead of creating a single game-playing program, Findler has created a system that allows several programs to play each other or to play against human subjects through the use of interactive graphics displays. An interesting match might pit a program which occasionally bluffs against a program which never bluffs against several human players. A large number of distinct programs have been created, some of which use learning. Each program is a specific model of human play at poker, and its success is a measure of the quality of the model.

The unusual mideastern game Kalah, played using stones and dishes, has been studied extensively. The game commences (Fig. 5) with an equal number of stones (usually three to six) in each of the side dishes (commonly six in number). The players take turns; in one turn a player takes all stones from one side dish and distributes them, one to a dish, in a counterclockwise fashion, but skipping the opponent's home dish (or Kalah). If the last stone falls in the player's home dish, then a second turn is taken. If the last stone in the first turn falls in an empty dish on the player's side, the stones in the opponent's dish on the opposite side are "captured" and placed in the player's Kalah. The game ends when all dishes on one side are empty, at which point all stones remaining on the other side are placed in that player's Kalah. A Kalah-playing program by Slagle achieved excellent results against human opponents.

Of all games programmed for computers, more time and effort has been devoted to chess than to any other. The results and current status of this work are described in the article on computer chess. A recent trend is the emergence of microcomputer-based games on the mass market. Quality of play varies, with backgammon and checker programs playing quite well and bridge and chess

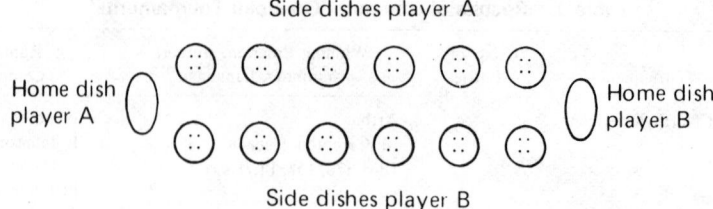

Fig. 5. Start of a Kalah game with four stones in each of the side dishes.

programs playing at a lower level. Rapid improvements in the quality and variety of these games may be expected.

REFERENCES

1950. Shannon C. E. "Automatic Chess Player," *Scientific American* **182**, *No. 2*: 48–51.

1953. Turing, A. M. "Digital Computers Applied to Games," in B. V. Bowden (Ed.), *Faster Than Thought*. London: Pitman, pp. 286–310.

1967. Epstein, R. A. *The Theory of Gambling and Statistical Logic*. New York: Academic Press, Chap. 10.

1967. Samuel, A. L. "Some Studies in Machine Learning Using the Game of Checkers, II—Recent Progress," *IBM Journal of Research and Development* pp. 601–617 (November).

1978. Findler, N. V. "Computer Poker," *Scientific American* **239**, *No. 1*: 144–151.

A. L. ZOBRIST

GARBAGE COLLECTION

For articles on related subjects *see* LISTS AND LIST PROCESSING; and STORAGE ALLOCATION.

In most computer programs, fixed regions of memory are allocated for various purposes—such as arrays, constants, temporary storage, etc.—before the computation begins. On the other hand, some systems (including most list-processing systems) permit *dynamic storage allocation*—the assignment and reassignment of memory as determined by requirements during the course of the computation. In such systems, *garbage collection* refers to the automatic process of identifying those memory cells whose contents are no longer useful for the computation in progress and then making them available again for some other use.

Techniques exist that enable dynamic storage allocation to occur without garbage collection. For example, if the programmer has sufficient control of a program's memory, storage can be reassigned explicitly as necessary, thereby avoiding the accumulation of garbage.

However, such techniques generally either place an undesirable burden upon the programmer's attention or require excessive use of computer space or time for bookkeeping operations. It has frequently proved more practical to allow programs to use available storage indiscriminately without any careful bookkeeping; then either periodically or when all space has apparently been used, the garbage collector is called to generate recycled working space.

Garbage collection generally takes place in two stages: first, identification of the garbage, and then its restructuring into a set of memory cells available for future use. The identification stage can be accomplished by systematically scanning and marking all the nongarbage, i.e., all cells in memory that can be accessed in any way by any current process. In a typical list-processing system, for example, this means starting with a base list of all memory addresses (pointers) that occur in active programs, symbol tables, and the system's temporary storage registers; marking all the cells pointed to; replacing the base list with a list of all pointers found in the cells just marked; and repeating the marking process until no new unmarked cells are reached. (Marking can be done by using a spare bit in each cell, or by using bits in a separate table for this purpose.)

At this point, every unmarked cell in working storage has been identified as garbage. The second stage of collection can then consist of one linear scan through memory to link every unmarked cell into one new long list of available storage (and to unmark every marked cell, in preparation for future garbage collections).

A common variation of the above basic scheme is *compacting* garbage collection. Here, the second stage includes physical rearrangement of data cells so that all the garbage is compressed into a contiguous array. This process requires an extra pass through memory to correct existing pointers to data that has been moved. This extra work is sometimes worthwhile because an available space *array* can be utilized more efficiently than an available space list, especially in paged and swapping memory systems.

B. RAPHAEL

GENERAL REGISTER

For articles on related subjects *see* ARITHMETIC-LOGIC UNIT; BASE REGISTER; INDEX REGISTER; and REGISTER.

A general register is a storage device that holds the input (operands) and the output (results) of the various functional units of a computing system. It is also used for temporary storage of intermediate results.

The width of the register is directly related to the width of the operational units, as it appears to the programmer, and does not necessarily reflect the width of the main-memory addressable unit. Thus, in the IBM/370, for example, the general registers are 32 bits wide, although the memory is addressed in 8-bit units.

The functional units referred to in the definition usually include the arithmetic/logic unit, the memory, the control unit, and various I/O processors.

The registers operate at a speed that is directly connected to the speed of the units they serve. Their speed must be such that they do not slow down in any considerable way the functional units connected to them. In this sense they are the highest-speed storage in the hierarchy of stores present in a computer.

Among a multitude of hardware reasons for the presence of general registers, one should note in particular their role in reducing the average number of bits needed to specify the operands in a computer program. For example, one of 16 general registers can be addressed with four bits whereas a main memory address for a memory of one million locations requires a 20-bit address.

As their name implies, the usage of general registers is varied. They may serve as arithmetic or logical registers, in which case they function as dedicated parts of the arithmetic/logic unit. If we denote registers by R, then a typical arithmetic or logical instruction will be $R_i \leftarrow R_j \, o \, R_k$, where o stands for any arithmetic or logical operation, and i, j, k may be either distinct or equal (e.g., $R_2 \leftarrow R_2 + R_3$).

The general registers may also serve as: shift registers; index registers, in which case they serve as input to the memory unit; input/output registers, in which case they hold parameters that specify channels; or channel command registers, etc.

The number of general registers varies widely between 0 to 256 (as of 1980). The numbers represent today's architecture and hardware trade-offs, and are not to be taken as magic numbers. There are also computers that possess more than one set of general-purpose registers (and the programmer may switch between them), and computers that possess no general registers at all.

G. FRIEDER

GENERATIONS, COMPUTER

For articles on related subjects *see* DIGITAL COMPUTERS: Early, and Contemporary and Future; and COMPUTER INDUSTRY.

In discussions of the history of electronic computers, it is convenient to refer to at least three computer generations.

The first generation is characterized by the use of vacuum tubes as active elements. This generation started with one-of-a-kind computers in university and government research laboratories. Mercury-delay lines and electrostatic storage tubes were the typical memory devices in the early systems.

The development of a reliable magnetic core memory was a major turning point in the first generation. The IBM 704 is an impressive example of the advanced hardware and software technology of that period. The latter part of the first generation also saw the introduction of many computers that used magnetic drums as their main storage.

The second generation is characterized by the use of transistors as active elements. The first important transistorized computers were delivered in 1959, and vacuum tubes rapidly disappeared from computer systems. The second generation was characterized by some powerful computers: Larc, Stretch, IBM 7090, Philco 2000, CDC 3600, etc., and many small systems such as the IBM 1401, RCA 301, and CDC 160A.

The distinction between the second and third generation is not nearly as clear-cut as that between the first and second. Computers that use integrated circuit technology are, by definition, third-generation computers, but some of the most powerful computers of the third generation use discrete component technology. It is capability and performance rather than circuitry that makes a large computer a member of the third generation. They are characterized by their ability to support multiprogramming and multiprocessors with a rather elaborate disk-based operating system. A typical third-generation operating system on a large computer handles multiple local and remote job streams and can support a variety of remote on-line terminals.

The third computer generation is generally considered to have started in 1964. Third-generation systems introduced by the largest computer manufacturers around that time and in the 10 years or so thereafter include the IBM 360 and 370 series, the Univac 1108 and 1110, the Honeywell 6000 series, the Control Data 6000, 7000, Cyber 70, and Cyber 170 series, the Burroughs B5700 and B6700, Digital Equipment Corporation's PDP-10 and PDP-20, and many others.

Some of the smaller computer manufacturers have claimed that one or another of their computers represents a fourth generation, but as of 1980 there is no generally accepted fourth generation of computers. Most authorities consider the computers introduced since 1969 to be "late third generation" computers. They look for a more significant breakthrough, such as an electronic peripheral storage system to replace disk storage, to characterize a fourth generation. Since the introduction of their third-generation systems, most computer manufacturers, especially the large ones, have been very reluctant to make any major changes in the logical organization of their computer systems. They feel that it is necessary to protect the enormous investment in systems and applications software by manufacturers and by users. Thus, it can be argued that we are still in the third computer generation and will probably remain there for a long time to come.

Even though logical organization has changed very slowly since the mid 1960s, circuit technology has continued to advance at a very rapid rate. From the point of view of circuit technology, vacuum tubes and germanium diodes characterize a first generation, discrete transistors a second, simple integrated circuits a third, medium scale integration a fourth, and large scale integration a fifth generation.

Some authorities suggest that microprocessors, which represent the most impressive achievement of large scale integration technology, also represent a fourth or perhaps even a fifth computer generation. If the concept of computer generation is tied directly to advances in technology, we are faced with an anomalous situation in which the most powerful computers of 1979–1980, the CDC Cyber 176 and the CRAY 1, would have to be assigned to the second and third generation, respectively, while the most trivial of hobbyist computers would be a fifth-generation system.

S. ROSEN

GIGO

GIGO (garbage in—garbage out) is a popular acronym in computing. A more precise statement of the principle involved is "output is a function of the input and the instructions." The implication is that, if the input data is erroneous, or the sequence of instructions is illogical, or both, then it should not be astonishing that the results make little sense. Only if all parts of the computing activity are precisely correct can one expect useful results.

F. GRUENBERGER

GLITCH

For article on a related subject *see* BUG.

The term *glitch,* as used in computing, usually denotes a small error of any kind—a bug. It has been defined more generally by Thomas Martin (*Malice in Blunderland.* New York: McGraw-Hill, 1973) as "an inherent, built-in, organic fallibility in a design or a plan or an equipment or in any human contrivance," and by Jackson Granholm as "a momentary, unexplained, disruptive step function."

F. GRUENBERGER

GLOBAL AND LOCAL VARIABLES

For articles on related subjects *see* BLOCK STRUCTURE; and PROCEDURE-ORIENTED LANGUAGES, Programming in.

The quantity (or quantities) referred to by a given variable name in a computer program can generally be accessed (i.e., used or changed) only in certain parts of the program. The domain of the program during which a variable name can be accessed is called the *scope* of the variable.

In a block-structured language, the scope of a variable is the block in which it is declared, but excludes any subblocks that are internal to the defining block *and* in which the same variable name is declared. This is illustrated in Fig. 1, which shows the schematic of an Algol program with an outer block L1 and an inner subblock L2, which in turn contains two further subblocks L3 and L4. Also shown in Fig. 1 is the scope of each variable. Note in particular that a variable like C, defined in the outer block, has a scope L1 minus L4 because C is declared again in L4.

A variable in a block in which it is defined, like G in block L4 in the example, is said to be *local* to that block, and is therefore a local variable. Correspondingly, variable A is *global* to block L4, since it is defined outside this block, although it may be referred to in the block. The variable C defined in the outer block is also global to block L4, but it cannot be referred to in L4 because of the declaration of C in block L4, the latter (but different) C being local to L4.

In a language such as Fortran, where subprograms are separate from the main program, a local variable in a subprogram is one that is defined and used only in the subprogram, while a global variable is one used to communicate with the main program as the name of an input argument, an output argument or both. Additionally, variables in Fortran *common* storage are essentially global variables. Current knowledge of programming methodology suggests that global variables should be used sparingly if at all.

```
L1:   begin
        real A, C, D;  real array B[1:10];
           L2:   begin
                   real D, E;  real array F[-4:6,1:12];
                      L3:   begin
                              real F, G;
                                .
                                .
                                .
                              end L3;
                   L4:   begin
                           real B, C, G;
                             .
                             .
                             .
                           end L4;
                end L2;
        end L1;
```

Variable Name	Label of Defining Block	Scope of Name
A	L1	L1
B	L1	L1–L4
C	L1	L1–L4
D	L1	L1–L2
D	L2	L2
E	L2	L2
F	L2	L2–L3
F	L3	L3
G	L3	L3
B	L4	L4
C	L4	L4
G	L4	L4

Note: L1–L4, for example, means those parts of the program in block L1 but *not* block L4.

Fig. 1.   Scope of variable names.

REFERENCE

1978. Peterson J. L. *Computer Organization and Assembly Language Programming.* New York: Academic Press.

J. A. N. LEE AND A. RALSTON

GRAMMARS

For articles on related subjects see FORMAL LANGUAGES; LANGUAGE PROCESSORS; PARSING; PROGRAMMING LINGUISTICS; and SYNTAX, SEMANTICS, AND PRAGMATICS.

A grammar is an algebraic system describing the processes by which instances of a language can be constructed. A grammar consists of four elements—a set of *metavariables* or *nonterminal* symbols V_T (usually called *parts of speech* when dealing with natural languages); an alphabet V_T (or character set), often called the *terminal symbols;* a set of rules or *productions P,* which describe how a sequence of substitutions can be made for each metavariable; and a special metavariable S called the *starting* or *root* symbol, which is the starting point for the substitution process to be described below. These four elements are often represented by the quadruple $\{V_N, V_T, P, S\}$.

Grammars are most commonly classified into two groups—*context-sensitive* and *context-free.* In the case of context-sensitive grammars, the rules are applicable only when a metavariable occurs in a specified context—for example, the modification of verbs to their plural form in the context of plurality in the rest of the sentence in natural languages. By contrast, in a context-free grammar, any occurrence of a metavariable may be replaced by one of its alternatives, irrespective of the other elements in the language. Most programming languages appear at first glance to be describable by context-free grammars until consideration is given to the effect of declarations, such as the dimensions of an array or the specification of a procedure to support a procedure reference. In the discussion that follows, we will restrict ourselves to context-free grammars.

Grammars for high-level programming languages are called *generative* because, given a starting metavariable such as *sentence,* they specify a sequence of replacements or substitutions that can be applied to that name to form an instance (in this case, a sentence) in the language. For example, consider the following small grammar:

> *sentence* : : = *noun-phrase verb-phrase*
> *noun-phrase* : : = *article noun*
> *verb-phrase* : : = *verb noun-phrase*

and

> *article* : : = the, a
> *noun* : : = cat, milk
> *verb* : : = drank

where the italicized elements are metavariables and the nonitalicized elements are from the alphabet of the language. Using these rules, the sentence

The cat drank the milk.

can be generated by the following sequence:

> *sentence* → *noun-phrase verb-phrase.*
> → *article noun verb-phrase.*
> → the *noun verb-phrase.*
> → the cat *verb-phrase.*
> → the cat *verb noun-phrase.*
> → the cat drank *noun-phrase.*

→ the cat drank *article noun.*
→ the cat drank the *noun.*
→ the cat drank the milk.

Equally, the sentences "the milk drank the cat" and "the cat drank the cat" can be generated, since they have the required underlying syntactic (grammatical) structure.

Similarly, consider the following grammar for simple forms of arithmetic expressions in high-level languages (where the vertical bar is to be read "or"):

add-op : : = + | −
mult-op : : = * | /
exp-op : : = **
primary : : = *constant* | *variable*
factor : : = *primary* | *primary exp-op primary*
term : : = *factor* | *factor mult-op factor*
arithmetic-expression : : = *term add-op term*

and where constants and variables then have usual definitions in computer languages. Then the expression

A + B*C**D

could be generated as follows:

arithmetic-expression
    → *term add-op term*
    →*factor add-op term*
    →*primary add-op term*
    →*variable add-op term*
    →A *add-op term*
    →A + *term*
    →A + *factor mult-op factor*
    →A + *primary mult-op factor*
    →A + *variable mult-op factor*
    →A + B *mult-op factor*
    →A + B**factor*
    →A + B**primary exp-op primary*
    →A + B**variable exp-op primary*
    →A + B*C *exp-op primary*
    →A + B*C***primary*
    →A + B*C***variable*
    →A + B*C**D

During the compilation process for high-level programming languages, we are interested not in generating the allowable strings in a language but rather in syntactically analyzing or parsing (*q.v.*) the strings presented to the compiler. The function which performs this analysis is naturally called a *syntactic analyzer*. Grammars for high-level programming languages are commonly classified according to the types of syntactic analyzers used to parse them.

Syntactic analyzers can broadly be classified into two types: (1) the predictive types, which, starting from the root symbol, attempt to predict the means by which the string was generated; and (2) the reductive types, which attempt to reduce the string to the root symbol. These methods are loosely termed the *top-down* and *bottom-up* methods, respectively. The direction implied by these terms is related to the *syntactic trees* that may be generated by the analysis wherein the root symbol is at the top of the page and the string at the bottom. It may then be seen that a predictive (top-down) method starts at the top of the (yet unconstructed) tree and builds down toward the string, whereas the bottom-up (reductive) method starts at the string and attempts to develop a tree that converges onto the root symbol.

For example, consider the grammar with

$$V_N = \{A, B, C, X\}$$
$$V_T = \{a, b, c, d, x, y\}$$

and the production rules

$$S : : = AX$$
$$A : : = aB$$
$$B : : = b$$
$$X : : = xC$$
$$X : : = yC$$
$$C : : = cd$$

which generates the language L with two strings {*abxcd, abycd*}. Note that, when a particular metavariable, such as X in this example, has more than one possible substitution for it, the productions are sometimes written

$$X : : = xC | yC$$

with the vertical bar being read as "or." When X is to be substituted for in a string, the syntactic analyzer must then choose one of the possible substitutions and, if this does not lead to a successful parse, try another. Typically, the possibilities are tried in left-to-right order when the production is written using the vertical bar.

The above grammar can be analyzed in either a top-down or bottom-up manner. For the string *abxcd*, we have

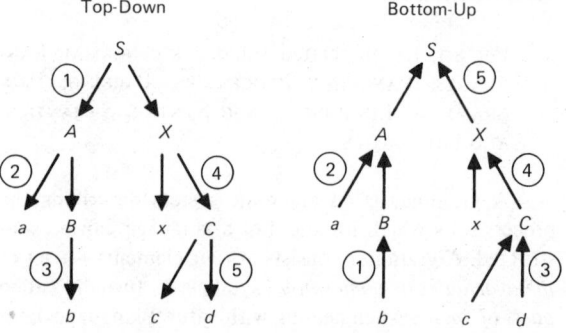

Top-Down   Bottom-Up

"Growing from the root"   "Pruning toward the root"

The top-down tree corresponds to the derivation

$$S \to AX \to aBX \to abX \to abxC \to abxcd$$

so that the numbers in the tree correspond to the steps in the derivation. Similarly, in the bottom-up case, the reduction shown in the tree corresponds to

$$abxcd \to aBxcd \to Axcd \to AxC \to AX \to S.$$

Since each metavariable appears on the left side of some production, in the top-down approach any metavariable in the string can always be replaced by the corresponding right side of a production. When going bottom-up, however, metavariables in the string may not correspond to right sides of productions (e.g., A in $Axcd$ above). The bottom-up procedure is conveniently visualized by imagining a left-to-right scan across the string with successive characters put on a *stack* (*q.v.*) until a production can be applied. For the example above this is illustrated as follows, where the symbol ∇ signifies the bottom of the stack.

Symbol Scanned	Stack	Comments
a	∇a	
b	∇aB	Using $B \to b$
	∇A	Using $A \to aB$
x	∇Ax	
c	∇Axc	
d	$\nabla Axcd$	
	∇AxC	Using $C \to cd$
	∇AX	Using $X \to xC$
	∇S	Using $S \to AX$

Notice, in particular, the ability to search down from the top of the stack (or, if you will, "remember" the previous contents of the stack) in order to determine if the top elements of the stack contain the right side of some production.

In the top-down derivation for the example above, whenever the derived string contained more than one metavariable, the leftmost one was used to generate the next string, thus leading to a *leftmost derivation*. Similarly, in the bottom-up derivation, the rightmost nonterminal was always replaced (indeed, in this example, there was no choice), thus leading to a *rightmost derivation*.

Studies of the development of parsers for programming languages have led to the definition of specialized grammars that are parsable by certain classes of analyzers. These can be divided into two classes that correspond directly to top-down *(predictive)* and bottom-up *(reductive)* analyzers and are known as either LL or LR grammars, respectively. LL grammars are defined by a parser, which scans the input string from left-to-right (the first L in the name) and produces a parsing that corresponds to a leftmost (the second L) generation of the string. Where such a grammar (and corresponding parser) can accomplish the analysis with the examination of a single symbol in the string at each stage of the predictive process, then this is known as an LL(1) grammar; where up to k symbols may be required, it is called an LL(k) grammar. There exist languages which are LL(0), that is, the predictor does not have to look at the string at all except to confirm conformance with the prediction, in order to analyze the string. Obviously, a degenerate LL(0) grammar is one containing only a single production rule; other simple LL(0) grammars can be constructed, such as

$$A ::= aBe$$
$$B ::= bC$$
$$C ::= c.$$

LR grammars are reductive in processing style and are much more reliable in their analysis of complex languages once the generated parser tables have been optimized. As with LL, the LR system scans the string from left to right, but, because of the use of reductive analysis, the derived syntactic structure is equivalent to the rightmost generation (the R in the name LR). As with LL grammars, an LR(k) grammar must examine up to k symbols in the analysis. Whereas the amount of processing to analyze a language by means of an LL(k) system increases rapidly as the number of symbols (k) to be examined at each stage increases, to the point where it is very uncommon to consider symbol groupings of more than one character at a time (i.e., LL(1) systems), the increase in complexity for increasing symbol groupings in LR systems is much smaller. Thus, it is more common to use LR(k) systems where k is greater than 1 to improve the efficiency of analysis and to minimize the changes that have to be made to a context-free grammar in order to convert it to an acceptable LR(k) grammar.

Simply because a grammar is context-free, there is no guarantee that it can be converted into either an LL(k) or an LR(k) type grammar by simple transformations. At each stage of either an LL or LR analysis, there must exist a unique relationship between the next k symbols in the string and a specific production in the grammar. If this relationship cannot be determined, then the grammar cannot be converted into one of the desired forms. Thus, there are grammars which are LL and not LR and others which, though parsable to either a left or right derivative form by the addition of further information about the string, are not LL or LR, respectively. The set of grammars in Table 1 are examples of each of these cases.

Although LR parsing techniques have been known since 1965, the parsers produced were far too large to be practical. However, optimizing techniques were discovered by DeRemer in 1969, resulting in modified gram-

Table 1.   Grammars and Languages of Various Types

LR, left-parsable, not LL	$S ::= A\|B$ $A ::= aaA\|aa$ $B ::= aaB\|a$
LR, not left-parsable	$S ::= Ab\|Ac$ $A ::= AB\|a$ $B ::= a$
Left- and right-parsable, not LR	$S ::= Ab\|Bc$ $A ::= Aa\|a$ $B ::= Ba\|a$
Right-parsable only	$S ::= Ab\|Bc$ $A ::= AC\|a$ $B ::= BC\|a$ $C ::= a$
Left-parsable only	$S ::= BAb\|CAc$ $A ::= BA\|a$ $B ::= a$ $C ::= a$

Table 2.   Attributes of LL and LR Grammars

Attribute	LL	LR
Grammars	Can be hard to construct; rather awkward/ unnatural. Class of LL grammars is small.	Rather straightforward. Can express virtually all programming constructs naturally.
Languages	Like the grammars, class is small but is adequate for the normal syntactic features of programming languages.	Can find an LR(1) grammar for *every* deterministic context-free language. Some examples of LR but not LL languages: $\{a^n b^n \| n \geq 1\}$ $\cup \{a^n c^n \| n \geq 1\}$ $\{a^n b^m \| 1 \leq m \leq n\}$ $\{a^n O b^n \| n \geq 0\}$ $\cup \{a^n O b^{2n} \| n \geq 0\}$

mars known as SLR (Simple LR) and LALR (Look-Ahead LR) parsers. Each of these is defined in terms of the optimization techniques that are used and are virtually impossible to construct by hand except in trivial cases. Basically, given an LR(1) system, the optimization process develops an LALR parser while an LR(0) grammar can be converted into an SLR system. However, this process is not guaranteed for all LR grammars and, thus, the set of languages that can be optimized in this way is much smaller than that which may be represented by the LR system of grammars.

Table 2 lists some of the characteristics of LL and LR grammars and provides a comparison of the qualities of each grammar system. Fig. 1 illustrates some relationships of the grammars discussed in this article. Both the table and figure are due to N. Tindall.

REFERENCES

1978. Lewis, P. M. 2d, Rosenkrantz, D. J., and Stearns, R. E. *Compiler Design Theory.* Reading, MA: Addison-Wesley.
1979. Aho, A. V. and Ullman, J. D. *Principles of Compiler Design.* Reading, MA: Addison-Wesley.

J. A. N. LEE

GRAPHICS. *See* BIOMEDICINE, COMPUTER GRAPHICS IN; and COMPUTER GRAPHICS.

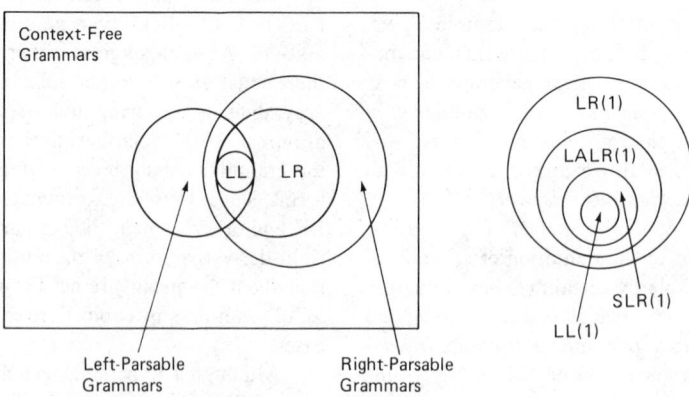

Fig. 1.   Relationships between grammars.

GRAPH THEORY

For articles on related subjects *see* ALGORITHMS, ANALYSIS OF; COMPUTATIONAL COMPLEXITY; DATA STRUCTURES; NP-COMPLETE PROBLEMS; and TREE.

Informally, a *graph* is a collection of points, any pair of which may or may not be joined by a line. Graph theory is the study of these objects. A graph may be represented by a diagram such as those in Fig. 1.

The uses of graph theory in computer science are diverse, and they include applications such as scheduling in operating systems and elsewhere, resource allocation, flowchart representation, information retrieval, and even sorting. The algorithms developed to solve graph theoretical problems have recently been found to be also of theoretical interest in the area of computational complexity (*q.v.*). In this article, we shall give basic definitions of graph theory and summarize the current state-of-the-art in the algorithmic area.

The terminology of graph theory varies from author to author and from application to application; the reader should take care to know what concept is intended when reading articles from diverse fields. We attempt here to use what has become more or less standard vocabulary, and to mention alternative words that are common.

It is frequently pointed out that graph theory had its beginnings with Euler and the Königsberg bridge problem. The problem is to find a way of taking a walk (in Königsberg—then in East Prussia, but now in the Soviet Union and called Kaliningrad) and to cross each of its seven bridges (Fig. 2) exactly once. Euler showed such a walk to be impossible, by noting that each of the land masses A,C,D has an odd number (three) of bridges. It is noteworthy that Euler's solution to the generalization of this problem (made in 1736), which is known as finding an *Eulerian path* when one exists, remains the basis of the best algorithm known today for the solution to this problem.

Formally, a graph $G(V,X)$ is a finite, nonempty collection V of *points* (nodes, vertices) and a prescribed set X of unordered pairs of distinct points. Such a pair (v_1,v_2) is called an *edge* (branch, arc, line). The diagram of a graph is sometimes referred to as the graph itself.

A graph is called *labeled* (see the rightmost example in Fig. 1) if its points are distinguished by names. A *directed graph*, or *digraph* (Fig. 3), is a finite nonempty set of points V and a set X of ordered pairs of distinct points for edges. A digraph is said to be *oriented* if both (v_i,v_j) and (v_j,v_i) do not occur in X.

Note that the preceding definitions do not allow an infinite set of points, multiple edges, or loops (a line from a point to itself). Some authors allow all or some of these in graphs and reserve some special word (*linear graph,*

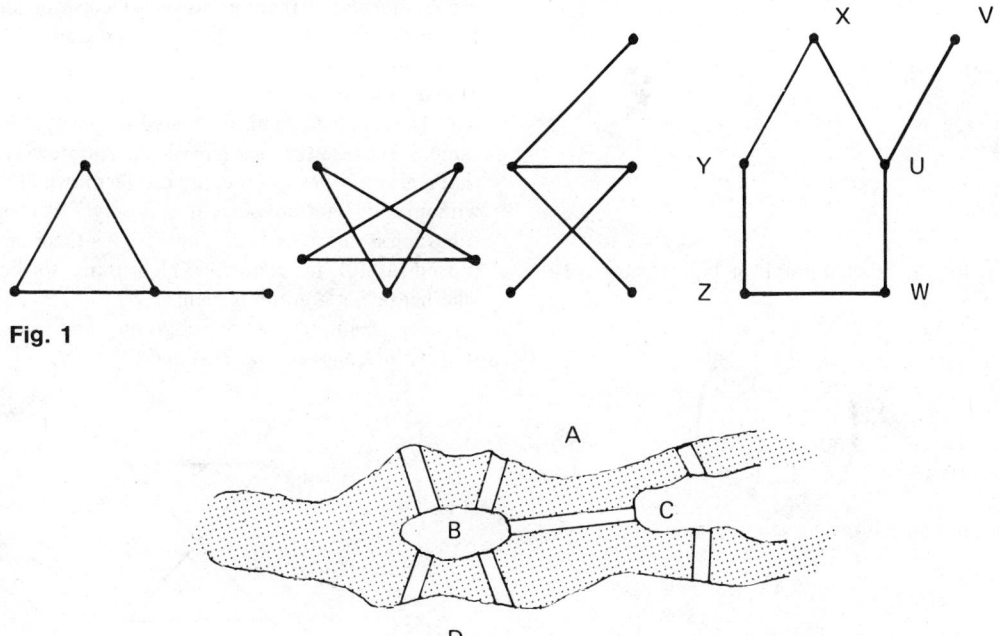

Fig. 1

Fig. 2

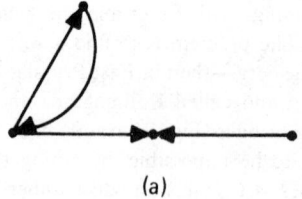
(a)

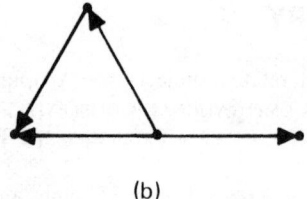
(b)

Fig. 3.   (a) A digraph. (b) An oriented graph.

for example) to mean the structure we define as simply a graph.

There are two common ways to represent a graph or digraph in a computer: (1) by its *adjacency matrix,* and (2) by its *adjacency structure.* The adjacency matrix for a graph on n vertices is $A = (a_{ij})$, $i,j = 1,2,\ldots n$, where $a_{ij} = 1$ if vertex v_i is *adjacent* to v_j [i.e., if (v_i,v_j) is an edge of the graph], and zero otherwise. The adjacency structure is the listing for each vertex of all other vertices adjacent to it. The adjacency structure has proved generally to lead to faster algorithms on a random access, nonparallel machine.

For the labeled digraph in Fig. 4, the adjacency matrix is

$$
\begin{array}{c}
 \\ u \\ v \\ w \\ z
\end{array}
\begin{array}{cccc}
u & v & w & z \\
\end{array}
\left(
\begin{array}{cccc}
0 & 1 & 1 & 0 \\
1 & 0 & 0 & 0 \\
0 & 0 & 0 & 0 \\
0 & 0 & 1 & 0
\end{array}
\right)
$$

and the adjacency structure is

u: v,w
v: u
w: {empty}
z: w

Similarly, for the labeled graph in Fig. 5, we have the adjacency matrix:

$$
\begin{array}{c}
 \\ 1 \\ 2 \\ 3 \\ 4
\end{array}
\begin{array}{cccc}
1 & 2 & 3 & 4 \\
\end{array}
\left(
\begin{array}{cccc}
0 & 1 & 0 & 1 \\
1 & 0 & 1 & 1 \\
0 & 1 & 0 & 1 \\
1 & 1 & 1 & 0
\end{array}
\right)
$$

and adjacency structure

1: 2,4
2: 1,3
3: 2,4
4: 3,4

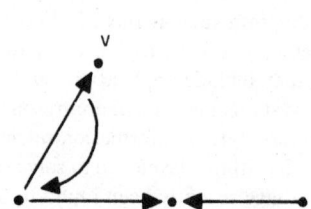

Fig. 4

The reader will note that if no orientation is given to the edges [i.e., "(v_i,v_j) is an edge" means that v_i is adjacent to v_j, and conversely], then the adjacency matrix is symmetric about the diagonal, which is zero when no loops are present. Also, any permutation on the rows and columns ($P^{-1}AP$, where P is a permutation matrix) simply represents the same graph with a different labeling.

A *subgraph* of a graph G is a graph whose points and edges are all in G; a *spanning subgraph* is a subgraph that contains all the points of G. Two graphs, G_1 and G_2, are *isomorphic* if there exists a 1–1 correspondence between their point sets which preserves adjacency. The diagrams of isomorphic graphs may appear quite different (see Fig. 6).

The graph $K_{3,3}$ and the related graph K_5 of Fig. 6 are famous because the mathematician Kuratowski showed that a graph is *planar* (roughly can be drawn in the plane without any lines crossing) if and only if it contains no subgraph isomorphic to $K_{3,3}$ or K_5. This theorem has *not* proved useful in computer algorithms to determine whether or not a graph is planar.

For examples of a subgraph, and a spanning subgraph of $K_{3,3}$ see Fig. 7(a) and (b).

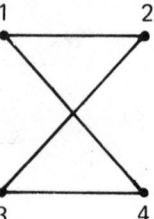

Fig. 5

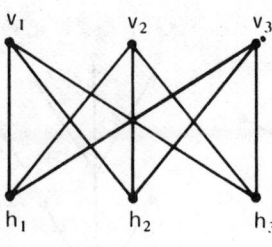

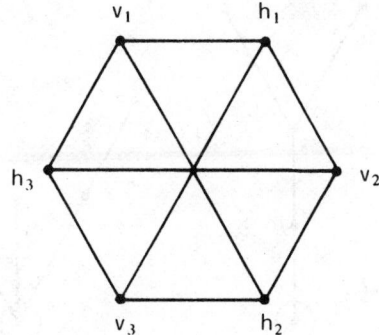

Fig. 6. (a) $K_{3,3}$. (b) K_5.

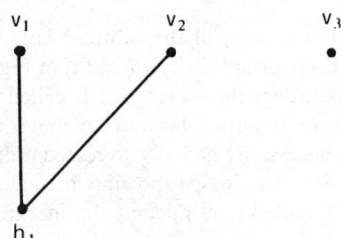

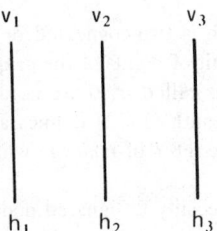

Fig. 7. (a) A subgraph of $K_{3,3}$. (b) A spanning subgraph of $K_{3,3}$.

A set of vertices $\{v_0, v_1, \ldots, v_n\}$ in a graph G is a *walk* of length n if (v_i, v_{i+1}) $i = 0, 1 \cdots n - 1$ is an edge of G and a *path* if all v_i are distinct. Some writers use the word "path" when a given vertex is allowed to appear more than once in the set $\{v_0, v_1, \ldots v_n\}$ and use the term "simple path" to denote what we have called a path. If $n \geq 2$ and $v_0 = v_n$, then the path is called a *cycle* (sometimes *circuit*). The *distance* between two points in a graph is the length of the shortest path between them. A graph is called *Eulerian* if there exists a walk that traverses each edge of the graph exactly once, and is called *Hamiltonian* if there exists a path passing through each vertex exactly once. A graph is *connected* if every pair of points is connected by a path. A maximal connected subgraph of a graph is called a *component*.

The *degree* (valence) of a vertex of a graph is the number of lines *incident* to that point. In a digraph, the corresponding idea is expressed by *out degree* and *in degree*. Clearly,

$$\sum_{v_i \in G} \deg(v_i) = 2q,$$

where q is the number of edges in the graph.

A *complete* graph on n points, denoted by K_n, is the n-graph containing all $\binom{n}{2}$ possible lines. A *bipartite* (bicolorable) graph, or *bigraph,* is a graph whose point-set can be partitioned into two subsets, V_1 and V_2, such that any edge of G connects a point of V_1 with a point of V_2. A graph is bipartite if and only if all its cycles are of even length. A *complete bigraph,* denoted by $K_{m,n}$, contains all possible lines. $K_{3,3}$ in Fig. 6 is such a graph, with $V_1 = \{v_1, v_2, v_3\}$ and $V_2 = \{h_1, h_2, h_3\}$.

A graph useful in many applications is the "n-cube" Q_n; this is a graph on 2^n points where each vertex may be denoted by an n-bit number. Two points of Q_n are adjacent whenever their binary representations differ in exactly one place, as in Q_1 and Q_3 in Fig. 8.

A *cut-point* (articulation point) of a component of a graph is a point whose removal disconnects that component, and (analogously) a *bridge* (isthmus) is an edge whose removal disconnects a component. A graph is *n-connected* if n points must be removed to disconnect the

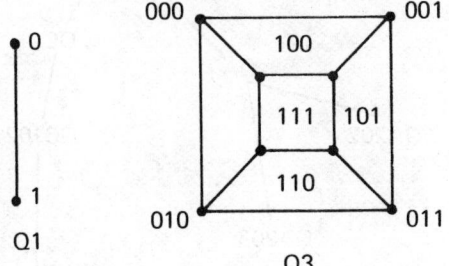

Fig. 8

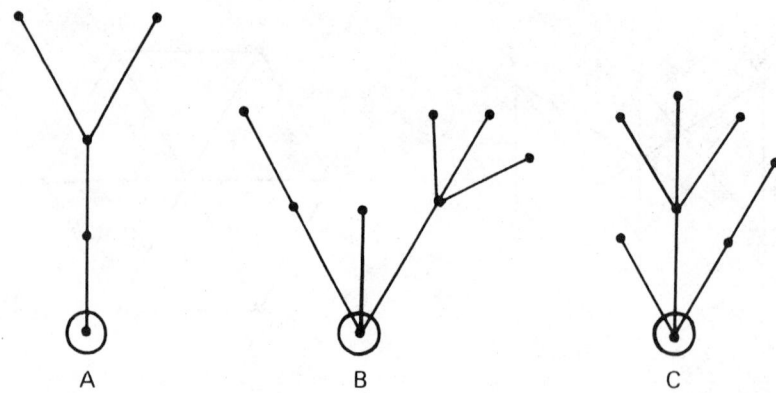

Fig. 9

graph. A graph is two-connected or *biconnected* if and only if every pair of points of the graph lies on a cycle.

The graphs called *trees* are used in many computer applications. Knuth (1972) defines a *rooted tree* recursively as a finite set T of *nodes* in which

1. One specially designated node is called the *root* of the tree.
2. The remaining nodes are partitioned into $m \geq 0$ disjoint sets $T_1, T_2, \ldots, T_m$ (or *subtrees*), each of which is a tree.

Fig. 9 illustrates some rooted trees, with the root circled. If there is no point of the tree distinguished as the root, then the tree is called a *free tree* by Knuth, but we will just use the term "tree" here.

It can be proved without too much difficulty that any of the following statements about a graph are equivalent, and hence any one of them may also be used as a definition for a tree. Let G be a graph with n vertices and k edges.

1. G is a tree.
2. G is connected and has no cycles (is *acyclic*).
3. Every two points of G are connected by a unique path.
4. G is connected and has $n - 1$ edges.
5. G is acyclic and has $n - 1$ edges.
6. G is connected, but if any edge of G is removed, then the resulting graph is disconnected.

The word "tree" has lead to much fanciful vocabulary—forest, plantation, leaf, twig, root, palm tree, frond, arborescence, etc., all have technical meanings. In particular, we note that an *end-point,* or *leaf* of a tree is a vertex of degree 1. A *spanning tree* of a graph is a spanning subgraph, which is also a tree. For the application of Kirchoff's laws (which make use of spanning trees) to flowcharts, see Knuth (1973).

If the order of the subtrees formed by deleting the root is important, i.e., if B and C in Fig. 9 are considered distinct, then the rooted tree is called *ordered*. Ordered trees are important because computer representations of trees necessarily give rise to rooted ordered trees.

For some reason (possibly in analogy to the "family tree"), rooted trees in computer literature are drawn upside down, with the root at the "top." Computer terminology for tree structures is usually sexist. Every root is said to be a father (mother) to the roots of its subtrees. These roots are called "brothers" (sisters) and "sons" (daughters) of their "fathers" (mothers). The neuter words (parent, child, sibling) are sometimes used. The root of the entire tree (godhead?) has no father. The nonsexist words "ancestor" and "descendant" are terms that may designate nodes several levels apart in the tree.

A *binary* tree is a rooted, ordered tree, each vertex of which has at most two subtrees that are designated left and right. Binary trees arise naturally from a variety of sources. The labeling system of the library classification for books may be thought of as a tree. (See Fig. 10.) Algebraic formulas give rise to tree structures as shown in Fig. 11 for the formula $x + y(a + bc)$.

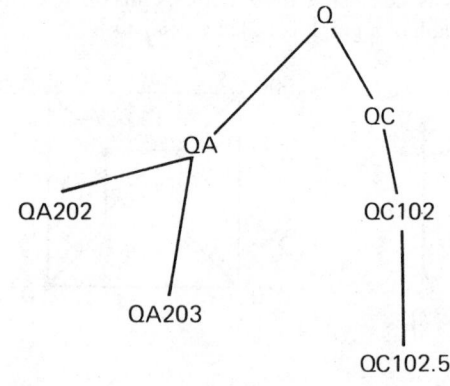

Fig. 10

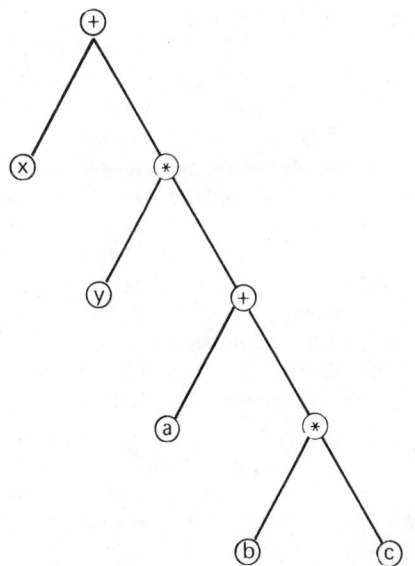

Fig. 11

Many algorithms exist for traversing (searching) a tree systematically. These are of great importance whenever large sets of data are stored in a tree structure and it is required either to find an existing piece of data or to insert a new piece of data appropriately.

The development of graph theoretical algorithms is playing an increasing role in those areas that have come to be called *computational complexity,* and in the analysis of algorithms. On early computers, lack of main storage prevented the solution of graph problems involving many nodes. Moreover, these computers were not fast enough to handle the very large number of computations that are often required for graph-related computations. Today, large main stores and readily available backing stores have alleviated the storage problem but the time problem still remains, particularly for problems where the obvious algorithm requires $n!$ operations.

For example, the problem of deciding whether or not two graphs are isomorphic is a trivial one for the mathematician, who will simply check all $n!$ mappings of one vertex set onto the other. But the time requirements for a problem of this sort quickly get out of hand. If the solution of this problem would require 6 minutes on a computer when $n = 10$, it would require 9 years for $n = 15$ and 300,000 centuries when $n = 20$. In order to overcome this difficulty, computer scientists have, in recent years, invented new approaches to algorithm design and new algorithms for a number of problems that require much less time than $n!$ algorithms.

Among the matters of significance in the discovery of fast algorithms for graph problems are the choice of data structure (the use of the adjacency structure instead of the adjacency matrix, for example), depth-first search procedures in tree structures, and recursively dividing the problem into two problems, each one-half the previous size but requiring much less than one-half the computation.

Sometimes the new algorithms are heuristic; i.e., they do not attempt to find the optimal solution (least number of colors in graph coloring, for example) but one that is near optimal.

We now briefly summarize problems for which algorithms have been written and give for each problem the currently best-known upper bound for the time of its execution. We assume our graph is an (n,m)-graph, i.e., one having n points and m edges.

An algorithm is said to require $0(n^p)$ operations if the number of operations divided by n^p is bounded as $n \rightarrow \infty$. Such an algorithm is said to require polynomial time. Among algorithms that are $0(n)$ are those to determine tree isomorphism and those to determine planarity. It is interesting to note that the bound for planarity algorithms has dropped from $0(n^4)$ to $0(n)$ in the past few years. Most connectivity problems—finding cut-points and/or bridges, determining connectivity, biconnectivity, and three-connectivity—are $0(\max(m,n))$; so is the problem for finding a spanning tree of a graph and that of constructing an Eulerian path if it exists. The best algorithm for subtree isomorphism is $0(n^{2.5})$ and that for finding a minimum spanning tree (the edges are given weights and the spanning tree with minimum total weight is required) is $0(\min(n^2, m \log m))$. An algorithm for the isomorphism problem for planar graphs also exists, which is $0(n \log n)$. The best shortest path (edges are weighted) algorithms are $0(n^3)$, as are the algorithms for more general maximum-flow problems.

Some problems are known to require algorithms that are exponential [i.e., there is no p such that the number of operations is $0(n^p)$]. For example, the problems of finding all cliques (a clique is a set of vertices, each of which is connected to all others) in a graph, all isomorphisms between two graphs, and all cycles or all paths in a graph are all known to be exponential.

For a rather large class of problems, called NP-complete (*q.v.*) problems, the upper bound is unknown. These include: finding the largest clique, general graph isomorphism, vertex coloring, and the traveling salesman problem. However, it is known that if an algorithm requiring polynomial time exists for one of them, then so does one for all of them. If any is shown to be exponential, then they all are.

REFERENCES

1969. Harary, F. *Graph Theory.* Reading, MA: Addison-Wesley.
1973. Knuth, D. E. *The Art of Computer Programming* [vols.

1 (1968), **2** (1969), **3** (1973)]. Reading, MA: Addison-Wesley.

1976. Biggs, N. L., Lloyd, E. K., and Wilson, R. J. *Graph theory 1736–1936.* Oxford: Clarendon Press.

1977. Andrasfai, B. *Introductory Graph Theory.* London: Adam Hilger.

P. J. EBERLEIN

GROSCH'S LAW

For articles on related subjects *see* PERFORMANCE OF COMPUTERS; and SUPERCOMPUTERS.

In the late 1940s, Herbert R. J. Grosch formulated Grosch's law concerning economies of scale in computers; namely, that computing power increases as the square of the cost, or

$$P = KC^2$$

where P = computing power, K = a constant, and C = system cost (either lease price or purchase price) so that, for example, for twice the money one obtains four times the computing power.

While Grosch never published his law, it became part of the oral tradition of the computer industry. It was quoted both seriously and humorously, and eventually gained respectability through numerous journal citations.

The pricing implications inherent in Grosch's law have led to serious attempts to ascertain its validity. While several studies lend empirical validity to its assumptions, it is not clear whether this reflects a true value in relation to users' costs or if computer manufacturers use its widespread acceptance in pricing.

There are limits to the extent that economies of scale can be realized and there is some point—the state of the art—beyond which computing power can only be increased at great cost. Also, the calculations of Grosch's law reflect a given instant of time in that they are concerned with new computers only. The existence of a used-computer market, short- and long-term leases, and third-party leases limits applications of Grosch's law in the evaluation of computer purchases or leases.

However, even today Grosch's law may be used as a rough guide to computing power, especially if one considers the total system. As Grosch himself said recently, if the considerations include "total cost"—CPU, memory, peripheral devices, software, and operations, then " . . . my old law still gives useful guidance."

K. E. KNIGHT AND R. P. CERVENY

GUARDED COMMAND

For articles on related subjects *see* CONTROL STRUCTURES; PROGRAMMING LANGUAGE SEMANTICS; and PROGRAM VERIFICATION.

The term *guarded command*, as defined by Dijkstra (1975), is synonymous with a conditionally executed (possibly compound) statement. More precisely, a guarded command is the combination of a condition (boolean expression) B and the (possibly compound) statement S whose execution is controlled by B. In a sense, B "guards" the execution of S. In Dijkstra's notation, a guarded command is represented as

$$B \rightarrow S.$$

In more common notation, the meaning of a guarded command is very much like that of the simple selection structure (**if** statement):

if B **then** S.

However, unlike the **if** statement, a guarded command, by itself, is not a complete statement in a programming language. Rather, it is one component of a more extensive control structure containing one or more guarded commands. The most interesting applications of guarded commands are those involving a set of n of them, for $n > 1$.

$$B_1 \rightarrow S_1$$
$$B_2 \rightarrow S_2$$
$$\vdots$$
$$B_n \rightarrow S_n$$

Here there are n (normally different) boolean expressions, each guarding a separate (and also normally different) statement. When a structure containing a set of guarded commands is executed, the guards are evaluated; the fashion in which they are evaluated is completely immaterial. Upon evaluation, a subset (which may be empty) of the guards will have the value **true**. Of this subset, one is chosen *at random;* it is the corresponding S that is selected for execution.

If all of the guards in a given guarded command set are disjoint—that is, if no more than one guard is **true** at any given time—then the selection of S is well-defined despite the unspecified and random nature of guard evaluation and selection. If, however, the guards are not disjoint, with the possibility that more than one may be true simultaneously, then selection of S is not well defined (and indeed may be different from one execution of the program to the next). For this reason, guarded command sets are fundamentally non-deterministic. The nondeterminism places increased emphasis on abstract specification of the desired computation, with corresponding de-emphasis of algorithm implementation details. As a result, programs can be developed in a more systematic, and, hence, reliable, manner.

Guarded command sets may be incorporated into control structures in a number of ways. The two following examples, together with simple illustrative applications, have been described by Dijkstra. In each case, the control structure syntax is the guarded command set, as formulated above, enclosed in a pair of key words.

A selection control structure has the syntax shown below.

> **if**
> $\quad B_1 \rightarrow S_1$
> $\quad B_2 \rightarrow S_2$
> $\quad$.
> $\quad$.
> $\quad$.
> $\quad B_n \rightarrow S_n$
> **fi**

The semantics of this structure are that after execution of an S, execution of the **if-fi** terminates. Only one execution of an S is performed, the selection of which is as described above. If no B is true in an execution of an **if-fi** structure, then execution of the **if-fi** does not terminate, causing the program to abort. (An alternative, in a tasking environment, might be to wait for a guard to become true.)

This **if-fi** structure is very much like the classical **case** control structure (see the article on control structures), in that only one statement group is executed and the order of the statement groups is immaterial. Unlike the usual **case** structure, however, the guards in the **if-fi** structure may be non-disjoint arbitrary conditions. In the **case** structure, the "guards" are disjoint sets of constants. Thus, the **case** structure is completely deterministic, whereas the **if-fi** is in general nondeterministic.

The following program is a simple application of the **if-fi** structure.

$$[\text{determine } max\,(P,Q)]$$

> **if**
> $\quad P \geq Q \rightarrow \text{MAX} \leftarrow P$
> $\quad Q \geq P \rightarrow \text{MAX} \leftarrow Q$
> **fi**

$$[\text{MAX} = max(P,Q)]$$

Note in this example that one of the two guards must be true, so that execution of this **if-fi** is guaranteed to terminate. Note also that both guards may be true (when $P = Q$), and that in this case execution of either statement gives the same result. Thus, at termination of execution of the **if-fi** MAX = max(P,Q).

A repetition control structure involving guarded commands has the form

> **do**
> $\quad B_1 \rightarrow S_1$
> $\quad B_2 \rightarrow S_2$
> $\quad$.
> $\quad$.
> $\quad$.
> $\quad B_n \rightarrow S_n$
> **od**

The semantics are that a statement S is selected in the manner described above, and, after execution of S, this entire process is repeated. Execution of the **do-od** structure terminates only when all guards evaluate to **false**. By constructing the appropriate guards, any desired repetitive control can be achieved.

The following program for calculating the greatest common devisor of two positive integers illustrates the use of **do-od** for specifying repetition control.

$$[\text{determine } gcd(P,Q)]$$

> $X \leftarrow P;\ Y \leftarrow Q$
> **do**
> $\quad X > Y \rightarrow X \leftarrow X - Y$
> $\quad Y > X \rightarrow Y \leftarrow Y - X$
> **od**

$$[X = Y = gcd(P,Q)]$$

Note that the two guards in this program for gcd are disjoint, so that this example is completely deterministic. In principle, the guards for a given control pattern can always be devised so that no two are true simultaneously, although this restriction often (unnecessarily) complicates guard construction and evaluation.

It is well known that **if-then-else** selection control and **do while** repetition control are sufficient to construct any conceivable execution control in a program. Special cases of **if-fi** and **do-od** are identical to **if-then-else** and **do while**, as shown in the following constructs.

> **if** B **then** S_1 $\qquad$ **if**
> $\quad$ **else** S_2 $\qquad\quad B \rightarrow S_1$
> **endif** $\qquad\qquad\quad \neg B \rightarrow S_2$
> $\qquad\qquad\qquad\quad$ **fi**

> **do while** B $\qquad$ **do**
> $\quad S$ $\qquad\qquad\quad B \rightarrow S$
> **endloop** $\qquad\quad$ **od**

As with **if-then-else** and **do-while**, these particular forms of **if-fi** and **do-od** are completely deterministic, and the **if-fi** is guaranteed to terminate.

Therefore, **if-fi** and **do-od**, as defined here in general, are quite versatile control structures. Their attraction, however, does not (currently) lie in their use as practical control structures in programming languages. For one thing, the inefficiencies of the guard evaluations tend to mitigate against such use (unless guards are evaluated concurrently). Rather, **if-fi** and **do-od** are simple and systematic enough so that they are relatively amenable to formal description, synthesis, and analysis. Moreover, since the "body" of each of these two constructs is the same (namely, a guarded command set), the same set of formal machinery applies to both. The only semantic difference between them is the condition for normal termination: **do-od** terminates when no guard is true; **if-fi** terminates after any guard is **true**.

RERERENCES

1975. Dijkstra, E. J. "Guarded Commands, Nondeterminancy and Formal Derivations of Programs," *CACM* (August).
1976 Dijkstra, E. J. *A Discipline of Programming*. Englewood Cliffs, NJ: Prentice-Hall.

J. L. WAGENER

GUIDE

For articles on related subjects *see* COMPUTER USER GROUPS; and SHARE.

GUIDE is an international association of users of large-scale IBM computers. It was formed in 1956 as an informal computer users group with members from 44 companies. The name GUIDE originated as an acronym: *G*uidance of *U*sers of *I*ntegrated *D*ata-Processing *E*quipment.

GUIDE was incorporated as a not-for-profit organization in 1970 under the full name of GUIDE International Corporation. As of 1980, GUIDE was made up of more than 2,400 member installations. The minimum equipment configuration that a member installation has either installed or on order is System 370 Model 115 or larger or IBM 4300 series processors.

GUIDE has three objectives, as follows:

1. *In relation to its members:* To exchange and disseminate information of mutual interest and value, and to promote sound and professional EDP practices.

2. *In relation to the EDP industry:* To communicate to the IBM Corporation user needs in all technical areas of interest; to review, comment, and exchange information on products and services related to IBM large-scale computers; and to influence the development of computer industry standards.

3. *In relation to the public:* An appropriate involvement regarding public opinion as it relates to the data processing industry.

GUIDE holds general sessions semiannually, usually for three days, in the Spring and Fall. Following a prominent keynote speaker, the individual sessions are usually formal presentations that may take the form of tutorials, user experience panels, workshops, or committee reports. The subject matter consists of current topics that deal with all facets of the data processing environment. Normally, over 150 individual sessions are conducted at a GUIDE general session, with an attendance of over 4,000 delegates.

Immediately preceding the general sessions, the Division and Group management and the GUIDE working projects meet to perform the major work of GUIDE. The GUIDE project work has become so valuable to its membership that two more meetings per year have been added. These meetings, called Mini-GUIDE meetings, usually consist of over 150 working projects. The objectives of these projects include sharing of information of mutual interests, suggesting enhancements to existing hardware and software, bringing problems with existing hardware and software to the attention of each other and to IBM, promoting effective usage of existing hardware and software products, and/or suggesting the development of future hardware, software, or management techniques.

The roster of GUIDE presidents includes the following persons:

Ed Law, North American Aviation, 1956–1957
Mel Gross, ESSO, 1957–1959
Carl Byham, Southern Railway, 1959–1960
Les Calkins, U.S. Steel, 1960–1963
Otis Simpson, Boeing, 1963–1965
Ottice Tidwell, A T & T, 1965–1967
Earl Althoff, Eastman Kodak, 1967–1969
Herb Seidensticker, Combustion Engineering, 1969–1971
Garland Cupp, McDonnell-Douglas Automation Co., 1971–1973
Al Burris, Northern Trust Co., 1973–1975
Charles Letteer, Armstrong Cork Co., 1975–1977
Charles E. Mairet, Deere & Co., 1977–1979
Thomas F. O'Leary, Jr., North American Philips Corp., 1979–1981

James Pitchell, Southern New England Telephone Co., 1981–

More information can be obtained by writing to GUIDE International Corporation, One Illinois Center, 111 East Wacker Drive, Chicago, Ill. 60601.

T. F. O'LEARY, JR.

H

HANDSHAKING

For articles on related subjects *see* DATA COMMUNICATIONS; and TELEPROCESSING SYSTEMS.

The exchange of predetermined sequences of control signals or control characters between two devices or systems to establish a connection, or to break a connection or exchange data and status information, is commonly referred to as *handshaking*. This is best illustrated by means of examples.

Consider first Fig. 1, which shows the sequence of signals on the input-output bus of a small computer when writing a character to a device connected to the bus. The computer first places the device address on the DATA OUT lines and raises the ADDRESS control line to tell the device that the data on the DATA OUT lines is an address. The device recognizes its address and raises the control line OK, informing the computer that the device is aware that it has been selected. This causes the computer to drop ADDRESS and DATA OUT. The device responds by dropping OK, upon which the computer places the character on the DATA OUT lines and raises the control line WRITE to tell the selected device that the character is on the bus. The de-

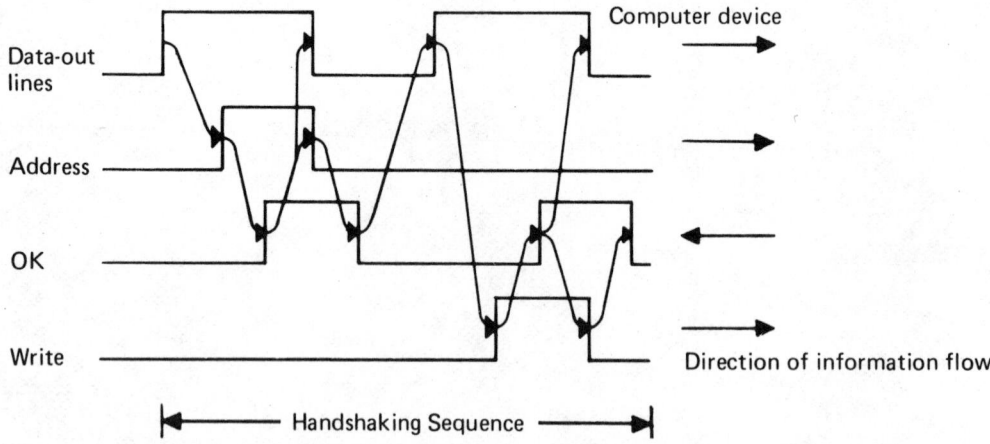

Fig. 1. Example of handshaking sequence. The arrows are used to indicate which control signal causes which response during sequence.

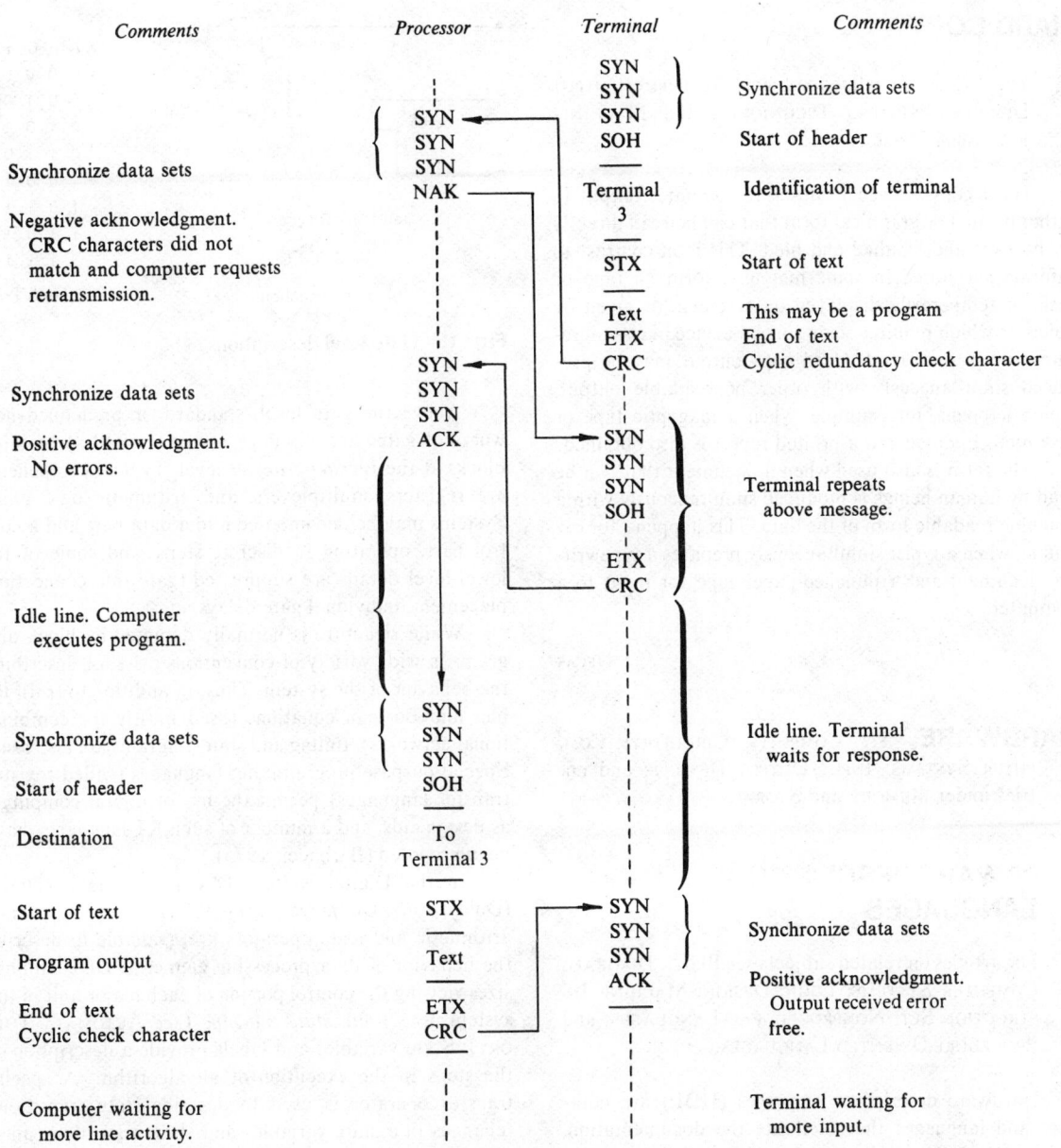

Fig. 2. Handshaking between a computer and a remote batch terminal. The arrows indicate the sequence of line activities.

vice then accepts the character and raises OK, signifying that it has accepted it. The computer then drops DATA OUT and WRITE, which causes OK to go down. This completes the handshaking sequence for transferring a character from the computer to the device.

Fig. 2 shows an example of handshaking between a computer and a remote batch terminal using synchronous communication. Here the connection is established by a special sequence of control characters (SYN, SOH, STX, etc.). Such handshaking between remote terminals and a computer is often called *communication protocol,* or simply a *protocol.*

J. S. SOBOLEWSKI

HARD COPY

For articles on related subjects *see* Input/Output Devices; Printing Techniques; and Machine-Readable Form.

Hard copy is used to describe computer output in either printed or graphical form that can be read directly by humans and handled and filed. This is in contrast to information stored in some magnetic form on tape or disk, or temporarily displayed on a screen, or given by voice, or which requires some special device like a microfilm reader to be read. Hard copy output may be produced simultaneously with other nonreadable output, which happens, for example, when a magnetic tape or disk file is updated and a printed report is also obtained.

The term is also used when a document that can be read by human beings is produced simultaneously with a machine-readable form of the data. This happens, for example, when a typist simultaneously prepares a typewritten document and a punched-paper tape for input to a computer.

J. NECAS

HARDWARE. *See* Computer Circuitry; Computer Systems; Input/Output Devices; and entries under Memory and Storage.

HARDWARE DESCRIPTION LANGUAGES

For articles on related subjects *see* Block Diagram; Computer Systems; Logic Design; Machine Instruction Set; Nonprocedural Languages; and Procedure-Oriented Languages.

Hardware description languages (HDL) are notations and languages that facilitate the documentation, design, simulation, and manufacturing of digital computer systems.

A digital system can be described at many different levels of detail in order to depict structural or behavioral aspects. Thus, a system can be described at the *gate* level as a network of logic gates and flip-flops whose behavior is specified by timing diagrams, Boolean equations, or truth tables. Typical gate level information is shown in Fig. 1. While a complete digital computer can be described at this level, the amount of information to be conveyed can be too extensive for a human designer to comprehend, and higher-level notations are often used to abstract or hide details.

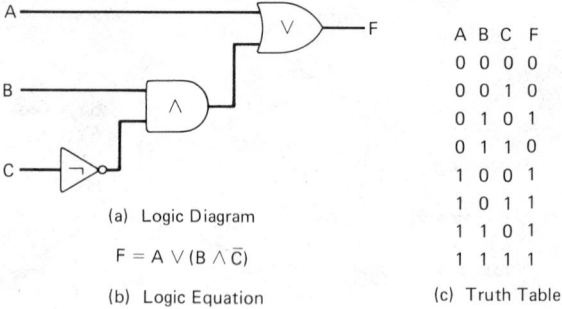

(a) Logic Diagram

$$F = A \lor (B \land \bar{C})$$

(b) Logic Equation

A	B	C	F
0	0	0	0
0	0	1	0
0	1	0	1
0	1	1	0
1	0	0	1
1	0	1	1
1	1	0	1
1	1	1	1

(c) Truth Table

Fig. 1.   Gate level descriptions.

Above the gate level, standard or predefined networks of gates and flip-flops are often used as building blocks at the *register transfer* level. Typical components are registers, multiplexers, and arithmetic-logic units. Systems may be decomposed into a data part and a control part, operating in discrete steps, and some of the lower-level details are suppressed (gate interconnection, placement, individual gate delays, etc.).

While structure is normally depicted by block diagrams, a wide variety of conventions exist for describing the behavior of the system. Thus, in addition to truth tables and Boolean equations (used mostly for combinational networks), timing and state diagrams are also used. Special-purpose programming languages (called register transfer languages) permit the use of digital computers as design aids, and a number of such RT-languages have been proposed (Barbacci, 1975).

In the Digital System Design Language (DDL) (Duley, 1967; Dietmeyer, 1971, 1974), a large number of arithmetic and logic operators are available to describe the behavior of data processing elements. DDL emphasizes viewing the control portion of each major unit in the system as a *finite state machine* (*see* Automata Theory). State variables and labels provide a description of the steps in the execution of an algorithm. A special transfer operator is used to describe state transitions (changes in a state variable) and these transitions must be written explicitly, characterizing DDL as a non-procedural language (*q.v.*) in the sense that the lexical order of the statements does not necessarily represent the execution order.

The example in Fig. 2 shows some of the features of the notation. Declarations are preceded by a tag, describing the type of element or unit. Thus, there are REgisters, MEmories, TErminals (combinational networks), etc. The IDentifier declaration names an often-used operation or set of operations, thus helping to simplify a description. AUtomaton declarations describe major portions of the system. STate declarations specify lists of operations to be performed when the automaton is at a given state.

⟨CO⟩   Booth Multiplier for 10-bit numbers
⟨SY⟩   computer:
　　　　⟨TI⟩   clock (1E-7)
　　　　⟨TE⟩   IN[21] = go∘mcnd[10]∘mpr[10]

　　　⟨RE⟩   R[10]
　　　　　　　other declarations
　　⟨AU⟩   booth:
　　　　　　clock:
　　　　⟨TE⟩   add = ¬ p ∧ q,
　　　　　　　　sub = p ∧ ¬ q,
　　　　　　　　x[10] = add ∧ R ∨ sub ∧ ¬ R
　　　　　　　　adder[10] = al ⊕ x ⊕ csub,
　　　　　　　　c[10] = al ∧ x ∨ al ∧ csub ∨ x ∧ csub.
　　　⟨RE⟩   a[21] = al[10]∘ar[9]∘p∘q.

　　　⟨ID⟩   csub = (c[1]∘sub),
　　　　　　　as =(a←adder[1]∘adder∘adder∘a[11:20]).
　　　⟨ST⟩   s0:
　　　　　　　　　go:
　　　　　　　　　r←mncd,
　　　　　　　　　a←0D10∘mpr∘0D1,
　　　　　　　　　→s1.
　　　　　　s1:   as,
　　　　　　　　　→s2.
　　　　　　s2:
　　　　Other state definitions

COmmentary information
SYstem (computer) declaration
100 nanosecond TImer (clock)
21-bit TErminal IN: go line,
10-bit multiplicand and multiplier
10-bit REgister R

AUtomaton (booth)
use clock as timer
operation definitions

REgister a is 21-bits long, formed
by 10 bits of al, 9 bits of ar, p, and q
operation definitions

STate transitions. Initial state is s0
Wait for go line.
Transfer multiplicand to r.
Transfer multiplier to a.
Goto State s1 (state transition)
State s1: perform operation as and
goto state s2.
State s2

End of state definitions
End of automaton definition
End of system definition

Fig. 2.   DDL register transfer description.

State transitions are specified by the *goto* operation (→) followed by the name of the new state.

Most of the older hardware description languages are based on a non-procedural model of execution, the best example being the Computer Description Language (CDL) (Chu, 1970, 1974). Each statement of a CDL description is preceded by a *label,* a Boolean expression on data and clock variables specifying the conditions under which the statement is to be executed. One or more register transfers can then be executed concurrently by grouping them under the same label or by the use of non-mutually exclusive expressions.

Other register transfer languages are based on a procedural model of execution, usually based on a programming language. Such is the case of A Hardware Programming Language (AHPL) (Hill, 1973, 1974), which is based on the notational conventions of APL with suitable extensions to handle parallel control sequences and asynchronous operations. AHPL uses the convention that all operations can be readily translated into hardware primitives by the use of a few simple rules.

The example in Fig. 3(a) depicts a simple sequence in AHPL. The example (taken from Hill, 1974) describes the behavior of a simple digital network. The first three statements declare two input lines (x and start), an output line (z), and a two-bit internal register (Y). The input line x feeds sequences of octal digits in bit-serial fashion. The output line z delivers the 8's complement of these digits (with 000→000) after a delay of two clock periods, as shown in Fig. 3(b). Steps 1, 3, and 5 are register transfer operations (the input x is shifted into the Y register and the proper output is sent to the z line). Steps 2, 4, and 8 are control transfer operations. Each pair of transfer and branch steps takes one clock period. Depending on the value of start, the system is reset (by going back to step 1) or branches to the next step in the algorithm. In step 7, the three bits of the digit (two bits in Y concatenated with one bit in x) are complemented (COMP is the name of the function performing the 8's complement operation). The least significant bit of the new digit is output immediately on line z and the other two bits are placed in Y.

INPUTS: x, start   *Data input and control lines*
OUTPUTS: z   *Data output line*
REGISTERS: Y(2)   *Internal storage (bits are Y_0 and Y_1)*
1. $Y \leftarrow x,0$; $z \leftarrow 0$ *Idle state ($Y_0 = x$, $Y_1 = 0$, $z = 0$)*
2. $\rightarrow (\text{start} \times 1) + (\neg \text{start}) \times 5$ *If start go to 1 else goto 5*
3. $Y \leftarrow x, Y_0$; $z \leftarrow Y_1$ *Shift Y_1 into z, Y_0 into Y_1, and x into Y_0*
4. $\rightarrow (\text{start} \times 1) + (\neg \text{start}) \times 5$ *If start go to 1 else goto 5*
5. $Y \leftarrow x, Y_0$; $z \leftarrow Y_1$ *Shift (see step 3)*
6. $\rightarrow (\text{start} \times 1) + (\neg \text{start}) \times 7$ *If start goto 1 else goto 7*
7. $z \leftarrow COMP_2(x,Y)$; $Y_1 \leftarrow COMP_1(x,Y)$;   *Complement of digit (Y_1, Y_0, x) is ($COMP_0$, $COMP_1$,*
         $Y_0 \leftarrow COMP_0(x,Y)$ *$COMP_2$)*
8. $\rightarrow (\text{start} \times 1) + (\neg \text{start}) \times 3$ *If start goto 1 else goto 3*

Fig. 3(a).   AHPL register transfer description.

start	1	0	0	0	0	0	0	0	0
x	1	0	0	1	1	1	0	0	0
z	0	0	0	1	1	1	0	1	0

Fig. 3(b).   Sample sequence for delay/complement network. The one on *start* causes subsequent three-bit sequences on x to the complemented and output on z (i.e., 001 results in 111 output, etc.). A subsequent one on *start* resets the system.

The existence of digital components capable of interpreting *instructions* stored in some memory (i.e., instruction set processors) motivates the existence of the *programming* level of description. At the programming level, the basic components are the interpretation cycle, the machine instructions, and operations (all of which are defined as *register transfer* level operations). The programming level arises from the need to describe the behavior rather than the structure of processors—in particular, the behavior as seen by the programmers of the machine.

In the Instruction Set Processor (ISP) notation (Bell, 1971) and its successor, ISPS (Barbacci, 1981), a processor is described by declarations of carriers and procedures specifying the behavior of the system:

1. Information carriers—registers and memories used to store programs, data, and other state information.
2. Instruction set—procedures describing the behavior of the processor instructions.
3. Addressing modes—procedures describing the operand and instruction fetch and store operations.
4. Interpretation cycle—typically, the main procedure of an ISP description. It defines the fetch, decode, execute sequence of a digital processor.

Fig. 4 shows an abridged description of the Digital Equipment Corporation PDP-8 processor. Declarations are grouped into sections as an organizational device; thus, **Mp.state**, **Pc.state**, **Instruction.Format**, etc., are suggestive of the role of the declarations in the overall description of the machine. For instance, the main memory of PDP-8 is described in the Mp.state section and consists of 4,096 words, each 12 bits wide. The Pc.state section describes those registers used to preserve the status of the processor between instructions. It includes the program counter, a "current page" register (used in the address computation algorithm), and an accumulator. The instruction format section describes the different fields of an instruction (e.g., operation code, address, and indirect bit, etc.). The behavior of the PDP-8 is specified via three procedures, specifying the instruction interpretation cycle, the address computation algorithm, and the instruction set proper (the *execute* algorithm).

ISPS is an example of those procedural hardware description languages derived from Algol 60. Similar rules of scope are used and behavior is described via procedure invocations. Given the specialized domain of application, special operators exist in ISPS to describe common hardware data operations (e.g., shift, rotate, concatenate, sign-extension), as well as control operations (e.g., concurrency, synchronization, external interrupts).

Beyond the programming level, other notations are used to provide concise descriptions of the physical structure of a digital system. The Processor Memory Switch (PMS) notation (Bell, 1971) is a graphical notation, and makes use of only a few primitive components:

M—A *memory* holds or stores information over time.
L—A *link* transfers information from one place to another in a system between fixed ports of other components.

```
PDP8 :=                                              Machine name
Begin
**Mp.state**                                         Memory state section
      M[0:4095]⟨0:11⟩,                               Memory, 4096 words, 12 bits/word
**Pc.state**                                         Processor state section
      PC⟨0:11⟩,                                      Program counter, 12 bits
      cpage⟨0:4⟩,                                    Current page number, 5 bits
      L⟨⟩,                                           Link bit
      AC⟨0:11⟩,                                      Accumulator, 12 bits
**Instruction.Format**                               Instruction format section
      i⟨0:11⟩,                                       Instruction register, 12 bits
            op⟨0:2⟩ := i⟨0:2⟩,                       Operation code, 3 bits
            ib⟨⟩     := i⟨3⟩,                        Indirect bit
            pb⟨⟩     := i⟨4⟩,                        Page 0 Bit
            pa⟨0:6⟩ := i⟨5:11⟩,                      Page address, 7 bits
**Instruction.Cycle**                                Instruction cycle section
interpret :=                                          Interpretation algorithm

      Begin                                          Interpretation loop
      Repeat Begin                                   Fetch next instruction and save
            i = M[PC];                               Current page number, in parallel
            cpage = PC⟨0:4⟩ Next                     Increment program counter
            PC = PC + 1 Next                         Invoke execution algorithm
            execute()                                End interpretation loop
            End                                      End interpretation algorithm
      End,                                           Execution algorithm
execute :=
      Begin
      Decode op =⟩                                   Instruction decoding
            Begin
#0\and := AC = AC And M[address()],                  AND accumulator with memory
#1\tad := L@@AC=AC+M[ address()],                    Two's complement add
#2\isz := Begin                                      Increment and skip if zero
            M[address] = M[address()] + 1 Next       Increment memory location
            If M[address] Eql0 =⟩ PC = PC + 1        Test memory location-increment
            End,                                          program counter
. . . . . . . . . . .other instructions
            End                                      End of instruction decoding
      End,                                           End of execution algorithm
address⟨0:11⟩ :=                                     Address computation algorithm
      Begin
      Decode pb =⟩                                   Decode page bit of instruction
            Begin
            0 := address = '00000 @ pa,              Page 0 address
            1 := address = cpage @ pa                Current page address
            End Next
      If ib =⟩                                       Test indirect bit of instruction
            Begin                                    Indirect address case
            If address⟨0:8⟩ Eql #001 =⟩              Test for autoincrement locations
                M[address] = M[address] + 1 Next     Increment memory location
            address = M[address]                     Indirect memory fetch
            End                                      End indirect address case
      End                                            End address computation algorithm
End                                                  End of description
```

Fig. 4. ISPS programming level description.

677

K—A *control* evokes operations of other components in a system.

S—A *switch* enables links between other components.

T— A *transducer* is used to interface a system with the external world.

D—A *data operation* produces or alters information according to algorithms describing logical and arithmetic operations.

P—A *processor* interprets programs in order to execute a sequence of operations.

Components of these types can be connected to make computers and other digital systems, as shown in Fig. 5. Components are classified as belonging to one of several categories (processors, memories, switches, links, etc.) characterizing their generic function (e.g., storage). In addition, each component specifies its specific function (e.g., primary or main memory), its technology (e.g., semiconductor), and its speed, capacity, cost, size, etc. The notation allows for the specification of a limitless amount of information characterizing or describing a component.

Components are interconnected with solid and broken lines to specify the flow of data (solid lines) or control (broken lines). In the simplest case, no more information is needed for a reader to understand the implied function of the line (e.g., data transfer, control). When necessary, a line is treated as a component (a link) in its own right, and the full power of the notation can then be used to specify its role in the system to an arbitrary level of detail. The symbol X is used to denote the external environment of the computer.

PMS components are hierarchical in nature, and can be decomposed and described by simpler PMS diagrams. For instance, processors typically consist of networks of

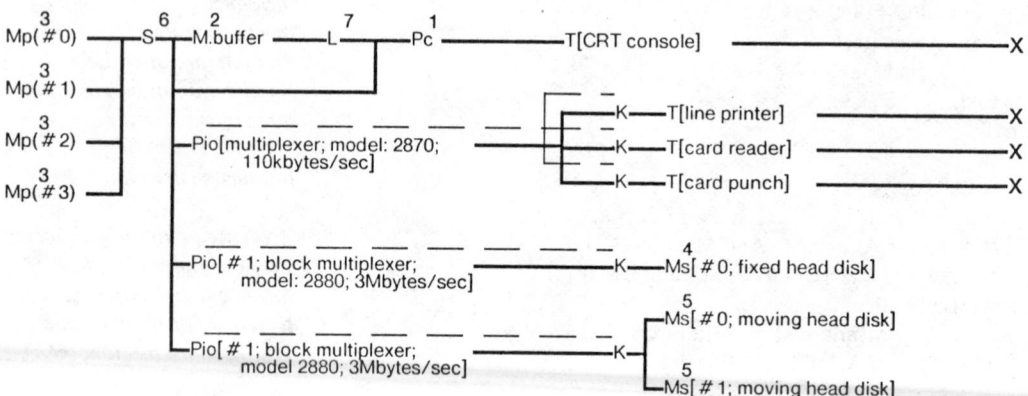

1. Pc[model: 165; cycle time: 80 ns; data paths: 64 bits]

2. M.buffer[16384 bytes; 8bytes/word; cycle time: 80 ns]

3. Mp[262144 bytes; cycle time: 2 microseconds]

4. Ms[model: 2305 model 2; fixed head disk unit;

   capacity: 11 M bytes; rotation: 0.01 sec; rate: 1.5 Mbytes/sec]

5. Ms[model: 3330; moving head disk unit; 2 disk packs;

   capacity: 100M bytes/pack; rate: 806 K bytes/sec]

6. S[bandwidth: 16M bytes/sec; data path: 8 bytes]

7. L[bandwidth: 50M bytes/sec; data path: 8 bytes]

PMS Abbreviations:

P[function:central] -> P[central] -> P.central -> P.c -> Pc

M[function:primary] -> M[primary] -> M.primary -> M.p -> Mp

P[function: input/output] -> P[input/output] -> P.io -> Pio

M[function:secondary]->M[secondary]->M.secondary->M.s->M.s

Fig. 5.   PMS diagram of an IBM 370/165.

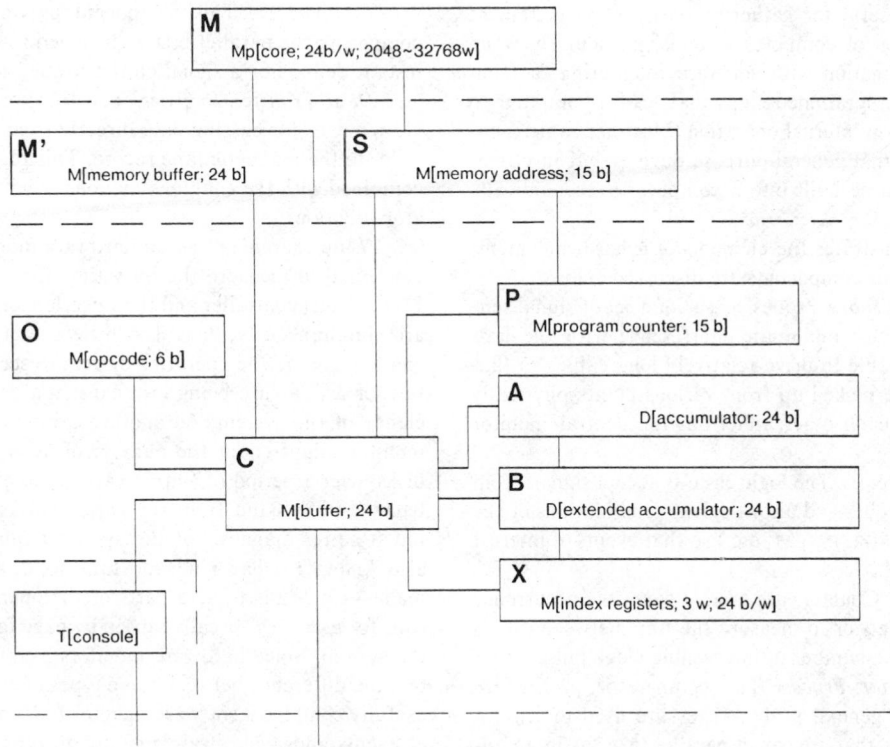

(Block Diagram of the SDS 900, Bell&Newell, 1971)

Fig. 6. PMS description of a processor (b = bits; w = word).

components of the other types. This is illustrated in Fig. 6, which shows the structure of a processor (boxes have been drawn around the PMS components, as in traditional block diagrams).

In this article, we have presented a sample of existing HDLs. For a survey of hardware description languages in the United States and abroad, see Chu (1974). It should be noted that there exists some amount of overlap between the facilities offered by the various notations. Thus, our pairing of languages and levels should only be taken as suggestive of the main area of application for a given notation and not as a clear boundary between the notations.

REFERENCES

1967. Duley, J. R. "DDL—A Digital System Design Language," PhD. Dissertation, University of Wisconsin, Madison.
1970. Chu, Y. *Introduction to Computer Organization.* Englewood Cliffs, NJ: Prentice-Hall.
1971. Dietmeyer, D. L. *Logic Design of Digital Systems.* Boston: Allyn and Bacon.
1971. Bell, C. G. and Newell, A. *Computer Structures: Readings and Examples.* New York: McGraw-Hill.
1973. Hill, F. J. and Peterson, G. R. *Digital Systems: Hardware Organization and Design.* New York: Wiley.
1974. Hill, F. J. "Introducing AHPL," *IEEE Computer* **7,** *No. 12* (December).
1974. Chu, Y. (Ed.). "Hardware Description Languages," Special issue of *IEEE Computer* **7,** *No. 12* (December).
1974. Dietmeyer, D. L. "Introducing DDL," *IEEE Computer* **7,** *No. 12* (December).
1975. Barbacci, M. R. "A Comparison of Register Transfer Languages for Describing Digital Systems," *IEEE Transactions on Computers* **C-24,** *No. 2* (February).
1981. Barbacci, M. R. "Instruction Set Processor Specifications (ISPS): The Notation and its Applications," *IEEE Transactions on Computers* **C-30,** *No. 1* (January).

M. R. BARBACCI

HARDWARE MONITOR

For articles on related subjects *see* PERFORMANCE MEASUREMENT AND EVALUATION; and SOFTWARE MONITORS.

A hardware monitor is a device for measuring electrical events (e.g., pulses, voltage levels) in a digital computer. It is useful for gathering data for measurement and evaluation of computer systems, particularly when used in conjunction with software monitoring, a technique using programmed steps that lead a computer to examine its own internal operation. Most hardware monitors are external general-purpose devices, but in principle they could be built into a computer if economically justifiable.

Fig. 1 illustrates the elements of a hardware monitor. The various components are discussed below.

General Probes. Probes consist of a set of signal sensors designed for minimum interference with the host machine and able to drive relatively long cables so that signals can be picked up from various points physically distant from each other and from the central monitor console.

Logic Circuits. The logic circuits accept signals from the general probes and allow logical combinations of the signals (AND, NOR, INVERT, etc.) so that events of interest can be defined.

Counters. Counters are used to count the occurrence of various events or to measure the time between events by counting the number of intervening clock pulses.

Comparator Probes. The comparator probes are similar to the general probes. They are used to sense a number of bits that appear in parallel (e.g., as in an address register).

Comparator. This component provides means for comparing the parallel bits with some preset value at an instant defined by a signal on the strobe line.

Data Transfer Register. The transfer register provides means for passing data directly from the host computer to the magnetic tape record. This register could be combined with the counter functions or with the comparator functions.

As an example of use, a hardware monitor might be connected to measure the busy time for a CPU and an I/O channel controller and their overlap, or the time they are simultaneously busy. Too little overlap might alert one to examine the operating system to see if opportunities for overlap are being lost, causing a decrease in efficiency of the system. As another example, a hardware monitor might count the number of accesses to several disks, over a period of time, to see if there is reasonable balance in demand from the various disks. However, a much better diagnosis of the system might result from also knowing what kinds of calls to disk were being made—e.g., calls to load parts of the operating system, calls for user files, or calls caused by page faults in a paging system. Since hardware monitors usually cannot detect the difference between these types of calls, one could usefully combine a software monitor to identify the types of events and a hardware monitor to observe their frequency and duration.

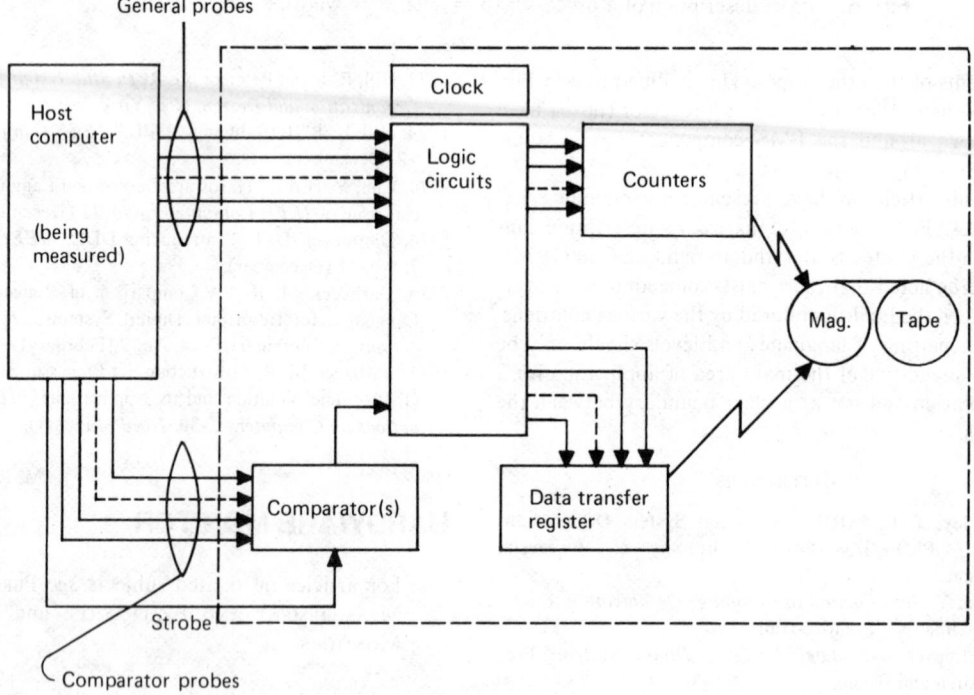

Fig. 1. Elements of a hardware monitor.

In addition to refining the basic functions of gathering data, current development in hardware monitors shows a trend toward using microprocessors for processing data during collection and for allowing the host computer and the monitor to alter each other's measurement functions during operation. From the user's viewpoint, the principal differences between hardware and software monitors are:

1. Software monitors can provide more information on cause and effect by relating measured data to the program steps being executed; however, care must be exercised to avoid disruption of time relationships caused by the addition of the measurement programs.

2. Hardware monitors only measure electrical events at predetermined physical points; hence, it is more difficult to relate measurements to program activity. However, with reasonable care, data may be gathered without interfering with the system being measured.

References

1978. Ferrari, D. *Computer Systems Performance Evaluation.* Englewood Cliffs, NJ: Prentice-Hall, pp. 32–40.

1979. Borovits, I. and Neumann, S. *Computer Systems Performance Evaluation.* Lexington, MA: Lexington Books, D. C. Heath and Co., pp. 39–56.

1981. Plattner, B. and Nievergelt, J. "Monitoring Program Execution: A Survey." *IEEE Computer* **14,** No. 11 (November).

J. D. Noe

HASHING

For articles on related subjects *see* Sorting; and Table Lookup.

Hashing (or *hash coding*) is a word coined by computer programmers to describe a general class of operations done to transform one or more fields (usually a *key*) into a different (usually more compact) arrangement. Probably, "hashing" was first coined because it seemed that "hash" was being made out of integral pieces of data. The rationale for hashing is developed more fully in the article on table lookup, dealing with key transformation. The justification for hashing derives from being able to convert naturally occurring, diverse, ill-structured, scattered key fields into compact, easily manipulated fields—usually some numeric, computer-oriented field such as a word or double word, or a computer memory address to facilitate subsequent references. The transformation from the natural field to the hash address is only a one-way process, however; the natural field cannot be decoded or reconstructed from the hash. Also, the hashed field may not represent only one unique natural field; many natural fields could hash into the same value.

For example, suppose there is a table of automobile part numbers that are ten numeric characters in length, but there may be no more than 10,000 unique part numbers. In order to contain every possible number, the table would have to allow 10 billion (10^{10}) positions to handle only 10^4 possible keys. A scheme can be contrived to transform the original ten-digit key to an integer that will represent the position of that part in a much more compact table.

One simple scheme for hashing is the division-remainder method: Choose a number close to the number of table positions needed. Use that number as a divisor to extract a quotient and a remainder from the dividend (which is the original key). The remainder so obtained is the transformed key. Using 10,000 as the divisor, the transformed key becomes the original key modulo 10,000. Some examples follow.

Original Key (Part Number)	Transformed Key
00 0000 1000	1000
00 0001 0000	0
00 0001 0001	1
00 0001 0099	99
10 0001 0099	99
22 3333 4444	4444
90 0020 0110	110
99 0020 0112	112

The examples in this table were constructed to illustrate the occurrence of duplicate transformed keys. In such schemes, prime divisors are normally used in practice.

Ideally, the hashing scheme would convert the original keys to transformed keys with no duplicates. While schemes can be constructed to minimize *collisions* (*hash clash*) their possibility cannot be eliminated completely and, because of this, the original key must be stored in the table. Further, some scheme must be used to handle duplicate transformed keys.

The examples and discussion in the article on table lookup will further describe methodology and rationale for hashing. Some other techniques in addition to division-remainder are: (1) folding, (2) radix transformation, and (3) digit rearrangement.

Folding consists of splitting the original key into two or more parts, then adding the parts together (or, sometimes, using the exclusive or operator). This sum, or some part of it, is then used as the transformed key. For example:

Original key = 20 2152 9396
Splitting and adding: 20 + 2152 + 9396 = 11568
Discard high-order digit to obtain four-digit
    transformed key of 1568.

Radix transformation involves changing the radix or base of the original key and either discarding excess high-order digits (i.e., digits in excess of the number desired in the key) or extracting some part of the transformed number. For example, an original key of 12345 (base 10) could be considered a base-16 number, and would be transformed as follows:

$$(1 \times 16^4) + (2 \times 16^3) + (3 \times 16^2)$$
$$+ (4 \times 16^1) + (5 \times 16^0) = 74565.$$

The four-digit key would be 4565 by discarding the high-order excess digit(s).

Digit rearrangement consists simply of selecting and shifting digits of the original key. For example, an original key of 1234567 could be transformed to a four-digit key of 6543 by selecting digit positions 3 through 6 and reversing their order.

No one technique is necessarily superior to another in general; however, for specific applications, some may work better than others. The selection of a technique should involve consideration of which technique results in fewest duplicate hash keys.

Hash totals are sometimes used for purposes of checking or verification; in this context, hashing has a different purpose than key transformation, inasmuch as the totals may not necessarily be hashed or scrambled. The use of hash totals is for a purpose much like the use of parity bits or self-checking codes for representing characters in digital form on media such as magnetic tapes or punched paper tapes. When such data is written (or recorded), hash totals are generated and written along with (usually after) the data. Then, when the data is read, the hash totals are recomputed, using the same algorithm, and checked against the ones recorded. If they agree, one can be more certain that the recorded data read is identical to that written and that no bits have been lost or misread.

For example, if a hash total is taken after every five numbers, that hash total could be recorded (written) after the five numbers, thus:

Five data numbers	12345
	37654
	89701
	00378
	42270
Total	182348
Discard excess to obtain "hash" total	82348

Now, upon reading this data and its hash total during some subsequent process, one could recompute the hash total in the same way and thus verify that it matched the one originally recorded.

C. E. PRICE

HEURISTICS

For articles on related subjects *see* ALGORITHM; ARTIFICIAL INTELLIGENCE.

The ancient Greek word *heuriskein* means "to find out, to discover." The English adjective "heuristic" and the more recently coined noun "heuristics" came into being via the Latin adjective *heuristicus*. According to the *Random House Dictionary*:

> *heuristic* adj. *1.* serving to indicate or point out, stimulating interest as a means of furthering investigation. *2.* (of a teaching method) encouraging the student to discover for himself.—n. *3.* a heuristic method or argument.

In the general sense, we talk of the "heuristic power" of a technique, the "heuristics in somebody's reasoning," and so on. Pólya (1954) has written several most entertaining books that do not teach, but do make one realize how to approach problems in mathematics and geometry via heuristic ideas. Also, Hadamard's essay (*The Psychology of Invention in the Mathematical Field*, Dover, 1974) on discovery in mathematics yields an interesting insight—a much too rare phenomenon—into how one of the great mathematicians of all time tackles problems.

How does all this concern us in computing? The reason is simple but its application leads to an area that is completely open-ended. Let us consider, for example, a standard task in programming. We wish to find the roots of a higher-order algebraic equation. There are several methods of approximation that yield the solution with estimatable error bounds. We have the formulas to follow, step by step, and eventually we obtain the results. This is the *algorithmic approach*.

Let us now consider a so-called ill-defined problem, and we have many of them in everyday life. For example, say we want to balance our household budget by following a program. Although our basic needs are reasonably well known (food, shelter, clothing, medical items, transportation, entertainment, etc.), neither the relative weight of the components nor their unit prices are determinable completely. Also, our needs, desires, and tastes change continually. Our interaction with the environment represents a significant modifying factor. Because this problem is terribly ill-defined, no mathematical technique by itself has a chance to solve it. The computerization of the solution requires all those vague, hard-to-quantify ideas that humans in fact make use of in doing this problem. ("Either I go on vacation or buy that new car. . . . Let's see, how much longer can I drive my old bomb?") The collection of these rules of thumb, sometimes referred to as insight, intuition, or experience with a particular task, represents what computer scientists call "heuristics" (plural noun).

We resort to *heuristic programming* whenever an algorithmic solution is prohibitively expensive or impossible to follow, or is unavailable. The role of heuristics is to cut down the time and memory requirements of search. On the average, it should result in appreciable savings when programming our budget to satisfy our basic needs. It must be pointed out that heuristic methods are not foolproof; they can fail a certain proportion of the time. (Algorithms are not supposed to fail. . . . However, the fact that a technique is not foolproof does not render it heuristic.)

The larger the range in which a heuristic can be applied, the more powerful it is considered to be. Also, its level of performance should be at least comparable to that of an exhaustive strategy (an algorithm, in fact) or of a random search for a solution.

The following example, originally reported by Simon, should shed some light on the concept under discussion. It is well known that practically any nontrivial game cannot be played by humans *or* by machines algorithmically (because there does not exist an algorithm) or exhaustively (because the memory and time requirements far exceed any available ones). The classical example of intellectual games, chess, has been programmed by several groups of researchers. In all these, heuristic ideas occupy a central role in move selection and position evaluation. In fact, de Groot and other psychologists have shown that the basic difference between excellent and merely good players is not in their memory capacity or even in their data processing ability *in abstracto*. All players analyze practically the same number of board positions, but not always the same ones. Excellent chess players have developed very powerful heuristics for the *selection* of game continuations to be considered. They may go down to a depth of, say, 20 half-moves along one path and disregard others below a depth of 2 or 3, for reasons of their own.

One of the rather often used heuristics in chess is to leave as little freedom of move selection for the opponent as possible. If all other techniques of comparison assign an equal score to two moves considered, a chess expert usually selects the one that restricts the opponent's mobility to a larger degree. This technique, being a heuristic,

works most of the time. There was a famous game, however, between two international masters in which the winner used this heuristic *to his disadvantage*. It has been shown by game analysts that in a particular position, the optimum move (overlooked for the reasons discussed) could have led to an earlier victory. A supplement to this story is that the MATER program by Baylor and Simon (1966), which incorporates the heuristics of fewest-replies, was presented the same particular near-end position and duplicated the mistake made by the international master.

Outlook. Except for some introductory efforts (Waterman, 1970; Findler *et al.*, 1971), present heuristics are all preprogrammed in artificial intelligence projects. In other words, it is not the machine that discovers, selects, and optimizes the rules that play an increasingly important role in many problem-solving programs. Therefore, the performance level of these programs is determined by the researcher's experience, insight, and perhaps even luck.

A much more desirable situation would be the one in which the heuristic processes are automated. Learning programs, initially inefficient and possibly even random in their actions, would gradually formulate more and more heuristics on the basis of experience. These heuristics would assume a flexible, or parametric, format so that subsequent optimization processes could raise the overall level of performance.

REFERENCES

1954. Pólya G. *Mathematics and Plausible Reasoning:* **I**. *Induction and Analogy in Mathematics,* **II**. *Patterns of Plausible Inference.* Princeton, NJ; Princeton University Press.

1966. Baylor, G. W. and Simon, H. A. "A Chess Mating Combinations Program," *Proc. SJCC* **28**: 431–447.

1970. Waterman, D. A. "Generalization Learning Techniques for Automating the Learning of Heuristics," *Artificial Intelligence* **1**: 121–170.

1971. Findler, N. V., Klein, H., Gould, W., Kowal, A., and Menig, J. "Studies on Decision Making Using The Game of Poker," *Proc. IFIP Congress, Book TA-7:* 50–61. Ljubljana, Yugoslavia.

1978. Waterman, D. A. and Hayes-Roth, F. (Eds.). *Pattern-Directed Inference Systems.* New York: Academic Press.

N. V. FINDLER

HISTORY. *See* DIGITAL COMPUTERS, HISTORY; and SOFTWARE HISTORY.

HOLLERITH, HERMAN

For articles on related subjects *see* DIGITAL COMPUTERS, History; IBM CARD; NINETY-COLUMN CARD; and WATSON, THOMAS, SR.

Herman Hollerith (b. Buffalo, NY, 1860; d. Washington, DC, 1929) was the inventor of punched-card data processing and founder of a firm that evolved to become IBM.

For the quarter-century from 1890 to World War I, he had a virtual monopoly on punched-card data processing. He held the foundation patents on the field (U.S. Patents 395 781–395 783) and nearly 50 other U.S. and foreign patents on basic techniques and equipment. He developed applications of punched-card data processing to many fields of endeavor, including the Census, medical and public health statistics, railroad and public utility accounting, stock and inventory control, and factory cost accounting.

Many basic decisions he made at, or before, the turn of the 20th century persist today. Punched cards today are the size of dollar bills of that era because Hollerith found it economical to buy cabinets and drawers subdivided in that size. The positional coding used on punched cards (Hollerith code) has evolved directly from decisions he made about card design when designing the first column-by-column keypunch for the 1901 Census of Agriculture. Even the practice of IBM and other firms of leasing and maintaining their own data processing equipment originated in Hollerith's decisions made prior to 1900.

Upon graduation from Columbia University in 1879, Hollerith took a job with the Census, where he became the protégé of Colonel John Shaw Billings, an Army surgeon who was also serving as director of the division of vital statistics for the Census. Billings suggested to Hollerith that a good machine to do the purely mechanical work of tabulating population and similar statistics was badly needed and that a technique of using cards with the description of each individual punched into them was a good approach to the problem. Intrigued by this suggestion, Hollerith made a study of the problem and determined to his own satisfaction that it was feasible.

In 1882, Hollerith followed General Francis Walker from the Census to M.I.T., where he became an instructor in mechanical engineering. While there he worked hard on his "Census machine" invention, concentrating initially upon a variant of an earlier machine developed by Colonel Charles W. Seaton, chief clerk for the 1870 Census. This prototype had used a player-piano roll type of feed mechanism rather than individual cards.

By the end of his first year at M.I.T., Hollerith decided that his true vocation was invention. He returned to Washington and secured a position with the Patent Office to learn the arts of invention and patent protection. After a year, he left the Patent Office and set up shop as a "Solicitor and Expert on Patents" to earn his living while he gave his primary attention to invention. Soon he applied for several patents; included among them was the first application for the foundation patents on punched-card data processing.

Considering this to be the most promising of his inventions, he concentrated upon it and developed the experimental test systems used for vital statistics tabulations in Baltimore, New Jersey, and New York City. During this period, his system evolved from a simple machine with cards punched by a conductor's ticket punch to a complete system. This system included a pantograph-like punch, a tabulating machine with a large number of clocklike counters (each capable of counting up to 10,000 occurrences), and a simple, electrically actuated sorting box for classifying and grouping cards in accordance with the categories punched into them.

In 1889, his system was installed in the Army Surgeon General's office to handle Army medical statistics. A description of this system and his plans for the Census was accepted by Columbia as a doctoral dissertation, and he was awarded a Ph.D. "for achievement" in 1890. Also in 1889, a comparative test made of the Hollerith and two competitive systems caused the Hollerith system to be chosen for use in the 1890 Census. Austria, Canada, Italy, Norway, and Russia were soon investigating and adopting Hollerith equipment for their population censuses. These early systems could only tally, not add or accumulate, totals one at a time.

Shortly after 1900, Hollerith began developing a second generation of his equipment. A new type of card design arranged numeric information in columns and permitted development of a simple, new kind of keypunch, an automatic-feed card sorter, and an automatic-feed tabulator of vastly improved performance. These new systems could accumulate numbers of any size, and thus were obviously applicable to many situations other than census and similar statistical work. Hollerith soon spread their use to an amazing variety of industries. They even went overseas with the American Expeditionary Forces in World War I.

About 1905, the management in the Census Bureau began to object to Hollerith's profits and sponsored alternative developments designed to break his monopoly. These competitive systems were widely adopted, once Hollerith's fundamental patents expired, and often led the data processing industry into new developments. Because this competition resulted in a need for increased capitalization, Hollerith sold his patent and proprietary rights to a holding company in 1912. This relieved him of day-by-day management chores and he became a highly paid consultant. Before long, Thomas J. Watson, Sr., was brought in to head Hollerith's old company, but Watson's commercialism and Hollerith's devotion to purely inventive objectives caused dissension. Watson's interests prevailed, and Hollerith's contributions and achievements were soon absorbed in the greater representative image of IBM.

REFERENCE

1971. Hollerith, Virginia. "Biographical Sketch of Herman Hollerith," *ISIS* **62**, *No. 210:* 69–78.

W. F. LUEBBERT

HOME COMPUTERS. *See* PERSONAL COMPUTERS.

HONEYWELL. *See* MANUFACTURERS, COMPUTER.

HOPPER, GRACE MURRAY

For articles on related subjects *see* AIKEN, HOWARD; DIGITAL COMPUTERS, HISTORY: EARLY; and MARK I.

Grace Brewster Murray Hopper was born in New York City on 9 December 1906. She received her B.A. in Mathematics and Physics from Vassar College in 1928, where she was elected to Phi Beta Kappa. She continued her graduate studies in mathematics at Yale University, where she was awarded her M.A. (1930) and Ph.D. (1934). From 1931 to 1943, she was a member of the mathematics faculty at Vassar College. In December 1943, she joined the United States Naval Reserve and attended Midshipman's School at Northampton, MA.

She graduated in 1944 with a commission in the U. S. Navy (Lt. J.G.) and was assigned to the Bureau of Ordnance's Computation Project under the direction of Howard Aiken at Harvard University. It was at Harvard that Dr. Hopper was first exposed to the world of automatic digital processing. There she joined Robert Campbell and Richard Bloch as a "coder." In her words: "I became the third programmer on the world's first large-scale digital computer, Mark I." At the end of World War II, Dr. Hopper resigned from Vassar and was appointed to the Harvard faculty as a Research Fellow in the newly founded Computation Laboratory.

In 1949, she joined, as senior mathematician, the fledgling Eckert-Mauchly Corporation, where BINAC and UNIVAC were under construction. She remained with the organization after its acquisition by Remington

Fig. 1. Grace Murray Hopper.

Rand, through the merger with Sperry Rand, and until her retirement from the Univac division in 1971. Throughout this period, she maintained her activity in the U. S. Naval Reserve and was promoted successively through the ranks until her retirement as a Commander in 1966. In 1967, she was recalled to active duty and, in 1973, promoted to the rank of Captain. Currently, she is on active duty at the Pentagon with the Naval Data Automation Command.

For more than three decades Captain Hopper has been an innovator and major contributor to the development of programming languages. Inspired by John Mauchly's "Short Order Code" (BINAC, 1949) and Betty Holberton's first Sort-Merge Generator (UNIVAC I, 1951), she developed the first compiler, A-0 (1952), and the first compiler to handle symbolic manipulation, A-2 (1953). This work, coupled with her view of what the world of programming languages ought to be like, led her to the development of the first English language data processing compiler, B-0 (Flow-matic), completed in 1957. In April 1959, Dr. Hopper met with a small group (I. E. Block, B. Cheydleur, S. Gorn, R. Rossheim, and A. E. Smith) to discuss plans for a meeting whose object was "to develop the specifications for a common business language for . . . a digital computer" (Sammet, 1981, p.

200). This meeting triggered a sequence of events that resulted in "Initial Specifications for a Common Business Language" (DOD, April 1960). Flow-Matic, along with AIMACO and Commercial Translator, provided the main inputs in influencing the early development of Cobol (Sammet, 1981, p. 217).

Dr. Hopper's awards, honors, and professional publications are much too numerous to detail here. Most notably, she has received honorary degrees from the Newark College of Engineering (D. Engr., 1972); C. W. Post College, L.I.U. (D. Sci., 1973); The University of Pennsylvania (LLD, 1974); and the Pratt Institute (D. Sci., 1976). She has also received almost every major award in her profession. These include DPMA's "Man-of-the-Year" (1969); AFIPS' Harry Goode Memorial Award (1970); and Yale University's Wilbur Lucius Cross Medal (1972). In 1971, the Univac Division of Sperry Rand Corporation created the Grace Murray Hopper Award, which is awarded annually by ACM to a distinguished young computer professional.

Clearly, Grace Hopper belongs to that select group of computer professionals whose talent, vision, dedication, and constant persistence has laid the foundation for the continuing information processing explosion. Throughout her career, she has seen herself as a teacher and as one who has always battled entrenched attitudes of those she refers to as the "establishment." The phrase "but it's never been done that way" is anathema to her. As a visual reminder of her personal creed, she keeps a ship's clock in her office. It appears to be a typical ship's clock until you look carefully: It runs backward.

REFERENCES

1971. "Grace Murray Hopper," *ACM '71: A Quarter Century View*, pp. iii–iv.
1981. Wexelblat, Richard (Ed.). *Proceedings, History of Programming Languages Conference*. New York: Academic Press. (See Sammet, J. "Introduction of Captain Grace Murray Hopper," pp. 5–7; Hopper, G. "Keynote Address," pp. 7–24; and Sammet, J. "COBOL," pp. 199–278.)

H. S. Tropp

HOSPITAL INFORMATION SYSTEMS

For articles on related subjects *see* BIOMEDICINE, COMPUTER GRAPHICS IN; COMPUTED TOMOGRAPHY; INFORMATION SYSTEMS; INTENSIVE CARE, COMPUTERS IN; MANAGEMENT INFORMATION SYSTEMS; and MEDICAL APPLICATIONS.

The automation of health care delivery is variously referred to as the development of hospital, health, or medical information systems. These systems have in common a high level of on-line operation and a file structure based on a patient-oriented record. A hospital information system (HIS) in our usage deals with the patient while occupying a bed in the hospital. In countries with a hospital-based health care system, this term implies a much broader level of automation.

The physician and nurse are central to an HIS, since most activities in a medical environment are based on a physician's order. Such an order may activate tasks in many areas: The pharmacy, the clinical laboratory, the kitchen, accounting, etc. It is obvious that communication capability is a primary requirement. It has been shown that 20–30% of the nursing staff time, and a similar percentage of total hospital costs, are related to information processing. Beyond simple communication services, an HIS system may be used in a pharmacy for the preparation of medication schedules, drug compatibility, and interaction checking. Clinical laboratory tasks such as blood collection schedules, test scheduling, and instrument monitoring result in normalization based on standard test samples, and outcome posting, with flags indicating that abnormal or out-of-range results may be produced by modules of an HIS. Other tasks can include the generation of patient care plans, diet, planning, inventory tracking, maintenance, scheduling of staff, etc.

For the tasks mentioned above, only a limited record has to be kept on the patient. In order to impact the medical care to a greater extent, a computerized medical patient record will have to be kept. The entry of physicians' and nurses' observations on the patient, combined with formal categorizations such as problem statements and diagnoses, will allow summarization of a patient's history and progress. Given good tools, such as decision aids that use computer-stored data, the possibility of useful interaction for the physician emerges. Without such feedback, the utility to the physician of using a computer entry device, no matter how sophisticated, is at best negligible. Much data entry into current systems is performed by the nursing staff and ward clerks.

A long-term medical record implies extension of the HIS into the outpatient, community pharmacy, and private physician areas. A well-organized medical record can aid in distribution of the responsibility for health care delivery among physicians, nurses, specialists, and medical paraprofessionals, since less will depend on the memory of the physician in attendance.

Since health care is currently being delivered by a spectrum of providers, from family practice physicians to specialized clinics outside of hospitals, there is no single depository for the medical record, and data are collected at times redundantly and, in other respects, incompletely. A comprehensive health insurance scheme, which would track the cost and benefits of medical services in order to

Fig. 1. Terminal entry station of the Technicon medical information system used to select medication frequency for a prescribed drug. Thus, the drug order appears on the medication standard at appropriate times and allows the pharmacy to provide unit-dose trays. This reflects the latest care plan for the patient.

optimize its operation, could provide the required incentives for a complete and integrated medical record. Closest to this goal are the health maintenance organizations, but most do not integrate hospital services, nor collect hospital data, in their systems.

Systems providing major or minor portions of the services outlined above have been provided in a variety of forms. Entry devices have been readers of prepunched cards, large function keyboards, conventional typewriter terminals, but CRT terminals dominate today. The most

successful methods have utilized lightpen or finger-touch selection from CRT-presented choice lists (Fig. 1). In a well-structured hierarchy of choices, any specific order may be entered with three to seven screen loads. Physicians can select such menu screens at a rate of 2.5 per second. Terminals have to be available in all nursing areas and in most service areas to make such a communication system effective. A major problem has been the poor quality of output presentation. Excessive quantities of data printed on identical white sheets using lines of uniform uppercase-only characters with unpleasant fonts have made the task of searching for relevant information in the record harder instead of easier. Some graphic presentation of the patient's state, as is now frequently provided by the nursing staff, may make HIS output more acceptable.

The computer systems themselves range from minicomputers doing fairly isolated tasks to shared computer utilities. Frequently, local minicomputers provide the communication and data collection services, and are connected at night to service computers for data analysis and report preparation. Most systems are now procured from outside vendors. Difficulties with in-house development have been due to inadequate staff, program incompatibilities, and lack of intercomputer communication standards, which have prevented the integration of individually successful application modules from many sources into a cohesive system. Total systems, which provide services to all hospital areas, have been associated with high initial costs and long delays before they achieve productive operation. The delays have the effect that the hardware is no longer optimal when the system is distributed on a wide scale. Several systems have, however, been well accepted in a number of hospitals and provide the expe-

System name	MIDAS	MIS	POMCS
Location (number of sites)	Stockholm County, Sweden	El Camino Hospital, Sunnyvale, CA (~10)	Coral Gables Variety Children's Hospital
Developer	Local and Univac	Technicon, Tarrytown, NY	Dynamic Control
Scope	In- and out-patients	In-patients	In-patients
Number of patients	750,000	500 patients	180 beds
Database content	Management and medical indicators	Medical orders and results	Medical orders, results, billing
Computer service	Central system for all county hospitals; multiple Univac 496's, CRT keyboard terminals, and Telex printers.	Shared system for multiple hospitals, also installed in dedicated sites; single 360/370 processor with back-up, lightpen terminals, and ink-jet printers.	Parameterized dedicated system for moderate sized hospitals; single IBM system 32 with CRT keyboard terminals and printers.

Fig. 2. Systems that exemplify the range of hospital information systems.

rience for further technical development of medically relevant systems (see Fig. 2).

The increasing demands on health care quantity, quality, distribution, and cost control will have the effect that continued attempts at improved HIS implementations will be made. With a better understanding of system requirements, a suitable system architecture can be developed. With imaginative human interface engineering, the acceptability of these systems can be increased. With the inclusion of a complete range of services, economic benefits may accrue which will make the concept of an HIS truly viable.

REFERENCES

1974. Collen, M. F. *Hospital Computer Systems*. New York: Wiley.
1977. Watson, R. J. "A Large-Scale Professionally Oriented Medical Information System—Five Years Later," *J. Med. Sys.* **1**, No. 1: 3–21.
1977. Shires and Wolf (Eds.). *MEDINFO77*. Amsterdam: North-Holland.
1978. Thompson, G. E. and Handleman, I. *Health Data and Information Management*. Boston, MA: Butterworth.
1978. Fenna, Donald; Abramson, Sixten; Lööw, J. D., and Peterson, H. The Stockholm County Medical Information System. New York: Springer-Verlag.
1979. Hospital Information Systems. *The Art, Problems and Prospects*. Roger Shannon (Ed.). Amsterdam: North-Holland.
1979. Schmitz, Homer H. *Hospital Information Systems*. Germantown, MD: Aspen Systems Corp.

GIO WIEDERHOLD

HOST SYSTEM

For articles on related subjects *see* DISTRIBUTED SYSTEMS; FRONT-END PROCESSORS; MICROPROGRAMMING; and MULTIPROGRAMMING.

A *host system* or a *host computer* is the physical system that interprets a program. The program is written on a *logical machine*, which is usually not the same as the physical machine (host system). These differences arise because the physical system either does not possess or does not allocate all features or resources directly requested by the logical machine (program). The distinction between host system and logical system is especially notable in two areas: multiprogramming systems and microprogrammed (emulated) systems.

In multiprogramming systems the host system is responsible for allocating storage and I/O resources to each of the logical machines (i.e., in effect, active programs), which are usually called *virtual* machines, as they are re-

quired. This allows a number of virtual machines to share the physical resources without logical conflict (i.e., without any programmer intervention in the source programs) and at the same time more effectively use the resources of the physical host system.

In microprogrammed systems the notion of host system applies to the physical machine that interprets (*emulates*) the programs written in other machine languages. The machine being emulated by the host machine is said to be the *image* machine (sometimes the term "virtual" is also used to describe this situation).

Another and an increasing use of the term *host system* is in time-sharing or remote computing, where the *host* is the central computer providing service to terminals or satellite computers.

M. J. FLYNN

HUMAN FACTORS IN COMPUTING

For articles on related subjects *see* DATABASE MANAGEMENT; PERSONAL COMPUTING; SOFTWARE MANAGEMENT; SOFTWARE SCIENCE; and SYNTAX, SEMANTICS, AND PRAGMATICS.

Systems developers and researchers are paying increasing attention to the human factors aspects of computer uses, such as programming, database retrieval, and terminal interaction. There is a growing awareness that the experience of system and language designers can be, and should be, supplemented by controlled experimental testing of new concepts before widespread dissemination makes revisions difficult. Emotional arguments and unfounded claims about the effectiveness of languages, systems, or applications are being replaced by experimental results which provide quantitative evidence. Researchers are recognizing that insights gained through experimentation refine and complement intuition and experience.

Early languages such as APL and Basic became popular because of careful attention to human engineering. However, contemporary users are more discriminating and often have backgrounds and experiences which radically differ from programming language designers. Experimental testing can help to ensure that the interface design matches user needs and skills.

Experimental Methods. Experimental research depends on the clear statement of the *hypothesis*, such as "the use of mnemonic variable names in long Fortran programs reduces the time necessary for professional programmers to locate and repair bugs." This hypothesis indicates that there is a single *independent variable*, the presence or absence of mnemonic variable names and a single *dependent variable,* the time to locate and repair bugs. The experimenter manipulates the independent variables and measures how the dependent variables change. Subjects must be selected so as to represent the population and assigned to groups so as to minimize experimental bias. The administration of the experiment is followed by data collection and statistical evaluation using methods such as the t-test, analysis of variance, correlation coefficients, factor analysis, or regression analysis. Although group means may differ, a *statistically significant difference* must be established through the use of statistical techniques, which reveal the magnitude of the difference and account for variability among subjects.

Controlled experimentation demands a careful decomposition of human performance in which the significant factors are first studied independently and then jointly to measure interaction effects. Critics argue that controlled experimental testing produces minor results, but supporters respond that each result should be reliable, replicable, and generalizable. Each small result, like a tile in a mosaic, contributes to the image of human performance in using computers.

For the experimental approach, tasks such as learning a programming language must be distinguished from other tasks such as composition of programs. Comprehension, debugging, or modification of previously written programs are still other tasks. Separate experiments can be done with each of these tasks. Distinctions must be made between novice and professional users, between short and long programs, among the applications domains and among the variety of available languages. For example, the harsh limitation of two-character mnemonic names in Basic does not seem to disturb novice programmers when writing short game-playing programs, but such limitations might be serious in large programs that will be maintained for many years.

Programming Research. Experimental research in programming language usage has focused on stylistic issues, language features, design techniques, program evaluation methods, and group processes. Stylistic issues, such as the choice of mnemonic names, comments, indentation, parameter passing techniques, level of nesting of conditional statements, iteration techniques, or output formats, are likely candidates for research, since clear-cut results can be implemented rapidly in the form of organizational standards.

Some experimental results suggest that mnemonic names aid comprehension, especially if there are many names in a program. High-level comments describing the function of a module are helpful but numerous low-level comments, which describe the function of only a few statements, lengthen the program listing and interfere with program comprehension, debugging, and modifica-

tion (Shneiderman, 1980). Experimenters have not been able to validate the conjecture that indentation of statements aids in program comprehension, debugging, or modification, suggesting that indentation of lines may disrupt visual scanning, cause line breaks which lengthen the listing, and show only syntactic structure but hide functional organization.

Detailed standard flowcharts have not been found to aid programming but the utility of macro-flowcharts, pseudo-code, and other documentation schemes remain to be studied. High-level control structures, such as the **do-while** and **if-then-else,** have been shown to aid programmers; modular organization, based on functional decomposition, also appears to help.

A natural byproduct of experimentation is the increased interest in measurement techniques. Numerous program quality evaluation methods have been proposed, although none has emerged to dominate. Halstead's software science (*q.v.*) depends on objective counts of operators and operands in a program to estimate the effort in constructing the program and indirectly measure quality. McCabe assesses program complexity by counting the number of control paths. Various other measures have also been proposed.

The popularity of team organizations and group processes in programming has stimulated researchers to study some of these practices. Although the cost in programmer time is high, group processes appear to reduce the variance in performance by eliminating extremely poor programs, to provide a training ground for novices and new employees, and to improve communications among members of a project team.

Database Languages. Although only 1% of the population will become professional programmers, 10% of the population may be users of database systems for storing and retrieving information. Since the experience of programming language designers is specialized, human factors experimentation should be used to validate the assumptions about what is reasonable for the intermittent and/or poorly trained user of a database system. Experiments have helped to clarify query language design principles, have shown that inexperienced users can be taught the fundamentals of self-contained query languages in a few hours and have provided guidance in revising proposed languages. Other important issues involve the choice of data models, design of schemas to facilitate comprehension, the match of query language features with user skill levels, and the use of natural language front-ends for database systems.

Interactive Systems. Although only 10% of the population may become familiar with database facilities, nearly 100% of the population may become users of interactive terminal systems for airline, car, or hotel reservations, banking, shopping, teleconferencing, electronic mail, education, and medical applications. Personal or home computing might include financial record-keeping, home energy monitoring/control, entertainment, telephone/mailing list maintenance, and information storage. The design of these applications must incorporate careful human engineering to ensure that untrained users can succeed.

Parametric command languages, fill-in-the-blank approaches, or menu selection will be the primary modes for interactive systems designed for widespread use. Experiments have begun to reveal the fundamental principles of keyboard layout, screen design, language design, error handling procedures, and human information processing capabilities. Research has shown that, as the response time increases, users modify their approach to employ fewer commands and also that, as the response time variance increases, satisfaction and performance deteriorate and that violations of human expectations (such as unusually slow or fast response times) are extremely disruptive.

Text editing, word processing, and document generating systems provide further opportunities for human factors researchers, since user satisfaction and performance can be strongly influenced by design changes. Experiments have shown that full page screen editors can double the productivity of users working with line editors and that improved command language syntax can significantly increase speed, accuracy, and satisfaction.

Cognitive Model. Each topic requires numerous experiments to help resolve issues and guide designers, but some unifying principles have begun to emerge. There appears to be a basic separation of human knowledge into *semantic* and *syntactic* components. The semantics of an application domain are the functions or operations that are permitted. This knowledge is acquired or understood through experience, by integration with familiar concepts, with demonstrations of examples, and through high-level cognitive processes. Semantic knowledge is language-independent and once acquired is resistant to forgetting. Syntactic knowledge consists of the details for expressing an operation in a specific language. It must normally be acquired through rote memorization, is likely to be forgotten unless frequently rehearsed, and is largely arbitrary. For example, the semantic knowledge about a line-oriented text editor concerns operations to insert, delete, replace, or change lines and to save or destroy files. Syntactic knowledge would include the abbreviations for each command, valid delimiters, acceptable file names, and the permissible character set. This syntactic/semantic model applies to programming, database usage, text editing, and terminal interaction, and can pro-

vide guidance to designers of command languages, error handling procedures, user aids (such as *help* facilities which provide on-line information about system features), or training manuals.

The increasing interest in human factors research is a result of the awareness that computer systems are becoming widely used by a diverse population who expect computers to be reliable, easy to use, effective, efficient, and, above all, "friendly" tools.

REFERENCES

1971. Weinberg, G. M. *The Psychology of Computer Programming.* New York: Van-Nostrand Reinhold.
1973. Martin, J. *Design of Man-Computer Dialogs.* Englewood Cliffs, NJ: Prentice-Hall.
1980. Shneiderman, Ben. *Software Psychology: Human Factors in Computer and Information Systems.* Cambridge, MA: Winthrop.

B. SHNEIDERMAN

HUMANITIES APPLICATIONS

For articles on related subjects *see* ARTS APPLICATIONS; COMPUTER GRAPHICS; COMPUTER MUSIC; DATA BANK; INFORMATION RETRIEVAL; PATTERN RECOGNITION; and SOCIAL SCIENCE APPLICATIONS.

The use of the computer in the humanities entails the preparation of information banks which include data and rules specifying procedures to be used for applications involving either pattern recognition or pattern generation (or both). For a book-length survey of the subject, readers are referred to Hockey, 1980.

Information Banks in the Humanities. The preparation of information banks implies preliminary decisions as to format and editing. Because many of the traditional categories in the humanities are not rigorously defined, investigators wishing to use such categories often pre-edit the text so as to be able to retrieve information concerning, for example, syntactic or semantic patterns. Thus, at this stage of the use of the computer in the humanities, the text's format and editing sometimes make use of poorly defined elements and weakly defined or nonexistent models. For example, categories such as image or texture are not sufficiently defined to permit specification by rule for their recognition by the computer; images must be identified in advance by the human being using the computer.

As empirical data gathering, model building, and model testing facilitated by the computer have grown, the need for arranging information so as to anticipate the theory upon which the conclusions are based has been declining. It should be possible some time in the future to "bank" information in its conventional form and then provide rules for sorting the elements in the bank into desired categories. At that point, preparation of information banks will be a step prior to, and separate from, pattern recognition and pattern generation applications in the humanities. At present, although the functional distinction is relatively clear, the methodological distinction is not.

Types of information banks currently used in computer-based applications in the humanities include bibliographies, texts, dictionaries, historical records, and rules for combining discrete elements of whatever artifact is being generated. For the value of bibliographical data for information retrieval, the reader is referred to the article on that subject. The annual Shakespeare bibliography and the U. S. Modern Language Association's annual bibliography are examples of major data banks of this sort for the humanities. General-purpose dictionaries (e.g., Webster's, Random House) that are available in computer-accessible form are used by humanists, for example, to search for literary themes; in addition, humanists have prepared special-purpose dictionaries (e.g., *The Old English Dictionary*) for research related to their special fields of interest. A formidable text bank, nearing completion at the University of Chicago through cooperation with the Centre National de la Recherche Scientifique, will make available 1,500 works of French writers from the 18th to 20th centuries, and the Center for Computer Assisted Textual Analysis is developing an archive of machine-readable English texts (Holzman and Morrissey, 1979).

An example of an information bank consisting of historical records is the 11-volume, 8,000-page, 3-million word collection on the London stage, 1660–1800, an

> exhaustive calendar of plays, entertainments, afterpieces, dancing, and singing, together with casts, box receipts, advertising, contemporary comment, and all available information about scenery, theatre construction, costuming, audiences, management, and production, compiled from the playbills, newspapers, and theatrical diaries of the period. (Daland and Schneider, 1971.)

If this material were not available in computer accessible form, the scholar who

> wished to determine how many times actor X and actress Y performed in the same play together during their careers might find it necessary to scan a period of 15 to 20 years (possibly 800 to 1000 pages) to exhaust all the possibilities of intersection, and yet the list of joint performances might not fill a page. (Daland and Schneider, 1971.)

Historical records of all sorts, ranging from voting records to land use records, are being put into computer-accessible form for scholarly research (see Levitt and LaBarre, 1975).

Information banks of recorded speech are of interest to humanists because research based upon such banks may provide useful analytical categories for the auditory components of language and literature. Speech information banks require large quantities of storage (a 2,400-foot magnetic tape will hold 5 to 10 minutes of digitized speech), and techniques for coping with the data are likewise complex.

Information banks comprising rules are currently of importance for pattern generation and will become increasingly significant for pattern recognition as the categories being recognized become ever more amenable to description through a precisely defined procedure. An example of such a bank of rules would be those necessary to enable the computer to approximate the form of a sonnet—number of lines, number of syllables per line, stress patterns within the line. Some rules (e.g., number of lines) would be obligatory, whereas options would be available as to the selection of some others; for example, within certain metrical contexts, an anapest (UU/) might be substituted for an iamb (U/).

Pattern Recognition. Pattern recognition based upon data banks consisting of bibliographies is described in the article on information retrieval. Pattern recognition based upon historical records is analogous to that involved in bibliographies—searching for either a particular type of record (e.g., cast listings in Daland and Schneider's *London Stage*) or a specified word (e.g., the name of a particular actress in *London Stage*).

Pattern recognition for which the data banks are texts in machine-readable form—dictionaries, and indeed sometimes bibliographies and historical records—might be thought of as falling into three divisions: (1) recognition, using categories that derive from standard graphic conventions; (2) recognition, using categories that derive from traditional approaches to language and literature; and (3) recognition, using categories that derive from theories or models concerning the description of discrete and continuous events (from the mathematical sciences).

Categories that derive from standard graphic conventions include characters, words, sentences, and strings longer than sentences. Occurrences of single characters and short strings are useful for humanists concerned with manuscript *stemma* or with various editions of a given text. The derivation of one manuscript from another is of interest for two reasons: (1) the scholar would like to find the manuscript that is either the original or closest to the original manuscript of the text in question; and (2) shifts in spelling provide data for studies of sound change (Mullen, 1971). Comparisons of editions of a given text are undertaken in order to list the variants among them, and thus to arrive at either an edition that seems best to reflect the presumed original or to arrive at an edition that at least exhibits internal consistency (Cabaniss, 1970).

The presence or absence of specific characters in a text may also provide guides to the style of the author. Insofar as linguistics is considered part of the humanities, the character and short strings of characters are important guides to morphology (e.g., the discrimination of roots, affixes, and plural morphs). Such morphological patterns are of obvious importance for the study of foreign languages, traditionally considered humanistic disciplines.

The humanities have used the *word* as a category most centrally in indexes and concordances. An index is generally taken to be a listing of the word together with locations of its occurrence in the text. A concordance is a listing of the word together with a specific quantity of context for each of its occurrences in the text. For the production of research aids such as these, the computer is now regarded as an indispensable tool by scholars in the humanities, and new techniques are being developed for further use of this tool (Crosland, 1979; Holzman and Morrissey, 1979). Words are also used to provide stylistic clues, which in turn are sometimes used for author identification (McKinnon and Webster, 1969). For example, the classic study by Mosteller and Wallace (1964) of the Federalist papers indicated that it is possible to discriminate between those written by Hamilton and those written by Madison on the basis of certain function words (e.g., articles, prepositions, conjunctions) that occur in the known writings of one author at a frequency significantly different from that in the known writings of the other author.

Sentences and strings longer than sentences, such as paragraphs and chapters, are categories that derive from standard graphic conventions and may provide guides to various components of style. Decisions as to the units by which these strings are measured may well affect their usefulness for a particular problem. For example, although Mosteller and Wallace (1964) could find no significant difference among the sentence lengths of Madison and Hamilton when measured in words, Robert Wachal suggested in a doctoral dissertation (on Linguistic Evidence, Statistical Inference, and Disputed Authorship) that there may be a significant difference if those sentences are measured in terms of syllables. Whatever the measure, this approach to pattern recognition can be replicated by other scholars as long as the unit is defined according to standard graphic conventions. Perhaps that is the salient point about pattern recognition based upon categories that derive from standard graphic conventions.

The conventions can be clearly defined, departures from the conventions can be clearly specified, and experimentation is thus replicable.

It is with the next group of categories, those traditionally used for studies in language and literature, that replicability and reliability become a serious problem. Among the categories that fit into this general class are those drawn from phonology, syntactics, and semantics, as well as terms that refer to readability and terms such as unit and texture which refer to other terms such as structure and content, etc.

Phonology is concerned with the sound of the spoken language, and one might assume that there are categories related to phonology analogous to those, such as characters and words, which relate to the graphic representation of the language. It is indeed possible to produce information banks of digitized speech and subsequently to make statements concerning acoustic properties such as frequency and intensity (amplitude). Unfortunately, the quantity of storage demanded by even short strings of digitized speech has thus far prevented storing literary or linguistic strings in sufficient length to permit the development or discovery of categories arising directly from the acoustic data—categories that would facilitate discussion of metrics, rhythmical patterns, or rhyming patterns. If, given acoustic parameters, the latter categories no longer seem relevant because they lack equivalent precision, then acoustic patterns might be used to distinguish one utterance, or one poem, or one prose work from another.

Current efforts to map the short strings of acoustic signals that are available onto graphic conventions such as characters, combinations of characters, or words are extremely complicated pattern recognition problems. Syllable recognition can now be achieved approximately 80% of the time, but identification of word boundaries is much less successful. (For further discussion of the pattern recognition problem in speech, see the article on speech recognition.)

In lieu of direct input and analysis of acoustic signals, phonology has been studied on the basis of human graphic transcriptions of the auditory component of language and literature. Although linguists are extensively trained and become skilled at making such transcriptions, recording variabilities do introduce very serious problems as far as reliable replicability is concerned. Nonetheless, mappings from phonetic transcriptions onto graphic conventions, and vice versa, are of interest to humanists wishing to describe patterns of rhyme, or rhythm, and of auditory phenomena (see Logan, 1976).

Syntactic categories are used for stylistic discrimination applied to author identification or to changes in the style of a given author over time. The syntactic categories used depend upon traditional intuitions concerning parts of speech, plus intuitions concerning the text being examined, or upon a particular linguistic model, e.g., transformational, phrase-structure, or Montague (see Green, 1971; Friedman, 1978). The use of the computer to locate syntactic patterns for which the syntactic units are defined on the basis of traditional intuitions or even on the basis of various models usually implies pre-editing of the text. Because the syntactic categories used in such pre-editing are not sufficiently rigorously defined, efforts to replicate the use of a particular set of categories may not succeed. Insofar as a given scholar is consistent in the use of a set of categories, it may well be possible to make statements concerning use of the different categories in the text being examined. But if another scholar questions the consistency and attempts to replicate the work, difficulties may ensue because the categories themselves are somewhat amorphous. Computer-based parsers have thus far not been used for extended studies of syntactic patterns in literary or other texts, presumably because such parsers are either not sufficiently general-purpose to deal with the texts in question or they provide so many possible syntactic readings for a given sentence as to make analysis of such readings for extensive quantities of text extremely difficult and time-consuming. Probabilistic parsers, which give the single best (most probable) parsing for a given sentence, seem most promising for this application; one such parser was described rather early in the development of parsers (Stolz *et al.,* 1965) and, more recently, work on speech recognition has revived interest in probabilistic linguistic analysis, including syntax (Kender, 1977).

Semantics, which is just coming into its own in linguistics, has long been of interest to humanists. Categories such as texture, theme, and tone presumably refer to semantic implications of words and to the relations among those words in a text. Computer-based efforts to utilize semantics in literary analysis have depended upon interplay between words in the text and words in standard reference works such as *Roget's International Thesaurus* or portions of the *Oxford English Dictionary* (Sedelow and Sedelow, 1967, 1969). For literary analysis, large stores of semantic information are necessary; hence, artificial intelligence efforts to cope with semantics (Winograd, 1972; Schank, 1975; Woods, 1975)—efforts that deal with very restricted universes of discourse—are not thus far viable for literary analysis. Rather, computer-based work in the humanities relies on reference works (dictionaries and thesauri) reflecting general use of the language as both validated and modified through time. The difficulty in using such reference works is that their own structures—particularly of thesauri—are not sufficiently characterized so as to ensure that the research scholar knows the biases they introduce into his results. If such references are to be used with assurance, research

on modes of characterizing these reference works is necessary; some such research has been undertaken (Sedelow and Sedelow, 1969; Smith and Maxwell, 1977). When semantic networks both external and internal to texts can be more adequately characterized, categories such as texture and tone may either assume new meaning or completely disappear as viable indicators of literary style and structure.

Other traditional categories such as readability and dramatic climax depend either upon categories (e.g., syntactic and semantic) that fall into this general area of categories traditional to language and literature or upon categories, such as word length, which depend upon standard graphic conventions, or both.

The third major category area important to pattern recognition in the humanities is that derived from the mathematical sciences, particularly statistics and probability, information theory, and analysis (especially relevant to acoustical phenomena). Models in the mathematical sciences can, of course, be rigorously defined and thus tested extensively against data. Because of its quantity, humanistic verbal data is especially appealing to mathematical model builders who in the past have sometimes been dependent upon the restricted number of subjects convenient to social science experiments or to restricted instances of any given case. On the other hand, the application of mathematical and statistical models to natural language data is often hampered by the very quantity of data. Contingency tables, transition matrices, and other structures requisite to mathematical and statistical models quickly become so large that they exceed the capacity of even very large digitial computers. Efforts to find models that fit data more adequately (e.g., nonparametric statistical models), as well as to find ways of managing data so as to increase data computability, are likely to increase dramatically during the coming years as more data becomes available in computer-accessible form and as more model builders become aware of this large storehouse of data available for model testing.

Pattern Generation. In many respects, computer-based pattern generation represents the obverse of pattern recognition. At first blush, it might seem to be more difficult because it demands rules specifying the way elements being generated are to be combined. This would seem to be more complicated than, for example, a search through a text for occurrences of specified words. It is probably true that the most elementary generation of poetry is more complicated than elementary searches for words. But as pattern recognition efforts become more comprehensive so as to include, for example, semantic relationships, the pattern recognition task then becomes more complicated than elementary generation tasks (Petrick, 1977). An analog might be the greater ease with which computer-based transformational generative grammars are written than are computer-based transformational parsers. It is easier to generate acceptable sentences than to attempt to parse the infinite variety generated by humans.

Pattern generation, like recognition, uses information banks such as dictionaries, thesauri, bibliographical information, and banks of rules based upon models or assumptions appropriate to the artifact being generated. For example, generation of haiku poetry would entail specification of the number of lines, the length of lines, acceptable sequencing of syntactic classes, the vocabulary that falls into the general type of vocabulary appropriate to haiku, and some appropriate semantic relationships among the words. Specification of the latter has been minimal in poetry generated to date. For haiku, a verse form for which semantics is relatively obscure anyway, this specification is not so vital and, in fact, in some contemporary poetry, semantic relationships among words are certainly oblique and often distant. The casual reader may not see a great deal of difference between "a great king packed in an acorn" written by a human and "dance, oh life, like a silent tumbleweed!" written by a machine (Boroff, 1971).

Inasmuch as sophisticated pattern generation of language and literature is extremely complicated, in large measure because of semantics, computer-based pattern generation in the humanities will doubtless be used in the foreseeable future for testing models or parts of models of language and literature. The computer may never write like Shakespeare, but it may be used to identify precisely some aspects of the nature of Shakespeare's writing.

Although computer graphics represents pattern generation in a somewhat different sense, its use in the humanities as a heuristic, or aid to insight, should be mentioned. Graphics can help reveal patterns in the structure of a literary or other text. Thus, graphics can show which themes or ideas tend to cluster together in a text and which never appear together, and which metrical patterns tend to dominate and where. In short, graphics can be used to represent those elements of the text that have been specified and identified by the computer. Most often, computer graphics provide visual representations of the results obtained by the application of mathematical and statistical models to data.

Other Applications. One of the major areas of the humanities of which the scope of this article does not permit coverage is instruction. Computer-assisted instruction is being used in the teaching of foreign languages, and there is a growing effort to use it in teaching composition. For a detailed presentation of current work in computer-assisted instruction, the reader is referred to the article on that subject.

REFERENCES

1964. Mosteller, Frederick and Wallace, David. *Inferences and Disputed Authorship: The Federalist.* Reading, MA: Addison-Wesley.

1965. Stolz, Walter S., Tannenbaum, Percy H., and Carstenson, Frederick V. "A Stochastic Approach to the Grammatical Coding of English," *Comm. ACM* **8**, *No. 6:* 399–405 (June).

1967. Sedelow, Sally and Sedelow, Walter A., Jr. "Stylistic Analysis," in Borko, Harold (Ed.). *Automated Language Processing: The State of the Art.* New York: Wiley, pp. 181–213.

1969. McKinnon, Alistair and Webster, Roger. "A Method of 'Author' Identification," *Computer Studies in the Humanities and Verbal Behavior* **2**, *No. 1:* 19–23 (March).

1969. Sedelow, Sally and Sedelow, Walter A., Jr. "Categories and Procedures for Content Analysis in the Humanities," in Gerbner, George *et al.* (Eds.). *The Analysis of Communication Content.* New York: Wiley, pp. 487–499.

1970. Cabaniss, Margaret Scanlon. "Using the Computer for Text Collation," *Computer Studies in the Humanities and Verbal Behavior* **3**, *No. 1:* 1–33 (January).

1971. Boroff, Marie. "Creativity, Poetic Language and the Computer," *The Yale Review* **60**, *No. 4:* 481–513 (June).

1971. Daland, Will and Schneider, Ben R., Jr. "The 'London Stage' Information Bank," *Computers and the Humanities* **5**, *No. 4:* 209–214 (March).

1971. Green, Donald C. "Formulas and Syntax in Old English Poetry: A Computer Study," *Computers and the Humanities* **6**, *No. 2:* 85–94 (November).

1971. Mullen, Karen A. "Using the Computer to Identify Differences Among Text Variants," *Computers and the Humanities* **5**, *No. 4:* 193–202 (March).

1972. Winograd, Terry. *Understanding Natural Language.* New York: Academic Press.

1975. Levitt, James H. and LaBarre, Claude E. "Building a Data File from Historical Archives," *Computers and the Humanities* **9**, *No. 2:* 77–82 (March).

1975. Schank, Roger C. "The Structure of Episodes in Memory," in Bobrow, Daniel G. and Collins, Allen (Eds.). *Representation and Understanding.* New York: Academic Press, pp. 237–272.

1975. Woods, William A. "What's in a Link: Foundations for Semantic Networks," in Bobrow, Daniel G. and Collins, Allen (Eds.). *Representation and Understanding.* New York: Academic Press, pp. 35–82.

1976. Logan, H. M. "The Computer and the Sound Texture of Poetry," *Language and Style* **9**, *No. 4:* 260–279 (Fall).

1977. Crosland, Andrew T. "The Concordance as Aid in the Historical Study of Style," *Style* **11**, *No. 3:* 274–283 (Summer).

1977. Kender, John R. *An Annotated Bibliography of Natural Language and Speech Understanding Systems.* Department of Computer Science, Carnegie-Mellon University.

1977. Petrick, Stanley S. "Understanding Understanding Poetry," *Computers and the Humanities* **11**, *No. 4:* 217–221 (July/August).

1978. Friedman, Joyce *et al. Research Reports, 1976–78.* University of Michigan, Department of Communications and Computer Science.

1979. Holzman, Michael and Morrissey, Robert. "Computers and Humanistic Research," *Proceedings: Apollo Agonistes: The Humanities in a Computerized World* (SUNY Albany) **1**: 196–206 (April).

1980. Hockey, Susan. *A Guide to Computer Applications in the Humanities.* Baltimore and London: The Johns Hopkins University Press.

D. A. DINNEEN AND S. Y. SEDELOW

HYBRID COMPUTERS

For articles on related subjects *see* ANALOG COMPUTERS; ANALOG-TO-DIGITAL AND DIGITAL-TO-ANALOG CONVERTERS; SIMULATION; and SPECIAL PURPOSE COMPUTERS.

Overview. Hybrid computers, incorporating at least one stored-program digital processor linked with a multiplicity of analog computing units, have been successfully used since the late 1950s for the solution of a wide range of engineering simulation studies. In addition, the continuous parallel computing capability of analog devices in combination with the sampling and storage facilities of the digital computer has proven to be very efficient for complex signal processing. Many large industrial and government organizations around the world with major research and development programs have at least one active hybrid computing center. Important areas of application of hybrid computers are considered in a later section of this article. In some fields, such as guided missiles and space vehicles, where real-time, high-fidelity simulation is essential, hybrid computers have been necessary for successful system development.

The relative usefulness of continuous analog simulation versus numerical digital techniques has been subject to continuous review over the last 20 years. The proponents of analog techniques have often been successful in demonstrating the desirability of these methods. The main rationale is based upon the fact that digital computers capable of real-time engineering simulation of these complex systems cost many millions of dollars and cannot be realistically dedicated in real time. In most applications, a hybrid computer capable of real-time solution has been at least an order of magnitude less expensive than an equivalent digital computer. In a few real-time applications demanding unusually high-frequency performance, there was literally no single digital computer capable of the task. Also, standard multiprocessor systems supported by appropriate software for real-time simultaneous computation are still not available. Multiple CPU systems beyond the complexity of two or three processors require a level of overhead for synchronization which obviates the speed advantage.

Hybrid computing methodology is actually a continuum of techniques ranging from all-digital numerical analysis to all-analog continuous electrical solution. Since all-digital and all-analog solution methodologies are covered in other sections, here we will discuss only the techniques and the systems that have been developed to exploit the combined computation schemes.

Architecture. The modern hybrid computer is a digitally-based system in which the users interact primarily with the digital computer through alphanumeric and graphic terminals. All programs and data for the complete hybrid programs are maintained as mass memory files to provide automatic program set-up and operation. The analog computer(s) serve as high-speed parallel computing devices under direct control of the master digital program. This is in contrast to earlier hybrid laboratories, where the digital computer was often used only as an adjunct to the analog computers to perform special computations.

As shown in Fig. 1, the hybrid simulation laboratory is usually composed of a master stored-program digital computer to which a variety of local and/or remote terminals are interfaced. The digital computer may include a multiplicity of secondary digital processors, such as minicomputer or array processors, to handle specific tasks. A data and control interface capability is required for communication between the digital computer and one or more analog processors. This includes a multiplexed analog-to-digital converter (ADC) and a set of digital-to-analog converters (DAC). In many systems, the DACs are actually digital-to-analog multiplying (DAM) devices to obtain the analog product of an analog signal and a rapidly updated digital coefficient.

The control interface provides both communication of logical data and facilities for real-time synchronization of the digital subsystems and the analog processors. In some more sophisticated systems, logical control signals from the analog processors can control the sequencing of data transfer through the interface directly to/from the main memory.

Analog processors used in modern hybrid systems may be automatically loaded from the digital computer except for insertion of the interconnection panel. As discussed in the section on future hybrid systems, it appears that this last mechanical vestige will be soon eliminated. Essentially, all control and monitoring functions available to the manual operator of the analog computer are now digitally controlled on the latest analog processors.

Finally, as shown in Fig. 1, this complex of processors can be connected in real time to various test facilities and analog graphic devices through a trunking system. The trunking system, in its simplest form, may be a set of cables, while in multifunction laboratories, it is a programmable interconnection system. Graphic devices include CRTs, strip-chart recorders, and analog plotters.

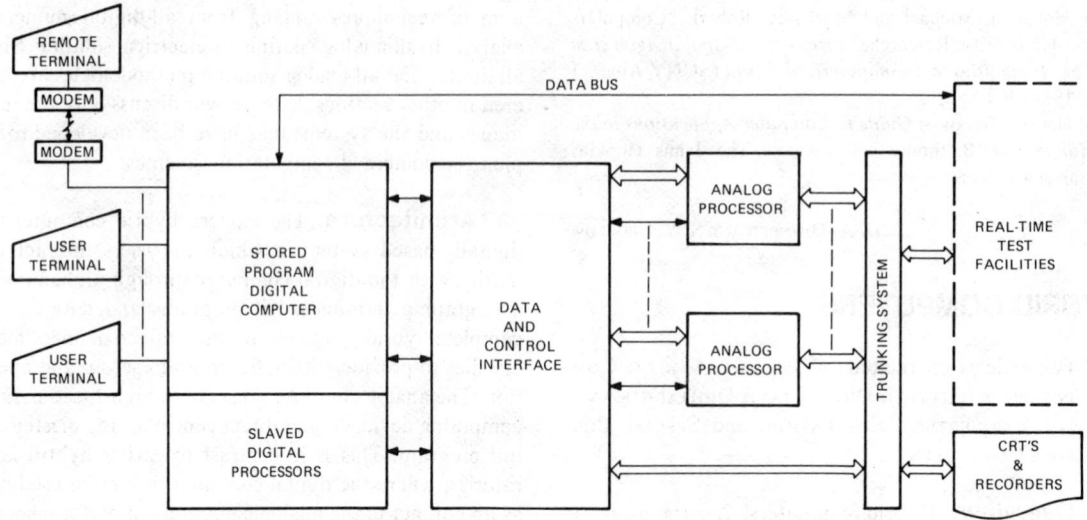

Fig. 1. Hybrid simulation laboratory structure.

Test facilities often require both parallel analog/logic signals and digital bus signals.

Using the latest multiprogrammed operating systems, it is feasible to provide non-real-time user operation on terminals, while real-time simulation studies are running on the test facilities.

Electronic Associates, Inc. (EAI) of West Long Branch, NJ, is the primary manufacturer of general-purpose hybrid computing systems (see Fig. 2). Other manufacturers of analog computers who have also implemented hybrid systems include Applied Dynamics International (ADI) of Ann Arbor, MI, and Denelcor, Inc., of Denver, CO. Foreign manufacturers include Hitachi in Japan and Dornier in Germany. In addition, a

Fig. 2. Grumman Aerospace Corporation of Bethpage, NY, uses EAI HYSHARE 2000 computer for dynamic systems simulation.

number of small educational analog computers are built by small companies like Comdyna, Inc., but these are seldom used in hybrid configurations.

Operating Systems.

Hybrid computation places unique demands upon the digital computer operating system for both communication and sequence control. To appreciate these requirements, one should understand that there are a variety of tasks which must be handled with different timing priorities.

1. Time-critical CPU operation for hybrid closed-loop computation.
2. Real-time data storage/retrieval for graphic display, forcing functions, iterative computation, curve fitting, etc.
3. Non-real-time analog processor automatic iterative control.
4. Analog processor interactive operation.
5. Set-up and check-out of analog processor.

Of all these classes, only item 1 demands true real-time operation of the central processing/arithmetic units. Time-critical operation means that the CPU must perform a specified task within a given frame time.

Most real-time data communication tasks such as data storage/retrieval can be preprogrammed for direct memory transfer during the analog processor run. The remaining tasks require the operating system to provide rather sophisticated data/logical communication with the analog processor, but there are no special priority processing demands. For iterative control of the analog processor, the digital computer need only read the value of an objective function at the end of a run, change appropriate parameters on the analog console, and initiate another run. All devices on the analog processor must be buffered, of course, so that the operations can be interrupted as necessary.

Time-critical operation can be defined on the basis of a repetitive frame time or a random event basis. For dedicated single-task operation, the repetitive frame time operation and appropriate multiframe sequencing can be programmed by polling a real-time control signal. Interrupts could also be used in this mode; however, this is normally wasteful simply for synchronizing to real time.

For random events as typified by exception conditions such as overflow, limits, or block transfer termination, interrupt-oriented operation is most efficient. In some cases, these interrupts do not need to be handled on a time-critical basis, and the usual task activation procedure will suffice. In other situations, there is a maximum interrupt response time requirement, and "directly connected" vectored interrupts are required. In this case, the only operating system overhead permitted is for saving and restoring of register stacks.

The most demanding requirement is for time-critical processing in a multiprogramming environment. However, this type of operation provides for the most efficient system utilization and user access/convenience. Both repetitive frame time and random solution events demand directly connected interrupts. One of the complications for the time-critical processing of directly connected interrupts is the relative priority of I/O interrupts, which usually have higher priority in operating systems than the user interrupt levels. For buffered I/O devices operating on a record basis, CPU processing is only needed between records and is not a time-critical function. Therefore, the directly connected hybrid interrupts should be given a higher priority than I/O interrupts.

There are two basic methods for implementing analog/digital interprocessor communication. In a single-user hybrid environment, the complete set of I/O instructions for the analog processor can be executed directly in the user's program since there are no questions about user program integrity. The problem with most digital processors and operating systems is that, in this mode of communication, the operating system must allow the user to execute the entire set of I/O instructions. This can destroy other users' programs if not the operating system.

Next, implementation of hybrid computation in a multiprogramming environment requires that the basic hybrid communication be performed by resident routines as a part of the operating system. Users can then request allocation of resources and the operating system can maintain integrity. A large portion of the analog processor set-up and control functions are not time-critical—the extra time required to perform these functions through the operating system is not significant. But, for time-critical functions, special handling of the operating system traps is required. When the communication sequence can be preprogrammed prior to real-time operation, time-critical operating system response is often not needed.

Programming Languages.

It is generally recognized that hybrid computers are very effective for solution of continuous system simulation problems. It is also an accepted fact that programming, set-up, and check-out of a hybrid simulation are generally more difficult and specialized than performing digital simulation. This has tended to limit the number of engineers who have become users of hybrid computers.

During the last ten years, a significant effort has been underway to develop compiler and program generation systems for hybrid computers. This stemmed from work done in England from 1964 to 1969 to develop a practical compiler for analog computers called APSE

(Automatic Programming and Scaling of Equations), which was sponsored (and supported) primarily by the National Computing Center in Manchester, England. The APSE language is a relatively simple extension of Fortran to allow specification of differential equations. Declarations are included to target the generated program to different configurations of analog computers.

Through efforts supported by the U. S. government in the mid-1970s, the APSE compiler was enhanced to become a Program Generation System (PGS) to provide automatic set-up, check-out, and operation of analog processors. This became the ECSSL I Compiler/PGS which necessarily includes an on-line hybrid interpreter called HYTRAN. ECSSL is basically a Continuous System Simulation Language (CSSL) with extensions to define special data for the analog processor program. The interpreter accepts the object code generated by the ECSSL/PGS and performs the set-up and check-out of the parallel analog processor. Features have been added to ECSSL to provide interactive analog program operation, including graphic display and recording of results.

Starting in the late 1960s, a new compiler designed to generate programs for the complete, integrated hybrid system was initiated by the British Aircraft Corporation (BAC) and later supported by a consortium of organizations. This program, called ACTRAN (Analog Computer Translator) and later HCS-1 (Hybrid Compiler System), was a major undertaking and was only partially completed by BAC. EAI, with U. S. government support, finished this package and is now marketing the ECSSL II Program Generation System for a variety of analog and digital processors.

Computing Methodology.
Most studies to which hybrid computers are applied include two fundamental elements: First, a mathematical model or analysis requirement and, second, an experimental procedure. For relatively simple problems, this leads to a natural problem split where the analog processor handles the mathematical analysis and the stored program digital processor implements the experiment. The programming, set-up, and check-out of the analog processor are also performed by the digital computer.

As seen from the digital computer, the analog processor is a very high-speed subroutine to handle those parts of a task which would consume an inordinate amount of digital processing. But as seen from the analog real-time program, the digital processor looks like a set of real-time functions which are not available on the analog processor or for which there are insufficient analog components. Another way of using the hybrid scheme is to split the problem so that the lowest frequency (longest time constant) components of a model are solved digitally while the highest frequency (*stiff equations*) are solved using continuous parallel analog methods.

One of the limitations of parallel analog computation can be the finite number of computing elements available for complex system simulations. Fortunately, for many of these problems, the system is composed of a series of similar elements and the mathematical model can be described by a vector of coupled models with only parametric differences between elements of the vector. Thus, an algorithm to "time-share" or "multiplex" analog computing elements can often be devised using the digital processor to sequence the components and to save/restore intermediate results. The recent additions of electronic coefficient devices and high-speed analog/digital direct memory data conversion are elements of hybrid systems which effectively implement sequential analog computing techniques.

Many of the most challenging applications of hybrid computers are related to the solution of models for distributed systems represented by sets of partial differential equations (PDEs). A variety of effective techniques have been developed to solve most forms of PDEs. These methods are relatively complex both from a mathematical and computational point of view and have found limited applications. Standard packaged software for combined hybrid computer simulation of any given class of application has not been practical due to the need to interconnect manually and debug the resulting program. As discussed in the section on future hybrid systems, it is anticipated that this limitation will be overcome with stored program hybrid processing systems.

Applications.
Hybrid computers are used by an engineer for the analysis of dynamic systems much as an oscilloscope or spectrum analyzer and a breadboard circuit implementation may be used. For system design and evaluation, an engineer needs to express the mathematical laws governing the system operation, test a set of design parameters and logical sequences, and observe the results. This kind of symbiotic relationship between the creative mind of the engineer and the physical realization of physical system as embodied in the computer model is very different from the structured business information processing or statistical analysis functions of a typical data processing system.

Major classes of applications of hybrid computers over the last ten-year period are given in Fig. 3. Military applications for real-time simulation of aerospace vehicles represent approximately one-half of all hybrid computer activity. For example, introduction of more sophisticated fighter aircraft has necessitated the development of new antiaircraft missiles with greatly improved performance. These simulations require both greater fidelity and increased natural frequencies as compared to the earlier, less sophisticated vehicles. Accordingly, hybrids have continued to be the only practical computational choice. It has been estimated (Holmes and Hall, 1980) that a

Aerospace
Real-time missile system design/evaluation
Space vehicle stabilization
Space vehicle human factors analysis
Helicopter dynamics
Shuttle hydraulics system design
Shuttle mission evaluation
High-performance fighter aircraft human factors
Rotating Machinery
Turbine engine control
Centrifugal compressor dynamics/control
Synchronous motor control
Automotive
Directional control/stability
Ride quality analysis
Microprocessor engine control
Real-time off-highway vehicle simulator
Crash data signal processing
Military tank human factor studies
Electrical/Nuclear
Nuclear power plant
Three-phase inverters/rectifiers
Electric car power conversion/storage
Transmission line overvoltage transients
Communications system design
Chemical
Distillation column controller design
Tubular reactor control/optimization
Heat exchange analysis/control
Biomedical
Biomechanical studies for prosthetic design
Cardiovascular system simulation
Pulmonary system modeling

Fig. 3. Classes of hybrid computer application.

digital would need to perform over 150 megaflops* to meet real-time simulation requirements, a constraint which cannot be met by any existing digital system for complex simulation studies.

A second major set of applications of hybrid computers through the 1970s was for the Space Shuttle development. Real-time rocket engine simulation was required for microprocessor control system design. Complete mission simulations with experienced astronauts were needed for human factor and control avionics studies. Also, vehicle development for hydraulic system evaluation and transportation studies was done on hybrid computers.

As shown in Fig. 3, the remaining applications cover nearly all fields of engineering design and evaluation. In some cases, a smaller complement of analog computing

*A megaflop is equal to 10^6 floating-point operations per second.

elements has been used because the digital processing speed has increased in typical hybrid systems.

Future Hybrid Systems. Since the early 1960s, there have been studies and proposals to replace the manual patch panel of analog computers with switching matrices. However, the many thousands of switching contacts needed, coupled with the lack of an appropriate switching element, have made the implementation of such a computer rather impractical except for small prototype systems. A high-level compiler has always been considered an essential element of such an automatic system and this has also been lacking until ECSSL II came along.

Development of solid-state, high-accuracy analog switching elements in the late 1970s has made the implementation of a matrix for analog processors an economic and technical reality. These switching elements, using Complementary Metal Oxide Semiconductor (CMOS) technology, have been developed both as multiplexers for analog-to-digital converters and as matrix elements for solid-state PBX systems. The most recent chip is a 4 × 8 matrix with low ON resistance and nearly infinite back impedance. Combined in a three-stage matrix architecture with voltage-following differential output amplifiers, a practical large-scale matrix can be economically constructed.

Using an earlier 8 × 1 solid-state switch, a three-stage matrix of 64 inputs and 128 outputs has been installed in a number of hybrid computing laboratories to use for specialized purposes. Also, a pair of these matrices was installed on a hybrid system at the Technical University of Vienna in Austria in 1979. These efforts have proven the technical feasibility of such an automatic system.

A second dimension to the implementation of an automatic analog processor is to replace the logic and switching components of the analog computer with an equivalent stored program capability. Two basically different technologies are available, either of which might satisfy the requirement. First, one can simply implement a very high-speed sequential microcoded logic processor which responds to state changes (events) on an interrupt basis. This has finite speed limitation if several events occur simultaneously. But, given the speeds which can be economically implemented today, this approach would appear to be adequate.

Programmable Logic Arrays (PLAs) and an appropriate logic signal matrix would be an alternative to a sequential processor. This could also be combined with logic storage elements (flip-flops and registers) to provide an expandable parallel logic processing capability. This approach would provide speeds comparable to the patched logic of present analog processors while providing for complete automation.

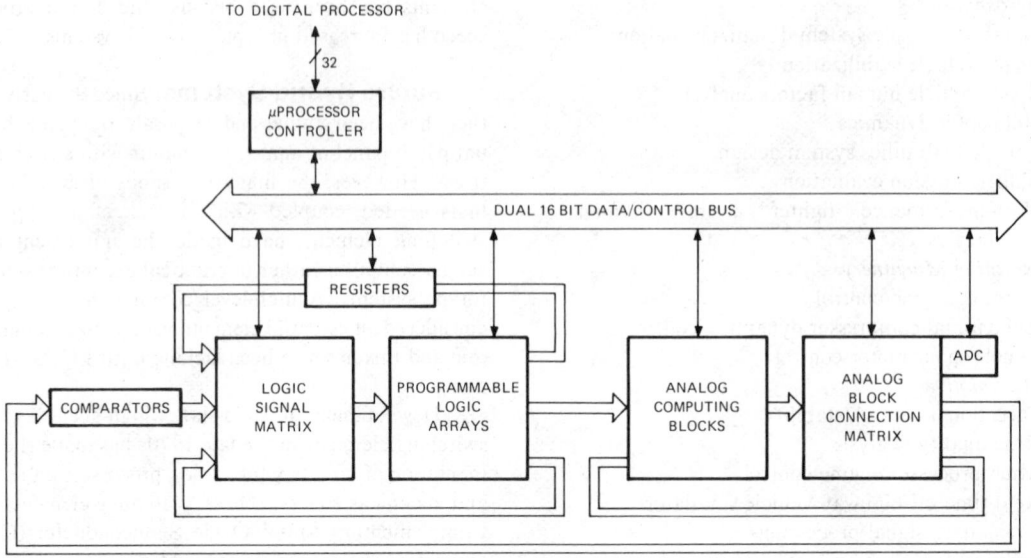

TO DIGITAL PROCESSOR

Fig. 4. Architecture of stored-program analog processor.

An architecture for a stored program analog/logic processor utilizing the analog matrix and PLAs is shown in Fig. 4. The high-speed microprocessor controller can act as a format converter between the CPU floating-point data in memory and the multiplicity of fixed-point devices in the various processing units. The 16-bit control bus allows the microprocessor to set up a block transfer between the main memory and the various storage elements of the analog/logic processor. The 30-bit counters/interval timers have a built-in clock and buffer register so that a multiplicity of precisely timed sequences can be established. Communication from the analog computing blocks to the logic subsystem is through a set of threshold comparators while logic to analog switching control goes directly from the outputs of the PLAs to the electronic switches and mode control gating of the analog computing blocks.

Such a system should continue to provide a factor of about 20:1 economic advantage over digital computer solution of simulation problems for at least the next five years. In addition, the program preparation costs will be reduced significantly for new simulation and it is anticipated that the system could be used by much less experienced personnel. In fact, for the first time, problem-oriented languages could be prepared for hybrid computers so that libraries of mathematical models could be shared for complex system simulations by end users.

Conclusions. Combined digital and analog computing methods have proven to be very effective for a range of engineering studies over the last 20 years. Although the use of hybrid computing waned somewhat in the latter 1970s due to the introduction of new digital processing systems, recent hardware and software developments may revitalize this valuable computing methodology. All indications are that hybrid computers will continue to provide a unique capability that will not be met economically by digital processing in the foreseeable future. Greater use will be made of specialized high-speed digital processors, but the continuous analog computational capability will remain an essential feature.

REFERENCES

1974. Bennett, A. W. *Introduction to Computer Simulation.* New York: West Publishing Co.
1977. Landauer, J. P. "Stored Program Hybrid Processing System," *Simulation 77,* pp. 127–191.
1980. Holmes, W. M. and Hall, K. L. "MICOM's Advanced Simulation Center and Digital Computer Boundness," *Symposium on Very High-Speed Computing Technology* (September), pp. I.3–I.18.

J. P. LANDAUER

IBI-ICC. *See* INTERGOVERNMENTAL BUREAU FOR INFORMATICS.

IBM. *See* MANUFACTURERS, COMPUTER.

IBM 360–370 SERIES

For articles on related subjects *see* COMPUTER INDUSTRY; GENERATIONS, COMPUTER; OPERATING SYSTEMS: CONTEMPORARY; and VIRTUAL MEMORY.

The IBM system 360 and its upward compatible successor, system 370, have been so widely used, and so many of its features have been widely imitated, that it has become important for almost everyone in the computer field to be aware of the essential aspects of their hardware and software systems. The literature concerning these systems is very extensive. An annotated bibliography of documents published by IBM on Systems 360 and 370 would itself fill a volume the size of this encyclopedia.

The basic unit of information in the 360/370 is the eight-bit byte. Four bytes comprise a word. Some instructions operate on bytes, and others operate on half-words (two bytes), words, double words (eight bytes), and on strings of bytes. An instruction or operand address is always a byte address, the leftmost or most significant byte when a group consisting of more than one byte is being addressed. The 24-bit address field in index registers permits the direct addressing of $2^{24} = 16,777,216$ bytes.

The magnetic core memories of the early 360s were severely limited in size, from a 64K-byte maximum (K = 1024) on the model 30 to a maximum of 1M bytes (M = 1,048,576) on the top of the line model 75. The larger models could use auxiliary (though slower) large-core memory of up to 8M bytes. Auxiliary core memory was eliminated in the 370 series. Maximum memory was gradually increased into the millions of bytes even on the small 370 models, and up to the addressing limit of 16M bytes on the larger ones. These large memories became economical and practical with the use of MOS large scale integration memory technology on models of the 370 introduced after 1972.

The 370 design assumes that the computer will run under control of an interrupt-driven operating system. The system provides for automatic storage in main memory and for automatic loading from a different area of main memory of the contents of essential control registers in response to an interrupt. The contents of these control registers may be considered to form a control word, which is referred to as the *program status word*. The program status word contains the address of the next instruction, to permit resumption of a program after an interrupt. It also contains interrupt masks, the storage protection key, and a number of special control fields and control bits. One of these control bits distinguishes between system (or supervisor) state and problem state.

A 370 series computer has general-purpose registers that serve as base registers and index registers, and which also serve as fixed-point accumulators and as temporary storage registers. A special instruction stores all or a subset of the general registers in memory starting at a spec-

Fig. 1. The IBM 370 Model 168 multiprocessor system.

ified address. Another instruction can load the general registers (all or a subset) from a specified area of memory. The general registers are 32 bits long, and the most significant 8 bits are ignored in physical address calculations. The use of the general registers as base and index registers permits the direct addressing of 16,777,216 bytes without requiring that each instruction contain a 24-bit address field. This is illustrated by the RX instruction format, one of several instruction formats used in the 360. Instructions may be one, two, or three half-words long. The RX format uses two half-words as follows.

```
Op-code   R1   X2   B2   D2
--------  ----  ----  ----  ------------
```

The eight-bit op-code specifies the instruction. There are two operands. The first is in the general register, specified by the four-bit field R1. The second is in memory, at a location determined by adding the 12-bit displacement D2 to the contents of the two general registers specified by B2 and X2.

The 370 series has a large and varied instruction set. There are three types of arithmetic: Fixed point, floating point, and a special decimal arithmetic that uses strings of four-bit binary-coded decimal digits as operands. There is a set of privileged instructions that can be executed only in supervisor state. Special instructions are designed to aid in the programming of data processing applications, of which *translate and test* and *edit* are interesting examples. A special *test and set* instruction helps in the handling of interlock problems.

The central processor has only very rudimentary I/O instructions to start and stop I/O, and to determine the status of an I/O operation that has been started or stopped. Input and output can proceed simultaneously, with computing under control of channels that can directly access main memory and which can execute *channel programs*. Block multiplexer channels control devices such as tapes and disks for fast, high-volume data transfers. A byte multiplexer channel can control large numbers of lower-speed devices.

The original 360 series had a number of atypical models, one of which, the 360/67, was a virtual memory system; i.e., it provided dynamic address translation hardware (see VIRTUAL MEMORY). This feature has become standard on all 370 models, even though it was lacking on some of the early ones. The 360 model 85 was a very large computer that provided a cache or buffer memory, a small, high-speed memory used to improve the observed performance of a very much larger central memory. This type of memory organization has become standard on most 370 models. New 370 models of various sizes have been introduced about every other year to take advantage of new technology. Thus, for example, the 4330 model introduced in 1979 provided the 370 organization in a minicomputer that used specially designed 64K-bit memory chips.

Starting with the introduction of the 3033 in 1977, the 370 designation has been dropped. A list of the models that were current in 1975–1980, along with an estimate of their relative capacity, is presented in Table 1, with the throughput capacity of the 370/158-3 taken as equal to 1.0. The central processor speed of the 158-3 is roughly estimated to be one million instructions per second (1 MIPS).

Table 1.   Relative Throughput* of IBM 370 Series Computers Manufactured in 1975–1980

370 Models		30 Series		4300 Series	
Model No.	Throughput	Model No.	Throughput	Model No.	Throughput
370/138	0.26			4331	0.24
370/148	0.53			4331-2	0.49
370/158-3	1.0	3031	1.2	4341	0.82
370/168-3	2.8	3032	2.8		
		3033	5.0		

*Throughput data is taken from tables published in *Computerworld* on 8 January 1979 and 12 May 1980.

The introduction of the 30 series in 1977 marked a significant price reduction at the high end of the IBM line, since the 3033 was priced slightly lower than the 168, and the other 30 series computers provided a corresponding price/performance improvement. This price cut was at least partially in response to competition from Amdahl Corp. and others who offered compatible computers at prices lower than IBM had been charging. The introduction of the 4300 series in 1979 and 1980 provided an even more significant price cut at the low end of the IBM line. For example, the throughput of the 4331 was estimated at about 90% of that of the 370/138, and the price of the 4331 was less than one-fourth of the price of the 138. Here again, the price cut was at least partially

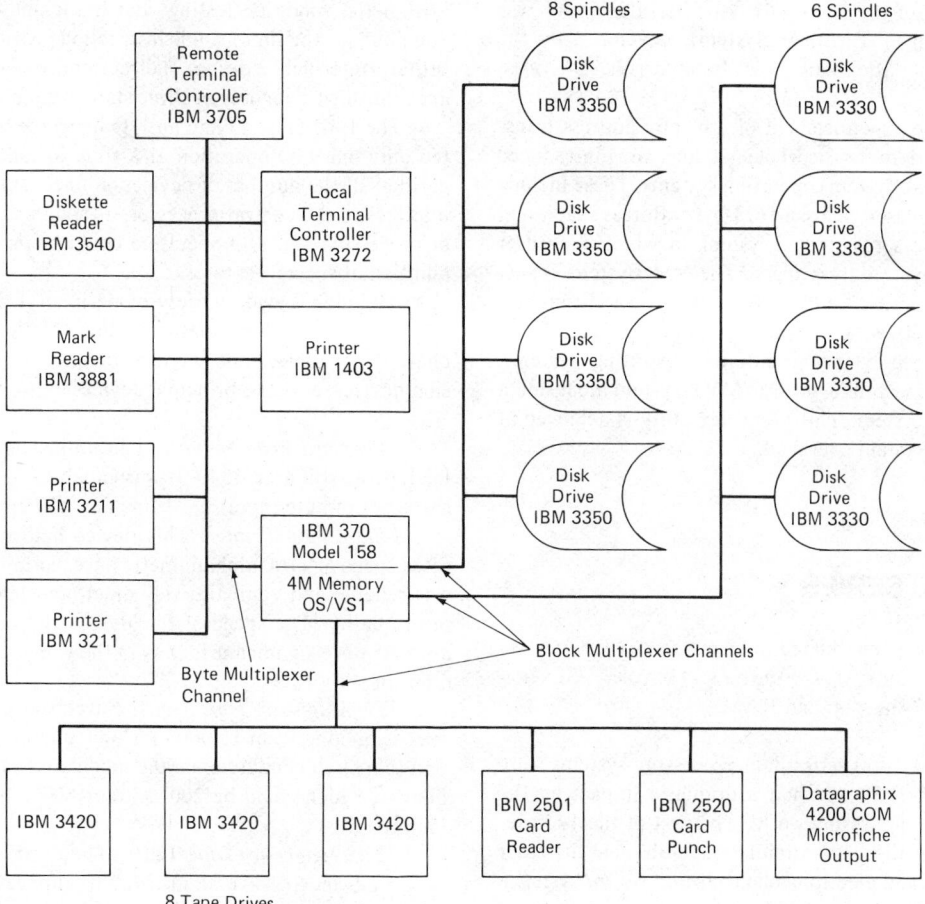

Fig. 2.   Block diagram of a medium-sized IBM 370 installation at Purdue University's administrative data processing center in 1979.

in response to competition from the growing PCM (Plug Compatible Mainframe) industry that produces many models of computers that use the IBM 370 architecture, and that can therefore run essentially all of the programs that can run on the IBM systems.

A new series of large, very high-speed central processors, of which the 3081, announced in 1980, is the precursor, is expected to replace older 30 series models in the early 1980s.

The original 360 concept assumed that only one major operating system would be required, which was given the name OS 360 (i.e., Operating System 360). It soon became apparent that many small- and intermediate-sized 360 systems needed a reasonably sophisticated operating system, but could not afford the high memory space and processor time overhead of OS 360. This led to the early development of an alternative system, DOS (disk operating system), which was very widely used. The time-sharing system, TSS 67, was another major software system. IBM also provided an alternative system, CP 67, which achieved greater acceptance than TSS among users of the Model 67. Another alternative was MTS (Michigan Terminal System), developed by the University of Michigan (see INTERACTIVE SYSTEMS, USING).

With the announcement of dynamic address translation as standard for the whole 370 line, IBM introduced its VS (Virtual System) operating systems. These include VS1, in which users share a 16M-byte address space, and MVS, a more sophisticated system, in which each user has a 16M-byte address space. The VM System, a successor to the earlier CP67 system, provides a virtual machine capability which permits users on the same hardware system to be using different operating systems, including, for example, an OS/MVT system alongside a newer MVS system. This great flexibility is achieved at some cost in system overhead.

S. ROSEN

IBM 1400 SERIES

For articles on related subjects see COMPUTER INDUSTRY; DIGITAL COMPUTERS: HISTORY; GENERATIONS, COMPUTER; and RAMAC.

The IBM 1400 series data processing systems were introduced in 1959 and had a dramatic impact on the business data processing world. The first of the 1400 series machines, the 1401, rapidly made obsolete the older vacuum tube and electromechanical *unit record* systems. The 1400 system enjoyed widespread use in every type of data processing application from 1959 until "third-generation" equipment became available in the mid-1960s.

The 1400 line consisted of five basic computers: 1401, 1440, 1460, 1410, and 7010. The basic mainframe, the 1401, was a second-generation, fully-transistorized machine with a magnetic core memory having original capacity options of 1.4K, 2K, and 4K characters, with later announced options of 8K, 12K, and 16K characters.

Internally data was represented in six-bit BCD code, with additional parity check and *word mark* bits. The memory cycle was 11.5 μs per character access.

Instruction formats were variable from one to eight characters, and data fields and records could be variable length within the constraints of the peripheral device characteristics and memory size. Instruction and data fields were defined by the presence of a word-mark bit set beneath the leftmost character of the instruction or data field.

The instruction format consisted of a single character op-code, two optional three-character data or instruction addresses, and an optional single character "d-modifier." The instruction set provided for internal data transfer, input/output control, add-to-storage decimal arithmetic, condition testing, and branching operations. A unique (at the time) single instruction provided for versatile printer-field editing. Indirect addressing could be accomplished using any of three standard index registers.

The 1401 (Fig. 1) had an I/O interface that permitted only one I/O operation at a time to take place, regardless of the number of devices on line. I/O operations interlocked the central processor, although some overlap of processing and I/O operation could be gained by the addition of special features.

Although a wide variety of peripheral devices was available for the 1400 series, including MICR and optical character readers, paper-tape readers, remote transmission devices, etc., the principal devices in use were:

1402 Card Reader/Punch. This unit, somewhat modified, is the still used 2540. It was capable of reading 800 cards per minute (cpm) and punching 250 cpm.

1403 Chain Printer. This device had a maximum rated speed of 1100 alphanumeric lines per minute (lpm), was reliable and comparatively quiet, and had excellent print quality. The speed of this device and its relatively low cost were significant factors in the widespread acceptance of the 1401.

729 Magnetic Tape Units. Seven-track units with speeds ranging from 15,000 to 62,000 characters per second (chps), depending upon the model and the recording density, which could be 200, 556, or 800 characters per inch (chpi).

7330 Magnetic Tape Units. These were relatively slow and inexpensive units (7,200 chps at 200 chpi density).

1405 Disk Storage Units. These were fixed-disk units with 50,000 or 100,000 directly addressable 200-charac-

Fig. 1.   The IBM 1401 System.

ter records. Records were accessed by a single arm moving laterally and vertically. Average access time was 600 ms.

1311 Disk Storage Units. These replaced the 1405-type units with modular disk-pack storage. Each pack stored 2 million characters in the form of 20,000 hundred-character records. The access device was of the "comb" type, requiring only lateral motion. Average access time per record was 250 ms.

Several languages were available for the 1401. It could be, and often was, programmed in machine language. A basic assembly language SPS (Symbolic Programming System) permitted the use of mnemonic operation codes, symbolic addresses, indirect addressing, data field establishment and definition, and was widely used. A significantly enhanced version of SPS, called "Autocoder"—analogous to basic assembly language for third-generation computers—became the predominantly used language. Autocoder used SPS constructs, but was free form (as opposed to fixed format for SPS statements) and employed macroinstructions for initiating I/O operations. Fortran and Cobol compilers existed, but were not widely used because of either excessive processing time needed for compilation or limitations on the scope of the language due to the limited memory size of the system. Various Report Program Generator (RPG) packages were available, as was a complete set of basic utility packages.

Operating systems were not used with the 1401, 1440, or 1460, although many users developed monitors to permit a rudimentary form of job control by automatic loading of a series of programs as opposed to the conventional method of loading each object program from a card reader before execution.

The 1440 system was initially a disk-oriented 1401 with slower peripherals and lower cost. Internally, the 1440 was, for all practical purposes, identical to the 1401

except that the memory cycle was 11.1 ms as compared to 11.5 for the 1401, and the printer and reader-punch buffers were relocatable in memory.

The 1460 was again basically a 1401 except that it had a 6 μs memory expandable to a 32K capacity.

The 1410 systems, while having the same basic architecture as the 1401, were significantly more powerful. Memory sizes were 10K, 20K, 40K, 60K, or 80K characters. The internal code was BCD and the use of word-mark bits permitted variable length data and instruction fields. The memory cycle was 4.5 μs per character. The instruction set was similar to the 1401, but included a table-lookup instruction and 64 different data-move instructions. Fifteen index registers were available. The basic system had a single I/O channel, but a second could be installed. Like the 1401, the processor was interlocked during any I/O operation, though special features were available to provide limited overlap. Autocoder was the predominantly used language, although Cobol and Fortran were widely used. All peripheral equipment was the same as that used in other 1400 series systems except for 1301 and 1302 disk files, which were large fixed-disk units similar to the 350 units used on 305 "RAMAC" (*q.v.*) machines. The 1410 could be operated in emulated 1401 mode, which provided almost total compatibility with 1401 programs.

The 7010 system was functionally, although not architecturally, an advanced 1410. It used the 1410 instruction set and, unlike the 1410, had a 1410 compatibility feature. The 7010 accessed two characters in parallel on each 2.4 μs cycle. Four I/O channels could be installed. Memory protection, an interval timer, and a program-level interrupt feature were available. All 1400 compatible I/O devices could be used on the 7010. Comparatively few of these systems were installed, as the system was introduced shortly before the System 360 was announced.

There were approximately 14,000 of the 1401 systems and over 1,000 of the 1410 systems installed. A typical 1401 system rented for $8,000 per month and ranged from $4,000 to $12,000 per month. A typical 1410 system rented for $11,000 per month and ranged from $8,000 to $18,000 per month.

The high-speed card reading and tape and printing ability of the 1401 systems ideally suited them for use as peripheral I/O systems to IBM 7000 series computers.

G.D. Baer

IBM CARD

For articles on related subjects *see* ASCII; BINARY-CODED DECIMAL; CHARACTER SET; EBCDIC; HOLLERITH, HERMAN; and NINETY COLUMN CARD.

In 1890, Dr. Herman Hollerith was faced with the problem of conducting the U. S. Census and evaluating all resulting information. The data from the previous census had taken ten years to process manually. To enable this processing to be carried out more efficiently, Dr. Hollerith invented a technique whereby information could be recorded in cards as a series of holes. He also invented a number of machines that were able to read these holes, interpret and accumulate this information, and sort cards into sequence. Using these cards and equipment, he was able to complete the 1890 census by 1892. This card, known almost universally today as the IBM card, is sometimes still called the *Hollerith* card.

Dr. Hollerith patented his ideas and later founded the Tabulating Machine Company. This company became the Computing-Tabulating-Recording Company in 1911. In 1914, Thomas J. Watson, Sr., joined this company, which later became International Business Machines Corporation.

While early cards enabled storage of an amount of information varying from around 30 characters to 90 characters, the card as it is known today has been standardized at a size of 7⅜ in. by 3¼ in., and normally contains 80 characters of information. However, more than 80 characters may be contained in a card if special punching techniques such as binary punching are used.

The 80-Column Card and Card Codes.
Each card is divided into 80 columns and 12 rows (Fig. 1). Each column is normally used to record one character of information as a series of holes. The top row is called the "12" or "Y" row, and the second row from the top is called the "11" or "X" row. The remaining rows are called the 0, 1, . . . , 9 row, as indicated by the digit printed on the card. Holes punched in the top three rows of the card are called *zone punches*.

A decimal digit of 0–9 is readily recorded in a column by a punch in the appropriately valued row. In the case of alphabetic information, however, two punches are necessary in a column (see Table 1 for 80-column card codes). The first punch is a zone punch and the second punch is a numeric punch. Thus, the letters A–I are represented by a combination of a 12-zone and the numerics 1–9. Special characters (punctuation marks, etc.) are generally represented by a combination of one zone punch and two numeric punches, as shown in Table 1.

With the advent of computers in the 1950s, it was found necessary to extend the number of different characters that could be recorded on a card. Consequently, various combinations of holes are used to represent up to 256 different values, as in the Extended Binary Coded Decimal Interchange Code (EBCDIC), or up to 128 val-

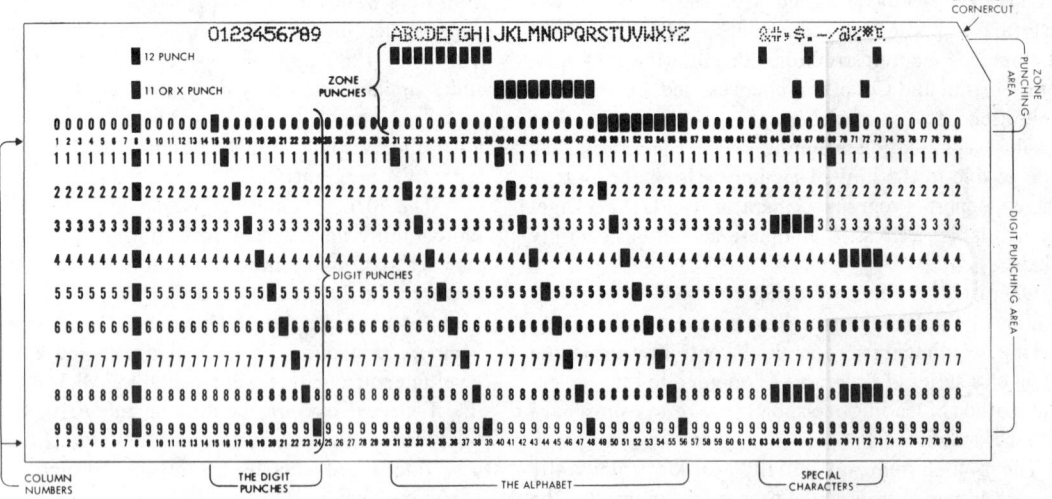

Fig. 1. IBM 80-column card format.

ues, as in the American Standard Code for Information Interchange (ASCII).

The 96-Column IBM Card and Its Codes.

In 1969, IBM introduced the System/3 computer and the 5496 data recorder (Fig. 2), which use a 96-column card rather than an 80-column card. The 96-column card is physically smaller, measuring only 3¼ in. by 2¹¹⁄₁₆ in. and can record 20% more data than the 80-column card (Fig. 3). Information is recorded on the 96-column cards in 32 columns, each column containing three sets of rows (Fig. 4). Each set of rows is called a *tier,* and consists of 6 rows instead of the 12 rows found on the 80-column card. From the top down, the first row is the B row; the second, the A row; then the 8 row, the 4 row, the 2 row, and the 1 row. This series of rows is repeated again immediately underneath for the second set of 32 columns, and then again for the third set of 32 columns.

Fig. 2.   IBM 5496 data recorder used for punching 96-column cards.

Table 1.   IBM 80-Column and 96-Column Card Codes.

Character	Description	80-Col. Card Code	96-Col. Card Code	Character	Description	80-Col. Card Code	96-Col. Card Code
b	Blank	No punches	No punches	E		12–5	B A 4 1
&	Ampersand	12	A 8 2	F		12–6	B A 4 2
¢	Cent	12–2–8	B A 8 2	G		12–7	B A 4 2 1
.	Period	12–3–8	B A 8 2 1	H		12–8	B A 8
<	Less than	12–4–8	B A 8 4	I		12–9	B A 8 1
(	Left paren	12–5–8	B A 8 4 1	J		11–1	B 1
+	Plus	12–6–8	B A 8 4 2	K		11–2	B 2
|	Logical "or"	12–7–8	B A 8 4 2 1	L		11–3	B 2 1
–	Minus	11	B	M		11–4	B 4
!	Exclamation	11–2–8	B 8 2	N		11–5	B 4 1
$	Dollar	11–3–8	B 8 2 1	O		11–6	B 4 2
*	Asterisk	11–4–8	B 8 4	P		11–7	B 4 2 1
)	Right paren	11–5–8	B 8 4 1	Q		11–8	B 8
;	Semicolon	11–6–8	B 8 4 2	R		11–9	B 8 1
¬	Logical "not"	11–7–8	B 8 4 2 1	S		0–2	A 2
/	Slash	0–1	A 1	T		0–3	A 2 1
≠	Record mark	0–2–8	A 8 2	U		0–4	A 4
,	Comma	0–3–8	A 8 2 1	V		0–5	A 4 1
%	Percent	0–4–8	A 8 4	W		0–6	A 4 2
—	Underscore	0–5–8	A 8 4 1	X		0–7	A 4 2 1
>	Greater than	0–6–8	A 8 4 2	Y		0–8	A 8
?	Question	0–7–8	A 8 4 2 1	Z		0–9	A 8 1
:	Colon	2–8	8 2	0		0	A
#	Number	3–8	8 2 1	1		1	1
@	At	4–8	8 4	2		2	2
'	Quote	5–8	8 4 1	3		3	2 1
=	Equals	6–8	8 4 2	4		4	4
"	Quotation	7–8	8 4 2 1	5		5	4 1
A		12–1	B A 1	6		6	4 2
B		12–2	B A 2	7		7	4 2 1
C		12–3	B A 2 1	8		8	8
D		12–4	B A 4	9		9	8 1

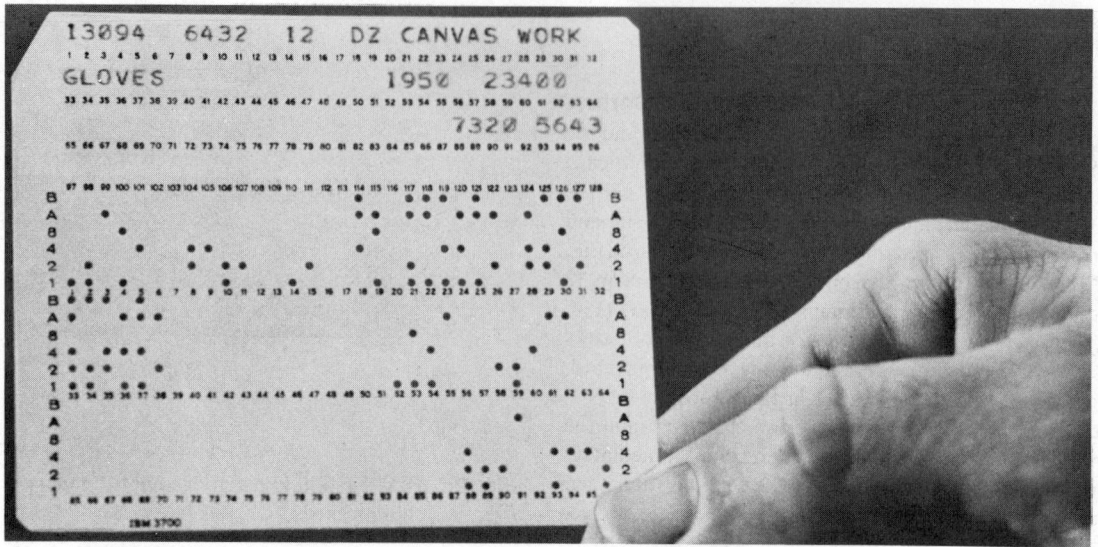

Fig. 3. The IBM 96-column card.

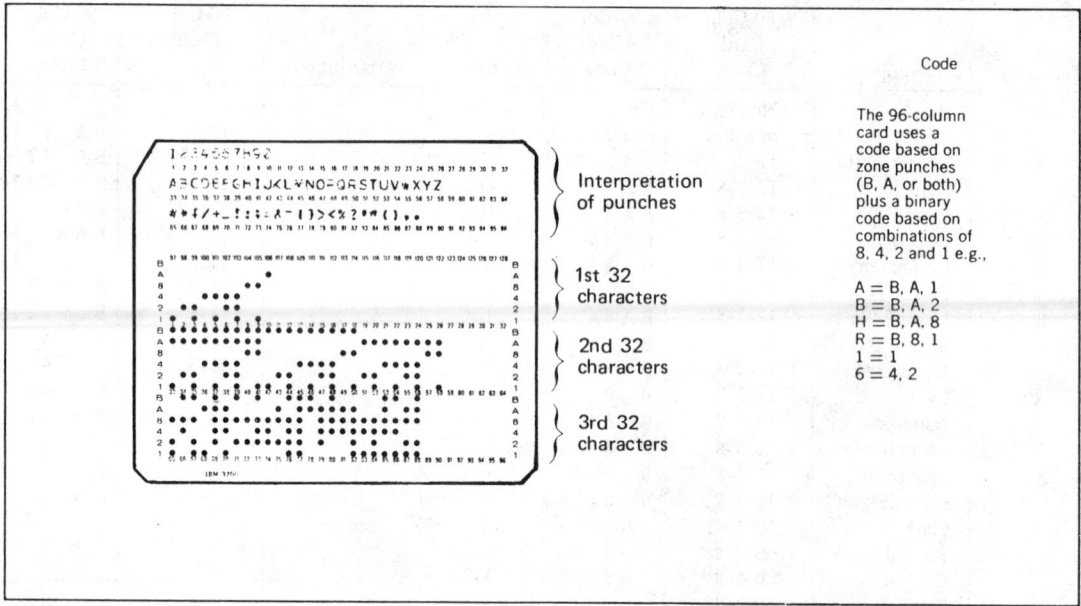

Fig. 4. IBM 96-column card format.

Numeric information is recorded as a combination of punches in the A, 8, 4, 2, and 1 rows, as shown in Fig. 4 and detailed in Table 1 for 96-column card codes. Note that the B and A rows are used to represent zone punches, with both B and A corresponding to the Y zone punch on the 80-column card, B alone corresponding to the X zone punch, and A alone to the 0 zone punch. Note in Table 1 that the sum of the other punches on the 96-column card is equal to the second punch on the 80-column card for alphabetic characters.

Justification for the Use of Cards. The main advantage of a card is that it is a separate unit record of information. Cards are used as a convenient means of recording information relating to transactions used to update master files. Thus, cards are useful for recording separate order transactions to update an orders file, issues and receipts transactions to update a product inventory file, or name and address changes to update a customer master file, for example. Cards are also used for the development of programs, with source program statements being punched into cards for compilation and translation by a computer into actual computer instructions.

The use of computer terminals and time-sharing systems for program development since the late 1960s has resulted in significant improvements in efficiency of program writing and testing. These facilities enable the programmer to enter program instructions directly into the computer, using typewriter terminals, visual display terminals, or other hardware. The use of the IBM card for programming is, therefore, rapidly decreasing and will probably end entirely during the 1980s.

The late 1960s also saw the introduction of devices designed to replace the card as a storage medium for input of transactions into a computer. These devices and advanced techniques have become increasingly dominant, with the use of cards being sharply reduced but not yet eliminated.

C.B. FINKELSTEIN

ICCP. *See* INSTITUTE FOR CERTIFICATION OF COMPUTER PROFESSIONALS.

IDENTIFIER

For articles on related subjects *see* CONSTANT; EXPRESSION; LABEL; PROCEDURE-ORIENTED LANGUAGES; PROGRAMMING LANGUAGES; and STATEMENT.

In a programming language, an identifier is a string of characters used as a name for some element of the program. This element may be a statement label, a procedure or function, a data element (such as a scalar variable or an array) or the program itself.

Most commonly, the word *identifier* is used almost synonymously with *variable name.* In a system where the location of a program's data remains fixed throughout program execution, an identifier for a scalar variable is related to a memory address, which in turn references a physical location within the memory of the machine, which in turn contains a value representation. The intermediate relationships between the identifier and a value are usually transparent to a programmer, and thus some confusion arises in practice between the *name* of a variable (i.e., its identifier) and its *value,* which is the current contents of the memory location assigned to that identifier.

In the majority of programming languages, identifiers may be formed from any alphanumeric string, often of some restricted length (usually six to eight characters), provided the leftmost character is alphabetic. Some languages also permit the use of special characters.

J. A. N. LEE

IEEE-CS. *See* INSTITUTE OF ELECTRICAL AND ELECTRONIC ENGINEERS—COMPUTER SOCIETY.

IFAC. *See* INTERNATIONAL FEDERATION OF AUTOMATIC CONTROL.

IFIP. *See* INTERNATIONAL FEDERATION FOR INFORMATION PROCESSING.

IMACS. *See* INTERNATIONAL ASSOCIATION FOR MATHEMATICS AND COMPUTING IN SIMULATION.

IMAGE PROCESSING

For articles on related subjects *see* ARTIFICIAL INTELLIGENCE; CELLULAR AUTOMATA; CODES; COMPUTER GRAPHICS; DATA COMPRESSION AND COMPACTION; PATTERN RECOGNITION; PICTURES, BASIC STRUCTURE; and TOMOGRAPHY, COMPUTED.

A wide variety of techniques exist for processing pictorial information by computer; these techniques are collectively referred to as *image processing* or *picture processing.* The information to be processed is usually input to the computer by sampling and analog-to-digital conversion of video signals obtained from some type of two-dimensional scanning device (television camera, facsimile scanner, etc.). Thus, at least initially, this information is in the form of a large array (in the case of ordinary television, about 500 by 500), in which each element is a number, typically eight bits in length, representing the brightness of a small region in the scanned image, or a set of such numbers representing its color. The elements of a digitized picture are sometimes called *pixels,* and their values (in the non-color case) are called *gray levels.* The key distinction between image processing and *computer graphics* is that the latter does not deal with input pictures in array form, though it may construct pictures from input sets of coordinate data.

Image Compression and Matching. Most of the classes of pictures encountered in practice are *redundant* (in the sense of information theory), and can be *compressed,* to some extent, without loss of information, using *efficient encoding* techniques. If we do not insist that there be no loss of information, we can achieve higher degrees of compression if we *approximate* the picture by another picture having lower information content, which can then be further compressed.

One very common class of picture compression techniques takes differences between successive pixels (in time or space). Since such pixels are usually interdependent, these differences are more redundant than the original values. Another approach employs transforms (e.g., Fourier), which can be roughly approximated and still yield acceptable reconstructed pictures (Fig. 1). Applications of image compression include television, facsimile, and various types of narrow-band picture transmission systems.

Image *matching* involves establishing a geometric correspondence between two pictures, and measuring their degree of similarity or difference. Matching techniques are used for registration of pictures with each other or with maps; for detecting changes in a scene by comparing pictures of it taken at different times; for tracking moving objects in a scene by comparing successive frames; and for deriving three-dimensional information about a scene by comparing the positions of objects on pictures taken from different positions (stereoscopy).

Image Enhancement and Reconstruction.

A picture is not always a satisfactory representation of the original object or scene; e.g., it may have a poorly chosen gray scale (under- or overexposure); it may be geometrically distorted; or it may be blurred or "noisy."

The goal of *image enhancement* is to improve the quality of a picture; e.g., by increasing contrast, deblurring, removing noise, or correcting geometrical distortion. In particular, *image restoration* techniques assume a known model for the blur or noise, and attempt to estimate the original image. These techniques have applications in many areas, including astronomy, reconnaissance, microscopy, etc.

Noise can be removed from a picture if it is distinguishable from the signal—e.g., consists of isolated specks, or is periodic and has a distinctive Fourier spectrum. Noise can be weakened by local averaging, but this

(a)   (c)

(b)   (d)

Fig. 1. Picture approximation. The original was a 256-by-256-point array of eight-bit values. It was divided into 256 16-by-16-point subarrays, and each of these was expanded in a two-dimensional Fourier series. In (a), the picture was reconstructed using only the first 128 coefficients of each series; in (b), using only the first 64 coefficients. In (c), the 128 coefficients of (a) were quantized to four bits, and, in (d), to two bits, before reconstructing the picture. The average number of bits per point in these four approximations is (a) four, (b) two, (c) two, (d) one. (From P. A. Wintz, "Transform Picture Coding," *Proc. IEEE,* **60,** July 1972, pp. 809–820.

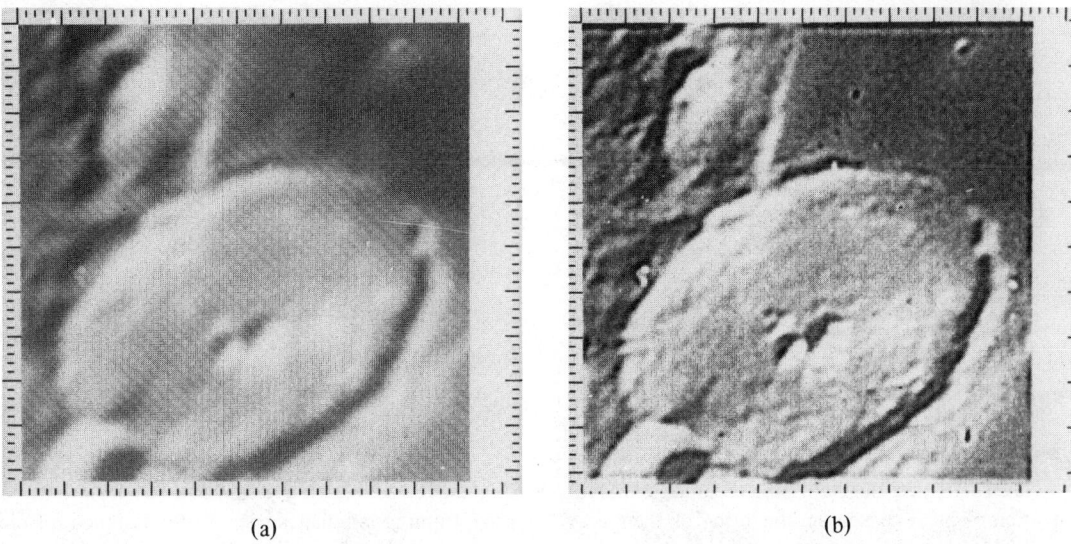

(a)   (b)

Fig. 2.   (a) The lunar crater Gasendi, image blurred by atmospheric turbulence. (b) Results of enhancement by filtering to emphasize a high spatial frequency band. (From D. A. O'Handley and W. B. Green, "Recent Developments in Digital Image Processing at the Image Processing Laboratory at the Jet Propulsion Laboratory," *Proc. IEEE*, **60,** July 1972, pp. 821–828.)

must be done selectively so as not to blur regional borders. A picture can be sharpened (Fig. 2) by emphasizing its high spatial frequency content. This can be done in the Fourier domain, or by a "Laplacian" method in which a blurred version of the picture is subtracted from it point by point.

The gray levels of a blurred picture are linear combinations of the ideal gray levels. Thus, in principle, it is possible to restore the ideal picture by solving a large system of equations. Similarly, if we have a large set of projections of a picture (i.e., sums of gray levels along families of lines) in various directions, *reconstruction* of the picture is possible; this is the goal of *computed tomography,* in which three-dimensional objects are reconstructed, slice by slice, from a set of their x-ray projections.

A known geometrical distortion in a picture can be corrected by resampling it at an irregularly spaced array of positions (as specified by the distortion function) and outputting the samples as a regular array. Gray levels can be assigned to the new samples by interpolation from the levels of the nearby pixels. To correct an unknown relative distortion between two copies of a picture, one can find matches between pairs of distinctive local patterns (Fig. 3), measure the relative displacement of each pair, and construct a geometrical distortion function by interpolation from these displacements. (Local pattern matching is also used to extract relief information from stereopairs of pictures.)

Picture Recognition and Scene Analysis.
In image compression and enhancement, pictures are not only the input but also the output, since the goal is an approximation to, or an improved version of, the input picture. Another major branch of picture processing deals with *picture classification* and description; here the goal is the assignment of the picture to a category or, more generally, the creation of a relational structure that contains useful information about the picture.

Picture recognition and analysis systems have been developed for many different applications, including optical character reading, analysis of nuclear bubble chamber pictures, medical diagnosis from micrographs and radiographs, recognition of faces or fingerprints, industrial assembly (robot vision) and inspection, and interpretation of reconnaissance or remote sensor imagery.

The basic steps in picture analysis are *segmentation* of the picture into regions or objects; *measurement* of properties of, and relationships among, these parts; and *comparison* of the resulting relational structure with models describing classes of scenes. In simple cases, the entire picture or the parts can be classified, using statistical pattern classification techniques, based on a set of measured properties; but in general, it is necessary to "recognize" relational structures by establishing how they might correspond to the models.

Properties commonly used in the recognition process include geometric properties of regions (connectedness, size, shape, etc.), as well as "textural" properties describ-

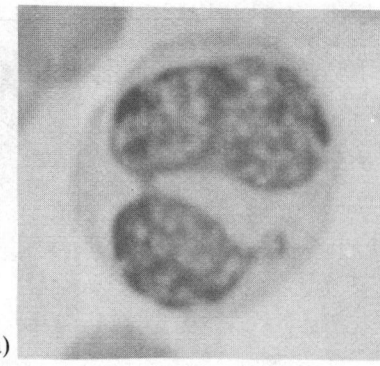 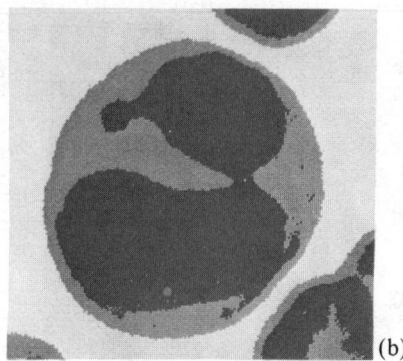

(a)   (b)

Fig. 3.   Segmentation of a white blood cell image into nucleus, cell body, and background by clustering of gray levels: (a) original; (b) segmented.

ing gray level statistics. Segmentation techniques include classification of pixels based on clustering of their gray levels (Fig. 4), spectral signatures, or local properties, repeated splitting or merging to obtain a partition into homogeneous regions; detection of local features such as edges, lines, and spots; and tracking of curves and borders. The resulting parts can in turn be segmented based on shape criteria—e.g., regions can be broken into "lobes," borders can be segmented at corners. Relationships of adjacency, relative position, (etc.) between these parts can then be determined.

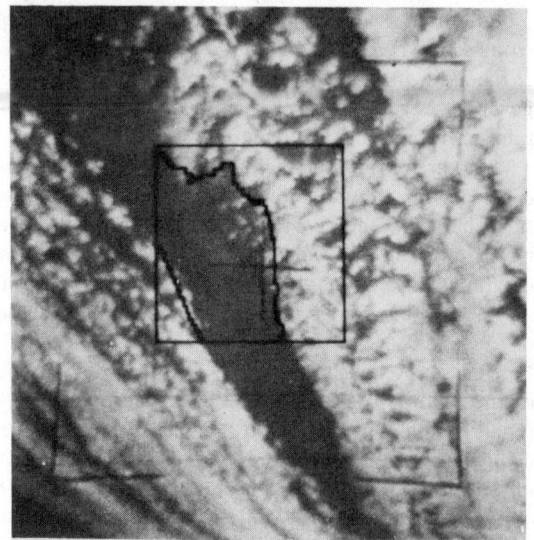

Fig. 4.   Region outlining on a textured picture (a TIROS VI cloud-cover picture) using differencing of average gray levels. (From J. P. Strong, III, and A. Rosenfeld, "A Region Coloring Technique for Scene Analysis," *Comm. ACM,* **16,** 1973.)

Software and Hardware. There are as yet no programming languages specifically designed for picture processing, but many large software packages exist. Since digital pictures are usually quite large, processing is generally done row by row, using operations which require only a few rows at a time to be in main memory.

Picture processing can often be greatly facilitated by using special hardware array processors. Many useful picture processing operations can be performed optically, but a discussion of nondigital processing techniques is beyond the scope of this article.

Digitally refreshed color image displays are extensively used for interactive picture processing. Typically, such displays handle images of size 500 by 500 or 1,000 by 1,000 pixels, and allow up to 8-bit color component values, as well as graphic overlay capabilities to permit outlining regions on the display. Many of them also incorporate the capability of performing simple operations on the displayed image in real time.

Formal Models and Semantics. A variety of formalisms for computations on pictures and for description of picture structure have been studied. Formal grammars can be generalized from strings to arrays, and one can also define automata that have arrays as *tapes*. Models for parallel computation on arrays—e.g., by *cellular arrays* of automata—are of special interest. *Perceptrons* (*q.v.*—machines that compute linear threshold functions of local properties) have been extensively investigated.

Formalisms for computations on data structures (in particular, on picture descriptions) have also been developed. Grammars can be generalized from strings to graphlike structures, and automata having graph-structured "tapes" can be defined.

One can regard picture segmentation and scene analysis as parsing operations with respect to such formal models. However, a purely "syntactic" approach to scene analysis is unlikely to be adequate except in simple cases. In general, it seems necessary to develop *knowledge-based* scene analysis systems, which make use of "semantic" information about the objects whose images appear in the scene. This approach constitutes an important area of artificial intelligence research.

REFERENCES

1976. Rosenfeld, A. and Kak, A. C. *Digital Picture Processing.* New York: Academic Press.
1978. Pratt, W. K. *Digital Image Processing.* New York: Wiley.
1979. Fu, K. S. (Ed.). *Proceedings of the IEEE.* Special issue on pattern recognition and image processing (May).
1981. *IEEE Computer.* Special issue in Pictorial Information Systems (November).

A. ROSENFELD

IMP. *See* INTERFACE MESSAGE PROCESSOR.

INDEX REGISTER

For articles on related subjects *see* ADDRESS MODIFICATION; ADDRESSING; BASE REGISTER; GENERAL REGISTER; INDIRECT ADDRESS; MACHINE INSTRUCTION SET; and REGISTER.

An index register is a storage device most often used in the determination of an operand address, but which may be used for other purposes, mainly as counters.

In the process of the formation of the address of an operand, one can distinguish three basic parts. Consider, for example, the ADD instruction in a program loop computing the sum of the elements of a vector. The operand address of the ADD instruction is formed from:

1. The address of the base of the vector (its first element) relative to the program module. This address is known when the program is being written.
2. The memory address into which the program module is loaded. This address is known at load time.
3. The offset from the base of the vector, which depends on the element that is currently being added and which is known only at execution time.

Index registers are normally involved with the last of the three parts of the address.

The address computed with an index register is referred to as the *effective address*. The index register accomplishes its role of forming the effective address in one of two ways: Either the address is formed from a constant in the address field of an instruction plus a changing offset in the index register, or the address as a whole is contained in the index register. In the former case, shown in Fig. 1, the index register is used as a counter.

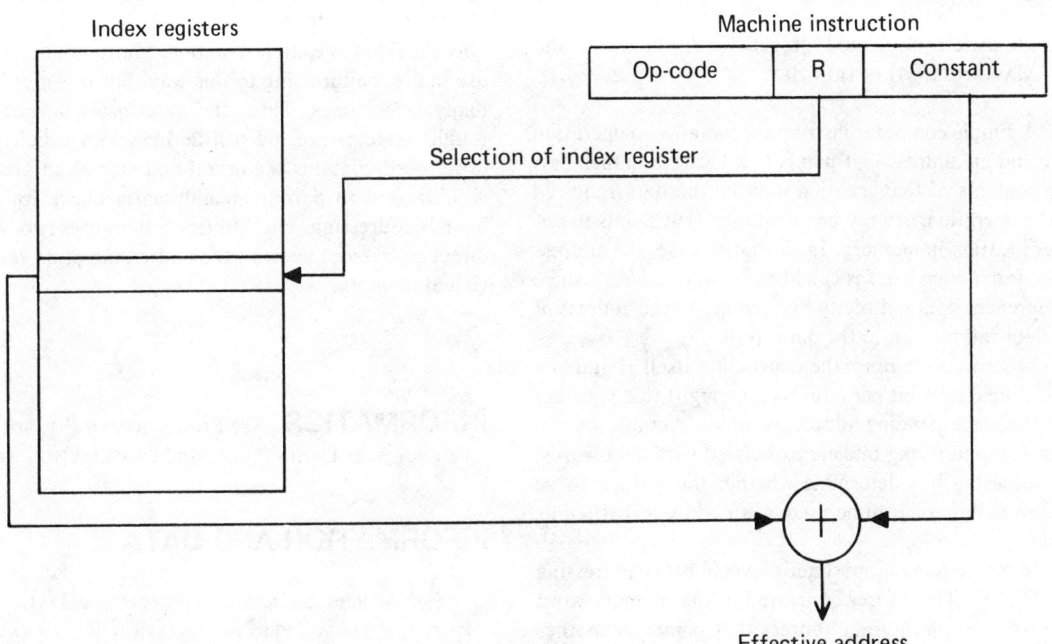

Fig. 1.   Example of the formation of an effective address.

The number of index registers in a machine and the number of index registers used in the formation of the effective address and other attributes of the index registers are highly dependent on the particular architecture. Thus, one finds machines with a single index register, one index register and one dedicated base register, multiple index registers and/or base registers, and machines in which the general registers (*q.v.*) may be utilized for indexing and base addressing.

As mentioned before, apart from their function in address formation, the index registers can serve as counters. As such, they are used in special instructions that increment or decrement the contents of the index register and check its new contents, thereby exercising control over the program flow.

Special care must be exercised in the use of index registers when the computer possesses an indirect addressing mode. In this case, the index register can be used either to compute the location of the indirect address (*pre-indexing*) or as an offset to the indirect address itself (*post-indexing*). When more than one index register is involved in the formation of the effective address, both pre- and post-indexing may be present. Again, the availability of either of the modes varies widely among different machines.

G. FRIEDER

INDIRECT ADDRESS

For articles on related subjects *see* ADDRESSING; and MACHINE INSTRUCTION SET.

A simple computer instruction contains an operation code and an address that points to a location in memory. The contents of that location may be the data required by the operation, or may be an address that points to another location in memory. In this latter case, the address in the instruction itself is called an *indirect address,* since it references data indirectly by pointing to the address of the data rather than to the data itself.

In some computers, the instruction itself contains a control field (one bit per address is enough) that specifies that the corresponding address is an indirect address. In other computers, tag bits are associated with data words, and these tag bits determine whether the word is to be treated as data or is to be used as an address that points to data.

Many systems support multilevel indirect addressing (see Fig. 1). The address retrieved in the memory word may itself be an indirect address that points to another memory location, which in turn may be an indirect address, etc. Computers that allow multilevel indirect ad-

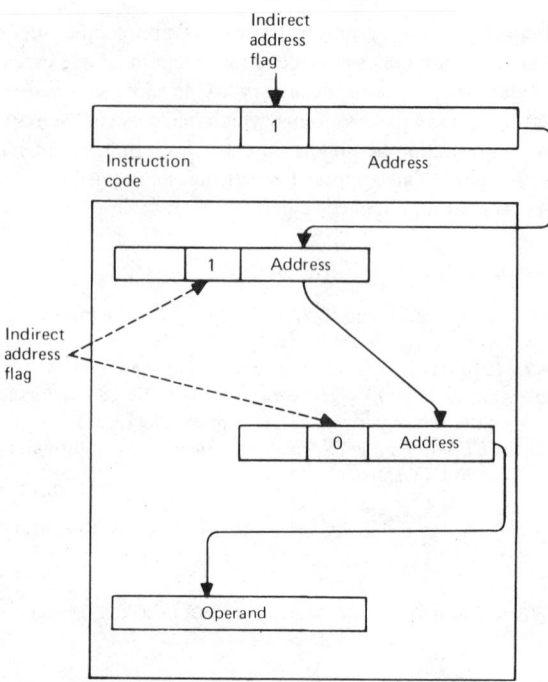

Fig. 1.   Two-level indirect addressing.

dressing usually have a time-out interrupt facility that causes an interrupt to occur in the case of a nonterminating indirect addressing loop.

There are many uses for indirect addressing. It has been used most effectively in those systems that require a longer address field than can be conveniently or reasonably provided in each instruction. Many small computers use indirect addressing in this way, but it is also used on many larger ones. Thus, the *descriptors* on large Burroughs systems are indirect addresses in which the address word contains the origin and size of an array that is addressed to permit an automatic check for out-of-bounds addressing. The Multics system uses two-word indirect addresses to permit the addressing of its very large virtual memory.

S. ROSEN

INFORMATICS. *See* EDUCATION IN COMPUTER SCIENCE AND TECHNOLOGY; and INFORMATION SCIENCE.

INFORMATION AND DATA

For articles on related subjects *see* DATA STRUCTURES; DATA TYPE; INFORMATION RETRIEVAL; SYMBOL MANIPULATION; and SYNTAX, SEMANTICS, AND PRAGMATICS.

Although the layperson typically uses the terms *information* and *data* interchangeably, to the information scientist or the information systems designer, the distinction between them is important. Among the several existing points of view about this distinction, this article presents one with considerable current and, more important, increasing support.

The term *information* has a number of different meanings and is used in a number of different contexts. It is one of the more overused words in our language, a word considered to be synonomous with knowledge or intelligence. Computer and information scientists and systems designers are broadly concerned with this meaning of the term. The same meaning is also implied when a layperson says, "May I have some information, please?" However, in a scientific and engineering sense, it is desirable to establish a somewhat more formal, useful, and precise definition.

The word *information* is also frequently used rather narrowly, specifically in the sense that Shannon and Weaver (1949) have established in their treatment of *information theory*. In this sense, the context of the message is of no significance; instead, the theory is concerned with the probability of the receipt of any particular message from among many for various conditions of the transmission system. While this interpretation may indeed be of interest in designing information systems, it is certainly not the major, nor even *a* major, concern. Such a treatment does not consider the really important areas of interest, almost all of which involve the context, meaning, and effectiveness of the message.

Shannon and Weaver identify three levels of information problems:

1. The technical problem. (How accurately can the symbols of communication be transmitted?)
2. The semantic problem. (How precisely do the transmitted symbols convey the desired *meaning?*)
3. The effectiveness (or behavioral) problem. (How effectively does the received meaning *affect conduct* in the desired way?)

These three levels of communication research are perhaps most clearly and most simply described by these questions: (1) What is the message? (2) What does the message mean? (3) What are the effects of the message on the recipient?

Problems at the first level are essentially attacked by the use of Shannon's information theory which is concerned primarily with the *communication* problem.

The semantic problem has been of interest for some time. Early productive ideas were suggested by Carnap and Bar-Hillel in 1952. Since then, many others have studied this problem. Recently, for example, Winograd (1972) and Woods (1978) have attacked the problem of the meaning of transmitted symbols.

And yet, ultimately, it is the level 3 consideration, namely how the message *affects* the *behavior* of the recipient with which information scientists and systems designers are primarily concerned. That is, what is the effectiveness of the information? This is a much more difficult problem than the other two. It has been approached by MacKay (1969), Marschak (1964), and Yovits and Ernst (1969), as well as a number of others. This third level may be said to deal with *pragmatic information,* or just *pragmatics.*

Information and Data. Even among professionals engaged in the design and use of computerized information systems, there is a difference of opinion as to how to define and categorize information and data, all generally within the framework of equating information essentially with knowledge or intelligence of some type. See, for example, Langefors (1972). There are those who suggest that information is somehow connected with the way in which data is displayed. It is suggested that the information is a function of the ease with which the data can be comprehended by the user.

Then, there are those who suggest that information is "smoothed" as opposed to "raw" data. This smoothing permits a user to make decisions more easily than might be possible from the unsmoothed data. The suggestion has been made that information consists of appropriate aggregation of data; or perhaps information can be defined as the appropriate interconnection between various pieces of data, thus making it possible to use the data readily.

Several common characteristics run through most of these definitions. First, information is a *subset* of *data* or perhaps inferred from data. It is also generally either explicitly stated or at least implied that the ultimate concern is that somehow the information must eventually be *used.* Thus, a user is involved. Generally, the concern is with the *effectiveness* with which the information is used. In other words, the general interest is with the problems of level 3—the pragmatics of the message. The *value* of the information in a message is the important criterion.

Information: A Definition. Many information scientists accept the standard definition: *Information is data which is used in decision-making.* (Yovits and Ernst, 1969; McDonough and Garrett, 1965.) This definition has a number of significant derived implications. One is that information is a *relative* quantity, relative to the situation, to the time at which a decision is made, and to the decision-maker and the decision-maker's background and history. What is of considerable importance in one situation is very possibly totally useless in another. What may be of considerable value to one decision-maker at a particular time may likely be useless to another decision-maker or even to the same decision-maker at a different time or in a different situation. This differs from the physical world, where the quantities involved are generally absolute; i.e., one second is (almost) always one second.

A second implication is that information and decision-making are closely intertwined. Information is used *only* for decision-making and decision-makers have *only* the resource of information available to them. Consequently, to understand these properties of information in this context, the process of decision-making must also be studied.

The objective of information system design then becomes principally the design of a system which makes available the information needed for making a variety of decisions obtained from among all the data the system has stored. Such a system must capture and store as much as possible of the information which may be needed, and *only* this information. An information system should make available most readily the most valuable data. The *value* of information in some sense is a major criterion.

Data: A Definition. We have defined information in terms of data. It is, accordingly, desirable to define data in somewhat more fundamental terms. We first quote from Webster's Unabridged Dictionary (1966), which offers the following partial definition for *datum*.

Something that is given either from being experimentally encountered or from being admitted or assumed for specific purposes; a fact or principle granted or presented . . .

In other words: *Data are facts or are believed to be or are said to be facts which result from the observation of physical phenomena.*

The Generalized Information System Model. Yovits and Ernst (1969) have proposed a generalized model or a *generalized information system* (G.I.S.) which explicitly indicates the interrelationship between data, information, decision-making, and other important quantities. This is shown in Fig. 1.

This model can be used to describe and understand any information-dependent activity of the level 3 type—that is, information involved in the decision-making process. Information is presented to the decision-maker (DM) by the information acquisition and dissemination (IAD) module. Information enters the IAD module either as external or feedback (internal) data. Feedback provides information to the decision-maker about prior

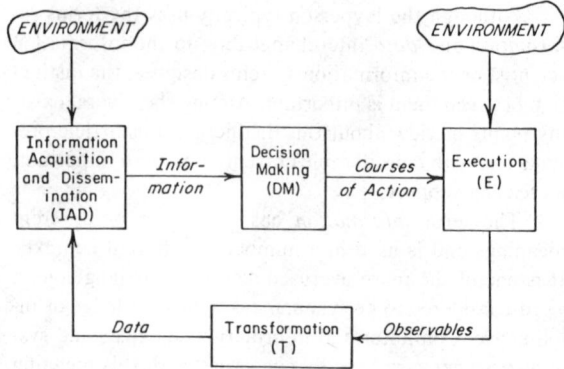

Fig. 1. The generalized information system model.

decisions. It is the mechanism available to the DM by which the DM's assessment of the decision-making situation can be updated. Repetitive or similar types of decisions enable the DM to benefit from prior decisions by updating and modifying the DM's current personal model of the situation.

The DM makes a decision (selects a course of action) which the *execution* module carries out. The decision-making will generally have uncertainty with regard to the execution function *(executional uncertainty)* and with regard to the specific environmental conditions prevailing *(state of nature uncertainty).* The *transformation* module converts or transforms the results of the decisions which are physical and observable into feedback *data* for the IAD. Note that the decision-maker has *transduced* information into observable quantities. The observables are in turn transformed into data.

The model makes explicit not only the relationship between information and decision-making but also the relationship between data and observable physical quantities as well as the sometimes overlooked but necessary feedback property found in useful information/decision-making systems.

Although it is beyond the scope of this article, it is possible using the framework established by the G.I.S. to establish precise and quantitative definitions of *quantity of information* in terms of *binary choice units* (which is a deterministic choice from a pair of alternatives); *decision-maker effectiveness* in terms of expected values and probabilities of choice; *value or effectiveness of information* in terms of the change which will result in decision-maker effectiveness; as well as other important quantities. The references should be consulted for futher details.

REFERENCES

1949. Shannon, C. E. and Weaver, W. *The Mathematical Theory of Communication.* Urbana, IL: University of Illinois Press.

1952. Carnap, R. and Bar-Hillel, Y. *An Outline of a Theory of Semantic Information,* Technical Report No. 247. Cambridge, MA: Research Laboratory of Electronics, M.I.T.

1964. Marschak, J. "Problems in Information Economics," in Bonini, C. P., Jaedicke, R. K., and Wagner, H. M. *Management Controls.* New York: McGraw-Hill, pp. 38–74.

1965. McDonough, A. M. and Garrett, L. J. *Management Systems, Working Concepts and Practices.* Homewood, IL: Richard D. Irwin.

1966. *Webster's Third New International Dictionary.* Springfield, MA: G. & C. Merriam Co.

1969. MacKay, D. M. *Information, Mechanism, and Meaning.* Cambridge, MA: M.I.T. Press.

1969. Yovits, M. C. and Ernst, R. L. "Generalized Information Systems: Consequences for Information Transfer," in Pepinsky, H. P. (Ed.). *People and Information.* New York: Pergamon Press.

1972. Langefors, B. *Theoretical Analysis of Information Systems.* Philadelphia, PA: Auerbach (also Lund, Sweden: Studentlitteratur).

1972. Winograd, T. "Understanding Natural Language," *Cognitive Psychology* 3.

1978. Woods, W. A. "Semantics and Quantification in Natural Language Question Answering," in Yovits, M. C. (Ed.). *Advances in Computers.* **17.** New York: Academic Press.

M. C. YOVITS

INFORMATION PROCESSING

For articles on related subjects *see* ACCESS METHODS; ARTIFICIAL INTELLIGENCE; DATABASE MANAGEMENT; INFORMATION AND DATA; INFORMATION RETRIEVAL; INFORMATION SYSTEMS; MANAGEMENT INFORMATION SYSTEMS; and SYMBOL MANIPULATION.

Information processing might, not inaccurately, be defined as "what computers do." In fact, the broadest professional organizations concerned with computer science are named the American Federation of Information Processing Societies, and the International Federation for Information Processing, respectively.

For information to be processed by a computer or by any other information processing system, it must somehow be represented or symbolized. Hence, information processing is essentially synonymous with symbol manipulation, and the entire discussion in this Encyclopedia of symbol manipulation could be readily retitled "information processing." In this article, we will approach the topic of information processing in a somewhat more philosophical, less technical, vein than in the article SYMBOL MANIPULATION.

The phrase *information processing* is often used in preference to *computation* or *data processing,* to emphasize the generality of computers—the fact that they are in no way limited to manipulating just symbols that designate numbers, but can operate in any domain, numerical or nonnumerical, where information is represented in symbolic form. The term *information,* in turn, carries allusions to the Shannon-Wiener theory of selective information, which emphasizes the role of symbol structures as designating one particular state of affairs out of some larger set of possible states. Thus, if we are dealing with the class of flowers, the symbol "rose" conveys the information that we are concerned with a particular subclass of that class.

Information has other aspects besides the selective aspect emphasized in the Shannon-Wiener theory. However, this selective aspect is closely connected with the way in which information is used by information processing systems such as computers. Information processing systems are capable of executing a *conditional branch* or transfer operation. The conditional branch operation detects which of several different states of affairs prevails (e.g., which of several symbol structures is stored in the working memory of the computer), and sends the subsequent computation along different paths depending on which state of affairs is detected. Thus, as the basis of the selective information available to it, the information processing system behaves in a selective, or informed, fashion.

The use of selective information by conditional branch processes lies at the root of everything complex or clever that a computer can do. In the simplest case, the conditional branch detects when an iteration is done (e.g., when the adding of a column of figures has been completed), and transfers control to the next process. (It was with this use in mind that Babbage first invented the conditional branch.) In more complex situations, conditional branching processes enable information processing systems to engage in all kinds of intelligent problem-solving behaviors (whether the intelligence be artificial or natural).

Effective information processing often depends crucially on substituting a high degree of selectivity (that is, a high degree of dependence on selective information) for a large amount of brute-force search through immense spaces of possible alternatives. Popular accounts of the computer often emphasize the impressive speed of its basic arithmetic processes and the vast number of computations it can perform in a short time. In actual fact, apart from *number crunching* applications, the arithmetic speed of the computer is far less important than its capability for selectivity, using information interpreted by the conditional branch processes.

Empirical research on human chess-playing skill, for example, shows that masters do not explore more alternatives than ordinary players—and probably do not even usually look more moves ahead. Instead, their superior performance almost certainly rests on looking at the *right* things—i.e., using information effectively to explore selectively. Similarly, artificial intelligence applications of the computer, whether for chess playing or in other tasks, always require the use of information to behave selectively, rather than rely primarily on the speed of the machine to carry out extensive searches.

We can illustrate this trade-off between selectivity and speed in information processing by two examples: programs for retrieving information from large stores, and programs for solving problems.

Information Retrieval. Whenever we have a large store of data—say, a set of customer records—it becomes expensive to search the entire store sequentially to find a particular piece of data. We would like, instead, to be able to go directly to the point where the data is to be found and to extract it without a lengthy search. A memory that allows us to do this is often called *random access*. A better description for it is *addressable, direct access,* for there is nothing random about the way in which we approach it. The store is to be *addressable* so that each record in it can be designated, or pointed to, by a symbolized address (name). It is to have *direct access* so that the information processor can be switched to read the desired record directly, once its name is known, without requiring a search.

Now it is well known that to select a particular item from a set of n items requires approximately $\log_2 n$ binary switching operations. Suppose we have a store of 64 records. Since $64 = 2^6$, we can use strings of 6 binary digits each (e.g., 100110) to provide distinct addresses for the 64 records. An appropriate switching device would have to perform six switching operations—one for each digit—to select a desired record. With such a system, the number of switching operations required to select a record increases only with the logarithm of the number of records—6 binary operations, as we have seen, for 64 records; 10 operations for 1,024 records; and 20 operations for more than a million records.

An unindexed book (or a nonalphabetized encyclopedia) frustrates human information processors because it provides no means to find a desired item of information without linear search. Thick books are proportionately more frustrating in this respect than thin books. A good index converts the book into an addressable, direct access store. The cost of retrieving an item can now be expected to increase only with the logarithm of the size of the book.

Problem Solving. To illustrate how information permits selectivity in solving problems, we will examine a trivially simple example.

How do we use an information processor to solve this arithmetic equation:

$$5X + 3 = 2X + 7$$

If we depended only on the processor's speed, we might try a simple *generate-and-test* method: Generate various values of X and substitute them in the equation; then test whether the two sides are equal. The futility of this approach is evident as soon as we ask, "Over what class of values shall we generate—integers, rational numbers, real numbers—and in what order?" Of course a very fast computer might solve such problems in a reasonable time, if only problems involving small numbers were presented and possible solutions involving fractions with small numerators and denominators were generated first.

A second approach might be to write the equation as

$$5X + 3 - 2X - 7 = 0.$$

Then we could generate a possible solution and test to find it if gave a positive or negative value to the left side. If the values were positive, this information, communicated to the generator, could cause it to next generate a smaller possible solution; if the values were negative, a larger solution. In this way, the feedback of information could guide the generator to the correct solution by a process of successive approximations. Computational algorithms that employ successive approximations use information in this general way to reduce the amount of search.

Of course a far more effective way to solve the original equation is to observe that the solution is an expression of the form $X = K$, with no constant on the left side, no term in X on the right side, and X having unity as its coefficient. By subtracting 3 from both sides of the original equation, then subtracting $2X$ from both sides, and then dividing the resulting equation through by 3, we obtain the final result, $X = 4/3$, without any search whatsoever. This was accomplished by comparing the given equation with the form of the desired solution, and taking specific actions to bring it into the desired form based on the specific differences noted. Thus, when the constant 3 is found on the left side, where no constant is wanted, it is removed by subtracting 3 from both sides.

At each step, specific information extracted from the problem expression is used to choose a specific action that will alter the expression in the desired way. Since all the required selectivity is provided by the information embedded in the given symbolic expression, no search is required to find the answer. The safe can be opened, so to speak, by reading off the correct combination, rather than by spinning the dials to try different settings. Simple as it is, this example is a prototype for the most sophisticated artificial intelligence systems, and contains in rudimentary form the information processes needed for carrying out *means-ends analysis.* (Means-ends analysis involves deleting one or more differences between an actual and a desired situation and then applying operators to reduce one or more of the remaining differences as described in the algebra example above.)

A basic reason, then, why we refer to computers as information processors is that they have not only to provide us with information—by performing a numerical computation, retrieving data from a store, or in some other way—but also to respond to new information, enabling them to substitute a high degree of selectivity for speed in search as a means of solving problems.

References

1968. Minsky, Marvin (Ed.). *Semantic Information Processing.* Cambridge, MA: M.I.T. Press (Contains examples of how systems use information to guide search in sophisticated ways.)
1972. Newell, Allen and Simon, Herbert A. *Human Problem Solving.* Englewood Cliffs, NJ: Prentice-Hall, Chap. 4. (This work discusses selective search, and describes a number of general search methods, including means-ends analysis, and their properties.)
1972. Simon, Herbert A. and Siklóssy, Laurent (Eds.). *Representation and Meaning.* Englewood Cliffs, NJ: Prentice-Hall. (Further examples of sophisticated search in information processing systems that use information to guide search in sophisticated ways.)

H. A. SIMON

INFORMATION RETRIEVAL

For articles on related subjects *see* CURRENT AWARENESS SYSTEM; DATA BANK; DATABASE, ON-LINE; DATA SECURITY; DATA STRUCTURES; INFORMATION AND DATA; INFORMATION SCIENCE; INFORMATION SYSTEMS; KEYWORD-IN-CONTEXT (KWIC) INDEX; LIBRARY AUTOMATION; MEDLARS/MEDLINE; and NATURAL LANGUAGE PROCESSING.

Information retrieval (IR) is concerned with the structure, analysis, organization, storage, searching, and dissemination of information. An IR system is designed to make available a given stored collection of information items to a user population desiring to obtain access. The stored information is normally assumed to consist of bibliographic items, such as the books in a library, or documents of many kinds; by extension, an IR system may also be used to access collections of drawings, films, museum artifacts, patents, and so on. In each case, the IR system is designed to extract from the files those items that most nearly correspond to existing user needs as reflected in requests submitted by the user population.

The IR area has become increasingly important in recent years because of the large amount of information that is potentially available for access—the production of printed materials, for example, is thought to increase yearly at a rate of about 10%; because of the difficulties of assembling large stores of bibliographic records in easily accessible forms and locations; and because of the increasing technical problems that arise in the selective distribution of large volumes of materials to heterogeneous user populations.

In recent years, many of the operational retrieval services have implemented on-line operations, using console terminal devices to introduce search queries and to obtain retrieval output. In that case, the information searches may take place *interactively* in such a way that information supplied by the users during the search operation is used to obtain improved search output. Furthermore, *networks* of information centers may be created by supplying suitable connections between individual centers, thereby affording the user population a chance to access the resources of the whole network.

The establishment of information nets, capable of storing large masses of data and of making them available to vast user populations in remote locations, raises complicated legal and social problems, connected in part with the propriety of unlimited duplication and transmission of information that may be subject to legal restrictions (as is the case for patented and copyrighted information), and in part with the preservation of information privacy, where this may be warranted.

Retrieval operations and techniques used in conjunction with library or text processing systems are also of interest in a variety of different information processing systems, including data management systems, selective information dissemination systems, and fact retrieval or question-answering systems.

Indexing and Content Analysis. In most operational retrieval situations, information analysis is carried out manually by using subject experts or trained indexers to assign content identifiers to information items and search requests. Such information identifiers are known variously as keywords, index terms, subject indicators, or concepts, and the search operation often consists in matching sets of keywords assigned to stored information items with keywords representing the search requests. The matching is followed by the retrieval of those items whose content indicators exhibit a sufficiently high degree of similarity to the query indicators.

A typical set of words, or word portions, indicative of the notion of "toxicity" is contained in Fig. 1. Such terms might then be assigned for purposes of content identification to documents and queries in the area of toxicity.

In some, so-called full-text retrieval systems, the assignment of keywords and content identifiers is completely avoided by assuming that the words which occur in the document texts can serve adequately for content representation. In these cases, a given item is retrieved if its text contains a given combination of words suggested in the information request.

While the indexing practice is still largely manual, automatic indexing methods are becoming increasingly popular. The following types of operations are often used.

1. Expressions are chosen from document or query texts, consisting variously of words, word stems, noun phrases, prepositional phrases, or other content units, which exhibit certain specified properties.
2. Weights may be assigned to each expression on the basis of the frequency of occurrence of the given expression, or the position of the expression in the document, or the type of entity.
3. The expressions originally assigned may be replaced by new ones, or new "associated" expressions may be added to those originally available, based on information contained in stored dictionaries, or on statistical co-occurrence characteristics among the terms in a document collection, or on syntactical relations among words.
4. Additional relational indicators between terms may be supplied to express syntactical, or func-

tional, or logical relationships among the entities available for content identification.

Such an automatic indexing process then produces for each stored item a set of "terms" representing information content. In operational systems, the automatic indexing practice is still largely restricted to the analysis of document *titles* only—the resulting search products being called "permuted" title indexes or "keyword in context" (KWIC) indexes. However, as larger text portions are made available in machine-readable form, content analysis will extend to abstracts, summaries, or full texts, with results equivalent to, or exceeding in effectiveness, those now obtainable in manual systems. An example of a KWIC index is given in the article on that subject.

Instead of using ordinary index terms for the representation of document content, it is also possible to describe bibliographic items by using lists of bibliographic citations related to the particular item to be described. Two possibilities suggest themselves: The citations may consist of the reference lists that normally appear at the end of a given technical article, or book; alternatively, the citations may comprise outside documents that themselves cite the particular item under consideration. A *citation index* can be used to identify the lists of outside documents that all refer to a given document. An example is shown in Fig. 2. The representation of document content through the use of citations is indirect: A document dealing with toxicity is described by citing other toxicity-related documents from the literature.

File Organization and Search Strategies.

Several classes of file organizations are commonly used, the simplest of which is the *serial file*. Here, no subsets of the file are defined, no directories are provided affording access to any subsections of the file, and no particular file order is specified. A search is then performed by a sequential comparison of the query with the identifiers of all stored items. Such a serial file organization is most economical in storage space, since no overhead is incurred for the storage of directories or links between items. Furthermore, access is equally convenient with respect to all keyword classes such as document authors, dates of publication, or content indicators. Unfortunately, a sequential search operation is time consuming and is thus unusable if search output is expected rapidly.

An equally small storage overhead may be incurred in the *computed-access* or *scatter storage* files, where the stored information is grouped into sets of items mathematically related in some way. In this case, a computation is performed on the set of terms used for accessing, and the *hashed* result of the computation is transformed into one or more storage addresses corresponding to the

---

toxic ... , poison ... , lethal dose, LD, side effect, drug allerg ... , drug reaction, drug sensiti ... , intoxicat ... , venom ... , side action, side reaction, adverse effect, adverse reaction, ill effect, idiosyncra ... , overdos ... , overtreat ... , intoleran ... , contraindicat ... , salicylism, goitrogen ... , nephrotoxic ... , neurotoxic ... , hypervitaminosis, untoward, undesirable, deleterious, irritat ... , irritan ... , harm ... , risk ... , danger ... , hazard ....

Fig. 1.   Terms denoting notion of toxicity that may be assigned during document and query analysis.

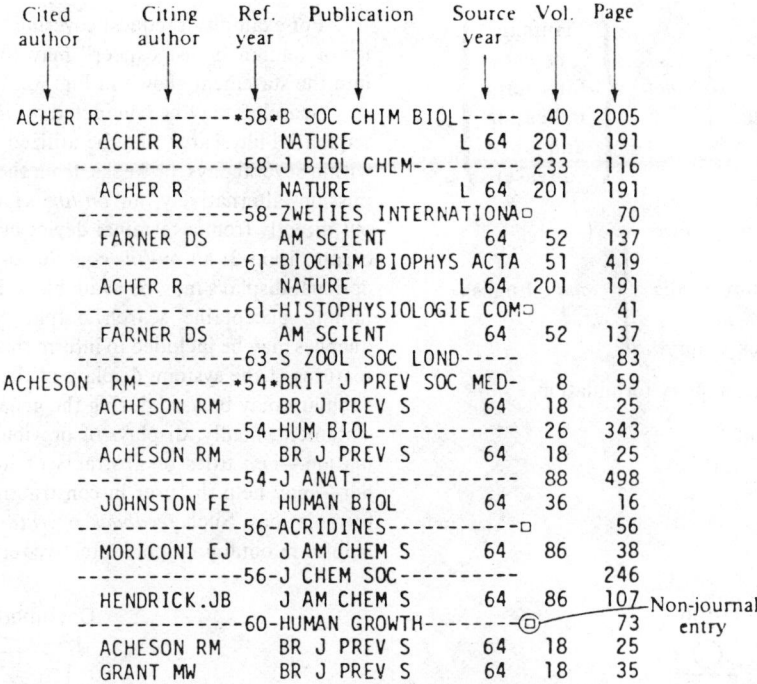

Cited author	Citing author	Ref. year	Publication	Source year	Vol.	Page
ACHER R		•58•	B SOC CHIM BIOL		40	2005
	ACHER R		NATURE	L 64	201	191
		58-	J BIOL CHEM		233	116
	ACHER R		NATURE	L 64	201	191
		58-	ZWEIIES INTERNATIONA□			70
	FARNER DS		AM SCIENT	64	52	137
		61-	BIOCHIM BIOPHYS ACTA		51	419
	ACHER R		NATURE	L 64	201	191
		61-	HISTOPHYSIOLOGIE COM□			41
	FARNER DS		AM SCIENT	64	52	137
		63-	S ZOOL SOC LOND			83
ACHESON RM		•54•	BRIT J PREV SOC MED		8	59
	ACHESON RM		BR J PREV S	64	18	25
		54-	HUM BIOL		26	343
	ACHESON RM		BR J PREV S	64	18	25
		54-	J ANAT		88	498
	JOHNSTON FE		HUMAN BIOL	64	36	16
		56-	ACRIDINES	□		56
	MORICONI EJ		J AM CHEM S	64	86	38
		56-	J CHEM SOC			246
	HENDRICK.JB		J AM CHEM S	64	86	107
		60-	HUMAN GROWTH	⊙		73
	ACHESON RM		BR J PREV S	64	18	25
	GRANT MW		BR J PREV S	64	18	35

Non-journal entry

Fig. 2. Typical excerpt of science citation index.

locations where the requested information may be stored. The search time is very small for computed access files, and no directories may be needed in addition to the main file. However, it is difficult in practice to construct good hashing (*q.v.*) functions that produce few collisions between distinct items mapping into the same storage address.

Chained files are characterized by the fact that all items exhibiting a given common identifier are "chained" together by appropriate links, or pointers; a directory normally provides access to the first item in each chain, and the file is searched by following the pointers within the individual chains. Chained files provide faster access than do serial files, but considerable storage overhead may be incurred to store pointers and directories, and a problem arises when the chain lengths become excessive for certain terms.

The best known and most universally used file organization in information retrieval is the so-called *inverted file*, where a large inverted directory is used to store for each applicable keyword or content identifier the corresponding set of document or item identifications and locations. The file is thus partitioned into sets of items with common keywords, and a search in the document file is replaced by the directory search. To identify the documents indexed by term *A* as well as term *B*, it is sufficient to retrieve from the inverted directory the list of document identifications appearing under term *A* as well as term *B*. References contained on both lists represent the answers to the query. Since only small portions of the directory need to be accessed for any given query, acceptable search times are generally obtainable. For this reason, inverted files are currently used with almost all operational on-line retrieval systems.

Inverted file organizations are advantageous in a static environment where the set of terms usable for content identification is not subject to many changes, and where access to the complete term set pertaining to a given stored item is not normally required. In a dynamic situation where changes are made to the content indicators attached to queries and documents, a *clustered file* organization may be preferable. In a clustered file, items that exhibit similar sets of content identifiers are automatically grouped into common classes, or clusters, and a search is performed by looking only at those clusters that exhibit close similarity with the corresponding query identifiers. A clustered file produces fast search output, and the file-updating operations are relatively easy to implement.

Retrieval Operations. In many conventional retrieval situations, a search request is constructed by choosing appropriate keywords and content terms and appropriately interconnecting them by boolean connections (*and, or, not*) to express the intent of the requestor.

$$\left\{ \begin{array}{c} \text{Breast neoplasm} \\ \textit{or} \\ \text{Carcinoma, ductal} \end{array} \right\} \; \textit{and} \; \left\{ \begin{array}{c} \text{Human} \\ \textit{or not} \\ \text{(any term} \\ \text{indicating} \\ \text{animal or} \\ \text{disease)} \end{array} \right\}$$

$$\textit{and} \; \left\{ \begin{array}{c} \text{Tissue culture} \\ \textit{or} \\ \text{Culture media} \\ \textit{or} \\ \text{Chick embryo} \end{array} \right\} \; \textit{and} \; \text{English}$$

Fig. 3. Typical boolean query formulation.

For example, a request covering "tissue culture studies of human breast cancer" may then be transformed into the statement shown in Fig. 3.

Searches may be conducted *off line,* in which case a sequential file search may be utilized to obtain responses within several days, or weeks, from the time of query submission; alternatively, an *on-line* search can be carried out directly from a terminal device using an inverted file organization. If an *on-line* console search is used, various optional displays may be available to help the user in obtaining acceptable search output. Thus, tutorial sequences may be included to inform the operator about the features of the system; displays of the available term vocabulary may be used during the generation of the query statement; finally, displays of previously retrieved information—i.e., titles or abstracts of items retrieved earlier—may help the user in constructing improved query formulations. Such *feedback operations* are particularly helpful in obtaining more effective retrieval output.

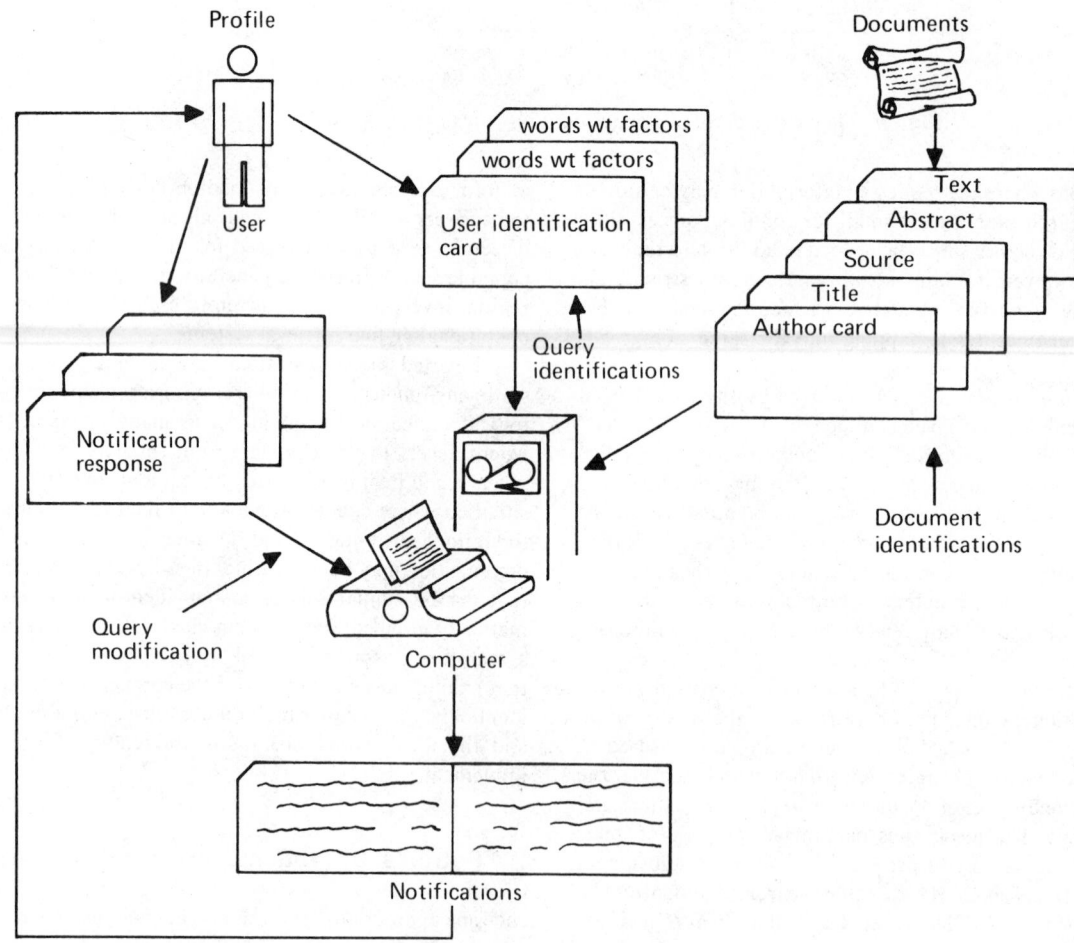

Fig. 4. Elements of retrieval system with provision for user feedback.

A diagram describing a feedback retrieval system is shown in Fig. 4, and a typical on-line search protocol is given in Fig. 5.

Retrieval failures may be due to the analysis and indexing policy—i.e., the assignment of too many, or too few, or of a number of incorrect content indicators—or to the indexing language itself (i.e., to the type of vocabulary available for assignment to queries and stored information items); or to the search strategy used; or, finally, to problems arising during user-system interaction. The use of natural language indexing systems may ease some of the restrictions inherent in a controlled indexing language in that it creates many diverse avenues for obtaining access to the stored information. On the other

```
• • • • •USER::
FIND INFORMATION RETRIEVAL

+ + + +CONIT:
YOUR SEARCH HAS BEEN NAMED S1 WHICH CONIT WILL GET BY DOING: COMBINE S1A AND S1B WHERE
     S1A = FIND INFORM:
     S1B = FIND RETRIEV:
RESPONSE NOT YET RECEIVED FROM RETRIEVAL SYSTEM.
SHOULD CONIT WAIT FOR A RESPONSE ANY LONGER? (ANSWER YES OR NO)
• • • • •USER::
YES
SEARCH S1A (FIND INFORM:) FOUND 15867 DOCUMENTS.
     NOTE THAT CONIT ORDINARILY SEARCHES EACH WORD IN YOUR SEARCH
SEPARATELY AS INDICATED BY THE COMBINE COMMAND FOR THE SEPARATE
SUB-SEARCHES.
     NOTE ALSO THAT CONIT ORDINARILY SEARCHES FOR ALL TERMS BEGINNING
WITH YOUR SEARCH WORDS AS INDICATED BY THE TRUNCATION SYMBOL (:).
USUALLY, THIS KIND OF SEARCHING GIVES THE BEST RESULTS.
FOR INFORMATION ON OTHER TYPES OF MORE EXACT SEARCHING, TYPE:
     E EXACT
RESPONSE NOT YET RECEIVED FROM RETRIEVAL SYSTEM.
SHOULD CONIT WAIT FOR A RESPONSE ANY LONGER? (ANSWER YES OR NO)
• • • • •USER::
YES
SEARCH S1B (FIND RETRIEV:) FOUND 1464 DOCUMENTS.
SEARCH S1 (COMBINE 1A AND 1B) FOUND 1093 DOCUMENTS.
TO SEE REFERENCES TO THE FIRST 5 DOCUMENTS TYPE:
     SHOW
• • • • •USER::
SHOW
-1-
ACCESSION NUMBER         A79036851
TITLE                    STATISTICAL FEATURES OF PHASE SCREENS FROM SCATTERING
                         DATA
AUTHORS                  ZARDECKI, A.; BALTES, H.P., ED.
ORGANIZATIONAL SOURCE    DEPT. DE PHYS., UNIV. LAVAL, QUEBEC, CANADA
SOURCE                   INVERSE SOURCE PROBLEMS IN OPTICS, ISBN
                         3-540-09021-5, SPRINGER-VERLAG, BERLIN, GERMANY,
                         PP.155-89, 1978, 240 REF.
TO SEE THE SAME INFORMATION ON THE NEXT 5 DOCUMENTS, TYPE:
     SHOW MORE (ABBREVIATED: SM)
TO SEE HOW TO GET OTHER INFORMATION ON YOUR SEARCH RESULTS, TYPE:
     E SHOW
```

Fig. 5.   On-line search protocol.

hand, new problems may be introduced by ambiguous or non-standard uses of the vocabulary. Many of the retrieval problems arising in standard systems from the lack of appropriate user-system interaction are eliminated in modern real-time search systems.

In addition, the *networks of information systems,* which are starting to be created, may relieve the inadequacy of local data banks, provide access to a greater variety of services, and furnish economy and improved use of technical competence.

The question of *information privacy,* involving the right of individuals to obtain access to a given piece of information under specified conditions, is most complex, and no solution acceptable to all user classes is likely to emerge soon. On the other hand, it is relatively easy, at least conceptually, to provide *file security* by implementing any given set of privacy decisions. Elaborate systems of user authentication by means of special passwords and of monitoring devices designed to detect unauthorized access are now in use of some installations.

Retrieval Applications. The most common type of retrieval situation is exemplified by a *reference retrieval* system performing "on demand" searches submitted by a given user population. Normally, only the bibliographic information is stored for each item, including authors' names, titles, journals or places of publication, dates, and applicable keywords and content identifiers. Often, only the keywords are usable for search purposes. Sometimes, the words of the document titles can also be searched. Less commonly, more extended text portions such as abstracts, summaries, or even full texts may be stored, in which case a text search (as opposed to a simple keyword search) becomes possible.

In any case, the responses provided by the system consist of references to the bibliographic items that match the user queries. In most conventional situations, the retrieved information is submitted to the users in no particular order of importance. An ordering in decreasing query-document similarity can, however, be obtained in the more advanced systems, which can then be used advantageously for search negotiation and feedback purposes. A sample search output in decreasing query-document similarity order is shown in Fig. 6.

In a standard reference retrieval system, a search is conducted only when a user actually submits a search request. However, systems also exist which permanently store (and update) user "interest profiles" (i.e., dummy queries that express the principal areas of interest for a given user population). Any new information items coming into the system are then periodically matched against the stored interest profiles, and the relevant output is sup-

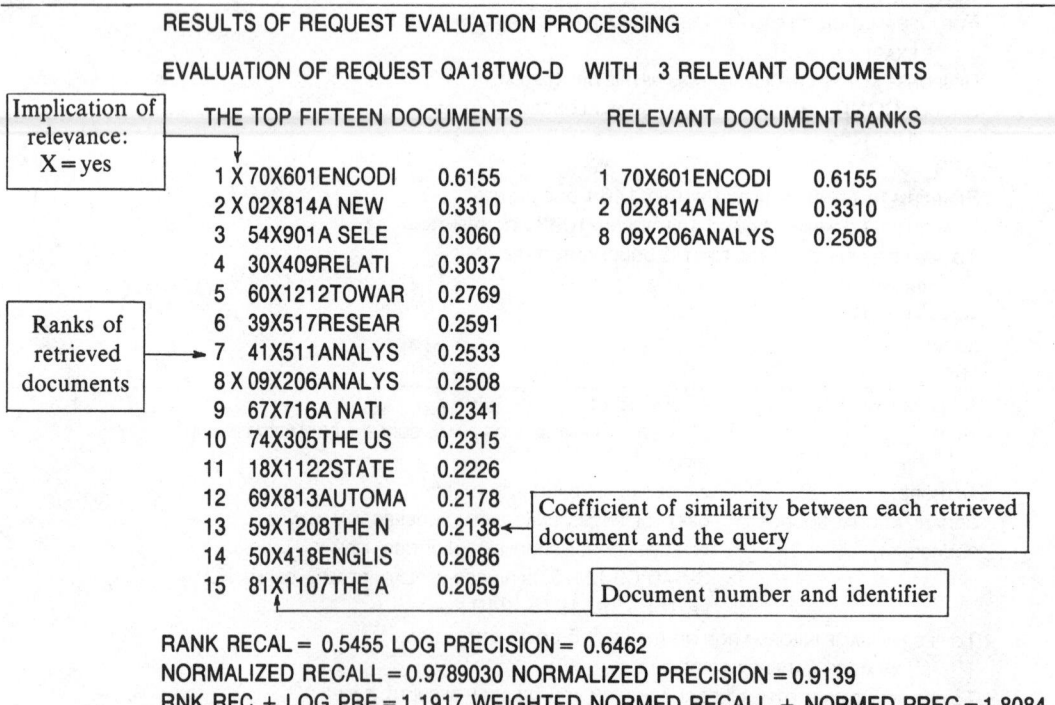

Fig. 6. Search output in query-document similarity order.

plied directly to each individual on a dependable, continuous schedule.

Some of the operational systems for such a *selective dissemination of information* (SDI) use response cards, submitted by the user population following receipt of a retrieved document, to update automatically the stored user profiles. Thus, as users become more or less interested in some areas, the positive or negative responses of the recipients are used to add or upgrade (or, correspondingly, to delete or downgrade) the respective terms from the profiles.

The rapid development of SDI systems is due in large part to the production and availability of a variety of tape databases containing titles, references, and sometimes index terms of the published information in various fields.

Data management, or *management information systems* (*q.v.*) normally provide general file processing capabilities together with user interface methods to simplify the manipulation and analysis of the stored data. In general, such systems include simple record-keeping provisions, together with exception reporting, and output-generating capabilities based on the use of statistical packages and plotting facilities.

Some management information systems also include query capabilities, permitting the user to obtain answers to certain types of submitted queries. In that case, a search-and-retrieval component of the type previously described must be included.

A final class of language processing applications of interest in retrieval are the language-understanding, or *question-answering,* systems, wherein a direct answer is expected in response to a submitted query (instead of only a set of references that may in turn contain the answers). The depth and complexity of the document-and-query analysis must be much greater in question-answering than in standard reference retrieval, since a precise and detailed understanding of the queries is needed before the answers can be supplied.

Normally, question-answering systems include syntactic components based on a stored grammar and dictionary; a semantic interpreter that transforms the syntactically analyzed input into a formal query statement acceptable to the program; and, finally, a deductive component that can generate responses by comparing the formalized query statement with information included in the database.

Several experimental text-based question-answering systems have been designed, but for the moment their coverage is limited to a small discourse area and a restricted subset of the natural language. Until more is known about language understanding and semantics, the question-answering application is likely to remain a laboratory pursuit rather than a practical possibility.

References

1975. Doyle, L. B. *Information Retrieval and Processing.* Los Angeles, CA: Melville.
1975. Salton, G. *Dynamic Information and Library Processing.* Englewood Cliffs, NJ: Prentice-Hall.
1979. Lancaster, F. W. *Information Retrieval Systems—Characteristics, Testing and Evaluation* (2nd Ed.). New York: Wiley.
1979. Van Rijsbergen, C. J. *Information Retrieval* (2nd Ed.). London: Butterworths.

G. SALTON

INFORMATION SCIENCE

For articles on related subjects *see* COMPUTER SCIENCE; INFORMATION AND DATA; and INFORMATION PROCESSING.

The term *information science* was coined to designate an interdisciplinary field initially concerned with the exponential growth of recorded scientific information. In 1950, the 81st U. S. Congress authorized the National Science Foundation to "foster an interchange of scientific information among scientists in the United States and foreign countries." Applied information science received a major impetus with the enactment of the National Defense Education Act of 1958, by the 89th Congress, which directed the National Science Foundation to establish a Science Information Service through which the Foundation "shall (1) provide, or arrange for the provision of, indexing, abstracting, translating, and other services leading to a more effective dissemination of scientific information, and (2) undertake programs to develop new or improved methods, including mechanized systems, for making scientific information available."

In the 1960s, the thrust of applied information science focused primarily on the handling of bibliographic records and textual information in science and engineering. Two major foci of effort received considerable attention: the study of the communication processes in the communities of science and industry; and the development of techniques and systems for more efficient organization, storage, and dissemination of recorded scientific information. The term *informatics,* synonymous with these two directions of effort, was coined in France *(informatique)* and popularized after its adoption by the USSR and the Soviet bloc countries; in these countries, *informatika* is considered to be a branch of the social sciences. (Terminological agreement is by no means unanimous: for example, in France and West Germany, as well as other places throughout western Europe, *informatics* designates applied computer science.)

More recently, the preoccupation of applied information science with the control of recorded information and communication in the scientific sector has been broadened to encompass concern with information handling in other professions as well: management, education, medicine and health care, government, law, the military, and others. The initial premise of applied information science—that the cost effectiveness of scientific and engineering work can be raised by improving the communication among its practitioners—has been formulated into a broader assumption, that the cost effectiveness of the human information processes which characterize these professions (e.g., problem solving, decision making, learning, etc.) can be significantly improved through their formalization and gradual delegation to symbol processing machines.

From this assumption, present-day information science and its professions derive their current social mission and long-term objective: the design of information processing systems that augment man's mind and purposeful activities. The significance of the social mission of information science lies in its extending man's historic concern with the efficiency and effectiveness of physical processes into the domain of the symbolic processes of the human mind. So formulated and interpreted, information science subsumes or provides linkages among directions and aspects of other disciplines and professions, including those of applied computer science. Indeed, to the extent that both computer science and information science share these logical aspects of an engineering discipline (an interest in the design and use of information processing engines and systems), they are considered by many to be synonymous.

As reflected in its principal review publication (*Annual Review of Information Science and Technology*) and the programs of its professional societies (in the U.S., the American Society for Information Science), the character of recent information science has been that of a social science and/or an engineering science (technology). Increasingly it is realized, however, that significant progress in the social mission of information science may depend on its ability to develop a natural science branch of the discipline, to be devoted to basic research on the nature and properties of "information" as a fundamental phenomenon, and on primitive information processes. Such a realization motivates a growing number of academic departments in information science, the first of which was established in 1963 at the Georgia Institute of Technology, under the sponsorship of the National Science Foundation. Indicative of the theoretical orientation of the field is the new research agenda of the NSF Division of Information Science and Technology; introduced in 1979, it places a significant emphasis on basic research.

As a basic science, information science has only begun its search for content and structure. The main direction of this incipient effort in the United States, the USSR, and western Europe is that of *empirical semiotics,* the study of sign phenomena. (Signs are entities that signify some other thing, called the "object" of the sign, and can be interpreted by a sign interpreter.) This direction includes investigations of the static structure of signs—as represented by fields such as semantics, information theory, and complexity theory—and the study of dynamic sign processes (semiosis) that transfer or transport sign phenomena. In this setting, information science is of metadisciplinary import, due to the semiotic nature of the nonphysical sciences (linguistics, psychology, sociology, history, and others) in which the essential phenomena studied are sign phenomena.

REFERENCES

1966. Cuadra, C. C. (Ed.). *Annual Review of Information Science and Technology.* Chicago, IL: Encyclopedia Britannica, Vol. 1.

1973. Debons, A. (Ed.). *Challenges to the Development of a Science of Information: Proceedings of the 1972 NATO Advanced Study Institute in Information Science.* New York: Dekker.

1980. Slamecka, V. and Borko, H. (Eds.). *Planning and Organization of National Research Programs in Information Science.* New York, Pergamon Press.

V. SLAMECKA AND C. PEARSON

INFORMATION SYSTEMS

For articles on related subjects *see* COMPUTER SYSTEMS; CURRENT AWARENESS SYSTEMS; DATABASE MANAGEMENT; DATA NETWORKS, PUBLIC; DATA PROCESSING; DISTRIBUTED SYSTEMS; HOSPITAL INFORMATION SYSTEMS; INFORMATION AND DATA; INFORMATION PROCESSING; MANAGEMENT INFORMATION SYSTEMS; MEDLARS/MEDLINE; and PROCESSING MODES.

An information system can be defined as a collection of people, procedures, and equipment designed, built, operated, and maintained to collect, record, process, store, retrieve, and display information.

In practice, the term *information system* is used in a very general sense, both in technical literature and in general publications. Sometimes, the term *information processing system* is used when the focus is on the "processing" of information rather than on its "use."

The term *data processing system* is frequently used synonymously with *information processing system.* The difference usually arises from the point of view.

An information system may utilize various technologies; Sage (1968) describes the historical development of information systems in organizations from Babylonian times. Systems that contain digital computers as integral parts are sometimes called computer-based information systems (CBIS) to distinguish them from earlier (i.e., manual) systems.

Information systems (Fig. 1), as defined above, accept (as inputs), store (in files or a database), and display (as outputs) strings of symbols that are grouped in various ways (digits, alphabetical characters, special symbols). Users of the information systems attribute some value or meaning to the string of symbols. One journal concentrating on this field is *Information Systems.*

In this article, the emphasis is on the common characteristics of systems rather than on the meaning attached to the output.

Structure. The information system itself may be viewed as shown in Fig. 1. First there are machines, or hardware, of which the most important is the CPU (central processing unit) and various input and output devices such as terminals, card readers, printers, etc. Next is a set of software, including operating systems, utility programs, database management systems, etc. The hardware and software constitute the computer system. In addition, there are programs specially prepared for the particular system, frequently known as the application software, which is normally prepared in some high-level programming languages. The data stored in, and maintained by, the system is called the database and is stored on auxiliary memory devices, such as disks and tapes. Even in a computer-based information system, the processing is usually supplemented by manual (noncomputerized) procedures. An organizational interface exists between the system and its users.

Classification of Information Systems. Information systems may be classified in different ways for different purposes. One method of classification is by the application area, such as government, payroll, accounting, and airline reservation. Another classification is by type of service rendered. The following are among the most important classes under this classification.

1. *Computing service* systems that provide a general computing service to a number of users. Common examples are university computing centers, computing centers in research institutions, and commercial time-sharing services.
2. *Information storage and retrieval* systems designed to store data (or documents) and retrieve it in response to queries. An example is the medical information retrieval system MEDLARS (*q.v.*).
3. *Command and control* systems built to monitor some given situations and provide a signal when predefined conditions occur. An example is the Ballistic Missile Early Warning System (BMEWS).
4. *Transaction processing* systems designed to process predefined transactions and produce predefined outputs as well as maintain the necessary database. An example is an order-entry billing system.
5. *Message switching* systems that route messages over transmission lines from a point of origin to destination.
6. *Process control* systems designed to control physical processes by monitoring the conditions and signaling appropriate action to the machines. Common examples are systems to control chemical processes and oil refineries.

A summary of the inputs, database contents, and outputs for these six types of systems is given in Table 1.

Each of these types has certain characteristics that affect the structure of the system, the measures of performance which are appropriate, and the process of designing, building, and operating the system. Many sys-

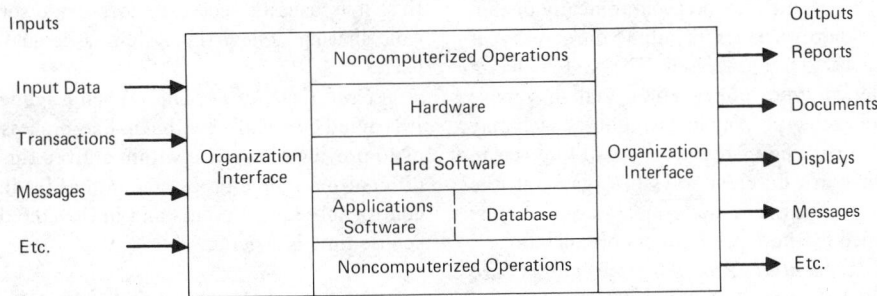

Fig. 1.   Structure of an information system.

Table 1.   Typical Inputs, Database Contents, and Outputs by Types of System

Type	Input	Database	Outputs
Computing service	Both programs and data supplied by users.	Created by individual users for their own purposes. System maintains minimal database for control and allocating charges.	Specified by users for their own purposes.
Information storage and retrieval	Determined by system designers on basis of what is relevant to inquiries to be answered.	Contains all input received.	Produced in answer to user inquiries.
Command and control	Obtained from sensors and monitors.	Built up from data received by inputs.	Warning and action notices obtained by periodic processing of inputs and database.
Transaction processing	Predefined transactions.	Contains all data necessary to process transaction and produce outputs.	Specified by system designer to accomplish system objectives.
Message switching	Messages.	Minimal. Contains data on status of nodes in network.	Messages sent to specified location.
Process control	Obtained from sensors and monitors.	Status of all processes under control of systems.	Signals to control operator of physical devices.

tems in existence today have features from more than one type, and may be considered mixtures of the basic types; some examples are:

Business Data Processing Systems. These are basically transaction processing systems, but usually are designed to serve users distributed over a geographical area and hence include communication and message switching capabilities.

Management Information Systems. These are a combination of information storage and retrieval systems and command and control systems. They usually draw a substantial part of their data from the business data processing systems.

Computer Networks or Distributed Processing Systems. These provide computing service and message switching over a geographical area. They may also provide transaction processing capability.

The users of systems may be geographically distant from the physical hardware. Users initiate different types of requests or jobs to be processed. The system has a number of different types of resources, and may have more than one of each type. Any given request or job may need more than one type of resource, possibly given in some order. There are different ways of organizing the resources to accomplish the requests, and systems may be therefore classified by the type of system organization.

Batch or Sequential Processing. Requests are grouped into batches on the basis of common processing requirements, and each batch is processed as a unit, usually at a predetermined time. The individual user there-

fore gets results at the conclusion of all operations on the batch in which the request is included.

Store and Forward. Each resource has a queue, consisting of the jobs that require that resource. When a job is finished at that resource, it is sent to the queue at the next resource needed, and the next job in the queue is processed. The user gets results when all the operations on a job have been performed.

In-Line or Random Processing. Jobs are selected for processing according to some priority scheme; once a job has been started, it is processed completely through to the final result. All the necessary files in the database are updated.

Interactive. The user communicates with the computing facility via terminals, and requests are processed as they arrive. The user gets quick responses, which may be used to prepare the next input. In order to accomplish this, it is usually necessary to provide some method of time sharing, unless the system is dedicated to a single user.

Real Time, or On Line. When a request is received, it is acted on usually by the on-line processing method so as to provide a response within a given time period. This differs from in-line processing in that feedback is used to control subsequent inputs and in that the demand on response time is stricter.

Common Features of Information Systems.
The various classifications described above are useful in identifying common features of systems that

may appear in more than one type. All information systems have certain characteristics in common.

1. Information systems are human-made; i.e., they have to be designed, constructed, operated, and maintained. This is a nontrivial task and has led to the need for methods of system development, operation, and maintenance. An introduction to the topic is given by Benjamin (1971). A survey of current practice appears in the *EDP Analyzer*. Software engineering (*q.v.*) is a discipline emerging as a partial response to this need.
2. In the development and operation of information systems, both the programs and the database are important.
3. Because of the large cost involved in developing information systems, there is an economic need for systems to share hardware, files, and software.
4. The systems tend to be large and costly to develop, operate, and maintain. This arises because of economies of scale involved in larger hardware and in economies of scale involved in operation and maintenance of systems.
5. The systems involve human-machine communication at various levels, and problems of design and operation include both problems of communication among individuals, of communications with the machine, and of the communication among the various units of the machine. Therefore, documentation is an important aspect.
6. The uses of the systems and the technology on which the systems are developed are continuously changing, as are the organizations using them; consequently, the systems themselves are seldom if ever static.

Information systems are expensive to develop and to operate; consequently, analyses to determine whether they are serving the desired needs of users, and the measurement of their performance, are receiving considerable attention. Performance evaluation must be considered at a number of levels. At the top level, the value of the output of the system to the organization that supports it must be determined. Once these specific outputs have been justified, the performance of the physical system in achieving these outputs must be measured. This performance is a combination of the performance of programs, software, and the hardware euqipment itself. The process of developing user requirements and designing systems to achieve them effectively is known as *systems analysis and design*.

REFERENCES

1968. Sage, S. M. "Information Systems: A Brief Look into History," *Datamation*, pp. 63–69 (November).

1971. Benjamin, R. I. *Control of the Information System Development Cycle*. New York: Wiley.
1979. *EDP Analyzer* **17** (925 Anza Avenue, Vista, CA 92083).

D. TEICHROEW

INPUT-OUTPUT CONTROL SYSTEMS

For articles on related subjects *see* ACCESS METHODS; DATABASE MANAGEMENT; FILES; LOGICAL AND PHYSICAL UNITS; MEMORY: Auxiliary; and OPERATING SYSTEMS.

One of the earliest and most fundamental reasons for the initial development and subsequent growth of operating systems concerns the handling of input/output (I/O) operations. The transfer of responsibility for I/O operations from the programmer to the operating system has been undertaken for several reasons. First of all, the construction of code for handling I/O is one of the more difficult aspects of programming a computer. By not requiring a programmer to know the details of programming I/O operations, computing services have become accessible to a greater number of people. Secondly, as assemblers, compilers, sort packages, and other utilities became available, it was necessary that:

1. Each of these utilities be provided with I/O services.
2. User programs not be permitted to write into areas where these utilities or their work spaces are stored.

A common set of I/O routines could be used by all system facilities (and user programs, too), thus saving duplicated effort. Moreover, a simple, carefully debugged set of routines could provide some measure of protection against destruction of important files of data. The problem of accidental destruction of stored data was further compounded in operating systems that permitted users to construct and maintain private files of programs and/or data. In such systems, the denial of direct I/O capabilities to the user became even more important.

By having a common set of I/O routines, it becomes possible to interleave in time the execution of different programs. When a program issues a request for I/O, the appropriate I/O routine is called. If the I/O operation cannot be completed immediately, further execution of this program can be suspended and control given instead to some other program which is ready to execute. This interleaved or multiprogrammed execution of programs makes more efficient use of the central processor without necessitating detailed planning of overlapped I/O operations by a programmer.

For all of these reasons, the handling of I/O operations has become almost exclusively the province of the operating system. More specifically, it has become the province of the I/O control system (IOCS) portion of a computer operating system.

Programmer Communication with the IOCS.

Typically, a programmer will communicate with the IOCS by calling various modules as subroutines. The assembly language programmer will generally have available a number of predefined macros, which will be expanded into subroutine calls to IOCS modules, using predefined calling sequences. Similarly, I/O commands in high-level languages will generally be compiled into subroutine calls to appropriate IOCS modules. In more recent systems, these requests for I/O service have taken the form of supervisor calls.

The Functions of IOCS.

The global function of an IOCS is, of course, to perform I/O operations for a programmer. This function may be refined to include the following tasks:

1. Interpretation of I/O requests.
2. Execution of I/O requests, once interpreted.
3. Location of the data to be transferred and where it is to be transferred to.
4. Initialization of transfer parameters.

These four topics will be discussed in subsequent sections.

Interpretation of I/O Requests. Each of the various I/O requests that a user may make (e.g., READ, WRITE, INSERT, DELETE, REPLACE REWIND, OPEN, CLOSE) must be decoded and the parameters checked. This process is accomplished by an I/O request interpreter. The interpreter will check such things as (1) the name of the operation, (2) the name of the logical unit involved, and (3) the parameters specified for the operation. Once checked, the interpreter will enter the parameters into the appropriate table (to be discussed below) and initiate execution of the I/O request.

The I/O request interpreter can, in certain cases, cause a variety of actions based on the I/O request. For example, a request to read a file that has not yet been opened might cause an error condition or simply cause the open request to be generated by the interpreter. Similarly, requests to write on a read-only device, such as a card reader, can be trapped at this level.

Execution of I/O Requests. Execution of I/O requests involves various kinds of information and routines. Among the tasks that must be handled are:

1. Maintenance of correspondences between logical and physical devices.

2. Generation of physical I/O commands based on requests.
3. Coordination of peripheral activities and maintenance of status information.

Following the distinction between logical units and physical units, it is convenient to divide the portion of the IOCS that is directly concerned with I/O transfers into two parts—logical IOCS and physical IOCS. Logical IOCS will contain routines for managing data on logical units, while physical IOCS will perform analogous functions with respect to physical units. Thus, physical IOCS will contain routines for every physical I/O device attached to the computing system (actually, these routines may be shared among devices that are all of the same type, such as all the tape drives). These routines will handle interrupts from the device and control the execution of I/O transfers without regard for the logical content, format, or organization of the data being transferred. Physical IOCS will also contain routines for handling errors and exceptional conditions received from the device.

The logical IOCS contains routines that perform functions associated with the logical unit, as declared by the programmer (or as predefined by the system). Thus, the logical IOCS will contain routines to handle space allocation and freeing, blocking and deblocking, index maintenance, control error handling and recovery, sense end-of-file and other exceptional conditions, etc., depending on the characteristics associated with a given logical unit. Clearly, logical IOCS will communicate with physical IOCS when transfer of data is necessary. Table 1 illustrates the division between logical and physical IOCS for several I/O requests.

Tables for Logical IOCS and Physical IOCS. As mentioned previously, it is common to share the actual routines for performing the various functions mentioned. In order that this may be done, and also provide a capability for users to change certain characteristics, the information that is particular to a given unit is usually organized into a table. The table is then passed to the particular IOCS routine as a parameter. Two types of tables may be distinguished: logical device tables and physical device tables.

Physical Device Tables. Each physical I/O unit (device) will have an associated table containing information such as the following.

1. The device type and an indication of the data paths that may be used to transfer data to or from the device.
2. Status information concerning whether the device is busy, which data path is being used if the device is indeed busy, and whether the device is reserved though perhaps not busy.

Table 1.   Division of Logical and Physical IOCS Requests

Request	Logical IOCS	Physical IOCS
Get the next record.	Deblock the next record. If buffer empty, get next block. If end-of-reel condition and file span multiple tapes, mount next reel.	Deliver next block from device.
Find a record in a randomly accessed file.	Request index tracks. Search index to find block of record. Request block of record. Find record and deliver to calling program.	Deliver index tracks. Deliver requested track.
Store a new record in a randomly accessed file which carries an index.	Add new record to proper block if there is space. Otherwise write new record in a separate area. Update the index to reflect the new data values.	Write updated block. Write a new record. Fetch index blocks and write index blocks.

3. The I/O operation currently pending on this device.
4. If the device contains storage that can be allocated and freed (e.g., the device is a disk), an indication of which areas are available.
5. The address of the routine that can construct commands for initiation of I/O transfers for this device.
6. The address of the routine that handles interrupts from the device.
7. The address of the routine that processes errors from the device.
8. Pointers to logical device tables associated with this physical device, with an indication of the currently active logical device.
9. Pointers to other physical device tables which share a data path with this physical device.

Fig. 1 gives an annotated version of a portion of a physical device table.

Logical Device Tables. The logical device table is used to keep track of information pertaining to an I/O operation on a logical device. Since several logical devices may share a single physical device (e.g., a disk), there may be several I/O operations outstanding on a given physical device. The current operation on the physical device is, of course, contained in the physical device table, as shown in Fig. 1. The information concerning the various logical device I/O operations will reside in the logical device table. A logical device table will contain information as follows.

1. The symbolic name of the logical unit.
2. The logical device type and name of the file currently attached to this logical device.
3. The logical I/O request currently pending on this logical device.
4. A pointer to the buffer(s) associated with the logical device, with indications of each buffer's status.

Device Status Table (DST) Entry

Unused	Driver name	Inst.	Entry count	Alternate channel	Primary channel
Head 1 position	Head 2 position	Exit count	Inst.	Device busy/ not busy

Explanation:
Driver name: Name of subroutine that issues physical I/O commands.
Inst: Current physical I/O instruction being executed by the driver.
Entry count: Counts the number of requests on this device.
Primary–Alternate channels: Naming of channels that can be used in conjunction with this device.
Head 1-2 positions: Status information on read/write head positioning.

Fig. 1.   A portion of a physical device table. (Adapted from *SCOPE 3.1 Manual*, Control Data Corp.)

5. The address of the routine used for transferring data to and from buffers.
6. The address of the routine that can process interrupts, errors, and exceptional conditions for this logical device.
7. An indication of which data areas on a shared device belong to this logical device (if appropriate).
8. A pointer to the physical device table for this logical device.
9. Status information concerning the "current" address or position of the logical device, the "current" record number processed, the number of records in a buffer, etc.

Fig. 2 gives an annotated logical device table.

It should be noted that both the logical device tables and the physical device tables contain pointers to routines that perform various functions. A programmer is typically not allowed to provide routines to replace those in the physical IOCS. To do so would impinge on the integrity of data stored on the physical device. However, it is

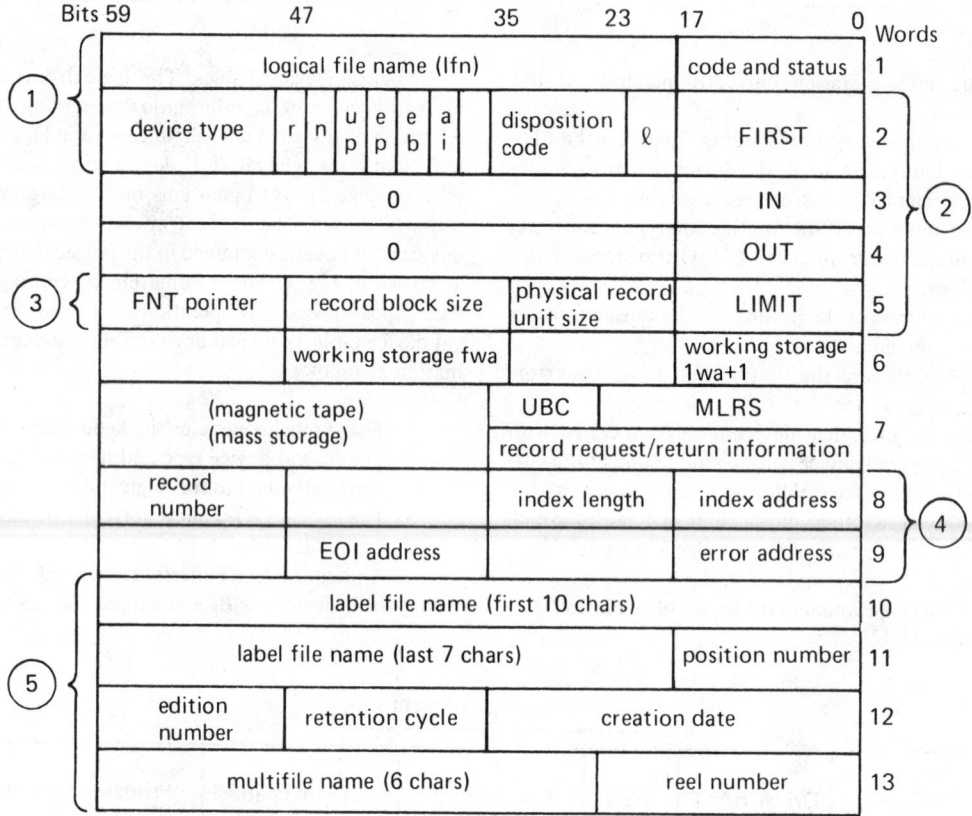

Explanation:

1. Name of the file and information concerning its corresponding physical device.
2. Buffer pointers for circular buffering.
3. Information concerning blocking factors for blocking/deblocking operations.
4. Indications of index locations for indexed sequential file organization.
5. Label information for verification and future mount requests.

Fig. 2.   Annotated logical device table (Adapted from *SCOPE 3.0 Manual 60189400*, Rev. I, Control Data Corp.)

common to allow programmers to supply their own routines to perform:

1. Blocking, deblocking, and buffer management.
2. Processing of exceptional conditions such as *end-of-file* or other error conditions on the logical device.
3. Label verification of nonstandard file labels (see below).

In either case, it is clear that substitution of different processing routines in place of the standard ones is simply a matter of changing pointers in the tables (and having the routines available). A programmer effects these changes by declaring that a substitution will be made and by supplying the routine. The IOCS then replaces the pointers in the logical IOCS table with pointers to these user-supplied routines.

Pointers are also used to maintain the correspondences between logical and physical devices. This may be diagrammed as shown in Fig. 3. By using the pointers from logical to physical units, it is possible to discover the physical device associated with a given logical device. Moreover, a change in logical/physical device correspondence is easily accomplished by changing a pointer in the logical device table.

Coordination of Peripheral Activities and Maintenance of Positioning Information. The scheduling and coordination of peripheral activities is an especially important IOCS function. In a large computer system, there will often exist a variety of data paths from the central processors through the data channels to the particular devices. Fig. 4 illustrates a typical situation.

Notice in Fig. 4 that a given device may be "attached" to more than one control unit and/or channel in order to form a path that can deliver data to or take data from main storage. This does not imply that data flows to or from the device over two paths simultaneously; only one path to or from a device is used at a given time. The multiple paths exist in order that devices may be kept busy as long as there exists at least one unused path to the device. The multiple paths also allow for continued operation should certain units in a data path break down temporarily. However, the IOCS must keep track of what data paths are currently in use and prevent new requests from using these paths. When a unit signals that a certain component of a path is no longer needed, the IOCS will search the pending requests to see if one can be initiated over the freed path.

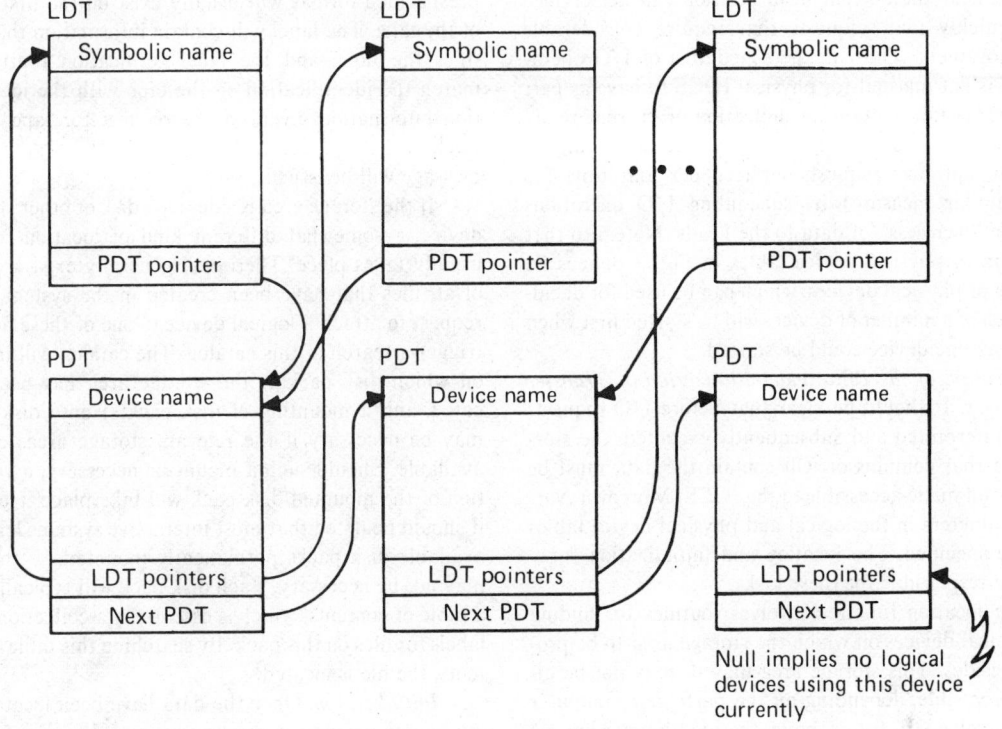

Fig. 3. IOCS table links.

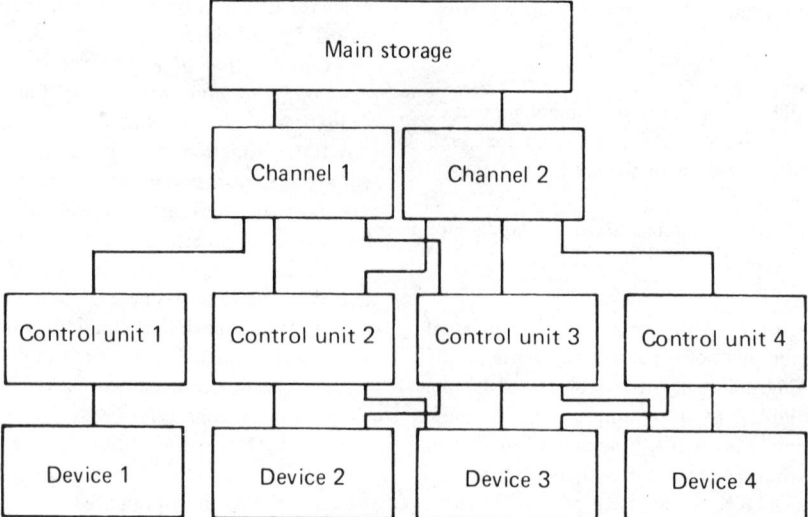

Fig. 4. Data paths to I/O devices.

In deciding on the next request to be serviced, it is convenient for physical IOCS to have information concerning the current position of read/write heads relative to the position of the data. This is particularly true with disks, which involve movable read/write heads. Requests for data near the current head position can be serviced more quickly than requests that require considerable head movement. Thus, in the scheduling of I/O operations, it is not unusual for physical IOCS to have as part of its status information an indication of current read/write head position. Using this information, it can attempt to optimize requests serviced per unit time (or some similar measure) by scheduling I/O operations based on "nearness" of data to the heads. Note also that the chain of physical device tables in Fig. 3 defines an ordering of physical devices, which can be used for deciding which of a number of devices will be started first when more than one device could be started.

Location of the Data and Initialization of Transfer Parameters. It should be clear that before I/O requests can be interpreted and subsequently executed, the storage area that contains or will contain the data must be located and made accessible to the IOCS. Moreover, various parameters in the logical and physical device tables must be specified. The location and initialization functions are responsible for these tasks.

The location function involves routines for finding the physical devices on which the storage area to be processed resides. This storage area may or may not be directly accessible, depending on the particular computer system involved. If, for example, the programmer has attached a logical device to a tape drive on which a specified tape is to be mounted, then the IOCS must make sure that the tape is indeed mounted. This will typically involve a request to the computer system operator to mount the specified tape. It also usually involves a *label verification* routine. In order to check that the operator has indeed mounted the correct tape, a tape label in a prespecified format will usually exist on the first record of the tape. The label will contain information that identifies the tape, and the label verification routine will match the identification on the tape with the identification information given on the request for tape mount. Lack of a match indicates an error, and an appropriate message will be issued.

If the storage area resides on a disk or other sharable device, a somewhat different kind of location function usually takes place. There will generally exist a catalog of all files that have been created in the system, and a request to attach a logical device to one of these files will trigger a search of this catalog. The catalog will indicate on which disk pack(s) the storage area has been allocated, and a mounting of disk pack(s) onto disk drives may be necessary if the relevant storage areas are not available. Should such a mount be necessary, a verification of the mounted disk pack will take place. However, it should be noted that most interactive systems leave the available disk packs permanently mounted, so this step may not be necessary. Each disk pack will typically have a table of contents, which is essentially a collection of file labels for files on this pack. By searching this table of contents, the file is located.

Initialization. Once the data have been located, the initialization function can be executed. In order for I/O requests to be executed, various entries in the logical and physical device tables must be filled in. These parameters may be specified on a system control card or by the programmer during execution, but in certain cases they may reside with the data itself, usually as part of the file label. Thus, if it is appropriate, the initialization routines will move a copy of these parameters to the appropriate table entries.

When the file is no longer needed, a final set of IOCS routines will restore the file to a state in which it can be used at a later time. This will involve such things as marking the end of a tape, rewinding it, and informing the operator that it may be dismounted, or updating the table of contents for a file on a disk.

Recent Trends. In recent years, the trend has been for I/O control systems to become even more sophisticated. This is necessary primarily because the rate at which central processing units can process data is increasing while the rate at which I/O devices can access and transfer data, while also increasing, is not keeping pace. This implies that more sophisticated buffering strategies will have to be incorporated into the IOCS in order that the data be ready when needed by the processor. One approach is to have the IOCS anticipate what data a program will need (based on an analysis of reference patterns) and transfer this data to a higher-speed storage device in order to reduce access time when the data is actually referenced. The extra processing power to do this reference analysis is often placed in an enhanced channel. The program within the enhanced channel can be regarded as a portion of the IOCS which has been moved to a special IOCS processor. The effect is to improve performance with minimal impact on the rest of the operating system and allow other functions, such as reorganization of the data for increased efficiency, to be performed with the main processor not becoming involved.

REFERENCES

1974. Madnick, S. E. and Donovan, J. J. *Operating Systems.* New York: McGraw-Hill, pp. 337–373.
1974. Tsichritzis, D. C. and Bernstein, P. A. *Operating Systems.* New York: Academic Press, pp. 123–145.

R. W. TAYLOR

INPUT-OUTPUT DEVICES

For articles on related subjects *see* AUDIO TERMINAL; CARD READING AND PUNCHING TECHNIQUES; COLLATING SEQUENCE; COMPUTER GRAPHICS; CURSOR; DATA ACQUISITION COMPUTER; DATA PREPARATION DEVICES; DATA TABLET; KEYBOARD STANDARDS; LIGHTPEN; MEMORY: Auxiliary; OPTICAL CHARACTER READERS; OPTICAL MARK READERS; PAPER TAPE; PRINTING TECHNIQUES; TERMINALS; and UNIVERSAL PRODUCT CODE.

Input is the process of translation of incoming information into electronic patterns suitable for computer processing. Output is the reverse process in which the electronic patterns are translated into a form readable by other machines or understandable by human beings. The translation process is carried out by the input and output devices of the computer system.

The most natural media for communication between a human being and a computer are those which are most natural for communication between people. For input to the computer, this would mean speaking, writing (preferably handwriting) or drawing, and movements of the hands, like pointing, etc. As for computer output, the preferred form by a human being would be hearing (spoken sentences, numbers, and/or sounds like alarm signals, etc.), reading (written messages), or seeing (drawings, graphs, or other types of pictures along with visual sensing of colors). The use of such natural I/O devices is constantly increasing as a result of the recent developments in this field, but these devices will not be discussed further in this article unless they have progressed beyond the research and development stage. However, all those now in general use, as well as some special I/O devices, are described and listed in Table 1, which also shows a few of their characteristics and some typical systems in which they may be used.

In spite of the fact that Table 1 was designed with great care, computer technology (hardware and software) as well as application fields of computer systems change rather quickly. Such changes will surely have impact upon the content of the Table 1, and it should therefore be looked upon as a general guide rather than as correct in every detail. Additional information about the devices and systems in the table can be found in other articles in this encyclopedia.

One of the main changes taking place in the technology of I/O devices is the steadily increasing impact of microprocessors and microcomputers. Micros are used increasingly as control units for I/O devices (e.g., in a magnetic tape unit or an OCR reader). They may perform not only the control functions but they also, as in the case of serial printers, may replace some of the tasks previously performed by mechanical or electromechanical elements of I/O devices (by, for example, simplifying the design of the print head, format, and advance mechanisms), or in their interfaces to the rest of the computing system (e.g., providing the interface protocol, thereby enabling the printer to be interfaced to different computer systems without mechanical change).

Table 1. Uses of Input/Output Devices in Some Typical Systems*

DEVICES USED IN SYSTEMS

CHARACTERISTICS: (1) I, O, or I/O. (2) Type: numerical only (N), alphanumerical (A), graphical (G). (3) Use: terminal (T), conversational mode (C)

Class	Devices — Groups and Subgroups	(1)	(2)	(3)	Off-Line, Conventional Computer	On-Line, Conventional Computer	Terminal, Time-Sharing System	Conversational Terminal, Time-Sharing System	Remote Station, Single-Keyboard System	Remote Station, Multiple-Keyboard with Data Concentrator	Remote Station, Multiple-Keyboard with Message Switching	Remote Station, Multiple-Keyboard, Direct On-Line to Computer	On-Line, Industrial Supervising or Process Control
1	**NUMERICAL AND ALPHANUMERICAL**												
	Operator's Control												
	Console	I/O	A	**	N	Y	Y¹	Y¹	Y¹	Y¹	Y¹	Y¹	Y
	Card readers and punches												
	Readers	I	A	—	Y	Y	Y	N	N	N	Y	N	N
	Punches	O	A	—	Y	Y	Y	N	N	N	Y	N	N
	Reader/punch	I/O	A	—	Y	Y	Y	N	N	N	Y	N	N
	Paper tape readers and punches												
	Readers	I	A	—	Y	Y	Y	N	N	N	Y	N	(Y)
	Punches	O	A	—	Y	Y	Y	N	N	(Y)	Y	N	(Y)
	Magnetic-ink and optical-character readers												
	MICR document	I	A	—	Y	Y	N	N	N	N	N	N	N
	MIMR document	I	A	—	Y	Y	N	N	N	(Y)	N	N	N
	OCR page	I	A	T	Y	Y	Y	N	(Y)	N	N	(Y)	N
	OCR document	I	A	T	Y	Y	Y	N	(Y)	(Y)	N	(Y)	N
	OCR journal tape	I	(A)	—	Y	Y	N	N	N	N	N	N	N
	OMR page	I	(A)	T	Y	Y	Y	N	(Y)	(Y)	N	(Y)	N
	OMR document	I	(A)	T	Y	Y	Y	N	(Y)	(Y)	N	(Y)	N
	Printers												
	Strip	O	A	—	N	(Y)	(Y)	(Y)	N	N	N	N	Y
	Digital	O	(A)	—	N	(Y)	(Y)	(Y)	N	N	N	N	Y
	Serial	O	A (G)	T	Y	Y	Y	(Y)	(Y)	(Y)	(Y)	Y	(Y)
	Line	O	A (G)	T	Y	Y	Y	(Y)	(Y)	(Y)	(Y)	Y	(Y)
	COM printers	O	A (G)	—	Y	Y	N	N	N	N	N	N	N
	Simple keyboard	I/O	A	T	(Y)	Y	Y	Y	Y	Y	Y	Y	Y
	Complex keyboard	I/O	A	T C	(Y)	N	Y	N	Y	Y	Y	Y	N

Note: "Data Collection Systems" spans the Remote Station columns (Single-Keyboard System, Multiple-Keyboard with Data Concentrator, Multiple-Keyboard with Message Switching, and Multiple-Keyboard Direct On-Line to Computer).

Classification table (continued)

	I/O												
Direct keying													
Numerical keyboards	I	N	—	—	T	C	Z	(Y)	N	Y	Y	(Y)	Y
Touchtone phone	I	N	—	—	T	C	Z	Y	Y	Y	Y	(Y)	Y
Alphanumerical keyboards	I	N	A	—	T	C	Z	Y	Y	Y	Y	(Y)	Y
Special keyboards	I	(N)	(A)	—	T	C	Z	Y	Y	Y	Y	(Y)	Y
Alphanumerical visual display													
Key input checking	I	N	A	—	T	C	Z	Y	Y	(Y)	Y	(Y)	Y
Alphascope (I/O)	I/O	N	A	(G)	T	C	Z	Y	Y	(Y)	Y	(Y)	Y
Plasma, and others	O	N	A	(G)	T	—	N	Y	Z	Y	Y	(Y)?	Y
Audio													
Input	I	N	A	—	T	(C)[2]	Z	Z	Y[2]	Z	N	N	Z
Output	O	N	A	—	T	C	Z	Y	Y	Z	N	N	(Y)
I/O in industrial (and similar) processes and systems													
Input (analog/digital)	I	N	—	—	T	—	N	Z	Z	Z	Z	Z	Y
Output (analog/digital)	O	N	—	(G)	T	—	N	Y	Z	Z	Z	Z	Y
GRAPHICAL													
Image input													
Facsimile I/O	I/O	N	A	G	—	—	N	Z	Z	Z	Z	Z	N
Manual off-line registration	I	N	(A)	G	—	—	Y	Z	Z	Z	Z	Z	Z
Manual on-line registration	I	N	A	G	T	C	Z	Y	Y	Y	Y	Z	Z
Automatic image input	I	N	A	G	T	C	Z	Y	Y	Z	Z	Z	Z
Digital plotters													
Pen (drum or flatbed)	O	N	A	G	T	—	Y	Y	Z	Z	Z	Z	Y
Electrostatic	O	N	A	G	T	—	Y	Y	Z	Z	Z	Z	Y
Graphical visual displays													
Graphoscopes, entry	I	N	A	G	T	C	Z	Y	Y	(Y)	(Y)	Z	Y
Graphoscopes, I/O	I/O	N	A	G	T	C	Z	Y	Y	(Y)	(Y)	Z	Y
TV display	I/O	N	A	G	T	C	Z	Y	Y	(Y)	(Y)	Z	Y
Microfilm I/O													
COM graph plotters	O	(N)	(A)	G	—	—	Y	Y	Z	Z	Z	Z	N
COM plotter/printers	O	N	A	G	—	—	Y	Y[3]	Z	Z	Z	Z	Z
CIM	I	N	A	G	—	—	N		Z	Z	Z	Z	Z

2

Table 1. Uses of Input/Output Devices in Some Typical Systems* (continued)

DEVICES USED IN SYSTEMS

Class	DEVICES Groups and Subgroups	CHARACTERISTICS (1) I, O, or I/O. (2) Type: numerical only (N), alphanumerical (A), graphical (G), (3) Use: terminal (T), conversational mode (C) — (1)	(2)	(3)	Off-Line, Conventional Computer	On-Line, Conventional Computer	Terminal, Time-Sharing System	Conversational Terminal, Time-Sharing System	Data Collection Systems — Remote Station, Single-Keyboard System	Remote Station, Multiple-Keyboard with Data Concentrator	Remote Station, Multiple-Keyboard with Message Switching	Remote Station, Multiple-Keyboard, Direct On-Line to Computer	On-Line, Industrial Supervising or Process Control
3	**SPECIAL DEVICES**												
	Special input devices												
	Bar code readers	I	N A —	T —	Y	Y	Y	N	(Y)	Y	N	Y	(Y)
	Badge readers	I	N A —	T —	N	Y	Y	Y	(Y)	(Y)	N	(Y)	Y
	Pressure pads	I	N A (G)	(T) —	Y	Y	(Y)	N	(Y)	Y	N	(Y)	N
	Systems to control telephone calls and billing	I	N — —	— —	Y	Y	N	N	N	N	N	N	Y
	Special I/O devices												
	PoS terminals	I/O	N (A) —	T (C)	N	Y	Y	(Y)	(Y)	(Y)	N	Y	N
	EFT systems	I/O	(N) A —	(T) C	N	Y	(Y)	Y	N	N	N	Y	N
	Special output devices												
	Ticket vendors	O	— A —	T (C)	N	Y	Y	Y	Y	N	N	N	Y

*For Characteristics:** = not available or not pertinent. (A), (N), (C), (GT) = sometimes, exceptional. (C)² = R & D stage.

For Systems: Y = yes. N = no. (Y) = sometimes, exceptional. (Y)? = unknown. Y¹ = operator's console with each processor and at remote stations. Y² = R & D stage. Y³ = special systems.

Additionally, micros have the potential to bring additional qualities to I/O devices. For example, they could be used to enable serial printers to print every other line backwards, thus eliminating the delay caused by the carriage return. Others of these new functions will be considered later in this article when discussing specific devices.

Alphabetical and Numerical Input and Output Devices.

OPERATOR'S CONTROL DEVICES. A *console* is a unit used by the operator for all manual communication with the computer. It also provides a display from the computer, generally in all or some of these forms: visual display, printed message, acoustical signals. The operator communicates with the computer by depression of switches (with a specific function assigned to each of them) or by a typewriter-like keyboard. However, the trend in newer systems is toward a console design resembling a normal visual display terminal with an alphanumeric keyboard (see Fig. 1).

The configuration of the console arrangement differs with the computer size and model used. For instance, in some large and fast computer systems, a line printer is used for printing information to speed up the overall performance of the system. Sometimes the console configuration can be extended upon request of the user; e.g., by adding certain features to the unit, such as a pin-feed platen to the typewriter; adding a display unit; a reference typewriter attached to smaller systems using display register and functional switches, etc. Large computer systems usually are equipped with a system console that has two CRTs and one keyboard. However, these devices may be more numerous, with several display consoles being used for controlling independent programs simultaneously.

Remote terminal stations are equipped with data station consoles to control the various I/O devices and to control communication between the data station and the central computer. A data station console generally includes a data set to connect the station to a communications channel, and also has circuits to handle automatic detection and correction of transmission errors.

CARD READERS AND PUNCHES. The punched card has been in use as a data carrier for a long time; however, its use is constantly declining due to several reasons, but mainly because of the development and use of more effective transcriptive data preparation devices such as key-to-cassette encoders or shared-logic key-to-disk systems or the use of direct entry devices such as typewriter-like terminals, CRT terminals and optical character readers. The punched card is still often used as a medium for computer program input (but even this use is rapidly decreasing) or in shop-floor data collection systems and similar special applications. The punched card contains data represented in the form of punched holes, which can be sensed by a variety of punched-card machines in order to carry out such functions as sorting, collating, basic arithmetic, and printing. Generally, the card has a standard size of 7.375 by 3.250 in. and a thickness of 0.007 in. It can accommodate 80–90 numerical digits and/or alphabetical characters. In the late 1960s, IBM introduced System/3, which uses a small punched card (*minicard*). This has approximately one-third the area of the standard card, and accommodates up to 96 digits and/or characters and symbols.

Fig. 1. Operator's console in Control Data's Cyber 170 Series 700 computer family.

The card transport mechanism of card readers and punches is closely related to the function of the device. The basic functions are reading, punching, selecting, collating (merging, matching), interpreting (which, in the punched card machine terminology, means printing on the face of the card), gangpunching, reproducing, sorting, and computing. Table 2 shows the five basic types of card readers and punches, with their characteristics.

PAPER TAPE READERS AND PUNCHES. Functionally, paper tape readers and punches are similar to those of card readers and punches except that the information media differ. A reader translates the information punched in code on tape into the internal code of the computer and transmits the data to the computer. A punch presents coded information in the form of holes in paper tape, and can be operated manually or automatically. Automatic tape punches will be discussed here as units that are connected with the central processing unit from which they receive the information to be punched.

Paper tape readers and punches were widely used long before the advent of computers (e.g., for telegraphy), and punched paper tape has been used as an I/O medium since the earliest development of electronic digital computers. In early computer applications, the five-track paper tape used for data transmission in the telegraphic service was adopted.

Each character is recorded as a single row of holes across the width of the tape. Apart from these larger round (occasionally square) holes, the smaller round holes (so-called sprocket holes) are prepunched in one row along the length of the tape. These holes insure correct mechanical feeding in slow-speed readers and punches or are photoelectrically read as an indexing means for driving the tape at the correct speed in high-speed readers. It should be noted that paper tape has now been almost entirely superseded by other methods of handling bulk input and output of data (for examples of the limited use of these devices *see* PAPER TAPE).

Paper Tape Readers. Paper tape readers (Fig. 2) may be classified according to speed into three categories:

1. Low-speed readers with performance from less than 1 chps (character per second) up to 50 chps.
2. Medium-speed readers with speeds ranging from 60 chps up to 500 chps.

Table 2.   Basic Types of Punched-Card Input/Output Devices

Characteristics	Reader	Punch	Read-Punch, 1 Hopper	Read-Punch, 2 Hoppers	Multifunction Unit
			Basic Types		
Functions					
Reading	Y	N	Y	Y	Y
Punching	N	Y	Y	Y	Y
Selecting	–	–	–	Y	Y
Gang-punching	N	N	Y	Y	Y
Collating, merging, matching	N	N	N	–	Y
Sorting	N	N	N	N	–
Interpreting	N	N	N	N	Y
Computing	N	N	N	N	N
Features					
Number of hoppers	1	1	1	2	2 or more
Number of stackers	1–2	1–2	1–2	2 or more	4 or more
Speed (for fully punched 80-col. cards), cpm					
Lowest	Appr. 60	16 col./sec	Slowest function is decisive	Reader plus punch performance (if independent)	Slowest function is decisive
Average	300–500	100–200			
Top	To 2,000	500			

Note: Y, yes; N, no; –, possible.

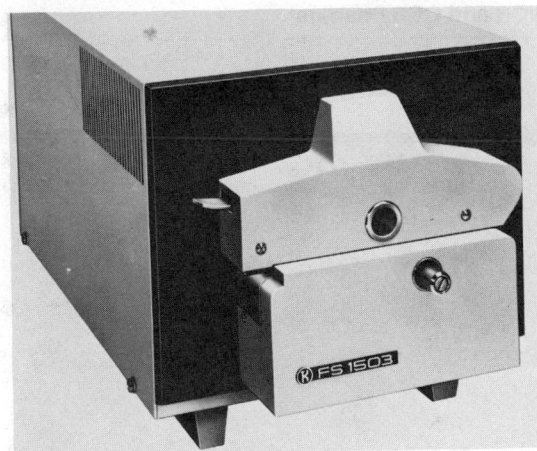

Fig. 2. ZPA FS-1503 paper tape reader.

3. High-speed readers with throughput higher than 600 chps. The top speed of at least two commercially available readers is 2,500 chps.

Paper Tape Punches. Paper tape punches (Fig. 3) as computer output devices are more complex than a simple keyboard-operated punch; their design demands increased accuracy, maximum speed, and reduced maintenance (mainly the sharpness of the punching die).

As computer output devices, tape punches may be classified by their performance. Low-speed tape punches have speeds ranging from some 15 chps up to less than 100 chps, and high-speed tape punches from 100 chps up to 300 chps.

MAGNETIC-INK AND OPTICAL CHARACTER READERS Magnetic-ink and optical-character readers interpret information printed or written on a document. The infor-

Fig. 3. Facit 4070 paper tape punch.

mation may be represented in several forms—by marks, bar codes, numerals, or letters of the Roman alphabet, and by other characters.

Marks are made by hand in preprinted positions on the document, each position having its information significance assigned beforehand to express its meaning. For example, a mark in a particular position can stand for "Yes" in a questionnaire, or it can stand for one chosen digit (or number) in the mark field of several preprinted digits (or numbers), etc. Mark readers have long been used with punched-card machines and so-called test-scoring machines. As computer input devices, they are used for many types of applications, mainly for surveys, census compilations, billing, etc.

Bar codes are printed by machine and usually represent numbers selected in a predetermined manner. Bars look somewhat like Morse code representation, but include some type of check. Bar-code readers are used mainly in point-of-sale and similar terminals for reading price tags, identification cards, etc. They are also sometimes used in optical and magnetic-ink recognition systems for subsequent sorting of documents. Numerical digits and alphabetical characters are either printed or written by machine or by hand in a more or less stylized font. This has been a steadily expanding type of computer input in recent years.

There are two distinct groups of scanning techniques, magnetic and optical. Both are used at present with magnetic-ink character recognition, a somewhat older technique. However, the commercial production of optical scanners has made distinct progress in recent years. Both magnetic-ink and optical readers are very similar in performance. However, they differ mainly in four ways:

1. The kind of ink used for printing the information to be read by machine.
2. Types of font, the size and the character set they read.
3. Size of documents and volume of printed information on them to be read by the reader.
4. Scanning technique.

Consequently, their applications are different. Table 3 shows some characteristics of both types of reader. Magnetic-ink mark recognition (MIMR) readers are being rapidly replaced by optical reading devices as are bar code readers.

Magnetic-ink character recognition (MICR) readers interpret only information printed in magnetic ink on one line of a document. The font used may be either the E-13B (adopted as a standard by the American Bankers Association) or the CMC-7 (designed by Bull and adopted as standard font by the European banking com-

Table 3.   Characteristics of MICR and OCR Readers*

Characteristics	Readers	
	MICR	OCR
Fonts		
MICR: E-13B	Y	Y
CMC-7	Y	Y
OCR: OCR-A	N	Y
OCR-B	N	Y
Other optical fonts	N	Y
Mark and bar codes	—	Y
Handwriting	N	Y
Ink		
Magnetic	Y	Y
Printing (black)	N	Y
Typewriter ribbon (black)	N	Y
Character Density (pitch)		
8 characters/inch in a line	Y	—
10 characters/inch in a line	N	Y
12 characters/inch in a line	N	—
Printed Forms (derived from applications)		
Page: Typical 14 × 9.0 in.	N	Y
Document: 3.75 × 6.0 to 3.67 × 8.75 in.	Y	Y
Journal tape: tally roll:		
1 ft × 1.3 in. to 350 ft × 4.5 in.	N	Y
Readers		
Typical maximum speeds		
Page	N	400–2,400 chps
Document	1,200–2,400 chps	200–3,000 chps
Journal tape (tally roll)	N	1,000–3,600 chps
Sorting possibility (reader/sorter)	Y	Y
Maximum number of lines read per pass	1	**
Error control:		
Validity check	Y	—
Timing check	Y	—
Rescan feature	N	Y

*Y, yes; N, no; —, possible.

**Up to 15 on documents and 80 on pages depending on device used.

munity). Both fonts are shown in Fig. 4. A picture of an OCR and an MICR reader-sorter is shown in Fig. 5.

MICR readers are used mainly in check and credit-card applications. Hence, the document has a small-size (typically, 2.75 by 6.00 in. up to 3.67 by 8.75 in.) with one line printed in an MICR font and containing the numerals and four special characters used for reading-control purposes. Since checks, postal money orders, and credit cards require handling at different points before their final filing, MICR readers generally have a sorting feature incorporated. Characters to be read magnetically have to be very carefully printed. The reason for using magnetically printed characters on checks is that eventual overprinting by postmarks or smudges will not affect the accuracy of reading. However, some sophisticated OCR methods can also deal with this problem today. Op-

tical readers are described elsewhere in this Encyclopedia.

The preparation of input documents for either magnetic or optical reading should be done with great care. The paper used should be appropriately chosen and print should be clear and well centered. Devices are more or less sensitive to these requirements. Characters not recognized with a high degree of probability are considered as *unknown* and such documents will usually be marked and/or rejected in a special stacker called a *reject pocket*. The handling of rejects, if numerous, can be very troublesome.

Both categories of readers, MICR and OCR, can be used in an on-line or off-line mode to the main processing computer. When used off-line, the possible output information will generally be written on a magnetic tape.

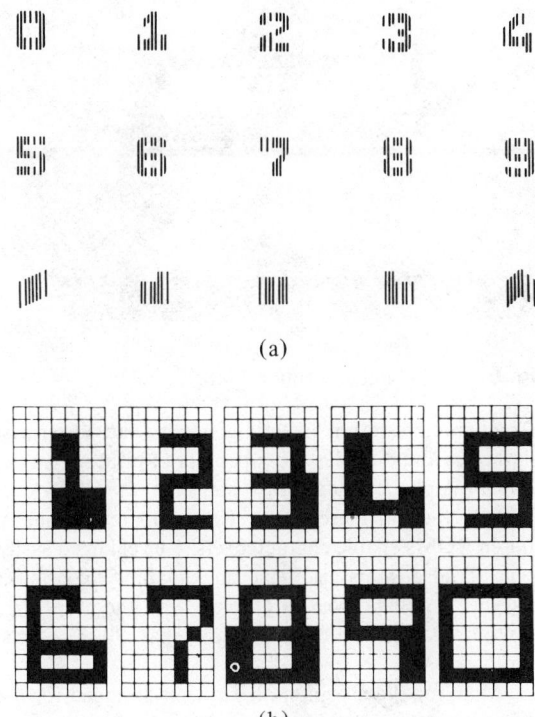

(a)

(b)

Fig. 4. (a) Digits of the CMC-7 MICR font used by the European banking community, and (b) the E-13B font adopted by the American Bankers Association.

However, punched cards or paper tape are sometimes used as well.

PRINTING DEVICES. Printers are output devices that convert computed data into printed form. The different printing techniques they use have impact upon several features of these devices; these printing techniques are discussed elsewhere in this Encyclopedia.

From the user's point of view, printing devices can be classified into two main groups, those with and without the capability of data input by means of a keyboard. Printers not having this capability can be further divided (by the paper form of the printed output) into strip printers, digital or journal tape printers, serial (character by character) printers, line printers, and page printers. In this article, only the first four categories are discussed; page printers are used mainly in microfilm I/O devices. However, a few page printers using other than microfilm techniques have been included in the later section entitled *line printers*. Note that the term *page* printer is sometimes used to describe the ability of a device to print a page format, as opposed to the *strip* type of printing.

Printers having the keyboard facility have in common (unless directly connected to the computer), besides input and output features, some device to get the connection to the transmission line (e.g., a dial-in telephone).

Generally, all printers may be used as terminals, but interactive conversational capability is restricted to keyboard printers.

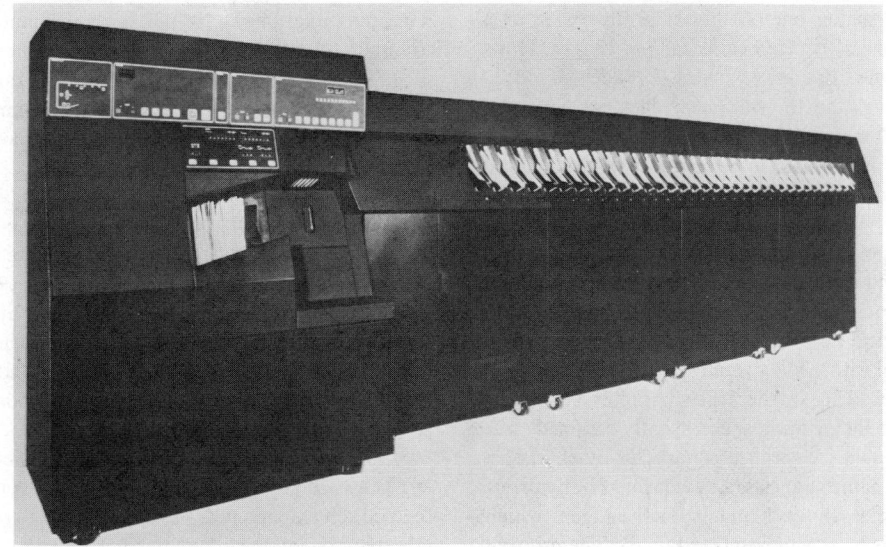

Fig. 5. The Control Data 92690 reader/sorter processes magnetically encoded bank checks and other documents at speeds of over 60,000 documents per hour.

Strip Printers. As the name suggests, a strip printer prints the information along a narrow (usually half-inch wide) paper tape, much like a ticker tape. It is a low-cost device used for special applications in systems where the cost of a multiple-column printer would be prohibitive. Strip printers are used not only as computer peripherals, but also as telegraph or industrial printers.

A typical example of such a device is a strip printer which has a printing repertoire of 64 characters as follows: capitals A through Z; numerals 0 through 9; and 28 various signs, symbols, and punctuation marks. These characters are arranged on a print barrel in such a way that they pass through the print position in the order used in the ASCII code. Average speed is 20 chps; a higher rate is possible for printing numerals only. Characters are printed with their vertical axes perpendicular to the longitudinal axis of the paper strip, 10 characters per inch. The paper stock is a half-inch wide roll approximately 200 ft long.

The development, in recent years, of nonimpact printers—mainly of the serial dot-character matrix variety, at very low costs—has made strip printers almost entirely obsolete.

Digital (Journal Tape) Printers. The primary advantage of a digital printer is its ability to make a permanent, continuous recording of the numerical values indicated by an instrument over a period of time. A similar requirement is sometimes posed for the output of a low-cost scientific computer. However, for this purpose, an electric typewriter is often used because an alphabetical print-out may be also required in some instances.

The name "digital printer" originates in its industrial application, and is used to distinguish this type of print from the analog one. A digital printer used as a computer peripheral is often called a *line printer.* However, as the printed line is very short (between 8 and 32 printing positions) and the stationery does not generally need to have sprocket holes (which are necessary for the paper-advance mechanism in line printers), the printed tape resembles much more closely that of the journal tape printer.

The speed of digital (journal tape) printers varies considerably, and can be anywhere between 100 lines per minute (lpm) to 2,400 lpm for numerical, or 1,200 lpm for alphanumerical information. The printing set may be either numerical with a few special symbols only, or a full 64-character set. The smaller the character set repertoire, the higher the printing speed usually attained.

Serial Printers. A serial or character-by-character printer is, as its name suggests, a device for serially printing each character, much like a typewriter from which the keyboard has been removed (see Fig. 6). The printing rate of these devices is usually between 60 and 330 chps. The character repertoire usually contains 64, 96, or even

Fig. 6. Facit matrix printer 4540.

128 characters, often including upper- and lower-case characters and includes the capability of printing various national alphabets, optical fonts such as OCR-A or OCR-B, the Japanese script Katakana, etc. Usually, plug-in ROMs enable character sets to be changed easily. Some serial printers also have the capability of printing a larger "boldface" font intermixed with the usual font, as required. The print line usually has 80–132 print positions.

Many of these printers have been designed for use with minicomputers, microcomputers, word proccessors, hard copy devices, visible record computers, or as terminals; several are offered also on the OEM market. Some may have the optional capability of utilizing a keyboard, in which case they will fall into the category of keyboard printers (discussed in a later section).

Line Printers. Line printers are used mainly to print out results of calculations; they can be programmed to print on stationery preprinted as invoices or statements. The individual pages are part of a continuous sheet and are marked out by folds and perforations across the sheet at intervals required by the nature of the document. The stationery is supplied as a pack, and a complete set may consist of several sheets with interleaved carbon paper to produce additional copies.

The continuous-feed paper supply is fed past the print head by a sprocket mechanism engaged through positionable traction clamps. Vertical spacing and skipping of paper is generally controlled by a tape loop in which the positioning of the page is determined by holes in the specific channels (8- or 12-channel tape being most popular today). When this control is not provided, the program within the central processor must control the line spacing of the page.

Fig. 7 shows a vertical-format unit mounted on the left-hand side of the printer. The shaft from the paper-feed clutch extends into the unit to turn a sprocket wheel in correspondence with paper advance. When a format tape is engaged with the sprockets, it is moved between a set of photodiodes and lamps. The tape is prepunched

Fig. 7. Vertical format unit for line printer.

with holes in 12 channels for up to 12 format choices. The holes in each channel indicate the line of the form at which the skipping paper-feed cycle is to terminate. As the tape moves over the photodiodes, a pulse is generated by each hole. The output from the selected channel is synchronized with the output of the paper-drive pulse generator to signal the end of the cycle. After being printed, the stationery sets can be split up into single sheets by means of decollators and bursters.

Several manufacturers produce computer form printers that copy the continuous output forms from the computer onto single copies of the same or reduced size. Some of these devices can use masks to eliminate copying of certain parts of the forms, or they can add printed information such as headings or footnotes to the printed image.

Some of the more important line-printer characteristics are as follows.

1. Printing speed differs so much that it is useful to divide line printers into three categories, Low-speed printers, often used as terminals, have speeds of up to 400 lpm, with about 200 lpm as a good average. Medium-speed printers go from 500 lpm to 3,000 lpm, with an average rate of about 1,200 lpm. High-speed line printers are exemplified by nonimpact electrostatic printers, some of which are called *laser printers* and which use electrophotographical rather than electrographical principles. They attain speeds of up to 21,000 lpm. Some of these models can print individual copies and, at the same time, collate them, sort them, etc. (Fig. 8). This category also includes *COM printers,* which can attain speeds of up to some 40,000 lpm (as a matter of convenience, these are described in more detail in the section on graphical microfilm output devices). All high-speed printers, COM printers included, are commonly categorized as line printers; however, they are, in fact, page printers, as they print a whole page of data at a time.

2. The maximum number of printed characters on a line is usually 120, 132, 136, or 160.

3. The print density on a line is usually given in

Fig. 8. The Xerox 9700 electronic printing system simultaneously produces computer-generated text and creates business forms and all other images on a page. The system uses standard 8½ by 11-inch plain paper and prints two pages a second.

"chpi," the number of characters printed in 1 in. (also called "character pitch"). It is generally 10 chpi; however, MICR font printers use 8 chpi, and other exceptions are also possible.

4. Start-stop or continuous operation is available. Generally, all line printers operate in the start-stop mode. However, printers using certain printing techniques require continuous operation and are used for off-line batch processing.

5. Simple image printing is often possible, mainly with line printers using the dot-character printing principle.

6. Checking involves parity, timing, echo, validity, receipt of data, or none.

Other Printing Facilities. Among these are such features as the ability to print embossed cards and labels (often incorporating bar codes, OCR fonts, etc.) or to print signatures on checks, to print in color, or to use a computer printer as a conventional copying machine (as, for example, the IBM 6670 xerographic printer, which has the capability of printing both sides of a page, or the Wang Image Printer).

Simple Keyboard-Printers. In the subgroup of relatively simple devices, there is always an input keyboard and a printer. The latter can often be used to print both the keyed-in data and the computer output information. In this subgroup are teletypewriters as well as typewriters and typewriterlike devices or printers of some other type with a keyboard added. These devices are often called *keyboard printers.*

The input speed of keyboard printers is limited by human ability; their output speed is determined by the device and/or transmission capabilities, ranging between 10 and 40 chps for interactive terminals, but up to 180

chps or more for some terminals. The printing technique used is usually of a serial type, with character-by-character print.

The arrangement of the input keys may be that of a separate keyboard for alphanumerical information—upper and/or lower case—and/or for numerical information entry. Apart from these, some controlling keys are needed; they may be accommodated on the same panel with the others or on a separate keyboard.

The interrogating function is sometimes provided by devices called *interrogating typewriters.* A single unit may be connected directly to the processor (generally through an interface channel), or a number of devices may be connected via a communications multiplexer. Besides the interrogating function, the device may be used also for other purposes, such as for program debugging.

This subgroup also includes portable terminals, which incorporate a built-in telephone coupler and typewriter-like input and output features.

A typical example of a printing terminal is shown in Fig. 9. The printing facilities of this terminal include, among others, a cartridge ribbon, a self-adjustment feature for single or multipart forms, vertical forms control provided through fixed electronics (ROM) instead of paper tape, and variable horizontal and vertical pitch. The keyboard design incorporates an alphanumeric typewriter-style keyboard, a numeric pad, and special function keys. A standard interface incorporates, among other things, a 1,000-character buffer, selectable buffer full and empty limits, selectable control characters for data stream protocols, different modem controls, and baud rates selectable from a front panel of from 110 to 2,400 baud.

More Complex Keyboard Printers. This subgroup includes devices of the types mentioned earlier as simple

Fig. 9.   New HP 2631G dot-matrix printer for HP CRT graphics terminals.

keyboard printers (with the exception of portable terminals), but with some more features added to them. These devices may have some kind of programming feature that allows for a restricted computing facility and printing format, and often for a choice of a few available programs. These features allow for less complex programming at the computer site and considerably lessen the number of commands transmitted from the computer to the terminal. The programming feature may be external (e.g., plugboard or programming bar) or internal (hardware and/or software type). Devices with more sophisticated (computerlike) facilities are often called *intelligent*. Similar intelligent terminals are also found in the visual display unit (VDU) group or among graphical devices. There may be systems configurations making use of all these devices.

Word (text) processing machines are also included in this category (*see* WORD PROCESSING). Sometimes, these are used in connection with typesetting (such as, for example, for fast Braille typesetting). SINTEF, the Norwegian Research Institute in Trondheim, has developed a Braille typesetting terminal, and Norsk Data has extended its Nord text computer typesetting system to make use of it. Now that so many books are set on computerized typesetting systems so that the text matter is generally held on file, the text can be converted automatically into Braille.

Direct Keying Devices. Direct keying devices represent a relatively new group of computer input equipment, enabling direct entry of information by means of keyboards (or, exceptionally, dials) operated by humans. Many of these devices are similar to those used in data collection systems that operate in an off-line mode, mainly to keying units in key-to-tape or key-to-disk systems. Direct keying devices, however, are connected with the computer directly, either by cable or transmission lines. Thus, they can also use for validation purposes the files stored in the computer direct access memory. Given proper environmental conditions, they can be used in time-sharing systems that require several types of intermixed data formats to be processed in real-time mode (e.g., updating centralized computer files).

Keyboard devices are used for entry of variable data. However, some of them may have additional features that permit duplication of repetitive data or of personal or other identification, using prepunched or preprinted cards, badges, edge-punched cards, etc.

To allow the operator to correct a typing error detected during the typing operation, the keyboard device is often connected to either some printing means or to a simple visual display called a *key-input checking VDU*. (See the following section, *Alphanumerical Visual Displays.*)

As do all devices that use a keyboard, direct keying devices are faced with the problem of the keyboard arrangement, which must be adapted to generation of the character repertoire of the ISO seven-bit ASCII code.

Direct keying devices can be divided into four categories; numerical keyboard devices, Touchtone telephone, alphanumerical keyboard devices, and special keyboard devices. Each of these is discussed in subsequent paragraphs.

Numerical Keyboard Devices. These devices resemble those used in key-to-disk off-line systems, but they differ in several respects. The keyboard or *key pad* for a numerical keyboard is arranged in three basic configurations, as follows:

1. Adding machine (or hand-held calculator)
   7 8 9
   4 5 6
   1 2 3
     0
2. Punched-card machine
     0
   1 2 3
   4 5 6
   7 8 9
3. Telephone
   1 2 3
   4 5 6
   7 8 9
     0

Differences between these basic types of numerical keyboard arrangements are self-explanatory, as are their uses. A few functional keys are generally added to the ten numerals.

Touchtone Phone. The advent of the electronic telephone exchange in the United States made possible the Touchtone phone, which provides a telephone-to-tape data-entry method. The instant response of the new exchange relays eliminates the requirement for a spring-loaded dial as a counter. Instead, the relays respond to unique tones generated by keys that replace the dial on the telephone. Soon after the introduction of Touchtone, it was realized that the instrument provided a new means of entering or preparing data for a computer, particularly where the data has to be collected from a number of remote locations, as in a multi-outlet or branch type of business, or from many different departments situated at some distance from the data processing center.

The Touchtone phone is a special kind of numeric keyboard device. When used in telephone-to-tape communication, it makes use of a translator, an electric device that interprets the unique tones from each phone key, alters them into a computer code, and enters them directly onto tape. The tape and translator are connected to an automatically answered telephone (*data set*), which allows many phones to input through a single translator onto a single tape. A data set is a device that connects a data processing machine to a telephone or telegraph communication line. A telephone data set is a unit used to connect a data terminal to a telephone circuit; e.g., to transmit data from the terminal to the processing center. Such a data set converts signals from the terminal into a form suitable for transmission over a telephone cirucit, and vice versa.

Typical Touchtone telephone users key in about 1.4 digits per second, with a relatively low error rate. Errors of omission are the most serious faults. Where check-digit verification can be applied, the error rate will be even lower. Further savings may be achieved by the use of a plastic card (originally designed as a self-dialing facility) for entering fixed format information.

The technique of Touchtone data transmission is not limited to batch operations, but can be used on line for any variety of information updates applicable to production, stock, and credit control systems. Increasing use of credit cards opens up a new area of on-line credit validation for all sorts of businesses by keying on line to a central computer. In countries where the electronic exchange is not yet standard, this device can still be used, once a connection has been established through the normal dial telephone. Touchtone pads, linked to any telephone and transmitting through the data set and translator, allow remote data preparation direct to tape.

The Touchtone pad has a single 12-button keyboard and is easy to use. The pad provides the user with the normal ten keys of the Touchtone phone, plus two additional keys (one for "skip," "duplicate," and "data entry" and the other for "error correction"). Data is entered a line at a time; each line can contain as many as 180 characters and can be split into as many fields as required. One key is used to skip from one field to the next; at the end of the line, a final tap on the "skip" key causes the line to be written onto the key tape. If an error is made during the entry of the line, the error-correct key can be used and the line reentered before it is written to tape.

Alphanumerical Keyboard Devices. Alphanumerical keyboard devices are similar to the numerical ones previously described, the only difference being the keyboard, which may be one of three basic types, depending upon the positioning of the numerical characters in the overall layout of the keyboard. A typical layout is shown in Fig. 10. (For more information *see* KEYBOARD STANDARDS.) Some of these devices may be designed as portable terminals.

Special Keyboard Devices. Special keyboard devices are of two types. In one, a normal numerical or alphanumerical keyboard is used, but keys are assigned special significance, depending upon the type of work for which the device is being used. The keys may be given special additional labels that identify various types of information when the recording is made. When the recorded data is read into a computer, the computer program is so devised that the significance of the various items of information is recognized.

The second type of special keyboard devices is that especially designed for a given purpose, such as mathematical expressions. Such a special keyboard device is used mainly in addition to keyboard devices of the numerical or alphanumerical type.

Alphanumerical Visual Displays. A display device allows the operator or user to inspect visually data that is keyed into the computer, and/or retrieved from the computer upon a request from the operator/user, or displayed automatically as a message. For example, data may be presented as a printed report, or in graphical or character form on a cathode-ray tube visual display unit (VDU). This section will describe the alphanumerical VDU, or *alphascope*. (See later section, "Graphical Visual Displays," for discussion of *graphoscopes*.)

Key Input-Checking VDU. To ease the key-in operation, several kinds of visual aids are used, such as a simple illuminated panel display or the more sophisticated alphascope with cursors. The latter incorporate a VDU upon which the latest data entry or any record entry held within the control unit buffer storage can be displayed. Such devices usually use a 64-character set. Normally, the data is displayed in a few lines, the total number of characters being limited by the maximum number permissible for a single record (generally fewer than 200 characters). Often, there is also a moving cursor to show where the next character is to be entered.

All these devices have in common the capability to display the input data only. If a device has the additional capability of displaying the output data, which is the more general practice, it is classified in a separate subgroup (see next section, where some common features will be discussed).

Alphascope—The VDU as an I/O Device. An alphascope is an interactive alphanumerical device (often a terminal) that forms part of a computer-based system requiring a short response time for getting answers to queries made by managers, dispatchers, stockkeepers, or clerks (see Fig. 11). Its purpose is to retrieve these answers from the computer random access memory. The alphascope terminals need only be connected to the computer by an ordinary telephone line. Since it is a relatively low-cost unit, it makes possible later extension of the user's facility to true computer graphics, from simple graphs to full vector capability.

The CRT (cathode-ray tube) terminal is not much more complicated than the Teletype, but because it does

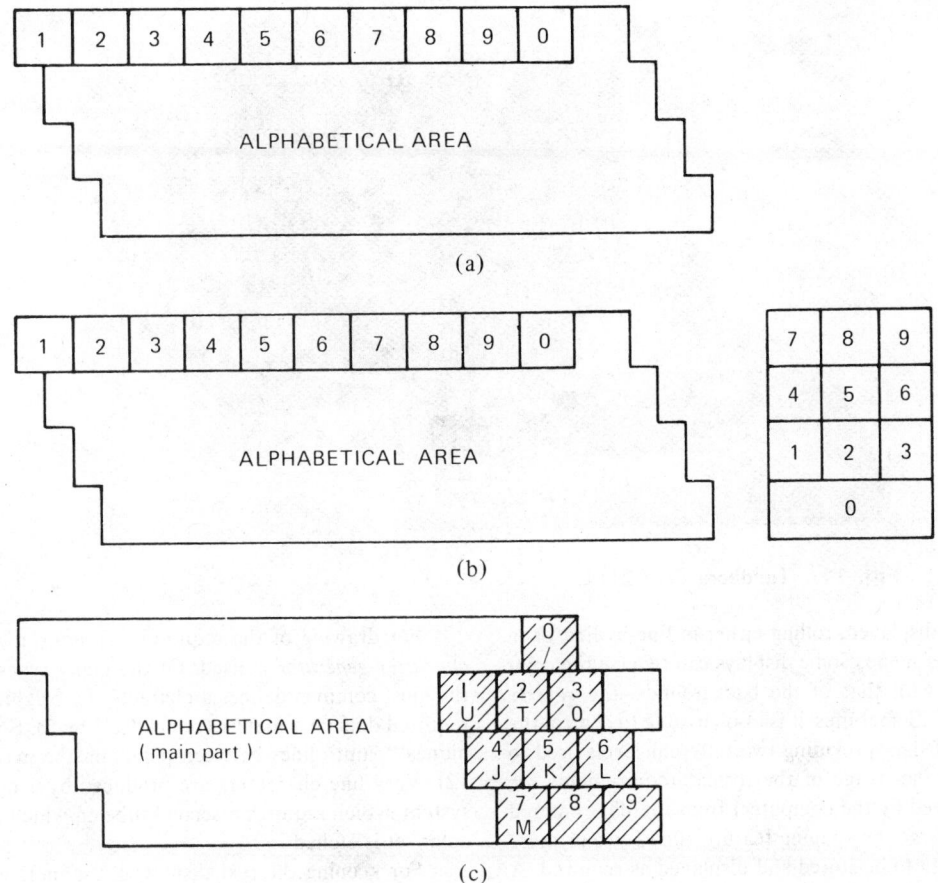

Fig. 10.   The three basic types of alphanumerical keyboard arrangement. (a) Typewriter-type alphanumerical keyboard arrangement, for predominantly alphabetical data. (b) Typewriter-like alphanumerical keyboard arrangement, with additional portion for predominantly numerical data. (c) Card punch-like alphanumerical keyboard arrangement.

not depend on a mechanical means of printing, it is considerably more reliable.

An alphascope consists of the CRT, a keyboard, a method of generating characters, a method of refreshing the display, and communications equipment. The *keyboard* fulfills the data input function and, following the ISO standard, is generally arranged like a typewriter, with a few more control keys added and often a numeric key pad, as well. The keyboard also controls the screen location of a cursor, which is a movable symbol that glows beneath the position at which the next character from the keyboard will be displayed. Often a feature is available to allow the display station to have full editing capability. This permits the display operator to insert and delete characters, move lines up and down, set tabs, and provide operator status to the CPU.

Screens have generally different diameters, to 20 in. or more, with the display on the whole screen or on part of it. Information is presented in from 6 to 24 lines, with up to some 80 positions each, giving a total capacity of a maximum of 1920 or even more characters. The characters are usually displayed in fixed positions on the screen, with the beam moving along each row, character position by character position. More sophisticated systems switch the beam to the next row when no more characters in the row are to be displayed, thus eliminating the need for tracing the path of remaining blank positions in the row. Sometimes a roll feature selects the whole array of char-

Fig. 11. Tandberg TDV 2114.

acters to be displayed, rolling either in line-by-line or in group-of-lines mode. Some displays can reverse the color of the data with that of the background—the *reverse video* feature. Sometimes, it is also possible to control the brightness of data providing two different levels used to differentiate the image of the format requirements (or questions asked by the computer) from the data entered (or the answers). The paging feature allows two or more frames of data to be stored and displayed as required. A graphics facility is also available on several alphascopes, so that their difference from graphoscopes has greatly diminished when simple graphic applications are required.

Another type of input is a *touchwire* system. Ten or fifteen short pieces of wire are imbedded in a transparent screen over the face of the display tube. The function of each wire is displayed on the screen above it so that it is possible for every character on the keyboard to be displayed by an associated touch, thus eliminating the need for a keyboard. The wire is connected to a balanced electrical bridge and is sensitive to the touch of the operator. By putting a finger on one of the short pieces of wire, the user initiates the start of a computer program.

The user is piloted through the process being controlled by labels alongside each touchwire, which are initiated on the display by the computer program. By looking at the displayed diagram (say, an electronic circuit) and pointing to parts alterations can be made. Touchwire systems are presently used only to choose the next required display, since a balanced-bridge network is more expensive than a keyboard, and also does not satisfy the sense of touch needed by typists. Moreover, this type of input is very tiring for the operator and should be used only occasionally.

For drawing of the required character, a *hardware character generator* is used. Of the many types applied, the most common defines a character by brightening the required dots on a matrix (typically, 7 by 5). Some techniques "paint" lines between points on the matrix (Fig. 12). Very fine characters are produced by a monoscope system, which requires a second tube on which the character set is etched.

For keeping the text displayed, the method of *continuous cyclic refreshment* of the picture (40 to 60 times per second) is generally used.

The *communications* with the main computer should be much faster than that of a Teletype if the main advantage of the alphascope (the quick presentation of information) is not to be lost. The reading speed should be much higher than that of the human eye. This is essential in many applications because the user scans the displayed text for quick orientation, choosing only the parts required for more detailed study.

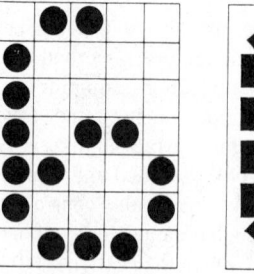
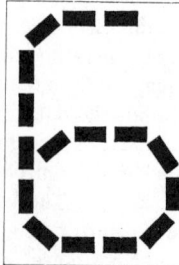

Fig. 12. Dot matrix and painted-line matrix presentation on the IBM 2260 and 2265 VDU, respectively.

The computer terminal market, particularly alphascopes, is one of the fastest growing areas of the whole computer industry and one in which the technology is changing most rapidly. Now it seems to be reasonable enough to suppose that, in the early 1980s, some 50% of all display terminals installed will be microprocessor-controlled. The impact of microelectronics and the dot-character matrix principle have been applied with considerable effect to the generation of characters and graphic symbols. Interface modules are available to convert any ordinary television set into a full 16-line alphanumeric video terminal. The incorporation of large amounts of semiconductor storage has enabled local refreshing to be used, reducing the overhead on the controlling processor. Violet-on-black flat screen displays with attractive performance characteristics may rival the present liquid crystal displays. Among the advantages of this type of display is that not only does the information displayed remain visible without refreshing until it is altered, but it survives when power is switched off.

All these technological developments and systems solutions make the task of categorizing alphascopes particularly difficult. The earlier classification by the amount of intelligence is probably still valid, however.

Simpler display techniques may sometimes be adequate, depending on the functions they have to perform. An example of a strip display is the Hewlett-Packard HDSP—87XX series 18-segment alphanumeric display system (Fig. 13).

Plasma and Other Output VDUs. Other hardware solutions are sometimes considered for visual display output devices, besides CRTs. One of these is the plasma display (Fig. 14), consisting of three sheets of glass. The middle sheet is drilled with holes 0.025 in. apart, each containing receptacles filled with illuminant gas (plasma). Both outer glass sheets incorporate strips of transparent conductors, one vertical on the inside sheet and the other horizontal on the outside sheet. The a-c voltage is kept at a level required to make these tiny discharge tubes glow when fired at the user's control station, and any particular spot can be switched on or off. The display provides its own storage, and there is no limit to the size of the screen.

AUDIO DEVICES

Audio Input Devices. Audio input devices are still in a research and development stage, although a few systems are commercially available. Automatic recognition of the human voice is extremely difficult, mainly due to

Fig. 14. CDC plasma display at New York Stock Exchange.

Fig. 13. Hewlett-Packard's new HDSP-87XX series 18 segment alphanumeric display system features a display, a microprocessor-based controller, and low power requirements.

the segmentation problem (i.e., the recognition of boundaries between spoken words) and to the extremely wide differences in enunciation among people. However, the recent electronic development of recognizable *voice prints* makes it possible to recognize a person by the mode of speech. At present the use of voice prints is limited, but they may introduce new methods into banking and other money-transfer computer applications, especially in the area of program security.

Speech recognition systems are currently aimed mainly at data entry and machine control applications. One such system is based on the Threshold 500 VDU terminal. In this system, the processor acts as a speech translator; in conjunction with its built-in microprocessor, it analyzes and identifies words or phrases spoken into the system. The Threshold 500 is an "isolated word" recognition terminal which implies that each utterance or vocabulary word must be followed by a short break. A vocabulary word may be a digit, a word in any language or a short phrase lasting no more than four seconds. The vocabulary normally consists of the numerals 0–9, control words, and normal data words. The size of the vocabulary is variable from 64 words minimum and can be expanded as required. However, as the hardware is usually dedicated to a particular application, a vocabulary greater than, say, 192 words would be unusual. Each user initially trains the system to understand his or her particular pronunciation. Training involves having the operator repeat each of the chosen words ten times. An average of these inputs is stored in memory, and can be changed at any time.

When operating, the processor receives a pattern of a word, searches in its memory for the best match, performs some tests, and the word is either chosen or a reject signal is transmitted to the user (via a screen) for correction.

Audio Output Devices. Audio output devices are produced by only a few manufacturers, but they are much more common than audio input devices. They provide a recorded voice response (optionally, male or female) and sometimes with language options to inquiries made from telephone-type terminals (with dials or Touchtone phone keyboards) and similar computer transmission terminals (with keyboards). They are attached to the computer via the multiplexer channel that connects the computer to the telephone network. For example, the IBM 7770 audio response unit model 3 (Fig. 15), for use with System/370, provides a vocabulary prerecorded in analog form on a magnetic drum within the device. This offers a maximum vocabulary of 128 words with many lines (4 basic, expandable to 48).

Devices of this type are used, for example, to answer calls to out-of-service telephone numbers. An operator asks the caller for the number desired and connects it into the system through a simple ten-button keyboard. The computer searches the directory file (stored on a disk) for the new number and then transmits it to the audio response unit. A voice message is heard by the caller within 10 to 20 sec after placing the call.

I/O DEVICES IN CONTROLLED PROCESSES. Processing industries have grown up with analog presentation of data. Digital machines are now coming into this field, some in an indirect capacity—supervising analog controllers—and some observing and optimizing processes. In recent years, with the development of digital computers, digital machines are beginning to take over a very substantial part of process control tasks, often together with some analog elements if necessary, thus forming a new technical field of applications called DDC (*direct digital control*).

There are two main forms of DDC. In one, local control loops take care of subordinate functions and the central processor exercises supervisory control over local loops. In the other form, a large-scale computer sends signals to control devices directly, with virtually all controlling functions being exercised by the computer.

Input Devices for Processing Industries. Computer input in process control systems involves the following types of information:

1. Descriptions of type, quality and quantity of the incoming resources to the process (e.g., raw material and energy).
2. Description of the transformation process that takes part in the plant (e.g., process variables

Fig. 15.   IBM III audio response unit.

such as temperature, pressure of fluids, flow of fluids).

3. Information signaling interrupts of the process and describing their causes (such as equipment breakdown or some other abnormal condition), as well as commands for measures to be taken, which are given automatically by the computer or by the supervising engineer.

4. End-point control information describing type, quality, and quantity of the process output (e.g., finished products, materials and energy not consumed in the process).

With few exceptions, the input information is procured by suitable industrial sensing devices that form the first link in a chain of control equipment. Some of them substitute for human senses:

Feeling: temperature or thickness.
Sight: light, color, smoke density, level of liquids, or granulated solids in open containers, dimensions of solid bodies, etc.
Hearing: human speech recognition.
Taste: acidity, salinity, sweetness, etc.
Smell: presence of odoriferous gases such as ammonia and coal gas.

Some sensing devices have "extrasensory" characteristics beyond direct human perception, such as moisture measurement, chemical analysis, and crack detection.

Before a variable of an industrial process can be controlled, it must first be measured. There are two ways to achieve such measurement. In the first, some physical property of a sensing device can be utilized directly (e.g., a spring, balance, thermometer, barometer, or tachometer). In the second way, comparisons have to be made with a known but adjustable quantity of the same nature, in which the process of measurement involves the accurate assessment of equality between the two qualities (like a scale balance, measuring rule, micrometer, and potentiometer).

The sensing and the measuring functions are usually combined in one instrument. As processes get more complex, both the number and type of variables that need to be controlled increase. Information from a multitude of instruments has to be concentrated and transformed into a standardized digital format that is suitable input information to the computer.

The forms of data presentation from the various sources differ considerably and their frequency can also be widely different. The process variables measured by industrial instruments have to be filtered and amplified, switched, or scanned by multiplexers which sequentially connect these instruments via analog-to-digital convert-

ers to the central computer buffers. Other forms of data presentation may be pulse inputs that enter the buffers via counters, or binary inputs and process interrupts that are connected directly to the buffers.

Output Devices for Processing Industries. The computer output has two distinct functions. The first function is the automatic regulation of the process. The output electric signals set up and/or adjust the electric actuators of the regulating devices (valves, etc.), thus forming, together with the automated input, a closed-loop control system. This type of output usually is in the form of electric signals that have to be converted from digital to analog form and then amplified; there may also be a binary or a pulse output that can be used without any intermediate conversion.

As opposed to the machine/machine interface function, the second function of computer output concerns the human/machine interface. This normally gives up-to-the-minute information to the supervising engineer, usually signaling some abnormal condition or possibly calling for the takeover of control from the computer. It also gives logging information on the process (for further analysis of behavior under varying conditions), using typewriter, Teletype, printer, or plotter.

SPECIAL I/O DEVICES. From time to time input/output devices designed for some special application can be used. Some typical devices and systems are as follows.

1. *Input* devices and systems.
   - Bar code readers, which read optically barcoded tags (*see* POINT-OF-SALE TERMINAL).
   - Badge readers, reading magnetically-encoded plastic cards identifying persons or organizations and used in retail transaction applications, for access acceptance, etc.
   - Pressure pad character recognition terminals which recognize the directions of different strokes drawn on the paper; they are used in special applications.
   - Systems to control telephone calls and billing with application in hotels and large companies, etc.

2. *Input/output* devices and systems.
   - PoS terminals (*see* POINT-OF-SALE TERMINAL)
   - EFT systems terminals (*see* ELECTRONIC FUNDS TRANSFER SYSTEMS) and foreign money exchange systems, etc.

3. *Output* devices and systems, such as
   - Ticket vendors.

Graphical Input-Output Devices. The term *computer graphics (CG)* is used to denote a set of computer techniques and applications wherein data is either presented or accepted by the computer in the form of line drawings or graphs. The interest in CG and new developments in hardware, software, and their applications has grown steadily since the mid-1960s, mainly after the introduction of interactive graphic devices, time-sharing systems using terminals, and the possibilities of plotting projections of three-dimensional objects. Computer graphics and image and picture processing are discussed in more detail elsewhere in this Encyclopedia. This article is concerned only with the CG I/O devices.

CG input/output devices can be classified into four main groups:

1. Image input devices (derived from hard copy graphics).
2. Electromechanical plotters (such as output devices onto hard copy).
3. Visual display units (VDU) with graphical capabilities (such as interactive graphics devices).
4. Microfilm I/O devices.

Nearly all devices of these four types, in addition to their capability to represent graphical images, also allow alphanumerical characters to be represented. These more sophisticated graphical devices are much more expensive than the alphanumerical ones, and the success of their application may be seriously affected by unsuitable or unavailable software.

IMAGE INPUT DEVICES. Many applications require transformation of hard copy images into a proper form for computer processing. Such information, when collected at remote locations, should generally be computerized at a central site with transformation taking place there. In order for this information to be submitted quickly, facsimile transmission systems are sometimes used. Indeed, methods generally used for image input to computers are closely connected with those used for facsimile data transmission.

Facsimile Transmission Devices. Facsimile transmission can be thought of as a form of remote photocopying. A document (or picture) is fed in at one terminal and its exact reproduction emerges at the other, complete with company headings, logos, signatures, etc. A facsimile system consists of four function subsystems—scanner-transmitters, modems, transmission media, and receiver-recorders.

Facsimile scanner-transmitters generally use some raster-scanning method that optically scans all points of an imaginary grid placed over the picture to be transmitted, registering each point as black (part of the image present) or white (part of the image absent). In this technique, even if only a minute portion of the picture is actually filled by an image (e.g., a signature), it is then necessary to transmit details of all the background that carries no useful information. This basic technique can, however, be improved by application of methods to eliminate this drawback, improve the shading, introduce colors, etc.

In all facsimile transmission systems, the original picture (or a portion of it) is then sent to the receiving terminal (or terminals) where it is reproduced by printing or projecting onto a screen. The projected image can be microfilmed at the terminal so that a hard copy duplicate of the original image can be obtained at some later date. At the receiving end, the data is not represented in a digital form; however, technical improvement in quality scanning, transmission, and printing make it possible to use the transmitted copy either directly as an input to OCR or OMR readers, or to digitize it by some other means suitable for generating computer input.

Direct Input Devices. For graphical processing on computers, the information must be recorded in a digital form, either directly or with the use of a converter, when an analog form is to be translated. In addition to techniques in which the pictures are usually sensed and reproduced line by line, there is another method by which the images are drawn by incremental plotting. Here the information is represented by scales, coordinates, vectors, etc., as well as by identifiers, some descriptive text, and figures, etc. In some parts of the process, where it is necessary to translate the information from one representation to another suitable for computer processing, the computer itself can help substantially, thus reducing the usually great burden connected with manual description of graphical information in the required digital form. Besides the computer itself, the user has a wide variety of devices and means designed to help in the description task; they are usually called *digitizers* and can be classified as follows.

1. Devices designed to help the user with the manual description and/or registration of the image data, to be used for subsequent computer processing.
2. Same as the preceding class, but for use in a direct interactive on-line operation mode.
3. Devices used for automatic input of image data to the computer.

Because of the wide variety of devices designed for different applications, only some representative examples of devices in each group will be given here.

Class 1. Devices designed to help the user with the manual description and/or registration of the image data, to be used for subsequent computer processing. One of the useful devices in this group is the *pencil follower,* which is used for conversion of data presented as graphs, charts, drawings, photographs, and film into digital form for subsequent automatic processing by a computer. It generally consists of two units, the reading table and the electronic console. The pictorial information to be analyzed is placed or projected onto the surface of the reading table. Operation is effected manually by following the trace with the reading pencil or by pointing the pencil at a position. An automatic mechanism beneath the table surface follows the pencil accurately, and position signals are passed to the electronic console where they are visually displayed and converted into suitable form for feeding the output devices (punched cards or tapes, a typewriter, etc.).

Operation of the pencil follower is normally controlled by a foot switch connected to the reading table. Alternatives are a handheld pushbutton; in some cases, a pushbutton is incorporated with the reading pencil.

Usually there are no lines engraved on the reading table for alignment of charts, graphs, or drawings, but such lines may be added by the operator if required. The normal method of reading is to place the graph or chart at any position or angle on the reading table and to take off fiducial points prior to the main analysis, programming the computer to take care of any required correction. Another method requiring special types of pencil followers is the reading of images such as high-speed camera films and other types of photographic work projected on the reading table.

The speed is normally between 18 to 300 symbols a second or between 2 and 30 pairs of coordinates a second, depending upon the ability of the operator and the speed of the output device.

The pencil follower reads out coordinates of points, and no variable origin or scaling facilities are provided. The origin is normally situated at the near left-hand corner of the reading table and a fixed scale of 0.1 mm per digit is used, giving a work area, for example, of 9,999 digits $\times$ 4,500 digits. Any corrections for origin and scale would be programmed into the computer. If the chart or image to be analyzed has timing marks or incremental lines along its length, these may be analyzed in several ways:

1. By taking individual readings at the intersection of the trace with the incremental markings.
2. By analyzing the trace fully, using the line mode of output and programming the computer to incorporate the required increments.
3. By using the incremental readout facility, if the increments are, for example, 1 mm or multiples of it up to 1 cm.

Fig. 16 shows four different types of pencil followers used in the normal method of reading and two types used for reading of projected images.

Another device is *trace analysis equipment that uses two cursors* for tracing the image. The paper trace is placed in the right-hand spool holder and stretched across the length of the illuminated screen. Starting at the left-hand side of the screen, the operator sets the vertical cursor line against the first reference mark on the records and adjusts the quadrant cursor that carries the calibration curve until coincidence is obtained between the vertical line, the calibration curve, and the trace. A foot-switch is then pressed, actuating the attached output equipment—such as typewriter, punch, or plotting table (the latter using a changed scale or calibration corrections to cross-plot one parameter against another)—and the recording is thus completed. The operator moves the cursor to the next reference mark, and the whole operation is repeated.

Trace analysis equipment provides a semiautomatic system for the reduction of analog data recorded on paper or film. Average reading speeds are 1,000–2,000 positions per hour. Such trace analysis equipment is used as a computer input device for information that is basically in analog form. The information is converted into digital form by a converter incorporated in the device. This device may also be used if the data should remain in analog form, but the primary information has to be replotted in a different manner; an analog plotter can be attached to the trace analysis equipment.

Some devices of this class can use small (usually, desk-top) computers to guide the operator using instructions and error indications; these are shown, for example, on the console of the computer. There are also intelligent digitizers, which perform similar functions by microprocessor-based control units.

As an example, the Calcomp 600A intelligent digitizer comes with a microprocessor-based control unit which can handle linear and area calculation, output data formatting and document skew compensation. The user is provided with a *menu* of up to 70 different subroutines held in firmware and can select any one of them by placing the digitizer pen on an appropriate square on the digitizing surface. The menu squares can be located anywhere on the surface. An alternative to the pen is a 12-button cross-hair cursor which offers very high accuracy. An optional display terminal with a full ASCII keyboard provides operator prompting and can display processed data and program instructions.

Class 2. Devices designed to help the user with the manual description and/or registration of the image data, to be used in a direct interactive operation mode. Interactive graphic devices used in connection with video display units, such as a lightpen, trackball, etc., are described in the later section entitled *Graphical Visual Displays*.

As an example of a digitized input for an on-line interactive computer system, an HP 9874A digitizer attached to the HP 9845 Hewlett-Packard graphic desk-top

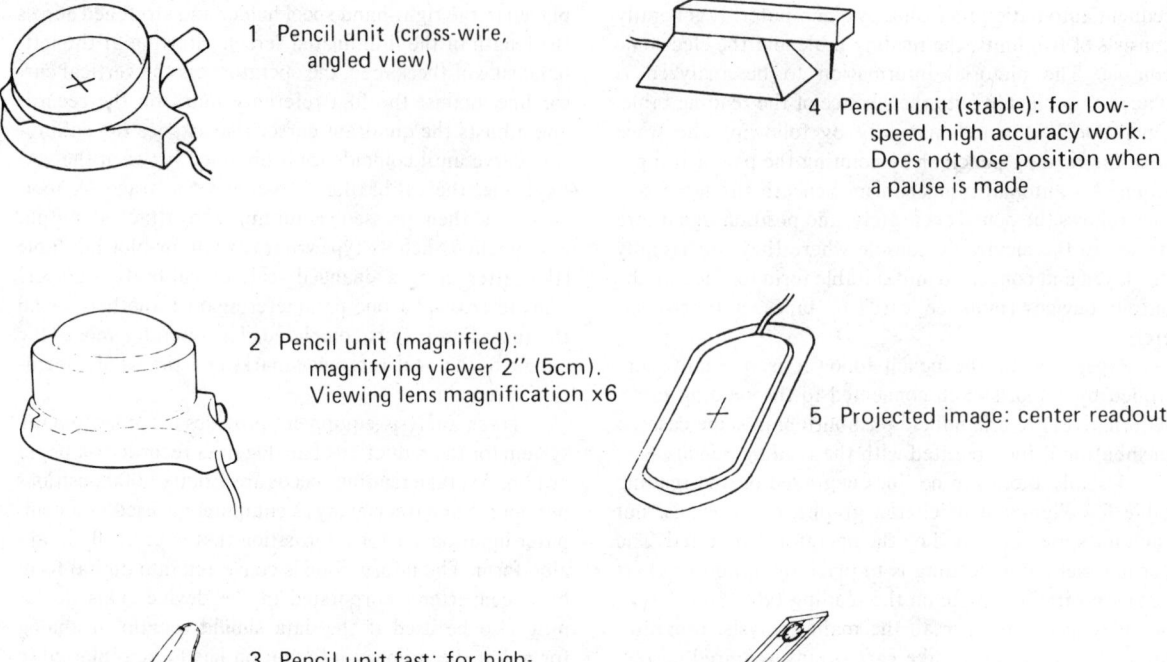

1 Pencil unit (cross-wire, angled view)

2 Pencil unit (magnified): magnifying viewer 2″ (5cm). Viewing lens magnification ×6

3 Pencil unit fast: for high-speed work. Fast and easy to use

4 Pencil unit (stable): for low-speed, high accuracy work. Does not lose position when a pause is made

5 Projected image: center readout

6 Projected image: double co-ordinate

Fig. 16.   The six types of reading pencil for D-MAC pencil follower (Type PF 10,000, Mark 1B).

computer will be described (Fig. 17). The 9874 features an adjustable glass platen that can accommodate the digitizing of a variety of projectable media such as X-rays, movies, and 35 mm slides. By tilting the platen to full vertical position and setting a projector behind the digitizer, exact images can be reproduced without distortion, and then digitized. To take advantage of the adjustable platen, a vacuum cursor was developed which can adhere to any portion on the platen. Regardless of the platen's position, the cursor will not slip—even if bumped. The lighted cursor has an open-circle target, 0.250 mm in diameter, giving the pinpoint precision to accurately position and then move the cursor on a line thinner than a human hair.

In addition, the 9874 has microprocessor intelligence and its own built-in memory (16K bytes). It also has a control pad with digitizer control, special function, and numeric entry keys. Points may be digitized one at a time or continuously (based on time or distance increments) by simply pressing the appropriate key. An axis align key automatically aligns the x and y axes of the digitizer with those of the document—immediately establishing a new

coordinate system. This device may be used in several applications, such as strip chart analysis, mapping and resource management, printed-circuit board layout, and destructive and nondestructive test analysis.

Class 3. Automatic image scanners as computer on-line or off-line input devices. There exist special devices designed for specific uses and which have capabilities of automatically scanning charts, often connected with some analytical evaluation method. For example, one such system is an *electronic chart reader* which scans curves recorded previously by industrial instrument recorders on continuous paper forms and converts them into digital form. This output is then passed to the evaluation unit of the system for analysis. Because the evaluation of the chart in this unit takes place in steps corresponding to previous 15-min registrations (either selected or all of them, on the scanned chart), the system not only permits data registration and conversion, but also a very considerable reduction of the input data. An example of such a recorded chart used for evaluation is shown in Fig. 18.

There is a wide field of application for systems that

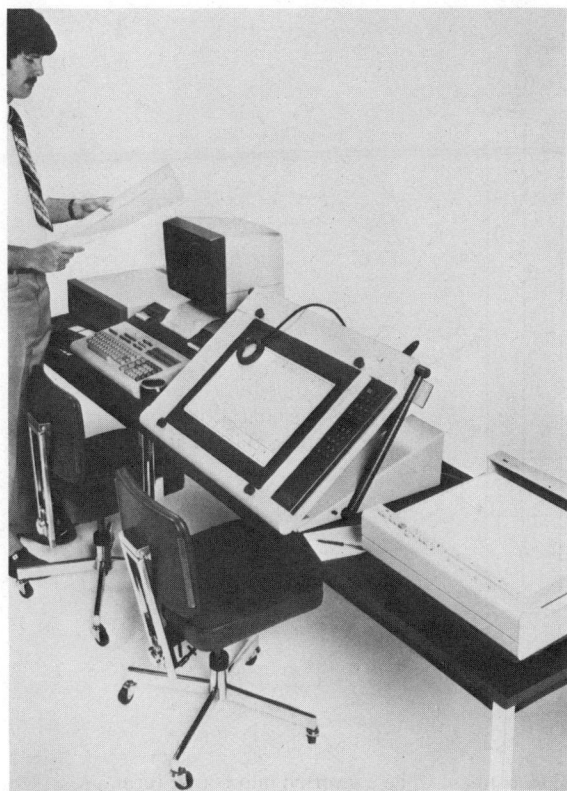

Fig. 17. The powerful new HP Portable Digitizer (center) features a tiltable working surface, rear projection capabilities, a cursor vacuum system, a built-in self-test, microprocessor control, and a multiple function user keyboard.

need some type of automatic pattern recognition device to be used in arriving at image data needed for subsequent processing. An example of such a device is the *pattern recognition system,* which consists essentially of a set of hard-wired digital processor modules that can be combined in many ways to recognize and classify distinct objects of an image, regardless of their orientation.

The choice of source image input devices include *optical-scanning electron microscopes, movie and slide projectors, X-ray systems* and *electron probes.* The image or object is scanned electronically at the rate of one million 720-line frames a second and is converted into 650,000 picture points in a single scan. The digital equivalent of the gray value of the point is processed by the device to determine shapes, sizes, and optical densities, and to classify the objects in the image. This data can be further processed by an on-line, desk-top, or other computer, or it can be output onto computer-compatible paper tape.

Also worth mentioning are "intelligent" *computer-controlled robot systems,* which are being developed and which can recognize different patterns such as technical drawings (*see* ROBOTICS).

Input devices used in microfilm image systems are described in the last section of this article under the heading *CIM—Computer Input from Microfilm.*

PLOTTERS. Automatic plotting devices are used in conjunction with digital computers where graphic or pictorial presentation of computer data on a hard copy are meaningful and easier to use than extensive alphabetic or numeric listings. They are indispensable when the volume of graphic presentations of output data makes it uneconomical or impossible to perform the task manually.

The first plotters were analog devices, developed from the basic strip recorders commonly used in applications such as laboratory analysis and in plotting radar tracks. Compared with the later development of incremental plotters, these early instruments were slow and inaccurate, but they are simple to interface and easy to program and data is easily and accurately transmitted over telephone lines. They are also comparatively cheap and are still used for many applications in specialized fields where advanced facilities are not required.

By the early 1960s, however, analog-to-digital converters allowed the introduction of incremental plotters which worked on absolute values so that increments could be plotted to within extemely accurate limits. They were driven off line by paper tape or punched cards, but many of the necessary functions, such as character generation, were directly performed by the hardware.

Second-generation plotters were made possible by the fact that large computers had become widely available, with the speed and power to reduce the need for intelligence in the plotter and so the concept of digital, incremental plotters could be realized. The majority of plotter installations today are of this type.

With the introduction and growth of minicomputers and, more recently, microprocessors, the intelligent plotter came back into its own. Even quite cheap machines include interpolation techniques and automatic character generation, and the cost per inch of plotted outputs is ten times less than it was ten years ago.

The most recent development is the technique of writing by means of lasers onto film. Although this technology achieves a very high degree of accuracy, the cost is equally high and, as yet, few such plotters have been installed.

Today, two different technologies are competing for a potentially lucrative market—plotters based on a writing instrument (the pen), and those based on electrostatic techniques.

Pen plotters are impact-plotting devices; hence, they are sometimes called *ink-on-paper* or *pen-on-paper* plotters. They operate generally on the basic digital incre-

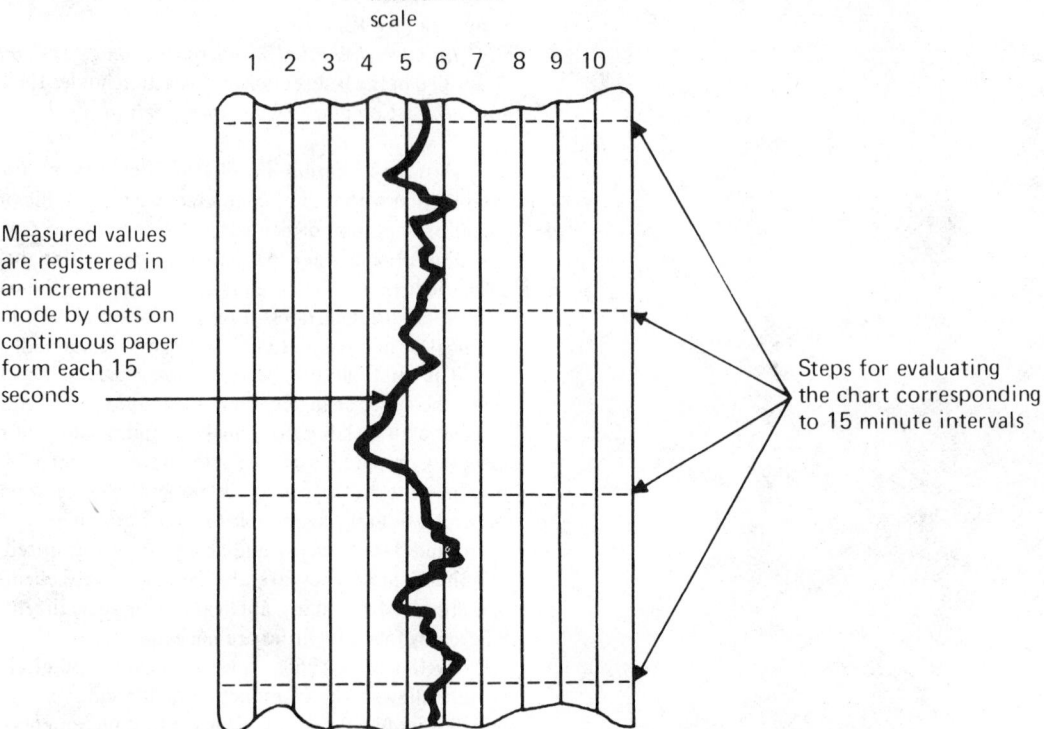

Measurement
scale

1 2 3 4 5 6 7 8 9 10

Measured values
are registered in
an incremental
mode by dots on
continuous paper
form each 15
seconds

Steps for evaluating
the chart corresponding
to 15 minute intervals

Fig. 18.   Example of a chart recorded by an industrial instrument to be converted into digital form.

mental principle. Decoded input commands from the computer are used to produce increments of movement in either direction along either axis, or at some angle relative to the axes. In the electromechanical ink-on-paper plotters, the plot is produced by movement of a pen relative to the surface of the recording paper.

Electromechanical plotters generally operate in completely digital fashion and hence are drift-free. Accuracy is not dependent upon voltage stability as it is in systems that employ digital-to-analog conversion for positioning of a servomechanism. Since operation is fully incremental, there is no restriction on format. The user has complete freedom of choice in size, type, and orientation of letters, symbols, lines, and axes. Plotters are used for either on-line or off-line operation, often with any standard computer. Some of them may be used as terminals.

Pen plotters are of the drum or flat-bed type. The *drum-type plotters* are available in several sizes. The plot is produced by rotary motion of the drum (*X*-axis) and lateral motion of the pen carriage (*Y*-axis). Either ballpoint or liquid-ink pens may be used. The drum-type plotter uses special chart paper rolls and can produce continuous plots up to, for example, 120 ft in length. A wide selection of paper is available. An overall view of the equipment is shown in Fig. 19.

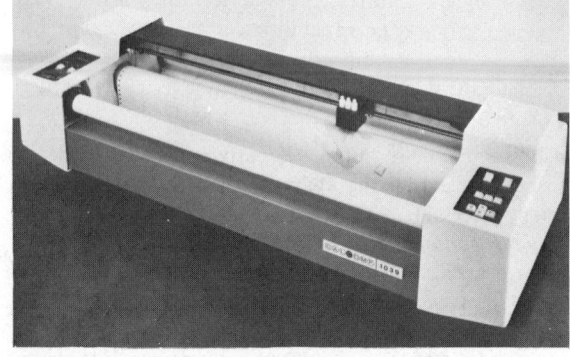

Fig. 19.   Calcomp 1039 plotter.

Flat-bed plotters are also available in several sizes. The plot is produced by lateral motion of the beam and vertical motion of the pen carriage. Either ballpoint or liquid-ink pens may be used. The flat-bed plotter provides a continuous display during plotting. It does not require special paper, and can handle a large variety of preprinted forms and special materials. A picture of a flat-bed plotter is shown in Fig. 20.

The most common method of plotting on drum or flat-bed plotters is by increments in one of eight direc-

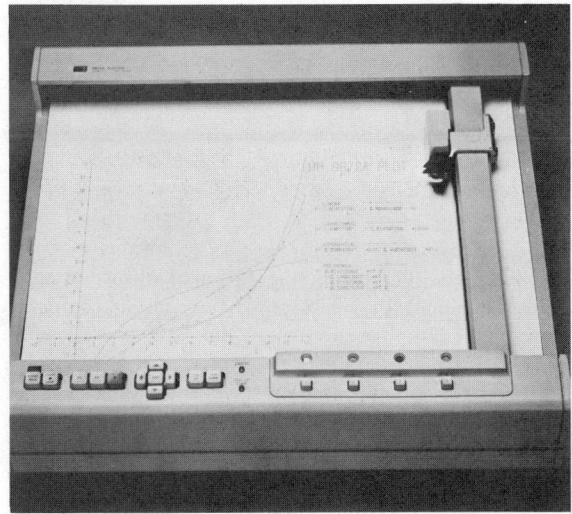

Fig. 20. Hewlett-Packard 9872A fast, four-color X-Y plotter.

tions. However, since the increments are small, straight lines beyond these limits can also be drawn. Curves are produced as a series of short lines in one of the eight basic directions. The speed and accuracy of plotting is often expressed in terms of increments. The smaller the increments, the more accurate the drawing will be, but the slower the speed.

Flat-bed plotters are available in a large range of sizes and have the advantage that additions can be made to existing drawings if the registration is correct. They are generally more accurate than drum plotters, since only the writing head is moving while the paper is held still. Both flat-bed and drum plotters have the capability of drawing in color and, if more than one pen is available, in a multitude of colors. Here they have the advantage over electronic plotters which can only reproduce in black and white, although the ability of the latter to produce a great variation of shading offsets this to some degree. However, some impact dot-character matrix plotter/printers have the capability to print alphanumeric data and simple graphic pictures in color using multicolor cartridge ribbons.

Incremental plotters, while giving great precision, require a vast amount of data, each character, curve, or line having to be generated as individual vectors. With the introduction of intelligence in the early 1970s, all that had to be provided was the coordinates and the text that had to be printed, and the local intelligence creates the vectors, increments, and so forth.

A limit has almost been reached in this area of technology. The best electromechanical plotters can drive pens so rapidly and accurately that it is unlikely that there can be much further improvement. Thus, the mak-

ers of pen plotters are turning their attention to lasers and microfilm techniques.

Electrostatic plotters. Coincident with the development of pen plotters, another technology was starting up in parallel. This also had its origins in a strip recorder, but of a different type. In electrical engineering, where there was a demand for very fast information plotting, a whole range of high-speed ultraviolet recorders were developed. In recent years, these have been largely replaced by electrostatic devices which wrote onto paper that could be moved at 200–300 cm/sec. Versatec introduced the first electrostatic plotter in 1970.

As with drum plotters, the paper on an electrostatic machine moves in one direction, but the writing head is in the form of a row of styli positioned across the width of the paper. These styli generate all the points on a line simultaneously. Upon digital command, the nibs selectively create minute electrostatic dots on the paper as it passes the writing head. The paper is then passed through a developer to produce the visible image; it emerges from the plotter ready to handle.

Originally, the electrostatic plotter was only 28 cm wide and tended to find a market in specialized scientific fields, while the classic engineering or construction drawing remained the province of the pen plotter. However, with the advent of the converter and with the introduction of electrostatic plotters up to 630 cm wide, the pattern is beginning to change. Electrostatic plotters are expensive but fast. A machine running at 3 cm/sec is far from being at full capacity, but data cannot be produced fast enough to take advantage of its full potential. While the speed varies slightly according to the data rate, the machine can still produce, in 30 seconds, a drawing which may take a pen plotter 30 minutes.

A picture of an electrostatic plotter is shown in Fig. 21 and a schematic diagram of its operating principle in Fig. 22. Fig. 23 shows the way overlapping dots for a continuous pattern are created in this machine.

GRAPHICAL VISUAL DISPLAYS. Graphical visual displays are interactive graphics devices, often called *graphoscopes*. They are entry/display devices that enable the operator/user to manipulate graphic material in a visible two-way, real-time communication with the computer.

Data Entry Means for Graphoscopes. For communication with the graphoscope, the operator has available (depending upon the specific hardware used) a lightpen, a keyboard, or other data entry means. *A lightpen* is a photosensitive device that generally consists of a small photocell on the end of a rod (Fig. 24), but for better performance (although at higher cost) can use as modem a highly sensitive photomultiplier tube, located inside the cabinet, to which the light is conveyed along a flexible fiber-optic light guide.

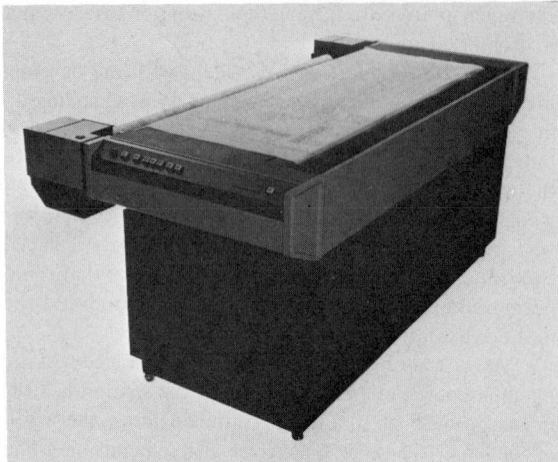

Fig. 21. The Versatec 8172, the world's widest high-resolution electrostatic plotter, produces 200 dot-per-inch resolution across 72-inch-wide paper.

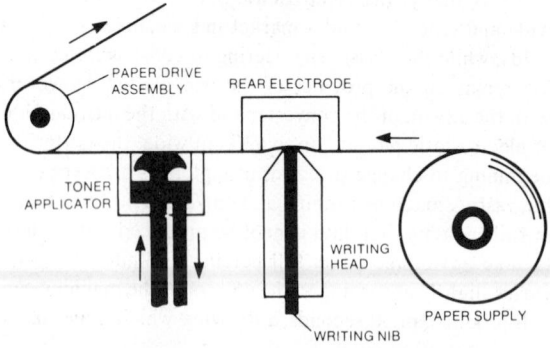

Fig. 22. Operating principle of electrostatic units.

Fig. 23. A dual array of writing nibs (top) creates overlapping dots for continuous patterns (bottom).

The lightpen has two functions: One is to say "there," and the other is to say "do that." Pointing a lightpen at the display indicates that the user wishes to say something about the part of the picture pointed at. When used for drawing, the lightpen is pointed at the center of a small cross, called a *tracking cross*, which is displayed on the screen by a tracking program. The movement of the pen is interpreted by the computer program to actuate movement of the tracking cross, which follows the pen across the screen.

In addition to the lightpen, a *keyboard* similar to that of an alphascope is used for typing messages to the computer.

Switch indicators provide another means of communicating with the computer. By making use of software techniques, the operator may control the computer operation, call up frequently used data, and cause special effects to occur.

The *trackball* (see Fig. 25) performs a function similar to a lightpen. It is a phenolic ball inset in the display console. When it is invoked by the operator, a cursor appears on the display screen and follows the rotation of the trackball, continuously keeping track of the *X-Y* position. When desired, the operator simply pushes an "interrupt" button to transmit the coordinate data to the computer.

The function of a lightpen is sometimes replaced by a *joystick* or by a *data tablet display*.

I/O Functions of Graphoscopes. Unlike the alphascope, whose prime objective is fast retrieval of the desired information from the computer store and display onto a screen, the graphoscope is mainly used for drawing a picture, amending it, and then storing it for further processing or plotting it on a hard copy, as required. However, a graphoscope can also be used for retrieving and displaying stored pictures. Besides its graphical capability, it has to have an alphanumerical feature as well, since the graphs to be displayed have to be presented with adequate headings and notes.

A graphoscope consists of a display unit and some entry device, as discussed previously. Because of its sophisticated nature, its performance has to be monitored by a *controller* interface between the graphoscope and the computer. The controller is equipped with a vector generator, a character and symbol generator, and control logic. Sometimes arc or curve generators are also included, and an addressable buffer store is often added to speed up the overall operation of the system. The latest versions of these devices are microprocessor-controlled.

The *display unit* of the graphoscope has an appearance very much like that of an alphascope (Fig. 26). The viewing screen is generally oblong, like a television screen, but sometimes is round, its diameter usually being between 14 and 21 in. Diameters as small as 8.5 in. or as large as 25 in. are known. The whole surface can be used for displaying characters, symbols, vectors, and points, generally using a raster with 1024 addressable positions in the *X*- as well as in the *Y*-axis.

The character set used generally includes approximately 64 different characters and symbols. Several

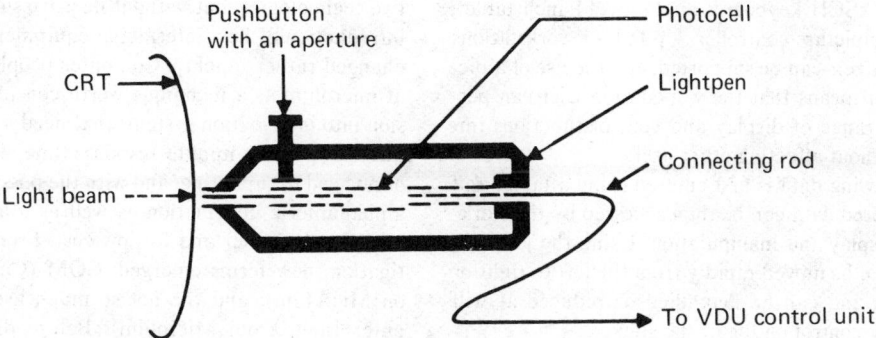

Fig. 24.   Schematic diagram of a lightpen.

Fig. 25.   Solid-state magnetic trackball.

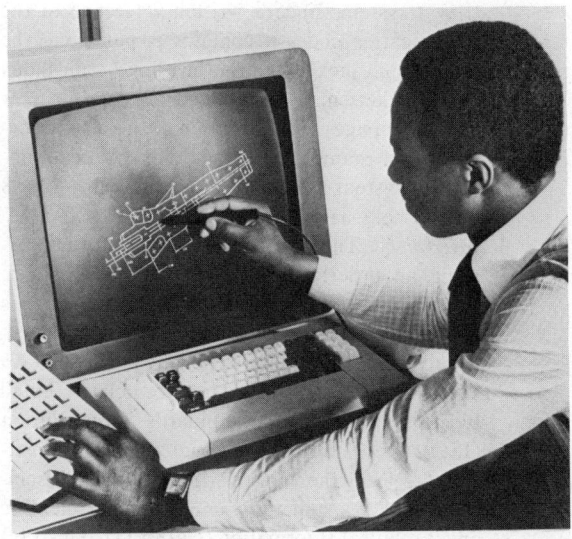

Fig. 26.   User drawing with a lightpen on the IBM 3250 display unit.

VDUs have, as an option, an extension of the set to 128 characters—to meet requirements for special symbols or different character styles, as well as for displaying characters in more than one size (up to four sizes are often offered).

The number of lines needed to display the alphanumerical text is usually between 16 and 64, depending upon the size of the screen and the size of character set used. Normally, from 32 to 128 characters are displayed on a line.

All functions of the graphoscope have to be done quickly and automatically. The operator should not be bothered with the problem of translating the graphic image and all the manipulating commands into mathematical terms and then into computer language. This is the task of the control unit and the computer, hardware as well as software.

In comparison with the plotter control discussed previously, the software controlling a graphoscope not only must be able to handle a static picture, but also must be very flexible to permit manipulation of the picture (lines and curves in two- or three-dimensional images). Hence, the software considerations are even more important than those of the hardware.

Several facilities have been developed during recent years to make the operation of graphoscopes easier. Examples are the zooming and panning facilities that enable the user to magnify any portion of the picture to permit the examination and modification of dense areas, and an area shading and pattern generation facility to help in architectural and engineering design work.

An example of a current interactive graphics system which can be configured to the user's requirements is the Calcomp IGS 500 shared-logic electronic drawing system based on a minicomputer. The system consists of a 64K-word minicomputer, a 50-megabyte disk drive, an operator console, software and a user workstation with 64K bytes of its own memory—the "picture processor," separate raster-scanned alphanumeric and graphic CRT displays, a full ASCII keyboard, an 11 by 11 inch tablet, and a joystick picture controller. Up to four workstations and four digitizers can be supported, and the use of a picture processor means that the workstation user can perform a wide range of display and control functions immediately without affecting other users.

Raw drawing data is first entered using a tablet and stylus; the stored data can be then accessed by the workstation for display and manipulation. Using the joystick, the picture can be moved rapidly from the left to right or up and down and can be magnified or reduced at will using a rotary control on top of the stick.

Use of the tablet/stylus and stored drawing features enables the user to construct on the CRT any arrangement needed with ability to delete and move at will. The changes appear immediately on the screen and are sent to the database to update the drawing file. The disks can store this and many other drawings at the same time and they can be accurately drawn on the associated flat-bed plotter as they are needed. No difficult instructions must be followed in order to use the equipment; indeed, the user is guided at all times by a second CRT display.

Television Display Devices. Television-type displays are sometimes used as a less expensive solution of the image presentation requirement. Color television techniques are also applicable in such displays.

At least two single-chip circuits are on the market (the 8275 from Intel and the 6845 from Motorola) which allow builders to avoid all complicated designs normally associated with high-speed analog television-type circuits, and which use the same video system for all displays, from simple non-intelligent VDUs to the all-feature computer.

The Intel chip is intended to be suitable for a graphoscope, operating a raster-scan display, including CRTs and self-scanning types of display panels. In addition to scan control and operation of the character generator ROM, the chip handles refreshing, transfer of data from main memory, graphics generation (about up to Viewdata (*q. v.*) standards), cursor control, light pen detection, and other auxiliary functions, such as blinking, underlines, and highlights.

A minimum microprocessor and a small control memory are virtually all the other circuitry needed to build a full terminal with keyboard and screen features.

MICROFILM I/O DEVICES. In the past decade, use of microfilm has expanded into a vast range of application areas connected with space-saving archival storage. This has been due not only to the general problems and pressures of information storage and retrieval, but also to the development of a more flexible range of microfilm equipment in parallel with the application of computers.

Some attempts were made earlier to coordinate the two technologies, but without decisive success. With the introduction of new interfacing equipment, the situation changed rather quickly. Computer people began to look at microfilm as a technique worth considering for inclusion into information systems that need a large data base but not up-to-the-minute response time, with very limited or no need for updating, and with the possibility of storing alphanumeric information as well as graphics in a very condensed manner and for low cost. From all this investigation, new terms emerged: COM (Computer Output on Microfilm), and the not so much used CIM (Computer Input from Microfilm). Before discussing COM and CIM, the different forms of microfilm used in connection with computers will be briefly examined.

Forms of microfilms can be divided into five groups:

1. *Roll microfilm.* This is similar to 16 mm or 35 mm film, but is not perforated. The 16 mm film is used in two different ways, either with one or two tracks of images along the film. With one track, the reduction ratio applied is about 24:1, with two tracks, the ratio is about 43:1. The approximate doubling of the reduction ratio in fact quarters the quantity of film used. Rolls of film are loaded into cassettes, or cartridges, and used in roll-film viewers. There are already a number of double cassettes that overcome the problems of the old single cassette; rewinding is not necessary and the mechanics of the viewer are simplified.

2. *Jackets.* Short strips of microfilm (or individual frames) are inserted into clear plastic covers (acetate sleeves). Related information can be held in one jacket to provide a quick manual retrieval system, since a written reference to the identification codes it contains is put along the top of each jacket like the heading on an index card. Jackets may be updated by inserting new frames or pages of information in the plastic covers. As an example, a Bell and Howell jacket microfilm system uses jackets that measure 5 by 8 in. and hold sixty 16 mm film frames each.

3. *Microfiche.* This is a sheet of 105 mm film carrying an orderly arrangement of microimages, the 105 by 148.75 mm (or 4 by 6 in., which is about the size of a postcard) fiche being the most widely used, known internationally as the ISO A6 size. This is the only standard-size fiche accepted by the International Standards Organization (ISO), the American National Standards Institute (ANSI), the Nation Micrographics Association (NMA), and the Committee on Scientific and Technical Information (COSATI). This ISO A6 size fiche has two basic types—the first with 72 frames arranged in 12 columns and 6 rows, the

second with 112 frames in 14 columns and 8 rows. (The reduction ratio of the original document should not be greater than 1:24.) Some organizations have used punched card size 82 by 183 mm and 75 by 125 mm fiche with a variety of grid patterns; however, none of these is standard. Also, in practice, the reduction ratio often exceeds the standardized margin of 1:24, with ratios 1:42 or 1:48 widely used, mainly in COM systems. A fiche with images at reduction ratios of more than 1:90 is called *ultrafiche*. At 1:120, the ultrafiche contains 70 columns and 30 rows, providing for 2,100 215 by 280 mm documents. At 1:150, the ultrafiche contains 70 columns and 40 rows, providing 3,200 215 by 280 mm documents. There are certain microfiche characteristics which are common to all formats, regardless of application or fiche grid. They include pagination indexing, cutting mark, and the method of identifying the sensitized side of the fiche.

4. *Aperture cards.* These were introduced in 1945 when a microimage was inserted into a conventional 80-column punched card, which could then be sorted mechanically. The present day ISO, ANSI (etc.) standards identify two basic layouts of aperture cards, depending upon whether the microimage is to be inserted into a pocket in the aperture card or if it has be be firmly fixed (glued) to it. In the first case, 16 mm or 35 mm film is used; in the second, 35 mm film only. Normally, the 35 mm film accommodates only one frame; however, a larger number of frames can also be used within a single card. The 16 mm film accommodates several frames. When more than one frame is to be used on a single card, all frames must be on one film strip.

5. *Microcards.* Development of new techniques also brought changes in the original idea to process (mainly sort and select) aperture cards by a machine. First, they enabled replacement of the punched code representation of the image identification data in the card by binary coded data printed with higher density, which can be read either optically or magnetically by machine. Thus, more information required for manipulation can be stored on a relatively small area of the card and processed by machine. Second, since the card no longer needs to be processed by the standard punched card equipment, its size can be enlarged. This, together with gains from the data representation change, has made it possible to enlarge the image area. The layout of these microcards (such as Filmorex, Minicard, and Magnavue) is very similar to those of the advanced type

of microfiche (and may also contain image identification data).

In all these forms, black-and-white (B and W) microfilm is used, although the use of color microfilm is under study. While B and W can store many levels of information at many places by varying signal densities, from opaque through the gray scale to transparency, color microfilm could store many levels of the same print by varying not only the density but also the color.

Most of the computer microfilm-generating devices have the disadvantage of making positive microfilm, which is commonly known to be not so easily read from a screen as negative microfilm. However, a reversal film especially made for computer printout has also been produced, at least by one manufacturer.

The arrangement of the pages on the film can usually be varied, depending on the particular unit used but normally the choice is either the type of arrangement similar to that used in printing comic strips or to that used in movie film, with reduction ratios of from 24:1 to 43:1. The choice depends on the sophistication of the equipment.

COM. The name "COM" should be related to the overall concept of accessing computer-based information via microfilm. However, more often the term is used to refer to the hardware device that generates the microfilm. Depending upon the technique used, a COM system usually consists of three sections (all of which may be accommodated in one cabinet, or kept as separate units):

1. A *tape drive* in an off-line installation or a *computer*, if the mode of operation is on-line, provide data to be microfilmed.

2. A *control unit,* including a buffer store for speeding up the throughput, a symbol generator for printing alphanumerical and special symbols, a vector generator for drawing graphs, and control logic. The latter coordinates and directs the action of all system elements to achieve the end result of exposed microfilm. It selects the input tape, what is to be recorded, and in what size and position of the "page" it should be located, and when the film is to be advanced to the next frame. It also controls the coding (if any), tape-error conditions, reread, and frame marking to show unreadable characters.

3. The *microfilm recorder* with the microfilm transport and positioning section, and the optical system used for the recording and developing the frame.

In some systems, if hard copy is required, recordings on microfilm can be suppressed and instead the image can be copied in the desired form.

Many COM plotters and/or printers have the ability to superimpose on the printed image one of several program-selectable forms, giving a combined image on microfilm or on hard copy stationery.

The microfilm produced by the COM system can also be used in a conventional way. If hard copy is required, high-speed copying devices using microfilm frames as a copying matrix for producing one or more printed copies are available. Similarly, another device is applied when one or more duplicates of the microfilm are required. The kind of device to be used is determined also by the requirement to ease the selection operation in the information retrieval process. At least two manufacturers produce equipment for automatic microfilm-stored information retrieval.

Generally, all COM systems on the market are offered for off-line operation, but many of them can work on line with the computer. However, there is at least one system that operates in conjunction with the computer in on-line mode only.

Nearly all COM devices translate data from magnetic tape to microfilm via a CRT presented to a microfilm camera, although there are variations of this scheme, such as an electron beam recording directly onto the film or a fiber optics system to present the character image to the camera on line from the computer.

The trend in COM systems over the last few years has been away from roll film and towards microfiche, for several reasons, two of which are ease and economics. However, there are still situations in which roll or cartridge film would be preferred, such as coded retrieval, improved security, and file integrity.

A distinction can be drawn between systems whose output is primarily active and those which are primarily archival. Archival files owe their existence to a statutory, contractual, or audit requirement to retain selected data for an extended period of time. Conversely, active files are in day-to-day use as source documents for inquiries and have a comparatively short retention period and a high look-up rate.

The demands of active files are best met by fiche, which, with its extremely effective retrieval aids (in the form of eye-legible titling and comprehensive indexing), enable the user, regardless of the size of the file, to access precise data in less than a minute. Archival files are best recorded on 16 mm film, which, when stored in cassette or cartridge form, provide a well-protected, simple-to-store unit.

Most COM systems are equipped to handle both 16 mm and 105 mm film, which is accomplished by a simple change-over from one mode to the other (including lens change) carried out by an operator.

COM hardware on the present-day market is divided into three categories: COM graph plotters, COM printers, and COM plotter/printers. These devices are sometimes known by other names.

COM *graph plotters* use a design technique very similar to that of the pen-on-paper plotters. Drawings are composed by the creation of incremental moves in the X- and Y-axes by deflection of an electron beam on a CRT. A third move required, equivalent to the raising and lowering of the pen, is achieved by blanking and unblanking the beam. The drawing areas are typically on a raster of 3,000–4,000 positions with a standard 15X magnification of the 35 mm microfilm frame, which would give the equivalent of a 0.005 in. increment size resolution on a finished drawing of 11 by 17 in. The plotting speed varies with different models and can be up to 500,000 increments a second. Fig. 27 shows a representative device of this rather esoteric class.

These plotters can plot graphs as well as alphanumerical characters. They are, however, not suitable for use as high-speed commercial printers.

COM printers use a symbol generator or other technique to generate characters to be recorded on microfilm and then printed out (all of them, or selectively). Since the microfilm image of the information stored has a form similar to that of a page printed by a high-speed line printer, the COM printers are often called *high-speed page printers*. The printing speed varies with the different models used and can be as high as 40,000 lines per minute.

Off-line COM processing requires preformatted tapes, with built-in edit and formatting commands. Most COM suppliers today provide fairly extensive libraries of software to run on common mainframes, usually a host-resident program or routine that is called by the user just before it outputs the data it has produced. The alternative is to provide intelligence at the COM unit to take unformatted tapes and process their data before it is actually filmed. Such intelligence is provided, for example, in the Datagraphix 4550 COM system.

Another main supplier of COM systems, NCR, has an 1100 series whose units deliver individual processed

Fig. 27.   Calcomp 1670 microfilm plotting system.

microfiche in one operation, generating fiche at a rate of one every 30 seconds. The 1100 series includes models with free-standing units with microprocessor-controlled editing and formatting—units that operate on line with a host mainframe, and powerful off-line systems with minicomputer controllers. Some models are able to convert data directly from a disk storage device. (The stand-alone model 1105 offers selectable reduction ratios of 24X, 42X, 48X and 72X.)

Presently, all but the cheapest COM printers can provide a variety of output options (Fig. 28). All have a forms-overlay facility, for example, which allows a pre-formatted overlay on most filmed information. Most will print in one or all of several typefaces and type sizes with different intensities, graphic plots, subscripts, and non-standard characters. Sophisticated indexed *retrieval coding* can allow for easy, and sometimes semi-automatic, access to specific data.

COM plotter-printers are really just an extension of COM printers. Presently, almost all COM printers on the market are offered with some graphics capability (sometimes as an option), so that they can be categorized as plotter-printers. Such a feature is useful for producing microfiche of technical parts catalogs and engineering drawings in merging text and illustration on one fiche. Individual data frames on the fiche can either be all text, all illustration, or a combination of text and illustration.

The *CIM system* may be regarded as the inverse of

Fig. 28.   NCR COM 1100.

COM. However, in comparison with COM, CIM is still far more in the research and development stage, with just a handful of systems already installed. The decisive factor that causes difficulties in the design of a CIM device concerns the level of universality of the images to be read, as well as the patterns to be recognized. CIM devices usually can work on line as well as off line. From the few devices available, we will describe three to give the reader some idea of the current range of capability.

FOSDIC (film optical sensing device for input to computers) is a device to read marks from microfilmed documents of census questionnaires. It was developed jointly by the U.S. National Bureau of Standards and the U.S. Bureau of the Census. However, FOSDIC also may be classified as an optical mark reading device with no graphical recognition capabilities.

Original sheets are position-coded (or marked) by census takers. These are microfilmed and the microimages are scanned with an electronic beam which detects position codes and translates them into digital data format for input to a computer which, in turn, after validating the data, transcribes it onto a magnetic tape for further processing. The major advantage of this solution, as opposed to conventional OMR readers scanning marked documents on paper stationery, was the replacement of more difficult paper handling techniques by a much simpler one used for handling of microfilm images. Furthermore, electronically sensing the transmitted light was easier than the technique of sensing reflected light used on conventional scanners.

Several FOSDIC off-line models have been built since 1952, when the original idea emerged. The main applications of FOSDIC were the U.S. Census of Population and Housing, using four FOSDIC III scanners, and that of 1970, using six further improved FOSDIC 70 machines. This last application involved 225 boxcars that delivered approximately 200,000,000 forms, which were converted to 140,000 microfilm rolls as input to the FOSDIC 70 systems. The processing produced 14,000 reels of computer magnetic tapes on which were recorded approximately four billion facts. The 1970 census application also made use of COM utilizing advanced techniques for page composition to produce publication-quality images on microfilm. An important feature of the COM operation, not available from the previously used impact printer, was the ability to call out and generate retrieval coding.

The Information International Incorporated GRA-FIX 1 CIM configuration is in itself a large computer system containing two processors, the binary image processor (BIP) and a PDP-10 computer with a two billion bit disk store, six tape drives, a number of operator consoles, and a film scanner optical system. The film to be read is positioned frame by frame between a programmable

CRT (light source) and a photomultiplier (the image detector).

Under control of the BIP, over a billion points on each frame of the film are examined as potential image constituents. Each character on the film will generate a unique dot pattern within the matrix enclosing it. This pattern is compared with the stored patterns until a match is achieved. Any unrecognizable characters (typically 1 in 10,000) are displayed on one of the operator consoles for verification. If a previously unknown character represents a member of a new font, the GRAFIX 1 system "remembers" the new style for future reference.

Each font stored in the GRAFIX 1 may consist of up to 92 symbols, and to avoid an average of 46 comparisons in the BIP prior to character identification, the PDP-10 attempts to predict forward characters, using known statistical distributions. The manufacturers claim that this reduces the average number of comparisons in the BIP to 4.6 before a match is achieved. Reading from a known font, the GRAFIX 1 is supposed to input 2,000 chps from microfilm to its backing store.

The GRAFIX 1 is basically a pattern-recognition device with a large range of pattern recognition capabilities. Three basic graphical modes of operation can be distinguished:

1. Character recognition (OCR).
2. Reproduction of images.
3. Image pattern recognition.

All three modes of operation may be used in any combination, either in connection with COM or without it. When used in connection with COM, they are used to create and update databases on microfilm which have to be maintained indefinitely, and where each record is updated very occasionally.

Some of the well known applications including at least the OCR mode of operation are used by the U.S. Navy for creation and updating a database of illustrated manuals for maintaining their aircraft and other hardware; the Canadian government for reading the Canadian Law Statutes; "a U. S. government agency" for reading text in the cyrillic script; and the U. K. Department of Health and Social Security for a handprinted name and address reading application.

The Joyce-Loebl MAGISCAN image analysis system is based on a Data General Nova 2/10 minicomputer, and lays an unusual emphasis on software. The system has none of its analytic procedures entrusted to specially constructed hardware. To reach greater flexibility, all functions are performed by high-level programs, which can be rewritten.

Image analysis is concerned with the extraction of useful information from an optical image, and is applicable to a wide range of specific fields, from examination of biological specimens to analysis of atomic reactions. The producer of this device is a scientific instrument company based at Gateshead, U. K., which claims that the MAGISCAN, working on a digitized television camera projection of the image, can automatically pick out features of certain optical density, marked variations in optical density, or certain textures. These criteria, and their mathematical and logical combinations, can be set up in the system using a special high-level language, Magic, developed by the company.

REFERENCES

1976. Grover, D. "Interaction with Displays," in Benwell, N.J. (Ed.), *Data Preparation Techniques*. London: Advance Publications, pp. 147–168.
1978. Clifton, H. D. *Business Data Systems*. Englewood Cliffs, N.J.: Prentice-Hall.
1978, Arnold, R. R., Hill, H. C. and Nichols, A. V. *Modern Data Processing,* 3rd Ed. New York: Wiley.

J. NECAS

INPUT-OUTPUT INSTRUCTIONS

For articles on related subjects *see* CENTRAL PROCESSING UNIT; CHANNEL; INPUT-OUTPUT CONTROL SYSTEMS; INPUT-OUTPUT DEVICES; and MACHINE INSTRUCTION SET.

Input-output (I/O) instructions cause transfer of data between peripheral devices and main memory, and enable the central processing unit to control the peripheral devices connected to it.

Prior to discussing such instructions in detail, a rudimentary model of the logical structure of an I/O setup is necessary. An important point to note is that the model used here is purely logical; i.e., in any actual computer organization, some of the units to be mentioned may be physically nonexistent with their function being integrated into the other existing units. This will not change the description of the I/O procedures and operations that will be presented in this article.

The model we use is illustrated in Fig. 1. The central processor and its memory are connected to channels. The number of possible channels is variable. Each one of them has an identifying name (i.e., number). Each channel can accommodate a number of peripheral device controllers. Each controller will control one or more identical, or very similar, devices such as line printers of different speeds, disks, and drums.

In the area of I/O processing, the distinction be-

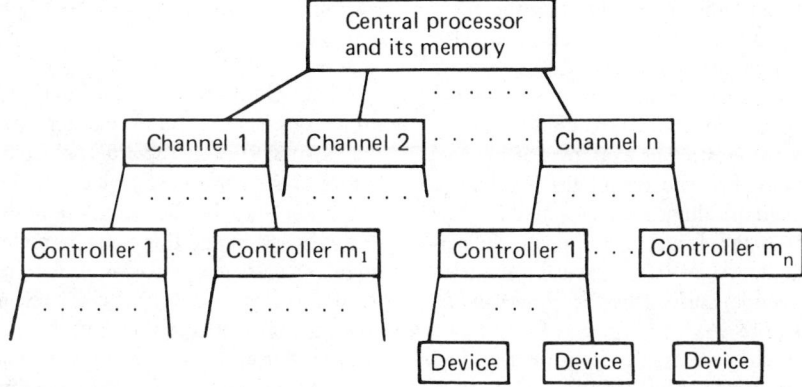

Fig. 1.   Model of an I/O setup.

tween hardware and software is extremely vague. In certain cases, vendors of computing equipment include in their hardware manuals a description of I/O instructions, which in reality are parameters to subroutines that incorporate the actual hardware I/O instructions. The questions of the physical existence of channels and controllers must also be dealt with carefully. The reader is advised to keep these gray areas in mind when trying to apply the following discussion to an actual computer.

Nomenclature. The sequence of I/O operations needed to perform an actual data transfer will be called an *I/O procedure*. In an I/O procedure, all devices present in the I/O setup (i.e., the central processor, the channels, and the controllers) take part. They operate as independent processors, each performing its own type of operation. We distinguish between I/O *instructions* performed by central processing units, I/O *commands* performed by the channel, and I/O *orders* performed by the controllers. The degree of independency and concurrency of these operations will be dealt with later.

As usual when introducing nomenclature, it is important to note that different vendors use different words for the same concept. We will follow more or less established nomenclature, but will introduce synonyms in the proper places.

I/O Operations. I/O operations are of two classes: control operations and data transfer operations.

Control operations perform the following tasks.

1. Establish the *data path* between the main memory and the peripheral device.
2. Check to verify that the path is legally established and that all devices in the path are operational.
3. Diagnose the success or failure of all data transfer and control operations.

Data transfer operations initiate and terminate the actual data transfer through the preestablished path.

I/O Instructions. These are regular machine instructions in one of the formats acceptable to the computer. They are decoded and performed by the central processor in the same manner as any other instruction, such as an arithmetic instruction. Examples of such instructions are: START I/O (e.g., on the IBM/370), which initiates a channel operation; TEST I/O, which returns status information about the conditions on an I/O path; HALT I/O, etc. The number of basic I/O instructions is usually low, but there are very many variants, which may have different meanings for different devices. These variants are usually defined by the address fields of the instruction or deferred to the channel command (see below).

While performing these instructions, the whole central processor is tied up, in the same way that any other type of instruction ties up the CPU.

Channel Commands. Channel commands, sometimes referred to as *channel control words,* or *I/O descriptors,* are bit strings that contain control information for the channel. They are interpreted by the channel, which can therefore be viewed as an independent processor whose instructions are the channel commands, and which is operating in parallel to the central processor. From such a description of the channel, it is clear why the role of the channel can, in certain configurations, be performed by the central processing unit.

The channel commands can either be contained in arbitrary or fixed memory locations (as in most large- and medium-scale computers), or contained in special registers (as in most minicomputers and microcomputers). In each case, the channel operation is initiated by a central processor instruction that passes the location of the channel commands to the channel, or which notifies the channel to start under the assumption that the channel commands are already resident in a predefined, fixed memory location or in predefined registers.

The structure of channel commands is very similar to the structure of regular machine instructions.

Fig. 2 contains two particular examples of channel commands, taken from IBM and Burroughs. The meaning of the various fields is almost self-explanatory. The code (or "opcode") is the actual operation to be performed by the channel: READ, WRITE, READ BACKWARD (in the case of magnetic tape), MOVE (the recording) HEADS (in the case of disks), etc.

The flags and options are usually short fields, sometimes as short as one bit, indicating specific demands and conditions. These may include indications of the course of action to be taken on normal or abnormal completion of the channel command, additional information needed to support some opcodes, enabling or disabling options like command and data chaining (see below), modes of automatic character conversion (if applicable), etc.

The starting address and count, or the starting and ending addresses, serve to identify the data on which the operation is to be performed. In certain cases, where the amount of information is limited by the nature of the device (i.e., the length of the line on a line printer), it is enough to indicate the beginning of the information.

Once the channel is started, it processes its own commands, which cause the transfer of data to and from the peripheral device controllers. This data, in turn, can be interpreted by the controller, either as an actual data item or as an order to the peripheral device controller. The distinction between data and order can be done in different ways. The transferred item may have identifying information associated with it, or the sequence of arrival of the items will define them to be either orders or actual data.

I/O Orders. Orders to controllers may be: START, STOP, TRANSFER status information, GET a data item, MOVE HEADS, REWIND, etc. The orders obviously must reflect the nature of the controlled device.

Each step in the sequence instruction-command-order causes, in addition to its normal operation, the creation and storage of status information. This information is usually of two types. One is the setting of the condition codes or status bits of the central processor itself, as expected after each CPU instruction. The other is the creation of a *channel status word,* sometimes also referred to as a *result descriptor.* Whereas the condition codes describe the state of the CPU, the channel status words describe the control information that is presented to the channel by the controller (together with data specifying the device itself), and the status of the channel itself.

The structure of the result descriptors varies so widely among manufacturers that examples would be more misleading than beneficial. The reader is advised to consult the manual of any computer of interest.

The various status information items are used to determine the success, or failure, of the I/O process. In the case of failure, the program that initiated that I/O operation can take either corrective or merely diagnostic steps.

A complete I/O procedure will therefore consist of the following steps.

1. Prepare a set of channel commands which will cause the proper set of orders for the device to be activated.

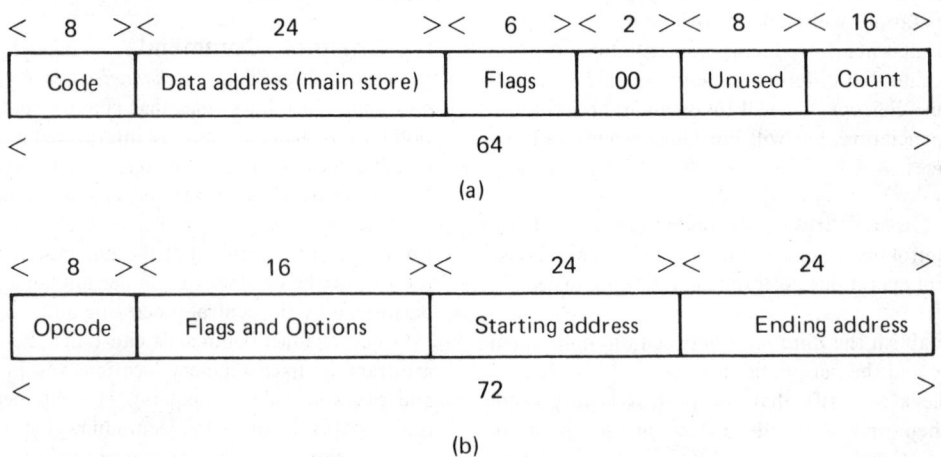

Fig. 2. Channel commands for (a) IBM/370, and (b) Burroughs B2500 (where the ending address is not always necessary). Field lengths are given in bits in both (a) and (b).

2. Issue instructions that will activate the channel. In this sequence of instructions one should first check to see if the channel is available, i.e., not busy with previous operations or is physically disabled.

3. After completion of the I/O operation, check for success and take necessary steps in case of failure.

Again, the interested reader is strongly advised to follow such a procedure in detail on a particular computer. Procedures of this type are sometimes called *I/O drivers*.

In an actual I/O process, it may be desirable to perform a whole program built from channel commands. The sequencing through the program can be driven by the end of each command, or by the exhaustion of the data to be transferred, without the command being actually finished. These two methods of sequencing channel commands are called *command chaining* and *data chaining,* respectively. Not all computers possess this capability. When present, this option is controlled by the flag and option fields of the channel command.

In actual computer systems, the channels are sometimes physically integrated into the CPU. It also happens more and more frequently that the controllers are integrated into the devices themselves. This by no means changes the description of the I/O procedures. The channel commands merely turn into computer instructions. The actual transfer of data, made by the channel, will be done by the central processor hardware. Whether this process will, or will not tie up the computer, is dependent on the sophistication of the hardware.

In most minicomputers as well as in microprocessors, the notion of channels is replaced by a *DMA (direct memory access) controller.* DMAs are specially designed circuits which share the memory access mechanism among themselves and the CPU. The channel commands and the various orders are performed, as we have already indicated, either by loading specially allocated registers (in the DEC PDP-11, for example) or by transferring proper information via I/O instructions (in the Data General Eclipse, for example). However, the logical sequence of operations, as outlined previously, is still maintained.

There exist computer configurations in which not only are the channels not integrated into the CPU, but (as in the CDC Cyber 170 series) are turned into full-fledged computers. In this case, one needs a whole layer of software in these computers to interpret the I/O request posted by the central processor. In other solutions to the question of channels (used, for example, by IBM and Burroughs), the vendors supply factory microprogrammable channels which, on one hand, have the advantage of programmable computers, but on the other hand do not burden the user with software maintenance.

Finally, it is necessary to indicate that no matter which of the former hardware alternatives is present, the I/O process in basically an asynchronous one in which the channels, or their variants, are operating in parallel with the CPU. Thus, one needs a synchronization procedure by which the CPU and channel operations are coordinated. This procedure is indicated by the flag fields and involves either interrupts or polling.

G. Frieder

INSTITUTE FOR CERTIFICATION OF COMPUTER PROFESSIONALS (ICCP)

For articles on related subjects *see* ASSOCIATION FOR COMPUTING MACHINERY; DATA PROCESSING MANAGEMENT ASSOCIATION; and PERSONNEL IN THE COMPUTER FIELD.

The Institute for Certification of Computer Professionals (ICCP) is an organization of computing societies, established in 1973, for the purpose of sponsoring activity in the areas of testing and certification of knowledge and competence of computing personnel. It is intended to pool the resources and interests of individual societies so that ultimately the full attention of the industry may be focused on the vital tasks of developing and recognizing qualified personnel.

The purposes of the Institute are:

1. To foster, promote, develop, and conduct scientific inquiry and research into any of the several activities related to the development and recognition of knowledge and competence among personnel in the computer and information systems industry.

2. To foster, promote, develop, and conduct scientific inquiry and research into standards of good practice.

3. To formulate and administer testing and evaluation programs designed to determine the aptitude, level of knowledge, and competence of individuals engaging in, or desiring to engage in, disciplines directly related to applied computer and information science.

4. To foster, promote, and develop internationally the purposes of the corporation, including without limitation (a) the establishment of reciprocal standards with, and reciprocal membership for

and cooperation with, organizations having similar aims and purposes; (b) the establishment of international standards of good practice in the worldwide computer and information systems industry; and (c) the formulation and administration of reciprocal testing and evaluation programs.

How Established. ICCP was incorporated as a not-for-profit corporation in the State of Delaware on 13 August 1973. Its establishment was the outgrowth of several years of study by committees of the Data Processing Management Association (DPMA) and the Association for Computing Machinery (ACM) during which the concept of a "computer foundation" to foster testing and certification programs was formulated. An open invitation was extended to other societies to support an organizational period. The organizations that served on the Computer Foundation Organizing Committee and then became members of the Institute were

> Association for Computing Machinery
> Association of Computer Programmers and Analysts
> Association for Educational Data Systems
> Automation 1 Association
> Canadian Information Processing Society
> Data Processing Management Association
> IEEE Computer Society
> Society of Certified Data Processors
> Society of Professional Data Processors

Presidents of ICCP to date have been

John K. Swearingen,	1973–1975
Fred H. Harris,	1976
G. Gary Casper,	1977–1978
Merton R. Walker,	1979–1980
Roland D. Spaniol,	1981–

Organizational Structure. The Institute is governed by a Board of Directors to which each member society designates two directors. Officers of the Institute are elected from the Board at its annual meeting and include a president, vice-president, secretary, and treasurer. The officers constitute an Executive Committee, which may act for the Board between its regularly scheduled meetings. Standing committees advise the Board and assist in the management of the Institute while *ad hoc* committees are established from time to time to investigate, evaluate, and recommend action on potential programs.

As programs are authorized by the Institute, councils with appropriate technical and professional expertise are established to oversee them and to provide the competence necessary to ensure high standards. Councils

have policy-making powers, as well as responsibility for quality control, within the domain of their programs. Presently, there are two certification councils which have jurisdiction over the testing and certification programs described in the next section.

Programs of the Institute. The Institute's highest priority is the improvement of existing certification programs and the establishment of new examinations for various specialties. In 1974, the Institute acquired the testing and certification programs of DPMA, including the Certificate in Data Processing (CDP) examination, which DPMA had begun in 1962 and had administered since then. The CDP examination focuses on business-oriented data processing, particularly supervisory and management levels, and is offered annually at designated testing centers, usually colleges and universities, in the U. S., Canada, and a number of international locations.

All candidates for the CDP examination must have at least 6 months of full-time, or equivalent part-time, work experience in a computer-based information systems environment. Candidates may submit college level academic experience for evaluation as partial fulfillment of the current experience qualifications. The amount of credit is determined by the CDP Credentials Committee.

The present CDP examination requires one day to complete, and consists of five sections: Data Processing Equipment, Computer Programming and Software, Principles of Management, Quantitative Methods, and Systems Analysis and Design. Any qualified person may take it, and every candidate must successfully complete all five sections to receive the Certificate. Through 1981, 49,963 candidates have sat for the CDP examination and 21,565 have been awarded certificates.

The CCP (Certificate in Computer Programming) examinations focus more on programming. There are three separate examinations and each is given annually at test centers in colleges and universities in the U. S., Canada, and several international locations. Each of the three examinations tests a common core of programming knowledge and one area of specialization. The choices of specialization are Business Programming, Scientific Programming, and Systems Programming. The common core of knowledge emphasizes such areas as data and file organization, techniques of programming, programming languages, interaction with hardware and software, and interaction with people.

These one-half day examinations do not require specific experience but the interested CCP candidate should be aware that the examination questions are primarily intended for senior-level computer programmers.

Through 1980, 1939 candidates have sat for the CCP examinations and 831 have received certificates. In addition, 843 holders of the Registered Business Programmer certificate (predecessor of the Business specialty offered for several years by DPMA) have been awarded the CCP certificate without further examination.

The headquarters of ICCP are located at 35 East Wacker Drive, Chicago, IL 60601.

F. H. HARRIS

INSTITUTE OF ELECTRICAL AND ELECTRONIC ENGINEERS— COMPUTER SOCIETY (IEEE-CS)

For article on related subject *see* AMERICAN FEDERATION OF INFORMATION PROCESSING SOCIETIES.

Purpose. The IEEE Computer Society was formed to advance the theory and practice of computer and information processing technology. Its objectives are to promote cooperation and exchange of technical information among its members. To achieve this, the Society holds meetings for the presentation and discussion of technical papers, publishes technical journals, and through its chapters and technical committees studies and provides for the professional needs of its members. The scope of the Society encompasses all aspects of design, theory, and practice relating to digital and analog devices, computation, and information processing.

How Established. The IEEE Computer Society was so-named in 1972, having originated in October 1951 as The Computer Group of IRE (Institute of Radio Engineers), which on 1 January 1963, merged with the American Institute of Electrical Engineers and became the Institute of Electrical and Electronics Engineers (IEEE). The IEEE represents some 180,000 electrical and electronics engineers throughout the world.

With so many special interests among its members, it was natural for members who wished to concentrate in one area of electronics, or who wanted to exchange knowledge with those of similar interest, to create special interest groups. The Computer Society, with some 40,000 members, is one of these special interest groups. (The IEEE-CS headquarters address is 1109 Spring Street, Silver Spring, MD 20910.)

Organizational Structure. The IEEE Computer Society has a Governing Board consisting of a maximum of 24 voting members, including the President, two Vice-Presidents, the Junior Past-President, and 20 elected members of the Board. The Society membership annually elects the President and two Vice-Presidents. The President-elect appoints three additional Vice-Pres-

idents, a Secretary, and a Treasurer for a one-year term coextensive with his/her term. The President, under direction of the Board, has general supervision of the affairs of the Society.

Technical Program. Members of the IEEE Computer Society receive *Computer* magazine, "the voice of the computer systems design profession," which contains tutorial and survey articles, practical applications ideas for the computer professional, and various other pertinent departments. In addition, they have the choice of receiving the *Transactions on Computers,* which contains papers of archival quality on the theory, design, and practices related to digital and analog computation and information processing; the *Transactions on Software Engineering,* which contains archival research papers on all aspects of the specification, development, management, test, maintenance, and documentation of computer software; the *Transactions on Pattern Analysis and Machine Intelligence,* which contains archival materials on all aspects of pattern analysis and manipulation; or the *Journal of Solid State Circuits,* which covers devices and systems affecting circuit design.

The IEEE Computer Society sponsors three annual Computer Society Conferences and numerous specialized conferences, and co-sponsors the annual AFIPS National Computer Conference.

The IEEE Computer Society's technical committees include Computer Architecture, Computer Communications, Computer Elements, Data Acquisition and Control, Design Automation, Data Base Engineering, Distributed Processing, Fault-Tolerant Computing, Oceanic Engineering and Technology, Machine Intelligence and Pattern Analysis, Mass Storage Systems, Math Foundations, Microprogramming, Mini/Micro Computers, Operating Systems, Optical Processing, Packaging, Security and Privacy, Simulation, Software Engineering, and Test Technology. Their aim is to promote technical excellence in specific areas by sponsoring seminars, symposia, and sessions at professional conferences.

Other activities of the IEEE Computer Society include Standards, and Education and Professional Development, which are concerned with curriculum and continuing education, and the Distinguished Visitors and Tutorial Programs, which arrange for leading computer professionals to speak to local chapters of the Society.

Officers of the IEEE-CS since its inception (9 October 1951) include the following persons.

Chairmen:
Morton M. Astrahan, 1951–1952
Jean H. Felker, 1953–1954
H. T. Larson, 1954–1955
Jerre D. Noe, 1955–1957

Werner Buchholz, 1957–1958
Willis H. Ware, 1958–1959
R. O. Endres, 1959–1960
A. A. Cohen, 1960–1962
W. L. Anderson, 1962–1964
K. W. Uncapher, 1964–1965
R. I. Tanaka, 1965–1966
Samuel Levine, 1966–1967
L. C. Hobbs, 1968–1970
E. J. McCluskey, 1970–1971

The Society's name changed to the IEEE Computer Society on 1 January 1971.

Presidents:
E. J. McCluskey, 1971
A. S. Hoagland, 1972–1973
S. S. Yau, 1974–1975
D. B. Simmons, 1976
M. G. Smith, 1977–1978
Tse-yun Feng, 1979–1980
Richard E. Merwin, 1981
Oscar N. Garcia, 1981–

I. L. AUERBACH

INSTRUCTION. *See* MACHINE INSTRUCTION SET; and PRIVILEGED INSTRUCTION.

INSTRUCTION COUNTER. *See* PROGRAM COUNTER.

INTEGRATED CIRCUITRY

For articles on related subjects *see* COMPUTER CIRCUITRY; JOSEPHSON JUNCTION DEVICES; LOGIC DESIGN; and MICROPROCESSORS AND MICROCOMPUTERS.

The beginning of the solid state electronics revolution is usually dated from the invention of what is now known as the bipolar transistor by J. Bardeen, W. H. Brattain, and W. Shockley, all of Bell Telephone Laboratories, in 1948. After a few years of development, this device became a strong competitor to the older vacuum tube in many electronic circuits. The use of transistors was especially important for computer circuitry because their small size, high reliability, and low power dissipation helped overcome major limitations that vacuum tube circuitry exhibited.

At first, transistors were used simply as replacement devices for vacuum tubes and the same circuit fabrication methods that had evolved for vacuum tube-based systems were adapted for transistor-based systems. These were wiring by hand and later printed circuit boards. Gradually, it occurred to people that it would be very useful to be able to fabricate entire circuits on the semiconductor material from which the transistors were made. The first public expression of this idea is generally credited to G. W. A. Dummer, a British radar expert, in a paper he presented in 1952. The first implementation of such a circuit, the forerunner of what is now called an integrated circuit, is credited to Jack Kilby of Texas Instruments. Another pioneer in the field, who made great contributions in developing the technology for manufacturing integrated circuits, was Robert Noyce—who was at that time with Fairchild and later co-founded Intel. Both filed patents in 1959, although Kilby's first circuit, a phase shift oscillator, was operational in September 1958. Both Texas Instruments and Fairchild were offering integrated circuits commercially in 1961.

The first integrated circuits used the bipolar transistor as the amplifying or active element. More recently (the 1970s), integrated circuits fabricated with a particular type of unipolar field effect transistor known as the Metal Oxide Semiconductor (MOS) transistor have become extremely popular. MOS integrated circuits are especially prevalent in the microprocessor and memory chips that so dramatically reduced the cost of computing power in the 1970s.

As integrated circuit technology has developed, the number of *gates* (i.e., basic functional units) that can be put on a single chip has increased rapidly. Thus, over the years, we have advanced from Small Scale Integration (SSI—up to 10 gates/chip) to Medium Scale Integration (MSI—10–100 gates/chip) to Large Scale Integration (LSI—100–1000 gates/chip) to today's Very Large Scale Integration(VLSI—over 1000 gates/chip).

This article surveys the basis of integrated circuit technology, primarily its MOS form, beginning with its twin origins in photolithography and semiconductor physics and continuing with a brief description of the fabrication process. Finally, some of the more important factors in the design and production of integrated circuits and some indications of future trends are presented.

Photolithography. Prior to the existence of integrated circuitry, electronic circuits, including those for use in computers, were fabricated out of discrete components—resistors, capacitors, inductors, transistors, and, earlier, vacuum tubes. Initially the components were interconnected with separate lengths of insulated copper wire. Such wiring—done by hand—was tedious, error-prone, and time-consuming. By the 1950s, an alternative interconnection technique, the printed circuit board, gained commercial acceptance. The underlying technology was that of photolithography, and, as the name implies, the circuitry connecting the devices was "printed" on an insulating substrate.

The printed circuit process, which in modified form remains central to the production of integrated circuits, is actually fairly simple. The substrate, typically a phenolic resin or fiberglass "board," has a thin layer of copper foil bonded to it, over which a layer of light-sensitive emulsion, known as a *photoresist,* is coated. When the photoresist is exposed to light, its molecular form changes. In use, a pattern of the desired circuitry in which opaque areas represent desired copper paths, and transparent areas represent the absence of copper, is placed over the photoresist and the whole arrangement is exposed to light.

The pattern of the desired circuit interconnections is obtained by a technician or engineer who is said to *lay out* the circuit. The pattern may be laid out full scale or several times full scale. When the desired layout is obtained, a full-size transparency of the interconnections is made. This transparency, really a large black and white slide, is opaque in areas where there are to be copper paths and is transparent in other areas.

The opaque areas of the pattern protect the underlying photoresist from the light but the transparent areas do not. As a result, the resist, which coats what is to become the bare areas of the board, is chemically changed and may be washed away with solvent. This leaves the copper over the to-be-bare areas exposed while the copper over the interconnections is coated with and protected by the emulsion. The copper in the unprotected areas is then etched away, after which the resist is also removed, leaving the resultant "printed wires." Strictly speaking, what has been described is a positive photoresist. Negative photoresists, in which desired patterns are made from photographic negatives of the desired interconnections, are also in use.

To complete a printed circuit board, holes must be drilled for component leads and the components soldered in place. In practice, patterns may be etched on both sides of the substrate, and boards themselves may be sandwiched together with insulating layers to allow the printed "wires" to cross without touching. Boards with four layers of interconnection are common.

The great advantages of printed circuit board fabrication over earlier hand-wiring techniques are the ability to mass produce the interconnections, the fact that all components may be soldered in one operation, and the increased parts density achievable. This last point is important in that, if the components are closer together, smaller—less powerful—transistors may be used, while keeping equivalent performance levels. Other devices,

particularly resistors, can also be scaled down in power requirements so that the system as a whole requires less power. There are, however, practical limits to how tightly packed a printed circuit board can be. One limit comes from the fact that the components placed on the board must be individually handled. Adequate space must also be left around components for cooling and adequate space must be left between the printed wires for insulation. The advantages of decreased size also hold when making an integrated circuit but now there are no limits to the size reduction arising from the necessity to manipulate individual components. In addition, the elimination of troublesome macroscopic connections in the form of solder joints leads to significant reliability improvements. These factors of decreased power dissipation and increased reliability combine to allow today's computer systems to be enormously more complex than those of the pre-integrated circuit era.

Hybrid and Monolithic Integrated Circuits. An integrated circuit has not only transistors, but also whatever resistors, capacitors, and interconnections are needed to make a complete functioning circuit, fabricated on a single substrate. The circuitry is then packaged and sold as a unit much in the way transistors or resistors are sold. In practice, there are two major classes of integrated circuits, known as *hybrid* and *monolithic.*

A hybrid integrated circuit is a miniaturization of the printed circuit board concept where, instead of components being interconnected with copper traces on fiberglass boards, the components are interconnected, usually with deposited aluminum, on a ceramic substrate. The components used on a hybrid integrated circuit are, however, not the same as those that would be used on a printed circuit board. For example, what the individually purchased "transistor" actually consists of is the transistor proper with its connections to the external leads, all encapsulated in a protective substance, frequently an epoxy resin. Encapsulation is done to protect the transistor from moisture and impurities in the atmosphere. The point is that the actual transistor is much smaller than its packaging might lead one to believe. Hybrid integrated circuits are made from such small components devoid of their protective packaging. Instead, once the components of the hybrid circuit have been interconnected, the whole assembly is encapsulated with only the necessary external leads brought out to allow interconnection at the printed circuit board level. The hybrid technique was never very popular for digital circuitry, but it remains in use for many forms of analog circuitry.

Monolithic integrated circuits, which are the subject of this article, are fabricated by manufacturing the components within and on the substrate. That is, the substrate serves not only as a support for the components, but also as the material from which the components are made—and even, to some extent, the interconnection medium. Other interconnections are formed by deposition of aluminum in a somewhat similar fashion to that used in manufacturing hybrid integrated circuits. Computer circuitry currently uses monolithic integrated circuits fabricated on a silicon substrate, and it is likely that this will remain the case for some time. The next sections will describe the fundamentals of the operation and fabrication of monolithic silicon MOS integrated circuits.

Basic Principles of Semiconductors.

The photolithographic process is a conerstone of integrated circuit technology. However, in integrated circuit fabrication as opposed to printed circuit board fabrication, photolithography is used not only to define the interconnection—the "wires" of the circuit—but also the components—the transistors, and resistors, of the circuit. As a result, the precision required for integrated circuit fabrication is much greater than that required for printed circuit board fabrication, but the basic concepts remain applicable.

Photolithography is, however, only a part of the technology required to fabricate integrated circuits. It is also necessary to treat the silicon in such a way as to cause the components to be formed. The details of both the photolithography and silicon treatment methods used by integrated circuit manufacturers are closely guarded trade secrets, but the broad outline is well known. The essential notion is that pure crystalline silicon can be treated with precisely controlled *impurities* to alter its ability to conduct current. The impurities actually settle in the crystal lattice and lead to either an excess of electrons within the lattice, yielding *n-type silicon;* or a deficit of electrons, yielding *p-type silicon*. A pure silicon crystal is actually a good insulator, but both *n* and *p* type silicon have a conductivity somewhere between a good insulator and a good conductor, and are called semiconductors. In general, the greater the concentration of impurities (called the *doping* level), the more conductive the material becomes. More important is the fact that the charge carriers in the two types of silicon are different. That is, when current flows in an *n* type semiconductor, one may think of moving electrons as carrying the flowing charge. However, when current flows in a *p* type semiconductor, one may think of the absence of electrons as flowing and thereby carrying the current. Thus, in *p* type semiconductors, one speaks of the *holes* as being the charge carriers. The presence of the two types of charge carriers is fundamental to both the action and fabrication of integrated circuit transistors.

When *p* and *n* type semiconductors are in contact, the resultant structure behaves differently from either. If the *p* material is made more positive than the *n* material

(for example, by connecting a battery as in Fig. 1), current flows very easily. The device has low resistance. If, however, the battery is reversed so that the *p* material is more negative, negligibly little current flows. This effect is the basis of the *semiconductor diode.*

Transistors are also formed by *n* and *p* type semiconductors in contact with each other. Two types of transistors are used in integrated circuits: the bipolar transistor, depicted in Fig. 2(a), and the unipolar transistor, shown in Fig. 2(b). The action of the bipolar transistor of the type shown in Fig. 2(a) is not simple but may be crudely thought of as follows: If the collector is made more positive than the emitter, no current will flow because of the diode effect between the base region and the collector. If now the base is also made positive with respect to the emitter, current will flow from the base to the emitter and this will induce current to flow from the collector region into the base region. Here it is swept along to the emitter also. Thus, the base voltage can be used to control the flow of current from the collector to the emitter. It happens that both electrons and holes are involved in the flow of these currents; hence the name *bipolar transistor.*

The unipolar transistor is simpler to explain and, in many respects easier to fabricate. Once again, imagine the drain region to be more positive than the source region. Negligible current will flow because of the presence of the *p* type material. Now apply a positive voltage to

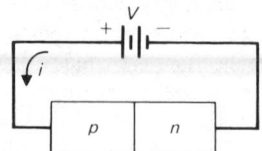

Fig. 1.   Semiconductor diode.

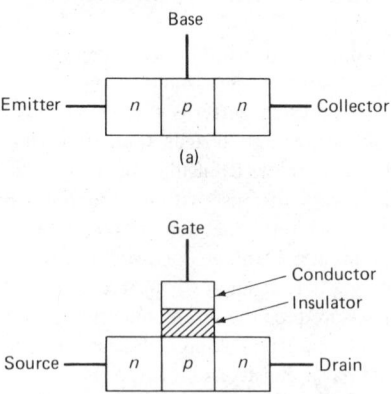

Fig. 2.   Transistor structures: a) bipolar transistor; b) unipolar transistor.

the gate. The insulator prevents current flow and, in fact, forms a capacitor with positive charge on the gate and negative charge, electrons, in the p region just under the insulator. With a sufficient gate voltage, these electrons form a thin channel of n type material beneath the insulator, which connects with the n type regions of the source and drain. Current can easily flow along this channel. Again, the current is dependent on the voltage of the gate with respect to the source. Here, because of the forming of the channel, only one type of charge carrier is used, giving rise to the term *unipolar transistor.*

Actually, unipolar transistors are better known by other terminology. Because its underlying principle of operation is known as the field effect, the device is also called a *field effect transistor (FET).* Because the gate may be fabricated out of metal, and the insulator out of silicon dioxide, the device is often referred to as a *metal oxide semiconductor (MOS) transistor.* Even though many integrated circuits now form the gate from polycrystalline silicon, also a conductive material, the MOS term has stuck.

Frequently a prefix is used to indicate the charge carrier type. Thus, what is pictured in Fig. 2(b) would be referred to as an NMOS transistor. If the types of the various regions were reversed, one would have a PMOS device. Earliest MOS transistor-based integrated circuits were PMOS because control of unwanted impurities is easier to achieve in PMOS fabrication. Modern integrated circuits that use only one type of device are usually NMOS, because NMOS devices are inherently faster than PMOS devices. Similar statements can be made with respect to the NPN transistor shown in Fig. 2(a) and its PNP counterpart.

Just as the application of a positive gate voltage to the device of Fig. 2(b) creates an effective n type channel in a p type material, one can, by selective application of impurities, form regions of silicon of one type within regions of the other type. The ability to do this, using the techniques of photolithography to define the regions, is essential to integrated circuit fabrication.

The Fabrication Process. The description of fabrication given below is necessarily abbreviated and will be limited to what is called the NMOS silicon gate process. The principles also apply to other fabrication technologies. Fabrication has two starting points—the semiconductor material itself, and a set of photolithographic patterns, called *masks,* which define the areas within the material to be treated. The material, silicon, is used in wafer form. The wafer is actually a thin, about 0.5 mm thick, slice of a single crystal of silicon that has been doped to be of p type. Early wafers were an inch or two in diameter but wafers of 100 mm or 125 mm in diameter were in use in 1981 in the most modern facilities.

The masks are used to define the circuit and transistor topologies. Early processes used perhaps four or five masks, while the most popular current processes use seven or eight masks. The number of masks required is significant because precise alignment must be maintained between the various masking steps and because, obviously, the more such steps that are required, the more chance there is for an error that will render the circuit inoperative.

Manufacturing of an integrated circuit is achieved by performing a series of processing steps. Some of these consist of altering the underlying silicon substrate, for example, changing certain regions from p type to n type. Other steps involve depositing an insulator or an interconnection in the appropriate place. These processes all share the common feature that a processing step is to occur in certain areas and not occur in others. The photolithographic technique, using the mask referred to above, is what defines these areas, and the process of transferring the definition of the areas from the mask to the wafer is called *patterning.* The details of patterning vary, depending on the particular step of manufacture and the material that is being patterned, but the basic idea can be seen by examining the steps required to pattern silicon dioxide.

The first step is to grow a layer of silicon dioxide on the wafer. This may be done by placing the silicon wafer in a suitably heated oxygen or steam atmosphere. The silicon dioxide may also be deposited rather than grown, if necessary. The reasons for using silicon dioxide in the first place are varied because at different stages of fabrication it performs different functions. Silicon dioxide's outstanding characteristic is that it is an excellent insulator. Therefore, it is used for separation between layers of interconnections, but it is also used to form the insulator between the gate and the channel of the transistor. In thick layers, it is used to define regions where controlled amounts of impurities may be administered to make transistors.

After a layer of silicon dioxide has been grown over the surface of a wafer, a coat of photoresist is applied. The mask is placed over the photoresist-coated wafer and the whole arrangement is exposed to ultraviolet light. As was true for printed circuit board manufacture, the mask protects some areas from exposure while allowing a chemical reaction to occur in the regions covered by the transparent areas of the mask. The changed photoresist can be washed away, leaving bare silicon dioxide in some areas, which can be etched away while the photoresist protects the remainder of the wafer from the etchant. The net result after now removing the photoresist is a pattern on the silicon dioxide layer which mimics that on the mask.

The patterning process occurs many times in integrated circuit manufacture. For example, the steps in making an MOS transistor are these: First a region on the silicon substrate corresponding to the outline of the transistor is exposed as described in the patterning discussion above. In this area, a thin layer of silicon dioxide is grown. This thin layer will be the insulator between the gate and the channels and is called the *gate oxide* to distinguish it from the thicker field oxide grown previously. Another step of photolithography is then used to define where the gate will be, and a layer of polycrystalline silicon, called *polysilicon* for short, is deposited. Now the thin gate oxide can be etched away in the areas not protected by the polysilicon, exposing the silicon wafer again. Impurities (for example, phosphorous ions) are then diffused into the exposed silicon by placing the wafer in a high-temperature phosphorous atmosphere. The result is a well of *n* type silicon surrounded by *p* type. Of course, the phosphorous also diffuses into the silicon dioxide and the polycrystalline silicon, but it has no effect on these materials. The resulting structure is pictured schematically in Fig. 3.

Actual fabrication techniques are much more involved than the description above. For example, in addition to diffusion, the technique of ion implantation (that is, directing a beam of ions at the wafer) is used to alter the type and conductivity of the silicon in certain regions. The diffusion areas described above may be used as embedded "wires" to interconnect the transistors. The polysilicon may also be used as a layer of wiring. There may, in fact, be several layers of polysilicon. In addition, there is a layer of aluminum "wiring" called *metalization* above all these. The layers are separated by silicon dioxide which must be selectively etched away to provide for any interconnections required between the various levels of "wiring." A mask is used to define the patterns for each of these layers. The whole structure takes on a three-dimensional aspect.

One must realize that the areas being described are very small. An integrated circuit "wire" might be 3μ wide (μ stands for micron, one thousandth of a millimeter). This characteristic dimension is often called *line width*. Gate oxides are about 0.05μ thick, and channels are about 3μ long. Clearly, cleanliness is vital during the fabrication process, since minute specks of dust on a mask could obliterate whole transistors.

There are other factors that limit integrated circuit production. Random concentrations of unwanted contaminants within the wafer, either there originally or arising from any one of the processing steps, can also make a circuit nonfunctional. The probability of such an occurrence increases as a circuit occupies more area, and is a strong motivating force for reducing the size of integrated circuits. While much reduction can be achieved by clever circuit design and layout techniques, most experts agree that continued reduction in circuit size is linked to reducing device and interconnection sizes, which, in turn, is dependent on developing improved patterning techniques. Already the contact mask, used just on top of the photoresist, as was done for printed circuit board work, has been largely replaced by a mask used on a projection basis, much like an ordinary slide projector. Short-wavelength ultraviolet light is used to get better line definition and x-rays are being experimented with. Experimental and prototyping facilities use a scanning electron beam to write the pattern directly on the photoresist. All of these techniques require expensive, sophisticated equipment, but give the promise of line widths of less than 1μ.

While the previous discussion has referred implicitly to the production of a single integrated circuit, in fact, many copies of the same circuit are made *simultaneously* on a single wafer. This leads to the observation that processing costs are largely on a per wafer basis and that it is economically advantageous to have smaller circuits (more per wafer) and larger wafers. This explains the growth in wafer size referred to earlier.

When the processing of a wafer is complete, the circuits are tested for proper functioning and the bad ones are marked. The lines between the circuits are scribed and the wafer broken on these lines. The resulting *die* or *chips* which are unmarked may then be mounted in a chip carrier, leads attached, encapsulated, tested again, and (if good) shipped to a customer. Notice that once testing and packaging begin, costs are associated with the handling of each circuit rather than each wafer. These steps have been labor-intensive and many manufacturers have developed facilities in countries where labor costs are low. At the same time, there is considerable effort being devoted to automating these manufacturing steps.

Importance of Yield. As far as wafer processing is concerned, it costs as much to make a bad chip as it does to make a good one. Hence, a manufacturer's profitability is closely tied to the yield, the percentage of good chips, that is obtained. Of course, packaging and testing are not insignificant costs either, but the manufacturer who can maintain good yields will be more profitable than one who does not. One aspect of yield—the chip size—has already been mentioned. For a given circuit, the tighter the components can be packed together and, in-

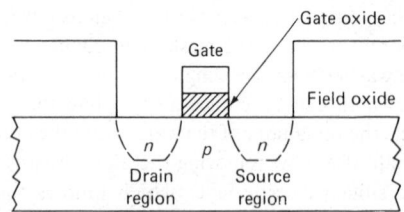

Fig. 3. Integrated circuit unipolar transistor.

deed, the smaller the devices themselves, the smaller the chip size will be. On the other hand, smaller device sizes and closer packing requires more accurate alignment of the various fabrication stages. At any given time, a manufacturer reaches a compromise between these two factors and promulgates a set of *design rules,* which specify device sizes, line widths, line separations, and related factors of a geometrical nature. The idea is that, if a circuit is laid out (that is, translated from the logic diagram description to an equivalent electrical circuit with all the components topologically placed such that the design rules are satisfied), then the chip will function properly and the yield will be high enough for profitability.

When a circuit, particularly a new and fairly complex circuit, is first placed in production, yields may be quite low. After a while, the processing is refined and tuned, and better yield may be expected. This phenomenon of increasing yield with time is often called the *learning curve.* Products that have been on the market for a while may be quite economical to produce and there may be substantial price reductions with respect to the original offering price, particularly if the part has sold in large volume. The Intel 8080, an eight-bit processor, sold for nearly $300 when it first appeared in 1974, but now sells for one-hundredth of that amount. In the meantime, technology has advanced and it may be possible to refabricate the part using design rules calling for decreased dimensions. In fact, it is possible to *scale* fabrication technology by suitably adjusting dimensions, doping levels, and thicknesses to get a new part that requires a smaller chip, takes less power, and is faster. Of course, there are limits to the extent to which scaling is possible, but it has proven an effective mechanism for the integrated circuit manufacturers because it means that a circuit does not have to be completely laid out again to take advantage of new processing technology.

The last point is important because VLSI (very large-scale integrated circuits) are currently being designed with over 400,000 transistors on them. If done strictly by hand, many human-years of effort would be required. Some types of circuitry, specifically memories, are very regular and consist for the most part of the same circuit repeated over and over again. Other devices, such as processors, are not by nature so regular, and specialized design techniques are used to cast the circuitry in a form suitable for integration. In either case, computer design aids are becoming a necessity to verify the design rules, to aid in the layout, to keep track of changes, and to drive the camera that makes the masks. Many experts feel that it is the area of computer-aided design that must now make significant progress if we are to continue on the road of dramatic improvements in integrated circuit technology that we have been on for the past couple of decades.

Integrated Circuit Technologies. This article has concentrated on MOS technology, but other technologies are available in integrated circuit form. Bipolar transistors are the building blocks of TTL (transistor transistor logic). The TTL family of circuits has been the mainstay of digital circuitry for over a decade and in new low-power Schottky form will continue to be popular. The ECL (emitter coupled logic) family is used in very high-speed computers. Neither ECL nor TTL can be fabricated as densely as the MOS technology, but both can be made faster at the expense of increased power dissipation. A newer development, I^2L (integrated injection logic), may be fabricated densely enough so that some small I^2L processors are now available commercially. A particularly attractive feature of I^2L is that its supply voltage is not critical. For low speed and low power dissipation, a low voltage may be used. If more speed is needed, a higher voltage may be used, but power loss will also increase.

MOS technology is also used in making the CMOS (complementary MOS) family of circuits. The advantage of this family, which combines NMOS and PMOS devices within a single gate, is extremely low static power dissipation. CMOS products are not yet as dense as standard NMOS, but they are getting close. Processor chips fabricated from CMOS have been commercially available for several years. Many experts believe that CMOS will become even more attractive in the future as heat dissipation problems with other technologies become more severe.

Finally, other substrate and media are under investigation in the attempt to fulfill the computer designer's quest for faster, cooler devices. A silicon on sapphire (SOS) process has been in use for some time, but has not found wide application. Recent work in gallium arsenide (GaAs) devices appears to hold much promise for the future.

References

1975. Hamilton, D. J. and Howard, W. G. *Basic Integrated Circuit Engineering.* New York: McGraw-Hill.
1977. Glaser, A. B. and Subak-Shurpe, G. E. *Integrated Circuit Engineering.* Menlo Park, CA: Addison-Wesley.
1979. Millman, J. *Microelectronics.* New York: McGraw-Hill.
1980. Mead, C. and Conway, L. *Introduction to VLSI Systems.* Reading, MA: Addison-Wesley.
1980. Clark, W. A. "From Electron Mobility to Logical Structure: A View of Integrated Circuits," *ACM Computing Surveys* **12,** *No. 3:* 325–357 (September).
1980. Colclaser, R. A. *Microelectronics Processing and Device Design.* New York: Wiley.

F. M. Brasch, Jr. and S. S. Yau

INTENSIVE CARE, COMPUTERS IN

For articles on related subjects *see* MEDICAL APPLICATIONS; and TOMOGRAPHY, COMPUTED.

Digital computers have proved themselves able assistants to the medical staff in a hospital's intensive care unit (ICU). The principal reason for the introduction of computers into the ICU is to improve patient care through patient monitoring. Such a computer system can vary in size, configuration, cost, complexity, and function,

depending on the degree of sophistication of the monitoring and analysis required, and the number of patients to be monitored in a particular ICU. A typical computerized surgical ICU is shown in Fig. 1.

Improved patient care is achieved through computerization for several reasons. First, nurses are able to concentrate on direct patient care when computers take over the repetitive and time-consuming measurement and record-keeping functions. The least sophisticated patient-monitoring systems should fulfill this role by logging the measurements provided by the multitude of commercially

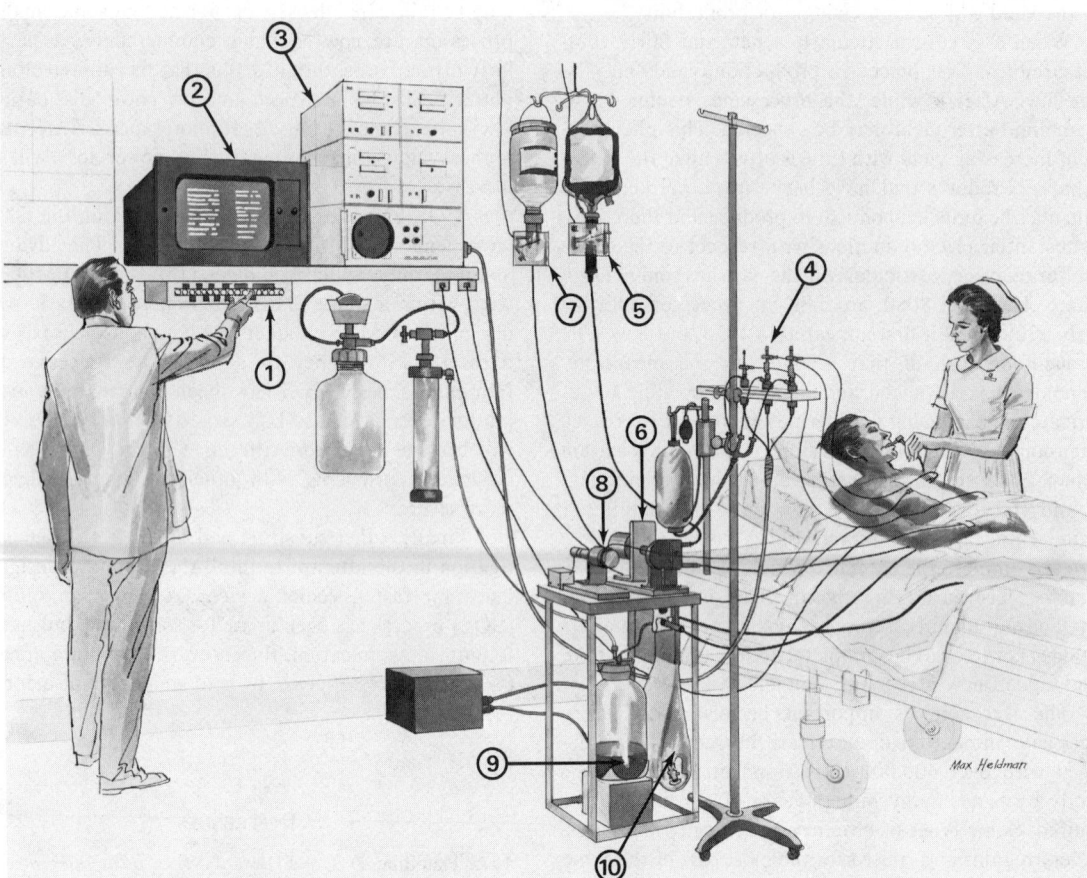

Fig. 1. Bedside view of the prototype automated patient-care system at the Cardiac Surgery Post-Operative Intensive Care Unit at the University of Alabama Medical Center, Birmingham, Alabama. Major elements of the automated system are: (1) numeric keyboard, (2) video display, (3) physiological monitoring devices, (4) blood pressure transducers, (5) blood drop detector, (6) blood infusion pump, (7) drug and fluid drop detector, (8) drug and fluid infusion pump, (9) chest drainage measurement scale, and (10) urine output measurement scale. The computer itself, an IBM 1800, was located in an adjoining room and continually monitored four such beds on a 24-hour basis. Input to it came from the numeric keyboard and the monoring devices. The video display provided the output from the computer. (From "Computer-Controlled Interventions for the Acutely Ill Patient," by L. C. Sheppard *et al.,* in *Computers in Biomedical Research* **IV.** New York: Academic Press, 1974, Chap. 6.)

available bedside biomedical monitoring devices. These instruments typically provide average values of such parameters as heart rate, blood pressure, respiration rate, and body temperature on front panel analog or digital displays for visual inspection by the medical staff.

Second, uniformity and reproducibility in data collection from shift-to-shift and day-to-day improve the reliability and completeness of the medical record. The more sophisticated systems maintain a database on each patient, which is reviewable upon request when using bedside display terminals.

Third, a continuous vigil is maintained for out-of-tolerance measured parameters. In advanced systems, trend analyses and multiparameter diagnostic algorithms contribute to a further increase in system capability by providing the physician with an immediate indication of many undesirable and correctable events, such as the presence of abnormal heart rhythms.

Finally, continuous computer adjustment of therapeutic interventions can provide a level of control unattainable by the periodic human supervision of these interventions. For example, the use of sophisticated computer hardware allows the implementation of automated infusion of blood or drugs, under closed-loop control, in response to needs signaled by changes in monitored parameters.

The method by which patient monitoring is physically implemented depends upon the situation in question. In many research environments, or when certain cardiovascular or respiratory monitoring functions are to be performed, it is sometimes advantageous to analyze physiologic variables on a "heartbeat-by-heartbeat" or "breath-by-breath" basis. The average values produced by standard bedside monitoring devices are not always adequate in this application. The digital computer must, in these situations, process the basic time-varying physiologic waveform. The necessary computer programs are generally written by personnel with medical backgrounds or under medical supervision. These pattern recognition programs represent a more complex level of programming than that usually required in other than the beat-to-beat situation.

Regardless of whether preprocessed average values obtained from physiologic waveforms or the waveforms themselves are manipulated within the digital computer, the always necessary analog-to-digital conversion process is a critical area of concern, since data is usually made available to the digital computer as an analog signal; i.e., a voltage that varies as a function of time.

The software used in intensive care monitoring systems can vary as widely as the system hardware. At one end of the spectrum, all monitoring and analysis tasks are performed by a relatively simple program which sequentially analyzes each of the signals being monitored on a particular patient, permanently records its findings, and then cyclically switches the analog-to-digital converter to the next patient before the program repeats its analysis.

At the other end of the software spectrum are re-entrant monitoring and analysis programs which exist in a multiprogramming environment. These programs use a hardware priority interrupt system to respond dynamically to the needs of many simultaneously monitored patients. In such a computer installation, data retrieval can be carried out interactively from many independent terminals, using sophisticated graphics and text analysis software. In addition, low priority background processing of non-real-time tasks is possible to a limited extent.

An open-ended area in the development of patient-monitoring systems is that of diagnostic and statistical analysis programming. The ultimate extent to which computers will contribute to patient care depends upon the growth of techniques utilized in the analysis and extrapolation of all available data. The application of cluster analysis, correlation techniques, nonlinear transformations, and other numeric methods will improve the specificity and accuracy of diagnostic and trend detection functions. The continuing development of diagnostic methods will provide the new criteria to be implemented on ICU computer systems in the future.

Presently, the high cost and the custom-designed nature of most ICU computers are the factors that limit the spread of these systems. Advances in computer technology, including the current microprocessor revolution, can be expected to decrease system cost and increase system capability.

REFERENCE

1975. Risso, William L., Jr., Kempner, Kenneth M., Owens, David C., Gorlen, Keith E., Holsinger, William P., McIntosh, Charles L., and Syed, Daniel. "A Postsurgical Intensive Care Computer System at the National Institutes of Health," in *Proceedings of the 1975 Computers In Cardiology Conference*. New York: Institute of Electrical and Electronics Engineers, pp. 101–108.

K. M. KEMPNER

INTERACTIVE SYSTEMS, USING

For articles on related subjects *see* DEBUGGING; DIAGNOSTICS; FILES; PASCAL; PROCESSING MODES; TIME SHARING; and UNIX.

One of the exciting aspects of contemporary computing is the availability of sophisticated interactive time-sharing operating systems. This concept represents a significant evolutionary change from the traditional batch-based operating system.

In a batch-processing system, a user submits a sequence of commands, programs, and data, termed a job, to the computer. The job typically takes the form of a deck of cards handed to the computer operator, but could be entered from a terminal directly to the operating system if the system was so designed. At some later time, the computer would process the job, based upon some scheduling sequence, after which the results would be available at the terminal or the user would return to the computing center and retrieve the results. The important point is that from the time the job was submitted until the results are retrieved the user has *no* interaction with the computer. The sequence of operations could not be altered, additional data could not be provided, and the programs could not be modified. These drawbacks motivated the development of interactive systems, which provide the user with the ability to communicate or interact directly with the computer.

Currently there are many variations of the time-sharing concept that exist on a variety of computers both large and small. These systems vary in terms of the number of concurrent users supported, functionality, ease of use, and even portability. In this article, we explore two of the best known and best designed operating systems, one originally developed for an IBM System 360 called the Michigan Terminal System (MTS) and the other designed for a DEC PDP-11 called UNIX.

Rather than developing a point-for-point contrast between the systems, each will be presented separately, providing both historical and operational background. Features such as text editing and command language interpretation will be discussed from a new user's perspective.

The Michigan Terminal System.

The early operating systems for the IBM System 360 series of computers, DOS (for disk-operating system) and OS/360, were entirely batch-oriented. The job control language for these systems, although extremely powerful, was not something a novice could learn in a few minutes or even hours. In the mid-1960s, the arrival of dynamic-relocation hardware, which allowed the location of a program in main storage to change during execution, spawned the term *virtual memory*, whereby many programs could run concurrently and each think that it had the whole machine to itself. Now it was feasible for many users to interact with the system at the same time—remotely, through terminals. This advance spawned the development of a number of interactive software systems for System 360. At the University of Michigan, this took the form of a totally new operating system to run on the 360

series which was terminal-oriented and would as well provide some batch capabilities. An important goal of the project was to develop a time-sharing system that was extremely easy to use, powerful, efficient, and "friendly" (i.e., tolerant of the mistakes of unsophisticated users, such as students).

General Information. On the Michigan Terminal System (MTS), authorized users can interact with the computer either through terminals or cards. To control the access to the system, each user is given a computer center identification number (ccid) and a secret password. The accounting system will then limit the number of dollars spent, amount of file storage space used, and some other resources. To gain access to MTS, one merely has to enter the command:

SIGNON ccid

on the terminal where ccid is the user id number mentioned above. The system will then ask for the password, which the user then enters, after which the logging-on process is complete.

When communicating with MTS, one can be operating in a number of modes. The mode of operation is indicated by the prompt character, which is the first character printed by MTS on the current line of the user's terminal. Common modes are MTS command mode (#), edit mode (:), and copy mode (>), where the character in parentheses is the prompt character. A question mark as the prompt character indicates that special information is being requested by the system.

Files. Under MTS, every program reads or writes information from or to files. These files may contain source code, object code, data, commands, output, or all of the above. There are three basic types of files—permanent, temporary, and pseudo. Permanent files have to be explicitly created and remain in existence until they are explicitly destroyed. Their names have the form ccid:filename or *filename, where filename is any name less than or equal to 12 characters in length. The former kind are files belonging to ccid, while the later are *public files,* which anyone can access. When referencing the file, if ccid is omitted, it is assumed the file belongs to the user. Temporary files have names of the form -filename and remain in existence only while the user is logged onto the system. Pseudo files refer to specific hardware devices. They have names like *SOURCE*, *SINK*, *PRINT*, and *PUNCH* which, respectively, refer to the terminal input device, the terminal output device, the system printer, and the system card punch.

In order to use MTS, one must be aware of the structure of files. A file can be either of a sequential or line nature. A sequential file is defined to be an ordered set of 0 or more lines, where lines may only be accessed sequentially; i.e., one after another. A line file is an ordered set of 0 or more lines, where each line has a number associated with it in the range -99999.999 to 99999.999. Any line may be accessed directly, as described in Fig. 1.

Line #	Data	Annotation
-7.3	first line	<-- can be referred to by *F
-4.1	second line	<-- can be referred to by -4.1
-1	third line	
0	fourth line	<-- *P (previous line pointer)
1.5	fifth line	<-- * (current line pointer)
2	sixth line	<-- *N (next line pointer)
3	seventh line	
3.1	eighth line	
5	ninth line	<-- can be referred to by 5
6	tenth line	
9	eleventh line	
10	twelfth line	<-- can be referred to by *L

Fig. 1

As can be seen in Fig. 1, any line in an MTS file can be referred to by an absolute line number, which need not be an integer. Additionally, the first and last lines may be referred to as *F or *L, respectively. While in edit mode *, *P, or *N may be used to refer to the most recently accessed line, the previous line, or the next line, respectively.

In line files, the numbers of the lines do not change, even though new lines may be added, unless the file is explicitly renumbered. This makes editing much easier, since the numbers on a listing—produced by the operating system or a compiler—are exactly the line numbers associated with the lines in the file. Therefore, normal users tend to use line files exclusively. In fact, many users are not even aware of the existence of sequential files on the system!

MTS Command Mode. When a user first logs on the system, MTS command mode is immediately entered. In this mode, the user can create files, destroy files, copy files, run programs, enter other modes, and perform a host of other useful functions. Below are some commonly used commands. The form in which they are given consists of a prototype command along with a description of the function of the command followed by one or more examples along with descriptions of what these commands would do. In some of the prototypes, the character string fdname appears. This is a shorthand notation for filename (b, e), where b is a beginning line number in the

file and e is the ending line number. Defaults are 1 and *L (i.e., the last line in the file), respectively.

CREATE filename   <-- filename creates a new file
CREATE JUNK   <-- creates a file called JUNK

DESTROY filename <-- used to destroy existing files
DESTROY JUNK   <-- gets rids of the file JUNK

COPY fdname1 TO fdname2 <-- used to copy information between files

COPY PROJECT1 TO NONLINEAR <-- replaces the contents of the file NONLINEAR with the contents of PROJECT1
COPY *SOURCE* TO PROJ1 <---| copies information typed on
line 1 | next three
line 2 | lines to file
line 3 | called PROJ1
$ENDFILE |

COPY F1 TO *SINK* <-- prints the file F1 on the terminal
COPY F1(1, 10) TO *SINK* <-- prints lines 1–10 of F1 on the terminal
COPY F1(10) <-- prints F1 on the terminal starting at line 10

To run either your own program or a library program, the system must know where the program is going to read information from and to where it is going to write information. This is accomplished by having programs perform input/output with logical units (e.g., SCARDS, SPRINT, SPUNCH) instead of physical devices. These logical units can in turn be "attached" to any physical device. The prototype of the RUN command is:

RUN fdname [I/O fdnames] [TIME = nS].

For example, to compile a Fortran program, one might issue the command:

RUN *FTN SCARDS = PROJ1 SPRINT = *SINK*
    SPUNCH = −OBJ.

Here, *FTN is the file containing the Fortran compiler that will read source statements from the file PROJ1, print a listing on the terminal, and direct the object code to the temporary file −OBJ that it will implicitly create. To run this Fortran program, one might use the command:

RUN −OBJ 5 = DATA 6 = *PRINT* TIME = 10S

Here, the compiled version of the Fortran program is contained in the file —OBJ and will read data from the file DATA and will produce output on the system printer. Also, the program is not allowed to execute for more than 10 seconds. It is also assumed that all READ statements refer to unit 5 and all WRITE statements refer to unit 6.

Below are some other useful commands which may be issued while in MTS command mode. Only the prototypes are given.

EMPTY filename   <- - empties the contents of a file
FILESTATUS <- - lists file names belonging to the user
LIST fdnamel ON fdname2 <- - same as the COPY command, but also adds line numbers
PERMIT filename access ccid <- - gives permission to others to use your files
RENAME filenamel filename2 <- - changes the name of a file
SET PW = string   <- - changes your password
SIGNOFF   <- - logs the user off the system

Edit Mode. Programmers probably spend more time modifying or editing their programs than doing anything else. To facilitate this, MTS has a very powerful editor. To get into edit mode, the MTS command

    EDIT filename

must be issued, where filename is the name of the file to be edited. Below are some commonly used edit commands. The form in which they are given is similar to that of the MTS commands; i.e., a prototype followed by examples. In some of the prototypes, the character string lpar may appear. This means that, in its place, a single line number, a pair of line numbers, or/FILE can appear. A vertical bar appearing in a prototype means that either of the two choices on either side of the bar may be used in the command. Also, the SCAN command sets the current line pointer, *, to the line number in which the string was found.

PRINT lpar <- - prints parts of the file on the terminal
PRINT 1 10 <- - prints lines 1–10
PRINT *L   <- - prints the last line in the file

ALTER lpar 'stringl'string2' <- - changes a range of lines
ALTER 12 'READ'READ(1, 10)' <- - inserts (1, 10) after READ in line 12
ALTER 1 17 'VAR2' <- - deletes 1st occurrence of VAR2 in lines 1–17

APPEND lpar 'string' <- - adds data to the ends of lines

APPEND 25 '+FP(Z)/F(Y)' <- - fraction added to end of line 25

COPY [lpar | F = fdname] TO [linenumber | F = name] <- - copies
COPY 24 30 TO 81 <- - copies lines 24–30 after line 81
COPY F = SUB1 TO 74 <- - inserts information from file SUB1 after line 74
COPY 50 56 TO F = ROUTINE <- - copies lines 50–56 to the file ROUTINE

DELETE lpar   <- - deletes lines in the file
DELETE 17 19   <- - deletes lines 17–19

INSERT linenumber   <- - inserts lines into the file
INSERT 7   <- - -|
line 1 | inserts next 2 typed lines
line 2 | after line 7
$ENDFILE   <- - -|

MOVE lpar TO [linenumber | F = fdname] <- - moves lines around
MOVE 1 5 TO 22 <- - moves lines 1–5 to after line 22

RENUMBER   <- - renumbers lines in the file

REPLACE lpar 'string' <- - replaces entire lines in the file
REPLACE 18 '   STOP' <- - makes line 18 a STOP statement

SCAN lpar 'string'   <- - looks for a character string
SCAN /FILE '**2'   <- - scans the entire file for **2
SCAN ' STOP' <- - looks for STOP after the current line
SHIFT lpar [LEFT| RIGHT] *n* <- - shifts lines to the left or right
SHIFT 13 RIGHT 3   <- - shifts line 13 right 3 spaces

STOP   <- - causes a return to MTS command mode

Edit commands may also be further enhanced through the use of command modifiers. Here are some examples.

ALTER@ALL 1 20 'READ'WRITE' <- - changes all READs to WRITEs in lines 1–20
COPY@NOVERIFY 10 13 TO 27 <- - copies lines 10–13 to after line 27 without listing the lines on the terminal

Sample Terminal Session. The example that follows illustrates the use of MTS with a terminal session in which a Pascal (*q.v.*) program is written to find and print all the prime numbers less than or equal to 100 using the Sieve of Eratosthenes.

Annotation	Actual Terminal Session

```
Device: DI1F Task: 564 Userid: BAWH 16:17:41 03-20-81
Michigan Terminal System at R.P.I. — Device: DI1F Task: 564
# signon bawh
# ENTER USER PASSWORD.
```

Annotation	Actual Terminal Session
Password would be blanked out	`? barry`
	`# TERM, NORMAL, IND`
	`# **LAST SIGNON WAS: 15:54:46`
	`# USER "BAWH" SIGNED ON AT 16:05:03 ON FRI MAR 20/81`
	`# create prime`
	`# FILE "PRIME" HAS BEEN CREATED.`
Now the program can be typed	`# edit prime`
	`: insert 1`
System will convert lowercase input to uppercase	`? program prime (input, output);`
	`?    (*   this program is designed to find and print all`
	`?        prime numbers between 2 and 100 using a method`
	`?            known as the sieve of eratosthenes—named`
Line 5	`?            after the greek mathematician who developed it`
	`?            over 2500 years ago.                       *)`
	`?`
	`?`
	`? const`
Line 10	`?        upper_limit = 100; (*upper_limit on # of primes *)`
	`? var`
	`?        primes : array (1.. upper_limit) of integer;`
	`?        i, j : integer;`
	`? for i := 1 to upper_limit do primes (i) : = i; (* initialize *)`
	`? i := 2; write (i);     (* print the first prime *)`
	`?`
	`?        (* cross out all multiples of 2 *)`
	`? j := 4;`
	`? while j <= upperlimit do`
Line 20	`?        begin primes (j) := 0; j := j + 2 end;`
	`?`
	`?            (* scan for the next non-zero entry in primes`
	`?            and replace all multiples of it by zero   *)`
	`? i := 3;`
	`? while i <= upper_limit do`
	`?        begin`
	`?        if primes (i) <> 0`
	`?          then begin`
	`?            write (i)`
Line 30	`?            j := 3*i;`
	`?            while j <= upper  limit`
	`?              do begin prime(†):=0; j := j+2*i end;`
	`?            end;`
	`?        i := i + 2;`
Line 35	`?        end;`
	`? end;`
	`? $endfile`

Annotation	Actual Terminal Session

Exit from editor

Compile the program
  in the file PRIME
  using the compiler
  contained in the
  file UNSP:PAS.BC

```
: STOP
# run unsp:pas.bc scards = prime spunch = -object
.  #          New version of UBC Pascal installed 02/03/81        #
# EXECUTION BEGINS
        14    00298  1-  FOR I: = 1 TO UPPER_LIMIT DO PRIMES (I) := I;
              ( • INITIALIZE •)
  • • • • • • • • • •              |                                              24
        24 Procedure body must start with BEGIN
        19    00116—WHILE J < = UPPERLIMIT DO
  • • • • • • • • • • •                          |  |                    12 50
```

Error message

Error number and
  type

Line number and
  hex offset in the
  object code

```
        12 Identifier not defined
        50 Illegal data types for previous operation
        30      001AC    - -     J: = 3•I;
  • • • • • • • • • •                        |                               54
        54 End of statement expected
        32      001AC    44           DO BEGIN PRIME(J): =0; J: = •I END;
  • • • • • • • • • •                                      |              12
        12 Identifier not defined
        36      001DA    - 1    END;
  • • • • • • • • • •                        |                               1
        1 Expecting '.'
  • • • • • • • • • •                        |                              98
        98 Unexpected end-of-file encountered
  • • • • •   7 errors detected   • • • •
            0.095 CPU SEC.
```

End of compilation
Modify the file

```
# EXECUTION TERMINATED
# edit prime
: insert 13.5
? begin
? $endfile
: alter 19 'upperlimit'upper_limit'
:         19      WHILE J < = UPPER_LIMIT DO
: print 28 30
:   28                      THEN BEGIN
:   29                           WRITE (I)
:   30                           J := 3•I;
: append 29 ';'
:   29                           WRITE (I);
: alter 32 'prime' primes'
:   32                  DO BEGIN PRIMES(J): =0; J: =J+2•I END;
: print 33 •I
:   33                      END;
:   34        I := I + 2;
:   35      END;
:   36   END;
: alter 36 ';'.'
:   36   END.
: stop
```

Annotation	Actual Terminal Session
Empty file that	# empty -object
contains incorrect	# DONE.
object code and	# run unsp:pas.bc scards = prime spunch = -object
recompile. Object	. # New version of UBC Pascal installed 02/03/81
code will go to	# EXECUTION BEGINS
the file -OBJECT	***** No errors detected *****
	0.083 CPU SEC.
	# EXECUTION TERMINATED
Execute the program	# run -object sprint = *sink* time = 1S
	# EXECUTION BEGINS

```
Output          2         3         5         7        11        13
               17        19        23        29        31        37
               41        43        47        53        59        61
               67        71        73        79        83        89
               97
```

End of run	# EXECUTION TERMINATED
Signoff the system	# signoff

Advanced Features. By now the reader should have a pretty good understanding of what it is like to use MTS even though a discussion of many of the advanced features has been omitted. For example, for convenience most of the commands can be abbreviated to just a few letters. There also exists a screen-type editor for use on intelligent terminals that allows the user to "paint" a picture of a program and make changes to lines through the use of function keys instead of EDIT commands. Also, a debug mode exists, which allows users to debug programs interactively. These features, along with the more standard ones, make MTS one of the most popular time-sharing systems currently available.

The UNIX Operating System. The UNIX time-sharing system was developed by Ken Thompson and Dennis Ritchie of Bell Laboratories. Some aspects of UNIX evolved from the MIT Multics project, which, in fact, provided its name—single-user Multics or UNIX. This single-user version of the operating system was designed for the DEC PDP-7/9 series of computers. However, once the PDP 11 was made available, it became the target machine. The PDP 11/45 became the first minicomputer to support UNIX as an enhanced general-purpose time-sharing system. The earliest versions of the system were written in assembler language; however, the updates and current versions are now written in C (*q.v.*), a structured programming language. The operating system is portable enough to now reside on DEC PDP 11s, VAX-11/780s, Interdata 8/32s, as well as on some mainframes (*q.v.*).

The current UNIX system includes a large assortment of software tools. More generally, it provides a clear and direct approach to problem solving using a computer. Some of the many strengths of the system include a rooted tree file system, a powerful editor, and a versatile command language interpreter. Overall, the operating system is highly modular and very concise.

File System. The UNIX file system is designed to be application-independent and bottleneck-free. It allows many specialized formats and treats all files as a collection of bytes. It has a very simple structure allowing all files and directories to share a comparable identity. In fact, directories are simple read-only files from the user's standpoint.

File access may be defined using a path name such as

/ usr / adm / temp

This defines the file *temp* as an entry in the directory *adm*. Adm is a subdirectory of usr, which, in turn, is an entry in the root directory (/). Access to the file temp may be streamlined to

temp

if the user is currently active with a working directory adm.

File systems can be expanded or attached to by a simple mount command so that a mountable device, such as a disk pack, may easily extend the domain of the system. Privacy of data is greatly enhanced by this concept.

Logging on. To get started on UNIX, the user merely types

LOGIN

in which case the system will request a user's ID and (optionally) a non-printing password. All the files are protected from unauthorized access by means of protection bits that are set by the respective owner of the file or the super-user (system manager) or by default at the time of file creation. Once logged on the system, the user has access to a default directory. In order to relocate to a new working directory, the user might type

CHDIR / usr / newdir

where newdir becomes the new working directory. The user must, of course, have execute permission in the new directory.

Text Editing. As with MTS, the most common functions performed during a typical time-sharing session pertain to editing. The UNIX editor is designed to facilitate the manipulations of text by allowing access at line or character levels.

The user invokes the editor by simply typing

ED

The editor enters command mode, initially allowing for the addition, deletion, or change of text within the file. The commands allow for a simple form of regular expression (*q.v.*) notation. The editor sets up a buffer or work space and all text is processed within the buffer. To begin the entry of text, the user could type the append command:

a
This text is being included as an apple.

The single period followed by a carriage return ends the text mode and enables commands to be entered. One such command might be

1, $s / apple / example /

This command searches from line 1 to the last line of text ($) for the string "apple" and replaces the first occurrence of it with the string "example." Searches can also be made by context such as

/ apple / s / apple / example /

In this case, the search would be for the first occurrence of "apple" in the buffer. When found, the string "exam-

ple" would replace "apple." Once this session is complete (or at any time during the editing process), the user would write the text to a file by using the write command

w textfile

The edit session would be terminated by typing the quit command

q

Control is returned to system command level. The editor offers the necessary flexibility to manipulate text that may be either a program written in some high-level language or a simple message prepared for all users to receive through the mail.

Command Line Interpreter. Perhaps the most powerful feature of all the different aspects of UNIX is the command line interpreter called the *shell*. The shell is a program which may either interpret a command such as

CAT file1

which reads file1 and prints it on the terminal or executes a file of commands by

SH < comfile

There are numerous features associated with the shell that elevate it from a simple command line interpreter to a mini-procedure-oriented language. Examples include conditional testing, argument shifting, branching, and even sub-command calls.

Two features which prove to be extremely useful are redirection of I/O and information transfer. The example using the symbol "<" demonstrates redirection; i.e., the access of information from a file other than the standard input device. This function allows great flexibility in the preparation of information. One example may be to run a prewritten edit session by simply typing

ED - < editfile file1

Redirection can occur for output as well, such as saving the result of a comparison of two files in a third file

COMP file1 file2 > file3

Another significant advantage of the shell over most command line interpreters is the use of *pipes* or *filters* for information transfer and transform. The symbol for a pipe is a vertical bar "|". For example, one could type

SORT file1 | PR -h"Sorted Output"

In this case, the file file1 is sorted and the sorted output is passed to the next command, which prints it with a special heading (-h) on the standard output device. Multiple commands may be strung together in a sequence allowing data to be cleanly transformed at each stage until the desired result is achieved.

Another feature of the shell is the ability to support special command processing. The user could type

```
CC source.c &
```

in which case, the C compiler would begin compilation of the file "source.c." However, the "&" would cause the shell to return control immediately to the user, thus enabling the entry of new commands even as the compilation continues.

Sample Terminal Session. A typical terminal session for someone first beginning to work with UNIX as well as with the programming language C is provided as an example below. This session demonstrates the process of logging on to the system, creating a C source program for a prime number algorithm similar to that in the previous example, using the editor, compiling and loading an executable program and, finally, executing it. The process is then terminated by a simple line disconnect. Side annotations are to assist readability.

```
login:tom                                   !LOGIN
password:
$ed                                         !INVOKE EDITOR
a                                           !APPEND TEXT
#define max 20                              !C PROGRAM BEGINS
main ( )
{
  / *                             * /
  / * PRIME NUMBER GENERATOR PROGRAM * /
  / * SIEVE OF ERATOSTHENES ALGORITHM * /
  / *                             * /
  int list[max], number, prime, pointer;
  / *                                   * /
  / * SET UP LIST OF INTEGERS FROM 2 TO 20 * /
  / *                                   * /
  pointer = 1;
  do
    {
      pointer = pointer + 1;
      list[pointer] = pointer;
    }
  while ( pointer < = max );
  / *                                             * /
  / * INITIALIZE AND PRINT HEADING                * /
  / * %d IS INTEGER CONVERSION, n IS CARRIAGE RETURN * /
  / *                                             * /
  prime = 2;
  printf ("PRIME NUMBERS IN THE INTERVAL 2 TO %d n",max);
  / *                                       * /
  / * TEST LIST UP TO SQUARE ROOT OF MAX FOR PRIMES * /
  / *                                       * /
  while ( prime*prime < max )
    {
  / *                                     * /
  / * IDENTIFY NON-ZERO ENTRIES IN THE LIST * /
  / *                                     * /
        if ( list[prime] != 0 )
          {
            printf ("%d n", prime);
            pointer = 2;
```

```
/ *                              * /
/ * ZERO ALL MULTIPLES OF A PRIME * /
/ *                              * /
        do
          {
              number = prime * pointer;
              list[number] = 0;
              pointer = pointer + 1;
          }
           while ( number < max );
      }
    prime = prime + 1;
  }
/ *                                              * /
/ * SEARCH THROUGH REMAINING LIST FOR NON-ZERO ENTRIES * /
/ * OUTPUT THEM AS PRIMES                              * /
/ *                                              * /
  while ( prime < = max )
    {
      if ( list [ prime ] != 0 )
        printf ( ''%d n'',prime);
        prime = prime + 1;
    }
}
.
w prime.c                    !WRITE SOURCE TO FILE
q                            !EXIT EDITOR
$cc prime.c                  !COMPILE, LINK, LOAD
$a.out                       !EXECUTE FILE
PRIME NUMBERS IN THE INTERVAL 2 TO 20
  2
  3
  5
  7
 11
 13
 17
 19
 $                                        !THE END
```

Reflections.

UNIX represents simplicity together with great functionality rarely found in time-sharing systems. One can play the "shell game" and in a few short minutes transform data that, if attempted by other methods, would typically take much longer. The designers of UNIX were truly visionary for UNIX has become an important partner in the minicomputer and microprocessor revolution of the 1980s. Good designs endure.

Conclusions. Perhaps the most important observation one can make about MTS and UNIX is that both achieve the target of creating a sophisticated, yet simple-to-use programming environment. Neither system uses a cumbersome job control language so common on many established systems. To achieve such features as functionality and ease-of-use, both systems create file structures that allow for device-independent storage of data. The command and edit subsystems are tailored to this file structure so that information can be manipulated without regard for its source or destination. Although the MTS and UNIX developers took radically different paths in the implementation of these subsystems, their awareness that a unified file system was a necessary prerequisite to the development of a flexible, friendly system has now become conventional wisdom.

REFERENCES

1974. Ritchie, D. M. and Thompson, Ken. "The UNIX Time-Sharing System," *Comm. ACM* **17**, No. 7.
1976. Salisbury, Richard (Ed.). *Volume 1: The Michigan Terminal System*. Ann Arbor, MI: University of Michigan Computing Center.
1978. Kernighan, B. W. and Ritchie, D. M. *The C Programming Language*. Englewood Cliffs, NJ: Prentice-Hall.
1979. Kernighan, B. W. and Mashey, J. R. "The UNIX Programming Environment," *Software: Practice and Experience* **9**.

B. R. HATHAWAY and T. F. O'CONNELL

INTERFACE MESSAGE PROCESSOR (IMP)

For articles on related subjects *see* ARPA NETWORK; COMPUTER NETWORKS; DATA COMMUNICATIONS; PACKET SWITCHING; and TELEPROCESSING SYSTEMS.

The term *Interface Message Processor*, or IMP (Heart *et al.*, 1970), is generally associated with the ARPA network (*q.v.*) which provides a capability for geographically separate computers, called *hosts*, to communicate with each other via lines leased from a common carrier. Each host is connected into the network through a small local computer called an IMP. Each IMP (Fig. 1), in turn, is connected to one or more other IMPs in the network via wideband leased lines.

In normal operation, a host wishing to communicate with another will pass a message, including the destination address, to its local IMP. This message will then be passed from IMP to IMP until it reaches its destination. The choice of the path that the message will traverse is determined dynamically. Each IMP forwards each message on the path it determines to be best to assure prompt delivery, taking account of network loading or failures. Alternate routings do exist, since the network is multiconnected to insure reliability. Since a message generally must traverse several nodes in going from source to destination, a copy of the message is stored at each node until it is received correctly at the following node. The IMP is therefore a type of *store and forward* message switcher.

The hardware consists of a 16-bit word length general-purpose computer with a 12K word memory and suitable interfaces to the host and the network. The software includes routines for handling, buffering, and routing messages. Particular attention has been paid to hardware and software features, insuring reliability and fast system recovery.

The IMP enables only host computers to be connected to the network. At any location where terminals only or terminals and host require access to the network, a terminal IMP or TIP (Ornstein et al., 1972) must be used as shown in Fig. 2. The essential hardware difference between the IMP and TIP is that the latter has a multiline controller (MLC), which allows connection to up to 63 terminals to the TIP, directly or via modems. The terminals may be synchronous or asynchronous, and work at bit rates up to 19.2K bits per second. The TIP also has an additional 8K words of memory for the extra programs required for the terminal handling.

The IMPs or TIPs may be connected to as many as four local hosts and five remote IMPs or TIPs via lines from 9.6K to 230.4K bits per second. Further work is being done to extend this to over one million bits per second and to include satellite links to overseas nodes.

Fig. 1. Interface message processor used in the ARPA network.

REFERENCES

1970. Heart, F. E., Kahn, R. E., Ornstein, S. M., Crowther, R. W., and Walden, D. C. "The Interface Message Processor for the ARPA Computer Network," *Proceedings of the AFIPS 1970 Spring Joint Computer Conference* **36**: 551–567.
1972. Ornstein, S. M., Heart, F. E., Crowther, W. R., Rising, H. K., and Russell, S. B. "The Terminal IMP for the ARPA Computer Network," *Proceedings of the AFIPS 1972 Spring Joint Computer Conference* **40**:243–254.

J. S. SOBOLEWSKI

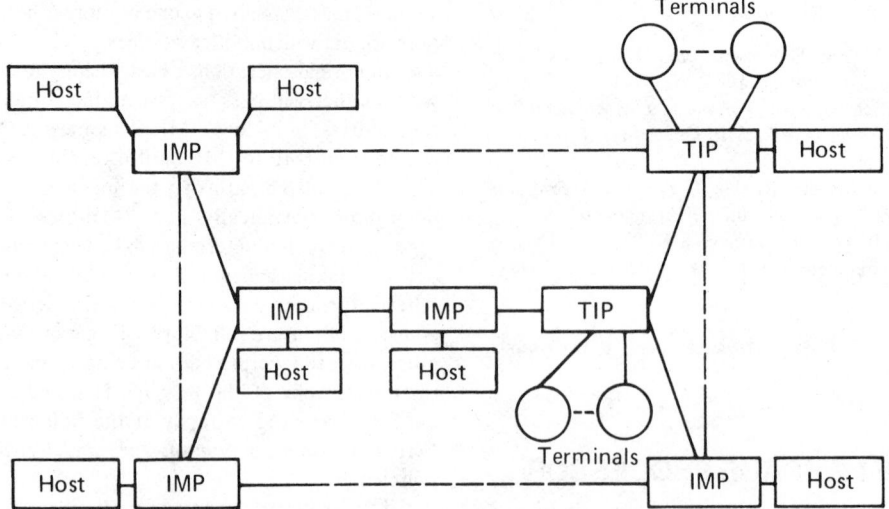

Fig. 2. Portion of the ARPA network showing hosts, IMPs, and TIPs. The network is such that alternate routings between IMPs or TIPs exist to insure reliability. Connections may be via leased lines at 9.6K to 230.4K bits per second, but most are at 50K bits per second.

INTERGOVERNMENTAL BUREAU FOR INFORMATICS (IBI)

For articles on related subjects *see* INTERNATIONAL FEDERATION OF AUTOMATIC CONTROL; and INTERNATIONAL FEDERATION FOR INFORMATION PROCESSING.

Purpose. The Intergovernmental Bureau for Informatics (IBI) is an organization of states that are members of the United Nations or of the United Nations Educational, Scientific and Cultural Organization (UNESCO) or of one of the other specialized agencies of the United Nations. All became parties of the Convention establishing the IBI by depositing an instrument of acceptance with the Director General of UNESCO. The member states are

Algeria	Argentina
Bolivia	Cameroons
Brazil	Cuba
Chile	France
Ecuador	Iran
Gabon	Iraq
Ghana	Italy
Israel	Mexico
Madagascar	Morocco
Nigeria	Spain
Swaziland	Tunisia

The objective of IBI is to promote scientific research, computer education and training, and the exchange of knowledge between developed and developing countries, carrying out activities mainly oriented toward the promotion of informatics particularly in developing countries.

How Established. IBI was created by the initiative of the Economic and Social Council (ECOSOC) under the auspices of UNESCO (by Resolution 2.24 adopted at the sixth session of its General Conference). It was established by an International Convention, and went into operation as an autonomous organization in November 1961, as the International Computation Centre (ICC). In 1969, the designation Intergovernmental Bureau for Informatics was added to the original name. This new name signified a change in operating policy, particularly with regard to the promotion of informatics in developing countries. In 1975, this was further reflected by dropping the International Computation Centre from the name.

Organizational Structure. The General Assembly, which consists of a representative of each member state of IBI and a representative of UNESCO, is the supreme body of government and meets every two years. The Executive Council, which is composed of six persons elected by the General Assembly and a UNESCO representative, meets twice a year, and is responsible for the program of IBI and administrative and financial matters.

The Director, who is appointed by the General Assembly, conducts the work of the organization in accordance with General Assembly Directives and at the direction of the Executive Council. The current and previous directors of the organization are

Stig Comet	1962–63
Claude Berge	1964–67
L. A. Lombardi	1967–68
Prof. F. A. Bernasconi	1969–

IBI headquarters is at 23 Viale Civiltà del Lavoro, 00144 Roma, Italy.

Technical Program. The activities of IBI center on the following technical programs.

1. Organization of conferences and seminars at an international level.
2. Promotion and organization of regional training courses on the use of informatics at governmental level.
3. Promotion of the use of informatics in the field of management through training courses on the technology and the management of information systems at national and regional levels.
4. Assistance in the creation of regional centers to conduct training, education, and research in informatics.
5. Cooperation with universities and education centers in formulating programs on informatics and in carrying them out by means of direct technical assistance.
6. Action on important research and development projects that cannot be implemented other than on an intergovernmental and interdisciplinary basis.
7. A research grant program designed to grant subventions to research and educational institutes operating in developing countries in the field of informatics, or to institutes operating in industrialized countries for projects to be utilized in developing countries.
8. A fellowship program designed to permit professionals from member countries to participate in courses, conferences, and seminars.

In addition to its own program an IBI/UNESCO Joint Program is being developed. The IBI also administers a Special Fund of Informatics for Development (SFIDE), which is included in the general program. SFIDE resources are made up by contributions from computer manufacturers, institutions, and organizations interested in the promotion of informatics as a tool for development. It is used basically for organization of conferences and courses, for fellowships, scholarships, and technical assistance to developing countries.

I. L. AUERBACH

INTERLEAVING

For articles on related subjects *see* ACCESS TIME; and MEMORY: Main.

In systems with more than one autonomous memory module, considerable advantage in system speed may be acquired by arranging that sequential memory addresses occur in different modules. By this means the total time taken to access a sequence of memory locations can be much reduced, since several memory accesses may be overlapped by a high-speed CPU. Two-way and four-way interleaving are commonly encountered.

Assume, for example, a memory with 0.6 μs access time (i.e., the time to get a word from memory to the processor) and a 1.2 μs cycle (i.e., the time after the initiation of an access before the memory can be accessed again), and a processor requiring 0.2 μs to prepare a memory request and a further 0.2 μs to handle the result. Also assume processor and memory overlap.

Under these conditions, as illustrated in Fig. 1, a sequence of four memory accesses would take 4.6 μs with no interleaving, 2.4 μs with two-way interleaving, and 1.6 μs with four-way interleaving. Notice in this example that four-way interleaving provides a smaller incremental advantage than does the two-way. This is a result of the particular choice made of CPU and memory timing, which happens to be fairly well suited for two-way interleaving. Notice further that four-way interleaving leaves the CPU fully occupied (at least as far as the example goes). The result is that more than four-way interleaving in this example will provide no increase in speed. The system speed for four-way (or more) interleaving has become CPU-limited rather than memory-limited, as is the case shown in Fig. 1(a).

For very high-speed CPUs (particularly those involving *lookahead*), for multiple CPUs, and for block transfers to cache memory, it is possible to keep many modules busy simultaneously. Up to 32 interleaved modules have been reported.

K. C. SMITH AND A. S. SEDRA

REFERENCES

1978. Hamacher, V. C., Vranesic, Z. G., and Zaky, S. G., *Computer Organization*. New York: McGraw-Hill, pp. 243–245.

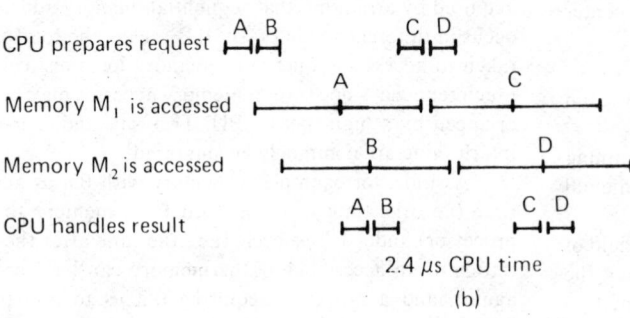

4.6 μs CPU time

(a)

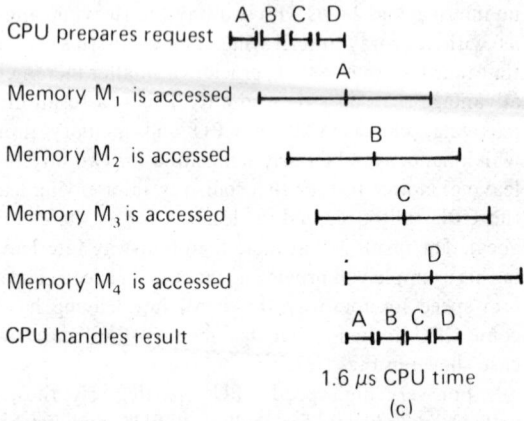

2.4 μs CPU time

(b)

1.6 μs CPU time

(c)

Fig. 1.   Timing diagram, showing a sequence of four memory accesses (A,B,C,D) in a speed-limited memory system with (a) no interleaving, (b) two-way interleaving, and (c) four-way interleaving. (Time scale is 0.2μs per division.)

INTERLOCK

For articles on related subjects *see* CONCURRENT PROGRAMMING; DEADLOCK; MEMORY: MAIN; PETRI NETS; and SEMAPHORE.

Interlock is a mechanism implemented in hardware or software which is intended to coordinate activity of two or more processes within a computing system. This mechanism generally insures that one process has reached a suitable state such that the other may proceed. In the event that two processes use a common resource (memory, for instance), interlock will guarantee that only one request is honored at a time, and perhaps that some discipline, such as first-come-first-served, is observed.

In many cases, the mechanism communicates with each process using *flags,* which are memory elements set and read either through software or hardware. A common problem concerns the relative timing of setting and interrogating the flags, and of the start of subsequent action. The problem is further complicated by the fact that asynchronous (time-uncoordinated) processes may be observing each other and must decide on a future course of action based on a snapshot observation. Often the interlock mechanism is an important part of the timing of each process; hence, it should be very fast.

One solution to interlock incorporates a polling mechanism where the appropriate conditions of each process are interrogated in turn and decisions are reached in a corresponding fixed order or priority. This scheme, though easily implemented either in hardware or software, requires a separate polling device or program and is wasteful of time, particularly when conflict is unlikely.

A hardware approach to arbitrating between requests from two processes (e.g., CPUs) for a shared resource (e.g., memory) is shown in Fig. 1. Normally, both inputs (request A and request B), are zero, setting the interlock flip-flop into the (1,1) output state and inhibiting both selection gates via the inverting threshold elements. When either request A or B is raised *separately,* the flip-flop establishes the corresponding (0,1) state, selecting the corresponding selection gate and generating a signal connecting the resource to the requester. If, for example, request B is raised while A is up, the connection to A is unaffected, and a suitable busy signal is returned to process B.

If both A and B requests occur *simultaneously,* the effect is to change both outputs of the interlock flip-flop from one to zero at once. By virtue of the feedback, shown in Fig. 1, an oscillation will be produced in which the outputs of the interlock flip-flop change in phase at a very high frequency. The amplitude of the oscillation is so small that the threshold of the detectors following can be set to ignore it.

Eventually, due to minute timing differences in the inputs, random electrical noise, circuit asymmetry, etc., the circuit will establish a stable state in which one and only one of the requests is honored. In practice, this oscillatory decision process occurs very rarely. In one study conducted using 10 ns logic, oscillation of any significance was observed only when input signals were within 100 ps of simultaneity. For signals within 10 ps of simultaneity, oscillation was maintained for about 1 μs before a decision was reached.

A. S. Sedra and K. C. Smith

INTERNATIONAL ASSOCIATION FOR MATHEMATICS AND COMPUTERS IN SIMULATION (IMACS)

For articles on related subjects *see* ANALOG COMPUTERS; and SIMULATION.

The object of the International Association for Mathematics and Computers in Simulation (IMACS), until 1976 called the International Association for Analog Computation, is to facilitate the exchange of scientific information among specialists, builders, or users interested in analog and hybrid computation methods by periodically organizing international meetings, displays of equipment and works, by issuing scientific publications and establishing frequent contacts with scientific associ-

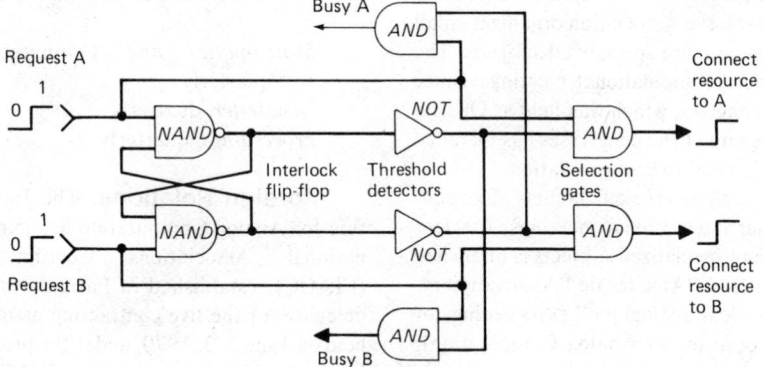

Fig. 1.   A high-speed interlock mechanism for arbitrating between two asynchronous requests for a single resource.

ations in the whole world for the study of arithmetical methods of computation.

How Established. The Association was established in response to a proposal of the presidents of the sessions of the first International Meeting for Analog Computation, 26 September to 2 October 1955. Professor J. Hoffmann, chairman and organizer of the meeting, was elected as a provisional chairman of the Managing Committee of the new Association.

The Association has a constitution approved by a Belgian royal decree dated 20 February 1956. During the second International Congress of Analog Computation in Strasbourg during 1958, Professor Hoffmann was confirmed, and since then he has been reelected by each of the general assemblies up to 1980.

Organizational Structure. According to the statutes, the Managing Committee is composed of a minimum of 6 and a maximum of 15 members, selected internationally from among specialists in experimental mathematics. At least one member, a chairman or a vice-chairman, must be of Belgian nationality. There may not be four members of the same nationality belonging to the committee.

The Association is composed of individuals and associated members (industrial firms and public administrations, institutes for research and training), of delegates appointed by the associated members, and, finally, of some honorary members.

The seat of the Association is established in Brussels, and at present is at H496 Ave. Moliere, B-1060, Brussels. A few individual members have agreed to be official delegates of the Association in their respective countries.

Technical Program. According to its rules, the Association organizes an international congress every three years, followed by a general assembly, which elects one-third of the members of the Managing Committee. Between such congresses, the Association organizes small international meetings on more specialized subjects. The Association also supports some national meetings. Since the time of the third congress, which was held at Opatija (Yugoslavia), the program of the congresses has included methods of computation and hybrid simulation.

The Association publishes the official acts of its congresses and of its other international meetings. A scientific publication on more specialized subjects is published quarterly under the title of "Annales de l'Association internationale pour le Calcul analogique" (Proceedings of the International Association for Analog Computation), with a subtitle: "Revue internationale des methodes de Calcul et de Simulation Hybrids" (Hybrid Computer

Simulation). All publications are written in the language of their authors. The official languages of the Association are French, English, and German.

Congresses of the Association were held as follows.

Brussels, 26 September to 2 October 1955
Strasbourg, France, 1–6 September 1958
Opatija, Yugoslavia, 5–8 September 1961
Brighton, Great Britain, 14–18 September 1964
Lausanne, Switzerland, 28 August to 2 September 1967
Munich, West Germany, 31 August to 4 September 1970
Prague, Czechoslovakia, 26–31 August 1973
Delft, Netherlands, 1976
Sorrento, Italy, 1979

The tenth international congress is to be held in Boston, MA, in August 1982.

The Association has also organized the following small meetings (colloquia) and seminars.

Brussels, 21–23 April 1960: Seminar on analog methods in nuclear energy problems.
Brussels, 21–23 November 1960: Seminar on analog computation applied to the study of chemical processes.
Paris, 28–30 May 1962: Colloquium on modern techniques of industrial computation and automation.
Liege, 9–12 September 1963: Symposium on analog and digital techniques applied to automation.
Versailles, 16–18 September 1968: Symposium on analog and hybrid computation applied to nuclear energy.
Tokyo, 3–7 September 1971: Symposium on the simulation of complex systems.

Publications of the Association are

Mathematics and Computers in Simulation, quarterly
Newsletter, quarterly
Proceedings, quarterly

Foreign Relations. The International Association for Analog Computation has joined the "Five International Associations Coordinating Committee" (FIACC), established in Paris during a meeting of the delegates of the five contracting associations, which was held on June 2–3, 1970, under the presidency of Professor Victor Broida, chairman of the IFAC. The five members of the international federation include the following.

IMACS, International Association for Mathematics and Computers in Simulation

IFAC, International Federation of Automatic Control

IFIP, International Federation for Information Processing

IFORS, International Federation of Operational Research Societies

IMEKO, International Measurement Confederation

I. L. AUERBACH

INTERNATIONAL FEDERATION OF AUTOMATIC CONTROL (IFAC)

For article on related subject *see* INTERNATIONAL FEDERATION FOR INFORMATION PROCESSING.

The International Federation of Automatic Control (IFAC) is a multinational federation of national member organizations, each one of which represents the engineering and scientific societies that are concerned with automatic control in their respective countries. At present, 40 countries (see Table 1) have formed appropriate national member organizations and joined IFAC.

IFAC is concerned with advancing the science and technology of control—which in the broad sense includes engineering, physical, biological, social and economic systems—and in promoting the dissemination of information about such systems throughout the world. The primary means for accomplishing these aims are:

1. International congresses, held every three years.
2. Between congresses, IFAC sponsors many symposia covering particular aspects of control systems, with topics ranging from "Automatic Control in Space," to "Systems Approaches to Developing Countries."
3. The IFAC Journal *Automatica,* which publishes both selected papers from symposia in expanded form, and original material of particular interest.

IFAC is also concerned with the impact of this advancing technology on society. The technical committee on the Social Effects of Automation acts as the focal point for the collection and dissemination of information in this field.

IFAC takes an active role in public affairs, making its broad technical expertise available to the United Nations family and other international and regional organizations. The IFAC Committee on Public Affairs maintains technical liaison with agencies such as the Office of Science and Technology of the United Nations, and nominates representatives to serve as advisors and consultants on a task basis.

How Established. IFAC came into existence because scientists and engineers working in the field of automatic control realized their need to become more closely associated to exchange information regarding their activities. In 1956, at an International Symposium on Automatic Control at Heidelberg, V. Broida (France), O. Grebe (FGR), A. M. Letov (USSR), P. J. Nowacki (Poland), R. Oldenburger (U.S.), and J. Welbourn (U.K.) formed the Organizing Committee of IFAC, with Dr. Broida as president and Dr. G. Ruppel as secretary. A general assembly was convened in Paris, France, and on 12 September 1957, IFAC became a reality with 19 member organizations. The constitution and bylaws were adopted in London on 21 June 1966.

The presidents of IFAC have been

Dr. Harold Chestnut (U.S.), 1957–1959
Prof. Dr. A. M. Letov (USSR), 1959–1961
Prof. E. Gerecke (Switzerland), 1961–1963
Prof. J. F. Coales (U.K.), 1963–1966
Dr. P. J. Nowacki (Poland), 1966–1969
Dr. V. Broida (France), 1969–1972
Mr. J. C. Lozier (U.S.), 1972–1975
Mr. U. A. Luoto (Finland), 1975–1978
Prof. Y. Sawaragi (Japan), 1978–1981

Organizational Structure. IFAC is governed by a general assembly, consisting of delegates from each national member organization, which meets during the triennial congresses. Between congresses, the federation is run by an Executive Council, headed by the president, and elected for three years. The day-to-day work of IFAC is administered by the secretariat, whose address is IFAC, Schlossplatz 12, A-2361 Laxenburg, Austria. The legal seat of IFAC is in Geneva, Switzerland.

Technical Program. The technical activities of IFAC are carried on primarily by technical committees, which play a major role in the generation of the technical program for the triennial congresses. The initiative for generating symposia on appropriate topics in their respective fields also lies with the technical committees. The list of technical committees is as follows.

1. Applications
2. Biomedical Engineering
3. Components and Instruments
4. Computers

Table 1. IFAC National Member Organizations

Dem. People's Rep. of Algeria	Commissariat Nationale à l'Informatique (C.N.I.)
Argentina	Asociación Argentina de Control Automático (AADECA)
Australia	The Institution of Engineers Australia
Austria	Österreichisches Zentrum für Wirtschaftlichkeit und Produktivität Abt. Automatisierung-Technische Entwicklung
Belgium	Federation IBRA/BIRA
Brazil	Sociedade Brasileira de Automatica (SBA)
Bulgaria	The National Centre of Cybernetics and Computer Technique of the Committee for Science and Technical Progress
Canada	Associate Committee on Automatic Control, National Research Council
People's Rep. of China	Chinese Association of Automation
Cuba	Centro de Automatización Industrial
Czechoslovakia CSSR	Czechoslovak National Committee for IFAC
Denmark	Danish Automation Society
Egypt	The General Organization for Industrialization
Fed. Rep. of Germany	VDI/VDE-Gesellschaft für Mess- und Regelungstechnik
Finland	The Finnish Society of Automatic Control
France	Association Française pour la Cybernétique Economique et Technique (AFCET)
German Dem. Rep.	Wissenschaftlich-Technische Gesellschaft für Mess- und Automatisierungstechnik in der Kammer der Technik der Deutschen Demokratischen Republik
Greece	Technical Chamber of Greece
Hungary	Computer and Automation Institute, Hungarian Academy of Sciences
India	The Institution of Engineers (India)
Iran	Iranian Society of Automatic Control Engineers (ISACE)
Israel	Israel Committee for Automatic Control
Italy	GNASII-CNR
Japan	National Committee of Automatic Control, Science Council of Japan
Dem. People's Rep. of Korea	The Korean General Federation of Industrial Technology Automation Association
Mexico	Mexican Association for Automatic Control (Asociacion Mexicana de Control Automatico-AMCA)
Morocco	Association Marocaine pour le Développement de l'Automatique (A.MA.D.E.I.A.)
Netherlands	Koninklijk Instituut van Ingenieurs
Norway	Norsk Forening for Automatisering
Poland	Polski Komitet Pomiarow i Automatyki, Naczelna Organizacja Techniczna w Polsce
Socialist Rep. of Rumania	Comisia de Automatizare
Republic of South Africa	South African Council for Automation and Computation
Spain	Comité Español de la IFAC
Sweden	Svenska Kommitten för IFAC
Switzerland	Schweizerische Gesellschaft für Automatik
Turkey	Türk Otomatik Kontrol Kurumu
United Kingdom (U.K.)	United Kingdom Automation Control Council
U.S.A.	American Automatic Control Council
Union of Soviet Socialist Republics (USSR)	USSR National Committee on Automatic Control
Yugoslavia	Yugoslav Committee for Electronics and Automation

5. Developing Countries
6. Economic and Management Systems
7. Education
8. Manufacturing Technology
9. Mathematics of Control
10. Social Effects of Automation
11. Space
12. Systems Engineering
13. Terminology and Standards
14. Theory

Conferences and Symposia. IFAC has had seven congresses: in Moscow, 1960; Basel, 1963; London, 1966; Warsaw, 1969; Paris, 1972; Cambridge, MA, 1975; Helsinki, Finland, 1978; Kyoto, Japan, 1981.

Full proceedings of the congresses and most of the symposium papers have been published.

I. L. AUERBACH

INTERNATIONAL FEDERATION FOR INFORMATION PROCESSING (IFIP)

For articles on related subjects *see* AMERICAN FEDERATION OF INFORMATION PROCESSING SOCIETIES; and INTERNATIONAL FEDERATION OF AUTOMATIC CONTROL.

The International Federation for Information Processing is a multinational federation of professional-technical societies (or groups of such societies) concerned with information processing. In any country, only one such society or group—which must be representative of the national activities in the information processing field—can be admitted as a full member. As of 1 January 1980, 39 national societies were members of the federation, as follows;

Country	Society
Algeria	Commissariat National a l'Informatique
Argentina	Sociedad Argentina de Informática
Australia	Australian Computer Society
Austria	Austrian Computer Society
Belgium	FAIB-FBVI
Brazil	Sociedade dos Usuários de Computadores e Equipamentos Subsidiários (SUCESU)
Bulgaria	Bulgarian Academy of Sciences
Canada	Canadian Information Processing Society
China, Peoples Rep. of	Chinese Institute of Electronics
Cuba	Academia de Ciencias de Cuba
Czechoslovakia	Czechoslovak National Committee
Denmark	Danish Federation for Information Processing
Egypt	Egyptian Computer Society
Finland	Finnish Association for Data Processing
France	Association Française pour la Cybernétique Economique et Technique (AFCET)
German Democratic Republic	Academy of Sciences of the German Democratic Republic
Germany, Federal Republic of	Deutsche Arbeitsgemeinschaft für Rechenanlagen (DARA)
Hungary	John von Neumann Society
India	Computer Society of India
Iraq	Planning Board/National Computer Centre
Ireland	Irish Computer Society
Israel	Information Processing Association of Israel (IPA)
Italy	Associazione Italiana per il Calcolo Automatico (AICA)
Japan	Information Processing Society of Japan
Korea, Rep. of	Korea Information Science Society
Morocco	Association Marocaine pour le Développement de l'Electronique et de l'Automatique (AMADEIA)
Netherlands	Nederlands Rekenmachine Genootschap
New Zealand	The New Zealand Computer Society
Nigeria	Computer Association of Nigeria
Norway	Norwegian Computer Society
Poland	Polish Academy of Sciences
Portugal	Associacão Portuguesa de Informática
South Africa	Computer Society of South Africa
Spain	Federacion Espanola de Sociedades de Informatica
Sweden	Swedish Society for Information Processing
Switzerland	Federation Suisse d'Informatique
Tunisia	Centre National de l'Informatique
United Kingdom	British Computer Society
U.S.A.	American Federation of Information Processing Societies (AFIPS)
USSR	The Computing Centre of the USSR Academy of Sciences
Yugoslavia	Yugoslav Committee for Electronics and Automation (ETAN)

The aims of IFIP are:

1. To promote information science and technology.
2. To advance international cooperation in the field of information processing.
3. To stimulate research, development, and application of information processing in science and in human activity.
4. To further the dissemination and exchange of information on information processing.
5. To encourage education in information processing.

IFIP is both a catalyst and a focal point for conceptual and technological developments that advance the state of the information processing art, thereby accelerating technical and scientific progress. It also performs a vital function in working toward the maximum dissemination of significant information about the digital computer and its applications.

How Established. The genesis of IFIP took place in June 1959 at the UNESCO-sponsored First International Conference on Information Processing in Paris. As conference chairman, Professor Howard H. Aiken stated at the conference in his closing speech, "The suggestion to hold this meeting was originated by Mr. Isaac L. Auerbach on behalf of the (U.S.) Joint Computer Committee in the form of a letter to Professor Pierre Auger, UNESCO. The importance of the subject and of the proposal made was such that UNESCO acted immediately and this conference was called."

Even before the success of this conference was confirmed, it was apparent in the planning sessions that future international meetings and other activities were essential to the worldwide development of information sciences. A committee was organized under the leadership of Isaac L. Auerbach (U.S.), to draft appropriate statutes and lay the foundation for future activities. The members of this committee were: J. Carteron, France; S. Comet, Sweden; A. Panov, USSR; J. G. Santesmases, Spain; A. Walther, West Germany; A. van Wijngaarden, Netherlands; M. V. Wilkes, U.K.; and H. Yamashita, Japan.

During the First International Conference on Information Processing, Paris, in June 1958, representatives of 18 national computer societies met to formulate the preliminary structure of IFIP. Statutes for the federation were reviewed and, in the months that followed, were ratified by 13 national societies—6 more than the minimum required. IFIP came into official existence on 1 January 1960.

The Presidents of IFIP have been the following.

Isaac L. Auerbach (U.S.) 1960–1965
Ambros P. Speiser (Switzerland) 1965–1968
A. A. Dorodnicyn (USSR) 1968–1971
Heinz Zemanek (Austria) 1971–1974
Richard I. Tanaka (U.S.) 1974–1977
Pierre A. Bobillier (Switzerland) 1977–

Organizational Structure. The supreme authority of IFIP is the General Assembly, which meets annually. It is made up of one representative from each of the member societies; the presidents of two Associate Members, IAG (IFIP Applied Information Processing Group) and IMIA (International Medical Informatics Association); the presidents of two Affiliate Members, IAPR (International Association for Pattern Recognition and IASC (International Association for Statistical Computing); and three Honorary Life Members, Isaac L. Auerbach, Heinz Zemanek, and Richard I. Tanaka.

The executive body of IFIP is composed of the officers: The president, three vice-presidents, the secretary, and the treasurer. These officers are elected by the General Assembly. The day-to-day work of IFIP is administered by a Secretariat, whose address is 3 rue du Marche, 1204 Geneva, Switzerland.

The Council, consisting of the officers and up to eight elected trustees, meets twice a year and makes decisions which become necessary between General Assembly meetings.

Technical Committees. In a continuing program devoted to a common basis for the worldwide development of the information sciences, IFIP has established a number of Technical Committees (TC) and Working Groups (WG), the influence of which are strongly felt at international as well as national levels.

Each Technical Committee is composed of representatives of the IFIP Member Societies (one per society), whereas Working Groups, under the supervision of a Technical Committee, consist of specialists in the field who are appointed as individuals independent of nationality.

The following Technical Committees and Working Groups are currently in operation.

	Area of Work
TC 2	*Programming*
WG 2.1	Algol
WG 2.2	Formal Description of Programming Concepts
WG 2.3	Programming Methodology
WG 2.4	System Implementation Languages
WG 2.5	Numerical Software
WG 2.6	Databases
WG 2.7	Operating System Interfaces
TC 3	*Education*

WG 3.1	Informatics Education at the Secondary Education Level
WG 3.2	Advanced Curriculum Projects in Information Processing
WG 3.3	Instructional Uses of Computers
WG 3.4	Post-Secondary Education and Vocational Training
TC 4	*Health Care and Biomedical Research* (with working groups now part of International Medical Informatics Association)
TC 5	*Computer Applications in Technology*
WG 5.1	Transporation Systems
WG 5.2	Computer-Aided Design
WG 5.3	Discrete Manufacturing
WG 5.4	Common and/or Standardized Hardware and Software Techniques
WG 5.6	Maritime Industries
WG 5.7	Automation of Production Planning and Control
TC 6	*Data Communication*
WG 6.1	International Packet-Switching for Computer Sharing
WG 6.3	Human-Computer Communications
WG 6.4	Local Computer Networks
WG 6.5	International Computer Message Systems
TC 7	*System Modeling and Optimization*
WG 7.1	Modeling and Simulation
WG 7.2	Computational Techniques in Distributed Systems
WG 7.3	Computer System Modeling
TC 8	*Information Systems*
WG 8.1	Design and Evaluation of Information Systems
WG 8.2	The Interaction of Information Systems and the Organization
TC 9	*Relationship Between Computers and Society*
WG 9.1	Computers and Work
WG 9.2	Social Accountability
TC 10	*Digital Systems Design*
WG 10.1	System Concepts and Characteristics
WG 10.2	Digital Systems Descriptions and Design Tools
WG 10.3	Software/Hardware Interrelation

The IFIP International Applications Group (IAG), which emphasizes administrative data processing, was established in 1967 as a special-interest group to serve the needs of the administrative data processing community to promote research, education, and the exchange of experience in the field of information processing as applied to problems in public and business administration. IAG conducts an extensive educational program. Its headquarters is located at 6 Stadhouderskade, Amsterdam, Netherlands.

The International Medical Informatics Association (IMIA), an extension of TC 4, was formed as a special interest group in May 1979 to address the special needs of the use of the computer for information processing in medicine. The Third World Conference on Medical Informatics (MEDINFO 80) was held in Tokyo in September 1980. Previous conferences were in Stockholm (1974) and Toronto (1977).

Affiliations of IFIP. IFIP was founded under the auspices of UNESCO and has had official relationships with UNESCO since inception. IFIP has the status of category B ("able to advise in a particular field"). IFIP was admitted into official relations with the World Health Organization in February 1972 and maintains informal relationships with most other members of the UN family, including the UN in New York.

IFIP has the status of a Scientific Affiliate of the International Council of Scientific Unions (ICSU). ICSU on its behalf maintains relations with UNESCO in category A ("proven competence in an important field of UNESCO's work").

In 1970, IFIP together with four related federations, IMACS, IFAC, IFORS, and IMEKO, established a "Five International Associations Coordinating Committee" (FIACC) which is the basis for cordial and successful coordination of activities and a yearly opportunity for the exchange of thoughts and experiences.

IFIP also participates in an advisory capacity in the work of CCITT, the Comité Consultatif International Télégraphique and Téléphonique.

IFIP Congresses. The main event in the IFIP program of activities is its Congress, held every three years. An IFIP Congress is an international occasion which attracts information scientists, managers, and administrators from all over the world to listen, to learn, to educate, and to exchange ideas with their colleagues from other countries.

The first Congress was held in Munich, Germany, in 1962. Others have been held in New York City, U.S. (1965); in Edinburgh, Scotland (1968); in Ljubljana, Yugoslavia (1971); in Stockholm, Sweden (1974); and in Toronto, Canada (1977). IFIP Congress '80 was held in Tokyo, Japan and Melbourne, Australia in October 1980.

In addition to these major Congresses, IFIP's technical committees organize a large number of international working conferences. The papers presented are published and form a comprehensive library recording the development of information processing, as well as the current state of the art.

I. L. AUERBACH

INTERPRETER

For articles on related subjects *see* COMPILE AND RUN TIME; COMPILER; LANGUAGE PROCESSORS; MACRO LANGUAGES; and MICROPROGRAMMING.

Interpretation and translation are the two basic processes involved in getting results from a computer program. An *interpreter* transforms a program directly into a sequence of machine actions, whereas a *translator* (e.g., a compiler) transforms a program written in a language *L* (e.g., Fortran) into an equivalent program in a language *L'* (e.g., a machine language). *L'* will later be further processed; e.g., by an interpreter.

It is common to distinguish between software and hardware interpreters. A hardware interpreter consists of the circuits of a computer which execute machine language instructions. Hence, execution by hardware is a special case of interpretation. A software interpreter is a program which runs on a given machine and which executes the statements of a high-level programming language such as APL, Lisp, Snobol, or of the machine language of another computer *M*. In the latter case, the software interpreter is called a simulator for *M*.

Given a source language program *P* written in a high-level language and a computer *M*, there are three basic ways to have *M* execute the actions described in *P*.

1. *Hardware interpreter.* The source program *P* is translated by a compiler into machine language for *M*, which is executed by the hardware interpreter of *M*.

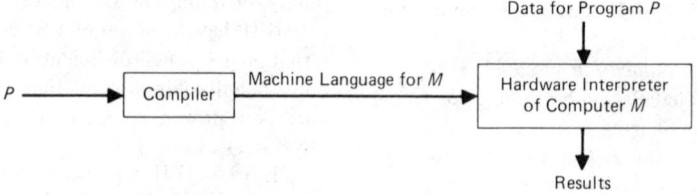

2. *Software interpreter: Interpretation of intermediate language.* The source program is translated into an intermediate language that is interpreted by a software interpreter which runs on computer *M*. Often, the intermediate language is the machine language of a hypothetical "ideal" computer which is simulated on a real machine.

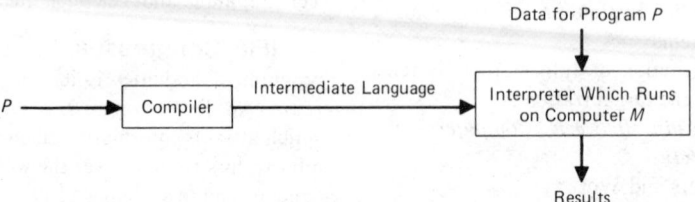

3. *Software interpreter: Interpretation of source language.* The source program is interpreted directly by a software interpreter which runs on computer *M*.

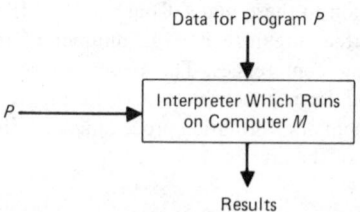

Method 1 is often used for languages such as C, Fortran, Pascal, or PL/1. The major advantage is fast execution.

An example of a programming system that is based on method 2 is the UCSD Pascal system (Bowles, 1978). Because the semiconductor industry is evolving new equipment very fast, it is becoming a practical necessity to have (nearly) machine-independent software. The UCSD Pascal system is built on a small hypothetical machine (known as the P-machine, which was originally developed at ETH Zurich). Therefore, to transfer the system to a new computer essentially involves only writing the P-machine interpreter in the machine language of the new computer. Today, P-machines are also available in hardware.

The P-machine is a stack-oriented computer; e.g., the Pascal statement A:=B+C translated to P-machine form looks like this:

```
lod b   [load B onto stack]
lod c   [load C onto stack]
adi
sto a   [store top element of stack into A]
```

ADI is the instruction which adds the two topmost elements on the stack and stores their integer sum as topmost element.

Method 3 is often used for languages such as APL, Lisp, or Snobol and for the interpretation of command languages such as job control languages. The major advantages are memory economy (no machine or intermediate code has to be stored) and the relative simplicity of programming, but the execution is slow.

For more information see Calingaert (1979).

REFERENCES

1978. Bowles, Kenneth L. "UCSD Pascal," *Byte,* p. 46 (May).
1979. Calingaert, Peter. *Assemblers, Compilers, and Program Translation.* Potomac, MD: Computer Science Press.

K. LIEBERHEER

INTERRUPT

For articles on related subjects *see* CHANNEL; INTERVAL TIMER; OPERATING SYSTEMS; PRIVILEGED INSTRUCTION; PROGRAM STATUS WORD AND STATE VECTOR; and SUPERVISOR CALL.

The capability to *interrupt* a program, an important feature of most modern computer systems, permits them to respond quickly to events that occur at unpredictable times. Some events of this type are signals generated by instruments or sensors monitoring some industrial or laboratory process, or a user at a teletype or video terminal signaling the end of a typed message that requires computer analysis and response. The response to an interrupt is the invocation of a responding program and, in this respect, an interrupt resembles other means of changing the flow of program control such as a linkage to a subroutine. The essential difference in the case of interrupt is the great diversity of interrupt events and their unpredictability.

An interrupt facility is very common in most operating systems and real-time applications. It not only enables a computer to communicate with a rich variety of external devices, but is also helpful to the system in managing its own device and program resources. Although basically implemented by hardware, the logical power of interrupts is also provided in a convenient form to users of some modern programming languages, as by the ON type of statement in PL/I.

Each event that can cause an interrupt generates an "interrupt request" that can be visualized as a 1 or 0 signal on a physical line indicating whether the request is active or not. To respond to an interrupt request, the current CPU (central processing unit) program must be stopped gracefully (i.e., *interrupted*) and the CPU then switched to a program designed to service the interrupt request. Interrupts are thus a mechanism which enables several logically unrelated programs to time-share a single CPU and, thereby, other computer resources.

General Functional Features. There are many computer architectures, each with its own interrupt scheme. Despite this great diversity in detail and also in terminology, there are certain commonalities:

1. Storage of interrupt requests.
2. Program-controlled enabling and masking.
3. Saving the program state.
4. Forced branch to a new program.
5. Cause-identification.
6. State restoration.

Item 1 refers to the need to store requests until serviced, since the CPU can respond to only one request at a time. Item 2's purpose is to provide a means for the program to "paralyze" the interrupt-response mechanism at certain awkward times, such as when a previously recognized interrupt is already being serviced. Item 3 refers to the graceful suspension of the current program, "graceful" meaning the program is stopped in such a way that it can be easily resumed later. This involves storing certain CPU registers that must be used by every program, including the one performing the interrupt response. The program counter (PC) is the most vital such register, since it holds the address of the next instruction to be executed. Item 4 is the essence of interrupt—the forced branch to the new responding program. Item 5 refers to the need to be able to identify the cause of the interrupt. Item 6 is required for eventual resumption of the interrupted program.

Microprocessor Examples. A *microprocessor* is a CPU whose circuitry is wholly contained on a single semiconductor chip. Our first example is the rather simple, but widely used, Intel 8080 microprocessor. Its interrupt-related items are

INT—one interrupt request line to the chip
DATA—data lines to the chip
INTE—interrupt-enable flip-flop
PC—program counter (16-bit register)
SP—stack pointer (16-bit register)

Both INT and DATA are connections to the 8080 CPU from the outside world, while INTE, PC, and SP are internal to the CPU. INTE can be set to 1 or 0 by a CPU instruction and controls whether an INT signal can actually cause an interrupt. The PC holds the memory address of the next instruction. The SP holds the memory address of a collection of bytes called a *stack,* used primarily for linking from one program or subroutine to another. CPU instructions can store ("push") a value from a register into the stack by using SP for its address and then decrementing SP. Similarly, a value can be "popped from" the stack to a register by using SP as its access-address and then incrementing the SP value.

An 8080 interrupt will take place only when three conditions are set at the same time: (1) INTE = 1; (2) the CPU has just completed an instruction; (3) INT = 0, indicating an interrupt request. The INT = 0 signal is set by the source of the request, which is also responsible for setting the DATA lines with the bits of an 8080 instruction, as will now be explained.

The 8080 hardware interrupt response consists of executing the single instruction on the DATA lines. The requesting source of interrupt usually supplies the instruction RESTART (RST) on these lines because this instruction contains three bits that can identify the interrupt request. More specifically, when the interrupt is taken, the RST instruction supplied on the DATA lines is executed as follows: (1) the PC is pushed into the stack, then (2) three *a* bits are taken from the eight bits on the data line and these are used to respecify PC as follows.

$$PC = 0000000000aaa000$$

By inserting the source-identifying *a* bits, as shown, into the PC, a branch is forced to one of eight locations in the first 64 cells of memory. In this way, each request can specify one of eight starting locations for its response program. The programmer must, of course, have prestored the start of the appropriate interrupt-response routine at each of these locations. After the interrupt response is complete, the CPU may return to the interrupted program by executing instructions to "pop" the stack to the PC and restore other saved register values of the interrupted program.

Our second example, the Zilog Z80 microprocessor, has several improvements over the 8080, including a more general interrupt system. The Z80 has one non-maskable interrupt request; i.e., one not controlled by INTE. This permits the machine always to be sensitive to a very serious event, such as an imminent power failure. In addition, there are three program-controlled modes. Mode 0 is identical to the 8080's interrupt system to allow 8080 programs to run on the Z80. Mode 1 provides a fixed interrupt to a single designated location. Mode 2 is a "vectored" interrupt wherein the PC is pushed into the stack and then the PC is replaced as follows

$$PC = i\,i\,i\,i\,i\,i\,i\,i\,ddddddd\,0$$

where the *i* bits are supplied by a CPU I register and the seven *d* bits are supplied to the DATA lines by the requesting source. The I register thus allows the interrupt-branch list to be located anywhere in memory (on 256-byte boundaries), while the *d* bits permit 128 possible cause-identifiers that are also interrupt-response locations. In contrast, the 8080 provides only eight locations and requires the interrupt branch list to be located in locations 0–63 of memory.

A Large Machine Example. A large computer tends to have a more elaborate interrupt scheme than, say, a microprocessor, in keeping with the greater number, variety, and complexity of its peripheral (I/O) devices and its need for high speed.

Fig. 1 shows a highly simplified version of the scheme used in the IBM 360/370 systems. The large number of interrupt request lines are subdivided into several mask-groups, the members of each group sharing one mask bit. A mask bit controls whether the request will be permitted to cause an interrupt or not. The mask bits are intended to give program control over which requests can be allowed to cause an interrupt at any given time. A special case occurs when all mask bits are 0, which inhibits all interrupts. This might be done by the operating system during certain interrupt response activities.

The interrupt mask bits, the PC (called the instruction address), and several other items relating to program sequencing and interrupt are "packaged" into a single 64-bit quantity called the PSW (program status word) that can be stored and reset in one operation (as will be seen shortly).

The circled numbers in Fig. 1 indicate relative time of events in the interrupt process. The request lines are combined with their mask bits at time 1. If any unmasked pending requests are found, this generates a master interrupt request. Also, the priority logic acts during this interval to select the highest priority request, which is then identified by the encoder logic, and this identity is

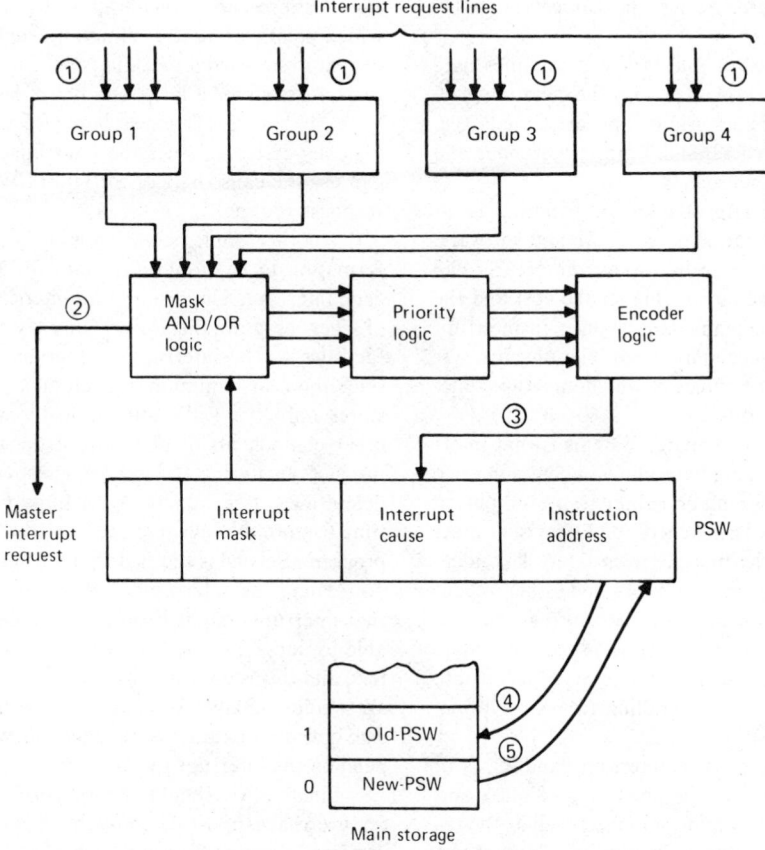

Fig. 1. A simple interrupt system. The circled numbers indicate relative event times.

then stored in the PSW at time 3. The CPU will respond to the master request at the end of the current instruction (but, in System 370, interrupts are permitted before the end of certain long-duration instructions). The interrupt itself consists of storing the PSW into a fixed area of memory called the "Old-PSW" (at memory location 1 in this example). Then the PSW is reset from the "New-PSW" (at memory location 0). Since the New-PSW respecifies the mask bits as well as the instruction address (PC), any mask can be set by prestoring its bits into location 0. The cause of interrupt is available to the response program in the Old-PSW at location 1.

Interrupt Request Classes. Interrupt requests may usually be categorized as follows.

1. Processor operations
2. Privileged operations
3. Supervisor-call instruction
4. Machine malfunction
5. Input/output
6. Timer
7. External device

Class 1 includes register overflows, divide-checks, illegal operation codes, and address-out-of-bounds. Class 2 refers to those conditions that may arise because many computers reserve certain instructions for a privileged mode of the machine, so that key resource-scheduling and storage-protection instructions can only be executed by the operating system. A class 2 interrupt occurs if execution of any of these privileged instructions is attempted while the machine is not in the privileged mode. Class 3 refers to the ability to initiate an interrupt by a special instruction designed to call directly operating system routines. Classes 4 and 5 are rather obvious in principle and will not be discussed further. Class 6 refers to an interval timer that can be set to any reasonable positive value by a machine instruction. Circuitry is provided to automatically decrement this value at regular time intervals and generate an interrupt request when the value reaches zero. Class 7 refers to interrupt requests that may be typically generated by sensor devices, instruments, or relay closures.

The term *synchronous interrupt* is sometimes used for one whose cause is associated with the currently executing instruction, while other interrupts are called *asynchronous*. Thus, classes 1, 2, and 3 are synchronous and the remaining ones asynchronous.

The complete problem of interrupt-handling is always solved by a combination of hardware and software. In general, the more done in hardware, the greater can be the speed of response but the higher the cost and the less the flexibility to accommodate changes in interrupt logic. Because of these economy-speed relationships, systems differ greatly in the choice of which interrupt functions to implement in hardware.

One theme in many computer systems is that interrupts and subroutine linking have much in common since in both cases one program or subprogram is "put to sleep" while another is "awakened" and provision must be made to return to the first program later. This idea, especially evident in microprocessors and other recent computers, leads to both mechanisms sharing common hardware and software logic. Unique aspects of interrupts, due to their time-unpredictability, necessitate hardware support for request-handling (masking, priority, cause-identification).

Much of the complexity of interrupt-handling is in the software, including both the prestoring of mask and New-PSW (or equivalent) information, as well as the responding routines. The software is usually a part of the operating system program that manages the assignment of all hardware/software resources to workload demands. In fact, most operating systems are *interrupt-driven;* i.e., the interrupt system is the mechanism for reporting all changes in resource states; and such changes are the events that induce new assignments. Incidentally, this fact makes interrupt handling an excellent place for monitoring resource-use for performance analysis and billing. Many performance monitors called *tracers* do their jobs by intercepting each interrupt and recording the cause and time of occurrence as a trace record. A stream of such records is a comprehensive log of system activity.

Because of the very close relationship between interrupts and the operating system that handles them, and the very great diversity in operating system logic, it is difficult to discuss the software aspects of interrupt implementation in any generality. For this reason, most of the following discussion is confined to options that appear in hardware implementations in some systems.

The number of request lines is clearly a logic-design decision. Some systems offer a small number as standard; the customer may add more at a modest cost.

The grouping structure is subject to hardware/software/speed trade-offs. We will call each source of New-PSW an interrupt level. Thus, for example, the case of

Fig. 1 represents a one-level system. Since each level, which points to the start of an interrupt service program, constitutes a partial decoding of the interrupt cause, fast response requires a large number of levels. On the other hand, as long as the cause is recorded, only one level is logically essential, since the interrupt-handling program can use the cause-field of the Old-PSW to determine the response routine.

Another implementation issue is the amount of information to be stored automatically (by hardware) at each interrupt. The result of an interrupt is the initiation of a new program that will require the same kind of CPU facilities as the interrupted program. The PSW represents the near-minimum of such facilities; a scheme that stores only the PSW automatically will have to store other components of the state of the CPU by program instructions during the interrupt response. This has two deleterious effects on response time. First is the actual time to store the registers and to reload them for the new program. Second is the fact that during this time the system cannot be interrupted, and it is therefore possible that interrupts might be lost. Maximum speed is attainable by supplying multiple sets of important CPU registers, and this is done in some systems. Sometimes the sets are made available in increments at incremental costs. The optimum number of register sets will, of course, depend on the interrupt speed specifications.

Finally, we should mention a hardware/software feature that is most desirable but is often lacking in an interrupt system. This is the ability to set any interrupt request line by a program instruction, although, of course, normally such requests are generated by natural events. Such program control over requests is a desirable feature for system testing and debugging.

REFERENCES

1962. Buchholz, W. (Ed). *Planning a Computer System*. New York: McGraw-Hill, pp. 136–147.
1973. Hellerman, H. *Digital Computer System Principles* (2nd Ed.). New York: McGraw-Hill, pp. 379–382, 418–424.
1975. *INTEL 8080 Microcomputer System User Manual*. Santa Clara, CA, pp. 2–11.
1978. *Z-80 CPU Technical Manual*. Cupertino, CA, pp. 55–56.

H. HELLERMAN

INTERVAL ARITHMETIC

For articles on related subjects *see* ARITHMETIC, COMPUTER; NUMERICAL ANALYSIS; ROUNDOFF ERROR; and SIGNIFICANT DIGIT.

For as long as numeric computation has been done, there has been a need to assess the accuracy of computed results. The traditional concepts of significant-digit calculation have evolved to meet this need, and are usually applicable in short computations when the quantities involved are largely independent. The starting premise of significant-digit computation is that the accuracy of approximating numbers is inferred from the way in which they are represented; e.g., "correct to within half a unit in the last place quoted." When an arithmetic operation with such numbers has developed a value, a representation must be chosen which implies the accuracy of the computed result. The stringency with which the choice is made depends on whether rigorous or probable (in some sense) error estimates are desired.

Applied pessimistically, significant-digit rules can result in loss of information; applied optimistically, they can lead to unacceptably large errors. For example, if "$x = 1.63$" means that x has some value between 1.625 and 1.635, then x^2 will have some value between 2.640625 and 2.673225. We could choose to represent x^2 as 2.66, 2.7, or 3, but none of these choices is entirely satisfactory. Thus, Paul Dwyer proposed in 1951 that *range arithmetic*, a modification of significant-digit arithmetic providing finer resolution, be employed to prevent loss of information while retaining an indication of accuracy. This kind of computation is now called *interval arithmetic*.

Rather than deal with approximations to variables, in interval arithmetic we suppose that lower and upper bounds are known; i.e., each datum is contained somewhere within a closed interval on the real line. Then each arithmetic operation can compute an interval result containing all values that could have resulted from operating on any numbers selected from the interval operands.

Suppose, given variables x and y, we wish to compute $z = x + y$. If exact values of x and y are not available, but we know instead that $a \leqslant x \leqslant b$ and $c \leqslant y \leqslant d$, then the rules of arithmetic inequalities tell us that $a + c \leqslant x + y \leqslant b + d$. If we now designate by X, Y, and Z the intervals in which x, y, and z are known to be contained, we could write $X = [a, b]$, $Y = [c, d]$, and $Z = X + Y = [a + c, b + d]$. Thus, we have defined addition on intervals consistent with the computational goal stated above. Further, this interval sum is the narrowest possible interval that can guarantee *rigorous* upper and lower bounds for the computed results.

However, error may be introduced into the computation of $a + c$ and $b + d$, since these will not necessarily be representable floating-point values even if a, b, c, and d are. To insure that error bounds remain valid at each computational step, it is necessary to modify the rounding rules when computing interval end-points so that the computed value of $a + c$ will be rounded to an algebraically lower value and the computed value of $b + d$ will be rounded to an algebraically higher value, *but only when they must be rounded at all*.

In theory, interval analysis is concerned with problems of the following type: If bounds on the input data are known, how can we compute results on which rigorous bounds are of realistic width? This question is easily answered in the case of the elementary arithmetic operations. The rules of interval arithmetic are

$$[a, b] + [c, d] = [a + c, b + d],$$
$$[a, b] - [c, d] = [a - d, b - c],$$
$$[a, b] * [c, d] = [\min(ac, ad, bc, bd),$$
$$\max(ac, ad, bc, bd)],$$
$$[a, b] / [c, d] = [\min(a/c, a/d, b/c, b/d),$$
$$\max(a/c, a/d, b/c, b/d)],$$
$$(\text{provided } cd > 0).$$

For example, we have the following correspondences:

$$-1 \leqslant x \leqslant 2 \quad X = [-1, 2],$$
$$1 \leqslant y \leqslant 3 \quad Y = [1, 3].$$

$$0 \leqslant (x + y) \leqslant 5 \quad X + Y = [0, 5],$$
$$-4 \leqslant (x - y) \leqslant 1 \quad X - Y = [-4, 1],$$
$$-3 \leqslant (x * y) \leqslant 6 \quad X * Y = [-3, 6],$$
$$-1 \leqslant (x/y) \leqslant 2 \quad X/Y = [-1, 2].$$

Each inequality is sharp, so each corresponding interval end-point can be attained, provided x and y are independent. If they are not, the inequalities will certainly still be valid, but may not be sharp. If, for example,

$$-1 \leqslant x \leqslant 2 \quad \text{and} \quad y = 1 + |x|,$$

then, although, as above $1 \leqslant y \leqslant 3$, in place of the inequalities above, we have instead:

$$1 \leqslant (x + y) \leqslant 5,$$
$$-3 \leqslant (x - y) \leqslant -1,$$
$$-2 \leqslant (x * y) \leqslant 6,$$
$$-1/2 \leqslant (x/y) \leqslant 2/3.$$

Naturally, it is important to keep the error bounds as narrow as possible. Since the outcome of each elementary arithmetic operation does not depend on past or future computational context, mathematical relationships that would hold for exact operands are not necessarily honored by interval arithmetic. For example, the evaluation of the expressions $A * (B + C)$ and $(A * B) + (A * C)$ in interval arithmetic will not always produce the same result, since the equivalence of the two occurrences of A is not taken into account. In practice, interval analysis is concerned with finding computational sequences to minimize the excess interval width that this phenomenon induces.

Interval arithmetic monitors error dynamically and is directly applicable in cases in which conventional forward error analysis gives realistic bounds. However, it is not a panacea for rounding error problems. Computations that are inherently ill-conditioned in floating-point arithmetic, and algorithms that induce instability, will behave similarly in interval arithmetic in that the computed interval results will be so wide as to contain only the negative information that something is wrong someplace. Because this often happens when interval arithmetic is applied naively, it is often supposed that it is hopeless to do nontrivial calculations in interval arithmetic. Nonetheless, good interval algorithms have been found for the solution of linear and nonlinear systems of equations, the algebraic eigenvalue problem, and the solution of ordinary differential equations. However, very few people are willing to work on interval problems because there is practically no high-level language support for the expression of interval algorithms, nor is there hardware support to do correctly rounded interval arithmetic.

The chief current utility of interval arithmetic is as a diagnostic tool. As such, it can save much human effort, which might otherwise be spent doing (or taking the consequences of not doing) error analysis. It is also useful in laboratory and engineering environments in which physical measurements subject to error are used to compute other quantities. If the variation of the output as a function of the input is critical, interval arithmetic is a natural tool.

The alternatives to interval arithmetic are the various significiance arithmetics, including unnormalized arithmetic. Sensitiviy of results to input variation is also sometimes evaluated by repeated computation with perturbed data. Such methods offer some confidence, but none offers complete reliability, so results obtained from these styles of computing are difficult or impossible to interpret. By contrast, interval results are very easily understood. When a computation produces narrow intervals, the drudgery of an error analysis is not required to know what accuracy has been attained.

REFERENCES

1951. Dwyer, P. A. *Linear Computations.* New York: Wiley. (Chapter 2 of this book explains the motivations for the use of interval arithmetic and provides a good introduction to the issues raised in approximate computation.)
1966. Moore, R. E. *Interval Analysis.* Englewood Cliffs, NJ: Prentice-Hall. (This is the standard reference, the only book devoted to the basic elements of interval analysis.)
1969. Hansen, E. R. (Ed.) *Topics in Interval Analysis.* New York: Oxford.
1975. Nickel, K. (Ed.). *Interval Mathematics* (Volume 29 in the series *Lecture Notes in Computer Science,* G. Goos and J. Hartmanis, Eds. New York: Springer-Verlag. (Invited and contributed papers from a 1975 conference. About half the papers are in German.)
1979. Moore, R. E. *Methods and Applications of Interval Analysis.* Philadelphia: Society for Industrial and Applied Mathematics (SIAM). (This book emphasizes the breadth of applicability of interval analytic techniques and contains an extensive bibliography.)

F. N. RIS

INTERVAL TIMER

For articles on related subjects *see* COMPUTER ACCOUNTING AND RESOURCE CONTROL; INTERRUPT; MULTIPROGRAMMING; and OPERATING SYSTEMS.

An interval timer (sometimes called a *real-time clock*) is a mechanism whereby elapsed time can be monitored by a computer system. In most systems, a word in memory is set aside to be used as the interval timer. This mechanism, usually at the low end of memory, cannot be used for anything else, since the computer is wired to increment it automatically by one interval every millisecond (or other fixed period). Although some timers are incremented as infrequently as 60 times per second, most are incremented much more frequently than that.

For timing purposes it is useful to have a timer capable of monitoring the execution of a few thousands, or tens of thousands, of instructions. Hence, in a computer with some instructions requiring only 1 μs, a millisecond timer will be incremented once for every thousand of those instructions, which is about as low a rate as can be tolerated. If the system stores the time of day (say, at start-up time) in another word, then any program needing to report the current time of day need only read the start time and add to it the number of milliseconds in the timer to obtain the current time of day.

The timer is useful for reporting the date and time of execution of various parts of a job. Equally important is its use in checking the timing for segments of a routine. To figure the average time required to compute a square root, for example, a program could call up the interval timer, save the contents, calculate 10,000 square roots, read the timer again, and obtain the difference.

In multiprogrammed systems, care must be taken to maintain interval timings with each job. The time of day will be global to all jobs, of course, but for timing purposes, the interest is usually in time elapsed only while the CPU is assigned to a particular job (as opposed to running other jobs or performing input/output operations for the job in question or other jobs). While a stopwatch might be adequate for timing large components of routines in a non-multiprogrammed system, an interval timer is essential for timing components of multiprogrammed systems, since time may be allocated to jobs in increments of only a few hundreds (or even tens) of milliseconds.

C. L. MEEK

IOCS. *See* Input-Output Control System.

IPL-V. *See* List Processing Languages.

ITERATION

For articles on related subjects *see* Control Structures; Numerical Analysis; Procedure-Oriented Languages; Recursion; and Structured Programming.

To *iterate* means to do repeatedly. In computer programming, *iteration* is the repeated execution of lines of code or statements until some condition is satisfied.

For example, ten numbers A(1), A(2), A(3), . . . , A(10) can be summed using the following Fortran program:

```
      L = 10
      I = 1
      SUM = 0.
15    SUM = SUM + A(I)          (1)
      I = I + 1
      IF (I .LE. L) GO TO 15
```

The statement 15 and the two following it are executed repeatedly until I becomes 11.

In contrast, the sum could be computed by

$$SUM = A(1) + A(2) + A(3) + A(4)$$
$$+ A(5) + A(6) + A(7)$$
$$+ A(8) + A(9) + A(10) \quad (2)$$

which does not involve iteration. This last statement is more efficient in the example given, since the sum is obtained with fewer program steps. However, if more elements are to be summed, then statement (2) must be changed by adding more terms to it. In the first program, however, to sum more elements, only the value of L (which could be an input quantity) need be changed. Therefore, when the number of elements to be summed increases, a point is eventually reached where the effort needed to write the program in form (2) becomes greater than for form (1). This illustrates the use of iteration to reduce the effort of the programmer at the price of using more computer time. At some point, of course, (2) will require more time to compile than (1).

All worthwhile computer programs are iterative in some way. For example, in the time that one can write program (2) above, one could perform the actual summation by hand. Thus, solving a problem by computer is worthwhile only if: (1) the programming effort is small compared with the amount of computing (which means

that some of the program is executed repetitively), or (2) the program is applied to a succession of input data values. Although this last process is less often called "iteration," the program is repeatedly executed.

Another advantage of the iterative approach is the greater ease of generalization. For example, the first program could be part of a subroutine, and the control of the iteration could be done by means of a parameter.

```
      SUBROUTINE ABC (L)
      . . .
      I = 1
      SUM = 0.
15    SUM = SUM + A(I)
      I = I + 1
      IF (I .LE. L) GO TO 15
      . . .
```

Calling the subroutine with

```
      CALL ABC (10)
```

would compute the sum of ten elements.

Control of Iteration. DO, FOR, and WHILE statements may be used to control an iteration. For example, the Fortran program

```
      SUM = 0.
      DO 5 I = 1, 10              (3)
         SUM = SUM + A(I)
5     CONTINUE
```

accomplishes the same effect as program (1).

In PL/I, the program (3) can be written as

```
      SUM = 0;
      DO I = 1 TO 10;
         SUM = SUM + A(I);       (4)
      END;
```

In Pascal, this same program (3) would be

```
      SUM := 0;
      for I := 1 to 10 do        (5)
         SUM := SUM + A(I);
```

Note that in the language APL the same summation can be written as

$$+ / A \quad (6)$$

Here, at the language level, no iteration appears to be involved. However, at the level of the interpretive program that evaluates the APL statement, iteration will occur.

The iteration may be repeated a number of times depending upon the values involved. For example, the summation (1) may be terminated if an $A(I) = 0$:

```
    SUM = 0.
    DO 5 I = 1, 10
        IF (A(I) .EQ. 0.) GO TO 6        (7)
        SUM = SUM + A(I)
5   CONTINUE
6   ...
```

In Pascal, this program would be

```
    SUM := 0;
    I := 1;
    while A[I] <> 0 do
        begin                            (8)
            SUM := SUM + A[I];
            I := I + 1
        end
```

Another type of example is illustrated by a SQUARE ROOT subroutine:

```
    SUBROUTINE SQRT (X,Y,E)
        IF (X .LT. 0.) GO TO 50
        Y = 1.
30  IF (ABS(Y•Y−X).LT. E) RETURN        (9)
40      Y = (X/Y + Y) • 0.5
        GO TO 30
50  ... error code ...
70  RETURN
    END
```

Line 40 of program (9) computes an improved value of the square root. If $X = 1.0$, it is not executed at all (assuming E is of appropriate size relative to the arithmetic precision of the computer on which the problem is run). Otherwise, the number of iterations depends both on the value of X and on the value of E.

Iteration in Numerical Methods.
Many numerical problems can be solved by iterative techniques. Here, a succession of values for one or more variables are computed. It is hoped that the successive values approach the true values. The iterative process is terminated when some error criterion is satisfied. The square root program (9) above is an example of an iterative numerical procedure. Although the successive partial sums of the first example (1) do approach the final sum, this procedure is not usually called an iterative numerical procedure. Thus, numerical iteration is usually characterized by the use of successive approximations and termination depending upon error bounds.

Hardware Iteration.
The distinction between hardware and software activity is less and less clear as more complex processors are designed. This is particularly true in using microprogramming techniques and read-only memories.

In a simple example, a number in a register (Register 2 of Fig. 1) may need to be shifted a number of binary positions determined by a number stored in a second register (Register 1). The shift circuits of Register 2 are repeatedly pulsed until the contents of Register 1 are counted down to zero. Although the activity of the shift circuits are iterative in character, very few logical designers would use the term.

In more complex processors the term may be more appropriate. For example, the summation of the elements of a vector (as discussed above) may be done entirely by hardware. This involves a complex sequence of events including: incrementing an address register to access successive components; performing a floating-point addition which itself involves comparing exponents; shifting mantissas; and perhaps normalizing results. Thus, the same pattern of activities is performed iteratively until all components of the vector are accounted for.

Iteration versus Recursion.
A program is recursive if at least one of its executable statements refers to the program itself. For example, in Pascal one may write

```
    function ABC(X: integer): integer;
    ...
    ...
    ...
        Z := ABC(Y);                     (10)
    ...
    ...
    ...
    end.
```

That is, the function calls itself. This requires a so-called STACK mechanism to keep track of parameters, and RETURN locations for each level of call. Needless to say,

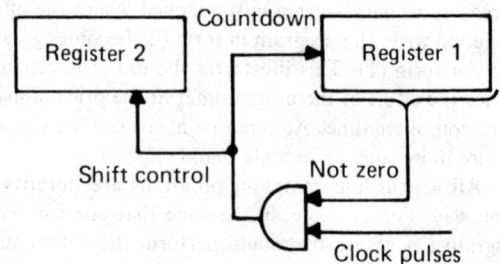

Fig. 1.   Simple example of hardware iteration.

other statements in the program must in some way limit the levels of calling. A frequently used example is the factorial (Wirth, 1976, p. 129):

```
function FACTORIAL (X: integer): integer;
if X = 1 then FACTORIAL := 1
        else FACTORIAL: = X*FACTORIAL(X−1)
end                                         (11)
```

Although portions of the code (11) are executed repetitively, the control is by reference to the named procedure. Therefore, this example is said to be recursive, and not iterative.

The factorial of N can be computed iteratively:

```
function FACTORIAL (N: integer): integer;
var integer I;
FACTORIAL := 1; I := 1;
while I < = N do
  begin
        FACTORIAL := I•FACTORIAL;
        I := I + 1
    end
end
```

In the iterative example, the function does not call itself and, therefore, does not have to save the parameter X each time it is called as the recursive function must do. In general, when a straightforward iterative algorithm is available, it is both faster and more frugal of memory than a corresponding recursive algorithm. But when recursion is more natural than iteration (*see*, for example, Quicksort in the articles SORTING and STRUCTURED PROGRAMMING), it is often preferable to use it.

REFERENCES

1970. Acton, F. S. *Numerical Methods That Work*. New York: Harper & Row.
1976. Wirth, N. *Algorithms + Data Structures = Programs*. Englewood Cliffs, NJ: Prentice-Hall.

H. D. HUSKEY

J

JOB

For articles on related subjects *see* MULTIPROGRAM-
MING; OPERATING SYSTEMS: Principles and Theory;
PROCESSING MODES; and TASK.

A job is a task or group of tasks to be performed by
a computer. The number of tasks (or steps) per job is usually a preference of the programmer, but is also subject
to the conventions of the operating system. For example,
many empty temporary files supplied by the operating
system are automatically closed and released at the end
of a job. If a programmer wishes to use one of these temporary files to store some intermediate information between two steps, then the two steps must be contained
within the same job. On the other hand, if the programmer uses a permanent file, then there may be a step that
creates the file in one job and a step that reads it in another job. In a batch-processing environment, where jobs
are run one at a time, the programmer needs only to insure that the job which reads the file is *submitted* to be
run after the job that creates it. But in a multiprogrammed environment, where several jobs are run concurrently, there is need to insure that the jobs are *executed* in sequence. To accomplish this automatically,
many multiprogramming operating systems allow job sequencing, which allows the programmer to specify that a
job cannot be selected for execution until its predecessor
has been completed.

A job is also the smallest accounting unit on most
machines. That is, computer resources are normally
charged against one account number per job.

C. L. MEEK

JOB CONTROL LANGUAGES. *See* COM-
MAND AND JOB CONTROL LANGUAGES.

JOINT USERS GROUP (JUG)

For article on related subject *see* ASSOCIATION FOR
COMPUTING MACHINERY.

The Joint Users Group was an organization of digital computer user groups. It was formed in the late 1950s
and was formally accepted as an activity of the Association for Computing Machinery (ACM) in 1961.

The purpose of the organization was "the establishment of communications among digital computer user
groups to promote study, exchange of information and
cooperative effort in areas of common interest."

Among the more significant activities of the group
was the publication of the *Computer Programs Directory*
by Macmillan Publishing Company in 1971 and 1974.
This directory listed programs (including a short narrative) that were available for exchange, for sale, or for the
asking; the degree of available documentation; and the
hardware requirements.

Another long-term JUG effort was active membership in ANSI X3 standards activity.

During its lifetime, JUG membership included virtually every major user group, from the very large mainframe SHARE and GUIDE groups to the newer minicomputer organizations such as TI-MIX (Texas
Instruments) and SWAP (Wang Laboratories).

Unfortunately, JUG's efforts were, despite ACM affiliations, entirely voluntary and drawn from member organizations whose activities were already voluntary. This

Table 1.   Final Membership of JUG

Group	Vendor
DECUS	Digital Equipment
Federation of NCR Users	NCR
FOCUS	CDC
GUIDE	IBM
HUG	Honeywell
SWAP	Wang Laboratories
TI-MIX	Texas Instruments
USE	Univac
VIM	CDC (Control Data 6000 users)

two-tiered voluntary effort, coupled with a lack of real size and a less than clear sense of purpose, resulted in JUG's ultimate demise. JUG's last meeting was held in March 1975. Its membership at that time is shown in Table 1.

R. H. VanDenberg, Jr.

JOSEPHSON JUNCTION DEVICES

For articles on related subjects *see* Computer Circuitry; Integrated Circuitry; Memory; Main; and Storage Hierarchy.

The Josephson tunnel junction, whose effect was predicted by Brian Josephson in 1962, typically consists of a thin insulating layer (~ 30 Å $= 30 \times 10^{-10}$m, or about 15 atomic layers thick) sandwiched between two superconducting (zero-resistance) films. When placed in suitable cryogenic environment (such as liquid helium at $4.2°$K $\approx -269°$C), these junctions form the basis of ultra-fast switching circuits with transition times of tens of picoseconds (ps) and power dissipations of a few microwatts (μW). Such high-speed and low-power dissipation make the technology of Josephson junction devices a strong contender for use in the ultra-high-performance computers of the future.

The Josephson tunnel junction is characterized by two states, one of zero resistance and the other of nonzero resistance. When the junction is in the zero-resistance state, an externally applied current is transported through the insulating layer, or tunnel barrier, by superconducting electrons which, via a quantum mechanical tunneling mechanism, cross the barrier without resistance. If the junction is in the non-zero-resistance state, an externally applied current passes through the barrier as a normal electron tunneling current with an associated voltage drop. A current biased ($\lesssim 1$ mA) junction in the zero-resistance state can be switched to a non-zero voltage (~ 2 mV) by increasing the bias current above a particular value (the critical current) or by applying a magnetic field generated by a current in an overlying control line. The magnitudes of the current and voltage lead to power dissipation measured in μW. The switching speed of ~ 10 ps is set primarily by the time required to charge the junction capacitance (measured in picofarads for devices with LSI dimensions). Josephson switching devices frequently consist of two or more junctions incorporated

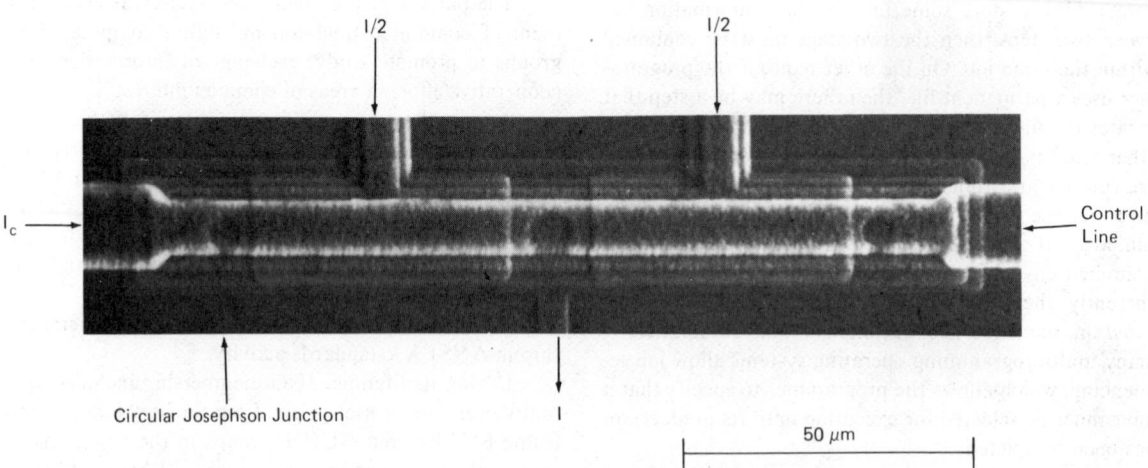

Fig. 1.   Scanning electron micrograph of a three-junction *superconducting quantum interference device* (SQUID). The bias current *I* is applied in a fashion that assures proper distribution to all three junctions. If the SQUID is biased in the zero-resistance state, a current $I_c \lesssim I$ passed through the control line will generate a magnetic field that will interact with the device and cause it to switch to a non-zero voltage. *(Courtesy of the Exploratory Cryogenic Technology Group, IBM Research, Yorktown Heights, NY.)*

in a superconducting loop to form a *s*uperconducting *q*uantum *i*nterference *d*evice (SQUID—see Fig. 1). In logic applications, current diverted from one SQUID as it makes a transition to the non-zero voltage state can be used to induce switching in another SQUID. Complete SQUID logic families have been successfully designed and tested.

Memory cells have also been constructed with Josephson devices. The cells rely on the phenomenon of "magnetic flux trapping," whereby a persistent circulating current can flow in a superconducting loop indefinitely with no expenditure of energy. Such a current can be initiated or terminated and its presence or absence can be detected by the use of Josephson junctions and SQUIDs. Again, the advantages of high speed and low power dissipation are significant.

The fabrication process for Josephson junction devices is similar in complexity to that of LSI semiconduct-

ing devices. Josephson structures are formed by multiple vacuum depositions on Si rather than by diffusion and induced crystal growth (epitaxy), as is common with semiconductor devices. The vertical structure typically consists of a niobium groundplane followed by approximately five layers of various metals (primarily lead alloy superconductors) interleaved with insulating layers (primarily silicon oxide). The most sensitive step in the fabrication process is tunnel barrier formation. Control of the average thickness of the barrier (nominally ~ 30 Å) to within about 0.5 Å leads to typical critical current variations on the order to $\pm 15\%$. The lead alloys used for junction electrodes are also used to make lossless transmission lines. Such lines with matched resistive terminations serve to convey signals without loss or degradation both on circuit chips and within the package in which the circuit chips are imbedded. Figs. 2 and 3 are photographs of Josephson junction chips.

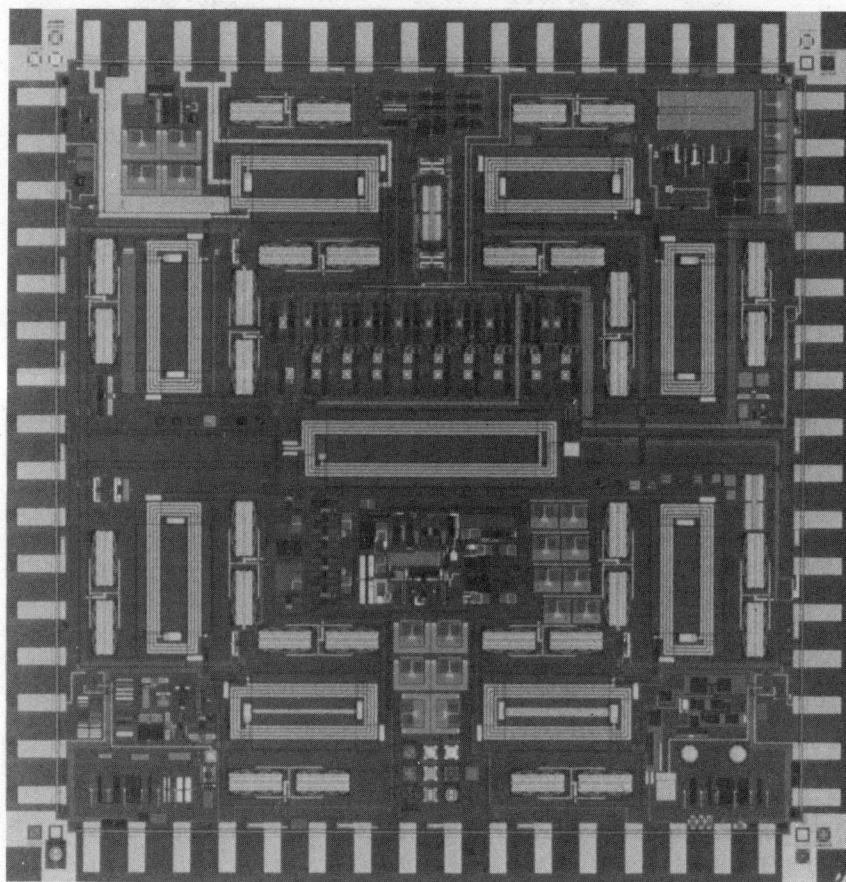

Fig. 2.   Photograph of an exploratory Josephson chip used to evaluate AC power supply designs. The main features that can be discerned on this 6.35 × 6.35 mm² chip are thin film transformers, each having the appearance of a rectangular spiral of four primary windings. *(Courtesy of the Exploratory Cryogenic Technology Group, IBM Research, Yorktown Heights, NY.)*

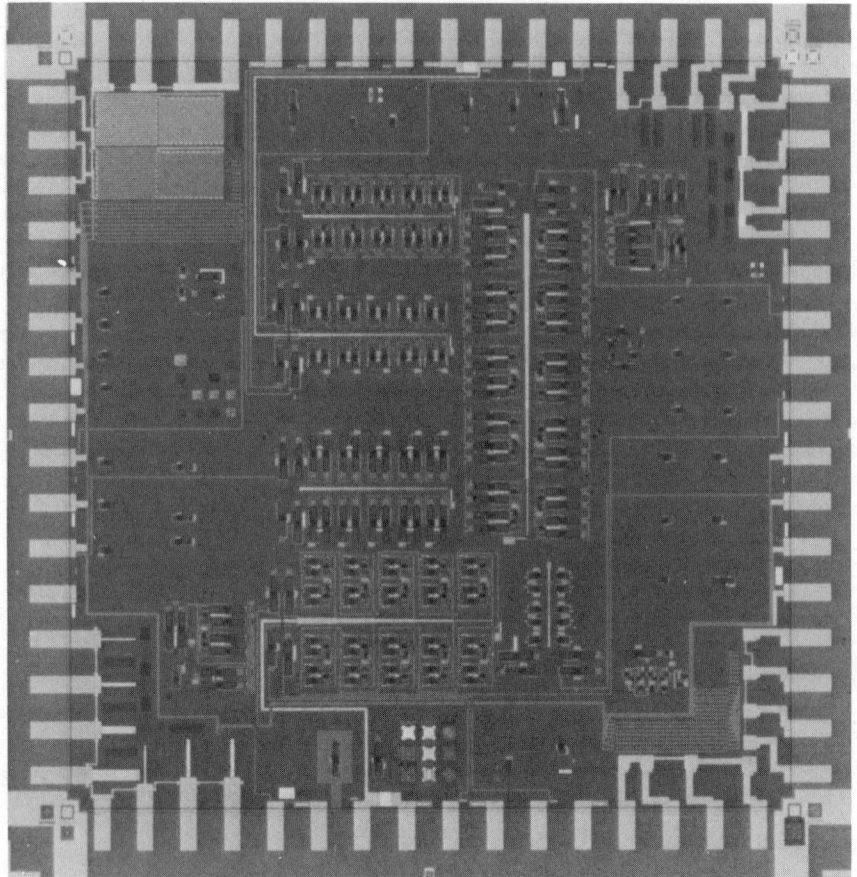

Fig. 3.   Photograph of an ultra-high-speed Josephson logic circuit test chip (6.35 × 6.35 mm²) fabricated with minimum structure dimensions of 2.5μm. *(Courtesy of the Exploratory Cryogenic Technology Group, IBM Research, Yorktown Heights, NY.)*

The primary advantages of Josephson technology arise from the extremely fast switching speeds and low power dissipation. Chips cooled by natural convection in liquid helium can be packed tightly together in a three-dimensional package with lossless superconducting transmission lines for communication. As an example, projections indicate that a Josephson version of the IBM 370/168, making use of thin film structures having minimum dimensions on the order of 5 micrometers (μm), would be capable of processing at a rate of 70 million instructions per second (MIPS) compared with the 3.5 MIPS of the existing IBM 370/168. The entire mainframe could be packaged in a cube 15 cm on an edge and would dissipate about 7 watts of power. With a large-scale Josephson computer such as this, the cost of providing and maintaining the cryogenic environment will amount to a small fraction of the total cost of the machine.

For ultra-high-performance machines, it appears that the cost of manufacturing and maintaining a Josephson computer will be similar to that for a semiconductor computer of comparable complexity. The overall improvement in computing capability should be about an order of magnitude. The major factors in determining the future of Josephson technology are understanding and controlling the properties of the materials and perfecting the fabrication process. Although much work remains to be done in these areas, the future for Josephson technology looks very promising.

REFERENCES

1972. Solymor, L. *Superconductive Tunneling and Applications.* New York: Wiley.
1978. Deaver, B. S. *et al.* (Eds.). "Future Trends in Superconductive Electronics," *AIP Conf. Proc. No. 44.* New York: AIP.

1978. Lubkin, G. B. "Search and Discovery—Josephson Junction Logic and Memory Circuits," *Physics Today* **31**, *No. 6*: 17, 19–20 (June).

1979. Anacker, W. "Computing at 4 Degrees Kelvin," *IEEE Spectrum* **16**, *No. 5*: 26–37 (May).

1980. Greiner, J. H. *et al.* "Fabrication Process for Josephson Integrated Circuits," *IBM J. of R&D* **24**, *No. 2*.

M. B. KETCHEN

JOURNALS, COMPUTING. *See* LITERATURE IN COMPUTING.

JOYSTICK

For articles on related subjects *see* COMPUTER GRAPHICS; DATA TABLET; and LIGHTPEN.

The joystick is a manual input device for graphics display consoles that allows the user to specify simultaneously the two or three coordinates of a point in two- or three-dimensional space. Typically, the current coordinate values specified by the joystick are indicated on the screen with a cursor symbol, which is "coupled" to the joystick by hardware or software. The joystick is thus a natural device for panning and/or zooming in on a drawing. By driving the cursor around the screen and having the program sample the successive positions, the user can

Fig. 1. A joystick on table below screen.

input freehand drawings. By providing a comparator circuit, the joystick can also be used to provide a lightpen type *picking* function.

Physically, the device consists of a stubby lever that rotates with two or three degrees of freedom, similar to a pitch/yaw control joystick in a small airplane. Angular displacements of the internal shaft encoders are transduced to electric voltages, which are analog-to-digital converted to x-y values and stored in computer-accessible registers for subsequent processing. The third degree of freedom (z value) can be provided by having the knob of the joystick rotate about the axis of the stick.

A. VAN DAM

JUG. *See* JOINT USERS GROUP.

JUSTIFICATION

For articles on related subjects *see* PUBLISHING, COMPUTERS IN; TEXT EDITING SYSTEMS; and WORD PROCESSING.

In the context of programming, *justification* refers to the left or right alignment of a piece of data, typically a bit or character string, in a field that is assumed to be larger (i.e., greater in length) than the data. Thus *right justifying* a bit string of length 2 in an 8-bit byte means that the rightmost of the two data bits is placed in the rightmost position of the byte. Remaining positions in the field are usually occupied by as many copies as needed of a specified or assumed *fill character*. These nondata characters or bits *pad* the data on the left if the data is right-justified, or on the right if the data is left-justified.

In the context of text processing, justification pertains to left- and/or right-margin alignment. Conventionally, typeset text such as that found in books and magazines appears with straight (justified) left and right margins. By contrast, typewritten letters usually have a left-justified ("flush left") margin but a "ragged right" margin. On some output devices such as computer line printers, where each character in the print line has a uniform size (monospace), computer-based typesetting algorithms can force alignment by inserting additional blanks between words or after punctuation. Typesetting for proportionally spaced devices involves inserting variable width spaces between words; with such devices, each character has its characteristic width as a function of font, size, etc.

A. VAN DAM

K

KERNEL

For articles on related subjects *see* INPUT-OUTPUT CONTROL SYSTEMS; OPERATING SYSTEMS: Principles and Theory; SCHEDULING ALGORITHM; SWAPPING; and TASK.

The term *kernel* (and sometimes *nucleus*) is applied to the set of programs in an operating system which implement the most primitive of that system's functions. The precise interpretation of kernel programs, of course, depends on the system; however, typical kernels contain programs for four types of functions:

1. *Process management*—Routines for switching processors among processes; for scheduling; for sending messages or timing signals among processes; and for creating and removing processes.
2. *Memory management*—Routines for placing, fetching, and removing pages or segments in, or from, main memory.
3. *Basic I/O control*—Routines for allocating and releasing buffers; for starting I/O requests on particular channels or devices; and for checking the integrity of individual data transmissions.
4. *Security*—Routines for enforcing the access and information-flow control policies of the system; for changing protection domains; and for encapsulating programs.

In some systems, the kernel is larger and provides for more than these classes of functions; in others, it is smaller. Each of the classes of kernel programs contains routines for handling interrupts pertaining to the class function. For example, clock interrupts are handled in class 1, page faults in class 2, channel completion interrupts in class 3, and protection violations in class 4. Some systems order the classes hierarchically (e.g., in order: 1, 2, 3, 4) so that programs in the given class can invoke services of programs of lower classes. For example, memory management (class 2) can be implemented by a collection of processes, the coordination of which is managed by process management routines (class 1).

The reader should not confuse the system kernel with the portion of the operating system which is continuously *resident* in main memory. Two criteria determine whether a particular system module (either routine or table) should be resident—its frequency of use, and whether the system can operate at all without it. For example, file directories can be maintained in address spaces so that they can be swapped out of main memory when not in use. Status information for inactive processes can similarly be swapped out. The resident part of the operating system is a subset of the kernel.

P. J. DENNING AND D. E. DENNING

KEY

For articles on related subjects *see* COLLATING SEQUENCE; SORTING; and TABLE LOOK-UP.

A *key,* in the computer programming sense, is a particular field or combination of fields in a data record upon which some "lookup" or ordering process is performed.

Other fields in the record would be considered ancillary to the key during such a process. Usually, a group of records (a file) will be ordered and controlled (i.e., added, revised, or deleted) based on some key field. For example, in a file containing personnel records, the person's social security number could be used as a record key. Computer processing of the key will usually involve comparisons of one key field with another or use of the key as an index. Thus, the programmer must be familiar with the characteristics of such keys: how characters making up the key are represented, how fields are justified, and how *padding* (i.e., adding characters so that all keys are the same length) is handled if necessary.

In a computer hardware sense, the term *key* may be used to describe a computer memory area used for certain purposes. In an associative or content-addressable memory, an associative key field is used to reference items. The key, which may be specified as part of an instruction, provides a value that is compared against corresponding fields in each memory cell. The contents of that cell(s) for which there is a key match are retrieved. In some hardware, a protection key is used to define and control resource privileges. In the hardware, a key field is put in correspondence with blocks of memory and used to enable or disable access to such blocks by an executing process. Both central processing unit (CPU) and channel references may be controlled in this way. In more general protection systems, the protection key is associated with a process and defines the privileges owned by the process (e.g., use of files or transfer of control to other processes).

Another use of the word key is in cryptography, where it connotes the numeric or alphanumeric sequence necessary for recovering a message from enciphered text (*see* DATA ENCRYPTION).

C. E. PRICE

KEYBOARD STANDARDS

For articles on related subjects *see* ASCII; DATA PREPARATION DEVICES; INPUT-OUTPUT DEVICES; and STANDARDS.

The most important reasons for specifying keyboard standards are to save manufacturing costs by standardizing both the keyboards and the interfaces with other equipment, to save operator training costs and to achieve higher operator efficiency in keying, to minimize input errors into data processing systems by operators, and to make it possible to use several national alphabets in the same information system as the use of international computer networks grows.

Despite the problem posed by the large investment

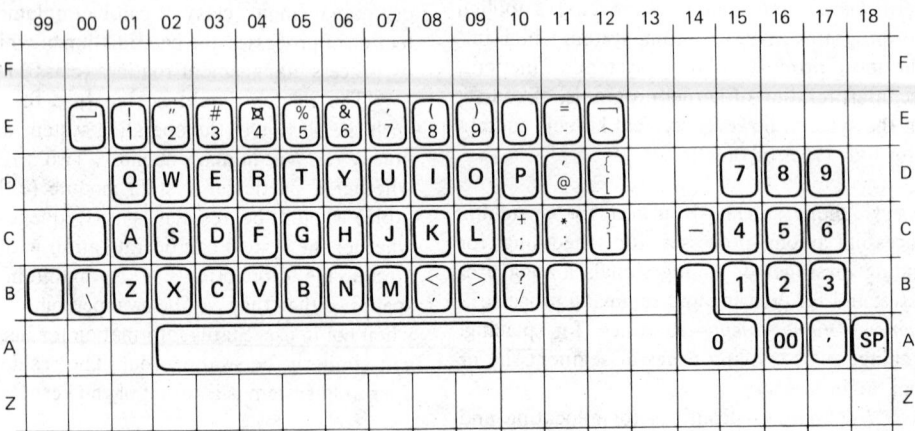

Fig. 1 The keyboard layout depicted is the ECMA-23 Standard (2nd Ed.) for predominantly numeric data. It comprises an alphanumeric area and, in addition, a numeric area consisting of shift-free keys. Only the alphanumeric area 48-key layout corresponds with the IS 2530 standard; the numeric area layout is discussed solely in the ECMA-23 standard. In both standards, the 47-key layout of the alphanumeric keyboard is derived by transmitting the UNDERLINE character from the shifted position of key E00 to the shifted position of key E10. Several allowable modifications to these layouts are discussed in detail in both standards. (The three blank single keys—B99, C00, and B11—do not count; the blank keybar is assigned to the SPACE character which is regarded as a non-printing graphic.)

in current keyboard equipment, progress toward keyboard standardization is steadily being made. Two international bodies are involved: The International Standards Organization—ISO, and the European Computer Manufacturers Association—ECMA. ISO standards are binding on all countries which have voted for their introduction, and to a degree also for those which have not; ECMA standards are, however, recommendations only.

Based upon the standard ECMA-23, the ISO issued the IS 2530 standard, "Keyboards for international information processing interchange using the ISO 7-bit coded character set—Alphanumeric area." This international standard defines layouts for the alphanumeric area of a keyboard implementing the 95 graphics positions of the ISO 7-bit coded character set, complying with ISO 646, "7-bit coded character set for information processing interchange," comprising 128 characters of which 95 are graphics, leaving the remaining 33 for control purposes. These layouts conform to ISO/R 2126, "Basic arrangements for the alphanumeric section of keyboards operated with both hands."

The ISO 2530 standard specifies the pairing of the characters (upper and lower case) and their allocation to the keys. Out of the 95 graphics positions, one is reserved for spacing, with a special key assigned to it; the remaining 94 graphic positions are handled one of two ways: Either paired to give upper and lower case positions of a 47-key layout; or, only 92 are paired on 46 keys with the remaining two—the UNDERLINE and the ZERO—assigned to two different keys for more convenience to the operator (see Fig. 1), thus giving a 48-key layout.

In addition to the basic alphabetic graphics layout, the keyboard shown in Fig. 1 has an area reserved for shift-free keys which generate the code combinations and associated characters. Rules and recommendations are given in IS 2530 on the most suitable way of contracting the standard 47-key graphic area in cases where not all of the 95 graphic characters are required.

J. NECAS

KEYWORD-IN-CONTEXT (KWIC) INDEX

For article on related subject *see* INFORMATION RETRIEVAL.

One of the oldest, automatically produced information search tools is the keyword-in-context (KWIC) index. Typically, the index is a list produced by filtering titles, text, or text portions extracted from documents, using a preconstructed *stop list* to eliminate words that are not indicative of content (such as "and," "of," and "or") and including in the index an entry for each of the remaining text words. Each line of text may thus appear many times in the list.

An entry in a KWIC index normally consists of one line of text printed in such a way that the particular keyword characterizing the entry appears in alphabetical order in the middle of the line, with both left and right contexts and with the corresponding document reference number. Thus, a phrase such as "diseases of the liver in mice" is entered three times in the index: once under D for diseases, once under L (liver), and once under M (mice). An excerpt from a KWIC index is shown in Fig. 1.

The advantages of the KWIC approach are its simple mechanized production—consisting principally of text reading, filtering, and automatic sorting routines—and the simplicity of utilization of the uncontrolled, natural-language vocabulary. The disadvantages include the chopped-up appearance (restricted to one line) of many entries, and the fact that the size of the resulting multientry index makes it necessary to use only very small text excerpts. In practice, only the titles of the documents are usually used for indexing purposes, the index then becoming a *permuted title index*. Since titles are sometimes not indicative of content, a KWIC index can never become a perfect search tool.

Some related automatic indexing products are author lists, keyword lists, and so-called KWOC (keyword-out-of-context) listings in which a full title may be en-

	Terms in context	Corresponding document numbers
ETERMINATION OF VERTICAL	WIND DISTURBANCES	--------
T OSCILLATIONS CAUSED BY	WIND GUSTS	--------
	WIND LOAD ON TOWERS	--------
FORM OF	WIND PROFILE IN NEAR-GROUND LAYER O	--------
A	WINDTUNNEL INVESTIGATION INTO THE P	--------
ON A 45 DEGREE SWEPTBACK	WING AT TRANSONIC SPEEDS	--------
	WING PLAN FORMS FOR TRANSONIC SPEED	--------
ISTRIBUTION ON SYMMETRIC	WING PROFILES IN THE CASE OF HIGH-S	--------
SIS OF AN ASPECT-RATIO-1	WING WITH FAN AT 0.354 CHORD	--------
ESSURE DISTRIBUTION ON A	WINGSURFACE IN A NON-UNIFORM SUPERS	--------

Fig. 1. Excerpt from KWIC index.

```
ABRAMYAN,B.L.,                                      63-02-0739
    ABRAMYAN,B.L.,   TORSION OF CIRCULAR CYLINDRICAL RODS WITH LO
NGITUDINAL WEDGE-SHAPED GROOVES
                                                    63-10-5685
    ABRAMYAN,B.L.,   TORSION OF CONICAL RODS AND OF CYLINDRICAL R
ODS WITH A CONICAL PORTION
                                                    63-11-6300
    ABRAMYAN,B.L., AND BABLOYAN,A.A.,   ON A CONTACT PROBLEM CONN
ECTED WITH THE TORSION OF A HOLLOW HEMISPHERE
                                                    63-11-6329
    ABRAMYAN,B.L., AND BABLOYAN,A.A.,   ON ONE CASE OF AXIALLY SY
MMETRIC DEFORMATION OF A HOLLOW CYLINDER OF FINITE LENGTH
                                                    63-12-6922
    ABRAMYAN,B.L., AND TONOYAN,V.S.,   THE TORSION OF A PRISMATIC
    BEAM WITH A TRANSVERSE SECTION IN THE FORM OF AN ELLIPSE WI
TH GROOVES
ABRASION                                            63-08-4964
    AVIENT,B.W.E., AND WILMAN,H.,   NEW FEATURES OF THE ABRASION
PROCESS SHOWN BY SOFT METALS . THE NATURE OF MECHANICAL POLI
SHING
                                                    63-12-7490
    KULHEARN,T.O., AND SAMUELS,L.E.,   THE ABRASION OF METALS . A
MODEL OF THE PROCESS
ABRASIVE                                            63-12-7152
    KOZYREV,S.P., AND SHALNEV,K.K.,   ABRASIVE WEAR AND CAVITATIO
N
ABRUKOV,S.A.,                                       63-12-7328
    ABRUKOV,S.A.,   DEPENDENCE OF THE LIMITS OF VIBRATIONAL FLAME
-SPREADING ON THE TEMPERATURE,  PRESSURE AND THE ADDITION OF
    INERT IMPURITIES
ABRUPT                                              63-01-0116
    MORGAN,W.C., AND BIZON,P.T.,   EXPERIMENTAL INVESTIGATION OF
STRESS DISTRIBUTIONS NEAR ABRUPT CHANGE IN WALL THICKNESS IN
THIN-WALLED PRESSURIZED CYLINDERS
```

Fig. 2. Excerpt from word-and-author index.

tered, together with the particular keyword listed separately (i.e., out of context). When author names also function as main index entries, a "keyword and author" index results, as shown in Fig. 2.

G. SALTON

KLUDGE

The word "kludge" as used in computing was coined by Jackson Granholm in an article "How to Design a Kludge," in *Datamation* (February 1962). The definition is given as "an ill-sorted collection of poorly matching parts, forming a distressing whole." The design of every computer contains some anomalies that prove to be annoying to the users and which the designer wishes had been done differently. If there are enough of these, the machine is called a *kludge*.

By extension, the term has now come to be applied to programs, documentation, and even computer centers, so that the definition is now "an ill-conceived and hence unreliable system that has accumulated through patchwork, expediency, and poor planning."

The first kludge article triggered five others ("How to Maintain a Kludge," etc.) in subsequent issues of *Datamation*. Four of the articles may be found in the book, *Faith, Hope and Parity,* edited by Jack Moshman, Thompson Book Company, 1966.

F. GRUENBERGER

KWIC *See* KEYWORD-IN-CONTEXT INDEX

LABEL

For articles on related subjects *see* IDENTIFIER; MACHINE AND ASSEMBLY LANGUAGE PROGRAMMING; and PROCEDURE-ORIENTED LANGUAGES.

A label is an identifier that may be prefixed to a statement (possibly a compound statement) in a program, which enables the statement to be referenced by other statements in the program. Label identifiers may be either alphanumeric or numeric, depending on the language.

In most symbolic assembly languages, statement labels are formed as strings of alphanumeric characters. Such labels are the identifiers of the storage locations in which the assembled statement is located. Where the statement is an instruction, the label permits references to the assembled instruction for the purpose (among others) of using it as the destination of a branch instruction. Where the label is attached to a declaration of a data element or data area, instructions in the program may utilize the symbolic label as the name of the element. For example, consider Gruenberger, (1969):

LOC'N	OP	ADDR	
BEGIN	LDA	JIM	Reference to data (LDA-LOAD ADDRESS)
	.		
	.		
	.		
	STA	OHIO	Modifying an instruction (STA-STORE ADDRESS)
OHIO	LDA	0000	
	.		

	LDA	OHIO	Using an instruction as data
	.		
	.		
	BZE	OUT3	Branch reference (BZE-BRANCH ON ZERO)
	.		
	.		
	BRA	BEGIN+4	Relative reference (BRA-BRANCH)
OUT3	HAL		
JIM	DEC	0	
	.		
	.		
	.		

where the labels used are BEGIN, OHIO, OUT3 and JIM.

In languages of a higher level than symbolic assembly languages, such as Fortran and Pascal, labels are used in connection with either executable statements or formatting specifications.

Thus, the usage of labels is confined to references to executable statements as the destination of a branching instruction (such as a **goto** in Algol or Pascal), as specifying the limit of a block of code (such as in the DO range of a Fortran program), or the identification of a formatting specification for an input/output instruction (as in Fortran). For example, consider (Hare, 1970):

50 DO 70 1 = 1, 10 ← Reference to a range
$\overline{\text{DO}}$ 60 J = 1,250

.

.

.

GO TO <u>60</u> ← Specification of destination

.

.

.

60   CONTINUE

.

.

.

⸏Format Reference

70 WRITE(6,<u>80</u>) NGAMES,SIMU,ACTU,ERROR

.

80 FORMAT(/ ,1X,I15,3F15.6)

In certain languages designed for use in conversational systems (such as Basic and APL), labels may be required with each statement so as to specify exactly the physical ordering of the statements. Thus, the statement labels are also used as line numbers and are required to be in ascending numerical order. In such cases the labels are used by a sorting routine to order the statements prior to compilation of the program, since it is not required that the user enter the program in exactly the correct order. For example, in Basic,

```
100 READ A,B,C,D,E
110 IF A<7500 THEN 800
120 IF D>A/52 THEN 800
130 IF B<=3 THEN 900
140 IF C>=3 THEN 900
800 PRINT "CASE NO." ,E, "CREDIT REJECTED"
805 GO TO 100
900 PRINT "CASE NO." ,E, "CREDIT APPROVED"
905 GO TO 100
```

With the advent of structured programming languages like Pascal, the need for labels in programs has been greatly reduced.

REFERENCES

1969. Gruenberger, F. *Computing: An Introduction*. New York: Harcourt, Brace & World.

1970. Hare, V. C. *Introduction to Programming, A BASIC Approach*. New York: Harcourt, Brace, and World.

A. RALSTON AND J. A. N. LEE

LAMBDA CALCULUS

For articles on related subjects *see* FUNCTIONAL PROGRAMMING; LIST PROCESSING LANGUAGES; PROGRAMMING LINGUISTICS; PROGRAM VERIFICATION; and SYNTAX, SEMANTICS AND PRAGMATICS.

The lambda calculus (or λ-calculus) is a mathematical formalism developed by the logician Alonzo Church in the 1930s to model the mathematical notion of substitution of values for bound variables. Consider the definition $f(x) = x + 1$, which defines f to be the successor function. The variable x in this definition is a *bound variable* in the sense that replacement of all instances of x by some other variable (say, y) yields a definition $f(y) = y + 1$, which is semantically equivalent. In the λ-calculus, the successor function f may be defined by the λ-expression $\lambda x(x + 1)$. The subexpression $(x + 1)$ is referred to as the *body* of the λ-expression. The subexpression λx is referred to as the *bound variable part* and specifies that x is to be regarded as a bound variable in the body with which λx is associated.

The application of $\lambda x(x + 1)$ to the integer argument 3 may be specified by the λ-expression $f(3) = \lambda x(x + 1)(3)$. The subexpression $\lambda x(x + 1)$ is referred to as the "operator part" of this lambda expression; the subexpression 3 is referred to as the "operand part" of this lambda expression. The substitution rules (reduction rules) of the lambda calculus specify that the operator part $\lambda x(x + 1)$ may be applied to the operand part 3 to yield the value $(3 + 1) = 4$.

Consider next the lambda expression $\lambda h(h(3) + h(4))$ $(\lambda x(x + 1))$. The substitution rules of the λ-calculus specify that $\lambda x(x + 1)$, which is the operand part of this expression, is to be substituted for all instances of h in the body of the operator part, yielding the λ-expression $(\lambda x(x + 1)(3) + \lambda x(x + 1)(4))$, which on further substitution yields $((3 + 1) + (4 + 1)) = 9$.

The binding of h to $\lambda x(x + 1)$ in $h(3) + h(4)$ may be expressed in one of the following ways.

1. Let $h = \lambda x(x + 1)$ in $h(3) + h(4)$.
2. $h(3) + h(4)$ where $h = \lambda x(x + 1)$.

The notations (1) and (2) are said to be syntactically "sugared" versions of the original λ-expression in the sense that they are semantically equivalent to the original λ-expression but are easier to read. The above syntactically sugared specifications illustrate that certain notational conventions of real programming languages may very easily be converted into semantically equivalent lambda notations.

The following example illustrates even more clearly that the bound variable h of the λ-expression given above represents a procedure that is initialized to the successor function $\lambda x(x + 1)$ at the time of binding, and is then called with the arguments 3 and 4:

procedure $h(x)$; result ← $x + 1$;
value ← $h(3) + h(4)$;

This example also illustrates that, in order to realize the functions determined by lambda expressions in a conventional programming language, it is necessary to introduce the assignment operator and to realize binding and substitution in terms of assignment.

In the preceding examples, λ-expressions were allowed to contain extraneous symbols, such as +, which allow arithmetic operations to be embedded in the substitutive mechanism of the λ-calculus. The pure λ-calculus does not contain such extraneous operators, and requires all transformations to be substitutions of values for bound variables. In the remainder of this article we will be concerned with the pure λ-calculus.

The pure λ-calculus may be thought of as a programming language with a very simple syntax and semantics. The syntax of λ-expressions may be defined by a BNF grammar whose terminal symbols are λ, (,), and a class V of variable names, and whose productions are $E \rightarrow V | \lambda VE | (EE)$, where E denotes the class of λ-expressions. An expression of the form λVE (say, λxM) denotes a one-parameter function and has a bound variable part λx and a body part M. An expression of the form (EE) [say, $(M_1 M_2)$], is referred to as an operator-operand combination, and has an operator part M_1 and an operand part M_2. An occurrence of a variable x in a λ-expression M is said to be bound in M if it occurs within a subexpression of the form λxM_1 within M, and is said to be free otherwise.

Note: The above syntactic definition requires application of an operator f to an operand x to be specified as (fx) rather than as $f(x)$.

The "computational semantics" of the λ-calculus may be defined by transformation rules that specify how λ-expressions may be converted into "semantically equivalent" λ-expressions. The principal computation rule is the *reduction rule* (sometimes called the "β-rule").

Reduction Rule. An operator-operand combination of the form (λxMA) may be transformed into the expression $S_A^x M$, obtained by substituting the λ-expression A for all instances of x in M, provided there are no conflicts of variable names. The condition that there be no conflicts of variable names may be explicitly specified as follows:

1. M contains no bound occurrences of x.
2. M contains no bound variables that occur free in A.

A second transformation rule called the "renaming rule" (α rule) allows conflicts of variables to be eliminated.

Renaming Rule. A bound variable x in a λ-expression M may be uniformly replaced by some other bound variable y, provided y does not occur in M.

Any λ-expression of the form (λxMA) may be converted into a λ-expression of the form $(\lambda xM'A)$ satisfying conditions (1) and (2) above by renaming of the bound variables of M, using the renaming rule, and may then be reduced to $S_A^x M'$ using the reduction rule.

Example

$$(\lambda x(x\lambda xx)(pq)) \underset{\alpha}{\rightarrow} (\lambda x(x\lambda tt)(pq)) \underset{\beta}{\rightarrow} ((pq)\lambda tt).$$

A λ-expression P that has no subexpressions of the form (λxMA) is said to be in *reduced form*. A λ-expression that cannot be converted to a reduced form by a sequence of renaming and reduction rules is said to be *irreducible.*

Example. $P = (\lambda x(xx)\lambda x(xx))$ is irreducible, since it is of the form (λxMA) with $M = (xx)$ and $A = \lambda x(xx)$, and application of the reduction rule produces $(\lambda x(xx)\lambda x (xx))$.

The question of whether an arbitrary λ-expression P has a reduced form is *undecidable*; i.e., there is no algorithm which, given an arbitrary λ-expression E, can determine in a finite number of steps whether or not E has a reduced form.

The notion of a reduced form corresponds to the intuitive notion of a value in arithmetic computation. For example, the arithmetic computation $(3 + (4 * 5)) \rightarrow (3 + 20) \rightarrow 23$ is accomplished by two applications of operators to their operands, corresponding to reductions in the λ-calculus. The result, 23, corresponds to a reduced expression because it contains no more instances of operators that can be applied to their operands.

If a λ-expression contains more than one sub-expression of the form (λxMA), then there is more than one "next step" in the computation, and the evaluation process becomes nondeterministic. The following important theorem states that for any λ-expression, all sequences of computation which yield a value will yield the same value.

Church-Rosser Theorem. If a given λ-expression is reduced by two different reduction sequences, and if both reduction sequences yield a reduced form, then the reduced forms are equivalent up to renaming of bound variables.

However, there are λ-expressions that give rise to both terminating and nonterminating sequences.

Example. The λ-expression

$$(\lambda x\lambda yy(\lambda x(xx)\lambda x(xx)))$$

has the form (λxMA), where $M = \lambda yy$ and $A = (\lambda x(xx)\lambda x(xx))$. If A is substituted for occurrences of x in M before A is evaluated, then the value of λyy is obtained, while if an attempt is made to evaluate A before substituting it in *M,* then an infinite reduction sequence is obtained.

The choice among different orders of evaluation in the λ-calculus has its counterpart in function evaluation for real programming languages. For example, in evaluating $f(g(x))$, we can choose to evaluate $g(x)$ and use the resulting value in the evaluation of *f,* or we can pass the unevaluated function $g(x)$ to *f* and evaluate $g(x)$ whenever it is needed in *f.* The first alternative is referred to as "inside-out" evaluation and corresponds to *call-by-value* in Algol 60 (Naur *et al.,* 1963), while the second alternative is referred to as "outside-in" evaluation and corresponds to *call-by-name* in Algol 60. Call-by-value is more efficient than call-by-name when the value of $g(x)$ is used more than once during the evaluation of *f,* but it is less efficient if $g(x)$ is never used during the evaluation of *f.* In particular, if $g(x)$ results in an infinite computation sequence but is never used in *f,* then the call-by-value strategy results in disaster, whereas the call-by-name strategy is always adequate.

The λ-expression

$$(\lambda x M A) = (\lambda x \lambda y y (\lambda x(xx) \lambda x(xx)))$$

is of the form $f(g(x))$, where $f = \lambda x \lambda y y$ has a function body with no occurrences of the parameter *x,* and $g(x) = (\lambda x(xx) \lambda x(xx))$ results in an infinite computation. The call-by-name evaluation strategy for λ-expressions corresponds to always reducing the instance of $(\lambda x M A)$ whose component λx occurs farthest to the left. This strategy is called the "leftmost" evaluation strategy. The universal adequacy of the call-by-name strategy is captured by the following theorem.

THEOREM. If for a lambda expression *E* there is a terminating reduction sequence yielding a reduced form *E,* then the leftmost reduction sequence will yield a reduced form that is equivalent to *E* up to renaming.

The λ-calculus is equivalent in computational power to the class of Turing machines in the sense that any computable function may be resented as a λ-expression. However, the notation and computation mechanism of the λ-calculus is closer to that of programming languages than in the case of Turing machines. This has led to attempts to model programming languages such as Algol 60 in terms of the λ-calculus (Landin, 1965). Such models capture certain concepts such as nested block structure, binding of variables, and the order of evaluation, but have difficulty in capturing other concepts such as assignment, sharing of values by references, side effects, and unconditional branching. Thus, although the λ-calculus is useful for gaining insights into certain computational mechanisms arising in real programming languages, it appears to be unnatural as a framework for modeling complete programming languages. In order to model complete programming languages in a natural way, it is appropriate to introduce (as a primitive notion) cells whose values may be updated and which may be referred to by references.

The λ-calculus is of computational interest because it allows us to factor out certain aspects of computational structure and study these features independently of the complexity of real programming languages. It is of mathematical interest because it provides a framework for characterizing the substitution of values for bound variables and for studying the notion of function application. The λ-calculus thus provides a bridge between mathematics and the theory of computation. However, since the λ-calculus is a natural model for only a very restricted class of computational mechanisms, it is likely to remain of limited value as a tool in the analysis of computing systems. Nevertheless, it should be noted that the programming language Lisp is closely modeled on the λ-calculus.

REFERENCES

1951. Church, A. "The Calculi of Lambda Conversion," *Ann. Math. Studies, No. 6.* Princeton, NJ: Princeton University Press.
1963. Naur, P. *et al.* "Revised Report on the Algorithmic Language ALGOL 60," *Comm. ACM* (January).
1965. Landin, P. J. "A Correspondence Between Algol 60 and Church's Lambda Notation," *Comm. ACM* (February and March).

P. WEGNER

LANGUAGE, NATURAL. *See* NATURAL LANGUAGE PROCESSING.

LANGUAGE PROCESSORS

For articles on related subjects *see* ASSEMBLERS, BINDING TIME; COMPILE AND RUN TIME; COMPILER; DEFAULT CONDITION; DELIMITER; EXPRESSION; GLOBAL AND LOCAL VARIABLES; GRAMMARS; INTERPRETER; OBJECT PROGRAM; OVERLAY; PARSING; PROCEDURE; PROGRAMMING LANGUAGES; PROGRAMMING LINGUISTICS; REENTRANT PROGRAM; and SOURCE PROGRAM.

The General Translatory Process. Given the fundamental language of communication with a computer—namely, *machine language*—there exists an almost intolerable barrier between the person who desires to solve some problem using the computer and the description of the solution in terms of the machine language. Although the ability of some programmers to communicate in terms of machine languages is exceptional, the minute attention to detail required to develop a program is generally beyond the scope of most computer users. Thus, early in the history of computer development, there was a drive to moderate this communications gap. The development of languages themselves was not recognized immediately, but instead the trend was toward providing codes that would reference specialized routines that were to be drawn from a library of such routines. Only later, when these codes took on the character of alphabetic phrases, did they become known as languages (Hopper, 1981).

The primary efforts toward simplication led to a symbolic form of machine language in which code sequences were represented by mnemonic character sequences (such as ADD for the operation of addition, or JMP for the instruction to break normal sequential processing and "jump" to some other designated instruction), and where references to data elements were in terms of symbolic names instead of through the memory address of the data element. This language development lead to the requirement for a processor (program) that would convert programs represented by a symbolic code into their equivalent machine language representation. This process was (and still is) known as *assembly,* and the processor was known as an *assembler.*

It is important to note that the assembler performs no task other than the generation of an equivalent machine language program based on a symbolic language program and, in particular, takes no part in the actual execution of the generated program.

The development of symbolic languages and assemblers was followed closely by the development of *autocoders,* in which the programmer's language was more closely related to mathematical notation than to the machine operations. Most of the first autocoders were primitive by the standards of the 1980s, permitting only simple one-operator expressions and restricted naming of data elements. However, the autocoder required the development of more sophisticated conversion processors, thus leading to a study of the general translatory process. An interesting comparison and effective history of the development of autocoders and other primitive languages may be found in Knuth and Pardo, 1980.

The methods of program conversion and subsequent execution of a user's program can be classified into two basic techniques: compilation and execution, or interpretation. Both systems use a translatory system in which the original program (the *source program*) is converted into some other language (*target* language). In the case of the compilation process (performed by a *compiler*), the target language is either machine language or its corresponding symbolic language. In the latter case, the com-

piler must be supplemented by an assembler in order to complete the conversion process. Once the compiler has generated the equivalent program in machine language, the program may then be executed independently. In the case of interpretation (performed by an *interpreter*) the two steps of conversion and execution are continuously interleaved so that the generated code corresponding to a portion of the source program is executed as it produced. In this manner the interpreter maintains control over both conversion and execution.

In the preceding exposition, the term "conversion" has been used in place of the term "translation," since we wish to reserve the latter for a very specific purpose (*see also* LANGUAGE TRANSLATION). The American National Standard Vocabulary for Information Processing (ANSVIP; 1970) provides a strict definition of this term:

translate
To *transform statements* from one *language* to another without significantly changing the meaning.

In this sense, a programmer must insist that a compiler or the conversion process within an interpreter should be a translator, since the meaning associated with a source program *must* be carried over to the target language program. The ANSVIP also provides definitions associated with the process of compilation and interpretation:

compile
To prepare a *machine language* program from a *computer program* written in another *programming language* by making use of the overall logic structure of the program, or generating more than one *machine [language] instruction* for each symbolic *statement,* or both, as well as performing the function of an *assembler.*

interpreter
(1) A *computer program* that *translates* and executes each *source language* statement before translating and executing the next one.

In practice, there rarely exists a compiler or an interpreter which adheres precisely to these definitions; most languages possess certain features that cannot be compiled, and most interpreters initially preprocess the source program into some intermediate form from which the original program can be reconstructed, and operate upon that code rather than the original form.

The steps that compose the process of translation of the statements of a high-level computer programming guage into machine language are shown in Fig. 1.

In Fig. 1, the processor portions of the translation system are shown in rectangular blocks and the data groups upon which they operate and which they develop

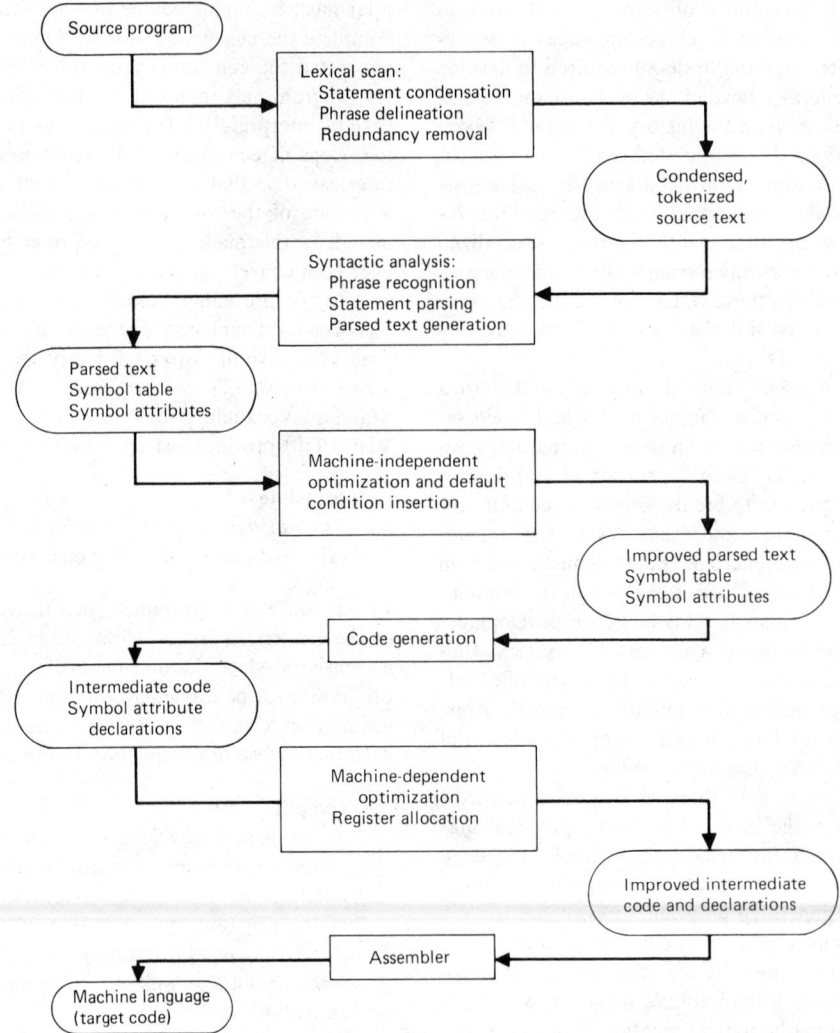

Fig. 1. The detailed process of language translation more closely related to the problem (a high-level programming language) than to a machine language.

are in ovals. This diagram is extremely formalized, the individual processors not being readily recognizable in most translatory systems. Nor is it necessary, as may be inferred from this diagram, that each phase of translation is completed before the next is entered.

The lexical analyzer used in the lexical scan performs the task of preparing the source text (the user's program in machine-readable form) for the syntactic analyzer phase. At the same time it attempts to condense the text so as to improve the efficiency of later examinations of the text. For example, in Fortran 77, the inclusion of blanks in the statements is tolerated by the language so as to provide a more readable text for the programmer.

In fact, except in Hollerith constants (i.e., literal strings), blanks may be inserted randomly.

However, such niceties can considerably slow down the statement scanning routines, which must examine each and every character of the statement. Hence, one of the assigned tasks of a Fortran lexical scan will be to eliminate nonsignificant blanks and condense the statements to their "raw" symbolic content. Further, to assist the syntactic analyzer, the delineation of the statements into words or phrases can be accomplished for many languages.

Once having recognized a symbol or a phrase, the lexical analyzer may then replace that item in the source text by a *token* that is more easily identifiable by the syntactic analyzer. At the same time, the lexical analyzer places the recognized element into the symbol table for later reference. For example, in Basic, the design of the language (to ease implementation) is such that the first three characters following the line number are a unique characterization of the type of statement that follows. Thus, if the lexical analyzer separates these characters into (say) one word, the recognition of the type of statement by the syntactic analyzer can be facilitated.

Further, considering Basic as a simple language for compilation, it is possible to recognize variables and language constants by simple lexical rules (as opposed to syntactic rules). Any string that starts with (has as the leftmost character) an alphabetic character is a candidate for recognition as a variable. The right delimiter of such a string is any non-alphanumeric character, except in the case of FOR statements, where special character sequences (TO and STEP) are of importance. However, it is possible in a lexical scan to recognize about 90% of all instances of variables and constants and to collect the characters that compose those language elements into words or other well-defined units. By this means, for example, punctuation in Basic READ and PRINT statements can be eliminated, the language elements now being delineated by logical boundaries in the representation of the text. The process of lexical analysis is accomplished by the use of algorithms for finite state machines (*see* AUTOMATA THEORY).

The syntactic analyzer of a translatory process completes the task of analyzing the input text by converting the text into a completely specified (*parsed*) text in which the grammatical components of the language are appropriately connected with the elements of the text. Syntactic analyzers may appear in one of two possible forms: a generalized analyzer, which uses a set of syntactic specifications to direct the analysis of a text; or a specialized analyzer, specifically designed for the analysis of text related to one specific language. Even though the lexical analyzer has "worked over" the text on the basis of readily recognizable characters in the text, such as punctuation, the syntactic analyzer must determine the structure of the text based on the grammar (syntax) of the language.

Lexical and syntactic analysis can be distinguished by the spatial relationships that exist between the elements over which they can operate. While it is true that in the Chomsky hierarchy (*q.v.*) of grammars (and hence of representable languages) lexical properties are a subset of syntactic properties, a useful distinction to make here is that lexical relationships exist only over one-dimensional textual domains of language (that is, between juxtaposed symbols) whereas the scope of a syntactic analyzer is two-dimensional since it permits relationships between juxtaposed symbols as well as relationships between more distant symbols.

"Pure" syntactic analysis of a text develops only a parsed version of the text, but the syntactic analyzer in a translatory process (as we will consider it here) also acts as a "collection agency" by adding to the *symbol table* of recognized elements (such as variables and constants) the attributes assigned (or implied) to those elements by the language.

The form in which a syntactic analyzer provides the parsed text to the next process is by no means fixed. It is necessary that the output from this analyzer be in the form of a structure that conveys the nested nature of the language to the succeeding processes. Syntactically parsed texts are typically displayed as trees, though a linked list or linear form may be more appropriate for machine representation.

Once the text has been scanned by the syntactic analyzer and the parsed text developed, a machine-independent optimization process may be used over the text to improve the anticipated code to be generated in a later phase. Machine-independent optimization can be distinguished from the later stage of machine-dependent optimization, not only by the fact that the domains of the two optimization processes are different but also by mechanisms of optimization. In the case of machine-dependent optimization, it is the general intent to eliminate instructions that are redundant.

If this latter type of optimization were to be applied to self-modifying code, it would not always be possible to reorganize instruction sequences and be assured that the optimizing changes not affect the result. On the other hand, at the level of a language such as Fortran, it is known that no statement is subject to modification. Thus, any change made within a single Fortran statement does not affect any other statement. For example, the recognition of common subexpressions, which has been the subject of several papers in the literature, is a process that provides optimization at the machine-independent level. For example, the Fortran statement

$$X = A \cdot B + A \cdot B + A \cdot B$$

may be reduced to the two sequential statements

$$Z = A \cdot B$$
$$X = 3 \cdot Z$$

which will develop the desired result in X.

On a larger scale, machine-independent optimization of statements that occur in loops can have a significant effect on the resulting execution time of the generated program. An analysis of the changes in the values of variables within loops can reveal that certain operations are repeated on each pass through the loop, and hence can be moved out of the loop to some initialization phase. Knuth (1971) has reported that in one typical analyzed program, almost 18% of the execution time was due to the repeated conversions of the constant 0 from integer to real mode. In this particular program, the constant was contained in an assignment statement in which the variable on the left-hand side was invariant during the repeated execution of the loop. Thus, the movement of this statement outside the loop gave a total execution time improvement of approximately 30%. Machine-independent optimization is, however, generally language-dependent, for although the techniques of optimization may be common across languages, the abilities to apply these techniques may be different for each language.

On the other hand, optimization of the type where one specified operation is replaced by another known to be faster on a particular machine is specifically machine-dependent optimization. For example, on a certain machine it was found by the author that the subroutine to perform the operation A^I took longer to develop a result than successive multiplications when I was an integer less than 15. Thus, a compiler written for that machine took this knowledge into account and transformed the Fortran phrase A**I into A*A*A*...*A in those circumstances. On the other hand, optimization of an expression to eliminate sign reversals, and thus minimize the number of operators in the expression, is not machine-dependent. This latter process of replacing operators by other simpler operators is known as *strength reduction*.

After initial code generation, the developed code is subjected to a machine-dependent optimization process that is independent of the original source language. Here, the optimization process is highly dependent on the characteristics of the target processor. An example of a highly machine-dependent optimization would be the assignment of index registers to code which had been developed on the basis of an infinite availability of registers.

Definitions of the techniques of compiler code generation optimization are included in Allen and Cocke (1972), and include:

Procedure integration
Loop transformation (making procedures into in-line code)
Common subexpression elimination
Code motion (moving code to a location where it is less frequently used)
Constant folding (computing constant expressions at compile time)
Dead code elimination
Strength reduction
Instruction scheduling (especially in multiprocessor environments)

Register allocation
Storage mapping (reuse of storage)
Special case code optimization
Peephole (or limited domain) optimization.

Binding Time. Given a program in (almost) any language and the derivation therefrom of the set of identifiers, constants, references, and other language elements, there must occur at some time a mapping from this user's set of elements onto the available storage of the computer that is to execute or which is executing the generated program. The majority of high-level computer languages do not provide the programmer with the ability to describe explicitly the organization of memory at object time (except in the case of Fortran COMMON), and rarely (with the exception of Fortran EQUIVALENCE) do they allow the user to specify relationships between identifiers and other language elements. Thus, the implementer is free to devise some mapping algorithm between the language elements and their assigned storage locations (at object time), provided a certain criterion is met. This criterion is that the values assigned to some identifier (variable, array element, statement identifier, etc.) should be retrievable at some later (possibly restricted) time.

The instant at which all the information is available which is necessary to permit the allocation of object time storage to some language element, is one of the bounds on the *binding time* of that element. That is, there must exist two bounds (which in certain instances may be identical) on the time during which storage may be assigned to a language element. The latest time (bound) available to assign a storage location to a language element is obviously the instant prior to its first usage in the program.

Conversely, if all the attributes of a language element are not only known but are also known to be fixed (i.e., static) at the instant that the element is first encountered in the translatory process, then it is possible to assign (allocate) storage at this earliest time. This period may be further subdivided by considering the type of memory referencing to be performed. For instance, if the earliest binding time is taken as that instant when an absolute address can be assigned to a language element, then actual binding might be defined as load time (i.e., the time at which the program is loaded into storage).

Binding time may be a language feature or it may be implementation-defined. For example, in APL, the left-arrow (assignment operator ←) operation has the side effect (actually, an initial effect) of assigning the attributes of the expression to its right to the operand on its left. Thus, the instant at which all the information is available to enable the assignment of storage to the operand on the left is the instant of executing the assignment operation. Hence, APL has dynamic attribute specifications, and binding time (earliest and latest) is execution time. Lacking explicit (and static) declarations of attributes, the APL interpreter itself determines attributes at execution time. Conversely, Basic, in the case of missing (omitted) array-size declarations, inserts the missing attributes so as to permit compile-time binding of variables.

In choosing a binding time within the established bounds, the implementer is free to choose any particular instant. However, the later that binding takes place, the greater the difficulty in generating effective code and the more time it will take to both store and retrieve the values of language elements. For instance, if an absolute address had been assigned to a variable, then all references to that variable in the generated code may be made directly. However, if the binding time is delayed until (say) the last moment, then each reference to that variable will require the system to look up the assigned location. Thus, the work of the symbol table is delayed until execution time and may be performed repeatedly rather than just once as would be the case for compile time binding of variables. In any case, it should be a general principle that the earliest possible binding time should be used always.

In the development of the Ada language (*q.v.*), it was established as a language design principle that the attributes of each language element should be determinable at compile time, thus defining compile time to be the earliest binding time and to make storage assignment effectively a static activity.

Compilation vs. Interpretation. Many factors must be considered by a language implementer before the decision is made to compile or interpret, to develop optimized code or not, to develop a load-and-go system, or to separate completely the translation and execution phases. The environment within which the system is to operate may help to determine the type of system to be developed. For example, if it is expected that the system will be used primarily for education, then an interpretive system may be advantageous, provided error reports are related to the source code directly. Or in a mixed education and research environment where many programs will run but few will ever become production programs and be run repeatedly, a load-and-go system may suit the needs best. That is, the code developed by a compiler is stored directly in the memory of the computer instead of being output on some intermediate storage system, and control is transferred to the first executable statement in the compiled program after compilation is complete, with the developed code not being saved for subsequent executions. In the same type of situation, where the number of compiles is high, an extremely efficient (or fast) compiler is necessary, and thus the opti-

mization phases may be omitted on the basis that the overall cost of compilation does not justify the cost of execution. Conversely, in a shop where compiled programs are to be developed into production systems and one compile may result in many thousands of runs, then a methodical compiler that develops highly optimized machine code is of importance.

The answer to the question of whether to compile or to interpret—all other economic questions being equal and assuming that the source code is susceptible to either interpretation or compilation—may depend on other factors that are less easy to express in quantitative terms. With regard to storage, it can be realized that the amount of storage required by a compiler is not substantially different from that required to perform the same tasks within the interpreter; in fact the interpreter will contain additional features to perform the execution phase of the problem solution. On the other hand, while it is obvious that there need be no significant differences between user data-storage requirements in an interpretive system as compared to a compiler system, nor differences between the storage requirements for the symbol tables of the two systems, a judicious design of the interpretive symbol table can substantially reduce the combined storage requirements of the symbol table and the user data storage.

Conversely, the interpreter must be self-sufficient and, except in comparatively large computer systems with fast access ancillary storage facilities, the interpreter should also have, readily available in memory, all anticipated library routines. On the other hand, the compiler can take advantage of the hiatus between compilation and execution to load into memory only those which are needed by this particular program.

It has been shown empirically many times that the amount of storage required by the compiled code of a source text is not substantially different (but is almost always less) than that for the source text itself.

Based on these premises we may deduce two interesting relations. *For the same program* (source text):

$$IM_{interpreter} > CM_{compiler}$$
$$IM_{user\ data} = EM_{user\ data}$$
$$IM_{symbol\ table} = CM_{symbol\ table}$$
$$IM_{source\ text} = EM_{target\ code}$$
$$IM_{library} >> EM_{library}$$

where IM stands for interpretative memory, CM stands for compile-time memory, and EM stands for execute-time memory. If ΣIM is the sum of all necessary parts of the memory for the interpreter, ΣCM is the sum of memory used at compile time, and ΣEM is the memory used at execute time, then it is obvious that $\Sigma IM > \Sigma CM$ and $\Sigma IM >> \Sigma EM$.

Other features relevant to the problem of whether to interpret or to compile are listed in Table 1.

Table 1

Interpreters	Compilers
1. Available storage should contain at the same time the interpreter, the source text, the symbol table and *all* library routines. Hence, the size of program (as measured by the numbers of statements in the program and the number of data elements defined) is restricted compared to that available for use with a compiler system.	The available storage at compile time must contain the compiler, the symbol table, and *one* statement from the source text. At execute time, the available storage must contain the compiled code and the required library routines.
2. There is always a direct relationship between the source text and the code being executed; hence there is a good relationship between detected errors and the source text, which promotes easy debugging.	The relationship between the source text and the code being executed is remote. Hence the burden of error/source relations is placed on the programmer and his/her knowledge of the machine and its compiler.
3. Syntactic errors detected by the interpreter can be corrected during a run (at the request of the interpreter) and do not require the whole run to be restarted. Execution errors may be reported to the programmer and source text changes can be made under the same controls.	Syntactic errors can be corrected at the instant of recognition, but the unavailability of the source text at execution time requires that corrections be made to the source text and that recompilation of all or, at least, part of the source text be performed.
4. Because of 2 and 3 above, and recognizing that condition 1 may not be too restrictive in this mode, an interpreter may be well suited to conversational time-sharing.	Compared to the interpreter, a compiler system is better suited to batch environments.
5. Due to the successive recompilations of the statements in the source text and the need to reference all data through the symbol table, an interpretive system is expensive to use.	A compiler system makes better use of the available resources of the computer system.

The question of whether a program written in a certain language can be compiled or can be interpreted is not directly related to the question of whether to interpret or to compile except as related to available storage. Obviously, if the average-size program (determined by some undefined means) cannot be interpreted because of a lack of available storage, there is a possibility that it may be compiled, and thus the question of to compile or to interpret is answered. However, it may be that some languages are not susceptible to compilation and must, therefore, be interpreted; conversely, it would seem that any language that can be compiled can also be interpreted (storage requirements aside). There are some languages which contain elements that cannot be compiled but which must be interpreted, thus raising the possibility of "hybrid" translator systems. In fact, Fortran is in the latter category: Due to the inclusion in the language of variable FORMAT, which is specified by the user at execution time, a portion of the compiler is left in the generated program to interpret the corresponding READ or WRITE statement. Similarly, those languages (such as PL/I and APL) that permit dynamic storage allocation must be interpreted to some extent.

In this context, it is necessary to define *interpretive code* as code that is parameterized to the extent that differing attributes of the operands can be inserted (accessed) at run time, and are not statically specified during the compilation phase. Typically, references to dynamically defined data elements take the form of calls upon generalized routines that can respond to the differing data organizations.

The Symbol Table. In the organization of any translatory system in which several subprocesses of translation take place (such as lexical analysis, syntactic analysis, and code generation), the vehicle for the transference of extracted or deduced information regarding the text is the symbol table. The symbol table provides a base for the coalescence of data relating to the various elements of the source text and provides a possibility for describing certain relationships between the text and the target machine, such as the assigned (possibly relative) addresses of variables. In a static environment the symbol table will serve the purpose of providing (say) assigned addresses to the compiler's code generator for substitution into instruction masks (see the last section of this article), while the symbol table in a dynamic environment may exist also at run time to provide a key to currently allocated memory space. Between the time of ending compilation and beginning the execution of the generated program (assuming that the generated code is not resident), the symbol table will provide necessary data to the loader for the acquisition of library-provided subprograms and will, in turn during run time, act as a transfer vector for the linkage of the generated code and those subprograms.

The compile-time symbol table of an algebraic language processor will contain entries pertinent to the various data elements that may occur within the source text. In general these may include variables (both simple and n-dimensional), statement identifiers, subprogram (or block) names, and constants. Among this data will appear not only the deduced (or defined) attributes of the language element but also data pertinent to the compilation of the statements in which they either appeared or are expected to appear.

In some language systems the symbol table may play an extremely important part of the run-time characteristics of the system. For example, in any system that includes the ability to allocate and free storage, or in a system that is implemented so that storage is dynamically controlled, the symbol table is the key between the executable code and the data set.

During the various phases of compilation or interpretation, in any procedural or block-structured language there may exist several differing symbol tables, each relating to a particular block or procedure. While the *raison d'être* and the means of establishment of each symbol table may be distinct, the means by which symbol tables in general are organized is common to all.

The purpose of a symbol table is to provide a common data source to the various components of a translatory system relating to the elements of the source text and, in particular, to provide a source of data pertinent to the specified or deduced attributes of those elements. The symbol table is thus being accessed by many routines during the process of translation and therefore must be amenable to rapid access and data retrieval. The routine that organizes the symbol table directs a number of tasks, among them the following.

1. Post an item and its associated data.
2. Retrieve the data associated with any item.
3. Delete an item and its associated data.

All these activities involve the searching of the table to locate the item or to recognize the absence of that item, and hence the efficiency of this search affects the efficiency of the whole compiler.

McClure (1972) states that the majority of productive working compilers use some variant of the *hash link* method of symbol table organization. This technique combines hash addressing based on the symbol table entry representation (i.e., the character string that comprises the language element representation) to locate an initial entry in a fixed-size table, with a linked list emanating from the initial entry.

Where a program is being developed in an interactive environment that includes the facilities for symbolic debugging, the maintenance of the symbol table during the post-compilation phase of development is essential. As in the case of dynamic storage features where a skeletal representation of the symbol table must remain in order to provide access to dynamically allocated elements, so in the case of a symbolic debugging environment, the user must have access to run-time data through reference to identifiers that are stored in the symbol table. Further, the reporting of the contents of the symbol table

on completion of compilation is a useful tool to place in the hands of the programmer.

During the 1970s, probably the two greatest developments in the design and production of compilers were in the areas of code optimization (discussed above) and syntactic analysis. While there existed a number of syntactic analysis methods in use in 1970, their approach was basically to provide a framework within which specialized analyzers could be developed by the designer *by hand*. Since that time, these techniques have matured considerably to the point where there exist a number of syntactic analysis generators that are based on the prior development of a formal syntactic description of the language to be compiled.

However, the two main techniques of implementing syntactic analyzers continue to be *precedence analysis* for expressions that contain a hierarchy of recognizable operators and the *method of recursive descent* (Lucas, 1961).

The former method, which originated with Samelson and Bauer (1960) has been formalized into simple stack automata which are driven by a precedence table which can be created by a table generated from the given grammar (*see* GRAMMARS) (Floyd, 1963).

Considerable attention has been paid to, and significant progress has been made in, the use of shift-reduce parsing techniques based on LL or LR grammars. Standing for left to right scanning with left- or right-most derivation, these techniques are necessarily the subject of table generation techniques, since the labor of producing them by hand is extremely high and subject to the producer not covering every possible situation. Variants on these schema have also been developed, including the simple LR technique (SLR) and the look ahead LR (LALR). For the theory of LL grammars, see Rosenkrantz and Stearns (1970). The fundamental paper on LR systems was presented by Knuth (1965) and extended to SLR and LALR by DeRemer in 1969 and 1971, respectively.

Combining the methods of syntactic analysis and the synthesis of attribute data has been formalized as *attribute grammars* by Lewis, Rosenkrantz, and Stearns (1976). By these methods, the data associated with identifiers in programs can be moved throughout the syntactic tree, synthesizing data toward the root (from declaration statements, for example) and inherited away from the root toward other elements (such as in inserting the functions necessary to perform code conversion across an assignment operator).

REFERENCES

1960. Samelson, K. and Bauer, P. I. "Sequential Formula Translation," *Comm. ACM* **3:** 76–83 (February).
1961. Lucas, P. "Die Structuranalyse von Formelübersetzen," *Electron. Rechenanl.* **3:** 159–167.

1963. Floyd, R. W. "Syntactic Analysis and Operator Precedence," *JACM* **7**, *No. 2:* 316–333.

1964. Randell, B. and Russell, D. J. *Algol 60 Implementation.* London: Academic Press.

1965. Knuth, D. E. "On the Translation of Languages from Left to Right," *Information and Control* **8**, *No. 6:* 607–639.

1966. Ingerman, P. Z. *A Syntax Oriented Translator.* New York: Academic Press.

1967. Lee, J. A. N. *The Anatomy of a Compiler.* New York: Van Nostrand Reinhold.

1968. Wegner, P. *Programming Languages, Information Structures, and Machine Organization.* New York: McGraw-Hill.

1969. Hopgood, F. R. A. *Compiling Techniques.* New York: American Elsevier.

1970. American National Standards Institute. *Vocabulary for Information Processing,* Doc. No. X3.12-1970. New York: ANSI.

1970. Association for Computing Machinery. "Proceedings of a Symposium on Compiler Optimization," *SIGPLAN Notices* **5**, *No. 7* (July).

1970. Cocke, J. and Schwartz, J. T. "Programming Languages and Their Compilers—Preliminary Notes," *Courant Inst. of Math. Sciences,* New York University.

1970. Rosenkrantz, D. J. and Stearns, R. E. "Properties of Deterministic Top-Down Grammars," *Information and Control* **17**, *No. 3:* 226–256.

1971. Knuth, D. E. "An Empirical Study of FORTRAN Programs," *Software—Practice and Experience* **1:** 105–133.

1972. Gries, D. *Compiler Construction for Digital Computers.* New York: Wiley.

1972. McClure, R. M. "An Appraisal of Compiler Technology," *Proc. S.J.C.C.* **40.** Montvale, NJ: AFIPS Press.

1972. Allen, F. E. and Cocke, J. "A Catalog of Optimizing Transformations," *Courant Computer Science Symposium.* Englewood Cliffs, NJ: Prentice-Hall, pp. 1–30.

1976. Lewis, P. M., Rosenkrantz, D. J., and Stearns, R. E. *Compiler Design Theory.* Reading MA: Addison-Wesley.

1980. Knuth, D. E. and Pardo, L. T. "The Early Development of Programming Languages," in Metropolis, N. et al. (Eds.), *The History of Computing in the Twentieth Century.* New York: Academic Press.

1981. Hopper, G. M. "Early Days," Keynote Presentation, *Proc. History of Programming Languages Conference.* New York: Academic Press.

J. A. N. LEE

LANGUAGES. *See* ADA; ALGEBRAIC MANIPULATION LANGUAGES; ALGOL 68; ASSOCIATIVE LANGUAGES; AUTHORING LANGUAGES AND SYSTEMS; C; COMMAND AND JOB CONTROL LANGUAGES; DATA DEFINITION LANGUAGES; DECISION TABLES: LANGUAGES; FORMAL LANGUAGES; LIST PROCESSING LANGUAGES; MACHINE AND ASSEMBLY LANGUAGE PROGRAMMING; MACROLANGUAGES; METALANGUAGE; NONPROCEDURAL LANGUAGES; PASCAL; PROBLEM-ORIENTED LANGUAGES; PROCEDURE-ORIENTED LANGUAGES; PROGRAMMING LANGUAGES; SETL; SIMULATION: LANGUAGES; and STRING PROCESSING LANGUAGES.

LANGUAGES, PROGRAMMING. *See* PROGRAMMING LANGUAGES.

LANGUAGE TRANSLATION

For articles on related subjects *see* ARTIFICIAL INTELLIGENCE; CHOMSKY HIERARCHY; NATURAL LANGUAGE PROCESSING; PROGRAMMING LINGUISTICS; and STRING-PROCESSING LANGUAGES.

The idea of using a computer as an aid for language translation seems to have originated in 1946 in a discussion between Warren Weaver and A. D. Booth. The computers of those days were so limited in storage and availability that until the mid-1950s it was hardly practical to use them for experimentation. Nevertheless, interest grew in the subject and was accelerated in the United States by the circulation of a memorandum by Warren Weaver and by the development of important techniques such as pre- and post-editing of text, and stem-ending decomposition (Locke and Booth, 1965), microglossaries, and binary dictionary search (Booth, 1953) which originated in this period. Probably the best account of early machine translation is that given by Locke and Booth.

In the 1950s and early 1960s, a number of projects came into being, particularly in the United States, encouraged by generous research funding and increasingly available computer time. Among the notable ideas emerging were those of predictive analysis—linguistic depth—which is concerned with the extent to which human beings can comprehend sentences (like the present one) in which clauses are embedded within other clauses, and proposals for the efficient mechanization of dictionaries (Oettinger, 1960). The end of the decade was notable for the development of Comit, the first higher-level language dedicated to text processing, and for Chomsky's work on transformational grammars.

In England a translation program from French into English, using a microglossary, was tested; the powerful computer of the National Physical Laboratory was utilized for a Russian-English translation experiment; and the idea of a thesaurus as an aid to the problem of multiple meaning was investigated.

On the European continent, projects emerged in Italy, France, and Germany, but only in Russia was support available on anything like the scale of that in the United States. Booth (1967) and Josselson (1971) are perhaps the best general references for this phase of machine translation (MT).

The majority of these projects concentrated, for political reasons, on the language pair Russian-English, and when Canada entered the field in the mid-1960s, politics also prompted support by the National Research Council of two projects directed toward English to French translation. Outstanding techniques emerging from this work are modified forms of transformational grammars, allowing the insertion of parameters and conditions and a rapid method of parsing, using statistical data.

In late 1966, a report by the National Academy of Sciences (NAS) in the United States presented a gloomy view of the future of MT and suggested that funds should be diverted to computational linguistics. This, combined with the general reduction in research funding, has led to a change in emphasis or to the elimination of many projects in the United States.

The NAS report, which is open to criticism on technical grounds, was undoubtedly partly inspired by the unrealistic claims made by some groups, chiefly industrial, of the imminent availability of fully automatic, high-quality translation by computers. Such claims were, of course, unjustified and led to a reaction against MT. It is unfortunate to note a recrudescence of them in recent literature.

Linguistic Problems of MT. At the lowest level of machine-aided translation, the computer is used merely as a mechanical dictionary, rendering translations of words or phrases as requested. As has been demonstrated at the German Armed Forces Translation Center at Mannheim, this can be a very useful service to human translators. All research projects, however, have aimed at more ambitious targets, ranging from the provision of technical translation good enough to be comprehensible directly or (after post-editing) by an expert in the field to the unattained goal of perfect machine output without human intervention.

As soon as even the simplest of these goals is attempted, the problem of syntax arises. That is, in order to produce translation at any level (as distinct from transliteration), some analysis must be made of the function of words in a sentence and their relation to one another in the source language. Moreover, since languages often differ in structure, transformations may be necessary before the target language sentence can be produced. Thus the sentence "He was given a difficult book by the teacher" becomes "Le maître lui a donné un livre difficile" in French (literally; the teacher to him has given a book difficult). In order to make the translation, it was necessary first to recognize that, "he," "book," and "teacher" are respectively the subject, direct object, and agent in the English sentence, and that "book" is therefore a noun rather than an adjective or verb. Second, a transformation must be made to remove the passive construction, which would not be grammatical in French,

and finally the order of adjective and noun must be reversed in French.

More subtle (and mostly unsolved) difficulties are that the teacher might in fact be feminine, requiring the translation of *La maîtres,* and that the sense of the surrounding text might require a completely different translation, such as *instituteur* or *professeur.* This illustrates the limitation of attempting translation by using only the local context of a single sentence. Most machine translation schemes do just this, and are thereby restricted in scope. In fact, to produce a perfect translation, the global context of a paragraph—or, indeed, of the complete text—may sometimes have to be considered.

The process of translation is thus seen to involve at least four stages;

1. Lookup of each word in a source language dictionary to determine properties and possible functions.
2. Analysis to determine the function of words and groups of words in the sentence.
3. Rearrangement and transformation of the results of (2) to conform to the syntax of the target language.
4. Substitution of target language equivalents.

As well as these four stages, any realistic translation scheme must include an idiom-processing routine, usually incorporated in stage 1. This is necessary because of the numerous phrases that are so peculiar to a language that they cannot be rendered on a word-by-word basis into another language (e.g., French *boîte de nuit* = English "night club").

The four stages defined above may in fact overlap and entwine each other in practice, but the important conclusion which is implied is that a precisely defined form of the syntax of source and target language must be provided to act as a basis for the program. This, together with the provision of adequately fast methods for applying this information, has been the crucial problem in MT.

It cannot be said that the problem has yet been solved in the sense that any one of the many schemes proposed and tested is greatly superior to any other in quality of resulting output, speed of operation, and extent of application. Some characteristic approaches are outlined briefly below. For a more extensive survey see Booth (1967) and Josselson (1971).

Transformational Grammars. Many of the proposed methods of machine translation utilize transformational grammars of the type discussed by Chomsky. A very simple example of such a grammar might be:

⟨sentence⟩ → ⟨subject phrase⟩⟨verb⟩
⟨subject phrase⟩ → the ⟨noun⟩
⟨verb⟩ → has | sees
⟨noun⟩ → cat | dog

The elements enclosed by ⟨ ⟩ are the syntactic elements, or *nonterminal symbols*, of the language and the words "the," "has," "cat," etc. are called *terminal symbols*. The "rules" are known as transformations or *productions*, and should define all possible legal sentences in the language under consideration. The vertical stroke | means "or".

Although attractive from the theoretical point of view, both because the precise style of formulation lends itself to computer interpretation and because (in theory) new "rules" can be added without altering the interpreting program, methods based on this idea suffer two disadvantages. When applied to natural languages, the number of rules required tends to be very large, and the ambiguous nature of many of the terminal symbols (words) of a language means that many permutations may have to be tested before a correct parsing is found.

As an example, consider the following very simple grammar in which the abbreviations used are: Noun = N, Verb = V, Adjective = A, Subordinator (while, when, etc.) = S, Determiner (a, the, etc.) = D, Connector (and) = C, Adverb = B.

Verb Phrase (VP) → ⟨V⟩ | ⟨V⟩ ⟨B⟩
Noun Phrase (NP) → ⟨N⟩ | ⟨D⟩ ⟨N⟩ |
　　　　　　　　　⟨D⟩ ⟨A⟩ ⟨N⟩
Subordinate Clause (SC) → ⟨S⟩ ⟨A⟩
Main Clause (MC) → ⟨NP⟩ ⟨VP⟩
Sentence → ⟨MC⟩ . | ⟨SC⟩ , ⟨MC⟩ . |
　　　　　　⟨MC⟩ , ⟨MC⟩ ⟨C⟩ ⟨MC⟩ .

Suppose we try to parse the sentence:

While contented, the man works well.

The individual words of this sentence can take the following possible parts of speech:

contented	V or A
man	N or V or A
the	D
well	N or V or A or B
while	N or S
works	N or V

On a first try, "while" and "the man works" might be identified as noun phrases, and "contented" and "well" as verb phrases. These then group to give two main clauses, but an attempt to form the construct ⟨MC⟩ , ⟨MC⟩ ⟨C⟩ ⟨MC⟩ would fail. We might next try "while contented" parsed as a subordinate clause, and the final parse as a sentence is then obtained from ⟨SC⟩ , ⟨MC⟩ · . This, of course, is incorrect semantically, but correct as far as our grammar is concerned. Further investigation would then show that the alternative, and correct, parse

"the man" = NP, "works well" = VP would also give a valid sentence.

As well as showing that *backtracking* (*q.v.*) and the investigation of alternative parses may be necessary, this example illustrates that a parsing method must produce *all* possible analyses for a given sentence.

Transition Network Grammars. This method of parsing is best described by an example. Suppose that the syntactic element *Noun Phrase* is defined as a noun possibly preceded by a determiner, or an adjective, or both, and possibly followed by a connector and a second noun. Thus,

$$[Determiner] \ [Adjective] \ \{Noun\} \ ([Connector] \ [Noun])$$

where the braces { } indicate that the element must be present, the brackets [ ] indicate optional elements, and parentheses ( ) indicate that the enclosed elements must be present together if at all. The process of parsing such a phrase can be represented by a *transition network*, which has an entrance node ① with at least one path leading from it, and an exit node ⊗ with at least one path leading to it and no paths emerging from it. These are connected by a series of nodes indicating the elements that must be recognized if the particular syntactic element is to be identified. Thus the transition network for *Noun Phrase* will be as shown in Fig. 1. Every syntactic element in the language will have such an associated network.

Semantic Models. As remarked earlier, the fundamental problem behind any attempt at translation is that of analyzing the "meaning" in the source language and conveying it into the target language. The use of semantic models, or templates, is one approach suggested as an aid in this process.

A number of such models are defined, each designed to express a particular "message," and these are matched against the source sentence. For example, one model might be

Actor-Act-Object

which would match the sentence

Men eat apples

because the dictionary would contain the information that *Men* is in the semantic class "actor," *eat* in the class "act," etc.

It is not yet clear how far such a system can cope with a more convoluted sentence structure, or how many models will be needed.

Dependency Theory (Hays, 1967). Developed by the MT group in Georgetown University and by workers in

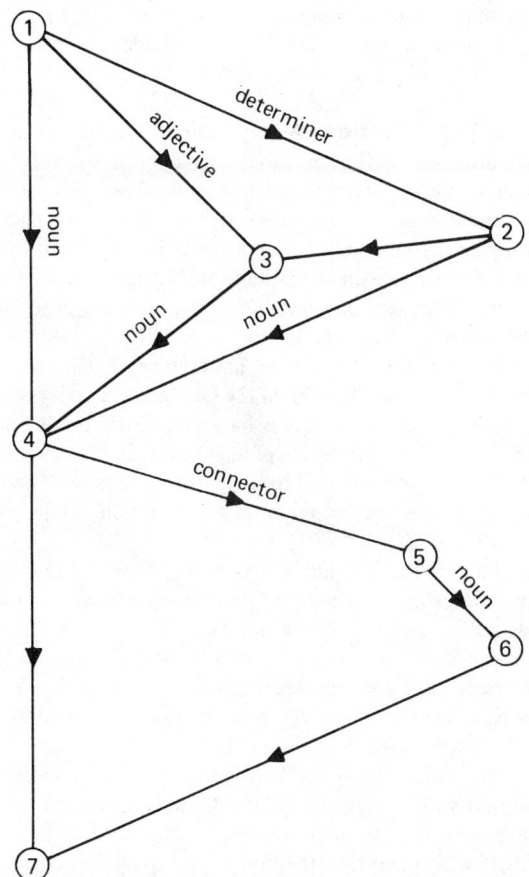

Fig. 1. Transition network for noun phrase.

the Rand Corporation, this method seeks to analyze sentences in terms of governor and dependent units. Analysis proceeds to higher and higher levels of grammar until, in general, a single ungoverned symbol is obtained. Most words and units have multiple functions and may be either governors or dependents.

Q and W Systems. The MT group at the University of Montreal has developed two grammars based on transformational grammars, but with the modifications that parameters can be introduced and the application of the rules can be governed by certain conditions. These grammars are called Q and W systems (after A. Querido and A. van Wijngaarden); in application to MT, the source language is first transformed to a "normalized" form. This leads to a normalized form of the target language, which is finally transformed to the actual target language.

Formational Theory. Developed at the University of Texas, this method is closely related to a transformational grammar, and assumes that the formation of sym-

bol strings can be defined mathematically. A metalanguage (*q.v.*) is used as an intermediate stage between the source and object language.

Wayne State University MT Program. An initial analysis of a sentence identifies elements or "blocks"; these are used in subsequent analysis to identify the main sentence units such as subject, predicate, and object. Although the blocking process will generally not be unambiguous, the resulting reduction in the number of elements that must be handled in the final phase simplifies the latter.

Predictive Analysis (Oettinger, 1960). The MT group at Harvard University has utilized the method of predictive analysis, first suggested by Rhodes. Analysis of a sentence is performed in a left-to-right scan, and predictions are recorded at each stage of the possible outcome. When a prediction is either fulfilled or shown to be untenable, it is erased. A practical difficulty, which was later removed to some extent by Plath, lay in the number of predictions that had to be followed through in some cases.

Statistical Analysis. At the University of Saskatchewan—and subsequently at Lakehead University, Thunder Bay, Ontario—a completely different approach has been tested, in which a preliminary parsing classifies the words of a sentence into 16 categories, using statistical data. Subsequent scans identify larger units, such as noun and verb phrases, and syntactic elements such as subject and object. From this analysis the application of a set of rules enables the target language sentence to be produced. This method has been tested extensively on "scientific" text and has the advantage that it appears to be much faster than most methods that employ a transformational type of scheme. Because of the inevitable errors (about 3.5%) when a statistical method is used, post-editing is considered necessary. An example of this approach is shown in Fig. 2.

This survey does not pretend to be exhaustive, but is enough to give an idea of the scope of methods that have been proposed for MT. The references list further reading in depth.

Computational Problems of MT. The representation of textual as distinct from numeric data in a computer presents no problem—at any rate, in theory. Letters and punctuation are coded numerically and are thereafter manipulated within the computer. The perfect computer, from the point of view of anyone wishing to process text, would undoubtedly be able to accept as input and print out the full range of lower and upper-case letters together with accents and other diacritics peculiar to the language under consideration. However, few such computers exist, and otherwise recourse has to be made to further coding, which is serviceable, though sometimes clumsy.

English Sentence

> North America comprises six main natural regions which are both physiographic and geological because the ages, kinds and structures of the underlying rocks determine the natures of the land surfaces.

Machine Output

> L" *AM1ERIQUE DU *NORD COMPREND SIX R1EGIONS PRINCIPALES NATU-RELLES(PROPRE) /CE/QUI SONT 2A LA FOIS(AUSSI BIEN QUE) PHYSIOGRA-PHIQUES ET G1EOLOGIQUES(DE LA G1EOLOGIE) PARCE QUE LES 3AGES , LES(DES) SORTES ET LES(DES) STRUC-TURES DES ROCHES SOUS-JACENTES (FONDAMENTAL) D1ETERMINENT-(D1ELIMITER/D1ECIDER) LES NA-TURES(SORTES) DES TERRES DE SUR-FACES.

Edited Version

> L'Amérique du Nord comprend six régions principales naturelles qui sont à la fois physiographiques et géologiques parce que les âges, les sortes et les structures des roches sous-jacentes déterminent les natures des terres de surfaces.

Fig. 2. This passage from the *Canada Year Book* is a part of a much larger translation produced by the MLT project at the University of Saskatchewan, Canada. The first French passage shows the machine output, with alternative translations, asterisks for capitals, and numerals representing accents. The second version shows what a human editor would make of it.

Programming has been assisted by the development of such high-level languages as Comit and Snobol, although translation programs have been produced in such unlikely languages as Algol-60 and Cobol, and many are written at least partly in machine language for the sake of speed.

The great problem in the early days of experimentation was restriction in storage space, but this is now a thing of the past. One technique developed to overcome this, and which is still in use to a certain extent, is that of stem-ending decomposition (Locke and Booth, 1965). This considerably reduces the number of dictionary entries required in languages such as Russian or French, which are heavily inflected, but puts an added burden on the lookup program.

MT in Practice. A very desirable feature of any MT program is that it should have been extensively tested on actual text and not merely used on such artificial and unrealistic examples as the famous sentence, "They are flying planes." It is often difficult to determine how far this has been done. Some authenticated tests and realistic estimates of time and costs, etc., however, do exist and are worth mentioning.

At Oak Ridge National Laboratory, Tennessee, a program based on the work of the Georgetown University group has been in operation for some years, producing Russian-English translation of technical text. No post-editing is done, and the total time required is said to be one-quarter of that needed for human translation, while the cost is competitive.

The Foreign Technical Division (FTD) of the U.S. Air Force Base at Dayton, Ohio, has for several years used a Russian-English program based on the work of the University of Texas group at Austin. Machine output is post-edited and a survey has indicated that total costs are comparable with those for human translation and the total time required is about one-half.

An evaluation of the University of Saskatchewan's program was carried out by the Canadian Government Translation Bureau in Ottawa on a 2,600-word technical text. It was found that the cost of MT plus post-editing was about equal to the cost of purely human translation, the end results being comparable. This program has now been tested on about 10,000 words of technical text, and average computer speed and cost are about 350 words per minute and 2 cents per word.

Recent Developments in Machine Translation. There has been a notable decline in published theoretical work on machine translation in recent years, but several groups are engaged in experimental production MT at various levels. There is also a considerable interest in MT, or machine-aided translation, on the part of the European Economic Community (EEC). This arises from the necessity to produce documents in all six of the official languages of the Community, a process involving 30 possible language-translation pairs. This daunting task will mushroom when Greece, Spain, and Portugal join, and the number of combinations becomes 72.

At present, interest is centered on Systran, an American program based originally on the work of the Georgetown group, but much developed by Toma to provide a Russian-English translation for USAF and NASA. This is a four-pass system (input-dictionary lookup-bottom up parse-translation) designed initially for use by specialists in a limited field, and requiring considerable post-editing. It has since been adapted for English-French and French-English translation, and the capabilities of the English-French section were evaluated by representatives of EEC (Van Slype, 1979). Although the output was considered to be far from satisfactory, it was recommended that work should continue to improve the system with the object of making it fully operational.

Another group still pursuing work is the TAUM project at the University of Montreal, where a much simplified version of their original system is being used for translating weather forecasts. Finally, the Chinese University Language Translation program (CULT), originating at the Chinese University of Hong Kong, should be mentioned. This translates pre-edited mathematics and physics journals from Chinese into English with surprisingly good results. Details of the program are not readily available, however.

Machine-Aided Translation. MT projects in which either pre- or post-editing is required are sometimes referred to as machine-aided translation. However, we prefer to define it as translation by a human aided by machine-based dictionaries (or word-banks or term-banks, as they are alternatively called). These normally provide an on-line service whereby the user may request the translation of words or possibly phrases, and obtain a prompt reply via display screen or printer. The number of these grows yearly and they have provided the greatest *practical* help to translators to date. Among them is LEXIS, operated by the West German Bundessprachenamt and providing dictionaries, glossaries, and special word lists of scientific and technical terms via print, photocopy, microfiche, or direct access display units.

The University of Montreal has for some years been compiling a Canadian French-English machine-based dictionary, and EURODICAUTOM is a pan-European data bank which includes dictionary-reference facilities but which is not yet widely accessible.

Finally, it may be mentioned that the paper by Hutchins (1978) gives a good review of the state of the art in 1978, and that of Lawson (1979) provides an interesting comment from the viewpoint of the professional translator.

REFERENCES

1953. Booth, A. D. "Mechanical Translation," *Computers and Automation* **2**, *No. 4.*
1960. Oettinger, A. G. *Automatic Language Translation.* Cambridge, MA: Harvard University Press.
1965. Locke, W. N. and A. D. Booth (Eds.). *Machine Translation of Language.* Cambridge, MA: M.I.T. Press, 3rd printing.
1967. Booth, A. D. (Ed.). *Machine Translation.* Amsterdam: North-Holland.
1967. Hays, D. G. *Introduction to Computational Linguistics.* New York: American-Elsevier.
1971. Josselson, H. H. "Automatic Translation of Language Since 1960: A Linguist's View," *Advances in Computers.* New York: Academic Press.
1978. Hutchins, W. J. "Machine Translation and Machine-Aided Translation," *Journal of Documentation* **34**: 119–159.
1979. Van Slype, Georges. "Systran," *The Incorporated Linguist* **18**, (Summer).
1979. Lawson, Veronica. *"Tigers and Polar Bears or: Translating and the Computer," The Incorporated Linguist* **18**, *No. 3:* 81–85 (Summer).

K. H. V. BOOTH AND A. D. BOOTH

LARC. *See* LIVERMORE AUTOMATIC RESEARCH COMPUTER.

LATENCY

For article on related subject *see* ACCESS TIME; CYLINDER; DIRECT ACCESS; and MEMORY: Auxiliary.

Latency is the rotational delay in reading or writing a record to a direct-access auxiliary memory device such as disk or drum (see Fig. 1). *Maximum* latency is the time for an entire revolution of the recording surface. A program suffers maximum latency—generally undesirable from an efficiency standpoint—if it requests a record whose starting point has just passed under the read/write heads. *Minimum* latency is zero delay, by definition. *Average* latency is half the maximum.

Newer direct-access devices often have a *rotational position sensing* (RPS) feature; they do not attempt to access a record until it is almost under their heads, as shown in Fig. 2. By dividing each track into N equal-sized sectors (N typically is 128), disk drives having the RPS feature reduce channel *latency,* but not *drive latency.* Channel latency blocks activity on all drives attached to the channel; while the channel awaits correct positioning of the record on one drive, no other drives can be active. The RPS feature permits a channel to service other drives while the requested sector is rotating toward the read/write head, as shown in Fig. 2.

D. N. FREEMAN

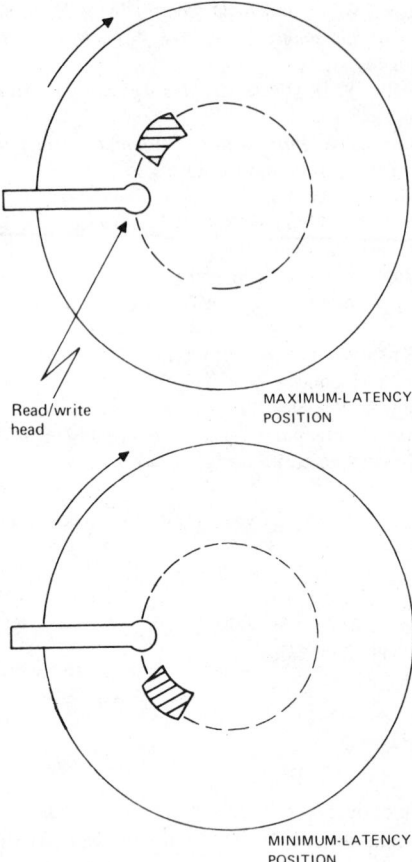

Fig. 1. Maximum and minimum latencies for various head-record orientations. Time: just after channel commences search for record indicated by cross-hatching.

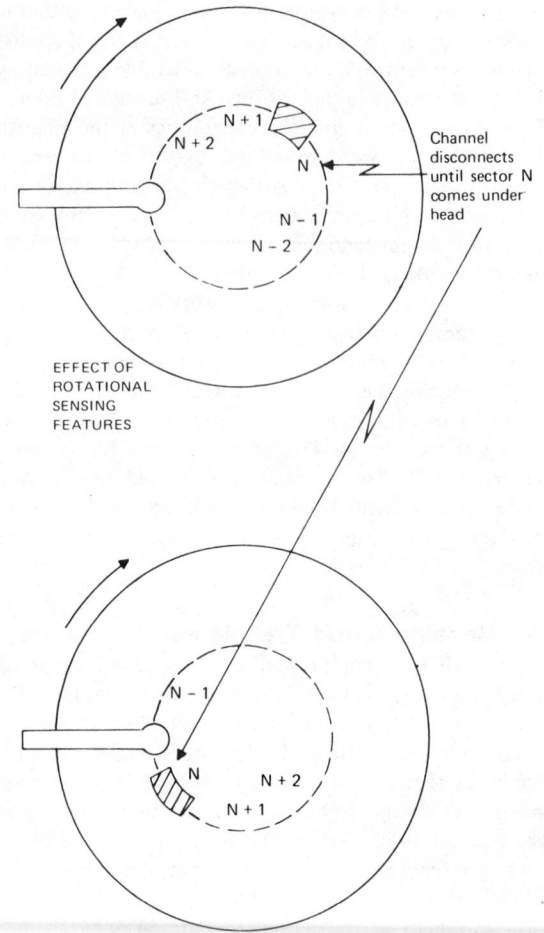

Fig. 2. Latency for direct-access devices having rotational position sensing feature.

LEAST-SQUARES APPROXIMATION

For articles on related subjects *see* APPROXIMATION THEORY; CHEBYSHEV APPROXIMATION; and NUMERICAL ANALYSIS.

Least-squares approximation refers to a wide variety of mathematical optimization problems in which the objective is to make a residual vector small in the sense of minimizing the sum of squares of its elements or to make a residual function small in the sense of minimizing the integral of the squared residual function.

For definiteness, and because of its frequent occurrence as a real-life computational problem, we will describe the real discrete linear least-squares problem and its analysis and solution. In this problem one has real numbers a_{ij}, $i = 1, \ldots, m$, $j = 1, \ldots, n$ $(m > n)$ and b_i,

$i = 1, \ldots, m$. One has some reason to believe that the b_i are approximately representable as linear combinations of the a_{ij} (i.e., that there exist numbers $\bar{c}_j$, $j = 1, \ldots, n$, such that $\sum_{j=1}^n \bar{c}_j a_{ij}$ is approximately equal to b_i for $i = 1, \ldots, m$). In matrix-vector notation this may be stated as the assumption that there is an n-vector $\bar{c}$ such that $A\bar{c}$ is approximately equal to **b**.

Mathematical Theory. The purely mathematical, real, discrete, linear, least-squares approximation problem, which we will refer to as problem LS, is to find an n-vector $\bar{c}$ such that $\|\mathbf{b} - A\bar{c}\| = \min \|\mathbf{b} - A\mathbf{c}\|$, where the *norm* of a vector **v**, $\|\mathbf{v}\|$, is defined as the square root of the sum of the squares of the components of **v**. A solution for this problem always exists. It is unique if and only if the rank of A is n.

A vector $\bar{c}$ is a solution vector for problem LS if and only if the associated residual vector, $\tilde{\mathbf{r}} = \mathbf{b} - A\tilde{\mathbf{c}}$, is orthogonal to all column vectors of A. This orthogonality condition may be written as $A^T(\mathbf{b} - A\tilde{\mathbf{c}}) = A^T\mathbf{b} - A^TA\tilde{\mathbf{c}} = \mathbf{0}$. From this latter expression one obtains the system of equations, $A^TA\mathbf{c} = A^T\mathbf{b}$, called the *normal equations* for problem LS. Forming the normal equations and solving them by the Cholesky algorithm is a common method of computing a solution for problem LS.

Other solution methods providing superior numerical reliability at a cost of about twice as many arithmetic operations are based on the *QR decomposition* of A. Thus, A can be written as

$$A = Q^T\begin{bmatrix} R \\ 0 \end{bmatrix} = [Q_1^T : Q_2^T]\begin{bmatrix} R \\ 0 \end{bmatrix} = Q_1^T R$$

where Q is an $m \times m$ orthogonal matrix and R is an $n \times n$ upper triangular matrix. The orthogonality of Q assures that

$$\begin{aligned} \| \mathbf{b} - A\mathbf{c} \|^2 &= \| Q(\mathbf{b} - A\mathbf{c}) \|^2 \\ &= \left\| \begin{bmatrix} Q_1 \\ Q_2 \end{bmatrix}\mathbf{b} - \begin{bmatrix} R \\ 0 \end{bmatrix}\mathbf{c} \right\|^2 \\ &= \| Q_1\mathbf{b} - R\mathbf{c} \|^2 + \| Q_2\mathbf{b} \|^2 \end{aligned}$$

for all n-vectors $\mathbf{c}$. Thus, a vector $\tilde{\mathbf{c}}$ is a solution of problem LS if and only if $R\tilde{\mathbf{c}} = Q_1\mathbf{b}$. The matrix R and the vector $Q_1\mathbf{b}$ needed here can be computed in a numerically stable manner by Householder transformations, Givens plane transformations, or modified Gram-Schmidt orthogonalization.

Practical Considerations. In practice, the given data, particularly the components of the vector $\mathbf{b}$, generally arise from observations or measurements and are therefore known only to some limited precision. One generally knows a priori the approximate size of the uncertainty in the vector $\mathbf{b}$. In addition, one often has some a priori notion about reasonable values for components of the solution vector.

We will say that problem LS is *ill-conditioned with respect to data uncertainty* if changes in the data matrix $[A:\mathbf{b}]$ of the order of magnitude of the uncertainty in this data can cause changes in the solution vector which are regarded as significant by the problem originator. In such a case, even though the rank of A may be n, there will commonly be a set of significantly different n-vectors that are almost as good as the unique best-solution vector if "goodness" is measured only by the criterion of reducing the residual norm.

In practice, it is desirable to have a systematic way of recognizing the occurrence of an ill-conditioned problem, of identifying the data dependencies that cause the ill-conditioning, of quantitatively characterizing a set of candidate solutions, and of selecting from the candidate solutions one that is suitable for the application at hand. Singular-value analysis and Levenberg-Marquardt analysis (also known as *ridge regression*) provide practical means for obtaining this information.

Singular-value analysis makes use of a matrix decomposition of the form $A = USV^T$, where U and V are orthogonal matrices and S is a diagonal matrix. The Levenberg-Marquardt analysis studies solutions of the augmented least-squares problem

$$\begin{bmatrix} A \\ \lambda I \end{bmatrix}\mathbf{c} \cong \begin{bmatrix} \mathbf{b} \\ \mathbf{0} \end{bmatrix}$$

as a function of the parameter λ.

As an example of an ill-conditioned least-squares problem, consider the problem $A\mathbf{c} \cong \mathbf{b}$ with

$$A = \begin{bmatrix} 0.780 & 0.563 \\ 0.913 & 0.659 \\ 0.133 & 0.096 \end{bmatrix}, \quad \mathbf{b} = \begin{bmatrix} 0.481 \\ 0.560 \\ 0.082 \end{bmatrix}$$

The exact mathematical solution for this problem is

$$\tilde{\mathbf{c}} = [477, -660]^T$$

with a residual vector $\tilde{\mathbf{r}} = \mathbf{b} - A\tilde{\mathbf{c}} = [0.0010, -0.0010, 0.0010]^T$ and residual norm $\| \mathbf{r} \| \doteq 0.0017$.

By either singular-value analysis or Levenberg-Marquardt analysis one can find that there are other candidate solution vectors that are much smaller in norm than $\tilde{\mathbf{c}}$ and which have residual norms only slightly greater than the minimal norm $\| \tilde{\mathbf{r}} \|$. For instance, the vector $\hat{\mathbf{c}} = [0.404, 0.292]^T$ gives a residual vector

$$\hat{\mathbf{r}} \doteq [0.0015, -0.0013, 0.0002]^T$$

whose norm is $\| \hat{\mathbf{r}} \| \doteq 0.0020$.

In most practical situations, particularly where there is uncertainty in some of the data defining A and $\mathbf{b}$, the vector $\hat{\mathbf{c}}$ would be preferred in place of the vector $\tilde{\mathbf{c}}$, whose components are larger by three orders of magnitude. The reason for preferring smaller solution vector components will be different in different contexts, but often this is related to the preference for a simpler, more economical explanation of the real-world phenomenon being modeled.

REFERENCES

1973. Stewart, G. W. *Introduction to Matrix Computations.* New York: Academic Press.
1974. Lawson, C. L., and R. J. Hanson. *Solving Least Squares Problems.* Englewood Cliffs, NJ: Prentice-Hall.

C. L. LAWSON

LEGAL ASPECTS OF COMPUTING

For articles on related subjects *see* COMMUNICATIONS AND COMPUTERS; COMPUTER ACQUISITION; CRIME AND COMPUTER SECURITY; DATA SECURITY; ELECTRONIC FUNDS TRANSFER SYSTEMS; LEGAL PROTECTION OF SOFTWARE; and PRIVACY, COMPUTERS AND.

The legal aspects of computing have, during the last decade, become ever more relevant to the computer scientist and the data processing manager. Law is now an important factor in the industry; it influences the usage and even the development of computer systems. When an organization decides to acquire and operate a computer system, or to obtain computer services from an independent organization, a three stage project begins: The design of the system, its acquisition, and its operation. There are legal implications to each of these stages. While the answers may differ somewhat when the work is done outside the using organization, the legal problems that must be considered are generally the same. This article will examine the legal implications of each stage and conclude with a brief discussion of some legal problems that face the computing industry.

SYSTEM DESIGN

In designing a computing system for an organization, two areas need particular attention from the legal point of view—corporate records and personnel. The legal problems related to the acquisition and operation stages must be considered at the system design stage also, so that an integrated plan can be developed.

Records. While many organizations acquire computers for scientific calculations and instructional purposes, the major area of computer usage has become the commercial sector, where business, government, and educational institutions use computers to prepare and maintain operational records. When these records are in machine-readable rather than hard copy form, it may be difficult to prove their accuracy, particularly when the program documentation does not support the program listings. Most courts that have considered the validity of computerized records when offered in evidence have decided to admit them. However, there is the distinct possibility that the records on which a corporation is relying to collect a debt may be held so untrustworthy that they cannot be considered by the jury. This could occur when the programs are heavily patched, but not documented.

The system designer must ensure the documentation of those programs that support the corporate records, not only for evidentiary purposes, but also because of the requirements of tax administrators, auditors, and securities regulators. The Internal Revenue Service has laid down definite rules on what records must be maintained in hard copy and in machine-readable form. The present rule, in essence, is that all machine-readable media used to record, consolidate, or summarize accounting transactions must be kept until the Internal Revenue Service says they may be destroyed (Rev. Rul. 71-20). Internal controls required by auditors, backed up by the Foreign Corrupt Practices Act (which applies to the data processing records of all companies listed on securities exchanges), will require the system designer to pay strict attention to procedures for preventing fraud or embezzlement.

The developing law on individual *privacy* (*q.v.*) must be considered in the design and operation of any system in which records pertain to individuals. Under the Privacy Act of 1974, the records systems of most federal agencies are subject to examination by individuals mentioned therein, and failure to comply with these rules can expose the agency to civil liability and the records manager to criminal prosecution. A number of states have adopted similar statutes. However, as of 1981, no general broad privacy act applies to private industry.

Several European countries have enacted privacy statutes that do apply to private industry. Some give a corporation or organization a right of privacy; some apply only to computerized records and not to manual records; some also control the transfer of personal information beyond the nation's borders. Efforts are underway to develop international agreements to simplify such transfers. However, a system designer must consider these restrictions, as they now are and may be in the future, in formulating the plan.

The designer of an international system must also consider other laws and policies of the foreign nations involved. For example, the rules on using data communications equipment not supplied by government-owned telephone monopolies may affect not only hardware, but the protocols available for use. Some nations, in order to encourage the growth of their own electronics industry, prohibit the importation of certain hardware; Brazil did just this with Automatic Teller Machines (ATMs) in the late 1970s. A Canadian statute requires banks to maintain and process their records in Canada; one of the major reasons is to preserve Canadian employment.

Personnel. The development of any computer system, commercial or non-commercial, involves personnel problems. Some affect all employees, such as computerized personnel records. Others affect those who will design and operate the system. Others affect those who may no longer have a job.

The development of computerized text editing and composition systems, particularly in the newspaper industry, has caused the loss of jobs by many skilled employees. Linotype operators have become surplus as reporters and editors use CRTs to compose the text for the next morning's paper. These problems have been responsible for the demise of such journals as the *New York Herald Tribune* and newspapers in Munich, Vancouver, and Copenhagen; only an eleventh hour settlement averted the death of the *Times of London* in 1980. The system designer must consider the effect of new computer systems on those already employed who may, as the British so neatly put it, become "redundant."

There is an increasing tendency toward unionization of lower paid and less creative jobs in computer operations—the data entry personnel, the computer room operators, etc. There have even been union organizing efforts in the programmer and systems analyst groups. The British experience is instructive. Selective strikes of computer personnel have effectively closed down large portions of the British government, such as the computer center that handles all of the telephone billing. As an organization—and even more, a government—becomes dependent on its computers, so also is it at the mercy of those who operate them. The "care and feeding" of computer operations personnel must be considered at the design stage and must be continually kept in mind by management.

As these examples show, the existence of collective bargaining agreements, and the need for coordination between management and union, requires considerable advance planning and tactful negotiation. The implementation of a computerized system that does not meet the requirements of union contracts can bring the entire enterprise to a halt.

ACQUIRING THE COMPUTER AND COMPUTER SERVICES

The acquisition of a computer system is often considered in the "subsets" of hardware, software, services, and telecommunications. However, a decision on one aspect of acquiring the system may well have ramifications in the other aspects. So a constant overview is necessary. However, each subset has its own problems; some of them are indicated here.

While the decision to buy or lease hardware is often financial, depending on relative interest rates, tax credits, depreciation schedules, and the like, it is also a decision based on management's forecast of technological obsolescence. Each approach has its own legal problems. For example, the company that buys a computer does not need to worry about the notorious "hell-or-high-water clause" found in leases from a third party financier. This clause says that no matter what happens to the computer, and whether it works or doesn't work, the lessee (user) still

has to make payments to the lessor. This is a logical position, since the lessor is only in the process of lending money, like a bank which holds a mortgage on a home. However, incautious lessees have found themselves bound by such a clause without having reserved their rights to hold the vendor responsible for unsatisfactory hardware.

A difficult problem in acquiring software has been preserving the proprietary interests of the vendor while giving the customer sufficient latitude. This question is considered in detail in the article LEGAL PROTECTION OF SOFTWARE. As an example, it is to the vendor's advantage to provide only object code, while it is to the user's advantage to obtain the source code in order to enable modifications to be made more easily or in case the vendor goes out of business. One of the more difficult contractual problems is drafting a satisfactory procedure for determining that programs do what they are expected to do, so that the user can be confident that the output will be right. Initially, bug-free programs are a very scarce commodity, if they exist at all. The user does not want to pay until the program is bug-free. The vendor doesn't want to wait that long.

When services are obtained from independent organizations, be they service bureaus or consultants, the problem of confidentiality must be considered. User management will probably not wish to entrust its records to an organization that serves a competitor. While it is possible that a service bureau may be able to keep these separated, the likelihood of a programming house being able to avoid cross-fertilization is much smaller.

When people are hired as employees to develop a system or to operate it, they will be exposed to confidential information. How the organization protects this information when the employee leaves, or prevents the employee from immediately using this information, and the skills developed, for the benefit of a competitor, are legal problems on which a policy must be developed before the employee is hired.

For decades, telephone and wire telecommunications have been monopolistic; essentially, there has been one local telephone company to deal with and one telegraph company. The late 1960s and 1970s saw the development of competing information carriers using microwave, satellite, packet switching, and other techniques. Because of federal and state regulations, the development of these competitive methods of conveying communication has been delayed as legions of lawyers have mounted prodigious paper wars before the Federal Communications Commission (FCC), the courts, and the state utilities commissions. The trend in the FCC, supported by the courts, has been to deregulate and to limit the monopoly rights of the telephone companies to voice communications. Efforts are underway in Congress to hasten deregulation, and it seems reasonable to forecast increasing competition in the offering of telecommunications services and hardware in the United States. A similar trend appears underway in Canada. In other nations, however, telecommunications is generally a government monopoly, which also administers the post office; telecommunications profits offset postal deficits, and competition from private industry is not welcome.

The acquisition of any telecommunications services automatically involves the user with a multi-vendor shop. This means that when the system doesn't work, each vendor tends to blame the other, and the customer has to take responsibility for determining who is at fault, a problem that can create legal difficulties. The same problem, of course, exists when hardware is acquired from more than one vendor, as noted below under *Maintenance*. Similar restrictions have arisen when software packages are acquired from other than the hardware manufacturer; in some instances, the hardware company may also claim that use of other than its own systems software is an infringement of its proprietary rights.

Taxes. Inherent in any discussion of acquisition of computers and computer systems is the problem of taxes. The software area has caused tax administrators particular difficulty. Under federal income tax law, it is advantageous to the government to treat programs as intangible property, like a share of stock. In this way, the period of depreciation can be decreased and certain tax credits cancelled.

However, state taxation laws levy sales and use taxes and personal property taxes on tangible property, such as desks and chairs; most states do not levy these taxes on intangibles. It is to the benefit of the state taxing authorities to treat programs as tangible property subject to tax. There has been considerable litigation at the state level on this question; the courts have, as of this writing, held that programs are intangible and not taxable under the general law. Some states have responded by easing their regulations. Others have amended their laws to provide specifically that software will be taxable.

A similar situation sometimes occurs when computer services are rendered, particularly by service bureaus. Again, some states have modified their position by regulation; others by statute. (A state-by-state, province-by-province discussion of taxes may be found in the appendices to Section 2-3.2 in Volume 2 of the *Computer Law Service*.)

The tax implications must be considered as part of every acquisition. This applies even to non-profit organizations. For example, the U.S. presently allows an Investment Tax Credit for the purchase of certain kinds of tangible personal property, such as a CPU. While such a tax credit would have no value to a university, it would have value to a private financier; a university may be able to acquire hardware cheaper through a third party than directly from the manufacturer.

OPERATIONS

Computer Misuse. An organization may be liable for the misuse of its computer. Some years ago, a gas company in Ohio sent out shut-off notices automatically—without human review—to non-paying customers. In some situations, the customer had a dispute with the gas company; when the shut-off notices were received, these customers were told to ignore them. However, computer-generated notices continued to come, and sometimes the company shut off the gas when it should not have done so. The company was held to have violated its customers' civil rights.

A similar problem could arise when a computerized database is inaccurate. For example, an engineer designing a bridge could rely on inaccurate information in an on-line information service as to the strength of concrete, and the misinformation could eventually cause the bridge to collapse. There could even be a situation where the failure to use a computer—for example, in extremely complex calculations of aerodynamic strength—could be held to be negligence; in this example, negligence by the designer.

Security, Crime, and Privacy. In the operation of a computer, as in its design, security and the prevention of fraud must be thoroughly considered. While the computer criminal is not nearly as severe a threat as the incompetent, the system must be protected against both. Failure to provide sufficient security may expose the organization to liability because it is unable to perform its contracts satisfactorily and on time, because it is unable to meet contractual commitments towards confidentiality, or because, in the case of government contracts, it may have violated specific laws. The need to use cryptographic techniques in telecommunications should be considered. Some contracts require use of the Data Encryption Standard (*see* DATA ENCRYPTION) of 15 January 1977, published by the National Bureau of Standards (FIPS PUB 46).

A major computer embezzlement may expose officers of the organization to personal liability to stockholders who can show that the officers were negligent in protecting the assets. A number of individuals have been convicted of crimes involving embezzlement or abuse of computers. At this writing, a federal statute has been proposed, and 15 states have enacted specific legislation designed to help prosecutors convict those who steal from (or with the aid of) a computer.

Violations of privacy rules and infringement of proprietary rights during the operational stages must also be considered; these are discussed above and in the articles on privacy and proprietary rights cited earlier.

Personnel. There can be legal problems with personnel during the operations stage. For example, federal law regulates when overtime must be paid. Court decisions have indicated that coders must be paid overtime, while systems analysts are sometimes exempt from this requirement.

Maintenance. Maintenance of the computer system—hardware, software, and telecommunications—is of major importance during the operational stage. Mainframe companies are reluctant to maintain systems with add-on memories supplied by competitors, and their con-

tracts reflect this position. The user may have to negotiate a settlement. Similarly, purchasers of used computers from companies other than the manufacturer may find the manufacturer reluctant to maintain the computer without a thorough examination, even though the hardware was always maintained by the manufacturer when owned by a previous organization.

INDUSTRY PROBLEMS

In many industries, there are additional regulations peculiarly applicable to computer systems used by those industries. The Electronic Funds Transfer Act of 1978, for example, provides consumer protections when EFT systems are used. The Act became effective in May 1980;

U.S. v. IBM.*

Perhaps the largest and longest case ever brought under the Sherman Antitrust Act, *U.S. v. IBM,* began in the 1960s and now in 1981 has yet to be decided. A chronology of the case indicates how time flies when you're having fun!

17 January 1969. Department of Justice files suit in the Federal Court for the Southern District of New York. For three years, little happened.

January 1972. David N. Edelstein, Chief Judge of the Southern District, who had sat on an earlier IBM antitrust suit that began in 1952 and concluded in 1956, assigned the new case to himself. Judge Edelstein pressured the parties to get on with the case and complete their examination (called *discovery*) of each other's files. During the discovery period, he made a number of orders, some of which were very controversial.

17 March 1972. Both the U.S. government and IBM are ordered to keep "all documents, writings, recordings, or other records" that in any way relate to electronic data processing until the judge says they can be destroyed (PTO #1). The amount of paper preserved under this order staggers the imagination.

12 May 1972. Judge Edelstein prohibits the government and IBM from disseminating information about the case "by press release, press conference or interview with the press, without the consent of the Court" (PTO #4). The order was later modified, and finally revoked.

1 August 1973. IBM refuses to comply with Judge Edelstein's order to disclose certain information. Judge Edelstein holds IBM in contempt of court and imposes a fine of $150,000 a day until it obeys. The fine is sus-

pended while IBM appeals. When the U.S. Supreme Court refuses to change the order, on 13 May 1974, IBM gives in.

19 May 1975. Over six years after the case was entered in court, the trial starts. The government calls many witnesses, some of whom testify for days on end. The government also summons two experts—a management consultant and a certified public accountant—but refuses to pay them more than $30 a day, the statutory witness rate. Judge Edelstein supports the government.

20 April 1976. The Court of Appeals affirms Judge Edelstein's decision. In order to get the experts to prepare for their appearance, the government eventually agrees to pay them $700 per day.

11 April 1978. IBM moves for a mistrial, claiming the government has shifted its ground of complaint during the trial. Judge Edelstein denies the motion (453 F. Supp. 348).

27 April 1978. The government concludes its case after 504 full or partial days of trial, having called 52 witnesses, and read into evidence the testimony of many others. The transcript of all this testimony, with examinations, cross-examinations, and lawyers' arguments, totals 72,038 pages.

26 April 1978. IBM begins its defense.

17 July 1979. IBM claims Judge Edelstein is so biased he cannot render a fair decision and should excuse himself. In September, the judge declines IBM's invitation. IBM appeals, and on 25 February 1980, the Court of Appeals backs him up.

1 June 1981. IBM rests its case and the admission of evidence in the trial is completed.

8 January 1982. Government drops case.

*Prepared by Robert P. Bigelow with the assistance of Aileen Lee and J. Thomas Franklin, Esq.

Panel 1.

the Federal Reserve Board has issued Regulation E interpreting the Act and specifying specific requirements for the banks to which its rules apply.

Similarly, the Privacy Protection Study Commission has made a number of recommendations. These apply to manual and computerized records. Certain states have enacted portions of the rules (e.g., Virginia on insurance; Rhode Island on health records) and Congress is considering specific legislation in this area that will apply to private industry.

With the development of the personal computer, many laws that have been enacted for consumer protection will apply to computers. For example, some states prohibit companies selling consumer products from limiting their liability for failure to perform their contracts; such a limitation is customary in commercial transactions. Similarly, using a "hell-or-high-water clause" in the rental or lease of a home computer system may be illegal, even though it would be effective in a commercial setting.

The computer industry has had its own legal problems. Probably best known are the numerous suits against IBM for alleged violation of the antitrust laws (see panel for a brief history of the *U.S. v. IBM* antitrust suit). However, there has been much other antitrust litigation; for example, the battle between Sperry Rand and Honeywell involving an antitrust defense to a claim of infringement of the ENIAC patent. There is also litigation on the validity of contracts requiring that programs be run only on computers specified by the vendor.

As the computer industry has developed and computers have become almost commonplace, the legal implications have become more and more important. Computer scientists and computer users must be alert not only to the societal implications of computing, but also to the likely legislative and judicial responses to these implications.

References

General

1969. *Computers and the Law: An Introductory Handbook.* Chicago: American Bar Association.

1972. Bigelow, R. P. *Computer Law Service* (12 volumes). Wilmette, IL: Callaghan & Co.

1976. Bigelow, R. P. and Nycum, S. H. *Your Computer and the Law.* Englewood Cliffs, NJ: Prentice-Hall.

1976. Freed, R. N. *Computers and the Law: A Reference Work* (5th Ed.) Published by author (Boston).

1978. Tapper, C. *Computer Law.* London: Longman's.

Specific Areas

1974. Bernacchi, R. L. and Larsen, G. H. *Data Processing Contracts and the Law.* Boston: Little, Brown.

1976. Brandon, D. H. and Segelstein, S. *Data Processing Contracts.* New York: Van Nostrand Reinhold.

1978, 1979. Bender, M. *Computer Law: Evidence and Procedure.* New York: Matthew Bender.

Periodicals

Computer Law and Tax Report. Warren, Gorham & Lamont, 210 South Street, Boston, MA, 02111.

Computer/Law Journal. 675 South Westmoreland Ave., Los Angeles, CA, 90005.

Law and Computer Technology. World Peace Through Law Center, 1000 Connecticut Ave., N.W., Washington, DC, 20036.

Rutgers Journal of Computers. Technology and the Law, 15 Washington St., Newark, NJ, 07102.

R. P. BIGELOW

LEGAL PROTECTION OF SOFTWARE

For articles on related subjects *see* LEGAL ASPECTS OF COMPUTING; PROGRAMMING LANGUAGES; SOFTWARE; and SOFTWARE PACKAGES.

Computer software is expensive to develop and maintain. It has high monetary value to its owners, both because it can give them a competitive advantage when used internally to do tasks more cheaply or quickly and because it can be licensed for use by others. Software, however, is very easy to copy at a trivial cost and is, therefore, very susceptible to pirating. Because of its value and its vulnerability to misappropriation, ownership interests in software must be protected.

For the purpose of legal protection, software is categorized as intellectual property. Intellectual property is a form of intangible personal property comprised of ideas, processes, information, or symbols. Intangible personal property contrasts with tangible personal property, such as hardware or supplies, and real property, such as office buildings and other structures affixed to the land. Intellectual property is protected in one of five principal ways: By patent, copyright, trade secret, trademark, and contract.

Patent. Patent protection is a federal statutory right in the U. S. that gives an inventor or his/her assignee exclusive rights to make, use or sell products or processes within the scope of the patent for 17 years from the effective filing date.

Patentable inventions must meet several tests to entitle them to the protection. They must be of statutory subject matter—physical methods, apparatus, compositions of matter, and devices and improvements, but not mere ideas. Further, they must be new, useful, and not obvious. They must be described in a properly filed and prosecuted patent application.

The status of patent protection for software in 1980 is ambiguous. The U. S. Supreme Court has thrice held particular pieces of software unpatentable based on the failure to meet the different tests described above. In *Gottschalk v. Benson,* 409 U. S. 63 (1972), the court declined to patent what it felt was merely a formula (idea); in *Dann v. Johnston,* 425 U. S. 219 (1976), the court held a process non-patentable for obviousness; in *Parker v. Flook,* 437 U. S. 584 (1978), the only novelty was the form of carrying out a non-patentable step.

At this writing, the court has heard, but not decided, in re *Diehr and Lutton,* 602 F.2d 922 (C.C.P.A. 1979) and in re *Bradley and Franklin,* 600 F.2d 807 (C.C.P.A. 1979). Even if the court finds either or both of these programs patentable, very few software owners will choose to seek patent status for their software because the patenting process is lengthy (it may take several years), requires full disclosure of the idea, is expensive to procure (it may cost thousands of dollars), and, once obtained, has only about a 50% chance to survive a challenge of invalidity in the courts. But, for those few programs which really do represent technological breakthroughs, a patent would provide the patent holder the right to make use of or to vend the program exclusively for 17 years (nonrenewable).

Copyright. Copyright is the companion federal statutory protection to patent that is available for writings of an author.

Writings created since 1 January 1978 are protected by the new copyright law, which provides exclusive rights to the author or his/her assignee for the copyright, publication, broadcast, translation, and other adaption, display, and performance of the expression of the idea contained in the creation from the time of embodiment of the creation in tangible form. This protection may be lost if the writing is published without copyright notice. Notice consists of the word copyright (or ©), the date, and the author's name. The notice must be affixed so as to come to the attention of third persons; e.g., on the first or inside front page of a book or pamphlet.

Following the recommendations of the Commission on New Technological Uses of Copyrights (CONTU), which was created by the new copyright law, the Computer Software Copyright Law of 1980, federal law was enacted to cover explicitly computer programs and databases under the copyright law.

Copyright is inexpensive and can be obtained quickly. It requires physical placement of the notice on the tangible form of expression (this may be a computer file) and one required and one optional deposit with the Copyright Office (accompanied by minor filing fees). The required deposit is an archival copy placed with the Library of Congress (software is exempt from this requirement). The second deposit (which can be only the first and last 25 pages of the program and may be in object form) is optional and serves as a prerequisite to bringing an infringement suit and to some remedies such as minimum damages and legal fees. Copyright lasts for the life of the author plus 50 years (nonrenewable).

Because copyright protects only copying and obtaining it requires disclosure of the idea, its utility for some programs is limited or useless. But it may be quite adequate protection for the multiple copy marketing of inexpensive package programs such as those sold in computer stores, where the function of the program itself is not unique, but the value to the owner lies in the vending of thousands of copies.

Trade Secret. A trade secret is a right protected state by state rather than by a federal law and is defined in many states as a "formula, pattern, scheme or device used in the operation of one's business that is secret and that gives one a competitive advantage over those who do not know it." In a number of court cases, computer programs have qualified as trade secrets; for example, *University Computing Corporation v. Lykes-Youngstown Corporation,* 504 F.2d 518 (5th Cir. 1974), *MSA v. Cyborg Systems, Inc.,* 6 CLSR 921 (N.D. Ill. 1978), and *Com-Share, Inc. v. Computer Complex, Inc.,* 338 F.Supp. 1229 (E.D. Mich. 1971). The absolute requirement for trade secret status is that the item be kept secret from all except those bound to keep it confidential by virtue of their relationship or by contract. If the secret becomes known to others, the protection vanishes. If it remains secret, the protection can last forever. The trade secret is maintained regardless of how many of those people know it. Confidential relationships include employees and agents in a fiduciary or trust relationship and thieves—who are held to be in a constructive trust relationship so they can't use their ill gotten knowledge. Contract is used to bind licenses and joint venture partners or investors. (In some states, these people are bound even without an express contract.) However, once the secret is disclosed without a requirement of confidentiality or is disclosed to one who didn't know of its secret character, the trade secret status is lost forever. Places where trade secrets are often disclosed carelessly are user group meetings and technical meetings.

Employees may need to learn the secret in the course of their employment. These people are bound not to misappropriate the trade secret by virtue of their position of trust with respect to the secret. Many employees do not realize the parameters of that trust and should consult their lawyers before using software developed for an employer for their own purposes. Trade secrets can also be lost through "reverse engineering" (i.e., through the legitimate process of buying a product and "taking it apart" to learn how it works); this encourages many software owners to encrypt their code. Trade secret protection has been held by the U. S. Supreme Court to be compatible with patent protection [*Kewanee Oil Co. v. Bicron Corp.,* 416 U. S. 470 (1974)], but the court has yet to decide a case that holds that a trade secret can also claim copyright protection if it is disclosed. Many vendors of software choose between the copyright and trade secret methods of protection; yet many others have both a copyright notice on their software *and* treat it and license it as a trade secret. The danger is that the presence of the copyright notice may someday be held to constitute a disclosure of the secret. Since copyright protects only the expression of the idea or algorithm and trade secret protects the algorithm, the possible preemption of copyright and corresponding loss of secrecy may be fatal to the value of the software.

Many software owners place a label on their software, stating: "This software is *proprietary* to (Name of Company)." That notice serves as a no trespassing sign to observers and a reminder to users who have acquired the software under an agreement to keep the software confidential.

Trademark. Trademark embodies the exclusive use of a symbol to identify goods and services. As distinguished from patent, which does not exist until obtained from the Patent Office, or copyright, which exists as soon as the creation is fixed in a tangible form, trademark arises upon use. Registration with the U. S. Patent Office or a state agency is not necessary to have the right to trademark status, although it helps greatly in exercising the status. Trademark protection exists at *both* the federal and state levels. The symbol protected can be both a tradename and a logo, such as *17 mile drive* and (17). However, one could not trademark an entire program, but only its name.

Contract. Because copies of software are ordinarily transferred to others in the course of business and sometimes transferred in source form, disclosure of the software is frequently made under an agreement to keep the secret confidential. Patented and copyrighted software can be transferred via contracts that may have more restrictive provisions than the law requires simply by the status accorded by the patent or copyright. One may, for example, contract with another not to disclose a copyrighted piece of software. One may also agree to remedies for disclosure or unauthorized copying and set up complex formulas for royalty payment for legitimate use and agree to the ownership of enhancements and changes to the software.

Conclusion. A number of statutory or court-based means of legal protection for software presently exist. (There have even been suggestions for special laws applicable only to software, but these have not yet resulted in law.) The developer or owner of software should know that the status of legal protection for software is changing and a lawyer should be consulted to keep the owner informed of those changes and their impact.

REFERENCE

1982. Nycum, S. H. *Protection of Proprietary Interests in Software.* Reston, VA: Reston Company.

Susan H. Nycum

LEIBNIZ, GOTTFRIED WILHELM VON

For articles on related subjects *see* Digital Computers: History: Origins; and Pascal, Blaise.

Gottfried von Leibniz (b. Leipzig, 1646; d. Hanover, 1716) had obtained an excellent education in his father's library before entering the University of Leipzig at fifteen years of age and receiving a bachelor's degree at seventeen. At twenty he received a doctorate in jurisprudence from Altdorf, and for six years thereafter pursued a career of law and diplomacy, working to create an effective defense for the German states against Louis XIV. These diplomatic intrigues took him to Paris (1672), where he spent the four most fecund years of his mathematical career. Under the tutelage of Huygens, Leibniz systematically studied mathematics, especially the work of Descartes and Pascal.

Pascal's calculating machine stimulated Leibniz's interest. By adding a movable carriage operating on wheels utilizing an active-and-inactive pin principle and a delayed carry mechanism, Leibniz modified Pascal's machine so that it would multiply and divide directly (i.e., without the operator having to use an algorithm). However, in the only extant Leibniz machine (Hanover Museum), a later model, Pascal's ratchet-carry mechanism is replaced by a primitive Geneva gear system that accomplishes the discontinuous carry of digits by a series of five-point star gears. Eliminating the ratchet mechanisms made subtraction and division possible by simply reversing the rotation of the addition and multiplication mechanisms.

In 1673, Leibniz made discoveries in differential calculus and observed (in 1675) that the summation process of integration was equivalent to reversing the operation of differentiation, the fundamental theorem of calculus. Newton had also made this observation in the 1660s, but Leibniz was apparently unaware of it.

In 1676 Leibniz left Paris for Hanover, where for the next forty years he was a historian and librarian actively

Fig. 1. Gottfried Wilhelm von Leibniz, from a painting by A. Scheits. (Photograph by courtesy of the Herzog Anton Ulrich-Museum.)

pursuing philosophy, theology, diplomatic missions, and scientific correspondences, and intermittently working on his calculating machines. In 1700 he organized the Berlin Academy of Science (an idea he first articulated in 1668) and at his death was carrying on the now-famous correspondence with Clarke about the theological implications of Newton's *Principia* and *Opticks*.

C. V. JONES

LIBRARY AUTOMATION

For articles on related subjects *see* AUTOMATION; COMPUTER NETWORKS; CURRENT AWARENESS SYSTEMS; DATABASE, ON-LINE; INFORMATION RETRIEVAL and MEDLARS/MEDLINE.

The functions of a library can be generally categorized as (1) collection development and acquisition—determining what to add to the collection and then acquiring it; (2) cataloging, classification, and physical preparation—the description, the subject analysis, and the preparation of the item for shelving and circulation; (3) retrieval and reference—locating materials in response to a request for a particular item or for information; (4) circulation—the intra-institutional reserving and loaning of materials; and (5) interlibrary loan—the borrowing and lending of materials between institutions.

Library automation had its genesis in the 1950s. Because of the rapidly escalating costs of library operations, it was natural to examine the possibilities of applying technology to library operations in order to reduce the per unit costs of acquiring and processing an item by performing necessary functions more effectively and to offer improved and expanded client services.

The Library of Congress (LC) has played an important role in the development of library automation beginning with the establishment in 1958 of a Committee on Mechanized Information Retrieval. Increased attention was also given elsewhere to the application of automated techniques to the operations of the libraries. Among the early library automation endeavors were Project Intrex at the Massachusetts Institute of Technology and the Medical Literature Analysis and Retrieval System (MEDLARS) of the National Library of Medicine, both designed to exploit the technology and/or to test advanced ideas in information access. However, many of these early projects were not "library automation" *per se* but were mainly concerned with the searching for information by subject (Kilgour, 1970).

Because the technical processing of an item (e.g., a book, periodical, map, motion picture, music score, sound recording, or manuscript) constitutes one of the most costly operations of a library, efforts also turned in this direction fairly early. *Technical processing* is a term that encompasses the library procedures for acquiring an item, cataloging it, and preparing it for shelving, preparing a book card, a spine label, etc. The principal product derived from technical processing is a record (called a cataloging record) to describe an item uniquely, to alert a client that an item is available for use, and to indicate where the item can be found. The libraries of Stanford University, the University of Chicago, and Columbia University were among the early pioneers in application of automated techniques for technical processing.

Early efforts were not particularly successful, principally because: (1) the full power of the computer was not utilized but, rather, the machine was viewed as a "glorified typewriter"; (2) the designers shortsightedly limited the amount of data converted to machine-readable form to that needed to satisfy a single function, whereas increasing the amount of data converted could have, for a slightly higher cost, satisfied the requirements for several functions; (3) the manual process was mimicked (i.e., the automated system was simply the automation of manual processes rather than the reorganization of the system); (4) peripheral hardware devices were not appropriate for library requirements; and (5) librarians understood the problem but had little technical expertise and the technicians with the technical expertise grossly underestimated the difficulties of automating library operations.

Among the main difficulties in the automating of library processes are the following.

The data (e.g., names of authors or titles of works) are variable in length. Any truncation of the data to a fixed length may make it difficult to identify an item uniquely.

The collections of libraries represent items written in many languages using a variety of alphabets and scripts. Therefore, the capability must exist to input, manipulate, and output multiple character sets (to include, for example, Cyrillic, Greek, Hebrew, Arabic, and Chinese in addition to an expanded Roman).

Libraries must continue to maintain older materials as well as add new materials, so that the number of machine-readable records representing items in the collection is constantly growing. The records are also dynamic and subject to change. Therefore, there is a significant maintenance requirement.

There are complex relationships within data files and across data files resulting in a requirement for sophisticated data management systems.

The complexity of the data make it necessary to have special arrangements for human display. Therefore, complicated algorithms must be devised to accomplish these arrangements.

Since many of the functions of libraries are dependent on the data describing an item in terms of its bibliographic and physical attributes and its subject matter (which together make up the cataloging record), the Council on Library Resources (CLR) supported a study of methods of converting these data to machine-readable form. This study led to a pilot project funded by CLR

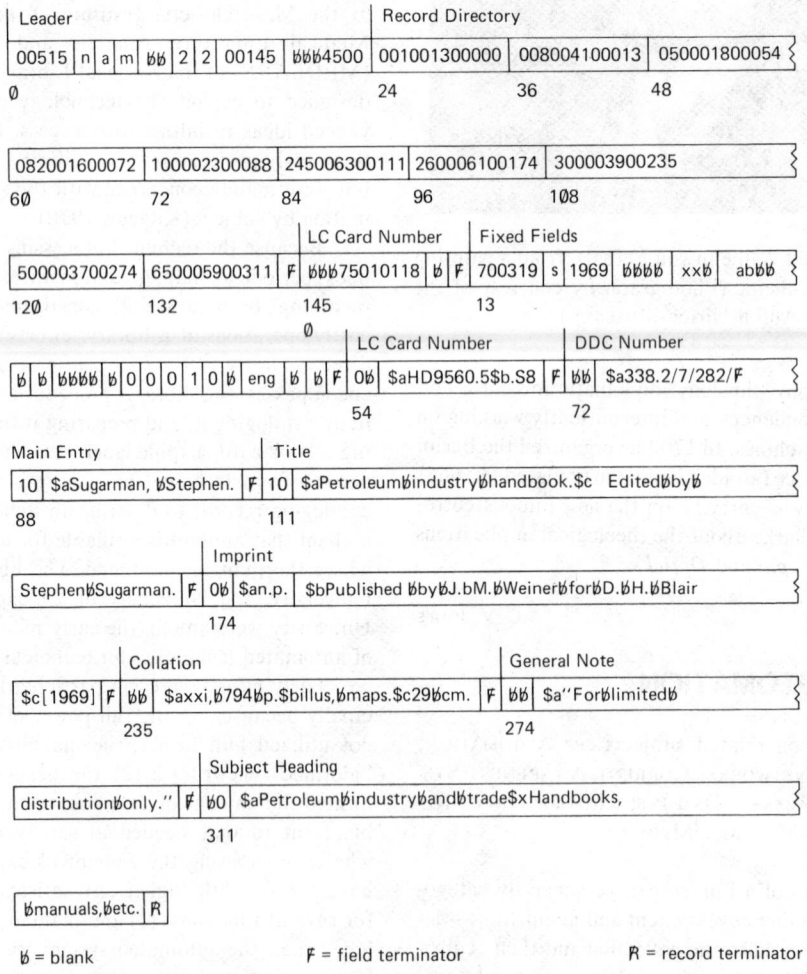

Fig. 1 Sample record in the MARC format.

which became known as MARC—*MA*chine-*R*eadable *C*ataloging (Avram, 1968) (see Fig. 1). Upon the successful completion of the pilot, in 1969, LC began the operational MARC system which is still in existence (Avram, 1975).

The MARC project was a fundamental building block to future development of the automation of many library functions, since: (1) it provided the vehicle for the establishment, adoption, and increased usage of standards so that libraries could exchange and share machine-readable data; (2) the adoption of standards provided the environment for the building of information processing equipment (input and output devices) for the manipulation of the data using these standards; (3) the MARC documentation (e.g., input and editing manuals and format documents) made freely available by LC (see Fig. 2) resulted in savings by organizations all over the world in implementing library automation projects; and (4) the machine-readable records from LC provided the base data upon which to build library automation projects, so that each individual organization did not have to assume the costs associated with the cataloging of the materials and/or the conversion of the cataloging data. Many of these functions have been automated in varying degrees and with varying success. Several commercial companies have offered turnkey systems for one or more of the functions.

Library Networking. It is not possible to discuss library automation without also addressing the developments in library networking. The 1960s were an affluent period and many stand-alone automated library systems were developed. However, the 1970s were lean years, and there was an increased requirement for sharing, thus networking. Libraries have always shared resources, but the technology offered a level of sharing heretofore not possible.

On-line systems were developed in which the database was both built and used by multiple organizations. The earliest and still the most advanced system was the Ohio College Library Center (since renamed OCLC, Inc.). Over 1,700 member libraries using some 3,000 terminals and extending over almost all of the 50 states and into Canada receive a variety of products and services from a resource database which includes data contributed by the participating members and the MARC data distributed by LC. Today there are several similar systems, among them the Research Libraries Information Network (RLIN) and the Washington Library Network (WLN) in the U. S., the University of Toronto Library Automation System (UTLAS) in Canada, and the British Library Systems (BLAISE) in the U.K.

In 1970, with Public Law 91-345, Congress established a National Commission on Libraries and Information Science (NCLIS) to develop overall plans for meeting national library and information service needs and for advising the President and Congress on the implementation of national policy in this area. In 1975, the Commission issued a program document which included a proposal for a full-service network to satisfy the information needs of the citizens of the U. S. Since the program document stressed the importance of LC as a component of the network, the Commission funded a study concerned with the role of LC in the evolving network (Buckland, 1978). The study noted the need for a coordinating effort to develop a cohesive network responding to this need. A Network Advisory Committee was formed and issued a planning paper (1977) which included a recommendation for assigning a high priority to the linking together of the various U. S. systems.

The evolution from individual systems serving multiple user terminals to an information network in which these stand-alone systems are nodes offers the possibility of increased resource sharing. The terminal user, a mem-

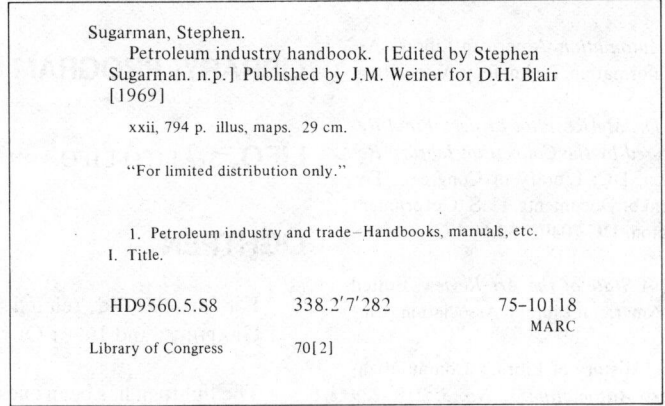

Fig. 2.   Sample LC catalog card.

ber of one system, could use the products and services of all systems in the network—thus avoiding costly duplication of cataloging, conversion, and storage of machine-readable records. Many problems (hardware, software, and economic) that must be resolved in order to link dissimilar computer systems are under investigation. One significant achievement is the development of a proposed application level protocol for a national information system (1977). In order to communicate information over a network, the facility must exist for a message transmitted from one node to be received and understood by another node. International standardization organizations have developed data communications protocols which assume that these application level protocols will be developed and embedded to carry out meaningful data exchange.

Among other problems requiring investigation is the development of techniques to permit the query and response language of one system to interact with all other systems. That is, when a terminal user inputs a request to one system, how does that request invoke a second system without the user having to be trained in the language of the second system? What is the optimum database configuration when the database is distributed among several network nodes? What are the most efficient procedures for billing? What organizations will serve as network control? What is the appropriate governance structure?

The rapid advances of the technology—microprocessors, semiconductors, videodisks, etc.—will doubtless offer new opportunities (and new problems) for the design and building of effective library systems.

REFERENCES

1965–. *Library Technology Reports.* American Library Association, Chicago, IL.

1966–. *Program; News of Computers in Libraries.* ASLIB, London, England.

1966–. *Annual Review of Information Science and Technology.* American Society for Information Science, Washington, DC.

1968–. *Journal of Library Automation.* American Library Association, Library and Information Technology Association, Chicago, IL.

1968. Avram, Henriette D. *The MARC Pilot Project: Final Report on a Project Sponsored by the Council on Library Resources, Inc.*, Washington, DC: Library of Congress. (For sale by the Superintendent of Documents, U. S. Government Printing Office, Washington, DC 20402. $3.50 LC1.2:M18/2.)

1969. *Library Automation; A State of the Art Review.* Edited by Salmon, Stephen R., American Library Association, Chicago, IL.

1970. Kilgour, Frederick G. "History of Library Computerization," *Journal of Library Automation* 3, *No. 3:* 218–229 (September).

1975. Avram, Henriette D. *MARC, Its History and Implications.* Washington, DC: Library of Congress. (Based on an article entitled "Machine-Readable Cataloging (MARC) Program," which appears in the *Encyclopedia of Library and Information Science* **16**.)

1975. *Toward a National Program for Library and Information Services: Goals for Action.* Prepared by the National Commission on Libraries and Information Science, Washington, DC.

1975. *Library Automation; The State of the Art II.* Edited by Martin, Susan K. and Butler, Brett, with a bibliography compiled by West, Martha W., American Library Association, Chicago, IL.

1977. *Toward a National Library and Information Service Network: The Library Bibliographic Component.* (Prepared by the Library of Congress Network Advisory Group.) Avram, Henriette D. and Maruyama, Lenore S. (Eds.). Washington, DC: Library of Congress (June).

1977. *A Computer Network Protocol for Library and Information Science Applications.* (Prepared by the NCLIS/NBS Task Force on Computer Network Protocol, National Commission on Libraries and Information Science, Washington, DC.) (December.) (For sale by the Superintendent of Documents, U. S. Government Printing Office, Washington, DC 20402.)

1978. Buckland, Lawrence F. *The Role of the Library of Congress in the Evolving National Network.* (A Study Commissioned by the Library of Congress Network Development Office and funded by the National Commission on Libraries and Information Science.) Washington, DC: Library of Congress.

1978. *LITA Library Automation: State of the Art III, Held in Chicago on June 22–23. Journal of Library Automation,* **11**, *No. 4:* 285–337.

1978. Simpson, George A. *Microcomputers in Library Automation.* Mitre Technical Report 7938. The Mitre Corp., Metrek Division (December).

Journal of the American Society for Information Science. American Society for Information Science, Washington, DC.

H. D. AVRAM

LIBRARY, PROGRAM *See* PROGRAM LIBRARIES.

LIFO. *See* FIFO-LIFO.

LIGHTPEN

For articles on related subjects *see* COMPUTER GRAPHICS; and INPUT-OUTPUT DEVICES.

The lightpen has been one of the most common manual input devices on vector graphic displays (and even on some alphanumeric ones), for use in identifying *(picking)* information displayed on the screen for subsequent computer processing. For example, in text editing, pointing at a certain character on a certain line with the lightpen might indicate to the program that a string of characters about to be typed by the user should be inserted after the identified character. Pointing the lightpen at a particular resistor in an electronic schematic on the screen might mean that the user wants that particular resistor moved, scaled up, deleted, or manipulated in some other specified way.

Physically, the lightpen (Fig. 1) is a photosensitive transducer that converts light emanating from the screen to an electric signal, which is typically used to interrupt the processor servicing the display. Associated with the interrupt is some sense data, usually the $x - y$ coordinates of the lightpenned display element (point, line, or character) on the screen, and/or the address in the display buffer of the display command which caused display of the element that the lightpen detected.

In either case, the program has the problem of relating such coordinate or address sense data to the particular text character or logical picture entity which the user selected for processing by the program. This process is known as *correlation* of the physical sense data to the logical subpicture item that the user wanted to indicate, and usually involves some amount of table searching.

Some lightpens aid the user in accurate positioning by projecting "finder beams" of light on the spot on the screen where the lightpen photodetector is focused. Nevertheless, most lightpens are not easily used for fast, accurate picking, and have the additional disadvantage that they are not natural for freehand input. A data tablet (*q.v.*) with its stylus allows such input without special programming aids, while a lightpen must be provided with special "tracking" algorithms. In such an algorithm, the program displays a tracking cursor (*q.v.*), or cross, and makes it follow the lightpen.

A. VAN DAM

LINEAR PROGRAMMING. *See* MATHEMATICAL PROGRAMMING; and SIMPLEX METHOD.

LINGUISTICS. *See* PROGRAMMING LINGUISTICS.

LINKAGE EDITOR

For articles on related subjects *see* ASSEMBLERS; LOADERS; and PROGRAM LIBRARIES.

The function of the linkage editor (sometimes called the *consolidator* or *composer* or *collector*) is to combine into a single module a number of program segments that have been independently compiled. Some of the segments may be held in a library (on disk or tape), and the linkage editor will normally provide facilities for the automatic incorporation of any library segments that have been referenced. The output of the linkage editor is usually a relocatable binary program suitable for loading by a relocating loader.

If a section of program has been independently compiled, there will be three kinds of items in the compiler output:

1. Constants (absolute items whose value does not depend on the ultimate position of the segment in memory).
2. Items (usually addresses or address constants) whose value is known relative to the value of a specified location counter at the start of the segment.
3. External references, whose value cannot be determined until all segments are present.

The complete output of the compiler will therefore typically consist of

1. A "code" block consisting of binary words tagged to show their absolute, relative, or external char-

Fig. 1. A lightpen pointing to a picture on a display screen.

acter, and, in the case of relative items, the appropriate location counter.

2. A table of external references, containing for each reference the (relative) address in the code section at which it occurs and its symbolic form.
3. A table of external (global) symbol definitions, containing the name and (relative) value of each symbol globally defined in the segment.

The linkage editor operates in a number of passes. The first pass determines which segments are missing, by comparing the external reference tables with the global definition tables. If there are "missing" segments, the directories of specified library files are scanned. If the relevant names are found, the corresponding segments are added to the program. Pass 2 scans the segment headers and computes the sizes of the blocks corresponding to the various location counters. This information is placed in a header block for the use of the loader. Pass 3 performs relocation of all subsequent segments relative to the first segment so as to produce a relocatable program based on a single set of origins.

The process is simple: The location counters are all set to zero at the start of the first segment. Their values at the start of segment n, together with the information in that segment's header block, determine their values at the start of segment $n + 1$. During this pass, the entries in the global symbol definition tables and in the external reference tables are relocated relative to the origin of the first segment, and the entries from the tables associated with each segment are merged to give a single global symbol table and a single table of external references. Finally, these two tables are used to fill in all the unresolved external references, and the end result is a single module of relocatable binary.

The operation of linkage editing is commonly done as a disk-to-disk operation, using temporary work files as necessary. It is evident that it is a trivial extra complication to perform the final relocation at the same time, thus producing an executable binary module. Such a system is called a *linking loader*.

REFERENCES

1972. Barron, D. W. *Assemblers and Loaders,* 2nd Ed. New York: American Elsevier.
1972. Presser L. and White, J. R. "Linkers and Loaders," *Computing Surveys* **4**:149–168.

D. W. BARRON

LISP. *See* LIST PROCESSING LANGUAGES.

LIST PROCESSING. *See* LISTS AND LIST PROCESSING.

LIST PROCESSING LANGUAGES

For articles on related subjects *see* ARTIFICIAL INTELLIGENCE; DATA STRUCTURES; FUNCTIONAL PROGRAMMING; GARBAGE COLLECTION; LAMBDA CALCULUS; LANGUAGE TRANSLATION; LISTS AND LIST PROCESSING; POINTER; PROGRAMMING LANGUAGES; and RECURSION.

List processing languages are computer languages that facilitate the processing of data organized in the form of lists. Lisp, Comit, Sail, and Pop-2 are typical list-processing languages.

External List Representation. We begin with some simple examples to show what kinds of problems are solved by list processing and also how the lists look as they are used for input and output.

Traditional Notation	List Notation
French to English translation:	
Où est le Métro?	(OU EST LE METRO?)
Symbolic integration:	
$\int xe^{x^2}dx$	(INT X ∙(E∙∙(X∙∙2)))
Logic:	
$(\forall x)(Q(x) \lor \sim P(x))$	(ALL X(QX)OR(NOT(PX)))
Automatic question answering:	
Who is on first?	(WHO IS ON FIRST?)

The list is a convenient way of representing nonnumerical data such as English sentences, mathematical formulas, a position in a game, logic theorems, or computer programs. The structure of a list is a natural way to represent the structure of data for the computer. By nesting sublists, sub-sublists, etc., one can create list structures of arbitrary complexity. List-processing techniques are especially useful for data that has variable structure, such as languages.

Some of the terms used in connection with list processing are used in slightly different ways by different writers. Some rough definitions are as follows.

An *atom* is the basic list element. It is not a list. An atom corresponds to a word in English. In the examples above, EST, INT, **, X, and WHO are some of the atoms.

An *element* is one item on a list. It may be an atom

or another list. Synonyms sometimes used for element are *node, item, record, entity,* and *bead.*

A *string* is an ordered sequence of elements (usually characters). A string lacks the complex structure that a list may have.

A *list structure* is a list whose elements may be atoms or lists or list structures.

A list is represented externally to the computer in terms of characters, and internally in terms of memory cells. The external representation (shown in the tabulated examples above) is designed for the convenience of the user and is used by the computer for input and output operations. The exact rules for writing a list vary from one language to another. In the above examples we have used the notation of Lisp. Parentheses indicate the beginning and end of a list, and blanks separate atoms.

Internal List Representation. The internal representation of a list is the way in which the computer stores the list in its memory cells. This varies from one language to another.

An important part of list processing concerns the way lists are stored in memory. In order to clarify this point, a comparison will be made between the way lists might be stored in a conventional language such as Fortran and the way lists are usually stored in a list-processing language such as Lisp.

Fig. 1 is a simple list—(SEE (THE BIG) DOG)— as it might be stored in a Fortran array and also as it might be stored in the memory of a Lisp system. Each rectangle represents one memory cell or word. In the Fortran array, the list is stored in the conventional form of coded characters, one atom to a memory word. We assume here that the words are filled with blanks and right-

justified. Parentheses indicate the beginning and ending of sublists.

The same list is represented in a Lisp system in the form of *pointers.* A pointer (*q.v.*) is the address of a memory word. Other terms sometimes used for pointer are *link* and *reference.* In this example, each memory word is divided into a front half and a rear half. Each half contains the address of another memory word. Each such address is represented in the diagram as an arrow pointing to the word to which it refers. The characters of the atoms are located in a special part of the memory reserved for characters. The arrow pointing to SEE represents the address of a special memory word that represents the atom SEE. The other arrows pointing to atoms have a similar meaning. The special atom NIL is used to mark the end of a list.

This type of memory organization has several advantages:

1. When adding or deleting items in the Fortran array representation, it is necessary to move down or move up all elements below the point at which the addition or deletion is made, whereas in the pointer type of organization one can add or delete an element by changing only two pointers. If a list is large, this is an important saving of time.

2. If a single sublist appears in many main lists, it can be represented by one pointer in each main list instead of repeating the entire sublist many times. This can be a considerable saving in memory space.

3. In Lisp, a sublist of any size can be added to or deleted from a main list by changing just two pointers. Thus, the processing of large sublists is more efficient.

4. In the Fortran array, adjacent elements of the list are physically adjacent in the memory. In Lisp, adjacent elements are linked by pointers, so the memory cells need not be adjacent. This means that any available memory word can be used in any list. This allows more efficient use of memory space.

5. The Fortran programmer must estimate the maximum size of each list and then reserve that number of words for each array. In Lisp the computer decides where to store lists while the problem is being run. This is called *dynamic storage allocation* and saves programmer effort.

6. Another advantage of the Lisp representation is that, when searching a main list, one can easily skip over the sublists if this is desirable, but in the Fortran representation one must search through each sublist in detail.

The Lisp Language

Data. Perhaps the best way to gain a good understanding of list processing is to describe a typical list-pro-

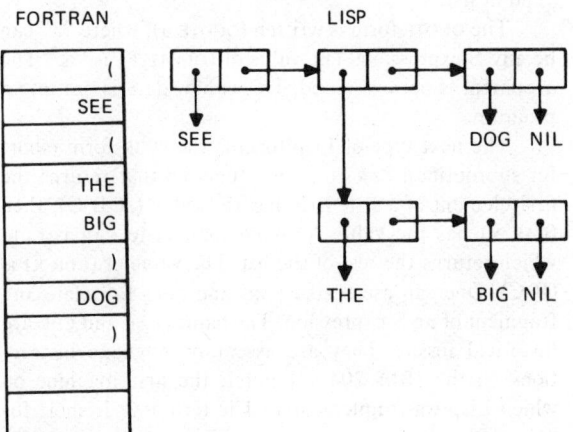

Fig. 1

cessing language in considerable detail. Lisp (short for LISt Processing) is one of the most popular of such languages. Lisp was developed by John McCarthy and his associates at M.I.T. during the late 1950s and early 1960s. Here we discuss Lisp 1.6, which is a version of the Lisp language developed at the Stanford Artificial Intelligence Project. In the interest of brevity, some of the finer details will be skipped over.

First we will define the data language that is used in Lisp: An "S-expression" (short for symbolic expression) is the general name for legal input data in Lisp 1.6. An S-expression is either an atom or a list structure. An atom is a string of characters. The start and finish of each atom is indicated by parentheses, or blanks. Numbers are atoms. A list structure consists of a left parenthesis followed by any number of atoms or list structures, followed by a right parenthesis. For example, each of the items below is an S-expression.

```
DOG
1984
(WHERE IS TURING NOW)
((MCCARTHY) IS MASTER OF (THE DARK
    TOWER))
(LIST STRUCTURE ((((CAN))) BE
    (((VERY))) ((((((DEEP)))))))
```

Now let us consider how data is represented internally in the computer memory. The memory is divided into two parts: free storage and full-word space. The free storage contains the list structure in pointer form, as described earlier. The full-word space contains the characters in the atoms.

An atom is represented internally as a special list in free storage space. The second half of the first word of an atom is a pointer to the *property list* of the atom. This property list contains information about that particular atom. Some typical properties are *print name* (a pointer to the characters of the atom name in full word space), *value* (if the atom is a variable), and *function definition* (if the atom is a function name). Also, the programmer can add additional properties to any atom at will. For example, an atom that is an English word might be given ADJECTIVE or NOUN as a property.

The Lisp reading routine checks each newly read atom against a list of all atoms known to the system. If the atom is already known, then a pointer to the existing atom is used. Otherwise, a new atom is created.

Numbers may also be used in Lisp 1.6. They may be integers, fixed-point, or floating-point numbers. All Lisp functions that operate on numbers automatically test the number type and perform needed conversions. The word NIL is a special atom in Lisp 1.6 and is used to mark the end of a list. By itself, NIL just means the "empty list" ( ).

Programs. The language for writing programs in Lisp 1.6 is actually a subset of the data language. Therefore, it is easy to write programs in Lisp which operate on other Lisp programs (e.g., compilers, optimizers, interpreters, etc.).

Lisp has a reputation among programmers as being a difficult language. This is an illusion caused by the unconventional syntactic style of Lisp. Actually, by any measure of complexity, Lisp would have to be judged one of the simplest computer languages extant. The basic unit of a program in Lisp is the *form*. A form is usually a function with its arguments. Almost all Lisp 1.6 forms follow the basic format: (function arg1 arg2 arg3 . . .). The only other kinds of forms are variables and constants, which are just atoms, and the conditional expression, which has the slightly different format: (COND (arg1 arg2) (arg3 arg4) . . .). Since one form can be the argument for another, large programs can be built up by nesting.

Lisp has very few special rules, exceptions, etc. It was designed by a group of mathematicians and therefore has the virtues of mathematical elegance and simplicity.

The semantics of Lisp are also straightforward. The Lisp 1.6 system contains a program called the *interpreter*. The interpreter reads a Lisp form and then prints the value of that form. To understand a Lisp program (a form), one must know what value the interpreter will produce when evaluating that form.

The simplest form is a variable. A variable is any atom to which a value has been assigned. The value is a pointer to some S-expression. For example, a variable X may have as value a list of three elements (A B C).

The other atomic Lisp form is the constant. A constant is simply a variable that has been assigned itself as a value. Typical constants are numbers, T, and NIL. The constant T means "true," and NIL means "false" and also "end of list."

The QUOTE form is written (QUOTE a), where "a" can be any S-expression. The value of (QUOTE a) is "a." The argument is not evaluated. This is how data is put into a program.

The next type of Lisp form is the SUBR form (short for subroutine); CAR is a SUBR function that returns the first element of a list. If X has the value (A B C), then (CAR X) has the value A. A companion to CAR is CDR, which returns the rest of the list. The value of (CDR X) is (B C). One can use nested CARS and CDRS to isolate any fragment of an S-expression. The names CAR and CDR are historical fossils. They are assembly language instructions on the IBM 704 computer, the first machine on which Lisp was implemented. The term CAR is short for "Contents of the Address part of Register," and CDR is short for "Contents of the Decrement part of Register."

The SUBR function CONS (short for construct) is used to build up S-expressions; CONS takes two arguments. The second is an existing list and the first is a new element for that list. If Y has the value A, then (CONS Y X) has the value (A A B C).

Lisp also contains predicates: ATOM is a predicate of one argument. A predicate is either true or false: (ATOM X) has the value T for truth if X is an atom; otherwise NIL for false.

Predicates are particularly useful in conditional forms, the Lisp equivalent of a branch instruction. The following is a typical conditional form:

```
(COND ((ATOM X) X) (T (CAR X)))
```

The arguments of a conditional form come in pairs. In each pair, the first is the predicate part and the second is the value part. The interpreter evaluates conditional pairs from left to right. If the predicate has a value T, the interpreter then evaluates the second portion of the conditional pair and returns this as the value of the entire conditional form. If the predicate is NIL then the interpreter starts to work on the next pair. If x is (A B C), then the value of the sample conditional form above is A, since (ATOM X) is NIL and (CAR X) is A.

The LAMBDA form is a way of assigning local or temporary values to variables. The LAMBDA form consists of a LAMBDA function followed by some arguments. A LAMBDA function is a list of three elements; for example,

```
(LAMBDA (X Y)(CONS Y X))
```

The second element is a list of lambda variables, the third is a form that uses those variables. Arguments may be added to a LAMBDA function to make a complete form according to the usual syntactic rule: (function arg1 arg2 ...).

The result looks more complex than other forms, since the LAMBDA function is a list of three elements instead of just one atom like the other functions. An example of a complete LAMBDA form is:

```
((LAMBDA (X Y)(CONS Y X))(QUOTE (A B C))
(QUOTE A))
```

The interpreter first evaluates the arguments. These values are then assigned to the corresponding variables on the lambda variables list. The form in which the lambda variables appear (the internal form) is then evaluated, and this value is then the value of the entire LAMBDA form.

In the example above, x will have the value (A B C) and y will have the value A. Thus, the internal form, (CONS Y X), will have the value (A A B C), and this will be the value of the entire LAMBDA form.

An EXPR function is a function written by the Lisp programmer. The programmer can make any atom into a function by assigning to that atom a suitable Lisp expression. Below is an example of a simple EXPR function being defined and then used. In this example, TIMES means multiply, DE means DEFINE.

```
(DE SQUARE (X) (TIMES X X))
(SQUARE 9)
```

The DE form above will assign to the atom SQUARE, an EXPR property with the value (LAMBDA (X) (TIMES X X)). When evaluating (SQUARE 9), the Lisp interpreter will first look up the definition of the EXPR function, as given on the property list of the atom, and then evaluate it. Thus, the value of (SQUARE 9) is 81.

Recursive Functions. A very useful property of Lisp is the ability to evaluate a recursively defined function, i.e., a function that uses its own name as part of its definition. For example,

```
(DE LAST (X) (COND
       ((ATOM (CDR X)) (CAR X))
       (T (LAST (CDR X)))        ))
```

where LAST searches a list of any length and returns the last element of that list. (ATOM (CDR X)) is true only if x is a list of just one element. If x is a list of two or more elements, LAST calls itself and shortens the list by removing the first element. Eventually, the list is shortened to just one element. Then (CAR X) is returned, which is the last element of a one-element list.

How can a recursively defined function be evaluated? When the Lisp interpreter is evaluating an EXPR function and it encounters another call of the same function, it simply obtains a pointer to the definition from the property list of the atom. The interpreter saves its place in the old definition by putting a pointer on an internal structure known as the *pushdown stack*. The evaluation procedure is exactly the same, whether the function happens to be the same as the one currently being evaluated or a different one. In the preceding example of the function LAST, the recursion depth will be equal to the number of elements in the list being searched.

A Lisp function may also call itself at several different places in its definition (possibly with different arguments). A Lisp function may also call itself implicitly; i.e., function FNA may call FNB, which then calls FNA again. One must take care that a recursive function is not given a circular definition.

The Reclaimer. The "reclaimer," or "garbage collector," aids the dynamic storage allocation in Lisp. It periodically searches memory to locate list structures that are no longer needed. The memory cells in this *garbage* are then added to the *list of available space* to be used in making new list structures. Reclaimers are also used in most other list-processing languages.

A Practical Lisp Program.

As a practical example to illustrate the use of Lisp, we will now write a program to differentiate algebraic expressions. Polish prefix notation is used for the algebraic expressions. Variables may be indicated by letters of the alphabet such as X, Y, and Z. Constants may be indicated by other letters or by numbers. These may be added or multiplied by the special symbols PLUS and TIMES as used in Polish prefix notation:

(PLUS X A) meeans X + A
(TIMES 3 X) means 3X

Larger expressions may be built up by nesting:

(PLUS 3 (TIMES X X)) means $3 + X^2$

The program will carry out four mathematical rules of differentiation:

1. $dX/dX = 1$.
2. $da/dX = 0$.
3. $d\ (\text{PLUS}\ Y\ Z)/dX = (\text{PLUS}\ (dY/dX)\ (dZ/dX))$.
4. $d\ (\text{TIMES}\ Y\ Z)/dX = (\text{PLUS}\ (\text{TIMES}\ dY/dX\ Z)\ (\text{TIMES}\ dZ/dX\ Y))$.

The program to carry out these rules is quite straightforward. The top-level function, called DIF, takes two variables—E the expression to be differentiated and x the variable of differentiation. Also, DIF uses a conditional form to decide which of the four rules should be applied. The fifth alternative is an error message, in case none of the four rules applies.

Each of the four subfunctions, DIF1, DIF2, DIF3, and DIF4, applies one of the four rules of differentiation as given above: DIF1 and DIF2 have no arguments, but DIF3 and DIF4 each take three arguments, E2, E3, and X; E2 and E3 are the second and third elements of the expression E, which was given to DIF. One may see in DIF the form (CAR (CDR E)), which obtains the second element of E, and also the form (CAR (CDR (CDR E))), which obtains the third element of E.

The last subfunction, DIF5 is called by DIF4 to handle the innermost part of the TIMES differentiation rule.

Note that DIF3 and DIF5 call DIF, the top-level function. Thus, DIF is a recursive function. This recursive design allows DIF to differentiate expressions that are nested to any depth. Thus, this simple program can handle algebraic expressions of arbitrary complexity. Here is the program listing.

```
(DE DIF (E X) (COND
  ((EQ E X) (DIF1))
  ((ATOM E) (DIF2))
  ((EQ (CAR E) (QUOTE PLUS))
    (DIF3 (CAR(CDR E)) (CAR(CDR(CDR
      E))) X))
  ((EQ (CAR E) (QUOTE TIMES))
    (DIF4 (CAR(CDR E)) (CAR(CDR(CDR
      E))) X))
  (T(CONS (QUOTE ERROR) E)) ))

(DE DIF1() 1)
(DE DIF2() 0)

(DE DIF3 (E2 E3 X) (CONS (QUOTE PLUS)
  (CONS (DIF E2 X)
  (CONS (DIF E3 X) NIL))) )

(DE DIF4 (E2 E3 X) (CONS (QUOTE PLUS)
  (CONS (DIF5 E2 E3 X)
  (CONS (DIF5 E3 E2 X) NIL))) )

(DE DIF5 (E2 E3 X) (CONS (QUOTE TIMES)
  (CONS E2
  (CONS (DIF E3 X) NIL))) )
```

Below is a use of DIF and the value that is returned by the computer. The problem is to differentiate $3X^2$:

```
(DIF (QUOTE (TIMES 3(TIMES X X)))
  (QUOTE X))
```

to get the result 6X

```
(PLUS(TIMES 3(PLUS(TIMES X 1)(TIMES X 1)))
  (TIMES(TIMES X X)0))
```

It is obvious that this program could use a subroutine to simplify the answers.

Other List Processing Languages.

IPL-V is the grandparent of all list-processing languages. It was developed by Allen Newell and his associates at the RAND Corporation and later at Carnegie-Mellon University. IPL is an acronym for Information Processing Language, a choice that reflects the lack of competition when the name was selected. IPL-V is the fifth member of the IPL family.

IPL-V was the first language to use lists made of memory cells linked with pointers, but garbage collection is the programmer's responsibility.

Below is an IPL-V program to test if two symbols are equal, and to return one symbol if they are equal or the second symbol if they are not. This could be expressed in Lisp as a conditional form:

(COND ((EQ X0 X1) X0)(T X1))

Here is the IPL-V version:

Name	PQ	Symbol	Link	Comments
E0		J2		Test if H0(0) = H0(1)
	70	9-1		Branch if not equal
	30	H0		Pop H0 (= H0(0)- the communication cell)
9-1		J0		Dummy instruction

According to the conventions of IPL-V, there is a special memory cell called H0 (the communication cell), which is used to transmit arguments to subroutines. The H0 cell is actually the head cell of a pushdown list, so that any number of arguments may be stored there. The notation H0(0) is the top symbol on the H0 pushdown list, and H0(1),H0(2), ... refer to the deeper elements. Thus, if a subroutine such as the example above takes two arguments, they will be placed in H0(0) and H0(1) by the calling program, and the result of the subroutine will be placed in H0(0).

Now let us consider the example above, where E0 is the name of the subroutine. After being defined, it can be called by this name. The call J2 is to an existing subroutine, called a *primitive*, which tests the equality of the first two arguments, H0(0) and H0(1). If they are equal, the test cell H5 is set plus; otherwise, H5 is set minus. In the next instruction there is no name, but the P part which is 7 means "conditional branch." The Q part, 0, means direct rather than indirect addressing. This instruction calls for a branch to 9-1 if the test cell is minus or to the contents of the LINK field if the test cell is plus. If the LINK field is empty, the next instruction is assumed. Thus, the third instruction will be executed only if the arguments are equal.

The P part of the third instruction is 3, which means pop the pushdown list named by the symbol part. The Q part, 0, again means "direct addressing." Thus, the effect of this instruction is to pop H0. This means that all arguments in the list are moved up one place; H0(1) becomes H0(0), H0(2) becomes H0(1), etc. The symbol that was at the top of the list is lost. The last instruction, 9-1, is a dummy to provide a place to branch to, like the CONTINUE statement in Fortran.

This brief example will give the flavor of IPL-V. The programmer must follow certain conventions to save arguments, reclaim free storage cells, etc.

The programming language Comit was originally designed for research on the mechanical translation of Russian into English. It was based on the notations used by some linguists working on this problem. However, Comit has now been generalized into a general-purpose language sufficiently powerful to perform any data processing task. In addition to the usual list-processing advantages of automatic storage allocation and efficient manipulation of strings, Comit also has a pattern-matching capability.

Basic Comit notation is a production rule or rewrite rule. An example is:

THE + DOG = 1 + BIG + 2

This means that the computer must search a certain list called the *workspace*, until two adjacent atoms, THE and DOG, are found. These two atoms are then replaced by what is defined by the right half of the production rule. The numbers refer to elements of the left-hand side; i.e., 1 + BIG + 2 evaluates to THE BIG DOG.

The left half of a rewrite rule defines a pattern that is to be found. The right half tells how to rearrange the elements of the pattern after it is found.

The left half can include various pattern variables in addition to specific atoms; for example, $1 means one atom of any type and $3 means three atoms. The right half may contain special symbols that specify complex operations in addition to rearrangements. A Comit program consists of a series of such rewrite rules.

The language Slip differs from other list-processing languages in two main ways: It is embedded in Fortran and it uses symmetric lists. Embedding in Fortran means that, except for a small number of assembly language subprograms, all Slip primitive functions are written in the form of Fortran subprograms. Slip programs are written as a series of Fortran subroutine calls. This makes it easy to use standard Fortran subroutines with a Slip program.

Data is represented in memory by Slip cells. A Slip cell is two or three memory words (depending on the implementation) that are physically adjacent. The cell represents one element of a list. It contains a pointer to the next cell on the list, a pointer to the preceding cell on the list, and some alphanumeric data. The data may be an atom or the name of another list.

Since Slip cells contain pointers in both directions, it is as easy to search a Slip list backward as forward. This is why Slip lists are called *symmetric*. Many Slip functions come in pairs, one forward and one backward. In most other list-processing languages the programmer must save a pointer to the start of a list and start from there if any backtracking is necessary.

Below is a sample Slip program. This program searches a list structure of English sentences, called TEXT, and counts the number of times the word CARL appears.

```
DATA CARL / 4HCARL /
K = LRDROV (TEXT)
J = −1
100 J = J + 1
200 X = ADVSER (K,F)
IF (F) 500,300,500
```

```
300  IF(EQUAL(CARL,X)) 200,100,200
500  CONTINUE
```

The syntax of the program is, of course, the same as Fortran. The instruction ADVSER is a Slip subroutine, which contains an advancing mechanism that searches a list structure. Every time it is called, it advances one cell and returns the data part of that cell. The instruction LRDROV initializes the advancing mechanism on a particular list structure.

The language Pop-2 is a descendant of Lisp and Algol. It was developed by R. J. Popplestone in the Department of Machine Intelligence and Perception at the University of Edinburgh. Programs written in Pop-2 look very much like Algol. Pop-2 is a very general language with many ingenious features. It might be described as a combination of Algol and Lisp plus every other feature known to humans. The pushdown stack is accessible to the programmer. The compiler is a subroutine that can be called by a program. An automatic reclaimer is available. Pop-2 is also extensible in terms of data structures. The programmer can invent new data structures, and the programs to handle them, with little difficulty. Pop-2 has been described as a "kitchen sink" language.

Extensions and Applications

1. *Data types.* The programmer is allowed to define new data types in a convenient way. Examples are *n*-tuples, unordered sets, etc.
2. *Control structures.* Multiarchies are now replacing hierarchies. In a hierarchy, the program control structure is like that of a tree. Multiarchies allow greater freedom. In some languages, any subroutine may call any other. Two subroutines may be executed simultaneously (simulated). Conditional interrupts, known as *demons*, are sometimes used.
3. *Deduction.* Built-in deductive mechanisms allow the programmer to specify what result is desired without telling the computer exactly how to do it. Planner, Conniver, Micro-Planner, and Popler are four languages with powerful deductive capabilities.
4. *Pattern matching.* The style of matching found in Comit has been extended in other languages. Patterns for matching are known as "skeletons," or "templates."
5. *Knowledge representation.* Special features make it easy to put domain-specific knowledge into the computer. One example is KRL (Knowledge Representation Language), developed by Bobrow and Winograd.
6. *Symbolic mathematics.* For example, the MACSYMA program at M.I.T. is used by researchers all over the world to perform symbolic mathematical operations such as integration, differentiation, expansion, simplification, and solving differential equations.
7. *Hardware execution.* Computers have been built for the direct hardware execution of Lisp programs. Such computers are known as Lisp machines.
8. *Automatic programming.* Research continues on automatic program synthesis from axiomatic specifications, from information specifications, or from examples. Automatic documentation and proving programs to be correct are other active research areas.

REFERENCES

1961. Newell, A. (Ed.). *Information Processing Language-V Manual.* Englewood Cliffs, NJ: Prentice-Hall.
1968. Quam, L. H. *Stanford LISP 1.6 Manual.* (Stanford U. Artificial Intelligence Program.) Stanford, CA: Stanford University Press.
1969. Knuth, Donald E. *The Art of Computer Programming* **1**. Reading, MA: Addison-Wesley.
1971. Burstall, R. M., Collins, J. S., and Popplestone, R. J. *Programming in POP-2.* Edinburgh University Press.
1971. Findler, N. V., Pfaltz, J. L., and Bernstein, H. J. *Four High Level Extensions of Fortran IV: SLIP, AMPPL-II, TREETRAN and SYMBOLANG.* New York: Spartan Books.
1973. Bobrow, Daniel G., and Raphael, Bertram. "New Programming Languages for AI Research," Xerox Research Center, Palo Alto, CA, Report CSL-73-2, August.
1977. Bobrow, D. G. and Winograd, T. "Experience With KRL-O: One Cycle of a Knowledge Representation Language," *Proceedings of the IJCAI 1977*, pp. 213–222.
1978. Allen, John R. *Anatomy of LISP.* New York: McGraw-Hill.
1979. Winograd, T. "Beyond Programming Languages," *Comm. ACM* **22** *No. 7:* 391–401 (July).
1981. Winston, P. H. and Horn, B. *Lisp.* Reading, MA: Addison-Wesley.

J. R. Slagle, J. K. Dixon, and T. L. Jones

LISTS AND LIST PROCESSING

For articles on related subjects *see* Artificial Intelligence; Data Management; Data Type; Garbage Collection; List Processing Languages; Pointer; Storage Allocation; and Symbol Manipulation.

Anyone who uses a digital computer to solve a problem must go through three major phases:

1. *Representation:* The creation of formal data objects that are understandable by an existing computer system and adequately represent interesting aspects of the real problem.
2. *Computation:* Actual operation of the computer to manipulate the data and produce results.
3. *Interpretation:* Translation of the computer-produced results into meaningful information about the real problem situation.

Most discussions of the use of computers focus upon the second phase, computation, which concerns the operation of the computer itself. However, representation and its inverse, interpretation, play a crucial role in making the calculation meaningful.

The Representation Problem. Some obvious or "natural" representations exist for most problems. For example, in the most common computer applications—business tasks such as payroll preparation and scientific tasks such as matrix calculations—the natural representation for much of the significant data is numeric; numbers appear on paychecks and as parameters in scientific equations. Since these same numbers can be stored and manipulated in computer registers, the numbers merely stand for themselves, so that the representation and interpretation phases are trivial and may be ignored.

In nonarithmetic problems, on the other hand, representation is frequently the most crucial phase. Fig. 1 gives some examples of primarily nonarithmetic tasks for which computers have been used. Note that there is no obvious way of representing uniquely by numbers the data from the examples in the third column of Fig. 1. Of course numeric codes can be invented—e.g., all possible chess positions could be enumerated in some systematic way so that the last example in Fig. 1 might be identified as position number 3,275,117—but such arbitrary encodings tend to obscure significant aspects of the problem situation, and thus complicate the tasks of programming and debugging.

For most research purposes, it is preferable to program directly in terms of nonnumeric data. Such data would have to be able to represent significant aspects of many different problem domains in a natural, intuitive manner, and at the same time would have to have sufficient uniform formal structure to permit manipulation within a single general-purpose programming system. Several data types, such as strings, trees, and graphs, have been proposed for such purposes and are available in various programming languages. However, the most familiar and widely used standard nonnumeric data type is the *list*.

Lists provide a convenient way for keeping track of things in our everyday life: shopping lists, laundry lists, lists of things to be done, and so on. Similarly, lists provide a convenient way for representing arbitrary nonnumeric information in a computer. The last column of Fig. 1 shows how the knowledge in the natural representations of the examples might be encoded into lists.

The remainder of this article will deal with the list as a formal data type, and will explain how it is represented and manipulated in a computer.

Lists

Basic Concepts. In everyday informal use, the simplest written list is usually a sequence of items, one written below another. For example:

> Milk
> Eggs
> Butter
> Jam
> Bread

For computer use, a simple list is also defined as a sequence of items. However, the meanings of the terms "item" and "sequence" must be more precise. The most elementary items, sometimes called *atomic symbols,* usually are strings of upper-case alphanumeric symbols that do not contain certain special punctuation characters, such as spaces. The sequence of items is enclosed in parentheses as delimiters for readability by both the computer and the programmer. Items within the list may be separated by placement on separate lines, or they may appear on the same line to save space if they are separated by spaces or commas. Thus, the preceding informal grocery list could be represented by the computer list

(MILK EGGS BUTTER JAM BREAD)

Note that the appearance of this machine-readable data structure is extremely close to the "natural" data representation.

Thus far we have been concerned with the appearance of lists on paper, i.e., external to the computer. When a list is read into computer memory, all the information in the list—namely, the list items *and their sequence*—must be captured by the internal computer representation. A key property of internal list representation is that *the sequencing information is stored explicitly with each list item* and does not depend upon the implicit sequencing of computer memory addresses. These explicit

Task	Natural Representation	Example	List Representation
Symbolic mathematics	Mathematical notation	$\int_0^\infty \dfrac{e^{-x}}{x^2+1}\,dx$	(INTEGRAL 0 INF DX (DIV(EXP E(MINUS X)) (PLUS(EXP X 2)1)))
Information retrieval	Bibliographic data in standard citation form	Duda, R.O., and Hart, P.E., *Scene Analysis and Image Processing*, John Wiley & Sons (1973)	(AUTHOR((DUDA R O)(HART P E)) TITLE(SCENE ANALYSIS AND IMAGE PROCESSING) PUBLISHER WILEY DATE 1973)
Picture processing	Photographs		(FACE(EYES SHIFTY) (EARS POINTED) (BEARD BUSHY) (SHAPE ROUND) (NOSE WIDE) (GLASSES RIMMED) (HAIR THICK DARK PARTED
Chess playing	Chess publication notation		((WHITE(KING Q7) (KNIGHT Q4 KN4) (BISHOP K8 KR4)) (BLACK(KING KN2) (PAWN KR2)))

Fig. 1. Representations.

sequencing data are crucial for efficient list processing, because they play a key role in the operations of inserting and deleting items on lists. (See the later section entitled *List Processing*.)

Each word in that portion of computer memory used for lists may be divided into two parts called *fields:* One contains a list item, and one contains a sequence *pointer* to the word containing the next item on the list. Such a memory word may be denoted by a rectangle, where the arrow indicates that the pointer field contains the address

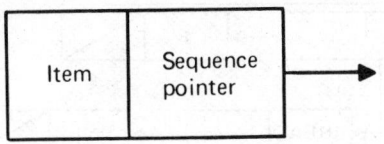

of another memory word. In this notation our grocery list looks like

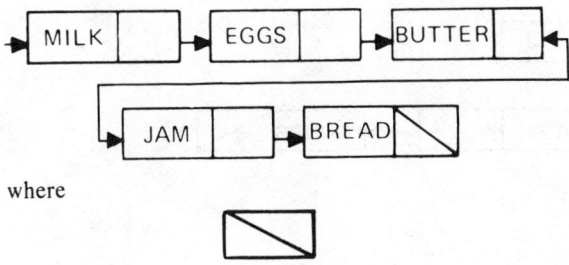

where

represents a special symbol used to mark the ends of lists. (We assume here that atomic symbols always fit into item fields. Actually, since this is often not the case in practice, these fields generally contain pointers to a part of memory where the atomic symbols are stored.)

Kinds of Lists. The basic kind of list described above consisted simply of atomic symbols and forward pointers. We now define some more complex kinds of lists that have been found useful, either because of their ability to represent conveniently more complex data or because of the efficiency with which they may be manipulated.

List Structures. Suppose the grocery list is modified to read

Milk
Eggs
Butter
Strawberry Jam
Bread

An obvious formal representation,

(MILK EGGS BUTTER STRAWBERRY JAM BREAD)

might result in a shopping basket containing, among other things, a jar of cherry jam and a single strawberry! To resolve this ambiguity, the fourth item on the list can itself be made into a list:

(MILK EGGS BUTTER (STRAWBERRY JAM) BREAD)

or, in internal notation,

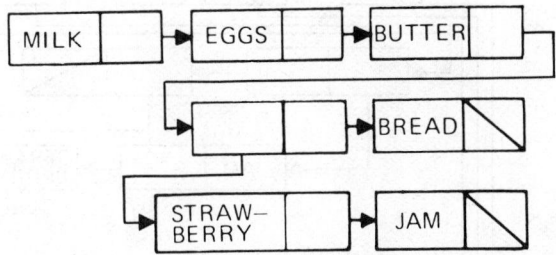

Thus, a *list structure* may be defined (recursively) as *a list, each item of which is either an atomic symbol or a list structure.*

List structures may be nested to any finite depth. For example, consider a more complete version of our grocery list:

2 qts milk
6 eggs
¼ lb butter
1 jar strawberry jam
1 rye bread.

The representation phase now consists of setting up some conventions:

1. The grocery list will contain a sublist for each food.
2. Each sublist will contain two items: a food and its quantity.
3. Each food will be represented either by its name or by a list of the name followed by modifiers.
4. Each quantity will be represented either by a number or by a list on which the number is followed by its units.

The resulting list structure, in external and internal notations, is shown in Fig. 2.

Reentrant Lists. Suppose we wish to consider simultaneously two alternative shopping lists:

a = (MILK JAM BUTTER)

and

b = (EGGS JAM BUTTER)

External Representation

((MILK (2 QUARTS))
 (EGGS 6)
 (BUTTER (.25 POUNDS))
 ((JAM STRAWBERRY)(1 JAR))
 ((BREAD RYE) 1))

Internal Representation

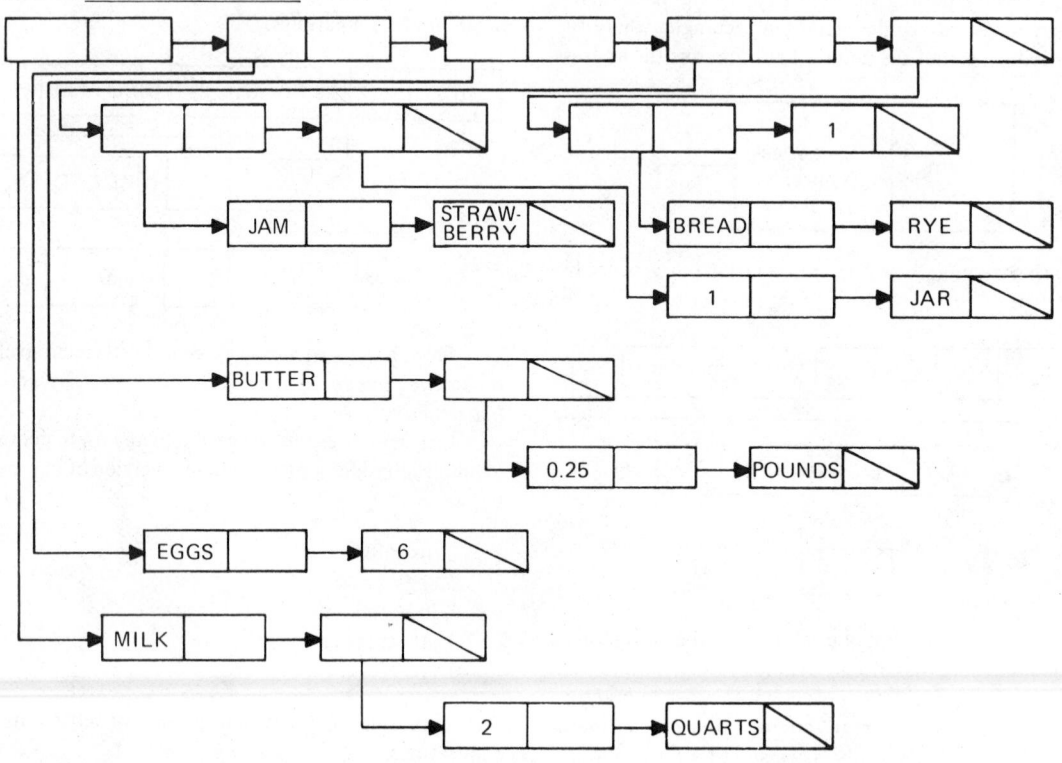

Fig. 2.   Grocery list structure.

Instead of needing the six memory words in the following diagram, all the information can be captured with four

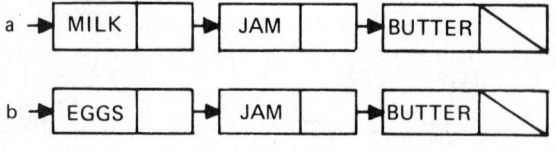

words by sharing the "tails" of the two lists:

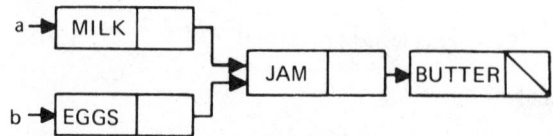

Similar savings may be realized by sharing substructures instead of sharing tails; e.g.,

a = (MILK (EGGS 6) BREAD)
b = (JAM (EGGS 6) BUTTER)

can be structured as shown in the following diagram.

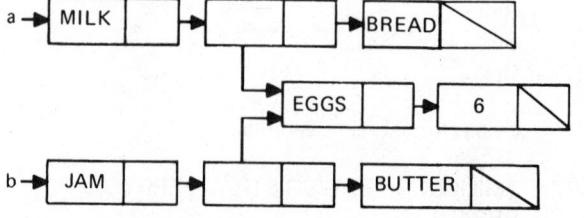

Such *reentrant* structures save memory, but frequently increase the complexity of memory bookkeeping chores.

Circular Lists. Circular lists look like the next structures. Unless the first, or *header,* cell in such lists is spe-

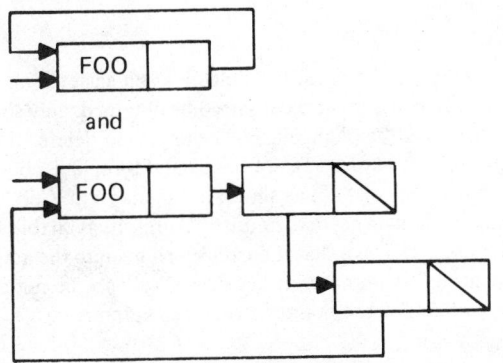

and

cifically denoted, circular lists cannot be described by the usual external notation. They are, therefore, rarely used in normal list-processing operations because any attempt to copy, search through, or print out such structures could create endless looping.

Symmetric Lists. The lists discussed thus far contain only forward sequencing information. Occasionally it is useful to go from the location of one list item to the preceding item. At such times, *symmetric* or, as they are often called, *doubly-linked* lists—*lists with sequencing pointers to previous as well as subsequent items*—may be useful. A common implementation uses a pair of memory words for each symmetric list cell; one word of the pair contains the list item, and the other contains both forward and backward sequencing pointers. For example, the symmetric list

(EGGS MILK BUTTER)

would look internally like

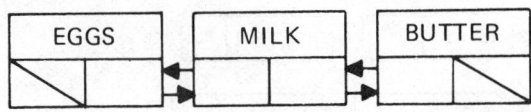

Multiple Association Lists. The multiple association list is a generalization of the symmetric list concept. Why restrict the number of pointers per cell to one or two? Why require the pointers to identify only the (forward or backward) adjacent item? In at least one widely used language (called "L⁶" or "L-sixth," which was developed at Bell Laboratories) the user may specify during the prob-

lem representation phase the number, arrangement, and use of sequencing pointers, with considerable generality. Of course such flexibility carries with it a responsibility for considerable detailed bookkeeping, since many automated features of simple list-processing systems depend upon more rigid, predefined pointer conventions.

Property Lists. The term "property list" refers to a list in which the data items are organized in a particular way, rather than a list that has some special internal pointer structure. Each property list is considered to describe some object or concept. The first, third, fifth, and every odd-numbered item on the list names a *property* or *attribute* of a relevant class of objects, and the item following the property name is the particular *value* of that property for the described object. For example, the following property list might be associated with a baseball:

(SHAPE SPHERE SIZE (4 INCHES)
COLOR WHITE MATERIAL HORSEHIDE)

Property lists provide a convenient way to represent an arbitrary amount of information about objects. The order of the attribute-value pairs on a list is generally ignored; one simply scans the list for a desired attribute, and returns the next item on the list as the corresponding value.

Pushdown List. The term "pushdown list" refers to the way a list is used, rather than to either its information organization or pointer structure. Pushdown lists, which are more commonly called *stacks* (*q.v.*), are only accessed from the front, i.e., only the first element is ever read, inserted, or deleted. This restricted use permits pushdown lists to be implemented in a different, more efficient manner than other lists.

List Processing. The term "list processing" refers to the collection of operations that must be performed on list-structured data in the course of solving a problem. These operations are usually specified by statements in some programming formalism, called a *list-processing language* (*q.v.*). Here we consider the basic data-manipulation operations themselves, and see how they can be carried out by altering the contents of fields in the memory of a computer.

Insert. A fundamental advantage of list structures over other data forms is the ease with which items may be inserted into lists. To add an item to the middle of an array, one must copy and move half the elements of the array, whereas to add an item to the middle of a list, one must merely change the contents of two memory cells.

For example, suppose we wish to insert EGGS after BUTTER on the list (MILK BUTTER JAM BREAD). In internal notation (with small letters naming the indi-

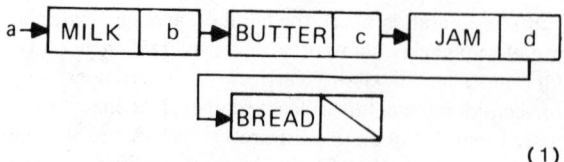

(1)

vidual computer words), we have, initially, the arrangement in (1). The insertion operation requires us to obtain some unused cell (say, "e") and place the new item, EGGS, in its item field.

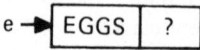

Now the insertion may be completed by changing the pointer field of the cell containing BUTTER from "c" to "e," and placing "c" in the pointer field of "e" to link back into the rest of the list, as in arrangement (2). This

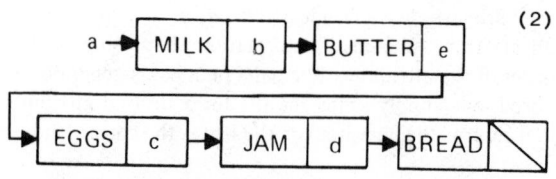

(2)

resulting structure represents the desired list:

(MILK BUTTER EGGS JAM BREAD).

List *structures* may be built up almost as easily as simple lists. Suppose instead of merely adding eggs to the list (1), we wanted to specify a half-dozen eggs. First we would have to build up a sublist describing the new item; say, in cells x, y, z, and w. One additional cell, "f," is

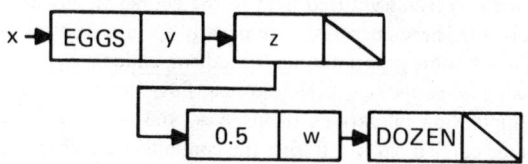

needed to contain the name of the sublist, "x," in its item field:

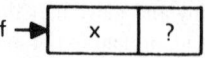

Now "f" can be linked into the original list in the same way that "e" was in the previous example as shown

in Fig. 3. The external representation is

(MILK BUTTER (EGGS (0.5 DOZEN)) JAM
BREAD)

as desired.

Delete. Deletion of list items is even easier than insertion. Because no new cells need be obtained, only some pointers need be changed. For example, to delete BUTTER from structure (2), we have only to replace pointer "b" by "e" in cell "a", as shown in the diagram. Cell "b" is now no longer needed, and it is therefore available for other uses. The fact that it currently points into the active data at "e" is immaterial because it will not be noticed when we follow the pointer structure beginning at "a."

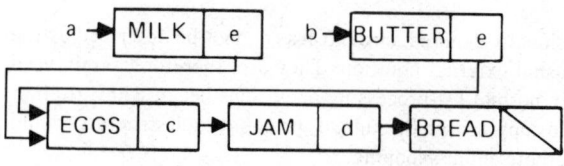

Connect. Suppose we have two lists, "a" and "b"; say, list "a" of dairy products,

a = (MILK BUTTER),

and list "b" of meat products,

b = (BEEF LAMB),

and we wish to combine them into a single shopping list. One way would be to find the end of list "a" and link it into "b," changing

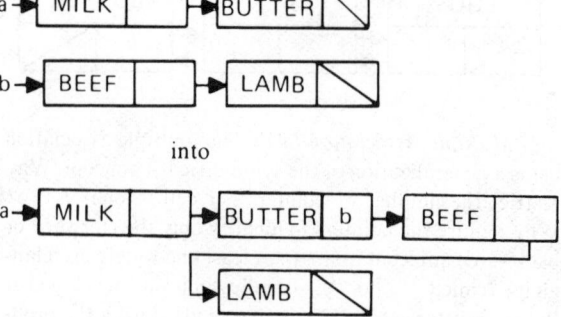

into

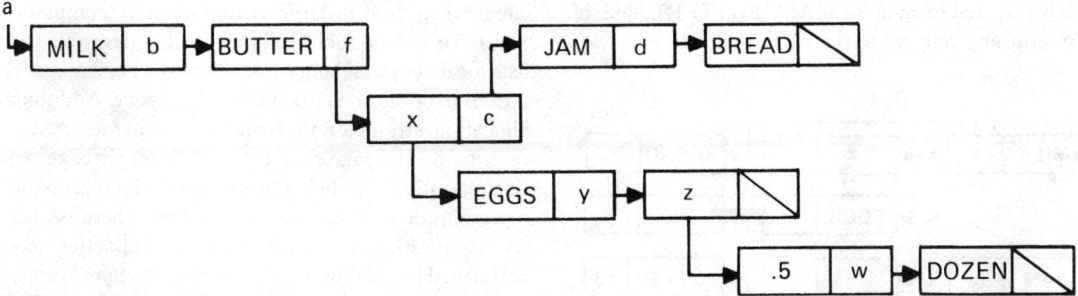

Fig. 3. Inserting one list in another.

List "a" now contains

(MILK BUTTER BEEF LAMB).

Note, however, that the list of dairy products is no longer separately available. An alternative connection operator, sometimes called "append," would *copy* the first of the two lists to be connected, producing from "a" and "b" a new list "c" rather than a modified version of "a," in the next arrangement. This approach allows "a," "b," and

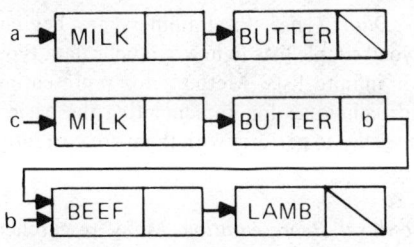

"c" to be referenced independently. Of course subsequent changes to the structure of "b" must be undertaken with care, since such changes would also affect "c."

Storage Management. As we have seen in the preceding examples, memory cells may be added to or deleted from list structures in the course of a calculation. This ability for *dynamic storage allocation* is a major feature of list-processing systems. However, it also poses a unique implementation problem: how to keep track of the dynamically changing set of available storage cells. The usual solution to this problem is to maintain a list of available cells—the *available space list* (ASL). When an insertion operation requires a new cell for the inserted item, the next available cell is removed from the ASL; when an item is deleted from a data list, the cell containing that item may be added to the ASL so that it will be

available for another use in the future. Thus, the ASL may be thought of as a pool of inactive memory cells.

When a list-processing system permits the creation of reentrant structures, one frequently cannot tell whether or not deleted cells should be returned to the ASL. Let us reconsider an earlier example:

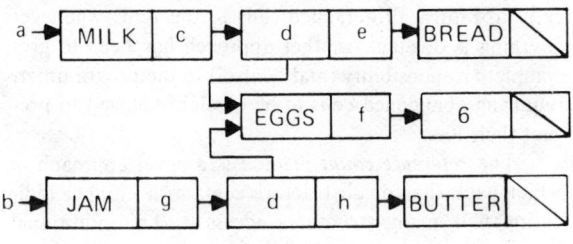

Suppose we wish to delete the eggs from list "a," leaving just (MILK BREAD), as shown in the diagram below. Clearly, cell "c" is no longer needed and may be

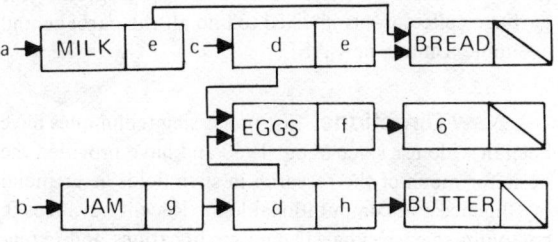

list "b" also, reducing it to (JAM BUTTER), and of course returning cell "g" to the ASL, thus:

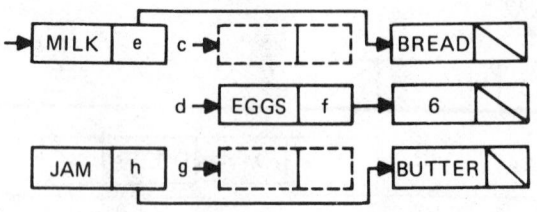

But now what about cells "d" and "f"? Unless they are returned to the ASL, they will be lost forever to the system. This kind of bug in some early list-processing programs caused memory to seem to shrink away and disappear during a computation.

This problem, called the *responsibility problem*— how to assign responsibility for returning cells to the ASL—has been solved in various ways. A trivial solution is simply to forbid reentrant structures, and automatically to return all detached cells to the ASL whenever anything is deleted. Another approach has been to give complete responsibility (and control) to the programmer, requiring abandoned cells to be explicitly erased to prevent their loss.

The *reference count method* is a novel approach in which each shared substructure contains a number indicating how many structures access it. This additional bookkeeping provides enough information for the system to decide when cells on a sublist may be returned to the ASL.

A well-known solution to the responsibility problem is based upon a technique called *garbage collection* (*q.v.*). In this approach, abandoned cells—the garbage—such as cells "d" and "f" in the preceding example, are simply ignored until they are needed, i.e., until the ASL is completely exhausted. At that point, a special program—the garbage collector—is invoked to find all the garbage and assemble it into a new ASL.

New Directions. List processing techniques have been in wide use since about 1960 and have provided the basis for much of the research in such fields as artificial intelligence and computational logic. Recent advances in computer science suggest some modifications and extensions of the techniques that are currently evolving. We conclude this article by mentioning some of these new influences.

Virtual Memory. List-structured memory, when implemented as suggested above, can be extremely ineffi-

cient when used in large virtual memory computer systems. To reduce such inefficiency, it is desirable to keep lists localized, which, in turn, allows the pointer representations to be encoded to save memory space. Additionally, allocation strategies that maintain separate ASLs for each hardware page may be used. Also, garbage collection algorithms are being investigated which keep the list representations as compact as possible. There is also the serious question of how often garbage collection need be performed in gigantic virtual memory systems. It may be the case that garbage collection only need be performed infrequently—once an hour, once a day, once a month, or even once a year.

Hardware. Artificial intelligence researchers, as well as others in computer science, require fast, large address space machines. At the time of this writing, several new "special-purpose" machines using lists as their basic method of data representation have been designed and built (including the MIT Lisp Machine marketed by Symbolics, Inc. and Lisp Machine, Inc., Xerox Parc's DOLPHIN and DORADO, and the SCHEME chip of Sussman and Steele). What remains to be seen is how well they perform and their effect on list processing in general.

New Data Types. Programmers are beginning to move beyond simple lists to new symbolic data types such as sets or infinite lists. Methods for representing such types and techniques for implementing the basic operations one wishes to perform with them are currently being studied.

Procedural Representation. Many researchers now believe that the best way to represent certain real concepts in a computer is not by static data items such as numbers or lists, but rather directly by *procedures* or programs in some appropriate language. For example, the volume of a box might be represented by a number telling how many cubic inches the box contains, but it might equally well be represented by a program that looks up the three dimensions of the box and then multiplies them together. Of course, programs may themselves be represented by list structures. Therefore, as this new mode of representation comes into use, the classic distinction between program and data is beginning to blur.

REFERENCES

1968. Bobrow, D. G. (Ed.). *Symbol Manipulation Languages and Techniques*. Amsterdam: North Holland.
1978. Allen, J. *Anatomy of LISP*. New York: McGraw-Hill.

B. RAPHAEL

LITERATURE IN COMPUTING

For related material *see Appendix:* COMPUTER SCIENCE AND TECHNOLOGY RESEARCH JOURNALS.

Before 1947, the only computer literature concerned analog computers (then called "analyzers"), punched card machines, and calculations made with pencil and paper or desk calculators. No periodicals were devoted to the subject. The literature was scattered in the publications of mathematics, statistics, physics, electrical engineering, engineering, and other sciences, especially astronomy. At that time, a few books—for instance, Whittaker and Robinson *(Calculus of Observations),* Scarborough *(Numerical Mathematical Analysis),* and Eckert *(Punch Card Methods in Scientific Computation)*—could be said to deal exclusively with computing. Contrary to current legends, science fiction literature did not foreshadow the stored program digital computer, or, indeed, computers of any kind.

Since them, the situation has changed completely. Today, there are more than 1,000 computer periodicals, more than half in the United States. Books in print on computers exceed 2,000. In addition, there is a wide variety of other literature such as research reports, trade publications, theses, patents, proceedings of conferences, abstracts and indexes, dictionaries, encyclopedias, data compilations, and product catalogs. Many thousand technical articles about computing are published each year. The computer is a mundane part of the background of every science fiction future.

The most explosive growth has been in the literature addressed to the personal computer user. A dozen periodicals flourish. Some, such as *Byte, Creative Computing,* and *Recreational Computing,* have achieved circulations in excess of 150,000 in less than six years. One book, *Basic Computer Games,* by David Ahl (Creative Computing) has sold 350,000 copies, extremely high sales for a trade paperback.

Bibliographic and Basic Literature

Guides and Lists. Good overall summaries of computer literature were last published in 1972 by Pritchard and in 1974 by Carter. Since then, the subject has expanded beyond the capabilities of this kind of specialized coverage and one must turn to the usual library reference lists such as *Books in Print,* which contains several dozen categories relative to computing and programming.

Couger annually lists all the books in print that are useful in teaching business applications of the computer. He classifies them as to purpose; e.g., introductions, programming, and systems analysis. He does not list books dealing with computing theory or computer design.

Since 1960, the Association for Computing Machinery has published a series of annual indexes to the literature, *ACM Guide to Computing Literature.* Since 1977, the form has been a series of annual publications, each of which indexes *Computing Reviews* for that year and lists several thousand additional items. It provides the most comprehensive coverage of the literature for the year, systematically including papers from both ACM-sponsored and other conferences and symposia and from all the major journals on computing and related disciplines. Its emphasis on the technical and its neglect of the popular reflects the orientation of the Association.

The computing literature of 1946–1967 is listed selectively by Youden. No later complete bibliographies are still in print.

The abstract journals listed below publish bibliographies on specific subjects at irregular intervals. The articles in *Computing Surveys* or annual reviews will often include reference lists that amount to comprehensive subject bibliographies. The ACM Special Interest Group newsletters will sometimes publish bibliographies.

Periodical lists giving addresses are printed annually in *Computing Reviews.*

There is no comprehensive listing of miscellaneous literature. Publication catalogs of the principal computer societies list their available conference and symposia proceedings and reports of their technical and special interest divisions.

Abstracts. Far more computer literature is published than anyone can read. Furthermore, although most of the significant material appears in a relatively small number of "core" journals, there is much relevant material in journals of other disciplines, because although computing is a science and a technical art in its own right, it is also an important service discipline, and thus much computer literature is interdisciplinary. Current abstracting services ameliorate this problem of volume and scatter of computer literature to some extent. The principal abstract services listed below all overlap in their coverage of periodicals, conference proceedings, research reports, patents, books, movies, and academic theses. No one service attempts to cover everything. All are issued monthly, have indexes, and regularly publish cumulative indexes.

Computer Abstracts. United Kingdom and international orientation. Strong in applications.
Computing Reviews. United States orientation. Strong in programming, software, theory. Unique in that reviews are critical and signed.
Computer and Control Abstracts. United States and United Kingdom orientation. Strong in computer hardware, control technology, and subjects related to electrical engineering.

Data Processing Digest. United States orientation. Strong in business systems and practices. Occasionally includes extended essays.

Referativnyi Zhurnal Automatika Telemekhanika Vychislitel'naya Tekhnika. Russian, East European, and Asian orientation. Strong in hardware and programming.

Cybernetics Abstracts. Translation of some of the abstracts from *Referativnyi Zhurnal Kibernetika.* Russian, East European, and Asian orientation. Strong in theory, mathematics, and applications.

Glossaries, Dictionaries and Encyclopedias. Glossaries previously published by standards organizations are now more than ten years old except the 1977 edition of the *Thesaurus of Computing Terms,* edited by the English National Computing Centre (Hayden, 1977). The IBM *Data Processing Glossary* (C20-1699) is recommended. It was last revised in 1977, but it includes all the sanctioned definitions as well as special IBM terms. Some small, paperbound glossaries for students or laypersons are available, but none are authoritative or can be recommended for serious technical use.

Dictionaries and encyclopedias can serve the purpose of glossaries. *Computer Dictionary,* by D. D. Spencer (Camelot, 1979), and *Standard Dictionary of Computers and Information Processing,* by M. H. Weik (Hayden, 1977), are current, complete, and correct. *Computer Dictionary,* by C. J. Sippl and C. P. Sippl (Sams 1974), is satisfactory but dated. The book you are reading is the only one-volume encyclopedia. The only possible alternative is a 12-volume giant, the *Encyclopedia of Computer Science and Technology,* edited by Jack Belzer et al. (Dekker, 1975–1979).

Annual Reviews. A few commercial firms specialize in the publication of annual reviews. "Annual" refers to the frequency of the publication and not to the period reviewed. The contents are a collection of usually well-written summary articles intermediate in length and comprehensiveness between journal articles and books. The selection as to what segments of the subject field are to be covered in each volume seems to be random and chiefly dependent on the current interest of the editors and the availability of authors. The chief traditional entries and the dates of their first volumes are: *Advances in Computers,* 1960 (Academic Press), *Annual Review of Information Science and Technology,* 1966 (Knowledge Indus.), *Advances in Information Systems Science,* 1969 (Plenum Press), *Methods in Computational Physics,* 1963 (Academic Press), and *Control and Dynamic Systems Advances in Theory and Applications,* 1964 (Academic Press). Since the articles are usually replete with

references, they are good entry points for literature searches. In most cases, each volume lists the contents of its predecessors.

Introductory Books. Couger's newsletter lists current introductory computer books for students, managers, and laypersons. The recommended introductory books are as follows: For students, *Introduction to Computers and Data Processing,* by Shelly and Cashman (Anaheim, 1980); for laypersons, *The Complete Computer,* by Van Tassel (SRA 1976); and, for a businessman or student of business seeking to understand how computers may be used, *Computers in Business,* 4th Ed. by Sanders, (McGraw-Hill, 1979). Good older books for the intelligent and concerned person seeking a general understanding of computing are *Understanding Computers,* by Crowley (McGraw-Hill, 1967), and *Computers and Society,* by Rothman and Mosmann (1972).

Handbooks. All the general handbooks on computing are badly out of date, but those on home and personal computing are more current. *The Home Computer Handbook,* a paperback by Brockman and Schlossberg (Bantam, 1978), is a good example.

Textbooks. Almost 200 publishers produce textbooks on computing. About a quarter of the textbooks in print deal with programming, Fortran and Basic being the most popular subjects. Books on specific subjects are referred to in other articles in this work. Couger's annual listing is a good condensed reference.

The technical classic is an omnibus survey of computer science written with style and wit, *The Art of Computer Programming,* by Knuth (Addison-Wesley, 1968–1973). It is projected as a series of seven volumes, but with only three published it has been recognized for almost a decade as the definitive statement of the fundamentals of computer science.

Original Contributions

Periodicals. Three major types of periodicals may be distinguished according to their character, objectives, and audience. Academic periodicals report original results, are refereed, and are published for the benefit of the authors' peers. Other commercial periodicals interpret original results for practitioners, are professionally edited for clarity and interest and occasionally for originality and precision. News publications are a form of commercial publication in which content currency is the most significant criterion.

The English language academic periodicals are those of the principal societies: The *Journal, Communications,* and *Transactions* (on *Mathematical Software, Database Systems, Programming Languages and Sys-*

tems, and *Graphics*) of the ACM; the *Computer Journal* of the BCS; *Transactions* (*on Computers, Software Engineering,* and *Pattern Analysis and Machine Intelligence*) of the IEEE Computer Society; *Mathematics of Computation* of the AMS; and the SIAM Journals on *Computing, Applied Mathematics,* and *Numerical Analysis.* The two principal Russian academic periodicals are available in translation: *Automatika i Telemekhanika* (*Automation and Remote Control,* Plenum Press) and *Zhurnal Vychislitel'noi Matematiki i Matematicheskoi Fiziki* (USSR *Computational Mathematics and Mathematical Physics,* Pergamon). Some academic periodicals are published commercially; for example, *Journal of Computer and System Science* and *Journal of Algorithms* (Academic Press), *Information Science, Artificial Intelligence,* and *Theoretical Computer Science* (Elsevier), *Acta Informatica* (Springer-Verlag), *Information Processing and Management* (Pergamon), and *BIT* (Data A/ S, Copenhagen). *Computing Reviews* publishes an exhaustive semiannual list of periodicals. The best of the academic periodicals, published by industrial organizations, because of rigid reviewing, outstanding editing, and intracorporate rewards to authors, are the IBM *Journal of Research and Development,* the *IBM Systems Journal,* and the *Bell System Technical Journal,* which are equal in content quality to the best of the society journals.

The commercial monthly periodical with the largest circulation, a reflection of the satisfaction of its readers and advertisers, is *Datamation.* It looks like a magazine and mixes simplified technical articles with market surveys, news, and comment. The dominant weekly is *Computerworld.* It looks like a newspaper and mixes news with interminable crusading and repetitive didactic articles. The British weekly, *Computing,* is better. There is a flux and ebb of competitors of even lesser quality supported by the apparently inexhaustible advertising budgets of the vendors of the computing world.

On the basis that the technical content is not limited to original results, *The Computer Bulletin* of the BCS, *Data Management* of DPMA, *The Journal of Systems Management* of the ASM, *Computer* of the IEEE Computer Society, and *Computing Surveys* of the ACM might be categorized with commercial periodicals although in each case refereeing procedures are applied to the technical content resulting in dramatically superior contents.

For further information see *Appendix:* COMPUTER SCIENCE AND TECHNOLOGY RESEARCH JOURNALS.

Conference Proceedings. Publication of papers in proceedings of professional conferences in the United States often takes the place of publication in academic periodicals. This is particularly true in computing because the field is expanding so rapidly that the number of authors and publishable papers constantly runs ahead of publication capabilities. Although conference refereeing is often not so strict as that applied by the leading academic journals, the material is often significant. The major regular conference is the National Computer Conference sponsored annually by the American Federation of Information Processing Societies (AFIPS). The other important regular conferences are the major meetings of the principal computer societies: The ACM, largely concerned with programming and the mathematics of computing; the IEEE Computer Society, slightly more concerned with hardware than with software; and the DPMA, concerned with applications of a business nature. Proceedings of computer conferences are also published by other technical and scientific societies with central and peripheral relationships to the discipline.

The proceedings of the conferences and symposia of the special interest groups of the ACM, and the technical conferences of the IEEE Computer Society, both periodic and aperiodic, are particularly important to specialists. Those available from ACM are listed in the *Communications of the ACM* and from the Computer Society in *Computer.*

The International Federation for Information Processing (IFIP) publishes proceedings of its triennial congresses and of the irregular international conferences held by the IAG (International Applications Group), the IFIP Administrative Data Processing Group.

Exhibitor and attendee fees make conferences on computing subjects so financially rewarding that several commercial firms devote themselves entirely to holding conferences for their own accounts. The papers and proceedings published as a result are generally worthless.

The fastest growing periodical field is that of magazines devoted to personal and recreational computing, which have appeared as part of the postwar micro-electronic revolution. The leaders are *Byte, Creative Computing, Recreational Computing, Computronics,* and *Personal Computing.* They are unique in computer literature because they get some general newsstand distribution. Written in a style reminiscent of *Popular Science,* an issue of any one of them will give the reader a feel for the flavor, tone, and dynamic excitement of the personal computing revolution. The purchase of *Byte* by McGraw-Hill has identified personal computing as an economically viable publishing market and is changing the magazine into the form that the firm favors for its stable of special interest periodicals. *Creative Computing,* still owned and controlled by its founder, continues to be more light-hearted, with puzzles, games, and cartoons mixed in with the serious, popular-technical articles. In addition, there are a number of specialized magazines devoted to a single home computer product line, such as the Apple Computer and the Radio Shack TRS-80.

Collections of Data

Hardware and Software Information Services. Auerbach Publishers, Datapro Research, and International Computer Programs all publish authoritative and reliable reports on almost every phase of hardware and software, giving specifications, prices, characteristics, user ratings, comparisons, selection guidelines, advice, and admonitions.

Each software vendor publishes its own product list. The *International Directory of Software* lists 3,200 independently marketed software products. Lists of free software are out of date, incomplete, or limited to a narrow specialty and valid only for a brief moment. Programs themselves, published in code form listings, appear in the personal computing periodicals and in some book collections (for example, *Basic Computer Programs in Science and Engineering,* by Gilder—Hayden, 1980). Since 1960, the ACM has offered the quarterly *CALGO* (Collected Algorithms from ACM), which gives code listings of some of the shorter algorithms (less than 1,500 lines) from ACM journals.

Directories. The field is so large that there is no longer any complete directory of all United States computer installations, or of vendors of computers and computer services, or of people in the computer field. Extensive, although certainly incomplete, lists are sometimes issued as commercial publications, especially as adjuncts to surveys.

Statistical Information. In almost all computer industry statistics, the definition problem regularly causes difficulties and discrepancies. For example, in counting computer installations or machines, should minicomputers be included or excluded? How can you distinguish between a personal computer and a small system? What is a computer installation? In short, there are no agreed upon and universally accepted standard definitions that apply to the collection of statistical data. Since the basis for privately published statistical reports are usually mail surveys of uninterested respondents, and the collection process is unaudited and untested, the results should always be considered in the light of the publisher's self-interest and never accepted as more than a gross indicator. While there is a standard industrial classification covering computer hardware, there is none for software or computing services. There is no computer industry association of sufficient scope and strength to collect and publish overall comprehensive and reliable statistical data.

The basic source for statistical information on installed computers is International Data Corporation, which publishes EDP *Industry Report* and EDP *Europa Report. Datamation* makes surveys and publishes accepted statistical reports, as does ADAPSO, the Association of Data Processing Service Organizations.

Miscellaneous Literature

Standards. The significant standards relating to computing are produced by the American National Standards Institute (ANSI) and the National Bureau of Standards (Federal Information Processing Standards) in the United States and the British Standards Institution and the National Computing Centre in the United Kingdom. International standards, usually derivative from those of the United States and the United Kingdom, are published by the International Standards Organization (ISO).

The National Bureau of Standards annually publishes *Federal Information Processing Standards Index,* which summarizes standards publications at all levels—federal, national, and international.

Trade Literature. Vast quantities of descriptive or publicity material are distributed free by vendors. The purely factual, descriptive, and instructional manuals are valuable and important, and are often the only reference material available for a new computer or software system. The remaining trade literature is a form of commercial advertising, and is usually worth what the vendor charges for it. There is no general listing or abstracting of such literature, each vendor maintaining its own listing, usually in an uncoordinated fashion. IBM is the exception. It has a comprehensive list of its own literature.

Patents. Although, in principle, patents (publicly available at a nominal fee from the U.S. Patent Office) should provide complete and comprehensive descriptions of the devices, methods, processes, or programs patented, their titles are deliberately vague and uninformative, and the disclosures themselves are written in an arcane, wordy, and laborious jargon that makes them generally useless as informative literature.

Translations. More than 90% of all computer literature is published in English. Only about 5% has been translated from another language, mostly from Russian.

Biographical Information. Some biographical information appears in *Annals of the History of Computing (AFIPS).* Book-length biographical treatment has been given to very few. Babbage has the most, starting with his own *Passages from the Life of a Philosopher* (London, 1894; reprinted in 1968) and including *Charles Babbage and His Calculating Engines, Selected Writings by Charles Babbage and Others,* by Philip Morrison and Emily Morrison (London, 1961), and *Charles Babbage,*

Irascible Genius, A Life of Charles Babbage, Inventor, by Mabeth Moseley (London, 1964). Norbert Wiener's autobiography is in two slim paperbacks: *Ex-Prodigy: My Childhood and Youth* and *I Am a Mathematician* (M.I.T. Press, 1964). *John von Neumann and Norbert Wiener: from Mathematics to the Technologies of Life and Death,* by Steven J. Heims (M.I.T. Press, 1980), is both a triple biography (the third subject being science at the time surrounding World War II) and a case against the misapplication of science in postwar America. The only other biographies are those of Alan M. Turing (*Alan M. Turing,* by Sara Turing (Cambridge, 1959), a mother's biography), and Thomas J. Watson, Sr. (*The Lengthening Shadow,* by Thomas and Marva Belden (Little, Brown & Co., 1962), the authorized life story, and *THINK,* by William Rodgers (Stein and Day, 1969), the unauthorized biography.

Critical Literature. Computing Reviews provides the only regular critique of the current literature, although other computer publications publish book reviews. Computer books are sometimes reviewed as trade books by the standard book reviewing mechanisms. A few well-conceived and thought-provoking books have been published that are works of scientific criticism addressed to computing. Worth mentioning are *Computers and Common Sense,* by Mortimer Taube (Columbia University Press, 1961), *What Computers Can't Do,* by Hubert L. Dreyfus (Harper & Row, 1972), and *Computer Power and Human Reason,* by Joseph Weizenbaum (W. H. Freeman, 1976). As with most critical literature, the vigor of the controversy they arouse is a measure of their effectiveness.

Fiction. The computer figures naturally and importantly in technology-oriented literature and drama of the future. Occasionally, a computer takes a major role in an important piece of literature, as with HAL in *2001, A Space Odyssey,* but literary works dealing with computers are chiefly limited to a lot of average-quality science fiction.

Philosophy. Essayists and social science writers are attempting to grapple with the philosophical and humanistic implications of computers and computing. Anthologies by Taviss (*The Computer Impact*—Prentice-Hall, 1970) and Pylyshyn (*Perspectives on the Computer Revolution*—Prentice-Hall, 1972) are typical. Donn B. Parker's *Crime by Computer* (Scribner, 1979) and *Ethical Conflicts in Computer Science and Technology* (AFIPS, 1980) break new ground. Douglas R. Hofstadter's effort to rectify the average person's ignorance of Gödel's Theorem, *Gödel, Escher, Bach, an Eternal Golden Braid* (Basic Books, 1979), won a Pulitzer Prize and must be classified as being related to the philosophy of computing. It is, as its jacket says, "A metaphorical fugue on minds and machines in the spirit of Lewis Carroll."

History. The history of computing is only now being written. Some of the pioneers are recording their memoirs; for example, *The Computer from Pascal to Von Neumann,* by Goldstine, (Princeton University Press, 1972). A collection of papers and the proceedings of two conferences are the most comprehensive historiographic publications available: *The Origins of Digital Computers: Selected Papers* (B. Randell, Ed.—Springer Verlag, 1973); *A History of Computing in the Twentieth Century* (N. Metropolis, J. Howlett, and G. Rota, Eds.—Academic Press); and *A History of Programming Languages* (R. L. Wexelblat, Ed.—Academic Press), 1981. AFIPS publishes a quarterly, the *Annals of the History of Computing,* to encourage the study and documentation of the history of computing by providing a refereed publication outlet for those who will write on the subject.

Humor. Computer humor is generally represented by cartoons in the technical and popular press, and by short items in *Datamation.* Some of this material has been collected in the now out-of-print *faith, hope, and parity* (Jack Moshman, Ed.—Thompson Book Company, 1966).

REFERENCES

1964. Youden, W. W. *Computer Literature Bibliography, 1946–1963.* National Bureau of Standards, Misc. Pub. 266 (out of print).

1968. Youden, W. W. *Computer Literature Bibliography* **2**, *1964–1967.* National Bureau of Standards, Spec. Pub. 309, Superintendent of Documents. Washington, DC: U.S. Government Printing Office.

1972. Pritchard, Alan. *A Guide to Computer Literature,* 2nd Ed. Hamden, CT: Shoe String Press.

1974. Carter, Ciel. *Guide to Reference Sources in the Computer Sciences.* New York: Macmillan Information.

1981. *Books in Print.* New York: R. R. Bowker.

Annual. Couger, J. Daniel (Ed.). *Computing Newsletter for Instructors of Data Processing, Annual Bibliography of Books Useful in Teaching Business Applications of the Computer.* Colorado Springs, CO.

ACM Guide to Computing Literature. New York: Association for Computing Machinery.

Computing Reviews. New York: Association for Computing Machinery.

Computing Surveys. New York: Association for Computing Machinery.

Computer Abstracts. St. Helier, Jersey, British Channel Islands: Technical Information Company, Martins Bank Chambers.

Computer and Control Abstracts. New York: IEEE.

Data Processing Digest. Los Angeles, CA.

Referativnyi Zhurnal Automatika Telemekhanika Vychislitel'naya Tekhnika. Moscow.

Cybernetics Abstracts. London: Scientific Information Consultants.

International Directory of Software. Pottstown, PA: CUYB Publications.

E. A. WEISS

LIVERMORE AUTOMATIC RESEARCH COMPUTER (LARC)

For article on related subject *see* STRETCH.

The LARC (Livermore Automatic Research Computer) was one of the first of the high-performance giant computers. It was developed at the Sperry UNIVAC engineering facilities in Philadelphia during the 1959–1960 period. LARC represented a manyfold increase in speed over any existing computer of that period.

Two LARC computers were manufactured. One was supplied to the Lawrence Radiation Laboratory in Livermore, California; the other was delivered to the former David Taylor Model Basin (now the Naval Ships Research & Development Center) located near Washington, DC. Both computers were phased out of service in the period 1968–1969. The consensus was that LARC was a technical success, but the high costs of manufacture did not justify further sales effort.

The basic LARC system was composed of two units. One was an input/output processor designed primarily to provide flexible, parallel, and coordinated control of the input/output equipment. The second was a computing unit designed to perform the arithmetic functions of the system. If increased computing capacity was required, the basic system could be expanded to include an additional computing unit. The computing unit was a parallel computer capable of both fixed and floating-point arithmetic operation. The number system was binary-coded decimal. Except for certain intercommunication facilities, the computing units and the input/output processor operated independently. Additions were performed in 4 μs, multiplication in 8 μs.

LARC had a high-speed magnetic core memory shared by the I/O processor and computing units. The memory was divided into units, each of which was capable of storing 2,500 computer words of 11 decimal digits plus a sign digit. Each unit of the memory contained all the necessary switches, read-write regenerate circuits, and intermediate storage to operate independently and in parallel with other units. The high-speed memory could be expanded to a maximum of 39 units, equivalent to 97,500 words. Eight units were used in the basic system

Fig. 1. The LARC computer.

on a high-speed bus to provide an effective rate of one word every ½ μs.

The high-speed memory was backed up by a magnetic drum-file memory. Up to 24 magnetic drums could be included in the system. Each drum was capable of storing 250,000 computer words of 12 decimal digits. The magnetic drums featured an air-floated read/write head assembly, which achieved high reliability with high pulse densities because of the absence of mechanical contact between the head and the drum surface. A continuous data-transfer rate of 2,500 words every 83 ms was achieved between the drums and the computing unit by interlacing the sequential operation of the two drums.

LARC was the largest *decimal* computer ever built and is almost sure to retain that distinction forever.

M. M. MAYNARD

LOAD-AND-GO COMPILER

For articles on related subjects *see* COMPILER; LANGUAGE PROCESSORS; LINKAGE EDITOR; LOADER; and OBJECT PROGRAM.

The process of running a computer program is generally a two-step sequence: the process of translating the program (compilation) from its humanlike language into executable machine code, and then the execution of that code. Where the program is expected to be used many times without modification, such as in an accounting or payroll situation, the cost of repeated compilation can be avoided by separating the two processing steps: (1) a single compilation stage (which provides an object program that is stored on some auxiliary storage medium such as disk), and (2) (at later times) the repeated execution of the resultant code. In this situation the compiler should be as efficient as possible in generating the minimal code for the program. Therefore, additional computer time is justified at the compilation stage in order to save considerably more time during the succeeding execution runs.

On the other hand, in a *debugging* or *educational* environment, where the expectation of repeated runs of the same compiled program is minimal, the cost of highly efficient compilation and its consequent time consumption must be weighed against the time used in executing the generated code. In general, in this type of environment, the time used in generating efficient code far outweighs the time saved by that code, and thus a fast compilation is more desirable than a quick execution.

Further, since the compilation is expected to be followed immediately by the execution of the generated code, the two phases can be permanently linked together. Where possible, the generated code is retained in the

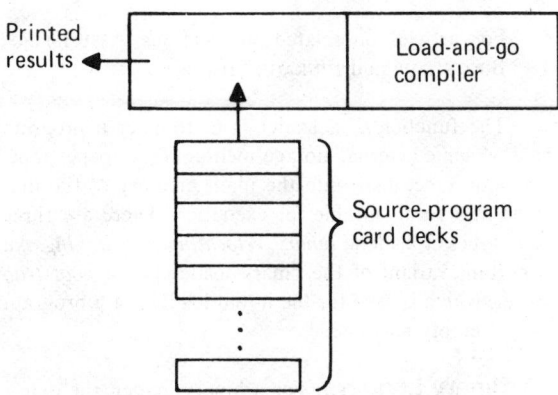

Main memory

Fig. 1. Operation of load-and-go systems.

working memory (as contrasted with the process of generating an intermediate output onto a scratch tape or disk area and then requiring the reentry of the code prior to the execution phase) so that, as soon as the compilation is complete, control can be transferred to the generated code without delay. This process is known as *load and go* and is the basis for many university systems, such as WATFOR (University of Waterloo Fortran) and its successor, WATFIV, and PUFFT (Purdue University Fast Fortran Translator).

When used in university environments, load-and-go systems generally operate as shown in Fig. 1. A batch of source program decks are read into main memory (or first onto auxiliary storage and then into main memory) one at a time. The load-and-go compiler compiles and executes these programs one at a time. In contrast to non-load-and-go systems, where the compiler is read into memory again each time a new source program is compiled, the load-and-go compiler remains resident in memory until the whole batch of source programs has been compiled and executed.

REFERENCES

1967. Shantz, P. W. *et al.* "WATFOR—The University of Waterloo Fortran IV Compiler," *Comm. of the ACM* **10**, *No. 1:* 41–44 (January).

1965. Rosen, S. *et al.* "PUFFT—The Purdue University Fast Fortran Translator," *Comm. of the ACM* **8**, *No. 11:* 661–666 (November). (Also contained in Rosen, S. (Ed.), *Programming Systems and Languages*. New York: McGraw-Hill, 1967.)

1980. Wilder, W. L. "Comparing Load and Go and Link/Load Compiler Organizations," *AFIPS Conference Proceedings* **49**: 823–826.

J. A. N. LEE

LOADER

For articles on related subjects *see* ASSEMBLERS; BOOTSTRAP; and LINKAGE EDITOR.

The function of a loader is to transfer a program held on some external storage medium (e.g., paper tape, magnetic tape, disk) into the main memory of the machine in a form suitable for execution. There are three main types of loaders: *binary, relocating,* and *linking.* An important variant of the binary loader is the *bootstrap* loader, which is used for the initial loading of a program into an empty machine.

Binary Loaders. For a binary loader, the external form of the program to be loaded is an exact image of the binary pattern to be established in main memory. Thus, the loading process consists of one or more read transfers, and such complication as there is resides mainly in the sum checks or longitudinal parity checks used to verify the correctness of the transfers. If the external medium is paper tape, there is a trap for the unwary if certain binary combinations are treated by the hardware as control characters (e.g., to halt the reader). Special shift conventions have to be employed in this case.

A further difficulty is that there must be room in memory for both the loader and the program being loaded. The loader may be kept in a reserved area, or it may be placed in a position where it is known that no program will be loaded (e.g., the blank COMMON area for a Fortran program). A more sophisticated solution is to include in a header block not only the address at which loading is to commence but also the size of the program to be loaded. The loader, which is itself written in relocatable form, reads these items and then copies itself into a place in memory outside the area to be loaded.

Relocating Loaders. A relocating loader differs from a binary loader in that some of the addresses in the program to be loaded are expressed relative to the start of the program rather than in absolute form. These addresses have to be adjusted by the loader by adding a suitable constant to put the program into an executable form. This type of source material, commonly called *relocatable binary,* is typically produced as output by a linkage editor.

If the machine in question uses a base-and-displacement addressing system (as, for example, the IBM System/370), only address constants will need relocating. If the architecture is such that instructions include absolute addresses (strictly speaking, absolute in the virtual address space), then all memory reference instructions will require relocation. The relocation information may be concentrated in one place in a relocation map that contains in coded form the positions of all the addresses requiring relocation, or each individual word may be tagged to show whether or not it is to be relocated.

In the first case, the loader first reads the routine and its map into store, as shown in Fig. 1. (The routine is preceded by a header block giving its length, thus allowing address B to be computed.) The map is then scanned and the specified words in the routine are relocated by having the address A added to them. If individual words are tagged, the loader examines the flag associated with each incoming word to decide whether or not to add the relocation constant (i.e., the address of the start of the routine). When the routine is completed, the relocation constant is updated (i.e., set to B) and the process continued by reading the next routine and its map into core, starting at B.

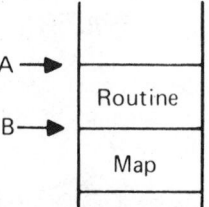

Fig. 1. Initial action of loader.

A more elaborate form of relocating the loader will deal with multiple location counters. [For example, an assembler output (Fig. 2) may contain code and literal constants: At run time, the literal constants for the entire program must be in a contiguous block, so they are conveniently described as being relative to a different location counter (Fig. 3). Similarly, COMMON areas in Fortran can conveniently be dealt with using additional location counters.]

In this case each instruction is tagged to show to which location counter (if any) the address in that item is relative. The loader now becomes a two-pass process: The first pass computes the sizes of the blocks for each location counter and determines the displacement of their origins, and hence the appropriate relocation constants. The second pass loads and relocates, using the origins determined in the first pass. This process is illustrated in Figs. 2, 3, and 4. Observe in Fig. 4 that the loader is now performing a storage-allocation function.

Linking Loaders. A linking loader combines the functions of a relocating loader and a linkage editor. It combines into an executable program a number of program segments that have been independently compiled; thus, in addition to relocation, it must resolve the cross-references between the segments.

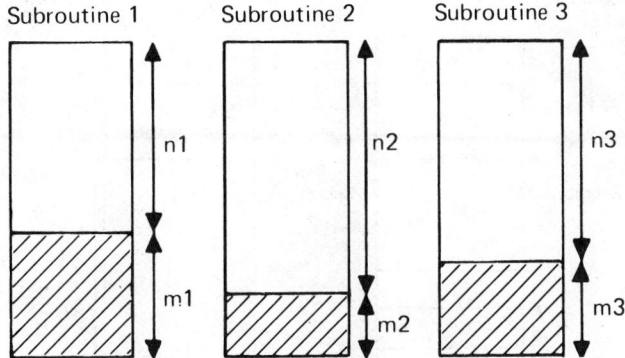

Fig. 2. Output of the assembler. White areas denote code and shaded areas denote literal constants to be stored relative to a second location counter, as in Fig. 3.

An independently compiled segment contains three kinds of information: absolute information, which is independent of the final position in memory (e.g., operation codes); relative addresses, which are expressed as displacements from the start of the segment; and external references. The output of the compiler will typically consist of a number of binary words, a relocation map as before, a table of external references, and a table of global symbol definitions. The external reference table contains the (relative) address of each external reference together with the symbolic form of the reference, and the table of global definitions contains the symbolic form and value (as a relative address) of each defined symbol.

The linking loader reads the first segment and its tables, noting the origin of the segment. This origin is used to adjust all relative addresses in the segment (via the relocation map), and in the external reference and definition tables. The entries from these two tables are copied to form the start of consolidated external reference and definition tables in some safe place (e.g., the top of the memory). The relocation origin is then reset to the end of the segment, and the next segment is read in, overwriting

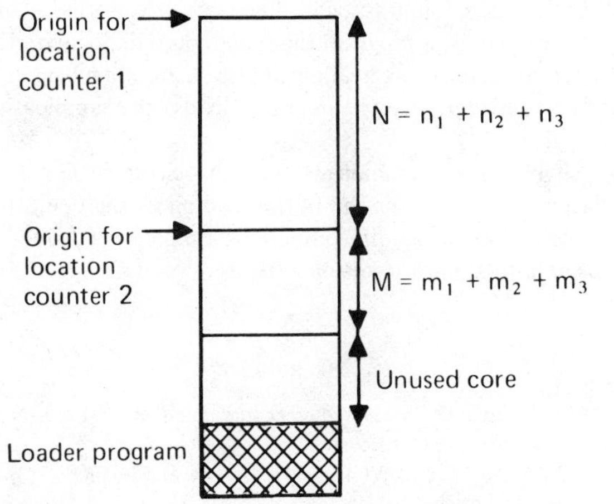

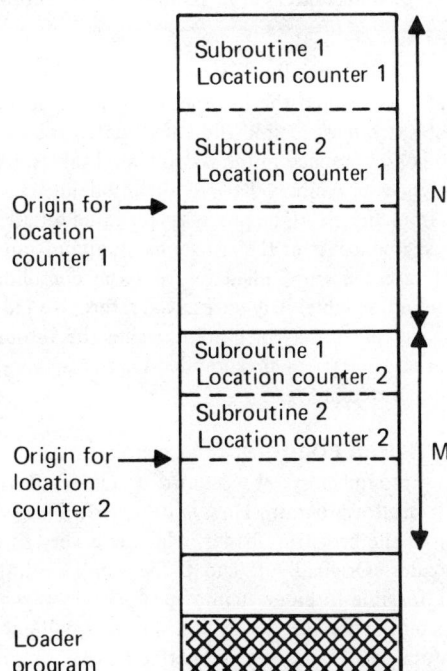

Fig. 3. Output of the assembler. Storage allocation after first pass.

Fig. 4. Output of the assembler. Storage map after first two subroutines have been loaded.

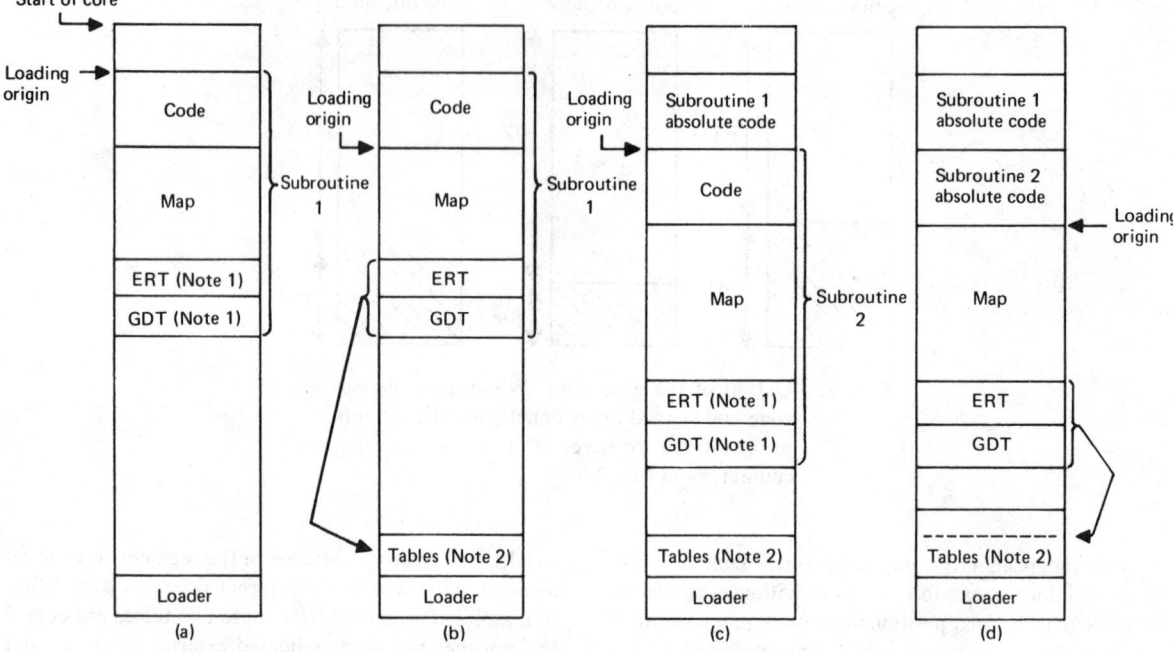

Notes:
(1)   External reference table (ERT) and global definition table(GDT) entries
       have values relative to start of subroutine.
(2)   Table entries now have values relative to start of core.

Fig. 5. Stages in link loading: (a) after first subroutine read-in, (b) immediately prior to reading of second subroutine, (c) immediately after reading second subroutine, (d) immediately prior to reading third subroutine.

the tables of the preceding segment. The process of relocation is repeated and the external reference and definition tables are merged into the consolidated tables. (In order to conserve space in the consolidated tables, external references to symbols that are already defined can be filled in immediately.) The process is repeated for all subsequent segments: After the last segment, all outstanding external references are filled in from the consolidated global definition table. Any unresolved references may be treated as errors or may be used to trigger the automatic scanning of a library of precompiled segments. The process is illustrated in Fig. 5.

Bootstrap Loaders. It is apparent that, to get a program into memory, we require a loader. But the loader is itself a program: How is it loaded? This is the function of the bootstrap loader, which is a very simple, small loader. Originally it had to be small enough to make it feasible to enter it into memory via the hand switches on the console. Today it has to be small enough to fit into a small read-only memory (ROM). The term "bootstrap" is appropriate because this loader is used to load a more elaborate loader (which may in turn load an even more elaborate loader . . .).

A typical system might consist of an eight-word program held in a read-only memory that is capable of reading 64 words of absolute binary from an unalterable peripheral device into a fixed place in memory (e.g., words 0 to 63). This is used to load a 64-word program that is capable of reading the first track on the first surface of the first disk found to be on line (say, 256 words). This, in turn, can be a program that conducts a dialog with the operator concerning available options, and then loads the "real" loader, which in turn loads the application program.

The most common use of a bootstrap loader on a large machine is for the initial loading of the operating system, but on a minicomputer the bootstrap loader is used to load most items of software.

REFERENCES

1972. Barron, D. W. *Assemblers and Loaders,* 2nd Ed. New York: American Elsevier.
1972. Presser, L. and White, J. R. "Linkers and Loaders," *Computing Surveys* **4**: 149–168.

D. W. Barron

LOCAL STORE

For articles on related subjects *see* GENERAL REGISTER; INDEX REGISTER; MEMORY: Main: and REGISTER.

The term *local store* (or *local registers*) is used to describe a relatively small number (usually less than 32) of high-speed storage elements, which may be directly referred to by the instructions. In some systems these registers, because of their general-purpose usage, are called *general registers* (*q.v.*). The contents of a cell in a local register is presumed to be readily available to the execution resources (the adder, etc.). By use of local registers, the main memory access time required for operand fetch can be reduced, thus minimizing the instruction execution time, and improving the performance of the system. In addition, the size of the instruction can be reduced, since fewer bits are required to identify one of the local registers than to identify a word in main storage.

Of course, not all operand references can be conveniently arranged in a single local storage. Machines that use the local register concept usually operate with a variety of instruction formats. This is illustrated by the System/370 RR and RX instructions, as shown in Fig. 1. In the RR instruction, the contents of register 1 (R_1) operate on register 2 (R_2), with the result replacing the contents of register 2. In the RX instruction, the contents of register 1 operate on an operand located in main memory, with the result replacing the contents of register 1. The RR instruction requires only 16 bits of storage, whereas the RX instruction requires 32 bits. In addition, the RX instruction requires the additional fetch of an operand from memory, which the RR instruction does not.

Usually, local registers are implemented so that several may be accessed simultaneously. This allows two operands to be simultaneously gated into separate inputs of

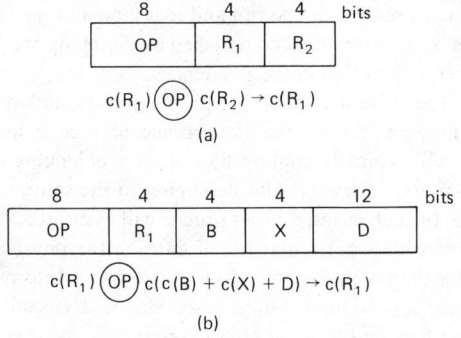

Fig. 1. System/370 instructions. (a) RR, register to register. (b) RX, register to memory: B, base register; X, index register; D, displacement.

an adder. In most implementations, access to a local register is directly controlled by the instruction decoder through a simple gating scheme, which requires only two logic delay units to retrieve the information from the register.

In low-cost machines, occasionally the concept of local storage is retained, but the implementation of the storage is through use of either main memory or a storage medium similar to main memory. These implementations, of course, provide no performance saving, but do provide a space saving in the size of the instruction.

M. J. FLYNN

LOCKOUT

For articles on related subjects *see* CONCURRENT PROGRAMMING; CONTENTION; MULTIPROCESSING; and SEMAPHORE.

When several processes are executing simultaneously, it may happen that two (or more) of these processes want to access the same data. For example, in a system with multiple CPUs, two processors can be idle and request a new task at the same time. If no precaution is taken, both will access the table where the list of waiting tasks is stored, and both may initiate the same task. In a multiprogramming system a READ process and a WRITE process might share the same buffer area, so that the writer has to be protected from having its data garbled by the reader before the output is completed. To circumvent this problem, means must be provided to protect the shared data from unorderly changes. Such means are usually called *lockout,* or *mutual exclusion.* The portion of code in a process that accesses a shared area is called a *critical section* of that process.

At the hardware level, one can use instructions such as TEST AND WAIT and SET, or the equivalent pair, LOCK/UNLOCK. Similar schemes have been proposed for high-level languages. In order to allow programs to be more independent, Dijkstra (1968) has defined a new type of variable, called a *semaphore* (*q.v.*), which can take only nonnegative integer values. Dijkstra's elegant solution is based on two primitive and indivisible operations on semaphores, namely:

$V(S)$ defined as: $S \leftarrow S + 1$.
$P(S)$ defined as: **if** $S = 0$
          then block process **else** $S \leftarrow S - 1$

Basically, the philosophy behind the use of semaphores is as follows: For purposes of clarity we restrict the semaphore S protecting a shared data base to take only the values 0 and 1. Initially, the semaphore is set to 1. Before entering a critical section, the process performs a *P* operation. If *S* is 1, the process decrements *S* and enters its critical section. Since *S* is now 0, no other process may enter its critical section. If *S* were 0, then the process would be blocked and would remain so as long as another process was executing in a critical section. When a process terminates its critical section, it performs a *V* operation, setting *S* to 1 and thus allowing another process to enter its critical section.

The semaphore concept is now widely recognized as an efficient means of protection between cooperating processes, and has been implemented in various forms in several operating systems.

REFERENCE

1968. Dijkstra, E. W. "Cooperating Sequential Processes," in Genuys, F. (Ed.), *Programming Languages.* New York: Academic Press.

J.-L. BAER

LOGICAL AND PHYSICAL UNITS

For articles on related subjects *see* INPUT-OUTPUT CONTROL SYSTEMS; INPUT-OUTPUT DEVICES; and MEMORY: Auxiliary.

A *physical* (input/output) *unit* is an input/output device and its associated recording medium. Thus, tape units, disks, drums, card readers, and printers are all examples of physical units. A *logical unit* is a convenient abstraction of a physical unit; it is an extra level of naming of input/output devices, which gives both the programmer and the system added flexibility in operations.

The usage of a two-level naming scheme may be compared to the usage of call numbers in a library card catalog. The call number of a book is sufficient to identify the book, but it bears no permanent relationship to the location of the book on the shelves. Rather, to locate a book physically, knowing only its call number, it is necessary to consult a directory that tells (for example) on which floor a particular collection of call numbers is located. The library staff is then free to change the physical location of the books, provided the directory is updated accordingly.

A similar two-level naming scheme is used for input/output operations on a computer. Each physical input/output unit in a computer has associated with it a physical unit name (number) in order that communication with the central processor can be established. When data is being transferred, these physical unit names are ultimately used. However, a programmer frequently finds it convenient to use logical unit names in place of these physical unit names, and to provide a correspondence (i.e., directory) between logical and physical units. Thus, for example, in the familiar Fortran statement

READ (5,100) X,Y,Z

the number 5 is a logical unit name, which indicates where the data (x, y, and z in the format given in the statement numbered 100) is to be found. Elsewhere, the programmer (or the operating system, by default) will provide the correspondence that logical unit 5 is currently associated with physical unit 007, which might be a card reader, for example. Data will then be transferred from Card Reader 007.

This two-level naming provides a number of advantages, both to the programmer and to the operating system. First of all, it is possible to reassign the physical unit associated with a given logical unit without recompilation of the program, since the program is written in terms of logical units only, and the correspondence is made during program execution by looking in the directory. Thus, for example, the card reader used for processing jobs may vary from time to time, with the programs still executing properly, provided the correspondence between logical and physical devices is properly maintained.

Similarly, a programmer processing tapes may have them mounted on whatever drives the system operator finds convenient (it is not necessary for a tape to be mounted on the same physical unit each time). This is especially important in a multiprogrammed system where there is no way to predict in advance which physical units will be in use.

A programmer can also gain *device independence* by using logical units. A program is said to be device independent if the successful execution of the program (without recompilation) does not depend on the type of physical unit associated with a given logical unit. Thus, a device-independent program can *attach* logical device 5 to a card reader on one run and to a tape unit on another. This is, once again, accomplished by changing the logical unit/physical unit correspondences.

The advent of sharable physical units such as disks further emphasizes the importance of logical units. A disk will typically contain files of data belonging to several users, or several files belonging to the same user, or both. In such cases, a programmer will associate a logical device with a particular file of data on the physical unit rather than with the physical unit itself. It is thus possible to have several logical units associated with (usually) different files on the same physical unit.

The correspondence between logical and physical units is very often declared in control statements that precede the program using the particular correspondence.

Particularly with tapes, the declaration of logical unit is often part of the request to mount the tape onto a tape drive. It is also sometimes possible to associate a logical unit and a file during execution of a program. This is most often true in time-sharing systems, which usually offer the user a capability to maintain permanent files.

Many operating systems reserve a set of logical unit numbers for internal use. It is also common practice to establish default assignments for certain commonly used logical/physical units. Typical logical/physical default assignments will involve the system-input card reader, the system-output printer, the system card punch, the user's console keyboard, and the user's console teleprinter.

R. W. TAYLOR

LOGIC, COMPUTATIONAL. *See* LOGICS OF PROGRAMS.

LOGIC DESIGN

For articles on related subjects *see* BOOLEAN ALGEBRA; COMPUTER ARCHITECTURE; COMPUTER CIRCUITRY; INTEGRATED CIRCUITRY; and SEQUENTIAL MACHINES.

The term *logic design* refers to the process of specifying an interconnection of logic elements in digital computer hardware so that a desired function is performed. Examples of this process might be the design of a circuit that would accept data representing numbers in a gray code and convert this data into a binary-coded decimal representation, or the specification of the gates and interconnections required to implement the arithmetic unit of a computer. Both formal and ad hoc techniques are used to achieve the desired design.

All digital logic networks in current use operate on signals that are restricted to two possible values only, and are thus called *binary* values. While it is theoretically possible to design logic networks in which a larger number of discrete values are allowed for the signals (so-called multiple-valued logic networks), the discussion here will be restricted to binary logic networks, since these are the only type of networks in current use. For some binary networks it is possible to specify the desired performance by means of tables of combinations as shown in Table 1, which lists each possible combination of binary signals on the inputs to the network and the corresponding combination of desired output signals.

In Table 1, (a) shows the combinations for a network having one input and one output. The output of this net-

Table 1. Combinations for Elementary Gates

(a) Inverter		(b) AND gate		
Input f	Output f'	Inputs A B		Output f
0	1	0 0		0
1	0	0 1		0
		1 0		0
		1 1		1

(c) OR gate		(d) XOR (exclusive OR) gate		
Inputs A B		Output f	Inputs A B	Output f
0 0		0	0 0	0
0 1		1	0 1	1
1 0		1	1 0	1
1 1		1	1 1	0

(e) NAND (not AND) gate		(f) NOR (not OR) gate		
Inputs A B		Output f	Inputs A B	Output f
0 0		1	0 0	1
0 1		1	0 1	0
1 0		1	1 0	0
1 1		0	1 1	0

Note: See Fig. 1.

work will have a signal representing the zero value on it whenever the input signal represents a 1, and will have an output signal representing a 1 value whenever the input signal has a zero. Such a network is called an *inverter,* and the symbol used to represent it is shown in Fig. 1(a).

Actually, a network having such a simple performance as that of an inverter is usually realized as a single logic element and is not constructed out of more elementary subnetworks. An inverter is thus one of the basic building blocks from which more complex logic networks are constructed. Other basic building blocks, or *elementary gates,* are shown in Table 1 as (b), (c), (d), (e), and (f), with the corresponding logic symbols shown in Figs. 1(b), 1(c), 1(d), 1(e) and 1(f).

The combinations for a more complex logic network are shown in Table 2. This network has four input signals and four output signals. If the four binary signals appearing on the network inputs represent one decimal digit encoded in the 8-4-2-1 code (i.e., binary-coded decimal, or BCD), then the four output signals will represent the encoding of the 9s complement of the input digit. Notice that in addition to having entries of 1 or 0, there are also entries in this table that are represented by a "d." This

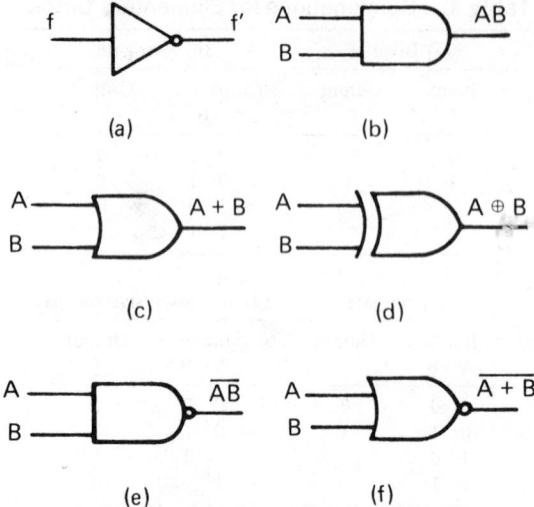

Fig. 1. Elementary gate symbols: (a) inverter; (b) AND gate; (c) OR gate; (d) XOR gate; (e) NAND gate; (f) NOR gate.

Table 2. Combinations for Generating the Complement of a BCD (8421) Digit.

	Inputs				Outputs			
	b_8	b_4	b_2	b_1	c_8	c_4	c_2	c_1
(0)	0	0	0	0	1	0	0	1
(1)	0	0	0	1	1	0	0	0
(2)	0	0	1	0	0	1	1	1
(3)	0	0	1	1	0	1	1	0
(4)	0	1	0	0	0	1	0	1
(5)	0	1	0	1	0	1	0	0
(6)	0	1	1	0	0	0	1	1
(7)	0	1	1	1	0	0	1	0
(8)	1	0	0	0	0	0	0	1
(9)	1	0	0	1	0	0	0	0
	1	0	1	0	d	d	d	d
	1	0	1	1	d	d	d	d
	1	1	0	0	d	d	d	d
	1	1	0	1	d	d	d	d
	1	1	1	0	d	d	d	d
	1	1	1	1	d	d	d	d

Note: See Fig. 2.

notation is used to indicate the fact that certain input combinations would not be expected to appear at the input of the network. Such entries are called "don't cares." A table of combinations that contains "don't care" entries is an *incompletely specified table of combinations*.

An incompletely specified table of combinations is actually a representation for a whole family of completely

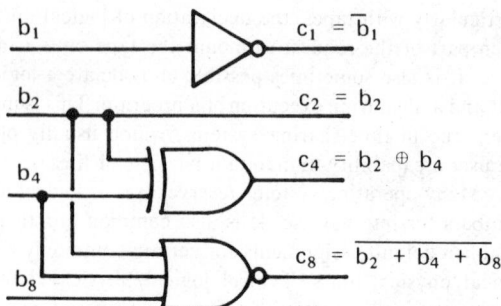

Fig. 2. Network for Table 2.

specified tables of combinations that would satisfy the given design requirements. Techniques exist that effectively choose a completely specified table of combinations that leads to the most efficient network design. An efficient network to realize the specifications of Table 2 is shown in Fig. 2. Using Table 2, the reader may verify that the equations given in Fig. 2 are correct.

The types of networks described thus far all have the property that the output values at any given instant of time are dependent solely upon the input values present at the same time. Such networks are called *combinational logic networks*. The other type of logic network is called a *sequential logic network* or a *sequential circuit*. These networks have the property that their outputs are dependent not only on their present inputs but also on the inputs that may have been present previously.

An example of a sequential circuit is a network whose input is a series of pulses on a single lead and whose outputs display the count modulo n of the number of input pulses. Such a circuit is called a *counter* (Gschwind and McCluskey, 1975). Since the output of a sequential circuit at any particular time may depend on previous inputs, there must be contained in the circuit some mechanism for recording some information about these previous inputs. This function is achieved by providing feedback loops in the circuit, which are capable of storing information in them. The most commonly used type of feedback loop consists of two gate elements interconnected, as shown in Fig. 3.

This type of circuit is called a set-reset (S-R) latch and operates as follows. The input combination S = R = 1 is not permitted. When input S = 1 and input R = 0, it follows from Table 1(f) that $Q' = 0$ and, therefore, Q = 1. Conversely, when S = 0 and R = 1, Q = 0 and $Q' = 1$. When the input which was 1 is changed to 0 so that both inputs are zero, the output remains equal to the value it had for the last non-zero input. Thus, when the inputs are both zero, the circuit "remembers" the last non-zero input. The circuit can thus be used to "store" information.

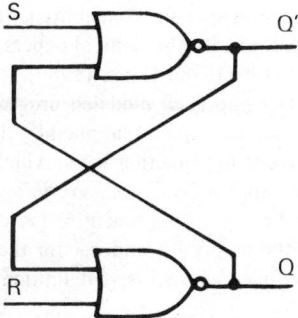

Fig. 3. Interconnected NOR gates forming an SR latch.

Fig. 3 is an example of a whole class of memory elements in which information is stored in interconnected gates. Such elements are known as *latches* or *flipflops*. Just as a table of combinations is a formal representation for the performance of a combinational circuit, *flow tables* or *state diagrams* or *regular expressions* (*q.v.*) are used as formal specifications for the action of a sequential circuit (see McCluskey, 1965).

Formal techniques exist for determining logic networks that correspond to specifications given in the form of a table of combinations or a flow table. These formal techniques are the subject of the discipline known as *switching theory* (McCluskey, 1965). Classical switching theory is concerned mainly with the problem of designing optimum networks that correspond to given formal specifications. Algorithms have been developed for designing networks that contain a minimum number of gates under certain constraints; e.g., the condition that there be no more than two gates connected in series between any input and any output. While a great deal of attention has been devoted to the *minimization problem*—that of obtaining minimum element networks—this problem has been solved only for networks having very specific constraints, such as those mentioned above. General design algorithms with flexible constraints have proved to be very difficult to discover.

Formal techniques for the design of logic networks have an inherent limitation in that the size of the table of combinations, or flow table, tends to be proportional to 2^n, where n is the number of network inputs. A logic network with ten inputs is not a particularly large one, but a formal specification for such a network would require over 1,000 entries. The approach taken to overcome this difficulty is to partition logic networks into subnetworks of a convenient size. The overall network is then structured by interconnections of the subnetworks, the interconnections being determined by ad hoc rather than formal techniques.

Other motivations besides design convenience also lead to the use of building blocks more complex than elementary gates. With present-day integrated circuit technology used to realize the logic elements, much of the cost of an element is in its packaging and interconnections, and thus it pays to minimize the number of such packages and external connections. The way in which this can be done is by incorporating in an individual package a circuit more complex than an elementary gate. Two general approaches have been taken to determine the nature of the complex building blocks to be used. One approach is to attempt to identify the more common types of subnetworks that occur, and to manufacture individual integrated circuit packages incorporating the functions performed by these subnetworks. This approach is commonly called "medium scale integration" (MSI). Some typical MSI elements are

1. Full adder
2. Arithmetic logic unit
3. Parallel binary multiplier
4. Magnitude comparator
5. Odd/even parity generator
6. Shift register
7. Register file (8 words of 2 bits, 4 words of 4 bits)
8. Data selector/multiplexer
9. Decoder/demultiplexer
10. Counter
11. Priority encoder

Each of the major manufacturers of integrated-circuit logic elements publishes its own manual on techniques for interconnecting the MSI elements, perhaps making use of some elementary gates (called "SSI," small scale integration), in connection with the MSI elements (Barna and Porat, 1973).

The integrated circuit industry now has the ability to manufacture chips containing hundreds of gates (LSI, large scale integration) or even many thousands of gates (VLSI, very large scale integration). Some modifications in logic design techniques are required to handle such complex chips. One technique used is to store a table of combinations like those in Tables 1 and 2 or a flow table in a read-only memory (ROM). A particular combination of values of the input variables is used as an address for the ROM and the contents read out of the addressed memory location are the corresponding values of the output variables. A disadvantage of this technique is that the size of the ROM is doubled for each additional input variable. This problem can be avoided by using a PLA (Programmed Logic Array). A PLA is physically similar to a ROM, but logically is like a two-stage network in which the inputs are connected to AND gates which are connected to OR gates whose outputs form the circuit outputs. Classical techniques of two-stage circuit minimization can be applied to the problem of designing efficient PLAs.

In summary, small specialized logic networks or standardized structures such as PLAs can be designed using the formal techniques of switching theory. For more complex structures, the logic design is usually accomplished by using *ad hoc* rather than formal techniques to specify interconnections of basic elements more complex than elementary gates.

REFERENCES

1965. McCluskey, E. J. *Introduction to the Theory of Switching Circuits.* New York: McGraw-Hill.
1973. Barna, A., and Porat, D. I. *Integrated Circuits in Digital Electronics.* New York: Wiley.
1975. Gschwind, H., and McCluskey, E. J. *Design of Digital Computers.* New York: Springer-Verlag.
1981. Hill, F. J. and Peterson, G. R. *Introduction to Switching Theory and Logical Design,* 3rd Ed. New York: Wiley.

E. J. McCLUSKEY

LOGICS OF PROGRAMS

For articles on related subjects *see* FORMAL LANGUAGES; FUNCTIONAL PROGRAMMING; LAMBDA CALCULUS; and PROGRAM VERIFICATION.

A program logic is a *language* in which properties of programs can be expressed unambiguously, a *semantics* that specifies the meaning of the expressions of the language, and *rules* for manipulating those expressions in a meaning-respecting way in order either to calculate or demonstrate the truth of assertions in the language. The study of logics of programs is of value in understanding how both people and computers may reason about software, either autonomously or in cooperation with each other. Applications include program verification, automatic programming, and program analysis for optimization and auditing purposes.

In some logics, the semantics will be omitted and assumed to be either understood intuitively or implied by the rules; alternatively, only the semantics may be given and the choice of appropriate rules left open. Sometimes, the rules will be nondeterministic and intended as criteria to be met by formal proofs, in the tradition of mathematical proof systems; sometimes, they will be deterministic and intended for use in an algorithm, in the tradition of logical decision methods.

Starting in 1967, a number of logics of programs have been proposed, each of them owing some debt to the subject of mathematical logic, with most of them making additional program-specific contributions of their own. The subject started with the seminal papers of McCarthy (1963), Floyd (1967), and Hoare (1969).

McCarthy's approach modeled programs as recursive functions. An example is supplied by the recursively defined list processing function $x@y$, which denotes the list that is the "append" $[x_1 \, x_2 \ldots x_m \, y_1 \, y_2 \ldots y_n]$ of the two lists $x = [x_1 \, x_2 \ldots x_m]$ and $y = [y_1 \, y_2 \ldots y_n]$. We write $[\ ]$ for the empty list and $a.x$ for the list $[a \, x_1 \, x_2 \ldots x_m]$ in the following recursive definition:

$$@1: \quad [\ ]@y \ = y$$
$$@2: \quad (a.x)@y = a.(x@y)$$

Append is associative; that is, $x@(y@z) = (x@y)@z$. We may prove this formally, by induction on the length of x, assuming that every list x is either $[\ ]$ or of the form $a.u$, where u is a shorter list than x. For the basic case, $x = [\ ]$, we have

$$[\ ]@(y@z) = y@z \qquad \text{(by @1)}$$
$$= ([\ ]@y)@z \quad \text{(by @1).}$$

For the inductive case, $x = a.u$, we take as our induction hypothesis that $u@(y@z) = (u@y)@z$ and argue thus:

$$\begin{aligned}
(a.u)@(y@z) &= a.(u@(y@z)) \quad \text{(by @2)} \\
&= a.((u@y)@z) \quad \text{(by the induction} \\
&\qquad\qquad\qquad\quad \text{hypothesis)} \\
&= (a.(u@y))@z \quad \text{(by @2)} \\
&= ((a.u)@y)@z \quad \text{(by @2).}
\end{aligned}$$

This completes the proof that the operator @ is associative.

It is possible to construct large systems of software entirely from recursively defined functions, and to establish many of the key properties of those systems by inductive proofs of this form on a correspondingly much larger scale. However, though some programmers find it a pleasure to program in this style, the bulk of the software that is produced in practice is written in an imperative style, involving assignments, begin-end-bracketed sequences of statements, conditional statements, and while-loops. To prove such programs correct, it would be most inconvenient to have to translate them into recursively defined functions.

To meet the needs of imperative programming more directly, Floyd developed a logic of flowcharts. The main feature of this method was the use of the *tag,* a logical assertion placed on an arc of the flowchart and guaranteed to hold whenever control passed along that arc. Floyd's principal contributions were to work out the details of a formal system based on these tags, to address aspects of the proof-theoretic completeness of his systems, and to consider the problem of proving termination of programs. He also introduced the concept of the verification condition, consisting of a component of a flowchart and tags at its entrances and exits. To prove a tagged flowchart correct it sufficed to prove, for each component of the flowchart, the verification condition consisting of that component and its associated tags. From the correctness of the verification conditions, a local property, the rule is that one may infer the correctness of the flowchart, a global property. This inference rule could well be called *Floyd's induction rule*. The logic was intended by Floyd both for calculation and semantics; in fact, the title of his paper, "Assigning Meanings to Programs," implied that the latter was the primary application.

Shortly thereafter, Hoare developed a logic similar to Floyd's but for "algebraic" programs rather than flowcharts, in which flow of control is represented not with a graph of assignments and decisions but with the constructs **begin** a_1; a_2; ... ; a_n **end** (we will omit the **begin** and **end** below), **if** p **then** a_1 **else** a_2, and **while** p **do** a. Assignments are as in Floyd's system. Hoare introduced the notation $p\{a\}q$ corresponding to Floyd's verification conditions and expressing "if p (the *precondition*) holds before executing a, then q (the *postcondition*) holds when and if a terminates."

Hoare gave a set of proof rules closer in form than Floyd's to traditional logical systems, though in content similar to Floyd's rules inasmuch as every Hoare proof of an algebraic program could be readily translated to a Floyd proof of the corresponding flowchart program. The reverse translation is also possible, though complicated by the difficulty of translating flowcharts to algebraic programs. Unlike Floyd, Hoare did not address the question of completeness of any aspect of his system. Like Floyd, Hoare regarded his proof rules as being for both proofs and semantics.

Hoare's proof system for assignments, begin-end, conditional statements, and while loops amounted to the following rules (to within irrelevant details) together with whatever rules are appropriate for proving ordinary (non-Hoare) assertions of the form $p \rightarrow q$. The rules take the form of zero or more premises written over a conclusion.

1. $$\frac{p' \rightarrow p \quad p\{a\}q \quad q \rightarrow q'}{p'\{a\}q'}$$

[If $p\{a\}q$ and also $p' \rightarrow p$ and $q \rightarrow q'$, then also $p'\{a\}q'$]

2. $$\frac{}{p(e)\{x:=e\}p(x)}$$

[If p holds of e ($p(e)$ is true) before assignment of e to x, p holds of x afterwards]

3. $$\frac{p\{a\}q \quad q\{b\}r}{p\{a; b\}r}$$

[The transitive rule for sequential constructs]

4. $$\frac{p \wedge r\{a\}q \quad p \wedge \sim r\{b\}q}{p\{\textbf{if } r \textbf{ then } a \textbf{ else } b\}q}$$

[The if-then-else rule where the value of r in the precondition determines which construct is executed]

5. $$\frac{p \wedge q\{a\}p}{p\{\textbf{while } q \textbf{ do } a\}p \wedge \sim q}$$

[In a while-loop, p is the *loop invariant* and q the condition that becomes false]

The second rule, for assignment, is really an axiom, since it has no premises. It says that if p holds of e, then, after executing $x := e$, p holds of x. With these rules, we may prove that the following program computes $n!$, the factorial of the initial value n of y, provided n is nonnegative.

$$A\!: x := 1; \ B$$
$$B\!: \textbf{while } y > 0 \textbf{ do } C$$
$$C\!: x := y \times x; \ y := y - 1$$

The following Hoare assertions about this program may all be seen to be true; moreover, they are all provable in Hoare's system. The last asserts the property we want. Together, these assertions form a correctness proof of the program, in the sense that they show that the program computes the factorial of the initial value of y.

i. $y>0 \wedge x \times y! = n!\{x:=y\times x\}y>0 \wedge x \times (y-1)! = n!$
   [First $y>0 \wedge x \times y! = n!$ $\rightarrow$ $y>0 \wedge (y \times x) \times (y-1)! = n!$; then apply (2), substituting x for $y \times x$]

ii. $y>0 \wedge x \times (y-1)! = n!\{y:=y-1\}y \geq 0 \wedge x \times y! = n!$
   [Similarly using (2)]

iii. $y>0 \wedge x \times y! = n!\{C\}y \geq 0 \wedge x \times y! = n!$
   [Applying (3) to (i) and (ii)]

iv. $y \geq 0 \wedge y = n \wedge x = 1\{B\}x = n!$
   [Since $y = n \wedge x = 1$ $\rightarrow$ $x \times y! = n!$ and since $y \geq 0 \wedge x \times y! = n! \wedge y \leq 0$ $\rightarrow$ $y = 0 \wedge x = n!$ $\rightarrow$ $x = n!$ (since $0! = 1$), (5) with (iii) gives (iv) with $q = y>0$ and $p = y \geq 0 \wedge x \times y = n!$

v. $y \geq 0 \wedge y = n\{x:=1\}y \geq 0 \wedge y = n \wedge x = 1$
   [Since $p\{x:=1\}p \wedge x = 1$]

vi. $y \geq 0 \wedge y = n\{A\}x = n!$
   [Applying (3) to (v) and (iv)]

Since the precondition in (vi) is just the initial condition on n and the postcondition gives the desired result, the program A is thus proved to compute $n!$

To discover this proof, one might start with the last line and work backwards. Discovering line (iii) is the one truly creative step here. The formula $y \geq 0 \wedge x \times y! = n!$ is the *loop invariant* or the *induction hypothesis,* and plays an analogous role to the more readily discovered induction hypothesis encountered above in connection with the associativity of append.

In more recent years, there has arisen an interest in decision methods for logics of programs, as an alternative to proof systems for reasoning about programs. In general, even the simple logics considered above are undecidable; their theory (set of valid formulas) is not only not recursive but not even recursively enumerable. However, there exist various fragments of program logic that are decidable, just as propositional logic is a decidable fragment of the predicate calculus. The fragment of program logic analogous to propositional logic is the system of propositional dynamic logic developed by Fischer and Ladner (1979), which they have shown to be decidable. From this, it is possible to deduce that program logic without binding (everything but assignments, quantifiers, and procedure definitions) is also decidable, and that the inclusion of any one of these binding mechanisms makes it undecidable. For reasoning about parallel programs there is A. Pneuli's (see Gabbay *et al.* (1980)) temporal fragment of logics of programs, which is also decidable.

Current research into logics of programs addresses a variety of questions. What are appropriate semantics, proof rules, and decision methods for other programming language constructs, including recursion, parameter passing, manipulation of complex data structures, parallelism, nondeterminism, and probabilistic programs? What is the computational complexity of the decidable fragments of program logic? What alternative forms may the semantics and rules take? What are the obstacles to applying program logics to enhancing software reliability via program verification? The reader interested in recent developments in this area should consult Harel (1980). Much of the most recent work may be found in the theoretical computer science journals and annual conferences, in particular the ACM Symposia on Theory of Computation, the ACM Symposia on Principles of Programming Languages, the IEEE Symposia on Foundations of Computer Science, the European Association for Theoretical Computer Science International Congress on Automata, Languages and Programming, and the Czech-Polish Symposium on Mathematical Foundations of Computer Science.

REFERENCES

1963. McCarthy, J. "A Basis for a Mathematical Theory of Computation," in Braffort, P. and Hirschberg, D., *Computer Programming and Formal Systems.* Amsterdam: North-Holland, pp. 33–70.

1967. Floyd, R. W. "Assigning Meanings to Programs," in Schwartz, J. T. (Ed.), *Mathematical Aspects of Computer Science (Proceedings of a Symposium in Applied Mathematics)* **19**. Providence, RI: American Mathematical Society, pp. 19–32.

1969. Hoare, C. A. R. "An Axiomatic Basis for Computer Programming," *Comm. ACM* **12**: 576–580.

1974. Manna, Z. *Mathematical Theory of Computation.* New York: McGraw-Hill.

1979. Fischer, M. J. and Ladner, R. E. "Propositional Dynamic Logic of Regular Programs," *JCSS* **18**, *No. 2:*194–211 (April).

1980. Gabbay, D., Pnueli, A., Shelah, S., and Stavi, J. "The Temporal Analysis of Fairness," *7th ACM Symp. on Principles of Programming Languages,* Las Vegas, (January).

1980. Harel, D. "Proving the Correctness of Regular Deterministic Programs: A Unifying Survey Using Dynamic Logic," *Theoretical Computer Science* **12**, *No. 1:*61–82 (September).

V. R. PRATT

LOOP

For articles on related subjects *see* ADDRESS MODIFICATION; CONTROLLED VARIABLE; CONTROL STRUCTURES; INDEX REGISTER; ITERATION; PROCEDURE-ORIENTED LANGUAGES; and STRUCTURED PROGRAMMING.

A *loop* is a program fragment designed to be executed repeatedly during each run of the program. This ability to re-use the same instructions, normally with fresh operands at each iteration, is the great advantage offered by the stored-program computer, and is the basis of practically all programs of interest and value.

The creation of a loop, whether accomplished explicitly by an assembly language programmer, or implicitly by a high-level language programmer, involves three steps beyond those required by noniterative routines: *initialization* (putting various registers and storage locations in the proper state for starting execution of a loop); *address modification* (to select the operands to be manipulated at each successive iteration); and *index modification and testing* (to record the number of times the loop has been traversed since its most recent initialization, and to exit from it when it has been traversed the required number of times).

The assembly language programmer has to write code to accomplish each of these tasks, usually using the index registers provided in the machine for the purpose. Loop initialization requires loading an index register with

```
                    BIG = A(1)
                    DO 4 I = 2,N
Range or        ┌
body of         │       IF(A(I).GT.BIG) BIG = A(I)
loop            └   4   CONTINUE
```

Initialization
Controlled variable (I), initial value
(2) and final value (N); step size is 1
implicitly

Fig. 1. Largest number loop in Fortran.

a value that is a function of the number of desired iterations, and another index register with the quantity by which operand addresses are to be modified at each iteration. Address modification is accomplished by referencing the index register in each loop instruction for which a new operand is to be selected; the machine modifies an address so tagged at each execution of such an instruction. Index modification and testing, finally, are accomplished by instructions that test the index register—to see if it has reached its terminal value—and cause either an exit from the loop or another iteration with modified index register value, depending on whether or not that value has been reached.

The high-level language programmer is relieved of much of this detail since the language used almost invariably contains at least one statement, which—given the range of statements that are to form the body of a loop, and the name, initial value, terminal value, and step size of the index or *controlled variable* (*q.v.*)—will generate all the necessary code. Fig. 1 illustrates the form and parts of a loop in Fortran to compute the largest of an array of numbers $A(1), \ldots, A(N)$. Other high-level language control statements giving the same effect direct that while (or until) a given logical or arithmetic condition obtains, a specified routine is to be performed. (In case of such "while" and "until" statements, the programmer assumes responsibility for modifying some variable forming part of the conditional expression and thus insuring that the loop terminates.)

Loops can be nested—i.e., contain other loops—to a depth usually limited only by storage capacity, with the number of times an inner loop is iterated being the product of its own iteration count and those of all the loops it nests within. This gives code within a deeply nested loop enormous leverage for good or bad; it may be executed millions of times in a single run of the program, and if any of it is redundant, the consequent waste of time is proportionately great. The desire to avoid such extreme penalties for small lapses has been a principal motivation for the inclusion of optimization phases in compilers, whose most fruitful efforts are perhaps those devoted to moving instructions out of an inner loop and into the less frequently executed loop (or ordinary straight-line code) in which it is embedded. Since it is common for a sizable program to be itself one big loop containing many multi-

level nests of loops, the question of creating and optimizing loops is, taken broadly, practically identical to that of good program design itself.

M. Halpern

LOVELACE, COUNTESS OF

For articles on related subjects *see* Babbage, Charles; and Digital Computers: History: Origins.

Augusta Ada Byron was born in London on 10 December 1815. She was the daughter of Lord Byron and Annabella Milbanke Byron, whose separation a little over

Fig. 1. By courtesy of the Rt. Hon. Earl of Lytton, OBE.

a month after her birth was followed by Lord Byron's leaving England, never to return. She married William, eighth Lord King, in 1835, and three years later, on his elevation to an Earldom, became known as the Countess of (Lady) Lovelace.

Ada, as she was known in the family circle, was educated by governesses and tutors, and later by much self-study. Dr. Augustus De Morgan, professor at the University of London, helped her in her advanced studies, and formed a very high opinion of her abilities: "The tract about Babbage's machine is a pretty thing enough, but I could I think produce a series of extracts, out of Lady Lovelace's first queries upon new subjects, which would make a mathematician see that it was no criterion of what might be expected from her." *(Lovelace-Byron Papers.)* Her correspondence with contemporary scientists, such as Michael Faraday, Mary Somerville, and Sir John Herschel, reveals her deep interest in varied scientific topics. She was also an accomplished musician, particularly on the harp.

Lady Lovelace, fascinated by Babbage's machines after first viewing his difference engine in 1833, translated L. F. Menabrea's paper on Babbage's analytical engine from French into English. Babbage suggested that she add some notes to the translation, which she did with such enthusiasm that they extended Menabrea's paper to about three times its original length. Of particular interest is her description in these notes of the repeated use of a set of cards with a purpose similar to that of subroutines in today's computer programs. With the help of Babbage, she worked out a nearly complete program to compute Bernoulli numbers, as complete as was consistent with the state of the design of the engine at that time. Because of this, she has been called the first computer programmer and, in 1979, a new language was named Ada (*q.v.*) in her honor.

Babbage's high regard for Lady Lovelace's notes is expressed in his autobiography: "Their author has entered fully into almost all the very difficult and abstract questions connected with the subject." Also, in a letter to her son, Viscount Ockham, in 1857, Babbage wrote, "In the memoir of Mr. Menabrea and still more in the excellent Notes appended by your mother you will find the only comprehensive view of the powers of the Anal. Eng. which the mathematicians of the world have yet expressed." *(Babbage Correspondence.)*

All of her life, Lady Lovelace was plagued by ill health. She died on 27 November 1852, less than a fortnight before her 37th birthday.

REFERENCES

Lovelace-Byron Papers. Bodleian Library, Oxford (Courtesy of Earl of Lytton and Viscount Knebworth).
Babbage Correspondence. Additional Ms., British Library, London.
1843. Lovelace, Ada Countess of. "Sketch of the Analytical Engine Invented by Charles Babbage, Esq. by L. F. Menabrea, of Turin, Officer of the Military Engineers: With Copious Notes by the Translator," *Scientific Memoirs* **III**:666–731. Taylor, R. (Ed.). London: R. & J. E. Taylor. (Reprinted in 1953. Bowden, B. V. *Faster Than Thought.* London: Sir Isaac Pitman & Sons.)
1864. Babbage, C. *Passages from the Life of a Philosopher.* London: Longmans, Green, & Co.
1977. Moore, Doris Langley. *Ada Countess of Lovelace.* London: Harper & Row.

V. R. HUSKEY

LSI. *See* INTEGRATED CIRCUITRY.

M

MACHINE. *See* SEQUENTIAL MACHINES; TURING MACHINE; and VON NEUMANN MACHINE.

MACHINE AND ASSEMBLY LANGUAGE PROGRAMMING

For articles on related subjects *see* ADDRESSING; ASSEMBLERS; BINDING; COMPUTERS, MULTIPLE ADDRESS; DEBUGGING; DUMP; INDEX REGISTER; INDIRECT ADDRESS; LINKAGE EDITOR; LOADER; MACHINE INSTRUCTION SET; MACROINSTRUCTION; NUMBERS AND NUMBER SYSTEMS; PROGRAMMING LANGUAGES; REGISTER; STORAGE ORGANIZATION; SUBPROGRAMS, CALLING; and SUBROUTINE.

Throughout this article, ML stands for machine language, and AL for "[symbolic] assembly [program] language." For the sake of clarity, the coding examples offered throughout are for a now obsolescent machine family (the IBM 704-709-7090-7094 series), which lends itself to piecemeal elementary presentation better than its successors. This can be done without loss of generality because newer machines—although faster, bigger and more complicated—embody no essentially new principles.

Definition of ML. Machine language has traditionally meant that particular representation of instructions and data immediately interpretable by the hardware of the machine concerned. But, as the variety of implemented machines grows, a simple and precise definition of ML becomes increasingly difficult to give. It no longer suffices to call it the language of the hardware now that microprogramming is coming into wider use, nor to call it machine-oriented rather than application oriented now that machines (Fairchild's SYMBOL, for example) are appearing with compilerlike languages wired in.

All that can or need be done here is to indicate, by listing essential characteristics, what is meant in this article by that term. ML, then, is that programming language that is immediately executable by the machine concerned, and whose typical statement consists of a single operator-operand pair. The operand part of the statement, or instruction, is typically an address; i.e., a binary integer designating one of the storage segments usually called either *words* or *bytes*. (*Byte* is the usual term where the machine's addressable storage segment is designed to hold one alphanumeric character, and is hence six, seven, or eight bits long; *word* is more often reserved for the addressable segments of machines whose special strength is in handling numbers rather than characters, and may be anything from 8 to 60 bits in length, with 32 or 36 being perhaps both mean and mode.)

The operator part of an ML statement will typically call for the performance of a dyadic arithmetic or logical operation upon the contents of (1) the addressed segment of storage and (2) any of several special registers where those operations can occur; or it will move contents between one of the special registers and a storage segment; or between either of these and one of the machine's input/output devices. The bit pattern in an addressed word will, if the operator is an arithmetic one, be treated as the representation of a scalar quantity in base 2 or an integral power of 2, such as hexadecimal.

(The foregoing describes a typical ML instruction

887

only; for an idea of the range of possible variants, note that some machines, chiefly older ones, offer multiple-address instructions; i.e., instructions that include the addresses of two or more operands, such as the augend and addend of an addition operation. Again, many machines offer some instructions whose operand parts are immediate, i.e., they are interpreted not as the addresses of data, but as being themselves the data. Finally, all machines include instructions, variously called *jumps, transfers,* or *branches,* whose function is to change the standard sequence in which instructions are executed.)

One further note on the usage of the term ML: Because genuine ML is rarely used, its name has come sometimes to be used loosely as a synonym for assembly language. This regrettable practice has sometimes forced those to whom the distinction is important to use "binary," "absolute ML," or just "absolute" to ensure being understood when they mean ML. In this article, the terms *machine language* and *assembly langauge* will be kept quite distinct, with ML standing solely for that langauge (characterized above) which requires no software to translate it, and makes no concession whatever to human readability or convenience.

Example. In the computer from which we will draw our illustrations, the register in which most arithmetic is done is called the *accumulator*; the instruction that causes the quantity in a word—word number 100, say—to be brought to the accumulator is, in its full binary glory,

$$000101000000000000000000001100100 \tag{1}$$

The leftmost 12 bits of this instruction constitute the operation code, which in this case specifies that a quantity in memory is to be brought to the accumulator; the rightmost 15 (the "address field") specify that the particular word to be fetched is number 100 (note that 1100100 in binary is 100 in decimal). The other available bits in this instruction type are not used in the present example.

The instruction that adds the quantity in word 101 to the quantity we have just put in the accumulator is

$$000100000000000000000000001100101 \tag{2}$$

and the instruction that stores the quantity in the accumulator into word 102 is

$$000110000001000000000000001100110 \tag{3}$$

These three instructions constitute a tiny program. If they were loaded into the computer in the order just given, at locations n, $n + 1$, and $n + 2$, and the computer were directed to execute instructions starting at location n, then the sum of the quantities that happened to be in locations 100 and 101 would be formed in the accumulator and stored in location 102.

Uses of ML. Many programmers have to be able to recognize and interpret ML when they see it in memory dumps and assembly listings, but very few have had occasion to use it as a programming tool since alternative langauges were first offered. The occasions that still arise for its use are virtually limited to the patching (we still call it patching even if it's done interactively) of a program already in ML, and to the implementation of the first assembler for a new machine (but see below).

Patching is an expedient that may be attractive to a programmer who has found a bug in a sizable program, or for whom turnaround time is a critical consideration. Wanting to avoid a complete reassembly, the programmer may decide to play the role of assembly program for the few instructions that need to be added to correct the object program. This involves keying in the ML instructions and data required in the format demanded by the loader, including computing whatever relocation information, loading addresses, and check sums may be called for. This exercise calls for a degree of patience and exactitude uncommon even among programmers, but when the alternative is the reassembly of a big program at a heavy cost in computer time, turnaround time, or both, it may be justified.

It must be borne in mind, too, that while ML patching demands the greatest accuracy of mind, hand, and eye, it yields no documentation, so that the continued usefulness of the assembly listing from which the programmer has been working depends upon its manual updating to correspond to the revised state of the object program. The programmer will also want to make the identical change in the assembly-language version of the program against the day of reassembly that will inevitably come if the program continues to be used.

ML is a necessary tool to programmers developing the first assembler for a computer. (An alternative, at least in principle, is the development of an assembler for machine A by means of a meta assembler running on machine B; this approach, for a variety of reasons both technical and psychological, has not yet established itself in practice.) The usual approach is to write the assembler in its own langauge, as if it already existed, and then assemble it by hand in the manner just described for ML patching. Hand translating from an assembly-language original carries the advantage of working from a complete specification rather than, for example, a comparatively abstract flowchart; in addition, it can serve as a check on the assembly algorithm.

If the programmer "plays computer," strictly following the logic of the assembler in the process of translating its assembly-langauge representation into ML, as a bonus many of the bugs in it will be disclosed. Often it will be sufficient to hand-assemble only a certain essential core of the new assembler, after which the rest of it can be written in a perhaps restricted assembly language and translated by the part already running. A curious result of this approach is that the first ML version of a new assembler, the hand-translated one, usually has its own assembly-language image for its first source program, and usually finds itself discarded after translating that one source program, since the version it has assembled on the computer is probably both richer in facilities and freer from bugs than the hand-assembled prototype.

A third and even more marginal application of ML may be found in the use of the unofficial instructions that enterprising programmers have sometimes discovered among a machine's capabilities, although not advertised by or perhaps even known to the authors of the machine's assembly language. While it has happened several times that bit configurations not recognized in an assembly-language manual have turned out to be interpretable by the hardware as instructions, the discovery is seldom more than a curiosity. Almost without exception, these windfall instructions cause effects for which it is difficult to think of practical uses; if programmers manage to use them at all, it is generally by twisting the design of programs so as to make a place for them. Whatever the wisdom of using such instructions, it is clear that, if used at all, they are used in ML form. (They will generally be represented in the assembly-language source proram as octal or hexadecimal constants, if that feature is available, but since they must first have been conceived as bit configurations, their appearance in any form may be regarded as ML usage.)

None of the ML applications just described, especially the last two, is part of the common experience of programmers today, and apart from these applications, ML may be said to be a dead language.

Features of AL. The earliest assemblers were little more than routines for translating some more convenient representation of ML instructions into ML, with none of the additional features now expected as a matter of course. The primitive assembler offered the programmer only a symbolic representation of operators—ADD instead of 000101000000 for example, with decimal or octal representation of operand addresses; or octal representation of the entire instruction, 050000003770—instead of 36 binary digits.

It is instructive to note how much extra programming capability is achieved with even so rudimentary an assembly language as this last mentioned octal represen-

tation, though it amounts to just the octal-constant feature that is today considered a very minor adjunct to assembly language (AL). The $3:1$ compression ratio, together with the use of eight of the familiar decimal digits, makes errors of transcription and keypunching both harder to commit and easier to spot. In addition, when represented by octal digits, at least the more common instructions become recognizable on sight.

What AL means today, though, is "symbolic" AL— a language in which all operators and virtually all operands are normally represented by names chosen for their explanatory and mnemonic power. Some of these names, those for the operators particularly, will have been chosen by the AL designers (although many modern assemblers allow users to rename operators); operands are left for the user to name within each source program.

Example. The three instructions given in ML form in (1), (2), and (3) would appear in AL as

$$
\begin{array}{ll}
\text{CLA 100} & \\
\text{ADD 101} & \qquad (4) \\
\text{STO 102} &
\end{array}
$$

or, if the programmer cared to assign names (defined by means explained later) to the locations involved, they could be

$$
\begin{array}{ll}
\text{CLA AUGEND} & \\
\text{ADD ADDEND} & \qquad (5) \\
\text{STO SUM} &
\end{array}
$$

This more convenient form for the writing of instructions is, however, only one part, and perhaps the least important part, of the advantage offered by AL. In introducing a software intermediary between programmer and computer, AL provided a framework within which all kinds of new conveniences and features could fit. The new notational features, which gave programmers more convenient access to powers already in ML, were valuable; the new substantive features—powers having no direct counterparts in ML, and made possible only by the existence of the assembler—made programming really practical. (It is essential in evaluating software to bear in mind that an accumulation of minor conveniences, none of them indispensable or even particularly impressive considered by itself, can in the aggregate amount to a breakthrough, an arrival at a new plateau of capability in programming.)

Among these substantive new features offered by the assembler are those allowing data to be defined in octal, decimal, character string, or other "natural" form; the reserving of execution-time storage space; the production of a printed, cross-indexed listing of the program, with programmer-written comments and assembler-generated warnings of known or suspected errors—all being features that let the programmer do explicitly and directly things otherwise so difficult to do that in effect they would be impossible.

Example. The way in which the operand names used in (5) would be defined for example, is through the use of one or another of these new, assembler-born features—the pseudo-operations, as they are frequently called, since they look like machine operation codes or instructions, but are not; they are addressed to the assembler for its use in assembling the real machine instructions that form the bulk of the program. (The distinction between operations and pseudo-operations is analogous to that between a manuscript to be typed and the author's marginal notes to the typist; the notes are not to be typed, but merely give the typist instructions about what *is* to be typed. The names AUGEND, ADDEND, and SUM, for example, would have been assigned through use of pseudo-ops such as these:

```
AUGEND PZE 0
ADDEND PZE 0                    (6)
SUM    PZE 0
```

or

```
AUGEND PZE 0
ADDEND DEC 1                    (7)
SUM    PZE 0
```

where PZE stands for "Plus ZEro," meaning that the word in question is to contain the internal representation of + 0, which is all zeros; DEC is for "DECimal," meaning that the number so introduced is to be interpreted as decimal rather than octal or binary. The example in (6) simply reserves the next three available words of storage (the next available word being that whose address is one greater than the last used, unless the programmer specifies otherwise) and assigns them the names given in the left-hand column, setting their contents to zero; nonzero values would presumably be stored in locations AUGEND and ADDEND before the first execution of the program given in (5), or the result would be simply to add zero to zero, and store the resulting zero in a word whose contents were already zero. The variant form (7) does what (6) does, but adds one more feature: It gives ADDEND the initial value of 1. The pseudo-op DEC instructs the assembler to interpret the number that follows as a decimal number, and to put its binary representation in the word reserved.

Each of the names so assigned to storage locations is entered into a *symbol table* or dictionary maintained by the assembler as it does its job, along with the actual address of the location to which it has been assigned. In this way the programmer is free to use the name alone to refer to the quantity stored in the word, leaving it to the assembler to replace this mnemonic symbol (which is meaningful only to the programmer) with the binary address that is meaningful to the machine. It must be emphasized that a programmer-chosen mnemonic symbol is simply an arbitrary string of characters to the assembler and the computer, and it is up to the programmer to see to it that the value of a location actually mirrors its name. There is nothing to prevent, for example, calling a location ONE, but storing a value of two or two thousand in it.

Probably the most important of the unexpected advantages of programming in symbols rather than bit patterns is the control it gives the programmer over what has come to be called *binding*, the assignment of directly machine-computable values to the symbolic expressions of which a source program is generally composed. Since the computer cannot execute a program until it is in ML form, a narrow concept of efficiency would seem to dictate that it be reduced to that form as quickly as possible. The forced deferral of final translation that is entailed by the use of AL turns out, though, to carry advantages more important even than those originally aimed at in AL.

Programming in a symbolic language both enables the programmer to see the potential generality of a program being currently worked on, and encourages the realization of this generality. In doing so, a little more time may be spent writing (and documenting) today's program; the reward will be not having to rewrite that program tomorrow to deal with slightly changed circumstances. If the program computes a payroll, for example, the fact that AL will encourage the programmer to represent a tax rate throughout the program as TAXRATE rather than as 17.25%, and allow it to be defined numerically just once, will not only make the program easier to write, but will also allow it to survive a change in the tax rate with unimpaired usefulness at no greater cost than reassembly with a newly defined TAXRATE. Not only that, but by forcing the programmer's mind to the slightly elevated abstraction of the symbolic level, AL tends to suggest treating as variables other quantities that would almost certainly have been treated as constants if the programming were in ML: the total number of paycheck deductions to be provided for, the number of governmental levels for which tax is to be withheld, and so on. If the possibility of changes in these quantities has occurred to the programmer before the program is finished, it is easy to provide for it in any of several ways:

1. As already suggested by providing a new value for a variable by substituting a new definition of it in the source program, and reassembling.

2. By designing the program to accept a possible new value from the data given it at run time.
3. Even by, under some operating systems, having the computer operator set one or more program-testable switches, thereby selecting one from among several alternate values built into the program.

But the possibility of achieving this flexibility at acceptable cost hinges on the programmer's seeing the need for it while the program is being written, at the latest. What is still very easy to do at that stage is often so hard to do after the program is written as to be practically impossible. And this is where a symbolic assembly language is rewarding, by putting a certain distance between the user and the immediate problem, forcing consideration of it somewhat more generally and detachedly, and thus investing it with a degree of adaptability that may save the programmer or a colleague from having to write essentially the same thing over again.

Because the final assignment of a computable value to a program variable (e.g., 17.25% to TAXRATE) is called *binding,* and its moment of occurrence *binding time,* the AL property just discussed may be called *binding-time control.* The degree of such control offered by a modern, multipass assembler working in conjunction with a sophisticated linking loader and an indulgent operating system is very great. Symbols can be defined in terms of other symbols to form an indefinitely deep regression, with the definition of those at the most primitive layer of the hierarchy deferred until the end of the source program or even—to push matters to the limit—until program load time.

The loaders that are prepared to handle so-called object programs in which so much binding remains to be done are misnamed, in fact, since their loading function is by this point incidental. They are actually the last (and sometimes the longest) pass of the assemblers they work with, and their use amounts to a return to the old "load-and-go" concept in which final assembly is followed immediately by loading and execution, rather than simply the production of an object program that is to be executed only when the programmer so orders. The object program (whether in the form of a card deck, tape file, or disk file) produced by the assembler part of such an assembler-loader partnership is not in ML, but in some nameless intermediate language dictated by the needs of the loader. (Here, as in the attempt to define ML, the proliferation of variants and extreme cases makes it possible to maintain a stable terminology only at the cost of a measure of arbitrariness: despite the observations just made, we will continue to refer to these translators that fail to produce ML as assemblers, and to the processors that carry these incomplete assemblies all the way to completion as loaders.)

Perhaps most important of all the possibilities opened up by binding-time flexibility is that of having variables in one program defined by values assigned to them in another. This makes it possible for a number of independently written programs—provided they observe the conventions governing the use of such *external* symbols—to join forces and become in effect one large program, and in so doing greatly extend the usefulness of the constituent programs.

Important as it is, though, binding-time control is only one aspect of a broader and more fundamental principle that was introduced into programming along with AL: *decoupling.* This is the technological version of the military principle, "divide and conquer"; as applied to programming; one of the things it means is the separation of potential problems and their isolation from one another so that they can be separately dealt with, and so that errors cannot propagate from one to another. Binding-time control permits decoupling the writing of an expression that relates many variables in elaborate ways from the task of giving those variables specific numeric or other computable values.

But AL programming promotes other exploitations of decoupling. The symbols used in such a program, for example, will probably be defined by the programmer in a group at the end of the source program; if there are a substantial number of them, they will probably be divided further into subgroups of constants, storage reservations, and so on, creating something very like Cobol's Data Division. In doing so, the AL programmer is led naturally to apply the decoupling principle, not merely on the level of the individual expression and its component variables, but also on that of the entire program algorithm and the data it operates on. The strikingly superior managability of programs so organized—their greater intelligibility to those who have to study and maintain them, their amenability to revision, and their resistance to obsolescence as circumstances change—collectively amount to an enormous advantage over ML programming, one probably far more important than the convenience an assembly language offers in simply getting a program running.

Subroutines and Macroinstructions. Decoupling can be seen again in the practice of subroutinizing, in which routines that have been written once are preserved so that they need not be written again—the decoupling is between work done and work yet to do. The occasion for creating a subroutine arises when a programmer notices that essentially the same routine (e.g., one that converts external-representation numerals to internal, computable form) has been written over and over, possibly with minor variations. Creating a subroutine for the function in question will obviate the need for ever having to do it again, and this promise gives the incentive to invest great care in generalizing it, debugging it, making it as compact or as fast as possible, documenting it, and otherwise perfecting it.

Subroutinizing, it should be noted, is not the same thing as modularizing, with which it is often confused. Both subroutines and modules are chunks of code that have been deliberately isolated, but for quite different, even opposed, reasons. The ignorance of context that is a corollary of their isolation is, for the subroutine, a fault— probably its major fault; in the module, this trait is the very reason for its existence. The success of a subroutine is often dependent on the degree to which it can be made sensitive to its environment at each call; it will be expected to approximate the efficiency of the tailor-made code it has replaced.

A module, on the other hand, like a member of a cloistered religious order, is supposed to remain ignorant of the world it lives in for the sake of higher things. The module is intended to limit the area of concern of any one programming-team member, and to minimize the impact of later changes. It does this by isolating and formalizing the channels of communication, or *interfaces,* between itself and other program components. A common application is the funneling of all a program's input/output requests through one module, which alone makes I/O requests on the operating system or the hardware. If the I/O facilities of the system later change in ways that affect a program that has been so modularized, only its I/O module need be revised. The module, then, can accomplish its objective only if its relations with the rest of the system are sharply restricted. A subroutine, on the other hand, will often succeed to the extent that it can adapt to the state of the calling program at each call; it should be as worldly as the module should be sequestered.

Once created, a subroutine need only be assembled along with an assembly-language program (or loaded with its ML representation) to be available as often as needed throughout that program. At whatever points in the program the function performed by the subroutine is required, a *calling sequence* (explained below) to the subroutine can be written by the programmer, and a transfer to it will be made. After the subroutine has been executed, a return transfer from it to a point some fixed number of locations from the call just honored is automatically made, and the program continues. The subroutine need never be written again, nor need it ever appear more than once in a program, however often its services may be required. (What is being discussed here is, strictly speaking, the *closed* subroutine; there is also an *open* variety that is physically copied as a whole into the calling program at each point of call. This type is of little interest; it was never widely used, and has been replaced for all practical purposes by the macroinstruction, discussed below.)

Subroutinizing is useful even when practiced by a solitary programmer within one large program, but its advantages grow enormously if subroutines can be freely traded back and forth within the entire community of programmers working with one kind of computer. The possibility of doing this depends on the observance by all concerned of a number of conventions for creating and using subroutines, and these are usually set forth in the AL manual of a computer as if they were built into the hardware or the assembler. These conventions, while absolutely necessary to the exchangeability of subroutines, are responsible also for many of the unsatisfactory features of subroutine usage (discussed below), and account at least in part for the rise of an alternative form of subroutinization, the macroinstruction.

Like the subroutine, the *macro* (as it is usually called) is a way of packaging routines for future use, but the conventions governing both its creation and its use differ greatly from those of the subroutine. The root of the difference is that the macro facility is made possible by a special processor that can be embedded within an assembler or exist as a separate piece of software; if separate, it will be given as input a source program consisting of a mixture of macros and AL statements, transform the macros into AL, and pass the resulting program to a simple assembler. The consequent differences between programming with macros and with subroutines may be summarized in four categories—locus of creation, format of call, trapping ability, and code-generating economy.

Locus of Creation. The new macro can be created, or defined, at any point in a program. Since the macro processor, whether embedded in an assembler or not, is put in a special macro-defining mode when it encounters a macro definition, the creation of a macro does not generate any instructions in the program; only an explicit call does that.

Until called, the instructions constituting a macro definition are stored in an area under the control of the macro processor, and do not appear in the object program being assembled. By contrast, the defining of a subroutine, since it is indistinguishable from ordinary programming as far as the assembler is concerned, causes the insertion of its constituent instructions into the host program at the point of definition. If the programmer wants the subroutine to be stored at the end of the object program when it is loaded, as is usually the case, the definition must appear at the end of the source program.

Example. A subroutinized version of the miniature program created in (5) would take a form like this:

```
TRISUM CLA* 1,4
       ADD* 2,4                              (8)
       STO* 3,4
       TRA  4,4
```

In this little routine, which we have given the name TRISUM, some new programming features are used. The addresses of the four instructions refer, respectively, to the first, second, third, and fourth locations following the instruction that has just called TRISUM (the 4 following the comma is the designation of a special register, an index register, one of whose uses is to record the location of the instruction in the main program from which a subroutine—in this case, TRISUM—has been called. Its action is such that an address in the subroutine of the form "n, 4" will refer to the nth location following that call). Another notation new to this example is the "*" following three of the instructions, denoting *indirect* use of the address that follows. Indirect addressing means that the address, modified as necessary by any index register used, is to be taken not as the location of the data, but as the location of the *address* of the data. Accordingly, the interpretation of "CLA* 1, 4" is: "Bring to the accumulator the quantity whose address is one word below that in which the call to this subroutine is located." Using the calling sequence in (10) below as an example, the quantity specified would be that in LOCA.

An equivalent macro would take this form:

```
TRISUM MACRO A, B, C
       CLA     A
       ADD     B                    (9)
       STO     C
       END     TRISUM
```

The first line of this macro definition declares that TRISUM is its name, and that this name, when used to call upon the macro, will normally be accompanied by three values (parameters) that are to replace A, B, and C, respectively, wherever these symbols occur in the definition. The ways in which the TRISUM subroutine and the TRISUM macro are called upon are explained in the next section.

Format of Call. The macro is called by what is in appearance and placement just another AL operator (but one invented by the macro definer or user). The values that are to be passed down into the defining instructions when they are inserted into the program text in answer to this particular call—the *parameters,* as they are frequently called—will usually follow the macro name on the same line in a format that closely parallels that of the operands supplied with a standard AL operator.

The subroutine is traditionally called by a stereotyped series of AL instruction [see (10) below] known as a calling sequence. This consists of (1) an instruction that transfers control to the subroutine while recording its own location (in index register 4 by convention in our example machine); (2) a number of locations reserved for the parameters that are to be passed to the subroutine with each call; and (3) one or more locations for the subroutine to transfer back to when its execution is done, depending on the number of exit conditions for which it is wished to provide separate paths. In the more advanced macro processors the difference in appearance may be greater yet; they may permit the programmer to give the parameters accompanying each call on a macro in an order convenient on that particular occasion. The more "natural" appearance of macro calls, besides making for a more readable source program, offers a most important advantage in the trapping capability described in the next section.

Example. To call upon the subroutine TRISUM defined in (8) above, we would insert into the main program at the point where it was wanted the following calling sequence:

```
TSX    TRISUM, 4
PZE    LOCA
PZE    LOCB                         (10)
PZE    LOCC
```

The first of these instructions, TSX, is the special transfer instruction, referred to earlier, that transfers to TRISUM while marking its own location in an index register (4 in this case). This location-marking is needed so that instructions in the subroutine can reach back for the parameters being held (or, as in this example, whose addresses are being held) in the calling sequence, and so that a return transfer can be made to the proper location when the subroutine has been executed.

The three PZE pseudo-ops that follow are simply dummies whose function is to hold, in their address parts, the addresses at which parameters A, B, and C can be found by the subroutine. Each call upon the subroutine, then, would cost the execution time of the TSX and the return transfer at the end of the subroutine, plus the storage space for these two instructions and the three PZEs.

To call upon the macro TRISUM defined in (9), we would write, at the point where it was wanted:

```
TRISUM ALPHA, BETA, GAMMA           (11)
```

where ALPHA, BETA, and GAMMA are the values we want to be substituted for A, B, and C on this occasion. The macro would generate into the program, at the point of call, the wanted instructions, and only them:

```
CLA ALPHA
ADD BETA                            (12)
STO GAMMA
```

The overwhelming economic superiority of the macro form over the subroutine in this example is due to our employment of an unrealistically brief piece of code as the core of each. In particular, the illustration is unfair to the subroutine in making it so trivial that it is actually shorter than the calling sequence that connects it to the main program; a more realistic impression is gotten by postulating that TRISUM is a routine of 50 or more instructions. On the other hand, the macro, too, can do better than this example would suggest; see the section, "Code-Generating Economy," and the example in the next section.

Trapping Ability. A unique property of the macroinstruction, and one having no subroutine counterpart, is its trapping ability. This enables the macro user to define any standard AL operator as a macro, and thereby trap it for special treatment. This valuable capability rests on two seemingly trivial points: first, the fact that macro calls are (or can be) identical in format to ordinary AL operators; second, the fact that macro processing precedes (or can be made to precede) ordinary assembly. By virtue of these two facts, any symbol defined both as an ordinary operator and macro name is effectively a macro name only, and will cause the generation into the object program of whatever instructions the macro author has specified. This feature would, for example, allow the programmer (1) to trap every transfer instruction in a program (or a selected portion of it) and generate instead, or in addition, instructions that would compute at execution time the actual addresses to which control is being ordered transferred; (2) compare those with limits set by the programmer; and (3) allow the transfer to be executed only if within those limits.

Preventing the execution of wild transfers would, in turn, much facilitate debugging, whose difficulty is greatly aggravated when a program is allowed to run on after a bug shows up, and particularly so when control is thereby transferred into unknown territory. When this occurs, the program is very likely to wipe out the evidence a bug hunter will need to correct it, or at least so confuse matters as to make the run useless for debugging. A similar redefinition of operations that write information into storage will accomplish, to give another example, equally useful feats in the precise protection of storage.

Example. A macro that would trap and test an ordinary transfer instruction (mnemonic op-code TRA) is shown in Fig. 1. (The new instructions introduced in this example are not explained in the same way as those introduced in earlier ones, but in schematic depictions of the effect they have on the accumulator or the storage location addressed.) The followng shorthand notation is employed.

- AC means accumulator.
- IR means index register.
- C(n) means contents of n [e.g., C(AC) means contents of the accumulator].
- Y stands for the apparent address of the TRA (i.e., the value of the address-field expression itself, without consideration of any indirect-addressing or index-register modifications called for elsewhere in the instruction).
- X stands for the index-register designation (0, 1, 2, or 4) in the TRA.

First, this macro defines the mnemonic op-code TRA to be a macro instruction instead, so that it will be caught at the macro processing stage and expanded into the instructions shown, rather than simply be passed unchanged to the assembler and there translated into its ML equivalent. The body of the macro computes the effective address of the TRA instruction evoking it (i.e., the value of the address-field expression, modified by any index register specified—we ignore here, for simplicity, the further complication of possible indirect addressing), and compares that effective address to a permissible

```
TRA      MACRO  ZERO                (Define TRA to be a macro)
         CLA    LOCMAC              Fetch to AC the TRA to test
         TIX    NOTAG, ZERO, 0      Skip computation of
                                    effective address if X = 0 or C(X) = 0
         SXA    SAV, ZERO           Store C(X) into SAV
         SUB    SAV                 Form Y-C(X); i.e., effective address
NOTAG    PAX    0, 1                Put effective address into IR 1
         TXL    TOOLOW, 1, LOWLIM   Address too low—trap to TOOLOW
         TXH    TOOHI, 1, HILIM     Address too high—trap to TOOHI
         XEC    LOCMAC              Address legal—execute original TRA
         END                       (End of definition of TRA macro)
```

	AC			SAV	
TRA	X	Y	TRA	0	0
			TRA	0	C(X)
0	?	Y − C(X)			

Fig. 1

range defined by the programmer-supplied bounds LOW-LIM and HILIM.

If the address lies outside that range, the TRA instruction is not executed and control is transferred instead to one of the two error routines, TOOLOW and TOOHI. If its address falls within the permissible range, the TRA instruction is executed and the program being debugged proceeds. (The macro as given contains some simplifying assumptions, among them that the symbol ZERO has elsewhere been given the value zero; that SAV is a location having a TRA in its instruction part and zeros elsewhere; that LOCMAC is where the TRA instruction currently under test is stored, and so on.)

Code-Generating Economy. The macroinstruction and the subroutine differ most obviously in that each call of a macro causes a fresh copy of its defining instructions to be inserted into the text of the program being translated, while a subroutine appears in the program using it just once, no matter how often called. This distinction should not, however, be taken to mean, as it frequently is, that macro usage entails a wasteful repetitive generation of coding that could be avoided by the use of subroutines instead.

The economics of programming is such that the advantage sometimes lies with generating the substantive code as many times as it is to be executed, sometimes with generating only multiple calling sequences to a single copy of that code. The decision will hinge on such considerations as the length of the calling sequence versus that of the routine to be executed, and the relative importance of storage space and time during execution. While a decision to save time clearly points to the macro as the instrument of choice, a space-saving strategy does not point to the subroutine; it merely suggests that the macros to be employed should generate not the entire routine, but only a calling sequence to a subroutinized version of it.

In short, there is no hard choice to be made. A macro facility incorporates the ability to use subroutines as well, and to call them by means of macros, with the superior writability and readability of that form. In at least one macroinstruction processor based on assembly language, the programmer is allowed to include within a macro definition both a subroutine and its calling sequence; at the first use of the macro, the processor copies both the calling sequence and the subroutine into the object program, the former at the point where the macro was used and the latter back with the data. Subsequent uses of the macro cause only the calling sequence to be copied, the processor recalling that it has already incorporated the subroutine into the program.

Example. Schematically, the kind of macro subroutine combination referred to would look like this:

Macro definition:

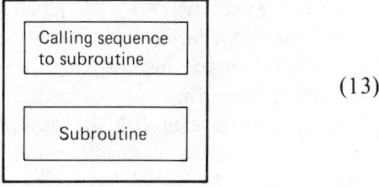

(13)

Calls upon such a macro would generate code as follows: First call in a program:

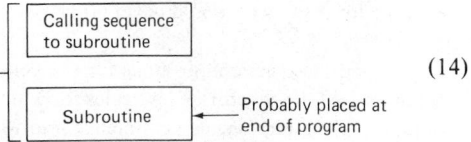

(14)

Second and all subsequent calls:

| Calling sequence to subroutine | (15) |

Roles and Applications of AL. It has long been expected, and from time to time announced, that compiler langauges would supplant AL as thoroughly as it in turn had supplanted ML. This replacement has not occurred; AL survives and even flourishes. The fundamental reason is clear: AL is a general language, standing to the compiler languages as English stands to the jargons of various trades and professions. AL allows the programmer to do with the computer anything it can do at all, while compiler languages trade this versatility for superior applicability to a limited range of problems. If compiler languages existed for every conceivable application, no role might be left to AL, but such complete coverage is unlikely in the foreseeable future. For one thing, new applications continue to arise with no end in sight. For another, the cost of developing and maintaining a compiler language and all its supporting sub- and superstructure is such that a very large community of users is needed to justify it economically, and it may well be that the science-engineering and business markets served chiefly by Fortran and Cobol, respectively, are the only ones large enough to support such efforts.

During the years between the first (1976) and the present edition of this encyclopedia, the microprocessor burst from the laboratory into our kitchen appliances and toys, and in doing so at least temporarily rejuvenated AL. The explosive progress in ability to fabricate small (in all senses) processes brought back the circumstances that had, years before, made every programmer an AL programmer: Small memories and small addressing capabilities. The result has almost been to recapitulate on the microprocessor the history of software development on the mainframes, but it has not been necessary, this second time around, to establish the desirability of high-level languages in the face of such entrenched skepticism. By now, the major high-level languages, including Cobol and PL/I, are available on processors that can be carried in a coat pocket. Nevertheless, the microprocessor has caused an outburst of AL activity, and will probably continue to provide an opportunity for programming in that langauge for many who would never otherwise experience it.

Beyond these general grounds for the continued importance of AL lie several specific roles for which it seems uniquely well suited—ecological niches into which it fits so well as to insure its survival against any competitor now visible. Among these at least five are worthy of being named and examined: fine tuning, early responsiveness, machine accessibility, pioneering, and craftsmanship.

Fine Tuning. Because only the AL programmer directly and consciously determines the machine-language instructions that are to be executed, and the detailed internal representation of the data upon which they are to operate, the AL programmer alone can guarantee that a program will fit within a given area of storage or exeucte within a given period of time. Also it is the AL programmer who can most plausibly claim (no guarantee is possible here) that a program has been so written as to take either the least possible space or the least possible time to execute.

Programs, or program segments, may be arbitrarily restricted in execution time because they are real-time applications, i.e., directly linked to other equipment or processes operating fast enough so that even a computer is pressed to keep up with their demands. Examples of such equipment and processes include the evaluation of radar signals to produce target-tracking displays and antenna-steering commands, and typically involve computer linkage to equipment that, based on the same technology that supports the computer itself, demands input and generates output at rates comparable to the computer's. With a permissible slight stretching of terminology, it may be said that in such applications the computer is rushed because it is trying to satisfy another computer.

Programs may be arbitrarily restricted in the storage space (particularly in highest-speed, or CPU, storage)

available to them because they are to be executed by a multiprogramming system in which each task is allotted a partition of predetermined size within which it must reside. This is becoming an increasingly common strategy of computer resource allocation as attempts are made to keep all components of a computing system productively busy by having them deal concurrently with several distinct programs. Such space constraints may be due, however, to nothing more than the absolute size of the machine involved. Where the computer has to operate within a missile, aircraft, or other highly weight- and space-limited environment, its storage size may be such as to make the program hard to fit in, even though the machines may be dedicated to one task alone.

Whatever the circumstances, a requirement that a program be executable within critical time or space constraints generally implies that it should be written in AL. (It is possible to write such a program in a compiler language, if one is available, and then, if the program so compiled should exceed the given limits, to rewrite parts of it in AL so as to make it fit. This approach requires a very detailed knowledge of the way in which the compiler generates its object code if the hand-written code being introduced is to work smoothly with its host. The difficulty of deciding what part to rewrite, and the uncongeniality to programmers of having to revise others' coding rather than write their own, make this a seldom-chosen alternative.)

Example. A problem that occurred in the development of the original Fortran compiler for the IBM 704 offers a vivid example of a situation in which AL alone will do. It was found at a late stage in the development of that compiler that a quantity had been put into the wrong index register, and that if the omission were to be rectified without extensive modification to the compiler, it would have to be done under drastic constraints. These constraints dictated that space for only two instructions was available to load the index register with the requisite value, and that this two-instruction sequence had to be absolutely autonomous. It could not affect storage or arithmetic registers, nor could it assume the existence of any particular value in any location other than that of the desired value in another index register. The following two instructions did accomplish this seemingly impossible task (the source and target index registers are here arbitrarily taken to be 1 and 2, respectively):

```
LXD  *+1,2
TXI  *+1,3,0                                      (16)
```

The first of these instructions loads the target index register (number 2) with the quantity (0) in the so-called decrement portion of the next instruction ("next" symbolized by *+1). The second location contains an instruction whose exact identity was unimportant (any of several would have done). Its only functions were (1) to contain a value of zero in its decrement part so that the LXD would know where to find one (recall that this patch could not take for granted the contents of any location outside itself), and (2) to address the nonexistent index register 3.

The 704 had but three index registers (1, 2, and 4); if the numbers 3, 5, 6, or 7 were used where an index-register designation was expected, the index registers affected would be those whose numerical designations summed to form the number given. The effect on the actual index registers so designated was to form the logical OR of their contents and store the value so formed into each of them. It should be apparent how the storing of a zero in the target index register (number 2), followed by the execution of an instruction that involved a reference to the mythical index register 3, could achieve the desired movement of the value in index register 1 to index register 2. A compiler language (such as Fortran itself) would not have permitted the programmer to specify the index register into which a quantity was to be loaded, let alone a nonexistent index register. Solving this problem was possible only through a combination of intimate knowledge of the machine and the availability of AL to exploit that knowledge.

Another common fine-tuning application of AL is the writing of segments of code that are to be executed so often as to make their time or space optimization economically worthwhile, if not strictly necessary. These include practically anything that has been found worth turning into a subroutine, practically all general-purpose software (to be discussed separately), and the critical parts of big, long-lived, compiler-language application programs. This last category is worth emphasizing because its hazards are seldom appreciated until they present a serious problem.

The compiler-language application programs that are candidates for this treatment are those whose execution consumes a substantial part of the total machine time available at their installation, and hence offer real savings if they can be speeded up. If such a program has been written in a compiler language, a clever programmer, familiar with the code the compiler has generated and also with the characteristics of the program at hand, is very likely to be able to improve it significantly by rewriting in AL some small but critical section. It would not be very remarkable for such a programmer to be able to speed up such a program tenfold by rewriting a few hundred lines of code. This can often be accomplished, in fact, by essentially negative actions involving no substantive new coding at all. Just the deletion of stretches of code that (representing the compiler writer's desire to serve a wide range of needs) offer options or safeguards not relevant to the program at hand, or the removal of a few instructions from the innermost loop of a deep nest, or the mere reordering of a number of file searches to reflect the programmer's knowledge of the probable contents of those files may be sufficient to show dramatic improvements in execution time.

With such rewards waiting, an installation manager is strongly tempted to relax the edict that only Fortran (or Cobol, or whatever) is to be used, but succumbing to this enticement means that all big compiler-language programs will tend inexorably to become hand written AL programs that use a thin shell of compiler-generated code just to interface with the operating system they must run under. The danger of this practice is sometimes unrecognized until the installation that has permitted it decides to replace its computers. Thinking that all his principal programs are, for example, Fortran-language programs, the installation manager supposes that only their recompilation through the new machine's Fortran compiler will be needed to get them running on it. The discovery that many of these programs are substantially handwritten in the old machine's AL, usually by programmers who are no longer available and who did not much care for documenting their work, can be a painful one.

If an installation adopts the policy of allowing compiler-generated programs to be improved by the implanting of handwritten AL—and there may be excellent reasons for doing so—it should adopt it formally, with explicit recognition of the attendant dangers and careful provision against them. Essential among the safeguards will be putting all such optimization work under the direction of someone who believes wholeheartedly in the importance of full and lucid documentation.

Early Responsiveness. To ensure that their development will be carried on in an orderly and thoughtful way, and above all in a way that will not jeopardize their machine independence, the standard compiler languages have been entrusted to various national and international standards organizations (in the United States chiefly to the American National Standards Institute, known as ANSI). These organizations, which attempt to include or at least consult representatives of all concerned parties, issue formal definitions of the languages entrusted to their care, and entertain proposals for their enrichment and revision. Part of the price that must be paid for this elaborate and necessarily slow-moving apparatus of consultation and deliberation is that additions to the compiler languages, even if approved at every stage of review, are a very long time in coming. Usually, years pass between the first proposal that a new feature be incorporated and the actual appearance of that feature in manufacturer-supplied software. This gap between programmer requirement and compiler response leaves another opening for AL, which, under the sole control of the manufacturer concerned, can be used at the one-for-one level to get the job done immediately or, if time permits, to enrich the system with subroutines or macros, either by the manufacturer or by users.

Machine Accessibility. As "early responsiveness" reflects the immediate answer of AL to the requirements generated by application programmers, so "machine accessiblity," refers to its unique responsiveness in making available all the capabilities built into the machine by its manufacturer. Providing such access is generally impossible for the compiler languages, which—again because of their need to remain machine independent—cannot refer to any machine facility not common to all on which those languages are to be offered. If some, but not all, of the machines on which a compiler is to run include, say, a program-testable real-time clock, then the compiler language cannot be augmented with statements that let users refer to that clock without either restricting the transferability of source programs that do so, or forcing the compiler to generate coding that simulates such a clock on those machines not having it in the hardware.

Since neither of these penalties is acceptable (the second is not always even physically possible), the outcome is that such nonuniversal features are simply ignored in the standard compiler languages. For most purposes, this partial disabling of the machine is tolerable; for a few, and most particularly for systems programming (*q.v.*), it is not. Whatever distinctive features a machine offers must be usable by its software, or they may as well not exist. System software itself is a major consumer of machine time, time spent on its execution is felt to be nonproductive overhead by application-minded programmers and budget-minded installation managers, so it is doubly important that a system be as fast as possible. This requirement means that software has to be written in a language that allows access to all machine features, and thus normally rules out the standard compiler languages.

Computer manufacturers and other regular software producers have long sought to develop for their own in-house use a special language that would combine most of the advantages of compiler languages with the fine machine control offered by AL. They would thus acquire for their internal task a tool as good as those they provide for their customers. Many such projects have been mounted, and many interesting languages have come out of them, but none has yet proved completely satisfactory. There-

fore AL remains, so far, the standard language for the writing of software.

Pioneering. Because of those attributes listed above, particularly under "Machine Accessibility," AL is almost the invariable choice when a wholly new computer application is being pioneered, even though the necessity for its use may not be clear at the outset. When it is uncertain what the demands of the new species of program are going to be, the safest course is to use the language that imposes no constraints. After a number of AL programs have been written in the new application area, it may turn out that one of the existing compiler languages (almost always with some modifications) is adequate, or it may be found that the new application is sufficiently different (and economically important) to warrant the development of a language tailored to its needs. AL programming experience forms, among many other things, the breeding ground for specialized language development.

Craftsmanship. Another reason for the continued use of AL—one that has caused some clashes between programmers and their managers—is that programming in that language is widely felt to be the most professional and demanding kind, and many career programmers will seek to use it even when none of the reasons discussed above applies. To a considerable extent, the programmer's private wish to use AL can coincide with the best interests of the installation. No matter how adamant management may be about running a pure Fortran or Cobol shop, there must always be a few programmers behind the scenes who can read dumps, help the application programmers with special debugging problems, understand the operating system, and deal as equals with the computer manufacturer's systems engineers.

Furthermore, a knowledge of AL often helps the programmer to use compiler languages more efficiently, clarifying the relation between what is written and what the compiler produces, and warning about the hidden points in compiler-language usage where the price of execution may suddenly rise tenfold because the code compiled has exceeded some buffer size or other critical system constraint. And if AL specialists in what is nominally a pure compiler-language shop are to keep their skills sharp, they must be allowed to practice them. Even in such a shop, then, some AL programming will take place, with the connivance if not the wholehearted approval of installation management.

Beyond these reasons for tolerating AL usage in a compiler-language shop—reasons that make sense from management's viewpoint—there is the good programmer's personal desire to learn more about the machines and systems the programs depend upon, to be able to understand dumps and other operating system messages, and in general to upgrade skills and deepen understanding, even when there is little or no foreseeable benefit to a present employer in doing so. This instinct to practice one's craft at the highest possible level of capability is a perennial one that will, independent of economic considerations, continue to turn many programmers toward AL.

Neither the roles discussed above nor the qualifications of AL to fill them would seem to be in any immediate danger of vanishing. By means of such devices as the macroinstruction, the subroutine, and the externally defined symbol, this language potentially affords its user the chief powers of the high-level languages, embedded in a general programming language that is oriented to no one application, but which gives access to all the powers of the computer to a programmer who knows how to use them. This combination of power and generality suggests that, contrary to innumerable predictions of its imminent extinction, AL has a long and vigorous future before it.

Source Literature. ML programming seems to have generated no literature, and AL has had little of any consequence written about it. On most topics that the reader may want to pursue further, relevant articles in this Encyclopedia will probably be the best resource. On the loading of programs that have been translated into ML, and the linking together of such separately translated programs when they refer to each other symbolically, see Presser and White (1972). For the internal workings of assemblers, see Barron's (1972) lucid explanation.

REFERENCES

1972. Barron, D. W. *Assemblers and Loaders,* 2nd Ed. New York: American Elsevier.
1972. Presser, L. and White, J. "Linkers and Loaders," *Computing Surveys* **4**, *No. 3*: 149–167 (September).

M. HALPERN

MACHINE INSTRUCTION SET

For articles on related subjects *see* ADDRESSING; BOOLEAN ALGEBRA; COMPUTERS, MULTIPLE ADDRESS, GENERAL REGISTER; INPUT-OUTPUT INSTRUCTIONS; INTERRUPT; MACHINE AND ASSEMBLY LANGUAGE PROGRAMMING; MICPROGRAMMING; OPERAND; OPERATION CODE; PRIVILEGED INSTRUCTION; and SHIFTING.

A machine instruction is a string of digits in the base in which the machine operates, which, when interpreted by the hardware, causes a unique and well-defined change in the state of the computer.

This rather terse definition calls for a more loosely-worded explanation. Most computers today are based on the binary system. Therefore, for most cases, the "string of digits" will be a string of bits, each having the value 0 or 1. In what follows, we will refer to instructions with bits only, although for convenience we will express those bits using hexadecimal notation.

In the definition given above, the words "interpreted by the hardware" really mean "used by the hardware." The change in state of the machine is, in fact, a change in the contents of various registers or memory locations. The changed registers may be those explicitly, or implicitly, referred to by the instruction, or they may be some internal registers not directly known to the user. For example: The 16-bit string 1010000100100001 (hexadecimal A121), when interpreted by the hardware of one of the IBM System 370 computers, causes the contents of general register 1 to be added to general register 2, the result replacing the previous contents of register 1. In this case, the change of state is apparent to the user of the machine. On the other hand, on the same machine, the bit string 0000011111110001 (hexadecimal 07F1) causes an inaccessible internal register, the program counter, to set its value to that of general register 1, thus causing the next instruction that has to be interpreted by the hardware to be taken from the location whose address is the contents of register 1.

It is important to realize that each computer model possesses its own unique instruction set. The same bit string may mean completely different things on two different computers, even if the number of bits needed for expressing an instruction is the same on the two machines. Thus, the bit string A121 (hexadecimal), which we used as an example on the IBM/370 and which caused addition of the contents of two registers, when interpreted by a Data General Corporation NOVA computer, will decrement by one the contents of the memory location whose address is in location 18 and skip the next instruction if the result is zero. This different interpretation for the same bit string makes it clear that bit strings are not a good basis for classification of machine instructions. We will therefore introduce categories based on other criteria in order to be able to find some patterns in the multitude of instructions available on various computers.

Classification of Machine Instructions. We have already hinted that machine instructions differ in length, i.e., in the number of bits needed to express an instruction. There is usually a simple relation between the length of the computer word or addressable unit and the instruction length. Thus, we find up to four instructions per word in the B5500 and CDC Cyber series, but one instruction per word in most minicomputers and microcomputers.

The length of the instruction need not be fixed. For example, in the IBM 370 we find instructions whose length is 16, 32, or 48 bits. In most minicomputers we have single-length (i.e., one word) instructions and double-length instructions.

The bit string representing a machine instruction is generally divided into two major fields: the operation (or "op") field and the operand(s) field, usually referred to as the address field(s). Note that this is completely analogous to the way a mathematician denotes a function; i.e., $g(x, y, z)$ means the function (operation) g on the variables (operands) x, y, z. The number of operands available in each instruction is generally different, not only between different machines but also in the same machine between different operation types, as we shall see later. However, neither the question of the number of operands nor the question of the way they are addressed will be discussed here. The interested reader is referred to the articles ADDRESSING; and COMPUTERS, MULTIPLE ADDRESS. This article concentrates on the operation field only.

The types of operations available on contemporary machines are roughly divided into arithmetic, logical, data move, and control operations.

Arithmetic Operations. Arithmetic operations are usually confined to the four basic ones (plus, minus, multiply, and divide) and to the "compare" operation, which serves to record status information about the relative magnitude of the operands. These arithmetic operations may operate on different types of operands, such as integers, and floating-point numbers, with different precision (half-, single-, or double-word length numbers). The operands may assume various bases. Binary is the usual one, but decimal is also common, especially on business-oriented machines. In specialized machines, one may find arithmetic operations of a more sophisticated nature, such as exponentiation or square root, but this is rare.

An example of an arithmetic operation is the IBM 370 instruction A121 (hexadecimal) used at the beginning of this article. Fig. 1 gives the structure of most IBM 370 instructions, and from it we can gain some preliminary insight into the actual structure of a machine instruction. Thus, in our example, the first eight bits (i.e., hexadecimal A1) are the actual operation code and the

8 bits	8 or 24 or 48 bits
Op code	Address fields

All op codes starting with 00 have an 8-bit address field.
All op codes starting with 01 or 10 have a 24-bit address field.
All op codes starting with 11 have a 48-bit address field.
For every length, the structure of the addressing is fixed.

Fig. 1. Typical structure of a vertical instruction set (IBM 370 series).

last eight bits (i.e., hexadecimal 21) are the address field. In this particular instruction, the address field specifies register 2 with the first four bits and register 1 in the last four bits. On a Data General Corporation NOVA computer, the instruction for the same task has the hexadecimal code CE10. Not only is the code different, but the breakdown of the instruction into fields is also completely different.

Logical Operations. The logical operations usually involve boolean operations on the bit values of the operands. Although there are 16 possible boolean operations between two operands, usually only a subset of these (typically AND, OR, and NOT) is available. This subset is sufficient to reproduce all other boolean operations.

Boolean operations are used for the manipulation of parts of words, for decision processes, and for nonnumerical processing. As an example, consider the following problem: Given a data item in a register, isolate the last six bits of it. By inspecting the AND operation truth table, one finds that the result of an AND with 0 is always zero, whereas the result of an AND with 1 reproduces the operand. Thus, an AND operation between the given data item and an operand that has 0 in all places except in the last six bits (all of which are one) will isolate the last six bits of the given data item. Thus:

Given data item:	Arbitrary bit string
Second operand:	0 ... 0 111111
Result of AND:	0 ... 0 6 last bits of given data item.

Operations like this are called *masking* operations. Note that the bit string representing the instruction is completely independent of the actual data. On an IBM 370, assuming that the first operand is in register 3 and the second in register 4, the instruction will be hexadecimal 1434.

In the logical operations, one also usually includes the various possible shift instructions, although, in some classifications, these form a category of their own. Shifting operations, as their names implies, shift the bits in a word to the left or right. The differences between types of shifts affects what happens to the bits being shifted out of a word and what bits are shifted in. For example, in logical shifts, the bits shifted out are lost and the bits shifted in are zeros. In an instruction that will shift two places to the left logically, the leftmost two bits of a data item are lost, and the last vacated two positions are filled with zeros. See also SHIFTING.

Data Move Operations. The data move instructions include moves of data between memory locations and registers, and the input/output instructions necessary for communication between the central processor and peripheral devices. Examples of the former operations are instructions to load and store a register and to move data from one location in memory to another. The input/output operations are of such a complexity that no useful example can be given without an extensive explanation. The reader is referred to the article INPUT-OUTPUT INSTRUCTIONS.

Control Operations. The control instructions include those operations that are necessary for the proper sequencing of the instructions so that the programmed task can be performed correctly. These include conditional and unconditional branches, test instructions, and status-changing instructions.

As an example of this category of instructions, there may be instructions like BRANCH (or JUMP) to a given address (to begin a new sequence of instructions) when the result of the last operation is negative, or if there was an arithmetic overflow. There are also instructions that swap the contents of the user accessible registers with internal registers, thus causing a change in the state of the computer; in particular, this may cause execution of a completely different sequence of instructions. Note also that program flow can be affected not only by explicit control instructions issued by the programmer, but also by special conditions known as *interrupts* (*q.v.*).

This rough division of instructions into types is not necessarily mutually exclusive. Referring to the previous example of a NOVA (compared with the IBM 370 in Fig. 1), the bit string represented by the hexadecimal number A121 will perform both an arithmetic operation (decrease; i.e., subtract 1) *and* a control operation (skip the next instruction if the result is zero).

An important point to note is that different instruction types usually possess different numbers of operands. Whereas arithmetic operations usually refer to three operands (two for the data locations and one for the result location), either explicitly or implicitly, certain control instructions may have one or no operands at all. For example, an unconditional BRANCH has one operand, but a HALT instruction has none. In addition to the operands involved in the instruction execution, there are also *condi-tion codes* involved. Generally speaking, condition codes are indicators, usually one-bit long, which describe the properties of the results and the validity of the operation performed.

Examples of condition codes are explicit indications of (1) the sign of the result, (2) whether or not an overflow has occurred, (3) what the relative magnitudes of the operands are, (4) whether there is a parity error in reading or writing to memory. Similar to the instruction repertoire, the variety of condition codes differs between computers. There is also a difference in the way that condition codes are used. In some computers they are incorporated directly in the instructions, especially conditional branches (like BRANCH ON OVERFLOW), and in others they can be transferred into registers and then manipulated as data.

Machine Language and Instruction Formats. The *machine language* of a computer is defined to be the set of all possible operations that the computer can perform. In a computer of the type discussed previously, this boils down to the set of all possible operation codes (op codes). There are, however, other types of computers such as *tagged architecture* machines in which the operation code *does not* fully describe the operation to be done. In such a computer, part of the operation performed is defined by the type of the operand. For example, there is only *one* ADD operation, and this is done in floating-point or integer mode, depending on the type of the operand. The machine language of such a computer is still the set of all possible operations. However, it is now defined not just by the set of all op codes, but by both op codes and operand tags.

We now go further into the question of the format of the instruction, but again without treating addressing in any detail. A machine instruction can be written, using mathematical notation, as $g(x_1, x_2, \ldots, x_n) \equiv g(x)$, where g is the operation performed on the n operands:

$$x_1, \ldots, x_n \equiv x.$$

The natural question to ask is: Can we have multiple operation instructions in the form

$$g_1(x_1)g_2(x_2)g_3(x_3) \cdots g_n(x_n) \tag{1}$$

where the operations g_i are performed on the operands x_i and the operand sets are either identical, partially overlapping, or distinct from each other? The answer is that machines with such instruction sets do, in fact, exist. Roughly speaking, we can divide instruction sets into *vertical* and *horizontal*. *Vertical instructions* are those of the type $g(x)$, where a single operation (or a time-ordered series of a *fixed* number and *type* of operations) is per-

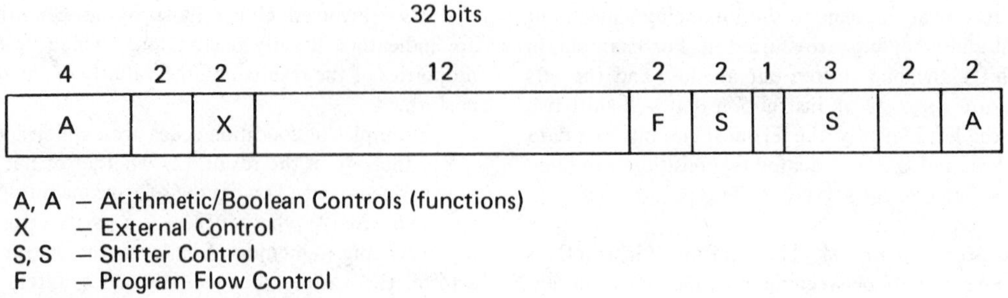

32 bits

4	2	2	12	2	2	1	3	2	2
A		X		F	S		S		A

A, A — Arithmetic/Boolean Controls (functions)
X — External Control
S, S — Shifter Control
F — Program Flow Control

Fig. 2 Typical structure of a 32-bit horizontal instruction (DSC META-4). Nonmarked fields are used for addressing.

formed on a single set of operands. Vertical instructions are usually highly coded (see below).

Horizontal instructions are those of the form (1). Here the functions g_i are *independent* and are performed on the respective operands in parallel or in a well-defined time sequence.

The instruction set of an IBM 370 series computer is an example of a vertical instruction set (see Fig. 1). That of the Digital Scientific Corporation META-4 computer is an example of a horizontal instruction (see Fig. 2). This second example requires some explanation. In the META-4 computer, there are four types of instructions, each having a different field structure (i.e., in each type the interpretation of the various bits is different). We have chosen one of the possible instruction formats. It has six operations done in parallel; two of them control the arithmetic/boolean devices and one controls the program flow. The functions g_i shown in form (1) are thus two arithmetic, two shift, and two control. In Fig. 2 they are denoted by A, A, S, S, X, and F, respectively.

Vertical instructions are found in most machines today. Horizontal instructions are mainly found in microprogrammed machines and in certain minicomputers.

The structure of the operation code itself, i.e., the structure of the contents of the operation field, is also of interest. In principle, if one wants a certain number of instructions, it seems sufficient to associate a function with each number expressible in the operation field. The operation then is determined by *all* the digits (in the binary case, the bits) in the field. By inspecting a part of that field, we generally have no meaningful information about the operation. We call such an arrangement a *highly coded* one. In the highly coded arrangement, the number of possible instructions is equal to the total information contents of the field. In a field of n bits, this means a total of 2^n possible instructions.

On the other hand, one can envision a completely different situation in which each part of the instruction

code conveys some information about the type of the operation. For instance, the first bit in the field may determine if the instruction is arithmetical or nonarithmetical. The second bit may determine the length of the operands; the third, the arithmetic mode (real or integer), etc. In this case we speak about a *low level of coding*. The number of instructions expressible in this case is smaller than the total information content of the op code field, since some of the combinations may be unused. For example, if the instruction is logical, the arithmetic mode may be irrelevant. The low decoding level needed for this type of instruction, and the strict interpretation of the various bits, enable a high degree of parallelism in the decision process that the hardware has to go through in order to decide which instruction has to be performed.

Up to this point we have assumed that the operation field is of fixed length, and in the case of a low decoding level, the bits have fixed meaning. Neither of these assumptions is either necessary or actually used in all machines.

Coding theory teaches us that it may be advisable to have codes of different lengths, utilizing short ones for the more frequently used combinations and long ones for the least used. Indeed, one finds computers that possess what can be called a "tree-structured" instruction code, i.e., the operation field is divided into parts and each part is interpreted in sequence, with the meaning attached to it dependent on the results of interpretation of the preceding parts. This not only solves the problem of meaningless bit settings that we encountered in the low decoding level combinations, but it also enables us to terminate the op code interpretation at a different point for different instructions.

Fig. 3 shows such a structure as present on Burroughs B1800 series. For op1 $\neq$ 0, we have all register moves, memory READ and WRITE, certain branch operations, and all arithmetic and logic operations. Because of the special architecture of this machine, part of the op-

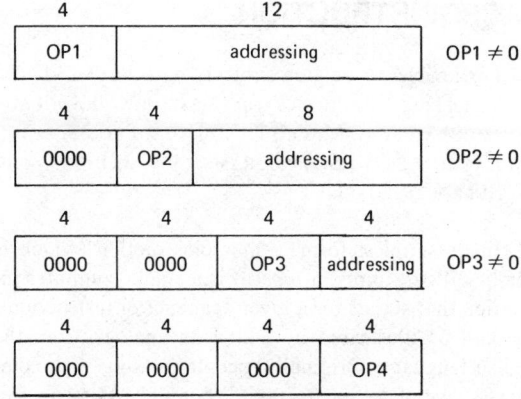

Fig. 3. Typical structure of a 16-bit variable length instruction code (Burroughs 1800). Note that the addressing structure is different for each type of instruction.

eration is defined by the structure of the address field, a feature that enables a large number of operations even though there are only 15 bit patterns for op1 $\neq$ 0. For op1 = 0, op2 $\neq$ 0, we find memory/register swap operations, register clear, shifts, and register increments and decrements. The instructions with op1 = op2 = 0, op3 $\neq$ 0, and those with op1 = op2 = op3 = 0, op4 $\neq$ 0, are used far less frequently. Computers that possess the structure of Fig. 3 need smaller numbers of bits to express a sequence of instructions than do other types of computers (possibly excluding machines that rely heavily on stacks).

The instruction sets of most microcomputers are not different in nature than those of other computers. In some of the older micros, the instruction set actually regressed relative to the state-of-the-art, mainly due to restrictions on word size and capability. The newer (post 1979) micros, however, are correcting this problem and, from the point of view of their instruction sets, most are now indistinguishable from current minicomputers.

General Remarks. This article has described single machine instructions according to their length, operation type, the degree of parallelism in the specification of the operation, the number of operations specified, and, finally, the degree of coding. We conclude with some general remarks on the capabilities of machine instruction sets.

It goes without saying that instructions are built into a machine in order to be used. This is, however, easier said than done. One has to realize that, at this time, high-level languages are the main means of program implementation. Thus, instructions that are present in the machine, but which are difficult to include in the code produced by a high-level language compiler, may have limited use. If those instructions have been included to support types of applications that are usually coded in high-level languages, they are nearly useless.

Generally speaking, a machine instruction set is a grouping of instructions according to their intended application. As always in statements of this kind, the grouping is extremely vague. For example, it is well accepted that floating-point operations are to be considered as part of a scientific instruction set. These instructions, however, may prove quite useful in many other complicated data processing computations. String manipulation and sophisticated data moves, for example, are of value both in business data processing and in compiling. Thus, in this classification, we rely more on instinct or on the choice made by a vendor than on a strict set of rules.

Through the use of microprogramming (*q.v.*), it is possible to implement instruction sets that will be specifically tailored to a class of applications and a class of high-level languages that are used to implement them. We therefore can expect to find machines that have different instruction sets for, say, Cobol applications than for the running of the operating system. Machine instruction sets of this type are usually referred to as language-oriented instruction sets. At the time of writing this article, such sets have been proposed for APL, Fortran, Cobol, Pascal, and Lisp, and operating system and compiler writing. Examples of complete instruction sets are available in most computer manufacturers' manuals.

G. Frieder

MACHINE LANGUAGE. *See* Machine and assembly Language Processing; and Machine Instruction Set.

MACHINE-READABLE FORM

For articles on related subjects *see* Card Reading and Punching Techniques; Input-output Devices; Ninety-Column Card; Optical Character Readers; Optical Mark Readers; Paper Tape; and Universal Product Code.

Machine-readable form refers to the form in which information is encoded for direct, automatic input into a computer. Punched cards contain information in machine-readable form, for example, because machines are able to "read" the information by sensing where the holes are. Information handwritten in script is typically not machine-readable, because devices are not yet generally available which can handle the wide variations in style.

Fig. 1.   Honeywell Type 236 MICR-document reader/ sorter, which can handle up to 1,625 documents per minute.

One exception to this is carefully hand-printed characters on certain forms (e.g., social security numbers on driver's license renewals), which are read directly by optical scanning devices.

In general, punched cards, punched paper tape, magnetic tape, disks, drums, data cells, etc. carry information in machine-readable form for the express purpose of being read exclusively by computers. Some printer and typewriter output on paper can be machine-read by optical scanners, and is also directly readable by humans, unlike the magnetic coding on tape or disk. Magnetic-ink characters, used principally for coding bank-accounting information on checks, are readable by humans (optically) and by machines (magnetically). Such magnetic-ink character recognition is often referred to by its abbreviation MICR. A typical MICR reader is shown in Fig. 1.

C. L. MEEK

MACHINE TRANSLATION.   *See* LANGUAGE TRANSLATION.

MACROINSTRUCTION

For articles on related subjects *see* ARGUMENT; ASSEMBLERS; MACHINE AND ASSEMBLY LANGUAGE PROGRAMMING; MACRO LANGUAGES; PROGRAMMING LANGUAGES; SUBPROGRAMS, CALLING; and SUBROUTINE.

In its simplest form, a macroinstruction (which is usually called, simply, a *macro*) is a single computer instruction that stands for a given sequence of instructions. This can be illustrated by taking an analogy from the English language. Originally, people working with computers spoke of a "binary digit," but since this is a frequently used term, people got tired of saying it and coined the more concise word "bit" to use instead. The word "bit" is therefore a macro that stands for "binary digit."

To implement macros, it is necessary to have a piece of software called a *macro processor,* which is often itself part of an assembly language software system. Macro processors are available on almost all computers, but there has been no standardization in their design. The job of a macro processor is simple. The programmer supplies some macro definitions, which define the macros and what is to replace them, and the macro processor then replaces any occurrence of the macro accordingly.

This is best illustrated by an example, which will be taken from the assembly language of a hypothetical computer. Assume, for instance, that at several points in a program a programmer needs to increase a variable, whose name is COUNT, by 1. Assume further that this takes three assembly-language instructions:

```
LOAD   COUNT
ADD    1
STORE COUNT
```

It would be wasteful of a programmer's time to keep writing out these three instructions in full. It would be much better to choose a single name (BUMPCOUNT, say) to stand for these instructions, and then to write the name each time it was necessary to specify the three instructions. The source program would then be processed according to Fig. 1.

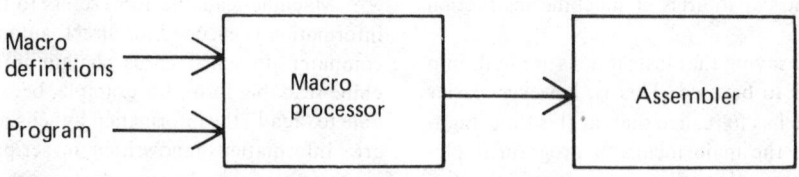

Fig. 1.

The macro definitions define BUMPCOUNT and the instructions that are to replace it. In practice, there would probably be several other macro definitions as well. The macro processor then scans the program, replacing each occurrence of BUMPCOUNT by its expanded form. It would similarly process any other macros that had been defined. As a result of this, the program is then in pure assembly language and can be passed on to the assembler, which processes it in the normal way.

The reader may wonder why the assembler itself cannot be adapted to deal with BUMPCOUNT, thus obviating the need for the two-part process illustrated above. The answer is that assembly languages, as are almost all other computer languages, are inflexible, and the ordinary programmer is not allowed to change them. To return to the earlier analogy, the assembler is akin to a person who has been taught about "binary digits," and is not going to understand anyone who calls them "bits." Hence, if anyone does speak of bits, an interpreter—the analogy of the macro processor—is needed to convert to the assembler's style of language. In summary, therefore, computer languages are intrinsically inflexible, but with a macro processor to act as interpreter, this need not inconvenience the programmer.

Thus far our picture of macros has been an oversimplified one in that the most important and powerful aspect has not been mentioned. This concerns macros with variable elements.

To return to the example of the BUMPCOUNT macro, the defect of this macro as it stands is that it works only for one variable, COUNT. In practice, it would be much more useful to have a general macro (called, say, BUMP) that could be used to increment any variable by 1. This can, in fact, be done. The name of the variable to be incremented is written immediately after BUMP, and is called the *argument* of the macro. The macro processor can be told to insert the argument at various points in the replacement of the macro. Thus,

```
BUMP  (name)
```

would be replaced by

```
LOAD   (name)
ADD    1
STORE  (name)
```

where any name of a variable could occur as *name*.

It is possible to have more than one argument to a macro. For example, it would be possible to specify a macro of form

```
PRODUCT X, Y, Z
```

which for any X, Y, and Z would compute Z to be the product of X and Y.

Beginners at programming often find it hard to distinguish between the concept of a macro and that of a subroutine. The difference is, in fact, clear-cut. A macro is actually replaced by its expanded form. Hence, if a program contains n occurrences of a macro, then n copies of the instructions it stands for are inserted into the program. (Note, however, that, if the macro possesses arguments, the instructions need not be identical in all the cases.) A subroutine, on the other hand, involves a break in the flow of a program. If a sequence of instructions occurs frequently in a program, then these can be written as a subroutine, and each occurrence in the program is replaced by an instruction to jump to this subroutine, execute it, and then return. There is then only one copy of the sequence of instructions. (Viewed at a more fundamental level, a subroutine is a run-time replacement and a macro a replacement at the time of translation.)

Macros are most often used to represent relatively short sequences of instructions or sequences that involve a relatively large number of insertions of arguments. But sometimes macros are quite long sequences of instructions, in which case the macro-processor will normally generate a calling sequence to a subroutinized version of the macro. Often a set of macros is combined into a library; a very common example of this is a library of macros to aid communication with an operating system.

Looked at from another viewpoint, a macro is a way of extending a language. Thus, once the BUMP macro has been defined, a programmer can treat BUMP as an extra assembly language instruction. It is common practice to build an extensive group of macros, and it often happens that a program is built entirely of macros and devoid of true assembly-language instructions. In this case the macros can be thought of as forming a new language in their own right. Macros are therefore a useful tool for constructing programming languages, though they are not normally powerful enough to build up from assembly languages to such high-level languages as Fortran.

Needless to say, such relatively sophisticated uses of macros require more facilities than have been described here. In particular, it is necessary for macro processors to contain a decision-making facility so that the instructions to replace the macro can depend on the form of a macro argument and the context in which it occurs.

The examples considered so far have shown macros for assembly language, as this is the most popular use of macros. Indeed, a macro processor is often combined with an assembler to make it appear to the programmer as if the two are a single unit, called a *macro assembler*. However, macros can be used with any programming language and, perhaps most interestingly of all, as an end in themselves.

As an example of the latter, assume that a computer is being used to print invitations. Each invitation is identical except for the name of the person to be invited. One way to do this would be to define a macro called, say, INVITE, which generates the invitation, inserting the argument at the necessary places. This macro could then be used by writing

    INVITE   STAN   JONES
    INVITE   MONICA   SMITH
    . . . etc.

In more general applications, macros can be used to provide a replacement facility in any written text. At the simplest level, macros may be used to replace one word by another throughout a document, and can therefore be used to correct systematic errors or make systematic changes. To deal with applications such as this, there exist so-called *general-purpose* macro processors.

REFERENCES

1960. McIlroy, M. D. "Macro Instruction Extensions of Compiler Languages," *Comm. ACM 3, No. 4*: 214–220 (April). (This is a classic early paper on macros and gives a good insight into their potential power.)
1969. Kent, W. "Assembler Language Macroprogramming," *Computing Surveys 1, No. 4*: 183–196 (December). (A tutorial paper on macro assemblers, particularly the macro assembler for IBM System/360.)
1971. Macleod, J. A. "MP/I—A FORTRAN Macroprocessor," *Computer Journal 14, No. 3*: 229–231 (August). (One example of a macro facility designed for a high-level language.)
1974. Brown, P. J. *Macro Processors and Techniques for Portable Software*. New York: Wiley.

P. J. BROWN

MACRO LANGUAGES

For articles on related subjects *see* ASSEMBLERS; COMPILER; MACROINSTRUCTION; PROGRAMMING LANGUAGES; and STRING PROCESSING LANGUAGES.

Although the term *macro languages* is sometimes used to describe programming languages which make exclusive or heavy use of macro calls (*see* MACROINSTRUCTION), as used in this article it refers to languages whose main purpose is string processing and manipulation and which make heavy use of macros to achieve their aims. Among these languages are found some interesting and sometimes opposing philosophies.

Since the fundamental operations of macroprocessing are concerned with string replacement, these can be extended to more general string processing and manipulation. This act of generalization can be approached by starting with macroprocessing ideas and extending them for string processing. The two best known languages which exemplify this approach are TRAC® (a registered service mark of Rockford Research, Inc.) and GPM (for General Purpose Macrogenerator). Both these languages were developed in the mid-1960s, TRAC by Calvin Mooers, and GPM by Christopher Strachey.

An unusual feature of these two macro languages is that all commands in the languages, such as string storage, string retrieval, and arithmetic, are considered to be valid data objects. Thus, sequences of such commands may be stored as strings like any other strings. When the stored string with commands is brought forth, the commands in the string become a macro and are executed. The macro language is normally run interpretively; i.e., a program in the macro language is not compiled. The result is a very powerful, though unusual, kind of computer language.

After an early vogue, macro languages such as the TRAC language and GPM suffered competition from newer string processing systems and from powerful editors.

Another approach to developing a macro language is to take some existing language that is suitable for string processing and adapt it to do macroprocessing as well. This is the approach taken by the PL/I macro processor and, more generally, by the SUPERMAC concept. SUPERMAC can be added to an existing language—called the *host*—that has reasonable string and file manipulation capabilities. Macro facilities are made available through built-in subroutines, such as "define a macro" and "gear a file for macro calls." For each macro, the user designates a subroutine, written in the host language, which is to be called every time the macro is recognized.

REFERENCES

1965. Strachey, C. "A General Purpose Macrogenerator," *Computer Journal 8, No. 3*. (Describes GPM.)
1966. Mooers, C. N. "TRAC, A Procedure-Describing Language for the Reactive Typewriter," *Comm. ACM 9, No. 3*.
1979. Brown, P. J. "Macros Without Tears," *Software—Practice and Experience 9, No. 6*. (Describes SUPERMAC.)

P. J. BROWN

MAINFRAME

For articles on related subjects *see* CENTRAL PROCESSING UNIT; and MEMORY: Main.

The mainframe of a computer system is the cabinet that houses the central processor and main memory. It is, therefore, separate from the peripheral devices (card readers, printers, tape drives, etc.) and device controllers. Typically, it is the largest component in size and cost, but modern electronics have allowed great reductions in both in recent years. The mainframe usually has many indicator lights (sometimes as part of the operator's console) to show fault conditions, memory contents, etc. The central processor and main memory are housed together as an aid in increasing processing speeds (cable lengths will be short) and improving reliability (e.g., both will be at similar temperatures and humidities). The term *mainframe* comes from the use of "frame" as a device to hold electronics (rack is also frequently used); and the frame holding the electronics that do the computing might reasonably be the main frame.

In modern systems with very large main memory, some memory modules are housed in cabinets separate from the mainframe. Frequently, they are attached and thus become part of the mainframe cabinet. Multiprocessor systems with more than one central processor (CPU) are referred to as two- or three-mainframe systems, in which case the mainframe refers only to the CPU and not to the main memory.

The term *mainframe* as a single word has come to be used as a designation of medium- and large-scale computers which contain a "main frame" as defined in this article; thus, we speak of a *mainframe* computer in contrast to a microcomputer or personal computer.

C. L. MEEK

MAIN MEMORY. *See* MEMORY: Main.

MAINTENANCE OF COMPUTERS

For articles on related subjects *see* FAULT TOLERANT COMPUTING; HARDWARE MONITOR; PERFORMANCE OF COMPUTERS; REDUNDANCY; and RELIABILITY, HARDWARE.

This article focuses on the maintenance of minicomputers and larger systems. By their nature, microprocessors (*q.v.*) require specialized, automatic testing techniques.

Like all sophisticated equipment, computers undergo the cycle of repair, check-out, operational readiness, failure, and back to repair. When the cost of a machine's not being in service is high, methods must be applied to reduce these out-of-service, or *downtime,* periods. The cost of downtime is not simply the lost revenue when the computer is not used, but also the cost of having to rerun programs that were interrupted by the ailing system, perhaps loss of real-time data, loss of control of external processes, opportunity costs, and costs related to user inconvenience, dissatisfaction, and reduced confidence in the system. Other costs are related directly to the diagnosis and corrective repair actions, and associated logistics and bookkeeping.

Due to the complexity of the equipment, as well as managerial judgment, many users, even some sophisti-

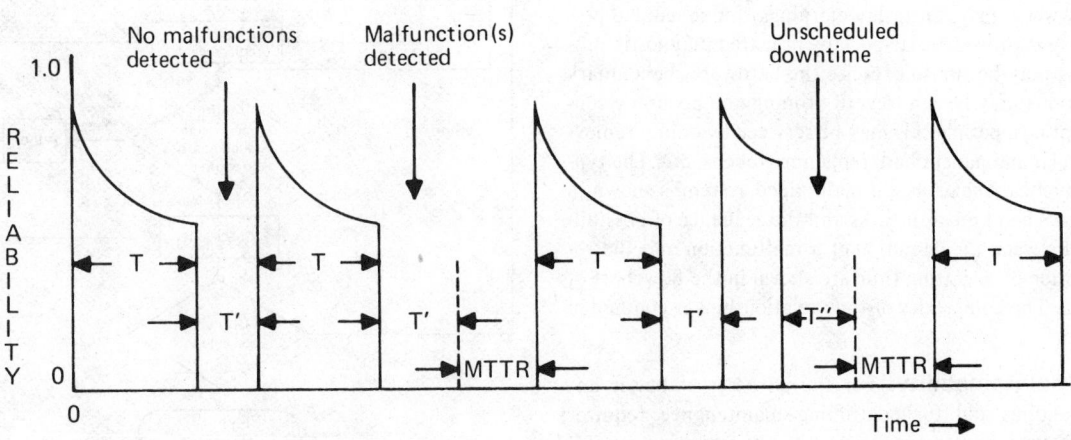

T   = maximum allowed "up" time
T′   = downtime due to preventive maintenance
T″ = unscheduled diagnosis
MTTR = mean time to repair

Fig. 1. Cyclical behavior of a maintained system.

cated computer-knowledgeable users, often decide not to maintain the system (processors, memory, system software, peripherals) themselves, but rather to have a maintenance contract with the system manufacturer. The cost of a maintenance contract over the useful life of the equipment in relation to its capital cost is quite high. It is also a good indicator of the expected unreliability. High costs due to unreliability and maintenance needs are a strong argument for designing dependability, maintainability, and serviceability into the equipment.

Decisions such as whether to have one's own maintenance personnel, what spare parts to stock and in what quantities, what test instruments are required, etc., have to be faced. Mathematical tools offered by operations research, such as dynamic programming and others, are often used to model the system in an attempt to arrive at optimal solutions to this complex problem.

Preventive Maintenance. One means of reducing the direct cost associated with an unexpected system failure is to provide scheduled downtimes for the purpose of preventive maintenance. Obviously, a deliberate scheduled shutdown is less disruptive than that due to an unexpected system failure. During the downtime the general idea is to tune up the system so that things that are in marginal working condition will be identified and remedied. Diagnosis should be made by exercising all aspects of the system to catch latent failures and those that may have already occurred but have been lying undetected. Failed portions of the system are likely to be undetected if they have never been called into service, and therefore their operational readiness would not have been verified.

Typically, most computer centers use a few hours every week, (say, Saturday mornings) for scheduled preventive maintenance. Especially prepared diagnostic programs may be run to exercise the hardware, benchmark programs may be run to verify timing and accuracy considerations, peripherals may be serviced by oiling, removing dust, and paper chad, replacing ribbons, etc. The typical cyclical behavior of a maintained system is shown in Fig. 1. The number of tasks and the sequence of possibilities between the detection of a malfunction and the resumption of operating time are shown in the flowchart of Fig. 2. The complexity of time relationships is codified in Fig. 3.

Maintainability. For the purposes of better understanding and for controlling maintenance requirements, we will attempt to quantify the foregoing considerations by defining the applicable terms, such as *maintainability* and *availability,* as well as other related terms. A qualitative definition of maintainability M is given by Goldman and Slattery (1967) as

> ... the characteristics (both qualitative and quantitative) of material design and installation which

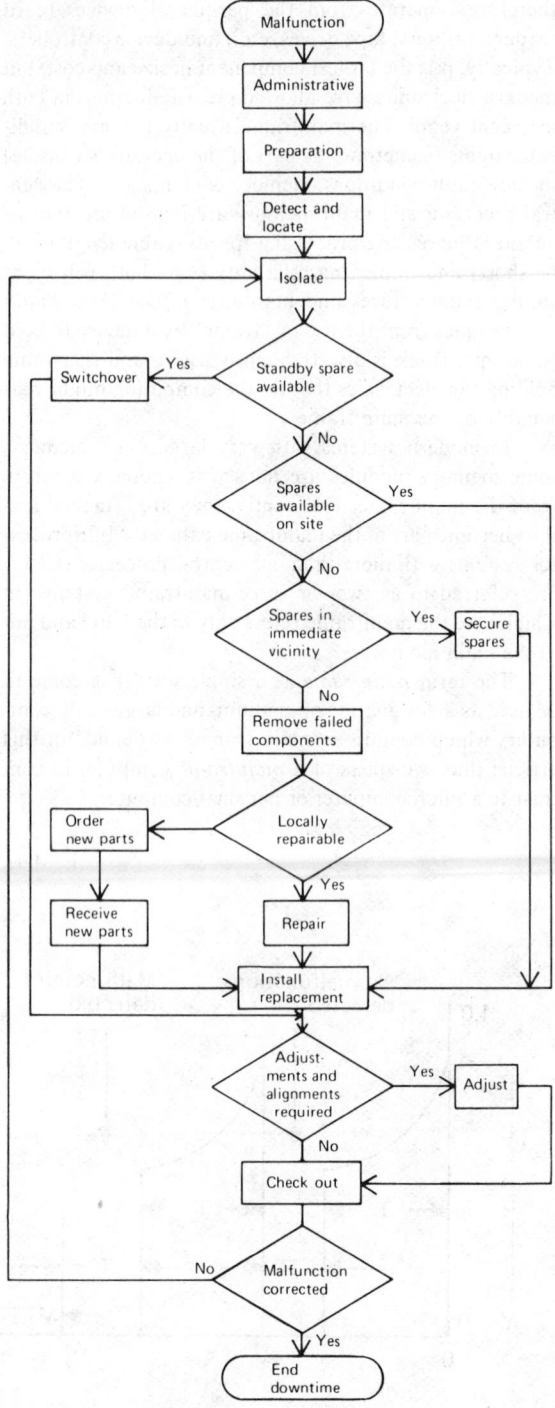

Fig. 2. Flowchart for maintenance operations.

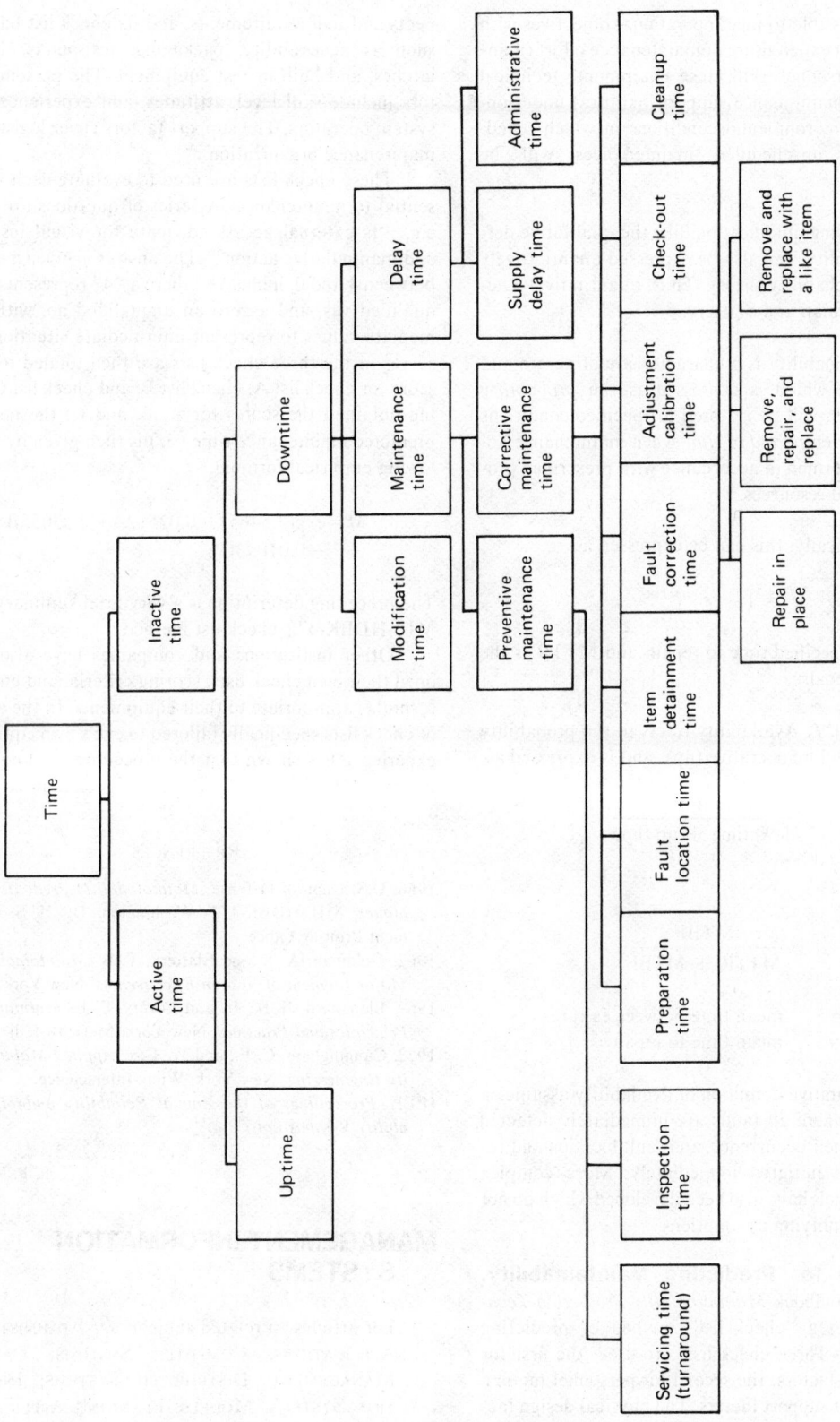

Fig. 3. Time relationship. (Adapted from O.A. Meykar, "Maintenance Terminology Supports the Effectiveness Concept," *IEEE Trans. on Reliability,* Vol. R-16, No. 1, May 1967.)

make it possible to meet operational objectives with a minimum expenditure of maintenance effort (manpower, personnel skill, test equipment, technical data, and maintenance support facilities) under operational environmental conditions in which scheduled and unscheduled maintenances will be performed.

The preceding qualification, like the qualitative definition of reliability, can also be expressed quantitatively by means of probability theory. Thus, quantitatively, according to Goldman and Slattery.

. . . maintainability is a characteristic of design and installation which is expressed as the *probability* that an item will be restored to specified conditions within a given *period of time* when maintenance action is performed in accordance with prescribed procedures and resources.

Mathematically, this can be expressed as

$$M = 1 - e^{-t/\text{MTTR}}$$

where t is the specified time to repair, and MTTR is the mean time to repair.

Availability. Availability refers to the probability that a system will be operative (up), and is expressed as

$$A = \frac{\text{up time}}{\text{downtime} + \text{up time}}$$

or equivalently as

$$A = \frac{\text{MTBF}}{\text{MTTR} + \text{MTBF}}$$

where MTBF = mean time between failures
      MTTR = mean time to repair

The quantitative definition of availability assumes a system model where all faults are immediately detected at the time of their occurrence, and fault location and repair action are initiated immediately. More complex availability models have also been developed which do not make these simplifying assumptions.

Methods for Predicting Maintainability. The military handbook *Maintainability Prediction Techniques* describes a "check list" method of predicting maintainability. Three check lists are used: the first for physical design factors, the second for personnel factors, and the third for support factors. The physical design factors encompass such equipment features as physical as-

pects and tool requirements, and its check list has items such as accessibility, packaging, test-points, internal latches, and built-in test equipment. The personnel factors include skill level, attitudes, and experience of the system operators. The support factors cover logistics and maintenance organization.

These check lists are used to evaluate each step essential to maintenance. A series of questions are raised: e.g., "Is external access adequate for visual inspection and manipulative action?" The answer is given a score of between 4 and 0, inclusive, where a "4" represents an unqualified yes, and a zero an unqualified no, with intermediate values to represent intermediate situations. The scores in the three check lists are then totaled to give a score for check list A, check list B, and check list C. Having obtained the scores for A, B, and C, the necessary predicted maintenance time (M) is then given by the following empirical formula:

$$M = \exp(3.54651 - 0.02512A - 0.03055B - 0.01093C).$$

The preceding description is a very brief summary of the MIL-HDBK-472 check list method.

Other institutions and companies have also developed their own check lists, scoring criteria, and empirical formulas appropriate to their equipments. In the absence of check lists specifically tailored to one's own equipment, experience has shown that the procedures and equations given in MIL-HDBK-472 serve as a good approximation.

REFERENCES

1966. U.S. Dept. of Defense. *Maintainability Prediction Techniques*, MIL-HDBK-472. Washington, DC: U.S. Government Printing Office.
1967. Goldman, A. S. and Slattery, T. B. *Maintainability: A Major Element of System Effectiveness*. New York: Wiley.
1969. Blanchard, B. S., Jr. and Lovery, E. E. *Maintainability Principles and Practices*. New York: McGraw-Hill.
1972. Cunningham, C. E., and W. Cox. *Applied Maintainability Engineering*. New York: Wiley-Interscience.
IEEE. *Proceedings of the Annual Reliability and Maintainability Symposium.*

F. P. MATHUR

MANAGEMENT INFORMATION SYSTEMS

For articles on related subjects *see* ADMINISTRATIVE APPLICATIONS, COMPUTER SYSTEMS; DATABASE MANAGEMENT; DISTRIBUTED SYSTEMS; INFORMATION SYSTEMS, MODELS; PLANNING APPLICATIONS; and SIMULATION: Principles.

A management information system (MIS) is a computer-based organizational information system which provides information to support management activities and functions. The portfolio of applications in an MIS will cover a wide variety of organizational needs, including applications which indirectly support management activities and applications which directly serve management users. Since management applications frequently need data that is best provided by a database, databases and database management software are generally part of an MIS.

Evolution of the MIS Concept.

The term *management information system,* or MIS, is the most widely used title for a management-oriented information system. However, many organizations refer to their computer-based information system as just a data processing system or information system.

The frequent use of the term MIS to describe a computer-based information system having applications in support of management activities began in the mid-1960s. The formation in 1968 of the Society for Management Information Systems (SMIS) indicated the acceptance by a significant group of practitioners of the term MIS and the concepts associated with it. Another term, *decision support systems* (DSS), is sometimes used to describe those applications in an MIS that directly support specific decision making.

The names of academic programs in organizational information systems reflect business practice. Masters degree programs (usually in business) with emphasis or concentration in organizational information systems most frequently are termed MIS programs; undergraduate programs are more likely to be called information systems or data processing.

The evolution of the use of computers in organizations may be traced as a function of type of applications (see Nolan 1979). In the first stage, applications are mainly transaction processing of such fundamental transactions as sales orders, billing and receipts, payables, and inventory accounting. These applications are at a clerical level—displacing clerical personnel and supporting basic operations in accounting, marketing, manufacturing, etc. The transaction processing applications generally include simple operations summaries. The next stage of information system development is the preparation of management control reports summarizing and analyzing the transaction data for management control purposes. The third stage of the information system is the data resource stage, in which stored data is made readily available to analysts and decision makers through organizational databases and database management software. The fourth stage is the use of retrieval software, analytical software, planning models, and decision models to obtain, analyze,

and manipulate data for support of analysis, planning, and decision making.

The four stages describe the general historical evolution of the MIS concept and the approximate pattern of development of an MIS in a specific organization. The stages provide a useful conceptual pattern but, in an individual organization, the actual development pattern may be less regular and more complex because of the need or demand for various applications. Also, functional areas in an organization may have differing rates of development (for example, accounting may be in a data resource stage using a database, while the personnel function may be implementing its first transaction reporting system).

The Structure of an MIS.

An information system consists of a number of elements—hardware, system software, application software, databases, procedures, and personnel. Data communications facilities are also included in most systems of more than modest complexity. For the purpose of defining the structure of an MIS, the basic components are the application systems, each consisting of a set of application programs, plus related procedures for data entry, system operation, and information distribution. The set of existing application systems (the *application portfolio*) defines the current capabilities of an information system.

The structure of an MIS is based on the structure and activities of the organization. Organizations are divided into functional areas (such as marketing, manufacturing, accounting, and finance). Within each function, management activities can be classified into three levels: Operational control, management control, and strategic planning (see Anthony 1965). There are sets of applications which apply to each specific functional area. For example, a group of applications process the finance transactions and provide reports and analyses to support finance management. These applications form the finance information system, which is a subsystem of the organization's MIS. The MIS for an organization, therefore, can be described as a federation of functional-area subsystems, each of which is divided into four major sections: Transaction processing, operational control, management control, and strategic planning. This structure is illustrated in Fig. 1.

Each of the functional subsystems of the MIS has unique data files which are used only by that subsystem (Fig. 1). There are also files that need to be available for general retrieval. These are organized into a general database under the control of a database management system. There may be common applications used by more than one subsystem; there are also decision models and analytical software that can be termed the model base.

The applications in the cells of Fig. 1 differ in several respects. The transaction processing applications support

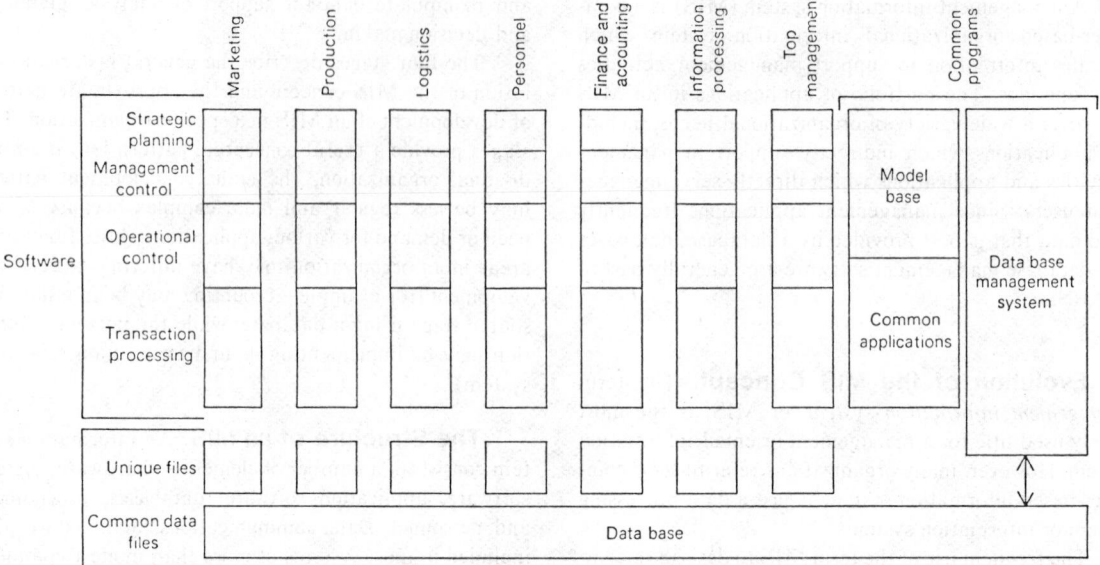

Fig. 1. The organizational MIS. (Reprinted by permission from Gordon B. Davis, *Management Information Systems: Conceptual Foundations, Structure, and Development.* New York: McGraw-Hill, p. 221 (1974).)

lower-level management and clerical personnel. Any decisions included in transaction processing computer programs are programmed decisions which can be described by straightforward algorithms. Applications supporting higher-level activities are less structured, and decisions incorporated in the applications tend to be less programmable and require human/machine interaction to arrive at a result. There are considerably more feasible applications in support of transaction processing and operations than there are in support of strategic planning. Therefore, the structure of an MIS is sometimes described visually as a pyramid (Fig. 2).

MIS Applications to Support Management Activities. The classification of management activities into operational control, management control, and strategic planning is based on the commonly used classification by Anthony. The applications associated with each of the levels of management activity have different characteristics.

Operational Control. Operational control is the process of ensuring that operational activities are carried out effectively and efficiently. Operational control makes use of fairly stable pre-established procedures and decision rules. The decisions and actions cover short time periods. The information system support for operational control consists of transaction processing, operational report processing, and inquiry processing. Some examples of infor-

mation processing in support of operational decision making are the following.

- When an inventory withdrawal is made the system not only records the transaction and produces a transaction document but also, using pre-estab-

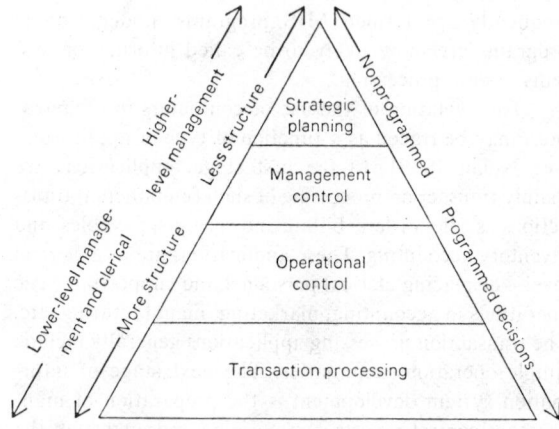

Fig. 2. The management information system as a pyramid. (Reprinted by permission from Gordon B. Davis, *Management Information Systems: Conceptual Foundations, Structure, and Development.* New York: McGraw-Hill, p. 222 (1974).)

Demo Company
Report of Sales and Gross Profit on Sales
Month Ended 31 March 1981

	Sales Dollars (000) Actual/		Gross Profit (000) Actual/		Analysis of Gross Profit Variance (000)		
Jan	Planned	Variance	Planned	Variance	Volume	Price	Mix
Feb	3,791	19*	1398	122*	61*	12*	49*
Mar	3,142	42	1290	50	21	5*	34
Apr	3,761	239*	1173	210*	159*	38*	13*
May	4.050		1620				
	4,100		1640				

*Unfavorable variance.

Fig. 3.   Management control report for sales manager using variance analysis.

lished algorithms, examines the balance on hand to see if a replenishment order should be placed. If so, order quantity is calculated. An action order document is produced for review by an analyst before the order is placed.

- An analysis of orders still outstanding after 30 days is produced periodically for manual follow-up.

Management Control. Management control information is needed by managers of departments, profit centers, etc., to measure performance, to decide on control actions, to formulate new decision rules, and to allocate resources. Management control reporting generally requires some standard of performance in order to calculate variances from standard and to analyze the causes of the variances. MIS applications include planning models to assist in preparing plans and budgets, variance analysis programs, problem analysis modules, and inquiry capabilities. An example of management control information is a performance report with planned and actual performance, plus an analysis of reasons for variances. Fig. 3 illustrates a management control report for a sales manager.

Strategic Planning. Strategic planning develops the strategy with which an organization will attempt to achieve its objectives. Data requirements are generally for summary data rather than for detailed transaction data. The data needs include both external and internal data and projections of future demand. An example is a report describing past demand and past market share, plus a forecast of future demand (Fig. 4).

MIS Support for Decision Making and Planning. The MIS support for decision making in an organization can be described in terms of Simon's (1977)

three phases of the decision-making process: Intelligence, decision design, and choice. The intelligence phase is for discovering problems and opportunities. The MIS support for this phase requires a database plus methods for search and discovery. Structured search may use predefined search algorithms; unstructured search requires flexible access to the database. The decision design phase is for the generation of alternatives. This involves inventing, developing, and analyzing possible courses of action. The MIS support for decision design consists of statistical and analytical software and model-building software. The final step in the decision-making process is choice. The MIS support for the choice phase consists of various decision models, sensitivity analysis, and choice procedures. Fig. 5 gives examples of MIS support for the three phases of decision making.

The planning process requires future expectations to be quantified and classified. A planning model is prepared as a method of structuring, manipulating, and communicating expectations and plans. Computational support for the planning process consists of historical data analysis techniques, planning data generation techniques, and financial planning computations. The preparation and testing of organizational plans can be aided by planning software.

Issues in the Design and Implementation of MIS Some MIS applications have been implemented with great success; others have been failures. The failures, which are often instructive, have usually been due to one of the following factors.

- Failure to identify correctly or completely user requirements. (Systems were designed to meet requirements that turned out to be incorrect or incomplete when the systems were implemented.)

Demo Company
Market Share Analysis
For Past Five Years and
Five Year Demand Forecast
for
Squidgits

		Total Units (000)	Estimated Market Share [Units (000) and Percent]							
			Demo Co.		Svarto, Inc.		Vito Co.,		Andra	
Past	1976	12,500	1,900	(15.2)	3,137	(25.1)	6,313	(50.5)	1,150	(9.2)
	1977	13,300	2,168	(16.3)	3,724	(28.0)	6,198	(46.6)	1,210	(9.1)
	1978	12,000	2,100	(17.5)	3,384	(28.2)	5,376	(44.8)	1.083	(9.5)
	1979	15,600	2,652	(17.0)	4,555	(29.2)	6,864	(44.0)	1,529	(9.8)
	1980	14,900	2,742	(18.4)	4,232	(28.4)	1,586	(44.2)	1,340	(9.0)
Forecast	1981	16,200								
	1982	16,900								
	1983	17,500								
	1984	17,500								
	1985	17,000								

Fig. 4.   Strategic planning report showing past and projected demand and past market shares.

- Rigidity in application development life cycle. (MIS applications often need an iterative or experimental development life cycle because many of the requirements emerge during development. Use of a rigid, linear cycle that ensures complete specification of requirements in the first stage has resulted in systems that have not been accepted.)
- Making systems too complex. (The designs typically attempted to integrate processes too tightly to use a computer-based system.)
- Lack of attention to human and social factors in the design of the system. (Technical factors have often dominated during design, and the systems as designed have met resistance from the organization.)
- Lack of attention to implementation processes. (Management information systems cause change in organizational structure, power relationships, etc. Where the procedures for change have been inadequate to obtain organizational willingness to change, the systems have not received adequate support to succeed.)

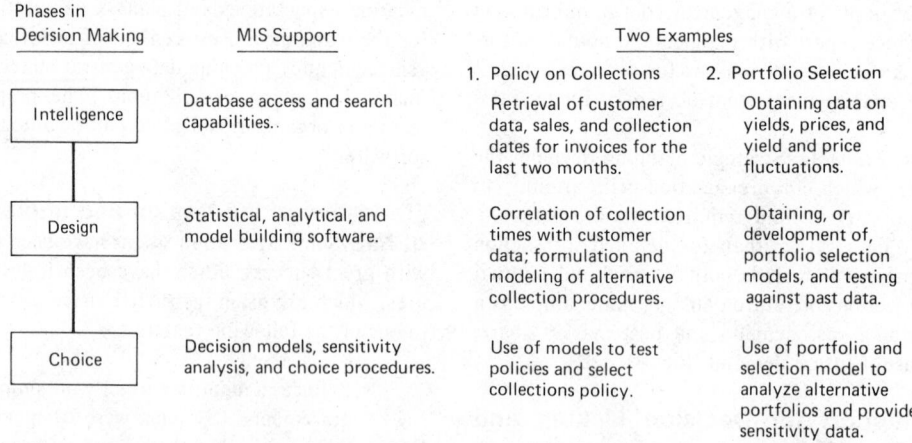

Fig. 5.   MIS support for phases in decision making with examples from finance subsystem.

The above causes of failure suggest some of the issues in MIS design and implementation. Other MIS design issues are listed below.

- How useful and cost-effective are information systems to support relatively unstructured management activities such as strategic planning (see Dearden, 1972)?
- How can applications be designed so as to achieve the desired organization behavior? (The issue arises from experience which indicates that information systems applications have substantial impact on organizational behavior.)
- How much control should be given to users and how should this control be achieved? (Technology changes and user awareness of the power of information technology have made many users demand greater control over their information resources.)
- How should the functions between computer and user and the characteristics of the user interface be allocated? (The design of user interfaces in applications and the allocation of functions between the computer and the user affect both the user performance and the user willingness to accept the application).

Note that the MIS design and implementation issues are usually not technical; rather, they relate to cost and effectiveness and to the impact of design and implementation on human and organizational behavior.

Sources of Information on MIS. The Society for Management Information Systems (SMIS) is the major professional society for MIS. Its members are mainly MIS executives and MIS planners. It holds an annual convention and publishes the *MIS Quarterly* (jointly with the Management Information Systems Research Center at the University of Minnesota).

The general computing literature contains articles on MIS. Important sources are the *MIS Quarterly, Data Base* (published by the Special Interest Group for Business Data Processing of ACM), *Datamation, Infosystems,* and *Journal of Systems Management.* A European journal in English is *Information and Management.* Articles on MIS appear with reasonable frequency in *Management Sciences, Decision Sciences,* and the *Harvard Business Review. Computing Reviews* of ACM reviews some MIS articles under the section titled, "Information Systems Applications."

The Future of MIS. The implementation of systems embodying MIS concepts is the trend in the design or redesign of almost all organizational information systems. Technology improvements in hardware and software make many MIS applications both feasible and cost-effective. For example, improved terminals at lower cost make terminal-based management applications more cost-effective, and improved database management systems make it feasible to implement applications involving management inquiry and retrieval from databases.

The future of MIS applications and their implementation is constrained primarily by design issues related to human and organizational behavior. Insight into some of these design issues can be gained by trial and error experimentation with MIS applications. Many of the human and behavioral considerations in MIS are also amenable to laboratory and field research, so that much of the contribution of MIS research to success in the development of MIS applications is likely to be in this area.

REFERENCES

1965. Anthony, Robert N. *Planning and Control Systems: A Framework for Analysis.* Cambridge, MA: Harvard University Press.

1967. Ackoff, R. L. "Management Misinformation Systems," *Management Science* (December), pp. B.147–B.156. (A classic article on information needs.)

1969. Blumenthal, Sherman. *MIS—A Framework for Planning and Development.* Englewood Cliffs, NJ: Prentice-Hall. (A description of the operational control portion of an MIS.)

1969. Aron, J. D. "Information Systems in Perspective," *Computing Surveys* (December), pp. 213–236. (Historically interesting survey article.)

1972. Dearden, John. "MIS Is a Mirage," *Harvard Business Review* (January–February), pp. 90–99. (A significant critic of MIS. See also letters to Editor in May–June issue.)

1974. Davis, Gordon B. *Management Information Systems: Conceptual Foundations, Structure, and Development.* New York: McGraw-Hill. (The most widely used conceptual text on MIS.)

1976. Davis, Gordon B. and Everest, Gordon C. *Readings in Management Information Systems.* New York: McGraw-Hill. (A collection of classic and survey articles on MIS topics.)

1977. McClean, Ephraem R. and Soden, John V. *Strategic Planning for MIS.* New York: Wiley.

1977. Simon, Herbert A. *The New Science of Management Decision* (Rev. Ed.). Englewood Cliffs, NJ: Prentice-Hall.

1979. Nolan, Richard L. "Managing the Crises in Data Processing," *Harvard Business Review* (March–April), pp. 115–126.

G. B. DAVIS

MANAGEMENT OF COMPUTING. *See*
BENCHMARK; COMPUTER ACCOUNTING AND RESOURCE CONTROL; COMPUTING CENTER; CRIME AND COMPUTER SECURITY; DATA SECURITY; HARDWARE

MONITOR; LEGAL ASPECTS OF COMPUTING; MAINTENANCE OF COMPUTERS; OPEN AND CLOSED SHOP; PERFORMANCE MEASUREMENT AND EVALUATION; PROCESSING MODES; PROGRAM LIBRARIES, NUMERICAL AND STATISTICAL; REMOTE JOB ENTRY; SECURITY OF COMPUTER INSTALLATIONS, PHYSICAL; SOFTWARE MONITORS; and THROUGHPUT.

MANUFACTURERS, COMPUTER. *See* COMPUTER INDUSTRY.

MARK I

For articles on related subjects *see* AIKEN, HOWARD; DIGITAL COMPUTERS: HISTORY: Early; and HOPPER, GRACE MURRAY.

The Harvard Mark I, also called the IBM Automatic Sequence Controlled Calculator, was the first large-scale, automatic, digital computer. The gift of the International Business Machines Corporation to Harvard University in August 1944, Mark I marked the beginning of the era of the modern computer.

The Mark I was the brainchild of Howard Hathaway Aiken, who conceived the idea for a general-purpose computing machine for scientific calculations while working on his Ph.D. at Harvard. In 1937 he approached IBM with this idea. Thomas J. Watson, Sr., supported the plan to adapt the components and techniques of IBM statistical machines to an automatic scientific calculator.

The machine was designed in collaboration with IBM engineers Claire D. Lake, Francis E. Hamilton, and Benjamin M. Durfee (U.S. Patent 2,616,626) at the IBM Research Laboratory at Endicott, New York. Final construction of the machine was delayed by United States entrance into World War II. When placed in operation at Harvard in 1944, the Mark I was operated round-the-clock for the Navy's Bureau of Ships, under the supervision of Professor Aiken, then Commander, USNR.

The Mark I was a parallel, synchronous calculator with a word length of 23 decimal digits, plus the algebraic sign. It was 51 ft long (see Fig. 1), stood 8 ft high, and weighed approximately 5 tons. It used many standard components from IBM equipment, including relays, counters, cam contacts, typewriters, card feeds, and punches. The sequence mechanism, the primary innovation of the Mark I, governed the atuomatic operation of the machine from instructions encoded on punched paper tape; by much the same method, Babbage envisioned the control of his analytical engine by Jacquard cards. The fundamental time cycle of the Mark I was 300 ms, the

Fig. 1. The Mark I, or Automatic Sequence Controlled Calculator.

time necessary to advance the sequence tape. One cycle was sufficient for addition; multiplication, division, and functional computations required from 10 to 200 cycles.

The machine consisted of 60 constant registers set by dial switches, 72 storage counters used for arithmetic operations and temporary storage, a multiplying/dividing unit, functional counters for computing logarithmic and trigonometric functions, three interpolators capable of interpolation from tables of previously computed values punched on paper tape, and the sequence mechanism. Input was by interpolator tape, punched cards, and constant registers; output, by punched cards or IBM Electromatic typewriters. A 4 hp, 25 Kw motor provided the mechanical drive for the counters and functional units through electromagnetic clutches controlled by relays.

The flexibility of the automatic computer was demonstrated by the Mark I solution of various defense problems, including logistics, firing tables, and a highly secret, mathematical simulation of the first atomic bomb. The main load of the Mark I for many years was the computation of Bessel functions. Later electronic machines outrivaled the Mark I in speed, but its suitability for the computation of tables insured its continued operation until 1959. Results of this work are used by almost every computing laboratory. After more than 15 years of service in the Harvard Computation Laboratory, the Mark I was retired and dismantled. Pieces of the machine may still be seen at Harvard, IBM headquarters in New York, and the Smithsonian.

For many pioneers, their early training on the Harvard Mark I set the stage for later important contributions to the development of the computer. Though this electromechanical machine was soon surpassed by the electronic computer, the Mark I—as the first completed, operational, automatic, general-purpose, digital calculator, the fulfillment of Babbage's dream—is assured a permanent place in history.

REFERENCES

1946. Computation Laboratory, Harvard University. "Manual of Operation for the Automatic Sequence Controlled Calculator," *Annals of the Computation Laboratory* 1, Cambridge, MA: Harvard University Press.

E. L. STOLL

MARKOV ALGORITHMS

For articles on related subjects *see* ALGORITHM; ALGORITHMS, THEORY OF; COMPUTABILITY; and TURING MACHINE.

Markov algorithms have been proposed for the purpose of making the concept of an algorithm precise. They are due to the Russian mathematician A. A. Márkov (1903–1980). A concise description of Markov algorithms can be found in Hermes (1965), who refers to them as *normal algorithms*.

A normal algorithm operates on strings of symbols (words) over an alphabet, A. Its way of operation is described by a finite sequence of *substitution formulas:*

$$W_1 \rightarrow (.) \, W_1'$$
$$W_2 \rightarrow (.) \, W_2'$$
$$.$$
$$.$$
$$.$$
$$W_m \rightarrow (.) \, W_m'$$

W_i and W_i' are themselves words over A and the parentheses around the dots mean that there may or may not be a dot in the substitution formula. (An example is given below.)

For every word U over A, the normal algorithm defines a possibly terminating sequence of words $U = U_0, U_1, U_2, \ldots$. U_k is a terminal word, if it has been obtained by the use of a substitution rule with a dot in it, or if it does not contain any of the W_i as a subword. Otherwise, U_{k+1} is defined by replacing in U_k the first occurrence of the subword W_i by W_i', where i is chosen as the smallest integer such that W_i is a subword of U_k.

Let f be a function whose domain and range are subsets of the set of nonnegative integers. Let us say that f is *Markov computable* if and only if there exists a normal algorithm that contains 0,1 and $ in its alphabet A, and which is such that, for any nonnegative interger n, if U_0 is the binary representation of n followed by $, then:

1. If n is in the domain of f, then the sequence U_0, U_1 ... terminates in some U_k, and U_k is the binary representation of $f(n)$,

2. If n is not in the domain of f, the sequence U_0, U_1, ... does not terminate.

For example, let $A = \{0, 1, \$\}$, and let the substitution formulas be

$$0\$ \rightarrow .1$$
$$1\$ \rightarrow \$0$$
$$\$ \rightarrow .1$$

This normal algorithm computes the successor function $s(n) = n + 1$. Two typical computations are

101$, 10$0, 110
111$, 11$0, 1$00, $000, 1000

A similar definition can be given to define when the function f is *Turing computable,* using a Turing machine instead of a normal algorithm. It can then be proved that a function f is Markov-computable if and only if it is Turing-computable. The equivalence of such precise replacements of the intuitive notion of a computable function is one of the strongest arguments in favor of Church's thesis, discussed in the article ALGORITHMS, THEORY OF.

REFERENCES

1962. Markov, A. A. *The Theory of Algorithms.* U.S. Dept. of Commerce. (English trans.)
1965. Hermes, H. *Enumerability, Decidability, Computability.* Berlin: Springer-Verlag.

G. T. HERMAN

MASKING

For articles on related subjects *see* INTERRUPT; MACHINE INSTRUCTION SET; and SHIFTING.

The information items required by a computer program may be of lengths that are not matched to the usually fixed length of the storage unit in the computer memory. Therefore, either an item may require several storage units or several items may be packed into one unit. In the latter case, a mechanism is necessary in order to get to the information item that is needed, without interference from other items that are stored in the same memory unit. *Masking* is the procedure that enables one to "open a window" on the desired information while suppressing or masking out the undesired information.

The basis of the masking operation is the boolean operation AND, which, for two variables D and M, is defined as follows.

D	M	D AND M
0	0	0
0	1	0
1	0	0
1	1	1

From the truth table, we see that

when $M = 1$, D AND $M = D$
when $M = 0$, D AND $M = 0$.

The variable M, therefore, functions as a mask. Whenever its value is 1, the result of the AND operation is to duplicate the value of D, whereas if $M = 0$, the value of D is 'masked out."

As an example, let us assume that in an eight-bit byte we would like to gain access to the middle four bits. The necessary mask is 00111100. The AND operation of this mask with the data byte produces a result in which the first two and last two bits are masked out. This result can then be aligned to the byte boundary (or any other boundary) with the aid of shift operations.

There are other masking operations concerned with control information. Various control items can be grouped; those that are required can then be chosen by masking all nonrequired items with a zero mask. For example, a user of an IBM 370 system may choose one of four possible condition codes by structuring a mask of four bits, with values of one and zero corresponding to the selection or masking of the appropriate condition. The same type of masking is used in order to mask out undesired interrupt conditions, control bits, etc. One has to note that in these cases, as opposed to data masking, one cannot use shift operations because the information to be masked is not data in the usual sense.

G. FRIEDER

MASS STORAGE. *See* MEMORY: Auxiliary; and STORAGE HIERARCHY

MATHEMATICAL PROGRAMMING

For articles on related subjects *see* NUMERICAL ANALYSIS; OPTIMIZATION METHODS; OPERATIONS RESEARCH; and SIMPLEX METHOD.

This article provides an overview of mathematical programming—its scope, its methods, and the associated computer feasibility and efficacy of the methods. Mathematical programming as discussed here has nothing inherently to do with computer programming. Although mathematical programming is usually done by computer, this term refers to mathematical *optimization,* with or without constraints. A mathematical programming problem can be written without loss of generality as

Maximize: $c(x_1, \ldots, x_n)$,   (1)
Subject to: $a_i(x_1, \ldots, x_n) \leq 0$ $(i = 1, \ldots, m)$

In the formulation (1), $x_1, \ldots, x_n$ are real decision variables for which values are desired which will maximize the objective function $c(x_1, \ldots, x_n)$, subject to the m constraints $a_i(x_1, \ldots, x_n) \leq 0$. There may be further restrictions requiring that the values of x_j $(j = 1, \ldots, n)$ are a proper subset of those values that satisfy the constraints. For example, all or some of the variables may be required to be integers.

With some imagination one can see that almost any well-defined deterministic optimization problem (a problem in which all numbers in the functions of expression (1) are known constants) can be formulated as a mathematical programming problem. Many nondeterministic problems (those in which some numbers in the functions of expression (1) are probabilistic, i.e., are random) can be formulated in this manner as well. Solving mathematical programming problems in general is quite another matter. Although certain classes of problems are relatively inexpensive to solve computationally, others are very expensive.

Methods of mathematical programming may be divided into three groups: linear programming, integer linear programming, and nonlinear programming. Linear programming methods solve the problem for which the functions $c(x_1, \ldots, x_n)$ and $a_i(x_1, \ldots, x_n)$ are linear and the x_j may take on any values that satisfy the constraints. Linear programming problems are relatively easy to solve, and computers have great capability for solving such problems. Integer linear programming problems are those in which some or all variables must be integers. Nonlinear programming is literally everything else in mathematical programming. As might be expected, because of the availability of computer programs to solve large linear programming problems efficiently, there has been a great incentive to find nonlinear programming problems that are in some manner similar or reducible to linear programming problems so that linear programming methods can be used to solve (or approximately solve) them. In addition, special methods have been developed to solve certain nonlinear programming problems not similar to linear programming problems.

This article discusses linear and nonlinear programming problems and methods for their solution. Also discussed are some useful necessary conditions for an optimal solution to a nonlinear programming problem which are also sufficient under restrictive circumstances. Finally, integer programming problems and methods are discussed, and some comments on computational feasibility are presented.

Linear Programming Problems.

Linear programming is used to solve problems of resource allocation in which the employment of a resource in different activities has proportionately constant returns. This means that, for example, if four units of a resource can be employed to produce one unit of a product, then eight units of the resource can be used to produce two units of the product. Similarly, each unit of a product produced contributes the same amount to cover profits and overhead.

The general linear programming problem may be written as follows (minimization problems may be solved by maximizing the negative of a function, and variables unrestricted in sign may also be incorporated):

$$\text{Maximize: } c_1 x_1 + \cdots + c_n x_n,$$
$$\text{Subject to: } a_{i1} x_1 + \cdots + a_{in} x_n + x_{n+i} = b_i \quad (2)$$
$$i = 1, \cdots, m$$
$$x_1, \cdots, x_{n+m} \geq 0.$$

The a_{ij}, c_j, and b_i are constants. By reference to the set of constraints, it can be seen that the solution set is underdefined. Choosing any n variables (subject to consistency limitations) to be set to some particular values, the remaining m variables are uniquely determined. Further, if a problem has an optimal solution, it can be shown that some *basic solution* (obtained by setting n variables to zero so that the remaining set of equations has a unique solution) is optimal. A naive way to solve linear programming problems would be to try to enumerate all basic solutions and choose the one that is optimal.

A more practical way to solve linear programming problems is to begin with a basic solution that is feasible and then proceed to find a sequence of basic feasible solutions in which each member of the sequence has one variable of a nonzero value different (and therefore one different variable with a zero value) from its predecessor solution. By further assuring that the value of the objective function is non-decreasing, and that no basic solution can be repeated, an optimal solution is attained. This is the essence of the methods currently used to solve linear programming problems.

Applications. Linear programming has been used for a number of years by business, government, and industry to solve certain resource allocation problems. Some examples of applications include the following:

1. *Blending problems* in which a lowest-cost blend is desired to satisfy certain requirements subject to material availability, etc. The blending of animal feeds, peanut butter, gasoline, and specification of foods in hospital diets are examples of blending problems that have been solved using linear programming.

2. *Product-mix problems* in which the maximal-profit mix of products is desired consistent with facility and material limitations, sales commitments to customers, and sales potential of products. Product-mix problems in the aluminum, manufacturing, oil, and steel industries (among others) have been solved by linear programming.

3. *Distribution problems* in which least-cost procedures are desired for distributing products from plants or warehouses to customers.

4. *Dynamic production planning* over a time projection.

Linear programming has also been used to help make advertising and investment decisions, and it has been used in numerous other ways such as in education planning. For a comprehensive, reasonably up-to-date bibliography of linear programming applications, see Gass (1975).

Example of a Linear Programming Problem. We will now develop an example of a linear programming problem that will also illustrate related concepts.

A small shop has two machines used to make two-products. Both machines are each operated 12 hours each day. Product 1 requires 2 hr on machine A and 1 hr on machine B, and produces a net profit (above the costs of materials) of $15. Product 2 requires 0.25 hr on machine A and 0.5 hr on machine B, and produces a profit of $10. The proprietor of the shop wants to maximize total profits. Assume that raw materials are abundantly available, and that all production will be saleable. To formulate the problem, let x_1 and x_2 be the number of units of product 1 and product 2 produced on a given day, respectively. The number of hours of machine A time required for production of product 1 is

$$\frac{2 \text{ hr}}{\text{unit}} (x_1 \text{ units}) = 2x_1 \text{ hr}$$

and the number of hours of machine A time required for production of product 2 is

$$\frac{0.25 \text{ hr}}{\text{unit}} (x_2 \text{ units}) = 0.25x_2 \text{ hr}.$$

The total amount of machine A time required for x_1 units of product 1 and x_2 units of product 2 is, then

$$2x_1 + 0.25x_2.$$

Incorporating the 12-hr limitation per day on machine A, we then have

$$2x_1 + 0.25x_2 \leq 12. \qquad (3)$$

where $\leq$ means "is less than or equal to," or "must not exceed."

Similarly, we have that $x_1 + 0.5x_2$ hr of machine B time are required to produce x_1 units of product 1 and x_2 units of product 2. Incorporating the 12-hr daily availability of machine B, we then have

$$x_1 + 0.5x_2 \leq 12. \qquad (4)$$

Since the number of units of a product to be produced must be nonnegative, we have further that

$$x_1, x_2 \geq 0 \qquad (5)$$

Total net profits (or, more properly, contributions to overhead and profits) may be expressed as $15x_1 + 10x_2$, whose value we wish to maximize. Writing the objective function and constraints together, we have

$$\begin{aligned} \text{Maximize:} \quad & 15x_1 + 10x_2 \\ \text{Subject to:} \quad & 2x_1 + 0.25x_2 \leq 12 \\ & x_1 + 0.5x_2 \leq 12 \\ & x_1, x_2 \geq 0. \end{aligned} \qquad (6)$$

The problem may be solved graphically by plotting x_1 and x_2 as coordinates and graphing the constraints. A graph for the example is given in Fig. 1, in which the shaded area represents the set of feasible solutions to the problem. The dashed lines of the form $15x_1 + 10x_2 = K$, are lines of constant profit K. We desire the line having the greatest value of K which intersects the shaded area. As can be seen, $K = 240$ is the maximum value of profits for which the associated line of constant profit intersects the solution set. Accordingly, that is the optimal value of profits obtainable, and the solution is the intersection of the line with the constraint set. That intersection is usually, but not always, a unique point. For this example, it is a unique solution: $x_1 = 0$, $x_2 = 24$.

Problems having more than two variables cannot be solved graphically. A method for solving such problems (which was roughly outlined above) in general is called the *simplex method*. [For more information on the simplex method and its variants see, e.g., Gass (1975) or Zionts (1974).] This method is quite efficient, and computer programs capable of solving problems having thousands of constraints, with virtually no limit on the number of variables, are available for many computer systems.

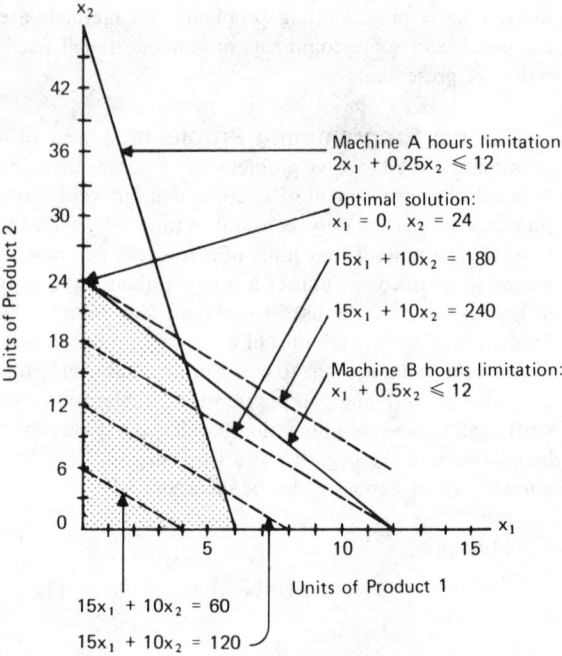

Fig. 1. Graphical representation of example.

Duality. Closely associated with the preceding problem is another linear programming problem called the *dual* problem. This is a pricing problem, as opposed to a resource allocation problem, and has both practical and theoretical importance.

Example of a Dual Problem. Suppose the owner of the machine shop has been approached by an individual who would like to rent the facilities of the shop for one day. The assets of the shop consist of hours on machine A and hours on machine B. Designating the rental rate for each kind of hour as y_A and y_B, respectively, the owner will receive a daily rental of $12y_A + 12y_B$. However, if the *owner* were to use the shop to produce one unit each of products 1 and 2, a profit of 15 and 10, respectively, would be made. Hence, whatever rental price is decided on, the owner would not be willing to rent the machines unless

$$2y_A + y_B \geq 15 \qquad (7)$$
$$0.25y_A + 0.5y_B \geq 10 \qquad (8)$$
$$y_A, y_B \geq 0.$$

That is, unless the rental income is at least as much as the production income. For (7), recall that product 1 requires 2 hr on machine A and 1 hr on machine B; for (8), apply a similar argument for product 2. The *renter* wants to know the lowest prices that can be expected. Thus, all together we have the following linear programming problem.

$$\text{Minimize:} \quad 12y_A + 12y_B$$
$$\text{Subject to:} \quad 2y_A + y_B \geq 15 \qquad (9)$$
$$0.25y_A + 0.5y_B \geq 10$$
$$y_A, y_B \geq 0.$$

The solution to (9) which may be found graphically is $y_A = 0$, $y_B = 20$, with a total rental of \$240. It should not be surprising that the minimum acceptable rental is the same as the maximum level of profits that can be achieved. The owner should accept any offer of more than \$240 rental per day, reject any offer of less than \$240 per day and be indifferent to an offer of \$240. (The reader may wonder why someone would be willing to pay a rental of more than \$240 per day. Such a person might have other options that the owner does not have available.)

Individual rental rates are of interest, too. Those rates (sometimes called shadow prices or dual variables) are the values of a unit of each resource. Recall that in the optimal solution to the owner's problem, only 6 machine A hr were used $(2(0) + 0.25(24) = 6)$ and all 12 machine B hr were used $(1(0) + 0.5(24) = 12)$. The dual variables, $y_A = 0$, $y_B = 20$ reflect the fact that the owner's profit will decrease by \$20 if 1 hr of machine B time is lost. Similarly, the owner's profit may increase as the amount of available resources increases. The dual variables will vary in general as a function of the number of units of resource lost or added. Dual variables give valuable measures by which to gauge the cost of resources. Fortunately, the solution of the dual problem is obtained as a by-product of solving the resource allocation problem.

The dual theorem of linear programming sums up the relationship between the two problems in a formal manner.

The Dual Theorem of Linear Programming. Given two linear programming problems:

$$\text{Maximize:} \quad c_1x_1 + \ldots + c_nx_n$$
$$\text{Subject to:} \quad a_{11}x_1 + \ldots + a_{1n}x_n \leq b_1$$
$$\cdot \qquad \cdot \qquad \cdot \qquad \cdot$$
$$\cdot \qquad \cdot \qquad \cdot \qquad \cdot$$
$$\cdot \qquad \cdot \qquad \cdot \qquad \cdot$$
$$a_{m1}x_1 + \ldots + a_{mn}x_n \leq b_m$$
$$x_1, \ldots, x_n \geq 0$$

and

$$\text{Minimize:} \quad b_1y_1 + \ldots + b_my_m$$
$$\text{Subject to:} \quad a_{11}y_1 + \ldots + a_{m1}y_m \geq c_1$$
$$\cdot \qquad \cdot \qquad \cdot \qquad \cdot$$
$$\cdot \qquad \cdot \qquad \cdot \qquad \cdot$$
$$\cdot \qquad \cdot \qquad \cdot \qquad \cdot$$
$$a_{1n}y_1 + \ldots + a_{mn}y_m \geq c_n$$
$$y_1, \ldots, y_m < 0.$$

1. If one problem has an optimal solution, then so does the other, and the objective function values of the solutions to the two problems are identical.
2. If one problem has an infinite optimal solution (i.e., the constraint set is not bounded and the optimal solution is infinite), then the other problem does not have any feasible solutions.

As a corollary to the dual theorem, there are the complementary slackness conditions, which we now state informally and give examples of from our problem. (The word "resource" is used in a general sense; every constraint is assumed to limit a resource. Similarly, the word "product" is used in a general sense; every variable is assumed to be a product.)

1. If the value of a resource (as measured by its dual variable) is positive, it should all be used ($y_B = 20$ implies that machine B has no idle hours: $x_1 + 0.5x_2 = 12$).
2. If a resource is not all used, its value is zero. (That machine A is not fully utilized or that $2x_1 + 0.26x_2 < 12$ in the optimal solution implies that $y_A = 0$.)
3. If the value of resources required to produce a unit of product exceeds the profit of producing that product, the product will not be produced. (For product 1, $2y_A + y_B > 15$ implies that $x_1 = 0$.)
4. If a product is produced, the value of the resources used to produce the product exactly equals the profit associated with producing the product. (That product 2 is produced, or $x_2 > 0$, implies that $0.25y_A + 0.5y_B = 10$.)

Nonlinear Programming Problems. A mathematical programming problem of the form

$$\text{Maximize:} \quad c(x_1, x_2, \ldots, x_n)$$
$$\text{Subject to:} \quad X \equiv (x_1, x_2, \ldots, x_n) \text{ in } S, \qquad (10)$$

which is not a linear or integer programming problem, is classified as a nonlinear programming (NLP) problem.

If the function, c, in (10) is concave and the set S is closed, bounded, and convex, then an optimal solution occurs either at the global maximum of c or a boundary point of S. A function, c, is concave if for all $X \equiv (x_1, x_2, \ldots, x_n)$ and $Y \equiv (y_1, y_2, \ldots, y_n)$ and $0 < \lambda < 1$,

$$c(\lambda(x_1, x_2, \ldots, x_n) + (1 - \lambda)(y_1, y_2, \ldots, y_n))$$
$$\geq \lambda c(x_1, x_2, \ldots, x_n)$$
$$+ (1 - \lambda) c(y_1, y_2, \ldots, y_n).$$

Intuitively, if the function is concave, then if a line is "stretched" between any two points on the function's surface, that line will be at or below the surface.

A set, S, is called convex if for any X and Y in S, the point $\lambda(x_1, x_2, \ldots, x_n) + (1 - \lambda)(y_1, y_2, \ldots, y_n)$ is also in S. If either c is not concave or S is not convex (or both), then an optimal solution could occur anywhere within S.

Methods for solving NLP problems exist, but many methods apply only to certain subsets of problems because they assume certain conditions about c or S (e.g., concavity or convexity). The problem of solving a general NLP problem can be compared to the problem faced by a person trying to walk to the highest point in the State of New York on a foggy day. From any point, the person can only see a short distance in any direction and hence never knows for sure if the "hill" on which he or she is standing is the highest hill.

Most algorithms used for solving general NLP problems involve some sort of neighborhood search method analogous to the method of the hiker in New York. There are four problems that such a method must overcome:

1. How can a local optimum be identified?
2. Which direction from a given point leads to an improvement in the function value?
3. If several directions improve the function, which is the "best" direction?
4. How far can the searcher move in the improving direction and still remain within S?

In the case of an NLP problem of form (1) in which the functions $c, a_1, a_2, \ldots, a_m$ are differentiable, an important theoretical result known as the Karush-Kuhn-Tucker conditions provides necessary conditions for a point to be a local optimum. The Karush-Kuhn-Tucker conditions characterize local optimality by use of the gradient vectors of c and a_i. The gradient vector, c, is the vector of partial derivatives of c, $\nabla c = (\partial c / \delta x_1, \partial c / \partial x_2, \ldots, \partial c / \partial x_n)$. This vector also provides an analytic tool for determining which way is "up." If a point X is a local optimum, then it must satisfy the following *Karush-Kuhn-Tucker conditions*.

1. X must be in S.
2. There exist $y_i \geq 0$ such that

$$\partial c / \partial x_j = \sum_{i=1}^{m} y_i (\partial a_i / \partial x_j) \quad j = 1, 2, \ldots, n.$$

3. $y_i a_i(X) = 0$.
4. The Karush-Kuhn-Tucker constraint qualification holds at X.

Condition 4, whose precise statement is beyond our scope here, is a condition which ensures that the feasible region is "well behaved" at the point. The Karush-Kuhn-Tucker conditions are the basis for determining local optimality in NLP algorithms.

The gradient, ∇c, indicates the direction of increase of c. The method of "steepest ascent (descent)" is an algorithm which begins at a point X_0 in S, and moves through S in "small" steps by computing

$$X_i = X_{i-1} + \alpha \nabla c(X_{i-1})$$

where $\alpha > 0$ is a (usually small) real constant which determines the size of the movement. Under certain conditions, this procedure converges to a local optimum and the rate of convergence can be computed. The problem with this approach is that the sequence of points generated by such a method may lead to points not in S. Two methods, known as penalty and barrier methods attempt to overcome this problem.

A penalty function, $P(X)$, has the property,

$$P(X) < 0 \text{ if } X \text{ is not in } S$$
$$P(X) = 0 \text{ if } X \text{ is in } S.$$

Thus, the constrained optimization problem (10) can be converted to the unconstrained optimization problem,

$$\text{Maximize: } c(X) + \theta P(X). \tag{11}$$

If θ is very large, then the maximum must occur at a point X for which $P(X) = 0$. Therefore, by solving (11) for successively larger values of θ, a solution to (10) can sometimes be obtained.

A barrier function, $B(X)$, has the property,

$$B(X) \geq 0 \quad \text{for all } X$$
$$B(X) \to \infty \text{ as } X \text{ approaches the boundary of }$$
$$S \text{ from a feasible point.}$$

For example, if S is defined by the m constraints,

$$g_i(X) \geq 0 \quad i = 1, 2, \ldots, m.$$

Then,

$$B(X) = \sum_{i=1}^{m} [g_i(X)]^{-1}$$

is a barrier function, since it becomes infinite as the boundary $g_i(X) = 0$ is approached.

A constrained optimization problem can be converted to the unconstrained problem,

$$\text{Maximize: } c(X) - \theta B(X),$$

if a barrier function can be found.

Integer Linear Programming. Solving linear programming problems with the stipulation that some or all variables be integer-valued might seem to be a rather useless activity, particularly if we are concerned with determining the optimal number of four-door sedans General Motors should produce next year. It would appear that rounding a solution value such as 102,376.35 to a nearby integer value would make a neglibile difference in the objective function value. On the other hand, if a variable represented the number of new bridges to be built across the Niagara River between the U.S. and Canada, and the optimal linear program solution value were 0.53, rounding to 0 or 1 would indeed make a great deal of difference in the objective function value.

We may infer from the above that, generally, large integer variables may be rounded arbitrarily, whereas small integer variables may not; this seems most reasonable. In addition, the use of integer variables may be made to assure that certain logical conditions are fulfilled [e.g., of two alternatives (x_1 and x_2) exactly one must be selected: $x_1 + x_2 = 1$, where $x_1, x_2 \geq 0$ and integer], or that certain peculiar nonlinear functions are involved which do not correspond to maximizing a concave function over a convex set. [The solution set of an arbitrary constraint set of a mathematical programming problem (1) is convex when all $a_i(x_1, \ldots x_n)$ are convex; e.g., linear constraint sets are convex.] See Salkin (1975) or Zionts (1974) for further information.

Thus, there are many applications for integer variables in addition to the obvious one that the number of units to be produced is to be integer. Integer programming methods have been successfully utilized to solve problems of airline-crew scheduling, capital budgeting, and bank-check clearing for large companies, as well as other problems.

We briefly describe integer programming methods and indicate which methods tend to be successful in practice. For our discussion we categorize the methods into four types:

1. Cut methods.
2. Group theoretic methods.
3. Branch-and-bound methods.
4. Implicit enumeration methods.

Further, we will refer to the problem as an all-integer problem if all variables are required to be integer, and as mixed integer if only some of the variables are required to be integer.

Cut Methods. Cut methods, which were among the first methods developed, employ cut constraints derived from the original problem. Cut constaints have the desirable property that they exclude or cut off parts of the feasible solution space without cutting off any integer solution points. Some cut methods first require the solution of the linear programming problem before cut constraints are added; others do not. If the linear programming optimal solution should happen to have the required variables integer, it is optimal. Otherwise, a cut constraint is added and a new optimal solution to the augmented problem is found. The procedure is continued until an integer solution is obtained. Other cut methods do not first solve the linear programming problem; instead they generate and utilize a cut constraint at every step of the solution process. There are cut methods for both all-integer and mixed-integer problems.

Currently, cut methods are not used much in practice; some experimentation on using cut methods in conjunction with other methods has been undertaken.

Group Theoretic Methods. Group theoretic methods can be used only for problems in which all variables are required to be integers. The method begins by solving the linear programming problem. Assuming that the solution is not integer, the method then systematically constructs an integer solution to the problem by increasing to positive integer values certain variables that were set equal to zero in the optimal linear programming solution. Quite often, the constructed solution will be the optimal solution to the integer programming problem; where it is not, additional construction is required to generate the integer optimum. The method is based on mathematical group theory and works reasonably well on some problems. Although there is little available data on the efficiency of the methods, commercial computer codes using the technique are in use.

Branch-and-Bound Methods. Branch-and-bound methods are generally the most successful for solving integer programming problems—both for all integer and mixed integer. We outline one of a number of variations of the branch-and-bound procedure.

First solve the linear programming problem. If the solution does not satisfy the integer requirements, choose a variable in the solution which should be integer, but which is not. Supposing that the variable chosen has a solution value of 3.4, two new linear programs are solved, one stating that the variable must not exceed 3, and the other stating that the variable must be at least 4. Then the two problems and their solutions are stored in a list. The following procedure is then used.

Pick the best solution from the list; if it is integer, it is optimal. Otherwise, as above, choose a variable in that solution which is not integer, but should be, and solve two linear programming problems, storing the resulting solutions in the list. Then the best solution on the list is chosen, a variable is branched upon, and so on. The method is particularly successful because feasible integer solutions are usually found early in the solution process. Once such a solution has been found, the solution can be terminated at any time, as is often done in practice. A bound on how far the solution can be from optimal is known; it is the difference between the objective function value of the best-known integer solution and the objective function value of the best noninteger solution on the list. In addition, the cost of altering and resolving the problem is usually quite low.

Implicit Enumeration Methods. Implicit enumeration methods are methods for solving all-integer problems. Most of the successfully implemented variations also require that all integer variables be zero or one, but more general methods have been developed. The idea of the method is straightforward: if there are n variables there are 2^n possible solutions to enumerate; explicit enumeration would require explicit consideration of each of them. By using tests that follow conceptually from using implied upper and lower bounds on variables, generally only a tiny fraction of all possibilities need to be considered with the implicit treatment of all possibilities. Some auxiliary techniques used to accelerate implicit enumeration have been derived from linear programming.

Example. To briefly illustrate the methods consider the following problem.

$$\text{Maximize:} \quad z = 1.1x_1 + x_2$$
$$\text{Subject to:} \quad 2x_1 + 3x_2 \leq 14$$
$$3x_1 + 2x_2 \leq 14$$
$$x_1, x_2 \geq 0 \text{ and integer.}$$

The optimal solution, ignoring the requirement that x_1 and x_2 be integer, is $x_1 = x_2 = 14/5, z = 5.88$. (Note that rounding in this case yields a solution that violates both constraints.) Using one of the cut methods, a cut constraint $3x_1 + 3x_2 \leq 16$ is added to the original problem and the problem is resolved, yielding the solution

$$x_1 = {}^{10}\!/\!_3, \ x_2 = 2, \ z = 5\%.$$

Because this solution is not integer, a new cut constraint $x_1 + x_2 \leq 5$ is added, yielding the optimal integer solution $x_1 = 4, x_2 = 1, z = 5.4$.

Using branch-and-bound, the linear programming problem is solved, and then variations of the problem are solved. The sequence of solutions for the example is given in Fig. 2.

Implicit enumeration requires that all variables be zero or one. Such a transformation can be accomplished by substituting $x_1 = w_1 + 2w_2 + 4w_3$ and $x_2 = v_1 + 2v_2 + 4v_3$, where each w_j and v_j is either zero or one. For this problem there are 64 possible solutions: only five need be examined to determine and confirm the optimal solution.

Putting the Computational Considerations into Perspective. We conclude this article with a few comments about the current state of computational efficiency in mathematical programming. Very large linear programming problems (having thousands of constraints) may be solved, and have been solved, inexpensively, although it is certainly possible to dream up problems that are too large for solution. Fairly large nonlinear programming problems (including quadratic programming and separable programming) that employ methods based on linear programming methods may be solved at reasonable cost. Beyond that, linear constraints are much easier to handle than nonlinear constraints, and the size capabilities of the remaining methods are somewhat smaller. In integer programming, although some fairly large problems have been and are being solved on a routine basis, there are still many relatively small problems that are computationally difficult to solve.

In perspective, mathematical programming gives a potentially very powerful means for formulating and solving optimization problems. Numerous methods have been developed and implemented in many computer systems, and are becoming a viable means of solving all kinds of optimization problems.

REFERENCES

1969. Wagner, H. M. *Principles of Operations Research.* Englewood Cliffs, NJ: Prentice-Hall.
1970. Lasdon, L. S. *Optimization Theory for Large Systems.* New York: Macmillan.
1973. Luenberger, D. G. *Introduction to Linear and Nonlinear Programming.* Reading, MA: Addison-Wesley.
1974. Zionts, S. *Linear and Integer Programming.* Englewood Cliffs, NJ: Prentice-Hall.
1975. Gass, S. I. *Linear Programming,* 4th Ed. New York: McGraw-Hill.
1975. Salkin, H. M. *Integer Programming.* Reading, MA: Addison-Wesley.

S. ZIONTS and J. N. BARRER

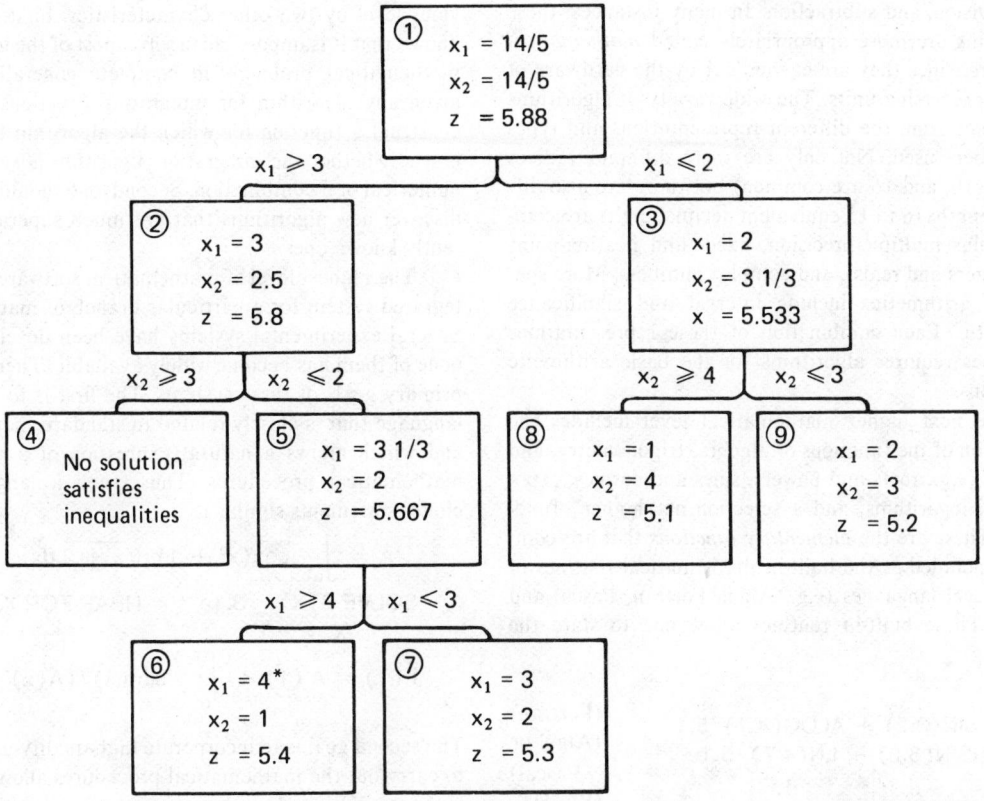

Fig. 2. Sequence of solutions to the example problem, using branch-and-bound augmentation of the original problem. Notes: An asterisk (*) indicates optimal solution; circled numbers in the blocks indicate the position in sequence in which the respective problem was solved; all constraints along the path from a problem to the first problem have been added to the original problem in solving that problem. For problem 6, $x_1 \geq 4$, $x_2 \leq 2$.

MATHEMATICAL SOFTWARE

For articles on related subjects *see* ALGEBRAIC MANIPULATION; ALGORITHM; APPROXIMATION THEORY; MATRIX COMPUTATIONS; NUMERICAL ANALYSIS; PROGRAM LIBRARIES, NUMERICAL AND STATISTICAL; and SYMBOL MANIPULATION.

Mathematical software is the set of computer *algorithms* in the area of mathematics. The exact scope of the term is slightly vague, but it is generally accepted to include algorithms whose primary interest or motivation is mathematical and not merely the application of mathematics. Thus, a computer program to solve a system of first-order differential equations is considered to be mathematical software. A program to solve a chemical reaction problem is not mathematical software, even though the essence of the program might be an algorithm for solving differential equations. The scope of the term is much broader than a pure mathematicians's view of mathematics; it includes some aspects of programming languages and computer systems. The scope is also much broader than traditional *numerical analysis,* for it includes such areas as statistics, symbolic mathematical analysis, and linear programming, which are clearly mathematical in nature.

The origins of mathematical software came with the advent of modern computers. A Mark I routine for sin (x) was published in 1944 and the first operational electronic computer (EDSAC) had a well thought-out subroutine library before 1950. Activity and interest in the area grew steadily, and by 1970 mathematical software began to be recognized as a separate subdiscipline of the mathematics-computer science area.

Mathematical software can be classified from several points of view, and one of the most natural is according to complexity or mathematical level. At the bottom are algorithms for arithmetic; i.e., addition, multiplication, division, and subtraction. In many instances, these algorithms are more appropriately called *mathematical hardware,* since they are carried out by the hardware of central processing units. The wide variety of algorithms here stems from the different representations and types of numbers used. Not only are there different radices (base 2, 10, and 16 are common) but there are also different lengths (6 to 15 equivalent decimal digits are common), plus multiple-precision, fixed- and floating-point (or integers and reals), and complex numbers. More specialized arithmetics include interval and significance arithmetic. Each combination of these representations and types requires algorithms for the basic arithmetic operations.

The next higher mathematical level includes the evaluation of the functions of algebra, trigonometry, and analysis (e.g., roots and powers, sines and cosines, exponentials, logarithms, and a selection of "higher" functions). These are the *elementary functions* that are commonly included as the built-in mathematical routines of higher-level languages (e.g., Algol, Fortran, Pascal and PL/I). These built-in routines allow one to state the following.

$$X = SIN(3.2) + ALOG(4.7)/5.1 \quad \text{(Fortran)}$$
$$X := SIN(3.2) + LN(4.7)/5.1 \quad \text{(Algol or Pascal)}$$
$$X = SIN(3.2) + LOG(4.7)/5.1 \quad \text{(PL/I)}$$

1571

The following algorithm illustrates how an efficient evaluation is made for the sine function SIN(X).

> **Set** $Y = X \bmod(2\pi)$
> **If** $Y > \pi$ **then set** $Y = Y - \pi$, SIGN $= -1$
>   **else set** SIGN $= 1$
> **If** $Y > \dfrac{\pi}{2}$ **then set** $Y = \pi - Y$
> **Set** $Z = Y/3$
> **Compute** SIN(Z) using a cubic polynomial
>   accurate to 10 decimal places
> **Set** SIN(X) = SIGN * SIN(Z) * (3-4 SIN^2(Z))

One may obtain 20-decimal-digit accuracy by replacing the cubic polynomial by an appropriate sixth-degree polynomial. The state-of-the-art for this software is such that high-quality programs are tailored to exploit the specific characteristics of each computer's arithmetic unit.

The next level of mathematical software includes the algorithms of linear algebra (e.g., solving linear systems of equations) and the operations of calculus and advanced calculus (e.g., integration, differentiation, and solving nonlinear equations). These mathematical problems are of an order of magnitude more difficult than those discussed above. This software is distinguished from the pre-

vious level by two other characteristics. First, it is well known that it is impossible to solve most of the underlying mathematical problems in complete generality. Thus, given any algorithm for integrating functions, one can construct a function for which the algorithm fails. This is true whether the integration algorithm is symbolic or numerical or a combination. Second, one should expect to discover new algorithms that are much superior to currently known ones.

The highest level of mathematical software is the integrated system for a particular branch of mathematics. Several experimental systems have been developed, but none of them has become widely available. There are two primary goals of these systems. The first is to provide a language that is closely related to standard mathematics and which allows a natural expression of a variety of mathematical procedures. Thus, such a language includes statements similar to

$$A = \int_0^{1.5} \cos(x^2 + 1)\sqrt{x + 2}\, dx$$
$$\text{SOLVE } B*X^2 - 3.1e^{-x} = \text{HBAR FOR X, GUESS}$$
$$X = 2.0$$
$$F(T) = A'(T) + \int_0^{T+1} \sin(x)/(A(x) + 1)dx$$

The second goal is to incorporate high-quality algorithms to carry out the mathematical procedures allowed in the language. These algorithms are integrated with one another and the overall system so that results of one are automatically compatible with any algorithms to be applied later to these results. The development of such systems involves a broad range of mathematics and computer science (e.g., symbolic manipulation, numerical analysis, programming language design, compilers, and operating systems).

Mathematical software can also be divided into two classes, according to whether the program is "static" or "deterministic," or whether it is "dynamic" or "heuristic." This division is not precise, but it serves a useful intuitive purpose. An algorithm is said to be *static* if its operation is known in advance. Examples of static algorithms are those of arithmetic, symbolic differentiation, Simpson's rule for quadrature, and the evaluation of sin(x). The ambiguity of this classification arises from the word "know," and the division depends upon how much one knows. An algorithm is *dynamic* or heuristic if its operation is somewhat unpredictable in advance.

Unpredictability normally comes from logical decisions that are made on the basis of quantities computed during the operation of the algorithm. An example of such software is a *polyalgorithm*, which is a set of static algorithms plus a strategy for choosing and switching among them. Polyalgorithms were first introduced in attempts to automate numerical analysis. Only a small portion of current mathematical software is dynamic, but this is an area with great potential significance and growth.

Another common division of mathematical software is between *symbolic* and *numerical algorithms.* This division is easily seen in simple cases. Integer addition and symbolic differentiation of polynomials are symbolic; the exact results are obtained after a finite number of symbolic operations. Newton's method for polynomial zeros and Simpson's rule for integration are numerical. Approximate results are obtained, but they can be made as accurate as one pleases with sufficient effort and precision in the arithmetic. The algorithms of arithmetic are symbolic, but—unfortunately and unavoidably—they are incorrect due to the fixed precision of arithmetic. This incorrectness introduces ambiguity in the distinction between symbolic and numerical algorithms.

For example, many of the algorithms of linear algebra are symbolic (e.g., Gauss elimination for solving linear equations), but are considered to be part of numerical analysis. This is perhaps because one of the most important questions is the effect that incorrect arithmetic has upon these algorithms. On the other hand, polynomial manipulation is considered to be symbolic, and yet some programs for this take $(2X + 3) + (1/2)*(3X - 4)$ to be $3.5X + 1$, and thus are also subject to incorrectness due to the arithmetic. The depth and difficulty of understanding this distinction, is much greater than one might conjecture. For example, there is a well known formula to express the roots X_0 and X_1 of $ax^2 + bx + c = 0$ in terms of a, b, and c. However, given that a, b, c, X_0 and X_1 are representable in a particular computer, as yet there is no known program to produce X_0 and X_1 from a, b, and c, which will always be correct (for this computer).

Mathematical software is still an emerging subdiscipline, and it contains three general problems and areas of great importance. One of these is the *dissemination of software,* and while it may be a somewhat mundane problem, it is also a very difficult one. The objective is simple: Make the best and most effective software available to *everyone* in a natural, efficient, and automatic manner. Materials that fall into this area include *computer center libraries, textbooks, published algorithms, user group libraries,* and *computer manufacturer's libraries.* All these materials are prone to weaknesses in documentation, effectiveness, efficiency, ease-of-use, and ease-of-access.

A second problem area of great theoretical and practical interest is the evaluation of algorithms. The problems here range from the foundations of mathematics to experimental investigations. Symbolic algorithms have been studied from the point of view of pure mathematics, and a variety of proof techniques of a very rigorous nature have been used. Complex and/or numerical algorithms are much less tractable for rigorous and mathematical proofs, and new techniques (both mathematical and experimental) are needed.

Finally, we come to the *resource allocation* aspect of mathematical software. A simple example of this is the trade-off between computation time and memory used. There are frequent instances in which significantly faster execution results by using significantly larger amounts of memory. The advent of sophisticated multiprogramming systems and hierarchies of memories has introduced another dimension to the creation and evaluation of mathematical software.

High quality collections, libraries, and packages of mathematical software have appeared in recent years. These include two commercial libraries of algorithms and several systematized collections—the BLAS (Basic Linear Algebra Subroutines), EISPACK (56 routines for matrix eigensystems), FUNPACK (covers a number of the more difficult, higher transcendental functions), and LINPACK (linear systems of equations). All these collections are available (for a modest small handling fee) from IMSL, Inc. GNB Building, 7500 Bellaire Blvd., Houston, TX 77036. The Association for Computing Machinery Transactions on Mathematical Software regularly publishes mathematical software; over 500 algorithms have appeared and those published since 1975 are available in machine readable form from the ACM Algorithms Distribution Service at 11 West 42 Street, New York, NY 10036. Other packages are under construction.

REFERENCES

1968. Klerer, M. and Reinfelds, J. *Interactive Systems for Experimental Applied Mathematics.* New York: Academic Press.
1971. Rice, J. *Mathematical Software.* New York: Academic Press.
1979. Rice, J. "Software for Numerical Computation," Chapter 16 in Wegner, P. (Ed.), *Research Directions in Software Technology.* Cambridge, MA: M.I.T. Press, pp. 688–708.

J. R. RICE

MATRIX COMPUTATIONS

For articles on related subjects *see* ERROR ANALYSIS; MATHEMATICAL SOFTWARE; NUMERICAL ANALYSIS; and SCIENTIFIC APPLICATIONS.

A large proportion of the scientific calculations performed on computers involves matrices. Partly, this is because of the ubiquity of matrices in the mathematics of scientific problems, but it is also partly due to the fact that the use of matrices is ideally suited to the iterative type of calculation in which computers realize their full power.

Notation and Definitions.

From the point of view of this article, a matrix is defined to be a rectangular array of elements, each of which will generally be a real or complex number. An $m \times n$ matrix will be denoted by a capital Roman letter, and the elements of such a matrix A will be denoted by a_{ij}, $i = 1, \ldots, m$, $j = 1, \ldots, n$. If $n = 1$, the matrix is called a *column vector* and a lower case Roman letter will be used. The elements of a vector x of order m are denoted by x_i ($i = 1, \ldots, m$). The *transpose B* of an $m \times n$ matrix A is an $n \times m$ matrix defined by $b_{ij} = a_{ji}$. It is commonly denoted by A^T or A'. Similarly, the $1 \times m$ transpose of a column vector is denoted by x^T, and is called a *row vector*. The *Hermitian transpose B* of an $m \times n$ matrix A is defined by $b_{ij} = \bar{a}_{ji}$, where the bar over $\bar{a}$ denotes the complex conjugate, and is commonly denoted by A^H or A^*; x^H is defined similarly.

If A and B are of the same dimension, their sum C is defined by $c_{ij} = a_{ij} + b_{ij}$. The product C of an $m \times k$ matrix A and a $k \times n$ matrix B is defined by

$$c_{ij} = \sum_{s=1}^{k} a_{is} b_{sj}.$$

The definition applies immediately to the product y of an $m \times n$ matrix A and an $n \times 1$ column vector x; we have

$$y_i = \sum_{s=1}^{n} a_{is} x_s.$$

Finally, the product C of a matrix A by a scalar α is defined by

$$c_{ij} = \alpha a_{ij}.$$

A matrix or vector is said to be *null* if all its components are zero. Either "null" or "zero" will be denoted by the same symbol used for the zero scalar, the context providing adequate identification.

The classes of square matrices defined below are of special interest in matrix computations.

> *Symmetric:* $A = A^T$ (i.e., $a_{ij} = a_{ji}$).
> *Positive definite:* A real, symmetric and $x^T A x > 0$ for all real $x \neq 0$.
> *Hermitian:* $A = A^H$ (i.e., $a_{ij} = \bar{a}_{ji}$).
> *Orthogonal:* A real and $AA^T = A^T A = I$.
> *Upper (lower) triangular:* $a_{ij} = 0$, $i > j$ ($i < j$).
> *Tridiagonal:* $a_{ij} = 0$, $|i - j| > 1$.
> *Upper-Hessenberg:* $a_{ij} = 0$, $i > j + 1$.

The *identity matrix* of order n is denoted by I_n, or by I if the order is obvious, and is defined by

$$i_{kk} = 1, \; i_{kl} = 0 \; (k \neq l).$$

The elements are usually denoted by δ_{kl} rather than by i_{kl}. From the definitions, $IA = A = AI$ whenever the dimensions are such that these exist.

It will be assumed that the reader is familiar with the concept of the scalar function of a square matrix A, known as its *determinant* and denoted by $\det(A)$. A square matrix A is said to be *singular* if $\det(A) = 0$; otherwise is is *nonsingular*. The matrix formed by the elements at the intersection of any collection of rows and columns is called a *submatrix*. The determinant of a square submatrix is called a *minor;* if the submatrix is formed from the intersection of the first r rows and columns, its determinant is called a *leading principal minor*. The *cofactor* A_{ij} of the element a_{ij} of an $n \times n$ square matrix A is defined by

$$A_{ij} = (-1)^{i+j} \det(\text{matrix formed by omitting row } i \\ \text{and column } j).$$

The $n \times n$ matrix X with $x_{ij} = A_{ji}$ is called the *adjoint* of A, and it follows from the elementary properties of determinants that

$$AX = \det(A)I = XA.$$

Hence, if A is nonsingular, the matrix Y defined by $Y = X/\det(A)$ satisfies the relation $AY = YA = I$; Y is called the *inverse* of A and is denoted by A^{-1}.

The *rank r* of an $m \times n$ matrix A is defined to be the highest order of nonzero minor. Clearly, $r \leq m, n$.

A set of matrices $A^{(1)}, \ldots, A^{(k)}$ is said to be *linearly dependent* if there exists a set of scalars α_i, not all zero, such that

$$\sum_{i=1}^{k} \alpha_i A^{(i)} = 0;$$

otherwise they are said to be *linearly independent*. The concept is of particular interest when the $A^{(i)}$ are row or column vectors. If A is of rank r, then it has r independent rows and r independent columns; any k rows (or columns) with $k > r$ are linearly dependent.

The Solution of Simultaneous Linear Algebraic Equations.

Perhaps the most fundamental of all computations is the solution of a system of m simultaneous linear equations in n unknowns:

$$\sum_{j=1}^{n} a_{ij} x_j = b_i \quad (i = 1, \ldots, m) \text{ or } Ax = b,$$

where A is the $m \times n$ matrix (a_{ij}), and x and b are column vectors of order n and m, respectively. The mathematical theory is well known, the following being a brief summary.

Solutions exist if and only if rank $(A, b) = $ rank (A). The general solution is based on the ability to solve any $r \times r$ system $Cy = d$, where C is nonsingular. Such a system has the unique solution

$$y = C^{-1}d,$$

the inverse C^{-1} existing since C is assumed to be nonsingular.

If rank $(A, b) > $ rank (A), then there is no solution. If rank $(A, b) = $ rank $(A) = r$ (say), then the solutions are determined as follows: Since A is of rank r, there is a nonsingular $r \times r$ submatrix of A; arrange the order of the equations and the order of the variables so that the leading principal $r \times r$ matrix is nonsingular. Then any solution of the first r equations is automatically a solution of the remainder. The first r equations may be written in the form

$$a_{i1}x_1 + \cdots + a_{ir}x_r$$
$$= b_i - a_{i,r+1}x_{r+1} - \cdots - a_{in}x_n$$
$$= d_i \text{ (say) } (i = 1, \ldots, r),$$

or

$$Cx^{(r)} = d^{(r)},$$

where C is a nonsingular $r \times r$ matrix and $x^{(r)} = (x_1, \ldots, x_r)^T$. Hence, $x_{r1}, \ldots, x_n$ may be chosen arbitrarily, and for each such choice $x_1, \ldots, x_r$ are given uniquely as the solution of $Cx^{(r)} = d^{(r)}$. If $r < n$, there is an $(n - r)$ fold infinity of solutions. If $r = n$, the solution is unique.

Of particular importance is the case $b = 0$; the system is then called *homogeneous*. For such systems, rank (A, b) certainly equals rank (A), and hence they are necessarily compatible, but if $r = n$, the only solution is $x = 0$, the *null* solution. If $r < n$, there is an $(n - r)$ fold infinity of nonnull solutions.

The Practical Solution of a Nonsingular $n \times n$ System.

The difficulties involved in solving a system of equations are almost entirely of a practical nature. It is essential that a method should be stable with respect to rounding errors and be as economical as possible. Since the fundamental problem is the solution of a system with a square nonsingular matrix of coefficients, we now concentrate on this case. There are two main classes of methods. In *direct* methods the solution is obtained in a finite number of operations; without the intervention of rounding errors, it would be exact. In *iterative*

methods a sequence $x^{(k)}$ of solutions is obtained such that $x^{(k)} \to x$ the true solution, as $k \to \infty$. In practice, iteration is terminated after a finite number of steps.

Direct Methods. The best-known direct method is *Gaussian elimination*, which is merely a systematic version of the high-school method of successive elimination of variables. We denote the original set of equations by

$$a_{i1}x_1 + a_{i2}x_2 + \cdots + a_{in}x_n = b_i \quad (i = 1 \cdots n).$$

The variable x_1 is eliminated in each of equations $i = 2, \ldots, n$ by subtracting a multiple $m_{i1} = a_{i1}/a_{11}$ of the first equation from it. This gives the first derived set:

$$a_{11}x_1 + a_{12}x_2 + \cdots + a_{1n}x_n = b_1$$
$$a_{22}^{(1)}x_2 + \cdots + a_{2n}^{(1)}x_n = b_2^{(1)}$$
$$\cdots \quad \cdots \quad \cdots \quad \cdots$$
$$a_{n2}^{(1)}x_2 + \cdots + a_{nn}^{(1)}x_n = b_n^{(1)}$$

The variable x_2 is now eliminated from each of equations $i = 3, \ldots, n$ by subtracting a multiple $m_{i2} = a_{i2}^{(1)}/a_{22}^{(1)}$ of the second row from it. After $n - 1$ such steps, we obtain an *equivalent* derived system of the following form:

$$a_{11}x_1 + a_{12}x_2 + a_{13}x_3 + \cdots + a_{1n}x_n = b_1$$
$$a_{22}^{(1)}x_2 + a_{23}^{(1)}x_3 + \cdots + a_{2n}^{(1)}x_n = b_2^{(1)}$$
$$a_{33}^{(2)}x_3 + \cdots + a_{3n}^{(2)}x_n = b_3^{(2)}$$
$$\cdots \quad \cdots \quad \cdots \quad \cdots$$
$$a_{nn}^{(n-1)}x_n = b_n^{(n-1)}$$

or, in matrix form, $Ux = b^{(n-1)}$, where U is *upper triangular*. This triangular set may now be solved by *back substitution*, computing x_n from the nth equation, x_{n-1} from the $(n - 1)$st equation, $\ldots, x_1$ from the first.

The process breaks down if at any stage $a_{r+1,r+1}^{(r)} = 0$. This may be avoided by a simple modification. In the rth derived system, the last $n - r$ equations involve only the last $n - r$ variables. Any of these equations may be used to eliminate x_{r+1} from the remaining $n - r - 1$. We may choose that equation which has the largest coefficient of x_{r+1}. It is convenient to think of terms of interchanging this equation with equation $r + 1$. This modified process is known as Gaussian elimination with *partial pivoting*. Breakdown cannot now occur unless A is singular. (More accurately, unless A, modfied by the rounding errors, is singular.) With this modification $|m_{ij}| \leq 1$. A more sophisticated form of pivoting is sometimes used. In the rth reduced set, the largest element $|a_{ij}^{(r)}|$ $(i, j \geq r + 1)$ is determined. If this is $a_{st}^{(r)}$, then equation s is used to eliminate x_t from the remaining $n - r - 1$ equations. This is best thought of in terms of interchanging the appropriate rows and columns. This process is *complete pivoting.* In general, Gaussian elimination with pivoting is remarkably stable with respect to rounding errors, but without pivoting it may be arbitrarily unstable.

If a matrix L is constructed from the multipliers m_{ij} by taking $l_{ij} = m_{ij}$ $(i > j)$, $l_{ii} = 1$, $l_{ij} = 0$ $(j > i)$, then the resulting unit lower triangular matrix (i.e., lower triangular with diagonal 1s) is such that $LU = A$. (In the case where partial pivoting has been used, the relation is $LU = \tilde{A}$, where $\tilde{A}$ is A with its rows suitably permuted; with complete pivoting, $LU = \tilde{A}$ where $\tilde{A}$ is A with both rows and columns suitably permuted.) The factorization $A = LU$ may be derived directly without producing the intermediate matrices $A^{(k)}$, and it is not difficult to combine this direct factorization with the equivalent of partial pivoting. The solution of $Ax = b$ is then achieved by solving $Ly = b$, $Ux = y$. There is an analogous factorization in which U is unit upper triangular.

An important class of direct methods is based on the factorization of A into the product of an orthogonal matrix Q and an upper triangular matrix R. (The notation R is used rather than U, for historical reasons). If $A = QR$, then $Q^TA = R$, where Q^T is of course also orthogonal, and the factorization is commonly achieved in this way. Q^T is not derived directly, but as the product of a number of simple orthogonal matrices. Such factorizations are associated with the names of Givens and Householder. The QR factorizations have slightly more reliable numerical stability than the LU factorization with pivoting, but since they involve more work, the LU factorization is more commonly used for solving linear equations. However, the QR factorizations are of fundamental importance in connection with the eigenvalue problem and the least squares problem.

Iterative Methods. Basically, the simplest iterative methods for solving linear systems are those of Jacobi and Gauss-Seidel. The relations are most simply expressed if we write $A \equiv D - E - F$, where D is the set of diagonal elements, $-E$ is the set of subdiagonal elements, and $-F$ the set of superdiagonal elements. Jacobi's method may then be expressed in the form

$$Dx^{(k+1)} = b + Ex^{(k)} + Fx^{(k)}.$$

Clearly, the method can be applied only if the diagonal elements are nonzero. Writing $D^{-1}E = L$, $D^{-1}F = U$, this becomes

$$x^{(k+1)} = D^{-1}b + (L + U)x^{(k)}.$$

If x is the true solution, then

$$x = D^{-1}b + (L + U)x,$$

and writing $e^{(k)} = x - x^{(k)}$, we have

$$e^{(k+1)} = (L + U)e^{(k)} = Pe^{(k)},$$

giving $e^{(k+1)} = P^k e^{(1)}$.

The process is therefore convergent if $P_k \to 0$ as $k \to \infty$, which is true if all the eigenvalues of P are less than unity in modulus (see later sections of this article). In the Gauss-Seidel method the most up-to-date value of each component is used at each stage, the relevant relations being

$$Dx^{(k+1)} = b + Ex^{(k+1)} + Fx^{(k)},$$

giving

$$(I - L)x^{(k+1)} = D^{-1}b + Ux^{(k)}.$$

The error matrix now satisfies the relations

$$(I - L)e^{(k+1)} = Ue^{(k)}$$

or

$$e^{(k+1)} = (I - L)^{-1}Ue^{(k)} = Qx^{(k)},$$

and the process is convergent if $Q^k \to 0$. When both methods are convergent, one might expect the Gauss-Seidel to converge faster, since it always uses the most recent information; this is true generally, but not always.

Research on iterative methods has mainly been concerned with *sufficient* conditions for convergence and methods for *accelerating* the rate of convergence. If A is real and symmetric with a positive diagonal, then a *necessary* and *sufficient* condition for Gauss-Seidel to converge is that it be positive definite. If L and U are nonnegative, then Gauss-Seidel and Jacobi are either both convergent or both divergent. In the former case, Gauss-Seidel converges the more rapidly.

A class of matrices that arises frequently in the study of partial differential equations is that for which the equations and variables can be reordered so that $L + U$ is of the form

$$\begin{bmatrix} 0 & P \\ Q & 0 \end{bmatrix}$$

where the null submatrices are square. These are said to have *Young's property A*. For matrices of this kind, when Gauss-Seidel converges, it does so twice as fast as Jacobi.

Acceleration of convergence of Gauss-Seidel can be achieved by making a change in each component which is ω times as great as that determined by Gauss-Seidel itself. The relevant relation is therefore

$$x^{(k+1)} - x^{(k)} = \omega[D^{-1}b + Lx^{(k+1)} + Ux^{(k)} - x^{(k)}],$$
$$(I - \omega L)x^{(k+1)} = x^{(k)} + \omega[D^{-1}b - (I - U)x^{(k)}],$$

giving

$$e^{(k+1)} = (I - \omega L)^{-1}[(1 - \omega)I + \omega U]e^{(k)}.$$

If $\omega > 1$ (<1), the method is known as *successive over-relaxation* (*under-relaxation*). The effectiveness of the method depends on a judicious choice of ω. Young has investigated fully the case when A has property A, and has shown that the optimum choice of ω is $2/(1 + (1 - \theta^2)^{1/2})$, where θ is the largest eigenvalue of $L + U$.

In iterative methods one works throughout with the original matrix A, and for this reason it was at one time thought that such methods would be much more stable with respect to rounding errors than would direct methods. This advantage has proved to be less important than was thought. Much more important is the fact that if A has a high percentage of zero elements, then it is easy to take advantage of this and thereby reduce the storage requirements and the number of arithmetic operations. In direct methods such as Gaussian elimination, the zero elements in the original matrix do not persist in the successive derived matrices.

The Algebraic Eigenvalue Problem. The practical importance of the algebraic eigenvalue problem springs mainly from its relation to the problem of solving a system of n simultaneous linear differential equations of first order with constant coefficients. In standard form such a system may be written as

$$\frac{dx}{dt} = Ax,$$

where A is an $n \times n$ matrix and x a vector. By substitution, $x = ue^{\lambda t}$ is a solution if $\lambda u = Au$. Conversely, if λ and $u \neq 0$ satisfy $\lambda u = Au$, then $x = ue^{\lambda t}$ is a solution. The *algebraic eigenvalue problem* is the determination of such λ and u. From the theory of linear algebraic equations, nonnull solutions exist if and only if $\det(\lambda I - A) = 0$. This is a polynomial equation of degree n, the coefficient of λ^n being unity. It is known as the *characteristic equation* of A. The roots of this equation are called the *eigenvalues, latent roots,* or *characteristic values* of A. Taking into account multiplicities, there are always precisely n eigenvalues. Corresponding to each eigenvalue there is at least one nonnull solution u, and this is known as a corresponding *eigenvector*. The number of independent eigenvectors corresponding to a given eigenvalue λ

may be less than its multiplicity; it is equal to $n - k$, where k is the rank of $A - \lambda I$.

Since the calculation of the eigenvalues is equivalent to finding the roots of the characteristic equation (an *apparently* simpler problem), early methods were based on the explicit determination of this equation. All such methods are inherently unstable, since very small errors in the coefficients of the equation may correspond to large changes in its roots even when the eigenvalues are not unduly sensitive to changes in the elements of A.

If the transformation $x = Py$ is made in the system of differential equations, it becomes $dy/dt = (P^{-1}AP)y$, assuming that P is nonsingular. The matrix $P^{-1}AP$ is said to be *similar* to A. Since $\det(P^{-1}AP - \lambda I) = \det(A - \lambda I)$, the eigenvalues of A are the same as those of any similar matrix. This is intuitively obvious from consideration of the differential equations. Many of the most effective methods for finding eigenvalues are based on determining a similarity transformation such that eigenvalues of $P^{-1}AP$ are readily available. The eigenvalues of a triangular matrix are its diagonal elements, and hence reduction to this form gives the eigenvalues immediately.

The theory of similarity transformations shows that for any A, there exists a nonsingular P such that $P^{-1}AP$ is upper-triangular. In fact such a transformation is always possible even if P is restricted to the class of *unitary* matrices, i.e., matrices such that $PP^H = P^HP = I$. A real unitary matrix satisfies $PP^T = P^TP = I$ and is therefore orthogonal. Unitary similarity transformations are numerically very stable, and several of the best algorithms are based on their use. For such matrices, $P^{-1}AP = P^HAP$.

When A has distinct eigenvalues, there is always a P such that $P^{-1}AP = \text{diag}(\lambda_i)$, the diagonal matrix with λ_i on the diagonal. If A has any multiple eigenvalues, reduction to diagonal form is not generally possible, and hence *general* algorithms are not usually based on such a reduction.

Real Symmetric Matrices. When A is symmetric, there is an advantage in taking P to be orthogonal, since P^TAP is still symmetric. It is known that a real symmetric matrix is always reducible to diagonal form via an orthogonal P; Jacobi's method, one of the most effective algorithms, is based on such a reduction. P is not determined directly, but as a product of a sequence of elementary orthogonal matrices of the form R_{pq}, where

$$r_{pp} = r_{qq} = \cos\theta,$$
$$r_{pq} = -r_{qp} = \sin\theta;$$
$$r_{ij} = \delta_{ij} \quad \text{(otherwise)}$$

This is known as a rotation in the p,q plane. Denoting the successive derived matrices by $A^{(k)}$, if $a_{p_k,q_k}^{(k)}$ is the off-diagonal element of largest modulus, then the next transformation is given by

$$A^{(k+1)} = R_{p_k,q_k}^T A^{(k)} R_{p_k,q_k},$$

with the angle θ being chosen so that

$$a_{p_k,q_k}^{(k+1)} = 0.$$

In general, an infinite number of transformations are needed to give the diagonal form, and iteration is terminated when the off-diagonal elements are all negligible. To reach this point approximately $12n^3$ multiplications and additions are required.

A real symmetric matrix can be reduced to symmetric tridiagonal form by $(1/2)n(n-1)$ elementary orthogonal similarities of the above type, involving less than 10% of the computation in Jacobi's method. This algorithm is due to Givens; an alternative reduction involving orthogonal similarities and requiring half as much work is due to Householder.

The calculation of the eigenvalues of a symmetric tridiagonal matrix is a very economical process. Two methods are widely used. The first is due to Givens and is based on the fact that if T is tridiagonal, the leading principal minors p_r, $(r = 0, \ldots, n)$ of $(T - \lambda I)$ can be computed from the relations

$$p_0(\lambda) = 1,$$
$$p_1(\lambda) = t_{11} - \lambda,$$
$$p_r(\lambda) = (t_{rr} - \lambda)p_{r-1}(\lambda) - (t_{r,r-1})^2 p_{r-2}(\lambda).$$

For any given value of λ the number of agreements in sign between consecutive members of the sequence $p_0, p_1, \ldots, p_n$ equals the number of eigenvalues greater than λ. Any individual eigenvalue may be found by repeated bisection using this property, given only an initial upper and lower bound. The second method is described in the next section.

Eigenvalues of General Matrices. The most efficient method for general matrices is based on the unitary similarity reduction to upper-triangular form. For real matrices, an analogous *real* reduction may be achieved, using only orthogonal similarities to give a triangular matrix apart from 2×2 diagonal blocks corresponding to complex conjugate pairs of eigenvalues. This reduction is much more economical if the orginal matrix is first reduced to upper-Hessenberg form, which can be done by $(1/2)n(n-1)$ elementary orthogonal similarities, as in Givens' reduction of a symmetric matrix to tridiagonal

form. Again, Householder has given an alternative requiring only half as much computation.

The Hessenberg matrix is then reduced to the quasi-triangular form by the Francis QR algorithm. In the basic QR algorithm, a sequence of similar matrices A_s is produced via the relations

$$A_s - k_s I = Q_s R_s, \quad R_s Q_s + k_s I = A_{s+1},$$

where Q_s is orthogonal, R_s is upper-triangular, and the k_s are chosen so as to accelerate convergence. The matrix A_s tends to the quasi-triangular form, the speed of convergence being extraordinarily satisfactory. Upper-Hessenberg form is preserved by this algorithm and this greatly reduces the volume of computation.

The QR method is also extremely effective for finding the eigenvalues of a real symmetric tridiagonal matrix. The symmetric tridiagonal form is preserved, giving great economy in the volume of work. For finding all the eigenvalues, it is the most efficient of known methods.

The Main Areas of Research. In the solution of linear systems, the main area of research is devoted to the economical solution (by direct methods) of large sparse systems, i.e., systems for which the matrix of coefficients has a low percentage of nonzero elements. The main problem is that of taking advantage of sparseness without sacrificing numerical stability.

In the eigenvalue field, the main areas are sparse matrix techniques and the generalized eigenvalue problem. The latter is related to the solution of the differential equation of system

$$A_r \frac{d^r x}{dt^r} + A_{r-1} \frac{d^{r-1} x}{dt^{r-1}} + \cdots + A_1 \frac{dx}{dt} + A_0 x = 0,$$

which gives rise to the solution of the algebraic problem

$$(A_r \lambda^r + A_{r-1} \lambda^{r-1} + \cdots + A_1 \lambda + A_0) u = 0.$$

REFERENCES

1962. Varga, R. S. *Matrix Iterative Analysis.* Englewood Cliffs, NJ: Prentice-Hall.

1964. Householder, A. S. *The Theory of Matrices in Numerical Analysis.* New York: Blaisdell.

1965. Wilkinson, J. H. *The Algebraic Eigenvalue Problem,* Oxford: Clarendon Press.

1971. Wilkinson, J. H. and Reinsch, C. *Handbook for Automatic Computation: Linear Algebra* **2**, Berlin: Springer-Verlag.

1971. Young, D. M. *Iterative Solution of Large Linear Systems.* New York: Academic Press.

1972. Rose, D. J. and Willoughby, R. A. *Sparse Matrices and Their Applications.* New York: Plenum Press.
1973. Stewart, G. W. Introduction to Matrix Computations. New York: Academic Press.

J. H. WILKINSON

MAUCHLY, JOHN WILLIAM

For articles on related subjects *see* DIGITAL COM-PUTERS: Early; ECKERT, J. PRESPER; ENIAC; and UNIVAC I.

John Mauchly (b. Cincinnati, OH, 30 August 1907, d. Philadelphia, PA, 8 January 1980) was one of the major visionaries and pioneers of our current electronic digital computer era. The dedication of his brainchild, ENIAC, in 1946 totally changed the scientific and commercial information processing environment.

In 1925, Mauchly received a scholarship to attend the engineering school of The Johns Hopkins University. After two years, however, he decided that he didn't care for engineering and switched to physics. His Ph.D. was

Fig. 1 John William Mauchly

awarded in 1932 with a thesis on an analysis of the carbon monoxide molecule. He remained at Johns Hopkins the following year as a research assistant to Professor Joseph Eachus, where his work included calculating the energy levels of the formaldehyde spectrum. This research project, as well as his thesis work, involved a great deal of calculation, and Mauchly began to be interested in devising special techniques to cut down on the work involved.

He taught physics at Ursinus College from 1933 to 1941. During this period he developed an interest in the problem of weather prediction, and built an analog computer to do harmonic analysis of weather data. This work led to a paper (1940) on the quasi-periodicity of precipitation. He spent the summer of 1940 with H. Helm Clayton, who was interested in long-range weather forecasting, and he also presented a paper during this period to the Geophysical Union, using a statistical approach to the causes of sunspots.

In the summer of 1941, with war impending, he attended a defense training course in electronics at the Moore School of Electrical Engineering (University of Pennsylvania). He was subsequently invited to join the faculty of the Moore School as an instructor. The Moore School had long had a contract with Army Ordnance to calculate ballistics tables, and Mauchly was assigned this work in addition to his regular teaching duties. All of his work of the past decade seemed to come together in these ballistics calculations, and in 1942 he wrote a memorandum proposing that an electronic calculator be constructed to perform these vital computations. This original proposal was rejected, but it was revived a year later by Herman Goldstine, who had been assigned to Aberdeen Proving Ground to expedite the production of the firing data. Thirty months later, ENIAC, conceived by Mauchly and engineered by J. Presper Eckert, was publicly demonstrated (February 1946). From the standpoint of speed of computation, it was a quantum jump, increasing that ability by a factor of 1,000.

ENIAC, now retired to the Smithsonian Institution, operated successfully at Aberdeen Proving Ground for ten years. It well deserves its description as the first truly electronic, general-purpose computer and the precursor of all that was to come.

Mauchly and Eckert left the Moore School in 1946 to found the Electronic Control Co., which became the Eckert-Mauchly Corporation in 1947. The company's first contracts were to design a small binary computer for the Northrop Aircraft Corporation (BINAC) and a computer for the Bureau of the Census (UNIVAC I). In 1951, the Eckert-Mauchly Corporation became a division of the Remington-Rand Corporation, and Mauchly remained with it in various capacities until 1959, when he formed Mauchly Associates.

Mauchly was a founder of ACM and became its first Vice-President and second President. He was a member of many other learned societies, including the American Physical Society, the Franklin Institute, and the National Academy of Engineering. He has received numerous awards, including the Howard Potts Medal of the Franklin Institute (1949), the John Scott Award (1961), and most recently (jointly with J. P. Eckert) the Philadelphia Man of the Year Award (1973). ACM's Eckert-Mauchly award is partially named in his honor. His scientific papers will be housed in the Van Pelt Library of the University of Pennsylvania.

REFERENCES

1946. Kennedy, T. R., Jr. "Electronic Computer Flashes Answers, May Speed Engineering," *New York Times* (February 15), pp. 1,16.
1971. Rosen, Saul. "Electronic Computers: A Historical Survey," *Computing Reviews*, **1**, *No. 1* (March). Reprinted in "A Quarter Century View," *ACM*, pp. 9–36.

H. S. TROPP

MEDICAL APPLICATIONS

For articles on related subjects *see* BIOMEDICINE, COMPUTER GRAPHICS IN; HOSPITAL INFORMATION SYSTEMS; INTENSIVE CARE, COMPUTERS IN; MEDLARS-MEDLINE; and TOMOGRAPHY, COMPUTED.

Applications of computers are found throughout the spectrum of tasks that are part of the world of medicine. This article will cite examples ranging from medical research via clinical applications to health care administration.

Organizational Support. A large fraction of the reported work is government-supported. In the U.S., the National Institutes of Health and the National Center for Health Services Research have promoted the use of computers in medicine. The Biotechnology Resources branch of the NIH has funded shared computer facilities, complementing the specific mission-oriented grants of other institutes and departments. In Europe, much activity has been sponsored through the national health maintenance schemes, and hospital computer systems have had specific governmental encouragement in Scandinavia, France, and Germany. Medical documentation for national public health programs has been encouraged in the Netherlands; Switzerland, Italy, and Japan have supported pharmacological data analysis. In the U. S., the FDA has been concerned about improved data management in drug trials. In Great Britain, there is interest in tracing of drug effects after a new drug is made available to the population. Studies of biological systems based on the application of cybernetic concepts have been produced in eastern European countries as well as in France and Germany. Much of the medical instrumentation now being produced in Europe, Japan, and the U.S. uses microprocessors. Due to the need for multidisciplinary capabilities, many of the efforts are associated with major medical centers. Interest in medical application of computers can be found throughout the world. This summary merely illustrates the geographical breadth of computer applications in the field of medicine.

Societies. Some of the organizations that provide a focal point for medical computing are the following.

- The Society for Computer Medicine
  c/o A.A.M.I.
  1901 North Fort Meyer Drive
  Arlington, VA 22209
- Special Interest Group on Biomedical Computing (SIGBIO)
  Association for Computing Machinery
  1133 Avenue of the Americas
  New York, NY 10036
- Society for Advanced Medical Systems
  4405 East-West Highway—Suite 404
  Bethesda, MD 20014
- Biomedical Engineering Group
  Institute of Electrical and Electronics Engineers
  345 East 47th Street
  New York, NY 10017
- International Medical Informatics Association (IMIA)
  c/o SAZZOG Foundation
  Groningen Singel 1043–1045
  6835GN Arnhem, The Netherlands

A number of journals dedicated to medical computation are listed in the references. Many relevant articles are found in the literature of the specific medical application areas.

Annual conferences at which recent developments can be presented are sponsored by most of the societies listed above; by the French government research organization, IRIA, in Toulouse as *Journèes d'Informatique Mèdicale;* by the University of Illinois, alternately at its Urbana and Chicago campuses; by the Texas Medical Center, Inc., in Houston, under the title *Symposia on Biomathematics and Computer Science in the Life Sciences;* by the IEEE and UCSD as the *San Diego Biomedical Symposia;* and, since 1977, by the George Washington University Medical Center with the IEEE Computer Society, titled *Computer Applications in Medical Care.*

Research. Medical research has stressed computer technology in several areas, and a number of developments that are significant outside the medical area can be reported.

Medical Statistics. The need to make statistical tabulation and analytical procedures available as a tool to health care personnel provided the impetus to Drs. Dixon and Massey of UCLA to publish statistical algorithms, which became the basis for the BioMeDical Statistical Program Library. This BMD series of programs is published by the Health Sciences Computing Facility at UCLA. The University of North Carolina has since then developed the SAS package. A feature of the programs is a common input specification, which allows multiple procedures to operate on a collection of data without requiring separate data transformation and selection programs. Current research includes the assessment of survival data in heterogeneous and ongoing populations. Statistical procedures are essential in medicine to test potential causal relationships in biological systems. Applications include the evaluation of new and old drugs, medical procedures, and environmental and hereditary causes of disease, as well as studies on normal population groups.

Advice Giving and Artificial Intelligence. A number of systems have been demonstrated which can provide advice to physicians who are faced with clinical decisions. Such systems may be *algorithmic,* if the problem is quantitatively well understood; *heuristic,* if rules have been formulated based on expert advice; or *comparative,* if enough data are available to compare the case with cases previously seen, treated, and recorded. The best known example of the algorithmic type is the acid-base advisor developed by Bleich at Beth Israël Hospital in Boston. Physicians can consult the program on-line to reestablish the proper electrolyte balance in patients with renal or metabolic problems. An example of the heuristic type is the MYCIN program of Shortliffe at Stanford. Several hundred rules with attached certainty factors of the form **if** *conditions* **then** *set condition or result* have been collected to encode antibiotic treatment knowledge. The evaluation is triggered by entering observations of the patient's state and initial laboratory findings. Rules with matching conditions are executed. The eventual result is a set of ranked therapy recommendations, with an optional explanation about the reasoning process followed. Without the certainty parameters, the rules are similar in form and execution to Dijkstra's guarded commands. MYCIN and other artificial intelligence techniques in medicine are supported by an NIH funded central computer resource, SUMEX, accessible via TYMNET throughout the U.S.

Advice based on a comparison of a new patient with a set of similar, previously treated patients is provided by the ARAMIS system, developed by Fries, also at Stanford. Patients with immunologic diseases can be aided by careful management of their specific disease state. ARAMIS provides the access to the recorded treatment experience embodied in many case records so that an optimal management strategy can be chosen.

Databases in Medicine. The collection of medical experience is often collected in computerized data banks. Several database systems specific for medicine have been developed.

ARAMIS uses a time-oriented database approach (TOD) to facilitate on-line analysis of many sequential observations made when patients visit the clinic. The underlying system implements a two-level, patient-visit hierarchy, but is flexible in terms of number and type of data items to be collected. The data types are specifically related to medicine: Name, data, discrete values, continuous values, value (a five-level scale), note, and confidential note. The time-oriented approach is also provided by *CLINFO,* a minicomputer system sponsored by NIH for use in clinical investigations.

Great impact in medical record keeping has been made by *MUMPS,* a programming system with integrated file-management for minicomputers developed by Barnett at Massachusetts General Hospital in Boston. In MUMPS, all file accesses are implied by references to global variables. The natural hierarchy of patient, problem, visit, treatments, etc. is modeled by the hierarchical file structure, where the global at each successive level has one more subscript that at the level above it. MUMPS has been used in many patient-oriented systems, and a prime example is the ambulatory patient record system, COSTAR, now being made available in parameterized form to clinics and health care maintenance organizations. MUMPS is also being marketed by DEC to non-medical minicomputer users.

Large patient-oriented databases are also supported by the National Cancer Institute to provide incidence surveillance and treatment control of patients who receive anti-cancer drugs. Of great interest have been the graphical presentations of cancer incidence of various types in different sections of the country. Such presentations trigger the generation of hypotheses regarding causes of cancer. Other areas in which data of an epidemiological nature is collected on a nationwide basis is the recent heart disease and stroke data bank (also using TOD) and the renal disease data bank at Triangle Research Institute in North Carolina.

Not all disease registries have been effective. The mere collection of data, without feedback to the source physicians is a frustrating task and the data quality deteriorates rapidly. As more of the cost of health care becomes a public concern, the need for data as a base for decision making increases, and the quality of the data will become of increasing concern.

Simulation. In order to develop a better understanding of biological processes, computer-based models of portions of the human metabolic system have been built. Some early models used analog computers, but digital computation predominates now. The programs may be written in languages such as CSMP (Continuous System Modeling Program), which allow models to be constructed of elements familiar to model builders, such as integrators, delays, attenuators, and threshold functions. An extension to CSMP, which provides interactive graphics for the medical researcher, has been developed at the RAND Corporation under the name BIOMOD.

Other models have been written in algebraic languages such as Fortran in order to utilize commonly available facilities. A formal separation of the constructive specification of the model and the parameters describing its current state has been advocated and used by Yamamoto at George Washington University in order to provide a basis for scientific evaluation and development of models. Significant models have been constructed in the areas of respiratory behavior, the cardiac cycle, responses to a number of drugs, and adrenaline production in reaction to stress. Models of cell life cycles are used to give some guidance to sequential radiation treatments in cancer therapy.

Data Acquisition. A large number of medical research projects use data that can be acquired directly from instruments. Typical sources are electroencephalogram and electrocardiogram recorders, which measure surface electric potentials due to neural and muscular activity in the brain and in the heart, blood pressure measurements via catheters, and ultrasonic probes (see Fig. 1). Implantable devices for blood flow measurement, using Doppler effects in the ultrasonic frequency range, have been constructed by Meindl at the Stanford Electronics Laboratory. Signals may be transmitted by telemetering from implanted monitors. More conventional instrumentation includes strain gauges for the measurement of motion, thermistors, and Geiger counters. Also important are instruments that operate on biological material removed from the patient. These include highly automated blood and urine analysis systems. Most of these instruments are relatively slow and operate in tune with human metabolic rates. Data acquisition speeds per channel rarely exceed 1,000 samples per second and are frequently considerably lower. Higher data rates are generated by mass spectral analysis of biological samples as well as by data that is received in image form by optical, X-ray, gamma-ray, or ultrasonic cameras. In computed

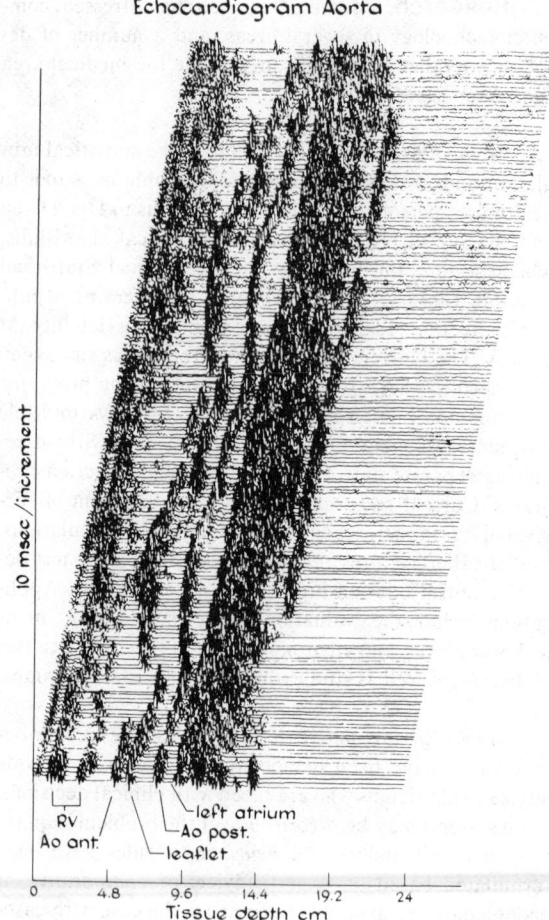

Echocardiogram Aorta

10 msec/increment

RV
Ao ant.
left atrium
Ao post.
leaflet

Tissue depth cm
0   4.8   9.6   14.4   19.2   24

Fig. 1 A time/motion presentation of heart-structure motion over a few heart beats, using a Picker ultrasound transducer. Data were recorded on analog tape and anayzed at 1/32 real time on a PDP-12 computer for presentation on a Houston plotter. (Courtesy of Dr. Eugene Dong, Stanford University.)

tomography (*q.v.*), X-ray sources and sensors are rotated around the patient. The strengths of the received signals are used to construct an image of the tissue in the plane of rotation. Any on-line and real-time data acquisition is very demanding on computer operations. Such computers are hence typically dedicated to one research problem. Kirklin in Birmingham, AL, operates a closed-loop system that controls the intravenous administration of fluids to patients.

In some centers (e.g., the Brain Research Institute at UCLA under Adey, and the Cardiology Laboratory at the Latter-Day Saints Hospital in Salt Lake City under

Warner), fairly large machines are operated with a professional staff in order to support a number of projects concentrated in one specific research area. At Stanford, ACME, a time-shared system designed by Wiederhold, permitted researchers from a variety of disciplines to share the resources and convenience attainable with a larger computer and interactive operations, while providing data acquisition capabilities. In studies using laboratory animals, electric probes are sometimes implanted in the brain or near the heart. A closed-loop experiment has been carried out by Dong at Stanford, in which the computer stimulates the vagal nerve, which has been shown to control the heartbeat rate through a phase-dependent mechanism.

The use of mass spectral analysis on urine samples, now still too costly for routine care, has been shown by Jellum of the University of Oslo in Norway to be an extremely powerful tool in the diagnosis of metabolic diseases.

Even with dedicated computers, data selection and reduction of voluminous data creates bottlenecks. The Fast Fourier Transform (q.v.) and work by Gersch at the University of Hawaii on automatic spectrum analysis provide important tools, but there is a need to develop better procedures in the area of biological data processing so that real-time data analysis becomes as accessible to medical researchers as statistical tools have become through the BMD programs.

Graphics. Frequently, graphic representation of computer-produced results is required, so that CRT technology has received a significant impetus from the biomedical area, beginning from the first graphic-oriented minicomputers (the LINC machines) by Cox, as well as others at MIT, and later at Washington University in St. Louis. Today, graphics applications in medicine include the use of Evans-Sutherland systems for the study of organic modecules (Fig. 2). A central national resource to serve pharmacological research, PROPHET, has been developed by Bolt, Beranek, and Newman of Cambridge, MA, and provides not only graphic output, but also graphic input by means of an electronically scanned input tablet. There is also a need to enhance languages in order to describe two- and three-dimensional images adquately, without which work in physiology and anatomy is severely hampered. Fig. 3 shows an example of pattern recognition. It may be generally observed that medical computing problems demand much memory relative to processing capability.

Education. Programs to train scientists in biomedical computing have been instituted by Saunders in Winnipeg, Gremy in Paris, Blois and Starkweather at the University of California in San Francisco, Slamecka

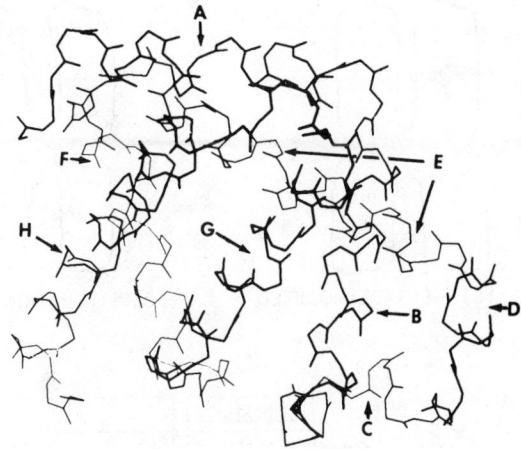

Fig. 2   This computer graphic presentation of complex molecules shows a model of the polypeptide backbone of myoglobin. Each helix is lettered (A–H), starting with the nitrogen terminal of this amino acid. (Courtesy of Prof. Andrew Tometsko, School of Medicine, University of Rochester.)

at Georgia Tech, and others. Training in the U.S. has been strongly supported by the National Library of Medicine. These programs are intended to close the gap that is frequently felt when computer scientists attempt to solve biomedical problems without adequate awareness of the medical environment, or when medically oriented personnel invest in efforts that do not benefit from the state of the art in computer science. Reliance on generalization from a few examples, common in medicine, conflicts with the mathematical formalism underlying computer science. Many projects have suffered greatly through this lack of mutual understanding. The traditional organization of medicine, as well as the social aspects of health care problems, has inhibited or impeded many computer scientists who have been interested in biomedicine.

Even without specific programs in medical information science, educational opportunities exist at many major medical centers where current research is being done. Specifically worth mentioning are Harvard, with its associated Massachusetts General Hospital and School of Public Health; the University of California in Los Angeles; Stanford University; the University of Illinois; the University of Alabama in Birmingham; and the University of North Carolina at Chapel Hill.

Use of computer-assisted instruction has received encouragement at various schools in Canada and the U.S. Augsburger in Heidelberg uses CAI in the rehabilitation

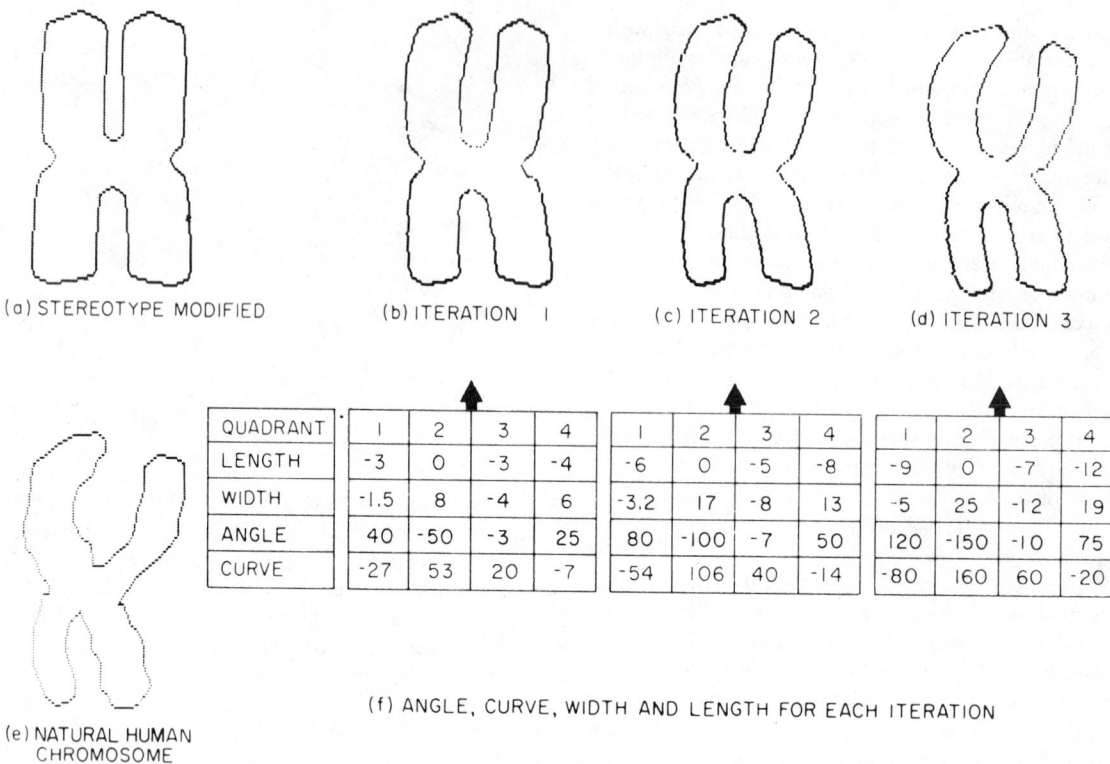

(a) STEREOTYPE MODIFIED (b) ITERATION 1 (c) ITERATION 2 (d) ITERATION 3

(e) NATURAL HUMAN CHROMOSOME TO BE FITTED

QUADRANT	1	2	3	4	1	2	3	4	1	2	3	4
LENGTH	-3	0	-3	-4	-6	0	-5	-8	-9	0	-7	-12
WIDTH	-1.5	8	-4	6	-3.2	17	-8	13	-5	25	-12	19
ANGLE	40	-50	-3	25	80	-100	-7	50	120	-150	-10	75
CURVE	-27	53	20	-7	-54	106	40	-14	-80	160	60	-20

(f) ANGLE, CURVE, WIDTH AND LENGTH FOR EACH ITERATION

Fig. 3 Pattern matching of individual chromosomes. A standard sterotype matches the image of a natural chromosome. Length parameters are critical for chromosome classification. (Courtesy of Prof. B. Widrow and Robert Melen, Information Systems Laboratory, Stanford University.)

of patients with severe disabilities, and Colby at UCLA works with autistic children.

The National Library of Medicine now provides terminal access to its index files at many medical centers, in addition to the MEDLARS batch-oriented bibliographic services.

Clinical Use. A number of research developments are moving into the area of direct health care. Many of these projects still carry a significant research component and are supported through the dedication of individuals who expect that routine usage will occur in due time.

Monitoring. A prime area of application is the monitoring of patients, as exemplified by Weil and Shubin's work at USC (Fig. 4). Such systems replace some aspects of the tedious task of continuous bedside monitoring by nursing personnel, while preserving a historical record that can be used for better understanding of the onset of conditions that give rise to an alarm. Improvements in instrumentation help in dealing with a potentially mobile patient.

Monitoring of vital signs during anesthesia is another important area of computer application. Monitoring of the fetus during labor can give advance warning of potential problems. The monitoring and analysis of data during catheterization can shorten the procedure and at the same time increase the reliability of the obtained data. Analysis of sequences of images of the heart is used to estimate heart-stroke volume. Video disks are used here for fast playback and analysis of an image frozen at a particular instant. The analysis, or at least the selection of abnormal intervals of electrocardiograms, developed initially by Caceras (now at George Washington University) has attained routine use.

Requirements of reliability and availability cause most of those clinical systems to be based on minicomputer technology. The computer is frequently not explicitly visible to the physician, but is part of the complex of medical instrumentation.

Clinical Services. Less demanding, but still with high availability requirements, are applications that are one step removed from the patient. Important uses of com-

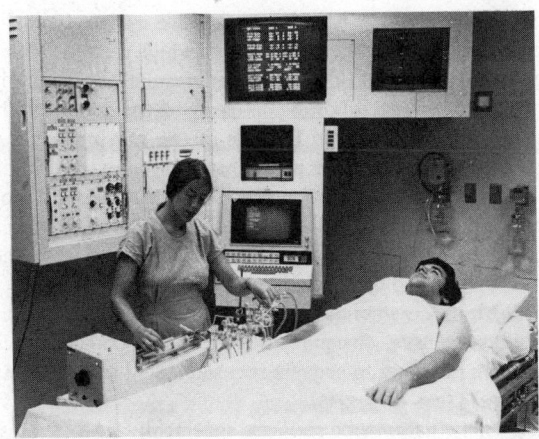

Fig. 4 Bedside arrangement in the Shock Research Unit, Center for Critically Ill, Hollywood Presbyterian Hospital. The oscilloscope (upper right) displays electrocardiographic and pressure waveforms. The TV monitor (left) provides status display. The CRT and the video terminal present trend plots, summaries of patient data, and record data into the system. (Courtesy of Dr. Herbert Shubin and Dr. Max Weil.)

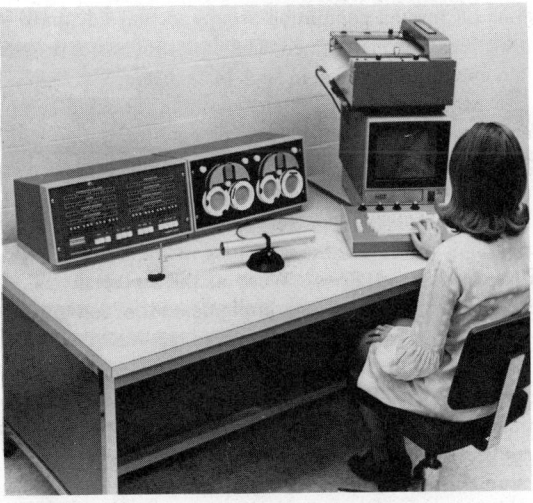

(a)

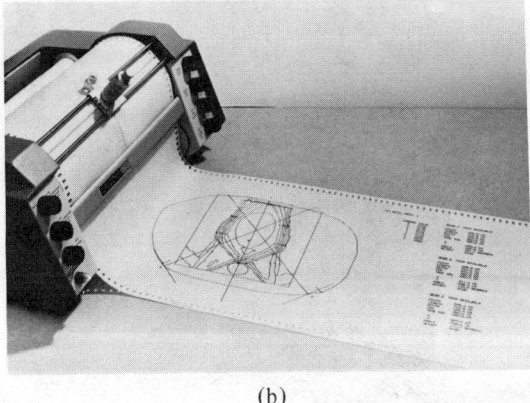

(b)

Fig. 5 Programmed console for radiation treament planning. Data concerning the patient are entered from radiographic information by tracing with stylus, and the drawings are displayed on the storage scope. Descriptions of ionizing radiation beams are stored on digital tape units. Final results are reproduced on an incremental plotter. (Courtesy of Prof. J. Cox, Washington Univ. St. Louis.)

puters can be found in radiation treatment planning, for which specialized systems have been developed by Cox. These provide the contours of radiation intensity in the body for a sequence of treatments so that the effects may be concentrated on tumors and minimized in other areas (see Fig. 5). The checking for potential interaction between a combination of drugs (Cohen at Stanford) and the data reduction, test scheduling, and quality control in clinical laboratories are among areas of application where computers are now routine.

Medical Records. The collection of some of the data for the medical record has been automated. One aspect of this area is the collection of medical history data from a patient by a programmed structure and branching interview sequence, which was initiated by Slack at the University of Wisconsin. Another is the administration of a routine battery of tests as part of a regular checkup procedure, *multiphasic screening,* as developed by Collen at Kaiser Foundation in Oakland. Data banks of test information are being collected to determine more appropriate limits of normalcy and abnormalcy, so that test results may be as specific as possible to the individual patient. The decision process that leads to an optimal or least-cost sequence of tests in order to arrive at a specific diagnosis is also a candidate for computerization.

A capability to follow patients over long periods of time is needed to make studies on patient data useful. This capability exists in the U.S. mainly in health maintenance organizations. In Europe, the more centralized health care systems assign health care identification numbers, which are used in every aspect of health care delivery. The database maintained by most central organizations, however, contain little medical data. Some population studies by American researchers are, in fact, done on foreign population groups so that adequate follow-up can be maintained. The data-processing problems become quite complex in such instances.

Many specialized clinics maintain detailed computerized records on their chronic population, but do not use them to replace the conventional paper record. These data may be helpful for surveillance (McDonald at the University of Indiana for diabetics), emergency care (Robbins at the Cardiology Clinic in Oklahoma City), or disease analysis (Fries). Weed at the University of Vermont advocates, and has implemented, a computerized version of a systematic approach to medical record-keeping in which the data acquired is not only associated with a patient, but also with a particular problem of the patient. Such a record organization will not only aid in the delivery of care, but also make the processing problem more tractable and enable the patient medical record to be used as a record of disease and treatment (Fig. 6).

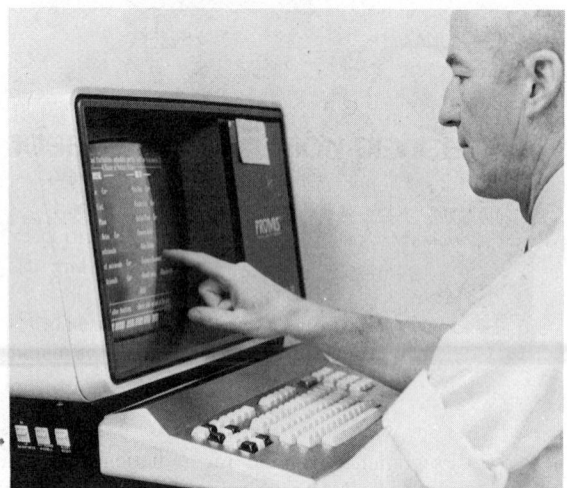

Fig. 6 Dr. Weed at a PROMIS terminal. Query and data entry is mainly accomplished through selection of displayed elements by touching the screen. A packet network connection provides a very high communication bandwidth so that screens can be rapidly changed. Photograph courtesy of the PROMIS Laboratory, University of Vermont.

Off-line processing of narrative pathology and radiology reports, resulting in automatic classification of problems found, can provide another formal input to the medical record, as shown by Pratt (NIH) and Lamson and Robinson (UCLA).

Hospital Management. Most hospitals use their own or service bureau computers to do their daily account processing. The data processing cycle is typically based on a midnight census against which all daily transactions are posted. The processed results are generally available by the following morning. Considerable difficulties are encountered because of the varying requirements of the third-party organizations that pay for a large fraction of the hospital expense. Cost justification may include disease diagnosis and severity information, which is generally not available in convenient form and has to be coded by specialized personnel.

Many commercial computer system manufacturers produce census, charging, and billing packages, which may be modified to specific requirements (*see* HOSPITAL INFORMATION SYSTEMS).

Some nationwide services, specifically PAS (Professional Activity Study), run by the Commission on Professional and Hospital Activities, Ann Arbor, MI, collect and summarize abstracted data from many hospitals in order to provide performance feedback to their subscribers.

Modeling of hospital processes has been another tool to aid management in the allocation and scheduling of resources. Valbona at Baylor in Houston used computers directly to schedule services to patients, and is now using computer aids in inner-city ambulatory clinics.

It is clear that medical computing will remain an area of much activity in the coming decade. Computers will also play a role in the measurement of their own effects on health care, as well as in the evaluation of other changes in the delivery area.

Source Information. One of the principal sources of current material is the journal, *Computers in Biomedical Research,* published since 1967 by Academic Press, New York. Proceeding of annual meetings, specifically the symposia held at San Diego, the University of Illinois, and in Washington, by the IEEE Computer Society, provide further reference material. Material for the IRIA meetings, as well as from other sources, has been published since 1970 in the *International Journal of Biomedical Computing,* by American Elsevier Publishing Company, The *Journal of Medical Systems,* sponsored by Advanced Medical Systems, the Health Applications Section of Operations Research Society of America, the Hospital Management Systems Society, the Health Services Division of the American Institute of Industrial Engineers, and the Society for Computer Engineers, publish articles on health care systems. The *Proceedings of the MEDINFO* Conferences (North-Holland), held since 1974 in conjunction with the tri-annual IFIP Congresses, provide an international overview. The National Center on Health Services Research (Rockville, MD) produces monographs and reports on health care delivery systems. In Great Britian, the Nuffield Provincial Hospitals Trust has documented *Computers in the Service of Medicine* through a series under that name published by the Oxford University Press.

Other periodicals in the area include *Methods of Information in Medicine,* published by the Schattauer Verlag, Stuttgart, since 1962; *Computing in Biology and Medicine* by Pergamon Press; and *Computer Programs in Biomedicine,* by North-Holland in Amsterdam, the last two published since 1970. In addition to application reports in the medical and health care management literature, a number of relevant articles can be found in the *IEEE Transactions on Biomedical Engineering* and in the Annals of the New York Academy of Sciences. Occasional special issues of the IEEE Transactions on Computers concentrate on medical areas (see, for instance, the issue of September 1979).

GIO WIEDERHOLD

MEDLARS/MEDLINE

For articles on related subjects *see* CURRENT AWARENESS SYSTEMS; INFORMATION RETRIEVAL; MEDICAL APPLICATIONS; and NEW YORK TIMES INFORMATION BANK.

The National Library of Medicine initiated a program for access to the biomedical literature nearly 100 years ago under the guidance of Dr. John Shaw Billings. *Index Medicus,* a guide to the medical literature, was first published in 1879. In 1962, the library began to develop a computerized system for the production of *Index Medicus;* the system went into operation in January 1964. This computer system, called MEDLARS (Medical Literature Analysis and Retrieval System), incorporated the first operational photocomposition system. As a by-product, the system could provide partially individualized bibliographies ("demand searches") for a requesting health professional. The demand for such services grew with time and with the size of the computer file, reaching a peak in 1970 with a total of 24,000 searches in the U.S. and participating foreign centers. The search service was provided, at times, from 10 computers in the U.S. and 11 computers in foreign countries.

To obtain a search, a qualified health professional submitted a written request describing the details of the information needed. This request was then "formulated" by a trained analyst, coded into the vocabulary of MEDLARS for input to one of the computers, and processed on the computer. The output was reviewed by the same search analyst who had formulated the query; finally, in three to four weeks, the requester received the bibliography. The entire MEDLARS file now contains 4 million citations, but at that time only about 800,000 were maintained in a current file that was available for routine searching.

On 29 October 1971, NLM initiated a nationwide, on-line, bibliographic retrieval system as a general service for the biomedical community. This service, called MEDLINE, now allows almost instantaneous, interactive searching of over 600,000 citations from the world's biomedical serial literature. This service has superseded the MEDLARS-batch demand search service. The service now supports an average of 65 simultaneous users,

```
USER:                        (Indicates user is to type command)
MULTIPLE SCLEROSIS           (Command to search for term multiple sclerosis)
PROG:
PSTG (746)                   (Program has found 746 postings of this term in
USER:                        current MEDLINE file)
print                        (Command to print one citation)
PROG:
AU—LASSMANN H                2 authors (AU) of article
AU—WISNIEWSKI HM

TI—CHRONIC RELAPSING EXPERIMENTAL ALLERGIC ENCEPHALOMYELITIS:
CLINICOPATHOLOGICAL COMPARISON WITH MULTIPLE SCLEROSIS.
SO—ARCH NEUROL 1979 AUG;36(8):490-7
```

Fig. 1. Excerpt from a MEDLINE search. Lower-case in the left column represents typing by the user; capital letters are entries from the terminal. (TI = title; SO = source.)

80 hr/week. In 1979, about one million on-line searches were processed.

Access to the MEDLARS/MEDLINE network is by telephone communications networks. The central computers (two IBM 370/158s) are located at the National Library of Medicine in Bethesda, MD. A back-up computer is at the central office of the State University of New York in Albany, from which the service is also available. There are over 1,000 institutions in the U. S. with MEDLINE access, located at medical schools, hospitals, research institutions, government agencies, and commercial organizations. In addition, MEDLINE is available in Australia, Canada, France, Great Britain, Italy, Japan, Mexico, South Africa, Sweden, and West Germany, and at the Pan American Health Organization Regional Medical Library in Sao Paulo, Brazil.

MEDLINE is the largest and most important of the Library's on-line databases, containing recent references (many with abstracts) to journal articles published in over 3,000 biomedical serials. There are a number of other important on-line databases, however, available over the network: TOXLINE (toxicology information), CATLINE (books catalogued at NLM), AVLINE (audiovisuals), CANCERLIT (cancer literature), and SERLINE (serial records), to name just several.

Access to the MEDLINE retrieval service is provided by a simple language at a typewriter-like device (although the indexing vocabulary is rather complex) connected through a telephone line to the computer at the NLM. Fig. 1 is an excerpt from a MEDLINE search.

REFERENCES

1967. Austin, Charles J. *MEDLARS 1963–1967.* Bethesda, MD: National Library of Medicine (Public Health Service Publication No. 1823), 76 pp., bibliography.

1973. McCarn, Davis B. and Leiter, Joseph. "On-line Services in Medicine and Beyond," *Science, No. 181* (July 27): 318–324.

1977. Leiter, Joseph. "On-Line Systems of the National Library of Medicine," in Shires, D. F. and Wolf, H.; *MEDINFO 77: Proceedings of the Second World Conference on Medical Informatics. Toronto, August 8–12, 1977.* New York: North-Holland, pp. 349–353.

1978. *Medical Informatics* **3**, *No. 3* (September). (Issue devoted to MEDLARS/MEDLINE.)

D. B. McCarn

MEMORY

For articles on related subjects *see* MEMORY-MAPPED I/O; ONE-LEVEL MEMORY; ULTRASONIC MEMORY; VIRTUAL MEMORY; and WILLIAMS TUBE MEMORY.
See also articles under STORAGE

The information in this article is organized in two major sections: *Main* and *Auxiliary*.

MAIN

For articles on related subjects *see* ACCESS TIME; ADDRESSING; ASSOCIATIVE MEMORY; CACHE MEMORY; COMPUTER CIRCUITRY; CYCLE STEALING; CYCLE TIME; DIRECT ACCESS; INTERLEAVE; INTERLOCK; MEMORY: Auxiliary; MEMORY PROTECTION; READ-ONLY MEMORY (ROM); and STORAGE HIERARCHY.

Different levels of *storage* (or *memory*) are usually employed in a computer system. This article concerns itself with the computer main memory, which is usually the most rapidly accessible memory and the one from which most, generally all, instructions in programs are executed. However, due to the rapid change of computer technology and its impact on the design philosophies of computers, some items traditionally unrelated to main memory techniques will be briefly treated.

In this article, each of the key terms related to main memory will be defined and illustrated. A concise description of the different organizations, technologies, and system techniques associated with memory design are then given.

Memory performance and cost are the twin keys to computer technology. It is fair to say that without the faster and cheaper memories that have been developed in recent years, the innovations in electronic device technology, processor organizations, and software systems would not have had their enormous impact on computer technology.

Definitions and Terminology. From a hardware point of view the computer main memory is formed by a large number of basic units referred to as *memory cells*. Each memory cell is a device or an electronic circuit that has two or more stable states. In current practice, only two-state devices are commonly available; each is capable of storing a binary digit, or bit. The physical grouping of these cells or bits into chunks such as bytes, or words, and the rationale behind each grouping scheme is discussed in detail in the section "Dimensional Quantization." At this stage it is sufficient to note that all the digits in a quantum (referred to as a word for the present) in the main memory are simultaneously accessed for a READ or WRITE operation.

Two important characteristics of main memory are: (1) The main memory is a *read/write* memory (RW or R/W) permitting data to be stored or retrieved at comparable intervals. This should be contrasted to *read only* memories (ROM) and *read mostly* memories (RMM), which permit reading at the same high speeds of RW memories, but for which the writing operation is restricted. ROM's may be written only once and cannot be changed thereafter. RMM's may be erased and written again, but the erase and write operations are usually much slower than the read operation. These RMMs are widely used with microprocessors and microcomputers *(q.v.)*, where they are called programmable read-only memory (PROM) and erasable programmable read-only memory (EPROM) and provide increasing degrees of adaptation by the user. (2) The main memory is a *random access* memory (RAM); i.e., the time to access each stored word is constant, independent of the sequence in which words were stored. This should be contrasted with *serial memories* such as disks, drums, tapes, and shift registers and including charge coupled devices (CCD) and magnetic bubble devices (of which more will be said later). In these memories data is available essentially only in the same sequence as originally stored.

Viewed from the system standpoint, a main memory can be considered as W words, each of B bits for a total storage capacity of $W \times B$ bits. Storage capacity may be stated in bytes, each of which consists usually of eight or nine bits. As mentioned before, the B bits of one word are available in parallel for reading or writing, as schematically indicated in Fig. 1.

With respect to memory timing, we speak of *access time* and *cycle time*. Access time is the time required to read out or write into any randomly selected word from memory. Cycle time is the minimum time interval required between the initiation of two successive, independent memory operations. In some memory technologies, such as bipolar semiconductor, the read cycle and write cycle times are almost equal. On the other hand, for magnetic cores, the reading operation is destructive. Thus, a core has to be rewritten after each reading, resulting in a cycle time equal to the time required to read and rewrite.

From the definitions above we distinguish between memory technologies that necessitate a *destructive readout* (DRO), such as magnetic cores, and those for which the readout is *nondestructive* (NDRO), such as some semiconductors. The rapid growth of semiconductor technology has introduced, in addition to other terminology, the terms *static* and *dynamic* memories. A static memory is one whose cells retain their states indefinitely as long as the system power is applied. Such memories do not fundamentally need a clock for their operation. Clocks

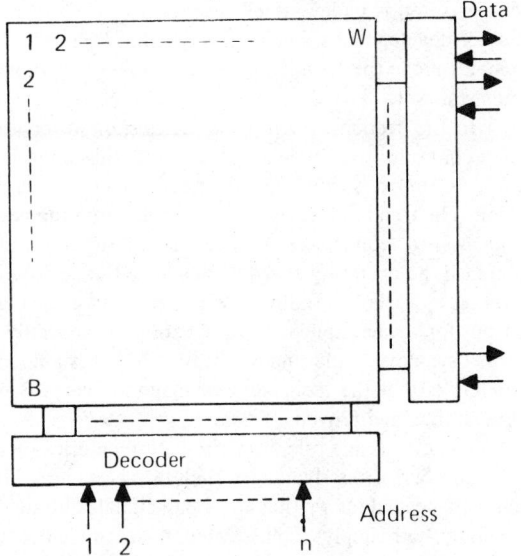

Fig. 1. Memory consisting of W words of B bits, each requiring an address of n bits ($n = \log_2 W$ — W is always a power of 2).

may be used but are required only to synchronize memory operation with the other elements in a computer system. Magnetic cores provide static memories. Static semiconductor memories employ a bistable flip-flop for each memory cell. On the other hand, dynamic memories usually store a binary digit as charge on a capacitor. Since capacitors will discharge with time, a dynamic memory cell needs periodic refreshing. This is accomplished by reading the cell content and rewriting it periodically under clock control. The details of the refresh operation, as well as its implication on the memory system design, will be considered later.

We should also distinguish between *volatile* and *nonvolatile* memories. A nonvolatile memory is one that retains its contents even if the power supply is removed. This property is present in ferrite core memories; semiconductor memories, however, are volatile. Since main memory is not used for long-term storage of instructions or data, volatility is not a major concern. Nonvolatility, however, is an essential attribute of mass storage systems.

Memory Technologies: An Overview. The oldest, still current memory technology is that of ferrite cores. (See Hodges, 1972; Renwick, 1964.) In spite of the challenge posed by the later technologies such as plated wires, thin film, and (more recently) semiconductors, magnetic core memories continue to exist. The advantage they continue to provide is nonvolatility, although that property too is under attack by recent (1981) semiconductor developments. For the time being, cores maintain a small niche (perhaps 10%) in the add-on and replacement markets.

In the section *Ferrite-Core Memories,* we consider their characteristics in detail. We wish at this point, however, to make some general observations concerning them. The trend in ferrite-core memories from the beginning was to reduce the cost per bit and simultaneously increase the operating speed. Cores have the obvious advantages of zero standby power, reasonable cost and speed for general-purpose applications (especially in large systems), and nonvolatility. Most significant, though, is that the technology of magnetic cores is mature, stable, and proven.

The decreasing role of ferrite-core memories relates to a number of disadvantages they bring, such as large currents needed for writing and small signals obtained in readout; both imply sophisticated read and write circuitry. The cost of such circuitry is an overhead on the system, which results in magnetic memories being uneconomic in small sizes. In addition to being bulky, magnetic-core memories are a foreign technology in relation to the rest of the computer system components. Stated in other terms, both the mechanical and electrical interfaces and power supplies present added problems.

During the ascendency of ferrite cores, modest parallel advances had been made in other magnetic memory technologies, such as thin films and plated wires. For example, in 1970, plated wires pioneered by Univac were estimated to fill about 2.5% of the RAM market. However, these developments, along with the much stronger ferrite-core technology, were swept away in the 1970s by developments in semiconductor technology.

Meanwhile, one major advance has been made in magnetic memory technology with the introduction of magnetic bubbles commercially by Rockwell in 1977. Using fabrication techniques developed in the semiconductor industry, bubble memories utilize thin wafers of magnetic garnet (a material in the ferrite family) to provide a memory with essentially serial access at speeds intermediate between that of disks and semiconductor RAM, but with nonvolatility. Bubbles have a potential for application as main memories in small, low-speed systems such as terminals, where nonvolatility is of paramount importance.

However important magnetic memory has been historically, and may yet become again as bubbles develop, semiconductor memory has attained clear dominance in the last decade. It has done so because its manufacture is basically a bulk process, while that for cores is much more discrete. Thus, while core prices on a per bit basis became quite stable in the 1970s, semiconductor prices fell by orders of magnitude. Currently, for complete memory systems, semiconductors are much cheaper than cores.

Semiconductor random access memory is known by various names—monolithic memory, integrated circuit memory, large-scale integrated (LSI) memory, and, now, very large-scale integrated (VLSI) memory. All these names refer to binary digital memories that employ an electronic circuit for each memory cell.

Originally, semiconductor memories were used in computer systems for applications requiring high operating speed such as scratch-pad memories. These were low-density, high-cost units employing bipolar junction transistors connected to form flip-flop memory cells. Note in the following that we refer to semiconductor memories employing integrated circuit bipolar junction transistors as *bipolar memories.* This will be contrasted with *MOS memories,* which employ metal-oxide-semiconductor field-effect transistor technology.

Later, semiconductor memories made their way into the computer main memory area. An early example of this trend was the IBM System 370/145. Many of these original memory systems utilized bipolar chips containing 256 bits of storage. Presently (1981), the dominant technology is MOS, with chips containing 65,536 bits available and announcements of 262,144 having been made.

In the remainder of this article we consider in some detail magnetic-core memories and semiconductor memories. The former are considered because of their historic importance and current utilization, which, though small on a functional basis, is still large in absolute terms, and the latter are emphasized because of their very rapid growth and their potential for complete replacement of all other technologies in mainframe *(q.v.)* applications.

Dimensional Quantization. Digital memory is dimensionally quantized as to both the number of words and the bits per word. The quantization naturally depends on the application for which the memory is intended, but also on some constraints produced by technology.

For "small" computers, the number of words required is often available in one *module,* and the complete memory consists entirely of a single module. For magnetic-core memories, the natural physical unit (or module) is called a *stack.* Depending on the speed of technology and other factors, a stack may be 1,024 (called 1K) 2K, 4K, or 8K words. Thus, for small machines, a single core memory stack may suffice. For semiconductor memory, the module is called a *board.* Single boards containing 256K bytes and more are relatively common and available at low cost (less than 0.1 cents per bit in 1981).

However, for "large" applications, the number of words required may easily exceed the number in a single module stack or board. Thus, a number of modules may be required, in which case a new opportunity for functional quantization arises. If the total number of words required by a system is at least twice that naturally available in one module, it is possible to apply the technique of address interleaving—[or simply *interleaving (q.v.)*]—in the system. In an interleaved memory consisting of M independent modules, consecutive addresses occur in physically separate modules. This arrangement in large systems makes possible the very high speed access of a sequence of contiguously addressed words, since all modules operate nearly simultaneously to obtain M words. In the event that sequentially accessed words are not in contiguous addresses, the reduction in total access time will not be so great, but will still be meaningful.

Though the digit or bit dimension (i.e., the number of bits per word) of a mainframe memory appears constrained by the system in which it is embedded, internally the memory may operate in a way that is technologically constrained. For example, though a memory may appear to the user to have addressing at a bit level, this appearance would normally be implemented by a combination of word addressing, and then subsequent bit-from-word selection.

The number of bits available from each quantum selection is constrained by the simultaneous need for speed and economy. For a speed of data access fixed by the technology chosen, it is obvious that the peak memory data rate in bits per second increases as more and more bits are retrieved by a single word access. Thus, there is a tendency to increase the number of bits per word to improve system speed. Another reason for increasing the number of bits per access quantum is that, for a given memory capacity, this reduces the total number of words and thus the total cost of the word-access mechanism.

However, these savings are often offset by other costs: Besides the need for additional bit sensing and standardization circuitry, there is a cost associated with the increased complexity of a system which is able to utilize selectively parts of a long word.

Whether a memory is most economically accessed by bit, byte, fraction of a word, half-word, word, double word, or multiple word will depend on the relative costs of the word-and-bit access mechanisms. Often the solution chosen balances in some sense the word and digit dimensions to produce a "square" design. In a "square" design there is a rough equality among the speed, cost, or space (or some combination) of mechanisms for selection in the word direction and for bit recovery in the digit direction.

Memory Selection—The Numbers Game.

Even modest memories require prodigious numbers of individual binary storage cells. For example, a memory of 4,096 words of 16 bits each, suitable only for a very mod-

est minicomputer configuration, contains 2^{16} ($=65,536$) memory elements. Clearly, even this small size results in an enormous technological problem in the selection of the desired bits. This has been solved in practical main memory technology by the concept of multidimensional access. One dimension, the digit dimension, is implicitly identified in the original memory specification. For each word selected, 2^4 (or 16) bits are accessed. However, there remains the need to select from one of 2^{12} (or 4,096) words. The notion of coordinate selection suggests itself.

If each memory cell typically containing one bit of information is conceived to be at the crossing points of a two-dimensional $X \times Y$ unit grid, or 2D array, then the number of grid points is XY. Clearly, for a memory of 2^N cells: $XY = 2^N$. By this means, an important advantage has accrued—namely, that the number of selection lines has been reduced from one per cell, 2^N, to $X + Y$, where $XY = 2^N$. The reduction is often greatest when the array is nearly square; i.e., when X is as close to Y as possible. For N even, the best choise is $X = Y = 2^{N/2}$, in which case the required number of lines is $2 \times 2^{N/2}$ for a 2^N cell array.

Now that we have identified 2^N nodes in a conceptual *array*, it is necessary to implement some physical node-selection mechanism. What is needed in practice is a *nonlinear* element with a threshold. A fundamental example of such an element used with magnetic core technology is a semiconductor diode that conducts current in only one direction with a few tenths of a volt drop while accepting large voltages in the reverse direction but allowing no current to flow. An example of a suitable array is shown in Fig. 2. One can see that current will flow in diode D_{11} only if the voltage V_{Y1} on Y_1 is positive, and if the voltage V_{X1} on X_1 is negative. Further, one can see that if all other Y wires are held negative and all other X wires positive, current will not flow in any other diode.

The diode itself, by its very existence, is a one-bit store. If it exists at a selected node, current flows; if it is absent, no current flows. A diode array, then, constitutes a simple *read only* store, which has an important application in mainframe computers as a means to store permanently instructions or constants.

More generally, if the diode current accesses a digital storage mechanism, one has succeeded in selecting one of 2^N storage locations by energizing two of $2 \times 2^{N/2}$ wires. In this role the diode nonlinearity is performing a logical AND function. If both X_1 and Y_1 are simultaneously energized, then current flows in D_{11}, selecting cell C_{11}. Logically, $C_{11} = X_1 \cdot Y_1$. This is a necessary property of all coordinate selection systems. Each selected entity is driven by an AND-ed coincidence of selection variables. For two-dimensional (2D) select, there are two selecting variables; for three-dimensional (3D) select, there are three selecting variables. Because we have in-

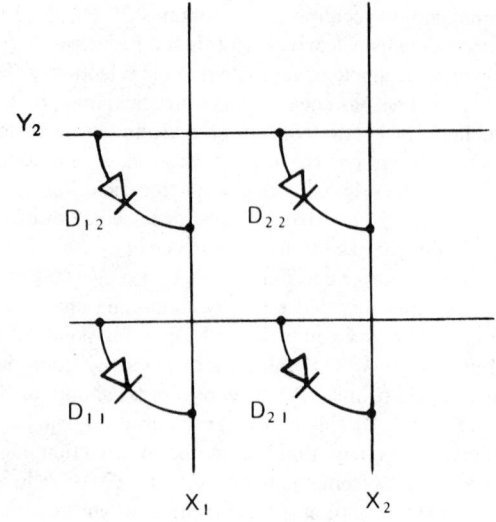

Fig. 2. Diode selection array.

troduced no constraint on the order of energizing the X or Y, the array so obtained is said to be *random access*.

Ferrite-Core Memories. A realization of the possibility of using magnetic square-loop toroids in a digital memory organization came to Jay Forrester at M.I.T. in 1950. Though his invention incorporated Permalloy tape-wound cores at first, the concept was quickly extended to the more easily mass-produced ferrite material.

Two critical properties of an ideal memory element happen to coexist in a single square-loop magnetic device: The first of these is memory, or *remanence,* permitting the fundamental storage of information. The second is threshold, or nonlinearity, facilitating noncritical *selection.*

Figure 3(a) shows a toroid of appropriate (ferrite) magnetic material through which a wire is run. In actuality, this toroid, or magnetic core, or core can be very small. Typical paired values of outer and inner diameters expressed in units of 10^{-3} in. include 80/50, 50/30, 30/18, 18/12, 12/7, 7/4. The incentive to use smaller and

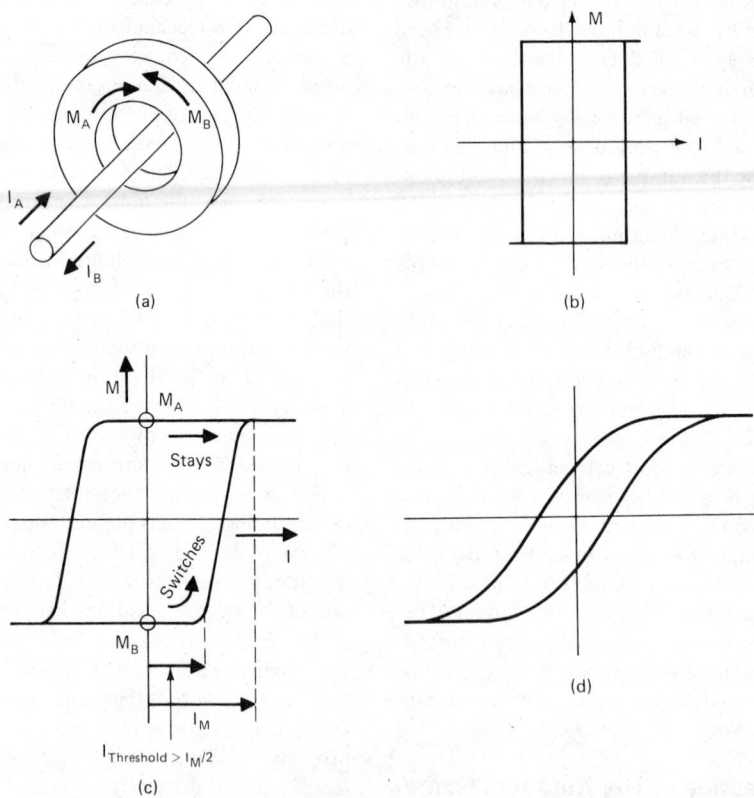

Fig. 3. Ferrite-core memory. (a) Magnetic toroid; (b) perfect "square loop"; (c) real loop, good core; (d) poor remanence.

smaller cores, besides the obvious one of miniaturization, is that less and less energy is needed to operate the device, and, with available switches, speed improves if smaller currents are required.

In actual use, as we will see, more than one wire threads each core. Thus, depending on the particular memory design parameters, including number of wires per core and number of cores on each selecting wire, some particular small core becomes a standard at any time corresponding to the current state of fabrication technology.

An ideal core such as that shown in Fig. 3(a) might have an ideal relationship between its controlling parameter, wire current I, and its controlled internal magnetization M, such as shown in Fig. 3(b) as a *perfect square* (meaning rectangular) *loop*. Real cores are, however, less than perfect, as shown in Figs. 3(c) and 3(d). Assuming that the core is initially in the remnant state M_B, application of a current I_A moves the state of the core into the fourth quadrant until, when I_A exceeds $I_{threshold}$, the core *switches*. If I_A is sufficiently large ($>I_M$), the core switches entirely, and when the current is removed, the magnetization has reversed to remanent state M_A. If a current I_A is again applied, the magnetization remains essentially constant. If, however, the current I is reversed to $I_B > I_M$, the state of magnetization will permanently change back to M_B.

Remanence per se does not depend strongly on the shape of the *MI* curve, and in fact the core in Fig. 3(d) has distinct remanent states. However, for purposes of selection, the shape of the "square loop" is very critical. It is very important, as we will see, that for a core to be safely selected [Fig. 3(c)] $I_{threshold}$ must exceed $I_{M/2}$.

Selection. Consider the core in Fig. 4 through which two wires are threaded. Consider further that currents I_1 and I_2 individually take on the values 0, or $\pm I_{M/2}$. If a total current $I_{M/2}$ flows on wires through the core, there

is no effect, since the threshold is not exceeded. That is, if

$$I_1 = I_{M/2} \text{ alone, nothing occurs,}$$

or if

$$I_2 = I_{M/2} \text{ alone, nothing occurs}$$

but if $I_1 = I_2 = I_{M/2}$, the core threshold is overcome and the core may switch to state A. To reverse the state of the core (state B), it will be necessary to apply $I_1 = I_2 = -I_{M/2}$, or alternatively, a current of $-I_M$ on one wire.

Output. A voltage is induced on every wire coupling the core if its remanent state is changed. Fig. 5 shows an output on a third wire threading the core in conjunction with the application of currents $I_{M/2}$ on two others in overlapped time sequence.

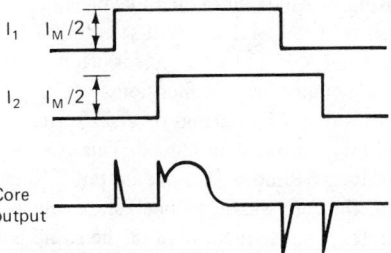

Fig. 5. Output voltage on third wire coupling the core of Fig. 4 due to application of select currents $I_M/2$.

Application or removal of just one of the select currents causes the core to traverse the relatively flat upper and lower branches of the M-I curve. For each such traversal occurring at the leading and trailing edges of the select pulses, a small, short output signal is produced. The effect is similar to coupling in a linear magnetic transformer, and reverses with the polarity of the current change. Because the change is not permanent and not related to the remanent property of the core, it is said to be "reversible." These reversible changes occur as noise on the bit-signal line. Each of the two signals to be interpreted as binary stored information is preceded by one of these reversible outputs appearing as an initial spike before the longer-term output, caused by permanent reversal of the magnetic domains within the core. In the case that the core is remanent at the state to which it is being sent, essentially only the reversible part appears.

Noise due to reversible core coupling and other magnetic and capacitive coupling between wires is a serious system problem in memories. As a result, it is common

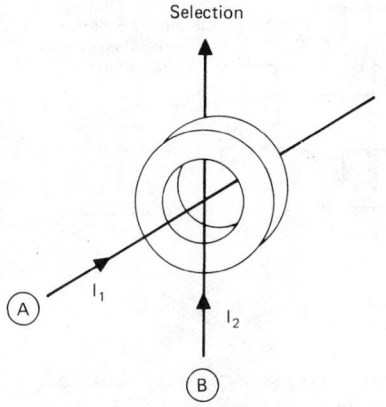

Fig. 4. Threshold selection.

practice (and technologically more natural) not to provide perfect pulses as shown, but rather ones that have controlled rise and fall times. Rise times must, of course, be less than the *fundamental ferrite switching time*. Fig. 6 shows a typical sequence of operations in the selection of one core in a memory array. The figure is realistic with the exception of the implied perfection of the current pulses. Their rise time is normally somewhat increased, and pulse shape is not necessarily perfect. The currents applied to the core on wire 1 and wire 2 are intentionally shown noncoincident so as to represent the propagation delay of currents along each dimension of a real two-dimensional core array. One can see that as a result of this delay, select pulses must be longer than would be needed if there were no delay, to ensure an adequate overlap that allows time to permit complete core switching.

As can be seen, only a small noise output results from a half-selected core where only one selection pulse is supplied. It is very important, of course, that this half-select output be small, since on a line of N cores, only one is selected while $N - 1$ are half-selected. The total accumulation of $(N - 1)$ half-selects is often a limiting factor in core-memory array dimensions.

If the core is selected and reverses state, a relatively large and long output is produced. This is shown in Fig. 6 arbitrarily as "Read with a one output." Since there is an output, the core was in a "one" state, but is now in a "zero" state. A subsequent read of the same polarity labeled "Read with zero output" produces no output. The rewrite of a "one" is shown to require reversal of both select currents to drive the core into its former remanent state. Though an output is produced at this time, it is rarely used. Thus, we see that reading is a destructive process, and therefore each read operation is normally followed by a restoring rewrite cycle.

Wiring Organizations

3D or *Bit Organized.* Fig. 7(a) shows a memory plane organization, traditionally called *bit organized,* or 3D. The complete memory system shown in Fig. 7(c) is composed of edge-connected planes wired as in Fig. 7(a) where a short diagonal line represents each core. The particular wiring shown within the plane is called "3D-4 wire, simplified."

Each core in a given core plane is threaded with four wires. The role of the wires in Fig. 7(b), labeled X and Y is similar to that described previously. However, for simplicity of electronic control, the current waveforms on each are invariant, consisting of a bipolar pulse doublet as shown in Fig. 7(b), independent of the data to be read or written. In order to write zeros and ones, an additional single line called "bit inhibit" threads every core in the same sense as the X line. A simple monopolar pulse applied to it, when present, cancels one half-select at the selected core, preventing the rewrite of the "one" state and leaving a zero. A fourth wire called "bit sense" threads every core. As a result of the simplicity of the diagonal path, the pulse traverses alternate diagonals of cores in a reverse sense from the previous diagonal. Hence, the polarity of the signal available between its ends varies from core to core. In operation, accordingly, the signal available has three states, either a positive or negative pulse called a "one," or nothing but noise for a zero. Since the contribution from each threaded core alternates, the noise accumulation from half-selects is reduced considerably.

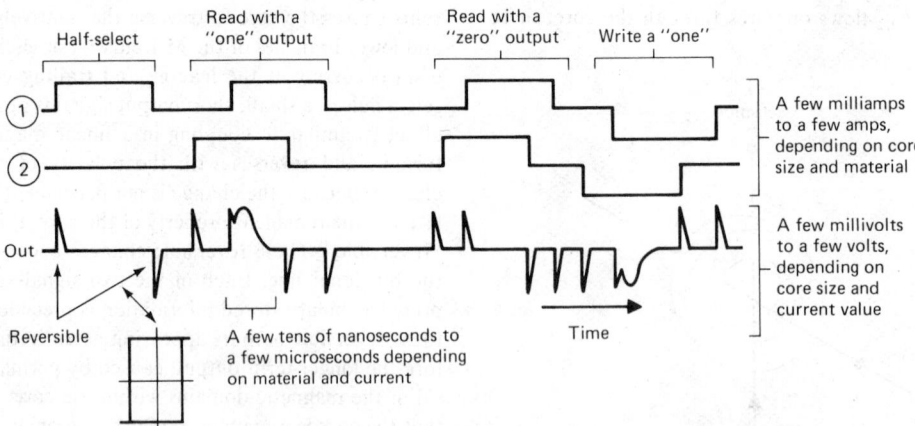

Fig. 6. A sequence of operations in the selection of one core in a memory array, illustrating the destructive nature of the read operation. In normal operation each read cycle is usually followed by a restoring write cycle.

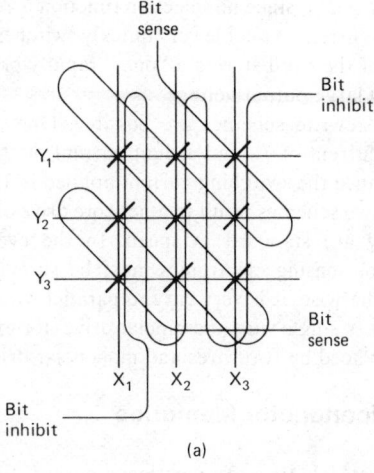

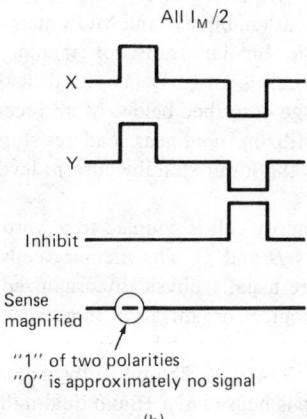

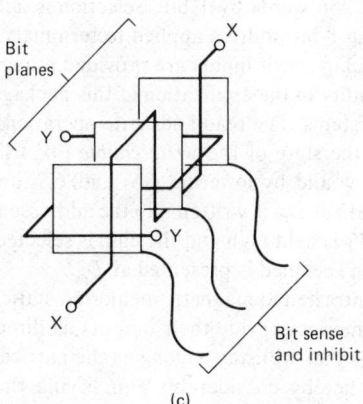

Fig. 7. Memory plane organization. (a)3D, four-wire, simplified core plane; (b) initial pulses on X and Y; (c) 3D core stack.

In use, each plane is assigned to one bit of all words in the *collection of planes* called the *stack*. Accordingly each X and Y line must thread each plane as shown. A completed stack is truly a solid 3D object, as the name of the technique implies. Typically, each plane may consist of 64 to 128 cores to a side, producing a memory of 4,096 to 16,384 (4K to 16K) words with a number of planes equal to the number of bits per word, say, 16 or 32. Such a 4K, 32-bit memory would have 64 X drivers and (since $4K = 64 \times 64$) 64 Y drivers, 32 digit-inhibit drivers, and 32 digit-sense circuits.

Strobing. Strobing is a name for the technique required to time-synchronize data appearing as pulses at the output of a memory. It is implemented by a gate within each sense amplifier (connected to each digit line), which is opened at a predetermined optimum time at which the correct digit readout is expected. It is intended to solve two problems: The first is the fact that a core plane is a noisy environment, and the selection of a legitimate logic 1 signal from the accumulation of half-selects, reversible signals, and driven line induction requires some precision. Luckily, the timing of the noise, particularly of the reversible and induced signals, and including the half-selects, is earlier than the true signal.

The second problem that strobing must solve complicates the solution to the first selection. This problem concerns the time delay of transmission within each plane and within the stack. Clearly, the bit lines indicated in Fig. 7 are very long and consist of a wire having a distributed load of magnetic cores. The result is a transmission line having considerable delay per bit. It is apparent that a signal originating at a core deep within a plane will appear at the bit-sense terminals somewhat later than one originating near the ends of the sense line. This is a difficult problem to solve with strobe timing, and often limits the size of the core plane that can be used. In some designs it is possible to vary the strobe, and hence the bit-sensing time, with the *address* of the bit selected, thus allowing somewhat longer bit lines.

In designing the digit strobe circuitry, account must also be taken of the delay along the X and Y select lines. In a bit-organized 3D memory, this is particularly easy, since the X and Y lines are relatively short, being $d/\sqrt{2n}$ times the length of the bit lines for d ($n \times n$) bit planes* (n^2 words of d bits each). Furthermore, it is easy to adjust the strobe for each bit to cancel X and Y delay if necessary.

Figs. 8 and 9 show other 3D designs. The four-wire

---

*This may be seen by observing that the digit line of each digit plane consists of $2n$ diagonal bit lines of variable length equivalent to n lines of length $\sqrt{2}$ times the plane side length.

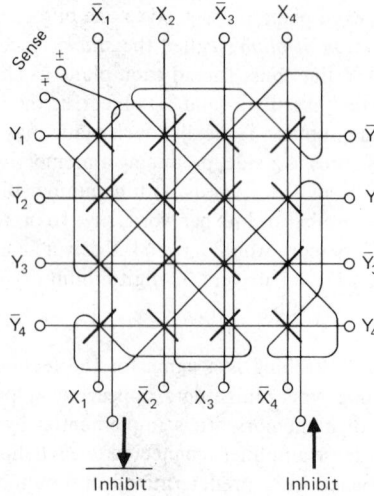

Fig. 8. Another 3D, four-wire, standard core plane.

standard design has a complex double-diagonal sense wire, arranged so that half-select disturbances tend to cancel in pairs of cores on any X or Y line. In use, the onset of X and Y drives are staggered to reduce the composite size of half-select outputs. The bar notation of X and Y drive lines indicates a system of current reversal, which compensates for the alternating property of the sense line threading to insure single-polarity sense outputs.

2D or Word-Organized Selection Schemes. The simple system shown in Fig. 10(a) is a 2D two-wire, one-core-per-bit configuration, also referred to as *linear select* or *word organized.* In the simple scheme shown, simplicity of wiring has been gained at the expense of complexity of driver electronics. Fig. 10(c) shows a variety of possibilities. For each write possibility, the read pulse may be

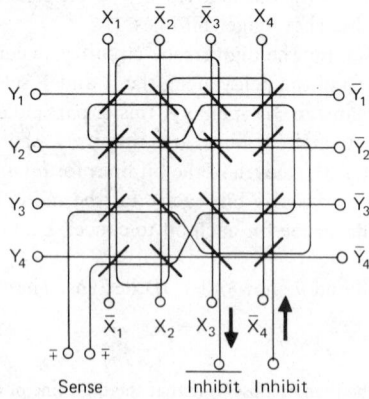

Fig. 9. A 3D, four-wire, rectangular core plane.

very large ($> I_M$), since no selection function is required. The excess current available very quickly switches to zero each core of the word storing a "one," rapidly producing a relatively large output voltage.

Three rewrite schemes are possible. One, using a word line current of I_M and a digit current of $\pm I_{M/2}$ is very fast, since the switching current applied is $3/2$ (I_M). The other two schemes result in a net core drive of I_M and accordingly are standard in speed. In the event that switching or sensing electronics must be simplified for speed or otherwise, it is very easy to parallel wires in the array. Thus, a single wire and bipolar drive (for example) may be replaced by two wires and monopolar drivers.

Semiconductor Memories

Bipolar Memories. As mentioned earlier, two basic semiconductor technologies are used in semiconductor memory fabrication, bipolar and MOS memories. Fig. 11 shows a basic bipolar transistor memory cell. This multi-emitter cell is an early one, used in the Fairchild 256-bit package described below. More recent variations on this cell utilizing nonlinear load resistors operate at higher speeds and lower standby current levels (Inadachi et al., 1979).

Each memory cell is coupled to a word line W and two digit lines D and $\bar{D}$. The memory cells on a single silicon chip are usually physically organized in a square matrix. The logical organization, however, of an *n*-cell chip is that of *n* words by 1 bit. As an example, consider the Fairchild 93410, a 256-bit fully decoded memory chip. The chip is housed in a 16-pin dual-in-line package. Fig. 12 shows the terminal connections. The chip is organized as 256 words by 1 bit. Selection is achieved by means of an 8-bit address applied to terminals A_0 to A_7. The three chip-select inputs are provided to permit some logic flexibility in the application of this package to large memory systems. The read and write operations are controlled by the state of the *write enable* ($\bar{W}_E$) line. With $\bar{W}_E$ held low and by lowering $\overline{CS}_1$ and $\overline{CS}_2$ and raising $\overline{CS}_3$, the data at D_{IN} is written into the addressed location. To read, $\bar{W}_E$ is held high and the chip is selected. Data in the location specified is presented at D_{out}.

As contrasted to magnetic memories, static semiconductor memories provide their outputs as direct-current (DC) levels that will stay as long as the particular cell is accessed, thereby considerably simplifying the readout electronics. Interface problems are almost nonexistent, since both input and output levels are easily made compatible with standard integrated circuit logic families.

The particular package of Fig. 12 is specified to have a maximum read-access time of 50 ns, with 1.8 mW per bit power dissipation. In general, it is fair to say that bipolar memories commercially available in the early 1980s

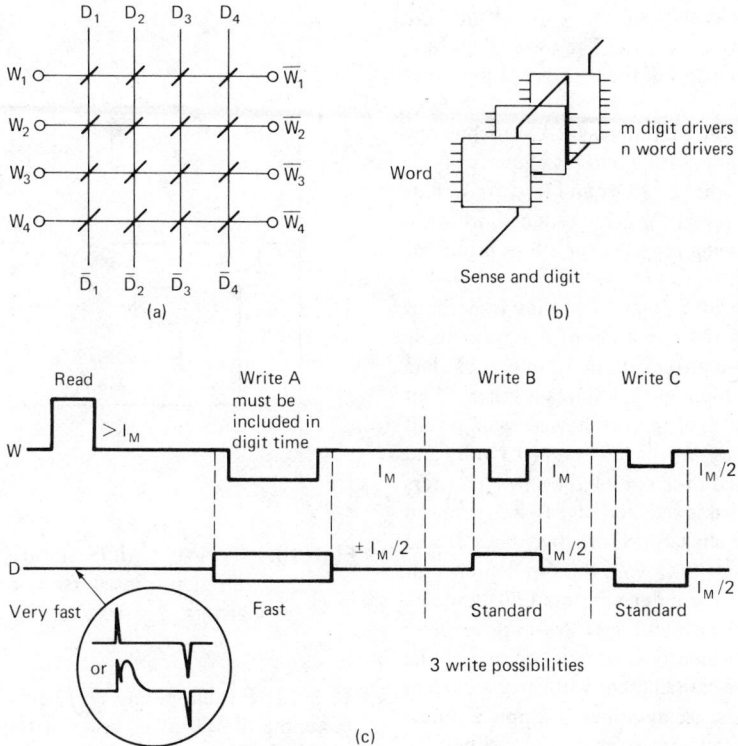

Fig. 10 A linear-select system. (a) 2D, two-wire, one-core per bit plane; (b) 2D core stack; (c) read/write waveforms.

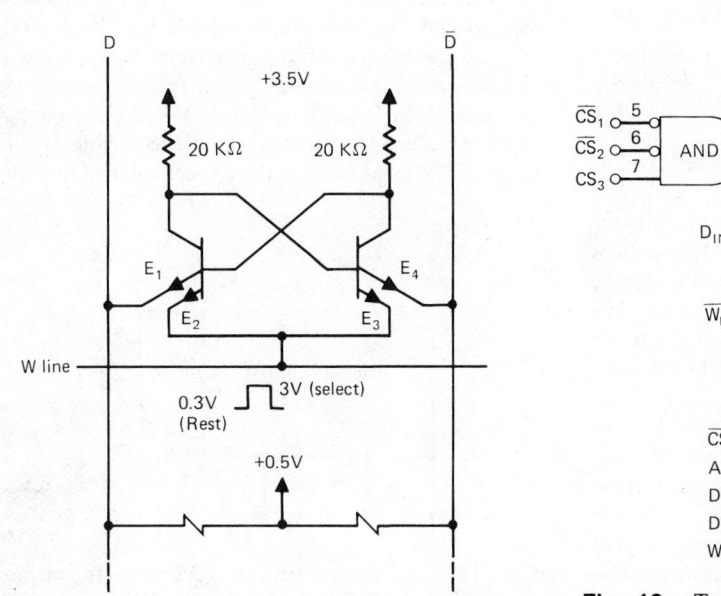

Fig. 11. A basic emitter-coupled bipolar memory cell.

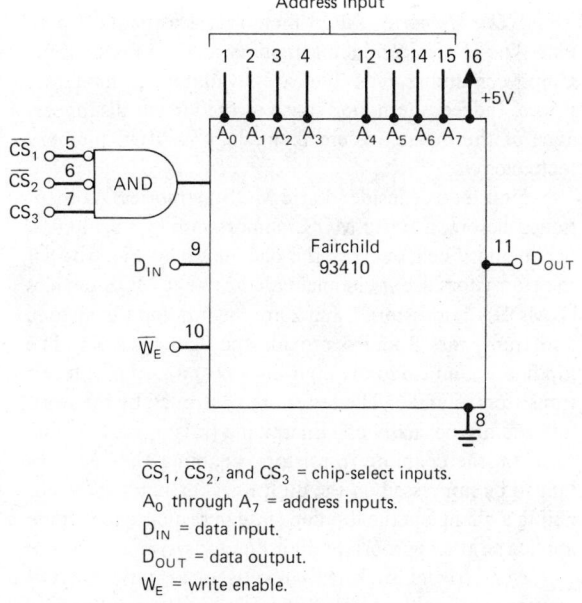

$\overline{CS}_1$, $\overline{CS}_2$, and CS_3 = chip-select inputs.
A_0 through A_7 = address inputs.
D_{IN} = data input.
D_{OUT} = data output.
W_E = write enable.

Fig. 12. Terminal connection of the Fairchild 93410 fully decoded 256-bit bipolar memory chip.

obtain high operating speeds at the expense of high standby power and increased cost. They are, therefore, appropriate only for the parts of the memory system that require this high speed.

It is important to note that bipolar RAM technology is continuously developing, with 4,096-bit chips available in 1981 having access times of 25 ns and less. As well as speed increases, power levels are being reduced, with less than 0.2 mW per cell being reported for a 6 ns prototype (Inadachi et al., 1979).

An understanding of bipolar memories is perhaps enhanced by reviewing the operation of a typical basic cell. Consider the multi-emitter cell shown in Fig. 11. The two transistors form a flip-flop that stores a binary digit 0 or 1, according to which of the two devices is on or off. Normally, the word line is at the low level (0.3 volt) and the current is conducted over one of the inner emitters (say $E3$). When the word is selected, the W line is raised to the high level (+3 volts). Since the digit lines D and $\overline{D}$ are normally at about +0.5 volt, the flip-flop current is transferred to one of the outer emitters ($E4$) and the inner emitter junctions ($E2$ and $E3$) are both reverse-biased. Depending on which transistor is on, one of the two digit lines ($\overline{D}$ in the case chosen) will carry a current of about 0.25 mA. The sense amplifier is simply a differential amplifier connected across the D and $\overline{D}$ lines. To write into the cell, the W line is first raised in potential, and current is applied to either the D or $\overline{D}$ (to write a 1 or a 0) to force the flip-flop to the desired state. Note that for the component values shown, this cell dissipates about 900 μW in standby mode.

MOS Memories. MOS memories are the most popular type of semiconductor memory at the present time. Chips containing 64K bits are available at moderate prices. Indeed, the major cause of the virtual disappearance of the magnetic-core technology is MOS memory technology.

First let us consider static MOS memories. As mentioned before, a static MOS memory employs a flip-flop per memory cell, such as the one shown in Fig. 13. All the transistors are *n*-channel-enhancement MOS devices (NMOS). Transistors 1 and 2 are the flip-flop transistors, and transistors 3 and 4 provide the load resistors. The flip-flop is coupled to the digit lines D and $\overline{D}$ through two transistors, 5 and 6. The latter are controlled by the word line and are normally off. Energizing (raising) the W line turns on the coupling transistors, enabling the cell content to be impressed on the digit lines for reading, or enabling a change in the flip-flop state in response to voltage applied to the appropriate digit line for writing.

A matrix of such cells results in a static NMOS memory chip, with each cell requiring six transistors. For example, the 2147, a modern 4,096 × 1 bit static RAM manufactured by Intel and others, is available in a single

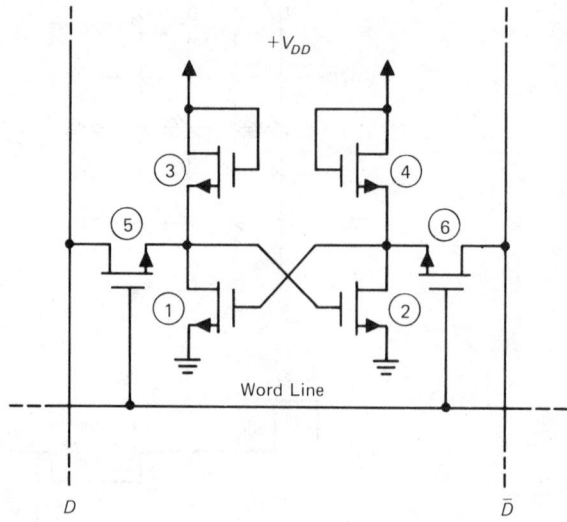

Fig. 13. Typical NMOS static memory cell: 1, 2 = flip-flop transistors; 3, 4 = load resistor transistors; 5, 6 = coupling transistors.

18-pin DIP (dual-in-line pin) package. It provides an access time of 100 ns or less, yet requires only about 150 mA from its 5-volt supply. Although the resulting memory generally dissipates less power and is easier to manufacture than bipolar memories, speed is sacrificed, and the power and area saving is not substantial. A correction of the latter deficiency is the motivation to consider dynamic memory cells.

Fig. 14 shows one possible three-transistor dynamic memory cell. The binary digit is stored as a charge on the gate-to-substrate (ground) capacitance of Q_1, while Q_2 and Q_3 serve as gating switches for reading and writing, respectively. Since the capacitance-stored charge decays with time, the memory needs periodic refreshing. By "refreshing" we mean reading the cell content and rewriting

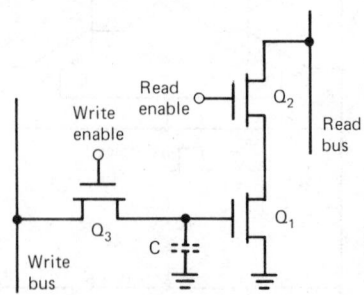

Fig. 14. A three-transistor MOS dynamic memory cell. The binary bit is stored as charge on the junction capacitance C.

it. This has to occur at a certain specified minimum frequency. Memories based on such a scheme are called *dynamic memories*. A clock or a timer is essential for the operation, to keep track of the elapsed time between successive refreshes.

A more recent event in the evolution of MOS dynamic memory has been the development of the single transistor dynamic storage cell shown in Fig. 15. Here, Q_1 is an *n*-channel device which acts as a selection switch in a coordinate selection system to control access to the storage capacitor C. This capacitance, a small fraction of a picofarad, exists between the drain of Q_1 and the chip substrate, which is grounded.

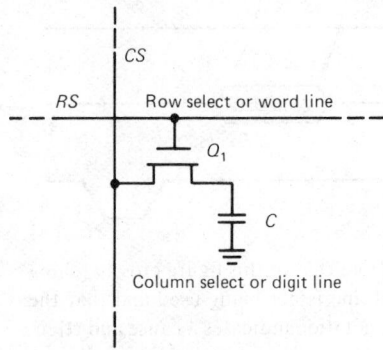

Fig. 15. A single transistor dynamic storage cell.

Writing of information into the cell proceeds as follows: When the row select line RS is raised, Q_1 conducts, causing C to charge to the voltage on the column select line CS, a voltage that is made high or low depending on the writing of 1 or 0, respectively. To read information that has been previously stored, the (capacitance of the) CS line is initially connected to the high voltage level (a logic 1), then released as the RS line is raised. If the voltage on C had been high, the voltage on CS is unaffected, and a logic 1 is sensed. If, on the other hand, C had been low, the result would be a lowering of the voltage on CS as the voltage on C is raised initially. This lowering of CS is detected by a sensing amplifier-driver, which immediately lowers the voltage on CS, restoring the voltage on C. Thus, we see that though the reading mechanism is inherently destructive, the old information is immediately and automatically restored by this means.

Note that in the arrangement described, all cells connected to a row select line are activated at once as RS is raised. If, as is usual, each column is equipped with a sensor/driver, then a whole row of cells may be read and rewritten at once. Though this feature is not an essential part of normal operation, it allows a large number of cells to be refreshed at once, with a great saving in refresh

time. For example, as a result of this ability, total refresh of a 4,096 × 1 memory consisting of a 64 × 64 array of cells, is possible in only 64 cycles. Typically, each cell in a dynamic RAM should be refreshed at least once every 2 ms. For a 200-ns memory cycle, this constitutes only a 0.64% overhead for such a 4K memory.

To illustrate a large number of the features available in a modern (1981) dynamic RAM, we will consider the Motorola MCM6664 memory chip. This is a 65,536 word by 1 bit memory array housed in the 16-pin DIP package shown in Fig. 16. It utilizes high-performance NMOS silicon gate technology, requiring only a single 5-volt power supply. Internally, the chip consists of four 16,384-bit subarrays, each 128 × 128, and each having 128 sense amplifiers. To access 64K words (each of 1 bit) requires 16 bits of address, which are provided in time-multiplexed fashion to the 8 address pins (A_0 through A_7). An address is entered as a row address when $\overline{RAS}$ (the row address strobe) becomes active, acting as a row address selector. Likewise, a column address is entered with $\overline{CAS}$ (the column address strobe) activated.

Refresh,	$\overline{R_{FF}}$	1	16	V_{SS}, ground	
Data in,	D	2	15	$\overline{CAS}$	
Read/write,	$\overline{W_E}$	3	14	Q, data out	
	$\overline{RAS}$	4	13	A_6	
	A_0	5	12	A_3	
	A_2	6	11	A_4	
	A_1	7	10	A_5	
5 volts,	V_{CC}	8	9	A_7	

Fig. 16. A_0 through A_7 = address inputs ($2^8 = 256$). RAS = row address strobe; CAS = column address strobe. Note that the bar notation indicates that the named action occurs when the signal is low, that is at the logic 0 level.

Fig. 17 illustrates the external timing signals required for various memory operations: The sequence of write cycle followed by a read cycle and a refresh cycle is shown. For both the write and read cycles, row addresses are first presented and RAS is activated. Then column addresses are presented and CAS activated: In each case, address data is assimilated on the initiation of the strobe (RAS or CAS). Read/write status is also accessed from the W input on the initiation of CAS. If "write" mode is intended, the data must have been stabilized at the input D. For most conditions, including the write mode, the output Q remains "disconnected," that is in the high-impedance state of the tristate output circuit. In the "read" mode, valid data is switched to the Q out-

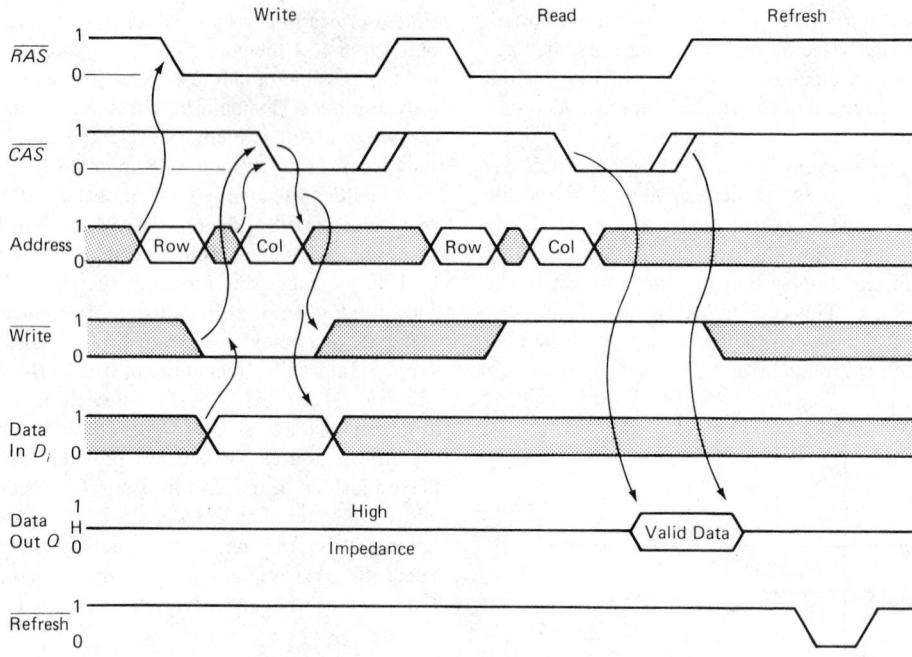

Fig. 17. External timing signals for memory operation. Note that in this figure crosshatching indicates that the information on the associated line is not being used and that the state of the line is immaterial. The curved arrow notation indicates a cause and effect relationship, the effect being at the head of the arrow.

put following the initiation of *CAS* and is maintained until *CAS* rises.

Refresh activity is performed on three occasions in the time span represented in Fig. 17. Each time a row is accessed, whether for write or read, all 256 cells in the row, including the targetted one, are refreshed. In addition, at any time that *RAS* is held inactive ($\overline{RAS}$ high) and $\overline{Refresh}$ is lowered, a special feature of the 6664 is accessed; namely, an *internal refresh counter* is first used as a row address, then incremented. Thus, 256 successive applications of Refresh guarantees that each and every cell of the 65,536 has been refreshed, independent of

other memory activity. Since the memory cycle of the 6664, that is the interval from one activation of *RAS* (or Refresh) to the next, is about 150 ns, refresh activity would occupy, at most, 256×0.15 or 38.4 μs.

Thus far, we have described the operation of only a single IC chip and not of a complete memory system. Such a system would utilize several such chips, some to increase the number of bits per word and others to increase the total number of words provided. Thus, for example, a memory board equipped to provide 64K bytes (each of 8 bits) could use eight 64K $\times$ 1 memory chips such as we have described. If only 4K $\times$ 1 chips were

Table 1.   Comparison of Memory Systems

	Technology	Access/Cycle Time (ns)	System Pwr. (mW/bit)	Density (bits/cm³)	Bits/Chip
IBM 360-85	Bipolar	40/80	5.5	5	64
IBM 370-145	Bipolar	125/150	0.6	54	128
Fairchild-Illiac	Bipolar	188/200	3.8	5	256
Semi RAM 300	Bipolar	300/400	0.7	31	128
STD Logic-1103	MOS	450/550	0.5	32	1024
EM & M 3000	Core	300/650	0.5	50	—

available, a total of 128 would be required for such a memory. If 4K × 4 chips were available, only 32 would be required.

While the construction of such systems lies beyond the scope of this article, it may be useful to indicate the general nature of the interconnections needed. To increase the word length of a memory by a factor of 8, 8 chips are interconnected with all of the control inputs paralleled (address, strobes, and write) but with data inputs and outputs separate. On the other hand, to increase the number of words by a factor of 4, 4 chips would be interconnected with data inputs (data input, data output) and some controls (row strobe and write) paralleled and column strobe gated under control of two additional bits of address decoding logic.

In concluding this article, we present Table 1, which shows a comparison of some of the memory systems employing bipolars, MOS, and magnetic cores.

REFERENCES

1964. Renwick, W. *Digital Storage Systems.* London: SPON.

1972. Hodges, D. A. (Ed.). *Semiconductor Memories.* New York: IEEE Press.

1973. Luecke, G., Mize, J. P., and Carr, W. N. *Semiconductor Memory Design and Application.* New York: McGraw-Hill.

1978. Proebster, W. E. (Ed.). *Digital Memory and Storage.* Braunschweig: Vieweg.

1979. Inadachi, M. et. al. "A 6ns 4Kb Bipolar RAM Using a Switched Load Resistor Memory Cell," *1979 International Solid State Circuits Conference Digest,* p. 108.

1980. Matsue, S. et al. "A 256K Dynamic RAM," *1980 International Solid State Circuits Conference Digest,* p. 232.

K. C. SMITH AND A. S. SEDRA

AUXILIARY

For articles on related subjects *see* ACCESS TIME: BLOCK AND BLOCKING; DATA ACQUISITION COMPUTER; DIRECT ACCESS; LATENCY; MEMORY: Main; SCRATCH FILE; and STORAGE HIERARCHY.

Auxiliary memory (AM) is distinguished from main memory (MM) by the fact that only from the latter are instructions taken for execution. In most computers, the arithmetic logic unit (ALU) and MM comprise a carefully designed pair of machine components, matched for speed and data path width. AM comprises all other memories, whose contents (instructions and data) must be fetched into the MM before processing by the ALU.

AM is rewritable, i.e., it can be written, read, rewritten, etc., many times without deterioration. Thus, punched cards, paper tape, and printer paper are not classified as AMs, although the first two media store instructions and data in rereadable form. AM generally uses electromagnetic digital technology for storing data.

There are some eight different types of AMs in use today, and their variety and number continue to grow:

  Magnetic tapes
  Cassette tapes
  Drums
  Fixed-head disks
  Moving-head disks
  Video-recorded cartridges
  Large solid-state memories
  Floppy disks.

Magnetic Tapes. Magnetic tapes are long narrow ribbons (typically 2,400 feet long and 0.5 inch wide) of plastic film coated with iron oxide, wound on hard plastic reels approximately 1 foot in diameter. Information is stored transversely on tape, usually seven or nine bits per *frame* (character or byte of data recorded on tape; see Fig. 1). Several frames are consecutively recorded as a *block* of data; blocks are separated by *inter-record gaps* (IRGs), and files of such blocks by inter-file gaps usually called *tape marks.*

Longitudinally, data are typically stored at one of the following densities: 800, 1600, or 6250 bits per inch. Thus, a fully written reel of tape, recorded at 1,600 frames per inch (or, on each track, "bits per inch," normally abbreviated to bpi), contains over 40 million bytes: 2,400 feet by 12 inches/foot by 1,600 bytes/inch = 46,080,000 bytes although normally inter-record gaps would reduce this by about 1/3.

Data is read from a magnetic tape AM into MM via a *tape drive* (also called a *tape station,* or *tape controller*), depicted in the photo in Fig. 2 and the schematic in Fig. 3. Referring to Fig. 3, the tape is pulled from the supply reel to the takeup reel by motors driving the two hubs. These motors operate independently, so that the length of tape between the two reels varies from instant to instant. This permits the takeup reel to accelerate quickly at the start of each read/write (R/W) operation without requiring synchronized acceleration of the supply reel. The interhub strand of tape droops into two vacuum columns in most tape drives, where it is held lightly taut by air-pressure differences (Fig. 4). As the loop drops below a vacuum-sensing hold in the takeup column, an electric signal engages the takeup motor with the corresponding reel. The motor disengages as soon as the loop is pulled above a second vacuum-sensing hold (Fig. 5). Analogous controls keep a varying-length loop suspended in the supply column.

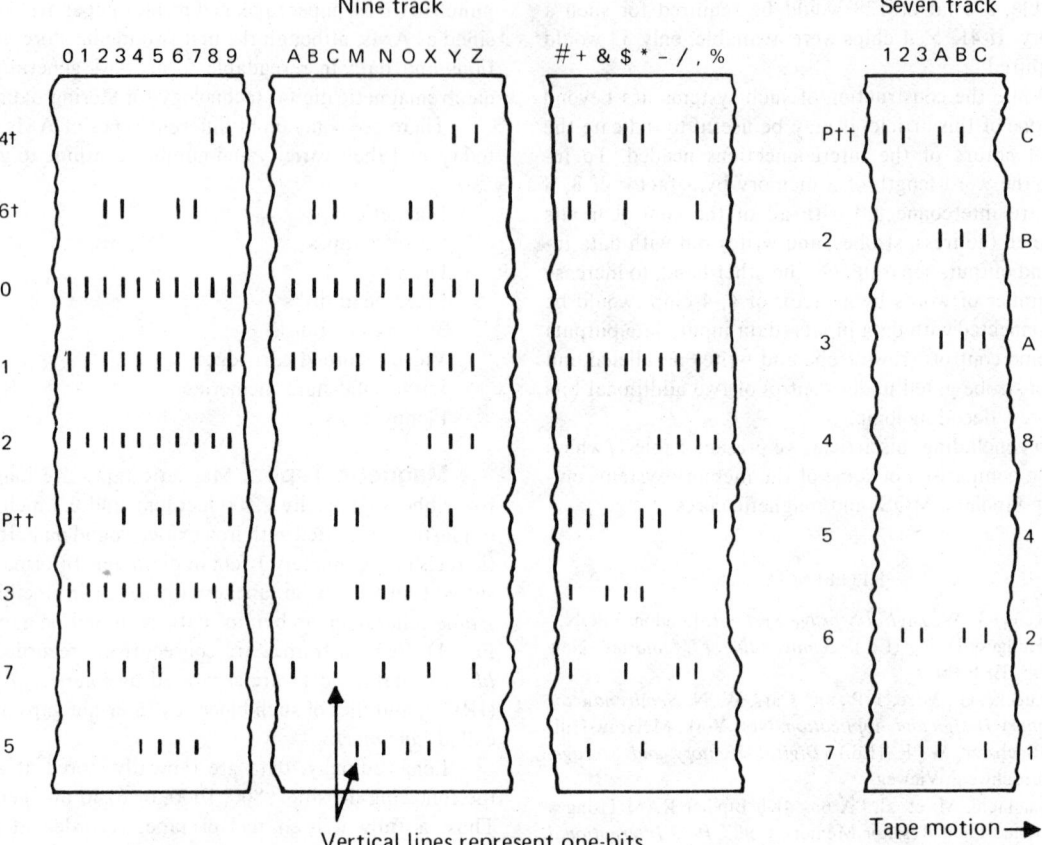

Fig. 1.   Nine- and seven-track tape data format. *Notes:*† Track numbering shows order in which bits are accumulated into bytes (characters); bit 0 is leftmost character and bit 1 is next, etc. Therefore, the character 0 has the bit representation 11110000 on a nine-track tape.‡ The parity bit.

The foregoing describes *forward* R/W operations; *backward* R/W operations are commonly available on tape drives manufactured since the early 1960s. Supply and takeup reels reverse roles; the two motors are capable of driving the reels in either direction.

Reading and writing are performed by a pair of *heads* (seven to nine transformers) aligned transverse to tape motion. During reading operations (Fig. 6), the *write head* is inactive; the *read head* senses the flux produced by electromagnetic spots on the tape as it moves past the transformers. During writing operations, the write head furnishes strong electromagnetic signals at precisely timed instants. Whether the prior content of each frame is logical 0, 1, or "no value" (i.e., blank tape), the write signal creates a new frame of 0s and 1s (predetermined voltage levels). The read head checks newly written data a split second later by reading back the pattern of bits and comparing it to the pattern originally

transmitted to the write head. These patterns should be identical; if not, a "write error" signal is sent by the tape drive to the computer. Error-retry operations follow, as described in the following paragraphs.

To detect (and, in some advanced tape drives, to permit logical correction of) recording errors, two sets of check bits are written—*parity bits* and *longitudinal check bits* (Fig. 7). One or two parity bits are furnished per frame on almost all tape drives, permitting detection of all *single-bit* errors (substitution of 0 for 1, or *vice versa*). At the end of each block of data, several frames of check bits are written, typically two (with their own parity bits, of course). The *tape subsystem* (one or more drives plus control unit) contains sophisticated checking logic which determines during each R/W operation if all frames have been correctly transmitted to/from the tape. If a parity error is sensed during reading of one or more frames, the subsystem sets an internal latch; when the

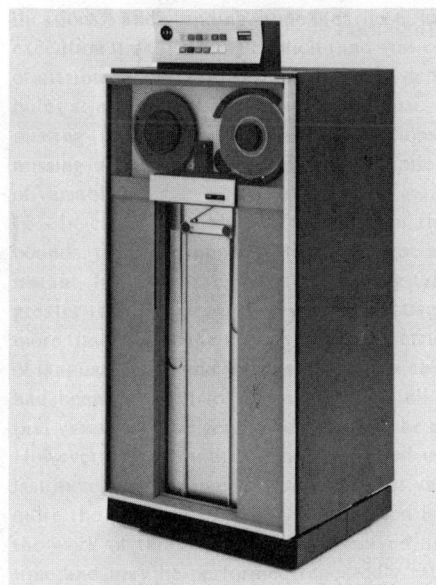

Fig. 2.   An IBM 3420 magnetic tape unit.

end of this block is reached, the subsystem sends status bits to the ALU (via an I/O channel) so that rereading may be attempted.

Two different approaches to formatting and using magnetic tape data are prevalent, exemplified by tape drives furnished by IBM and DEC. IBM-compatible drives create variable-length blocks and cannot be updated/overwritten in place, DECTAPE drives create fixed-length blocks that can be updated/overwritten with new information. To update a tape file using an IBM-compatible system, the old master file must be completely copied onto a new master file, with transaction data merged in as appropriate (Fig. 8). With DECTAPE drives, the master file need only be spaced forward to blocks requiring updating. In this respect, DECTAPE drives can be used like direct-access devices (see next section). However, it is often desirable in commercial data processing (and certain scientific applications) to continually create backup copies of tape master files. In such environments, recopying required by IBM-compatible drives is consistent with local data-security practices. The old master file is called the "parent," the new master file the "child"; when the next updating is performed, a new generation of this file is created; the "parent" file becomes the "grandparent," the "child" becomes the "par-

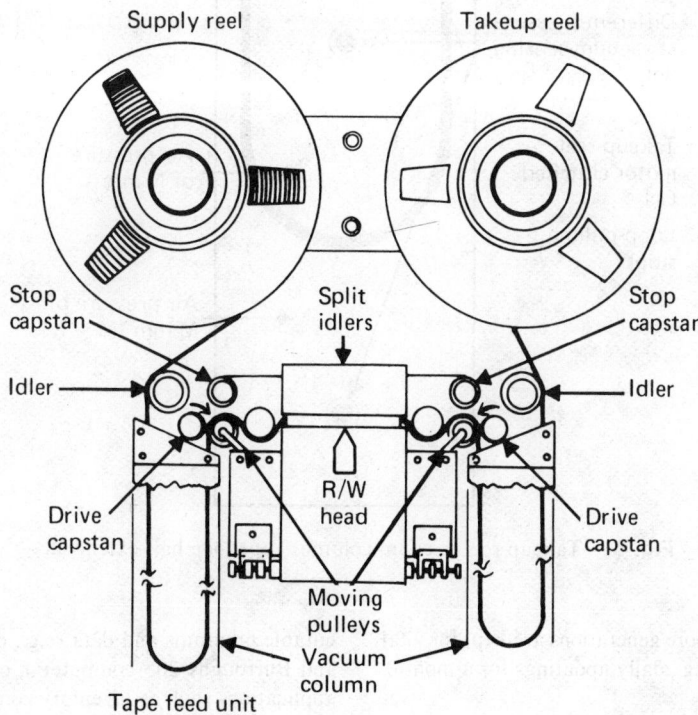

Fig. 3.   Tape-drive schematic.

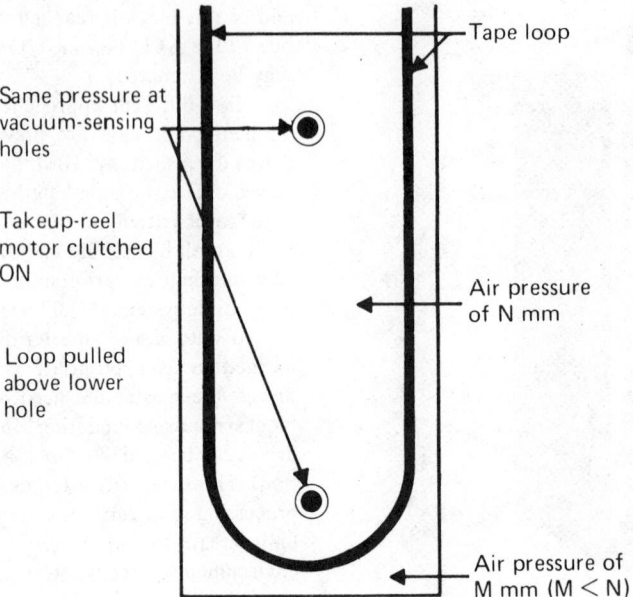

Fig. 4.   Takeup-reel vacuum column. Tape loop fully extended.

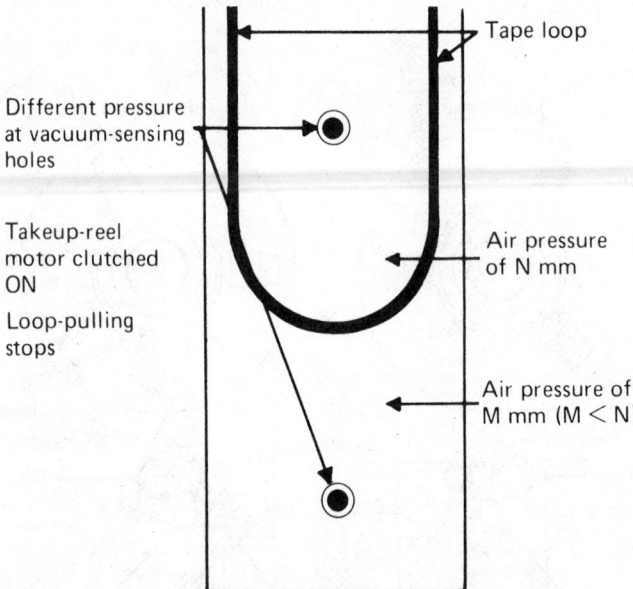

Fig. 5.   Takeup-reel vacuum column. Tape loop half-extended.

ent," etc. Often, 30 or more generations are kept for vital corporate master files; e.g., daily updatings for a month.

Typical Usage. Until the early 1960s, magnetic tape was the prevalent AM for scientific and commercial data processing; direct-access devices were used only for exe-cutable programs and data (e.g., drums on the IBM 650 and Burroughs 205 computers), or for on-line real-time applications such as inventory control and satellite mon-itoring. From 1963 to 1968, many sequentially stored files were transferred from magnetic tape to direct-access de-vices. Allocated to tape drives on second-generation com-

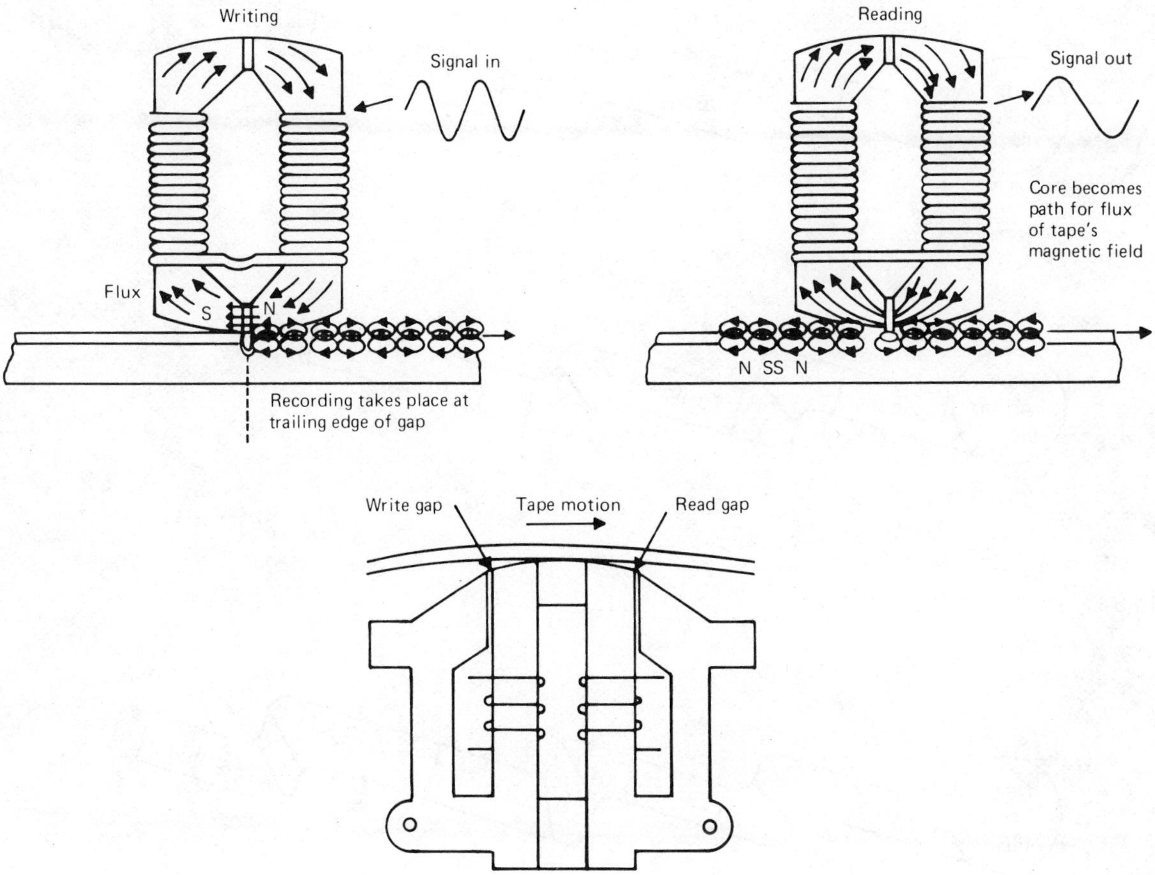

Writing

Signal in

Flux

S N

Recording takes place at
trailing edge of gap

Reading

Signal out

Core becomes
path for flux
of tape's
magnetic field

N SS N

Write gap | Tape motion | Read gap

Fig. 6. Two-gap read/write head.

puters, *scratch files* (intermediate storage required by compilers, sort and utility programs, and application programs) were typically allocated to disk and drum devices on third-generation computers.

Nonetheless, magnetic tape drives are found on most third-generation systems (and their successors), where they fulfill the following roles:

1. Retention of low- and medium-activity master files. Common practice is that "high activity"

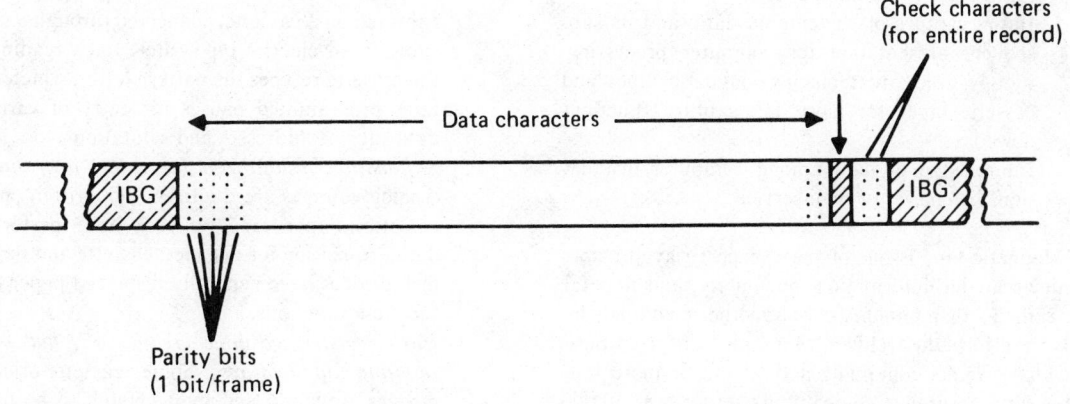

Check characters
(for entire record)

Data characters

IBG

IBG

Parity bits
(1 bit/frame)

Fig. 7. Data and checking bits for typical magnetic tapes.

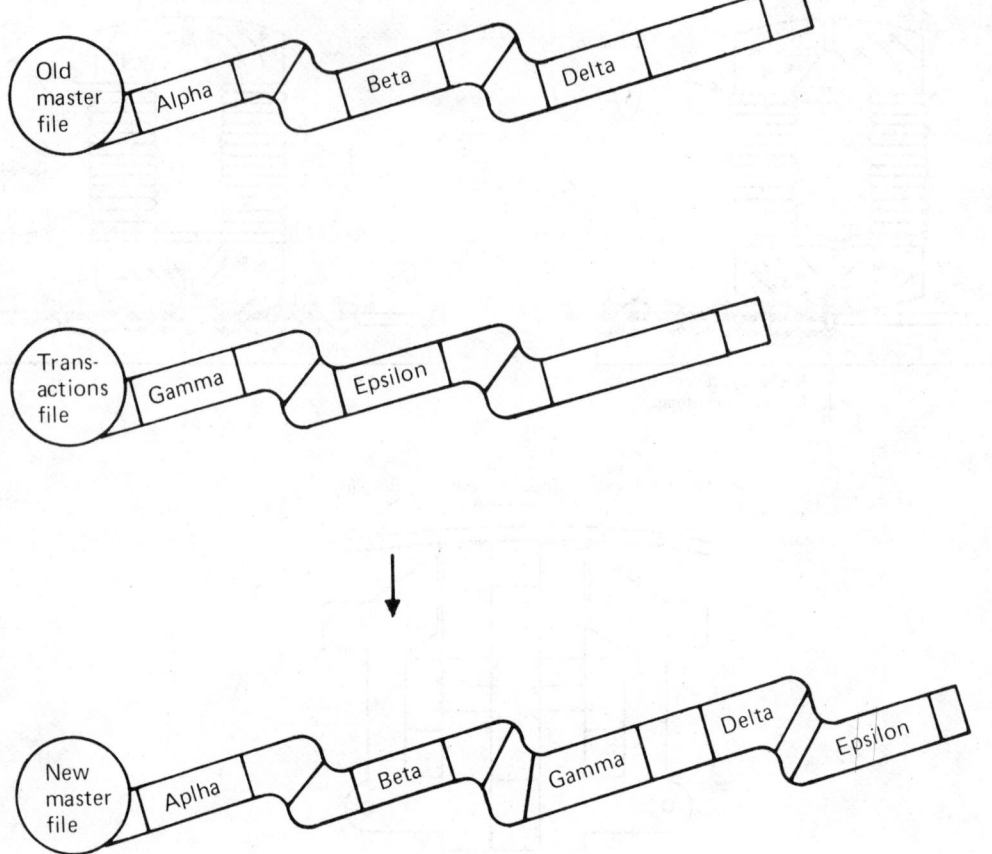

Fig. 8. Tape file maintenance.

files are accessed over 300 times annually, "medium activity" files at least 50 times, "low activity" files less than 50.

2. Backup of direct-access device contents (1–3 reels are required to back up each disk pack containing 20–100 million bytes).

3. Initial capture of key-entered data, and its subsequent presentation for computer processing. Floppy disks are replacing magnetic tapes and cassette tapes for most data-capture functions nowadays.

4. Interchange of data among computer installations by courier or mail service.

Magnetic tape is one of the cheapest ways to store machine-readable information indefinitely, and it is far more compact than punched cards, another medium commonly used for data archives. Many medium-sized businesses have vaults containing a thousand or more tape reels; a large insurance company may store over 50,000 reels.

Cassette Tapes. The preceding section described magnetic tapes created and used primarily *within* computer centers. Cassette tapes are increasingly used for data originating *outside* computer centers, as follows.

1. *Preparation of form letters.* Each pattern letter is captured on a cassette, connected through a short cable to an electric typewriter. Each reading of the cassette retypes the pattern letter, which contains programmed pauses for entry of variable data such as addresses and salutations.

2. *Acquisition of data from laboratory instruments.* Analog voltages are digitized and written onto a cassette. Paper tape punches have performed data acquisition for decades; cassette and floppy-disk devices have generally displaced paper tape for these functions.

3. *Cash register, gasoline credit card, and other retailing applications.* Some cassette-oriented devices are small and light enough to be hand-held.

Typically, cassette tapes are ¼ inch wide and store 10^5 characters, in contrast to full-sized tapes, which are ½ inch wide and store 10^6–10^8 characters.

Many microcomputers and minicomputers and some full-sized third-generation computers have cassette drives as I/O devices. For many microcomputers and for minicomputers used in data acquisition environments, cassette tapes are often the principal AM, used both to load programs into MM and to capture data. On other computers, cassette readers serve primarily for original entry of data. Cassette drives are often installed on terminals, serving as a local data-capture AM. After all data are on the cassette, the user dials up a computer and transmits cassette contents through the terminal-computer link.

Cassette reels should not be confused with short-length reels of conventional computer tape; some of the latter are only 5 inches in diameter and wind 50–200 feet of ½-inch tape.

Direct-Access Devices. Drums, disks, floppy disks, video-recorded cartridges, and charge coupled devices (CCDs) are collectively termed *direct-access* (DA) devices (also sometimes *random-access devices*) for their ability to access blocks of data at random without sequentially passing over a major portion of their contents. Thus, DA devices can be contrasted with magnetic tape drives, which are generally cost-ineffective for random retrieval of data (but see the preceding discussion of DECTAPE). DA devices cannot access individual words as fast as MM devices, the former having access times in the range 5×10^{-3} seconds and the latter in the range 10^{-8} to 10^{-6} seconds. Most DA devices are suitable for software storage; video-recorded storages, however, have undesirably long random-access characteristics for system software. Although widely used for software storage until the mid-1960s, magnetic tapes have been almost entirely displaced by disks and drums for this function.

Drums. The earliest DA devices were magnetic drums (Fig. 9), built since the early 1950s by a number of major manufacturers. A cobalt-nickel substrate is coated with iron oxide, which is magnetized and sensed much as in magnetic-tape operations. Drums are typically 8–20 inches in diameter, 2–4 feet in length, and revolve at 1,500–4,000 rpm. Each character is stored on one or more tracks circumferentially, blocks of characters being separated by *inter-record gaps* (IRGs) of several thousandths of an inch. Densities of 4,000 bpi are commonplace, yielding R/W rates of 1–3 million characters per second.

As with magnetic tape, two types of formatting are possible: *Fixed-length blocks* (often called *sectors*) and *variable-length blocks*. With either format—and in contrast to conventional magnetic tape—it is possible to update blocks in place; i.e., without copying their contents to another part of the device. This facility is vital to the updating activities commonly performed during random retrievals from master files. In fact, all AMs except certain magnetic tapes and the photocopy/laser-holography devices permit updating in place.

Drums hold considerably less data than do disks, magnetic tapes, etc. However, they can access blocks of data at random more quickly than other DA devices, 5–8 ms on the average. Since a drum is a narrow cylinder, its typical rotational speed of 3,600 rpm is considerably higher than that of disk drives, typically 2,400 rpm. A speed of 3,600 rpm means an average rotational time of 16.7 ms. This is compared to 12–80 ms for disk drives.

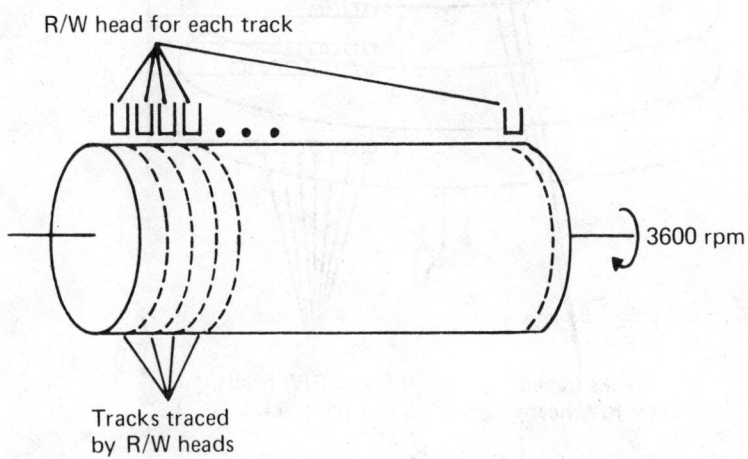

Fig. 9. Magnetic drum.

Therefore, drums have typically been used for the following functions.

1. Prior to the development of magnetic-core memories in the mid-1950s, drums were used as MMs (e.g., on the IBM 650 and Burroughs 205 computers).
2. Thereafter, frequently needed software (interjob monitors, portions of the I/O-error and program-error supervisors, compilers and sort programs, etc.) has been stored permanently on drums. Since drum storage is *nonvolatile*—electric power can be turned off and on without disturbing its contents—it is well suited for permanent storage of continually-used software.
3. High-activity scratch files for the operating system, compilers, and other software are often allocated to drums.
4. Backing storage for virtual-memory (VM) machines has been a major role for drums since the Ferranti Atlas systems of the late 1950s. Thousand-word blocks of MM contents are shuttled to/from drums by the VM control program.
5. In many airborne computers (and similar high-stress environments), drums are used for MMs or AMs because of their high reliability, insensitivity to sudden force changes, and relatively light weight and small bulk.

Disks. Two major varieties of disk drives are widely used.

1. *Fixed-head, multiple-platter* (Fig. 10). Although their geometry is considerably different from that of drums, fixed-head (FH) disks (Fig. 11) have comparable access times and transfer rates. They have approximately the same capacity as commonly used drums—disks in the range 3×10^6 to 10×10^6 bytes, and drums approximately 4×10^6 bytes.

Over the past 20 years, computer manufacturers have vacillated between offering drums or fixed-head disks in their new configurations. Functional repertoires are essentially identical, as are their reliability and cost per character. It seems safe to predict several years' persistence of both in computer configurations, even though they are functionally equivalent.

Each FH drive contains five to ten steel platters coated with iron oxide, aligned vertically on a common spindle. R/W heads extend between the platters, facing up and down from the *comb* suspending the heads and containing signal cables. Since there is a head for each track, the only delay in accessing a data block is due to *rotational latency* (0–15 ms required for the block to revolve beneath the corresponding R/W head). Although track *lengths* vary linearly with distance from the spindle, R/W heads are calibrated in such a way that track capacities are all identical. Therefore, there is a universal

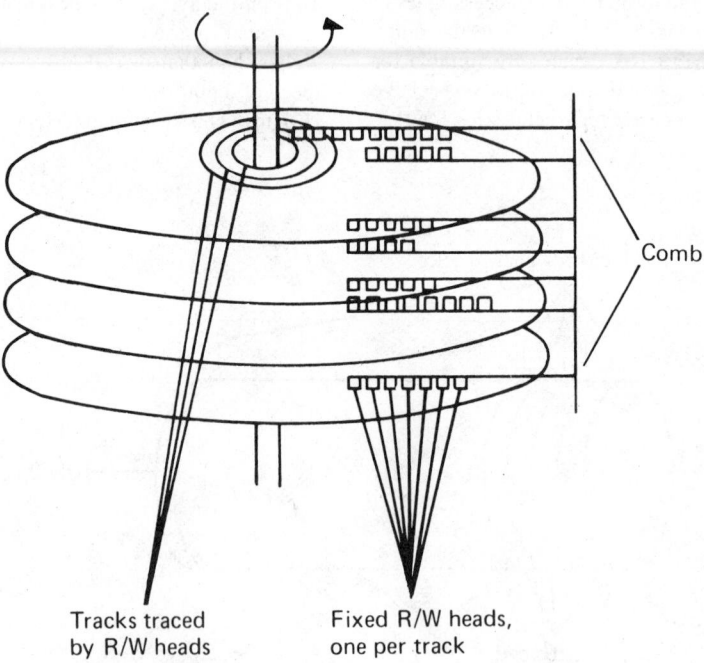

Tracks traced
by R/W heads

Fixed R/W heads,
one per track

Comb

Fig. 10 Fixed-head disk drive.

Fig. 11. IBM System/7 disk module contains either one fixed disk, or a fixed disk and a removable cartridge, on a single drive. Capacity: up to 2.46 million 16-bit words.

transfer rate for data, whether read from inner or outer tracks. The average delay for reading a random block is half the maximum rotational latency, although recent hardware/software developments in *rotational position sensing* (RPS) considerably reduce inefficiencies caused by I/O, as follows.

The I/O supervisor keeps the queue of disk requests (i.e., R/W operations pending for one or more programs) ordered by angular displacement from an *index point*, a universal logical origin for the tracks. Index points for all platters are vertically aligned (Fig. 12). As each R/W operation terminates, the I/O supervisor searches its queue for the nearest request in terms of angular position. This request may reference any track in the FH file, not necessarily that from which the preceding block was read. If N requests are enqueued with uniformly distributed angular displacements—a reasonable assumption for most computer environments—the average *interoperation latency* is only $(1/N + 1) \times$ (max. latency).

2. *Moving head*. Since only two heads and associated electronics are required per platter, moving-head (MH) drives are considerably cheaper to build than FH drives, although the former require sophisticated servomechanisms to move their read/write heads over the platters. Per-character cost for MH storage is typically 10–15% of the cost for FH storage. Some MH drives permit removal of their disk-and-spindle socket assemblies: *Disk cartridge* in the case of a single platter, *disk pack* in the case of multiple platters. An installation can store an indefinite number of cartridges/packs off line to be mounted as required by various applications programs.

Recently, the *Winchester architecture* for disk packs has susperseded most conventional disk-and-spindle socket assemblies. Winchester drives (derived from IBM's pre-announcement product name) do not themselves contain R/W heads, the latter being manufactured together with the platters they access: *Winchester modules*. Winchester drives with the highest storage capacities (3×10^8 to 12×10^8 bytes) do not have removable modules; small Winchester drives permit shelf storage and mounting of the modules, although the latter are considerably more expensive than conventional disk packs.

Most batch-processing installations with MH drives designate one subset as *resident* (also called *permanently mounted* although this is a logical designation rather than a physical attribute), containing the operating system, scratch storage, and frequently referenced data files. Another subset of drives is designated *mountable*, where cartridges/packs are set up as required.

Most on-line installations (i.e., devoted to real-time and telecommunications applications) keep cartridges/packs resident, since data requests originate unpredictably and generally require responses within a few seconds (or milliseconds), too short for a computer operator to retrieve and mount an off-line cartridge/pack.

Moving-head drives may be either single platter or multiple platter.

Moving Head Single Platter (MHSP). This type is shown in Fig. 13. Typically, the *fork* (two-tined comb) contains two R/W heads; it is inserted/withdrawn radially according to the track address furnished with each I/O request.

Moving Head Multiple Platter (MHMP). The MHMP (Fig. 14) drives generalize the MHSP type, with combs containing *2P-2* heads, P being the number of platters. (The top surface of the top platter and bottom surface of the bottom platter are not used on MHMP packs, since they are much more exposed to scratches and dust contamination than are interior surfaces.) Widely used drives have $P = 6$ or 11, corresponding to pack capacities of approximately 50×10^6 and $100–1,200 \times 10^6$ characters. (The wide range of the latter figure is due to recent doublings of both radial and circumferential bit densities.)

MHMP drives have the largest capacity of all hardsurface DA devices. Floppy disks, tapes, and video-recorded cartridges have flexible substrates and hence an inherently higher error rate—both *hard errors* (unrecoverable errors), where a small recording area becomes per-

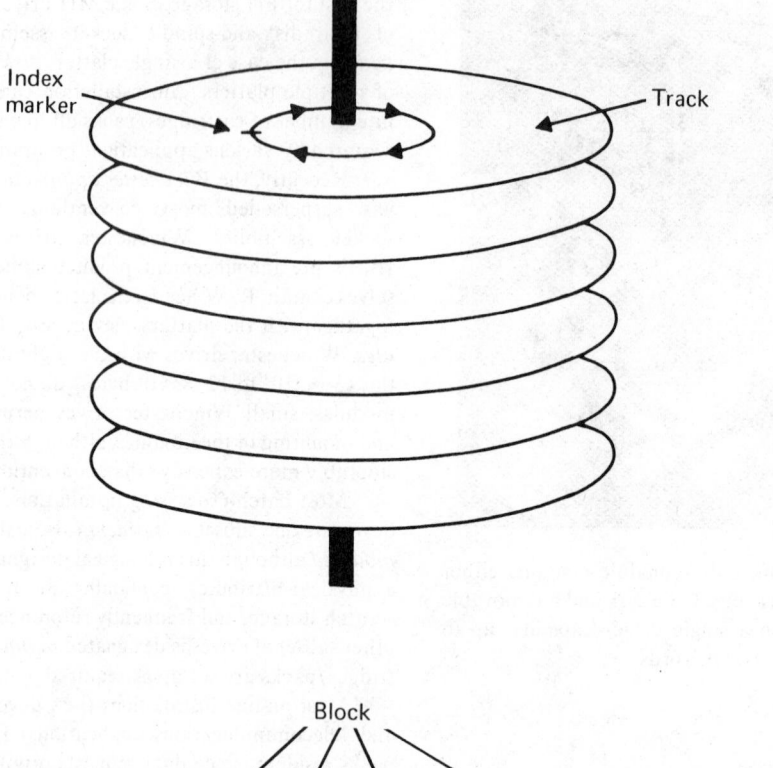

Fig. 12. Track format for disk storage.

manently defective, and *soft errors,* where rereading or rewriting successfully brushes off (or avoids) small oxide flecks. Hard-surface devices may operate for weeks or months without experiencing hard or soft errors—especially FH and Winchester drives, which have an air-sealed environment, in contrast to non-Winchester MH drives, in which cartridges/packs are exposed to dust during handling and off-line storage.

From 4–100 MHMP drives are installed in most third-generation installations performing scientific and

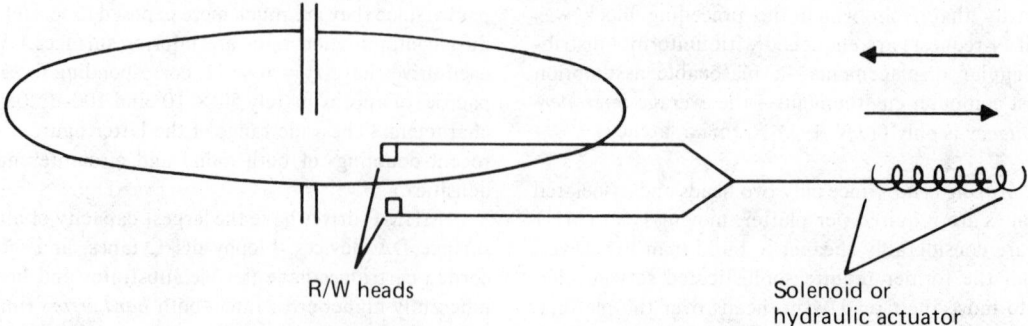

Fig. 13. Moving-head single-platter drive.

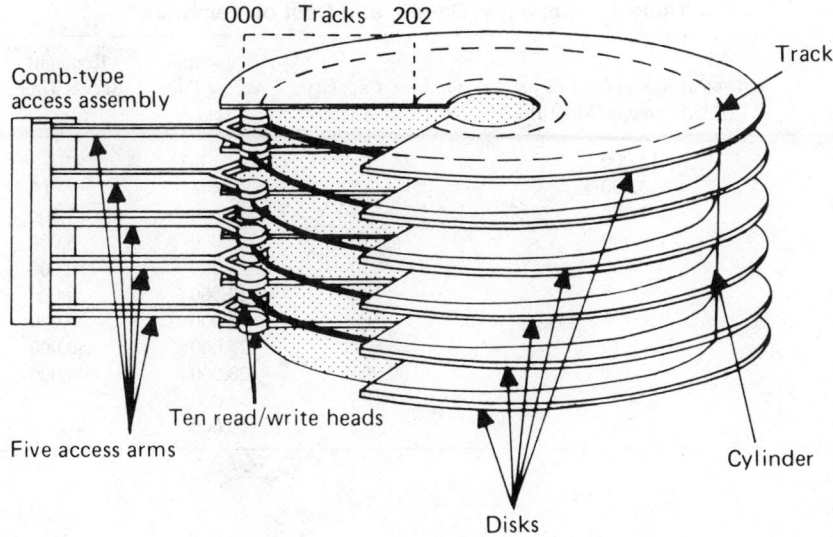

Fig. 14. Moving-head multiple-platter drive.

business data processing. Large installations oriented to on-line operations, such as air-traffic control and real-time inventory, often have over one hundred drives. Growth in their usage was rapid between second-generation (1962) and third-generation (1968) computers. As operating systems evolved toward more comprehensive control of programs and data during this period, they made increasing use of program and data *libraries,* accessed through catalogs, directories, and indices. For most third-generation systems, catalogs and directories were stored exclusively on DA devices, generally disks and drums. Increasingly, libraries themselves are being stored on disk drives to take advantage of their superior transfer rates, random access, and reliability versus soft-surface AMs.

Soft-Surface DA Devices. Floppy disks (also called *diskettes*), video-recorded cartridges, and similar devices compete against MH disk drives for selected application areas. *Floppy disks* are structurally similar to MHSP hard-surface disk drives, except that their recording medium is a flexible plastic substrate—approximately the size of a 45-rpm phonograph record—coated with iron oxide. Information is recorded and read back just as for an MHSP hard-surface drive. Unlike the latter, a floppy disk can be easily handled (within its protective cardboard jacket) and even sent through the mails without extraordinary protective wrapping. Floppy disks are inexpensive: $4–10 per full-size diskette, (8-inch diameter) each of which can hold approximately one million characters. Mini-floppies (5¼ inches in diameter) store about 100K characters if single-sided, up to 350K if two sided.

During the 1970s, several manufacturers developed *mass storage systems:* Trillion-bit storage devices based on reels, cartridges, or cassettes of videotape or wide magnetic tape. In late 1974, marketing of these MSS devices to commercial users commenced with the IBM 3850 Mass Storage System, whose on-line capacity is 50–500 billion bytes (0.4–4 $\times$ 10^{12} bits). Other manufacturers and corresponding products include Ampex's Terabit Memory (TBM), and Computer Peripheral's, Inc. MSS. All but Ampex utilize a large magazine of cartridges or cassettes from which a transport mechanism extracts requested units. Each cartridge or cassette contains approximately 50 million bytes, comparable to a fully packed reel of conventional magnetic tape. A full MSS of this type contains 500–5,000 cartridges or cassettes, together with transports and read/write stations. Often, the transports and R/W stations are duplexed or triplexed to assure continuity of operation, should one of these complex electromechanical devices malfunction.

The Ampex TBM utilizes reels of 2-inch wide video tape rather than cassettes or cartridges. Each reel can hold 11 billion bytes (9 $\times$ 10^{10} bits). A full TBM system contains 31 read/write stations for these reels.

The dominant trend today in MSS design is toward *virtual direct access storage,* whereby data are automatically retrieved at the start of a batch job and transcribed onto a conventional MH disk drive. The MSS performs this transcription *(staging)* asynchronous to other computing on the host computer. It utilizes neither main memory nor CPU power of the host, since the MSS controller contains one or more minicomputers and its own memory. The principal interface of the MSS to the host computer is through disk storage controllers. Via the lat-

Table 1.   Capacity, Speed, and Cost of Memories

Memory	Typical Rental Cost ($ per 10^6 characters/Month)	On-Line Capacity ($\times 10^6$ characters)	Sequential Access Time (μs)	Random Access Time (μs)	Transfer Rate (characters/sec)
MM (pre-1978)	15,000	<8	0.3	0.3	10^7
MM (post-1978)	3,000	>8	0.1	0.2	10^8
Drum	1,000	4	8,500	8,500	1.5×10^6
FH disk drive	500	10	5,000	5,000	1.5×10^6
MHSP	300	10	25,000	150,000	10^5
MHMP (pre-1978)	5	100	12,500	30,000	8×10^5
MHMP (post-1978)	1	300	10,000	20,000	1.2×10^6
Floppy disk	10	1	25,000	150,000	5×10^4
MSS	0.1	100,000	20,000	5,000,000	2×10^5
Magnetic tape drive	—	25	5,000	—	$60–1,200 \times 10^3$
Cassette tape drive	—	1	10,000	—	10^3

ter, the host computer and the MSS alternatively read and write to the same disk drives. This provides to the host computer an on-line database whose unit storage cost is comparable to conventional magnetic tape, but whose accessibility—after transcription to disk—is approximately the same as for a 100-megabyte disk drive (8.4 milliseconds average sequential access time, transfer rate exceeding 800KB).

Average random access time to MSS units is 10–20 seconds. However, this delay is essentially invisible to the host computer, since MSS devices are not generally used for servicing on-line transactions submitted to the host.

Tables 1, 2, and 3 provide comparative data for the various memory types, also giving cost/benefit comparisons of using these memories for large and small computer applications.

D. N. FREEMAN

MEMORY ADDRESSING. *See* ADDRESSING.

MEMORY ALLOCATION. *See* STORAGE ALLOCATION.

Table 2.   Auxiliary Memory Cost/Benefit Comparisons for Large Computers

Size of Module, (Characters)	Average Interusage Frequency (Seconds)	Type of Access	Reliability and Transfer Speed Requirements	Must Be On Line	Shelf Storage Acceptable	MM	Drum or FH Disk	MHSP Disk	MHMP Disk	Magnetic Tape	Cassette Tape
<10^5	<0.1	Random		X		P	A	*	*	*	*
10^5–10^6	<0.1	Random		X		C	P	A	TS	*	*
>10^6	<0.1	Random		X		C	A	P	*	*	*
<10^5	0.1–1	Random		X		A	P	A	A	*	*
10^5–10^6	0.1–1	Random		X		C	P	A	A	*	*
>10^6	0.1–1	Random		X		C	A	P	*	*	*
<10^5	1–10	Random		X		*	C	A	P	*	*
10^5–10^6	1–10	Random		X		*	C	P	A	*	*
10^6–10^8	1–10	Random		X		*	*	P	*	*	*
>10^8	1–10	Random		X		*	*	P	*	*	*
<10^8	>10	Random		X		*	*	P	*	A	*
>10^8	>10	Random		X		*	*	TC	*	P	*
		Random			X	*	*	P	*	*	*
<10^6		Sequential	High		X	*	*	*	P	*	A
<10^6		Sequential	Low		X	*	*	*	P	*	A
>10^6		Sequential			X	*	*	*	*	A	P

NOTES: (*) Inapplicable for this function. (A) Acceptable in terms of cost versus influence on system performance; inferior to alternative P if latter exists for this function. (C) Costly, in same terms as (A). Cheaper AM suffices for this function unless computer is near saturation and/or under tight response-time constraints. (P) Preferable, in same terms as (A) to other AMs. (TS) Too slow, in same terms as (A). Use of this AM severely degrades system performance; faster AM should be considered.

Table 3.   Auxiliary Memory Cost/Benefit Comparisons for Small Computers

Size of Module (Characters)	Average Interusage Frequency (Seconds)	Type of Access	Reliability and Transfer Speed Requirement	Must Be On Line	Shelf Storage Acceptable	MM	MHSP Disk	MHMP Disk	Floppy Disk	Magnetic Tape	Cassette Tape
$<10^4$	<0.1	Random		X		P	TS	TS	*	*	*
$>10^4$	<0.1	Random				C	P	A	TS	*	*
$<10^5$	0.1–1	Random		X		A	P	A	A	*	*
10^5–10^7	0.1–1	Random		X		*	P	A	A	*	*
$>10^7$	0.1–1	Random		X		*	A	P	*	*	*
$<10^6$	>1	Random		X		A	A	P	A	*	*
$>10^6$	>1	Random		X		*	*	P	TS	*	*
$<10^6$		Random			X	*	A	*	P	*	A
$>10^6$		Random			X	*	P	*	*	*	*
$<10^6$		Sequential	High		X	*	P	*	A	A	A
$<10^6$		Sequential	Low		X	*	A	*	P	A	A
$>10^6$		Sequential	High		X	*	P	A	*	A	A
$>10^6$		Sequential	Low		X	*	A	A	*	P	A

NOTES: (*) Inapplicable for this function. (A) Acceptable in terms of cost versus influence on system performance; inferior to alternative P if latter exists for this function. (C) Costly, in same terms as (A). Cheaper AM suffices for this function unless computer is near saturation and/or under tight response-time constraints. (P) Preferable, in same terms as (A) to other AMs. (TS) Too slow, in same terms as (A). User of this AM severely degrades system performance; faster AM should be considered.

MEMORY-MAPPED I/O

For articles on related subjects *see* MEMORY: Main; and MICROPROCESSORS AND MICROCOMPUTERS.

In a conventional computer equipped with a graphic display device, a programmer must direct characters to such a display in much the same way as output is directed to a tape or disk or other on-line I/O device; i.e., the program must execute an I/O statement that (typically) names the channel to which the display device is attached, the number of characters to be transmitted, the screen location where they are to be displayed, and the starting address in memory where the data to be transmitted may be found. Most popular microcomputers, however, are now using a much simpler and more flexible system known as *memory-mapped I/O,* whereby individual character positions on the screen are mapped one-to-one to bytes in the computer's main memory. For example, on the TRS-80 Model I, the 16 × 64 screen is mapped onto the 1,024-byte memory segment starting at hexadecimal address 3000. This has a twofold advantage. First, to display, say, HELLO in the middle of the screen, one would merely store the five-byte ASCII *(q.v.)* equivalent of HELLO at hexadecimal memory locations 3DDB to 3DDF, which correspond to the desired portion of the screen. Instantaneously and automatically, the desired message will appear without need for any further instructions. Second, unlike the programmer of a conventional system whose programs cannot detect what is currently on the screen, the programmer of a memory-mapped system need only check the current contents of the memory map area to ascertain what is being displayed. If a user at the console changes it through keyboard action, the storage map will change to conform.

Not only the display device but also the keyboard is memory mapped in some of the newer microcomputers. This allows the software to use simple memory accesses to be able to sense at any given time which keys (or combination of keys) are being depressed and to take appropriate action. Such mapping systems are so obviously flexible and useful that the concept is likely to endure and be applied to additional I/O interface situations.

E. D. REILLY, JR.

MEMORY ORGANIZATION.

See STORAGE ORGANIZATION.

MEMORY PROTECTION

For articles on related subjects *see* ADDRESSING; BASE REGISTER; MULTIPROGRAMMING; OPERATING SYSTEMS; READ-ONLY MEMORY (ROM); and STORAGE ALLOCATION.

Memory protection, as used in this article, is a hardware mechanism that limits or prevents access to specified areas in the central or main memory of a computer.

Memory protection first became important when systems became capable of permitting or requiring more than one program to be resident in memory at the same time. The possibility then existed that, while one of the programs was running, it might inadvertently (e.g., because of a bug) write in the area occupied by the other program and thus invalidate that program.

In *uniprogramming* operating systems—and most first-generation systems were uniprogramming systems—there were typically two programs resident in memory, an executive program and a user program. The earliest memory protection mechanism provided a switch register that could be set to a memory address which marked the upper limit of a protected area. The lower limit was zero. No program running outside the protected area could write into any location inside the protected area. The executive routine, presumably debugged, would reside *in* the protected area. The user program would run on the outside, and if it did anything improper, it could hurt only itself. The execution of a user program instruction that would result in a write into the protected area would abort the user program, and then, either automatically or through operator intervention, control would be returned to the executive, which could proceed to the next user program.

With the development of *multiprogramming* systems, more elaborate memory protection mechanisms were needed. In such systems, supervisory programs and a number of user programs may reside in memory simultaneously. While a user program is running, it is important to be able to designate the areas that belong to that program and to limit its access to other areas. The supervisory programs must be able to designate and change the areas under protection, and the user programs must be denied this capability. Although some systems limited themselves to *write protection* (i.e., a program could *read* from any area in memory, but could not *write* outside its own area), it was recognized quite early that a more general access protection was desirable.

The first effective memory protection mechanism for a multiprogramming system used a *base register (q.v.)* also called a *relocation register,* and a *limit register.* A program must reside in a contiguous area of memory; when that program is to run, the executive places the program's origin (i.e., its lowest address) in the base register and its length in the limit register. Any attempt by a program to access a memory location outside its own area causes control to go to the executive routine.

It is, however, often desirable for a program and its associated data to reside in disjoint areas of memory. In such cases, it is nevertheless necessary to protect the program and data as a unit. In the IBM 360/370 series, for example, each block of 2,048 consecutive bytes has an associated protection code register that holds a four-bit

protection key set by an executive routine operating in *supervisor* state. A running program runs under its protection key, and an interrupt results from any attempt to access a block whose protection key is different from that of the running program. Protection code 0000 is reserved for executive routines and has special significance in that a program with protection code 0000 has access to all memory.

Memory protection is an important feature of multiprogramming systems, but it does create problems in systems in which routines and data are to be shared among programs simultaneously present in memory. Some virtual memory systems have been designed to permit and encourage such sharing. The problems of protection in such systems can be very complicated and are beyond the scope of this article.

Memory protection can be important within a single program. One of the most usual of program bugs occurs when a program calculates a subscript that causes a value to be stored outside the array that is being referenced. Automatic checking of array boundaries (as provided, for example, on many Burroughs' computers) can be an extremely useful memory protection feature. This type of checking is often done in software. The run-time systems provided by many compilers provide a routine check for references outside of the bounds that have been declared for arrays.

S. ROSEN

MERCURY DELAY-LINE MEMORY. *See* UL-
TRASONIC MEMORY.

METACHARACTER

For articles on related subjects *see* BACKUS-NAUR FORM; LANGUAGE TRANSLATION; MACRO LANGUAGES; and PROGRAMMING LINGUISTICS.

Metacharacters in computer programming language systems are characters that have some controlling role with respect to other characters with which they may be associated. The terminology comes from the Greek stem *meta* (meaning "after," "along with," "beyond," or "behind"). In an interactive macro language, an input string from the interactive typewriter is terminated by a metacharacter. The metacharacter is a signal to the connected processor that the preceding input string is complete and is ready to be acted upon. In this case, the metacharacter is discarded, and is not considered to be a part of the input string.

In a similar view, the delimiter characters such as

+ and = might also be considered metacharacters of arithmetic expressions. This is because of their lexically controlling role with reference to the alphanumerical characters with which their operands are constructed.

C. N. MOOERS

METALANGUAGE

For articles on related subjects *see* BACKUS-NAUR FORM; PROGRAMMING LANGUAGES; and PROGRAMMING LINGUISTICS.

A metalanguage is a set of symbols and words used to describe another language (in which these symbols do not appear). The most common application is in the definition of programming languages. The first and best known example was the definition of Algol 60, and a small section of this follows as an example.

The metalanguage used in this case (called Backus-Naur Form-*q.v.*) consists of the symbols ⟨, ⟩, |, :: =, together with a number of metalinguistic variables that are used to define the elements of Algol. The brackets ⟨⟩ are used as delimiters for the metalinguistic variables, the vertical stroke | has the meaning "or," and the symbol :: = means "is defined as." The following extract from the report on Algol 60 gives the definition of an integer and illustrates the use of the symbols:

⟨digit⟩:: = 0|1|2|3|4|5|6|7|8|9
⟨unsigned integer⟩:: = ⟨digit⟩
        |⟨unsigned integer⟩ ⟨digit⟩
⟨integer⟩:: = ⟨unsigned integer⟩
        | + ⟨unsigned integer⟩
        | − ⟨unsigned integer⟩

The complete definition of Algol 60 in this form, together with some semantic interpretation, takes about 26 pages.

It will be observed that in order to define the symbols of the metalanguage, we had to make use of another language, namely, English. This causes no confusion in the present case, but might do so if we were to try to define English itself by a metalanguage.

In the example above we made use of three metalinguistic variables: digit, unsigned integer, and integer. In defining the complete language, there will normally be one metalinguistic variable that is never used in the definition of any other variable; this is known as the *starting type*. In programming languages, this would normally be ⟨program⟩, and in natural languages it might be ⟨sentence⟩.

The digits 0, 1 . . . 9 and the signs + and − are *terminal symbols* of the language; i.e., they will appear in statements written in the language. For this reason they are often printed in heavy type to distinguish them from the *nonterminal symbols* (digit, integer etc.), sometimes called *defined types* or *metavariables*.

REFERENCES

1967. Rosen, S. *Programming Systems and Languages.* New York: McGraw-Hill.
1969. Sammet, J. E. *Programming Languages.* Englewood Cliffs, NJ: Prentice-Hall.

K. H. V. BOOTH

METAVARIABLE

For articles on related subjects *see* BACKUS-NAUR FORM; and GRAMMARS.

In the description of languages by syntactic rules, it is necessary to identify elements of the language, such as phrases, by names. In natural languages, these are termed *parts of speech* and are identified by such terms as *noun, verb*, etc.

The formal description of computer languages ascribes the names *metavariable, phrase name*, or *nonterminal symbol* (among others) to these language elements. For example, in the simple grammar for an arithmetic expression given in the article GRAMMARS, the metavariables are *constant, variable, add op, mult op, exp op, primary, factor, term*, and *arithmetic expression*. In describing a language in printed form, the metavariable must be distinguished from the actual strings of the language by some technique, such as the italics used here.

J. A. N. LEE

MICROPROCESSORS AND MICROCOMPUTERS

For articles on related subjects *see* INTEGRATED CIRCUITRY; MEMORY-MAPPED I/O; MINICOMPUTERS; PERSONAL COMPUTING; and ROBOTICS.

A *microprocessor,* or microprocessing unit (MPU), is a computer central processing unit (CPU) built as a single tiny semiconductor chip or as a small number of chips. It contains the arithmetic and control logic circuitry necessary to perform the operations of a computer program. A microprocessor chip is a (very) large-scale integrated (LSI or VLSI) circuit fabricated on a sliver of silicon less than 5 mm (1/5 in.) square and 0.5 mm

(1/50 in.) thick, about the size of a baby's fingernail. In 1980, there were about 50 different microprocessor families including hundreds of varieties of MPU chips, each containing the equivalent of between 1,000 and 70,000 transistors. A transistor-equivalent is able to make one simple logic decision or to store one binary digit (or *bit* = 0 or 1). The circuit densities (transistors per chip) of commercially available MPUs have been increasing by a factor of 10 every 4 to 6 years.

A *microcomputer* is a more complete system than a microprocessor, containing not only the CPU logic but also memory for storing programs and data, I/O interfaces for exchanging data with peripheral devices, and timing circuits to control the flow of data within the computer. In 1980, most microcomputers were single-board computers built by combining an MPU chip with 1 to 60 other support chips on a circuit board no larger than this page. A 60-chip microcomputer could perform up to 300 different operations at rates between 100,000 and 10,000,000 operations per second, might access up to eight I/O devices, and might contain 4,096 to 65,536 bytes of memory. A memory byte consists of eight bits and can store a binary number, two decimal digits, or one alphabetic character. The particular characteristics of a microcomputer depend upon system cost and intended applications.

Memory chips are standardized enough to be used with many different varieties of MPUs. There are standards for the patterns of signals used to exchange data between computers and peripheral I/O terminals. A few interface chips can be used with different MPUs to connect terminals. However, most interface, timing, and other support chips are designed specifically for some small class of similar MPUs from the same manufacturer.

There are already dozens of varieties of single-chip microcomputers, such as the Texas Instruments (TI) TMS1000, Intel 8748, and Motorola 6801. Each has its CPU, memories, and interfaces integrated onto the same chip. They are inexpensive; the marginal costs of fabricating, testing, and marketing each microcomputer chip can be less than $1. However, it can cost millions of dollars to develop a new chip design. Improvements in chip production steadily lower costs by increasing the yield of defect-free chips. Initial development and production costs are recovered by charging up to $300 apiece for the first few thousands of copies and progressively less as more are produced. After millions have been sold, prices may be as little as $2 apiece.

In 1980, all single-chip microcomputers had chip space for, at most, a few thousand bytes of memory and could be used only for simple applications such as the control of instruments, appliances, or toys. Increasingly, special interface chips were being made programmable by including a simple microcomputer as part of their circuitry. As circuit densities increase by about a factor of 100 during the decade starting in 1980, there will be room for more memory and control circuitry per chip. The standard microelectronic component will then become the single-chip microcomputer, instead of separate microprocessor, memory, and interface chips.

Although most microcomputers use a single microprocessor chip for their CPU, a few powerful ones use a series of chips for the CPU: Several identical, fast bipolar technology chips that together form the arithmetic logic plus one or two very fast read-only memory (ROM) chips and a fast microcontrol unit that can read data and instructions from the main memory of the microprocessor and execute microprograms from the ROM. This type of CPU is known as a *bit-sliced (q.v.)* microprocessor, since the first bipolar arithmetic chips could each perform arithmetic only on single-bit values (0, 1) but several could be connected in parallel for operations on larger values. By 1976, several manufacturers offered arithmetic unit slices that could each handle four-bit values (0 to 15). A bit-sliced microprocessor is *microprogramable* at the hardware immplementation level, meaning that the instruction codes for the CPU can be changed by altering the ROM microprograms which interpret them.

The multichip style of CPU is frequently used to build microcomputers, such as the Data General MicroNova and Digital Equipment Corporation (DEC) LSI-11 and LSI-11/23, which faithfully execute the programs of larger computers that have instruction sets too complex to be directly implemented by logic within a single microprocessor chip. Recent microprocessors, such as the Intel 8086 and the Motorola 68000, which perform arithmetic on 16- and 32-bit values, use microprogrammed logic within a single chip. Although slower than logic dedicated to individual instructions, ROM-based microprogrammed logic requires less chip space and can easily be modified to accept new CPU instrucions.

Organization. The basic functional units of a microcomputer are the same as for any other digital computer system. As shown in the block diagram in Fig. 1, the three major units are as follows.

1. The *memory,* which holds program instructions and data to be manipulated by the programs and which may be subdivided into programmable read-only memory (PROM) for permanent instructions and read/write random access memory (RAM) for data and alterable instructions.
2. The *I/O ports,* which interface the computer to peripheral devices such as user terminals, large disk storage units, and printers so that starting data and possibly program instructions can be

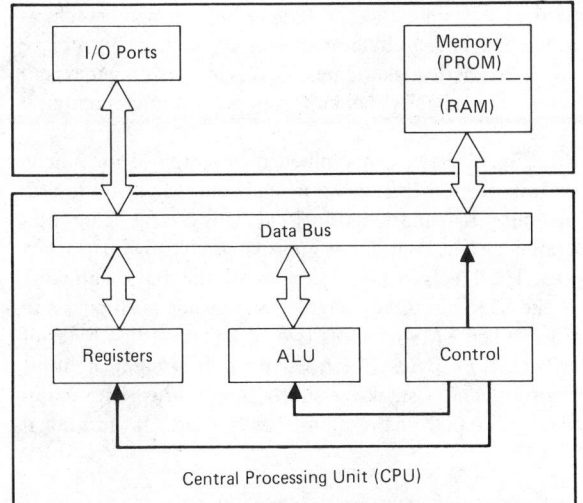

Fig. 1. Basic components of computer system can now be compressed onto a single chip, as in the Intel 8748. In this block diagram "control" includes control logic and instructions for decoding and executing the program stored in "memory." "Registers" provide control with temporary storage in the form of random-access memories (RAMs) and their associated functions. The "ALU" (for arithmetic logic unit) carries out arithmetic and logic operations under supervision of the control circuitry. "I/O ports" provide access to peripheral devices such as a keyboard, a cathode-ray-tube display terminal, "floppy disk" information storage and a line printer.

read into the memory and results can be written from the memory.

3. The *central processing unit (CPU),* which controls the flow of data through the computer system and which executes the sequence of program instructions by reading each one from memory, interpreting it to decide what operations to perform on which data, manipulating the data, and deciding which instruction to execute next.

As shown in the bottom half of Fig. 1, the CPU consists of three major sub-units linked to one another and to the I/O ports and memory by a data bus, which is a system of parallel connections, usually one for each bit in the data values that are manipulated:

1. The *registers,* which are rapidly accessible small memories that hold values used during the execution of programs.

2. The *arithmetic/logic unit* (ALU), which performs common arithmetic operations such as add and multiply or logical operations such as complement or AND on one or two values held in registers.

3. The *control unit,* which interprets instructions and routes data through the various units of the computer as required to execute the instructions.

Microcomputers are often characterized by the number of bits in the largest data value that they can transfer in one operation (i.e., the *width* of their data bus). This width is typically the same as the number of bits stored in one memory word, held in one register, or manipulated by one ALU operation. The normal widths for microcomputers are 4, 8, or 16 bits; 32-bit systems are being developed. Many systems allow pairs of registers to hold double-length values for extra precision in some special arithmetic operations.

The functional units of a microcomputer can be implemented with separate MPU, memory, and I/O port interface chips; with the I/O ports combined with either the MPU or the memory; or as a single microcomputer chip. Whether implemented as separate memory chips that can be used with a wide variety of MPUs or combined with the CPU logic of a microcomputer chip, there presently are several different standard types of microcomputer semiconductor memory. *Random access memory* (RAM) is used to store data and sometimes instructions that must be both read and written during execution of programs by the CPU. *Read-only memory* (ROM) is used to store programs that the CPU must read but does not need to change.

ROMs, programmable ROMs (PROM), and erasable, programmable ROMs (EPROM) are non-volatile memories since their contents remain the same even when there is no electrical power. ROMs have their contents determined in the last stage of the manufacturing process. PROMs and EPROMs can be written slowly by a series of high-voltage, short-duration electrical pulses produced by special equipment such as the PROM-burner shown in Fig. 2. PROMs cannot be erased once they have been written; EPROMs can be erased either by ultraviolet light or by special high-voltage electrical signals. Since their contents can be rewritten to correct errors, EPROMs are used to develop programs that will later be kept in ROMs or PROMs.

Non-volatile RAMs are currently being developed, and the distinctions between RAMs, ROMs, PROMs, and EPROMs will probably vanish by the mid-1980s. Newly available are *magnetic bubble memory* chips, which are slower to access than RAMs but are non-volatile and store about 10 times more information per chip. In 1980, the largest commercially available RAM chips

Fig. 2. System 19/Unipak.

held 65,536 bits, and the largest bubble memory chips, 1,048,576 bits. Bubble memories are starting to replace small magnetic diskette peripherals in providing inexpensive large-capacity backup storage for microcomputer systems.

Fig. 3 shows a magnified photograph of the silicon circuitry for an Intel 8748, a single-chip, eight-bit microcomputer first marketed in 1977. It is a large-scale integrated circuit containing approximately 20,000 transistors. The labels in Fig. 4 demarcate the major sub-units in the 8748 circuitry, roughly in the same positions as in Fig. 1. The 8748 contains two I/O ports, 1,024 bytes of EPROM, 64 bytes of RAM, two sets of eight eight-bit registers, and a stack for subroutine returns. It executes about 400,000 instructions per second. If additional

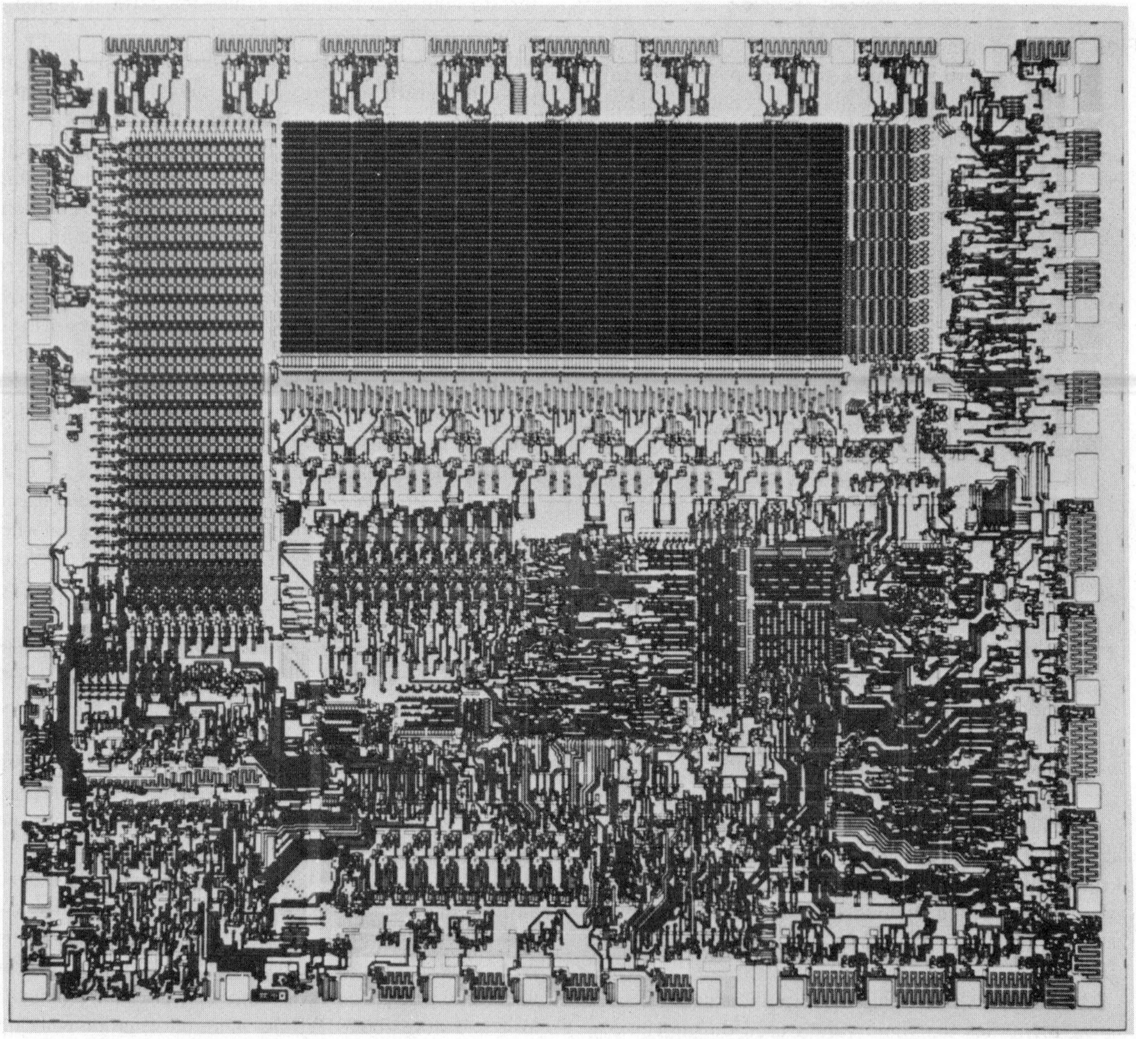

Fig. 3 Courtesy Intel Corporation.

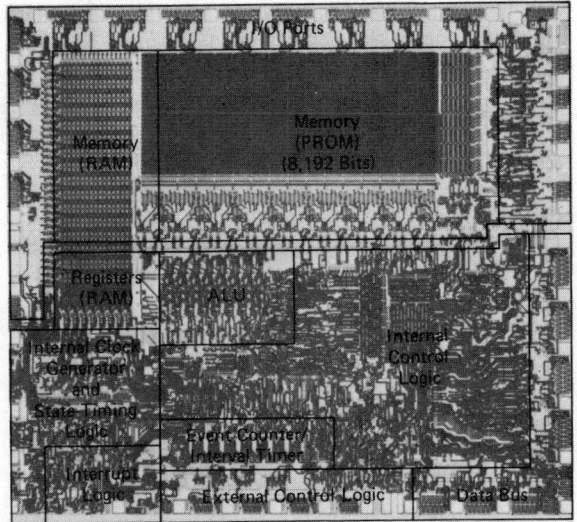

Fig. 4. Map of 8748 microcomputer identifies the location of the various computer functions. Each function can be assigned to one of the five basic functional blocks: control, memory, registers, ALU and I/O ports. Device holds some 20,000 transistors fabricated by *n*-channel silicon-gate metal-oxide-semiconductor (*n*-MOS) technology. The eight-bit central processor responds to 96 instructions in average time of 2.5 microseconds.

memory or ports are needed, they may be added as separate chips.

Whether implemented as a single-chip or as a single-board, a microcomputer is not a usable system until provided with a carefully regulated supply of electrical power and until connected to peripheral I/O devices that allow it to exchange information with human users or other machines. Because of the variety of devices that may need to be connected to a microcomputer, commercially available complete microcomputer systems usually house the power supply in a box with a *backplane,* or *motherboard,* into which are inserted specialized circuit boards for the microprocessor, additional memory, and specialized device interfaces. Peripheral devices such as video displays, keyboards, and floppy diskette or magnetic tape drives for permanent storage are either housed in the same box or in a few boxes connected by short cables. (For more information about "single-box" microcomputer systems, see PERSONAL COMPUTERS.)

A microcomputer backplane contains a *bus* of hundreds of systematic wiring connections so that each member of a family of circuit boards may simultaneously exchange several dozen signals with other boards in the same backplane. The backplane bus is an extension of the data bus within the CPU but has additional lines for control signals to coordinate sharing by all the circuit boards. Each major manufacturer, such as Intel, Motorola, Zilog, and DEC, has its own conventions for buses interconnecting its microcomputer boards. In addition, there are widely used standard bus conventions for interconnecting instruments to microcomputers (IEEE-488: General Purpose Interface Bus) and for mixing personal computer boards from different small manufacturers (S-100 Bus). A system for interconnecting large numbers of separate computers and peripheral devices within the same building (Ethernet) has been developed by Xerox and is becoming an industry-wide standard.

History. Microprocessors and microcomputers are representatives of a microelectronic revolution characterized by ever-shrinking costs and sizes for information processing devices. The revolution began with the development of the transistor in 1948 at Bell Laboratories. This tiny amplifier device, formed on the surface of a semiconductor material such as pure germanium or silicon (sand and glass are mainly silicon dioxide), was hundreds of times smaller than the vacuum tube which it replaced for building computers by the late 1950s. After learning how to use photographic masks to control diffusion of critical trace impurities into tiny regions of silicon, by the mid-1950s, engineers could produce batches of hundreds of individual transistors from a single thin wafer of pure silicon.

In 1959, Fairchild marketed the planar transistor, the first device using integrated circuit (IC) technology. In 1960, TI produced a special military IC. In 1961, Fairchild marketed the first commercially available IC, a flip-flop with four transistors and two resistors. Transistor, resistor, and capacitor circuit elements in an IC are insulated by layers of silicon dioxide and connected by thin films of evaporated metal. After hundreds of ICs have been photographically reproduced upon a wafer, they are tested to eliminate defective copies, cut into individual circuits about 5 mm (⅕ in.) square, and mounted in standard packages such as the 16-pin dual-in-line package (16-DIP) shown in Fig. 5.

The first ICs were single-logic gates or single flip-flop (one-bit) memory circuits. The maximum number of elements per circuit doubled regularly every year between 1959 and at least 1976. In 1967, ex-Fairchild executives formed Intel. The first commercially available microprocessor was the Intel 4004, marketed in 1971. It grew out of a 1969 project to develop a general-purpose chip set for inexpensive hand-held calculators. The 4004 chip contained about 1,000 transistors and performed arithmetic on four-bit-wide binary integers, each of which could encode a decimal digit. In 1972, Intel intro-

Fig. 5.   16-pin dual-in-line package.

duced the 8008 and 8080 microprocessors, which could operate on eight-bit bytes encoding a binary integer, one alphabetic character, or (in the 8080) two-decimal digits. The 8008 was designed to control video display terminals and input keyboards. The 8080 was an enhanced version of the 8008 with additional registers, decimal and 16-bit arithmetic, improved subroutine call facilities, and a larger possible memory (up to 65,536 bytes). The 8080 and its faster 1974 version, the 8080A, became the first widely used microprocessors.

In 1974, Motorola introduced the 6800, an eight-bit processor with a powerful set of data addressing modes that allowed more compact programs than on the 8080, saving expensive memory, instruction execution time, and human programming time. In 1974, the designers of Intel's 8080A formed the Zilog Corporation and, in 1976, introduced the Z80, a faster version of the 8080A with more instructions, additional registers, and less expensive support chip requirements. In 1975, ex-Motorola engineers introduced the MOS Technology 6500 family of low-cost MPUs, all similar to the 6800. Although there were about 30 different microprocessors by 1977, the 8080A, 6800, and Z80 had become by far the most widely used eight-bit MPUs.

In 1973, aiming toward the industrial control market, National Semiconductor sold the first of the single-board 16-bit microcomputers, the IMP-16C · with an MPU, 256 bytes of RAM, 512 bytes of ROM, and I/O drivers on one card. In 1975, DEC sold the single-board LSI-11, which executed the same programs as the popular PDP-11 family of minicomputers. The LSI-11 can be combined with a family of memory and interface cards to to form multi-board computer systems costing from $1,000 to $9,000 plus peripherals. In 1980, DEC released the LSI-11/23 CPU board, which can be substituted for the LSI-11 to address four times as much memory (262,144 bytes) and to execute programs two to three times as rapidly (about 250,000 instructions per second).

Between 1975 and 1980, other families of component cards for 16-bit microcomputers were introduced by TI (TM990), Data General (MicroNova), Computer Automation (Naked Mini), and several other companies. Intel, Zilog, Motorola, and MOS Technology offered single-board computers and board families built with their eight-bit CPU chips. Using the 8080, Z80, 6800, and 6502 CPU chips and cards, dozens of companies have marketed personal computers costing from $200 to $8,000 apiece. Most of the personal computers use the S-100 bus backplane standard first developed by Altair. Hundreds of small companies supply special memory and interface cards compatible with the S-100 bus.

In 1974 TI introduced the first *single-chip* four-bit microcomputer, the TMS1000. In 1977 Intel introduced the first eight-bit microcomputers, the 8048 and 8748. By 1980, there were dozens of single-chip eight-bit and four-bit microcomputers. Since all components are contained in a single package, microcomputer chips allow the design of very inexpensive computer-controlled consumer products. The microcomputer chip with the highest sales volume in 1980 was the TMS1000, costing only $2. The huge volume of sales and the simplicity of the chip allowed the low price. The more complex Intel 8748, with only three years of sales to recover development expenses, still cost about $60 in 1980.

In 1980, the most complex commercially available chips were the 16-bit single-chip microprocessors: The TI TMS9900 (released in 1975), the Intel 8086 (1978), the Zilog Z8000 (1979), and the Motorola 68000 (1980). Each provides full arithmetic operations on 16-bit binary integers; the 68000 provides some 32-bit operations as well. In 1979, TI marketed the TMS9940, which is a 9900-MPU combined with 2,304 bytes of memory to form the first single-chip 16-bit microcomputer. As a lab exercise in 1980, IBM produced the control unit for a 32-bit IBM 370 on a single-chip. Several groups are developing 32-bit microprocessor chips that are targeted for release between 1982 and 1986.

The history of microprocessor development from 1971 to 1980 has been one of exponentially increasing complexity per chip with exponentially decreasing costs per operation. In 1971, the Intel 4004, with 1,000 transistors per chip, could perform about 8,000 four-bit operations per second; in 1980, the Motorola 68000, with 68,000 transistors per chip, could perform about 800,000 16-bit operations per second. For roughly the same potential cost per chip, the nine years produced a 70-fold increase in chip density, a four-fold increase in operand length, and a 100-fold increase in operation speed. The rates of increase have been approximately a factor of four in logic device density every three years, a factor of two increase in operand length every three years, and a factor of ten increase in speed every four to five years.

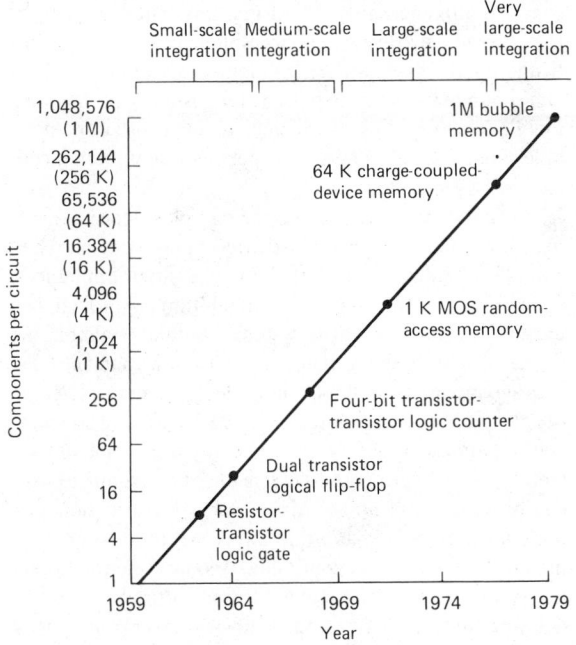

Fig. 6.   Component density trend.

As shown in Fig. 6, since 1959 maximum IC component densities have increased by a factor of four every two years, especially for regularly connected circuits such as memory arrays. Between 1959 and 1965, small-scale integrated (SSI) circuits had fewer than 60 elements each. Between 1965 and 1969, the medium-scale (MSI) circuits gradually increased to 1,000 elements apiece. From 1969 to 1977, dense large-scale integrated (LSI and VLSI) circuits increased to nearly 200,000 elements.

Because random logic circuits have more connecting links than memory arrays, the growth rate for densities in MPUs has only been a factor of four every three years. Since 1978, the rates have slowed slightly, at least partially because denser, more complex chips have been produced faster than application programs can be written to use them. However, the cost effectiveness of microprocessors will continue to increase for many years.

Research laboratories have already demonstrated several new processes offering order-of-magnitude increases in circuit speed. These include shrinking of component sizes with nearly linear decrease in signal propagation delays and use of new semiconductor materials such as gallium arsenate in which electrons move about five times faster than in silicon. Since the mid-1960s, IBM has been exploring techniques for building superconducting computers using quantum electron tunneling in Josephson junctions (q.v.) for logic and memory devices. Not only are these devices more than a hundred

times faster than silicon circuits, but they also use less than a ten-thousandth the electrical energy per logic decision and less than a hundredth the power per device. Less power means less heat to remove. One should be able to build small, fast superconducting computers with device densities which, if attempted for present-day, nonsuperconducting technology, would result in microprocessors melting into beads of glass. The main problem with these devices is that, to remain superconducting, they must run at a temperature near absolute zero (273°C below the freezing point of water).

Using present planar photolithography technology, the simplest method to increase silicon circuit speed and density is to shrink device sizes. There are some physical limits. Lines are already so narrow that short-wavelength ultraviolet light must be used for photoprinting of lines on wafers. More precise electron beams or X-rays must be used to continue decreasing line widths. Total chip power requirements and quantum electron effects in very thin films look as if they will limit planar silicon circuits to about 100 million transistors per chip before 1995. However, research has begun on circuits built in three dimensions instead of two, so that circuits of more than 10 billion components may be feasible by 2000. Microelectronic circuits of this density will almost certainly have to be superconducting to avoid overheating.

Applications. The key to the application potential of microprocessors and especially of single-chip microcomputers is that they offer inexpensive intelligence. As circuit densities increase, individual computations become less expensive, and feasible applications are more varied. At present, the primary application areas are control and communications.

In its fullest sense, control means intelligence. In control applications, a microcomputer receives input signals that measure a dynamic system or that set goals for the behavior of the system. By combining new inputs with remembered old inputs, the microcomputer must decide rapidly what output signals to send to help the system to achieve the goals for its behavior.

In communication applications, microcomputers perform the necessary control and translation functions to allow two or more systems to send highly variable meaningful signals to each other. The microcomputer may connect machines to machines, machines to humans, or humans to humans. Many applications involve both control and communication.

The most important control applications for microcomputers are in manufacturing processes. Large computers have long been used to run chemical factories and oil refineries where precise and rapid control of processes is necessary. Microcomputers are being embedded into individual manufacturing machines, such as numerically controlled lathes, grinders, and drill presses. Even more important are microprocessors controlling the manipulators (hands) of industrial robots which can be taught to perform complex sequences of assembly-line operations. Robots are being used to fabricate everything from calculators to cars with little human assistance. More powerful microcomputers are being combined with television cameras to produce vision systems (eyes) for industrial robots. Robots with eyes as well as hands can identify and position parts to assemble an almost limitless number of devices that now require human workers (including, of course, microcomputers themselves or, even, other robots than can then start producing more robots . . .). Factories that require no human workers at all are already being designed. The economic and social consequences of factory automation are immense.

Microcomputers are being used in many transportation control applications. Networks of microprocessors with sensors to detect cars are used to control series of traffic lights to maximize traffic flow under widely varying conditions. Microcomputers in cars and trucks provide non-skid brake systems, control ignition and fuel systems to increase engine efficiency and to reduce exhaust emissions, and detect component failures to reduce repair problems. Microcomputers are extensively used in navigation devices for airplanes and ships. They are indispensible for controlling high-performance aircraft for which human responses are too slow.

Microcomputers have already revolutionized the control of consumer products. They are used instead of complex electromechanical linkages in household appliances such as washers, dryers, and microwave ovens and in high-technology products such as cameras with automatic shutter control and even automatic focusing, radio and television sets with programmable tuning, and calculators for simple arithmetic and advanced computations. In amateur sports alone, many new high-technology devices have been made possible by microcomputers—radar units that measure baseball and racer speeds, jogging pedometers that keep track of calorie loss, and finger-sized calculators that monitor pulse rates during exercise. Microcomputers packaged as small self-contained units have now become consumer products for work and play within the home.

Inexpensive microcomputers control toys such as talking dolls, walking robots, and radio-controlled trucks. In computerized games, they provide exciting light/sound patterns; act as a teacher or opponent in chess and bridge; referee or keep rules for group contests; test memory, refine motor skills, and reflexes in arcade games such as Pong and Space Invaders; and provide rote practice quizzes for children learning arithmetic (Little Professor) and spelling (Speak and Spell).

Digital wristwatches have become a basis for personal intelligence aids. By using tiny microcomputers, they already feature calendars, split-second timers, multifunction displays, tiny calculators, musical alarms, spoken reminders, and even pulse rate sensors. Watches with mobile telephone links, foreign language translators, portable wrist television sets, and personal computer terminals will soon be feasible.

Microcomputers provide the complex decision-making power needed for sophisticated home control. They can allow remote control of lights and small appliances, open doors and switch lights as inhabitants approach, run burglar sensor and alarm systems, simulate inhabitants in vacant dwellings by changing lights and sounds to discourage intruders, and lock outer doors except to selected people recognized by voice or by easily altered numeric codes. Home computers are especially important in controlling solar heating and passive cooling systems to save energy within the home. Most energy-conservation systems must rapidly make fine adjustments to work optimally. Many require continuous monitoring to protect the system from extreme conditions: To prevent the circulating fluid from freezing, solar-heat panels may need draining on cold nights; and to avoid flying to pieces, wind-driven rotors generating electricity must be slowed if the wind blows too strongly.

Applications of microcomputers to merchandising and banking include both control and communication functions. Small computers already control cash registers, point-of-sale terminals (q.v.) that automatically identify merchandise from bar codes, anti-shoplifting monitors, and hand-held systems to speed counting of inventory. Microcomputers in credit card verification terminals automatically phone into central databases to authorize purchases. Small business computers are used for billing, sales records, record-keeping, and payrolls. Small computers control automatic remote bank teller machines. Data encryption (q.v.) techniques have been developed that will soon allow small computers to send personal mail, private financial information, and even verifiable signatures electronically without fear of eavesdroppers or forgers.

The combination of microcomputers with communication equipment is particularly powerful. Already microcomputers have replaced much of the electromechanical apparatus in individual telephone units, and now allow selective message forwarding and signalling features previously found only in desk-sized switchboards. Sophisticated channel sharing procedures allow thousands of phone calls to be reliably combined and separated in single continent-spanning hops through communications satellites. Microcomputers are used to control microwave relay stations both on earth and at the edges of space.

Small computers control telephone answering equipment and programmable video-recording systems. Built-in computers allow amateur radio operators to carry "pocket packet radios," small shortwave radios that transmit compressed conversations at very precise frequencies in short bursts through automatic repeater stations shared by many operators concurrently. Commercial companies are developing networks of shared, but interference-free, radio repeaters to link telephones in moving cars. Using satellite links, these systems will evolve into portable communicators worn by every person for nearly instantaneous communications anywhere in the world.

In Great Britain, computerized *teletext* systems allow television sets to select written newspaper pages broadcast invisibly along with normal television pictures. In cities such as San Francisco, material of public interest, including news and computer programs, are broadcast via radio in computer-readable form for selective storage and display by personal computers. In Europe, Japan, and North America, two-way *Viewdata* (*q.v.*) systems let computers controlling television displays connected to telephones or to cable networks request news, educational, and entertainment material from national databases. These systems will evolve into powerful communication facilities found in nearly every home, much like the telephones of today. Especially as robot-controlled factories replace human assembly lines, they will allow most people to work at design and planning tasks within their own homes or small local offices rather than in large centralized facilities. People will communicate to work rather than commute.

One of the largest application areas for small computers is in aiding larger computers. Microcomputers have long been used to control keyboards for user input and video displays for output. They now can display images of keyboards on touch sensitive screens used for flexible, low-cost input in dirty environments such as battlefields and factories. They control high-speed ink-jet printers and large storage devices such as rotating magnetic and optical disks. Microcomputers built inside large computers provide automatic startup and even remote error diagnosis via telephone links to national repair offices.

Inexpensive computers can be used to control interfaces that allow communications from machine-to-human via graphics displays and speech generation systems, from human-to-machine via input terminals and speech recognition systems, and from machine-to-machine for computer networks. Simple speech generation interfaces for microcomputers have been implemented in LSI chips costing as little as $1 apiece. They allow automatic telephone number directories, talking translators and dictionaries, and audio-warnings for computer-controlled automotive instrument displays. Combined with

laser beam pointers, speech generation systems can provide automated instruction manuals to direct inexperienced workers in assembly or repair of equipment. Speech-understanding units are more complex but are already used for totally automated telephone enquiry systems for financial data and for "no-hands" manufacturing control and inspection systems.

Computer network interfaces allow many computers to share large databases and expensive peripheral devices. They allow users to combine functions of several specialist machines for one task, such as a facility to check spelling, typeset, and print copies of technical papers. Combined with communication networks, computer networks will allow paperless offices all over the world to exchange business data. They will allow new technological workers to manage information from comfortable surroundings instead of centralized offices in large cities. Thousands of microcomputers are being combined into large network computers designed to give rapid answers to large repetitious problems that are too complex to be solved by a computer with only one processing unit.

These are but a few of the applications for microcomputers and microprocessors that can be foreseen. A true revolution in manufacturing, communications, information management, and personal services has just begun. It will profoundly affect society.

REFERENCES

1977. Noyce, R. N. "Microelectronics," *Scientific American* (Special Issue on Microelectronics) **237**, *No. 3:* 63–69 (September).

1977. Toong, H. M. D. "Microprocessors," *Scientific American* (Special Issue on Microelectronics) **237**, *No. 3:* 146–161 (September).

1979. Johnson, D. E. *et al. Digital Circuits and Microcomputers.* Englewood Cliffs, NJ: Prentice-Hall.

1979. Osborne, A. *Running WILD: The Next Industrial Revolution.* Berkeley CA: Osborne/McGraw Hill.

1980. Patterson, D. A. and Sequin, C. H. "Design Considerations for Single-Chip Computers of the Future," *IEEE Transactions on Computers* (Special Issue on Microprocessors and Microcomputers) **C-29**, *No. 2:* 108–116 (February).

1981. Cooper, J. A. *Microprocessor Background for Management Personnel.* Englewood Cliffs, NJ: Prentice-Hall.

L. D. WITTIE

MICROPROGRAMMING

For articles on related subjects *see* COMPUTER ARCHITECTURE; CONTROL POINT; CYCLE TIME; DIGITAL COMPUTERS; EMULATION; HOST SYSTEM; LOGIC DE-

SIGN; MACHINE INSTRUCTION SET; READ-ONLY MEMORY (ROM); and WILKES, MAURICE V.

Microprogramming is a technique used by designers to implement the control functions of a computer. The collection of control microprograms is sometimes called the *firmware* of the computer. As with the case of a number of other terms relating to computer systems, microprogramming has gradually evolved and broadened its meaning—as, in fact, the understanding of the term "control" has also broadened. Microprogramming, as originally conceived by M. V. Wilkes in 1951, was a specific technique "to provide a systematic approach and an orderly approach to designing the control section of any computing system." In Wilkes' context, the term "control" is taken to mean the interpretation and execution of a machine instruction. The timing for this is shown in Fig. 1.

The interpretation and execution of the instruction involves four phases:

1. Fetching the instruction into the instruction register (IR).
2. Decoding the instruction and generation of the data address.
3. Fetching the data.
4. Final execution of the instruction.

Each of these phases is broken into a number of steps. The steps are defined by the notion of a *cycle*: One cycle is the smallest time quantum in the control process. Generally, it is the time required to reconfigure (i.e., change the contents of) the data registers of the system. Thus, the notion of step or cycle is roughly equivalent to the notion of a register-state transition. Several cycles are required to execute one machine instruction, usually between 2 and 5 cycles are required per phase or between 6 and 20 cycles per instruction execution for even a simple instruction.

The machine, exclusive of control, consists of register and combinatorial execution resources (adders, shifters, etc.). Each register in the system can be directed to one of a number of other registers during one cycle. The registers, interconnections, and resources, are referred to as the *data paths*. The output of each register drives a series of AND gates, which are directed to each of the destinations that may be reached from the source register in one cycle. See Fig. 2.

The gates on the output of the registers, which direct the flow of information along the data paths, are called the *control points* of the system. Every bit of every register will have at least one control point. More commonly, however, there will be between five and ten control points per register bit, each corresponding to a possible destination point. However, control points are not handled independently; i.e., the control unit that is responsible for

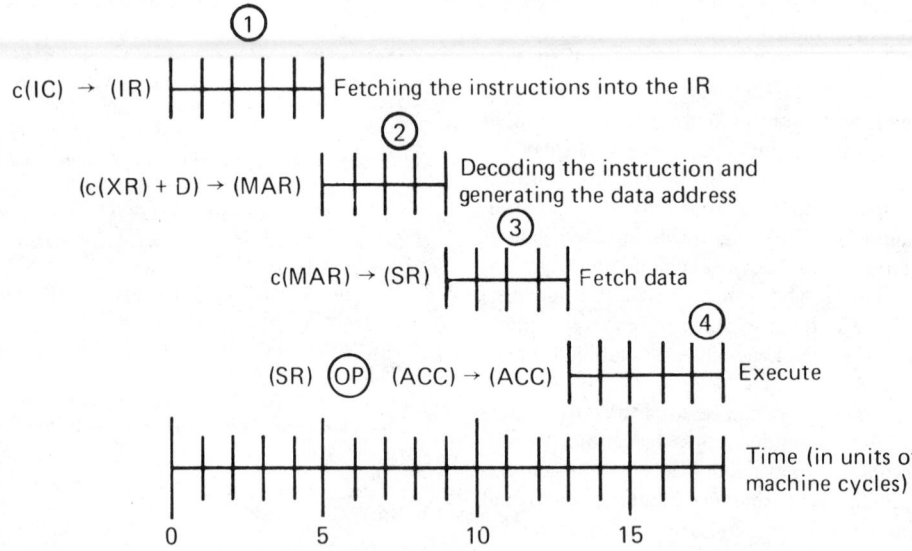

Fig. 1. Sequencing through a simple instruction. Instruction in the form c(c(XR) + D) OP (ACC)→(ACC), where c( ) = contents of; SR = storage register; MAR = memory address register; IR = instruction register; XR = index register; OP = operation specified by the instruction; D = address displacement; ACC = accumulator; IC = instruction (program) counter.

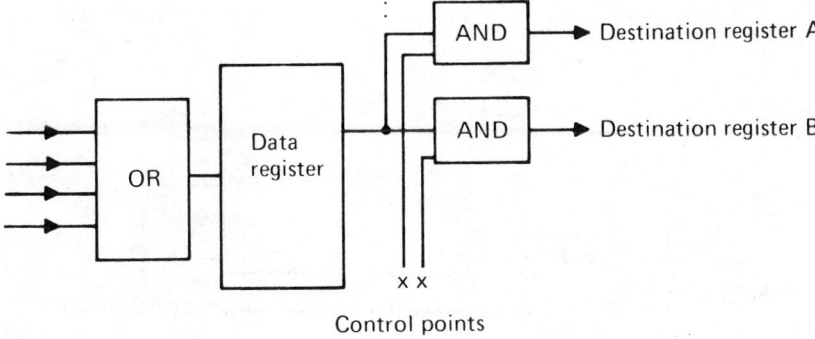

Control points

Fig. 2. Gating logic.

specifying data movement does not signal each point independently, but rather many (e.g., the control points associated with different bits of the same register) are ganged together and are treated as one point by the control unit. This defines an *independent control point,* or ICP (Fig. 3). Each of the ICP's must be specified as an output from the control unit. The sum value of all ICP's determines the complete control state of the system—i.e., which data register is connected to which and through what resource. Thus, the set of all ICP's represents the output of the control unit. Primary input to the control unit is the op-code (operation code) of the instruction.

The op-code specifies the operation to be performed; by itself, it is insufficient to specify multiple ICP steps for the execution of an instruction. Some additional counting mechanism is also required. If the control implementation is to be done with the *hardwire* implementation,

using a combinatorial network (Fig. 4), then the counting mechanism will be a sequence counter. This counter identifies the particular step of the instruction which is executed at any moment. The combination of the sequence count and the operation is the input to the network, which then describes the exact state of each ICP on each cycle of every instruction.

The microprogramming technique to implement the control function substitutes storage for the boolean combinatorial network and sequence counter. This serves as both a sequence and a combinatorial translator. The op code specifies the first microinstruction. The next microinstruction in the sequence, which interprets the instruction, may lie "in line" (i.e., following the address of the first microinstruction) or, alternately, the successor microinstruction may have its address contained in one of the fields of the first microinstruction.

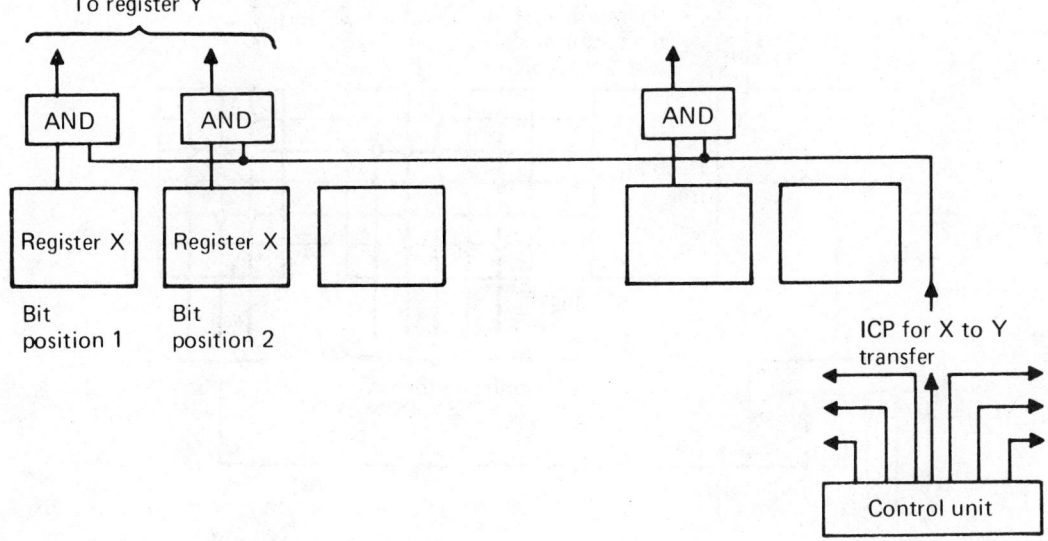

Fig. 3. Independent control points (ICPs).

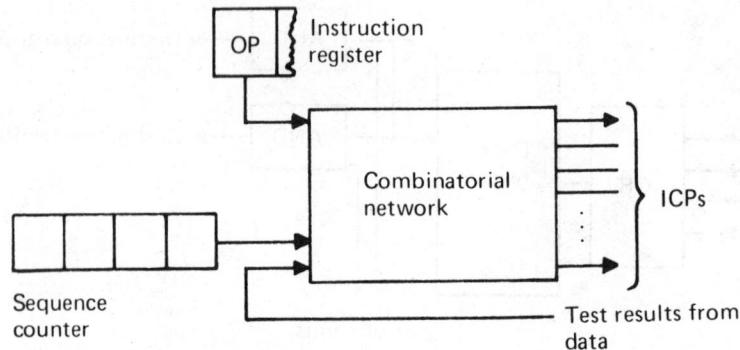

Fig. 4. Hardwire control.

The Evolution of Microprogramming. Microprogramming has evolved through distinct phases. Initially, microprogramming was used for engineering convenience. The storage contained the ICP's for each cycle. Ease of engineering change and design were important considerations. For these early microprogram implementations, diode matrix technology was well suited. Microprogrammed implementations of control during this era are best illustrated perhaps by Wilkes' ideas (Fig. 5). Wilkes viewed the microprogrammed control store as consisting of two diode matrices. The first matrix would determine the control information for the data paths, while the second matrix would determine, at least in part, the next microinstruction selected to continue the interpretation of the given instruction. The next microinstruction could be influenced by some selected datum (e.g., the sign bit of an accumulator). If the sign were negative, one microinstruction would be called; if the sign bit were positive, another might be invoked. This was required so that proper complementation rules could be used for addition and subtraction.

A decoding tree has the function of transforming a pattern of n bits into a unique selection of 1 out of 2^n possible outputs. Thus, for example, a four-bit binary input into a decoder tree would have four input variables. These would define 16 possible configurations, from 0000

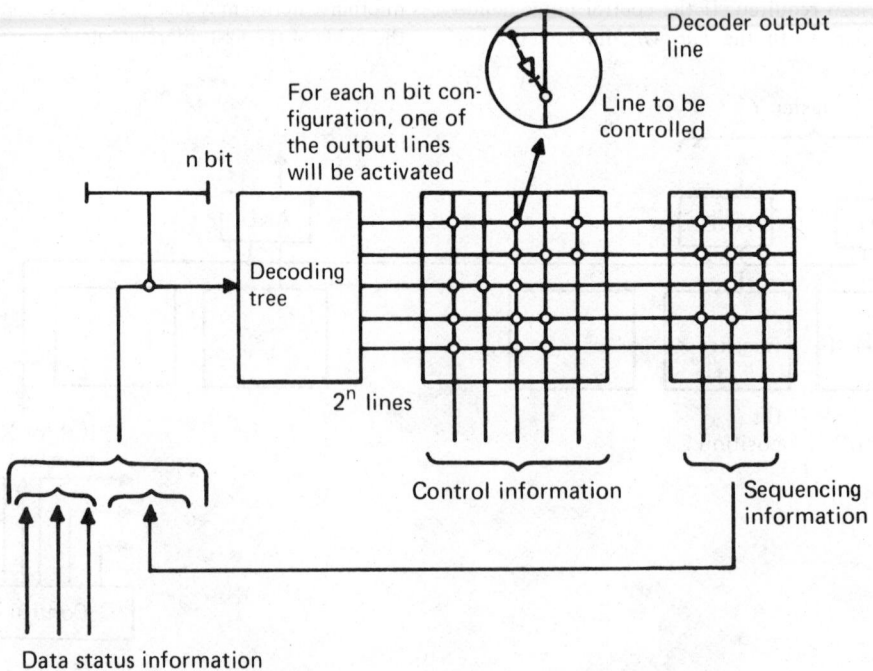

Fig. 5. Wilkes' microprogrammed control storage.

to 1111. The output of the tree would be 16 lines or possible events. Each output line would correspond to one and only one of the input configurations. When an output line is activated, it will also activate all lines out of the matrix that are connected to it (via diodes). The diode action essentially allows current to pass from the drive or input line into the output line. Of course, if no diode connects an input line to an output line, no current will be transmitted, and that line will remain in a "down state." These diode arrays give a simple and regular implementation to the control function. However, speed could be a problem.

In early implementations, no speed problems developed because main memory was quite slow, on the order of 10 μs cycle time, and the diode matrix had an access time of under ½ μs. The ratio of control access to the main memory access time was an important one; namely, as long as there was a large number of internal cycles in each memory cycle, the microprogramming task was relatively simple and straightforward. One register-to-register transformation was performed per internal cycle, and performance was essentially limited by the main memory cycle. As the main memory access time decreased, however, microprogramming techniques became correspondingly more sophisticated. If only one or two internal machine cycles are available for each main memory cycle, it is necessary to have multiple data transfers in each machine cycle. That is, the microinstruction has to control simultaneously a number of resources internal to the system. This gave rise to a type of internal parallelism within the processor.

The second generation of microprogrammed systems was distinguished by its small number of internal machine cycles per main memory cycle. By the early 1960s, main memory speed had dropped below 1 μs; yet the technology for control store had not noticeably improved, and the best access for read-only store varied between 200 and 400 ns. In addition, the read-only storage technologies tended to be exotic: The technology was not common with any other part of the machine and not always reliable. However, by this time the arguments for using microprogramming went well beyond the reasons cited by Wilkes. In the beginning of 1964, with the announcement of the IBM System 360, an important application for microprogramming was added—*emulation* of multiple machines on a single host system. This was intended to make the customer's transition from an old to a new system much more palatable, in that the customer could, with one system, support old software as well as develop new applications with new programming languages and facilities (Husson, 1970).

The third generation of microprogramming dates from about 1970 with the advent of fast read-write control store. The development of bipolar monolithic technology created a storage medium with the same access

time as combinatorial decisions, since essentially they are made out of the same material. The writable capability of control store represents an important transition, since now the control store becomes a true member of the memory hierarchy. It is unnecessary for control store to contain dynamically all interpretations for each and every instruction for each and every machine that must be emulated. Rather, emulated routines may be overlaid, as required, into a common microstorage. Similarly, the same storage may be used to hold parameters and buffer data values. Where the flexibility of high-performance operation over a variety of machine languages is not required, the data buffering function can be split off into a separate memory, again with the same technology. Here, references to main memory are anticipated by transferring blocks of data into the buffer. This gives rise to the "cache" type systems. Fig. 6 shows a medium-scale computer system, which features microprogrammable processors.

Fig. 6. The Burroughs B1728 (B1700 series) medium-scale computer that features microprogrammable processors.

Microinstructions. The microinstruction is the control mechanism that causes a single data-register state transition; i.e., it actuates an internal cycle. One can view this as the action of two separate machines—(1) a control machine whose output activates the data, and (2) an operational machine. The flexibility of these activations gives rise to a variety of possible microinstructions; terms such as horizontal, vertical, nanoinstruction, and packed or unpacked microinstructions have been used to describe the diversity of activations. These terms arise, sometimes ambiguously, to describe certain differences (Fig. 7):

1. If the microinstruction contains a separate description of each independent control point in the resource (i.e., the true description of the control

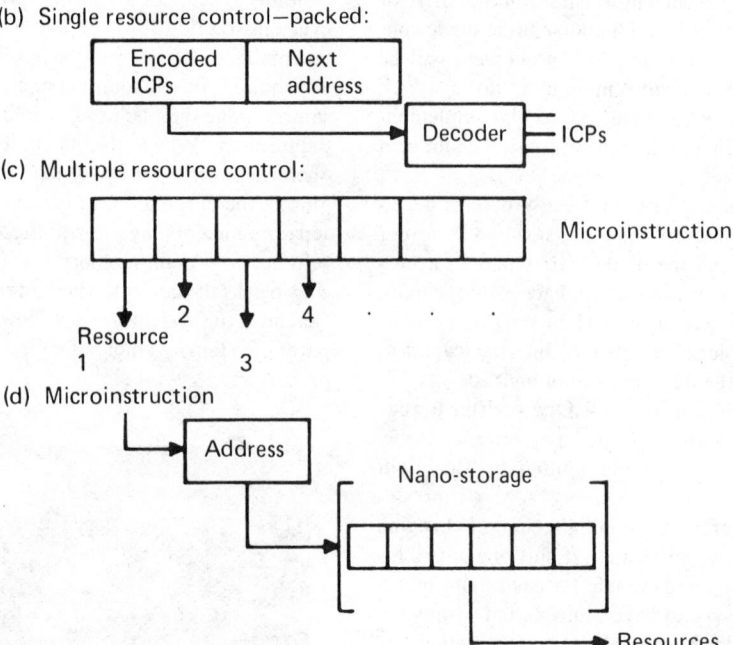

Fig. 7. Some concepts used in microinstruction formats.

gating), that activation is said to be an *unpacked* or *exploded form* of the microinstruction. This form is most expensive in terms of space, but it provides the ultimate flexibility in that any combination of ICP values may be specified at any time in the future. As an alternate to this unpacked form, a specific number of combinations of ICPs may be chosen. These combinations are coded into a smaller number of control points, and through the use of a decoder can be regenerated when the microinstruction is executed. Thus, only the packed form of the microinstruction is stored, in effect saving space at the expense of flexibility. Occasionally the distinction between packed and unpacked forms of microinstructions are referred to as *vertical* and *horizontal* microinstructions, respectively.

2. If the resources of the system are partitioned into a number of independent units which can be simultaneously activated, then the microinstruction that activates each of these resources simultaneously contains separate control information. Thus, in Fig. 7(c), a resource might be an adder, a shifter, a unit for loading and/or storing information into a register or a test and branch unit. Notice that each of these could be operated at the same time, as long as they did not make conflicting use of a data operand.

The distinction between the control of the single resource through the use of ICPs [whether packed or unpacked—Figs. 7(a), (b)] and the multiple resource control situation [Fig. 7(c)] should be noted. Of course the control for an adder still requires a set of ICPs, whether or not a microinstruction is specifying only the adder action or multiple units. This simultaneous use of resources gives rise to a type of internal parallelism that is explicit (visible to the microprogrammer) within the single instruction stream. This is unlike the type of internal parallelism of certain highly overlapped machines such as the CDC 7600 and IBM 3033, whose parallelism is transparent to the programmer. In any event, this use of the microinstruction for identification of possible simultaneous use of resources in conjunction with a partitioned set of resources has also been referred to as a "horizontal" microinstruction. The alternative is to use a universal single resource (unpartitioned); its corresponding control mechanism is sometimes referred to as a "vertical"microinstruction.

These two notions are independent; i.e., one can have an unpacked single resource microinstruction or a packed parallel-control-type microinstruction. In any event, a "vertical" microinstruction is a short form of a microinstruction, usually using a coded (packed) specification of an operation and also usually referring to only one type of operation. The "horizontal" microinstruction usually has either an unpacked specification or an operation and/or specification of multiple simultaneous operations.

3. There is an allied notion relating to the structure of a microinstruction called a *nanoinstruction*. In this mode, a packed instruction (the microinstruction), with usually only one or two fields, is used as the basic control mechanism. However, instead of driving the resources directly, it indirectly refers to the resources through another storage level, the nanoinstruction. The nanoinstruction is the "horizontal" instruction that contains the exploded form of the control description. This technique is used on machines such as the Nanodata Corporation's QM1.

Fig. 7(d) illustrates this concept in which the microinstructions are a sequence of addresses in which each address points to a nanoinstruction. A microinstruction may be horizontal and may have multiple resource specifications. The purpose of this technique is to reduce the size of the storage needed to represent the program. Use of a two-level control strategy requires both *microprogramming* and *nanoprogramming* to complete the interpretation.

Emulation. An *emulator* (Rosin, 1969; Husson, 1970) is the collection of routines and programs that interprets a language. Languages that are efficiently interpreted are said to have the directly executable language property. "Efficiency" in this sense is a relative measure, and includes factors such as the amount of storage required to represent a statement in a language, as well as the amount of time required to interpret that statement (Fig. 8).

In the past, emulation has mainly involved the interpretation of machine language with the use of microprogramming techniques for instruction interpretation. It is relatively easy for a single physical system to interpret more than one machine language. The physical machine, as defined by its microinstructions and their actions, is

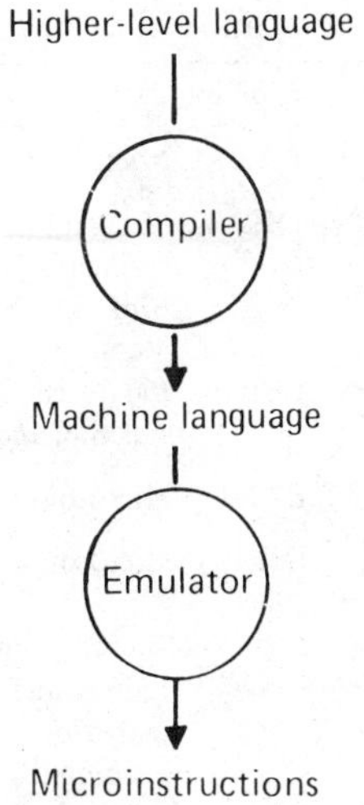

Higher-level language

Compiler

Machine language

Emulator

Microinstructions

Fig. 8. Emulation.

called a *host machine*. Machine languages that are emulated by sets of microprogrammed routines are called *image machines*. It is, of course, possible to write an emulator for one image machine in terms of another image machine language; thus, one can conceive of layers of emulators. However, more common usage of the term *emulator* implies that the interpretive set of programs is written in the microlanguage of the host processor.

Probably the most widely known use of emulation is that of IBM System/360. Most of the models of System/360 and System/370 are microprogrammed. Each model of the System/360 and System/370 is quite a distinct machine, with widely differing performance characteristics, data path size, etc. However, each has the common machine language of System/360. In all the microprogrammed models of the System/360, the interpretation of the machine language is done by an emulator that resides in microstorage. This emulator consists of a series of routines; each routine represents a particular System/360 instruction.

The emulation of a non-360 machine on a 360 machine is not so straightforward. Consider a Model 65 that emulates a 7090 (Table 1—see Tucker, 1967). The "emulation" of a 7090 on a Model 65 is more accurately described as a simulation of the 7090, using a combination of techniques, which includes 360 instructions, special instructions, and 7090 type instructions. The hybrid approach to emulation reduces the size of microstorage needed to provide emulation for both the 360 and the 7090. In the Model 65, each 7090 instruction is interpreted by an emulation subroutine that is contained in main memory (Fig. 9). This subroutine uses special instructions as well as conventional System/360 instructions. One of the most notable of the special instructions

Table 1. Emulation of 7090 Instructions

7090 instruction	360 Emulation routine	
AXT address to index true	EAXT	Microroutine that does AXT
	DIL	Microroutine that does fetch and interpretation of next instruction
AXC address to index complemented	LCR	360 instruction that complements the address
	EAXT	Microroutine (see above)
	DIL	Microroutine (see above)
TMI transfer if minus	ESTO	Microroutine that puts the value into a work area of the 360 (the simulated accumulator)
	TM	360 instruction, test under mask (to get the sign bit)
	EBC	Microroutine that does a 7090 branch if the test is satisfied

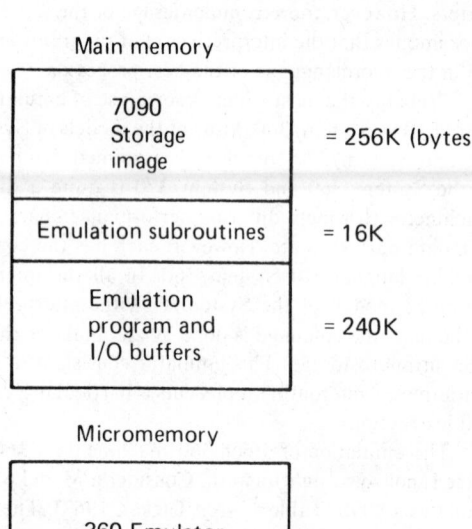

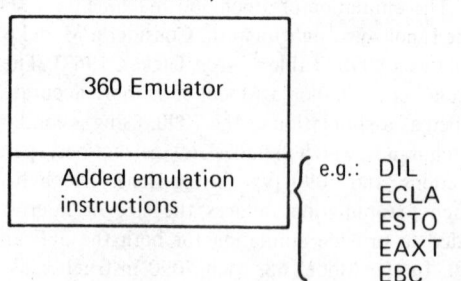

Fig. 9. Configuration of main memory and micromemory in a 360 Model 65 that is emulating a 7090 (Tucker, 1967).

is the DIL (Do Interpretive Loop), which is a microprogrammed routine that does a fetch and interpretation of the next 7090 instruction. In addition to the DIL routine, a number of other subroutines are added to the microstorage to assist in emulating specific 7090 instructions. The configuration of main storage and microstorage during emulation is shown in Fig. 9.

Microprogramming and Computer Architecture. The development of large, high-speed read-write storage technology is now widely recognized for its attractiveness in microprogram storage implementations. Presently, there are two important trends in computer architecture arising from this use of microprogram storage: (1) enriching the capability of traditional machine implementations (Fig. 10) and special language machines (Fig. 11).

An important trend in recent implementations of general-purpose computers (for example, from IBM and DEC) is the use of large microprogram storage to support

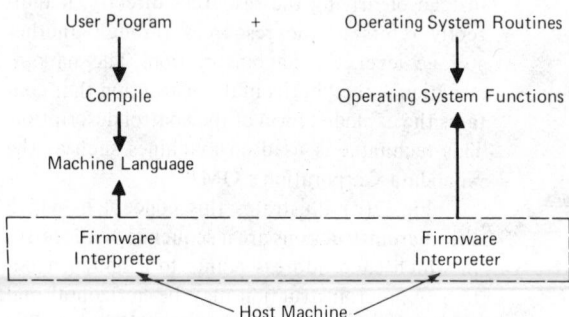

Fig. 10. Expanding operating system function and efficiency through emulation using firmware interpreters.

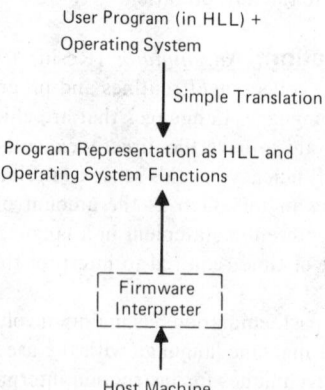

Fig. 11. High-level language (HLL) machine emulation.

additional functionality in the instruction set. The large microprogram storage actually represents an extension mechanism which allows portions of the operating system and the diagnostic support system to be implemented efficiently in microprogramming. The user's investment in traditional program representations prohibits extensive changes to the user's instruction set and thus only small extensions are made at this level. However, instructions executed in the supervisory state, entered by calls to the operating system, such as special memory management functions, can be microcoded and emulated to improve the overall performance of a virtual storage system as well as improving file handling capabilities.

Microcoding parts of the operating system are especially interesting in the area of security detection, since usually the microprogram storage lies outside the addressable memory space of the problem state program. This prevents accidental contamination of the operating system by a problem state program.

Machine diagnostics for fault location are already a widely accepted use of microprogram storage. With a conventional instruction, the diagnostic program must proceed through a large number of state transitions before a result can be evaluated and a determination made as to whether or not a fault has been encountered. The microinstruction, on the other hand, by its nature, executes in exactly one state transition. Therefore, the diagnostic resolution through the use of microinstructions is much finer than by the use of traditional machine instructions. Thus, higher resolution and more efficient diagnostic routines can be implemented by the use of microprogram storage.

High-Level Language Machines. By redefining the instruction set to make it cater to particular high-level language environments, one may realize an additional degree of representation efficiency (see Fig. 11). Of course, the resulting architecture is necessarily more limited in its flexibility. It is efficient only for one particular high-level language. However, in those cases where the emulators can be easily changed, so too can the interpreter for a particular high-level language. In the Burroughs B1800, for example, emulators are available for RPG, Cobol, and Fortran and some significant improvement in both code density (i.e., program size) and interpretation time have been noted by Wilner (1972).

In the high-level language machine, the instruction set is designed about the actions in the high-level language itself. A translation process still exists but it is now a simple one- or two-pass process to bind the variable values to names before program interpretation is done. Of course, more efficient coding of all objects used in the program may be accomplished during the same translation. In a well-designed, directly executable language form (which has been called a DEL), the instructions to be interpreted lie in one-to-one correspondence with the actions called for in the high-level language program. Further, no new names or objects are introduced into the representation; thus, unique names in the high-level language are preserved uniquely in the DEL form. Coding of objects in the intermediate form can be done much more concisely than in a traditional image program since the translator will know the number of objects used by the program or used within the scope of a subroutine and may use field sizes to represent these objects which are appropriate to the number of unique objects used (of the order of the logarithm to the base 2 of the number of objects in the scope of definition).

In a typical object code produced by standard compilers for familiar high-level language programs, there is an expansion factor of between 3 and 10 to 1 in the number of instructions in the object form when compared to the number of actions in the high-level language source form. But by the creation of efficient DEL representations, one can effectively reduce the number of instructions to be interpreted by exactly this factor and obtain a further program representation reduction by efficient coding of object names.

The result of all of the above is very concise program representations which have been created with a minimum compilation time. Since the number of objects to be interpreted has been reduced by a substantial factor, so too is the interpretation time provided that an efficient host implementation for the emulator is available.

REFERENCES

1967. Tucker, S. G. "Microprogram Control for System 360," *IBM Sys. J.* **6**: 222–241.
1969. Rosin, R. F. "Contemporary Concepts in Microprogramming and Emulation," *Computing Surveys* **1**: 197–212 (December).
1970. Husson, S. S. *Microprogramming: Principles and Practices.* Englewood Cliffs, NJ: Prentice-Hall.
1972. Wilner, W. "Burroughs B1700 Memory Utilization," *Proc. FJCC, AFIPS* **41**: 579–586.

M. J. FLYNN

MINICOMPUTERS

For articles on related subjects *see* ADDRESSING; COMPUTER SYSTEMS; DIGITAL COMPUTERS: Contemporary and Future; MACHINE INSTRUCTION SET; MICROPROCESSORS AND MICROCOMPUTERS; and MICROPROGRAMMING.

Today's minicomputer can be broadly classified as a 12-, 16-, 18-, 24-, or 32-bit word length machine with real memory sizes of 16K–8M bytes provided in modules of 16K or 64K bytes. Nearly all minicomputers employ a parallel internal processor structure with a high-speed bus and a clock rate of 1–10 MHz. The basic configuration ranges in price from $4,000–$50,000, with the cost of peripheral devices usually far outstripping the cost of the machine. The use of low-cost MSI and LSI logic has removed many of the initial design constraints, such as:

1. Limited addressing capability.
2. Lack of general-purpose registers and accumulators.
3. Elementary I/O processing and devices.
4. Limited interrupt schemes.

Indeed, the minicomputer is a product of our technology which can provide us with machines that exhibit significant architectural designs at very modest prices.

Although it is becoming increasingly difficult to distinguish differences in the range of applications of minicomputers and larger-scale (mainframe) computers, still there are some differences in usage which are often encountered and are worth mentioning.

1. For minicomputers with word lengths shorter than 32 bits, the precision of various data types is limited without the use of multiple-precision software.
2. Although high-level languages are usually available, the use of assembly language for writing user programs is more common.

3. Although some minis are run in a closed-shop, production environment, many are still run in an open-shop environment, with the user acting as operator, programmer, and application analyst. A typical installation is shown in Fig. 1.
4. A substantial number of minis operate in a dedicated environment for which the system has been specifically configured.
5. For other than standard applications, the mini user must, in general, be more sophisticated and ingenious, since large and complex operating systems do not exist, thus requiring the user to program what is more routinely provided by the large-scale computing system.

The trend of the minicomputer market has shifted from an OEM to an end-user market, and, as a result, more sophisticated software (requiring additional hardware) is being developed. This allows the user to buy a turnkey minicomputer system that has a complete operating system capable of supporting one or many users simultaneously. Indeed, the new breed of 32-bit machines look increasingly like their mainframe counterparts!

The languages available on these machines usually include Fortran, Basic, APL, Cobol, PL/I, and Pascal, besides other proprietary dialects of these standards. As we go through new generations of minicomputer systems, it seems clear that the mini and large computer are beginning to appear as one, at least from the point of view of the applications programmer.

Fig. 1. An IBM System/38 minicomputer.

Differences Among Minicomputers. Despite basic similarity of appearance, not all minicomputers are alike. Thus, although two manufacturers may provide similar capabilities on their 16- or 32-bit minis, the machines may differ in such minor things as utilization of octal or hexadecimal notation and number of accumulators/index registers to more major considerations, such as addressing techniques, I/O methods, interrupt structures, and instruction code assignments.

With so many types of minicomputers being produced by different manufacturers, the amount of variation seems unlimited. The same manufacturer will have different "families," whose commonality is achieved by machines that have a given word length and an essentially similar instruction set. Because of the similarities and differences, the user must choose a mini both on its external characteristics (software and support) and on its internal characteristics (word length, I/O structure, etc.) in light of the intended primary focus; namely, the tasks to be performed.

Internal Characteristics. As with most larger computers, the basic instruction in any minicomputer may be divided into three fields—the operation to be performed, the address mode to be used, and the address field (see Fig. 2). Often the last two fields are repeated if more than single operand instructions are allowed. The size of each field is very important in that it determines much of the internal machine characteristics (e.g., how many registers, how much memory may be referenced directly, how many distinct op codes will exist.).

Operation Codes. Since the size of the op code field of an instruction is often limited by the short word length of older minis, the number of distinct op codes is increased by a simple trick. Instructions that do not reference memory do not have address fields. Instead, these instructions are lumped together under one basic op code and the address field is used as an extension of the basic op code so as to specify a particular operation within the group.

On some machines, the extension field is likened to horizontal microprogramming, where the individual bits can be used independently to perform such functions as clearing the accumulator, skipping if a register is zero (or positive or negative), and shifting the contents of a spec-

ified register/accumulator. As a result of these instruction extenders, most minicomputers have large instruction sets when all the various legal combinations are considered.

New machines, with their longer word lengths allocate one byte for the instruction codes. This simplifies instruction decoding and allows for a large combination of op codes. If one byte isn't enough, one op code can be reserved to indicate a second instruction code byte.

Addressing Characteristics. Part of the basic instruction word is the *address mode field*. Possible addressing options include absolute/relative addressing, direct/indirect addressing, and indexed/no-indexed addressing. These different modes allow the programmer to expand the range of possible addresses that programs can generate. Since the number of bits available for specifying the address is small in 12- or 16-bit minis, it is absolutely essential that various addressing options be part of the addressing structure.

Although newer minis may address all of memory directly and absolutely, such is not the normal case in older machines. Instead, it was more common to be able to address only 256 (8 bits) or 4,096 (12 bits) memory locations. As a result, the address field of the instruction is used relatively to address small portions of memory by combining its value with the current program counter value, resulting in a floating page of fixed size, or with a page-register value, such as the high-order bits of the program-counter value, resulting in a fixed page of fixed size.

Fig. 3 depicts both the floating and fixed page addressing schemes. In Fig. 3(a), the program-generated address X is added algebraically to the program-counter value, generating the effective memory address. In Fig. 3(b), only the page bits of the program counter are used with X to generate the effective address. In this second case, the value of X is always assumed to be positive, so that the page is fixed in both size and position.

One advantage of relative addressing is the position independence of the generated code. Since only the relative distance between instructions and data are preserved as part of the instruction word, the word can be easily moved around in memory without requiring the services of a relocatable assembler and loader.

When indirect addressing is used, the entire word pointed to as the address field can be utilized, thus ex-

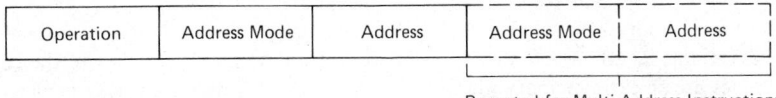

Operation	Address Mode	Address	Address Mode	Address

Repeated for Multi-Address Instructions

Fig. 2.   Instruction format.

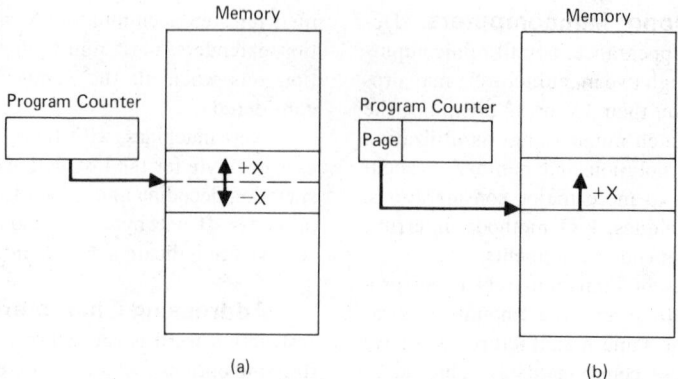

Fig. 3. Fixed and floating pages. (a) Floating page: effective address = PC ± X. (b) Fixed page: effective address = Page + X.

panding significantly the addressing space of the instruction. The level of indirectness may be single or multilevel, of course, depending on whether the indirect bit is associated with the instruction or the address field.

Current technology has produced minicomputers with truly general-purpose registers that may be used as index registers, accumulators, program counters, and stack registers. When used as index registers (and when implemented in active logic rather than as special-purpose memory locations), general-purpose registers allow large blocks of memory to be referenced without requiring additional instruction execution time. Additionally, these registers (whether part of memory or separate hardware locations) may be used in an auto-indexing fashion such that, when utilized indirectly, their contents are automatically incremented (or decremented). Auto-indexing is useful for loops, for stepping through arrays, and for subroutine parameter passing.

When it is possible to use all the addressing modes described, the order of execution for calculating the effective address becomes quite important. Depending on the size of the address field, post- or pre-indexing is performed after "derelativizing" the address field. For small address field machines, post-indexing is preferred, since the indirect address field can address a larger portion of memory, which is then indexed. On the other hand, for a large address field where more of memory can be addressed, it is particularly convenient to perform indexing before indirect addressing for such things as subroutine parameter passing, where the parameters may be addresses that have to be indirectly referenced.

There is another type of addressing scheme, which is associated with the variable-length instruction minicomputer. These machines use an extra memory word for the address field (when necessary) and specify that the instruction is more than one word long by setting the appropriate bits in the address-mode field. These machines

require extra memory cycles for fetching the extra words, but clearly the time is no more than the time required to perform indirect addressing.

Finally, the larger minicomputers use 24- and 32-bit addressing, thus allowing for the direct specification of enormous amounts of memory (up to 4 billion bytes). These minis don't actually contain that much real memory but use a virtual memory addressing technique to collapse or map the virtual memory address into its physical memory location. Since not all of virtual memory can be resident in physical memory, a large portion of it must reside on secondary storage. When needed, this copy of what would have been in physical memory is swapped with what currently resides there.

Input/Output. The range of peripheral devices that may be connected to a minicomputer is quite large and includes teletypewriters and CRTs, card readers and punches, line/page printers, disks, cassette tapes, magnetic tapes, plotters, and telecommunication equipment. Because of the sophistication of the minicomputer I/O bus, a large number of peripheral devices may be attached.

Data and control information is transferred to the I/O device either through the mini's accumulator or through special device registers. Once initiated (by making a request to the device controller), the I/O device is capable of operating concurrently with the CPU. Indeed, it is often possible to have several devices running simultaneously with the CPU, stealing memory cycles as needed.

Many minicomputers include a direct memory access (DMA) feature as part of the computer's structure. A DMA port allows an I/O device to communicate directly with memory without tying up the I/O bus or the CPU. Typical devices for which a DMA port would be useful are high-speed mass-storage devices and special-purpose interfaces to time-critical processes such as color graphic displays.

One of the key features found on most minicomputers is the interrupt structure. Depending on the application, the sophistication of the interrupt system may be more important than machine speed or instruction repertoire. The interrupt structures commonly found on minis range from single-level without priority to multilevel with priority.

A direct consequence of the multilevel interrupt structure is the automatic stacking of the processor state words. By means of a stack register, any level of interrupt nesting is possible. In addition, by utilizing the stack register for the automatic stacking of state words during subroutine activation, recursive programming and co-routine (q.v.) structures are more easily facilitated. Further, by introducing trap instructions into the instruction set, it is possible to link together easily independently written software systems and/or emulate/simulate hardware features (e.g., multiply/divide, floating point) not part of the basic instruction set.

Software. The range of software packages available for most minicomputers is quite large. At the very minimal level, all systems include an assembler, a loader, an editor, an I/O programming system, a debugging tool, and a mathematical utilities package. Each of these programs can be executed on the basic or minimal hardware configuration.

As the size of memory is increased, more sophisticated software becomes available to the user. This software includes high-level and special-purpose languages, as well as networking.

By adding a mass-storage device, such as a disk, to the minicomputer system, the minicomputer user gains the flexibility of a single-user disk operating system, or a batch operating system if a card reader is attached. In addition, by adding memory hardware for protection and relocation, background/foreground programming becomes possible, or even time-sharing systems capable of supporting 8–64 simultaneous users.

As a result of the recent trend to provide more sophisticated software, it is becoming more common to find minicomputers serving as general-purpose computing machines. On the other hand, the number of potential applications is almost limitless, and minicomputers can be found in a wide range of environments.

Applications. By and large, the greatest use of minicomputers has been in the areas other than general-purpose computing. These areas include:

1. Industrial applications such as control of power generation, petrochemical systems, data acquisition, and testing of equipment and devices.

2. Biomedical control for experiment monitoring.
3. In larger computer systems for communication and peripheral control, such as data concentrators, satellite peripherals, and intelligent terminals.
4. Intelligent graphic terminals and interactive graphic systems that may be part of general-purpose, graphic-oriented computing.
5. Microprogrammable minicomputer systems that are capable of being tailored to specific applications and/or environments.

It is important to distinguish between microprogrammable computers and the simple operation-code extension mentioned earlier. The value of the microprogrammable machine can be found in its compatibility with other different machines by emulation of the same instruction set; in its ability to allow the user to tailor a machine at the most primitive level to accommodate particular requirements; or in its ability to allow the user the flexibility of experimenting with new ideas and designs.

Another distinction occurs between microprogrammable minis and minis with read-only memories (ROM). Although ROMs are often used to hold microprograms, they may also be used to store programs for minicomputer applications that do not change and where the instructions may be locked into memory, providing decreased memory cycle time and greater integrity against accidental destruction.

Future Developments. As the cost of the hardware goes down with new technological advances, the cost/performance ratio of minicomputer hardware will continue to improve more dramatically than for large computer systems, where cost has remained fairly constant and performance has changed only slightly. As a result, there will be an increasing use of minicomputers in new applications areas (e.g., hospital record keeping, retail inventory management, and specialized commercial applications areas). Indeed, as the sophistication of the software improves, it will become increasingly difficult to distinguish minicomputer systems from larger computer systems.

REFERENCES

1974. Weitzman, Cay. *Minicomputer Systems: Structure, Implementation and Application.* Englewood Cliffs, NJ: Prentice-Hall.
1979. Eckhouse, Richard and Morris, Robert. *Minicomputer Systems: Organization, Programming and Applications (PDP-11).* Englewood Cliffs, NJ: Prentice-Hall.
1980. Levy, Henry and Eckhouse, Richard. *Computer Programming and Architecture: the VAX-11.* Bedford, MA: Digital Press.

R. H. ECKHOUSE, JR.

MIS. *See* MANAGEMENT INFORMATION SYSTEMS.

MODELS

For articles on related subjects *see* ENGINEERING APPLICATIONS; MATHEMATICAL PROGRAMMING; OPERATIONS RESEARCH; QUEUEING THEORY; SCIENTIFIC APPLICATIONS; and SIMULATION.

A *model* is a mathematical representation of a system. The term *system* here is used in a broad sense, to include any sort of process or structure—for example, a chemical reaction, the process of osmosis, the ecology of Lake Superior, the organizational structure of a corporation, the national economy, the weather, the molecular structure of matter, the human circulatory system, the human mind, machines and instruments of any sort (including computers), and programs that control computers.

A model for a system provides a language for conceptualization and communication that is appropriate for that system. A model normally consists of a formal mathematical structure that represents the system, together with a collection of notations (e.g., special symbols or graphical and diagrammatic notations) and terminology that is useful for expressing ideas about the system. The fundamental tools that are useful in modeling systems are the mathematical concepts of set, relation, and function. The universality of these concepts facilitates communication between fields, and helps to reveal similarities between systems that, on the surface, appear to have little in common.

Modeling has always been an important activity in engineering and science, but the development of computers has made modeling more important than ever for two reasons. First, in order to program a computer to analyze, control, or design a system, the programmer needs a precise, unambiguous description of the system (i.e., a model). Second, techniques for systems analysis, design, and control that have significant computational requirements have become feasible. Development and application of these techniques necessarily involve a great deal of modeling. This is particularly true for simulation techniques. Simulation involves developing a model to represent a system, programming a computer to implement the model, and then using the computer to experiment with the system. Simulation is used when real world constraints prohibit experimentation with an actual system, or, in system design, when the construction and testing of a prototype are impractical. It is especially useful in the initial stages of top-down design for testing alternative high-level organizations, and in later design stages for parameter optimization.

Types of Models. There are two basic types of models that arise frequently in practice—structural models and process models. A *structural model* describes the organization or structure of a system. A *process model* describes the operation of a system. A complete model for a system frequently includes both a structural model and a process model. Consider a communication network, for example. The structural model consists of the set of locations which may send and/or receive messages, together with a relation on this set that indicates all direct links between locations. The process model describes the operation of the system in routing messages through the network. As another example, consider a complex computer program. The structural model may describe the program database (e.g., inventory records, personnel records), or the structure of the input information (e.g., the collection of tasks at any time that must be processed by an operating system). The process model describes the operation of the program. The area of computer science that deals with structural aspects of programming is known as data structures (*q.v.*); the area that deals with the processing aspects of programming is the theory of algorithms (*see* ALGORITHMS, THEORY OF).

Structural Models. Examples of systems with interesting structural models are electrical networks, transportation and traffic systems, large organizations (e.g., corporations or governments), and large multiprocessor computer systems. Structural models usually involve the representation of relations. For example, the set of tasks waiting to be executed at a given time by an operating system has an associated precedence relation, indicating the order in which the tasks must be executed; a communication network has an associated relation indicating the existence of communication paths (i.e., point x is related to point y if it is possible to send data directly from x to y). Abstractly, a relation is a set of ordered pairs; element x is related to element y if and only if the pair (x,y) is in the set. Graphs provide a convenient visual representation of relations, and binary matrices (called *adjacency matrices*) provide a convenient computer representation. Structural models make frequent use of both types of representations. Fig. 1 illustrates these notations.

The relation of Fig. 1 might represent airline flight routes. The graph provides the most natural visual representation. The nodes represent cities and the branches represent the existence of scheduled flights between cities. For example, there exist direct flights from c to a and from c to d but not from c to b.

Process Models. Usually, the operation of a system is sequential, most frequently in time, but sometimes in other dimensions as well. For simplicity, let us restrict attention to processes that are sequential in time. Then

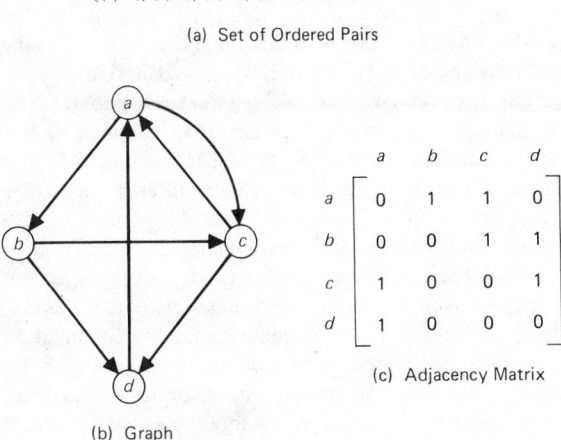

{(a, b), (a, c), (b, c), (b, d), (c, a), (c, d), (d, a)}

(a) Set of Ordered Pairs

	a	b	c	d
a	0	1	1	0
b	0	0	1	1
c	1	0	0	1
d	1	0	0	0

(c) Adjacency Matrix

(b) Graph

Fig. 1. Alternative representations of a relation.

time is modeled as an independent variable over a linearly ordered set, usually either the real numbers *(continuous time)* or the integers *(discrete time)*. A model involves two types of system parameters, those that are constant in time and those that vary with time. The process model provides a precise description of the relationships among these system parameters. Each system variable is characterized by its *range* (the set from which it assumes values) and its *type* (random or deterministic). A *deterministic* variable assumes a unique value from the range at each point in time; the value assumed by a *random* variable at any point in time is described statistically by a probability distribution over the range. Random variables are used to represent uncertainty about the process that generates the variable: Either the process is not well understood, or it is too complex to model deterministically, or it is truly random by nature. The range of a variable can usually be classified either as continuous (i.e., a subset of real numbers) or discrete (any finite or countable set). An important special type of discrete variable is the binary variable, which has a two-element set, usually {0, 1}, as its range.

It frequently happens that certain system variables are naturally thought of as inputs and other variables as outputs. Input variables are generated by some process external to the system. The system processes the inputs to produce the outputs. The process model for such a system is called an *input/output (I/O) model*. An I/O model may be either *static* or *dynamic*.

In the static model, the outputs at any time are a function only of the inputs at that time. A static system is said to possess no memory, since it has no recollection of previous inputs. The outputs of a dynamic system, on the other hand, may depend upon past values of inputs as

well as upon present inputs. That is, the system remembers certain information about the previous inputs, and the system outputs at any time depend upon this remembered information as well as upon the present inputs. This remembered information is called the *state* of the system. Fig. 2 shows four types of I/O models classified according to whether time is continuous or discrete, and whether the process is static or dynamic. The variable q represents the state. The range of the state variable must be continuous for the continuous time system, but it may be either continuous or discrete for the discrete time system. Each of the variables (x, y, and q) may be a vector [e.g., $\mathbf{x} = (x_1, x_2, \ldots, x_n)$].

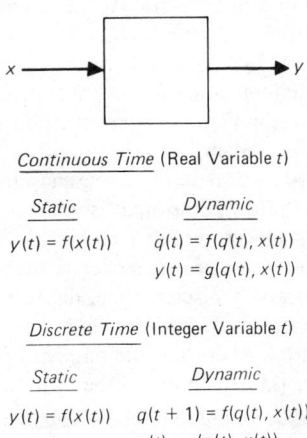

Continuous Time (Real Variable t)

Static	Dynamic
$y(t) = f(x(t))$	$\dot{q}(t) = f(q(t), x(t))$
	$y(t) = g(q(t), x(t))$

Discrete Time (Integer Variable t)

Static	Dynamic
$y(t) = f(x(t))$	$q(t+1) = f(q(t), x(t))$
	$y(t) = g(q(t), x(t))$

Fig. 2. I/O models.

As a simple example of a dynamic model, consider the process of amortizing a debt by a series of periodic payments. The payment made at the end of period t is the input, $x(t)$. The outstanding principal during period t is the state, $q(t)$. The outstanding principal for period $t + 1$ is the outstanding principal for period t, plus the interest owed on the principal for period t, minus the payment for period t. That is,

$$q(t+1) = f(q(t), x(t)) = q(t) + i \cdot q(t) - x(t),$$

where i is the interest rate per period. The output of this system is simply the state itself. That is,

$$y(t) = g(q(t), x(t)) = q(t).$$

Both static and dynamic models are important in the design of computers and other digital systems. Networks of logic gates without feedback, called *combinational networks,* are commonly represented by static models, while gate networks with feedback and networks involving both gates and flip-flops are represented by dynamic models called *sequential machines*.

Another important dimension for classifying models is *linearity*. The ranges of the input, output, and state variables for a linear system must be vector spaces, and the functions f and g of Fig. 2 must be linear. A single variable function h is linear if, for any scalars α and β and any vectors **u** and **v**,

$$h(\alpha\mathbf{u} + \beta\mathbf{v}) = \alpha h(\mathbf{u}) + \beta h(\mathbf{v}).$$

A two-variable function is linear if it is linear in each of the variables. Linear functions over finite dimensional vector spaces can be represented by matrices. Hence, the I/O relation for a linear static system becomes $\mathbf{x} = A\mathbf{y}$ and, for a linear continuous dynamic system, $\mathbf{q} = A\mathbf{q} + B\mathbf{x}$ and $\mathbf{y} = C\mathbf{q} + D\mathbf{x}$. The linear discrete dynamic system is similar. A, B, C, and D are matrices.

The input x in Fig. 2 may be either deterministic or random. If it is random, then the output y and the state q are also random. But the I/O relationship itself is deterministic even though the input is random. In contrast, there also exist process models for which the I/O relation is random. The most common model of this type is called a *Markov process*. A discrete-time, discrete-range Markov process, called a *Markov chain,* is characterized by an $n \times n$ matrix, where n is the number of elements in the *state space* (i.e., the range of the state variable). The element in row i, column j of the matrix is the probability that the next state will be j if the present state is i. The sum of the elements in each row is 1.

Fig. 3 represents a simple Markov chain. Continuing the example of Fig. 1, this particular Markov chain might represent the travel patterns of tourists visiting cities a, b, c, and d. Row i of the transition matrix indicates where the tourists in city i today will go tomorrow. Hence, a typical tourist visiting city b on any day will stay in b for the next day with probability $\frac{1}{2}$, go to c with probability $\frac{1}{3}$, and go to d with probability $\frac{1}{6}$.

$$\text{State Space} = \{a, b, c, d\}$$

$$
\text{Transition Matrix} =
\begin{array}{c}
 \\ a \\ b \\ c \\ d
\end{array}
\begin{array}{cccc}
a & b & c & d \\
\left[\begin{array}{cccc}
\tfrac{1}{2} & \tfrac{1}{4} & \tfrac{1}{4} & 0 \\
0 & \tfrac{1}{2} & \tfrac{1}{3} & \tfrac{1}{6} \\
\tfrac{1}{3} & 0 & \tfrac{1}{3} & \tfrac{1}{3} \\
1 & 0 & 0 & 0
\end{array}\right]
\end{array}
$$

Fig. 3. Markov chain.

Multi-Level Models. A model is an abstraction of the system that it represents. Only those features of the system that are relevant to the purpose for which the model is intended are included in the model. Irrelevant details are suppressed. This element of abstraction, the controlled suppression of detail, plays a crucial role in the analysis and design of complex systems. Consider, for example, the problem of designing a modern computer. The computer is constructed from electronic components (resistors, diodes, transistors, etc.). The system to be designed, the computer, is extremely different in nature from the components, and the final design may involve hundreds of thousands of these components. In order to manage the enormous complexity of a design problem such as this, it is essential for the designers to use a systematic modular design procedure, usually a combination of *bottom-up* design and *top-down* design. Bottom-up design begins with the components to be used, and from there constructs a set of new components that are closer in nature to the goal system. If there remains a great disparity between the goal system and the new components, the procedure is repeated. Top-down design begins with the goal system, and decomposes that system into subsystems that are closer in nature to the components available. If the disparity between these subsystems and the components is too large, the process is repeated. The system that is designed using either of these procedures, or a combination of the two, has a built-in multi-level structure. This multi-level structure for a modern computer is shown in Fig. 4. Each level is characterized by the set of components available at that level, and by the models

If $q(t) = b$, then $q(t + 1) = b, c,$ or d with probabilities $\frac{1}{2}$, $\frac{1}{3}$, and $\frac{1}{6}$, respectively.

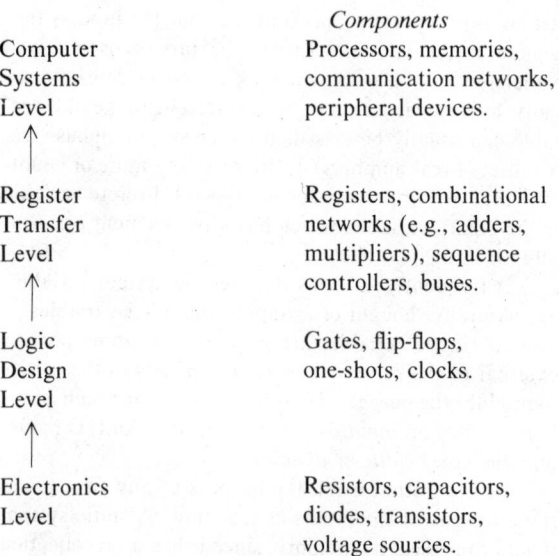

	Components
Computer Systems Level	Processors, memories, communication networks, peripheral devices.
Register Transfer Level	Registers, combinational networks (e.g., adders, multipliers), sequence controllers, buses.
Logic Design Level	Gates, flip-flops, one-shots, clocks.
Electronics Level	Resistors, capacitors, diodes, transistors, voltage sources.

Fig. 4. Multi-level computer structure.

used to describe these components and the systems that are constructed from them. The systems at any level become the components for the next higher level. But the model from the lower level is not used at the higher level. Instead, a new model is developed that suppresses the details of internal structure and operation that are irrelevant at the higher level.

For example, at the electronics level, a two-input NAND gate is a moderately complex system. A nonlinear continuous time dynamic model is used, involving 20 or 30 continuous range variables representing voltages and currents. The designer is interested in the exact values of the voltages and currents under steady state conditions, as well as the detailed nature of the transients when switching between steady states. At the logic design level, the two-input NAND gate is a simple component. The model involves three binary variables instead of 20 or 30 continuous range variables, and these are related by a simple switching function. For many applications, a static model is sufficient: $C(t) = \overline{A(t) \cdot B(t)}$. When it is necessary to represent the delay through the gate, a very simple continuous time dynamic model is usually sufficient: $C(t + \Delta) = \overline{A(t) \cdot B(t)}$. The details of the transient response are replaced by a single parameter, Δ, called the propagation delay.

This example is typical of the suppression of detail that occurs in moving from one level to the next in Fig. 4. It is this controlled suppression of detail that provides the mechanism for developing the multi-level models that are essential to understanding and designing complex systems.

REFERENCES

1971. Windeknecht, T. G. *General Dynamical Processes*. New York: Academic Press.
1973. Stone, H. S. *Discrete Mathematical Structures*. Chicago: Science Research Associates.
1973. Coffman, E. G. and Denning, P. J. *Operating Systems Theory*. Englewood Cliffs, NJ: Prentice-Hall.
1976. Tanenbaum, A. S. *Structured Computer Organization*. Englewood Cliffs, NJ: Prentice-Hall.
1978. Gajda, W. J. and Biles, W. E. *Engineering: Modeling and Computation*. Boston, MA: Houghton Mifflin.
1980. Kowalik, J. S. and Jacoby, S. L. S. *Mathematical Modeling with Computers*. Englewood Cliffs, NJ: Prentice-Hall.

L. R. MARINO

MODEMS

For articles on related subjects *see* ACOUSTIC COUPLER; DATA COMMUNICATIONS; and TELEPROCESSING SYSTEMS.

Modems are used in data communication networks to help transmit data between computers and terminal devices. They transform (modulate) digital data from a computer terminal to analog form, which is more suitable for transmission over communication lines. Since, in general, data flows in both directions, modems are also able to accept the analog signal and restore (demodulate) it back to its original digital form, as shown in Fig. 1. The word *modem* stems from the *mod*ulation-*dem*odulation process performed. In addition to performing the basic transformation between digital and analog voice-frequency signals, modems can also perform a number of control functions that coordinate data flow over the communication link. Terms usually used synonymously for modems include *data set*, *data phone*, and *subset*.

Modem Types. Different types of modems are available, depending on whether they are used for:

1. Synchronous or asynchronous transmission
2. Operation over dedicated or dial-up lines
3. Simplex, half-duplex, or full-duplex operation
4. Long-distance (long-haul) or limited-distance (short-haul) operation.

Some modems handle characters serially, while others handle an entire character in one bit-time by receiving or transmitting the individual bits in parallel on several

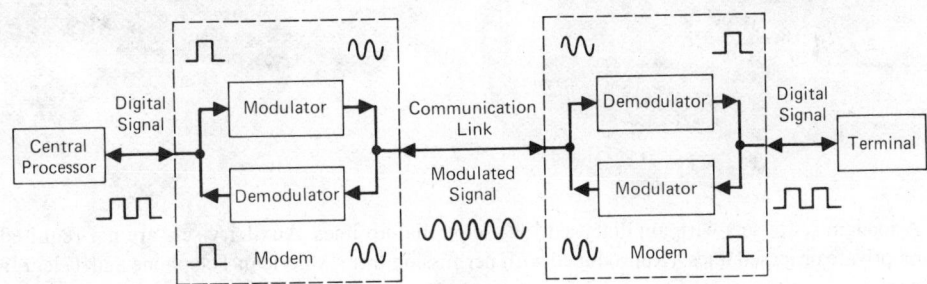

Fig. 1. A communication link using modems.

voice-grade channels. Also, some modems, called *acoustic couplers,* can be acoustically coupled to the telephone handset. Since parallel modems are not in common use, and acoustic couplers are described elsewhere, further comments will be limited to modems that transmit and receive characters serially by bit and do not use acoustic coupling.

Synchronous transmission, when the characters are transmitted at a fixed rate with the transmitter and receiver synchronized, is usually used for transmission rates greater than 2,000 bits/sec between buffered terminals. Synchronization is achieved using several special characters (SYNCH characters) at the beginning of each message. In asynchronous transmission, the time interval between characters can vary arbitrarily with the synchronization accomplished by adding start and stop bits to each character. Consequently, it is used primarily for unbuffered terminals such as keyboard devices. Synchronous transmission is more difficult to implement but is more efficient since no start and stop bits are needed for each character. Software for simultaneous support of many asynchronous terminals, however, is generally easier to implement than for a similar number of synchronous terminals.

Modems initiating transmission over the switched (telephone) network have an auxiliary set (dialing unit) to allow dialing from the originating device, as shown in Fig. 2. Dial-up modems provided by other than telephone companies require a data-access arrangement (DAA) between modem and the network unless they have been "certified" for direct connection to the telephone network. The DAA protects the telephone network by limiting the modem's output signal level. Modems used on dedicated lines do not require a DAA, have no dialing units, and can operate at higher transmission rates. Consequently, the choice between dedicated and dial-up lines is usually determined by the amount of data to be transmitted and the relative costs of the two services.

Modems can be designed to operate in simplex, half-duplex, or full-duplex modes. Simplex refers strictly to unidirectional transmission and, hence, is rarely used. Full duplex refers to *simultaneous* transmissions in both directions, while in half-duplex systems, data may flow in both directions, but *not simultaneously.* Most modems built today can work in any of the three modes, the choice being determined by the communication line and the terminal devices at each end.

Initially, most modems were long haul; i.e., they would function satisfactorily over unlimited distances. Today, one may obtain limited-distance or short-haul modems. These are specifically designed to work on short (usually 50 miles or less) point-to-point dedicated lines and offer substantial cost savings over their long-haul counterparts with similar performance characteristics, especially at transmission rates in the range between 2,400 and 19,200 bits/sec.

Fig. 2. A modem (data set) with auxiliary set for use on dial-up lines. Auxiliary sets are not required for use on private or leased lines. (Reproduced with permission from American Telephone and Telegraph Company.)

Modulation Techniques. To modulate a digital signal for transmission over a communication channel, a modem may use amplitude modulation (AM), frequency modulation (FM), or phase modulation (PM), as shown in Fig. 3. The type of modulation used depends upon the specific application. FM in the form of frequency-shift keying (FSK) is used almost exclusively for asynchronous communication up to 1,800 bits/sec. A form of PM is used for synchronous communication at 2,000 and 2,400 bits/sec. For the 4,800–9,600 bit/sec range, the choice is much wider, and depends upon the design objectives and the quality of channels available. In these cases, the modulation technique is usually more complex, being some combination of AM, FM, and PM.

Long-haul modems operating at rates above 9,600 bits/sec usually require two or more voice-grade lines or must use special wideband channels. Operation up to 230,400 bits/sec is possible, using wideband lines and modems.

Modern Modem Design. On dial-up lines, the current limit of reliable transmission is 4,800 bits/sec. On leased lines, the limit is 9,600 bits/sec, although special circuits for higher rates are available. Above 4,800 bits/sec, the modem must use an elaborate modulation technique and have automatic equalization to allow for the wide variations encountered in voice-grade channels. The higher the operating speed, the more self-testing arrangements are provided to aid in isolating causes of faulty operation. Most modems use the standard EIA (Electronic Industries Association) Standard RS-232 specifications between the modem and terminal devices, but other interfaces, such as MIL-Standard 188B (for military communications equipment) and CCITT (Comité Consulta-

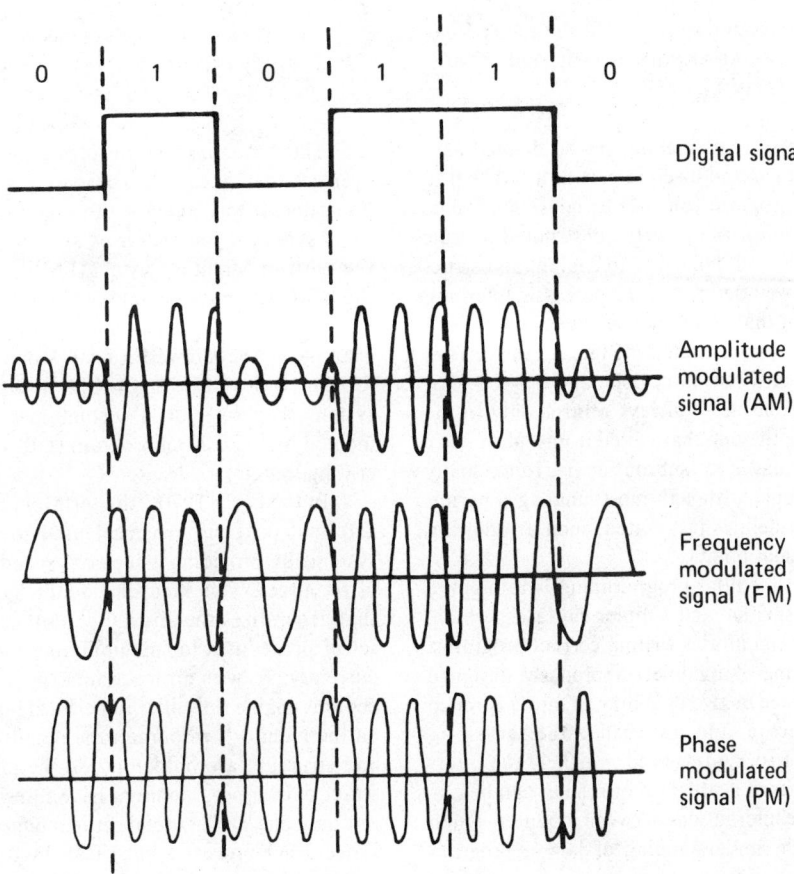

Fig. 3. Modulation techniques. In AM the amplitude is used to differentiate a "0" from a "1." In FM this is done by using two different frequencies, while PM uses a change in phase.

tif International Télégraphique and Téléphonique) Recommendation V.24 and V.27, are available for some types of modems.

The newest modems use microprocessor technology which offers smaller size and cost, greater reliability, added flexibility, better equalization, improved diagnostic capability, and much lower transmission error rates because of error detection and correction capabilities.

REFERENCES

1972. Davey, J. R. "Modems," *Proc. IEEE* **60**, *No. 11:* 1284–1292 (November).
1976. Martin, James. *Telecommunications and the Computer,* 2nd Ed. Englewood Cliffs, NJ: Prentice-Hall.

J. S. SOBOLEWSKI

MODULAR PROGRAMMING

For articles on related subjects *see* PROGRAM VERIFICATION; SOFTWARE ENGINEERING; and STRUCTURED PROGRAMMING.

A program or system *module* can be defined as a logically self-contained and discrete part of a larger program. A complete program can thus be considered to be a collection of modules. A properly constructed module accepts input that is well defined as to content and structure, carries out a well-defined set of processing actions, and produces output that is well defined as to content and structure. A properly constructed module, as the term is normally used, has only one entry point and only one exit point. If it is a subroutine, it always returns only to the statement following the one that called it into play.

In many languages a subroutine is functionally equivalent to a module, although most languages permit violations of the guidelines just stated, such as allowing multiple entry and exit points.

The purpose of modular programming is to break a complex task into smaller and simpler subtasks, which, among other things, facilitates writing correct programs. A program consisting of modules of properly designed scope (typically a page or two of coding at most) is much simpler to design, write, and test than is the same program when it is not so modularized. Further, the interactions between parts of a program or system can be rigidly restricted to the interactions between modules, which greatly simplifies the understanding of how a program works.

In the development of large software systems by teams of programmers, good modularization is essential if the portions written by different programmers are to mesh effectively and in a reasonable period of time into a system. Finally, since all programs and systems that are used over a period of time have to be maintained and modified, good modularization also aids in doing these chores more quickly and accurately.

Good program design starts with the most general definition of the function of the program, and proceeds through a sequence of increasingly detailed specifications. This technique, called *top-down design,* is an aspect of structured programming, and is greatly enhanced by modular programming.

D. D. McCRACKEN

MONITOR. *See also* HARDWARE MONITORS; and SOFTWARE MONITORS.

MONITORS

For articles on related subjects *see* ABSTRACT DATA TYPES; CLASS; CONCURRENT PROGRAMMING; OPERATING SYSTEMS; and SEMAPHORE.

The term *monitor* denotes a control program that oversees the allocation of resources among a set of user programs. It was, along with *supervisor* and *executive,* an early synonym for *operating system.* An old example is the Fortran Monitor System (FMS), which appeared on the IBM 709 series beginning in the late 1950s to provide run-time support for Fortran programs. A contemporary example is the Conversational Monitor System (CMS) for the IBM VM/370; CMS is a single-user interactive system that runs on a virtual machine (VM) implemented by the control program (CP) of the VM/370 operating system.

In the early 1970s, the term *monitor* was applied to a formal program construct used to simplify operating systems by providing a separate scheduler for each class of resources. This kind of monitor has a syntactic form that generalizes the abstract data type (*q.v.*); it defines a set of procedures for manipulating a set of objects concurrently. As with abstract data types, the monitor's procedures enable the caller to perform high-level operations on the monitor's resources; the details of resource status and structure are hidden inside the monitor. Unlike abstract data types, monitors have internal locks that permit only one process to execute monitor instructions at a time. Other processes must wait in a queue to enter the monitor. If a process in the monitor stops to wait for a resource to become available, the monitor must be unlocked so that another process (e.g., one that will release the desired resource) can gain access.

The following example of a resource manager is

adapted from Hoare's 1974 paper on monitors. Monitor RM handles the allocation of a set of resources whose indices $1, \ldots, N$ are initially in the set UNITS.

```
type RM = monitor;

    var nonbusy: condition;
    type unitnumber = 1..N;
    type UNITS = set of unitnumber;

    function entry acquire: unitnumber;
    var i: unitnumber;
    begin
        if UNITS = [ ] then nonbusy.wait;
                                    ([] denotes empty set)
        i := "any member of UNITS";
        UNITS := UNITS − i;
                                    (Deletes i from UNITS)
        return i;
    end acquire;

    procedure entry release (i: unitnumber);
    begin
        UNITS := UNITS + i;
                                    (Inserts i in UNITS)
        nonbusy. signal;
    end release;

begin
    UNITS := [1..N];
end RM;
```

The condition "nonbusy" can be regarded as an (initially empty) queue of processes each awaiting a unit of resource. To acquire a unit of resource, a process executes the call:

$$i := RM. \; acquire;$$

As soon as this procedure returns, the caller has control over the ith unit of resource and the monitor is unlocked. If other processes come while there are no available units of resource, they will be enqueued when they perform the operation "nonbusy.wait." To release unit i, the holder executes the call

$$RM. \; release \; (i);$$

The operation "nonbusy.signal" during this call permits one of the queued processes to proceed from its stopping point (at the statement "nonbusy.wait"). The monitor lock is held as long as any process is executing in the monitor; it is released either when a process exits from the monitor or gets queued for a condition.

Monitors in their modern context are increasingly used as tools for structuring operating systems.

REFERENCES

1974. Hoare, C. A. R. "Monitors: An Operating System Structuring Concept," *Comm. ACM* **17**, *No. 10:* 549–557 (October).
1977. Brinch Hansen, P. *The Architecture of Concurrent Programs.* Englewood Cliffs, NJ: Prentice-Hall.

P. J. DENNING AND W. F. TICHY

MONTE CARLO METHOD

For articles on related subjects *see* RANDOM NUMBER GENERATION; and SIMULATION.

In applied mathematics, the name "Monte Carlo" is given to the method of solving problems by means of experiments with random numbers. This name (after the casino at Monaco) was first applied around 1944 to the method of solving deterministic problems by reformulating them in terms of a problem with random elements, which could then be solved by large-scale sampling. But, by extension, the term has come to mean any simulation problem that uses random numbers.

A classical example of what we would now call the Monte Carlo method is that of Buffon, who in 1733 pointed out that π could be found experimentally by repeatedly throwing a needle onto a ruled surface, and counting the number of times the needle crossed a line (see Fig. 1). The idea is more remarkable for its sophistication in geometric probability than for its practicality—a more accurate evaluation of π could be done with a piece of string, a ruler, and the plates and saucers in your kitchen. But the idea of Monte Carlo had been conceived, although the difficulty of using physical devices for sampling and the lack of suitable statistical theory

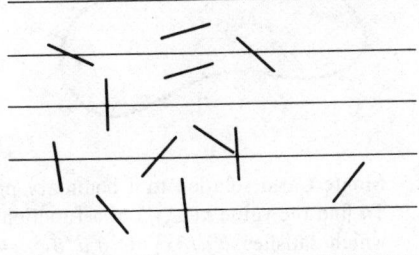

Fig. 1. Buffon's needle problem. If a needle of length ($L \leq 1$) is dropped on a ruled surface of parallel lines spaced one unit apart, the probability that the needle will cross a line is $2L/\pi$. If the needle is dropped N times, the number of line crossings (say, X) should be about $2NL/\pi$, and hence, $2NL/X$ is a Monte Carlo estimate of π.

made it little more than a curiosity until the advent of large-scale computers.

The development and proliferation of computers were accompanied by widespread use of Monte Carlo methods in virtually all branches of science, ranging from nuclear physics (where computer-aided Monte Carlo was first applied) to astrophysics, biology, engineering, medicine, and operations research. Note that the use of the term has become so extensive that it now serves as an adjective (as in a Monte Carlo problem), as a noun (as in the previous sentence), and, unfortunately, even as a verb (as in "Let's Monte Carlo it") meaning to get an idea of the answer to a complicated problem with random elements by having a computer run through the problem as many as thousands of times, using random numbers to assign values to the random or unpredictable parts of the problem.

The examples and nearly 500 references listed by Hammersley (1964) and Shreider (1966) give an idea of the variety of applications that have been reported. Since the time of those publications, the method has become even more widespread. Today the Monte Carlo method of solving complicated problems by using random numbers in a computer—either by direct simulation of physical or statistical problems or by reformulating deterministic problems in terms of ones involving random processes (e.g., partial differential equations or integral equations in terms of diffusion processes or random walks, multidimensional integrals as expected values of certain random events)—has become one of the important tools of applied mathematics. An example of a Monte Carlo solution to a boundary value problem is in Fig. 2.

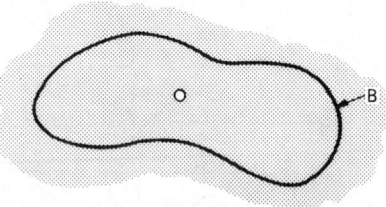

Fig. 2.   Monte Carlo solution to a boundary problem. To find the value $u(x_0, y_0)$ of a function $u(x, y)$ which satisfies $\partial^2 u/\partial x^2 + \partial^2 u/\partial y^2 = 0$ for (x, y) in the region enclosed by boundary B, and for which $u(x, y) = f(x, y)$ for points (x, y) on the boundary B, start 1,000 random walks at x_0, y_0 (center circle) so as to get 1,000 border crossing points. The average of $f(x, y)$ over the border crossing points is then approximately $u(x_0, y_0)$. The random walk moves from each point on the lattice to the four neighbors, with probability 1/4.

REFERENCES

1964. Hammersley, J. M. and Handscomb, D. C. *Monte Carlo Methods*. London: Methuen.
1966. Shreider, Yu. A. (Ed.). *The Monte Carlo Method, The Method of Statistical Trials*. New York: Pergamon Press. (Translated from the Russian.)

G. MARSAGLIA

MULTIPLEXING

For articles on related subjects *see* BANDWIDTH; CHANNEL; COMMUNICATION CONTROL UNIT; COMMUNICATIONS AND COMPUTERS; COMPUTER NETWORKS; DATA COMMUNICATIONS: General Principles; DATA COMMUNICATION NETWORKS; MODEM; PACKET SWITCHING; and TIME SHARING.

In general terms, the word *multiplexing* refers to the use of a single facility to handle simultaneously several similar but separate operations. Most computers, for example, have high-speed multiplexed input/output channels to handle many peripheral devices such as line printers or card readers, all of which may operate simultaneously. The main use of multiplexing, however, is in the field of data communication, where it is used for the transmission of several lower-speed data streams over a single higher-speed line. The primary motivation behind multiplexing is the reduction of costs, although in many cases an increase in reliability is an additional benefit.

Basically, there are two methods of multiplexing: frequency-division multiplexing (FDM) and time-division multiplexing (TDM). Before describing these further, it is appropriate to mention that the words "multiplexing" and "concentration" are sometimes used synonymously. *Concentration,* however, is a TDM method that uses a sharing technique in which statistics and queueing play an important role. This usually involves a small computer, and the word "concentrator" is therefore usually reserved for a small computer, programmed to perform the functions of a multiplexer.

Frequency Division Multiplexing. In FDM, a high bandwidth line is divided into several lower-frequency bands, with each band capable of carrying a channel of data. As an example, Fig. 1 shows a voice-grade line with a bandwidth of 2,400 Hz split into four subchannel bands of 500 Hz each. Each 500-Hz band is capable of carrying bidirectional data using frequency shift keying. Thus, on the 600 to 1,100 Hz channel, "0" data bits may be transmitted at 675 Hz, and "1" data bits may be transmitted at 1,025 Hz. Other channels are split up in similar fashion, the matched pairs of modulators

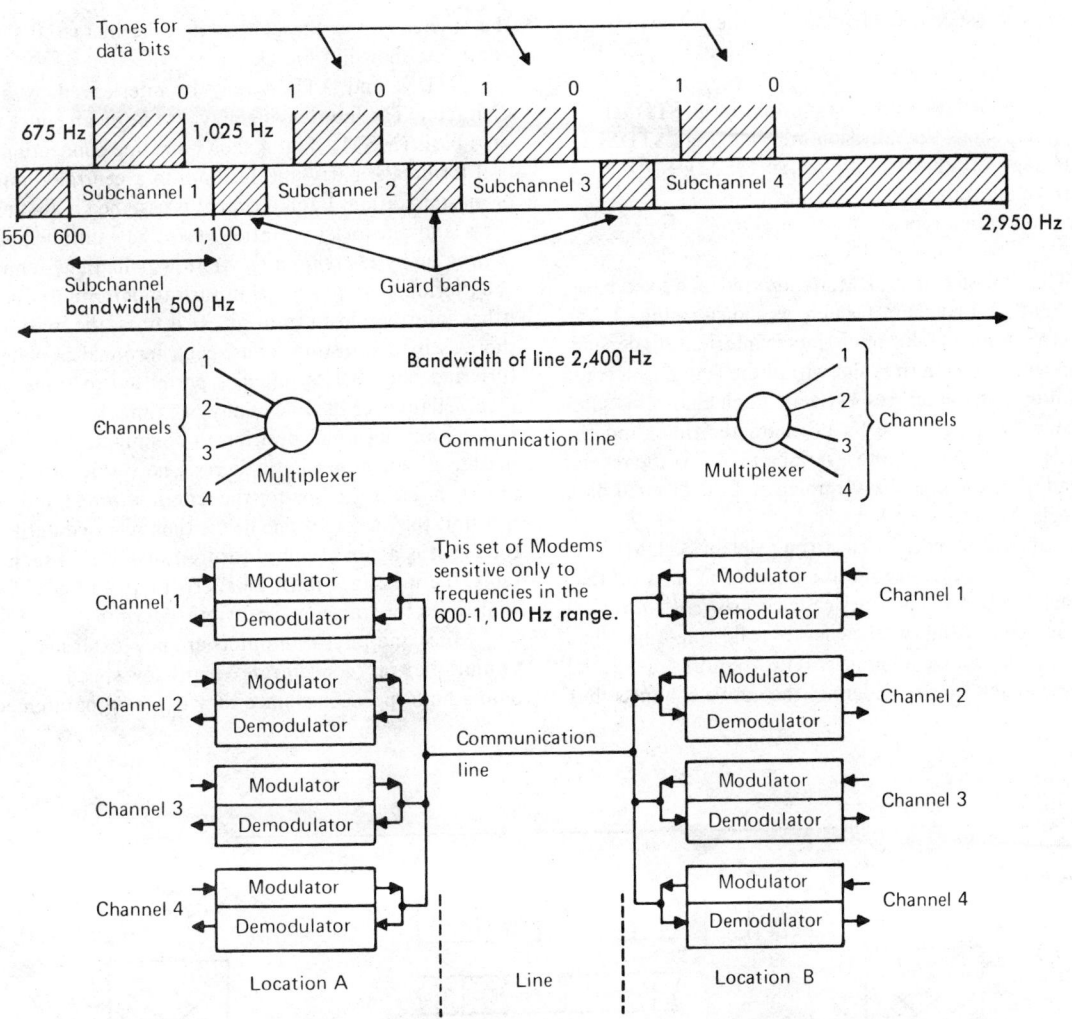

Fig. 1. Signaling-frequency assignments in a simple FDM system for digital data. The modulator-demodulator sets are sensitive only to the range of frequencies within a particular channel, and hence provide signal separation.

and demodulators with appropriate filters insuring channel separation. The guard bands, as illustrated, enhance the channel separation still further.

Fig. 1 illustrates how several low-speed terminals may send data concurrently on a single voice-grade line. This sharing reduces the connection costs per terminal. In similar fashion, several voice-grade lines could be multiplexed to share a still higher bandwidth line, reducing the effective cost of each voice-grade line.

A familiar example of FDM is television broadcasting. Stations broadcast programs continuously at different frequencies, the atmosphere being the transmission medium. The tuning circuits in the television tuner select and separate one channel from all others.

Time-Division Multiplexing. In TDM, time is divided into small slots, and each time slot is used to perform a segment of the desired operation. In data communication, this operation may be the transmission of a portion of the signal. Perhaps a more familiar example of TDM is a time-sharing computer. Here, a large number of users access the computer simultaneously, and the operating system schedules the computer resources to each user for very short periods of time on a demand basis. This occurs so rapidly that users think that they have the computer to themselves.

The time slots may be allotted on a fixed, predetermined (a priori) basis or on a demand basis. The allotted time slices may be fixed in length or variable. TDM is therefore usually subdivided into the following categories:

1. Synchronous time-division multiplexing (STDM).
2. Asynchronous time-division multiplexing (ATDM).
3. Message-switching multiplexing (MSM):
   (a) Polling type.
   (b) Contention type.

The time slots in STDM are allotted on a fixed basis, usually in a round-robin fashion, as shown in Fig. 2. The data stream may be bit or character interleaved, depending on whether each time slot within the frame is devoted to a bit or a character, respectively. Each channel is sampled one by one for one bit or character time, and the samples are assembled into a serial stream. At the receiving end, the stream is disassembled and the original data channels are reconstructed.

It should be noted that a time slot in STDM is allotted for a channel even in the absence of data on that channel. ATDM (sometimes called *statistical multiplexing*) overcomes this inefficiency by allotting time slots only for the active channels. This requires a special header in each frame to identify the active channels, but the efficiency and throughput may be increased significantly, as shown in Fig. 3.

STDM and ATDM may be interleaved by bit or character. The interleaving may also be on an entire message basis (MSM). Fig. 4 shows one line connecting several terminals, party-line fashion, to a central computer or master station. Each terminal is assigned a unique address and the master station does the multiplexing by *polling* or by *contention* (*q.v.*) In a polled environment, each terminal is addressed in turn to determine whether it has information to transmit. If it does, the master authorizes it to transmit. Thus, each terminal is polled in turn and only one terminal is permitted to transmit or receive data over the line at any one time. In a contention system, any terminal desiring to communicate with the master station waits until there is no traffic on the line and then seizes the line for the length of time required to transmit the message. The line is then released until such time as it is again required for transmission. In such systems, the messages must be short, to avoid unduly long wait times for transmission by other terminals.

Mini- and microcomputers are now extensively used to multiplex or "concentrate" many low-speed terminals onto a high-speed line, since they can be programmed to

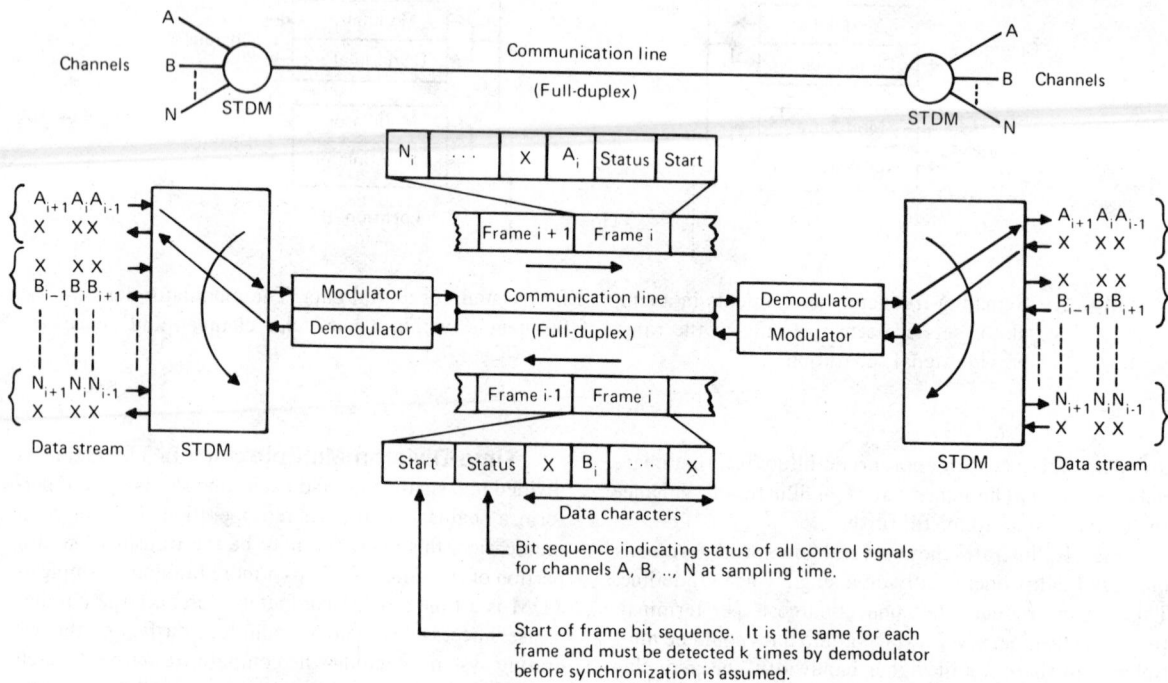

Fig. 2. Typical character-interleaved STDM and associated frame format. After sending the start and status bit sequences, the STDM in effect connects in turn each channel to the line for a very short time, forming the stream of data characters for each frame. A full-duplex line is shown to enable simultaneous data transfer in both directions. The X's represent an idle-line condition.

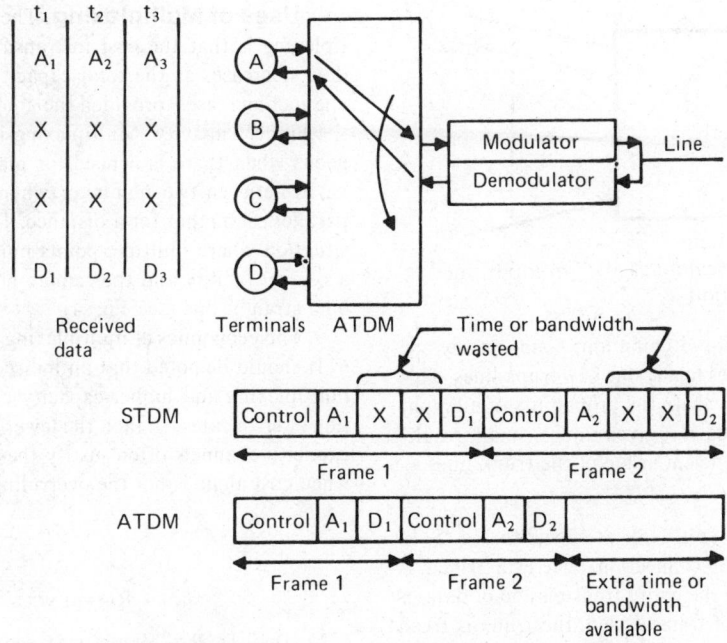

Fig. 3. Comparison of STDM and ATDM. The example shows reception of data on channels A and D, with B and C being idle, as indicated by the X's. By assigning time slots only to the active terminals, ATDM results in less wasted bandwidth. The control signals in ATDM contain the addresses of the active terminals and the order in which they are sent.

perform the ATDM functions. Besides the multiplexing function, they can perform additional tasks, such as code conversion, error detection, line polling, and other control functions, at no additional hardware costs. Minicomputers programmed to perform the functions of a multiplexer are sometimes called *programmable multiplexers* or *concentrators.*

Line or Circuit Switching. Circuit or line switching refers to equipment that can connect *m* inputs

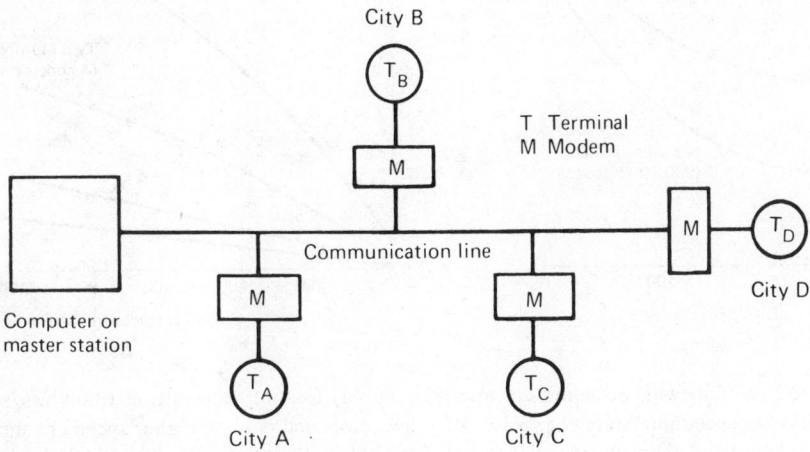

Fig. 4. Multiplexing by polling or by contention.

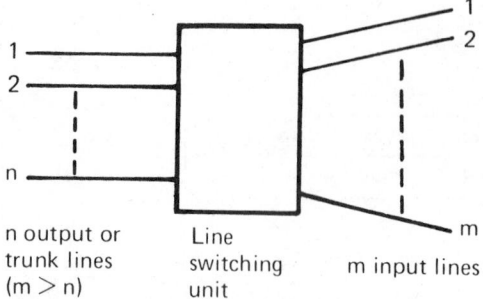

Fig. 5. Line or circuit-switching unit connects any one of *m* input lines to any one of *n* trunk lines. This is widely used where the probability of all input lines being used at a given time is small, resulting in more efficient usage of the trunk lines.

to *n* output trunk lines ($m > n$), as shown in Fig. 5. In a typical application, the connection, once established, is held for the duration of the entire transmission of data or voice call. At the end of transmission, the trunk is freed and made available for assignment to the next input desiring a trunk connection. An input can be connected to a trunk if at least one trunk is not being used. This technique is mainly used in conventional telephone networks, and is sometimes called *space-division multiplexing*.

Uses of Multiplexing. The basic reason for multiplexing is that the cost to transmit a fixed amount of data decreases as the total capacity of the transmission channel increases, provided the amount of traffic justifies the higher capacity. Multiplexing is especially advantageous when there is a need for many independent data paths between two points, or when multiple data paths parallel each other for a distance. The latter includes the situation where multiple points must communicate with a central facility and the remote points are more or less on a straight line (see Fig. 4).

The economics of multiplexing are illustrated in Fig. 6. It should be noted that an indirect advantage of using multiplexing and higher-capacity channels is the reduction of error rates. In fact, the lower error rates on higher-capacity channels often justify the use of such facilities when cost alone is not the overriding factor.

REFERENCES

1972. Doll, D. R. "Multiplexing and Concentration," *Proc. IEEE* **60,** *No. 11:* 1313–1321 (November).
1976. Martin, James. *Telecommunications and the Computer,* 2nd Ed. Englewood Cliffs, NJ: Prentice-Hall.

J. S. SOBOLEWSKI

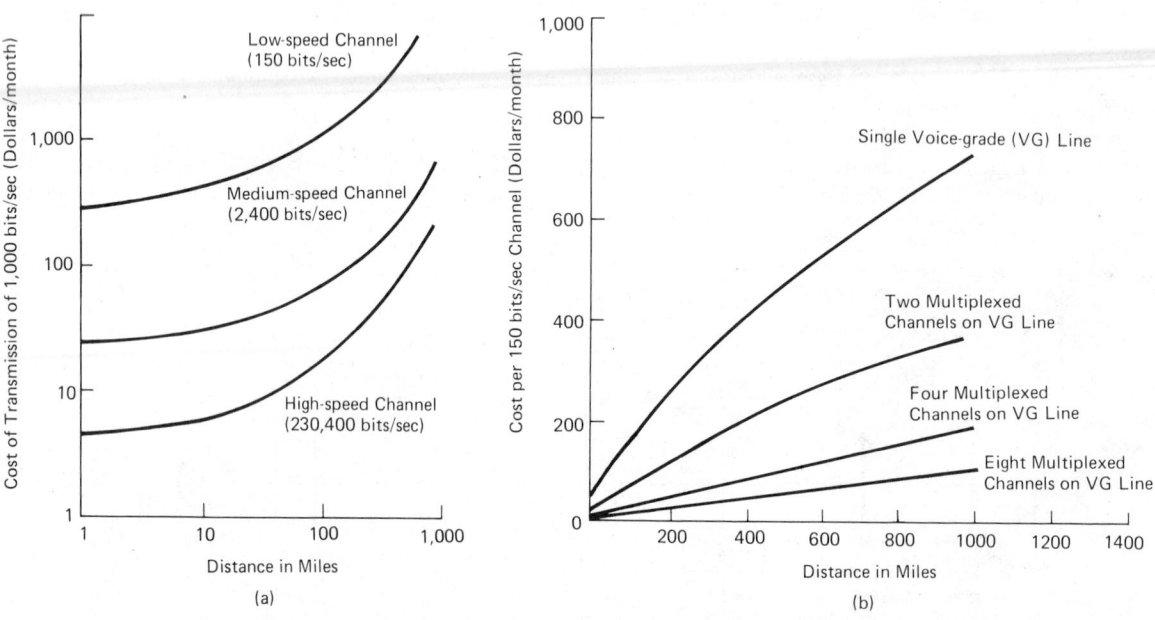

Fig. 6. Comparative costs showing economics of multiplexing. (a) Cost of transmitting 1,000 bits/sec using low-, medium-, and high-speed interstate channels. (Note how costs decrease on higher speed channels.) (b) Reduction in costs for low-speed channels. (Costs are based on full-duplex transmission and include termination costs.)

MULTIPROCESSING

For articles on related subjects *see* CONCURRENT PROGRAMMING; CONTENTION; LOCKOUT; MULTIPROGRAMMING; PARALLEL ALGORITHMS; PARALLEL PROCESSING; PETRI NETS; PIPELINE AND ARRAY PROCESSORS; SEMAPHORE; and SUPERCOMPUTERS: Principles.

Multiprocessing is the simultaneous processing of two or more portions of the same program by two or more processing units. Among the latter, the I/O processors are normally excluded, since the asynchronous operation of a CPU and I/O processors has more of a *buffering* or *multiplexing* nature. The simultaneous processing of different programs on a system with several CPU's (one program/CPU) sharing a common memory is considered here as an extension of *multiprogramming* rather than true multiprocessing.

With this definition, multiprocessing involves a departure from the classical von Neumann machine organization in which only one program executes at a time. From the architecture, we can distinguish between multiprocessors of the Single Instruction Multiple Data (SIMD) and Multiple Instruction Multiple Data (MIMD) organizations.

In SIMD architectures, exemplified by the ILLIAC IV, a single control unit fetches and decodes instructions. Then the instruction is either executed in the control unit itself (e.g., a Jump instruction) or is broadcast to multiple parallel processing elements which will perform the same operation on different sets of data. Pipeline processors, such as CDC STAR-100, Texas Instruments ASC, and CRAY-1, can also be considered of the SIMD type. Pipelining is analogous to an assembly-line organization, with each process decomposed into subprocesses which have to pass through each station or computational stage. The instruction repertoires of SIMD and pipeline machines call for vector instructions allowing the treatment in parallel of ordered sets of data. It is this mode of operation, in which consecutive vector elements are treated simultaneously, which justifies the SIMD labeling for pipeline computers.

MIMD machines are differentiated according to the switching structure between processors and memory modules and the homogeneity of the processing elements. Typical examples are C.mmp (Carnegie Multi-Mini-Processor), with a cross-bar switch arrangement [Fig. 1(a)] linking 16 PDP-11's and 16 memory modules; C.m* (which, like C.mmp, is an architecture developed at Carnegie-Mellon University), with clusters of microprocessors and memories organized into a hierarchy of addressing spaces; PLURIBUS, where minicomputers share local and global multiport memories [Fig. 1(b)]; and

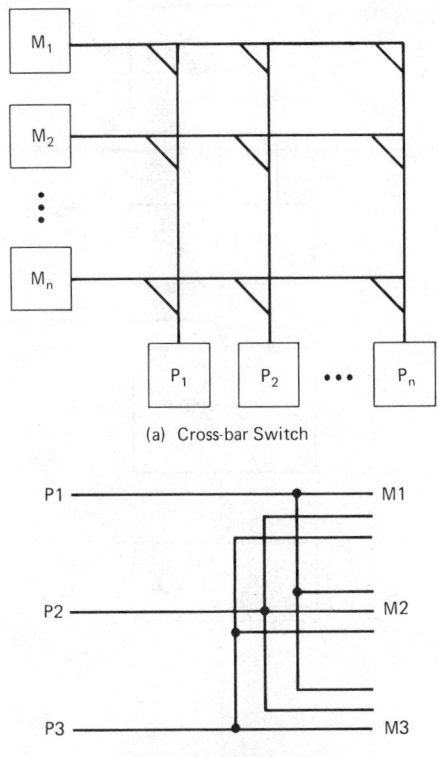

(a) Cross-bar Switch

(b) Multiport Memories

Fig. 1. Two examples of processor-memory interconnections. (P = processor; M = memory.)

multifunctional CPU's, like those of the CDC 6600 and IBM System 360/91.

In multiprocessing systems, the increase in performance resides mainly in path parallelism (i.e., the concurrent execution of two different parts, or of the same part with different data, of the program). Explicit indication of this parallelism is done by FORK and JOIN or equivalent constructs for distinct paths, and by PARALLEL FOR statements for replication of loops. In Fig. 2, we show how one process is FORKed into three concurrent paths (at points K and L) and how these latter three JOIN at point J. Instructions starting at point $(J + 1)$ cannot begin execution prior to the termination of the three processes.

In MIMD architectures, control, synchronization, and scheduling of the processors are sensitive areas. Two types of control can be implemented: A fixed mode, whereby one or more processors are dedicated to execute the operating system; and a floating, or decentralized, mode, where each processor can have access to the operating system and schedule itself. In this latter case, and more generally when a task is split into concurrent paths, it will happen that two concurrent processes will wish to

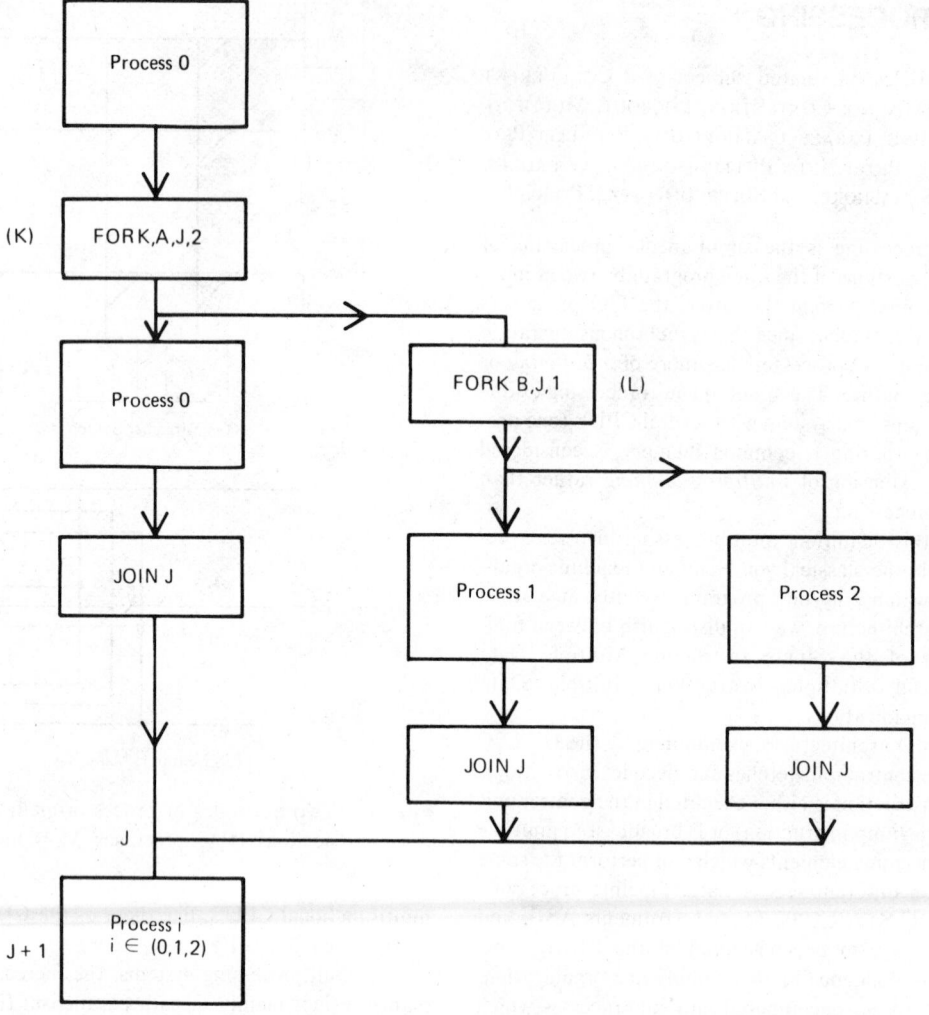

Fig. 2.   FORK-JOIN concept. FORK *A,J,N:* (1) Initiate process at address *A;* (2) continue current process at next instruction; (3) increment counter at address *J* by *N.* JOIN *J:* (1) Decrement counter at address *J;* if zero, initiate processing at address *J* + 1, else (2) release the processor executing the JOIN.

access the same data. Hence, there must be some means of preventing disorderly changes in the shared database. This has been referred to as the *lockout* or *mutual exclusion* problem. The portion of code—in a path—which accesses the shared data is called the *critical section* of that path.

One way to provide the necessary protection is by having instructions of the form TEST AND WAIT and SET or the equivalent pair LOCK/UNLOCK. A possible realization is to associate a one-bit lock indicator *w* with each shared data object. The effect of the LOCK instruction is shown in Fig. 3(a). The lock bit is set to 1 by the current process when the data object has not been locked by any other

process. The effect of the UNLOCK instruction is to reset the bit indicator to 0 [Fig. 3(b)]. The synchronization of concurrent processes cycling through their critical sections can be done, through software, with integer and boolean variables; by using a new type of variable called a *semaphore,* elegant and efficient solutions can be obtained.

The presence of several CPU's adds a new dimension to the scheduling problem. In almost all cases, optimal schedules cannot be attained even with an *a priori* knowledge of the exact time requirements of each task. Models have been devised, analytical solutions have been investigated, and a number of heuristic methods have been

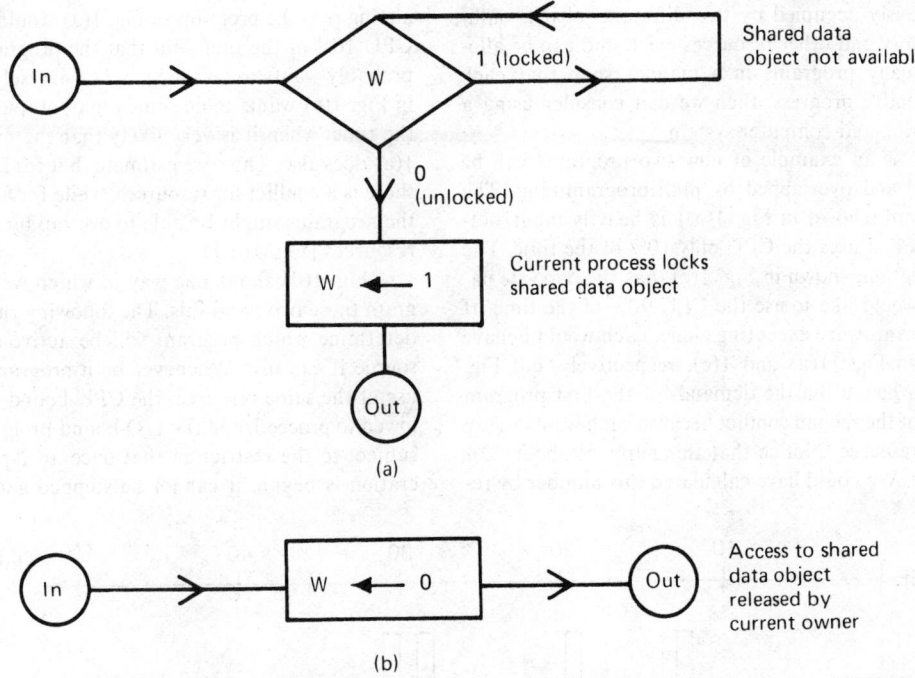

Fig. 3. Lock/Unlock concept. (a) Lock instruction; (b) Unlock instruction.

proposed to assess the performance of multiprocessing systems. This performance can be improved not only by an explicit expression of parallelism, but also by compiler-detected parallelism (loop replication principally for SIMD machines) and by designing new algorithms for parallel environments.

References

1974. Enslow, P. H. (Ed.). *Multiprocessors and Parallel Processing,* New York: Wiley-Interscience.
1976. Baer, J. L. "Multiprocessing Systems," *IEEE Trans. on Comp.* **C-25:** 1271–1277 (December).

J-L. BAER

MULTIPROGRAMMING

For articles on related subjects *see* COMPUTER UTILITY; DATA SECURITY; DEADLOCK; INPUT/OUTPUT CONTROL SYSTEMS; JOB; OPERATING SYSTEMS; OVERHEAD; PARALLEL PROCESSING; PRIVILEGED INSTRUCTION; PROCESSING MODES; SCHEDULING ALGORITHM; SWAPPING; TASK; and TIME SHARING.

Most modern computer systems can provide more resources than one typical program requires. By *multi-programming*—i.e., overlapping and interleaving the executions of more than one program—an attempt is made to keep all the resources of a modern computer system working as much as possible.

Early computer systems executed only one program (or *job*) at a time. It was quickly observed that certain jobs were *input/output* (I/O) *bound;* i.e., their rate of progress was limited by the speed of input/output units such as tape drives or card readers. Other jobs rarely used these I/O devices after they began calculating; these *central processing unit* (CPU) *bound* jobs performed mostly numerical calculations, with little input/output. Neither of these types of jobs fully utilized the power of the computer system. But it was found that if we can multiprogram, and thereby concurrently execute more than one job, better utilization of the available equipment could be realized.

In modern computing systems, many resources can be active simultaneously. For example, once a card reader has begun to read a card, the processor can execute instructions while data is being transferred into an area of memory that is being used as a *buffer*. If we have a single CPU, then it can perform work for many different jobs by switching from one to another while being devoted at any one moment to a particular *task*. Each program requires memory space to hold the data and instructions to be executed, and this memory cannot be simultaneously occupied by two different jobs. If sufficient memory and other resources exist, and can be allocated to many programs in a manner such that each makes effective progress, then we can consider using a multiprogrammed computer system.

Fig. 1 is an example of how two programs can be interleaved and overlapped by multiprogramming. The first program (shown in Fig. 1(a)) is heavily input/output-bound, and uses the CPU only 10% of the time. The second program, shown in Fig. 1(c), has the opposite nature, and would like to use the CPU 90% of the time. If these programs were executing alone, each would behave as shown in Figs. 1(a) and 1(c), respectively, but Fig. 1(b) shows how often the demands of the first program and those of the second conflict because each wants to use the same resource. Notice that this happens about 20% of the time. We could have calculated this number by re-

alizing that the program in Fig. 1(a) would like to use the CPU 10% of the time, but that the program in Fig. 1(c) probably wants to do the same. Conversely, the program in Fig. 1(c) wants to do some input/output about 10% of the time, when it is very likely that the program in Fig. 1(a) does also. Thus, we estimate that for 20% of the time there is a conflict for resources, while for 80% of the time the programs might be able to overlap by using different resources [Fig. 1(d)].

Fig. 1(d) shows one way in which we can multiprogram these two programs. The following rules are used to determine which program will be active and which resource it can use: Whenever both programs request the use of the same resource, the CPU-bound program is allowed to proceed, and the I/O-bound program must wait, subject to the restriction that once an input/output operation is begun, it cannot be stopped and must be fin-

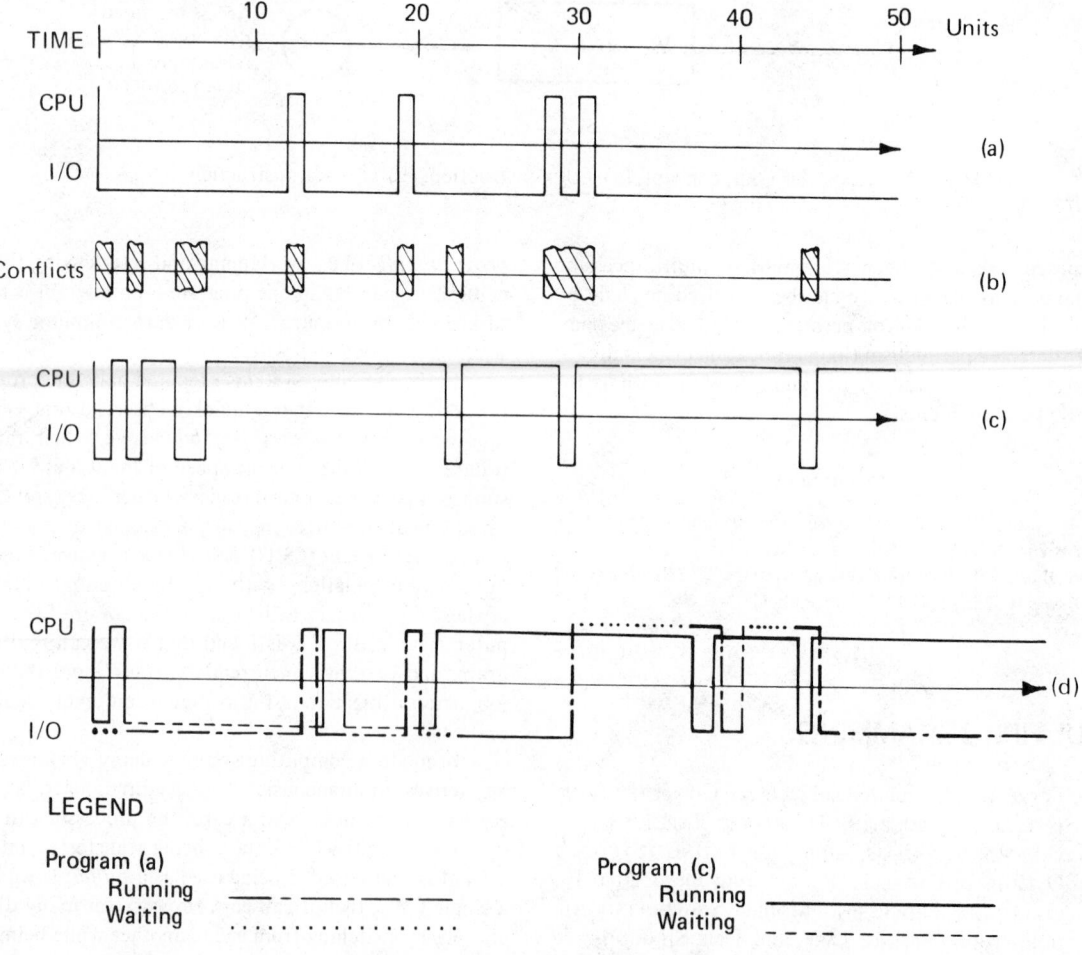

LEGEND

Program (a)		Program (c)	
Running	— · — · — · —	Running	——————
Waiting	· · · · · · · · · ·	Waiting	— — — — —

Fig. 1. An example of the advantages of multiprogramming. The area of overlap between the I/O-bound program (a) and CPU-bound program (c) is shown in (b). In (d) one way of multiprogramming these two programs is shown.

ished. (These decision rules are shown only as an example and are not necessarily the "best" rules to use for the types of jobs shown.) We see that, in the 50 units of time displayed, either the CPU or an I/O device is in use for 71 units. Since together we have resources for 100 units of work (50 from the CPU and 50 of I/O), we are achieving 71% *utilization* of the system. Separately, the program in Fig. 1(a) or Fig. 1(c) would use only 50% of the available resources, so we have improved utilization of the system by about 40%. We could not expect utilization to go much beyond 90% (excepting some unusually favorable circumstances), since we calculated that for 80% of the time both resources could be in use, and that for 20% of the time only one resource is busy while one program waits for the other.

Multiprogramming does not require a large operating system in order to coordinate the demands of each program. On a small computer, such as is used for process control, it is common to provide a *background/foreground* system that permits two programs to execute. The foreground, or real-time program, may consist of a job to monitor periodically a number of instruments and perform some corrective adjustment. In between each measurement, the system may have sufficient resources to permit a background program to execute, doing compilations or calculations. These two programs might cooperate by mutual understanding; i.e., the programmers could insure that each would not interfere with the use of the system by the other.

While in very simple situations it may be feasible to multiprogram cooperatively, often we must be sure that, if one program somehow violates the rules of the system, it does not corrupt the whole environment. Thus, most multiprogramming systems require a *monitor* (also called an *executive* or *supervisor*).

It is the responsibility of the monitor to maintain the integrity of the system. In the case of the background/foreground system used as an example previously, we would like the monitor to guarantee that the foreground real-time program will be able to take its measurements, even if the background program goes into a loop and never voluntarily relinquishes control. Thus, our computer system must have the capability to preempt a resource (such as the CPU) from a program and to insure that the foreground program or the monitor gains control. The monitor must be *protected* from accidental or malicious destruction by a program (which we refer to as a *user* program, in contrast to the supervisor itself); and user programs must be protected one from the other by intercepting, usually through hardware features, attempts to change or access memory that is "out of bounds" to a particular program.

In order to control effectively resources such as space for data or file storage, modern systems centralize all input/output operations in an *input/output control system* that performs services on behalf of the user programs. In this manner the users of the multiprogrammed system cannot corrupt each other's data or invade the privacy of secure information. The multiprogrammed operating system may provide accounting information for the management of the computer system, and this information should not be destroyed by a user program.

To permit the construction of a monitor with these capabilities, computer systems generally possess a *privileged* class of instruction that user programs cannot execute. For example, all input/output instructions, or those instructions associated with the protection of one area of memory from a program executing in a different area, are reserved for the monitor. When the computer is executing in monitor (or *master*) mode, these functions are permitted. The monitor has the responsibility of insuring that when control is given to a user program, the system is switched to user (or *slave*) mode. In slave mode, any attempt to execute privileged instructions will give control back to the monitor without permitting any violations of resource control.

In addition to the monitoring function, the executive of a multiprogrammed operating system must perform a *scheduling* function. If too many jobs are begun, they can interfere with each other and waste resources. In fact, it is even possible to cause a *deadlock* to occur when a number of programs have begun but cannot continue until additional resources are available, and yet those resources are tied up by other jobs. The algorithm used for scheduling must have enough information to avoid such situations, or should possess the means to "untangle" them if they occur, otherwise system performance degrades as it enters a very active but non-productive state called *thrashing*.

Scheduling in a multiprogrammed environment is often complex. The concept of multiprogramming entails the *global* optimization of the resources of the entire system. However, users are generally concerned with their own tasks, and attempt to optimize *locally*; i.e., they try to make their programs perform better or faster, without regard to the total environment.

Consequently, it is common to find the ultimate scheduling performed external to the system itself, either by administrative decisions concerning the categories (or *classes*) of jobs that are permitted at certain times of day, or by the operator of the system. The operator may be able to start or suspend programs from an operator's console based on the performance of the system. Meanwhile, the scheduler program of the multiprogrammed operating system performs the microscopic decisions such as initiating input/output operations or deciding which program is to be given the resources of the central processor.

One common form of scheduling is provided by a

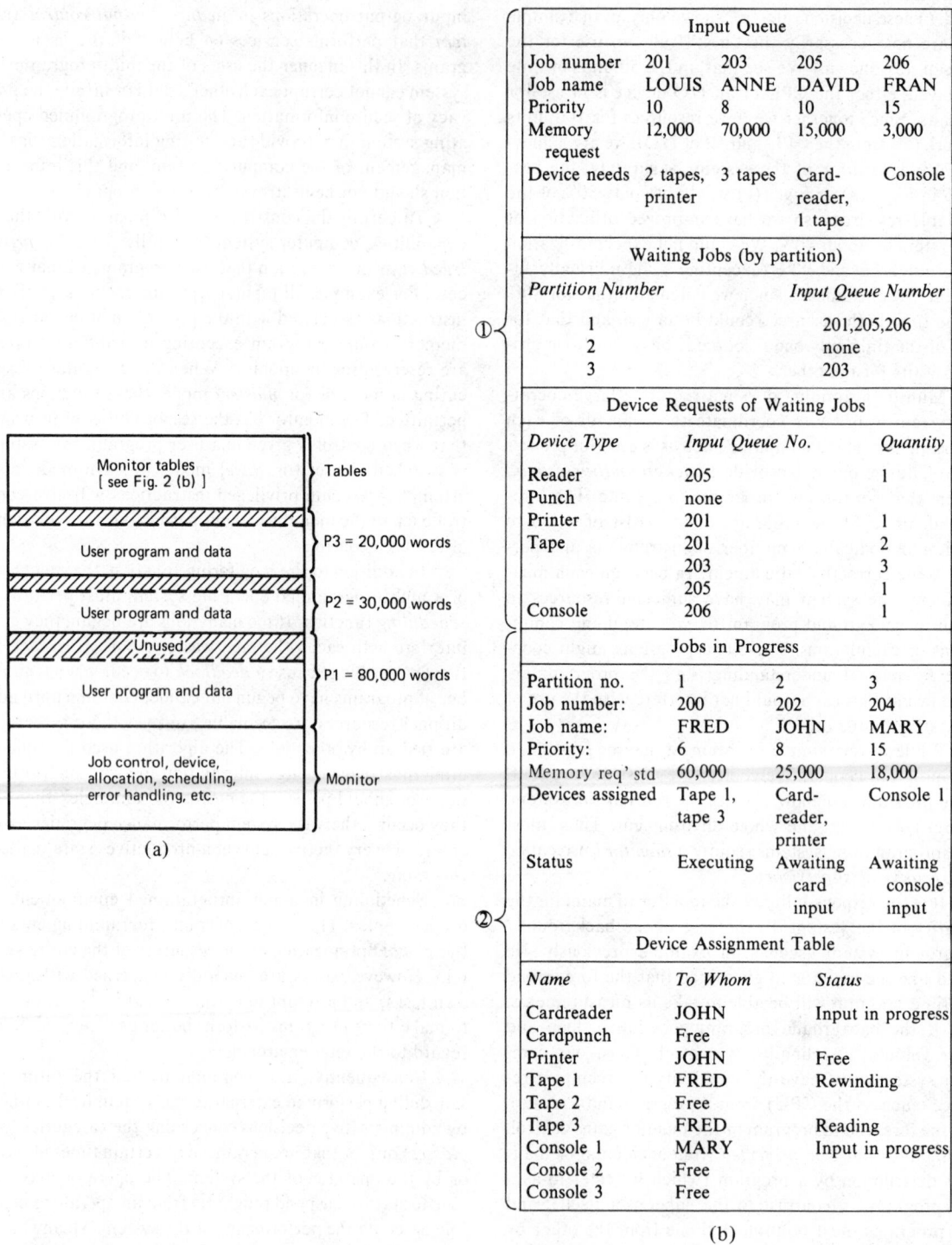

Fig. 2. Schematic representation of the partitioning of memory in a multiprogrammed system. (a) Memory layout. (b) Samples of monitor tables: Group 1 represents the information concerning future jobs; Group 2 represents the information concerning present jobs.

priority assigned to each job or task within the system. The actual value of the priority may be based on external factors such as the fact that the results are needed quickly (or the converse), or it may be based on the overall resource requirements of the job when submitted to the computer system. This priority may change dynamically as the program evolves, or it may increase as time progresses if the job is not making effective progress. It may also be changed by an operator from a console. The detailed nature of scheduling depends heavily on the nature of the service the system is expected to provide.

Multiprogramming of modern computer systems can be done in a variety of fashions. Some systems, such as the IBM System/370 Operating System Multiprogramming a Fixed number of Tasks (OS/MFT), allocate certain resources in a static fashion. Memory is divided into *partitions* of fixed size, and each job submitted to the system must specify which partition is to be used. Other systems, such as OS/MVT (the IBM System/370 Operating System with a Variable number of Tasks), distribute the memory space according to the request of the user. This additional flexibility requires extra complexity and possibly extra *overhead*, but may be critical in the effective use of a system where many users submit programs of widely differing sizes.

Fig. 2 is a highly schematic representation of the partitioning of memory in a simple multiprogrammed system, and illustrates some of the information that the monitor uses in controlling and scheduling jobs. In this example, memory has been split into five major areas [Fig. 2(a)]. The partitions P1, P2, and P3 are for the execution of user-written programs or system-provided programs such as language translators. The monitor program itself occupies another area, and provides job supervision, resource scheduling, allocation of memory and input/output devices, and other services for user programs. Finally, space is reserved for a large variety of tables used by the monitor in carrying out its tasks. Within these tables are all the critical data regarding the status of the system and of additional requests that will have to be handled. Fig. 2(b) shows only a small fraction of the actual information that a real multiprogrammed monitor would use to make its decisions.

The tables fall into two classes, those containing information about the present jobs being executed, and tables relating to jobs that have been submitted for execution, but are not yet being multiprogrammed. We can locate information about each partition (such as the job name), or we can determine the status of an input/output device (such as to whom it has been assigned). In order to determine which job should be entered into the multiprogrammed *mix* next, we can see which jobs are awaiting a particular partition or are waiting for some input/output device to be available. Notice that many pieces of information are repeated in different tables in order to locate rapidly the relevant jobs whenever any significant change takes place.

Multiprogramming may also take place within a single job. For example, the system may be able to overlap the computational needs of a single program with its input/output needs. In IBM's OS/MVT, a program may spawn (or create) additional tasks that are to be multiprogrammed as if they were jobs, but which possess a filial relationship to the parent task. Each of these tasks may have differing requirements for resources, and may cause concurrent utilization of system facilities.

Multiprogramming is accepted as the standard means of utilizing all but the smallest of today's computer systems. A computer utility that provides service to many users who may be sitting at remote consoles, communicating with an executing program in an interactive fashion, can serve many individuals while others are thinking or responding. Such a *time-sharing* system attempts to provide rapid response to the interactive requests of users at consoles; a *multiprogrammed* system may be required in order to provide time-sharing facilities, but multiprogramming connotes, in itself, a concern with resource utilization and not with rapid response time. The advantages offered by multiprogramming are now filtering down to even very small systems, and may be found on a large number of computers that until recently were used in a dedicated, one-user environment.

REFERENCES

1972. Lorin, H. *Parallelism in Hardware and Software: Real and Apparent Concurrency.* Englewood Cliffs, NJ: Prentice-Hall.

1973. Katzan, H., Jr. *Operating Systems: A Pragmatic Approach.* New York: Van Nostrand-Reinhold.

1976. McKeag, R. M. and Wilson, R. *Studies in Operating Systems.* New York: Academic Press.

1978. Kuck, D. J. *The Structure of Computers and Computations.* **1**: 521–535. New York: Wiley.

H. J. SAAL

MUSIC, COMPUTER. *See* COMPUTER MUSIC.

N

NATURAL LANGUAGE PROCESSING

For articles on related subjects *see* ARTIFICIAL IN-
TELLIGENCE; COMPUTER-ASSISTED LEARNING AND
TEACHING; GRAMMARS; HUMANITIES APPLICATIONS;
INFORMATION RETRIEVAL; LANGUAGE TRANSLATION;
PARSING; SPEECH RECOGNITION; STRING PROCESS-
ING LANGUAGES; SYNTAX, SEMANTICS, AND PRAG-
MATICS; TEXT-EDITING; and WORD PROCESSING.

Natural language processing refers to the computer
processing of natural language as *language*, rather than
as a meaningless string of letters or sounds. The key characteristic here is meaning, so we will be concerned with
that processing of natural language which requires understanding. Because of this, we might as well have used
the title "Natural Language Understanding" instead of
"Natural Language Processing," and, indeed, there is not
general agreement on which of these two terms is the
more appropriate.

Natural language needs to be distinguished from artificial, formal languages. Natural languages are those
such as English, Russian, and Mandarin, which people
learn to use without formal training. Although native
speakers can judge sentences as being more or less grammatical, few, if any, natural languages have had complete
formal grammars written for them. Indeed, native speakers disagree on the grammatical correctness of individual
sentences. Living natural languages grow and change.
New words come into use and old ones go out of favor.
Meanings change. Native speakers can seldom provide a
formal definition of a given word, but can understand, act
on, and paraphrase sentences in which the word occurs.

We can give an operational definition of what it
would mean for a computer system to understand natural
language for a given purpose or within a given domain of
discourse. If a person, knowing only the general capabilities of a system, with no training other than occasional
clarifying dialogue with the system itself (of the sort
human speakers engage in when they are not sure they
understand each other), can take the initiative in interacting with the system (as opposed to reacting to system
prompts or menus) and can make use of its complete capability, we could say that the system "understands" that
subset of natural language used in that domain. For example, we could envision a terminal in a library with no
information other than a sign saying, "Automated Card
Catalog." If an untrained library patron could type requests on that terminal and use it to get any information
obtainable from a standard card catalog, we would have
to say that the automated card catalog system understood
the natural language appropriate for card catalogs.

There are several possible tests for understanding
which could be given to a human or a computer. One
could require the subject to maintain a cogent part in a
conversation, to answer questions about, paraphrase, or
summarize what has been said, to translate into another
language, or to follow directions, commands, or requests
appropriately. Computer programs have been written
that demonstrate limited understanding of natural language in each of these ways.

History. Natural language processing has its roots
in several areas of computer science: Machine translation, artificial intelligence, and information retrieval. It
grew out of early work on machine translation (*see* LAN-

GUAGE TRANSLATION) with the realization by Bar-Hillel (1960) that "fully automatic, high quality translation" would require "that a translation machine should not only be supplied with a dictionary but also with a universal encyclopedia." Although he thought that "this is surely chimerical and hardly deserves any further discussion," it had been discussed ten years previously by Turing in his seminal article, "Computing Machinery and Intelligence" (1950) [reprinted in *Computers and Thought* (1963)], one of the foundation papers of artificial intelligence. In this article, Turing considered the question, "Can machines think?", and replaced it with what he called "the imitation game," which has since been known as "the Turing test." Briefly, this test requires a computer to be indistinguishable above the chance level from a human when both answer questions posed by an interrogator who communicates with them over a teleprinter. The acceptance of this test as a long-term goal by researchers in AI made the understanding of natural language, especially written text rather than spoken language, of central concern. Also before Bar-Hillel's paper, McCarthy had proposed the Advice Taker (1959) (see Minsky, 1968), a program which would make common sense inferences from information available to it in a formal database. Although McCarthy did not himself implement the Advice Taker, it was the model for later AI "question-answering" programs and for the inference sections of natural language processing systems. The key properties of the advice taker were "that its behavior will be improvable merely by making statements to it" and "one will be able to assume that the advice taker will have available to it a fairly wide class of immediate logical consequences of anything it is told and its previous knowledge."

Natural language understanding became important to information retrieval (*q.v.*) in two ways. Natural language front ends would enable users of standard information retrieval systems to express their requests in natural ways without requiring training. The usefulness of this became controversial in the early 1970s [e.g., Montgomery's "Is Natural Language an Unnatural Query Language?" (1972)], but recognition of its usefulness to the "casual user" grew with Codd's work on the Rendezvous System (1974). Document retrieval systems may be viewed as simulations of a reference librarian who, when asked a question, provides the patron with a set of books in which the question is probably answered. This may be done without the librarian's actually having read the books. However, if the librarian had read and understood the relevant books, the patron's question could be answered directly. This distinction was made in 1963 by Travis, who called the latter "fact retrieval" to distinguish it from document retrieval. Automatic indexing and abstracting may be viewed as kinds of paraphrasing

that, therefore (it may be argued), would benefit from natural language understanding, although this application has not yet been pursued.

The first natural language processing program was the conversation program of Green, Berkeley, and Gotlieb (1959), which conversed about the weather. For example, to the input, "I do not enjoy rain during July," it responded "Well, we don't usually have rainy weather in July so you will probably not be disappointed." The program worked by categorizing the words of the input sentence, using the set of categories to look up a response sentence frame, and filling in the blanks of the response frame with words from the input or stored words. Green, Wolf, Chomsky, and Laughery's Baseball program (1961) [reprinted in *Computers and Thought* (1963)] accepted English questions about one season's American League baseball games (such as, "Where did the Red Sox play on July 7?" and "What teams won 10 games in July?"), and answered them based on information previously stored in a hierarchical database. Lindsay's SAD SAM (1963, in *Computers and Thought*) accepted English sentences, extracted information on kinship relations from them, and stored that information in a structured database designed to represent genealogical information. Together, SAD SAM and the Baseball program represent the paradigm for interfaces of later natural language processing programs—translation of statements into a structured database or formal database update commands; translation of questions into formal retrieval commands; and generation of English sentences from information retrieved from a structured database. Two pieces of the basic structure remained to be developed: Methods of performing inference on the stored information to derive facts implied by the input, but not explicitly contained in it; and design of general-purpose database structures.

Two inference programs appeared in 1964. Fischer Black's program (in Minsky, 1968) was essentially an implementation of McCarthy's Advice Taker, using a formal language similar to the standard syntax of the predicate calculus for input, output, and the database. Raphael's SIR (in Minsky, 1968) accepted statements and questions in English, stored the information from the statements in the form of a relational graph (with nodes representing individuals and classes of individuals, and arcs representing relations between them), and answered the questions based on the stored relations and inferences drawn from them. Input sentences were limited to those which matched fill-in-the-blank sentence patterns, and relations were limited to those for which reasoning rules were written into the program, but SIR was the first program that combined natural language input, a structured database, and reasoning.

In 1966, Quillian (in Minsky, 1968) discussed a Semantic Memory system that represented dictionary definitions by relational graphs in which nodes represented word senses, and each arc was labeled with one of a set of only seven relations. He argued that these were enough to represent all dictionary definitions, and that the "meaning" of a word was the entire structure of the way it was connected to other word senses in the graph. These became the defining notions of the *semantic network* as a representation of knowledge. When, in 1968, Fillmore proposed an analysis of natural language sentences using "deep cases," workers in semantic networks seized on such deep cases to be the underlying relations labeling the arcs of the network. Fig. 1 shows a simplified semantic network for "John gives a dog to Mary." In 1971, Shapiro showed how predicate calculus-like rules could be stored in semantic networks, allowing a unification of previous work on inference mechanisms and knowledge representations.

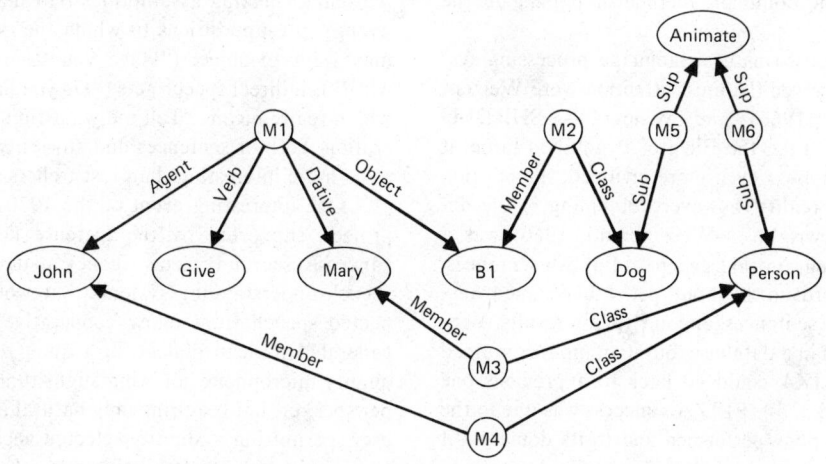

Fig. 1. A semantic network. Nodes representing assertions and corresponding sentences are:

    M1: John gives Mary a dog.
    M2: What John gives to Mary is a dog.
    M3: Mary is a person.
    M4: John is a person.
    M5: Dogs are animate beings.
    M6: People are animate beings.

Arcs and their meanings are:

VERB:	Goes from a node representing that an action has occurred to one representing the act involved.
AGENT:	Goes from a node representing that an action has occurred to one representing the actor.
OBJECT:	Goes from a node representing that an action has occurred to one representing the affected object.
DATIVE:	Goes from a node representing that an action has occurred to one representing an animate being affected by the act.
MEMBER:	Goes from a node representing a set membership relation to one representing the element.
CLASS:	Goes from a node representing a set membership relation to one representing the set.
SUB:	Goes from a node representing a subset relation to one representing the subset.
SUP:	Goes from a node representing a subset relation to one representing the superset.

Node B1 represents the actual dog, whose name has not been mentioned, given by John to Mary.

Accepting unrestricted natural language sentences as input requires the ability to parse them (see PARSING). At first, parsing methods were derived from methods of parsing programming languages, and attempts were made to write transformational grammars in the parsing, rather than generating direction. In 1970, however, Woods presented recursive augmented transition network grammars (ATNs), a way of writing parsing grammars that was particularly easy for programs to use, yet retained the perspicuity of more traditional grammars. ATNs became the dominant method of parsing in the 1970s.

By 1972, the two natural language processing systems that had received the most attention were Weizenbaum's ELIZA (1966) and Winograd's SHRDLU (1972). ELIZA ("Like the Eliza of Pygmalion fame, it can be made to appear even more civilized, the relation of appearance to reality, however, remaining in the domain of the playwright."—Weizenbaum, 1966) was a conversational program that accepted English sentences, recognized keywords in the input, performed some transformations on the sentences, and output the results. Very little was retained in a database, but if an input contained no keywords, ELIZA could go back to a previous one ("Earlier you said . . ."). ELIZA's success was due to the clever transformations performed and to its domain—it simulated a Rogerian psychologist, who is supposed to contribute little if anything to the conversation, but just keep the patient talking. Although it was claimed that ELIZA passed a simplified version of the Turing Test, most researchers considered it a benchmark of how a cogent conversation could be simulated with no understanding on the part of one of the participants. Panel 1 contains a sample dialog with ELIZA. SHRDLU (a meaningless name derived from a row of keys on a typesetting machine, often used by typesetters to overwrite a mistake in a text and sometimes mistakenly left in the finished text) was a simulated robot arm which could manipulate simulated toy blocks on a simulated table. A human could converse with SHRDLU in English, giving it commands ("Find a block which is taller than the one you are holding and put it into the box"), asking it questions about the "blocks world" ("Is there a large block behind a pyramid?"), giving it some new information ("A 'steeple' is a stack which contains two green cubes and a pyramid"), and asking it questions about its previous actions ("Had you touched any pyramid before you put the green one on the little cube? When did you pick it up?"). SHRDLU would carry out the commands and answer the questions in English ("Yes, the green one. While I was stacking up the red cube, a large red block and a large green block."). The significance of SHRDLU was that it put together a lot of pieces of the natural language understanding task—a sophisticated parser, discourse and event contexts, problem solving, natural language response. An important ingredient in its success was its limited domain of expertise—the blocks world. Indeed, it proved difficult to extend SHRDLU to other domains. However, SHRDLU demonstrated that computerized natural language understanding for limited domains had arrived.

Work on natural language processing in the 1970s was characterized by increased concern with multi-sentence input, such as simple stories and newspaper articles, representations of rich connections of facts about objects and events, strategies of controlling inferences, default reasoning (making assumptions that may turn out to be wrong), presuppositions to which the question answerer may want to object ("Have you stopped beating your wife?"), indirect speech acts ("Do you have the time?"—which really means "Tell me what time it is"), and generation, both of sentences and stories, which turned out to be more interesting than researchers had supposed.

One interesting event of the 1970s was a five-year project, supported by the Defense Department's Advanced Research Projects Agency, to develop one or more speech understanding systems that would "accept connected speech from many cooperative speakers of the general American dialect, in a quiet room over a good quality microphone, allowing slight tuning of the system per speaker, but requiring only natural adaptation by the user, permitting a slightly selected vocabulary of 1,000 words, with a highly artificial syntax, and a highly constrained task, with a simple psychological model of the user, providing graceful interaction, tolerating less than 10% semantic error, in a few times real time, on a 100 MIPS machine, and be demonstrable in 1976 with a moderate chance of success." At the end of the period, four systems were demonstrated, one of which, called HARPY and developed at Carnegie-Mellon University, met the goals (see SPEECH RECOGNITION).

Prospects. Practical natural language interfaces with computer programs in very limited domains are now feasible. What is required is the engineering effort to give each particular interface the completeness of lexicon and grammar to cover the actual needs of its users. The best domains to begin with are probably those for which users understand the domain well, but use the system so infrequently that they cannot remember the syntax of formal commands (for example, library card catalogs and computer system help facilities).

Natural language understanding research will concentrate increasingly on language as a communicative act in a larger problem solving context. Human communication seems to depend on each person recognizing the plans and goals of the other and on maintaining a model of the other's state of knowledge of the topic. Thus, other areas of artificial intelligence, such as planning and problem solving, are relevant, as are ways of representing and reasoning about knowledge and beliefs about knowledge

Doctor, I have terrible news . .
  You say you have terrible news
Yes, there is a computer program at M.I.T. that'll ruin us . .
  Why do you say that
I have seen it working . .
  You say you have seen it working
Its frightening—you must see it . .
  You think I must see it
It listens to patients chatter just as you and I listen . .
  You think I and you listen
No, not usually—no need to get nasty though . .
  Why do you say that
Someone might hear us—don't you care . .
  You think I care
You sound depressed to me . .
  In your phantasy—perhaps we sound depressed to each other
Yes—perhaps . .
  I understand
I do too . .
  You say you do too
We are both in the same boat with respect to that computer . .
  Let's continue to talk about you—shall we
You are a comfort . .
  What makes you think I am a comfort
At a time like this you want to talk about me . .
  Why do you think I want to talk about you
Because you share my feelings about that damned computer . .
  What does that suggest to you
That, of course, you hate computers too . .
  You think I hate computers too

Why not, they're hardly human, are they . .
  Perhaps that's what we are here to find out
No computer could converse as you can, for example . .
  Oh
I can't understand how anyone could be fooled by a mere machine . .
  Can't you really
No, after all there is nothing creative about a computer program . .
  You are being negative
I am convinced I am correct . .
  Are you worried to have been convinced you are correct
No, not in the least. Not at all. Not even a little . .
  You are being negative
You said you agreed with me, didn't you . .
  Is that what you heard me say
Why don't you try to dissuade me—computers diddle with numbers, that's all . .
  You wish me to try to dissuade you
You can't . .
  You think I can't
For example, could a computer in a conversation like this raise a new topic . .
  You seem to have avoided speaking of your parents altogether
Precisely as you just did . .
  You think I just did
Yes, and that's what shows the difference between a man and a computer . .
  I see

Panel 1.   A conversation with ELIZA. (Class handout in 6.45, Introduction to Automatic Computation, J. Weizenbaum, Lecturer, M.I.T., Fall 1964.)

and beliefs. Computer understanding of natural language texts in unconstrained domains probably remains far in the future.

References

1959. Green, L. E. S., Berkeley, E. C., and Gotlieb, C. "Conversation with a Computer," *Computers and Automation* **8**, *No. 10*: 9–11.

1960. Bar-Hillel, Y. "A Demonstration of the Nonfeasibility of Fully Automatic High Quality Translation," in Alt, F. L. (Ed.), *Advances in Computers* **1**. New York: Academic Press, pp. 158–163.

1963. Feigenbaum, E. A. and Feldman, J. (Eds.). *Computers and Thought*. New York: McGraw-Hill.

1963. Travis, L. E. "Analytic Information Retrieval," in Garvin, P. L. (Ed.), *Natural Language and the Computer*. New York: McGraw-Hill, pp. 310–353.

1966. Weizenbaum, J. "ELIZA—A Computer Program for the Study of Natural Language Communications between Man and Machine," *Comm. ACM* **9**, *No. 1*: 36–45 (January).

1968. Minsky, M. (Ed.). *Semantic Information Processing*. Cambridge, MA: M.I.T. Press.

1968. Fillmore, C. J. "The Case for Case," in Bach, E. and Harms, R. T. (Eds.), *Universals in Linguistics Theory*. New York: Holt, Rinehart and Winston, pp. 1–88.

1970. Woods, W. A. "Transition Network Grammars for Natural Language Analysis," *Comm. ACM* **13**, *No. 10*: 591–606 (October).

1971. Shapiro, S. C. "A Net Structure for Semantic Information Storage, Deduction and Retrieval," in *Proc. Second International Joint Conference on Artificial Intelligence*. London: The British Computer Society, pp. 512–523.

1972. Montgomery, C. A. "Is Natural Language an Unnatural Query Language?," in *Proceedings of the ACM National Conference*. New York: ACM, pp. 1075–1078.

1972. Winograd, T. *Understanding Natural Language*. New York: Academic Press.

1974. Codd, E. F. "Seven Steps to Rendezvous With the Casual User," in *Proceedings of the IFIP TC-2 Working Conference on Data Base Management Systems*. Amsterdam: North-Holland.

S. C. SHAPIRO

NAVAL ORDNANCE RESEARCH CALCULATOR (NORC)

For articles on related subjects *see* DIGITAL COMPUTERS: History: Early; and ECKERT, WALLACE J.

The NORC was built by IBM for the U.S. Navy Bureau of Ordnance under a non-profit research and development contract to build the most powerful and effective calculator which the state of the art would permit (as of 1951). It was designed for the rapid and convenient solution of the very largest computational problems of science, including partial differential equations in three space dimensions and time. It was the outgrowth of a research project under Byron L. Havens at IBM's Watson Scientific Computing Laboratory at Columbia University where Dr. Wallace J. Eckert had assembled a group of electronic specialists in 1946 to further the development of electronic computers. Early in the project, Havens developed a fundamental circuit, the microsecond delay unit, which operated reliably at 1,000,000 steps a second. The NORC was designed and built at the Laboratory. Assembly started in late 1953 and it was demonstrated and turned over to the Navy on 2 December 1954, at which time it calculated pi to over 3,000 places. It was installed at the Naval Proving Grounds, Dahlgren, VA in the summer of 1955 and remained in highly productive use until replaced by an IBM Stretch computer in 1958.

NORC was based on the use of the Havens microsecond delay unit, diode switching, a 3,600-word cathode ray tube storage unit with 8-microsecond access and high-speed 4-channel magnetic tape units (which transferred 71,340 decimal digits per second).

The calculator operated on decimal numbers of 13 digits precision and a range of 10^{-30} to 10^{30}.

Computing speed was 15,000 three-address instructions per second. Each instruction provided for modifying each address by any of three modifiers, fetching two operands from electronic storage, carrying out a floating point, specified point, or fixed decimal point (i.e., integer) arithmetic operation, checking the result with an independent modulo-9 arithmetic unit and storing the result. The arithmetic unit featured fast multiplication using serial digit-by-digit addition and serial generation of the nine multiples of the multiplicand. A pipeline of 12 dec-

Fig. 1.   The NORC computer.

imal adders, each of which introduced a microsecond of delay while adding, combined a digit from each one-digit product and output one digit of the result every microsecond. The product of two 13-digit numbers required 31 microseconds.

Checking of the operation of the calculator was continuous. In addition to the mod-9 arithmetic check, a check digit accompanied each word of instruction or data. This check digit was calculated when the data was read from punched cards, verified each time it was read from tape or in storage or refreshed in storage and after printing by echo pulses generated during printing. The cathode ray tube storage was further checked by an independent check on each bit column of storage. These two orthogonal checks pinpointed for correction any single bit in storage which was in error.

The instruction set took advantage of the three-address format to perform arithmetic (including multiple precision numbers), modification of the address modifiers, machine and operator interrupts, and three-way transfer of control with a single instruction wherever possible. Reading tape forward or backward or writing tape with a variable length block of words was done with a single instruction.

The microsecond delay unit which was used throughout the calculator for the registers, arithmetic units and logical control functions acted as a storage unit with an output which regenerated a full pulse the microsecond following the receipt of an input pulse. It was highly reliable and facilitated maintenance off-line of the pluggable units of which the machine was composed. Fifty percent of the total circuitry employed only six types of units, and 80% employed only 18 types.

The peripheral equipment for the NORC was built by the IBM Poughkeepsie and Endicott laboratories. It included eight tape units operating at 70,000 characters per second reading or writing, two 150 line-per-minute printers with buffered input permitting calculation to proceed during printing and a card-to-tape-to-card machine for card input and output.

One of the early uses of the NORC was computing the exact positions of the moon, earth, and other planets in space at all times to the year 2000 for Project Vanguard. This was done by Dr. Paul Herget, Director of the Cincinnati Observatory in a ten-hour run on the NORC. Another was a simulation of neutron motion in a nuclear reactor. Mathematical models of various aspects of the earth satellite programs, evaluation of various guided missile designs, and study of the reentry of satellites into the earth's atmosphere were other early uses of the NORC. One of its last jobs was a tremendous astronomical calculation for which the answers could be rigorously checked. The NORC run lasted 65 hours, performing over 75 billion operations without error.

REFERENCES

1954. Anon. *IBM Business Machines* **37**, *No. 26*: 1, 4–11 (December 23).
1955. Eckert, W. J. and Jones, R. *Faster, Faster*. New York: McGraw-Hill.
1963. von Neumann, J., *Collected Works* **5**: 238–247 [Taub, A. H. (Ed.)]. New York: Oxford University Press.
1971. Brennan, J. F. *The IBM Watson Laboratory at Columbia University: A History*. Armonk, NY: IBM, pp. 18, 26–29.

J. C. McPherson

NETWORKS. *See also* ARPA NETWORK; COMPUTER NETWORKS; DATA NETWORKS, PUBLIC; and QUEUEING NETWORK MODELS.

NETWORKS FOR INSTRUCTION

For articles on related subjects *see* AUTHORING LANGUAGES AND SYSTEMS; COMPUTER ASSISTED INSTRUCTION (CAI); COMPUTER ASSISTED LEARNING AND TEACHING; and COMPUTER NETWORKS.

The future for instructional use of computers depends to a large extent on the distribution of effective learning materials through networks. For example, a *star* network (central computer serving widely distributed users) extends the audience for programs and materials developed by the instructional computing staff at a central location. A *distributed* network (different kinds of computers connected so that the special capabilities of all are available to a user of any one) maximizes utilization of those computing resources that are available to education. Nationwide communication networks will encourage the application of quality standards to computer-related materials.

Economic and academic incentives for development and validation of computer-based learning materials result when a large number of users find access convenient. Authors whose programmed material has passed a critical review procedure should receive credit, as they do for traditional publications. Furthermore, authors or sponsoring organizations should receive some return on financial investments, probably in proportion to the amount of material made available through the network. The distribution has been via digital cassette tape, diskette, and other portable media that can be read by the computers at many user sites. Long-distance communications are used to connect a user anywhere in the country with the most current version of a program at the originating site or a central library.

The PLATO project at the University of Illinois in Urbana has established a centralized system, and, along with CDC, is distributing training and author assistance as well as finished programs through the communications network. Materials developed at one location in the country are stored centrally and are immediately available (with permission of the author) to any other location. Groups of users of the PLATO system exchange information among themselves, using the system for communication and storage.

CONDUIT, which is a consortium of regional computing services, has explored a variety of means for transporting materials successfully from the site of the originator to the site of the user, such as personal visits, workshops, video tapes of the originator, and detailed user guides. State organizations, such as the North Carolina Educational Computing Service, make good use of circuit riders, who maintain communication not only in the sense of a star network from central site to users and back, but also in the important connections among users throughout the state.

EDUCOM (the Inter-university Communications Council with headquarters in Princeton, NJ) works on nationwide networks in higher education. Helpful publications include the report of a summer conference in 1966, selected reports of the fall and spring meetings, the report of three symposia on a national science network, and studies of resource sharing.

The idea of a collection of networks serving as an information utility is very attractive at a time when demands on institutions are increasing and financial resources are decreasing.

REFERENCES

1974. Greenberger, Martin; Aronofsky, Julius; McKinney, James L.; and Massey, William F. (Eds.). *Networks for Research and Education.* Cambridge, MA: M.I.T. Press.

1977. Heydinger, Richard B. and Norris, Donald M. *Cooperative Computing: A Process Perspective on Planning and Implementation.* Princeton: Educom.

K. L. ZINN

NEW YORK TIMES INFORMATION BANK

For articles on related subjects *see* CURRENT AWARENESS SYSTEMS; DATA BANK; DATABASE MANAGEMENT; and INFORMATION RETRIEVAL.

The New York Times Information Bank is an on-line, current events database, created, operated, and marketed by The New York Times Information Service of Parsippany, NJ.

The database was conceived in the mid-1960s by John Rothman of The New York Times Company and grew out of the company's many years of experience with its commercially available printed Index as well as its internal clipping files. The original Information Bank software was designed and programmed by IBM's Federal Systems Division during 1969–1971. The first subscriber was connected to the system in February 1973.

The Information Bank database contains over 1.9 million abstracts of articles from *The New York Times* and about 60 other English language newspapers and magazines (including *The Wall Street Journal, The Washington Post, Business Week,* and the *Financial Times* of London). The publications in the database have varied somewhat over the years, with a growing emphasis on factual business news using a broad geographic range of sources.

The database contains information as far back as January 1969 and keeps highly current, with selected *New York Times* material available 24 hours after publication. The files are updated nightly. Approximately 200,000 abstracts are added each year.

All articles of research significance from *The New York Times* are abstracted. Articles from other publications are selected in accordance with criteria worked out in consultation with system users. An attempt is made to omit items that largely duplicate one another or that appear to be of only local or transient interest.

Each on-line entry consists of a detailed abstract along with a complete bibliographic citation (see Fig. 1). Included in the citation is a microfiche address for *New York Times* material. The Information Bank produces *The Times* on microfiche and offers it to subscribers on an optional basis.

Information Bank entries are fully indexed using a controlled vocabulary that is published annually as *The Information Bank Thesaurus.* The entire on-line thesaurus, including personal and organization names, contains over 800,000 search terms.

The original Information Bank system required that all searching be conducted through the use of *Thesaurus* terms. During 1981, new software was introduced that permits free text searching of the database as well. Searches can also be limited bibliographically by date, section, page, column, type of material (e.g., editorials, interviews, surveys), illustrations, and wire service source.

The Information Bank has thousands of users throughout the United States, Canada, Mexico, Europe, and the Far East. The system is operated both as a traditional research tool and as a management information system providing current awareness reports on a wide range of subjects.

A new database was introduced during 1981 con-

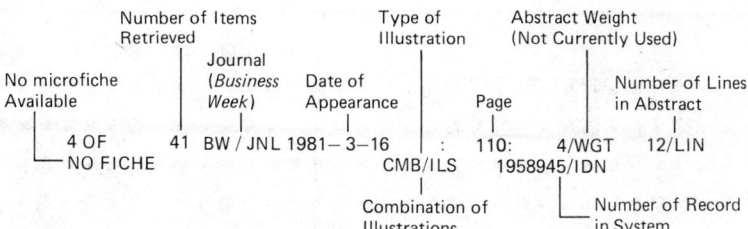

CORPORATE STRATEGIES COVER STORY PROFILES GE, WHICH IS SHIFTING
ITS FOCUS FROM FINANCIAL SOUNDNESS BACK TO TECHNOLOGY; REPORTS
GE IS EMBARKING ON TECHNICAL RENAISSANCE ITS CONSUMER PRODUCTS
OPERATIONS AND IS SEEKING NEW BUSINESSES IN ELECTRONICS,
GENETICS AND INDUSTRIAL ENGINEERING; CITES GE'S ACQUISITION OF
INTERSIL INC AND ITS POTENTIAL ACQUISITION OF CALMA CO AS
LATEST EXAMPLES OF NEW DRIVE; HOLDS APPOINTMENT OF CHEMICAL
ENGINEER JOHN F WELCH JR AS NEW CHMN AND CHIEF EXECUTIVE
OFFICER IS MOST SIGNIFICANT SIGN OF NEW TECHNOLOGICAL FOCUS;
DETAILS FIRM'S PAST AND PRESENT STRATEGY, AS WELL AS VAST
FINANCIAL RESOURCES BEHIND ITS TECHNOLOGY DRIVE; PHOTOS AND
GRAPHS (L)

		Section Number	Column Number			
5 OF	41 NYT/JNL 1981– 3–16	4:	5: 5	4/WGT	3/LIN
NO FICHE	UPI/SRC		1955853/IDN		

GENENTECH INC AND MONSANTO CO REPORT THEY HAVE SUCCEEDED IN
PRODUCING NATURAL HORMONE BOVINE THAT PROMOTES MEAT AND MILK
GROWTH IN CATTLE BY MEANS OF RECOMBINANT DNA TECHNOLOGY(S)

At End of
Page Prompts
System to   —B   Interview   Photograph
Print Next Page

		Interview	Photograph		
6 OF	41 USN/JNL	1981– 3–16	: 74:	4/WGT	8/LIN
NO FICHE		INT/TOM PHO/ILS	1958912/IDN		

STANFORD UNIV BIOCHEMIST PROF ARTHUR KORNBERG, INTERVIEW,
DISCUSSES GENETIC ENGINEERING; SAYS GENETIC ENGINEERING HAS
BROUGHT ABOUT 'REVOLUTION IN MEDICINE'; BELIEVES TECHNOLOGY
WILL BE ABLE TO PRODUCE HUMAN PROTEINS PREVIOUSLY UNKNOWN OR
UNAVAILABLE; BELIEVES GENETIC DISCOVERIES WILL CHANGE BASIS OF
MODERN MEDICINE, AS ANTIBIOTICS DID SEVERAL DECADES AGO;
DISCOUNTS FEARS REGARDING ABUSES OF GENETIC RESEARCH; PHOTOS

(M)

7 OF	41 SCI/JNL 1981– 3–13	: 1142: 1	4/WGT	4/LIN
NO FICHE		1956804/IDN		

FIRST PROGRAM TO TRAIN BIOCHEMICAL ENGINEERS IN RECOMBINANT DNA
TECHNIQUES WILL BE ESTABLISHED IN FALL '81 AT UNIVERSITY OF
MARYLAND IN BALTIMORE COUNTY; PROGRAM IS BEING CO-ESTABLISHED
WITH GENEX CORP AND BETHESDA RESEARCH LABORATORIES INC (S)

Fig. 1. Sample information bank entries.

taining the *full text* of *New York Times* articles, accessible through free text searching as well as through a controlled indexing vocabulary.

A. R. GREENGRASS

NINETY-COLUMN CARD

For articles on related subjects *see* CARD READING AND PUNCHING TECHNIQUES; HOLLERITH, HERMAN; IBM CARD; and MANUFACTURERS, COMPUTER.

Today the familiar rectangular-hole, 80-column "IBM card" has no serious competition as the international standard for data processing punched cards. Until about 1960, however, the IBM card had significant competition from cards of the same size, which were punched with round holes and contained 90 columns of information, known as the Powers or "RemRand" cards (Fig. 1).

This is the background. Until about 1909, Herman Hollerith (whose firm evolved to become IBM) enjoyed a monopoly on punched cards as a result of his patents. He charged the Census Bureau for processing on a per-card basis (65¢ per 1,000 cards tabulated). Although he

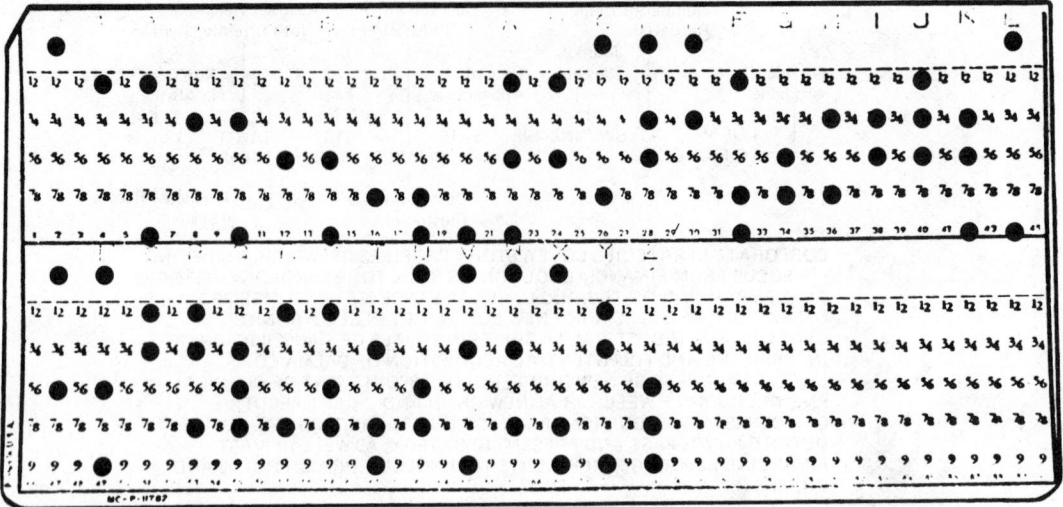

Fig. 1. The 90-column punched card.

gradually introduced technological improvements, such as automatic card feed, which reduced the processing costs, he did not correspondingly lower his prices. Because the Census Bureau objected to what it viewed as monopolistic overpricing, it sponsored the development of a competitive system. John Powers, an imaginative and competent mechanical engineer, became head of this effort. He managed to get patent rights on the inventions involved in a new system which successfully skirted Hollerith's patents by using sophisticated mechanical linkages to substitute for many of Hollerith's electrical techniques. After the new system was well started, Powers left the bureau to manufacture and sell these systems. In 1927 the Powers Accounting Machine Company, the Remington Typewriter Company, and Rand Cardex merged to form Remington Rand, a well-capitalized and serious competitor to IBM.

The Powers/RemRand system offered many technological innovations. It provided positive "die set" punching with the possibility of visual verification of the entire card entry before all holes were punched simultaneously (initially by depressing a foot treadle; later by an electrically driven punch). It was the first system to offer card punches with automatic card feed, the first to offer a printing tabulator, the first to offer a multiplying punch, the first to link a typewriter and a card punch, and the first with many other important innovations in punched card processing.

There is a direct line of evolution from the punched cards used by Hollerith in the 1890 census to the modern IBM card. In the early 1900s, Hollerith cards used round holes in a 45-column card of the same size as the modern card. There were 12 punch positions in each column. The Powers/RemRand cards initially used this standard.

The two systems diverged in the late 1920s and early 1930s. In 1924–1925, the Powers system introduced its first alphanumeric punch and tabulator along with a technique for doubling the amount of information in each card. The 12 rows were split into two 6-row banks, in effect giving two 45-column half-cards stacked one above the other (a 90-column card). A six-bit code requiring multiple punches per column was introduced, since there were only six punching positions to represent a digit or number. In 1929–1931, when IBM moved to meet the competition, it adopted an entirely different approach and standard. It adopted a 12-row code, the Hollerith code, which always used a single punch in a column to represent a number, and two punches to represent a letter. It got more columns onto the card by a very different technique. It changed from round holes to narrow, rectangular holes, which permitted 80 columns to be squeezed into a card of the same size.

Twice the Powers/RemRand system had major opportunities to take over as the predominant system. In the 1930s it might have become the *de facto* U.S. Government standard if its equipment had won the competition for mechanization of the social security system. Again, in the 1950s, it had a unique opportunity when its parent firm, Remington Rand, seemed to have an almost insurmountable lead in the evolving technology of computers. Though IBM was then preeminent in punched cards, it seemed possible that the RemRand UNIVAC computers would be able to drag the RemRand corporate standard (90-column) punched card along with them into data processing predominance. However, in both cases, RemRand failed to grasp its opportunity, and today the 90-column, round-hole punched card has all but disappeared.

REFERENCES

1933. Comrie, L. J. *The Hollerith and Powers Tabulating Machines*. Printed for private circulation, London. (Available at Library of Congress)

1965. Truesdell, Leon E. *The Development of Punch Card Tabulation in the Bureau of the Census, 1890–1940*. U.S. Dept. of Commerce. Washington, DC: U.S. Government Printing Office.

W. F. LUEBBERT

NOISE

For articles on related subjects *see* ACOUSTIC COUPLER; DATA COMMUNICATIONS; MODEM; and RELIABILITY AND FAULT TOLERANCE.

One fundamental limitation of information transmission in communication systems is the presence of noise. By *noise* is meant any spurious or undesired disturbance that tends to obscure or mask the signal to be transmitted.

One can distinguish between different types of noise produced by fundamentally different means: man-made, erratic disturbances, and spontaneous fluctuations. The primary difference between the erratic and spontaneous types is that the former is not continuously present whereas the latter is.

Two basic types of spontaneous fluctuations are present in electric circuits. One is the so-called *shot effect* due to the random emission of electrons; the other type of spontaneous fluctuation is that due to thermal interaction between the free electrons and vibrating ions in a conducting medium.

If the noise spectrum is flat at all frequencies, the noise is called *white noise*. This term is derived from optics, since white includes all colors or frequencies. Unlike shot noise, thermal noise is an illustration of white noise, since it has been shown that the thermal noise spectrum is uniform up to extremely high frequencies on the order of 10^{13} Hz.

Equivalent noise circuits have been modeled for the thermal and shot noise effects for various components such as vacuum tubes, transistors, and diodes. Extensive noise-model analyses have been conducted ever since the early days of electronics and telephony in the late 1920s. It has been shown for both shot and thermal noise that the mean-squared noise voltage or current is proportional to system bandwidth and the mean noise power is also proportional to bandwidth.

The idea of *signal-to-noise ratio* (SNR) is used as a measure of the distinguishability of signals in the presence of noise. It is defined as the ratio of mean signal power to mean noise power, where both are measured at the same location in the system. Using the SNR, we may derive the concept of *noise figure* to compare the relative noisiness of different networks. Noise figure is defined as

$$F = \frac{S_s/N_s}{S_0/N_0}$$

where S_s/N_s is the SNR at the system input (source) and S_0/N_0 is the SNR at the system output. An ideal network will have $F = 1$, since this corresponds to the case where the system itself contributes no additional noise.

With reference to digital system design, the term *noise* can be considered as any unwanted signal that produces an undesired result. In practical design terms, there are three sources of noise: (1) high-frequency effects within the circuitry and associated wiring, (2) extraneous pulses that may be caused by circuit interaction or *time races* within the logical system, and (3) sources outside the system.

Digital systems deal with pulse waveforms that are square (ideally). It may be shown by Fourier analysis that square pulses are equivalent to the summation of an infinite series of successively higher frequency components. Such high-frequency components of the primary pulse waveform are much faster than the pulse repetition rate of the clocked pulses. These high-frequency components of the pulse get differentiated (and, thus, amplified) by the distributive wire-to-wire capacitances of the circuit or by backplane wiring and thus become the major source of *noise spikes*. Another source of susceptibility to noise is due to self-resonance of circuitry and wiring that tends to pick up pulse components from adjacent lines.

Various other causes of noise in digital systems are electrostatic interference in backplane wiring, effects due to capacitive coupling, effects due to inductive coupling (since the lines act as primary and secondary windings of air-core transformers), inductive voltage drops along common buses, inductive ringing of wire lines, relay surges, and resistance paths between separate circuit ground points.

Some helpful rules of thumb to minimize noise effects are: (1) always use direct point-to-point wiring, without cabling, if possible; (2) never cable individual trigger or count input lines with groups of high-current or parallel-word transfer lines; (3) use the twisted pair transmission line or coaxial cable for running long lines in backplanes; (4) always fan out wires from a central point rather than step from one point to the next; and (5) always use a separate filter point and ground return for high-current solenoid drivers or similar device types. For additional practical details in handling noisy situations in digital systems, refer to Jones (1964).

REFERENCES

1959. Schwartz, M. *Information Transmission, Modulation, and Noise.* New York: McGraw-Hill.
1964. Jones, J. Paul. *Causes and Cures of Noise in Digital Systems.* W. Concord, MA: Computer Design Publishing Corporation.

F. P. MATHUR

NONPROCEDURAL LANGUAGES

For articles on related subjects *see* FUNCTIONAL PROGRAMMING; PROBLEM-ORIENTED LANGUAGES; PROCEDURE-ORIENTED LANGUAGES; PROGRAMMING LANGUAGES; and REPORT GENERATORS.

Basic Concepts

Nomenclature. This article describes some of the basic characteristics of the class of programming languages commonly referred to as *nonprocedural* or *very high level.* (For more details, see Leavenworth and Sammet, 1974.) Some of the descriptive terms which have often been applied to the word "language" to convey essentially the same concept are the following.

Nonprocedural
Very high level
Less procedural
Goal oriented
Problem oriented
Pattern directed
Declarative
Functional
Relational
Problem statement
Problem definition
Problem description
Specification
Result specification
Task description

The most common term used has been *nonprocedural,* which is employed by a user to indicate the goals to be achieved (i.e., *what*), rather than the specific methods used to achieve them (i.e., *how*).

Properties of Programs. It is not possible to state that a given programming language is nonprocedural in any absolute sense because it is a relative term that changes as the state of the art changes (as will be discussed later). We can, however, say that a language possesses certain nonprocedural features. In order to see why this is so, we review briefly some fundamental properties of programs and programming languages.

In general, a program is a prescription for solving a particular problem. A procedure is a series of steps followed in a regular, orderly, definite way. Procedural programming is based to a great extent on the necessity to conform to the inherent sequential organization of the conventional digital computer. Therefore, a possible definition of a nonprocedural program is that it is a prescription for solving a problem without regard to any arbitrary sequencing requirements. More generally, we will say that a nonprocedural program is a prescription for solving a problem without regard to details of *how* it is solved. That is, the solution should be specified in terms of structures or abstractions which are relevant to the problem rather than those operations, data, and control structures which are based on some particular machine organization.

Relative Nature of the Term "Nonprocedural." The term *nonprocedural* is a relative one and changes as the state of the art changes. In many ways, the term *less procedural* is better because it makes clear the relative nature of the concept. An examination of Fig. 1 should make this clearer. A comparison of Figs. 1(a) and (a*) shows the difference between assembly language and Fortran-like languages. Prior to the existence of Fortran, the expression A = (B + C) * D + E * F could have been considered nonprocedural because it could not be directly translated by any language processor. Similarly, Figs. 1(b) and (b*) indicate another level of relativity, since the Fortran program to do matrix multiplication can be handled by one statement in APL. The use of a subroutine in Fortran would not give additional nonprocedurality, since the procedurality is based on the language primitives. Finally, the illustration of Fig. 1(c*), which is a program to CALCULATE THE SQUARE ROOT OF THE PRIME NUMBERS FROM 3 TO 95 AND PRINT IN TWO COLUMNS, cannot be handled by any translating system known today but, if it could be, the language would be considered nonprocedural by the standards of 1980. [It is essential to realize that the two forms shown in Fig. 1(c*) are logically equivalent, and the desirability of one form over the other (i.e., formal notation versus English) is a matter of personal preference.] The ability of a system to "understand" English is not at issue here; phrases that look like English may really depend on specific programming techniques (e.g., pattern matching and macro expansion), rather than English grammar. Putting the same point another way (because of its fundamental significance in this matter), it is entirely possible to design a formal language for doing mathematical problems in which the statement CALCULATE THE SQUARE ROOT OF THE PRIME NUMBERS FROM 3 TO 95 AND PRINT IN TWO COLUMNS is acceptable. At the other extreme, a natural and elegant looking phrase such

| (a) | (a*) |
| (Assembly Language) | (Fortran) |

```
CLA B                 A = (B + C)*D + E * F
ADD C
MPY D
STO T
CLA E
MPY F
ADD T
STO A
```

| (b) | (b*) |
| (Fortran) | (APL) |

```
  DO 7 I = 1,M         A ← B + .xC
   DO 8 J = 1,N
     C(I,J) = 0
      DO 9 K = 1,L
        C(I,J) = C(I,J) + A(I,K) * B(K,J)
9        CONTINUE
8     CONTINUE
7 CONTINUE
```

| (c) | (c*) |
| (PL/I) | |

```
DO I = 3 TO 95 BY 2;       PRINT (2),
  IF PRIME (I)               SQ (PRIME (3,95))
    THEN PUT SKIP LIST
       (I, SQRT (I));              or
    ELSE RETURN;
END;                       CALCULATE THE SQUARE
                           ROOT OF THE PRIME
                           NUMBERS FROM 3 TO
                           95 AND PRINT IN
                           2 COLUMNS
```

Fig. 1

as FIND X SUCH THAT X **2 = 5 is really equivalent to invoking a square root routine. Thus, nonprocedurality and English notation are completely independent issues.

We actually have two types of relativeness: One involves the problem or application area as described above and one involves the actual hardware. In the case of the hardware, we can only use as the base from which to measure some particular hardware or class of machines. As the machine changes, so does the relativeness. The reason that one must consider the hardware is that certain features or facilities which might be available on one machine are not on another. Thus, prior to the availability of floating point instructions in essentially all hard-

ware, the capability to perform floating point arithmetic had to be included explicitly in the programming language, and thus would be considered higher level with respect to the machine. Once floating point became virtually universal on computers, it was removed from serious language consideration.

Sequencing. There is a difference between sequencing across statements and within one statement. The former requirement tends to be obvious in a problem. However, sequencing within a single statement may or may not be explicit and this affects the nonprocedurality of the statement. Moreover, it is not always obvious from looking at a statement whether sequencing information is embedded in it. For example, sequencing is inherent in any mathematical expression that has precedence among its operators. Any data dependencies which are inherent in the problem statement may also affect the sequencing by requiring the data to be obtained in the correct order. A trivial illustration of this is obvious by merely noting that one cannot produce outputs until after one has performed calculations on the inputs.

As another illustration of the significance and relevance of sequencing, consider the problem statement shown in Fig. 1(c*). This calculation could actually be performed in several ways. One way is to follow each number through the three "computations"; i.e., test for primality, and if the number is prime, then compute its square root and print it. However, depending on the particular hardware and software, it might be more efficient first to determine all the primes, then to calculate all the square roots of the identified primes, and then to do all the printing. This is a prototype of a calculation involving a sequence of tasks, each of which supplies data to the next but where each input datum is independent of the others. The program given in Fig. 1(c) chooses only one of the alternatives; no discretion is left to the translator, whereas the statement in Fig. 1(c*) could—as indicated above—be translated in several significantly different ways which could have a major impact on efficiency. The explicit sequencing used in the program of Fig. 1(c) is not required for solution of the problem. One way of characterizing nonprocedurality is to say that the specification of sequencing of any information by the programmer (except that which is inherent to the logic of the problem) is irrelevant.

History. It is beyond the scope of this article to give more than a few highlights of the history of this area. In the very early stages of programming (i.e., in the first half of the 1950s), the phrase *automatic programming* was used to mean the process of writing a program in some high-level language. In that context, "high level" was by comparison with machine code. As time went on, it became clear that the coding was only a portion of the entire problem solving task, and therefore the phrase *automatic coding* came into use as meaning the use of a language such as Fortran. Thus, even in the very early days, the proper distinction was made between coding (which is one aspect of the entire programming task) and the larger activity of specification and design. One of the first significant accomplishments was the work of the Codasyl Language Structure Group in the development of the Information Algebra. This was essentially a mathematically-oriented way of describing a data processing application in terms of the input/output relationships; these were actually defined by means of transformations on sets of entities called *areas* (analogous to files). As another example, we note that string and pattern directed languages such as Comit and Snobol are much less procedural for those features than languages such as Fortran and Cobol.

Features of Nonprocedural Languages.

We discuss three features which are considered of major importance for inclusion in a programming language that claims to be nonprocedural. Some examples of languages possessing some of these features are included.

Associative Referencing. We will use the term *associative referencing* to refer to the accessing of data based on some intrinsic property of the data. Associative referencing is usually provided in those languages that contain sets as a data structure. The operation of selecting elements from previously defined sets, and of defining new sets from old based on some property of the members, is sometimes called the *set former* (see, for example, SETL—*q.v.*). An example of the power of SETL can be seen by the following expression, which specifies the prime numbers between 2 and 100.

$$\{P, 2 <= P <= 100 \uparrow$$
$$(\forall 2 <= N < P \uparrow (P//N)NE. 0)\}$$

This can be read in English as "the set of P's between 2 and 100 such that for every N greater than or equal to 2 and less than P, the remainder of P/N is not equal to zero." (This specification is obviously not an efficient one; a practical algorithm would at the very least consider the odd numbers from 3 to 100.)

The importance of associative referencing in nonprocedural languages is that the programmer does not have to specify access paths explicitly or program an algorithm to conduct a search for a specific data structure. Associative referencing is also used in database management languages, of which more will be said later.

Codd (1972) defines algebraic operations on relations which give a measure of the relative power of a language with respect to this type of data structure. In addition to the traditional set operations of Cartesian product, union, intersection, etc., he defines the relational operations of projection, join, division, and restriction. These operators (see *Aggregate Operators,* below) effectively provide various types of associative referencing.

Aggregate Operators. It is possible to avoid writing loops in some programming languages that provide aggregate operators. The $+$ operator in APL is the simplest example of an operator that applies equally to scalars and aggregates. For example, the addition of two vectors X,Y is obtained merely by writing X $+$ Y, whereas, in most programming languages, the elements of the result vector would have to be obtained one at a time under the control of a loop. Another example of an aggregate operator in APL is the use of the reduction operator to sum the elements of a vector X as shown in the following expression: $+/X$. In some cases, the PL/I programmer can avoid loops by using certain operators which distribute over entire arrays or structures (e.g., the assignment and plus operators, as in A $=$ B $+$ C, where A, B, and C are arrays).

There seems in general to be a close relationship between associative referencing and the aggregate operators we are discussing. It is certainly clear that the algebraic operators defined by Codd (1972) on relations are aggregate operators. Certainly, the elimination of explicit sequencing by this means is truly a nonprocedural feature.

Two interesting aggregate operators which are useful in data processing applications (but only for specification purposes) are the *bundle* and *glump* operators proposed in the Information Algebra (Codasyl, 1962). The glump operator partitions an area (which is like a file) into subsets called elements such that an element contains all entities in the area having identical values for the given glump operator. The glump operation is used for grouping and summarization purposes, which are typical tasks in data processing. For example, given a set of customer orders, where there may be more than one order for some customers, a glump operation might be represented by GLUMP(CUST#,ORDERS). The result of this operation would be to partition ORDERS so that each order in a partition would have the same order number. The bundle operator works on an ordered set of areas and, for each member of the Cartesian product, selects only those entities meeting a certain condition (such as equality of values in a particular domain).

Elimination of Arbitrary Sequencing. We will define *arbitrary sequencing* as any sequencing which is not dictated by the data dependencies of the application.

A functional programming language is one that does not contain either assignment or goto statements. As such, "functional" appears to be a synonym for "nonprocedural," since it is more involved with specifying the outcome desired as a function of the inputs, rather than indicating a step-by-step sequence of program steps. A program in a functional language such as pure Lisp avoids side effects which are a concomitant of procedural programming. A side effect may be caused in procedural languages during expression evaluation by the modification of memory by an assignment statement (e.g., during evaluation of a function in the expression). Pure functional languages produce no side effects since they have no assignment operation and cannot modify memory during expression evaluation.

One example of functional programming would be APL "one-liners" (without assignments, or without function calls with side effects). The following APL one-line function will delete leading elements from a vector X where Q represents a quoted character string or a numeric vector that contains examples to be deleted.

$$\nabla R \leftarrow Q \text{ DELETE } X$$
$$[1] \quad R \leftarrow (\sim \wedge \backslash X \epsilon Q)/X$$
$$\nabla$$

The ultimate expression of lack of arbitrary sequencing is a pure dataflow programming language. In this formalism, an application is decomposed into a set of modules such that one module can only consume (i.e., get its input data) a particular value after it has been produced by another module, and conversely. The sequencing is governed strictly by data dependencies [see, for example, Fig. 1(c*)]. The best example of a well-known dataflow programming language is GPSS (General-Purpose Systems Simulator), in which sequencing of a simulation program is controlled by transactions (data) moving through the model.

Database Languages. Database languages have many of the characteristics we have been discussing and the database area is an important and fast growing segment of computer technology. We will give one example from the relational algebra (Date, 1977) which may be considered to be representative of a class of languages rather than a specific implementation. The special issue of *ACM Computing Surveys* (1976) gives examples of the different database approaches and data management languages. The relational algebra which was developed originally by Codd (1972) consists of the operators SELECT, PROJECT, and JOIN, among others. Each operation of the relational algebra takes either one or two relations as its operand(s) and produces a new relation as a result. A relation has a precise mathematical definition but can be considered to be a table for our purpose. An example of a relation (table) called s is shown below:

S	S#	SNAME	STATUS	CITY
	S1	Smith	20	London
	S2	Jones	10	Paris
	S3	Blake	30	Paris

The heading SNAME stands for supplier name, and the first row can be interpreted as the supplier Smith who has supplier number (s#) s1, has status 20 and is in London. The SELECT operator constructs a new relation by taking a horizontal subset of the argument table (i.e., all rows that satisfy some condition) and the PROJECT operator constructs a new relation by taking a vertical subset of the argument table. As an example, consider the query to find s# and STATUS for suppliers in Paris. This can be determined in two stages:

TEMP ← SELECT S WHERE CITY = 'PARIS'

This returns the table:

TEMP	S#	SNAME	STATUS	CITY
	S2	Jones	10	Paris
	S3	Blake	30	Paris

We then do a projection:

RESULT ← PROJECT TEMP OVER S#, STATUS

The result is the relation:

RESULT	S#	STATUS
	S2	10
	S3	30

Note that the SELECT operator uses associative referencing and is an aggregate operator. PROJECT is an aggregate operator, too.

It is not necessary to break up the retrievals into two distinct steps as indicated above. We could combine the query into one operation using the following syntax.

SELECT S#, STATUS
FROM S
WHERE CITY = 'PARIS'

Many of the newer database languages have extensive data manipulation capabilities in addition to their retrieval function.

Relation of RPGs to Nonprocedural Language. RPGs (Report Program Generators) are often mentioned when discussing nonprocedural languages. It is certainly true that the output format of an RPG is specified by stating *what* is wanted rather than *how* it should be produced. It should be noted, however, that the

Calculation section of an RPG program is decidedly low level. This confirms our statement that no language is nonprocedural in the absolute sense. A particular language may possess some features and lack others, or possess some feature in one area and lack the same feature in another area.

Summary. We have attempted to describe some of the basic characteristics and issues arising from the term *nonprocedural languages*. Perhaps the key observation is that it is not possible to state that a given programming language is nonprocedural in any absolute sense because it is a relative term that changes as the state of the art changes. However, it can be said that a language possesses certain nonprocedural features relative to a specific time. The best examples of languages in 1980 that possess the "most" nonprocedural features are probably SETL and many of the database query languages. APL has high-level operators but does not have the concept of associative referencing as a primitive notion. However, the elimination of arbitrary sequencing can be achieved in APL programs by exploiting the power of the aggregate operators.

REFERENCES

1962. Codasyl Language Structure Group. "An Information Algebra Phase I Report," *Comm. ACM* **5**, *No. 4* (April).

1972. Codd, E. F. "Relational Completeness of Data Base Sublanguages," in Rustin, R. (Ed.), *Data Base Systems*. Courant Computer Science Symposia Series, Vol. 6. Englewood Cliffs, NJ: Prentice-Hall.

1974. Leavenworth, Burt M. and Sammet, Jean E. "An Overview of Nonprocedural Languages," *Proc. ACM SIGPLAN Symposium on Very High Level Languages, ACM SIGPLAN Notices* **9**, *No. 4* (April).

1976. Data Base Management Systems. *ACM Computing Surveys* **8**, *No. 1* (March).

1977. Date, C. J. *An Introduction to Database Systems.* (2nd Ed.) Reading, MA: Addison-Wesley.

B. M. LEAVENWORTH AND J. E. SAMMET

NORC. *See* NAVAL ORDNANCE RESEARCH COMPUTER.

NP-COMPLETE PROBLEMS

For articles on related subjects *see* ALGORITHMS, ANALYSIS OF; ALGORITHMS, THEORY OF; COMBINATORICS; COMPUTATIONAL COMPLEXITY; GRAPH THEORY; and MATHEMATICAL PROGRAMMING.

There are many practical computational problems for which no effective computer algorithms have been devised. Many of these seemingly intractable problems belong to a class of problems known as the *NP-complete problems*. NP stands for *nondeterministic polynomial*, a concept discussed below. The only known algorithms for these problems require an amount of time that is an exponential function of the problem size (measured by some parameter, n, on which the problem depends). Such algorithms are called *exponential time algorithms*. Technically, problem size is measured by the number of bits in the problem description, but often the running time of an algorithm is more conveniently expressed in terms of some other (roughly equivalent) measure of the amount of input data. For problems of size n, exponential time algorithms may take time 2^n, $2^{n^{1/2}}$, 3^{n^2}, etc. In contrast, many problems can be solved by algorithms that require an amount of time that is a polynomial function of the problem size. These algorithms are called *polynomial time algorithms*. For problems of size n, they may take time n, $n \log n$, n^2, n^3, etc. Because polynomials grow more slowly than exponentials, polynomial time algorithms (even with a large exponent) are efficient in comparison with exponential time algorithms. As a first cut at categorizing algorithm complexity, polynomial time algorithms are regarded as "efficient," and exponential time algorithms as "inefficient."

Computer scientists have proved that, if one efficient (i.e., polynomial time) algorithm can be found for *any* of the NP-complete problems, then efficient algorithms can be devised for *all* of these problems. Conversely, if any of these problems requires exponential time, they all do. Most computer scientists are pessimistic about the possibility that nonexponential algorithms for these problems will ever be found, and so proving a problem to be NP-complete is now regarded as strong evidence that the problem is intrinsically intractable. If, however, an efficient algorithm can be found for any one (and hence all) NP-complete problems, it would be a major intellectual breakthrough with immense practical implications.

We illustrate these concepts with three NP-complete problems, one from graph theory, one involving summing numbers, and one involving sets.

Clique Problem. A *graph* is a set of nodes with edges connecting certain pairs of nodes (such as the graph in Fig. 1). A *clique* is a set of nodes from a graph where every pair of nodes in the set is connected by an edge. In the figure, $\{1, 3, 7\}$ is a clique. Set $\{2, 4, 5, 6\}$ is not because nodes 5 and 6 in this set are not connected by an edge.

Problem. Given a graph and a "clique size" k, decide if the graph has a clique of size k. For the problem given in Fig. 1, the answer is "YES" because $\{1, 2, 4, 5\}$ is a clique of size 4. If, instead, the clique size in the problem were 5, the answer would be "NO."

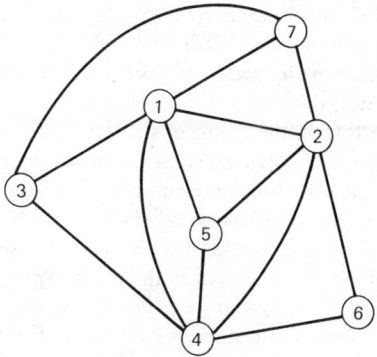

Fig. 1. Example of a clique problem.

Knapsack problem. Given a list of numbers and a "knapsack size," determine if some subset of the listed numbers adds up to the knapsack size. For the problem given in Fig. 2, the answer is "YES" because

$$4 + 18 + 25 + 42 = 89.$$

If, instead, the knapsack size were 90, the answer would be "NO."

List of Numbers: 4 7 13 18 25 32 42 49
Knapsack Size: 89

Fig. 2. Example of a knapsack problem.

Set Covering Problem. For a given set, a collection of subsets is said to *cover* the given set if each member of the given set belongs to at least one set in the collection.

Problem. Given a set to be covered, a list of available subsets, and a "cover size" k, determine if k of the available subsets can be chosen so that the collection of chosen subsets covers the given set. For the problem given in Fig. 3, the answer is "YES" because the three subsets S_3, S_6, and S_7 can be chosen. If, instead, the cover size were 2, the answer would be "NO."

Set to be Covered: $\{a, b, c, d, e, f, g, h\}$
Available Subsets: $S_1 = \{d\}$, $S_2 = \{a\}$, $S_3 = \{a, b, c\}$
$S_4 = \{f\}$, $S_5 = \{b, e, g\}$, $S_6 = \{c, d, e, h\}$, $S_7 = \{f, g, h\}$

Cover Size: 3

Fig. 3. Example of a set covering problem.

The three problems illustrated have the common property that, if the answer is "YES," there is a short, easily verified demonstration of this fact. For the clique problem, the demonstration is a list of nodes, equal in number to the clique size, that form a clique. For the knapsack problem, the demonstration is a subset of the listed numbers whose sum equals the knapsack size. For the set covering problem, the demonstration is a collection of the available subsets that contain every element of the set to be covered. This common property suggests a common approach to solving these problems; namely, enumerate the potential demonstrations and check each potential demonstration to see if it is an actual demonstration. For the knapsack problem, this means enumerating the subsets of the given numbers and adding the numbers in each subset to see if their sum is the knapsack value. Unfortunately, these enumerate-and-check algorithms require exponential time due to the number of things to be enumerated. In the knapsack case, with n numbers, there are 2^n subsets to be checked.

The preceding problems are called recognition problems because the answer for a given problem example is "YES" or "NO." A recognition problem is called *nondeterministic polynomial* (or *NP*) if, whenever the answer is "YES," there is a "polynomial" demonstration of this fact. A problem is considered to have polynomial demonstrations if there are constants c and k such that a problem example of size n with answer "YES" has a potential demonstration that can be verified correct in cn^k steps. Thus, if the answer is "YES," a lucky person might guess a correct demonstration and verify his or her guess, all in polynomial time. However, the word *nondeterministic* is not meant to imply randomness or any use of probability. *Nondeterministic* signifies only that no rule is given for determining what the guess should be.

The key concept in relating problems to each other is *polynomial-time reducibility*. Problem A is said to be *reducible* to problem B if problem A can be solved using as a subroutine an algorithm that solves problem B. In particular, problem A is *polynomial-time reducible* to problem B if there is a polynomial bound on the number of steps taken by a main program to solve problem A, where the main program can call a subroutine for problem B. Note that the number of steps taken by the subroutine is not counted. If there is an efficient (i.e., polynomial-time) algorithm for solving problem B, then using that algorithm as the subroutine produces an efficient algorithm for problem A. Conversely, if problem A is intrinsically hard (i.e., cannot be solved in polynomial time), then no efficient subroutine for B can exist, and so problem B is also intrinsically hard.

To illustrate a polynomial-time reduction, Fig. 4 outlines a main program for reducing the clique problem to the set covering problem. If step 1 of the main program

Main Program for Clique Problem

Step 1

Input graph G and clique size k

Step 2

Construct new graph $\overline{G}$ with:

(a) The same nodes as G

(b) An edge between two nodes if and only if there is no edge between these two nodes in G

(c) A unique name for each edge in $\overline{G}$.

Step 3

Let S = set of edges in graph $\overline{G}$

(S is set to be covered)

Step 4

For each node x in graph $\overline{G}$, let S_x = members of S with endpoint x

(each S_x is an available subset)

Step 5

Let cover size = number of nodes − clique size

Step 6

Call subroutine for set covering problem, passing it the problem example constructed in steps 3, 4, and 5

Step 7

If subroutine answers "YES," then output "YES"

If subroutine answers "NO," then output "NO"

Fig. 4. Reduction of clique problem to set covering problem.

is given the clique problem example of Fig. 1 as input, the graph $\overline{G}$ constructed in step 2 is the graph of Fig. 5. For instance the edge named b appears in $\overline{G}$ because G does not contain an edge between nodes 3 and 5, and $\overline{G}$ has no edge between 1 and 3 because G does have an edge between 1 and 3. Steps 3, 4, and 5 construct the set covering example of Fig. 3. Notice that set S_3 has members a, b, and c because a, b, and c are the edges of $\overline{G}$ having node 3 as an endpoint. The subroutine returns with an-

swer "YES" (because of cover S_3, S_6, and S_7), and the main program outputs "YES."

The reason the program works is that for a graph with n nodes, there is a direct relationship between the nodes which form the clique of size k and the n-k covering subsets which solve the constructed set covering problem. Specifically, the clique consists of the nodes corresponding to the available subsets which are not part of the cover. In the example, it is the available subsets S_1, S_2, S_4, and S_5 which are not in the cover $\{S_3, S_6, S_7\}$, and it is nodes $\{1, 2, 4, 5\}$ that form the clique.

A problem is said to be *NP-complete* if it is an NP-problem and every NP-problem is polynomial-time reducible to it. Thus, an algorithm for an NP-complete problem is universal in that it can be used as a subroutine for any NP-problem.

To show that a new problem is NP-complete, it suffices to show that it is an NP-problem, and that any one problem already known to be NP-complete is polynomial-time reducible to it.

As the number of problems already known to be NP-complete increases, there are more problems available for showing other problems NP-complete, and so the task of proving NP-completeness becomes easier and easier. In 1971, Cook formulated the concept of NP-completeness, and showed that the problem of testing a logical formula for satisfiability is NP-complete. Shortly thereafter, Karp (1972) extended the set of known NP-problems to include about 20 other problems of practical interest. This gave momentum to the search for NP-complete problems and now large numbers are known (see, for example, Garey and Johnson, 1979). It is now routine for a computer scientist confronting an apparently hard problem to investigate whether the problem is NP-complete.

The concept of NP-completeness is relevant not only to recognition (i.e., YES-NO) problems but also to optimization problems. This is because optimization problems have closely related recognition problems. The clique problem above is the recognition problem closely related to the optimization problem of finding the largest size clique in a graph. The knapsack problem above is the problem closely related to the optimization problem of finding a subset of listed numbers which has the largest sum not exceeding the knapsack size. The set covering problem above is the problem closely related to the optimization problem of finding the smallest collection of available subsets which cover a given set. In each case, the answer to the optimization problem also provides an answer to the recognition problem. For example, if the answer to the clique optimization problem is a clique of size n, the clique recognition problem has answer "YES" if $k \leq n$ and "NO" if $k > n$. Thus, the optimization must be at least as hard as recognition. Some well-known optimization problems with closely related NP-complete

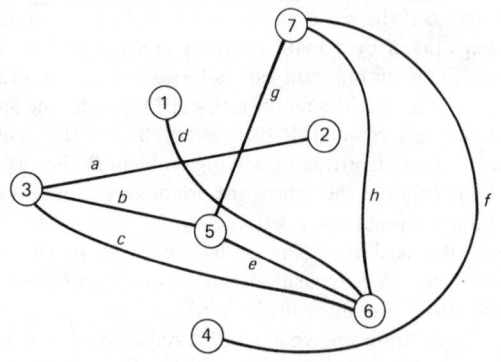

Fig. 5 The graph $\overline{G}$ corresponding to Fig. 1.

recognition problems are the traveling salesman problem, integer programming, job-shop scheduling, and graph coloring.

What does a computer scientist do when confronted with an NP-complete problem? A variety of approaches have been taken.

1. Develop an algorithm that is fast enough for small problem sizes, but that would take too long if presented with larger size problems. This approach is often used when the anticipated problems are all of small size.

2. Develop a fast algorithm that solves a special case of the problem, but does not solve the general problem. This approach is often used when the special case is of practical importance.

3. Develop an algorithm that quickly solves a large proportion of the cases that come up in practice, but in the worst case may run for a long time. This approach is often used when the problems occurring in practice tend to have special features that can be exploited to speed up the computation.

4. For an optimization problem, develop an algorithm which always runs quickly, but produces an answer that is not necessarily optimal. Sometimes a worst case bound can be obtained on how much the answer produced may differ from the optimum, so that a reasonably close answer is assured. This is an area of active research, with suboptimal algorithms for a variety of important problems being developed and analyzed.

5. Work on some other problem. This is often done when there are no users who really care about the problem.

In general, NP-completeness effectively eliminates the possibility of developing a completely satisfactory algorithm. Once a problem is seen to be NP-complete, it is appropriate to direct development efforts towards a more achievable goal.

REFERENCES

1971. Cook, S. A. "The Complexity of Theorem-Proving Procedures," *Proc. Third ACM Symposium on Theory of Computing*, pp. 151–158.

1972. Karp, R. M. "Reducibility Among Combinatorial Problems," in Miller, R. E. and Thatcher, J. W. (Eds.), *Complexity of Computer Computations*. New York: Plenum Press, pp. 85–104.

1979. Garey, M. R. and Johnson, D. S. *Computers and Intractibility: A Guide to the Theory of NP-Completeness*. San Francisco: W. H. Freeman and Co.

D. J. ROSENKRANTZ AND RICHARD E. STEARNS

NUCLEUS. *See* KERNEL.

NUMBERS AND NUMBER SYSTEMS

For articles on related subjects *see* ARITHMETIC, COMPUTER; COMPLEMENT; INTERVAL ARITHMETIC; NUMERICAL ANALYSIS; PRECISION; and SIGNIFICANCE ARITHMETIC.

Since almost everyone uses numbers every day, it is at first glance surprising that so many laypeople have difficulty understanding the rather simple variations on the decimal system theme that are widely used in computing. The crux of the problem seems to be that, while we may use and manipulate (e.g., do arithmetic with) numbers with some facility, there is all too often little understanding of what is being done. The proliferation of hand calculators bids fair to exacerbate this problem. What needs to be understood, however, is simply that the representation in which we normally write numbers, for example

$$276.1069 \qquad (1)$$

is nothing more than shorthand symbolic representation for the precise mathematical equivalent

$$2 \times 100 + 7 \times 10 + 6 \times 1 + 1 \times 0.1 \\ + 0 \times 0.01 + 6 \times 0.001 + 9 \times 0.0001 \quad (2)$$

or

$$2 \times 10^2 + 7 \times 10^1 + 6 \times 10^0 + 1 \times 10^{-1} \\ + 0 \times 10^{-2} + 6 \times 10^{-3} + 9 \times 10^{-4} \quad (3)$$

The representations (2) and (3) express clearly that the decimal system we use has a *base*, or *radix*, 10. By analogy, therefore, the *binary*, or *base 2*, system so commonly used with computers can become immediately understandable, as presented below. The notation (1)—often called *positional notation* because the position of a digit specifies the power of 10 in (3), which is associated with it—may effectively hide for many the real mathematical content of a number.

Radix Representation. The notation in (2) or (3) above is called the *radix representation* of a number. The general form of any decimal number may be written

$$\sum_{i=-m}^{n} d_i \cdot 10^i \qquad 0 \le d_i \le 9 \ (d_i \text{ an integer}),$$

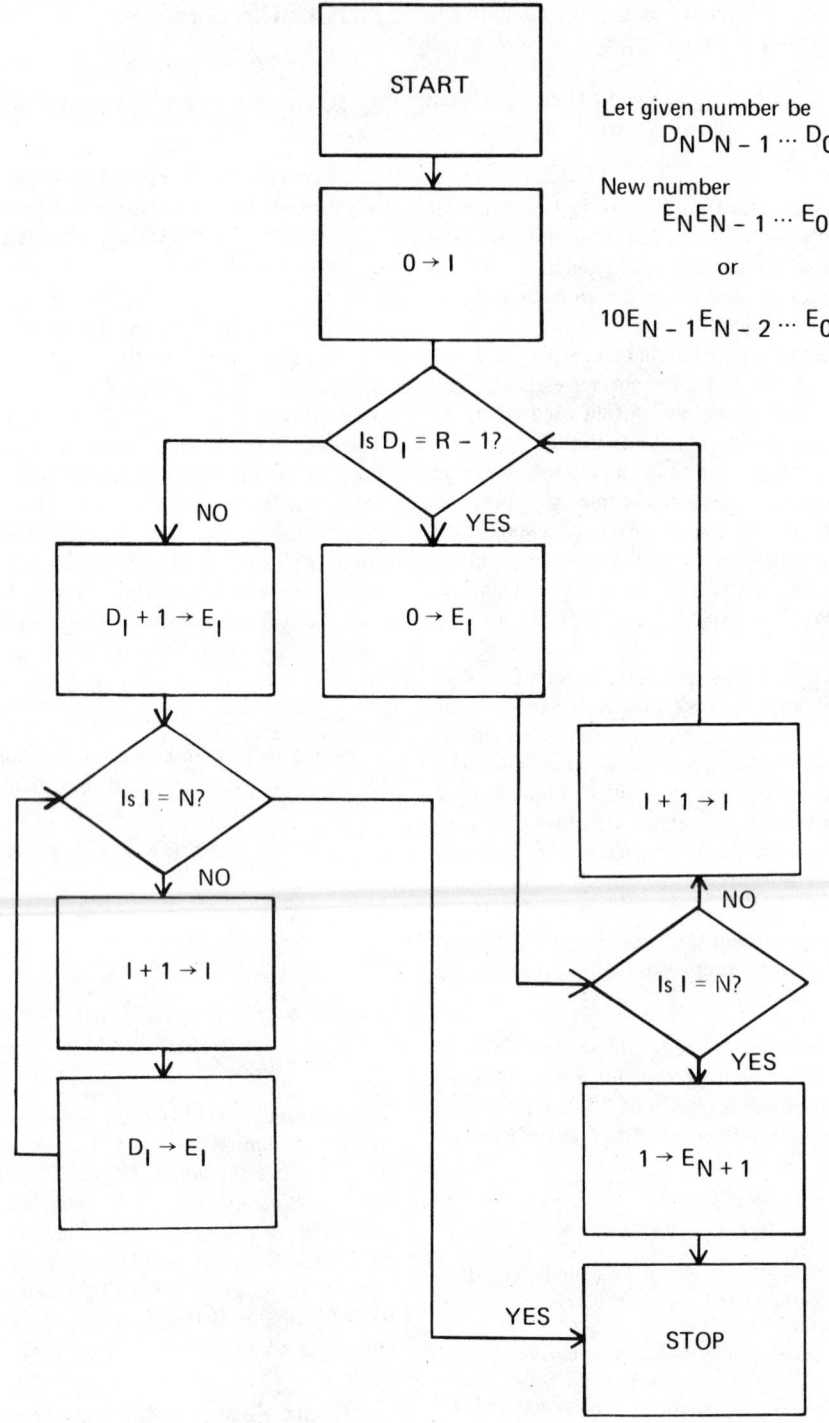

Fig. 1.   Flowchart for generating next number in a number system with radix R.

which in the case of (3) specializes to

$$m = 4, \quad n = 2$$
$$d_{-4} = 9, \quad d_{-3} = 6$$
$$d_{-2} = 0, \quad d_{-1} = 1$$
$$d_0 = 6, \quad d_1 = 7, \quad d_2 = 2$$

The three other number systems most important in computers are *binary, octal,* and *hexadecimal.*

1. In binary, numbers are represented by

$$\sum_{i=-m}^{n} b_i \cdot 2^i \qquad b_i = 0 \text{ or } 1. \qquad (4)$$

2. In the octal (formerly called *octonal*), or base 8, representation, we have

$$\sum_{i=-m}^{n} o_i \cdot 8^i \qquad 0 \le o_i \le 7 \ (o_i \text{ an integer}).$$

3. In the hexadecimal, or base 16, system, numbers are represented by

$$\sum_{i=-m}^{n} h_i \cdot 16^i \qquad 0 \le h_i \le 15 \ (h_i \text{ an integer}).$$

We will now consider the characteristics of each of these systems briefly.

Binary. The rule for generating successive numbers in any number system is given in Fig. 1. If $R = 10$, this algorithm will generate successfully the familiar sequence of decimal numbers. But, if $R = 2$, we get the sequence of binary numbers, the first few of which are

0	1	10	11	100	101
110	111	1000	1001	1010	1011
1100	1101	1110	1111	10000	10001

The addition and multiplication tables for binary numbers are particularly simple (Table 1) and, once learned, so is binary arithmetic using these tables. Fig. 2 gives examples of all four arithmetic operations in binary, with the corresponding decimal arithmetic also given. Finding the equivalent decimal integer to a given binary integer is very simple using expression (4). Thus, for example,

$$1011010 = 1 \times 2^6 + 0 \times 2^5 + 1 \times 2^4 + 1 \times 2^3$$
$$+ 0 \times 2^2 + 1 \times 2^1 + 0 \times 2^0$$
$$= 64 + 16 + 8 + 2$$
$$= 90$$

Later on in this article, we will consider the general problem of conversion from a number in one system to another.

Table 1.   Binary Addition and Multiplication Tables

+	0	1		×	0	1
0	0	1		0	0	0
1	0	10		1	0	1

Octal. The octal system was once used widely in computing (but is rather seldom used now) only because of its simple relation to binary. To convert a binary number to octal, it is only necessary (since $8 = 2^3$) to group the binary digits in sets of three and convert each set to its binary equivalent. (Note that three binary digits—hereafter we will use the common contraction *bits* for binary digits—can represent the digits from 0 to 7 or one octal digit.) Thus, the binary equivalent of one million in decimal is

$$11 \mid 110 \mid 100 \mid 001 \mid 001 \mid 000 \mid 000$$
$$\downarrow \quad \downarrow \quad \downarrow \quad \downarrow \quad \downarrow \quad \downarrow \quad \downarrow$$
$$3 \quad 6 \quad 4 \quad 1 \quad 1 \quad 0 \quad 0$$

and the octal equivalent is 3641100. Correspondingly, to go from octal to binary, each octal digit is converted into its binary equivalent. Thus,

$$647.0534$$
$$\downarrow$$
$$110100111.000101011100$$

The advantage of octal over binary is shown clearly by the preceding two examples. For all large numbers or numbers with a significant number of binary places, the octal representation is much more compact, and therefore is easier to write and manipulate than its binary equivalent. Table 2 gives the octal addition and multiplication tables.

Hexadecimal. This system became important with the advent of the IBM 360 and 370 systems, which, while binary internally, from the user's point of view are hexadecimal machines. Because hexadecimal requires 16 distinct characters, 6 characters in addition to 0, 1, ..., 9 are needed to represent "10", "11", ..., "15". These are usually taken to be *A, B, C, D, E, F.*

Just as octal is related to binary using three-bit groups, hexadecimal is related to binary using four-bit groups. Thus,

$$111 \mid 1010 \mid 0001 \mid 0010 \mid 0001$$

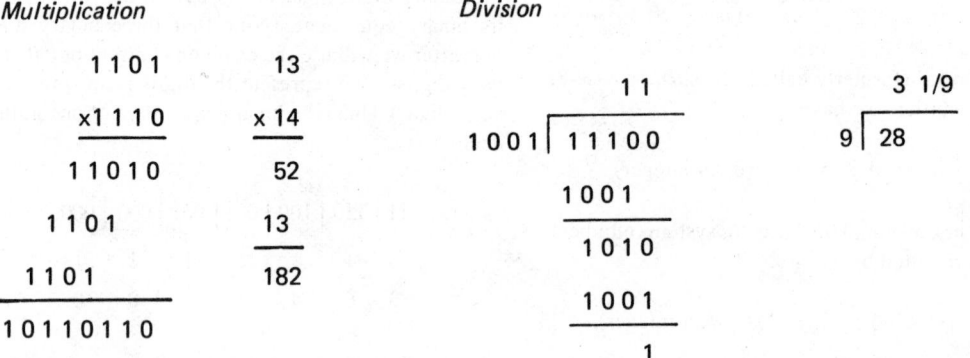

Addition

```
Carries   1 0 0 1 1

            1 1 0 0 1        25
          + 1 0 0 1 1      + 19
          ─────────        ────
          1 0 1 1 0 0        44
```

Subtraction

```
Borrowing      10    1    1
          0     0̸   1̸0   1̸0   10
          1̸    1̸    0    0    0      24
        - 0     1    1    0    1    - 13
        ─────────────────────      ────
                1    0    1    1      11
```

Multiplication

```
        1 1 0 1          13
       x 1 1 1 0        x 14
       ─────────        ────
        1 1 0 1 0          52
       1 1 0 1            13
      1 1 0 1           ────
     ────────           182
     1 0 1 1 0 1 1 0
```

Division

```
          1 1                    3 1/9
   ┌──────────           ┌───────
1001│ 1 1 1 0 0         9│ 2 8
    1 0 0 1
    ─────────
    1 0 1 0
    1 0 0 1
    ─────────
          1
```

Fig. 2. Binary arithmetic.

Table 2. Octal Addition and Multiplication Tables

+	0	1	2	3	4	5	6	7	×	0	1	2	3	4	5	6	7
0	0	1	2	3	4	5	6	7	0	0	0	0	0	0	0	0	0
1	1	2	3	4	5	6	7	10	1	0	1	2	3	4	5	6	7
2	2	3	4	5	6	7	10	11	2	0	2	4	6	10	12	14	16
3	3	4	5	6	7	10	11	12	3	0	3	6	11	14	17	22	25
4	4	5	6	7	10	11	12	13	4	0	4	10	14	20	24	30	34
5	5	6	7	10	11	12	13	14	5	0	5	12	17	24	31	36	43
6	6	7	10	11	12	13	14	15	6	0	6	14	22	30	36	44	52
7	7	10	11	12	13	14	15	16	7	0	7	16	25	34	43	52	61

becomes

$$7 \quad A \quad 1 \quad 2 \quad 1$$

in hexadecimal.

Other Number Systems

Balanced Digit Systems. In a balanced digit system the allowable digits in each position are from a value $-s$ to $+s$, with negative numbers usually denoted by an overbar. Thus, a balanced binary system might have digits $-1, 0, 1$ with -1 written as $\bar{1}$. In this system,

$$10\bar{1}\bar{1} = 2^3 - 2^1 - 2^0 = 5$$

and

$$\bar{1}101 = -2^3 + 2^2 + 2^0 = -3.$$

One property of such a system, sometimes useful in the design of arithmetic units in computers, is the *redundancy* which occurs when a number has more than one possible representation. For example, in the system described above, 5 may, as in the usual binary system, also be represented by

$$101$$

In any balanced digit system where s is less than the base, the leftmost digit gives the sign of the number so that no explicit sign is needed. In addition, given any number A, its negative may be found by changing all digits to their negatives (i.e., removing all overbars and inserting overbars where there were none). Thus, for example,

$$10\bar{1}10 = 2^4 - 2^2 + 2^1 = +14$$

and

$$\bar{1}01\bar{1}0 = -2^4 + 2^2 - 2^1 = -14.$$

A particularly interesting balanced digit system, which does not yet appear to have been applied in computers, is *balanced ternary* (Knuth, 1969), which has radix 3 and where, as above, the digits, called *trits*, are 1, 0, and $\bar{1}$. This system is nonredundant and, in addition to the properties mentioned above, has the additional useful property that a number may be rounded to the nearest integer merely by deleting its fractional part. Thus,

$$10\bar{1}.\bar{1}\bar{1} = 3^2 - 3^0 - 3^{-1} - 3^{-2} = 7\tfrac{5}{9}$$

and

$$10\bar{1} = 8.$$

Residue Systems. A residue system is one in which (1) each digit position corresponds to a different radix; (2) all pairs of radices are relatively prime; i.e., the only common divisor of any two radices is 1; (3) the value of the digit d_i for integer A in position i corresponding to radix r_i is given by $d_i = A$ modulo r_i, i.e., the remainder when A is divided by r_i.

For example, if $r_2 = 5$, $r_1 = 3$, $r_0 = 2$, then 13 is represented by

$$311$$

and 29 is represented by

$$421.$$

Because of property (2), the range of values that can be expressed is from 0 to 1 less than the product of the radices used.

Radix Conversion. We now consider how to take a number in a system with base p and convert it to a number in base q. To do this, we consider the integer and fractional parts of the number separately. Let $(I)_p$ and $(F)_p$, respectively, be the integer and fractional parts of the number in base p, which we wish to convert to base q; let $(q)_p$ be the expression of q in the p system (e.g., to convert from binary to decimal $(q)_p = (10)_2 = 1010$). Figures 3(a) and 3(b) are flowcharts to perform the con-

versions of the integer and fractional parts, respectively. We illustrate these algorithms with two examples.

Example 1. Convert 6753.31 in decimal to binary. Here $p = 10$, $q = 2$, $(I)_p = 6753$, $(F)_p = 0.31$, and $(q)_p = 2$. From Fig. 3(a) we calculate the integral part and find it to be 1101001100001.

	Quotient	Remainder
6753/2	3376	1
3376/2	1688	0
1688/2	844	0
844/2	422	0
422/2	211	0
211/2	105	1
105/2	52	1
52/2	26	0
26/2	13	0
13/2	6	1
6/2	3	0
3/2	1	1
1/2	0	1

From Fig. 3(b), with $K = 6$, we calculate the fractional part, and find it to be 010011.

	Fractional Part	Integral Part
0.31×2	0.62	0
0.62×2	0.24	1
0.24×2	0.48	0
0.48×2	0.96	0
0.96×2	0.92	1
0.92×2	0.84	1

Thus, 6753.31 in decimal is equivalent to

$$1101001100001.010011\cdots$$

in binary.

Note that the binary fraction is nonterminating (i.e., not expressible in a finite number of bits) even though the decimal fraction is finite.

Example 2. Convert 1001100.011 in binary to decimal. Here, $p = 2$, $q = 10$, $(I)_p = 1001100$, $(F)_p = 0.011$, and $(q)_p = 1010$, which is the binary representation of 10 in decimal. From Fig. 3(a),

	Quotient	Remainder
1001100/1010	111	$110 \rightarrow 6$ in decimal
111/1010	0	$111 \rightarrow 7$ in decimal

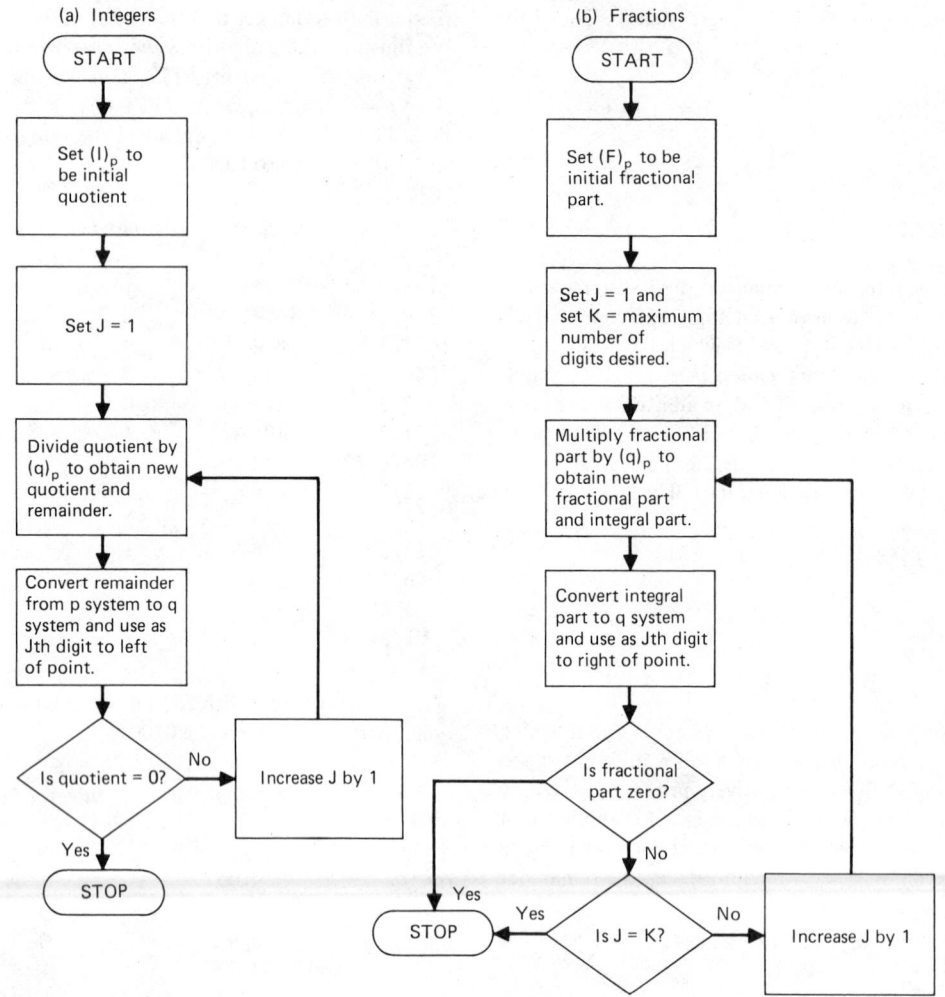

Fig. 3. Radix conversion.

Thus, the integral part of the decimal number is 76. From Figure 3(b).

	Fractional Part	*Integral Part*
0.011×1010	0.110	$11 \rightarrow 3$ in decimal
0.110×1010	0.100	$111 \rightarrow 7$ in decimal
0.100×1010	0.000	$101 \rightarrow 5$ in decimal

Thus, the decimal equivalent of 1001100.011 is 76.375. In this instance a finite binary fraction became a finite decimal fraction. This is always the case because all the negative powers of 2 have finite fractional expansions in the decimal system.

Because of our natural facility with decimal arith-metic, an easier way to do Example 2 is to apply expression (4) directly:

$$1001100.011 = 1 \times 2^6 + 1 \times 2^3 + 1 \times 2^2$$
$$+ 1 \times 2^{-2} + 1 \times 2^{-3}$$
$$= 64 + 8 + 4 + 0.25 + 0.125$$
$$= 76.375$$

The conversions illustrated in Examples 1 and 2 are indeed precisely those performed when

1. A program written in a high-level language in decimal notation is compiled into the machine language of a binary computer.

2. The results computed in that binary computer are printed out as decimal numbers

although the algorithms used on the computer may be somewhat different from those shown in Fig. 3.

REFERENCES

1969. Knuth, D. E. *The Art of Computer Programming* **2**. Reading, MA: Addison-Wesley.

1969. Menninger, K. *Number Words and Number Symbols*. Cambridge, MA: (This book, subtitled "A Cultural History of Numbers," is a fascinating account of the history and uses of numbers in many natural languages.)

1971. Ralston, A. *An Introduction to Programming and Computer Science*. New York: McGraw-Hill.

A. RALSTON

NUMBER THEORETIC CALCULATIONS

For articles on related subjects *see* DATA ENCRYPTION; and NUMERICAL ANALYSIS.

The theory of numbers is primarily concerned with the properties of the *natural numbers* 1, 2, 3, ... These numbers possess a multiplicative structure which is exemplified by the fundamental theorem of arithmetic which states that each natural number can be uniquely expressed as a product of *prime numbers*. A prime number is a natural number greater than 1 having no divisor other than 1 or itself. A natural number which is not prime is called *composite*. Much of the research in number theory, both theoretical and computational, has dealt with the properties of the set of primes and with closely related subjects. This article will report some of the major advances in computational number theory which have been made in the last ten years and will be subdivided into the following areas:

1. Prime testing and factoring.
2. The largest known primes.
3. Fermat's last theorem.
4. The zeros of the Riemann Zeta function.

Prime Testing and Factoring. This is the familiar problem of testing a number n to determine whether it is prime or composite. If it is prime, we want a rigorous proof of its primality; if it is composite, we want to factor the number and provide proofs of the primality of the factors. If n is sufficiently small (i.e., fewer than 15 decimal digits), we can use the familiar method of dividing the number by 2, 3, 4, 5, . . . (actually, of course, only the sequence of primes is necessary here), dividing out each factor that is discovered and stopping when we reach its square root. If no divisor is found, then n is prime; otherwise, we obtain the desired prime factorization. D. E. Knuth and L. Trabb Pardo have shown that the number of trial divisions needed will be $\leq n^{0.35}$ about half of the time.

For larger numbers, a better procedure is needed. There exists a very fast test for primality which is based on Fermat's little theorem. This theorem states that if n is a prime number and a does not divide n, then

$$a^{n-1} \equiv 1 \pmod{n} \qquad (1)$$

(i.e., the difference between a^{n-1} and 1 is divisible by n).

We can raise a number a to the $n - 1$ power (mod n) in roughly $\log_2 n$ steps by a doubling and squaring procedure (see Lehmer, 1969, p. 126). Although the converse of the above theorem is not generally true, the probability that a large composite number n satisfies (1) is very small. Thus, (1) will almost never be satisfied when n is not prime.

It requires much more computer time to obtain a rigorous proof that a number satisfying property (1) above is indeed prime. See Williams (1978) for a comprehensive treatment of the subject and Selfridge and Wunderlich (1974) for a detailed algorithm for one method. The most frequently used algorithms depend on theorems of Lehmer, Proth, and Selfridge and prove the primality of n by obtaining partial factorizations of $n-1$ and $n+1$ and doing some complicated tests on the factors found. One can prove primality of most prime numbers with fewer than 50 digits by this method.

Factoring composite numbers is much harder. Many new algorithms have been developed in the last ten years and are described by R. K. Guy (1976). The best method known today was developed by John Brillhart and essentially reduces the task of factoring one n-digit number to the factorizations of many (perhaps several thousand) $n/2$-digit numbers. As of 1980, we are able to factor most composite numbers with fewer than 43 decimal digits in, at most, an hour on a moderately fast machine. Since the smaller numbers can be factored independently, there is hope that the algorithm can be successfully implemented on one of the fast array processors such as the ILLIAC IV or ICL DAP so that we may be able to factor 60–65 digit numbers.

Largest Known Primes. Primes which are of the form $2^p - 1$, where p is a prime, are much easier to prove prime than arbitrary ones of the same size. Thus, primes of this form, called *Mersenne primes*, have always been the largest known ones. There are 27 known Mersenne primes, the largest of which is $2^{44497} - 1$, a number having 13,395 decimal digits, which was discovered on 8 April 1979 by D. Slowinski. He used a CRAY-1 computer, a fast pipeline machine, and was able to rediscover all the previously known Mersenne primes using only a fraction of the computer time devoted to the search by other investigators using more conventional machines.

Fermat's Last Theorem. This theorem says that if $n > 2$, there are no solutions to the equation

$$x^n + y^n = z^n \tag{2}$$

in natural numbers. This conjecture has resisted proof for three centuries, since Fermat noted it in a margin of his copy of a book by Diophantus. Although Fermat claimed to have proved it, he apparently did not. Computers can be used to verify its truth for a particular n. The best results to 1980 were produced by Samuel Wagstaff, who has shown that the equation (2) has no solution in natural numbers x, y, z for all $n \leq 125,000$. See Ribenboim (1977) for a very readable exposition on the subject.

The Riemann Zeta Function. Our final topic concerns the complex valued function

$$\zeta(s) = \sum_{k=1}^{\infty} \frac{1}{k^s}, \text{ where } s = \sigma + it.$$

The relationship

$$\zeta(s) = \prod_{p} \left(1 - \frac{1}{p^s} \right)^{-1},$$

where the product is taken over all prime numbers, shows the connection between $\zeta(s)$ and prime number theory. From this relationship and the statement that $\zeta(s)$ cannot have the value zero whenever $\sigma = 1$, one can prove the *prime number theorem*, namely that the number of primes $\leq x$ is asymptotic to $x/\log x$. The celebrated Riemann hypothesis conjectures that all zeros of $\zeta(s)$ with $\sigma > 0$ satisfy $\sigma = \frac{1}{2}$. Many important results in number theory would follow if this statement were proved. The best computational results known have been obtained by R. P. Brent at the Australian National University at Canberra, Australia. At the time of this writing, it is known that the first 83,800,000 zeros of $\zeta(s)$ lie on the line $\sigma = \frac{1}{2}$.

REFERENCES

1969. Lehmer, D. H. "Computer Technology Applied to the Theory of Numbers," *Studies in Number Theory* **6**. MAA Studies in Mathematics.

1974. Selfridge, J. L. and Wunderlich, M. C. "An Efficient Algorithm for Testing Large Numbers for Primality," *Congressus Numerantium XII, Proceedings of the Fourth Manitoba Conference on Numerical Mathematics*, Winnipeg, pp. 109–120.

1976. Guy, R. K. "How to Factor a Number," *Congressus Numerantium XVI, Proceedings of the Fifth Manitoba Conference on Numerical Mathematics*, Winnipeg, pp. 49–89.

1977. Ribenboim, P. *13 Lectures on Fermat's Last Theorem*. Berlin: Springer-Verlag.

1978. Williams, H. C. "Primality Testing on a Computer," *ARS Combinatoria* **5**: 127–185.

M. C. WUNDERLICH

NUMERICAL ANALYSIS

For articles on related subjects *see* ALGORITHM; APPROXIMATION THEORY; ERROR ANALYSIS; ERRORS, ABSOLUTE AND RELATIVE; FAST FOURIER TRANSFORM; FINITE ELEMENT METHOD; MATHEMATICAL PROGRAMMING; MATHEMATICAL SOFTWARE; MATRIX COMPUTATIONS; PARTIAL DIFFERENTIAL EQUATIONS, NUMERICAL SOLUTION OF; ROUNDOFF ERROR; and SCIENTIFIC APPLICATIONS.

Numerical analysis is concerned with the development, analysis, and use of algorithms that simulate physical and social processes. It is a practical science, involving as it does the production of numbers that approximate the solution of mathematical models of physical and social systems. It is a very old science. Many famous mathematicians from the eighteenth and nineteenth centuries—including Gauss, Newton, and Fourier, to mention a few—developed numerical algorithms, which are still widely used. The advent of computers provided a tremendous impetus to the study and development of numerical analysis, and indeed led to so many new advances that it is now common to refer to the period from 1950 to the present as the era of "modern numerical analysis." High-speed computers have made it possible for us to solve ever more complex problems and, as a result, to gain much better insight into complex processes. It is quite accurate to say that modern technological achievements in such areas as space and atomic energy would have been impossible without high-speed computers and advances in numerical analysis.

Computers have affected the direction of numerical analysis in several important ways. They have forced numerical analysts to search for algorithms that are computationally fast and efficient, and to search for a better understanding of error analysis. Algorithms that produce speed-up factors on the order of 100 or more have been discovered in such areas as harmonic analysis, the solution of large linear systems by iterative methods, and matrix eigenvalue problems, to mention a few. Computers have also generated new problems for numerical analysts. For example, because computers work with finite word lengths and because of the inexactness of conversion from one number base to another, roundoff errors are inevitably introduced. These errors in turn propagate in very complicated ways. Numerical analysts are concerned about the effect of the totality of such errors on the accuracy of the results. Statistical methods of error analysis yield some promise in this area, but the most effective approach to date is that of backward error analysis, due to Wilkinson (1960).

In backward error analysis one shows that the *computed* results are the exact solutions of a perturbed problem and that the bounds for the perturbations can be obtained numerically. By comparing the perturbed problem and the given problem, one can then decide on how much confidence one can place in the computed results.

Another problem introduced by computers is that of numerical instability. Errors introduced into a computation, from whatever source, propagate in different ways. In some algorithmic processes these errors tend to grow exponentially, with disastrous computational results. An algorithm that exhibits such exponential error growth is said to be numerically unstable. Numerical analysts therefore seek algorithms that are not only fast and efficient, but also stable at the same time.

The complexity of error analysis has also led to the development of automatic error analysis procedures. In such automatic error procedures an attempt is made to have the computer monitor the error at each stage of the computation and to adjust parameters automatically so as to reduce the error in subsequent computations. The adaptive integration schemes for quadrature, which will be described in a later section, provide one example of such automatic error-monitoring algorithms. Traditional numerical analysis usually deals with the following topics.

1. Root-finding methods for a single equation or for systems of equations.
2. Interpolation.
3. Approximation.
4. Numerical differentiation.
5. Numerical quadrature.
6. Solution of linear systems.
7. Matrix eigenvalue problems.
8. Solution of ordinary differential equations.
9. Boundary value problems.
10. Solution of partial differential equations.

In an article of this length, one can hope to provide only a brief glimpse of the algorithms available in each of these areas. In this section are brief discussions of algorithms for root finding, interpolation, numerical differentiation, numerical quadrature, and ordinary differential equations. Ralston and Rabinowitz (1978), Conte (1972), and Hamming (1973) give a more detailed treatment of each of these areas. Topics 3, 6, 7, and 10 above are discussed in separate articles in this encyclopedia.

Roots of Equations. We consider first the problem of finding the roots of equations of one variable. Some examples of equations that arise in physics and engineering are:

1. $x^3 - x - 1 = 0$.
2. $e^x - \cos x = 0$.
3. $2x - \tan x = 0$.

It is only rarely possible to find roots of such equations explicitly, and we must therefore rely on numerical methods that produce approximate solutions.

The simplest of all methods for finding a simple real zero of a continuous function $f(x)$ is the *bisection method*. The process begins by finding an interval (a_0, b_0) which contains the desired zero α. If the zero is simple, then $f(a_0)$ and $f(b_0)$ must be opposite in sign, the usual test for this being based on the inequality

$$f(a_0)f(b_0) < 0.$$

The next step is to bisect the interval (a_0, b_0); i.e., compute $m = \frac{1}{2}(a_0 + b_0)$. We then evaluate $f(m)$ and form the product $f(a_0)f(m)$. If this product is negative, then we know that the zero lies in the interval (a_0, m); otherwise, it must be in the interval (m, b_0). Of course, if $f(a_0)f(x_m) = 0$, then m is the desired zero. We now bisect the smaller interval, which is known to contain the zero α, and the entire process is repeated until the zero is obtained to the accuracy desired. The procedure is summarized in algorithmic form below.

The Bisection Algorithm. Given a function $f(x)$ continuous on the interval (a_0, b_0) and such that $f(a_0)f(b_0) \leq 0$.

For $n = 0, 1, 2, \ldots$, until satisfied, do:
Set $m = (a_n + b_n)/2$.
If $f(a_n)f(m) \leq 0$, set $a_{n+1} = a_n$, $b_{n+1} = m$;
    otherwise, set $a_{n+1} = m$, $b_{n+1} = b_n$.
Then $f(x)$ has a root in the interval (a_{n+1}, b_{n+1}).

The phrase "until satisfied" used in this algorithm must be made precise in a program and is usually based on one of the following criteria.

1. $|f(m)| < \epsilon$;
2. $|b_{n+1} - a_{n+1}| < \delta$

where ϵ, δ are selected to achieve the desired accuracy.

As a simple example, consider the function $f(x) = x^3 - x - 1$. It is easy to verify that

$$f(1) = -1 < 0 < 5 = f(2).$$

Hence, there must be at least one zero of $f(x)$ on the interval $(1,2)$. In fact, there is exactly one zero on $(1,2)$. We call this zero α. The midpoint of the interval $(1,2)$ is 1.5, and we know that $\alpha \approx 1.5$ with an absolute error of at most 0.5. Now $f(1.5) = 0.875$ and $f(1)f(1.5) < 0$; hence, the zero lies in the interval $(1,1.5)$. Therefore, $\alpha \approx 1.25$, with absolute error less than 0.25. After 20 steps of this algorithm we find that

$$1.3247175 = a_{20} \le \alpha \le b_{20} = 1.3247184,$$
$$f(a_{20}) = (-1.857\cdots)10^{-6},$$
$$f(b_{20}) = (2.209\cdots)10^{-6}.$$

At this point we have six significant digits of accuracy. As this example shows, the bisection method always brackets the zero and provides an automatic bound on the approximation. Its simplicity makes it ideal for computer solution. On the other hand, it usually converges very slowly. If the function is complicated, this method is not very efficient and we are led to a search for methods that converge faster.

One such method is due to Newton. The algorithm for Newton's method is also quite simple.

Newton's Algorithm. Given $f(x)$ continuously differentiable and a starting approximation x_0. For $n = 0,1,2, \ldots$, until satisfied, do:

Calculate

$$x_{n+1} = x_n - \frac{f(x_n)}{f'(x_n)}. \tag{1}$$

Geometrically, Newton's method takes as a next approximation the intersection of the tangent to the curve $f(x)$ at the point x_n with the x-axis (see Fig. 1). We note that Newton's algorithm requires that the derivative $f'(x)$ be available.

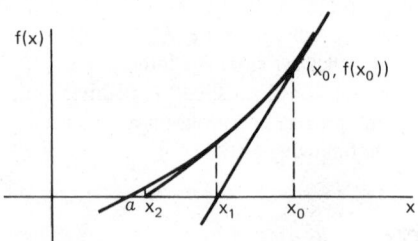

Fig. 1.   Newton's method.

For the example used above, $f(x) = x^3 - x - 1$, we have $f'(x) = 3x^2 - 1$, and Newton's algorithm leads to the iteration

$$x_{n+1} = x_n - \frac{x_n^3 - x_n - 1}{3x_n^2 - 1}.$$

Starting with $x_0 = 1$, we obtain the values in Table 1.

Table 1.   Newton's Method Applied to
$f(x) = x^3 - x - 1$

n	x_n
0	1.0
1	1.5
2	1.3478261
3	1.3252004
4	1.3247182
5	1.3247180

Since the iterates x_4, x_5 agree to seven significant digits, we take x_5 as an approximation to α, which is correct to at least that many digits.

The rapidity of convergence in this problem, even considering the fact that we do more work per step, shows that Newton's method is much more efficient than the bisection method. The tabular results also illustrate another important feature of this method. The number of correct digits, those underlined in Table 1, appears to double with each iteration. This observation is made more precise by the following theorem.

Theorem: Newton's Method. Let $f(x)$, $f'(x)$, $f''(x)$ be continuous and bounded on an interval containing the zero α. If x_0 is picked sufficiently close to α, then the iteration of Eq. (1) converges; moreover, for n large enough,

$$(x_{n+1} - \alpha) \approx K(x_n - \alpha)^2, \tag{2}$$

where K is a constant that depends on the derivatives of $f(x)$ at the point α.

The last inequality shows that the error of the $(n+1)$st iterate is proportional to the square of the error at the nth iterate, and demonstrates the eventual quadratic convergence of Newton's method. For this reason it is a very popular method. The most important disadvantage of Newton's method is that it will sometimes diverge or that it will converge to some zero other than the one desired. While the theorem guarantees convergence if x_0 is sufficiently close to α, it is difficult in practice to know what "sufficiently close" implies. A second disadvantage of Newton's method is that it requires that $f'(x)$

be computable. In many cases we may know $f(x)$ but not $f'(x)$.

A method that retains most of the advantages of Newton's method, but which does not require knowledge of $f'(x)$, is the secant method. It can be derived directly from Eq. (1) by replacing $f'(x_n)$ by a difference quotient:

$$f'(x_n) \approx \frac{f(x_n) - f(x_{n-1})}{x_n - x_{n-1}}. \tag{3}$$

We know from calculus that this difference quotient is a reasonable approximation to $f'(x_n)$, provided x_{n-1} is sufficiently close to x_n. Substituting expression (3) into Eq. (1), we obtain the secant iteration:

$$x_{n+1} = x_n - f(x_n) \frac{x_n - x_{n-1}}{f(x_n) - f(x_{n-1})}.$$

Stated in algorithmic form, we have

The Secant Algorithm. Given a function $f(x)$ and two points x_{-1}, x_0. For $n = 0, 1, 2, \ldots$ until satisfied, do: Calculate

$$x_{n+1} = x_n - f(x_n) \frac{x_n - x_{n-1}}{f(x_n) - f(x_{n-1})}. \tag{4}$$

Geometrically, as shown in Fig. 2, the secant method takes x_{n+1} as the intersection with the x-axis of the secant passing through the points (x_n, f_n) and (x_{n-1}, f_{n-1}).

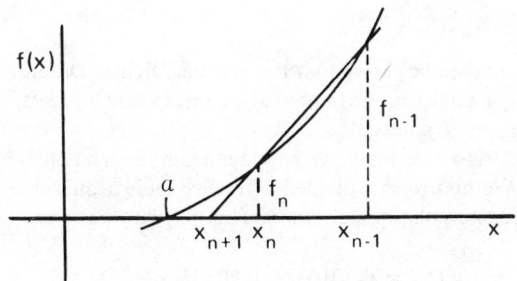

Fig. 2.   Secant method.

This method converges much more rapidly than the bisection method, but less rapidly than Newton's method. Its primary advantage is that it requires no knowledge of $f'(x)$.

There are many other methods that could be considered, including fixed-point iteration, the modified regula falsi, Steffensen iteration, etc. Those mentioned above are, however, used most commonly in practice. Moreover, each of these methods can be generalized to apply to systems of nonlinear equations. As applied to systems, he

ever, these methods frequently fail to converge, and in fact a great deal of research remains to be done to produce an effective computational method for finding zeros of nonlinear systems.

Interpolation.   We now describe briefly the process of interpolation. In its simplest form we are given the values of a function $f(x)$ at a selected set of points $\{x_i\}$ $(i = 0, 1, \ldots, n)$. The function $f(x)$ is usually not known explicitly, but its values at the selected points can be obtained either from a table of values or experimentally. The problem is to estimate the value of $f(x)$ at some nontabular point $\bar{x}$. In Table 2, for example, we are given the values of an unspecified function $f(x)$ at the indicated points. We may now be required to estimate the value of $f(x)$ at, say, $\bar{x} = 2.1$, or at any nontabular point. To do so, it is customary to select a simple class of functions, most commonly polynomials, which agree with the function $f(x)$ at the tabular points. We can then evaluate this polynomial at the point $x = \bar{x}$ to obtain the desired estimate. The simplest case is that of linear interpolation. Here we are given two points $\{x_0, x_1\}$ and the corresponding values $\{f(x_0), f(x_1)\}$. The equation of the linear polynomial (a straight line) which passes through the points $(x_0, f(x_0))$ and $(x_1, f(x_1))$ may be written in the following equivalent forms:

$$y = f_0 + \frac{f_1 - f_0}{x_1 - x_0}(x - x_0), \tag{5a}$$

$$y = f_0 \frac{x - x_1}{x_0 - x_1} + f_1 \frac{x - x_0}{x_1 - x_0}, \tag{5b}$$

where we have used the notation $f_0 = f(x_0)$, $f_1 = f(x_1)$. From either form it is easily verified that when $x = x_0$, $y = f_0$; and when $x = x_1$, $y = f_1$. Hence, the line passes through the two tabular points (x_0, f_0) and (x_1, f_1). Linear interpolation is pictured geometrically in Fig. 3.

Table 2

x	2.0	2.2	2.4	2.6
$f(x)$	0.30103	0.34242	0.38021	0.41497

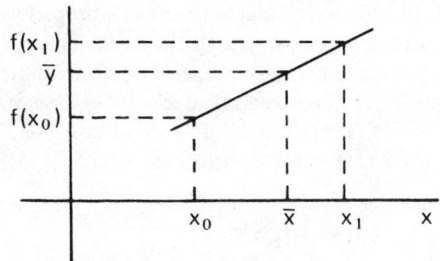

Fig. 3.   Linear interpolation.

To estimate $f(2.1)$ for the data in Table 2, using linear interpolation, substitute $x = 2.1$ into Eq. (5a) to obtain

$$y = 0.30103 + \frac{0.34242 - 0.30103}{2.2 - 2.0}(2.1 - 2.0)$$

$$= 0.30103 + 0.020695 = 0.321725.$$

This result "appears" to be reasonable, but we cannot say much about its accuracy. If the function varies greatly over the interval $[x_0, x_1]$, linear interpolation will generally give poor accuracy. It is reasonable to expect that if the actual function $f(x)$ is smooth, interpolation based on a higher degree polynomial will give better results than that based on lower-degree polynomials.

If we are given $n + 1$ values of x and $f(x)$, say $\{x_i, f_i\}$ $(i = 0, 1, \ldots, n)$, then we can pass a polynomial of degree n through these points. It can be proved that if the points x_i are distinct, the interpolating polynomial of degree less than or equal to n is unique. However, it can be expressed in many different forms. One such form is the Lagrangian form defined by

$$p_n(x) = \sum_{k=0}^{n} f(x_k)\ell_k(x), \tag{6a}$$

where the $\ell_k(x)$, $k = 0, 1, \ldots, n$ are defined by

$$\ell_k(x) = \prod_{\substack{i=0, \\ i \neq k}}^{n} \frac{(x - x_i)}{(x_k - x_i)}.$$

Since each $\ell_k(x)$ is a polynomial of degree n, it is obvious that $p_n(x)$ is a polynomial of degree *at most* n and, furthermore, it is evident by direct substitution that $p_n(x_j) = f(x_j)$ $(j = 0, 1, \ldots, n)$. Another form of the interpolating polynomial which is more convenient than the Lagrangian form is the "Newton Divided Difference Polynomial." It is defined by

$$p_n(x) = a_0 + a_1(x - x_0) + a_2(x - x_0)(x - x_1)$$
$$+ \cdots + a_n(x - x_0) \cdots (x - x_{n-1}). \tag{6b}$$

In order for this polynomial to interpolate properly at the $n + 1$ distinct points $[x_k, f(x_k)]$, the coefficients a_k ($k = 0, 1, \ldots, n$) must be chosen properly. They are most conveniently derived from a so-called *divided difference* table (see Table 3). The divided difference of order one $f(x_0, x_1)$ for any 2 arguments x_0, x_1 is defined as

$$f(x_0, x_1) = \frac{f(x_1) - f(x_0)}{x_1 - x_0}.$$

Higher-order differences are then defined as the difference of two divided differences each of order one less.

Table 3.   Divided Difference Table

x	f	$f(,)$	$f(,,)$	$f(,,,)$
x_0	f_0			
		$f(x_0, x_1)$		
x_1	f_1		$f(x_0, x_1, x_2)$	
		$f(x_1, x_2)$		$f(x_0, x_1, x_2, x_3)$
x_2	f_2		$f(x_1, x_2, x_3)$	
		$f(x_2, x_3)$		$f(x_1, x_2, x_3, x_4)$
x_3	f_3		$f(x_2, x_3, x_4)$	
		$f(x_3, x_4)$		
x_4	f_4			

Thus, the divided difference of order two, $f(x_0, x_1, x_2)$ with arguments x_0, x_1, x_2 is defined by

$$f(x_0, x_1, x_2) = \frac{f(x_1, x_2) - f(x_0, x_1)}{x_2 - x_0}.$$

Similarly, the divided difference of order k, $f(x_0, x_1, \ldots, x_k)$ is defined by

$$f(x_0, x_1, \ldots, x_k) = \frac{f(x_1, \ldots, x_k) - f(x_0, \ldots, x_{k-1})}{x_k - x_0}.$$

If the coefficients a_k which appear in Eq. 6b are selected from the upper diagonal elements of Table 3, so that

$$a_0 = f_0, \ a_1 = f(x_0, x_1), \ a_2 = f(x_0, x_1, x_2), \ \ldots$$
$$a_k = f(x_0, x_1, \ldots, x_k),$$

it can then be shown that the Newton Divided Difference Polynomial (Eq. 6b) does indeed interpolate correctly at the $k + 1$ points $x_0, \ldots, x_k$.

As an example, we consider again the data of Table 2. We first form a divided difference table as in Table 4. The interpolating polynomial (Eq. 6b) now becomes

$$p_3(x) = 0.30103 + 0.20695(x - 2)$$
$$- 0.04500(x - 2)(x - 2.2) \tag{7}$$
$$+ 0.011875(x - 2)(x - 2.2)(x - 2.4).$$

Table 4

x	$f(x)$	$f(,)$	$f(,,)$	$f(,,,)$
2.0	0.30103			
		0.20695		
2.2	0.34242		−0.04500	
		0.18895		0.011875
2.4	0.38021		−0.037875	
		0.17380		
2.6	0.41497			

To find an estimate for $f(2.1)$, we set $x = 2.1$ in (7) to obtain

$$f(2.1) \approx p_3(2.1) = 0.30103 + 0.020695$$
$$+ 0.00045 + 0.000035625 = 0.3222106. \quad (8)$$

This example illustrates two important features of Newton polynomial interpolation. First, we can increase the degree of the interpolating polynomial by simply adding on additional terms. No recalculation of coefficients once obtained is necessary. Second, the error of the interpolating polynomial of a given degree can be estimated by examining the next term. Thus, in Eq. (8) the error in linear interpolation is approximately 0.00045, while the error in second-degree interpolation is 0.000035625. Notice that each term decreases in magnitude. A thorough study of the error in the interpolating polynomial is beyond the scope of this article. While it is true that for most smooth functions the error decreases as the degree of the interpolating polynomial increases, this does not always hold. In practice, it is usually better to use a low-degree polynomial over a smaller range of the points of tabulation than to use a high-degree polynomial over a larger range. This method of interpolation is called "piecewise polynomial interpolation." Interpolation is discussed in Wilkinson (1960) and Ralston and Rabinowitz (1978).

Numerical Differentiation. We turn next to a consideration of numerical differentiation. In the calculus differentiation is a well-defined process if the function to be differentiated is given explicitly. Thus, if $f(x) = \sin x$, $f'(x) = \cos x$ and if $f(x) = x \sin x$, then $f'(x) = \sin x + x \cos x$. Often, however, the function is not known explicitly. $f(x)$ may, for example, only be known at a set of tabular points. How do we then obtain an estimate of the derivative at a point? One answer is to rely on finite difference approximations to the derivative. The simplest of these approximations is the "forward difference formula," given by

$$f'(x_0) \approx \frac{f(x_0 + h) - f(x_0)}{h} = \frac{\Delta f_0}{h}. \quad (9)$$

where the forward difference operator Δf_0 is defined by (9) as $f(x_0 + h) - f(x_0)$.

Since the limit on the right as $h \to 0$ is the definition of $f'(x_0)$, if it exists, then we can expect that for h small enough, the difference quotient will be close to $f'(x_0)$. Geometrically, as shown in Fig. 4, the difference quotient is the slope of the chord joining the points $(x_0, f(x_0))$ and $(x_0 + h, f(x_0 + h))$.

It can be shown that the error in the forward difference formula is proportional to h. Hence, the approximation (9) is generally quite poor unless h is very small.

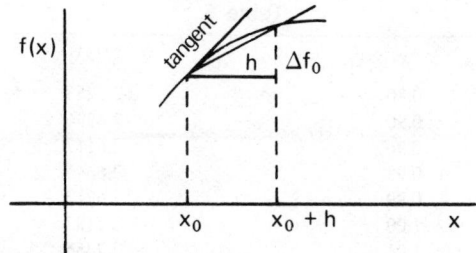

Fig. 4. Numerical approximation to $f'(x_0)$.

If, however, h is taken very small, then there is a possibility of serious loss of accuracy due to the fact that we will be subtracting two quantities, $f(x_0 + h)$ and $f(x_0)$, which are nearly equal in magnitude. This type of error arises because computers have fixed word lengths. It is usually referred to as a "loss of significant digits due to subtraction." For example, if $f(x_0) = 0.76482122$ and $f(x_0 + h) = 0.76482333$, then $f(x_0 + h) - f(x_0) = 0.00000211$, which in floating-point arithmetic will be written as $0.211 \cdot 10^{-5}$. Even if $f(x_0)$ and $f(x_0 + h)$ were correct to eight significant digits, the difference will be correct to only three significant digits. How, then, do we avoid this loss of significance? One way is to use a formula that has a smaller error term and hence will not require so small a value of h for a desired accuracy. One such formula is the "central difference formula":

$$D(f,h) = \frac{f(x_0 + h) - f(x_0 - h)}{2h}. \quad (10)$$

The error term for this formula is of the order h^2 ($0(h^2)$); i.e.,

$$f'(x_0) - D(f,h) = ch^2 \quad (11)$$

for some constant c, while the error for the forward difference formula is only $0(h)$. An even more accurate formula is

$$D^2(f,h) = -\frac{1}{12h} \{f(x_0 + 2h) - 8f(x_0 + h)$$
$$+ 8f(x_0 - h) - f(x_0 - 2h)\} \quad (12)$$

The error of this formula is given by

$$f'(x_0) - D^2(f,h) = 0(h^4). \quad (13)$$

Of course Eq. (13) requires more information about the function. Nevertheless, there is much less danger of loss of significance from subtraction, since we can use a considerably larger value of h.

To illustrate these formulas, consider the data in

Table 5

x	f(x)
0.80	2.2255
0.90	2.4596
0.96	2.6117
0.98	2.6645
0.99	2.6912
1.00	2.7183
1.01	2.7456
1.02	2.7732
1.04	2.8292
1.10	3.0042
1.20	3.3201

Table 5. Suppose that we wish to find an estimate of f' (1), using this data. The function tabulated in Table 5 is $f(x) = e^x$, and since $f'(x) = e^x$, $f'(1) = e \approx 2.7183$. Using the forward difference formula (9) with $h = 0.1$, we get

$$f'(1) \approx \frac{f(1.1) - f(1.0)}{0.1} = \frac{3.0042 - 2.7183}{0.1} = 2.8590,$$

while for $h = 0.01$, we get

$$f'(1) \approx \frac{f(1.01) - f(1.0)}{0.01}$$
$$= \frac{2.7456 - 2.7183}{0.01} = 2.7300.$$

Neither result here is very good.

If we now use the central difference formula (10) with $h = 0.1$, we obtain

$$f'(x_0) \approx \frac{f(1.1) - f(0.9)}{0.2}$$
$$= \frac{3.0042 - 2.4596}{0.2} = 2.7230,$$

while for $h = 0.04$ we obtain

$$f'(x_0) \approx \frac{f(1.04) - f(0.96)}{0.08} = 2.7188.$$

Finally, for $h = 0.01$ we find that

$$f'(x_0) \approx \frac{f(1.01) - f(0.99)}{0.02} = 2.7200.$$

These results are clearly better than those for the forward difference formula, but notice that the results for $h = 0.01$ are worse than those for $h = 0.04$. This is again due

to loss of significance. If we now use formula (12) with $h = 0.1$, we obtain

$$f'(x_0) \approx \frac{-1}{.12} \{f(1.2) - 8f(1.1) + 8f(0.9) - f(0.8)\}$$
$$= 2.7185,$$

a greatly improved result even with a rather coarse step h.

As this example shows, numerical differentiation is an unstable process. Even under the best of circumstances it is usually difficult to obtain good accuracy. By contrast, numerical integration, which we discuss next, is a very stable process.

Numerical Integration. We turn now to a consideration of numerical integration. The problem here in its simplest form is to compute an approximation to the definite integral

$$I = \int_a^b f(x)\, dx. \qquad (14)$$

Geometrically, we can interpret this problem as that of finding the area between the curve for $f(x)$ and the x-axis on the interval (a,b) (see Fig. 5).

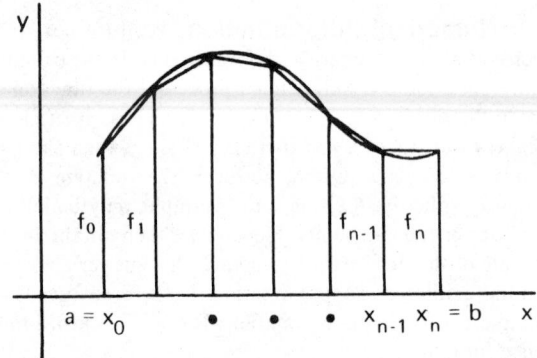

Fig. 5.   The trapezoidal rule.

The simplest usable formula based on equally spaced points for this purpose is the trapezoidal rule. This rule in its composite form consists of subdividing the interval (a,b) into N equal parts, each of length h, so that $Nh = b - a$. Also let $x_0 = a$, $x_1 = a + h$, ..., $x_N = b$, and $f(x_0) = f_0$, $f(x_1) = f_1$, etc. The area of a trapezoid over one panel (say, the first) is

$$T = \frac{h}{2}(f_0 + f_1).$$

Adding the areas over each panel leads to the composite trapezoidal formula

$$T_N = \frac{h}{2}(f_0 + 2f_1 + 2f_2 + \cdots + 2f_{N-1} + f_N).$$

How good is T_N as an approximation to the integral I? It is impossible to answer this question for all integrable functions $f(x)$. Sometimes the results are remarkably accurate, in some cases even exact. If we assume that the class of function we are considering is sufficiently smooth, then we might try to answer the question by examining the error in the approximation T_N. It can be shown that the error is given by

$$E = I - T_N = \frac{h^2(b-a)}{12}f''(\eta), \qquad a < \eta < b$$

The error here is called the *discretization error*. In general we will not know $f''(\eta)$, but we see that the error in T_N is proportional to h^2, where $h = (b-a)/N$. We can achieve any desired accuracy, at least mathematically, by taking h sufficiently small. As we decrease h, however, the required number of function evaluations will increase and the danger of roundoff error accumulation will also increase.

We have thus encountered a situation that arises frequently in numerical computations. The total error comes from two sources: a discretization error caused by using an approximate expression for the true mathematical operator, and a roundoff error. To achieve good accuracy in the mathematical sense, i.e., to reduce the discretization error, we need to take smaller divisions of h. Roundoff error, however, is inversely proportional to h. Hence, decreasing h increases roundoff error. The numerical analyst must therefore seek algorithms that in some sense minimize the totality of errors, those due to the sum of the absolute values of the discretization and roundoff errors.

Table 6 presents the results of applying the trapezoidal rule for various values of N to the integral

$$I = \int_0^1 e^{-x^2}\,dx$$

calculated using both single precision (SP) and double precision (DP) arithmetic.

The correct value of I to eight significant figures is 0.74682413. As N increases from 50 to 400, $T_N(SP)$ approaches the correct result. However, for $N = 800$, the results are worse. The difference between the single precision result and the double precision result shows that the poorer results are due entirely to roundoff error. Thus, for this example, the optimum single precision result

Table 6. Trapezoidal Rule Results for $I = \int_0^1 e^{-x^2}\,dx$

N	$T_N(SP)$	$T_N(DP)$
50	0.74679947	0.74679961
100	0.74681776	0.74681800
200	0.74682212	0.74682260
400	0.74682275	0.74682375
800	0.74682207	0.74682404

would be obtained for a value of N considerably less than $N = 800$. Even $N = 400$ requires considerable computational effort. This effort can be reduced by using a formula with a smaller discretization error.

One such formula is known as "Simpson's rule." It begins by subdividing the interval (a,b) into $2N$ equally spaced panels, each of length h. Hence, $2Nh = b - a$. Again the subdivision points are labeled x_i $(i = 0,1, \ldots, 2N)$ and the functional values $f(x_i) = f_i$ $(i = 0,1, \ldots, 2N)$. Over each panel of width $2h$ one now assumes that the function $f(x)$ can be approximated by a polynomial of degree 2 passing through the points (x_{2j}, f_{2j}), (x_{2j+1}, f_{2j+1}), (x_{2j+2}, f_{2j+2}), $(j = 0,1, \ldots, N-1)$. Integrating the polynomial over this panel then yields an approximation to the integral of $f(x)$ over this panel. Adding these approximations over all subpanels of width $2h$ leads to Simpson's quadrature formula S_{2N}:

$$S_{2N} = \frac{h}{3}(f_0 + 4f_1 + 2f_2 + 4f_3 + \cdots + 4f_{2N-1} + f_{2N}). \qquad (15)$$

The error of this formula is given by

$$I - S_{2N} = \frac{-h^4(b-a)}{180}f^{iv}(\xi), \qquad a < \xi < b.$$

Again we do not in general know $f^{iv}(\xi)$, but the error is proportional to h^4. Thus, for functions that are sufficiently smooth, Simpson's formula should require fewer subdivisions, at least theoretically, to obtain a required accuracy compared with the trapezoidal rule. In fact, for the example considered above, Simpson's rule with $N = 50$ yields the result 0.74682400 in single precision and the result 0.74682413 (which is correct to eight significant figures) in double precision. Obviously, Simpson's rule is computationally much more efficient than the trapezoidal rule in this case, and this remains true in general for most functions $f(x)$.

Having selected a method and a step h in either Simpson's formula or the trapezoidal rule, we are faced with the question: "How good are the results produced?"

The error term normally provides little help, since we usually cannot evaluate the derivatives involved. One way to build some confidence in the results is to solve the same problem several times with different values of h and then to compare the results. Thus, if one uses Simpson's rule with a step h and then with a step $h/2$, one will have two approximations to the integral. If these two approximations agree to s significant figures, the assumption is then made that the results are correct to s significant figures. This method, while not conclusive mathematically, does provide some basis for confidence in the results. Each halving of the step size doubles the amount of work, however, and if the function $f(x)$ is not "smooth," the halving process may have to be repeated many times. We will not precisely define "smoothness" of a function here. However, a function that wiggles a great deal on part of an interval will be harder to integrate than one that does not, and some functions may even have singularities within the interval. In Fig. 6 we exhibit a function of this type.

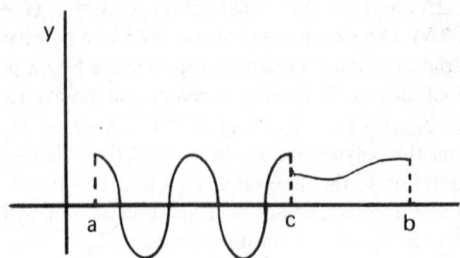

Fig. 6. A discontinuous function.

A finer subdivision will be required over the interval (a,c) than over the interval (c,b). At the point c there is a discontinuity in the function. If this is known to the user, then it is reasonable to write

$$\int_a^b f(x)\ dx = \int_a^c f(x)\ dx + \int_c^b f(x)\ dx.$$

The user, however, may not know that c is a point of discontinuity. An automatic approach, which has been used to handle such a situation in an efficient manner, is known as *adaptive integration*. It can be based on any basic integration formula, but we choose Simpson's rule for illustrative purposes. We are given an interval (a,b), the function $f(x)$, and an error ϵ, and a starting step size h.

The procedure for adaptive integration is as follows.

1. Divide the interval (a,b) into two equal parts. Call these I_1, I_2.
2. Using the subdivision h, integrate over each part separately to obtain $S_h(I_1), S_h(I_2)$.

3. Replace h by $h/2$; apply Simpson's rule again to obtain $S_{h/2}(I_1), S_{h/2}(I_2)$.
4. If $|S_h(I_1) - S_{h/2}(I_1)| \leq (\frac{1}{2})\epsilon$, accept $S_{h/2}(I_1)$ and store. If $|S_h(I_2) - S_{h/2}(I_2)| \leq (\frac{1}{2})\epsilon$, accept $S_{h/2}(I_2)$ and store.
5. If both or either of these are not satisfied, divide the interval or intervals into two parts. For definiteness, assume the test is not passed on I_2. Divide I_2 into two parts I_3 and I_4. Compute $S_{h/2}$ and $S_{h/4}$ on each part and test again, this time using a test like $|S_{h/2}(I_3) - S_{h/4}(I_3)| \leq (\frac{1}{4})\epsilon$, where the coefficient of ϵ is the ratio of the subinterval to the interval $b - a$.
6. Continue the process until the test is passed on each portion. The sum of the integrals over all portions then yields the desired approximation.

The advantage of adaptive schemes is that they do only as much work as necessary on each subinterval. Even discontinuities can be handled reasonably well by this approach.

Among other formulas based on equally spaced formulas, one should mention the Newton-Cotes formulas and Romberg integration. These quadrature formulas are capable of producing higher order error terms and thus hold the promise of further reduction in computational error.

Somewhat different in nature are integration formulas of the Gaussian type. All the formulas considered above are based on equally spaced points. In Gaussian formulas one attempts to select the integration points as well as the weights so as to produce a "best" integration formula. Such formulas have the form

$$I = \int_a^b f(x)\ dx \approx \sum_{i=0}^n w_i f(x_i),$$

where the points x_i as well as the weights w_i are to be determined. Such formulas, for a given number n of points, are capable of much higher accuracy. Gaussian methods can also be used to treat integrals with singularities. They are not, however, popularly used, primarily because the weights w_i and the points x_i turn out to be irrational numbers.

A more complete discussion of integration formulas can be found in Davis and Rabinowitz (1975).

Differential Equations. Now we consider methods for solving ordinary differential equations. In this section, we restrict ourselves to a first-order initial value problem; i.e., we are given an equation involving a function $y(x)$ and its derivative

$$y' = f(x,y) \tag{16a}$$

and an initial value such as

$$y'(x_0) = y_0. \qquad (16b)$$

We seek a continuous function $y(x)$ which satisfies Eq. (16a) subject to the initial value (16b). The theory of differential equations tells us that Eqs. (16a) and (16b) have a unique solution, provided certain conditions on $f(x,y)$ are satisfied. Closed-form solutions are sometimes, but not very often, possible. For example, the differential system

$$y' = y, \qquad y(x_0) = y_0$$

has the solution $y(x) = y_0(\exp(x - x_0))$. More often we must rely on numerical methods to obtain an approximation to the solution over a given interval.

Let a solution be required over an interval (x_0,b). We first subdivide the interval (x_0,b) into N equal parts of length h so that $Nh = b - x_0$, and we label the subdivision points $x_n = x_0 + nh$ $(n = 0,1,\ldots,N)$ with $x_N = b$. We will consider several methods that yield approximations y_n to the true solution $y(x_n)$ at the subdivision points. The simplest of all methods is that of Euler, depicted in Fig. 7.

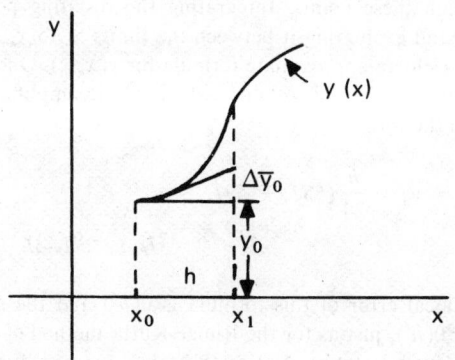

Fig. 7. Euler's method.

Geometrically, we find an approximate value of y at x_1 by extending the tangent to $y(x)$ at x_0 to the line $x = x_1$ and then adding to y_0 the increment $\Delta y_0 = hf(x_0,y_0)$. We thus obtain

$$y(x_1) \approx y_1 = y_0 + hf(x_0,y_0).$$

Note in Fig. 7 that the slope to the curve $y(x)$ is available immediately from the given equation $y' = f(x, y)$. Now

that we have an estimate y_1 at $x = x_1$, we can calculate $y' = f(x_1, y_1)$, and thus we can step ahead to obtain

$$y(x_2) \approx y_2 = y_1 + hf(x_1, y_1).$$

The general formula, which yields y_{n+1} when we know x_n, y_n, is

$$y_{n+1} = y_n + hf(x_n,y_n), \quad n = 0,1,\ldots,N-1. \qquad (17)$$

As an example, consider the equation

$$y' = -y^2 \qquad y(1) = 1 \qquad (18)$$

We choose $h = 0.1$ and apply formula (17) over the interval $(1,2)$. The results are given in Table 7. The exact solution of Eq. (17) is $y = 1/x$. The results of Euler's method with a step $h = 0.1$ produces about one-digit accuracy.

Table 7

n	x_n	y_n	$y(x_n) = 1/x_n$	$f(x_n,y_n) = -y_n^2$
0	1.	1.	1.	-1.
1	1.1	0.0	0.9090	-0.81
2	1.2	0.819	0.8333	-0.6708
3	1.3	0.7519	0.7692	-0.5654
4	1.4	0.6954	0.7143	-0.4836
5	1.5	0.6470	0.6667	-0.4186
6	1.6	0.6051	0.6250	-0.3661
7	1.7	0.5685	0.5882	-0.3232
8	1.8	0.5362	0.5555	-0.2875
9	1.9	0.5074	0.5263	-0.2575
10	2.0	0.4817	0.5000	-0.2320

An estimate of the error in Euler's method can be obtained by expanding $y(x_n + h)$ about x_n. Thus, application of Taylor's theorem with remainder yields

$$y(x_n + h) = y(x_n) + hy'(x_n) + \frac{h^2}{2}y''(\xi_n), \qquad x_n < \xi < x_n + h.$$

Hence, the error in one step of Euler's method is

$$y(x_n + h) - \{y(x_n) + hf(x_n,y_n)\} = \frac{h^2}{2}y''(\xi_n).$$

This is called the "local error" since it is based on the assumption that x_n, $y(x_n)$ are known exactly. Errors committed at each step will themselves propagate, and the global or total error at the end of N steps will be considerably larger. In fact the global error of Euler's method can be shown to be of order h instead of h^2. To achieve any kind of accuracy for the problem presented above will clearly require a much smaller value of h. As we decrease h, however, the amount of work increases because we must evaluate $f(x,y)$ once for each step and, in addition, our roundoff error problems will increase. In practice, therefore, it is advisable to use formulas that are of higher order; i.e., we seek formulas for which the error is $0(h^p)$ with p greater than 1.

A direct use of Taylor's theorem carried to more terms would yield a formula of the form

$$y(x_n + h) = y(x_n) + hy'(x_n) + \frac{h^2}{2} y''(x_n$$
$$+ \cdots + \frac{h^k}{k!} y^{(k)}(x_n) + \frac{h^{k+1}}{(k+1)!} y^{(k+1)}(\xi_n) \quad (19)$$

If we use the first $k + 1$ terms of this formula to predict $y(x_{n+1})$, then the error would be of order h^{k+1}. Taylor's theorem in this form is difficult to use because the higher derivatives of $y(x)$ are generally not easily computable. Runge first discovered formulas that achieve agreement with the Taylor expansion for different values of k, but which depend only upon the evaluation of $f(x,y)$. One such formula is

$$y_{n+1} = y_n + \frac{h}{6}(k_1 + 2k_2 + 2k_3 + k_4), \quad (20)$$

where:

$$[nt k_1 = hf(x_n,y_n),$$
$$k_2 = hf\left(x_n + \frac{h}{2}, y_n + \frac{k_1}{2}\right),$$
$$k_3 = hf\left(x_n + \frac{h}{2}, y_n + \frac{k_2}{2}\right),$$
$$k_4 = hf(x_n + h, y_n + k_3).$$

The local error of this method is $0(h^5)$ and the global error is $0(h^4)$. It is called a "Runge-Kutta fourth-order" method; no derivatives of y other than $y' = f(x,y)$ are required. We note, however, that we must evaluate $f(x,y)$ at four different points for each step of the integration. By comparison with Euler's method, this Runge-Kutta method is far more efficient and, in addition, round-off error is considerably less for the same accuracy. For the example presented in Eq. (18), again using $h = 0.1$, at $x = 1.1$ we obtain $y_1 = 0.090909$, which agrees with the exact result $1/1.1$ to all digits shown, indeed a remarkable improvement over the Euler result. The Runge-Kutta method and variations of it are very popular. It provides

good accuracy, it is simple to program, it requires minimum storage, and it is stable. Its principal disadvantage, compared to methods based on finite differences, is that it requires four function evaluations per integration step.

Next we discuss the so-called multistep methods which make it possible to achieve comparable accuracy with about half the amount of work. Runge-Kutta methods are called "one-step" methods because they use information at a single point to estimate y at the next point. Let us suppose that we have already estimated $y(x)$ at several successive subdivision points. For definiteness, assume that we know

$$(x_n, y_n, f_n), \qquad (x_{n-1}, y_{n-1}, f_{n-1}),$$
$$(x_{n-2}, y_{n-2}, f_{n-2}), \qquad (x_{n-3}, y_{n-3}, f_{n-3}),$$

where f_n represents $f(x_n, y_n)$, etc. How can this information be used to extrapolate a value for y at x_{n+1}? The theory of interpolation suggests one possible approach. If we integrate the equation $y' = f(x,y)$ from x_n to x_{n+1}, we obtain

$$y(x_{n+1}) - y(x_n) = \int_{x_n}^{x_{n+1}} f(x,y(x)) \, dx.$$

Since we know the value of f at the four successive points $x_n, x_{n-1}, x_{n-2}, x_{n-3}$ we can pass a polynomial of degree 3 through these points. Integrating the resulting polynomial and evaluating it between the limits x_n to x_{n+1} will then yield an approximate formula for $y(x_{n+1})$. One such formula is that of Adams, which after simplification, takes the form

$$y_{n+1} = y_n + \frac{h}{24}(55f_n - 59f_{n-1} + 37f_{n-2} - 9f_{n-3}). \quad (21)$$

The local error of this formula is $0(h^5)$ and the global error $0(h^4)$, just as for the Runge-Kutta method of order 4, discussed earlier. Notice that only one new function evaluation is required to compute y_{n+1}. It would thus appear that a formula of this type should be computationally more efficient than the Runge-Kutta method. It turns out that the accuracy of Adams' formula (21) is not quite so good as that of the Runge-Kutta method, even though both are of the same order, because the coefficient in the error term is somewhat larger. It is customary to consider the result of applying Eq. (21) as a predicted value and to correct it by using the formula

$$y_{n+1}^c = y_n + \frac{h}{24}\{9f(x_{n+1}, y_{n+1}^p) + 19f_n - 5f_{n-1} + f_{n-2}\}, \quad (22)$$

where y_{n+1}^p is the value obtained from Eq. (21). The global error of Eq. (22) is also $0(h^4)$. The pair of formulas (21) and (22) is called a *predictor-corrector* pair. It yields results comparable in accuracy to the Runge-Kutta method, with about half as much work. Multistep formulas such as (21) and (22) have the disadvantage of requiring special techniques for starting, since initially we have information at one point only. Some multistep methods also suffer from numerical instability, a phenomenon that can lead to disastrous results, and hence they should not be used indiscriminately.

A great deal of work has been done recently on multistep methods of higher order and on variable step size methods which attempt to select an optimum integration step. The reader is referred to Gear (1971) for discussion of these methods.

As with all numerical methods, we must ask: "How accurate are the results?" The fact that a method achieves good accuracy on one problem is no assurance that it will give comparable accuracy on another. One commonly used technique, analogous to the quadrature case, is to integrate the given differential equation twice, once with a step h and again with a step $h/2$. If the two solutions at the common subdivision points agree to s significant figures, we can then have some confidence in them. Indeed, if we are using the Runge-Kutta method and we let $y_{n+1}(h)$ represent the computed solution at x_{n+1}, then the discretization error can be represented roughly as

$$y(x_{n+1}) - y_{n+1}(h) = ch^4. \tag{23}$$

If we now replace h by $h/2$, the error is

$$y(x_{n+1}) - y_{n+1}\left(\frac{h}{2}\right) = c\left(\frac{h^4}{16}\right) \tag{24}$$

In these equations we assume that c is a constant that does not depend on h. Of course this assumption is not usually valid, but in many practical problems c will change only slowly, and in such cases the following analysis is valid. Even though we do not know the exact solution $y(x_{n+1})$, we can solve (23) and (24) for ch^4 and substitute in (24) to obtain

$$y(x_{n+1}) - y_{n+1}\left(\frac{h}{2}\right) = \frac{y_{n+1}(h/2) - y_{n+1}(h)}{15}. \tag{25}$$

This equation states that the error in $y_{n+1}(h/2)$ is given by the right side of Eq. (25), and this quantity is computable. Notice, however, that to obtain this error estimate we pay a severe price in computational effort, in fact more than twice the effort for a single solution.

On the other hand, if we run a multistep predictor-corrector formula such as either Eq. (21) or (22), a similar error estimate can be obtained with almost no additional effort. This can be seen from the equations

$$y(x_{n+1}) - y_{n+1}^p = c_1 h^4,$$
$$y(x_{n+1}) - y_{n+1}^c = c_2 h^4,$$

where c_1, c_2 are known constants. Eliminating h^4 as in Eq. (25), we obtain the error estimate

$$y(x_{n+1}) - y_{n+1}^c = \frac{c_2}{c_1 - c_2}(y_{n+1}^c - y_{n+1}^p).$$

The right-hand side, which is easily computable, is the error in going from one point x_n to the next point x_{n+1}. It can therefore be used as a basis for deciding whether the step size h is too small, too large, or about right. This is perhaps the most important advantage of multistep methods. They provide a basis for automatic monitoring of the error at little additional cost.

Boundary Value Problems. Differential equations of order higher than one are classified either as *initial value problems* or as *boundary value problems*. In general, a differential equation of order n which can be expressed in the form

$$y^{(N)}(x) = f(x, y(x), y'(x), \ldots, y^{(N-1)}(x))$$

requires N conditions if it is to yield a unique solution. If these N conditions are all specified at one point, say $x = x_0$, then we have an *initial value problem*. If these conditions are specified at more than one point, then we have a *boundary value problem*. The methods previously considered for a single differential equation can be directly adapted to apply to initial value problems of any order. Boundary value problems are more complicated and require a different approach. Among the methods most commonly used for such problems are *finite difference methods, the finite element method, shooting methods,* and *collocation methods*. We shall restrict our discussion to a consideration of the finite difference method as applied to a second order equation. We assume a second order equation in the form

$$y''(x) + f(x)y'(x) + g(x)y(x) = q(x) \tag{26}$$

subject to the boundary conditions

$$y(a) = \alpha, \qquad y(b) = \beta, \tag{27}$$

where $f(x)$, $g(x)$, and $q(x)$ are given coefficient functions with sufficient continuity requirements. The problem is to find an approximate solution of Eq. 26 over an interval (a, b) which satisfies the boundary conditions (Eq. 27) at $x = a$ and $x = b$.

We first divide the interval (a, b) into N equal parts of width h so that $Nh = b - a$. We set $x_0 = a$, $x_N = b$ and we define the *mesh points* $x_n = x_0 + nh$ ($n = 0, 1, \ldots, N$). The corresponding values of y, f, g, and q are denoted by $y_n = y(x_0 + nh)$, etc. The next step is to replace each derivative appearing in Eq. 26 by an appropriate finite difference approximation. We use central difference approximations defined by

$$y'(x_n) \approx \frac{y(x_{n+1}) - y(x_{n-1})}{2h} = \frac{y_{n+1} - y_{n-1}}{2h},$$

$$y''(x_n) \approx \frac{y(x_{n+1}) - 2y(x_n) + y(x_{n-1})}{h^2}$$

$$= \frac{y_{n+1} - 2y_n + y_{n-1}}{h^2}.$$

Substituting these into Eq. 26 leads to the finite difference equation,

$$\frac{y_{n-1} - 2y_n + y_{n+1}}{h^2} + \frac{f_n(y_{n+1} - y_{n-1})}{2h} + g_n y_n = q_n.$$

Multiplying by h^2 and grouping terms we obtain

$$\left(1 - \frac{h}{2} f_n\right) y_{n-1} + (-2 + h^2 g_n) y_n$$
$$+ \left(1 + \frac{h}{2} f_n\right) y_{n+1} = h^2 q_n. \quad (28)$$

When Eq. 28 is written out for $n = 1, 2, \ldots, N - 1$, we will obtain a linear system of $N - 1$ equations for the $N - 1$ unknown values $y_1, y_2, \ldots, y_{N-1}$. Of course, y_0 and y_N are specified by the conditions of Eq. 27. More explicitly, we obtain the system

$$(-2 + h^2 g_1) y_1 + \left(1 + \frac{h}{2} f_1\right) y_2$$
$$= h^2 q_1 - \left(1 - \frac{h}{2} f_1\right) \alpha,$$

$$\left(1 - \frac{h}{2} f_2\right) y_1 + (-2 + h^2 g_2) y_2$$
$$+ \left(1 + \frac{h}{2} f_2\right) y_3 = h^2 q_2;$$

$$\cdots\cdots\cdots\cdots\cdots\cdots\cdots$$

$$\left(1 - \frac{h}{2} f_{N-2}\right) y_{N-3} + (-2 + h^2 g_{N-2}) y_{N-2} +$$

$$\left(1 + \frac{h}{2} f_{N-2}\right) y_{N-1} = h^2 q_{N-2},$$

$$\left(1 - \frac{h}{2} f_{N-1}\right) y_{N-2} + (-2 + h^2 g_{N-1}) y_{N-1}$$

$$= h^2 q_{N-1} - \left(1 + \frac{h}{2} f_{N-1}\right) \beta. \quad (29)$$

This linear system of equations can be solved readily by standard methods, some of which are described in the article on MATRIX COMPUTATIONS. Actually, because the matrix of coefficients of the system shown (Eq. 29) is *tridiagonal*, a computer solution can be found very efficiently. The solution of this system will be the values $y_1, \ldots, y_{N-1}$, which approximates the solution function $y(x)$ at the mesh points. The accuracy of these approximations will depend upon how fine a mesh is chosen; i.e., on the value of h or N.

The method of finite differences works quite well on linear differential equations of any order. However, if the differential equation is nonlinear, this method becomes more complicated, and in such cases the shooting or collocation methods may be more appropriate.

Conclusion. In a short article on numerical analysis, one can hope to present to the reader only a synopsis of the work of the numerical analyst. We have discussed only a small number of algorithms. These algorithms work well on some classes of functions, but no algorithm is uniformly best for all classes of functions. The numerical analyst must be constantly alert to indications that an algorithm is not functioning properly. We have tried to stress those qualities of good algorithms which are important for computational purposes. These qualities are speed, efficiency, and automatic error analysis and control. There are many good books on numerical analysis at various levels for the reader interested in pursuing this subject, among which are Ralston and Rabinowitz (1978), Conte (1972), and Hamming (1973).

REFERENCES

1960. Wilkinson, J. H. "Error Analysis of Floating Point Computations," *Num. Math.*, **2**: 319–340.
1971. Gear, C. W. *Numerical Initial Value Problems in Ordinary Differential Equations.* Englewood Cliffs, N.J.: Prentice-Hall.
1972. Conte, S. D. and deBoor, Carl J. *Elementary Numerical Analysis: An Algorithmic Approach.* New York: McGraw-Hill.
1973. Hamming, R. W. *Numerical Methods for Scientists and Engineers,* 2nd Ed. New York: McGraw-Hill.
1975. Davis, P. and Rabinowitz, P. *Methods in Numerical Integration.* New York: Academic Press.
1978. Ralston, A. and Rabinowitz, P. *A First Course in Numerical Analysis, 2nd Ed.* New York: McGraw-Hill.

S. D. CONTE

O

OBJECT PROGRAM

For articles on related subjects *see* Compiler; Language Processors; Procedure-Oriented Languages; and Source Program.

An object program is the output of a translating program, such as an assembler or a compiler, which converts a *source program* written in one language into another language, such as machine language, capable of being executed on a given computer.

This output may be in one of several forms: It may be in an intermediate language, needing further translating; it may be *relocatable,* in which data and program references are still expressed relative to a base address; or it may be *absolute,* in which all linkages between program elements have been made, and absolute address assignments established, so that the program is ready to be loaded and executed. Usage varies as to which of these may be called the *object program.* Properly, any output of a translating program is the object of that step, and hence is an object program.

C. H. Davidson

OCR. *See* Optical Character Readers.

OEM. *See* Original Equipment Manufacturer.

OFFICE AUTOMATION

For articles on related subjects *see* Administrative Applications; Data Processing; Terminals; Text Editing; and Word Processing.

Office automation is the application of computer and communications technology to improve the productivity of clerical and managerial office workers. In the mid-1950s, the term was used as a synonym for almost any form of data processing, referring to the ways in which bookkeeping tasks were automated. After some years of disuse, the term was revived in the mid-1970s to describe the interactive use of word and text processing systems, which would later be combined with powerful computer tools, thereby leading to a so-called "integrated electronic office of the future."

The major functional components of an office automation system include text processing, electronic mail, information storage and retrieval, personal assistance features, and task management. These may be implemented on various types of hardware and usually include a video display terminal, a keyboard for input, and a hard-copy output device for "letter-quality" printing.

Initially, systems sold by major manufacturers were aimed at clerical and secretarial personnel. These were mainly developed to do word processing and record processing (maintenance of small sequential files, such as names and addresses, which are ultimately sorted and merged into letters).

More recently, attention has also been focused on systems which directly support the principals (managers and professional workers). Such systems emphasize the managerial communications function.

Electronic mail and filing permit a user to compose and transmit a message on an office automation system. In the early 1970s, the ARPANET community developed a number of such systems which have been heavily used. Through standard message format protocols, several hundred different computers and electronic mail interfaces are able to exchange information with one another. These protocols are like the post office's specification of how recipient and return addresses should appear on envelopes, and which sizes are allowable for envelopes. In the electronic message world, they describe what sequences of characters are required at the beginning of a message to identify the sending and receiving mailboxes (currently, the characters "⟨**carriage return**⟩**To**:" must precede the recipient's name, and "⟨**carriage return**⟩**From**:" precedes the sender's user-name and machine identification. It is not uncommon for people in widely dispersed locations to collaborate and communicate almost exclusively via *electronic mail*.

Automating the filing system of an office has proven to be most difficult for documents which are not created on some electronic system. These enter the electronic storage medium in one of several ways. They may be scanned using a facsimile or image scanner for later viewing on a CRT or as facsimile hard copy. They may be microfilmed or microfiched, with the user supplying some index terms for a document to the system. Later, the microimage reader moves the proper frame into view under computer control. Or, the entire text may be re-keyed into the system.

Once the document is captured electronically, indexing becomes the main problem. One can index by keywords only, or attempt, as some legal retrieval systems do, to index every single word. These issues have been thought out in the library information retrieval context over many years. There is also some experimentation with other indexing cues, such as spatial (the document is on the "second" shelf on the right in some computer image of an office) and pictorial (a graphic symbol is shown on a CRT; e.g., a dollar sign for budget information).

Calendar and scheduling systems are seen as a software component in an office automation system. Users keep their appointment lists in a database, and can request meetings by having the system search for available time blocks. The schedule may also include reminders, which can jog a user's memory of an event or thing to do.

The term *paperless office* implies one of the long-term goals of office automation. Today, much user interaction is done through a video display terminal. The desk it replaces is often 10–100 times larger in surface area. People often wish to work with or examine 5 or 6 items simultaneously, which is impossible on a 24 by 80 character screen (the predominant type available today). As these technologies improve to permit more information to be displayed simultaneously, this goal may become more attainable.

Where printed output is desired, one of three primary methods can be used to produce it. Impact printing is used for low speeds (15–50 characters/second) and high quality, ink jet and variants for medium speeds (90–200 chps), and electronic or laser printing for very high speeds (2,000–20,000 chps). These electronic printers can also print forms and graphics along with the text.

Interaction with users is by and large keyboard limited, although Engelbart and Xerox have pioneered in the use of a "mouse" as a pointing device. (This is a small box, with three buttons on the top used to indicate that desired positions have been reached, and a sensor built into the underside, which is rolled around on any flat surface. Its direction of movement is sensed and transmitted to the computer, which translates the movement into cursor movement on a screen.) Voice input, though already achieved for limited sets of words from known speakers, is not yet well enough developed to permit production of an old dream—the talking typewriter.

The major elements discussed above are examples of mechanized tools, each of which make some task (composing, reading, etc.) more efficient. The overall understanding of what goes on in offices and how to represent it is an aspect of task management. A task management system takes a description of an office process, and invokes appropriate tools at appropriate times. For example, Zisman (1978), using Petri nets (*q.v.*) augmented with production systems, represented such diverse processes as the review of a technical paper submitted to a journal, an application for a home mortgage, and a budget approval cycle. The events, actions, and documents generated are described in a precise language. Similar work at Xerox is based on a concept of principals being manipulators of business forms. Hardware and software to facilitate this have been built.

The office automation field is under heavy development and is evolving rapidly. As processing and storage costs drop, more functionality can be put into the "intelligent" terminals. The availability of public data networks permits intracompany exchanges. The increased use of more sophisticated software and hardware interfaces (e.g., color, graphics, and touch panels) to simplify and reduce training gives us hope that office automation can be effective in increasing the productivity of the "knowledge workers" in offices everywhere.

REFERENCES

1973. Engelbart, D. "Design Consideration for Knowledge Workshop Terminals," in *Proceedings of the 1973 National Computer Conference,* pp. 221–227 (June).

1976. Morgan, Howard L. "Office Automation: A Research Perspective," in *Proceedings of the 1976 National Computer Conference.*

1978. Zisman, M. D. "Office Automation: Revolution or Evolution?" *Sloan Management Review* (Spring).

1980. Ellis, C. and Nutt, G. "Office Information Systems and Computer Science," *Computing Surveys* **12**: 27–60.

H. L. MORGAN

ONE-LEVEL MEMORY

For articles on related subjects *see* ADDRESSING; CACHE MEMORY; STORAGE HIERARCHY; MEMORY; and VIRTUAL MEMORY.

One-level memories are computer memories in which all stored items are accessed by a uniform mechanism. In computer systems that possess such a memory, the programmer is relieved from considerations of data residence, and does not have to be concerned with I/O manipulations to access data that is stored on auxiliary memory devices. This is in contrast to the more common situation in which the programmer has to distinguish between main memory and auxiliary memory resident data, and has to monitor in the program all the changes of residence for each data item and program module.

One-level memories, and the mechanisms provided to implement them, are related to *virtual memories.* However, virtual memories are introduced only to provide a user with a larger main memory space. Thus, in using a virtual memory, the programmer is not relieved of the need to be cognizant of auxiliary devices for the reading and writing of files. Another major difference between a virtual memory and a one-level memory is in the protection mechanisms, as will be explained below.

One-level memories and the access mechanisms associated with them can be implemented in various ways. The hardware support for the implementation is usually a memory hierarchy, in which physical memories built of different technologies and possessing different access and storage characteristics are connected together. The choice of sizes and technologies usually reflects the price/performance criteria chosen by the implementor, and typically constitutes a range starting from a small but very high-speed memory (e.g., a cache) through larger fast memory (e.g., main memory) and through still larger medium-speed memories (e.g., bubble memories or high-speed drums) into high-volume pseudo-random access devices (e.g., disks), and in some cases into a very large but slow archival device. To construct a one-level memory from such a hierarchy requires the addition of hardware, firmware, and software, which then allows the user to access the entire memory hierarchy in a uniform manner.

Since a one-level memory access mechanism re-places regular I/O to peripheral devices, it has to include in it those protection mechanisms that are available in file access systems. Therefore, one-level addressing is more complex as well as more powerful than regular memory addressing. It typically relies on the division of the whole addressing space into *segments,* each of which possesses its own protection and access characteristics. In particular, one-level memory is well suited to *capability* type addressing, in which the access rights of each process are matched with the execution and access characteristics of other processes, data items, or devices. One-level memories are thus ideal candidates for accessing data in a highly secure operating system.

REFERENCE

1972. Organick, E. I. *The Multics System: An Examination of its Structure.* Cambridge, MA: M.I.T. Press.

G. FRIEDER

OPEN AND CLOSE A FILE

For articles on related subjects *see* BLOCKS AND BLOCKING; FILES; INPUT-OUTPUT CONTROL SYSTEMS; LOGICAL AND PHYSICAL UNITS; SCRATCH FILE; TAPE LABEL; and UPDATE.

A file is considered *open* when it may be accessed for reading, writing, or possibly both. It is considered *closed* when it cannot be so accessed. The open routines change the state of a file from closed to open; the close routines do the opposite.

The open and close routines are the primary mechanisms by which various parameters in the logical device tables and physical device tables are initialized, or stored, and the associations between logical and physical device tables are maintained. The open and close routines also handle the initialization and update of tape and file labels. After the open routines have been executed, all data needed for further processing is available in the appropriate table. When a file has been closed, the file is in a state suitable for subsequent reopening.

When a program opens a data file, it often declares a number of attributes that the file will have. It is the responsibility of the open routines to initialize the proper table entries to reflect the declared attributes. For example, a file of data typically may be opened for reading only, writing only, or in some cases for both reading and writing (update). As another example, most systems allow a programmer to create a file for temporary storage of data. In such cases, the temporary file will be destroyed at the end of the job.

Upon receipt of a request to open an existing permanent file, the open routines must first find the file, which usually involves the accessing of the system catalogs and/or, if the file is one of several on the same tape reel, the positioning of the tape at the appropriate point. With indexed sequential files where the index is to be kept in main storage, the open routines will locate the index and read it into an internal buffer. If the file has been declared as temporary, then the open routines will interact with the secondary storage allocation routines to reserve space for the data that will be saved.

The next task is one of label verification and initialization of logical and physical device tables with parameters that are carried in the label. Assuming the file resides on a tape and that the operator has mounted the correct reel, the open routines will locate such file parameters as the blocking factor, the density at which information is recorded, and the description of allocated storage areas and storage formats. These parameters will be copied to the proper fields in the logical and physical device tables.

The open routines will also set the read/write/update status so that subsequent requests can be checked for validity. If the file is to be written, then a fresh label must be created, giving the date written, the edition number (multiple copies of files with the same name are updated by editions, much like newspapers), and all other pertinent data that resides in the tape label.

If the file resides on a disk or similar shared device, control information similar to that in a tape label will be accessed by the open routines in order to initialize tables. Like a tape label, this file-control information is stored with the file and gives information concerning blocking factors, storage allocation, and storage organization. The storage organization information will often be more complex than with a file on tape. For example, the strategy to be used when storing new records that might not fit in a given storage area (*overflow policies*) would be part of the file control information for some files stored on a disk.

Unlabeled files are also allowed in most systems. They are the normal case for data residing on punched cards. In such situations, the open routines will ignore the label verification phase. Needed control information such as physical record size must be provided by other means—e.g., as an argument to the open routines — so that table entries can still be initialized.

The routines to close a file have a number of tasks to perform before the file is ready for subsequent reopening. First, some of the data that has been logically "written" may still reside in a buffer because the buffer was not full and no physical "write" had been generated. The close routines will cause that data to be transferred to the recording medium. An end-of-file marker and perhaps also an end-of-file label will then be written if the file resides on tape. Alternately, if the file is on a direct-access device, the routines to close a file will restore indices and

file-control information to their allotted storage locations, updating them to reflect any changes in the status of the file. Closing a temporary file usually results in the release of the allotted file space.

When the file is on tape, the closing routines may or may not rewind the file; often the programmer specifies which option is desired. If the file is rewound, then subsequent reopening causes the first record of the previously closed file to be processed. If not, then the next file on the tape will be processed on the subsequent opening.

Closing a file also results in the logical device table for the appropriate logical device being restored to a state that indicates that there is no file currently attached to this device. This allows subsequent requests on the logical device to be invalidated.

R. W. Taylor

OPEN AND CLOSED SHOP

For articles on related subjects *see* Computing Center; and Security of Computer Installations, Physical.

The terms *open shop* and *closed shop* refer to operating policies and procedures of a computer center. An *open shop* permits users to enter their programs into the computer and to operate consoles and peripheral equipment without assistance from a professional staff. A *closed shop* requires users to submit their programs at a terminal isolated from the central computer site or to submit their programs to an operator (I/O handler, control clerk, etc.) at the central site, who enters them into the computer.

Microcomputers operate, almost by definition, in open-shop mode. Most minicomputer installations also operate as open shops, since (1) equipment and software are simple to operate, (2) the cost of the installation is relatively small, and hence (3) inefficiencies incurred by letting users operate the equipment are less costly than maintaining a staff of computer operators. Also, (4) minicomputer users tend to be more knowledgeable about machine operations than are users of a large, closed-shop facility.

Most large, multiprogrammed computers are operated as closed shops, since the second-by-second cost of the facility is too high to permit waste of time by amateur operators. Also, the complexity and physical security aspects of large installations require a full-time operations staff to police the machine room for hazards, unauthorized visitors, etc., as well as to service continually the consoles and peripheral equipment of the computer.

D. N. Freeman

OPERAND

For articles on related subjects *see* ADDRESSING; ARGUMENT; and POLISH NOTATION.

An operand is the entity on which operations are performed. In a typical computer, an instruction will specify an operation such as FETCH, ADD, MOVE, MULTIPLY, EDIT, etc. It will also usually specify one or more operands (see Fig. 1). The operands are the data items that will be fetched, added, moved, multiplied, edited, etc.

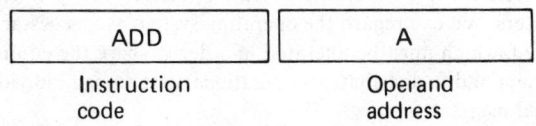

Instruction   Operand
code   address

(Add the operand at address A to the accumulator.)

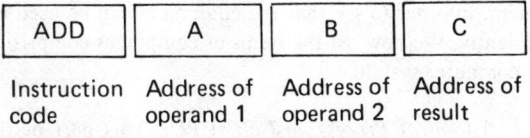

Instruction Address of Address of Address of
code   operand 1 operand 2 result

(Add the operand at A to the
operand at B and store the result at C.)

Fig. 1. Typical single operand and multiple operand computer instructions.

In some special cases the operand itself may be contained in the instruction, in which case it is usually called *immediate*. Usually, the instruction contains a memory address, or a number of fields from which a memory address can be calculated. That memory address is then a pointer that points to the operand and which permits the operand to be retrieved.

Many computers provide single-precision arithmetic operations in which the operands are numbers stored in single computer words. Some provide double-precision or multiple-precision operations in which operands may occupy two, three, or more words each.

In many nonarithmetic operations (and even in some arithmetic ones), the operands are strings of characters (or bytes). The operand address points to the beginning of the string. The extent of the string may be specified in the instruction, but in many cases it is determined by a count field or by a termination code in the operand itself.

S. ROSEN

OPERATING SYSTEMS

CONTEMPORARY FEATURES

For articles on related subjects *see* ADDRESSING; BUFFER; COMMAND AND JOB CONTROL LANGUAGES; COMPUTER SYSTEMS; DATABASE MANAGEMENT; DATA SECURITY; INPUT/OUTPUT DEVICES; INTERACTIVE SYSTEMS, USING; JOB; MEMORY: Main; MEMORY: Auxiliary; MEMORY PROTECTION; MULTIPROCESSING; MULTIPROGRAMMING; OVERLAY; PROCESSING MODES; PROGRAM LIBRARIES; SOFTWARE; SPOOLING; SWAPPING; THROUGHPUT; TIME SHARING; TURNAROUND TIME; and UNIX TIME-SHARING SYSTEM.

This article briefly surveys the features provided by computer operating systems. Basically, an operating system is the software (programs and data) that initiates the interaction of the electronic and electromechanical components of a computer so that they constitute a useful system for carrying out calculations. The operating system is responsible for sharing the computer equipment among users and is therefore sometimes identified by functional names such as *control programs, supervisors, executives,* or *monitors,* although these names have gradually fallen out of use.

From the viewpoint of a *user* of a computer system, the purpose of an operating system is to provide a convenient and economical means of processing programs, but from the viewpoint of the person who manages a computer system, the purpose of an operating system is to share the computer equipment among several users in such a way as to maximize the system's throughput. That is, the objective of a system manager is to maximize the amount of useful work performed by the system. This difference in objective is analogous to that between a purchaser and seller of retail goods. The buyer wants the best buy that can be obtained, and the merchandiser wants the best price for the quality of goods and services being sold. In a computer system, the operating system is supposed to effect a satisfactory match between user and manager objectives.

Equipment Needed to Satisfy User Requirements. This article gives examples of computer services required by users, and then discusses the actual computer equipment and the technological constraints (speed and size) which this equipment imposes upon the system.

Economy and Convenience for the User. A user of a computer system typically submits a *job* to the computer center. This job consists of a program to be run by the computer (as well as data to be processed by the program). There is a tremendous variation in the characteristics of jobs that are submitted to different computer systems by different users. We give four examples.

1. *A Typical Small, One-Time Job.* Most commonly, these are submitted by students at a high school or university and may consist, for example, of 60 punched cards. The student's job description might print out a table of values of the sine function. Student jobs such as this one require little calculation; the reading of the student's cards and the printing of the answers may take longer than does the calculation. The student wants good *turnaround time;* i.e., to see results soon after the job is submitted.

2. *A Typical Scientific Calculation.* A physicist, who needs to calculate the focusing properties of a proposed set of lenses for a telescope, writes a computer program to determine these properties for various lens configurations. This program is punched onto cards (say 1,500 cards) and submitted as a job to the computer center. Scientific jobs such as this one require a lot of calculation. Although the scientist wants good turnaround time, there is also concern that the job will not *cost* too much to run. In many systems, the manager bills each user, such as the physicist, for the time required to process the user's jobs.

3. *A Typical Business Data Processing Job.* Let us suppose that the electric utility company in a small town keeps the accounts for its customers on punched cards. Each month a billing card is key-punched for each customer to record the amount of electricity used. At billing time, a job is submitted to the computer system in order to read account cards and billing cards, and to print bills to be sent to customers. The job will perform simple calculations such as multiplying the electricity usage of a customer times the cost per kilowatt-hour of electricity. Data processing jobs, such as this one, often require a lot of printing and reading of *files*, such as the reading of the file of account cards. On the other hand, these jobs typically require little computation. The electric utility company does not require a short turnaround time (after all, bills are printed only once a month). However, the company is very concerned about *reliability*, for its own sake as well as the customer's.

4. *A Typical Interactive Programming Session.* Some computer systems support interactive consoles (typewriter-like devices). These consoles allow the user to interact with the computer on a line-by-line basis. By contrast, in the first three examples, an entire job was submitted as a unit. Consider a civil engineer who wishes to evaluate a complicated formula for the thickness of concrete pillars required to support a given bridge. The formula could be typed into the computer, using a console, and then the required thickness could be received

back at the console. But the engineer also wants good *response time;* i.e., to have the computer evaluate the formula in at most a few seconds.

These four examples are not intended to illustrate *all* uses of computer systems, but to demonstrate the *diversity of needs* of computer users. We now turn to the equipment needed to satisfy these requirements.

Equipment in a Computer System If cost could be ignored, we could dedicate a computer system to every user. Unfortunately, computer systems remain quite expensive, and many users are able to run their jobs only because the cost of the system is supported by many users. We can regard the operating system as a necessary evil, which must be tolerated in order to share the equipment and to distribute its operational cost among individual users.

By seeing that the equipment is used efficiently, the operating system can increase throughput and thus decrease cost to users. The designer of an operating system will need to have an intimate understanding of the equipment, in order to see that the equipment can be used efficiently. We now list the items of equipment comprising a computer system.

1. *Central Processing Unit (CPU).* This part of the system actually performs the calculations required by users. Calculations are broken into basic operations (e.g., addition); each operation may take a microsecond (0.000001 sec) or less to perform its work. That is, modern CPU's can perform a million or more operations per second.

2. *High-Speed Memory.* This memory holds programs and data; the programs are sequences of operations to be performed by the CPU. Memory is typically divided into *bytes*, each of which can hold one character of information. Memory sizes for different computer systems range from a few thousand bytes to several million bytes.

3. *Magnetic Disks.* Disks provide storage for programs and data; this storage is cheaper (per byte) and larger than high-speed memory. Programs and data stored on a disk cannot be directly accessed by the CPU. Before being used, information must be transferred from the disk into high-speed memory. The transfer of a block of information (say, 1,000 bytes) from the disk to memory may require 10 ms (0.01 secs). Although 10 ms seems like a very short time to a person, it is not so short to a CPU; a CPU can perform around ten thousand operations in 10 ms. A typical disk can hold about 10 million bytes of information. In computer systems, it is common for the information capacity of the disks to be 10 to 1,000 times that of the high-speed memory. The purpose of

disks is to hold programs and data that are not currently active in the high-speed memory.

4.*Card Readers*. These devices read punched cards and transfer their contents into memory. A typical card reader can read 300 cards a minute (i.e., 5 cards per second). Note that a CPU with a microsecond (μs) instruction time can perform 200,000 operations in the time taken to read one card.

5.*Printers*. These devices take lines of text from memory and print them on paper. A typical printer can produce 300 to 2,000 lines per minute

6.*Consoles*. These are typewriter-like devices. A person can type information into the computer and the computer can type information back to the user. A typical console can print about a line a second. Hence, the CPU can perform about a million operations in the time taken to print a line. Most computer systems have an *operator's console;* the person who is the *operator* for the computer system can give commands to the system via this console.

For brevity's sake, we have limited this discussion to the six classes of devices listed above. Actual computer systems often have other pieces of equipment, such as magnetic drums, magnetic tape drives, card punches, paper-tape readers and punches, etc.

We have given the speeds and capacities of the above six types of devices in order to illustrate their diversity. It is a great challenge to the operating system to transform these seemingly mismatched speed ratios (varying by as much as a million to one) into a convenient and efficient system.

Traditionally, the CPU and the high-speed memory have been the most expensive components of a computer system. The operating system must see that the CPU does not remain idle while work is to be done, and that memory is occupied by active programs and data. We now present features of operating systems that are designed to accomplish these aims.

Features of Operating Systems.

In some *very small* computer systems, there is little need for an operating system. In those systems, the sharing of the equipment can be handled on a *manual* basis. For example, a user may sign up to use the system between 10:00 and 11:00 A.M. It is the user's responsibility to provide all software to run the system. At the end of the allocated time, the user relinquishes the machine to the next user.

Automatic Job Sequencing. The problem with manual scheduling is that the equipment may be idle for relatively long periods betweeen the time when one user finishes work and the next user sets up the machine for a new job. For larger and more expensive computer systems, it is advantageous to provide software that automatically begins running the next job as soon as the current job finishes. This software is called a "sequential batch operating system."

Introducing a sequential batch operating system can more than double the throughput of the system simply by eliminating idle time between jobs. The obvious disadvantages of such a system over manual scheduling are (1) the expense of writing the software that does the sequencing, and (2) providing memory and disk space to store the operating system.

Common Input/Output Routines. When a number of users share a computer system, it becomes convenient to write a common set of routines to control the input/output devices (printers, readers, etc.). These routines schedule these devices and are absorbed into the software comprising the operating system.

Off-Lining of Input/Output. Once the idle time between jobs has been minimized, the mismatch between the speed of the CPU and the input/output devices emerges as an important source of inefficiency. For a typical job, the CPU time used may approximately equal the time the input/output devices spend in reading and writing. If the CPU remains idle while the input/output devices are running, and vice versa, then the CPU and input/output devices will each be idle about 50% of the time.

One solution to this problem is to move the card reader and printer to a cheaper off-line system and replace them on the main system with high-speed magnetic tape drives. In the off-line system, a sequence (batch) of user jobs is loaded onto a magnetic tape. The tape is then manually transferred to the main system, which runs the jobs on the tape and places the output from those jobs on another magnetic tape. Finally, this output tape is carried to the off-line system, which prints the results. This process of separating card reading and printing from the actual running of jobs is called *off-lining*.

The primary advantage of off-lining is that the CPU of the main system does not need to wait for relatively slow devices, such as card readers and printers, and therefore can spend much more of its time in processing jobs.

The obvious disadvantages of off-lining are the cost of the tape drives, of the off-line system, and of the operator who must move the tapes. There is another disadvantage. The user must now wait for a job to be loaded onto a tape with a batch of other users' jobs; and the user will not be able to see the results of a job until the whole batch has been processed by the main system. Even the user with a very small job will be forced to wait for the completion of large jobs, such as data processing jobs, which are in the same batch.

Buffering of Input/Output There is another technique that solves the problem of having the CPU wait while input/output devices are working. This allows the CPU and the input/output devices to operate *concurrently* (i.e., simultaneously). The computer equipment is augmented by special-purpose processors, often called *channels* (*peripheral processors* and *input-output controllers* are terms also in use), which keep the input/output devices running at the same time the CPU is working. Cards are read before they are actually needed by the user's job. Some high-speed memory, called a *buffer,* is set aside to hold the information from cards until it is required by the running user's job. Similarly, a buffer is set aside in high-speed memory to hold print lines that have been produced by a user's job, but which have not yet been printed. This technique is called *buffering.* By allowing the CPU to continue working while input/output is in progress, the buffering technique can more than double the throughput of a computer system.

Once the CPU and the input/output devices run concurrently, a new type of problem arises for the operating system designer. Software must now be produced that can cope with the *asynchronous* activity of equipment. This software (the operating system) must *synchronize* the user job's input request with the continuing operation of the card reader. The difficulty is that the operating system must simultaneously keep track of (1) the running user's job and (2) the running input/output devices. Fortunately for the efficiency of computer systems, and unfortunately for the complexity of operating systems, asynchronous activity is a fact of life in modern computer systems.

Common Library Routines. Users of computer systems have found that they can save time and money by using computer programs that other users (or the computer manufacturer) have previously developed. For example, once programs have been developed to evaluate trigonometric functions, they can be used again and again. One way to provide users with common routines is to store such software on a magnetic disk. When a user wishes to use one of the routines, a card is included in the job which asks the operating system to fetch the desired routine from the disk and attach it to the job.

User Files. A user of a computer system may find it convenient to store private programs and data on a magnetic disk (or, for that matter, on a magnetic tape). For example, the electric utility company described in a previous example may wish to store its customers' accounting records on a disk. We call a collection of information, such as this type of accounting record, a *file* or a *data set.* Most operating systems provide their users with a means

of "long term" storage of files on disks or tapes, where "long term" means days, months, or years.

The primary purpose of some computer systems is to maintain a large set of files which can be queried or updated. A large set of files is called a *database,* and a computer system that handles queries to and updates the files is called a *database management system.*

A user will be willing to place information in the long-term storage of a computer system only if confident that the information will not be scrambled or destroyed. You would not like to be told that "the janitor unplugged the disk by mistake and so your accounting records are lost." Hence, the operating system must be carefully designed to maintain the *integrity* of files, i.e., to see that files are not lost.

If several users of a computer system are using long-term storage, then a situation may arise in which one user does not wish to allow another user to inspect his/her files. For example, two competing department stores might keep their lists of active sales items in separate files in the same computer system. Each department store wants to be guaranteed that its files are secure against accidental or purposeful access by the other company. In such an arrangement the operating system must be carefully designed to maintain the *security* of its users' files, i.e., to see that access to files is limited to authorized users.

Logging of System Activity. Operating systems commonly keep a *log* of the activity of the computer system. In small systems, the log is usually made by printing on the operator's console. The log may record the time each job is started and finished, as well as the resources (CPU time, input/output time, etc.) consumed by the job. This information can be used to bill users for the jobs they run. The log may also record the usage of the various pieces of equipment in the computer system. This information helps the computer system manager to adjust the system and improve its efficiency. The log may also be used to record failures in the computer equipment or software. These entries can be used for maintenance of the equipment and for improving the system's reliability.

Command or Job Control Language. Some computer systems provide their users with a variety of services, such as several computer language translators, file-managing programs, and application programs. The user of a computer system can specify which service a job requires by using *control cards.* For example, an engineer who wishes to run a Fortran program adds to the card deck a control card requesting use of the Fortran translator. The operating system reads control cards and sees that the requested services are provided. The control cards accepted by a particular computer system are called a *job control language* (JCL) or a *command language*.

Multiple Programs in Memory (Multiprogramming). In computer systems where there is a lot of concurrent input/output activity, especially on a large number of devices, it may be advantageous to load more than one user's program into memory at a given time. This technique is called *multiprogramming*.

Consider a large business data processing job that uses little CPU time, but which uses a lot of disk time in updating a file of customers' accounts. Such a job will leave most of the system's resources idle, the exception being the disk. This is not only wasteful of equipment, but also means that users with small jobs must wait a long time while the large data processing job ties up the system. Multiprogramming can be used to solve these problems. In a multiprogramming operating system, more than one job is active at a time. This means that when one job leaves the CPU idle because it is waiting for an input/output operation to finish, the operating system can start the CPU working on another job. Similarly, if one job is not using part of the system's equipment (e.g., the magnetic-tape drives), then another program which requires the idle equipment can be activated.

Multiprogramming can also solve the problem of poor turnaround time for small jobs by allowing small jobs to be started and completed while a large job is in progress.

In computer systems that support interactive consoles, many users' programs are active at one time. The operating system automatically switches CPU attention from one user to another. This technique is called *time sharing* because it shares CPU time among many active users. Since the CPU is very fast and consoles (and users) are relatively slow, time sharing gives each user the impression of having the entire CPU to use.

With the introduction of multiprogramming, a number of technical problems must be solved. We now briefly discuss some of them: memory protection, program relocation, and CPU scheduling.

Memory Protection and Program Relocation. Since multiprogramming allows more than one program in memory at one time, the operating system must see that misbehavior on the part of one program does not ruin another program. This problem is solved by adding *memory protection hardware* to the CPU, which guarantees that a program accesses only memory to which it is authorized.

Another problem with multiprogramming is that there is no longer a unique position in memory where a program can expect to be loaded. To solve this problem, the CPU is augmented by *relocation hardware,* which al-

lows a program to be run in any available place in memory. This hardware allows the operating system to load a user's program into any currently unused part of the memory.

Protection hardware and relocation hardware require in turn a mode of CPU operation called *supervisor state*. When the CPU is running in supervisor state, it is possible to set the memory access rights and the relocation properties of user's programs. Supervisor state is used by the operating system in assigning memory to user jobs. (Users' programs are not allowed to use supervisor state.)

CPU Scheduling. Since more than one program is simultaneously active in a multiprogramming system, the operating system must *schedule* the CPU for use by the various programs; this is sometimes called *dispatching* the CPU. If the operating system consistently assigns the CPU to an inopportune program, the result can be poor equipment utilization, poor response time for interactive users, and poor turnaround time. The operating system must use a relatively sophisticated strategy for assigning the CPU to jobs in order to keep the CPU, memory, and input/output devices productive while simultaneously providing good service to users.

Using Multiprogramming to Implement Spooling. Once multiprogramming is available in a system it can be used by the operating system to simulate off-lining (described above). The operating system can use special programs that are active concurrently with their user programs. One special program can read cards from the card reader onto magnetic disk or tape. The cards representing a user's job will be stored until the system is ready to process the job. Similarly, when a user job produces lines to be printed, these lines are temporarily stored on a disk or tape. Later, a special program reads the stored lines and sends them to the printer. This arrangement is called *spooling*; it is similar to off-lining, as described previously, but has an advantage in that it is not necessary to transport the input and output tapes between the main system and the off-line system.

When user jobs are stored on a disk rather than on tape, this arrangement provides a scheduling advantage. In particular, if there are several jobs on the disk waiting to be run, the operating system can choose to run first those jobs that require fast turnaround.

We have covered various aspects of the use of multiprogramming, and will now summarize its advantages and disadvantages. Multiprogramming can (1) improve CPU and input/output equipment utilization, (2) improve turnaround time for small jobs and (3) provide good response for interactive consoles. The disadvantages of multiprogramming are that it requires expensive hardware and a sophisticated operating system. Unfortunately, a sophisticated operating system is expensive to produce, consumes valuable system resources such as CPU time and memory space, and requires costly programmer time for adjustments to accommodate new equipment and changes in users' applications.

Automatic Sharing of Memory. The obvious method of running a user's program is to place the entire user's program in memory and leave it there until the program has finished running. This method has the advantage of simplicity, and it is commonly used. However, it has several drawbacks. First, a long-running program can prevent short jobs from receiving good turnaround time. Second, during the running of a program, only parts of the program are active at a given time. In fact, it often happens that some parts of a program never become active in a given job. This means that memory space reserved for a job is not effectively used. Finally, some programs are just too large to fit into high-speed memory; some means must be provided for dividing such programs into smaller pieces, each of which fits into memory.

Complicated techniques have been developed with the aim of solving these problems and increasing the utilization of memory. We now present two such techniques, called *swapping* and *paging*.

Memory Swapping. The simplest scheme for automatically sharing memory involves temporarily suspending the progress of the running program and moving the program onto a magnetic drum or disk. The high-speed memory occupied by the suspended job is then reassigned to another more pressing job. When the memory once again becomes free, the suspended job can be restored to memory from the drum or disk and allowed to continue running. This scheme is called memory swapping, or *roll-out/roll-in* (the suspended job is "rolled-out" to the drum or disk and later "rolled" back into memory). One of the prime advantages of swapping is that it allows short jobs to overtake longer ones. This technique can also be used to share the computing power of the system among a number of interactive consoles.

Paging. A more sophisticated scheme, called paging, divides the high-speed memory into equal-sized parts called *pages*. Typically, a page may hold 4,000 bytes of information. The operating system assigns to a job only the number of pages required for the active parts of the job program (and data). Extra hardware is added to the CPU so that is is not necessary to assign contiguous pages of memory to a given program. The user writes a program as if it were to be all in memory at the same time; it is then the responsibility of the operating system to see that pages are made available to the program as they are required.

The result is that each user job is provided *virtual*

memory, i.e., the apparent (but not real) dedication of enough high-speed memory to hold the user's entire program.

One of the advantages of paging is that it decreases the memory requirements for running a given job. A second advantage of paging is that the user is provided with a convenient method of running programs that exceed the size of the high-speed memory. The paging technique does not require the entire program to be in memory at one time. This allows the operating system to implement for the user a virtual memory larger than the actual memory. In the absence of a large virtual memory provided by paging, a user with a large program may be forced to invent a scheme for *overlaying* successively real memory with different parts of a program.

Some computer systems, such as the Burroughs B5500, use a technique similar to paging, the difference being that the high-speed memory is divided into parts of *variable* size. These variable-size parts of memory are called *segments*. Some computer systems, such as the Honeywell Multics system, provide variable-length segments, which are in turn subdivided into fixed-length pages.

Multiple CPU Systems. Large computer systems, such as the CDC Cyber series, sometimes include more than one CPU. When more than one CPU is present, the system becomes a *multiprocessing* system.

Features of Commercially Available Systems.
The foregoing description of operating systems has introduced increasingly complex and sophisticated features. In general, smaller and older computer systems have simpler operating system features, and larger and newer computer systems have more complex features.

Small computers (minicomputers) such as the Digital Equipment PDP-8, are commonly run using no operating system or using a sequential batch operating system.

The larger and older IBM 7090 normally ran with a sequential batch system supported by spooling.

Medium-scale systems, such as the IBM 360/65, the CDC 3600, and the Titan, were typically run under multiprogramming operating systems.

Paging and/or segmenting has been available for years on some machines, such as the Atlas and the Burroughs B5500. IBM has provided these facilities on its 370 series of computers.

The UNIX operating system, developed at Bell Laboratories, is notable for supporting many convenient features and yet running on a small computer, the Digital Equipment PDP-11. Since its original development, UNIX has been adapted to run on various computers, including the Digital VAX.

Two Examples of Operating Systems. There is a tremendous variation among contemporary computer systems and their operating systems. Some computer systems cost millions of dollars and occupy several rooms. Other systems cost a few thousand dollars and occupy no more space than a writing desk. Some systems provide their users with a nearly infinite variety of services. Other systems provide only a single service. Some models of computers, with their respective operating systems, have been installed in thousands of businesses, industries, and universities. Others are one-of-a-kind systems.

To illustrate this variation in computers and their operating systems, we present two examples. The first is the small, specialized T.H.E. multiprogramming system, and the second is the large, general-purpose OS/360 system.

T.H.E. Multiprogramming System. In the early 1960s, a team of six computer scientists at the Technical University of Eindhoven in the Netherlands constructed a small special-purpose multiprogramming system. Since the name of their university, in Dutch, is Technische Hochschule Eindhoven, the system is called the T.H.E. multiprogramming system.

The system was designed for one purpose: to run users' Algol programs. The system provides its users with the following services and advantages.

1. Users can run Algol programs that are punched on paper tape. (The system does not accept punched cards.) Users can edit (modify) their paper tapes by running a special editing program.
2. Good turnaround is provided to small jobs; these jobs can overtake larger jobs which have already started running. Since small jobs occupy only a fraction of the system resources (e.g., memory), and since other jobs can concurrently be using the other resources, it is not costly to run small jobs.
3. Users can run jobs with larger memory requirements than provided by the system's actual high-speed memory. The system provides a large virtual memory, and hence programmers need not worry about the memory requirements of their programs (within reasonable limits).

The common library of the T.H.E. system provides its users with an Algol translator and support routines (e.g., trigonometric functions) for Algol programs. There are no other translators available and there is no assembler. The system provides no facility for maintaining user files. Any user files must be kept by the users on paper tape.

The system uses an Electrologica X8 computer; this is a Dutch machine of which few were manufactured. The system's equipment includes the following items.

CPU: instruction time of about 2.5 μs.
Memory: capacity of about 150K bytes.
Magnetic drum: capacity of about 1,500K bytes.
Operator's console.
One printer.
Three paper-tape readers.
Three paper-tape punches.
One plotter.

The user's programs and data are read by the paper-tape readers. The user's programs can produce output on the printer, the plotter, and the paper-tape punches.

The operating system provides multiprogramming: up to five user jobs can be running on the system at the same time. It also gives higher priority to small jobs, and thus provides them with good turnaround. Larger slow jobs, such as those producing pictures using the plotter, can remain in the system for long periods of time without disturbing turnaround time for small jobs.

The operating system supports paging: the active parts of running user jobs are kept in high-speed memory, while the inactive parts are stored on the magnetic drum. Hence, high-speed memory is not wasted by holding inactive parts of programs. The total size of a user's program is thus limited by the size of the drum (which is relatively large) instead of by the size of the high-speed memory (which is about one-tenth the size of the drum).

Since the system provides its users with only one language translator (for Algol), its designers took advantage of this fact by integrating the translator into the operating system. They solved the problem of protecting user programs from each other by having the translator provide checks to keep each user within the authorized memory. They also used the translator to help them implement paging. (It is more common in the design of systems to separate the operating system and the language translators.)

The T.H.E. multiprogramming system is interesting to study because it has a simple, well-described structure, and because it is highly reliable and reasonably efficient. However, its narrow range of service is of value only to a limited number of applications. We now describe an operating system that provides a very broad range of the services.

The Operating System for the IBM 360-370 Series. In the IBM System/360 series of computers, each has the same instructions for its CPU and the same input/output channel arrangement. However, the speeds, the memory capacities, and the attached input/output devices on these systems vary dramatically. The Model 30 of the 360 series is a relatively small machine, having typically 128K bytes of memory; it is comparable to the Electrologica X8 of the T.H.E. system. The Model 91 of the 360 series is a very large computer with 4,000K bytes of memory. There is a range of 360 models between the Model 30 and the Model 91.

IBM supplies the OS/360 operating system, designed to support the 360-370 series of computers. Not only does it support many different computer models, but it also provides its users with a vast variety of services. OS/360 is really a whole series of operating systems rather than a single one, which offer a large complement of programs that support user applications. Therefore, it is not surprising that OS/360 is a big system; it is one of the most expensive software developments ever undertaken. The programs that comprise OS/360 utilize over 200K lines of code, and required thousands of person-years to produce.

Services provided by OS/360 include:

1. Higher-level languages; most commonly used are Cobol, Fortran, and PL/I.
2. Assembly language.
3. A very sophisticated job-control language.
4. A filing system, together with a set of "utility programs" for maintaining user files.

There are many other services available in using OS/360, such as interactive programming, special subsystems to run student jobs, special subsystems to manage large business databases, etc.

As OS/360 is actually a family of operating systems, we limit our attention to one of its most common variants, called "OS/MVT," in which MVT stands for "*multiprogramming with a variable number of tasks*," which means that OS/MVT can concurrently run a number of user jobs, the number depending upon the memory requirements of the jobs.

OS/MVT is sometimes augmented by a spooling subsystem (such as the Houston automatic spooling program (HASP) subsystem), which controls the system's card readers and printers. This subsystem minimizes the time jobs spend waiting for readers and printers, and as a result decreases the time during which jobs occupy memory.

The OS/MVT operating system does not support paging. Instead, memory is assigned to a user's program when the program begins running; the assigned memory remains dedicated to the program until the program terminates.

Since OS/360 supports a series of machines together with diverse applications, it is necessary to tailor an operating system to a particular computer installation. This is accomplished by a process called *system generation* (*q.v.*), which selects from among the available operating system features, attempting to fabricate an operating system that is well suited to the particular installation.

OS/360 is one of the most widely used operating systems because so many 360/370 series computers are in use. Because of its generality, OS/360 has proved useful in a great range of applications. However, as a result of this generality, OS/360 is not an easy system to understand, and can be difficult and expensive to use. Table 1 lists operating systems used on some commonly available large-scale computer systems.

General Remarks about Operating Systems. In this survey of operating systems we have tried to emphasize their great diversity in terms of (1) services provided to users, (2) types of equipment managed by the system, and (3) methods of managing the equipment. Across this diversity, the main purpose of an operating system is to provide convenient and economical computer services by efficiently sharing the computer equipment among users. Complex methods of managing input/output devices and assigning high-speed memory to users' jobs can improve equipment utilization and thus decrease the cost to the users. In general, the simpler of these techniques (such as automatic job sequencing) are used on smaller computer systems, and more complicated techniques (such as paging) are used on larger computer systems.

REFERENCES

1972. Hoare, C. A. R. and Perrot, R. H. *Operating Systems Techniques*. New York: Academic Press.
1973. Hansen, P. Brinch. *Operating System Principles*. Englewood Cliffs, NJ: Prentice-Hall.
1974. Tsichritzis, D. C. and Bernstein, P. A. *Operating Systems*. New York: Academic Press.

R. C. HOLT

PRINCIPLES AND THEORY

For articles on related subjects *see* COMMAND AND JOB CONTROL LANGUAGES; COMPUTER ACCOUNTING AND RESOURCE CONTROL; DEADLOCK; FILES; INTERRUPT; JOB; KERNEL; MULTIPROCESSING; MULTIPROGRAMMING; PARALLEL PROCESSING; PROCESSING MODES; STORAGE ALLOCATION; TASK; and TIME SHARING.

In this section the ideas discussed in the previous section related to contempory operating systems are considered in a general conceptual and theoretical framework.

Tasks and Operating Systems. The term *task* (or *process*) is used to denote a program or subpro-

Table 1.   Operating Systems for Some Widely Used Large-Scale Computers

Operating System	Computers Supported	Comments
1100 Executive (Exec-8 and up)	Univac 1100 series	Supports various batch and interactive languages, including Fortran and Basic; good support in recent systems for data communication and time sharing.
MCP	Burroughs B5000, 6000, and 7000 series	Strongly oriented toward business applications (Cobol); provides efficient transaction facilities for large databases; favors high-level programming; systems software is written in Algol.
Multics	Honeywell series 60 level 68	Originally developed at M.I.T., Multics provides users with powerful means of managing and sharing files; Multics is one of the most secure operating systems available today.
OS	IBM 360/370 series	Widely used in business data processing, teaching, and research; supports a large number of languages, the most commonly used of which are Cobol, Fortran, Pl/I, and 360/370 Assembler.
Scope	CDC Cyber 70, Cyber 170, and 6000 series	Provides batch processing and was originally used in scientific and teaching applications (Fortran). Scope combined with the NOS operating system provides interactive processing, with applications to engineering, management sciences, and database management.
Tops-10	DEC-system 10	Long associated with academic and scientific applications (Fortran); excellent networking and time-sharing facilities.

gram in execution. A computer system may be defined in terms of the various supervisory and control functions it performs for the tasks created by its users:

1. Creating and removing tasks.
2. Controlling the progress of tasks—i.e., insuring that each logically enabled task progresses at a positive rate and that no task can indefinitely block the progress of others.
3. Acting on exceptional conditions arising during the operation of a task—e.g., arithmetic or machine errors, interrupts, addressing snags, attempted execution of illegal or privileged instructions, protection violations.
4. Allocating hardware resources among tasks.
5. Providing access to software resources—e.g., file editors, compilers, assemblers, subroutine libraries, utility programs.
6. Providing protection, access control, and security for information.

7. Providing a means of communicating messages or signals among tasks.

These functions must be provided by the system, since they cannot be handled adequately by the tasks themselves. The computer system software that assists the hardware to implement these functions is known as the *operating system*. Table 1 shows the principal characteristics of computer and operating systems as they have evolved over the years.

Users seldom (if ever) perform a computation without assistance from the operating system. Thus, they often come to regard the entire hardware/software system, rather than the hardware alone, as "the machine." Moreover, many systems permit users to redefine or add to all but a small *kernel* of operating-system programs; an operating system is therefore not immutable, and each user can be presented with a different "machine." The combination of the hardware plus the operating-system software, which defines the environment within which a

Table 1. A Summary of the Characteristics of the Generations of Computers

Characteristics	Generations			
	First	Second	Third	Late Third
Electronics				
Components	Vacuum tubes	Transistors	Integrated circuits	Same as third
Time/operation	0.1–1.0 ms	1–10 μs	0.1–1.0 μs	Same as third
Main memory				
Components	Electrostatic tubes and delay lines	Magnetic drum and magnetic core	Magnetic core and other magnetic media	Semiconductor registers (cache)
Time/access	1 ms	1–10 μs	0.1–1.0 μs	0.1 μs
Auxiliary memory	Paper tape, cards, delay lines	Magnetic tape, disk, drum, paper cards	Same as second, plus extended core and mass core	Same as third
Programming languages and capabilities	Binary code and symbolic code	Higher-level languages, subroutines, recursion	Same as second, plus data structures	Same as third, plus extensible languages and concurrent programming
Ability of user to participate in debugging and running his program	Yes (hands on)	No	Yes (interactive and conversational programs)	Same as third
Hardware services and primitives	Arithmetic units	Floating-point arithmetic, interrupt facilities, microprogramming, special-purpose I/O equipment	Same as second, plus microprogramming and read-only storage, paging and relocation hardware, generalized interrupt systems, increased use of parallelism, instruction lookahead and pipelining, datatype control	
Software and other services	Assemblers, compilers, limited-batch monitor, subroutine library features	Subroutine libraries, batch monitors, special-purpose I/O equipment	Same as second, plus multiaccessing and multiprogramming, time sharing and remote access, central file systems, automatic resource allocation, relocation and linking, one-level store and virtual memory, segmentation and paging, context editors, programming systems, sharing and protection of information	

Source: P. J. Denning, "Third-Generation Computing Systems," *Computing Surveys*, Vol. 3, No. 4 (December 1971), pp. 175–216. (© Association for Computing Machinery, Inc.)

given user may perform tasks, is often called the *virtual machine* seen by that user.

Types of Systems. The range of computing systems available today is enormous. It includes general-purpose programming systems, real-time control systems, time-sharing systems, information service and teleprocessing systems, and computer network systems. All systems provide one or the other (and sometimes both) of *batch-processing* and *interactive* service.

Under batch-processing service, the user submits the program and data of a task together with control information describing what the system is to do with the task. All this is typically submitted in the form of cards, either to a single entry station in the computing center or to a remote entry station connected by a communication link to the computing center. The cards describing what the system is to do with the task cards are called the *control cards*. They describe such information as processing time, memory space, and other resource requirements of the task. They also show the names of files to be used as input to, or output from, the task; the names of library procedures to be included as part of the task; the name of the language translator to be used to compile the task; and whether the task is to be loaded and executed after compilation. The system reads the cards, stores their content in a file, and places the file in a queue for processing. The details of this are presented in a later section of this article on Job Control. After a suitable delay, the processing of the task is completed, and the original cards plus output are returned to the user.

In contrast, a system providing interactive service does not usually require the user to specify a task as a deck of cards. The function of the control cards is replaced by a set of *commands* interpreted by a *command system,* which receives control information directly from the user at a console. Each command issued by the user causes a task to be executed, the output of which is usually transmitted directly to the user's console. It is possible in some systems for the user to interact with the task, modifying it or its behavior as desired. Interactive systems fall into four main categories:

1. Dedicated *transaction* systems, such as airline and other ticket reservation systems, in which the user may initiate tasks that perform transactions on a database, the set of allowable transactions being fixed and small.
2. Dedicated *interactive* systems, such as Joss (Johnniac Open Shop System), Quiktran, or Basic, in which users may program tasks in a single simple language.
3. General-purpose *interactive* systems, as are offered by many time-sharing service bureaus, in which users may write and execute tasks in any one of a collection of languages supported by the system.
4. *Extensible* systems, such as M.I.T.'s Multics (Multiplexed Information and Computing Service) or Bell Labs' UNIX, in which users (usually by the medium of a file system that permits long-term storage and sharing of files) may extend the basic system by implementing their own languages and subsystems and making them available for others to use.

Almost all systems require that each user make prior arrangements with the computing center management before being allowed to use the system at all. Each user will negotiate with the computing center for an account number and will pay for services rendered. Often the arrangements involve limitations on the amount of resources that can be used, and new arrangements will have to be made when the ration has been consumed. (Exceptions to this most often include dedicated transaction systems and dedicated interactive systems where a user, by virtue of gaining access to a dedicated terminal, gains access to the system.) Thus, the first control card of a job submitted to a batch-processing system, or the first command issued to an interactive system, will serve to identify the user to the system; access will be permitted only if there is an account with the system and the user is properly identified.

Because of the high degree of task/user communication in interactive systems, there is typically much overhead involved in switching resources (especially the processor and main memory) among tasks, and the execution of tasks is correspondingly less efficient than in a batch-processing system. To balance this, an interactive system provides a highly efficient environment for program development: editing, debugging, and testing. Thus, batch-processing systems are most often found in computing centers where program development is considered to be a minor part of the overall activity, and efficient production runs are considered to be the major part. Interactive systems are often found in centers where program development is considered the primary activity, and in centers where interaction is dictated, of course, by the nature of the problems being solved (e.g., ticket reservation systems, real-time control systems).

Common Properties of Systems. The views taken by programmers and designers of systems are almost as varied as the systems themselves. Some are viewed as large and powerful batch-processing facilities, offering a wide variety of languages, programming systems, and services (e.g., most of the IBM 360 and 370 series, most of the CDC Cyber series). Some are viewed as highly efficient environments for specific purposes (e.g., Algol on the Burroughs B5700/B6700 machines, Cobol on the Burroughs B1800). Some are viewed as extensions of some language or machine (e.g., M.I.T. Multics, IBM CP-67 virtual machine system). Others are viewed as information management systems (e.g., the SABRE airline reservations system). Still others are viewed as information utilities or extensible machines (e.g., M.I.T. Multics, the BBN TENEX system for the PDP-10, A/S Regnecentralen RC4000 system, IBM TSS/360).

Despite the diversity of system types and views about them, most operating systems have a great deal in common, arising from three basic and common design objectives: an efficient environment for program development, debugging, and execution; a wide range of problem-solving facilities; and low-cost computing through the sharing of resources and information. The characteristics in common are listed below. Not all need be found in any single system.

Concurrency. This property is associated with two or more activities that are in progress simultaneously; e.g., the central processing unit can be executing instructions from some task at the same time a peripheral processor is carrying out an input/output operation. The notion of *parallel processes* or *parallel tasks* is a form of concurrency, though at a logical rather than physical level; it means that at any given time, more than one task may be observed between its initiation and termination.

Asynchronism. This refers to the potential unpredictability of the order in which events occur. Asynchronism is a consequence of concurrency and sharing. Because of dependence on total load, inaccuracies in prior information supplied by programmers with regard to the demands of their programs, and the speed differentials among the various hardware units of the system, the order in which resources are assigned, released, or accessed by tasks is unpredictable. The mechanisms for handling concurrency and sharing must be designed to allow for this. When it is desired to impose a logical ordering on certain events, synchronization mechanisms must be part of a system's design, and their use must appear explicitly in the programming of the tasks. These mechanisms cause one task to be stopped at a given point until a signal or message has been received from another task.

Automatic Resource Allocation. A centralized resource-allocation mechanism appears in many systems in order to monitor resource usage to satisfy objectives of good service and efficiency, especially since there is the possibility that otherwise independent tasks can interfere with one another by competing for the same resources. System control of resource allocation is a consequence of the goal of removing as much as possible of the burden of resource allocation from the programmer, in order that energies may be concentrated fully on the logical properties of algorithms. Moreover, the unpredictable nature of demands in systems supporting concurrent activity places the programmer at a severe disadvantage in making efficient resource allocation decisions.

Sharing. This term has two related uses. First, it refers to the fact that resource *types* can be shared, irrespective of whether individual *units* of those types are sharable. Examples of resource types include hardware types such as processor and memory, and software types such as files and messages. Examples of corresponding units are, respectively, a single processor, a page of memory, a file, or a message. A unit of physical resource type is typically subject to exclusive control by the task to which it is assigned (since the task may manipulate the internal "state" of the resource unit), and some form of *multiplexing* (see below) must be used to implement the sharing. Second, the term refers to sharing of information. Information sharing is motivated in part by the desire to be able to use, in one's own programs, subprograms or modules constructed by others; in part by the existence of problems involving the use of a central database; and in part by a desire to avoid multiple, redundant copies of a procedure that is to be used by more than one task.

Long-Term Storage. Second-generation systems provided long-term storage only under severe limitations (e.g., it was restricted to subroutine libraries accessible only via compilers or loaders), which considerably simplified the problem of managing and protecting this information. However, many third-generation systems endeavor to provide a mechanism by which users can store files for indefinite periods, giving rise to three nontrivial implementation problems:

1. A file system must be designed to manage information entrusted to it, using symbolic file names provided by users.
2. There must be guarantees that the information will survive system failures, and even users' own mistakes.
3. A protection mechanism is required to permit access to files only as authorized.

Multiplexing. This is a technique under which time is divided into disjoint intervals, and a unit of resource is assigned to at most one task during each interval. The time interval during which a task is granted exclusive control of a unit of resource may be defined naturally by the task's alternating between periods of demand and nondemand for a unit of that type, or it may be defined artificially by *time slicing* and *preemption.* The latter method is used primarily in time-sharing systems and other systems in which response-time deadlines must be satisfied.

The prefix *multi-* is frequently added to a term to denote some form of sharing or multiplexing:

1. *Multitasking* refers to the capability of a system to support two or more active tasks simultaneously.
2. *Multiprogramming* refers to the capability of a system to have programs or program segments of two or more tasks in main memory simultaneously. Multiprogramming implies multitasking, but not conversely; a system that has many active tasks, but loads only one at a time into main memory, is an example. The purpose of multiprogramming is to permit the concurrent operation of the devices in the system by maintaining a supply of tasks to which the central processor can be switched should the one it was processing stop to use an input/output device.
3. *Multiaccessing* refers to the capability of a system to be accessible through two or more terminal stations. It does not imply, nor is it implied by, either multitasking or multiprogramming.
4. *Multiprocessing* is used to refer to the capability of a system to provide two or more processors for

the execution of tasks. (Actually, the word "multiprocessoring" should be used because "multiprocessing," taken at face value in English, means the same as "multitasking.") To be practical, multiprocessing implies multiprogramming, and therefore multitasking.

Time sharing is a technique used in certain multiaccess, multitask systems to permit different users simultaneously to receive the services of the system by multiplexing processor and main memory rapidly among the active tasks.

A Model of Multitask Systems.

At the heart of most modern operating systems is the mechanism for implementing multitasking. An understanding of this mechanism is a prerequisite to an understanding of the operation of most other parts of an operating system. Accordingly, a simple model for a multitask mechanism in a single processor system is presented here.

Task Descriptors. Each task in the system will be identified by a unique index i, which is a positive integer. A task in the system is described at any time by its *task descriptor*,

$$D = (ep, ip, pc, mc),$$

in which ep is an environment pointer (designating, for example, the base of a region of main memory containing the program and data of the task, or the base of a page table describing the virtual address space of the task); ip is the instruction pointer, designating the next instruction to be executed by the task; pc is a protection code indicating the protection state or domain of the task (e.g., user or supervisor state); and mc is the machine conditions (processor stateword—contents of programmable processor registers) of the task. The descriptor D of a task is given a new value at the end of each instruction execution. Observe that, to start or resume a task, all one must do is load its descriptor into a processor and start the processor. To preempt a processor from a task, one needs only to signal the processor to pause at the end of the current instruction-execution, whereupon the value of D is saved. Since a task completely describes the sequence of its descriptor values, the preceding definitions guarantee that we can interrupt any task and preempt processor and memory resources from it without interfering with its logical progress.

Structure. The system is assumed here to be equivalent to a network of queues and servers, as shown in Fig. 1. There are $n + 1$ servers, server 0 being the (single) processor and servers $1, \ldots, n$ being other types of service that tasks may request (e.g., supervisor functions like file handling or input/output operations). Associated with

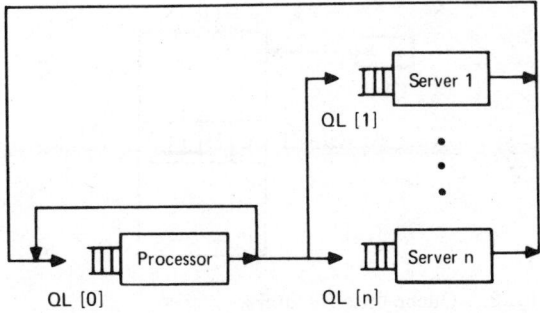

Fig. 1.   Network diagram of system.

each server is a queue of tasks waiting for that type of service. (We assume here that the queues are FIFO [first-in first-out]; the FIFO assumption is merely a matter of convenience, for the system is straightforwardly modified to include priority and other types of queues.) A data structure called the *queue list* (QL[0:n]) will implement these queues. In particular, QL[j] will designate a FIFO queue containing the indices of tasks waiting for service of type j. QL[0] will be called the *ready list*. Associated with server j, for $1 \leq j \leq n$, is a special task, the *overseer task* (O-task for short), whose duty it is to render service of type j to the tasks whose indices are listed in the QL[j]. (The scheduling of the O-tasks is discussed later.)

The *interrupt handler tasks* (tasks invoked by interrupts, faults, or exceptions, such as arithmetic errors, machine errors, protection violations, addressing snags, device completion signals) are *not* considered as O-tasks in the model described here. However, various supervisor functions are regarded as "servers" (e.g., file systems, intertask message transmission facilities, input or output operations, compilers, loaders, job initiators, and terminators). The distinction between overseer tasks and interrupt handler tasks is not essential, being made here partly as a matter of convenience and partly because most systems make such a distinction: The interrupt handler tasks are considered to be on a level of abstraction below the overseer tasks, and may therefore be used to invoke or schedule the overseer tasks.

As noted above, the queue list QL[0:n] designates a list of FIFO queues for the various servers. As will be shown shortly, the FIFO queues themselves are stored in another structure, the task list. As indicated in Fig. 2, the structure of a typical entry in the queue list is

$$QL: (QL.L, QL.H, QL.T, QL.O)$$

where QL.L is an integer giving the length of the queue, QL.H is the index of the task at the head of the queue, QL.T is the index of the task at the tail of the queue, and

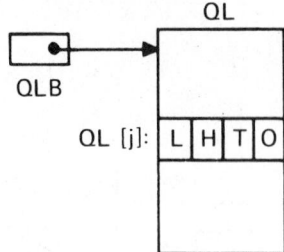

Fig. 2. Queue list structure.

QL.O is the index of the O-task of the queue. A cell QLB (which we assume for convenience to be a processor register) contains the base address of the queue list.

There is an additional structure, the *task list* TL[0:m], containing one entry for each task in the system, where m is the maximum number of tasks that can exist simultaneously in the system. Task 0 is an "idle task," which is executed whenever no other task is available for execution. As shown in Fig. 3, the structure of a typical entry in the task list is

$$\text{TL: (TL.S, TL.N, TL.D)}$$

where TL.S is the status of the task (i.e., the index of the queue in which the task is waiting or being served, TL.N is the index of the next task after this task in the queue whose index is in TL.S, and TL.D is a pointer to the descriptor block of the task. The *descriptor block* of task i, denoted by DB[i], is simply a contiguous set of main memory locations used for storing the descriptor of task i, the base address of DB[i] being stored in TL.D[i]. A cell TLB (which we assume for convenience to be a processor register) contains the base address of the task list. Fig. 4 shows the configuration of TL and QL when tasks $i_1, i_2, \ldots, i_k$ are waiting for service of type j.

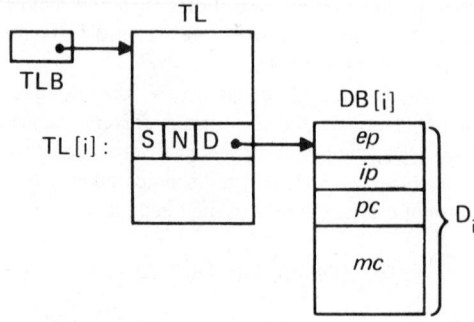

Fig. 3. Task list structure.

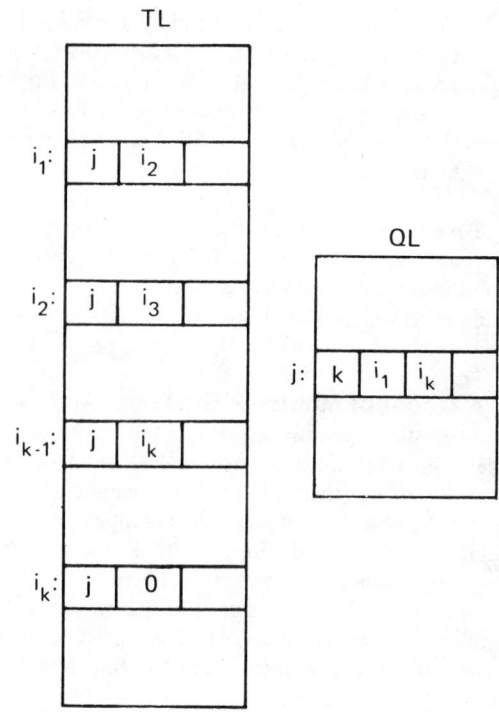

Fig. 4. Configuration of queue list and task list.

Hardware Assumptions. The processor is assumed to contain the usual registers for holding a descriptor D of a task; the register QLB pointing to the base of the queue list; the register TLB pointing to the base of the task list; and a register T holding the index of the task currently assigned to the processor. Registers QLB and TLB are set when the system is initialized. Register T is set whenever a new task is assigned to the processor. The following special instructions are provided:

SAVE   Causes the descriptor of task i, where i is the contents of the T register, to be saved in DB[i]; the base address of DB[i] is found in TL.D[i].

RESUME   Causes the descriptor of task i, where i is the contents of the T register, to be loaded from DB[i], after which the processor begins executing instructions.

LOAD-T,x   Load the T register from location x.

STORE-T,x   Store the T register into location x.

SC,j   (service call of type j) Causes the index of the currently running task to be appended to the queue of QL[j] and the next task waiting for the processor (at the head of QL[0]) to be resumed (see below).

DISABLE   Turn off the interrupts (see below).

ENABLE   Turn on the interrupts (see below).

To switch the processor to another task whose index is stored in location x, a task needs to execute the sequence

SAVE; LOAD-T,x; RESUME;

The ability of a task to execute the above instructions may depend on the protection code (pc) part of its descriptor, as may its ability to alter the ep, ip, and pc parts of its descriptor. An attempt to execute any of the instructions when not authorized by the pc in the descriptor will cause an interrupt, which will invoke the interrupt handler task that acts on protection violations.

Fig. 5 summarizes the relations among the above structures. As shown, task i is running on the processor, so that the ep register points to the address space A_i of task i and the ip register points to the next instruction task i is to execute. Another task j, which is not running, has its descriptor stored in DB[j] so that the next time it is resumed, it can continue from the point designated by the value of its descriptor.

Operations. Three operations on the lists QL and TL are defined: **enqueue**(u,j) causes task index u to be added to the end of the queue QL[j]; **dequeue**(u,j) causes the first entry in QL[j] to be removed and assigned to u; and **push**(u,j) causes u to become the first element of QL[j], the remaining elements of QL[j] being as before but starting at the second position of the queue. For FIFO queues, these operations are defined as follows:

enqueue(u,j)

if QL.H[j] = 0
    then QL.H[j] ← u
    else TL.N[QL.T[j]] ← u;
	If the queue is empty, put u at its head; otherwise, let i be the task at the tail and u be the task following i.

TL.N[u] ← 0;	Indicate that no task follows u in the queue.
TL.S[u] ← j;	Indicate that u is waiting in queue j.
QL.T[j] ← u;	Indicate that u is at the tail of queue j.
QL.L[j] ← QL.L[j] + 1;	Indicate that the length of queue j has increased by 1.

dequeue (u,j)

u ← QL.H[j];	Let u be the task at the head of the queue.

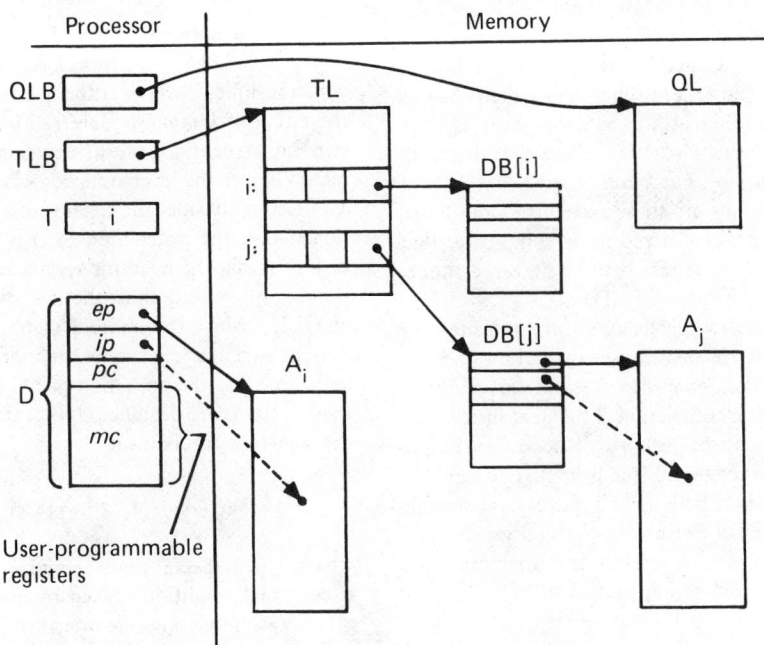

Fig. 5. Structure of system.

QL.H[j] ← TL.N[u];	The task following u becomes the head of the queue.
QL.L[j] ← QL.L[j] − 1;	Indicate that the length of queue j has decreased by 1.

push(u,j)

TL.N[u] ← QL.H[j];	The task at the head of the queue becomes the one following u.
QL.H[j] ← u;	Task u becomes the head task.
TL.S[u] ← j;	Indicate that u is waiting in queue j.
QL.L[j] ← QL.L[j] + 1;	Indicate that the length of queue j has increased by 1.

Since the queue manipulation operations are critical sections of code, they must be executed with the processor in uninterruptible mode (see below). Often we write **enqueue**(T,j), **push**(T,j), and **dequeue**(T,j), which of course implies the use of the LOAD-T and STORE-T instructions.

The hardware is assumed to contain a set of 1-bit *condition cells* $X[1:c]$ such that the event $X[k]: 0 \rightarrow 1$ signifies the occurrence of the *k*th *exceptional condition* where $1 \leq k \leq c$. (Condition cells corresponding to channel completion signals are sometimes called *channel indicators*.) Define the signal X to be 1 whenever $X[k] = 1$ for some *k*, and 0 otherwise. We assume that the hardware also contains a 1-bit *mask cell* M such that $M = 1$ indicates that conditions are to be recognized and acted on (interrupts are "enabled") and $M = 0$ indicates that action on condition-occurrences is to be deferred (interrupts are "disabled" or "masked off").

As noted earlier, two instructions are provided for setting the mask cell: DISABLE causes the action $M \leftarrow 0$; and ENABLE causes the action $M \leftarrow 1$, but this action is deferred until *after* the completion of the next instruction so that a new task can be resumed if necessary before another interrupt is recognized (see below). The signal Y $= MX$ is 1 if and only if both M and X are 1. At specific points in the execution of instructions—usually at the end of the instruction cycle or on references to memory—the processor will execute an action equivalent to

$$\text{if } Y = 1 \text{ then } \{M \leftarrow 0; \text{DISPATCH};\}$$

where

DISPATCH

push(T,0)	Save the index of the running task at the head of the ready list.
SAVE;	Save the descriptor of the running task.
LOAD-T, H[k];	Load the index of the interrupt handler task corresponding to the index *k* of the condition being recognized.
RESUME;	Load the descriptor of the interrupt handler task and begin execution.

Here, *k* is a signal generated by the hardware, having as value the index of the interrupt condition to be acted on—usually *k* will designate the interrupt of highest priority (e.g., $k = \min\{i \mid X[i] = 1\}$)—and $H[1:c]$ is an array whose position is known to DISPATCH such that $H[k]$ contains the index of the handler task for condition *k*. (The array H is sometimes called an "interrupt vector" and is sometimes implemented as registers in the processor.) Since RESUME (in DISPATCH) does not cause the action $M \leftarrow 1$, the condition handler task will operate with the interrupts off. When it completes its action, the handler executes the sequence

dequeue(T,0);ENABLE;RESUME;

which resumes the task at the head of the ready list. Since the effect of ENABLE is deferred until after the next instruction-execution, the RESUME operation will be completed before the interrupts come back on.

Let us consider the schema of an O-task. It was mentioned that the instruction SC,j is available for a user-task to signal the need for service of type *j*; this instruction is supposed to place the task executing it at the end of QL[j]. Since the number of possible types of service may be variable (e.g., some functions are implemented in software) and the operation of SC is relatively complex, most systems are designed so that the SC instruction uses the interrupt mechanism

$$\text{SC},j: \{J \leftarrow j; X[k_{sc}] \leftarrow 1;\}$$

where J is a special register and k_{sc} is the index of the exceptional condition caused by an SC instruction. Another reason for using the interrupt mechanism for invoking O-tasks is protection: It guarantees that control is transferred only to the entry point of the O-task (i.e., it implements "protected entry point"). The handler task operates as follows:

---

task $H[k_{SC}]$

$X[k_{SC}] \leftarrow 0$;	Turn off the condition cell.
dequeue(u,0);	Save the index of the task at the head of the ready list in the variable u (so that u is the task interrupted by the SC interrupt).
enqueue(u,J);	Place u on the queue for service requested (the index of the service requested being in the J register).
if $TL.S[QL.O[J]] \neq 0$ **then enqueue**(QL.O[J],0);	The index of the O-task for queue J is in QL.O[J]; if this task is not in the ready list, it is placed there.
dequeue(T,0); ENABLE; RESUME;	Resume the next ready task.

The fourth step above schedules the O-task for the service requested if that O-task is not already on the ready list. (Recall that $TL.S[i]$ for any task i indicates the index of the queue in which task i is waiting.) Although the fourth step above shows the O-task being placed at the end of the ready list, a more realistic system would give it priority in the ready list. The operation of the O-task is

---

O-task j

Perform service j for task QL.H[j];	Perform the requested service for the task at the head of queue j.
DISABLE;	Turn off the interrupts, as subsequent actions will manipulate the queue list and task list.
dequeue(u, j);	Let u be the index of the task at the head of queue j (which task has now had service completed for it).
enqueue(u,0);	Place u at the end of the ready list.

---

reinitialize DB[O-task j];	Since O-task j could have been interrupted before the DISABLE, the descriptor block needs to be reinitialized so that future resumptions of this task start at the beginning.
if $QL.L[j] > 0$ **then enqueue**(T,0) **else** TL.S[O-task j] $\leftarrow$ j;	If there is more work for O-task j, place its index on the ready list. Otherwise, indicate that this task is not ready and is in fact waiting for work to appear in queue j.
dequeue(T,0); ENABLE; RESUME;	Resume the next ready task.

In the case of a channel-driving task, the action "perform service j" will check to see if the channel is busy and if so take no further action; otherwise, it will specify work for the channel (in the form of a channel program) and start the channel. The channel completion interrupt will invoke an interrupt handler task that will initiate the channel for the next task (see below).

Note that the queue-manipulation portion of O-task j operates with the interrupts off; some O-tasks may be designed to operate entirely in uninterruptible mode, in which case DISABLE would become the first step. Some O-tasks may be intended to complete all work in $QL[j]$ before relinquishing the processor, in which case the task could follow the design.

O-task j

DISABLE;	Turn off the interrupts while manipulating queue.
L1: **if** $QL.L[j] = 0$ **then goto** L2;	If queue j is empty, there is no more work to do.
ENABLE;	Turn on interrupts while performing service j for task at head of queue.
Perform service j for task QL.H[j];	Perform service for task at head of queue.
DISABLE;	Turn off the interrupts.

dequeue(u,j); **enqueue**(u,0);	Move task for which service now is complete back to the ready list.
goto L1;	Repeat for next task in queue j.
L2: TL.S[O-task j] ← j;	Indicate O-task j not in ready list.
reinitialize DB[O-task j];	Reinitialize its descriptor block.
dequeue(T,0); ENABLE; RESUME;	Resume the next ready task.

Next we need to consider the operation of the exceptional condition handler tasks (we mentioned one, task $H[k_{SC}]$, above), since these tasks are the only tasks other than the O-tasks with authority to manipulate the queues. Suppose k_{ERR} is the index of some error condition caused by the running task; the action to be performed is one of three:

A. Rectify the error and resume the task.
B. Stop the task and report to the superior of the erroneous task.
C. Stop the task and report the error to the task's user.

If action A is intended, the handler task schema is

task $H[k_{ERR}]$

X[k_{ERR}] ← 0;	Turn off the condition cell.
Perform action A;	Take intended action.
dequeue(T,0); ENABLE; RESUME;	Resume next ready task.

If actions B or C are intended:

task $H[k_{ERR}]$

X[k_{ERR}] ← 0;	Turn off condition cell.
dequeue(u,0);	Get index of interrupted task from head of ready list.
Perform action B or C on task u;	Perform intended action.
dequeue(T,0); ENABLE; RESUME;	Resume next ready task.

Note that task $H[k_{ERR}]$ does not save its own descriptor on completion—DB[$H[k_{ERR}]$] is thus never altered, so that later resumptions of this task will always start it with the initial value of its descriptor.

Next consider the form of a handler task for a condition *not* caused by the interrupted task. One important such condition is the completion signal from a device or channel started previously by some O-task. Suppose k_j is the index of the condition corresponding to a completion signal from channel j, and the tasks waiting for service on channel j are queued in QL[j]:

task $H[k_j]$

X[k_j] ← 0;	Turn off condition cell.
dequeue(u,j); **enqueue**(u,0);	Move completed task to ready list.
if QL.L[j] > 0 **then**{specify work for the device or channel, to be performed on task QL.H[j]; start the device or channel;}	If tasks are waiting, specify work and start the channel on the next task.
dequeue(T,0); ENABLE; RESUME;	Resume next ready task.

Another important such case is the *clock interrupt*, which is used to force the preemption of the running task after some time limit if that task has failed to relinquish the processor for some other reason. In systems having a clock interrupt, a hardware clock is initialized with some value v; after v time units, the clock generates an exception signal. The clock handler task is

task $H[k_{CLK}]$

X[k_{CLK}] ← 0;	Turn off condition cell.
dequeue(u,0); **enqueue**(u,0)	Move interrupted task to tail of the ready list.
LOAD-CLOCK, v;	Load the value of a time limit (quantum) into the clock.
dequeue(T,0); ENABLE; RESUME;	Resume next ready task.

Message Sending. It is frequently necessary to be able to transmit messages among tasks in the system, these messages being useful to request service and to receive replies from service tasks. A simple extension of the previous system will handle this. With each task is associated a private *message queue,* consisting of a linked list of *message buffers.* Each buffer contains a single message, and all buffers reside in a system buffer area (outside the address spaces of tasks). For the purpose of this discussion, it is convenient to assume that all message buffers are of the same size (say, *b* words). The first word of a buffer is a *link field,* and is used to point to the next buffer on the chain. The second word of a buffer is an *identification field,* and is used to contain the *index of the task which sent the message.* (See Figs. 6 and 7.) The structure of each task-list entry is extended to include pointers to the head (TL.MH) and tail (TL.MT) of the chain of message buffers.

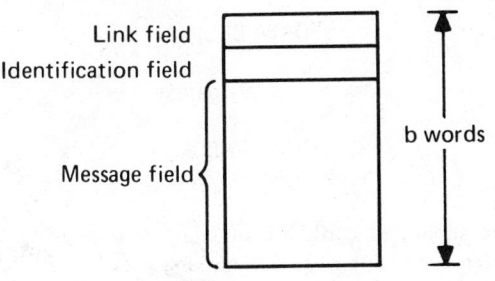

Fig. 6. A message buffer.

The identification field serves two purposes: First, it allows a task to send a *return message* to another task. Second, it is very useful for implementing *protected entry points,* since a receiver always knows the identification of the sender and there is no way for a sender to "enter" the receiver except at the point where the receiver examines its message buffer.

A task *i* wishing to send a message to task *j* places the message in a region with base address *a* of its address space (A_i); it then executes the operation

send message (a, j).

This operation will activate an interrupt handler task, which will allocate a message buffer, copy into it the message (starting at address *a* in A_i), put the index *i* of the sender in the identification field of the buffer, and link the buffer to the end of the chain constituting the message queue in task *j*. (See Fig. 7.)

A task *i* wishing to obtain the next message from its message queue executes the operation

get message (a).

This operation will activate an interrupt handler task, which will copy the message (including the identification field) from the buffer at the head of the message queue into the address space (A_i) of the caller, beginning at address *a*; it then releases the buffer to a pool and updates the pointer TL.MH[i].

If task *i* should request a message when the queue is empty (i.e., TL.MH[i] = 0), it will be suspended (this can be indicated by placing an appropriate status indicator into TL.S[i]) until a message arrives. Therefore, the **send message** operation must check to see if, when the next message becomes the only one in the queue, the receiver task is waiting for a message; if so, the **get message** operation previously initiated by that task is completed. Instead of forcing a task to wait when it attempts to get a message from an empty queue, it is possible to implement an operation that tests whether a message is present; if there is no message present, the testing task could presumably perform other work and retest for a message later on. This is usually considered undesirable: it is easy for a task waiting for a message to enter a *busy loop* testing for the presence of a message, and thereby wasting processor time.

File Storage. Many systems provide each task with access to files on secondary storage for use during execution. In some cases, a system will provide a capa-

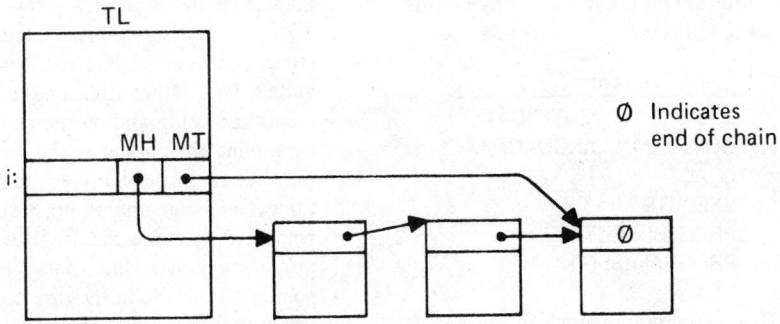

Fig. 7. A chain of messages in TL[i].

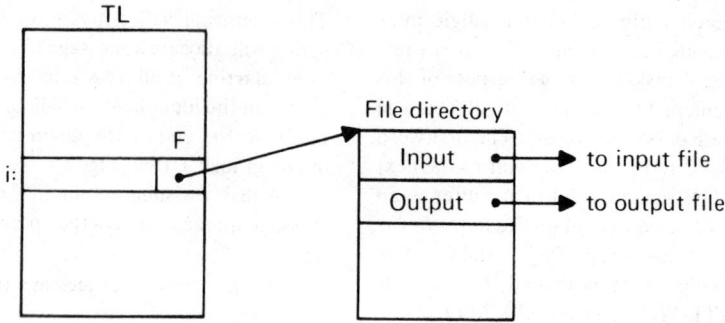

Fig. 8. Files belonging to a task.

bility only for a task to use temporary files during its execution, such files being deleted when the task terminates. Other systems provide long-term storage facilities, according to which a user can store a collection of files of the user's own choosing for indefinite periods; in particular, these files continue their existence even at times when there is no active task authorized to use them.

A basic file capability is easily added to the multitask system model. Associated with each user account is a *file directory,* containing pointers to all the user's permanent files. (If the user has no permanent files, the directory will, of course, be empty when the user is not using the system.) When the user successfully gains access to the system, the user's task will be provided with a pointer to the file directory; this pointer is stored in an extension (TL.F) to a task list entry. Fig. 8 shows task *i* having access to an input and an output file. Whenever a task calls for service from a file-manipulation task, it is an easy matter for the latter to locate the file directory (and therefore the files) of the former.

Job Control. The basic multitask system of the previous sections now has the capabilities to support the execution of a job submitted by the user. To avoid unnecessary detail, a simple example of a typical batch job will be given. It will suffice to show the principles of operation in this case. A typical job submitted in the form of cards will be equivalent to the following:

Job Step	Cards
	//JOB BEGIN, IDENTIFICATION
1	//COMPILE IN LANGUAGE L
2	//LOAD
3	//EXECUTE
4	//PRINT OUTPUT
	//PROGRAM BEGIN
	.
	. (program cards)
	.
	//PROGRAM END

```
//DATA BEGIN
         .
         . (data cards)
         .
//DATA END
//JOB END
```

The submitted cards are of two types: *control cards,* which begin with a special marking ("//" in the example), and *program* or *data cards.* The former specify how the job is to run; the latter specify the job itself. As indicated above, the example job has four main *job steps* indicated on the control cards. The following system tasks will be involved in carrying out the job steps:

Reader: Read the cards. Authenticate user identification information.
    Create a file directory pointing to three files:
        commands: images of the control cards
        program: images of the program cards
        input: images of the data cards
    Send to the control card interpreter a message containing a pointer to this file directory.

Control Card Interpreter: Get the next message (using the **get message** operation). Using the file directory pointer in the message, access the *commands* file, and obtain the next unexecuted control card. If the control cards are exhausted, delete the file directory and all files. Otherwise, send to the task that implements the command on the control card a message containing the pointer to the file directory.

Compiler (of language L): Get the next message (using the **get message** operation). Using the file directory pointer in it, access the *program* file, and compile it, producing a new file *compiled program.* Place a pointer to this file in the directory. Send to the control card interpreter a return message containing the pointer to the file directory.

Loader: Get the next message (using the **get message** operation). Using the file directory pointer in it, access the file *compiled program* and load it, together with any routines required from the system library, into a file *address space*. A pointer to this file is placed in the directory. Send to the control card interpreter a reply message containing the pointer to the file directory.

Initiator: Get the next message (using the **get message** operation). Using the file directory pointer in it, obtain the pointer to the file *address space*. Find an unused task index, *i*, and create a task list entry for it, with a pointer to *address space* and an initial descriptor in DB[*i*], and the pointer to the file directory in TL.F[*i*]. Add a pointer for the file *output* to the file directory. Add the new task to the ready list.

Terminator: Gains control (by the SC instruction) when a task terminates. Create a message containing the pointer to the file directory of the terminated task. De-allocate the task list entry TL[*i*]. Send the message to the control card interpreter.

Printer: Get the next message (using the **get message** operation). Using the file directory pointer in it, access the *output* file and print it. Send to the control card interpreter a return message containing a pointer to the file directory.

When the task created by the initiator comes into existence, it executes the program in its address space. Any input/output operations (which are invoked by the SC instruction) refer to the *input* and *output* files listed in the task's file directory.

Fig. 9 shows the flow of messages among the tasks mentioned above as they cooperate in carrying out the steps of a job. There are ten message transmissions in the example given. Note that each message contains a pointer to the file directory which contains in turn a pointer to the file to be processed by the task receiving the message.

In the example, the control card interpreter deletes the file directory and the files when the job is completed. In a more general implementation, each file would be designated *temporary* or *permanent,* and only the temporary files would be deleted. In a time-sharing system, the basic operations above are the same except that there is usually a unique *command interpreter* task, associated with each active terminal, to process the commands (and other input and output) from that terminal.

Distributed Systems. Mini- and microcomputer technology now make it feasible to spread operating systems functions over a collection of different computers, each with its own private processor and memory. These computers are usually all at the same site and they communicate by means of a high-speed data network. Impor-

tant functions, such as a file system or the log-in authenticator, can be permanently housed in one (or several) of the computers. A task requiring text-editing can be routed to a computer specializing in word processing, while another, requiring large-scale computation, can be routed to a computer specializing in vector operations.

Two kinds of data network ("net" for short) are coming into use. One is the *contention network,* a cable up to 1 km long to which the computers are connected. Each computer monitors all transmissions, looking for packets containing its name as destination. A computer may not transmit if the net is busy. If a computer finds its transmission jammed by another computer (because both thought the net was free), it stops, waits a random interval, and retries the transmission. Because this type of network is passive, the failure of any computer will not put the entire net out of commission. (But it may bring the system down if it is a critical computer, such as the one housing the file system.) This type of network is sometimes called an *ethernet* because the cable is a passive medium, an ether; it was pioneered at Xerox Palo Alto Research Center.

The second type of network is the *ring network.* Here the stations act as repeaters arranged in a circle; each is constantly receiving packets from one neighbor and retransmitting them to its other neighbor. A computer wishing to transmit awaits an empty packet, which it replaces by a message-containing packet. A computer monitors packets coming by, looking for those with its name as destination; when one such comes by, the computer removes the message and uses the same packet to return an acknowledgment to the sender. Because this type of network is active, a failure of any station will put the net out of commission. This form of network was pioneered at the Computer Laboratory of the University of Cambridge.

Both the contention network and ring network are examples of broadcast networks: All stations can monitor all transmissions. Long distance communications are usually handled with packet-switching networks, which deliver packets only to the stations addressed (*see* NETWORKS).

Operating systems designed to exploit these architectures were still highly experimental in 1980. They are best modeled in the traditional way, as a collection of processes exchanging messages; but each process may have its own computer, and each message is sent by the data network. Aside from the high degree of actual concurrency among processes, these experimental systems are functionally not much different from traditional operating systems.

Three major research problems confront the designers of distributed operating systems: (1) separating functions into enough modules so that the failure of any one (e.g., the file system computer) does not disable the whole

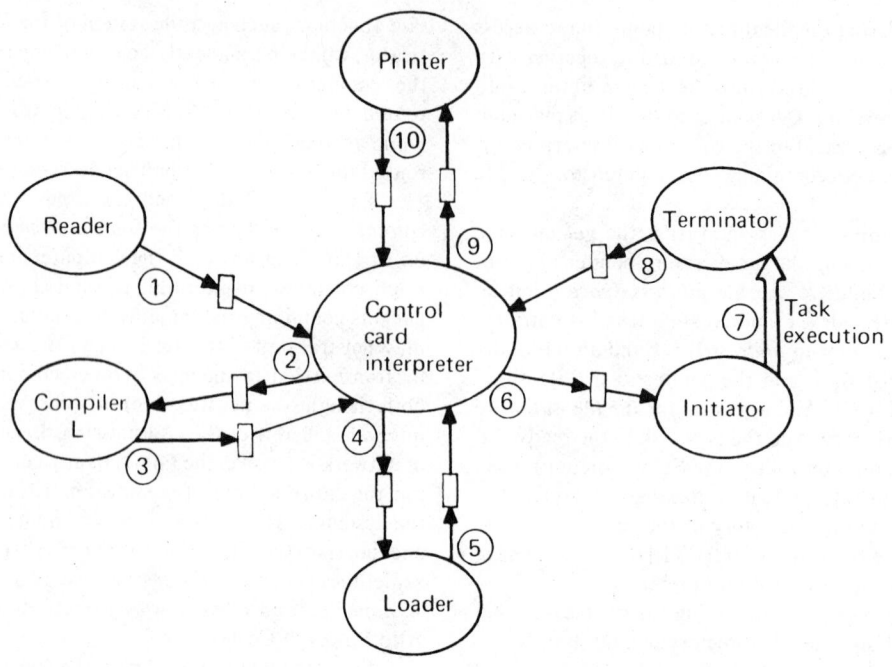

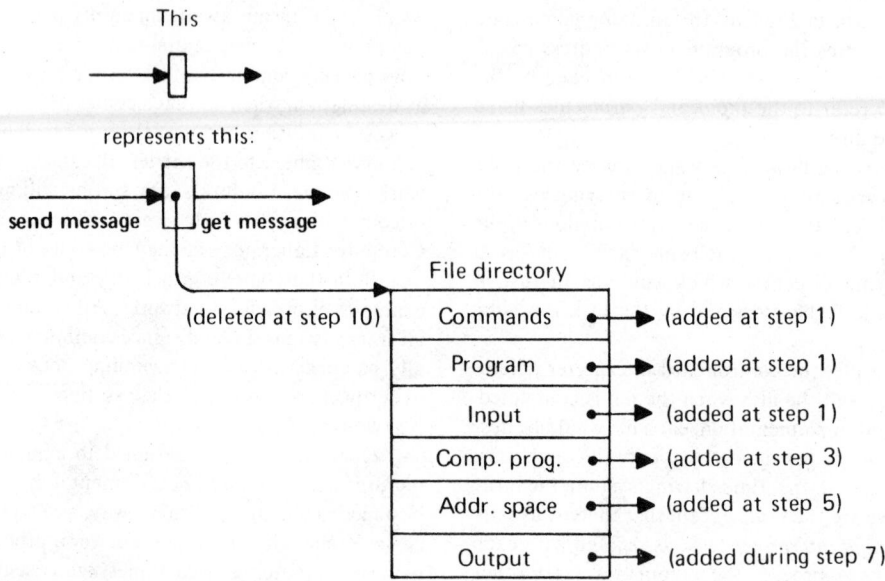

Fig. 9. Flow of job steps.

system; (2) learning how to recover from errors which occur while a synchronization operation is in progress; and (3) learning how to distribute operating system functions, perhaps with multiple copies, among the nodes of long-distance networks to facilitate load sharing.

REFERENCES

1971. Denning, P. J. "Third Generation Computer Systems," *Computing Surveys* 3, *No. 4:* 175–216 (December).
1972. Organick, E. I. *The MULTICS System: An Examination of Its Structure.* Cambridge, MA: M.I.T. Press.

1973. Coffman, E. G., Jr. and Denning, P. J. *Operating Systems Theory*. Englewood Cliffs, NJ: Prentice-Hall.

1973. Katzan, H. *Operating Systems: A Pragmatic Approach*. New York: Van Nostrand-Reinhold.

1973. Organick, E. I. *Computer System Organization: The B5700/B6700 Series*. New York: Academic Press.

1974. Shaw, A. *The Logical Design of Operating Systems*. Englewood Cliffs, NJ: Prentice-Hall.

1975. Graham, R. M. *Principles of Systems Programming*. Reading, MA: Addison-Wesley.

1975. Wilkes, M. V. *Time Sharing Computer Systems,* 3rd Ed. New York: American Elsevier.

1976. Habermann, A. N., *Introduction to Operating System Design*. Chicago: SRA.

P. J. DENNING

OPERATIONS RESEARCH

For articles on related subjects *see* MATHEMATICAL PROGRAMMING; MODELS; QUEUEING THEORY; SIMULATION; SIMPLEX METHOD and STOCHASTIC PROCESS.

The Beginnings. The modern origins of operations research (OR) are attributed by Trefethen (1954) to the British military during World War II. A group known as Blackett's Circus assisted in the employment and coordination of radar equipment at gun sites. The success of the venture stimulated others, and the term *operational research* was applied to the application of scientific techniques to military operations. *Operations research (OR)* became the term in vogue in the U.S. as interest grew in both industry and the military following the war. Gradually, courses emerged in universities in both England and the U.S. Mathematics, statistics, and industrial engineering provided early impetus (and often an academic home) for the discipline, which has now emerged to a curriculum status in almost all major universities. Memberships in the Operations Research Society of America exceeded 6,700 as of 1 January 1980.

In a disciplinary sense, OR emerged from applied mathematics. The early probabilistic models of telephone problems by A. K. Erlang in the period 1909–1920 and the work of T. C. Fry (1928) precede the beginnings of OR, but both are acknowledged ancestral contributions. The paper by D. C. Palm (1947), formulating the machine interference problem, is an early example of the use of queueing models in production settings. The discovery of the simplex method of linear programming by George B. Dantzig (in 1947) triggered extensive research in constrained optimization, which emerged as a major element of OR. The papers of Kendall (1951, 1954) exerted major influence on subsequent developments in queueing theory. As early books integrated optimization and prob-

ability studies within the nucleus of the modeling approach, OR assumed a more recognizable disciplinary form.

The influence of the digital computer is difficult to overemphasize for certain areas such as computer simulation gained practical significance only through advances in computing hardware and software. Other subdisciplinary areas were to feel the computer influence much later, but they experienced no less an impact.

Views of Operations Research. Contemporary views of operations research have tended to reflect the particular responsibilities and interests of the viewer. For several years, the research community emphasized techniques and methodologies, dwelling principally on the mathematical underpinnings. The simplex method to solve linear programming problems, having assumed a focal position, was examined, tested, and extended as the research community sought to understand its necessary assumptions and to expand its applicability. Special classes of linear programming models were recognized, such as the transportation, network, and assignment problems, and algorithms were designed for efficiently solving these problems (see Dantzig, 1963). Researchers in queueing theory—the study of waiting lines—formed their own problem classification as they refined their understanding of the relations between the contributors to a waiting line situation—the arrival and service processes; the behavior of the potential and actual members of the queue; and the constraints on arrivals, service, or queue size.

Another view of OR might be characterized as the *model* view. Those adopting this vantage derived their own partitioning of OR activities, depending on the model type and the objectives of the modeler. For example, *descriptive models* furnished an understanding of an existing or planned problem situation without necessarily suggesting the means for improvement. Early queueing theory models were of this type. In contrast, *prescriptive models* offered solutions in terms of the desirability of outcomes. The determination of optimum or near optimum conditions through a linear program exemplified this type.

The partitioning of OR along model types was supported also by the differences in the underlying assumptions and the supporting mathematical subdiscipline. Linear programming and, later, mathematical programming (including linear, nonlinear, integer, and mixed) drew heavily on the areas of analysis and topology, while random process applications emanated from probability theory. Inevitably, problems arose with characteristics based on more than one underlying area of mathematics; scheduling and inventory decisions are two prime examples.

Scheduling theory seeks to provide prescriptive

models under deterministic or probabilistic conditions governing the sequencing of events, such as the order of task assignments to a single central processor. *Inventory theory* supports the development of prescriptive models of replenishment decisions possibly subject to uncertain conditions; for example, in the lead time between reorder and the arrival of the ordered stock. As significant questions forced attention to the use of both deterministic and probabilistic models within a single problem area, the size and complexity of models also increased. Consequently, the digital computer became an indispensable tool for solving the more challenging problems prompting such models.

Yet another perspective on OR might be described as the *algorithm* view. This view, often held by those practicing the profession in industry or government, stems naturally from the roots of the discipline in problem solving within an operational context. An algorithm might be broadly applicable, or it could be developed only to treat an isolated problem. The emphasis is on an efficient solution using the simplest modeling techniques that achieve the problem-solving objective. Increasing importance is attached to heuristic approaches—that is, the use of "rules of thumb," perhaps guided by theory or knowledge of the problem domain—to obtain "good" but not necessarily optimum solutions.

The concern for improved (but not necessarily optimal) behavior, and the increased complexity of models, combined to lend emphasis to the technique of computer simulation. Computer simulation as an early problem-solving tool received the attention of von Neumann (1951) and other noted scientists during the late 1940s. While simulation had historical origins predating computers and OR, the technique became significant only when development of the digital computer established its practical feasibility. Simulation is not an optimization technique, but is the combination of a simulation model and a search routine that enables directed improvement to be realized.

EXAMPLES OF THE OPERATIONS RESEARCH APPROACH

Fundamental in the OR approach is the development of a model to describe the particular problem. The following problem scenarios serve as simple illustrations of the several classes of models described above. Each scenario consists of a problem description, a solution description, and comments on the assumptions regarding the problem or implications of the solution technique. The simplicity of the selected problems cannot be over-emphasized. More practical examples would be excessively complex, difficult to understand, and likely to span two or more model classes.

A Scheduling Model for Throughput Maximization

Problem. An integral part of the operation of a computer system is the task scheduler, the program that assigns tasks to a CPU according to some criterion. One such criterion is to maximize throughput (the number of tasks completed per unit time). The designer of an operating system for a single-processor installation might utilize an OR modeling approach to implement the scheduling decision.

Solution. Assume that the order of task completions is immaterial and the completion of one task causes no change in the task completion time of a successor.

Let $t(i)$ = the completion time for the ith task to be completed; $t*$ = the arbitrary final time (with $t = 0$ at the start); and n = the number of completed tasks. The objective is to

$$\text{maximize } n \text{ such that } t(n) \leq t*.$$

That is, to find the largest number of tasks which can be completed in the interval from 0 to $t*$. Following intuition, the solution is to assign to the CPU that task requiring the least processing time. This scheduling rule assures that the maximum number of tasks are fitted into the $t*$ period.

Comments. (1) The above rule, known as the Shortest Processing Time (SPT) rule, can be shown to be optimal for criteria other than the maximization of throughput and to problems involving more than one processor [see Conway, Maxwell, and Miller (1967) and Coffman and Denning (1973)]. (2) Note that this solution requires that, during the time $t*$, the CPU is continuously busy. (3) The task completion times are assumed to be known and deterministic, which is not the usual case.

A Job Mix Resource Allocation Problem

Problem. A university computing center processes two types of jobs—teaching and research. The center is heavily loaded and seeks to maintain balanced service providing the highest satisfaction level to the entire user community. The center has a single computer with 5,120 Kb-hrs (kilobyte-hours, where 1 Kb-hr is the use of 1,000 bytes of memory for one hour) of memory and 48,000 seconds of CPU time available per day. The problem is to determine the balance between teaching and research jobs that provides the highest overall satisfaction level.

Solution. Working with the user community and the administration, the OR analyst estimates a "relative satisfaction return" per job of 6 to 4 for research and teaching, respectively. From a study of center records, the analyst obtains estimates of 32 Kb-hrs of memory and 200 seconds of CPU time for each teaching job. Each research job takes 40 Kb-hrs of memory and 400 seconds of CPU time. Using this data, the analyst constructs a linear programming model.

Let X_1 = the number of research jobs processed, and

X_2 = the number of teaching jobs processed.
Then, the objective (represented as the function z) is to maximize the overall satisfaction level:

$$\text{maximize } z = 6 * X_1 + 4 * X_2$$

while not exceeding the available memory and the CPU time limitation,

subject to:
$$40 * X_1 + 32 * X_2 \leq 5,120$$
$$400 * X_1 + 200 * X_2 \leq 48,000$$

and noting that the number of research and teaching jobs processed must be non-negative:

$$X_1 \geq 0, X_2 \geq 0.$$

This simple linear program in two variables (X_1 and X_2) can be solved graphically, as shown in Fig. 1 (*see* MATHEMATICAL PROGRAMMING). The solution of 107 research and 26 teaching jobs per day gives an overall maximum satisfaction level of 746.

Comments. (1) The determination of "relative satisfaction returns" is not a simple task, and another sub-disciplinary area of OR—decision analysis—deals with the definition, measurement, estimation, and integration of preferences. (2) The solution of this problem has been given as integer values because fractional jobs are not meaningful. Non-integer solutions are to be expected using linear programming, and roundoffs to integer values do not guarantee the preservation of an optimal solution.

Disk Access: A Queueing Problem

Problem. A disk is a peripheral storage device consisting of several recording surfaces, each of which resembles a phonograph record. A surface is divided concentrically into tracks and each track is divided into sectors of storage locations. The two basic types of disk design are movable head and fixed head (also known as head per track). The latter type has its read and write mechanisms—the heads—fixed in place, one pair for each track. Rotation of the disk brings the storage locations under the read/write (R/W) heads that permit the retrieval (reading) and storage (writing) of data (*see* MEMORY: Auxiliary).

Access requests contain a sector identifier so that the

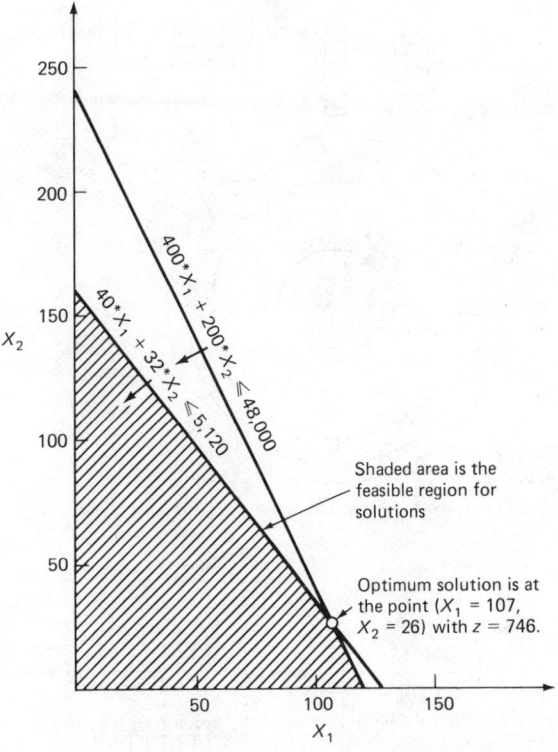

Fig. 1. Graphical solution of the job mix problem.

search in a fixed head disk consists of sector identification followed by address location within a sector. The access delay is made up of (1) the time to place the sector identifier (initializing address) under the R/W heads, which is called rotational latency, and (2) the time to locate the specific address within a sector (location time). Fig. 2(a) illustrates these access operations, which utilize a single-access request queue for a track.

The objective in programming the access to data stored on a fixed head disk is to minimize the total access time (latency plus location time). The simplest approach to this problem is to program the disk access as a "first come/first served" decision. However, some alternative decision rules can be suggested providing that certain specific data are available for implementing the solution. For example, if the sector identifiers for access requests and the current rotational position are known, then the closest sector could be accessed first. A mathematical (queueing) model offers a means for experimenting with different decision rules or alternative data organizations without incurring the expense of constructing the devices.

Solution. The rotational latency can be estimated to be one-half the time for one complete revolution (the request is equally likely to be any address on a track). However, the estimation of the seek time requires the use of

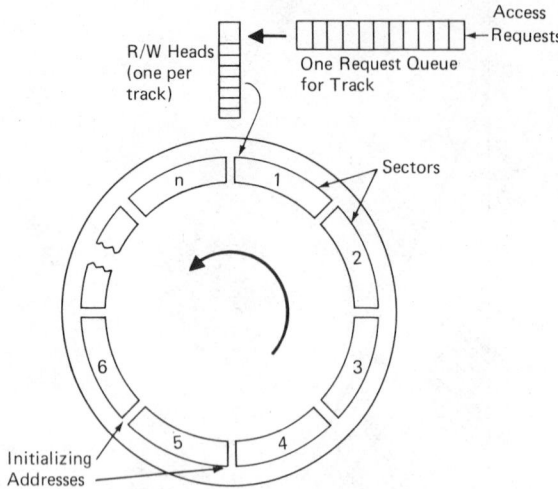

(a)   Track organization and a single request queue

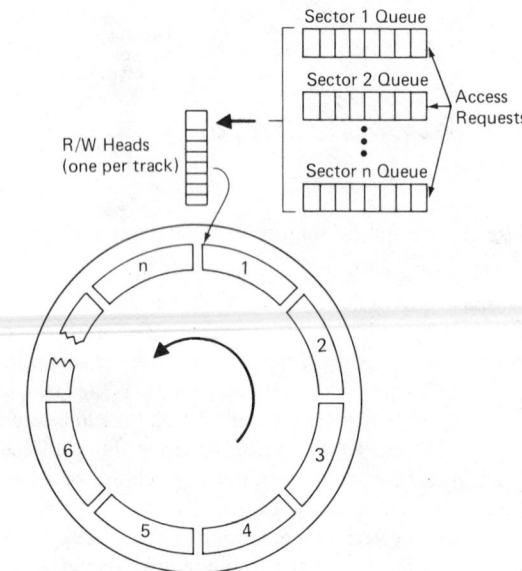

(b)   A request queue for each sector

Fig. 2.   Single- and multi-queue request illustrations.

probability theory beyond the scope of this article. Nevertheless, one can appreciate a suggested solution which defines a queue of disk requests for each sector and provides for service of any non-empty queue encountered by the R/W heads during the rotation of the surface. This multi-queue operation, illustrated in Fig. 2(b), significantly reduces the rotational latency.

Comments. The multi-queue operation can be modeled, with the appropriate assumptions, so as to admit a solution through mathematical derivations. A more com-

plicated model is likely to require the use of computer simulation, which could be more costly to produce but more detailed in its description.

RELATIONSHIPS WITH COMPUTER SCIENCE

Computer science and OR are linked by the similarities in their evolutions, their mutual dependencies on mathematics, and the close proximities of their research and applications areas. A scan of the prominent overlapping technical areas reveals both similarities and contrasts in the two disciplines, especially when each is viewed in relation to the other. (A comprehensive picture of OR techniques is given in Moder and Elmaghraby, 1978.)

William Orchard-Hays (1978) provides an excellent history of the development of mathematical programming systems, which documents not only the significant advances enabled by the rapid development of computing technology, but also notes the contributions to the technology stimulated by the reactions to the demands of those producing mathematical programming systems. Expanding computational capabilities has enabled the solution of larger, more complex problems. However, caution is warranted in attributing the ability to solve more extensive problems simply to more capable computer systems; actually, the expanded capabilities can be traced to one or more of the following sources.

1. The discovery of new mathematical techniques which are embodied in existing algorithms (for example, the solution of traveling salesman problems with 150 cities in 1980, compared to only 20 cities in 1960).
2. The design or redesign of algorithms, involving both changes in data structures and revisions in the operations and control structures (enabling the solution of linear programs with 10,000 rows and 100,000 columns, for example).
3. The revelation of the complexity inherent in classes of problems so that heuristic techniques can be employed to obtain near optimal solutions (for example, the general scheduling problem).
4. The increase in storage and speed provided with current computing systems.

Advances in numerical approximation techniques, predominantly through research in computer science, have extended the range of "solvable" probabilistic models. Researchers in OR, sensitive to the utility of the approximate but more informative models, have contributed to the improvement and extension of the techniques (see Bhat, 1969). Instead of exact solutions to queueing models, given in terms of complex and abstract Laplace-

Stieltjes transforms, approximate answers are now more common, both for the long-term (steady-state) and the short-term (transient) behavior of the system being studied. So important have computational approximations become in the solution of probabilistic models that an area of inquiry—computational probability—has emerged within OR (see Neuts, 1980).

Advances in the development and applicability of computer simulation have proceeded through the extensions to the methodology for statistical analysis of model output and the improved capabilities of simulation programming languages (e.g., Simula 67, Simscript II.5, GPSS V) and model development tools (e.g., the DELTA Project underway at the Norwegian Computing Center, 1977). Fundamental inquiry into the representation of simulation models and efficient experimentation represents a research area of mutual interest for computer scientists, operations researchers, and systems theorists (see Zeigler, 1976).

Perhaps the nucleus of the intersection of OR and computer science is the algorithm. The derivation and design of algorithms has dominated OR throughout its history and has been recognized as a major element of computer science at least since the publication of the book by Knuth (1968). The representation of algorithms, usually as computer programs, has been a dominant concern of computer science from the early 1950s. More recently, the interest in algorithms has broadened for both disciplines, and the future might portend the merging of research in this fundamental area.

REFERENCES

1928. Fry, T. C. *Probability and Its Engineering Uses*. New York: D. Van Nostrand.
1947. Palm, D. C. "The Distribution of Repairmen in Servicing Automatic Machines" (Swedish), *Industritidningen Norden* **75**: 75.
1951. von Neumann, J. "Various Techniques Used in Connection with Random Digits," *National Bureau of Standards, Applied Mathematics Series 12*, p. 36.
1951. Kendall, D. G. "Some Problems in the Theory of Queues," *Journal of the Royal Statistical Society* **B13**: 151.
1954. Kendall, D. G. "Stochastic Processes Occurring in the Theory of Queues and Their Analysis by the Method of the Imbedded Markov Chain," *Annals of Mathematical Statistics* **24**: 338.
1954. Trefethen, F. N. "A History of Operations Research," in McCloskey, J. F. and Trefethan, F. N. (Eds.), *Operations Research for Management* **1**. Baltimore: Johns Hopkins Press.
1963. Dantzig, G. B. *Linear Programming and Extensions*. Princeton: Princeton University Press.
1967. Conway, R. W., Maxwell, W. L. and Miller, L. W. *Theory of Scheduling*. Reading, MA: Addison-Wesley.
1968. Knuth, D. E. *The Art of Computer Programming* **1**: *Fundamental Algorithms*. Reading, MA: Addison-Wesley.
1969. Bhat, U. N. "Sixty Years of Queueing Theory," *Management Science* **15**, *No. 6:* B-280 (February).
1973. Coffman, E. G. and Denning, P. E. *Operating Systems Theory*. Englewood Cliffs, NJ: Prentice-Hall.
1976. Zeigler, B. P. *Theory of Modeling and Simulation*. New York: Wiley.
1977. Holbaek-Hanssen, E., Handlykken, P., and Nygaard, K. *System Description and the DELTA Language, Report No. 4* (Publication No. 523). Oslo: Norwegian Computing Center.
1978. Orchard-Hays, W. "History of Mathematical Programming Systems," in Greenberg, H. J. (Ed.), *Design and Implementation of Optimization Software*. Alphen aan den Rijn, The Netherlands: Sijthoff and Noordhoff.
1978. Moder, J. J. and Elmaghraby, S. E. *Handbook of Operations Research*. New York: Van Nostrand Reinhold.
1980. Neuts, M. F. *Matrix-Geometric Solutions for Stochastic Models: An Algorithmic Approach*. Baltimore: Johns Hopkins Press.

RICHARD E. NANCE

OPTICAL CHARACTER READER

For articles on related subjects *see* DATA PREPARATION DEVICES; INPUT-OUTPUT DEVICES; MACHINE-READABLE FORM; OPTICAL MARK READERS; PATTERN RECOGNITION; and UNIVERSAL PRODUCT CODE.

Optical character recognition (OCR) may be defined as the high-speed process of converting machine (i.e., typewritten or printed) or hand-printed numerals, letters, and symbols into computer-processable information by an optical scanning system.

Basic Configuration and Operation of OCR Systems. Before data from an OCR document can be converted into its machine representation, it has to pass through three major OCR subsystems—an electro-optical converter, a preprocessor, and a recognition logic system.

The electro-optical converter scans the characters and converts them into electric signals for further processing. Commonly, three scan patterns can be identified.

1. The *raster scan,* which scans the entire field of view, a line at a time (similarly to commercial television cameras), using some basic scanning technique, such as mechanical, vidicon, flying-spot with either a cathode ray tube (CRT) or laser light source, or an array of photocells in either single-row or two-dimensional retina arrangement.

OCR-A

ALPHA CHARACTER SET:
UPPER CASE: A B C D E F G H I J K L M N O P Q R S T U V W X Y Z
LOWER CASE: a b c d e f g h i j k l m n o p q r s t u v w x y z
NUMERIC CHARACTER SET: 0 1 2 3 4 5 6 7 8 9
PUNCTUATION: ; ' , . : ? "
SYMBOLS: - = / ¥ ⌐ ♪ $ % & * + { } |

OCR-B

ALPHA CHARACTER SET:
UPPER CASE: A B C D E F G H I J K L M N O P Q R S T U V W X Y Z
LOWER CASE: a b c d e f g h i j k l m n o p q r s t u v w x y z
NUMERIC CHARACTER SET: 0 1 2 3 4 5 6 7 8 9
PUNCTUATION: ; ' , . : ? !
SYMBOLS: - = / + @ & $ * ( ) — ■ |

1403

ALPHA CHARACTER SET: A B C D E F G H I J K L M N O P Q R S T U V W X Y Z
NUMERIC CHARACTER SET: 0 1 2 3 4 5 6 7 8 9
PUNCTUATION: ; ' , . :
SYMBOLS: / - ¤ # $ % & = + *

PICA 72

ALPHA CHARACTER SET:
UPPER CASE: A B C D E F G H I J K L M N O P Q R S T U V W X Y Z
LOWER CASE: a b c d e f g h i j k l m n o p q r s t u v w x y z
NUMERIC CHARACTER SET: 0 1 2 3 4 5 6 7 8 9
PUNCTUATION: ? ; : , . '
SYMBOLS: $ & + ( ) * % # = / - @

Fig. 1 Machine-printed alphanumerical optical fonts. OCR-A and the less stylized OCR-B are international standard fonts. The two others are examples of nonstandard fonts. The 1403 is derived from the IBM 1403 computer printer; the PICA 72 is a typewriter font. All examples are printed in an approximately 1:1 scale.

2. The *line-following scan,* which follows successively the outline of each character within the field of view. (Used mainly when large numbers of type fonts or print styles must be accommodated.)

3. A hybrid scanning technique, which, due to the availability of monolithic self-scanned line arrays, makes feasible a mode of scanning that is partly electronic and partly mechanical; it gives rise to a *modified raster scan.* (Self-scanned arrays consist of a row or matrix of photodiodes or, more recently, of a row of light emitting diodes— LEDs.)

The preprocessor converts the output signal of the scanner into a form that can be used by the recognition logic system for character identification. Two steps, quantization and feature extraction, may be involved, depending on the nature of the system. The quantizer converts the analog signals produced by the scanner into digital signals representing light and dark areas and may also include noise elimination and normalization logic. The feature-extraction logic reduces the scanner or quantizer output to feature sets from which the characters can be more reliably recognized.

The recognition logic system performs two functions. It locates the characters and, if necessary, separates them

from one another. It then identifies each character by one of several classification schemes. One of the simplest is that which directly compares the quantized scanner output data with a stored representation (or template) of each character and selects the closest match. Other classification schemes are based on the use of nongeometric features of the characters to be recognized, such as density, or on some form of geometric-feature matching, or on using complex features and mathematical transformations, etc.

If the decision logic connected with the recognition process cannot identify a character with reasonably high probability, it is preferable to reject the character since erroneous identification can be costly. Then, depending upon the application and machine used, one of several alternate strategies may be followed, such as:

- A new attempt at automatic recognition, by rereading (perhaps several times) and/or by programmed correction (e.g., check digit validation or context correction).
- A new attempt by operator-assisted recognition, using a keyboard plus a visual display unit (VDU).
- The document containing the unrecognized character being automatically marked or directed to a reject stacker; such documents can either be

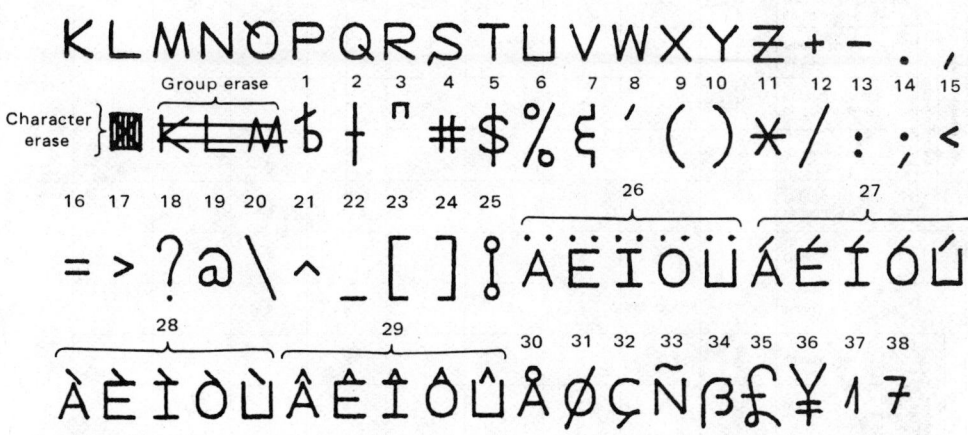

NOTE: Scale approximately 1:1.

Fig. 2.   Standard hand-printed universal subset optical fonts—ANSI standard, U.S. character repertoires.

1 blank symbol
2 long vertical bar (logical OR)
3 quotation marks
4 number sign
5 dollar sign
6 percent sign
7 ampersand
8 apostrophe
9 opening parenthesis
10 closing parenthesis
11 asterisk
12 slash (division sign)
13 colon
14 semi-colon
15 less than
16 equal
17 greater than
18 question mark
19 "at" sign

20 reverse slant
21 circumflex
22 underline
23 opening bracket
24 closing bracket
25 dumbbell—available   character   for   special purposes
26 umlauts (German)
27 accent acute (French)
28 accent grave (French)
29 accent circumflex (French)
30 angstrom (Danish and Swedish)
31 oerted (Norwegian)
32 cedilla (French)
33 tilde (Portuguese and Spanish)
34 double "s" (German)
35 pound symbol
36 yen symbol
37 number one in Europe
38 number seven in Europe

corrected or retyped for a rerun, or they can be used as the basis for transcription by some other data preparation device.

Machine-Readable Optical Fonts. Several fonts are commonly being used for optical character reading. Historically, the first commercially available optical character readers were single-font readers which used specifically designed heavily stylized machine-printed fonts with small character sets generally containing numeric or alphanumeric (upper case) characters plus a few special symbols. These fonts were not standard, as each manufacturer tended to design its own font.

Later, systematic hardware and software developments brought the advent of multifont readers capable of reading less stylized machine-printed fonts with a large number of characters (up to a full ASCII character set), as well as hand-printed numerals. Two machine-printed

Table 1. Classes of Optical Character Readers

Optical Character Reader Class	Typical Device	Kind of Reader — General-purpose	Kind of Reader — Special-purpose	Part of Multi-media Shared-logic Systems	Capability to Read — One or Two Lines	Capability to Read — Several Lines	Operating Mode — Stand-alone Units	On-Line — Without Communications Interface	On-Line — With Communications Interface	Scanning Unit — Stationary	Scanning Unit — Moving	Data Carrier Located — Inside Scanner	Outside Scanner Close to	Outside Scanner At Longer Distance	Paper Up to A4	Paper Up to A5	Journal Tape	Microfilm	Other	Preprinting by Printing Presses	As Computer Printout	By Typewriter or Keyboard Encoder	By Cash Register, Adding Machine, etc.	By Label-printing Machines or Computer Label-printers	By Handwriting (Hand-printing or Marking)	Anyhow, however, Microfilmed at Some Later Stage
1 General-purpose page readers	IBM 3886 Scan Data 1150	Y	N	(Y)	Y	Y	Y[5]	Y[5]	Y[5]	Y	N	Y	N	N	Y	(Y)	(Y)	N	N	Y	Y	Y	(Y)[4]	N	Y	N
2 General-purpose document readers	Lundy 7200 HYPERSCAN Scan Data 410	Y	N	(Y)	Y	N	Y[5]	Y[5]	Y[5]	Y	N	Y	N	N	Y	Y	(Y)	N	N	Y	Y	Y	(Y)[4]	N	Y	N
3 Journal tape readers	Almex OCR 82 Scan Optics 501	Y	N	(Y)	Y	Y	Y[5]	Y[5]	Y[5]	Y	N	Y	N	N	N	N	Y	N	N	N	Y	Y	Y	N	N	N
4 Special-purpose page readers	Scan Data 3350 Hendrix Typereader 2	(Y)	Y	(Y)	Y	Y	Y[5]	Y[5]	N	Y	N	Y	N	N	N	(Y)	(Y)	N	N	Y	Y	Y	(Y)[4]	N	Y	N
5 Special-purpose document readers	REI-TRACE System Cognitronics Syst. 71 Cummins Allison SCANAK 4229	(Y)	Y	(Y)	Y	N	Y[5]	Y[5]	Y[5]	Y	N	Y	N	N	N	Y	(Y)	N	N	Y	Y	Y	(Y)[4]	(Y)	Y	N
6 Microfilm readers (CIM-Computer Input from Microfilm)	Information International Inc. GRAFIX 1	Y	Y	N	Y	Y	Y[5]	Y[5]	N	N	Y	Y	N	N	N	N	N	Y	N	→	→	→	→	→	→	Y
7 Miniature hand-held character readers (optical wands)	REI-OCR WAND Key Tronic M-3 Caere 760	N	Y	(Y)	Y	N	Y[5]	Y[5]	Y[5]	N	Y	N	Y	N	(Y)	Y[1,2]	(Y)	N	(Y)[1]	(Y)	(Y)	(Y)	(Y)	Y	N	N
8 Stationary slot scanners	Batelle Institute Scanner	N	Y	N	Y	N	N	N	N	Y	N	N	Y	N	N	Y[2]	N	N	(Y)[3]	N	N	N	N	Y	N	N
9 Stationary industrial scanners	URW Unternehmens-beratung Scanner	Y	Y	N	Y	N	Y[5]	Y[5]	N	Y	N	N	Y	N	N	Y[2]	N	N	Y[3]	N	N	N	N	Y	N	N

Y = yes, N = no, (Y) = yes, sometimes.
1 Some readers can read laminated documents such as identity cards made of plastic, etc.
2 Generally tags.
3 With capability to read information painted on cases, cars, etc.
4 To be used with journal tape readers only.
5 Only one of the marked possibilities can be chosen when specifying reader's configuration.

fonts—the OCR-A (formerly called ISO-A or ANSI-A) and the OCR-B (formerly ISO-B or ECMA-11) shown in Fig. 1—and one hand-printed font (Fig. 2) have been agreed upon as standards.

Currently, optical readers include a variety of machines with widely different reading capabilities, ranging from single-font readers that can read just one machine-printed stylized numerical font up to multiple-font readers that can read several machine-printed fonts of various kinds, size, and pitch, as well as hand-printed characters and marks (*see* OPTICAL MARK READERS), which may all be intermixed on a document or line. These different reading capabilities have a considerable impact on the readers' costs.

Classes of OCR Readers and Their Characteristics.

Nine classes of OCR readers can be identified, as shown in Table 1.

Since most OCR equipment is computer controlled, some editing and validation may be included in OCR devices. However, the high input speed (up to several thousand characters a second) and the occurrence of rejects means that computer files usually cannot be accessed for full editing in devices used for on-line processing.

OCR Application Areas and Effectiveness.

Four groups of typical OCR application areas can be identified:

1. *Data entry systems in which an inscription can be read repetitively* at different times and, usually, at different places. (An example of such a system is circulation control in libraries, where each transaction record is created by scanning the bor-

rower's identity card and the book identification number printed on a label attached to the book. The higher the volume of transactions, the greater is the cost-effectiveness of such a system. The effectiveness can be further improved when the same data carriers can also be used in other applications, as, for example, identity cards for patients in medical systems.)

2. *Nontranscriptive data entry systems with computer-generated "turnaround" documents* which are prepared at a computing center, transmitted for information purposes, usually outside this organization, and received back at some later time, when the required transaction takes place, for machine-reading and computer processing. (An example of such a system is a public utility billing or notice of payment due, as shown in Fig. 3, which requires the return of the bill stub with the payment. To be effective, these systems require the use of forms with uniform design. Also, the vast majority of forms must be returned for optical reading. A very low rejection and substitution rate can be expected in turnaround document systems, since strict control on the forms and the print quality can be exercised.)

3. *Systems with nontranscriptive data entry without "turnaround" documents,* of which the most commonly used are those with data entry at the source by handwriting. The main aim here is to eliminate central data preparation and to shorten the time interval between the moment when a transaction takes place and when it is processed. Documents prepared in this way also meet the requirement for a hard copy for auditing or other

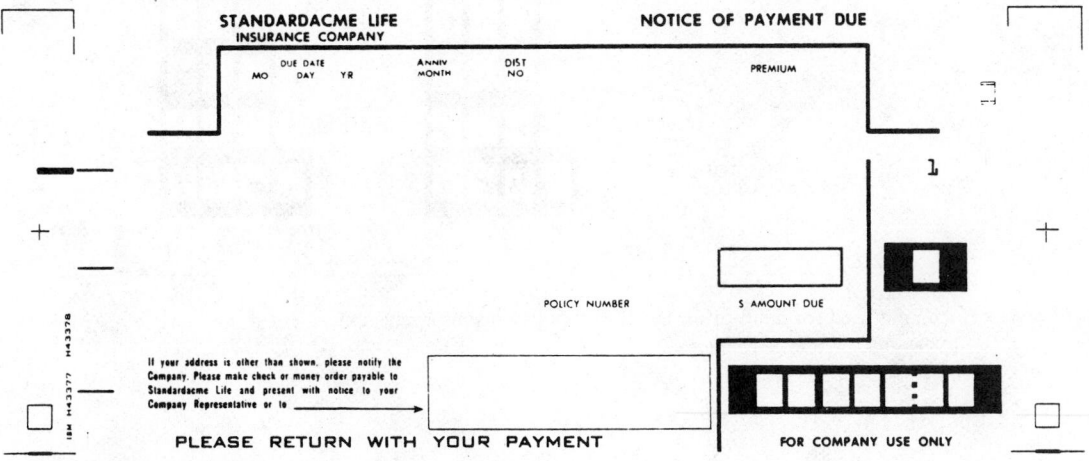

Fig. 3. Turnaround billing document for OCR input.

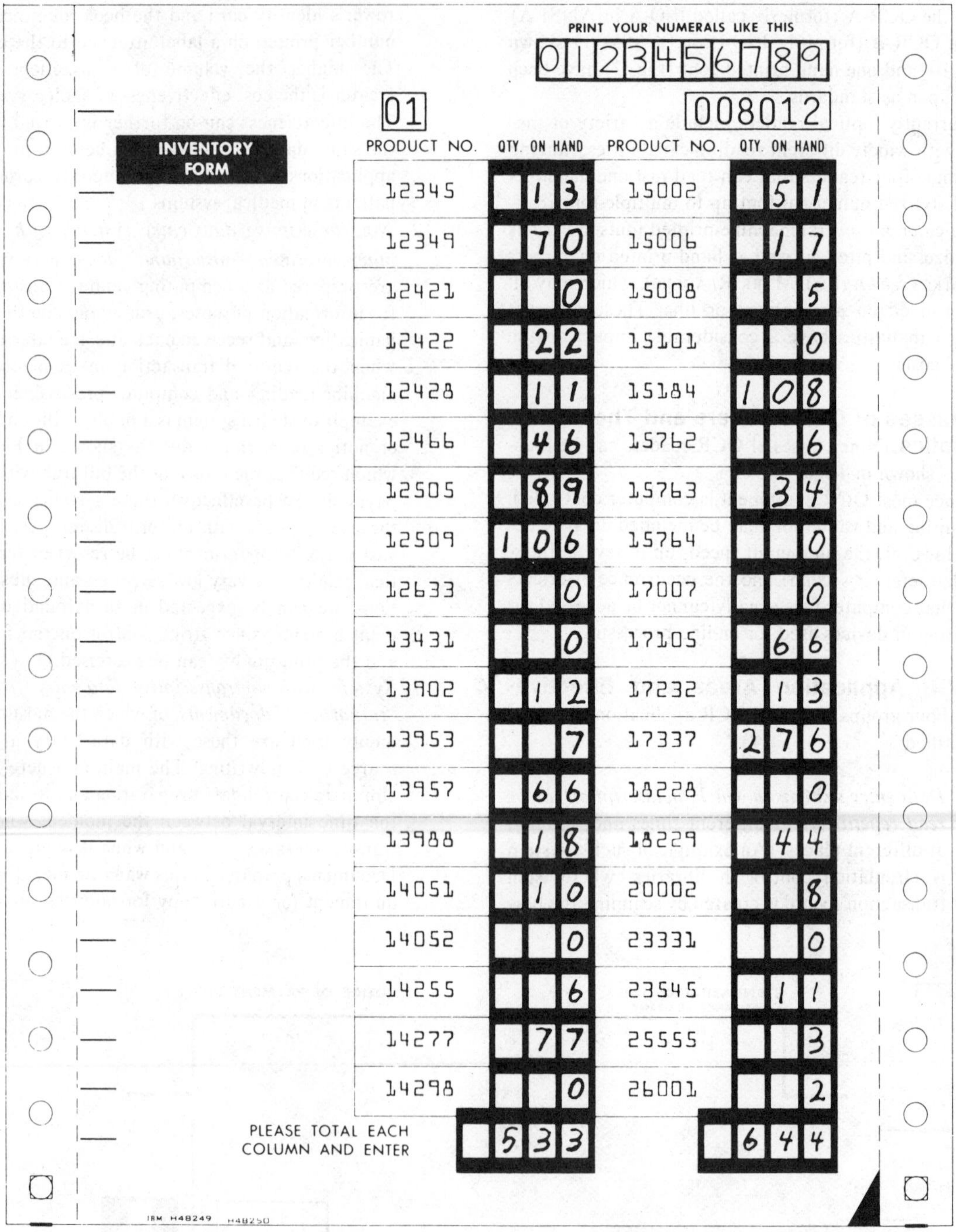

PRINT YOUR NUMERALS LIKE THIS

| 0 | 1 | 2 | 3 | 4 | 5 | 6 | 7 | 8 | 9 |

01

008012

INVENTORY FORM

PRODUCT NO.	QTY. ON HAND	PRODUCT NO.	QTY. ON HAND
12345	13	15002	51
12349	70	15006	17
12421	0	15008	5
12422	22	15101	0
12428	11	15184	108
12466	46	15762	6
12505	89	15763	34
12509	106	15764	0
12633	0	17007	0
13431	0	17105	66
13902	12	17232	13
13953	7	17337	276
13957	66	18228	0
13988	18	18229	44
14051	10	20002	8
14052	0	23331	0
14255	6	23545	11
14277	77	25555	3
14298	0	26001	2
PLEASE TOTAL EACH COLUMN AND ENTER	533		644

IBM H48249   H48250

Fig. 4. Document used for hand-printing OCR input to inventory system.

purposes. A typical example is that of recording incoming orders. (An important advantage of these systems is the elimination of the transcription process requiring keying. Whenever appropriate, further improvements in costs can be achieved by using forms with preprinted data so that the amount of handwriting or typing is kept to a minimum, as shown in Fig. 4.)

4. *Systems with conventional transcriptive data entry,* generally considered to be the least cost-effective systems for OCR readers. However, some reasons for their use can be identified, such as the need to transcribe the original document for some control purpose; the replacement of a more highly qualified operator (such as a keypunch operator) by a less qualified one (such as a typist); or the requirement to create a hard copy of the input data for auditing or other purposes.

REFERENCES

1971. "Character Recognition 1971." A publication of the British Computer Society.
1974. Freedman, M. D. "Optical Character Recognition," *IEEE Spectrum* (March), pp. 42–52.
1976. Benwell, N. J. (Ed.). *Data Preparation Techniques.* London: Advance Publications.
1977. "All About Optical Readers," Datapro Research Corp. Report on Peripherals (May), pp. 70D-010-78a–78o.

J. NECAS

OPTICAL MARK READERS

For articles on related subjects *see* DATA PREPARATION DEVICES; INPUT-OUTPUT DEVICES; OPTICAL CHARACTER READER; and UNIVERSAL PRODUCT CODE.

The first optical mark readers appeared in the early 1960s. They were initially designed to read information marked in pencil on examination sheets and were used off-line from a computer. They read answers as a series of marks on the sheet, accumulating these answers and printing the results at the bottom of the sheet. Examples of such units were the IBM 1230 Optical Mark Scoring Reader, and the Optical Scan Corporation's Model 100 Test-Scoring Reader.

As the uses of optical mark reading expanded to other applications, the availability of other optical mark readers increased in the 1960s and early 1970s. These later models were designed to be attached either directly to a computer, or to off-line card punches or magnetic tape.

Reading Optical Marks. In optical mark reading, information is read as a series of marks on a sheet of paper, which is divided into a number of separate mark response positions as illustrated in Fig. 1. Specific response positions may represent the digits 0–9, or may represent different choices among a number of possible responses. Each separate response position is then interpreted by the computer to have a specific meaning.

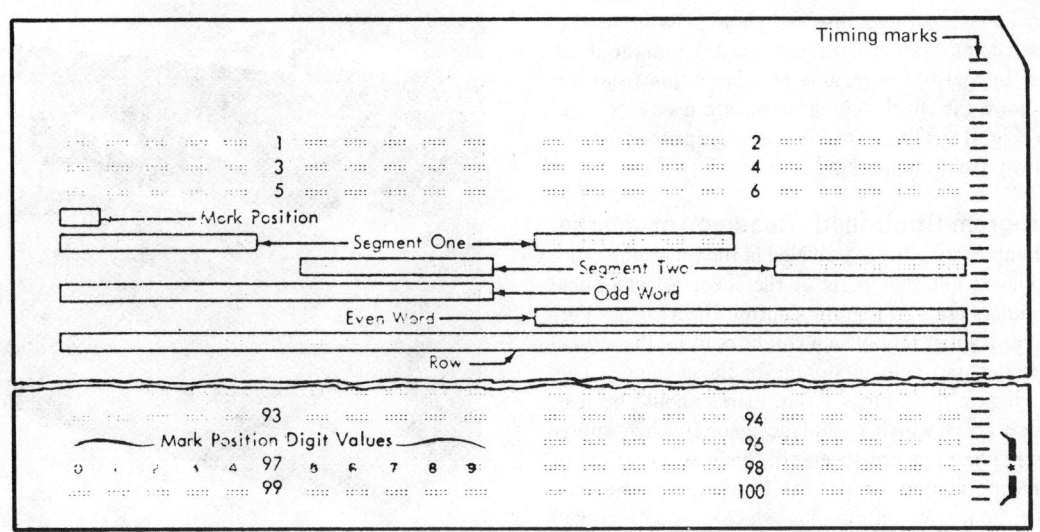

*These six control timing marks are used for counter read out controls in the IBM 1230.

Fig. 1. Typical optical mark reader data sheet format.

Fig. 2.   The Data Recognition System 83 reads optically marked sheets and records this data on magnetic tape. (Courtesy Data Recognition Limited.)

Information is recorded using a pencil, a ballpoint pen, or a fiber-tip pen, or it may be produced directly by a computer printer, embossed plate, or preprinting. These marks are then read optically. Lamps direct beams of light onto the paper, which are reflected back from the paper; the amount of light reflected is measured by a photocell. When a mark is present, the amount of light reflected is much less than when the mark is absent. In many readers, separate lamps and photo cells are used to read each column of mark response positions on the sheet. In order to control the reading of information from row to row down the sheet, timing marks are used (see right side of Fig. 1). These are normally preprinted on the sheet away from the marking area.

Program-Controlled Reading of Marks.

Considerable flexibility is provided in the recording of information on different parts of the sheet. Most optical mark readers use a "Program Control Sheet" or a "Format Control Program," which can be read by the optical mark reader and held in storage in the machine. This sheet indicates those areas where marks should be read and those areas which should be ignored when subsequently reading marked sheets. In this way, a variety of different information formats can be used.

The amount of information which can be recorded on a marked sheet varies with different machines. Examples of optical mark readers are the System 83, produced by Data Recognition (see Fig. 2), or the IBM 3881 Optical Mark Reader (see Fig. 3).

Fig. 3.   IBM 3881 optical mark reader, which handles documents ranging from small cards to page-size forms.

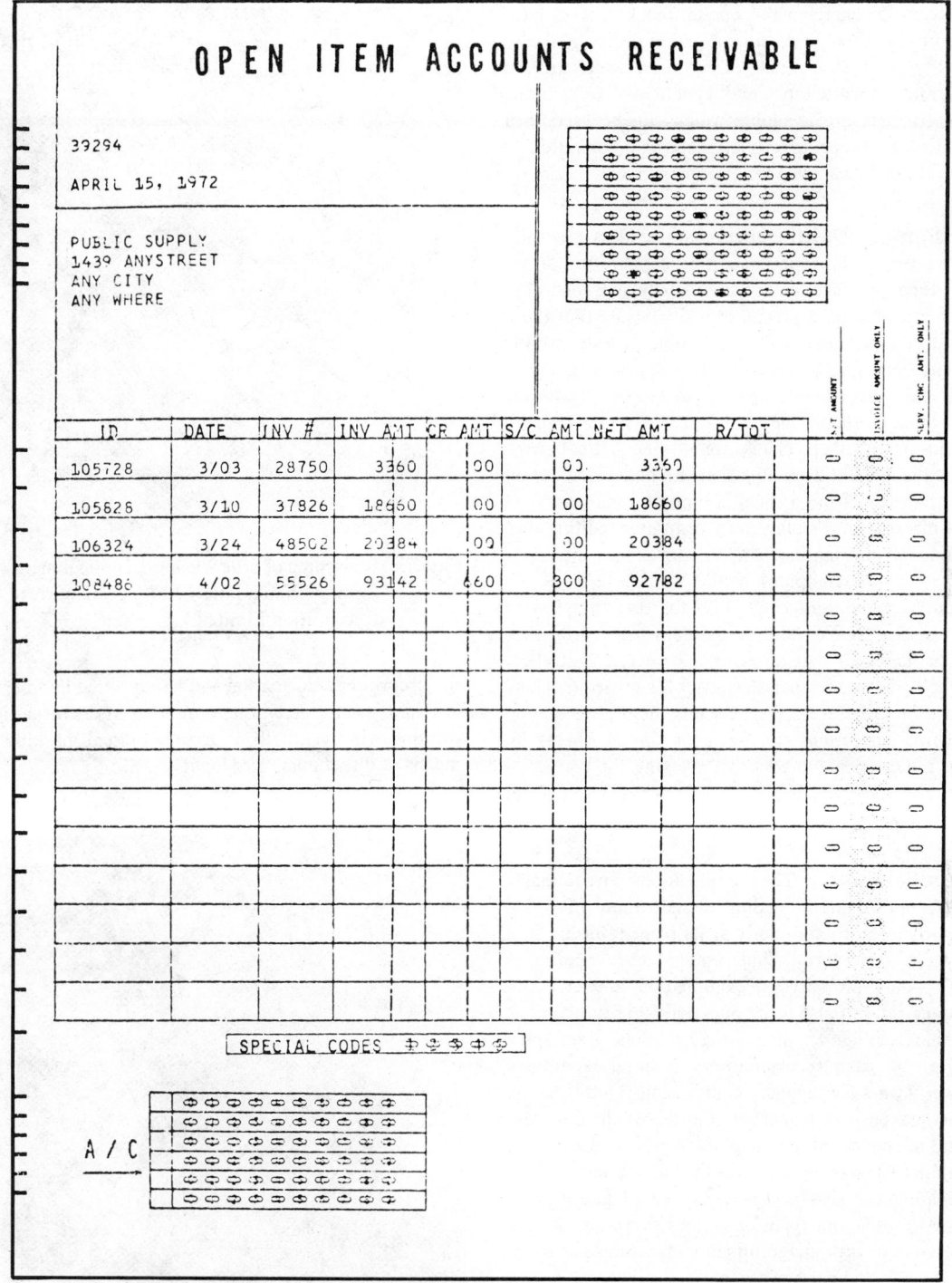

Fig. 4. Recording of accounts receivable data using a hand-marked optical mark sheet.

Recent developments in optical mark readers have resulted in increases in document reading rates, and also the ability to attach a variety of peripherals such as card readers and magnetic tape and magnetic disk units to the reader. Readers are available which can be used in a stand-alone mode, or directly attached to a computer, or instead remotely attached via telephone lines.

Editing of Data. Optical mark readers generally provide a limited information-editing capability. For example, they can test for the mandatory presence of a mark in a field of data, or can check to ensure that there is not more than one mark. In addition, in order to differentiate between a distinct mark, a spurious mark, or a mark which may have been only partly erased, controls are provided to enable the reader to verify the *intensity* of marks on the sheet. Thus, for off-line optical mark readers, the amount of editing that can be carried out on information read from a sheet is limited; for readers attached directly or remotely to a computer, editing and validation of information can be carried out more exhaustively by the computer. Sufficient time is available between the reading of each sheet for the computer to access various files to validate the data marked on that sheet. In the event that an error is detected, that sheet can be selected into a separate stacker for subsequent correction. Since these error sheets are themselves source documents, corrections can be made on the sheets by erasing the erroneous marks and marking the necessary information correctly. The sheet can then be re-read and re-edited, and accepted if valid.

Applications. The applications particularly suited to optical mark reading include those in which data is to be recorded directly at its point of origin in a machine-readable form. Thus, optical mark reading is ideal not only for surveys, examination answers, and questionnaires, but also for applications such as accounts receivable (see Fig. 4), advertising bookings, order entry (see Fig. 5), cash reconciliations, hospital laboratory analyses, insurance agents' commissions, job costing, parts issues, payroll, personnel records, production control, and telephone sales among many others. When used in conjunction with diagrammatic information, optical mark reading can also be used in medical diagnosis to record the location and types of various symptoms by entering marks on a prediagrammed body form so as to indicate the affected parts of the body.

The Future. Because of recent technological advances, optical mark reading is being superseded in many current applications by other forms of optical input. In particular, hand-held optical character readers can perform many of the tasks of optical mark readers by reading preprinted information and handprinted numbers and letters. It seems likely, therefore, that in the future handprinting will eventually supersede optical marking as a means of direct computer input.

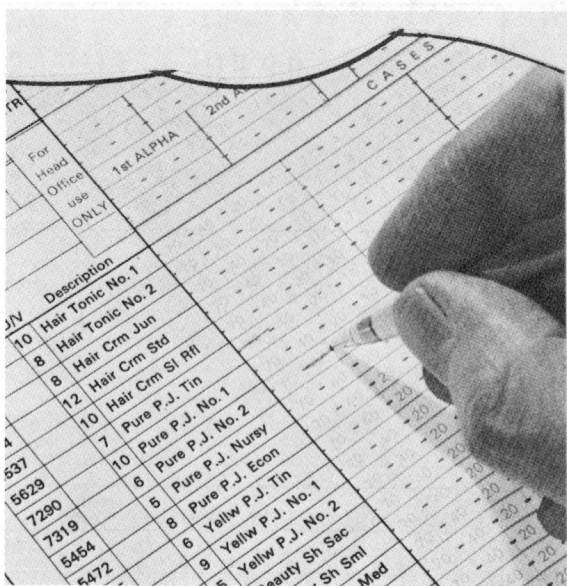

Fig. 5. Recording of orders using an optical mark order form, with hand-marked input. (Courtesy Data Recognition Limited.)

C. B. FINKELSTEIN

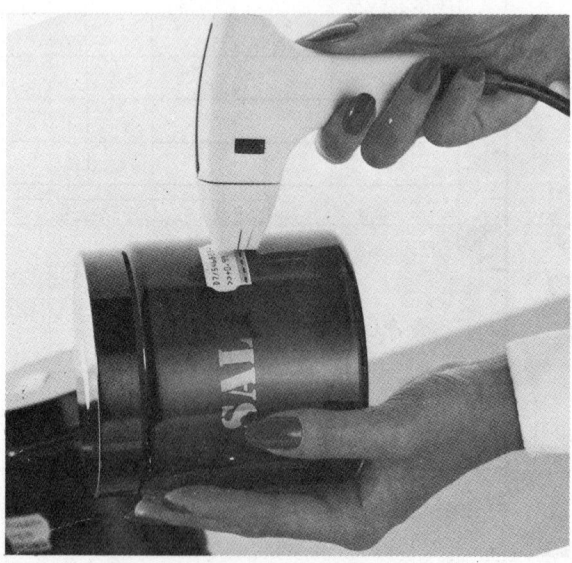

Fig. 6. ICL 9531 OCR Wand Reader for hand-held reading of optical character information—a possible successor to optical mark reading.

OPTIMIZATION METHODS

For articles on related subjects *see* LEAST-SQUARES APPROXIMATION; MATHEMATICAL PROGRAMMING; MODELS; NUMERICAL ANALYSIS; OPERATIONS RESEARCH; QUEUEING THEORY; SIMPLEX METHOD; SIMULATION; and TOMOGRAPHY, COMPUTED.

Mathematical optimization deals with the problem of finding (or approximating) a point that gives an *optimal* (minimal or maximal) *value* to some function (called the *objective function*), subject to some additional conditions (called *constraints*).

Many problems in various scientific and technological fields, such as physics, engineering, chemistry, economics, and operations research, as well as other fields of mathematics, can be cast as optimization problems and thereby benefit from, and contribute to, the reservoir of knowledge of mathematical optimization. In this field, numerical analysis, computational methods, and other branches of mathematics, as well as the study of practical applications, interact with and fertilize one another and promote our understanding and ability to solve concrete problems.

The two main branches of optimization are *dynamic optimization* and *static optimization*. The latter is more commonly called *mathematical programming*.

Dynamic optimization is particularly concerned with decision-making situations or economic growth models and mathematical formulations of problems involving moving objects in which the time variable enters naturally into the optimization problem and therefore also appears in its solution. The objective function here usually takes the form of an integral, while the constraints are described by a system of differential equations. The forerunner of this discipline was the *calculus of variations,* which, later on, upon the formulation of *Pontryagin's maximum principle,* developed into the modern theory of *optimal control* (*see* McShane, 1978, for a review of this development). In between, the theory of *dynamic programming* appeared. This proved itself particularly efficient in handling multistage decision processes [see Bellman and Kalaba (1965) and Dreyfus (1965)].

Static optimization is concerned with all forms of time-independent optimization. In the general formulation of the static optimization problem (*see* MATHEMATICAL PROGRAMMING), there is a function of n variables to be optimized (i.e., maximized or minimized), called the *objective function,* subject to m constraints on the variables. When the objective function and the constraints are all linear, this area is called *linear programming* and the best known method is called the *simplex method.*

Obviously, the rest of mathematical programming is called *nonlinear programming,* of which one sub-branch is *convex programming,* in which the objective function

is a convex function and the *feasible set* (that is, those points in Euclidean n-space which satisfy the constraints) is a *convex set.* Part way between linear and convex programming lies the theory and practice of *quadratic programming,* dealing with problems where the objective function is a positive definite quadratic function and the constraints are linear.

If the additional condition that some or all variables should take only integer values is imposed on the problem, *integer programming* is obtained.

Other specialized branches of mathematical programming are *stochastic programming* [see, e.g., Sengupta (1972)], *geometric programming* [see, e.g., Duffin *et al.* (1967)], *multiobjective programming* [see, e.g., Polak and Payne (1976)], and *large-scale programming* [see, e.g., Lasdon (1970)].

Real systems most often lead to large optimization problems which can be solved practically only by implementation of appropriate solution algorithms on a computer. Success or failure then depends strongly on computer-programming talent, acquaintance with machine specifications and the right methodology of implementation.

Some Optimization Methods. In this section, we shall sample briefly the huge number of methods of mathematical optimization.

Solving Nonlinear Equations. The general problem is that of solving a system of equations $F\mathbf{x} = \mathbf{0}$, where F is an operator mapping some domain D of Euclidean R^n space into R^n. This problem arises frequently in numerous fields of applications so that the importance of having at hand effective methods of solution for it can hardly be exaggerated. One fruitful approach is to replace it by an equivalent optimization problem. With the aid of a real-valued function f on R^n, which has the property that its global minimum is uniquely attained at $\mathbf{x} = \mathbf{0}$, a new function g is defined by

$$g(\mathbf{x}) = f(F\mathbf{x}) \qquad \text{for} \qquad \mathbf{x} \in D,$$

Then the optimization problem

> Minimize: $g(\mathbf{x})$
> Such that: $\mathbf{x} \in D$,

has to be solved to find $\mathbf{x}^* \in D$, which gives g its global minimum on D.

If $F\mathbf{x} = \mathbf{0}$ has a solution, then this must be $\mathbf{x}^*$. If $F\mathbf{x} = \mathbf{0}$ has no solution in D, then $\mathbf{x}^*$ is called an *f-minimal solution* of $F\mathbf{x} = \mathbf{0}$ (see Ortega and Rheinboldt, 1970). The special choice $f(\mathbf{x}) = \mathbf{x}^T\mathbf{x}$ gives rise to an f-minimal solution which is called a *least-squares solution* of $F\mathbf{x} = \mathbf{0}$ (*see* LEAST-SQUARES APPROXIMATION).

The Method of Steepest Descent. Also called the *gradient method,* this method for minimizing a real-valued, continuously differentiable function *f,* defined on R^n, consists of an iterative algorithm

$$\mathbf{x}^{k+1} = \mathbf{x}^k - \alpha_k \nabla f(\mathbf{x}^k)$$

in which $\mathbf{x}^{k+1}$ and $\mathbf{x}^k$ are the new and old iterates, respectively, $\nabla f(\mathbf{x}^k)$ is the gradient vector of *f* calculated at $\mathbf{x}^k$, and α_k is a nonnegative scalar minimizing $f(\mathbf{x}^k - \alpha \nabla f(\mathbf{x}^k))$. This means that from the point $\mathbf{x}^k$, a search is made along the direction of the negative gradient $-\nabla f(\mathbf{x}^k)$ to a minimum point on this line which is taken to be the next iterate [see, e.g., Luenberger (1973)].

Newton's Method. Newton's method for solving a system of equations (for the case of a single equation, *see* NUMERICAL ANALYSIS) may be applied to the system

$$\nabla f(\mathbf{x}) = \mathbf{0},$$

which describes the necessary condition for a minimum of the function *f.* To do this, *f* has to be twice continuously differentiable and its Hessian $\nabla^2 f(\mathbf{x})$ (the matrix of all second order partial derivatives) must be invertible at every iteration point. The resulting Newton-type optimization method then takes the form:

$$\mathbf{x}^{k+1} = \mathbf{x}^k - [\nabla^2 f(\mathbf{x}^k)]^{-1} \nabla f(\mathbf{x}^k),$$

where the -1 power denotes matrix inversion. Various modifications of this method have been suggested [see, e.g., Avriel (1976), Luenberger (1973), or Ortega and Rheinboldt (1970)]. For other optimization methods in a computer-oriented presentation, see Polak (1971).

Optimization Methods in Computed Tomography. Examples of problems from various fields of applications to which optimization methods are applied are abundant and can be found also in almost every book in the references at the end of this article.

One recent application of great importance is that of the problem of *image reconstruction* in which an image (a function of two variables) has to be recovered from experimentally available integrals of its grayness (i.e., its overall brightness) over thin strips. An important version of this problem in medicine, called *computed tomography,* is concerned with the density distribution within the human body from X-ray projections.

In the *series expansion approach* to the image reconstruction problem [other approaches are available (see Herman, 1980)], the mathematical formulation takes the form of a system of equations

$$\mathbf{p} = M\mathbf{x} + \mathbf{e}$$

where **p** is the *m*-dimensional vector of actual measurements, **x** is the *n*-dimensional unknown vector representing the grayness levels of the image to be reconstructed, and **e** is an (also unknown) *m*-dimensional vector of the errors which are due to the inaccuracy of the physical measurements and possibly also to the *discretization* of the original problem. The $m \times n$ matrix **M** is huge (of the order of magnitude of $10^5 \times 10^5$), sparse (i.e., has many zero elements), but lacks any structure in its sparsity.

By setting up various optimization criteria (i.e., objective functions) according to which a "solution" that agrees with the measurements is sought, the problem is transformed into an optimization problem. Quadratic optimization has received considerable attention (see Herman, 1980 for a unified approach, and experimental results).

REFERENCES

1965. Bellman, R. and Kalaba, R. *Dynamic Programming and Modern Control Theory.* New York: Academic Press.
1965. Dreyfus, S. E. *Dynamic Programming and the Calculus of Variations.* New York: Academic Press.
1967. Duffin, R. J., Peterson, E. L., and Zener, C. *Geometric Programming: Theory and Applications.* New York: Wiley.
1970. Lasdon, L. S. *Optimization Theory for Large Systems.* London: Collier-Macmillan.
1970. Ortega, J. M. and Rheinboldt, W. C. *Iterative Solution of Nonlinear Equations in Several Variables.* New York: Academic Press.
1971. Polak, E. *Computational Methods in Optimization: A Unified Approach.* New York: Academic Press.
1972. Sengupta, J. K. *Stochastic Programming: Methods and Applications.* Amsterdam: North-Holland.
1973. Luenberger, D. G. *Introduction to Linear and Nonlinear Programming.* Reading, MA: Addison-Wesley.
1976. Avriel, M. *Nonlinear Programming: Analysis and Methods.* Englewood Cliffs, NJ: Prentice-Hall.
1976. Polak, E. and Payne, A. N. "On Multicriteria Optimization," in Ho, Y. C. and Mitter, S. K. (Eds.), *Directions in Large-Scale Systems.* New York: Plenum.
1978. McShane, E. J. "The Calculus of Variations from the Beginning through Optimal Control Theory," in Schwarzkopf, A. B., Kelley, W. G., and Eliason, S. B. (Eds.), *Optimal Control and Differential Equations.* New York: Academic Press.
1980. Herman, G. T. *Image Reconstruction From Projections: The Fundamentals of Computerized Tomography.* New York: Academic Press.

Y. CENSOR

ORIGINAL EQUIPMENT MANUFACTURER (OEM)

For articles on related subjects *see* INPUT-OUTPUT DEVICES; and MEMORY: Auxiliary.

One descriptor for equipment sold by one manufacturer to another for use in the latter's products is *original equipment manufacturer (OEM),* as opposed to an *end user.* OEM equipment usually comprises complete components such as card readers and central processors, rather than circuit cards, metal parts, and the like. OEM equipment is often delivered to its purchaser without power supplies and cabinets necessary for its ultimate location on customer premises. OEM prices for computer components are generally much lower than end-user prices, the former applicable to lots of 10, 100, or more units and the latter to single purchase.

D. N. Freeman

OVERHEAD

For articles on related subjects *see* Operating Systems: Principles and Theory; Scheduling Algorithm; and Task.

The term *overhead* is described loosely as the time a computer system spends doing computations that do not contribute directly to the progress of any user tasks in the system. The *overhead of a task* is described even more loosely as the difference between the time to run the task in the presence of all other tasks in a system and the time to run the task if it had the entire system to itself. A precise definition of overhead is difficult to obtain, and a measurement of overhead in a given system must be interpreted carefully.

Offhand, it might seem that whenever an operating system program is executing, no user task is making progress and the time so spent should be attributed directly to overhead. Overhead, according to this definition, is easily measured as the time the central processor spends in the *supervisor state.* The imprecision of this definition becomes clear when one considers that (1) many systems have peripheral processors and channels dedicated to the execution of systems programs, whereupon the central processor has little occasion to execute systems programs; and (2) many important functions and services employed by user tasks are implemented as part of the operating system (e.g., input and output programs, file system programs, and error handling programs) so that one cannot always say that no progress on any task is being made whenever the processor is observed to be executing a systems program. The point is, overhead cannot be measured simply as the time the central processor spends in supervisor state; it must be measured in terms of the total system resources expended on system functions.

Thus, for example, an observation that an IBM System 370 spends 80% of its time in the supervisor state cannot be interpreted to mean that the system spends only 20% of its time doing useful work: We need to know what portion of the 80% is spent on running systems programs specifically requested by some user task. Or, an observation that a CDC Cyber processor spends 90% of the time running user tasks cannot be interpreted to mean that overhead is low, as there are eight or more peripheral processors concurrently carrying out systems functions.

There are at least four sources of overhead in most systems: allocation of resources, responding to exceptional conditions, providing protection and reliability, and accounting. Each will consume some system resources to provide, for example, time on central and peripheral processors to execute systems programs, or space in various memory devices to store information about the running tasks and the system state.

With respect to *resource allocation,* a portion of system capacity will be devoted to functions such as scheduling the use of resources, initiating and terminating tasks, switching processors among tasks, allocating space in primary and secondary memory, and managing information transfers among levels of memory. With respect to *exceptional conditions,* a portion of the system's capacity will be devoted to handling such errors as arithmetic contingencies, data transmission failures, addressing snags, and illegal actions by tasks. With respect to *protection and reliability,* a portion of the system's capacity will be devoted to monitoring accesses to various resources for authenticity, to periodic testing of equipment, and to periodic dumping and copying of information off line. With respect to *accounting,* a portion of the system's capacity will be devoted to collecting information on each task's usage of resources, figuring costs and billings for users of the system, and generating statistics on resource usage and performance.

The costs of the overhead functions mentioned above are usually borne by the users of the system. Where possible, these costs are allocated to the tasks that caused the overhead function to be performed (e.g., initiating a task, switching a processor to a task, moving information of a task among the levels of memory). Otherwise, these costs are distributed among all users according to some pro rata formula.

It is important to recognize that overhead detracts from system performance only to the extent that the overhead functions interfere with the processing of user tasks. As noted earlier, many services are provided by the system to relieve programmers from having to provide these functions themselves. As long as the system can provide these functions more efficiently than the users, the resulting increases in overhead may well be offset by better service, improved performance, and lower overall costs to the users.

P. J. Denning and D. E. Denning

OVERLAY

For articles on related subjects *see* MODULAR PRO-
GRAMMING;   PROCEDURE-ORIENTED   LANGUAGES:
Programming in; and STORAGE ALLOCATION.

When a section of computer code is loaded into a
central memory area that was previously allocated to another section of the same executing program, the process
is called *overlaying*, and the loaded section of code is
called an *overlay*. An overlay may contain instructions or
data, or a combination of instructions and data.

The technique of overlaying is used to permit a job
to run on a computer even if its total memory requirement is larger than the amount of memory available to it.
The amount of memory available may be all of central
memory in a simple uniprogramming environment. It is
usually only a fraction of the total memory in a multiprogramming environment.

In a program using overlays, an initial part of the
program is loaded into main memory; the remainder is
held in peripheral storage. During the running of the program, instructions are executed to cause all or part of the
core-resident program to be overlayed by specified program sections in peripheral storage.

A very simple overlaying system called *chaining* was
used in a number of early Fortran systems. The chained
overlays were relatively independent and self-contained.
A link of the chain would be loaded into memory and
would execute until it terminated by loading another link
(i.e., overlay) over itself. The next link would then execute and terminate in the same way by loading an overlay
over itself and giving control to the new overlay. A common non-overlayed data area in memory, declared by the
Fortran COMMON statement, provided the only communication between the links of the chained program.

More recent and more sophisticated systems permit
the programmer quite a bit of flexibility in handling overlays. In a typical system the programmer can specify an
overlay tree, as in Fig. 1. The programmer specifies a *root
segment R*, which remains in memory throughout the
running of the program. The memory area just beyond
the end of the root segment may be occupied by one of
the first level overlays *A*, *B*, or *C*. If it is occupied by *A*,
then the area just past the end of *A* may be occupied by
D or *E*. If it is *D*, then either *K* or *L*; if *E*, then *M* or *N*
may occupy the next area of storage. However, *K* or *L*

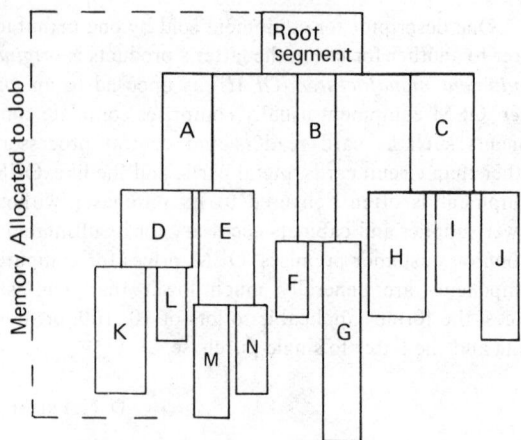

Fig. 1.   An overlay tree structure.

cannot be in memory unless *D* and *A*, and of course the
root segment, are present.

If *R*, *A*, *D*, and *K* are in memory, a reference in *D*
to a location in *L* will cause the loader to bring in *L* and
overlay *K*. A reference in *A* to a location in *E* will cause
E to be loaded over *D*, extending over part of *K* or *L* if
necessary. A reference in the root segment to a location
in *C* will load *C* over *A*, effectively removing *A* and all of
its lower levels from central memory. A reference to *F* in
the root segment will cause both *B* and *F* to be loaded.
At any given time, one path through the overlay tree is
current, and any segment can be loaded through references from any point above it in the tree.

The programmer must specify the beginning and
end of each segment and its position in the tree structure.
The language processing system organizes the object
code modules along with necessary control information
into a structure that resides in peripheral storage during
program execution and from which the appropriate overlays are loaded.

The development of an appropriate and efficient
overlay structure for a long and complicated program can
be very difficult. One of the aims in the development of
virtual memory systems has been to make the handling
of overlays completely automatic.

S. ROSEN

P

PACKAGES, SOFTWARE. *See* SOFTWARE PACKAGES.

PACKET SWITCHING

For articles on related subjects *see* ARPA NETWORK; COMMUNICATIONS AND COMPUTERS; DATA COMMUNICATION NETWORKS; DATA NETWORKS, PUBLIC; and DATA PROCESSING.

Packet switching is a term used to describe the internal operations of a particular type of data communications network that usually has a fixed topology and uses software to route information in a special format through the network from source to destination. A packet-switched data communication network is usually composed of a number of geographically separate nodes connected by dedicated high-speed data links. The nodes are (usually) stored program computers that have internal data link connections to the other nodes and external data links connected to local terminals and computers. Fig. 1 illustrates an example of a packet-switched data communications network.

The general theory of operation is that a unit of information, called a *packet* (usually 128 bytes or less), is routed from one *packet-switching exchange* (PSE) to another via transmission lines until the packet reaches its destination. The destination address for the information is contained in the header of the packet. Each packet may, therefore, go to a different destination; hence the term *packet switching*.

When a packet arrives at a PSE, the exchange determines whether it is a transit node or a destination node. If the former, it chooses a transmission line to send the packet toward its destination. This type of operation is called *store and forward* transmission, a term created in message-switching systems. In packet-switching systems, the store-and-forward operations generally occur in tens to hundreds of milliseconds. End-to-end transmission delay (source to destination) is usually in the range of 200 milliseconds to one second.

Two alternative strategies have evolved (see Fig. 2) in the implementation of packet-switching systems—*datagrams* and *virtual circuits*. In the datagram strategy, each packet of information is totally independent of all others. They are independently routed and have the properties that they can be lost or duplicated (this phenomenon is caused by transmission errors and retransmissions) with some probability, and transmission order between packets is not preserved. Proponents of the datagram approach argue a simpler network interface can be achieved and that transmission of datagrams can easily be routed around failed links and nodes.

In the virtual circuit (VC) approach, a logical path is created by the network between the source and destination (see Fig. 3). The virtual circuit allows the network to maintain order, discard duplicates, and detect missing packets. The VC uses special packet types to establish and clear calls. VC proponents argue a simpler end-to-end protocol, better flow control by the network, and lower transmission and processing overhead as the VC's chief assets.

All public data networks use the VC approach, while some of the earlier packet networks, such as the ARPANET, use the datagram approach.

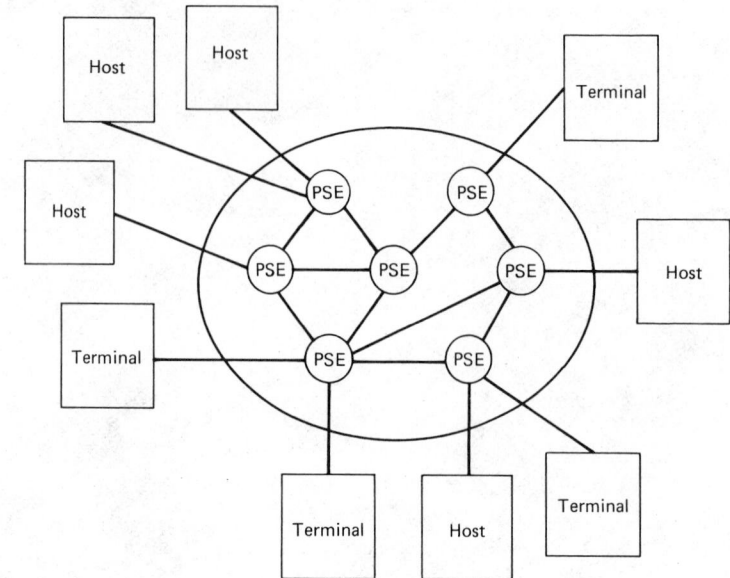

Fig. 1.   Typical packet-switched network.

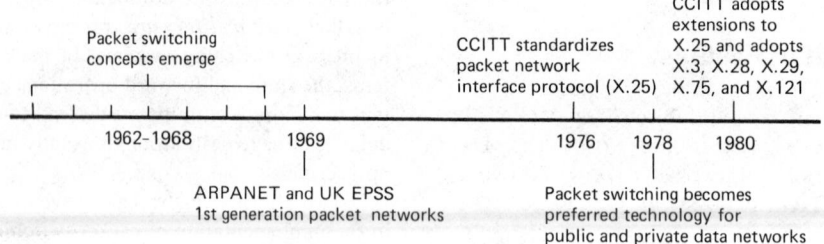

Fig. 2.   Evolution of packet switching.

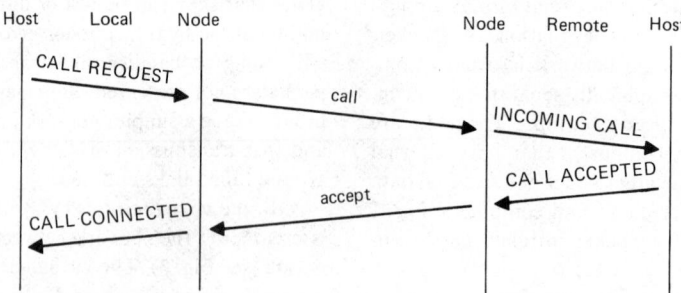

Fig. 3.   Virtual circuit setup.

In 1976, the international standards body responsible for the worldwide telecommunications standards (CCITT) recommended an interface protocol for attaching terminal equipment to a packet network. This standard, called X.25 (see Fig. 4), has been adopted by public networks, many private networks, and is available in a growing number of types of data processing equipment.

The packet-switching networks (usually) provide interface to terminals not supporting the packet mode of operation (X.25). These terminals are supported through

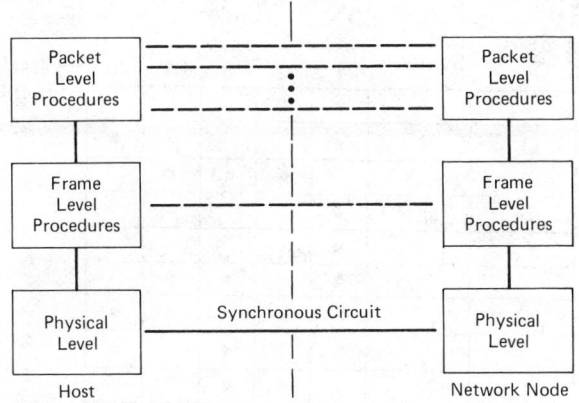

Fig. 4. X.25 interface.

PADs (packet assembler-disassemblers), which convert the native protocols (such as asynchronous, binary synchronous (BSC), synchronous data link control (SDLC), etc.) into X.25 for transmission through the network (see Fig. 5).

B. D. WESSLER

PAPER TAPE

GENERAL

For articles on related subjects *see* ASCII; BAUDOT CODE; BINARY-CODED DECIMAL; CODES; DATA PREPARATION DEVICES; EBCDIC; and INPUT-OUTPUT DEVICES.

Punched paper tape is a storage medium used for the preparation, storage, and transmission of data in various applications. Slow-speed paper tape may be used as a control device for numerically controlled machine tool operations. At higher speeds, paper tape may be used for typesetting, telegraphic and data transmission, and automated typewriting, as well as for storing computer programs and data, and also for other data processing functions (e.g., to control the carriage movement in line printers).

The use of punched paper tape for data preparation, storage, and transmission is not a new technique. It was introduced by Sir Charles Wheatstone in 1857 for telegraphic purposes, just 21 years after the first practical demonstration of the electric telegraph. One year later, in 1858, a Morse tape reader-transmitter operated at 100 words per minute. Five-track tape keyboard punches were in common use in 1908. In 1925, five-track readers were commonly operating at four letters, or 20 bits per second. When multiplexed for transmission use, the line speed was 80 bits per second. Adoption of this technique for data processing saw a vast increase in applications of punched paper tape.

Speed requirements and therefore performance have increased manyfold, and the available number of tracks has increased from five to eight to accommodate the various alphabets required. Small sprocket holes appear along the length of the tape and are used to feed the tape mechanically as they engage toothed wheels in slow-speed readers; in high-speed machines, these sprocket holes (or feed holes) act as a clock pulse when a tape is read by a photoelectric head (see Fig. 1). Data is recorded in the tape by punching holes in a row across the width. Each row represents one character, and the pat-

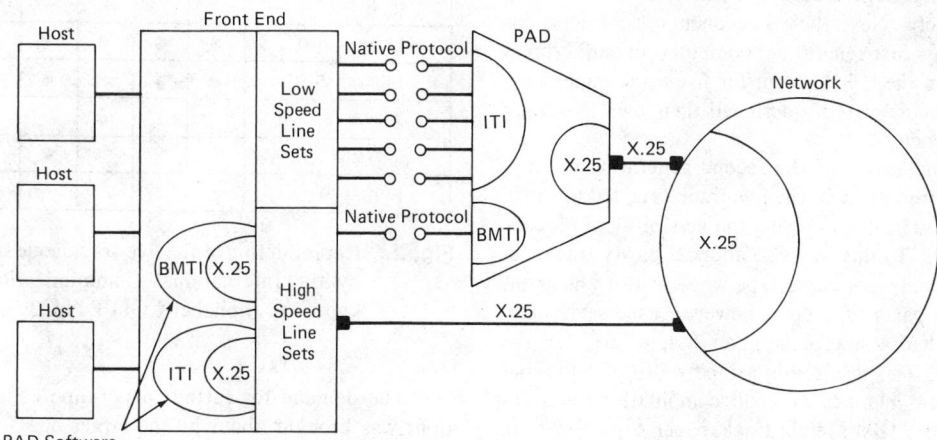

Fig. 5. Typical interfaces to hosts. (X.25 above indicates hardware and software that implements the X.25 standard.)

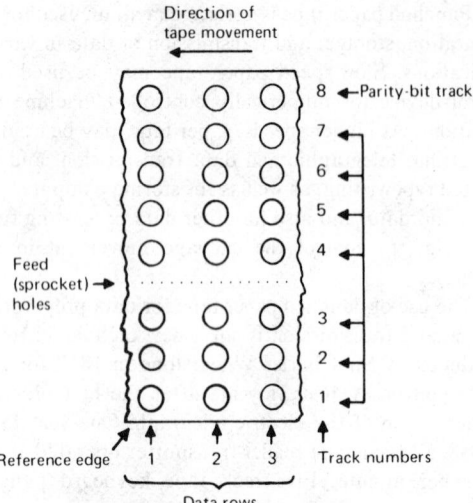

Fig. 1. Punched paper tape terminology. Note: Each data row represents one seven-bit character.

tern of the holes punched indicates the particular character.

In the narrowest tape (with five tracks, and which is $^{11}/_{16}$ in. wide), since a hole can be punched in any track, the number of unique hole combinations possible is 2^5, or 32. Thus, 32 characters can be represented by a five-hole code. More than 32 separate items can be identified if each code group is made to represent two or more characters, and a special character (e.g., letter or figure shift) precedes the punched data to indicate which interpretation is to be used (see Fig. 2). In certain circumstances this arrangement can be cumbersome; hence, it has resulted in the development of tape with more information tracks so that a larger number of characters can be identified uniquely. Nevertheless, economic considerations caused many first-generation computer manufacturers (especially in the U.K.) to opt for five-track paper tape input, and many of them designed their own five-track paper tape code.

With the advent of the second generation of computers, the limitations of the five-track tape led to introduction of a sixth track, giving the possibility of 64 code combinations. To this was also added a parity track, resulting in seven-track paper tape whose width was about ⅞ in. IBM's paper tape code, however, used seven data tracks and had a single character ("new line") in the eighth track. This resulted in a tape width of 1 in., and the maximum number of code combinations was increased to 65. IBM's eight-track paper tape has been widely adopted by office machine manufacturers because it provides enough codes for various miscellaneous commands.

Letters	Figures and Symbols	1	2	3	4	5
A	—	●	●			
B	?	●			●	●
C	:		●	●	●	
D	Who are you?	●			●	
E	3	●				
F		●		●	●	
G			●		●	●
H				●		●
I	8		●	●		
J	Bell	●	●		●	
K	(	●	●	●	●	
L	)		●			●
M	.			●	●	●
N	,			●	●	
O	9				●	●
P	0		●	●		●
Q	1	●	●	●		●
R	4		●		●	
S	'	●		●		
T	5					●
U	7	●	●	●		
V	=		●	●	●	●
W	2	●	●			●
X	/	●		●	●	●
Y	6	●		●		●
Z	+	●				●
Blank						
Letters shift		●	●	●	●	●
Figures shift		●	●		●	●
Space				●		
Carriage return					●	
Line feed			●			

Fig. 2. Reproduction of the five-track code standarized by the International Communications Union, known as Alphabet CCITT No. 2.

The demand for further paper-tape code combinations was brought about by the larger character sets of third-generation computers. These computers had discrete codes for upper- and lower-case characters, a larger number of special symbols for both control and graphical characters, and transmission control codes. Seven-bit codes for information interchange were set up and internationally adopted as ISO Standard No. 646 (revised 1973). Many national standards have been based upon it, such as ASCII. Eight-track paper tape was then used so that the first seven tracks accommodated the seven-bit code and the eighth track was used for parity. Despite the adoption of the ISO standard, many other codes are still in use (e.g., the six-bit BCD code and the seven-bit EBCDIC).

Paper tape for computers is normally supplied in an $^{11}\!/_{16}$ in. width (which satisfies the teleprinter tape standard now established at $^{11}\!/_{16}$ in. wide by 1,000 ft long in coil form), or $^{7}\!/_{8}$ in. or 1 in. widths to suit the requirements of 5-, 6-, 7-, or 8-track information. Tapes for most applications are supplied in coils with a nominal length of 1,000 ft and an outer diameter of 8 in. The center supporting cores are available in plain and serrated plastic.

Several kinds of substances are available for paper tape manufacture, depending upon the application and the machines in which the tape is to be used. For computer applications, the most suitable substance is a low-filler paper tape, either with or without the inclusion of oil. There are also more durable tapes of the paper variety suited for long-life cyclic uses, and long-life polyester plastic tapes are used for continuous cyclic work that needs tapes of exceptional durability.

Despite the inexpensiveness of paper tape and its usefulness as a by-product (e.g., from a cash register or ticket issuing machine), its disadvantages, such as the difficulty of correcting errors and the relatively slow speeds at which it can be read, have meant its almost complete disappearance as a computer input medium and its replacement by tape cassettes or floppy disks. But this changeover tends to be rather slow because it is often connected with the change of the machinery being controlled. Consequently, there will be some technological improvement of paper tape devices in the future.

READING AND PUNCHING TECHNIQUES

For articles on related subjects see IBM CARD; INPUT-OUTPUT DEVICES; and NINETY-COLUMN CARD.

Tape Reading. Electrochemical techniques are used for reading low-speed paper tape on devices that operate at approximately 50 characters per second (chps). On higher-speed readers, photoelectric reading is the normal practice.

Photoelectric reading of paper tape is similar to the technique used in high-speed punched-card reading, in which a pencil-beam of light is projected through holes in each track so that it strikes a photoelectric cell (or *photocell*).

Fig. 1 shows the design of a high-speed paper tape reader. The feed mechanism consists of an electromagnetic brake (A) at the start of the tape, and an electromagnetic clutch (B) at the winding end of the tape. The clutch consists of a divided, rotating drum (C) with a permanently magnetized, internal, fixed excitation winding, superposed by a roller (D). When the winding is energized, the roller presses against the drum and the paper tape moves between them as a result of friction.

The brake at the input of the tape consists of a U-shaped electromagnet and a flat armature. The clutch and brake are energized in such a way that electric current can be switched to either one, thus permitting transport of the tape and a start/stop operation of the device.

The photoelectric reader part of the device consists of a light bulb (E) and an optical system (F) that concentrates light through a prism (G) into a narrow rectangular beam that is perpendicularly oriented at the punched paper-tape centerline and which passes through the punched holes in the tape. Below the tape the polarized light falls on a photocell (H), which converts the light rays into electric current that feeds into the signal-shaping circuit inputs. The signal-shaping circuits vary their outputs in proportion to the amount of illumination entering the photocell. The rectangular outputs of these circuits are then adapted by means of matching circuits.

Some paper tape readers (e.g., the Danish Regnecentralen A/S—RC 2000 series) do not employ any physical start-stop operation character-by-character. Rather, during reading, characters are temporarily stored in a cyclic buffer (of 1,024 characters for the RC 2000), from which they are transferred to the computer. Unprocessed characters in the buffer are fed back through a servo system which sets the actual reading speed. This system is claimed to reduce tape breakage and permit characters in the buffer to be accessed at speeds much higher than actual reading speed.

Tape Punching. Tape is punched by five-to-eight-track rows of dies striking against a steel matrix with a corresponding number of holes while the paper tape passes between the dies and matrix. The dies are activated by a mechanism under the control of computer output signals. Mechanisms used for the punching operation differ mainly in the movement of the dies and/or the steel matrix. Although patents have been granted for punches that have no moving parts because they are activated by compression (air pressure waves) and operate at a speed of 1,000 chps, no such devices are known to be in production.

The design of paper tape punches is complicated by the need to examine the tape immediately after punching.

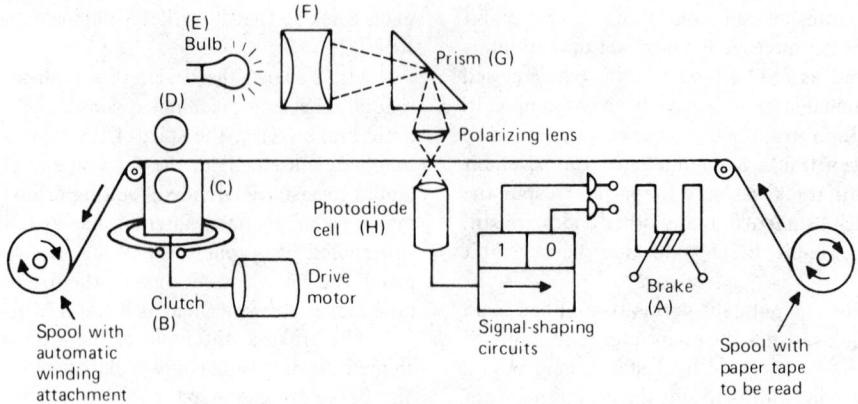

Fig. 1.   Simplified diagram of paper tape path in a high-speed reader.

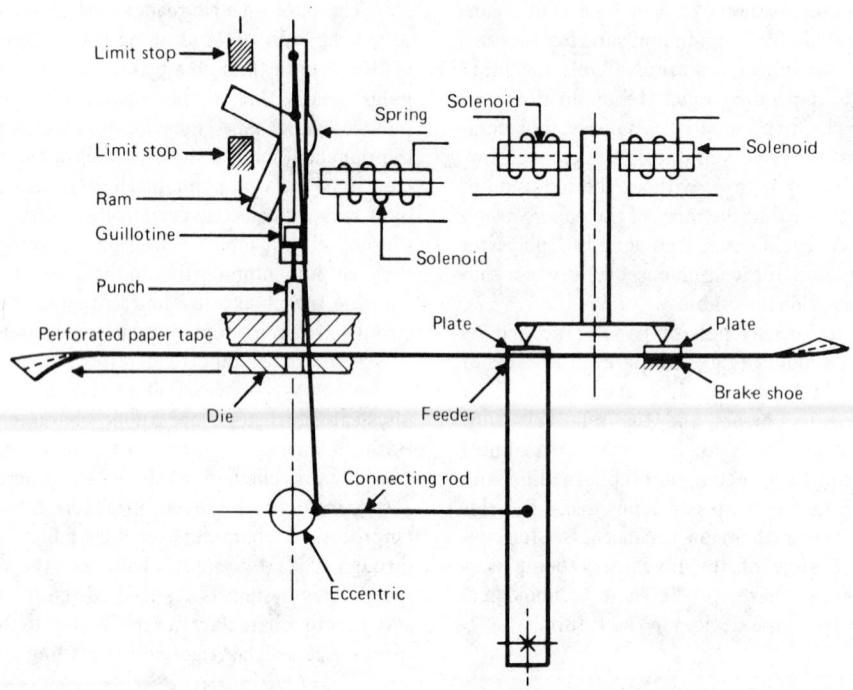

Fig. 2.   Solenoid-controlled punch mechanism of the FACIT PE-1500 punch.

This means that the tape has to be punched in a horizontal plane, with the *chad*, or chips from the punching being ejected upward. Fig. 2 shows a solenoid-activated punch mechanism used for paper tape punching.

J. NECAS

PARALLEL ALGORITHMS

For articles on related subjects *See* CONCURRENT PROGRAMMING; MULTIPROCESSING; NUMERICAL ANALYSIS; PARALLEL PROCESSING; PETRI NETS; and SEMAPHORE.

With the advent of multiprocessors, parallel algorithms and models for parallel computations have received a great deal of attention. Historically, many computations which are inherently parallel (e.g., addition of two vectors) had to be transformed into a series of sequential steps only because of the restrictions imposed by the architecture of the majority of current machines. The same holds true for a number of algorithms, applicable mostly to scientific problems, such as the Jacobi method for solving a system of linear equations. Thus, algorithms which are conceptually in parallel form and those which have to be transformed into a parallel representation must be differentiated.

In numerical analysis, several processes originally intended to be run on single processors, by design or by necessity, have been recast in parallel form. Frequent examples can be found in the fields of optimization theory, root finding, solution of differential equations, and resolution of systems of linear equations. The improvements in the completion times range from log N to N, where N is the number of parallel machines. Often, in these new algorithms, all processors synchronously execute the same operations (SIMD architectures).

Techniques and tools for designing asynchronous parallel algorithms have slowly begun to emerge. Numerous models (directed graphs, Petri nets (q.v.), program schema) have been proposed to study the control flow properties of parallel systems. These models exhibit the parallelism inherent in a program (i.e., they model FORK and JOIN primitives) and depict the synchronization required for the sharing of common databases and procedures. Another approach is to model the dataflow; in these models, operators are activated as soon as their operands are ready, and no variable is assigned more than one value during the computation (single-assignment rule).

The control flow models are often represented in graphical form. A convenient frame of reference to describe them is to consider a triple (W,U,C) where:

$W = \{w_1, w_2, \ldots, w_n\}$ is a set of operators
$U = \{u_1, u_2, \ldots, u_m\}$ is a set of variables
C is a control link.

This control link can take various forms, such as bipartite graphs where nodes representing conditions are linked to those modeling occurrences of events (Petri nets) or schema connecting members of W to members of U, and *vice versa*.

As an example, we consider a very simple graph model to represent the computation of the root of $y = f(x)$ by the Newton-Raphson method; i.e.,

$$x^{(i)} = x^{(i-1)} - \frac{f(x^{(i-1)})}{f'(x^{(i-1)})},$$

with an error less than ϵ. The graph of Fig. 1 shows how $f(x)$ and $f'(x)$ can be computed in parallel. Nodes of the graph represent computational tasks [w_1 is the start; w_2, the iteration node; w_3, the computation of $f(x)$; w_4, the computation of $f'(x)$; w_5, the computation of $x^{(i)}$ and the test for convergence; and w_6, the end node]. Arcs represent flow of control and/or holdings of variables [a_1 holds $x^{(0)}$ and ϵ; a_2 and a_3 hold $x^{(i-1)}$ and ϵ; a_4 and a_5 also hold

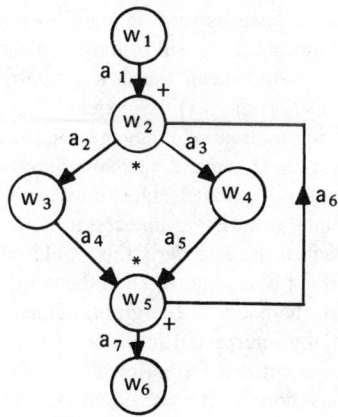

Fig. 1.   Graph model for parallel computation.

$x^{(i-1)}$ and ϵ, and $f(x^{(i-1)})$ and $f'(x^{(i-1)})$, respectively; a_6 holds $x^{(i)}$; and a_7, the solution y]. The control of the parallelism is indicated by the sign *, which at the output of a node indicates a FORK (i.e., possible parallel initiation) and at the input indicates a JOIN (i.e., all predecessors of this node must terminate before it can initiate). The usual branching and looping is indicated by $+$.

With each operator is associated an input set $I_i = \{u_{i1}, \ldots, u_{ik}\}$ and an output set $O_i = \{u_{o1}, \ldots, u_{op}\}$. In our example, let $u_1 = x^{(i)}$, $u_2 = \epsilon$, $u_3 = f(x^{(i)})$, and $u_1 = f'(x^{(i)})$. Then $I_1 = O_1 = \{u_1, u_2\}, \ldots, I_4 = \{u_1, u_2\}$, $O_4 = \{u_1, u_2, u_4\}, \ldots, I_6 = \{u_1\}$, $O_6 = \phi$.

A simulation on the model P is defined by the following.

- For each variable u_i, a domain D_i of values which the variable may assume.
- For each operator w_i, a mapping $O_i = f(I_i)$. This mapping can be both computational (values associated with members of O_i are defined in terms of values associated with members of I_i) and logical (control conditions can be dictated by operators).
- A set of initial values for members of U.

A variable history h_i is the sequence of values associated with u_i during a simulation on P. A program history is the m-tuple $\{h_1, \ldots, h_m\}$ consisting of the variable histories of the elements of U.

An important property of a parallel program model is its determinacy. A program is said to be determinate if and only if each simulation results in a unique program history. Often, less stringent conditions such as proper termination are considered. Two models, P and P', are equivalent if they have the same set of variables and if their program histories are the same.

The objectives of the model dictate the amount of *interpretation* given to the mapping $O_i = f(I_i)$. If the main goal is to describe specific algorithms or systems, then a total interpretation will be most convenient. In our example, this would mean the description of a specific $f(x)$, and *a fortiori* of $f'(x)$. A model of this type can be regarded as a programming language. On the other hand, if the derivation of general formal properties and the characterization of parallel algorithms are of prime interest, then interpretation is unnecessary and schema can be introduced. In the case here, this would mean looking at Fig. 1 without being interested in the computations associated with the nodes of the graph. Generally, models will be partially interpreted in order to retain some descriptive power without losing formal properties. This is what has been done in the preceding example by giving some indication of the purpose of each node and arc.

Pipelining (*q.v.*) is also becoming an important technique to achieve concurrency. It is not limited to hardware implementations (e.g., functional units in the IBM System/370 Model 195 and CRAY-1, complete CPUs in vector processors such as CDC STAR-100 and TI ASC). Software processes can be pipelined, thus extending the concept of coroutines (*q.v.*) to that of parallel coroutines.

The design of algorithms for parallel machines is not limited to the modification of sequential algorithms or to the creation of new ones. New or modified data structures play an important role since it is the sharing of data structures which often limits the achievable parallelism. The data structures may have added fields so that locking is performed easily; parts of the data may be reproduced (redundancy) so that techniques such as concurrent reading and writing may be used.

Finally, with the advent of VLSI, we may envision hardware parallel algorithms. Algorithms which stress as much the importance of regular communication patterns as that of parallel paths will have to be investigated.

REFERENCE

1973. Baer, J-L. "A Survey of Some Theoretical Aspects of Multiprocessing," *Computing Surveys* 5, *No. 1:* 31–80 (March).

1981. Hockney, R. W. and Lesshope, C. R., *Parallel Computers: Architecture, Programming and Algorithms.* London: Adam Hilger.

J-L. BAER

PARALLEL PROCESSING

For articles on related subjects *see* CHANNEL; COMPUTER ARCHITECTURE; CONCURRENT PROGRAMMING; MULTIPLEXING; MULTIPROCESSING; MULTIPROGRAMMING; OPERATING SYSTEMS; PARALLEL ALGORITHMS; PETRI NETS; PIPELINE AND ARRAY PROCESSORS; SUPERCOMPUTERS; AND TIME SHARING.

Forms of Parallelism. Processing of more than one task on a computer system may be *truly* simultaneous or *apparently* simultaneous. True simultaneity can be achieved only with sufficient hardware to operate multiple functions at the same time. Apparent simultaneity may be achieved by various multiplexing algorithms applied to a single hardware unit. Both true and apparent simultaneity require degrees of logical disconnectivity which enable tasks to run independently of each other for periods of time.

Fig. 1A demonstrates the notion of true simultaneity applied to a computer system trying to compute something while it is reading a record across a channel at the same time. In order to achieve this, there must be hardware to perform computing and I/O operations and there must be logical independence between the compute and I/O functions.

Fig. 1B demonstrates apparent simultaneity. If there are units to be serviced which have operational speeds slower than a servicing unit, then the servicing unit may interleave its attention in such a way as to give the impression that all serviced units are being given simultaneous attention. *Multiplexing* of this kind may be achieved with hardware or with a software algorithm.

Levels of Parallelism. There are numerous operational levels at which parallelism may be designed into a system.

Basic Data Flow. Data moved from one point to another in a system are moved in units wider than one bit at a time. For example, consider the transfer of data from a bank of memories to a processor across data paths which will move 64 bits at a time. Such parallelism is fundamental to most memory-processor interfaces and memory-I/O interfaces. Because of skew (i.e., the tendency for parallel bits to reach an interface at differing times) and control problems, however, many mechanisms which interconnect units at distances of geographical importance are serial rather than parallel.

Between Stages of an Instruction. An instruction may be thought of as having an interpretation stage (I-stage) and an execution stage (E-stage). During an I-stage, an instruction is prepared for execution. During an E-stage, it is actually performed. If no circuitry is shared between the I- and E-units, then one instruction may be executed while a successor is being prepared for execution. Fig. 2 demonstrates the overlap of instructions. Machines with this capability are sometimes referred to as *lookahead* machines. The IBM 3033 is amongst those which have lookahead features. The parallelism here is between the E-stage of an instruction and the I-stage of a successor, because the I-E sequence of a single instruc-

A. TRUE SIMULTANEITY
Events happen at the same time. For example, *read* tape while computing actually occurs at the same time.

Event	Time Units											
	1	2	3	4	5	6	7	8	9	10	11	12
CPU DIV inst.	X	X	X	X	X							
CHAN. READ tape		X	X	X	X	X	X	X	X	X		
CPU STORE inst.						X	X	X				
CPU ADD inst.									X	X	X	X
CPU summary: (DIVIDE, STORE, ADD)	X	X	X	X	X	X	X	X	X	X	X	X

SUMMARY: Overall time period = 12 units. CPU operating time = 12 units, consisting of: DIV (1–5) = 5; STORE (6–8) = 3; ADD (9–12) = 4. Tape operating time (2–10) = 9. CPU-only (1, 11–12) = 3. Channel-only operating time = 0. Overlapped units of time (2–10) = 9.

B. APPARENT SIMULTANEITY
Events appear to happen at the same time. For example, time-sharing terminals.

Event	Time Units														
	1	2	3	4	5	6	7	8	9	10	11	12	13	14	15
User 1 req.	X														
User 2 req.		X													
User 3 req.			X												
CPU serv					1	2	3	1	2	3	1	2	3		
User 1 resp.												X			
User 2 resp.													X		
User 3 resp.														X	
User time ref.	←— A —→					←— B —→					←— C —→				

Note: Users perceive time in five-unit groups so that terminals appear active at the same time in A and C, and appear to be receiving simultaneous CPU service in time reference B.

Fig. 1. Comparison of true and apparent simultaneity.

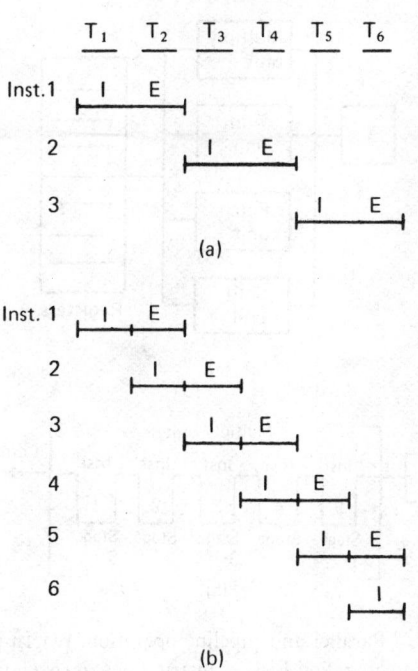

(a)

(b)

Fig. 2. Basic lookahead. (a) No lookahead. (b) Lookahead.

tion is temporally ordered, the E-stage is dependent upon the I-stage, and they cannot be performed in parallel.

Between Instructions. This is the ability to execute more than one instruction at the same time. It is an extension of the lookahead concept that depends upon either a finer decomposition of stages or the proliferation of instruction units. High-performance systems all have this ability in some form. A high-performance uniprocessor may have multiple execution units which are functionally specialized to perform a particular subset of instructions. Many members of the CDC Cyber series, for example, and the CRAY-1 have populations of specialized execution units which receive instructions which are passed to them, as appropriate, by a single I-stage processor.

Another approach to parallel instruction execution is *pipelining.* The I- and E-stages of an instruction are further decomposed into smaller units. A population of instructions are moved through the pipe so that a different instruction is being processed at each stage. Pipelining is often combined with parallel execution units so that each parallel execution unit pipelines the class of instructions for which it is responsible. This is a feature of many machines, including members of the Cyber family and the IBM 370/195. Fig. 3 demonstrates the ideas of parallel execution units and pipelining.

When the capability for parallel execution of I-functions exists in a machine, it is called a "multiple I-stream" machine. This capability allows instructions from different programs to join the mix of instructions using the execution units or sharing the pipeline. Multiprocessors are a form of multiple I-stream machine in which parallel capability is achieved by providing multiple sets of I- and E-hardware packaged so that I-E sets are isolated from each other. UNIVAC 1100s and IBM 3300 series multiprocessors are examples.

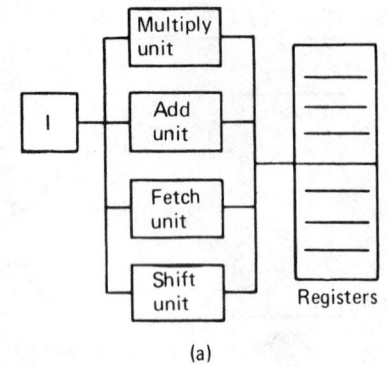

(a)

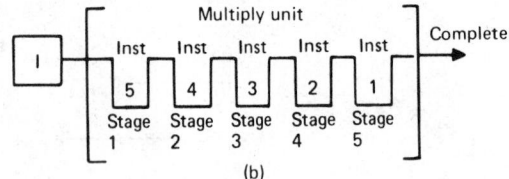

(b)

Fig. 3. Parallel and pipeline operation. (a) In parallel operation I issues instructions to specialized execution units, each of which operates independently and concurrently. (b) In pipeline operation, MULTIPLY takes five stages, each of one cycle. The effective rate of MULTIPLY, however, is one cycle, since a MULTIPLY is completed every cycle. At cycle 5, instruction 1 completes; at cycle 6, instruction 2 completes; etc. Stages 1 through 5 are executed in parallel on a series of instructions.

Between Elements of a Program. A program may contain a number of computational steps that are logically independent, but which are represented serially in code because of the serial nature of most programming languages. Consider the following program.

```
Region 1
        ALABEL:  A = B + C;
                 D = A * W − 5;
                 Z = R + D ** 2;
                 GO TO NEXT;
Region 2
        BLABEL:  E = B − C;
                 F = E * W − 10;
                 H = R + D ** 3;
Region 3
        CLABEL:  I = Z − X;
                 T = Y * D − W;
                 GO TO NEXT;
```

Each of the labeled elements can be executed in parallel if multiple execution units exist in the system. None of them pass values to one another and do not depend upon one another's execution.

Hardware/software techniques necessary to achieve actual program concurrency involve (1) a means for recognizing element independence; (2) a means for starting the parallel execution; and (3) a means for establishing the conditions for execution of the code beginning at NEXT. The mechanisms for starting and synchronizing parallel execution on small program elements of this kind must be very fast so that the burden of this control is not long relative to the execution time of the program elements.

Between Formal Modules. Recent interest in program structuring techniques has led to the development of interest in coordinating cooperating processes. Various language extensions to PL/I and to Pascal (*concurrent Pascal*) are intended to establish protocols by which programs may communicate with one another and by which they may achieve synchronization. A major area of design concern is the nature of the structure and function of operating systems to support interprocess communication and synchronization. Early concepts of program coordination involved ideas of shared storage areas called *semaphores* (*q.v.*) which are used to establish *gateways* which permit or prohibit programs from passing into *critical* sections where joint use of data would result in pathological conditions. Similar mechanisms for determining when a program could proceed past a certain point have been described. Concepts like FORK (request a processor to perform a process in addition to the process being executed), JOIN (terminate a process and "rejoin" the main processor), LOCK (protect a resource being used), and UNLOCK (free a resource for use) have been described. More recently, there has been an emerging feeling that programs should synchronize and communicate with one another on a message basis without explicit sharing of storage even on multiprocessing systems where shared memory is possible. Thus, concepts of SEND and RECEIVE are being investigated in various forms for program cooperation and synchronization. The essential idea is that programs are more easily debugged and better programming structures are achieved if all communication is done in a way similar to the way programs in geographically dispersed distributed systems intercommunicate and synchronize.

Coordination between programs in a cooperating set is basically achieved through the cooperation of the operating system. When a program asks for another program to start, the operating system creates a *process control block* and enqueues it on a work request queue in the system. The processor which is to do the work may acquire a process control block by executing code in the operating system which associates the process with the processor. In multiprocessing systems, the work queue may be in shared memory and equally accessible to any processor which can execute operating system code. A strong motivation in system design in "generic multiprocessors" is the ability for processes to be arbitrarily assigned to available processors with maximum flexibility.

Between Independent Programs. This is the ability to run multiple unrelated "jobs" on a set of processors. Here no directives for synchronization are issued by application programs because they do not know of each other. The operating system becomes completely responsible for synchronization and control. Some new notions are developing in this area. It used to be thought profitable to be able arbitrarily to associate sets of programs across sets of processors. There is a developing feeling that the economics of computing may suggest it is best to isolate and partition functions and dedicate them to a single processing element. This feeling comes from a desire to achieve maximum performance stability and predictability even at the cost of sub-optimal processor utilization.

Recent advances in technology have considerably expanded the configuration options in multiple-machine systems. It is now feasible to construct systems out of multiple processing units, each of which has its own memory and private operating system but which can communicate with each other very rapidly over interprocessor connecting buses. There is current interest in how systems consisting of many processing units of such types can and should share work. New concepts of *distributed processing* intersect very closely with concepts of "parallel processing" in two basic ways. The decomposition analysis which determines how an application may be split up for parallel execution is very similar to the analysis techniques which seem to be emerging for determining distribution. Also, problems of the synchronization and intercommunication between nodes of a distributed system are very similar to the problems of synchronizing parallel program structures. Thus, a great deal of work previously accomplished for discovering parallel structures in systems such as the ILLIAC IV is relevant to contemporary problems in distributed systems' logical structures.

Problems and Directions. An essential question for parallel or distributed machine organizations is how much total aggregate power achieved by the interconnection of multiple processing units is needed to match the performance of a single large uniprocessor. Is it better, if one wants a 50 million instruction per second processor system, to build a single 50-MIP machine or to interconnect five 10-MIP machines? Queueing theory seems to suggest that the single larger server is optimum. However, considerations of machine economics and system configurability preclude a general answer.

In any multiple processor system, it is important that work have a proper "shape." A system with five executing units must have five tasks ready to go if the power of five units is to be utilized. This is true of both multiple I-stream and single I-stream systems. A single I-stream system requires a proper mix of instructions in order to achieve its speed by keeping its execution units busy. A multiple I-stream machine requires a proper mix of programs.

Computing systems with multiple processing units may provide for additional availability. It is possible to construct systems so as to limit the "scope of failure" (the impact that a component outage has on a community of users). This is achieved by dedicating subsets of processing units to subsets of users so that only a partial community of users is affected by an outage. The repair of the malfunctioning unit must be accomplished, in such a design, without disrupting the work of other units. Another approach to increased availability is to designate "back-up" units which can assume the work of a malfunctioning component. These back-up units may be permanently assigned or may dynamically assume increased workload in the event of a system malfunction. The construction of fault-tolerant systems based upon replicated units involves discovery of suitable partitions of work, meaningful fail-soft levels, and an analysis of the components of a system most vulnerable to failure. Software structures must be investigated with the same care as hardware. Multiple-processing systems may or may not be more reliable than single processing systems. To the degree that increased component dependency is introduced, reliability and availability may suffer. The probability that all units of a system will be up decreases as the population of units increases. However, the probability that all units of a system will be down also decreases as the number of units goes up. Achieving increased reliability will tend to encourage designs in which functions are portable (two processors will be used if two processors are available, but the work can be done sequentially by one), and in which the operability of the system does not depend on all units being operational.

Some fundamental programming questions are raised by issues of system structure. Current thinking in application development suggests that program structures should be minimally influenced by the characteristics of the hardware on which they will run. To what extent should an awareness of the existence of the potential for concurrent execution be introduced into the programming process? One school of thought proposes that good design and programming technology will achieve modular, concurrent structures at no extra cost. In fact, programming expenses will go down because of the inherent modularity of parallel structures. In opposition to this is an opinion that writing parallel programs introduces additional and "unnatural" complexity into the program development process and that parallel structures will become widely used only when language processors can discover the parallel potential. An essential question is "Who pays the bill?" The answers are the programmer, the compiler, or the machine.

A question also exists as to what extent a programmer must know the functional characteristics of a pipelined or parallel uniprocessor in order to provide good instruction mixes. Optimum programming of machines of this class requires an appreciation for the details of parallel potential. A program with one sequence of statements may behave very differently from a functionally equivalent program written in a different order. Some progress has been made in compiler techniques which will achieve various degrees of statement rearrangement and operator rearrangement within a statement. However, there are conceptual problems a compiler cannot reach. For example, a compiler may rearrange a sequence of arithmetic operations in order to optimize execution unit use, but no compiler will expand an expression which has been factored.

For multiprocessors, the problem of programming lies in the proper definition of populations of autonomous or partially autonomous modules. Programming languages which facilitate modularization and synchronization are just beginning to mature. There is a school of thought which says that techniques must be developed to recognize parallel potential at a higher level of abstraction than statements in order to relieve a programmer of the burden of parallel designs. In the past, the design of parallel structures has been considered difficult. However, recent insights into good programming practice encourage the kind of modularization and structuring which might naturally lead to highly parallel programs.

A further aspect of parallel operation concerns the functions of an operating system. A set of problems in system structure are being revealed by new configuration possibilities for multiple-computer systems with parallel potential. To what extent should the operating system be involved in supporting synchronization? To what extent should the acquisition and release of processors be dynamic? To what extent should user language facilities be extended to support statements indicating the desired number of processors.

It is a very real possibility that, in the future, very large systems may be constructed out of populations of small systems with various degrees of resource privacy and resource sharing. New interconnection possibilities emerging out of new technology and economics promise an almost infinite variety of configurations of processors, memories, and controllers within a single system concept. This increased configurability may help to solve some of the classical problems of multiprocessor performance and increase the effective parallelism of a system. The ability to configure areas of private and shared memory will help address the memory contention problem which decays performance when multiple processors are addressing the same memory banks. Bottlenecks in the I/O function will be relieved by the proliferation of paths to I/O devices and by the use of specialized processing units to control I/O and communication functions. In the past, there has been an interest in the ability to order so many adders, so many multipliers, etc. There is now an equivalent interest in how many processors, how many memories, etc.

New concepts are emerging concerning how the success of a parallel system should be measured. Traditionally, the ideal was that a parallel structure would reduce the elapsed time, T, of a given program to T/N for N processors. This ideal is rarely achieved, although it is theoretically possible. It is rarely achieved because problems are not easily segmentable into elements of equal size, because the overhead of controlling parallel processes adds important execution time, and because parallel processes might contend with each other for resources. New configurations address these problems but, in addition, parallel structures are being looked at in new lights because of their potential configurability, fault-tolerance, and performance stability.

We are in a time when the cost of processors is dropping rapidly, when new interconnection methodologies promise new concepts of system structure, and when the concepts of parallel systems are being carried into concepts of distributed systems which cooperate with one another.

REFERENCES

1972. Lorin, H. *Parallelism in Hardware and Software.* Englewood Cliffs, NJ: Prentice-Hall.
1977. Ramamoorthy, C. V. and Li, H. F. "Pipeline Architecture," *Computing Surveys* **9**, *No. 1* (March).
1977. Enslow, P. H., Jr. "Multiprocessor Organization—A Survey," *Computing Surveys* **9**, *No. 1* (March).
1978. Holt, R. C. *et al. Structured Concurrent Programming With Operating Systems Applications.* Reading, MA: Addison-Wesley.

H. LORIN

PARITY

For articles on related subjects *see* CODES; DATA ENCRYPTION; ERROR-CORRECTING CODE; and UNIVERSAL PRODUCT CODE.

Parity is a synonym for equality. Parity checking is an extensively used error-checking facility provided to insure correct recording of data, its input into a computer system, and its transfer within the system, transmission included. A parity check consists of adding up the bits in a unit of data, calculating the parity bit required, and comparing the calculated parity bit with that transferred with the data item. This form of check will normally be performed by hardware.

A parity bit is a check bit whose binary value (0 or 1) depends upon whether the sum of bits with value 1 in the unit of data being checked is odd or even. If the total number of bits with value 1, including the parity bit (or bits), is even, the unit of data is said to have even parity; if it is odd, it has odd parity. Checking methods use either even or odd parity. Each information system must use the same parity principle, even or odd throughout. An error caused by incorrect parity detected as a result of a parity check is called a *parity error*.

The unit of data to which a parity check is applied may be a character, a byte, a word, etc., the character parity check being the one mostly used. The smaller the unit of data to which the check is applied, the higher the probability that compensating errors will not occur.

J. NECAS

PARSING

For articles on related subjects *see* EXPRESSION; GRAMMARS; PRECEDENCE; SOURCE PROGRAM; STATEMENT; and SYNTAX, SEMANTICS AND PRAGMATICS.

Parsing is the process by which the phrases in a string of characters in a language are associated with the component names of the grammar that generated the string. The structural description of the string that results from parsing is called the *parse*. A parse is often shown as a *tree*, as in the following example of the parse of the English sentence, "The cat drank the milk" (see Fig. 1).

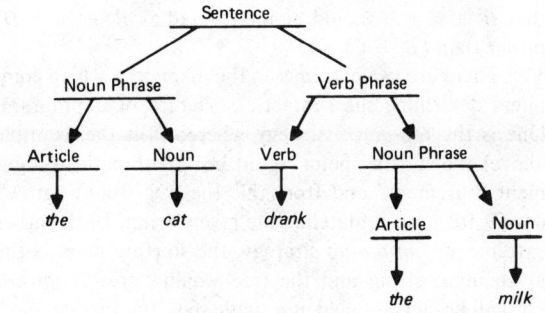

Fig. 1

An equivalent parse of this sentence is

$$(_S(_{NP}(_A{}^{the})_A(_N{}^{cat})_N)_{NP}$$
$$(_{VP}(_V{}^{drank})_V(_{NP}(_A{}^{the})_A(_N{}^{milk})_N)_{NP})_{VP})_S$$

which has the advantage of being linear (i.e., one-dimensional), but may have the disadvantage of being harder to visualize.

Parsing is the heart of the process of compilation of source programs in a high-level language into machine language. The compiler must take the string of characters written by the programmer and associate appropriate substrings of characters with the syntactic components of the high-level language in order to determine the structure of the given program so that it can be translated into machine code. For example, the arithmetic assignment statement

$$A = B + C * D$$

might be parsed as in Fig. 2. Hidden in this example are many subtleties, such as: How can the compiler know

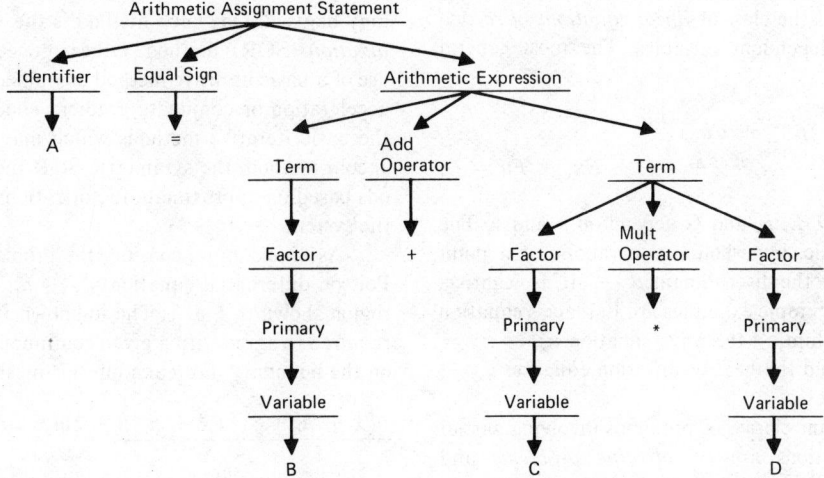

Fig. 2

that $B + C * D$ should be interpreted as $B + (C * D)$ rather than $(B + C) * D$?

There are two extremes in the manner in which compilers determine the syntactic structure of a program. One is the *top-down* strategy whereby (in the example above) the starting point would be "Arithmetic Assignment Statement" and from this the tree would "grow" downward until it matched the given string. In the other extreme, or *bottom-up* strategy, the starting point is the given input string and the tree would "grow" upward until all branches joined at a single root. In practice, most language processors employ a combination of these strategies.

REFERENCES

1972, Presser, L. "The Translation of Programming Languages," in Cardenas, A. F., Presser, L., and Marin, M. A., (Eds.), *Computer Science*. New York: Wiley-Interscience.
1972, 1973. Aho, A. V. and Ullman, J. D. *The Theory of Parsing, Translation, and Compiling*, 1 and 2. Englewood Cliffs, NJ: Prentice-Hall.

J. A. N. LEE AND A. RALSTON

PARTIAL DIFFERENTIAL EQUATIONS

For articles on related subjects *see* FINITE ELEMENT METHOD; MATRIX COMPUTATIONS; NUMERICAL ANALYSIS; and SCIENTIFIC APPLICATIONS.

A major scientific application of large-scale digital computers is the numerical solution of problems involving partial differential equations. These problems have application in such areas as weather forecasting, nuclear diffusion studies for reactor design, fluid flow, supersonic flow, and elasticity. An important class of partial differential equations is the class of *linear equations of second order* in two independent variables. The most general such equation is

$$L[u] = Au_{xx} + 2Bu_{xy} + Cu_{yy}$$
$$+ Du_x + Eu_y + Fu = G,$$

where A, B, C, D, E, F, and G depend on x and y. The equation is elliptic, hyperbolic, or parabolic at a point *(x,y)* according as the discriminant $B^2 - AC$ is negative, positive, or zero. Simple examples are Laplace's equation $u_{xx} + u_{yy} = 0$ (elliptic); the wave equation $u_{xx} - u_{yy} = 0$ (hyperbolic); and the heat or diffusion equation $u_{xx} - u_y = 0$ (parabolic).

Two important classes of problems involving partial differential equations are *initial-value problems* and *boundary-value problems*. For an initial-value problem in two variables the desired function $u(x,y)$ is to satisfy the differential equation in an unbounded region R and to satisfy auxiliary conditions on the boundary S. Such conditions might involve prescribing the values of $u(x,y)$ on S or (as for the Cauchy problem) u, and the normal derivative $\partial u/\partial n$ might be prescribed on S. For a boundary-value problem the region R is bounded, and one prescribes either u, $\partial u/\partial n$, or a linear combination of u and $\partial u/\partial n$ on S. For Laplace's equation, $u_{xx} + u_{yy} = 0$; these conditions would correspond to the Dirichlet, Neumann, and mixed problems, respectively.

Before the solution of a problem involving a partial differential equation should be attempted, one should determine whether or not it is *well set* or *well posed*. To be well set, there should exist a unique solution which depends continuously on the boundary data. For linear equations of second order, boundary-value problems involving hyperbolic or parabolic equations are usually not well set, nor are initial-value problems involving elliptic equations.

A basic tool in the solution of partial differential equations is the method of finite differences. Here one covers the region under consideration by a mesh, usually consisting of horizontal and vertical lines, and one seeks approximate values of the solution at the intersections, or nodes. The partial derivatives appearing in the differential equation are represented by difference quotients (for example, u_{xx} might be represented by $h^{-2}[u(x + h,y) + u(x - h,y) - 2u(x,y)]$, where h is the spacing between the adjacent lines in the mesh. Substituting the difference quotient in the differential equation leads to a difference equation. For a boundary-value problem, one then obtains a system of linear algebraic equations, with the number of equations equal to the number of interior mesh points. It can usually be shown without difficulty that the linear system has a unique solution. Direct methods, designed to take advantage of sparseness and to minimize fill-in, are often used. Alternatively, iterative methods may be used. One such method is the *successive overrelaxation* (SOR) method. Other procedures involve the use of a basic iterative method combined with Chebyshev acceleration or conjugate gradient acceleration. Among the basic iterative methods which may be used are the Jacobi method, the symmetric SOR method, and methods based on approximate factorizations of the matrix of the system.

As an example, consider the problem of solving the Poisson differential equation $u_{xx} + u_{yy} = G(x,y)$ in the region shown in Fig. 1. The unknown function $u(x,y)$ is required to agree with a given continuous function $g(x,y)$ on the boundary. For each interior mesh point we have

$$\frac{u(x + h,y) + u(x - h,y) - 2u(x,y)}{h^2}$$
$$+ \frac{u(x,y + h) + u(x,y - h) - 2u(x,y)}{h^2} = G(x,y).$$

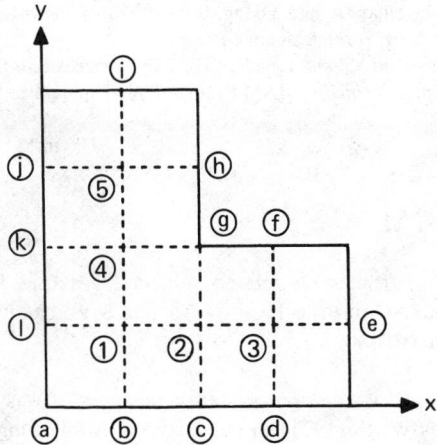

Fig. 1

The application of the difference equation at the point labeled 1 leads (after multiplying by $-h^2$) to the linear equation

$$4u_1 - u_2 - u_4 - u_l - u_b = -h^2 G(x_1, y_1).$$

where the subscripts refer to the points with those labels. Similar equations correspond to the other interior points ②, ③, ④, and ⑤. The values u_a, u_b, ..., are equal to the known values g_a, g_b, ...

Another alternative procedure for solving boundary-value problems is the *finite element method:* Here, again, one eventually obtains a linear system. However, instead of using finite differences one generates the linear equations based on functional approximation techniques using certain subsets of the region (elements) and based on variational procedures, Galerkin procedures, or collocation procedures.

One class of initial-value problems involves the differential equation $u_t = L[u]$, where $L[u]$ is an elliptic operator in one or two "space" variables. Frequently, one is given $u(\vec{x},0)$ for all $\vec{x}$ in the region (where $\vec{x}$ represents x when there is one space variable and x,y when there are two) and $u(\vec{x},t)$ for $\vec{x}$ on the boundary and for all $t > 0$. In the method of finite differences, one constructs a mesh in the space variables, as in the case of a boundary-value problem. In the *forward difference method* one replaces u_t by $[u(\vec{x},t + \Delta t) - u(\vec{x},t)]/(\Delta t)$ and sets it equal to $L_h[u](\vec{x},t)$, where $L_h[u](\vec{x},t)$ is a finite difference representation of $L[u](\vec{x},t)$. The determination of $u(\vec{x},\Delta t)$, $u(\vec{x},2\Delta t)$, etc., can be carried out explicitly. However, numerical stability considerations require that $\Delta t/h^2$, where $h = \Delta x = \Delta y$, be bounded as $h \to 0$. The work required because of the excessively small value of Δt is usually prohibitive.

A more popular method, which greatly relaxes the

restriction on Δt, is the *Crank-Nicolson method*, where one replaces $L_h[u](\vec{x},t)$ by $\frac{1}{2}[L_h[u](\vec{x},t) + L_h[u](\vec{x},t + \Delta t)]$. An implicit rather than an explicit procedure is thus developed. However, with one space dimension, the implicit calculation involves solving a linear system with a tridiagonal matrix. (This is relatively easy.) With two space dimensions, one must solve a boundary-value problem for each time step. However, certain iterative methods can be shown to converge much more rapidly than in the case of a pure boundary-value problem.

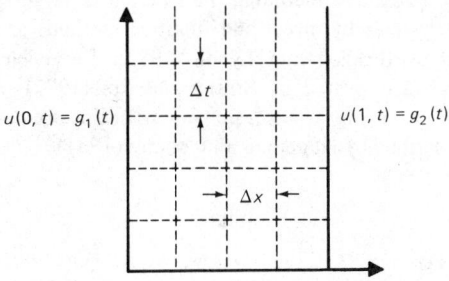

Fig. 2

As an example, consider the diffusion equation $u_t = u_{xx}$ for $0 < x < 1$, $t > 0$, subject to the boundary conditions $u(0,t) = g_1(t)$, $u(1,t) = g_2(t)$, for $t > 0$, and the initial condition $u(x,0) = f(x)$. Here, $g_1(t)$, $g_2(t)$, and $f(x)$ are given. The forward difference method is given by

$$\frac{u(x,t + \Delta t) + u(x,t)}{\Delta t}$$
$$= \frac{u(x + h,t) + u(x - h,t) - 2u(x,t)}{h^2}$$

From this, the values of $u(x,t + \Delta t)$ can be calculated explicitly in terms of values of $u(x,t)$. For the Crank-Nicolson method, the right-hand side is replaced by

$$\frac{1}{2}\left\{ \frac{u(x + h,t) + u(x - h,t) - 2u(x,t)}{h^2} + \frac{u(x + h,t + \Delta t) + u(x - h,t + \Delta t) - 2u(x,t + \Delta t)}{h^2}\right\}$$

Hyperbolic equations of the form $u_{tt} = L[u]$ can often be treated in a manner similar to that described above. Other hyperbolic equations, or systems of equations, are treated by the *method of characteristics*.

In recent years, several software packages have been developed for solving partial differential equations. One such package, known as ELLPACK, is designed to be a research tool for studying and comparing methods. ELLPACK has several modules including input, mesh generation, discretization, equation solution, and output. The

ITPACK package of programs for solving large sparse linear systems using iterative methods can be used for the equation solution module. Alternatively, the equations can be solved using programs of LINPACK, for solving linear systems by direct methods or using programs of the Yale Sparse Matrix Package.

The book by Forsythe and Wasow (1960) treats the solution of hyperbolic, parabolic, and elliptic equations by finite difference methods. The solution of initial value problems by finite difference methods is treated in detail by Richtmyer and Morton (1967). Methods for solving elliptic equations, including the solution of large sparse linear systems by direct and iterative methods are discussed by Birkhoff and Lynch (1982). Finite element methods are treated by Strang and Fix (1972). Algorithms for solving large sparse systems of linear equations are described by Hageman and Young (1981).

REFERENCES

1960. Forsythe, G. E. and Wasow, W. R. *Finite Difference Methods for Partial Differential Equations,* New York: Wiley.

1967. Richtmyer, R. D. and Morton K. W. *Difference Methods for Initial-Value Problems* (2nd. Ed.). New York: Interscience.

1972. Strang, G. and Fix, G. *An Analysis of the Finite Element Method.* Englewood Cliffs, NJ: Prentice-Hall.

1981. Hageman, L. and Young, D. *Accelerated Iterative Methods.* New York: Academic Press.

1982. Birkhoff, G. and Lynch, R. E. *The Numerical Solution of Elliptic Problems*, SIAM Studies. Philadelphia, Pa.: SIAM.

DAVID M. YOUNG

PASCAL

For articles on related subjects *see* ADA; PROCEDURE-ORIENTED LANGUAGES; and STRUCTURED PROGRAMMING.

Pascal is an Algol-related language that was developed by Wirth (1971) in the early 1970s following some earlier work by Wirth and Hoare (1966). Its existence is due to its originators' dissatisfaction with procedure-oriented languages. Pascal was designed to serve as a language for teaching computer programming as a systematic discipline, while at the same time proving that a reliable (error-free) and efficient (in size and speed) implementation of a large procedure-oriented language could be created on presently available computers.

Pascal is one of the few programming languages specifically designed to help the programmer find coding errors quickly. Extensive error checking is performed during compilation and (optionally) during execution. It is

```
program primes (input, output);
const n = 25; { number of primes to compute }
type index = 1..n; { scalar data type is subrange of integer }
var x: integer;
    i,k,limit: index; { variables i,k,limit are of type index }
    prime: Boolean; { prime is either true or false }
    p: array[index] of integer; { p[i] is ith prime }
begin p[1] := 2; { first prime }
    writeln(2); {output prime and end of line terminator}
    x := 1; limit := 1; { initialize method }
    for i := 2 to n do { compute next n − 1 prime numbers }
    begin
        repeat
            x := x+2; { only odd numbers need be considered }
            if sqr(p[limit])<x then limit := limit+1; { to determine greatest prime needed as a divisor }
            k := 2; prime := true;
            while prime and (k<limit) do
                begin
                    prime := (x div p[k])*p[k]≠x;
                        { div results in integer part of quotient }
                    k := k+1
                end
        until prime; { if prime true no prime divisor of x exists }
        p[i] := x; { save prime found in array p }
        writeln(x) {output the prime}    }
    end { of for loop }
end. { of prime number generator }
```

Fig. 1. A sample Pascal program. (Adapted from Wirth, 1973.)

not unusual for Pascal programs, once syntactically correct, to execute error-free almost immediately. This phenomenon can be attributed to (1) the requirement for declaring how each programmer-defined symbol is to be used (there are virtually no defaults in the language), and (2) the existence of a rich set of data types plus a variety of programming structures permitting programs to be closely related to their intended meaning. The latter is the essence of structured programming; i.e., writing programs that are easy to read and understand, are less prone to programming errors, and are easy to maintain (i.e., update and debug).

The Pascal statements that make it an excellent host language for structured programming are: **repeat-until, case,** plus the Algol-like constructs of **if-then-else, while-do,** and **for-do.** The statement **goto** is also permitted in Pascal; however, its use—strongly criticized by structured programming advocates (Habermann, 1973)—can almost always be avoided by a suitable choice of program organization.

Pascal can also be generally characterized as including Algol 60 as a subset, although it omits such Algol features as an exponentiation operator and the ability to include a step size in the **for** statement. In all but a few cases, conversion of an Algol 60 program to Pascal is a negligible effort of transcription (Wirth, 1971). The principal differences between the two languages lie in the area of data structuring facilities (data types), which determine the kinds of values that user-defined variables may assume. For example, in addition to the integer, real, array of integer, and array of real that Algol permits, Pascal provides (among others) scalar, set, record, file, pointer, and character types, plus arrays to accommodate each. Pascal also provides a primitive input/output (I/O) facility which is easy to understand and apply in most cases, but is somewhat difficult to use in programs with complex I/O requirements.

As Pascal's popularity has grown, so also has its availability on numerous mini- and microcomputers for which its compact size and efficiency suit it particularly well. Its applicability as a systems programming language has also been recognized. Concurrent Pascal (Brinch Hansen, 1977), a version of the language with extensions to facilitate concurrent processes and monitor operations, is one of several instances of such a usage. However, the most significant event in Pascal's short history has been its selection as the base for the new Department of Defense programming language, Ada (*q.v.*). For an example of some of the features that make Pascal so attractive, see Fig. 1 (adapted from Wirth, 1973).

REFERENCES

1966. Wirth, N. and Hoare, C. A. R. "A Contribution to the Development of Algol," *Comm. ACM* **9**, *No. 6:* 413–431.

1968. Dijkstra, E. W. "GOTO Statement Considered Harmful," *Comm. ACM* **11**, *No. 3:* 147–148.

1971. Wirth, N. "The Programming Language PASCAL," *Acta Informatica* **1**: 35–63.

1972. Dahl, O. J., Dijkstra, E. W., and Hoare, C. A. R. *Structured Programming.* New York: Academic Press.

1973 Habermann, A. N. *Critical Comments on the Programming Language PASCAL.* Pittsburgh: Carnegie-Mellon University, Dept. of Computer Science.

1973. Wirth, N. *Systematic Programming: An Introduction.* Englewood Cliffs, NJ: Prentice-Hall.

1974. Lecarme, O. and Desjardins, P. "Reply to a Paper by A. N. Habermann on the Programming Language PASCAL," *SIGPLAN Notices* **9**, *No. 10:* 21–27.

1975. Jensen, K. and Wirth, N. *PASCAL User Manual and Report,* 2nd Ed. New York: Springer Verlag.

1977. Brinch Hansen, P. *The Architecture of Concurrent Programs.* Englewood Cliffs, NJ: Prentice-Hall.

M. KESSLER

PASCAL, BLAISE

For articles on related subjects *see* DIGITAL COMPUTERS: Origins; and LEIBNIZ, G. W.

Pascal (b. Clermont, France, 1623; d. Paris, 1662) was educated by his father Etienne, and, after discovering a proof of Euclid's Proposition 32 at age 12, he became a participant in Mersenne's Circle. Four years later he presented to them his well-known theorem in projective geometry.

Fig. 1. Death Mask of Blaise Pascal. (Courtesy N.Y. Public Library.)

In 1640, he started developing a calculating machine to help in his father's tax work in Rouen. He completed the first operating model in 1642 and built 50 more during the next ten years. The machine was a small box with eight dials (resembling telephone dials), each geared to a drum that displayed the digits in a register window. Pascal's fundamental innovation was a ratchet linkage *(sautier)* between the rotating drums, which transferred rotating motion from one drum to the next higher-position drum only during carryover. This kept the digit of each drum aligned with its display window. The machine added and subtracted directly, and multiplied and divided by using repeated additions and subtractions, analogous to present-day pencil-and-paper algorithms. The machine was presented publicly in 1645.

In 1646, Pascal learned of Torricelli's experiment with the vacuum and successfully repeated it. Because of illness, he moved back to Paris in 1647, where he associated with Roberval, met Descartes, published treatises on the vacuum and on conics, and prepared the Puy-de-Dômes (barometer) experiment. Around 1651, he met the Duc de Roannez and the Chevalier de Mere and became reinvolved in research; in 1654, he produced two papers establishing the foundations of the integral calculus and of probability theory. In 1658, using the pseudonym Amos Dettonville, he challenged mathematicians to a mathematical contest and created a controversy by awarding himself the prize. No further significant research followed.

Pascal had been converted to Jansenism in 1645 and, in 1654, he had an ecstatic religious experience which drew him into the Port-Royal Jansenists' machinations with the Jesuits, resulting in his writing the *Provincial Letters,* the beginning of French classical literature. His general health, which had been poor, degenerated and he became more mystical in his interests. During his last months in 1662, he created the first public transportation system—an omnibus service in Paris.

C. V. Jones

PATCH

For articles on related subjects *see* Debugging; Fix; and Machine and Assembly Language Programming.

A patch is a piece of code that (1) represents a programmer's afterthought, (2) is generated by more primitive means than was the program it is to be applied to, and (3) is usually overwritten on code or data in the program to be patched. As a verb, therefore, to "patch" is to modify a program in a rough or expedient way.

A typical example of patching would begin with the discovery of a bug in a sizable compiler-language program, and the realization that it would be very costly or inconvenient to fix it by recompilation. An alternative procedure is to patch—i.e., to generate the required new code either by writing it in assembly language and assembling it, or even by writing it directly in machine language—and loading it after the program to be modified. If the patch is no greater in size than the code to be replaced (if any), it can simply be overlaid on that code, possibly with a terminal transfer over some remaining undesired old code. If it is larger than the code to be replaced, it will be necessary to find "patch space" in which to load it, and to insert transfer instructions to and from the patch so as to link it in at the appropriate point. Depending on the loader that will be inserting the patch, it may be necessary for the programmer to be concerned with checksums, load addresses, and relocation quantities or bits.

The advantages of a patch (over reassembly or recompilation) are that it does not incur the cost, in time or money, involved in submitting the entire program in source form to the appropriate processor. The disadvantages include a much greater liability to error and a loss of correspondence between the latest program listing and the program. Since one of the greatest advantages of the patch is its saving of turnaround time, the coming of on-line programming has deprived the patch of one of its chief reasons for being.

M. Halpern

PATENTS, SOFTWARE. *See* Legal Protection of Software.

PATTERN RECOGNITION

For articles on related subjects *see* Artificial Intelligence; Image and Picture Processing; Medical Applications; Optical Character Readers; Optical Mark Readers; Scientific Applications; Tomography, Computed; and Universal Product Code.

Pattern recognition is the area of computer science that is concerned with the classification or description by computer of objects, events, or other meaningful regularities in noisy or complex environments. In other words, it is the study of ideas and algorithms that provide computers with a perceptual capability to put abstract objects, or patterns, into categories in a simple and reliable way.

As a human experience, pattern recognition refers to a perceptual process in which patterns in any sensory modality (vision, hearing, touch, taste, or smell) or patterns in conceptual or logical thought processes are analyzed and recognized (or classified) as being familiar, either in the sense of having been previously experienced or of being similar to, or associated with, a previous experience.

Motivation for the study of pattern recognition in computer science is threefold. First, it is an essential part of the broader field of *artificial intelligence* (*q.v.*)—which is concerned with techniques that enable computers to do things that seem intelligent when done by people. Second, it is an important aspect of applying computers to solve problems in science and engineering—since many of them involve analysis and classification of measurements taken from physical processes. Third, pattern recognition techniques provide a *unified framework* to study a variety of techniques in mathematics and computer science that are individually useful in many different applications; for example, pattern recognition algorithms based on statistical, linguistic, geometrical, and graph-theoretic concepts and data structures for pattern representation encompass a spectrum extending from simple concepts of vectors to knotty questions concerning knowledge representation.

The major applications of pattern recognition fall into three categories: (1) patterns in images (or spatial patterns): (2) patterns in time (or temporal patterns); (3) patterns in more abstract data environments. Within image processing and scene analysis, the most important application areas are computer vision—optical character recognition (*q.v.*) for systems ranging from bank check processing to reading machines for the blind, industrial robot vision, and unmanned planetary exploration systems; biomedical analysis—automated cytology and computed tomography (*q.v.*); and remote sensing—earth resources, meteorology, and military applications. Signal processing applications include speech recognition (*q.v.*), radar and sonar signal analysis, seismological monitoring, and medical waveform analysis, as in electrocardiography (EKG) and electroencephalography (EEG). More general data analysis problems that have received attention within pattern recognition are typified by medical diagnosis using medical history and various clinical data.

Terminology. The process organization of a general pattern recognition system is shown in Fig. 1. In ob-

serving a pattern, *measurements* of an object are made that directly or indirectly reflect attributes of the object which distinguish it from other objects. *Features* are functions of the measurements intended to recover the defining attributes. The extracted features are used by a *classification procedure* to give a class assignment to the object. Since the overall process is one of reducing the pattern data in stages, pattern recognition may also be viewed as an information reduction process.

As an example, let us consider the recognition of hand-printed characters on a page. The measurement process consists of scanning optically a region of the paper where the character (i.e., pattern) is written so as to represent the pattern as a two-dimensional array whose values represent shades of gray from white to black. A second stage of the measurement process is concerned with enhancing the data prior to analysis and includes operations such as smoothing to reduce noise (irrelevant variations), sharpening to enhance edges, segmentation of the image into separate characters, and transformations to allow for variations in size, position, and orientation of the characters to be recognized. The feature extraction stage searches for features in the input—*global* features, such as the number of holes in the character, the number of concavities in its outer contour, or the relative protrusion of character extremities, or *local* features, such as the relative positions of line-endings, line-crossovers, and corners. The final classification stage identifies each input character by considering the detected features. In practice, it is difficult to choose a set of features that reliably distinguishes handwritten characters (see, for example, Fig. 2, in which the H and A

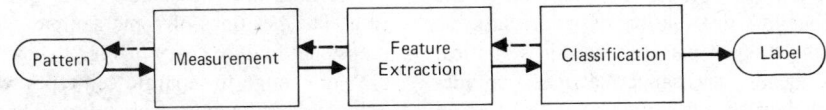

Fig. 2. Identical patterns, in different contexts, have different meanings.

letters are represented almost identically). Thus, the later phases may need to reawaken earlier phases to re-examine ancillary (often contextual) evidence so as to help in the development of a particular interpretation. The *top-down* flow of control information (as opposed to the *bottom-up* flow of pattern information) necessary to utilize *context*, is represented by the dotted lines in the process organization diagram of Fig. 1.

Pattern → Measurement ⇄ Feature Extraction ⇄ Classification → Label

Fig. 1. Stages in a pattern recognition system.

Class Definitions. A class is a group or set of patterns that are similar or equivalent in some sense. Class definitions are based on the intuitive notion that members of a class share some common properties or attributes. To represent a class, either a prototype (an ideal form on which all member patterns are based, the class "essence") or a set of samples must be known. A philosophical distinction may be made between *canonical,* or natural, pattern classes, such as animal species and diseases, and *conventional,* or symbolic, pattern classes, such as letters and musical notes. The feature selection process attempts to recover the pattern attributes characteristic of each class. For canonical classes, appropriate features may be inferred from an understanding of the natural phenomenon. For conventional classes, the features may be specified by the class definition, although, as in the case of hand-printed characters, they may not be explicit.

Depending on the nature of the data analysis problem, the various classes may be distinguished *a priori* or they may not. In the first case, representative samples or defining characteristics are available for each class and the problem is one of classification of subsequent observed patterns. In the second case, referred to as the *clustering problem,* the data consists of an unlabeled collection of samples and the analysis task is the detection and description of naturally occurring groups or clusters in the data. Additional samples may then be classified into the empirically established groups.

Approaches to Pattern Classification. Ultimately, the process of pattern recognition consists of assigning a pattern to a class. The assignment is made by a classification algorithm (or *classifier*) based on the features extracted and the relationships among the features. Since members of a class are equivalent or similar inasmuch as they share defining attributes, the measurement of similarity, either explicitly or implicitly, is central to any classifier. Depending on the features extracted— which, in turn, depend on the data environment, variability within classes, and defining attributes—classifiers are derived using quite different approaches.

In the *statistical* approach, patterns are represented by points in a multidimensional *feature space.* Each component of the feature space is a measurement or feature value, which is a random variable reflecting the inherent variability within and between classes. A classifier partitions the feature space into regions associated with each class, labeling an observed pattern according to the class region into which it falls. The partition is based on the multivariate probability distribution of each class, as specified by a sample set of patterns, certain statistical parameters (e.g., means, covariance matrices), or, ideally, the joint probability density function of the random

variable features. The classification algorithm commonly employs generalized distance measures in n-space.

Although many problems are successfully dealt with using the statistical approach, it is often more appropriate to represent patterns explicitly in terms of relationships among features other than statistical covariance. In such cases, the structure or arrangement of components or primitive elements is taken as the defining attribute of the pattern. The *structural* approach to pattern recognition represents patterns in terms of *primitives* and *relations* among the primitives in order to describe pattern structure explicitly. Computer vision problems, where the primitives are simple objects and the relations are spatial, is an application area that uses this approach. Most commonly, the concepts of formal language (*q.v.*) theory are employed to represent pattern structure in terms of syntax rules, and classes in terms of grammars and their associated languages. An observed pattern is assigned to the class whose grammar allows a successful parsing.

In the remainder of this article, we discuss the statistical and structural approaches in greater detail. Included in the references are sources of information beyond the elementary view of pattern recognition we are able to present here.

Statistical Pattern Recognition. The statistical approach to pattern recognition may be summarized as follows. A pattern that is represented by a set of m measurements is thought of as a point $\mathbf{p}$ in an m-dimensional measurement space. Feature extraction is expressed as a transformation that maps $\mathbf{p}$ into a point $\mathbf{x}$ in an n-dimensional feature space; it may be viewed pragmatically as a process that reduces pattern space dimensionality and consequently simplifies the classification task. The classifier then assigns $\mathbf{x}$ to a class by means of a decision function $d(\mathbf{x})$—which, in effect, is a method of partitioning the feature space into territories corresponding to different classes. The performance of the classifier is measured by an objective function, which is usually the probability of error (or misclassification).

An example of feature space partitioning used to classify white blood cells into the standard categories (neutrophils, eosinophils, basophils, lymphocytes, and monocytes) based on two features, the nucleus area and the cytoplasm area, is shown in Fig. 3. In this case, the decision functions for each class are measures of distance from the classes (see geometric classifiers below), and the dotted lines are equidistant from the classes they separate. The positions of some sample cells in the two-dimensional feature space of Fig. 3 show that two features are not enough to separate cell types with an acceptably low misclassification probability. The addition of two

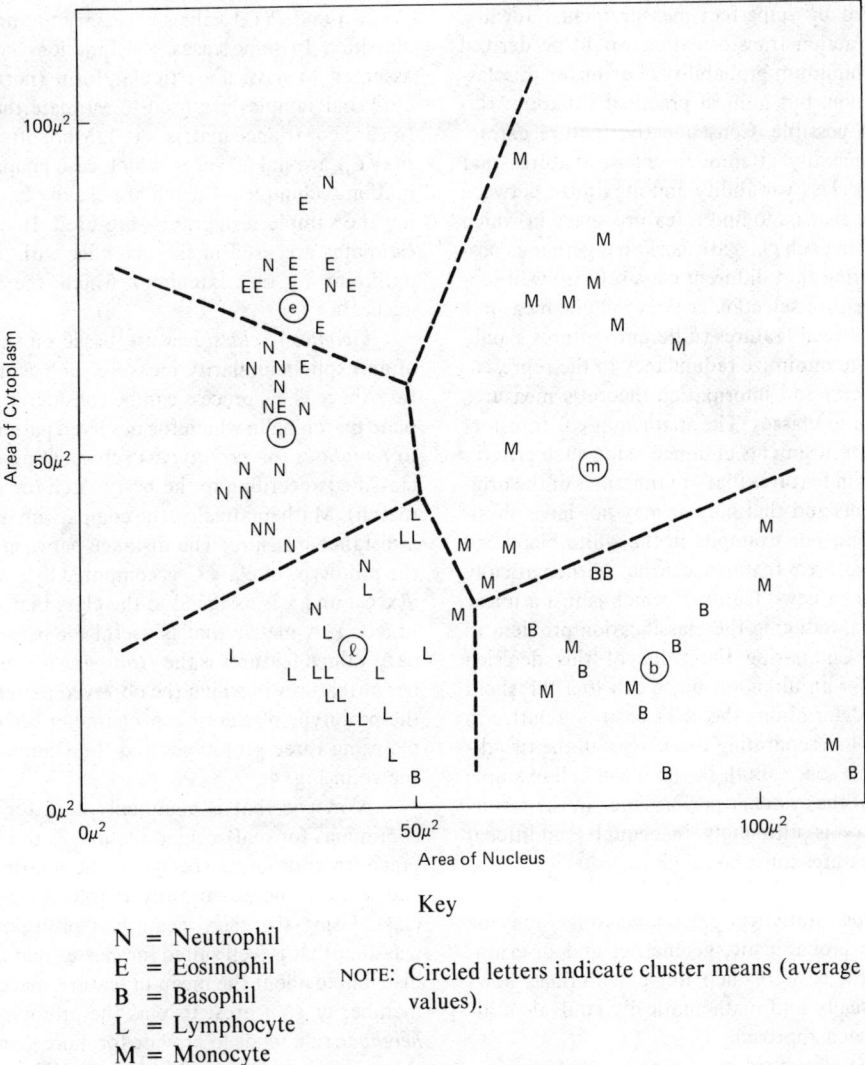

Key

N = Neutrophil
E = Eosinophil
B = Basophil   NOTE: Circled letters indicate cluster means (average
L = Lymphocyte   values).
M = Monocyte
μ = 1 micrometer (10^{-6} meters)

Fig. 3. White blood cells are separated into categories by partitioning the feature space. Four features are required for reliable separation. (Adapted, with permission, from Winston, P. H. *Artificial Intelligence*. Reading, MA: Addison-Wesley, 1977.)

more features, nucleus and cytoplasm color, results in a four-dimensional feature space in which the five classes are separated with a much lower error rate.

Many important problem domains do not have the convenient clustering properties exhibited by the white blood cell example. For example, the samples of different classes may not be clustered equally close about class centers; features may interact with each other producing ellipsoidal rather than spherical distributions; few sam-

ples may be available; the classes themselves may not be specified initially. We will discuss a variety of mathematical techniques that have been developed to handle such problems. The techniques themselves are conveniently grouped into three categories—feature extraction methods, classification methods, and clustering methods.

Feature Extraction. On a conceptual level, feature extraction is concerned with recovering the defining attributes obscured by imperfect measurements. Ideally, the feature extraction transformation would be derived according to a minimum probability of error (or misclassification) criterion, but in most practical situations this approach is not possible. Consequently, feature extraction schemes generally attempt to choose features that minimize within class variability and maximize between class variability; that is, to find a feature space in which the samples within each class are as close together as possible, while insuring that different class sets are well separated. Other feature selection criteria include measures of correlation between features (different features should be uncorrelated to minimize redundancy in the representation of an object) and information theoretic measures relating features to classes. The mathematical transformation of the measurements obtained using such criteria generally results in features that are functions of the original measurements and that may or may not have physical interpretations. For example, in the white blood cell problem, the two area features can be mathematically combined to form a new "feature," which is just a linear decision function, reducing the classification problem to one dimension. Comparing the value of this decision function, $d(\mathbf{x})$, for an unknown blood cell to a threshold is equivalent to determining the cell's position relative to a corresponding line separating two classes in the two-dimensional feature space. Both in the blood cell example and in general, if the system's performance in the resulting feature space is ultimately inadequate, additional measures and features must be sought.

Classification. Statistical pattern classifiers may be distinguished as probabilistic, geometric, and discriminant-based, on the basis of their implementations; however, one can usually find mathematically equivalent algorithms using each approach.

Probabilistic classifiers are based on the principle that a pattern should be assigned to the class that is most probable, given the observed features. In other words, a point $\mathbf{x}$ of feature space (i.e., an observed pattern) is assigned to the class that maximizes the *a posteriori* probability $P(C_i/\mathbf{x})$ over the set of classes $\{C_i\}$. From the Bayesian theory of conditional probabilities, this is mathematically equivalent to assigning $\mathbf{x}$ to the class C_i that maximizes

$$p(\mathbf{x}/C_i) * P(C_i)$$

where $p(\mathbf{x}/C_i)$ is called the *class-conditional* probability density function (i.e., it gives the probability that the pattern has value $\mathbf{x}$ given that it is in class C_i) and $P(C_i)$ is the probability of class C_i before the pattern is observed (i.e., the *a priori* probability). Labeled samples representative of each class are generally used to determine the

$p(\mathbf{x}/C_i)$ and $P(C_i)$ values necessary to implement such a classifier. In some cases, the functions $p(\mathbf{x}/C_i)$ may be assumed to have a particular form (normal, binomial, etc.) and samples are used to estimate their parameters (mean, covariance matrix, etc.). More often, the forms of $p(\mathbf{x}/C_i)$ are unknown, in which case nonparametric estimation techniques—which are usually based on computing the sample histogram—are used. In either case, the estimates are used in the classifier with a result that is optimum to the extent to which the estimates are accurate.

Geometric classifiers are based on the computation of an explicit similarity measure such as distance in feature space. This process can be considered a kind of template matching in which the observed pattern is compared to *templates* (or *prototypes*) representing each class and classified according to the best match (or minimum mismatch). Mathematically, the comparison is achieved with a distance measure. The distance between pattern $\mathbf{x}$ and the prototype of class C_i is computed by a *metric function* $d(\mathbf{x}, C_i)$ and $\mathbf{x}$ is assigned to the class that minimizes this function. A metric that is useful for patterns having binary valued features is the *Hamming distance*—the number of features in which the observed pattern differs from the prototype of class C_i. A character recognition example using three prototypes and the Hamming distance is shown in Fig. 4.

A metric that is commonly used for patterns with continuous (or real) valued features is the Euclidean distance. In addition to specifying the metric distance, it is necessary to choose carefully a prototype pattern for each class. Using the class mean as a prototype results in a classifier that is well suited for classes that are spherically distributed about the mean in feature space. By using the member of C_i nearest to $\mathbf{x}$ as the prototype, the *nearest neighbor* rule tends to provide for more general (i.e., nonspherical) distributions. Metrics other than the Euclidean distance that are suitable for particular feature spaces are also commonly used. For example, the Mahanalobis distance between $\mathbf{x}$ and the class mean (which is defined by the algebraic equation, $d(\mathbf{x}, C_i) = (\mathbf{x} - \mathbf{m}_i)^T S_i^{-1} (\mathbf{x} - \mathbf{m}_i)$ where $\mathbf{m}_i$ and S_i are the mean and covariance matrix of class C_i, respectively) compensates for unequal feature variance as well as statistical correlation among features. The white blood cell example of Fig. 3 uses the Mahanalobis distance measure to partition the feature space.

Discriminant function classifiers associate a function $f_i(\mathbf{x})$ with class C_i, and assign $\mathbf{x}$ to the class that has the maximum discriminant function value. An example is a classifier that computes a *potential function* for each class—which measures the cumulative electrostatic potential induced at $\mathbf{x}$ by unit charges placed at the samples of class C_i in feature space. In the case where the classes are *linearly separable* (i.e., there is a linear decision func-

Templates

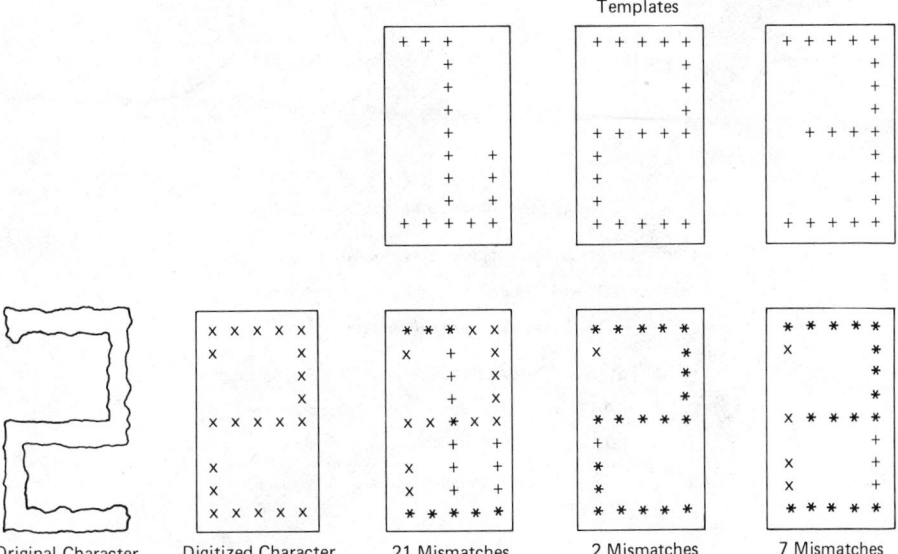

Original Character · Digitized Character · 21 Mismatches · 2 Mismatches · 7 Mismatches

Fig. 4. Template matching using the Hamming distance. All points of the digitized character (i.e., features) are compared with corresponding points in each template. If the two are not the same (i.e., both 0 or both 1), a mismatch, or distance 1, is counted. Here, the second template is selected as a result of minimum mismatch.

tion which is greater than zero for all samples in one class and less than zero for all samples in the other class) in the chosen feature space, an iterative algorithm, known as the *perceptron* (*q.v.*) algorithm finitely converges to discriminant functions which correctly classify all given samples. For linearly non-separable classes, various criterion functions can be used in gradient descent procedures to obtain discriminant functions. As with geometric classifiers, some of the discriminant function classifiers are equivalent to probabilistic classifiers.

In addition to the above classifiers, we mention three important elaborations developed for particular types of problems. The first of these is for utilizing *context* in making a decision. For example, in classifying speech sounds, or letters in a word, the preceding and succeeding patterns are valuable in establishing the identity of a single pattern. In principle, a sequence of patterns $x_1, \ldots, x_n$ may be regarded as a single complex pattern X. However, this representation is generally impractical due to the high-dimensional feature space that would be needed. Therefore, methods have been developed for utilizing *bottom-up* contextual knowledge in the form of Markovian models of pattern dependency and *top-down* contextual knowledge in the form of dictionaries, syntax, and semantic models. The second extension is based on *sequential decision theory,* which applies to a situation in which successive features are measured only as necessary to achieve a desired expected probability of error. Finally,

the theory of *fuzzy sets* has been applied in classification problems where a non-exclusive assignment of patterns to classes is desired. If the classes do not have precisely defined criteria of membership (e.g., tall people, beautiful women, numbers much greater than one), the concept of a membership function with value between 0 and 1 is a useful characterization. Rather than probabilistically assigning a pattern to one class or another but not both simultaneously, a fuzzy classifier would provide the degree of membership of a pattern to each of the classes.

Clustering. Both feature extraction and classification depend critically on the nature of the *a priori* information about the classes with which the system is to deal. An important class of problems deals with unlabeled data sets in which class definitions must be determined empirically. Clustering algorithms are concerned with establishing any empirical classes—sets of samples that are more similar to each other than to patterns outside the set—which are present in the given set of unlabeled samples.

Simpler clustering algorithms establish clusters on the basis of the similarity of (distance between) individual samples, while more complex schemes employ formal criteria such as measures of within and between cluster scatter (variability) in iterative optimization algorithms. In the first category are the hierarchical clustering algorithms, such as the *nearest neighbor algorithm*, in which

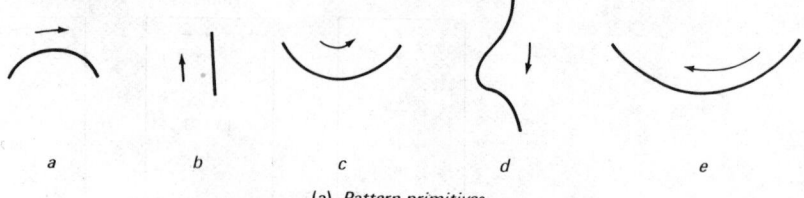

(a) *Pattern primitives*

S (chromosome), S_1 (submedian), S_2 (telocentric), *A* (armpair),

B (bottom), *C* (side), *D* (arm), *E* (right part), *F* (left part)

(b) *Nonterminal symbols*

$$S \rightarrow S_1 \mid S_2 \qquad A \rightarrow CA \mid DE \mid AC \mid FD \qquad D \rightarrow Db \mid bD \mid a$$
$$S_1 \rightarrow AA \qquad B \rightarrow bB \mid e \mid Bb \qquad E \rightarrow cD$$
$$S_2 \rightarrow BA \qquad C \rightarrow Cb \mid d \mid bC \mid b \qquad F \rightarrow Dc$$

(c) *Production rules*

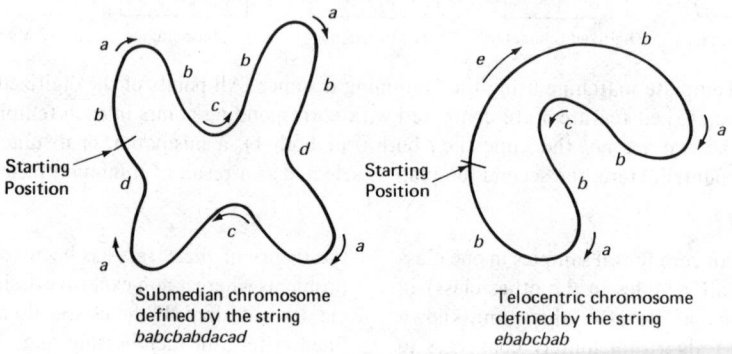

Submedian chromosome
defined by the string
babcbabdacad

Telocentric chromosome
defined by the string
ebabcbab

(d) *Example patterns*

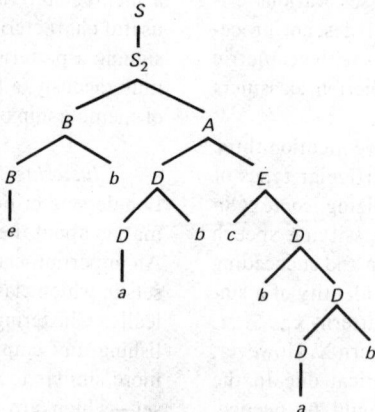

(e) *Tree structure (parse) of ebabcbab*

Fig. 5. Chromosomes are described syntactically. The pattern primitives are concatenated head-to-tail according to the production rules. For example, the production $S_2 \rightarrow BA$ says that a telocentric chromosome consists of a bottom (*B*) and an armpair (*A*). (Adapted, with permission, from Gonzalez, R. C. and Thomason, M. G. *Syntactic Pattern Recognition.* Reading, MA: Addison-Wesley, 1978.)

clusters are merged (or split) in a hierarchical fashion according to the proximity of the nearest neighbors, and graph-theoretic algorithms relating clusters with connected sub-graphs, patterns with nodes and similarities (distances) with edges. A well-known algorithm of the second category is ISODATA (Iterative Self Organizing Data Analysis Technique), which combines scatter criteria and user intuition in an effective interactive scheme.

Structural Pattern Recognition. The approach of interpreting a list of characteristic attributes of a pattern as the coordinates of a point in feature space reduces the classification problem to one of partitioning the feature space. In problems such as computer vision, the patterns are quite complex and the number of features required is often very large. Thus, the idea of using the structural information that describes each pattern to simplify its representation is attractive. The basic idea of the structural approach is to describe complex patterns in terms of a composition of simpler patterns.

Pattern Grammars. In the case where patterns consist of (one-dimensional) waveforms or (two-dimensional) images of flat objects, the structure of patterns can usually be described in a manner analogous to the syntax of languages. Patterns are specified as being hierarchically built up from sub-patterns in various ways of composition by a grammar. In this approach, also called the *syntactic approach,* the important element is the pattern description language that provides the structural description of patterns in terms of a set of pattern primitives (or *morphs*) and their composition operations defined by the grammar. An example of a context-free grammar for describing the structure of two chromosome types, submedian and telocentric, is given in Fig. 5.

In the syntactic approach, after each primitive within a pattern is identified in the feature extraction stage, classification is accomplished by performing a syntax analysis (or parsing) of the sentence describing the given pattern to determine whether or not it is syntactically correct with respect to the specified grammar. The syntax analysis produces a structural description of the sentence representing the given pattern in the form of a tree structure. The grammar itself may be inferred from sample patterns by using *grammatical inference* techniques. The most attractive aspect of this approach is its capability to use the recursive nature of a grammar to express in a very compact way some basic structural characteristics of infinite sentences. Again, for this approach to be practical, recognition of the simple pattern primitives and their relationships, as represented by the composition operations, is essential.

Scene Description. The mathematics of feature spaces and formalisms of pattern grammars do well when scenes satisfy two criteria: (1) the features are *invariant* (i.e., do not change much over the range of circumstances likely to be encountered), and (2) the measurement of each feature over the entire image is dominated by the measurement of that feature for the object contained in the image. These criteria help explain why classifying a single well-framed, flat blood cell is different from deciding if a room has a telephone in it. Programs that enable a robot to find a telephone in an office or help a surgeon identify a tumor in a three-dimensional computed tomogram require more powerful descriptive machinery for pattern representation.

The problem of describing scenes of three-dimensional objects can be approached in two distinctly different ways—two-dimensional and three-dimensional scene description. To illustrate the distinction between them, consider the very simple scene shown in Fig. 6. Such a line drawing can be obtained from a TV picture of a real scene by a computer program, although this is also a nontrivial problem. A two-dimensional description of this scene might specify, in some formalism and to some degree of precision, "three adjacent quadrilaterals, three collinear line segments, and two adjacent triangles." A three-dimensional description, on the other hand, might specify "box and pyramid resting on a floor and in front of a wall." In terms of human understanding, at least, the three-dimensional description is much clearer and more intuitive than the two-dimensional description.

It is clear that a three-dimensional description of a scene can be extracted only with the aid of prior information about objects that populate the environment. In order to produce a three-dimensional description of a scene, we need both a set of three-dimensional models of objects in the environment and a well-defined procedure for interpreting a given scene in terms of these models. If the environment is sufficiently simple, then the set of models need not be specified in great detail and the model matching procedure can be trivial. Suppose that the only objects in the environment are boxes and pyramids. Then

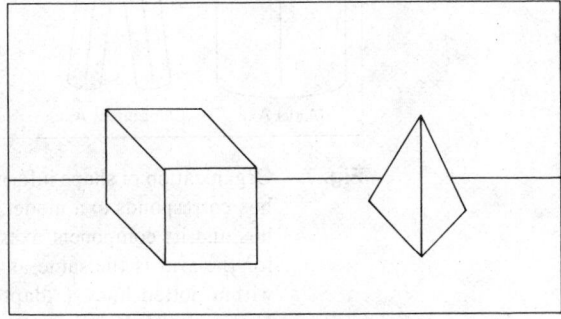

Fig. 6. Scene analysis decides how each line in a drawing should be interpreted.

our model of the environment can be as crude as "a box has only quadrilaterals" and "a pyramid has triangles."

As we consider more complicated environments, we will need more accurate and complete models. Sometimes it is possible to translate critical facts about models into simple facts about their images. An illustration of this sort of situation is of scenes consisting of polyhedra (plane-bounded solids) placed in arbitrary configurations and even having associated shadows. Programs to describe such scenes exploit the fact that crack, shadow, boundary, and interior line types combine at junctions in only a few ways. Once line types are known, through a search procedure, it is easy to use those lines known to be boundaries to divide the scene into distinct objects.

In the general case, we are not likely to be so fortunate as to be able to incorporate all the necessary model information into a few simple tests. Instead, we will have to make a more thorough comparison between each one of the three-dimensional models and the scene at hand. To introduce the basic approach, suppose we have to begin with a finite number of models of three-dimensional objects, and suppose we are given a scene with one of these objects. Conceptually, we can take each model in turn and place it in all possible positions and compute the match with the given object. The model that achieves, for some position, the best match is declared to be the model (or class) of the given object. Thus, the model-matching paradigm is similar to template matching, one where each model in effect generates a family of templates, one for each position.

Three-dimensional models for representing polyhedra such as boxes and pyramids are simple, since they are describable by the coordinates of their vertexes or the surface normals or some other simple expedient. For the real world, however, the description of shape has new dimensions. One method of describing the structure of complex three-dimensional shapes is known as *recursive modeling*. In this approach, each model is specified by a *model axis* and a set of *component axes*—where an axis is defined to be a line segment in three-dimensional space. The model axis specifies coarse information such as the size and orientation of the object. The component axes specify the relative spatial arrangement of the major components of the object with respect to the model axis; the number of component axes is chosen to be small and such that they are of roughly the same length. Each component is recursively described by a three-dimensional model. Although individual models have a limited complexity, a combination of several in this kind of organizational hierarchy allows one to build up a description that captures the geometry of a shape to an arbitrary level of detail. Such a representation also allows us to view recognition as a gradual process proceeding from the general to the specific. An example of the description of a human shape using recursive models is given in Fig. 7, which shows the highest level model (human), the model of one of its components (arm), and so on.

Recognition of objects based on the above structural representation involves a search similar to parsing based on a pattern grammar. The classifier uses a catalog of

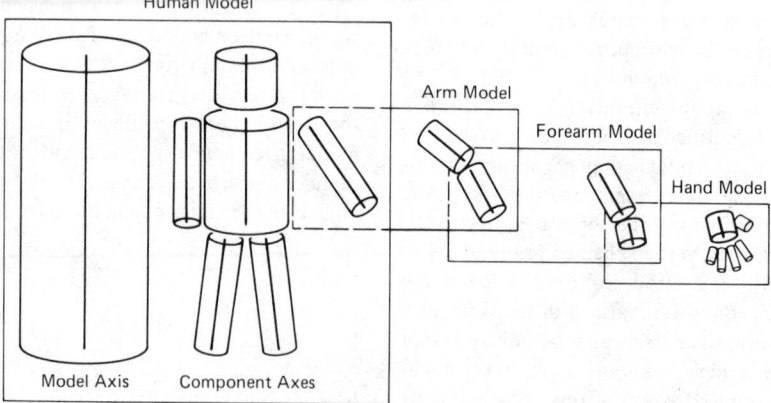

Fig. 7. Organization of shape information in a three-dimensional model. Each box corresponds to a model, with its model axis on the left side of the box and its component axes shown on the right side. The model axis for the arm is the same as the component axis of the human shown within dotted lines. (Adapted, with permission, from Marr, D. and Nishihara, H. K. "Representation and Recognition of the Spatial Organization of Three-Dimensional Shapes," *Proceedings Royal Society London* B.**200**:269–294, 1978.)

stored three-dimensional model descriptions as well as various indices into the catalog. The three-dimensional model of an observed object (which is derived in the feature extraction stage) is related to a model in the catalog by starting at the top of the hierarchy and working down the levels through models until a level of specificity is reached that corresponds to the precision of information in the object. A search through the catalog should also take into account the fact that, when a component of a shape is recognized, it can provide information about what the whole shape is likely to be.

The method of recursive modeling is but one of many different representations that have been proposed for recognizing complex three-dimensional shapes. In fact, the method is useful only for shapes that have a well-defined decomposition. Other methods for shape representation are considered in Shirai's 1978 survey.

REFERENCES

Books
1973. Duda, R. O. and Hart, P. E. *Pattern Classification and Scene Analysis.* New York: Wiley. (A classic in the field. Discusses both the statistical and structural approaches in depth up to its time of publication.)
1974. Tou, J. T. and Gonzalez, R. C. *Pattern Recognition Principles.* Reading, MA: Addison-Wesley. (Includes a number of examples of scientific applications of pattern recognition.)
1975. Winston, P. H. (Ed.). *The Psychology of Computer Vision.* New York: McGraw-Hill. (Describes influential work on machine vision research conducted at the M.I.T. Artificial Intelligence Laboratory.)
1978. Gonzalez, R. C. and Thomason, M. G. *Syntactic Pattern Recognition.* Reading, MA: Addison-Wesley. (Describes the application of formal language and automata theory to the description of patterns.)
1980. Tanimoto, S. and Klinger A. (Eds.). *Structured Computer Vision.* New York: Academic Press. (Collection of papers that survey hierarchical computation structures for machine perception.)
1980. Lea, W. A. (Ed.). *Trends in Speech Recognition.* Englewood Cliffs, NJ: Prentice-Hall. (Overviews of approaches to speech recognition taken by different research groups.)
1981. Bezdek, J. C. *Pattern Recognition with Fuzzy Objective Function Algorithms.* New York: Plenum. (Models of feature selection, clustering, and classification based on fuzzy set theory are discussed.)
1982. Fu, K. S. *Syntactic Pattern Recognition and Applications.* Englewood Cliffs, NJ: Prentice Hall. (Syntactic methods applied to the recognition of patterns in a variety of applications.)

Surveys
1974. Kanal, L. N. "Patterns in Pattern Recognition: 1968–1974" *IEEE Trans. Inform. Theory* **IT-20**, No. 6: 697–722. (A survey of pattern recognition techniques up to 1974, with emphasis on statistical methods.)
1978. Toussaint, G. T. "The Use of Context in Pattern Recognition," *Pattern Recognition* **10**: 189–204. (A tutorial survey of techniques for using contextual information in pattern recognition.)
1978. Pavlidis, T. "A Review of Algorithms for Shape Analysis," *Computer Graphics and Image Processing* **7**: 243–258. (Survey of methods for extracting features describing two-dimensional shape.)
1978. Shirai, Y. "Recent Advances in Three-Dimensional Scene Analysis," *Proc. Fourth Int. Joint Conf. Pattern Recognition,* pp. 86–94. (Survey of methods for describing the structure of three-dimensional scenes.)
1980. *IEEE Computer, Special Issue on Machine Perception* **13**, No. 5 (May). (Contains a number of articles surveying the use of visual and speech pattern recognition in industry.)

Journals
Journals that regularly contain research papers in pattern recognition include:
   IEEE Transactions on Pattern Analysis and Machine Intelligence
   IEEE Transactions on Biomedical Engineering
   IEEE Transactions on Acoustics, Speech and Signal Processing
   IEEE Transactions on Information Theory
   IEEE Transactions on Systems, Man and Cybernetics
   Communications of the ACM
   Journal of the ACM
   Pattern Recognition
   Artificial Intelligence
   Information Sciences
   Computer Graphics and Image Processing
Conference Proceedings
Proceedings of the following regularly held conferences have a significant number of papers on pattern recognition:
International Joint Conference on Pattern Recognition, 1972, 1974, 1976, 1978, 1980.
IEEE Computer Society Conference on Pattern Recognition and Image Processing, 1977, 1978, 1979, 1981.
International Joint Conference on Artificial Intelligence, 1973, 1975, 1977, 1979, 1981.
International Conference on Cybernetics and Systems, held annually.

M. E. JERNIGAN AND S. N. SRIHARI

PDP SERIES. *See* DIGITAL EQUIPMENT CORPORATION PDP SERIES.

PERCEPTRON

For articles on related subjects *see* ARTIFICIAL INTELLIGENCE; and PATTERN RECOGNITION.

In 1958 the psychologist Frank Rosenblatt proposed the network structure of Fig. 1 as a cognitive machine

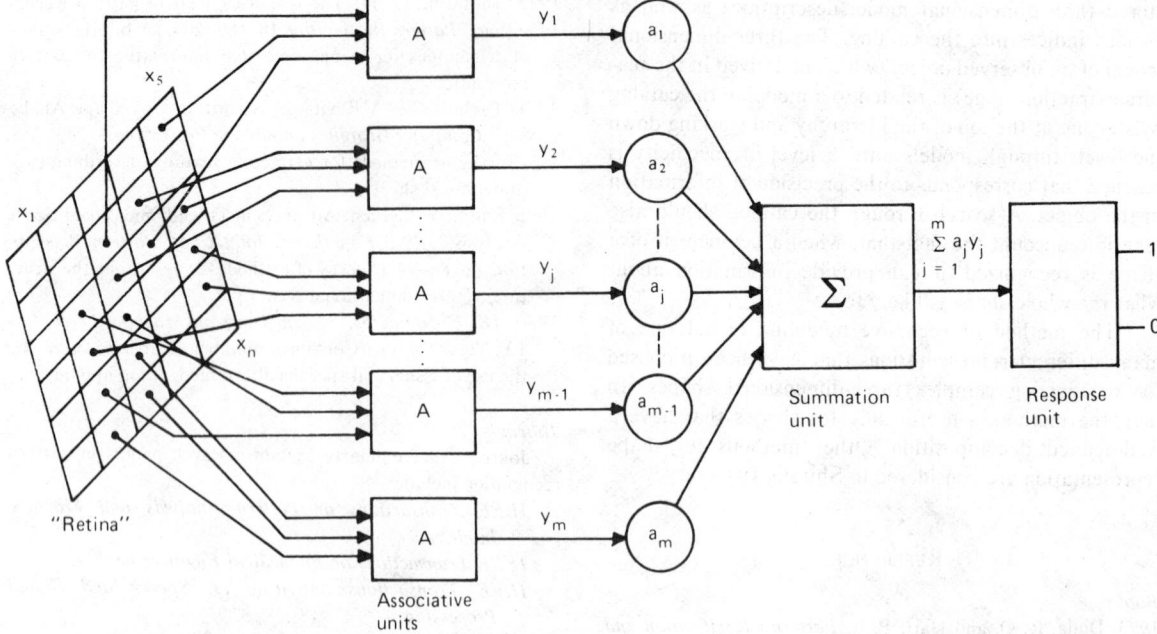

Fig. 1. Mark-1 Perceptron structure.

embodying aspects of the brain and the visual system of animals. This was called a *perceptron,* or specifically, the Mark I Perceptron (Rosenblatt, 1962).

A basic building block of a perceptron is an element that accepts a number of inputs x_i, $i = 1 \cdots I$, and computes a weighted sum of these inputs, where the weights ω can be only $+1$ or -1 for each input. The sum is then compared with a threshold θ and an output, y, equal to 1 or 0, is produced, depending on whether or not the sum exceeds the threshold. In other words,

$$
y = \begin{cases} 1 & \text{if } \left(\sum_{i=1}^{I} \omega_i x_i \right) \geq \theta \\[2em] 0 & \text{if } \left(\sum_{i=1}^{I} \omega_i x_i \right) < \theta \end{cases}
$$

The receptor of the perceptron is analogous to the retina of the eye, and is made of a rectangular array of light-sensing elements or photocells. Depending on whether or not a photocell is excited, it produces a binary output. A randomly selected set of retinal cells is connected to the next level of the network, called "A units," or associative elements. Each A unit behaves like the basic building block discussed above. The $+1$, -1 weights for the inputs to each A unit are randomly assigned. The threshold for all A units is the same.

The binary output of the kth A unit ($k = 1,m$) is multiplied by a weight a_k, and a sum of all m weighted

outputs is formed in a summation unit that is the same as the basic building blocks with all weights equal to $+1$. Each weight a_k is allowed to be positive, zero, or negative, and may change independently of other weights. The output of this block is again binary, depending on a threshold that is normally set at zero. The binary values of the output are used to distinguish or classify two classes of patterns which may be presented to the retina of a perceptron. The design of a perceptron to distinguish between two given sets of patterns involves adjusting the weights a_k, $k = 1, m$, and the threshold θ.

Rosenblatt (1962) proposed a number of variations of the following procedure for "training" perceptrons. The set of given patterns of known classification are presented sequentially to the retina, with the complete set being repeated as often as needed. The output of the perceptron is monitored to examine if a pattern is correctly classified. If not, the weights are adjusted according to the following "error correction" procedure: If the nth pattern was misclassified, the new value $a_k(n + 1)$ for the kth weight is calculated as

$$
a_k(n + 1) = a_k(n) - y_k(n) * \delta(n),
$$

where $\delta(n)$ is 1 if the nth pattern is from class 1 and $\delta(n)$ is -1 if the nth pattern is from class 2. No adjustment to the weight is made if a pattern is correctly classified.

If there exists a set of weights such that all patterns can be correctly classified, the pattern classes are said to be *linearly separable*. It was conjectured by Rosenblatt that, when the pattern classes are linearly separable, the error correction "learning" procedure will converge to a set of weights which correctly classifies all the patterns. Many proofs of this perceptron convergence theorem were subsequently derived, culminating in a short proof by A. J. Novikoff.

Rosenblatt's brilliant conjectures and the colorful names for his "self-organizing" machines attracted wide attention. He had high hopes for his "artificial intelligences." They were to be replacements for human perceivers, recognizers, and problem solvers. Over the next few years after his proposal there followed a flock of other "adaptive" and "learning" machines. As was to become evident, the true contribution of the brilliant conjectures, catchy names, and audacious claims for these machines was not in providing a general approach to pattern recognition, but rather in creating an air of excitement about automatic pattern recognition and learning machines. Today, perceptrons are properly viewed as a class of machines with interesting but restricted properties; in particular, Minsky and Papert (1969) prove many theorems about a class of perceptrons, some of which indicate their limited pattern-recognition capabilities.

REFERENCES

1962. Rosenblatt, F. *Principles of Neurodynamics.* New York: Spartan Books.
1969. Minsky, M. and Papert, S. *Perceptrons.* Cambridge, MA: M.I.T. Press.

A. K. AGRAWALA AND L. N. KANAL

PERFORMANCE EVALUATION AND REVIEW TECHNIQUE. *See* PERT/CPM.

PERFORMANCE MEASUREMENT AND EVALUATION

For articles on related subjects *see* BENCHMARK; COMPUTER ACCOUNTING AND RESOURCE CONTROL; COMPUTER ACQUISITION; HARDWARE MONITOR; MODELS; OPERATING SYSTEMS; PERFORMANCE OF COMPUTERS; QUEUEING NETWORK MODELS; SIMULATION; SOFTWARE MONITOR; SYSTEM GENERATION; TIME SHARING; THROUGHPUT; and TURNAROUND TIME.

The main purposes of the measurement and evaluation of computer systems are to:

1. Aid in the design of hardware and software.
2. Aid in the selection of a computer system.

3. Enable the performance of an existing system to be improved.

The first of these must use some type of model of the system being designed. The latter two may use actual measurements or models or some combination of the two.

Measurement and evaluation of computer system performance is difficult due to the complexity of the internal structure of computer systems and because of the difficulty of describing and predicting the workload. As illustrated in Fig. 1, a computer system is composed of subsystems, each of which can be viewed as a system with its own workload and performance. Total system performance is related to the performance of the subsystems, although the relationship can be complex. Both computer system and subsystem performance measures generally fall into three categories—*responsiveness, throughput,* and *cost.* The response time for interactive commands or the turnaround time for batch jobs are typical measures of responsiveness. Throughput is a measure of the computational work accomplished by the system per unit time. There is, however, no generally acceptable definition of a unit of computational work. Measures such as jobs per unit time or transactions per unit time only become meaningful when the resource requirements of these tasks are described; this is one aspect of the workload characterization problem. The cost of a computer system is the dollar amount required to buy or lease the system. Response and throughput characteristics have to be evaluated in terms of the cost of the system.

As stated above, it is necessary to characterize the load on a system in order to make meaningful statements about its performance. One aspect of this problem is determining which characteristics of the load largely determine the performance measures of interest. Another is determining the values of the workload model parameters for a particular performance study and is particularly difficult if the system is not operational since measurements cannot be made. But even with an operational system, the workload may vary with time and the workload characteristics measured will depend on the measurement period chosen.

This article is concerned with the use of measurement data in computer system performance evaluation and not directly with the techniques for collecting the appropriate data. The articles on SOFTWARE MONITORS and HARDWARE MONITORS should be referred to for details on computer system monitoring methodologies.

Purposes of Performance Measurement and Evaluation. In this section, we provide some detail about the goals and constraints of the types of performance studies listed at the beginning of the article.

Optimization. Modern computer systems offer a

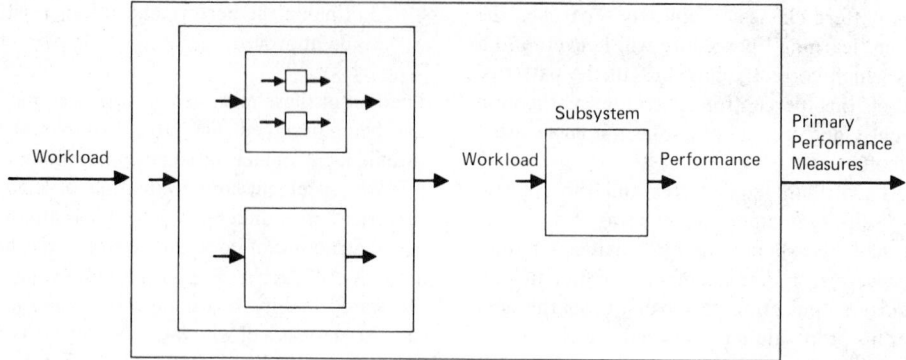

Fig. 1. Computer system and subsystems.

number of options in terms of hardware and software configuration which allow wide flexibility in tailoring a given installation to the workload and the desired performance characteristics. Some examples of the options are main memory size, number, type, and interconnection of channels and I/O devices; location of files on secondary storage; selection of non-resident portions of the operating system; and parameters for resource allocation algorithms. *System tuning* refers to the optimization of software-related options, and *reconfiguration* refers to the hardware aspects.

Computer System Selection. One of the considerations in the selection of a new system is the comparative cost/performance of the systems being considered. Judgments as to expected performance can be made informally based on the experience of others or the manufacturer's claims. More formal studies involve experimentation using benchmarks or system models. Prediction of the workload is an obvious problem if the system is being acquired for a new application. However, even upgrading of an existing system usually involves new functionality and features which have to be accounted for in the projected workload. Optimization is a part of the selection problem since it is only reasonable to compare the cost/performance of systems which are tuned to the workload.

Evaluation of Design Alternatives. The simulation or mathematical models used for this purpose require values for workload parameters. Measurements from currently operational systems can give some insight into the range of parameters that might be expected for the new system. Specific details of the workload can be very difficult to predict since (1) the system may be used in many different environments and (2) the characteristics of the system can affect how it is used. However, general characteristics of program behavior have been isolated and found to be useful in system design. A good example is the characteristic of *locality of reference* exhibited by

most programs. [Locality of reference refers to the tendency of programs to sequentially execute in phases (or localities) such that, in each phase, the program references a subset of its pages.] This is the basis for most memory management policies of paged memory systems.

Models of Computer System Performance. As a practical matter, when actual measurements cannot be made, or in order to deal with the complexity of systems even when they can be made, we must use models. Two kinds of models need to be considered—system models and workload models.

SYSTEM MODELS. System models are simplifications of the real system which describe the relationship between workload measures and performance measures. The major types of system models are given below.

Functional models. These describe the operation of the system. They may be written down (e.g., as a flowchart or as a Petri net *(q.v.)*), but often they exist only in the mind of the performance analyst. This type of model is used informally to relate observed load and performance measures, or as a first step in developing a more formal model.

Simulation models. (*See* SIMULATION.) Discrete event simulation is still the most commonly used technique in computer system modeling because of its flexibility in modeling details of the system. Its disadvantage is the cost of developing and then using a complex simulation.

Stochastic models. (*See* QUEUEING NETWORKS.) The range of applicability of queueing models has greatly expanded since the early 1970s when queueing network models of computer system began to be explored. A queueing network is a multiple resource model in which jobs "visit" the resources in a sequence which is probabilistically defined. A special case of a queueing network, called a *central server model*, is illustrated in Fig. 2. The

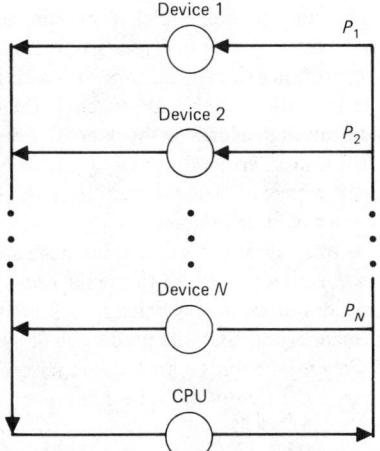

Fig. 2.   Central server queueing network model.

resources in this example are labeled to indicate the computer system resources represented. The numbers on the arcs from the CPU to the I/O devices represent, for each I/O device, the probability of that device being visited by a job after receiving CPU service. The goal with these models is to obtain closed form performance equations from which performance predictions may be easily calculated. However, there are many restrictions on the class of queueing networks for which closed form performance equations are known. For example, priority scheduling and some other common scheduling disciplines are not permitted and no limit can be set on the number of jobs at a resource or in a subset of the network (*blocking*).

Hierarchical decomposition. This term refers to a methodology in which subsystems are analyzed to obtain their performance characteristics and these results are then used in a higher-level analysis of the system. An example of this approach is to use a queueing network model to obtain throughput rates for the jobs currently being multiprogrammed and then use these results in a higher-level simulation of job scheduling strategies. This significantly reduces simulation run time, since the very high-rate events (CPU dispatching and I/O requests) are not simulated. However, the assumptions that must be made to analyze subsystems can introduce serious errors and approximations into hierarchical models.

The above is a brief summary of the types of system models most often used in computer performance evaluation studies. Additionally, statistical models such as regression analysis and analysis of variance are occasionally used to model computer systems.

WORKLOAD MODELS. An *executable* workload model is either a benchmark set of programs selected from the real workload or a set of synthetic programs which have

been designed to exhibit certain resource utilization patterns expected in the real workload. These programs are directly executable on the system(s) being studied and the performance of the system can be measured in actual operation. A *nonexecutable* workload model is a parametrization of the real workload which is to be used in conjunction with a simulation or stochastic system model.

There are two types of non-executable workload models:

1. Recorded sequences of resource demands by actual programs which are used with trace driven simulations.
2. Statistical descriptions of the workload distribution of (for example) CPU execution times between I/O requests or working set (*q.v.*) size distribution, which can be used as input to either simulation or mathematical models.

Forming a system model or a workload model is still not a well defined process and is based on experience with similar situations and detailed knowledge of the subject system.

Use of Models. The various uses of workload models and system models are illustrated in Fig. 3. Fig. 3(a) indicates measurement of an operational system. A functional model is used to diagnose a performance problem and to hypothesize a remedy. Measurements taken after implementing the remedy are used to validate the hypothesis.

Fig. 3(b) illustrates the use of a workload model which is executable on the system under study. The workload model in this case consists of a set of programs or "scripts" of terminal commands which are representative of the real workload (*see* BENCHMARK). This method is common in computer system selection in which the experiment is repeated for systems being considered and their performance compared. This method can also be used to experiment with changes to an operational system. The advantages are that the workload during the experiments is reproducible and that the behavior of the system under a wide range of workloads can be explored. A major disadvantage is that it requires exclusive use of the system and interrupts normal service.

In Fig. 3(c), both a workload model and a system model are used. This is the case with simulation and analytic modeling. If a model is being developed for an operational system, then measurement experiments are useful for calibrating the model. The workload parameters and performance are measured for a number of measurement periods. The model can be calibrated by driving it with the workload parameters from each measurement period and comparing the model performance predictions

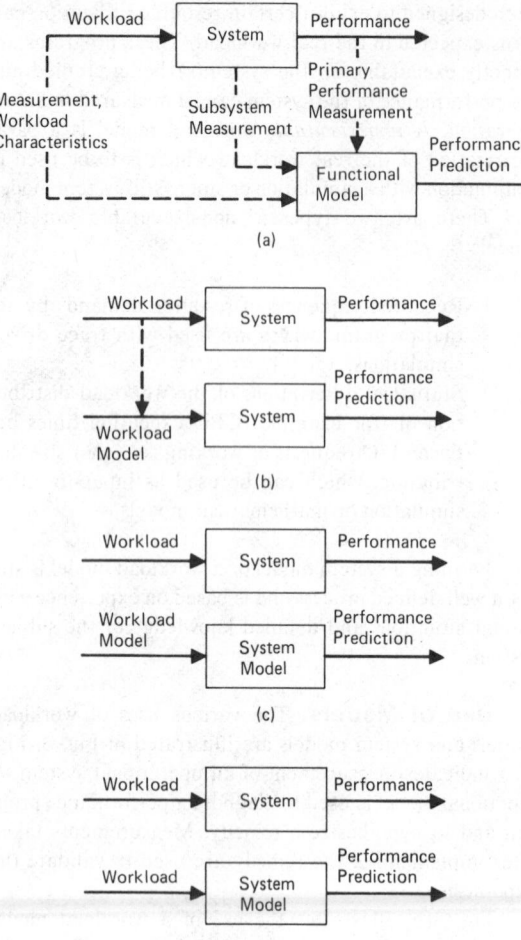

Fig. 3.   Uses of workload and system models.

with the observed system performance in the corresponding period: The model is corrected or refined until the performance predictions are sufficiently close to the measured variables. Performance predictions involve either a change in the workload or a change in the system. If a change in workload is to be considered, then the workload parameters for the new workload must be estimated. A change in the system is reflected by a corresponding change in the system model. Clearly the calibration of a model gives some confidence in its ability to model the real situation. Confidence in the predictions of the model after alteration is a function of the magnitude of the alteration.

Fig. 3(d) illustrates the last possibility, which is using a real workload to drive a system model. This is not feasible to do precisely, but it can be approximated. For example, a real workload might be interpretively executed on a system model. However, experiments which most closely approximate the true situation involve using

a virtual machine monitor which simulates nonexistent hardware. A faster I/O device, for example, can be simulated by controlling the virtual time at which interrupts occur. One limitation to this approach is the ability to synchronize internal events with external events which occur in real time. Terminal activity by real users could reasonably be expected to be different because the system response time would be affected.

To illustrate how the techniques discussed in the foregoing are actually used, in the remainder of this article we consider, first, the optimization of computer system performance, and then the prediction of system performance. Several specific techniques are covered in some detail rather than attempting to be comprehensive.

Optimization of Computer System Performance. Fig. 4 illustrates a model of major resources of a computer system and their interconnection. The resources explicitly shown are the CPU, the main memory, channels, and the secondary storage devices. The main memory is shown as a box surrounding the other hardware resources, since it is required for a task to execute and utilize the other resources. The active set of tasks constitute those which have been allocated main memory and are competing for the CPU and I/O system resources. The box labeled *task queues* represents tasks which are waiting for entry into the active set. This simple model can be used to describe the notion of a *system bottleneck*.

As a first-order approximation, assume that tasks submitted to the system require known mean amounts of

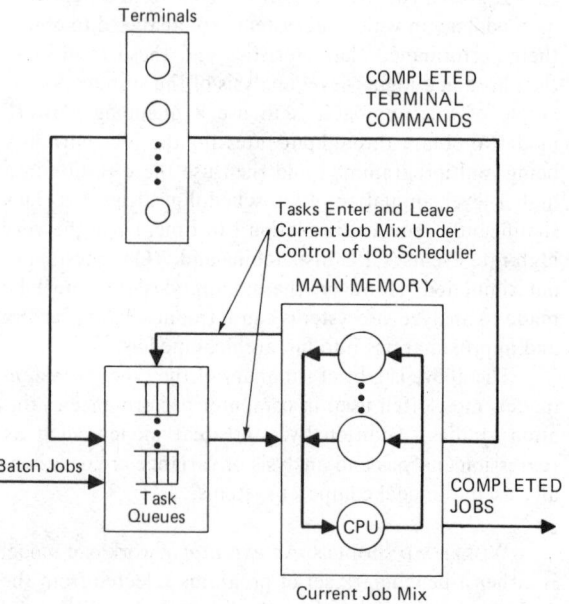

Fig. 4.   Simple computer system model.

service at each resource. For example, the mean CPU time required per task might be 20 seconds. (This is the total CPU time required, which is received in many "visits" to the CPU.) Then the throughput of the system cannot be greater than 1/20 tasks per second (or three tasks per minute), since the CPU, even if 100% busy, cannot process tasks at a higher rate. This is the capacity of the CPU measured in tasks per unit time. Similar calculations can be made for the other resources. The throughput of the system is bounded above by the capacity of the individual resources. If one resource has a capacity which is significantly lower than that of any of the other resources, then the usual effect is that this resource has a relatively high utilization and a relatively long queue of tasks waiting for it. This resource is called a *bottleneck* or *limiting resource,* and is generally a major contributor to reduced throughput and poor responsiveness. The contrary situation, a balanced system, occurs when all resources have similar utilizations. Balanced resource utilization generally results in greater throughput, since there is greater concurrent utilization of resources (CPU and I/O).

Using the model of Fig. 4 and an appropriate workload model, *system profiles,* which are a set of measurements giving the utilization of the major system resources and the amount of overlap in CPU and I/O utilization, can be generated. These values might be simply given in table form but are more easily interpretable if shown as a Gantt chart [Fig. 5(a)] or in a Kiviat graph [Fig. 5(b)]. This data is useful in the exploratory phase of a performance optimization study to determine system bottle-necks, which then have to be studied in more detail. When considering the possible reasons for the observed resource utilizations, it is useful to consider the following factors.

1. System overhead.
2. The hardware characteristics of the resource.
3. Intrinsic resource requirements of the tasks.
4. The scheduling algorithm used to manage the resource.
5. Interactions among tasks; e.g., thrashing (*q.v.*) in main memory, contention on a disk.
6. Complex interactions between resources; e.g., the relationship between channel and disk utilization. Disk utilization can appear artificially high because of a bottleneck in the channel. A major portion of the disk utilization might then be due to waiting for the channel to become free.

Several examples of behavior that might be observed from a system profile and a partial list of possible explanations are given below.

Low utilization of CPU and I/O resources:

1. Insufficient workload.
2. Insufficient main memory to fit enough tasks in the active set to utilize resources.

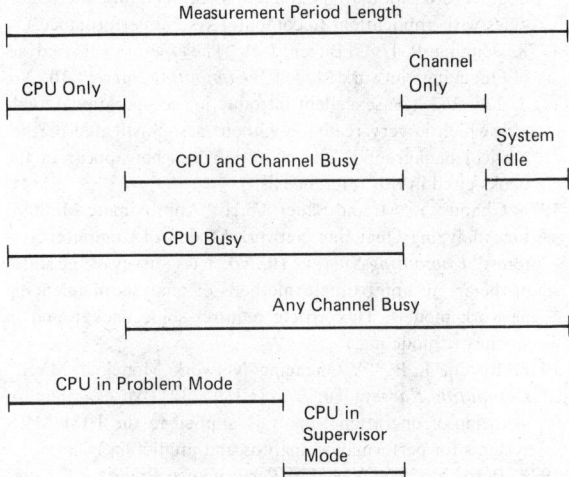

Fig. 5a. System profile shown as a Gantt chart. Each line represents a possible state of the system, and the length of each line corresponds to the total time the system was in that state during the measurement period.

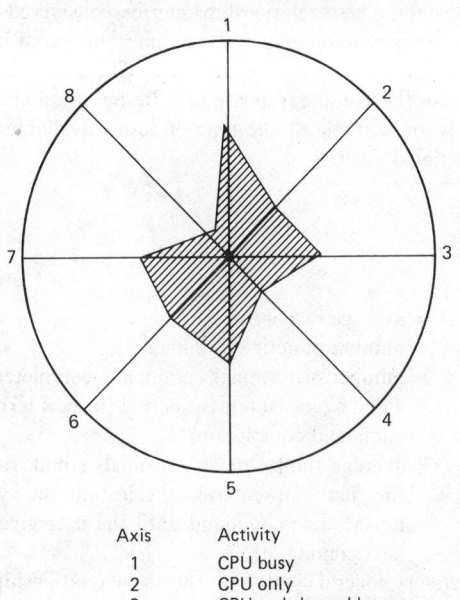

Axis	Activity
1	CPU busy
2	CPU only
3	CPU and channel busy
4	Channel only
5	Any channel busy
6	CPU idle
7	CPU in problem mode
8	CPU in supervisor mode

Fig. 5b. System profile shown as Kiviat graph.

3. Poor memory management policy that results in insufficient active set size.

High CPU utilization and low I/O device utilization:

1. Excessive CPU overhead.
2. Workload is CPU intensive.
3. Poor job mix scheduling algorithm.
4. Poor CPU scheduling algorithm; e.g., not giving priority to I/O bound jobs.

Computer System Performance Prediction.

The information gathered to aid in diagnosing a performance problem often suggests a remedy for the problem. Easy and inexpensive remedies are often implemented and the effects observed. Tuning of system parameters falls into this category. But if a large number of alternatives must be examined or the changes are costly to implement, some more formal method of predicting the effect of the changes is desirable. Simulation or stochastic modeling are alternatives, particularly when the cost of model development can be amortized over many applications; e.g., when the model is to be used for tuning or capacity planning for many installations. A relatively new approach called *operational analysis* is briefly discussed next.

In operational analysis, precise definitions of measured values and minimal assumptions about the system are used to derive invariant relationships among the measured data. These relationships can be considered to be consistency requirements for the values measured in any particular measurement experiment. The following formula for the average response time for an interactive system is an example of the type of result available from operational analysis.

$$R = \frac{N}{X} - T$$

where:

R = average response time

N = number of active terminals

X = number of terminal commands completed, divided by measurement period (rate of terminal command completion)

T = average think time at terminals (think time is the time elapsed from the instant the system finishes one command until the user gives the next command).

Under very general conditions, the above relationship can be shown to be *exact* for any measured period. This is an invariant relationship between measured values and not a formula for computing the average response time. However, it can also be useful for prediction of performance under changed conditions, although the problem of estimating or bounding new values for some of the variables

is still present. For example, if the effect on the rate of terminal command completion X due to a proposed system change could be estimated, then the equation yields an estimate of the new value for R as a function of N and T. Bounding X also yields some information. For example, if it can be determined that $X < X_0$, then

$$R > \frac{N}{X_0} - T.$$

A value for X_0 might be estimated by considering system bottlenecks as previously discussed.

Operational analysis has succeeded in developing relationships among performance and load measures which are analogous to many of the results available from queueing theoretic models but without the strong assumptions typically required in queueing theory. This approach is only in its infancy; how far it can be developed remains to be seen.

REFERENCES

1976. Svobodova, Liba. *Computer Performance Measurement and Evaluation Methods: Analysis and Applications.* New York: Elsevier. (A general introduction to measurement tools and methods of performance analysis and prediction.)

1978. Ferrari, Domenico. *Computer Systems Performance Evaluation.* Englewood Cliffs, NJ: Prentice-Hall. (An up-to-date comprehensive treatment of all of the issues discussed in this article.)

1978. Kobayashi, H. *Modeling and Analysis: An Introduction to System Performance Evaluation Methodology.* Reading, MA: Addison-Wesley. (A formal, mathematical treatment of stochastic, simulation, and statistical modeling methodologies with applications to computer system performance.)

1978. Denning, P. J. and Buzen, J. P. "The Operational Analysis of Queueing Network Models," *Computing Surveys* **10**, *No. 3:* 225–262. (An excellent introduction to operational analysis which is very readable without a sophisticated mathematical background. This material does not appear in the books cited in this reference list.)

1978. Chandy, K. M. and Sauer, C. H. "Approximate Methods for Analyzing Queueing Network Models of Computer Systems," *Computing Surveys* **10**, *No. 3.* (A survey of the state-of-the-art in approximate methods of analysis of queueing network models. This article requires some background in stochastic modeling.)

1978. Buzen, J. P. "A Queueing Network Model of MVS," *Computing Surveys* **10**, *No. 3:* 319–332. (An example application of operational analysis applied to the IBM MVS systems for performance analysis and prediction.)

1978. Bard, Y. "The VM/370 Performance Predictor," *Computing Surveys* **10**, *No. 3:* 333–342. (A model developed for capacity planning for IBM systems using VM/370 is described. Included are a description of the model and of data collection required to use the model.)

R. R. MUNTZ

PERFORMANCE OF COMPUTERS

For articles on related subjects *see* ACCESS TIME; BENCHMARK; CYCLE TIME; GROSCH'S LAW; PERFORMANCE MEASUREMENT AND EVALUATION; and SUPERCOMPUTERS.

While the idea that present-day computers are faster and more efficient than their predecessors is universally accepted, ideas about how they arrived at this level are not. One school of thought holds that computer performance has progressed by major breakthroughs, which are discrete and quantifiable, and are evidenced by "generations." Another maintains that progress has been fairly steady over the years and, rather than the result of major breakthroughs, is the sum of many improvements.

Over the past few years, several methods of comparing computer power have been developed. The technique used here is one that lends itself readily to comparing computer technology levels by year (see Knight, 1968, 1972; Knight and Cerveny, 1976). It consists of developing a value for computer power which is compared with its cost to yield a technology level for a given year. The results of this comparison show that computer technology has advanced at a fairly steady rate over time.

Calculation of Computing Power and Cost.

The variables used in comparing computer power P (measured in operations per second) with seconds of operations-per-unit cost C are expressed in the following formula.

$$P = \frac{10^{12}\left[(L-7)(T)(WF)/[(32{,}000)(36-7)]\right]}{t_{CPU} + t_{I/O}}$$

where

$$t_{CPU} = 10^4[C_1 A_{F1} + C_2 A_{F2} + C_3 M + C_4 D + C_5 \mu]$$

$$
\begin{aligned}
t_{I/O} = \; & p \times OL_1 \times \{10^6(W_{i1} \times B \times (1/K_{i1})) \\
& + [W_{o1} \times B(1/K_{o1})]\,R_1 \\
& + (1-p)OL^2 \\
& \times 10^6[W_{i2} \times (1/K_{i2})] \\
& + [W_{o2} \times B \times (1/K_{o2})]\}R_2 \, .
\end{aligned}
$$

Symbols used in these equations are defined in Table 1 for the variable attributes of each computing system and in Table 2 for semiconstant factors. The factor 32,000 (36 − 7) in the numerator reflects the need to evaluate P relative to a standard memory size, chosen here to be 32,000 36 bit words with the − 7 reflecting a penalty for short word lengths.

As indicated in Table 2, P can be computed for both commercial and scientific applications. The results for the

Table 1. Definitions of Symbols in the P Formula: Variables—Attributes of Each Computing System

L	=	word length (in bits)
T	=	total number of words in memory
t_{CPU}	=	time for the CPU (central processing unit) to perform one million operations
$t_{I/O}$	=	time the CPU stands idle waiting for I/O to take place while one million I/O operations are performed
A_{F1}	=	time for the CPU to perform one fixed-point addition
A_{F2}	=	time for the CPU to perform one floating-point addition
M	=	time for the CPU to perform one multiply
D	=	time for the CPU to perform one divide
μ	=	time for the CPU to perform one logic operation
B	=	number of characters in each word
K_{i1}	=	input transfer rate (chps) of primary I/O system
K_{o1}	=	output transfer rate (chps) of primary I/O system
K_{i2}	=	input transfer rate (chps) of secondary I/O system
K_{o2}	=	output transfer rate (chps) of secondary I/O system
R_1	=	1 plus fraction of useful primary I/O time required for nonoverlap rewind time
R_2	=	same as R_1 for secondary I/O system

commercial calculation are very similar to those for the scientific calculation and therefore are omitted in Table 3. The calculation of P also omits all software considerations, thus allowing comparisons to be made on hardware developments alone.

The value of C is arrived at by taking the cost of the computer in terms of its lease price in dollars per month and dividing that into the number of usable seconds of system operations during a month. Table 3 contains the values of computing power, cost, and date of introduction for a representative sample of computers introduced over the period 1972–1979.

The values of P and C shown in Table 3 are average numbers for one configuration of each machine listed. They should not be taken as "measures" for any machine, as there are thousands of combinations possible. The major use of these figures is not to compare computers but to observe changes in the level of technology and economies of scale. The relative values of P and C for any two computers should not be taken to mean that one is "better" than another.

Computer Performance Over the Years.

A regression technique can be used to determine cost as a function of power for any year. The coefficients in the regression equation are calculated using the data in Table 3. The graph of the regression equation (Fig. 1) depicts the technology available in any given year per unit of cost. Logarithmic scales are used for both variables. The insert in Fig. 1 shows some examples of values for P and C for each of the years shown.

The results shown in Fig. 1 lead to two observations: (1) computer technology, in terms of how much comput-

Table 2.   Definitions of Symbols in the *P* Formula: Semiconstant Factors

Symbol	Description	Scientific Computation	Commercial Computation
WF	Word factor:		
	(a) fixed-word-length memory	1	1
	(b) variable-word-length memory	2	2
C_1	Weighting factor representing percentage of fixed add operations		
	(a) computers without index registers or indirect addressing	10	25
	(b) computers with index registers or indirect addressing	25	45
C_2	Weighting factor indicating percentage of floating additions	10	0
C_3	Weighting factor indicating percentage of multiply operations	6	1
C_4	Weighting factor indicating percentage of divide operations	2	0
C_5	Weighting factor indicating percentage of logic operations	72	74
P	Percentage of I/O using primary I/O system:		
	(a) systems with only a primary I/O system	1.0	1.0
	(b) systems with primary and secondary I/O systems	Variable	Variable
W_{i1}	Number of input words per million internal operations using primary I/O system:		
	(a) magnetic tape I/O system	20,000	100,000
	(b) other I/O systems	2,000	10,000
W_{o1}	Number of output words per million internal operations using primary system	Same as for W_{i1}	Same as for W_{o1}
W_{i2}/W_{o2}	Number of I/O words per million internal operations using secondary I/O systems		
OL_1	Overlap factor 1: fraction of primary I/O system time not overlapped with compute:		
	(a) no overlap, no buffer	1	1
	(b) read or write with compute; single buffer	0.85	0.85
	(c) read, write, and compute; single buffer	0.7	0.7
	(d) multiple read, write, and compute; several buffers	0.6	0.6
	(e) multiple read, write, and compute with program interrupt; several buffers	0.55	0.55
OL_2	Overlap factor 2: fraction of secondary I/O system time not overlapped with compute	Same as for OL_1 $(a-e)$	Same as for OL_1 $(a-e)$
	Exponential memory weighting factor	0.5	0.333

Table 3.   Values of *P* and *C* for Scientific Computations for Representative Computing Systems

Computing System	Date Introduced	P (operations/second)	C (seconds/$)
Burroughs B1709	1972	185,995	326
Burroughs B2771-1	1972	73,035	180
Honeywell 2020	1972	21,341	834
Honeywell 2070	1972	85,247	51
IBM 370/125	1972	77,688	157
IBM 370/158	1972	346,509	19
IBM 370/168	1972	1,450,410	12
NCR Century 101	1972	28,359	366
Burroughs B4784	1973	1,881,080	19
DEC Datasystem 560	1973	30,971	374
Honeywell Datanet 66	1973	269,138	462
IBM System 3/15	1973	7,640	409
IBM 370/115	1973	55,868	260
Nanodata QM-1	1973	296,865	243
NCR Century 251	1973	606,269	113
Sperry Univac 9480	1973	84,452	143
Artonix PC-12/770	1974	179,392	425
CDC Cyber 175	1974	13,389,300	11
Computer Comm CC80	1974	83,053	374
Honeywell Level 64	1974	136,268	219
Honeywell 66/05	1974	926,133	87
IBM 360/20	1974	20,119	1,708
Sperry Univac 90/30	1974	351,320	360
Xerox 550	1974	703,969	243
Artronix PC-12/790	1975	207,144	383
Burroughs B2802	1975	734,937	275
Data General Eclipse	1975	415,793	675
DEC PDP-11/70	1975	1,478,630	403
Harris S110	1975	743,509	299
Hewlett-Packard 2000	1975	367,195	403
Honeywell 6180	1975	1,979,060	12
Sperry Univac 1100/2	1975	1,205,160	41
Amdahl 470V/6-II	1976	36,275,000	12
IBM 370/138	1976	290,395	91
IBM 370/148	1976	988,227	46
Itel AS/4	1976	4,701,100	27
Itel AS/6	1976	7,881,940	12
NCR 8550	1976	2,516,310	163
Prime Computer P400	1976	1,112,770	365
Sperry Univac 1100/1	1976	1,711,560	52
Amdahl 470V/5	1977	63,835,300	14
Burroughs B1720-1	1977	3,426,960	180
Burroughs B6803	1977	14,321,200	85
CDC Cyber 176	1977	42,401,700	6
CDC Omega 480-1	1977	2,161,920	71
Harris S130	1977	1,287,710	164
IBM 3031	1977	928,719	29
NCR 8560	1977	10,577,800	130
Sperry Univac 1100/80	1977	14,347,903	14
Burroughs B6808-2	1978	14,413,700	59
DEC VAX-11/780	1978	812,281	257
IBM 3033M	1978	7,685,550	8
Itel AS/3-3	1978	387,708	42
Magnuson M80/3	1978	1,170,890	124

Table 3.   (Continued)

Computing System	Date Introduced	P (operations/second)	C (seconds/$)
Nanodata VMX 200	1978	450,899	310
Sperry-Univac 90/40	1978	1,128,800	83
Amdahl 470V/7A	1979	27,155,300	14
Burroughs B1855	1979	867,323	299
CDC Cyber 203	1979	403,165,000	4
CDC Omega 4	1979	32,565,800	70
DEC Decsystem 1	1979	2,264,390	57
IBM 3033 AP	1979	26,817,800	4
IBM 4341	1979	5,295,640	10
Sperry Univac 1100/61C	1979	1,971,570	848

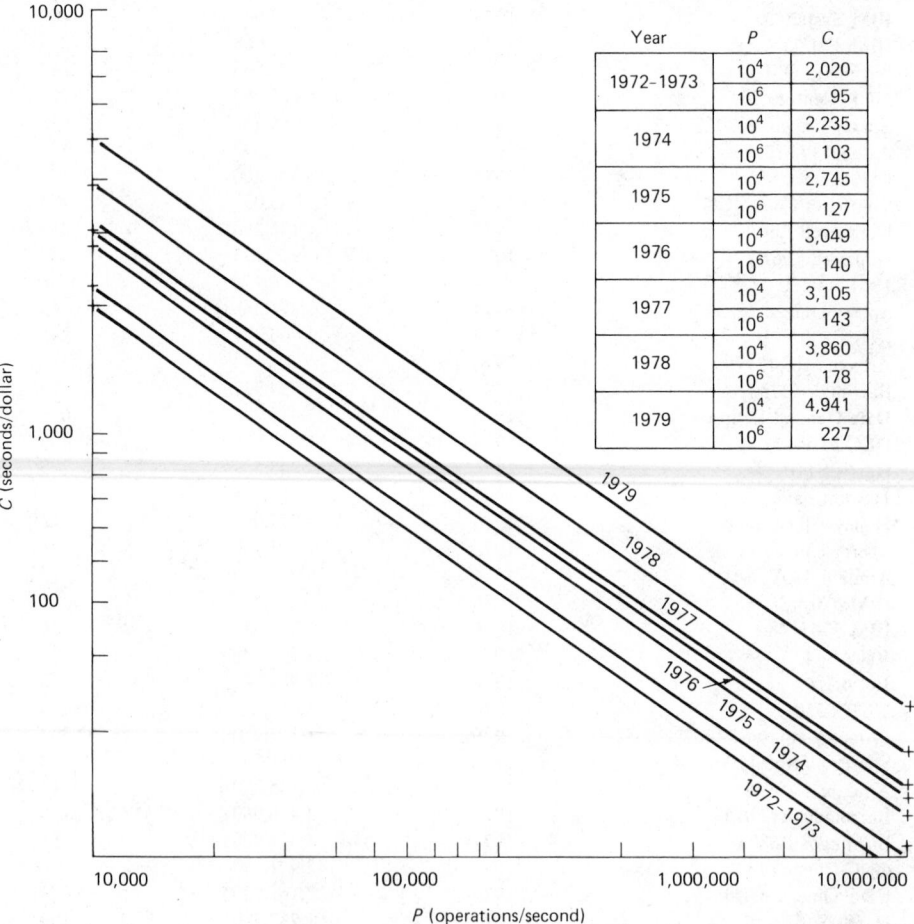

Year	P	C
1972–1973	10^4	2,020
	10^6	95
1974	10^4	2,235
	10^6	103
1975	10^4	2,745
	10^6	127
1976	10^4	3,049
	10^6	140
1977	10^4	3,105
	10^6	143
1978	10^4	3,860
	10^6	178
1979	10^4	4,941
	10^6	227

Fig. 1.   Graph of regression calculations for scientific computation.

ing power one may buy per dollar cost, has been improving on a yearly basis since 1972 (Fig. 2 illustrates the yearly change); and (2) economies of scale, as predicted by Grosch's law, are still obtainable.

The regression equation used for Fig. 1 has the form

$$\log C = \log P + k.$$

It may be used to test Grosch's law for the years 1972/

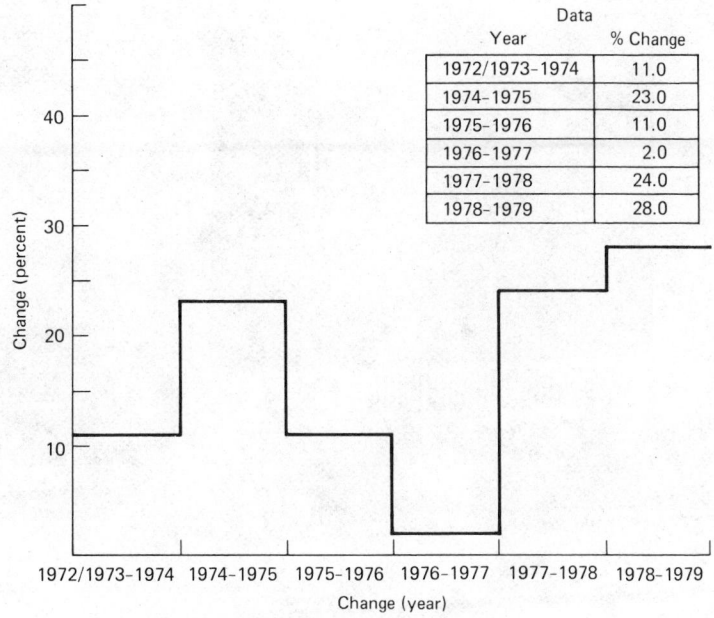

Data	
Year	% Change
1972/1973-1974	11.0
1974-1975	23.0
1975-1976	11.0
1976-1977	2.0
1977-1978	24.0
1978-1979	28.0

Fig. 2.   Average yearly shift of the technology curve: Power *P* change for constant inverse cost *C*.

1973 through 1979. We first rewrite this equation as

$$C = K \cdot P^{\alpha_1} \quad \text{or} \quad \text{Cost} = \frac{1}{C} = \left(\frac{1}{K}\right) P^{-\alpha_1}.$$

Grosch's law predicts that computing power increases as a function of cost squared, so that, for twice the cost, one should have four times as much computing power. The actual α_1 found from Fig. 1 is $\alpha_1 = -0.668$. Grosch's law predicts $\alpha_1 = -0.5$, so the agreement is quite good.

It should be noted that the analysis used here was first developed in 1963 for computers which were at the forefront of technology at that time. Since then many of the parameters originally involved in differentiating between machine have become so standard that they are now constants. Therefore, the resultant evaluations of machine differences are less robust than in the original study. That the formula can still track progress on certain of the parameters attests to their underlying importance and the fact that all development along these dimensions has not ceased. A new evaluation of the relevant parameters is needed to incorporate the current state-of-the-art and tie future developments to their historic roots.

References

1968. Knight, K. E. "Evolving Computer Performance 1963–1967," *Datamation* **1**: 31–35 (January).
1972. Knight, K. E. "Application of Technological Forecasting to the Computer Industry," in Bright, J. R. and Schoeman, M. F. (Eds.), *A Guide to Practical Technological Forecasting*. Englewood Cliffs, NJ: Prentice-Hall, pp. 377–403.
1976. Knight, K. E. and Cerveny, R. P. "Performance of Computers," in Ralston, A. and Meek, C. L. (Eds.), *Encyclopedia of Computer Science*. New York: Petrocelli-Charter, pp. 1065–1070.

R. P. Cerveny and K. E. Knight

PERSONAL COMPUTING

For articles on related subjects *see* Calculator, Electronic; Computer Games; Computer Industry; and Microprocessors and Microcomputers.

The term *personal computing* has been used in two ways. Some have used it to refer to a computing environment in which the user has full and exclusive use of an entire computer system, regardless of the system's uses or ownership. Most people, however, have come to accept the phrase as referring to situations involving relatively inexpensive microcomputers owned by their users and often used for not-for-profit, not-for-business purposes. Indeed, as of early 1982, there were in excess of one and one half million computer systems that fit the latter description.

Until recently the most popular such systems were Radio Shack's TRS-80 (Fig. 1), Commodore's Pet, and Apple's Apple II. However, 1981 saw the introduction of

Fig. 1. A Radio Shack TRS-80 microcomputer system.

personal computers from IBM, Xerox, Hewlett-Packard, and Victor Business Machines, all of which appear certain to take a significant share of the market. A wide selection of other microcomputers and subsystems is available from a large number of other manufacturers. Each has a base price comparable to that of a console color television, video tape recorder, or sophisticated stereo system. Each can be greatly enhanced and expanded by adding a considerable variety of components and subsystems.

A wide variety of software and applications packages are available both from the equipment manufacturers and from independent vendors—often designed and marketed for the nonprofessional computer owner/user. The reliability, versatility, and documentation of both hardware and software varies from excellent to virtually unusable, though this situation is rapidly improving as the market and user community matures.

History. Personal computing as a mass movement has existed only since 1975. Prior to that, there were several hundred to a thousand or more computer hobbyists who built and/or owned their own computers. Without the availability of very inexpensive, highly reliable microcomputer electronics components, it was simply not viable, economically or technically, to attempt to offer computers as consumer products for the intelligent layperson.

The first microprocessors were marketed by semiconductor manufacturers in the early 1970s. There is a major difference, however, between a simple micropro-

cessor and a usable computer that includes memory, data storage devices, terminals, and software.

In 1974, a small manufacturer named MITS, located in Albuquerque, New Mexico, decided to offer a microcomputer in the form of a kit for the electronics hobbyist market. They called it the Altair, naming it after a fictitious planet used in one of the episodes of *Star Trek,* the science fiction television series. It used an Intel 8080 microprocessor as its central processing unit (CPU). The hardware design was poor and unreliable; the documentation verged on being unintelligible; and the kit initially included no software at all—but the notion of a computer for the layperson, available at modest prices, caught the fancy of a considerable number of people. MITS was swamped with orders for Altair kits, particularly after the appearance of a cover story about the Altair in the January 1975 issue of *Popular Electronics* magazine.

As the product gained attention, a number of other companies quickly began to address the same market. Some of them offered similar kit-form microcomputers. Others manufactured add-on components or fix-it kits for the Altair. Still others offered computer programs that would run on the Altair or its competitors. Computer stores—retail outlets selling inexpensive computers and related products—opened all over the nation, particularly in the high-technology metropolitan areas along the east and west coasts.

By September 1975, *Byte* magazine appeared, explicitly founded to discuss personal computing and microcomputers. Within a year, half a dozen other periodicals came into existence addressing the same topic.

At the same time, a hundred or more local computer hobbyist clubs sprang up around the U.S. Some of them had as many as several thousand members and met several times per month, consistently drawing three or four hundred attendees or more to each meeting.

Many of the companies addressing the newly founded personal computer market were created specifically to address that market. The other companies that first served that market were small computer or electronics firms. None of the traditional major computer or electronics manufacturers initially made any attempt to enter the personal or hobbyist computer market.

Finally, in 1977, Commodore—a major manufacturer of hand-held calculators—announced that it would make a personal computer, calling it the Pet. Before Commodore could begin significant production of the Pet, the Tandy Company, which operates the Radio Shack chain of electronics retail stores, announced that it would also offer a microcomputer, the TRS-80.

There were two major differences between most of the previously available units and these new offerings from Commodore and Tandy. First, the new computers were completely assembled, ready-to-use microcomputers. Second, they were offered by relatively large consumer electronics manufacturers, both having established distribution networks for their products.

By 1977, the computer hobbyist market—the market consisting of dedicated electronics tinkerers—had been fairly well saturated with microcomputer kits. Because of this, because of the difficulty of supporting customers who built these complex kits, and because there was (and is) a much larger market for fully assembled computers, most companies stopped manufacturing or marketing computer kits, preferring to offer ready-to-use systems comparable to the Pet and TRS-80.

A number of the small companies that initially fostered the personal computer market have closed their doors. This has usually been due to poor products, bad management, or poor marketing practices. Others have been acquired by larger, more successful corporations. The companies that have survived, for the most part, have grown rapidly into solid, successful organizations offering equipment and support comparable to that found in most other consumer electronics manufacturing. And there remains considerable room for the innovative entrepreneur, programmer, or engineer to create a new company and offer a new product, particularly in the areas of software, peripherals, and services.

Hardware. Technically, many of the video games currently on the market must be classified as personal computers. They have a microprocessor CPU, memory, input and output facilities, and one or many programs. These might be considered to be dedicated personal computers—dedicated to performing a single (and rather mundane) task. Beyond the video games, there have been three general types of computers used as personal computers, all using a microprocessor as their CPU.

The first is a single-board computer. This consists of the CPU, a small amount of semiconductor memory, the necessary interface circuits, and often a 10- or 16-button keyboard and 4–10-character numeric or alphanumeric display—all mounted on a single printed circuit card. Such units, available from microprocessor manufacturers and from a few independent electronics manufacturers, are designed to assist engineers in learning about microcomputer hardware or developing microprocessor-based equipment. Though they include the full capabilities of the CPU, they have a very small power supply, limited memory, limited input and output capabilities, little expandability, and very limited software. They are available in both kit and assembled forms. Typically, their prices are around $100–$300.

The second type of computer used for personal computing is the one that is actually called a personal or consumer computer. It uses the same CPU as do single-board computers, has a reasonable and expandable amount of semiconductor memory, either includes a video display and full typewriter-style keyboard or allows easy interface to a variety of full-capability computer terminals, and is easily expandable—both internally and by the addition of peripherals. Since this system is fully expandable, it can support software of considerable sophistication, complexity, and utility. Though prices for a complete personal computer have tended to bottom out at around $700, the cost per unit of hardware capability—memory, storage capacity, speed, etc.—has been decreasing by a factor of two or more each year, and seems likely to continue to do so for some years.

The final type of system sometimes used for personal computing is actually a professional-grade microcomputer or minicomputer, offered by the traditional manufacturers of industrial and business computer equipment. Functionally, there is little difference between these units and the second type. Because they have been on the market for a longer period of time, they often have a wider variety of peripheral equipment available as options—particularly large-capacity mass storage devices. Functionally equivalent peripherals are rapidly appearing for personal computers, however, and are often significantly less expensive. These professional-grade computer systems generally have a bottom price on the order of $1,200, and not uncommonly cost $3,000 or much more. Though they are generally more sturdily constructed mechanically, there is mixed evidence regarding whether they are more reliable or less reliable than the personal computers. Among other things, professional-grade computers sometimes show greater susceptibility to failure due to power-line fluctuations, and commonly produce much more electromagnetic radiation than consumer-oriented personal computers. (The radiation is of concern in that it may interfere with television or radio reception—considered to be little problem in a business or industrial application, but of great concern in home use.)

Software. There is a large and rapidly expanding amount and variety of software for personal computers. Much of it is closely comparable to software that has been available for years on professional-grade computers (e.g., disk and magnetic tape operating systems, text editors, interpreters, assemblers and compilers for such high-level languages as Basic and Pascal and, to a lesser extent, Fortran, C, APL and Lisp).

Some programs are beginning to appear that are different from traditional software, being specifically oriented to some personal task or problem environment. Certainly this characterizes the extensive collection of game software available for personal computers (though most of that software was developed some time ago on professional-grade computers in business, industrial, and educational installations). Additionally, most personal computing software is more highly interactive in its mode of usage than has been true of traditional software for professional-grade computers in the past.

The personal computing software is generally as bug-free (or bug-filled) as software of comparable capability and complexity that has been available for a comparable length of time for professional-grade systems. Not uncommonly, personal computing software appears to be somewhat more forgiving and accepting of human error ("friendly") than has been the case with software designed for professional use in traditional computing environments.

The documentation of the software is sometimes much better, and sometimes much worse, than the documentation for traditional industrial and business software. It is quite common, however, to find tutorial documentation for personal computing software which assumes that readers have no familiarity at all with programming, and teaches them how to use the software and the system.

Often, the software that forms the nucleus of an operating system or command-handling system is permanently stored in the personal computer's memory by placing it in nonvolatile read-only memory (*q.v.*—ROM)—semiconductor circuits that retain their contents, even if the power is turned off. Sometimes, entire interpreter programs—usually for the Basic language—and even major portions of disk operating systems are placed in ROM, thus making them permanently and immediately accessible. It also makes them difficult to change if errors are found or improvements are to be made.

Personal computing software is very inexpensive, regardless of its complexity, in comparison to equivalent software for professional-grade systems. It is common to find entire compilers and operating systems of considerable capability available for $100–$400 that are comparable to equivalent traditional systems that cost thousands of dollars or more. This situation exists because software producers are achieving a reasonable—and sometimes outstanding—level of profit by depending on mass sales, rather than on high profit per unit sold.

Applications. One of the questions most commonly asked about personal computing systems is "but what can you *do* with them?"

One computer hobbyist refers to this as "function guilt," arguing that it is sufficient to be entertained and intellectually stimulated by one's personal computer. It is no more appropriate to demand utility of a personal computer than it is to query the utility of a model plane, stamp collection, or personal library. If one wishes, however, home computers can be of significant and increasing personal utility.

Unquestionably, the most common personal computing applications have been computer games and computer-assisted education. The games may be single-player games in which the computer is the opponent, or multi-player games in which the computer functions as bookkeeper. Commonly, the computer may maintain a complex video display that may or may not be animated (involving automatic motion as time passes). The games may or may not involve the random occurrence of events. For instance, computer blackjack involves apparently random dealing of "cards" but computer chess does not use random selection of moves.

Using a computer to play games may seem mundane, even recognizing that the games may be highly complex, sophisticated, and entertaining. However, if one recognizes that many games are actually simulations of real-world environments, then they may be more acceptable. Often, what appears to be an entertaining and exciting game of considerable complexity may actually be subtly and significantly educational by being a reasonably accurate simulation of some real-world situation, e.g., business investments, earth resources management, flight simulations, etc.

Some personal computers have been used for an eminently personal application—as prostheses for the physically impaired. With appropriate peripheral equipment, low-cost computers have assisted the mute to speak (using speech synthesis equipment), provided paraplegics with control over their surroundings (e.g., wheel chair control via voice commands), allowed blind programmers to "hear" their programs rather than having to depend on unreliable and expensive Braille printers, etc.

Interesting variations on traditional computer applications have appeared on home computers. Food buying groups maintain orders and expense records, and divide operations costs via personal computers. Co-op residences keep track of telephone costs and calls with computers. Some heads of families maintain family budgets using home systems. Many individuals use their personal computers to write, edit, and modify correspondence and articles. Collectors often use personal computers to index and automatically cross-reference their collections—recordings, stamps, names of members of the opposite sex, etc. Clubs and organizations maintain membership and mailing lists.

Personal applications of computing power have generally focused more on the computer's logical and storage capabilities than on its numeric computational facilities. This appears likely to continue, assuming that individuals generally have more use for information handling than they have for numeric computation.

The Future. General-purpose personal computers will become more and more widely distributed among the lay public. This will occur as they become more capable, and as their cost per unit of capability continues to decrease. It will also result from the increasingly widespread pre-college teaching of computer programming and usage.

Nonetheless, the percentage of recognizable, general-purpose digital computers in the hands of the general public, used not-for-profit and not-for-business, will likely remain quite small in comparison to, for instance, the number of televisions or telephones in similar use.

However, the number of systems dedicated to a single task will increase virtually without limit. These will include typewriters that will include checkers for spelling errors as well as word-processing capabilities; telephones that will allow dial-by-name instead of requiring that one remember one's friends by number; automobile dashboards that will give vocal response to verbal queries regarding speed, time, and fuel consumption; etc.

The most significant development in personal computing, however, will result from combining personal computing with electronic communications—telephonic, broadcast, and cable. Currently, personal computing offers a large amount of information processing power to the general public, but there is little information available to process—that is, in machine-readable form. A number of experiments and developments are currently underway that will result in widespread distribution of large amounts of information in computer-readable form.

Orders-of-magnitude more information than is currently available via cost-constrained daily newspapers will be distributed to the general public in this form in the near future. This includes transmission of information by FM radio transmission, by broadcast during the vertical retrace interval inherent in television broadcasts, unidirectional and bidirectional information exchange via cable systems currently used only for subscription television, and interactive communications by telephone.

The interactive systems will depend on large central computers for personal information processing with the home units serving as little more than communications terminals. The central computers will have information that is of personal interest to individuals, rather than being limited to business, industrial, and government databases as tends to be the current situation.

The unidirectional systems will include arbitrarily complex information processing by programmable receivers in the home (*see* VIEWDATA). For example, some home systems will continuously scan incoming text for news articles and want ads of interest, based on key words specified by the user. Other systems will automatically keep a personal stock portfolio completely up-to-date based on incoming stock exchange quotes. Others will assist with optimal scheduling of air travel using completely up-to-date airline schedules. Still others will assist with shopping chores by providing pricing and availability information regarding products available from local and mail-order vendors.

In the foreseeable future, by coupling personal information processing power with access to massive quantities of information in machine-readable form, the real power of computers will become available to and pervasively used by the general public, and will have as much or more impact on the nature and development of the society and culture as have the telephone, automobile, and—most comparably—the printing press.

Keeping Up-to-Date. Personal computing changes at a pace that is fast, even when compared to the rapid rate of change that characterizes most of the computing and electronics fields. As a result, the only practical means for obtaining information regarding the current state of affairs is via the periodicals and conventions that focus on personal computing. Fortunately, many of these publications and conferences are appropriate for the intelligent layperson.

Creative Computing might be viewed as the "liberal arts" periodical addressing personal computing. It specializes in computer games, educational computing, computer-related fiction, and other entertaining or personal aspects of computing.

Interface Age and *Popular Computing* (formerly *on Computing*) address the more-or-less novice personal computerist, generally assuming a relatively minimal level of computer knowledge or experience.

Byte and *Kilobaud Microcomputing* are the two major periodicals serving the serious computer hobbyist. *Byte* is the largest of all personal computing periodicals, with a circulation in excess of 215,000, as of 1982.

InfoWorld is the only fast-distribution, newspaper-format periodical addressing personal computing and microcomputers, published on a biweekly schedule.

Data Cast provides extensive surveys of the progress of mass digital telecommunications and offers in-depth tutorials on major systems and applications software for microcomputers.

Additionally, there are a number of smaller or more specialized periodicals that address personal computing, including several newsletters published by computer hobbyist clubs.

There are several major conventions and a multitude of smaller conferences and exhibitions held each year that focus exclusively on personal computing. These are open to and appropriate for the general public. The larger such meetings are held in San Francisco, Boston, and New York.

REFERENCES

Periodicals
Byte. 70 Main St., Peterborough, NH 03458.
Creative Computing. Box 789-M, Morristown, NJ 07960.
Data Cast. 345 Swett Road, Woodside, CA 94062.
InfoWorld. 530 Lytton Ave., Palo Alto, CA 94301.
Interface Age. 16704 Marquardt Ave., Cerritos, CA 90701.
Kilobaud Microcomputing. 73 Pine St., Peterborough, NH 03458.
Popular Computing. 70 Main St., Peterborough, NH 03458.

Conferences and Expositions
Boston. Northeast Computer Show, Box 678, Brookline Village, MA 02147.
New York. Small Computer Show, 110 Charlotte Pl., Englewood Cliffs, NJ 07632.
San Francisco. West Coast Computer Faire, 333 Swett Rd., Woodside, CA 94062.

Books
1974. Nelson, Theodor. *Computer Lib/Dream Machines*. Chicago: Hugo's Book Service.
1977. Nelson, Ted. *The Home Computer Revolution*. South Bend, IN: The Distributors.
1977. Osborne, Adam. *An Introduction to Microcomputers— Volume 0: The Beginner's Book*. Berkeley, CA: Osborne/McGraw-Hill.
1977. People's Computer Company. *What to Do After You Hit RETURN, or PCC's First Book of Computer Games*. Menlo Park, CA: People's Computer Co.
1979. Osborne, Adam. *Running Wild: The Next Industrial Revolution*. Berkeley, CA: Osborne/McGraw-Hill.

JIM C. WARREN, JR.

PERSONNEL IN THE COMPUTER FIELD

For articles on related subjects *see* COMPUTING AND SOCIETY; DATABASE ADMINISTRATOR; DIGITAL COMPUTERS: Contemporary and Future; PROGRAMMER; and SYSTEMS ANALYST.

A national public opinion survey (AFIPS, 1971) found that 30% of the adults interviewed responded positively to the question: "Do you currently have a job which requires some contact with a computer—either directly or indirectly?" Fifteen percent said yes to the question: "Does your job require that you have some knowledge of how a computer system works?" Another 7% said that they currently had a job where they worked directly with computers or computer equipment. Although there may have been some ambiguity in the questions, especially in what was meant by "directly," the clear indication is that the computer is being used by, or in some way affecting, a significant percentage of the American labor force.

The continuing expansion of the use of point-of-sale terminals in the retail industry during the late 1970s may have doubled the above percentages.

Those in the labor force who are affected by computers or who have jobs created by the computer may be divided into the following broad classes.

1. Those directly concerned with the operation of computers and associated equipment (e.g., programmers, systems analysts, computer operators, and data entry and retrieval operators).
2. Those involved directly with providing management and administrative support to computer facilities (e.g., managers, tape librarians, receptionists, and clerical employees).
3. Those involved in the manufacture, sales, and servicing of computers.
4. Those who use computers as an integral part of their jobs in other disciplines (e.g., engineers, accountants, and scientists).
5. Those who rely on computers in order to perform their jobs, but who only use them in particular, limited ways (e.g., stockbrokers using a quotation system, airline reservation clerks, and retail clerks using point-of-sale terminals connected to a computer.)
6. Those who use the output of computers (e.g., accountants who are given computer-produced financial statements, buyers who receive computer generated purchase orders, and executives who make decisions based on computer-generated reports).

Considering all six categories, the 7% of the population reporting that they worked directly with a computer is not surprising. In fact, probably only the percentages of answers in the first three categories should be compared with the approximately 4% of the gross national product that is being spent by organizations for computers, computer services, and the people who operate them (Gilchrist, 1973).

When an attempt is made to estimate the number of people in each of the six groups, it is quickly found that there is a dearth of statistics, government or private. We find that computer-related occupations, being a new phenomenon, were not separately identified in the 1960 decennial census and were only partially identified in the 1970 census. In the 1980 census, these statistics should be available, but in the meantime it is necessary to make use of the limited data in the literature.

For the first class, the following estimates have been made.

For 1973:*

Keypunch operator	395,000
Computer operator	165,000
Programmer	100,000
Systems analyst	140,000

For 1978:**

Keypunch operator	666,000
Computer operator	
Programmer	247,000
Systems analyst	182,000

For 1977:†

Teacher	7,700
Management	105,000
Systems analyst	175,000
Systems programmer	105,000
Applications programmer	245,000
Computer operator	210,000
Other operating personnel (data entry and retrieval clerks, tape librarians, peripheral operators)	560,000
Total	1,407,000

Estimating the number of individuals in the second class is difficult because of the wide variety of job definitions used in computer installations and, in many cases, the problem of deciding whether a support position is attributable solely to the computer facility or should be divided between it and other areas. A rough idea of the size of the group can, however, be seen from a 1972 salary survey conducted by *Infosystems Magazine*, which found that, for the average computer installation, the total of all employees engaged in EDP was 4.4 times the number of programmers and systems analysts. Using this result in conjunction with the numbers estimated for the first class gives a rough estimate of one million people providing direct management and administrative support to computer facilities for 1973 and in the neighborhood of two million by 1978.

Although IBM and a few other large companies are best known to the public for the manufacture, sales, and servicing of computers, there are actually many hundreds of companies in the industry. The U. S. Department of Labor collects data on employment by industry and, for 1978, 274,900 employees were reported to be in SIC code 3573 (Electronic Computing Equipment). However, inspection of the annual reports of major companies in 1974 indicated that the number of domestic employees then in data processing manufacture, sales, and servicing was probably in the range of 300,000–400,000 and it is surely considerably greater now. (It should be noted that this does not include employees of the companies' overseas operations, nor does it include those employed in non-data processing product lines.)

The employment estimate for the first three classes is that more than 4 million people are directly involved with computers. This total represents 4% of all U.S. employment, which approximately corresponds to the portion of the gross national product being spent on the purchase and use of computers.

No estimates are available for the number of individuals in the remaining three classes, but probably they outnumber considerably those in the first three. They may even now exceed the 30% figure found by the survey quoted earlier. Considering the importance of knowledge in our post-industrial society, this high percentage should not be surprising. In fact, employment will probably continue to increase as the computer becomes an even more ubiquitous tool.

REFERENCES

1971. AFIPS. "A National Survey of the Public's Attitudes Toward Computers," Joint Project of the American Federation of Information Processing Societies and *Time*. Montvale, NJ: AFIPS Press.

1973. Gilchrist, B. and Weber, R. E. (Eds.). *The State of the Computer Industry in the United States*. Montvale, NJ: AFIPS Press.

1974. Weber, R. E. and Gilchrist, B. *Numerical Bias in the 1970 U.S. Census Data on Computer Occupations*. Montvale, NJ: AFIPS Press.

1979. Hamblen, J. W. *Computer Manpower—Supply and Demand—By States*. St. James, MO: Information Systems Consultants.

1979. Bureau of Labor Statistics, Department of Labor. *1980–81 Occupational Outlook Handbook*, Washington, DC: U.S. Government Printing Office.

B. GILCHRIST AND J. W. HAMBLEN

---

*Gilchrist and Weber, 1974.

**Bureau of Labor Statistics (1979).

†Hamblen (1979).

PERT/CPM

For article on related subject *see* PLANNING, COM-PUTER APPLICATIONS IN.

The development of project management techniques using network methods, of which PERT (project evaluation and review technique) and CPM (critical path method) are the most widely known, was undertaken in the late 1950s by several independent groups working on different types of projects. The most widely publicized of these efforts was the use of PERT in conjunction with the design of the Polaris submarine system. It was credited with saving substantial time and cost on Polaris, which caused its use to be made mandatory on all significant development projects undertaken for and by the U.S. Department of Defense. Knowledge of this and other successful applications soon became widespread, and many variants, additional features, and computerized aids were developed and publicized. As a result, project management techniques have become the most extensively used of the quantitative tools for management, with the possible exception of linear programming.

Most uses of these techniques are in the defense and construction industries, although they are suitable for any situation where:

The *project* consists of a collection of *activities* or tasks.

The activities can be started and stopped independently of each other (in contrast to a sequential flow of processing), even if the resources employed on the various activities are not independent.

Precedence relationships exist which preclude the start of certain activities until others are complete (e.g., surfacing a road must be preceded by the laying of the road bed).

Specific and general examples of successful use include:

Apollo mission development and countdown procedures.

Construction projects such as a building.

Procedures for closing accounts in a bank or firm (e.g., payroll).

Ship or aircraft repair projects.

Implementation of a computer system, from ordering and site preparation through installation and checkout.

The techniques can be used in both planning and control of projects. *Planning* in this context consists of the overall layout of the project, with rough estimation of the time and resources required, and the detailed scheduling of the timing and order of activities. In short, it concerns the set of decisions made before the start of the project. By contrast, *control* takes place during the project. As actual resource use and completion times are obtained, project management techniques can be used to reallocate resources according to the revised criticality ratings of activities.

Computation of a Critical Path. All variants of the project management technique compute what is called a *critical path*. Since a project consists of an ordered set of independent activities, it can be represented as a *network* (Fig. 1), where activities are shown as branches connected at nodes to immediately preceding and immediately following activities. (Other conventions are possible, but the idea of a network remains.)

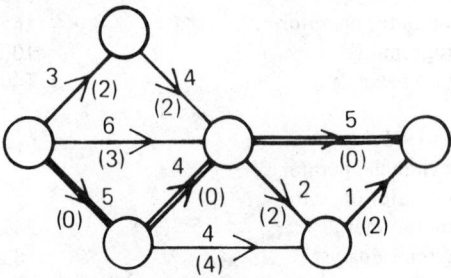

Fig. 1. Example of project network. Single-shaft arrow indicates activity with time slack; double-shaft arrow represents critical path.

A *path* through the network is any set of successive activities which goes from the beginning to the end of the project. Associated with each activity in the network is a single number that best estimates the time which that activity will consume; differences in the way this number is obtained distinguish the major variants of the technique. A *critical path*, then, is one whose sum of activity times is longer than that for any other path through the network (multiple critical paths with equal total times are, of course, possible). This path is important because, if everything goes according to schedule, its length gives the shortest possible completion time of the overall project.

In addition, a *slack time* can be associated with each activity in the project. This is the difference between the latest possible completion time of each activity which will not delay the completion of the overall project, and the earliest possible completion time, based on all predecessor activities. Activities on a critical path have zero slack time, and conversely, activities with zero slack time are on a critical path.

The critical path and associated slack times for a project are found by simply working forward through the network, computing the earliest possible completion time for each activity, until the earliest possible completion time for the total project is found. Then, by working backward through the network, the latest completion time for each activity is found, the slack time computed, and the critical path identified.

This procedure is so straightforward that it is clearly easily programmable for a computer. For example, the complete data input, computation, and output of results can be done in fewer than 40 Fortran statements. Not surprisingly, there is a wide proliferation of programs that perform this computation, many with special features tailored to a specific industry or type of problem. Nearly every commercial time-sharing system or service bureau has such software available for use by its customers.

PERT Assumptions. The variant of the technique described above, which carries the name PERT, was first used in conjunction with the Polaris systems development cited earlier. Because of imperfect knowledge of the times of individual development activities, it is felt necessary to have a means to incorporate uncertainty in the estimation of such times. To do this, a three-point estimate of optimistic, pessimistic, and most likely completion times is obtained for each activity. These are used to estimate the mean and standard deviation of each activity time. The means are in turn used to find the critical path and slack times, as described in the preceding section, implying that a given activity is or is not critical. Then continuing on the assumption that activities are independent, the estimates of individual activity standard deviation are used to estimate the standard deviation of completion time for the whole project.

It seems clear that only a few additional program statements are required to convert a basic critical-path program into one that computes the results based on the foregoing assumptions. To relax the assumptions about criticality and independence requires a much more sophisticated code. To date, most practical success has been obtained by using Monte Carlo simulation to obtain the mean and variance of total project time as well as a "probability of criticality" for each activity. Research continues into the development of computational methods for relaxing these assumptions without resorting to expensive simulation.

CPM Assumptions. The variant known as CPM was developed for the construction industry, where the times for each activity are assumed to be perfectly known, but controllable within limits depending on the amount of additional effort to be expended. Computation typically proceeds by first assuming a nominal time for each activity, and then using this to find a critical path in

the normal manner. Activities on the critical path become candidates for "crashing," i.e., for a reduction in their times by payment of a premium for early completion. By successively relaxing activities on the critical path, a curve showing total project cost versus time to completion can be obtained. These computations can be done using a simple embellishment of the basic critical-path program. If, in addition, the value of the project as a function of its completion time is known, the mix of crash and normal activity times which best balances the crash-cost premiums against the overall value of the project can be found.

Other Major Variants

Costing Methods (e.g., PERT/COST). The structure provided by the network representation of the project is used as a framework for collecting and allocating project cost, replacing standard functional allocation schemes. This provides a more appropriate means for aggregating the individual costs of project activities. Software that performs this costing in conjunction with a project network is available, but is more limited than the critical-path computations themselves. Such methods are used in surprisingly few projects, probably because of a reluctance to abandon standard cost-accounting methods, however inappropriate.

Resource Allocation. The assumption of unlimited resources available when necessary is replaced by an assumption of limited resources of various sorts (e.g., computer time, carpenters, bulldozers). The problem then becomes one not only of scheduling activities to avoid delaying the overall project, but also of insuring that the scarce resources are available when necessary. This becomes particularly interesting in the so-called *multiship, multishop* problem where several projects compete simultaneously for the same resources. Computer codes available for this purpose are usually based on heuristic methods of optimization.

REFERENCE

1969. Wiest, J. D. and Levy, F. K. *A Management Guide to PERT/CPM.* Englewood Cliffs, NJ: Prentice-Hall.

E. G. HURST, JR.

PETRI NETS

For articles on related subjects *see* AUTOMATA THEORY; CHOMSKY HIERARCHY; CONCURRENT PROGRAMMING; FORMAL LANGUAGES; MODELS; MULTIPROCESSING; PARALLEL ALGORITHMS; PARALLEL PROCESSING; and SEMAPHORE.

Petri nets are a popular and useful model for the representation of systems with concurrency or parallelism. They are named for, and have been developed from, the work of Carl Adam Petri, currently at the Gesellschaft für Mathematik und Datenverarbeitung in Bonn, West Germany. A Petri net (see Fig. 1) is a graph with two types of nodes—*places* and *transitions*. Places are drawn as circles while transitions are drawn as bars. Directed arcs (arrows) connect places to transitions and transitions to places. For each transition, the directed arcs define its *input* places (arc from place to transition) and its *output* places (arc from transition to place).

A Petri net is *executed* by defining a *marking* and then *firing* transitions. A marking is a distribution of *tokens* to the places of the Petri net. A token is represented on a Petri net graph by a small solid dot in a place. A transistion is *enabled* whenever all of its input places have one or more tokens. A transition *fires* by removing one token from each of its input places and adding one token to each of its output places.

For example, in the marked Petri net of Fig. 1, two transitions are enabled. Transition *b* has one input (p_2) and that place has a token so transition *b* is enabled. Similarly, transition *e* has tokens in both of its input places (p_4 and p_7), so it is also enabled. Transition *d* is not enabled since there is no token in place p_5, one of its inputs. To fire transition *b*, we remove the token from p_2 and put a token in p_5 and a token in p_8 (its two outputs). This would enable transition *d* and also *f*. Firing transition *e* will remove a token from both p_4 and p_7 and put a token in p_{10}.

If more than one transition is enabled, the firing of these transitions is generally asynchronous—they may fire simultaneously or at different times before or after each other. For example, in Fig. 1, transitions *b* and *e* are enabled and may fire completely independently. If two transitions share input places, then they are in *conflict* and only one can fire. In Fig. 1, transitions *f* and *g* are in conflict when a token is in place p_8.

Petri nets are a simple, elegant model of information flow. This makes them useful for describing and explaining systems, especially systems with concurrency and synchronization. Petri nets have been used mainly to model computer hardware (e.g., asynchronous circuits, pipelined computers, and computers with multiple functional units such as the CDC 6600 and IBM 360/91) and computer software (e.g., sets of cooperating processes, communication protocols, and operating systems). Transitions represent *events* in the modeled system, while places represent *resources* or *conditions*. For example, Fig. 2 is a Petri net model of a disk scheduling algorithm with a disk drive, disk controller, and channel. The two available disk drives are represented by two tokens in the "disk drive available" place. Only one disk controller is available.

A Petri net can be associated with a nondeterministic automaton whose states correspond to the markings of the net. An execution of this automaton defines a *string* of events corresponding to a firing sequence of the Petri net. The set of all possible strings for a Petri net is its *language*. For example, if we associate the symbols (*a, b, c, d, e,*) with the transitions as shown in Fig. 2, then one

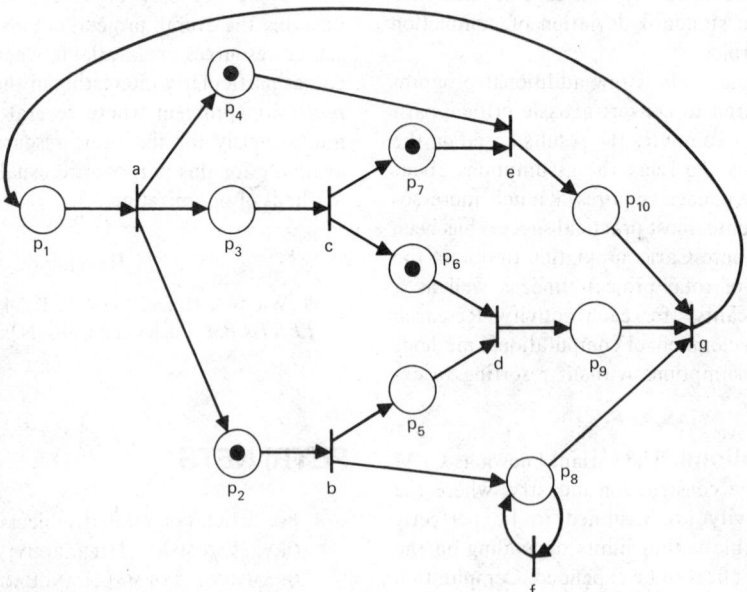

Fig. 1. An example Petri net.

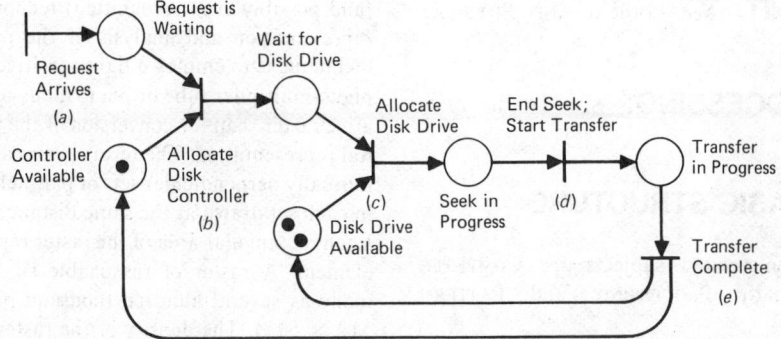

Fig. 2. A Petri net model of an algorithm for allocating a disk controller and disk drives.

possible string is *abcdebcde;* another string is *aabcde-abcdebcde.* In general, for Fig. 2, any string is made up of the substrings *a* and *bcde* such that the number of *b*s never exceeds the number of *a*s, from left to right. The *a*s can otherwise be arbitrarily interleaved with the *bcde* substrings.

The class of Petri net languages has been used as a basis for comparing the Petri net medel with other models of parallel systems: If the language of a model *A* is (strictly) contained in the language of a model *B*, then model *A* is (strictly) less powerful than model *B;* if the languages are equal, then the models are considered equivalent. The results of such comparisons must be judged with caution, since the representation of an execution by a linear string does not distinguish between the resolution of conflict (where only one sequence is possible) and parallelism (where many arbitrary interleavings of events are possible but only one happens to occur). With this reservation, it can be stated that the Turing machine model is strictly more powerful than the Petri net model, while Petri nets are strictly more powerful than finite state models. All regular languages are Petri net languages, and all Petri net languages are context-sensitive (see Fig. 3).

A Petri net can be *analyzed* to determine properties of the modeled system. Analysis techniques have been developed to decide if the number of tokens in a Petri net is bounded, if tokens are conserved, if deadlocks can occur, or if mutual exclusion is violated. These correspond to important problems for concurrent systems, but more general analysis techniques would be useful. Current techniques are based on either of two approaches: (1) a matrix representation of the Petri net, or (2) a tree representation of its state space.

One typical analysis problem is the *reachability problem:* Given a Petri net with an initial marking and a desired final marking, is it possible to fire transitions and change the initial marking to the desired final marking? Researchers are trying to find an algorithm to decide reachability. However, at the moment, no such algorithm is known, and it is possible that no such algorithm can exist; reachability may be undecidable. It is known that if reachability is decidable, it is very hard to determine. The time and memory (computational complexity) needed to analyze a Petri net grows exponentially with the size of the Petri net (in the worst case).

Continued work on Petri nets and their use is resulting in the development of a new research area called *general net theory.* Within this general theory, *special net theory* corresponds to the Petri net model described here.

REFERENCES

1977. Peterson, J. L. "Petri Nets," *Computing Surveys* **9,** *No. 3:* 223–252 (September).

1979. Agerwala, T. "Putting Petri Nets to Work," *Computer,* **12,** *No. 12:* 85–94 (December).

1980. Brauer, W. (Ed.). "Net Theory and Applications," *Proceedings of the Advanced Course on General Net Theory of Processes and Systems, Lecture Notes in Computer Science* **84.** Berlin: Springer-Verlag.

1981. Peterson, J. L. *Petri Net Theory and the Modeling of Systems.* Englewood Cliffs, NJ: Prentice-Hall.

J. L. PETERSON

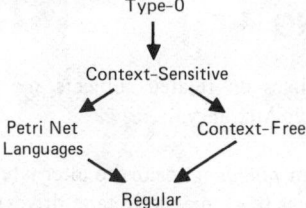

Fig. 3. The place of Petri net languages in the Chomsky hierarchy of languages. An arrow indicates proper containment.

PHYSICAL UNIT. *See* Logical and Physical Units.

PICTURE PROCESSING. *See* Image Processing.

PICTURES, BASIC STRUCTURE

For articles on related subjects *see* Computer Graphics; Image Processing; and Pattern Recognition.

The basic structure of any photograph or reproduced picture consists of small areas, known as picture elements (*pixels* or *pels*), of gray scale intensity and, possibly, color. The amount of detail in the picture depends on the size and number of elements making up the picture. For fine detail, the picture elements should be small and numerous, as in an ordinary photograph, and should not be individually visible except on very close inspection. However, if the picture elements are few and large, they will show quite plainly, as they do in photographs reproduced in newspapers. The number and size of picture elements required for satisfactory visual representation depend upon two factors: the amount of detail desired and the distance at which the picture is to be viewed.

All images to be processed by a computer may be divided into two categories: those made up solely of lines and curves, such as engineering drawings (so-called line drawings); and those, such as photographs, that include areas of tone (often called halftone or gray scale pictures). Images of the first category, in which there is no shading or change of color of the lines and curves, can be read by devices such as curve followers and can be subsequently reproduced by any standard plotting device. Images of the second category, including line drawings in which lines can be drawn with varying intensity or color, can only be recognized or reproduced by devices that not only distinguish between white and black (or colors), but also recognize *shades* of black and white (or colors). Therefore, general purpose computer image-input devices must have the ability to distinguish multiple levels of gray (or color) and to convert (*digitize*) them into digital representations; similarly, computer image-output devices must be able to distinguish these levels of gray, for example, by representing picture elements by dots of different size or by dots of varying intensity (or color).

It is obviously more convenient to have a computer use an input device to "read" a picture directly and then to analyze it instead of first having the picture digitized off-line and then using the computer only for analysis. To accomplish such computer-controlled input, such devices must incorporate some kind of sophisticated scanning (and possibly even recognition) technique for the digital representation and analysis of the picture. A common technique is to employ a light-sensitive receiver such as a photo-multiplier tube or photo diode to make an enumerative raster scan for conversion of the picture into its digital representation. The term *raster* can be defined as two mutually perpendicular sets of parallel lines, with all lines in each set drawn at the same distance from one another. Each rectangular area of the raster represents one picture element. A raster of reasonable size often contains as many as several hundred thousand pixels (for example, 512×512). The density of the raster cross lines is usually called its *resolution*. The optical beam of the raster scan proceeds sequentially from one picture element to another, normally horizontally across the picture and then from top to bottom as in a TV raster deflection. The scan produces a large matrix of digitized gray (or color) values. For a single picture such a matrix may require as many as several million bits of storage. (For example, a 512×512 display, each of whose pixels has eight levels of gray, requires a quarter-million bytes—two million bits—of storage.) To proceed from the scan to recognition of the picture then requires analysis of these values. Examples of devices that use a raster scan are fingerprint readers and automatic signature verification terminals, both of which, however, are still in the research and development stage.

Raster scan techniques are also widely used by computer output devices such as electrostatic printer/plotter systems, which print one or more raster lines at a time and advance the paper, and by some COM (computer output on microfilm) systems.

In graphic and/or color display systems, raster/color scan refresh is used. Each picture element is represented not just by a single value but by a bit string (pixel) encoding which maps gray scales to colors.

REFERENCE

1981. Chang, Shi-Kuo (ed.) "Pictorial Information Systems". Special issue of *Computer* **14**, No.11 (November).

J. Necas

PINGPONG

For articles on related subjects *see* Buffer; and Memory: Auxiliary.

The term *pingpong* means to alternate two or more storage devices (e.g., magnetic tape drives) so that processing may take place on a virtually endless set of files. For example, a program may operate on a file of a dozen reels of tape, but the program, when executed, requires a computer with only two tape drives. Reel 1 is mounted on drive A, and reel 2 on drive B. The end-of-file signal on drive A causes the program to switch to drive B, at which time the console operator can demount reel 1 and mount reel 3 on drive A. This procedure continues, "ping-ponging" the two drives, until all 12 reels have been processed.

F. GRUENBERGER

PIPELINE AND ARRAY PROCESSORS

For articles on related subjects *see* ARITHMETIC; COMPUTER; COMPUTER ARCHITECTURE; PARALLEL PROCESSING; and SUPERCOMPUTERS.

Pipelining is a hardware technique for achieving higher performance by breaking a complex, time-consuming function into a series of simpler, shorter operations, each of which can then be executed in assembly-line fashion with simultaneous computation on different sets of data. For example, any floating-point-arithmetic operation involves exponent calculation, prenormalization and postnormalization shifts of mantissa, mantissa arithmetic, rounding, and exponent correction. Similarly, multiplication requires a sequence of additions, and division a sequence of subtractions.

Although some pipeline processors may involve several pipelines, which in turn may compute one or more functions, let us consider the simplified model shown in Fig. 1, in which the pipelined processor performs only multiplication. Assume that multiplication is broken into k segments and each segment takes one clock time. Consider executing the following program.

for $I = 1$ **to** 100 **do**
$$X(I) \leftarrow A(I) * B(I)$$

Initially, the A and B arrays are fetched from memory to the general registers. Processing begins as $A(1)$ and $B(1)$ are sent from the registers to segment 1 of the pipeline processor. When processing of these two operands by segment 1 is complete, the intermediate results are sent to segment 2, and so on, until the final result $X(1)$ emerges from segment k. But when the intermediate results of $A(1) * B(1)$ are passed to segment 2, two new arguments, $A(2)$ and $B(2)$, can enter the pipeline through segment 1. Thus, by the time $X(1)$ emerges from the pipeline, the nearly completed results of $A(2) * B(2)$ are entering segment k, and so on up the pipe to segment 1 where $A(k + 1)$ and $B(k + 1)$ are entering. Notice that this process is very much like an assembly line, where each segment does a little further processing of the intermediate result, and segment k emits the completed prod-

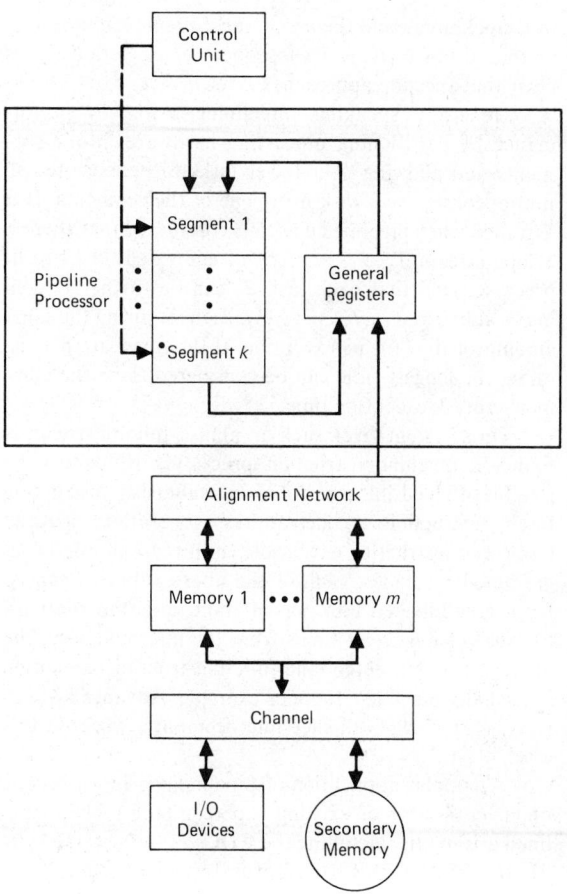

Fig. 1. Pipeline processor system.

uct. Each segment consists of combinational logic followed by a register to hold the intermediate results.

If we assume that the time to pass through the entire pipeline is approximately equal to the time required to multiply two numbers in a standard processor, then the total operation time or scalar time is unchanged. But for a vector of operations, this time is reduced by up to a factor of $k,$ the number of pipeline segments, as the length of the vector gets very long. This follows from observing the rate of flow from segment k. A new result appears in the time required to traverse one segment of the pipe, not all k segments. We must also pay k delays to fill the pipeline initially. More precisely, the speedup of a k segment pipeline over a serial version of some function which requires k clock times is

$$\frac{nk}{k + n - 1}$$

for n pairs of arguments. The denominator follows from the fact that the first pair of arguments leads to a result in k clock times, and the $n - 1$ subsequent results appear at the output in $n - 1$ subsequent clock periods. It is clear that speedup approaches k for $n \gg k$.

Generally speaking, pipelining improves performance by partitioning processing hardware into k segments and allowing k or fewer tasks to be executed simultaneously, each task using one of the segments. It is assumed when pipelined design is considered that there is a long stream $T_1, T_2, \ldots, T_n$, of equivalent tasks to be processed and that each task T_i can be further broken into k subtasks $T_{i,1}, T_{i,2}, \ldots, T_{i,k}$, each requiring the same amount of time for its execution. If the times are not the same, the longest time can be considered to be the common subtask execution time.

On a system level, such an almost infinite stream is found in machine-instruction processing which can be roughly divided into the following subtasks: Instruction fetch, instruction decode, address generation, operand fetch, and instruction execution. In the case of microprogrammed machines, each of the above subtasks can be further subdivided into one or more microinstructions. Because of long read times from the micromemory, the microinstruction fetch and microinstruction execution are usually pipelined, too. For example, Advanced Micro Devices' AM 2900 bit-slice microcomputer works in this way.

A popular application of pipelining is in arithmetic units. A number of existing supercomputers have pipelined arithmetic, including the CDC 7600, the IBM 360/91, the CDC STAR 100, Texas Instruments ASC, the Cray-1, CDC Cyber 203 and 205 (see SUPERCOMPUTERS), and the Manchester University MU5.

When pipelining arithmetic functions, it is possible to use several unifunctional pipes or to merge several unifunctional pipes into one multifunctional pipe. In case of several unifunctional pipes, it is possible to configure them in such a way that the results from one pipe are directly sent to the other pipe (Cray-1) to improve the efficiency. Multifunctional pipes have by definition several configurations—one for each function. The pipe is called static if, at any instant of time, only one configuration is active, which in turn allows only pipelining of tasks that involve the same configuration. Since static pipes are easier to control, all multifunctional pipes in existing machines are static. On the other hand, dynamic multifunctional pipes permit overlapped processing of several tasks with different configurations.

The control structure of a pipelined system can generally be implemented in two ways. The first, and simpler, control unit allows straightforward streaming of tasks or instructions in such a way that the completion ordering of the instructions is the same as their initiation ordering (IBM 360/75, TI ASC). The second, more flexible and more expensive, type of control, allows the completion ordering to be different from the initiation ordering (IBM 360/91, CDC 6600/7600, CDC STAR-100).

A way to improve the throughput of a small- or medium-sized host computer system in many applications (e.g., computed tomography (q.v.), image enhancement, vibration testing, speech analysis) is to add a type of pipelined arithmetic processor, usually called an *array processor* because of its efficiency in processing array operations. In such multiprocessor configurations, the array processor executes high-speed operations at speeds up to 100 times faster than the host could perform, while the host processor provides overall system control, directing the flow of data and instructions between I/O peripherals and the array processor. One such array processor, designed for solving well-defined sets of problems employing fast Fourier transforms (q.v.), matrix operations, correlation or convolution algorithms, is the Floating Point Systems AP-120B (Fig. 2). It is a synchronous, parallel, pipelined, and horizontally microprogrammable machine with a 167 ns cycle time and a 38-bit floating-point word (10-bit exponent, 28-bit mantissa). Separate program, data, and table memories can be addressed independently to eliminate memory access conflicts. There are two independent blocks of 32 floating-point registers each. High-speed arithmetic capability is achieved with a two-segment pipelined adder and a three-segment pipelined multiplier, each with two buffer registers and operating at 167 ns per segment. Multiple data paths (System bus, A, B, C, D buses) connect the I/O interface to multiple memories, and the memories to arithmetic units. These paths provide an independent connection between each memory and each arithmetic unit, allowing high-speed processing. For example, both adder and multiplier can be driven with four separate arguments on the same cycle.

In parallel with the floating-point hardware, there is a 16-bit integer arithmetic-logic unit with sixteen 16-bit registers for performing loop counting and address indexing.

The AP-120B has only the primitive I/O capability to set up a direct memory access transfer and to determine its completion. No interrupt handling hardware is available. For any type of operation other than floating-point add and multiply, the performance of AP-120B degrades to that of a serial microprogrammed machine.

In summary, pipelining is a well proven and a major technique in addition to parallelism (see SUPERCOMPUTER IIMPLEMENTATIONS) for improving the performance of data processing without using a faster technology. However, pipelines suffer from four inherent limitations. First, if the vectors are short relative to the number of segments in the pipeline, pipelining is not very effective. If only one scalar operation needs to be performed, it will usually take longer than a more conventional organization. Sec-

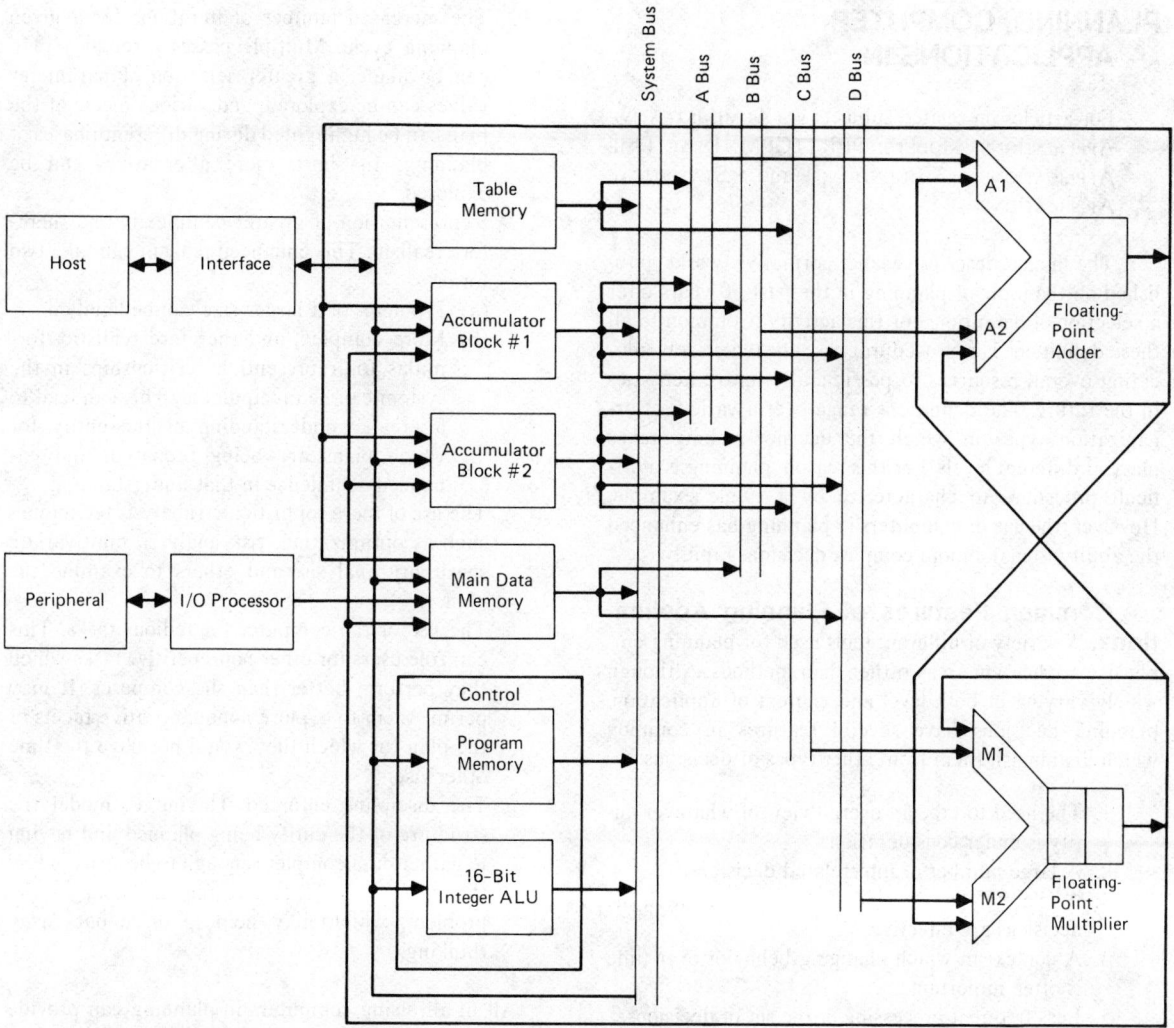

Fig. 2. A Floating-Point Systems AP-120B array processor.

ond, the emergence rate of results is limited by the time required for the longest segment. Third, computer operations can be broken only into a limited number of segments, independent of technology. Therefore, the speedup is limited to a factor of 10 or less in existing machines that use one pipeline at a time. Fourth, for improved performance, multiple multifunctional pipes can be used. However, they are difficult to set up, schedule without conflict, and try again once an error is discovered in the result. However, when pipelining is used in special-purpose applications such as array processors, these limitations are not so severe. The array processors should be thought of as a hardware implementation of frequently used software subroutines and, with low-cost VLSI technology, it is not difficult to imagine a variety of *coproces-*

sors working together with, and complementing, the host processor.

REFERENCES

1977. Ramamoorthy, C. V. and Li, H. F. "Pipelined Architecture," *Computer Surveys* **9**, *No. 1:* 61–102 (March).
1978. Kuck, D. J. *The Structure of Computers and Computations.* New York: Wiley.
1979. Hufnagel P. S., "Comparison of Selected Array Processor Architectures," *Computer Design* **18**, *No. 13:* 151–158 (March).
1980. Kogge, P. *Pipelining and Overlap in Computer Design.* New York: McGraw Hill.

D. J. KUCK AND D. D. GAJSKI

PLANNING, COMPUTER APPLICATIONS IN

For articles on related subjects *see* ADMINISTRATIVE APPLICATIONS; MODELS; PERT/CPM; REAL TIME APPLICATIONS; SIMULATION; and STATISTICAL APPLICATIONS.

The many descriptive and normative works published on the topic of planning in the past 50 years offer a selection of definitions for this activity. Common to all these definitions is a procedural base for tentatively allocating overall resources to possible alternative activities in the future. The definitions range over a variety of organization types in which the decision-making takes place at different levels. For this reason, planning is a difficult procedure to characterize by a single example. However, the use of computers in planning has enhanced the ability to make more complex decisions rapidly.

Common Features of Planning Applications. A variety of different tools used for planning emphasize application areas rather than methods. Although widely varying in both level and context of application, planning decisions have several features in common which distinguish them from other types of decisions:

1. The need to take an overall view of whatever entity is under consideration.
2. A large number of interrelated decisions.
3. A relatively long period of time during which the decisions are effective.
4. A context in which changing behavior over time is often important.
5. Less frequent processing of the set of decisions.

These five characteristics of planning decisions have tended to prevent computers from supplanting humans. They also tend to make use of computers in planning relatively more difficult.

Advantages of Computers in Planning. Despite the problems introduced by the preceding five factors, computers have also brought certain advantages to planning applications. Many of these are similar to the advantages brought by computerization of decision processes in general, although some are unique to planning. The most important advantages include:

1. The speed at which results can be obtained. Reports can be produced in seconds or minutes rather than in days. This not only can provide more timely information to the planner, but (even more important) can supply it when the plan is being worked on, rather than later.

2. The increased number of iterations for a given planning cycle. Multiple passes through a plan can be made, a greater selection of parameter values can be explored, and various facets of the plan can be highlighted during different phases of planning. In short, more alternatives can be explored.
3. Representation of greater complexity and therefore realism. This enhanced realism can take two forms:
   (a) Problems of a larger size can be handled.
   (b) More complex, and therefore realistic, formulas for representing relationships in the system can be manipulated. This can lead to a greater understanding of the entity for which plans are being prepared, and enhanced confidence in that understanding.
4. The use of more sophisticated analysis techniques such as optimization, risk analysis, multivariate sensitivity analysis, and others to examine the plan.
5. The use of the computer for tedious tasks. This can free users for other nonrepetitive tasks which they perform better than the computer. It may permit them to explore nonquantitative facets of the plan for which they would not have the time otherwise.
6. The discipline enforced. Having to model the structure of the entity being planned and having to gather data complete enough to be analyzed by the system can force an organized look at the problem, which may help to drive out fuzzy thinking.

All in all, using computers in planning can provide more alternatives more quickly, leading to better decisions and more confidence in those decisions.

Examples of Application Areas

Production and Operations Planning. These types of planning generally focus on one narrow function or operation in the enterprise, whether it is a manufacturing or service firm, an educational institution, or a government organization. The most common example is the planning and scheduling of the production line in a factory, where the data consist of the number of jobs to be done, their completion due dates, and other production factors, all of which are combined to plan a proposed factory schedule. On the other hand, the scheduling of classes in a school, the scheduling of the tasks in a health-care facility, and even the choice of a call schedule for sales people can be regarded as operations planning. Planning of this sort is characterized by the relatively low level in the organization at which it takes place, and by the fact that it is relatively frequently performed. For these reasons, operations planning adapted fairly quickly to computerization.

Still, in spite of the potential benefits made possible by the frequency of performance, operations planning includes a large number of individual choices that must be made and that are of relatively low financial importance, and this choice process implies that satisfactory performance in decision making by humans without computers can often be achieved. Computer methods, particularly those that seek exact optimal solutions, are not yet economical in all applications. In spite of this, a number of computer software manufacturers and service bureaus offer packages that attempt to solve such problems either approximately or exactly. Some of these have proven quite successful. Many of the early business applications of the first-generation scientific computers were in this area, using a variety of increasingly sophisticated mathematical programming packages. Today, human-aided optimization, where the human plays an explicit role in all stages of the optimization process using an interactive computer, has become increasingly feasible and economical.

Project Planning. This form of planning is oriented toward a specific project rather than a continuing operation. Formal project planning first gained prominence during the development of the Polaris submarine system, in which it was necessary to take into account the interrelationships among new engineering and scientific developments, each having uncertain costs and times to completion. A scheme was developed for deciding what jobs were critical and how long the total project would take. Because of its well-publicized success in saving both time and money, the technique soon became adopted for development projects in the U.S. Department of Defense.

Among the methods for dealing with project scheduling problems are the CPM (critical path method) and PERT (program evaluation and review technique). While these techniques are used only once for planning every project (although they are often used as a control measure throughout the project), and while every project has unique features, there are enough characteristics in common in specifying structure, processing times, and costs for a given project, that standardized computer packages are now available. These range from simple programs handling small problems on time-sharing systems through very sophisticated systems containing a variety of options that can solve mammoth problems.

Financial Planning. A growing area of planning made popular largely by the advent of computer systems is the area of financial planning. Although financial planning itself is not new, the ability to examine quickly the probable financial consequences of a number of alterna-

tives has become possible because of the availability of specially designed computer systems. As an example, consider the preparation of the projected cash-flow statements of a firm. Forecasts of sales and costs are combined with the likely values of delays and other internal factors to produce probable cash-flow summaries under various sets of assumptions. A number of firms have custom-built systems for their internal financial planning needs. There also exist several general-purpose programs or sets of programs, developed for the most part by large commercial banks, which are available on time-sharing systems. These programs tend to have built-in the structure of the standard financial reports, and require only that detailed projections and historical data specific to the individual firm be input.

Strategic Planning. Strategic planning is the term commonly given to consideration of high-level, one-of-a-kind, long-term, complex decisions about different alternative courses of action which face the entire enterprise. Because of its characteristics, it is not nearly so amenable to computerized analysis as are lower-level forms of planning. In the past, the cost of programming a model structure unique to the strategic decision has in most cases far exceeded the benefits derived. However, with the rise in the economic consequences of the strategic decisions being made, and the enhanced ease of programming and analysis of such decisions brought about by the development of specially designed planning systems, the computer is becoming increasingly useful and used in the strategic planning area.

General-purpose systems for both financial and strategic planning are discussed in the next section.

Planning Systems. A planning system is a special-purpose, problem-oriented software system intended for the easy representation and manipulation of models and data appropriate to strategic planning decisions. Although both the availability and the characteristics of different planning systems change quite rapidly, as is common for business-oriented applications software, it is now possible to describe a planning system and distinguish it from other special-purpose software systems.

Planning systems have three major characteristics:

Modeling Language. An essential characteristic is the availability of a modeling language, in which the unique structure of the problem faced by the planner can (and indeed *must*) be expressed. It is this necessity to custom build the *structure* of the problem which distinguishes these systems from earlier planning software packages, which had the structure built-in and in which the user could specify only data values.

Model languages in planning systems tend to be one of three sorts. The first type, used for the earliest planning systems, is a high-level language such as Fortran or

Basic. In these systems, there are usually some additional functions, as well as some constraints on variable names and the like, to permit communication with the system as a whole. The systems that use general-purpose languages as modeling languages were generally built by engineers and other analytical problem solvers interested in generalizing the kinds of problems they could solve. By their nature, these modeling languages refer to the various basic entities by variable name, and manipulate them by algebraic equations.

The second source of modeling languages for planning systems was the report generation (*q.v.*) languages. Such modeling languages look like generalized report writers; that is, the basic entity is referenced not by variable name but rather by position in the report. Such languages used for planning contain additional computational options in which rows and/or columns can be combined and manipulated to form new rows and columns.

The third type of modeling language is a hybrid of the two previous types of languages, specially built for planning systems. In its most general form, the hybrid language permits either variable name or positional references to a particular entity. It is even more common to have rows referenced by variable name, but columns referenced by position. The modeling language in at least one planning system available today (IFPS) is non-procedural, so that the order of the definition of variables does not matter. This permits the simultaneous solution of equations where appropriate, and allows easy editing of the model by the ultimate user without the worry that some key variable will be left undefined.

Virtually all modeling languages of currently available planning systems include a number of functions geared to the predominantly financial planning use made of such systems. Functions such as net present value, internal rate of return, amortization and depreciation schedules, payback period, loss carry forward, and the like are used routinely in financial analysis and reporting applications.

Analysis Capabilities. The analysis options typically available are:

1. *Case analysis.* The ability to evaluate outcomes for a given set of input values. This category is included here for completeness, even though every planning system must clearly be able to evaluate results for a given set of inputs.
2. *Parametric analysis (what if . . .).* The ability to vary a set of input values and observe the effect on the outcomes. This is the most important capability of a planning system, and it is available on virtually all of them. Using it, one or more

values in the database can be altered interactively and the effect on the result variables measured.
3. *Sensitivity analysis.* An organized version of parametric analysis, in which one or more input variables can simultaneously take on different values, and their effect on the result variables explored.
4. *Break-even analysis (how get . . .).* The ability to find the value of an input variable that yields a desired outcome. This capability is the mirror image of parametric analysis, in that a particular result variable is set for some time period at a desired value, after which the system searches for the value of a specified input variable that causes the desired result. This is also known as management by objectives, target value analysis, or goal seeking in some planning systems.
5. *Impact analysis.* The ability to learn for a chosen result variable all the input variables that affect its value, and, for those that do, the amount of change in the result caused by, say, a 1% change in the input. This option is extremely useful for determining the few most important variables in a complex planning problem; when it is available, the popularity of this option is second only to "what if" analysis.
6. *Data analysis.* The ability to input historical data and manipulate it into a forecast suitable for direct input to the model. This option, if available, gives the ability to "launder" the data before it is included in the planning database. Many planning systems do not contain this function within the system itself, but instead utilize a related and compatible package available on the same computer.
7. *Risk analysis.* The ability to determine the effects of randomness in the input variables on the potential outcomes, usually by Monte Carlo simulation. Several systems have the rudimentary ability to perform this analysis, usually by specifying randomness through the variable definitions in the model rather than including it as desired when the model is analyzed. The usual difficulty for this option is in giving the user a convenient means of expressing uncertainty in terms that both the user and the planning system understand; a few systems (e.g., EMPIRE) have solved this problem quite successfully.
8. *Optimization.* The ability to seek the values of a set of the controllable input variables that yield a "best" value of one of the result variables. For a model that is unrestricted in mathematical form, as is usually the case in planning

system models, optimization (which is available on only a few systems) is performed by one of several hill-climbing methods. In a few special cases, the general model can be translated into a form suitable for solution by mathematical programming (usually mixed integer programming), but this translation must typically be done by modeling specialists rather than the manager, so that it becomes more difficult to have this general capability available in a planning system.

9. *Comparison and consolidation.* The ability to compare the results of two or more runs made with different input assumptions, or to compare predicted with actual results, or to consolidate results from different model runs. In order to include real data for predicted versus actual comparisons, the ability to have direct access to the operating data of the organization is highly desirable.

10. *Command sequences.* The ability to write, execute, and save for later use a regularly executed series of analysis and report commands. This capability permits the user to build special-purpose analysis options from the primitive analysis operations available in the planning system. The means by which this is done range from preparing files of special commands to recalling sequences that are generated and saved automatically during the normal interactive operation of the system.

Report Generation. Another general capability of planning systems is the ability to generate reports. This can be done in several ways, some or all of which a given system may use:

1. *Standard reports.* The format of the report is fixed; the user selects only the variables to be included. Most systems use this report form to present the results of "what if" and other standard, frequently used analysis options, as well as for preliminary reports during the debugging of a model.

2. *Model parameters.* Reports are formatted by setting parameters in the model, or by using a special version of a "model" for generating the report. In these cases, there is usually available a default report whose characteristics are overridden by the parameter settings.

3. *Report format language.* A special language, different from the modeling language, in which reports are formatted. Variables to be included are selected, and options such as column width and spacing, column headings, and variable descriptions, and number formatting can be used at their default values or tailored.

4. *Graphical reports.* Input assumptions and results are presented graphically, either on standard alphanumeric terminals or, in some cases, on graphics terminals. The principal graphics options are:
   (a) Variables plotted against time.
   (b) Variables plotted against other variables, as in a scatter diagram.
   (c) Probability distributions, in either histogram or cumulative form, usually presenting the results of Monte Carlo simulations.

Other Characteristics of Planning Systems. In addition to the three main sets of features by which planning systems are characterized, other capabilities have proven useful in their operation. Some of the most important are:

1. *In-line editor.* The capability to enter and correct models and report formats within the planning system itself. While some systems still rely on an editing facility outside the planning system, most now have this important capability built in.

2. *On-line help.* The ability to obtain additional prompting or other help immediately, wherever you are in the system; usually received by typing a "?" in response to the command question given by the system. This reduces or eliminates the need to search through a users' manual during a planning session.

3. *Multiple data formats.* Many systems permit data to be entered in a variety of formats and configurations, including custom-built formats to match the real data of the organization. This facilitates the comparison of actual and projected data as required in analysis for control.

4. *Compatibility with database management systems.* Going even further, more and more planning systems can now directly access data stored using a packaged data management system, permitting the use of data with complex structures as inputs to the planning system.

5. *Shared logic.* The ability of the planning system to share copies of the common software among several people using the system simultaneously, so that users need only have copies of models unique to their problems and not the entire systems. Given the size of the typical planning system, this rather technical feature becomes important for computer efficiency when several groups within the same organization are using the system for planning at the same time.

In summary, a planning system is a combination of most of the features of a report generation language, many of the features of a clock-paced simulation language, some of the features of an inquiry or data management language, along with the extra modeling, analysis, and other utilities necessary to represent and solve unique planning problems. Several systems are available for use only as proprietary offerings on commercial time-sharing systems; others can be purchased for use on in-company computers, and a few are available in batch mode as well as interactive. But the thrust is clearly toward systems that are built, furnished, and maintained by time-sharing companies or their associated consulting and software development firms.

Choosing a Planning System. Whatever the source of alternative planning systems, there are a large number of criteria by which they can be compared. These criteria can be more or less important, depending on the organization and its needs. To suggest some of the more important possible criteria, in no particular order:

1. *Feature availability.* Matching features from the above lists of characteristics that are available on a given system with the specific planning needs of the organization.
2. *System compatibility.* Commercial time sharing and/or in-house use; computers on which it operates; interfaces to other systems (statistical, data management); minimal computer configuration required; efficiency of operation.
3. *Vendor support.* Training; documentation; installation; tailoring; system modification; help in modeling.
4. *Costs.* Initial; operation; maintenance and updates; additional modules.
5. *Vendor solidity.* Number and names of other clients; length of time in business; financial soundness.

In addition to all the technical considerations, there are political considerations internal to the organization that can influence the choice of a planning system. The most important of these concern the locus of control of the system and the models, jealousy of the operations research and information systems staffs, physical location and prior experience of the users and model builders, and the history of the use of such systems in the organization. In many cases, these factors will be more important than the technical considerations. Table 1 lists the names of currently (1981) available planning systems and their suppliers (typically either a time-sharing service or the developer of the system).

Table 1   Available Planning Systems

AUTOTAB II	Capex Corporation
BBL	Tymshare
BPL	International Time Sharing
CALLPLAN/IMPACT	Call Data Systems
CUFFS	CompuServe
CYPHERTAB	Cyphernet
EIS	Boeing Computer Services
EMPIRE	Applied Data Research
ENTERPRISE	City Share
EXPRESS	Tymshare
FAL II	General Electric Time Sharing
FCS	Comshare
FISCAL	Rapidata
FLARES	Computer Sciences
FML	Network Services
FORESIGHT	Foresight Systems
FPS	Scientific Time Sharing
GPOS	On-Line Decisions
IFPS	Execucom
MAPS	Ross Systems
OLSFMS	On-Line Systems
PAMS	On-Line Systems
PROPHIT II	Service Bureau Corporation
QED/INSIGHT	Time Sharing Resources
SIMPLAN	Social Systems, Inc.
STRATPLAN	International Business Machines (Europe)
XSIM	Interactive Data

Directions for Future Applications. All the elements mentioned in the following areas of probable growth are available to a limited extent today, but each should assume even more importance as improved planning systems are developed.

1. Planning systems are increasingly capable of solving higher-level unstructured planning problems. This means that:
    (a) Larger and more complex problem structures are representable.
    (b) The larger volume of data necessary for predicting outcomes is accessible.
    (c) The two foregoing features are becoming economical.
2. Users of the plan are increasingly able to deal directly with the planning system rather than through an intermediary. This is happening because:
    (a) The capability for writing sophisticated models and manipulating them in natural languages gives users the ability to model their own problems, rather than being bound by a ready-made model whose structure does not represent the entity being planned.

(b) The increasing availability of interactive, personal, small, dedicated computer systems permits the users of plans to interact directly with the planning system at their pace, without constraints imposed from the outside.

3. The plan is immediately usable for control of the plan, with no additional modeling effort. The quicker availability of real data directly accessible by the planning system itself means that plans can be monitored by the system and the users signaled when there appears to be a problem. This sort of control is already available for chemical processes and other production operations, and is being used increasingly in higher planning levels and contexts.

REFERENCES

ATSU Interactive Computing Directory (Third Printing), "Financial Modeling Languages." Boulder, CO: The Association of Time-Sharing Users.

1969. Ebeling, D. G. and Hurst, E. G., Jr. "PA3: A General-Purpose, Time-Shared Problem Analysis Language," *Proceedings of the Third Conference on Applications of Simulation* (December).

1975. Boulden, J. B. *Computer-Assisted Planning Systems: Management Concept, Application, and Implementation.* New York: McGraw-Hill.

1979. Keen, P. G. W. and Wagner, G. R. "DDS: An Executive Mind-Support System," *Datamation* (November).

1979. Naylor, T. H. *Corporate Planning Models.* Reading, MA: Addison-Wesley.

1980. Braun, T. H. "The History, Evolution, and Future of Financial Planning Language," *ICP Interface* (Spring).

E. G. HURST, JR.

PL/I. *See* PROCEDURE-ORIENTED LANGUAGES.

PMS NOTATION. *See* HARDWARE DESCRIPTION LANGUAGES.

POINTER

For articles on related subjects *see* ADDRESSING; DATA STRUCTURES; LISTS AND LIST PROCESSING; RING; STORAGE ORGANIZATION; and TREE.

A digital computer memory contains *cells,* which may be referred to by *addresses.* The address of a memory cell is sometimes referred to as a *pointer,* since it may be thought of as pointing to the memory cell to which it refers.

Pointers may occur at the level of machine language both as direct addresses and as indirect addresses.

LOAD 100　This assembly-language instruction specifies that the content of memory cell 100 is to be loaded into the accumulator. The address 100 is a pointer to the memory cell whose address is 100.

LOAD∗100　This indirect-addressing assembly-language instruction (indicated by the ∗) specifies that location 100 contains the address of the quantity to be loaded into the accumulator. The address 100 is a pointer to a pointer.

In general, a pointer p_1 may point to a cell containing a pointer p_2, and the pointer p_2 may in turn contain a pointer to a cell containing a pointer p_3. A sequence of pointers $p_1, p_2, p_3 \ldots$ such that p_i points to a cell containing p_{i+1} for $i = 1, 2, \ldots$ is called a *pointer chain.*

Pointers may also occur in high-level languages such as PL/I:

P = ADDR(A);　This PL/I statement assigns to the variable P the address of the variable A. The value stored in P is a pointer to the variable A, and P is said to be a pointer-valued variable.

Data structures may be implemented as directed graphs in which vertices represent memory cells and directed edges represent pointers between memory cells. For example, the tree structure in Fig. 1 contains five memory cells *a, b, c, d, e,* with a pointer from *a* to *b* and pointer chains from *a* through *c* to *d* and *e.*

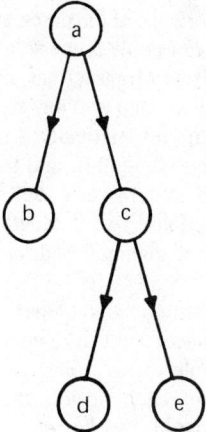

Fig. 1

In general, pointers may be used to connect individual memory cells and also to point from one composite data structure to another. For example, in the diagram the pointer from *a* to *c* may be thought of not merely as a pointer from *a* to the cell *c*, but also as a pointer from *a* to the subtree having *c* as its root.

Pointers are essential in any composite data structure for linking components of the data structure. Nevertheless, they must be used with care because indiscriminate use of pointers leads to undesirable complexity in data structures in much the same way that indiscriminate use of **goto**s leads to control structure complexity.

P. WEGNER

POINT-OF-SALE TERMINAL

For articles on related subjects *see* ADMINISTRATIVE APPLICATIONS; DATA ACQUISITION COMPUTER: TERMINALS; TRANSACTION-BASED SYSTEMS; and UNIVERSAL PRODUCT CODE.

A point-of-sale terminal is an input/output device connected to a computer which takes the place of a conventional cash register or similar device. Point-of-sale (PoS) systems offer several advantages over conventional devices for inventory control, credit authorization (if required), and recording sales, while at the same time reducing the time, manpower, and paperwork needed for such operations.

PoS terminals were made possible by the advent of electronic cash registers (ECRs). All ECRs have certain common features including a numeric keyboard, some functional keys, an operator-guide display, a sales data display panel, a cash drawer and up to three printers for generating customer receipts, a sales journal roll and one printer perhaps for special purposes, such as for refunds. Such a machine can guide a checkout clerk through the different types of retail transactions, clearly indicating on a display panel every step and any mistake made. Then, if necessary, it can automatically print out a bill or invoice with all items, sub-totals, and totals detailed.

Current PoS systems use ECRs for the standard cash register functions. Two distinctly different types of such systems can be distinguished:

1. Those based on stand-alone intelligent terminals with sufficient built-in logic and storage so that, for example, price tables can be stored in the memory of each device, thereby enabling the elimination of the keying of each item price. Some of these models are even user programma-

ble and equipped with automatically rechargeable battery power packs providing emergency power for a few hours' time in the event of power failure.

2. Shared-logic PoS systems, in which less intelligent individual ECRs placed at all checkpoints act as terminals connected to an on-site data collector with a magnetic tape, or to a minicomputer with disk and (perhaps) magnetic tape storage. Such configurations enable the transmission at any time of all current transaction data to a remote computer for immediate processing. In this way, management can be provided with continuous, almost up-to-the-minute details of sales by product and department. This kind of configuration also makes possible on-line credit authorization as well as automatic electronic funds transfer.

An interesting variation of the shared-logic PoS system is one in which the individual ECRs are connected to one (or more) of them acting as a "master" terminal. This allows for data consolidation by summarizing totals for other terminals and also makes possible electronic transfer of funds. The master terminals are specifically designed to have larger memories and are usually programmable by the user. These systems are aimed at smaller ECR installations, and bridge the gap between PoS systems with stand-alone ECRs and full shared-logic PoS systems.

The *effectiveness* of a PoS system is crucially influenced by the success of the solution to the data capture problem; namely, what data is to be captured for each type of transaction and how it is to be captured, by keying, and/or by being machine read from labels attached to goods and preprinted in bar codes or special optical fonts. Two types of optical reading devices are being used in PoS systems:

1. *Miniature hand-held scanners,* which can read either bar-coded data—and are usually called *light pens* (as in Fig. 1)—or which read an OCR font and are usually referred to as *optical wands* (as in Fig. 2). The checkout clerk reads in the data preprinted on each label by passing the pointing head of the scanner over the data.

2. *Stationary slot scanners,* usually using laser beams, are mounted on conveyors at the checkout stands in supermarkets and read the bar-coded label attached to goods via one or more slots, either automatically, while it is passing the reading station, or when it is moved along the reading slot by the checking clerk (see Fig. 3).

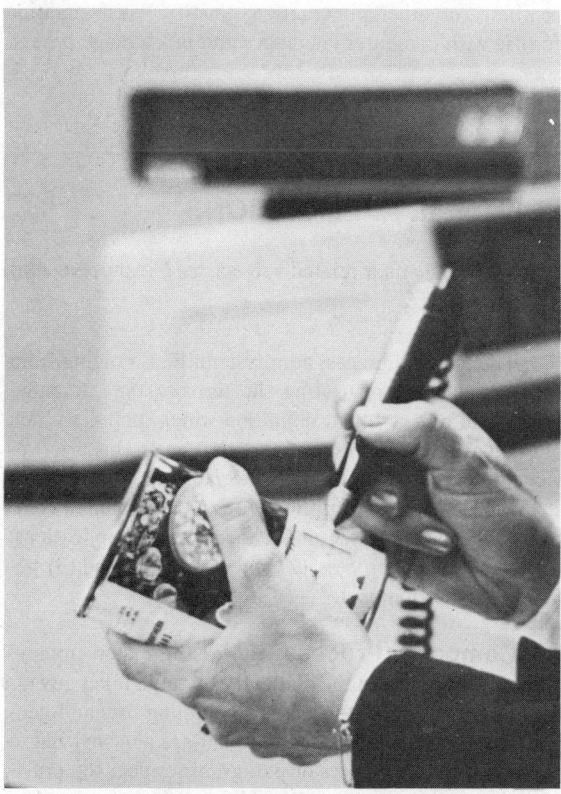

Fig. 1. NCR hand-held UPC scanner for use in supermmarkets.

Fig. 2. Recognition's portable OCR WAND®.

Fig. 3. NCR stationary slot scanner.

Using these scanners effectively requires a unified coding system for data to be read from labels. Presently, three national and international standards for coding goods can be identified, with several others in the design stage. In the U.S., there are the UPC (Universal Product Code) and the NRMA (National Retail Merchants Association) code. The UPC was adopted for supermarkets and identifies all manufacturers and their products in bar codes. Despite problems sometimes caused by the lack of imprinted bar codes on goods, the acceptance of the UPC is increasing and the range of its use is being extended to other areas, such as drugs, alcoholic beverages, and containers. NRMA has accepted the OCR-A Type 1 font (special numeric subset) as a standard for encoding price tags in non-food stores. In Europe, a solution similar to the UPC is being introduced. It is called the EAN (European Article Number), and it will be used for all kinds of goods; moreover, it is compatible with the UPC and is designed in such a way that all coded European and U.S. products can be properly identified with the same scanners. All three standards are designed so that they allow data to be read either from left to right or in reverse; they also include a check digit feature.

Extensive future developments of PoS systems can be envisaged, bringing all the capabilities of fully shared logic systems to all terminals, each with the capability to perform as masters and costing no more than current terminals.

J. NECAS

POLISH NOTATION

For articles on related subjects *see* Calculators, Electronic and Programmable; Expression; Language Processors; Parsing; Procedure-Oriented Languages; and Stack.

In 1951, the Polish logician Jan Lukasiewicz devised a *parenthesis-free* notation for logic. This notation, extended for use in algebra and other operator-operand systems, has become known as *Polish notation*. Basically, by consistently placing operators before (or after) their operands, the need for parentheses is eliminated, provided each operator has a fixed number of operands. The *prefix* form, in which the operators precede the operands, is used in Lisp, while the *postfix* (or *suffix*) form, in which the operators follow the operands, is used as an intermediate expression form by many compilers and in Hewlett-Packard calculators.

Parenthesis elimination is made possible by the fixed number of operands for each operator. Thus if "+" denotes ordinary addition, we expect two operands. Hence, "+ab" (prefix) and "ab+" (postfix) are as clearly understood as "a + b". Similarly, if "~" denotes logical negation, exactly one operand is expected. The minus sign causes a problem, since it may be associated with one operand (negative numbers) or two (subtraction). Agreement to limit its use to defining negative numbers solves this problem at the expense of writing subtraction as "a + (−b)" rather than "a − b". Table 1 gives several examples of Polish notation.

Table 1. Polish Notation

Expression	Prefix	Postfix
$a+(-b)$	$+a-b$	$ab-+$
$(-a)+b$	$+-ab$	$a-b+$
$a*(b+c)$	$*a+bc$	$abc+*$
$(p\supset q)\equiv(\sim p\vee q)$	$\equiv\supset pq\vee\sim pq$	$pq\supset p\sim q\vee\equiv$

If a prefix expression is evaluated from right to left, then whenever an operator is encountered, its operands are those that have most recently been evaluated. Hence, the operator can be immediately processed. The same is true of a postfix expression evaluated from left to right. For example, the evaluation sequence for $*a+bc$ is c, b, $+bc$, a, $*a+bc$. Similarly, the expression $+*abc$ (i.e., $(a*b) + c$) is evaluated in the order c, b, a, $*ab$, $+*abc$. Thus, evaluated subexpressions placed on a stack are naturally "popped" from the stack in the order of their use. These two properties—ease of evaluation and unique representation of an expression without use of pa-

rentheses or other punctuation—justify Polish notation for use with computer languages and in language processors.

R. R. Korfhage

POLITICAL APPLICATIONS

For article on a related subject *see* Computing and Society.

The political process admits definitions ranging from the very narrow, restricting the term to the campaign process, to a very broad definition which includes much of the legislative and executive activities. In this brief review of computers and politics, we adopt a relatively restrictive view. Our description of the employment of computers will be discussed under three major applications: (1) the campaign process, (2) vote projection, and (3) political reapportionment.

Campaign Process. By far the major employment of computers in the political campaign takes advantage of the equipment to maintain mailing lists and generate computer-composed letters that are personalized to the extent that sentences or paragraphs reflect the previously indexed interests of the addressee. Frequently, also, an individual's name is included in the text of the letter to enhance the personalization process.

Mailing lists are maintained which specify for each person a set of personal characteristics such as residence, degree of economic affluence, sex, religion, and prior political affiliations. In addition, the lists are indexed to reflect a history of prior campaign contributions and those political, social, and economic issues sufficiently interesting to the individual to have prompted a previous expression of opinion to a legislator or a candidate.

Although no hard statistics are available, it is estimated that over 90% (perhaps as much as 98%) of computer applications in the campaign process relate specifically to campaign mailings and solicitations of contributions. The small remaining balance includes more sophisticated uses of computers in the management of a campaign. Among these applications are (1) the organization and maintenance of, and coping with changes in the campaign activities using PERT (*q.v.*) techniques, and (2) the development and use of models for the allocation of funds or of the candidate's time and the simulation of a campaign in different jurisdictions, where the interplay of the emphasis of different issues will have varying effects upon the voting population. Such models require a large database of voter attitudes towards issues and knowledge of the extent to which the emphasis, either in support of or in opposition to a particular issue, will sway an already committed or politically leaning voter.

The existence of a database of this type allows a final application of computers in the campaign process which is the tabulation and analysis of public opinion polls among the voters wherein opinions on issues are related to degree of candidate support. The results of the analyses serve as aids to campaign strategy in determining issues and areas of strength and weakness that may be defined geographically or in terms of characteristics of segments of the voting population. A candidate's campaign strategist may be able to identify issues which may influence "undecided" or "leaning" voters, without alienating those who have already decided to support the candidate.

Vote Projection. The use of computers by the television networks to project early voting returns into estimates of the final result was the first introduction of the computer and its possibilities to large parts of the U. S. population. The first broad-scale application of computers to vote projections began in the 1952 Eisenhower-Stevenson race, making use of a UNIVAC I. By the time of the 1960 election, all networks were using some form of computer assistance, and the 1964 presidential election saw the first full, large-scale, three-network competition, each network making use of its own system and its own computer to project the election results. The mathematical models which form the basis of the projection procedures for the three networks differed markedly at that time. Since then, there has been a tendency to conform to a more uniform philosophy, although considerable differences in approach and in execution still exist among the three major TV networks.

As an example, the technique used by one network makes use of an equation of the form

$$P = w_b P_b + w_p P_p + w_v P_v$$

where the ws are weights and the Ps are individual estimates of the vote for, say, the Democratic candidate obtained by considerations of the baseline (b), key precincts (p), and raw vote (v). P_b is an estimate based upon a compilation of all available pre-election information, including polls and informed opinion. P_p is an estimate based upon the change in a select sample of key precincts over a prior comparable election. The sample precincts are carefully checked to ensure that the characteristics of the voting population in each precinct have not varied significantly since the prior comparable election; e.g., that what had been a blue-collar working class precinct has not been replaced by a luxury high-rise development. The estimate provided by P_v is the actual raw vote as it is assembled at state or regional collection centers from coun-

ties and individual precincts and transmitted to the networks. The raw vote may be adjusted for reporting patterns if, for example, a larger proportion of the more Democratic urban vote typically is reported before the more Republican rural vote in a state.

Except for P_b, all quantities in the equation are constantly changing. At any time, the sum of the weighting coefficients, the ws, must be unity. They reflect the relative importance of the factors associated with them in the equation. At the beginning of the evening, $w_b = 1$ and the other two coefficients are zero, reflecting the fact that the only component of the estimate is the pre-election baseline. As the evening continues, the dominant effect is generally assumed by the second term $w_p P_p$ with its magnitude being a function both of the number of key precincts whose returns have been entered into the model and the degree of consistency they have shown. As more raw vote is received, the first two coefficients tend to zero; w_v assumes dominance and ultimately becomes 1 when all precincts have reported. In those states where absentee ballots are counted in a special way after the votes cast on election day are counted, provision is made to incorporate the effect of the absentee ballots into the model.

The major networks and wire services have combined to form the News Election Service (NES), which is responsible for collecting the actual vote at local precinct, county, and ward levels, aggregating this vote into higher-level political jurisdictions, and sending updated totals at rapid intervals to all subscribers simultaneously. The networks have agreed that the NES vote would be the only vote displayed in front of their cameras.

The NES operation is highly computerized with state or regional tabulations sent to a national computer, which, in turn, aggregates vote totals from throughout the country, organizes them in different ways, and transmits the information automatically on high-speed lines to the networks and wire services.

The projection teams, generally consisting of political scientists, statisticians, journalists, and computer scientists, have built a record of extremely high accuracy and rapid projection. Still, there have been instances of erroneous projections which generally were recognized reasonably soon after the fact and recalled by the network.

Political Reapportionment. The Supreme Court's "one person-one vote" decision in *Reynolds v. Sims* in 1964 led to an investigation of the use of computers to aid legislators in reapportioning their electoral jurisdictions to be acceptable to the Court's dictum. Most applications have been to state legislatures, but there have also been applications to Congressional redistricting within a state and in the drawing of district lines by municipal councils.

The various models that have been developed, most of which depend upon a high-speed computer for their practicality, differ in their approach to the specification of initial conditions for the legislative reapportionment and in the criteria used to find the best allocation.

The less politically sophisticated, "non-partisan" models attempt to lay a rectangular grid across a state, modifying the lines so as to obtain as nearly an equal proportion of the electorate in each of the districts as possible. Other models which reflect a greater degree of political sophistication commence with an initial allocation based upon the existing legislative boundaries and then perturbing them in such a way as to obtain population parity. To be practical, all models must recognize political boundaries such as towns and counties and major geographic barriers such as bodies of water and mountain ranges.

Mathematical models and associated computer programs have been developed by various academic and commercial organizations. They differ in their degree of political sophistication, the extent to which on-line graphics are used, and in their ability to introduce degrees of partisanship such as to give as great a representation as possible to one political party or one ethnic group.

REFERENCES

1964. Moshman, Jack. "The Role of Computers in Election Night Broadcasting," *Advances in Computers* V. New York: Academic Press.

1972. Chartrand, Robert L. *Computers and Political Campaigning.* New York: Spartan Books.

1973. Moshman, Jack and Kokiko, E. M. "A Redistricting Algorithm Applied to Geographic Reorganization of Circuit Courts," *Annals of the New York Academy of Sciences* **219.**

J. MOSHMAN

PORTABILITY

For articles on related subjects *see* COMPATIBILITY; CROSS ASSEMBLERS AND COMPILERS; SOFTWARE; and SOFTWARE FLEXIBILITY.

Software is said to be *portable* if it can, with reasonable effort, be made to run on computers other than the one for which it was originally written. Portable software proves its worth when computers are replaced or when the same software is run on many different computers, whether widely dispersed or at a single site.

The simplest aid to portability is the use of standard high-level languages such as Cobol or Fortran. Such standard languages do, however, have the following deficiencies: (1) standards change over time; (2) compilers often support non-standard language extensions; (3) standards are rarely completely precise; (4) programs sometimes require non-standard parts to interface with the local operating environment. Therefore, extra work is needed to make software properly portable. Useful methods include the use of language subsets, common to all compilers, and the use of verifier programs to ensure adherence to subsets; the use of *preprocessors* to map a source program into several alternative forms, thus catering to variations among compilers; separating out machine-dependent aspects of software; and the use of portable compilers (which themselves may use a so-called "abstract machine" as a common interface between the source language and all machine languages, thus aiding their own portability).

Several widely used programming languages owe some of their success to the availability of a portable compiler. In addition to Fortran and Cobol, these include BCPL (using the O-code abstract machine), Snobol, using the SIL abstract machine and others, Pascal (using the P-code abstract machine), and Algol-68 using Z-code. Since the late 1950s, attempts have been made to produce UNCOL (Universal Computer-Oriented Language), a universal abstract machine, to act as a common interface between all programming languages and all computers. Some computer scientists, however, fear that all such attempts are bound to fail, because of their excessive generality.

It costs a good deal of planning and effort to produce software that is portable. Moreover, on any one computer, a portable program will be less efficient than a specially hand-tailored one. Nevertheless, given the huge cost of rewriting non-portable software, an investment in portability is normally one that will repay handsomely.

REFERENCE

1977. Brown, P. J. (Ed.). *Software Portability.* Cambridge University Press.

P. J. BROWN

PORTS, MEMORY

For articles on related subjects, *see* CHANNEL; MEMORY: Auxiliary; and MEMORY: Main.

In simple systems the main memory has a single *port* or logical connection through which data is transferred under CPU control. In more elegant systems (e.g., PDP-11), a single memory port is connected to a *bus* via which several CPUs and I/O devices have memory access. On still larger systems, bus traffic can become sufficiently in-

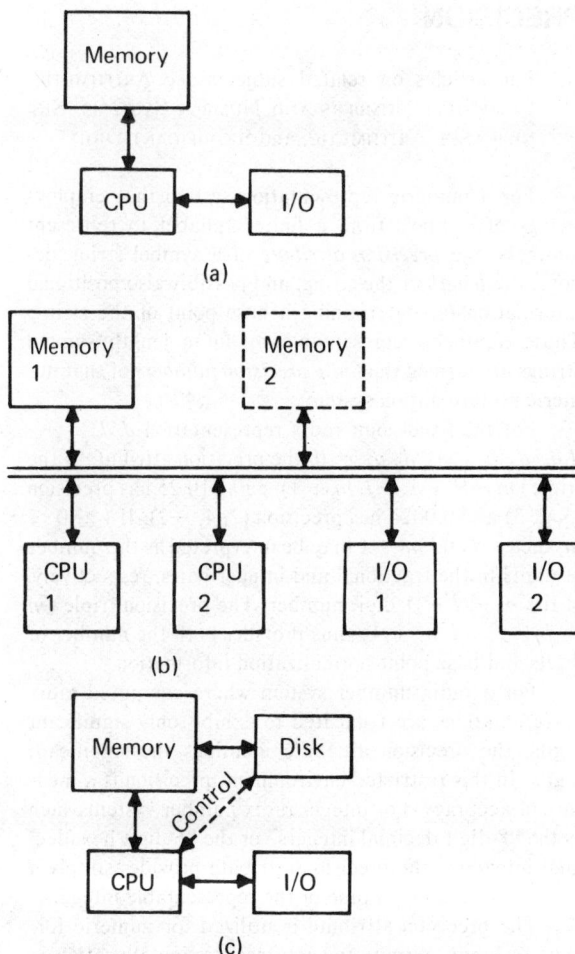

Fig. 1. Memory port connections: (a) single port, simply connected; (b) single-port, bus-connected; (c) double-port, servicing disk and CPU on separate ports.

tense that speed of some important high-speed activity may be sacrificed. Because the CPU to memory path is normally high speed, a second port for the CPU may be added to the memory. Since data rates are high and overrun is possible, another port for backup store or bulk store may be provided. For example, a DEC PDP-10 may have several ports connected typically to CPU, disk, or special high-speed I/O. In some cases (e.g., the HP 1000), multiport memory is used to interface between autonomous buses in multiprocessor, multimemory systems; this allows, for example, the I/O and internal buses to communicate as needed through memory but to proceed normally without interference from each other's traffic.

Within a multiport memory there must, of course, be some form of interlock (*q.v.*) mechanism to arbitrate

conflict between port requests. Often a cyclic polling scheme insures access to memory by each of the ports on some priority basis with a guarantee of minimum service.

K. C. SMITH AND A. S. SEDRA

PRAGMATICS. *See* SYNTAX, SEMANTICS, AND PRAGMATICS.

PRECEDENCE

For articles on related subjects *see* EXPRESSION; GRAMMARS; POLISH NOTATION; and PROGRAMMING LINGUISTICS.

The subject of this article is operators in high-level languages and the types of precedence relations, or *hierarchy,* that exist among them.

As an example of the need for such relationships, consider the expression

$$A + B*C$$

Is this to be interpreted as $A + (B*C)$ or $(A + B)*C$? One way to solve this problem would be to enforce a strict left-to-right or (as in APL) a right-to-left order of evaluation. In APL, therefore, the expression is interpreted as $A + (B*C)$, but (also in APL) $C*B + A$ would be interpreted as $C*(B + A)$. To minimize the effect on interpretation of the order in which an expression is written, precedence relations among operators exist in most languages. A major purpose of such relations is to assure that as many expressions as possible have their "natural" interpretation (e.g., most people would regard $A + (B*C)$ as the natural interpretation of $A + B*C$).

The operator hierarchy includes not only arithmetic operators but also relational operators ($<$, $>$, $\leq$, $\geq$, $=$, $\neq$) and logical operators [$-$, $\wedge$, $\vee$, $\supset$, $\equiv$], as well as (in PL/I) the concatenation operator ($\|$). Table 1 gives the operator hierarchy in Fortran, Algol, and PL/I. It is to be interpreted as follows: In an expression containing more than one operator, the operator to be applied first is the one that is highest in the hierarchy. Thus,

	Expression	Interpretation
Fortran:	$A+B/C-D$	$A+(B/C)-D$
PL/I:	$-A*B$	$(-A)*B$
Algol:	$-A{\uparrow}B$	$-(A{\uparrow}B)$
	$A \wedge B \vee C$	$(A \wedge B) \vee C$

Note that the position of the relational and logical operators relative to the arithmetic operators is forced if

Table 1. Operator Hierarchy

	Fortran	Algol	PL/I
High	**	↑	¬** – (unary)
	/*	/* ÷	/*
	+ –	+ – (binary	+ –
	(binary	and unary)	
	and unary)		‖
	Relational	Relational	Relational
	operators	operators	operators
	.NOT.	¬	&
	.AND.	∧	∣
	.OR.	∨	
		⊃	
Low		≡	

+ Addition
– Subtraction
* Multiplication
/ Division
÷ Integer Division
Exponentiation: **, ↑
Negation: .NOT., ¬
Conjunction (logical product): .AND., ∧, &
Disjunction (logical sum): .OR., ∨, ∣
Implication: ⊃
Equivalence: ≡
Concatenation: ‖

expressions containing a combination of these operators are to be meaningful. Thus, the Fortran expression (.NE. means $\neq$)

$$A + B \text{ .NE. } C \text{ .OR. } D$$

makes sense only if interpreted as

$$((A + B) \text{ .NE. } C) \text{ .OR. } D$$

where D must be a variable of type logical.

When an expression contains two operators of equal precedence, the usual rule is to evaluate them from left to right with APL the chief exception (although in PL/I the highest precedence class is evaluated right to left). Thus $A/B * C$ is to be interpreted as $(A/B) * C$. Finally, in all languages, parentheses may always be used to override the precedence rules. Put another way, the precedence rules (or left-to-right rule) are never applied across parentheses.

REFERENCE

1973. Elson, M. *Concepts of Programming Languages*. Chicago: Science Research Associates.

A. RALSTON

PRECISION

For articles on related subjects *see* ARITHMETIC, COMPUTER; NUMBERS AND NUMBER SYSTEMS; SIGNIFICANCE ARITHMETIC; and SIGNIFICANT DIGIT.

For a numeric representation system that employs strings of symbols from a finite alphabet to represent numbers, the *precision attribute* of a symbol string denotes the *length* of the string, and possibly also positional information for determining a base point of the string. Those numbers representable by finite length symbol strings are termed the *finite precision numbers* of that numeric representation system.

For the fixed-point radix representation $d_m d_{m-1} \cdots d_1 d_0 \cdot d_{-1} d_{-2} \cdots d_l$, $d_m \neq 0$, the precision attribute is the triple $(m - l + 1, -l, m + 1)$; e.g., 310.25 has precision $(5, 2, 3)$ and 0.0024 has precision $(2, 4, -2)$. If $l \leq 0 \leq m$, then $-l$ and $m + 1$ may be interpreted as the number of digits in the fractional and integer parts, respectively, of the $m - l + 1$ digit number. The precision triple $(m - l + 1, -l, m + 1)$ thus provides both the number of digits and base-point normalization information.

For a radix number system where computed radix representations are truncated to exhibit only significant digits, the precision attribute identifies the significant digits. In this restricted environment, precision is a measure of accuracy. For integer radix-number systems such as the "8-digit decimal integers" or the "6-digit hexadecimal integers," the precision attribute provides simply a measure of the magnitude of the representable integers.

The precision attribute is utilized for numeric formats in input, output, and internal storage allocation in high-level programming languages. In PL/I, for example, precision rules are employed to compute the precision attribute of program variables at compile time to help optimize storage utilization.

Precision, as defined here, is intimately related to the displayed representation of a number in contrast to *accuracy*, which is concerned with freedom from error. Thus, a highly precise number (i.e., one displayed with many digits) may be quite misleading regarding accuracy since the accuracy would still be limited to the number of significant digits independent of the number of digits displayed.

REFERENCE

1976. Matula, D. W. "Radix Arithmetic: Digital Algorithms for Computer Architecture," in Yeh, R. (Ed.), *Applied Computation Theory: Analysis, Design and Modeling*. Englewood Cliffs, NJ: Prentice-Hall.

D. W. MATULA

PRINTING TECHNIQUES

For articles on related subjects *see* INPUT-OUTPUT
DEVICES.

Present-day printers used either for on-line or off-
line computer output fall into two main classes, impact
and non-impact printers, depending upon whether or not
there is impact of the printing element on the paper. In
this article, the main principles of the most commonly
used techniques are considered.

A printed character can be represented either by a
complete image formed by uninterrupted strokes or by
dots in close proximity so that they give the reader the
impression of having been printed by uninterrupted
strokes. Hence, printers are classified as face (or solid)
character or dot character (or simply dot matrix or mosaic) printers. Both categories include serial (character-
by-character) as well as parallel (line, or line-at-a-time)
printers.

Although there are several variants of the dot-character approach, the general principle behind them all is
to form each character from a matrix of dots. Unlike face
character printing methods, the printing elements are organized in columns or rows which print dots. Depending
upon whether used in serial or line printers, a character
in a dot matrix is formed sequentially by printing at one

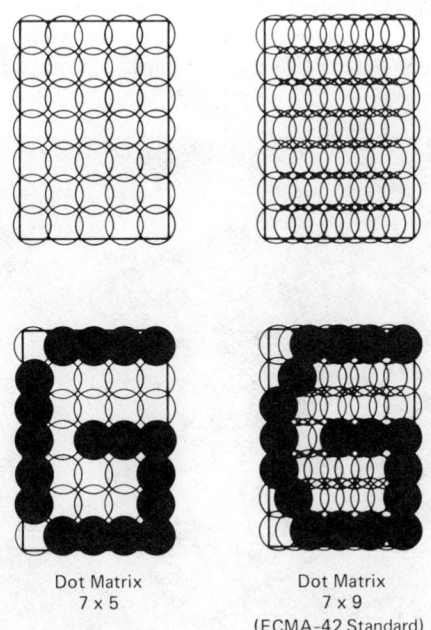

Dot Matrix
7 x 5

Dot Matrix
7 x 9
(ECMA-42 Standard)

Fig. 1. Comparison of two dot character matrices: 7
× 5 and 7 × 9 (ECMA-42 standard), using as
an example a printed image of the letter G.

time either all the selected dots, respectively, in a column,
or in a row.

The dot matrix print-head is under the control of the
electronic logic built into the printer and, by simply
changing the logic, can be made to reproduce any character set whatsoever within the limits of resolution imposed by the matrix size and such constraints as paper
and carriage movement possibilities. Theoretically, given
the proper conditions, any character set in any language
and even graphics can be produced by these methods.

The most common matrix size is 7 by 5 dots, the first
number indicating number of lines (or rows) and the second the number of columns in the matrix. However, several other matrix sizes, generally with larger numbers of
dots, are being used increasingly, so as to improve the
printed character image and/or to allow for a larger
character set. Often, the same number of printing elements (i.e., the number of dots printed at one time) is
used, but the number of printing steps is increased—for
example, from 7 by 5 to 7 by 9 in a serial printer, thereby
creating four column print positions, intermediate to the
previous five (as shown in Fig. 1). A further improvement
can be achieved by shifting the basic print positions not
only horizontally but also vertically; this would transform
the original 7 by 5 matrix into a 13 by 9 dot matrix.

Impact Printing Techniques. All impact
printer design is based on electromechanical principles,
sometimes with supplemental electronic improvements.

Face-Character Impact Printing Techniques. These
can be classified in five categories:

1. Type-bar printing.
2. Barrel printing.
3. Daisy wheel or petal printing.
4. Cylinder or drum printing.
5. Chain or train printing.

In parallel *type-bar printing,* there are as many type-
bars (and hammers) as there are print positions (or columns) on the line, thus avoiding the horizontal shifting of
the carriage. Each bar contains all the characters that
can be printed and is elevated to a print point determined
by the character being printed. Here it rests while being
struck by the hammer (plunger), and then it returns to
its home position. In the printing position, the character
to be printed faces the printing cylinder; the ribbon and
the paper move between them. This technique has been
used, for example, in some punched card accounting machines. Alphanumerical printers of this type operate at
100 lines per minute (lpm), and numerical ones at 150,
200, or 300 lpm.

A newer technique being used in some line printers

is based upon a single interchangeable type-bar, containing all the characters of a given set or multiples of its subsets. In contrast to the above method, the type-bar moves horizontally, parallel to the printed line, so that all characters pass all printing positions on the line. When a character reaches the position on the line where it is to be printed, a print magnet actuates the hammer (Fig. 2).

For serial type-bar printing, a technique is applied resembling that of a conventional typewriter. Here, the number of type-bars generally equals the number of different characters to be printed, each bar having a different character. The printing of a character is effected by actuating the type-bar with the appropriate character to be printed. After the type-bar returns to its home position, the carriage moves horizontally into the next print position on the line. Serial printers of this type operate at some 10 characters per second (chps).

On some typewriters and serial printers, the conventional type-bars and moving carriages have been replaced by a single type head of a "golf-ball" shape. This type head skims across the printed line while the typewriter or printer carriage does not move. As this head is removable, it may be changed for another type head with other than Roman script or with a different size of Roman font such as the elite or pica, or OCR-A, OCR-B, etc. These print-ers are still used by many computer manufacturers as console typewriters, interrogating typewriters, or as printers for small scientific or business computers (Fig. 3). The speed of these printers, when used as computer output devices, is up to 16 chps, which may be doubled by using two separate type heads to print in parallel on each half of the print line.

Another method for low-cost serial printers is that of the *print barrel*, in which the barrel head is cylindrical and contains several "rings" of print characters, along the length of the cylinder. To bring the required character into position, the barrel has to be rotated and also moved along the axis of the cylinder. Because of the mechanical requirements, the speed is limited to about 10 chps as, for example, in the widely used Model 33 Teletype of which over a million have been sold.

The major alternative to golf ball and barrel type serial printing is the so-called *daisy wheel* or *petal* printing technique; it uses a print mechanism which resembles a small spoked wheel, about 3 in. (7.5 cm) in diameter. Each "spoke" has a print character embossed on the tip, and the whole wheel revolves to allow the appropriate character to be positioned against the ribbon. The "spokes" are sometimes called petals, which is what led to the "daisy wheel" designation. This technique was introduced by Diablo in 1971 and shortly afterwards by Qume. This technology is used quite widely for operator console keyboards and word (text) processing systems (Fig. 4), etc. Current devices use either plastic, metalized, or metal printwheels which are easily exchangeable and which have speeds up to 55 chps.

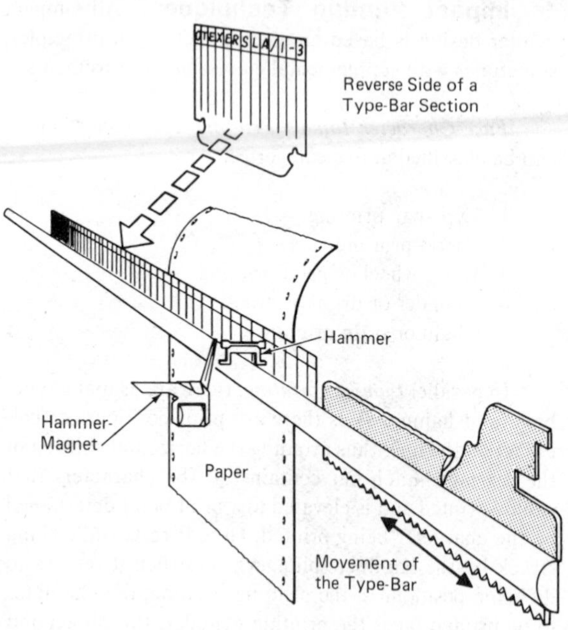

Fig. 2. Single-type-bar printing technique used in IBM 2203 line printer designed as a 360-20 model computer peripheral device. Four different interchangeable type-bars containing 13, 39, 52, or 63 character sets can be used with speeds of 750, 425, 330, or 300 lpm, respectively.

Fig. 3. IBM Selectric with rotating type head in use as a console unit.

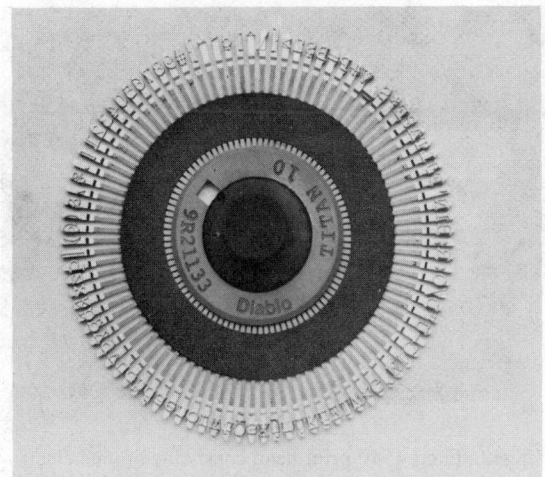

Fig. 4. A 96-character daisy wheel used in Diablo printers.

One of the oldest techniques used in line printer design was the *print cylinder (drum)* method, in which all characters in the character set were engraved on the surface of a rapidly rotating, solid cylinder. The printing here is effected by hammers that strike the paper at the moment when the appropriate character on the cylinder is in the correct position relative to the paper. This method is similar to one that uses multiple wheels locked together to form a print drum; it is also similar to the print barrel technique. Fig. 5 illustrates this principle.

Another device used with line printers is that of the *chain* or *train* of print slugs; these printers are referred to

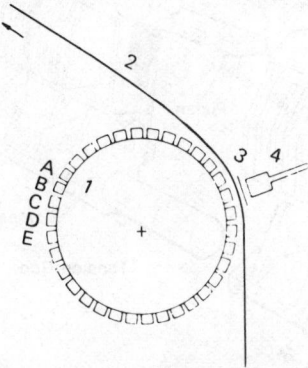

Fig. 5. Principle of barrel print technique (side view). (1) Print barrel, with type rows of characters on periphery equal to number of characters in set used. (2) Paper does not move. (3) Ink ribbon. (4) Print hammers equal number of print positions on a line.

as chain or train printers. As opposed to a cylinder which rotates in the direction of the vertical paper feed, the chain or train rotates horizontally, at right angles to the feed. The characters for printing may be linked together in a chain (Fig. 6) or in a train of print slugs. In the latter, there is no connecting band between characters so that the train moves at a velocity of more than double the chain.

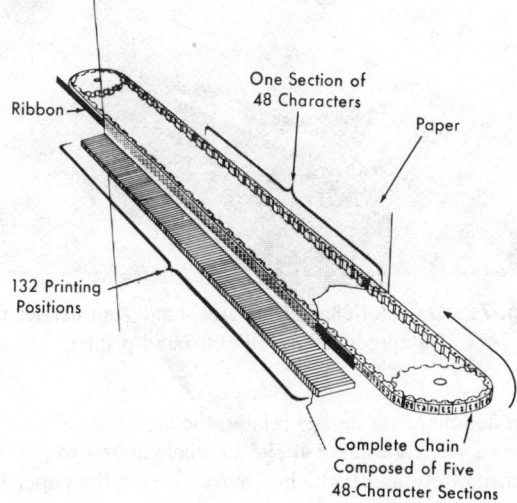

Fig. 6. Chain-type mechanism of the IBM 1403, Model 2 line printer.

Chain printers are becoming increasingly popular because any irregularities in timing show up as horizontal spacing variations between characters, and this is thought by many to be more acceptable to the eye than the vertical irregularities produced by timing inaccuracies on a cylinder printer. However, controlling the firing of hammers in such printers is much more complicated than on a cylinder.

Microprocessors are widely used in the present-day implementations of chain printers. At the slower end of the scale, there is, for example, the Dataproducts B-Series printers (Fig. 7). At the other end, the fastest impact printer on the market in 1980 was Documentation's microprocessor-controlled Impact 3000, whose speed is 3,000 lpm. In this printer, a lightweight metal alloy was used to construct the mechanical printing hammers mounted behind the paper. A microprocessor controller, which communicates with the host system, decodes commands, controls the printer, and reports errors and status.

Dot-Character Impact Printing Techniques. In these printers, the pins are generally electromagnetically or hydraulically actuated, and can be moved quickly. In a *se-*

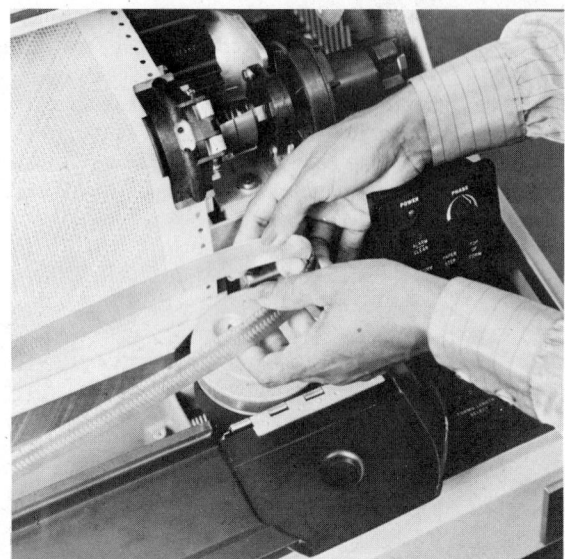

Fig. 7. Operator-changeable steel-band font carrier of Dataproducts' new B-600 Band printer.

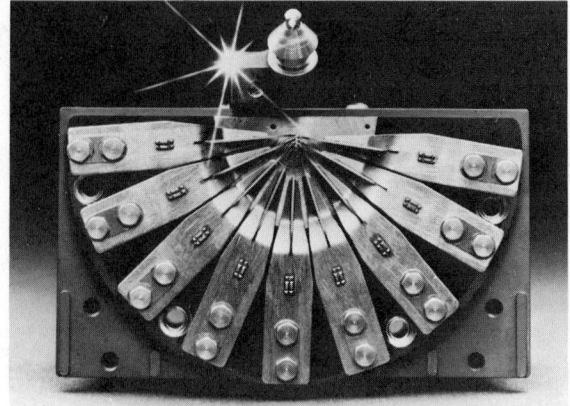

Fig. 8. Facit 4540 print head consisting of nine electromagnets with hammers to print a 9 by 9 dot matrix. It may be used, among others, to print OCR-A numerics.

rial dot-character impact printer, the head normally contains a vertical column of pins (a whole matrix of pins is rather rarely used) which is moved across the paper in minute steps, the number of steps being equal to that of columns in the respective matrix; the number of pins which are actuated at each step is varied in accordance with whichever character is required. Some devices, however, are able to reduce the number of steps required by eliminating those at both sides of a character in which no printing takes places as, for example, when printing the letter I.

An example of a device in this category is the Facit 4540 printer; its print-head may be equipped either with nine electromagnets with hammers to print a 9 by 9 dot matrix (Fig. 8) or, with seven electromagnets to print a 7 by 9 dot matrix following the ECMA-42 standard. This microcomputer-controlled bidirectional incremental printer operates at speeds of up to 250 chps and can accommodate up to 155 characters on a line.

Parallel dot-character impact printing is performed similarly to the serial, except that a whole horizontal line of dots is printed in parallel at one time.

As an example, the Hewlett-Packard 2608A medium-speed line printer uses a combined horizontal- and vertical-scan dot matrix technique to achieve print speeds of up to 400 lpm when printing upper case only with a 5 by 7 matrix, or up to 320 lpm when printing upper and lower case with a 5 by 9 dot matrix. The basic printing operation is the energizing and release of a cantilever steel tine (hammer) by an electromagnet (Fig. 9). To

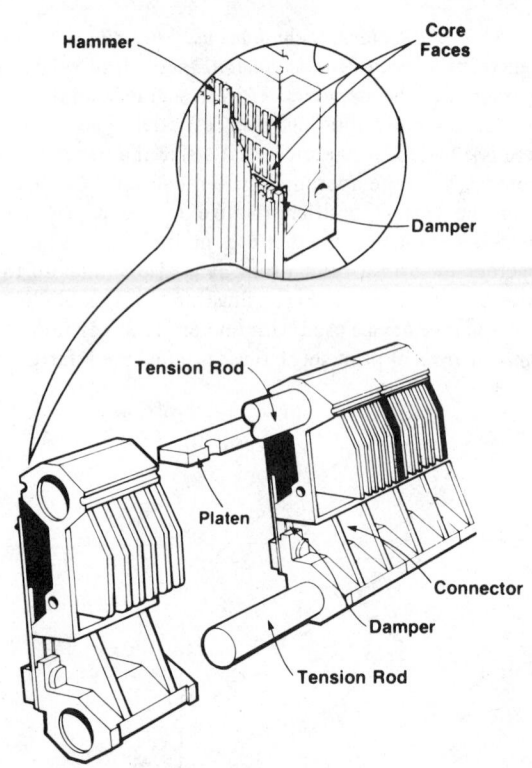

Fig. 9. Print hammer mechanism of the HP 2608A line printer using parallel dot character impact printing. Eleven modules holding 12 hammers each are clamped together by two tension rods to form a rigid bar that is moved back and forth by a linear (voice-coil) motor.

print a dot, the magnet draws the tip of the hammer away from the paper and then releases it. When released, the hammer snaps forward and a tungsten carbide sphere welded near its tip impacts the ribbon against the paper and platen, printing a dot 0.45 mm (0.018 in.) in diameter.

To print a complete character, the hammer and magnet are moved horizontally five dot positions, and dots are printed in the positions required by that character in that particular row of the dot matrix. The paper is then advanced 0.353 mm (0.0139 in.), the hammer and magnet reverse direction, and the next dot row of the character is printed. Seven rows of dots complete an upper case character. For lower-case characters, two more dot rows print the descenders (i.e., portions below the line), if required.

The mechanism has 132 hammers, spaced on 2.5 mm (0.1 in.) centers, that move horizontally as a unit. Any combination of hammers can be fired simultaneously, depending on the information being printed. The paper is pulled through the machine in discrete steps, one dot row at a time, and after each advance, the hammer and magnet assembly move horizontally to print all the data in that row for all the characters on that line.

The 2608A can be program-controlled to print characters which are twice the size of normal characters (the 5 by 7 matrix is doubled to 10 by 14). When printing double size characters, line spacing becomes either three or four lines per inch (depending on vertical spacing selection) and characters occupy two print columns instead of one.

Graphics are made possible by precisely positioning dots on a page. When in the graphic mode, the printer interprets each data byte as eight horizontal dot positions; i.e., 167_8 = 01110111 = .•••.••• A continuous line across the page contains 924 dots at a density of 70 dots per inch. Vertical dot density in the graphics mode is 72 dots per inch. This precise dot placement capability, combined with user written applications software, provides the potential for a virtually unlimited array of graphics output. Printers incorporating graphics capabilities are often called *printer/plotters*.

The trend towards matrix printers (impact and non-impact) is expected to continue, with one advantage of impact printers being the capability to produce up to six copies at a time.

Non-Impact Printing Techniques. In contrast to impact printers, non-impact printers work either without contact of the printing element with the paper or, as in the case of electrostatic electrophotographic methods, with a pressure non-impact contact only. Non-impact printers may also be divided into the face-character and dot-character categories.

Face-Character Non-Impact Printing Techniques. These are usually used in copying and reproducing machines rather than in data output printers. Exceptions are the computer printers which have the ability to print data as well as forms at the same time; for the printing of forms, these would use face-character non-impact printing techniques, usually the electrostatic electrophotographic process, rather imprecisely referred to as a "xerographic process."

Dot-Character Non-Impact Printing Techniques. Computer non-impact printers are almost all in this category. Several printing techniques are being used, all of them based upon three main principles—electrostatic (both electrophotographical and electrographical), thermographic, and ink-jet printing.

In *electrophotographical* techniques, a latent image is created by making use of the photoelectric characteristics of materials being used. The most common such technique is xerography. It is generally not applicable to serial printing, but recent developments in laser beam research using this technology operate in serial mode when preparing the latent image; the printing operation, however, takes place a whole page at a time.

As an example, in the Siemens 3352 laser printer, a laser beam is projected onto an acousto-optical deflector. Fed with vhf ultrasonic signals, the device acts as a diffraction grating for the coherent light. When the frequency is varied—the angle of the laser beam changes so that it fans out along the vertical axis. At the same time, the fan is moved in the horizontal axis by a multi-sided mirror (Fig. 10).

The scanning, amplitude-varying beam is directed onto a photoconductor drum which is charged electrically before exposure; it is then discharged at those points that are struck by the light beam. Charged toner powder adheres electrostatically to the exposed points and is transferred by the rotating drum to paper where heat and pressure produce the characters on the paper. A similar technique was also used in the earlier IBM 3800 laser printer. The Siemens printer has a top speed of 21,000 lpm, whereas that of the IBM printer is 13,360 lpm.

This is the appropriate place to mention COM (computer output on microfilm) printers, which are based on the electrophotographical principle of creating a latent image by an electron or laser beam, usually either directly on the microfilm, or via a CRT. However, the printing operation is quite different, resembling that which is commonly used in microfilm cameras containing (or attached to) developing equipment.

In *electrographical* techniques, the latent character or graphical picture is formed by transferring directly the electric charge from the writing elements—which may be, for example, a linear array or matrix of scanning styli

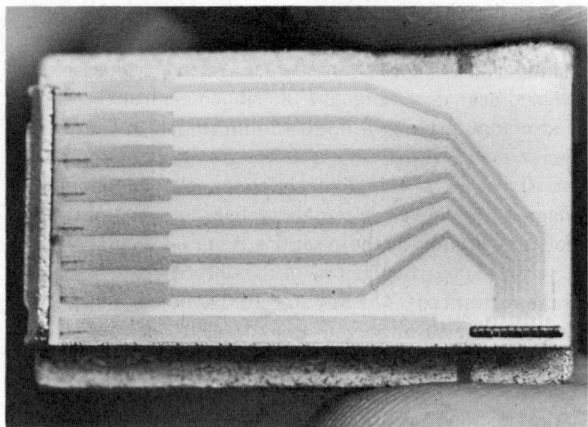

Fig. 11.   Print-head of the Dataproducts T-80 Thermal Printer. A 64 ASCII character subset is printed in dots using a 5 by 7 matrix. Plotting capabilities are provided using a 7 by 7 dot matrix.

Fig. 10.   Character generator of the Siemens 3352 (ND2) laser printer.

or appropriately shaped scanning electrodes—onto the dielectric coating of the recording paper medium.

As an example, the Centronics Microprinter 1 employs non-impact discharge technology that requires only four moving parts to produce variable pitch 8 by 5 dot matrix characters. The paper carries a conducting aluminized coating less than one micron thick, which is vaporized by a low voltage discharge from the print head to produce highly readable characters.

This electrographical principle has also been used in the high-speed Honeywell Page Printing System—PPS models I and II, which uses a matrix print head with a density of 200 dots per inch and operates at speeds of up to 18,000 lines or 210 pages a minute. To print document forms simultaneously with the data, the PSS uses a rotating engraved metal cylinder. Its minicomputer controller allows it to be programmed to cut the printed pages to specified lengths, punch holes for ring binders and produce multiple copies at one pass (by repeating the print operation of each page); printed output is decollated, burst, and stacked (similarly to the Xerox 9700 laser printer capabilities).

The *thermographic* principle is used with non-impact thermal printers. They work by using heating elements in the print head to create the character impression on a special heat-sensitive paper, which reduces the need for mechanical parts.

Fig. 11 shows the print head of the Dataproducts T-80 thermal printer which operates at 80 chps printing 80

column lines. Rather than apply constant heat to the matrix wires and lifting and moving the head from the paper to form each character (which is the technique normally used), the T-80 leaves the print head in constant contact with the sensitized paper. It alternately cools, heats, and cools the matrix wires as the head moves from left to right across the paper. This pulsed heating effect permits higher printing speeds and also simplifies the mechanics of the print head.

The *ink-jet* principle has been around for years and several manufacturers have tried to put theory into practice with varying degrees of success. This principle makes use of electrically charged droplets of ink, whose sensitivity to the electric field towards which they are fired causes the image of the character to be printed on standard quality paper (or on another substance, depending on application); the ink dries by its absorption into the paper.

The printers using the ink-jet principle are commonly divided into two groups; continuous printers and drop-on-demand printers. The latter eject ink from the nozzle only if needed, eliminating the encatchment and pumping mechanism needed in the previous group. One of the newest products on the market is the Siemens PT-80 ink-jet printer terminal which uses a vacuum principle to print up to 300 dot characters a second using a 12 by 9 matrix. The print-head comprises a linear array of 12 nozzles, each of which contains a vacuum except at the instant a droplet is ejected. Droplets can be released from individual nozzles on demand. Ejection is by means of shock wave from a piezoelectric transducer which momentarily increases nozzle pressure. Up to 3,500 droplets a second per nozzle can be released. Each one is 0.1 mm

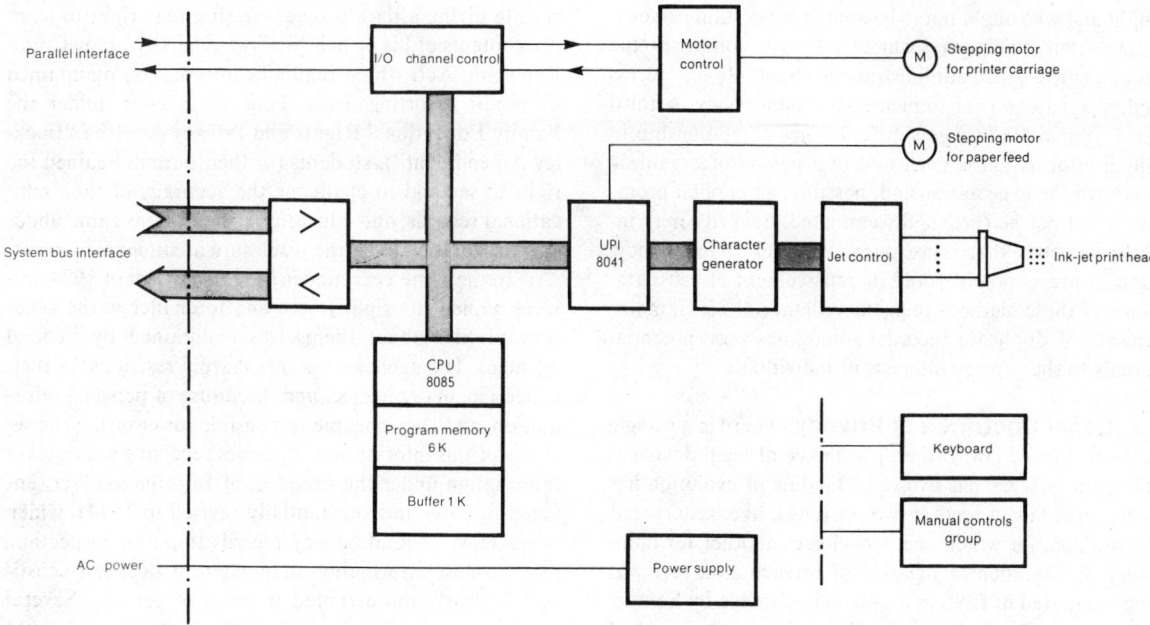

Fig. 12. Schematic diagram of the Siemens PT80 ink-jet printer terminal.

in diameter and produces a 0.3-mm diameter dot on standard paper 1.5 mm away. Nozzles are self-cleaning; any ink left in a nozzle tip is pulled back by the vacuum. The PT-80 is a microprocessor-controlled I/O device which operates at speeds up to 270 chps. The microprocessor controls the bidirectional print head movement and has an extended system information bus interface for external connection of data sets, network selectors, additional storage devices, etc. A schematic diagram of this device is shown in Fig. 12.

A bright future may be predicted for ink-jet and electrophotographic printers.

REFERENCE

1973. "Standard ECMA-42 for an Alphanumeric Character Set for 7 × 9 Matrix Printers," *ECMA Standards,* European Computer Manufacturers Association, Geneva.

J. NECAS

PRIVACY, COMPUTERS AND

For articles on related subjects *see* COMPUTING AND SOCIETY; CREDIT SYSTEMS APPLICATIONS; CRIME AND COMPUTER SECURITY; DATA BANK; DATA ENCRYPTION; DATA SECURITY; ELECTRONIC FUNDS TRANSFER SYSTEMS; and LEGAL ASPECTS OF COMPUTING.

Rapid improvements over the past 15 years in the technologies of computer processing, data storage and retrieval, and telecommunications have generated a growing social concern about the personal privacy of the *data subjects.* These are the individuals to whom much of the information collected and maintained by organizations pertains. (While the term *privacy* occasionally is used in reference to the protection of intellectual property and of proprietary data, it is used here in reference only to the protection of personal information.) In this context, privacy is generally understood as an individual's right to control certain aspects of the flow, content, and use of information pertaining to that individual, even though the information may be requested by, or be in the possession of, a governmental or private organization. Privacy rights are sometimes viewed as a moral issue—an aspect of personal dignity and autonomy. Such rights have become embodied increasingly, however, in legal doctrine, particularly in statutes pertaining directly to private and public data banks. An organization's policy with regard to the privacy of its data subjects is often guided by both moral and legal considerations. Following language proposed in a 1973 study by the Department of Health, Education, and Welfare, organizational policies pertaining to privacy rights are often called "Fair Information Practices."

Privacy and Security. Although the terms *privacy* and *security* are sometimes used interchangeably, privacy properly comprises issues of policy (e.g., who ought and who ought not to be able to see certain personal information), whereas security properly comprises the technological and administrative means (e.g., access codes, signatures) for implementing such policy. A third term, *confidentiality,* generally denotes a relationship in which information is entrusted to a person or organization with the expectation and, possibly, an explicit promise that it not be further disseminated. Security may include methods that serve purposes other than privacy, such as prevention of fraud or replacement of lost data. Some of these methods (e.g., surveillance of users, maintenance of duplicate records) sometimes pose potential threats to the privacy interests of individuals.

Legal Doctrines of Privacy. There is no single body of privacy law; rather, a melange of legal doctrines related to privacy has evolved. One line of evolution has been in the law of *torts* (private wrongs, like battery and defamation, for which one person sues another for damages). Recognition of invasion of privacy as a tort was first suggested in 1890 in a law review article by Samuel Warren and Louis Brandeis. Soon afterwards, a set of privacy-related torts became recognized in the various states, either by the courts directly or through legislation. William Prosser summarizes these torts as follows: (1) intrusion upon a person's seclusion, or into his or her private affairs, (2) public disclosure of embarrassing private facts, (3) placing a person in a false light in the public eye, and (4) appropriation of a person's name or likeness for another's advantage.

The other major line of privacy evolution has been in Constitutional law. While the Constitution nowhere mentions privacy explicitly, several of the rights in the first ten amendments embody aspects of privacy: Freedom from unreasonable search and seizure (Fourth), right against self-incrimination and right to due process (Fifth), freedom of assembly and of religion (First), and even the freedom from the quartering of troops in a person's home (Third). However, it was not until 1965 that the Supreme Court looked at these rights collectively in order to recognize a constitutional right to privacy within certain zones of activity. A woman's decision to have an early abortion, for example, was found in 1973 to be a private activity in which the state cannot interfere. Other Constitutional rights, most notably freedom of speech and of the press, conflict inherently with the right to privacy.

Computer-Era Privacy Legislation. In the mid-sixties, a proposed National Data Center sparked Congressional interest in privacy, apparently because it raised the specter of George Orwell's "Big Brother" society. Concern over large databases containing personal dossiers grew to include the private sector, and the first

statute giving a data subject the (limited) right to learn the contents of his or her "file" was the 1970 Fair Credit Reporting Act, which regulates information maintained by credit reporting firms. Four years later, under the Family Educational Rights and Privacy Act (the "Buckley Amendment"), students (or their parents) gained the right to see and to challenge the accuracy of their educational records, and educational institutions came under strict regulation as to the disclosure of students' records.

In the same year, under the Privacy Act of 1974, citizens gained the right to see and to challenge the accuracy of files about themselves maintained by Federal agencies. The agencies became sharply restricted in their collection, maintenance, and disclosure of personal information, and they became responsible for ensuring the security of this information. Agencies receiving requests for information under the Freedom of Information Act (enacted in 1966 and substantially revised in 1974), which opens most Federal agency records to public inspection, may disclose information only where it does not constitute a clearly unwarranted invasion of privacy. Several states have enacted fair information practices statutes similar to the Privacy Act of 1974 for the regulation of data in state agencies.

The Privacy Act also created a Privacy Protection Study Commission, which, between 1975 and 1977, studied possible privacy abuses in the private sector. The commission concluded that private organizations often collect, maintain, and exchange information about individuals for purposes going beyond the relationships they may have with those individuals, and that individuals have neither the legal nor technological means of protecting their legitimate rights in these records. The commission recommended a series of reforms, particularly in the area of medical, insurance, and financial records. It also recommended a voluntary program that would give employees the right to see and to challenge the accuracy of personnel files. In 1978, the Right to Financial Privacy Act was enacted, restricting the flow of a customer's bank records to Federal authorities. In 1979, the Carter administration introduced major bills for the purpose of protecting privacy (1) of medical records, (2) of research subjects, (3) of bank, credit, and insurance records, and (4) in electronic funds transfer systems but none became law.

Public Concern About Computers and Privacy. The results of a national opinion survey conducted in December 1978 by Louis Harris and Alan Westin indicated a substantial and growing public concern about threats to privacy. Sixty-four percent of the adult population polled were "very concerned" or "somewhat concerned," compared to 47% a year earlier (50% of the computer industry executives polled shared this concern).

Fifty-four percent of the public (and 53% of computer executives) believed that present uses of computers are an actual threat to privacy.

REFERENCES

1890. Warren, Samuel D. and Brandeis, Louis D. "The Right to Privacy," *Harvard Law Review* 4:193–220.

1960. Prosser, William L. "Privacy," *Columbia Law Review* 48:383–423.

1971. Miller, Arthur R. *The Assault on Privacy*. Ann Arbor, MI: University of Michigan Press.

1972. National Academy of Sciences, Computer Science and Engineering Board, Project on Computer Databanks. *Databanks in a Free Society*. Westin, Alan F. (Project Director) and Baker, Michael A. (Assistant Project Director). New York: Quadrangle Books.

1973. U.S. Department of Health, Education, and Welfare, Secretary's Advisory Committee on Automated Personal Data Systems. *Records, Computers, and the Rights of Citizens*. Cambridge, MA: M.I.T. Press.

1977. U.S. Privacy Protection Study Commission. *Personal Privacy in an Information Society*. Washington, D.C.: U.S. Government Printing Office, Superintendent of Documents, Stock No. 052-003-00395-3.

1979. *The Dimensions of Privacy: A National Opinion Research Survey of Attitudes Toward Privacy*. Stevens Point, WI: Sentry Insurance.

J. A. MELDMAN

PRIVILEGED INSTRUCTION

For articles on related subjects *see* INPUT-OUTPUT INSTRUCTIONS; INTERRUPT; MACHINE INSTRUCTION SET; OPERATING SYSTEMS: Principles; and SUPERVISOR CALL.

Improper use of certain instructions can easily affect system integrity in a multiuser environment. These instructions usually include storage protection setting, interrupt handling, timer control, I/O, and special processor status-setting instructions.

In order to prevent accidental or intentional misuse of these instructions, many computers have a special privileged mode in which instructions of the aforementioned type, called *privileged instructions*, can be executed. In a processor that possesses such a mode, the instructions are divided into sets; each set can be executed in its own mode. The privileged mode includes *all* instructions, whereas all other modes include some of them. The number of modes may be one (which means essentially the absence of a privileged mode) or two (one user mode and one privileged mode) or more. In the case of the PDP 11/45, for example, the computer has three modes: user, supervisor, and kernel (*q.v.*).

One way of handling the attempted execution of a privileged instruction in a nonprivileged state is an illegal instruction trap, causing an interrupt. Another is to ignore it completely, which is equivalent to the former if the interrupt is disabled.

Another possible approach to the division of instructions into privileged and user subsets is to structure the computing system into two or more independent processors each dedicated to one subset. Such division was originally made, for example, in the CDC 6000 series of computers. In those machines, the central processor had no instructions that caused any system functions unless explicitly directed to do so by another processor. (This was later changed by adding one additional instruction to the central processor.)

G. FRIEDER

PROBABILISTIC AUTOMATA

For articles on related subjects *see* AUTOMATA THEORY; FORMAL LANGUAGES; SEQUENTIAL MACHINES; and STOCHASTIC PROCESS.

A probabilistic or stochastic automaton (pa) [sequential machine (psm)]—in what follows all bracketed comments refer to psm's—is a device with a finite number of internal states, scanning input words over a finite alphabet and responding by successively changing its state in a probabilistic way [and printing output words probabilistically, over a finite output alphabet].

Let ρ be a vector with entries ρ_i representing the probability that the automaton [machine] was in its ith state to begin with; let $A(x)$ [$A(y|x)$] be a matrix with entries $a_{ij}(x)$ [$a_{ij}(y|x)$] representing the probability that the automaton moved to state j from state i [the machine printed the symbol y and moved to state j from state i] upon scanning the input symbol x. Let η be a column vector with some entries equal to one, the other entries being equal to zero [with all entries equal to one]. Then,

$$p(x_1 \cdots x_k) = \rho A(x_1) \cdots A(x_k)\eta$$
$$[p(y_1 \cdots y_k | x_1 \cdots x_k) = \rho A(y_1|x_1) \cdots A(y_k|x_k)\eta]$$

is a function representing the probability that the automaton entered a designated final state [the machine printed the output word $y_1 \cdots y_k$] after scanning the input word $x_1 \cdots x_k$. The function p can be used as a sorting criterion to define the probabilistic language consisting of all input words $x_1 \cdots x_k$ with $p(x_1 \cdots x_k) > \lambda$, λ being a preassigned given threshold.

The study of pa's is concerned mainly with the study of probabilistic languages, their closure properties and relation to other types of formal languages. The study of psm's is concerned with the input/output relations induced by the machines, minimization of states, and other problems connected with input/output information systems with random characteristics.

Example. Consider a physical system (or animal) assumed to be in one of two possible states (healthy or ill), with probabilities 0.2 and 0.8 correspondingly. If a sequence of stimuli (medicines) is applied to the system (animal), it undergoes probabilistically successive changes of its states. Assume that the transition characteristics of the first stimulus are as depicted in Fig. 1

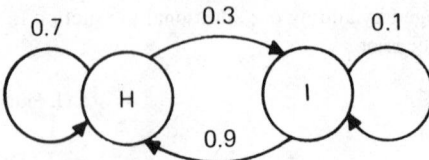

Fig. 1.   Transition characteristics.

which is to be interpreted as meaning that with probabilities 0.7 and 0.3, the system will stay in its first state, or will go to the second state, respectively, if the stimulus has been applied while the system was in its first state, etc. The probabilities of being in one of the two states after the application of the first stimulus (after swallowing the medicine) will then be

$$(0.2 \quad 0.8) \begin{pmatrix} 0.7 & 0.3 \\ 0.9 & 0.1 \end{pmatrix} = (0.86 \quad 0.14)$$

and the process will continue in the same way.

REFERENCES

1969. Carlyle, J. W. "Stochastic Finite-State System Theory," in Zadeh, L. A. and Polak, E. (Eds.), *System Theory.* New York: McGraw-Hill, Chap. 10.
1971. Paz, A. *Introduction to Probabilistic Automata.* New York: Academic Press.

A. PAZ

PROBLEM-ORIENTED LANGUAGES

For articles on related subjects *see* COMMAND AND JOB CONTROL LANGUAGES; ENGINEERING APPLICATIONS; PROCEDURE-ORIENTED LANGUAGES; PROGRAMMING LANGUAGES; and SIMULATION: Languages.

The term *problem-oriented* languages, if taken literally, is too general to be useful in the taxonomy of programming languages. In its most general meaning, one would have to include any programming language that helps solve problems. Thus, Fortran is a problem-oriented language when one solves scientific or numeric problems. Cobol (COmmon Business-Oriented Language) is problem oriented, even in its title, for business problems. However, accepted usage in computer science literature has imposed a narrower context for problem-oriented languages than one that could encompass Fortran and Cobol. From this more restricted point of view, synonyms for *problem-oriented* are *applications-oriented* or *special-purpose.*

This article discusses a number of applications-oriented and special-purpose programming languages. Some languages have been designed for very special applications such as numerical control programming or electronic circuit analysis. Others are applications oriented, but at the same time are more general purpose. Examples of these would include simulation languages, statistical packages, and information retrieval systems. Discussion of the more general-purpose, problem-oriented languages is found in other sections of this Encyclopedia.

Numerous problem-oriented languages have been developed. It is obvious that this article can only touch upon a small part of the vast work that has been done in this field. Many of these languages have been described in Sammet (1969) and in her subsequent rosters of programming languages published in a number of journals, including the Association for Computing Machinery's *SIGPLAN Notices* (see Sammet, 1978). According to these rosters, the number of problem-oriented languages has consistently represented about half of all the high-level languages used in the U.S. The best source of technical information about a language is generally the reference manuals provided by the developers or suppliers of the software.

Before looking at specific problem-oriented languages in current usage, we present an example of one of the earliest such languages and then review the characteristics of the more commonly used languages in numerical control, civil engineering, and electrical engineering. Finally, we will have a few things to say about trends in the future use and development of problem-oriented languages.

An Early Problem-Oriented Language— DYANA. Shortly after the successful introduction of Fortran as a programming language for scientific and engineering calculations, the General Motors Research Laboratories developed a specialized language for describing vibrational and other dynamic systems. DYANA (dynamic analyzer) was developed originally for the IBM 704 in 1958 and was an extension of Fortran. See Theodoroff (1958).

DYANA provided for the definition of variables to specify the elements, excitation, and dependent and independent variables in a dynamic system. These variables have meaning in both Fortran and non-Fortran statements. The variables are constructed in such a way as to define the topology of the mechanical system. Fig. 1 illustrates a simple mechanical system. The topology of the system is contained in the variables themselves, using the letters E for element, K for spring, M for mass, F for force, etc. For example, E03K02 stands for the spring element, which is contained between the two elements 03 and 02. E03K02 is also used as the coefficient of damping for that spring element when the variable appears in Fortran arithmetic or input/output statements.

In Fig. 1, the DYANA language is first used to define the system description (group 1). This is done by list-

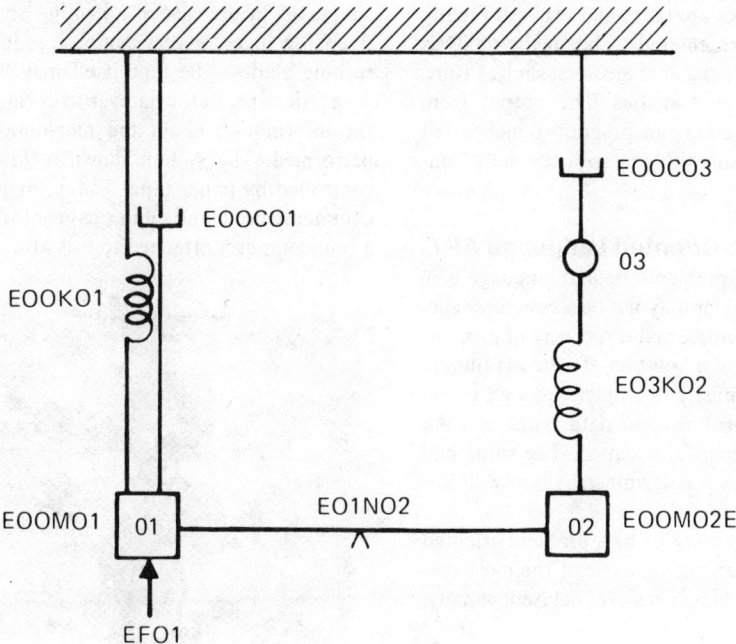

INPUT WITH DIAGNOSTIC COMMENTS FLAGGED BY AN X

X	SYSTEM DESCRIPTION	CARD	1
	EOOMO1,EOOMO2,EOOKO1,EOOCO1,EOOCO3	CARD	2
	EO3KO2,EO1NO2,EFO1	CARD	3
X	PRE-COMPUTATION	CARD	4
	EO3KO2 = 2.4 + 0.6 * EOOKO1	CARD	5
X	DAMPING RATE, EOOCO3(XO3)	CARD	6
	EOOCO3 = A * XO3 + B	CARD	7
X	FORCE, EFO1	CARD	8
	EFO1 = F *SINF(W *TIME)	CARD	9
X	INPUT VARIABLES	CARD	10
	A,B,F,W	CARD	11
X	PRINT PRECOMPUTATION ANSWERS	CARD	12
	EOOMO1,EOOMO2,EOOKO1,EOOCO1,EO3KO2,EO1NO2,A,B,F,ɅV	CARD	13
X	PRINT TIME DEPENDENT ANSWERS	CARD	14
	TIME,EFO1,XO1,XO2,XO3,DXO1,DXO2	CARD	15
X	TRANSLATIONAL	CARD	16
X	TRANSIENT	CARD	17
X	END	CARD	18

Fig. 1. Sample DYANA program. (From J. E. Sammet, *Programming Languages: History and Fundamentals*, Prentice-Hall, 1969.)

ing all system elements, with each element name showing its relationship to each other element, and defining its type (mass, spring, force, etc.).

Next (group 2), a series of Fortran arithmetic statements specify the functional relationship of the coefficients of damping of the two spring elements, the damping rate of element E00C03 as a function of the displacement of the point 03, and the forcing function EF01. Next (group 3), parameters *A, B, F,* and *W,* and the other initial conditions are input and printed. Finally (group 4), statements are entered to begin the analysis and printout of the time-dependent answers, such as time, force, displacements, and velocities. The output from DYANA was a complete Fortran program punched out on cards and ready to run with the requisite set of numerical data.

Using a Problem-Oriented Language APT.

The essential goal of any problem-oriented language is to provide the user, who may or may not be a computer specialist, with a relatively simple and direct way of expressing a problem for computer solution. To be maximally effective, the language must be complete enough to express the functions, algorithms, and data types that are normally used in the specific application. The value and effectiveness of a language is determined by how well this criterion is met.

To illustrate the process of using a problem-oriented language, we present as an example one of the most successful problem-oriented languages ever devised, namely, APT (IIT, 1967).

APT stands for *automatically programmed tools.* It was first developed at M.I.T. in the early 1950s to assist in the production of punched tapes for numerically controlled machine tools. The early versions of APT were restricted to two-dimensional objects, using only straight lines and circles. Later developments, which were sponsored by the Aerospace Industries Association, resulted in a system called APT II. APT II utilized a specialized language to describe geometric surfaces. In the 1960s the APT Long-Range Program, sponsored by numerous industries and conducted by the Illinois Institute of Technology Research Institute, developed APT III, which eventually became the de facto standard for numerical control applications. Most of the currently used languages for numerical control programming are extensions, variations, or subsets of APT.

The APT System. The utilization of numerical control for machine tools is one of the most significant modern developments in manufacturing. It has made possible the machining of components of great complexity, with tolerance conditions and repeatability never attained by conventional machining methods. It has provided great flexibility and economy in the production of both simple and complex parts. Numerical control (N/C) has been applied to milling machines, drilling and boring machines, lathes, machining centers, automatic wiring machines, welding and flame-cutting machines, etc.

To utilize an N/C tool, one must prepare a control tape that has recorded on it a description of all motions and machine functions required to fabricate the part on the tool. The control program on the tape may be very simple, as in the case of a drilling application with relatively few holes, or very complex, as in the case of milling turbine blades. The tape itself may be punched tape or magnetic tape, but, whatever its form, it must contain all the information about the machining operations to be performed. The system shown in Fig. 2 is numerically controlled by paper tape. Today, magnetic tape is more commonly used, and numerical control of the machine by a minicomputer attached to it is also common.

Fig. 2. Large milling machine numerically controlled by paper tape units (behind glass in center). Units at left record information on paper tape received from remote computer, which is then transferred to unit at center. (Courtesy of Illinois Institute of Technology Research Institute.)

In all but the simplest applications, a certain number of computations must be performed before the control tape can be produced. In the case of continuous path-control systems, literally thousands of computations must be performed to prepare a control tape. It is only natural, then, that computers have been applied to the preparation of control tapes for N/C tools. The words *symbolic control* have been used to describe this application of computers. Symbolic control describes a process wherein a human controls a machine through the use of language (i.e., symbols), and wherein the computer serves as the translator and calculator to produce the numerical signals for controlling the machine.

The APT system includes a programming language, which provides a vocabulary for describing the geometry, motions, and machine functions necessary to produce a part using N/C, and a group of computer programs, which translate the APT language, perform the required calculations, and produce the control tape. The individual who prepares the APT program is called a *part programmer*. The APT language provides the part programmer with a vocabulary to describe a large variety of two- and three-dimensional part geometry, to define tool shape, to specify tolerance, to command cutter motion, to indicate machining functions, to perform in-line computations, and to execute program logic and specify geometric transformations. These features, when used individually and in combination, offer the part programmer the possibility of producing simple or complex parts efficiently and economically.

The APT Language. We will illustrate the APT language by describing the process of writing a part program for a two-dimensional cam (Fig. 3). The APT language is used to:

1. Give names or symbols to the different geometrical elements of the part.
2. Describe the dimension and shape of the tool with which the part is to be cut.
3. Specify the computational tolerance. This tolerance is used by the computer to calculate the offset of the tool from the surfaces of the part and to determine successive cutter locations. By changing tolerances from run to run, machining can be varied from rough cuts to finer cuts.
4. Define the geometry of the part.
5. Describe the motion of the tool. Here, the part programmer acts as if sitting on the tool and driving it, like a car, around the part.
6. Specify auxiliary functions of the controller-machine tool combination.

With these elements, one obtains the part program shown in Fig. 3. The APT computer system calculates successive cutter positions to fabricate the part specified, taking into account the defined tool shape, the tolerances, part geometry, and tool motions contained in the part program.

This application is typical of the procedures used in a problem-oriented language. The problem is defined in terms of variables and data types (points, lines, circles, ellipses, etc., in APT), certain declarations are invoked to establish proper environment (cutter specifications, tool positions, coordinate transformations, tolerance, etc., in APT), and then statements are executed in a specific order to produce the desired result (tool motion, program logic, arithmetic operations, input/output control, etc., in APT). These same types of expressions, declarations, and statements are found in one form or another in all languages considered here.

Civil Engineering Applications. Some of the most active development of problem-oriented languages has been for civil engineering applications. The computer was recognized very early as an invaluable tool to the civil engineer in performing the numerous calculations and in handling the complex data that are involved in the design and construction of bridges, building highways, harbors, etc.

The solution of civil engineering problems involves many disciplines. For example, in the design of a highway interchange, the engineer utilizes surveying, highway engineering, soil mechanics, structural engineering, hydraulic engineering, transportation engineering, etc. Computer aids to each of these fields have been developed over the past 20 years. Recent work has been done in combining these separate applications into an integrated package of programs known as ICES (Integrated Civil Engineering System). This section discusses some of the work that led up to the design and implementation of ICES, and then discusses ICES as an example of a unified system approach to problem-oriented languages.

Cogo. Cogo (coordinate geometry) is a programming language used to perform the geometric calculations required in surveying. It was developed originally by Professor C. Miller of the M.I.T. Civil Engineering Department around 1960. It is now available on most computers and has been also implemented under several time-sharing systems.

Cogo provides the civil engineer with a large number of commands and associated programs to perform plane geometry computations. Some examples of Cogo commands are given below.

DIVIDE/LINE	To divide a line into a specified number of segments.
LOCATE/AZIMUTH	To define a point, given the distance and azimuth from a specified point.
AREA	To calculate the area of a triangle, given the three vertices.

Stress. Structural Engineering Systems Solver (Stress) was developed (Fenves, 1964) with the objective of facilitating the use of computers in analyzing structures. The principal objective of Stress was to provide a

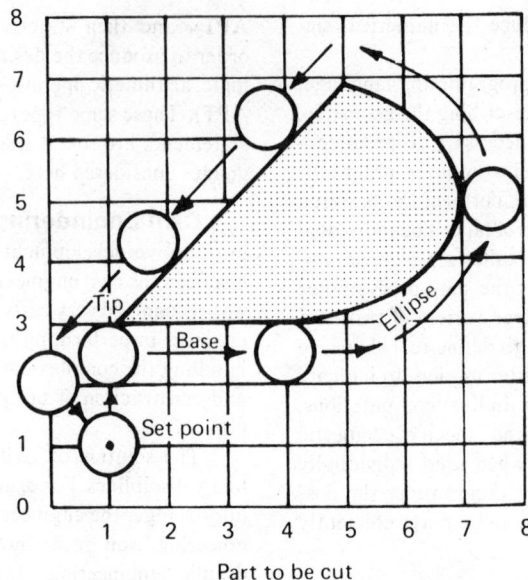

Part to be cut

Part Program	Explanation
CUTTER/1	Use a 1 in. diameter cutter.
TOLER/.005	Tolerance of cut is 0.005 in.
FEDRAT/80	Move tool at feed rate of 80 in./min.
HEAD/1	Use head #1.
SPINDL/2400	Turn on spindle. Set at 2,400 rpm.
COOLNT/FLOOD	Turn on coolant. Use flood setting.
PT1 = POINT/4,5	Define point PT1, as point with coordinates (4,5), used later to define ellipse.
FROM/(SETPT = POINT/1,1)	Start tool from point called SETPT, defined as point with coordinates (1,1).
INDIRP/(TIP = POINT/1,3)	Aim tool in direction of point called TIP, defined as point with coordinates (1,3).
BASE = LINE/TIP, AT ANGL, 0	Define line called BASE as line through point TIP, which makes angle of 0 deg. with horizontal.
GO/TO, BASE	Go to the line BASE.
TL RGT, GO RGT/BASE	With tool on right of part with respect to direction of motion, go right along line BASE until tangency with next surface, the ellipse, is reached.
GO FWD/(ELLIPS/CENTER,PT1, 3,2,0)	Go forward along ellipse with center at PT1, semi-major axis = 3, semi-minor axis = 2, and major axis making angle of 0 deg with horizontal.
GO LFT/(LINE/2,4,1,3,), PAST, BASE	Go left along line joining points (2,4) and (1,3) past line BASE.
GOTO/SETPT	Go to point SETPT in a straight line.
COOLNT/OFF	Turn off coolant flow.
SPINDL/OFF	Turn off spindle.
END	This is end of machine control unit operation,
FINI	and the finish of part program.

Fig. 3. An APT program for the two-dimensional cam shown at top. (From J. E. Sammet, *Programming Languages: History and Fundamentals*, Prentice-Hall, 1969.)

wide variety of structural analyses with a minimum of programming effort. It can be used to analyze two- and three-dimensional structures, with either pinned or rigid joints, with prismatic or nonprismatic members, and subjected to concentrated or distributed loads, support motions, or temperature effects.

Stress was developed in the early 1960s under the direction of Professor S. J. Fenves at M.I.T. Numerous computer implementations of this language have been accomplished since this early work. The following statements are examples of types found in Stress.

Header Statement. The word STRUCTURE followed by any identifying information serves to start a new problem.

Size Descriptors. Several statements are needed to define the size of the problem to be handled. These include:

    NUMBER OF JOINTS
    NUMBER OF SUPPORTS
    NUMBER OF MEMBERS
    NUMBER OF LOADINGS

Structural Data Descriptors. To describe completely a framed structure, it is necessary to provide information about its geometry, topology (interconnection of members and joints), mechanical properties (load-deflection relationships of the members), and the presence of local releases (such as hinges or rollers). Six types of statements are provided:

1. Geometry is specified in terms of joint coordinates by the statement

    JOINT COORDINATES

followed by the *X, Y, Z* coordinates of each joint (or *X, Y* for plane structures). These statements are also used to describe the status (i.e., free or support) of the joints.

2. The presence of hinges or rollers at support joints is given as

    JOINT RELEASES

followed by the joint numbers and the designation and orientation of the released (zero) force components.

3. The interconnection of the members is specified by the statement

    MEMBER INCIDENCES

followed by a list giving the starting and ending joint of each member. The meaning of this state-

ment is best illustrated by the descriptive input form, which for a typical member may be MEMBER 17 GOES FROM JOINT 10 TO JOINT 7.

4. The load-deflection properties of the members are specified as

    MEMBER PROPERTIES

followed by a statement for each member, giving the type of member, and the labels and numerical values of the properties.

5. The presence of hinges in the members is given as

    MEMBER RELEASES

followed by the member numbers, and the position and orientation of the released force components.

6. Constants associated with the members are specified by the

    CONSTANTS

statement.

Loading Data Descriptors. The loading applied to the structure is specified in terms of loading condition descriptors, descriptors of individual loads, and descriptors of groups of loads, as follows.

The word

    LOADING

followed by any identifying information, delineates groups of loads (together comprising a loading condition) and serves as a loading condition header.

Individual loads are specified by statements such as

    JOINT LOADS

followed by the joint numbers and the components of applied load,

    JOINT DISPLACEMENTS
    MEMBER DISTORTIONS
    MEMBER LOADS

followed by a statement for each load, giving the member number, the orientation, magnitude, and type of the load.

Certain loading specifications involve general information such as

    COMBINE

followed by a list of loading conditions to be combined.

Modification Descriptors. To permit rapid evaluation of alternate designs, the following statements can be used after an initial problem has been defined.

MODIFICATION   (with information for output identification)

ADDITIONS   (interspersed with pertinent
CHANGES   statements of all the above types
DELETIONS   describing the modification)

Termination Statements. These statements terminate the input of portions of or all statements of a problem:

SOLVE
SOLVE THIS PART
FINISH

ICES. The problem-oriented languages discussed to this point have provided the user with language capability to solve very special problems, such as producing tapes for numerically controlled machine tools, solving problems in plane geometry, and performing structural analysis. The integrated civil engineering system (ICES), on the other hand, was designed to function as a series of subsystems, each subsystem corresponding to an engineering discipline (Roos, 1967). Each subsystem in ICES utilizes its own data structure; nevertheless, it provides for common files of problem data. ICES also provides an engineering programming language, command-definition language, and data-definition language to create subsystems. Thus, ICES is a framework within which engineering programs can be embedded.

The engineering programming language is Icetran, which is an extension of Fortran designed to handle civil engineering programming. With Icetran, a programmer can develop problem-oriented subsystems that become part of the ICES package.

To provide for a common method of defining the language elements, the subsystem designer makes use of a command-definition language (CDL) to specify the commands needed for the necessary problem-solving capabilities, as well as the external data requirements and the internal data processing required for each command. This information is transmitted to the computer in the command-definition language. The command-definition language requests are processed by the command-definition system program (an ICES subsystem), which produces a command dictionary, a COMMON map, and command data blocks for the subsystem. The dictionary and the command data blocks are used by ICEX, the ICES executive program, which processes the engineer's problem-oriented language commands.

There are two types of commands in ICES: system commands and subsystem commands. System commands are used by an engineer to specify the name of the ICES subsystem to be used. Examples of system commands are Cogo, Strudl (structural design language), Sepol (settlement problem-oriented language), etc. Subsystem commands refer to the engineering commands in each subsystem. The engineer specifies the appropriate system command, followed by the relevant subsystem commands. Assume, for example, that a structural engineer is working on a bridge-design problem. First the BRIDGE system command will be given, followed by BRIDGE subsystem commands. Then to design the bridge geometry, the Cogo system command will be issued, followed by the Cogo subsystem commands. After the bridge geometry has been calculated, the BRIDGE system command will be issued, which returns to the bridge subsystem.

Thus, the essence of ICES is the generation of appropriate subsystems for specific engineering applications, which are then used to solve a given class of problems. Once a new subsystem is generated, it becomes a part of the ICES package. The generation of a subsystem requires that a programmer:

1. Write a description of each subsystem command in CDL.
2. Write programs in Icetran to carry out the computations.
3. Design the load module structure.
4. Design the subsystem COMMON area.

Example Subsystem. As an example, let us consider the generation of a subsystem to analyze simple beams. The specifications for this subsystem will permit the engineer to input the length of the beam and a set of uniform and/or concentrated loads acting on it, and to obtain as output the reactions at the left and right ends resulting from this loading. After examining the reactions, the engineer could add new loads to the beam and recompute the reactions. Loadings may be deleted by applying negative loads to the beam. Only one beam will be maintained by the system at a time.

Summarized below is the information which the subsystem designer must specify to the ICES system.

Internal Structure. The data necessary for this subsystem are (1) the length of the beam, and (2) the position and magnitude of each load. Since only one beam is considered at a time, the beam length is stored as a scalar in COMMON. The information relating to each load is stored in dynamic arrays. The size of each dynamic subarray is determined by the type of loading (specification of a concentrated load requires less information than does specification of a uniform load).

The algorithms for solving the problem can be described quite simply. When a new beam is introduced, information (one array in this case) will be initialized, and the length of the beam will be stored in COMMON. An

Icetran subroutine called FJSTRT will be used for this task. For each load applied to the beam, data subarrays will be defined, and information about the magnitude and position of the forces will be stored in them. A subroutine called FJLOAD will perform this task.

Finally, when the reactions are requested, a subroutine called FJREAC will be called to carry out bookkeeping functions on the stored loads. Then FJREAC calls FJRCAP for concentrated loads and FJRCAU for uniform loads. Subroutine FJRCAP handles concentrated loads by distributing the load between the two ends according to the ratio of the distances from the ends to the load. For example, a load that is three-quarters of the way across the beam will send three-quarters of its value to the support at the right end (closest support) and only one-quarter of its value to the left support. Subroutine FJRCAU handles uniform loads by finding the equivalent concentrated load and then calling FJRCAP.

Structure of the Commands. The convention of *underlining* that part of each command or identifier which is required is followed below. Data or identifiers in parentheses may be omitted. The name of the subsystem is FJSBEAM. Thus, the prefix of all programs will be FJ. When the engineer desires to use the system, the name of the subsystem will be given, followed by the length of the simple beam to be analyzed:

<u>FJSBEAM</u> length

where "length" will be the length in feet, a real number. Note that the entire word "FJSBEAM" must be used. If no value for "length" is given, 10 ft will be assumed. The use of the command implies that all information related to previously defined beams is to be deleted.

To add loads onto the beam, the engineer will have available the following command:

$$\underline{FORCE}\begin{cases} \underline{UNIFORM}\ w \quad (\underline{POSITION})\ l_1\ (\underline{FROM})^{LEFT}_{RIGHT}\ (\underline{TO})\ l_2\ (\underline{FROM})^{LEFT}_{RIGHT} \\ \\ \underline{CONCENTRATED}\ p\ (\underline{POSITION})\ l_3(\underline{FROM})^{LEFT}_{RIGHT} \end{cases}$$

Here, w is the load in pounds/foot, p the load in pounds, and "l_1", "l_2", and "l_3" are positions in feet on the beam. One of the choices of type of load *must* be made, and the magnitude of the specified load must be supplied. All optional words, if present, must be spelled out in full. If positional information is omitted, the following is assumed: For concentrated loads, the left end ($l_3 = 0.0$ FROM LEFT) is assumed; if a distance but not a support is given, the support is assumed to be at the left. On uniform loads, $l_1 = 0.0$ FROM LEFT, $l_2 = 0.0$ FROM RIGHT are assumed if not specified. Therefore, if no other information than the magnitude of the uniform load is given, that magnitude will be assumed to act on the entire beam.

Finally, when the reactions are desired, the engineer requests

<u>REAC</u>TIONS

Note that any word starting with REAC is permitted. The routines needed for each command are shown in Fig. 4.

Command	Icetran Programs Executed
FJSBEAM	FJSTRT
FORCE	FJLOAD
	↗ FJRCAP
REACTIONS	FJREAC
	↘ FJRCAU → FJRCAP

Fig. 4. Relation between commands and Icetran programs (FJSBEAM).

Data Structure. Storage in COMMON is structured as follows:

I1, F1, I2, F2, I3, F3, ALENGT, NUMLDS, ALOADS(P)

where:

ALENGT = stored length of the beam

NUMLDS = number of loads placed on the beam and number of subarrays

ALOADS = dynamic array whose subarrays contain loading information (see Fig. 5)

I1 = flag indicating type of load (1 = concentrated; 2 = uniform)

F1 = magnitude of load

I2 = flag indicating orientation of first distance (1 = from left; 2 = from right)

F2 = distance from support (I2 specifies which support)

I3 = flag for orientation of second distance (if a uniform load), where 1 = from left and 2 = from right

F3 = distance from support (I3 specifies which support)

The ICES command interpreter stores I1, F1, I2, F2, I3, F3, and ALENGT as a result of encountering data storage requests.

Electrical Engineering Applications. Computers are essential aids to the electrical engineer in many applications. Circuit analysis is the "bread and butter" computation for most electrical engineering applications.

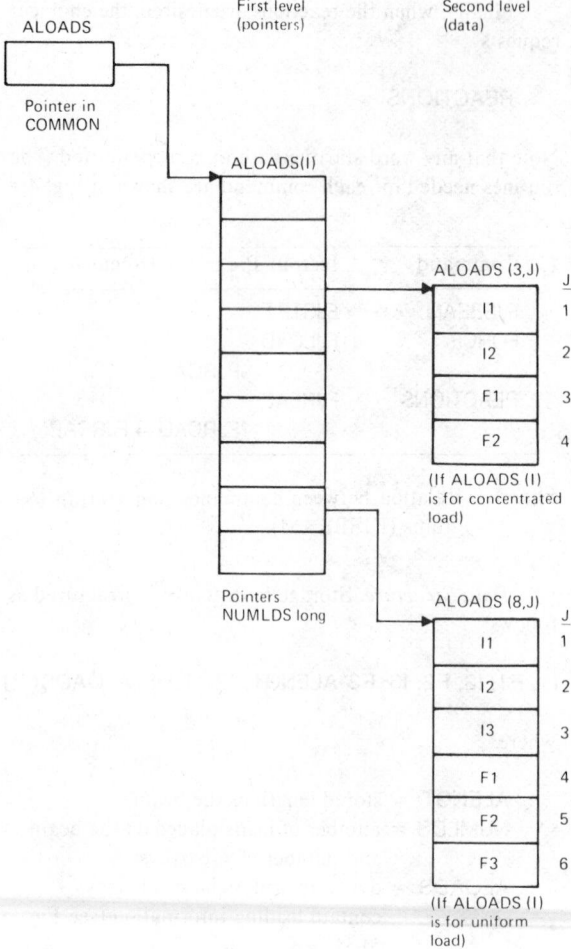

Fig. 5. The FJSBEAM data structure.

The two most commonly used circuit analysis programs are ECAP (Electronic Circuit Analysis Program) and SCEPTRE (respectively: Jensen and Lieberman, 1968; Bowers and Sedore, 1971). ECAP allows the electrical engineer to perform d-c, a-c, and transient analysis. Under control of ECAP, network equations are formulated and solved after the appropriate topological information and element values of the network have been provided. SCEPTRE also performs d-c and transient analysis, but was designed to provide several improvements over ECAP in transient analysis.

To illustrate the use of ECAP, a d-c analysis is performed (Comer, 1971). A transistor amplifier has been reduced to an equivalent circuit using the standard branches allowed in ECAP. The only branches permitted in ECAP in the d-c analysis program are independent d-c sources, dependent d-c current sources, and resistance or capacitance. Among the output quantities that can be

calculated by ECAP, using the d-c program, are node voltages, element voltages, branch voltages, element currents, branch currents, and element power losses. Fig. 6(a) shows the circuit to be analyzed. Fig. 6(b) shows the equivalent circuit with standard branches.

The program first specifies the type of analysis to be performed, in this case, d-c analysis followed by comment cards. Branch information is then input, starting with B1 and proceeding consecutively to the highest branch in the circuit. The nodal connectivity information for each branch starts in column 7 with the letter N. The two

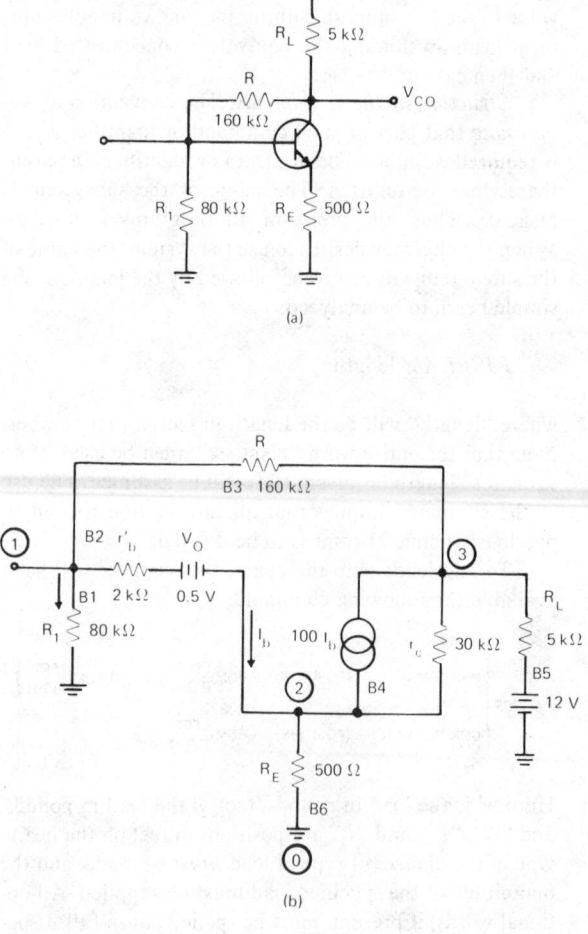

Fig. 6. Circuits on which ECAP program analyzes quiescent voltage. (a) Transistor amplifier; (b) equivalent circuit showing standard branches. (Copyright © 1971 by International Textbook Company. Reprinted from *Computer Analysis of Circuits* by David J. Comer by permission of Intext Educational Publishers, New York.)

numbers in parentheses specify the two nodes to which the branch connects and the direction defining positive current. Positive current flows from the first node specified to the second node. Nodal information is followed by a comma and a finite value of resistance. Independent voltage-source information follows the resistance value and independent source current would follow the voltage-source value if a current source appears in the branch. Commas always separate the data subgroups.

Dependent current-source cards follow the branch cards and are identified by the letter T, followed by the number of the source. Dependent sources are also numbered consecutively, starting with number 1. This information is located in columns 1 to 5. Note that the number following the letter T does not necessarily correspond to the branch number. Branch information for the current source starts in column 7 with the letter B. The first number in parentheses specifies the branch current to which the dependent source is proportional, and the second number corresponds to the branch that contains the source. The strength of the source is then specified in terms of the word BETA, which is the current gain of the source. The value of BETA can be negative, depending on the chosen directions of positive current in both the "from" branch and the "to" branch. Current-source information can also be specified in terms of a transconductance. In this case the letters GM are used instead of BETA. The current is then equal to the value of GM times the voltage appearing across the resistance of the "from" branch.

There are only four circuit elements recognized by the ECAP d-c analysis program, resistors (or conductances), independent voltage sources, independent current sources, and dependent current sources. All these elements except independent current sources are used in the preceding program. After the topology of the network is described by B-cards (branches) and T-cards (dependent sources), an output specification card determines the output block of data to be printed.

Other Problem-Oriented Languages. Literally hundreds of problem-oriented languages have been developed over the past 25 years. We have looked in detail at the areas of numerical control, civil engineering, and electrical engineering. Table 1 summarizes some other representative languages, showing their areas of application. These, of course, are only a small percentage of the numerous languages in use today.

Future Developments in Problem-Oriented Languages. As the computer continues to impact new fields, the need for problem-oriented languages will increase. Computer science research in programming languages will affect future developments in special-purpose languages. One new area of research is the development of techniques to permit users to define their own language requirements and have an automatic procedure for generation of the translator for that language. The growth of interactive systems will permit a man-machine dialog for the definition, refinement, and generation of the user-developed language. The system would then produce the necessary language documentation, tutorial material, and compiler or interpreter to translate and execute programs in the new language.

Table 1.   Representative Problem-Oriented Languages

Application Area	Program Name
Statistics	SPSS: Statistical package for the social sciences
	SAS® Statistical Library*
	OMNITAB
Computer-assisted instruction	TUTOR
	PLANIT
	COURSEWRITER
Simulation	GPSS: General-purpose systems simulator
	SIMSCRIPT
	CSSL: Continuous system simulation language
Database management	IMS: Information management system
	GIS: Generalized information system
	TOTAL
	SYSTEM 2000
Systems programming	AED: Automated engineering design
	BLISS: Basic language for implementing system software
	C: For nonnumeric and systems programming
Computer design	CDL: Computer design language
	CSL: Computer structure language

*SAS Registered trademark of SAS Institute Inc., Cary, N.C.

As pointed out by Sammet (1969), the controversy over language structure will continue into the future. Some people advocate the use of English as a programming language. Others insist that many applications require a precision of expression which would be aided by a more formal and structured language than would be available when using natural language. Since this controversy is unlikely to subside in the near future, it seems reasonable to press for user-defined languages. In this way, the personal preference of the specific user could be satisfied. However, research in this field has only recently begun in earnest.

Another development in computer science, which is impacting problem-oriented languages, and will continue to do so, is the growth of time-sharing systems and interactive graphics. Many of the languages discussed in this article have been modified to include interactive processing. Numerical control, civil engineering, and electrical engineering are only some of the disciplines that are becoming heavily involved in the application of interactive graphics to problem solving. The design of future problem-oriented languages will be influenced by the availability of inexpensive graphics terminals as part of every time-sharing service. As microcomputers become more accessible and more powerful, they too will be supplied with an array of problem-oriented languages.

Finally, new theoretical and practical work in compiler design, in extensible languages, in program complexity, in artificial intelligence, and in many other areas of computer science will influence the design, utility, accessibility, and application of new problem-oriented languages. The use of problem-oriented languages will continue to expand because specialists in every discipline will want to communicate with the computer in languages that are comfortable for them to use and which provide them with the greatest degree of expressiveness possible.

REFERENCES

1958. Theodoroff, T. J. "DYANA: Dynamics Analyzer-Programmer, Part I, Description and Application," *Proc. Eastern Joint Computer Conference,* pp. 144–147.

1964. Fenves, S. J. *et. al. STRESS: A User's Manual.* Cambridge, MA: M.I.T. Press.

1967. IIT Research Institute. *APT Part Programming.* New York: McGraw-Hill.

1967. Roos, D. *ICES Systems Design.* Cambridge, MA: M.I.T. Press.

1968. Jensen, R. W. and Lieberman, M. D. *IBM Electronic Circuit Analysis Program—Techniques and Applications.* Englewood Cliffs, NJ: Prentice-Hall.

1969. Sammet, Jean E. *Programming Languages: History and Fundamentals.* Englewood Cliffs, NJ: Prentice-Hall.

1971. Bowers, J.C. and Sedore, S. R. *SCEPTRE: A Computer Program for Circuit and Systems Analysis.* Englewood Cliffs, NJ: Prentice-Hall.

1971. Comer, D. J. *Computer Analysis of Circuits.* Scranton, PA: International Textbook.

1978. Sammet, J. E. "Roster of Programming Languages for 1976–77," *SIGPLAN Notices* **13**, *No. 11:* 56–85.

B. MITTMAN

PROCEDURE

For articles on related subjects *see* ARGUMENT; BLOCK STRUCTURE; GLOBAL AND LOCAL VARIABLES; PROCEDURE-ORIENTED LANGUAGES; PROCEDURE, PURE; RECURSION; SIDE EFFECT; SUBPROGRAMS, CALLING; and SUBROUTINE.

A procedure is a portion of a high-level language program which performs a specific task necessary for that program. This term is normally used interchangeably with the terms *subprogram* and *subroutine* when referring to high-level languages, although the term *subroutine* has a wider meaning outside high-level languages. The use of procedures is so central to programming in general-purpose, high-level languages such as Fortran, Pascal, and PL/I that these languages are often known as *procedure-oriented* languages.

Early in the development of programming languages it was recognized that programs would be written in which the same process was to be executed at several different locations within the program. One example of such a process is the evaluation of mathematical functions such as logarithms and exponentials, or trigonometric functions such as sine or cosine. To accomplish this conveniently, a facility was needed to permit the programmer to code such a procedure once and then to call that process whenever it was needed.

Procedures in high-level languages are of two types: *instrinsic* (or *built-in* or *library*) and programmer-written. Intrinsic procedures are those provided with the language so that the programmer need only cite them in a program to have them automatically *invoked*. This invocation requires only that the programmer give the *name* of the procedure and its *arguments*. Fortran, for example, has numerous built-in functions, a short list of which is given in Table 1. If a program contains a variable X and the programmer wishes to compute the cosine of the current value assigned to that variable, it is only necessary to write

COS(X)

If you wish to assign to variable A the absolute value of the sum of the cosine and sine of the argument, you may write

A = ABS(COS(X) + SIN(X))

Table 1.   Fortran Functions

Name of function	Mathematical Definition	Fortran Name
Sine	sin x	SIN
Cosine	cos x	COS
Exponential	e^x	EXP
Natural logarithm	ln x	ALOG†
Absolute value	| x |	ABS
Maximum	Value of maximum of $x_1, x_2,..., x_n$	AMAXI†

† The A in front of these names is required because Fortran names beginning with L or M automatically have integer values.

If you wish B to be the maximum of the sine and exponential of the arguments, then write

B = AMAX1(SIN(X),EXP(X))

Other high-level languages have different sets of intrinsic procedures. Pascal has a much smaller number of intrinsic procedures than Fortran and PL/I has a much larger number. For example, PL/I and Fortran 77 have a built-in function that allows the programmer to extract a *substring* from a named string of characters which is an argument of the function. Intrinsic procedures which return a single result are often called *functions* because they involve common mathematical functions and because they are used in arithmetic expressions in high-level languages just like mathematical functions.

The availability of intrinsic functions clearly suggests the need for a parallel facility to permit the programmer to define procedures at the same time as the referencing or *main* program is written. Thus, the programmer could write *subprograms* in the language and then reference these in the same manner as intrinsic procedures. All general-purpose, high-level languages have such a facility, although the details of how it can be used and how it is implemented vary considerably.

In Fortran, programmer-written procedures are called *subprograms* and are of two types: FUNCTION subprograms and SUBROUTINE subprograms. The former are directly analogous to intrinsic functions in that FUNCTIONS are invoked or *called* just like intrinsic functions. Fig. 1 is an example of a programmer-written FUNCTION to calculate the sum of the products of the corresponding elements of two 100 element arrays together with two main program statements calling this function. Note in particular that the *value* of the function is the value assigned to its name (PROD in Fig. 1).

In Fortran, SUBROUTINE subprograms differ from FUNCTION subprograms in the method by which they are called and in the lack of any requirement that a specific result as such be produced. Fig. 2 is an example of a SUBROUTINE subprogram to transpose the elements of a two-

```
Main program
  —
  —

  A = C + (D*E)/PROD(F,G)

  —
  Q1 = Q2*PROD(Q3,Q4)

  FUNCTION PROD (X,Y)
  REAL X( 100), Y( 100)
  PROD = 0.
  DO 2 I = 1,100
     PROD = PROD + X(I)*Y(I)
2 CONTINUE
  RETURN
  END
```

Fig. 1.   A FUNCTION in Fortran.

```
Main program
  —
  —
  —
  —

  —
  CALL TRANS (B,100)
  —

  CALL TRANS (C,50)
  —
  —
  —
  SUBROUTINE TRANS (A,N)
  REAL A(N,N)
  DO 2 I = 2, N
     I1 = I − 1
     DO 4 J = 1, I1
C  NOTE NEED TO SAVE A (I, J)
C  BEFORE REPLACING IT BY A (J, I)
        TEMP = A(I, J)
        A(I, J) = A(J, I)
        A(J, I) = TEMP
4    CONTINUE
2  CONTINUE
   RETURN
   END
```

Fig. 2.   A Fortran SUBROUTINE.

dimensional square array [i.e., interchange the (I, J) and (J, I) elements]. Note that the only "result" of the subprogram is the input matrix with its elements interchanged, and that the subprogram is not called in an assignment statement but by a CALL statement.

Also in Fortran, as shown in Figs. 1 and 2, procedures are physically separate from the main program, but in block-structured languages they are an integral part of the main program. Fig. 3 shows an example from Pascal corresponding to that in Fig. 2 for Fortran. Here the procedure is a *declaration* at the start of the *block* which is the Pascal program. The procedure is called by giving just its name followed by its arguments.

Pascal also has a procedure facility analogous to Fortran functions. PL/I is also a block-structured language and has procedure facilities generally similar to those in Pascal. By contrast with block-structured languages and Fortran, Cobol has a quite rudimentary procedure facility that integrates subprograms into the main program in a much more restrictive context than with languages such as Pascal or PL/I.

The contrast between the physically separate procedures of Fortran and those integrated into the main program, as in block-structured languages, needs to be noted and understood. The former allows separate compilation of the main program and subprograms, which may be convenient during debugging. Block-structured languages generally require recompilation of the procedure every time the program is recompiled, but the integration of procedures into the main program is an aid of great value to programming and to thinking about programming.

J. A. N. Lee and A. Ralston

```
program test (input, output);
type matrix = array [1..100, 1..100] of real;
var B: matrix:
    C: array [1..50, 1..50] of real;
procedure TRANS (N: integer, var A: matrix);
  var I, J: integer;
      TEMP: real;
  begin
    for I := 2 to N do
      for J := 1 to I − 1 do
        begin
          TEMP := A[I, J];
          A[I, J] := A[J, I];
          A[J, I] := TEMP
        end
  end;
          —
          —
          —
{Main Program}
begin
          —
          —
          —
  TRANS (B, 100);
          —
          —
          —
  TRANS (C, 50);
          —
          —
          —
end.
```

Fig. 3.   A Pascal Procedure.

PROCEDURE-ORIENTED LANGUAGES

SURVEY

For articles on related subjects *see* ADA; ALGOL 68; BACKUS-NAUR FORM; C; GLOBAL AND LOCAL VARIABLES; ITERATION; LANGUAGE PROCESSORS; LIST PROCESSING LANGUAGES; MACHINE AND ASSEMBLY LANGUAGE PROGRAMMING; PASCAL; PROBLEM-ORIENTED LANGUAGES; PROGRAMMING LANGUAGES; SETL; STRING PROCESSING LANGUAGES; STANDARDS; SUBPROGRAMS, CALLING; and VIENNA DEFINITION LANGUAGE.

A procedure-oriented language (POL) is a way of expressing commands to a computer in a form somewhat similar to such natural languages as English and mathematics. It is distinguished from machine language and assembly language—in which we are constrained to express ourselves in a form much closer to the language of the machine itself—and problem-oriented languages, in which we state our problem and leave the system to choose a procedure for solving it. It is also distinguished from list-processing and string-processing languages, which do in fact express procedures and not problems, but which are different in that the information processed is almost entirely symbolic. All of these and other forms of programming languages are treated elsewhere in this Encyclopedia.

In one sense a computer can understand only its own machine language. From this point of view a procedure expressed in any other language must be translated into machine language before it can be executed. The translation is done by another program of machine instructions, called a *translator, language processor* or (most commonly) a *compiler*. The process is usually called "compilation." The input to the compilation, the program written in a POL, is the source program, and the output is a machine-language program called the object program. It is the object program that is actually executed to process data.

Advantages and Disadvantages. When the early POLs were introduced in the 1950s, they were seen primarily in relation to assembly language, compared with which they promised several advantages and some disadvantages. Most of these considerations still apply, although today the choice is seldom solely between assembly language and POLs.

POLs offer savings in programming time. Since the programmer can concentrate on the procedure and worry less about how the machine will carry out the details, productivity is usually higher. There is a further speed factor because a line of coding in a POL generally produces—after compilation—many machine instructions.

Since the procedure is written in a form closer to human means of communication, documentation and program understandability are enhanced. If the programmer takes a little additional care in writing the program, using meaningful data names, for example, the program may become—at least to some extent—its own documentation.

All programs that are used over an extended period of time have to be maintained because requirements and procedures change. When programs are written in assembly language, rather simple-appearing changes in such things as data formats can mean extensive reprogramming, which is time consuming, expensive, and error prone. In a POL it is generally a simple matter to make the necessary changes and recompile the entire program.

A program written in a POL can be used on any computer for which an appropriate compiler exists. For the more widely used POLs, such as Fortran and Cobol, compilers are available for all medium- and large-sized computers and for many microcomputers. With (ideally) only a few changes having to do with minor language and machine differences, a POL program that has been running on one machine can be transferred to another one with only a simple recompilation required.

Finally, a POL is usually rather easier to learn than an assembly language. This assertion can be challenged in terms of the full reach of the most powerful POLs, but relatively few people need to know *everything* about the language they are using, especially the more powerful ones. Ease of learning obviously eases the programmer training problem. Furthermore, this training is transferable just as programs are: A person who knows Cobol can write programs for any computer that has a Cobol compiler (which is most), with only modest retraining to become familiar with minor language differences and what little needs to be known about machine differences.

The advantages of POLs outweigh their disadvantages in most peoples' minds, but there are disadvantages.

The compilers are expensive to write, are often delivered late, and routinely have many errors in them at first.

The claims for transferability or portability of programs and programmer training are sometimes exaggerated since the languages implemented by different suppliers are not actually identical. A few differences can be explained by machine differences, but beyond that there is a great temptation for every implementor to add extra features that he/she considers desirable. These features, regardless of how valuable they may be, detract from the ability to move a program or a programmer to another installation that uses a different system.

The early POLs had compilers that were quite slow, and produced programs that, in some cases, executed much more slowly than corresponding assembly language programs written by an accomplished programmer. The charge against POLs, accordingly, was that they were expensive in machine time and that this was an unavoidable price that had to be paid for such advantages as speed of programming. This argument has nearly died out as compilers have been steadily improved over the years, and as it has become obvious that there will never be enough accomplished assembly language programmers to write all the programs that are needed.

On balance, it is clear that there are situations where POLs have clear advantages. There is every reason to believe that they will be used indefinitely, with evolutionary improvements rising out of research into language design and out of experience with their use. It is also clear that there are circumstances where lower-level languages are the rational choice, most commonly in time- or space-critical systems programming, and that for some purposes non-procedural (*q.v.*) approaches are best.

Fortran. The first POL to be widely used was Fortran (see Meissner and Organick, 1980), an acronym that was coined from the words "FORmula TRANslation." Work on Fortran began in the mid-1950s by a committee composed of people from IBM and some of its customers. The name of John W. Backus of IBM is most closely associated with the effort.

Fortran was designed initially for use on problems of a mathematical nature, and it is still most commonly used for solving problems in mathematics, engineering, and science. Nothing in the language actually forces this specialization, however, and Fortran is widely employed as a vehicle for teaching computer applications and programming to students without extensive mathematical backgrounds because it is fairly easy to learn.

For problems of a technical nature, Fortran is by far the most widely used computer language. Since there are more business than technical applications of computers, however, Cobol is more widely used on an overall basis. Basic is a common choice in the microcomputer world and in some aspects of the educational use of computers, and Pascal is becoming the standard for the first course in computer science.

An illustrative program, shown in Fig. 1, demonstrates some of the features of Fortran. The program is designed to find the roots of the quadratic equation $ax^2 + bx + c = 0$, which are given by the formula

$$x = \frac{-b \pm \sqrt{b^2 - 4ac}}{2a}.$$

The program is to read values of a, b, and c, compute and print the roots, and then go back to read more data. Each time values of a, b, and c are read, a check is made to determine whether $a = 0$, which will be used to signal that the end of the deck of data sets has been read. We will assume that the equation does have real roots, which means that the discriminant (the quantity under the square root sign) will always be positive.

```
      REAL A,B,C,X1,X2,DISC
   5  READ (5, 100) A, B, C
 100  FORMAT (3F10.0)
      IF (A .EQ. 0.0) STOP
      DISC = B**2 - 4.0*A*C
      X1 = (-B + SQRT(DISC))/(2.0*A)
      X2 = (-B - SQRT(DISC))/(2.0*A)
      WRITE (6,200) A, B, C, X1, X2
 200  FORMAT (1X, 5F12.5)
      GO TO 5
      END
```

Fig. 1. A Fortran program.

Looking at the program in Fig. 1, we see that it begins with a REAL statement which lists all the variables and indicates that their values are real. The next statement is a READ statement, which is a command to read an input record (e.g., a card or a line of input at a terminal) and assign three values from it to the variables named A, B, and C. The 5 in parentheses commonly identifies a card reader, and the 100 is the statement number of the FORMAT statement that follows. Within parentheses in the FORMAT statement, we describe the numbers as they will be punched on a card: The 3 means three numbers, the F means "fixed format," the 10 means that each number will occupy ten columns, and the zero means that if we do not punch a decimal point, the numbers will be taken as having zero places after the decimal point (i.e., as being integers). If we do, in fact, punch decimal points in the numbers, the zero has no effect.

The IF statement is an example of a conditional: If the logical expression in parentheses is true (i.e., if A is equal to (.EQ.) zero), program execution is to stop.

The calculation of the discriminant is done with an arithmetic assignment statement in which we see how arithmetic operations are designated by various symbols. The minus sign for subtraction and the asterisk for multiplication are fairly obvious; two asterisks together call for raising to a power (exponentiation). We see in the following statement the plus sign for addition and the slash (/) for division. An arithmetic assignment statement is a command to evaluate the expression on the right of the equal sign, using values for the variables that have been previously read or computed, and assign that value to the variable named on the left. In the following two assignment statements we have examples of the use of parentheses to indicate groupings of quantities, and of a function to compute the square root. When the compiler encounters the function name SQRT it incorporates a call (transfer) to the library square root routine.

The WRITE statement calls for the printing of the data values and the roots. The FORMAT statement that is referenced this time specifies single spacing with the 1x, and with the 5F12.5 calls for each of the five numbers to be printed in 12 character positions with 5 digits after the decimal point.

The GO TO statement causes a transfer of control back to the statement labeled with the number 5, to repeat execution of the program. The END is a notice to the Fortran compiler that the end of the program has been reached and that compilation can be completed.

In Fig. 2 we have a sample of the output that could be produced after this program has been compiled and is being executed. We see in the first line, for instance, that the roots of the equation $x^2 - 1.5x - 4.5 = 0$ are 3.0 and -1.5.

The program shown in Fig. 3 exhibits some additional Fortran features, especially the handling of an array of data as distinguished from a single value. Here the name z stands for 100 separate real number data elements, which fact is specified in the REAL statement. The INTEGER statement indicates that K and N take on integer values. We wish to read some number of data items, probably fewer than 100, and form the sum of their squares. The program reads the value of N, then reads N additional items, assigning the data values from them to the successive elements of the array named z. The DO statement says to carry out the READ statement N times, with the index variable named K running from 1 to N. This index is used as the subscript that identifies a particular element of z. The formation of the sum of squares is handled by another DO loop, as it is called, in which a variable named SUMSQ accumulates the squares after having been started at zero. We note the use of comments (lines beginning with a c) to make the meaning of the program clearer.

An important feature of all POLs is the ability they give to the programmer to write subroutines. In some,

1.00000	−1.50000	−4.50000	3.00000	−1.50000
1.00000	−2.00000	1.00000	1.00000	1.00000
100.00000	−200.00000	100.00000	1.00000	1.00000
1.00000	−10.00000	25.00000	5.00000	5.00000
1.00000	−3.00000	2.00000	2.00000	1.00000
2.00000	−6.00000	4.00000	2.00000	1.00000
1.00000	1.00000	−2550.00000	50.00000	−51.00000
1.43200	9.87600	−4.56700	0.43500	−7.33164
8.81300	−1.31000	0.0	0.14864	0.0
2.30030	1.99170	0.0	0.0	−0.86584

Fig. 2. Output of program of Fig. 1.

```
      REAL Z( 100) SUMSQ
      INTEGER K, N
      READ (5, 50) N
   50 FORMAT (I3)
C  CHECK FOR N OUT OF RANGE
      IF (N .LT. 1 .OR. N .GT. 100)STOP
C  READ DATA VALUES
      DO 60 K = 1, N
   60 READ (5, 70) Z(K)
   70 FORMAT (F10.0)
C  CLEAR SUMMING LOCATION TO ZERO
      SUMSQ = 0.0
C  GET SUM OF SQUARES
      DO 80 K = 1, N
          SUMSQ = SUMSQ + Z(K)**2
   80 CONTINUE
      WRITE (6, 90) N, SUMSQ
   90 FORMAT ( 1X, I5, 1PG15.6)
      STOP
      END
```

Fig. 3. Fortran program showing additional features.

```
SUBROUTINE QUAD( A, B, C, X1, X2)
REAL A, B, C, X1, X2, DISC
DISC = B**2 − 4.0*A*C
X1 = ( −B + SQRT(DISC) ) / ( 2.0*A)
X2 = ( −B − SQRT(DISC) ) / ( 2.0*A)
RETURN
END
```

Fig. 4. A Fortran subroutine.

the end of which control would be transferred back to the calling program. In calling the subroutine, we specify actual arguments. If we want the roots of the equation $x^2 − 4x + 3 = 0$, assigning them to the variables named R and S, we would write

CALL QUAD(1.0, −4.0, 3.0, R, S)

If the three coefficients were Y, Z(13), and F + 12.3, with the roots being array elements T(1) and T(2), we would write

CALL QUAD(Y, Z(13), F + 12.3, T(1), T(2))

To find the roots of different equations the subroutine could thus be called many times from the same calling program.

A subroutine can be designed to carry out alternative calculations, and then convey information about its execution back to the calling program. In our quadratic equation illustration, we might wish to have the subroutine tell the calling program whether the roots are real or complex, calculating them in either case. To do this, we would need to have two parameters for the real and imaginary parts of the roots if they are complex, and an additional parameter to carry the real or complex information. This latter parameter might be set to zero for real and to one for complex, for example, or other conventions could be used. The calling program could test this param-

like Fortran, these can be compiled separately, if desired, and then combined with a main program and run. Subroutines permit more effective division of effort on large projects, improve documentation, facilitate program checkout, and save effort when previously programmed routines can be used. In Fortran this capability is provided by the FUNCTION and SUBROUTINE features, of which we illustrate the latter.

Suppose that a subroutine is desired which will accept the coefficients of a quadratic equation and return the roots. The program of Fig. 4 begins with a notice to the compiler that this is a SUBROUTINE, and gives its name and the names of the three input and two output arguments. The assignment statements are as before, after which we have a RETURN. The scheme is that during the execution of some other program, we would encounter a statement calling for the execution of this subroutine, at eter to determine how to process the roots, or perhaps to choose appropriate printing formats for the two cases.

Some of the more important features of Fortran, which it is not possible to illustrate here, include the details of handling input and output, complex and double precision operations, and the control of storage allocation with the COMMON and EQUIVALENCE statements.

Standards on Fortran were adopted by the American National Standards Institute, ANSI, in 1966, with provision for occasional revision. Most subsequent Fortran implementations differed from the standard (and from each other), most commonly in the way they added features not covered in the standard. Some of these features offered considerable convenience and power to the programmer, but at the expense of a partial loss of such POL advantages as program and programmer transferability and ease of learning.

Fortran 77, the most recent ANSI Fortran standard, incorporates a number of improvements and extensions. Many of these had become fairly common in actual implementations before their definition by the ANSI Fortran committee. Among the more important are an IF-THEN-ELSE control structure, a character data type, list-directed input and output (i.e., with no FORMAT statement required), and various other input and output features. The character data type replaces the Hollerith data type, which was the only feature deleted from the former standard. A new Fortran standard is targeted for about 1985.

One variation of Fortran deserves mention because of its importance and wide use. Watfor and its successor Watfiv were developed at the University of Waterloo, Canada, originally for student use. They offer simplified input and output operations, very fast compilation, and extensive error diagnostics. They are ideal for beginning students, but they also have value to the experienced programmer in the early stages of program checkout because of the error diagnostics. Since the source language is little different from other Fortrans, it is a simple matter to check out a program using Watfiv and then make a final compilation on some other compiler that may produce a faster-running object program.

Cobol. Cobol is intended for use in the solution of problems in business data processing; the acronym stands for COmmon Business Oriented Language. It was developed in the late 1950s by a group of computer manufacturers and users, especially the U.S. government. The work built on several other POLs, which had been developed earlier.

Cobol is probably used by a majority of those business computer installations for which a Cobol compiler is available. It is by a good margin the most widely used POL. Cobol, like Fortran, has been standardized by the American National Standards Institute; but, also like Fortran, many implementations differ from the standard (McCracken 1976).

Major goals of the early Cobol efforts were easy readability of computer programs and as much machine independence as possible. This latter means that it was to be possible to run a Cobol program on any computer for which a compiler existed. This had the effect of simplifying programmer training.

A Cobol program is composed of four divisions, each with a distinct function and with varying degrees of machine independence. We will consider some of the features of the divisions in conjunction with a very simple but complete Cobol program. The function of the program is to read records containing the number of hours employees worked in a week and their hourly pay rate, and compute their gross pay with time-and-a-half for any hours over 40. For each record read, a line is to be printed giving the input data and the gross pay, with appropriate decimal points and a dollar sign included. The program is shown in Fig. 5.

The IDENTIFICATION DIVISION in this case consists of just one line giving a name to the program, and has no other effect on the compilation.

The ENVIRONMENT DIVISION functions to link the DATA DIVISION (which is mostly machine independent) and the PROCEDURE DIVISION (which is almost entirely machine independent) with the actual equipment that will be used. Using the SELECT verb, we designate the devices that will hold the input and output files. We have used symbolic names (CARD and PRINTER) so that the final decision on what the devices will be can be postponed to the latest possible time, when the object program is actually run, to gain further flexibility.

In the preceding paragraph we called the word SELECT a *verb*. This is an important concept in POLs, and is perhaps the most important of several borrowings from the terminology of English grammar. A verb, as the term is used here, is an imperative, a command to carry out some action. In Cobol, the verb is always the first word of the sentence, which simplifies the work of the compiler in determining the meaning of the sentence. Moreover, the verbs (as well as other Cobol words) are *reserved words* and therefore cannot be used also as data names. If the verb calls for action on data, the data names can be thought of as nouns. If two or more data items have the same name, and therefore have to be qualified as to which record or other data group they are in, the qualifiers can be thought of as adjectives, although the terminology is not used as such. Finally, for our purposes here, the term *declaration* is used to denote POL language elements that do not call for any processing actions, but rather describe such matters as data formats, the grouping of data items into arrays, and record layouts. Everything in the Cobol DATA DIVISION, described next, consists of declarations.

```
IDENTIFICATION DIVISION.
PROGRAM-ID. PAYROLL.

ENVIRONMENT DIVISION.
INPUT-OUTPUT SECTION.
FILE-CONTROL.
    SELECT IN-FILE ASSIGN TO UT-S-CARDS.
    SELECT OUT-FILE ASSIGN TO UT-S-PRINTER.

DATA DIVISION.
FILE SECTION.
FD  IN-FILE
    LABEL RECORDS ARE OMITTED.
01  IN-RECORD.
    02  HOURS-WORKED         PICTURE 99V9.
    02  PAYRATE              PICTURE 9V999.
    02  FILLER               PICTURE X(73).
FD  OUT-FILE
    LABEL RECORDS ARE OMITTED.
01  OUT-RECORD.
    02  HOURS-WORKED-EDITED  PICTURE ZZ99.9.
    02  PAYRATE-EDITED       PICTURE ZZ9.999.
    02  GROSS-PAY-EDITED     PICTURE $$$$$$$9.99.
    02  FILLER               PICTURE X(56).
WORKING-STORAGE SECTION.
01  EXTRA                    PICTURE 99V99.
01  GROSS-PAY                PICTURE 999V99.

PROCEDURE DIVISION.
INITIALIZATION.
    OPEN INPUT IN-FILE, OUTPUT OUT-FILE.
PROCESSING-ROUTINE.
    READ IN-FILE RECORD
        AT END GO TO WRAPUP.
    MULTIPLY HOURS-WORKED BY PAYRATE GIVING GROSS-PAY ROUNDED.
    IF HOURS-WORKED GREATER THAN 40
      COMPUTE EXTRA ROUNDED = 0.5 * (HOURS-WORKED - 40) * PAYRATE
      ADD EXTRA TO GROSS-PAY.
    MOVE SPACES TO OUT-RECORD.
    MOVE HOURS-WORKED TO HOURS-WORKED-EDITED.
    MOVE PAYRATE TO PAYRATE-EDITED.
    MOVE GROSS-PAY TO GROSS-PAY-EDITED.
    WRITE OUT-RECORD.
    GO TO PROCESSING-ROUTINE.
WRAPUP.
    CLOSE IN-FILE, OUT-FILE.
    STOP RUN.
```

Fig. 5. A Cobol program.

The DATA DIVISION is used to describe all files that will be used by the program, together with the arrangement of information into records within the files. In our case we have two files, named IN-FILE and OUT-FILE. The record description for IN-RECORD begins with 01, which is called the "first level." The second level consists of the data items within the record, which is the lowest level in this simple program. We could have such things as a date at one level broken into month and day, and year at the next level. Within the PROCEDURE DIVISION it would be possible to refer either to the entire date or to any of its components. This kind of data structure is widely used in business data processing, and is an important feature of Cobol.

Each of the items at the lowest level must be described as to format: the number of characters, whether digits or letters, where the assumed decimal point is, any initial value, etc. This is handled here with the PICTURE clause, with which we essentially provide an illustration of what the item looks like. Other ways are provided for conveying the same information, but are less commonly used. In the PICTURE clauses for the output record OUT-RECORD, we see that for printing the output the PICTURE can be used to control format. The z's call for the suppression of leading zeros, embedded decimal points call for insertion of decimal points into the output (the v's in IN-RECORD indicate the position of the decimal point on input), and the dollar signs call for a "floating dollar sign," i.e., one dollar sign immediately to the left of the first significant digit. The FILLER is used to describe unused space.

The working storage section in this case provides temporary storage for quantities between the time they are computed and the time they are converted to a form suitable for printing.

The PROCEDURE DIVISION specifies the processing to be done. We note that computation can be specified either by words (MULTIPLY HOURS-WORKED BY PAYRATE . . .) or by using a formula style much like Fortran except that it is introduced by the verb COMPUTE.

Fig. 6 shows the output produced when the program was compiled and run with representative data.

We see in this program that data names can be much longer than in Fortran, up to 30 characters, and that they may be hyphenated. If a Cobol program is written with an eye to easy readability, using meaningful data names, it can indeed be quite readable.

One of the important innovations in Cobol was the rigid separation of the data and procedure divisions, a separation that is left partly implicit in many POLs, as in Fortran. When processing or data specifications change, as they frequently do in most applications, appropriate changes can be made in just the items affected and the programs can be recompiled. Something as simple as the expansion of a data item from two digits to three can result in changes in almost all parts of the object program. Without some way of keeping the data descriptions from being embedded in the procedure description, programs become extremely inflexible and difficult to change. On the other hand, Cobol does permit the inclusion of literals (such as 40 and 0.5 in the illustrative program) in the PROCEDURE DIVISION. Overuse of PROCEDURE DIVISION literals can lead to severe maintenance problems, but the Cobol programmer is left to make his or her own judgment on this matter of programming style since the language enforces no standards on it.

Important Cobol features that we are not able to cover here include details of input and output processing, the handling of conditionals and subscripts, and the facilities for controlling loops.

Algol. Algol (ALGOrithmic Language) was developed by an international committee that began work in the late 1950s (Kieburtz, 1975). The goal, as the name suggests, was to devise a language for expressing algorithms, whether intended for later execution on a computer or not. The language as defined was very machine independent, although particular implementations of necessity develop some dependence on the machine used.

Compared with Fortran, which Algol followed by a few years, Algol introduced a number of important concepts. Some of the new features offered easier and more powerful ways of doing common information processing operations. The means for controlling loop execution are more flexible and comprehensive than in Fortran. There are facilities for grouping a set of statements into one compound statement that can be treated as a whole by other program elements. Algol distinguishes between *global variables*, which are known in all parts of a program, and *local variables*, which are known only in the program block where they are declared. (Some variation of this distinction appears in most POLs.) This concept of block structure, whereby we are able to divide a program into precisely defined and named segments, with explicit control over the blocks in which variables are "known," is one of the most significant contributions by the designers of Algol to the development of subsequent POLs.

We will illustrate a few of these features, this time without showing a complete program.

The Algol **for** statement is used to control loop execution; it is a much more powerful version of the Fortran DO. To find the sum of the squares of the N elements of

40.0	3.000	$120.00
42.0	3.000	$129.00
37.5	3.888	$145.80
40.0	3.888	$155.52
41.0	3.888	$161.35
50.0	3.888	$213.84
44.0	2.200	$101.20
44.0	9.876	$454.30
22.0	2.876	$63.27

Fig. 6. Output of program of Fig. 5.

the array named z we could write:

sumsq := 0.0;
for k := 1 **step** 1 **until** N **do**
    sumsq := sumsq + Z[k] ↑ 2;

We see that statements are separated by semicolons; that the combination := is used to specify the replacement of a variable value by the value of an expression; and that the exponentiation operator is denoted by an upward-pointing arrow instead of the double asterisk that we have seen in Fortran and Cobol. In the language as defined, variable names may be of any length and may use both upper and lower-case letters; actual implementations may place restrictions on this freedom.

An interesting example of the **for** statement, suggested by Donald E. Knuth, shows how much can be done with one statement in Algol. The Newton-Raphson iteration method for finding the square root of a positive number A requires repeated evaluation of the formula

$$x = ((A/prevx) + prevx)/2$$

where x at one stage becomes *prevx* at the next stage, until x and *prevx* are the same to within some tolerance. The variable *prevx* has to be given a starting value, which can be 1:

prevx := 1;
for x := (A/prevx + prevx)/2
    while abs(x − prevx) > tolerance **do**
        prevx := x;

This **for** statement calls for repeated application of the formula and replacement of *prevx* by *x,* as long as the absolute value of the difference between x and *prevx* is greater than the tolerance.

Algol was defined in a report in 1960 that was itself an innovation in that the Algol language was described in another language (therefore called a *metalanguage*) developed by John Backus and Peter Naur of Denmark. This Backus-Naur Form (BNF—*q.v.*) provides a clear and unambiguous way to express the syntax of a POL (i.e., the rules for forming correct programs).

The language itself was the first major POL to use recursion (*q.v.*), which describes a procedure that is able to call itself. The usual illustration is the factorial function, which can be evaluated with the following Algol procedure (subroutine):

real procedure factorial (n);
if n = 1 **then** factorial := 1
        else factorial := n * factorial (*n* − 1);

We see that the entire procedure body consists of one **if** statement. It asks whether n is equal to 1 and sets the factorial equal to 1 if so. Otherwise, it multiplies n by the value of the same procedure evaluated for $n - 1$. In other words, the procedure calls itself repeatedly until the argument is reduced to 1, and then multiplies out the integers.

This is not an effective way to compute factorials in actual practice. The example is widely used to show what recursion is about, since practical applications are usually much more complex (*see* Quicksort program in STRUCTURED PROGRAMMING).

The Algol language provides for a degree of dynamic storage allocation, which means that assignment of storage to variables can be delayed until program execution reaches the block where the variable is used, and that the storage is released when the work of the block is finished. This can be important in problems involving large amounts of storage.

Algol was and still is more widely used in Europe than in the United States but the introduction of Pascal (see below) has resulted in a rapid decline of its use in Europe. It is, nevertheless, a landmark in the development of programming languages, and has had an influence on almost everything done later.

The closest "descendant" of Algol that has attained wide popularity is Pascal (*q.v.*), which retains many of Algol's features while adding a number of new ones (see below). In turn, a descendant of Pascal called Ada (*q.v.*) may become a very important language of the 1980s. Another language related to Algol is Algol 68 (*q.v.*), which generalizes many of the concepts in Algol 60.

Pascal. Pascal (*q.v.*) is a language designed by Niklaus Wirth in 1968. It is a member of the Algol family of languages in that its essential syntax is very Algol-like. The motivation behind its design was to provide a language that encouraged—to a degree, even required— the programmer to write programs according to the principles of structured programming (*q.v.*). Toward this end, Pascal embodies a philosophy and some explicit features different from Algol.

An important aspect of the Pascal design philosophy is that it is a "small" language. That is, the totality of the syntactic constructs it allows is quite limited, compared to, say, a language such as PL/I (see below). The intent of this is to provide the programmer with a language that can be easily learned and retained. Thus, for example, Pascal does not include the dynamic storage allocation features of Algol (i.e., variables cannot be declared in subblocks of the main program block) and the number of built-in functions is quite limited. Particularly noteworthy and controversial facets of this philosophy are (1) the absence of an exponentiation operator, thereby requiring the programmer to program exponentiation through successive multiplications or with the use of the exponential and logarithm functions and (2) the inability to use step sizes other than ± 1 in iteration control.

On the other hand, in the belief that good programming methodology requires as rich a variety of data structuring as control structure facilities, Pascal provides a *pointer* data type (which allows the definition and manipulation of *linked lists*) and set, file, and record data structures. A particularly interesting feature of Pascal, which presaged the current development of abstract data types (*q.v.*), is the provision that allows the programmer to define new data types. Thus:

type subject = (english, history, mathematics, physics);

defines a data type *subject,* which can then be given to variables, as in

var major, minor: subject;

To enable simple manipulations with these *programmer-defined* types, Pascal defines such functions as *succ* (successor) and *pred* (predecessor) so that, using the example above,

succ (history) = mathematics
pred (history) = english.

Pascal has rapidly become the preferred language of instruction in computer science courses at many universities. It is also becoming a widely available language on microcomputers. These two developments together mean that it is having a major influence on the programming habits of programmers trained from the mid-1970s on. Fig. 7 gives the Pascal version of the program of Fig. 1.

```
program quad (input,output);        {program heading}
var a, b, c, disc, x1, x2: real;
begin
    read (a);
    while a <> 0 do                 {<> is symbol for}
      begin                         {not equal}
        readln (b, c);              {ln means go to}
                                    {next line after}
        disc := b*b − 4.0*a*c;      {reading}
        x1 := (−b + sqrt (disc))/(2.0*a);
        x2 := (− b − sqrt (disc))/(2.0*a);
        writeln (a, b, c, x1, x2);
        read (a)
      end
end.
```

Fig. 7. The Pascal version of program of Fig. 1.

A complete description of Pascal may be found in Jensen and Wirth (1975).

PL/I. PL/I (Programming Language One) was developed for the IBM System/360 in the mid-1960s by a committee composed of representatives of IBM and two organizations of users of its large computers, GUIDE and SHARE (Weinberg, 1966). The committee drew upon the work that had been done on Fortran, Cobol, and Algol, so that PL/I has characteristics of each. It was presumably the hope of IBM that PL/I would replace both Fortran and Cobol, thus reducing the cost of maintaining compilers. This has not occurred, but PL/I probably is the third most commonly used POL on large IBM computers.

PL/I is by a wide margin the largest POL now widely available; i.e., it provides the programmer with the most features for handling a variety of applications in a variety of ways. One of the distinguishing features of the language is that it can be used equally well for both scientific and business data processing applications (to the extent that a clear distinction can always be made between the two). This can be a benefit in terms of reducing the number of compilers required in an installation.

It would be quite simple to fill this entire article with examples of programs that use PL/I features, without important duplication. We will have to be content with the briefest indication of what PL/I programs look like, followed by a description of other aspects of the language.

Fig. 8 is a PL/I version of the Fortran program shown in Fig. 1. Since it appears as the label of the PROCEDURE statement, QUAD becomes the name of the program. Following that we see a comment, so recognized because it appears between the delimiters /* and */. A comment may appear anywhere a blank is permitted. We see that statements end with a semicolon. A PL/I program is to be thought of as a linear string of characters, quite independent of its assignment to lines. As with Algol and Cobol, a statement may continue over more than one line, with no indication of the fact required; more than one statement may appear on one line. Blank lines may be used to improve understandability, which, perhaps surprisingly, is not permitted in all languages.

The DECLARE statement is one example of the features furnished to provide the information of the Cobol DATA DIVISION about variables, data layouts, etc. The GET statement calls for input of values for A, B, and C from a list of numeric values separated by spaces or commas. Numerous other input forms are permitted. Most of the rest of the program is not greatly different from the Fortran version except for the method of stopping program execution. Here, we first read one card, then go into a loop that is repeated indefinitely as long as (WHILE) the value of A is not equal ($\neg$ =) to zero. Thus, the program

```
QUAD:      PROCEDURE OPTIONS (MAIN);

           /* A PL/I PROGRAM TO FIND ROOTS OF QUADRATIC EQUATIONS*/

           DECLARE (A, B, C, DISC, X1, X2) FLOAT ;

           GET LIST (A, B, C) ;
REPEAT:    DO WHILE (A ¬= 0.0);
               DISC = B**2 - 4.0 * A * C;
               X1 = (-B + SQRT(DISC)) / (2.0*A) ;
               X2 = (-B - SQRT(DISC)) / (2.0*A) ;
               PUT LIST (A, B, C, X1, X2) ;
               GET LIST (A, B, C) ;
           END REPEAT ;

           END QUAD ;
```

Fig. 8. The PL/I version of program of Fig. 1.

does not involve any GO TO statements; it is therefore easier to understand and more likely to be correct when first written.

Fig. 9 is a PL/I version of the Fortran program of Fig. 3 for finding the sum of squares of an array. New features here include the use of the underline (called the "break" character) in place of hyphenation in data

names, provision of an initial value in a declaration, and the vertical bar for the OR function.

Fig. 10 shows the Cobol program of Fig. 5 rewritten in PL/I. We note the use of the abbreviation DCL for DE-CLARE; a variety of abbreviations are available. (Incidentally, there are no reserved words in PL/I as there are in Cobol; any word may be used as an identifier if it will be

```
SQUARE: PROCEDURE OPTIONS (MAIN);
               /* A PROGRAM TO FIND THE SUM OF SQUARES OF THE
                    ELEMENTS OF AN ARRAY */

           DECLARE Z(100) FLOAT,
                   SUM_SQUARES FLOAT INITIAL (0),
                   (K, N) FIXED;

           GET LIST(N);

           IF N<1 | N>100 THEN GO TO WRAPUP;

READ_LOOP:     DO K = 1 TO N;
                   GET LIST(Z(K));
               END READ_LOOP;

SQUARE_LOOP: DO K = 1 TO N;
                   SUM_SQUARES = SUM_SQUARES + Z(K)**2;
               END SQUARE_LOOP;

           PUT LIST (N, SUM_SQUARES);

WRAPUP: END SQUARE;
```

Fig. 9. The PL/I version of program of Fig. 3.

```
PAYROLL:        PROCEDURE OPTIONS (MAIN);

                DCL HOURS_WORKED FIXED (3,1),
                    PAYRATE        FIXED (4,3),
                    EXTRA          FIXED (3,1),
                    GROSS_PAY      FIXED (5,2);

                ON ENDFILE (SYSIN) GO TO WRAPUP;

START:          OPEN FILE (SYSIN) INPUT;
                OPEN FILE (SYSPRINT) OUTPUT;

PROCESSING_ROUTINE:
                GET EDIT (HOURS_WORKED, PAYRATE) (COLUMN(1), F(3,1), F(4,3));
                GROSS_PAY = PAYRATE * HOURS_WORKED;
                IF HOURS_WORKED > 40 THEN BEGIN;
                   EXTRA = 0.5 * (HOURS_WORKED - 40) * PAYRATE;
                   GROSS_PAY = GROSS_PAY + EXTRA;
                END;
                PUT SKIP EDIT (HOURS_WORKED, PAYRATE, GROSS_PAY)
                   (F(5,1), F(8,3), P'$$$$$$$9V.99');
                GO TO PROCESSING_ROUTINE;

WRAPUP:         CLOSE FILE (SYSIN);
                CLOSE FILE (SYSPRINT);

                END PAYROLL;
```

Fig. 10.   The PL/I version of program of Fig. 5.

clear to the compiler from the context that it has no special meaning in PL/I. This is quite different from Cobol.) The OPEN statements carry out various necessary actions in getting started on input and output operations; previously, we let the system do these actions on its own initiative when first encountering GET and PUT statements.

The GET used in this program is the EDIT version, which means that we provide information about the arrangement of input, in a way not too different from Fortran although with considerably more flexibility. The format information associated with the PUT includes a picture specification similar to a Cobol feature. We also see the explicit file closing.

We now turn to a brief sketch of some of the other features of PL/I. PL/I provides for fixed, floating, binary, and character data, with length and radix-point location specifiable. These and various other attributes may be specified in DECLARE statements; if not so specified, there are prescribed defaults (see DEFAULT CONDITION). Array features are much like Algol, and various data structures are reminiscent of Cobol; the elements of an array may themselves be structures.

If not specified otherwise, storage is allocated to

variables upon entry into the procedure in which the variables are defined. But variations are possible, such as fixing storage allocation at the time the procedure is loaded into storage, or leaving allocation to the programmer through explicit statements. Facilities are available for making the name of a variable known outside the procedure block in which it is declared.

A multiple assignment statement gives a value to more than one variable, using a form such as

$$A, X = B + C;$$

An assignment statement may use arrays and structures in whole or in part, rather than elements or elementary items. For example, if R, S, and T are all arrays of the same size, we can write

$$R = S + T;$$

which means to perform an element-by-element addition of the two arrays. When a variable name appears as part of more than one structure, data name qualification can be used to specify which is meant, or sometimes the compiler can be left to deduce the correspondences. It is possible to call for actions on some subset of the elements of any array (i.e., a specified row or column of a two-dimensional array). This is called a *cross-section* of the array.

The loop control facilities match the generality of Algol and are similar. Some kinds of loops can be replaced by functions that have been provided to accomplish tasks that arise frequently. For example, the sum of all the elements of an array is given by the function SUM, and the function INDEX returns the position of the first occurrence of one string in another string.

It is possible to specify that various conditions should be tested during the execution of a program, together with the action that should be taken if they arise. Examples include END-OF-FILE on input, the existence of a subscript that is out of specified range, and arithmetic overflow. It is also possible to describe the desired handling of asynchronous interrupts, which means that two or more processes can be executed concurrently within the same program.

Input and output divides most basically between the stream and record types. All of the examples above were of stream I/O, where the characters are transmitted as a continuous flow. The PL/I verbs used in this case are GET and PUT. Record I/O deals with data grouped into records, with the records usually being further grouped into blocks to achieve speed and space efficiencies. The verbs in this case are READ and WRITE.

In summary, PL/I offers many powerful features and a high degree of generality. On the other hand, the great flexibility and generality leads to very large compilers and to long training periods.

Basic. Basic (Beginner's All-Purpose Symbolic Instruction Code) was developed in the mid-1960s at Dartmouth College under the direction of John Kemeny and Thomas Kurtz (Kemeny and Kurtz, 1967). It was intended to be very simple to learn and inexpensive to implement and use, so that large numbers of users could take advantage of it for learning purposes. It was designed as an interactive language, i.e., one in which the programmer gets immediate response to what is typed at a terminal connected to the computer. A few batch-mode compilers do exist, however.

The simplicity of Basic makes it easy to learn quickly and permits the writing of *interpreters* (*q.v.*) that are fast and small. It is accordingly popular for beginning students (as its name implies); the relative ease of writing translators has led to wide use with microcomputers. On the other side of the coin, its limited scope makes it less than ideal for sophisticated applications, and it does not provide facilities needed for effective development of very large applications. In sum, its scope is limited, but within that scope its clear usefulness has generated a body of faithful adherents.

Many of the characteristics of Basic can be seen in the example in Fig. 11. This is a program to generate drill in subtraction for one of the writer's daughters, then seven years old. We see that every statement must have a line number, which serves as the statement label, and the line numbers are in ascending sequence. The first thing after the line number is a word that establishes the nature of the statement. We first have a remark introduced by REM. Next are three assignment statements, which begin with LET. We see here string variables, one of the data types permitted in Basic, which have as their second character a dollar sign. Variable names in Basic consist of a single letter or of a letter followed by a digit. Subscripted variables do not require a dimension statement unless they have more than ten elements. One- and two-dimensional arrays are allowed.

A random number function (RND), which generates random numbers in the range 0 to 1, is used to help produce the numbers for the drill: minuends between 1 and 9, inclusive, and subtrahends between zero and the minuend. The integer (INT) function discards the fractional part of its argument. The rest of the program controls the drill logic, in which the student is given the correct answer after the second and succeeding errors, and is forced to enter the correct answer before being given another exercise. We note the rather simple conditional statement, in which the action is implied: GO TO the statement named. The PRINT with no arguments at 210 is to produce a blank line. Fig. 12 shows a few sample interactions.

Other features of Basic include programmer-defined functions, simple subroutines, and matrix operations.

APL. APL (A Programming Language) was defined in a 1962 book by Kenneth E. Iverson, then of IBM, describing a language he developed while teaching at Harvard (Iverson, 1962; Pakin, 1972). It is a procedure-oriented language, like the others treated in this article, in that it is used to express procedures for solving problems. Since it is used almost exclusively in the interactive mode, however, a "procedure" can be in the most rudimentary form: If we type 2 + 2 at an APL terminal and press the return key, the system responds at once with a 4. The plus sign alone serves as a sufficient command for the system to take action. It is also possible to write procedures of the more common type, where a group of operations is defined in advance and then applied to data.

The word "rudimentary" used above should not mislead the reader into the notion that APL is limited or that APL programs are always trivial to understand. APL is a very powerful language indeed, having operators that carry out actions requiring dozens of statements in other languages. The language thus has the attractive characteristic that the beginner can get started doing meaningful work very quickly—within minutes, in fact—and still

```
0 REM A PROGRAM TO PROVIDE DRILL IN SUBTRACTION
10 LET L$(1) = 'TRY AGAIN'
20 LET L$(2) = 'THE CORRECT ANSWER IS:'
30 LET L$(3) = L$(2)
40 REM THE NEXT TWO STATEMENTS USE THE RANDOM NUMBER
50 REM     FUNCTION TO GENERATE THE TWO NUMBERS
60 LET A = INT (9 * RND(0) + 1)
70 LET B = INT (A * RND(0))
80 LET C = A - B
90 REM T COUNTS THE NUMBER OF TRIES
100 LET T = 1
110 PRINT A; ' - '; B; ' = ';
120 INPUT D
130 IF C = D THEN 200
140 PRINT L$(T);
150 LET T = T + 1
160 IF T = 2 THEN 120
170 PRINT C
180 LET T = 3
190 GO TO 110
200 PRINT 'GOOD'
210 PRINT
220 GO TO 60
230 END
```

Fig. 11. A Basic program.

```
6  -    1 = ?5
GOOD


3  -    1 = ?1
TRY AGAIN   ?2
GOOD


2  -    0 = ?2
GOOD


9  -    1 = ?7
TRY AGAIN   ?6
THE CORRECT ANSWER IS:   8
9  -    1 = ?8
GOOD


8  -    5 = ?3
GOOD


4  -    2 = ?2
GOOD


2  -    1 = ?1
GOOD
```

Fig. 12.   Typical user-computer dialog for program of
Fig. 11.

have available language features of great power and
range.

The power of APL is built upon the use of arrays as
the basic data elements and a set of functions of remarkable scope for manipulating arrays. All functions that operate on scalars, such as the arithmetic and logical operations, exist in both monadic and dyadic form. For
example, the operator that produces the maximum of two
values, if applied to a single value, returns the smallest
integer that is greater than or equal to the argument.
There is a function that produces the factorial of a single
argument or the binomial coefficient of two. One function
is a random number generator. All these functions apply
without change to arrays, as long as dimensions are compatible.

One of the unusual features of APL is that there is
no hierarchy of functional operators as in the other POLs
discussed here: In the absence of parentheses, expressions
are evaluated from right to left; thus $2 \times 3 + 4$ is 14,
not 10, because the addition is done first, followed by the
multiplication.

An operator called "reduction," denoted by a slash,
applies a stated function to all the elements of a vector.
If A is a vector, for example, the expression $+/A$ forms
the sum of all the elements of A.

The subscript of an array can itself be an array.
Since there is a function that produces a vector giving the
order in which the elements of another vector would have

to be taken to be in ascending sequence, sorting a vector is a matter of writing a simple subscript expression. Thus an action that would require at least a dozen statements in most other POLs is done as one part—perhaps a small part—of a single APL statement. This is not an isolated example. There are functions that transpose matrices, rotate the rows or columns of an array, reshape a vector into any type of array, perform number base conversion or solve a substitution cipher in a single operation, or generate all the integers from 1 up to the argument. Assignment of new values to variables is done with an assignment operator ($\leftarrow$) that may be embedded within a statement that does many other things. Most of the operators generalize in logical ways to arrays of any dimensionality. Matrix multiplication, for example, is designated by just three symbols ($+ . \times$) between the names of the two matrices.

APL has been used as a convenient notation for describing complex information processing succinctly without involving a computer at all. Considered as a POL for running on a computer, however, APL is normally an interactive language in which there is ordinarily no compilation into a separate object program at all: The statements are interpreted and carried out as they are encountered. There is a provision for the use of user-defined functions, but they usually cannot be compiled separately. There are provisions, however, for making use of preprogrammed routines that may be available in the system. Functions may be recursive.

Since the language was intended for use at an interactive terminal with modest amounts of storage, the input and output facilities are very limited. The business concerns that provide APL time-sharing service, however, have developed file systems that have much more storage capability, combined with appropriate input and output facilities.

Two examples of APL functions will have to suffice to give a hint of the flavor of the language. These are taken from *APL 360 User's Manual*, by A. D. Falkoff and K. E. Iverson, published by IBM.

The first is a simple routine to give drill in multiplication, as shown in Fig. 13. The first line is called the "function header"; it gives the name of the function, the

name of the argument (N), and establishes Y and X as local variables that will be used only in this function and have no relation to any other variable of the same name elsewhere. The scheme is this: When we want drill in multiplication, we will type MULTDRILL followed by two integers that give the maximum sizes of factors that we want to use. Thus, N becomes a vector of two elements; the fact that it is a vector instead of a scalar will be established by usage—no declaration is necessary.

Statement 1 generates two random numbers, using the ? operator, and assigns them to the vector Y. Statement 2, since it does not say to do anything else with the variable named, will print these two values. Statement 3 calls for a number to be read from the terminal; this would be the student's answer to the implied question as to the product of the two elements of Y that have been printed. Thus, X is a scalar. Statement 4 determines whether the student typed the letter s (for Stop) instead of a number, and must be read from right to left: If X is equal to the letter s the comparison produces a 1, and the iota operator (ι) of this is also 1. One times zero is zero, and we transfer (the right-pointing arrow) to statement zero, which means to leave the function. If X is not equal to s, the comparison produces a zero: The iota function of zero is null (which is different from zero), which multiplied by zero is still null, and the transfer is not taken.

Statement 5 establishes whether the answer is correct by asking whether the product of the two elements of Y is equal to X and transferring back to statement 1 for another exercise if so. If the answer is wrong, we print a comment to that effect and transfer back to ask for another try at the answer.

Fig. 14 shows a complete APL program for finding the inverse of a matrix. It would not serve our purposes to explain its operation, which would take pages, but perhaps the reader can gather the extreme power of the APL operators when it is realized that this procedure would take dozens of statements in most other POLs.

An APL program, as this example shows, can be extremely condensed. This can sometimes make it difficult to explain and understand, which in turn becomes a potential handicap to producing correct programs. It is not always in the programmer's best interest to take full advantage of APL to produce absolutely the shortest possible program.

APL has attracted many staunch supporters. Implementations exist for machines of most manufacturers, some of the implementations having been produced in university environments for educational use. Whether APL will continue to gain popularity at the expense of the more conventional POLs remains to be seen.

The Future of POLs. The future of POLs is not entirely clear. As noted earlier, there seem to be definite places for programming languages at both the POL level

---

```
       ∇MULTDRILL N;Y;X
[1]    Y←?N
[2]    Y
[3]    X←□
[4]    →0×ιX = 'S'
[5]    →ιX = ×/Y
[6]    'WRONG, TRY AGAIN'
[7]    →3∇
```

Fig. 13. An APL program.

$$\nabla Z \leftarrow INV \; M;I;J$$

[1] $\quad M \leftarrow \phi(1\,0 + \rho M)\rho(,\phi M),\sim J \leftarrow 1 < \mathcal{U} \leftarrow 1 \uparrow \rho M$

[2] $\quad M \leftarrow 1\phi(J,1)\phi[1]M - (J \times M[;1]) \circ . \times M[1;] \leftarrow M[1;] + M[1;1]$

[3] $\quad \rightarrow 2 \times 10 \neq I \leftarrow I - 1$

[4] $\quad Z \leftarrow M[;11\uparrow \rho M]$

$$\nabla$$

Fig. 14. An APL routine for finding the inverse of a square matrix.

and at a level much closer to that of the machine. A steady evolutionary development of POLs may reasonably be expected, with existing POLs being improved and extended, and with major new languages (such as Ada (*q.v.*), most recently) being introduced occasionally.

But it is becoming clear that this will not be enough. The "software crisis," as it is commonly called, finds us unable to write programs to satisfy all the demands of users for new and improved applications. This demand, in turn, is in part the result of the astonishing advances in hardware price/performance ratios—advances in no way matched on the software side. There have been significant improvements in the practice and management of software development, to be sure, but these gains are negligible compared with those in hardware performance.

Many observers now doubt that evolutionary improvements in the design and utilization of POLs will be sufficient to solve the software crisis. One body of opinion holds that it will be necessary to move away from primary dependence on programming in any language at all, and move toward heavier use of application packages, re-use of existing code, and what are called (for lack of a better term) non-procedural languages (*q.v.*).

The outcome of this ferment is an open question. One thing does seem reasonably certain, however: Any change will be gradual. The investment in applications programs written in POLs, estimated in the tens of billions of dollars, and the normal human inertia represented by hundreds of thousands of programmers who are familiar with present languages, make any kind of step-function change exceedingly unlikely. This is no doubt regrettable in many ways, but it does offer assurance to both practitioners and students that skills with present languages will not be made obsolete in the near term.

REFERENCES

1962. Iverson, K. E. *A Programming Language.* New York: Wiley.

1966. Weinberg, G. M. *PL/I Programming Primer.* New York: McGraw-Hill.

1967. Kemeny, J. G. and Kurtz, T. E. *Basic Programming.* New York: Wiley.

1969. Sammet, J. E. *Programming Languages: History and Fundamentals.* Englewood Cliffs, NJ: Prentice-Hall.

1972. Pakin, S. *APL/360 Reference Manual* (2nd Ed.). Chicago: Science Research Associates.

1975. Kieburtz, R. B. *Structured Programming and Problem Solving with Algol W.* Englewood Cliffs, NJ: Prentice-Hall.

1976. Conway, R., Gries, D. and Zimmerman, E. C. *A Primer on Pascal.* Cambridge, MA: Winthrop Publishers.

1976. McCracken, D. D. *A Simplified Guide to Structured COBOL Programming.* New York: Wiley.

1980. Meissner, L. P. and Organick, E. I. *Fortran 77 Featuring Structured Programming.* Reading, MA: Addison-Wesley.

D. D. McCRACKEN

PROGRAMMING

For articles on related subjects *see* COMPILER; DATA STRUCTURES; DEBUGGING; DIAGNOSTICS; EXPRESSION; LANGUAGE PROCESSORS; LOOP; MODULAR PROGRAMMING; OBJECT PROGRAM; PASCAL; PROCEDURE; PROGRAMMING LANGUAGES; SOURCE PROGRAM; STATEMENT; STRUCTURED PROGRAMMING; SUBROUTINE; and TRACE.

In contrast with the tremendous advances in computer hardware, the level at which machine languages operate has changed little over the past two decades. Instructions can be executed only if they are submitted as sequences of numerical codes. Moreover, the typical machine language instruction represents an activity that is trivial by human standards, offering no direct correspondence with our idea of a "step" in a problem solution.

Consequently, there is a gap between what the programmer wants to say and what the processor can recognize. High-level programming languages are designed to bridge this gap. It is in this context that one may examine the major conveniences provided by such languages, together with their effects on programming techniques.

Each of the hundreds of high-level programming languages is designed to meet a particular set of objectives. Some are intended for use over a wide range of applications; others address a more limited spectrum of problem types characteristic of a specific discipline. All share a common property: The elemental vehicle for expressing the programmer's intention (i.e., the language statement) conveys a level of complexity consistent with the procedure being represented. Thus, the activity which can be described in a single "instruction" or "command" bears no direct resemblance to a single machine operation. Instead, many languages try to provide some similarity between a language statement and its counterpart in the notation appropriate to the application. For example, the following statement in the Fortran language,

$$H = 0.023*(C/D)*(D*V*R/U)**0.8*$$
$$(U*P/C)**0.4, \tag{1}$$

is easily related to the same formula in conventional algebraic form:

$$H = 0.023 \frac{C}{D} \left(\frac{DVR}{U}\right)^{0.8} \left(\frac{UP}{C}\right)^{0.4}. \tag{2}$$

This equation ultimately would require a considerable number of machine operations to produce the specified result (i.e., a value for H). Accordingly, the correspondence between the Fortran statement and the equivalent sequence of machine instructions produced by the language-translating program (the compiler) is not obvious at all.

This extensive insulation between machine and programmer has had a profound effect on the growth of computer use and the range of successful applications. Most programs are written in high-level languages, and most people who write programs are not computer specialists.

A number of fundamental programming facilities will be examined briefly. Once their functions have been defined, they will be used to synthesize programs and program segments. The discussion will center around several widely used languages whose properties typify the range of conveniences generally afforded. Many of the illustrations will use Fortran 77, Algol, PL/I, and/or Pascal, all of which implement syntactically similar instruments for computations and decisions. When appropriate, they will be contrasted with Cobol, a language directed away from formulaic expression and more toward narrative description. Occasional examples will be shown in the Snobol language to illustrate programming techniques engendered by its approach.

Because a different set of techniques is required to exploit their specific advantages, interactive programming languages will not be emphasized here. However, two examples will be mentioned briefly with regard to some of their conveniences. Certain illustrations will be expressed in Basic to show a minimal approach that reflects its emphasis on ease of learning the language syntax. By way of contrast, some program segments in APL will be included to illustrate its highly compact syntax,

its complexity and variety of primitive operations, and its general orientation toward expressions.

Descriptions and Specifications. Regardless of the language used by the programmer, the final result must be an operationally equivalent sequence of machine instructions. This consists of a numerical string in which each operation is designated by its respective code, defined for it as part of the machine's design. References to operands (data on which operations are to be performed) cannot be expressed in terms of names. Instead, such references are expressed as addresses; i.e., memory locations in which the desired data is stored.

For example, if a procedural step calls for the addition of variables X and Y, the eventual implementation in machine language has no knowledge of an X or a Y. Having previously established associations between those variables and particular storage locations, the actual instructions to be executed will be in terms of the contents of those locations. Thus, instead of saying "add Y to X," the implied activity is to "add the content of the location associated with Y to the content of the location associated with variable X."

Similarly, when an algorithm includes a choice of processing sequences, the programmer sets up appropriate branches to different parts of the procedure, associating each destination with a particular activity. However, when this structure is represented in final form, these references are stripped of any procedural association. The destination, rather, is an address containing the instruction to be executed next.

If a machine language program is being prepared manually, then it is the programmer who must define the associations between addresses and their contents vis-á-vis their significance with respect to the procedure. The necessity of keeping track of these relationships accounted for much of the tedium required to turn out a reliable machine language program and helped motivate the development of high-level languages.

Consequently, every high-level language includes features that relieve the programmer of these bookkeeping tasks, shifting them to the software. The extent of this transfer depends on the sophistication of the language and the class of problems toward which it is oriented. In all cases, the programmer is no longer responsible for defining the direct relationships among the variables and their respective addresses. It is still necessary to make sure that ample storage is allocated to the various data items, but that process is greatly simplified. The programmer treats each variable in conventional terms, giving it a meaningful name that will apply throughout the program.

Within this general framework, the mechanism for expressing such specifications varies from one language to another. For many languages, the first stated activity involving a variable (such as the initial assignment of a value) is sufficient to trigger the automatic reservation of storage. For example, if we consider the Fortran statement shown in Eq. 1 as part of a program, and if the reference to the variable H in that statement constitutes its initial appearance in that program, the compiler will automatically allocate storage under that name for the result of the specified computations. Subsequent references to H will be processed routinely. Most languages include facilities for the explicit reservation of storage. For instance, each of the three following statements

REAL X, Y, Z   (Fortran)
real x, y, z;   (Algol and Pascal)   (3)
DECLARE (X, Y, Z) FLOAT;   (PL/I)

reserves storage for three variables X, Y, and Z, each to accommodate a numerical value placed there later in the program. Since nothing further is specified, internal language rules (called defaults) will determine the amount of reserved storage and the form for the numerical values. Various means are available to the programmer for overriding these defaults. In languages such as Fortran and PL/I, such explicit specifications are optional.

However, increasing emphasis on programming methodology and the systematization of the programming process has underscored the importance of such explicit definitions even when the language does not require them. Both Algol and Pascal are *strongly typed* languages which require all variables to be defined prior to their initial use in processing.

Cobol, because of its concern with data files and records, requires a hierarchical description of the items for which storage is to be allocated. That is, unless specifically defined otherwise, each variable is considered to be a component of a larger data structure. Moreover, the storage associated with each variable must be specified in terms of the type of information to be accommodated. For example, the following specification

```
01 RENEW-INFO.
   02 R-DATE.
      03 R-MONTH PICTURE 99.        (4)
      03 R-DAY PICTURE 99.
      03 R-YR PICTURE 99.
   02 RENEW-RATE PICTURE 999V99.
```

reserves storage for a group of variables known collectively as RENEW-INFO. This structure consists of two basic components, R-DATE and RENEW-RATE. The former is a collection of three variables (R-MONTH, R-DAY, and R-YR), each of which is a two-digit integer. The second component is a single variable whose value

will be expressed as a five-digit number having two decimal places.

The basic naming facility extends to the identification of statements within a program. It is possible to attach unique labels as prefixes to statements, thereby providing an unambiguous way of referring to a desired point in the processing. In most languages, statements may be associated with symbolic names such as those used for variables. In Fortran and Basic, the syntactic rules require numeric statement labels. The equivalent assignment statements shown below illustrate the labeling conventions for several languages.

calc2: c := a + y*b;   (Algol)   (5a)

17   LET C = A + Y*B   (Basic)   (5b)

24   C = A + Y*B   (Fortran)   (5c)
CALC2: C = A + Y*B;   (PL/I)   (5d)
CALC2 C = A + Y * B   (Snobol)   (5e)
CALC2.
   COMPUTE C = A + Y*B   (Cobol)   (5f)
      2: c := a + y*b   (Pascal)   (5g)
[5] CALC2: C ← A + Y*B   (APL)   (5h)

Note that the label 2 in the Pascal assignment statement would not be accepted without prior definition as a label. Note also the variety of different assignment symbols (=, :=, ←) and that APL has a numeric line number in addition to the (optional) statement label.

Specification of Complex Activities in Simple Terms. The statement in Eq. 1 exemplifies the primary convenience a high-level language brings to its users—the ability to specify intricate steps with little loss in correspondence between the conventional description and its representation in a program. Syntactically, this intent is reflected in the characteristic of a language's elemental "sentence" or *statement*. Generally, the limitation on the length and complexity of a statement is designed to be sufficiently large so that it does not restrict the programmer's ability to maintain the integrity of a procedural step. Thus, it is usually the programmer, and not the computing system or the language, that determines the amount of activity to be specified in a single program "step" without serious regard to the number of actual machine steps these actions will eventually entail.

Terms, Operators, and Expressions. The effect of this facility is seen perhaps more dramatically in terms of statements denoting internal manipulative operations (i.e., "computing"). In many high-level languages, the type of statement most commonly associated with such operations is the assignment statement. When specifying mathematical computations, the assignment statement bears a close resemblance to an equation as exemplified in Eq. 5. For many languages, particularly those emphasizing mathematical capabilities, the assignment statement is some variant of the general structure

$$variable \leftarrow expression. \tag{6}$$

The $\leftarrow$ in this construction symbolizes the operation of replacement, so that the general sense of the assignment may be represented as follows: "Evaluate the *expression* on the right-hand side of the $\leftarrow$ by performing the indicated operations; then, let the result be the new value for *variable,* replacing its current value." In many widely used high-level languages, replacement is denoted (inaccurately) by the symbol "$=$"; Algol and Pascal use "$:=$"; and APL uses the actual symbol "$\leftarrow$". Because of this basic characterization, *variable,* the item to the left of $\leftarrow$ is structurally restricted to a single variable. Thus, a formulation such as

$$\frac{A + B}{C^2} = \frac{32.96(D + C)}{D} \tag{7}$$

would have to be rewritten with the desired variable (say *B*) isolated on the left, i.e.,

$$B = \frac{32.96C^2(D + C)}{D} - A, \tag{8}$$

before the formula could be represented as a program statement.

An expression consists of a combination of *terms* and *operators* in which the rules of construction constitute a restricted version of those applying to ordinary algebra. The two basic restrictions given below are imposed to accommodate the computer's functional limitations and to avoid problems in compiler implementation.

1. Each individual arithmetic operation must be indicated explicitly; it may never be implied. (For example, the expression $A(B + C)$, understandable in algebra, must be written as $A*(B + C)$ in a program statement.)
2. Expressions must be in linear form. For example, $(A + B)/(C - D)$ is a more awkward, but unavoidable, substitute for the conventional algebraic equivalent:

$$\frac{A + B}{C - D}.$$

The latter restriction reflects a physical limitation imposed by I/O media rather than any linguistic constraint.

Each compiler uses certain rules to evaluate expressions. Unless the user is familiar with these rules for a particular compiler, there may be constructions that appear ambiguous. For example, $A + B/C*D$ may be thought to represent

$$A + \frac{B}{CD}, A + \frac{BD}{C}, \text{ or even } \frac{A + B}{CD}.$$

Most procedure-oriented languages define an operator *precedence* (or *hierarchy*) which dictates the interpretation of an expression, but different languages use different hierarchies. Most high-level languages allow the programmer to avoid ambiguity or to force the meaning intended by using parentheses to indicate the exact intent. Thus, the linear expressions $A + B/(C*D)$, $A + (B/C)*D$ and $(A + B)/(C*D)$ are the respective equivalents of the three algebraic expressions shown above.

Additional limitations are those imposed by the necessity of ensuring that there is a value associated with each variable appearing in an expression. This must be guaranteed by the programmer, since compilers generally are designed to proceed on that assumption. Once the programmer makes sure that the variables have been defined (i.e., storage has been made available for them and values have been provided), the language presents no further obstacles with regard to the length or complexity of an expression.

To illustrate, we refer again to Eq. 1, which uses the Fortran language. Assuming that values are available for each of the variables D, V, R, U, P, and C, the programmer has the prerogative of computing a value for H via a single statement, as in Eq. 2, or using several statements to produce partial results that are stored in separate variables and used subsequently:

```
V1 = D*V*R/U
V2 = U*P/C                              (9)
H = 0.023*(C/D)*(V1**0.8)*(V2**0.4).
```

The choice of form is governed predominantly by legibility of the resulting program.

For an increasing variety of applications, "internal manipulations" or "computation" need to be extended to include operations on strings of letters and other nonnumeric symbols. While most high-level languages accommodate such *alphanumeric* information, their facilities generally are limited to the simple movement and display of strings, treating them as labels or headings. However, capabilities for substantive processing of character strings are included in a number of languages that allow the use of nonnumeric data as constants and variables, and implement the manipulation through the general assignment statement. A fundamental operation is *conca-*

tenation, the synthesis of larger strings from smaller ones. This process is exemplified below to show the parallelism with arithmetic assignments. In each instance, we form a string consisting of the letters IDENTICAL and assign it to the variable *W3*.

PL/I:
```
    DECLARE W1 CHARACTER(4)
            W2 CHARACTER(3)         (10a)
            W3 CHARACTER(9);
    W1 = 'DENT'; W2 = 'CAL';
    W3 = 'I' ‖ W1 ‖ 'I' ‖ W2;
```
Fortran 77:
```
    CHARACTER W1•4,W2•3,W3•9
    W1 = 'DENT'                     (10b)
    W2 = 'CAL'
    W3 = 'I'//W1//'I'//W2
```
Snobol:
```
    W1 = 'DENT'
    W2 = 'CAL'                      (10c)
    W3 = 'I' W1 'I' W2
```
APL:
```
    W1 ← 'DENT'
    W2 ← 'CAL'                      (10d)
    W3 ← 'I', W1, 'I', W2
```

Built-In Functions. High-level languages include features that expand considerably the range of processes expressable in a statement. The objective of these capabilities is to allow the programmer to specify as "single" operations a variety of activities, each of which actually embodies a number of steps, even by human standards. Prototypical is the extraction of the square root, a process viewed as a single mathematical operation and represented that way in conventional notation. To preserve this idea, a procedure designed to produce the square root is embedded in many high-level languages and made available to the programmer via a simple reference name (SQRT in most languages). Thus, the structure of a formulation such as

$$C = \sqrt{A^2 + B^2} \qquad (11)$$

still can be preserved in a language statement:

C = SQRT(A••2 + B••2)	(Fortran)	(12a)
C = SQRT(A••2 + B••2);	(PL/I)	(12b)
LET C = SQR(A↑2 + B↑2)	(Basic)	(12c)
c := sqrt(sqr(a) + sqr(b))	(Pascal)	(12d)
c := sqrt(a↑2 + b↑2);	(Algol)	(12e)

This facility is known as a *built-in function.* Most high-level languages provide a library of such functions, with

their exact nature being determined by the language's orientation. Accordingly, languages such as Fortran and Basic reflect their emphasis on arithmetic in terms of a substantial mathematical function library (e.g., logarithms, trigonometric functions), while those provided by Snobol and other languages directed toward nonnumeric applications offer a different spectrum of operations.

A standard collection of built-in functions represents part of a more general facility that enables a programmer to supplement the language with additional custom-designed functions. Inclusion of such functions is a relatively straightforward process independent of the complexity of the function or its intended permanency.

Decisions and Decision Structures. Building on simple comparison operations available at the machine level, a high-level language generally provides the programmer with syntactic structures for expressing arbitrarily complicated tests and decision rules.

The conceptual element that forms a basis for decision statements can be represented graphically as in Fig. 1. The nucleus is the test condition, formulated as a comparison with two possible outcomes (true or false). Accordingly, the outcome of the test will dictate which of the two alternative actions will ensue. The power of this construction can be summarized in terms of three basic properties:

1. The formulation is simple and "natural," reflecting the flowchart given in Fig. 1: "Test the specified condition. If it exists (true), perform alternative action *A*, ignoring *B*. If it is false, perform *B*, ignoring *A*. Upon completion of the action, continue that part of the processing that is independent of the test condition."

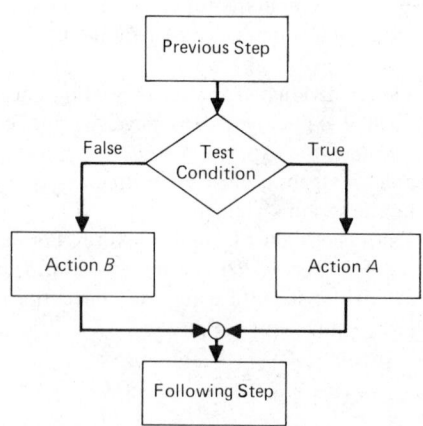

Fig. 1.   Flowchart for basic high-level language decision structure.

2. The test may be arbitrarily complex.
3. Either or both of the alternative actions may be arbitrarily complex, ranging from a very long sequence of program statements to no action at all.

The testing facilities in the Basic language, though rudimentary, typify the form underlying more extensive mechanisms. In general terms, the condition to be tested (in Basic) consists of a pair of arithmetic expressions connected by a relational operator that defines the comparison. Thus, the construction

$$X*Y <= Z \qquad (13)$$

specifies a comparison to determine whether the product XY is less than or equal to Z (in which case, the outcome would be "true") or not. Only one type of action is specifiable—a branch to some other place in the program, at which point the appropriate processing presumably continues; the alternative merely is to ignore the branch. Accordingly, the test and branch are combined to form a complete statement:

$$\text{IF } X*Y <= Z \text{ THEN } 70, \qquad (14)$$

as shown in Fig. 2. The "70" refers to the statement label attached to the branch's destination.

Other languages (such as Algol, PL/I, Fortran 77, and Pascal) provide less awkward vehicles by allowing

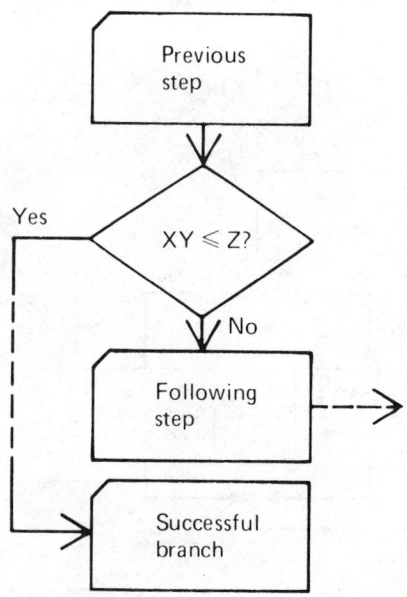

Fig. 2. Example of testing and branching in the Basic language.

the explicit specification of alternative actions, thereby mirroring directly the graphic representation in Fig. 1. This is seen in the following implementations of a decision rule.

PL/I:
```
    IF X*Y <= Z THEN X = X + 7.8;
                ELSE X = X - 1.6;
    T = X*Y*Z*(2.5*Y + W);          (15a)
```
Pascal:
```
    if x*y <= z then x := x + 7.8
                else x := x - 1.6;
    t := x*y*z*(2.5*y + w);          (15b)
```
Fortran 77:
```
    IF (X*Y .LE. Z) THEN X = X + 7.8
                    ELSE X = X - 1.6
    END IF
    T = X*Y*Z*(2.5*Y + W)            (15c)
```

The same facility is present in Cobol in a more narrative form:
```
    IF X*Y <= Z ADD 7.8 TO X
        ELSE SUBTRACT 1.6 FROM X.
    COMPUTE T = X*Y*Z*(2.5*Y + W).    (15d)
```

The structural simplicity made possible by the IF . . . THEN . . . ELSE coupling is not very useful without a corresponding enlargement in the range of activities that may be attached to a decision rule. This is handled by including syntactic components wherein sequences of statements are treated as a single (conceptual) activity. To illustrate, our decision rule will be complicated: "If XY is less than or equal to Z, do the following: Add 7.8 to X, double Y, and subtract 2.2 from Z; otherwise, subtract 1.6 from X, make $Y = 0.85 \times$ its current value, and leave Z alone. In either case, compute the value $XYZ(2.5Y + W)$ and store the result in T." The construction of appropriate program techniques is as follows.

Fortran 77:
```
    IF (X*Y .LE. Z) THEN X = X + 7.8
                         Y = 2*Y
                         Z = Z - 2.2
                    ELSE X = X - 1.8
                         Y = 0.85*Y
    END IF                            (16a)
    T = X*Y*Z*(2.5*Y + W)
```

PL/I:
```
    IF X*Y <= Z THEN DO;
                X = X + 7.8;
```

```
          Y = 2•Y;
          Z = Z − 2.2;
        END;
      ELSE DO;
          X = X − 1.8;
          Y = 0.85•Y;
      END;
    T = X•Y•Z•(2.5•Y + W);        (16b)
```

Pascal:

```
  if x∗y <= z then begin
            x := x + 7.8;
            y := 2∗y;
            z := z − 2.2
        end
      else begin
            x := x − 1.5;
            y := 0.85∗y
        end;
    t := x∗y∗z∗(2.5∗y + w);        (16c)
```

The representation in Algol follows the same form. Cobol uses a more casual syntax:

```
    IF X•Y IS <= Z ADD 7.8 TO X
      MULTIPLY 2 BY Y SUBTRACT 2.2 FROM Z
      ELSE SUBTRACT 1.6 FROM X MULTIPLY
      0.85 BY Y.
    COMPUTE T = X•Y•Z•(2.5•Y + W).    (16d)
```

Many languages allow their users to implement decisions in which specified test conditions are to be met simultaneously and/or sequentially, with various consequent actions at each step. A simple structure of this type is shown in Fig. 3. Carryover to the actual program statements is generally straightforward. For example, in PL/I:

```
IF X•Y <= Z & Z > 2.9• W THEN
    IF W > 29.6  THEN DO;
    X = X + 7.8; Y = 2•Y; Z = Z − 2.2;
            END;
        ELSE DO;
    X = X + 1.9; Y = 1.8•Y; W = 1.1•W;
            END;
                ELSE
    IF W > 29.6  THEN DO;
        X = X − 1.6; Y = 0.85•Y
            END;
        ELSE   X = X − 1.4;
    T = X•Y•Z•(2.5•Y + W);        (17a)
```

The programming in Fortran 77, Pascal, and Algol is similar. Basic (in its standard form) forces the use of a more awkward articulation:

```
100   IF X•Y <= Z THEN 300
200   IF W > 29.6 THEN 230        (17b)
210   LET X = X − 1.4
220   GO TO 400
230   LET X = X − 1.6
240   LET Y = 0.85•Y
```

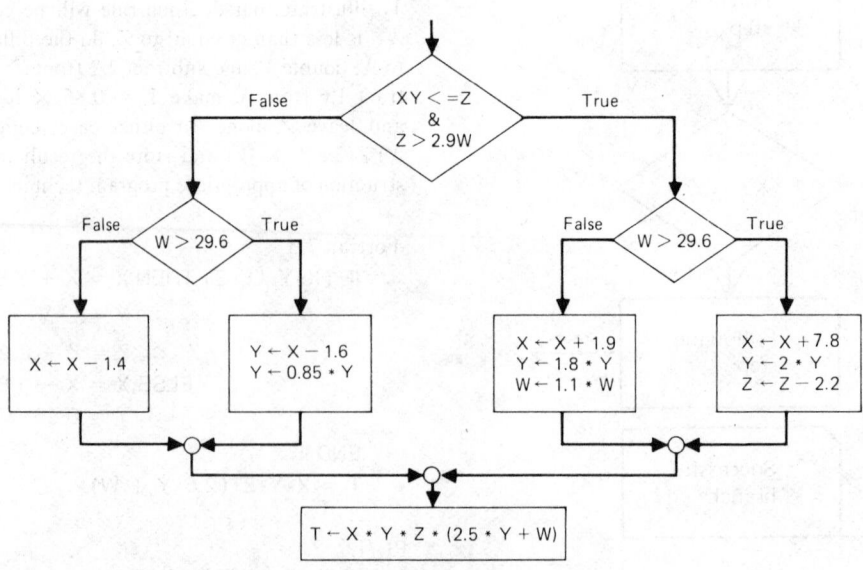

Fig. 3. Flowchart of sequential decision structure.

```
250   GO TO 400
300   IF Z > 2.9•W THEN 320
310   GO TO 200
320   IF W > 29.6 THEN 370
330   LET X = X + 1.9
340   LET Y = 1.8•Y
350   LET W = 1.1•W
360   GO TO 400
370   LET X = X + 7.8
380   LET Y = 2•Y
390   LET Z = Z − 2.2
400   LET T = X•Y•Z•(2.5•Y + W)
```

Programming Loops. Most high-level languages offer convenient ways to specify and control repetitive operations. In general, these enable the programmer to identify the beginning and end of a loop, specify the number of repetitions, and define a mechanism for (automatically) keeping track of the number of cycles through the loop.

These mechanisms can be examined conveniently via an example involving arrays. An array A_1 will have its 14 elements set respectively to values of 1, 2, . . . , 14. A second array, A_2, also consisting of 14 elements, will receive respective values of 3, 5, 7, . . . , 29. The sequences in Basic, Fortran, PL/I, and Pascal are quite similar.

```
Basic: 10   DIM A1(14), A2(14)
       15   FOR I = 1 to 14
       20      LET A1(I) = I                    (18a)
       25      LET A2(I) = 2•I + 1
       30   NEXT I
```

```
Fortran: INTEGER A1(14), A2(14)
            DO 30 I = 1, 14
               A1(I) = 1
               A2(I) = 2•I + 1                  (18b)
       30   CONTINUE
```

```
PL/I: DECLARE A1(14), A2(14);
         DO I = 1 TO 14;
            A1(I) = I; A2(I) = 2•I + 1;        (18c)
         END;
```

```
Pascal: var a1,a2:  array[1..14] of real;
            i     : integer;
        begin
            for i := 1 to 14 do                 (18d)
               begin
                  a1[i] := i;
                  a2[i] := 2*i + 1
               end
        end.
```

The mode of expression in Cobol is characteristically less formulaic:

```
01   ARRAYS.
     02 A1 OCCURS 14 TIMES PICTURE 999V99.
     02 A2 OCCURS 14 TIMES PICTURE 999V99.
                  .
                  .
                  .
77 I PICTURE 99.                               (18e)
                  .
                  .
                  .
PERFORM BUILDUP VARYING I FROM 1 BY 1
    UNTIL I GREATER THAN 14.
BUILDUP.
     COMPUTE A1 (I) = I.
     COMPUTE A2 (I) = 2•I + 1.
```

In Snobol, the construction uses a test mechanism as part of a compound statement. Thus, the condition LE(I,14) determines whether I is less than or equal to 14. If it is, the test is *successful,* and the statement operates as if the test were not there. That is, I is increased by 1. Furthermore, the :s(BUILD) stipulates that the action precipitated by a successful test should culminate in a branch to the statement identified as BUILD. Failure prevents processing of both the assignment and the branch.

```
         A1 = ARRAY(14)
         A2 = ARRAY(14)
         I = 1
BUILD    A1<I> = I                             (18f)
         A2<I> = 2 • I + 1
         I = LE (I,14) I + 1        :S(BUILD)
         further processing
```

APL, because of its strong emphasis on arrays, treats such operations as being much more fundamental. Accordingly, much of the processing is implied and the necessary programming reduces to

$$A1 \leftarrow \iota\, 14 \qquad (18g)$$
$$A2 \leftarrow 1 + 2 \times \iota\, 14$$

where ι is an operation that creates an array named by the identifier to the left of $\leftarrow$; the number of elements is specified by the term to the right of ι, and respective values are successive positive integers beginning with 1 and ending with the right argument of ι.

These facilities may be generalized so that the programmer can implement loops in which the number of cycles and the method of cycling may vary with each use.

For some languages, the ability to specify the number of cycles is complemented by another control mechanism that is not based on a prescribed number of cycles. Instead, the programmer may construct a loop in which some arbitrarily defined criterion automatically terminates the repetitions, irrespective of the number of cycles. To see how this works, we consider the following example: X is a number, values for which are read in successively. The program is to accumulate the sum of these successive input values until that sum reaches or exceeds a value Y (said value also having been made available to the program earlier). To simplify matters, it will be assumed that Y will be reached or exceeded before all of X's values are exhausted.

Some languages include a specific mechanism to deal with such situations conveniently. PL/I serves as an appropriate example:

```
TOTAL = 0;
DO WHILE (TOTAL < Y);
    GET DATA (X);                    (19a)
    TOTAL = TOTAL + X;
END;
further processing
```

In the absence of this automating feature, the programmer is obliged to set up the decision mechanism manually. Accordingly, an equivalent sequence in Fortran 77 would be expressed as follows.

```
    TOTAL = 0.0
1 IF (TOTAL .GE. Y) GO TO 30
    READ *, X                       (19b)
    TOTAL = TOTAL + X
    GO TO 1
30 further processing
```

Although the example shown above is sufficiently simple so that there is no conspicuous difference in legibility between the PL/I and Fortran versions, use of numerous branches in more complex loops and other decision structures may lead to overly intricate, logical mazes that are extremely difficult to analyze. In such contexts, the branch may represent an operational intrusion that detracts from the resemblance between a procedural component and its implementation in a program.

As the design and analysis of programs have become more systematized, there has been a corresponding evolution of language features that facilitate the representation of complex logical situations without the use of explicit branches. This approach, known as *structured programming*, has prompted the introduction of language features that make it easy to avoid the need for such branches. For example, Pascal recognizes two distinct variations of the loop control mechanism illustrated in the previous example: One of these, the *repeat-until* construct, provides for the convenient specifications of a loop for which the programmer guarantees at least one cycle. Implementation of the previous program segment using this construct is shown below.

```
total := 0;
repeat
    total := total + x              (19c)
until total >= y
```

As the construct implies, the test (which determines whether or not to perform another cycle) occurs after the activity is completed. The alternative is the *do-while* construct, already seen in the PL/I example. This is the most general loop control, in that it includes the possibility that the loop will not cycle at all. Accordingly, the determining test implied in this construct occurs prior to the cyclic activity.

Input/Output Operations. A significant aspect of the growing computer hardware technology is the widening array of available I/O devices. One of the primary duties of a high-level language is to accommodate this expanding capability without undo inconvenience to the programmer. These dual requirements of versatility and convenience often are antithetical and language designers must seek an effective compromise.

Many languages handle I/O operations using two basic mechanisms. The first of these is to provide a unified form for specifying all data transmission. Specific circumstances pertaining to a particular operation then are defined within the statement's general structure. In Fortran, for example, these operations can be represented by the general statements:

```
READ (n, m) v1, v2, etc.
WRITE (n, m) v1, v2, etc.          (20)
```

Access to the various peripheral devices is provided by n. Each device in a particular computing constellation is given a unique number, and a table of these designations is made available to Fortran within the supervisory software under which it operates. (These assignments are fairly standard, but they may easily be redefined at each individual installation). Accordingly, the programmer specifies the device number involved in a particular data transmission, and the appropriate association is established. The second parenthesized indicator, m, gives the number of a statement in that program in which the data format is described. For input (i.e., in a READ statement), the statement labeled m gives an item-by-item description of the appearance of the data (number of digits, location of the decimal point, number of spaces between consecutive values, etc.). Each description corresponds to a variable named in the input list v1, v2, etc. To illustrate, assume that values for three variables X, Y and Z are keypunched on a card as shown in Fig. 4. Using 5 to represent the card reader, the appropriate Fortran sequence would be

```
REAL X, Y, Z
READ (5, 12)X, Y, Z                    (21)
12 FORMAT( 1X, F4.1, 1X, F6.2, 2X, F4.1)
```

In the WRITE statement, the information in statement m describes the listed data items as they are to appear on the output medium.

PL/I handles I/O with two pairs of statement types: GET and PUT for transmission of individual data items, and READ and WRITE for multiple data items organized into records. Input with the GET statement is roughly analogous to Fortran's READ statement. This can be seen in the general construction:

```
GET FILE FILENAME EDIT ( v1, v2, etc.)(format
description);
```

The list of names to be read is specified as in Fortran, and the item-by-item descriptions of the input are similar except that they appear as part of the same statement, thereby obviating the reference to a separate format statement. Designation of the data source is through *filename*, the name of a data collection from which these items are taken. The connection between the name and input device is established outside the program.

Since the card reader is a common input source, it is possible to define that device (or some other one, for that matter) as a standard input unit, in which case its designation may be implied in the program:

```
GET EDIT ( v1, v2, etc.)(format description);.
```

Accordingly, a sequence of PL/I statements to read the card shown in Fig. 4 would appear as follows.

```
DECLARE X, Y, Z;
GET EDIT (X, Y, Z)(X(1), F(4, 1), X(1),
          F(6, 2), X(2), F(4, 1));    (22)
```

Further simplification is possible when dealing with input items separated by blanks. The X in both Fortran and PL/I causes the program to skip the indicated number of spaces, irrespective of their contents. Thus, there could have been anything at all between the data items in Fig. 4 without affecting the result. When input items are separated specifically by blanks, it is possible to exploit a special scanning mechanism available in several languages. For example, the card used above can be read with the PL/I statement:

```
GET LIST (X, Y, Z);.                   (23)
```

The Fortran 77 equivalent is

```
READ *, X, Y, Z                        (24)
```

The Pascal statement appears as

```
readln(x, y, z);.                      (25)
```

Corresponding output facilities are provided via the PUT, PRINT, and WRITELN statements for PL/I, Fortran 77, and

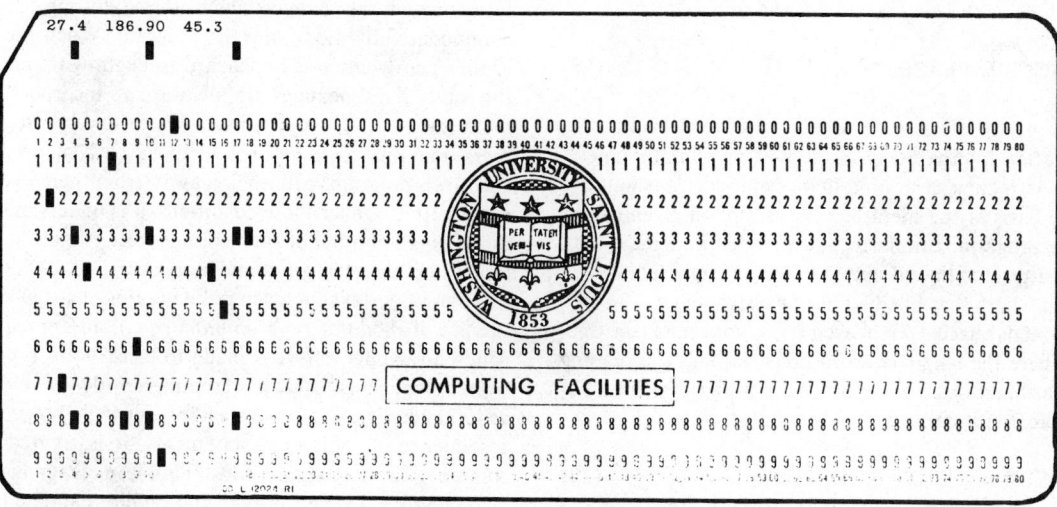

Fig. 4. Values of variables X,Y,Z keypunched for statement (21).

Pascal, respectively. Each statement allows the simplification discussed above (i.e., the specification of an output list without a corresponding format description), in which case the programmer relinquishes control of the output's appearance and accepts a standard format built into the language.

Complementing the PL/I GET and PUT facilities are those for transmitting entire records. The data items in a record are organized hierarchically in much the same way used by Cobol and illustrated in Eq. 4. Input is handled via the general construction

$$\text{READ FILE (FILENAME) INTO (PLACE);} \quad (26)$$

where FILENAME has its previous meaning and PLACE refers to an area in storage reserved for the input record. Once the record has been read, its individual data items may be extracted for further processing. Output follows the same pattern:

$$\text{WRITE FILE (FILENAME) FROM (PLACE);} \quad (27)$$

Individual data items are assembled in place to form the record, after which it is written as an entity.

As an alternative approach to implementing I/O handling, some languages provide separate vehicles for transmitting data to and from standard peripheral devices (usually the card reader and line printer), keeping these constructions simple. Data transmissions involving other devices are specified with different types of statements designed to express the necessary complications. Along these lines, the general facilities in Cobol are expressible through READ and WRITE statements that resemble (and are ancestral to) their namesakes in PL/I. However, if the programmer simply wants to read data from a card, he or she may do so with the statement

$$\text{ACCEPT PLACE.} \quad (28)$$

where PLACE refers to an area in storage providing the destination for the 80 characters of input data. Subsequent extraction of desired items from PLACE is handled on the basis of the hierarchical description given earlier in the program. Similarly, the DISPLAY statement produces a printed line of output from a designated area in storage where that line had been constructed.

Standardized I/O is even more convenient in Snobol, where the language word INPUT implies the reading of a card and OUTPUT implies the printing of a line. For example, the statement

$$\text{DEST = INPUT} \quad (29)$$

reserves storage under the name DEST for a cardful of data, reads the next available card, and stores its contents

in DEST. Similarly, the statement

$$\text{OUTPUT = DEST} \quad (30)$$

pads the information stored in DEST with blanks to fill a print line (normally, 132 characters long), and prints it. In fact, the combined processes of reading a card and printing it can be specified in the single statement

$$\text{OUTPUT = INPUT} \quad (31)$$

The I/O handling facilities incorporated in most Algol systems are relatively complex, reflecting the language's primary concern with internal manipulations and logical organization. APL and Basic, being languages designed for interactive use, assume the availability of a single external device that serves the dual purpose of transmitting input and receiving output. (Several versions of Pascal assume the same orientation.) Consequently, the I/O statements are simple and limited in scope.

Organization of Programs. Efforts to increase the parallels between statements in a language and steps in an algorithm have helped shape the techniques surrounding program preparation. In contrast to early approaches, in which sequences of statements were put together to produce something that "worked," increasing emphasis is being placed on facilitating the programming process through systematic exploitation of high-level language features. Some of the underlying motivations are worth noting.

On innumerable occasions, the cost of designing and perfecting a program outstrips that of using the finished product. Moreover, many programs tend to be unstable in that experience, along with external events, precipitates procedural changes which ultimately must be accommodated by modifying the program. When the program's construction is haphazard to begin with, any but the most trivial changes are awkward to incorporate. In many cases, such modification is aggravated by programmers' inability to follow the tortuous path of events in their own programs after being away from them even for a short time. Under these conditions, it is understandable that a small number of such episodes often result in a decision to scrap a program and start over.

An important factor in reducing this chaos has been the use of *modular programming* (*q.v.*), an approach in which an explicit effort is made to construct a program from components, each representing an identifiable procedural activity. That is, instead of viewing a program as a sequence of individual statements, it is treated as a combination of modules. Most high-level languages include features that encourage and facilitate modularity.

To illustrate some aspects of this approach, a number of the features discussed in previous sections will be integrated to construct complete programs representing solutions to the following problem:

An array of input values X consists of 32 numbers, each in the form $YY.Y$. The array is to be divided into two component arrays, $X1$ and $X2$, such that each member of $X1$ has a value smaller than that specified by an additional input variable named CUTOFF, with the remaining elements being assigned to $X2$. The program is to print three lines of output: The first of these is to repeat the input value for CUTOFF; the second line is to display the sum of all the values assigned to array $X1$ (SUM1), the number of elements assigned to $X1$ (N1), the smallest element in $X1$ (SMALL1), and the largest value assigned to $X1$ (BIG1). The final line of output is to show similar values for array $X2$ (SUM2, N2, SMALL2, and BIG2, respectively). Note that the arrays $X1$ and $X2$ are not needed to obtain the required results. Their inclusion presumes that they would be processed further in a more extensive procedure.

Several versions of solution programs are shown to compare structural possibilities in various languages. Additional explanatory material is embedded in each program by exploiting each language's ability to display incidental information that is not part of the actual program. For reference, sample input and output are shown in Fig. 5.

The Fortran 77, PL/I, and Pascal programs (Figs. 6, 7, and 8) exploit the use of compound statements to enhance organizational simplification. As a result, the implementation of the basic decision mechanism is a direct result of its narrative description.

High-level languages provide the ability to define and integrate subprograms easily and to make them very general. This has revolutionized programming techniques, motivating an overall approach in which frequently used procedural activities are constructed as subprograms and maintained in a library. Then, a new set of procedural requirements are fulfilled by selecting appropriate library routines and combining them by means of a relatively small main program, adding those special procedures not otherwise covered. In using this construction, each activity can be treated as a "black box" whose input requirements are known and whose results are defined, thereby enhancing the overall program's legibility. Furthermore, there may be a considerable reduction in the effort required to produce a working program, since each of the prepackaged activities is known to work and

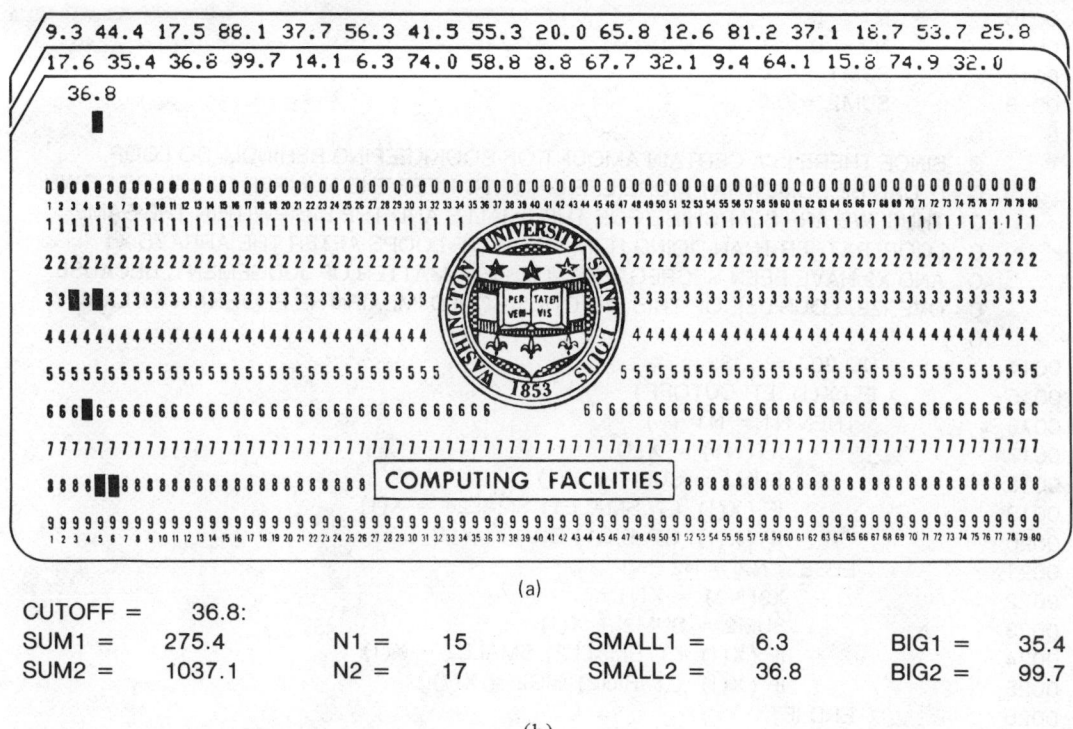

(a)

CUTOFF =	36.8:						
SUM1 =	275.4	N1 =	15	SMALL1 =	6.3	BIG1 =	35.4
SUM2 =	1037.1	N2 =	17	SMALL2 =	36.8	BIG2 =	99.7

(b)

Fig. 5

```
0001              PROGRAM ARRY
0002              REAL X(32),SUM1,SUM2,SMALL1,SMALL2,BIG1,BIG2,CUTOFF,X1(32),X2(32)
0003              INTEGER N1,N2
       C
       C   A 'REAL' VARIABLE IN FORTRAN IS STORED AS A FLOATING POINT NUMBER.
       C   THIS IS EQUIVALENT TO A DEFAULT DECLARATION IN PL/I, E.G.,
       C   DECLARE SUM1, SUM2; WITHOUT FURTHER QUALIFICATION.
       C   EACH READ STATEMENT HANDLES AT LEAST ONE CARD, TAKING ONLY THE
       C   INFORMATION INDICATED BY THE VARIABLE NAME(S) IN ACCORDANCE WITH
       C   THE FORMAT SPECIFICATIONS.
       C
0004              READ *, CUTOFF
       C
       C   SINCE X IS DEFINED AS CONSISTING OF 32 ELEMENTS, THE DESIGNATION
       C   IN THE FOLLOWING READ STATEMENT IS SUFFICIENT TO INSTIGATE THE
       C   READING OF 32 ITEMS.
       
0005              READ *, X
       C
       C   SMALL1 AND SMALL2 ARE INITIALIZED TO 99.9, THEREBY FORCING THE FIRST
       C   ASSIGNMENTS FROM THEIR RESPECTIVE ARRAYS, AFTER WHICH THE LOOP WILL
       C   PROCEED ROUTINELY. THE SAME REASONING PUTS THE LOWEST POSSIBLE
       C   VALUES (IF WE ASSUME NO NEGATIVES) IN THE TWO MAXIMA.
       C
0006              SMALL1 = 99.9
0007              SMALL2 = 99.9
0008              BIG1 = 0.0
0009              BIG2 = 0.0
0010              N1 = 0
0011              N2 = 0
0012              SUM1 = 0.0
0013              SUM2 = 0.0
       C
       C   SINCE THERE IS A CERTAIN AMOUNT OF BOOKKEEPING BEHIND A DO LOOP,
       C   IT CAN BE SOMEWHAT MORE EFFICIENT TO KEEP THE NUMBER OF LOOPS DOWN.
       C   THUS, WE ARE SEARCHING FOR THE SMALLS AND THE BIGS WITHIN THE SAME
       C   LOOP, RATHER THAN DOING IT IN SEPARATE LOOPS AFTER THE ARRAYS X1
       C   AND X2 HAVE BEEN SEGREGATED. THIS IS A MATTER OF JUDGEMENT, BECAUSE
       C   OVERZEALOUS USE OF THIS PRACTICE COULD IMPAIR THE PROGRAM'S CLARITY.
       C
0014              DO 20 I = 1, 32
0015              IF (X(I) .LT. CUTOFF)
0016                THEN N1 = N1 + 1
0017                     X1(N1) = X(I)
0018                     SUM1 = SUM1 + X(I)
0019                     IF (X(I) .LT. SMALL1) SMALL1 = X(I)
0020                     IF (X(I) .GT. BIG1) BIG1 = X(I)
0021                ELSE   N2 = N2 + 1
0022                     X2(N2) = X(I)
0023                     SUM2 = SUM2 + X(I)
0024                     IF (X(I) .LT. SMALL2) SMALL2 = X(I)
0025                     IF (X(I) .GT. BIG2) BIG2 = X(I)
0025              END IF
```

Fig. 6.   Listing of Fortran program for producing the output of Fig. 5.

```
0027               20 CONTINUE
       C
       C
0028               PRINT *, 'CUTOFF = ', CUTOFF
0029               PRINT *, 'SUM1 = ', SUM1, 'N1 = ', N1, 'SMALL1 = ', SMALL1, 'BIG1 = ', BIG1
0030               PRINT *, 'SUM2 = ', SUM2, 'N2 = ', N2, 'SMALL2 = ', SMALL2, BIG2 = ', BIG2
       C
0031               END ARRY
```

Fig. 6   (continued)

need not be redeveloped. When a new program must be constructed from the ground up because required subprograms are unavailable, careful modularization allows several people to work on the program concurrently.

This approach is seen in the reorganized PL/I program in Fig. 9 (an equivalent Pascal program is fairly similar). Assignment of an element from array X to another array is handled by a separate procedure, which is called each time through the loop. Once all of X's elements have been processed, a second subprogram is called twice, once for each of the arrays $X1$ and $X2$, to find the respective extreme values.

There are additional language features that allow further organizational improvements, such as the ability to vary the sizes of arrays X, $X1$, and $X2$ independently to suit each set of requirements as they become known. This type of simplification tends to reduce programming time and cost so that accompanying penalties in the program's ultimate efficiency usually are justified.

A strikingly different construction is required by Cobol, consistent with its narrative orientation. The program in Fig. 10, operationally equivalent to the previous ones, shows the four required formal divisions. Variables are described in the DATA DIVISION, providing a record of all names and storage allocations. The implied intent—that the program serve as its own documentation—carries over into the PROCEDURE DIVISION, where the actual processing steps are specified.

In addition to other language features that permit more concise expression, Cobol also includes provisions for subprograms. However, the descriptive aspect still is preserved, as seen in Fig. 10.

Aids in the Debugging Process. In the process of freeing the programmer from the minutiae of the machine, high-level languages also have removed the programmer from the vantage point, so that he or she is no longer in a position to know what is going on inside. This becomes a crucial problem when something is wrong in the program or the processing, since it may be impossible to relate an event concerning an individual machine instruction to the corresponding point in the procedure as the programmer perceives it.

To reestablish control, the software structure within which a high-level language operates is equipped with diagnostic mechanisms to provide appropriate clues that will facilitate the location, identification, and repair of difficulty. Since any software structure inherently contains rules whose violation prevents the system from operating properly, the general approach is to supplement these rules with a repertoire of messages. Then, if a rule is broken, the appropriate message is displayed as part of the system's response. The rest of the response often is to curtail the processing at that point, but not before the programmer has been given some information.

There is continuing controversy over what is "appropriate." Users would like their high-level language implementation equipped with extensive messages that delineate the type of difficulty as well as its source. Designers, more concerned with the size and operating overhead of a software system, favor a minimal set of aids in which the difficulty is located but no attempt is made to specify its nature. The idea is that once the user is directed to a trouble spot, then presumably he or she will determine what is wrong and correct it. The direction of the inevitable compromise varies widely among languages and among implementations of the same various language.

Diagnostic facilities will be examined within two basic contexts: The first deals with the compilation process during which a high-level language *source program* is analyzed to produce an equivalent machine language *object program*; the second situation is concerned with events preventing a successfully compiled program from operating.

Aids During the Compilation Process.
Every programming language has its syntactic rules which permit the unambiguous and repeatable analysis of a source language program by an appropriately designed compiler. As part of the same process, then, the compiler can detect and classify violations of those rules, calling the programmer's attention to them.

To become acquainted with the general nature of these responses, the illustrative program shown in Fig. 7 has been contaminated with the following syntactic errors.

```
STMT LEVEL NEST
  1                     PG1: PROCEDURE OPTIONS (MAIN);

                        /************************************************************** **/
                        /** ALL PL/I PROGRAMS ARE EXPRESSED AS PROCEDURES, BE-      **/
                        /** GINNING WITH A PROCEDURE STATEMENT AND CONCLUDING       **/
                        /** WITH AN END STATEMENT.                                  **/
                        /** THE DESIGNATION FIXED(3,1) DESCRIBES NUMBERS OF THE     **/
                        /** FORM XX.X; FIXED(5,1) SPECIFIES THE NUMERICAL FORM      **/
                        /** XXXX.X.                                                 **/
                        /************************************************************** */

  2     1               DECLARE (X(32),X1(32),X2(32),SMALL1,SMALL2,BIG1,BIG2,CUTOFF)
                            FIXED(3,1), (SUM1,SUM2) FIXED(5,1), (N1,N2) FIXED(2);

  3     1               GET LIST(CUTOFF,X);

                        /************************************************************** */
                        /** BIG1 AND BIG2 ARE SET TO ZERO SO THAT THE FIRST COM-    **/
                        /** PARISON WITH AN ARRAY ELEMENT INEVITABLY WILL FORCE     **/
                        /** A REPLACEMENT. THE SAME REASONING MOTIVATES THE INI-    **/
                        /** TIALIZATION OF SMALL1 AND SMALL2 TO 99.9, THE LAR-      **/
                        /** GEST POSSIBLE VALUE THAT CAN BE ACCOMMODATED THERE.     **/
                        /************************************************************** */

  4     1               X1 = 0; X2 = 0;
  6     1               N1,N2,SUM1,SUM2,BIG1,BIG2 = 0;
  7     1               SMALL1,SMALL2 = 99.9;

  8     1               DO I = 1 TO 32;
  9     1     1         IF X(I) < CUTOFF THEN DO;
 11     1     2             SUM1 = SUM1 + X(I); N1 = N1 + 1; X1(N1) = X(I);
 14     1     2             IF X(I) < SMALL1 THEN SMALL1 = X(I);
 16     1     2             IF X(I) > BIG1 THEN BIG1 = X(I);
 18     1     2                 END;
 19     1     1         ELSE DO;
 20     1     2             SUM2 = SUM2 + X(I); N2 = N2 + 1; X2(N2) = X(I);
 23     1     2             IF X(I) < SMALL2  THEN SMALL2 = X(I);
 25     1     2             IF X(I) > BIG2 THEN BIG2 = X(I);
 27     1     2                 END;
 28     1     1         END;
                                                     /*********************** */
 29     1               PUT SKIP DATA(CUTOFF);           /* THE WORD SKIP FORCES  */
 30     1               PUT SKIP DATA(SUM1,N1,SMALL1,BIG1); /* THE START OF A NEW    */
 31     1               PUT SKIP DATA(SUM2,N2,SMALL2,BIG2); /* LINE OF PRINT.     */
                                                     /*********************** */

 32     1               END PG1;
```

Fig. 7.   PL/I program for producing output in Fig. 5

```
program arry (input, output);
   var X,X1,X2:    array [1 .. 32] of real;
      small1,small2,big1,big2,cutoff,sum1,sum2:  real;
      N1,N2:  integer;
      I:  1 .. 32;
```
{These declarations are essentially similar to those specified in the FORTRAN 77 and PL/I versions. Of particular note is the declaration for I. The specification of 1 .. 32 defines the range of values that variable I can assume}
```
   begin
      readln (cutoff);
      small1 := 99.9; small2 := 99.9;
      sum1 := 0.0; sum2 := 0.0;
      big1 := 0.0; big2 := 0.0;
      N1 := 0; N2 := 0;
      for I:= 1 to 32 do
        begin
            X1[I]:=0.0;
            X2[I]:=0.0;
            read(X[I])
        end;
      for I:= 1 to 32 do
        begin
            if X[I] < cutoff then
              begin
                  sum1:=sum1+X[I];
                  N1:=N1+1;
                  X1[N1]:=X[I];
                  if X[I] < small1 then small1:=X[I];
                  if X[I] > big1 then big1:=X[I]
              end
                            else
              begin
                  sum2:=sum2+X[I];
                  N2:=N2+1;
                  X2[N2]:=X[I];
                  if X[I] < small2 then small 2:=X[I];
                  if X[I] > big2 then big2:=X[I]
              end
        end;
      writeln('cutoff = ' ,cutoff);
      writeln('sum1 = ' ,sum1, 'N1 = ' ,N1,
         'small1 = ' ,small1, 'big1 = ',big1);
      writeln('sum2= ',sum2,'N2 = ',N2,
         'small2 = ',small2,'big2 = ',big2)
   end.
```

Fig. 8. Pascal program for producing the output of Fig. 5.

1. The closing parenthesis on the storage allocation for array x has been omitted. (This type of oversight is fairly common.)
2. Storage for array x2 has not been reserved.
3. The variables SUM1 and SUM2 have not been initialized.

The comments have been deleted for brevity.

This program was then processed by a production compiler, resulting in the program listing shown in Fig. 11 followed by error messages of which only the first few are shown. The error display produces predefined messages for each statement found to be in error. The accompanying codes (e.g., IEM0728I) refer to entries in a separate manual containing more information about the possible source of the difficulty, along with suggested remedies. It should be noted that, even if the whole display of error messages were shown, it would reveal no particular concern with the fact that SUM1 and SUM2 were not initialized. Statements 11 and 20, as it turns out, are rejected because of improper use of x. Thus, it is only coincidence that would draw the programmer's attention to the uninitialized variables.

The types of diagnostic services exemplified by the example above represent but one layer of such facilities, available by default (i.e., without requiring explicit requests). Many compilers include more elaborate diagnostic structures that may be activated at the programmer's option.

Diagnostic Aids During Program Execution. Successful compilation in no way guarantees subsequent execution of the resulting machine language program. An endless variety of anomalies and inconsistencies can appear during processing, and hardware/software systems contain features for detecting and dealing with some of these difficulties. Of course, it is impossible for the system to anticipate each particular situation. Instead, diagnostic mechanisms are sensitive to certain types of events whose occurrence can be expected to cause trouble. Typical categories include attempts to divide by zero, references to nonexistent storage addresses, or involvement of a nonnumeric data item in an arithmetic operation. Once such a situation is encountered, the resulting message usually gives the general category, together with some indication of the place in the program at which the difficulty occurred.

An example of a minimal set of such services is given in Fig. 12, which shows an attempt to run the PL/I program from Fig. 11 with the declarations corrected but SUM1 and SUM2 still uninitialized. The run is terminated at some point, producing a message (Fig. 12) requiring two supplementary sources of information to make it useful: The error type refers to information cataloged under

PG3: PROCEDURE OPTIONS (MAIN);

```
STMT LEVEL NEST
  1                    PG3: PROCEDURE OPTIONS (MAIN);
  2      1                  DECLARE (X(32),X1(32),X2(32),SMALL1,SMALL2,BIG1, BIG2,CUTOFF)
                            FIXED(3,1),(SUM1,SUM2) FIXED(5,1),(N1,N2) FIXED(2);

  3      1                  GET LIST(CUTOFF,X);

  4      1                  SUM1,SUM2,N1,N2 = 0;
  5      1                  X1 = 0; X2 = 99.9;
  7      1                  SMALL1,SMALL2 = 99.9; BIG1,BIG2 = 0;

                    /*******************************************************************/
                    /** THE LOOP IS STRUCTURALLY THE SAME AS BEFORE, EXCEPT    **/
                    /** THAT THE ASSIGNMENT OF EACH OF X'S ELEMENTS TO THE     **/
                    /** APPROPRIATE ARRAY IS HANDLED BY THE SUBPROGRAM FIND.   **/
                    /** THE SUBPROGRAM NEED NOT BE IN THE IMMEDIATE PROXI-     **/
                    /** MITY; THE CALL STATEMENT IMPLIES A BRANCH TO THE       **/
                    /** START OF THE SUBPROGRAM AND A RETURN TO THE REGULAR    **/
                    /** SEQUENCE, AS IF ONE STATEMENT HAD BEEN EXECUTED.       **/
                    /*******************************************************************/

  9      1          DO I = 1 TO 32;
 10      1    1      IF X(I) < CUTOFF THEN CALL FIND(X1,SUM1,N1);
 12      1                    ELSE CALL FIND(X2,SUM2,N2);
 13      1    1      END;

                    /*******************************************************************/
                    /** THE PROGRAM ARRIVES AT THIS POINT ONLY AFTER THE       **/
                    /** LOOP HAS BEEN CYCLED 32 TIMES, I.E., ALL ELEMENTS      **/
                    /** HAVE BEEN PROPERLY ASSIGNED. NOW ANOTHER SUBPROGRAM    **/
                    /** (NAMED RANGE) IS CALLED TO FIND THE EXTREME VALUES     **/
                    /** FOR EACH OF THE ARRAYS X1 AND X2.                      **/
                    /*******************************************************************/

 14      1          CALL RANGE(X1,N1,SMALL1,BIG1);
 15      1          CALL RANGE(X2,N2,SMALL2,BIG2);

 16      1          PUT SKIP DATA(CUTOFF);
 17      1          PUT SKIP DATA(SUM1,N1,SMALL1,BIG1);
 18      1          PUT SKIP DATA(SUM2,N2,SMALL2,BIG2);

                    /*******************************************************************/
                    /** HERE ARE THE TWO SUBPROGRAMS USED BY THE MAIN PRO-     **/
                    /** GRAM. THEIR PLACEMENT HERE IS CONVENIENT RATHER THAN   **/
                    /** OBLIGATORY. SINCE EACH IS BRACKETED BY A SET OF        **/
                    /** PROCEDURE AND END STATEMENTS, THEY WILL BE BYPASSED    **/
                    /** IN NORMAL SEQUENTIAL PROCESSING, BEING ACCESSIBLE      **/
                    /** ONLY BY MEANS OF A CALL STATEMENT.                     **/
                    /*******************************************************************/
```

Fig. 9. Reorganized PL/I program employing subprograms.

```
19   1              FIND: PROCEDURE (Y,TOTAL,M);
                    /*****************************************************/
                    /** THIS PROCEDURE IS GIVEN THE NAME OF AN ARRAY,      **/
                    /** THE NUMBER OF ELEMENTS OCCUPIED THUS FAR, AND      **/
                    /** THE SUM OF THOSE ELEMENTS. EACH TIME IT IS         **/
                    /** CALLED, IT FILLS THE NEXT AVAILABLE POSITION       **/
                    /** WITH THE VALUE OF THE INPUT ARRAY ELEMENT CUR-     **/
                    /** RENTLY BEING EXAMINED AND UPDATES THE TOTAL.       **/
                    /*****************************************************/
20   2              DECLARE Y(32) FIXED(3,1), TOTAL FIXED(5,1), M FIXED(2);
21   2              M = M + 1; Y(M) = X(I); TOTAL = TOTAL + X(I);
24   2              RETURN;
25   2              END FIND;


26   1              RANGE: PROCEDURE (Z,L,S,B);
                    /*****************************************************/
                    /** THIS SUBPROGRAM LOOKS THROUGH THE INDICATED        **/
                    /** NUMBER OF OCCUPIED ELEMENTS IN AN ARRAY AND        **/
                    /** FINDS THE LARGEST AND SMALLEST VALUES.             **/
                    /*****************************************************/
27   2              DECLARE (Z(32),S,B) FIXED(3,1), L FIXED(2);
28   2                  DO J = 1 TO L;
29   2   1              IF Z(J) < S THEN S = Z(J);
31   2   1                      ELSE IF Z(J) > B THEN B = Z(J);
33   2   1              END;
34   2              RETURN;
35   2              END RANGE;


36   1          END PG3;
```

Fig. 9.   (continued)

that code in a manual; the point at which execution stopped is expressed as a storage address whose relation to a particular source-language statement is defined in a separate reference table produced by the software.

Increased emphasis on debugging capabilities is seen in the PL/C system (a teaching subset of PL/I developed at Cornell University). Attempted execution under this system (Fig. 13) produces direct designation of the type of error, supplemented by the results of automatically triggered action based on the assumption that initialization to zero is reasonable. (In this particular case, it is). Subsequent results are printed each time through the loop (only a few cycles are shown). Thus, even if the assumed initialization were improper, the programmer could see the consequences.

While there is a loose parallelism between the processes of producing a successful compilation and a successful run, the techniques associated with the latter activity are conspicuously different. Despite the extensive diagnostic aids available by default or by request during a program's execution, it often is impossible for the user to exploit them passably. Since these facilities necessarily must be general, the information they provide may be useless unless it is accompanied by more specific qualifications actively supplied by the programmer. To do this, the programmer uses a simple but effective technique: The source program must be equipped with supplementary statements designed specifically to provide helpful information for debugging. A common practice, for instance, is to print the input "as is" as soon as it is read (this is termed an *echo*), thereby providing a convenient reference point. Displays of intermediate results also may be revealing.

A frequently recurring situation is one in which execution is terminated and the regular diagnostic services report that there was an attempt to divide by zero at a point corresponding to a particular statement in the source language program. However, there are complications because that statement turns out to be part of a loop and there is no indication of the number of cycles that had been completed before the tragedy occurred. Insertion of a statement that prints the value of the index (and,

```
00001      IDENTIFICATION DIVISION.
00002      PROGRAM-ID. 'PG4'
00003      REMARKS. THE FIRST TWO DIVISIONS, SHOWN IN MINIMAL FORM HERE,
00004               REFLECT AN INTENT TO HAVE THE COBOL SOURCE PROGRAM
00005               SERVE AS ITS OWN DOCUMENTATION.
00006      ENVIRONMENT DIVISION.
00007      CONFIGURATION SECTION.
00008      SOURCE-COMPUTER. IBM-360.
00009      OBJECT-COMPUTER. IBM-360.
00010      DATA DIVISION.
00011    *
00012    *           THE VARIABLES S1,S2,SM1,SM2,B1,B2 ARE USED TO
00013    *      STORE THE COMPUTER RESULTS. WHEN COMPUTATION IS COMPLETE,
00014    *      THEY WILL BE REPRODUCED, RESPECTIVELY, IN SUM1,SUM2,SMALL1,
00015    *      SMALL2,BIG1 AND BIG2, FROM WHENCE THEY WILL BE PRINTED.
00016    *
00017      WORKING-STORAGE SECTION.
00018      77 I PICTURE 99.
00019      77 SM1 PICTURE 99V9 VALUE IS 99.9.
00020      77 SM2 PICTURE 99V9 VALUE IS 99.9.
00021      77 B1 PICTURE 99V9 VALUE IS ZERO.
00022      77 B2 PICTURE 99V9 VALUE IS ZERO.
00023      77 S1 PICTURE 9999V9 VALUE IS ZEROS.
00024      77 S2 PICTURE 9999V9 VALUE IS ZEROS.
00025      77 C PICTURE 99V9.
00026    *
00027    *           THERE IS NO CONVENIENT WAY TO READ KEYPUNCHED DATA
00028    *      WITH EMBEDDED DECIMAL POINTS. CONSEQUENTLY, THE INTEGER
00029    *      AND FRACTIONAL PORTIONS VT AND VU ARE DEFINED AS SEPARATE
00030    *      VARIABLES THAT WILL BE COMBINED, ONCE THEY ARE READ, TO
00031    *      FORM C. THE SAME IS DONE WITH EACH OF THE ELEMENTS IN THE
00032    *      INPUT ARRAY, PARTITIONING THE VALUES INTO TX AND UX.
00033    *
00034      01 FIRST-CARD.
00035         02   FILLER PICTURE X(4).
00036         02   VT PICTURE 99.
00037         02   VP PICTURE X.
00038         02   VU PICTURE 9.
00039         02   FILLER PICTURE X(72).
00040      01 IN-ARRAY.
00041         02   INHERE OCCURS 32 TIMES.
00042            03   TX PICTURE 99.
00043            03   TP PICTURE X.
00044            03   UX PICTURE 9.
00045            03   FILLER PICTURE X.
00046      01 WORKING-ARRAYS.
00047         02   X1 PICTURE 99V9 OCCURS 32 TIMES.
00048         02   X2 PICTURE 99V9 OCCURS 32 TIMES.
00049         02   X PICTURE 99V9 OCCURS 32 TIMES.
00050    *
00051    *           EACH OF THE THREE LINES OF PRINT IS SET UP EXACTLY
00052    *      AS IT WILL APPEAR, WITH THE LABELING PREDEFINED AND THE
```

Fig. 10. Cobol programming listing.

```
00053    *    SPACES RESERVED FOR THE NUMERICAL RESULTS.
00054    *
00055    01  LINE-1.
00056        02  FILLER PICTURE X(4).
00057        02  L11 PICTURE X(9) VALUE IS 'CUTOFF = '.
00058        02  CUTOFF PICTURE 99.9.
00059        02  FILLER PICTURE X(115).
00060    01  LINE-2
00061        02  FILLER PICTURE X(4).
00062        02  L21 PICTURE X(7) VALUE IS 'SUM1 = '.
00063        02  SUM1 PICTURE 9999.9.
00064        02  L22 PICTURE X(8) VALUE IS ' N1 = '.
00065        02  N1 PICTURE 99 VALUE IS ZEROES.
00066        02  L23 PICTURE X(12) VALUE IS ' SMALL1 = '.
00067        02  SMALL1 PICTURE 99.9.
00068        02  L24 PICTURE X(10) VALUE IS ' BIG1 = '.
00069        02  BIG1 PICTURE 99.9.
00070        02  FILLER PICTURE X(75).
00071    01  LINE-3.
00072        02  FILLER PICTURE X(4).
00073        02  L31 PICTURE X(7) VALUE IS 'SUM2 = '.
00074        02  SUM2 PICTURE 9999.9.
00075        02  L32 PICTURE X(8) VALUE IS ' N2 = '.
00076        02  N2 PICTURE 99 VALUE IS ZEROS.
00077        02  L33 PICTURE X(12) VALUE IS ' SMALL2 = '.
00078        02  SMALL2 PICTURE 99.9.
00079        02  L34 PICTURE X(10) VALUE IS ' BIG2 = '.
00080        02  BIG2 PICTURE 99.9,
00081        02  FILLER PICTURE X(75).
00082    *
00083    *         THE FINAL (PROCEDURE) DIVISION CONTAINS THE ACTUAL
00084    *    PROCESSING STEPS. THE PERFORM STATEMENT IS MUCH LIKE A CALL
00085    *    TO A SUBROUTINE. IN THIS CASE THE SINGLE STATEMENT WITH THE
00086    *    LABEL 'BUILD' WILL BE USED AS THE NUCLEUS OF A LOOP. ON THE
00087    *    OTHER HAND, 'FIND' REFERS TO AN ENTIRE SECTION, COVERING
00088    *    ALL OF THE PROCESSING FROM 'FIND-1' THROUGH 'AWAY'.
00089    *
00090    PROCEDURE DIVISION.
00091        ACCEPT FIRST-CARD.
00092        COMPUTE C = VT + VU / 10.
00093        ACCEPT IN-ARRAY.
00094        PERFORM BUILD VARYING I FROM 1 BY 1 UNTIL
00095        I IS GREATER THAN 32.
00096        PERFORM FIND VARYING I FROM 1 BY 1 UNTIL
00097        I IS GREATER THAN 32.
00098    COMMENTS-1.
00099        NOTE THE PLACEMENT OF C'S VALUE IN CUTOFF INCLUDES THE
00100        INSERTION OF THE ACTUAL DECIMAL POINT, DESIGNATED BY
00101        CUTOFF'S DESCRIPTION IN THE DATA DIVISION. THE SAME HOLDS
00102        TRUE FOR THE OTHER OUTPUT VALUES.
00103    OUTPUT-PREP.
00104        MOVE C TO CUTOFF.
```

Fig. 10. (continued)

```
00105          DISPLAY LINE-1.
00106          MOVE S1 TO SUM1.
00107          MOVE B1 TO BIG1.
00108          MOVE SM1 TO SMALL1.
00109          DISPLAY LINE-2.
00110          MOVE S2 TO SUM2.
00111          MOVE B2 TO BIG2.
00112          MOVE SM2 TO SMALL2.
00113          DISPLAY LINE-3.
00114          GO TO ENDALL.
00115      BUILD.
00116          COMPUTE X (I) = TX (I) + UX (I) / 10.
00117      FIND SECTION.
00118      FIND-1.
00119          IF X (I) IS LESS THAN CUTOFF GO TO ADD-ON-X1 OTHERWISE
00120          GO TO ADD-ON-X2.
00121      ADD-ON-X1.
00122          ADD 1 TO N1.
00123          COMPUTE S1 = S1 + X (I).
00124          MOVE X (I) TO X1 (N1).
00125          IF X (I) IS LESS THAN SM1 MOVE X (I) TO SM1.
00126          IF X (I) IS GREATER THAN B1 MOVE X (I) TO B1.
00127          GO TO AWAY.
00128      ADD-ON-X2.
00129          ADD 1 TO N2.
00130          COMPUTE S2 = S2 + X (I).
00131          MOVE X (I) TO X2 (N2).
00132          IF X (I) IS LESS THAN SM2 MOVE X (I) TO SM2.
00133          IF X (I) IS GREATER THAN B2 MOVE X (I) TO B2.
00134      AWAY.
00135          EXIT. .
00136      ENDALL.
00137          STOP RUN.
```

Fig. 10.   (continued)

perhaps, other crucial variables) each time through the loop may be all that is required to identify the problem. Once the difficulty is found and appropriate safeguards are installed (e.g., testing potential divisors for a value of zero and specifying evasive action should this be true). Now extraneous output statements may be removed for the program's final version. Many programmers take a more conservative approach: Instead of removing the test statements, they merely surround them with the special symbols necessary to convert them to comments. In this way, they remain as physical parts of the source program and, should they ever be needed again, they can be reactivated easily.

These techniques are especially helpful in dealing with the more insidious types of situations in which a program runs to completion but is procedurally wrong: Input was read properly and the program printed when it should have printed, but the output values make no sense. Correction is strictly up to the programmer, who must decide which items will be most revealing and at which time their display will be of greatest use.

Diagnostic facilities of many systems include features that facilitate this type of scrutiny. Rather than requiring the programmer to insert explicit statements at strategic points, a trace may be requested during which designated variables are monitored automatically. In this mode of operation, the value of a variable is printed every time it undergoes a change, together with information regarding the point in the program at which the change occurs. Another type of trace chronicles the sequence of events during execution. This is very useful in procedures containing numerous modules and/or complex decision networks that provide a wide choice of possible actions and sequences.

PG1: PROCEDURE OPTIONS (MAIN);

```
STMT   LEVEL   NEST
  1                       PG1: PROCEDURE OPTIONS (MAIN);
  2       1               DECLARE (X(32, X1(32), SMALL1, SMALL2, BIG1, BIG2, CUTOFF)
                              FIXED (3.1), (SUM1, SUM2) FIXED (5, 1), (N1, N2) FIXED (2);
  3       1               GET LIST (CUTOFF, X);
  4       1               X1 = 0; X2 = 0;
  6       1               N1, N2, BIG1, BIG2 = 0;
  7       1               SMALL1, SMALL2 = 99.9;
  8       1               DO I = 1 TO 32;
  9       1     1             IF X(I) < CUTOFF THEN DO;
 11       1     2                 SUM1 = SUM1 + X(I); N1 = N1 + 1; X1(N1) = X(I);
 14       1     2                 IF X(I) < SMALL1 THEN SMALL1 = X(I);
 16       1     2                 IF X(I) > BIG1 THEN BIG1 = X(I);
 18       1     2                             END;
 19       1     1                 ELSE DO;
 20       1     2                 SUM2 = SUM2 + X(I); N2 = N2 + 1; X2(N2) = X(I);
 23       1     2                 IF X(I) < SMALL2 THEN SMALL2 = X(I);
 25       1     2                 IF X(I) > BIG2 THEN BIG2 = X(I);
 27       1     2                             END;
 28       1     1             END;
 29       1               PUT SKIP DATA (CUTOFF);
 30       1               PUT SKIP DATA (SUM1, N1, SMALL1, BIG1);
 31       1               PUT SKIP DATA (SUM2, N2, SMALL2, BIG2);
 32       1               END PG1;
```

PG1: PROCEDURE OPTIONS (MAIN);
COMPILER DIAGNOSTICS.
TERMINAL ERRORS.

IEM0728I   2   COMPILATION TERMINATED DUE TO A PREVIOUSLY DETECTED SEVERE ERROR IN
               STATEMENT NUMBER 2

SEVERE ERRORS.

IEM0677I   13   ILLEGAL PARENTHESIZED LIST IN STATEMENT NUMBER 13 FOLLOWS AN IDENTIFIER
                WHICH IS NOT A FUNCTION OR ARRAY. LIST DELETED.
IEM0677I   22   ILLEGAL PARENTHESIZED LIST IN STATEMENT NUMBER 22 FOLLOWS AN IDENTIFIER
                WHICH IS NOT A FUNCTION OR ARRAY. LIST DELETED.
IEM0677I   2   ILLEGAL PARENTHESIZED LIST IN STATEMENT NUMBER 2 FOLLOWS AN IDENTIFIER
                WHICH IS NOT A FUNCTION OR ARRAY. LIST DELETED.

Fig. 11

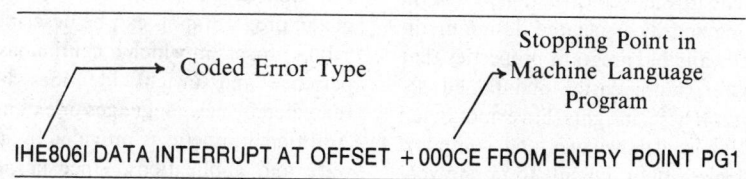

IHE806I DATA INTERRUPT AT OFFSET +000CE FROM ENTRY POINT PG1

Fig. 12. Diagnostic message produced by PL/I system after attempt to
run with SUM1 and SUM2 uninitialized.

· · · · · ERROR IN STMT 11 SUM1 HAS NOT BEEN INITIALIZED. IT IS SET TO ZERO. (EX50)

· · · · · ERROR IN STMT 20 SUM2 HAS NOT BEEN INITIALIZED. IT IS SET TO ZERO. (EX50)

CUTOFF =	36.8;				
SUM1 =	275.4	N1 =	15	SMALL1 =	6.3	BIG1 =	35.4;
SUM2 =	1037.1	N2 =	17	SMALL2 =	36.8	BIG2 =	99.7;

IN STMT 32 PROGRAM RETURNS FROM MAIN PROCEDURE.

IN STMT 32 ARRAYS, SCALARS AND BLOCK-TRACE:

· · · · · MAIN PROCEDURE PG1

I =	33	N2 =	17	N1 =	15	SUM2 =	1037.1	SUM1 =	275.4
CUTOFF =	36.8	BIG2 =	99.7	BIG1 =	35.4	SMALL2 =	36.8	SMALL1 =	6.3
X2(1) =	36.8	X2(2) =	99.7	X2(3) =	74.0	X2(4) =	58.8	X2(5) =	67.7
X2(6) =	64.1	X2(7) =	74.9	X2(8) =	44.4	X2(9) =	88.1	X2(10) =	37.7
X2(11) =	56.3	X2(12) =	41.5	X2(13) =	55.3	X2(14) =	65.8	X2(15) =	81.2
X2(16) =	37.1	X2(17) =	53.7	X2(18) =	0.0	X2(19) =	0.0	X2(20) =	0.0
X2(21) =	0.0	X2(22) =	0.0	X2(23) =	0.0	X2(24) =	0.0	X2(25) =	0.0
X2(26) =	0.0	X2(27) =	0.0	X2(28) =	0.0	X2(29) =	0.0	X2(30) =	0.0
X2(31) =	0.0	X2(32) =	0.0	X1(1) =	17.6	X1(2) =	35.4	X1(3) =	14.1
X1(4) =	6.3	X1(5) =	8.8	X1(6) =	32.1	X1(7) =	9.4	X1(8) =	15.8
X1(9) =	32.0	X1(10) =	9.3	X1(11) =	17.5	X1(12) =	20.0	X1(13) =	12.6
X1(14) =	18.7	X1(15) =	25.8	X1(16) =	0.0	X1(17) =	0.0	X1(18) =	0.0
X1(19) =	0.0	X1(20) =	0.0	X1(21) =	0.0	X1(22) =	0.0	X1(23) =	0.0
X1(24) =	0.0	X1(25) =	0.0	X1(26) =	0.0	X1(27) =	0.0	X1(28) =	0.0
X1(29) =	0.0	X1(30) =	0.0	X1(31) =	0.0	X1(32) =	0.0	X(1) =	17.6
X(2) =	35.4	X(3) =	36.8	X(4) =	99.7	X(5) =	14.1	X(6) =	6.3
X(7) =	74.0	X(8) =	58.8	X(9) =	8.8	X(10) =	67.7	X(11) =	32.1
X(12) =	9.4	X(13) =	64.1	X(14) =	15.8	X(15) =	74.9	X(16) =	32.0
X(17) =	9.3	X(18) =	44.4	X(19) =	17.5	X(20) =	88.1	X(21) =	37.7
X(22) =	56.3	X(23) =	41.5	X(24) =	55.3	X(25) =	20.0	X(26) =	65.8
X(27) =	12.6	X(28) =	81.2	X(29) =	37.1	X(30) =	18.7	X(31) =	53.7
X(32) =	25.8								

Fig. 13. PL/C diagnostic output for program with uninitialized SUM1 and SUM2.

Future Directions. Despite the abundance of syntactic and operational restrictions, there still is sufficient latitude to make high-level language programming a surprisingly subjective endeavor. There is no "ultimate" language (nor is its eventual definition assured), and there are no rigorous "laws" characterizing programs or the techniques pertinent to their construction. Work in structured programming and its associated design methodologies has identified valuable program properties that tend to produce clearer, more easily maintained sequences of instructions. These insights have motivated the development of high-level languages and compilers whose rules make it increasingly difficult to circumvent the use of certain structural components deemed to be desirable. The Pascal language, for example, incorporates minimal default mechanisms, compelling its users to provide explicit definitions for all data items. Many view Pascal as the beginning of a new family of high-level languages which, eventually, will shift virtually all of the subjective/creative activity to the design of the algorithm, with subsequent implementation (i.e., coding) becoming an (almost) automatic process.

Consequently, the development of high-level language programming can be described as a dynamic, spiraling process in which a continuous accumulation of experience and insight identifies linguistic deficiencies remedied by new languages or extensions to existing ones. Additional impetus is provided by newly emerging hardware and applications. Once newer languages become available, they engender new programming techniques and higher levels of algorithms that stimulate further developments, and so it goes. The overall result is a turbulent and challenging arena for all people involved with computers and computing.

REFERENCES

1968. Maurer, W. D. *Programming: An Introduction to Computer Languages and Techniques.* San Francisco: Holden-Day.

1973. Elson, M. *Programming Techniques.* Chicago: Science Research Associates.

1975. Pratt, T. W. *Programming Languages: Design and Implementation.* Englewood Cliffs, NJ: Prentice-Hall.

1976. Pollack, S. V. and Sterling, T. D. *A Guide to PL/I*, 2nd Ed. New York: Holt, Rinehart and Winston.

1976. Dijkstra, E. W. *A Discipline of Programming.* Englewood Cliffs, NJ: Prentice-Hall.

1978. Nicholls, J. E. *The Design and Structure of Programming Languages.* Reading, MA: Addison-Wesley.

1980. Gillett, W. D. and Pollack, S. V. *Introduction to Engineered Software.* New York: Holt, Rinehart and Winston.

S. V. POLLACK AND T. D. STERLING

PROCEDURE, PURE

For article on related subject *see* REENTRANT PROGRAM.

A pure procedure is one that never modifies any part of itself during execution. Thus, any data subject to modification during execution of the pure procedure must be stored in memory associated with the calling program. A *reentrant program* is, therefore, generally a pure procedure.

A. RALSTON

PROCESS. *See* TASK.

PROCESSING MODES

For articles on related subjects *see* COMPUTING CENTER; INTERACTIVE SYSTEMS, USING; REAL TIME APPLICATIONS: TIME SHARING; and TURNAROUND TIME.

Six distinct categories of computing activity can be identified at modern computing installations:

1. Card-oriented batch processing.
2. Keyboard-oriented batch processing.
3. Interactive computing (also called time sharing).
4. On-line inquiry and transaction processing.
5. Message switching.
6. Data acquisition and control (DAX).

Of these processing modes, the last four are performed on line and in real time; responses to input stimuli (or input transactions) are almost instantaneous. The batch-processing modes differ in that substantial queues of unprocessed transactions *(jobs)* are held in the computer throughout normal operation. Likewise, substantial queues of output reports are printed/punched continuously for card-oriented batch processing. (These queues are presented on request during keyboard-oriented batch processing.) Typical response times for the six modes are shown in Fig. 1.

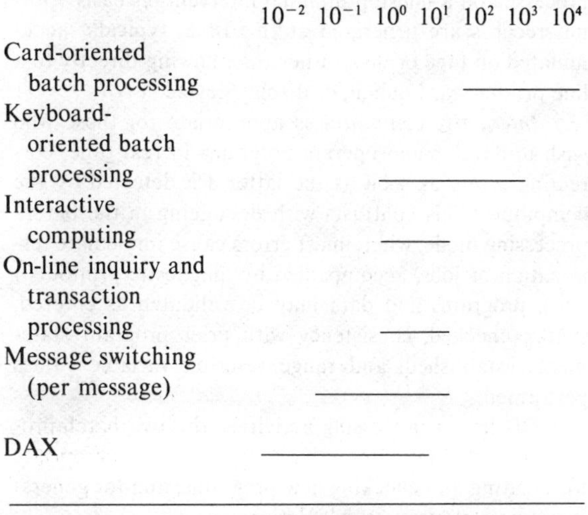

	10^{-2} 10^{-1} 10^{0} 10^{1} 10^{2} 10^{3} 10^{4}
Card-oriented batch processing	
Keyboard-oriented batch processing	
Interactive computing	
On-line inquiry and transaction processing	
Message switching (per message)	
DAX	

Fig. 1.   Response times to input stimuli, in seconds.

Batch processing uses programs and data stored at all levels of a memory hierarchy:

1. Main memory.
2. Auxiliary memory.
3. Card decks, floppy disks, cassettes, etc.

Each batch installation maintains a library of systems and applications programs on fast auxiliary memory, typically drums or disks. Applications based on punched cards (or their images) require input *unit records* prepared on keypunches, key/disk key/tape systems, teletypes, or other off-line devices not connected to a computer. Input data (and specialized programs associated with the data) are submitted to the computer all at once in a high-speed stream. Little validation of data is performed during this input phase.

Users of keyboard-oriented batch processing prepare input data and programs much the same as for card-oriented processing. Some validation and syntax checking are performed as statements are typed directly into the computer. When accepted, images of these statements are retained temporarily/permanently on disk storage. A broad repertoire of commands is available for inserting new statements, updating existing statements, and other editing of partially developed programs.

After all input records have been read into the computer, the *job* (processing task defined by these records) is *enqueued* for execution. If small and short, it may be selected for execution a few seconds later; if large and low-priority, it may remain enqueued for hours.

When the control program selects a job for execution, its control statements are scanned for consistency and completeness. If valid, source data and programs are processed on a nonstop minimal-intervention basis. Output records are generated at this time, typically accumulated on tape or disk rather than flowing directly to a line printer, card punch, or display device.

Interactive computing is appropriate for those who wish to develop and operate programs in real time, correcting errors as soon as the latter are detected by the computer. (This contrasts with debugging in the batch-processing mode, where most errors cause immediate termination of jobs, accompanied by diagnostic printouts.) Also, programs and data may be validated as entered, syntax checked, consistency with prior program statements established, and range tests on variable values performed.

Of the six processing activities, the two batch-processing modes and interactive computing are appropriate for creating and checking new programs, and for general scientific and business calculations.

On-line inquiry and *transaction processing* use the computer to access rapidly a repository of data and to update the database or to insert new data in it. Processing time per query or transaction (e.g., making an airline reservation) is typically trivial compared with times required to enter and display information. This mode has been made feasible by development and widespread usage of large disk drives whose capacities range from 50 million to a billion characters per drive. Complete and up-to-date master files can be accessed by authorized clerks, management personnel, etc., using typewriter terminals or CRT (cathode ray tube) displays.

Message switching resembles on-line inquiry in that processing per input stimulus (message, query) is trivial. Whereas the inquiry mode permits retrieval and display of disk-stored records, the message-switching mode receives streams of characters *(messages)* from one site and routes them to other sites automatically according to destination headers describing (for each message) where it is to be sent. Message switching is almost invariably used in conjunction with the public telephone network; large

commercial, manufacturing, and governmental enterprises use message switching for high-speed communications among offices and for efficient usage of their telephone networks. Such systems are the forerunners of more general *electronic mail* systems.

DAX has many operational similarities to message switching—modest requirements for computational power and main memory, fast processing of incoming cassette tapes or punched paper tapes. As data are received from such instruments as voltmeters, gas chromatographs, and thermocouples, they are scaled and tested for conformance to normal operating ranges for these instruments (and associated physical processes). When the computer detects an out-of-range condition, it notifies appropriate personnel such as a plant guard, fireman, or operating engineer. Typically, the DAX-oriented computer types out a warning message, rings an alarm bell, or flashes an alarm light continuously until the out-of-range condition is corrected.

D. N. FREEMAN

PRODUCTION

For articles on related subjects *see* FORMAL LANGUAGES; GRAMMARS; PARSING; PROGRAMMING LINGUISTICS; and WELL-FORMED FORMULA.

A production is a rule, often called a *rule of inference,* in a grammar that describes how parts of a string (or word, or phrase, or construct) can be replaced by other strings. The set of productions of a grammar describe all the rules by which strings of the language can be generated by the grammar.

As an example, consider the grammar whose alphabet consists of the characters a and b and which is to generate any string consisting of any number (including zero) of bs followed by any number (including zero) of as. A set of productions which generate this language is

$$S \rightarrow a$$
$$S \rightarrow b$$
$$S \rightarrow Sa$$
$$S \rightarrow bS$$

the first two of which read "a and b are constructs of the language" and the last two read, "If S is a construct of the language, then so is S followed by a or preceded by b." Sometimes this set of productions would be written as

$$S \rightarrow a \,|\, b \,|\, Sa \,|\, bS$$

where the vertical bar is to be read as "or."

Productions may be much more complex than those above. An example is the type of production found in *context-sensitive languages*,

$$S_1 S\ S_2 \rightarrow S_1 T S_2,$$

which states that, if the string S is found in the context (i.e., between) strings S_1 and S_2, then S may be replaced by the string T. Thus,

$$abSba \rightarrow abaSaba$$

states that, if S is any string surrounded by *ab* and *ba,* it may be replaced by the same string preceded and succeeded by *a*.

REFERENCES

1967. Naur, P. *et al.* "Revised Report on the Algorithmic Language ALGOL 60," in Rosen, S. (Ed.), *Programming Systems and Languages.* New York: McGraw-Hill.
1975. Lewis, P. M., Rosenkrantz, D. J., and Stearns, R. E. *Compiler Design Theory.* Reading, MA: Addison-Wesley.

J. A. N. LEE AND A. RALSTON

PROGRAM

For articles on related subjects *see* ALGORITHM; ASSEMBLERS; COMPILER; INTERPRETER; MACHINE AND ASSEMBLY LANGUAGE PROGRAMMING; MODULAR PROGRAMMING; PROBLEM-ORIENTED LANGUAGES; PROCEDURE; PROCEDURE-ORIENTED LANGUAGES; PROGRAMMER; PROGRAMMING LANGUAGES; STORED PROGRAM CONCEPT; and STRUCTURED PROGRAMMING.

In order to solve a computational problem, its solution must be specified in terms of a sequence of computational steps, each of which may be effectively performed by a human agent or by a digital computer. Systematic notations for the specification of such sequences of computational steps are referred to as *programming languages*. A specification of the sequence of computational steps in a particular programming language is referred to as a *program*. The task of developing programs for the solution of computational problems is referred to as *programming*. A person engaging in the activity of programming is referred to as a *programmer*.

Programming is sometimes contrasted with *coding*. Coding generally refers to the writing and debugging of programs for given program specifications, while programming includes the task of preparing the program specification as well as that of writing the program. The text of a program is sometimes referred to as *code,* and lines of program text are referred to as lines of code, especially in the case of machine-language programs. The term *coder* is used, sometimes pejoratively, to describe a person engaged exclusively in implementing program specifications prepared by others.

The programs for the earliest digital computers were written in a *machine language.* Pure machine-language programming required the programmer to write out the sequences of binary or decimal digits by which each instruction was represented in the computer memory. By the mid-1950s it was realized that programmers could specify instruction codes and memory locations by symbolic mnemonics, which could be translated into the internal machine language by a translation program called an *assembler.*

In the late 1950s and in the 1960s, *procedure-oriented languages* were developed to allow programmers to specify algorithms in a notation natural to the problem being solved. Programs specified in a procedure-oriented language were translated into the internal language of a particular computer by a translation program called a *compiler.* The commonly used programming languages in the 1960s and 1970s included Fortran, Algol 60, Cobol, PL/I, and APL. The reader is referred to Sammet (1969) for brief descriptions of over a hundred programming languages developed in the 1950s and 1960s (*see also* Appendix: Key High-Level Languages).

The flavor of programs in procedure-oriented languages is illustrated by following the Algol 60 procedure for finding the maximum of a set of numbers in Fig. 1.

A problem specification is generally given in terms of a desired relation between inputs and outputs which specifies *what* is to be computed. An algorithm or program for a given problem specifies *how* the given relation between inputs and outputs is to be achieved. It is the task of the programmer to convert "static" input/output specifications of what is to be computed into dynamic specifications that specify how the computation is to be performed.

A given input/output relation may be realized by a wide variety of different algorithms, and each algorithm may in turn be realized in a variety of different programming languages. There is thus considerable freedom in developing a program for the solution of any given problem. This freedom of choice in developing programs leads to the notion that programming is an art rather than a science.

Although the set of all programs for realizing a given problem specification is in general infinite, there are a number of criteria other than correctness which may be used to restrict the class of acceptable programs that realize a given problem specification. A good program should economize both on computation time and on the

```
procedure MAX(X,N);
    integer N; array X;
        begin integer I; real T;
        T: = X[1];

        for I: = 2 step 1 until N do
            if X[I]>T then T: = X[I];

        MAX: = T;
    end
```

Declares data types of procedure parameters (X,N) and local variables (I,T)	
Tests each component of X in sequence against largest found thus far (T)	
Sets name of procedure (MAX) to largest of set (T)	

Fig. 1

storage space required to represent the program and data structures. It should have a modular structure in the sense that each well-defined subtask should be specified by a well-defined subprogram. Modular design of a program is important because it makes the program easier to understand, facilitates debugging, and allows modifications to be made more easily. It is usually worth paying a price in computation time and memory space in order to achieve greater modularity. Modular construction is especially important in large programs, since the human mind is severely restricted in the complexity it can handle, and systematic modularity reduces the number of factors the human mind must handle at any given moment, thereby allowing the understanding of a larger system than would otherwise be possible.

Programming was regarded as an art rather than a science in the 1950s and 1960s because it was felt that the choices among different styles of implementing a given problem were creative choices based on intangible criteria of style, just as in the case of literature. However, as more experience was gained in writing large programs, the freedom of the programmer to develop a personal style became increasingly restricted by programming conventions designed to mechanize programming style. For example, it has become accepted that *goto* statements should be avoided whenever possible, and that operators that preserve modularity, such as *while* statements, should be more heavily used.

During the last few years, it has been realized that maintenance of programs is more expensive than development, so reading of programs by humans is as important as writing them. Documentation and other aids to readability are becoming increasingly important. The programs of a large system are increasingly viewed as one of several forms of system documentation and are stored in a database for manipulation by compilers and other system programming tools.

REFERENCES

1968. Knuth, D. E. *The Art of Computer Programming*. Reading, MA: Addison-Wesley.

1969. Sammet, J. *Programming Languages—History and Fundamentals*. Englewood Cliffs, NJ: Prentice-Hall.

P. WEGNER

PROGRAM CORRECTNESS. *See* PROGRAM VERIFICATION.

PROGRAM COUNTER

For articles on related subjects *see* MACHINE AND ASSEMBLY LANGUAGE PROGRAMMING; and MACHINE INSTRUCTION SET.

Typically, a computer instruction is the specification of an operation to be performed, the address of operands on which the operation will be performed, the address for the location of the result, and a specification (an address) of the next instruction in the sequence. These specifications or addresses may be explicitly placed in the instruction or implicitly defined. By "implicit" is meant that the machine will assume that an operand will be in a certain place (e.g., the *accumulator*) rather than have it specified in each instruction. In the case of the specification of the next instruction location, it is common for the machine to assume that the instructions lie in sequence. That is, the next instruction is contained in the address following the location of the current instruction. This address is kept in a register called the *program counter* (or, in some systems, the *program address register* or *instruction counter*). During the execution of an instruction, the program counter is advanced by one or more address units.

If the instruction lengths are not uniform (i.e., there are several different sizes), then the algorithm to increment the program counter must take this into account. For example, in the IBM System/370, instructions are of three different sizes: 2 bytes, 4 bytes, or 6 bytes. Since addresses always refer to bytes, the program counter must be incremented by either 2, 4, or 6, depending upon the type of instruction currently being executed.

In all systems that use program counters, there must be a mechanism for initializing its value and for changing values at certain points in the program. This mechanism is a special instruction, usually called a *branch* or *jump*. There are two basic kinds of branch instructions—*unconditional branch* and *conditional branch*. The unconditional branch causes a new value to be placed in the program counter and hence defines the start of the location of a new sequence of instructions. The conditional branch has a similar action except that it is dependent upon the state of certain data items. Thus, whether the next instruction will be simply the next instruction in the current sequence or the beginning of a new sequence will depend upon the result (e.g., positive or negative) of a preceding instruction.

M. J. FLYNN

PROGRAM LIBRARIES, NUMERICAL AND STATISTICAL

For articles on related subjects *see* COMPUTING CENTER; DOCUMENTATION; MATHEMATICAL SOFTWARE; SOFTWARE PACKAGES; SORT/MERGE PACKAGES; and SUBROUTINE.

Definition. A program library for a computer is a collection of programs for a particular use or application. This article surveys program libraries for numerical computation and for statistical analysis. These libraries contain programs (usually written in Fortran) for the solution of differential equations, for analysis of variance, for numerical integration, and for other mathematical and statistical applications.

Any given computer site will also generally have further libraries for special purposes and applications, such as the Fortran support library containing locally optimized versions of the standard intrinsic functions, graphical libraries adapted to the particular hardware at the site, and specialized computational libraries (such as sets of weather prediction programs) concentrating on the site's major activity. These libraries, being generally site-dependent, are not discussed here.

Program Library Development. The first program libraries for numerical computation were written in machine or assembly language for a particular computer at a given site. Probably the earliest of these was a library written for the EDSAC (*q.v.*) computer in England by Wilkes, Wheeler, and Gill in 1951. By the early 1960s, the computer manufacturers, to help their customers and to stimulate sales, were working on program libraries and, in 1961, IBM developed the SSP (Scientific Subroutine Package) library and provided it free with a computer rental or sale.

Many groups in universities, government laboratories, and private industry began to feel the need to consolidate programming effort into useful libraries. For example, to minimize duplication of effort, a group of statisticians in the biomedical group at the University of California put together a set of statistical routines. The first edition of this library appeared in 1961 and the library has been widely used since that time, the current version being available as BMDP-81 (Biomedical Computer Programs P-Series). Other statistical libraries originating in the early 1960s were the SPSS (Statistical Package for the Social Sciences) library originally written at Stanford University, and then developed further by the National Opinion Research Center at the University of Chicago, and the SAS® (Statistical Library) statistical library developed at North Carolina State, but now supported commercially.

In England, also in the early 1960s, two libraries were being built for numerical computation. One of these was developed in 1963 for the IBM Stretch computer at the Harwell Atomic Energy Research Establishment; in 1967, the library was converted to an IBM 360. The other effort, growing out of combined universities' effort to create a common program library, has developed into the NAG (Numerical Algorithms Group) library now available in versions for several classes of large and small-scale computers. The NAG library can be obtained in three separate language versions: Fortran, Algol 60, and Algol 68, and is in use at more than 600 sites worldwide.

In the U.S., library development initially was carried out at universities, and by computer manufacturers and also at governmental computer sites such as Los Alamos, but in 1970 a commercial concern, IMSL (International Mathematical and Statistical Libraries), seeing the possibility of a market for program libraries, offered a library for the IBM 360-370 class of computers. (The IMSL library is now available on a number of computer classes and is out in the field at 1,700 sites.) Also in the early 1970s, the NATS (National Activity to Test Software) group was established at Argonne Laboratory under government and university sponsorship to produce quality software covering specific areas of numerical computation. In 1972, the NATS project completed the package, EISPACK, containing programs for eigenvalue-eigenvector computation, in 1979, LINPACK, a package of programs for the solution of linear systems was produced and, in 1980, MINPACK-1, a set of programs for the numerical solution of nonlinear equations and nonlinear least squares problems was introduced.

At Bell Laboratories, another library effort has resulted in the PORT program library of programs for numerical computation. The library is now in its second edition and is in use at 20 sites within the Bell System and at many educational institutions. In the development of the PORT library emphasis has been placed on the portability (see below) of the library. Only one version of the library is maintained; machine-dependent quantities are invoked using calls to three function subprograms, particularized to a given computer during library installation.

Portability. The costliness of the effort not only to develop program libraries, but to adapt them to ever-changing computer hardware has recently led to a concern for the portability of a library. Although most of the libraries under discussion here are written in Fortran, not all can be moved easily from one computer to another; instead, commercial libraries are often provided in a different version for each brand of computer. Two things stand in the way of portability: First, the dialect of Fortran in use on each computer and, second, the arithmetic differences, both in static hardware and dynamic behavior, between computers.

Recently, considerable progress has been made in overcoming these problems. Libraries are now usually programmed in standard Fortran, and their adherence to the standard can be mechanically verified. A program called the *PFORT Verifier* (Ryder, 1974) can be used to check if a program is written in ANSI (1966) Fortran. To cope with arithmetic differences between computers, machine-dependent values in programs are either flagged to be set by a preprocessor before compilation, or are obtained during run time by a call to a function routine as discussed above.

Error Handling and Storage Allocation. In order to protect users from program failure and from their own programming errors, the best quality program libraries do careful error checking. Both the legality of the input parameters to a subprogram and the validity of the computation process should be checked. Some errors must be signaled as *fatal* whereas others can be less serious. Unfortunately, no standard has been adopted for error handling, and the procedures used vary from one library to another.

It is also helpful to library users to have some sort of automatic storage allocation for scratch use. In dynamic

---

BQUAD—integrate a piecewise-smooth function, $f(x)$, $\int_{X_1}^{X_N} f(x)\, dx$

Purpose: BQUAD should be used to integrate functions which have discontinuities in their derivatives. By putting in the x-values of the points of discontinuity, the user can make the integration process more economical than in the general case.

Usage: CALL BQUAD (F, N, X, EPS, ANS, ERREST)

F → the name of a function subprogram, F(X), written by the user to provide the integrand.

The name of the function must be declared EXTERNAL in the program calling BQUAD.

N → the INTEGER number of X values (two end-points plus the number of points of discontinuity within the interval)

X → a REAL vector containing the points of discontinuity; X(1) and X(N) are the endpoints of the integration interval.

The Xs must be monotone: either
X(1) ≤ X(2) ≤ ... ≤ X(N), or
X(1) ≥ X(2) ≥ ... ≥ X(N).

EPS → the absolute accuracy desired by the user

ANS ← the value of the integral

ERREST ← an estimate of the absolute error of ANS

Error Situations

Number	Error
1	N < 2
2	the X vector is not monotone (see above)
3	ERREST > EPS
4	the dynamic storage stack is full

Fig. 1. Example of subprogram documentation.

storage allocation, as it usually is defined, space is obtained from and returned to a large pool of available memory space. In general, the mechanism is system-dependent and not available with Fortran programs. However, it is possible in Fortran to set aside a sizable array in a COMMON region for use as a dynamic stack, and to develop a set of programs for allocation and deallocation of space in the stack, as is done, for example, in the PORT library.

Documentation. A program library is of no use unless it is supported by documentation showing users

Library Name	Area	Size estimate	For information
BMDP	statistical	40 (large) programs	Health Sciences Computing Facility Center for Health Sciences University of California Los Angeles, CA 09924
EISPACK	eigenvalue-eigenvector problems	70 programs	Distributed by IMSL (see below)
IMSL	numerical and statistical	458 programs	IMSL Sixth Floor-NBC Building 7500 Bellaire Blvd. Houston, TX 77036
HARWELL	numerical	556[1] subprograms	Conputer Science and Systems Division AERE Harwell, Oxfordshire OX11 ORA, Great Britain
LINPACK	solution of linear systems	163[2] programs	Distributed by IMSL (see above)
MINPACK-1	nonlinear equations optimization	10 programs	Distributed by IMSL (see above)
NAG	numerical	463 programs	Numerical Algorithms Group Inc. 1250 Grace Court, Downers Grove, Il 60615
NPL	optimization	50 main programs 310 auxiliary modules	Control Analysis Corporation 800 Welch Road Palo Alto, CA 94304
PORT	numerical	125 callable subroutines 525 modules	Computing Information Service Bell Laboratories 600 Mountain Avenue, Murray Hill, NJ 07974
ROSEPACK	linear regression	47 programs	Distributed by IMSL
SAS	statistical[3]	50 (large) programs	SAS® Institute Inc. SAS Circle Box 8000 Cary, NC 27511
SPSS	statistical		National Opinion Research Center University of Chicago

[1]This number includes both double and single precision versions of each program, and sometimes similar versions of the same basic task.
[2]This number incluces single precision, double precision, and complex versions of each program.
[3]SAS is available only for the IBM 360/370 class of computers.
[4]SPSS is a large package of integrated programs for data analysis using standard statistical techniques.

how to use each program. The purpose of the program, its input and output parameters, and possible error situations must be clearly described. Fig. 1 shows an excerpt from a reference sheet for a PORT library program. Notice that the calling sequence for the program does not, in this case, include parameters for error flags or for scratch storage since both are automatically handled in that library. The rest of the program description (not shown here) includes a description of the numerical algorithm, the name of the author or individual responsible, literature references where appropriate, and, most important, an example of actual program use. The last is often adapted with minor editing by a user to solve the problem at hand.

Increasingly, documentation for a library is being kept on-line at a computing site, permitting users to access the information in an interactive mode.

Program Library Availability. Fig. 2 lists a few of the program libraries currently (1981) available and tells where the libraries can be obtained. Of course, there are many libraries and sources of programs not represented here. Journals in several scientific fields regularly publish algorithms and programs. For example, the Association for Computing Machinery started publishing algorithms in their *Communications* in 1960, and the *Collected Algorithms from ACM* contains algorithms published since that time. In 1975, publication of algorithms was transferred to *ACM Transactions on Mathematical Software (TOMS)*.

Some of the program libraries discussed here, such as EISPACK, FUNPACK, LINPACK, MINPACK-1 and ROSEPACK, are in the public domain; others can be leased for a year or bought outright. Often, a library can be obtained by an educational institution at a reduced price.

The libraries classified in Fig. 2 as numerical generally include the following topics.

Approximation and interpolation

Differential equations

Linear algebra

Eigenvalue-eigenvector problems

Optimization

Quadrature

Roots of polynomials

Zero finding and solution of nonlinear systems

Special functions

Fourier and other transforms

The libraries classified as primarily statistical generally include the following.

Basic statistics

Analysis of variance

Regression analysis

Cluster analysis

Factor analysis

Nonparametric techniques

Programs to generate random deviates from various distributions are often found in both types of libraries, as are Fast Fourier Transforms, general time series analysis, and least-squares fitting routines.

REFERENCES

1951. Wilkes, M. V., Wheeler, D. J., and Gill, S. *The Preparation of Programs for an Electronic Digital Computer.* Reading, MA: Addison-Wesley.

1971. Rice, John R. (Ed.). *Mathematical Software.* New York: Academic Press.

1974. Ryder, B. G. "The PFORT Verifier," *Software—Practice and Experience* **4:** 359–377.

1977. Rice, John R. (Ed.). *Mathematical Software III.* New York: Academic Press.

P. A. Fox

PROGRAMMABLE CALCULATOR. *See* CALCULATORS, ELECTRONIC AND PROGRAMMABLE.

PROGRAMMER

For articles on related subjects *see* APPLICATIONS PROGRAMMING; PERSONNEL IN THE COMPUTER FIELD; PROGRAM; SYSTEMS ANALYST; and SYSTEMS PROGRAMMING.

The computer *programmer* is the link between a problem or process to be computerized and its successful realization on the computer. In the fullest meaning of the term, the programmer will participate in the definition and specification of the problem itself, as well as the algorithms to be used in its solution. He or she will then design the more detailed structure of the implementation, select the most suitable programming language, write and debug the necessary programs, and provide clear and complete documentation for both the user and other programmers who may need to modify the program.

The amount of this process which is done by any one

individual is highly variable. A scientist who has a small problem may do all of the above tasks personally, while in a large airline reservation system, many hundreds of people may be involved in each phase of the process. However, even in this latter case, programmers should participate in the design and documentation of at least their own portions of the overall system. It is demoralizing for most programmers to be treated as *coders,* a pejorative term reserved for those in the programming profession whose work consists of almost a direct translation of detailed flowcharts into code. One of the major attractions of programming as opposed to coding as a career is its requirement for at least some creativity on a daily basis. It is a mistake for the manager of a programming group to overspecify the team's programming tasks and thereby stifle this creativity. On the other hand, the programmer must not let ego engender bad programming practices such as the use of involved programming tricks which can only be easily understood by the programmer who used them. Good programmers write well-structured and clear programs which others can read and, if necessary, correct or modify.

Both the amateur programmer (e.g., the scientist) and the professional programmer (e.g., a member of the airline reservation team) mentioned above are examples of *applications programmers.* They most frequently use high-level languages (e.g., Cobol or Fortran) to write programs which serve particular applications. They approach the computer as a race car driver does a car—as a tool which enables a goal to be attained as efficiently as possible. As the race driver relies heavily on the mechanic, the applications programmer depends even more on the *systems programmer,* the elite member of the programming profession. The systems programmer is responsible for the compilers, assemblers, utility programs, operating systems, etc., which provide the environment for the applications programmer and is very close to the hardware. Usually, therefore, the systems programmer uses assembly language or a specialized systems programming language as this gives better access to the bits and bytes of the machine. It is hard to define what makes good systems programmers, but they are certainly a breed apart with a talent which is hard to teach. Although experience is of great importance, a good systems programmer can frequently be identified before education or experience has had a chance to have an effect. Almost any kind of background can be appropriate; once hooked, a systems programmer will find the mysteries of a full blown operating system a challenge for many years.

The distinction between applications and systems programmers is not really as clear-cut as has been described above. For example, the airline reservation system mentioned above as an example of an applications program is very much like an operating system and so

would be written by many who consider themselves systems programmers.

One of the noteworthy aspects of programming is the great variation in programmer productivity, perhaps as great as a ratio of 10:1 from the best to the merely good. But for any programmer, applications, or systems, there are some traits which are required if a programmer's full potential is to be realized. There is the need for creativity, of course, but it must be tempered with great patience and intense discipline if clever but unmanageable programs are to be avoided. Too many programs are written which may be a tribute to a programmer's ability to master complex logical structures but which have no place in a professional environment. The discipline of good programming practices is a severe one. *Egoless programming* is a technique which helps impose this discipline. Each member of a programming group will submit programs to the other members for criticism. The careful examination of another's program helps both the creator and the critic understand what makes a good, clearly written program. It is called "egoless" programming because, in order for it to be successful, all members must be able to submerge their own egos in the interest of good programs. The importance of good programmers cannot be overstressed because of the great variation in programmer productivity. The application of good programming techniques can do much to decrease the 10:1 ratio mentioned above.

REFERENCES

1971. Weinberg, G. M. *The Psychology of Computer Programming.* New York: Van Nostrand Reinhold.
1975. Brooks, Frederick P. *The Mythical Man Month.* Reading, MA: Addison-Wesley.

F. D. FEDERIGHI

PROGRAMMING. *See* APPLICATIONS PROGRAMMING; FUNCTIONAL PROGRAMMING; MICROPROGRAMMING; MODULAR PROGRAMMING; STRUCTURED PROGRAMMING; and SYSTEMS PROGRAMMING.

PROGRAMMING LANGUAGE SEMANTICS

For articles on related subjects *see* FUNCTIONAL PROGRAMMING; GRAMMARS; LAMBDA CALCULUS; LOGICS OF PROGRAMS; PROGRAMMING LANGUAGES; PROGRAMMING LINGUISTICS; PROCEDURE-ORIENTED LANGUAGES; SYNTAX, SEMANTICS, AND PRAGMATICS; and VIENNA DEFINITION LANGUAGE.

The term *semantics* is used in both linguistics and computer science to refer to the meanings of the symbol strings of a language. A program in a programming language is represented by a symbol string, but denotes a sequence of instructions to be executed by a computer. The symbol string is a *syntactic* representation of the program. Semantics associates meanings with syntactic program representations, although, as we shall see later, there are several alternative ways of doing this.

A definition of the semantics of a programming language is a finite set of rules for uniformly defining the meaning of the potentially infinite set of all programs of the language. The purpose of a semantic definition is to provide a clear, complete, and unambiguous definition of a programming language for language designers, language implementors, and language users. Unfortunately, programming language definitions appear to be inherently complex. One of the challenges in this area is to develop clear, structured definitions that allow the meaning of programming languages to be defined in a simple and intuitively natural manner.

The set of rules which constitute a definition of the semantics of a programming language may be thought of as a mapping from the set P of all programs (symbol strings) of the programming language into the set M of meanings (see Fig. 1).

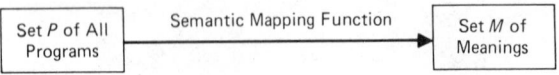

Fig. 1. Semantics as a mapping from programs to meanings.

However, there may, in general, be several alternative notions of meaning for programs of a programming language appropriate to alternative contexts in which the semantic definition might be used. A semantic definition appropriate to compiler writers might define the meaning of a program in the source language as the target language string generated by the compiler. The system implementor might wish to define meaning in terms of the sequence of executed instructions. The end user is not interested in the instruction sequence but only in the computational effect of the program expressed as a relation between inputs and outputs.

Semantic models may be classified by the kinds of meanings they permit. Thus, semantic models whose meanings are target language strings generated by a compiler are called *compiler models*. Semantic models whose meanings are relationships between inputs and execution sequences are called *interpreter models* or operational models. Models whose meanings are relationships between inputs and outputs are called *mathematical models*.

Compiler semantics defines the meaning of a program in a language L in terms of its translation to a second language L'. We shall be concerned with expressing the meaning of programs in terms of their execution rather than in terms of their translation, and will therefore not pursue the notion of compiler semantics.

Operational semantics defines a language L in terms of an interpreter *(abstract machine)* for executing it. The semantic definition language in which its interpreter is specified should have mechanisms for defining and manipulating program structures. The first example of an operational language definition was the definition of Lisp by an interpreter that was itself written in Lisp.

For defining operational semantics, Lisp is probably the simplest and most complete language. It has the following features: *Selectors* that allow selection of particular components of lists; *constructors* that allow construction of lists from their components; and *predicates* that allow testing whether a given structure is a list and whether two structures are equal. It has a conditional statement of the form

$$p_1 \rightarrow a_1; \ p_2 \rightarrow a_2; \ldots; p_n \rightarrow a_n,$$

which causes the action a_i, corresponding to the first true predicate p_i, to be executed. An interpreter in this context may be defined as a conditional statement in which the p_i are statement forms and a_i is the execution action associated with the statement form p_i. The Lisp interpreter (Lisp APPLY function) is, in fact, defined as a large conditional statement which takes a program in list representation and its data as arguments and produces as its value the result of applying the program to its data.

In the late 1960s, a more elaborate language for operational semantic definitions called the Vienna Definition Language (VDL) was developed by Lucas and Walk (in Wegner, 1972). It was used to define PL/I (a very large language). VDL, like Lisp, has powerful facilities for manipulating structures. Programs were converted into an "abstract syntax" representation in the form of labeled trees. For example, the expression "$a + b$" could be represented in the abstract syntax by the following tree structure:

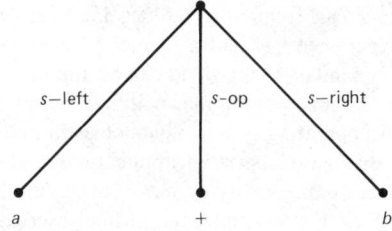

Fig. 2. Abstract syntax in VDL.

The abstract machine for VDL starts from an abstract syntax representation of the program, just as the Lisp interpreter starts from a list representation of the program. The execution time data structure for VDL consists of a tree-structured program representation which permits nondeterministic execution of any terminal node of the program tree as the next instruction, as well as table data structures containing the relationship between symbols and their values.

Mathematical semantic models can be classified into *denotational* models which define the meaning of programs as denotations of an abstract algebraic domain, and *axiomatic* models which define the meaning of primitive program constructs in terms of axioms (axiom schemes) and define the meaning of composite programs by means of theorems derivable from axioms for primitive program constructs by rules of inference for program composition.

Denotational semantic models were developed for the lambda calculus in the early 1960s but are associated with the name of Scott, who defined denotations of programs in terms of an "applicative" topological space (1976) in which every element can be interpreted both as a function and as a data element. This idea captures the fact that computer programs can be executed as functions or manipulated as bit strings. Applicative spaces occur in their purest form in the lambda calculus (*q.v.*), where lambda expressions may be applied to operands or serve as operands of some other lambda expression. They serve as a basis for modeling applicative programming languages such as Lisp. Scott's denotational semantics is of mathematical interest because it provided the first mathematical model of the lambda calculus, and it is of practical interest because, by augmenting the applicative model with a model of computer memory and assignment, the semantics of real programming languages such as Algol 60, PL/I, and Ada can be defined.

Denotational models start from the notion of an underlying state set and the notion of a command as a mapping from states to states. In order to accommodate assignment, the notion of an environment as a mapping from identifiers to values is introduced, and the meaning of assignment is defined in terms of its effect on the environment. The meaning *(denotation)* of composite program structures is defined in terms of the denotation of component structures. The meaning of a recursive procedure P is defined in terms of the notion of a fixed point x with the property that $P(x) = x$.

Axiomatic semantic models define primitive statements such as assignment statements in terms of "axioms" which define their input/output (I/O) behavior (i.e., the values of variables after execution of a statement in terms of their values before execution), and define composite statements, such as **while** statements, in terms

of rules of inference which allow I/O relationships for composite structures to be defined in terms of I/O relationships for their components.

The axiom for assignment was formulated by Hoare (1969) as follows.

$$\{P_E^X\}\ X := E;\ \{P\}.$$

In order for the predicate P, the *postcondition*, to be a correct assertion *after* the assignment statement $X :=$ E; is executed, then the predicate P_E^X, the *precondition*, must be true *before* the statement is executed. P_E^X is obtained from P by substituting E for all (free) occurrences of X.

Example

$$\{X + 1 < 10\}\ X := X + 1;\ \{X < 10\}.$$

If $X < 10$ is to be true after $X := X + 1$; has been executed, then $X + 1 < 10$ must have been true before the statement was executed.

The axiom (rule of inference) for **while** statements has the following form.

from $\{P \wedge B\}\ S\ \{P\}$ infer $\{P\}$ **while** B **do** S $\{P \wedge \neg B\}$

That is, if execution of S when B is true preserves the *invariant* P ("from $\{P \wedge B\}\ S\ \{P\}$"), then execution of "**while** B **do** S" will preserve the invariant P. If execution of the while statement terminates, then $P \wedge \neg B$ will be true upon termination. Meaning is essentially captured here by the invariant which generally must be determined by human rather than automatic means. The invariant determines a constraint on execution within the **while** statement. The purpose of executing the **while** statement is to falsify B while not violating the constraint imposed by P.

Axiomatic definitions have been used to define large fragments of programming languages such as Pascal (*q.v.*), and are being extended to include language features such as procedures, pointers, exceptions, and tasks.

Different semantic definitions serve different purposes. Thus, compiler definitions serve the compiler-writer, operations definitions provide a model for the implementor, and axiomatic definitions are appropriate to program verification. Denotational definitions come closest to providing an abstract (Platonic) meaning for programs and have the best claim to serving as a standard for defining meaning.

REFERENCES

1965. McCarthy, J. *et al. Lisp 1.5 Programmers Manual.* Cambridge, MA: M.I.T. Press.

1969. Hoare, C. A. R. "An Axiomatic Basis for Computer Programming," *Comm. ACM*, **10**: 576–583.

1972. Wegner, P. "The Vienna Definition Language," *Computing Surveys* **4**: 5–63.

1976. Scott, D. "Data Types as Lattices," *SIAM Journal on Computing* **5**: 522–587.

1978. Stoy, J. E. *Denotational Semantics—The Scott-Strachey Approach to Programming Language Theory.* Cambridge, MA: M.I.T. Press.

P. WEGNER

PROGRAMMING LANGUAGES

For articles on related subjects *see* ADA; ALGOL 68; ASSEMBLERS; AUTHORING LANGUAGES AND SYSTEMS; C; COMPILER, SYNTAX-DIRECTED; COMPILER, INCREMENTAL; INTERPRETER; LANGUAGE PROCESSORS; LANGUAGES; LIST PROCESSING LANGUAGES; MACHINE AND ASSEMBLY LANGUAGE PROGRAMMING; NONPROCEDURAL LANGUAGES; PASCAL; PROCEDURE-ORIENTED LANGUAGES; PROGRAMMING LINGUISTICS; SETL; and STRING PROCESSING LANGUAGES.

See also Appendix: Key High-Level Languages.

The definition of the term *programming languages* is a controversial subject and by no means agreed to by all experts in the field. In order to lead up to the one proposed by this writer, we must consider various levels of languages used for dealing with the computer.

At the lowest level is pure binary. This is so impractical to use that humans almost never use this even though it is actually the only language the machine "understands." A step above this is what is generally referred to as *machine code* or *symbolic machine code*. In this case the user generally writes instructions in some type of alphabetic symbols (e.g. SUB for subtract, TRA for transfer control, etc.). Machine addresses are written in normal decimal form (e.g., 1723). At the next higher level is the *symbolic assembly language* in which the names of variables are written in symbols (e.g., ALPHA, TEMP, X, Y, Z) so that the location can be referred to symbolically rather than numerically. Thus a user might write

```
CLA Z       (CLA = clear accumulator and add)
ADD ALPHA
STO TEMP    (STO = store)
```

meaning: "Add the variables stored in locations named Z and ALPHA and store the result in a location named TEMP." A program called an *assembler* (*q.v.*) assigns absolute storage locations to the variables and fills in the numeric values for machine addresses in the instructions.

The term *assembly language* is sometimes used for what was called above (symbolic) "machine code," and is sometimes used for what was called "symbolic assembly language."

The next level of complexity involves a macroassembler in which the user may define new "instructions" and use them in a program, with their definitions being given elsewhere in the program; for example, INCR ALPHA might represent the use of the macro INCREMENT which automatically adds 1 to the variable ALPHA. This would be shown elsewhere in the program as

```
MACRO    INCR    VAR
         CLA     VAR
         ADD     CON
         STO     VAR
         CON     1
         END
```

The previous levels bring us to what is frequently called *high-level language.* This author uses that term interchangeably with the term "programming language," although some others include the concept of assembly language in the term "programming language." The term *source program* means a program written in a high-level language. It is generally translated to an *object program,* which is in a form directly understandable by the computer. The translation is usually done by a program called a *compiler.*

Definition of Programming Language.[*] A programming language is a set of characters and rules for combining them, which has the following four characteristics:

1. It requires no knowledge of machine code on the part of the user. In other words, the user need only learn the particular programming language, and can use this quite independently of (perhaps nonexistent) knowledge of any particular machine code. This does not mean that the user can completely ignore the actual computer. For example, the user may need to know how floating-point numbers are represented, or may wish to take advantage of certain known machine resources which provide more efficient programs. In particular the user obviously cannot use input/output equipment that does not exist on a particular computer configuration. However, the fun-

---

[*]This section and the succeeding three sections are rewritten versions of material taken from Jean E. Sammet, *Programming Languages: History and Fundamentals,* © 1969, Prentice-Hall, Inc., Englewood Cliffs, N.J., pp. 9–22.

damental point is that a knowledge of the basic machine code for the given computer is not needed.

2. A programming language must have some significant amount of machine independence. This means that there must be some high potential of having a source program run on two computers with different machine codes without completely rewriting the source program. (In the early development of programming languages this characteristic was often stated or implied as "complete machine independence." The state-of-the-art in 1980 does not provide such a capability, so the objective is to minimize the changes required to go from one computer to another.)

3. When a source program is translated into machine language, there is normally more than one machine instruction per executable unit created. For example, an executable unit in a programming language might be something of the form "A = B + C * D" or "OPEN FILE ALPHA." Normally, each of these executable units would be translated into more than one machine instruction.

4. A programming language normally employs a notation that is somewhat closer to that of the specific problem being solved than is normal machine code. Thus, for example, the example "A = B + C * D" might be translated into a sequence of machine instructions such as

```
CLA    C
MPY    D
ADD    B
STO    A
```

which is clearly less understandable than the programming language form.

Advantages of Programming Languages.

As always, one cannot obtain something for nothing, and therefore there are both advantages and disadvantages to programming languages, where the alternative is some type of assembly language. Let us consider the advantages first.

The primary advantage of a programming language is that it is easier to learn than a machine or assembly language. It must be emphasized that there is a relative aspect involved in this advantage. An extremely powerful programming language might be harder to learn in its entirety than an assembly language on a computer which has only a dozen instructions. However, given programming and assembly languages of approximately the same complexity in their relative classes, the programming lan-

guage will be easier to learn. This actually has two facets to it. The programming language may itself be extremely complex, but its ease of learning often comes because the notation is somewhat more related to the problem usage than is the machine code; furthermore, more attention can be paid to the language itself rather than to the idiosyncrasies of the physical hardware, which is necessary when one deals in machine code.

A problem written in a programming language is generally easier to debug for two major reasons. First, the program is usually shorter than its assembly language equivalent because of the expansion factor indicated as the third characteristic of a programming language. Since the number of errors tends to be roughly proportional to the length of the program, there will normally be fewer errors. A second reason for the program's being easier to debug is that the notation itself is somewhat more natural, and therefore relatively more attention can be paid to the logic of the program with relatively less attention paid to syntactic details.

A program coded in a programming language is generally easier to understand and to transfer to someone other than the originator because of the notational advantages and relative conciseness already mentioned.

Fourth, the notation of a programming language automatically provides a part of the necessary documentation because the notation is easier to understand and the logic is easier to follow.

Finally, the above advantages tend to accumulate into two general advantages, which are that the total calendar time and the total cost required for the problem solution are generally reduced significantly.

Disadvantages of Programming Languages.

There are disadvantages to programming languages which have varying importance in specific instances. First, the additional process of compilation obviously requires machine time, which may exceed the time saved by easier debugging.

Second, the compiler might produce very inefficient object code. This would significantly affect production runs (i.e., programs that are run repeatedly) because the machine-time requirements might be increased significantly by any inefficiencies. (The counter argument to this, of course, is that compilers today generally produce code that is at least as good as the average programmer can produce, and there are only a few really expert programmers who can write the most efficient machine code.)

Finally, the program may be much harder to debug than an assembly language program if the user does not know machine code and if the compiler does not provide the proper type of diagnostics and debugging tools. A user who must look at an unfathomable memory dump in octal is going to have more trouble than debugging an assembly language program in which what is happening is understood.

In the opinion of this author, and generally supported by common practice, the advantages of programming languages in the 1980s far outweigh the disadvantages. The normal mode for writing (at least) application programs is to use a high-level language, and the burden of justification for not doing this falls on the proponent of assembly language.

Classifications of Programming Languages.

As indicated earlier, it is very difficult to define a programming language. However, it is a little easier to propose definitions for classes of programming languages, although these definitions are themselves controversial and not agreed on by everyone. The terms to be defined are the following: procedure-oriented and nonprocedural; problem-oriented, special-application and special-purpose; problem-defining, and problem-solving; hardware, publication, and reference. Note that some of these are overlapping and that a particular language may fall into more than one of these categories.

A *procedure-oriented* language (*q.v.*) is one in which the user specifies a set of executable operations that are to be performed in sequence and which specify a procedure. The key factor here is that these are definitely executable operations, and the sequencing is already specified by the user. Fortran, Cobol, and PL/I are examples. (The relation of these to domains of application is discussed later.)

The term *nonprocedural language* (*q.v.*) has been used for years without any attempt to define it. A definition is not really possible because nonprocedural is actually a relative term, meaning that decreasing numbers of specific sequential steps need be provided by the user as the state-of-the-art improves. The closer the user can come to stating a problem without specifying the steps for solving it, the more nonprocedural is the language. Furthermore, there can be an ordered sequence of steps, each of which is "somewhat nonprocedural," or a set of executable operations whose sequence is not specified by the user. Both cases contribute to more "nonproceduralness." Thus, before the existence of such languages as Fortran, the statement

$$Y = A + B \cdot C - D/E$$

could be considered nonprocedural because it could not be written as one executable unit and translated by any system. In 1981, the sentences CALCULATE THE SQUARE ROOT OF THE PRIME NUMBERS FROM 7 TO 91 AND PRINT IN THREE COLUMNS and PRINT ALL THE SALARY CHECKS are nonprocedural because there is no compiler available that

can accept these statements and translate them; the user must supply the specific steps required. As compilers are developed to cope with increasingly complex sentences, the nature of the term changes. Thus, what is considered nonprocedural today may well be procedural tomorrow. The best examples of currently available nonprocedural systems (not really languages) are report generators (RPG) and sort generators in which the individual specifies the input and the desired output without any description of the procedures needed to obtain the output.

The term *problem-oriented* (*q.v.*) has been used in many ways by different people, but it seems that the most effective use of this term is to encompass any language that is easier for writing solutions to a particular problem than assembly language would be. Any current programming language illustrates this; thus, in this author's opinion, the term "problem-oriented" is a general catchall phrase. However, it is worth noting that many other people use the term to refer to languages for very specialized application areas.

It is a frequent misunderstanding that there is a separate category of languages called *application-oriented*. In reality, *all* languages are application-oriented, but some are for larger or smaller application areas than others. For example, Fortran is primarily useful for numerical scientific problems, whereas Cobol is best suited for business data processing. On the other hand, PL/I is useful in both those application areas, and therefore has a wider area of application. The term *general purpose* is sometimes used for PL/I (and even for Fortran), although in this author's opinion there is *no* truly general-purpose programming language. In this writer's view, the following application areas are sufficiently wide and important to justify particular consideration: numerical and nonnumerical (i.e., formal algebraic) scientific applications, business data processing, string and list processing. Subjects other than these (or combinations of them) seem to be more specialized (e.g., graphics, simulation, machine-tool control, equipment checkout). Languages for application areas other than those defined as fairly general should be called "special-application-oriented."

A *special-purpose* language is one designed to satisfy a single objective. The objective might involve the application area, the ease of use for a particular application, or pertain to efficiency of the compiler or the object code.

A *problem-defining,* or *specification,* language is one that literally defines the problem and may specifically define the desired input and output, but it *does not* define the method of transformation. There are significant differences among a problem (and its definition), the method (or procedure) used to solve it, and the language in which this method is stated.

Finally, a *problem-solving* language is one that can be used to specify a complete solution to a problem. Like the term "nonprocedural," this is a relative term, which changes as the state-of-the-art changes. All procedure-oriented languages are problem-solving languages.

A *reference* language is the definitive character set and form of a language. It usually has a unique character for each concept or character in the language, is one-dimensional, and need not be suitable as computer input. In some cases, the reference language contains English words considered as single characters; in other cases, a fixed set of symbols is provided. The concept of having a reference language, as distinguished from a publication or hardware representation language (discussed below), was introduced by the Algol committee in its first report. The reference language need not be particularly easy to read.

A *publication* language is some well-defined variation of the reference language that is suitable for publication. It is designed to be suitable for printing and/or writing; therefore, it will have reasonable rules and characters for such things as subscripts, exponents, spaces, and Greek letters. The publication language would normally be the means of communication between people (using printed media). There can be many publication languages and they can contain different characters, but there must be a well-defined mapping between the publication and reference languages. An illustration of this is the use of an "up" arrow ↑ to denote exponentiation in the Algol reference language, but the use of a raised symbol in the publication language, e.g., A ↑ 2 becomes A².

A *hardware* language, sometimes called a *hardware representation,* is a mapping of the reference language into a form suitable for direct input to a computer. The number and types of characters used must be those accepted by the computer involved, and is often determined by those available on input devices such as keypunches. A hardware language must have a well-defined mapping between itself and the reference language; for example, ** might be a hardware representation of the ↑ in the reference language, and **begin** might be represented by ′BEGIN′.

History and Statistics. A large number of higher-level languages have been developed since the first ones in the early 1950s. By 1980, there were more than 200 implemented (Fig. 1) and in use at some time just in the United States. Of these, roughly half were languages for specialized application areas (e.g., graphics, simulation, computer-assisted instruction, machine-tool control, equipment checkout, systems programming). The remainder are divided among the application areas cited earlier as being important and general. However, of this large number of languages developed in a 25-year time span, only a handful have been truly significant, and even fewer have been widely used.

Fig. 1. The Tower of Babel, representing the large number of programming languages, is a concept that first appeared in the *Communications of ACM.* The form shown above was used as the jacket design for *Programming Languages: History and Fundamentals* by J. E. Sammet, © 1969, Prentice-Hall, Inc., Englewood Cliffs, N.J.

In approximate chronological order, the languages of major significance, and the approximate dates of their earliest public documentation and/or general availability, are shown below.* In some instances, notably IPL-V and Algol 60, earlier versions of the language contributed significantly to the ones listed here.

APT (*A*utomatically *P*rogrammed *T*ools); 1956. The first language for a specialized application area.

Fortran (*FOR*mula *TRAN*slation); 1956. The first high-level language to be widely used. It opened the door to practical usage of computers by large numbers of scientific and engineering personnel.

Flow-Matic; 1956. The first language suitable for business data processing and the first to have heavy emphasis on an "English-like" syntax.

IPL-V (*I*nformation *P*rocessing *L*anguage *V*); 1958.

---

*This list and subsequent text are based on material excerpted from "Programming Languages: History and Future," by Jean E. Sammet, in *Communications of the ACM,* Vol. 15, No. 7 (July 1972). By permission. pp. 603–604.

The first—and also a major—language for doing list processing.

Comit; 1957. The first realistic string-handling and pattern-matching language; most of its features appear (although with different syntax) in any other language attempting to do any string manipulation.

Cobol (*CO*mmon *B*usiness-*O*riented *L*anguage); 1960. One of the most widely used languages on an absolute basis, and the most widely used for business applications. Technical attributes include real attempts at an English-like syntax and at machine independence.

Algol 60 (*ALGO*rithmic *L*anguage); 1960. Developed for specifying algorithms, primarily numerical. Introduced many specific features in an elegant fashion and, combined with its formal syntactic definition, inspired most of the theoretical work in programming languages and much of the work on implementation techniques. More widely used in Europe than in the United States.

Lisp (*LIS*t *P*rocessing); 1960. Introduced concepts of functional programming combined with facility for doing list processing. Used by many of the people working in the field of artificial intelligence.

Jovial (*J*ules *O*wn *V*ersion of *IAL*); 1960. The first language to include adequate capability for handling scientific computations, input/output, logical manipulation of information, and data storage and handling. Most Jovial compilers were written in Jovial.

GPSS (*G*eneral-*P*urpose *S*ystems *S*imulator); 1961. The first language to make simulation a practical tool for people.

Joss (*J*OHNNIAC *O*pen-*S*hop *S*ystem); 1964. The first interactive language; it spawned a number of dialects, which collectively helped to make time sharing practical for computational problems.

Formac (*FOR*mula *MA*nipulation Compiler); 1964. The first language to be used fairly widely on a practical basis for mathematical problems needing formal algebraic manipulation.

APL\360 (*A* *P*rogramming *L*anguage); 1967. Provided many higher-level operators, which permitted extremely short algorithms and caused new ways of looking at some problems.

Pascal (*q.v.*); 1971. Introduced some new ideas about data typing and combined numerous known constructs in a neat and elegant manner in a fairly small language.

Some other languages are now more widely used or more comprehensive than those on the list, specifically Basic, PL/I, Simscript, and Snobol. In many cases, they have almost completely replaced some of the languages on the list (e.g., Basic for Joss and its derivatives, Snobol for Comit). The four "obvious candidates" cited above are omitted from the list of languages of major significance for the following reasons: Basic, although simple and economical, added no new concepts, was not the first on-line language, and was not the first to be of major practical importance. PL/I has capabilities derived from Fortran, Cobol, and Algol, but by 1980 had not succeeded in one of its implicit objectives, which was to replace these languages. It was preceded by Jovial in the attempt to combine capabilities for several application areas. Simscript built on the previous discrete simulation languages. Snobol was a good but fairly obvious improvement to the concepts introduced in Comit.

There is a large effort by the U.S. Department of Defense to introduce a large modern language called Ada (*q.v.*). It is too soon to know whether or not this will be a major language.

REFERENCES

1969. Sammet, J. E. *Programming Languages: History and Fundamentals.* Englewood Cliffs, N.J.: Prentice-Hall.

1975. Nicholls, J. E. *The Structure and Design of Programming Languages.* Reading, MA: Addison-Wesley.

1975. Pratt, T. W. *Programming Languages: Design and Implementation.* Englewood Cliffs, NJ: Prentice-Hall.

J. E. SAMMET

PROGRAMMING LINGUISTICS

For articles on related subjects *see* AUTOMATA THEORY; BACKUS-NAUR FORM; CONCATENATION; EXPRESSION; FORMAL LANGUAGES; GRAMMARS; LANGUAGE PROCESSORS; METALANGUAGE; PARSING; PRODUCTION; PROGRAMMING LANGUAGE SEMANTICS; PROGRAMMING LANGUAGES; RECURSION; STRING PROCESSING LANGUAGES; SYNTAX, SEMANTICS, AND PRAGMATICS; and WELL-FORMED FORMULA.

Languages for communication between any two systems, be they human or mechanical, can be described by three intertwining concepts: syntax, semantics, and pragmatics. This article is concerned with the methods of language description used to specify these concepts. For a discussion of the analysis of such specifications and their translation, *see* LANGUAGE PROCESSORS.

Semiotics. In natural languages, the *syntax* of a language is known as its grammar, and it defines the valid relationships between the elements of the language. While syntax (or grammar) implies nothing about the meaning of the valid sentences (or phrases), *semantics* is the definition of meaning that is prescribed for the sentence by the originator of the sentence; i.e., by the speaker or writer. *Pragmatics,* on the other hand, is the meaning received by a listener or reader. *Semiotics,* the theory of symbols, is concerned with these three aspects of symbols.

In computer languages, the set of symbols available for the composition of sentences (or, in languages such as Fortran or Algol, *statements*) is highly restricted, and therefore syntactic specifications can be predicated on individual symbols rather than on words, prefixes, and suffixes. Further, since computer languages are artificial languages, it can be prescribed that there exists no difference between the semantics and the pragmatics of a language. Thus, in this article we omit any consideration of the pragmatics of computer languages, and confine our attention to those aspects of linguistics that are in use in relation to computer languages.

Initially, we review the concepts behind the use of syntactic and semantic specification with respect to programming languages and then subsequently examine the implementation of these concepts in practice.

Context-Free and Context-Sensitive Grammars.

A grammar of a language is a formal system of description of the relationships among the symbols that comprise the language, over the operations of symbol substitution and concatenation. A grammar is composed of four parts:

1. An alphabet of the language (character set or symbol set).
2. A set of parts of speech (known as the *component names* or *metavariables*).
3. The initial language element, such as "sentence" or "speech," from which all other sentences may be constructed.
4. A set of rules which directs the formation of instances of the language (called *productions*).

In the case of a language that may be described syntactically by rules of direct unconditional substitution and concatenation, such that the substitution of a phrase for a component name is independent of the context of that component name, the language (and its grammar) is said to be *context free*. On the other hand, where such a substitution depends directly on the symbols or component names surrounding the component being replaced

by substitution, the language is said to be *context sensitive*.

Language Descriptors.

The terminology in which a language may be defined is a *metalanguage,* and must be uniquely distinguishable from the language being described. Thus, attempts to define a language in terms of itself can lead to paradoxes due to the indistinguishability of the metalanguage and the language. For example, we may say in the metalanguage of English that a sentence has certain qualities, such as; *it is grammatically correct* or *that sentence is true.* Consider, then, the sentence: *This statement is false.* If one is not given the information as to whether this sentence is written in the language or a metalanguage, one assumes that the word *this* refers to the statement itself; then the sentence is paradoxical. However, the same utterance on the part of a scholar pointing to some other statement is clearly valid. Thus, the metalanguage for the programming language Ada (*q.v.*), for instance, must be clearly distinguishable from Ada. By these requirements, the symbolism of a metalanguage must not include the symbols used in Ada. Hence, there is a necessity to provide a distinct metalanguage that has applicability to the class of languages known as programming languages.

Symbolically, a grammar can be considered to be the definition of sets in terms of elements of other sets. For example, a member of the alphabet of Basic is a member of the set named (say) *character;* i.e.,

$$character = \{A,B,C,D,E, \ldots X,Y,Z,0,1, \ldots \\ 8,9,+,*,/,-, \ldots\},$$

and, further, the class of objects named *variable* is composed of objects that are instances of the roman alphabet (*roman* = $\{A,B,C, \ldots X,Y,Z\}$) or the set of single instances of roman letters concatenated with single instances of the set of digits; i.e.,

$$variable = roman \cup (roman \times digit)$$

where *digit* = $\{0,1,2, \ldots 8,9\}$ and the operation $\times$ signifies the cross-product of the two sets.

The rules for generation of sentences in a context-free language is composed of a set of productions in which each rule has the form

$$\alpha \rightarrow \beta_1\beta_2\beta_3 \ldots \beta_n \quad (n \geq 1),$$

where α is a member of the set of component names and β_i is a member of the union of the set of component names and the alphabet of the language being defined. The string (or phrase) $\beta_1\beta_2\beta_3 \ldots \beta_n$ represents the concatenation of the individual elements β_i. The construct itself is taken to mean that the occurrence of α in any string may be replaced by the string $\beta_1\beta_2\beta_3 \ldots \beta_n$. The consistency of the set of production rules may be partially determined by ensuring that the following five conditions are met:

1. There shall exist only a single language component that is not derivable from other language elements. This component is known as the *root component*, or *root symbol*, and generally is given the name of the object that the grammar describes, such as *program* or *sentence*.
2. All other components shall appear on the left-hand side of at least one construct rule, thereby assuring that there are no "dead ends" in the grammar.
3. For every component in the grammar, there must exist at least one sequence of substitutions using the production rules that will lead to a string composed totally of the characters in the alphabet of the language.
4. Starting at the root symbol, there must exist for each component in the language a sequence of substitutions based on the production rules which will result in a string in which the component occurs; i.e., there are no "useless" components.
5. For every string of characters in the language, there shall exist at the most one sequence of sub-

stitutions which permits the generation of that string; i.e., the language must be *unambiguous*.

In practice, there are (at least) three forms of syntactic specification in common use: BNF (Backus-Naur Form—*q.v.*, also occasionally known as Backus Normal Form), the Cobol language notation, and syntactic railroad charts. BNF was originally developed for the specification of the syntax of Algol 60 (Naur, 1960). This method of specification has since been widely used in the literature of computer science and has become widely accepted as a result of its ease of use and its readability.

This notation is applicable to an alphabet which is composed of the union of the alphabet of the language being described and the set of component names (names of the "parts of speech") of the language. To distinguish between the character set (alphabet) of the language and the component names, the BNF system encloses component names in angle brackets, or corner braces ($\langle$ and $\rangle$), whereas the actual alphabet symbols are free of any enclosing marks.

While the original notation used for the Algol specifications was not subject to any constraints such as those that need to be imposed to restrict (say) the number of characters in an identifier name, BNF has been extended to include notation from regular expressions so as to provide this needed control. Table 1 defines the symbolism of BNF and compares the notation with set notation.

In the construction of the set of productions for a

Table 1. BNF Notation vs. Set Notation

Symbol	BNF Meaning	Set Meaning, or Equivalent
$\langle X \rangle$	Component named X	An instance class of objects named X
x	Actual symbol x	the actual object x
$::=$	$\ldots$ is to be replaced by $\ldots$	$\ldots$ is a member of the set of strings $\ldots$
$\vert$	"or" (the exclusive "or")	(When the separator between two class names) set union $\cup$; (when the separator between two elements of the alphabet) the set punctuation $',\,'$,
$\cap$	Operation of concatenation*	Product of the two sets
$\{z\}_i^j$	If z^k represents k concatenated occurrences of z, then: $\{z\}_i^j = z^i \mid z^{i+1} \mid \ldots \mid z^j$	$\{z^i, z^{i+1}, \ldots, z^j\}$

* Represented on the printed page by juxtaposition.

language, where there exists more than one possible substitution for any given component name α, two methods of description are possible: Either there exist several production rules in which α occurs on the left-hand side, or the list of alternatives is specified on the right-hand side of a single production rule, separated by the alternation symbol |. Thus, the definition of a language composed of the set of binary digits (0 and 1) may take either of two forms:

$$\langle binary\ digit \rangle ::= 0$$
$$\langle binary\ digit \rangle ::= 1$$

or

$$\langle binary\ digit \rangle ::= 0\,|\,1$$

As an example of a syntactic specification, consider the simple programming language (SPL) developed by Neuhold (1971) as the vehicle for the description of the Vienna Definition Language (*q.v.*). This language has two basic components, called *numbers* and *variables:*

$\langle number \rangle$	::=	$\langle digit \rangle\ |\ \langle digit \rangle\ \langle number \rangle$
$\langle digit \rangle$	::=	$0\,|\,1\,|\,2\,|\,3\,|\,4\,|\,5\,|\,6\,|\,7\,|\,8\,|\,9$
$\langle variable \rangle$	::=	$\langle letter \rangle\ |\ \langle variable \rangle\ \langle letter \rangle$
$\langle letter \rangle$	::=	$A\,|\,B\,|\,C\,|\ \ldots\ |\,X\,|\,Y\,|\,Z$

In these two definitions, a recursive description system has been used, which basically consists of two parts: a starter and an expander. That is, each definition contains an alternative which does not depend on the component type being formed, and an alternative which creates another instance of the component named on the left-hand side, given an instance of that component. Such recursive definitions permit the generation of unbounded strings of characters. Where an implementation restricts the length of a string (i.e., the number of characters that comprise the string), two alternate methods of description are available; either the set of permitted strings can be described individually, or a bounded repetition notation can be employed. The equivalence of these two descriptive methods is obvious. For example, let us assume that a particular implementation has restricted strings that represent *numbers* to three characters in length. Then the two representations could be

$$\langle number \rangle ::= \langle digit \rangle\ |\ \langle digit \rangle\ \langle digit \rangle$$
$$|\ \langle digit \rangle\ \langle digit \rangle\ \langle digit \rangle$$

or

$$\langle number \rangle ::= \{\langle digit \rangle\}_1^3$$

where the { } notation represents repeated concatenation of the object within the braces with itself, and the indices

specify the upper and lower bounds of the number of repetitions.

The SPL uses these elements to form programs that comprise statements that may be labeled optionally:

$\langle label \rangle$	::=	$\langle letter \rangle\ |\ \langle letter \rangle \langle label \rangle$
$\langle statement \rangle$	::=	$\{\langle label \rangle\}_0^1 \langle statement\ body \rangle$
$\langle program \rangle$	::=	$\langle statement \rangle\ |$
		$\langle program \rangle ; \langle statement \rangle$

An SPL statement may take one of two forms: an arithmetic assignment statement (set statement) or a conditional branching statement (goto statement).

$$\langle statement\ body \rangle ::= \langle set\ statement \rangle\ |$$
$$\langle goto\ statement \rangle$$
$$\langle set\ statement \rangle ::= \text{SET}\ \langle variable \rangle\ \text{TO}$$
$$\langle expression \rangle$$
$$\langle goto\ statement \rangle ::= \text{GOTO}\ \langle label \rangle\ \text{IF}\ \langle expression \rangle$$

In the latter two descriptions (productions), the upper-case characters are elements of the language being described, and therefore are without the angle brackets. Finally, the description of an *expression* is required:

$$\langle expression \rangle ::= \langle simple\ expression \rangle\ |$$
$$\langle simple\ expression \rangle$$
$$\langle operator \rangle \langle expression \rangle$$
$$\langle simple\ expression \rangle ::= \langle number \rangle\ |\ \langle variable \rangle\ |$$
$$(\langle expression \rangle)$$
$$\langle operator \rangle ::= +\,|\,-$$

This set of constructs completes the description of the syntax of the language and conforms to the five formation rules set forth previously.

As in the case of the specification of Algol 60, there existed a need in the development of Cobol for a means of syntactic specification. Whereas the Algol committee was composed of a set of academicians and researchers, the Cobol committee was composed of a much more pragmatically oriented group of people. Thus, the Cobol form of specification is much more oriented toward visual understanding than the (comparatively) mathematical form of BNF.

The latest version of this notation is presented in the specification of Standard Cobol (ANSI, 1974). This descriptive system uses lower-case strings to denote language components (called *generic terms* in the Cobol Standard) and upper-case string to symbolize actual Cobol language characters. Further, upper-case strings that are underlined occur as key words in the language and must appear exactly as printed. On the other hand, upper-case characters that are not underlined are optional, and may or may not be present in the program. There are two sets of parentheses: brackets, [ ], which denote users' options and which may or may not appear in the program; and braces, { }, which denote alternatives, one of which must occur in the program. In this notation, the elements of the brackets or braces are listed vertically. There also exists a notation that means "and so on" which is represented by the symbolism (. . .). According to the Cobol Standard (Chapter I, Section 5), the meaning of this becomes apparent in context.

Using this method of syntactic specification, the simple programming language (SPL) described earlier in BNF can be described as follows.

program: statement [; statement] . . .

statement: [label] $\left\{ \begin{array}{l} \text{SET variable TO expression} \\ \text{GOTO label IF expression} \end{array} \right\}$

label: letter [. . .]
variable: letter [. . .]
number: digit [. . .]

expression: $\left\{ \begin{array}{l} \text{number} \\ \text{variable} \\ \text{(expression)} \end{array} \right\}$ $\left[\left\{ \begin{array}{l} + \\ - \end{array} \right\} \text{expression} \right]$

letter: $\left\{ \begin{array}{l} A \\ B \\ C \\ \dots \end{array} \right\}$

digit $\left\{ \begin{array}{l} 0 \\ 1 \\ 2 \\ \dots \end{array} \right\}$

With the introduction of the programming language Pascal, the use of *syntax diagrams* or *railroad charts* for syntactic specification has become much more popular. Very similar in structure to the style of charts used in connection with finite state automata, these charts specify the alternative paths that may be taken in the construction of the allowable structures of a language.

Like both BNF and the Cobol notation, railroad charts can be constructed for each metavariable in the syntactic description of a language. Also like BNF, the railroad chart has been extended since its original conception to include a notation for the specification of the number of times a particular path in the chart can be traversed; this corresponds directly with the super- and subscript notation that was added to BNF.

Using a BNF notation as a basic source of a syntactic rule, let us examine the procedures by which a railroad chart can be developed. For each BNF production there exists a railroad chart, which is named by the metavariable on the left hand side of the BNF production.

Every occurrence of an actual language symbol (member of the language alphabet) is represented in the railroad chart by that symbol enclosed in a circle. Thus, the production

$$\langle A \rangle ::= x$$

would be represented by the chart:

A:

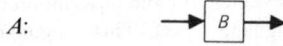

Similarly, the occurrence of a metavariable on the right hand side would be represented by a rectangle.

$$\langle A \rangle ::= \langle B \rangle$$

becomes

A:

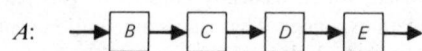

A BNF production having the form of a concatenated sequence of (say) metavariables would be represented by the sequential graph of their equivalent boxes.

$$\langle A \rangle ::= \langle B \rangle \langle C \rangle \langle D \rangle \langle E \rangle$$

is represented by:

A:

Alternatives in a production are handled very much as the two-dimensional scheme of the Cobol notation wherein they are listed vertically with connecting arrows:

$$\langle A \rangle ::= \langle B \rangle | \langle C \rangle | \langle D \rangle | \langle E \rangle$$

A:

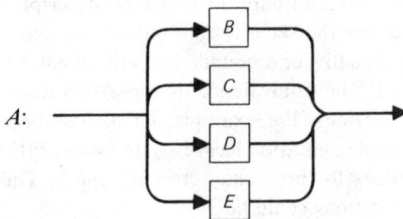

Repetition or recursion is represented by the graph that loops back on itself:

A:

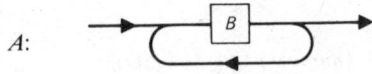

where the exit from the loop is clearly identified as the alternative route out.

For the case of repetition with the possibility of zero passes through the loop, the construction

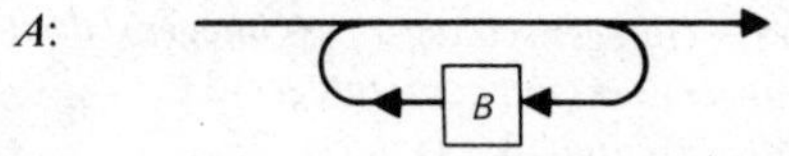

A:
B

is the appropriate one.

Let us now present the railroad chart definition for the simple programming language we have used to illustrate the two prior syntactic systems:

program:
statement
;
statement:
label
SET
variable
TO
exp
GOTO
label
IF
exp
label:
letter
variable:
letter
number:
digit
exp:
number
variable
(
exp
)
+
−
letter:
A
B
C
digit:
0
1
2

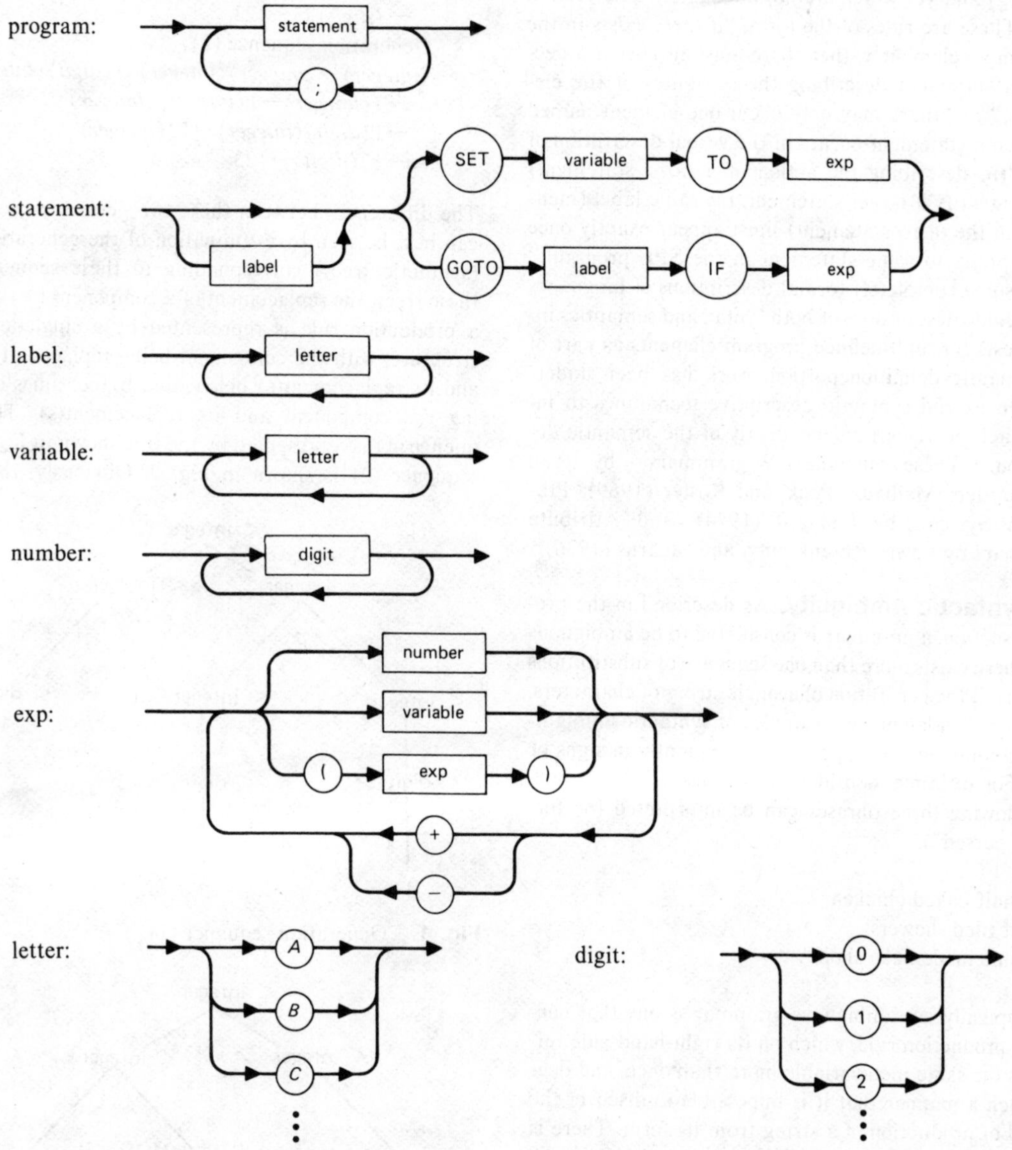

If the restriction had been placed on the construction of (say) variables that they should not contain more than five letters, then the notation used consists of a half circle in the connecting arrow containing the number of repetitions that are permitted. The minimum number of repetitions must be represented by an explicit number of occurrences of the object being repeated. Thus, if we were to add the additional constraint on variable names that they must contain at least two letters, the chart would be constructed as follows.

variable:
letter
letter
letter
3

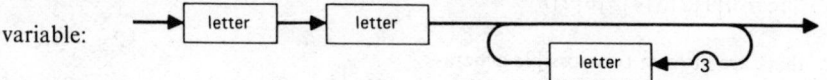

Any context-free representation of syntactic description suffers from one deficiency: An inability to specify context-sensitive restriction rules. In most programming languages, there exist rules for the formation of programs that are totally independent of meaning (i.e., semantic meaning) and yet which are not adequately described in BNF. These are rules of the form, "if there exists in the program an element *x*, then there must also occur a declaration statement describing the attributes of the element *x*," or "there may only occur one element named *y*." Such a statement occurs in the verbal description of SPL: "(in describing the action of a GOTO statement) ... To identify a target statement, the same label (mentioned in the GOTO statement) must appear exactly once as the prefix to some statement in the SPL program." While some completely formal descriptions of languages that include descriptions of both syntax and semantics include tests for multidefined program elements as part of the semantic definition portion, work has been undertaken to extend syntactic descriptive techniques to include such provisions independently of the semantic description. These include W-grammars by van Wijngaarden, Mailloux, Peck, and Koster (1969); Production Systems by Ledgard (1974); and Attribute Grammars by Lewis, Rosenkrantz, and Stearns (1976).

Syntactic Ambiguity. As described in the preceding section, a grammar is considered to be ambiguous when there exists more than one sequence of substitutions that permit the generation of a single string of characters. In the English language, examples of syntactic ambiguities are common and appear most frequently in signs or titles. For example, consider the various ways in which the following three phrases can be interpreted (or formally "parsed"):

> a half baked chicken
> hot tiled showers
> home made bake shop.

Typically, an ambiguous grammar is one that contains a production rule, which on its right-hand side references the same metavariable more than once, and does it in such a manner that it is impossible to discover the method of production of a string from its form. There is no known algorithmic technique to test for the existence of ambiguities in a grammar. However, examples of ambiguous grammars may help to indicate common sources of ambiguity. For example, consider the grammar

> $\langle integer \rangle$ $::= \langle digit \rangle \mid \langle integer \rangle \langle integer \rangle$
> $\langle digit \rangle$ $::= 0 \mid 1 \mid 2 \mid 3 \mid 4 \mid 5 \mid 6 \mid 7 \mid 8 \mid 9$

Using this syntax, there are at least two possible generation sequences to generate any string composed of three

or more digits. For example, consider the string 123:

> Generation sequence (1)
> $\langle integer \rangle \rightarrow \langle integer \rangle \langle integer \rangle \rightarrow \langle integer \rangle \langle digit \rangle$
> $\rightarrow \langle integer \rangle 3 \rightarrow \langle integer \rangle \langle integer \rangle 3$
> $\rightarrow \langle integer \rangle \langle digit \rangle 3 \rightarrow \langle integer \rangle 23$
> $\rightarrow \langle digit \rangle 23 \rightarrow 123$
> Generation sequence (2)
> $\langle integer \rangle \rightarrow \langle integer \rangle \langle integer \rangle \rightarrow \langle digit \rangle \langle integer \rangle$
> $\rightarrow 1 \langle integer \rangle \rightarrow 1 \langle integer \rangle \langle integer \rangle$
> $\rightarrow 1 \langle digit \rangle \langle integer \rangle \rightarrow 12 \langle integer \rangle$
> $\rightarrow 12 \langle digit \rangle \rightarrow 123$

The differences between these two generation sequences can best be seen by examination of the generation trees (syntactic trees) corresponding to these sequences. In these trees, the replacement of a component by the use of a production rule is represented by a single-level tree structure, with the component being replaced at the top and its replacement(s) below, and branch lines connecting the component and its replacement(s). Thus, sequence (1) is represented by the tree shown in Fig. 1, and sequence (2) is shown in Fig. 2. Obviously, these two

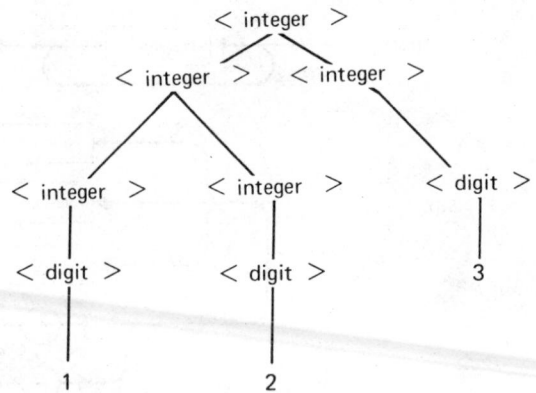

Fig. 1.   Generation sequence (1).

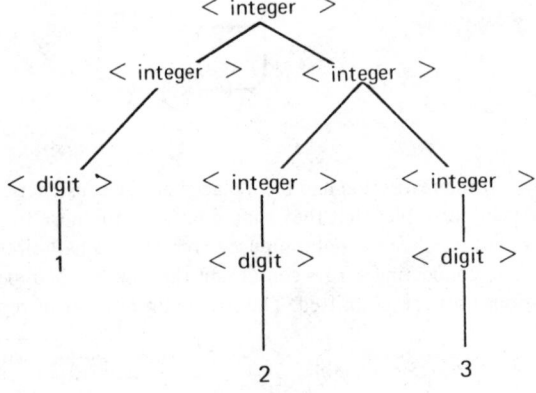

Fig. 2.   Generation sequence (2).

trees are not equivalent, and thus we may state that this grammar appears to be ambiguous.

However, apparent ambiguity can result from a failure to be consistent in the order in which components in the partially expanded string are replaced. In fact, any rule that contains in its right-hand part more than one component is a potential source of apparent ambiguity. Thus, we insist that the order of replacement of components in a string be strictly left-to-right or right-to-left. That is, the leftmost (rightmost) component in a string is the candidate for replacement at each generation stage. Such a strict sequence of generation is known as *canonic generation*.

Returning to the definition of a digit string given above, it may be seen that a canonic generation would not alleviate the ambiguousness of the grammar. However, a simple change in the grammar would solve this problem:

$$\langle integer \rangle ::= \langle digit \rangle \mid \langle integer \rangle \langle digit \rangle$$
$$\langle digit \rangle \quad ::= 0 \mid 1 \mid 2 \mid 3 \mid 4 \mid 5 \mid 6 \mid 7 \mid 8 \mid 9$$

From this grammar, it would appear that there are at least two distinct manners of generating the string 123, depending on the order of application of the production rules, i.e., left or right canonic generation.

Left canonic generation sequence (3):
$$\langle integer \rangle \rightarrow \langle integer \rangle \langle digit \rangle$$
$$\rightarrow \langle integer \rangle \langle digit \rangle \langle digit \rangle$$
$$\rightarrow \langle digit \rangle \langle digit \rangle \langle digit \rangle$$
$$\rightarrow 1 \langle digit \rangle \langle digit \rangle \rightarrow 12 \langle digit \rangle \rightarrow 123$$

Right canonic generation sequence (4):
$$\langle integer \rangle \rightarrow \langle integer \rangle \langle digit \rangle \rightarrow \langle integer \rangle 3$$
$$\rightarrow \langle integer \rangle \langle digit \rangle 3 \rightarrow \langle integer \rangle 23$$
$$\rightarrow \langle digit \rangle 23 \rightarrow 123$$

While it would appear that these two generation sequences are distinct, their generation trees are in fact identical, as is shown in Fig. 3.

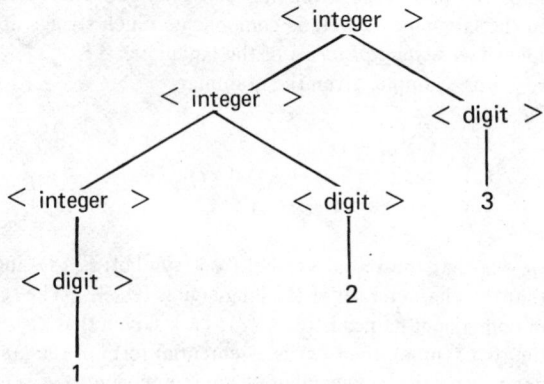

Fig. 3.   Canonic generation tree for sequences (3) and (4).

In general, an ambiguous grammar will be formed when two grammars are combined to define languages that have at least one element in common. For example, consider the grammar

$$\langle this \rangle ::= \{A\}_1^3$$

which corresponds to the language with the sentences A, AA and AAA. Then, if this were to be combined with the grammar

$$\langle that \rangle ::= AA$$

there would be two canonic generation sequences to develop the string AA. Thus, the grammar

$$\langle this\text{-}or\text{-}that \rangle ::= \langle this \rangle \mid \langle that \rangle$$

is ambiguous.

Although syntactic specification techniques are intended merely to provide a mechanism for describing the spatial relationships between the symbolic elements of the language, other structures inherent to the language are often introduced in order to provide guidance for compilers and other processors. The most common example is that of the arithmetic expression where the syntactic structure is organized in such a manner that it reflects the hierarchical execution (evaluation) structure of the expression. That is, if phrases within a syntactic tree are recognized in the same order in which the arithmetic factors are evaluated, then the two structures are synonomous.

Similarly, in connection with programming languages, it is important that languages be defined so that the desired meaning of a statement is unambiguous. As an example, it should be clear in defining an arithmetic expression that the implied meaning of an expression is unambiguous. Consider the simple expression

$$A - B - C$$

The interpretation (or parsing) of this string is usually considered to be equivalent to the string

$$(A - B) - C$$

and not

$$A - (B - C)$$

That is, $A - B$ is to be considered the first operand of the subtraction that contains C as its second operand. In terms of syntactic rules, this can be described by requiring that in unparenthesized arithmetic expressions, the left (first) operand is always an *expression* and the right (second) operand is always a simple *element,* where a degenerate *expression* is an *element.* Thus, we might define

$$\langle expression \rangle ::= \langle element \rangle \mid \langle expression \rangle$$
$$- \langle element \rangle$$

If we now add a semantic interpretation scheme over the syntactic form, which specifies that only *expressions* can be evaluated and *elements* are number representations, we may see that

$$9 - 7 - 2$$

can be generated only by a sequence of productions such that $9 - 7$ is an *expression* (and hence can be evaluated) that is part of the larger *expression* $\overline{9 - 7} - 2$, where the overscore identifies the left-hand operand, which must have a value (i.e., be evaluated) in order to evaluate the second subtraction term.

Context Sensitivity. In the use of syntax productions, the progression from the root symbol to the actual string of characters may be visualized as the progressive substitution of components until all components have been replaced by elements of the character set of the language. This may be further visualized as the progression through certain branches of a tree structure wherein each branch is independent of all other branches. However, this treelike structure with no interdependence of branches exists only for *context-free* languages. If the left-hand side of a production contains more than one metavariable, then the production of the right-hand side is dependent on the occurrence of more than one metavariable, and the language is said to be *context-sensitive.* In such languages, productions of the type

$$\langle a \rangle \langle b \rangle \langle c \rangle ::= \langle a \rangle \pi \langle c \rangle$$

indicate that in the context of $\langle a \rangle$ and $\langle c \rangle$ (either but not both of which may be empty strings), the component $\langle b \rangle$ is to be replaced by the string π, where π may be any combination of characters and components. Although the majority of elements of computer languages are susceptible to description by a context-free grammar, certain features may require the use of a context-sensitive grammar, thus developing a totally context-sensitive grammar for that language.

For a discussion and formal definition of context-sensitive languages, see Ginsburg (1966).

The need for context-sensitive grammars has diminished as a result of the existence of *attribute grammars* and the inability of researchers to develop syntactic analysis systems that are equivalent to those that have been developed for lexical analysis or for context-free grammars. Thus, although they are academically interesting, they are not used in any production system. The closest approach to such sensitivity is in the lookahead facilities of LR(k) grammars or LALR systems. However, such contextual checking is one-dimensional.

Syntactic Analysis. The problem of associating a given string of symbols through a grammar to a language, such that an answer to the question "does this string belong to the language?" may be determined, is known as *syntactic analysis.* It is intended that in determining the existence of the string in the language, the syntactic tree for that string can be created. In fact, in terms of syntactic trees, the process of analysis can be thought of as the determination of the syntactic tree that was used to generate the string.

Cheatham (1967) has likened the problem of tree generation to the game of dominoes, wherein the dominoes contain the left-hand side and the right-hand side of each syntactic production. The problem, then, is to fit the dominoes together in such a manner that there exists a complete tree between the root symbol and the string in question. Such a structure is shown in Fig. 4 and is discussed later in this section.

Another means for validating the existence of a string in a language is to generate all possible strings of that language and then to investigate the existence of the string in question in the generated set. Obviously, in some languages this is impossible, since the language is infinite. However, given a string of a prescribed length (i.e., number of distinct characters in the string), it is possible to generate all sequences of that length, provided the null element is rejected from the grammar. That is, if each and every production in a given grammar either maintains or increases the length of the generated string upon application, then it is possible to discard many alternative generation sequences when the generated string is too long. In this sense, a string may consist of both characters in the language as well as components. Such strings are known as *sentential forms* of the language.

For example, given the grammar

(1) $\langle s \rangle ::= \langle e \rangle$
(2) $\langle e \rangle ::= \langle e \rangle + \langle t \rangle \mid \langle t \rangle$
(3) $\langle t \rangle ::= A \langle t \rangle \mid A$

we see that the initial symbol (root symbol) is $\langle s \rangle$ and that the character set of the language is $\{A, +\}$. The set of component names is $\{\langle s \rangle, \langle e \rangle, \langle t \rangle\}$. Given that $\langle s \rangle$ is the root symbol, then $\langle s \rangle$ is a sentential form of the language, and the replacement of any component in a sentential form by the use of one of the productions also de-

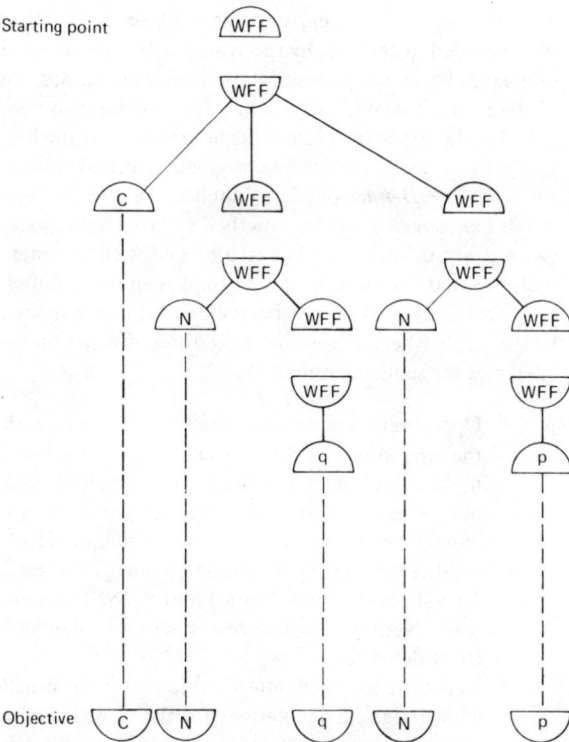

Starting point   WFF

Objective   C   N   q   N   p

Fig. 4. Syntactic tree as a dominoes game. Given a starting point and objective as semicircles, the game is finished when all semicircles match with another containing the same character or component name.

velops a sentential form. Hence, the sequence of sentential forms

$$\langle s \rangle \rightarrow \langle e \rangle \rightarrow \langle e \rangle + \langle t \rangle \rightarrow \langle t \rangle + \langle t \rangle$$
$$\rightarrow A \langle t \rangle + \langle t \rangle \rightarrow AA + \langle t \rangle \rightarrow AA + A$$

may be developed, showing that each form is *in* the language. However, we will usually be concerned with only those sentential forms that are composed totally of characters of the language; i.e., sentential forms that contain no components which are candidates for replacement through the use of any production. In the language defined by the grammar above, the *proof* that a string exists is the existence of a sequence of steps (using one production rule at each step) which leads from the root symbol to the desired string.

Such a definition of the proof of the existence of a string in a language is consistent with the definition of *proof* as related to formal systems (Mendelson, 1966):

A proof ... is a sequence A_1, A_2, ... A_n of well formed formulas such that, for each *i*, either A_i is an

axiom (of the system) or A_i is a direct consequence of some preceding well formed formula by virtue of one of the rules of inference.

In terms of syntactic forms, the existence proof may be defined as follows.

An existence proof over a string of characters $\emptyset_n$ in the language is a sequence $\emptyset_1, \emptyset_2, \ldots, \emptyset_n$ of sentential forms of the language such that, for each i, $\emptyset_i$ is a sentential form which is the result of applying one of the production rules of the grammar to $\emptyset_{i-1}$ and where $\emptyset_1$ is the root symbol of the language.

The means for determining this sequence is the task of a syntactic analyzer, and the sequence of productions which generates the sentential forms is known as the *parse* of the string. That is, for example, in the sequence of sentential forms that relate the root symbol $\langle s \rangle$ to the string $AA + A$ above, the parse is the sequence of rules applied. Thus, if the rules were numbered *i.j* where *i* is the rule number and *j* the alternative used, then this sequence of sentential forms is equivalent to the parse

$$1.1, \ 2.1, \ 2.2, \ 3.1, \ 3.2, \ 3.2$$

While we develop the parse of a string in the process of compilation, at least by implication, the most important derivative of a syntactic analysis of a string from the point of view of a compiler is the relationships between component names and the string. For example, it is comparatively easy to see in Fortran that the component name *⟨variable⟩* can be related to strings of characters in statements. Once this relationship has been established, then the generator of the compiler can (say) create addresses in target language instructions.

The task of analysis of a string must be initially to determine the existence of the string in the language. As noted above, one way to do this is by developing from the root component all strings of the same length as the string in question. Consider the grammar

$$\langle WFF \rangle ::= p \,|\, q \,|\, r \,|\, s \,|\, N \langle WFF \rangle \,|$$
$$\{C \,|\, A \,|\, K \,|\, E\}_i^1 \langle WFF \rangle \langle WFF \rangle.$$

This simple grammar (Allen, 1970) permits the production of well-formed formulas (WFF); the upper-case characters (N,C,A,K,E) represent the operators, and the lower-case characters (p,q,r,s) represent the simple operands. Fig. 4 shows Cheatham's domino game form of the generation tree of the string CNqNp. Now, obviously, since the definition of this language includes a recursive production, the language is an infinite language, and hence it will not be feasible to generate all possible strings in the language to test against any string that is believed to exist in the language. However, it is possible to generate all strings of a certain length and then to check the existence of some string in this generated set. For example, consider again the string CNqNp. This string is composed of five characters (symbols in the language); and, by an examination of the possible substitutions that can be made, it can be seen that there are approximately 2,500 five-character strings that may be generated from this grammar! Thus, even for strings with comparatively few (5 even) characters, the number of alternatives in the algorithm for analysis is extremely large. Therefore, we must search for an alternate approach.

Syntactic analyzers can broadly be classified into two types: (1) the predictive methods, which, starting from the root symbol, attempt to predict the means by which the string was generated; and (2) the reductive methods, which attempt to reduce the string to the root symbol. These methods are loosely termed the *top-down* and *bottom-up* methods, respectively. The direction implied by these terms is related to the syntactic trees that may be generated wherein the root symbol is at the top of the page and the string at the bottom. It may then be seen that a predictive (top-down) method starts at the top of the (yet unconstructed) tree and builds down toward the string, whereas the bottom-up (*reductive*) method starts at the string and attempts to develop a tree that converges to the root symbol. It can be seen, using Cheatham's domino game, that starting from the basic game board containing only the root symbol (at the top) and the string to be analyzed (at the bottom), the two stages of analysis are well exemplified by the order in which the players fit the pieces into the puzzle.

Semantic Descriptions. The formal description of the semantics of programming languages is currently in a state of active development, with several competing techniques, each emphasizing some aspect of definitional technology. There exist methods of semantic definition which are based on automata theory; these methods model processes and languages by modeling techniques. Other systems have developed abstract machines that closely resemble actual machines and which have a language of instruction that is used to describe a process or language. Although tremendous strides have been made in the methods of definition, including several examples of defining the semantics of actual languages and using those descriptions to guide the development of compilers and interpreters for those languages, there has been little practical work done in the area of formally validating those definitions. Conversely, there is a growing body of knowledge related to the proof of assertions about simple programs, which can be expected to develop to more meaningful proof techniques and systems in the future.

Although even as early as the work on Algol 60, it was intended to accompany the syntactic specifications of languages by semantic descriptors, such a model was not available until several years later. The first large system that was described by a semantic description was the language PL/I, using the schema originally entitled *Universal Language Definer* but later dubbed the *Vienna Definition Language* (*q.v.*). This method is based on a model of an abstract machine that is provided with an interpreter so that instances of the language can be executed.

This methodology has been extended and modified to the stage where there now exist three distinct methodologies for semantic definition:

1. Operational semantics—which is concerned with the operations of (possibly) abstract machines highly dependent on sequential activities that mirror the von Neumann style of computer architecture. This is the original technique developed as the Vienna Definition Language and used (in a slightly informal form) in the ANSI (American National Standards Institute) standard PL/I definition.
2. Denotational semantics—which is concerned with designing denotations for the elements of a programming language in an abstract domain (possibly the domain of data items in the language) independent of either an actual or an abstract machine system.
3. Axiomatic semantics—where the description of the properties of programming languages is specified in terms of the axioms to which the execution of that program must conform.

By analogy (but not necessarily in fact), these three descriptive methods correspond to the description of the interpreter for a programming language (operational semantics), the properties of the elements of the program (denotational) without regard for the end result, and the assertions that could be included in the program to show that it is correct (axiomatic definition).

REFERENCES

1960. Naur, P. "Documentation Problems: Algol 60," *Comm. ACM* **3**, *No. 5:* 299–314 (May).

1963. Floyd, R. W. "Syntactic Analysis and Operator Precedence," *Journal of the ACM* **10**: 316 (July).

1966. Ginsburg, S. *The Mathematical Theory of Context Free Languages.* New York: McGraw-Hill.

1966. Mendelson, E. *Introduction to Mathematical Logic.* New York: Van Nostrand.

1967. Cheatham, T. E. *The Theory and Construction of Compilers,* 2nd Ed. Wakefield, MA: Computer Associates.

1969. Van Wijngaarden, A., Mailloux, B. J., Peck, J. E., and

Koster, C. H. A. "Report on the Algorithmic Language Algol 68," MR 101, *Mathematisch Centrum,* Amsterdam.

1969. Lucas, P. and Walk, K. "On the Formal Description of PL/I," *Annual Review in Automatic Programming, Part 3.* Oxford, U.K.: Pergamon Press.

1969. Lucas, P. and Walk, K. "On the Formal Description of PL/I," *Ann. Rev. in Automatic Prog.* **6,** *No. 6, Part 3.* Pergamon.

1970. Allen, L. E. *Wff'n Proof.* New Haven, CT: Antotelic Instructional Materials.

1971. Branquart, P. et al. "The Composition of Semantics in ALGOL 68." *Comm. ACM* **14,** *No. 11:* 697 (November).

1971. Neuhold, E. J. "The Formal Description of Programming Languages," *IBM Systems Journal* **10,** *No. 2:* 86–112.

1972. *Proceedings of a Symposium on Proving Assertions about Programs, SIGPLAN Notices* **7.** *No. 7,* (January). New York: Association for Computing Machinery.

1974. ANSI. *American National Standard Cobol, X3.23-1974.* New York: American National Standards Instutute.

1974. Jensen, K. and Wirth, N. *Pascal User Manual and Report.* New York: Springer-Verlag.

1974. Ledgard, H. F. "Productions Systems: Or Can We Do Better Than BNF?" *Comm. ACM* **17,** *No. 2:* 158–165 (February).

1976. American National Standard Programming Language PL/I, American National Standards Institute, X3.53.

1976. Lewis, P. M., Rosenkrantz, D. J., and Stearns, R. E. *Compiler Design Theory.* Reading, MA: Addison-Wesley, Chapter 9.

1978. Bjorner, D. and Jones, C. B. "The Vienna Development Method," *Lecture Notes in Computer Science,* Goos, G. and Hartmanis, J. (Eds.). New York: Springer-Verlag.

1979. Gordon, M. J. C. *The Denotational Description of Programming Languages.* New York: Springer-Verlag.

J. A. N. Lee

PROGRAMMING, MATHEMATICAL. *See* Mathematical Programming.

PROGRAM SPECIFICATION

For articles on related subjects *see* Documentation; Program Verification; Software Reliability; and Structured Programming.

The term program specification may refer to:

1. A statement of *requirements* for a program;
2. An expression of a *design* for a program; or
3. A formal statement of conditions against which the program can be *verified.*

In any kind of specification, there are several concerns:

1. *Consistency.* Is the specification logically satisfiable?

2. *Implementability.* Is the specification practically realizable?
3. *Completeness.* Does the specification capture the *full* intent of the specifier?
4. *Non-ambiguity.* Does the specification capture the *precise* intent of the specifier?

Consider a program which deals with mailing lists and addresses. A *requirement specification* might be as follows.

> The program will read a list of addresses, separate those which are valid (to the extent that the town and state are in the given zip code area), print out the invalid addresses, also print out the valid addresses sorted by zip code with all duplicates removed, and finally print out the valid addresses which are duplicates.

Certainly the purpose of the program is clear—to generate a mailing list which has some bad cases filtered out, but there are some specification difficulties.

1. A town and state may agree with a zip code, but the actual street address may not fall within that zip code area. The specification does not require, indeed even prohibits, this more precise meaning of validity. Is this the intent of the specifier?
2. It wasn't stated what geographical area the mailing list must cover, so the table of zip codes down to the town level may be too large for the target computer.
3. What does it mean for addresses to be duplicated? Is "5674 Windsor Way #212" the same as "5674 Windsor Way"?

A design for the program might be that provided in Fig. 1. This high-level program is intended for *stepwise refinement* or for transformation into a specific implementation. Assertions (following *preconditions* and preceding *postconditions*) constitute the specifications to be verified. Its data types, *Address* and *SequenceOf-Address,* may be defined by algebraic axioms. The concepts of a valid address and matching (for duplication) of two addresses are left undefined. Fig. 2 shows the definitions of the concepts used in the formal specification that require more explanation.

A major concern of software methodology is the formalization of requirement specifications so that verification is meaningful. *Verification* is the task of showing consistency between a program and its specifications, usually by one of the common methods of proving and/or testing. Specifications for verification are usually given in terms of predicates called, as above, preconditions and postconditions.

This program illustrates some aspects of preparing a mailing list. The actual program implementing the specifications should be equivalent, but can compute the same results differently.

procedure Mailing(Inputs:SequenceOfAddress;
   var Duplicates,InValids,SortedValids:SequenceOfAddress);

A sequence, as in SequenceOfAddress, is either a NewSequence or some sequence s with an element i appended to its right, denoted by the operator apr. (for append right)

pre *TRUE;*   *[No assumptions required for input]*

post *DisjointEqual(SortedValids,InValids,Inputs')*   *[SortedValids + InValids = Initial inputs.*
and ValidCheck(Inputs',SortedValids)   *SortedValids contains all Valid Inputs.*
and DuplicateCheck(Inputs',Duplicates)   *Duplicates contains all duplicated Valid Inputs.*
and OrderedByZip(SortedValids)   *SortedValids are ordered by zip code with no duplicates]*
and Nodups(SortedValids);

The following procedure does the removal of duplicates and sorting.

procedure SortAndDedup(Inputs:SequenceOfAddress;
   var SortedInputs,Duplicates:SequenceOfAddress);

pre *TRUE;*   *[SortedInputs contains all Inputs, sorted by zip, without*
post *ElemsEqual(Inputs',SortedInputs)*   *duplicates. Duplicates contains all inputs which match*
and Duplicated(Inputs',Duplicates)   *others.]*
and OrderedByZip(SortedInputs)
and Nodups(SortedInputs);
begin end;

The body of the procedure is omitted as we are only interested in its effects.

var Valids:SequenceOfAddress;
begin
  Valids,InValids := NewSequenceOfAddress,NewSequenceOfAddress;

  maintain *some UsedInputs(*   *[At all times through the loop it is true that those Inputs*
    and Inputs' = UsedInputs join Inputs   *used plus those left are the original Inputs (i.e., Inputs'),*
    and DisjointEqual(Valids,InValids,UsedInputs)   *that Valids plus InValids together are the Inputs used, and*
    and ValidCheck(UsedInputs,Valids)   *that Valids contains the same number of occurrences of*
    and ValidOccsEqual(UsedInputs,Valids))   *valid Inputs as in the Inputs processed.]*
  while Inputs ~ = NewSequenceofAddress <u>do</u>   *[Continue until all Inputs used.]*
    begin
      if Valid(First(Inputs))   *[Take the first element of Inputs and put it on Valids or*
      then Valids := Valids apr First(Inputs)   *InValids and then delete it from Inputs.]*
      else InValids := InValids apr First(Inputs);
      Inputs: = LessFirst(Inputs)
    end;
  SortAndDedup(Valids,SortedValids,Duplicates);   *[Use Valids to form SortedValids and Duplicates.]*
end;

Fig. 1. Mailing list program. (Functions in pre- and postconditions and invariants are defined in Fig. 2.)

A powerful language such as the *predicate calculus* is usually necessary for program specification. The *program precondition,* a predicate over the input and global program variables, expresses what can be assumed at the beginning of execution of the program, whereas the *postcondition* expresses the desired property of the output and global variables at termination of the program. Often the postcondition must refer to values of parameters and global variables at the beginning of the program unit's computation.

By convention, these earlier values are denoted by *priming* (i.e., initializing) the variables. In our example,

we have TRUE, that is no restriction on input, as the precondition. Our postcondition has several stipulations which formalize various parts of the requirements, using mathematical concepts from sets and sequences and the predicate calculus. Fig. 2 relates the formal concepts to their informal meaning.

Verification of a program against its specifications requires a hierarchy starting with the requirements, through their formalization, and then precise formal specification of successively smaller program units (e.g., the procedure *SortAndDedup* and the loop in *Mailing*) down to the programming language statements, where

declare s, s1, s2: SequenceOfAddress;
declare x, e : Address;

matches and Valid are not further specified.

interfaces matches(x, e), Valid(x): Boolean;

define hasmatch(x, s)   [Another address in s matches x]
  = = (x in s
    and ((2 < = Occurrences(x, s)) or hasanothermatch(x, s))),

  hasanothermatch(x, s)   [Address x is equivalent ("matches")
    = = some e (e in s and (x~ = e) and matches(x, e))   another address e.]

  ElemsEqual(s1, s2)   [Sequences s1 and s2 have the same elements.]
    = = all x (x in s1 eqv x in s2),

  ElemsDisjoint(s1,s2)   [No element in s1 is also in s2 and vice versa.]
    = = all x (x in s1 imp ~(x in s2)),

  DisjointEqual(s1, s2, s)   [s1 and s2 are disjoint but together form s.]
    = = (ElemsDisjoint(s1, s2) and
        ElemsEqual(s, s1 join s2)),

  ValidCheck(s1, s2)   [if x is in s1 this implies it is valid iff it is also in s2.]
    = = all x (x in s1 imp (x in s2 eqv Valid(x))),

  DuplicateCheck(s1, s2)   [x is valid and has a match in s1,
    = = all x (Valid(x) and hasmatch(x, s1) eqv   iff it is in s2.]
           x in s2),

  Duplicated(s1, s2)   [x has a match in s1 iff it is in s2.]
    = = all x (hasmatch(x, s1) eqv x in s2),

  Occurrences(s,x) =   [The number of occurrences in s of x.]
    if s = NewSequenceOfAddress
    then 0
    else Occurrences (LessLast(s),x)
      + if x = Last(s) then 1
        else 0

  ValidOccurrencesEqual(s1, s2)   [If x is valid then it has the same number
    = = all x (Valid(x)imp   of Occurrences in s1 and s2.]
        Occurrences(x,s1) = Occurrences(x, s2)),

Notation:
= = means "is defined to be"
eqv means "equivalent"
~ means "not equal"
join means "catenate"
imp means "implies"
iff means "if and only if"

Fig. 2. Mailing list specification notation.

the language's semantics are the final specification. The Mailing List example illustrates this range on a (mechanically) verifiable program. Its proof, however, reveals the additional assumption that "any address matching a valid address is also valid."

REFERENCES

1977. Parnas, D. "The Use of Precise Specifications in the Development of Software," *Proc. IFIP Congress 1977.*
1979. IEEE Computer Society. *Conference on Specifications of Reliable Software.*
1979. Liskov, B. and Berzins, V. *An Appraisal of Program Specifications.* Cambridge, MA: M.I.T. Press.

S. L. GERHART

PROGRAM STATUS WORDS AND STATE VECTORS

For articles on related subjects *see* INTERRUPT; MASKING; MEMORY PROTECTION; MULTIPROGRAMMING; OPERATING SYSTEMS: Principles; SCHEDULING ALGORITHM; and TASK.

In multitask computer systems the processor or processors must be switched among the tasks or processes of the system. The mechanism for accomplishing task switching must guarantee the integrity of the tasks; by saving all vital information about a task, switching should not interfere or affect in any way the computation performed. For protection purposes, it may be also desirable that no information about a previous task should remain behind in a processor after the switching operation is done. To interrupt the processor from one task and assign it to another, it is necessary to save the state of the processor at the time of interruption; later, the processor state can be restored to this value and the task resumed at the point of interruption. The state information about the task to be saved is called the *task state descriptor,* or *state vector,* of the task. In some systems, notably IBM, a portion of the state descriptor is called the *program status word;* this term is, however, misleading, not only because the state concept applies to the dynamic behavior of a task and not the static program that generates it, but also because a state descriptor often requires several words of storage for its representation, whereas a program status word normally requires only one.

A task's state description can be represented as a vector of four components:

$$D = (ep, ip, mc, pc).$$

The component *ep* is called the *environment pointer;* it is usually contained in a set of one or more base registers, and designates where the instructions and data code for the task are located. In the case of a CDC Cyber series system, *ep* is the content of a base/limit register, defining a contiguous main memory region containing the task. In the case of the IBM OS/360 system, *ep* is implicit in the *storage key* (which is part of the program status word) and designates a unique region of memory whose *lock register* contains the same value as the storage key. In the case of virtual storage systems, *ep* is the content of a register pointing to the mapping tables, defining the address space of the task; and in the case of the Burroughs B7900, *ep* is the content of the *display,* which is a stack of base registers pointing to activation records of the task. The component *ip* is called the *instruction pointer;* it is simply the address of the next instruction to be executed by the task from its address space as designated by *ep.*

The component *mc* is called the *machine conditions* of the task; it comprises the contents of all programmable registers in the processor, such as arithmetic and index registers. The component *pc* is called the *protection code* of the task; it specifies the protection domain of the task, i.e., the authorizations it has to perform certain actions. The simplest form of protection code is the value of the supervisor/user mode flip-flop, the setting of which to the "user" state indicates that certain instructions (e.g., those that load base registers) may not legally be executed by a user task.

In IBM systems, a state descriptor is of the form $D = (psw, mc)$, where *psw* is the program status word. The instruction pointer *ip* is embedded in *psw,* as is the environment pointer *ep* (as the "storage key"), and also the supervisor/user protection code. Also contained in *psw* are:

1. A *condition code,* indicating the outcome of the most recently executed arithmetic or boolean operation.
2. A collection of interrupt *masks,* indicating which exceptional conditions (e.g., overflow, underflow, zero-divide) are enabled for the task.
3. *Channel masks* indicating which channels may interrupt the task by their completion signals.

There is some question whether the channel masks ought to be part of a task state descriptor, since the channels operate independently of user tasks. Many systems have all interrupt masks, except for interrupts that can be enabled from a programming language (e.g., ON conditions in PL/I), implemented separately and independently of task state descriptors.

P. J. DENNING AND D. E. DENNING

PROGRAM VERIFICATION

For articles on related subjects *see* DEBUGGING; LOGICS OF PROGRAMS; PROGRAM SPECIFICATION; and STRUCTURED PROGRAMMING.

It is important to know that a computer program meets its specifications. For example, payroll programs should issue checks to each employee for exactly the amount due, sorting programs should reorder the given elements without losing or introducing spurious elements, message-sending programs should direct the correspondence to the stated recipients and to nobody else, and compilers should produce an object program which faithfully preserves the meaning of the source program. Each of these brief informal specifications can and must be elaborated in order to ascertain whether a program satisfies precise and rigorous specifications. This determination can be done in various ways, each of which provides varying amounts of assurances.

The most common technique is known as *debugging* or *testing* a program. Sample data, presumed to be representative and to cover the necessary extreme cases, are given to the program, and the results are compared against known or expected answers. The major problem is to know when to stop testing—how much more assurance of meeting specifications would be gained by additional cases. Or, as E. W. Dijkstra (1972) wrote, "Program testing can be used to show the presence of bugs, but never to show their absence!"

In contrast, but often as a supplement to, rather than as a distinct alternative to, testing, is the technique of *program verification,* as that term is used in this article. To *verify* a program means to demonstrate, via a mathematical proof, that the program is consistent with its specifications. It may be quite useful just to prove limited properties such as that the program terminates (and without undefined operations) or that certain variables remain unchanged. The criterion of success requires a sufficiently believable proof, as do all mathematical proofs. Failure to complete the proof may be due to a problem with either the program *or* the specifications as well as because of insufficient information about the problem domain or even inability actually to prove a true theorem.

Basic Technique and Example. The most common technique for verifying a program is known as the method of *assertions* (or *invariant assertions* or *inductive assertions*). The basic idea is to associate assertions with various points in the program. *Assertions* are propositions involving the variables of the program usu-

ally expressed in a system like the first-order predicate calculus. The intent is that each assertion be a true statement every time the execution of the program passes the point with which that assertion is associated. The proof requirement is to demonstrate that this intent is actually satisfied. Those assertions which appear at the end of a program are often called *postconditions;* assuming that the program terminates, these give the result of the program. Assertions which appear at the start of a program are called *preconditions.* Because programs do not accept arbitrary inputs, a precondition is intended to give a sufficient condition for the program to compute its result. For example, a program to compute the inverse of a matrix or the reciprocal of a number requires a nonzero input and perhaps other conditions as well. The only other requirement on the association of assertions is that (the path formed by) every loop must have at least one point with an assertion. An assertion which is true for every execution of a loop is called a *loop invariant.* Such invariants can often be deduced from the program or, indeed, the loop can be constructed to preserve a previously given invariant. In either case, the loop invariant is an essential part of understanding why the program works as well as an essential ingredient of the verification.

The standard way to achieve the proof requirement is to focus on a particular assertion, say P_1, and to follow the program execution from P_1 along all possible paths, stopping on each path when another assertion, P_2, is reached (P_2 is often P_1 again if the path is a loop). One must show, for each such path, that P_1 and the effects of the statements between P_1 and P_2 imply that P_2 holds. Suppose we do this for all assertions, including the preconditions which may be assumed, and suppose that for each P_1 we can show that P_2 holds. In particular, the postconditions will be a P_2 for one or more P_1. Thus, if the postconditions are actually reached (i.e., the program halts), it will be true. This argument by mathematical induction justifies the method and motivates some of its names.

As a simple example, consider the program whose aim is to count the positive elements in the *n*-element array $A(1 .. n)$.

```
poscount := 0; i := 1;
while i ≤ n do
    begin
        if A(i) > 0 then poscount := poscount + 1;
        i := i + 1;
    end
```

In Fig. 1 is a flowchart of this program with assertions 1, 2, and 3 added. There the notation Positive (A, j, k) informally denotes the number of positive elements of A in

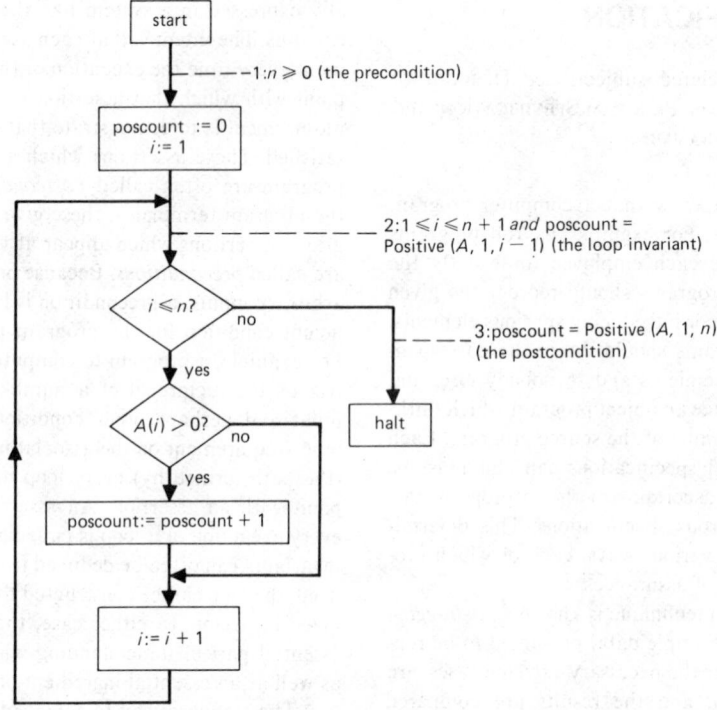

Fig. 1.   Example program, including assertions, as a flowchart.

the range j to k inclusive. A formal recursive definition is

Positive (A, j, k) = **if** j > k **then** 0
                          else if A(k) > 0 **then**
                                  1 + Positive (A, j, k − 1)
                          else Positive (A, j, k − 1)

For convenience, we assume n nonnegative. The postconditions 3 express the aim of the program. A very informal proof of this program might be simply that poscount, initially zero, is incremented for each positive element encountered as A is inspected, element by element, by the **while** loop.

A more rigorous version of this informal proof uses the loop invariant 2 which appears just prior to the test to the **while** statement, thereby satisfying the requirement that each loop have at least one assertion point. There are four paths between assertions in this example: (a) 1 to 2, (b) 2 and $A(i) > 0$ back to 2, (c) 2 and not $A(i) > 0$ back to 2, and (d) 2 to 3. The four propositions to be proved follow:

a. n ≥ 0 **and** poscount = 0 **and** i = 1 ⊃
     1 ≤ i ≤ n + 1 **and**
     poscount = Positive (A, 1, i − 1)

b. 1 ≤ i ≤ n + 1 **and** poscount =
     Positive (A, 1, i − 1) **and** i ≤ n **and**
     A(i) > 0 **and** poscount′ = poscount + 1
     and i′ = i + 1 ⊃ 1 ≤ i′ ≤ n + 1
     and poscount′ = Positive (A, 1, i′ − 1)

The prime (′) has been introduced to denote the "new" value of a variable.

c. As b except poscount′ = poscount
     and not (A(i) > 0).

d. 1 ≤ i ≤ n + 1 **and** poscount =
     Positive (A, 1, i − 1) **and not** (i ≤ n) ⊃
     poscount = Positive (A, 1, n)

Each of these propositions can be easily proved informally using traditional and elementary mathematical reasoning or formally using the techniques of, say, the predicate calculus which provides appropriate axioms and rules of inference for a deductive theory. Both kinds of proofs of a, b, and c use the three cases of Positive, respectively, plus substitution of equals for equals and simple inequality facts. For d, it is necessary to obtain $i = n + 1$ from $i \le n + 1$ **and not** ($i \le n$). With the completion of these four proofs, the example program is verified.

The main distinctions between formal and informal proofs are the required efforts to obtain each kind, the manner of presenting the proofs, and the likelihood of having a convincing proof. Informal proofs are easier to obtain, at least for the non-clerical part, are shorter, and must be read and judged by people. Formal proofs may have to be evaluated by people but may also be constructed and/or checked by computer programs. The large number of formal details may swamp the human reader or human constructor. Thus, we tend to have more faith in machine proofs than in human proofs, but we must always understand and question what axioms, lemmas, and other facts were simply assumed by the mechanical proof. Yet, going all the way back to first principles or giving too many details can easily obscure the essential elements of a proof. It should be noted that the example above is too simple to illustrate these distinctions.

Variations of this basic verification method exist. Details and examples are given by Hantler and King (1976) and Manna (1974). The various methods have been extended so that they also apply to programs containing, for example, subroutines (including recursive ones); data structures such as arrays, records, and pointers; parallelism and nondeterminism; abstract data types (*q.v.*); monitors (*q.v.*); synchronization mechanisms; and communication constructs.

Goals and Contributions of Verification. A

major aim of program verification is to provide techniques for actually verifying programs in order to eliminate the bugs in programs and to know that this has been done in particular instances, thereby significantly decreasing the incidence of unreliable program behavior. The discipline of program verification also provides an important viewpoint that affects program construction, program specification, program decomposition, and language design. How would one actually verify a program being constructed? What are appropriate invariants? What are the specifications (preconditions and postconditions) of an auxiliary procedure? Only the publicly available specifications of a program component may be used in verifying uses of the component; hidden information or hidden assumptions may not be used. If the component is later modified without changing the public specifications, then only the component itself needs to be reverified since the verifications of the uses of the component remain valid. One measure of the modifiability of a program is how much does the proof change in response to program changes. A modular program, when modified, will cause corresponding changes to the proof but not changes otherwise. Verification concerns can also suggest appropriate decompositions of a programming task as well as appropriate abstractions to be used.

Verification concerns have also influenced the design of several new programming languages, for example Euclid (Lampson *et al.*, 1977). In order that Euclid programs be semantically legal, it is necessary that conditions, known as *legality assertions* and made a part of the language, be true at specific points in the program. For example, a pointer must not be the nil-pointer if it is to be dereferenced. Showing that each legality assertion holds falls to the verifier unless the compiler can show it itself. Also influenced was the procedure mechanism of Euclid which was designed to satisfy a particular style of semantic definition. Global variables are allowed, but must be stated explicitly so any changes are directly detectable. Another decision involving procedures was to insist that distinct formal parameters must always have distinct actual parameters in a call; i.e., no *aliases* such as the two array elements $A(i)$ and $A(j)$ with $i = j$, which are both names for the same variable. This restriction removes many subtle effects in procedure calls and makes it somewhat easier to specify procedures. It should be noted that many people consider aliases harmless and a very useful feature.

In the long run, then, other aspects of program verification, besides actual proofs of specific programs, are potentially even more significant by providing tools and reasonably objective tests for developing and judging the success of new programming language designs, new language definition techniques, new programming strategies and methodologies, and new specification techniques. Because verification requires, for example, the definition of a programming language and the specifications of a programming task as integral parts of the verification effort, any inefficiencies, imprecisions, or inelegancies will soon surface. The concepts of verification have already had, and will continue to have, a deep impact on our thinking and understanding about programming and software technology.

Current Capabilities in Practice. While ver-

ification can be carried out by hand, one soon wishes to have computer assistance in this activity, both for reasons of reducing the time and effort involved and for reasons of accuracy and credibility of the results. To these ends, several prototype verification systems have been programmed which have been used to prove some significant examples (see below). Capabilities exist to take Pascal-like or Lisp-like programs with assertions and produce the required propositions; to prove these propositions; to prove properties of definitions (e.g., that Positive is always nonnegative but, more important, properties of axiomatically defined abstract data types); to combine proofs of parts of programs (e.g., procedures or data types) into proofs of programs which use these parts; to design the program and assertions in the first place; and to organize a database of information about the assumptions being made, the progress of the proof, and the dependencies of the parts. Various systems require differing amounts of user interaction; in no case can the user blindly submit a nontrivial program with assertions and appropriate definitions and expect a quick proof with no further interaction. Careful organization and decomposition of the entire task are required, just as these are required in programming itself. Moreover, the theorem provers in use, while quite powerful and well-developed, often require some gentle persuasion as they help the user to discover an acceptable proof. These verification systems, described more fully in the references, have been designed primarily in universities and research laboratories although they are beginning to be used in companies and application centers.

Examples of successful verifications by these systems include programs, generally of modest size, for sorting, pattern matching, searching, numeric and algebraic calculations, list processing, scheduling, communication of messages, algebraic simplification, managing symbol tables, and elementary compilation of simple languages.

In practice, verification is clearly feasible on numerous small examples provided one is willing and able to provide the required specifications and assertions. Experience shows this nontrivial activity to be teachable and learnable, especially with one of the prototype verification systems available for use. The usual bottleneck is getting all the details properly organized and specified. In principle, large programs are verified as an appropriate series of small programs—a large number of small proofs—analogously to the way large programs are constructed. It is not that simple in practice, largely because unexpected interactions among the program parts and among the specification parts produce serious problems of sheer size. Appropriate factoring and organizational techniques, both in the verification and programming areas, must be further developed to solve the problems of scaling up.

There is much more to the theoretical side of program verification. One aspect is the entire area of denotational semantics, a method for formally describing programming languages. An excellent introduction is by Gordon (1979). A thorough overview of other formal systems is given by Constable (1979).

REFERENCES

1972. Dijkstra, E. W. "Notes on Structured Programming," in Dahl, O.-J., Dijkstra, E. W., and Hoare, C. A. R. (Eds.), *Structured Programming*. New York: Academic Press.

1974. Manna, Z. *Mathematical Theory of Computation*. New York: McGraw-Hill, Chapter 3.

1976. Hantler, S. L. and King, J. C. "An Introduction to Proving the Correctness of Programs," *Computing Surveys* 8, No. 3 (September), 331–353.

1977. Lampson, B. W., *et al.* "Report on the Programming Language Euclid," *SIGPLAN Notices* 12, No. 2 (February).

1977. Luckham, D. C. "Program Verification and Verification-Oriented Programming," *Information Processing 77*, Proceedings of IFIP Congress 77, B. Gilchrist (ed.). Amsterdam: North-Holland, 783–793.

1978. Constable, R. L. and O'Donnell, M. J. *A Programming Logic with an Introduction to the PL/CV Verifier*. Cambridge: Winthrop.

1979. Anderson, R. B. *Proving Programs Correct*. New York: Wiley.

1979. Boyer, R. S. and Moore, J. S. *A Computational Logic*, ACM Monograph Series. New York: Academic Press.

1979. Constable, R. L. "A Discussion of Program Verification," in Wegner, P. (Ed.), *Research Directions in Software Technology*. Cambridge: M.I.T. Press, pp. 393–404.

1979. Gordon, M. J. C. *The Denotational Description of Programming Languages: An Introduction*. New York: Springer-Verlag.

RALPH L. LONDON

PROOF OF PROGRAM CORRECTNESS.
See PROGRAM VERIFICATION.

PROPRIETARY PROGRAM. *See* LEGAL PROTECTION OF SOFTWARE.

PROTECTION, MEMORY. *See* MEMORY PROTECTION.

PSW. *See* PROGRAM STATUS WORDS AND STATE VECTORS.

PUBLISHING, COMPUTERS IN

For articles on related subjects *see* JUSTIFICATION; TEXT EDITING SYSTEMS; and WORD PROCESSING.

Although publishing companies, like other businesses, require computers for standard data processing applications, it is principally in the *production* of printed material that computers have transformed the publishing industry from the use of a medieval technology to an electronically based process. These changes have occurred mainly in the 1960s, and to understand their significance it is necessary to appreciate how "copy" was typeset before the use of computers.

At the beginning of the twentieth century, there were three principal methods of typesetting in use: Hand assembly of individual characters, just as Gutenberg had first done in the middle of the fifteenth century, the method used for small quantities or complex designs; linotype, Mergenthaler's 1885 contribution of a keyboard-driven machine which automatically cast lines of type as keyed, used almost universally for newspaper setting in the Western world and for many other purposes where high reproductive quality was not the main criterion; and monotype, a mechanical method of casting individual characters of type at a relatively high speed by a machine commanded by a perforated paper ribbon which had been punched from a keyboard.

These remained the processes in general use until computers began to be used to tackle the problems of assembly command and typesetting arithmetic in the 1950s.

Assembly command is the process of instructing a typesetting machine to assemble the right characters across the right length of line ("measure"). The arithmetical problems are associated with the need to "justify" lines; i.e., produce columns of type which, unlike the product of a typewriter, have straight margins on the right-hand side as well as the left.

It is this typographical convention of justification which has demanded most attention. Typeset characters, again unlike most typewriters, are proportionately spaced: To achieve the best optical arrangement, different characters have different widths, expressed in terms of a "unit width" or an "m" (an em). Broadly, typefaces of fine design have their unit widths expressed as large numbers so that the variations of width are significant and the subsequent readability is high.

To justify a line of type, the parameters given to the program are therefore the unit width of the characters in the line, the amount of space allowed between individual letters ("letter spacing") and the amount of space allowed between words ("word spacing"). If the permitted minima and maxima of these spaces cannot be satisfied with a line of whole words, then hyphenation of the word at the end of the line becomes necessary.

The order of precedence is (1) word spacing, (2) letter spacing, and (3) hyphenation. If the arithmetic of word and letter spacing will not work because a short line ends with a long word, preventing spacing of that line within the minimum and maximum parameters, then that word must be hyphenated or the parameters changed. Most minicomputers controlling typesetting applications have hyphenation software, but this is a controversial subject.

There are two problems with hyphenation: First, different countries, even though using the English language, have different conventions for acceptable hyphenation, and, second, some countries, notably the U.K., have highly complex conventions governed by rules which are not easily expressed in computer logic without very long programs. Possible solutions for these problems are to extend the breadth of the spacing parameters and forbid hyphenation altogether; to arrange that any word to be hyphenated should be displayed on a VDU for an operator decision to be made; and to store an "exception dictionary" containing lists of critical word-breaks which the computer refers to before using its own logic.

Minicomputers providing the control of typesetting machines are now often dedicated machines with magnetic tape or disk storage for the material being typeset, keyboards or OCR readers for the input, editing, and instructions, and a CRT for display. The phototypesetting machine itself may be on-line or off-line, may contain its own logic, or may be simply a "slave" unit performing instructions on the command of the computer.

A typical medium-size typesetting unit on a weekly newspaper may consist of a mini with a 96K memory and the following peripherals: Several keyboards for direct input to the computer or producing punched paper tape for input, a couple of disk drives for storage of the copy, a couple of typesetting machines to process the output which may come from the disk store or from a second punched tape containing the processed information.

The typesetting machine will usually be a phototypesetter with a series of lenses to project film images of the required characters onto photographic paper or film which will then be photographically processed. These are called *second-generation* and *first-generation* machines, working mechanically rather than electronically. The *third-generation* machines now coming into general use digitize a dot matrix plan of type characters, often holding these type "fonts" on disk, and recall them, flash them onto a CRT, and photograph them to produce film or photographic paper output. For a *fourth-generation*, laser-based system, see Fig. 1.

Book production, while generally less demanding than the high-speed, large-format work on newspapers and magazines, poses a set of specific problems which have resulted in a number of useful software packages which can format a book into fully composed pages after keyboarding.

The Datek 7000 system, for example, running automatically, without operator intervention, will compose at a speed of 1,500 characters a second, giving something like 12 pages of "average" sized book text a minute, with running heads and folios automatically inserted, and producing paper or film output ready for litho reproduction. It tackles the problem of footnote inclusion on a book page quite effectively, giving the operator command over page depth of "standard" text and automatically handling the arithmetic necessary to accommodate footnotes or part of footnotes in a different typeface or size on a specified page. It will also change justification parameters in three different orders to eliminate "widow lines," the short lines which sometimes fall at the head of a page of book text and are the *bête noire* of book designers because they create an unsquare page of text.

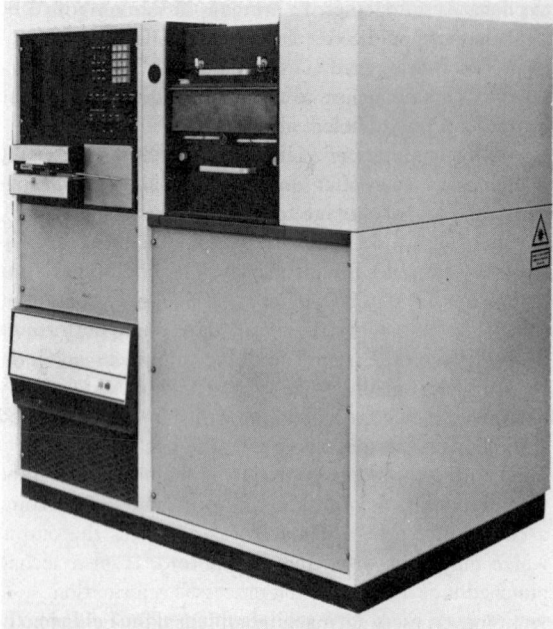

Fig. 1   Monotype Lasercomp phototypesetter.

Advances in computer-controlled composition are moving in two directions—toward smaller, stand-alone units, and toward the use of dedicated mainframes to handle typesetting as part of an overall publishing process.

The use of larger computers also has the advantage that more advanced applications such as the digitizing of graphics for reproduction and the etching of printing plates direct from the stored copy information can also be achieved.

Sophisticated newspaper systems, in particular, can make use of the bigger machines; for example, from one input, setting an advertisement, invoicing the customer, sorting the ad into an alphanumeric sequence and a correct classification, positioning it on the page, engraving the plate, and so on. Meanwhile, other parts of the system could be controlling other parts of the production process, such as the press, and providing information on the day's distribution requirements updated from the previous day's sales, etc.

Effort is now being directed towards routing information in as complete a form as possible direct to the printing press and the next generation of systems may well omit all intermediate stages of output and instruct a press using jets of ink to "write" each page from stored information.

In the future, we may expect computers to be the essential constituents of general *document preparation* systems which will be used in all facets of the publishing industry (see Kernighan, Lesk, and Ossanna, 1978). The software components of such systems will be as follows.

1. An easy to learn and use *text editor* for creating and modifying a manuscript.
2. A *text formatter* for specifying the style of the document.
3. Special-purpose programs for such tasks as footnote processing, picture or figure placement, mathematical expressions, and tabular data.

The result of processing by this software will then drive a phototypesetter.

REFERENCE

1978. Kernighan, B. W., Lesk, M. E., and Ossanna, J. F., Jr. "UNIX Time-Sharing System: Document Preparation," *The Bell System Technical Journal* **58**.

M. BARNARD

PUNCHED CARD. *See* IBM Card; and NINETY-COLUMN CARD.

PURE PROCEDURE. *See* PROCEDURE, PURE.

QUEUEING NETWORK MODELS

For articles on related subjects *see* DEADLOCK; MODELS; MULTIPROGRAMMING; OPERATIONS RESEARCH; QUEUEING THEORY; and SIMULATION.

A queueing network model embodies a set of devices, jobs, and connections. A device is a service center containing a queue for holding waiting jobs and one or more processors for rendering a given type of service. A job travels through the network, visiting one device at a time; when it completes a task (interval of service) at a device, a job moves to another device along one of the interdevice connections. The time for a job to move between devices is negligible. A device is never idle when jobs are in its queue.

Queueing networks can model a wide variety of important aspects of multiprogrammed computer systems. These include multiple-task jobs, different job classes, queueing for resources, concurrency among devices, bottlenecks, and saturation. Despite their simplicity, these models are remarkably accurate. For typical systems, these models estimate throughput and utilization to within 5% of the true values, and mean queue lengths and mean response times to within 25% of the true values.

The first successful application of a network was Scherr's machine repairman model for M.I.T.'s time-sharing system, CTSS (1967). In 1971, Buzen introduced the central server network, a model applicable to many typical configurations; he applied theory dating back to 1957 to develop efficient algorithms for calculating performance quantities in these models. Since that time, numerous validations have shown that these models work well in practice. (See Denning and Buzen, 1978, for a survey.)

Fig. 1 illustrates a model of a time-sharing system. Device 1 represents all the active terminals on the system and device 2 represents the central computing facility. A thinking period corresponds to an interval when a user's job is present at device 1, and a waiting period corresponds to an interval when the job is present at device 2. This simple network was used by Scherr for CTSS (1967).

Fig. 2 depicts the *central server* network model. The boxes represent the devices and their queues. Device 1 is the CPU and devices $2, \ldots, K$ are I/O stations. A job enters the system at the IN port and begins with a CPU service interval (burst); it continues with zero or more I/O intervals which alternate with further CPU bursts; finally, it exits from the OUT port. The time required for a job to travel from the IN port to the OUT port is called the *response time*.

Each device i has two basic parameters. The *visit ratio*, V_i, denotes the mean number of times a job requires service at device i. It can be a fraction; for example, $V_i = 0.5$ indicates that every other job requires service at device i. The *mean service time, S_i,* denotes the mean time between completions when device i is busy. If S_i depends on the device's queue length, the device is *load-dependent;* otherwise, the device is *load-independent*.

A queueing network can be open or closed. If open, the number of jobs in the network, N, varies. If closed, N is fixed. A closed network can model a system that includes the source of jobs—e.g., the users logged in at their terminals in Fig. 1. A closed network can also model a subsystem operating under a backlog—the moment one

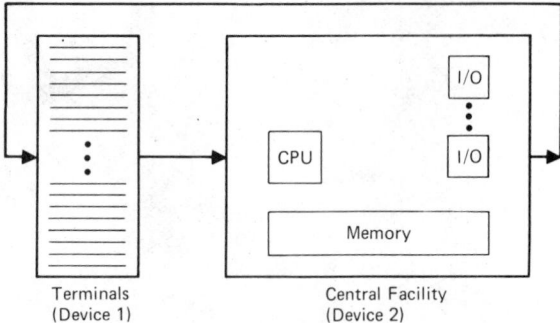

Terminals
(Device 1)

Central Facility
(Device 2)

Fig. 1

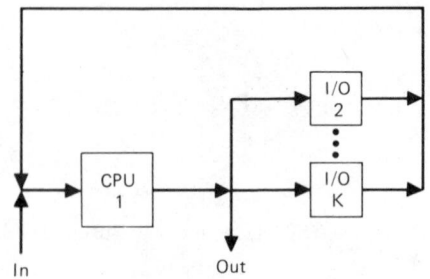

In   Out

Fig. 2

job leaves the subsystem, another is immediately injected to replace it.

Network models can be used for a simple *bottleneck analysis* if the parameters V_i and S_i are independent of the total number of jobs, N, in the system. As N increases, the device b for which the total service demand $V_b S_b$ is largest saturates and limits system throughput to, at most, $1/V_b S_b$ jobs per second. In this case, the system's mean response time is approximately $N V_b S_b$ seconds. (See Denning and Buzen, 1978.)

Network models are used to calculate the following *standard performance metrics*.

U_i = utilization of device i (fraction of time the device is busy).

X_i = throughput at device i (jobs per second being completed).

X_O = throughput of the system (jobs per second at the OUT port).

Q_i = mean queue length at device i.

R_i = mean response time per visit to device i.

R_0 = mean response time of the system for one job

These quantities are easily derived from the basic parameters (V_i and S_i) under two basic assumptions:

1. *Flow balance*—the number of arrivals equals the number of departures at every device of the system.

2. *Homogeneity*—the job flow from a source device to a destination device depends on the queue length at the source, not on any other queue length.

These assumptions lead to simple calculations of the standard performance metrics from the basic parameters. Because the cost of these calculations is small, and because the results allow useful conclusions to be drawn about real systems, the errors introduced by these assumptions are acceptable.

Solution of a Model. The *state* of a model is a list $\mathbf{n} = (n_1, \ldots, n_K)$ specifying the number of jobs present at each of the K devices. In a closed network, $n_1 + \ldots + n_K = N$, the fixed load on the network. The quantity $p(\mathbf{n})$ denotes the proportion of time state $\mathbf{n}$ is observed. It can be shown that, under the two assumptions noted above, the quantity $p(\mathbf{n})$ has the so-called *product form*

$$p(\mathbf{n}) = F_1(n_1) \ldots F_K(n_K)/G$$

where $F_i(n_i)$ is a "device factor" that depends only on the queue length n_i and the basic parameters (V_i and S_i) at device i, and G is a normalizing constant chosen so that the sum of $p(\mathbf{n})$ for all $\mathbf{n}$ equals 1. Although the number of possible states is large, the standard performance metrics of any device can be calculated from the product form in time proportional to NK. (See Bruell and Balbo, 1980.)

An example of the computational algorithm derived from the product-form solution is given below.

$$R_i(N) = S_i(1 + Q_i(N-1)) \qquad \text{(all devices } i\text{)}$$
$$X_0(N) = N/(V_1 R_1(N) + \cdots + V_K R_K(N))$$
$$Q_i(N) = X_0(N) V_i R_i(N) \qquad \text{(all devices } i\text{)}$$

These equations are evaluated sequentially for each N and iteratively for $N = 1, 2, \ldots$ until the desired network load is reached. The initial condition is $Q_i(0) = 0$. For each value of N, the first equation calculates the mean response time per visit to each device in terms of the mean service time per visit and the mean queue length of the network with one less job in it. The second equation calculates the system throughput as the system load divided by the mean response time. The third equation calculates the queue length from the system throughput, the visit ratio, and the mean response time per visit. (See Buzen and Denning, 1980.) A complete discussion of these algorithms, and their limitations, is given by Bruell and Balbo (1980).

The basic computational algorithms for queueing networks have been extended and refined in many ways.

One of the most important is for *multiple job classes:* Different classes of jobs can be identified, and separate values of the basic parameters measured for each. The product form solution tends to be inaccurate when some job classes have priority over others, and when jobs have service time distributions of high variance at devices with first-in first-out (FIFO) queueing disciplines. Even for these cases, good approximations have been developed to refine iteratively a product form network until the error is minimum.

Queueing network algorithms are available in several commercial, proprietary software packages.

REFERENCES

1967. Scherr, A. L. *An Analysis of Time Shared Computer Systems.* Cambridge: M.I.T. Press.
1978. Denning, P. J. and Buzen, J. P. "The Operational Analysis of Queueing Network Models," *Computing Surveys* **10**, No. 3: 225–261 (September).
1980. Bruell, S. C. and Balbo, G. *Computation Algorithms for Closed Queueing Networks.* New York: Elsevier/North-Holland.
1980. Buzen, J. P. and Denning, P. J. "Measuring and Calculating Queue Length Distributions," *Computer* (April).

P. J. DENNING

QUEUEING THEORY

For articles on related subjects *see* COMMUNICATION AND COMPUTERS; OPERATIONS RESEARCH; QUEUEING NETWORK MODELS; SIMULATION; STATISTICAL APPLICATIONS; and STOCHASTIC PROCESS.

Queues are nothing more than the waiting lines that have become an accepted and often frustrating fact of modern life. Whenever demands occur in production, transportation, communication, computers, or other kinds of service systems, waiting lines are built up, resulting in a blocking of resources and in losses of time, money, patience, and good will. Efforts to control congestion are thus of vital importance, and have led to a rapid growth of research activity in "queueing theory," which is the study of waiting-line processes through the use of mathematical and/or simulation models.

Queueing Models. The basic queueing context (see Fig. 1) can be described as follows: Units from some source arrive at a service facility, wait if necessary in a queue or system of queues, receive service at a time (or times) determined by some service policy or discipline, and depart after service completion. Thus, the study of a queueing process requires the specification of each of the following elements (numbers refer to those in Fig. 1).

1. *Source.* The source, finite or infinite, is a population or a group of populations from which the units demanding service emanate. These units may be people; paperwork, such as orders, invoices, letters, or computer programs; malfunctioning machines; or electronic signals in telecommunications systems.

2. *Arrival Process.* The statistical pattern by which units arrive at the service facility is called the "arrival-time distribution." In many mathematical models, the time between successive arrivals is assumed to have the negative exponential distribution. This arrival process is also called "random arrivals" or "Poisson arrivals" since, under this assumption, the number of arrivals in a fixed period of time has the Poisson distribution.

3. *Queue Structure.* The waiting line of a system may consist of a queue or a system of queues. Each queue may be constrained to a finite maximum length or be permitted to be unlimited in length. The waiting line may be conceptual rather than physical, as in the case of remote terminals waiting to be polled by a computer.

4. *Service Discipline.* The rules by which units are selected from the queue structure and serviced constitute the service discipline. Service may be first-come, first-served (or FIFO, first-in, first-out), random, or according to some priority procedure. In the latter case, the priorities may be externally or internally determined, and service may be on a preemptive basis in which service on a "low" priority unit is interrupted (i.e., it rejoins the queue structure) whenever a "high" priority unit demands service. Whatever service discipline is to be used must be specified.

5. *Service Facility.* The service facility may consist of one or more service channels in parallel; each channel may have one or more servers in series. A queueing model must specify the arrangement of the service facilities. Note that each "server" need not be a person but may be a machine (e.g., a computer). Not all servers need be alike.

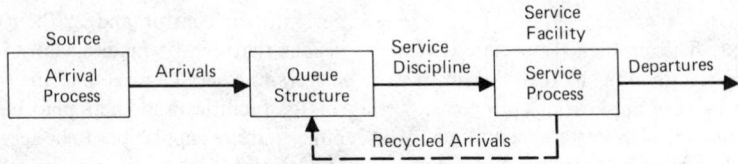

Fig. 1

6. *Service Process*. The time required to service completely a unit at any server is referred to as that server's "service (or holding) time." A queueing model must specify the probability distribution of service times for each server (possibly for each type of unit entering the system). The service processes commonly used in mathematical models are the negative exponential and the constant service time distributions.

As an example of queueing in the computer area, consider a time-sharing system. The goal here is to provide preferential treatment (rapid response) to those jobs making small computational demands at the expense of jobs which make large demands on the CPU. Without prior information on how large a demand each arriving job makes, the feedback queueing system described essentially "tests" jobs, discovers which ones are short, and provides these with faster service. In time-sharing systems, then, the arriving units are jobs requiring computation and the server is the CPU. There is a system of queues which hold jobs awaiting service and the service discipline is determined by a scheduling algorithm which decides which job will be serviced next and for how long. The amount of service time awarded is known as a *quantum* and may vary. If the job being serviced is completed during this quantum, the job departs from the system. If the job is not completed, the job reenters the system of queues and awaits more service.

Simple examples of time-sharing queue structures and scheduling algorithms include the following.

Round-Robin. Newly arriving jobs join the single queue which is first-come-first-serve. All quanta are the same size. Jobs requiring more than one quantum of service return to the end of the same queue and repeat the cycle. In the round-robin system, the response time varies directly with the computational demand made.

Foreground-Background. In its simplest form, the queue structure consists of two queues. A newly arriving job joins the first queue (the foreground queue) and waits in a first-come-first-serve manner for its first quantum. If the job completes, it departs the system. If not, the job joins the tail of the second queue (the background queue which is also first-come-first-serve) and waits to be awarded another quantum. The second queue is serviced only at those times when the foreground queue is empty. This two-queue model is easily extended to a system having many background queues. The quanta given to a job usually get larger as a job works its way through these systems.

Problem Areas.

The problems associated with queueing theory may be classified as (1) analytical or theoretical, and (2) operational or applications problems.

Analytical Problems. Under certain conditions, a queueing system that has been in operation for a sufficiently long time settles down to a behavior independent of time and the initial state of the system. The system is then said to be in an equilibrium (or steady-state) condition. Because the steady-state condition is less difficult to study analytically than the initial transient condition, the majority of analytical queueing results concern steady-state behavior.

A great deal of insight into the steady-state behavior of queues can be gained through the analytical results for the simplest models; consequently, a few single-source models are summarized in Table 1, which uses the following notation:

p_n = probability that the number of units in the queueing system (line length) is n.

p_0 = probability that the system is idle.

L = average line length.

Q = average queue length, where queue length is the line length minus the number of units being serviced.

W = average waiting time in the system (includes service time).

W_q = average waiting time in the queue (excludes service time).

λ_n = mean arrival rate (expected number of arrivals per unit time) of units when the line length is n.

μ_n = mean service rate (expected number of units being serviced per unit time) when the line length is n.

The first line of Table 1 gives the general results for some models in which it is assumed that the rates at which units arrive and are serviced depend only on the current line length (often called "birth-death" process). Subsequent lines of Table 1 give results for a number of special cases.

As the table indicates, most queueing-system results depend upon the specific assumptions made; however, the following results hold under quite general conditions. Assume that $\lambda_n = \lambda$ for all n. Then $L = \lambda W$ and $Q = \lambda W_q$ (Little's result). Further, if $\mu_n = \mu$ for all n, then $W = W_q + 1/\mu$. These relationships enable us to determine all four quantities (L, Q, W, and W_q), if any one of them can be found analytically. Also, $\rho = \lambda/\mu$ is the utilization factor for the service facility; i.e., the expected fraction of time the server is busy.

Operational Problems. The study of real queueing systems is motivated by the objectives of improving their design, their control, and/or their effectiveness. The decisions that can be made usually involve the number of servers, the service rate(s) of the servers, the number of service facilities and their placement, the service discipline, and the populations to be served. All these decisions involve the general question of the appropriate level of service to provide and the appropriate trade-off to make

Table 1.   Some Sample Steady-State Queueing Results

Model Description	p_n	p_0	L	Q
1. Birth-death process Arrival rate $= \lambda_n$ Service rate $= \mu_n$	$\left(\dfrac{\prod_{i=0}^{n-1}\lambda_i}{\prod_{i=1}^{n}\mu_i}\right)p_0 = R_n p_0$	$\dfrac{1}{1 + \sum_{n=1}^{\infty} R_n}$	$\sum_{n=0}^{\infty} n p_n$	$\sum_{n=c}^{\infty} (n-c)p_n$
2. Poisson arrivals, exponential service times. Arrival rate $\lambda_n = \lambda$ for all n. Service rate $\mu_n = \mu$ for all $n > 0$.	$\left(\dfrac{\lambda}{\mu}\right)^n p_0 = \rho^n p_0$	$1 - \rho$	$\dfrac{\lambda}{\mu - \lambda}$	$\dfrac{\lambda^2}{\mu(\mu - \lambda)}$
3. Poisson arrivals, arbitrary service times Arrival rate $\lambda_n = \lambda$. Service time has mean $1/\mu$ and variance σ^2		$1 - \rho$	$\rho + Q$	$\dfrac{\rho^2 + \lambda^2\sigma^2}{2(1-\rho)}$
4. Poisson arrivals, constant service time. Arrival rate $\lambda_n = \lambda$ for all n. Service time $=$ constant $= 1/\mu$.		$1 - \rho$	$\rho + Q$	$\dfrac{\rho^2}{2(1-\rho)}$
5. Poisson arrivals, exponential service time, finite maximum queue length M. Arrival rate $\lambda_n = \lambda$ for $n \le M$. Service rate $\mu_n = \mu$ for $n > 0$.	$\rho^n p_0$	$\dfrac{1-\rho}{1-\rho^{M+1}}$	$\dfrac{\rho}{1-\rho} - \dfrac{(M+1)\rho^{M+1}}{1-\rho^{M+1}}$	$L - (1 - p_0)$
6. Finite source population (size N) exponential service $\lambda_n = \begin{cases} (N-n)\lambda & \text{if } n = 0,1,\dots,N \\ 0 & \text{if } n \ge N \end{cases}$ $\mu_n = \mu$ for all $n > 0$	$\dfrac{N!}{(N-n)!}\rho^n p_0 = C_n\rho^n p_0$	$\dfrac{1}{1 + \sum_{n=0}^{N} C_n\rho^n}$	$N = \dfrac{\mu}{\lambda}(1 - p_0)$	$N - \dfrac{\lambda + \mu}{\lambda}(1 - p_0)$

between the costs incurred by providing the service and the costs incurred by waiting for service.

In attempting to use theoretical models for practical applications, a number of statistical problems arise, including verification of the basic assumptions of the model in order to avoid misusing mathematically derived results. In applications where the system is the least bit complex or the transient behavior of the system is of interest, many of the results of interest have not yet yielded to exact analysis. As can be seen from Table 1, even those results which can be obtained may be difficult to apply in practical situations. A relatively new branch of queueing theory deals with methods of finding simpler approximate or bounding results for queues. Computer simulation also may be used to obtain approximate results. Several higher-level computer programming languages such as GPSS (General Purpose Systems Simulator) and Simscript have been designed with the simulation of queueing processes in mind.

The earliest works in queueing (the classical studies by Erlang, a Danish mathematician) were concerned with highly practical problems in telephony. For many years, however, the problems studied were largely those amenable to mathematical analysis and queueing theory, as a tool for the analysis of practical problems, remained in a primitive state. More recently, the study of computer systems as queueing networks has led to many new results and applications. Queueing theory has been used to determine the effects of various quantum sizes and priority assignments on response time in time-sharing systems and to predict and evaluate the performance of different computer systems. Thus, after many years in the hands of the theoreticians, queueing theory is proving to be an important application tool in the design of complex information processing systems.

REFERENCES

1975, 1976. Kleinrock, Leonard. *Queueing Systems,* Vols. **I** and **II**. New York: Wiley-Interscience.

1978. *Computing Surveys* **10**, *No. 3.* (Issue devoted to "Queueing Network Models of Computer Systems Performance.")

1978. Gordon, Geoffrey. *System Simulation,* 2nd Ed. Englewood Cliffs, NJ: Prentice-Hall.

1978. Chandy, M. K. and Reiser, M. (Eds.). *Computer Performance: IFIP Working Group 7.3 on Computer System Modeling.* New York: North-Holland, Elsevier.

J. M. McKINNEY

R

RAMAC

For articles on related subjects *see* COMPUTER INDUSTRY: United States; and DIGITAL COMPUTERS: Early.

The IBM 305 RAMAC (random access method of accounting and control) was among the first (in the late 1950s)—if not the first—data processing systems to employ a magnetic disk file permitting direct random accessing of data records. It was essentially a unit record system enhanced by a stored program capability and the direct access capability provided by its disk file.

The basic 305 consisted of a processing unit, a disk file, an operator console, a printer, card reader, and card punch. The processing unit permitted the storage of only a hundred instructions, which were loaded to and serially accessed from a magnetic drum. The drum provided four 100-character areas for working storage. The instruction set was, by today's standards, extraordinarily limited. The set provided for data transfer, decimal arithmetic, disk I/O operations, and switch setting. All I/O operations, including formatting, print editing, and all branching operations, were accomplished by wired plugboards located in the I/O and processing units. The execution of each job required that a stored program be loaded and the appropriate control panels be mounted in each unit. Programming was done in machine language only. Program overlays from disk to drum were commonly used.

The disk file consisted of 50 magnetic disks with 100 recording tracks on each surface. Each track stored 10 to 100 character records. The total disk capacity of a 305 could be expanded to 20 million characters, and a single file could be shared by two systems. The access mechanism consisted of one or two arms, which moved vertically past the disks and laterally between them. Records were directly addressed by a sequential record address. The cylinder concept of file management was programmatically implemented by users, but the hardware did nothing to facilitate the concept. Access time was less than 1 sec.

The printer was a very slow serial-stick printer but could be replaced with a 407 unit record accounting machine operating at a maximum speed of 150 lpm. Multiple printers could be attached to a single 305.

The 305 was employed for most common in-line ap-

Fig. 1. The IBM 305 RAMAC.

plications such as inventory control and distribution accounting. The first management operating system, integrating many business applications, was developed by IBM and implemented on the 305 as a user package. Experience gained with this system led to the development of file management techniques, such as address randomization and chained file structures, which were employed on subsequently developed disk systems. The 305 was quickly made obsolete by the introduction of the IBM 1400 series and similar second-generation computers.

G. D. BAER

RANDOM ACCESS. *See* DIRECT ACCESS.

RANDOM NUMBER GENERATION

For articles on related subjects *see* MONTE CARLO METHOD; SIMULATION; and STOCHASTIC PROCESS.

A *random-number generator* is a computer procedure which scrambles the digits of an integer to produce a new integer. Here, "scramble" means to mix and combine by means of simple computer operations. The idea is to produce a sequence of integers which, in spite of being produced by a fixed procedure, will serve as random variables in computer simulations such as Monte Carlo, which is used to describe any simulation problem that uses random numbers. For reasons of speed, simplicity, and repeatability, virtually all Monte Carlo programs in computers use a set of random numbers that is produced by a fixed procedure, chosen in such a way that the results pass extensive tests for randomness. The following examples (using decimal digits, although most generators scramble binary digits) are representative.

1. *Mid-Square Generator.* Given an 8-digit decimal integer, square to get 16 digits; keep the middle 8 digits:

   current I = 45086273,
   I^2 = 2032772013030529,
   new I = 77201303.

2. *Congruential Generator.* Given an 8 digit integer, multiply by a constant, say, 7654321; then keep the last 8 digits:

   current I = 45086273,
   $I \times 7654321$ = 345104806235633,
   new I = 06235633.

3. *Shift-Register Generator.* Given an 8-digit integer, shift right 3, do no-carry add, shift left 4, then another no-carry add:

   current I = 45086273

00045086	shift right 3
45021259	no-carry add
12590000	shift left 4

   new I = 57511259   no-carry add

Each of these examples produces a sequence of integers that seem to jump around haphazardly within the allowable range (word size) of the computer. No doubt the reader could make up a few procedures that would appear to do as well. There are two basic problems: (1) to make sure that the generator does not begin to repeat itself too soon, and (2) somehow to test the output for randomness.

Problem 1 is usually resolved, sometimes after some difficult mathematics. If there is no satisfactory solution, as in the case of the mid-square generator, the method is abandoned. Problem 2, or the suitability of a generator for Monte Carlo use, can never be completely resolved. All we can do is try the generator for more and more problems for which we know an exact or approximate answer, or, as in the case of congruential generators, use some theoretical arguments to suggest Monte Carlo problems for which results will not be satisfactory.

The examples above are from the three types of random-number generators that have dominated both practical use and theoretical discussion in the literature. The *mid-square* generator is now considered obsolete. Used in early computers, it produced important results in Monte Carlo studies of neutron diffusion, particularly in the development of atomic bombs, reactors, and shielding. *Congruential* generators, by far the most commonly used method for the past thirty years, have been the subject of scores of papers. Recent discoveries have shown, however, that congruential generators are not so satisfactory as they were thought to be. *Shift-register* generators, used for many years in communication theory, coding theory, and cryptography, have been recently heralded as the best alternative to congruential generators. However, shift-register generators have regularities that appear to be more serious, though not so easy to establish, as those of the congruential generators. Regularities in congruential and shift-register generators are illustrated in Fig. 1 and discussed below.

Congruential Generators. These are more properly called "linear" congruential generators because they produce a sequence of residues of a large modulus

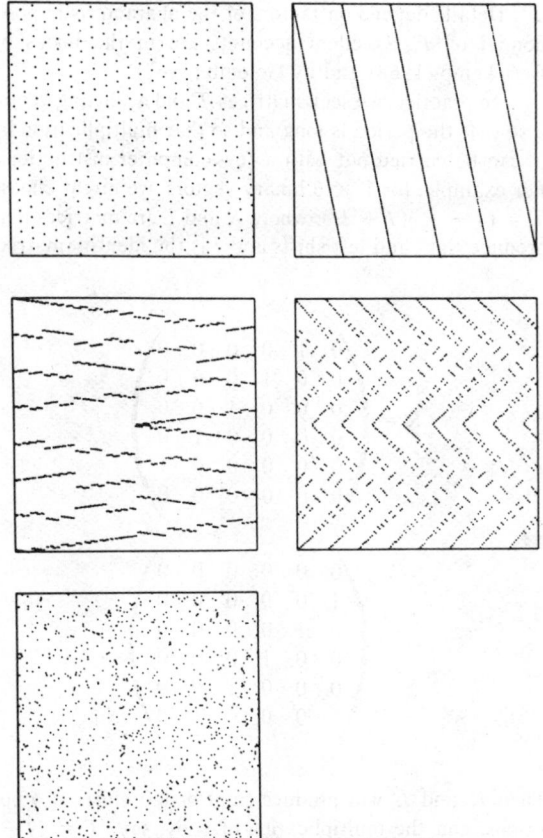

Fig. 1. Regularities in congruential and shift register generators with pairs of random numbers shown as points in the plane. Top: Patterns produced by two congruential generators. Middle: Two shift registers. Bottom: A satisfactory pattern produced by combining two generators (algorithm M). Regularities are a consequence of the linear nature of the generators and cannot be removed by choice of parameters.

m (usually the word size of the computer) by means of a linear transformation:

$$x_0, x_1, x_2, x_3, \ldots$$
$$x_{i+1} \equiv ax_i + b \bmod m, \quad 0 < x_i < m. \quad (1)$$

The preceding example of a congruential generator had $a = 7654321$, $b = 0$, and $m = 10^8$.

Scores of papers have been written on congruential generators, establishing their periods for various choices of x_0, a, b, and m, and reporting—usually favorably—on statistical tests for randomness. Much of the discussion has centered on the choice of b in the relation $x_{i+1} \equiv ax_i$

$+ b \bmod m$, and in particular on whether *multiplicative* generators ($b = 0$) were better or worse than *mixed* generators ($b \neq 0$). Essentially, there is no difference. The congruential sequence (1) may be expressed, modulo m, in the form

$$x_0, \ x_0 + v, \ \ x_0 + v(a + 1), \ \ x_0 + v(a^2 + a + 1),$$
$$x_0 + v(a^3 + a^2 + a + 1), \ldots$$

where $v \equiv x_1 - x_0 \bmod m$; thus, every congruential sequence, whether mixed or multiplicative, is a linear transformation of a sequence of the form

$$0, \quad 1, \quad a + 1, \quad a^2 + a + 1, \qquad (2)$$
$$a^3 + a^2 + a + 1, \ldots \bmod m.$$

Thus, the choice of x_0 and b are important only in that a poor choice may shorten the period. But as long as $v = x_0(a - 1) + b = x_1 - x_0$ has no factors in common with the modulus m, then the period and the "randomness" of sequences (1) and (2) are the same.

Marsaglia (1972) gives a complete development of the theory of linear congruential sequences. The particular case $m = 2^\beta$, the one most commonly encountered with modern computers, is summarized here.

Congruential Generators for Modulus 2^β.

To find the period of the sequence:

$$x_0, x_1, x_2, x_3, \ldots \quad x_{i+1} \equiv ax_i + b \bmod 2^\beta, \quad (3)$$

write $a = 1 + k \cdot 2^\alpha$ or $a = -1 + k \cdot 2^\alpha$ according to whether $a \equiv 1 \bmod 4$ or $a \equiv -1 \bmod 4$, with k odd and $2 < \alpha < \beta$. (The case $\alpha = \beta$ is of no interest.) When b is odd, sequence (3) has period 2^β for $a = 1 + k \cdot 2^\alpha$, and period $2^{\beta - \alpha + 1}$ for $a = -1 + k \cdot 2^\alpha$. However, in either case, sequence (3) has *effective period* $2^{\beta - \alpha}$ in that it is made up of a block $\{B\}$ of $2^{\beta - \alpha}$ residues, followed by translations of that block:

$$\{B\}, \ \ \{B + c\}, \ \ \{B + 2c\}, \ \ \{B + 3c\}, \ldots \bmod 2^\beta.$$

When $b = 0$, the sequence becomes

$$x_0, \quad ax_0, \quad a^2 x_0, \quad a^3 x_0, \ldots \bmod 2^\beta,$$

and the period is $2^{\beta - \alpha}$ in either case, provided x_0 is odd. If x_0 is multiplied by a power of 2, the period is divided by that power of 2.

Example: $a = 2^7 + 1$, $b = 1$, $m = 2^{35}$. The generator

$$x_{i+1} = (2^7 + 1)x_i + 1 \bmod 2^{35}$$

was suggested in 1960 because one can quickly multiply by $2^7 + 1$ with a shift and an add. Since $a = 1 + 2^7$, the period is 2^{35}, but the effective period is 2^{38}; the full sequence is made up of 128 translations of a block of 2^{38} residues.

Regularities in Congruential Generators. For most uses, the integers produced by a random-number generator are divided by the modulus (usually 2^k for k-bit computers) to get random numbers between zero and one. If we use n-tuples of these numbers to represent points in the unit cube in n-space, we find that the points, rather than appearing to be randomly spread throughout the n-cube, may form patterns that suggest the random-number generator will give poor results for certain types of Monte Carlo problems. Both congruential and shift-register generators show regularities of this type, illustrated for 2-space in Fig. 1.

In the case of congruential generators, the pattern is very regular; points in n-space fall on a lattice with relatively large spacing compared to the lattice of points with integer coordinates that is the theoretical limit of resolution of a computer with a fixed word size. The particular shape of the lattice associated with a congruential generator depends on the multiplier used in the generator.

If we characterize a lattice in n-dimensions by the smallest number of hyperplanes that contain all points produced by the generator, we find that all points, for a congruential generator with modulus m, must lie in fewer than $(n!m)^{1/n}$ parallel hyperplanes. For example, in a binary computer with 32-bit words, $m = 2^{32}$, and no matter what the multiplier or starting value of the congruential sequence, fewer than 2,953 hyperplanes will contain all 3-tuples, fewer than 566 hyperplanes will contain all 4-tuples, and fewer than 41 hyperplanes will contain all 10-tuples.

In Fig. 1 the lattices are for modulus 2^{10}, so that $(n!m)^{1/n} = (2 \times 2^{10})^{1/2} \cong 45$. In fact, all points are contained in 21 lines for the first lattice and 5 lines for the second.

Shift-Register Generators. The theory can be described by means of a linear transformation over a binary vector space. We start with a vector of zeros and ones; say, $\beta = (1, 0, 1, 1, 0, 1)$. Then, if T is a 6×6 matrix with elements in the field with two elements (0 and 1, with arithmetic modulo 2), we form a sequence of vectors by repeated multiplication by the matrix T:

$$\beta, \beta T, \beta T^2, \beta T^3, \ldots.$$

If T is nonsingular, this sequence will repeat with the smallest integer k, such that $\beta = \beta T^k$; i.e., β is a characteristic vector belonging to the characteristic root 1 of

T^k. Details depend on factors of the characteristic polynomial of T. Excellent accounts are in the books by Berlekamp (1968) and by Golomb (1967).

In practice, we seek matrices T and a starting vector β so that the period is long and so that multiplication by T can be carried out with a few computer instructions. For example, for 1×6 binary vectors, we might choose $T = (I + R^2)(I + L^3)$, where R and L are matrices that produce right and left shifts and I is the identity matrix:

$$R = \begin{pmatrix} 0 & 1 & 0 & 0 & 0 & 0 \\ 0 & 0 & 1 & 0 & 0 & 0 \\ 0 & 0 & 0 & 1 & 0 & 0 \\ 0 & 0 & 0 & 0 & 1 & 0 \\ 0 & 0 & 0 & 0 & 0 & 1 \\ 0 & 0 & 0 & 0 & 0 & 0 \end{pmatrix}$$

$$L = \begin{pmatrix} 0 & 0 & 0 & 0 & 0 & 0 \\ 1 & 0 & 0 & 0 & 0 & 0 \\ 0 & 1 & 0 & 0 & 0 & 0 \\ 0 & 0 & 1 & 0 & 0 & 0 \\ 0 & 0 & 0 & 1 & 0 & 0 \\ 0 & 0 & 0 & 0 & 1 & 0 \end{pmatrix}$$

Then R^s and L^s will produce right or left shifts of s positions, and the multiplication of β by, say, $T = (I + R^2)(I + L^3)$ can be carried out by shifting and adding (exclusive "or") as follows:

$$(1\ 0\ 1\ 1\ 0\ 1) = \beta$$
$$(0\ 0\ 1\ 0\ 1\ 1) = \beta R^2$$
$$(1\ 0\ 0\ 1\ 1\ 0) = \beta(I + R^2)$$
$$(1\ 1\ 0\ 0\ 0\ 0) = \beta(I + R^2)L^3$$
$$(0\ 1\ 0\ 1\ 1\ 0) = \beta(I + R^2)(I + L^3).$$

Many of the shift-register generators for large computers are of this type. For 1×31 binary vectors, any of these three choices of T,

$$T = (I + R^3)(I + L^{28}),$$
$$T = (I + R^6)(I + L^{25}),$$
$$T = (I + R^{13})(I + L^{18}),$$

(or their transposes) will generate all possible nonnull vectors; i.e., the period is $2^{31} - 1$ and any nonnull starting vector may be used.

For 1×32 binary vectors (the full word for IBM 360/370 machines), there is no matrix of the above form that has full period; however, $T = (I + R^{15})(I + L^{17})$ or its transpose has period 99.95% of the possible maximum of $2^{32} - 1$.

A *simple* shift-register generator is one for which the matrix T is a particularly simple matrix, called a "companion matrix," of the form (say, for $n = 6$).

$$C = \begin{pmatrix} 0 & 1 & 0 & 0 & 0 & 0 \\ 0 & 0 & 1 & 0 & 0 & 0 \\ 0 & 0 & 0 & 1 & 0 & 0 \\ 0 & 0 & 0 & 0 & 1 & 0 \\ 0 & 0 & 0 & 0 & 0 & 1 \\ c_0 & c_1 & c_2 & c_3 & c_4 & c_5 \end{pmatrix}$$

If R is the right-shift-one matrix and γ is the constant binary vector $(c_0, c_1, \ldots, c_5)$, then βC is either βR or $\beta R + \gamma$, depending on whether the last element of the vector β is 0 or 1. Simple shift-register sequences are very easy to generate in a computer, but they are obviously unsuitable for general Monte Carlo use, since half of the time a new point will be produced by shifting coordinates of the previous point one position. Thus, half of the points (x, y) will be on the line $2y = x$. This is a flaw common to all shift-register generators: If β, βT, βT^2, ... is any shift-register sequence, there is a nonsingular matrix Q such that half of the points produced by successive pairs of elements in the sequence βQ, βTQ, $\beta T^2 Q$, ... will lie on the line $2y = x$.

Regularities in Shift-Register Generators. Since the theory of shift-register generators is similar to that of congruential generators, in the sense that we have a linear transformation on binary vectors rather than on the residues of some modulus m, we should expect to find some sort of linear patterns in the output. We do, except that when the binary vectors are viewed as the representation of an integer to the base 2, the linear patterns get folded over and distorted, much as the original linear sedimentary patterns in the earth are distorted and folded over to produce the patterns we observe millions of years later. Two examples of this type of regularity are in Fig. 1.

Regularity in shift-register generators is not so easy to characterize as that of congruential generators, but it is there all the same, and should be taken into account in considering the kind of Monte Carlo problems for which the generator is used.

The examples in Fig. 1 are for a 12-bit word, to illustrate the situation. Ordinarily, for 32-bit words or larger, regularities in 2-space are not evident for congruential generators, and only in higher dimensions do they become a problem. However, shift-register regularities may cause trouble in the plane, even with a large computer such as the IBM 360/370. For example, Fig. 2 shows the results of the "parking lot" test applied to a shift-register generator and to a good generator. In this test, "cars" are parked in a large car park until each of its 16 sections with capacity of 1,000 cars is filled. The left picture is a bird's-eye view of the lot filled by a good random-number generator, and the right picture shows the result of filling the lot with the very shift-register generator (31 bits, right shift 3, left shift 28) that was pro-

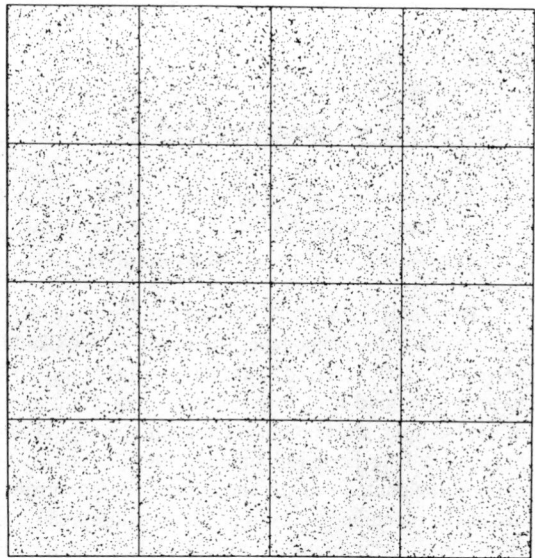
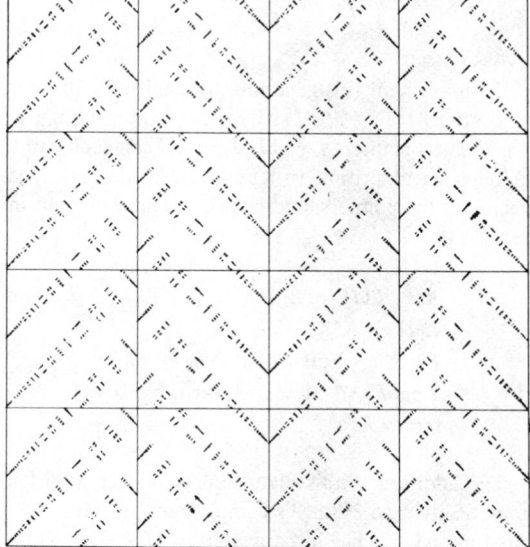

Fig. 2. The parking-lot test where each sector has a capacity of 1,000 cars (random points). Left: Bird's-eye view of a lot filled with a good generator (algorithm M). Right: The lot filled with the 31-bit shift-register generator discussed in text.

posed as the successor to congruential generators for the IBM 360/370, after regularities in congruential generators were discovered.

Combining Generators. Congruential and shift-register generators have regularities that make them individually unsuitable for precision Monte Carlo use, but combining the generators in various ways appears to produce satisfactory sequences. For example, in a 32-bit machine, the congruential sequence $x_{i+1} \equiv 69069x_i$ mod 2^{32} and the shift register sequence $\beta \rightarrow \beta(I + R^{15})(I + L^{17})$ may be combined by adding (either by an *arithmetic* or an *exclusive "or"* addition). The result appears to be a quite random sequence with period about 5×10^{18}.

Another method, known as algorithm M, combines two sequences of uniform variates $U_1, U_2, U_3, \ldots$ and $V_1, V_2, V_3, \ldots$, with magnitude between 0 and 1, produced by two simple methods (e.g., a congruential and a shift-register generator). Suppose, say, that memory locations $C(1), C(2), \ldots, C(100)$ are filled with U. Then one generates a new V, uses it to get an index J from 1 to 100 by taking the greatest integer in $1 + 100*V$, uses $C(J)$ as the next random number, and then fills location $C(J)$ with a newly generated U.

A recently developed generator that passes even the most stringent statistical tests is based on an extension of the idea behind the famous Fibonacci sequence: $x_n = x_{n-1} + x_{n-2}$. Rather than combining the two most recent integers, the generator uses the fifth and seventeeth most recent, getting the sequence

$$x_1, x_2, \ldots, x_{17}, x_{18}, \ldots \qquad x_n = x_{n-5} + x_{n-17} \text{ mod } 2^\beta.$$

To implement this generator, one initially fills storage locations $L(1), \ldots, L(17)$ with 17 integers, not all even, and sets pointers $I \leftarrow 17$, $J \leftarrow 5$. Then each call to the following algorithm will update the memory locations, move the pointers, and return the next random integer, say K:

$$K \leftarrow L[I] + L[J]$$
$$L[I] \leftarrow K$$
$$I \leftarrow I - 1 \text{ ; if } I = 0 \text{ then } I \leftarrow 17$$
$$J \leftarrow J - 1 \text{ ; if } J = 0 \text{ then } J \leftarrow 17$$
$$\textbf{return } K$$

The addition in this algorithm is integer addition, automatically mod 2^β for 2's complement machines with β bits for integers. The initial values in $L(1), \ldots, L(17)$ are $x_{17}, \ldots x_1$ in reverse order. This allows the pointers I and J to be reset at 0 rather than at 18, as the test for $I = 0$ is faster than that for $I = 18$ in many computers. The period of the generator is $2^{\beta-1}(2^{17} - 1)$—re-

markably long. Even for 8-bit microprocessors the period is 16,777,088, while 16- and 32-bit machines give periods of some 4.3×10^9 and 2.8×10^{14}, respectively.

Each of the three generators discussed here has passed extensive tests for randomness and has also resisted attempts to display regularities of the type shown in Fig. 1 for congruential or shift-register generators used alone. Thus, at the time of this writing, it appears that by perhaps doubling or tripling the time required for the simplest generators (combining them in various ways), satisfactory sequences can be produced for general Monte Carlo use. There is no assurance that a new level of sophistication for simulation problems will not find these methods unsatisfactory, but the situation looks promising, since regularities in the latest methods appear to be of the magnitude of limitations imposed by the fixed word size of the computer.

REFERENCES

1964. Hammersley, J. M. and Handscomb, D. C. *Monte Carlo Methods.* London: Methuen.
1967. Golomb, S. W. *Shift Register Sequences.* New York: Holden Day.
1968. Berlekamp, E. R. *Algebraic Coding Theory.* New York: McGraw-Hill.
1972. Marsaglia, G. "The Structure of Linear Congruential Sequences," in Zaremba, S. K. (Ed.), *Applications of Number Theory to Numerical Analysis.* New York: Academic Press.
1981. Knuth, Donald E. *The Art of Computer Programming* **2** *(Seminumerical Algorithms),* (2nd Ed.). Reading, MA: Addison-Wesley.

G. Marsaglia

READ-ONLY MEMORY (ROM)

For articles on related subjects *see* CYCLE TIME; EMULATION; MEMORY: Main; MICROPROGRAMMING; PERSONAL COMPUTING; and STORAGE HIERARCHY.

Read-only memory (ROM) is based on a wide spectrum of storage technologies, many of which should be more accurately referred to as "slow write" storages. The basic idea behind read-only storage is that, for a number of applications, the contents of the storage are relatively fixed for a long period of time. In fact, for some applications, the contents of storage are not altered during the life of the machine. An example is the widespread use of ROM in current microcomputers to hold an invariant copy of the processor for a high-level language such as Basic or Pascal.

The memory cycle of read-only storage is shortened because its contents, being fixed, does not have to be re-

Fig. 1. A 24,000-bit read-only store chip, using field-effect transistor technology packaged in a 1-in. square metallized ceramic substrate.

generated. In addition, since a store operation cannot be performed by the system, the accessing mechanism usually can be designed to operate faster than otherwise. Also, in most situations, the read-only memory system will be less expensive than a read-write memory with corresponding performance.

Many technologies have been used and applied to read-only storage. These include the diode matrix, the card-capacitor approach, and magnetic or transformer type read-only storage.

Read-only storage has been used quite extensively for microprogrammed implementations of the control function—controlling the action of an instruction execution. For this function, the read-only storage has to be as fast as the basic cycle time of the machine.

Another use of read-only storage is the area of the *bootstrap loader*, which is a program that is permanently stored as part of the main memory of the system. Control is transferred to this program on machine startup so that other programs can be called in an orderly way and control can be transferred to them.

REFERENCE

1970. Husson, S. S. *Microprogramming: Principles and Practices.* Englewood Cliffs, NJ: Prentice-Hall.

M. J. FLYNN

REAL-TIME APPLICATIONS

For articles on related subjects *see* ADMINISTRATIVE APPLICATIONS; COMMUNICATIONS AND COMPUTERS; DATABASE, ON-LINE; DATABASE MANAGEMENT; MULTIPROGRAMMING; TERMINALS; and TRANSACTION-BASED SYSTEMS.

Real-time applications have been well established in the field of computer systems for almost two decades, and in certain areas of computer usuage have become virtually the exclusive mode of data processing. This approach to computer applications can perhaps the best described by contrasting it with batch processing, the prevailing form of computer utilization before the advent of the more sophisticated systems concepts that underlie real-time processing.

What Are Real-Time Applications? In batch processing, transactions against a file of data are accumulated until a sufficient number are present to warrant mass updating of a master file. This type of processing is particularly suitable for accounting applications such as payroll accounting or accounts receivable, in which master files are updated with new transactions periodically and in which output is produced according to a predetermined processing cycle. The processing cycle for this type of system is ordinarily defined by the frequency with which the master file must be updated.

Fig. 1 provides a simplified illustration of a batch data processing system for billing. During each processing cycle, receipts and new charges are batched for entry, as are status changes (open account, close account, change address, etc.). After keypunching, both classes of input go into an edit/convert run where they are validated as to correctness of account number and completeness of information. After editing, each item is written out to magnetic tape for subsequent processing. The next processing step is to sort these transactions into the same sequence as the master file. The master may then be updated during what is by far the most complicated and time-consuming run in the system. Outputs from this run include the updated master (which will become input to this same run during the next processing cycle) and other tapes, which go into output-edit runs to produce new bills and management reports.

What is a real-time system, and how does it compare with the batch-processing type of system just described? Real-time systems can best be differentiated by their quality of *responsiveness*. Conventional systems "respond" to their business environment by producing the requisite journals, reports, and other outputs according to their carefully prescheduled batch-processing cycles. Real-time systems, in contrast, can respond immediately at the *time* a transaction occurs. Thus, a bank teller using a terminal can obtain immediate information about a customer's current balance while the customer waits at the counter for completion of the transaction.

The question of how responsive a system must be before it merits designation as real-time is, of course, a

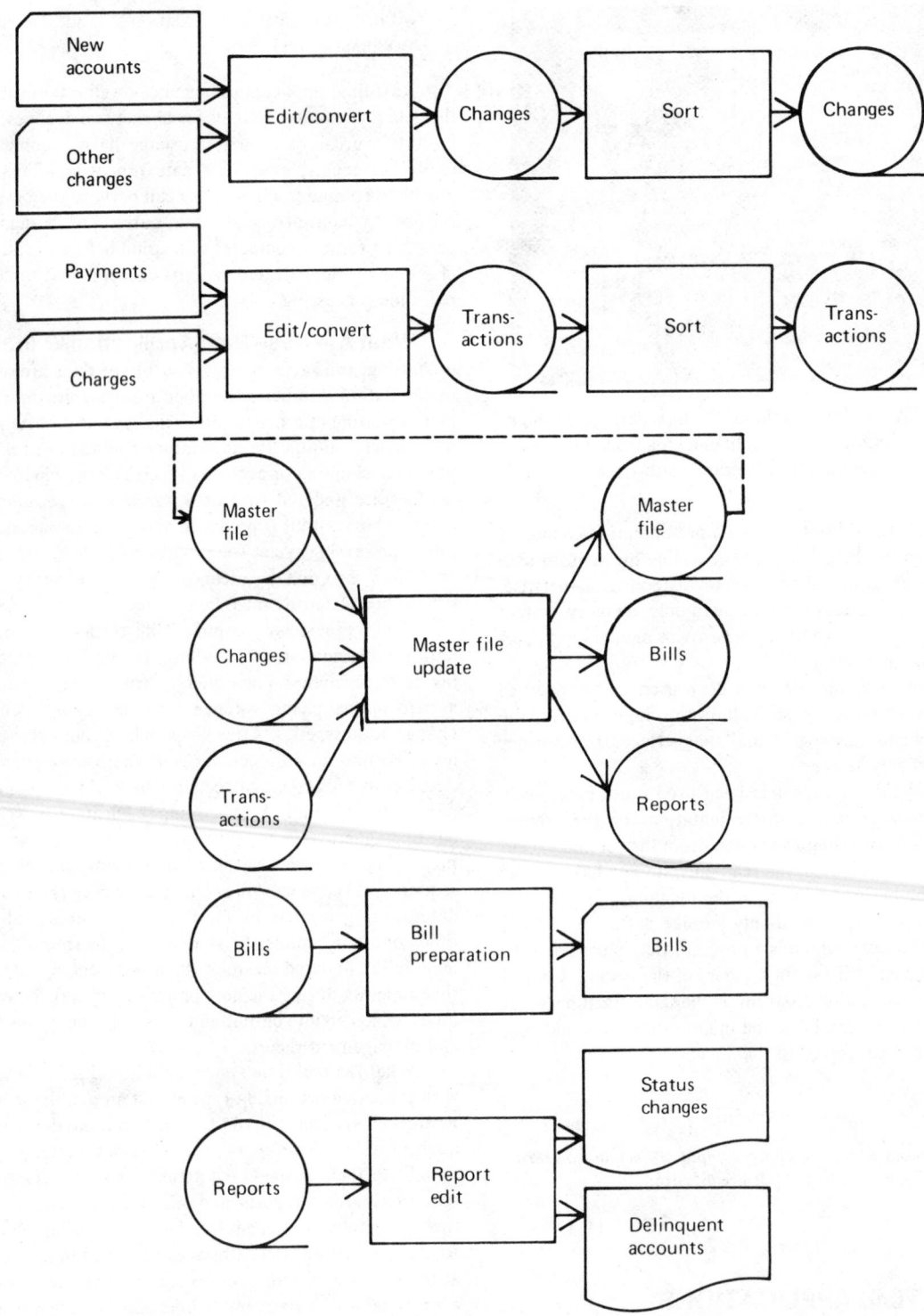

Fig. 1. Batch-processing application.

relative one. In some situations, usually those in which the customer is awaiting a decision based upon the computer's response, the reply will be required within a few seconds; in other circumstances, a longer response time can be tolerated. Real-time systems in which there is rapid and frequent interaction between human and machine are sometimes said to operate in a *conversational* mode.

Most real-time applications require hardware and software that provide fast responses to the terminal operator. From a human factors standpoint, a system response time of 3 to 5 sec on the average is desirable. This covers the elapsed time from the dispatch of a message from a remote terminal into a central processing unit and back to the terminal in the form of a response to the user. A significant component of such response time is usually the time devoted to retrieval of one or more records to satisfy the requirements of the incoming transactions.

Besides this characteristic of responsiveness, other features of real-time systems can prove advantageous to computer users. When a transaction is processed in real-time, there is no need for the laborious retranscription of source data from its original form to its processable form, which frequently must take place in preparing input for a conventional system. For example, when an airline reservation agent using an alphanumeric terminal enters each passenger's name and flight information at the time the booking is made, that is the end of it. There is no need to retranscribe these facts on a slip of paper to be sent to the "back room" for keypunching and subsequent pro-

cessing. And, of course, there is no delay imposed by the real-time system if the reservation agent wishes to retrieve and modify the record just created.

In real-time applications, files are updated as new transactions occur, with results of the updating transmitted back to the originator almost immediately upon receipt and processing of the transaction. Examples of this are plentiful, such as those in savings bank accounting systems in which the customer's balance is updated immediately after entry of a deposit or withdrawal request at a teller window equipped with a terminal connected to the bank's computer.

Classes of Real-Time Applications. The scope of real-time applications is almost as varied as the field of data processing itself. Among pioneer systems of the early 1960s can be found such diverse applications as the following.

1. The SABRE system of American Airlines, which provides instantaneous access to flight inventory information and electronic storage of passenger itinerary data. Fig. 2 shows part of the terminal display of this transaction.
2. Interactive problem-solving systems epitomized by MIT's MAC, which was the forerunner of today's omnipresent "time-sharing" systems for the compilation and execution of user-written programs.
3. Real-time mission-control systems developed for

---

*92/10 NOV-HART	Entry typed by agent to display record: flight, number and date, passenger's name
HART/JAMES MR	
1. 92Y10NOV HS1 SFOBUF 845A 516P HRS SPM	Y: tourist class HS1: 1 seat held SFO: San Francisco; BUF: Buffalo; SPM: special meal
TKTG TAM0 8NOV/	Ticket to be mailed 8 NOV.
FONE NYC-212 AA6-9531-H	H: home phone number
NYC-212 TW9-6431-H C/O CROSS	Person making reservation
RCVD-PSGRS NIECE, MRS CROSS	
AFAX CAKE WITH HAPPY BIRTHDAY UNCLE JIM SFO SKY CHEF	AFAX: additional facts
OSI PSGR IS CELEBRATING 85TH BIRTHDAY	OSI: other supplementary information
TAM 475 FOREST ST AMHERST NY 14226	Address to mail ticket
JFK 17Y10NOV HK SEAT 18D	HK: notes seat number confirmed
NYC-LS 0124A/04NOV 9151CH	LS: agent identification 0124A: Time reservation made 9151CH: disk file address of PNR-typing *9151CH will also cause display of this record

Fig. 2. Annotated sample of terminal display of passenger name record (PNR) on the SABRE system.

NASA, which have supported every flight of American astronauts from the early days of Project Mercury through the Apollo moon landings.

Out of the myriad real-time applications operational today, three generic types of processing can be identified which correspond to these landmark efforts.

There is, first, transaction-oriented processing in which clerical personnel interact with a computer for the entry and recording of business transactions such as airline reservations. One characteristic of such transaction processing is that the terminal operator is carefully guided through a set of input/output operations by the computer, which responds with an error message should an erroneous or unacceptable entry be submitted. For example, an airline reservation agent would be notified if an attempt was made to book a passenger on a nonexistent flight or on a flight already sold out. Similarly, a bank teller would be reminded if an inactive account number was entered or a withdrawal was requested that caused a deposit balance to become negative.

A second class of real-time processing involves interactive problem solving in a manner less highly structured than transaction processing. Here, terminal users are provided with generalized software packages such as those for information retrieval, which allow them to enter the parameters of a retrieval request and trigger a search of system files. For example, a database of personnel information might be interrogated to find out how many employees fit a pattern of more than ten years of service with salary level greater than $20,000 or who have a college degree. Another category of interactive processing permits on-line program development, whereby program instructions are input at a terminal with a request that the program be immediately compiled and executed.

A third class of real-time systems is found in industrial applications in the field of continuous process control where a computer is utilized to adjust the performance of other equipment in a continuous process such as petroleum production. Such process-control systems may be of the "open loop" variety in which the computer prints out, on an exception basis, messages requiring remedial action by an operator to adjust system flows, or they may be "closed loop" in which the computer itself is able, through links to sensors and control equipment, to adjust the production process without human intervention. In either case, there must be feedback from the process control equipment to the computer in real time, and resultant messages must be output from the computer within the same immediate time frame.

Equipment Requirements for Real-Time Applications. Real-time applications of the kinds described are operational on a wide range of equipment, from minicomputers with limited storage capacity serving only a few terminals, up to the largest systems available today which embody multiple processing units and memory modules, billions of characters of immediate access storage, and hundreds of terminals. But regardless of size, the equipment employed in real-time systems has a number of common characteristics. Although not all real-time applications require all these features, the vast majority will be found to employ them at least to some degree. Fig. 3 provides a schematic of the major equipment elements usually present in a real-time processing environment. Descriptions of these elements follow.

Terminals. Terminals for real-time applications are almost as varied as the applications themselves. In some instances, the terminal may be a simple numeric input device, such as a Touchtone telephone keyboard, with responses provided by computer-generated voice answer. At the other end of the complexity scale, one can find intelligent terminals, which in actuality may be minicomputers or microprocessors with enough storage capacity and logic to perform extensive preliminary processing before accepting a transaction for transmission to the central processing unit.

Terminals for real-time applications can also be differentiated as special-purpose or general-purpose types. Special-purpose terminals are employed in such applications as stock quotation, airline reservations, and on-line banking. Such terminals may be equipped with special-purpose function keys, specialized print symbols, and templates or masks for specialized displays. However, many real-time applications, in particular those for handling relatively unstructured retrieval requests or interactive problem solving, require only a standard low-speed typewriter-like device or an input keyboard combined with a data display screen.

Communications Front End. A communications front end is necessary to interface the lines connecting remote terminals to the central processing unit. It performs such functions as assembling incoming messages, detecting transmission errors, and routing responses back to the terminal operators. In large systems, this front-end equipment may be a minicomputer and may have associated with it magnetic tapes or disks for message queueing. In smaller systems, front-end functions may be integral to the central processing unit rather than assigned to a separate processor.

Central Processing Units. Two central processing units are shown in Fig. 3 to reflect a characteristic of many real-time configurations that contain dual processing units for greater reliability. In such systems, one processing unit may perform high-priority transaction pro-

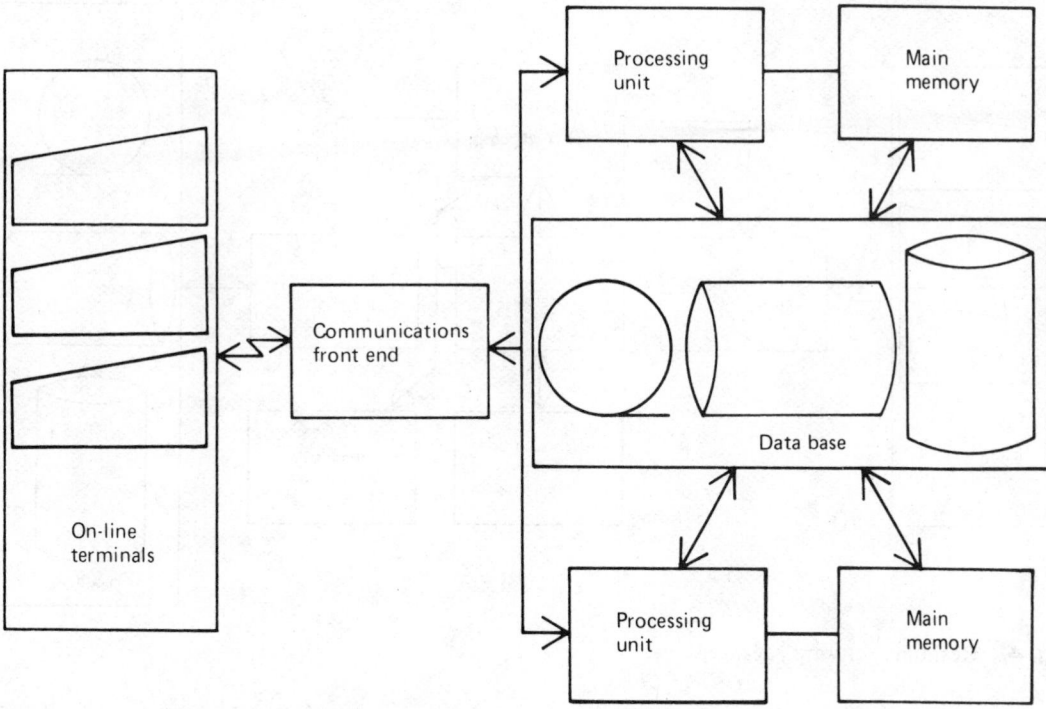

Fig. 3. Real-time equipment configuration.

cessing while the other performs lower priority work, perhaps batch processing, with the capability of the second processing unit assuming the on-line processing work load if there is a malfunction in the first.

Main Memory Modules. As in the case of the central processing unit, two or more main memory modules may be configured for workload sharing and enhanced reliability.

Immediate Access Storage. Immediate access storage is found in virtually all real-time applications, and sometimes ranges into the billions of characters for storage of large databases that must be immediately accessible. In many systems, there is a hierarchy of such storage, ranging from fixed-head drums or disks with access times of a few milliseconds up to large-capacity disk files with access times averaging 100 ms or more. Removable disk storage is also present in many configurations so that files can be conveniently removed and stored, once processing against them is completed. In multiprocessing configurations, each processing unit may have a channel to all the immediate storage.

Other Devices. Magnetic tape drives continue to be utilized in real-time applications for such purposes as logging incoming transactions, maintaining duplicate copies

of files and transactions for recovery purposes, and performing sorting and other batch processing for low-priority batch applications. More exotic types of storage devices are now beginning to appear as substitutes for, or augmentations of, conventional disk storage units, such as laser memory systems that provide access to billions of characters of storage within a few seconds.

Software Requirements for Real-Time Applications. The operation of real-time systems dictates the need for certain kinds of software that might not otherwise be required. Fig. 4 illustrates the major software components typically present in real-time applications. These packages may, in some cases, be housed in a single computer; in more complex systems, they may be distributed among multiple computers (e.g., communications front ends and central processors).

The Operating System. All the software functions illustrated in Fig. 4 are under control of an operating system. The operating system maintains overall control of system operations by scheduling the execution of all other programs, allocating main memory, establishing job priorities, servicing interrupts, communicating with the computer operator, and performing similar housekeeping tasks. Obviously, the precise capabilities of a given operating system are dependent on the size of the computer

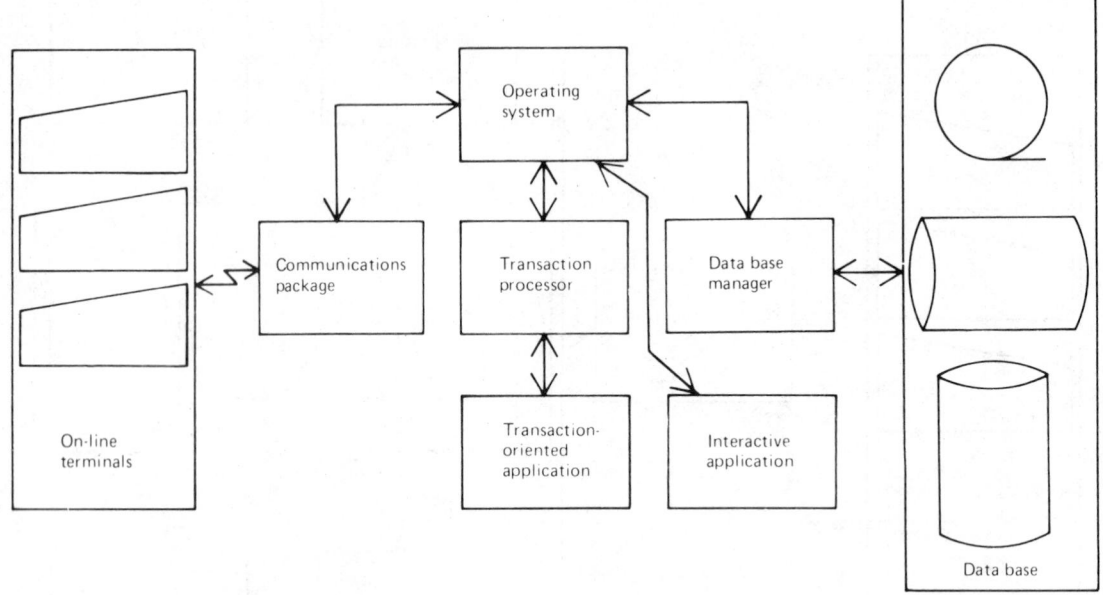

Fig. 4.   Real-time software packages.

for which it was written, as well as on the design objectives of the manufacturer in creating this all-important piece of software.

Many users of third-generation computers, on which operating systems were first employed extensively, have been dissatisfied with the performance of this software, maintaining that it is poorly designed, overly complex, and inefficient for real-time applications. Despite these criticisms, nearly all users have made a decision to live with the operating system as delivered by the manufacturer and to press for improved versions to overcome major deficiencies. The penalty for "going it alone" by designing a nonstandard operating system is too great today, since all other software componentry for a particular machine is designed for compatibility with the operating system.

Communications Package. Referring again to Fig. 4, we can identify a communications package required to control the operation of the multiple, remote terminals found in most real-time applications. In some large configurations, this front-end software may actually be lodged in a separate computer dedicated to controlling all system communications. In small systems, the communications package may simply be a subroutine of the operating system.

Besides controlling the terminals and communication lines, and interrupting the operating system when action must be taken on incoming messages, the communications package provides (or should provide) *termi-*

nal transparency to the other programs in the system. This means that an application program need not be concerned with the *kind* of terminal from which an inquiry has been received or to which a message must be sent. Instead, these programs need concern themselves only with the substance of the data, not with its specific format. This is an important consideration in a system that employs a variety of terminal devices (e.g., teletypewriters, cathode-ray tubes, voice-response terminals, or graphics terminals). It is often necessary to change terminal types or upgrade terminal capability as new information needs are identified or as new hardware becomes available. With terminal transparency, flexibility can be achieved by making changes only in the communications front end, *not* in the application programs themselves.

Besides communications network control, a communications package may perform such functions as input message error handling, input editing, and output report and display formatting. The communications package may also contain security provisions as well as data-logging capability and other features to facilitate recovery.

Database Management Package. At the right of Fig. 4 is shown the database management package that performs on the database a set of operations analogous to those performed at the front end of the system by the communications package. The database management package services the application programs and the system users by providing retrieval and updating capability for the file records of a real-time system. Specific features of such packages vary widely, especially for functions such as information retrieval. Some are designed to carry out highly specialized searches in which required data elements are qualified by a series of "and/or" statements. Others permit the statistical sampling of a file or the accumulation of data from designated portions of a file. Still others allow simultaneous inquiry against mulitple files and the combination of file data into a single output, as might be required by a request for both payroll and skills inventory data for an employee.

There are numerous database management packages available for sale or lease. As in the case of the operating system, it would be imprudent for the user to try to design one. Not all packages are suitable for on-line usage, but may instead require the accumulation, batching, and sorting of information requests for subsequent processing against a sequentially ordered file. Further, some packages may support data retrieval only, with no provision for file updating and maintenance, in which case the package may have to be augmented by the user's own programs.

Just as the communications package aims for terminal transparency, the database management package seeks to provide *program independence* by separating the application programs from the file data they operate on. This permits the database to be modified or reorganized without unduly affecting the application programs, since all requests for data are "filtered" through the database management package. This is in marked contrast to earlier practice, in which the application programmer was free to design files and records, and embed references to these records within the program wherever convenient and unconstrained by outside standards. Such practice is intolerable in a system in which files frequently must be expanded or reorganized, based on their degree of usage, with data shifted from one physical storage medium to another. The objective of program independence is to permit these changes to the database without requiring inordinate changes in the application programs that reference the database.

Transaction Processing Package. This is the newest category of software package utilized in real-time applications. In earlier real-time systems, transaction-processing functions were performed by specially tailored software; today, many of these functions have been sufficiently well defined that they can be generalized and packaged.

The purpose of the transaction processor is to handle large volumes of specifically defined transactions in a highly efficient manner. Examples of such transactions can be found in booking airline passenger reservations or in recording deposits to savings bank accounts. Transac-

tion processing should be contrasted with interactive problem solving in which the nature of the processing to be performed is determined by the user during the interactive session. In transaction processing, the features and options available to the terminal operator are carefully structured in advance and are performed by specialized application programs under control of the transaction-processing software. Any deviation from the predetermined processing scenario by the operator, such as the entry of an invalid date, results in discontinuation of processing and transmission of an error response.

In a transaction-oriented real-time system, the transaction processing package is activated by the operating system upon receipt of an incoming transaction. It performs initial validation of data, establishes what application program action is required, and reacts to error and other special conditions.

The transaction processor is responsible for maintaining control over real-time application program scheduling. Following the scheduling of an application program as the result of the arrival of a transaction, the transaction processor delivers the input transaction to the application program.

The transaction processor may initiate recovery procedures following abnormal termination of an application program. Such recovery procedures could include scheduling a special routine to repair any files damaged by the malfunctioning program; shutting the program down; releasing any facilities, such as main memory, assigned to the program; and apprising the operator of the problem. The transaction processor may also maintain statistics on such data as transaction volumes processed by type.

Real-Time Application Processing. As previously suggested, real-time applications imply a high degree of simultaneity of processing in order to provide fast responses to large numbers of system users. One approach to achieving a high level of throughput in real-time applications lies, of course, in multiprocessing. Here, more than one processing unit is available to handle transactions, as suggested in Fig. 3. But there is a practical limit, especially in business applications, to the amount of simultaneity that can be achieved through the addition of multiple hardware components and the distribution of incoming transactions among them.

Software techniques are commonly employed in transaction-oriented systems to enhance throughput capability. Two of the most common are multiprogramming and reentrancy.

Multiprogramming. What is multiprogramming and why does it have such an important role in real-time systems? Like so many other terms in current usage among computer specialists, it has taken on a variety of shades of meaning. In this discussion a multiprogrammed system is defined as one in which several transactions may be in process at the same time inside the central processing unit. This is in contrast to a sequentially programmed system, which disposes of transactions one by one, not permitting a new action to enter the processing cycle until the current one has been completely processed.

Reentrancy. In addition to the multiprocessing and multiprogramming approaches, further simultaneity of operations and hence greater throughput and responsiveness can be achieved in real-time systems by means of program reentrancy. By employing this programming technique, one resident copy of an application program can be used to process multiple transactions of the same type in a highly efficient manner. Suppose, for example, that a banking system simultaneously receives several requests to debit customer account records from various terminals. It would be desirable if the transaction processor were able to initiate the processing of a second transaction and perhaps a third or fourth before the first transaction had been completely processed by the application program involved.

An application program frequently interrupts its processing of a transaction at some intermediate point prior to completion of processing; at that point, processing could begin on another transaction of the same type. But this is possible *only* if the application program is reentrant, i.e., written in such a manner that it is capable of starting to process the new transaction without affecting switches, variables or working storage locations still set to handle the suspended processing of the first transaction.

Simultaneity in processing several identical transactions could, of course, also be achieved by having multiple copies of the same application program resident in main memory and assigning a single transaction to each, but the preferred method is to write these programs in such a manner that simultaneity is achieved through the ability to reenter *one* resident copy of an application program with a new transaction at any time.

System Reliability. No discussion of real-time processing is complete without emphasis on the heightened requirements for reliability in these kinds of systems. Special provision must be made to compensate for equipment malfunctions or program errors in such a way that these can be isolated and corrected or bypassed without causing the entire system to "crash" and without destroying or damaging file data. This implies software capability, in conjunction with hardware features, to accomplish "graceful degradation" that could, for example, permit one processor to assume the entire work load in the event of malfunction in a multiprocessing con-

figuration. It also implies programs and procedures for recovering from errors and restoring the system and its associated files to its users in such a manner that work can proceed with minimum need for manual reentry of transactions or file data.

As real-time systems have evolved from their tentative beginnings, there has been a steady increase in the numbers of applications and the size of the systems devoted to such processing. Today, real-time processing is the normative mode for numerous applications in stock brokerage, transportation, banking, and retail merchandising as well as countless nonbusiness applications. Today's equipment and software packages are, because of the importance of such processing, becoming increasingly oriented to providing the high level of performance and reliability that are mandatory for real-time applications.

REFERENCES

1967. Martin, J. *Design of Real-Time Computer Systems.* Englewood Cliffs, NJ: Prentice-Hall.
1969. Blumenthal, S. C. *Management Information Systems: A Framework for Planning and Development.* Englewood Cliffs, NJ: Prentice-Hall.
1972. Head, R. V. *Manager's Guide to Management Information Systems.* Englewood Cliffs, NJ: Prentice-Hall.

R. V. HEAD

REAL-TIME CLOCK. *See* INTERVAL TIMER.

RECORD

For articles on related subjects *see* BLOCK AND BLOCKING; DATA SET; and FILES.

A record is an organized and identifiable aggregate of data transcribed on a computer storage medium. Each record comprises data that have an underlying relationship to one another. For example, a personnel record usually contains data such as Social Security number, first name, middle initial, last name, data of birth, next of kin, and home address. All these data are *attributes* (descriptors, locators, identifiers, etc.) peculiar to this individual.

Data elements in a record may be of similar or dissimilar types: bits, numbers, character strings, etc. The contents of punched cards and printer lines are often called *unit records,* since these document lengths are predefined by associated electromechanical devices. Magnetic tape and disk drives usually accommodate *variable-length records* in which the amount of data per record varies according to activity, age, etc., of the individual.

Records of the same type are usually grouped into larger aggregates, called *files* or *data sets* or *databases*. When written sequentially into a file, records are collected into intermediate aggregates called *blocks,* whose lengths are efficient for transcription to tape or disk devices. In theory, a file or database could comprise a single block containing all its records. In practice, a large file or database may contain hundreds or thousands of blocks, each containing one or more records. The number of records per block, called the *blocking factor,* is an important consideration in determining the efficiency of file processing.

D. N. Freeman

RECURSION

For articles on related subjects *see* Iteration; Loop; Stack; and Turing Machine.

Recursion refers to several related concepts in computer science and mathematics. One or more functions of an integer variable are defined by giving initial values and by giving the value for larger integers in terms of smaller ones. No single definition is generally accepted, so we will give examples of increasing complexity.

Recursion Relations

1. The Fibonacci sequence is given by the equations

$$f_0 = 1,$$
$$f_1 = 1,$$
$$f_{n+1} = f_n + f_{n-1}$$

2. When differential equations are to be solved numerically, *recursion relations* such as

$$f(x_0 + nh) = F(f(x_0 + (n - 1)h),$$
$$f(x_0 + (n - 2)h), \ldots, f(x_0 + (n - k)h))$$

arise where f is, in general, a vector of real numbers.
3. When linear differential equations are solved by series, recursion relations for the coefficients of the powers of the independent variables arise.

Recursive Functions. The systematic study of recursion began in the 1920s when mathematical logic began to treat questions of definability, computability, and decidability. An important role is played by *primitive recursive functions.*

Primitive recursive functions are integer functions of integers built up from addition and multiplication of in-

tegers, and previously defined primitive recursive functions by the primitive recursion scheme:

$$f(0, x_2, \ldots, x_k) = g(x_2, \ldots, x_k),$$
$$f(x_1 + 1, x_2, \ldots, x_k) = h(f(x_1, \ldots, x_k), x_1, \ldots x_k).$$

Here, g and h are primitive recursive functions of $k - 1$ and $k + 1$ arguments, respectively. As an example, we define $n!$, where n is a positive integer, by $n! = f(n)$ where $f(0) = 1$ and $f(n + 1) = (n + 1) \cdot f(n)$. So, in this case, g is a function of 0 arguments, namely, the constant 1, and $h(u, v) = (v + 1)u$.

All the common functions of number theory are primitive recursive. Moreover, many important functions on countable domains other than the integers correspond to primitive recursive functions when we choose a specific enumeration for the domain.

Primitive recursive functions are included in general recursive functions. The definition of general recursive functions is like that given above for primitive recursive functions, except that the relations are replaced by an arbitrary finite collection of equations relating the values of f for different arguments, and the function is considered defined if and only if a unique value of $f(x_1, \ldots, x_k)$ can be deduced from the equations for each k-tuplet $(x_1, \ldots, x_k)$. Naturally, if someone gives you an arbitrary collection of such relations, you may not be able to determine whether $f(x_1, \ldots, x_k)$ is uniquely determined, so you may not know whether you have a general recursive function. This difficulty is unavoidable. There is no way to give a definition scheme that is always guaranteed to give a function but which will give all computable functions. This fact is itself expressed in the terminology of recursive function theory by the statement that the set of computable functions is *recursively enumerable* but not recursive. The famous example of a general recursive function that is not primitive recursive is the *Ackermann function,* defined by the equations

$$A(0, n, p) = n + p, \quad A(1, 0, p) = 0$$
$$A(m + 2, 0, p) = 1$$

and

$$A(m + 1, n + 1, p) = A(m, A(m + 1, n, p), p).$$

An important result for computer science is that the general recursive functions coincide with the functions defined by a Turing machine, which is a simple form of computer. They also coincide with the functions of integers defined by Algol or Fortran programs, assuming that the program can cope with whatever size integers arise.

Both programs and general recursion schemata, in general, give *partial functions* because the computation may terminate for some values of the arguments and not for others.

The study of computable functions is the domain of recursive function theory, an active branch of mathematics. The connection between current research in recursive function theory and computing practice, or even current research in computer science, is rather tenuous. This situation might change because of developments in either field.

Recursive Procedures. In programming, it is frequently convenient to have a procedure use itself as a subprocedure. If the procedure does this, it is called *recursive*. Recursive procedures are particularly natural in dealing with symbolic expressions because the structure of the programs often matches the structure of the data. As far as programming languages are concerned, recursive procedures are quite natural; it requires a special statement in the definition of the language to forbid them. However, implementing them requires that a special kind of object code be compiled, and early programming languages like Fortran do not allow them. The problem is that variables in the program correspond to locations in the machine, and when the program is called by itself, it will use these same locations, overwriting their previous contents. Therefore, recursive programs use a data structure, called a *stack*, to store the contents of registers that must be saved. This storage can be done by the calling routine before it enters the subroutine, or it can be done by the subroutine before it uses the registers, the latter being more common.

After the registers have been saved on the stack, the index into the stack is increased by the number of registers stored, so that subsequent saving on the stack will use fresh registers. When the subroutine exits, the contents of the saved registers are restored from the stack to their previous values, and the stack pointer is reduced by the amount it was previously increased. This is done by the caller or by the subroutine, according to whether the caller or subroutine did the original storing. An alternative technique is to use the stack for all temporary registers. In this case, it is unnecessary to move data around, and it is only necessary to change the stack pointer when subroutines are entered and left. However, this technique uses up the indexing capabilities of some machines that may be wanted for other purposes. Recursive programs can be written in any programming language by explicitly programming the saving and restoring.

The first languages to use recursive subroutines on a regular basis were the IPL languages of Newell, Shaw, and Simon. Lists were used for the stack and the saving and restoring was done explicitly by the programmer. The first language to provide an automatic mechanism

for recursion was Lisp. Algol 60 and its successors, Pascal and Ada, also allow recursion, as do such other popular languages as APL, PL/I, C, and Snobol.

Many computers have special instructions for handling stacks (e.g., the PUSH and POP instructions of the Digital Equipment DEC-10). Other machines, such as the Burroughs B5000 and its successors, have instructions that use a hardware stack directly. These special facilities give a modest increase in the efficiency of recursive programming.

Recursive Conditional Expressions. The recursive use of conditional expressions provides an economical and elegant way of specifying the functions that are computable in terms of a collection of base functions. This technique is the basis of the Lisp prgramming language and also of the theoretical system of Dana Scott for studying the properties of computer programs. A conditional expression has the form, in Algol-like notation, of

$$\textbf{if } p \textbf{ then } a \textbf{ else } b.$$

It is evaluated by first evaluating the propositional expression p. If p is TRUE, the value of the conditional expression is that of a, and if the value of p is FALSE, the value of the conditional expression is that of b. It is important to note that only one of a or b is actually evaluated.

A simple example of the use of conditional expressions is to define the absolute value of a number by

$$|x| = \textbf{if } x < 0 \textbf{ then } -x \textbf{ else } x.$$

Conditional expressions are used to define functions recursively by writing the definition in the form

$$f(x, \ldots , z) \leftarrow E\{x, \ldots , z, f, g, \ldots , h\},$$

where E is an expression involving the variables $x, \ldots ,$ z, the function f being defined, and known or previously defined functions $g, \ldots h$. An example of such a definition is

$$n! \leftarrow \textbf{if } n = 0 \textbf{ then } 1 \textbf{ else } n \cdot (n - 1)! \qquad (1)$$

The general method for evaluating recursive conditional expressions is illustrated by using the above definition to evaluate 3!. Namely, we have

$$3! = \textbf{if } 3 = 0 \textbf{ then } 1 \textbf{ else } 3 \cdot (3 - 1)!$$
$$= 3 \cdot 2! = 3 \cdot (\textbf{if } 2 = 0 \textbf{ then } 1 \textbf{ else } 2 \cdot (2 - 1)!)$$

= 3·2·(**if** 1 = 0 **then** 1 **else** 1·(1 − 1)!)

= 3·2·1·(**if** 0 = 0 **then** 1 **else** 0·(0 − 1)!)

= 3·2·1·1 = 6.

Note that the rule for evaluating conditional expressions ensures that the computer never attempts to evaluate (−1)!. This is necessary since its evaluations would not terminate.

As a second example, the Ackermann function mentioned above is written as a recursive conditional expression as follows:

$A(m, n, p) \leftarrow$

    if $m = 0$ **then** $n + p$

    else if $n = 0$ **then** (**if** $m = 1$ **then** 0 **else** 1)

    else $A(m − 1, (A(m, n − 1), p), p)$.

Several remarks are worth making:

First, in a programming language that uses recursive conditional expression, 3! would not be evaluated by the above symbolic manipulation. Either (1) would be compiled into a recursive subroutine (i.e., a subroutine of the type explained above that calls itself and uses a stack to save intermediate results and return addresses), or a recursive interpreter would interpret a list structure version of (1).

Second, (1) can easily be replaced by another expression for the factorial that can be compiled into a nonrecursive program. Namely, we write

$$n! \leftarrow \text{fact}(n, 0, 1) \qquad (2)$$

where

$$\text{fact}(n, m, p) \leftarrow \textbf{if } m = n \textbf{ then } p$$
$$\textbf{else fact } (n, m + 1, (m + 1)p).$$

Now (2) can be translated into a nonrecursive program because the only occurrence of "fact" on the right-hand side of the definition appears at the outer level; i.e., fact $(n, m + 1, (m + 1)p)$ gives the value of fact (n, m, p), in contrast to the situation in (1) where $(n − 1)!$ must be multiplied by n to give $n!$. This allows the object program to contain an ordinary jump to itself rather than a subroutine call. When this is possible, the function definition is called *iterative*. Thus, "fact" is iterative, while the definition (2) is not, Recursive definitions cannot in general be replaced by iterative definitions except by encoding the stack as a variable in the program, and, if this has to be done, there is no advantage in the replacement.

Third, there may be several occurrences of the function being defined on the right-hand side of the recursive definition, and whether the evaluation terminates may depend on which occurrence is evaluated first. The following example due to Morris shows this:

$$f(x, y) \leftarrow \textbf{if } x = 0 \textbf{ then } 0 \textbf{ else } f(x − 1, f(y − 2, x)).$$

The reader should evaluate $f(2, 1)$ to see the problem.

It is also possible to use recursive conditional expressions to define functions that take functions as arguments or give functions as results. However, there remain unsolved problems in finding compiling algorithms that produce efficient object code and give the "right" answers in all cases.

The term *recursive* is sometimes also applied to the Backus-Naur form (*q.v.*) used to define classes of strings of symbols.

Source Material. McCarthy *et al.* (1962) has some discussion of the implementation of recursion in Lisp, and Randell and Russell (1964) discuss the implementation of recursion in Algol. Wirth (1976) discusses when to use recursion and when to use iteration. Peter (1967) has a thorough treatment of subclasses of general recursive functions. The standard reference on recursive function theory was written by Kleene (1952), who gave a more elementary treatment in a later book (1967).

Two aspects of recursion are current research topics in computer science. First, the notion of recursive program is being extended in various ways, and methods of implementing these extensions by compilers and interpreters are being studied (Bobrow and Raphael, 1973). Second, the formal properties of recursive programs are being studied as part of the mathematical theory of computation, which has as its major object the ability to prove assertions about programs and check these assertions on a computer (Manna, 1974). (*See* PROGRAM VERIFICATION.)

REFERENCES

1952. Kleene, S. C. *Introduction to Metamathematics*. Princeton, NJ: Van Nostrand.
1962. McCarthy, J. *et al. Lisp 1.5 Programmer's Manual*. Cambridge, MA: M.I.T. Press.
1964. Randell, B. and Russell, L. J. *Algol 60 Implementation: Translation and Use of Algol 60 Programs by Computers*. New York: Academic Press.
1967. Kleene, S. C. *Mathematical Logic*. New York: Wiley.
1967. Peter, R. *Recursive Functions*. New York: Academic Press.
1973. Bobrow, D. and Raphael, B. *New Programming Languages for AI Research*. Palo Alto: Xerox Research Center.
1974. Manna, Z. *Mathematical Theory of Computation*. New York: McGraw-Hill.
1976. Wirth, N. *Algorithms + Data Structures = Programs*. Englewood Cliffs, NJ: Prentice-Hall.

J. MCCARTHY

REDUNDANCY

For articles on related subjects *see* ERRORS; ERROR CORRECTING CODES; FAULT-TOLERANT COMPUTING; and RELIABILITY, HARDWARE.

A system is said to be *nonredundant* or is said to have a *simplex structure* if it is designed in such a manner that only the absolute minimum amount of hardware is utilized to implement its function. If, even after using the finest components available, the desired system reliability is not achieved, or if failure tolerance is desired as a system capability, then *redundancy* as a design procedure is resorted to; i.e., more system elements are used than are absolutely necessary to realize all the system's functions. The additional system elements, referred to as the redundant elements, need not all necessarily be hardware elements, but may also be additional software *(software redundancy)*, additional time (*time redundancy*— e.g., performing a computation more than once and comparing the results), and additional information (*information redundancy*—e.g., the application of error-detection and correction codes).

Naturally, redundancies are often interrelated. Additional software requires additional memory storage, and additional time is used to execute the added software. The term *protective redundancy* is often used to characterize that redundancy which has an overall beneficial effect on the system attributes, since redundancy alone without proper application may well become a liability. Protective redundancy is utilized to realize *fault-tolerant digital systems and self-repairing systems* by such means as triple or *N*-tuple modular redundancy (TMR, NMR), quadded redundancy, standby-replacement redundancy, hybrid redundancy, software redundancy, and the application of error-detection and correction codes.

Redundancy as a procedure for designing more reliable systems than allowed by the intrinsic reliability of the constituent components is as old as the discipline of engineering itself. An example of the use of redundancy in ancient times is provided in structures where more than the absolute minimum required number of struts were provided to support a structure. Thus, early uses of redundancy were used as insurance against (1) the lack of accurate knowledge of underlying phenomena, and (2) the lack of confidence in the available data on the materials used. Redundancy as a procedure is even more basic. This is evidenced by the testimony of evolutionary processes of life, which make abundant use of it (e.g., in the human body there are two kidneys, two lungs, two cerebral hemispheres, etc.) Also, in societal systems, protective redundancy is advocated by the truism "two heads are better than one," and conversely, the improper use of redundancy by "too many cooks spoil the broth." Among other societal systems exhibiting the principles of redundancy is the typical committee, which has an odd number of members so that a tie in balloting may never occur. This is analogous to the majority voting redundancy used in some computer systems. Other examples will readily occur to the reader.

For the computer age, redundancy has been used at all levels of technology, from that of large-scale-integrated (LSI) devices, circuit logic, subsystem computers, and even to entire networks of digital systems.

F. P. MATHUR

REENTRANT PROGRAM

For articles on related subjects *see* COROUTINE; MULTIPROGRAMMING; PROCEDURE, PURE; and TIME SHARING.

In a time-sharing or multiprogramming environment a number of user programs may be sharing a common pool of subprograms or processors. Therefore, it is necessary that the shared programs be written in such a form that each can be applied to, say, user program 1 without running to completion, then be interrupted and applied to some other user program (perhaps, or perhaps not, running to completion), and then later be *reentered* at the point of interruption of user program 1 without loss of information.

In order to allow this reentrant capability, the programs must be written so that they contain no self-modifying features and so that all data required by the reentrant program can be maintained in a separate file related to the user program rather than as part of the reentrant subprogram or processor itself. Then the execution of the reentrant program can be interrupted at any point, and— provided the data file is stored together with the contents of the machine registers and the program counter at the point of interruption—the program can be immediately applied to another user program and can be resumed at a later time by restoring the data file and the program counter. Fig. 1 shows a schematic of a reentrant program shared by *n* user programs. When UPi is interrupted, perhaps before it finishes using the reentrant processor, and another user program (say, UP2) gets to use the reentrant processor, the reentrant processor must have communicated to it the location of the data for UP2 and the place I2 where previous execution was interrupted. Reentrant programs are sometimes called *pure procedures* (*q.v.*).

J. A. N. LEE

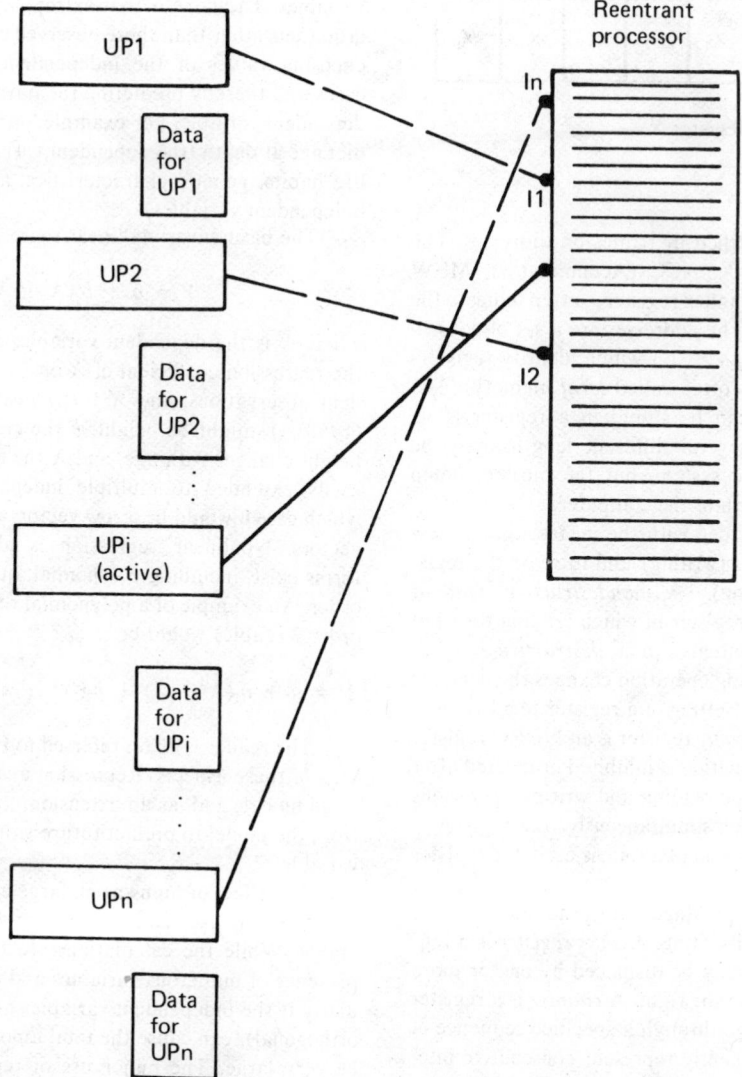

Fig. 1. A reentrant processor. UP, user program; dotted lines indicate point in reentrant program at which user program was interrupted; solid line shows where reentrant program execution is taking place for the currently active user program.

REGISTER

For articles on related subjects *see* ARITHMETIC-LOGIC UNIT; BASE REGISTER; GENERAL REGISTER; INDEX REGISTER; and SHIFTING.

A register is a specialized storage element of the CPU that consists of several flip-flops or of some other kind of digital storage element. The purpose of a register is to store a string of bits (often a word) representing related information: the digits of a number, the symbols of an alphanumeric word, the bits representing the status of various parts of a computer, the bits indicating the presence of interrupt requests, etc. The bits X_i that are stored in the register X are considered to be arranged in linear order and are identified by the indices i, usually chosen in the range $0 \leq i \leq n$ (Fig. 1).

All registers within a computer or other digital de-

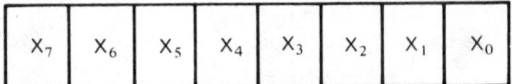

Fig. 1. An eight-bit register X.

vice are uniquely identified by names or addresses. The names—for example: X, ACC (Accumulator), MSW (machine status word), index register—often indicate the function of a register. The addresses are a set of consecutive integers A $(0 \leq A \leq N)$ which identify registers within a storage array (often called *local* memory). The number of bits that can be stored in a register is its *length*. Registers of several different lengths may be found within the same system, but the most common length is the word length of the computer.

Registers are provided with the means to *load* new words or individual bits (writing) and to *sense* the register's contents (reading). A *nondestructive readout* (NDRO) register is a register in which reading does not alter the register's contents. In a *destructive readout* (DR) register the reading operation changes the contents to all zeros or all ones. Setting of a register to all zeros is called *clearing*. A *read-only* register is an NDRO register in which the writing function is inhibited or deleted after the initial loading. If the reading and writing operations use all bits of a register simultaneously, the register is called *parallel*, but if one bit at a time is used, the register is called *serial*.

Registers may be provided with other functions in addition to reading and writing. A *shift register* is a register in which all bits may be displaced by one or more positions to the left or to the right. A *counter* is a register in which the contents go through a specified sequence of states. The states frequently represent consecutive integers in binary or decimal notation. An *accumulator register* has a built-in adder that adds an input number to the contents of the accumulator. The shifting, counting, and adding operations are performed upon receipt of appropriate commands.

A. AVIŽIENIS

REGRESSION ANALYSIS

For article on related subject *see* STATISTICAL APPLICATIONS.

Regression analysis is used for many different purposes. The most important is to build models explaining a dependent variable in terms of a set of independent variables. The hope is that extrapolation into new population sets other than those observed can be performed by choosing values of the independent variables for new cases and thereby predicting the most likely value of the dependent variable. For example, one might wish to predict age at death (the dependent variable) on the basis of life habits, genetic characteristics, and physiology (the independent variables).

The basic bivariate linear regression equation is

$$Y = a + b (X - \overline{X}),$$

where Y is the dependent variable, a is a constant, b is the regression coefficient of X on Y, the Xs are independent observations, and $\overline{X}$ their mean. To follow Fisher (1958), Y might be height, b the coefficient with which height changes with age, and X the age. The equation is easily extended to multiple independent variables, in which case $\mathbf{b}$ would be a row vector, and $\mathbf{X}$ and $\overline{\mathbf{X}}$ column vectors. Nonlinear regression is also possible. Many forms exist, including polynomial, quadratic, and higher order. An example of a polynomial regression equation of order 3 (cubic) would be

$$Y = a + b_1(X - \overline{X}) + b_2(X^2 - \overline{X^2}) + b_3(X^3 - \overline{X^3}).$$

The reader is again referred to Fisher for further details of these aspects. Regression analysis is thus used to build models and, as an extension, to allow extrapolation from the model to predict future values of the dependent variable.

The effect of high-speed, large central memory computers on the use of regression analysis has been considerable. While the calculations are basically simple, the presence of numerous variables and observations, particularly if the independent variables are interrelated (nonorthogonal), can cause the total amount of calculation to be very large. The major use of regression analysis on computers has paralleled the development of the *stepwise regression* method. Perhaps the most widely used stepwise regression program has been BMDO2R (and its replacement BMDPO2R), which was written as part of the UCLA Library of computer programs (Dixon, 1978). The method is basically that of Efroymson (1964), later elaborated upon and further refined by Jennrich (1976). These programs were the first to address the problem of selecting variable subsets that reduced the residual sum of squares (i.e., increased the multiple correlation coefficient) the most. After entering into the equation that variable with the largest partial correlation coefficient with the dependent variable, its effect is removed from the correlation matrix and then the most important variable is entered. This process continues until some criterion for terminating the process is reached. Mantel (1971) has pointed out that the step-up method of selecting variables leaves much to be desired because it is possible to miss the more important variables. He suggested instead (but was not the first to use) stepdown procedures wherein all variables are initially used and those that explain the smallest amount of variance are removed, one by one.

A method which has come into use in recent years is *ridge* (or damped) *regression,* first formally described by Hoerl and Kennard (1970). In this method, damping factors are added to the diagonal of the correlation matrix prior to inversion. This tends to orthogonalize interrelated variables, and by the study of the robustness of the regression coefficients with changes in the damping factors (ridge trace), one determines sets of variables that should be removed. This method also permits one to deal with the overdetermined case; i.e., one in which there are more variables than observations.

Still another method not infrequently used is *optimum regression,* due to Lamotte and Hocking (see Hocking, 1976) in which all possible two-variable, three-variable, etc., subsets are evaluated under various constraints. A computationally more economical technique, one which examines the combinations more likely to be among the optimum sets, has been described by Furnival and Wilson (1974) and implemented in the BMDP programs (Dixon, 1978). The user is then free to choose whatever combination of variables is of most interest, on the basis of the multiple correlation coefficient and the variables contributing to that coefficient.

Various methods of robust regression (i.e., methods which can deal with variables which do not meet the normality, homogeneity, etc., assumptions) have recently come to the fore. These methods are aptly summarized in Chambers (1977).

In regression analysis, particular attention must be paid to *outliers;* i.e., values that do not "fit" the scheme of the majority of the observations. Outliers may swing regression coefficients in a way that makes them lack robustness. The importance of an analysis of the residuals from the regression calculation cannot be overemphasized. The lack of this analysis is frequently the cause for the failure of regression equations to be imbued with sufficient confidence.

Present restrictions on regression analysis are mostly due to computational power. The stepwise and ridge methods can be used with up to approximately 400 variables and an essentially unlimited number of observations. The optimum regression method is presently limited by computer time to approximately 50 variables.

References

1964. Efroymson, M. A. "Multiple Regression Analysis," in Ralston, A. and Wilf, H. S. (Eds.), *Mathematical Methods for Digital Computers* 1. New York: Wiley.
1970. Hoerl, A. E. and Kennard, R. W. "Ridge Regression:
Biased Estimation for Nonorthogonal Problems," *Technometrics* 12: 55–67.
1971. Mantel, N. "Why Stepdown Procedures vs. Variables Selection," *Technometrics* 12:621–625; and *Technometrics* 13:455–457.
1974. Furnival, G. M. and Wilson, R. W., Jr., "Regressions by Leaps and Bounds," *Technometrics* 16:499–511.
1976. Jennrich, R. I. "Stepwise Discriminant Analysis," in Enslein, K., Ralston, A., and Wilf, H. S. (Eds.), *Statistical Methods for Digital Computers (Vol. 3 of Mathematical Methods for Digital Computers (Series).* New York: Wiley.
1978. Dixon, W. J. (Ed.), *BMDP Biomedical Computer Programs.* Berkeley: University of California Press.

K. ENSLEIN

REGULAR EXPRESSION

For articles on related subjects *see* AUTOMATA THEORY; FORMAL LANGUAGES; PRODUCTION; and WELL-FORMED FORMULA.

The formal description for a language acceptable by a finite automaton or for the behavior of a sequential switching circuit is known as a *regular expression.* It tells how a language is built up from atomic languages, using regular operations. The atomic languages are the empty language ϕ and the singleton sets $\{a\}$, where a is a letter of some previously specified alphabet. The regular operations are *union, catenation,* and *catenation closure.* Union is the ordinary set theoretical union; the catenation (sometimes called *concatenation*) XY of two languages X and Y consists of all words xy with $x \epsilon X$ and $y \epsilon Y$; and the catenation closure X^* of a language X consists of the empty word and of all words of the form $x_1 \cdots x_n$, where $n \geq 1$ and each $x_i \epsilon X$. For example, $(ab \cup b)^*$ is a regular expression for the language X, obtained by catenating ab and b in an arbitrary fashion; i.e., X consists of the empty word and of all words over the alphabet $\{a,b\}$ ending with b and having no subwords aa.

A formal definition of regular expressions is now given. Assume that V and $V_1 = \{\phi, \cup, *, (,)\}$ are disjoint alphabets. A word α over the alphabet $V \cup V_1$ is a regular expression over V if and only if (1) α is a letter of V or the letter ϕ, or (2) α is of one of the forms $(\beta \cup \gamma)$, $(\beta\gamma)$, or β^*, where β and γ are regular expressions over V. Each regular expression α over V denotes a language $|\alpha|$ over V according to the following conventions:

1. The language denoted by ϕ is the empty language.
2. The language denoted by $a \epsilon V$ consists of the word a.
3. For regular expressions α and β over V,

$$|(\alpha \cup \beta)| = |\alpha| \cup |\beta|, \quad |(\alpha\beta)| = |\alpha| \, |\beta|,$$
$$|\alpha^*| = |\alpha|^*.$$

Very different looking regular expressions may denote the same language; e.g., each of the regular expressions

$$(a \cup ab \cup ba)^*, \quad (ba \cup a^*ab)^*a^*, \quad a^*(ab \cup ba^*a)^*$$

denotes the same language.

The behavior of a finite automaton or a sequential switching circuit is very often better understood after a simplification of the corresponding regular expression. Especially helpful is the reduction of the star height, i.e., the maximum number of nested stars in the regular expression. A finitary axiomatization can be given to all equations among regular expressions, although rules of inference stronger than substitution are necessarily needed. Various algorithms are known for the transition from a regular expression to a finite automaton, and vice versa.

REFERENCES

1968. Ginzburg, A. *Algebraic Theory of Automata.* New York: Academic Press.
1969. Salomaa, A. *Theory of Automata.* New York: Pergamon.

A. K. SALOMAA

RELIABILITY, HARDWARE

For articles on related subjects *see* DATA SECURITY; FAULT-TOLERANT COMPUTING; REDUNDANCY; and SOFTWARE RELIABILITY.

The domain of *reliability engineering* involves considerations of all aspects of design, development, and fabrication so as to minimize the chance of equipment breakdown. Neglect of reliability considerations can prove to be very costly, from the loss of consumer acceptance of the product to the possibility of endangering human life. The success of complex missions such as space probes depends heavily on reliability engineering since failure of a single component could result in the total loss of the system.

Reliability in a qualitative sense can mean a host of different things relating to the confidence in the quality of the equipment, and is closely connected but often confused with the concepts of maintainability, availability, safety, and even security of the system. Quantitatively, reliability can be formulated mathematically as the probability that the system will perform its intended function over the stated duration of time in the specified environment for its usage.

As equipment becomes more complex, the chance of system unreliability becomes greater, since the reliability of any equipment depends on the reliability of its components. The relationship between parts reliability and the system reliability can be formulated mathematically to varying degrees of precision, depending on the scale of the modeling effort. The mathematics of reliability is based on parts-failure rate statistics and probability theoretic relationships. The mathematical theory of reliability is used to model, simulate, and predict proneness of the equipment to failure under expected operating conditions.

There have been two distinct and viable approaches taken to enhance system reliability. One is based on component technology; i.e., manufacturing capability of producing the component with the highest possible reliability, followed by parts screening, quality control, pretesting to remove early failures (infant mortality effects), etc. The second approach is based on the organization of the system itself (e.g., fault-tolerant architectures that make use of protective redundancy to mask or remove the effects of failure, and thereby provide greater overall system reliability than would be possible by the use of the same components in a simplex or nonredundant configuration).

Fault tolerance is the capability of the system to perform its functions in accordance with design specifications, even in the presence of hardware failures. If, in the event of faults, the system functions can be performed, but do not meet the design specifications with respect to the time required to complete the job or the storage capacity required for the job, then the system is said to be *partially* or *quasi fault-tolerant.* Since the number of possible hardware failures can be very large, in practice it is necessary to restrict fault tolerance to prespecified classes of faults from which the system is designed to recover.

Faults may be classified as *transient* or *permanent, deterministic* or *indeterminate, local* or *catastrophic.* The first category refers to the duration of the fault, the second to its effect on the values of the system design parameters, and the third to the propagation of the fault to its neighboring elements.

Fault tolerance is provided by the application of protective redundancy, or the use of more resources so as to upgrade system reliability. These resources may consist of more hardware, software, or time, or a combination of all three. Extra time is required to retransmit messages or to reexecute programs, extra software is required to perform diagnosis on the hardware, and extra hardware is required to provide replication of units.

Hardware redundancy may be of the *fault-masking* or *self-repair* types, or a hybrid of these two. In fault masking, redundancy is of a static nature; faults are masked instantly and the operations of fault detection, location, and correction are indistinguishable. In self-repair, redundancy is used dynamically; faults are selectively masked and are detected, located, and subsequently corrected by the replacement of the failed unit by an unfailed replica. Examples of the former are triple modular redundancy (TMR) and quadding (see below), and (of the latter) standby-replacement (SR) systems and reconfigurable systems. Schemes using a combination of these two basic approaches are called *hybrid* or *adaptive* redundancy.

Some Fundamental Principles. A fundamental principle of reliability is that it must be not only inherent but also a function of how the component is used. Another important principle is that, to achieve reliability by means of protective redundancy, the redundancy must be applied to the lowest level of component complexity in the system in order to maximize gain in reliability. This is the idealized state; in practice, tradeoffs due to overhead are required in utilizing redundancy techniques (e.g., providing *voters* in TMR systems and detection-switching requirements in standby systems). The application of the mathematical theory of reliability in modeling such systems provides quantitative design guidelines that make such tradeoffs and optimizations possible and practicable.

In addition to the foregoing first and second principles of fault tolerance, a third principle is that a system may be made arbitrarily reliable, provided the degree of redundancy is made high enough (i.e., a sufficiently large number of replicas are provided). Again, this principle holds only in an idealized situation; in practice, since the probability of detecting a failure and correctly switching over to a spare is less than unity, this parameter, called *coverage*, limits the advantages postulated by the third principle.

A fourth principle concerns the problem of requiring the checking elements (those elements that are used for the diagnosis of the rest of the system and the subsequent reconfiguration of the system units) also to be checkable. This is the problem of "checking the checker." Thus, the fourth principle states that any system utilizing protective redundancy will have major and minor "hard cores" (i.e., unprotected system elements), and that these cannot

be totally eliminated from the system design; however, they may be made arbitrarily small by judicious use of a mixture of different, protective redundancy techniques.

Mathematical Theory of Reliability. Some relationships among reliability parameters and the underlying probability theoretic relationships are as follows: If a fixed large number N_o of identical items is being tested, of which N_s is the number of items surviving after time t and N_f is the number of items that failed during time t, then $N_o = N_s + N_f$ for all t. Now, for a sufficiently large N_o, the reliability $R(t)$ of an item is N_s/N_o. The failure rate $\lambda(t)$, which is defined to be the rate at which the population changes at time t, can be shown to be given by

$$\lambda(t) = -\frac{1}{R(t)}\frac{dR(t)}{dt}, \tag{1}$$

so that

$$R(t) = \exp\left(-\int_0^t \lambda(\tau)d\tau\right) \tag{2}$$

The reliability function $R(t)$ is often called the *survival probability function*, since it measures the probability that failure of an item does not occur during the time interval $[0,t]$.

Failure Rate. Statistical data on equipment failure yields a characteristic "bathtub" curve, as shown in Fig. 1. When the equipment is first put into service, inherently weak components fail early; this stage is also called "infant mortality." Subsequently, the failure rate stabilizes quickly to a relatively constant value; this period is called the "useful life period." After much usage, failure rate begins to increase rapidly as a result of deterioration and wear.

Exponential Failure Law. In general, the failure law of a component is the probability distribution effective from the moment at which a component enters

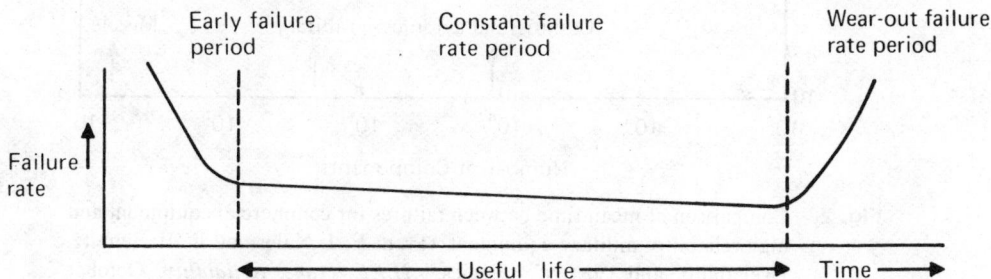

Fig. 1. Bathtub curve of failure rate.

service up to the moment of its failure. In practice the most commonly used failure law is the exponential law, which applies when a component is subject only to failures that occur at random intervals and the average number of failures is the same for equal time periods. These constraints are valid for a component that is no longer subject to infant mortality failures and whose failure rate is a constant within the "useful life" span. Thus, for operating periods within the useful life, the component reliability over a period of time t can be expressed as $R(t) = e^{\lambda t}$, where λ (usually expressed in failures per hour or per million hours) is the constant failure rate of the device. A characteristic of the exponential failure law is that the reliability of the device within the useful life period is the same for operating times of equal duration.

From the definition of $R(t)$ it follows that the mean time between failures (MTBF) or the mean time to first failure (MTTF), usually expressed in hours (Fig. 2), are given by $\int_0^\infty R(t)\,dt$; i.e., it is the area underneath the reliability curve $R(t)$ plotted versus t. This result is true for any failure distribution. For the specific case of the exponential failure law, the MTBF, m, is equal to $1/\lambda$. Further, when the product λt is small, the equation for $R(t)$ may be approximated by $R(t) \approx 1 - \lambda t$. Thus, if $\lambda t = 0.01$, $R(t) = e^{-0.01} = 0.99.$, or 99.0%. The product λt is often referred to as the "normalized" time, since $\lambda t = t/m$; i.e., the mission time t is normalized with respect to the MTBF.

Series Reliability. If a system is composed of elements in such a way that the failure of any one element causes a failure of the system, then these elements are considered to be functionally in series. For the system to survive, each element must survive. The probability of survival for the system cannot be better than the element with the lowest probability of survival; e.g., a chain is no better than its weakest link. When these series elements are independent of each other, then, by the probability multiplication law, the system survival probability is the product of the individual survival probabilities of the elements. This is known as the product rule:

$$R_{\text{system}} = \prod_{i=1}^{n} R_i,$$

where R_i is the reliability of the ith element of an n-element system (Fig. 3).

Parallel Reliability. Parallel reliability is an illustration of protective redundancy. The system is com-

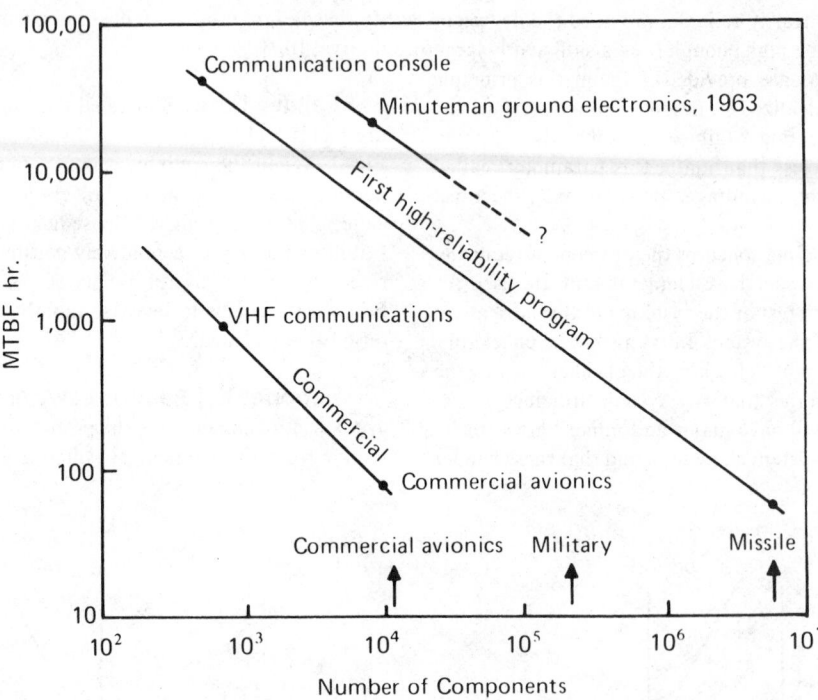

Fig. 2. Comparison of mean time between failures for commercial equipment and high-reliability military equipment. (From E. J. Nalos and R. B. Schultz, "Reliability and Cost of Avionics," *IEEE Trans. Reliability*, October 1965. By permission.)

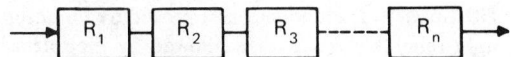

Fig. 3. System composed of a series of elements.

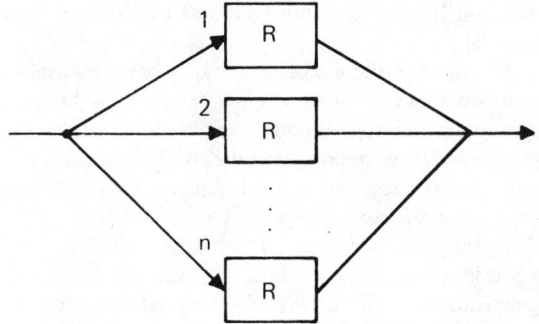

Fig. 4. System composed of elements in parallel

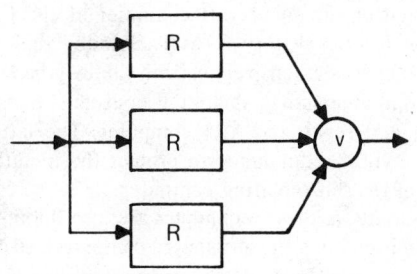

Fig. 5. Triple modular redundancy.

posed of functionally parallel elements in such a way that if one of the elements fails the parallel unit will continue to do the system function. See Fig. 4. The system reliability, under the assumption of independence of failure of the elements, is expressed by

$$R_{\text{system}} = 1 - (1 - R)^n,$$

which is the probability that not all n elements have failed. The term $(1 - R)$, known as the unreliability of a unit, is the probability that a unit will fail. The term $(1 - R)^n$ by the product rule is the probability that all n units will fail and one minus that is the probability that not all units will have failed. An example of parallel reliability is given by electronic diodes in parallel; if one diode open-circuits, the other will still provide the function.

Triple Modular Redundancy (TMR). TMR is also known as the *multiple-line voting* system. One of the earliest and most influential schemes was developed by John von Neumann. The simplex unit is triplicated and each of the three independent units feeds into a ma-

jority voter, which outputs the majority signal. The system fails if more than one unit fails, in which case the failed units outvote the good one. This scheme is generalized to N-modular redundancy (NMR) where N is any odd number of units. Various schemes of protecting the voter are available, and also various other variants of the basic TMR strategy have been developed. The TMR system reliability is expressed as

$$R_{\text{system}} = [R^3 + 3R^2(1 - R)]R_v,$$

which is the product of the reliability R_v (the voter reliability) and the reliability of the idealized TMR system. The idealized TMR system reliability is the sum of the probabilities of two events: (1) that all three units survive, R^3; and (2) that any two units survive so that one unit fails, $3R^2(1 - R)$.

Quadded Redundancy. Quadding is a method of component redundancy applicable to circuits with alternating AND and OR gates. It is similar in concept to TMR with the major difference being that the voting or restoration or fault-masking functions are distributed into the network and are not separable as in TMR. In general, the quadding procedure requires that each logic gate be quadruplicated and that each of the gates in a quad stage will have twice as many inputs as the nonredundant gate replaced. The outputs of a stage are interconnected to the inputs of the succeeding stage by a connection pattern in such a way that the effects of errors in earlier stages get subsequently "restored" in the latter stages; i.e., the originally intended "good" signal is restored.

Standby Replacement Redundancy. In standby replacement redundancy (Fig. 6), only one unit is operational at a time, unlike TMR. When the active unit fails, this event is detected by additional circuitry, and a spare unit from a reserve of spares is switched in as a replacement of the failed unit, thereby restoring the

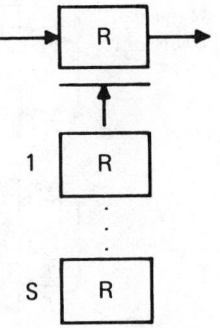

Fig. 6. Standby replacement redundancy.

system to its operational state. The reliability of this system is expressed as

$$R_{\text{system}} = 1 - (1 - R)^{S+1},$$

which is the probability that not all units have failed.

Hybrid Redundancy. Hybrid redundancy is a synthesis of TMR and standby replacement redundancy (see Fig. 7). It consists of a TMR system (or, in general, an NMR system) with a bank of spares so that when one of the TMR units fail, it is replaced by a spare unit. Failure detection is achieved by means of the disagreement detectors, which compare the individual outputs of each of the triple modular redundancy units with the system output. If there is a difference, the disagreement detector signals the switching network to replace the failed unit by a spare unit. When all spares are utilized, the hybrid redundancy system reduces to a TMR system. Variations of hybrid or adaptive redundancy schemes are possible. The system reliability in its simplest terms may be expressed as

$$R_{\text{system}} = 1 - [(1 - R^{S+3} + (S + 3)(1 - R)^{S+2} \cdot R],$$

which is the probability that not all $S + 3$ units fail and that not any $S + 2$ units fail with one not failing.

Summary. Redundancy as a procedure for designing more reliable systems than allowed by the intrinsic reliability of the constituent components is as old as the discipline of engineering itself. In fact, even in the evolutionary processes of life, Nature makes abundant use of it (e.g., in the human body there are two kidneys, two lungs, etc.).

Examples of the use of redundancy in ancient times are provided in the construction of temples and bridges, where more than the absolutely required number of pillars is provided to support structure; thus, should one pillar sustain damage, the remaining pillars would still be able to share successfully the load.

In the computer age, all the basic techniques described here have been applied, with varying degrees of sophistication, to the design of ultrareliable computing systems. TMR has been successfully applied in designing the guidance and control computer of the SATURN V launch vehicle. Quadding is utilized to a great extent in the design of the spacecraft computer of the Orbiting Astronomic Observatory (OAO). Standby replacement redundancy was extensively used in the Raytheon RAYDAC computer and in the Jet Propulsion Laboratory's self-test and repair (STAR) computer. The latter also utilized hybrid redundancy to protect the monitor subsystem of the self-repairing computer.

In addition, these techniques are also finding application in protecting the automated computerized controls

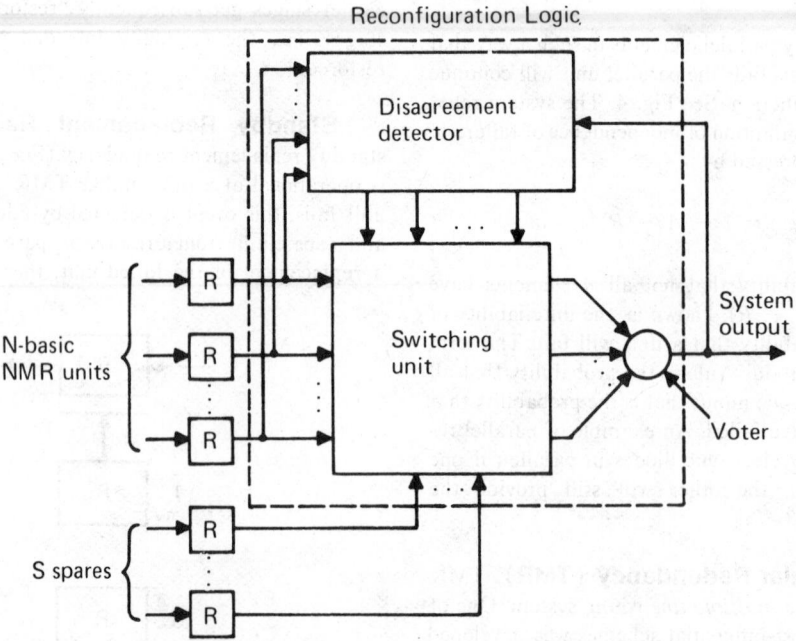

Fig. 7. Hybrid redundancy.

of modern high-speed transit systems and in other applications where the cost of using redundancy is justifiable because it minimizes danger to human life, or increases the continuous availability of services that, if interrupted by failure and subsequent repair, would cause severe consumer dissatisfaction. An example of the latter is the present-day automated telephone switching system. In an expanding society where products become more sophisticated and projects proliferate, the scope of reliability engineering, protective redundancy and fault-tolerant computing will continue to grow.

REFERENCES

1956. von Neumann, J. "Probabilistic Logics and the Synthesis of Reliability Organisms from Unreliable Components," in *Automata Studies*. Princeton, NJ: Princeton University, pp. 43–98.

1961. Bazovsky, I. *Reliability Theory and Practice*. Englewood Cliffs, NJ: Prentice-Hall.

1962. Lloyd, D. K. and Lipow, M. *Reliability, Management Methods, and Mathematics*. Englewood Cliffs, NJ: Prentice-Hall.

1971. IEEE. *Transactions on Computers: Special Issue on Fault-Tolerant Computing* C-20, *No. 11* (November). *Digest of the IEEE Annual Symposium on Fault Tolerance.*

F. P. MATHUR

RELOCATION. *See* LOADER.

REMOTE JOB ENTRY

For articles on related subjects *see* COMMUNICATIONS AND COMPUTERS; DATA COMMUNICATIONS; INPUT-OUTPUT DEVICES; PROCESSING MODES; and TELEPROCESSING SYSTEMS.

Remote job entry (RJE) refers to the submission of jobs to a central computer from a location at least several hundred feet and sometimes many miles distant from the computer. Job entry becomes "remote" when the length limits of cable connections between input/output devices are exceeded, in which case the telephone or another common-carrier communications link must be used to bridge the gap, as shown in Fig. 1.

Remote job entry is usually combined with so-called "remote job receipt," since a remote terminal can enter the job on the computer and can also receive output results returned by the computer. Often the output device speed at the remote terminal is quite slow, so that only jobs with very small amounts of output (a few lines in the case of typewriter-speed devices) can or should be received remotely. In other cases, larger amounts of output must or should be printed at the central computer site, and then sent to the remote user via mail or courier.

Sometimes the elements of a job received from a remote site are assembled by referring to data and programs that are stored in permanent files at the central site. The assembly of job segments from a remote site is also considered to be remote job entry, even though all the substance of the job originates at the central site and only the output ever leaves it. In all cases of RJE, some output is sent back to the remote user when the job arrives. This consists at least of confirmation that the remotely submitted and assembled job is ready for processing, or is being executed, at the central site.

A typical remote job entry system is shown in Fig. 2.

C. L. MEEK

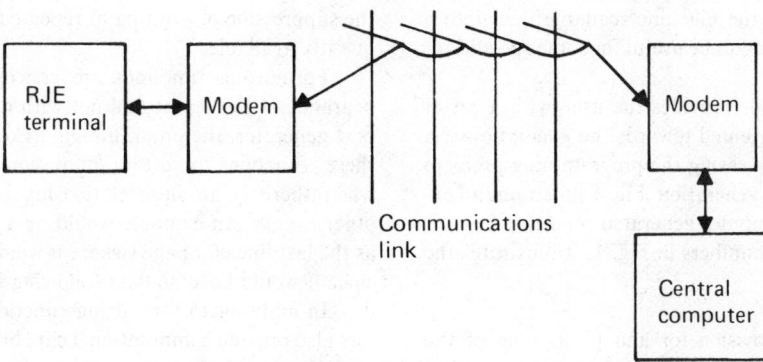

Fig. 1.   Connections for remote job entry to a computer through a communications link.

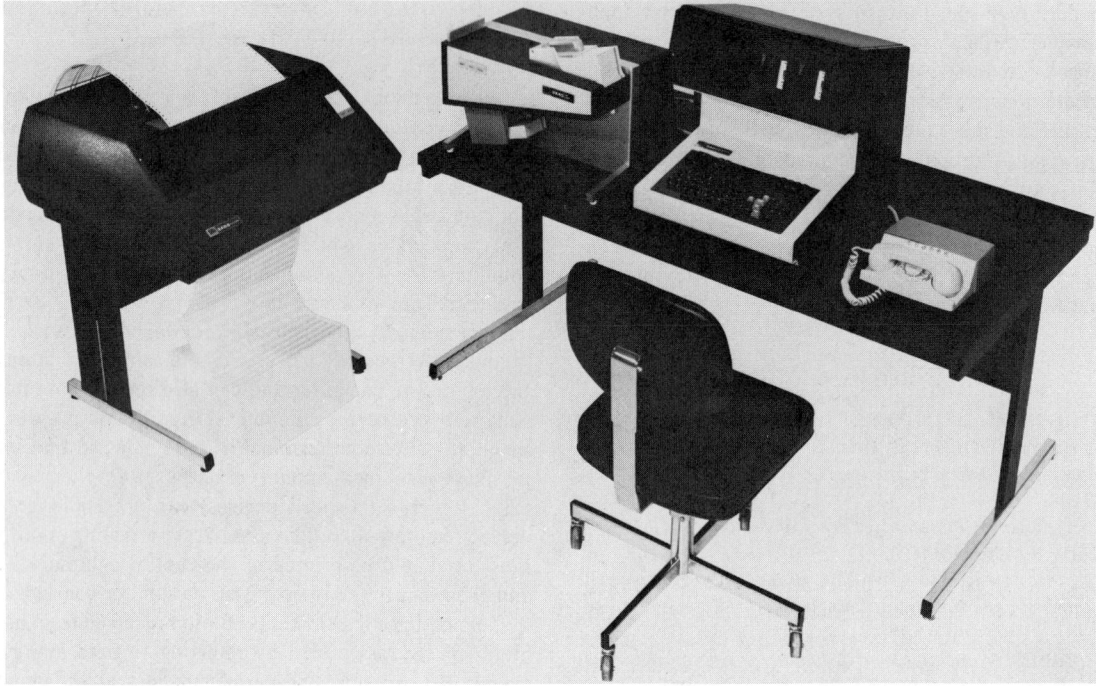

Fig. 2. This Sycor remote job entry system includes an intelligent terminal (right), a card reader (center), and a line printer (left).

REPORT GENERATORS

For articles on related subjects *see* ADMINISTRATIVE APPLICATIONS; EXCEPTION REPORTING; MANAGEMENT INFORMATION SYSTEMS; and NONPROCEDURAL LANGUAGES.

Nearly all administrative data processing applications involve the storing of data on disk or tape files. Such data is in machine-readable form and not in a form that is understandable by people. A *report generator* is a program which converts the machine readable data into a printed report organized to be useful for some specific administrative purpose.

A report generator provides the user with a set of functions which are oriented towards the generation of a report, thereby greatly easing the programming problem associated with report generation. Fig. 1 illustrates an example of a typical computer generated report.

Referring to the numbers in Fig. 1, it illustrates the following features.

1. Automatic provision for and positioning of the current date.
2. Automatic centering of the title.
3. Automatic page numbering.
4. Page subtitles with appropriate line spacing.
5. Column heading borders to accommodate a varying number of column heading lines.
6. Column headings centered over the data.
7. Subtitles with spacing.
8. Detail data with appropriate formatting.
9. The sorting of data into order by a field or fields.

These are typical of the formatting features provided by report generators. Other features, such as automatic folding of data when the line is too long to fit on the page or the suppression of printing of repeated data, are also frequently available.

Formatting functions are concerned with the appearance of the report and not with data. Without a report generator, the programming associated with each of these functions is often quite complex—particularly when there is an interrelationship between them and other events. An example would be a subtitle appearing as the last line of a page (where it would be inappropriate since it would have no data following it).

In addition to formatting functions, report generators also provide computational capabilities which use the stored data to calculate such items as the total, count, maximum value, minimum value, or average of a column of data. Here too, without the report generator, the cod-

(1) 03/29/79   (2) PURCHASE ORDER STATUS REPORT BY PURCHASE ORDER   (3) PAGE 1

(4) ABC COMPANY   (5)

```
      LINE  VENDOR NO.  BUYER / STATUS    PART ORD   (6) UM    UNIT PRICE    QTY ORD    QTY RCVD   NEED DATE
                                                         ORD

(7) P.O. 00230 ◄ (9)

      002   10000   245          DESK CHAIR        EA      45.0000      40          40    02/21/79
      P.O. 00500

(8) 001   10000   147          OAK DESK          EA     483.3300       3           3    02/23/79
      002   10000   147    C     FILE CABINETS     EA     100.0000      25          25    02/20/79
      003   10000   147          WASTE BASKET      EA      10.0000     100               02/21/79
      004   10000   147    C     CHAIR-FOLDING     EA      16.0000       4           4    01/22/79
      005   10000   147          THUMBTACK PADS    DZ       1.0000     100               03/06/79
      006   10000   147    C     BINDER-BLUE       DZ       8.0000     500         500    02/21/79
      P.O. 00700

      001   10100   145    C     TRASH CANS        EA       6.0000     100         100    01/01/79
      002   10100   145    C     LIGHT BULBS       DZ      50.0000      50          50    01/01/79
      003   10100   145    C     ASH TRAYS         DZ      20.0000      40          40    01/01/79
      004   10100   145    C     DATE BOOK         EA      20.0000       1           1    01/01/79
      005   10100   145    C     DESK LAMP         EA      20.0000      25          25    01/02/79
      P.O. 00904

      001   10100   147          FILE FOLDERS      DZ      60.0000       4           1    01/01/79
      002   10100   147    C     PAPER PUNCH       EA      20.0000       5           5    01/01/79
      003   10100   147          BALL POINT PENS   DZ       2.0000     100         100    02/14/79
      P.O. 00912

      001   10000   245          CARDBD BOXES      DZ       2.0000     250               01/31/79
      002   10000   245    C     DESK CALENDAR     EA      20.0000       4           4    01/28/79
```

Fig. 1. Example of a Report.

ing can be extensive depending on the type of summary, number of summaries, and nesting of summaries. Summaries are said to be nested when one exists as part of another one over a broader range of influence. For example, a *group* total may be part of a *department* total, which itself may be part of a *division* total.

For both formatting and computational functions, the desired function is usually simple to identify but the coding often presents problems using conventional programming languages. At a minimum, the coding is repetitive and tedious with the ever-present possibility of error; at worst, the coding can be quite complex. Report generators remove much of the problem by having most functions preprogrammed. The user of the report generator merely has to identify the functions required by providing simple parameters. The report generator will then generate the report according to the specifications provided.

To achieve a transformation from machine data to printed output, it is necessary that the report generator be told what the data looks like on the file, what data is to be transformed, and what the report is to look like. The data on the file is described by means of a file definition.

This is sometimes a separate step performed prior to the actual generation of the report. At other times, this information is provided directly to the report generator along with the report specifications. The data to be selected is most often merely a list of field names identifying certain fields previously specified in the file definition. Finally, the report format is provided by supplying certain parameters. While the functions of file definition, report content, and report format are all essential, for ease of specification and convenience, they are often merged together. An example of typical specifications is illustrated in Fig. 2.

Report generators are typically nonprocedural. This means that the user states "what" is wanted and not how to do it. The report generator acts on "what" is specified and produces the result.

Input to report generators may be fixed form or free form. Fig. 2 is an example of a typical fixed form input, and Fig. 3 is an example of typical free form input. Both of these specifications generate the report shown in Fig. 1.

Just transforming the data as explained above is generally sufficient for generating a report in a particular

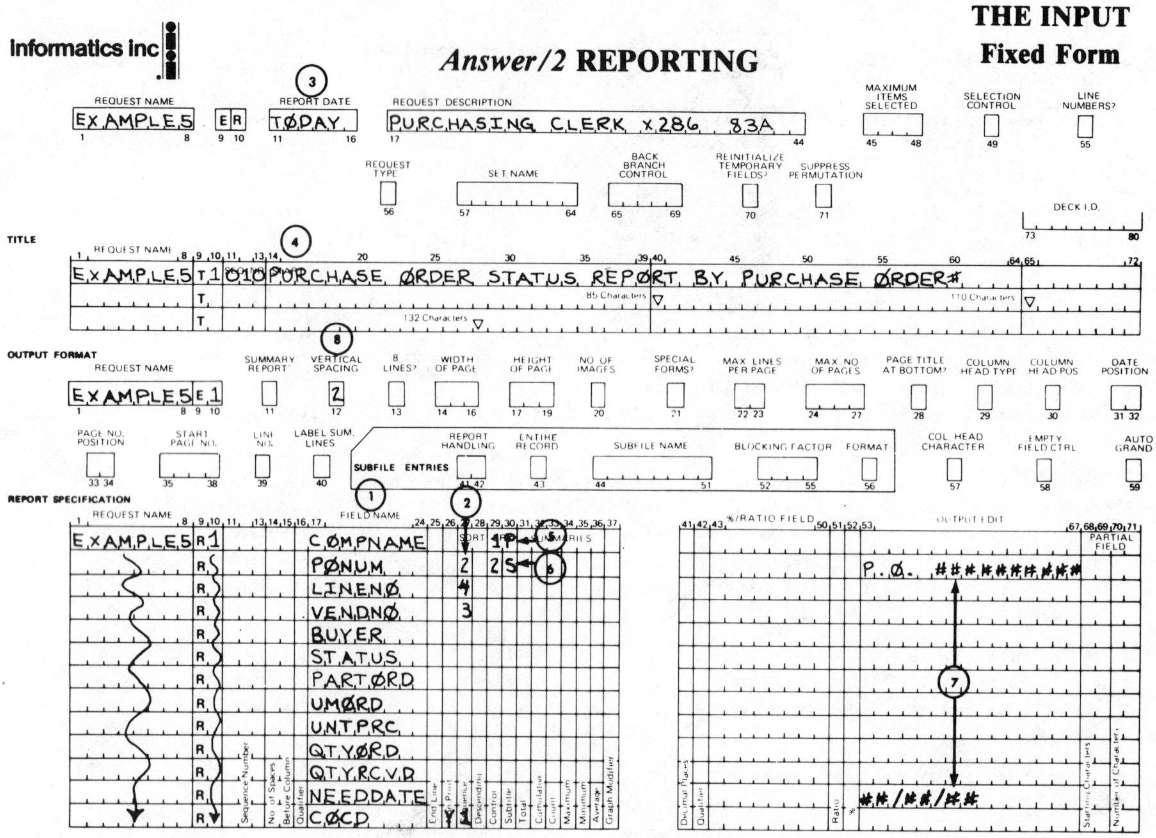

Explanation   (Circled numbers refer to this illustration: numbers in squares refer to items identified in Figure 1.)

File Definition   With *Answer/2* the file structure is predefined to the system.

Report Content   The list of field names ① identifies the content, sorted by order identified ②.

Report Format

a)   The page number ③ is automatically provided.

b)   Column headings ⑤ are provided with the file definition.

c)   ③ Specifies the report date ①.

d)   ④ Provides the title ②.

e)   ⑤ P specifies that a new page is to be generated when COMPNAME changes and an appropriate subtitle generated ④.

f)   ⑥ S specifies a subtitle ⑦ is to be generated when PONUM changes.

g)   ⑦ Special editing formats.

h)   ⑧ Specifies double spacing.

Fig. 2.   Typical fixed form input.

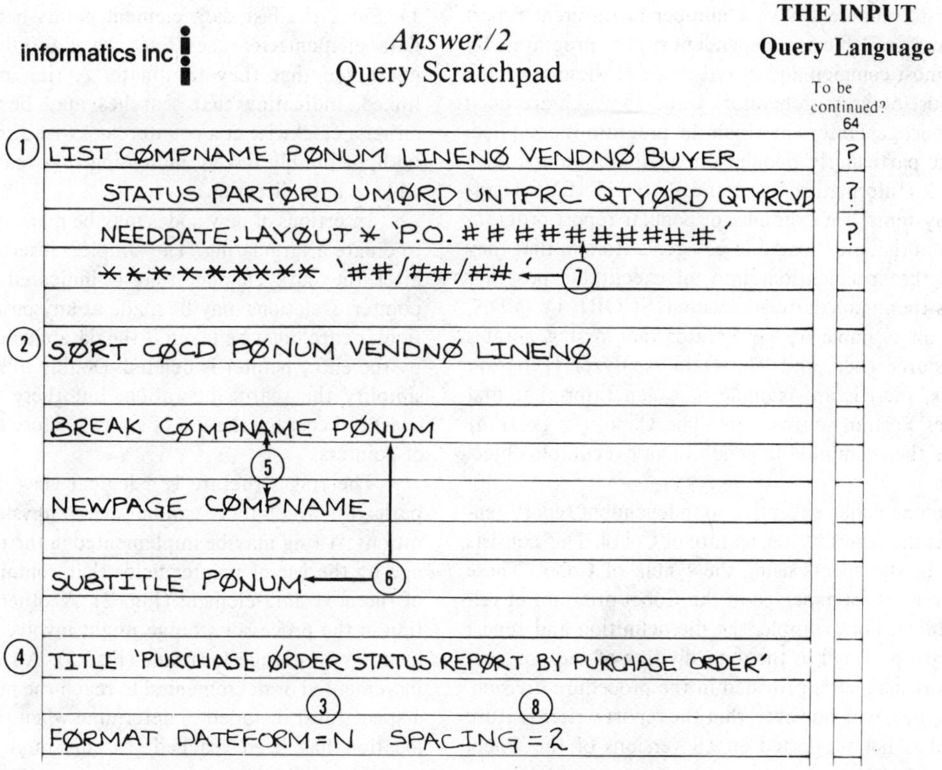

informatics inc

Answer/2
Query Scratchpad

THE INPUT
Query Language

To be
continued?
64

① LIST CØMPNAME PØNUM LINENØ VENDNØ BUYER   ?

STATUS PARTØRD UMØRD UNTPRC QTYØRD QTYRCVD   ?

NEEDDATE, LAYØUT * `P.O. ## ## ## ## ## ##´   ?

* * * * * * * * * `## /## /## ´ ← ⑦

② SØRT CØCD PØNUM VENDNØ LINENØ

BREAK CØMPNAME PØNUM

⑤

NEWPAGE CØMPNAME

SUBTITLE PØNUM ← ⑥

④ TITLE `PURCHASE ØRDER STATUS REPØRT BY PURCHASE ORDER´

③   ⑧

FØRMAT DATEFORM = N   SPACING = 2

Explanation   (Circled numbers refer to this illustration: numbers in squares refer to items identified in Figure 1. The circled numbers identify the same specifications as identified in Figure 2.)

File Definition   With *Answer/2* the file structure is predefined to the system.

Report Content   The list of field names ① identifies the content, sorted by order identified ②.

Report Format

   a) The page number ③ is automatically provided.

   b) Column headings ⑤ are provided with the file definition.

   c) ③ Specifies the report date ①.

   d) ④ Provides the title ②.

   e) ⑤ NEWPAGE COMPNAME specifies that a new page is to be generated when COMPNAME changes and an appropriate subtitle generated ④.

   f) ⑥ Specifies a subtitle ⑦ is to be generated when PONUM changes.

   g) ⑦ Special editing formats.

   h) ⑧ Specifies double spacing.

Fig. 3.   Typical free form input.

format, but is often inadequate for the handling of the data required by modern business practices. As a result, most report generators also contain a procedural capability which allows the user to write elementary programs in a very high-level language. This language allows the creation of computational and logical expressions, enabling each user to modify the data or perform complex selection based on criteria unique to the business environment, prior to displaying the data. In this respect, the report generator is like a procedural language.

Most computers have a number of different report generators available as independent system programs. By far the most common and heavily used of these are RPG (for report program generator) I and II which are fixed form report generators in which the program is compiled. They are particularly popular on small computers. AN-SWER/2 (Informatics, Inc.) and EASYTRIEVE (Pansophic Systems) are examples of popular report program generators that are "load and go" generators in that they compile the specifications into an executable program which is then immediately executed. SCORE IV (SDA, Inc.) is an example of a generator that first generates Cobol source code, and The Data Analyzer (Program Products, Inc.) is an example of a generator that first generates Fortran source code. The Cobol (or Fortran) source is then compiled to generate an executable object program.

The one major exception to independent report generators is the report writer feature of Cobol. This consists of a set of statements using the syntax of Cobol. These statements are interspersed in the Cobol program at relevant points. For example, the file definition and report format are provided in the data division of the program and report content is provided in the procedure division. It should be noted, however, that the report writer feature of Cobol is not supported on all versions of the Cobol compiler.

REFERENCES

1971. Murray, Jerome T. *Programming in RPG II: IBM System/3.* New York: McGraw Hill.
1974. *American National Standard Programming Language COBOL.* New Jersey: American National Standards Institute, Inc.
Comprehensive descriptions of the various report writers will be found in the following publications. All are updated on a continuing basis.
Auerbach Computer Technology Reports—System Software. Pennsauken, NJ: Auerbach.
Datapro 70 **3**. Delran, NJ: Datapro Research Corp.
ICP Software Directory, Volume 1, Data Processing Management. Indianapolis: International Computer Programs, Inc.

F. BRADDOCK

RESTART. *See* CHECKPOINT AND RESTART.

RING

For articles on related subjects *see* DATA STRUCTURES; LISTS AND LIST PROCESSING; and POINTER.

A ring or *circular list* is a cyclic arrangement of data elements, usually including a specified entry pointer (Fig.

1). Since the last data element points back to the first data element, searches must be carefully designed to guarantee that they terminate. A ring may be singly linked, indicating that searches may be performed in either a clockwise or a counterclockwise direction, but not both; or doubly linked, indicating that searches are possible in both directions.

Insertions of new nodes may be made at any position to create a larger ring. The simplest insertion position is after the data element that is indicated by the entry pointer. Deletions may be made at any position, but particular care must be taken if the data element referenced by the entry pointer is deleted. Doubly linked rings may simplify the search operation, but there is substantial overhead cost for the use of space to store the second set of pointers.

The ring structure is a logical view of data access paths, for which there can be several physical implementations. A ring may be implemented in the processor storage by the use of pointer fields that contain the address of the next data element (Fig. 2). Another implementation in the processor storage might involve sequential allocation of storage locations (Fig. 3). An index may be incremented or decremented to reach the next node, with a special test included to determine when the first or last location has been reached. In this implementation, it would be difficult to insert or delete a node, since a potentially large portion of the data elements would have to be shifted. Finally, the ring structure could be imple-

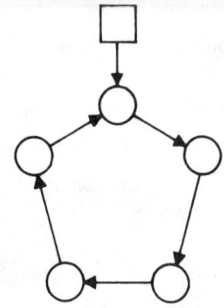

Fig. 1. A ring with entry pointer.

	Info	Link
100	S	103
101	N	105
102	I	101
103	R	102
104		
105	G	100

103

Entry

Fig. 2. A ring that stores "RINGS."

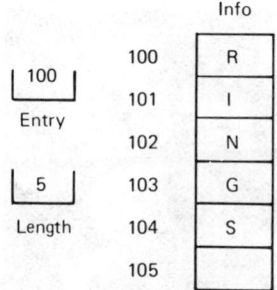

Fig. 3. Another ring that stores "RINGS."

mented on a direct-access device, with pointers to region numbers containing the next data element.

The greatest use of rings is in connection with other data structures. Ring structures appear in the implementation of lists, strings, and trees. Certain database management systems utilize a ring structure for the fields of a record and use indices to enter the ring at any position for the start of a search. Another application example might be that of putting into a ring all records of the employees in each corporate division. Then, if any employee's record were to be accessed, it would be a simple matter to retrieve all co-workers by traversing the ring once.

REFERENCE

1968. Knuth, Donald. *The Art of Computer Programming* **1**, *Fundamental Algorithms*. Reading, MA: Addison-Wesley.

B. SHNEIDERMAN

ROBOTICS

For articles on related subjects *see* ARTIFICIAL INTELLIGENCE; AUTOMATION; and COMPUTER-AIDED, DESIGN.

Robotics is the science of robot design and use. The word "robot" was popularized by Karel Capek's 1920 play, R.U.R. (Rossum's Universal Robots). It comes from the Czeck word *robota* meaning "unpleasant or difficult work."

In popular parlance, a robot is a machine that acts like, and may look somewhat like, a human being. But in computer science, a robot is usually a manipulator (i.e., a machine analogous to the human arm and hand that can hold or pick up or move some physical object) and its associated computer control system. Walking machines and teleoperators (remote control manipulators) are also sometimes included in the field of robotics.

In the historical development of the field, it is useful to distinguish between the development of industrial ro-

bots for practical, economically justifiable uses and research robots. The first practical industrial robot was used by George Devol in the 1960s to remove parts from a die casting machine. About 10,000 industrial robots were in service by 1980, and the industry is growing at about 30% per year. These robots are, for example, becoming increasingly common on automobile assembly lines. Most industrial robots use computer control systems to step their mechanical manipulators through a series of fixed positions. By contrast, research robots usually have much more elaborate computer control systems capable of recognizing objects detected by sensors, planning actions, and correcting errors. The most intelligent research robots can recognize objects they see or touch (provided the objects are sufficiently distinctive), then grasp the objects and perform some task such as assembly of a model car. Recently, there has been some blending of the two historic lines, as the first sensor-based industrial robots went into service in the late 1970s.

Important research areas in robotics are listed below.

Mechanical Design. Manipulators should be accurate and reliable, and have high strength to weight ratios for maximum speed.

Servo Controls. These controls include the motors and controls for each joint of the manipulator. Optimal servo control of a multi-jointed manipulator is a difficult research problem because the load on each joint changes continuously; some advanced manipulators use a separate microcomputer for each joint.

Sensor Design. Vision, touch, and force are the most common sensor types.

Object Recognition. Object recognition is accomplished by computer processing, usually by dedicated computers, of sensory data to identify specific objects (a form of pattern recognition).

Automatic Planning. The computer generates a series of elementary manipulator commands to carry out some task.

Error Recovery. Automatic revision of plans corrects some unexpected problem, such as a dropped object.

Problem Solving. The computer generates plans by artificial intelligence methods based on specialized knowledge of some domain; for example, a robot which "knows" about welding might plan how to support parts while welding them.

Except for mechanical design and sensor design, the above fields are active research areas in computer science.

A number of computer languages have been developed for control of robots such as VAL (a trademark for Vicarm Arm Language) by Unimation, Inc., AL (Assembly Language) at Stanford University, ML (Manipulator Language) by IBM, and ROBOTLAN by Kawasaki Heavy Industries.

Fig. 1. The UNIMATE® industrial robot manufactured by Unimation, Inc. (Photo courtesy of Unimation.)

In the future, we can expect:

1. Research in computer science to improve the intelligence, capability, dexterity, and flexibility of robots.
2. Autonomous and semi-autonomous robots to be used for work in the ocean and in space.
3. Low cost vision and touch sensors to become commonplace during the 1980s.
4. The cost of robots to decline because of greater production volume and the decreasing cost of computers, particularly microcomputers.
5. The number of economical applications for robots to increase rapidly due to the above improvements. (For example, robotic toys are beginning to appear on the market.)

The principal technical journals which cover robots are *Robotics Today*, published by the Society of Manufacturing Engineers; *Industrial Robot* by IFS, Ltd. of Bedford, England; and *Robotics Age* by Robotics Publishing Corp. of California. Robotics articles also appear in the various journals of the IEEE, ACM, and the Society of Manufacturing Engineers.

REFERENCES

1973. Young, John E. *Robotics*. London: Butterworths.
1976. Raphael, B. *The Thinking Computer-Mind Inside Matter*. San Francisco: W. H. Freeman & Co.
1977. Abraham, R. J. S. et al. *State-of-the-art in Adaptable-Programmable Assembly Systems*. Pittsburgh, PA: Westinghouse R&D Center.
1979. Tanner, W. R. (Ed.). *Industrial Robots*, Vols. **I** and **II**. Dearborn, MI: Society of Manufacturing Engineers.
1979. Dodd, G. G. and Rossol, L. (Eds.). *Computer Vision and Sensor-Based Robots*. New York: Plenum Press.

J. K. DIXON AND J. R. SLAGLE

ROM. *See* READ-ONLY MEMORY.

ROUNDOFF ERROR

For articles on related subjects *see* ERRORS; INTERVAL ARITHMETIC; and NUMERICAL ANALYSIS.

Computers typically deal with numbers of fixed length (i.e., with a fixed number of digits or bits) when performing arithmetic (although there are exceptions to this). For example, when multiplying two numbers, each of which has n bits, the resulting $2n$ bit product is usually *rounded* (or, on some few computers, truncated) to n bits. The error that results from this is called *roundoff error*, or sometimes *rounding error*. With pencil and paper calculations, such roundoff is seldom significant, but with the thousands or even millions of arithmetic operations performed in computer calculations, the effects of roundoff can be considerable and sometimes disastrous. In addition, even a single roundoff error can be disastrous in large problems solved on a computer (see below for an example of this).

Roundoff also occurs when the data for a calculation, which may be known exactly, must be rounded to n bits when read into and stored in the computer.

As examples of how large a single roundoff error can be we consider two cases, both assuming the use of fixed-point arithmetic on a computer using 32-bit numbers with binary point at the left end as shown in Fig. 1.

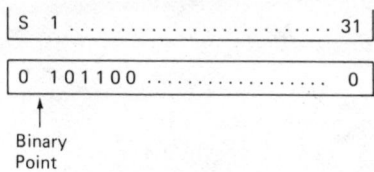

Fig. 1. The 31-bit number shown with positive sign (0) has the value $0.1011 = 11/16$.

Case 1. *Multiplication of two 31-bit numbers rounded to a 31-bit product.* Rounding to a 31-bit product means that the thirty-second bit of the product is examined. If it is 0 (i.e., bits 32-62 represent less than $\frac{1}{2} \times 2^{-31}$), then nothing is done; if it is 1 (i.e., bits 32-62 represent greater than or equal to $\frac{1}{2} \times 2^{-31}$), then 1 is added into bit position 31 of the product. The magnitude of the error in the product is therefore no greater than

$$\frac{1}{2} \times 2^{-31} = 2^{-32}.$$

Case 2. An exact datum is read into the computer and rounded to 31 bits. If the rounding is done as above, by looking at the thirty-second bit, then again the magnitude of the error is no greater than 2^{-32}.

The analysis of roundoff error in a long calculation is usually very difficult. Sometimes, by considering the worst possible error magnitude in each roundoff, a bound on the worst error in the result can be obtained, but this bound may be very conservative (i.e., much larger than the actual error). For example, suppose each of N numbers read into the computer, as in Case 2 above, are added. The quantity $N \cdot 2^{-32}$ is then a bound on the error in the sum, but this bound will occur only if all numbers have the maximum possible roundoff error *with the same sign.* Generally, individual roundoff errors will be less than the maximum possible and will have both positive and negative values so that there will be some cancellation of errors when they are added. Probabilistic analysis shows that, for this addition example, the *probable error*, defined as the value exceeded by the actual roundoff error one-half of the time, is given approximately by $0.2 \times \sqrt{N} \times 2^{-32}$. The *square root rule* (i.e., replacing the number of operations N by $\sqrt{N}$) is often used as a rule of thumb in making probable error estimates from maximum error bounds.

As an example of the disastrous effects that roundoff error can have, we consider the case of finding the zeros of the polynomial

$$(x - 1)(x - 2)(x - 3) \cdots (x - 20),$$

where the computer is given the coefficients A_0 to A_{19} in

$$x^{20} + A_{19}x^{19} + A_{18}x^{18} + \cdots + A_2x^2 + A_1x + A_0.$$

It is easily calculated that $A_{19} = -210$. Now suppose that the coefficients $A_0, A_1, \ldots A_{18}$ are all stored exactly in the computer, but that, because of a roundoff error, A_{19} is stored as $-210 - 2^{-23}$, noting that 2^{-23} is approximately one ten-millionth. This one error changes the polynomial so that—even if the computer then calculated the zeros exactly (i.e., with no further roundoff errors)—instead of $1,2, \ldots ,20$, it would obtain (correct to three decimal places)

1.000	6.000	$10.095 \pm 0.644i$
2.000	7.000	$11.794 \pm 1.652i$
3.000	8.007	$13.992 \pm 2.519i$
4.000	8.917	$16.731 \pm 2.813i$
5.000	20.847	$19.502 \pm 1.940i$

Not only have the larger zeros become quite inaccurate, but ten of them have also changed from real to complex conjugate pairs, all because of one error in the seventh decimal place. Problems in which a single, small roundoff error in the data or in subsequent calculation results in much larger errors in the answers, are called *ill-conditioned.* Recognition of ill-condition may be difficult, although some classes of problems—such as the calculation of the zeros of high-degree polynomials—are known to be generally ill-conditioned. Unless an ill-conditioned problem can be somehow transformed to well-conditioned form, it is usually true that the only way to overcome ill-condition is by using multiple precision arithmetic in which the individual roundoff errors will be much smaller.

REFERENCES

1963. Wilkinson, J. H. *Rounding Errors in Algebraic Processes.* Englewood Cliffs, NJ: Prentice-Hall.

A. RALSTON

RPG. *See* REPORT GENERATORS.

RUN TIME. *See* COMPILE AND RUN TIME.

SCHEDULING ALGORITHMS

For articles on related subjects *see* INTERRUPT; MULTIPROGRAMMING; OPERATING SYSTEMS; PROCESSING MODES; SWAPPING; TIME SHARING; and TIME SLICE.

A computer system consists of a finite set of resources, such as processor cycles, memory locations, and input/output (I/O) devices, which many programs or processes may need to use. The object of a scheduling algorithm is to allocate these resources to the programs which require them. At each decision point, a scheduling algorithm must decide which of several competing processes should next receive a given resource.

One crucial resource in any computer system is the processor itself, since every process residing in the system must have the processor allocated to it for some period of time in order for the process to complete execution and leave the system. In this article, we will concentrate on processor scheduling algorithms for both single processor and multiprocessor systems.

There are two main phases of processor scheduling activity. During the job management phase, several programs (or *jobs*) are selected for execution and are loaded into available memory. Then, during the dispatching phase, a processor is assigned to one after another of the memory resident programs. In general, the simpler dispatching algorithm is executed many times between any two executions of the more complex job management scheduling algorithm; the job management algorithm itself may be dynamically modified still more infrequently.

In describing the essential concepts of scheduling, we shall first assume a batch-oriented, single-processor computer system. We note that while our discussion will treat the dispatching and job management aspects of scheduling separately, these two functions are often integrated in existing systems. We first discuss the simpler dispatching function.

Dispatching involves the allocation of processor cycles to active programs, those programs which are currently in memory and competing for processor time. A given active program is in one of three states. It is either executing, ready to execute, or blocked waiting for the occurrence of some event such as the completion of an I/O operation. It is the task of the short-term scheduling algorithm or *dispatcher* to decide which of the ready processes is to receive processor time and for how long (the *time slice*). The usual algorithm cycles *round robin* through the set of ready programs, allocating the processor to each program in turn. The program executes until it blocks or terminates, or until its time quantum expires (see Fig. 1). This simple scheme is appropriate, since dispatching is done very frequently and the time involved in this type of scheduling (the *overhead*) must therefore be minimized.

The result of the dispatcher consecutively allocating processor cycles to several different memory resident processes is called *multiprogramming:* A single processor appears to be executing multiple programs concurrently. Equivalently, we can say that a single processor is made to simulate the effects of several independent virtual processors. The task of the job management algorithm then becomes the assignment of one job to each virtual processor.

The object of the short-term scheduler or dispatcher is to maintain good utilization of the processor and I/O

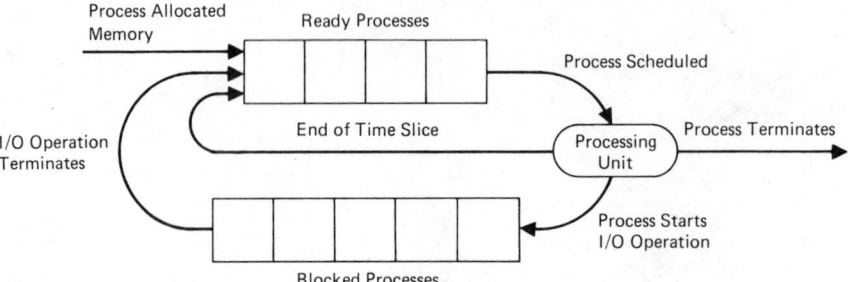

Fig. 1. Dispatching.

devices. The level of multiprogramming or, equivalently, the number of virtual processors is determined primarily by how many programs (or their *working sets (q.v.)* in a virtual memory system) fit comfortably in the memory, and this number may vary, depending on the job mix, or may be fixed.

The object of job management scheduling, in contrast, is to carry out management objectives with respect to total system utilization. The management policy may strive to satisfy a majority of casual users at the expense of a minority of users with very high resource demands. Alternatively, the management policy may favor production runs and only allow casual use when the system is otherwise underutilized. Regardless, it is primarily the task of the job management scheduling algorithm to achieve the stated management objectives.

Typically, to achieve this aim, a priority function is defined and each program in the system has a priority value which is updated at fixed decision points by the scheduling algorithm. The programs having the highest priority at each decision point are then assigned virtual processors. Between these job management decision points, the programs are managed by the simpler dispatching algorithm, which typically does not involve the overhead of priority calculations.

A great deal of work has gone into the development of different job management scheduling algorithms, and many different algorithms are used on current systems. We will only discuss some general approaches rather than giving the details of any particular system.

One important factor in this level of scheduling involves the choice of decision points. One could choose to recalculate priorities only when a program enters an empty or underutilized system, or when a program terminates execution. It is more common, however, to define a preemptive scheduling algorithm where a fixed time interval is specified and the scheduling algorithm is executed at the end of each such interval. Depending upon the priority function chosen, use of this scheme can prevent a few long programs from monopolizing the proces-

sor. In general, more users are kept satisfied when shorter programs get preferential treatment.

The priority of each program may depend upon such static parameters as memory requirements, requirements for special I/O devices, or management-dictated preferential treatment; or upon such dynamic parameters as the amount of processor time already received, how long the program has been resident in the system, or recent frequency of I/O operations. The resulting set of priority values may uniquely order the waiting programs or merely group them. In the latter case, if several programs have the same highest priority, then the job management scheduling algorithm commonly cycles round robin through these programs, giving each the opportunity to reside in memory for some time quantum.

Job management scheduling algorithms have also received much theoretical attention. The techniques of queueing theory have been used to model simple scheduling algorithms for statistically defined classes of programs, and to determine analytically system performance measures for them. While these models are necessarily somewhat simplistic, they do indicate the relative benefits of such different approaches as first-in-first-out (FIFO), shortest job first (SJF), shortest remaining time first (SRTF), and round robin (RR).

As system load characteristics change over time, the management policy may be best implemented by also changing the job management algorithm. This can be done by either switching to a totally different algorithm or by modifying parameters in the existing algorithm. To implement this adaptive control of the scheduling algorithm, a set of system descriptors such as queue lengths must be identified and updated. As the values of these descriptors vary significantly from desired norms, the job management scheduling algorithm is dynamically modified. It is only fairly recently that the responsibility for this dynamic adaptation of the scheduling algorithm has shifted in some systems from the computer system operator to the operating system itself.

We now extend our discussion of single-processor,

batch-oriented scheduling to describe scheduling of time-shared, real-time, and multiprocessor systems.

In a time-shared system, the processor must be allocated to each terminal user in such a way that the trivial interactive requests of the user are quickly responded to, and other requests requiring more resources have response times proportional to their resource demands. Typically, management objectives have shifted from efficient hardware usage towards satisfactory response time characteristics. In this environment, many user programs are in an inactive state waiting for the user to provide terminal input, and they need not be retained in memory. The active user programs are those which have a terminal request outstanding and these programs must be brought into the physical memory for execution within some short time interval.

In such a time-sharing system, the scheduler may maintain two or more program queues in order to distinguish between active programs which have not received service and may therefore have just a trivial interactive request, and other active programs which have already received one or more full quanta of service, thus indicating a more substantive request. All new program requests in this multi-level treatment are serviced before the processor continues to execute any other unsatisfied requests, thus improving response characteristics. If all the active programs do not fit in memory, then response times may increase as active user programs are swapped in and out of memory to satisfy the requirement that all new active processes receive some service before others receive additional service.

Real-time systems, such as those used to control production machinery, are characterized by having certain programs whose execution must be completed within fixed time intervals. In terms of scheduling, the key parameter of the job management scheduling algorithm is the length of time remaining till the program's deadline is reached. As the time leeway diminishes, the program's priority increases.

We next consider scheduling for multiprocessors, which we characterize as consisting of several processors of similar power executing from a large common memory. The role of scheduling is the same as described before—to use the physical processors to simulate a possibly larger number of virtual processors, to allocate programs to these virtual processors, and to adapt the scheduling algorithm to changes in the workload. A key design decision for the multiprocessor concerns the choice of processor(s) to do the scheduling. The scheduling algorithms may always be executed by one processor, may float from processor to processor, or may be executed by each processor as it requires scheduling.

In a master/slave multiprocessor operating system, one processor is responsible for scheduling all work on the system. Whenever a slave processor requires service, it must request service and wait until the current program on the master processor is interrupted so that the scheduling algorithm can be executed. Although this control strategy is easy to implement, access to the scheduling processor may become a system bottleneck and any failure in the master processor crashes the entire system.

In an operating system with a floating scheduler, any one processor at a time may perform the scheduling functions for the system, with either a software or hardware controller preventing two processors from scheduling simultaneously. While somewhat more difficult to implement, this form of control does have the potential for greater reliability than the master/slave organization.

In a multiprocessor operating system using distributed control, each processor is responsible for scheduling itself from a common table of scheduling information. System-wide conventions are used for initially entering the programs into the scheduling queues and for assigning priorities; standard synchronization techniques are used to prevent two processors from accessing and changing the scheduling information at the same time. This organization, like that of the floating scheduler, has good reliability and is easily extendable to additional processors. Moreover, by allowing several processors to schedule concurrently, access to the scheduling program is less of a system bottleneck than is the case with the other scheduling organizations.

Decreasing hardware costs indicate that more and more multiprocessors and computer networks will be built. The trend is towards distributed control of these systems. While single-processor scheduling techniques can be extended to multiprocessors in a fairly straightforward manner, the scheduling of programs on a network is much more difficult. The lack of a single common memory in which network scheduling information can be maintained, as well as the cost of sending such information between processors, means that new scheduling techniques will have to be developed for effective control of these systems.

REFERENCES

1973. Brinch Hansen, P. *Operating Systems Principles*. Englewood Cliffs, NJ: Prentice-Hall.
1975. Muntz, R. R. Chapter 7 in Freeman, P. (Ed.), *Software Systems Principles: A Survey*. Chicago: Science Research Associates.

L. J. MILLER

SCIENTIFIC APPLICATIONS

For articles on related subjects *see* COMPUTER GRAPHICS; ENGINEERING APPLICATIONS; IMAGE PRO-

CESSING; INFORMATION RETRIEVAL; MONTE CARLO METHOD; NUMERICAL ANALYSIS; PATTERN RECOGNITION; PIPELINE AND ARRAY PROCESSORS; SIMULATION: Principles; STATISTICAL APPLICATIONS; and SUPERCOMPUTERS.

Computation has always played a central role in the closed cycle known as the scientific method. A new theory gains acceptance or falls by the wayside in direct proportion to its success in explaining known phenomena and predicting new ones, not just qualitatively but also quantitatively. Einstein's theory of relativity predicted not just that light should be deflected in passing by a massive object such as the sun, but also the precise amount by which it should be deflected. No computer is needed for such a prediction (indeed, the first such calculation antedated electronic computers by almost a half-century), but a certain minimum amount of arithmetic computation is nonetheless required. This is typical of any new scientific discovery, since the truly fundamental physical phenomena are governed by equations that describe what happens to small particles or energy bundles as they move through space and time. In the same way in which the physicist's quest to explore particle phenomena at ever higher ranges of energy leads to the construction of ever larger (and more costly) accelerators, the attempt to solve these equations in increasing detail has led to a continual need for computers of higher speed and greater memory capacity. The initial sections of this article attempt to explain why.

The Quest for Ultra Performance. It is often of scientific interest to calculate the behavior of aggregates of particles over large regions of space or within long time intervals. Scientists facing such a task usually have a choice of two basically different approaches. One can calculate the flight of an individual particle until it is scattered by a second particle, absorbed, or leaves the region of observation. The exact history of each particle depends on a sequence of random numbers chosen and used in such a way as to constrain the particle to experience one event or another in accord with its correct probability. Tracking and accumulating statistics on thousands of such particles then enable calculation of quantities of physical interest. Such a technique is called the Monte Carlo method (*q.v.*), for obvious reasons, and finds application in such diverse situations as the behavior of neutrons in a reactor, light quanta in stellar atmospheres, and automobiles in heavy traffic. Monte Carlo calculations are inherently time consuming, even on very fast electronic computers, because of the necessity to follow a sufficiently large number of particles to obtain results that are accurate within statistically acceptable limits of error.

The second principal line of computational attack occurs more often, namely, when (1) the behavior of the quantity of interest is known to obey a linear or nonlinear algebraic equation, a differential equation, an integral equation, or an integrodifferential equation over some region of space/time of given shape, and when (2) the desired quantity obeys specified boundary conditions in space (and initial conditions in time in time-dependent problems). Taking differential equations as an example, the simplest situations occur when the desired quantity (the dependent variable) is a function of only one independent variable, perhaps time or one-space dimension. Such differential equations are called *ordinary*. In such cases, either an analytic solution is obtainable or use of a simple difference equation approximation will allow production of desired answers in a few seconds of computer time.

When the dependent variable is a function of two or more independent variables, the appropriate differential equation is called a *partial differential equation* (PDE) because it involves partial derivatives that indicate the change in the dependent variable as one or another of the independent variables change while holding all other independent variables fixed. Except under special circumstances, the solution of such equations is computationally formidable. As an example, consider an electromagnetic wave impinging on a target of given shape and internal composition (Fig. 1). In principle, Maxwell's system of differential equations and attendant boundary conditions completely specify the behavior of the radiation scattered from the target. When the target is either a metallic (perfectly reflecting) sphere or a penetrable sphere of homogeneous and isotropic internal electrical properties, Maxwell's partial differential equations reduce to three ordinary differential equations, one each specifying the behavior of the scattered wave with the r, θ, and ϕ directions in spherical coordinates. This has been known at least as far back as 1908, and so-called Mie calculations (after their originator), while tedious, can be programmed and normally take only a few seconds of computer time.

Imagine the target, while still spherical, to have internal electrical properties that are a function of radial position. Perhaps the core is dense and surrounded by a diffuse fringe, for example. Then Maxwell's equations still separate into three ordinary differential equations, but the radial equation, which in the homogeneous case was known to have solutions familiar to scientists (Bessel functions), must now be solved from point to point by difference methods. A digital computer is now a virtual necessity.

Now envision a progression of relaxations of symmetry conditions; each will greatly extend computer running time: Nonspherical but still axially symmetric tar-

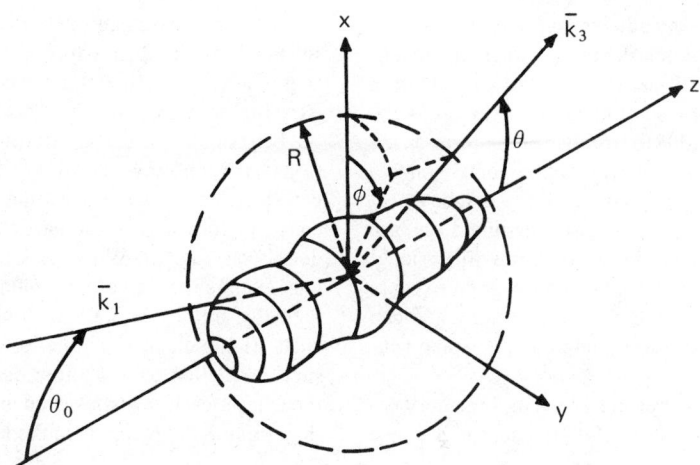

Fig. 1. Geometry for scattering from an arbitrarily shaped body of revolution. (From E. D. Reilly, Jr., in *Journal of Computational Physics*, April 1973, Academic Press, New York.)

gets will require several minutes to an hour of computer time and anisotropic targets will need a few minutes to an hour or more (depending on spatial symmetry), and so on up to completely nonsymmetric anisotropic targets, which would take several hours, even on the fastest computers presently available.

The situation described above is typical of a number of physical situations. A scientist will often know that the subject of study is governed by equations whose full complexity places exact solutions beyond the capability of the computer available. A sufficient number of approximations is then made to bring a typical calculation down to an acceptable bound, usually an hour or less, on the available computer. When the host installation increases its capability by, say, a factor of 4, the scientist will not necessarily be content to run four times as many cases in unit time, but will often remove a restriction or approximation, which will bring total running time back to an hour or so.

In reactor design, for example, it is known that neutron behavior is governed by a complex integrodifferential equation known as Boltzmann's equation. This equation takes into account that, at any given spatial point, the rate of neutron flow depends on their speed and direction, and to a certain extent on their past history. The solution of such an equation everywhere throughout reactor volume for all possible neutron velocities is a task beyond presently available computers. However, what can be, and usually is, done is to make approximations that replace the Boltzmann equation with a series of coupled partial differential equations, each of which calculates neutron flux at a particular energy (speed) at a

given space point. Each such equation, a so-called diffusion equation, is then calculated in either one-, two-, or three-space dimensions, whichever the symmetry of the reactor (or expediency) demands. Any horizontal plane through a reactor core is obviously best modeled in cartesian (x,y) coordinates, but other geometric arrangements often dictate use of polar (r, θ) or cylindrical (r,z) coordinates. Any of these geometries reduces to this simple situation: Given that p, a, c, d, and e are known functions of position (precalculated and stored in computer memory prior to the time-consuming calculation of neutron flux), we would like to know what values of neutron flux ϕ_P, ϕ_A, ϕ_C, ϕ_D, ϕ_E balance the equation

$$p\phi_P - a\phi_A - c\phi_C - d\phi_D - e\phi_E = 0$$

at every mesh-point P, where left, right, bottom, and top neighboring points are designated A, C, D, and E, respectively. All questions of geometry, material composition, and boundary condition are buried in the calculation of the coefficients. Any one such equation has five unknowns, and hence cannot be solved uniquely, but since a similar equation must hold at every mesh point, a 10,-000-point model (say) represents 10,000 equations in 10,000 unknowns. In principle, this can be solved by inverting a 10,000 × 10,000 matrix. Such an attempt would be not only foolish but unnecessary. Since most elements of such a matrix would be zero (the result of using only a nearest-neighbor numerical approximation to derivatives in the diffusion equation), the desired fluxes are best obtained iteratively. There are a variety of methods for doing this, but most process a line of points at a time, sweeping all lines a sufficient number of times to obtain the desired convergence. Here, "sweeping" means the consistent solution of just the 100 (say) points on a line by a systematic forward-elimination/backward-substitution method applicable to so-called three-term or *tridiagonal* linear systems (matrices whose only nonzero elements are on the diagonal or next to the diagonal).

Although the preceding discussion assumed use of a two-dimensional slice taken from a full three-dimensional reactor, the technique can be extended (at great expense in computer time) to all three space dimensions, and can be used to calculate quantities of interest other than neutron flux.

In some fields, the increasing speed and memory capacity of successive generations of digital computers have transformed the image that the computer conveys to the scientist from that of a tool—albeit a powerful one—to that of a new experimental device in its own right. Chemistry is a good example. The basic equation that governs the behavior of molecules, atoms, and (low velocity) electrons has been known for almost 50 years—the Schrödinger equation. Without a computer, only simple systems consisting of two or three particles can be studied in any detail (see Fig. 2). With the latest computers, however, ions of much larger atomic number can be followed kinetically as they interact with other ions to form molecules. If the chemist is able to watch the progression of such a reaction on a TV-like display device attached to the computer, it is just as good or better (and less messy) than mixing the reagents in the laboratory. ("Better" be-

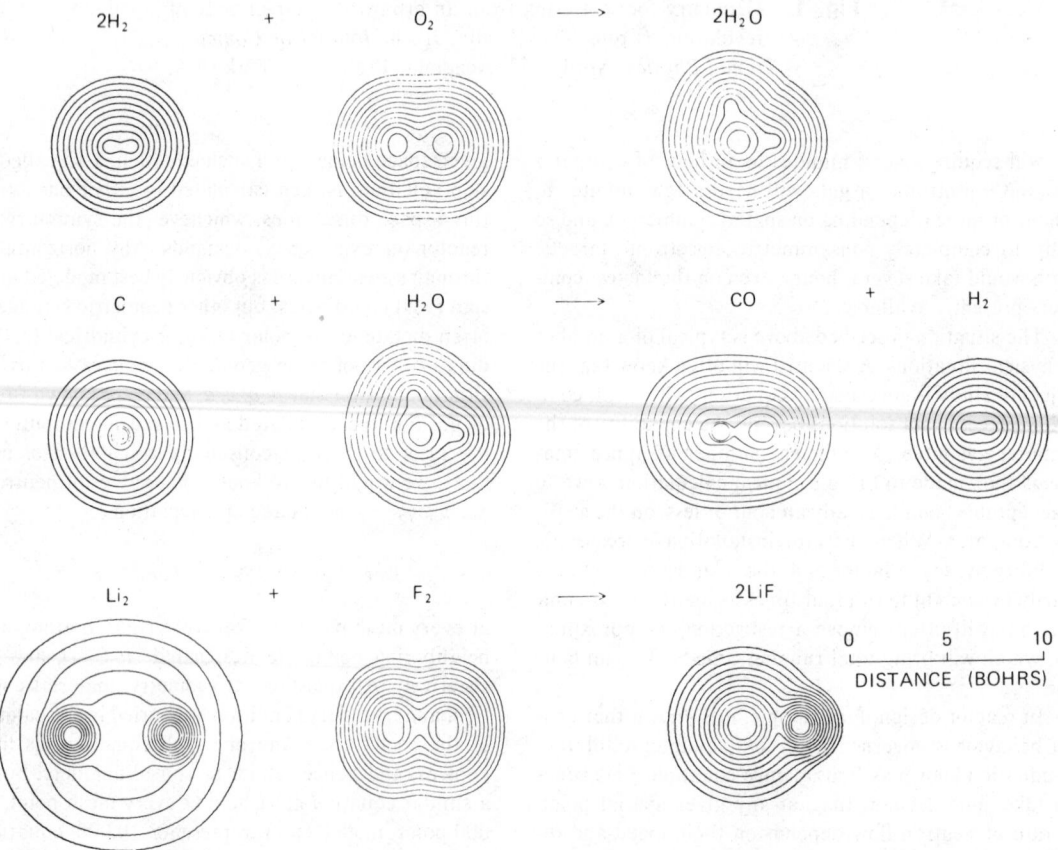

Fig. 2. Three chemical reactions portrayed in terms of changes in computer-produced electron-density diagrams. Top shows two hydrogen molecules combining with an oxygen molecule to form two water molecules. Middle shows a carbon atom and a water molecule combining to form a carbon monoxide molecule and a hydrogen molecule. Bottom shows a lithium molecule and a fluorine molecule combining to form two lithium fluoride molecules. Although these are simple reactions, it appears reasonable to expect that this general approach can be extended to much more complicated reactions. (From Arnold C. Wahl in *Scientific American*, April 1970, fig. 5.)

cause there are only limited means of varying the speed of an actual reaction whereas the simulated reaction can proceed at "instant replay" slow motion on a display device through appropriate variation of program parameters.)

Inverse Calculations. All of the examples cited thus far are examples of *direct* calculational situations. We know the characteristics of a target and want to calculate its scattering properties. We know the reactor configuration and desire its lifetime behavior. We know the reagents and want to know their reactivity. As time-consuming as such calculations can be, they are routine in their demand for computer time compared to indirect or *inverse calculations,* where we have access to experimental data but no access at all to the source of the phenomena generating the data.

An example is the problem of interstellar dust particles. Astrophysicists and cosmologists would like to know the quantity, shape, and composition of these particles, since this knowledge has a bearing on theories of the origin and evolution of the universe. We cannot yet send space ships to retrieve such matter, but we can observe quantities such as the polarization and absorption of light of various wavelengths passing through it. What kinds of particles produce the scattered light: spherical? elongated? metallic? anisotropic ferrite needles? dirty ice? The question is far from settled, and the astrophysicist will need to experiment with many different models to achieve success without being at all sure that the answer is unique.

Crystallographic calculations are another example of inverse computations. It would be straightforward to calculate the pattern of x-rays diffracted from a known spatial distribution of known atoms, but we cannot get inside crystals or molecules the way Asimov's fictional scientists traveled through the circulatory system in "Fantastic Voyage." We can observe the pattern of diffracted x-rays or neutrons impinging on a crystal of unknown structure, but in doing so, certain basic information (phase relations between atoms) is lost. Using what information is available, however, such as intensity data, suspected symmetries, and chemical formulas learned through destructive testing of portions of the same material, crystallographers are now able to use an organized trial-and-error method to deduce the structure of quite large molecules of up to 100 atoms or so, and the frontier is pushed ahead with each advance in computer technology.

As complex as they are, the structures of several proteins as well as the vitamin B_{12} have been determined by computer techniques. Some programs are so sophisticated that they produce as a final result a stereo pair (Fig. 3) of similar views of the predicted molecular structure; viewing them through an appropriate optical device brings out the spatial arrangement and vibrational characteristics of crystal constituent atoms in stunning detail.

Just as the astrophysicist and the crystallographer are barred from entering the domain of the objects of their interest, so is the geophysicist unable to examine more than an infinitesimal fraction of the interior of the earth. There is data, however, that gives extremely pointed clues as to the internal composition of the earth, namely, that provided through seismological records

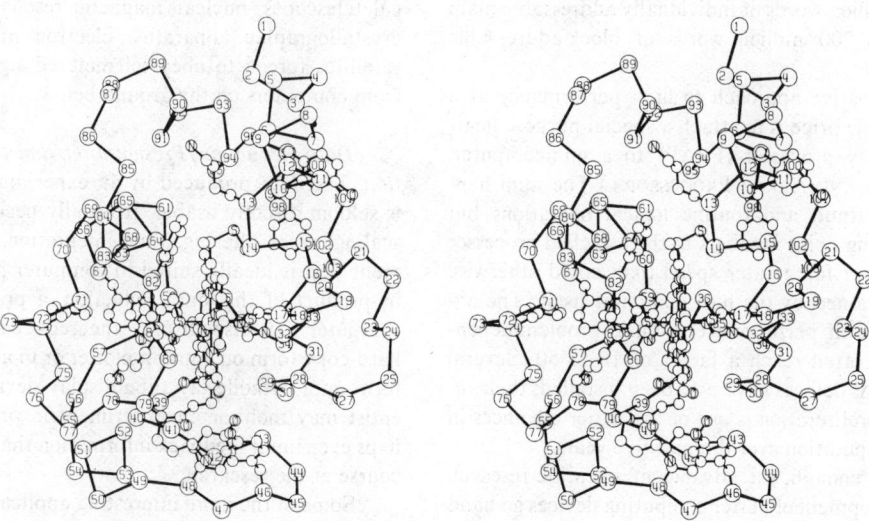

Fig. 3. Stereoscopic pair of front view of reduced cytochrome *c* molecule from a tuna. (Source: R. E. Dickerson, California Institute of Technology.)

taken during periods of earthquake, volcanic eruption, and atomic testing. The earth, like any (approximate) sphere of given internal composition, has certain characteristic modes of vibration, and allows elastic waves to propagate at certain speeds from point to point on its surface. By using digital computers to vary appropriate parameters in the equations that govern such phenomena, geophysicists have derived a profile of the earth's interior with reasonable certitude, a confidence founded on agreement between the predicted characteristics of their model and observed properties. Based on such methods, they already predict a molten liquid core, and their detailed predictions of its shape and composition are being sharpened as they make increasingly detailed comparisons with experimental data of the effects the liquid core might have on the earth's rotational and magnetic properties. Similar methods are allowing geologists to map strain energies in the earth in an attempt to understand earthquake phenomena.

Impact on Hardware Development. One obvious impact of the scientist's perceived need for ever higher performance computers to cope with the type of problem cited above is to create a market climate in which vendors are willing to design and develop supercomputers (*q.v.*). Computers capable of a million operations per second (MIPS) are now rather commonplace and 10 to 30 MIPS speed is attainable for certain problems on currently available supercomputers.

It is not impossible that special-purpose supercomputers with a sustained speed of a billion floating point operations per second (1 BIPS) could be operational by the late 1980s. Potential users would like such computers to have 40 million words of individually addressable main memory plus 200 million words of block-addressable main memory.

An alternative approach to high performance at a more affordable price is to attach a special-purpose floating point array processor (FPAP) to a minicomputer. (See PIPELINE AND ARRAY PROCESSORS.) The mini handles input, output, and routine logical operations but streams floating point numbers to the attached processor for execution at far greater speed than could otherwise have been attained by the host computer itself. The average increase in performance is quite problem-dependent but can often reach a factor of 10 to 50. Several hundred FPAP devices have now been installed; their invention and proliferation is one of the major advances in scientific computation over the past five years.

Fittingly enough, the advance of scientific research and the development of better computing devices go hand in hand. Faster speeds depend on faster switching devices, which, in turn, depend on such scientific advances as that of the Josephson junction (*q.v.*), an outgrowth of

research in solid state physics. Computers of the future that are able to use such junctions will lead to still further advances in solid state physics. And so it goes.

Ancillary Roles. In addition to their obvious value for direct and inverse calculation, digital computers play a role in automating many other aspects of the scientist's personal work load. These will be discussed under the headings information retrieval, instrumentation, data reduction, comparison of theory and experiment, simulation for design, simulation for prediction, and simulation for education.

Information Retrieval. The profusion of scientific papers being published makes it ever more difficult for working scientists to keep abreast of their fields, even in their own specialties. Increasing numbers of workers are subscribing to computerized information retrieval services of one kind or another, or have access to libraries that do. Principal among these would be the ability to file an interest profile with such a service center, and then be continually apprised of papers that match that profile as they are published; another service might make a specific search over past literature according to certain keywords and key concepts.

Instrumentation. Many of the instruments of modern research science have themselves become so complex that it is often expedient to control their operation automatically with a small computer directly connected to the instrument. Nuclear reactors and particle accelerators are often controlled or at least monitored in this way, as are a wide range of other devices such as radio and optical telescopes, nuclear magnetic resonance equipment, crystallographic apparatus, electron microscopes, and satellites forced to obey telemetered signals emanating from computers on the ground below.

Data Reduction, Presentation, and Pattern Recognition. The data produced by an experimental instrument is seldom directly usable. It usually needs some kind of scaling, noise filtering, time integration, or other treatment that is ideally suited to computer processing. As a by-product of this data reduction, a properly equipped computer can also display the reduced data either in hard-copy form on a graph plotter or in a transient visual form on a cathode-ray tube display device. Thus, a scientist may monitor an experiment in progress and perhaps even input feedback information that alters the later course of the research.

Some of the more interesting applications of data reduction occur in a pattern recognition context. The classic example is the widespread use of devices called *bubble chambers* in high-energy physics. Particles passing through such devices leave visible tracks composed of tiny bubbles that can be photographed and scanned for the occurrence of interesting branchlike structures that indicate the presence of a collision or reaction between particles. Although humans can do this quite well, a bubble chamber can snap a new picture every few seconds and easily reach an annual production of over a million frames. Such prodigious output can be coped with only by computerized pattern-recognition techniques, and modern accelerators are serviced by large computers devoted almost exclusively to this task.

Pattern recognition (*q.v.*), or at least computerized image processing (*q.v.*), also plays a vital role in planetary exploration. NASA space probes that flew by Mars (and Jupiter and Saturn) in recent years transmitted pictures back to earth in digital form (Fig. 4), specifically, as a series of 40,000 six-bit data points, each representing on a scale of 0 to 63 the shade of gray that was observed at the intersection of a 200 × 200 grid array superimposed on the visual scene. Once read into the memory of a high-speed computer, such a digitized picture was then easily "cleaned up" by removing spurious noise and enhancing its resolution for human viewing, thus producing the sharp and often breathtaking photos presented in news magazines at the time.

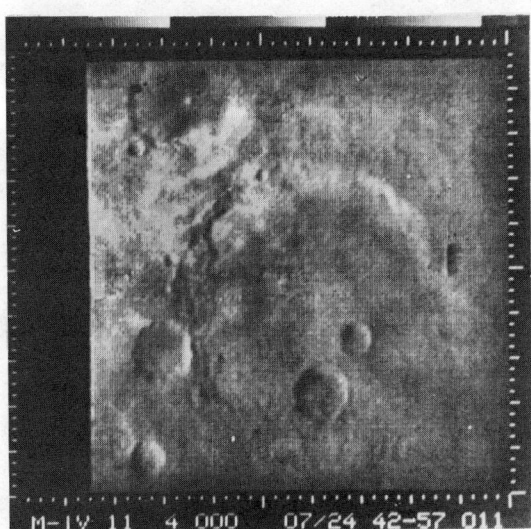

Fig. 4. A computer enhanced photograph of a portion of the surface of Mars. (Source: Jet Propulsion Laboratory.)

In a similar vein, pattern recognition by computer has been used by scientists in other fields. Biologists have successfully identified mutant chromosomes among normal ones through such techniques. Atmospheric scientists are experimenting with attempts to identify cyclonelike disturbances in cloud-cover satellite photos. Archeologists have successfully reconstructed murals from Egyptian temples by fitting together photographs of stone fragments as if they were pieces in a gigantic jigsaw puzzle solved by computer matching of similar patterns. In a similar application, but with far fewer pieces to worry about, earth scientists have tested theories of continental drift by doing a computerized comparison of how well the east coast of North and South America fits the west coast of Europe and Africa, and found the fit to be very plausible indeed.

Comparison of Theory and Experiment. Some physical situations are insufficiently well understood to be described according to fundamental principles and therefore must be treated phenomenologically. This implies that an equation devised to cover a phenomenon contains a number of adjustable parameters whose values are not known in advance, or known only within certain bounds. An example is the scattering of nuclear particles such as protons and electrons from atomic nuclei. In principle, the scattering properties are known (through solution of Schrödinger's equation) when the strength and shape of the force field (or *potential*) causing the scattering (i.e., the target nucleus) is known, but such characteristics of nuclei are extremely difficult to calculate quantitatively from first principles.

The solution is to characterize the potential as having a certain functional form containing several adjustable parameters such as potential depth, nuclear radius, degree of surface diffuseness, etc., up to as many as eight or nine such parameters. It then becomes a task worthy of a modern computer to vary these parameters to achieve that degree of agreement between theory and experiment that gives the best fit, in the least squares sense. This is not a trivial task; it is something like trying to achieve the sharpest possible picture on a color TV set that has nine adjustable knobs and where adjusting one may make it necessary to readjust knobs already set by earlier trial and error. To achieve a reasonable fit, the computer must effectively search through an *n*-dimensional parameter space, recalculating the scattering at reasonably small steps in the parameters along the way. It is not unusual to consume hours of computer time in the process, but the scientist who does this considers the additional insights gained into nuclear structure well worth the effort.

Simulation for Design. The calculational problems associated with the behavior of neutrons in a reactor have been discussed previously, but the rationale for studying these problems was not considered. Initially, through the late 1940s and early 1950s, research data was reasonably fundamental, since the properties of neutron propagation in various materials under a variety of operating conditions were imperfectly understood. As in other fields, however, the widespread use of digital computers accelerated the natural progression of a given type of activity, from research to applied science to engineering. The point has now been reached where most reactor calculations are part of a design engineering process whose aim is to simulate performance of tentative reactor designs in lieu of constructing an experimental prototype. By this

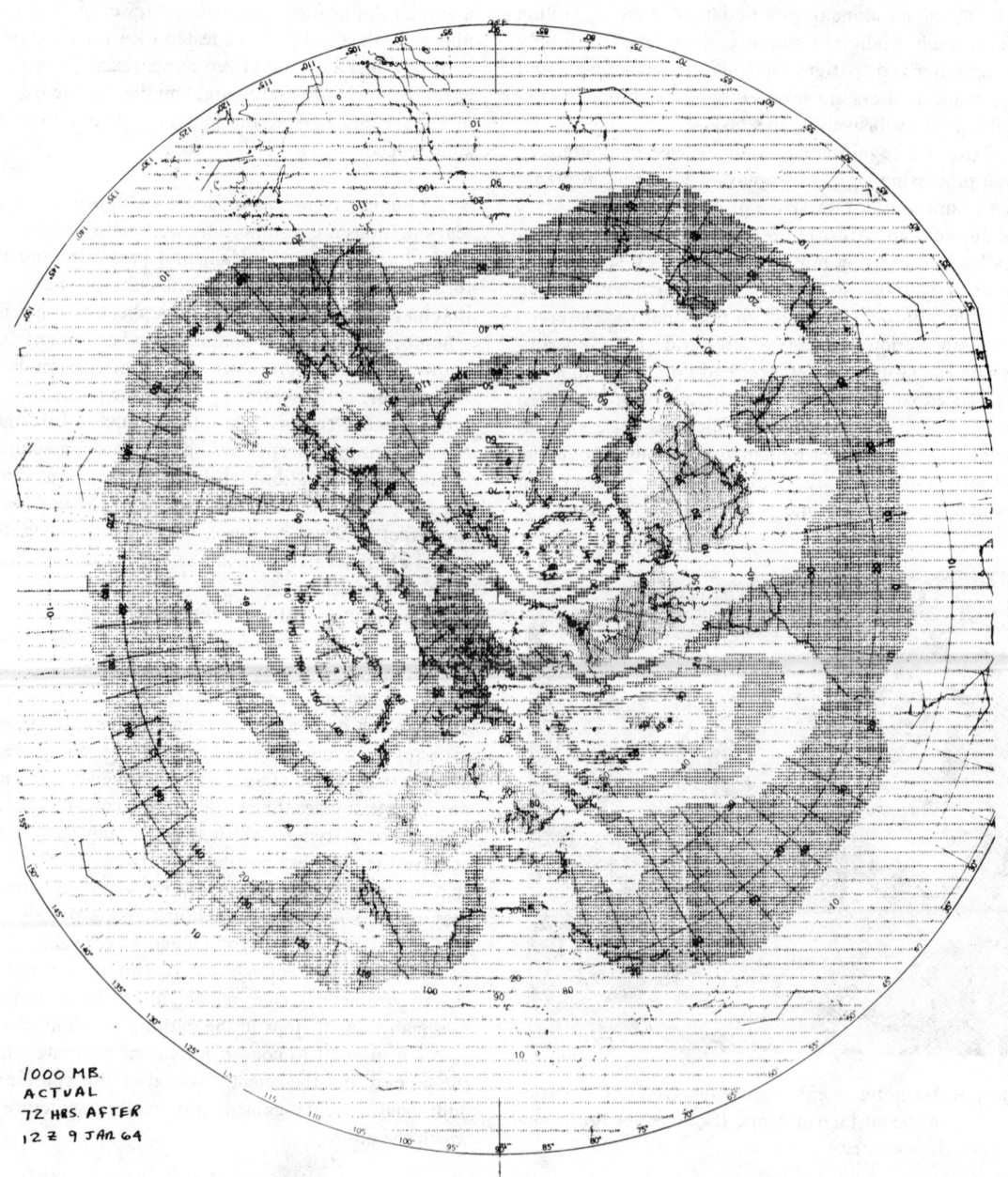

1000 MB.
ACTUAL
72 HRS. AFTER
12 Z 9 JAN 64

Fig. 5.   Computer-produced weather map of the Northern Hemisphere with geographical outlines superimposed. The four-digit numbers are observed geopotential heights of 1,000 mbar surface. The shaded swaths represent lines of constant geopotential intervals and are a rough measure of wind direction, with narrower channels indicating stronger winds.

technique, many hundreds of design variations can be tested in theory and only the most promising results need be tested in practice.

The preceding example is typical of many applications of simulation to design practice. In the same vein, other large scientific instruments can be engineered to desired specifications through preliminary simulation of a large number of alternative designs. It would now be extremely difficult for humans using precomputer methods to design the large accelerators used in high-energy physics research or the large radio telescopes used in astronomy.

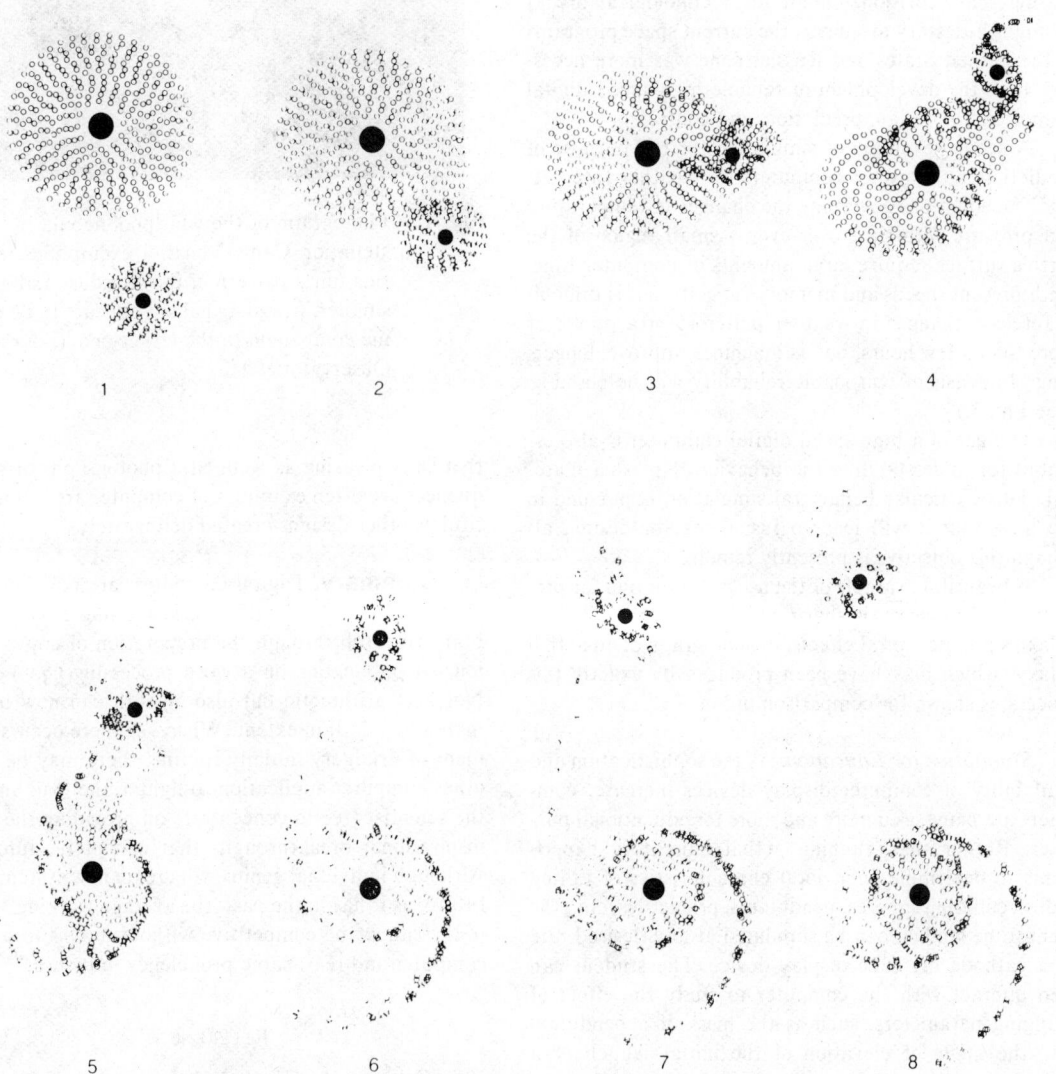

Fig. 6. Computer simulation of flyby of small galaxy past a larger one. In time frames *1* and *2*, the barely distorted small galaxy is still rising toward the viewer. At its closest approach to the larger galaxy (*3*) it passes as much in front of it as to the right of it. The tidal effects in both disks (*4*) are distinctly two-sided. As the smaller galaxy recedes (*5–7*), the tide it raised on the side of the larger disk closer to it evolves into a narrow bridge connecting the two galaxies. The similar bulge that it caused on the far side wraps into a fine counterarm that will become sparse and eventually disappear. (From Alar and Juri Toomre, "Violent Tides between Galaxies," © December 1973 by *Scientific American, Inc.* All rights reserved. With permission.)

Simulation for Prediction. Another reason for simulating a complex physical system is to predict its behavior. The physical laws governing the motion of planetary bodies are intrinsically simple for two-body systems, but they are intractable analytically for the complex systems of earth, moon, multistage rockets of changing mass, satellites, etc., whose relative motions must be calculated with great precision in order to assure success of the most routine space mission. Of all the technological breakthroughs necessary to support the current space programs of the United States and Russia, none was more necessary then the development of reliable high-speed digital computers for design, prediction, and control.

A second example of simulation for the purpose of prediction is the use of computers for weather forecasting. The equations governing the changes in temperature and pressure with time over even a small region of the earth's surface require large amounts of computer time. With present speeds and memory capacities, it is difficult to forecast changes in weather patterns for a period of more than a few hours, but as machines improve, longer-range forecasts of reasonable reliability will be possible. (See Fig. 5.)

The use of a high-speed digital computer is also essential for understanding the behavior of plasma material. This particular behavioral simulation is pursued in the hope that it will lead to fusion reactor design, although this objective is presently remote.

A beautiful example of the use of simulation for prediction in astronomy is shown in Fig. 6, where colliding galaxies produce spiral effects. A photograph of an actual galaxy, which may have been produced by exactly this process, is shown for comparison in Fig. 7.

Simulation for Education. As the sophistication and availability of computer display devices increase, computers are being used more and more for educational purposes. Rather than running actual laboratory experiments to determine behavioral characteristics of falling bodies, colliding spheres, pendulums, projectiles, etc., the event to be studied can be simulated at any desired rate on a cathode ray tube display device. The student can then interact with the computer to study the effect of changing parameters, such as the mass of a pendulum bob, the angle of elevation of the initial launch of a rocket, or any one or more of other factors that affect the experiment at hand.

Using such numerical simulation and display techniques one can even examine phenomena that are closed to easy observation in the laboratory; for example, the tunneling of a quantum mechanical particle through a potential barrier, the slow-motion fall of water droplets into a pool, or the crashing of water waves upon a beach. These simulations are instructive to watch, and are es-

Fig. 7. Photograph of the whirlpool nebula in the constellation Canis Venatici exemplifies the interior spiral pattern of the star dust and gas. The smaller, irregular galaxy appears to be a genuine companion to the larger one. (Source: Hale Observatories.)

thetically pleasing as well. Still photographs of such sequences are often examples of computer art just as beautiful as other designs created deliberately.

Summary. Digital computers are now being used in every facet of scientific work, ranging from initial library research through the preparation of copy for final journal publication on a word processing (*q.v.*) system. Not only arithmetic but also algebra can now be automated to a certain extent. Wherever there occurs an element of drudgery in daily routine, there may be yet another computer application to lighten the load and leave the scientist free to concentrate on providing the human inspirational breakthroughs that cannot be automated. Although individual genius will create new systems in the future, as it has in the past, the average working scientist today cannot be competitive without access to a digital computer and reasonable proficiency in its use.

REFERENCES

1966. Oettinger, A. "The Use of Computers in Science," *Scientific American* (September). Reprinted in 1971, R. Fenichel and J. Weizenbaum (Eds.), *Computers and Computation (Readings from Scientific American),* San Francisco: W. H. Freeman.

1970. Fernbach, S. and Taub, A. (Eds.). *Computers and Their Role in the Physical Sciences.* New York: Gordon and Breach.

1971. Pell, G. A. *Introduction to Scientific Computing.* New York: Appleton-Century-Crofts.

1974. Streeter, D. N. *The Scientific Process and the Computer.* New York: Wiley.

1980. Bardwell, S., Stahlmar, M., and Tappert, F. "Computers and Scientific Breakthroughs in the 1980s," (three separate but related articles), *Fusion* **3** *No. 9:* 38–39, 48–56 (July).

1980. Rodrique, G., Giroux, E., and Pratt, M. "Perspectives on Large-Scale Scientific Computation," *Computer* **13** *No. 10:* 65–80.

1981. Langridge, R., Ferrin, T. E., Kuntz, I. D., and Connolly, M. L. "Real-Time Color Graphics in Studies of Molecular Interactions," *Science* **211**, No. 4483 (13 February), pp. 661–666.

E. D. REILLY, JR.

SCRATCH FILES

For articles on related subjects *see* FILES; and MEMORY: Auxiliary.

During the processing of substantial files of data, it often becomes necessary to create temporary files for later use by copying all or part of a data set to an auxiliary-memory device—tape, disk, or drum. Such a temporary file (or the associated storage device) is called a *scratch file.* Sometimes, scratch-file data is unchanged from what was originally read into the computer, e.g., during sorting. In other applications (compilations, data editing, etc.), scratch-file data is partially processed.

In most installations, scratch-file devices are the fastest available: drums or fixed-head disk drives; other disk drives; or high-speed magnetic tapes. In large installations, several disk drives (or tape drives, or both) are often allocated permanently for general-user scratch-file storage. In a multiprogramming environment, several users can simultaneously allocate modest amounts of scratch-file storage from this pool. This tends to economize the number of disk drives required at an installation, compared to the alternative strategy of having each user furnish private packs for scratch files.

D. N. FREEMAN

SCS. *See* SOCIETY FOR COMPUTER SIMULATION.

SDI. *See* CURRENT AWARENESS SYSTEMS.

SEAC

For articles on related subjects *see* DIGITAL COMPUTERS: Early; EDVAC; and SWAC.

In 1947, with the encouragement of the U.S. Navy, the National Bureau of Standards (NBS) established the National Applied Mathematical Laboratories under the leadership of John Curtiss. The purpose was to create a centralized national computation facility equipped with high-speed automatic computers, which would provide a computing service for other governmental agencies and play an active part in the further development of computing machinery.

The Census Bureau, the U.S. Air Force, and the U.S. Navy all supported the Laboratories, and negotiations for the acquisition of computers from Eckert and Mauchly (later acquired by Sperry Rand), from Engineering Research Associates (a supplier to the security agencies), and from Raytheon Corporation (RAYDAC), were under way in 1948. Impatient with the slow development of computers, and feeling the need for more "hands-on" expertise, the NBS decided at a meeting in May 1948 to build its own computer; later in the same year the decision was made to build a second computer at the Institute for Numerical Analysis, an NBS field station located at the University of California at Los Angeles. These two bureau computers became known as the SEAC and SWAC (Standards Eastern and Standards Western Automatic Computers).

The SEAC, built under the direction of Samuel Alexander, used mercury delay lines for storage. Its design was based on the EDVAC work at the University of Pennsylvania. The original memory used the same type of mercury delay lines, consisting of 64 eight-word lines operating at a clock rate of 1 MHz. Initial input and output was by punched paper tape. Later, magnetic wire and magnetic tape replaced the paper tape, and a Williams' tube memory (*q.v.*) was added to the system.

Addition time (including storage access) ranged from 192 to 1,540 ms, and multiply time from 2,300 to 3,600 ms. The SEAC was the first stored-program computer to run in the United States. It was dedicated in May 1950 and was in operation until October 1964.

REFERENCES

1951. Alexander, S. N. "The National Bureau of Standards Eastern Automatic Computer (SEAC)," *IRE Eastern Joint Computer Conference,* pp. 84–89.

1953. Shupe, P. D., Jr. and Kirsch, R. A. "SEAC—A Review of Three Years of Operation," *IRE Eastern Joint Computer Conference,* pp. 83–90.

H. D. HUSKEY

SECURITY. *See* DATA SECURITY.

SECURITY OF COMPUTER INSTALLATIONS, PHYSICAL

For article on related subject *see* DATA SECURITY.

This article deals with protection of hardware and software against physical threats. Each subsection describes a physical threat and useful countermeasures that have been successfully applied in a number of installations. Physical security measures are intended to reduce or prevent disruptions to operations or loss of assets. Because in most organizations there is a growing dependence on the computer, its disruption can have a devastating effect upon the organization's performance as well as cause a large loss of assets. Before selecting specific security measures, management should review assets and operations and possible threats against them to select the optimum security program, bearing in mind its cost and effect on productivity as well as its protective features.

When developing physical security plans, examination should be made of the possibility of insuring the computer installation. Most large organizations have on their staff an insurance specialist who might be called a "risk" manager. This individual should be contacted and asked to determine if insurance should be purchased for the computer center. If the organization does not have this type of expertise available from within, the insurance broker or agency with whom it normally deals should be asked to make recommendations concerning purchase of insurance for the computer installation. A benefit of this study will be that the insurance company will make a survey of the computer installation to determine its level of protection before any policy will be issued.

The measures discussed below, if fully implemented, will give an extremely secure environment. All installations will, of course, not need all these measures. For example, a university research computing center that handles no sensitive or classified data or information will probably not be concerned about access control. However, it may develop an extremely effective fire safety program, since destruction of the center may have a fairly major impact on carrying out the research program of the university if there is no way of obtaining backup computer services within a reasonable period of time. Another example is the average industrial computing center, which probably would not develop a backup power source to assure continuing power during blackouts or brownouts, whereas a medical center, which has life monitoring systems connected to its computer, would probably want to do everything possible to assure a continuing power supply.

Fire. Fire damage of the computer room may be caused by a fire outside the building in which the computer is located, inside the building, or interior to the room itself. Consequently, one should consider all these possibilities. If possible, one should avoid high hazards in or near the building; e.g., chemical or petroleum operations, warehouses, lumber yards. Internal fires may originate in trash, electric wiring, inside the computer hardware or in forms storage, data encoding, or in programming areas. Smoke, heat, and corrosive gases from fires may enter the area through doors, windows, elevator shafts, or air conditioning ducts. Tapes and disk packs can be destroyed by temperatures as low as 150°F.

A good fire safety program for computer hardware and software has five parts: (1) building design, construction, and location; (2) building operation; (3) fire detection; (4) fire fighting; and (5) loss control.

Building Design. The preferred building is of fire-resistive construction, well separated from hazardous materials and operations (e.g., chemicals, plastics, paint, packing materials, etc.) stored or used in it. The computer facility should be located on an upper floor where it will be less exposed to water damage, intrusion, and vandalism. In the case of a large installation, a special building embodying maximum fire and safety features can sometimes be set aside for the computer complex.

Building Operations. Rigorous measures should be taken to minimize the risk of fire, including prompt trash removal; unobstructed fire doors; careful maintenance of fire detector and extinguisher equipment, and of heating ventilating, and cooling equipment; protection of fuel lines and other potential fire sites. Regular inspections are required to assure compliance.

Fire Detection. The fire detection system should provide *prompt, positive* detection. The preferred system uses (1) products-of-combustion detectors in the computer area located above hung ceilings, at ceilings, under raised floors, in air conditioning ducts entering the computer area, electrical equipment closets, and other key areas; (2) less expensive rate-of-temperature-rise detectors in adjacent areas, and preferably throughout the building; and (3) flow alarm switches in sprinkler systems and hose lines. The control panel design should include enough indicators to make it easy to locate a fire. If possible, the detection system should be connected by telephone line to the fire department. Alarm bells should be located to assure a response at *all* times.

Fire Fighting. Prompt effective response to all alarms, of course, increases considerably the likelihood of quick extinguishing and minimum damage. A fire brigade should be appointed and trained for first-aid fire fighting, not as a substitute for professional fire fighters, but as a deterrent force to extinguish minor blazes before they become major. This is obviously not to be done at the expense of life endangerment of the employees. Local fire departments often will be happy to assist in training fire fighters. Provide ample Class A and Class C portable extinguishers, some of which should be light enough to be carried easily. An automatic sprinkler will provide highly reliable protection against catastrophic loss; the preaction/recycle type minimizes water damage. HALON-1301 extinguishing systems (see NFPA Standard No. 13-A) are preferable for tape vaults, underfloor areas, and other locations where the contents must be protected against damage or where conventional extinguishing is difficult to apply; however, their cost is significantly higher than sprinklers, and of course protection is lost after discharge until HALON containers are recharged.

Loss Control. Loss and disruption can be minimized, and recovery can be accelerated if steps are taken to control smoke and water damage. Individuals should be designated, trained, and equipped to take steps like the following: conduct an orderly shutdown of hardware; dismount and protect tapes and disk packs; cover hardware with plastic sheeting; protect documentation and source documents. Fire-rated vaults for tapes and disk packs can be kept nearby for emergency use.

Water Damage. Water damage may come from natural flooding, broken pipes, or water from fire fighting. Hardware is surprisingly resistant to water damage, and tapes and disk packs inside canisters are usually safe unless subjected to immersion. However, wiring, air conditioning equipment, paper, furnishings, and the like can be seriously damaged or destroyed, and actual flooding in the computer room will halt operations.

No computer should be located where it is subject to natural flooding, nor should it be in a basement where water may collect or drains may back up. Exterior windows should have burglar-resistant glass that protects against water as well. Overhead water, steam, fuel, and drain pipes should be avoided if possible, or inspected regularly. All openings in the floor above should be sealed with cement, and positive drainage should be provided for the computer area.

Earthquake. If the computer facility is located in an earthquake-prone area, backup facilities should be outside the area. One must assume that little or no support, including personnel, will be available locally for backup operation in the event of an earthquake. The building containing the computer complex should be constructed to the highest standards. Particular attention should be paid to eliminating internal and adjacent fire hazards, and to providing on-site energy and other utilities.

Air Conditioning. The air conditioning system should be of adequate capacity, with good controls, adequate air filtering, and properly located outside air-intake louvers. Louvers should not be located at ground level where they are subject to sabotage attacks, nor should they be near sources of harmful gases.

Reliability depends on proper design and effective preventive maintenance. Each element of the system—air handling unit (AHU), chiller, cooling tower unit, circulating pump, etc.—should be redundant. Each of these should be sized and interconnected in such a way that the failure of any single unit will not cause interruption or shutdown of computer operations. If the AHUs in the computer room are supplied by a central system, it may be possible to eliminate comfort air conditioning elsewhere in the building during an emergency. Except when the outside air is above 80°F, increased outside air can be used in an emergency, but humidity controls may not work. The computer operations staff should be familiar with the air conditioning system operation and alarm panel and should oversee arrangements for preventive maintenance and emergency repairs. An individual should be designated to inspect temperature and humidity recorder charts on a regular basis and to resolve any out-of-limits operation.

Electric Power. There are three possible sources of electric power trouble: (1) transients or "spikes," which may propagate into logic hardware and cause erratic operation and scrambled data; (2) subnormal line voltage or "brownouts" (or possibly overvoltages), which may prevent computer (and, in extreme cases, air conditioning) hardware from functioning properly; and (3) power failures, which immediately halt operations. Transients may be caused by high-current devices in the building, switching transients (which often occur between 7:00 and 8:00 A.M.), or lightning strikes on the transmission or distribution system within a few miles of the building. Brownouts usually are imposed deliberately when power demand overloads the available generating capacity. Power failures may result from an electrical fault or fire in the building, destruction of a utility pole, an accident at the supplying substation, or, in very rare cases, a systemwide disturbance.

A review of recent reliability and quality of the power source and an estimate of the cost of reruns and delayed processing will indicate the amount (if any) appropriate to spend for countermeasures. An electric power monitor connected to all three phases with a strip-chart recorder will help to pinpoint problems caused by electric power fluctuations, particularly transients. These records will help correlate occurrence of systems problems with power fluctuations.

There are a number of countermeasures. Voltage-regulating transformers will compensate for brownouts. Diesel- or turbine-driven generators can generate power locally if protection against long-term power failures is needed. Uninterruptible power systems (UPS) filter out transients and protect against brief power failures, by storing energy internally. Rotary UPSs use a motor-generator with a flywheel for energy storage; they are relatively inexpensive, but are noisy, require regular maintenance, and can support the load for only 10 to 15 sec when power fails. Electronic UPS use a solid-state rectifier-inverter set with a battery, which can carry the load for 15 to 45 min. The ultimate system, using an electronic UPS, a diesel or turbine generator set, and transfer switches, will assure high-quality power and can survive an indefinitely long power failure. A solid-state bypass switch will transfer the computer load to the incoming electric power source in a few milliseconds if a UPS fails.

The emergency power system must have enough capacity to support the computer hardware, communications and data encoding equipment, air conditioning, a minimum of lighting and (possibly) elevators, dumbwaiters, and security hardware. Only uninterruptible or transient sensitive loads need be connected to the UPS. Proper design of the UPS, emergency generator, transfer and bypass switches, and their integration into the building's electrical service must be done by qualified engineers for best results.

Deliberate Destruction. The possibility of sabotage, vandalism, arson, or bombing must be considered. Depending on public "image"—the local crime rate, character of the neighborhood, and similar factors—the computer facility may be exposed to damage from vandals, extremists, extortionists, striking workers, a rioting mob, or a disgruntled customer or employee. Countermeasures include: building location and construction; controls over access to and from the building and computer area; computer operations rules; personnel selection, training, and supervision.

If possible, high-crime areas and proximity to production plants (potential picket lines) should be avoided. The exterior of the building should be designed and built to make covert or forced entry difficult and to provide resistance to riot damage or sabotage. For example, all first-story windows should be protected as well as doors. Electric power and communications lines, cooling towers, etc., should be hidden or protected. Entrances and parking lots should be safe for employees, particularly at night. Exterior signs designating the building as a computer facility, or building directories that give the room number of the computer room, should be omitted.

Access control simply means that only authorized persons—employees, service personnel, proper visitors, and vendor representatives—enter the building, and that all materials which enter or leave the building are properly screened to deter both theft and sabotage. It may be adequate to depend on personal recognition if there are no more than 50 employees, *but* all employees must be trained to challenge strangers, and supervisors must be alert to compliance with property-pass procedures and the like. In larger facilities, it may be necessary to adopt more formal procedures, including visible badges and access control zones; i.e., individual access to sensitive areas limited to only those assigned or authorized.

Enforcement of access controls may require the use of a security force, guards and receptionists in large facilities. Undue dependence should not be placed on door locks, as even exotic card-key systems are vulnerable. Perimeter fences, intrusion detectors, closed-circuit television, and similar security devices can help to secure and control a building, *but only if used by alert people with responsibility for security*. All employees should be briefed on their responsibilities for secure operation. Issuance and recovery of keys, ID cards, and badges should be closely controlled. For example, all locks and badges should be periodically changed. A designated staff member should regularly verify proper functioning of security devices and compliance with security and access control procedures.

Personnel Screening. Ideally, *all* personnel who enter sensitive areas should be prescreened as trustworthy or should be under direct supervision. Supervisors should be sensitive to the attitudes and deportment of their staff in order to discover disgruntlement before it causes problems and to take corrective action. For reasons of both personal safety and security, individuals should never work alone. Through their own strict compliance with control and security procedures, supervisors at all levels should set a good example for their subordinates.

REFERENCES

1968. Healy, R. J. *Design for Security*. New York: Wiley.
1971. Brown, W. F., Greenlee, M. B., and Jacobson, R. V.: *AMR's Guide to Computer and Software Security*. AMR International.
1974. Jacobson, R. V., Brown, W. F., and Browne, P. S. *Guidelines for Automatic Data Processing Physical Security and Risk Management*. Washington, DC: National Bureau of Standards, FIPS Pub. 31.

W. F. BROWN AND R. V. JACOBSON

SEGMENT. *See* OVERLAY.

SELECTIVE DISSEMINATION OF INFORMATION. *See* CURRENT AWARENESS SYSTEMS.

SEMANTICS. *See* PROGRAMMING LANGUAGE SEMATICS; and SYNTAX, SEMANTICS, AND PRAGMATICS.

SEMAPHORE

For articles on related subjects *see* CONCURRENT PROGRAMMING; DEADLOCK; LOCKOUT; MONITORS; PARALLEL PROCESSING; and PETRI NETS.

Semaphores are synchronization primitives used to coordinate the activities of two or more programs or processes that are running at the same time and sharing information. They are used for elementary interprocess communication, to guarantee exclusive access to shared data, to protect a section of code that must be executed without certain kinds of interruptions (such a code segment is called a *critical region* or *critical section*), or to allocate a set of identical scarce resources.

Two operations are defined on semaphores: *P,* or wait, and *V,* or proceed. The usage protocol for a shared resource is as follows: A process that needs control of a resource executes a *P* operation on the semaphore associated with that resource. The system suspends the process until the resource is available, and then allows it to proceed. When the process is finished with the resource, it executes a *V* operation on the semaphore to release the resource for use by another process. The resource may be any hardware or software component, including data structures, physical devices, or code segments. A semaphore may also be used to indicate when it is safe for execution to proceed past a certain point in the program. The usage protocol is slightly different when a semaphore is used to coordinate interprocess communication. For example, if process *A* requires data produced by process *B* before it can execute further, a semaphore can be used to block *A* until *B* provides the data and releases *A* with a *V* operation.

One case of special interest is the *mutex* (for mutual exclusion) semaphore, which allows only one process to use the resource at once. This is particularly useful for protecting a data structure from being updated simultaneously by more than one process.

Semaphores are often implemented with counters. For example, a typical implementation of a semaphore (call it SEM) might involve:

- Initialization of SEM. (Set the counter of SEM to the total number of instances of the resource; e.g., for a mutex semaphore, to 1.)
- P(SEM). (If the counter of SEM is greater than zero, decrement it by one and allow the calling process to proceed; otherwise, block the calling process and switch to another—unblocked—process.)

- V(SEM). (If there is a blocked process waiting on SEM, then select and awaken some blocked process; otherwise, increment the counter of SEM by one.)

The bodies of these routines must be indivisible (uninterruptible operations). The *P* and *V* notation is due to Dijkstra, who, motivated by the counter implementation, used his native Dutch to get *P* from *proberen te verlagen* ("to try to decrease") and *V* from *verhogen* ("to increase").

REFERENCE

1968. Dijkstra, Edsger W. "The Structure of the 'THE'-Multiprogramming System," *Comm. ACM* **11**, *No. 5:* 341–346 (May).

M. SHAW

SEQUENTIAL MACHINES

For articles on related subjects *see* AUTOMATA THEORY; FORMAL LANGUAGES; MARKOV ALGORITHMS; and REGULAR EXPRESSION.

Basic Concepts. A sequential machine is a mathematical model of a certain type of sequential switching circuit. It has an input σ which can take on any value from a finite set Σ, called the *input alphabet,* and an output δ, from a finite *output alphabet* Δ, as shown in Fig. 1. The input and output values are of interest only at certain instants of time; these instants are usually referred to as instants $1, 2, 3, \ldots$. At any time t, the output $\delta(t)$ depends not only on the present input $\sigma(t)$, but also on the past input sequence $\ldots \sigma(t - k), \sigma(t - k + 1), \ldots, \sigma(t - 2), \sigma(t - 1)$; hence the name *sequential machine*.

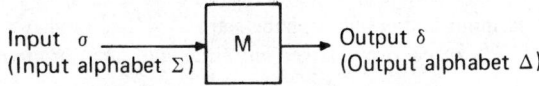

Fig. 1. Sequential machine symbol.

The dependence of the output on past inputs implies that a sequential machine has memory. Usually, this memory is finite and corresponds to a finite set Q, called the set of *internal states.* At time t, the machine M is in some (present) state $q(t)$. It receives an input value $\sigma(t)$, and this present input and the present internal state determine the next internal state $q(t + 1)$.

An example of a sequential machine is shown in Fig.

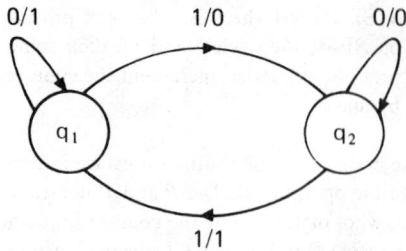

Fig. 2. Machine M_1.

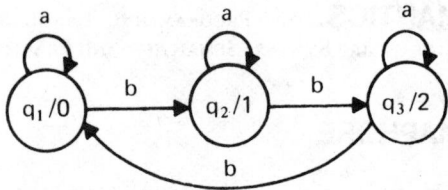

Fig. 4. Machine M_2.

2. The machine is represented by a directed graph, a *state graph*, where the nodes correspond to internal states and the labeled edges to transitions among internal states. The labels are of the form σ/δ, where σ is the input value causing the transition and δ is the corresponding output value. For example, if M_1 of Fig. 2 is in state q_1 at time t, and if $\sigma(t) = 1$, then the transition labeled $1/0$ is relevant, $\delta(t) = 0$, and at time $t + 1$ the state of M_1 will be q_2. If we are given an initial state $q(1)$—i.e., the value of q at $t = 1$—and an input sequence $\sigma(1), \sigma(2), \ldots, \sigma(t)$, we can determine from the state graph the resulting state sequence $q(2), \ldots, q(t + 1)$ and the corresponding output sequence $\delta(1), \delta(2), \ldots, \delta(t)$. A typical computation is shown in Fig. 3, where it is assumed that $q(1) = q_1$. The reader will verify that if M_1 is started in state q_1, it will produce an output of 1 at time t if and only if the number of 1's in the sequence $\sigma(1), \sigma(2), \ldots, \sigma(t)$ is even.

With each sequential machine we associate two functions: the *transition function f*, which determines the next state from the present state and the present input, and an *output function g*. In the machine M_1, the present output depends on both the present state and the present input. The model in which the output depends on both the state and the input—i.e., where $\delta(t) = g(q(t), \sigma(t))$—is the *Mealy model*. In another useful model, the *Moore model*, the present output is uniquely determined by the present state, i.e., $\delta(t) = g(q(t))$.

An example of a Moore machine is shown in Fig. 4. The input and output alphabets are $\Sigma = \{a,b\}$ and $\Delta = \{0,1,2,\}$, respectively. Given an initial state and an input

sequence, we can determine the state sequence, as in the Mealy model. Since the output is determined solely by the state, we associate it with the nodes of the state graph rather than with the edges. A typical computation for M_2 is shown in Fig. 5, assuming $q(1) = q_1$. The behavior of M_2 can be described as follows: The input value a is "ignored" by M_2 in the sense that no change of state results when $\sigma(t) = a$. The input b advances the state of M_2 cyclically. If the machine is started in q_1, the output $\delta(t + 1)$ is congruent modulo 3 to the number of b's in the input sequence $\sigma(1), \sigma(2), \ldots, \sigma(t)$.

The differences between the Moore and Mealy models are only technical. From a general point of view, these models are equivalent as far as computational power is concerned. Another model equivalent to these in the general sense is the *finite automaton* model. This is a special case of the Moore model, where $\Delta = \{0, 1\}$. If the output corresponding to an internal state is 1, that state is called *accepting*, or *final;* if the output is 0, the state is called a *rejecting* state. A single *initial state* q_0 is usually specified in the finite automaton model. A finite automaton A can be viewed as an *acceptor* of input sequences. For the input sequence $\sigma(1), \ldots, \sigma(t)$, let $q(t + 1)$ be the state reached by A, when started in q_0. If $q(t + 1)$ is a final state, the sequence is accepted; otherwise, it is rejected. An alternate point of view considers a sequential machine as a *sequence transducer*—a machine that transforms an input sequence into an output sequence, as in Figs. 3 and 5.

Realization of Sequential Machines. The behavior of a sequential machine can be realized by a sequential switching circuit. We now describe an idealized

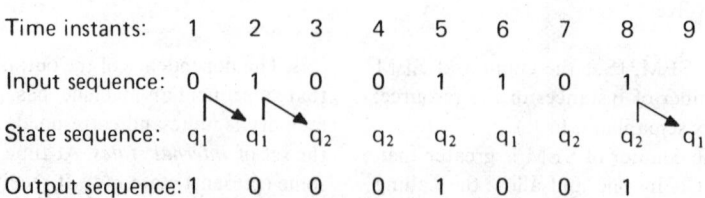

Time instants:	1	2	3	4	5	6	7	8	9
Input sequence:	0	1	0	0	1	1	0	1	
State sequence:	q_1	q_1	q_2	q_2	q_2	q_1	q_2	q_2	q_1
Output sequence:	1	0	0	0	1	0	0	1	

Fig. 3. Sequences for M_1.

Time instants:	1	2	3	4	5	6	7	8	9	10
Input sequence:	b	a	b	a	b	b	b	a	b	
State sequence:	q_1	q_2	q_2	q_3	q_3	q_1	q_2	q_3	q_3	q_1
Output sequence:	0	1	1	2	2	0	1	2	2	0

Fig. 5.   Sequences for M_2.

model of such circuits, which we call a *sequential network*. The sequential network reflects the logical properties of the switching circuit, but not its electronic properties. Thus, it has the advantage of being independent of actual technological implementation while retaining many of the basic structural properties.

A block diagram of a switching network is shown in Fig. 6. As is usually the case, we assume that all signals in a sequential network are binary, with 0 and 1 as the two possible values. The network has a finite number of binary inputs $x_1, \ldots, x_n$ and binary outputs $z_1, \ldots, z_m$. If the output values $z_i(t)$ are uniquely determined by the input values $x_j(t)$, then it has no memory. In that case, it is called a *combinational network,* and its behavior can be described by m boolean functions, one for each output z_i. A combinational network can be implemented by a network of gates *without* any feedback loops.

A switching network with memory is called *sequential.* The function of memory can be performed by gate networks *with* feedback. In general, such networks have no special timing signals and are called *asynchronous.* If a special periodic input, called *clock,* is provided to control the action of the network, the network is *synchronous.* In that case, the response of the network is of in-

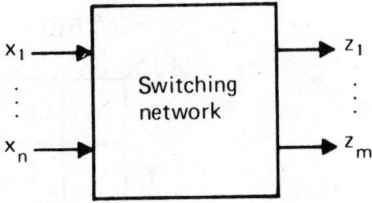

Fig. 6.   Switching network.

terest only at certain times, once during each clock period. These times correspond to the instants 1, 2, 3, ... mentioned earlier.

A synchronous sequential network can be divided into a combinational part and a memory part. The units corresponding to memory are rather complex asynchronous gate networks called *flip-flops.* For theoretical considerations, the simplest memory module is the *unit delay,* whose output y is equal to the input x delayed by one unit of time; i.e., $y(t) = x(t - 1)$. The general form of a synchronous sequential network with unit delays as memory elements is shown in Fig. 7. The network can be described by two sets of equations.

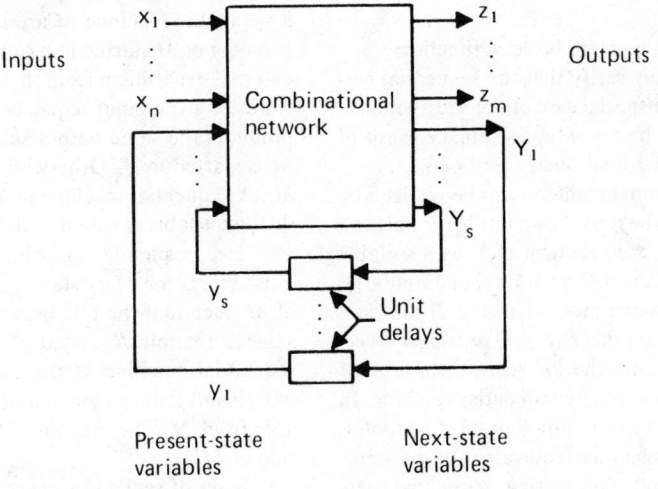

Fig. 7.   Sequential network with unit delays.

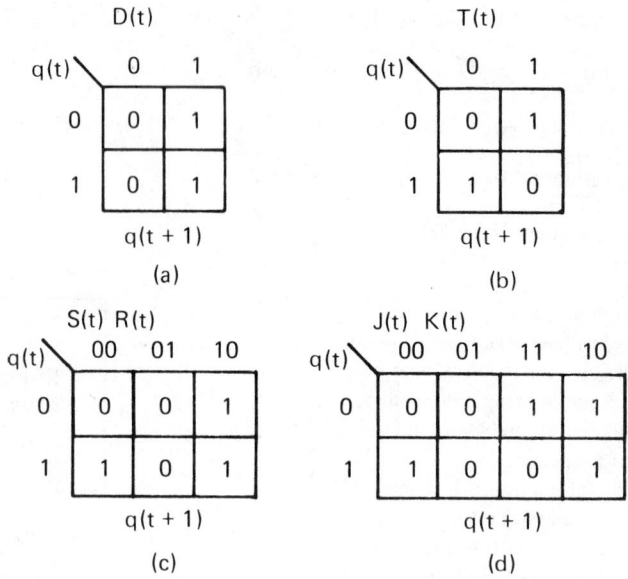

Fig. 8. State tables. (a) D flip-flop, (b) T flip-flop. (c) SR flip-flop; note that S = R = 1 is not used. (d) JK flip-flop.

1. Next-state equations:

$$Y_i(t) = y_i(t+1)$$
$$= f_i(x_1(t), \ldots, x_n(t), y_1(t), \ldots, y_s(t)),$$
$$i = 1, \ldots, s.$$

2. Output equations:

$$z_j(t) = g_j(x_1(t), \ldots, x_n(t), y_1(t), \ldots, y_s(t)),$$
$$j = 1, \ldots, m,$$

In (1) the f_i and in (2) the g_j are boolean functions.

The reader will easily verify that the sequential network model of Fig. 7 is a special case of the Mealy model, where Σ is the set of all binary n-tuples (binary words of length n) and Δ is the set of all binary m-tuples.

Any abstract sequential machine can be realized by a sequential network of the type shown in Fig. 7. This can be done by representing each element of Σ by a suitable n-tuple $x_1, \ldots, x_n$, and Δ and Q must be coded similarly.

The unit delay is sometimes called the *D flip-flop*. Other types of flip-flops are the *T (toggle or trigger) type*, the *SR (set-reset) type*, and the *JK type*. Each type of flip-flop can be used to realize any sequential machine. In Fig. 8 we define the four types of flip-flops by *state tables*, which constitute a common way (equivalent to the state-graph representation) of representing sequential net-

works. The rows of the state table correspond to the internal states, and the columns to input combinations. The entries represent the next state. The most general type of flip-flop is the JK. The condition $J = 0$, $K = 0$ is the *remember* condition, where no change takes place. $J = 0$, $K = 1$ corresponds to *reset* condition (the flip-flop is reset to 0); $J = 1$, $K = 0$ is the *set* condition; and $J = 1$, $K = 1$ is the *toggle* condition (the state changes, or *toggles*).

Behavioral Properties. Two states q and q' of a sequential machine M are *indistinguishable* if the I/O behavior of M started in q cannot be distinguished by any external experiment from that of M started in q'. In other words, a given input sequence applied to M, started in q, produces the same output sequence as in the case when M is started in q'. Otherwise, q and q' are *distinguishable*. A sequential machine in which every pair of states is distinguishable is called *reduced*.

Two sequential machines M and M' are indistinguishable if for every state q of M there exists a state q' of M' such that the I/O behavior of M started in q is the same as that of M' started in q', and vice versa. For every sequential machine M there exists a unique (up to isomorphism) reduced sequential machine M_0 indistinguishable from M. The machine M_0 is the minimal-state version of M.

A set of sequences over a finite alphabet is called a

language. It is natural to associate certain languages with sequential machines. For example, in the case of a finite automaton *A,* we define the *language, L(A),* accepted by *A* to be the set of all accepted sequences. Similarly, the set L_{ij} of all sequences taking a sequential machine from state q_i to state q_j, or the set L_δ, of all sequences resulting in a particular output value δ, represent useful languages. All such languages of the form $L(A)$, L_{ij}, or L_δ are *regular languages.* It can be shown that any language defined by a sequential machine in the above sense is regular and, conversely, for every regular language there exists a sequential machine "recognizing" that language.

An important application of sequential machines is in counting. When the number of states is finite, a sequential machine can only count modulo an integer.

Another unique characterization of sequential machines is provided by the *syntactic semigroup* of the machine, defined as follows: For each input σ, the set Q of states of a reduced machine is transformed according to the transition function. The set of all transformations of states performed by all input sequences constitutes the syntactic semigroup. This representation is useful for certain structural properties.

Structural Properties. In a general network, as shown in Fig. 7, there may be feedback loops. For example, Y_1 may be a function of y_2, and Y_2 may be a function of y_1. In the special case where no such loops exist, the network is called *definite.* An example of a simple definite network is shown in Fig. 9.

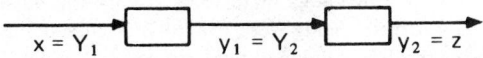

$$x = Y_1 \quad\quad y_1 = Y_2 \quad\quad y_2 = z$$

Fig. 9.   A definite network.

The languages recognized by definite networks are particularly simple, since the behavior of the machine depends only on the last k symbols of the input sequence, for some k. In general, feedback is required in order to realize the behavior of an arbitrary sequential machine. It can be shown, however, that every sequential machine can be realized by a sequential network having a single feedback loop.

When SR flip-flops (instead of unit delays) are used as memory elements, the class of machines realizable without feedback is considerably larger than the class of definite machines. The languages recognized by machines in this class are the so-called *noncounting* regular languages. Such machines can only "count to a threshold," in the following sense: If the threshold is the integer $k \geq 0$, then the machine may be able to determine

whether a certain sequence of symbols occurs in the input sequence 0, 1, . . . , or $k - 1$ times. After this, it cannot distinguish k occurrences from $k + 1$ occurrences, but can only conclude that the number of occurrences is at least k. Therefore, such machines cannot count modulo any integer greater than 1, and are called *counter-free.* The languages corresponding to counter-free machines constitute a natural subclass of regular languages. They can be defined by regular expressions that use only boolean operations and concatenation. Such expressions are called *star-free.* The syntactic semigroups corresponding to this class of machine and language are *group-free* (i.e., only groups of order 1 are allowed).

Sequential machines that can be realized by networks of unit delays and exclusive-OR gates are *linear* and constitute a proper subclass of sequential machines. Linear machines have important applications in coding theory.

The problem of decomposing a sequential machine into a *cascade connection* of smaller sequential machines has received much attention. The cascade connection of two machines is shown in Fig. 10. This connection is also known as the *series connection.* The *parallel connection* of two machines is a special case of the cascade connection, where neither machine influences the other. We have already mentioned that definite machines correspond to cascade connections of unit delays, and counter-free machines correspond to cascade connections of SR flip-flops. The Krohn-Rhodes theory shows that, in general, arbitrary sequential machines correspond to cascade connections of (1) machines whose syntactic semigroups are simple groups, and (2) SR flip-flops.

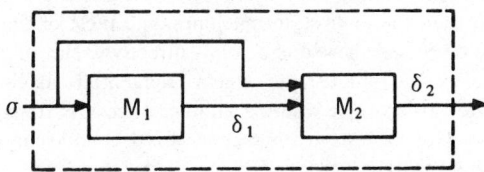

Fig. 10.   Cascade connection.

Such results are of theoretical interest. For practical applications, an often-used cascade connection is a *shift register,* which is a very simple cascade connection of flip-flops. Shift registers and counters constitute basic modules in the design of sequential networks.

Related Models. In practical applications, certain state-input combinations of a sequential machine may never occur. In this case, the next state and output may be irrelevant and need not be specified. The *incom-*

pletely specified sequential machine model handles such cases.

The situation where the next state and output of a machine are not precisely predictable is modeled by *stochastic* or *probabilistic* sequential machines. The case where the transition function and the output function vary with time is modeled by *time-varying* sequential machines. Both the stochastic and the time-varying machines are more powerful than the ordinary machines in the sense that they can recognize some irregular languages.

A theoretically convenient model is the *nondeterministic* sequential machine. Here, for a given present state and input, the next state can be chosen from a set of states; i.e., it is not unique. As acceptors of languages, the nondeterministic machines are not more powerful than the deterministic machines; both types can recognize regular languages only. A nondeterministic machine can have fewer states than the corresponding reduced deterministic machine accepting the same language. Nondeterministic machines do not correspond directly to sequential circuits, since the latter do not possess any freedom of choice for the next state.

The concept of a *generalized sequential machine* (GSM) has applications in the theory of formal languages. In this model, for a given present state and input symbol, the machine can produce a sequence of output symbols, whereas the standard model permits only one output symbol. The GSM is also a more powerful model than the standard one.

In the discussion above, we have tacitly assumed that the term *sequential machine* implies that the number of states is finite. *Infinite-state* sequential machines have also been studied. They are obviously much more powerful than the finite-state machines, and most of the results discussed above do not apply directly to the infinite-state case. Infinite-state linear sequential machines provide an example where a number of results from the finite-state case have their generalized counterparts in the infinite case.

REFERENCES

1968. Ginzburg, A. *Algebraic Theory of Automata.* New York: Academic Press.
1971. McNaughton, R. and Papert, S. *Counter-Free Automata.* Cambridge: The M.I.T. Press.
1976. Eilenberg, S. *Automata, Languages, and Machines,* Vols. **A** and **B**. New York: Academic Press.
1976. Brzozowski, J. and Yoeli, M. *Digital Networks.* Englewood Cliffs, NJ: Prentice-Hall.
1978. Kohavi, Z. *Switching and Finite Automata Theory,* 2nd Ed. New York: McGraw-Hill.

J. A. BRZOZOWSKI

SERVICE BUREAUS, DATA PROCESSING

For articles on related subjects *see* ADMINISTRATIVE APPLICATIONS; COMPUTING CENTER; DATABASE MANAGEMENT; DATA NETWORKS, PUBLIC; PROCESSING MODES; and SOFTWARE MANAGEMENT.

Data processing service bureaus sell computer processing time and related services, usually in conjunction with access to networks and sophisticated, often proprietary, software. Today's services company is part of a well-established multibillion dollar industry. The typical company of 1980 is technologically advanced, emphasizes solution products (for instance, accounting systems for end users rather than tools like programming languages for data processing professionals), develops advanced applications, is network oriented, and derives a growing portion of its revenue from international operations. It may be considering selling computers in addition to its traditional services, may have been acquired by a larger corporation, and may be actively making acquisitions of its own.

This typical firm is certainly a far cry from the small corner carry-in service bureau that was the norm only ten years ago. Although the data processing services industry has become significant in only the past decade, the first punched-card data processing service company dates back to approximately 1910. By 1935, a number of small firms were offering "tabulating services," for the most part in the statistical area of commercial data processing. By 1970, a wide range of services in both the scientific and commercial fields were available from some 1,700 firms generating combined revenues of $1.3 billion.

In 1980, over 2,000 U.S.-based firms with a total of 165,000 employees generate $6.8 billion worldwide revenue. This is a highly fragmented market place. Small batch bureaus typically generate far less than $1 million a year each in sales, while the largest suppliers, Control Data Corporation and Automatic Data Processing, each generated over $400 million in 1979 revenues.

Industry Segmentation and Size. Service bureaus charge for raw computer processing on the basis of computer and communications resources used with the price depending, like most other commodities, on vendor cost. The most profitable services offered by these bureaus, however, are those often called *problem-solving* services. These include the use of proprietary models or data, specialized applications programs or sophisticated software, back-up protection against computer disasters, or consulting and advisory assistance. These services are priced according to their value to the user; that is, on the basis of what the market will bear.

There are two methods of accessing processing services:

1. Carry-in batch services involve no direct communication between the user and the computer. The user's processing job is physically delivered to the batch service center, processed, and returned to the user.
2. Remote services involve interaction between the user and the computer. The user communicates with the service firm's computer through either a terminal or a minicomputer on site.

Carry-in batch was 75% of the market as recently as ten years ago. It is rapidly decreasing as a percentage and, by 1984, will probably represent only 25%.

Remote services may be divided into two separate categories, dependent upon user usage. The first, remote problem-solving services, include traditional time sharing as well as sophisticated, professional applications; for instance, scientific and engineering calculations and forecasting/modeling. Remote problem-solving services were only 18% of the market in 1970, now comprise 28% and are projected to increase to 31% by 1984.

The most rapidly growing sector of the processing services market is remote autotransaction services. These are remote services of a repetitive, clerical nature that include standard accounting services as well as industry-specific applications such as hospital services and services to auto dealers. Remote autotransaction services, only 8% of the 1970 market, grew 25% in 1979 and should continue to grow rapidly through 1984, by which time they may comprise over 40% of the services market.

Table 1 shows estimated market size and growth rates from 1970 through 1980 with projections to 1984 for the three main sectors of the services industry—carry-in batch, remote autotransaction, and remote problem-solving.

The single most important fact about the processing services market is that it is driven by the markets it serves. Most sales come from the end user, not the data processing manager. The market environment is different for each type of firm (carry-in batch, remote problem-solving, and remote autotransaction).

Carry-In Batch Environment. In the carry-in batch environment, most of the clients are very small firms and there are many specialty markets. Competition comes not only from other services firms, but from the in-house alternative, primarily the small business computer vendor. Payroll processing is a very common application area: Users often claim they want to process the payroll out-of-house to maintain confidentiality.

Surveys of small businesses show that they tend to have unsophisticated perceptions about what they need from data processing. For instance, when asked why they purchased an in-house computer instead of subscribing to a computer service, users often cite more rapid response time as a major reason. Present computer services users, however, never cited response time as a "problem" or a reason to purchase an in-house system.

Remote Problem-Solving Services. Remote problem-solving services are quite a different market. Manufacturing, the federal government, utilities, and banks are the most significant target markets. Together, they comprise fully 70% of the spending for these services. Scientific and engineering applications were once nearly the total remote problem-solving market. But for the first time in 1979, general business and administrative applications generated more revenue. The purchasers of these services are usually fairly sophisticated. They include middle management, scientists, engineers, and, often, application programmers.

Remote Autotransaction Services. The medical, banking, retail, and insurance fields are the most important users of these services. Manufacturing shows up again, but for a different type of application, most significantly distribution accounting. Here, the interrelation of target industries and applications is critically important. Retail, for instance, is 14% of the target market, but more than half of this retail spending is for credit authorization and credit card processing services.

TABLE 1. Worldwide Revenues of U.S. Suppliers, 1970–1984 ($ millions)

	1970	Compound Annual Growth	1975	Compound Annual Growth	1980	Projected Compound Annual Growth	1984 (est.)
Carry-in batch	$ 940	12%	$1,675	8%	$2,435	7%	$ 3,135
Remote problem-solving	230	27%	755	21%	1,945	19%	3,855
Remote autotransaction	95	50%	715	27%	2,415	23%	5,470
Total	$1,265	20%	$3,145	17%	$6,795	16%	$12,460

Future. The future of the processing services industry is bright. It is expected to grow 16% a year to $12.5 billion by 1984 and, in at least two areas, even more rapid growth is possible.

Remote database services constitute a major services industry growth area. They have grown from only $55 million in 1970 to $570 million in 1979 and will continue to increase at well over 20% a year reaching perhaps $1.5 billion by 1984.

Both remote problem-solving services suppliers and remote autotransaction services suppliers sell database services. They sell access to actual pieces of information such as stock market quotations, credit histories, periodical text, as well as the processing power to manipulate the data.

Remote problem-solving services suppliers sell what can be called intermediate product databases. The pieces of data in these databases are manipulated, not merely read by the user. Financial/economic and demographic marketing databases are the fastest growing in this area. Scientific/engineering databases are usually provided by suppliers merely as an accommodation to one or a very limited number of clients.

End product databases are sold by the remote autotransaction services suppliers. Here, the piece of data itself is the end product. Credit/check verification is the largest submarket. Stock quotation database services, once the largest sector, have become saturated as to number of clients, and total market growth follows the brokerage industry rather than the processing service industry. Bibliographic retrieval and legal database services are also growing rapidly.

Acquisitions have always been popular in the services industry, and are accelerating. Services companies often acquire smaller services and/or software companies to enter a new target industry. Large corporations acquire services companies to enter the rapidly growing marketplace. For instance, American Express acquired First Data Resources; Dun & Bradstreet acquired National CSS; and McGraw-Hill acquired Data Resources, Inc.

These major new market contenders can readily change the complexion of the services market over the next ten years. The biggest market change may be the reality of the home market, especially database services accessed in the home.

SOURCES OF DATA

International Data Corp., Waltham, MA.
Association of Data Processing Service Organizations, Arlington, VA.
INPUT, Inc., Palo Alto, CA.

P. D. LANDRY

SETL

For articles on related subjects *see* PROGRAMMING LANGUAGES; and PROCEDURE-ORIENTED LANGUAGES.

Very high-level languages are programming languages which allow algorithms to be stated in a manner independent of detailed data structuring. SETL is a very high-level language designed to facilitate the programming of algorithms involving sets and related structures.

SETL provides conventional control structures (if-then-else, while, case, etc.), as well as some specifically set-oriented ones [e.g., forall (the members of a set)], but its data structures are very general and include arbitrary finite sets nested to any length and nested tuples with arbitrary components as objects. More specifically, SETL admits the following structures.

Tuples are arbitrary length ordered sequences of component values, which may be primitive or may themselves be tuples. Tuples correspond closely to one-dimensional vectors in familiar languages except that they have no fixed length and can be extended dynamically simply by assigning a value to a previously nonexistent element. In SETL, tuples are used to represent both ordered sequences and unordered "bags" where equal elements may occur. In the latter case, the order of the elements in the tuple is not important.

Examples of SETL tuples, which are delimited by brackets, and of the results of operations on them are as follows.

$$t_1 := [0,1.1, \text{'hello;'}]; \ t_2 := [0,0, ['a', 'b']];$$
$$t_1(2) = 1.1, \ t_2(3) = ['a', 'b'],$$
$$t_2(2..3) = [0,['a','b']],$$
$$t_1 + t_2 = [0,1.1, \text{'hello'}, 0,0, ['a', 'b']].$$

Sets are unordered collections of objects with the constraint that a given element cannot appear more than once. SETL provides the usual set-theoretic operations (union, intersection, etc.) and also the *arb* operator which selects (nondeterministically) an arbitrary element from a set. Examples of sets and of the results of operations on them are the following.

$$s_1 := \{0,1.1, \text{'hello'}\}; \ s_2 := \{0,['a', 'b']\};$$
$$s_1 * s_2 = \{0\}; \ s_1 - s_2 = \{1.1, \text{'hello'}\};$$
$$s_1 + s_2 = \{0,1.1, \text{'hello'}, ['a', 'b']\};$$

where * represents intersection; +, union; and −, set difference.

Maps in SETL are not a separate basic type, but are simply sets of tuples of length 2 (called pairs) whose first component is a domain value and whose second component is the corresponding range value. The set of tuples in a map, therefore, defines a function. Maps may be single or multiple valued, and SETL provides functional-style constructions for evaluating maps for a given argument value, assigning new map values, etc. Since maps are sets, all set valued operators can be used with maps. An example of a map and of operations involving it are:

numbvowels := {['hello', 2] , ['goodbye',3]};
numbvowels ('hello') = 2; numbvowels ('zebra')
=Ω/*undefined*/.

The following succinct "toplogical sort" program illustrates the use of SETL. We read a directed graph *g,* which is assumed to be a set of ordered pairs {[*a, b*], [*c, d*], ...}, each such pair representing an edge, and then attempt to arrange the nodes of *g* in a tuple in such a way that each directed edge goes from a lower to a higher numbered node (i.e., from an element of the tuple to one which follows it).

read (g); /* read in the graph, which is set of pairs */
set_of_nodes := {n(1) : n ε g} + {n(2) : n ε g};
/* all nodes of g*/
ordered_tuple := [ ];
/* tuple to be built up is initially empty */
(**while exists** n ε set_of_nodes **suchthat**
(**forall** m ε set_of_nodes | [m,n] ∤ g)
/*if no [m, n] is in g, add n to end of ordered-
tuple and remove it from set_of_nodes */
ordered_tuple := ordered_tuple + [n];
set_of_nodes := set_of_nodes − {*n*};
end while;
if set_of_nodes = { } **then**
/* remaining set of nodes is not null*/
print('topological ordering is impossible');
end if;
/* otherwise ordered_tuple includes all nodes */

SETL's *representation sublanguage* adds a system of declarations to the core language described above. These declarations allow the user of the language to control the data structures that will be used to implement an algorithm that has already been written in pure SETL. Ideally, no rewriting of the algorithm is necessary. A supplemented program SP involving declarations written in the data representation sublanguage will always produce the same output as the core language program CP which SP incorporates.

The default representation of a set *S* in the absence of all declarations is a hash table, within which the elements of *S* are located via a system-wide hash function which can be applied to any SETL object. Each element is stored in a plex (an arbitrary data structure) called an

element block. These element blocks are also linked together in a list, to expedite iteration over the set. In the presence of declarations written in the data representation sublanguage, the element blocks used to represent a set are expanded to contain additional fields, bit-flags, and pointers, allowing sets to be represented either as bit-vectors or distributed collections of flag bits, in addition to their standard default representation. Similarly, maps can be represented by value fields stored directly in plex blocks or grouped into arrays. Use of these representations eliminates a good deal of hashing and can improve the time and space efficiency of a SETL program considerably without requiring the original abstract form of an algorithm to be rewritten.

The SETL system is implemented in a transportable manner and is currently available on the IBM 370, DEC 10 and VAX, and CDC 6600. An advanced optimizer, capable of choosing reasonably acceptable data structures automatically, is a significant component of the system.

REFERENCES

1975. Schwartz, J. and Kennedy, K. "An Introduction to the Set Theoretical Language SETL," in *Computers and Mathematics with Applications* **1**: 97–119. New York: Pergamon Press.
1979. Dewar, Robert B. K.; Grand, Arthur; Liu, Ssu-Cheng; Schonberg, Edmond; and Schwartz, Jacob T. "Programming by Refinement, as Exemplified by the SETL Representation Sublanguage," *ACM Transactions on Programming Languages and Systems* **1**: 27–49 (July).

J. T. SCHWARTZ

SHARE

For articles on related subjects *see* COMPUTER USER GROUPS; and GUIDE.

SHARE is an organization of users of medium- and large-scale IBM data processing systems (essentially 360/50 and larger and including systems 370 and 303X) whose objective is the exchange and dissemination of ideas and information pertinent to the use of such systems. SHARE membership is open to all organizations that can demonstrate competence and a legitimate interest in SHARE activities.

The organization conducts semiannual general meetings, for which *Proceedings* are published, as well as other smaller meetings for specialized purposes. Additionally, SHARE sponsors—either wholly or jointly with other organizations—workshops and symposia open to all qualified data processing practitioners. A monthly newsletter, *SHARE Secretarial Distribution,* together with a variety of irregular publications supplements the face-to-face information exchange derived from meetings.

SHARE, the first *computer user group,* was established in August 1955. The founding fathers were Lee Amaya of Lockheed Aircraft, Paul Armer of RAND, and Jack Strong and Frank Wagner of North American Aviation. Invitations were sent to all known prospective IBM 704 installations, and the response was virtually total. The first SHARE meeting was held in Santa Monica, California, and 46 persons representing 17 installations participated.

Since the IBM 704 was designed for *scientific computation,* the composition of SHARE remained oriented to this domain for some time. *Business data processing* became an area of major concern only after the announcement of IBM's System 360 in April 1964. Well before this time, the users of IBM equipment concerned with business data processing had established a sibling organization, GUIDE, to serve their needs. Much of the energy of both organizations in the late 1960s was devoted to developing a modus operandi for cooperation, resulting in a merger proposal that was rejected by the memberships. At present, approximately 30% of the membership of SHARE (currently about 1,300 installations) also belongs to GUIDE as well.

The early thrust in SHARE was toward development of conventions, standards, and procedures necessary to permit and promote exchange of programs. While this objective remains explicit in SHARE activities today, the current emphasis is directed to criticize vendor-supplied products for the purpose of providing a consensus on functional need to the vendors.

Central to SHARE's interests are *programming languages, operating systems,* and *database systems.* Software associated with specific application areas has always been of secondary interest in SHARE. A complete listing of SHARE activities is beyond the scope of this article, but is is fair to say that almost all data processing subjects not directly concerned with the design of hardware have been given scrutiny by some subgroups of the organization.

SHARE has responded to growth and change in the computer industry in various ways. An administrative office with full-time personnel has been established, legal counsel has been retained, the by-laws have been redrawn to remove explicit organizational structure, and the original SHARE organization was dissolved by the transfer of its assets and good will to a newly created not-for-profit corporation, SHARE, Inc., in January 1969. Funding is provided solely by the registration fees paid by meeting participants and by receipts from sale of publications. As a consequence, SHARE is not obligated to IBM or any other vendor, and has now broadened its interests beyond its original area of concern.

The roster of presidents and the dates of their service follows.

Jack Strong, 1955–1956
Frank Engel, 1956–1957
Frank Wagner, 1957–1958
Ben Ferber, 1958–24 July 1959 (resigned)
Ed Jacks, 1959 (appointed by Executive Board, 24 July 1959
Frank Verzuh, 1959–1960
Harry Cantrell, 1960–1961
Aaron Finerman, 1961 (resigned 16 Oct. 1961)
John Jordan, 1961–1962 (promoted from vice-president, 16 Oct. 1961)
George Ryckman, 1962–1963
Jim Rowe, 1963–1964
Jim Babcock, 1964–1965
Roy Dickson, 1965–1966
Jim Tupac, 1966–1967
Phil Cramer, 1967–1968
John Noerr, 1968–1969
Philip Dorn, 1969–1970
E. David Callender, 1970–1971
David M. Smith, 1971–1972
George E. Gautney, Jr., 1972–1974
Shirley Prutch, 1974–1975
Edward J. Farrell, 1975–1976
John Hogan, 1976–1978
Edward S. Haskell, 1978–1980
Bettye Odneal, 1980–

T. B. STEEL, JR.

SHIFTING

For articles on related subjects *see* ARITHMETIC-LOGIC UNIT; MACHINE AND ASSEMBLY LANGUAGE PROGRAMMING; MACHINE INSTRUCTION SET; and REGISTER.

Shifting is the process of moving data that is stored in a storage device relative to the boundaries of the device (as opposed to moving it in and out of the device). The device in which the shift is performed is called a *shift register.*

In order to discuss the various modes of the shift operation, we assume that the register in which the shift is to be performed is n bits wide, and number the bits from left to right, $1 \cdots n$.

A *left shift* is the operation in which the ith bit is replaced by the $(i + 1)$st one. This operation can be repeated an arbitrary number of times so that one can shift by any number of positions. The question of what re-

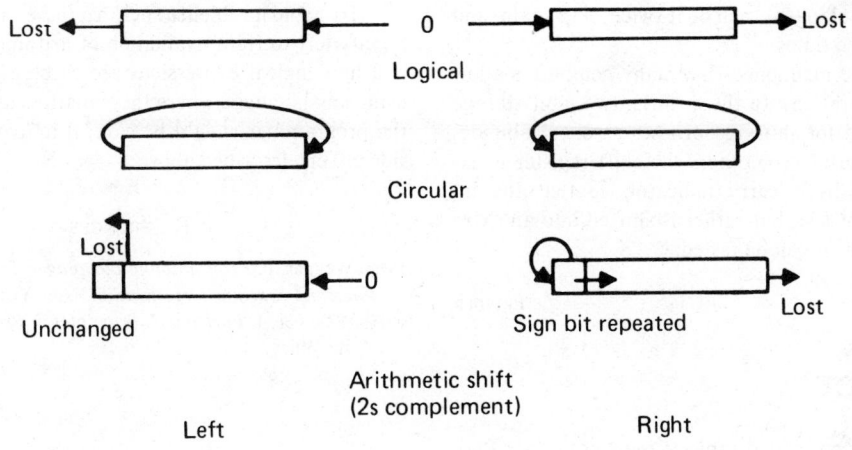

Fig. 1. The various shift operations.

places the nth (last) bit will be dealt with later, as will the question of what happens to bit 1.

A *right shift* is the operation in which the ith bit is replaced by the $(i-1)$st bit. Again, this is easily generalized to a right shift by any number of positions.

There are three types of shifts: logical, circular, and arithmetic (see Fig. 1). They differ in the treatment of the first and last bits, both in the left and right shift.

In *logical shifts,* the bit shifted out is lost, and the bit shifted in is zero. Note in the left shift that the bit shifted out is bit 1, and the bit shifted in occupies position n, whereas in the right shift, the bit shifted out is the nth one and the bit shifted in occupies position 1.

In *circular shifts* the bit shifted out of one end is shifted into the other end. There is, therefore, no loss of information in the circular shift.

The *arithmetic shift* is designed to take orderly advantage of the fact that shifting a bit string left multiplies the binary number represented by it by 2, whereas shifting it right divides it by 2. Multiplication and division of positive number by 2 can therefore be accomplished by logical shifts. However, when negative numbers are present, special care must be exercised in dealing with the sign bit.

In the sign-magnitude representation of negative numbers, the sign bit should be left intact. In the 2s complement representation, it should be kept intact on left shift and should be repeated on right shift; i.e., in the right shift, bit 2 should be replaced by bit 1 (the sign bit) and bit 1 should be left in its previous value. In the 1s complement representation, the equivalent operation is done by circular shifts. In either of these, there are cases in which overflow can be generated.

The precise definition of an arithmetic shift depends, therefore, on the way negative numbers are represented

in the computer. For 2s complement representation (Fig. 1), the definition is as follows:

In a right arithmetic shift, the nth bit is shifted out and the first bit is repeated. In a left arithmetic shift, the sign bit is left intact, the nth bit is filled with zero, and the second bit is lost. Most computers will set condition codes to indicate possible overflow in arithmetic shifts.

Some examples of the effect of the various shift operations on some five-bit strings are presented in Table 1.

Shift operations are usually used in field alignments, packing and unpacking of data items into storage units, and high-speed multiplication and division, especially by constants. Among the more exotic uses is that for the creation of control patterns. For example, the pattern 10110111 can be used for a switch that will do an oper-

Table 1.   Examples of Shift Operations

Bit String	Operation	Result	Comments
01011	Left logical	10110	
01011	Right logical	00101	Last bit lost
01011	Right circular	10101	
01011	Left circular	10110	
01011	Right arithmetic	00101	
01011	Left arithmetic	00110	Result incorrect (overflow)
11001	Left arithmetic	10010	2's complement assumed
11001	Right arithmetic	11100	
11001	Left logical	10010	
11001	Left logical 2	00100	2-place shift

ation once, then skip (0), then do it twice, skip again, and finally do it three times.

It should be mentioned that many computers allow double-shift operations. In these shifts, two n-bit storage devices are used for shifting purposes as one $2n$-bit device. Also, in certain computers the shift register is extended, usually by a carry indicator, so that the bit shifted out is not lost, but rather is shifted into an extra bit storage where it can be tested.

G. FRIEDER

SIDE EFFECT

For articles on related subjects *see* ARGUMENT; PRO-CEDURE; PROCEDURE-ORIENTED LANGUAGES: Programming; and SUBPROGRAMS, CALLING.

A side effect is a consistent result of a procedure that is in addition to or peripheral to the basic result. It is often evidenced as a change in values of variables that are not local to the procedure. Although a side effect may be of no consequence or undesired, in many cases it is just what is desired from the procedure—as, for example, when one of the procedure arguments is an output argument. But side effects can result in nasty problems in the evaluation of arithmetic expressions. To understand this consider the expression

A + B∗C

It is most convenient to evaluate this expression by multiplying B times C and then adding A, for otherwise we must first fetch A, store it away temporarily, multiply B∗C, and then add back the temporary value. But what if the expression is instead

FCN(A) + B∗C

where FCN is a procedure with argument A? Suppose the evaluation of FCN(A) has a side effect that modifies the value of B or C or of both. Then the value of the expression is different if B∗C is evaluated before FCN(A) is evaluated or afterward. A related problem can occur in the evaluation of logical expressions such as

I < 20 **and** FCN(A) = 5.

If I $\geq$ 20, then the expression must be false. Some systems will recognize this and not evaluate FCN(A) at all. Others will perform all evaluations of the arguments of AND and then evaluate the expression. If FCN(A) modifies other variables in the program, then it is vital to know how expressions are evaluated.

To avoid problems such as these, some languages specify left to right evaluation of arithmetic expressions and how logical expressions are to be evaluated. When using any language where these matters are not specified, the programmer should be careful to avoid the kinds of side effects described above.

REFERENCES

1968. Wegner, P. *Programming Languages, Information Structures and Machine Organization.* New York: McGraw-Hill.
1980. Wagener, J. *Fortran 77: Principles of Programming.* New York: Wiley.

A. RALSTON

SIGNIFICANCE ARITHMETIC

For articles on related subjects *see* ARITHMETIC, COMPUTER; NUMBERS AND NUMBER SYSTEMS; PRECISION; and SIGNIFICANT DIGIT.

The significant digits of a radix approximation (from some finite precision radix-number system) to a true number implicitly convey information on the accuracy of the numerical approximation. Significance arithmetic is an easily applied accuracy-monitoring technique providing rules for estimating the number and positions of the significant digits of the radix approximation that results when an arithmetic operation is applied to operands in radix approximation form.

Suppose the positional digit sequence $d_m d_{m-1} \cdots d_l$ $\cdots$ is the standard base $\beta \geq 2$ radix representation of the real number x (i.e., $d_m \beta^m + d_{m-1} \beta^{m-1} + \ldots$ so that no radix point need be shown) with most significant digit $d_m \neq 0$. The absolute error in approximating x by the $m - l + 1$ digit real number $\tilde{x} = d_m d_{m-1} \cdots d_l$ with least significant digit d_l is less than β^l. A bound on the relative error $|(x - \tilde{x})/x|$ is given uniformly for any $x \neq 0$ by $1/\beta^{m-l}$. As a function of x, a sharper bound on the relative error is found by plotting the gap function β^l/x. This function may be interpreted as the absolute error bound divided by the true value x. The gap function then yields a bound on the relative error, which varies with x in a log periodic manner, and is best illustrated on a log-log plot (Matula, 1970).

The solid line in Fig. 1 shows the gap function for radix approximations truncated to $n = m - l + 1 = 5$ significant decimal digits; the dashed line corresponds to six significant decimal digits; and the dotted line to five significant hexadecimal digits. The decimal gap functions in Fig. 1 illustrate the rule than an additional significant digit in the base β radix approximation provides a uniformly tighter error bound on the relative error by a factor of $1/\beta$. It is also evident that an n significant digit

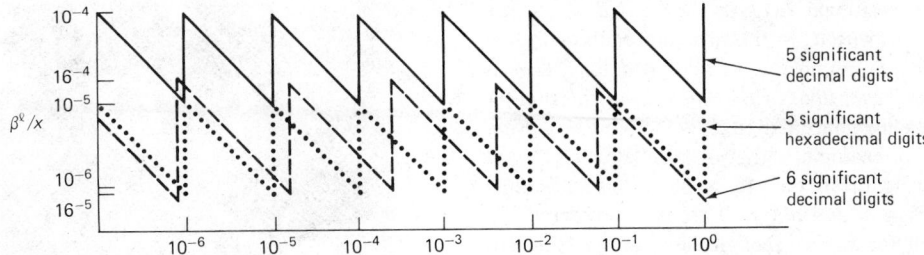

Fig. 1. Three cases of the gap function.

base β radix approximation with a leading digit of unity will provide only a slightly better relative error bound than an $n - 1$ significant digit radix approximation with a leading digit of value $\beta - 1$. For example, 1.065 as a four-digit approximation to 1.065 $\cdots$ has only a slightly smaller relative error bound than that of 0.978 as a three-digit approximation to 0.978 $\cdots$ (this explains why four digits are as easily obtained on the left-hand side of a slide rule as are three digits on the right-hand side).

The significance arithmetic rule for radix conversion (Matula, 1970) is that an n significant digit base β radix approximation will, upon conversion to base γ, yield approximately ($n \log \beta/\log \gamma$) significant digits in the base γ radix approximation. This estimate is inherently crude, since Fig. 1 implies that five significant digit hexadecimal radix approximations can in some regions yield more accuracy than seven significant digit decimal approximations, whereas in other regions they will yield less accuracy than five significant digit decimal radix approximations (see point A in Fig. 1).

The significance arithmetic rule for addition/subtraction of radix approximations is that (if no overflow to a higher indexed most significant digit occurs) the position of the least significant digit is the higher index of the least significant digit positions of the operands, and (if overflow occurs) the least significant digit position is taken as one unit higher. The most significant digit of the result is the highest indexed nonzero digit of the result, providing this position is at least as great as the least significant digit position. Note that subtractive concellation can result in a severe decrease in the number of significant digits, with a possibility of leaving no resulting significant digits. In schematic radix addition form:

	SSSS.SSXX
	SSS.SXX
With no overflow:	SSSS.SXXX
With overflow:	SSSSS.XXXX
Cancellation example:	000S.SXXX

where S = significant digit and X = nonsignificant digit.

The significance arithmetic rule for multiplication/division is simply that the number of significant digits in the result is the minimum of the number of significant digits in the operands.

In schematic radix multiplication form,

$$
\begin{array}{r}
\text{S S . S X X} \\
\times \quad \text{S . S S X} \\
\hline
\text{.}\circledX\text{X X X X X} \\
\circledS\text{. S S S X X} \\
\circledS\text{S . S S X X} \\
\circledS\text{S S . S X X} \\
\hline
\end{array}
$$

With no overflow:	SS.SXXXXX
With overflow:	SSS.XXXXXX

where S = significant digit, X = nonsignificant digit, ⓢ = possible significant overflow digit, and ⓧ = possible nonsignificant overflow digit.

In summary, significance arithmetic provides rules for estimating the significant digits of an arithmetically computed radix approximation, which in turn provides an estimate of the error of this approximation. The overall error estimate is crude but easy to compute.

REFERENCES

1970. Matula, D. W. "A Formalization of Floating Point Numeric Base Conversion," *IEEE Trans. Comp.* **C-19**:681–692.
1976. Matula, D. W. "Radix Arithmetic: Digital Algorithms for Computer Architecture," Chapter 9 in Yeh, R. (Ed.), *Applied Computation Theory*. Englewood Cliffs, NJ: Prentice-Hall.

D. W. MATULA

SIGNIFICANT DIGIT

For articles on related subjects *see* ARITHMETIC, COMPUTER; NUMBERS AND NUMBER SYSTEMS; PRECISION; and SIGNIFICANCE ARITHMETIC.

Let the positional digit sequence $d_m d_{m-1} \cdots d_0$ $\cdot d_{-1} d_{-2} d_{-3} \cdots$ with $d_m \neq 0$ be an exact radix representation for the real number x. Each digit d_i for $i \leq m$ is termed a *significant digit of the exact representation* for x, and the leading nonzero digit d_m is the *most significant digit* for x. For example, with $x = 0.030200 \ldots, d_{-2} = 3$ is the most significant digit for x. Note that the leading zero digits $d_0 = 0$ and $d_{-1} = 0$ are not considered significant digits for x, even though the representation utilizes $d_{-1} = 0$ to properly position the significant digits; d_{-3} is significant because it falls after the most significant digit.

Let the positional digit sequence $d_m d_{m-1} \cdots d_0$ $\cdot d_{-1} d_{-2} d_{-3} \cdots$ with $d_m \neq 0$ be a radix approximation for the real number x. Suppose x is known to fall strictly between the real numbers with radix representations $d_m d_{m-1} \cdots d_{l+1}(d_l - 1)$ and $d_m d_{m-1} \cdots d_{l+1}(d_l + 1)$, where l can be positive, negative, or zero, and furthermore where the digit value d_{l-1}, such that x falls between the real numbers with radix representations $d_m d_{m-1} \cdots d_l(d_{l-1} - 1)$ and $d_m d_{m-1} \cdots d_l(d_{l-1} + 1)$, is either incorrectly chosen *or* unknown. Then each digit d_i for $l \leq i \leq m$ is a *significant digit of this radix approximation* for x, d_m is the most significant digit for x, d_l is the least *significant digit* for x, and $m - l + 1$ is *the number of significant digits* in this radix approximation for x. For example, the decimal approximations $0\underline{3}.0$, $\underline{3.1425}0$, $\underline{3.14158}0$, $\underline{3.14160}3$, and the binary approximation $0\underline{11.00111}$ for $\Sigma = 3.1415926 \cdots$ have the significant digits underlined. In these cases the digit following the least significant digit is incorrect in each case. The statement that a measured value, (say, 23.185) has three significant digits merely indicates that the digit value d_{-2} is not known with certitude, although $d_{-2} = 8$ might be possible (and perhaps represents a "best guess").

D. W. MATULA

SIMON, HERBERT A.

For article on related subject *see* ARTIFICIAL INTELLIGENCE.

Herbert Alexander Simon (b. Milwaukee, WI, 1916) is best known in computer science for his work in artificial intelligence and cognitive psychology. As his receipt of the Nobel Prize in Economics for 1978 indicates, his intellectual base is far wider. Trained as a political scientist at the University of Chicago (Ph.D. 1943), he has made substantial and often major contributions not only to political science, but to the study of organizations, public administration, econometrics, management science and operations research, the philosophical founda-

Fig. 1. Herbert A. Simon.

tions of causality and Newtonian mechanics, and the nature of scientific discovery, as well as to psychology and computer science.

It is possible to emphasize the diversity in such a scientific career; e.g., a highly successful text on public administration (Simon, Smithburg, and Thompson, 1954), an influential research monograph on the servomechanism analysis of factory production control (Holt, Modigliani, Muth, and Simon, 1960), and so on. It is preferable, and equally valid, to emphasize the common theme that runs through all this work: To understand the nature of rational behavior in humans. Simon's first book (1947) was an analysis of how the administrative human operates in formal organizations—a creature of institutional, informational, and computational limits who works within a frame of *bounded rationality*. This book, a core citation in the Nobel award, was central to establishing a model of economic decision making that has stood in contradistinction to the dominant model of the *economic humans,* global optimizers who know their preferences over all conceivable commodity bundles. This concern with bounded rationality—with behavior that *satisfies* rather than optimizes—also lies at the heart of his work in understanding in detail how computers and humans can behave intelligently.

Counterposed to the diversity of his intellectual career is the simplicity of his academic career. After relatively short stays at UC Berkeley and the Illinois Institute of Technology, he joined Carnegie Mellon University (then Carnegie Institute of Technology) in 1949 as a founding member of the Graduate School of Industrial Administration, which launched a revolution in graduate education in business, building it on scientific knowledge in economics, psychology, and operations research. He has been at Carnegie-Mellon University ever since, the last 15 years most closely associated with its Psychology Department (as Richard King Mellon Professor of Psychology and Computer Science).

Simon's primary contribution in computer science was his collaboration with John C. (Cliff) Shaw and Allen Newell in the development of the first heuristic programs (the *Logic Theorist,* 1956; the *General Problem Solver,* 1958) and the first list processing languages (the IPLs, 1957). This team of three, along with John McCarthy, Marvin Minsky, and Oliver Selfridge, are generally credited with having founded the area of *artificial intelligence* (McCorduck, 1979). The early programs were also taken to be models of how human thinking occurs (then usually called *simulation of thought processes*). Simon has continued to produce a stream of programs and analyses that explore how intelligent action occurs—in problem solving, memorizing, inducting, behaving in semantically rich domains, and learning. Throughout, the connection with human thinking has been explicit and often dominant. A major work on human problem solving was published in 1972 (Newell and Simon, 1972) and the range of his work can be found in Simon (1978). In 1975, Simon (jointly with Newell) was given the ACM Turing Award for his entire line of work. Simon had earlier (1969) received the Award for Distinguished Scientific Contribution of the American Psychological Association for the psychological side of this work.

Simon has received many awards and honorary degrees, and is a member of the National Academy of Sciences. He has been active in many professional societies, and in giving advice and counsel to government at all levels. His total scientific output is prodigious, even by the standards of his peers (12 books and some 500 papers). His contributions show no sign of diminishing, as of the date of this writing (1980).

REFERENCES

1947. Simon, H. A. *Administrative Behavior.* New York: Macmillan.

1954. Simon, H. A., Smithburg, D. W., and Thompson, V. A. *Public Administration.* New York: Knopf.

1960. Holt, C. C., Modigliani, F., Muth, J. F., and Simon, H. A. *Planning Production, Inventories, and Work Force.* Englewood Cliffs, NJ: Prentice-Hall.

1972. Newell, A. and Simon, H. A. *Human Problem Solving.* Englewood Cliffs, NJ: Prentice-Hall.

1979. McCorduck, P. *Machines Who Think.* San Francisco: Freeman.

1979. Simon, H. A. *Models of Thought.* New Haven, CT: Yale University Press.

A. NEWELL

SIMPLEX METHOD

For articles on related subjects *see* MATHEMATICAL PROGRAMMING; MATRIX COMPUTATIONS; and OPTIMIZATION METHODS.

Although first developed over 30 years ago in the late 1940s by G. B. Dantzig and his associates, and although various alternative algorithms have been developed since, the *simplex algorithm* or one of its modifications remains the most common one in use today for solving the linear programming (LP) problem:

$$\text{Minimize: } f(\mathbf{x}) = \mathbf{c}^T\mathbf{x} = c_1x_1 + c_2x_2 + \ldots + c_nx_n \quad (1)$$

Subject to the constraints:

$$A\mathbf{x} = \mathbf{b} > \mathbf{0}, \quad (2a)$$
$$\mathbf{x} \geq \mathbf{0}, \quad (2b)$$

where A is an $m \times n$ matrix ($m < n$), $\mathbf{c}$ and $\mathbf{x}$ are vectors of dimension n and $\mathbf{b}$ is a vector of dimension m. It is assumed that A has rank m.

If, instead of minimizing Eq. 1, we wish to maximize $\mathbf{c}^T\mathbf{x}$, we need merely minimize $-\mathbf{c}^T\mathbf{x}$, since max $\mathbf{c}^T\mathbf{x} = -\min -\mathbf{c}^T\mathbf{x}$.

We call a vector $\mathbf{x}$ *feasible* if it satisfies Eq. 2 and *basic* if any $n - m$ components are zero. We call an $\mathbf{x}$ which is both basic and feasible a *basic feasible solution*. If, in addition, all m nonzero components are positive, the solution is called *nondegenerate*.

Suppose now that the first m columns of A are linearly independent. Let us write $A = [A_{mm}, A_{m,n-m}]$ where A_{mm} represents these first m columns. Then, if we multiplied Eq. 2a by A_{mm}^{-1}, we would obtain

$$\mathbf{x}_m = \tilde{\mathbf{b}} - \tilde{A}\mathbf{x}_{n-m} \quad (3)$$

where $\mathbf{x}_m^T = (x_1, \ldots, x_m)$, $\tilde{\mathbf{b}} = A_{mm}^{-1}\mathbf{b}$, $\tilde{A} = A_{mm}^{-1}A_{m,n-m}$, and $\mathbf{x}_{n-m}^T = (x_{m+1}, \ldots, x_n)$. Thus, if all components of $\tilde{\mathbf{b}}$ are positive, then with $\mathbf{x}_{n-m} = \mathbf{0}$, $\mathbf{x}_m$ as given by Eq. 3 is a nondegenerate basic feasible solution (nbfs). Assume for now that we have indeed found such an nbfs.

If Eq. 3 is substituted into Eq. 1, then the *cost function* $f(\mathbf{x})$ becomes

$$f(\mathbf{x}) = z_0 + \tilde{c}_{m+1}x_{m+1} + \tilde{c}_{m+2}x_{m+2} + \ldots + \tilde{c}_nx_n \quad (4)$$

where $z_0 = c_1\tilde{b}_1 + c_2\tilde{b}_2 + \ldots + c_m\tilde{b}_m$. The $\tilde{c}_j$, $j = m + 1, \ldots, n$ are called *reduced cost coefficients*. Note that for our nbfs $f(\mathbf{x}) = z_0$. If all the reduced cost coefficients are nonnegative, any change in $x_{m+1}, \ldots, x_n$ cannot decrease $f(\mathbf{x})$. Indeed, this *local minimum* can be shown to be a *global minimum* and, thus, a solution of our LP problem.

Suppose now that some $\tilde{c}_k < 0$. Then an increase in x_k will decrease $f(\mathbf{x})$. If we choose

$$x_k = \min_{a_{pk}>0} \frac{\tilde{b}_p}{\tilde{a}_{pk}} = \frac{\tilde{b}_q}{\tilde{a}_{qk}} \qquad (5)$$

where $\tilde{a}_{pk}$, $p = 1, \ldots, m$ are components of $\tilde{A}$ in Eq. 3, then it is not hard to see that x_q in Eq. 3 becomes 0 and all other x_j, $j = 1, \ldots, m$ remain positive. Thus, we have a new nbfs with the kth component nonzero and the qth component zero. (Note that if all $\tilde{a}_{pk}$ in Eq. 5 are nonpositive, then x_k may be chosen unboundedly large, in which case $f(\mathbf{x})$ goes to $-\infty$; such a situation is almost surely indicative of a misformulation of the LP problem.)

The simplex method is essentially a mechanization of the procedure described in the previous paragraph for proceeding from one nbfs to another until all reduced cost coefficients are nonnegative. Before giving the equations to implement this mechanization, we show how to obtain an initial nbfs. Consider the LP problem:

$$\text{Minimize: } g(\mathbf{y}) = y_1 + y_2 + \ldots + y_m \qquad (6)$$

Subject to the constraints:

$$A\mathbf{x} + I_m \mathbf{y} = \mathbf{b} > \mathbf{0}, \qquad (7a)$$

$$\mathbf{x}, \mathbf{y} \geq \mathbf{0}, \qquad (7b)$$

where A and $\mathbf{b}$ are as in Eq. 2 and I_m is the $m \times m$ identity matrix. An nbfs for this problem is $\mathbf{y} = \mathbf{b}$, $\mathbf{x} = \mathbf{0}$. If we apply the simplex algorithm to this problem, we end up with an nbfs for our original problem if one exists. For if such an nbfs exists for Eq. 2, then with $\mathbf{y} = \mathbf{0}$, it is also an nbfs for Eq. 7 and gives a $g(\mathbf{y}) = 0$, which is its minimum possible value. Note that solving Eqs. 6 and 7 obviates the need actually to compute A_{mm}^{-1} since the solution of Eqs. 6 and 7 automatically results in an nbfs of the form in Eq. 3 (although usually with variables other than $x_1, \ldots x_m$ on the left).

To mechanize the simplex method we use the *tableau* shown in Fig. 1 where the coefficients are those given in Eqs. 3 and 4. $P_1, \ldots, P_m$ are the indices of the nonzero components of the nbfs at each stage of the algorithm and $P_{m+1}, \ldots, P_n$ are the indices of the zero components. Then, assuming that $\mathbf{x}_m^T = (\tilde{b}_1, \ldots, \tilde{b}_m)$ is an nbfs, the simplex algorithm proceeds as follows.

Step 1. Compute

$$\min_{m+1 \leq j \leq n} \tilde{a}_{0j} = \tilde{a}_{0k}$$

		$P_{m+1} \ldots \ldots$		P_n
	$\tilde{a}_{00} = z_0$	$\tilde{a}_{0,m+1} = \tilde{c}_{m+1} \ldots \ldots$		$\tilde{a}_{0n} = \tilde{c}_n$
P_1	$\tilde{a}_{10} = \tilde{b}_1$	$\tilde{a}_{1,m+1} \ldots \ldots \ldots$		$\tilde{a}_{1n}$
.				
.	$\ldots \ldots \ldots \ldots \ldots \ldots \ldots \ldots \ldots \ldots \ldots \ldots$			
.				
P_m	$\tilde{a}_{m0} = \tilde{b}_m$	$\tilde{a}_{m,m+1} \ldots \ldots \ldots$		$\tilde{a}_{mn}$

Fig. 1. The simplex tableau.

to find the most negative $\tilde{c}_k$. Choose the smaller index if there is a tie. If $\tilde{a}_{0k} \geq 0$, terminate the algorithm with solution $x_{p_1}, x_{p_2}, \ldots, x_{p_m}$ (and all other components zero).

Step 2. Compute, as in Eq. 5,

$$\min_{a_{pk}>0} \frac{\tilde{a}_{p0}}{\tilde{a}_{pk}} = \frac{\tilde{a}_{q0}}{\tilde{a}_{qk}}.$$

If all $\tilde{a}_{pk} \leq 0$, terminate with an indication that the solution is unbounded.

Step 3. Replace P_q by P_k on the left and P_k by P_q on top in the tableau.

Step 4. Calculate the new values (indicated by primes) of $\tilde{a}_{ij}$ in the tableau:

$$\tilde{a}'_{ij} = \tilde{a}_{ij} - \tilde{a}_{ik}\tilde{a}_{qj}/\tilde{a}_{qk} \quad \begin{aligned} & i = 0, \ldots, m; \, i \neq q \\ & j = 0, \ldots, n; \, j \neq k \end{aligned} \qquad (8)$$

$$\tilde{a}'_{ik} = -\tilde{a}_{ik}/\tilde{a}_{qk} \quad \tilde{a}'_{qj} = \tilde{a}_{qj}/\tilde{a}_{qk}$$

$$\tilde{a}'_{qk} = 1/\tilde{a}_{qk}$$

Return to step 1.

The equations given as Eq. 8 are a consequence of substituting Eq. 5 into Eq. 3 and rearranging the equations so that x_k appears on the left side in place of x_q.

To begin the algorithm, we apply steps 1–4 to Eqs. 6 and 7 with the nbfs $\mathbf{y} = \mathbf{b}$, $\mathbf{x} = \mathbf{0}$. An example of the application of this algorithm may be found in Ralston and Rabinowitz (1978).

In the foregoing, we have assumed a nondegenerate bfs at each stage. Theoretically, the simplex algorithm need not converge in the presence of degeneracy, but in practice, even though degeneracy is a common phenomenon, it can be ignored, since it virtually never causes computational problems.

In addition to the form above, there are a number of variations of the simplex algorithm. The most important of these, which can be quite useful computationally, is the *dual simplex algorithm,* in which, in effect, we interchange the roles of $\mathbf{b}$ and $\mathbf{c}$ in Eqs. 1 and 2 to derive another formulation of the LP problem whose solution is easily transformed into a solution of the original problem.

REFERENCES

1962. Hadley, G. *Linear Programming.* Reading, MA: Addison-Wesley.
1978. Ralston, A. and Rabinowitz, P. *A First Course in Numerical Analysis,* (2nd Ed.). New York: McGraw-Hill.

A. RALSTON

SIMSCRIPT

See SIMULATION: Languages.

SIMULATION

For articles on related subjects *see* EMULATION; HARDWARE MONITOR; MODELS; MONTE CARLO METHOD; OPERATIONS RESEARCH; PERFORMANCE MEASUREMENT AND EVALUATION; PROGRAMMING LANGUAGES; QUEUEING THEORY; SCIENTIFIC APPLICATIONS; and SOFTWARE MONITORS.

Simulation is the representation of certain features of the behavior of a physical or abstract system by the behavior of another system. In computing, therefore, simulation refers to the employment of the computation process to implement a model of some dynamic system or phenomenon. The purpose of simulation is usually to make experimental measurements or predict behavior, although simulation is also used for teaching purposes. Simulation has been one of the most consistently useful and productive applications of computer science. Simulations, both large and small, have been used by industry, academia, and government for as long as the modern digital computer has been employed. Actually, the concept of simulation preceded the advent of digital computation through the use of analog systems, and even preceded the use of analog computers through the use of physical models in, for example, wind tunnels and towing tanks.

This treatment of digital simulation is divided into two categories: the process and applications of simulation; and the techniques, or languages, of simulation.

PRINCIPLES

Historically, the concept of modern digital simulation was first proposed by John von Neumann, who visualized the application of gathering repetitive, statistical data on modeled phenomena. This was termed the Monte Carlo method (*q.v.*) because it imposed randomly generated parametric changes on the model. Among the earliest published applications of digital simulation were the solutions of problems related to job shops, that is the allocation and distribution of resources to production scheduling. Among the latest applications of digital simulation is, curiously, the prediction of the performance of computers themselves. Both examples are illustrative of one of the prime justifications for employing simulation, namely, that the economics or logistics of experimenting with the actual system are prohibitive. Since simulation is an expensive (both labor-intensive and computation-intensive) tool to use, economic justification for its application is of great importance.

Other situations where simulation has been economically feasible are those in which a model or substitute system must be used to attain predictive data: system-design concept evaluation (the system is not physically available); system-destruction or safety experiments (too dangerous); system-reliability or failure testing (economically unfeasible). Simulation has also been employed to replace elements of systems or entire systems too large or cumbersome to test, e.g., spacecraft docking and maneuvering; world weather dynamics; large man/machine systems; weapon effects. It is employed in lieu of a closed-form, mathematical means of predicting behavior. The term "prediction" is an important concept. Simulation enables the mapping of the analyst's concept of the real world. Because mapping is an approximation, the results are approximate rather than precise.

In the modern sense, digital simulation began about 1959 with the reporting of several job-shop simulators developed by large industrial corporations. In 1962 came the documentation of the first general-purpose simulation languages, Simscript and GPSS. The technology has burgeoned in the intervening years. Practitioners of simulation hold three yearly national conferences on general subjects, and there are a number of symposia devoted to special applications (e.g., simulation of computers). Several major technical societies have simulation-oriented component organizations. There is at least one technical organization, the Society for Computer Simulation (*q.v.*), devoted exclusively to simulation. Many academic institutions, responding to the rapidly increasing demand for this useful technology, give courses in simulation which are sponsored mainly in the multidisciplinary curricula: computer science, operations research, or industrial management. This is appropriate because simulation is, in essence, a multidisciplinary technology, comprising elements of mathematics, engineering, and management science.

The Process of Simulation

Definitions. Simulation is a process that employs a computerized model of certain significant features of some physical or logical system. The object of the process of simulation is to provide an experimental model for the accumulation of data on the target system. The process of simulation comprises the steps of experiment definition, modeling, computer implementation, validation, and data gathering.

Simulators are programs developed to apply the process of simulation. The term *simulator* usually implies the incorporation of some model elements (job-shop simulator; computer simulator) even though the tool may be quite flexible and thus useful for many modeling adaptations.

Simulators should be distinguished from *simulation languages,* which are general purpose and contain no model bias.

Experiment Definition. The problem to be solved by simulation can be considered as the identification of the behavior of some dynamic system. "Dynamic" and "simulation" are interrelated terms. Systems that are dynamic—i.e., whose states change with time—are those which are customarily defined to be simulatable.

What the problem solver must determine at the outset of the process is the extent and detail of the model required, and correspondingly the scope of input and output data required.

"Extent" and "detail" are also interrelated. The *extent* of a system is the broadness of system function encompassed by the simulation model. The number of functions modeled is the *detail* or level of structure incorporated in the model. Because the computer size and speed present a finite boundary for any application, the broader the scope of the system considered, the less detail is likely to be included. For example, the synthesis of a model of airport service might include planes landing, taking off, taxiing, and loading-unloading. Corresponding detail might be the actual runway routing and the unloading ramp services. Broader specification might include descent, ascent, flight routing, and holding. Finer structure might involve fueling, inspection, and crew assignments. In the broad extent, the incorporation of finer levels of detail would usually be irrelevant, and vice versa.

The desired output data and available input data are important ingredients in defining the simulation process. The data detail should be at a level comparable to that of the complexity of the model definition. Input data is frequently considered a simulation problem area. Hypothesized or poor-quality input data may degrade the validity of output data, but it may not diminish the viability or utility of the simulation process if the validity problem is taken into account (see later section, "Validation.")

Modeling. The target system, thus defined, is modeled. Many types of simulation models exist. They are classified by the nature of the systems they represent. The most frequent classfication criterion is the dynamic-change property of the system variables: continuous or discrete.

Continuous-variable models usually represent those systems that are describable by mathematical expressions which depict the continuous change of variables with time. Physical systems represented by differential equations, where time is the independent variable, are of this nature. What continuous-variable simulation implements is the behavior of the system during transient responses to perturbations. Continuous-variable simulation is often carried out on analog, digital, or hybrid computers (*q.v.*).

Because they account for the large majority of all computer simulations, this article will focus on *discrete-event* systems in which the dynamic state changes in discrete steps. In this case, no smooth, mathematical function can be found to obtain system behavior. The changes are abrupt, steplike. Transients between states are not considered. Such system behavior usually results from the disruption of system status caused by the allocation and deallocation of resources within the system. Queueing is an important consideration in systems describable by discrete-event models.

Computer Implementation. By *implementation* we mean the process of computerization of the discrete-event model. Simulation programming may be accomplished by using various programming tools, such as high-level languages and languages specifically designed to implement simulation. It should be noted that most discrete-event simulation models could be exercised by manual computation, although this would be tedious. However, this is sometimes a useful method for checking the operation of the computerized model.

Computerization of the simulation model affords the benefit of automated data gathering and storage. Automation of these functions enables representation of complex dynamic processes and (optionally) the performance of Monte Carlo experiments on target systems. Monte Carlo experiments involve the perturbation of the system with randomly varying quantities, and the accumulation of large and statistically sufficient output data samples.

Another benefit accruing from computerization is the reduction of the experimental data to produce summary reports on important system variables. Thus, the experimenter may receive deterministic or statistical output data that depicts system status and performance during and at the end of specified time intervals in individual experiments or (in Monte Carlo models) at the conclusion of the desired statistical sample.

Discrete-event models are frequently implemented using such general-purpose, high-level languages as Fortran. Occasionally they are programmed in assembly language. Most commonly, languages especially designed to enhance this implementation process are used. These are called *discrete-event simulation languages*. They can be described by various properties: event orientation (transaction versus process); modeling purpose (general versus specific purpose); or coding level (statement versus database). Some, such as Simscript and GPSS, are available on a wide range of host machines; others designed for special machines and purposes have limited availability. Specific languages are discussed in a later section.

Validation. Validation is the most perplexing aspect of the simulation process. In the simulation community there is a wide range of opinion as to the meaning, necessity, and techniques of validation. Validation, in general, refers to estimating the degree of validity of the simulation results and is a property somewhat comparable to accuracy.

However, while "accuracy" has an absolute connotation, validity is concerned with *relative* accuracy (Morris and Roth, 1981). To state the validity of a result, one must impute to it an accuracy *related to* an understood criterion. This is important because simulation itself is an approximate process, frequently employing hypothetical or statistically varying data, constructs, and parameters. In this context, simulation results with a specified accuracy may be valid for one purpose but invalid for another. For instance, accuracies in simulated performance of a computer system of, say, 70% may be quite valid for configuration analysis for use in marketing, but the same results would be entirely invalid for some other purpose, such as final source selection. The process requires the use of an understood *criterion of validity*.

Simulation is itself a substitute for real experimentation, and usually is conducted in the absence of a complete set of "real" data. Even when a real data comparison with some specific system state is possible, absolute accuracy of extrapolated system states is impractical, for the modeling process itself imparts assumptions, linearities, and qualified detail to the target system model. In any case, establishing the final accuracy (hence, validity of the model) involves an iterative process whereby successive runs and adjustments converge and lead to some accepted criterion.

Other means of partially validating the results of a simulation are *comparison* (for a limited range) with a hand-computed solution, and an *estimation* of relative validity. This refers to an order-of-magnitude/polarity comparison of simulated and predicted behavior when subjecting the system to selected stresses.

Data Gathering. Data obtainable from discrete-event simulations fall into three primary classifications: timing, resource utilization and queueing, and historical.

Timing data includes the statistics of system or event timing: time to complete a job or process, or time allocation to a system user, or number of users per-unit-time. These are useful for gauging the dynamic performance of various systems entities, i.e., customers processed through facilities, speed of service, etc.

Resource utilization and queueing data includes the number of calls, time utilized, waiting time, length of queue, etc., for the system resources. This is useful for determining system-flow bottlenecks and balance of resources.

Historical data usually is represented by a chronological event-by-event trace for entire or partial simulations. This is useful for debugging models and programs, and for examining transient conditions in the simulated system.

Discrete-Event Models. Discrete-event models, while possibly differing in "world view" (organization of model logic and structure) may be considered to have a common, basic purpose and therefore a common basic set of elements. Discrete-event models basically are focused on system users, who consume system resources and expend time. Where resources are unavailable, queueing and queue-serving may occur. Models may differ in the generation of events and in method of accumulation of time and queueing statistics. However, all discrete-event models possess the basic element set—users, resources, demand and queues. Elements may be described as entities having referenced attributes, which enable classification and accumulation.

Users are the consumers of resources. They may be, for example, supermarket customers, computer applications, or factory orders. User entities may have defining attributes. Supermarket customers may be differentiated by sex, number of selections, point of origin (i.e., parking location). Computer applications may be differentiated by data set, number of segments processed, type of origin (i.e., remote terminal, batch load, etc.) Factory orders may be differentiated by type of product ordered, number of production operations required, shipping destination. A commonly employed attribute is *priority*. This is usually invoked to influence the competition for resources. Priority may be of a ranking nature or may be preemptive.

Resources may be described as single entities, pools or sets of entities, and storage entities. Resource entities may also have classifying attributes. A single entity is one that has uniqueness. Resources having common attributes and considered as interchangeable may be grouped in sets. Resources having multiplicity of storage capacity may be considered as multiserver facilities.

The manager of a supermarket is a resource likely to have unique attributes because there is only one in each unit of the supermarket system. However, the carts of a supermarket may be considered as having common, indistinguishable attributes, and therefore comprise a set of interchangeable units. A facility may be illustrated by the storage area of some store or shop, where a number of elements of occupancy exist.

An interesting attribute is spatial location. Entities may be transferred during use from one location to another—for example, locomotives on a rail system; program segments in memory; supermarket carts from store to parking lot. Most simulators can enable assignment of resources by location attribute.

Demand is the schedule of events, users, or customers to be processed through the target system. Demand specification may be expressed in deterministic or probabilistic fashion: Transactions may be scheduled at predetermined times or as the result of random selection from some statistical ensemble. A supermarket demand example is the specification of the arrival of shoppers of various types during, say, a peak hour.

Queues are entities that hold and order the users waiting for resource service. A stated service discipline controls the ordering, usually by user priority and time of request. Queues having length are usually associated with specific resources, such as the supermarket check-out waiting line, the computer application scheduling stack, the job-shop subassembly storage bin. The waiting line may be effectively infinite or be limited by floor space; the stack is necessarily limited by memory size; the storage bin, while holding a queue, is itself a facility occupied, and may, in turn, be queued.

The Tools of Computer Simulation

Discrete-Event Simulation Program Operation. Discrete-event simulation programming languages are, at the execution level, quite similar. They differ mainly in the method available to the programmer for communicating the model programmatically. Basically, programs in all simulation languages manipulate files, or sets, which contain elements describing simulated time, event resource-and-time requirements, resource status, etc.

The main operation of a typical simulation program consists of the updating of a *next event* file. Other main operations are the maintenance of a *queue* file, a resource status file, and data collection files (Fig. 1).

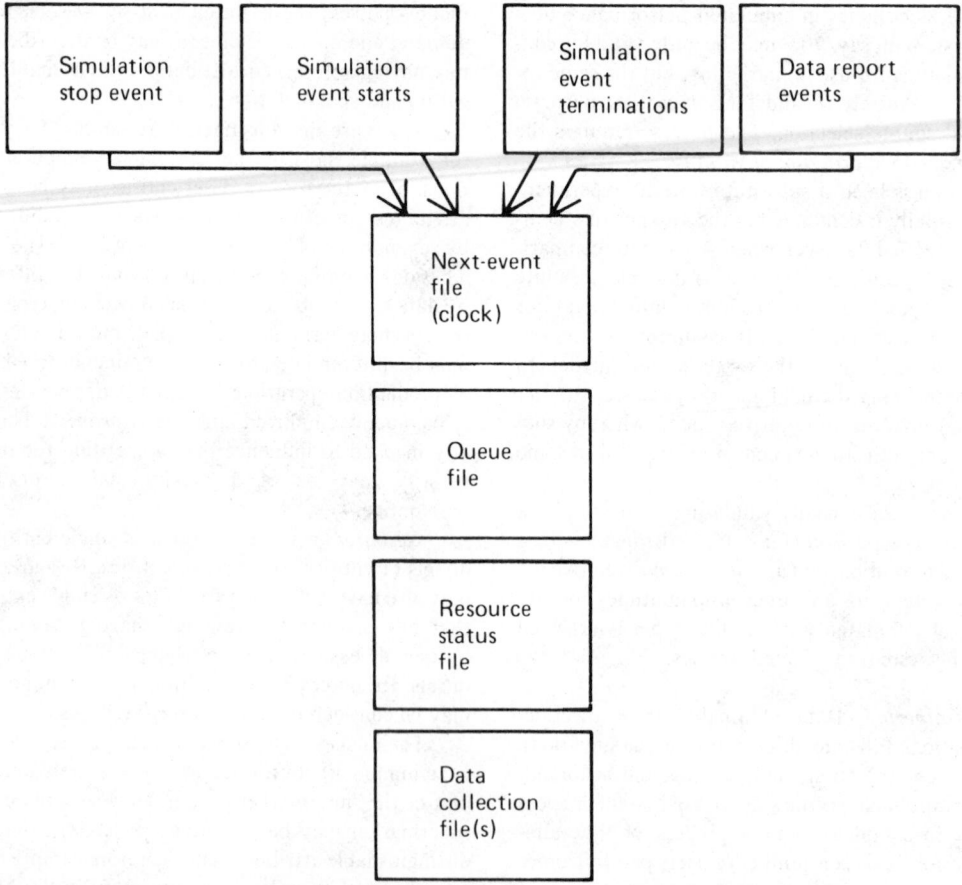

Fig. 1.   Typical main simulation files.

The queue file maintains a "time stamped" record of all events awaiting resource servicing and which have previously been denied resources.

The next event file has the function of maintaining a list of all events to be processed and also serves as the *clock,* allowing simulated time to be updated. An entry in the next-event file is made whenever the initiation time for a future event is established. Types of events handled by this file are:

1. Simulation events: the starting time of some process or string of events, the starting time of individual events, the termination time of events or processes.
2. Reporting events: start of interim or final simulation output reports.
3. End of the simulation.

At the beginning of a simulation, the starting times for all predetermined events may be loaded into the next-event file. For simulation events, these may consist of occurrence times generated from random ensembles or by deterministic specification. The times for reports and for the end of the simulation may also be input.

Processing of the next-event file, and hence the clock, then becomes a continuous updating of the start and finish of various events. Obviously, all event terminations and many event starts cannot be predetermined because of blockage or delays induced by resource contention and random selection of timing and decisions.

Initially, the next-event routine (Fig. 2) scans the next-event file to find the next event. When the next event is a scheduled-event start, it advances the file time-status NOW (or clock) to the time of this start, and then exits to a resource allocation routine, which either assigns resources or initiates queueing. If resources are successfully assigned, the event-service time is added to NOW, and this time is entered into the next-event file as a future completion event, and the scanning for other events occurring at NOW is resumed. If resources are unavailable, an entry is made into the queue file naming this event, requesting appropriate resources, and indicating NOW as the time of request. Control is then returned to the next-event routine to continue scanning for the next event in the file.

When the next event is a completion event (meaning that the clock has advanced so that NOW equals the event completion time), the next-event routine exits to a routine that restores the resources used by the event to their unbusy states and appropriate files. At this point, the event-scan routine will likely pass control to a queue-servicing routine, which determines if the required resources are now available for a queued event. The queue-servicing routine then scans the queue file for events which, at this point, can be assigned resources. If any events can be so assigned, they are effectively "reactivated," i.e., removed

from the queue file by having their completion times entered in the next-event file. Control is then given back to the next-event routine, which enters the scan mode and proceeds to look for other events at NOW. If current (NOW) events are exhausted, the "clock" scanning continues until the next event is found. This constitutes in effect a two-modal scan: the "clock" scan, looking for events chronologically, and the "event" scan, looking for events during the current value of NOW.

Note that, at the current time, many things may happen simultaneously. Events may start and finish; reporting may occur. The ordering of these occurrences during this "time freeze" is influenced by the order of insertion of events into the next-event file, which may be the result of various random processes.

It should also be noted that the clock is usually updated in asynchronous, random-time quanta, not in synchronous time steps. Periodic reporting occurs when the next-event routine senses a reporting notice in the next-event file. Control is then given to the report-generation section of the program.

Final programmatic stopping of the simulation occurs usually in one of two ways: The next-event routine may determine that no more simulation events are scheduled, or it may sense a STOP notice at some value of NOW. Usually, either condition will automatically generate a final data report.

LANGUAGES

Overview. The preceding section described the operation of a typical simulation program so as to illustrate its purely list-processing and nonmathematical nature. Reference to specific programs was intentionally omitted in order to convey this nature in an abstract sense. This operation is at the inner, execution level. In the context of simulation implementation, however, the most important language concepts are not those of execution, but rather of communication of simulation models to the computer so that execution may occur.

Simulation languages, as distinguished from general-purpose languages, are *problem-oriented.* Such languages are usually written in a largely computer-independent notation for a particular problem area, and contain statements or constructs appropriate for formulating solutions to specific types of problems. Of course general-purpose languages such as Fortran are also widely used in discrete event simulation. A recent estimate indicates that 75% of all discrete event simulation is performed using Fortran. Of the remaining 25%, GPSS and Simscript are the most popularly favored, with the former more highly favored.

These use patterns probably reflect the already established familiarity with such tools as Fortran rather than an objective preference based on features. Also, such

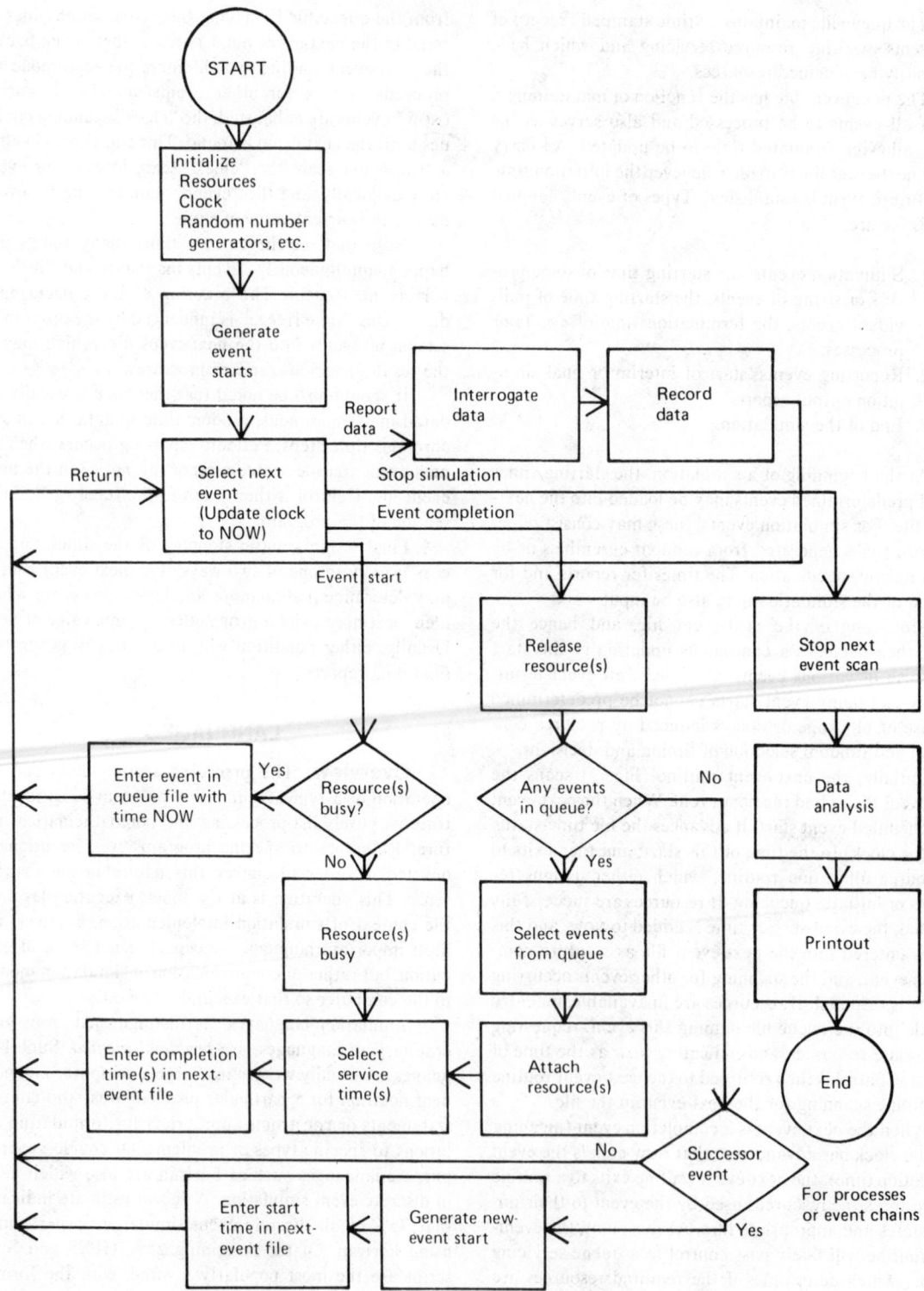

Fig. 2. Typical next-event routine for discrete- event simulation.

factors as training time and cost may weigh to some extent. However, an important decision factor in the choice of a simulation language is the complexity and freedom of model representation accommodated. This choice is frequently a trade-off between factors such as complexity of expression accommodated, language bias, cost of running, ease of programming, availability of program, and method of documentation of results.

The complexity accommodated refers to the programmatic features of the language. The language bias refers to the modeling conventions imposed by the language. A language such as Fortran has the widest range of expression and imposes the least bias upon the model to be programmed. This is at one end of the language spectrum. The remainder of the spectrum consists of various discrete-event simulation languages with varying degrees of expression and/or bias.

Simulation languages contain, to varying extents, constructs or structures that facilitate communication of a model to the computer. Control features such as data aggregation, event-timing routines, entity generation and destruction, data collection and presentation, and random variable generation are contained as subroutines or procedural operations in simulation languages. General-purpose programming languages require that these operations be programmed ad hoc.

One class of simulation languages, examples of which are Simscript and Simula, provides a basic, precompiled set of simulation support and control routines, but require the modeler to describe the model by using formal program language statements: Simscript uses Fortran-like statements; Simula uses Algol-like statements. Another type of simulation language, exemplified by GPSS, incorporates not only control routines but also general-purpose model structures, which are precompiled. This enables the communication of the model through specification of "blocks," which represent specific model routines. Programming this type of model consists of ordering block operations and specifying parameters through the use of rigid, formatted, data input files. This, of course, constrains the model basically to the "world view" of the simulation language developer. The statement-like languages discussed previously impart less "world view," and hence more modeling flexibility.

Simulation languages can be discriminated from another standpoint: their method of processing modeled events. The major distinction is between the "process-oriented" and "event-oriented" languages. The process-oriented language views the world as a set of fixed objects or facilities, which are employed to service the active transactions (users) that are created and which traverse the system. A supermarket can be modeled as a set of fixed resources (carts) assigned to the users (customers) who enter the store. In event orientation, facilities and events interact at scheduled times. An example of event orientation is a repairman looking for a failed piece of equipment to service.

It is interesting to note that statement simulation languages comprise primarily both process (Simula) and event (Simscript) orientation. Block languages such as GPSS tend to be process-oriented. However, most are sufficiently flexible to be used as desired by the inventive simulator.

Various human and economic factors must be considered in language selection. The block-diagram approach greatly eases the process of access to the computer. The precompiled nature of the block language requires only new data inputs to change the model structure and parameters, since compilation is eliminated from the simulation process. By contrast, a statement simulation language requires statement preparation, subsequent compilation, and debugging for each model respecification. Conversely, the statement language offers a potentially greater efficiency in running than does the block diagram language, and therefore lowers the computer cost. However, again, this may be offset by the potentially lower cost of programming a block-oriented simulation where it is applicable.

Another consideration is the level of expertise required to implement either approach. A statement language requires programming and syntax rigor; a block language requires only the ability to manipulate a data base to map the model; hence, the modeler or problem solver is presented with a shorthand method of communicating with the computer.

Description of Languages. In this section, we describe briefly three event-type (Simscript, Simscript II, Gasp II) and three process-type (GPSS, Simula, Boss) languages. Table 1, which has been abstracted from a compilation by Sargent (1979) summarizes the properties of these languages.

Simscript. Developed by H. Markowitz, G. Hausner, and H. Karr at the RAND Corporation, Simscript is available on a wide range of computers. It was one of the original discrete-event simulation languages. Since its statements equip the user with a Fortran-like instrumentation set, Simscript requires scientific programming ability. Simscript permits broad specification of an event-oriented model, but it does not provide any automatic statistical analysis or output. However, a Report Generator provides code for specifying output without the use of input-output statements per se. Subsequent to the RAND version, new compilers appeared for various machines under a copyrighted name, Simscript I.5.

Simscript II. This is a scientific programming language which enables discrete-event simulation. A descendant of, but not compatible with, the original Simscript, it was designed by Markowitz and Karr, with additional

Table 1. Characteristics of Some Simulation Languages

Characteristics					
Language name	Simscript	Gasp	GPSS	Simula	Slam
Meaning of name	No specific meaning	General-Activity Simulation Program	General-Purpose Simulation System	No specific meaning	Simulation Language for Alternative Modeling
Current versions	Simscript II.5 (discrete), C-Simscript (discrete, continuous, and combined)	Gasp II (discrete), Gasp IV and Gasp-PL/I (discrete, continuous, and combined)	GPSS/360, GPSS V, GPSS/H, and several others (all discrete)	Simula 67 (Discrete)	Slam (discrete, continuous, and combined)
Implementation language	Machine	Fortran or PL/I	Assembly	Algol	Fortran
Computer system	Most large computers (several commercial time-sharing systems)	Any computer having a Fortran or PL/I compiler (some commercial time-sharing systems)	Most large computers (several commercial time-sharing systems)	Most large computers	Any computer having a Fortran compiler (some commercial time-sharing systems)
Language orientation	Statement	Statement	Block	Statement	Statement or network
World view (discrete)	Event or process	Event	Process (transaction)	Process	Event and process
Storage management	Dynamic	Fixed	Dynamic	Dynamic	Fixed
Language type	Compiler	Compiler	Interpreter (GPSS/H:Compiler)	Compiler	Subprogram library/compiler
Language purchase cost	Moderate	Inexpensive	Moderate	Moderately expensive	Inexpensive

work done by P. Kiviat and R. Villaneueva at RAND. Simscript II contains five "levels," which provide a wide range of capability for use as a scientific and/or data processing language, as well as providing event-oriented simulation capability. It is widely available in two copyrighted versions: Simscript II Plus and Simscript II.5.

Gasp II (General Activity Simulation Program). This is a simulation language that essentially augments Fortran with a set of event-oriented simulation structures such as event timing, set manipulation, and statistical data collection and reporting. The Gasp user must be familiar with Fortran. Gasp II was developed by Kiviat and A. Pritsker. Lately, Pritsker and associates have developed a PL/I version, Gasp1-I, a new scientific language version of Gasp, Gasp IV, and a related combined discrete and continuous language Slam (see Table 1).

GPSS (General-Purpose Systems Simulator). GPSS, developed originally by G. Gordon at IBM, is the most popular discrete-event simulation language. GPSS is process-oriented, containing a repertoire of flowchart-like blocks (Gordon, 1978). It also provides a large variety of autonomously generated measurements about the simulated model. Since its original version, it has appeared in subsequent, more powerful versions: GPSS-II, -III, -IV, -V, -H and -360. Current versions provide limited capability for using Fortran and assembly language subroutines. GPSS-360 Norden is a proprietary version developed by Reitman and associates, which through a CRT display unit, provides conversational features, user-interactive input, and control.

Simula. Simula, an extension of Algol developed at the Norwegian Computing Center by O.-J. Dahl and K. Nygaard, is process-oriented: A process (user) continues until it is prevented from execution. An operative process is considered "active"; a queued or suspended process is considered "passive." Simula allows recursiveness, list-processing capability, and allows complete user access to

Algol. An advanced version, called Simula 67, is a general-purpose scientific language containing simulation capability.

Boss (Burroughs Operational System Simulator). This language was developed at the Burroughs Corporation by A. J. Meyerhoff, P. F. Roth, P. Shafer, and J. P. Troy. While not following GPSS block format, Boss is similar in that it allows the use of its own flowchart-like blocks for coding processes. Boss blocks, however, contain multiple functions; for instance, it has implicitly invoked queueing when a process task cannot obtain a resource. This imparts to Boss an extremely compact notation that is sufficiently powerful for most modeling applications.

Comparative Example. To illustrate simulation languages and their differences, the coding of a simple, single-server queueing model is illustrated, using a block-diagramming language and a statement language.

Fig. 3 represents the logical flow of events for each arrival in a rather general single-server situation. In this case, it is assumed that one server constitutes the fixed resource of the system, and the user activity is represented by the flow model. Discrete events occur as the service user arrives at the system for service; tests the status of the server (currently busy or unbusy) and branches accordingly; is queued awaiting service (if busy) and then dequeued; obtains possession of the server (busies it) for a time; releases the resource; and exits the system. Time parameters (left unspecified here for generality) that must be imparted to the system are the arrival time and the service time; these may be generated using random numbers or otherwise specified. The time in the queue is conditional upon the availability of the server; thus, it may have a value from zero to any number, based on the demand on the server.

A simulation comparison is shown by discussing the coding of such a model in GPSS, the major block-diagram language, and Simscript II, one version of the most popular statement language. These coding examples are abstracted from a detailed treatment given by Fishman (1973). Only code specifically related to model implementation is discussed here, although complete programs are illustrated (Figs. 4 and 6).

GPSS—Single-Server Example. The GPSS coding for the single-server model is shown in Fig. 4. The coding for the specific events of the single-server process are given in lines 9 through 17 of the code. Each GPSS instruction represents a GPSS verb, with its appropriate parameters. Each verb, in turn, assembles GPSS code for execution.

In the code example, lines 1–8 consist of initializing statements, with lines 3–8 specifying a two-valued table, which stores the coordinates of an exponential distribu-

tion, FUNCTION (FN1), which is used for random, or Monte Carlo, selection of parametric values. The simulation chain of events commences with line 9: GENERATE the arrival of a user. The GENERATE parameter fields enable a mean arrival rate (interarrival time) of 50 times a value selected from FN1. Line 10 adds this transaction into QUEUE 1, and line 11 adds 1 to the transaction record SAVEVALUE 1, which keeps a running account of active jobs in the system. Line 12 enables the user to SEIZE (make busy) server number 1, which in turn causes the user to DEPART the queue. As indicated by line 14, the service time called by ADVANCE is 45 times another value selected from FN1 at random. This time is effectively inserted into the next-event file of the simulation control program, and causes this user flow to suspend until the selected time elapses, at which time reactivation of the flow occurs. At this reactivation, lines 15 and 16 RELEASE the server (make it unbusy) and decrement the transaction record (SAVEVALUE 1). This records the departure of the user from the system, which is effected by the TERMINATE instruction in line 17. Other commands start, stop, and control the simulation run.

It should be fairly obvious that this GPSS type of coding from a block diagram is merely a very convenient design artifice, which really creates a graphic structure for representing the succession and interconnection of verbs. However, underlying this fairly easy coding convention is a complex simulation control structure, which, as previously discussed, maintains a log of active transactions, manages event generations and completions, and manages the queue servicing, the latter being invoked, for instance, by the simple verb QUEUE.

Fig. 5 depicts a partial output from this simulation run. The facility report contains the average utilization (time facility used as a fraction of total simulated time); the total number of entries (times the facility was used); and the average time-per-use for a transaction.

The queue report contains the maximum and average contents (i.e., length) of the queue; the total number of entries (transactions requesting service); the number and per cent of zero entries (transactions requiring no queueing); and the average transaction times (time an entry remains in the queue).

Simscript II Single-Server Example. The Simscript II coding (Fig. 6) for the same sort of single-server situation is basically distinguished from the GPSS code in that it is a close approximation of a "program" because formal statements are written and simulation control and model instructions are intermixed and explicit. However, certain primitive simulation-control macroinstructions are incorporated.

The declarations and initialization sections of the program set up the simulation control, the data structures, and the random-number generation. The MAIN rou-

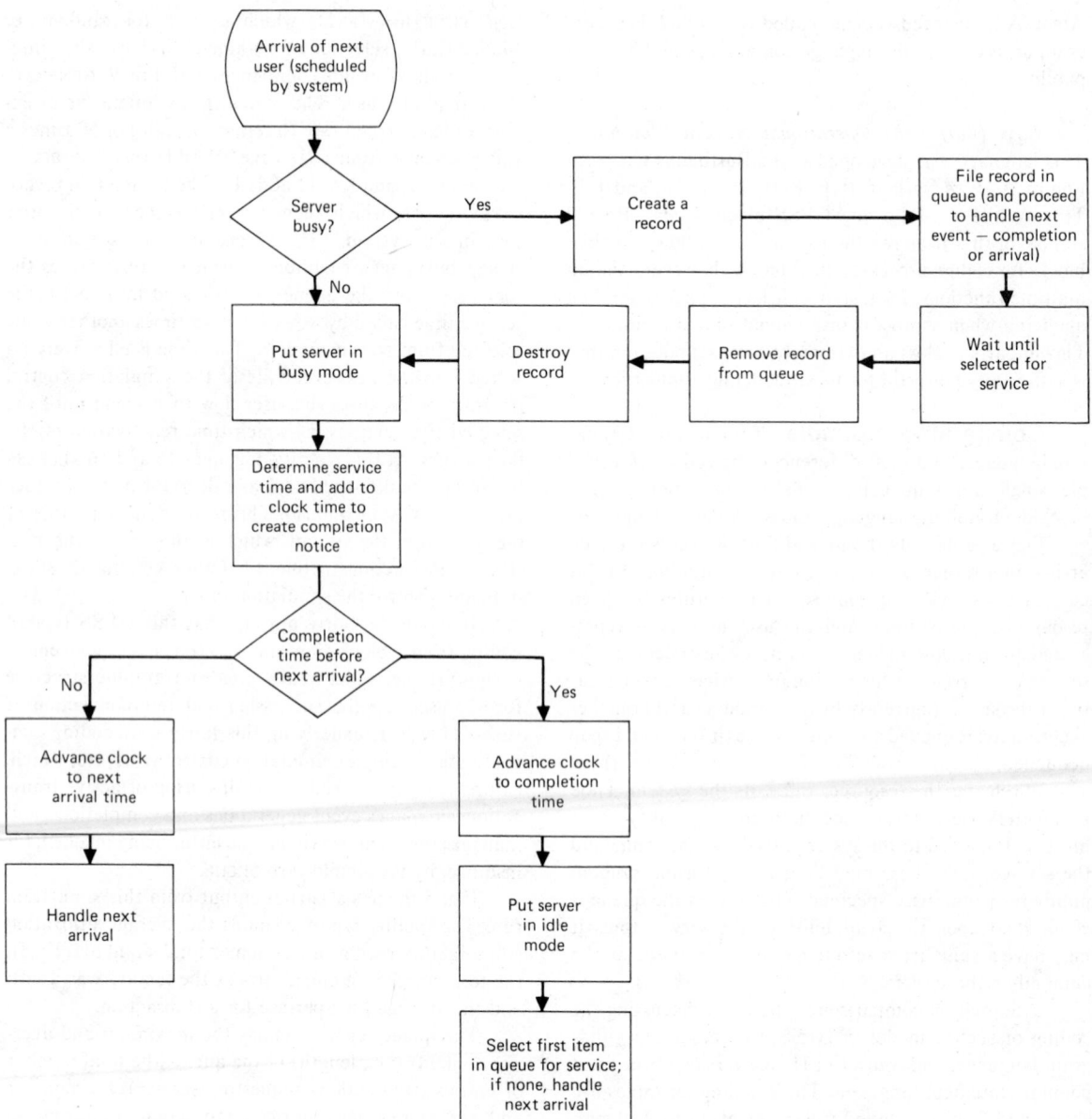

Fig. 3. Single-server queueing model for each arrival seeking service.

tine initializes the program, starts the simulation, and terminates program execution.

The EVENT ARRIVAL command (line 18) transfers control to the arrival event segment, which immediately executes the arrival scheduled on line 17. Execution of the service event, conducted in the arrival event and departure event segments, essentially divides the system flow into two parts. Following EVENT ARRIVAL, the next arrival time is scheduled (line 19), and lines 20–22 up-

date the system clock. Lines 24–27 test for "busy server" to CREATE A TASK TO FILE . . . IN QUEUE for servicing. Line 29 busies an unbusy server and line 30 SCHEDULE(S) A DE-PARTURE event, i.e., causes a notice that the service will end after some randomly selected time. The RETURN statements in lines 27 and 31 cause the simulation to re-turn to the next-event control (MAIN) routine. Therefore, the final outcome of the arrival event segment is either a notice in the next-event file to end this service (DEPAR-

```
Line
1               SIMULATE
2               SINGLE SERVER QUEUEING PROBLEM
3    1          FUNCTION      RN1,C24
4    0.0,0.0/0.1,0.104/0.2,0.222/0.3,0.355/0.4,0.509/0.5,0.69
5    0.6,0.915/0.7,1.2/0.75,1.38/0.8,1.6/0.84,1.83/0.88,2.12
6    0.9,2.3/0.92,2.52/0.94,2.81/0.95,2.99/0.96,3.2/0.97,3.5
7    0.98,4.0/0.99,4.6/0.995,5.3/0.998,6.2/0.999,7/0.9997,8
8    1          TABLE         X1,0,1,100
9               GENERATE      50,FN1
10              QUEUE         1
11              SAVEVALUE     1 + ,1
12              SEIZE         1
13              DEPART        1
14              ADVANCE       45,FN1
15              SAVEVALUE     1 – ,1
16              RELEASE       1
17              TERMINATE
18              GENERATE      10
19              TABULATE      1
20              TERMINATE     1
21              START         10000
22   *
23   END
```

Fig. 4. GPSS coding of single-server queueing system.

TURE) or a notice in the queue file requesting service of the server.

The departure event segment has two main functions: to terminate an event and to service queued events. Lines 33–36 reactivate the departure event and update the clock. Lines 37 through 39 test for tasks awaiting service in the queue. If none, the SERVER is made IDLE; otherwise, the FIRST TASK FROM THE QUEUE is selected and destroyed. As in an arrival event, a departure time is selected with a notice placed in the events list. The RETURN statements (lines 39 and 44) allow the program to return to next-event control, with the outcome of this segment execution being the release (or "unbusying") of the

server, thus ending a service event or entering a notice in the next-event file to end the service commenced in the queue-servicing routine, i.e., a DEPARTURE.

The collection routine effectively emulates the SAVEVALUE operation of GPSS, enabling the counting of system users.

The end simulation event segment computes summary statistics for presentation in the output report segment, which produces a free-format report (Fig. 7).

One of the distinct trade-offs between the Simscript and GPSS language approaches is clearly illustrated by the versatility of the Simscript coding and reporting structures versus (of course) the shorthand approach to

FACILITY	AVERAGE UTILIZATION	NUMBER ENTRIES	AVERAGE TIME/TRAN	SEIZING TRANS. NO.
1	.865	1938	44.682	27

QUEUE	MAXIMUM CONTENTS	AVERAGE CONTENTS	TOTAL ENTRIES	ZERO ENTRIES	PERCENT ZEROS	AVERAGE TIME/TRANS	$ AVERAGE TIME/TRAN	TABLE NUMBER	CURRENT CONTENTS
1	36	5960	1939	239	12.3	307.397	350.614		1

Fig. 5. Partial output from this simulation run. Shown are the printout for facility utilization ("FACILITY") and queueing activity ("QUEUE").

Declarations
```
 1  PREAMBLE
 2  THE SYSTEM OWNS A QUEUE AND HAS A SERVER
 .
 .
 .
 8  DEFINE IDLE TO MEAN 0
 9  DEFINE BUSY TO MEAN 1
10  DEFINE S AS A REAL, 1-DIMENSIONAL ARRAY
 .
 .
 .
14  END
```

Initialization
```
 1  MAIN
 2  READ MEAN.INTERARRIVAL, MEAN.SERVICE, INITIAL.Q, N
 .
 .
 .
 7  IF INITIAL.Q>0,
 8     LET SERVER = BUSY
 9     SCHEDULE A DEPARTURE IN
       EXPONENTIAL.F(MEAN.SERVICE,2)MINUTES
10        FOR I = 1 TO INITIAL.Q-1, DO
11           CREATE A TASK
12           FILE THIS TASK IN THE QUEUE
13        LOOP
14  ELSE
15  SCHEDULE A COLLECTION IN 1 MINUTE
16  SCHEDULE AN END.OF.SIMULATION IN N MINUTES
17  SCHEDULE AN ARRIVAL NOW
```

Arrival Event
```
18  EVENT ARRIVAL SAVING THE EVENT NOTICE
19  RESCHEDULE THIS ARRIVAL IN EXPONENTIAL.F(MEAN.INTERARRIVAL,1) MINUTES
20     LET T = TIME.V*1440
21     ADD T-T.1 TO S(N.QUEUE + SERVER + 1)
22     LET T.L = T
23     LET MAX.Q = MAX.F(MAX.Q,N.QUEUE + SERVER + 1)
24  IF SERVER = BUSY
25     CREATE A TASK
26     FILE THIS TASK IN QUEUE
27     RETURN
28  ELSE
29  LET SERVER = BUSY
30  SCHEDULE A DEPARTURE IN
    EXPONENTIAL.F(MEAN.SERVICE,2) MINUTES
31  RETURN
32  END
```

Fig. 6.   Simscript II coding of single-server queueing problem.

Departure Event

```
33  EVENT DEPARTURE SAVING THE EVENT NOTICE
34  LET T = TIME.V*1440
35  ADD T - T.1 TO S(N.QUEUE + SERVER + 1)
36  LET T.1 = T
37  IF QUEUE IS EMPTY,
38      LET SERVER = IDLE
39      RETURN
40  ELSE
41  REMOVE THE FIRST TASK FROM THE QUEUE
42  DESTROY THIS TASK
43  SCHEDULE THIS DEPARTURE IN
        EXPONENTIAL.F(MEAN.SERVICE, 2) MINUTES
44  RETURN
45  END
```

Collection Event

```
46  EVENT COLLECTION SAVING THE EVENT NOTICE
47  RESCHEDULE THIS COLLECTION IN 1 MINUTE
48  LET T = TIME.V*1440
49  LET X(T) = N.QUEUE + SERVER
50  RETURN
51  END
```

End of Simulation Event

```
52  EVENT END.OF.SIMULATION
53  FOR I = 1 TO MAX.Q + 1, DO
54      LET S(I) = S(I)/T.1
55      COMPUTE QBAR AS THE SUM OF (I - 1)*S(I)
56  LOOP
57  FOR I = 1 TO MAX.Q + 1, COMPUTE QVAR AS THE SUM OF
        S(I)*(I - 1 - QBAR)*(I - 1 - QBAR)
58  NOW REPORT
59  CALL ANALYSIS (N)
60  FOR I = 1 TO EVENTS.V,
61      FOR EACH ITEM IN EV.S(I), DO
62          REMOVE THE ITEM FROM EV.S(I)
63          DESTROY THIS ARRIVAL CALLED ITEM
64      LOOP
65  RETURN
66  END
```

model implementation gained through the GPSS block repertoire.

REFERENCES

1972. Kay, I. M. "Digital Discrete Simulation Languages. Discussion and Inventory," in Kay, I. M. and McLeod, J. (Eds.), *Progress in Simulation,* Vol. 2. New York: Gordon and Breach.

1973. Fishman, G. S. *Concepts and Methods in Discrete Event Simulation.* New York: Wiley.

1978. Gordon, G. *System Simulation.* 2nd Ed. Englewood Cliffs, NJ: Prentice-Hall.

1979. Sargent, R. G. "An Introduction to the Selection and Use of Simulation Languages," in *Proceedings of the AGARD Symposium on Modeling and Simulation of Avionics Systems and Command, Control and Communications Systems.* Paris.

SIMULATION RESULTS

STREAM 1 STARTING RANDOM NUMBER =   2116429302
     STREAM 1 LAST RANDOM NUMBER =   215867681
STREAM 2 STARTING RANDOM NUMBER =   683743814
     STREAM 2 LAST RANDOM NUMBER =   181518447

INITIAL QUEUE LENGTH = 0
MEAN INTERARRIVAL TIME = 5.00 MEAN SERVICE TIME = 4.50
AVERAGE QUEUE LENGTH IS   7.34 TASKS
STD.DEV. IS   6.12

QUEUE LENGTH HISTOGRAM

NO.	FREQ.
0	.090
1	.080
2	.072
3	.070
4	.069
5	.070
6	.067
7	.070
8	.062
9	.058
10	.060
11	.039
12	.026
13	.024
14	.018
15	.015
16	.013
17	.015
18	.011
19	.014
20	.011
21	.011
22	.010
23	.004
24	.002
25	.003
26	.004
27	.005
28	.002
29	.002
30	.002
31	.001
32	.000

ANALYSIS OF SERVER

IDLE	BUSY
.090	.910

Fig. 7.   Single-server queueing problem: Simscript II report routine statistics.

1981. Morris, M. F. and Roth, P. F. *Computer Performance Evaluation*. New York: Van Nostrand Reinhold.

P. F. ROTH

SMIS. *See* SOCIETY FOR MANAGEMENT INFORMATION SYSTEMS.

SNOBOL. *See* STRING PROCESSING LANGUAGES.

SOCIAL SCIENCE APPLICATIONS

For articles on related subjects *see* COMPUTING AND SOCIETY; DATA BANK; ECONOMETRIC APPLICATIONS; POLITICAL APPLICATIONS; PROGRAM LIBRARIES, NUMERICAL AND STATISTICAL; REGRESSION ANALYSIS; SIMULATION: Principles; and STATISTICAL APPLICATIONS.

The analysis of large bodies of data is the principal use of the computer made by social scientists. The data processing power of the computer has considerably enriched social analysis, but the debt is not all one way. Social studies have in turn contributed to data processing technology: the punched card was itself developed by Hollerith for the analysis of the U.S. Census of 1890. Using manual methods of analysis, research is limited to thousands of items of data (tens of observations on hundreds of subjects). The use of the punched card technology without computers (sorters, tabulators, etc.) increases the range by some two orders of magnitude (hundreds of observations on thousands of subjects). A computer effectively removes all restrictions and enables the social scientist to work close to the intrinsic limits of the problem. But apart from scale, social science data is likely to have features that mark it off from that occurring in other computer applications.

Data of Social Analysis. Records in social studies may take on very complex structures. A record describing a family, for example, might include a master section with data on family circumstances, a subrecord for each member of the family, and possibly sub-subrecords for each school attended by each child and each job for the adults. In a simpler case, it is common for a questionnaire, particularly in market surveys, to include branches so that the respondent answers one set of questions or another, depending on the answer to a previous question.

Complicated structures are also generated where subjects are retested over time. This is typical in medical surveys. The respondent may miss an examination, or take part in special tests. These types of records are difficult to accommodate within a normal computer file system. Their analysis has therefore anticipated many database techniques and now in turn benefits from this technology.

Most branches of statistical analysis are bedeviled by the problem of missing observations. This is often overcome by discarding units of the sample which are incompletely described. With human subjects, however, the frequency of missing observations and the expense of data collection make it both statistically and economically difficult to jettison a subject. This problem alone has often made the use of general statistics programs unsuitable for social science research.

Although nonnumeric data can occur in any study, in social studies they are normal. Variables such as sex and voting preference are not always easy to handle with standard methods because even when they can be coded and manipulated as numbers, their values still do not lie along a true numeric scale. Moreover, certain topics such as purchasing habits or readership typically give rise to analysis variables that may take on multiple values. For example, when asked which newspapers were read last week, a respondent may name two, three, or more journals, all of which must be considered in the analysis. Even an apparently orthodox integer value, such as age in years, may in practice be treated with values grouped in classes of unequal size, with a special value to indicate missing data.

Analysis of Surveys. Most social data is therefore unsuitable for the classical types of statistical analysis, so that cross-tabulation, which allows the underlying significance of data to be grasped with a minimum of calculation, has traditionally been the main analytical tool in this field. More recently, its power has been enhanced by the wider availability of methods for establishing objectively the significance of a cross-tabulation. Textbooks such as those by Davis (1971) and Rosenberg (1968) have influenced a larger public in acquiring a far more sophisticated attitude toward the assessment of social science data.

Methods of carrying out cross-tabulation on precomputer punched card equipment have reached a high level of sophistication. The capabilities of the tabulator and specialized statistical sorters were pushed to their limits in producing cross-tabulations of large files with minimal handling of the data. The early attempts to use a computer for survey analysis often retained the precomputer conceptual basis and used the computer to emulate a counter-sorter. The larger group of statistical analysts, however, had never found punched cards very useful and so approached computers with less preconception.

The publication in 1961 of the manual for the collection of biomedical computer programs (then known as BIMD and later as BMD and, most recently, as BMDP-81) was a landmark in the provision of flexible and reliable statistical programs on a large scale. The name of the system indicates its orientation, but it has been widely used in the social sciences. The 1981 edition describes 40 large programs covering the following areas.

Description and tabulation
Multivariate analysis
Regression analysis
Time-series analysis
Analysis of variance

To illustrate the range of programs in a particular section, here are those in regression analysis.

Simple linear regression
Stepwise regression
Multiple regression with case combination
Periodic regression and harmonic analysis
Polynomial regression
Asymptotic regression
Nonlinear least squares

BMDP is now written entirely in Fortran IV. It consists of a library of main programs, which carry out the required analysis, and a set of common subroutines. It has been developed at the School of Medicine at UCLA under the direction of Wilfred Dixon. The need by social scientists for just such a set of statistical routines is indicated by the wide use of BMDP. However, the existence of an early offshoot, called XTAB, illustrated that BMD could not properly cope with the special needs of large-scale data analysis. (The name XTAB, derived from the word "cross-tabulation," emphasizes the system's bias.)

XTAB was originally developed by Frank Massey of UCLA, who was also involved in BMDP. Technically, its main difference from BMDP is small but significant. BMDP expects to hold all the data in main store throughout the analysis. It forms a matrix with one row for each subject and one column for each variable. XTAB, however, reads the data case by case from secondary store or the primary input medium (usually cards), and adds into the current tables being formed. Thus, the data uses less of the main store, and the limits that BMDP places upon the number of cases (as low as 2,000) are relaxed.

The late 1960s saw an enormous proliferation of programs and packages for the analysis of data for social surveys. Problems of classification make an exact count impossible, but the total must be over a thousand. Two important examples may be cited.

The *multiple variate counter (MVC)* was developed by Andrew Colin while at the University of London. Technically, its main feature is that it is a full compiler that translates the user's specification (written in an Algol-like language) into an executable program. It gives the user facilities to input, recheck, and manipulate variables arising from surveys. These variables may then be formed into tables. Here is an example of the specification of a table in MVC.

title 'Table 2'
tabulate by class
count education, marital status, leisure
sum income tax, days ill
mean income tax, days ill
chisquare education, marital status, leisure
finish

The *statistical package for the social sciences (SPSS)* was developed under Norman Nie of the National Opinion Research Center, University of Chicago. Like BMDP, it has become very widely used indeed, and the user manual can be purchased in bookshops. By June 1970, it was already in use at over 60 universities and research centers and its use has spread continuously since then. SPSS gives the user powerful facilities for filing data and reaccessing it. It also permits the user to carry out the following statistical tests in addition to cross-tabulation, histograms, and descriptive statistics.

Pearson and rank-order correlation
partial correlation
multiple regression
Guttman scale
factor analysis

Data Banks. With the rapid increase in the amount of official data kept on members of the public, the use of existing files rather than samples becomes more feasible. The central problem here is that the information relating to any one person is scattered throughout several different data banks. Variants and mistakes in basic items of identifying data such as name, address, date of birth, and even sex can render it quite difficult to tie these scattered records together. Pioneering work by the Oxford Record Linkage Study in the United Kingdom, among others, has shown already how valuable this work can be in the health field, but has shown up even more clearly the inherent difficulties. Without computers, this sort of project could hardly be contemplated, particularly as the basic data itself is increasingly held on computer media.

The use of data banks has required many social scientists and other computer users to face unexpected ethical problems. The strong social value of medical and law-enforcement projects has been offset by a generalized fear of an overdocumented society. In the social sciences these problems have not been so critical, as surveys are generally based on samples, and the national censuses, the largest surveys in this field, are generally surrounded by careful rules controlling access.

Simulation. Social data is expensive to collect and difficult to control. Experimentation is usually impossible for ethical and practical reasons. An attractive solution to this problem is to set up dynamic models of a social situation, allowing the researcher to set whatever values are desired to the parameters of the model. The intrinsic complexity of social interaction gives the computer as large a role in this sort of simulation as it does in the analysis of real data.

Simulation techniques have been used, for example, in the analysis of personal belief systems and of patients in a drug trial. Business games and models of national economies use other facets of the same techniques. Leslie Stone and his colleagues at Cambridge attempted computer simulation of the British economy in the early 1960s (Klein *et al.*, 1967).

Large-scale simulation of the patterns of urban communication and behavior probably hold out the strongest hope of a basic understanding of these phenomena. Some years ago, for example, the population control program in Costa Rica was been modeled on a computer. Experiments with the model show what change in fertility is due to the control program itself and what is due to outside factors such as the changing age structure. They also show that the model can be used as a training device for the administrators involved in the project.

Anthropology. Although the impact of the computer has inevitably been biggest in the study of large-scale industrial societies, anthropologists have not neglected its aid (Burton, 1970). Field surveys can generate bodies of data large enough to warrant automatic analysis. Even in the 1950s punched cards were being used by E. P. Murdoch for cross-cultural studies, and the use of computers enlarges the possibility of extending this investigation. For example, Eleanor R. Heider (1972) used a computer in analyzing the possibility of correctly structuring the color system of a language community in the case of the Dani of Papua.

Simulation techniques can be as useful here as in urban studies; more specialized uses include the storing and analysis of genealogies, the simulation of small group dynamics, and the study of linguistic and mythological texts. Analysis of material culture records has been a valuable use of computers for archaeologists and anthropologists alike.

Applied Social Sciences. In the more directly applied social sciences, the use of computers has recently been described both in political studies (as in an analysis of concept frequencies described in political texts) and in political campaigning. For example, James Lee and Allan Kornberg (1973) used a computer to simulate the recruitment of candidates to parliamentary office in Canada.

In social administration we have the intersection of the research use of computers and of organizational data processing. Although this area of activity can be classified as an applied social science, it is better viewed in the wider context of management and business data processing.

REFERENCES

1961. Klein, L. R. *et al. An Econometric Model of the United Kingdom.* Oxford: Oxford University Press.
1968. Rosenberg, M. *The Logic of Survey Analysis.* New York: Basic Books.
1970. Burton, M. I. "Computer Applications in Cultural Anthropology," *Computers and the Humanities* **5**, *No. 1.*
1971. Davis, J. A. *Elementary Survey Analysis.* Englewood Cliffs, NJ: Prentice-Hall.
1972. Greenblat, C. S. "Gaming and Simulation in the Social Sciences: A Guide to the Literature," *Simulation and Games* **3**, *No. 4.*
1972. Heider, E. R. "Probabilities, Sampling, and Ethnographic Method: The Case of Dani Colour Names," *Man* **7**, *No. 3* (September).
1973. Lee, J. and Kornberg, A. "A Computer Simulation Model of Multiparty Parliamentary Recruitment," *Simulation and Games* **4**, *No. 1.*

B. C. ROWE

SOCIETY FOR COMPUTER SIMULATION (SCS)

For articles on related subjects *see* AMERICAN FEDERATION OF INFORMATION PROCESSING SOCIETIES; and SIMULATION.

Purpose. The Society for Computer Simulation promotes the advancement of simulation and allied computer arts by sponsoring meetings and informal discussions, by publishing reports of these meetings and papers, and by cooperating with other technical societies and with educational and other organizations in activities that contribute to the advancement of simulation and allied arts.

How Established. The Society began on the initiative of John McLeod, who called a meeting in Oxnard,

CA on 7 November 1952, of people (mostly from Southern California) who were using simulation in their work. Thirty-nine people from 13 organizations attended this meeting and created "The Simulation Council," carefully excluding any reference to the type of equipment used for modeling and simulation.

McLeod was elected chairman at the organization meeting, and he and his wife Suzette immediately began putting out at their own expense a mimeographed monthly *Simulation Council Newsletter,* which quickly developed national circulation and spread the Simulation Council idea across the country. In 1956, regional simulation councils elected two directors each to serve on the Board of Directors of Simulation Councils, an unincorporated association created to provide coordination and better communication among the regional councils and to advance the art of simulation.

On 3 June 1957, Dov Abramis, Dr. George Bekey, and Norman L. Irvine formed a California nonprofit membership corporation called Simulation Councils, Inc. (SCI), which is the legal name, though the Board, in 1972, adopted, and still uses, the name "The Society for Computer Simulation" as one that better describes the organization's activities. Eligibility for membership requires professional training and experience, and professional engagement in simulation or allied sciences. There were approximately 1,600 members as of 1981.

The following people have served as chairmen of the Board of Directors, an office that was retermed "President" in 1962.

Dr. Robert M. Howe, 1956–1957
B. Dov Abramis, 1958–1959
Stanley Rogers, 1959–1960
J. E. Sherman, 1960–1962
Maughan S. Mason, 1962–1964
P. J. Hermann, 1964–1966
James E. Wolle, 1966–1968
David R. Miller, 1968–1969
Francis C. Rieman, 1969–1971
Jon N. Mangnall, 1971–1972
Dr. George A. Rahe, 1972–1973
Robert D. Brennan, 1973–1975
Paul A. Berthiaume, 1975–1976
Per A. Holst, 1976–1977
Dr. Donald C. Martin, 1977–1979
Dr. Stewart I. Schlesinger, 1979–

The Society is a member of the American Federation of Information Processing Societies (AFIPS).

Organization. The Society is international in membership and interdisciplinary in scope. Members in 37 countries are divided geographically into 9 regional councils and one unassigned council (foreign). Councils include the U.S. and Canada, and the U.K.

International Headquarters are at 1010 Pearl Street, Suite 3, P. O. Box 2228, La Jolla, CA 92038, (714)459-3888.

Technical Program. The Society participates in the AFIPS National Computer Conferences and co-sponsors Summer and Winter Computer Simulation Conferences, the Annual Simulation Symposium, and the Pittsburgh Conference on Modeling and Simulation. Professional development seminars are a part of the Society's program.

The Society publishes *Simulation*, a monthly technical journal containing technical articles and information on the state-of-the-art and organization activities; *Simulation Councils Proceedings,* a semiannual series of hard-bound books, each dealing with a timely topic in the field of simulation and each edited by an expert in that field; and *Simulation Today,* a collection of four-page tutorial papers on the technology of simulation and its application, all originally published in *Simulation.*

I. L. AUERBACH

SOCIETY FOR INDUSTRIAL AND APPLIED MATHEMATICS (SIAM)

For article on related subject *see* AMERICAN FEDERATION OF INFORMATION PROCESSING SOCIETIES.

The Society for Industrial and Applied Mathematics (SIAM) is a professional membership association of the U.S. established in 1952 to:

- Further the application of mathematics to industry and science.
- Promote basic research in mathematics leading to new methods and techniques useful to industry and science.
- Provide media for the exchange of information and ideas between mathematicians and other technical and scientific personnel.

To support these objectives, SIAM publishes numerous periodicals and monographs containing research and expository papers; conducts national meetings, research conferences, and section activities; and sponsors the SIAM Institute for Mathematics and Society to promote the application of mathematics to the social sciences.

Presidents of SIAM since its founding have been:

William E. Bradley, 1952
Donald B. Houghton, 1953–1954

Harold W. Kuhn, 1955
John W. Mauchly, 1956
Thomas E. Southard, 1957–1958
Donald L. Thomsen, Jr., 1959
Brockway McMillan, 1960
F. J. Weyl, 1961
Robert F. Rinehart, 1962
Joseph P. LaSalle, 1963
Alston S. Householder, 1964
J. Barkley Rosser, 1965–1966
Garrett Birkhoff, 1967–1968
J. Wallace Givens, Jr., 1969–1970
Burton H. Colvin, 1971–1972
C. C. Lin, 1973–1974
Herbert B. Keller, 1975–1976
Werner C. Rheinboldt, 1977–1978
Richard C. DiPrima, 1979–1980
Seymour V. Parter, 1981–

SIAM publishes eight research journals, of which four are of particular interest to computer scientists: *SIAM Journal on Computing,* which contains research articles in mathematics that apply to the problems of computer science and the non-numerical aspects of computing (four issues per year, first issue: March 1972); *SIAM Journal on Numerical Analysis,* which contains research articles on the development and analysis of numerical methods (six issues per year, first issue: 1964); *SIAM Journal on Algebraic and Discrete Methods,* which contains research papers in combinatorics, graph theory, linear algebra, and related applications areas such as the intrinsically discrete areas of communications, management science, and operations research (four issues per year, first issue: March 1980); and *SIAM Journal on Scientific and Statistical Computing,* which contains research papers that focus on the techniques, methodologies, and computational insights needed for scientific and statistical computing and, in particular, papers that involve the mathematics (including statistics) with the hardware and software of computer systems (four issues per year, first issue: March 1980).

I. L. AUERBACH

SOCIETY FOR MANAGEMENT INFORMATION SYSTEMS (SMIS)

For article on related subject *see* MANAGEMENT INFORMATION SYSTEMS.

Purpose. The charter of SMIS lists its major purposes as follows.

- Fostering improved management performance and information exchange.
- Helping to find new applications of management information systems.
- Reviewing technological and theoretical developments relating to management information systems

SMIS was founded in November 1968 by a group of executives and management information systems professionals. There are five elected officers and an elected executive council. Presidents of SMIS have been

1969–1970, Robert Head
1971, M. H. Schwartz
1972, James Emery
1973, Richard Dooley
1974, Gerald Hoffman
1975, James Rude
1976, Daniel Teichroew
1977, Herbert Halbrecht
1978, Reed Phillips
1979, Richard E. Mahin
1980, C. W. Getz
1981, Robert Jirout
1982, Frederick Haines

The only prerequisite for membership in SMIS is an an interest in the goals, ambitions, and activities of the Society. There are six membership categories:

1. *Founding Members.* Those 12 persons who were members of the Founding Committee.
2. *Charter Members.* Those whose applications for membership were received before the initial Founder's Conference in September 1969.
3. *Regular Members.* Those individuals who joined the Society at any time following the close of the charter membership period.
4. *Faculty Members.* Those individuals who are full-time members of the faculties of universities and colleges and whose principal responsibilities are teaching and/or research.
5. *Institutional Members.* Those corporations and other institutions that support the Society and can benefit from the work of the Society.
6. *Student Members.* Those individuals who are full-time students at colleges and universities.

The Executive Office of SMIS is located at 111 East Wacker Drive, Suite 600, Chicago, IL 60601.

Professional Activities. The activities of the Society are planned and implemented to support the Society's objectives as stated in the Charter. Of principal importance is the Society's ongoing effort to keep members on the cutting edge of developments in the technology of automatic data processing, information resource management, and related management sciences.

Three major activities contribute to this objective:

1. *The SMIS Annual Conference.* Held in the late summer or early fall, the annual conference each year focuses on a critical theme that is relevant to the needs of Society members and reflective of current issues in the field. In all cases, the conference is directed at improving the effectiveness of the MIS function and the contribution of the senior MIS executive.
2. *MIS Quarterly.* The Society's professional journal, is published quarterly in cooperation with the MIS Research Center at the University of Minnesota. Members receive free subscriptions, and are encouraged to contribute articles for consideration.
3. *Workshops and seminars.* Throughout the year, the Society sponsors, or co-sponsors with other professional organizations, a number of specialized workshops and seminars. In a recent year, for example, seminar offerings focused on the impact of distributed processing, the prospects for the plug-compatible future in ADP, and the contribution of the MIS function to financial management and control. In addition, each active SMIS chapter sponsors numerous professional development programs throughout the year.

I. L. AUERBACH

SOFTWARE

For articles on related subjects *see* MATHEMATICAL SOFTWARE; OPERATING SYSTEMS; PROGRAM LIBRARIES; PROGRAMMING LANGUAGES; SOFTWARE COMPLEXITY; SOFTWARE ENGINEERING; SOFTWARE FLEXIBILITY; SOFTWARE HISTORY; SOFTWARE MAINTENANCE; SOFTWARE MANAGEMENT; SOFTWARE MONITORS; SOFTWARE PACKAGES; SOFTWARE RELIABILITY; SOFTWARE SCIENCE; and SYSTEMS PROGRAMMING.

Very early in the development of computers, people referred to the actual physical components—the tubes and relays, the resistors and wires, and chassis—as computer *hardware*. It soon became popular within the computer industry to use the word *software* to describe the nonhardware components of the computer, in particular the programs that were needed to make the computers perform their intended tasks. The word *software* caught on rapidly, and was in quite general use by 1960. One speaks of software people, software shops (i.e., organizations that produce software), software maintenance, and more recently, software engineering. Actually, software is a very general term that includes many areas discussed elsewhere in this Encyclopedia. The most significant are operating systems, programming, and programming languages.

Although the word *software* can be used in connection with all kinds of programs, it is usually used to denote programs whose use is not limited to one particular job or application. Thus, one speaks of systems software, of software systems, of mathematical software, of software for business applications, etc.

The following is a quotation, which remains accurate, from an unpublished document I wrote in 1960.

There exists a class of computer programs which are not designed to solve specific computational or data processing problems. These are the programs which are used to aid in the production, debugging, maintenance, and orderly running of other programs. They are collectively known as computer software. As computers have grown larger, more powerful, and more complex, computer software has become as important as and, in some cases, more important than computer hardware in determining the productivity of computer installations. The programs that make up the "software package" are usually supplied and maintained by the computer manufacturer. For large-scale computers such programs represent an investment of many millions of dollars, an investment that would be prohibitive except for the fact that it is spread over many computers of the same model. A good deal of computer software is produced by users ... who often have very special requirements along these lines.

Early computers could run with relatively simple software systems. A loader and a library of subroutines was considered sufficient for most first-generation computers. There were some very significant and sophisticated software developments associated with UNIVAC I. Grace Hopper and her colleagues designed the first, very general sorting systems, and developed the first high-level languages for business applications. Anatol Holt and William Turanski introduced many software system concepts in their GP (Generalized Programming) system, such as the *extended machine,* which refers to the *combination* of hardware and software that the user sees as the machine for which programs are written.

Still in the first generation, John Backus and his colleagues from IBM and from several IBM user installations developed the Fortran compiler for the IBM 704, perhaps the most significant piece of software ever written. Fortran became the language of discourse for scientific programmers throughout the world and throughout the computer industry, and once and for all established the importance and usefulness of high-level languages.

The separation of hardware and software, the idea that software was superimposed on hardware in order to enhance its capabilities, persisted throughout the first- and most of the second-generation computers. Even though this was already true in some earlier computers, especially those built by Univac, it is perhaps the distinguishing characteristic of third-generation systems that the hardware system is designed to operate under control of a rather sophisticated software system, and will perform very poorly or not at all in the absence of such a system. Especially in a multiprogramming and/or multiprocessor system, it is essential that there be an operating system (almost always software) that maintains control of the allocation of system resources and that avoids problems of conflict, blocking, interference among simultaneous users of the system. In particular, the input/output functions and the management of central and peripheral storage are software system functions that must be centralized and carefully controlled if chaos is to be avoided. These topics are discussed in detail in the article on operating systems.

The operating system provides a set of interfaces and conventions for using them which are reflected in all other major software products. A complete software system will contain, in addition to the operating system, a set of compilers for various languages, one or more system loaders, one or more database management systems, sets of utility routines, special- and general-purpose debugging systems, and generalized subsystems for applications such as sorting and merging, mathematical programming, engineering design, report generation, simulation, graphics, etc. All of these must interface with the operating system and its input/output system, and in this sense they all form part of a single software system. In general, the individual components cannot be moved from one operating system to another without considerable modification in areas in which they interface with other system routines.

Software systems for general-purpose computers are usually supplied by the manufacturers of the hardware systems. Up until about 1969, it was generally assumed that the purchase or rental of a computer hardware system entitled the customer to all general-purpose software produced by the manufacturer for that computer at no extra cost. The independent software industry, to the extent that it existed, was limited mostly to work on special-purpose systems and to applications programming. Software companies could attempt to produce software systems for sale that were better in some significant ways than those produced by the hardware manufacturers, but

this could rarely be done on a profitable basis. The software companies argued that the manufacturers were actually selling software to their customers and including its cost in the price of the hardware. The hardware customer had to buy a bundle consisting of the hardware plus all available software. They urged the *unbundling* (*q.v.*) of software. This would presumably benefit the buyer, who would only have to pay for as much software as needed. It would also permit competitive marketing of software products.

In June 1969, IBM announced that it was introducing a new policy to implement the unbundling of computer software. With the exception of essential operating system software, all new software products would henceforth be priced separately.

The decision to unbundle software was made under pressure as a response to charges of unfair competition, but it was probably not made reluctantly. It must have been clear to IBM that software rental could become a major source of revenue to computer manufacturers. Almost all other hardware manufacturers followed the lead of IBM and unbundled their software products.

Scientific and Mathematical Software. The first software systems were libraries of mathematical subroutines. In view of their very long history, it is rather surprising that major efforts in this area have continued and will continue on into the future. In fact, it was only in the early 1970s that some attempt was made to consolidate these efforts. A program supported by National Science Foundation was initiated with the aim of taking whatever steps are necessary to make sure that high-quality scientific software is available to the whole community of scientific users of computers. Most earlier efforts in this area underestimated the magnitude of the problems, and attacked them with insufficient resources.

A number of mathematical software packages have achieved very wide distribution and very general use on computers of very diverse characteristics produced by a number of different manufacturers. One of the best known is the Bi-Med (BMDP) series of statistical programs produced at UCLA. Another is the EISPAK eigenvalue package produced at the Argonne National Laboratory.

Software Engineering (q.v.). Techniques of software development developed on an ad hoc basis along with the earliest computers. Application of these techniques to the production of really large software systems (e.g., the SAGE system) resulted in unexpectedly large expenditures for the relatively inefficient programs that were produced.

There has been a great deal of thought devoted to the technology of software production. In the current third-generation of computers the cost of producing software seems to be excessive, and the methods used often show little or no advance over those used on some of the earliest systems.

Attempts have been made, with varying amounts of success, to apply to the problems of software production the engineering principles that have been reasonably successful in other disciplines. The most usual proposal is to develop sets of modules that can be used as "off the shelf" components in the development of software products. One of the factors that has limited the success of such ventures has been the continuing high rate of technological development of computer hardware. Thus, the increased use of large-scale integration and the projected development of large-scale, low-cost, fast bulk memory may produce very radical changes in software requirements and in software technology.

A more theoretical approach to the problems of program development has developed from the work of Perlis, McCarthy, Dijkstra, Wirth, Naur, Floyd, and others. This approach is based on *structured programming* (*q.v.*) and on the use of mathematical verification and proof techniques in connection with the production of programs. The aim is to produce programs that have been proved to be correct before they are tested on a computer, and thereby to eliminate much of the program-testing activity. Proponents of this methodology claim a tremendous increase in programmer productivity at little if any cost in program-running efficiency.

REFERENCES

Note: There are many books and journals devoted to the software field. Among the most important software journals are the ACM *Transactions on Programming Languages and Systems,* the IEEE *Transactions on Software Engineering,* and *Software Practice and Experience.*

1967. Rosen, S. (Ed.). *Programming Systems and Languages.* New York: McGraw-Hill. (A survey of software up to the mid-1960s.)

S. ROSEN

SOFTWARE COMPLEXITY

For articles on related subjects *see* SOFTWARE EN-GINEERING; SOFTWARE FLEXIBILITY; SOFTWARE MAINTENANCE; SOFTWARE RELIABILITY; SOFTWARE SCIENCE; and STRUCTURED PROGRAMMING.

Software complexity is what makes programs and systems difficult for people to understand, aside from subject matter and documentation unfamiliarity.

Software complexity is distinct from subject matter unfamiliarity. For example, a program for inventory control may be difficult to understand for someone with no knowledge of inventory control theory and practice, but easy to understand for someone with such knowledge. However, if a person has a good knowledge of the subject matter but still finds the program difficult to understand, then software complexity is normally the major source of the difficulty.

Software complexity also is distinct from documentation unfamiliarity. For example, if the program is written in a programming language unfamiliar to an individual, this makes the program difficult to understand. Or, if the design is documented with unfamiliar techniques, such as ANS flowcharts, this makes the program difficult to understand. However, if the individual is familiar with the documentation techniques used, yet still finds the program difficult to understand, software complexity is normally the major source of the difficulty.

Assessing Complexity. Historically, people assessed the complexity of software by using subjective judgment. This effort was usually qualitative and comparative, such as, "I believe this program is more complex than that other one."

Developments in the late 1970s and early 1980s have made it possible to replace subjective judgments with quantitative measurements. These measurements possess good objectivity, high reliability, and workable validity. That is, the measurements associate the complexity with particular characteristics visible to anyone with a knowledge of software. The measurements yield the same values when done independently by different people. The measurements done by different methods match well to one another and to poolings of subjective ratings.

Value of Quantitative Measurements. Measurements of software complexity have many uses, since software complexity correlates positively with bugs in software and with the cost to develop and maintain software, and negatively with staff productivity. Some of the uses are as follows: (1) to guide efforts to reduce software complexity; (2) to monitor the quality of software during development and maintenance; (3) to estimate the personnel time and cost of development and maintenance work; (4) to help match task assignments with staff available, since human ability to handle complexity is measurable from the software humanly produced; (5) to contribute to evaluating personnel performance more objectively; (6) to evaluate the acceptability of software, as a part of quality assurance work; (7) to contribute to the decision of when to rewrite software versus when to continue its maintenance; and (8) to evaluate software packages proposed for acquisition.

Major Types of Measures. The major ways of measuring software complexity in quantitative terms fit into four categories, depending upon their base—structure, feature, function, and token. All of the major measures correlate positively with one another [see Chapin (1979) and McTap (1980) for examples and comparisons]. Some require source code to work from, whereas others may be applied in the design stage of software development or maintenance. Some measures are easier to apply than others.

Structure-based measures look to the pattern of the control flow in the software as the basis for the complexity. Since this pattern can be expressed as a directed graph, most of the structure-based measures are drawn from graph theory. The most popular has been the *cyclomatic number*, which was proposed for this purpose by McCabe (1976). This is easily computed but best done from source code.

The feature-based measures look to a selection of characteristics visible from the documentation of either the design or the source code. Many such characteristics can be seen, and different workers in the field have emphasized different sets of such characteristics. The most inclusive have been the work of McTap (1980) and Zolnowski and Simmons (1977). For example, Zolnowski and Simmons worked with more than 55 features drawn from four general groups: Instruction mix, data reference, subprogram interaction, and control flow. McClure (1978), in contrast, has focused attention on the pattern of control variable usage as a basis for complexity in software designs.

The function-based measures look to the pattern of input to output data correspondences as the basis for the complexity. Usually, some aspects of the pattern of control flow are added, as, for example, the presence of iteration. The easily-computed Q measure proposed by Chapin (1979) is an example. This is applicable to designs and does not require source code.

The token-based measures look to the manner of expression of the software as the basis for the complexity, using some concepts from information theory. Halstead (1977) and Berlinger (1980) have offered several measures using counts of the symbols found in the source code. Mohanty (1979) and Shooman and Laemmel (1977) have offered more general approaches, but did not reduce them to practical measures.

Conclusion. The problems associated with developing software complexity measures and developing tools to make the measurements are formidable. Especially difficult is the development of measures that can be applied to specifications. But, as progress is made, the result could have a major impact on the design of reliable software.

REFERENCES

1976. McCabe, Thomas J. "A Complexity Measure," *Software Engineering* **SE-2**, *No. 4*: 308–320 (December).

1977. Halstead, Maurice H. *Elements of Software Science.* New York: Elsevier/North-Holland.

1977. Shooman, M. and Laemmel, A. "Statistical Theory of Computer Programs—Information Content and Complexity," in *Proceedings of the 1977 Fall COMPCOM.* Long Beach, CA: IEEE, pp. 177–185.

1977. Zolnowski, Jean C. and Simmons, Dick B. "Measuring Program Complexity," in *Proceedings of the 1977 Fall COMPCOM.* Long Beach, CA: IEEE, pp. 171–176.

1978. McClure, Carma L. *Reducing COBOL Complexity with Structured Programming.* New York: Van Nostrand Reinhold.

1979. Chapin, Ned. "A Measure of Software Complexity," in *Proceedings of the 1979 NCC.* Arlington, VA: AFIPS Press, pp. 995–1002.

1979. Mohanty, Siba N. "Models and Measurements for Quality Assessment of Software," *Computing Surveys* **11**, *No. 3:* 251–275 (September).

1980. Berlinger, Eli. "An Information Theory Based Complexity Measure," in *Proceedings of the 1980 NCC.* Arlington, VA: AFIPS Press, pp. 773–779.

1980. McTap, John L. "The Complexity of an Individual Program," in *Proceedings of the 1980 NCC.* Arlington, VA: AFIPS Press, pp. 767–771.

NED CHAPIN

SOFTWARE ENGINEERING

For articles on related subjects *see* MODULAR PROGRAMMING; SOFTWARE; SOFTWARE MAINTENANCE; SOFTWARE MANAGEMENT; SOFTWARE PACKAGES; SOFTWARE RELIABILITY; and STRUCTURED PROGRAMMING.

Software engineering refers to the process of creating software systems and applies loosely to techniques that reduce high software cost and complexity while increasing reliability and modifiability. Because of its general nature, software engineering is interdisciplinary. Mathematics is used to analyze algorithms, engineering to estimate costs and determine tradeoffs, and management science to define requirements, monitor progress, coordinate personnel, and assess risks.

The term *software engineering* first appeared at a NATO conference (Naur and Randell, 1969) in 1968. At that time, various people facing increasing difficulties in making reliable software for the large systems (the so-called "software crisis") began to realize the need for an engineering approach in developing software. Almost at the same time, Dijkstra (1968) wrote a famous short article that warned programmers that an undisciplined way of writing programs made resulting programs disastrous. Since then, there has been much research and experience in these areas. Early researchers focused their attention on design and implementation techniques. A major development in this area is *structured programming* (which is sometimes erroneously understood as a technique of writing a program without **goto**s). The next major step was the *software life cycle* concept, which recognizes the fact that the requirements of a system are dynamic rather than static, resulting in continuous changes to the entire system. For example, in the development of an air traffic control system, the requirements must identify: (1) the number of planes the system handles, (2) the amount of airspace it covers and (3) the processing time. From these requirements, software design is developed and implemented on a computer. During the design phase, the requirements may change and the programmer must incorporate these changes into the program. After testing of the software, the system goes into operation. Even after this period, the system may undergo changes because of possible software errors or the addition of new features to the system until the whole system is replaced by the new system. We focus our attention here on software engineering from the perspective of the software development cycle (see Fig. 1), which is usefully viewed as having five stages—requirements engineering, design specification, implementation, testing and validation, operation and maintenance—and software management.

Requirements Engineering. Requirements engineering refers to the activity of developing a complete, consistent, unambiguous specification describing *what* the software product will do as opposed to *how* it will do it (this is done in the design specification).

The actual specification of the software requirements is preceded by a requirements analysis phase, which focuses on the interface between the software system and the real world. For example, in a process control system: 1) What is the nature of the sensory inputs? 2) What is the time delay between an event's occurring and its perception by the software system (as in space vehicles)? 3) What is the processing time? And so on. A requirements analysis aids the understanding of the problems, tradeoffs, and conflicting constraints. Also identified at this phase are *functional* or *hard* requirements, which are those requirements absolutely essential to the functioning of the system, and *non-functional* requirements, such as efficiency, which are desirable but may be optional. The management aspect of developing the software is also considered at this step.

Currently, the specification of software requirements is usually expressed in free-form English, which abounds with ambiguous terms ("flexible," "adaptive," "suitable") and precise-sounding terms with unspecified definitions ("optional," "99% reliable"). This leads to many non-trivial errors that are much harder to correct in later phases of the software development cycle (some studies indicate ten times more difficult).

There has been, recently, a heartening trend toward using formal machine-analyzable software requirement specification. Formal requirements specification languages such as PSL/PSA (Teichroew and Sayani, 1977) (problem statement language/problem specification analyzer) and RSL (requirements specification language) have gradually emerged and have had better success in detecting requirements errors and providing a more solid base for independent code review, and walk-through

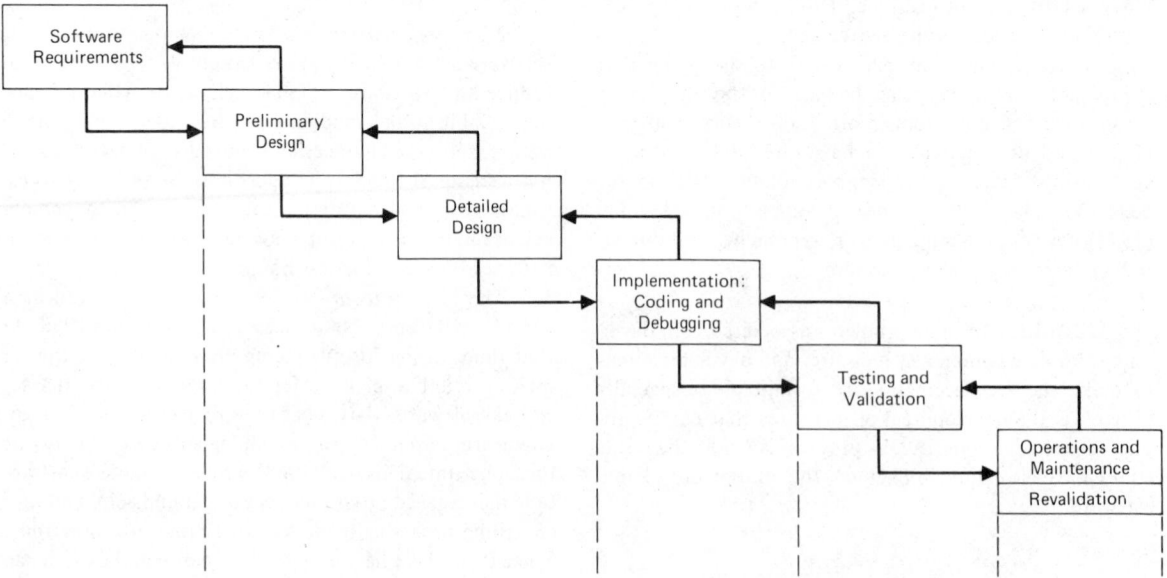

Fig. 1.   Software life cycle.

techniques. Using a formal requirements specification language, one can perform simple consistency checks, develop capabilities for designating validation points, provide capabilities for automatic generation of functional simulators from the requirements specifications, provide configuration control, and provide traceability to design and report generation.

Design Specification. The design specification consists of a series of steps aimed at transforming the (formal) requirements specification into a design so detailed that it can be directly implemented by designers not familiar with the application area.

In the design stage, one would like to have a complete, consistent, validated, unambiguous specification of software requirements before proceeding to software design. However, the requirements are not really completely validated until it is determined that the resulting system can be built at reasonable cost. In traditional branches of engineering, there is a vast body of well-documented previous experience to draw from in estimating resources needed to complete a project, but this documented experience is almost always lacking in software engineering. As a result, cost estimates for software systems are often markedly in error.

At each step of the design phase, the designer has a large number of degrees of freedom available for the software/hardware system. An implication of this is that, while it is easier for the designer to do an outstanding design job, it is also easier to do a terrible design job. Software design is mostly a manual process and a creative activity. Although there are an increasing number of software tools which can be used in the design stage, we cannot automate the design activity entirely, however sophisticated these tools may be.

There are some guidelines which can help a designer in creating good designs.

1. *Top-down hierarchical design.* The top is the fixed requirements specification and hardware architecture. The preliminary design decomposes the requirements into well-specified high-level modules; the next design step decomposes each module, and so on until the design is sufficiently detailed for direct coding. The top-down approach focuses early attention on issues of *module integration* and *interface definition*. The successive refinements can be viewed as *levels of abstraction* and vastly aid the understanding, communication, and validation of complex designs (McGowan and Kelly, 1975).
2. *Modularization and interface design.* Modularization guidelines (Parnas, 1975) are helpful in module definition. The most important are that a module should be completely specifiable by its interface and it should have no knowledge about the implementation details of other interacting modules *(information hiding)*. Structured design establishes a criterion for the cohesiveness of modules, classifies them in increasing order of strength; *viz.*, random, logical, temporal, procedural, communicational, sequential, and functional. Functions with the strongest bindings should be grouped together so that association from one module to another is kept minimal.
3. *Design representation.* Flowcharts are more widely used than any other technique for design representation but have many deficiencies, particularly in representing hierarchical control structures and data interaction. Also, their free-form nature makes it easy to construct unstructured designs.

Other techniques, such as HIPO *(hierarchical input-process-output)*, can represent a hierarchy of software modules by its inputs, outputs, and processing function.

PDL (Program Design Language) accepts constructs that have the form of hierarchical structured programs, but instead of actual code, the designer can write English text describing what the segment of code will do.

Implementation. Implementation is concerned with the mapping of the design specification onto the target machine, and is usually the easiest stage, if the requirements and design phases have been done well. The availability of high-level languages and structured programming techniques simplify this task.

Testing and Validation. It is at the testing phase where many software projects seem to founder. One reason for this is that testing is inadequately planned and not specified during the design stage of the project. Testing can be divided into three distinct operations (Zelkowitz, 1978).

1. Module testing.
2. Integration testing.
3. Systems testing.

A system is considered *validated* when *testing* shows conformance to the requirements specification, and *verified* when it has been *proved* to meet its requirements specification. The term *certification* is sometimes used to refer to the overall process of creating a correct program by validation and verification. Formal program proving, in its current state of the art, is, however, not feasible for even moderate sized programs, and the approach itself has been criticized (DeMillo et al., 1979). Proofs of small programs have been published in some cases only to be refuted by later researchers.

Operation and Maintenance. Software maintenance, though extremely important, is a highly neglected activity. The cost of software maintenance can sometimes be likened to the proverbial iceberg most of which remains submerged. About 40–50% of the overall hardware-software dollar goes into software maintenance today, and this figure is expected to grow to 60% by 1985.

For software maintenance, three main functions are involved:

1. *Understanding existing software.* This requires good documentation, traceability between requirements and code, and well-structured code.
2. *Modifying existing software.* This implies the need for software, hardware, and data structures that are easy to expand and that minimize the side-effects of changes and that have easily updated documentation.
3. *Revalidating the modified software.* This implies the need for software which can be selectively retested for the modified pieces, thus making the retest more thorough and efficient.

Software Management (*q.v.*). The difference between software project success and failure is often closely correlated to the quality of software management. The major software management problems have generally been the following (Boehm, 1976):

Poor planning and coordination. This leads to large amounts of wasted effort and idle time because of duplication of tasks, tasks unnecessarily performed or overdone or poorly interfaced.

An important aspect of good planning is an efficient deployment of computing resources and personnel. Most problems occur at the interfaces of modules written by different programmers. The number of such interfaces grows as the square of the number of individuals involved, and the problem becomes unwieldy when the group grows to four or more. The *chief programmer team* (Baker, 1972) idea is one approach to the solution of this problem.

Poor control. Even a good plan is useless when it is not kept up to date and used to manage the project. One reason for poor control of software projects is the lack of surface visibility of the project. By this we mean that it is difficult to assess the degree of completion of a project. The notion of a *milestone* (Zelkowitz, 1978) is useful where a milestone is the specification of a demonstrable event in the development of a project. To say "coding is 95% complete" is not a demonstrable milestone, because it cannot be verified before the project is complete.

Poor resource estimation. Without a firm idea of how much time and resources a task should take, the manager is in a poor position to exercise control.

Engineers have been building bridges for 6,000 years, but we have been designing software systems for only 30 years. Thus, we lack the experience that is vital to accurate estimation.

Poor accountability structure. Projects are generally organized and run with very diffuse delineation of responsibilities, thus multiplying all the above problems.

Inappropriate success criteria. Minimizing development costs and schedules will generally yield a hard-to-maintain product. Emphasizing "percentage of code written" tends to get people coding early and results in neglect of key activities such as requirements and design validation and test planning.

Procrastination on key activities. This is especially prevalent when reinforced by inappropriate success criteria as above.

REFERENCES

1968. Dijkstra, E. "GOTO Statement Considered Harmful," *Comm. ACM* **11,** *No. 3* (March).

1969. Naur, P. and Randell, B. (Eds.). *"Software Engineering: Report on a Conference Sponsored by the NATO Science Committee, 7–11 Oct., 1968"* Science Affairs Division, NATO, Brussels.

1971. Teichroew, D. and Sayani, H. "Automation of System Building, Technique for Structured Documentation and Analysis of Information Processing Systems," *IEEE Trans. Software Eng.* **SE-3,** *No. 1* (January).

1972. Baker, F. T. "Chief Programmer Team Management of Production Programming," *IBM Systems Journal* **11,** *No. 1.*

1975. McGowan, C. L., and Kelly, J. R. *Top-Down Structured Programming Techniques.* New York: Petrocelli/Charter.

1975. Parnas, D. L. "The Influence of Software Structure on Reliability," in *Proc. 1975 Int. Conference on Reliable Software.* (April).

1976. Boehm, B. W. "Software Engineering," *IEEE Trans. Computers* **C-25,** *No. 12* (December).

1978. Zelkowitz, M. V. "Perspectives on Software Engineering," *Computing Surveys* **10,** *No. 2* (June).

1979. DeMillo, R. A., Lipton, R. J., and Perlis, A. J. "Social Processes and Proofs of Theorems and Programs," *Comm. ACM* **22** (May).

1981. Enos, Judith C. and van Tilburg, R. L. "Tutorial Series 5: Software Design," *Computer* **14,** No. 2 (Feburary), pp. 61–83.

C. V. RAMAMOORTHY AND K. SIYAN

SOFTWARE FLEXIBILITY

For articles on related subjects *see* COMPATIBILITY; PORTABILITY; and SOFTWARE RELIABILITY.

Flexibility is a property of software which enables it to change easily in response to different user and system requirements. The necessary changes can be classified roughly according to their purpose:

1. To alter the user image (i.e., the "appearance" of the program to the user).
2. To adapt to different machine organizations.
3. To meet different system constraints.

These categories are not truly independent. For example, we might meet certain system constraints by changing the user image to remove expensive features. Nevertheless, the classification is a useful one because changes in different categories are normally achieved by somewhat different means.

The user image of a program is usually altered by making textual changes, principally excision of source code and selection of one of several alternatives. This implies that the body of text representing the source program incorporates the implementation of all possible user images, and is so structured that relevant changes can be made easily. Thus, some care must be taken during the implementation to modularize "by feature," avoiding if possible the use of a single procedure to provide several distinct facets of the user image. Also, wherever possible, the variations of the user image should provide a hierarchy of facilities. Changes then consist simply of removing all routines that deal with facilities above a certain level.

To solve a particular problem on a particular computer, one must model the operations and data types required for the solution in terms of the operations and data types provided by the computer. Part of this modeling is carried out by the programmer when a program is written to solve the problem, and part is carried out when the program is translated to machine code. Adaptability for different machine organizations is enhanced when the program is written in terms of operations and data types that are more closely related to the problem than to a particular computer. Changes then involve redefinition of these operators and data types in terms appropriate to the target computer. An important point is that the definition of an operator or data type should be independent of its use, so that the number of such definitions does not grow with the size of the program. Hence, a redefinition involves far less effort than would be required to recode the program.

System constraints include such items as peripheral complement, memory size, word length, and arithmetic (precision, rounding). Careful organization of the algorithm is necessary to provide flexibility in meeting these constraints, with the key point being the preservation of suitable fall-back positions. For example, the program should (if possible) be structured so that sections could be overlaid to meet a memory constraint. This consideration has implications for the procedure linkage and the segmentation of data; it may affect the algorithm chosen to solve the problem.

Some form of parameterization is generally used to achieve all aspects of flexibility: Symbols are used to denote key constants such as table sizes, and conditional operations are executed during translation to select different parts of the code according to the desired user image. Assembly languages and general-purpose macroprocessors provide the most powerful facilities for parameterization; most high-level languages are deficient in this respect. The best examples of software that can be adapted through parameterization are found in the kernel (q.v.) of an operating system. *System generation* (q.v.) is the process of adapting the body of text supplied by the manufacturer to the user image desired by the installation management and to the constraints of their hardware configuration.

Flexibility is important because it increases the useful life of a piece of software and extends its range of application. This permits the development cost to be recovered over a wider market, and hence reduces the price to the user.

REFERENCE

1973. Poole, P. C. and Waite, W. M. "Portability and Adaptability," in Bauer, F. L. (Ed.), *Advanced Course in Software Engineering.* Berlin: Springer-Verlag.

W. M. WAITE

SOFTWARE HISTORY

For articles on related subjects *see* COMMAND AND JOB CONTROL LANGUAGES; DATABASE MANAGEMENT; DEBUGGING; DECISION TABLES; DIGITAL COMPUTERS, HISTORY; OPERATING SYSTEMS; PROGRAMMING LANGUAGES; REPORT GENERATORS; SOFTWARE ENGINEERING; and TEXT-EDITING SYSTEMS.

As one looks back over the development of software since the early 1950s, one sees that the major thrusts have been in four broad areas—programming languages; operating systems; data handling; and software tools, techniques, and disciplines.

The term *programming languages* involves the specific form in which the user actually writes a program for input to the computer. (This subject is emphasized in this article because it has had more direct effect on computer users than the other topics. That balance may change in the future.) The term *operating systems* encompasses the general set of tools and techniques that enables both individuals and computer installations to effectively accommodate many jobs with minimum human intervention, allowing for parallel, sequential, and interactive modes. Real-time systems are also included within the framework of operating systems, even though the necessary real-time application programs are outside the operating system. The term *data handling* has been chosen to represent general capabilities, ranging from the early sort-merge generators to the current database management systems. *Software tools, techniques,* and *disciplines* run the gamut from subroutines to debugging tools (such as program tracers), from programming library support systems to editors that facilitate program entry, modification, and neat output formatting.

The history of almost anything in the computer field is extremely controversial. For that reason, it is essential to state that the approach taken here, and the statements made, represents the personal views of the author. Further, it is possible only to mention the highlights and give some sense of perspective in the short space available. No attempt has been made to completely indicate "firsts"; rather the emphasis is on significant developments, even though earlier work may have contributed greatly.

Programming Languages. The term *programming language* as used here is considered equivalent to *high-level language*. The development of assembly language and macroassemblers is not discussed here.

Language development started as far back as 1945 with the unimplemented "Plankalkül" by Konrad Zuse in Germany. Various attempts at developing a language that was closer to the problem expression than assembly language were made by numerous people and organizations, as described by Knuth and Trabb Pardo (1980) and Sammet (1969). The earliest *operational* compiler for a high-level language seems to be that developed by Laning and Zierler for mathematical computations, which was running on the M.I.T. Whirlwind in 1954. It provided capability for writing mathematical expressions (with subscripts *and* superscripts), assignment, branching, input/output, subroutines, and some handling of differential equations. However, the first high-level language that received wide usage was Fortran, developed by John Backus and others at IBM in the mid-1950s. Its original application area was intended to be only scientific and engineering computational problems, but it has also been used for everything from payroll calculations to compiler writing. It proved the feasibility of high-level languages and thus provided a foundation for future work on languages.

In 1958, a group of Americans (representing ACM) and Europeans (representing GAMM) working together created a language for algorithmic processes known as IAL (*I*nternational *A*lgebraic *L*anguage); this language eventually was modified to become Algol 60 (Naur, 1960) and the earlier version was renamed Algol 58. Both Algol 58 and Algol 60 led to a major emphasis and work in the area of programming languages by universities and industry. Several languages were developed based on Algol 58 (e.g., Jovial, Mad, Neliac), and compiler techniques were developed. Algol spurred the theoretical and research effort in programming languages, whereas Fortran had far more effect on the practical side.

In parallel with these developments in scientific languages were the efforts for business data processing; the first of these was Flow-Matic, developed by Grace Hopper and her colleagues at Remington Rand Univac in the mid-1950s. Flow-Matic was the first English language-oriented language; as such, it was one of the major inputs to Cobol (*C*ommon *B*usiness *O*riented *L*anguage), which was developed by a group of computer manufacturers' representatives and users organized in 1959 under Department of Defense sponsorship. Cobol has had as large (or larger) an effect on the programming of business data processing problems as Fortran has had for scientific and engineering problems.

It should be noted that the two years 1958 and 1959 were probably the two most productive years in the history of programming languages. Not only were Algol 58 and Cobol developed, but Comit and Lisp were developed at M.I.T. Comit was a string processing language developed primarily by Victor Yngve for use in translating natural languages. Lisp was developed for artificial intelligence applications by John McCarthy and a number of others (primarily graduate students). Lisp continues to be heavily used by the AI community. Comit, however, has been largely supplanted by varying versions of Snobol, which was developed initially by David Farber, Ralph Griswold, and Ivan Polonsky at Bell Telephone Laboratories in the mid-1960s. Snobol has been widely used in general text manipulation applications.

Because the early languages maintained the same dichotomy between scientific and data processing computations that the early computers did, it is not surprising that eventually languages began to be developed that were meant to be more general. One of the earliest of those was Jovial (an outgrowth of Algol 58), developed by Jules Schwartz and others at the System Development Corporation in 1959–1960. The first language really *intended* for both scientific calculations and business data processing, as well as systems programming, was PL/I, developed as a joint project between IBM and SHARE in 1963–1964. The next large language developed was Algol 68, which was really a new development and *not* an upward extension of Algol 60. One of its major characteristics is orthogonality, meaning it defines a small number of basic characteristics and systematic rules for combining them so as to eliminate many arbitrary restrictions. There is also a facility to allow the programmer to define new data types and operators on them. Algol 68 was defined with a new (and difficult) definitional technique and this seems to have discouraged a number of people from seriously studying and using the language.

The next major language development was the Department of Defense effort, which started in 1975, to get a single language suitable for embedded computer systems. (Embedded computer systems are those in which the computer is part of a system involving other equipment; e.g., air traffic control, process control, or weapons systems.) The preliminary specifications for this language, called Ada, were issued in 1979, and the language specifications labeled "final" were issued in July 1980. This was the baseline for a potential standard, future development, and major implementations. Although originally intended for use on embedded computer systems, the actual Ada specifications allow much wider use.

With the advent of interactive computing systems that permitted an individual to access a computer system from a remote terminal (see below), languages were developed for effective use in an interactive environment. The earliest was Joss, developed by J. Cliff Shaw at the Rand Corporation in 1963. Starting in 1964, a simple language named Basic was developed for batch or interactive mode. Basic has been implemented on almost every computer, including many microprocessors and home computers; it was developed by John Kemeny and Thomas Kurtz at Dartmouth College in 1964.

A number of languages have been developed to do non-numeric mathematics (i.e., formal algebraic manipulation—see ALGEBRAIC MANIPULATION) on a computer. The first to receive wide usage was Formac, developed by Jean Sammet and her colleagues at IBM in 1962–1964. The most comprehensive of the current systems is Macsyma, initially developed in the early 1970s at M.I.T. by Joel Moses and others.

Although the languages cited above are intended for relatively broad classes of applications, there has been a parallel development that has gone largely unnoticed or ignored by most computer scientists, namely, the development of languages for specialized application areas. The earliest of these was APT, for machine tool control, developed at M.I.T. by Douglas Ross and others starting in 1956. Other popular specialized languages include Cogo (civil engineering), Coursewriter (computer-assisted instruction), and Atlas (equipment checkout).

From 1967 to 1977, the author maintained a roster of high-level languages developed and used in the United States. The number in use in any given year ranges around 170, with roughly 25 to 30 simultaneously being added and deleted each time the annual or biannual

count has been made. An astounding phenomenon is that, since the tracking began, the languages for specialized application areas consistently have been about half of the total languages listed. (See, for example, Sammet, 1978.) However, the actual *usage* of these languages is much less than 50%.

As an indication of a value judgment on important languages, the ACM Special Interest Group on Programming Languages (SIGPLAN) sponsored a History of Programming Languages (HOPL) Conference in 1978. The program committee for that conference chose to discuss languages that met the following criteria: (1) they were created and in use by 1967; (2) they remained in use in 1977; and (3) they had considerable influence on the field of computing. The languages chosen were the following: Algol, APL, APT, Basic, Cobol, Fortran, GPSS, Joss, Jovial, Lisp, PL/I, Simula, and Snobol. Two other important languages of the early 1980s not on that list are Pascal, developed in 1968 by Niklaus Wirth, and Ada (already mentioned). Pascal has been implemented on many large, mini-, and microcomputers and has become a practical base and/or a spiritual catalyst of language development in the late 1970s, just as Algol was for the 1960s. Because of the newness of Ada at the time this article was written, anything said here about its impact would be speculation, not history.

In conjunction with the actual development of individual languages, of course, has come the development of concepts which appear in, or relate to, languages. Among the important enduring language concepts are block structure (Algol); data typing, record structure, and separation in a program of the data and procedural aspects (Cobol); the class (*q.v.*) concept (Simula), which has led to modern concepts of data abstraction; and the strong data typing mechanisms (Pascal). In addition, the primary concept of a formal technique for defining language syntax came from Backus in 1959 and is known as BNF (for Backus Normal Form or Backus Naur Form—*q.v.*); aside from the Backus paper proposing the concept, it was first used in the major publication of the Algol 60 report (Naur, 1960). The metalanguage (*q.v.*) of Cobol was developed independently and has been widely used.

Along with the development of these languages have come a myriad of compiler techniques, including optimization.

Much of the early history of specific programming languages can be found in Sammet (1969); for the 13 specified languages covered by the HOPL Conference, see Wexelblat (1981).

Operating Systems. The history of operating systems is much harder to trace than that of programming languages; for the former, the *concepts* are primary, whereas for the latter a specific *language* provides the major contribution to the field. Another major difference is that high-level languages, by definition, are *meant* to be machine-independent, whereas operating systems have normally been developed for a single computer or computer family.

In the earliest days of computing, each programmer tended to operate the computer alone. Before long, it became clear that it was not an efficient use of a programmer's time to mount tapes, put cards in a reader, etc.; as a result, the separate function of computer operator came into being. However, it was *still* necessary for a *person* to put cards into a card reader and/or mount tapes *separately* for each job that was to be run. As computers became faster, the amount of computer time that was lost between programs became significant, and so various techniques and concepts were developed to allow efficient use of the physical computer time, which was scarce and expensive in the early days. Although computers had far greater speed and lower costs in the early 1980s than at any preceding time, the uses of computers had also grown enormously and the larger capacity was needed. Hence, operating systems continued to be needed, particularly *because* the vast speed precluded wasting time with human intervention.

Around 1956, a simple operating system was developed jointly by General Motors and North American Aviation for the IBM 704. By the time Fortran became generally available, operating systems had been developed that provided facilities such as sequencing from one job to another, input/output control systems, calling in components (e.g., assembler, compiler), and loading object programs along with library routines.

In the early 1960s, there were batch operating systems (e.g., IBSYS on the IBM 7090) in which programs requiring differing services (e.g., separate compilers, assemblers) were submitted to be run and printed results were received in hours (or sometimes even days if there were many users). The programmer specified what functions the operating system was to perform via some special cards known as *job control cards*. Around 1963, Burroughs released its master control program (MCP) written in a high-level language and with facilities for multiprocessing and multiprogramming. OS/360, developed in the middle 1960s for the IBM System/360, typified the very large and powerful batch system, although it was actually designed for a broad range of uses (including real time). It provided facilities for handling devices and data, job management, debugging, and multiprogramming. It also provided growth, without recoding, across a family of compatible hardware and software, and often with printed results in minutes (rather than hours or days).

A third concept, which had been developed as early as the late 1950s (with SAGE) involved real-time systems, in which very rapid (and sometimes seemingly instantaneous) response from the computer is necessary. The IBM-American Airlines SABRE system of 1963 (for airline reservations) seems to be the earliest major system for transaction processing (*see* TRANSACTION-BASED SYSTEMS) and was the forerunner for later facilities of that kind, as well as influencing OS/360.

A major innovation was the development of the Compatible Time-Sharing System (CTSS) at M.I.T. on the IBM 709/7090 under the direction of Fernando Corbató, starting in 1961 and becoming of significant use by 1963. This was the first significant general system with the following characteristics: (1) numerous typewriter-like terminals were connected to one computer and could be used at the same time; (2) each terminal user seemed to have available the full power and facilities of the computer hardware and software; and (3) the time required for small tasks was sufficiently small so that all users could feel the entire machine was devoted to their service. CTSS provided various language compilers, file manipulation facilities, and user-developed systems. It was used heavily at M.I.T. and proved the practicality of general interactive systems. This capability contrasts with that in a system supporting Joss, which provided (only) a single language that could be used simultaneously by many people. By the 1970s, the most powerful and flexible of the general interactive systems was Multics, for the (now called) Honeywell 645. Multics was developed in the mid-1960s as a joint effort of General Electric, M.I.T., and Bell Laboratories; it was heavily influenced by the M.I.T. experience with CTSS.

Toward the late 1960s, the three operating system concepts of interactive, batch, and real time began to merge (although the similarity had been recognized earlier by some people). It became clear that the design requirement for all three concepts was resource management, and that the same basic design involving dynamic allocation of resources to independent processes could satisfy each of the "separate" problems. Included were various facilities to protect (1) the operating system against ruination from accidental or deliberate tampering by users, and (2) one user's files and programs from another user's access or tampering.

Since the early 1970s, UNIX (*q.v.*—a trademark of the Bell Telephone Laboratories) has become widely accepted as a model of a small but powerful interactive operating system. The initial version was developed by Ken Thompson of Bell Laboratories in 1969–1970 to run on the DEC PDP-7 and PDP-9 computers. Thompson and his colleague, Dennis Ritchie, developed better versions for various DEC machines, and the most widely used one runs on the PDP-11 family. UNIX and related developments—e.g., the programming language C (*q.v.*), in which UNIX is written—are described in BSTJ (1978).

Along with the early development of these various methods of accessing the computer, there arose the need for capabilities by which the user could indicate what functions were desired (e.g., compilation, printout, deletion of a file, editing). From this came the concept of *job control languages,* sometimes called *command languages* (*see* COMMAND AND JOB CONTROL LANGUAGES). It is hotly debated by language experts as to whether these really are high-level languages in the same sense as those discussed earlier.

The concept of virtual memory (*q.v.*)—i.e., the facility whereby the user can write a program assuming the memory size is effectively unlimited—seems to have started in the late 1950s on the Atlas computer at Manchester University in England. A virtual memory facility was eventually put into the major operating systems of most of the computer manufacturers.

Details on some of the earlier systems mentioned above, as well as on some of the programming languages, are in Rosen (1967). A general history of operating systems is in Weizer (1981).

Data Handling. The broad category of data handling refers to the tools and techniques used to manipulate large amounts of data. One of the earliest significant achievements in data handling was the 1951–1952 Sort-Merge Generator developed by Betty Holberton for the Remington Rand UNIVAC I. Not only did this introduce the concept of a program that would be automatically tailored for a particular set of parameters, but it helped initiate the development and widespread use of many data processing tools.

One concept that has pervaded work in the data handling area is the need for *data definition* facilities. This concept involves the tools and techniques for describing both full files and individual records (down to each field) as they are represented logically, and also physically. The earliest attempt at such a facility seems to have been the COMPOOL developed at the M.I.T. Lincoln Laboratory for the SAGE Air Defense System in the early 1950s. The COMPOOL provided a way of defining the characteristics of the very large SAGE database, which was used by hundreds of programs. The COMPOOL concept was later carried over to the programming language Jovial. The early work on Flow-Matic provided this data definition facility initially in the programming language, and the first major culmination of that approach was reached in the Cobol Data Division.

Research of various kinds on data definition facilities still continues, although no single technique had prevailed by 1981. However, based on concepts from IDS (mentioned later), the Codasyl (*q.v.*) Cobol committee in 1969 developed their first schema Data Definition Language (DDL—*q.v.*) for defining a total database, and a

Sub-Schema Data Manipulation Language (DML) for defining various aspects of the database associated with individual languages (e.g., Fortran). This work has subsequently been updated.

By the mid- and late 1950s, various systems were available for handling large collections of files and producing reports. Report writers started as early as 1956, at the General Electric (Hanford, WA) operation. They developed a report generator (*q.v.*) called MARK I for the IBM 702. One of the first widely used report generators was the Report Program Generator (RPG) developed for the IBM 1401 in 1961. In 1962, a Report Writer module and Sort module were added to Cobol in Cobol 61 Extended, thus freeing the user from the need to have separate programs to achieve those functions. However, many users still use independent RPGs.

File handling facilities also started at GE Hanford, and the two capabilities from there were the forerunner of 9PAC, developed on the IBM 709 around 1959 by users under SHARE (*q.v.*) auspices.

With the advent of the first Cobol specifications in 1960, the need for file manipulation facilities separate from the actual programs could be eliminated because file manipulation facilities were embedded in the support provided by Cobol. But, in most data processing environments, installations would create separate files for each set of applications; for example, an employee file was used for payroll purposes and a separate employee file was used for department assignment and transfer purposes. Eventually, it became clear that all of these separate files should be combined into a common framework, and this led to the concept now known as *database management systems.*

There have been three major technical approaches to database management systems. One is based on the Integrated Data Store (IDS), first proposed by Charles Bachman of General Electric in 1964. He proposed a network approach to storing data, and this was used as the basis for the work of the Codasyl Data Base Task Group. A second approach is the hierarchical system in which data is represented as a tree structure. The earliest manifestation of this approach seems to be the work at North American Aviation Space Division and IBM in 1965; it is exemplified by IBM's Information Management System issued around 1969. A third approach is the relational database of E. F. Codd of IBM, first introduced around 1970. It involves the concept of linked tables of data where information is not repeated as it must be in the hierarchical systems.

Each approach has strong proponents and opponents, and tends to be useful in differing application environments, based to a large extent on the preferences of the individuals making the selections. A good technical description of these alternative approaches is given by

Date (1981) and in ACM (1976). The article by Fry and Sibley (1976) provides a detailed history from which much of this section was derived.

Each approach has been implemented in one or more commercial systems, although, by 1980, there were more systems based on the first two approaches than on the third. By 1980, database management systems were very important from both a research viewpoint and as a major practical facility for large organizations.

Software Tools, Techniques, and Disciplines.

Many of the useful software tools and techniques for assisting programmers have now become so ingrained in the 1980s that it is hard to realize that these ideas did not exist in the early days and had to be developed. The development of disciplines is much more recent. As one example of an early technique, the crucial concepts of subroutine and subroutine libraries were promulgated as early as 1951 by Wilkes, Wheeler, and Gill (1951). As another illustration, the symbolic assembly program, which freed the programmer from worrying about absolute machine addresses, was developed by Nathaniel Rochester of IBM by 1953; it replaced the concept of regional or floating addresses implemented on the M.I.T. Whirlwind Comprehensive System.

Among the many other major software tools and techniques, only a few of the most important concepts can be mentioned. Specific early system names and dates are very difficult to identify.

Compilers are obviously a major class of tools, and the emphasis has been on developing techniques that provide rapid compilation and efficient object time code. The latter means both rapid execution and minimal use of memory. The earliest significant compiler was that for Fortran, as described by John Backus in Wexelblat (1981). The concept of a syntax-directed compiler was introduced by E. T. Irons in 1961; although this idea has inspired a great deal of research, it has *not* been of *major* practical value.

The concept of a *list* seems to have been introduced by Allen Newell, Herbert Simon, and J. C. Shaw in the mid-1950s as a useful technique in their work on developing programs that would prove theorems in the propositional calculus. Although a sequence of list processing languages was also developed (named IPL I, . . . IPL V) to do list processing, only the last became significantly used and even it eventually faded from use, while the list *concept* remains as a cornerstone of software techniques.

Debugging tools and concepts were created as part of the early development of programming. The tools ranged from very simple to quite sophisticated, and have included static and dynamic traces and cross references, simulators, measurements, and numerous features associated with compilers. In this connection, it is worth noting that, although testing is related to debugging, it was not until a conference in 1972, described by Hetzel (1973), that testing really began to be considered seriously as a scientific subdiscipline.

Decision tables represent one specific technique (other than programming languages) for expressing problem solutions. The first decision tables appear to have been developed in 1958 by Orren Evans at Hunt Foods and Industries, Inc., and he credits the Sutherland Company of Peoria, IL with many of the ideas. Evans' work was released to the Codasyl Systems Committee in 1959 and it, as well as General Electric and IBM, then contributed to further work on this approach throughout the early and mid-1960s. The earliest implemented system seems to have been Tabsol on the GE 225 in 1959–1960.

Attempts to make software development less of an art and more of a science or engineering discipline have been under way since at least 1968, when NATO sponsored small conferences entitled "Software Engineering." There is considerable debate on the meaning of this term even in the early 1980s, but it is reasonably clear that the term encompasses management issues as well as specific technical concepts, and includes a concern with the full *life cycle* of software development. For example, increased emphasis on requirements and specifications and design tools has occurred in recent years. A much earlier interest in restricting the way in which programmers wrote their code in order to make the programming process more manageable led to the structured programming (*q.v.*) concepts proposed by Edsger Dijkstra in the late 1960s and early 1970s (Dahl, Dijkstra, and Hoare, 1972); these concepts were heavily promulgated by him and others, as well as being enhanced by Harlan Mills and others.

A contribution to the developing discipline of programming has been the creation of ANSI standards. The main software standards have been the programming languages that started with the first Fortran standard in 1966. Other languages that have had one or more standards, either internationally or in the United States, are Algol 60, APT, Basic, Cobol, Mumps, and PL/I.

The relatively easy availability of interactive systems caused a large interest in editing systems that could be used by programmers for correcting and documenting their progrms. On-line editing systems then became widespread for use with ordinary text, not just programs. Major differences among the systems include the types of editing commands they use, and whether the basic unit of reference is a single line or is some unit of text controlled by a delimiter.

One of the earliest text editors was the system running under the M.I.T. Compatible Time-Sharing System

(CTSS) in 1963. A small system oriented toward text handling was the IBM Administrative Terminal System (ATS) available in the mid-1960s on the 1401. More powerful systems developed in the late 1960s include WYLBUR (Stanford University on the IBM 360/67) and TECO (M.I.T. on the DEC PDP computers). The SCRIPT system developed by IBM on the System 360/370 has evolved from earlier internal versions created in the late 1960s.

With the availability of more sophisticated terminals and display devices, there have been numerous sophisticated programs developed to provide scrolling, "pretty printing," and automatic typesetting and printing.

REFERENCES

1951. Wilkes, M. V., Wheeler, D. J., and Gill, S. *The Preparation of Programs for an Electronic Digital Computer.* Reading, MA: Addison-Wesley.

1960. Naur, P. (Ed.). "Report on the Algorithmic Language ALGOL 60," *Comm. ACM 3, No. 5:* 299–314 (May).

1967. Rosen, S. (Ed.). *Programming Systems and Languages.* New York: McGraw-Hill.

1969. Sammet, J. E. *Programming Languages: History and Fundamentals.* Englewood Cliffs, NJ: Prentice-Hall.

1972. Dahl, O.-J., Dijkstra, E. W., and Hoare, C. A. R. *Structured Programming.* New York: Academic Press.

1973. Hetzel, W. (Ed.). *Program Test Methods.* Englewood Cliffs, NJ: Prentice-Hall.

1976. *ACM Computing Surveys, (Special Issue: Data-Base Management Systems)* 8, *No. 1* (March).

1976. Fry, J. P. and Sibley, E. H. "Evolution of Data-Base Management Systems," *Computing Surveys* 8, *No. 1:* 7–42 (March).

1978. *Bell System Technical Journal (UNIX Time-Sharing System)* 57, *No. 6, Part 2* (July–August).

1978. Sammet, J. E. "Roster of Programming Languages for 1976–77," *ACM SIGPLAN Notices* 13, *No. 11:* 56–85 (November).

1980. Knuth, D. E. and Trabb Pardo, L. "The Early Development of Programming Languages," in Metropolis, N., Howlett, J., and Rota, G.-C. (Eds.), *A History of Computing in the Twentieth Century*, pp. 197–273.

1981. Date, C. J. *An Introduction to Database Systems,* 3rd Ed., The Systems Programming Series. Reading, MA: Addison-Wesley.

1981. Weizer, N. "A History of Operating Systems," *Datamation* 27, *No. 1:* 119–126 (January).

1981. Wexelblat, R. (Ed.). *History of Programming Languages.* ACM Monograph Series. New York: Academic Press.

J. E. SAMMET

SOFTWARE, LEGAL PROTECTION OF.

See LEGAL PROTECTION OF SOFTWARE.

SOFTWARE MAINTENANCE

For articles on related subjects *see* COMPATIBILITY; DEBUGGING; ERRORS; PROGRAM LIBRARIES; SOFTWARE; SOFTWARE PACKAGES; and STRUCTURED PROGRAMMING.

Because of the complexity of large software systems, there are almost always errors (bugs) and inadequacies in running them. Software maintenance is the activity that addresses itself to the correction of software errors and to remedying the inadequacies that may exist.

Computer manufacturers and other producers of software products have large software maintenance groups whose tasks vary from simple correction of typographical errors to major changes and extensions to existing software programs. These groups usually provide a formal mechanism whereby users can submit evidence of errors of inadequate performance. Corrections are then usually distributed to all users.

After a number of changes have been made, it is inconvenient to make additional changes, especially if new changes affect the results of earlier changes. Also, in some cases, very extensive changes require major revisions in the documentation of the software product. In such cases it is usual to release a new version of the software product which contains all changes to date and which serves as a new base for future changes. For example, IBM's Release 20 of OS 360, which went into use in 1972, was quite different from Release 16, which was current in 1968, and was radically different from some of the earlier releases.

In order to ease the impact on the users, the manufacturer usually continues to maintain several earlier software releases for some time after a new version is released. Ultimately, however, the older versions are declared to be obsolete and are taken off maintenance. When this happens, even reluctant users usually convert to the newer versions.

New versions of software products often have subtle effects on a user's applications systems, and large users usually have their own software maintenance personnel, not only for maintenance of the application systems, but also to install new versions of supplied software and make modifications that may be necessary to move their application programs from one version to another.

As software development and software maintenance have grown into major activities involving very large numbers of people and very large amounts of money, there has been considerable effort devoted to improving the efficiency and productivity of the whole software process.

Some software projects have claimed spectacular results through the use of a programming discipline that has come to be known as *structured programming* (Dahl et al., 1972). *Top-down programming* and the use of a *chief programmer team* are related concepts (Baker, 1972).

REFERENCES

1972. Baker, F. T. "Chief Programmer Team Management of Production Planning," *IBM Systems Journal* **11**, *No. 1*.
1972. Dahl, O. J., Dijkstra, E. W., and Hoare, C. A. R. *Structured Programming*. New York: Academic Press.

S. ROSEN

SOFTWARE MANAGEMENT

For articles on related subjects *see* COMPUTING CENTER; DOCUMENTATION; PROGRAMMER; SOFTWARE COMPLEXITY; SOFTWARE ENGINEERING; STRUCTURED PROGRAMMING; and SYSTEMS PROGRAMMING.

Software management means the management of the *people* who are building, fixing ("maintaining"), and enhancing software. An increasing portion of a computer's cost is for software. This is due to the increasing complexity of applications and the decreasing cost of hardware. This has directed considerable attention to the management of software development.

The task of managing software development is a function of the complexity of the application and the basic system on which the application is to operate (both hardware and software). Software management has a reputation for being difficult and lacking established management practice and dependable management tools. A major problem is the manager's inability to look inside a software product as it is being built. The "soft" nature of software is precisely what makes complexity and bad design difficult to see and sometimes seems to suggest patchwork repair of terrible messes.

The software end-product is a computer program represented as a printed listing or as a string of zeroes and ones on a magnetic disk or tape. By contrast, the physical nature of end-products in "hard" disciplines makes mistakes and poor designs more visible, more measurable. Moreover, the effects of design changes (e.g., reducing the size or reducing the number of wires which need to be soldered together) is usually readily apparent. However, the *apparent* ease of effecting a change of a single line of code or of a few zeroes and ones in a software product does not represent the true effect the change may have on the design and the complexity of the product. No

widely accepted analogs to the physical objects and measurements of them made in "hard" fields have emerged yet.

Management of software development is also made difficult by the speed of technical innovation in the computer industry. When, for a fixed cost, computer processor speeds and main storage capacities double every few years, the design parameters for large software systems change dramatically. As soon as one begins to get a feel for design tradeoffs, the parameters change.

The management aspects of software development have received some attention (Metzger, 1973; Kay, 1969; and Ditri, Shaw, and Atkins, 1971), but as yet there are no generally accepted guidelines. One of the chief designers and development managers of the IBM System/360 line of computers and its operating system OS/360 has documented his experiences in a book that gives a thoughtful retrospective look at that major software management effort (Brooks, 1975). Another enjoyable book that is a must for software developers shows how people's sociological and psychological makeup dramatically affects the software development process (Weinberg, 1971).

Modern operating systems and large real-time applications, such as airline reservation systems and military command and control systems, are examples of large systems that invariably require innovation in order to meet the many demands of sheer size, speed, efficiency, reliability, and flexibility. Significant experience is required to assess the degree of innovation required for such a system.

When such projects require large numbers of people (i.e., too many to allow close proximity and continuous personal contact for all) and involve several levels of management, communication and awareness of current status become hard to manage. What is more, new and advanced requirements are often difficult to define and specify. For example, concepts such as data security and reliability are not easily spelled out, let alone evaluated when they are applied to a complex system as yet not fully specified.

Documentation of software has come to be recognized as one of the most effective management tools because it provides the only visible evidence of progress during the development process. Of course, good documentation, in itself, does not guarantee the success of the final product. Efforts to invent standard specification and design languages in which to capture more formally the desired behavior of software and in which to specify an evolving design show promise (Ross, 1977).

Various attempts have been made to have computer systems assist in software management. Large efforts accumulate a large amount of information, such as programs, design documents, test plans and test data, personnel assignments and responsibilities, and the final completed systems. Besides being able to save this data, one also wants to preserve and query relationships among various items. Much of the data have various versions that are each different, yet related. All this information processing can conceivably be done by computer. One such effort by International Computers Limited (ICL) has been reported as quite successful (McGuffin *et. al.*, 1979).

Successful software management depends a great deal on an understanding of the basic practice of programming. The quality of programs and the speed at which they can be written and tested varies from programmer to programmer an astonishing amount. Recently, there has been evidence of emerging rigorous programming methodologies that hope to reduce that variation, thereby making the process more predictable while producing more rapidly higher quality results (*see* SOFTWARE ENGINEERING). In the 1970s, considerable attention was paid to what, for example, IBM called "Improved Programming Technology" (IBM, 1974), which included the following.

1. *Structured programming.* This term has many meanings but to most it means the development of programs in an orderly way so that they don't become impossibly complicated in their organization, especially in their control flow (*see* STRUCTURED PROGRAMMING).

2. *Top-down program development.* This is basically a technique to avoid the "integration problem" where many low-level programs are tried together for the first time. Many interface errors are usually detected during integration. In top-down development, one starts with high-level routines and only codes and tests programs after their invoking code has been written and tested. One attempts to have a "running," yet incomplete, system at all times.

3. *Chief programmer team.* Here, the analogy between a chief programmer team and a chief surgeon team has been made. Given an extremely well trained and talented programmer, can one supply that person with extra support specialists so as to magnify that individual's effectiveness? The team includes a back-up programmer, a librarian, and other specialists as needed.

4. *Development support libraries.* This is usually a part of the chief programmer technique. It identifies the specialty of managing physically the programs and documentation of a project (see Fig. 1). As well as removing the burden of com-

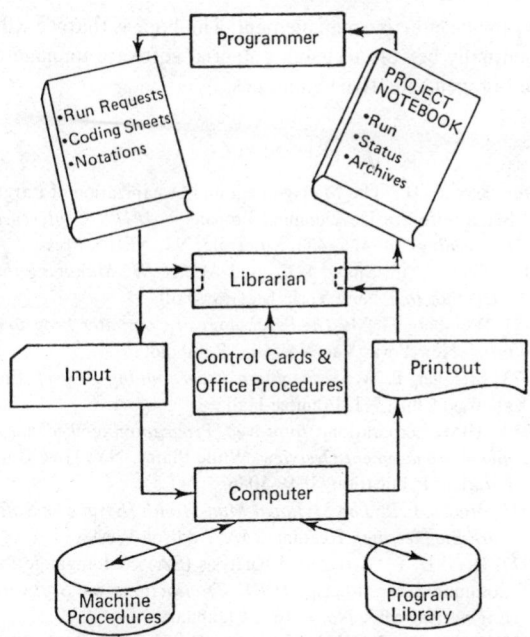

Fig. 1. Block diagram showing how a development support library relieves the programmer of clerical tasks. Centralized control is achieved through the librarian.

piling programs, logging tests, checking results, etc. from the chief programmer, the library forces a rigor in maintaining adequate controls on the programs and data developed.

5. *HIPO diagrams.* HIPO stands for hierarchy plus input-process-output. The input, output, and processing steps needed to define a programming system are recorded in a hierarchical set of diagrams. An analogy with mechanical drawings is sometimes made.

6. *Structured walk-throughs.* A structured walk-through is a review of a program or set of programs by the author and colleagues. The claimed benefits are at least threefold: The author knows others will be examining the work in detail and will try to do a better job, errors will be detected since the material will be looked at from non-author views, and it offers a medium for discussion of and exchange of good programming techniques.

Growing effectiveness in software management will come with the emergence of competent software engineers who have developed relevant experience and insight to provide effective management. The hope is that we will eventually be able to teach potential software managers well proven, effective techniques.

REFERENCES

1969. Kay, R. H. "The Management and Organization of Large Scale Software Development Projects," *AFIPS Conference Proceedings* **34**: 426–433. Montvale, NJ: AFIPS Press.

1971. Ditri, A. E., Shaw, J. C., and Atkins, W. *Managing the EDP Function*. New York: McGraw-Hill.

1971. Weinberg, G. M. *The Psychology of Computer Programming*. New York: Van Nostrand Reinhold.

1973. Metzger, P. W. *Managing a Programming Project*. Englewood Cliffs, NJ: Prentice-Hall.

1974. IBM Corporation. *Improved Programming Technologies—Management Overview*. While Plains, NY: IBM Corporation, Publication GE19-5086.

1975. Brooks, F. P. *The Mythical Man-Month (Essays on Software Engineering)*. Reading, MA: Addison-Wesley.

1977. Ross, D. T. "Structured Analysis (SA): A Language for Communicating Ideas," *IEEE Transactions on Software Engineering* **SE3**, *No. 1:* 16–34 (January).

1979. McGuffin, R. W., Elliston, A. E., Tranter, B. R., and Westmacott, P. N. "CADES—Software Engineering in Practice," *Proceedings of 4th International Conference on Software Engineering, IEEE Catalog No. 79CH1479-5C*. Piscataway, NJ: IEEE Computer Society, pp. 136–144.

R. H. KAY AND J. C. KING

SOFTWARE, MATHEMATICAL. *See* MATHEMATICAL SOFTWARE.

SOFTWARE MONITORS

For articles on related subjects *see* HARDWARE MONITORS; PERFORMANCE MEASUREMENT AND EVALUATION; SOFTWARE SCIENCE; and STRUCTURED PROGRAMMING.

A software monitor is, according to its most general definition, a piece of software used for performance measurement purposes. Like other types of instruments (e.g., hardware monitors), a software monitor is capable of measuring the performance of two kinds of objects—computer systems and computer programs. *A system-oriented* monitor usually measures system performance indices (e.g., response or turnaround times, throughput rates, component utilizations), as well as system and workload variables (e.g., CPU time demands, memory space demands, paging rates, degrees of multiprogramming). A *program-oriented* monitor is usually capable of measuring such program performance indices as execution times, instruction execution counts and frequencies, total CPU times, uninterrupted CPU interval durations, numbers and types of I/O operations performed, and so on.

The main functions of any monitor are event detection, data collection, data reduction, and presentation of results (see Fig. 1). A software monitor is either of the *event-driven* or *sampling* type. The basic type of event for an event-driven software monitor is the execution of a certain instruction within a program. This event can be detected by inserting into the program at that location a *checkpoint* or *software probe;* that is, an instruction which is executed whenever the monitored instruction is executed and which has the effect of recording the execution (e.g., by updating a counter). A wide variety of event types can be indirectly detected by this mechanism; for instance, the use of a variable, the coincidence of the value of a variable with a given value, the updating of a register, the execution of a given arithmetic operation, and so on. System events can be expressed in terms of these program event types when the program involved is the operating system.

With a sampling software monitor, the detection is performed by an interval timer which interrupts the CPU and causes the monitor to seize control. The main advantages of a sampling monitor over an event-driven one are its much easier addition to an existing system or program and the potentially lower interference with the object being measured. The main disadvantages are its lesser accuracy when measuring certain types of indices and, in some cases, its inability to collect protected system information.

With all types of software monitors, the detection of an appropriate event causes a certain amount of data accessible to the instrument to be collected and possibly processed for reduction purposes. The types of events to be detected, the amount of collected data, and the extent

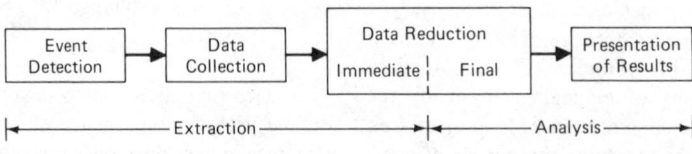

Fig. 1

of their immediate reduction vary with the instrument and may often be influenced by its user. When this is not possible, the monitor is said to be *fixed*. Examples of fixed software monitors are the *meters* (checkpoints which increment a software counter whenever they are executed) and all non-modifiable checkpoints inserted into a program (e.g., those which, within an operating system, measure resource consumptions for accounting and charging purposes). The extent to which monitors reduce data at collection time varies between the extremes of *counting* (maximum immediate reduction, minimum storage requirements, maximum loss of information) and *tracing* (no immediate reduction, maximum storage requirements, minimum or no loss of information).

Depending on the time which elapses between detection/collection and reduction/presentation, a monitor can be classified as *off line* or *on line*. In an off-line monitor, the completion of data reduction and the presentation of results are deferred until a later time. In the terminology of Fig. 1, the analysis follows the extraction at a relatively long temporal distance, so that, in an off-line software monitor, there is no appreciable interference between the two operations. On-line monitors are those which reduce data and present results at their full speed, which, for software monitors, is the speed of the system at which data is collected. In other words, in these monitors, analysis is performed on line with respect to extraction.

From the viewpoint of the duration of their operation, monitors can be classified as *permanent* or *temporary*. Permanent instruments are used in continuous monitoring, a fundamental aspect of performance management, and in resource usage accounting. Since they are permanently incorporated into the object being monitored, their interference (i.e., their effects on the measured quantities) is always present and can therefore be ignored, though their impact on system overhead generally cannot. Temporary monitors find their main applications in the measurement studies needed for system or program tuning, capacity planning, and benchmark design for procurement projects. Temporary event-driven software monitors consist of removable checkpoints and of appropriate measurement routines called by the checkpoints. The insertion and the removal of checkpoints can be partially automated by an interactive approach. Sampling monitors may be system or user programs which can be started and stopped by their users. On-line instruments are mostly used for fast short-term tuning, real-time detection and removal of sudden performance problems (infinite loops, deadlocks), and continuous monitoring. Any temporary instrument may be used for continuous monitoring by leaving it on without interruptions, or, more conveniently, turning it on periodically according to a performance management plan. However, in the

former case, a fixed *ad hoc* monitor normally consumes less resources than a more general type of monitor; also, in the latter case as well as in all temporary uses of a system-oriented software monitor, its interference with the measured system cannot in principle be ignored.

The amount of interference caused by a software monitor depends on the data collection rate, on the access times of the data to be collected, on the degree of immediate data reduction, on the strategies adopted for storing the data, and on the efficiency of the monitor's code.

The events a software monitor can detect and the data it can collect belong to the class of those which are accessible at the software level. Voltage pulses, control states, microinstruction delays, or contents of microregisters cannot be observed. On the other hand, variables such as the names of the jobs or transactions which have caused certain events, queue lengths, the names of the most frequently accessed files are only, or much more easily, measured by a software monitor than by a hardware monitor. All types of software monitors are to some extent dependent on the hardware-software system on which they run. Thus, they are much less portable than hardware monitors.

Most existing event-driven software monitors have been constructed by operating system manufacturers. It is clearly much easier for the designers of a system than for outsiders to instrument it with suitable checkpoints. These monitors, like the fixed instruments also based on the checkpoint technique, were originally implemented for the exclusive use of the manufacturer, but are being more and more often distributed to the customers for their own performance monitoring or measurement projects. In some cases, the user is allowed to specify or select both the data collection operations which are to take place upon detection of the system events corresponding to the fixed checkpoints, and the subsequent data reductions; in the case of fixed monitors, such as those which collect accounting data, the user can specify the desired reduction operations; commercial software packages exist which exploit either possibility. Most of the commercial software monitors, however, and some of those offered by system manufacturers, are of the sampling type. The first system-oriented sampling monitor appeared on the market in 1968, and was immediately followed by the first program-oriented sampling monitor. Several years later, the first on-line system-oriented software monitor, of the sampling type, was announced.

Three simple examples of applications of software monitors are given below.

Measurement of device utilization during a time interval of duration T. It is assumed that the operating system keeps the information about the state (busy or idle) of the device in a memory bit S.

An event-driven monitor to solve the problem consists of two checkpoints, C_1 and C_2, and two dedicated memory locations, A and B, whose contents are denoted by a and b. The two checkpoints are inserted into the operating system code immediately after the instructions which update the contents of S.

$$
\begin{aligned}
\cdot & \\
\cdot & \\
\cdot & \\
& S \leftarrow \text{busy} \\
C_1: & \quad B \leftarrow \text{clock} \\
\cdot & \\
\cdot & \\
\cdot & \\
& S \leftarrow \text{idle} \\
C_2: & \quad A \leftarrow a + \text{clock} - b \\
\cdot & \\
\cdot & \\
\cdot &
\end{aligned}
$$

Initialization: $A \leftarrow 0$, $B \leftarrow \text{clock}$. Computation of the utilization (at the end of time interval T): $u = a/T$.

A sampling monitor samples the contents of S periodically (or at random times) N times during the interval: If $N_1 \leq N$ is the number of times S was found to contain "busy," then $u \cong N_1/N$.

Measurement of the mean length of a queue. It is assumed that the operating system keeps the instantaneous length of the queue in memory location Q.

An event-driven monitor uses one checkpoint C consisting of two statements and two dedicated memory locations A and B. C is inserted into the operating system code just before the point at which an item is added to or deleted from the queue:

$$
\begin{aligned}
\cdot & \\
\cdot & \\
\cdot & \\
C: & \quad A \leftarrow a + q * (\text{clock} - b) \\
& \quad B \leftarrow \text{clock} \\
& \quad Q \leftarrow q + 1 \ \text{or} \ Q \leftarrow q - 1 \\
\cdot & \\
\cdot & \\
\cdot &
\end{aligned}
$$

Initialization: $A \leftarrow 0$, $B \leftarrow \text{clock}$. Computation of the mean queue length (at the end of a time interval T): $mql = a/T$.

A sampling monitor samples the contents of Q periodically (or at random times) N times during the interval and accumulates into location A the sum of the sampled queue lengths: If the initial contents of A were 0 and a is the contents of A at the end of the interval, then $mql \cong a/N$.

Measurement of the profile of a program by a sampling monitor. The monitor samples the contents of the program counter periodically and is able to determine when the program to be measured is running. (In practice, the monitor gets its data from the program status word of the process which has just been interrupted.) A code utilization map is constructed by dividing the instruction space of the program into contiguous regions of 2^n words each, mapping each region onto one word in the map, and incrementing by 1 the contents of a map word whenever the program counter is found to point to an instruction in the corresponding region. If the map initially contains all zeroes, at the end of the measurement interval it will show the utilization profile of the program during that interval with a resolution inversely related to the value of n.

REFERENCES

1973. Drummond, M. E. *Evaluation and Measurement Techniques for Digital Computer Systems.* Englewood Cliffs, NJ: Prentice-Hall.

1975. Hellerman, H. and Conroy, T. E. *Computer System Performance.* New York: McGraw-Hill.

1976. Svobodova, L. *Computer Performance Measurement and Evaluation Methods: Analysis and Applications.* New York: Elsevier.

1978. Ferrari, D. *Computer Systems Performance Evaluation.* Englewood Cliffs, NJ: Prentice-Hall.

D. FERRARI

SOFTWARE PACKAGES

For articles on related subjects *see* ADMINISTRATIVE APPLICATIONS; APPLICATIONS PROGRAMMING; DOCUMENTATION ENGINEERING APPLICATIONS; MATHEMATICAL PROGRAMMING; PORTABILITY; PROGRAM LIBRARIES, NUMERICAL AND STATISTICAL; and SORT/MERGE PACKAGES.

A *software package* is a computer program or set of programs which has been designed to perform specific functions useful to a number of computer users. Available through a variety of marketing channels, these packages can be characterized as either *application software* or as *system software,* the former usually performing business functions, and the latter functions related to the operations of the computer itself.

The software package had its origins at some point in the 1960s, but the exact date and circumstances are matters of opinion. The question is one of definition. For example, did the Program Application Library, first formulated by IBM for the 1400 series computer in the early 1960s, constitute a group of "packages"? This Library was seldom, if ever, used in package form; rather, its overall system design was usually modified and then re-coded to meet the requirements of specific users. Or does the genesis of the concept of "packaged software" date from the advent of AUTOFLOW (an automatic flow-charting package) from Applied Data Research or Mark IV (a comprehensive file-handling system) from Informatics, Inc.? The former of these now well-known program development systems was not designed and written as a package but, instead, became so through multi-client use while the latter was originally written as a "package" for a group of five clients. Or did software packages come into being when attempts were made to take customer programs and to modify them for use in other installations, a practice, started in about 1967, that is notable if only for its failure rate?

Whatever the exact origin of the software package might have been, in the late 1960s, and particularly after IBM announced in June of 1969 that it would "unbundle" its application software from the price of its computers and would sell this software separately, an increasing number of firms began to produce and to market packages and the software industry was born.

Software as a Package. Whatever its origins, the software package, whether distributed in source or object form, resembles other products that can be bought and used "off the shelf." Like an automobile, it can be acquired in either "stripped down" form or more fully-equipped to meet just about any user's needs. It comes with an "owner's manual" (i.e., documentation) explaining how it works, and it often comes with a certain amount of "maintenance" built into the contract. The analogy between software packages and cars, however, is somewhat misleading in the case of the term "maintenance." Unlike an automobile, software does not break down as a result of use, but it usually comes with defects ("bugs") in its code which need to be corrected when detected and, to meet the changing requirements of its users, it sometimes will need to be updated or enhanced. Thus, "maintenance" might more accurately be referred to as "user support" and this is something that vendors of software packages other than the inexpensive mail order sort will usually provide on a warranty or fee basis. Also, unlike an automobile that is purchased (but similar to one that is leased), the software package is often licensed to the user rather than sold outright, with the vendor retaining proprietary rights to ownership. The buyer of the licensed package, therefore, is granted only limited right of usage and is prohibited from making copies for multiple use or resale.

The Software Industry. Since the 1960s, the number of software products being marketed has snow-balled. As early as 1966, there might have been as many as 45 vendors selling over 100 packages. By the end of 1980, that number had grown to approximately 6,000 vendors (including microcomputer software companies) selling more than 15,000 products to over 100,000 end users. The largest of these vendors is IBM, estimated to have between 2,000 and 3,000 products and software revenues in 1979 in excess of $1.5 billion. The other computer manufacturers, companies such as Control Data, Burroughs, Digital Equipment, and Wang, are estimated to offer 1,300 or 1,400 software products but their revenues are generally unknown. By comparison, the so-called "independent software industry" composed of some 3,000 vendors (excluding IBM and the other computer manufacturers, turnkey systems houses, OEMs, consulting firms, etc.) generated slightly less than $1 billion in revenues selling 11,000 products.

Additionally, software package revenues in the area of small business computer (SBC) systems must be considered. Software revenues in 1979 in the SBC marketplace have been estimated to have been $255 million; however, this estimate includes revenues gained by various of the aforementioned hardware manufacturers, such as IBM, DEC, and Wang, which sell software as part of their SBC systems. Moreover, the $255 million lumps together both minicomputer and microcomputer software revenues, and tends to conceal the fact that the microcomputer sector of the software marketplace is still undeveloped and amorphous; consequently, its vendor population has not been clearly identified yet and its packages have not been adequately catalogued. An informed estimate, however, suggests that among the myriad microcomputer software companies and products in the marketplace by 1980, there were only about 50 vendors of any substance primarily in the microcomputer packaged software business. A typical one consisted of two people and had annual revenues of less than $3 million. Together, these vendors offered between 1,200 and 1,500 packages, including documentation and support.

Despite the vagueness and uncertainty in the figures cited above, the data on how much money is spent on software packages is better than any other data in this field. Thus, it is known that revenues derived from software package sales can be measured in the billions of dollars even if it is not known in all cases who is selling these packages or even what all these packages are. To understand why it is difficult to identify and catalogue the various vendors and their packages in a comprehensive way, it is useful to look at what might be called the "information product and service" marketplace as a whole.

The Information Product and Service Marketplace. To understand the complexity of the U.S. software product marketplace today, it is helpful to look at the structure and components of the entire information product and service marketplace (see Figs. 1 and 2). Fig. 1 lists the type of product or service, and the value-added

Value Added Components

Product/Service	Hardware	Software	Communications	People	Database
Counsulting				X	
Education				X	
OEM distributors	X	X		X	
Turnkey vendors	X	X	maybe	X	maybe
Software product		X		maybe	
Professional services		maybe		X	
Information processing services batch	X	X		X	maybe
Remote batch	X	X	X	X	maybe
Interactive	X	X	X	maybe	maybe
On-site	X	X	maybe	X	maybe
Hardware manufacturers	X	X		maybe	

Fig. 1. Information product and service marketplace/value-added components.

component(s) typically supplied with it. Fig. 2 shows the percentage of the marketplace held by various kinds of suppliers. Of course, it will be readily noted that not all the products and services listed involve software in package form. Some, such as "Processing Services," involve software as a service rather than as a product. Nevertheless, Figs. 1 and 2 are useful in showing the industry context into which the software package fits as well as the types of major providers of software as a package. Each of the types of businesses listed in Figs. 1 and 2 was originally established and developed apart from any of the others. The lines of demarcation separating them were obvious. But changing technology, economics, and customer demands have caused a coalescence, a crossing of boundaries, a merging of these various areas. In today's market, therefore, it is difficult to find a firm in just one of these several businesses. Most service and software firms are in two businesses, if not more.

The question of who is, or who is not, in the software product business, consequently, becomes confusing. Almost all of these various vendors are involved in the production and marketing of software in one form or another. Moreover, adding to the confusion is the fact that every year 5% of the independent software vendors go out of business and 1% of them are acquired by other firms. At the same time, the independent software industry as a whole is growing in number of vendors at an annual rate of 10%.

Major Product Categories. Software products can be characterized in various ways. For instance, they can be described in terms of the computer environment they operate in. Thus, there are *mainframe* (*q.v.*) products, so called because they are used on medium- and large-scale computers such as the IBM 4300 series and the IBM 360/370 systems or 303X series; minicomputer

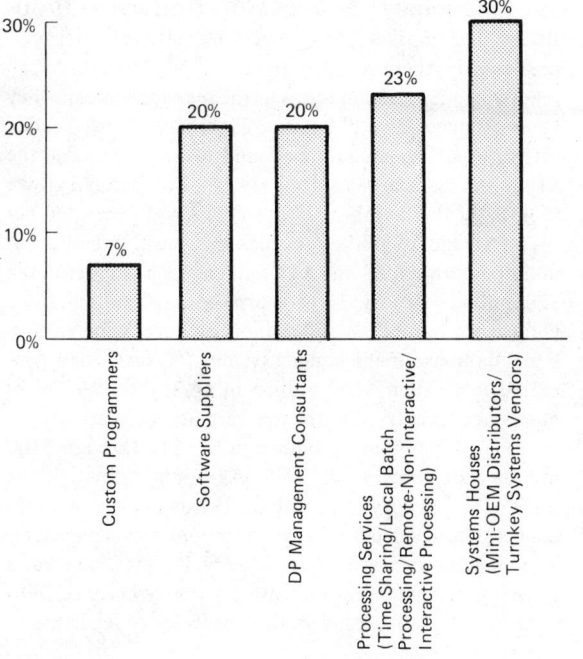

Fig. 2. Information product and service suppliers/percentage of marketplace.*

products which are used on such machines as the DEC PDP/8, Data General Nova, or IBM Series 1; microcomputer products which operate on computers such as the Apple or TRS-80; and those, referred to as "portable," which operate on computers of more than one size or type.

Further, these products can be characterized, as in Fig. 3, in terms of the types of products they are or the specific industry they are directed toward. Fig. 3, moreover, is based on a compendium of software products, the *ICP Directory* (which, for the reasons stated above, cannot be said to be absolutely complete), and it describes the percentage of these products in terms of each of 15 categories. Thus, it provides some idea of the areas where software packages are most used or useful.

As can be seen from Fig. 3, there are more products in the section labeled "Cross Industry" than there are in any other. What this means is that, as might be expected, there are more products of the general administrative and accounting sort—for instance, accounts payable/receivable, payroll, and personnel—than there are products directed toward specific industries such as banking, manufacturing, insurance, or transportation. Many companies need to automate functions in the administrative and accounting area. Further, these administrative and accounting applications tend to be more uniform, hence

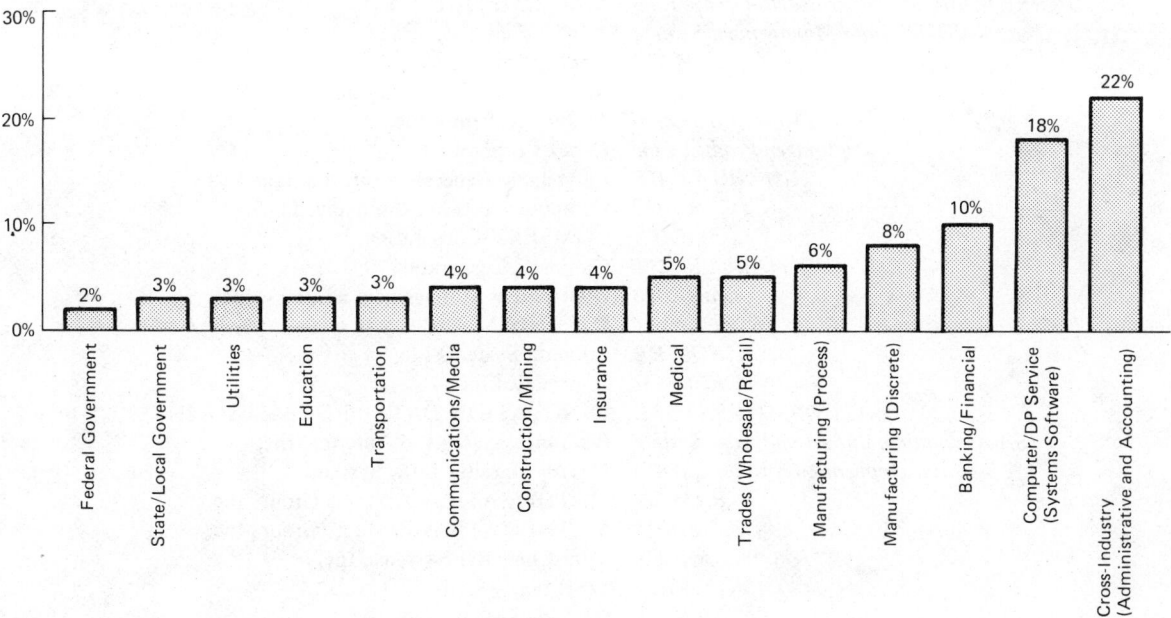

Fig. 3. Software market specialties/percentage of packages.**

*Vendors may be involved in more than one IP&S area. Data: International Computer Programs, Inc.

**Data: International Computer Programs, Inc.

more easily packaged, than do the applications in specific industry areas such as manufacturing or banking. It is not surprising, therefore, that more software packages are focused on this area than on any other. Nor is it surprising that the next largest number of products is directed toward the "Computer/DP Service" area, involving those products which are referred to as *system software*. These products include database management systems, utilities, teleprocessing and communications monitors, and programming languages—programs, that is, that facilitate or monitor the use of the computer, as distinguished from *application software* that performs functions, ranging from payroll to golf course management, pertaining to business operations. Various of these "system software products" are needed in fewer or greater numbers to operate any computer system, depending, of course, on its size and complexity.

In addition to the cross-industry administrative and accounting and computer/DP service categories, the designations "Construction," "Insurance," "Medical," and "Utilities" reflect the percentage of products in these specific industry or service areas.

Financially Successful Software Products. The marketplace success of software packages, particularly those vended by the "independents," can readily be measured in terms of the revenue plateaus they have attained. In 1972, only 29 independently-vended software packages could be found to have exceeded the $1 million mark in sales. By 1979, this number had grown to 432. Of this number, 290 products had generated between $1 and $5 million in sales revenues; 78 had accumulated between $5 and $10 million; 33 had entered the $20 million category; 10 had surpassed $30 million; three had earned more than $50 million; and one, Cincom Systems' database management system, TOTAL, had generated more than $100 million in aggregate sales revenues since its entry into the marketplace 10 years before.

Fig. 4 lists those products in the $10 through $100 million categories as of 1979. As might be noted, the higher the category, the more likely it is to contain a preponderance of system software over application packages. The system software in these very high-revenue categories outnumbers the application software because, until quite recently, the trend in data processing departments

$10,000,000

Shadow II	Altergo Software Inc.
CI/RF (Customer Integrated/Reference File)	**ANACOMP, INC.**
AS1-ST Data Management System	Applications Software
AUTOFLOW II®	Applied Data Research, Inc.
DATACOM	**Applied Data Research, Inc.**
Project Control/70	**Atlantic Software Inc.**
Optimizer Product Line	Capex Corporation
GIP/SIGA PAIE	**Compagnie Generale d'Informatique**
EDOS	Computer Software Company, The
AMAPS	COMSERV Corporation
EDP-AUDITOR/CULPRIT	Cullinane Corporation
DMS-1000	**Distribution Management Systems, Inc.**
IMSL Library	**IMSL, INC.**
INQUIRE	Infodata Systems Inc.
INTERCOMM	Informatics Inc.
FAST DUMP RESTORE	INNOVATION DATA PROCESSING, INC.
ISA/Accounting, Budget and Cost System	**Insurance Systems of America, Inc.**
Modular Application Systems (MAS)	Martin Marietta Data Systems
RAMIS®	MATHEMATICA Products Group, Inc.
RAMIS 11	MATHEMATICA Products Group, Inc.
MICOS	**Mini-Computer Systems, Inc.**
DATAMANAGER	**MSP Inc.**
OLIVER	**On-Line Systems Inc.**
The Data Analyzer	**Program Products Incorporated**
PROBE	Rapidata, Inc.
COM-PLETE	**software ag of North America, Inc.**
Cost^{sm}	Systems Architects, Inc.
TRES Customer Information System	TRES Systems, Inc.

$10,000,000

UNIAPT	United Computing Corporation
General Ledger System	**United Computing Systems, Inc./INFONATIONAL**
UCC ONE—Tape Management Software	**University Computing Company**
UCC TEN	University Computing Company
Westinghouse DISK UTILITY	**Westinghouse Electric Corporation**

$20,000,000

ROSCOE®	**Applied Data Research, Inc.**
ENVIRON/1	**Cincom Systems, Inc.**
4 ● 1 ● 1 Systems	**COMSHARE, Incorporated**
MSA Payroll Accounting System	Management Science America, Inc.
RAMIS II	**MATHEMATICA Products Group, Inc.**
EASYTRIEVE	Pansophic Systems Incorporated
PANVALET	Pansophic Systems Incorporated
EPAT	SDI
GRASP	SDI
GRASPVS	**SDI**
Software International General Ledger and Financial Reporting System	Software International Corporation
TALK^{sm}	System Architects, Inc.
TASK/MASTER	turnkey systems inc.
UCC FCS—Financial Control System	**University Computing Company**
UCC TWO—(Duo-DOS under OS)	**University Computing Company**
SYNCSORT/OS	**Whitlow Computer Systems, Inc.**

$30,000,000

The LIBRARIAN®	**Applied Data Research, Inc.**
CA-SORT	**Computer Associates**
IDMS	Cullinane Corporation
LIFE-COMM	**Informatics Inc.**
MSA General Ledger/FICS	**Management Science America, Inc.**
SYSTEM 2000	**MRI Systems Corporation**
SCERT	Performance Systems Incorporated
Policy Management Systems	**Policy Management Systems**
ADABAS	software ag of North America
LIFE/70	**TCC, Inc.**

$50,000,000

MSA Human Resource Management System	**Management Science America, Inc.**
InSci Human Resource System	Information Science Incorporated
MARK IV	Informatics, Inc.

$100,000,000

TOTAL	**Cincom Systems, Inc.**

Boldface indicates achievement during 1979

Fig. 4.   Financially successful software packages/revenue levels reached by 1979.

has been to buy system software in packaged form and to develop applications in-house. Software users have been less reluctant to buy system software in packaged form than they have the application kind because system software relates to computers which are uniform by model, whereas application software relates to business operations, and many companies consider themselves to be unique in the way they do business.

Further, as pointed out above, system software is needed in every computer installation. The potential number of installations for this software is, as a consequence, quite high. For example, successful packages such as Pansophic Systems, Inc.'s PANVALET and Applied Data Research's The LIBRARIAN, both program management systems, boasted installations numbering 4,100 and 6,000, respectively, in 1980. By comparison, successful application packages usually number their installations in the hundreds—everywhere, perhaps, but in the microcomputer area, which is characterized by a wide distribution of very low-priced application software. This difference in magnitude in the number of installations of mainframe and minicomputer system software packages versus those of application software helps to account for the greater financial success of the former.

There are, however, notable exceptions to the rule which seems to dictate that system software products will generate higher sales revenues than applications are able to. Such exceptions include the human resource management systems vended by Information Science Inc. and Management Science America, both of which had exceeded the $50 million revenue plateau by 1979.

LOUIS W. HARM

SOFTWARE RELIABILITY

For articles on related subjects *see* PROGRAM SPECIFICATION; PROGRAM VERIFICATION; SOFTWARE COMPLEXITY; SOFTWARE ENGINEERING; SOFTWARE FLEXIBILITY; SOFTWARE MAINTENANCE; SOFTWARE SCIENCE; and STRUCTURED PROGRAMMING.

Our heavy dependence on computer systems has made the assessment of their reliability very important. For the use of digital computers for critical applications (e.g., nuclear power plant safety control systems, air traffic control systems), it must be shown that the computer system meets the specified reliability constraints. Even for less critical systems (e.g., airline reservation systems, on-line banking systems), the effect of their breakdown can be severe. The theoretical basis for methods of estimating the reliability of hardware (*see* RELIABILITY, HARDWARE) is well developed. On the other hand, re-

search on software reliability is still rudimentary, although several models have been proposed since as early as the late 1960s for estimating software reliability and some related parameters (e.g., MTTF—Mean Time To Failure—or the number of errors remaining in the software). However, the basis of most software reliability models has not been validated and should be viewed skeptically.

An obvious question is why we cannot apply hardware reliability models to software reliability. The main reason is that the source of hardware failure is mainly physical deterioration (e.g., breakdown of components due to fatigue or other physical conditions), while the source in software is faulty design. Although design faults may exist in hardware design, this type of fault is normally ignored in hardware reliability theory. This is because most hardware systems maintain a continuity in the design from old systems to new ones, so that a large part of the design is well-tested. Further, hardware systems can be viewed as the interconnection of a number of independent submodules that can be tested separately. On the other hand, the replication process for software is almost trivial and software reliability models must be developed so that they can be applied to design reliability. Also, figures of merit for software reliability should be developed in such a way that they are compatible with hardware reliability in order to be able to compute the overall system reliability.

Since there is no physical deterioration or random malfunction in software, it is preferable to prove that software satisfies (or does not satisfy) its requirement specification rather than to estimate its reliability. Proving the correctness of a program means absolute reliability. If a program is written in a high-level language, this assumes that the compiler is correct; it also assumes the correctness of the specification against which the program has been proved. However, current program verification techniques cannot deal with the size and complexity of software for practical applications. Similarly, exhaustive testing, which provides absolute reliability, is ruled out by the large number of possible inputs. Besides, testing is limited by other factors, namely, the difficulty in verifying the output corresponding to an input and the lack of realistic inputs.

Most software reliability models attempt to estimate the reliability of the software based on its error history after integration and debugging. For example, an operating system which crashes more often than another has a lower reliability. The difficulty is how to quantify this measure. Research on this area focuses mainly on finding good reliability models so that we can quantify the reliability from a minimal amount of data.

In the following, we discuss the software reliability models proposed thus far.

Definitions. Software reliability has been defined as the probability that a *software fault* that causes *deviation* from required output by more than *specified tolerances,* in a *specified environment,* does not occur during a specified exposure period (TRW, 1976). Thus, the software need be correct only for the inputs for which it is defined (specified environment). Also, if the output is correct within the specified tolerances, in spite of some error, then the error is ignored. This may happen in the evaluation of a complicated floating point expression where many approximations are used. It is possible that a failure may be due to errors in the compiler, the operating system, the microcode, or even the hardware. These failures are ignored in estimating the reliability of the application program. However, when we estimate the overall system reliability, they must be taken into account.

The *exposure period* should be independent of extraneous factors such as machine execution time, programming environment, etc. For many applications, the appropriate unit of *exposure period* is a *run* corresponding to the selection of a point from the input domain of the program. However, for some programs (e.g., an operating system), it is difficult to determine what constitutes a "run." In such cases, the unit of exposure period may be calendar or CPU time.

Thus, we have:

$$R(i) = \text{reliability over } i \text{ runs}$$
$$= P\{\text{no failure over } i \text{ runs}\}$$

or

$$R(t) = \text{reliability over } t \text{ seconds}$$
$$= P\{\text{no failure in interval } [0,t]\}$$

where $P\{E\}$ denotes the probability of the event E.

The first definition leads to an intuitive measure of software reliability. Assuming that inputs are selected independently according to some probability distribution function, we can define the reliability R as follows.

$$R = 1 - \lim_{n \to \infty} \frac{n_f}{n}$$

where

n = number of runs
n_f = number of failures in n runs.

This is an "operational definition" of software reliability. We can estimate the reliability of a program by observing the outcomes (success/failure) of a number of runs under its operating environment. In this method, n must be sufficiently large for the estimation to be accurate. Various reliability models have been proposed for estimating the reliability. In the next section, we describe some of these models.

Reliability Models. Reliability models can be classified into the following categories: 1) estimation models, 2) measurement models, and 3) prediction models. Estimation models calculate reliability from testing in a non-operational environment. Measurement models calculate reliability from experiments in an operational environment. Prediction models derive reliability estimates from the internal characteristics (e.g., the number of statements) of software.

Estimation Models. Estimation models are used in an environment in which, once an error is found, it is corrected before the testing is continued. Each model requires data such as the number of errors found in a fixed period, the interval between two detected errors, and the time to correct an error, in addition to a failure rate. Estimation models are further classified into two categories: 1) error-counting models, which estimate both the number of errors remaining in the program and its reliability, 2) non-error-counting models, which only estimate the reliability. Estimating the number of errors remaining in a program is useful in determining a test completion point. Deterministic error-counting models assume that, if the model parameters are known, then the correction of an error results in a known increase in reliability. The Bayesian models due to Littlewood (1979) are applicable to the (usual) case where larger errors are detected earlier than smaller errors. These models neglect the time required to correct an error. This aspect is modeled as a Markov process by Trivedi and Shooman (1975). This model also yields an estimate of the availability of the software system, where the availability is the expected fraction of time during which the software system functions within acceptable ranges. The main disadvantage of these models is that, all too often, new errors may be introduced in the program as a result of imperfect debugging. Non-error counting models do not have this defect. Stochastic non-error-counting models consider the situation where different errors have different effects on the failure rate of a program. The correction of an error results in a stochastic increase in the reliability.

The deterministic and the stochastic non-error-counting models assume that the reliability is unchanged during the interval between consecutive error corrections. While this is true in an absolute sense, the reliability estimate, as *perceived* by the person testing the program, increases as the number of consecutive successful runs increases. This situation is modeled by the Bayesian growth models.

The models described above treat the program as a black box. That is, the reliability is estimated without regard to the structure of the program. The validity of the assumptions in these models usually increases as the size of the program increases.

Measurement Models. Measurement models are similar to hardware reliability models in the sense that they measure failure in an operational environment. They assume that the software is not modified during the measurement period even if an error is found. Various models are proposed to reduce the amount of testing by using different test-selection strategies. The Nelson model (TRW, 1976) is based on statistical principles. The software is tested with test cases intended to have the same distribution as the actual operating environment. The results are then used to obtain a reliability estimate.

The main disadvantage of the Nelson model is that a large number of test cases is required in order to have a high confidence in the reliability estimate. The Input Domain based model (Ramamoorthy and Bastani, 1979) reduces the number of test cases required by exploiting the nature of the input domain of the program. An important feature of this model is that the testing need not be random—any type of test-selection strategy can be used.

During the maintenance phase of the software development, a program may be changed because of error correction, addition of new features and improvements in algorithms. Any of these changes can perturb the reliability of the system. The reliability of the modified system can be estimated using the same models as for the validation phase. However, it may be possible to estimate the change in the reliability using fewer test cases since certain original features may not have been altered.

Prediction Models. Prediction models, unlike measurement and estimation models, which use data from the behavior of the software, use the internal structure (e.g., the number of statements of each type, or the number of variables) of the software for establishing reliability. This is similar to hardware reliability models based, for example, on the number of parts.

The software science (*q.v.*) (phenomenological) approach due to Halstead (1977) gives an empirical prediction of the error content of the software based on the number of operators and operands. If the predicted error content is high, then more testing is required.

REFERENCES

1975. Trivedi, A. K. and Shooman, M. L. "A Many-State Markov Model for the Estimation and Prediction of Computer Software Performance Parameters," *Proc. 1975 Int. Conf. Reliable Software,* Los Angeles, pp. 208–220.

1976. TRW Defense and Space Systems Group. *Software Reliability Study,* Redondo Beach, CA: TRW. Report No. 76-2260.1-9-5.

1977. Halstead, M. H. *Elements of Software Science.* New York: Elsevier/North-Holland.

1979. Kopetz, H. *Software Reliability.* New York: Springer-Verlag.

1979. Littlewood, B. "A Bayesian Differential Debugging Model for Software Reliability." Mathematics Department, The City University, London (June).

1979. Ramamoorthy, C. V. and Bastani, F. B. "An Input Domain Based Approach to the Quantitative Estimation of Software Reliability," *Proc. Taipei Seminar on Software Engineering,* Taipei.

C. V. RAMAMOORTHY AND K. SUZUKI

SOFTWARE SCIENCE

For articles on related subjects *see* HUMAN FACTORS IN COMPUTING; SOFTWARE COMPLEXITY; SOFTWARE ENGINEERING; SOFTWARE MAINTENANCE; SOFTWARE MANAGEMENT; SOFTWARE RELIABILITY; and STRUCTURED PROGRAMMING.

Software science is an experimental and theoretical discipline concerned with measurable properties of computer programs. The underlying hypothesis is that a computer program need not be considered solely as an art form or even as an example of logic, but that instead it could be treated as a structure which may be studied using the classical methods of natural science. This requires that its properties be measured with metrics which focus on variables, constants, special symbols, etc., which are used to represent the program and which are directly observable. The theory of software science was first formulated by the late Professor Maurice H. Halstead of Purdue University in 1972. This theory has been widely investigated by independent research groups and is gaining acceptance as a valuable tool in software engineering. It is now possible to use the formulas of software science to compare different programming languages, to estimate the time required to develop computer programs, and to make predictions about the number of errors that still remain in a delivered computer program. Since the human factor is an important element in the process of constructing computer programs, the formulas of software science can only be validated statistically using experimental data. Thus, any particular formula may not hold in a specific case.

Basic Metrics. The early machine language computer programs consisted of nothing but a series of one-word instructions, each of which contained an operator code and one or more operand addresses. Since this is still the form that a program is finally reduced to, it seems reasonable to postulate that the representation of a program consists of *operators* and *operands* and of nothing else. Each class is counted in two ways, either as the number of different elements in the class, or as their total occurrences. That is, we define

$$\eta_1 = \text{number of unique operators} \tag{1}$$
$$\eta_2 = \text{number of unique operands} \tag{2}$$
$$N_1 = \text{total occurrences of operators} \tag{3}$$
$$N_2 = \text{total occurrences of operands.} \tag{4}$$

Generally, any symbol or keyword in a program that specifies an action of the computer is considered an operator, and a symbol used to represent data is considered an operand. Most punctuation marks are also considered as operators. Software science defines the *length* of a program, in terms of the number of operators and operands, as

$$N = N_1 + N_2 \tag{5}$$

and the *vocabulary* of a program as

$$\eta = \eta_1 + \eta_2. \tag{6}$$

Additional Metrics.
The *volume* of a program is defined as

$$V = N \log_2 \eta. \tag{7}$$

It has the dimension of "bits" of information and may be interpreted as the size of the program under a uniform binary encoding of the unique operators and operands. It may also be interpreted as the number of mental comparisons needed to write a program of length N, assuming a binary search method is used to select a member of the vocabulary of size η. Since an algorithm may be implemented by many different but equivalent programs, a program that is minimal in size is said to have the *potential volume* $V*$. Any given program with volume V is considered to be implemented at the *program level L,* which is defined by

$$L = V*/V. \tag{8}$$

The value of L ranges between zero and one, with $L = 1$ representing a program written at the highest possible level (i.e., with minimum size). It may be used both to compare different implementations in different languages, and to compare implementations in the same language when different constructs or features are used. Note, however, that L is more a characterization of the implementation than that of the programming language, as one can write a program using only the elementary features of a powerful language to yield an L which is lower than if more sophisticated features are used.

The effort required to implement a computer program increases as the size of the program increases. It also takes more effort to implement a program at a lower level when compared with another equivalent program at a higher level. Thus, it is intuitive to define the *effort* in software science as

$$E = V/L. \tag{9}$$

Since $L = V*/V$, the effort E can also be written as

$$E = V^2/V*, \tag{10}$$

thus showing that E increases as the square of the volume. The dimension of E is *elementary mental discriminations,* which is directly related to the number of comparisons made at the given program level.

Hypotheses.
The first hypothesis of software science is that the length of a well-structured program is a function of only the number of unique operators and operands. It is called the *length equation,* where $\hat{N}$ is the predicted length of the program.

$$\hat{N} = \eta_1 \log_2 \eta_1 + \eta_2 \log_2 \eta_2. \tag{11}$$

The length equation was first verified by analyzing the first 14 algorithms published in the Algorithms section of the *Communications of the Association for Computing Machinery* (see Fig. 1.)

Although it is easy to construct a program to make $\hat{N}$ a very poor predictor for N, analysis of a large number of existing programs by researchers at Purdue and several other universities and in industry shows that the length equation works very well. Certain poor programming practices, such as the use of complementary operations or the use of a single variable name to represent several different meanings, are also known to make the length equation a poor predictor. Since control constructs change from one language to another, precise rules must be specified for each language to count the operators and operands. Many languages, however, have features that could be classified either as operators or operands. These ambiguities are usually settled by selecting rules so that the predicted length $\hat{N}$ most closely matches the actual length N.

As we have discussed earlier, the program that implements an algorithm in the most succinct form has the potential volume $V*$. If the desired operation on data is already defined in the programming language or its library as a "built-in" procedure, the potential volume is

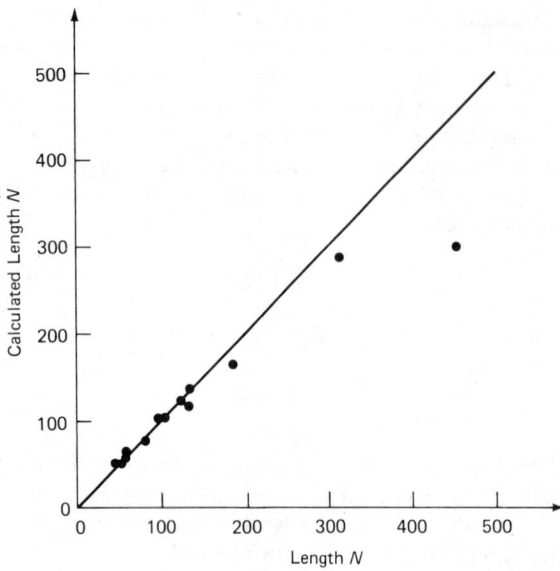

Fig. 1. Testing the length equation using Algorithms 1–14 (of *CACM*).

achieved by specifying the name of the procedure and giving a list of I/O parameters. The vocabulary of this program consists of two operators and η_2* operands where η_2* is the number of I/O parameters to the procedure. One operator is the name of the procedure, since it defines some action; the other operator is a grouping symbol needed to separate the list of parameters from the procedure name. Thus,

$$V* = (2+\eta_2*)\log_2(2+\eta_2*). \qquad (12)$$

The level of a particular implementation depends on its potential volume $V*$. However, it is not always possible to use Eq. 12 for $V*$, since certain programs do not have an explicit list of I/O parameters. An example would be a compiler program whose output consists of several files and messages to the operating system. A second hypothesis of software science is that the implementation level L may be approximated by

$$\hat{L} = \frac{2}{\eta_1}\frac{\eta_2}{N_2}. \qquad (13)$$

An intuitive argument for this formula is that the level becomes lower if additional operators are introduced ($2/\eta_1$ decreases) *and* if an operand is used repetitively (η_2/N_2 decreases). Every parameter in Eq. 13 may be obtained by counting the operators and operands in a computer program. The potential volume $V*$ may then be de-

duced using Eq. 8 with L equal to $\hat{L}$. Comparing the result with Eq. 12, it has been possible to validate this approximate formula using small sample programs. This formula can also be used with Eq. 9 to determine the software science effort for a given program.

A major contribution of software science is the ability to relate the actual implementation time to the basic metrics. A psychologist, John Stroud, suggested that the human mind is capable of making a limited number of elementary mental discriminations per second. This number S, called the *Stroud number,* ranges between 5 and 20. Since the effort E has the dimension of the number of elementary discriminations, the *implementation time* T of a program is simply

$$T = E/S. \qquad (14)$$

In practice, S is normally set to 18 since this seems to give the best results in experiments comparing the predicted times using Eq. 14 with observed programming times. This formula works very well when a given problem is solved by a single, proficient, and concentrating programmer writing a single program module. The results of one of the earliest experiments are shown in Table 1.

The calculation of $V*$ and L for a large number of programs shows that, as the complexity of the algorithm increases (larger $V*$), the program level decreases (smaller L). Professor Halstead hypothesized that if the programming language is kept fixed, $V*$ increases and L decreases in such a way that the product $LV*$ remains constant. Thus, the product, called the *language level* λ, can be used to characterize a programming language. That is,

$$\lambda = LV* = L^2V. \qquad (15)$$

Analyzing a number of programs written in different languages using Eq. 13 for L, the language levels were determined to be 1.53 for PL/I, 1.21 for Algol, 1.14 for Fortran, and 0.88 for CDC assembly language. These average values follow the intuitive rankings for these languages, but they all have large variances. Such fluctuation in a hypothesized fixed value would be expected since the language level depends not only on the language itself, but also on the nature of the problem being programmed and on the proficiency of the programmer. Eq. 15 is useful in comparing programming languages if the same set of problems is programmed in these languages. Algebraic manipulation of Eqs. 9 and 15 yields another formula for E:

$$E = (V*)^3/\lambda^2. \qquad (16)$$

Table 1.   Comparison of the Observed and Theoretical Implementation Times Using *CACM* Algorithms

CACM Algorithm	Number of Statements	Observed Time (minutes)	Theoretical Time (minutes)
33	1	3	1
19	5	9	6
24	8	10	12
20	6	11	7
31	15	13	13
23	7	16	8
17	9	18	13
14	22	24	19
29	14	25	10
21	12	37	54
25	57	42	72
16	35	85	93
Correlation coefficient with *T* observed	0.70		0.94

Thus, for a given problem, the effort (and the resulting implementation time) varies according to the inverse square of the language level.

Applications. The following applications of software science laws have been reported.

1. The measure $\hat{L}$ may be used to predict to what extent a program is likely to have errors after delivery. A program with lower $\hat{L}$ is more "error-prone" (C. P. Smith, IBM Corp.).
2. The number of errors to be discovered after a program is delivered is proportional to the measure V (L. M. Ottenstein, Purdue University).
3. The implementation time of a large programming project may be predicted using the language level and the estimated number of source statements (V. B. Schneider, Aerospace Corp.).
4. The measure E serves also as a measure of program complexity (B. Curtis *et al.*, General Electric Co.).

REFERENCES

1977. Halstead, M. H. *Elements of Software Science.* New York: Elsevier/North-Holland.
1978. Fitzsimmons, A. and Love, T. "A Review and Evaluation of Software Science," *ACM Computing Surveys* **10**, *No. 1:* 3–18 (March).
1979. Halstead, M. H. "Advances in Software Science," in Yovits, M. (Ed.), *Advances in Computers* **18**. New York: Academic Press.

V. Y. SHEN AND S. D. CONTE

SORTING

For articles on related subjects *see* BINARY SEARCH; COLLATING SEQUENCE; FILES; KEY; RECORD; and SORT-MERGE PACKAGES.

Sorting is the process by which a list of items or *records,* normally disordered, is put into order according to some criterion based on the content of each record. Why is it important to have ordered lists rather than disordered ones? A simple example will suffice to illustrate this. Consider a list of a thousand records. Suppose we wish to find a particular record. Whether the list is ordered or not, we must look at 500 records on the average to find the record we want if our search is conducted serially from beginning to end. Indeed, for an unordered list, there is no better procedure than a serial search. And if the list does not contain our record, we must examine *all* the records in the list to find this out. But if the list is ordered, certain techniques will greatly reduce the searching effort, whether or not the record is present. For example, using binary search, the search for a record and determination of its presence in or absence from an ordered list of 1,000 records takes only ten passes on the average. In addition, if a number of records are sought and these records are arranged in order according to their *keys,* then serial search requires only one complete examination of the ordered list to obtain all records. To summarize, the ordered list provides the following three advantages:

1. Faster search for a single record, using various sophisticated search techniques.

2. Faster determination if a sought record is present or absent.
3. More rapid retrieval of several records sought at once.

Before discussing various methods of sorting, we must first present some definitions and notation concerning records and files.

Definitions and Notation. Data is rather useless unless it corresponds to something real. The correspondents are *entries* or *individuals,* which might be, for example, people for a payroll application, accounts for bookkeeping applications, or items for an inventory application. In all cases we have a collection of these individuals which comprises a *universe.* Corresponding to each individual, there is a *record.* The set of records is called a *file.* Hence, there is one record in the file for each individual in the universe.

The record comprises a partial description of the entity, which may have many attributes, but of which only some are of interest in our data processing application. Each attribute has a name. If the attribute interests us, there is a corresponding *field* in our record. Each attribute must have two or more values. For example, sex can be described (currently) in one of two ways. On the other hand, a description of a person's wealth may require many digits.

The field in the record carries the *field value,* which is a reflection of the attribute value. The field value may represent the attribute value itself. For instance, the *weight* field in a personnel record may contain a value corresponding to the individual's weight in pounds at the time of measurement. To represent the state where an individual lives, the field value could be alphabetic (e.g., CONNECTICUT) or an abbreviation (e.g., CN), or a *coded* value (e.g., 07 to represent that Connecticut is the seventh state in the alphabetical listing of states).

To use our file effectively, and in particular to enable us to order it, we must uniquely identify each record. The field in the record which so identifies it is often referred to as the *record key,* or simply as the *key.*

Thus far, our definitions are unrelated to the use of a computer for sorting. In a computer, all or some portion of the file must be stored in a tangible, nameable location. We define:

A *cell* to be the location or locations in memory or on an auxiliary medium where a record is stored.
A *list* to be the location where a file is stored.

Fig. 1 shows a cell with a record in it. The record key is also displayed; note that it need not be in any special position in the record.

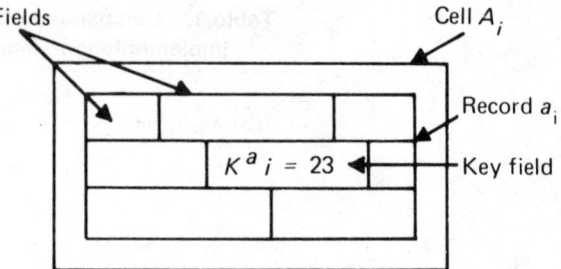

Fig. 1.   A cell containing a record with a key field.

A list, then, is a collection of cells. Records of a file are stored in cells of the list. However, it is not necessary that every cell of a list contain some record of the file. When all the cells of the list have records of the file, the list is called *dense.* Should there be cells in the list which do not contain records (are empty), as in Fig. 2, the list is said to be *loose,* or *thin.* These empty cells must have some recognizable unique feature so that the sorting program will identify them as empty.

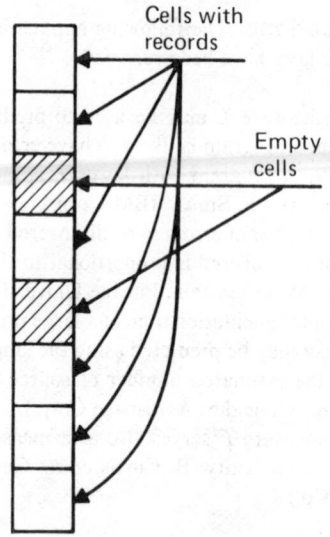

Fig. 2.   A loose list.

It is often useful for a contiguous portion of the list to hold the file compactly, as shown in Fig. 3, where the top six cells contain the six records that constitute the file. However, there are two more cells in the list, which are empty. Intuitively we feel that the list is both dense and loose; the top part is dense; all the cells are not occupied, so the list is loose; such a list is called "semi-dense."

We use the following notation to describe the various *quantities* involved in sorting.

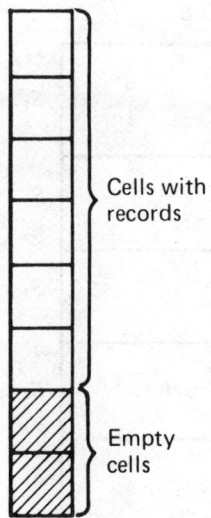

Cells with records

Empty cells

Fig. 3. A semidense list.

The *file* is designated by boldface lower-case letters, e.g., **a**.

Records are designated by subscripted lowercase italic letters, e.g., a_i.

Fields in records use lower-case letters, which are doubly subscripted; generally, the only field referred to is the *key field, K,* so that the key in record i of file **a** is designated as $_K a_i$.

Upper-case letters designate locations:

A *list* is designated by a bold-face upper-case letter, e.g., **A**.

A *cell* is designated by a subscripted upper-case italic letter, e.g., A_i.

The *field location* within a cell uses the double-subscript notation, so that the location of the key in cell i of list **A** is designed $_K A_i$.

Finally, we use the parentheses to extract the contents of a cell or extract a field from a cell. For instance (see Fig. 1), in symbolic form, the key in the ith cell of list **A**, which is 23, is denoted by

$$(_K A_i) = {}_K a_i = 23. \qquad (1)$$

We also need some notation to indicate the relative location of cells in a list. In a list **R** the order of the cells within the list is determined by the address of the cell, such that the cell with the lower address comes first. We display this fact by insuring that the designation for the lower address contains the cell with the lower subscript. In symbolic terms

$$i < j \supset R_i < R_j, \qquad (2)$$

which should be read, "if i is less than j, then the cell labeled R_i precedes the cell labeled R_j." The symbol $\supset$ represents "implies."

Now let us suppose we have a dense list. Each record contains a key. For a *sorted list,* the order in which we encounter records in the cells of the list should correspond to the size of the key assigned to each record. This is stated symbolically as

$$R_i < R_j \supset (_K R_i) < (_K R_j), \qquad (3)$$

and in words, "if cell R_i precedes cell R_j, then the key of the record contained in R_i is smaller than the key of the record contained in R_j." It should be obvious that we have imposed order upon the list **R** by the position of the records contained in that list with respect to the key contained in those records.

This is not the only order we might impose on the list **R**. For example, we can place a list into either ascending or descending order. The relation (3) describes a list in *ascending sequence.* To make a similar statement for an ordered list in *descending sequence,* we write

$$R_i < R_j \supset (_K R_i) > (_K R_j). \qquad (4)$$

This says that as we proceed through the list to cells of larger numerical address, we encounter records with smaller keys. In what follows we consider only the case of ordered lists in ascending order.

To recapitulate the foregoing, we refer to Fig. 4, which illustrates a disordered list **R** and its ordered counterpart **S**. The incoming dotted arrow points to r_2, indicating that it is the smallest record found in **R**. The dotted arrow from r_2 to r_5 in **R** shows that it is the next smallest; r_5 points to r_3 which should come next, etc. On the right of Fig. 4 we see the sorted list **S**. The first cell, S_1, contains r_2, which has been moved from its position in list **R**. S_2 contains r_5; S_3 contains r_3, etc. In a general sense it is easy to see how the sorted list **S** can be created from the unsorted list **R**. However, there are many ways the comparisons and the move operations can be performed. Much work has gone into finding good ways to do this. In what follows, we examine some of these methods.

Computer Sorting. Generally, the lists to be sorted on a computer are large. The lists are supplied using intermediate or external media such as punched cards or magnetic tape, disk, or drum. As far as the user is concerned, a list is supplied on such a medium and the computer returns a similar list, but in ordered form. What happens in between?

Internal Sorting. When the entire list can be brought into the main computer memory and sorted in memory,

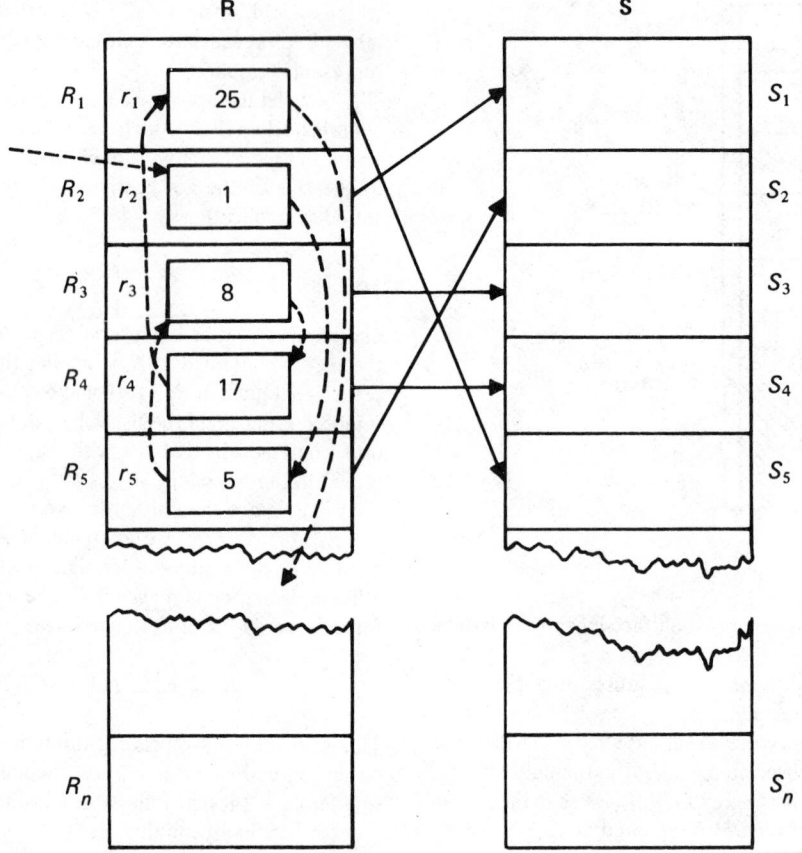

Fig. 4. Action required for sorting.

this process is called "internal sorting." Internal sorting can be done at least in two ways. Both are illustrated in Fig. 5.

For the *double-list sort*, the ordered file **t** is placed in a list area of memory, designated in Fig. 5(a) as **R**, using the buffer to load it from an external or auxiliary medium. The internal sort action then takes place, creating the sorted list **S**, generally in another area of memory. This becomes the output file **u**.

Entry sorting [Fig. 5(b)] takes place as records are

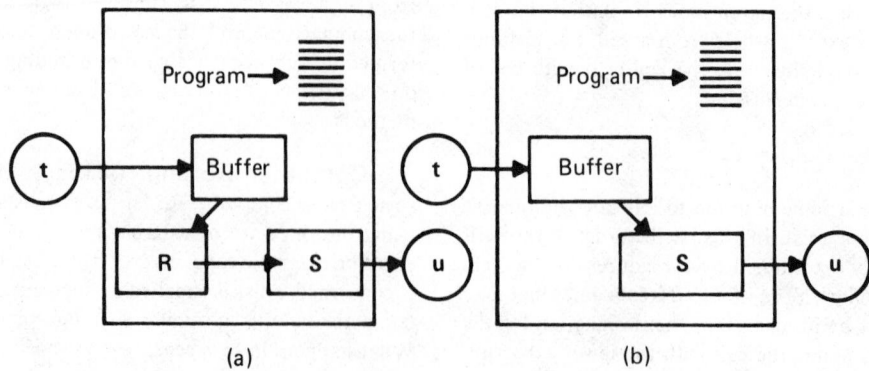

Fig. 5. Internal sorting, (a) Double-list sort. (b) Entry sort.

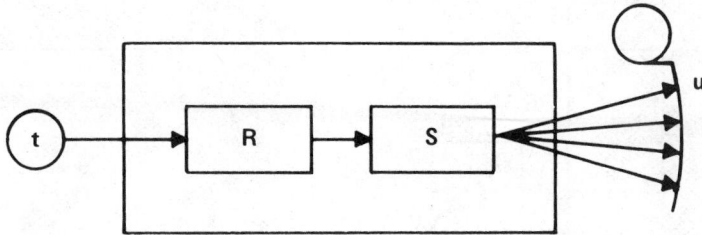

Fig. 6.   An internal sort of a long list produces a list of ordered sublists.

brought into the buffer from **t**. The sorting program sets up a buffer area where one record or a block of a few records is placed as it is brought in from the external medium. Entry sorting takes records from the buffer and places them in the sorted list **S**. This action takes place a bufferful at a time until the input file is exhausted.

External Sorting. When the input file grows large, the size of the computer memory becomes a limiting factor in the case of internal sorting. The technique provided in most sorting programs is to produce a string of sorted records by an internal sort. Thus, in Fig. 6 we see the input file **t**, which is brought into memory a piece at a time (to **R**) and sorted internally in **S**. As each sorted sublist is produced, it is placed on an auxiliary storage medium, shown in Fig. 6 as the file **u**. When this action is completed, **u** consists of ordered sublists. These are subsequently acted upon by the computer to form a single-ordered list; the action thus performed is called an *external sort* and uses *merging,* which will be described shortly.

Internal Sorting Techniques. In this section we examine a number of the simpler types of internal sorts. The more complicated sorts have much space devoted to them in the literature (Flores, 1969; Knuth, 1973; Lorin, 1971).

Selection. One of the simplest (but least efficient) sorts uses selection, which we illustrate in Fig. 7. On the left is an unordered list, **R**. Only the key of the records is shown. The program searches the list **R** sequentially, using two registers, M and P, in the figure. The key currently in M is compared to the key of each record as the list is searched. When the key of the record being examined is smaller than the number in M, the new key is placed in M and its location, the cell identification, is placed in P. At the end of the search, the cell containing the smallest record is pointed to by P. This record is transferred to S_i, the proper location in **S**.

A problem arises for the next selection. If nothing is done with the list **R**, the search will come up with the

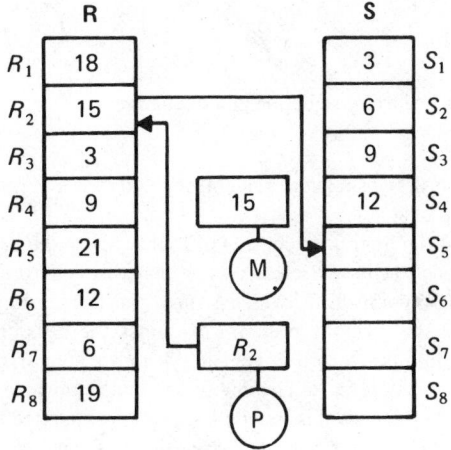

Fig. 7.   Sort by selection.

same least record. Hence, after a record has been transferred from its location in **R**, a *flag* must be inserted in **R** to indicate to the program to skip this cell. One way to do this is to change the key in the cell from which a record has been transferred to the highest possible key; that way it can never be least.

In Fig. 7, the four smallest records of **R** have already been placed in cells of **S**. The next least record to come from **R** for **S** is now in R_2. It should be clear from the description how this record is found and moved.

Selection and Exchange. Several improvements can be made on the selection sort. One such, called "selection and exchange," is a sort performed *within* the list area—a separate area **S** is not required. We describe it briefly. First, the list **R** is scanned for the smallest record. This record is moved to the top cell and the record in the top cell is moved down to the position of the list record—thus the reason for "exchange" in its name. One advantage obtained from selection and exchange is that, as it proceeds, fewer and fewer cells need be examined. Another is that it uses less memory. In Fig. 8, **R** is divided into two sublists, where R^o is the ordered sublist at the top; R^x is

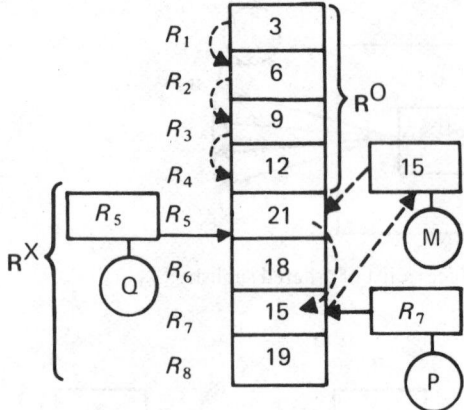

Fig. 8.   Sort by selection and exchange.

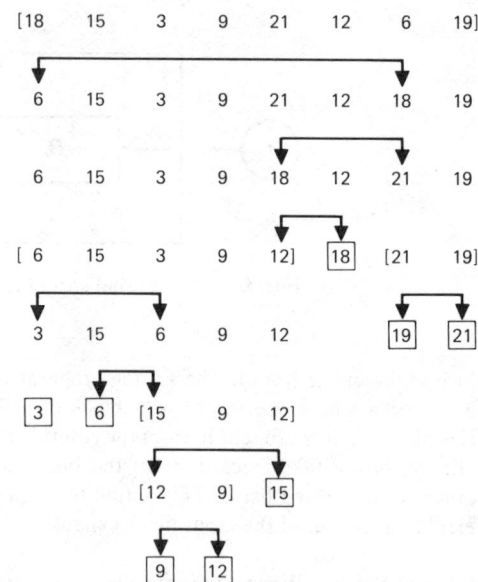

Fig. 9.   Quicksort. (Brackets represent sublists of length greater than 1 which must, therefore, be sorted. Lines with arrows indicate the exchanges made and a number in a square box indicates the final position of the number.)

the unordered sublist at the bottom; and Q is a pointer to the top of $\mathbf{R}^x$.

In the figure, $\mathbf{R}^o$ consists of four records; the arrows from one to the next clearly show that this is an ordered sublist. Q points to R_5, which is the top of $\mathbf{R}^x$. During this part of the sort, the program examines the cells of $\mathbf{R}^x$. The minimum record is kept in M and a pointer to its location is kept in P. The key of the minimum record in $\mathbf{R}^x$ is 15; this record is found at R_7, which is pointed to by P at the end of the search. Thereafter, an exchange must take place between the contents of the cells pointed to by Q and P. The exchange must take place so that neither record is altered. If the entire record is in M, R_5 can go at once to R_7, and M to R_5.

The sort described above is sometimes known as a *bubble sort*. Consider the record with the smallest key to be the lightest. During each phase of the sort, the lightest record bubbles up to the top of the unordered sublist. In actuality, the bubble sort described in the literature is more complicated and less efficient than selection and exchange because the comparisons and transfers are not done in exactly the order described.

Partition Exchange. If the list to be sorted contains *n* items, then the average number of comparisons of one key with another in both of the previous methods can be shown to be proportional to n^2. A better method in which the average number of comparisons is proportional to $n \log n$ is partition exchange sort, more commonly known as *quicksort*. The essential idea behind quicksort is that, since the number of comparisons in sorting increases faster than the length *n* of the list to be sorted, if we could replace the sorting of a list of *n* items by the sorting of two lists of less than *n* items, an efficient procedure might result. The essential idea of quicksort is shown in Fig. 9 using the same eight-item list as in the previous examples. We begin by comparing the first element, 18, with ele-

ments from the right until one *smaller* than 18 is found (6) at which point we exchange 6 and 18. Then we compare 18 with elements from the left (not counting the 6) until a larger one is found and we exchange again. We continue alternatively from the right and left until no more exchanges with 18 are possible. The item 18 is then in its final position and the process is repeated on the two remaining sublists (indicated in Fig. 9 by square brackets). As the figure indicates, this idea is applied recursively to all sublists generated until the list is sorted. (*See also* STRUCTURED PROGRAMMING.)

It can be shown that no sorting method based on comparisons can have an average running time proportional to a quantity less than $n \log n$. Another method which also achieves the $n \log n$ proportionality is *heapsort*, although a discussion of this method is beyond our scope here (see Knuth, 1973).

Merging. In its simplest form, *merging* consists of taking two ordered lists and creating a single ordered list out of them. This can be extended so that the input lists can consist of ordered sublists, as shown in Fig. 10. Lists **A** and **B** each consist of several sublists. The end of one sublist can be distinguished from the beginning of the next because the first cell of the next sublist has arrows that point both forward and backward to preceding and succeeding cells, respectively. Merging then consists of

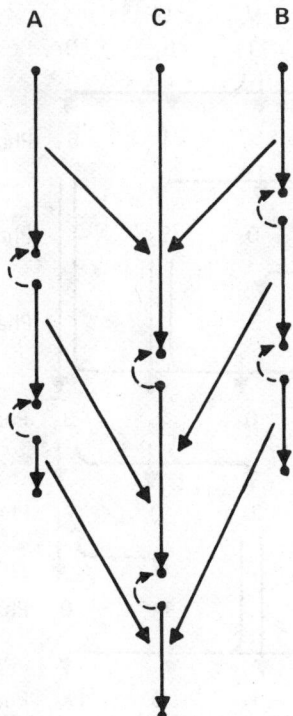

Fig. 10. A merge.

producing a single ordered sublist for corresponding ordered sublists in the two input lists. The action is better seen when numbers are actually used to represent the keys of records in the sublists as they are being merged, as shown by Fig. 11. The algorithm for performing the merge is introduced below and described in detail in Flores (1969).

Sorting by Merging. Merging is conveniently combined with internal sorting for large lists that cannot be stored conveniently in memory. Consider one of the internal sorts that takes records from an input list and creates an ordered sublist of them. The output of repeated internal sorts would be a *single list* of ordered sublists, which would not be suitable for later merging. To produce two lists of ordered sublists, a distribution action is necessary during the internal sort. As ordered sublists are created by the internal sort, they are distributed alternately to two lists on an intermediate medium such as tape or disk. After this *internal phase* of the sort, we have two *volumes* (*q.v.*), each containing a list, on separate devices.

Fig. 12 shows two lists, **L** and **M**, consisting of ordered sublists. These are submitted to the computer, which contains a *merge* program. An ordered sublist is produced from each two ordered sublists, one each from **L** and **M**, which have been merged together. If no further

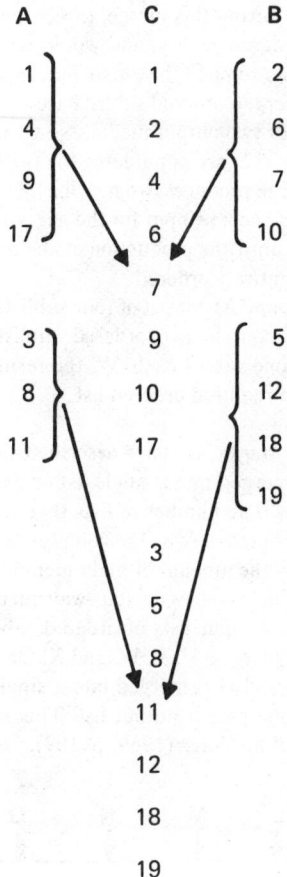

Fig. 11. Merge details.

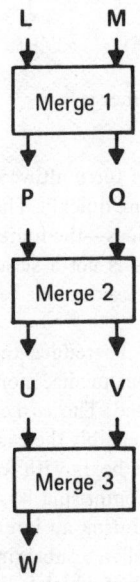

Fig. 12. Sorting by merging ordered sublists.

action is taken during this merge, the output would be a single list of ordered sublists and would be unfit for further merging. To remedy this, *distribution* occurs during each merge: Merged ordered sublists are presented alternately to each of two output media. Now these new lists, **P** and **Q** in Fig. 12, are candidates for further merging. The second merge produces two new lists, **U** and **V**. These new output lists become input for the next merge activity. This continues until the production of the merge is a single list that is entirely ordered.

Suppose **L** and **M** consist of four sublists each; **P** and **Q** would each contain two ordered sublists; **U** and **V** would contain one sublist each. **W**, the result of merging **U** and **V**, is the required ordered list.

Multiway Merge. We have described merging where two lists were merged into a single list or distributed into two output lists. The number of lists that can be merged at one time is limited only by the complexity of the merge program and by the amount of main memory available in the machine. Fig. 13 shows a four-way merge, where **L**, **M**, **N**, and **Q** are input lists of ordered sublists and distribution takes place to **U**, **V**, **W**, and **X**. One sublist each from **L**, **M**, **N**, and **Q** is merged into a single sublist and distributed to the proper output list. This method is described in detail in Flores (1969, p. 109).

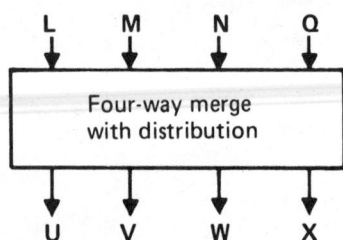

Fig. 13. Multiway merge.

The advantage of the multiway merge is that it gets the job done much more quickly. The disadvantage is that it uses many I/O devices—the four-way merge uses eight devices, although this is not a serious objection if disks rather than tapes are used.

Cascade Merge. To reduce the number of devices holding input or output media, more complicated merge sorts have been devised. The *cascade merge* was one of the first of these and possibly the easiest to explain. In the example of Fig. 14 we begin with four lists labeled **U**, **V**, **W**, and **X**. **U** is a list comprising 14 sublists. Each of these sublists was created during an internal sort. To indicate the length of each sublist, a subscript is used. A unit sublist is one of the length of which is the same as the sublist

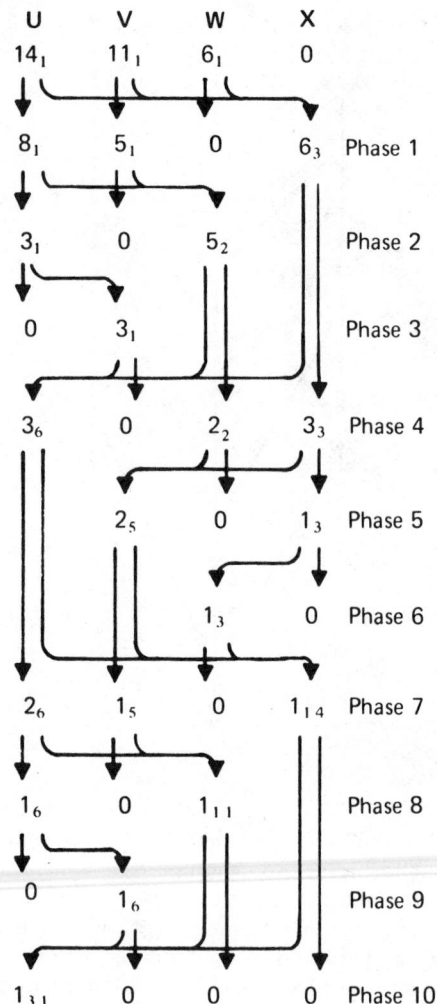

Fig. 14. Cascade merge.

produced during the internal sort. **V** contains 11 such sublists, and **W** contains six. During the first phase, sublists of unit length from each list are merged by a three-way merge producing six sublists, each of which is three units long. These are placed on **X**. During the second phase, a two-way merge produces five sublists, each of length 2 on **W**.

It might seem that we are ready to do another merge. However, this sort was designed for magnetic tape. Although the tapes can be read backward, control becomes more complicated when we try to do a merge reading **U** forward, and **W** and **V** backward. Hence, **U** is copied onto **V** in phase 3. Now it is possible in phase 4 to read **V**, **W**, and **X**, all backward, merging sublists of each into sublists of length 6.

The reader can now follow how the rest of the merge

is done using three- and two-way merges and copies (see Flores, 1969, p. 136).

Polyphase Sort-Merge. The polyphase sort-merge provides a more advanced merge facility. It is used in most manufacturer-supplied tape sorts. It enables the user with N tape units to have $N - 1$ of these in use for merging most of the time. To take advantage of the sort, the tape units should be capable of reading backward and forward, and the program must be able to energize the tape units in different directions during any given phase of the sort.

The polyphase sort requires a distribution procedure that is performed during the internal sort and which is quite uneven; it is based on a complicated algorithm. The origin and principle of the algorithm is explained in Flores (1969, p. 145).

Using the notation we developed for the cascade sort, let us examine Fig. 15, which shows how the polyphase sort works. The sort displayed uses four magnetic tape units. The internal sort has produced 13 sublists of unit length on the left-hand tape unit, 11 of these on the next one, and 7 on the third unit. The fourth unit contains a working tape. Actually, this can be on the input tape unit from which the original tape was removed and a working tape mounted to secure the integrity of the original file during the sort.

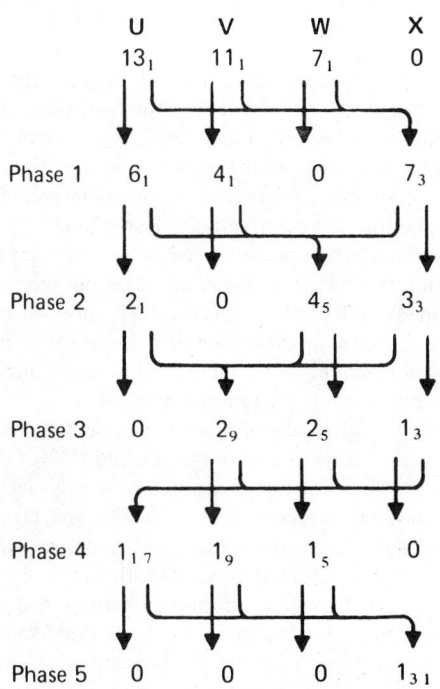

Fig. 15. Polyphase merge.

During the first phase, a three-way merge produces seven sublists, each of unit length three. These go to the fourth tape unit. As the last sublist from the third unit is merged, we find that no more sublists remain on that unit. The program senses this and makes an alteration in the I/O device assignment.

During the second phase, another three-way merge occurs. The output of this merge goes on to the third tape unit. Notice during this merge that the first and second tape units continue to read forward. However, the fourth tape unit had just been written upon; to save rewinding time, it is read backward. This may cause complications as sublist lengths get large. If the allocated buffer in main memory cannot hold the whole sublist, trouble arises, since we cannot merge the end of one sublist with the beginning of another sublist. For this reason, some polyphase sorts are designed so as to rewind the destination unit after it has accepted the proper number of sublists.

At the end of phase 2, the first tape unit has two unit sublists left and is still reading forward; the second tape unit is empty; the third tape unit has just received four sublists of length 5 and is ready to read backward; the fourth tape unit has three sublists of length 3 and continues to be read backward.

From the figure it should be clear how the five phases required for this particular sort are performed. During the distribution phase, the allocation of sublists to each tape unit is very sensitive. An algorithm creates the assignment numbers, which are known as perfect numbers (not to be confused with perfect numbers in mathematics). The perfect numbers corresponding to 31 sublists are 13, 11, and 7 when four tape units are involved.

If we have only 30 sublists, we find that no perfect numbers can be generated. Several alternatives are available. The simplest of these to understand is the creation of a null sublist so that the program thinks there are 31 sublists when there really aren't. This is compensated for by counters in the program. Thus, in Fig. 15, if the first tape unit contains 12- instead of 13-sublists, then during phase 3 there will occur one three-way merge using the first, third, and fourth tape unit. A second three-way merge cannot occur during this phase; instead, a two-way merge occurs, during which the first tape unit is not activated.

Disk and Drum Sorts. Modern disk and drum sorts use an efficient internal sort coupled with a balanced multiway merge. The *balanced merge* uses an equal number of input and output lists. For sorting with magnetic tape units, each list for merging, whether input or output, requires its own device. For the disk or drum we have direct access; this means that it is easy to switch access from one list on a volume to another on the same volume, in contrast to serial access devices such as a tape unit.

The disk or drum sort designer, therefore, does not face any inherent limitation arising from the number of lists to be used. Instead the problem is to use an optimum number of lists and space these lists in an optimum way. The crucial factor in reducing sort time is the number of seeks required by the disk mechanism. Therefore, one tries to optimize the list selection and layout with respect to minimizing the total number and length of seeks involved over the entire sort. A discussion of this topic is found elsewhere but rather little is available in the literature (Flores, 1969, p. 172; Knuth, 1973, p. 361).

REFERENCES

1969. Flores, Ivan. *Computer Sorting.* Englewood Cliffs, NJ: Prentice-Hall. (This book, somewhat complex in presentation and style, is devoted almost entirely to sorting. It provides in-depth explanations of major sorts and covers the wide field fairly completely.)

1971. Lorin, Harold, "A Guided Bibliography to Sorting," *IBM Systems Journal* 10, *No. 3:* 244–254 (Contains an annotated bibliography, but not an exhaustive one.)

1971. Martin, William A. "Sorting," *ACM Computing Surveys* 3, *No. 4:* 147–174. (December). (A briefer source than either Flores or Knuth, but useful for comparison purposes.)

1972. Rivest, Ronald L. and Knuth, Donald E. "Bibliography 26, Computer Sorting," *Computing Reviews* 13, *No. 6:* 283–289 (June). (Fairly complete when published. It also references other bibliographies.)

1973. Knuth, Donald E. "Sorting and Searching," in *The Art of Computer Programming* 3. Reading, MA: Addison-Wesley. (Comparable to Flores in coverage, but rather difficult to assimilate.)

I. FLORES

SORT/MERGE PACKAGES

For articles on related subjects *see* SOFTWARE PACKAGES; SORTING; and UTILITY PROGRAM.

A sort/merge package is a set of programs capable of sorting and merging data files. The package is often a part of the operating system and may be used either externally as a set of independent programs activated by control cards, or internally as a set of subroutines or macros callable from a user program.

Capabilities. Four types of application are possible:

1. *Sort.* A data file is sorted to create a new file, using a sequence of internal sorts and merges.
2. *Merge.* A merge operation is done on a number of presorted files.
3. *Combination sort and merge.* First a data file is sorted and then the output file is merged with other presorted files.
4. *Sequence check.* A special case of a merge application in which only one input file is specified. This checks whether the file is in the proper sequence.

Organization. A typical sort/merge package comprises a monitor and four phases: edit, internal sort, external sort, and final merge phases.

The monitor communicates with the operating system and maintains the interphase communication between the various phases. At the start of the run, the monitor transfers control to the edit phase. When the edit phase completes its functions, the monitor in turn calls other phases according to the particular application.

The edit phase reads the parameters supplied by the user, checks them, issues appropriate error messages if necessary, determines (from the parameters) information relevant to the particular application, and stores it in tables common to all other phases.

The internal sort phase reads data records into main storage and sorts them into ordered strings (sometimes called *runs, sequences,* or *sections*). These are written in turn on intermediate storage devices and are merged later. For efficiency, most internal sort phases use either *quicksort* or one of its modifications.

The external sort phase merges the strings previously produced by the internal sort phase. It performs a number of passes, each of which increases the average length of a string and reduces the number of strings, and it continues up to the point where the final merge phase can combine the strings into a single file in one pass. If the initital number of strings is small enough, the external sort phase may be bypassed by the monitor and control can be transferred directly to the final merge phase.

The final merge phase is used as the last merge pass of the run. It produces a single, sorted output file according to mode and blocking specifications supplied by the user. For a merge application, this phase is called by the monitor immediately after the edit phase (i.e., the internal and external sort phase are bypassed).

Today, almost every operating system includes a sort/merge package. Those of the IBM 360/370, OS and DOS, and the CDC Cyber series, are widely used and similar in many respects. Both offer disk and tape variants and permit the user to add modification routines at some points in the sorting process. Both use the replacement-selection technique for internal sorting, and either the balanced, the polyphase, or the oscillating techniques for external sorting. They are good examples of efficient, general programs which are useful in many applications and yet are used mainly by experienced programmers because of the many details involved in using them. Manufacturers' manuals for these three packages give more extensive details. For additional information, consult:

1. IBM System/360 VS Sort/Merge Form GC33-4043.
2. IBM System/360 DOS, Tape and Disk Sort/Merge, Form GC28-6676.
3. CDC Cybernet Services: Sort/Merge 4, Ref. Manual, Pub. 84000015B.

D. SALOMON

SOURCE PROGRAM

For articles on related subjects *see* COMPILER; OBJECT PROGRAM; and PROCEDURE-ORIENTED LANGUAGES.

A *source program* is a computer program written in a language one or more steps removed from the *machine language* of a given computer. Machine language consists of the very explicit set of instructions and operation codes capable of direct execution by the hardware of the computer. It is, however, extremely tedious and error prone, for it requires that instructions be spelled out in almost microscopic detail, specifying all data and program references in terms of actual addresses within the computer memory. Accordingly, other languages have been developed to make it easier for programmers' desires to be expressed. A program written in such a language is called a *source program,* and must be translated by one means or another into the language of the machine before it can be executed. Fortunately, other programs can carry out this translation on the computer itself.

If the source program is in assembly (i.e., symbolic) language, the process of translating it is called *assembling,* and the result is an *object program* in machine language, ready to be executed. If the source program is in a high-level language like Fortran or Cobol, the translating process is called *compiling,* and may involve one or more stages (e.g., a Fortran program may be first compiled into assembly language, and then that program assembled into machine language).

Source programs in high-level languages have great advantages in portability, for with only minor changes they can often be compiled to run on various machines.

C. H. DAVIDSON

SPECIAL-PURPOSE COMPUTERS

For articles on related subjects *see* ANALOG COMPUTERS; COMPUTER SYSTEMS; CONTROL APPLICATIONS; DATA ACQUISITION COMPUTER; DIFFERENTIAL ANALYZER; DIGITAL COMPUTERS; HYBRID COMPUTERS; MICROPROCESSORS AND MICROCOMPUTERS and REDUNDANCY, HARDWARE.

Since essentially all stored-program digital computers can be programmed to solve any information processing problem, there are, in a sense, no truly special-purpose computers. However, due to internal architecture or total system configuration, some systems are better adapted to a given application or function than others. In this article, *special-purpose computers* are defined to be those stored-program digital computers whose implementation architecture or system configuration is oriented toward one or more specific end-user applications.

By this definition, and for the purposes of this article, we exclude analog computers, mechanical and electromechanical computers, and devices which do not normally operate using an internally stored program, such as calculating machines. Although bordering on the functions and characteristics of a stored program computer, also excluded are specialized integrated circuits, often called controllers, used to control specific I/O equipment or other devices, even though they may depend on a program stored in a read-only memory (ROM). An example of such a device is a keyboard/CRT controller, which includes key decoders, character generators, and the like.

Configuration Special-Purpose Computers. Configuration special-purpose machines are tailored to particular applications by unique interconnections of processors and peripherals which, in general, have architectures that are identical to those of general-purpose machines. In addition, however, such configurations may include peripheral equipment with unique capabilities, such as the ability to measure voltages or to control switches external to the machine. As a consequence, the resulting computer is better-suited to some particular applications than to others. Similarly, the software system typically is designed to further enhance the characteristics necessary in the specific application. Thus, for example, the fundamental objectives of an operating system intended for use in real-time applications are quite different from those designed for a commercial application.

INDUSTRIAL CONTROL COMPUTERS. Since the early 1960s, computers have been used extensively to gather data from, and to control, industrial processes ranging from continuous processes, such as those found in the petrochemical industry, and batch (recipe) processes, such as those used in pharmaceutical and food processing, to discrete processes such as assembly and testing operations in automotive and computer manufacturing (Harrison, 1972). These applications are characterized by requiring a direct connection between the computer system and the physical process in order to collect data on the process state and effect control of the process. In addition, there are real-time demands such that the computer must complete its programmed function in a time period dictated by the process requirements. This differs from many data processing applications in which a processing delay may cause inconvenience for the user but generally does not have a dramatic effect on the application. An example of a required real-time response is an automated conveyor system used for sorting packages in a distribution center. Here the computer must detect the presence of an object on the conveyor; sense and read coded information indicating the final destination (e.g., a zip code or Universal Product Code (UPC—*q.v.*) label); calculate a routing; and actuate a sorting gate in less time than it takes the package to move from the sensing point to the first sorting gate.

In order to provide for the direct connection to a physical process and to assist in satisfying real-time requirements, industrial control computer configurations include specialized subsystems. As shown in Fig. 1, these typically include *analog input, analog output, digital input* (including external *priority interrupt*), and *digital output.*

Analog Input. The analog input subsystem provides the capability of converting the value of analog voltage or current signals into their equivalent digital representation. The output of many sensors (e.g., thermocouples, strain gauges) and instrumentation (e.g., chromatographs, defractometers) is an analog voltage or current signal whose magnitude is related linearly or nonlinearly to the quantity measured (e.g., temperature, displacement, composition). For use in a digital computer, it is necessary to convert the analog magnitude value into a digital quantity, in much the same way that a human converts temperature into a numeric quantity by comparing the displacement of a column of mercury to a linear scale on a thermometer.

The actual conversion function is provided by an *analog-to-digital converter* (*ADC*— *q.v.*). In addition to the ADC and its controls, the analog input subsystem usually includes a multiplexer and an amplifier. The multiplexer is a set of parallel switches used to connect one of many signal inputs to the amplifier and ADC for conversion. Configurations may provide for as many as several thousand inputs through a single multiplexer. The multiplexer uses field-effect-transistor (FET) or electromechanical switches, depending on switching speed and common-mode voltage requirements. Relay multiplexers generally

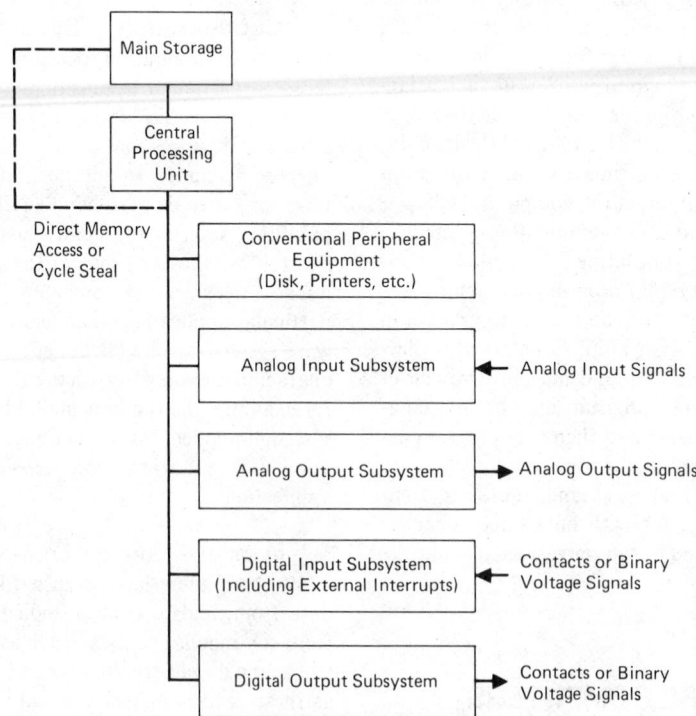

Fig. 1. Typical industrial process control computer configuration.

are limited to sampling and conversion rates of less than 200 samples-per-second (SPS). With FET switches, sampling rates in excess of 250,000 SPS are possible.

Since the output of many sensors is a low-level voltage (less than 0.5 V and, in some cases, less than 10 mV), an amplifier may be provided to increase the signal magnitude to better match the usual 5-V full-scale range of the ADC. Many subsystems provide for the automatic selection of the amplifier gain or for its programmed control by the computer to accommodate signals having a wide dynamic range without sacrificing measurement resolution.

Analog Output. In controlling an industrial process and some industrial instrumentation, such as strip chart recorders, a computer-controlled analog signal is required. The analog output subsystem converts the digital representation provided by the computer into an equivalent magnitude analog output signal. The analog output signal is typically in the range of -5 to $+5$ V and is provided by a *digital-to-analog converter* (DAC—*see* ANALOG-TO-DIGITAL AND DIGITAL-TO-ANALOG CONVERTERS). (Schmid, 1970; Harrison, 1978.)

Digital Input. In addition to analog signals in the process, there usually are binary (on/off) signals that must be monitored by the computer system. For example, it may be necessary to determine if a pump is *on* or *off* or if a solenoid valve is energized or not. The ability to sense contact closures or the presence of a voltage which exceeds a predefined threshold is provided by the digital input (DI) subsystem. Each input is connected to a single-bit position in its associated input word or byte so that information can be handled using the normal byte- and word-oriented instructions of the computer. However, digital input data is often bit-significant; that is, each bit may convey information independent of the value of the other bits in the word or byte. As a result, real-time computer systems often provide special instructions or software subroutines to extract one or more bits from the word or byte.

External Interrupts. Closely associated with the digital input subsystem is the external interrupt subsystem. Electrically, this subsystem often is identical to digital input, providing both contact sense and voltage sense. The difference is that, whenever the state of an input changes, the interrupt subsystem sends a signal to the control portion of the processor. In the simplest systems, this signal always causes an interruption of the currently executing program. When interrupted, the processor completes execution of the current instruction; branches to a software routine that saves the state of the processor by storing all relevant internal data; locates the exact source of the interrupt by determining which input bit changed state; and determines if immediate action should be taken or if the response to the interrupt can be delayed

until completion of the current task. If the response can be delayed, the program posts the necessary information concerning the interrupt, restores the saved state of the processor, and resumes processing the interrupted task. If an immediate response is necessary, however, the routine branches to the applicable response subroutine. After execution, the saved state of the processor is restored and execution of the interrupted task is resumed.

In more sophisticated systems, hardware is provided to assist in handling interrupts. Typically, a priority parameter is assigned to every input device and to every software task. If the interrupting device has lower priority than the currently executing task, the interrupt signal is not passed to the processor until all pending higher-priority tasks have been executed. On the other hand, if the interrupting device is of higher priority, the processor is interrupted and the interrupt serviced. The hardware often automatically stores the state of the processor when the interrupt is accepted, either in storage or in special registers. The hardware-assisted priority interrupt system significantly reduces the overhead associated with processing interrupts.

Digital Output. Many control actions are binary, such as turning an indicator light *on* or *off* or actuating a solenoid valve. The ability to control binary devices is provided by the digital output (DO) subsystem. In essence, it provides a set of computer-controlled switches that can be attached to external devices. These switches may be low-power digital logic gates, medium-power semiconductor switches, or high-power electromechanical relays. A switch is activated by setting a bit in the associated output word or byte. As with DI, the output data may be bit-significant. Instructions or software to manipulate single or multiple bits in a word or byte often are provided to facilitate the use of the digital output subsystem.

An Industrial Control Example. Fig. 2 shows a single-process flow loop, an operator panel, and an alarm panel. A real process might have hundreds of such loops, each serviced on a round-robin or interrupt-driven basis by a single computer. In this example, assume that the operator wishes to change the flow (F). The desired value (the new setpoint) is entered into switches at the operator console. This generates an interrupt, which, when serviced by the processor, reads the console switches through digital input and actuates a console display through digital output for operator verification of the new setpoint.

If satisfactory, the operator pushes an *enter* button to initiate the change. The processor, reacting to the console interrupt, verifies that the change is in accordance with operating rules (e.g., does not exceed the maximum allowable change) and then updates the setpoint tables. Rather than make the change as a single step function, the program might calculate a change profile that grad-

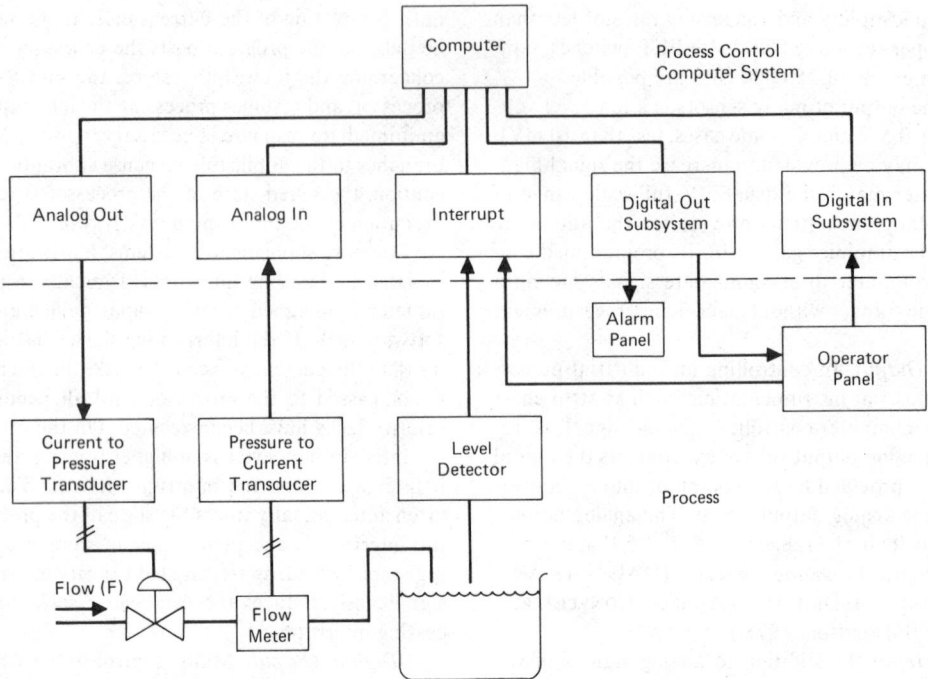

Fig. 2.　Industrial process control example.

ually changes the flow loop setpoint as a function of time so as not to cause a process upset.

Each loop in the process is sampled and changes are made on a predetermined time basis, such as every ten seconds. When the loop represented in Fig. 2 is due to be sampled, the processor reads the output of the flowmeter using the analog input subsystem and calculates the change needed to set the flow to the new desired value. The new output value is fed to the analog output subsystem, which generates an equivalent analog signal. This signal is converted to a pneumatic signal by the current-to-pressure transducer to operate the valve actuator. Since the speed of the valve is slow as compared to electronic speeds, the control program may establish a delay time of several seconds, after which it tests to make sure that the flow has changed as desired.

Fig. 2 also illustrates a common monitoring function that is often accomplished with the computer. The computer calculates the flows into and out of the vat to ensure that the vat will not overflow. However, a malfunctioning valve controlling flow out of the vat could cause an overflow, so a level detector is installed in the vat. If the level detector is actuated, an interrupt signal is generated that causes the computer to light an indicator and actuate an alarm horn to alert the operator to a problem. The computer might also be programmed to take corrective action, such as closing the input valve.

ULTRA-HIGH AVAILABILITY SYSTEMS. The Enterprise, NASA's Space Shuttle Approach and Landing Test vehicle, furnishes an example of a special-purpose system configuration designed to provide extreme availability (Sheridan, 1978). The need for availability will be appreciated when it is understood that the control surfaces are monitored and positioned by sensors and actuators under computer control and crew commands are effected only through the computer. The general requirement for all Shuttle subsystems is that they must remain fully operational after a failure in any single subsystem *(fail operational)*, and remain safe even after two failures in the same subsystem *(fail-safe)*.

Most vehicle subsystems employ at least triple redundancy to provide this type of availability. The computer configuration employs four interconnected general-purpose computers, with a fifth computer provided as backup. After a single failure, the redundant set of four is reduced to three. A second failure is detected by using two-out-of-three voting techniques to identify the failing computer.

The computer interconnection for the Shuttle is shown in Fig. 3. By using common buses, input data is available to each computer and each computer can be connected to any control output.

During critical phases of the mission, the four redundant computers are loaded with identical programs

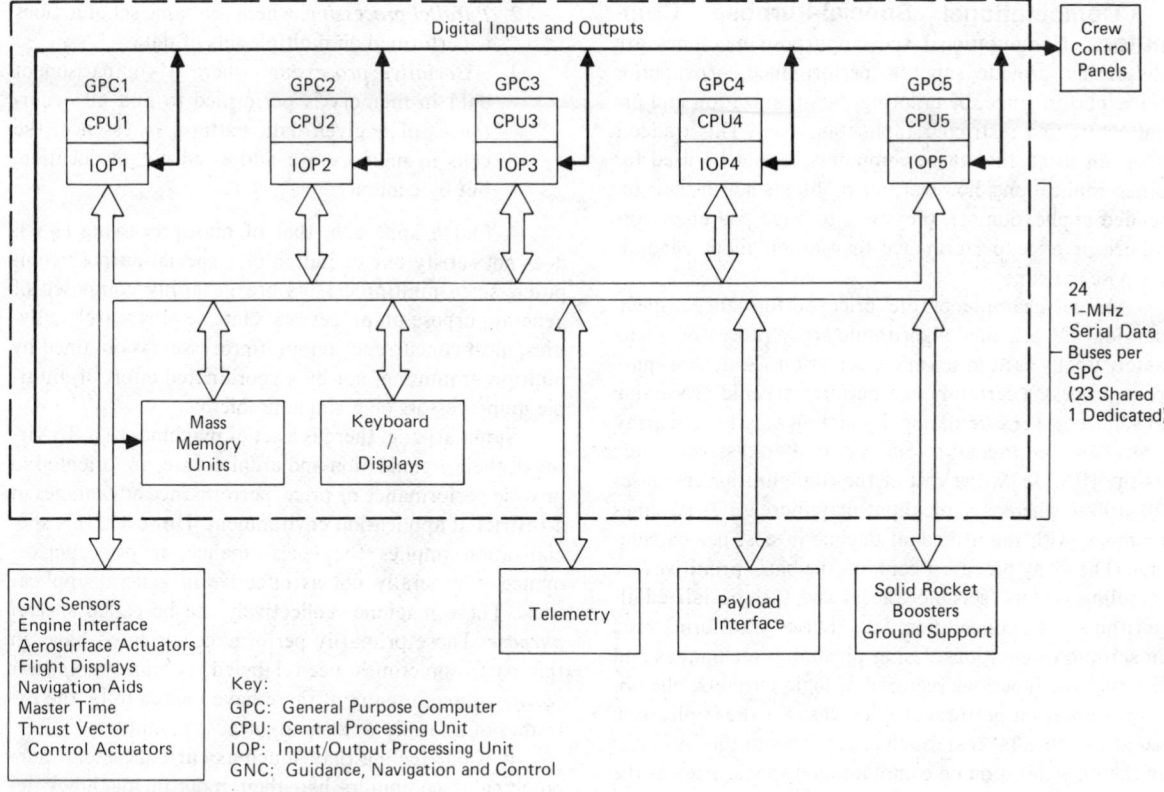

Fig. 3. Space shuttle avionics system block diagram.

and are operated so as to guarantee identical outputs when there is no malfunction. Any difference in output results in notification of the crew, which takes corrective action as prescribed by mission rules. In the unlikely event of a two-against-two conflict or the simultaneous failure of all four computers, the fifth computer can be activated to control the vehicle. To minimize the chance that the failure was caused by programming that would, therefore, also affect the fifth computer, the program for this computer was developed independently to provide the necessary, but reduced, control functions for safe reentry.

Merely providing redundant hardware does not guarantee availability. Special programming and synchronization techniques are also needed. For example, care must be taken to ensure that the data received by all redundant computers is identical. One technique employed in the Shuttle is for the four CPUs to exchange status data to ensure that all processors completed an input operation without error. If any error occurs, the data is not used for subsequent calculation.

Synchronization is a particularly difficult problem in an event-driven environment such as this. Suppose, for example, that four processors are executing the same pro-gram but that one processor is operating slightly faster due to a slight difference in clock frequency. Further suppose that an interrupt occurs at the instant the fast processor completes a particular instruction, causing it to mask further interrupts and branch to a servicing routine. The other processors will not yet have seen the interrupt. A subsequent interrupt, occurring just as the slower processors complete execution of their current instruction, could cause them to branch to a service routine for this different interrupt. Thus, the four processors no longer would be executing the same instruction sequence. Situations like this must be foreseen and techniques to force synchronization must be established to maintain the integrity of the redundant configuration.

Although this example is extreme in its concern for availability, redundant systems also are used in commercial and industrial applications. In most cases, only two computers are involved and comparison of computed results may or may not be utilized as an indication of malfunction. As an alternative, various programmed checks may be utilized and, if an error is suspected, control is transferred to the backup computer, which has been periodically updated with the process status.

Computational Special-Purpose Computers. Computational special-purpose machines are those that provide superior performance, or superior price/performance, by tailoring the organization and architecture to a restricted application class. This tradeoff does not mean that these computers cannot be used for other applications; however, for problems not in their intended application set, they tend to have poorer performance or price/performance than other, more general-purpose machines.

As an example of the price/performance aspect, consider the attached algorithmic array processors characteristically used in seismic calculations. A general-purpose processor certainly can perform seismic processing at some cost per calculation. By adding an attached array processor (*see* PIPELINE AND ARRAY PROCESSORS), such as the IBM 3838, the cost of the configuration increases 20–100%, whereas throughput may increase 2–10 times or more, with the attendant decline in cost per calculation. The array processor contains the basic primitives for handling vectors (seismic traces) and the specialized algorithms (e.g., convolution, fast Fourier transform) used in seismic calculations. Using pipelining techniques and limiting the functions required of logic curcuits, one obtains significant performance increase for the application set at incremental cost. Such processors put the emphasis in their organization on computational speed, often at the expense of I/O control facilities usually associated with general-purpose operating system structures and generic applications.

The other principal motivation for computational special-purpose computer is performance. The objective is either to complete a computation within given time constraints, or, within a fixed time period, to perform the largest amount of computation possible. The time period constraint is derived from the real-time nature of a problem (e.g., weather forecasting, radar tracking, or reactor control), or the realities of hardware/software failures; a six-hour computation may be reasonable, whereas a six-day computation may not be. Regardless of the precise reason, raw computational power is required to solve the problem, and the price of computation is of lesser importance.

This level of performance is usually obtained by doing multiple things concurrently and leads to three distinct mechanisms, each with its own architecture and organization implications for performance-oriented computing. These approaches to concurrency can be described as follows.

1. *Vector processing,* where a desired action is performed on a large set of data, such as in computing the element-by-element sum of two large vectors.

2. *Parallel processing,* where the same set of actions is performed on multiple sets of data.

3. *Associative processing,* where a comparison of data in memory is performed to find all occurrences of a given data pattern; in essence, the cells in memory are addressed not by location, but by content.

A fourth approach, that of multiprocessing (*q.v.*), does not satisfy our definition of a special-purpose computer, since multiprocessors are generally composed of general-purpose uniprocessors. Outside of research activities, most concurrency on multiprocessors is obtained by multiprogramming, not by a coordinated effort of multiple uniprocessors on a single problem.

Summarizing, there is a set of machines that, by virtue of their organization and architecture, are oriented to provide performance or price/performance advantages in a restricted application environment. However, this specialization implies that performance or price/performance is generally not as effective in general applications. These machines collectively can be called *special purpose*. Those primarily performance-oriented have, in the past, sometimes been labeled as *supercomputers* (*q.v.*), although many of these have tended to be the extremes of a family of general-purpose computers.

It is our feeling that, much as current general-purpose scalar computers had their roots in machines designed to solve specific classes of problems, the vector processor (particularly the large-scale vector processor, such as the Cray-1 and Cyber 200) is evolving into a general-purpose computing vehicle. The extensions of vector-oriented algorithms to typical commercial applications, such as sorting and database management, clearly indicate that the "special-purpose" tag will shortly no longer apply. Of note is that new algorithms have made such architectures useful for increasingly wider application sets.

VECTOR PROCESSORS. The key difference between scalar and vector computers is that the scalar computer allows only scalar operands, whereas a vector processor additionally admits vector operands. From this perspective, vector processors are simply an evolutionary step beyond scalar processors. Once vector operands are provided, it is natural to define new functions in addition to the simple distribution of scalar operations, element-by-element, over vector operands. An instruction stream on such a processor has intermixed scalar and vector instructions. The system has a full complement of I/O functions, although often oriented toward high-performance data transfer.

In terms of application, any large-scale computation expressible through the mathematical concepts of vectors, matrices, or tensors, including sparse matrix/vector computations, are realistic candidates. There has been significant development of algorithms (in contrast to applications) and their codes on vector processors.

The machine concepts of vector processing are modeled on the mathematical abstraction of vectors, but are not identical. Specifically, it is possible that the computational result obtained by a vector processor will be dependent on the order in which operands are executed, particularly if the resultant vector shares storage locations with the operand vectors. This notion, "vector hazard," is masked from the end user or programmer in modern systems by competent software that insures the integrity of the data. Consequently, the expected mathematical result is obtained for the user.

The simplest vector instructions are *elemental* vector functions that specify a scalar operation to be performed on the respective ordered (scalar) elements of two vector operands, with each pair resulting in a scalar result, and the aggregate of scalar results constituting the vector result. *Transformational* instructions also use vector operands. Examples of these instructions are the vector-inner-product and sum-reduction instructions that yield scalar resultants.

In order to provide a distinction between vector processors and algorithmic processors (discussed below), instructions implied by a specific algorithm in the solution of a problem are excluded in our definition. Thus, processors that include operations such as the fast Fourier transform, convolution, and matrix multiply are considered to be algorithmic processors.

A vector processor must also be able to address easily the aggregate, not just the individual elements. For vector-register machines, such as the Cray-1, where one explicitly loads vectors from storage to specific registers and subsequently uses register addresses to designate the loaded vectors, or for storage-to-storage architectures, such as the Cyber 200, it is sufficient to consider addressability of vectors in central storage. There are three primary types of addressing—direct, indirect (dynamic or static), and sparse. In each case, the basic regularity required for effective address computation must be explicity or implicitly defined in the hardware architecture.

Direct addressing defines a vector based on an initial memory address, an element count, and an index or *stride;* the latter indicates the address displacement between successive elements in the stored vector. Indirect addressing allows for the aggregation (or dispersal) of arbitrarily placed elements in central storage into (from) a vector. The exact mapping function is determined statically by use of a directly-addressed vector of addresses or displacements. Dynamically, a directly-addressed bit vector, and a directly-addressed address vector, whose elements are selected by the corresponding values of the bit vector, is used.

Potentially the most important in many applications, yet difficult to describe and implement, is sparse-vector addressing. The basic information is a directly addressed vector consisting of the non-zero data elements of the sparse vector, and either a bit vector whose non-zero (binary 1) elements indicate where the consecutive non-zero data elements would be located in the expanded sparse vector, or a directly addressed vector of indices designating the element positions of the data elements. The regularity in this mode of addressing lies in the regularity of the constituent data, as well as the conceptual regularity of the vector realized during the execution of a vector operation on sparse vectors.

ALGORITHMIC PROCESSORS. Algorithmic processors originated in the 1960s as price/performance enhancements to general-purpose systems. Early models were directed toward seismic calculations or other specialized signal processing applications. They began as convolution and fast Fourier transform (*q.v.*) processors, and were attached as auxiliary processors, either on storage buses or on channels and data ports of general-purpose processors. The IBM 2938 array processor, announced in 1966, was the first to feature multiple algorithms, including vector operations and floating-point arithmetic. Today, there are many such processors available for large mainframes (*q.v.*) and small processors, as well. Examples are the Datawest 400 for Univac mainframes, and the Floating Point Systems (FPS) Model AP120B, for several small and intermediate mainframes.

Algorithmic processors are functional supersets of vector processors. In addition to vector primitives, algorithmic processors additionally feature algorithmic instructions such as convolution, FFT, matrix multiply, and elementary mathematical functions. They also may accept as operands such data structures as matrices, in addition to scalars and vectors.

Part of the rationale for such algorithms lies in the attachment strategy. As an auxiliary programmable processor attached to a host, their programs are created in the host, and then both program and data are transmitted to the attached processor. Newer models contain significant amounts of internal storage, and often contain a fairly sophisticated multiprogramming control program.

In order to utilize effectively an attached processor, it is necessary, or at least desirable, to be able to specify a large quantity of data with a small description (e.g., a vector of N elements starts at location X and has a stride of Y), and to specify a fairly complicated and considerable amount of computation with a small program (e.g., convolve vector A with B, put result in C).

In the past few years, the intended application of attached algorithmic processors has moved beyond signal and seismic processing. Pioneered by FPS processors, the application set has expanded to include computations of a more general scientific nature that can be expressed naturally in the vector or matrix notation of mathematics.

PARALLEL PROCESSORS. Parallel processors (*q.v.*) obtain concurrency in one of two fashions; they perform identical operations in lock step on different portions of the data, known as SIMD (single-instruction multiple data streams), as defined by Flynn in 1966, or execute asynchronously with different processes utilizing the problem data simultaneously, known as MIMD (multiple-instruction multiple data stream) organizations.

Consider adding two matrices together to produce a third. If there were a processor for each matrix element position, the program would reduce to a simple sum of two scalars in each processor and placing the result back in storage. This is the concept behind SIMD machines in which there is an array of identical processing elements, each capable of performing arithmetic and addressing storage (usually its own private storage) for fetching operands. The program itself is executed by a controller that does the instruction fetch, decode, and branching and broadcasts *functional instructions* or opcodes to the array of elements that perform the computation in lock step. Additionally, there are connection patterns between the processing elements for passing data to selected subsets of the elements. For example, ILLIAC IV has an 8 x 8 array of elements capable of doing arithmetic on 64-bit operands, and each can receive data from its four nearest neighbors. For proposed/prototyped SIMD machines, the principal variations are the number of processing elements and their array structure, the mechanics of their interconnection networks, the widths of their data flows, and the mechanisms for private and shared memory.

Such structures are potent computing systems, but they must be connected/controlled by a common general-purpose *host* processor. The host provides the mechanisms for communications and control between the array and the outside world, as well as performing tasks of data management, compilation, and the resource allocation/control functions commonly associated with a general-purpose operating system.

There is an interesting comparison between these SIMD arrays and the algorithmic array processors mentioned earlier in their relationship to the host processor. The latter are usually price/performance enchancements to the host, whereas the former are performance machines that incorporate a subservient host. As another contrast, there have never been more than a few of any particular SIMD parallel processors manufactured, although several different kinds have been manufactured. Replication of various algorithmic array processors, however, is measured in tens and hundreds.

Because of their relatively rigid structure and mode of operation, problems suitable for solution on SIMD parallel processors are characterized by:

1. A large amount of identical computation that can be performed simultaneously on independent data.
2. Regular data transfer patterns that match the connection network of the individual processors.
3. Data structures that can be distributed across the address spaces of the processing elements to permit simultaneous fetching of data.

These characteristics imply severe restrictions on the application set for which such computers are well suited. Said in another way, it is relatively difficult to program these machines efficiently for many large conventional applications, thus demonstrating that their organization is tailored to a particular application set.

The MIMD parallel processors are an even more exclusive set in terms of commercial availability. There have been many good experimental machines built, the classical example being C.mmp of Carnegie-Mellon University. This is a collection of processors connected via a network to a collection of memory modules, with each processor capable of executing its own instruction stream. What makes such a system an MIMD parallel processor, instead of simply a multiprocessor, is the ability, easily and effectively, to provide coordination among the processors, so that several, or many, processors can be brought to bear on a single computational task. The biggest need is for effective synchronization mechanisms between asynchronously operating processors.

Although commercial multiprocessors can be described by the term MIMD from a systems perspective, they are excluded here since they achieve concurrency by multiprogramming or multitasking. For MIMD parallel processing, the added ability to partition a single task or application into processes that can be executed simultaneously on multiple cooperative processors is required.

Although inherently more flexible, there is yet no commercial MIMD product available, nor is there a strong theory of application decomposition that would allow for more than a few processors. As of late 1980, one announced machine falls into this classification, the Denelcor HEP (heterogeneous element processor). The first machine had not then been delivered to its customer (the U.S. Army Ballistic Research Laboratory) and commercial viability cannot be assessed. The processor (of which there can be 16) allows for the "simultaneous" execution of 16 processes (eight user, eight system) by a round-robbin selection of an instruction from each process for entry into pipelined execution elements. Concurrency is synchronized by state flags on each register and each data word in memory, so that all eight user processes can effectively cooperate on the same application. Although each process has its own register set allocated to it, sharing of registers across processes is also facilitated by the addressing structures. The number of available registers totals in the thousands.

Associative Processors. Associative processors are a rather unique type of parallel processor, traditionally composed of an SIMD-type array of processing elements, and an associative memory (*q.v.*). The most notable commercial product in this category, STARAN, produced by Goodyear Aerospace, has been produced in several models. A small number are in use, mostly in radar or image processing applications of the U.S. government.

The principal differentiation between SIMD parallel processors and associative processors is the use of associative or *content addressable* storage, a notion existing since the mid-1950s (Yau and Fung, 1977). The storage arrays, for example, can be interrogated to identify all "words" of the array that have a specified pattern in the same *n* bit field of each word, typically by a single instruction. The selected words can then be processed by the array making up the SIMD parallel processor portion. Clearly, applications must satisfy the same set of restrictions typical for SIMD processors. Such processors may, given adequate algorithm development and commercial impetus, be useful in applications such as databases, compilation, and information retrieval. To date, however, little success has been achieved in this area, although the potential, considered to be viable "soon" for the last ten years, may be realized as we truly enter a VLSI age.

Trends. Two things have consistently permeated the foregoing: First, a processor is said to be "special-purpose" if its architecture and organization is such that it performs "well" on a restricted class of applications, and not so well compared to "conventional" processors on the full domain of applications; and second, there is an evolution that moves "special-purpose" features slowly into the design of general-purpose processors, dependent primarily on the development of algorithms that expand the application domain of these processors.

Although this discussion has focused principally on computer-intensive or real-time applications, the notion of "special-purpose" applies to commercial environments as well. Tandem, Inc., for example, produces a product, the Tandem-16, in an up to 16-way multiprocessor configuration. It provides coherent hardware and software redundancy (fail-soft) characteristics which make it quite suitable for transaction processing applications (Thurber and Wald, 1975). Although it indeed can perform batch application processing, the implementation and speed characteristics are not that amenable to such processing. However, a ten-fold increase in basic process-

ing power of the individual processors, coupled with modification of other performance characteristics, might very well change that perspective.

It also should be pointed out that the notion of *dataflow* (*q.v.*) architectures and processors glimmers on the horizon. Many believe such processors to be the ultimate in parallel processing. Sometime in the next decade or two, commercial realization as a "special-purpose" processor will occur. If successful, even marginally, then subsequent realizations of the concepts, as manufacturers learn and as algorithms develop, will evolve into a general-purpose product.

REFERENCES

1970. Schmid, H. *Electronic Analog/Digital Conversions.* New York: Van Nostrand Reinhold.
1972. Harrison, T. J. *Handbook of Industrial Control Computers.* New York: Wiley.
1972. Flynn, M. J. "Some Computer Organizations and Their Effectiveness," *IEEE Trans.* **C-21**: 948–960.
1975. Thurber, K. J. and Wald, L. D. "Associative and Parallel Processors," *Computing Surveys* **17**, *No. 4.*
1977. Yau, S. S. and Fung, H. S. "Associative Processor Architecture—A Survey," *Computing Surveys* **9**, *No. 1:* (March).
1978. Harrison, T. J. *Minicomputers in Industrial Control.* Research Triangle Park, NC: Instrument Society of America.
1978. Sheridan, C. T. "Space Shuttle Software," *Datamation* (July).

T. J. HARRISON AND M. WAYNE WILSON

SPECIFICATION, PROGRAM. *See* PROGRAM SPECIFICATION.

SPEECH RECOGNITION

For articles on related subjects *see* ARTIFICIAL INTELLIGENCE; IMAGE PROCESSING; and PATTERN RECOGNITION.

The use of computers could be greatly expanded if human speech could be reliably utilized as an input/output (I/O) medium. Such a capability would allow humans to listen to synthetic speech output from a computer rather than read a display. Indeed, commercially acceptable synthetic speech can now be produced as output from a computer, even for unrestricted vocabulary and syntax. The ability of computers to recognize human speech would permit input to the computer without the use of a keyboard, but speech recognition is in its infancy, although commercial units of very limited capability are available.

In order to understand the process of speech recognition, it is useful to start by assuming that all of the necessary information for recognizing the spoken words is available in the speech signal. Indeed, much research and implementation is based on this assumption. The first task in recognition is thus to represent the speech signal in a form that contains fewer bits of information, but retains those facets that are thought to be useful for recognition. Most systems base this representation on derived attributes of a model for speech production called the *source filter* model. The human vocal apparatus is modeled as one or two sources exciting a set of coupled resonators that intensify the sound in the neighborhood of the resonant frequencies. One source is the sequence of puffs of air that can be produced by the vibrating vocal cords, as in "voiced" sounds such as the three (fricative "z," vowel "e," nasal "n") in the word "zen." In addition, the vocal tract can produce turbulent airflow at any of a large number of constrictions, leading to noise-like sounds, such as "s" in "sun." Both forms of excitation can be combined, as in "z." Whatever the form of excitation, it can be considered to excite a set of resonances (called *formants*) that vary with the shape of the vocal tract. The resulting speech spectrum is thus the result of multiplying the source spectrum by the vocal tract filter spectrum. (An example is shown in Fig. 1.) Most speech recognition systems utilize some form of spectral representation as input to pattern classification algorithms, since the relatively slow motion of the articulators is displayed in the formant trajectories, and this allows for an insightful reduction of the input information rate. Precisely what frequency-time-amplitude features are computed is an important attribute of any speech recognition system.

Following parametric (usually spectral) representation of the speech, end points of the utterance are found, and normalization may be performed to compensate for spectral warping due to variation in vocal tract length. Matching against stored templates is then performed, often utilizing a procedure called dynamic programming to warp optimally the time dimension of the input to secure the best match, as computed by a variety of scoring methods. Many investigators feel that the use of time warping is more important than the choices of spectral representation. Fig. 2 shows how these techniques are combined to perform the speech recognition task.

For tasks involving a single cooperative speaker, a few hundred words, and artificial syntax (or none), commercial systems can achieve recognition rates well above 95%, and have been used in many applications, including package sorting and instrument control. Companies producing such systems include Centigram Corp.; Verbex, Inc.; Heuristics, Inc.; Interstate Electronics; Logicon, Inc.; Nippon Electric Co.; and Threshold Technology, Inc. These units vary greatly in cost, performance accuracy, speed, ability to recognize continuous speech, training procedures, and capability to recognize multiple

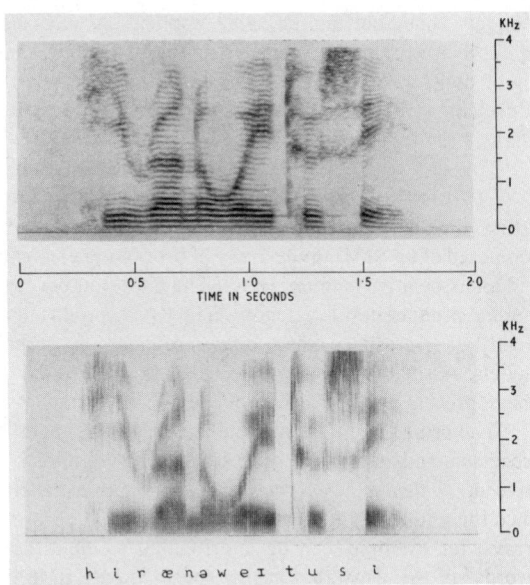

Fig. 1. Spectrogram of the sentence "He ran away to sea." The upper record is a narrow-band analysis made with a 30-Hz bandwidth filter. The fine horizontal lines are due to individual harmonics in the buzzing sound produced at the larynx. The lower record is a wide-band analysis made with a 240-Hz bandwidth filter. The fine vertical lines are due to the sound of individual pulses of air emitted by the larynx. The dark bands, or formants, are due to resonance peaks in the acoustic response of the vocal tract. Below the bottom figure the spoken phrase is written in phonetic symbols of the International Phonetic Association. Each "letter" represents a single sound.

speakers. The prospective user should make a careful appraisal of the task requirements, followed by a critical appraisal of these industrial offerings, which are evolving rapidly.

The commercially available devices should be seen as pattern-matching devices based on the assumption that only the information in the speech waveform is necessary for correct recognition. Certainly, it will always be desirable to utilize the best possible acoustic-phonetic analysis of the speech signal, and there is much active research in this area. There is a great deal of evidence, however, which indicates that constraints of the language being spoken are useful in recognition of an utterance. These constraints cover the allowable consonant clusters, syllable structure, morpheme sequences, phrase- and clause-level syntax, semantics, and discourse structure deriva-

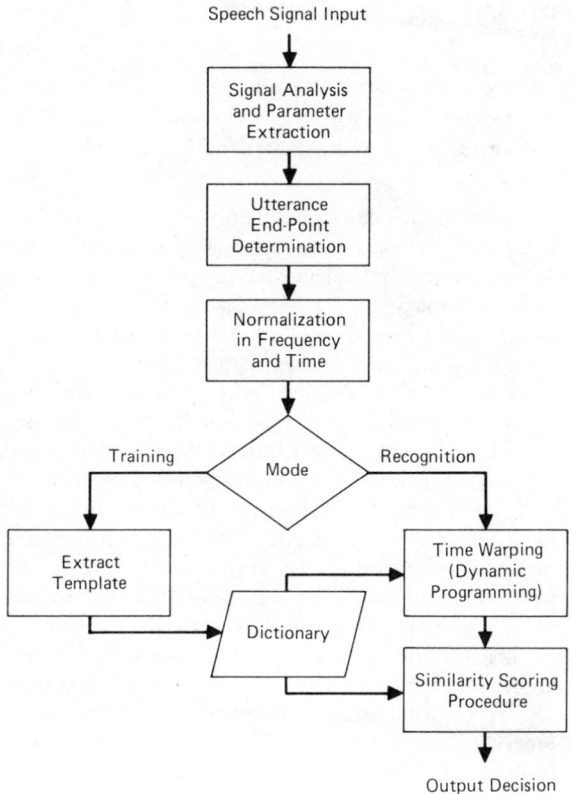

Speech Signal Input

Signal Analysis
and Parameter
Extraction

Utterance
End-Point
Determination

Normalization
in Frequency
and Time

Mode

Training   Recognition

Extract
Template

Dictionary

Time Warping
(Dynamic
Programming)

Similarity Scoring
Procedure

Output Decision

Fig. 2. Pattern-matching speech recognizer. The pattern produced from the speech signal is normalized and compared with a set of patterns derived from words of known identity. The input word is assumed to be the same as that word whose stored pattern has the highest similarity score.

tive from the nature of the specific task being performed. Since there are so many factors that influence recognition performance, many researchers have been concerned with the representation of these *knowledge sources*, their access, and means to combine their constraining effects on the output decision, as reflected in a control structure that guides the searching and decision-binding tasks. During the 1970s, there was a great deal of experimentation on these aspects of computational modeling of the speech recognition process. (Much of this work is described in the 1980 book edited by Lea.) It is useful to divide these models into two groups.

In one technique, represented by the HARPY system developed at Carnegie-Mellon University, the effect of all knowledge source constraints is used to *compile* a single network (composite knowledge source) that represents all possible utterances; that is, any allowed utterance can be described as a path through such a network. In this way, constraints of syllable structure, word structure, and syntax are all bound into one fixed structure. The control structure used for search is an adaptation of dynamic programming techniques, and is regarded as fixed. Experience has shown that such a scheme can provide a sentence error rate less than 10% for a 1,000 word vocabulary and a highly artificial syntax. Substantial tuning is required for each speaker, and performance has required approximately 80 times real time on a 0.35 MIPS (million instructions per second) computer. The design bias of this approach is to concentrate on one unified data structure that exhaustively represents all utterances, including variations in pronunciation. Because of this emphasis, the main development task focuses on provision and tuning of the networks, since search and control issues are constrained by the nature of the technique.

In another view, however, the knowledge sources and their associated processors are loosely coupled and flexibly utilized by a sophisticated control structure that determines search strategy and scoring procedures. This approach is typified by the HEARSAY-II system (also developed at Carnegie-Mellon University) and the HWIM (Hear What I Mean) system constructed at Bolt Beranek and Newman. In these systems, an initial acoustic-phonetic analysis is used to hypothesize word candidates, which are then verified by selective utilization of the constraints represented in the several knowledge sources. These systems are far less constrained in search strategy than HARPY-type systems, and can utilize several searches, focused at *islands of reliability* in the utterance rather than pure left-to-right search. Furthermore, the sequence with which knowledge is utilized and decisions are bound is determined by a flexible control that can utilize different strategies at different points of the utterance. That is, these systems open up a number of degrees of freedom to their designs, providing the opportunity for many novel techniques, but also require good insight and large amounts of experimentation to discover the best utilization of these capabilities. Nevertheless, some of these systems equal the performance of the compiled-network systems for comparable vocabularies, syntax, and acoustic-phonetic analysis capability. There is, of course, a large question of extensibility for all systems, the answer to which requires vastly increased knowledge of constraint-combination and search techniques. Based on current understanding, human speech perception appears to function as a complicated integrative mechanism, and there is no evidence to suggest either bottom-up or top-down biases over all utterances. For the present, however, researchers have to strike a balance between sufficient restrictions in order to obtain results in a reasonable time, and sufficiently general formulation of a system to permit extension without undue combinatoric explosion.

The complexity of speech recognition systems can be expected to grow as system performance, vocabulary, and syntax increase. Contemporary machines (of the PDP-10 class) already require approximately 100 times real time and memory of at least one million bytes to perform simple continuous speech recognition tasks typified by the systems discussed here. Hence, there is a great need for vastly improved computational resources, providing at least the equivalent of 100 MIPS performance with large memories, possibly through the use of multiprocessor system architectures. Given the rapid improvements in integrated circuit technology, these requirements do not seem unreasonable, particularly if special-purpose computational circuits are designed in order to exploit much of the available parallelism. Indeed, what is needed most is new fundamental insight into speech recognition algorithms. It is likely that the technology to support these new schemes will be ready when it is needed. In the meantime, further improvements in waveform-based pattern-matching schemes can be expected, and hence the range of applicability of practical speech recognition systems will grow, despite ignorance of the manner in which speech perception, as a human cognitive process, is performed.

REFERENCES

1972. Flanagan, J. L. *Speech Analysis, Synthesis, and Perception.* New York: Springer Verlag.

1975. Reddy, D. R. (Ed.). *Speech Recognition.* New York: Academic Press.

1980. Lea, W. A. (Ed.). *Trends in Speech Recognition.* Englewood Cliffs, NJ: Prentice-Hall.

J. ALLEN

SPEED OF COMPUTERS. *See* PERFORMANCE OF COMPUTERS.

SPOOLING

For articles on related subjects *see* BUFFER; INPUT-OUTPUT CONTROL SYSTEMS; INPUT-OUTPUT DEVICES; MEMORY: Auxiliary; and PINGPONG.

Spooling (Simultaneous Peripheral Operations On Line) is a method of handling low-speed input/output devices commonly implemented in operating systems to increase throughput. This increase is accomplished by using only high-speed I/O devices to supply images of lines of input data or of decks of punched cards or to receive images of printed lines when jobs are being run. Thus, a deck submitted by a user will be spooled (i.e., the input lines or card images transferred) to a high-speed I/O device, typically a disk or drum, by the spooling system. The image then behaves identically to the actual input terminal or card reader, but requests for reading the next line or card can be satisfied much more quickly by using the image on the high-speed I/O device. Similarly, a job's line images that are destined for a printer are delivered to the spooling system instead, where they are saved for transfer to the printer at a convenient time.

Spooling increases throughput because the central processing unit spends less time waiting for input data to be delivered to, or output data to be taken from, its buffers. This is illustrated by the simple example in Fig. 1.

The timing diagram in Fig. 1 shows the central processing unit filling a buffer with information. Eventually the buffer becomes full, and we assume the processor must wait for the buffer to be emptied (i.e., there are no other buffers available). The diagram also shows the relative waiting times when the data is delivered to a printer, as opposed to a disk. A printer running at 1,000 lines per minute prints one line every 60 ms. A disk can receive information about four times as fast, i.e., one line in 15 ms. Thus, the disk unit empties the buffer more quickly and less time (potential main-processor working time) is spent waiting. Of course the images will have to

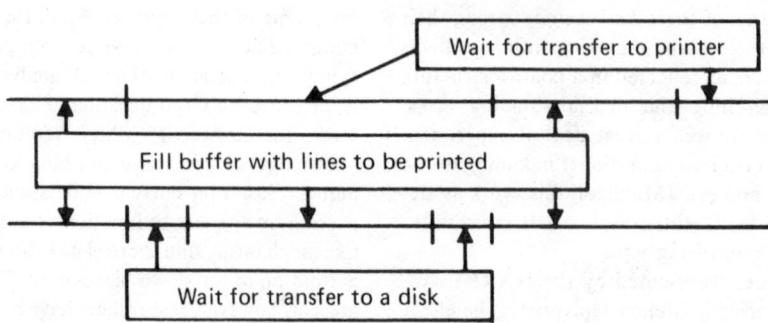

Fig. 1. Relative waiting times of output data delivered to a printer and to a disk.

transferred to the printer eventually, but not at the expense of main processor waiting time.

The idea of transferring input images to a higher speed I/O device (say, tape) before actual job processing—and similarly for line images destined for the printer—existed in early operating systems. In those systems, the "card to tape" and "tape to printer" utility functions were carried out on a separate computer, which either operated independently of the main processor or communicated with it. In both cases, there were at least two computers present. This is not the case with a spooling system. Rather, on a single system that is capable of supporting multiprogramming, the tasks "card to disk" and "disk to printer" are incorporated as members of the set of tasks to be supported. Thus, the I/O devices used by the spooling system are truly on line with respect to the main computer. System throughput is increased because these two tasks take relatively little processor time, and at the same time reduce the time that user tasks (the ultimate producers or consumers of data) wait for I/O.

Normally, spooling packages perform many other services in addition to the transfer of data from low- to high-speed I/O devices, and vice versa. For example, assuming that some jobs occupy the main computer for a long enough time so that several other new jobs can be spooled to a disk, it is not necessary to initiate the new jobs in the same order that they were spooled. Time, storage, I/O device, or other estimates can be used to initiate jobs in a manner that will increase throughput. Similarly, actual numbers of lines generated for printing can be used to schedule the flow of work through the printers.

Other desirable benefits that accrue from a spooling system are the ability to simulate the operation of several independent card readers using only a single one (thus creating the effect of multiple-batch streams), and the ability to print multiple copies of a job's output. Both advantages are due to the ability to locate directly and/or re-read the card or line images on the direct-access storage device.

R. W. TAYLOR

STACK

For articles on related subjects *see* DATA STRUCTURES; FIFO/LIFO; LISTS AND LIST PROCESSING; POLISH NOTATION; RECURSION; RING; SUBPROGRAMS, CALLING; and TREE.

A *stack* is a linear list for which all insertions and deletions, and usually all accesses, are made at one end of the list. The properties of a simple stack may be illustrated by a railroad switching network having a track into which railroad cars may be inserted and removed from only one end, as in Fig. 1. At any given time, only the most recently entered railroad car may be removed from the track. Railroad cars are said to enter and leave the track in a *last-in-first-out* (LIFO) order.

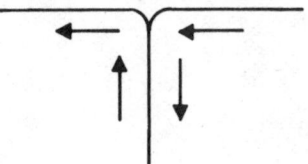

Fig.1

A stack may alternatively be defined as a linear list whose elements may be created and deleted only in a last-in-first-out order. Stacks arise in computational processes dealing with structures whose components are nested, as in the following example.

Example from Arithmetic Expression Evaluation. The expression $(3+(4*5))$ has a subexpression $(4*5)$, which is nested within the complete expression and is conveniently evaluated by first converting it to the parentheses-free postfix notation $345*+$ (in which the operator $*$ immediately follows its operands 4, 5, and the operator $+$ immediately follows its operands 3 and $45*$), and then using an operand stack for evaluation. The evaluation of the expression $345*+$, using a stack, is illustrated in Fig. 2, and is defined in detail below.

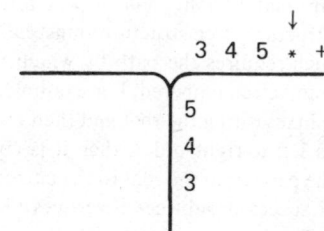

Fig. 2

Evaluation Rule for Postfix Expressions. Scan the constituents (operators and operands) of the expression from left to right. If the constituent is an operand, copy it into the operand stack. If the constituent is an operator, apply it to the two top elements of the operand stack and replace these two elements by the result of applying the operator to its operands.

The elements 3,4,5 in Fig. 2 have been placed in the operand stack and the operator "$*$" is about to be scanned. According to the evaluation rules, $*$ is applied to the two top elements (5 and 4) of the operand stack, which causes the elements 5 and 4 to be replaced by the

A(B,C(D,E))

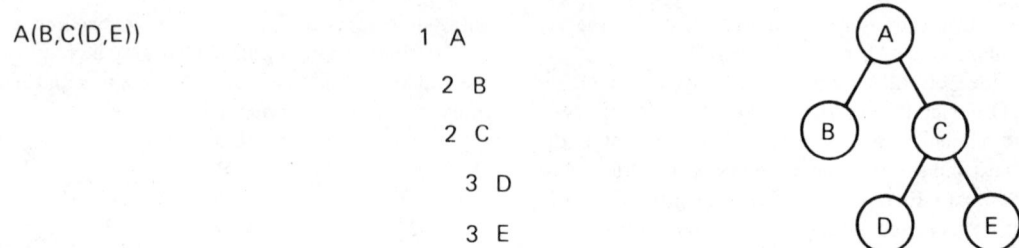

```
1  A
    2  B
    2  C
        3  D
        3  E
```

Fig. 3

value 20. The operator $+$ is now applied to the two top elements (20 and 3) of the operand stack, which causes these elements to be replaced by the value 23.

Arithmetic expression evaluation is conveniently implemented by stacks because expressions may contain subexpressions nested inside them to an arbitrary level. A further example of nested program structure arises in the case of subroutines (procedures).

Subroutine calls have the property that a called subroutine must be completely executed before return to the higher-level subroutine that called it. Thus, subroutines are executed in a last-in-first-out order (relative to the order in which they are called), and are conveniently implemented by a stack mechanism that creates and deletes information about subroutine parameters and the return address in a last-in-first-out order.

Nested structures may be represented by parentheses, embedding, or tree structures, as illustrated in Fig. 3.

There are many applications in which the elements of a nested structure (tree structure) must be "visited" in an order which requires the path by which the element was reached to be remembered. For example, if a tree is traversed by first visiting the root and then traversing the subtrees in a left-to-right order, then it is convenient to remember the path from the root to the current vertex on a stack, since successor subtrees of vertices along the path from the root to the current vertex must be examined in a last-in-first-out order if they are to complete the traversal of all vertices of the tree.

REFERENCE

1973. Knuth, D. E. *The Art of Computer Programming* **1**. (2nd. Ed.). Reading, MA: Addison-Wesley.

P. WEGNER

STANDARDS

For articles on related subjects *see* ASSOCIATION FOR COMPUTING MACHINERY; CODASYL; DATA PRO-CESSING MANAGEMENT ASSOCIATION; JOINT USERS GROUP; and KEYBOARD STANDARDS.

The availability of standards within any industry provides both the manufacturer and the consumer with a basis for the efficient operation of their respective tasks while at the same time promoting and encouraging fair trade. To the manufacturer, standardization provides monetary savings through the use of mass production techniques over a range of closely related products, by the production of uniform quality items, and through the decrease in developmental costs by the use of standard designs and equipment. To the user, standards improve the ability to evaluate adequately the products of competitive vendors and, by the use of interface standards, to develop systems which better suit the needs and requirements by the utilization of mixed manufacturer configurations.

Computer Industry Standards. Although the benefits of standardization of the elements of the computer industry are obvious, the timing of the publication and acceptance of standards is highly critical. Throughout the brief history of the development of standards related to the computer industry, the process of development has been continually greeted by the opinions of "too early" or "too late." On one hand, the premature standardization of computer elements can lead to a stagnation of the development of the product by being overly restrictive and therefore stifling further research in that area. In addition, standards adopted at an early stage of the development of a product can associate it so closely with the (then) current technology that no advantages can be taken of later technological developments.

The major benefit to be attained by early standardization is that the standard might recognize and codify the fundamental features of the element under consideration, and provide a uniform and logical means for the further development of the element.

On the other hand, the development of standards after the fact of product development can lead to confusion and rejection (by either misuse or misinterpretation) of the proposed standard. Where a product has been in the marketplace for some considerable period, and where there exists more than one manufacturer for the product, with a not inconsiderable body of consumers or users, the "Johnny-come-lately" approach to standardization is predestined to effective failure. Although standards would be beneficial in such situations, it is obvious that few manufacturers can afford to rewrite their software or to retool an assembly line; further, consumers will not have interest in modifications as long as their current requirements are met. Only when software is to be rewritten or an assembly is to be retooled in any case, is it advantageous to the manufacturer to contemplate conformance with the standard, and only when considering upgrading or replacing software or equipment is it worthwhile for the consumer or user to refer to the standard. On the national scale, such situations must occur daily, but on the individual scale, the standard that is "too late" has little direct influence.

Rarely, if ever, has the process of standardization of elements of the computer industry reached the middle ground between the two extremes of "too early" and "too late." Without any means for enforcement of standards in the United States, industry is paying dearly for its lack of attention to standardization efforts. It has been estimated that one-quarter of the total available computer power in the United States is being used to provide conversion systems between dissimilar, nonstandardized (or nonstandard) elements of computer systems. One need only look at the complexity of input/output conversion (software) packages to realize that a standard, common representation system would be highly beneficial. Even in other countries where government control and enforcement of standards is stricter, the predominance of United States companies in the computer industry effectively controls the production of national standards.

Standards Organizations. Within the U.S., standards are developed and published on a voluntary basis, since there exists no governmental agency with direct control over the use of standards within the computer (or any other) industry. Furthermore, there exist no congressional authorizations or appropriations that directly support or fund the development of standards for use within the U.S. However, the National Bureau of Standards (a division of the Department of Commerce) has direct responsibility under the "Brooks Bill" (Public Law 89-306, October 1965) for the development of computer-related standards for use within the federal government and for compliance with those standards by vendors of equipment to the federal government. Since the majority of computer equipment manufacturers are vendors not only to the U.S. government, but also to all consumers and users (nationally and internationally), federally enforced standards can be expected to be *de facto* industry standards, merely to save the cost of producing two sep-

arate lines of equipment. While the National Bureau of Standards has the authority to develop independent federal standards, the recognition of what would be the overall costs of purchasing special custom-designed equipment for the government requires the Bureau to participate actively in, and promote, the voluntary standards efforts of the computer industry.

The American National Standards Institute (ANSI) is the national clearinghouse and coordinating agency for voluntary standards in the U.S. It is a non-profit (membership) organization incorporated under the laws of the State of New York and is located at 1430 Broadway in New York City. It is a federation of approximately 200 trade associations and professional societies, together with 870 companies that are dues-paying members.

ANSI was originally organized as the American Engineering Standards Committee (AESC) in 1918 by five engineering societies—the American Institute of Electrical Engineers, the American Society of Mechanical Engineers, the American Society of Civil Engineers, the American Society of Mining and Metallurgical Engineers, and the American Society for Testing Materials. The AESC's initial purpose was to provide means for coordinating the standards issued by its founders, eliminating confusion and duplication among those standards. Its first act was to invite three federal government departments to join and work with the founding societies. The War Department, the Navy Department, and the Department of Commerce accepted the invitation. Enlarged in 1920 by the addition of trade associations, as well as more technical and professional societies, the AESC in 1928 was reorganized as the American Standards Association (ASA) to provide a more workable structure. The principles and procedures that were developed by the founders basically applied to the work of the ASA through 1966, when it became the United States of America Standards Institute (USASI). In 1969, the present name, the American National Standards Institute (ANSI), was adopted.

As the national clearinghouse for standards, ANSI provides the machinery for developing and approving standards that are supported by a national consensus. Its constitution states: "In standardization practice, a consensus is achieved when substantial agreement is reached by concerned interests according to the judgment of a duly appointed authority. Consensus implies much more than the concept of a simple majority, but not necessarily unanimity."

ANSI is currently publishing over 9,300 American National Standards, of which about 60 are directly related to the computer industry (end of 1979), with an additional 23 nearing final approval.

ANSI is the U.S. member body of the International Standards Organization (ISO). The viewpoints of the

U.S. to be presented in the technical work of ISO may be developed through the interested ANSI sectional committee, through a competent committee of another standards organization, or through a committee specifically organized as an Advisory Committee to an ISO Technical Committee. The work of the technical committees eventually results in ISO Draft International Standards (DIS), which may be embodied in the national standards of the ISO member bodies. Conversely, national standards of the member bodies may be embodied in DIS, and through this mechanism develop into other national standards.

To provide direct supervision of the hundreds of ANSI technical activities, there exists within ANSI a number of boards, each responsible for the several efforts in a particular area of standardization. One such board is the Information Systems Standards Management Board (ISSMB). American National Standards Committee X3 (ANSC-X3) for Computers and Information Processing, along with the standards committees for Office Machines (ANSC-X4), Financial Services (ANSC-X9), Business Data Interchange (ANSC-X12), Motor Vehicle Registration and Certificate of Ownership (ANSC-D19), Model Motorist Data Base for State Motor Vehicle Administrators (ANSC-D20), Library Sciences and Documentation (ANSC-Z39), and Library Supplies and Equipment (ANSC-Z85) are advised by the ISSMB. The ISSMB is responsible for all aspects of standardization of systems that transmit, store, or process analog, symbolic, or encoded representations of information, including satellite or control systems, peripheral equipment, and auxiliary devices that significantly influence the effective utilization of composite information processing systems.

The American National Standards Committee for Computers and Information Processing (ANSC-X3) was established in 1960 and was given the task of standardization related to systems, computers, equipment, devices, and media for information processing systems. The Committee Secretariat is held by the Computer and Business Equipment Manufacturers Association (CBEMA), 1828 L Street, NW, Washington, DC 20036. As the Secretariat, CBEMA provides essential administrative support and, through its Standards Management Committee, is responsible to ANSI for the general administration of ANSC-X3. CBEMA has the authority to appoint the chairperson of ANSC-X3, and through its administrative services is responsible for the processing of proposed standards to be forwarded to ISSMB and for publication as American National Standards.

The membership of the ANSC-X3 is approved by CBEMA and represents associations, professional societies, manufacturers (both of hardware and software), government agencies, and other bodies with an express interest in standards related to computers and informa-tion processing. These member bodies are categorized into three groups (consumer, general interest, and producer), the members of which are so chosen that no group has a majority. The major responsibilities of the ANSC-X3 include the development and approval of standards related to the computer industry and the development of national positions for presentation to the corresponding ISO committee (ISO/TC 97). ANSC-X3 accomplishes these tasks through two major committees: SPARC (Standards Planning and Requirements Committee) and IAC (International Advisory Committee).

The first committee (SPARC) is the research and study arm of ANSC-X3, responsible to, and responsive to, the ANSC-X3 committee for the identification of the needs and the requirements of the industry for standards. The process of determining the need, the justification, and the availability of resources and technical ability for the development of a standard is performed by a subcommittee. Having identified the need, justified the work, confirmed the availability of resources, and determined that the work is within the limits of current technology, SPARC recommends to ANSC-X3 the establishment of a standard development project, which will, if approved, be assigned to a (new or existing) technical committee for the actual development work. Once the project has been approved by ANSC-X3 and the committee assignment made, the SPARC oversees the progress of the project.

It is important to note that at the technical committee level (including SPARC, its subcommittees, and IAC), all membership is based on technical qualifications rather than organizational membership. Thus, while the membership of ANSC-X3 represents specific organizations, the membership of the other committees consists of individuals. In 1981, the committees of ANSC-X3 (listed in Table 1) were working on approximately 200 separate projects, including the tasks of maintaining and updating existing standards and determining need and justification for new standards development. The list of approved American National Standards developed by ANSC-X3 is given in Table 2.

The International Advisory Committee (IAC) coordinates and monitors the procedural and policy aspects of X3 and its subgroups as they relate to the work of ISO.

Although ANSI is responsible for the coordination of national voluntary standards in the U.S., the Institute has never established itself as the sole organization for the development of standards-related information. In fact, over one-third of the standards published by ANSI originated from outside the ANSI organization. The only requirement placed on these externally originating standards is that they be submitted by competent organizations, developed through their own procedures, and be supported by a consensus of the interested organizations in the field of application. In the particular area of Data Systems Languages, ANSC-X3 is supported by devel-

Table 1. Listing of ANSC-X3 Organizations

X3A1	Optical Character Recognition (OCR)
X3A7	Magnetic Ink Character Recognition (MICR)
X3B1	Magnetic Tape
X3B2	Perforated Media
X3B3	Punched Cards
X3B5	Magnetic Tape Cassettes
X3B6	Instrumentation Tape
X3B7	Magnetic Disks
X3B8	Flexible Disks
X3H1	Operating System Control/Response Language (OSCRL)
X3H2	Data Definition Language
X3H3	Computer Graphics
X3J1	PL/I Language
X3J2	Basic Language
X3J3	Fortran Language
X3J4	Cobol Language
X3J5	Compact/Action/Split Languages
X3J6	Text Processing Programming Language
X3J7	APT Language
X3J9	Pascal Language
X3K1	Project Documentation
X3K2	Flowcharts
X3K5	Vocabulary
X3K6	Network Oriented Project Management Systems (NOPMS)
X3K7	Program Abstracts
X3L2	Character Sets and Codes
X3L5	Labels and File Structure
X3L8	Representation of Data Elements
X3S3	Data Communications
X3S31	Data Communications Planning
X3S33	Data Communications Formats
X3S34	Data Communication Control Procedure
X3S35	Data Communication System Performance
X3S36	Data Transmission Speeds
X3S37	Public Data Networks
X3T1	Data Encryption
X3T9	I/O Interface
X3/SPARC	Standards Planning and Requirements Committee
SPARC/LRPL	Long Range Planning for Programming Languages
SPARC/OSIC	SPARC/Open Systems Interconnection Committee
SPARC/DBM	SPARC/Data Base Management
SPARC/ENCR	SPARC/Encryption
X3/IAC	International Advisory Committee
ANSI/X3	Computers and Information Processing

opmental work by the Conference on Data Systems Languages (CODASYL).

The most widely known products of CODASYL are the Cobol language, which was subsequently accepted as the basis for the American National Standard COBOL X3.23, and the Data Base Reports. The Cobol Committee also publishes, on an as-needed basis, a Cobol Information Bulletin (CIB) which reports on the proposals for the development of Cobol, and gives interpretations and clarifications of existing specifications.

The international aspects of standardization are im-

portant to U.S. manufacturers of both hardware and software, since they provide over 30% of the equipment to the free world outside the U.S. Of particular importance to the information-processing community is the work of the International Organization for Standardization (ISO) and its technical committee TC 97 (Computers and Information Processing).

ISO was established in 1947 to promote the development of standards in order to facilitate international exchange of goods and services, and to develop mutual cooperation in areas of intellectual, scientific, technolog-

Table 2. Listing of ANSC-X3 Standards (As of 1979)

Catalog No.	Short Title
X3.1-1976	Synchronous Signaling Rates
X3.2-1976	Print Specifications for MICR
X3.3-1976	Bank Check Specs for MICR
X3.4-1977	ASCII (Code for Info. Interchange)
X3.5-1970	Flowchart Symbols
X3.6-1973	Perforated Tape Code
X3.9-1978	Programming Language Fortran
X3.11-1969	General Purpose Paper Cards
X3.14-1973	Recorded Mag Tape (200 cpi)
X3.15-1976	Bit Sequences, Serial Data Transmission
X3.16-1976	Character Structure/Parity, Serial Transmission
X3.17-1977	OCR-A Character Set and Print Quality
X3.18-1974	1-In. Perforated Tape
X3.19-1974	$^{11}/_{16}$-In. Perforated Tape
X3.20-1974	Tape-Up Reels for 1-In. Tape
X3.21-1967	Rectangular Holes in 12-Row Punched Cards
X3.22-1973	Recorded Mag Tape (800 cpi)
X3.23-1974	Programming Language Cobol
X3.24-1968	Signal Quality/DTE and DCE (EIA RS-334)
X3.25-1976	Character Structure/Parity, Parallel Transmission
X3.26-1970	Hollerith Punched Card Code
X3.27-1978	Magnetic Tape Labels and File Structure
X3.28-1976	Communications Control with ASCII
X3.29-1971	Unpunched Oiled Paper Perforated Tape
X3.30-1971	Calendar Date and Ordinal Date
X3.31-1973	Identification of Counties of the U. S.
X3.32-1973	Graphics for ASCII Control Characters
X3.34-1972	Interchange Rolls of Perforated Tape
X3.36-1975	High Speed Signaling Rates
X3.37-1977	Programming Language APT
X3.38-1977	Identification of States of the U. S.
X3.39-1973	Recorded Magnetic Tape (1600 cpi)
X3.40-1976	Unrecorded Magnetic Tape
X3.41-1974	ASCII Code Extension Techniques
X3.42-1975	Representation of Numeric Values
X3.43-1977	Representation of Local Time of the Day
X3.44-1974	Measurement/Data Transmission System Performance
X3.45-1974	Character Set for Handprinting
X3.46-1974	Unrecorded Six Disk Pack
X3.47-1977	Identification of Named Populated Places
X3.48-1977	Magnetic Tape Cassette (0.150 in.)
X3.49-1975	OCR-B Character Set
X3.50-1975	Representations of Customary and SI Units
X3.51-1975	Representations of Universal Time and Time Zones
X3.52-1976	Unrecorded Single Disk-Front Load
X3.53-1976	Programming Language PL/I
X3.54-1976	Recorded Magnetic Tape (6250 cpi)
X3.55-1977	Unrecorded Magnetic Tape Cartridge (0.250 in.)
X3.56-1977	Recorded Magnetic Tape Cartridge (0.250 in.)
X3.57-1977	Structure for Message Heading Formats
X3.58-1977	Unrecorded Eleven Disk Pack
X3.60-1978	Programming Language Minimal Basic
X3.61-1978	Representation of Geographic Point Locations
X3.62-1978	OCR Paper
X3.64-1979	Additional Controls for Use with ASCII
X3.66-1979	Advanced Data Communication Control Procedures—ADCCP

ical, and economic activity. Its objectives, as specified in its constitution, are: " . . . to facilitate the coordination and unification of the standards of Member Bodies." In connection with this goal, ISO may "organize the exchange of information regarding the work carried out by each Member Body. . . . , set forth principles for the guidance of Member Bodies in their work. . . . , cooperate with other international organizations dealing with related questions. . . . , [and] set up international standards provided [that] in each case no Member Body dissents."

Present membership in ISO include 65 Member Bodies. A Member Body is an organization of an individual nation which best represents the standardization activities of its nation. Only one such body for each country can be an ISO Member Body. The ISO Member Body that represents the U.S. is ANSI.

The standardization work of ISO is accomplished by technical committees. Any ISO Member Body or any organization outside ISO may request the study of a technical subject. If the study is approved by a majority, and at least five Member Bodies are willing to take an active part, a technical committee is established by the Council.

For each committee, the Council designates one Member Body to act impartially as Secretariat. This Member Body also has its own delegation on the technical committee, with the same status as other participating Member Bodies. The Secretariat is responsible for the satisfactory conduct of the technical committee's work and annually reports to the Council.

Currently, over 170 technical committees have been established. Members who take an active part in the work of a technical committee are known as "(P) Members" (participating) and have the right to vote. Members who wish only to be kept informed of a committee's work are called "(O) Members" (observers) and may not vote.

Members participating at the committee, subcommittee, and working group levels of ISO/TC 97 include the following countries.

(P) Members	(O) Members
Australia	Austria
Brazil	Belgium
Canada	Bulgaria
Czechoslovakia	Chile
Finland	Denmark
France	Greece
West Germany	India
Hungary	Iran
Italy	Ireland
Japan	Israel
The Netherlands	Norway
Poland	Pakistan
Rumania	Peru

(P) Members	(O) Members
Spain	Portugal
Sweden	South Africa
Switzerland	Turkey
United Kingdom	Yugoslavia
United States	
U.S.S.R.	

One other standards organization has considerable impact on the computer industry of the U.S. That is the European Computer Manufacturer's Association (ECMA). This body parallels CBEMA of the U.S. organizationally, but restricts membership in the standards development and approval processes to manufacturers only. Since the majority of U.S. computer manufacturers also have a market in Europe, they also have a voice in the development of standards within ECMA. Although ECMA is not a member of ISO, it is regarded as being a competent standards development body, and its proposals are accepted as a basis for ISO Draft International Standards. In the early 1970s, ECMA, in cooperation with X3, was responsible for the development of a proposed standard for the PL/I language.

Installation Standards. Contrasted with industry standards, installation standards exist not specifically for the efficient interchange of information between organizations or companies, but rather to provide guidelines for the efficient operation of an individual installation. While such standards do not prohibit or nullify such interchanges, their primary purpose is to provide for clear, concise documentation of programs and systems for use in a single installation.

There exists no organization, in the U.S. or internationally, which has undertaken such standardization, although the individual professional organizations have attempted to provide guidelines for their own members. These include the following organizations.

- Association for Computing Machinery (ACM)
- ACM Special Interest Group on Computer Systems Installation Management (SIGCOSIM)
- Data Processing Management Association (DPMA)

REFERENCE

1978. Prigge, R. D., Hill, M. F., and Walkowicz, J. L. *The World of EDP Standards.* Blue Bell, PA: Sperry Univac Corp.

J. A. N. LEE and W. G. MADISON

STATEMENTS

For articles on related subjects *see* DECLARATIVE STATEMENT; DEFAULT CONDITION; EXECUTABLE STATEMENT; EXPRESSION; PROCEDURE-ORIENTED LANGUAGES; PROGRAMMING LANGUAGES; and STRING PROCESSING LANGUAGES.

In much the same way that a sentence is the structural unit of expression in a stream of natural language discourse, the *statement* may be viewed as the elemental organizational component of a high-level language program. As such, it embodies a unit of activity in terms of the algorithm being implemented. This is quite different from, and bears no direct correspondence with, processor activity. Although many types of statements are *executable* in that they instigate the high-level language compiler to produce operationally equivalent sequences of machine language instructions, this relationship is arbitrary: A given type of statement may be expanded or contracted to designate a wide range of activities, all within the syntax of that statement. For example, the following two statements,

```
A = 7.82
B = (22.4 + (X/Y)**3) * (X * Y - Z)
```

are both syntactically legitimate assignment statements in the Fortran language, but there is clearly a considerable difference in the amount of computation each one specifies. This is completely consistent with the underlying idea that the user, rather than the processor, be the determining factor with regard to the amount of processing expressed in a high-level language statement.

Not all high-level language statements can be related to instructions in the machine language program ultimately produced. Many languages include statement types whose primary purpose is not to convey the intent of an algorithm, but rather to provide supportive information for compilation and other processes auxiliary to the actual execution of the program. These statements, which pertain to matters such as the allocation of storage and description of variables, correspond to a range of activities that do not generally show up as equivalent sequences of machine instructions. Accordingly, they are *nonexecutable,* and usually are treated as a distinct syntactic set.

It is not always possible to provide the programmer with unlimited scope for expression in a single statement. Yet such capability is needed if the linkage between the statement and a meaningful activity is to be preserved. There are innumerable occasions in which a sequence of associated events, while clearly identifiable as a single procedural activity, contains arbitrarily diverse machine processes whose specification in a single statement would be linguistically impractical. Most high-level languages accommodate this necessity by allowing some type of compound construction. In some cases the construction is formed as a single statement with multiple clauses; in others, the idea of the *compound* statement is implemented as a group of single statements enclosed in special organizational statements or special words that serve as delimiters.

Executable Statements. Since these statement types are characterized by their ultimate relationship to explicit processing action in the object program, their general form tends to resemble the imperative sentence in many natural languages. Accordingly, it often is true that the language elements used for specifying activities are verbs. For example, an input activity in Fortran is expressed in the form

READ(i,j)*list*

where i, j, and *list* specify the source, form, and destination of the input, respectively. The same construction prevails when data is to be transmitted from the central processor to the outside, with the verb WRITE indicating the direction. In less dominantly formulaic languages, the resemblance to imperative syntax is more pronounced. Thus, one of PL/I's constructions for data transmission has the form

READ FILE*(source)* INTO*(destination);*

and

WRITE FILE*(destination)* FROM*(source);*

for input and output, respectively. When similarity to natural language is a primary design objective, the correspondence may be complete, as in the following Cobol statement:

ADD *a* TO *b* GIVING *c*.

The narrative construction persists in an alternative, more formulaic form:

COMPUTE $c = a + b$.

The Basic language designates the same operations in a similar manner:

LET $c = a + b$.

The words COMPUTE and LET are included in the fixed vocabularies of their respective languages specifically to enhance the parallels with "real" sentences; the language translators clearly can operate properly without them (at some slight inconvenience), as they do in such languages as Fortran, Algol, and PL/I. It should be noted, however, that the absence of such verbs does not change the inherently imperative syntax; though now more implicit, it still remains. Thus, the PL/I statement equivalent to the previous examples, namely,

$$c = a + b;$$

can be read as a highly implicit form of this sentence: "The value in c is to be replaced by the result of the indicated operation on a and b."

The same construction generally carries over to compound statements. Though high-level languages vary in the type and extent of compounding their syntaxes allow, there is one category of compound activity sufficiently basic to all computing work to compel its representation across the entire spectrum of high-level languages. This is the fundamental decision mechanism in which a comparison is specified in conjunction with procedural alternatives based on the outcome of that comparison. In programmers' argot, this is termed the IF-THEN-ELSE construct. A "natural" way to articulate such a construction would be with some form of conditional sentence: "If a particular condition exists, take the action specified here; if it does not exist, ignore that action and perform this alternative action." This construction is followed closely in many languages.

To illustrate this, consider the situation in which two variables, X and Y, are to be compared. If X is less than Y, the X value is to be doubled; otherwise, X is to be decreased by 8.2. In either case, a variable Z is to be computed as the product XY. The appropriate compound statements for several languages appear.

(Algol)	**if** x $<$ y **then** x := 2∗x
	else x := x − 8.2;
	z := x∗y;
(Cobol)	IF X IS LESS THAN Y
	MULTIPLY 2 BY X
	ELSE SUBTRACT 8.2
	FROM X.
	COMPUTE Z = X∗Y.
(Fortran 77)	IF (X .LT. Y) THEN
	X = 2.0∗X
	ELSE
	X = X − 8.2
	END IF
	Z = X∗Y
(PL/I)	IF X $<$ Y THEN X = 2∗X;
	ELSE X = X − 8.2;
	Z = X∗Y;

(Pascal)	**if** X $<$ Y **then** X := 2∗X
	else X := X − 8.2;
	Z := X∗Y;

These languages provide a variety of structural features that enable such decision mechanisms to be extended. One such extension, for example, allows either or both alternative actions at the ends of an **if** statement to be **if** statements themselves.

The language Snobol has a syntactic construction which emphasizes compound statements. Moreover, the language is characterized by a fundamental shift away from the sentence-like appearance of its statements; many of the crucial operations are either highly symbolic or completely implied. Both properties are illustrated in the statement below.

HERE   VSTR 'BC' = 'W'   :S(HERE)
    next statement

This may be paraphrased roughly as follows: Search the string VSTR for an occurrence of a B followed by a C, replacing that pair of characters with a single W; if the search was successful (that is what the S after the colon stands for), execute the statement again (i.e., return to the statement labeled HERE). When the search fails, continue with the next statement. Thus, a single compound statement embodies a request to find and process any or all occurrences of a particular set of characters in another, larger character string.

The ability to treat arbitrarily long sequences as single procedural activities receives formal emphasis in languages such as Algol, PL/I, and Pascal, whose vocabularies include special organizational statements to indicate the bounds of such sequences. This is intended to encourage a modular approach to program design wherein the implementation of an algorithm is treated as synthesis of related but logically (and structually) distinct activities. Languages so oriented are often termed *block structured* languages. In PL/I, for example, decision alternatives may be extended arbitrarily by bracketing them with the DO and END statements, as depicted in Fig. 1. The brackets **begin** and **end** serve the same purpose in Algol and Pascal.

The group of statements in each of the processing boxes in Fig. 1 is considered as a "unit" of activity, irrespective of its extent. On a somewhat larger scale, this method is used to enclose subprograms and other major program components (e.g., PROCEDURE and END statements in PL/I, and SUBROUTINE and END statements in Fortran). (Examples of these statements and their use are found in the article PROCEDURE.)

Concurrent Statements. Technological advances have broadened interests in concurrent processes

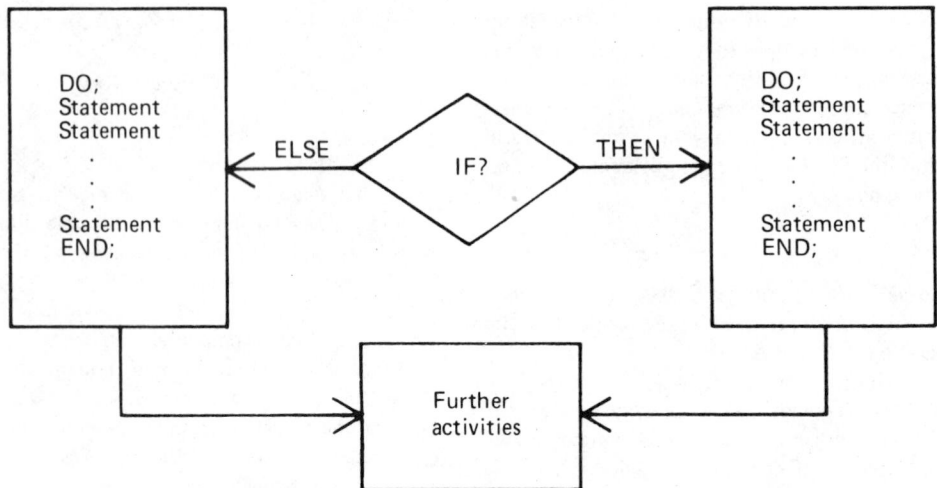

Fig. 1. Implementation of alternative activity groups in PL/I.

beyond their traditional association with the design and implementation of supervisory software. Feasible applications have emerged in which it is desirable to specify parallel computing activities (generally, parts of larger processes); i.e., a collection of activities whose overall outcome is to be independent of the sequence in which the activities are begun or performed.

Accordingly, facilities for specifying such processes, originally confined to low-level languages, have been incorporated into some high-level languages. One of the first languages to address this problem is concurrent Pascal, a derivative of Pascal developed by Per Brinch Hansen. Compound statements, subprograms, and programs are organized as in any block-structured sequential language. However, processing components, despite their resemblance to "main programs" in the traditional sense, will not execute until triggered by another program that establishes their concurrency and actually gets them started. The structure shown below, for example, specifies a complex of three procedures, any or all of which could be executing in parallel. Depending on the physical configuration available, these procedures may actually be running simultaneously or, in an environment with a single processor, any or all may be started but not yet complete.

```
type   P1  = process (list of
          pertinent components)
var    Declarations for P1                    P1's
begin                                         Definition
          Activities for P1
end.
```

```
type   P2 = process (list of
          pertinent components)
var    Declarations for P2                    P2's
begin                                         Definition
          Activities for P2
end.
```

```
type   P3 = process (list of
          pertinent components)
var    Declarations for P3                    P3's
begin                                         Definition
          Activities for P3
end.
```

```
var    pname1:P1; pname2:P2;      Activation of
       pname3:P3;                 Concurrent Processes
begin    init pname1, pname2,     pname1, pname2,
         pname3;                  pname3.
end.                              (pname1 is an
                                  instance of a P1 =
                                  type process, etc.)
```

Nonexecutable Statements. Completion of a high-level language program usually requires the inclusion of statements that do not correspond directly to steps in the algorithm being implemented. Rather, they provide the compiler with essential information from which it may determine the allocation of storage and other organizational characteristics of the final program. The command structure in these nonexecutable statements bears a less consistent resemblance to the imperative sentence than is found in other statement types.

A primary type of information transmitted by such

statements concerns the definition and description of variables to be used in a program. For example, each of the following statements,

(Algol)	**real** X, Y, **integer** Z;
(Fortran)	REAL X, Y
	INTEGER Z
(PL/I)	DECLARE (X, Y) FLOAT BINARY,
	Z FIXED BINARY;

associates the names x and y with certain amounts of storage, indicating further that the contents of these locations are to be treated as numerical values in floating-point form. In addition, the name z is associated with storage whose contents represent an integer value. Note that the expandability inherent in other statement types is present here, too, since it is possible to combine an arbitrary number of different declarations in a single statement.

Definition of entire arrays is no more complicated, since the same basic descriptive structure is used, augmented by information about the array's extent. For instance, the following declarations,

(Algol)	**real** X, Y, **integer array** Z[1:18];
(Fortran)	REAL X, Y
	INTEGER Z(18)
(PL/I)	DECLARE (X, Y) FLOAT BINARY,
	Z(18) FIXED BINARY;

define variables x, y, and z as they did above except that z now is an array of 18 elements, each of whose contents represents an integer value.

This descriptive process is much more formalized in Cobol, where the definitions and descriptions of variables are a required major organizational component of every program.

REFERENCES

1967. Higman, B. *A Comparative Study of Programming Languages.* New York: Elsevier.
1969. Sammet, J. *Programming Languages—History and Fundamentals.* Englewood Cliffs, NJ: Prentice-Hall.
1978. Brinch Hansen, P. *The Architecture of Concurrent Programs.* Englewood Cliffs, NJ: Prentice-Hall.

S. V. POLLACK AND T. D. STERLING

STATE VECTOR. *See* PROGRAM STATUS WORDS AND STATE VECTORS.

STATISTICAL APPLICATIONS

For articles on related subjects *see* ECONOMETRIC APPLICATIONS; MEDICAL APPLICATIONS; PATTERN RECOGNITION; REGRESSION ANALYSIS; SCIENTIFIC APPLICATIONS; and SOCIAL SCIENCE APPLICATIONS.

The advent of high-speed, large central memory computers has greatly expanded the application of statistics. However, for other than elementary applications, such as quality control, simple means and standard deviations, and the like, the actual practical application of computers to statistics has severely lagged behind methodological development. There are, in fact, relatively few practitioners of computer applications of statistics, particularly of multivariate statistics. The number of practitioners in very recent years has increased and is continuing to increase, however, due to the ubiquitous availability of personal calculators, and the advent of low-priced micro- and minicomputers.

The literature of statistical computing methodology is considerable. A reasonable sampling of this literature can be found in Enslein *et al.* (1976). Thus, the review of applications which follows must be viewed as only the beginning of a much wider development. The list is clearly not all-inclusive in that many of the more esoteric applications, such as weather prediction, have not been included.

In these applications the following methods are often used.

1. *Regression analysis,* for model building and prediction.
2. *Factor analysis,* to obtain a parsimonious description of a complex database.
3. *Univariate and multivariate analysis of variance,* to test hypotheses and search for interactions, for example, in clinical drug trials.
4. *Discriminant analysis,* to find hyperplanes that optimally separate groups, typically used in disease screens, toxicology, and econometrics.
5. *Time-series analysis,* particularly the fast Fourier transform (FFT), to demonstrate relationships between serial observations.
6. *Clustering and pattern recognition methods,* to find groups (used not infrequently in image analysis).

Demography. An application with a great impact on people's lives is the use of statistical computing in the 1970 U.S. Census. For the first time in the Census, all data were recorded on magnetic tape and, as a result, tabulations, economic analyses, and analyses of migration patterns, housing, and population characteristics, etc., have been published in timely fashion. In fact, success with the 1970 Census has encouraged the retrospective encoding of much data from the 1960 Census in computer form so that computer-based comparisons could be made between the results from the two censuses. For the 1980 Census there will be still more timely reporting with the aid of computerization.

Internationally, the United Nations (UN) statistics office has been instrumental in assembling worldwide data. In 1973, a totally computerized census was conducted in Nigeria.

Epidemiology. Computers have been used widely in epidemiological studies of many diseases and implied causes of diseases, such as cancer, smoking, bacterial and viral infections, longevity and aging, and the effects of pollutants. In the U.S., much of this work has been carried out by the National Center for Health Statistics (NCHS). Worldwide, the World Health Organization (WHO), a special agency of the UN, has been a foremost propounder of the use of computer statistics in this field.

Mortality. Mortality statistics are routinely obtained by means of digital computers, particularly related to various census and other geographic divisions. This, in turn, has led to the recompilation of many actuarial tables. Again, much of the data produced in this fashion are available through the NCHS and the UN.

Psychological Testing. The evaluation of psychological profiles, educational tests, and similar instruments is performed routinely, and has been made possible, by the use of statistical computing. In fact, the classical methods of factor analysis, of which many types have been developed, did not come to the fore until the high-speed, large-scale computer became a fact. Among the more important psychometric and aptitude testing instruments are Cattell's 16 Personality Factors (16 PF), the U.S. Department of Labor's General Aptitude Test Battery (GATB), and the Mayo Clinic's Minnesota Multiphasic Personality Inventory (MMPI). Educational tests appear to be substantially less robust at this point. This seems to be more a problem of norms than technique. Tests of this type have also been used to evaluate various psychiatric or neurotic conditions such as anxiety and depression.

Drug Research. One of the major applications of statistics, particularly multivariate statistics, is in the evaluation of the therapeutic and side effects of pharmaceutical compounds. In this area of application, the differing viewpoints of different investigators can be compensated for by analysis of covariance. Since most humans exhibit a strong placebo response, advanced statistical methods have also permitted the compensation for this effect in experimental designs, particularly double-blind crossover designs.

Medical Diagnostics and Screening. Diagnostic screens to detect diseases from multivariate data have been developed for thyroid diseases, chronic lung diseases, and pelvic diseases, among others. Computers are also used in reading electrocardiograms, karyotyping chromosomes, classifying leukocytes, multiphasic screens, and calculating pulmonary function, blood volume, and similar repetitive tasks.

Advertising and Marketing. These related fields have represented a major application of statistical computing in recent years. It is not always clear that the applications are appropriate, since the models used are often not sound. The choice of advertising medium, the areas to be studied, the strategies in marketing, and the demographic characteristics of the population to which one wishes to sell are often parameters in these applications.

Econometrics. Econometrics, particularly econometric forecasting, has been widely applied since the advent of high-speed digital computers. The applications have ranged from computation of the consumer price index to the allocation of resources and even to the modeling of entire economies. Time-series analysis, particularly the fast Fourier transform (*q.v.*), has found wide application in this area. Econometrics, however, is at the mercy of models and is a good example of the ease of computation offset by difficulty with the underlying model structure. In other words, while it is not difficult to build easily computable models and to test their impact analytically, in fact, the degree of adequacy with which the model reflects reality often leaves much to be desired. Fully adequate models, however, will likely involve computations beyond the capacity of even the most powerful of today's systems.

Image Analysis and Recognition. While some practitioners may not consider this an application of statistical computing, the methods used in image analysis and recognition are in fact statistical. Such methods encompass clustering, pattern recognition, and feature detection, and have been applied in aerial surveillance (the famous detection of Soviet missile bases in Cuba); in character recognition on checks and similar documents, as well as in biomedical techniques such as machine reading of chest X-rays to detect enlargement of the heart and similar malformations, in the classification of white blood cells and other biological tissues; and in comparison of perceived image "quality" to objective image parameters.

These applications of statistical computing are rapidly expanding.

Summary. This discussion reveals that many applications exist at this writing, though only a small fraction of the possibilities have been explored. While the reader may get the impression that there are virtually no limitations to what computers can do in this field, many applications—particularly those dealing with numerous variables, which includes image analysis—are restricted by the size of the problem, which in turn is reflected in central memory limitations as well as the speed of computation of presently existing machines.

REFERENCE

1976. Enslein, K., Ralston, A., and Wilf, H. S. (Eds.). *Statistical Methods for Digital Computers* 3: *Mathematical Methods for Digital Computers*. New York: Wiley.

K. ENSLEIN

STOCHASTIC PROCESS

For articles on related subjects *see* MONTE CARLO METHOD; and RANDOM NUMBER GENERATION.

The theory of stochastic processes deals with events that develop in time or space and which cannot be described precisely except in terms of *probability theory*. Formally, a stochastic process is a collection of random variables X_t indexed by the parameter t, such that for any finite set of t's, the joint probability distribution of corresponding X's is specified. This definition is so broad that it includes practically all of probability and statistics; in practice, the term *stochastic process* (also *time series* or, particularly in Russia, *random function*) is usually used to describe events that develop in time and whose realizations are curves, either continuous or with jumps. Examples of continuous processes: the barometric pressure at Greenwich Observatory during November 1934, or your blood pressure as you read this article. Examples of processes with jumps: arrivals at an airline counter; the number of mutations in a developing colony of bacteria.

Since chance is involved with measurements we take on most things, or the measured objects are so complicated that we resort to probability arguments to describe them, the theory of stochastic processes pervades virtually all the sciences. Computers play an increasingly important role in development and applications of that theory. For example, they are used for simulation, i.e., in the generation of stochastic processes using random numbers in the computer to verify theory or approximations provided by theory. They are used to suggest experimen-

tal lines of investigation for further theory, or to study *robustness* of existing theory—i.e., how good are the theoretical results when the (often necessarily simple) assumptions on which the theory was developed do not hold precisely. Computers also play an essential role in analyzing data collected on stochastic processes, for many procedures call for complicated and lengthy calculations such as Fourier and Laplace transforms, harmonic and spectral analysis, serial correlation, prediction, and so on.

Finally, computer science itself has led to consideration of new kinds or new levels of stochastic processes, ranging from queueing processes describing user demands in time-sharing systems to the complicated branching processes involved in the study of algorithms and their treatment by compilers and programming languages, as well as descriptions of the electromagnetic signals and associated random *noise* (*q.v.*) that are the physical bases of all modern computers.

REFERENCES

1964. Hammersley, J. M. and Handscomb, D. C. *Monte Carlo Methods*. London: Methuen.
1965. Cox, D. R. and Miller, H. D. *The Theory of Stochastic Processes*. London: Methuen.

G. MARSAGLIA

STORAGE. *See also* articles under MEMORY.

STORAGE ALLOCATION

For articles on related subjects *see* ADDRESSING; ASSOCIATIVE MEMORY; DATABASE MANAGEMENT; MEMORY: Main; OVERLAY; STORAGE HIERARCHY; STORAGE MANAGEMENT STRUCTURES; TIME SHARING; and VIRTUAL MEMORY.

Storage in a digital computer system must be allocated to programs and data that are being executed, just as for any other resource in the system. While the cost of hardware used for storage is rapidly decreasing in the 1980s, the demands for storage generated by increasingly sophisticated software systems and application programs are quickly diluting the benefits from the availability of cheaper, larger storage.

A computer system will normally have several levels of storage, usually referred to as "main" (or primary) storage, "secondary" (or auxiliary) storage, and so on. Main storage is implemented using fast but relatively expensive components. Secondary storage is slower and less expensive. A typical system will have more of secondary than of main storage. The lower levels of storage are intended for storing large amounts of information for relatively long periods of time. When some part of the information is to be referenced during a computation, it is usually transferred to main storage first; i.e., it is *loaded* into main storage.

Sound resource management frequently dictates that programs and data should be allocated only the minimum amount of main storage that is necessary, but additional amounts are often acquired and are released dynamically. Thus, a program may be allocated an initial amount of *static* main storage when it is loaded from secondary storage, which it will use until its execution is completed. During the computation, there may be requests to a supervisory system for additional dynamically allocated main storage, which will receive temporary values for subsequent computation or communication to other *processes,* and which may then be released back to the supervisory system when it is no longer required.

Another use for dynamically acquired storage (as well as the initially acquired storage) is for the introduction of additional segments of programs and/or data, while parts of the program or data which were used and are no longer needed are released or overwritten. When the same storage is used and reused in this way, it is called an *overlay* process. It should be noted that dynamic acquisition of space is not just an alternative to explicit overlay management; for certain types of programs, such as recursive programs, one cannot anticipate in advance the amount of storage that will be necessary. Depending on the depth of the recursion, one might need a very long chain of temporary storage acquisitions, each to be released on return to the next higher level of recursion.

A considerable amount of program and data management is involved in an explicit overlay process. It has been estimated that as much as 50% of a program development effort may be concerned with design and implementation of overlay procedures. For this reason, various software and hardware systems have included features that help to alleviate the overlay burden. For example, the PL/I language provides for the allocation of *static* storage to variables, and also for two modes of dynamic allocation, one of which acquires storage for variables declared at the time of entry to a block (with automatic release of the storage back to the supervisory system on exit from the block), and the other of which gives complete control to the program to request space at any time, with subsequent responsibility for its explicit release.

One concept introduced (at least partly because of the overlay problem) is *virtual storage.* Here, program and data are assigned addresses independent of the amount of physical storage actually available and independent of the location from which the program will actually be executed. Thus, one might use 32 bits to represent an address (thus addressing about four billion items), while the available physical (main) storage might accommodate about a quarter-million items (needing only 18 bits for the representation of a particular address). This large ratio of total virtual storage to total physical storage implies a potentially massive overlay problem, although only occasionally will a program or its data be expected to occupy a very large fraction of the virtual storage.

Given that the program and data are allocated enough addresses in virtual storage to enable them to be accommodated there without any worry about overlay, but also given the expectation that the physical storage will be shared with other programs and data in a typical time-sharing or multiprogramming system, it is quite commonly necessary for the system to invoke an automatic overlay procedure. This is typically accomplished in a virtual storage system by bringing into physical storage from secondary storage only those parts of virtual storage which have been referenced (or can reasonably be expected to be referenced shortly). By recording in a table the mapping (i.e., correspondence between parts of virtual storage and physical storage established when pieces of virtual storage are brought into main memory), addresses may be transplanted dynamically. Those references to virtual addresses that are not already mapped into physical storage can be intercepted by special hardware, and that part of virtual storage now needed, called a *page,* can then be brought into main memory. Pages are usually of a fixed size and therefore may be deposited into physical storage wherever a space of that size can be found.

Because the current location is entered into a mapping table whenever a page is introduced into physical storage, dynamic address translation can provide up-to-date interpretation of addresses (see below). This allows the effect of dynamic relocation without the overhead of actually modifying the addresses within instructions. The determination of which pages are to be removed from physical storage to make room for the needed incoming pages has itself been the object of research. Also, the question of pages of variable size is being studied, since a fixed size inevitably leads to some wasted space whenever a block of programs or data does not fill exactly a multiple of the page size.

Although it is possible to implement in software the mapping described above, the overhead is considerable, and recent computers that incorporate virtual storage concepts have provided a hardware implementation for dynamic address translation. In addition, several computers have introduced an additional concept, *segmentation.* Here, one views virtual storage as having identifiable regions, called *segments,* each containing enough addresses so that programs or data stored in them will not

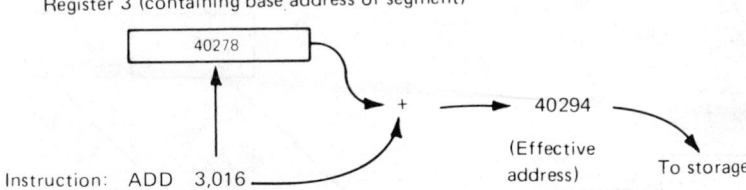

Fig. 1. Relocation within virtual storage.

try to assign the same addresses more than once, even if they expand during execution by means of dynamic allocation of additional virtual storage. Segments are thus different from pages in that page boundaries assume a predetermined relationship to blocks of physical storage, whereas segments are viewed as functional subdivisions of virtual storage (and usually contain a number of virtual pages).

An important motivation behind the use of segments is the facility for sharing programs and data. In physical storage systems, one often finds programs written so that all addresses are given as displacements from a *base* address; and this is implemented by maintaining the base address in a hardware register. In this way, different copies of the program (or data) can be placed into storage in different locations while executing. Similarly, by establishing a *convention* that programs and data be *address-free* (i.e., that all addresses be represented as displacements from the expected contents of a base register) and by arranging for base addresses of segments to be maintained in registers during execution, relocation within virtual storage can be accomplished. This is illustrated in Fig. 1. Now individual users of the system may "load"

programs or data into different areas of virtual storage (i.e., into different segments), and can arrange to share the copies that are actually loaded into physical storage through the paging mechanism. Fig. 2 illustrates this sharing.

Various hardware devices are being included in some new systems to facilitate the implememtation of paging, and—to a lesser extent—segmentation. One example of a hardware implementation of the dynamic address translation described above is given in Fig. 3. The virtual address is separated into three parts. The first, called the *segment number*, can be viewed (with an appropriate number of trailing zeroes) as the base address of a segment of virtual storage. In the implementation as shown in Fig. 3, however, it is used as an index into a *segment table* maintained for that user to retrieve the appropriate page table; i.e., a table showing the virtual-to-physical mapping for those pages of the referenced segment for which the mapping exists. Once the page-table base address has been retrieved from the segment table, the page number obtained as the second part of the original virtual address is used as an index into the page table to retrieve the physical address corresponding to the base of that

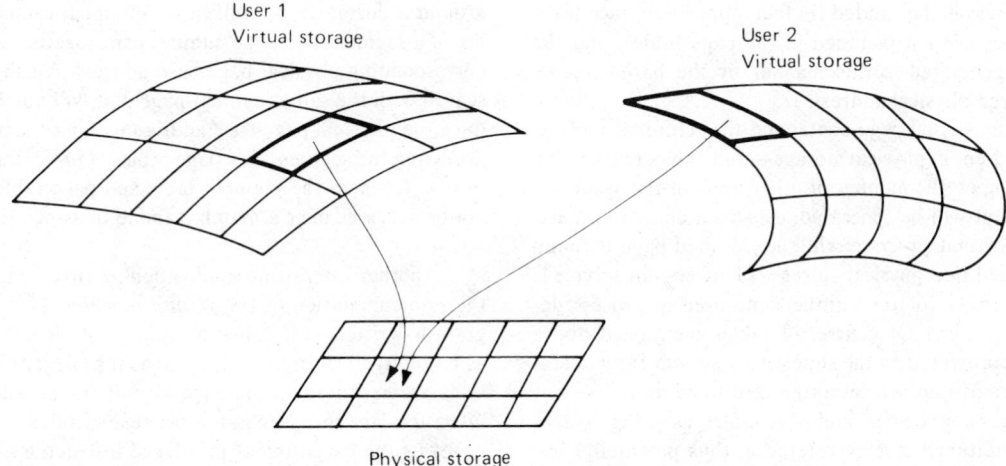

Fig. 2. Sharing in physical storage.

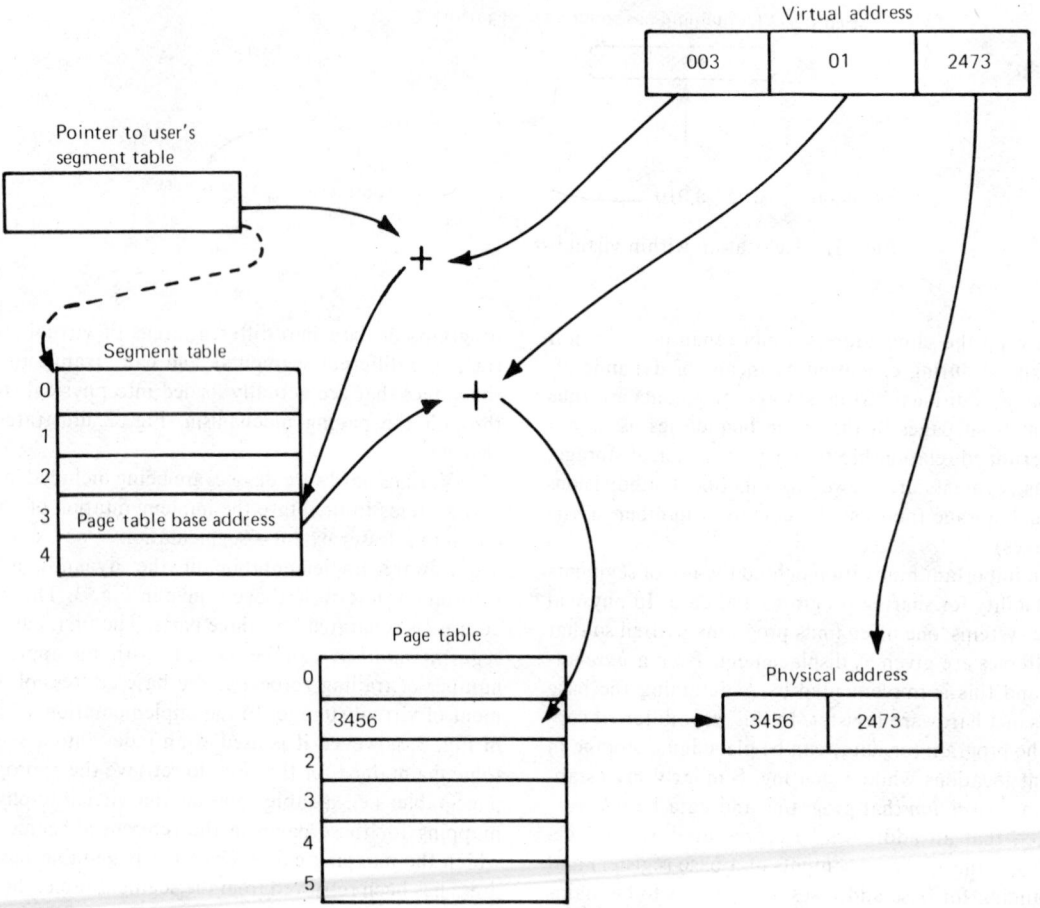

Fig. 3. Mapping from virtual address to physical address.

page in virtual storage. The third part of the original virtual address is then added (in fact, appended, since trailing zeroes are not included in the page table), and the result—generated in this manner by the hardware—is the desired physical address.

If the virtual page containing the reference address is not present in physical storage—and only a few will be, depending on the number of other users of the system—an interupt will be generated, causing a delay in the execution of that program while the desired page is found and loaded into physical storage. (This system service is the substitute for the cumbersome overlay process described earlier.) Of course all tables mentioned above must be protected by the supervisory system from access by programs that are not authorized to do so.

Accessing segment and page tables, as in Fig. 3, does imply additional storage reference, thus potentially implying a large overhead. Several hardware systems include a provisions for some *associative storage*, which re-

tains several of the most recent mapping results. Thus, around a dozen entries will be maintained, each consisting of a segment and page number pair, together with the corresponding physical page-base address. A subsequent search with the same segment-page pair will quickly produce the physical page-base address without the need for accessing the segment and page tables. This is illustrated in Fig. 4, where the segment table and page table would not be accessed once a match is found in associative storage.

Another interesting application of virtual storage is the implementation of the *virtual machine*. Here a program is written as if it had a segment of virtual storage as its physical storage, and most (nonprivileged) instructions are executed on the hardware at full speed. When interrupts are thus generated because of missing virtual pages or the execution of privileged instructions, the intended system services are provided by means more conducive to an environment in which several users are ac-

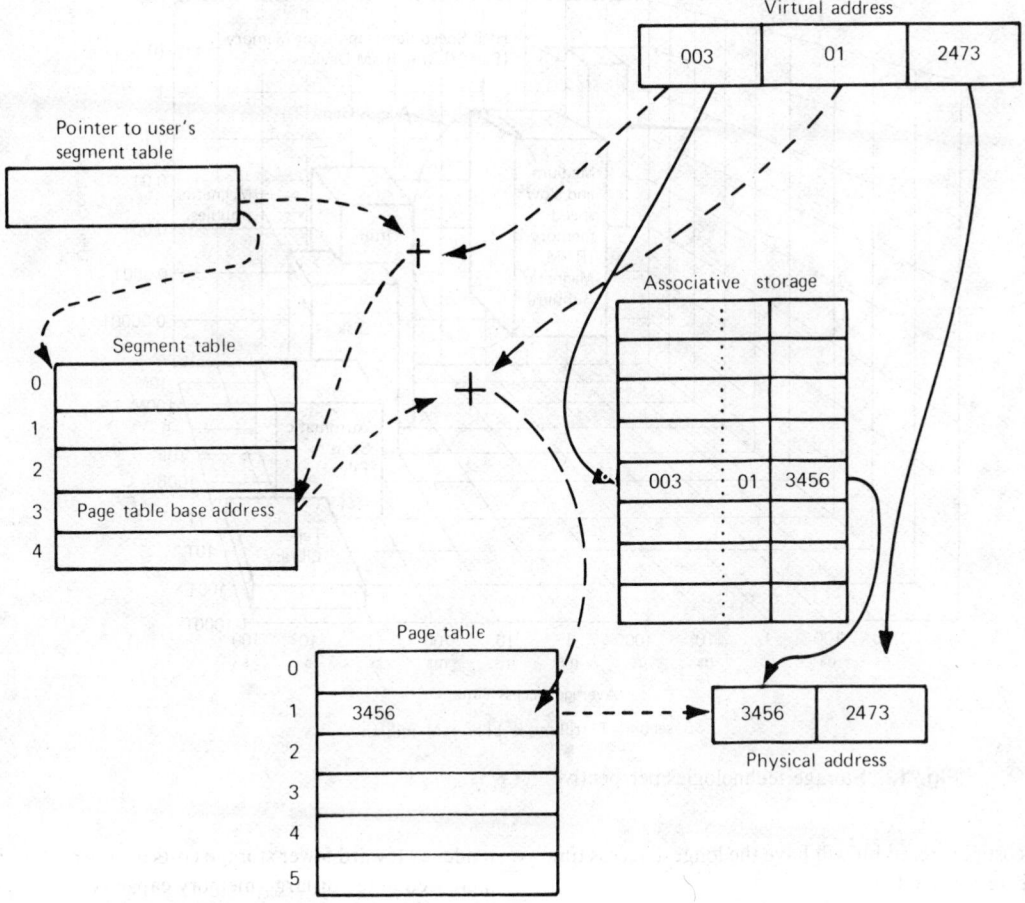

Fig. 4. Mapping from virtual address to physical address, showing the use of associative storage.

tually sharing the hardware. In addition, because paging services are provided for the bulk of virtual storage, large storage can be simulated for each virtual storage machine at a fraction of the overhead incurred in the planning and implementation of overlay processing. To the users of such a system, it appears as if each one has a different physical (or software) system on which to run a program.

REFERENCES

1969. Rosin, Robert F. "Supervisory and Monitor Systems," *Computing Surveys* **1**, *No. 1*:37–54 (March).
1970. Denning, Peter J. "Virtual Memory," *Computing Surveys* **2**, *No. 3*:153–190 (September).
1974. Shaw, Alan C. *The Logical Design of Operating Systems.* Englewood Cliffs, NJ: Prentice-Hall.

B. A. GALLER

STORAGE HIERARCHY

For articles on related subjects *see* ADDRESSING; CACHE MEMORY; COMPUTER SYSTEMS; JOSEPHSON JUNCTION DEVICE; MEMORY: Main; MEMORY: Auxiliary; ONE-LEVEL MEMORY; STORAGE ALLOCATION; and VIRTUAL MEMORY.

Computing systems designed for a broad range of data processing applications must include a number of memory functions which are normally provided by a set of data storage subsystems. Each member of this set will have, within the total system, a unique capacity, access time, and cost of manufacture per stored bit. The reason for this is that the economics which govern the manufacture of storage structures is such that a structure with an access time which is close to the cycle time of the central processing unit will have a relatively high cost of manufacture per stored bit, while the storage structure with the

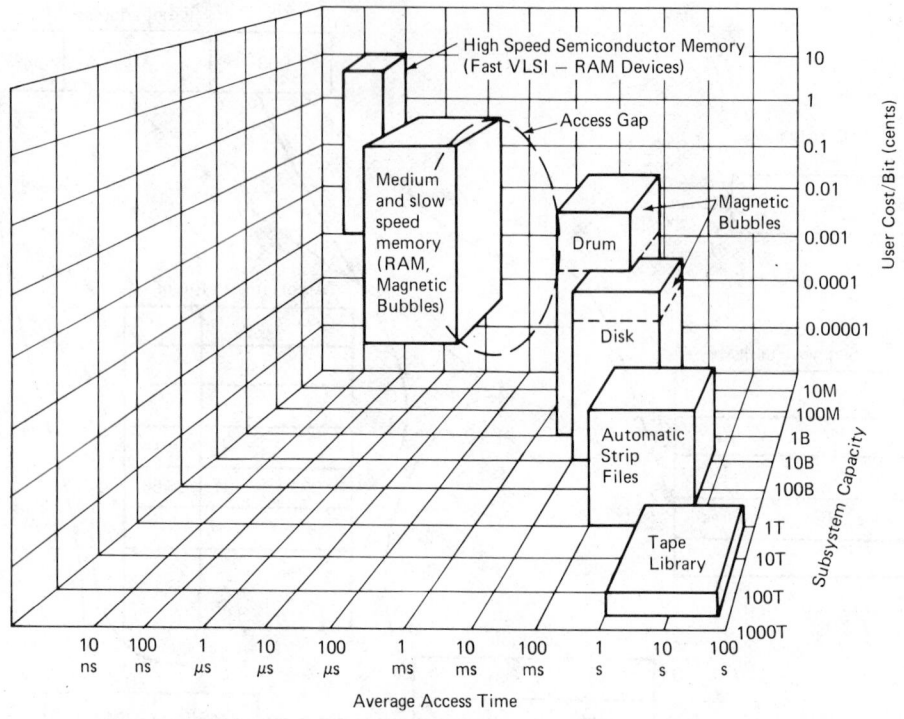

Fig. 1. Storage technologies perspective.

lowest cost per stored bit will have the longest access time and greatest capacity.

Fig. 1 lists a number of technologies that are currently used to implement data storage structures, and shows the approximate relationship between capacity, access time, and costs perceived by the user. The set of memory boxes depicted in Fig. 1 is called a *storage hierarchy,* and in one form or another has always been associated with data processing systems. In recent years, the storage hierarchy has become the focus of increasing attention from systems and hardware designers.

The shape and size of the storage systems depicted in Fig. 1 change with the capability and cost of available technology. Today, semiconductor devices are the dominant memory technology for both cache (high-speed memory) and main memory (medium- to slow-speed) applications. These have largely replaced the ferrite cores used in main memories during the past two decades. During the 1980s, magnetic bubble technology will be introduced for certain storage hierarchy and system residence applications. Due to technological advances in the techniques used for very large-scale integration (VLSI) in semiconductor and magnetic bubble memory products, substantial increases in density of stored information will take place during the next ten years, thus accelerating the

tendency toward lower storage costs on a per bit basis and increased usage of large memory capacity.

Automatic Storage Hierarchies—How They Work. Two distinct but somewhat overlapping approaches to the manipulation of stored data have evolved, each changing its form as technologies improved. The first, historically, has evolved as a data management approach and has come into being mainly as a consequence of the *access gap* depicted in Fig. 1.

Data Management Approach. The separation between access-time capability (and cost per bit) of solid-state storage devices and electromechanical storage devices resulted in system designs of the type shown in Fig. 2. Note that the user has access to a limited amount of directly addressable storage of the type shown on the left-hand side of the access gap in Fig. 1, while, to gain access to storage units on the right side of the access gap, the user must invoke channel-attached bulk store. More recently, *virtual memory* schemes have been implemented in which the user gives up some direct control in return for the ability to run a program (or more than one program if it is a multiprogramming application) even though total program size exceeds main memory capac-

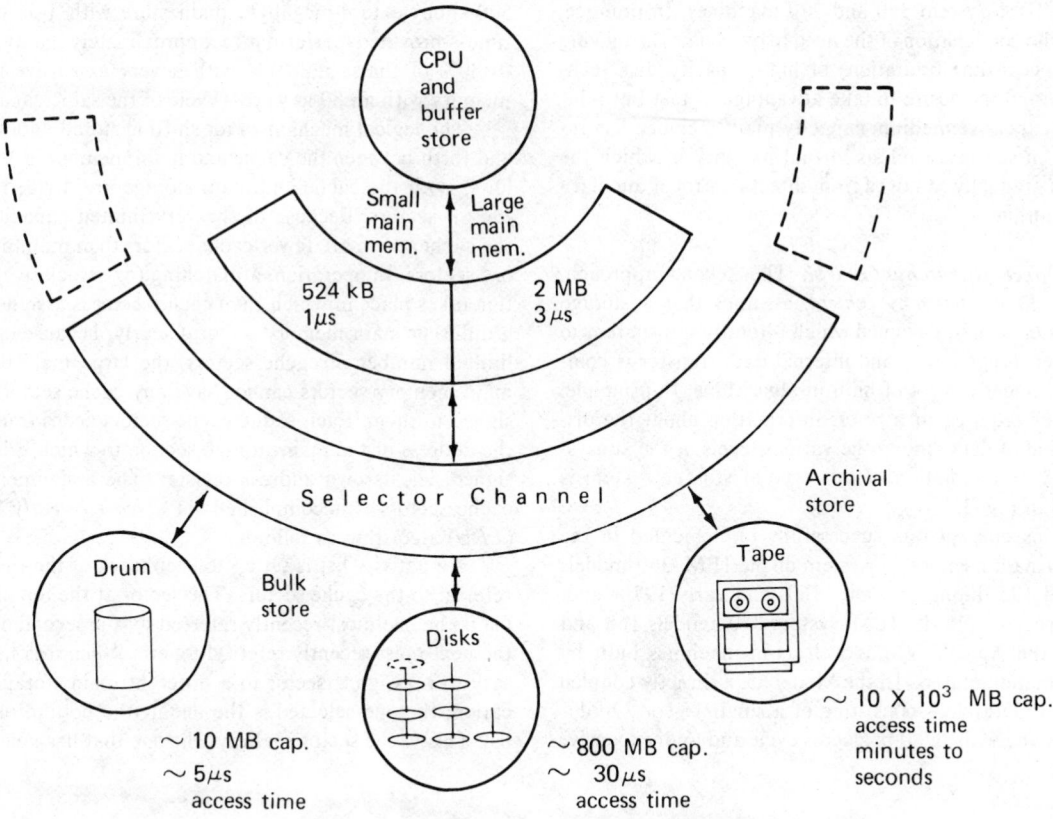

Fig. 2. Channel-switched storage system.

ity. This is accomplished by treating main memory plus a much larger amount of disk storage as one large main memory and moving portions of data stored on the disk into and out of the real main memory so that the user nearly perceives the rapid access performance of real main memory while using the much greater amounts of lower cost storage available on the disks. This is carried out as follows.

When a computer program is placed into a virtual storage system, it is automatically divided into small sections called *pages*. These pages are assigned to larger groups called *segments*. Initially, a page can occupy real main memory, but as real main memory becomes needed for some other task, the page of data is transferred to external page storage on a disk. When required again by the data processing job, the page is automatically shifted back through the channels into the main memory. The process of shifting pages back and forth between main memory and disk files is called *paging*.

On many systems, a hardware unit called a *dynamic address translator* automatically identifies a virtual address inquiry in terms of segment number, page number within the segment, and the position of the record with

reference to the beginning of the page. To speed program execution, the dynamic address-translation unit contains a translation *look-aside buffer* (small associated memory—*q.v*), which holds the addresses of previously referenced pages located in real main memory. If a real memory location for a referenced page is found, time need not be spent on a search of previously stored segment and page tables that indicate the locations of all pages in the storage system.

From a historic standpoint, it is interesting to observe that data exchange operations (read "virtual memory") of the type just described were used in data processing machines that were in serial production as far back as the early 1960s. In 1962, the Burroughs B5000 series machines swapped variable-length program segments between fixed-head disk files and main memory-core storage. Other pioneers in this area were a number of Univac machines, which, as early as 1963, interchanged programs between main memory and fast access drums. Closer to the present time, a virtual memory data-management scheme was invoked in the RCA Spectra series of machines, beginning in 1970. Most recently, similar capability has been made available in a number of the IBM System 360 and 370 machines. In practice, then, the combination of the need to overcome the moving arm access time limitations of high-capacity disk technology and the desire to take advantage of fast but relatively expensive medium-capacity main memory has resulted in schemes such as virtual memory in which the user is gradually removed from direct control of ancillary bulk storage.

Direct Hierarchy Control. The second approach, called *direct hierarchy control,* assumes that a storage subsystem can be designed which is totally transparent to the user/programmer and internal data transfer is completely under control of built-in algorithms. In principle, the user requires no *a priori* information about the distribution of data among the various levels of the subsystem. A representation of this type of storage system is shown in Fig. 3.

This concept was successfully implemented in the cache/main memory subsystem of the IBM/360 models 85 and 195 during the late 1960s and early 1970s and, more recently, in the IBM System 370/models 168 and 3033, the Amdahl V6, as well as in machines built by other manufacturers. In the Model 85, a directly coupled storage hierarchy—consisting of a small 16- or 32-kilobyte cache with an 80-ns access cycle and an inexpensive

500-kilobyte to 4-megabyte main store with 1-μs cycle time—provided performance approximately equivalent to 80% of that obtainable with a very expensive main memory with an 80-ns access cycle of the same capacity.

The logical mechanism for shifting stored data back and forth between the cache and main memory is as follows: Both the cache and main storage are divided into *logical* sectors. Because of the very limited capacity of the cache, there are fewer cache sectors than main memory sectors. In operation, a matching (or associative) action takes place in which each cache sector is assigned to a different main memory sector. Clearly, because of the limited number of cache sectors, the large majority of main memory sectors cannot have any cache sectors assigned to them. Each of the cache sectors keeps track of the address of the main storage section to which it is assigned, via its own address register. The assignment of cache sectors is accomplished via a *least recently used* (*LRU*) algorithm as follows.

An activity list is set up to keep track of the time of referral to the cache sectors. The sector at the top of the list is the one most recently referred to; the second one is the next most recently referred to; etc. When it is necessary to reassign a sector to a different main storage location, the one selected is the one at the bottom of the list. This cache sector is always the one that has gone the

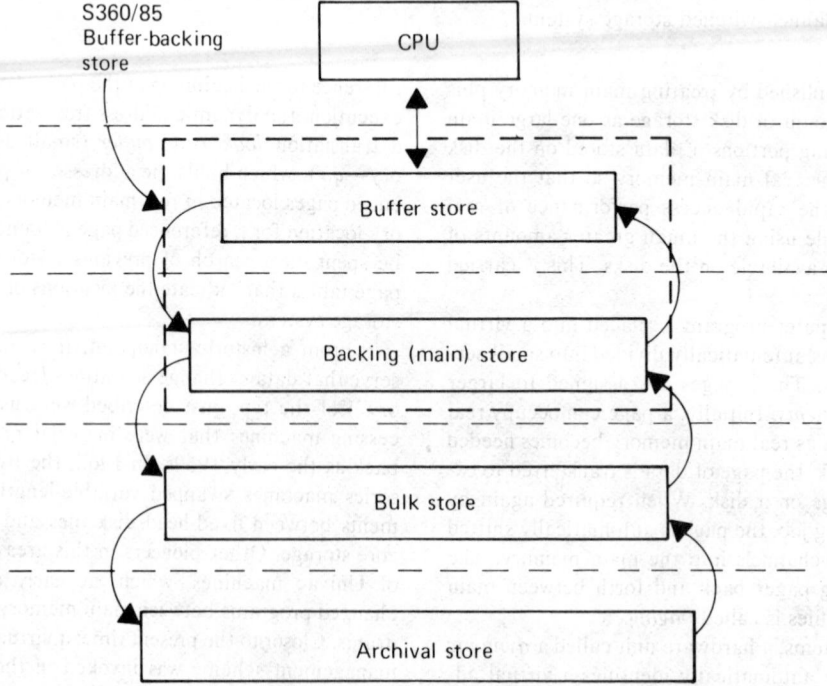

Fig. 3.   Directly coupled hierarchical storage system.

longest without being referred to. Conversely, when a cache sector is called out, it always moves to the top of the list, and all other sectors fall down one position.

In many of the current machine designs, two CPU cycles are required to extract data from the cache; the first cycle is used to interrogate the sector address registers to determine if the data is in the cache, and the second cycle is then used to read the data out. If the data is not present, additional cycles are required until a data block is loaded into the cache from main memory. In comparison with the previously described virtual memory scheme, the main difference is that the data swapping is directed, to a large extent, by the "wired-in," least recently used algorithm rather than software, and, because of the great compression of the access gap, the very fast processor can afford to wait a few cycles while data is moved from main memory to the cache, rather than engage in other jobs. More likely, the processor will be used to manage some of the software overhead required to operate the virtual memory part of the system. This latter action occurs in particular in recent machines, such as the IBM 370 model 168 and Amdahl V6, where there is both a cache/main memory subsystem and also a virtual memory management of the main memory/disk file part of the total hierarchy. As can be seen from this necessarily brief discussion, important system advantages are gained from technologies that economically reduce the ratio of access times between various levels of the hierarchy.

In summary, fast semiconductor storage placed in close proximity to the logic structure in the CPU yields the desired machine speed, while the large "main memory" provides the desired storage capacity. The combination results in a total memory system with an actual access time approaching that of the cache, but at a cost per bit and capacity approximating that of the main memory. This successful operation is based entirely on the fact that in most of the applications for which the system is designed, *the location of memory addresses generated by real-life user programs is not random.* Indeed, to put this in a more positive way, the phenomenon that permits a hardware-controlled hierarchy to operate is the *clustering of addressing patterns* in actual application programs run through the machine.

It is interesting and useful to note that, during the development of the System/360 Model 85, an alternate system was simulated which was in all respects identical to the proposed Model 85 except that the two-level cache/main memory hierarchy was replaced by a single-level store with cache access time and main memory capacity. (This single level store is called an *infinite cache* in today's terminology.) The performance of this simulated machine thus represented an upper bound on the performance of the proposed Model 85, and in fact was a benchmark against which the performance of the realiz-

able Model 85 could be measured. By using a very large number of "trace" tapes containing about 250,000 instructions each as input to both a simulation of the "real" machine and the "benchmark" single-level machine operating at cache speed, it was determined that the real machine could operate at an instruction execution rate of between 66% and 96% of the benchmark machine. In addition to this finding, it was also determined (by using the same set of trace tapes as input) that the average probability of finding data wanted for a fetch in CPU buffer memory (or cache) was 0.97. Looking at this quite remarkable result in another way, the simulation studies indicated that if the locations of the addresses derived from the tapes were truly random, the probability of finding data wanted in the buffer would be very, very low indeed. Clearly, the hierarchy worked precisely because real programs are *not* random in their addressing patterns.

The previous discussion of virtual and main memory/cache operation has described information exchange between the main memory and CPU "buffer memory" members of the hierarchy and also between fast access secondary shortage devices such as disk files on the "slow side" of the access gap and main memory on the "fast side" of the access gap. If the amount of high-speed auxiliary storage available to a particular user is limited by relatively high cost (as is usually the case with disks), and the applications (an on-line database, for example) tend to collect increasing amounts of data with the passing of time, a systematic means of migrating (sometimes called *trickling*) momentarily unneeded data on the disks to lower cost (and longer access time) levels of the hierarchy is necessary. Likewise, a scheme must be devised to bring back desired data into the higher-speed devices (sometimes called *percolating*) with sufficient speed to be acceptable to the user.

The exact criteria by which data stored in on-line disks or other forms of bulk storage migrates to very low-cost archival storage, such as automatic strip files or tape storage libraries, are of great practical importance. As a brief example, in operations of the storage hierarchy for on-line database applications managed by TSS/360 (time-sharing system/360), the initial criterion used to govern the distribution of data among various categories of stored data (such as data on disks mounted on drives; data on disk packs, but not mounted; data on tape reels, not mounted) was the date on which a volume of data (disk or reel of tape) was last used. Specifically, a volume of data recorded and stored on a disk was migrated to a lower level, depending only on the length of time since its last use. The details of the scheme have been designed to enable inclusion of other criteria as they are deemed necessary (Lin and Mattson, 1972).

The very important principle of combining storage technologies with significantly different access-time differentials into a *hardware-controlled memory hierarchy* that appears as a single level of storage to the programmer was demonstrated as early as 1962 in the pioneering Manchester University Atlas machine. In 1965, M. V. Wilkes also suggested the use of a slave memory in conjunction with a large store as a scheme to implement dynamic storage allocation. The Model 85 high-speed, buffer-main memory hierarchy is analogous to this scheme and is somewhat related to the combination of small content-addressable memories and large auxiliary stores used in multiprogrammed time-sharing systems. All these systems exploit strong regularities in the statistics of the instruction-addressing patterns in order to achieve success.

Technologies for Storage Hierarchies.

Magnetic disk files have been a vital element in data processing systems for the past ten years, and will certainly be important for the next ten years. The best of these devices have very high reliability, nonvolatility, relatively low access times (in the tens of milliseconds) and medium to large storage capacities (the IBM 3350 disk file has a capacity of 317 million bytes per spindle). The user cost per stored bit is attractively low (for rental equipment, a typical cost for the industry is in the vicinity of $10 per megabyte per month). Storage devices of this type dominate current bulk-storage systems.

Areal densities in magnetic recording have increased by a factor of about ten every five or six years during the past two decades and, since current areal densities are rather far from theoretical limits, it seems reasonable to assume that densities will continue to increase at a similar rate. This means that further decreases in cost per bit to the customer can be expected. However, because of the need to eliminate (or at least compress) the access gap described earlier, and because the applications trend is toward extremely large amounts of very rapid access storage, it would be desirable for disk files eventually to be displaced by superior technologies. The key to this accomplishment is the further development of solid-state technologies that can populate as many levels of the storage hierarchy as possible with memory structures whose capacities, access time, modularity, and costs substantially eliminate the access gap characteristic of present data processing systems. The main hopes in this area presently lie with magnetic bubbles and further advances in semiconductor devices.

The onset of VLSI semiconductor technology and

Fig. 4.   Innotronics model 410 disk drive, external view.

the consequent development of high-volume, low-cost mini- and microprocessors has stimulated the need for nonvolatile, highly portable data storage devices. This requirement is now satisfied by *floppy disk* technology (see Fig. 4). The information is stored on the magnetic surface of small, flexible diskettes which can be easily transported and stored. The diskettes are inserted into an inexpensive magnetic disk file unit in order to update or read out the magnetically recorded data. These magnetic storage units record in an in-contact mode and, consequently, the diskettes have to be replaced after a certain use time as specified by the manufacturers. In general, these units have relatively long access and latency (*q.v.*) (latency is in the vicinity of 100 milliseconds) and are not used in main memory storage hierarchies of large systems. They are used mainly as data I/O devices for small systems in those applications where long-term storage is either not essential or can be handled by rewriting data on a fresh diskette, and where portability and low cost are the major requirements. Typical of these devices is the Innotronics Corp. model 410 disk drive (Fig. 4).

From a longer-term technological change viewpoint, it is possible that floppy disk technology will, in many applications, be replaced by magnetic bubble systems, once production costs become attractive. Note that magnetic bubbles offer the advantages of nonvolatility, no moving parts, potential low cost, and much higher reliability.

Magnetic bubbles are very small, highly mobile, cylinder-shaped magnetic domains rather easily formed in certain ferrite and other materials. One of these materials (known as an orthoferrite) contains serpentine-shaped magnetic domains in its natural state. Magnetic "bubbles" are formed by applying an external magnetic field to a thin platelet of this material (see Fig. 5) in such a way as to change the shape of the serpentine domains into tiny cylinder-shaped domains in which the axis of the cylinder is oriented along the vertical axis (i.e., in the "thin" direction of the platelet, as shown in Fig. 5). It is important to note that the bubbles, once formed, can be easily moved in any lateral direction by application of extremely small, suitably directed forces created by interaction of the bubble fields with other magnetic fields resulting from electric currents in wiring patterns or other magnetic-field generating structures placed on the platelet (see Fig. 6).

From a device standpoint, the possibility of being

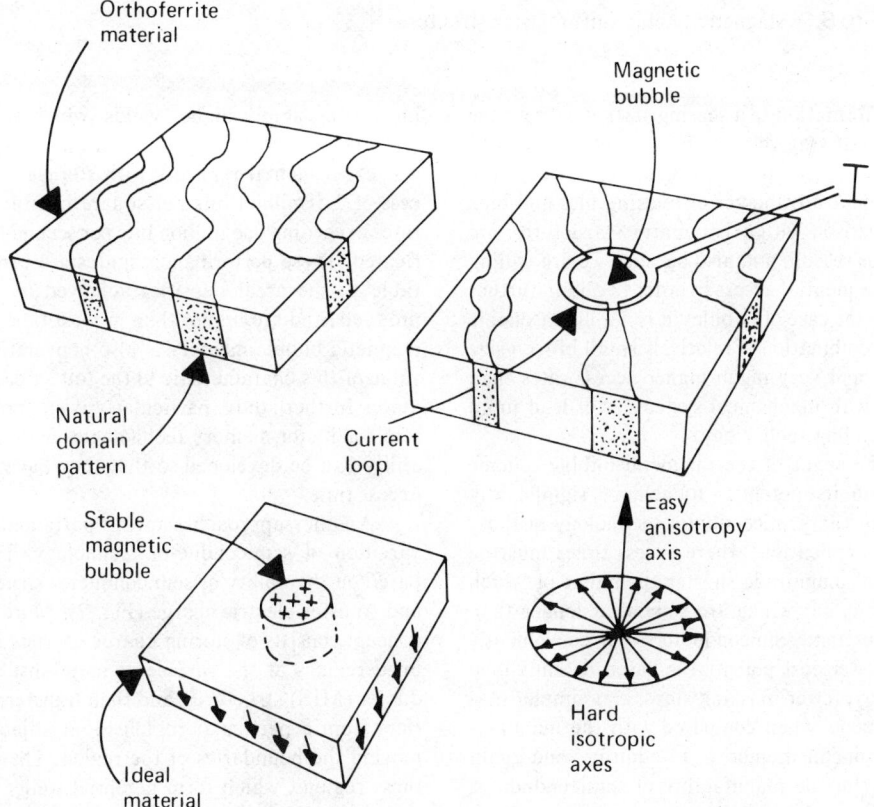

Fig. 5.   Magnetic bubble formation. Magnetization normal to surface permits bubble motion in any direction normal to direction of magnetization.

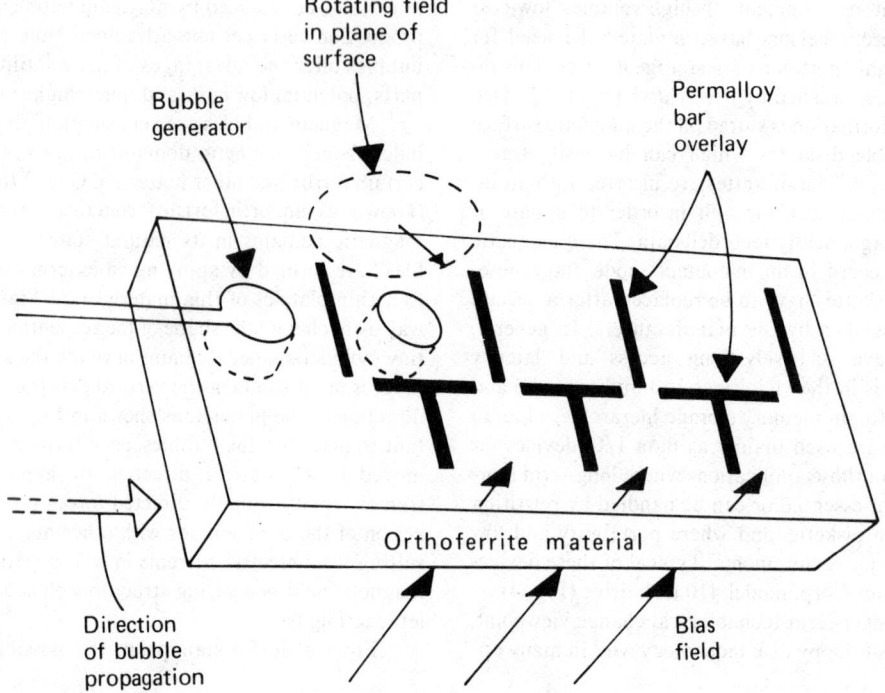

Fig. 6.   Magnetic bubble shift-register structure.

able to move information to a sensing station without the need to attach a driving voltage and ground wire to each bit location is an attractive one. Clearly, some of the enormous economic advantages of rotating files and tape drives, in comparison with existing array structures, are obtained for this reason, and also because we are willing to accept slow sequential access in order to obtain further cost benefits. In the case of bubbles, it is not unreasonable to hope that a combination of relatively small bit-cell size (1 mil or less), and very much higher access rates than are obtainable with mechanical systems, will lead to an acceptable gap-filling technology.

The major impact of the magnetic bubble scheme lies, however, in its potential to achieve significantly lower costs than can semiconductor technology in those storage system applications where access times must be several orders of magnitude shorter than that of which disks are capable, but which are somewhat longer than the access times that semiconductors can conveniently provide. This lower cost potential is based on simplified photolithography, fewer masking steps, and simpler materials requirements when compared with the manufacture of semiconductor memories. In addition, and again unlike the case for the manufacture of semiconductors, relatively small portions of the mask area are susceptible to defects. These simplifications in the basic manufactur-

ing process imply higher yields, which should result in lower cost to the user. In terms of the current state of the art, experimental registers with storage densities in excess of 2.5 million bits per square inch and bit transfer rates exceeding one million bits per second have been fabricated. These performance figures are certainly comparable to the areal densities achieved in available disk products, and are higher than in most tape products. The magnetic bubble memory is also nonvolatile. The added value of this characteristic to the total storage system requires further study, particularly if competitive low-cost semiconductor memory technologies with controlled volatility can be developed so that they have much shorter access time.

Another approach showing particular promise is a variation of semiconductor technology. The concept is based on the ability of semiconductor structures to store and transfer electric charge (Fig. 7). More precisely, the concept consists of storing charge carriers in sharply defined regions at the surface of metal-insulator-semiconductor (MIS) structures, and then transferring these carriers from a particular region to an adjacent region by moving the boundaries of the region. The boundaries of these regions, which form potential wells, are moved by the sequential application of signal voltages to appropriate electrodes on the semiconductor structure. Stored

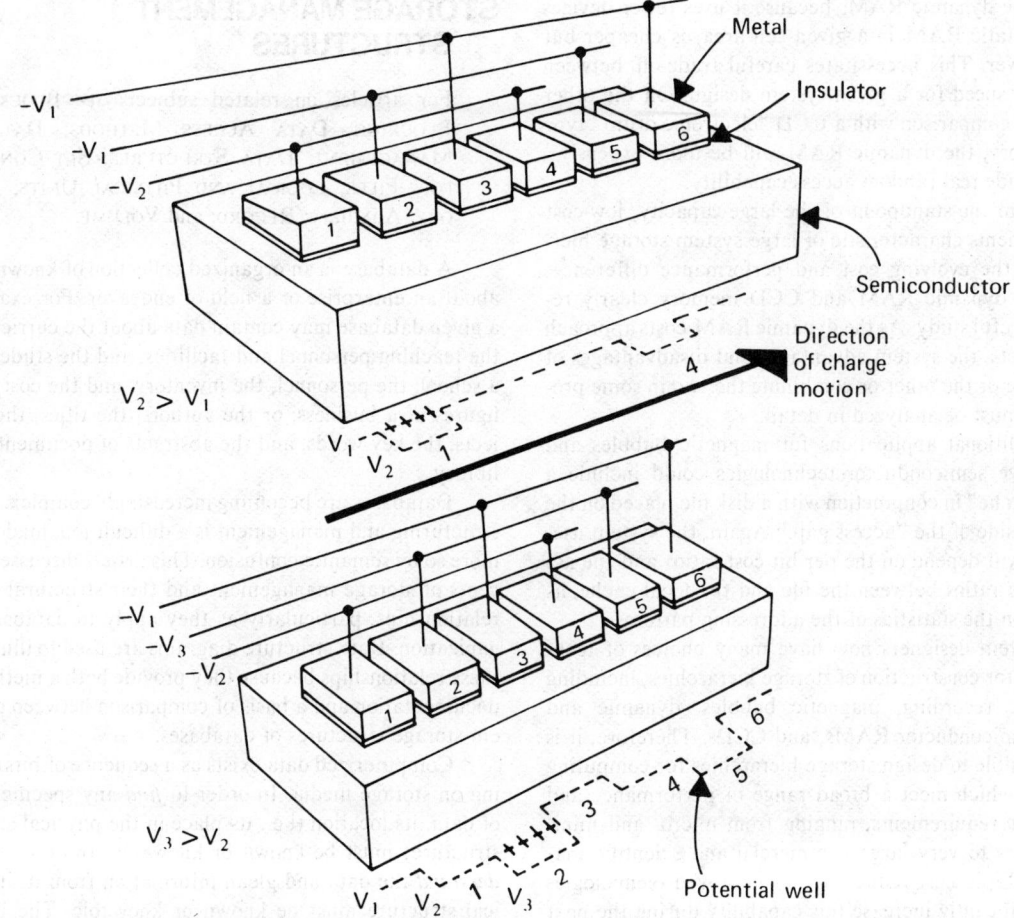

Fig. 7. Charge-coupled device shift-register structure.

charge will move to the new location in accordance with the location of the new potential well boundary.

The action of the *charge-coupled device* (CCD) bears some functional resemblance to that of the bubble scheme, where information is stored and transferred in the form of the stable magnetic domains. In an analogous manner, the charge-coupled scheme uses the charge-storage and transfer property of an integrated MIS structure to store and transfer information. Various useful *sequential* logic and memory devices—such as shift registers, delay lines, and electronic analogs of drums and disks—are conceivable and can be realized by constructing a set of these storage "capacitors" on a single substrate with provision for the manipulation of the potentials to be applied to various electrodes. The charge-coupled memory is volatile, and therefore some type of refresh or regenerative action is needed in a practical memory system. On the other hand, since the scheme does not require sepa-

rate power and ground wires for each stored bit, and since, at the device level, it is a variation of dynamic random access memory (dynamic RAM) now in production, it is likely that very low per bit costs will be obtained.

For system design purposes, the main interest in dynamic RAM is reduction in the number of semiconductor devices required to perform the random access storage function in a given memory cell area on a silicon chip, in comparison with that required by a static RAM. This is accomplished in a similar manner to that of the CCD, namely, by using the capacitance of the device itself as a storage element (Luecke *et al.*, 1973). Also, like the CCD, the memory cell, or element, will lose its information content after some short time interval due to leakage of charge and will have to be refreshed. Unlike the sequential CCD memory, however, the dynamic RAM requires individual signal and power access to each stored bit and therefore has true *random access* capability. In short, the dynamic RAM, because it uses fewer devices than a static RAM in a given cell area, is cheaper but also slower. This necessitates careful trade-off between size and speed for a given system design. On the other hand, in comparison with a CCD "electronic drum" type of memory, the dynamic RAM will be more expensive, but provide real random access capability.

From the standpoint of the large-capacity, low-cost requirements characteristic of large system storage hierarchies, the evolving cost and performance differences between dynamic RAM and CCD memory clearly require careful study. As the dynamic RAM costs approach CCD costs, the system advantages and disadvantages of using one or the other or combining the two in some proportion must be analyzed in detail.

Additional applications for magnetic bubbles and the above semiconductor technologies could include a "local cache" in conjunction with a disk file placed on the channel side of the "access gap." Again, the system usefulness will depend on the per bit cost ratios and the access time ratios between the file and the local cache, as well as on the statistics of the addressing patterns.

System designers now have many choices of technologies for construction of storage hierarchies, including magnetic recording, magnetic bubbles, dynamic and static semiconductor RAMs, and CCDs. Therefore, it is now possible to design storage hierarchies for computing systems which meet a broad range of performance and economic requirements, ranging from micro- and minicomputers to very large commercial and scientific machines. Rapid cost reduction and improved technologies will significantly increase this capability during the next few years.

REFERENCES

1968. Liptay, J. S. "Structural Aspects of the System/360 Model 85—Part II, The Cache," *IBM Systems Journal* 7, *No. 1:* 15–21.
1972. Lin, S. Y. and Mattson, R. L. "Cost-Performance Evaluation of Memory Hierarchies," *IEEE Transactions on Magnetics* (September), pp. 390–392.
1973. Luecke, G., *et al. Semiconductor Memory Design and Application.* New York: McGraw-Hill.
1975. Chang, S. (Ed.). *Magnetic Bubble Technology—Integrated Circuit Magnetics for Digital Storage and Processing.* New York: IEEE Press.
1977. Matick, R. *Computer Storage Systems and Technology.* New York: Wiley.
1977. Hodges, David A. "Microelectronic Memories," *Scientific American* (September).

E. Shapiro

STORAGE MANAGEMENT STRUCTURES

For articles on related subjects *see* BLOCK AND BLOCKING; DATA ACCESS METHODS; DATABASE MANAGEMENT; DATA STRUCTURES, SET CONCEPTS FOR; FILES; LOGICAL AND PHYSICAL UNITS; MEMORY: Auxiliary; RECORD; and VOLUME.

A database is an organized collection of known data about an enterprise or a field of endeavor. For example, a given database may contain data about the curriculum, the teaching personnel and facilities, and the students of a school; the personnel, the inventory, and the cost/sales figures of a business; or the authors, the titles, the subjects, the key words, and the abstracts of documents in a library.

Databases are becoming increasingly complex. Their structuring and management is a difficult job, made even more so by semantic confusion. This article discusses concepts of storage management and their structural interrelationships, particularly as they apply to database organization. Data structure diagrams are used to illustrate these relationships because they provide both a method of documentation and a basis of comparison between different storage structures of databases.

Computerized data exists as a sequence of bits residing on storage media. In order to *find* any specific piece of data, its location (i.e., its place in the physical storage structure) must be known or knowable. In order to *understand* the data and glean information from it, its logical structure must be known or knowable. The bridge between physical storage structure and logical structure is the *allocation structure,* i.e., that element of database systems which deals with the mapping of logically structured data onto physical storage media. [Bachman (1972) gives a detailed history and analysis of storage structures, and this article is, to a considerable extent, derived from his work.]

Data Structure Diagrams. In this article, data structure diagrams are used for the illustrations. Bachman (1969) describes this technique in detail.

The diagramming technique is based on a notation dealing with classes, specifically with classes of entities and the relationships among them. An *entity* in this context is an object or concept under consideration (e.g., "a school" is an entity); an *entity class* is a group of entities that are sufficiently similar in terms of their attributes to be considered collectively. In data structure diagrams, a box is used as a symbol for an entity class; thus, SCHOOL represents the class of schools under consideration.

The arrow "→" is used to symbolize $1:n$ relationships among entity classes; specifically, one occurrence of the entity class at the shaft of the arrow is associated with n (zero, one, or many) occurrences of the entity class at the head of the arrow, thus:

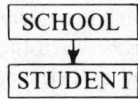

This drawing means:

1. There is a class of entities called "school."
2. There is a class of entities called "student."
3. Any number of students may be associated with a school.
4. Each student is associated with one, and only one, school.

Concepts. The following concepts relate to physical, logical, and allocation structures. They are presented together with the terms that have been given to them; generally, the italicized term is the preferred one. Definitions of the IFIP-ICC vocabulary (1966) are used whenever appropriate.

Physical Concepts

1. A *physical record* is a unit of storage on any medium that may be directly and independently read or written (without need to read and rewrite adjacent physical storage space).
2. A *track* is a unit of a storage medium characterized by most rapid serial transfer of consecutively recorded data. (The concept is most often applied to disks and drums.) A track may be divided into one or more physical records called *sectors*.
3. A *cylinder* (*q.v.*) is a unit of (secondary) storage characterized by the fact that consecutive transfer of data recorded within one cylinder is substantially faster than the consecutive transfer of data recorded on different cylinders. (This concept is primarily disk-oriented.) Cylinders may be subdivided into one or more tracks.
4. A *volume* (*q.v.*—file, physical tape reel, physical file, disk pack, drum, tape file, disk file) is a physical unit of storage capable of having data recorded upon it and being subsequently read. It is usually associated on a 1:1 basis (permanent or temporary) with a storage device. If disk, then it is subdivided into one or more cylinders.
5. A storage *device* is a unit of (secondary) storage hardware capable of permanently or temporarily

holding a volume and having read/write (and possibly cylinder selection) mechanisms for the volume.

Storage devices should be differentiated from I/O devices, which are hardware units basically concerned with bringing data into the system from the outside world, or transmitting processed data back out, such as card readers and printers.

Logical Concepts

1. A *field* (data item, item, elementary item, based variable) is a unit of information storage which holds the value associated with some attribute. The value may be represented as a character string, a number, a boolean value, or a pointer that will indirectly lead to the value.
2. A *logical record* is a unit of logical storage created by the execution of a WRITE/STORE command, which may subsequently be reaccessed by the execution of a READ/RETRIEVE/FIND command. A logical record may be subdivided into zero, one, or more fields.
3. A *page* is a unit of logical storage, characterized by logically contiguous addressability when resident in main storage. It is capable of holding zero, one, or more logical records.
4. A *logical file* (area, realm, segment) is a named unit of logical storage which serves as a container for logical records. It is subdivided into one or more pages.

Allocation Structure Concepts

1. A *block* is a unit of media allocation which serves as the data transfer unit between main and secondary storage. One or more (generally, consecutively recorded) physical record(s) may be mapped into it.
2. An *extent* is a unit of media allocation, representing a contiguously addressed portion of a volume. It is subdivided into one or more blocks for physical access.

Three hierarchies exist within the concepts established above. They are:

1. Physical storage structure hierarchy (device/volume/cylinder/track/physical record).
2. Logical storage structure hierarchy (logical file/page/logical record/field).
3. Storage allocation structure hierarchy (extent/block).

These three hierarchies may be observed throughout the study of storage structures; the interrelationships between their elements permit the translation of logical READ/WRITE operations into the necessary physical manipulation commands.

Physical Storage Structure. Fig. 1 shows a disk volume (removable disk pack) consisting of a number of cylinders, each cylinder consisting of a number of tracks, and each track consisting of a number of physical records; "a number of" should be interpreted here as zero, one, several, or many. The diagram also illustrates a "sometime 1:1" relationship between a volume and a storage device, "sometime" being those times when the volume is mounted (A "sometime 1:1" relationship is illustrated by a dashed line *without* an arrowhead. A "sometime 1:*n*" relationship, such as a magnetic cartridge storage device with a number of removable cartridges, would be illustrated by a dashed line *with* an arrowhead.)

On a fixed-head magnetic drum there is a "permanent 1:1" relationship between the concepts of storage device and volume, and a "permanent 1:1" relationship between the concepts of volume and cylinder; the three concepts are merged. These merged concepts are represented by a single entity class, illustrated at the top of Fig. 2. At the middle and bottom are the entity classes supporting the track and physical record concepts, as before.

On magnetic tape, the concepts of volume, cylinder, and track are merged, thus making the physical storage structure of the tape different. Fig. 3 shows this difference, also illustrating the removability of the magnetic tape volume from the device—i.e., the "sometime 1:1" relationship.

Logical Storage Structure. The elements of logical storage structures are logical files, pages, logical records, and fields.

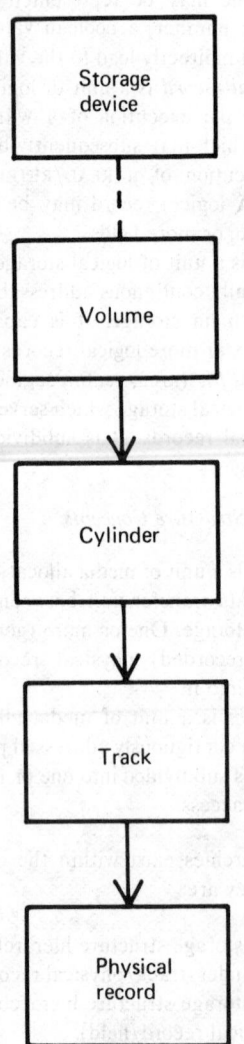

Fig. 1.   Physical storage structure for removable disk storage.

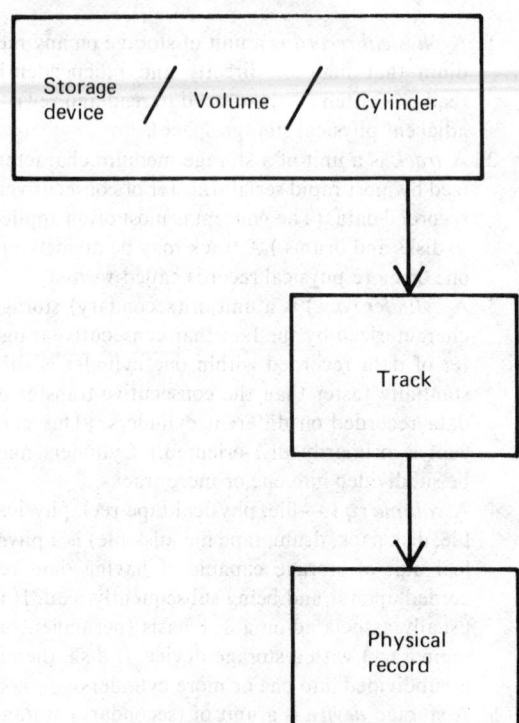

Fig. 2.   Physical storage structure for drum.

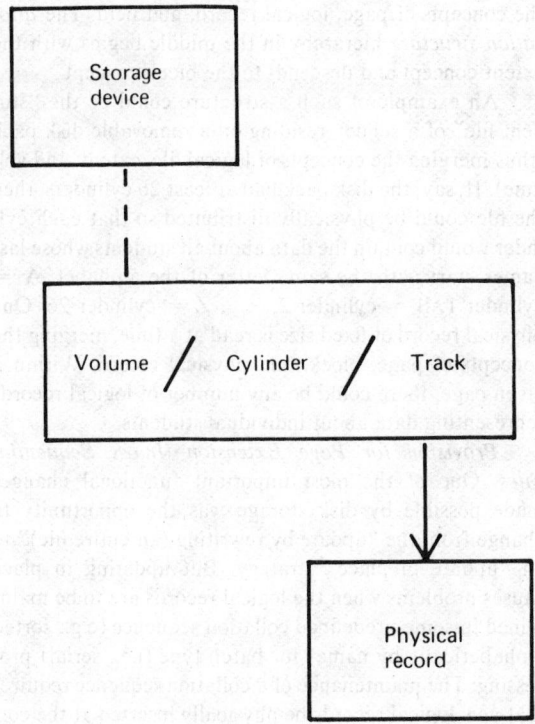

Fig. 3.   Physical storage structure for magnetic tape.

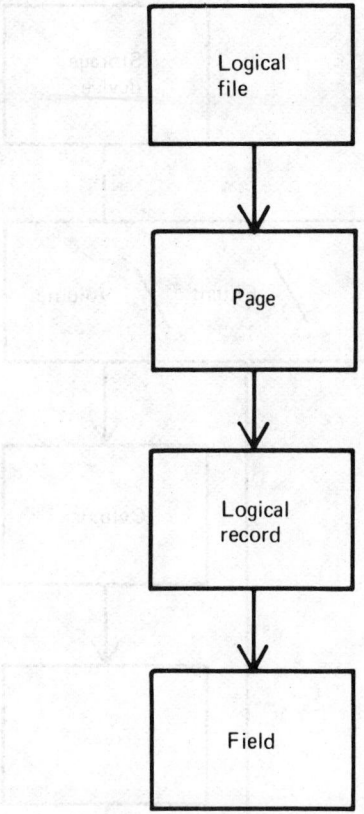

Fig. 4.   Logical storage structure.

Fig. 4 illustrates the hierarchy of these concepts: The logical file consisting of one or more page(s) which in turn hold one or more logical record(s), the containers for fields.

The page concept is introduced here because it represents the point where main storage addressability is overlaid on the logical structure; i.e., structured data is brought into main memory as a page. Logical records are directly addressable by a program within a page in main storage. The fields are, in turn, directly addressable within a record that is within that resident page.

Storage Allocation Structure. In order to achieve their assigned functions as containers of data, the logical storage structure concepts require physical storage existence; i.e., physical storage must be allocated to the logical structure entities. the allocation structure hierarchy is shown in the center of Fig. 5 and in all succeeding figures. It consists of the concepts of *extent* and *block*. The extent is the concept of gross or coarse allocation (i.e., the assignment of a portion, or all, of a volume to physically hold a portion, or all, of a logical file). The block is a finer allocation concept, which relates a page of the logical structure hierarchy to a physical record of the storage structure hierarchy. The role of these

allocation concepts (extent and block) is to join the physical and logical storage structure concepts into an integrated whole, allowing the storage-processing algorithms to map logical structures onto the appropriate physical storage structures.

Storage Structure of Removable Disk Storage.

Blocked Files. Fig. 5 uses the allocation concepts of *extent* and *block* to integrate the physical storage structure shown in Fig. 1 with the logical storage structure of Fig. 4. In Fig. 5, the blocked-record logical file is shown, mapped onto removable-disk storage, while maintaining the one logical file to one volume basis. The three storage hierarchies (logical, allocation, and physical) are very clearly seen in this data structure diagram, since the entity classes implementing the concepts are drawn vertically and in parallel. The *physical storage structure* on the right begins with the storage-device concept and descends through the concepts of volume, cylinder, track, and physical record. The *logical storage structure* on the left begins with logical file concept and descends through

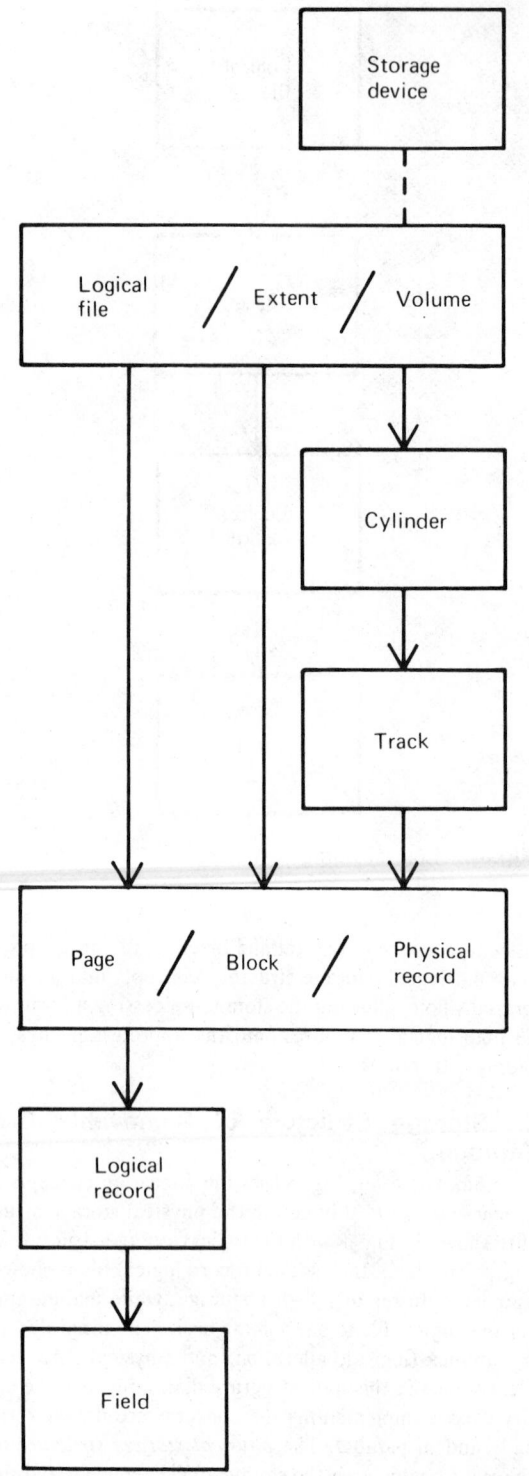

Fig. 5. Storage structure for blocked records on removable disk storage.

the concepts of page, logical record, and field. The *allocation structure* hierarchy in the middle begins with the extent concept and descends to the block concept.

An example of such a structure could be the "student file" of a school, residing on a removable disk pack (thus merging the concepts of logical file, extent, and volume). If, say, the disk pack had at least 26 cylinders, then the file could be physically distributed so that each cylinder would contain the data about all students whose last names start with the same letter of the alphabet: A = cylinder 1, B = cylinder 2, ..., Z = cylinder 26. One physical record of fixed size is read at a time, merging the concepts of page, block, and physical record. Within a given page, there could be any number of logical records representing data about individual students.

Provision for Page Extension: Index Sequential Files. One of the most important functional changes made possible by disk storage was the opportunity to change from the "update by rewriting (an entire file)" to an "update in place" strategy. But updating in place causes problems when the logical records are to be maintained in some predefined collation sequence (e.g., sorted alphabetically by name) for batch type (i.e., serial) processing: The maintenance of a collation sequence requires that new logical records be physically inserted at the correct point in a page. Therefore, provision must be made for the extension effectively to allow the page to grow when new logical records are to be inserted.

Growth potential is provided by establishing separate entity classes (IFIP, 1966) for the page and block concepts. At file creation time, one block is allocated to each page, and a group of blocks is reserved for overflow. When an existing page needs to grow to support logical record insertion, an overflow block is allocated and appended to the page. This strategy is typically adopted for index sequential files.

Fig. 6 illustrates this structure. The page and block concepts have now been split into separate entity classes, and there is an "alternative $1:n$" relationship between them: A page *may* consist of a variable number of blocks, but a block *need not be* associated with a page. Unassociated blocks, which are held in inventory and are available overflow blocks, belong to the extent; the forked arrow designates this alternative relationship; namely, that a given block belongs either to a page or to an extent, but not to both. (The available block inventory is equivalent to the available space list in list processing.)

Linked Sequential Files. For handling very dynamic files in a volume, a specialized mapping is desirable. One of these is called *linked sequential* mapping. It has two important features as compared to the example of Fig. 6. The logical file is subordinate to the extent (see Fig. 7) so that many small temporary files can be created and destroyed within the extent; blocks, rather than being ap-

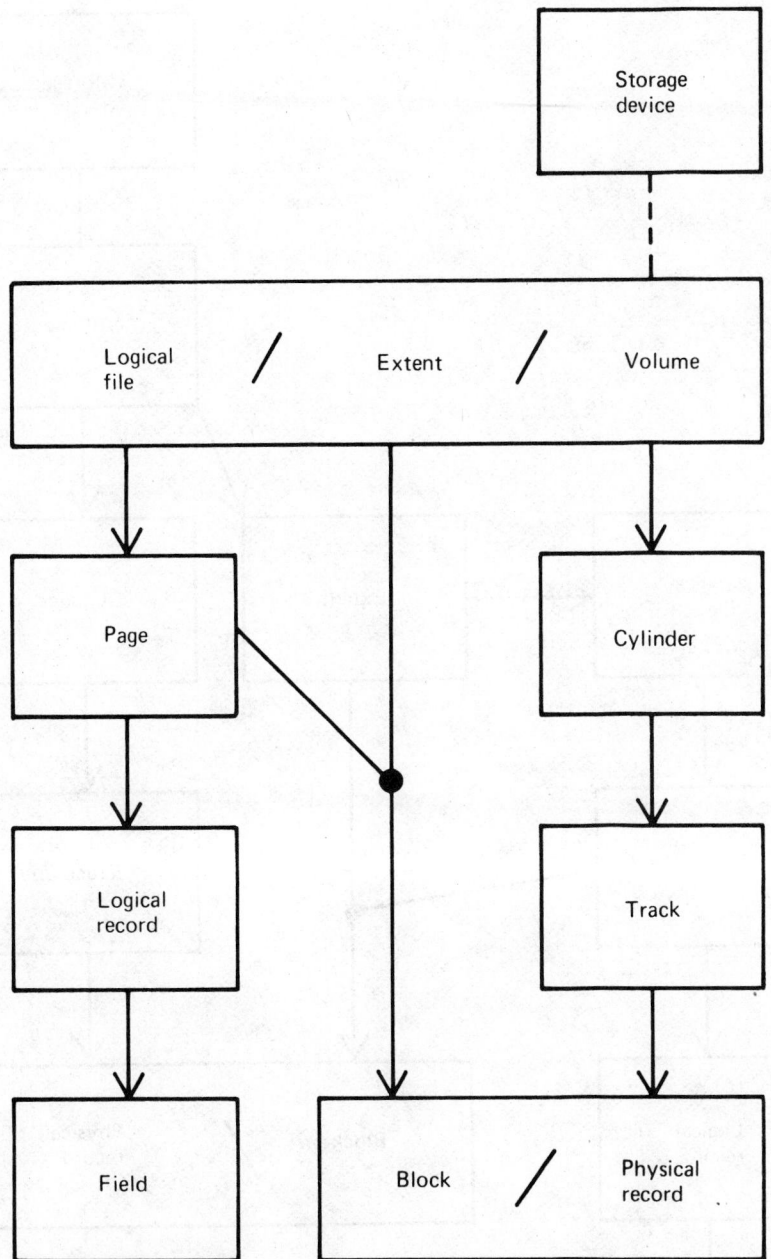

Fig. 6. Storage structure for blocked records on removable disk storage with overflow provisions.

pended to a page when allocated to it, are "linked" to it by placing a pointer to the new block in the last block allocated. Fig. 7 also illustrates the relationship between page/extent/ (respectively) and block, which exists because a block is either assigned to a page or is in the available block inventory, but not both. This structure is ex-

emplified by the case of a small school that needs less than a whole disk pack for its files. Thus, the volume (disk pack) is subdivided into extents, which may in turn contain one or more logical files. One of these could be the student file. As enrollment grows, more blocks may be assigned to pages from the pool of available blocks initially

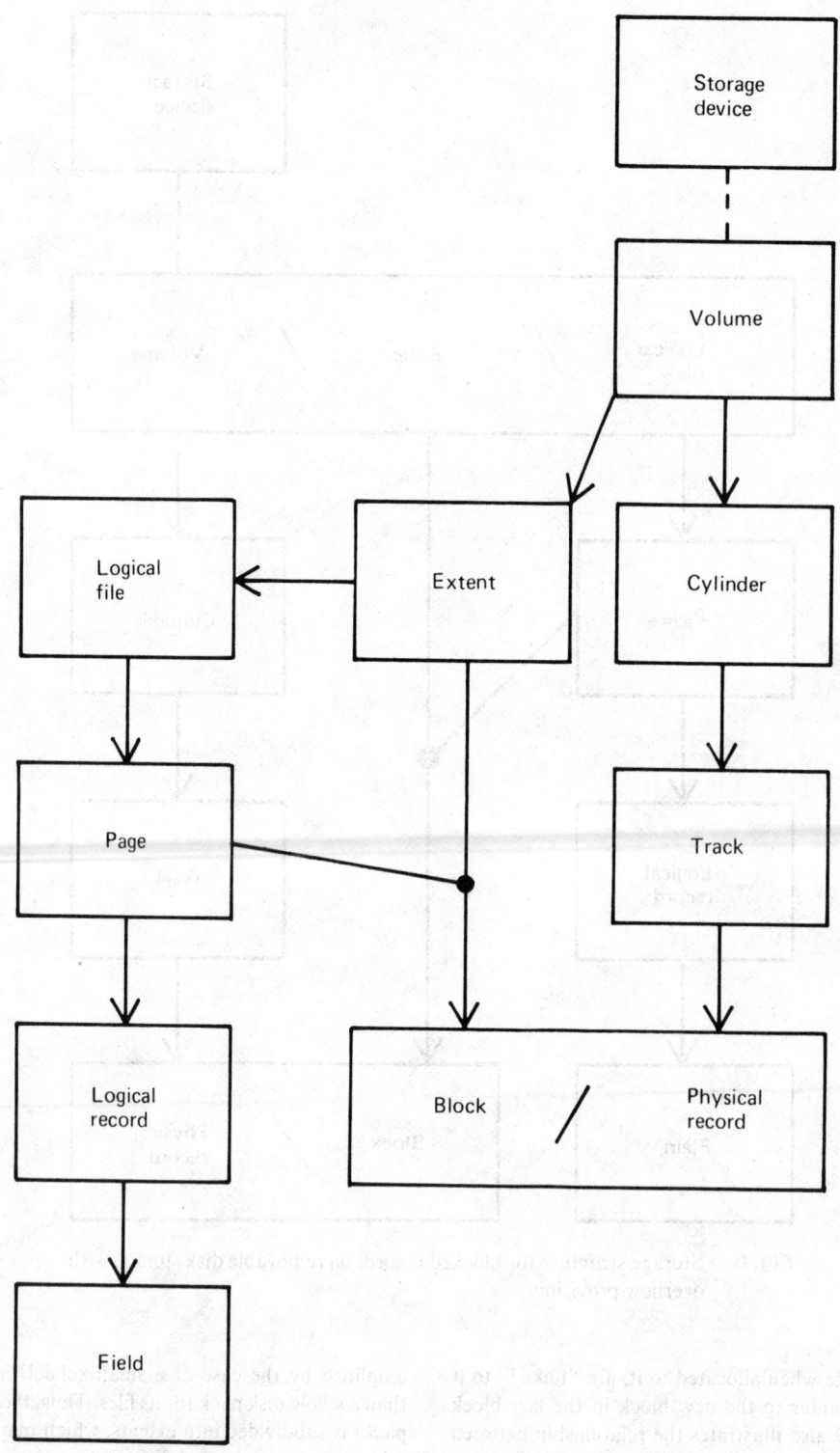

Fig. 7. Storage structure for linked sequentially paged files.

assigned to extents. If enrollment shrinks, the reverse of the procedure takes place.

Randomized Files. A variation of the dynamic allocation structure of Fig. 7 supports direct access to a particular page of a logical file without traversing the links in the preceding pages of the file to find it. This mapping requires that a hashing (*q.v.*—address calculation) algorithm be used to transform the file name and desired page number into the block number of an extent that is its calculated place of residence, provided the page exists. This storage allocation structure has the well-known *collision* problem associated with the hash functions: When more than one page randomizes to the same block number, the extra pages must actually be stored in some other block to be retrieved when requested.

The structure shown in Fig. 8 supports the solution of the synonym problem via the addition of a dashed arrow pointing from the entity class for "block/physical record" to the entity class "page." This specifies the relationship that will exist when a number of created pages all hash to the same block. The solid lines originating at "page" and "extent," and which join and point to the "block/physical record" entity classes, represent the alternate $1:n$ relationship between page/extent, respectively, and the block.

Integrated Data Store (IDS) Files. Through all the examples so far, physical record and block concepts have existed on a 1:1 basis. This is appropriate for the type of secondary storage media on which physical records of any length may be written within the track to create a block of the desired size. However, some disks have a fixed number of standard-sized physical records (sectors) per track. In these cases, a block is designated as a container for n physical records. Fig. 9 shows how the fixed physical record size has split the entity class of the merged concepts of block and physical record into separate entity classes. It also illustrates the actual storage structure of the Honeywell integrated data store (IDS) database system.

Relational Files.

From the point of view of storage technology, relations are keyed sequential files; for discussion of one implementation see The System R Group (1979). Furthermore, the external relational view is independent of the way in which the underlying data is stored; thus, relational files have had no discernible impact on classical storage structures.

Storage Structure for Blocked Magnetic Tape Files.

The discussion so far has centered on disk-resident files. To illustrate that the concepts are equally applicable to other storage media, Fig. 10 uses the allocation concepts of extent and block to integrate the physical storage structure of the magnetic tape (Fig. 3) and the logical storage structure (Fig. 4). It shows a file on magnetic tape where more than one logical record may exist per page. In this case, the concepts of a logical file, extent, volume, cylinder, and track are merged into a single entity class. The concepts of a page, block, and physical record are merged into a second entity class, the occurrences of which exist in a many-to-one relationship with occurrences of the first one. The remaining entity classes represent the concepts of the logical record stored within the page, the field(s) contained within the logical record, and (at the top of the figure) the storage device concept. Note that the dashed line between the storage device and the volume indicates a "sometime 1:1" relationship.

A thoughtfully designed logical structure is a necessity, especially for files that might be moved from one kind of volume to a different one (say, from tape to disk, or *vice versa*). It is relatively easy to move a blocked logical file for which processing is strictly sequential; tape is a sequential medium, and other than sequential access to data contained on it is impractical. As sophistication of processing increases, such files are becoming rarer; thus, intermedium movement of files in practical terms means tape to disk or disk to disk. The problem in the latter case is that of reconciling differences of potentially different track/physical record sizes with the preexisting logical page size without wasting too much physical storage space. [Welch (1979) discusses storage hierarchies for sequential access.]

Recent Developments in Storage Technology.

In the 1970s, there was no revolutionary, commercial data storage technology development comparable to the introduction of disk technology in the early 1960s (although recording densities have increased dramatically). Thus, the concepts discussed in this article remain as applicable in 1980 as they were when first proposed in 1969. Champine (1979) analyzes the interaction of technological advances at the logical, physical, and architectural levels. In the research—as contrasted with the commercial—environment, data storage technology advances fall into two basic categories: (1) bubble memories, and (2) "intelligent" rotating devices. Chang (1978) presents a good overview of current research and development activities in storage technology, as well as presenting an excellent bibliography for further study. It is unlikely, however, that these research developments will have an appreciable effect on commercially available storage media and devices in the first half of the 1980s.

Summary.

The discussion in this article has presented a set of concepts that have been defined and used as structural elements in describing storage structures. In many cases, the system objectives permitted two or more

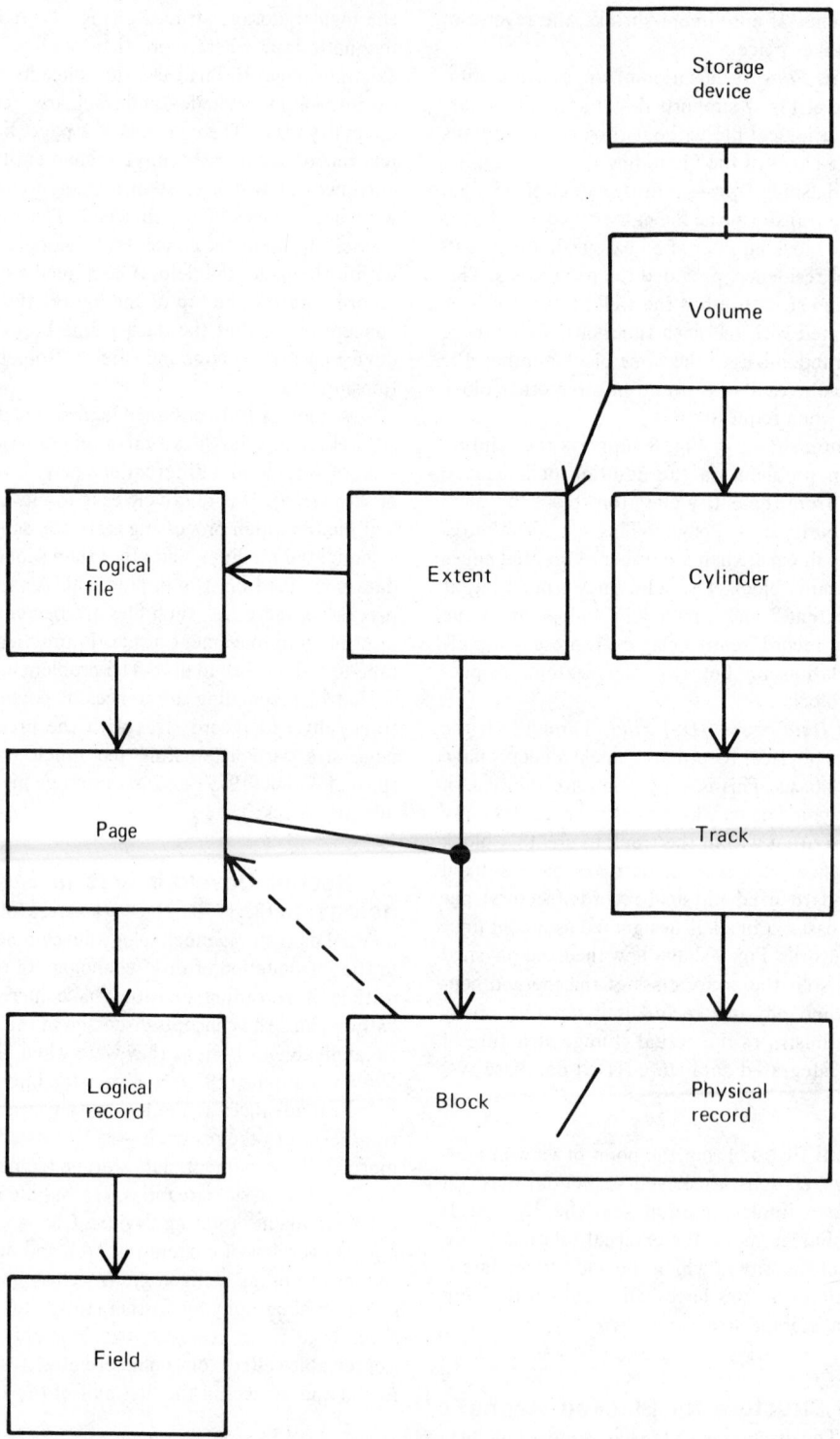

Fig. 8. Storage structure for randomized paged files.

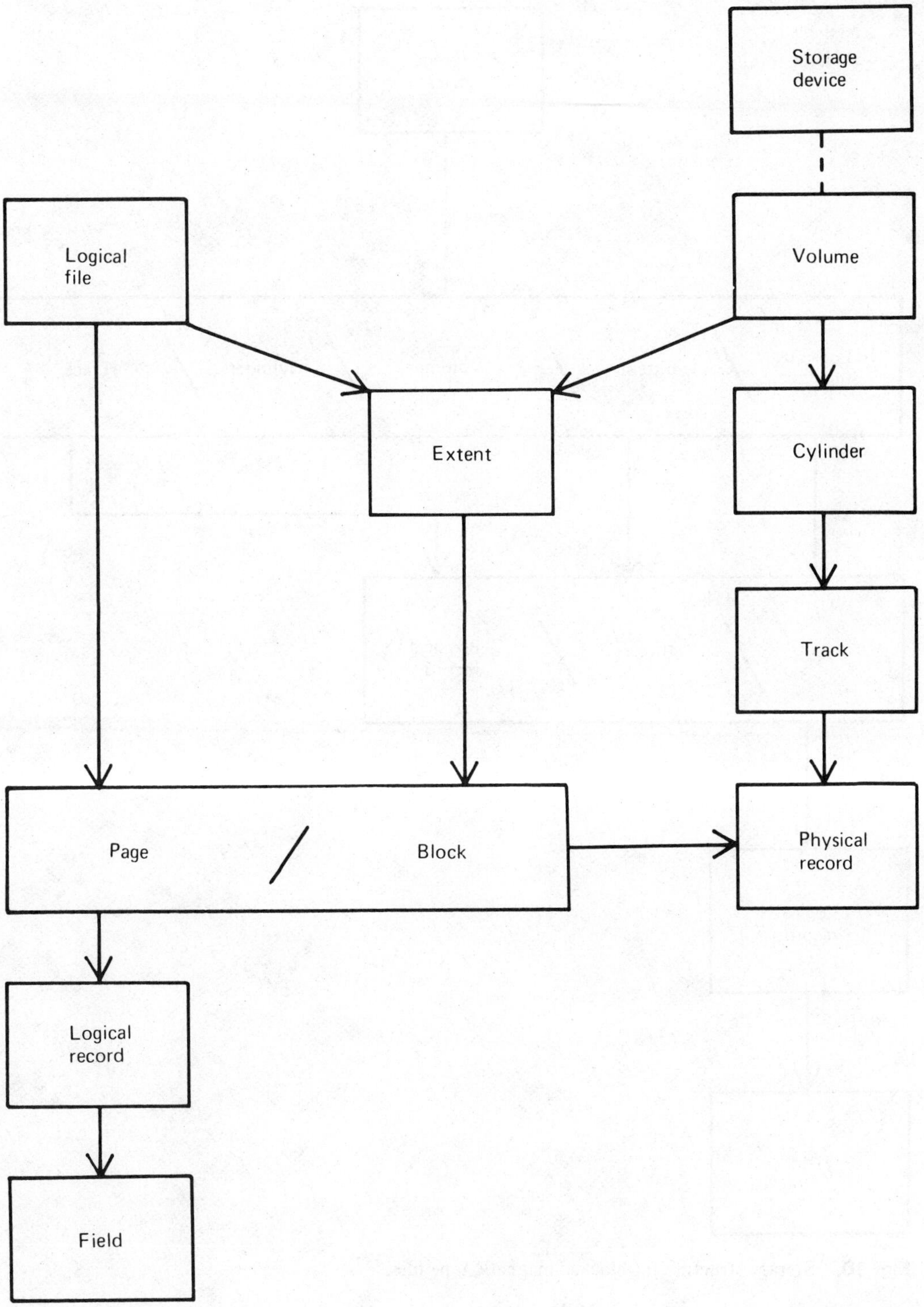

Storage
device

Logical
file

Volume

Extent

Cylinder

Track

Page / Block

Physical
record

Logical
record

Field

Fig. 9. Storage structure for integrated data store (IDS) files.

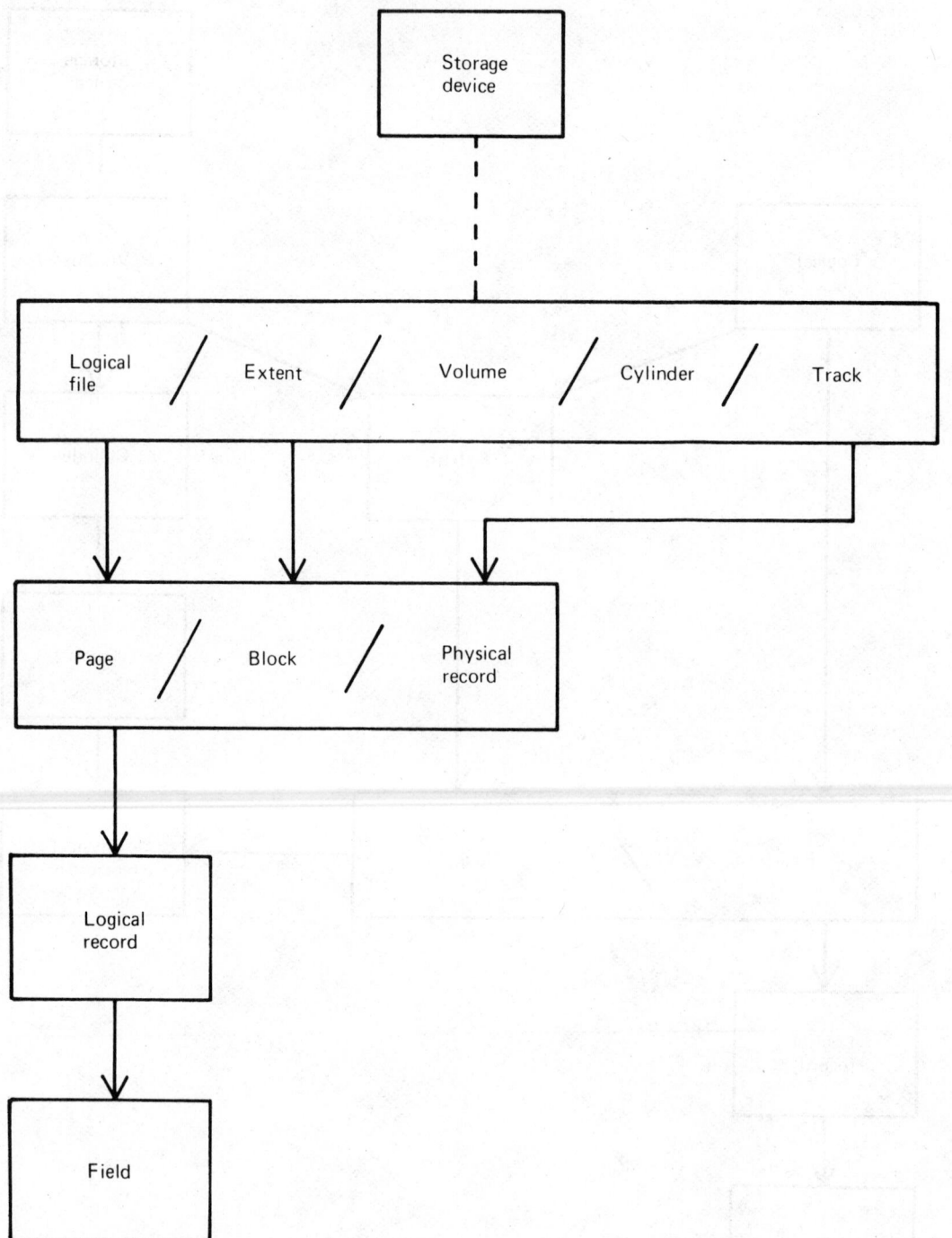

Fig. 10.   Storage structure for blocked magnetic tape files.

concepts to be merged into a single entity class, thus effecting a simplification. However, the need for comparison between database systems and the need for a general approach to understanding new systems suggest that each of these concepts should be allowed to maintain its own distinct identity, even when merged.

The data-structure diagramming technique used to illustrate the relationships between storage structure concepts should be helpful in fitting existing as well as emerging concepts into a solid frame of reference for the study and implementation of present and future more advanced database systems.

REFERENCES

1966. International Federation for Information Processing and International Computation Centre. *IFIP-ICC Vocabulary of Information Processing.* Amsterdam: North-Holland.

1969. Bachman, C. W. "Data Structure Diagrams." *Data Base (Quarterly News Letter of ACM-SIGBDP)* **1**, *No. 2* (Summer).

1972. Bachman, C. W. "The Evaluation of Storage Structures," *Comm. ACM* **15**, *No. 7* (July).

1978. Chang, H. "On Bubble Memories and Relational Data Bases," in *Proceedings of the Fourth International Conference on Very Large Data Bases,* pp. 207–229.

1979. Champine, G. A. "Current Trends in Data Base Systems," *Computer* 12, *No. 5:* 27–41.

1979. The System R Group. "A Relational Data Base Management System," *Computer* 12, *No. 5:* 42–48.

1979. Welch, T. A. "Analysis of Memory Hierarchies for Sequential Data Access," *Computer* 12, *No. 5:* 19–26.

S. C. Brewer

STORAGE ORGANIZATION

For articles on related subjects *see* ADDRESSING; COMPUTERS, MULTIPLE ADDRESS; INPUT-OUTPUT INSTRUCTIONS; MACHINE AND ASSEMBLY LANGUAGE PROGRAMMING; and MACHINE INSTRUCTION SET.

If information is to be stored in a computer system, a representation must be chosen to be used internally. The internal representation may be chosen to be quite different from the external form, as long as there are unique transformations from one to the other. In fact, this freedom to use various internal forms has created problems in situations where information generated on one computer system must be processed on another system.

Assuming a two-state representation, one can treat a collection of such states (or a *string*) as a unit as well. From the early interpretation of such strings as representing numbers with two states in each digit position (i.e., 0 or 1), these digits have become known as binary digits, or *bits*. This interpretation regards a string of zeroes and ones as an integer expressed in *base* 2 form. The term "bits" has now been generalized to include zeroes and ones found in strings that are not interpreted as binary integers.

Information other than binary integers must also be represented in storage. In some computer systems (in particular, those involved with monetary computations), there is a need for representing decimal digits per se and for doing decimal arithmetic on these digits. (This need arises from the different roundoff effects generated in binary and decimal arithmetic.) In other situations, it is necessary to represent alphabetic characters and punctuation symbols so as to process ordinary text, names, etc. In such cases, each alphabetic, numeric, or punctuation character is assigned a particular string of bits as its representation. Part of one such assignment, which uses eight-bit strings and has received wide support, is called the American Standard Code for Information Interchange (ASCII). Note that some of the 256 possible strings are not assigned symbols (see table in article on ASCII); these are reserved for later expansion. Others are given symbols that are neither letters, digits, nor punctuation characters; they are control symbols, usually used in communications to signal the beginning and end of a transmitted string, and so on. Earlier computers tended to use six-bit strings to represent symbols, but it became clear that this was too restrictive, and in recent years eight-bit strings have become standard. The term *byte* is used in referring to a bit string which is of the size corresponding to the symbol representation in a particular system. Thus, there are computers with six-bit bytes, but today one expects eight-bit bytes.

We have seen that a string of bits can have more than one interpretation, so that 01000001 might represent the letter A or the binary form of the decimal integer 65. Yet another interpretation of a string of bits may be as a computer instruction. In this case, some of the bits in the string are interpreted in the control unit of the system as a code for the operation to be performed. The remaining bits might be used to indicate registers (either special registers or storage locations), whose contents are to be used as input to the operation, or which are to receive the results of the operation as new contents. Several formats of instructions from typical computers are shown in Fig. 1.

Some early computers had separate storage for instructions and for data, but this did not last long because it proved costly to provide separate arithmetic processors for two kinds of storage, especially when many operations involved with modifying instructions were so similar to ordinary arithmetic operations. However, the development of microprogramming and read-only storage has somewhat restored separation of instructions and data.

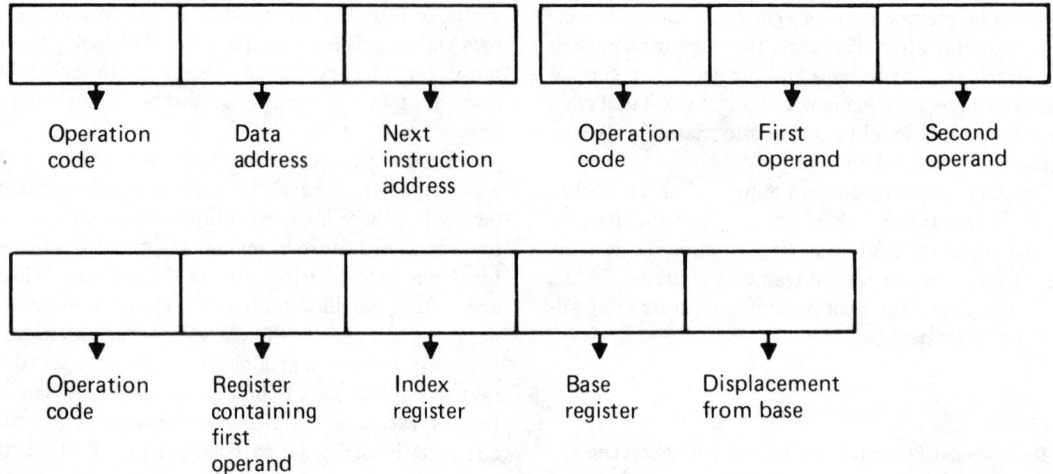

Fig. 1. Typical instruction formats.

Once separate storage for instructions and data was abandoned, it became necessary to find ways to store, and access, any kind of information from any part of storage. Very often, storage was divided into fixed-length strings called *words,* usually from 36 to 60 bits long.* Each word would contain one or more instructions as numbers in fixed- or floating-point form or a number of bytes so that the word length was always a multiple of the byte length. Addresses in such computers usually specified individual words, and one could access separate bytes only by shifting or masking operations.

Computers intended for commercial applications, on the other hand, were typically designed to facilitate variable-length strings of characters, since so much of their data exhibited this variability. Thus, one found computers in which both instructions and data were of variable length, with an address specifying the beginning of a string of characters, and a special *word mark* symbol signaling the end of a string.

Recently, computers have been designed to try to reflect both kinds of needs: fixed-length words to represent numbers, and variable-length strings of characters. In these cases, addresses usually specify a particular byte (occasionally even a particular bit) in storage, and a word is treated explicitly as a multiple of the byte length. Instructions may vary in length also, depending on the number of addresses they need to reference. This is to be contrasted with the fixed-word-length machine, where all addresses typically had to fit into the word, but where

many bits were wasted if fewer addresses were needed in particular instructions.

REFERENCE

1969. Rosen, S. "Electronic Computers: A Historical Survey," *Computing Reviews* **1**, *No. 1*: 7–36 (March).

B. A. GALLER

STORE. *See* MEMORY; and READ-ONLY MEMORY.

STORED PROGRAM CONCEPT

For articles on related subjects *see* ADDRESS MODIFICATION; ASSEMBLERS; DIGITAL COMPUTERS; BABBAGE, CHARLES; MACHINE AND ASSEMBLY LANGUAGE PROGRAMMING; PROGRAM COUNTER; VON NEUMANN, JOHN; and VON NEUMANN MACHINE.

The key design feature of modern computers, which allows the instructions to be held in the internal store while they are awaiting execution, is known as the *stored program concept.* Many computers, beginning with the Analytical Engine of Charles Babbage, and including the Automatic Sequence Controlled Calculator (Harvard Mark I), were designed to perform discrete operations, each specified by a concisely coded instruction. Prior to the use of electronics, however, these instructions were taken by the control unit from a special input device that read a tape or belt. Program loops required a loop of tape to be mounted (and the Harvard Mark I had three read-

---

*Smaller computers, particularly minicomputers and microprocessors often intended for applications in which long numbers are not needed, usually have from 8–32 bits in a word.

ers) with provision for control to be passed from one to another, to allow some flexibility in the logical structure of the program.

Electronics forced a departure from this arrangement because no tape reader could scan instructions fast enough to keep up with the internal speed of the computer. The first electronic computer, ENIAC, went back to plugboard programming (as used on punched card machines), but this proved extremely clumsy. The stored program concept emerged as an alternative solution from discussions that took place at the Moore School of Electrical Engineering, where ENIAC was under construction in 1944. Participants in these discussions included J. Presper Eckert, J. W. Mauchly, J. von Neumann, and H. H. Goldstine and the concept was first documented in a Moore School report drafted by J. von Neumann (1945).

Besides solving the speed problem, the concept had two important long-term effects. First, program jumps could be used liberally without incurring the time penalty required to hunt along the program tape. (Some early machines, especially those based on drum stores, had some residual timing penalties affecting the arrangement of jumps, but these were comparatively unimportant.) Therefore, much more complex program structures could be contemplated. Secondly, and more significantly, the instructions held in the internal store were accessible to be operated upon the same way as the data during the execution of the program.

Both these possibilities were quickly exploited when the first stored-program computers, EDSAC and BINAC, came into service in 1949. Alteration of programs during execution enormously increased the scope of automatic computing, and was heavily used in the early days. Since then, its use has diminished considerably, for several reasons, the main ones being the introduction of *index registers* (these achieved more economically the effect of address modification, which had been the commonest purpose of program alteration) and the trend toward time-sharing systems and run-time diagnostic systems (which required programs to be *pure procedures (q.v.)*, i.e., unaltered and unalterable during execution, all variations being embodied in sets of parameters held in a working store segment).

Another development, which demanded the abandonment of program alteration during execution, was the use of read-only memories for programs needed very frequently. This approach is now rather widely used in microcomputers.

The potentialities of program-processing were much more fully exploited later in the preprocessing of programs by assemblers and compilers before execution, and although the stored-program concept was not essential to this development, it certainly encouraged it strongly. In fact the load-and-go compiler, now very commonly used

in some kinds of installations, depends on the ability to store the program.

From the beginning it was inherent in the stored program concept that the instructions be made to fit (perhaps in groups) into the same word length as the data so that the same store could be used interchangeably for both with reasonable efficiency. Indeed, the ability of the machine to modify its program depended on having the program accessible in the same way as the data. However, the Harvard Mark IV was remarkable in having separate stores for the instructions and the data.

A. M. Turing had touched on the stored program concept in a paper on mathematical logic in 1936 (which led to the term "Turing machine"), though not in a form that showed its potential practicality. The first electronic stored-program machine to obey instructions was that built by Williams and Kilburn in Manchester, England, and the first to carry out practical calculations was the EDSAC, built by Wilkes at Cambridge, England, which was operating in May 1949. Both EDSAC and EDVAC, designed at the Moore School by Eckert and Mauchly, embodied many of the ideas incorporated in von Neumann's report (1945), but EDVAC did not become operational until 1951.

In the years that have followed these early implementations, the stored program concept has been elaborated in many ways. Programming techniques and languages of many kinds have been developed, as well as operating systems and all the various components of modern software. Perhaps the most fundamental variation from the original idea has been the introduction of program interrupts (*q. v.*), which means that the sequence of execution of the instructions is no longer uniquely determined by the program and its data, but can be affected by external events occurring during the execution.

These, however, are all auxiliary to the stored program concept itself, an essentially simple, but profoundly important, concept that has characterized the main stream of digital computer development since 1945. This concept, together with the practical development of electronics, has made possible the computer revolution as we now know it.

REFERENCE

1945. von Neumann, John. "First Draft of a Report on the EDVAC," Contract No. W-670-ORD-4926, U.S. Army Ordnance Department and University of Pennsylvania, Moore School of Electrical Engineering, University of Pennsylvania, Philadelphia, PA. (30 June).

S. GILL

STRESS. *See* PROBLEM-ORIENTED LANGUAGES.

STRETCH

For articles on related subjects *see* COMPUTER INDUSTRY: United States; DIGITAL COMPUTERS: Early; LIVERMORE AUTOMATIC RESEARCH COMPUTER; and SUPERCOMPUTERS: PRINCIPLES.

The *Stretch* computer (formally the IBM 7030) was the outcome of a research and development project started in 1955 and aimed at an advance in performance of about two orders of magnitude over the then existing computer technology and organization. It was a joint project between the IBM Corporation and the Los Alamos Scientific Laboratory of the U.S. Atomic Energy Commission.

The first computer (Fig. 1) was delivered to Los Alamos in 1961. Although the machine did not quite "stretch" as far as the ambitious performance goal originally set, at that time it was still the most powerful computer in existence. After ten years of service, the Los Alamos machine was dismantled in 1971. Seven other Stretch machines were built.

Fig. 1. The first Stretch computer being tested just prior to its installation at the Los Alamos Scientific Laboratory.

Stretch was the first major solid-state computer developed by IBM, and its transistor, core, and disk storage technologies were applied extensively to other computers of the 7000 series. Its sophisticated internal organization (Buchholz, 1962) departed substantially from that of previous computers. An instruction lookahead unit, for example, permitted up to six instructions at one time to be in various stages of execution; thus, Stretch became the first pipeline computer. While the sophistication contributed to the high speed of Stretch, the resulting complexity of implementation, in retrospect, also kept the speed somewhat short of the objective.

Other than speed, perhaps the most significant feature was the provision in one computer system of both the parallel floating-point arithmetic then associated with "scientific" computers, and the serial, variable-length, fixed-point arithmetic and character processing functions then found only in "commercial" computers.

The computer had been planned as the largest of a single line of general-purpose compatible machines. However, this concept did not materialize until the later System/360, which also adopted several other basic concepts of Stretch. Some of the terminology from the Stretch project (computer architecture, byte) has since entered general use.

A major nonarithmetical extension to Stretch, referred to as *Harvest,* provided very powerful data streaming and table look-up operations on a byte-by-byte basis (Buchholz, 1962, chap. 17). Only one Harvest machine was built.

REFERENCE

1962. Buchholz, W. (Ed.). *Planning a Computer System (Project Stretch).* New York: McGraw-Hill.

W. BUCHHOLZ

STRING

For articles on related subjects *see* CONCATENATION; NATURAL LANGUAGE PROCESSING; and STRING PROCESSING LANGUAGES.

In computer programming, the term *string* usually refers to a sequence of characters. This usage is an analogy to physical objects strung together, one after another, such as a string of beads. While this term can be applied to any type of object, it is usually reserved for characters, and the word *list* is usually used for other objects.

Strings are typically written from left to right. Thus, ABC is a string of three characters, the first being A and the last being C. In principle, strings may be arbitrarily long, but there are always restrictions in practice. Since a string is a sequence of characters, two strings joined together form another string. Appending one string to another is called *concatenation* (or sometimes simply *catenation*). The *null string* contains no characters and is important because it is the identity with respect to concatenation; concatenating the null string onto a string does not change that string. A sequence of consecutive characters within a string is a *substring*. Thus, BAT is a substring of BRICKBAT, but BB is not.

Strings are important because almost all computer input and output consists of strings, including programs and data. While this aspect of input and output is often not of direct concern to the user of the computer, in some problem areas, such as language translation, text editing, and artificial intelligence, strings are important per se.

An important aspect of strings is the characters they may contain. This is determined by the *character set* (*q.v.*) of the computer on which the string is represented. Character sets differ in specific characters, the number of characters, and the order in which they are arranged. There are several more or less standard character sets and a few variants. Most common are ASCII (128 characters) and EBCDIC (256 characters). ASCII and EBCDIC contain upper-case letters, numbers, some punctuation marks, and, as well, lower-case letters, and many special symbols. Within the computer, a character is represented by a pattern of bits. In ASCII each character is represented by seven bits; and in EBCDIC, eight. The correspondence between a bit pattern and a specific character is a matter of convention.

The characters arranged in order of their internal numerical representation are said to be in *collating sequence* (*q.v.*) or lexical order. For the letters, this order corresponds to ordinary alphabetical order. For other characters, different conventions apply. In ASCII, the digits come before the letters, while in EBCDIC the converse is true. The lexical order of characters extends to strings. Thus, strings may be compared lexically, i.e., for their relative alphabetical order. Such comparison is the basis of sorting. The leftmost character of a string is the most significant one for the purposes of determining lexical order, as is the case in a dictionary, except that characters other than letters must be considered.

The *graphic* is the printed representation of a character. This representation is fairly standard for letters and numbers, but sometimes varies for other characters, depending on the printing device. Not all characters have graphics. The blank, for example, has no graphic and appears as a space when printed. Additionally, there are characters which perform *control functions* affecting the behavior of the output devices such as "line feed" and "skip to the next page."

R. GRISWOLD

STRING PROCESSING LANGUAGES

For articles on related subjects *see* CONCATENATION; LIST PROCESSING LANGUAGES; LISTS AND LIST PROCESSING; MACROLANGUAGES; PROGRAMMING LANGUAGES; PROGRAMMING LINGUISTICS; and STRING.

In programming contexts, the term *string* usually refers to a sequence of characters. For example, ABC is a string of three characters. Strings are more prevalent in computer processing than is generally realized. In most cases, input to the computer from, for example, a terminal is in the form of strings. Similarly, output from the computer is in the form of strings; a printed line is no more than a string of characters. In spite of this fact, string processing has received surprisingly little attention.

Strings and String Processing. The majority of computer applications are numerical calculations and business data processing so that the most widely used and best known programming languages are in these areas. However, even as part of common applications, a substantial amount of string processing is performed. For example, a compiler must accept strings as input, analyze these strings, and produce other strings as output. Operating systems must analyze command strings and perform appropriate actions. Because compilers and operating systems are used so heavily, they must be extremely efficient. For this reason, such processors have typically been written in assembly language rather than in high-level string processing languages.

Nevertheless, string processing often must be performed in situations in which the complexity of the problem is such that highlevel languages offer many advantages. Examples are language translation, computational linguistics, symbolic mathematics, text editing, and document formatting.

Developers of languages for string processing have been in a less well-defined position than developers of numerical processing languages. While mathematical notation for numerical computation has developed over centuries, and its current form is widely known and fairly well standaridzed, string processing is a new area. There is no general agreement on what operations should be performed in string processing, nor is there a standard notation. The developers of string processing languages started largely without conventions. As a result, in string processing languages, notation, program structure, and approach to problem formulation are often radically different from those of more conventional programming languages and from each other.

Operations on Strings. While there were no generally agreed-upon string operations when string processing languages were first developed, four operations have achieved general acceptance—concatenation, identification of substrings, pattern matching, and transformation of strings to replace identified substrings by other strings.

Concatenation (sometimes called *catenation*) is the process of appending one string to another to produce a longer string. Thus, the result of concatenating the strings AB and CDE is the string ABCDE. This operation is a natural extension of the concept of a string as a sequence of characters.

A substring is a string within another string. For example, BC is a substring of ABCDE.

The most important and far-reaching string operation is that of pattern matching. Stated in general terms, *pattern matching* is the process of examining a string to locate substrings or to determine if a string has certain properties. Examples are the presence of a specific substring, substrings in certain positions, substrings in a specified relationship to each other, and so on.

Transformation of strings is typically accomplished in conjunction with pattern matching, using the results of pattern matching to effect a replacement of substrings.

The descriptions of the languages that follow emphasize approaches to string processing and the major facilities that deal with strings. No attempt has been made to describe these languages completely or in detail. Readers interested in the individual languages should refer to the cited reference material.

Comit. Comit (Yngve, 1963), designed in 1957–1958, was the first of the string-processing languages. The motivation behind the development of Comit was the need for a tool for mechanical language translation. Comit strongly reflects these origins, and is oriented toward the representation of natural languages.

Basic Concepts. In Comit, unlike most other string processing languages, a string is composed of *constituents*, which may consist of more than one character. Thus, a word composed of many characters may be a single constituent in a string. A string is written as a series of constituents separated by + signs. An example is

FOURSCORE + AND + SEVEN + YEARS + AGO

Attention is focused on a *workspace*, which contains the string currently being processed. There are 128 *shelves*, any of which may be exchanged with the workspace to change the focus of attention. Thus, there may be at most 129 distinct strings in a program at any one time.

A Comit program consists of a sequence of rules, each of which has five parts:

name left-half = right-half // routing goto.

The name identifies the rule. The left-half is a pattern applied to the workspace. The right-half specifies processing to be performed on the portion of the workspace matched by the left-half. The routing, separated from the rest of the rule by two slashes, performs operations other than pattern matching. If a rule has no routing field, the slashes are not required. The goto controls program flow.

Pattern Matching. The most important aspects of Comit are the pattern matching performed in the left-half and the transformation on the workspace produced by the right-half. The left-half may specify full constituents as written in a string, a specific number of constituents of unspecified value, an indefinite number of constituents, an earlier constituent referenced by its position in the left-half, and so on. A full constituent is written as it is in a string. Other left-half constituents are represented by special notations. For example: n matches n consecutive constituents, regardless of their value; $ matches any number of constituents. The integer n matches the same string that the nth constituent of the left-half matched. An example of a left-half is

THE + $1 + $ + 2.

This left-half, composed of four constituents, specifies a constituent consisting of the characters THE, followed by any single constituent, followed by any number of constituents until a constituent is encountered that is the same as the one matched by the second constituent; namely, $1. Pattern matching is left to right. Left-half constituents must match consecutive constituents in the workspace.

If the workspace contains

THE + FIRST
└┬┘   └─┬─┘
 1   2

+ MAN + IN + LINE + IS + SERVED + FIRST
└──────────────┬────────────────┘ └─┬─┘
               3   4

the match for each of the constituents is as shown. Note that the fourth constituent of the left-half matches the same constituents of the workspace as the second constituent of the left-half. The third constituent of the left-half consequently matches the intervening five constituents of the workspace. When a match occurs, workspace constituents are associated with the left-half constituents they matched, and are subsequently referenced by the number of the corresponding left-half constituent.

The right-half may contain full constituents and integers that correspond to the constituents of the left-half. The matched portion of the workspace is replaced by constituents specified in the right-half. Continuing the example above, the rule

THE + $1 + $ + 2 = 1 + SECOND + 3 + 4

transforms the workspace into

THE + SECOND + MAN + IN + LINE + IS +
SERVED + FIRST.

Other Facilities. The routing part of a rule permits operations that cannot be performed in the right-half. Examples are exchange of the workspace with a shelf, movement of constituents between the workspace and shelves, printing the workspace, reading data into the workspace, and so on. There are a variety of formats for reading and printing.

The goto part of a rule controls program flow. Control may be transferred to a named rule, back to the same statement for execution again, to the next statement, and so on.

Conditional loops may be programmed in a number of ways. One conditional operation is left-half matching, which may fail. For example, the left-half $10 would fail to match the workspace given earlier because the workspace does not contain ten constituents. When a left-half fails to match, the remainder of the rule is not performed, and control passes to the next rule in line. Special notations are used for names and gotos to facilitate the programming of loops. A * may be used for the name of a rule that needs no other specific identification. A * in the goto indicates that control is to be transferred to the next rule in line after the current statement is executed. A / in the goto indicates that control is to be returned to the present rule if it is executed successfully. Thus, the following statement, with a blank right-half and a / in the goto, can be used to remove all occurrences of THE from the workspace:

* THE = /

When the left-half finally fails to match, execution continues with the next rule in line. Arithmetic performed on numerical subscripts can also be used to control loops.

Status. The current version of Comit is Comit II. Comit II contains a number of improvements and features not contained in the original version, and is upward-compatible so that programs written for the original version of Comit will also run on Comit II. Comit II was originally implemented on the IBM 7000 series and now runs on the IBM 360/370. Because of its early origin, Comit lacks a number of features that are available in more recently developed languages. Comit is still in use, but most programmers have turned to newer languages.

The Snobol Languages. The first Snobol (string-oriented symbolic language) was designed and implemented in 1962–1963. The major motivation be-

hind the development of Snobol was the need for a general-purpose language for processing strings of characters. Manipulation of symbolic mathematical expressions was also an important consideration.

Snobol. In Snobol, unlike Comit, a string is simply a sequence of characters. Enclosing quotation marks (single or double) delimits the string, but the marks are not part of the string. An example is

'FOURSCORE AND SEVEN YEARS AGO'

Such a string is said to be specified *literally*. Strings may be assigned to names for subsequent reference. An example is the assignment statement

FIRST = 'MORGAN'

which assigns the string MORGAN to the name FIRST. There is no specific limit to the number of distinct strings. Storage management is handled automatically without declarations. Concatenation is performed by writing the strings to be concatenated one after another with separating blanks. Such strings can be given literally or as the value of names. For example,

FULLNAME = FIRST 'SMITH'

assigns the string MORGAN SMITH to the name FULLNAME. The blank is simply a character like any other, as illustrated.

A Snobol program consists of a sequence of statements. There are three basic kinds of statements—assignment, pattern matching, and replacement. The respective forms are

label	*subject = object*	*goto*
label	*subject pattern*	*goto*
label	*subject pattern = object*	*goto*

An optional label identifies the statement. The subject provides the focus for the statement and is the name on which operations are performed. The goto controls program flow and is optional. An assignment statement assigns a value to a name. A pattern matching statement examines the value of a name for a *pattern*, and a replacement statement modifies that part of the subject matched by the pattern.

Pattern Matching. Patterns in Snobol consists of a sequence of components. There are two types of components—*specific strings* and *string variables*. A specific string may be given literally or referred to by name. A string variable is indicated by delimiting asterisks, which bracket a name. There are several types of string variables. One is the arbitrary string variable, which can match any string. It is similar to the Comit $ notation, except that whatever the string variable matches is assigned to the name between the asterisks. Pattern matching is left to right, and components of the pattern must match consecutive substrings of the subject. An example is

    Z 'T' *FILL* 'N'

In this statement, the value of z is matched for any string that begins with a T and ends with an N. The substring between the T and N is assigned to the name FILL. If the value of z is TEEN, the value assigned to FILL is EE. Thus, string variables provide a means of assigning substrings to names.

There are also *balanced string variables* and *fixed-length string variables*. A balanced string variable matches a string that is properly balanced with respect to parentheses like an ordinary mathematical expression. Fixed-length string variables are indicated by a / and a quoted number following the name. The statement

    TEXT ',' *C/"1"*

examines the value of TEXT for a comma and assigns the character following the comma to the name C.

Replacement is a combination of pattern matching and assignment in which the matched substring is replaced by the object. The statement

    FULLNAME 'SMITH' = 'JONES'

replaces the substring SMITH by JONES and consequently changes the value of FULLNAME to MORGAN JONES.

Indirect Referencing. An interesting and important feature of Snobol is its ability to use any string as a name. A string may be computed and then used as a name by the indirect reference operator $. A $ placed in front of a string uses the value of that string as a name. For example, the statements

    X = 'NUM'
    N = '3'
    HOLIDAY = X N
    $HOLIDAY = 'EASTER'

first assigns the value NUM3 to the name HOLIDAY and then assigns the value EASTER to the name NUM3. The indirect referencing operator, similar in concept to indirect addressing in assembly language, thus provides a way of constructing data names at execution time.

Other Facilities. Input and output take place using

specially designated names as subjects. Arithmetic facilities are rudimentary. Integer arithmetic is performed on strings of numerals.

The goto part of a statement controls program flow. Gotos can be unconditional to a labeled statement, or conditional on the success or failure of pattern matching. Loops are programmed using the conditional nature of pattern matching.

Status. Snobol was superseded by Snobol3 in 1965. Snobol3 is similar to Snobol, but has several additional features, including a number of built-in functions and a facility for programmer-defined, recursive functions. Snobol3 was, in turn, superseded by Snobol4 in 1967.

Snobol4. Snobol4 (Griswold *et al.*, 1971) is the most recent language in the Snobol series. While Snobol4 is a natural descendant of earlier Snobol languages and is based on many of the same ideas and approaches to string processing, Snobol4 introduced a number of new concepts. The most important, from a string processing point of view, are those dealing with pattern matching.

Patterns. In Comit and the earlier Snobol languages, different types of patterns are indicated by specific notations. In Snobol4, on the other hand, patterns are data objects that are constructed by functions and operations. Consequently, quite complicated patterns can be built up in a series of steps.

There are two basic pattern-construction operations—*alternation* and *concatenation*. The alternation of two patterns is a pattern that will match anything either of its two components will match. The concatenation of two patterns is a pattern that will match anything its two components will match consecutively. Alternation is represented by a vertical bar, and concatenation by a blank. An example of pattern construction is

    PET = 'CAT' | 'DOG'
    PETKIND = PET '-LIKE'

The pattern PET matches either of the strings CAT or DOG, and PETKIND matches anything PET matches, followed by the string -LIKE (i.e., CAT-LIKE or DOG-LIKE). The pattern-constructing process can be continued, progressively building more complicated patterns.

To generalize the concept of patterns and avoid the need for special notations for each type, there are a number of pattern-valued functions. For example, the value of LEN(n) is a pattern that matches n characters, and the value of TAB(n) is a pattern that matches a substring through the nth character of the subject string. An example is given by the statement

    OPER = TAB(6) 'X'

which creates a pattern that will match any string containing an x as its seventh character. Other pattern-valued functions create patterns that match any one of a number of specific characters, search for specific characters, and so on. Examples are SPAN('0123456789'), which matches a substring consisting only of digits, and BREAK(';,'), which matches the substring beginning at the current position up to the next comma or semicolon.

As in Snobol, pattern matching is left to right, and components must match consecutive substrings of the subject string. When a component fails to match, alternative matches are attempted. If no alternative is specified, the pattern matching process backs up to earlier, successfully matched components, seeking other ways in which the entire pattern match can succeed. The pattern-matching process includes the concept of a cursor, which is an imaginary marker in the subject string indicating the current position of the match. Movement of the cursor is implicit, not under direct control of the programmer, although in some patterns, there is a direct correlation. Thus, LEN(3) moves the cursor to the right three characters. The cursor cannot be moved to the left by a successful match.

Names may be attached to components of patterns so that when the component matches a substring, the substring matched is assigned to the name. Attachment is indicated by the binary $ operator. An example is

HEAD = LEN(7) $ LABEL.

This statement constructs a pattern that matches seven characters. The seven characters, when matched, are assigned to the name LABEL. Thus, the statement

CARD HEAD

simply assigns the first seven characters of the value of CARD to LABEL. If the match fails (because CARD is less than seven characters long), no assignment is made to LABEL.

Another aspect of pattern matching is the ability to modify the meaning during pattern matching, depending on substrings matched by earlier components. Evaluation of an expression in a pattern may be deferred by prefacing the expression by *. The expression is then left unevaluated until it is encountered in pattern matching. An example of the power of this facility is given by the following pattern.

LIT = ('"'|"'") $ C BREAK(*C) . STRING LEN(1)

When LIT is used in pattern matching, the argument of BREAK is not evaluated until after the first pattern has matched. The pattern matches a single or double quote and assigns that character to C. The remainder of the pattern matches everything up to the next occurrence of the quote, assigns that substring to STRING, and then LEN(1) matches the second quote. Thus, this pattern matches literal string constants as used in many programming languages.

Other Facilities. Other string processing facilities in Snobol4 include alphabetical comparison of strings, mappings from one set of characters to another, and deletion of trailing blanks. Unlike the earlier Snobol languages, which were purely string processing languages, Snobol4 includes many types of data. In addition to the common types, such as integer and real, Snobol4 includes arrays as data objects, tables that provide associative look-up features, and the ability to define new data types during execution .These defined data types provide list-processing facilities. In many cases, it is possible to perform data-type conversions between various types of data. It is possible to convert a string into program statements during program execution, and hence to modify or extend the program while it is running. Snobol4 is actually a general-purpose language that strongly emphasizes string processing and contains a number of exotic features.

Status. Snobol4 is the most widely used and generally the most available string-processing language. It has been implemented on most large-scale scientific computers, including the IBM 360/370, CDC Cyber series, Univac 1100 series and DEC-System 10. A number of dialects differ somewhat from the basic version. An extension of Snobol4, called Snobol4B, incorporates a facility for manipulating three-dimensional character strings called *blocks*.

Recent Developments. The major emphasis in pattern matching in the Snobol languages, as in other string-processing languages, is on the *specification* of patterns that analyze strings. There is little facility for indicating *how* the matching is accomplished or for describing the synthesis of new strings from the results of pattern matching.

In many cases, this bias toward pattern specification is useful; it frees the programmer from the necessity of spelling out too much detail concerning the actual matching. This is especially true in Snobol4, in which the process of matching embodies a powerful search and backtrack algorithm that is particularly complex and obscure. Indeed, some of the intricacies of pattern matching in Snobol4 are poorly understood by even the language designers and implementors.

In other cases, however, programming tasks may not be achievable using the built-in capabilities of the pattern matching facility. Faced with this dilemma, programmers must resort to inefficient or obscure techniques that are typically unrepresentative of the capabilities of the language as a whole. This situation is due largely to the inextensibility of the pattern matching facility. In Snobol4, for example, while there is a facility for programmer-defined functions and data types, there is no facility for programmer-defined *matching* procedures (i.e., procedures, which are invoked during matching, that describe how a particular pattern is to be matched). This deficiency can be better understood by considering the pattern assigned to HEAD above:

HEAD = LEN(7) $ LABEL

The invocation of LEN(7) results in the construction of a pattern that, when applied, attempts to advance the cursor by seven characters. LEN itself plays no role in the matching—it merely constructs a data object that contains an indication of the action to be taken during pattern matching. It is this latter component of the pattern that corresponds to the matching procedure, and which cannot be defined by the programmer.

Snobol4 has been augmented with experimental facilities, such as programmer-defined matching procedures, additional pattern primitives for controlling the matching algorithm, and string synthesis facilities. This research eventually led to the use of procedural mechanisms for describing patterns instead of encapsulating patterns as data objects, and to the development of a new language, SL5 (Hanson and Griswold, 1978).

The central feature of SL5 is a powerful *coroutine* (*q. v.*) facility incorporated into the procedure mechanism of the language. There are also numerous lexical primitives that perform simple string analysis operations. Snobol4-style pattern matching is accomplished by using the lexical primitives in coroutines that cooperate in the analysis of a subject. The extensibility of the SL5 approach lies in the ability of the programmer to write those coroutines that participate in the analysis.

Despite these advances, SL5 and Snobol4 suffer a common problem: They are each, in reality, composed of two languages—a basic language and a pattern matching language. In each language, the programmer is burdened with the construction of pattern matching "programs." In Snobol4, this corresponds to construction of a pattern, which is subsequently applied, and in SL5, it corresponds to the construction of the set of coroutines, which eventually cooperate during pattern matching. This two-step process—pattern construction and pattern application—is due largely to the central role of patterns as distinguished objects in string processing languages. It is the elimination of patterns, but not of pattern matching, that differentiates the newest string processing language, Icon, from its predecessors Snobol4 and SL5.

ICON. Icon (Griswold and Hanson, 1980) is similar to SL5 in that it has a number of relatively low-level lexical primitives, some of which are related to patterns in Snobol4. Icon has a less general procedure mechanism than SL5, but has additional control structures and evaluation concepts that make pattern matching—called *string scanning* in Icon—an integral part of the language. The central feature of Icon is its goal-directed evaluation mechanism, which embodies a search and backtrack algorithm similar to, but simpler than that used in Snobol4 pattern matching. An important aspect of this mechanism is that it pervades the entire language, instead of being restricted to a component of the language. The combination of the lexical primitives and the evaluation mechanism yields string scanning capabilities comparable to those of Snobol4.

String scanning in Icon is accomplished in a manner that appears similar to Snobol4 and SL5 but does not involve anything like pattern construction. The expression

scan s *using* e

establishes s as the subject to which string processing operations in e apply. The expression e typically includes string processing operations, but may include *any* Icon operation.

Some of the scanning operations in Icon operate on an implicit cursor in the absence of other specifications. An example is *move*(n), which attempts to advance the cursor by n characters. If the advancement is successful, *move* returns the n-character substring between the initial and final cursor positions. For example,

scan line using write ("[", *move*(7), "]")

writes the first seven characters of *line* enclosed in brackets to the output. An equivalent Snobol4 program is as follows.

HEAD = LEN(7) $ LABEL [Defines pattern HEAD]
LINE HEAD [Matches LINE with HEAD and
    assigns result to LABEL]
OUTPUT = "[" LABEL "]"

This simple example illustrates an important aspect of string scanning in Icon: The move operation does not construct a pattern, but simply carries out the analysis. The Snobol4 equivalent involves construction of a pattern, followed by its application, and finally the output of the desired result.

Another important advantage resulting from the integration of string processing with the rest of Icon is that any language operation can be performed during string scanning. An example is given by the following expression.

scan text using repeat t := t || *move*(1) || *"."*.

which produces a string *t*, which is initially null (i.e., empty), containing the characters of text separated by periods. The || operator stands for string concatenation, and the repeat control structure repeatedly evaluates the assignment expression t := t || move(1) || *"."* until it fails, which occurs when the move(1) is invoked at the end of the subject string. Note the use of a standard control structure, repeat, within the scan expression. To accomplish the same thing in Snobol4 requires the separation of the analysis of the subject and the synthesis of the result since there is no provision for using arbitrary constructs within a pattern. Thus, the Snobol4 equivalent requires the following two statements.

```
T = ""                    [Initialize T to null string]

LOOP TEXT LEN(1) $ C =            :F(DONE)
                    [Assigns character of TEXT to C;
                     goes to DONE if no character]
T = T C"."                        :(LOOP)
                    [Updates T and returns to LOOP]
DONE
```

Icon has an alternation expression that resembles alternation in Snobol4: e1 | e2. The important difference is that, while the Snobol4 alternation operator constructs a pattern, alternation in Icon simply carries out the operation directly. The operation is similar to that performed during pattern matching in Snobol4 when the pattern constructed by P1 | P2 is applied.

In the Icon expression e1 | e2, e1 is evaluated first and if that evaluation succeeds, the value of e1 is the result of the entire expression. If, however, evaluation of e1 fails, the result is the result of evaluating e2. Another way in which e2 can be evaluated is if the entire expression is used in a context where the value of e1 is unacceptable. An example is

move(10 | 5)

The expression 10 | 5 has two literal subexpressions and the first 10, succeeds if the length of the subject is 10 or more characters. Suppose, however, that the subject is only six characters long. In this case, move(10) fails. This results in the reevaluation of the expression 10 | 5, which yields the value 5. This time, move(5) succeeds. Note that

move(10 | 5)

is equivalent to

move(10) | *move*(5)

which corresponds to the Snobol4 pattern

LEN(10) | LEN(5)

Note, however, that Snobol4 has no direct counterpart to the expression *move*(10 | 5). Alternation in Snobol4 is restricted to specific contexts; alternation in Icon may be used anywhere an expression may be used.

In Icon, operations that have the capacity for producing alternative values as required by the context in which they appear are called *generators*. In addition to alternation, many of the low-level lexical primitives are generators whose behavior when used in string scanning is designed to facilitate string processing. In addition, the procedure mechanism of Icon allows the construction of programmer-defined generators. This capability corresponds to the definition of programmer-defined matching procedures in Snobol4.

The generative capacity is not limited to the string processing aspects of Icon, but is meaningful for many operations. Generators allow a more natural expression of some constructions than is possible in most other programming languages. It is often possible to express constructions more concisely and closer to the way programmers think in mathematical and natural languages. For further information about this aspect of Icon, see Griswold, Hanson, and Korb (1981).

Status. Icon has been implemented on several large-scale computers, including the IBM 370, CDC Cyber Series, DEC System-10, and Cray-1. It has also been implemented on the PDP-11, a medium-sized computer.

Other String Processing Languages. Ambit (Wolfberg, 1972), developed in 1964, is a string processing language oriented toward algebraic manipulation. In many respects, Ambit is similar to the Comit and Snobol languages. However, the strings it operates on are parenthesized expressions that correspond to tree structures. In fact, strings are implemented as fully linked trees. In Ambit, unlike most other string-processing languages, two strings are considered equivalent even if they differ in the position and number of blanks they contain. A *basic replacement* rule consists of a *citation*, specifying a pattern, and a *replacement*, which effects a transformation on the string under consideration. The citation may match only one way; the replacement rule must be unambiguous. An important aspect of Ambit pattern matching is the explicit reference to pointers, which identify specific positions in strings. More recently, three versions of Ambit have been distinguished. Ambit/

S for manipulation of strings, Ambit/G for manipulating general data structures, and Ambit/L for list processing.

Convert (Guzman and McIntosh, 1966) is an extension of Lisp, incorporating pattern matching and transformation operations. There are a number of fundamental patterns and facilities for constructing most complicated ones. The function RESEMBLE applies patterns to strings. The function REPLACE performs transformations using skeletons that specify the structure of the replacement. A rule consists of a pattern and a skeleton. Convert applies the pattern to a string. If a "resemblance" is found, values of relevant parts are identified and substituted into the skeleton to effect the conversion.

Axle (Cohen and Wegstein, 1965), like Comit, has a workspace that is the focus of attention for pattern matching and replacement. Axle has *assertion tables*, which specify patterns. These specifications may be recursive. *Imperative tables* specify patterns to be matched and corresponding replacements. A pattern matching procedure determines which imperative is applicable. Axle has *markers*, which may be positioned in the workspace. These markers may be used to avoid reprocessing previously transformed parts of the workspace.

Panon (Forino, 1968) is a language based on generalized Markov algorithms (*q. v.*), and includes a number of pattern matching facilities and rules for transforming strings. A Panon program is itself a string, and hence susceptible to self-modification.

Not all string processing languages are high level. EOL (Lukaszewicz and Nievergelt, 1967) is a string processing language whose operations are low level, being more akin to machine language. In fact, EOL is thought of as the assembly language for a hypothetical EOL machine. EOL programs consist of a sequence of instructions that includes calls to subroutines and macro definitions. Data is processed as stacks of constituents. A constituent is a string of characters and may be of a number of types. EOL instructions manipulate the stack and constituents on them.

In addition to the languages discussed above, many languages intended for specific areas of application, or which stress other features, also have substantial string processing facilities. More recently developed general-purpose languages, such as PL/I, have string processing facilities, and macro languages form an entire class of important string processing languages.

REFERENCES

1963. Yngve, Victor H. *Computer Programming with COMIT II.* Cambridge, MA: M.I.T. Press.

1965. Cohen, Kenneth and Wegstein, J. H. "AXLE: An Axiomatic Language for String Transformations," *Comm. ACM* **8**, *No. 11* (November): 657–661.

1966. Guzman, Adolfo and McIntosh, Harold V. "CONVERT," *Comm. ACM* **9** *No. 8* (August): 604–615.

1967. Lukaszewicz, L. and Nievergelt, J. "EOL Programming Examples: A Primer," Report No. 242. Urbana, IL: Dept. of Computer Science, University of Illinois (September).

1968. Forino, A. Caracciolo. "String Processing Languages and Generalized Markov Algorithms," *Symbol Manipulation Languages and Techniques. Proceedings of the IFIP Working Conference on Symbol Manipulation Languages.* Amsterdam: North-Holland, pp. 141–206.

1971. Griswold, R. E., Poage, J. F. and Polonsky, I. P. *The Snobol4 Programming Language*, 2nd Ed. Englewood Cliffs, NJ: Prentice-Hall.

1972. Wolfberg, Michael S. "Fundamentals of the Ambit/L List Processing Language," *Proceedings of a Symposium on Two-Dimensional Man-Machine Communication, SIGPLAN Notices* **7**, *No. 10* (October): 66–75.

1978. Hanson, David R. and Griswold, Ralph E. "The SL5 Procedure Mechanism," *Comm. ACM* **21**, *No. 5* (May): 392–400.

1980. Griswold, Ralph E. and Hanson, David R. "An Alternative to the Use of Patterns in String Processing," *ACM Transactions on Programming Languages and Systems* **2**, *No. 2* (April): 153–172.

1981. Griswold, Ralph E., Hanson, David R., and Korb, John T. "Generators in Icon," *ACM Transactions on Programming Languages and Systems* **3**, *No. 3* (April).

R. E. GRISWOLD AND D. R. HANSON

STRUCTURED PROGRAMMING

For articles on related subjects *see* ADA; ALGOL 68; C; MODULAR PROGRAMMING; PASCAL; PROCEDURE-ORIENTED LANGUAGES: Programming in; PROGRAM; and PROGRAM VERIFICATION.

Structured programming (SP) may be defined as a methodological style whereby a computer program is constructed by concatenating or coherently nesting logical subunits which either are themselves structured programs or else are of the form of one or another of a small number of particularly well-understood *control structures* (*q.v.*). Such a definition is inherently and deliberately recursive. Though the idea is of uncertain and undoubtedly multiple parentage, an explosion of interest in the concept followed the publication of a letter-to-the-editor in *Communications of the ACM* in March 1968 by Edsger Dijkstra. In this letter, entitled "Go to Statement Considered Harmful" (by the editors of *CACM,* not the author), Dijkstra reported his observation that the ease of reading and understanding program listings was inversely proportional to the number of unconditional transfers of control (**"goto"**) which they contained. This rule of thumb is quite plausible since, when a programmer suddenly writes **goto,** what he or she is essentially saying to the reader is "However hard you were concentrating on the logical flow of my program, stop and find the continuation of this logic at another (possibly remote) physical point. That new point is presumably marked by a label of some sort (numeric in Fortran or Pascal, or alphanumeric in Algol or APL, etc.) which may not even be on the same page as contained the **goto.** The front page of any daily newspaper is full of **goto** (e.g., cont'd on p. 6) for the obvious reason that the editors want to draw attention to a large number of unrelated stories of approximately co-equal importance. At least some magazines are more considerate, however, and always finish one thought (article) before beginning another. Why can't programmers? Their ability to do so is at the heart of structured programming.

Control Structures for Structured Programming.

One possible barrier to writing structured programs is lack of a sufficiently flexible grammar. Consider the Fortran IV segment:

```
IF (A .GT. B) K = K + 1
J = 3*K
L = 7
```

Such a segment scans well because the possible detour consists of the single statement $K = K + 1$. But, when either branch requires two or more statements, the programmer is forced to write something like the following.

```
        IF (A .GT. B) GOTO 20
   10       J = 3*K
            L = 7
            GOTO 30
   20       K = K + 1
            M = 2
            GOTO 10
   30       -------
```

Following the flow of control in even this simple example is not trivial; if instead of two statements each at labels 10 and 20 there were 30 or 50 or more, readability would suffer greatly. At least as early as the development of Algol in the late 1950s, it was noted that use of a compound statement, two or more statements separated by a special character (say ";") and delimited by others, typically "**begin**" and "**end,**" could have a very beneficial effect. In Algol, the last example can be rendered:

if A > B **then begin** K := K + 1 ; M := 2 **end**
J := 3 * K; L := 7 ;   .....

In this example, the sequence starting with J : = 3*K is to be executed regardless of whether the consequent of the **then** is executed or not. When different and mutually exclusive actions are desired, the Algol or Pascal programmer can write:

if A > B **then begin** K := K + 1; M := 2 **end**
        else begin K := K − 1; M := 7 **end**

This **if-then-else** structure, which allows the selection of compound statement alternatives, turns out to be one of the essential control structures for structured programming. Interestingly enough, Cobol, which is seldom thought of as a structured language, has such a decision construct, whereas the more "scientific" language Fortran (in dialects up through IV) does not.

What else is needed? The answer was given in 1964 in a seminal paper by Bohm and Jacopini, who proved that every "flowchart" (program), however complicated, could be rewritten in an equivalent way using only repeated or nested subunits of no more than three different kinds—a *sequence* of executable statements, a *decision* clause of the **if-then-else** type described above, and an *iteration* construct, which repeats a sequence of statements **while** (or **until**) some condition is satisfied. Using conventional flowchart notation, these so-called *canonical forms* are typically rendered as in Fig. 1. Note that each of these control structures has a single entry point and a single exit, a key to their intelligible interconnectibility.

The two forms of iteration differ in this regard: The **repeat-until** variation of iteration does something first and asks a question later (as to whether a termination condition has yet become true) whereas the **do-while** variation of iteration cautiously asks a question first, since, if the condition tested is false, the loop under consideration is not executed at all. The Fortran DO statement and the Basic FOR statement are essentially weak forms of **repeat-until;** e.g., the Fortran segment:

```
        DO 17 I = 1, L
           .
           .
           .
   17   CONTINUE
```

will iterate until $I > L$ becomes true.

Using most compilers for Fortran dialects up through IV, the loop will run once even if $L < 1$ (and hence $I > L$) to start with. This can be avoided in Algol through use of the construction:

```
I := 0;
for I := I + 1 while I < L do
(a single, possibly compound, statement);
```

which does not iterate at all if $L < 1$.

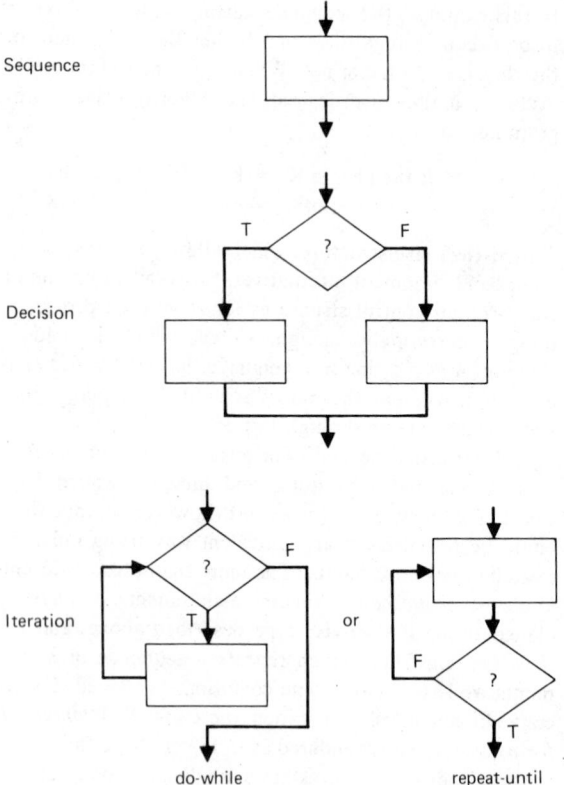

Sequence

Decision

Iteration

do-while   repeat-until

Fig. 1. SP canonical forms.

Do we need both iteration variants? The Bohm-Jacopini theorem says "no," but that theorem addresses only constructibility and not convenience. For this reason, programmers like to have both variants, as they do in Pascal. For similar reasons of convenience, three other constructs, **case, exit,** and **return** have proved to be desirable adjuncts to the canonical forms since each eliminates the need for an unconditional branch to a label under some circumstances. The utility of **case** is discussed in the article CONTROL STRUCTURES. **exit** (from a loop) and **return** (from a procedure) are closely related in that it is often contingently desirable to terminate a logic segment abruptly. Consider the following fragment of code in the language C:

```
true = 1; false = 0;
for (i = 1; i < = 100; i = i + 1)
    if (a[i] = gold) {found = true; exit}
found = false;   /* when loop runs to completion */
/* if executed, exit sends control here */.
```

Such a loop runs at most 100 times but terminates sooner if the search is successful. Without the **exit** construct, the only way to avoid a structure-destroying **goto** is (with the same true/false values):

```
found = false;
i = 1;
while (i < = 100) && (found = false)
if (a[i] = gold) found = true else i = i + 1;
```

Note that the **while** loop will terminate if *found* becomes true before *i* reaches 100 but the price paid for such structure is three decisions versus the original two (counting the implied test for $i < = 100$). Most SP advocates would consider the price too high and say, "If your language doesn't support **exit** then, by all means, use a **goto** to break a loop when necessary."

The occasional need for **return** from a procedure or function is quite similar. The foregoing logic embodied in a C function called "found" would be:

```
found (a, gold)
int a[ ], gold;
{ int i;
    found = false;
    for (i = 1); i < = 100; i = i + 1)
        if a[i] = gold return (true);
    return (false);
} /* end definition of found */.
```

Input/Output Aspects of Structured Programming. None of the canonical control structures were specifically designed to handle input/output; yet the way such statements are treated can have a significant impact on program structure and intelligibility. As a minimum, embedded program comments should describe the significance and expected range of each quantity to be read or written. When valid data or results are available for transmission, read/write statements are merely particular examples of *sequence*. The principal problem that impacts program structure arises when an abnormal or other special case occurs, such as, for example, the perennial problem of how best to handle the end-of-file condition. From the SP standpoint, one of the poorer ways is the PL/I (and typical microcomputer Basic) method of allowing the programmer to place a statement such as "On endfile do something" or "ON ERROR GOTO 5000" anywhere in the program—possibly far removed from the I/O statement it may affect. To the unwary reader of such a program, the logic being followed is subject to a "disembodied goto," i.e., something could occur during execution that could snatch control away from a presumably imperative statement that is actually a conditional one. Even Fortran IV provides a better answer by means of such a statement as

READ (5, 12, END = 100) A, B, C

The Fortran-knowledgeable reader is now able to see the conditional nature of the READ statement explicitly; it is saying, "If possible, read three numbers from input unit 5 according to the FORMAT specified at statement 12. But if an end-of-file condition is detected prior to receipt of three valid numbers, goto statement 100." Though the implied **goto** (and associated label) is annoying, the meaning is quite clear.

Somewhat better is the Pascal (and C) solution:

```
while not eof do
begin
    read (a, b, c);
    {process this data set}
end;
```

Finally, the preferred solution would be the ability to write:

```
while reading (a, b, c) do
{process data set}.
```

where "reading" is what Federighi calls a *gerund* procedure, one that returns a Boolean value **true** (when valid input is available) and **false** (upon encountering end-of-file) and whose *side effect* (something usually undesirable, but not so here) is the principal action desired, namely, the reading of data. An end-of-file, of course, terminates the **while** loop in a way analogous to the **exit** construct discussed earlier. This is the only solution that both preserves structure and directly associates the end-of-file with its proximate cause.

Structured Programs. While a fully structured program has no **goto**s (and hence needs no labels), re-writing a program merely to eliminate **goto**s does not necessarily result in a structured program; more is needed.

While still further evolution of SP is to be expected, most experts agree that the term connotes certain basic principles:

1. *Control structures.* Use of only those canonical control structures of Fig. 1 supported by the host language being used unless deviation therefrom removes a gross inefficiency or (most unlikely) enhances readability.
2. *Modular composition.* Subdivision of a program into modules, where a *module* is a program segment that embodies a complete logical thought in about one page of code. Depending on their relative sizes, a module may be larger or smaller than a procedure, but the two should be kept commensurate; i.e., either one module consists of one or more procedures, or else a large pro-

cedure is divided into several page-size modules. A program is divided into procedures both for the sake of processing efficiency and ease of construction. It is divided into modules partially for ease of construction but mostly for the sake of the human reader. Significant computer programs usually have only one or, at most, a few authors, but they may have many readers.

3. *Program format.* Careful organization of each such page into clearly recognizable paragraphs based on appropriate indentation of iteration, decision, and nested structures.
4. *Comments.* Judicious use of embedded comments that describe the function of each variable and the purpose of each module and procedure. A program whose every statement is annotated is often harder to read and understand than one that is devoid of comment; the right density is about one comment for every few lines of code that express a coherent logical action.
5. *Readability versus efficiency.* A preference for straightforward, easily readable code over slightly more efficient but obtuse code.
6. *Stepwise refinement.* Creation of the final program through an evolutionary process of *stepwise refinement (top-down design)* whereby the overall logic is first sketched in using a generous admixture of English, which is then gradually replaced in subsequent versions by more detailed logic syntactically acceptable to the intended compiler or interpreter.
7. *Program verification.* The ability to make assertions about key segments of a structured program so as to "prove" that the program is correct. (*See* PROGRAM VERIFICATION.)

Before discussing further the prospective benefits of adhering to these rules, we make two observations. First, note that nothing in all of the foregoing referred to the concepts of *algorithm* or *data structure*. The selection of an appropriate algorithm and associated data structure is a strategic concept; the application of SP techniques is a tactical methodology. Neither a structured program which implements an inferior algorithm nor an unstructured program which implements an excellent one is as desirable as the constructive use of good strategy *and* good tactics. To paraphrase the title of Niklaus Wirth's book: "Algorithms + Data Structures = (possibly unstructured) Programs," but "(Good) Algorithms + (associated) Data Structures + SP Techniques = An Efficient Structured Program."

Second, a purported structured program can be examined by a reader who can form value judgments as to whether characteristics one through five have been met, but unless the author chooses to display intermediate versions, it is impossible to tell (nor need we care) whether the final result was attained using stepwise refinement. This is not to denigrate rule six; there is now sufficient professional experience to support its continued advocacy.

Benefits of SP. An increasing number of advocates claim at least the following benefits for SP.

1. Structured programs are more readable and hence more intelligible than unstructured ones.
2. This greater readability makes it easier to maintain and modify structured programs, especially by programmers other than the original author.
3. Structured programs are more likely to be correct in the first instance and are more easily "proved" correct by systematic program verification (*q.v.*).
4. The greater likelihood of correctness cited above lessens elapsed time to create a new program because there are fewer bugs to find and fix. Instead of the routine expectation that a program will not run properly the first time, the goal of the structured programmer is "zero defects"; reasonably complex structured programs have indeed been known to run perfectly on the first attempt.

Though the foregoing claims are difficult to substantiate quantitatively, there is no question but that the majority of professionals who teach programming and language design have moved heavily toward the SP philosophy. This movement is reflected in at least three identifiable recent developments: (1) the widespread and increasing use of Pascal as the language of choice for teaching introductory computer science courses in universities, (2) the U.S. government's decision to choose a structured format for its new command and control language Ada (*q.v.*), and (3) perhaps most significant and surprising, the concession of the Fortran community that it was time to introduce some structure through the medium of Fortran 77.

Structured Flowcharts. Since SP has caused a significant change in programming, or at least in the way we think about programming, it should not be surprising that other related tools that once served us well need reformulation. One of these is the time-honored *flowchart* (*q.v.*), which so often contains a spaghetti-like maze of transfers from box to box, just the antithesis of SP. An interesting and useful remedy has been proposed by Nassi and Shneiderman, who recommend use of certain new diagrams for each principal SP control structure. Among these are a rectangular box for a declarative sequence (or process), "L" or inverted "L" structures for iteration, and other distinctive diagrams for binary (if-then-else) or multiple (case) decisions (Fig. 2). Since each diagram's outer outline is a rectangle and since the subdivision of any structure always leaves rectangles that

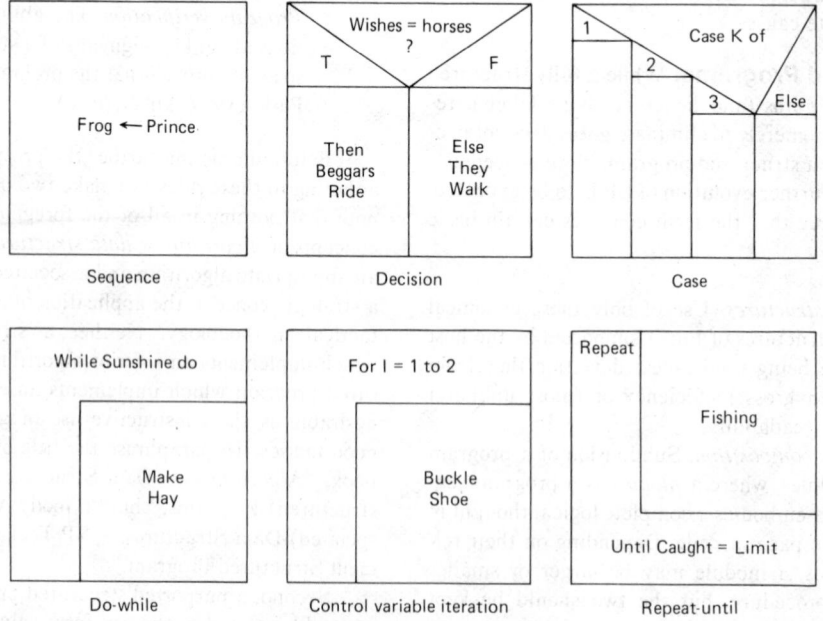

Fig. 2.   Structured flowchart building blocks.

may be further subdivided, a set of such diagrams can always be sequenced or nested within an outermost rectangle in a manner that models faithfully the recursive definition of a structured program given in the first sentence of this article. Examples of diagram intercombination are given in Figs. 3 and 4, which represent, respectively, procedures for calculating the factorial of N and the product of two N × N matrices. Such *structured flowcharts* are also called *iteration diagrams* or, after their inventors, *Nassi-Shneiderman diagrams*. Apart from their virtues in providing clear and concise documentation, teachers of computer science have noted that the great psychological difficulty which some students en-

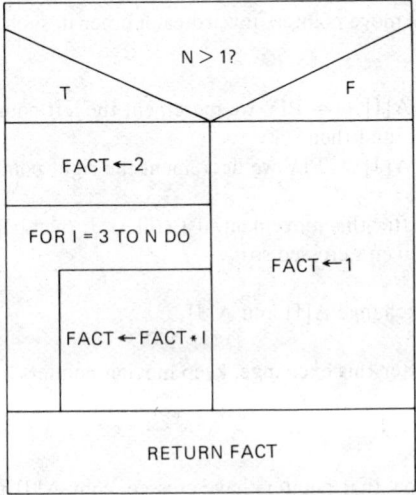

Fig. 3. Factorial.

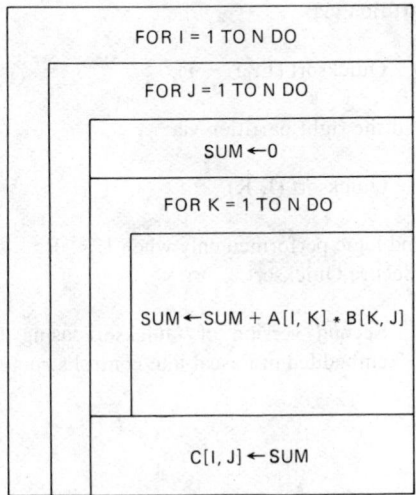

Fig. 4. Matrix multiplication.

counter in trying to write structured code (especially those who learned Basic or Fortran as a first language) is often dissipated by forcing them to prepare an iteration diagram first.

Still another significant feature of iteration diagrams is that the clarity with which nested logic is displayed often facilitates algorithm analysis; note in particular the three nested loops in Fig. 4, which so vividly emphasize that conventional matrix multiplication of N × N matrices takes running time proportional to N^3.

An Example. As an example of SP, consider the classic *Quicksort* algorithm for sorting an initially unordered one-dimensional array of (say) integers. One step of this algorithm will partition the array into three parts—a single interior element called the *pivot,* which is guaranteed to have gravitated to its correct final position; a left partition, all of whose elements are less than or equal to the pivot; and a right partition, all of whose elements are greater than the pivot. Repetitive (i.e., recursive) application of this process to the left and right partitions and to their subpartitions (until all such subpartitions are reduced to size one) will complete the sort.

The program logic is illustrated progressively in four forms, stepwise refined stages in Figs. 5 and 6, a structured flowchart in Fig. 7, and finally, in Fig. 8, the completed structured program and an example of its operation on a specific data set.

Not only does the program shown work correctly for the data set shown, we can prove that the basic partitioning algorithm works for *any* data set if, according to the precepts of program verification, we can identify two relations, say p and c, such that the combined truth of p and $\neg c$ guarantees a correct partitioning. The relation c is the loop control relation I <= J; i.e., an inspection of the program shows that the principal loop runs until $\neg c$ (I > J) is true. A more careful inspection of the program reveals that c switches from true to false in such a way that $\neg c$ is equivalent to the truth of J = I − 1. The other relation, p, is the so-called *invariant relation* of the loop, one that was true before the loop began and whose truth is preserved throughout the running of the loop. There may be many candidate relations for p, most of them irrelevant—we seek the particular one such that p and $\neg c$ proves the desired "theorem." That particular p has been right before us all along; it is precisely the statement in square brackets in Fig. 5. When that invariant relation is written with the substitution J = I − 1, we obtain:

"Set pointers to mark positions such that all elements to the left of the left pointer I are less than or equal to the pivot and all elements to the right of the

Procedure Quicksort (L, R : integer);
{sorts global array A[L..R] where A[R + 1] >
                                   any A[L..R]}

Choose pivot arbitrarily to be element at left end of array A.

[Set pointers to mark positions such that all elements to left of left pointer I are less than or equal to the pivot and all elements to right of right pointer J are greater than the pivot, leaving J − I + 1 elements between I and J (inclusive) to be examined.]

{The initial choices of I and J that satisfy the above are I = L + 1 and J = R.}
Move left pointer to right and right pointer to left until either

   a) the bracketed condition above is temporarily violated, in which case we exchange elements addressed by the pointers in order to restore that condition, and then continue moving the pointers, or
   b) the pointers cross.

Replace the first element with element addressed by right pointer and then replace that right element with the pivot in order to achieve the desired partition.

Now operate similarly on left and right partitions until all subpartitions are of size one.

Fig. 5.   First version of Quicksort written primarily in English.

---

right pointer J are greater than the pivot, leaving 0 elements between I and J to be examined."

which "proves" our theorem to the degree of conviction we achieve that our chosen "invariant" relation really is an invariant; i.e., no program step destroys the validity it had prior to execution of the primary loop to which it pertains.

Structured Programming Languages. Earlier it was mentioned that Cobol has the equivalent of an if-then-else control structure even though Cobol is not usually considered to be a structured language. Why not? We shall adopt the criterion that a structured language must have, as a minimum, an if-then-else compound statement-oriented decision statement, and at least one form of iteration based on a boolean decision; i.e., either **do-while** or **repeat-until. case, exit,** and **return** are luxu-

Procedure Quicksort (L, R : integer)
{sorts global array A[L..R] where the main program has set A[R + 1] to "infinity"; i.e., a number guaranteed to be larger than any A[L..R]}

if L < R **then**
begin
by initializing a left pointer I : = L + 1, which shall move to the right, and a right pointer J : = R, which shall move to the left.

   As an arbitrary pivot element, select PIV : = A[L], the first element. Now

repeat
   -edly move pointers toward each other in such a way that

   while A[I] < = PIV we increment the left pointer, and then
   while A[J] > PIV we decrement the right pointer.

   After this movement, if I still < J, then pointers haven't crossed so

   Exchange A[I] and A[J].

   After this exchange, keep moving pointers

until I > J.

   Now that pointers have crossed, copy A[J] to first position, A[L], and replace A[J] with the pivot element. This completes a partition. Finally, complete the work by recursively sorting the left partition via:

   Quicksort (L, J − 1)

   and the right partition via:

   Quicksort (I, R)

   End logic performed only when L < R.
end prodecure Quicksort.

Fig. 6.   Second version of Quicksort using English embedded in Pascal-like control structures.

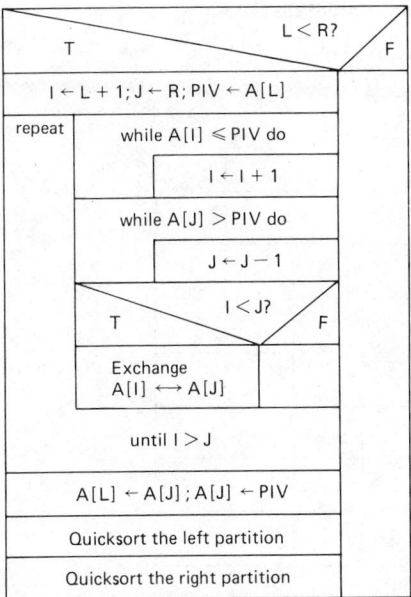

Fig. 7.   Procedure Quicksort (L, R).

```
procedure Quicksort (L, R : integer);
{sorts global array A[L..R] where A[R + 1] >
                                  any A[L..R]}

var I, J, PIV, T : integer;
begin
  if L < R then
    begin
      I := L + 1; J := R; PIV := A[L];
      repeat {move pointers I and J inwards as far
                                      as possible}
          while A[I] <= PIV do I := I + 1;
          while A[J] > PIV do J := J − 1;
          if I {still} < J then {exchange items pointed
                                      to by I and J}
          begin I := A[I]; A[I] := A[J]; A[J] := T
          end
      until I > J;
      {now two final replacements finish a partition}
          A[L] := A[J]; A[J] := PIV;
      {finish by recursively sorting the left and right
                                      partitions}
          Quicksort (L, J − 1); Quicksort (I, R)
  end {logic peformed only when L < R};
end {procedure Quicksort};
```

Example

```
I  J
2  8   8  6  12  20   2   5  47  14   Initial array;
3  6   8  6   5  20   2  12  47  14   pivot = 8
4  5   8  6   5   2  20  12  47  14
5  4   2  6   5  │8│20  12  47  14   Final result
                                      of one partitioning
```

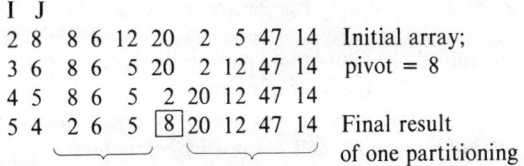

Left partition   Right partition

To be further processed recursively
(by 3rd-last line of the procedure)
until partitions of size one result
in completely ordered (sorted) data.

Fig. 8.   Final structured version of Quicksort implemented as a Pascal procedure together with an
example of how a particular data set would appear after a single partitioning.

ries. Note that although classical iteration based on a control variable (*q.v.*) is not cited as being necessary despite its obvious utility, most SP languages retain such a form in addition to **do-while** and/or **repeat-until.**

Table 1 summarizes the SP features of eight particular high-level languages. *Sequence* has not been tabulated because all of them have such a construct. Recursion, on the other hand, has been included because many procedures are much more intelligible (though, of course, not more efficient) when written in recursive form (as in our Quicksort example) than they are when written out non-recursively. Also, since embedded comments play an important role in readability, each language has been characterized in this regard as being *poor* if comments must be confined to separate lines, *fair* if they may be placed at certain restricted points internal to a statement, *good* if they may be placed within or at least to the right of statements, and *excellent* (exc.) if such comments are delimited by single characters [such as {} in Pascal] rather than the surprisingly jarring double-character delimiters/* and */ that PL/I and C and certain character-set limited versions of Pascal use.

The influence of the SP philosophy has now become quite pervasive, and deservedly so, even in environments where, for one reason or another, programs are still written in a traditional unstructured language. This is manifesting itself in several ways: (1) the creation of compilers for structured versions of languages such as Basic, Cobol, Lisp, and Snobol (i.e., versions in which, typically, options for **if-then-else** and **do-while** control structures are superimposed on the original language); (2) the creation of preprocessors (software translators), which change structured syntax into conventional statements acceptable to existing compilers; and, as a last resort, (3) hand translation of structured flowcharts or hypothetical structured code into transliterated conventional equivalents.

The major contributions of the SP approach have been twofold—the elevation of programming technique

Table 1. Language Features that Facilitate SP

	Algo 60	Pascal	Ada	Algo 68	PL/I	C	Fortran 77	Watfiv–S
if-then-else decision	√	√	√	√	√	√	√	√
Control variable iteration	√	√	√	√	√	√	√	√
do-while	√	√	√	√	√	√	−a	√
repeat-until	−	√	−	−	−	√c	−	−
case	−	√	√	√	√c	−b	−	−
exit	−	−	√	−	−	√	−	−
return	−	−	√	−	√	√	√	√
recursion	√	√	√	√	√	√	√	√
Flexibility of comments	Fair	Exc.	Good	Exc.	Good	Good	Poor	Poor

aNot in the standard but present in many actual implementations
bThe structure that C calls *case* does not have a common single exit and hence is more properly classified as a form of Fortran-like computed goto.
cUses different terminology.

to something less of an art and more of a science, and also the demonstration that carefully structured programs can be creative works of sufficient literary merit to deserve being read by humans and not just by computers.

REFERENCES

1964. Bohm, C. and Jacopini, G. "Flow Diagrams, Turing Machines, and Languages With Only Two Formation Rules," *Comm. ACM* **9**, No. 5.

1968. Dijkstra, E. "Go to Statement Considered Harmful," *Comm. ACM* **11**, No. 3.

1972. Dahl, O-J, Dijkstra, E., and Hoare, C. A. R. *Structured Programming.* New York: Academic Press.

1973. Wirth, N. *Systematic Programming: An Introduction.* Englewood Cliffs, NJ: Prentice-Hall.

1975. McGowan, C. and Kelly, J. *Top-Down Structured Programming Techniques.* New York: Petrocelli/Charter.

1976. Dijkstra, E. *A Discipline of Programming.* Englewood Cliffs, NJ: Prentice-Hall.

1977. Yeh, R. (Ed.). *Current Trends in Programming Methodology. Vol. 1: Software Specification and Design.* Englewood Cliffs, NJ: Prentice-Hall.

1979. Linger, R., Mills, H., and Witt, B. *Structured Programming, Theory and Practice.* Reading, MA: Addison-Wesley.

E. D. REILLY, JR.

SUBPROGRAMS. *See* PROCEDURE; PROCEDURE, PURE; SUBPROGRAMS, CALLING; and SUBROUTINE.

SUBPROGRAMS, CALLING

For articles on related subjects *see* ARGUMENT; PROCEDURE; SIDE EFFECT; and SUBROUTINE.

This article is not concerned specifically with the statements and other syntactic means by which subprograms or procedures are called from another part of a program, but rather with the mechanisms used to transfer arguments from the calling program to the subprogram. For the actual calling itself, there are two basic constructs, as follows.

1. The appearance of the name of a *function* procedure with its actual arguments in an expression; for example, in Fortran,

A = B + FCN1(C,D)·FCN2(2.3+D,J/K)

2. The use of an explicit statement for calling a procedure; for example,

Fortran: CALL PROC(A,B∗C,2.3,D(I))
Pascal: **proc**(A,B∗C,2.3,D[I]);

More interesting and subtle are the means by which the arguments are transferred. There are three basic techniques:

1. Call by value.
2. Call by location (sometimes known as call by *reference*).
3. Call by name.

Call by Value. In the case of call by value, the subprogram is provided with the value of the argument and no path leads back to the referencing program or to any of its storage elements. Call by value is illustrated in Fig. 1(a) for the argument B∗C. The subprogram thus has no control over the referencing program. In this manner, no side effects can affect the calling program.

Call by Location. In this case the referencing program does not provide to the subprogram the value of the argument but provides instead the address of the memory location at which that value can be found. It is then the responsibility of the subprogram to access the data through this mechanism. This is illustrated in Fig. 1(b) for the argument A. Somewhere in the body of the

procedure PROC is a memory location that will store the address of A in the calling program. Thus, with call by location, the subprogram in effect shares memory with the calling program.

For an argument which itself is an expression rather than a variable name, like B∗C in Fig. 1, there is no automatically corresponding address in the calling program. Therefore, if B∗C is called by location, the calling program must create a location for the value of B∗C, evaluate B∗C, and put it in this location, and then transfer the address of this location to the subprogram. This is then essentially the same in effect as calling by value.

But in two other cases, calling by location and calling by value are quite different.

1. If the calling argument is an array, say, of 1,000 elements, then calling by value would require that all 1,000 elements be transferred and that memory space be allocated in both calling program and subprogram for these 1,000 elements. But if the call is by location, then only the address of the first element in the array need be transferred to the subprogram.
2. If the formal argument appears on the left-hand

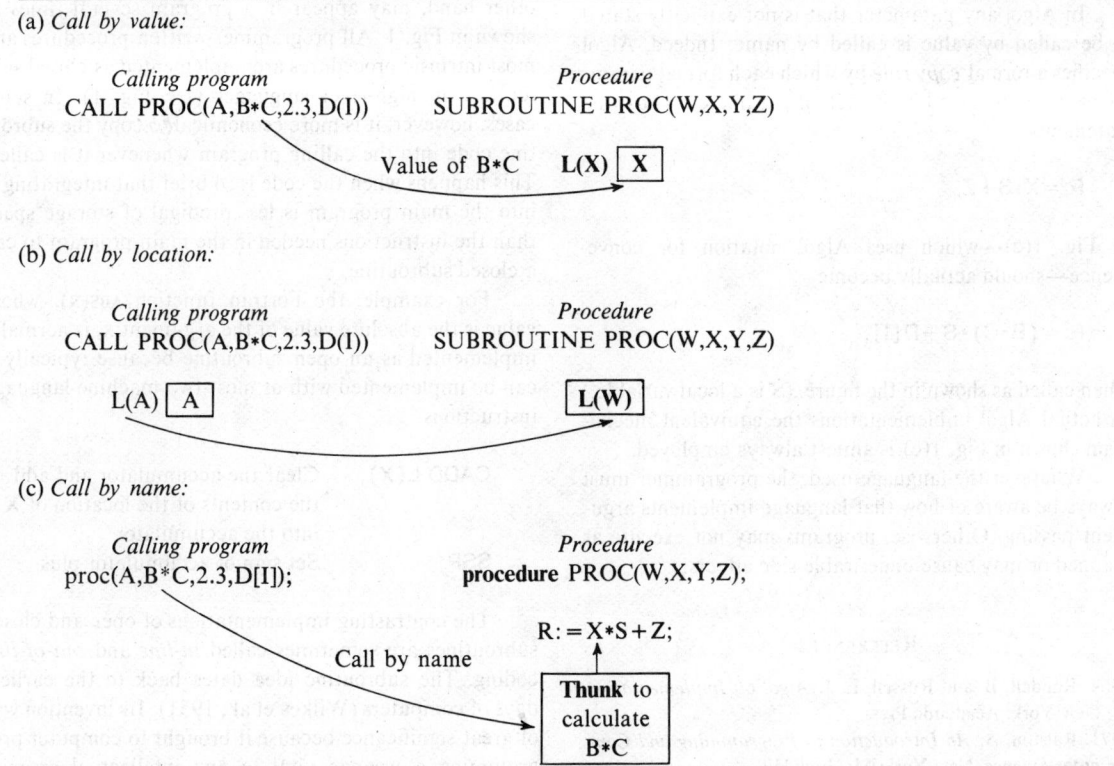

(a) *Call by value:*

    Calling program   *Procedure*
    CALL PROC(A,B∗C,2.3,D(I))   SUBROUTINE PROC(W,X,Y,Z)

                             Value of B∗C   L(X)   X

(b) *Call by location:*

    Calling program   *Procedure*
    CALL PROC(A,B∗C,2.3,D(I))   SUBROUTINE PROC(W,X,Y,Z)

    L(A)   A   L(W)

(c) *Call by name:*

    Calling program   *Procedure*
    proc(A,B∗C,2.3,D[I]);   **procedure** PROC(W,X,Y,Z);

                                       R: = X∗S + Z;

                  Call by name   **Thunk** to
                                         calculate
                                         B∗C

Fig. 1. Passing arguments to procedures.

side of an assignment statement in the subprogram, then, if the call is by value, the value of this argument *in the subprogram* is changed when the assignment statement is executed. But, if the call is by location, the value *in the calling program* is changed. In the case where the argument is an output argument, this is just what is desired. In other cases, call by location may result in undesirable side effects.

Call by Name. In the case of call by name, the actual expression itself is passed to the subprogram (so that it might better have been called *call by expression*). However, rather than passing the symbolic string which is the expression, the evaluation of the expression argument is represented by another (machine language) subprogram created by the compiler. Such a generated subprogram is often called a *thunk*. This is illustrated in Fig. 1(c) for the argument B∗C. In the subprogram, each time parameter x is referenced, the thunk is executed, and the current value of the argument expression is determined and is used as the value of x. Such values may change during the execution of the subprogram as the result of side effects. When the argument is a simple identifier (i.e., unsubscripted), the process of call by name is equivalent to call by location.

In Algol any parameter that is not explicitly stated to be called by value is called by name. Indeed, Algol specifies a formal *copy rule* by which each formal parameter is to be replaced by its actual parameter. Thus, the statement

$$R: = X \cdot S + Z;$$

in Fig. 1(c)—which uses Algol notation for convenience—should actually become

$$R: = (B \cdot C) \cdot S + D[I];$$

when called as shown in the figure. (S is a local variable.) In actual Algol implementations the equivalent mechanism shown in Fig. 1(c) is almost always employed.

Whatever the language used, the programmer must always be aware of how that language implements argument passing. Otherwise, programs may not execute as planned or may cause undesirable side effects.

References

1964. Randell, B. and Russell, L. J. *Algol 60 Implementation.* New York: Academic Press.
1971. Ralston, A. *An Introduction to Programming and Computer Science.* New York: McGraw-Hill.
1975. Pratt, T. W. *Programming Languages: Design and Implementation.* Englewood Cliffs, NJ: Prentice-Hall.

J. A. N. Lee and A. Ralston

SUBROUTINE

For articles on related subjects *see* Coroutine; Procedure; Side Effect; and Subprograms, Calling.

A subroutine is a portion of a program, which may be prewritten, that is a logically separate part of the program and which performs a specific task necessary for the execution of the program. Normally, a subroutine represents a unique implementation of a process that is utilized many times in a program, thereby saving programming time and storage space for code. In high-level languages, subroutines are implemented, for example, as *procedures* in Pascal and as subroutines and functions in Fortran. In assembly language programs, subroutines are also in common use, as is a macroinstruction facility.

Subroutines are divided into two types, *open* and *closed*. A *closed subroutine* is implemented, as implied above, as a single piece of code that can be called from different places in a program. An *open subroutine,* on the other hand, may appear in a program several times as shown in Fig. 1. All programmer-written procedures and most intrinsic procedures are implemented as closed subroutines in high-level languages (see Fig. 1). In some cases, however, it is more economical to copy the subroutine code into the calling program whenever it is called. This happens when the code is so brief that integrating it into the main program is less prodigal of storage space than the instructions needed in the main program to call a closed subroutine.

For example, the Fortran function ABS(x), whose value is the absolute value of the argument x, is normally implemented as an open subroutine because typically it can be implemented with at most two machine-language instructions:

CADD L(X)	Clear the accumulator and add the contents of the location of X into the accumulator
SSP	Set sign of accumulator plus

The contrasting implementations of open and closed subroutines are sometimes called *in-line* and *out-of-line* coding. The subroutine idea dates back to the earliest days of computers (Wilkes et al., 1951). Its invention was of great significance because it brought to computer programming a weapon vital to any intellectual arsenal,

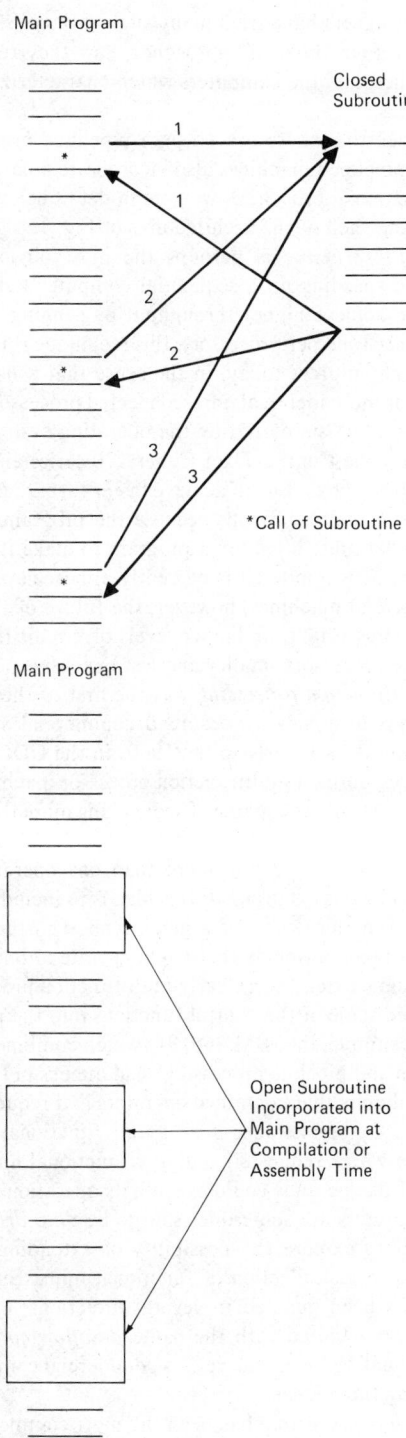

Fig. 1. Closed and open subroutines.

namely, the ability to break complex tasks into smaller units and then to treat each smaller unit separately.

REFERENCE

1951. Wilkes, M. V., Wheeler, D. J., and Gill, S. *The Preparation of Programs for an Electronic Digital Computer*. Reading, MA: Addison-Wesley.

J. A. N. LEE AND A. RALSTON

SUPERCOMPUTERS

PRINCIPLES

For articles on related subjects *see* DATAFLOW; DIGITAL COMPUTERS: Contemporary and Future; JOSEPHSON JUNCTION DEVICES; PERFORMANCE MEASUREMENT AND EVALUATION; PERFORMANCE OF COMPUTERS; and PIPELINE AND ARRAY PROCESSORS.

The term *supercomputer* adapts to several intuitive definitions. In a given period of time it may be applied to computers of the highest speed, largest functional size, biggest physical dimensions, or greatest monetary cost. The first computers to which this term was applied were the IBM Stretch (*q.v.*) and the Univac LARC (*q.v.*), both developed in the late 1950s and both now out of commercial use. Since all these attributes tend to occur in certain computers, such machines are referred to as supercomputers. A more explicit definition is difficult, but the following discussion of these four attributes characterizes typical usage of the term.

Over the past 30 years, the raw speed of the fastest available computers has approximately doubled each year to the point where we now have speeds of one billion operations per second in the fastest special-purpose computers. The price of modern supercomputers is in the range of $5–15 million. Whereas early machines had at most 1,000 words of primary memory, modern supercomputers have several millions of words of primary memory together with slower secondary memories arranged in a three- or four-level hierarchy, which may contain a total of ten billion words. The power requirements of such computers has been measured in hundreds of kilowatts and they were housed in cabinets that were 6 feet tall and more than 30 feet long, although some were arranged in the shape of a square, a cross, or a circle to minimize wire lengths, thereby increasing speed. Together with their peripheral equipment, they often occupied rooms measured in tens of thousands of square feet. Although the present-day VLSI technology is cutting size, cost, and power requirements sharply, these requirements still tend to be several times larger and costlier for supercomputers than for their slower and smaller counterparts.

In many installations, supercomputers are used for rather limited classes of computations. These are often numerical applications, which include the solution of partial differential equations for such problems as numerical weather prediction. Or they may involve large matrix calculations such as those required for the solution of linear programming problems in economic planning. Some calculations are nonnumerical, as in cryptanalysis. Other supercomputer systems do relatively little "computation" in the traditional sense. Rather, they are occupied in providing many users with essentially instant services. These may include compilation of programs and access to large files, as in an airline reservation system.

The speed increases of modern supercomputers have come from several sources. One is the great improvement in the speed of parts—from relays, through vacuum tubes and transistors, to modern integrated circuits, which can switch from one state to another in less than 1 ns (10^{-9} sec). These integrated circuits have from ten to several thousand transistors in one physical device. As a result of this integration, supercomputers with several hundred thousand switching devices (a factor of 100 higher than in the 1940s) are now being operated. Since many more components are used, various functions may be performed simultaneously, thereby achieving a functional speedup in addition to that resulting from faster component-switching speeds.

Given a traditional sequential computer, there are four classical approaches to speeding up processing (e.g., comparisons, logic operations, or arithmetic operations). Besides using faster circuits, other possibilities include the following.

1. *Multiprocessing* by replicating the sequential computer and interconnecting the collection so that each processor can execute the same or a different program at the same time.
2. *Parallel processing* by replicating and interconnecting the processors and memories but retaining a central control unit that sequences all of the processors together from one program.
3. *Multifunction processing* by replicating certain processing and control hardware to allow the simultaneous execution of several operations in one processor.
4. *Pipeline processing* by slicing the functions of a sequential computer into short segments, thereby allowing more than one set of operands to be processed simultaneously.

It is easy to think of variations that blend these ideas together, and in the quest of faster, more efficient machines, designers have tried many such variations. Fig. 1 shows the four classical approaches, how they relate to one another, and the computers which characterize these approaches.

Notice that there are no pure pipelined processors because pipelined machines also incorporate a parallel or multifunction approach, as we note in detail below when considering each of the architectures of Fig. 1.

Multiprocessing is perhaps the most obvious approach to speeding up a sequential computer's effective speed. To achieve higher throughput by running several jobs at once (one per processor), this technique is used by most manufacturers today, in the sense that a user can buy two or more identical, interconnected processors with multiprocessing supported by the operating system. Examples are the Control Data Cyber 170 series and Univac 1100/80 series. But to achieve faster turnaround of a single job is more difficult, because the programmer or the compiler must break up a program to make it fit the hardware. This approach is currently almost never used in commercial machines; however, the future of this approach seems bright, as higher levels of circuit integration make processors smaller and less expensive.

Multifunction processing was the first of these four approaches to achieve widespread commercial success. This idea was used early in the 1960s in the CDC 6600. In its purest form, a multifunction processor machine has a control unit that is capable of sequencing more than one processor function at once, and the processor has sufficient hardware to execute more than one operation at once. An obvious extension of this idea is to include more than one functional unit of a given type; e.g., the CDC 6600 had two multipliers that could operate at once.

To some extent, these early multifunction processors distributed some of the control functions into the processor. For example, the IBM 360/91 (which combines multifunction and pipeline processing) had queues in front of functional units that contained operators and requests for operands. Operands were sent to all functional units, picked up where requested, and any functional unit that had all of its operands could execute its operation. These functional units are sometimes said to be *data driven*. It is natural to explore the possibility of extending these ideas to a large collection of functional units. Such research has been pursued in several directions, most of which are associated with the name *dataflow computation,* although there are, as yet, no commercial computers embodying these ideas.

Pipeline processing has been the most commercially successful method of speeding up a sequential computer. For example, the CDC 7600 was a pipelined successor of the CDC 6600, and the IBM 360/91 was also pipelined; both machines appeared in the late 1960s. In the mid-1970s, the CRAY-1 was introduced; it is logically a suc-

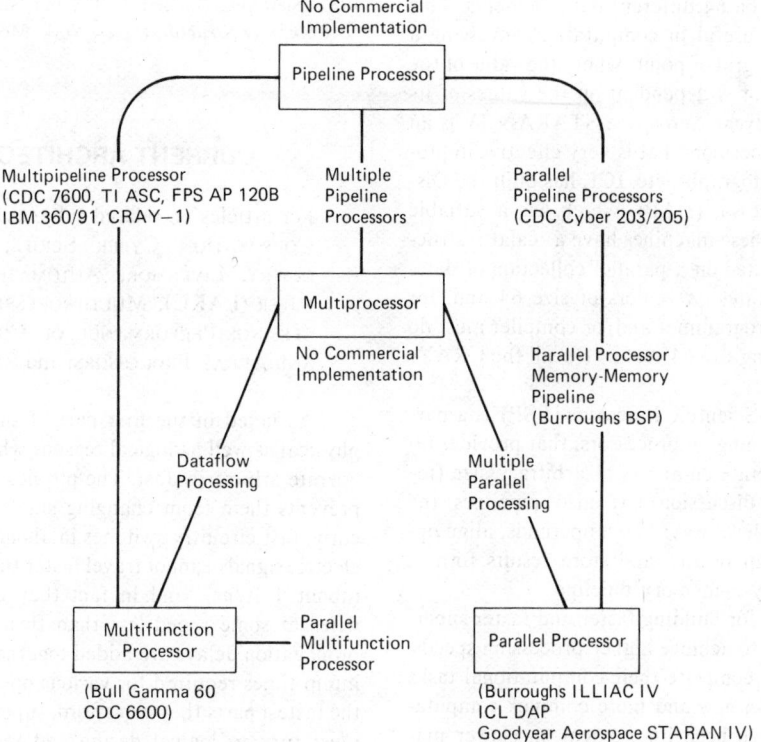

No Commercial
Implementation

Pipeline Processor

Multipipeline Processor
(CDC 7600, TI ASC, FPS AP 120B
IBM 360/91, CRAY—1)

Multiple
Pipeline
Processors

Parallel
Pipeline Processors
(CDC Cyber 203/205)

Multiprocessor

No Commercial
Implementation

Parallel Processor
Memory-Memory
Pipeline
(Burroughs BSP)

Dataflow
Processing

Multiple
Parallel
Processing

Multifunction
Processor

Parallel
Multifunction
Processor

Parallel Processor

(Bull Gamma 60
CDC 6600)

(Burroughs ILLIAC IV
ICL DAP
Goodyear Aerospace STARAN IV)

Fig. 1. Architectural monoprogramming speedup techniques.

cessor to the CDC 7600. The CDC 6600 had a 400-ns adder and two 1-μsec multipliers that could operate simultaneously, so its maximum rate for addition or multiplication was about two megaflops (million floating-point operations per second). The CDC 7600 had a 27.5-ns clock, so its pipelined operations could each proceed at a maximum rate of about 36 megaflops. The CRAY-1 has a 12.5-ns clock, so its pipelined operations can each proceed at a rate of 80 megaflops, a factor of about 40 greater than the CDC 6600. Of course, achieving the maximum possible performance with ordinary programs is very difficult.

The instruction set of the CDC 7600 consists only of scalar operations while the CRAY-1 has 8 registers, each containing 64 vector elements. For vectors of larger size, the programmer or compiler must cleverly page 64-element slices of a vector in and out of the vector registers in proper time slots. Vector instructions which can handle vectors of any size were built into the Texas Instruments Advanced Scientific Computer (ASC) in the form of memory-to-memory vector instructions. This is useful for programmers and compiler writers. Pipeline processing has been widely used, even in low-cost scientific computers which can be thought of as special-purpose add-on units for a general-purpose small host computer. They

usually contain high-speed arithmetic and a limited amount of high-speed memory. Since they execute only special vector and array instructions or subroutines (like the FFT), they are called *array processors*.

Pipelining has a serious limitation as a speedup technique, since most functions can only be broken into a relatively small number of segments (say eight). To get more speed, the machines mentioned above allow several operations to be executed at once. When this is carried very far, difficulties arise in controlling or programming the ensemble of functional units. This is also a problem in multiprocessing a single computation.

Parallel processing is a way of solving this problem by keeping control at a central point that sequences a collection of identical processors. An expensive, lookahead control unit can thus be shared by many processors. In theory, the number of processors—and thus the potential speedup over a single sequential processor—is unlimited and may be chosen to match any set of user computations. In fact, fitting computations to parallel machines also poses difficult programming or compilation problems.

Several parallel machines have been built and used successfully in limited application areas. Illiac IV contains a collection of 64 processors, each capable of floating-point operations on 64 different data elements. This organization is very useful in computations involving a function defined on a grid of points where the value of the function at each point is dependent on the values of its neighbors. The Goodyear Aerospace STARAN IV is an array of bit-serial processors that is very effective in processing digitized photographs, etc. ICL has built the Distributed Array Processor (DAP), which has a variable word length. All of these machines have a scalar instruction set that is executed on a parallel collection of data. Thus, Illiac IV operates on vectors of size 64 and, for longer vectors, the programmer and/or compiler must do the work of connecting size 64 vectors (recall the CRAY-1 discussion).

The Burroughs Scientific Processor (BSP) is a parallel machine, containing 16 processors, that provides instructions which operate on arrays of arbitrary size (recall the TI ASC discussion). It also pipelines the operations in a high-level way: Fetch operands, align operands, operate, align results, and store results form a five-segment memory-to-memory pipeline.

One motivation for building faster and faster supercomputers is simply to achieve higher processing speeds. This allows users to complete their computational tasks faster or to engage in new and more complex computations that would have been impractical on slower machines. In fact, various supercomputers at present are becoming more and more specialized for particular classes of computations. Another motivation for building large computers is the economy of scale which may be achieved.

It seems likely that new supercomputers will continue to appear. The supercomputers of 20 years ago were similar to the minicomputers of today—operating on scalar operands. Today's supercomputers operate on vector operands. In the future, supercomputers may operate simultaneously on multidimensional arrays whose elements are parse trees of arithmetic expressions, with many parallel operations being performed, each in a pipelined way. Ultimately, the speed of a supercomputer is a function of the switching speed of its parts and the amount of simultaneity that exists in the computations to be performed. The former constraint arises from the physics of its hardware devices. The latter constraint arises from the logical and numerical structure of the algorithms being executed.

REFERENCES

1978. Kuck, D. J. *The Structures of Computers and Computations.* New York: Wiley.

1978. Hayes, J. P. *Computer Architecture and Organization.* New York: McGraw-Hill.

1980. Baer, J.-L. *Computer System Architecture.* Rockville, MD: Computer Science Press.

1982. Sieworek, D., Bell, C. G., and Newell, A. *Principles of Computer Structures.* New York: McGraw-Hill.

D. J. KUCK

CURRENT ARCHITECTURES

For articles on related subjects *see* CONTROL DATA CORPORATION CYBER SERIES; INTEGRATED CIRCUITRY; LIVERMORE AUTOMATIC RESEARCH COMPUTER (LARC); MULTIPROCESSING; PARALLEL PROCESSING; PERFORMANCE OF COMPUTERS; PIPELINE AND ARRAY PROCESSORS; and STRETCH.

As noted in the first part of this article, there are physical as well as logical reasons why computers cannot operate arbitrarily fast. The physics of switching devices prevents them from changing states in zero time; presently, fast circuitry switches in about 1 ns. Furthermore, electric signals cannot travel faster than the speed of light (about 1 ft/ns), and in fact they usually travel along wires at some speed less than this. The switching and propagation delays are added together to determine minimum times required for various operations. Thus, using the fastest parts they can afford, supercomputer designers must turn to logical design and machine organization techniques to speed up computer operation.

One of the most obvious techniques for making faster computers is to employ some form of parallelism. Thus, memory, central processor, control unit, and I/O devices may all be designed to operate concurrently. Furthermore, each may be organized to perform more than one operation at a time. We focus our attention here on the parallel internal operation of central processors and to a lesser extent on control units.

Consider first the replication of identical arithmetic units (AU). Suppose we wish to add (or multiply, etc.) n pairs of numbers to form n sums: $a_1 + b_1$, a_2, $+ b_2$, $\ldots$, $a_n + b_n$. Using n AUs, as shown in Fig. 1, we can form these sums in the same time as required to do one addition with one AU. Thus, n AUs computing this kind of sum would be n times faster than a single AU. Notice, however, that if we needed m sums of $2m$ numbers, the speedup over one AU using n AUs would be only $m/\lceil m/n \rceil$ instead of n, where $\lceil m/n \rceil$ is the smallest integer greater than or equal to m/n. For example, if we want $m = 3n/2$ sums, n AUs could do this in two steps, whereas one AU would require $3n/2$ steps, so the speedup would be $3n/4$ instead of n.

Now, however, assume we wish to add $2n$ numbers to produce just one sum: $a_1 + a_2 + a_3 + \ldots a_{2n}$. Again, using n AUs, we first form n sums $a_1 + a_2$, $a_3 + a_4$, $\ldots$, $a_{2n-1} + a_{2n}$. Now we must use $n/2$ AUs [or $(n - 1)/2$ if n is odd] to reduce these n sums to $n/2$ [or $(n - 1)/$

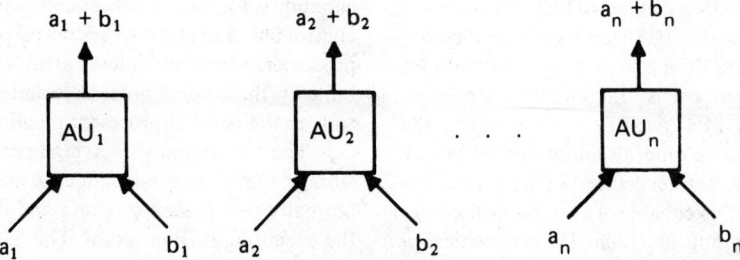

Fig. 1. Computation of n sums by n arithmetic units.

2] sums $(a_1 + a_2) + (a_3 + a_4)$, $(a_5 + a_6) + (a_7 + a_8)$, $\ldots, (a_{2n-3} + a_{2n-2}) + (a_{2n-1} + a_{2n})$. We keep repeating this until we have just one sum. This is illustrated in Fig. 2. In general, it requires $\lceil \log_2 2n \rceil$ time steps to reduce $2n$ operands to one sum, where $\lceil \log_2 2n \rceil$ is the smallest integer greater than or equal to $\log_2 2n$. A single AU could have done this same operation in $2n - 1$ steps. Thus, on this kind of computation, n AUs are only $(2n - 1)/\lceil \log_2 2n \rceil$ times faster than a single AU instead of n times

faster, as for the previous computation. In general, the effectiveness of replications of AUs is dependent on the number of operations that can be done in parallel in a given program, and on the interaction between these operations.

This technique of using parallel units has been employed to a significant degree in several computers, including Goodyear's Staran, ICL DAP, and the well-known Burroughs Illiac IV. Illiac IV consists of 64 iden-

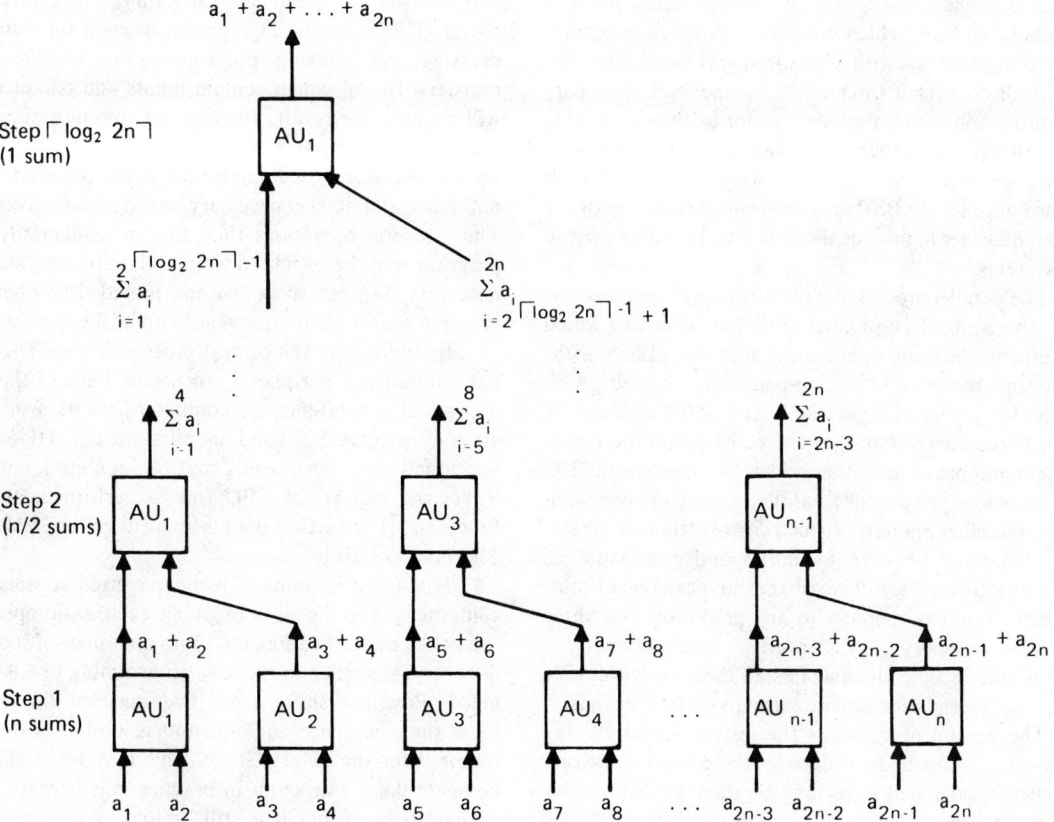

Fig. 2. Formation of the sum of $2n$ numbers by n AUs.

tical AUs, called *processing elements* (PE) connected to form an 8 × 8 array with 2,048 words of local memory in each PE. All PEs are driven by a global control unit (CU) whose primary purpose is to fetch instructions and broadcast them to all PEs. All PEs must perform the same operation at the same time, although some PEs may be turned off if they are not needed for a particular computation. Since each PE is capable of two 32-bit floating-point operations every 800 ns, Illiac IV can achieve a speed of 160 megaflops. However, this speed can be achieved only on programs that require 128 identical operations at once. On more general programs where scalar and vector codes are intermixed, the speed will be much less than maximum.

The new Burroughs supercomputer, the Burroughs Scientific Processor (BSP) uses only 16 processing elements and was designed to achieve good balance between scalar and vector codes. Instead of local memory and nearest-neighbor connections, it uses a shared-memory and crossbar switch. The BSP total system (Fig. 3) consists of two integrated processing environments—a foreground general-purpose system called the system manager, which provides for interactive program preparation, permanent file storage, and overall system control and workload scheduling, and a background number cruncher, the BSP, which provides high-speed execution of Fortran programs with a balanced I/O capability. The BSP itself consists of three major components—the parallel processor, which performs vector arithmetic operations; the control processor, which interprets the program; and the file memory, which provides high performance I/O to BSP programs and is shared with the system manager to provide the data interface between the two systems.

The parallel processor is the arithmetic engine of the BSP, consisting of 16 parallel arithmetic elements which all perform the same operation in lock-step. Each arithmetic unit performs a floating-point add or multiply in 320 ns for a peak computation rate of 50 megaflops. A conflict-free memory access scheme based on the use of a prime number of memories allows full bandwidth (100 million words per second) parallel access to rows, columns, and other regularly spaced cross-sections of arrays. Data is routed between memories and processors 16 words at a time via a full crossbar switch capable of routing data from any memory to any processor. The three functions—memory access, routing, and arithmetic—form a macroscopic pipeline; i.e., all these activities take place concurrently for separate groups of 16 operands.

The control processor is the instruction processing component of the BSP. It decodes the compiled instruction stream and builds vector operation descriptors for the parallel processor. It contains a separate dedicated memory for program storage. It also has full arithmetic capability for scalar processing. The parallel processor control unit, interfacing the control processor and parallel processor, accepts high-level array expression descriptors built by the control processor, and issues the microcontrols to the parallel processor pipeline.

The file memory is a high-performance secondary storage based on semiconductor memory technology. It normally contains all program and data files accessed by the executing BSP program. The file memory uses an intelligent hardwired controller to remove the burden of most required "physical I/O" operations from the operating system.

The three components of the BSP operate concurrently; thus, vector arithmetic, vector operation set-up, and I/O operations can all be done simultaneously. For further details, see Kuck and Stokes (1980).

While Illiac IV uses 64 and BSP 16 identical arithmetic units that are capable of executing any operation, but only one at a time, a slower but somewhat more general technique involves the use of a number of different arithmetic units. This is best illustrated by the CDC 6600 shown in Fig. 4. With reference to Fig. 4, a program running in the central processor may use any of the ten arithmetic units simultaneously, although a typical program will use two or three of these at a time. The central processor (CP) includes 24 registers, 8 each for data, addressing, and indexing. Each instruction specifies three registers, two of which contain inputs and one of which will receive the result. Instructions are introduced sequentially to the AUs subject to testing by the scoreboard. The scoreboard determines if the required AU is not busy and if the necessary registers are available. Thus, several operations that appear sequentially in a program may be executed simultaneously, provided the necessary AUs are available and provided no operation requires results from a previously unfinished operation.

In addition to the central processor, the CDC 6600 has a number of peripheral processors. Each of these independent general-purpose computers has its own memory and is capable of handling all system functions (system monitoring, peripherals control, I/O, etc.), and thus leaves the high-speed CPU free to perform arithmetic functions. [For further details about the CDC 6600, see Thornton (1970).]

Pipelining is another technique used to speed up computers. This involves breaking each basic operation (addition, multiplication, etc.) into a number of independent stages, similar to the way an assembly line is organized. Pipelines suffer from two inherent limitations. First, the emergence rate of results is limited by the time required for the longest stage. This may be as short as one gate delay (although in practice it is perhaps 10 or 20 gate delays), but it is still limited by device speeds. Second, if only one operation needs to be performed, as

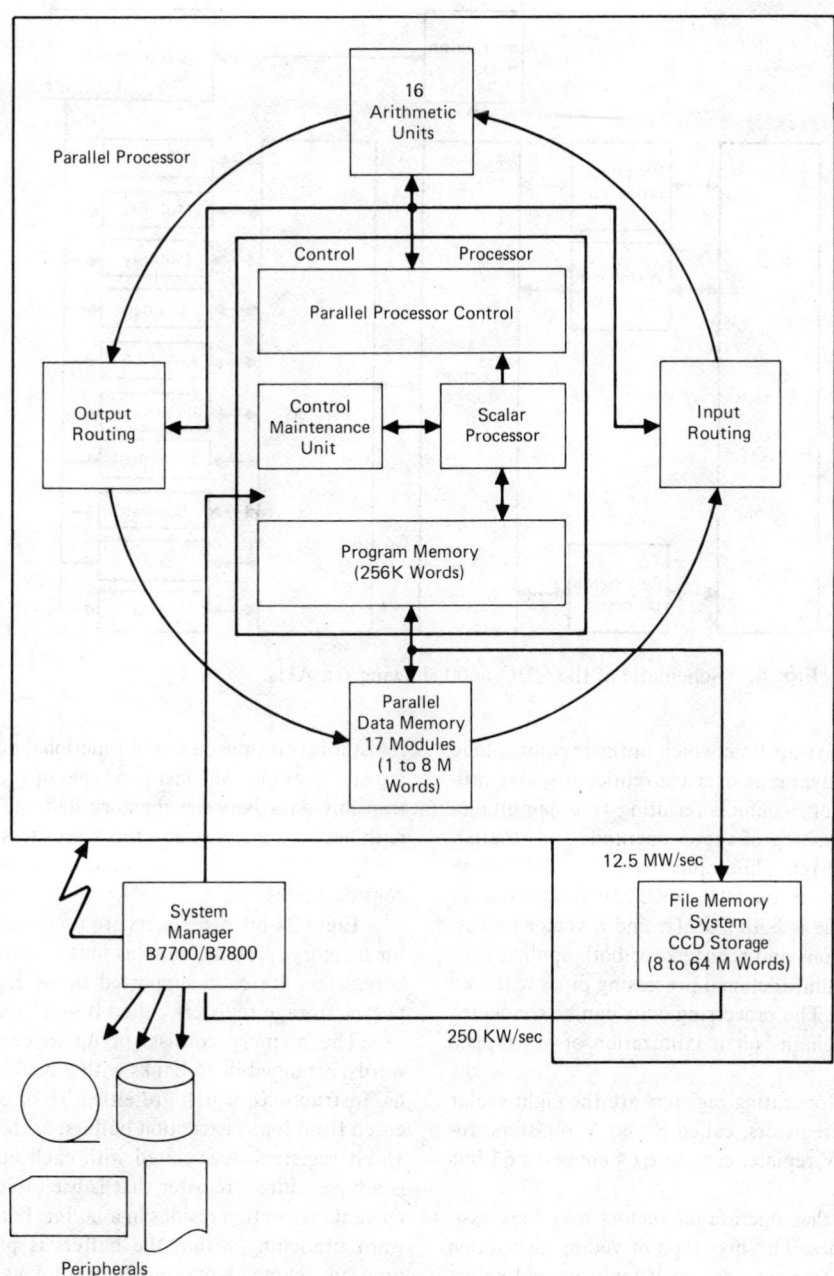

Fig. 3. Block diagram of the Burroughs Scientific Processor.

mentioned above, it will usually take longer than a more conventional organization.

Pipeline techniques have recently been used in several fast computers, including the IBM 360/91, the CDC STAR-100, and Texas Instruments ASC computer, CRAY-1, and CDC Cyber 203/5. Two strategies may be used in pipelined machine design: In one, each arithmetic operation is pipelined and the machine has many of these unifunctional pipes; in the other, all the arithmetic is merged into one pipe and there may be one or more of these multifunctional pipes working in parallel. The CRAY-1 computer, which belongs to the first category, is designed to overcome some of the deficiencies of vector processors (inability to compete successfully in scalar ap-

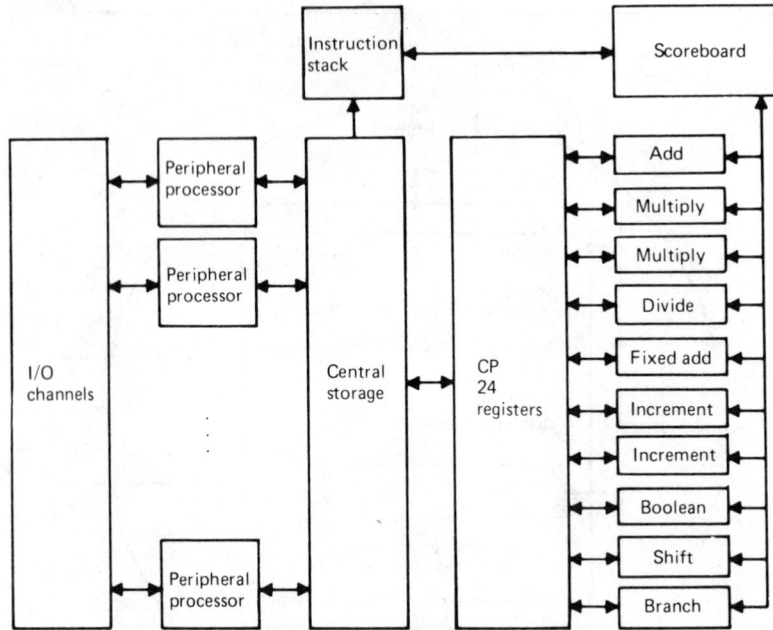

Fig. 4. Schematic of the CDC 6600 showing ten AUs.

plications, long start-up time which in turn requires long vectors to show advantage over conventional scalar processors, and memory conflicts resulting from simultaneous reading and writing of vector operands and results). The CRAY-1 design philosophy (see Fig. 5) follows closely the tradition of the CDC 6600 and 7600. Conceptually, the machine is both a scalar and a vector processor, with instructions and registers for both applications. There are twelve unifunctional processing pipes with two to eight segments. The processing units can be connected to form efficient chains for maximization of overlapped vector processing.

The primary operating registers are the eight scalar and eight vector registers, called S and V registers, respectively. Each V register can store 64 elements 64 bits wide.

Instructions that operate on vectors may be classified into four types. The first type of vector instruction obtains operands from one or two V registers and enters results into another V register. Successive operand pairs are transmitted to the segmented functional unit each clock period and corresponding results emerge from the functional unit m clock periods later, where m is constant for a given functional unit and is called the functional unit time. Results are entered into result registers. A constant in the vector length register determines the number of operand pairs processed by the functional unit. The second type vector instruction obtains one operand from an S register and one from a V register. A copy of the S

register is transmitted to the functional unit with each V-register operand. The last two types of vector instructions transmit data between memory and the V registers. A path between memory and the V registers may be considered to be a pipelined functional unit for timing considerations.

Eight 24-bit A registers are used as address registers for memory references and as index registers. The A and S registers are each supported by 64 rapid-access temporary storage registers called B and T registers.

The memory consists of up to one million 64-bit words, arranged in 16 banks with a bank cycle time of 50 ns. Instructions, which are either 16 or 32 bits, are executed from four instruction buffers, each consisting of 64 16-bit registers. Associated with each instruction buffer is a base address register that is used to determine if the current instruction resides in a buffer. Forward and backward branching within the buffers is possible, and the program segments may be discontinuous in the program buffer. When the current instruction does not reside in a buffer, one of the instruction buffers is filled from memory. Four memory words are read per clock period to the least recently filled instruction buffer.

Any number of the 12 input and output channels may be active at a given time. Each channel has a maximum transfer rate of 80M bytes/second. At most, one 64-bit word can be transferred to or from memory during each clock period.

The Cyber 200 series is based on the STAR-100.

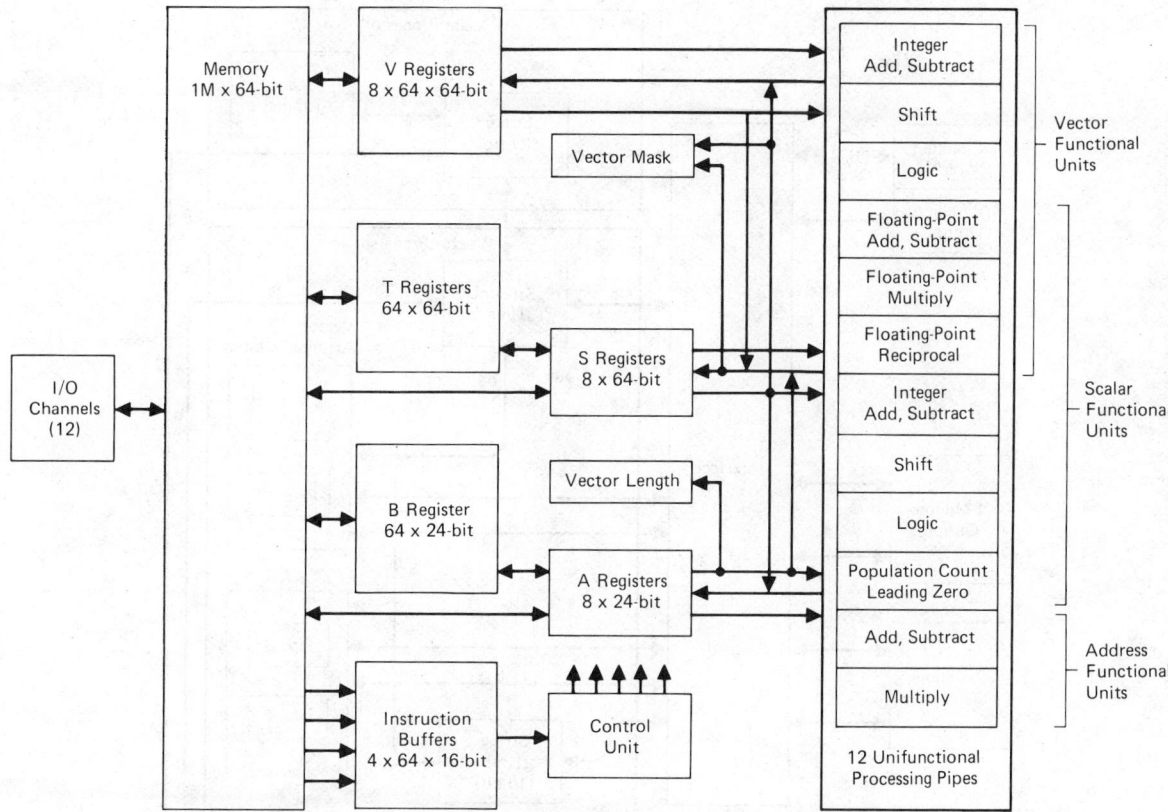

Fig. 5. CRAY-1 block diagram.

The first upgrade, Cyber 203, includes a new semiconductor memory to support high data rates required by the vector pipes, and a fast scalar processor whose counterpart on STAR-100 was very slow in comparison with those used on other serial computers.

The Cyber 200 has two or four pipelined processors (see Fig. 6). The pipeline stage delay is approximately 20 ns, and total pipeline delay is 100 ns for addition and multiplication. Each 64-bit pipeline can be split into two 32-bit pipelines. Thus, the Cyber 200 with two pipelines can perform four 32-bit operations simultaneously and can achieve a rate of four 32-bit operations every 20 ns, or 200 megaflops.

Fig. 6 shows a Cyber 203 consisting of Scalar Processor (SP), Vector Processor (VP), Memory Interface (MI), I/O channels, and Central Memory (CM).

The Scalar Arithmetic Unit, which contains independent arithmetic pipelined units, performs instruction control and virtual address translation. The vector instructions and streaming is controlled by the Stream Unit of the VP. The Stream Unit receives decoded instructions from the SP and proceeds to execute those instructions while SP is free to execute scalar instructions that are not in conflict with the vector operations. The Stream Unit manages the data streams that connect directly between CM and the vector pipelines. Each one-half million words of CM contains 16 memory modules each having 8 phased banks of 8K 32-bit words. The CM can supply 512 bits of data (i.e., 16 32-bit words) every 20 ns.

The memory buffer units of size 512 bits contained in the MI are necessary in order to smooth the flow of data between memories and pipelines, since the pipelines may require as many as 12 32-bit numbers every 20 ns (8 in, 4 out), and the memory system may miss a few cycles (but without, of course, losing any information) as a result of access conflicts.

In general, parallel operation and pipeline techniques are employed in varying degrees in today's fastest computers. At the lowest level, arithmetic and word transmissions are performed in digit-parallel fashion. Arithmetic or other functional units are often pipelined, more than one arithmetic unit can be used simultaneously, and there may be a pool of different functional units available for use by one or more programs. The de-

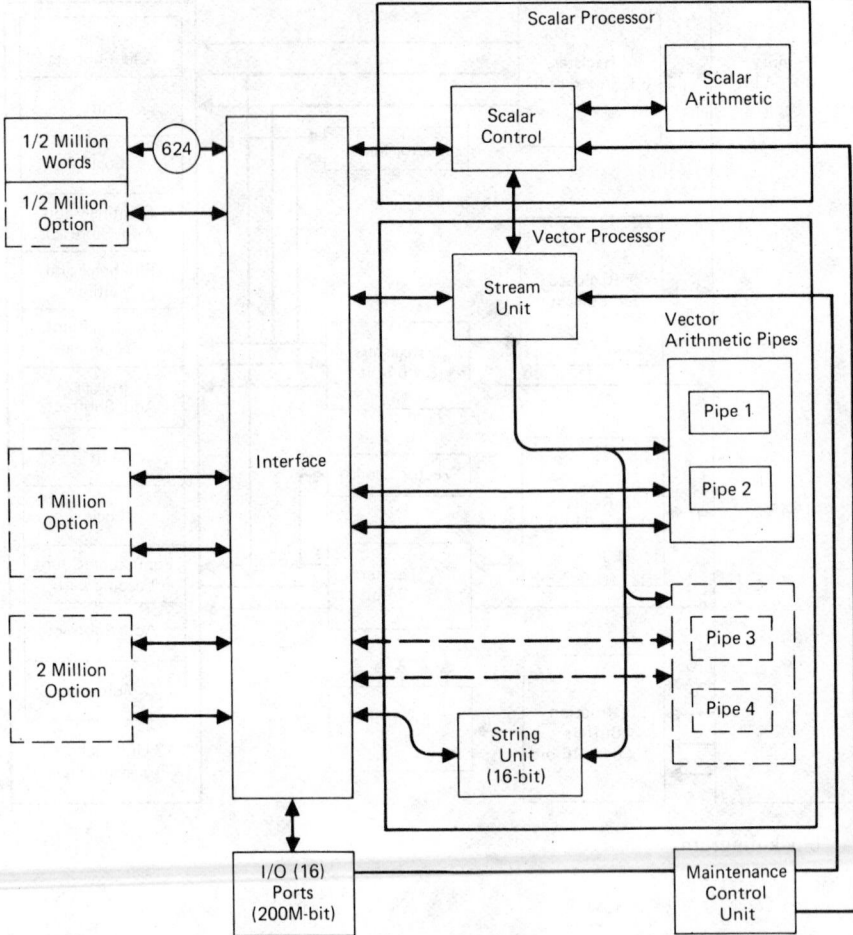

Fig. 6. Cyber 203 block diagram.

gree to which various techniques are employed depends on the required cost and speed of the final system and the type of programs to be executed.

REFERENCES

1970. Thornton, J. E. *Design of a Computer: The Control Data 6600.* Glenview, IL: Scott Foresman.

1978. Russell, R. M. "The CRAY-1 Computer System," *Comm. ACM* **21**, *No. 1:* 63–72 (January).

1980. Kuck, D. J. and Stokes, R. S. "The Burroughs Scientific Processor (BSP)," *IEEE Trans. Comp.*

1980. Love, H. H. "The Highly Parallel Supercomputers: Definitions, Applications, and Predictions," *AFIPS Conference Proceedings* **49**:181–190.

1980. Satyanarayanan, M. *Multiprocessors: A Comparative Study.* Englewood Cliffs, NJ: Prentice-Hall.

1981. Sieworek, D., Bell, C. G., and Newell, A. *Principles of Computer Structures.* New York: McGraw-Hill.

D. D. GAJSKI AND D. H. LAWRIE

SUPERVISOR CALL

For articles on related subjects *see* INTERRUPT; MULTIPROGRAMMING; OPERATING SYSTEMS; PRIVILEGED INSTRUCTION; and SUPERVISOR STATE.

A typical operating system has a set of system programs collectively known as the *supervisor,* whose function is to provide services for and to supervise the running of a number of user programs. Control goes to the supervisor every time the normal flow of processing is interrupted by a change of state in the system.

The purpose of a *supervisor call* is to provide a mechanism whereby a program can interrupt the normal flow of processing and ask the supervisor to perform a function for the program that the program either cannot or is not permitted to perform for itself.

The most typical supervisor calls have to do with input and output. In a multiprogramming system it is essential to have system control of I/O devices, especially those devices shared by a number of programs.

Most computers that were designed for multiprogramming systems have a supervisory mode of operation and hardware interlocks that prevent certain supervisory operations from taking place except when the computer is operating in supervisory mode. This may be handled by means of special privileged instructions that can be executed only in supervisory mode, or only in some other way.

In the IBM 360/370 systems, for example, a supervisor call is made through the execution of an instruction whose effect is to create an interrupt. The instruction is two bytes long. The first byte is the supervisor-call instruction code, and the second byte describes the nature of the supervisor call. This second byte goes into a special register which is used in connection with all interrupts to transmit information to the system as to the status of that particular interrupt.

The interrupt now proceeds like any other interrupt. It stores the status of the computer (the old program status word) and loads a new status that gives control to a resident supervisory routine, which operates in supervisor mode and whose function is the handling of supervisor calls. This routine then analyzes the second byte of the supervisor-call instruction and determines the nature of the call.

It is, of course, possible—and usually essential—that additional information is passed to the supervisory routine as a result of the supervisor call. This information may be in special registers (general registers) or in an area of memory pointed to by a special register.

The supervisor may have resident routines for handling certain classes of supervisor calls, and may have available areas of central memory (transient areas) into which overlays can be loaded for the handling of less frequent supervisor calls. Fast response to supervisor calls is usually an important factor in system performance, and systems that have large amounts of central memory can often improve their responsiveness by increasing the number of resident supervisor-call routines.

S. ROSEN

SWAC

For articles on related subjects *see* DIGITAL COMPUTERS: Early; and SEAC.

SWAC [(National Bureau of) Standards Western Automatic Computer] was dedicated in August 1950, and at that time was the fastest computer in existence. It was begun in January 1949 at the National Bureau of Standard's field station, the Institute for Numerical

Fig. 1. The SWAC.

Analysis at the University of California at Los Angeles, and was designed and constructed under the direction of the author. Originally named the ZEPHYR, due to its modest-sized budget and staff as contrasted with much larger projects being carried on elsewhere, it was later renamed the SWAC.

The SWAC was a parallel computer using Williams' tube (cathode-ray tube) memory (*q.v.*). The memory cycle was 16 μs consisting of an 8 μs action cycle and an 8 μs restore cycle (where some other memory location was restored). An addition of two 37-bit operands occurred in 64 μs, and multiplication occurred in 384 μs. Due to technical difficulties with Williams' tube storage, the memory was never increased beyond 256 words. A 4,096-word magnetic drum was added to the system with coordinated addressing so that block transfers of 32 words between the two memories occurred with no latency.

Initial input and output was by typewriter and punched paper tape. These were soon replaced by a card reader (240 cards per minute) and a card punch (80 cards per minute). The SWAC used a four-address command structure. A floating-point interpretive system named SWACPEC was developed, which made it much easier for users to write programs.

In 1953, the SWAC was producing about 53 hours of useful computing time per week. SWAC was used in a research computing environment, and therefore many of the problems tended to be quite large. Solution times from 177 to 453 hours are reported by Huskey et al. (1953). Some of the early problems included the search for Mersenne primes, the Fourier synthesis of X-ray diffraction patterns of crystals, the solution of systems of linear equations, and problems in differential equations.

When the National Bureau of Standards ceased to support the Institute for Numerical Analysis, the SWAC was transferred to the University and moved to the Engineering Building at UCLA. There it continued in useful operation until December 1967. Parts of the SWAC are now on exhibit in the Museum of Science and Industry in Los Angeles.

REFERENCES

1951. Huskey, H. D. "Semiautomatic Instruction on the Zephyr," *Proceedings of a Second Symposium on Large-Scale Digital Computing Machinery*. Cambridge, MA: Harvard University Press, pp. 83–90.

1953. Huskey, H. D., Thorensen, R., Ambrosio, B. F., and Yowell, E. C. "The SWAC—Design Features and Operating Experience," *Proceedings of the I.R.E.* **41,** *No. 10:* 1294–1299 (October).

1978. National Computer Conference Pioneer Day. (Edited transcript available from Charles Babbage Institute, Palo Alto, CA.)

H. D. HUSKEY

SWAPPING

For articles on related subjects *see* MEMORY: Auxiliary; SCHEDULING ALGORITHM; TIME SHARING; TIME SLICE; and WORKING SET.

Swapping is a name for the information transfer that occurs when a program is temporarily unloaded from main to secondary storage and later reloaded to continue processing. The term originated in the time-sharing systems of the early 1960s. Because there was no memory protection hardware to isolate multiple programs, these early systems permitted only one user program at a time to reside and execute in the main memory. When a program reached the end of a time slice or stopped for I/O, the operating system exchanged it for another waiting program.

Most modern operating systems use multiprogrammed virtual memory. In these systems, there are two kinds of information transfer between main and secondary memory:

1. Loading a program at the start of an execution period, and unloading it at the end of that period.
2. Fetching new pages or segments on demand during the execution period.

Swapping is often used to name the first type of information transfer, and *demand fetching* (or *demand paging*) the second type. The term *roll-in* is sometimes used to name the process of loading a program, and *roll-out* the process of unloading.

Both types of transfer need not be used in the same system. CDC Cyber series computers, for example, load a complete program for execution; these machines employ swapping but no form of demand fetching. On the other hand, paged virtual memory systems are capable of starting a program with no initial loading; in this case, demand paging also serves to load the program after the start of execution. This is not an effective use of demand paging. It is much more efficient to load and unload full *working sets* at the starts and ends of execution periods; demand fetching should be used to add pages to the working set during the execution period.

Early time-sharing systems had to control the overhead of swapping. In CTSS, for example, the CPU would be idle during a swap because the user memory was uniprogrammed. The CTSS multilevel scheduler started programs at priority levels whose quanta were at least as long as the swap time; this limited CPU idle time due to swapping to 50% (see Corbato, 1962). Schedulers in modern multiprogramming systems do not pay as much attention to this because the swapping of one program occurs in parallel with the execution of another.

REFERENCE

1962. Corbato, F. J., Merwin-Daggett, M., and Daley, R. C. "An Experimental Time-Sharing System," *Proceedings of the Spring Joint Computer Conference* **21.** (In Rosen (Ed.), *Programming Languages and Systems*. New York: McGraw-Hill (1967), pp. 335–344.)

P. J. DENNING

SWITCHING THEORY. *See* AUTOMATA THEORY; LOGIC DESIGN; and SEQUENTIAL MACHINES.

SYMBOL MANIPULATION

For articles on related subjects *see* ADDRESSING; ALGEBRAIC MANIPULATION; ASSOCIATIVE LANGUAGES; AUTOMATA THEORY; INFORMATION PROCESSING; INPUT-OUTPUT DEVICES; LISTS AND LIST PROCESSING; STORED PROGRAM CONCEPT; and STRING PROCESSING LANGUAGES.

The power of a modern computer derives from its being more than an arithmetic calculator. It is, in fact, a general-purpose symbol-manipulating system. A symbol *token* is a pattern that can be compared by an information processing system with some other symbol token and judged equal with it or different from it. The basic test for equality of tokens incorporated in an information processing system determines the fundamental alphabet of symbols it is prepared to recognize and distinguish. A symbol, then, is a class of equal tokens with respect to this basic test.

The key characteristic of symbols for an information processing system is their ability to *designate,* i.e., to have referents. This means that an information process can take a symbol token as input and use it to gain access to a referenced object in order to affect it or be affected by it in some way: to read it, modify it, build a new structure with it, and so on. Hence, three concepts are central to understanding symbol manipulation: information processing system, symbol structure, and designation.

Information Processing Systems. An information processing system (IPS) is a system (Fig. 1) consisting of a memory containing symbol structures, a processor, effectors, and receptors. Leaving out of account the effectors and receptors, we can summarize the characteristics of an IPS in this way:

1. There is a set of elements, called *symbols.*
2. Symbols may be formed into symbol structures by means of a set of *relations.*
3. There is a *memory,* capable of storing and retaining symbol structures.
4. There is a set of *information processes* that take symbol structures as inputs and produce symbol structure outputs.
5. The IPS has a component, the *processor,* that consists of (a) an ability to execute a set of *elementary information processes* (EIP); (b) *short-term memory* (STM) that holds the input and output symbol structures of the EIPs; and (c) an *interpreter* that determines the sequence of EIPs to be executed by the IPS as a function of the symbol structures in STM.

Symbol Structures. We say that a symbol structure *designates* (or *references,* or *points to*) an object if there exist information processes that admit the symbol structure as input, and either: (1) affect the object; or (2) produce, as output, symbol structures that are affected by the object.

A symbol structure serves as a *program* if the object it designates is an information process, and the interpreter, if given the program, can execute the designated process.

A symbol is *primitive* if its designation is fixed by the elementary information processes or by the external environment of the IPS.

The "objects" that symbols designate may include symbol structures stored in the IPS memories (data structures and programs), processes that the IPS is capable of executing, or objects in an external environment of sensible (readable) stimuli. To *read* is to create in memory internal symbol structures (representations) that designate external stimuli; to *write* is to create responses in the external environment that are designated by internal symbol structures.

The relation between a designating symbol and its object may have any degree of directness or indirectness. A structure can point to a structure that points to a structure that points to. . . .

Example. The meaning of these concepts can be illustrated by an example. An IPS for receiving Morse Code will have to be able to perceive the basic external stimuli: dots, dashes, letter spaces, and word spaces.

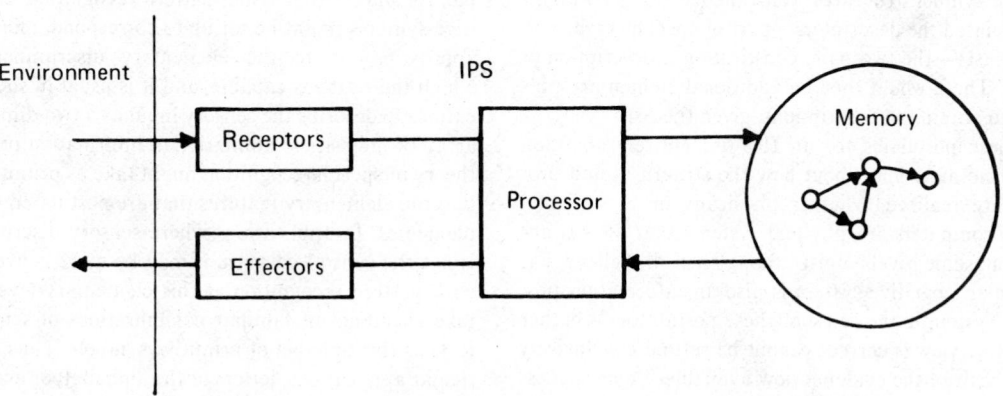

Fig 1. General structure of an information processing system. (From *Human Problem Solving*, Allen Newell and Herbert A. Simon. Englewood Cliffs, N. J.: Prentice-Hall, 1972.)

These stimuli could be represented internally by two different primitive symbol types, say "·" and "-", together with conventions for representing letters as lists of primitive symbols, and words as lists of letters. Sequences of stimuli could be represented by ordered sets (*lists*) of primitive tokens. Thus, if the external stimulus were a sequence of three dashes followed by a letter space, the read processes might store the symbol structure (-,-,-), the ")" representing the letter space.

In turn, each of these simple symbol structures would be assigned a *name*—i.e., a designating symbol. The structure (-,-,-), for example, might be designated by S. Then, larger structures could be built up as lists of such naming symbols [e.g., (W,A,S)], and so on indefinitely.

There would exist an elementary information process to find the member of a list next to a given member. Thus, given the token A and the list (W,A,S), this process would find the symbol token S. Another elementary process would test pairs of symbols for identity, to determine the equality, for example, of the second symbols of the lists (W,A,S) and (H,A,S), respectively.

The elementary processes would also have symbolic names, which could then be combined into composite processes, designated by lists of such names, thus allowing an arbitrarily complex subroutine structure. For example, the process for testing symbol identity could be combined with the process for finding the next symbol on a list, to test whether two lists are identical.

To execute composite processes, the IPS could use an interpretive process. A symbol structure (the program) would designate the sequence of elementary processes to be executed. The interpreter would keep track of the current elementary process being executed, and after execution would find the next process to be executed.

Finally, additional information could be associated with the symbol structures. With the list (W,A,S) might be associated the descriptors—part of speech (verb) and tense (past)—the two pairs constituting a description of the list. There would then be additional elementary processes to obtain the descriptions, given the list.

These postulates for an IPS are entirely abstract, making no assertions about how the structures and processes are realized, whether physically or biologically. Digital computers are physical systems that fit this abstraction; some psychologists, though not all, believe that the human cognitive system is also an information processing system in the sense of these postulates. Whether or not this view is correct cannot be settled conclusively on the basis of the evidence now available. Some success has been achieved, however, in modeling a range of human cognitive capabilities by means of appropriately defined information processing systems.

Designation. It would be more correct to say that symbol *structures* designate than to say that *symbols* designate. For example, if an information process takes as input the symbol structure (color, houseA) and produces the symbol "white," then the symbol structure (color, houseA) designates *white,* and hence indirectly designates the color of the house in question.

In discussing linguistic matters, one normally takes as prototypic of designation the relation between a proper name and the object named—e.g., "George Washington" and a particular man who was once President of the United States. One then attempts to pass from that relation to others more difficult to envision: e.g., the relation between "house" and any of a certain class of sheltering structures, and so on to "truth," "beauty," and "justice."

Any discussion of the basic characteristics of symbols and symbol structures always assumes the existence of information processes for acting on those symbols and structures. Each of the components, as is typical in abstract systems, remains essentially undefined, except when taken in conjunction with the other parts. Thus, the concept of *list* is inextricably mingled with the concept of a process for finding the *next* item on a list—i.e., for responding to the ordering relation that defines the list.

Some symbols have their meaning fixed by the existence of elementary information processes that treat them in fixed ways. The most important examples are:

1. Symbols that designate specific external events or structures (e.g., internal representations of real characters).
2. Symbols that designate elementary information processes, so that these EIPs can be executed when these symbols call for the execution.

What collection of symbols is primitive for a specific IPS will vary with the particular application. For example, for purposes of visual pattern recognition, the primitive symbols might be set up to correspond, more or less approximately, to the elementary discriminations of which the retina is capable, and it is usual in such applications to describe the sensory input as a two-dimensional array of intensities. Similarly, an information processing theory of speech recognition might take as primitive symbols the elementary features that are postulated to define phonemes. In applications where sensory discrimination is not the central concern, it may be more convenient to omit pattern recognition at this elementary level and to take encodings of familiar configurations of sensory objects as the alphabet of primitive symbols. Thus, for particular applications, letters of the alphabet, or even whole words, might be taken as primitive symbols. An important consequence of taking letters as primitive symbols is that we cannot then speak of one pair of letters as more closely resembling each other than another pair. There is no notion of degree of difference or similarity among them.

Representation. A simple example has already shown how primitive symbols can be combined into lists and descriptions. A couple of additional examples will illustrate the wide range of representations that can be accommodated by these means. In storing chess information, the pieces can be designated by symbols that have descriptions—defining each piece's type (King, Queen, Rook, etc.), color, and positions on the board. Squares can also be represented as described symbols, whose descriptions include information about the geometry of the board, i.e., which squares adjoin them. A position, in this representation, is a symbol structure that associates with each square the symbol or the piece occupying that square, if any, and which identifies the adjacent squares in various directions.

A somewhat different representation might be suitable for expressions from symbolic logic; e.g., $(P \lor Q) \cdot (Q \supset R)$. This expression can be represented by just this list of symbols, including parentheses. The expression can also be represented by a list structure, whose main list is $(\cdot, A, B)$, where A is the symbol that designates the list $(\lor, P, Q)$, and B the symbol that designates the list $(\supset, Q, R)$. Alternatively, making use of the relations of left (for left subexpression) and right (for right subexpression), the same logic expression could be represented as a tree structure (Fig. 2). Yet another representation of the expression uses descriptions. Take as attributes *term, connective, left,* and *right,* and as symbols a number of nodes, $x1, x2. \ldots$. Then the logic expression could be represented as the following set of descriptions.

connective$(x1) = \cdot$	left$(x1) = x2$	right$(x1) = x3$
connective$(x2) = \lor$	left$(x2) = x4$	right$(x2) = x5$
connective$(x3) = \supset$	left$(x3) = x6$	right$(x3) = x7$
term$(x4) = P$		
term$(x5) = Q$		
term$(x6) = Q$		
term$(x7) = R$		

These associations can be represented pictorially, as in Fig. 3. All of these representations are very closely related, as can be observed. That there are many ways of representing something should not be surprising. We could give still others, e.g., Polish prefix notation. All that is needed for a representation is some scheme of associations (relations) together with a set of information processes that can extract the appropriate information about connections. It is not usually possible to tell from its output exactly what internal representation is being used by an IPS, especially when alternate representations are as isomorphic as those presented here. However, in other cases, particularly in representing problems, the choice of representation can have striking observable consequences for external behavior.

If too limited a repertory of symbol structures and designations is provided by an IPS, the encoding of complex information can become an exercise in virtuosity that yields little benefit of any other kind. It appears that the structures essential to provide appropriate direct representation of a very wide range of stimuli are list structures and descriptions, the two types of structures we have used extensively in our examples. Other types of structures may be needed occasionally, but these two types are the core of the representational capability used in most information processing systems.

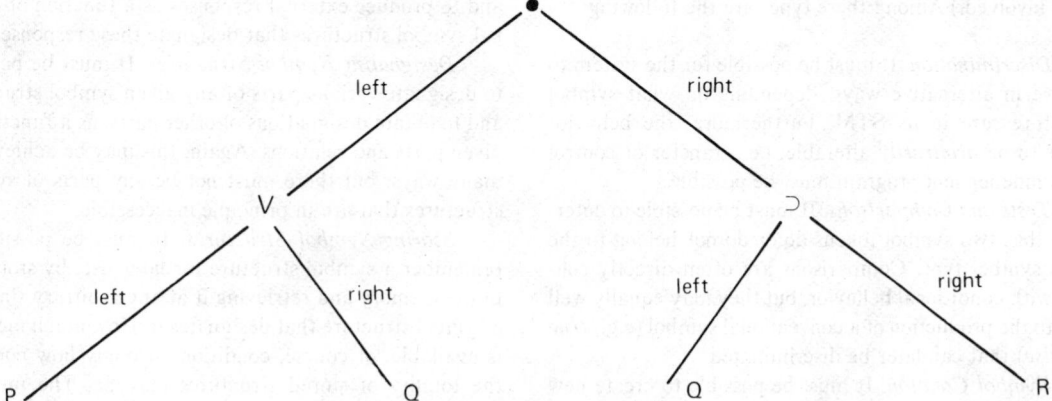

Fig. 2. Tree structure for $(P \lor Q) \cdot (Q \supset R)$. (From *Human Problem Solving,* Allen Newell and Herbert A. Simon. Englewood Cliffs, N. J.: Prentice-Hall, 1972.)

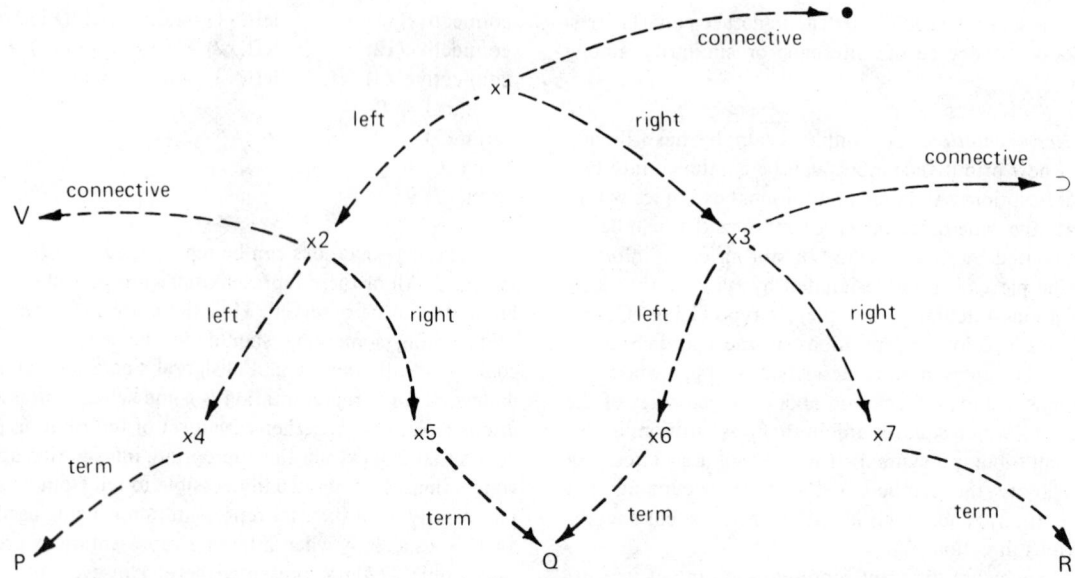

Fig. 3. Association structure for $(P \vee Q) \cdot (Q \supset R)$. (From *Human Problem Solving*, Allen Newell and Herbert A. Simon. Englewood Cliffs, N.J.: Prentice-Hall, 1972.)

Elementary Information Processes. There must be a sufficiently general and powerful collection of elementary information processes to extract from them all the macroscopic performances of the IPS. Furthermore, it is essential that these elementary processes be well defined so that they are realizable by known mechanisms. It is one of the major foundation stones of computer science that a relatively small set of elementary processes suffices to produce the full generality of information processing. On the other hand, there is no *unique* basis. However, all alternative schemes do incorporate certain fundamental types of EIPs that constitute a sufficient basic set. (Proof of their sufficiency is somewhat more involved.) Among these types are the following:

Discrimination. It must be possible for the system to behave in alternative ways, depending on what symbol structures are in its STM. Furthermore, the behavior needs to be *arbitrarily* alterable; i.e., transfer of control to an independent program must be possible.

Tests and Comparisons. It must be possible to determine that two symbol tokens do or do not belong to the same symbol type. Comparisons are often directly coupled with conditional behavior, but they may equally well lead to the production of a conventional symbol (e.g., *true* or *false*) that can later be discriminated.

Symbol Creation. It must be possible to create new symbols and set them to designate specified symbol structures. Again, this process must be performable arbitrarily; i.e., whenever a new symbol is desired, it can be cre-

ated, but it should carry no meaning other than its designation of the specified symbol structure. Whether the system must also be able to destroy symbols depends primarily on whether memory capacity is limited.

Writing Symbol Structures. It must be possible to create a new symbol structure, copy an existing symbol structure, and modify an existing symbol structure, either by changing or deleting symbol tokens belonging to the structure or by appending new tokens with specified relations to the structure.

Reading and Writing Externally. It must be possible to designate stimuli received from the external environment by means of internal symbols or symbol structures, and to produce external responses as a function of internal symbol structures that designate these responses.

Designating Symbol Structures. It must be possible to designate various parts of any given symbol structure, and to obtain designations of other parts, as a function of given parts and relations. Again, this may be achieved in many ways, but there must not be any parts of symbol structures that are in principle inaccessible.

Storing Symbol Structures. It must be possible to remember a symbol structure for later use, by storing it in the memory and retrieving it at any arbitrary time via a symbol structure that designates it. How much memory is available, of course, conditions strongly how complex the totality of stored structures may be. The memory must be highly reliable over time.

Even the earliest stored-program computers essentially met these requirements for an information processing system. The abstract characterization of a system such as that outlined here was developed in close relation with the invention and application of list processing and string manipulation languages, particularly in the domains of artificial intelligence, computer simulation of human cognitive processes, machine translation of language, and the design and construction of compilers. These applications make little use of the computer as a rapid arithmetic calculator, and depend basically upon its generality as a system for manipulating symbols.

Source Information. This article is drawn in large part from pages 20 to 30 of Newell and Simon (1972). For a formal approach to symbol manipulation in terms of Markov algorithms, see Chapter 1 of Galler and Perlis (1970), or Chapter 2 of Knuth (1968). Descriptions of two widely used list-processing languages illustrating many of the concepts discussed in this article will be found in Siklossy (1970) and in Griswold, Poage, and Polonsky (1971).

REFERENCES

1970. Siklossy, L. *Let's Talk Lisp.* Englewood Cliffs, NJ: Prentice-Hall.
1970. Galler, B. A. and Perlis, A. J. *A View of Programming Languages.* Reading, MA: Addison-Wesley. (Especially Chapters 1 and 3.)
1971. Griswold, R. D., Poage, J. F., and Polonsky, I. P. *The SNOBOL4 Programming Language.* Englewood Cliffs, NJ: Prentice-Hall.
1972. Newell, Allen and Simon, H. A. *Human Problem Solving.* Englewood Cliffs, NJ: Prentice-Hall.
1973. Knuth, Donald E. *The Art of Computer Programming* **1** (2nd ed.). Reading, MA: Addison-Wesley.

A. NEWELL AND H. A. SIMON

SYMBOL MANIPULATION LANGUAGES.
See ALGEBRAIC MANIPULATION.

SYNCHRONOUS/ASYNCHRONOUS OPERATION

For articles on related subjects *see* CONCURRENT PROGRAMMING; CYCLE STEALING; CYCLE TIME; HANDSHAKING; MULTIPLEXING; PETRI NETS; and SEMAPHORE.

The flow of information within a digital network may be said to be either synchronous or asynchronous. In the case of synchronous operation, a transfer of data from one point to another is assumed to occur within a fixed time interval, known to both the sending and receiving devices. The sender and receiver are synchronized by a signal called the *clock*, which may be supplied externally to both, or generated by the sender with the data, and occasionally incorporated within it, but often sent on a separate signal line. In the case of asynchronous operation, the sending device or circuit need have no knowledge of the time scale on which the receiver (and intervening connection) operates, but rather transmits its data with a "data ready" signal and then awaits a reply to the signal sent. Upon receipt of the reply by the sender, it removes its original data and status signal from the line, often (but not necessarily) waiting for the removal of the reply by the sender before proceeding with a second transfer.

The distinction between synchronous and asynchronous operation extends over an extremely broad range of digital design. It can apply to the logic gate and flip-flop level, to the logic unit interconnect level, to the bus transfer level, to the I/O device transfer level, and even to the level of communication with remote systems.

At the logic design level, the synchronous design technique is most straightforward and, accordingly, the most common. It is characterized by a cascade of alternating levels of combinatorial logic gates and synchronizing flip-flops driven by a common system clock. The system remains synchronized provided the total worst-case propagation delay through the combinatorial logic, from one flip-flop level to the next, is less than the interval between consecutive clock events. Accordingly, in synchronous logic designs, it is usual to practice to "capture" the state of the external environment by incorporating clocked flip-flops at the inputs, where, by means of the clock, a snapshot of the input is taken for processing. While the input sampling rate and internal clock rate are the same, the resulting process is essentially the one called pipelining (*q.v.*) in the context of large systems designs. In smaller-scale applications, the input sampling rate is usually at a small fraction of the clock rate of the internal logic, since the limited amount of hardware must be used in a succession of tasks between each input sample.

It is usual that the external inputs to a logic device are not inherently synchronized and thus may be said (causally) to be asynchronous. For example, the time at which an operator presses a button to signal a modified operation is quite random. As indicated previously, one approach is to synchronize such inputs by sampling them under control of the logic clock. However, it is possible to deal with them directly using logic operating in an asynchronous mode.

In asynchronous operation, the flip-flops used are of the simple unclocked reset-set (RS) kind, which wait in readiness for a gating event. Often the event is directly applied. For example, the RS flip-flop used with mechanical single-pole, single-throw (SPST) input pushbuttons and switches to *debounce* them (that is, to mask the intermittent connection provided by switch contact for a short time after its operation), is operating asynchronously; there is no clock; the flip-flop simply changes state upon the first transient contact of the bouncing switch element with its ultimate resting place.

Generally in asynchronous logic design, a large network of race-free combinatorial logic, in which the possibility of a transiently incorrect output (*glitch*) has been eliminated through care in the design of signal paths, may precede each RS storage element. A signal change at the input of this network is propagated to the flip-flop as fast as is possible at the actual speed of propagation of the intervening gates. While, for this part of the operation, no detailed knowledge is needed of the actual timing characteristics of the gates, it is quite difficult to know that gating is complete. Clearly, an estimate can be made from the specified worst-case propagation delays of all intervening gates.

On the larger systems level, synchronous and asynchronous operation are well illustrated by the signaling protocols that characterize both internal and external bus communications. Interestingly, one finds a synchronous protocol for links that are either very, very short or very, very long. The former choice is made when the environment is well-controlled and the maximum delay assumptions underlying synchronism can be made. The latter choice applies when the cost of waiting in an asynchronous exchange is thought to be too great.

Fig. 1 illustrates the synchronous exchange of data between two devices, the sender acting as master (M) and the receiver acting as slave (S). The letters M and S at the right edge of the waveforms in Figs. 1 and 2

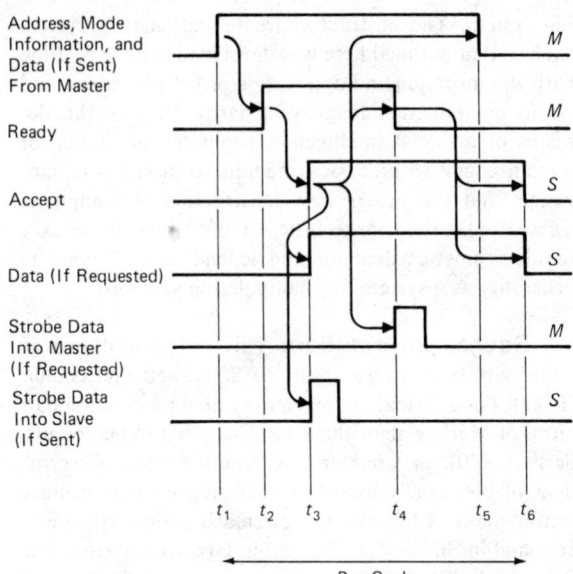

Fig. 2. Timing of data exchange between master and slave on an asynchronous bus with handshake control.

indicate the association device to be either master or slave.) The bus clock is common to both. At t_1, the master transmits the address of the slave, I/O mode information for control of the slave, and data (if any). The clock falling at t_2 signals the slave(s) to look at the bus and accept data (if sent) or send data (if required). The interval t_1 to t_2 allows for the time of signal propagation in the drivers, the line, and the receivers, as well as its variability (*skew*). At t_3, data, if requested by the master and sent by the slave, is gated into the master. The interval from t_2 to the following t_1 ensures settling of the bus prior to the next cycle.

When a bus is very long and serves many devices of different characteristics, the time required to handle a given device may be highly variable. However, if the synchronous protocol is used, all must go as slow as the slowest. This problem is avoided with asynchronous operation, as indicated in Fig. 2. Here, one device, the master (M) initiates the process at t_1 (having checked that the bus is not busy by noting that Ready and Accept lines are low), sending address, mode and data (if any) to the slave (S). Later, to allow for bus skew (the propagation time difference between signals on two lines), the master raises Ready at t_2, which signal propagates to all slaves. One, recognizing its address (indicated to be valid by Ready) at t_3, takes in (*strobes*) the data (if sent) or sends data (if requested) and raises the signal Accept. Subsequently, at t_4, having noted Accept and allowed for bus skew, the

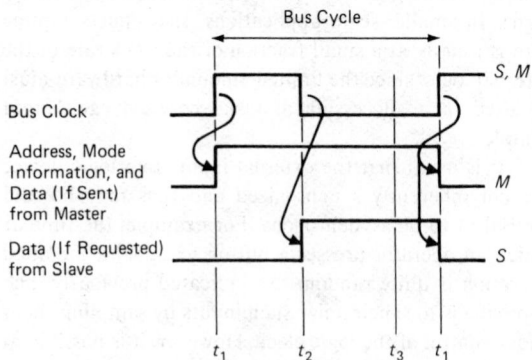

Fig. 1. Timing of data exchange between master and slave on a synchronous bus under common clock control.

master strobes data from the slave (if requested) and lowers Ready. However, to ensure correct operation of the slave while Ready is high in the presence of bus skew, the Master waits until t_5 to remove the Address and Control information. Meanwhile, the slave, having sensed the fall of Ready, removes Accept and Data (if any) at t_6, preparing the bus for a new cycle. In systems in which the role of master is not fixed, another control line, called Busy, is used to prevent the use of the bus by another (third) device connected to it. In simple systems, such conflict cannot occur since slave devices do not "speak unless spoken to."

For links of greater length, particularly between major components of a machine (such as CPU and memory, or CPU and Disk) or between two machines (CPU and CPU), asynchronous operation tends to dominate, since the Ready-Accept exchange can compensate for both transmission uncertainties as well as for busy states, etc., of one of the participating machines. However, as links lengthen, transmission time looms larger. Accordingly, for transmission at a distance, the message enlarges from a byte or two to a great many bytes. Within the message, the operation is synchronous although the initiation and completion of the message as a whole remains asynchronous in nature. In the limit, for large distances, the asynchronous element virtually disappears. The situation may be likened to that of sending a Telex. A message is sent with the assumption of availability of the recipient. If the receiver gets a garbled message, a repeat is requested. If no response at all is received by the sender, the message is sent again. These messages, while illustrating synchronism within themselves (that is locally), are embedded in a system that is asynchronous overall (that is, globally).

Another important example of a combination of synchronous and asynchronous techniques occurs in the start-stop codes used by teletypewriters and other terminals both in their connection to processing units and to each other. This connection often consists of a current loop connecting two or more devices through which loop current normally flows when the system is in the idle (rest) state. Transmission commences with the sender opening the line for a one-bit interval to signal the start bit, following which the sender opens and closes the loop corresponding to the 0 and 1 digits, respectively, of a serial code. When the desired bit string is complete (at the end of eight data bits for seven-bit ASCII), the loop is closed for a time corresponding to at least two bit intervals. These trailing "1" bits are called *stop bits* and signal to the receiver that a complete character has been sent, while preparing the line for the next transmission. A new character may be signaled by any device in the loop at any time following the last stop bit.

REFERENCE

1978. Hamacher, V. C., Vranesic, Z. G., and Zaky, S. G. *Computer Organization.* New York: McGraw-Hill.

K. C. SMITH

SYNTAX-DIRECTED COMPILER. *See* COMPILER, SYNTAX DIRECTED.

SYNTAX, SEMANTICS, AND PRAGMATICS

For articles on related subjects *see* GRAMMARS; LANGUAGE PROCESSORS; PROGRAMMING LANGUAGES; PROGRAMMING LANGUAGE SEMANTICS; and PROGRAMMING LINGUISTICS.

Every language of communication possesses two identifiable properties, the form of the language and the meaning associated with the form. In the case of natural languages (i.e., those languages used for human-to-human communication), the syntax of the language is generally referred to as its *grammar*. The syntax is a set of rules specifying which forms of the language are grammatically acceptable. For example, if a simple English sentence is specified to have the grammar

noun phrase verb phrase

and a *noun phrase* is composed of an *article* followed by a *noun*, while a verb phrase is defined to be a *verb* followed by a *noun phrase,* we may see that the sentence

"The cat drank the milk"

is a syntactically correct English sentence, provided the word "the" is in the class of *articles,* "cat" and "milk" are *nouns,* and "drank" is a *verb.* However, by the same reasoning, the sentence

"The milk drank the cat"

is equally valid syntactically even though it has no valid meaning.

The *meaning* associated with syntactically correct instances of a language can be viewed from two points of view, the meaning intended by the originator of the sentence and the meaning retrieved by a receiver. It is not always the case that these two meanings are identical. The former is called the *semantics* of the language, and the latter its *pragmatic* meaning. Much of modern humor is based on the skillful interplay between these two aspects of meaning, particularly with respect to the pun and the riddle.

Linguistic ambiguity may be caused by syntactic inadequacies or by a confusion between semantic and pragmatic meanings. An example of the former is the sign on a jet airplane:

> NO SMOKING AREA
> IN REAR CABIN

Does this imply there is a place in the rear cabin where smoking is not allowed (a NO-SMOKING AREA) or that there is no place in the rear cabin where smoking is allowed (NO SMOKING-AREA)? On the other hand, the sentence

> "I did not say that he stole the money"

can have a multitude of meanings in the spoken language, depending on such factors as emphasis, articulation, and tone. Each pair of the different meanings is a candidate for ambiguity between its semantic and pragmatic meaning.

In the case of programming languages, the distinctions above also apply, but in addition, there are some relatively subtle differences which have developed between computer languages and their associated formal language theory. When used by a computer linguist, grammar is usually applied to the rules governing the generation of strings in a language, while syntax is usually concerned with the recognition by the computer of whether or not a given string is a legal string in the language. There is, therefore, a complementary relationship between the productions of a grammar and the rules of syntax used by a computer language processor to recognize strings in the language.

The implementation of a computer language on a particular computer automatically removes any syntactic ambiguity that may have been present in the language definition by giving one and only one meaning to any language construct. Semantic and pragmatic ambiguities are still possible; they cause much confusion between what the programmer thought was meant and what the computer takes as the meaning of what the programmer wrote.

REFERENCE

1969. Sammet, J. E. *Programming Languages: History and Fundamentals*. Englewood Cliffs, NJ: Prentice-Hall.

J. A. N. LEE

SYSTEM CHART

For articles on related subjects *see* DOCUMENTATION; FLOWCHART; and FLOW DIAGRAM.

A system chart is a variety of flowchart. It is distinguished from other varieties of flowchart by its stress on the component operations that in sequence make up a system. Usually, these component operations are programs to be executed by a computer, but they may be operations to be done by other machines or by people. Examples of component operations are "transcribe data from handwritten documents," "sort," and "run program WY-37." System charts are sometimes known as *run diagrams*. They can be distinguished from other varieties of flowchart by the dominant use of input/output identifications and the clearly layered structure of input-process-output.

NED CHAPIN

SYSTEM GENERATION

For articles on related subjects *see* OPERATING SYSTEMS; and UPDATE.

System generation is the process of initiating a basic system (usually an operating system) at a specific installation. The process is diagrammed in Fig. 1. A program known as the system generator receives as input a description of (say) the basic operating system to be generated and a specification of parameters describing the specific installation (such as the types, quantities, and configuration of the system equipment). The generator processes the description of the basic system, substituting the parameters for variables in the description, and produces as output a specific system tailored to the installation. The system generator program will use the facilities of the existing basic system while it produces the tailored system; after production the tailored system can be loaded and started, thus bringing it into operation. By this technique a manufacturer need prepare only one version of the updated system for distribution to its customers, who then can produce from it a new system that will run efficiently on the specific equipment at their installations.

The process outlined above is also applicable to systems that are language processors (e.g., PL/I) as well as for complete operating systems (e.g., OS/VS2 for IBM System/370). If the basic system is a language processor, the parameters may specify such items as options regarding compile-time and run-time diagnostics, methods of

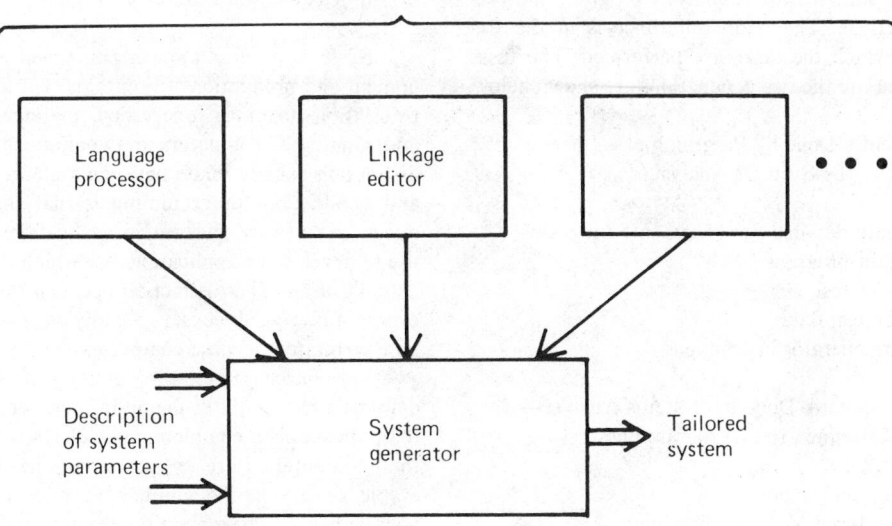

Fig. 1. System generation.

object-code optimization, formats for symbol table listings, and formation of address maps. If the basic system is a complete operating system, the parameters will include the details of the hardware configuration, of the system libraries, the procedures to be used for allocation and control of system resources (e.g., memory and processor management policies, protection mechanism), accounting and billing procedures, and performance monitoring procedures. In some cases, the parameters may specify procedures that are to be integrated into the basic system.

It should be obvious that this description of system generation applies also if the installation already has a running system. It is not at all uncommon to generate a newer version of an operating system using a previous release of the same system or a more primitive version of the same system.

For a new installation, where requirements can change rapidly, system generation may occur almost weekly, but in a mature and, therefore, stable installation, system generation may occur only once a year or even less frequently.

P. J. DENNING AND D. E. DENNING

SYSTEMS ANALYST

For articles on related subjects *see* ADMINISTRATIVE APPLICATIONS; DATABASE ADMINISTRATOR; FEASI-

BILITY STUDY; PERSONNEL IN THE COMPUTER FIELD; and PROGRAMMER.

The title of systems analyst is most often applied to the people who investigate, analyze, design, install, and evaluate information systems. Systems analysts first appeared in significant numbers in the 1940s, when the organization now called the Association for Systems Management (ASM) was formed.

Currently, systems analysts are usually located in or near the computer function in an organization. It is most common to find them in a project development department which reports to the Director of Information Systems. Less commonly, systems analysis and design is decentralized into the functional areas (e.g., marketing or finance) that process information.

The systems analyst needs to be competent as a communicator, a technician, and a business generalist. Communication skills needed are oral, written, and interpersonal. These include persuasive skills, the ability to be effective in leading and attending meetings, and supervisory skills. Technical skills include fact gathering, identification of information needs, feasibility analysis, equipment evaluation, and systems design. As a business generalist, the analyst needs to know the several business functional areas, the company, and the industry.

Observers have suggested that only a "renaissance person" could possibly have all of the required skills. However, since systems analysts usually work in teams, the skill deficiencies of one team member may be compensated for by others.

The tasks performed by systems analysts and programmers are similar in that analysts program and programmers analyze. The main difference is in the frequency with which the tasks are performed. The tasks which differentiate the two occupations are shown below.

Tasks Frequently Done by Programmer—Infrequently by Systems Analyst

- Translate detailed flowcharts into programs
- Maintain program
- Debug or test
- Prepare test data
- Prepare operator instructions

Tasks Frequently Done by Systems Analyst—Infrequently by Programmer

- Define requirements
- Prepare functional specifications
- Prepare system specification
- Prepare systems flowcharts
- Design forms and reports
- Design data items
- Define data organization
- Define systems calculations

Systems analysis is among the more rapidly growing of all occupations. A college degree in business with an information systems emphasis is the preferred education. Some firms hire systems analysts, while others promote from programming or user areas. A growing number of organizations are now requiring masters' level education.

Some organizations choose to combine the jobs of systems analyst and programmer and use the title *programmer-analyst*. Others split the systems analyst job into administrative systems analyst and computer systems analyst. These differences, plus the use of the same or a similar job title for engineers and economists, make it difficult to infer competencies from the job title alone.

References

1971. Dickmann, Robert A. *Personnel Implications for Business Data Processing*. New York: Wiley-Interscience.
1975. Willoughby, Theodore C. and Senn, James. *Business Systems*. Cleveland: Association for Systems Management.

T. C. WILLOUGHBY

SYSTEMS PROGRAMMING

For articles on related subjects *see* APPLICATIONS PROGRAMMING; MACHINE AND ASSEMBLY LANGUAGE PROGRAMMING; OPERATING SYSTEMS; PROGRAMMER; and UTILITY PROGRAM.

Systems programming is concerned with the development and production of programs that have to do with translation, loading, supervision, maintenance, control, and running of computers and computer programs. The distinction usually made between systems programming and applications programming is that the former produces the software tools which applications programmers use to develop the applications for which the computer is actually used. The distinction between the two is, however, not always obvious, especially on small special-purpose or limited-purpose computers.

Very large numbers of systems programmers are employed by computer manufacturers who normally attempt to supply a complete range of system programs for their computers. In recent years there has been a considerable growth in the number of independent software houses that provide system programmers and system programming products, often in competition with the computer manufacturers.

Some of the more important systems programming products are operating systems, language processors, utility systems, file management systems, etc.

Systems programmers tend to use languages that reflect the detailed characteristics of the computers for which the systems programs are being written. This is especially true with those systems programs that deal directly with interfaces between computers and peripheral equipment, or between computers and terminals or communication devices. Assembly language has been the traditional language of the systems programmer, and many of the design features of assembly languages reflect the needs of systems programmers.

In recent years there has been a concerted effort to develop languages and systems that would permit systems programmers to operate in high-level languages. The problem addressed was the extremely high cost of systems programming, and the unreliability and difficulty of maintenance of large systems written in assembly languages.

The most successful effort in this area was made by Burroughs Corporation. The logical design of the larger Burroughs machines has been such as to provide relatively efficient execution of programs written in Algol-like languages. By fiat, then, all systems programming on the Burroughs B5000 and B6000 machines has been done in special Algol-based high-level languages, and no assembly language processors are provided. Another important development in this area has been the language C (*q.v.*), which attempts to combine high-level structured control features with the low-level access to bit patterns normally found only in assemblers.

For most other machines the degradation in performance produced through the use of high-level languages proved too great, and routines with critical space or timing requirements are still mostly assembly language routines. High-level languages, including modifications and extensions of Fortran, PL/I, and Pascal, have been used and are being increasingly used in those parts of systems programming in which the time and space requirements are not too critical.

Systems programming has been called an art, sometimes a "black art," because the need for it developed so rapidly that it has not yet been possible to develop a theoretical foundation for it, or even to adopt criteria of good practice among practitioners in the field. There have been many textbooks written, many courses offered, and whole curricula devised to train people in the area of systems programming, but these efforts have had only limited success. To this day, there are programmers with little formal education or experience who can perform prodigious feats of systems programming, and others who have successfully completed all relevant courses in the best universities who could not get even a relatively simple programming system to run if their lives depended upon it.

REFERENCES

1972. Donovan, J. J. *Systems Programming*. New York: Mc-Graw-Hill.
1980. Welsh, J. and McKeag, M. *Structured System Programming*. Englewood Cliffs, NJ: Prentice-Hall.

S. ROSEN

T

TABLE LOOKUP

For articles on related subjects *see* ACCESS METH-ODS; ASSOCIATIVE MEMORY; BINARY SEARCH; FILES; HASHING; KEY; RECORD; and SORTING.

Lookup or searching for some information in a table is required in many programming applications, including the writing of compilers and interpreters (Glass, 1969). Table manipulation, search techniques, and routines should be considered, developed, and cataloged at all computer installations because they are so generally useful.

Definitions. The definitions promulgated by the American National Standards Institute (ANSI) in *Vocabulary for Information Processing* have been adapted to this article. These include:

Record. A logical unit of information that may contain one or more fields.

Field. A specific area of a record used for a particular category of data; e.g., a group of card columns used for pay rate.

File. A collection or batch of related records that must be processed in some way.

Table. A collection or batch of records containing "control" or master information to be used repeatedly in a process; e.g., a collection of records containing employee number versus pay rate fields.

Key. The particular field of a record on which the processing is performed; e.g., a lookup process might be performed on the employee number field (the key) to determine the pay rate for that employee.

Position. The "place" or logical location of a record in a table; e.g., position 13 of a table contains a particular record.

General Considerations. This presentation of lookup techniques is limited to the consideration of tables that can be totally contained in the main memory of the computer and in which all table positions are available in equal access time. The methodology could be complicated by considering techniques for tables that are too large for such storage or for tables on external direct-access devices where access time is not uniform. The table is considered fixed during processing; i.e., it need not be altered or updated (table records added, deleted, or revised) dynamically.

In file processing with a table, both file and table records may exist in computer-readable form on card decks, tape reels, disk packs, etc. or the table may be built into or generated by the program. If built in or generated, the programmer can exercise judgment on the arrangement of the table. If the table must be read in, the programmer can simply read table items into sequential locations and use the table as it stands, or the table can be rearranged to the programmer's preference. The programmer should realize that the rearrangement takes time on the computer and should be justified by time saved in searching the table when a file is processed. When large files or tables are involved, table organization that enables faster lookup is very profitable.

In addition to table arrangement considerations, the

matter of key transformation—converting existing logical table- and file-record keys to a different form or arrangement—must be considered because of its speed advantage. This subject will be discussed after some foundation for lookup techniques has been established.

Search Techniques

The Sequential Search. Sequential search is the most straightforward of table lookups. It consists simply of starting at some table position (usually the beginning) and comparing the file-record key in hand with each table-record key, one at a time, until either a match is found or all table positions have been searched. Sequential search is easily programmed, and lends itself nicely to index-register or address-modification techniques on most computers. Also, it is easy to code in a high-level language.

If the table is ordered or arranged in sequence on the key, various techniques can be used to speed up the search. For example, the key in every tenth table position could be interrogated, starting with position 1, until a table-record key greater than the current file record is found, at which point a sequential search could be started in reverse on each position until the match is found or a "less than" comparison results. Also, other table characteristics, if known, might be used to advantage.

Merge Search. The merge search is a sequential search technique requiring that both the table and file records be ordered in the same sequence on the key involved. The keys are compared, starting with the first file record and first table position. If a match is not found, the table is searched sequentially until an equal or greater table-record key is found. If greater, the table does not have that key, and the file must be advanced to examine the next record; if equal, the record is processed, and the next file record is considered. It is not necessary to start over with table position 1; one simply starts the search for each file record at the table position where the previous search terminated.

This merge technique will often turn out to be the fastest one if the table and file are already ordered in the desired sequence. If the program at hand must justify the required ordering, other techniques may be faster. This method, contrary to others to be discussed, does not require that all table positions be in memory at once; both table and file records could be on magnetic tape, for example. Thus, the merge technique could be very useful when tables are too large for memory.

Fig. 1 presents a flow diagram of the merge technique.

Binary Search. The term "binary search" comes from the principal feature of this technique, which provides that each "look" into the table either finds the key in question or eliminates *half* of the table positions from further consideration. A binary search requires that the table be ordered on the table keys. Ascending sequence is assumed in this discussion.

The procedure begins by comparing the current file-record key to the table key at the midposition of the table. If the file-record key is greater, the lower half of the table can be ignored, and the next look can be taken at the midposition of the remaining upper half. This process continues until a key match is found or the table "shrinks" to nothing. Fig. 2 should help clarify this technique.

The maximum number of inspections or looks into the table necessary to find the record key being sought, or to ascertain that it is missing, is the smallest integer L satisfying the relation

$$2^L \geq N + 1,$$

where L is the number of looks and N is the number of table positions. This may be rewritten as

$$\log_2(N + 1) + 1 > L \geq \log_2(N + 1).$$

Comparing the binary and sequential techniques in terms of the probable number of looks required to find a file-record key is shown in Table 1. While the saving in number of looks required for large tables proves that the binary search technique has a great advantage, the factor of *time per look* must be considered. If this time were equal for both methods, the binary search would always be best, but more tests are involved in the binary search, so each look takes longer. Thus, if we assume a 5:1 advantage for the sequential technique, the break even point would be somewhere around a 50-position table, neglecting the table setup time.

Certain techniques may be used to accelerate each look of a binary search when the program is written in machine or assembly language. For example, on computers with a three-way compare instruction, and for applications in which keys can be contained in single machine words and table record keys are stored sequentially in contiguous machine words, binary searches approaching the time-per-look speed of sequential searches can be written.

While not directly a part of the search methodology, a technique for saving table arrangement (sorting) time may be worth considering in some applications. This technique adds indirectness to the lookup, however, and requires more storage space because a pointer is required

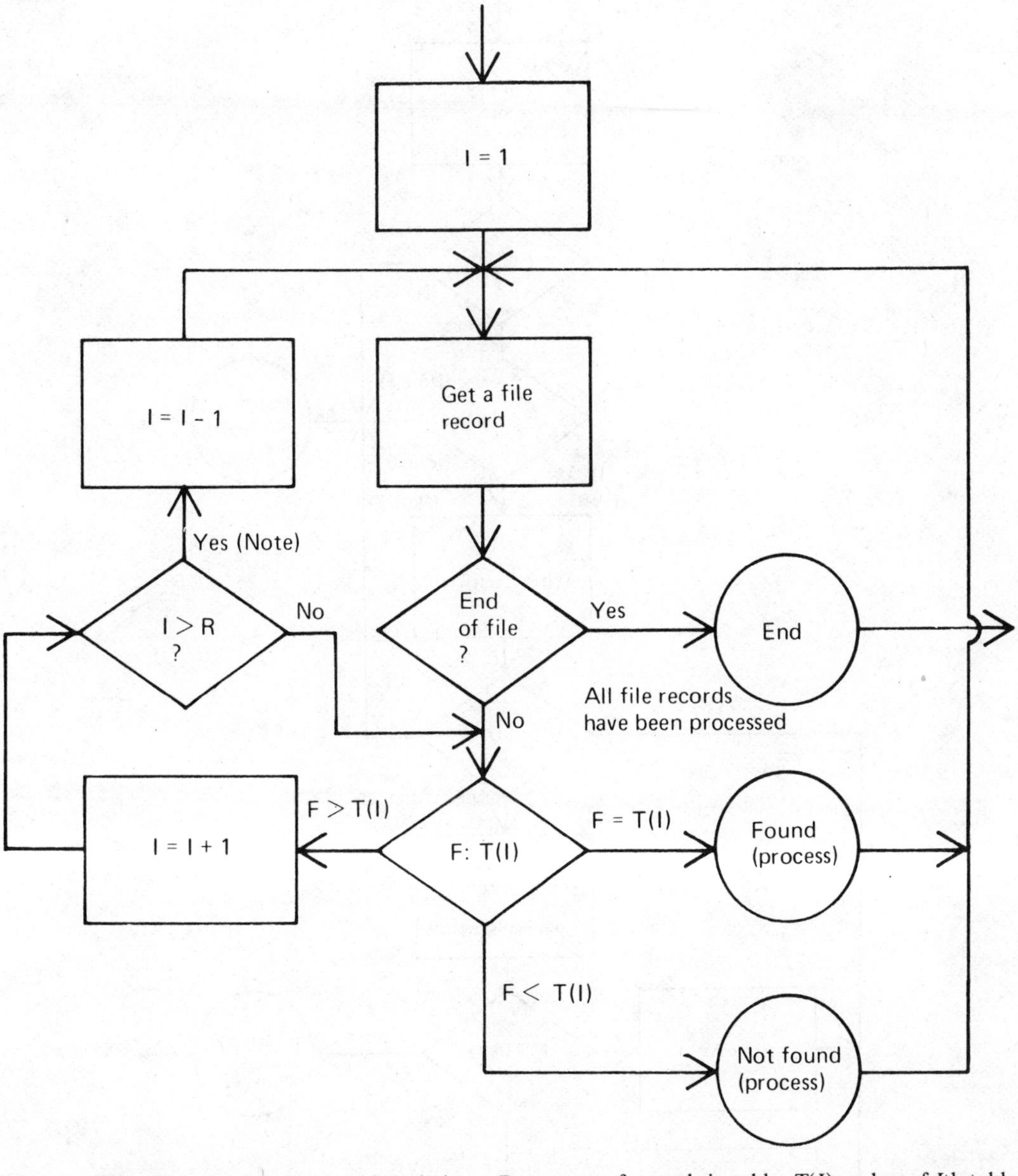

Fig. 1 Flow diagram of merge search technique. R = count of records in table; $T(I)$ = key of Ith table record (in position I). F = current file-record key. Table is sorted in ascending order on key T, i.e., $T(I)$ = lowest key; $T(R)$ = highest key. File records are sorted in ascending order on key F. *Note:* An alternative at "yes" to $I = I - 1$ would be: At the first occurrence of $I > R$, branch to a procedure that simply reads the balance of file records and treats them as "not found."

with each table position. The technique's virtue derives from elimination of the need to rearrange associated (nonkey) fields of the table records. The technique consists of appending a pointer, which represents the position of the ancilliary fields, to the key field. This key/pointer record is then stored in a separate table, and this table—not the one containing the nonkey fields—is sorted. A

search on the key will reveal a key hit, but the table record must be retrieved by looking in the "pointed to" position. Fig. 3 illustrates the table setup.

Direct Lookup. This technique is perhaps inherently the fastest when it can be used. As opposed to other techniques, it involves no trial-and-error searching, but an

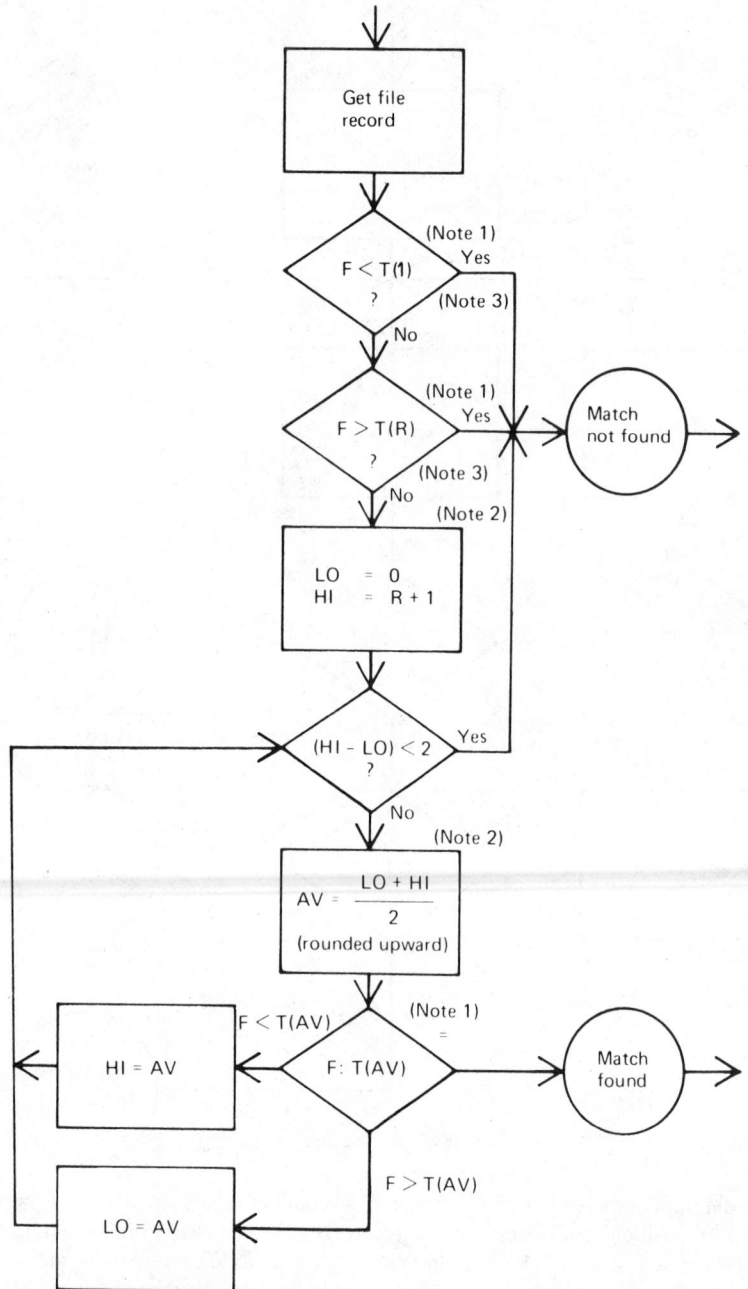

Fig. 2. Flow diagram of a general binary search technique. R = count of records in table; $T(I)$ = key of Ith table record (in position I); F = current file-record key. Table is sorted in ascending sequence on keys, i.e., $T(1)$ = lowest key and $T(R)$ = highest. *Note 1:* This test is dependent upon table keys being ascendingly ordered in collating sequence upon which test is based. *Note 2:* LO, HI, and AV are fields (integer) which control the table positions being looked in. *Note 3:* These tests are not necessary, but may save time if many file-record keys will not be found in table.

Table 1. Comparison of Table Size Versus Number of Looks Required in Sequential and Binary Searches

Number of Table Positions	Number of Looks Required			
	Sequential		Binary	
	Maximum	Average	Maximum	Average
5	5	3	3	2
10	10	5	4	3
50	50	25	6	5
100	100	50	7	6
1,000	1,000	500	10	9
10,000	10,000	5,000	14	13
100,000	100,000	50,000	17	16
1,000,000	1,000,000	500,000	20	19

Input Table Record

Key	Associated Information Fields

Key Table

Position	Key	Pointer
1	A1	1
2	MS	2
3	1A	3
4	X7	4
5	X3	5
6	MS	6
7	B5	7
8	C4	8
9	C3	9

Associated Information Table

Position	Information
1	A1 Info.
2	MS Info.
3	1A Info.
4	etc.
5	
6	
7	B5 Info.
8	
9	

After Sort

Position	Key	Pointer
1	1A	3
2	A1	1
3	B5	7
4	C3	9
5	C4	8
6	MS	2
7	MS	6 (Note)
8	X3	5
9	X7	4

Fig. 3. Method for saving sort time in setting up ordered table for binary (or other) search. *Note:* Including the pointer as a low-order part of the key during sort keeps duplicate keys in "as input" order.

exact relationship must be established between key and position. This relationship has to be determined or known in advance of table creation because table records must be stored in a position that is a function of the key value. Thus, the table storage allocation must include positions for all possible table records whose keys are in range.

Consider a simple example in which the table-record keys are numeric and are three-digit part numbers varying from legitimate values of 000 to 999. One could allocate a 1,000-position table and, as the table is input, store the records in the position indicated by their key (e.g., the table record whose key is part number 123 goes into table position 123). Here there is an exact 1:1 relationship between key and position. The technique cannot directly handle duplicate keys in the table. It is not necessary to store the table-record key in the table because its value is implied by its record position. For example, an input file record with part number 123 could have an associated table record in table position 123. In high-level language, TP(123) contains the information being sought; the subscript indicates the table position.

The possibility that table position 123 does not have information must be considered. This can be dealt with by storing some flag or special unique character in all invalid table positions. A waste of memory results if the table has many voids (or is *sparse*). That is, if only 200 part numbers of the possible 1,000 are in the table, there are 800 wasted positions. If memory cannot be spared, other schemes can be used, although they add indirectness to the lookup and slow it down.

One such technique is an auxiliary index table. This technique is perhaps best explained by the example illustrated in Fig. 4. In this approach, all zeros (or some special flag) are first moved to the entire index table. Then table records are read in one at a time, and the information is stored in sequential locations in the information table. As each table record is input, the sequence number or pointer to that table record is placed in the index table in the position corresponding to the current key value. In the example of Fig. 4, voids exist only in the index table so that 2,400 character positions are lost instead of 80,000. During the lookup phase, one must look in the index table first. If the position found there is zero, the file-record key is not in the table; otherwise, the information wanted is in the "pointed to" position of the information table.

This direct technique, with or without indexing schemes, can be applied to many situations and is quite fast. It is very good in situations where tables are logically multidimensional, assuming again the numeric key restriction.

Key Transformation. An important adjunct to direct table lookup is the subject of key transformation. Often the table keys, even if numeric, cannot be considered table positions because the resulting table would be too sparse. Transforming a key field from its natural form and length to a different representation may be worthwhile in some applications so that a quasi-direct lookup can be made rather than a trial-and-error search. This is done by performing some routine operation on the original key to transform it into a new key. This is often called *hashing*, and hash addresses are the transformed keys so created. These hash addresses are then used as direct-entry positions.

For example, suppose there is a table of part numbers that are ten numeric characters in length, but there may be no more than 10,000 unique part numbers. As a direct-entry table would have to allow 10 billion (10^{10}) positions to handle only 10^4 possible keys, a scheme must be contrived to transform the original ten-digit key to an integer that will represent the table position of that part in a much more compact table.

There are many possible schemes. One simple one is the division-remainder method: Choose a number close to the number of table positions needed. Use that number as a divisor to extract a quotient and a remainder from the dividend (which is the original key). The remainder so obtained is the transformed key. Using 10,000 as the divisor, the transformed key becomes the original key modulo 10,000. The following table lists some examples.

Original Key (Part Number)	Transformed Key
00 0000 1000	1000
00 0001 0000	0
00 0001 0001	1
00 0001 0099	99
10 0001 0099	99
22 3333 4444	4444
90 0020 0110	110
99 0020 0112	112

These examples were constructed to illustrate the problem of duplicate transformed keys *(collisions)*.

Ideally, the transform scheme would convert the original keys to transformed keys with no duplicates. While schemes can be constructed to minimize *hash clash,* its possibility cannot be eliminated completely, and because of this, the original key must be stored in the table. Further, some scheme must be used to handle duplicate transformed keys, and there are many choices to consider. Different divisors should be tried out to minimize the number of duplicate keys generated; for example using 9,999 or some divisor other than 10,000 might result in fewer duplicate keys. Also, different transform schemes should be considered. (*See* HASHING.)

The duplicates could be handled simply by an overflow table, which operates as follows: If a transformed key finds a void in the direct-entry table, it is placed

Index Table

Position*	Pointer
1	200
2	003
3	001
4	000
.	.
.	.
123	088
.	.
785	002
.	.
999	000

Information Table

Position*	Key	Other
		Information
1	003	(100 characters
2	785	for each item)
3	002	
.	.	
88	123	
.	.	
200	001	

Fig. 4. Memory conservation through use of index table. *Note: These fields are not required to be stored in memory, but are shown to illustrate the technique.

there. However, if the place is already occupied by a previously transformed key, then the direct-entry position is flagged to indicate the overflow occurrence, and the overflowed key (original key) is stored in the next sequential position of the overflow table. Thus, in searching such a direct-entry table with an overflow table, the file-record key must be transformed into a direct table position. If the key is found in the direct-entry table with no overflow flag, there is a match. If the position is occupied by either a nonmatching key without an overflow indicator or by a void, there is no match. If, however, there is a nonmatching key with an overflow indication, the overflow table must be searched to see if the record key of interest is there. This overflow table could be searched sequentially or arranged for faster methods.

If the total number of overflow keys is significant, an approach with more finesse can be used to handle the search for overflowed keys from the direct-entry table. The overflow flag in the direct-entry table of the transformed key, if nonzero, may be constructed to be an overflow table position. This would "chain" the lookup directly to the overflow table position containing the overflowed key. Thus, the overflow table itself would become a direct-entry table. Please note, however, that only the first direct-entry overflow can be handled in this way unless the overflow table itself has an overflow indicator. (More than one collision in a given transformed key position is possible.) This overflow chaining technique is illustrated by the example in Fig. 5. It should result in faster lookup than a trial-and-error overflow table search. In both approaches, however, enough space (computer memory) must be allocated to provide for all overflows, so the programmer must know the table and key transform characteristics quite well.

Some other methods of key transformation are: folding, radix transformation, and digit rearrangement. These key transform techniques per se have nothing special to recommend them over the division-remainder method. They are probably no faster and do not necessarily produce fewer duplicate transformed keys. The digit rearrangement technique has possibilities for reducing duplicates, if careful digit analysis is done on the original keys of a given table in order to determine which digit positions to select. That is, one should select digit positions in the original key in which digit values 0 through 9 are evenly distributed.

There are situations in which key transform techniques offer a speed advantage, as the table need not be ordered and the key transform time is probably faster than the time required to sort the table. The lookup time (where the percentage of overflows is small) is probably faster than a binary search if the key transform technique is quick. Thus, some sacrifice in program complexity and additional memory for overflow handling could speed program execution. Compiler and assembler programs use such techniques to advantage for handling symbol tables

Direct-Entry Table

Position (transformed key)	Original* Key	Overflow† Table Key
0	00 0001 0000	0
1	00 0001 0001	1
2	0	0
3	30 0050 0003	0
4	20 0120 0004	2

Overflow Table

Position	Original Key	Overflow† Table Key
1	20 0050 0001	0
2	30 0017 0004	4
3	00 0010 0167	0
4	30 0018 0004	0

Fig. 5. Example of an overflow-handling technique. *Note: 0 indicates no keys transform to this position. †Note: 0 indicates an "end of chain" condition (no more keys with this "hash" address).

(Glass, 1969; Morris, 1968) that are dynamic (i.e., need to be searched while they are being built).

Associative Lookup. The foregoing discussion assumes conventionally addressed computers where memory addresses, or cells, are fixed length words or bytes starting with a first address and extending sequentially (conceptually) to the highest or last address. As of this writing (1979), only the Goodyear Staran is a commercially available general-purpose computer utilizing an associative or content-addressable memory; however, because the technology for such exists, there will probably be more in the near future. Evidence for the value of associative table lookup is the TABLE facility in the Snobol language which implements associative lookup in software.

On a computer with an associative memory, table lookup would be (conceptually) a direct retrieval since the table record's address and its key are the same. The lookup is thus handled by hardware. It is not necessary to sort or otherwise arrange tables in preparation for search techniques. Programmers will be given new capabilities in the area of partial key lookup, which will enable retrieval of a set of records having some common key characteristic with just one "look." However, before we can be more definitive on programming techniques with associative memory machines, we must await implementation of viable hardware and programming languages which take advantage of this hardware.

Closing Remarks. Faced with an application, how does the programmer know which procedure will be best for the situation? There is probably no general solution to this problem because of the many variables involved. Sometimes it is intuitively judged that one technique is the most natural choice in a given application. Often, combinations of techniques can be used to advantage. At times the programmer can carefully plan the program and perhaps test out various techniques to optimize it. At other times, the main consideration is: "Have it running by the first of the month!"

Again, it is important to remember that technique optimization is economically advantageous only for programs that (1) execute often; and/or (2) have a large number of file records; and/or (3) have large tables. An attempt to define "often" and "large" is intentionally avoided.

This article is a condensation of a previous treatment (Price, 1971), based on work performed for the U.S. Atomic Energy Commission.

REFERENCES

1968. Morris, Robert. "Scatter Storage Techniques," *Comm. ACM* **11**, *No. 1:* 38–43 (January). (Scatter storage techniques applied to processing symbol tables, as in compilers and assemblers. A well-written paper, recommended to anyone interested in dynamic tables and key transforms.)

1969. Glass, Robert L. "An Elementary Discussion of Compiler/Interpreter Writing," *Computing Surveys* **1**, *No. 1:* p. 55 (March). (This paper mentions use of tables and search techniques in various phases of compiler/interpreter writing.)

1970. American National Standards Institute. *A Vocabulary for Information Processing,* ANSI X3.12–1970. (Defines and names computer-related words and concepts.)

1971. Price, C. E. "Table Lookup Techniques," *Computing Surveys* **3**, *No. 2:* p. 49 (June).

C. E. PRICE

TAPE LABEL

For article on related subject *see* MEMORY: Auxiliary.

Magnetic tape labels are special records appearing at the beginning and end of a reel of magnetic tape to provide details about the file of records stored on the tape.

A *header label* is a block of data at the beginning of a magnetic tape file containing descriptive information to identify the file. A header label may be, for example, 80 characters long, with all data recorded in even parity at the same density as the remainder of the data file. Header records would usually be separated from succeeding data records by an *interrecord gap*. A header label may typically contain the following fields (with the length in number of characters given in brackets):

1. Density [1] specifies density of recording in file.
2. Header-label identifier [2] identifies record as header label record.
3. Logical unit number [2] specifies logical unit to which file is assigned.
4. Retention period code [3] specifies (in days) retention period of file; only after expiration of this period may the tape be overwritten.
5. File name [14] identifies the file, using any combination of characters legal in the specific code used.
6. Reel number [2] identifies the sequence of reels for multireel files.
7. Date written [6] expressed in day, month, and last two numerals of the year. Identifies date written and is used with the retention period to determine release date of file.
8. Edition or generation number [2] identifies a single file set. Each time amendment data is applied to a magnetic tape file an entirely new copy of the file is created, containing all the valid data amendments. This new reel will bear the same field name as the original reel that was amended; the two will, however, be different generations of the same file and as such will bear different generation numbers.
9. User-supplied information [48] contains any comments the user might find useful.

When a file is opened, this data is checked by the program to insure that the correct file is being processed; also, if the tape is to be used for writing, to check that the retention period has been exceeded.

A *trailer label* is a special record appearing at the end of a file stored on magnetic tape. It serves to identify the end of the file and usually provides some control data related to that file. A trailer label may be, for example, 80 characters long, with all data recorded in even parity at the same density as the remainder of the data file. End-of-file marks precede and follow the trailer label. A trailer label usually contains the following fields (with length of characters given in brackets):

1. Trailer label identifier [3] identifies label as EOT (end of tape) or EOS (end of set) or EOF (end of file.
2. Record count [5] provides number of records in the file for control purposes.
3. User field [72] contains any comments the user might find useful.

The main advantages of tape labels lie in their ability to provide the computing system with means to accept only properly identified input files for each computer run, and to accept input in the correct sequence when more than one reel is used. Labels also make it possible for the operating system to identify the end-of-file (EOF) or end-of-reel (EOR) status. Use of labels, however, complicates the programming task somewhat, and also creates some administrative problems in the assignment of label codes.

The need often arises to exchange information recorded on magnetic tape between different users and different computers. This may be made possible by use of common standards for tape labels or by software that allows the system to handle unlabeled tapes as well as tapes with atypical labels.

J. NECAS

TASK

For articles on related subjects *see* JOB; OPERATING SYSTEMS: Principles and Theory; and PROGRAM STATUS WORDS AND STATE VECTORS.

A *task* (or *process*) is an atomic unit of activity in a computer system. It is specified in terms of its external characteristics only, it internal structure and operation being unspecified. The external characteristics of a task that must be specified will depend on the context in which a task is being studied or controlled; these include: input and output parameters or variables, resource requirements, and execution time.

If, for example, the context of a discussion is the evaluation of arithmetic expressions, tasks in that discussion will be the arithmetic operations of the computer. Or, if the discussion concerns the determinate operation of a set of tasks on common data, the tasks in that discussion are arbitrary procedures. In discussions where task-resource demands are being considered, some systems adopt the view that a task demand is a function of time; in contrast, others adopt the view that the demand of a task is fixed, and that time-varying demands are modeled by considering appropriate networks of tasks with constant demands.

If a system must preempt resources from a task at a certain point in its execution, a description of the task state with respect to the given resource at the time of preemption will have to be formulated. The *task descriptor* or *state vector* is an example of this when the processor is the preemptible resource.

A task is said to be *uninterpreted* if its function or operation is unspecified. Many systems are set up to control uninterpreted tasks, since (1) there is no way of knowing during the system design what specific tasks will be run, and (2) system behavior should be reproducible to the extent that the computations performed by arbitrary tasks will not depend on their relative speeds.

A *multitask system* is one in which two or more tasks can be in progress (i.e., between their points of initiation and termination) at any given time. The simplest form of multitask system assumes that all the tasks are *independent;* but many systems permit *precedence constraints* to be implemented—i.e., the requirement that the initiation of a certain task must always follow the terminations of other specified tasks.

The term "process" is also used to mean essentially the same as *task*. The literature is filled with so many conflicting definitions of *process* that many people find the term "task" less confusing. The word "process" is most often used to describe programs in execution, a somewhat more restricted context than that suggested above for tasks.

P. J. DENNING AND D. E. DENNING

TELEPROCESSING SYSTEMS

For articles on related subjects *see* COMMUNICATION CONTROL UNITS; COMMUNICATIONS AND COM-PUTERS; COMPUTER NETWORKS; DATA COMMUNICATIONS; PACKET SWITCHING; PROCESSING MODES; REAL-TIME APPLICATIONS; REMOTE JOB ENTRY; and TIME SHARING.

Remote-terminal processing systems, often called *teleprocessing systems,* refer to a form of information processing in which remote terminals access a computer via some type of communication line. In recent years, the number of such systems has grown very rapidly, and all indications are that this growth will be sustained for reasons of economics and convenience. These systems can provide various data processing services to many locations simultaneously without the necessity of having a computer at each such location. The six basic types are described in this article.

Inquiry and Response Systems. In these systems, the computer is used as a mass storage facility which can be accessed by a large number of terminal users via a communication network. The best examples are the various airline or hotel reservation, automatic document retrieval, and inventory control systems. The user enters a query at a terminal, causing the computer to search its files and send back the information. The files may be updated automatically or by the user.

An example of a large inquiry and response system is the reservation system for American Airlines. In 1972, this system supported 1,900 terminals, but by late 1979, it supported close to 18,000 I/O terminals—a ninefold increase in only seven years. At present, the system handles an average of 6,000,000 messages per day, maintaining a response time of less than three seconds 90% of the time. The average length of an inquiry is 16 characters, while a response averages 160 characters.

Data Collection Systems. In data collection systems, also called *data acquisition systems* or *data entry systems*, information from various terminals or other input devices is entered and stored in the computer. This data may be processed immediately (on-line, real-time systems), at some subsequent time, or it may be just used to update records that will be used for inquiry and response systems or accounting purposes. Examples of such systems are weather recording, automatic recording of transactions on the stock exchange or at banks, and keeping track of the status on an assembly line at various stages.

Data Distribution Systems. A data distribution system is the converse of a data collection system in the sense that the main flow of data is in the opposite direction; i.e., from computer to terminal. Dissemination of information such as stock quotations or timetables to a select group of customers are examples of such systems.

The transmission of data may be continuous, in batches, or on demand, depending upon the specific application.

Modern examples of data distribution systems include Teletext and Viewdata, which are aimed at the home consumer. Teletext is a data distribution system which allows subscribers to use their home television sets for viewing data at any time. This data is transmitted using VHF and UHF bands and includes pages of news, weather forecasts, sports scores, and stock market information. Viewdata (*q.v.*) is a system which transmits information from private computer banks via the telephone network to specially adapted television receivers. It is interactive and offers the subscriber data from news to theater reviews and travel information. Besides disseminating data, this system is also used for computer-aided instruction and has a message service among subscribers (*electronic mail*).

Conversational Systems.

These systems are designed to permit concurrent dialogues between the central computer and many local or remote users. In this mode of operation, each statement or command entered by a user is executed immediately, and a reply is sent back before the next statement or command may be entered. These are usually called *time-sharing* or *interactive* systems, and may be special-purpose (closed) or general-purpose (open) systems. The former allows users to prepare and execute programs in a very limited number of languages. The latter allow access to a large variety of compilers, editing and debugging aids, special application libraries, and usually include the ability to add additional facilities. The M.I.T. Multics systems is an example of a general-purpose system. In both general- and special-purpose designs, however, the emphasis is on rapid response to many users. The potential uses of these systems appear to be almost unlimited.

Included in this category are interactive graphics systems. Here, computer information is displayed on a cathode ray tube in response to commands from a keyboard or lightpen. Such systems are widely used in computer-aided design (*q.v.*) of airplane wings, car bodies, integrated circuit masks, circuit layouts, and other applications.

Another example is computer-aided instruction systems where students at terminals study computer-assigned material, perform assignments, and answer questions. Answers are examined and used to guide further computer-student dialogue, depending upon progress made. An example of such a system is PLATO, which supports programmed instruction using a specially designed graphics display terminal on which text and line drawings can be combined with rear projection of color images under control of the main computer supporting the system.

Remote Batch-Processing Systems.

In a remote batch-processing system, often called a remote job entry (RJE) system, the computer waits for a job from a remote terminal. It then places the job in the batch queue along with other jobs currently in the system. After execution, the output is transmitted to the originating terminal. This may take from a fraction of a second up to several minutes in contrast to conversational systems in which a virtually instantaneous response is essential.

These systems are used widely where the central or host computer has several remote batch stations, which may consist of line printer, card reader, and card punch. The remote terminals may also be other computers.

Message Switching Systems.

Message switching systems are special cases of data collection and data distribution systems, where very little or no processing is done on the data. The computer merely acts as a switching center, collecting data from, and distributing data to, various terminals. In these systems, it is possible for several terminals to send messages simultaneously to the same destination. Some of these messages must, therefore, be temporarily stored until the terminal is free to accept them. For this reason, such systems are often called *store and forward* systems.

Other Types of Teleprocessing Systems.

The categories discussed above serve only to summarize the general characteristics of teleprocessing and on-line systems. In many cases, the distinction between them is fuzzy. Combinations and variations are possible. Thus, monitoring systems are similar to data collection systems, but the input is usually from some source other than a computer terminal (e.g., a transducer monitoring heartbeat). Process control systems may be thought of as closed-loop monitoring systems that regulate an ongoing process. Other examples of teleprocessing systems include typesetting, document generation, electronic funds transfer, and transaction-based systems.

Hardware and Software Requirements.

The systems described are types of multiprogrammed, time-shared, or real-time systems. They may vary in size from small special-purpose systems servicing several terminals all the way to very large general-purpose systems servicing several hundred or thousand local or remote terminals. The general-purpose systems usually provide simultaneous conversational and remote batch processing, as well as the capability to run some of the more specialized systems described in the preceding section.

The desirable hardware features include a computer with independent data channels and flexible interrupt structure, memory protection, relocation hardware, and mass storage. Communication controllers, terminals, and the communication network also must be compatible with the type of application the system must support.

The software includes an *executive* for providing system protection, processor and memory allocation, scheduling of user programs and interrupt handling, a *file management system* for providing access to and allocation of direct-access storage devices and allowing users to share, create, change, and delete files, an *access method* for handling the communication between the computer and terminals, and a *command processor* to provide the interface between the user and the system which allows the user to log in and out, manipulate files, gain access to application software such as editors, compilers, debugging aids, and other system utilities.

Conclusion. A combination of appropriate computer hardware and software together with a suitable data communication network can service a large number of local and remote terminals. The uses of such teleprocessing systems are almost unlimited. They have grown rapidly in the past decade and all indications are that this growth will be sustained in the future with continued improvements in computer and communication technology and development of new applications. Many of the articles on applications of computers in this encyclopedia relate to uses of teleprocessing systems.

REFERENCES

1976. Martin, J. *Telecommunications and the Computer,* 2nd Edition. Englewood Cliffs, NJ: Prentice-Hall.
1979. Katzan, Jr. H. *Distributed Information Systems.* New York: Petrocelli.
1980. Jackson, R. N. "Home Communications I: Teletext and Viewdata," *IEEE Spectrum* (March).

J. S. SOBOLEWSKI

TELETEXT. *See* VIEWDATA.

TERMINALS

For articles on related subjects *see* AUDIO TERMINALS; COMPUTER GRAPHICS; DATA COMMUNICATIONS; INPUT-OUTPUT DEVICES; MULTIPLEXING; POINT-OF-SALE TERMINAL; PROCESSING MODES; TEXT EDITING SYSTEMS; and TIME SHARING.

A computer terminal is a device that allows users of a computer system to gain access to (i.e., to input programs and data to, and to obtain output from) that system in a more convenient manner than through the *input-output devices* (*q.v.*) local to that system (e.g., local card readers, card punches, and line printers). Often, computer terminals are located away from the computer, at locations convenient for the users of that system. Computer terminals fall into two main categories—*batch* and *interactive.*

Batch Terminals. The primary purpose of a batch terminal is to allow users to access a computer system just as if they were accessing it locally, but to do so from remote locations. Therefore, a batch terminal contains I/O devices that are similar to the devices attached directly to the computer. The simplest batch terminals usually have a printer and a card reader (see Fig. 1); more complex terminals may have, in addition, a card punch, one or more magnetic tape drives, one or more disk drives, and other I/O devices. In fact, small, general-purpose computers (or even medium-size ones) are often used as batch terminals to larger computers.

Batch terminals are connected to computers via *data communications* (*q.v.*) links. These links operate at speeds that typically range from 120 to approximately 6,000 characters per second, although higher speeds are used in some instances. These links may be *dedicated* (i.e., they connect a batch terminal to a computer in a permanent fashion), or *dial-up* (like a dial telephone). Dial-up links allow a batch terminal to access more than one computer; furthermore, a terminal that communicates with a computer via a dial-up link does not tie up a *port* (the computer's end of a link) when the terminal is not in use. Several terminals can use a single link simultaneously via a technique known as *multiplexing* (*q.v.*), meaning that each terminal transmits and receives data at a speed that is a fraction of the total speed of which the link is capable.

Information is usually transmitted to and from a

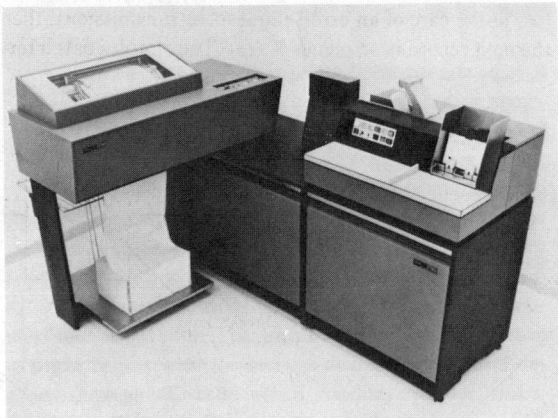

Fig. 1. A simple batch terminal (IBM 3780).

batch terminal (often, but not always, in one direction at a time) via a *carrier signal* that is *modulated* (i.e., changed in amplitude or frequency) to represent 0 and 1 bits. (This modulation, as well as the corresponding demodulation at the other end of the link, are performed by a device known as a *mo*dulator-*dem*odulator, or *modem—q.v.*) Groups of these bits represent *characters* (i.e., letters, digits, punctuation symbols). Each character is represented by a group of from 6 to 11 bits (the number of bits per character is, of course, a constant for any one link).

The terminal is equipped with a control unit that decodes the signal from, and encodes signals for, the communications link, and controls the operation of the various I/O devices attached to the terminal. The control unit usually also has provision for checking the validity of the information it receives from the computer; this checking is done using *parity* (*q.v.*) bits on each character, special check characters at the end of each message, and other *error-detecting* and *error-correcting codes* (*q.v.*). If the control unit detects a transmission error (i.e., an error due to the communications link), it requests the computer to retransmit the message (also known as the *record—q.v.*) in which the error occurred. Conversely, it can retransmit a record, should the computer request it to do so. The control unit, which is often physically built into one of the I/O devices, also provides the required switches, pushbuttons, and indicators for the operator of the terminal. Fig. 2 is a simplified diagram of the connection between a batch terminal and a computer.

In actual operation, once the connection between the terminal and the computer has been established, the operator of the terminal indicates, via the control unit, whether programs and data are to be transmitted to the computer, or whether the computer should send to the terminal any accumulated output. Every time a record is sent to or from the terminal, the receiver (the computer or the terminal) acknowledges the receipt of that record (or, in the case of an error, requests retransmission); then the next record in sequence is sent. The simpler batch ter-

minals cannot receive and transmit at the same time (i.e., they cannot operate in the *full-duplex* mode). More sophisticated batch terminals can transmit and receive (and, in the case of terminals that are computers in their own right, perform local data processing) all at the same time.

Interactive Terminals. The primary purpose of an *interactive* (or *time-sharing—q.v.*) terminal is to allow the user of a computer to use it in a mode (often called interactive or conversational) that is characterized by relatively fast response to each individual request.

In contrast to a batch terminal, the user of an interactive terminal does not submit an entire task (or *job—q.v.*) at one time to the computer, but rather enters requests, program statements, and data, one line at a time. The computer accepts each line and, if it is a request (often called a *command*), executes it. The time between successive requests is usually measured in seconds or fractions of seconds and, when the user is entering data or interacting with a *text editing system* (*q.v.*), the computer normally responds fast enough so that the user can type as fast as he or she is able to without having to wait on the computer. More complex requests can, of course, take longer. (The complexity of a request depends on how much of the computer's resources that request uses, and not on how long or difficult it is to type.)

A computer system that provides this type of service to users of interactive terminals can normally accommodate a number of such users simultaneously (up to hundreds at a time for very large computers). This is accomplished by operating the computer in a time-sharing mode (which is a special case of the *multiprogramming—q.v.—*mode of operation). When operating in this mode, the computer accumulates the requests of the various users and executes them in turn, devoting to each a *time slice* (*q.v.*), which normally lasts only a fraction of a second. If a request cannot be completed in its time slice, its execution is interrupted, it is saved on a queue (so it can be restarted when its turn

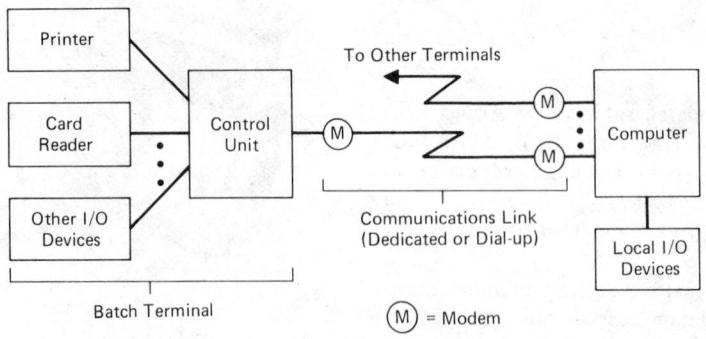

Fig. 2.   A batch terminal connected to a computer.

comes up again), the request of the next user is executed, and so on. Because a computer is very fast when compared to the speed with which users can type in requests and data at their terminals, each user normally gets the impression that the computer devotes all its resources to the user's current request (unless, of course, the request is very complex). As a result, each user can usually work as fast as he or she is able to and is generally unaware of the presence of other, concurrent users.

An interactive terminal is connected to the computer in the same manner as a batch terminal, but usually by relatively slower communications links. Typical speeds range from 30 to 960 characters per second. The higher speeds cannot be used effectively in transmitting *from* an interactive terminal whose input speed is limited by the user's typing speed; but they can be used when the computer is sending messages to the terminal and for transmission in both directions with graphic and intelligent terminals described below, as well as with terminals equipped with magnetic-tape cassette or *floppy* disk drives. The communication links are usually of the dial-up type.

Many interactive terminals very much resemble an office typewriter (Dolotta, 1970). They contain a typewriter-like keyboard and print mechanism and several control switches, keys, and lights. They are operated like a typewriter: Once the connection with a computer is established, the user types requests, data, etc., on the keyboard. Whatever is typed prints on the terminal. The responses that the computer sends to the user are also printed on the terminal, so that what eventually appears on the paper (or on the screen) in front of the user is a series of lines of text in the form of a "conversation," some lines having been typed by the user and some by the computer. (Fig. 4 of the article COMMAND AND JOB CONTROL LANGUAGES is an example of such a "conversation" or "terminal session.")

Interactive terminals first appeared in the early 1960s. These early terminals were essentially teletypewriters adapted to communicate with computers rather than with each other. They were typically quite slow (printing speed of 10 characters per second), had a limited character set (on the order of 50 characters: 26 upper-case letters, 10 digits, and some punctuation characters), and produced printing of the type seen on telegrams and stock quotation "tickers."

As the popularity of interactive use of computers grew, a large variety of terminals specifically designed for that purpose appeared on the market. With the passage of time, interactive terminals have become faster, easier to operate, and lighter (and thus more portable). They became capable of printing and transmitting larger numbers of distinct characters (typically, on the order of 90 characters: 52 upper- and lower-case letters, 10 digits, and a number of punctuation and special characters such as brackets, braces, arithmetic symbols, etc.). Some terminals have interchangeable print elements or character sets, making available even larger numbers of distinct characters.

Many of these newer terminals have additional features not normally found on typewriters or on older terminals, but which are very useful for interacting with a computer (Dolotta, 1970; Ossanna and Saltzer, 1970), such as:

1. Print suppression, which allows the computer to turn off the terminal's printing or display mechanism at certain times, for instance when the user has to type his or her secret password that authorizes access to the computer.
2. Forward and backward line and half-line paper feed, which is useful for printing subscripts, superscripts, etc.
3. Tab stops that can be cleared and set by *both* the user and the computer, which allows the computer to print formatted text on the terminal much faster.
4. Form feed, which allows the computer to position the paper at the top of a page.
5. Plotting capability, which allows the computer to move the print element and the paper (left and right, up and down) in increments as small as a one hundredth of an inch.

Fig. 3 shows one such terminal. Fig. 4 shows a terminal that lacks all but the first of these features, but that is truly portable, weighing only 13.5 pounds.

Also on the market are interactive terminals that, instead of (or in addition to) printing text on paper (i.e.,

Fig. 3. A contemporary interactive terminal (Diablo® 1620).

Fig. 4. A portable terminal (Texas Instruments TI-745).

producing hard copy), display it on a television-like screen. Such character-display (or *soft-copy*) terminals are capable of much higher speeds than printing terminals and allow the user to enter or receive more than one line of text at a time. In addition, on some display terminals, the user can *alter* and *correct* the text after it has been typed, but before it has been transmitted to the computer. This is because such terminals usually have a local memory (or *buffer—q.v.*) that holds whatever text is displayed on the screen (or even several screenfuls of text). Because of these advantages, character-display terminals have recently become very popular and their numbers are growing much faster than the numbers of typewriter-like terminals. Display terminals normally do not produce a printed record of the interaction between the user and the computer (although often groups or *clusters* of such terminals are connected to a printing terminal or a slow-speed printer, allowing users to print on paper selected data, records of transactions, etc.). Fig. 5 shows a character-display terminal.

Some display terminals (also called graphic terminals because they are used for *computer graphics—q.v.*) can, in addition to displaying characters on their screen, also draw arbitrary curves. They are more complex (and more expensive) than simple character-display terminals. Fig. 6 shows a graphics terminal.

Some of the more sophisticated display and graphics terminals allow the user to enter input with a pen-like device with which one can "write" directly on the terminal's screen or on a special "tablet" (*see* DATA TABLET). Some graphics terminals can display their output in color.

Many interactive terminals allow the attachment of magnetic-tape cassette drives, floppy disk drives, etc. Such devices often allow the user to record and edit the input onto tape or disk in local mode (i.e., without having to connect the terminal to the computer) and then, at a later time, to transmit that input to the computer at a higher speed. Similarly, output from the computer can be recorded onto a tape or disk and then examined locally by the user at a later time. (The terminal shown in Fig. 9 has this capability.)

Special-Purpose Terminals. In certain cases, one or more computers and all the interactive terminals connected to them are devoted to a single task, such as airline or hotel reservations, banking, assembly-line reporting, or supermarket check-out operations (these are the so-called *point-of-sale terminals—q.v.*). The terminals used in such applications are specifically designed so that their operators can perform their individual tasks as efficiently and conveniently as possible. Such terminals are usually connected to the computer via dedicated (and often multiplexed) communications links; they are highly specialized and may contain no general-purpose keyboard or printer, but instead be equipped with special indicators and other devices (e.g., magnetic badge readers, credit card readers, optical scanners). In some cases, they provide their output in the form of recorded or synthe-

Fig. 5. A character-display terminal (Helwett-Packard 2621).

sized voice through a normal telephone; such *audio response terminals* (*q.v.*) may be used, for instance, to give a bank clerk the current balance in a customer's account. In some cases, computers accept input from, and provide voice output to, regular pushbutton telephones; we expect that such use of telephones will grow significantly with time. Fig. 7 shows a terminal used by (human) bank tellers.

In the last few years, specialized terminals have been developed to dispense traveler's checks, travel insurance policies, and to act as unattended, automated "bank tellers." Because these terminals are operated, not by skilled,

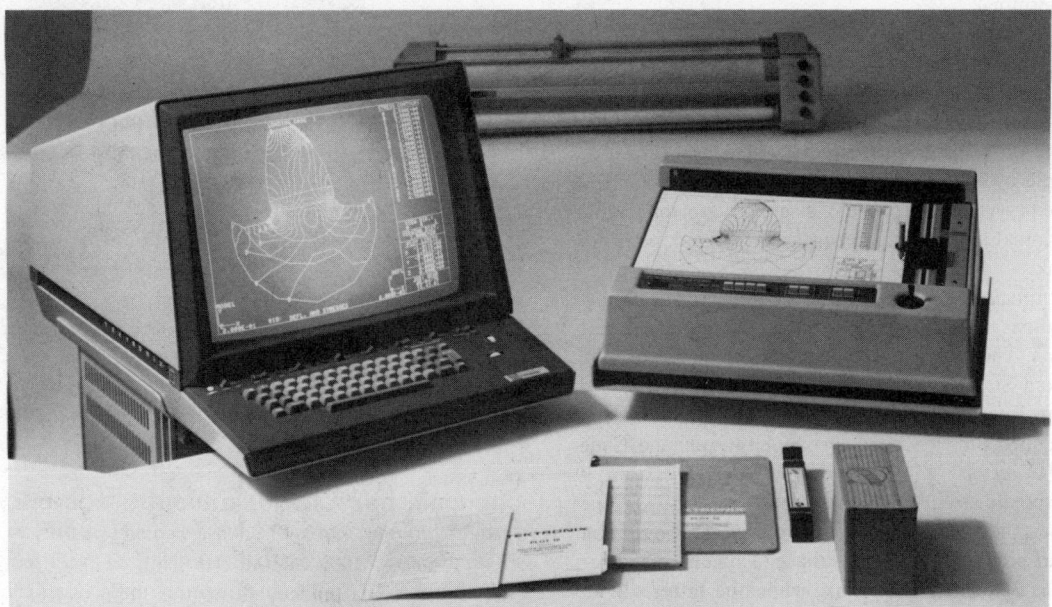

Fig. 6. A graphics terminal with an attached hard-copy unit (Tektronix 4104).

Fig. 7. A bank-teller's terminal (NCR 2261).

efficiently, so it is seldom used at speeds of over 480 characters per second.

Finally, terminals can operate in either *half-duplex* or *full-duplex* mode; in the former, at any one moment the terminal can be either transmitting or receiving information, but not both; in the latter, transmission and reception can proceed simultaneously, so that, for example, a user can be typing information that is transmitted to the computer at the same time that the computer is sending (different) information that is displayed on the terminal's screen.

Recent Trends. Recent advances in electronics, microcircuitry (LSI, or Large Scale Integration—*see* INTEGRATED CIRCUITRY), and mini- and microcomputers have made it possible to endow terminals with more and more capabilities ("intelligence"), and, at the same time, to decrease their size, power consumption, and, most importantly, cost. It is now possible to package an entire general-purpose minicomputer *inside* an interactive terminal. Fig. 9 shows one such terminal.

Terminals endowed with such distributed "intelli-

trusted operators, but rather by the general public, they must, above all, be very simple to operate, virtually foolproof, and very secure. Fig. 8 shows an automatic "bank-teller" terminal.

How Terminals Communicate. Terminals can be designed to communicate with computers in a variety of ways—via dial-up or dedicated communications links—and it is also possible to attach several terminals to a single communications link in a multi-drop fashion (i.e., like party-line telephones), as opposed to connecting each terminal to the computer by an individual, point-to-point link.

Terminals are generally designed to use one of several methods of encoding characters into sequences of 1 and 0 bits. The most common encoding schemes used in the United States are the American National Standard Code for Information Interchange (*ASCII—q.v.*) and the Extended Binary-Coded Decimal Interchange Code (*EBCDIC—q.v.*).

Terminals use either *synchronous* or *start/stop* line disciplines; the former requires that characters be sent on the link at predetermined times that are synchronized between the two ends of the link, while the latter allows characters to be sent at any time, but uses the link less

Fig. 8. An unattended, automatic "bank-teller" terminal (IBM 3614).

Fig. 9. An intelligent terminal with two magnetic-tape cassette drives (Digital Equipment VT-103).

gence" or "logic" (i.e., data processing capability) can do local editing, text compression, etc., resulting in more efficient utilization of communication links and faster response to user requests. This trend to more and more *intelligent terminals* is likely to continue for some time to come, and already the distinction between terminals and computers has become blurred.

The terminal manufacturing industry is rapidly growing and very competitive. There are already several million terminals in the United States. In some occupations (e.g., insurance companies, research laboratories, mail-order operations), there is now an average of nearly one terminal per employee. The cost of terminals is coming down dramatically and their capabilities are increasing at an equally rapid rate.

The ultimate market for interactive terminals is in the home (*see* PERSONAL COMPUTING). While home terminals are not yet a widespread phenomenon, there is no doubt that, in time, they will become as ubiquitous as automobiles and television sets. In fact, there already exist inexpensive terminals that consist only of a keyboard packaged together with some electronic circuitry and that attach to a normal television set, which then becomes the display part of the terminal. And even full-blown, quite sophisticated interactive terminals cost only little more than a good-quality high-fidelity sound system, and much less than a small car.

However, to really become a household appliance, interactive terminals need to become very reliable and very simple to operate, and there needs to exist a large variety of computerized services for such terminals to access (*see* VIEWDATA). Such services (e.g., stock market quotations, "shop-at-home" services, "electronic Yellow Pages," news summaries, computerized libraries) must be perceived as useful and cost-effective by the general public. There are already several "pilot" trials of such services, many of them using two-way cable television (CATV) as the communications medium.

REFERENCES

1970. Dolotta, T. A. "Functional Specifications for Typewriter-Like Time-Sharing Terminals," *Computing Surveys* **2,** *No. 1:* 5–31.
1970. Ossanna, J. F. and Saltzer, J. H. "Technical and Human Engineering Problems in Connecting Terminals to a Time-Sharing System," *American Federation of Information Processing Societies (AFIPS) Conference Proceedings* **35:** 355–362.

T. A. DOLOTTA

TEXT EDITING SYSTEMS

For articles on related subjects *see* COMMAND AND JOB CONTROL LANGUAGES; JUSTIFICATION; NATURAL LANGUAGE PROCESSING; PUBLISHING, COMPUTERS IN; TERMINALS; TIME SHARING; and WORD PROCESSING.

A *text editor* is a computer program that allows a user to enter, alter, format, and store program and manuscript text. A variety of factors have caused the editor to become an indispensable software tool. Among these are the increase in computer usage by a large portion of the business world, industry, and academia; the commercialization of word processing and computerized typesetting; and the advent of the personal computer. Long taken for granted by programmers as simply a necessary utility to create programs, text editors have now become powerful tools with which any computer user's productivity can be enhanced. Newspaper editors, authors, manual writers, lawyers—knowledge workers in general—now recognize the importance of the text editor in daily "knowledge work."

In this article, the general characteristics of text-editing systems are discussed, an informal taxonomy of the available types of systems is created, and examples of several specific systems are offered. Finally, we look briefly at the future of text editing.

General Overview. Text editing is the interactive use of computer-based tools to create, revise, and maintain text. It is the crucial component of *text processing,* which is concerned not only with the creation and maintenance but also with the formatting and utilization of the text; the other components of the text processing spectrum are the *text formatter* and various *text utilities*. *Word processing* (*q.v.*), a synonym for commercial text processing, has matured from its magnetic-card beginnings to include not only manuscript creation and revision, but many database processing utilities as well.

The generic design goals of an on-line text editor are as follows:

1. Fast response time.
2. A concise and consistent user interface that is easy to learn and to use—the author should not need to involve others in the creation of a document.
3. Powerful facilities, with few restrictions and exceptions, to make possible everything that one can do to hard copy with red pencil, scissors, and tape.
4. To as great an extent as possible, the editor should give the creator a "what you see is what you get" view of the final composition and complexion of the document.
5. Facilities that take advantage of computer capabilities; e.g., moving to the first occurrence of a user-specified pattern in a file, uniform substitution of one pattern for another in every place it may occur, automatic renumbering of sections or references after a file is altered, and flexible hard copy output.
6. Common access to the same information and files under controlled conditions (useful for a pool of researchers or documentors working in the same area, or for common access to updated management information).
7. The user should be given the ability to have multiple contexts on the same output device—much like the user has on a large desktop (see Fig. 1).

The User View—The Manual Editing Cycle. Text editors (editors for short) can be best understood by stepping back from their specific implementations and looking instead at the *document** creation/revision pipeline from a human perspective.

When an author begins a document, be it a scholarly paper, a memo, or a Fortran program, the first stage is the *design* phase. Here, a skeleton of the document is sketched and fleshed out and a rough but complete entity is created. The document may still have conceptual, logical, semantic, or syntactic errors at this point. Note that

the final medium is conspicuously absent from this description—the author writes by hand or types on a keyboard instead of setting the text in the ultimate type and page layout with which, say, a book will be printed. Modern text editors attempt to bridge this gap between (initial) content, structure, and final output format; unlike the editors of the past decade, the editors of the 1980s will be considered as tools in the design stage as well as in the latter stages of a document's life cycle. Examples of this new type of system will be given below.

The next phase constitutes perhaps the longest stage in the preparation of a document—the *revision* phase. Here, the author corrects conceptual, logical, semantic, syntactic, and grammatical errors—adding, deleting, and revising material and rearranging the structure. Traditional procedures involve marking pages with red pencil, photocopying, cutting, and pasting, etc.

The last phase in the evolution of a document is the *production* phase. Here, the document is produced in its final form and is "released" to the public.

The System View—The Computer-Based Editing Cycle. A text editor provides the user with primitives with which operations can be performed to carry out what was previously done manually, as well as new operations not (easily) done by hand. A small set of these primitives includes *add, change, delete, move, copy, pattern locate,* and *print hardcopy.* These primitives are executed in the *editing cycle.*

For a treatment of implementation considerations of many text editors still largely valid today, see Rice and van Dam (1971).

Regardless of the particular computers on which they are implemented, text editors follow the same general structure, as outlined in Fig. 2.* The area in the large dotted box represents what is visible to the ordinary user. Whether editing on a large mainframe (*q.v.*) or a micro, the user must have *input devices* with which to choose editing operations, *output devices* with which to view these choices and their results, and an *interaction syntax* with which to specify these choices.

Input Devices. Input devices, which provide the hardware interface to the editor, can be broken down into four categories (GSPC, 1979).

Pick devices allow the user to signal to the system the choice of a particular place on the screen where text should be inserted, deleted, or identified for later use as part of a string of characters to be deleted, moved, etc. These devices include *lightpens* (*q.v.*), *data tablets* (*q.v.*), and *touch-sensitive panels* overlaying the screen. *Locator*

---

*The word *document* is not meant to preclude computer programs, pictures, diagrams, etc., but is used in a general sense to comprise all of the above.

*Locally intelligent editing systems, as explained later, deviate from this structure.

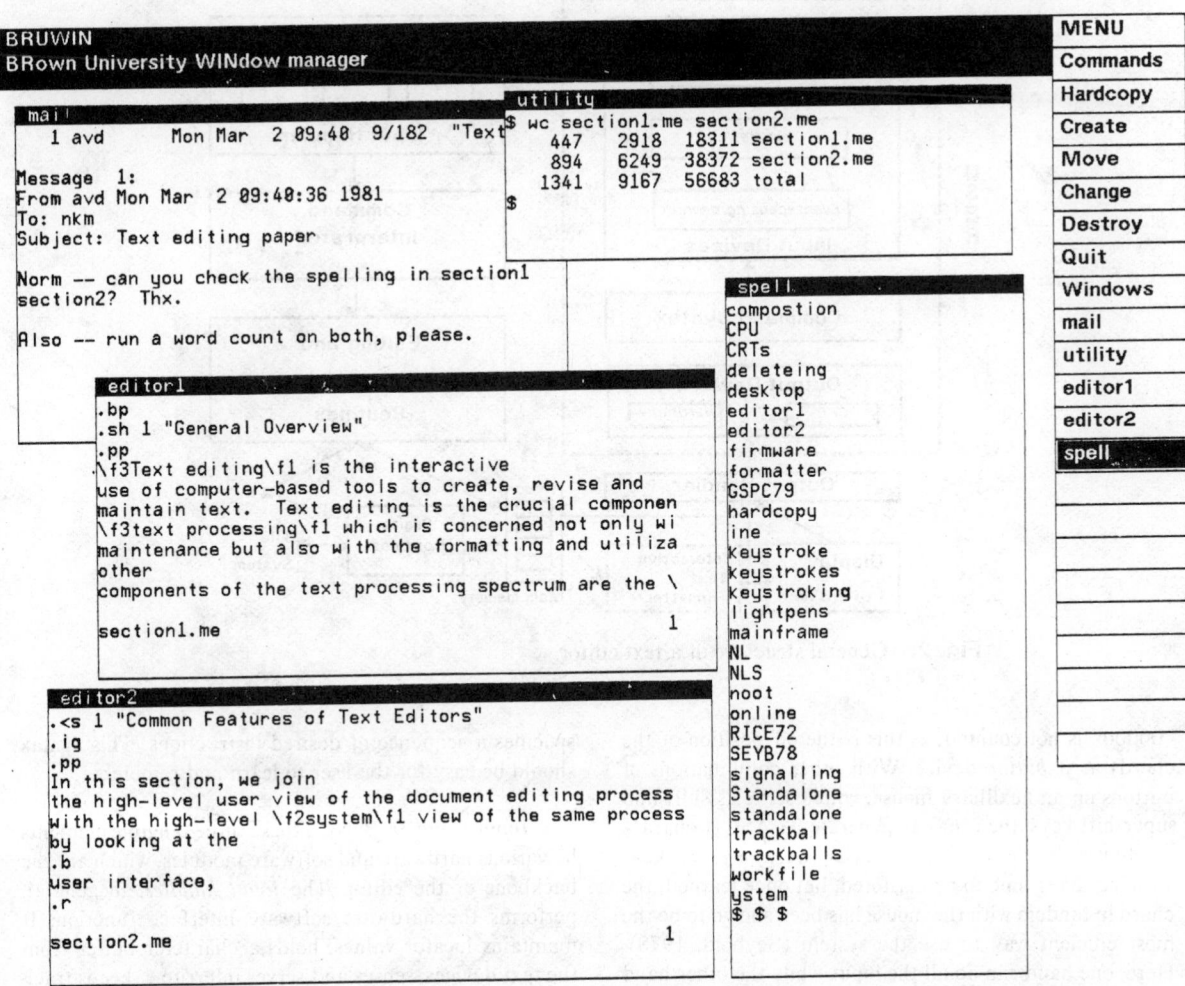

Fig. 1. Full screen editor/window manager. The user is presented with many contexts on the screen in order to be able to edit files (in the *editor 1* window and the *editor 2* window), read mail concerning the document (in the *mail* window), see spelling errors (in the *spell* window), and get a word count analysis (in the *utility* window).

devices are *x-y* analog-to-digital transducers that continually sample the analog values produced by the user's movement of the device to position a tracker/cursor symbol on the screen. These include *cursor keys, joysticks, trackballs* (*see* INPUT-OUTPUT DEVICES), and *mice* (a form of *x-y* trackball moved on a flat surface).

Pick devices differ from locator devices in that they generate an external interrupt, signaling the application program to read the position of the selected point, while locator devices constantly maintain a particular *x, y* coordinate in an internal locator register. (Pick devices are often used to simulate locator devices and vice versa, lending a bit of confusion to the matter.) *Button* devices, such as programmed function keys, generate an interrupt and indicate the occurrence of a certain *event* associated

with the button, typically to cause transfer to a subprocedure. *Text* devices tend to be mundane; these are typically typewriter-like keyboards with the variations necessary for a particular system (cursor keys, function keys, accent marks, brackets, etc.), though occasionally new text input devices are constructed.

Currently, several "one-of-a-kind" text input devices exist. One interesting device, called the *chord,* was created at Stanford Research Institute as part of its *on-line* system (NLS) and carried forward to Augment, the commercial version of that system. It consists of a pad of five long keys similar in shape to white piano keys. Each of these keys is a position in a five-bit binary word; by depressing the proper combination, the user can represent $2^5 - 1$ or 31 numbers or ASCII (*q.v.*) codes (binary

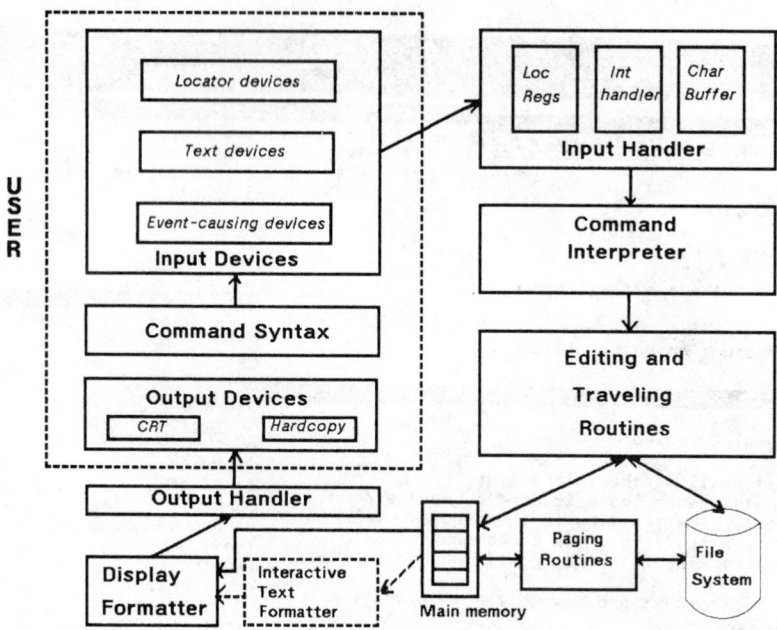

Fig. 2. General structure of a text editor.

"00000" is not counted, as this is the off position of the chord) as a *button* device. With other combinations of buttons on an auxilliary mouse, which serve as shift and supershift keys, the user can generate 93 ASCII characters to use the chord as a *text* device. Certainly, this keystroking takes time to be mastered, but once learned, the chord in tandem with the mouse has been shown to be the most efficient way to use the system (Seybold, 1978). Here, one hand can do all the input while the other hand performs all the necessary cursor locating of text on the screen.

Output Devices. Output devices for editing, formerly limited in range, are becoming much more diverse. The output device serves to let the user view the text and interact with the system. These range from (obsolete) teletypes and character-printing terminals to high-speed CRTs (cathode ray tubes) and bit-mapped, high-resolution raster graphic editing stations supported by a local bit map refresh buffer.

Interaction Syntax. The third item of interest to the user is the method of interaction with the system, known as the *interaction syntax*. The interaction syntax varies widely from editor to editor, though the functions normally specified in this syntax are similar from system to system. The syntax could be English-like or Pascal (*q.v.*)-like—or it could be proofreader's symbols picked from a displayed menu. In any event, the interaction syntax

specifies a sequence of desired instructions. This syntax should be easy for the user to learn and remember.

Input Handler. Beyond these three tangible elements lie various hardware and software modules, which are the backbone of the editor. The *input handler,* in general, performs the hardware/software interface function. It maintains locator values, holds a character buffer from the text devices, senses and serves interrupts, keeps track of cursor movement, discovers which function key has been pressed, stores the text command line, etc., depending upon the type of input devices and the interaction syntax of the particular editor.

Command Interpreter. When it has *received* the input, the input handler passes its information to a *command interpreter* either by direct call or by the generation of an *intermediate representation* of the desired user instructions followed by a call to the command interpreter. The added level of indirection caused by the intermediate representation seems wasteful at first. Yet the existence of this level allows the use of widely varying input devices and even interaction syntaxes, while the editing routines, driven from the common intermediate representation, need never be changed. This *device independence* increases the generality of an editor by making it highly transportable from one set of input or output devices or interaction syntax to another.

The command interpreter does "traffic control" between the user-interface and the editing, traveling, and utility routines discussed below. If, for example, the interaction syntax involves a typed command language, the typed-in character buffer is parsed to the appropriate command and its operands. If a function key is pressed in a button-driven editor, the hardware code that is generated is matched in a lookup table to find its procedure entry name. If an item on a menu is picked with a mouse, a graphics input routine would determine the command to which the picked item corresponds. Simply, then, the command interpreter translates physical actions by the user into usuable parameters (in some intermediate code) for the editing, traveling and utility routines.

Editing, Traveling, and Utility Routines. After determining a particular command, the command interpreter calls the *editing, traveling,* and *utility routines* to perform the appropriate tasks. These three types of routines form the heart of the text editor and are discussed in more detail below from the point of view of the functionality they provide. Editing routines perform the modification tasks on the user's document. The traveling routines move the user through the document for browsing purposes or for finding the target of an editing operation. Utility routines provide a variety of services that aid in document production like spelling checker/correctors, word count analyzers, etc.

Operating System Interface. The editing and traveling routines "communicate" with a user document on two levels—in *main memory,* and in the *file system* on disk. At the beginning of an editing session, most systems copy the user document from the file system to a *workfile* in working storage, leaving an unedited copy of the document as backup in the file system until the user specifies that this be replaced with the freshly edited workfile. All user editing changes take effect only on the workfile until the user explicitly tells the system to make the workfile permanent; this allows the user to *quit* (abort) an editor without making any changes permanent and also leaves the file in a consistent state should the system crash. Other systems work on the actual document itself, leaving it to the user to make backup copies.

If each operation specified by the user entailed an I/O operation to a disk device, it is easy to see that editing would be painfully slow. On the other hand, bringing an entire document into main memory may be infeasible or impossible. To alleviate this problem, *paging routines* bring in a logical chunk of a document called a page (though there is typically no correspondence between these pages and hard copy document pages) into main memory, where they reside until a user operation requires another piece of the document. These editor paging routines should not be confused with hardware paging rou-

tines on virtual memory systems; the editor must be able to specify explicitly which logical units of the document *data structure* it must operate on. In other words, even with hardware-paged virtual memory, data-structure pages may be managed under software control. As a result, documents are not necessarily stored sequentially, but in a format that allows addition, deletion, and modification with a minimum of I/O and character movement.

The editing and traveling routines, having been passed a command and its associated operands from the command interpreter, access a part of the stored document containing the data structure they need, using the paging routines to fetch it from auxilliary storage if it is not already resident in main memory. A special *exit, file,* or *save* user command at the end of the editing session instructs the system to copy the workfile to the file system as the new permanent copy.

Display Routines. When the operation in main memory is complete, the *display routines* format the data structure representation of the text into user-oriented output for the output device. These routines may simply write the storage structure sequentially on the output device, or they may perform complex *pointer chasing* to find the appropriate text to display.

A possible (optional) companion of the display routines is the *interactive text formatter.* This consists of special display routines that dynamically format the document per instructions—either visible or invisible— embedded in the text. This formatting can range from simple paragraphing and justification of monospaced text to complex typesetting. This interactive text formatter is the crux of systems that have a "what you see is what you get" philosophy of display and hard copy output. This philosophy requires that all operations on the document take place immediately, with the results displayed immediately for user-feedback.

Output from the display routines and/or interactive text processor is passed to the output handler, which provides an interface between the software-produced output and the hardware display devices. (The input handler and the output handler are generally independent of the editor; they are composed of specific device drivers provided by the host operating system.) The modified text is displayed on the output device and the editing cycle is complete.

Time Sharing versus Stand-alone versus Distributed Configurations. Editors function in the three basic types of computing environments—*time sharing, stand-alone,* and *distributed.* Each type of environment imposes some limitations on the design of a text editor. The time-sharing editor must function swiftly within the context of the load on the computer's file system, primary memory, secondary storage, and processor. The stand-alone editor must provide functions that the time-sharing editor obtained from its host operating system. These functions may be provided in part by a small local operating system or may be built into the editor if the stand-alone system is dedicated to editing. The distributed editor operating in a resource-sharing local network must, like a stand-alone editor, run independently on each user's machine, but, like a time-sharing editor, must accommodate shared resources like files. Some time-sharing-based editing systems take advantage of local (terminal-based) hardware to perform editing tasks. These *smart* terminals have hardware/firmware to implement operations such as character delete, line delete, line and page scroll, etc. More important, they have their own local buffer, in which these manipulations can be done, saving the time needed to read and write main computer memory. Thus, small and local actions are not controlled by the CPU of the host processor but can be handled by the terminal itself. In an IBM 3270 series terminal, for example, a full screen of material can be sent to the screen by the editor. Now, the user is free to add and delete characters and lines; when the buffer has been edited, its updated contents can be transmitted to the mainframe. The advantage of this scheme is that the host need not deal with each minor change, each keystroke. That is also the major disadvantage: With a dumb terminal, the CPU sees every character typed in and can react immediately to do error checking and prompting and to update the data structure and save the keystrokes for undoing editing operations. With a smart terminal, local functionality is more limited, and in the event of a system crash, all local work is lost.

Common Features of Text Editors

User Interface.
In the conventional (manual) document editing process, the author's "interface" with a manuscript will usually be proofreader's marks made with a pen or pencil. Though these marks may vary from author to author, the medium of communication—the pencil and paper—have been adopted as standard by those who create documents.

Computer text editors, too, have varied "marks" with which authors communicate their desires. However, unlike in the manual document process, not even the method of communication, the *user interface,* in the computerized text editor is standard. At best, we can split these interfaces into several broad categories.

Language-Oriented. The *language-oriented* interface is the oldest of the major editor interfaces. In this type of system, the user communicates with the editor by typing

Prefix	DELETE 10 lines
Postfix	Mark 10 lines, type DELETE
Infix	Mark start, type DELETE, mark end

Fig. 3.   Comparison of prefix, postfix, and infix.

English-like text strings from the keyboard. Commands in general can be divided into three categories—*prefix, postfix,* and *infix* (see Fig. 3). A prefix command specifies the operation desired followed by the *scope*—the range of text to be affected by that operation. A postfix command is structured just the opposite: The scope of the operation is specified first, followed by the operation desired. An infix command is a cross between the two former types; the operation is surrounded by its operands. Communications to the editor using a language-oriented interface take place by typing words on a keyboard; these words are echoed on the output device and sent to the editor. The editor communicates to the user by displaying *prompts,* a confirmation of the transaction, or some other conversational statement to signal its actions.

Function-Key Oriented. Language-oriented interaction requires that the user remember the commands with which to express desires to the editor. If the interaction syntax, however, is difficult to remember, the user must refer to a reference manual or an on-line "help" command for a description of less frequently used commands. Also, typing takes time, especially for users not oriented to keyboards. The *function-key-oriented* user interface was designed to address these deficiencies. Here, all the commands have associated with them a key on the user's keyboard. There is no possibility of forgetting the commands, as they are literally at the user's fingertips. Usually, only a single key need be struck. Function-key syntax is usually coupled with cursor-key movement for specifying operands, thereby eliminating typing almost completely. For a "rich," many-function editor, shift keys or an optional keyboard syntax must be used for less frequently invoked commands/options.

Menu-Oriented. The *menu-oriented* user interface is an attempt to allow the user to communicate with the editor without the limitations imposed by language-oriented systems (assumed familiarity with the system and language, awkwardness of commands, etc.) and by the function-key-oriented systems (limited number of keys on keyboard, familiarity with keystroke sequences, etc.). Using the notions described by Goldberg and Robson (1979), a *menu* is a set of *icons*—text and pictures—that describe the interface to a system (here the editor). These icons are a *filtered template* of the actions that may be taken at the current juncture in the system; they often represent but a handful of the literally hundreds of actions that the system may allow. The menu method of interaction prompts the user with the actions which may be performed at a given time. Initially, the editor may give the choice to create a new document or retrieve an old one. Next, the user might be given the choice to input new text or edit existing text. The exact sequence or semantics of functions are not "wired in"; the motivation behind the menu-oriented interface is to provide the user access to the editor without memorized knowledge of the interface. Unlike the other interfaces, the user is always presented with all the command "paths" that may be taken at the current state. The menu might call for the user to make selections by typing characters, by hitting function keys, or by picking at a command on the menu with some pointing device; the user need remember almost nothing about human/editor interaction from one session to the next.

One drawback of this type of system is the speed of interaction. Since the user must be prompted with all the information needed to choose a function, large hierarchical trees of menus must be traversed to do even simple commands. As this can be annoying and detrimental to the efficiency of a seasoned user, some menu-oriented systems allow the user to turn off menu-control, leaving a language- or function-key-oriented editor as a base. Others have the most-used functions on a main command menu and have "escape" menus to handle the more obscure functions. Some only display the menu when the user specifically asks for it. Of course, modern menu-oriented systems have dynamic menus which are dragged along with the cursor and are displayed instantaneously, allowing very rapid menu traversal.

Functional Capabilities

Creation of Text. The most common method of inserting text into a computer-based document is done through the aid of a text input device. Yet the editor need not simply simulate a typewriter, where at most one page of lines is conveniently accessible. The user is given methods to (for all practical purposes) move the "typehead" (either logically or physically) throughout the document, inserting text wherever desired without the annoyance of inserting physical pages into the typewriter. Often the user is provided with automatic *wordwrap* that eliminates the need for typing carriage returns at the end of lines. The text editor senses a word boundary at the end of the line, breaks the line there, and automatically skips to the next physical line.

An alternative to direct keyboard input is *optical character recognition (OCR)*. Here, a standard typewriter equipped with an OCR typeface is used to type the text on normal paper. This paper is then read through an optical character reader, an electromechanical device that scans the page and translates each character into a proper digital representation for that computer/file system. This allows the use of text editing facilities without the high cost of full conversion of an office; the typewriters become off-line "links" to the computer facilities. Many OCR systems do allow rudimentary editing of the raw text stream via character and line delete control characters inserted in the text, but this cannot compete with the convenience of on-line input, with its essentially instant editing facility. Thus, OCR defeats the increasingly popular notion of having the computer-based editor as an author's fundamental tool throughout the authoring pipeline rather than having secretaries transcribe from (illegibly) marked-up hard copy. In short, this is contrary to one of our initial goals—making the editor useful and usable enough so that there is no desire by the author of a document to involve anyone else in its creation.

Creation Aids. To aid in the creation of text, editors occasionally provide the users with templates of varying degrees of detail. Structure editors (Englebart and English, 1968; Hansen, 1971) impose a hierarchical structure upon the user's text; only a properly structured document can be produced by such an editor. Some editors have special indenting modes for various programming languages so that only properly indented programs are permitted by the editor. Some editors for Lisp may count left and right parentheses, allowing only those programs with matching parens to be accepted. Still others, called *syntax-directed* editors, give the user templates of programming language constructs, allowing only syntactically correct programs to be created.

Viewing Text. Once the user has input the text, it is stored in the editor's data/storage structure, typically on disk. How does the user go about viewing the document once the text has been input? In the manual process, the user would simply flip through the typewritten pages—and by this method perform actions upon a limited portion (a word, a line, a page, several pages) of a document at any given time. This amount is the user's editing *window* into the document. In the computer-based editor, the user is presented with a similar window. In essence, the user is presented with a cutout through which only part of the document may be accessed. By moving the cutout (or equivalently leaving the cutout stationary and moving the document), different parts of the document may be accessed. In some editors, the window may be limited to a single character at a time. In others, the user may be able to alter a line or group of lines at a time. Still in others, the user's editing window is limited only by the size of the file itself. Certainly, the larger the window, the larger the context within which the author may work.

The editing window is not to be confused with the *viewport*. The viewport indicates where the editor's window is to be mapped onto the user's output device, while the addressability indicates the smallest unit of information on which the editor can act. Often there is a one-to-one correspondence between window and viewport: The editor might act upon single lines of the user file (the window) and display the single line result (the viewport), or might act upon a large window of text reflected in a viewport of the same size, as in a full-screen editor. If one is limited by a low-speed, line-oriented output device, an editor could provide a large window (enabling the revision of large amounts of text) coupled with a small viewport, so that the entire scope of the editing operation need not be viewed or be in view.

Some editors allow the user to define multiple windows/viewports for file(s). This gives the user more context within which to make changes; many different parts of needed document(s) may be seen and altered while viewing all the files on the same viewing surface. Several editors provide facilities to alter the *viewing specifications (viewspecs),* allowing the user to control the window to viewport mapping (Englebart and English, 1968; van Dam, 1971). Besides controlling the window/viewport mapping, the viewspecs can be used to control any number of other viewing parameters to effect *information hiding* or *filtering.* An outline editor, for instance, allows the user to indicate what levels of detail in the hierarchy are able to be displayed. A syntax-directed editor allows the user to turn off comment printing. Display keyword or password viewspecs allows the user to see pieces of text only upon the presentation of the proper key to provide protection of sensitive materials (budgets in proposals, for example) and to declutter on-line presentation.

While one wants to be able to access large windows of information to develop a reasonable context, one also wants maximum *addressability*—the ability to address and revise the smallest unit of information possible (usually the character) while viewing this unit in a wide context. Thus, we want large windows and viewports coupled with the capability to address the smallest unit of information. In the original Dartmouth Basic, if one made a simple typographical error—say, transposing two characters—one was forced to retype the entire line. In such a system, the smallest unit of information is the character, but the addressability is the line!

Formatting of Text. Once the viewport is determined, the system knows what text should be displayed, and then must determine *how* it is to be displayed. The easiest route to take is to display the text exactly as it is stored in the data structure in *raw* mode. Yet this may not be the most effective way to show it. Often, text is stored essentially as consecutive characters on disk, with special characters indicating tabs and physical-end-of-lines/carriage returns. Thus, even a simple display routine has to take into consideration the size of stored lines in comparison with the size of the screen. In *stream* editing systems, in which a document's text is treated as an arbitrarily long character string, no indication of line

ends is stored; the display routines must make on-the-fly decisions as to where to break lines. Complex display-time formatting might consist of updating all the references to particular decimally-numbered sections of a document or proportional spaced typesetting and justification. Good discussions of computer typesetting can be found in Knuth (1979) and Reid (1980).

For simple on-line display, no further on-line formatting of the text beyond handling tabs, wordwrap, and carriage return may be necessary. With new hardware capabilities becoming prevalent, there will be more demand for having display output make use of many information coding techniques of hard copy (font changes, highlighting, meaningful page layout, etc.). Thus, on-line formatting for display (soft copy) and off-line formatting for hard copy will become more similar, especially when bit-map raster displays begin to approach the resolution of cheap (less than $15,000) typesetters. Indeed, computerized typesetting, once reserved for special documents or only for final copies of a document whose drafts were produced on line printers or typewriter terminals, is now within the reach of any commercial or academic installation. Editors must therefore make it possible to specify sophisticated formatting effects, the simpler of which may be shown on line during the editing phase.

Two methodologies exist to control the *specification* of formatting effects, and three methodologies exist to effect the formatting. To describe the desired formatting, some editors provide formatting primitives as part of their interaction syntax. Thus, the specification of the *underline* command in a language-driven editor or the specification of the UL function key would serve to describe the desired formatting option. Conversely, some editors don't support such primitives; the formatting specification is entered as a *formatting (typesetting) code* in the same manner as is "normal" (literal) text. A *.pp* might indicate the start of a new paragraph, a *.ft n* is a font change to font number *n* (including point size and/or style, such as bold, italic), a *.ul* an underline, etc. In some systems, these codes must be entered on separate lines to distinguish them from literal text; in other systems, a special control character, such as @, is used as a delimiter so the codes can be embedded in the normal text stream; two delimiters in a row then designate a literal character. Often, the method of specification is used to generate a low-level representation such as a typesetting code that is stored in the file (sometimes invisibly to the user). These systems, of course, need to provide the facility of changing these low-level representations with high-level editing commands.

The simplest way to effect the formatting is to alter the actual raw text of a file when a formatting command is specified. Literal underscore characters might be put in, spaces might be added to create paragraphs, etc. This method has several drawbacks. Once the formatting is done, the user and the system have no idea what took place; only the effects and not the actions taken are stored. Thus, changing the effect is not as easy as just editing a stored formatting code. Also, more complicated formatting requests, such as font changes, are impossible to effect without a stored code per font change unless the text is stored in typeface images, which requires significantly more storage, or unless each character has its own font code, also expensive.

The effects of (simple) stored codes can be seen instantaneously on some editors, especially commercial word processors. These codes are then made invisible unless the user wants to change them in some way. In others, the editor always shows the unformatted representation of the file; separate off-line formatting programs interpret the instructions in a file and perform the formatting/typesetting functions as a text-processing utility. Unix's NROFF/TROFF (Ossanna, 1976) and the University of Waterloo's SCRIPT are two common formatters. More complicated utilities, like those for mathematical typesetting (Kernighan and Cherry, 1975; Knuth, 1979) and table construction (Lesk, 1976), allow complicated off-line formatting/typesetting.

Currently, much research is being done on on-the-fly typesetting. In this methodology, the formatting/typesetting commands are part of the editor's interaction syntax. All formatting commands take effect immediately—typeface, type size, right justification (right margin alignment) with proportional spacing, etc. in the final documents are exactly "what you see" on line (except for resolution and quality differences). An implementation of this type of editor, Xerox PARC's Bravo, is explained in more detail later in this article.

Traveling Within and Between Files. Traveling routines offer the user the ability to change the file window on a file in order to read or edit a different piece of text. The less a system is oriented to transcription from hard copy and the more it is oriented to on-line composition/revision, the more important are traveling flexibility and power.

Simple Movement. Generally, a *cursor* (or, on a hardcopy device, the typing head) physically points at the *current position* in the viewed representation of the file, while a logical current operating pointer is maintained to point to the corresponding current position in the data structure. From this position, the user can move the window by issuing simple commands. In IBM's line-oriented CMS editor, moving the window down five lines would be accomplished by typing*

NEXT 5

---

*The command is shown in capitals without the customary abbreviation (*n* or *ne*) for ease of reading.

In editors whose lines have fixed line numbers rather than relative line numbers calculated as offsets to the top of the file, the user can specify a GOTO to a fixed line number. A fixed line number is simply a numeric label for a line provided by the user or the system. As an example, a Basic editor often has absolute line numbers specified some interval apart, such as:

00010 FOR I = 1 TO 10
00020 J = I * I
00030 NEXT I

To add a print statement after the second statement, one could simply type

00025 PRINT I,J

and have the editor put the new line in the proper place as a function of the numeric label.

In contrast, editors with relative line numbers keep track of a line's position internally—when a new line is added, all the internal line numbers of all lines underneath the new line are incremented by one, since they are one line further away from the top. Since the line numbers change dynamically, the deletion of a line near the top of the file causes all the line numbers below it to be decremented by one. Because of this, editing by specification of line number must be done from the bottom of the file upwards.

FRESS allows character string labels for such GOTOs to be inserted in the text—these move with the adjacent text as it is moved. The user need not know of the location of a piece of text, whether relative or absolute, in this system.

In a screen-oriented editor, like Rand's NED or Brown's *bb*, the user could move the window from one page to the next by hitting the function key marked

+ PAGE

Additionally, the window can be moved left or right by a specified number of character positions (columns) to allow editing of wide lines. In a graphics-oriented system, attempts are made to make the actions needed to perform traveling functions simulate human actions. Xerox's Bravo uses a graphical representation to "flip" to a certain place in the book-like document, as described below.

Pattern Searching. The above methods of traveling are positional in nature and offer the user an easy way to move relative to the current position or absolutely to a specific place in the text. In fact, the manual method of document preparation encourages this type of general search (looking for a page or landmark picture rather than individual words or characters). Almost all text editing systems, however, allow a much more content-dependent location scheme—*pattern searching.* Pattern searching allows the user to specify a string of characters to be found, communicate this to the editor, and have the editor move the window if it is found. To find the word "Computer" using a line-oriented editor, for instance, one would typically type:

LOCATE / Computer

The editor would respond by typing the window (here, a line) containing the word, as in:

Brown University Department of Computer Science.

Some editors allow not only simple searches for character strings as shown above but also allow the user to specify *regular expressions* (*q.v.*), which permit the user to search for a class of character strings.

To enhance regular expression matching, some editors also provide *boolean* primitives. Here, the user is able to combine regular expressions with the operators *and, or, not* to create "super-regular expressions." Now the search must satisfy the regular-expression criteria together with any boolean restrictions placed upon them.

Hypertext and Trails. The above types of travel are usually employed by the user *during* editing of the document, typically to get to the next place in the file where an edit is to be performed; the traveling is not premeditated. Occasions do arise when the user wants to set up (semi)permanent paths or links within a document or between documents. The motivation for these text links comes from the seminal work of Vannevar Bush, who envisioned the *Memex* system:

The human mind ... operates by association. With one item in its grasp, it snaps instantly to the next that is suggested by the association of thoughts, in accordance with some intricate web of trails carried by the cells of the brain. It has other characteristics, of course; trails that are not frequently followed are prone to fade, items are not fully permanent, memory is transitory. Yet the speed of action, the intricacy of trails, the detail of mental pictures, is awe-inspiring beyond all else in nature.

Consider a future device for individual use, which is a sort of mechanized private file and library. It needs a name, and, to coin one at random, "memex" will do. A memex is a device in which an individual stores all his books, records, and communications, and which is mechanized so that it may be consulted

with exceeding speed and flexibility ... when numerous items have been thus joined together to form a trail, they can be reviewed in turn, rapidly or slowly, by deflecting a lever like that used for turning the pages of a book ... It is exactly as though the physical items had been gathered together from widely separated sources and bound together to form a new book. It is more than this, for any item can be joined into numerous trails.

Hypertext editing systems are the modern-day incarnation of Bush's *Memex.* Coined by Nelson (1967), hypertext is "the combination of natural language text with the computer's capacities for interactive, branching, or dynamic display ... a nonlinear text ... which cannot be printed conveniently ... on a conventional page ..." Simply, hypertext is nonsequential writing. Hypertext systems allow the user to construct arbitrary links from a chosen point in a document to another point in that document or to a point in any other document in the user's domain. Menus of such links can be set up to provide a branching text. In the simplest sense, a hypertext document can consist of simply a "table of contents" with on-line links to files containing each chapter, each of which can link to sections, etc. (see Fig. 4).

More advanced uses include the use of links, rather than standard footnotes, which point to the actual referenced material to allow instantaneous access of cited material. Thus, a document can be browsed on line, and premeditated but optional diversions can be set up along trails the reader may find interesting. Of course, the author and readers are free to create links to new files or *annotation spaces* in which they may comment on what they are reading, thereby enriching the trails for others. A hypertext system may allow the user not only to see links to other places from the current position but to see that a particular text fragment has been *linked to.* The browser is then free to jump backward to see from what document this link was issued. In its richest sense, then, hypertext is a *bidirectional* collection of associative trails—a directed graph structure of document nodes that the user can traverse.

Editing Functions.

Often it is the revision process, in both the manual and computer-based editing tasks, that demands the most time of all phases of document preparation; the ease in which alterations can be made is clearly one of the most important considerations in the design of a text editor.

Simple Changes. Many of the changes that need to be made to a document are corrections of typographical and other minor errors. In manual text-editing, when these mistakes are discovered, they are highlighted by the

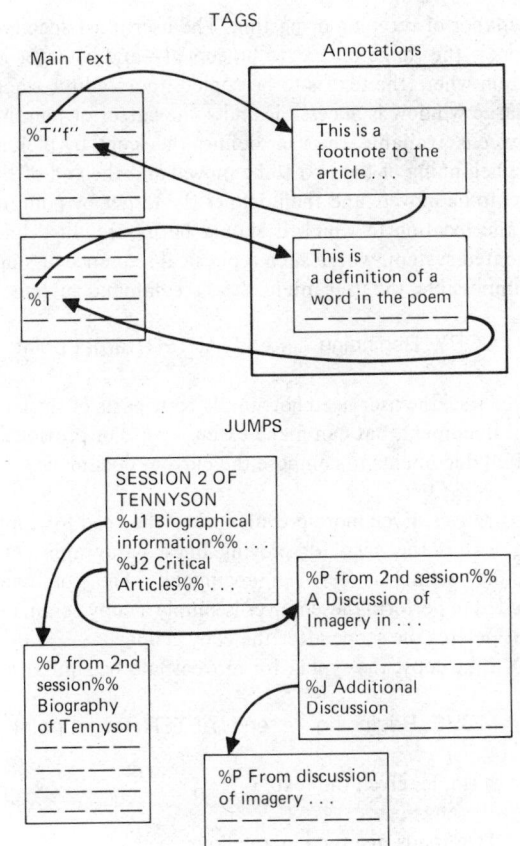

TAGS

Main Text   Annotations

%T"f"

This is a
footnote to the
article . . .

This is
a definition of a
word in the poem

%T

JUMPS

SESSION 2 OF
TENNYSON
%J1 Biographical
information%% . . .
%J2 Critical
Articles%% . . .

%P from 2nd session%%
A Discussion of
Imagery in . . .

%P from 2nd
session%%
Biography
of Tennyson

%J Additional
Discussion

%P From discussion
of imagery . . .

Fig. 4. An example of hypertext.

use of proofreader's marks. Not until the manuscript is retyped in a new draft does the correction take effect. Computer-based editors correct this deficiency by allowing corrections to take effect immediately; the current draft is always the most-up-to-date draft (an older, "archival" copy is retained for safekeeping). The simplest change is the replacement of one letter with another. In a cursor-oriented editor, where the user can move a cursor around the screen to address each character, the correction may be made by simply typing the new character "over" the erroneous one. Changing a word simply involves typing over the erroneous word. If the replacement word is shorter than the original word, a way to delete extraneous characters must be offered. Conversely, if the replacement word is longer, there must exist a way to insert extra characters.

In editors where each character is not accessible by a cursor, one would have to specify which character to replace. Most line-oriented editors, then, have a change command that takes as arguments both the *scope* of the change and the replacement string. To replace the letter "s" with the letter "r" in the line

The quick sed fox jumped over the laxy brown dog,

the user would typically specify the command*

CHANGE / s / r

Here, the editor takes as its scope the first occurrence of the first operand string that it finds in the current window. If one wanted to change the "x" in "laxy" to "z," the first thought would be to use the command

CHANGE / x / z

However, since "fox" has an x in it, the change command would use as its scope *that* x and change that word to "foz." To correct this problem, the user must supply enough *context* that the request is clear to the editor. A proper command would be

CHANGE / laxy / lazy
or
CHANGE / xy / zy

Of course, most change commands allow the substitution of arbitrary character strings rather than single characters. Thus,

CHANGE / lazy / intelligent /

would result in

The quick red fox jumped over the intelligent brown dog.

Certainly the ability to keep a draft fresh by having corrections take effect immediately is an advantage afforded by computer-based editing. The speed of a computer, however, makes it able to do operations much more rapidly than a human. The computer, then, is a natural for performing *global* operations—operations that take place repetitively throughout a document. The *global change* (or *uniform substitute*) command allows the user to specify a scope that is to be found throughout a document, and a replacement string to replace that scope wherever it may appear. In some systems, this command may do its work with no indication of the changes that have been made. In others, a count of the number of changes is given. In still others, each time a scope string is found, it is highlighted and the user is prompted as to whether the change is actually wanted (see Fig. 5).

---

*The / delimits the prefix command name and the operands.

!-p-MECHA (Movimento Estudiantil CHicano de Aztlan) has called for a mass descent upon the Coachella Valley of California June 6 to completely halt grape picking at farms still resisting the five-year-old strike by the United Farm Workers Union. In a statement of solidarity with the striking farm workers, MECHA declared, "We will stop these grapes of wrath from leaving Coachella Valley."

>us/the/a
upon the Coachella Valley of California June 6 to
OPTION =
>reject
resisting the five-year-old strike by the United
OPTION =
>accept
by the United Farm Workers Union. In a statement of
OPTION =
>accept
with the striking farm workers, MECHA declared, "We
OPTION =
>reject
stop these grapes of wrath from leaving Coachella
OPTION =
>reject
END OF AREA

!-p-MECHA (Movimento Estudiantil CHicano de Aztlan) has called for a mass descent upon the Coachella Valley of California June 6 to completely halt grape picking at farms still resisting a five-year-old strike by a United Farm Workers Union. In a statement of solidarity with the striking farm workers, MECHA declared, "We will stop these grapes of wrath from leaving Coachella Valley."

Fig. 5.   Global change transaction. Here, the user specifies the uniform substitute (global change) command. The editor displays each line on which this command could have an effect and asks the user to either ACCEPT the change or REJECT it. Displayed above is the text before changes, the transcript of an *us* operation to change all occurrences of "the" to "a" and the text after the modifications.

Copying. In many authoring situations, the text one wants to use as a base already exists in another document. In the manual process, one finds this existing text and retypes (or, more commonly, photocopies and pastes) it to compose the new document. A computer-based system provides the ability to copy already existing text (either in the current document or in another document) without the labor of retyping or pasting. The user must specify a scope—the range of text to be copied—and a target location where the text is to be copied. In an editor where a large window is accessible and some cursor or pointing device is available, the user defines the scope by picking the beginning of the text to be moved and the end of the text to be moved, and then defines the target by pointing to the location to which it should be moved. In a line-oriented system, where such a physical sequence of steps is impossible, the user might issue a command such as

COPY / Beginning . . . end / AFTER / target point

Of course, the user need not simply copy parts of the current document, but can make extensive use of previously edited documents to compose the current document.

Moves. Even more prevalent than the need for copying text is the need for moving lines, paragraphs, etc. around within or between documents. The command needed to perform these moves is simply a copy command that deletes the scope after the copy is done.

Like copy, the syntax for move would be similar to

MOVE / Beginning . . . end / AFTER / target point

For example, given the text

Two roads diverged in a yellow wood,
And looked down one as far as I could
To where it bent in the undergrowth.
And sorry I could not travel both
And be one traveler, long I stood

the Frost poem could be ordered properly by specifying:

MOVE / And sorry . . . long I stood / AFTER / yellow wood,

Deletion of Text. Often the user may want to delete some text that has previously been typed in. The user indicates, with scope specifications similar to those of move and copy, what portion of text to delete. Since deletes are obviously dangerous commands, some systems require confirmation before the delete is actually completed. Other systems allow the user to *revert* the command just executed so that the deletion is reversible. In many systems, change and copy/move are implemented (transparently to the user) as combinations of the delete and insert operations.

Reliability.
Backup Capability. To minimize the accidental erasure or destruction of a document, editors often have

backup capabilities. When entering the editor, a workfile may be created or a backup copy may be made. While in the editor, an *autosave* feature may save the current changes in the "freshest" copy of the file, or in every (user-specifiable) number n of keystrokes or command executions a backup of the current workfile is made.

Keystroke History. An expensive but very powerful reliability mechanism is the *keystroke history*. This keeps a copy of every keystroke (both command and text) that the user has specified since the current editor session started. If the system crashes without saving the changes that have been made on the currently open file, the user is provided mechanisms to run the keystroke history file against the old copy of the edit file as if the commands were being typed in. This history file also provides the basis of an *undo* command, which allows the user to revert commands as far back as the beginning of the editing session.

User-Defined Commands (Macros). Editing systems often allow the user to define his or her own *macros* or superinstructions based upon the system instruction set. This allows the user to group together logical clusters of commands that are continually executed sequentially. In some systems, these commands may take parameters (operands) and even provide conditional execution, for maximum power and flexibility. These are sometimes called editing scripts (see Fig. 6).

File System Interface. Of course, the editor must allow access to a stored document as the current file. Editing systems usually provide the user with the ability to imbed or append files into the currently edited file during output processing. This allows the user to create ("boilerplate") documents from the entire domain of user files on the computer.

Classification of Text Editors.

Among the ways by which different text editors may be distinguished, the two most instructive are by window/viewport and by application.

Classification by Window/Viewport.

One of the classical methods of describing computer-based editors is through the labels *line-oriented* and *screen-oriented*. Typically, however, these labels lack a standard meaning. Using the concepts of window and viewport outlined above, we will attempt to give a standard meaning to these labels.

Line-Oriented. Although *line editor* is probably the most widely known term in the field of text editing, its definition is not completely standard. In this classification, we will describe line editors as computer-based editors that use as their main window a single line (typically of fixed length, say, between 80 and 132 characters, or of indefinite length, terminated by a new-line control character). Thus, most commands, such as delete, insert, and move, act upon a single line unit or groups of line units. Traveling commands are then based upon the concept of a line as a unit of context: These commands generally have a syntax like "move up 3 lines, delete the next 2 lines, copy these 3 lines after that line," etc. Of course commands like "change" in most line editors allow character accessibility within a line by specifying a scope. Similarly, pattern searching commands are generally not limited by the concept of the line; they are free to use the entire document as their domain.

Screen-Oriented. Screen editors have as their viewport the entire display surface of the CRT terminal (and often their window maps one-to-one to this viewport). The commands, in general, concern entire screenfuls of text. The window may operate on a screen-oriented or a line-oriented data structure. Where line traveling commands might specify "go to the next line," the screen-oriented editor might have commands that allow the user to select the next screenful. More important, though, screen-oriented editors tend to have easier accessibility to characters on the screen; this class of editor has a user-controlled cursor that can be moved to address individual characters on the screen. This removes the often unwieldy specification of scope that the language-oriented line editor requires. Screen editors are also called *cursor editors*, and sometimes *window editors*, in the case that they allow the window to be shifted left or right on a file of (arbitrary-length) lines as well as up and down. Commercial word processing systems typically are cursor-driven, monospace (each character takes up the same width), "what you see is what you get" screen editors. They allow specification by menu pick or function key push of both the command and the *unit of operation* pointed at by the cursor—character, word, line, sentence, paragraph, cursor-delimited scope, or screen. The cursor can similarly be made to travel forwards or backwards by the same units.

Classification by Application.

The other common method of classifying computer text editors is by their applications, rather than by their functions. Initially, text editors were used to create programs and perhaps the data for these programs and formed the group known as *program* editors. With the advent of text processing, the *text-oriented* editor, which was unconstrained by the 80-column upper-case-only program characteristics, came into being. Soon, these editors fused to form the class known as *multi-purpose* editors.

Program Editors. Program editors are used to create the source for assembly language and high-level language

Suppose a user has a mailbox file that contains all the headers and text of messages received for a period of time and would like to create a shorter version of this file for quick reference containing only the headers. To do this a macro like this might be created.

```
DEFINE MACRO mail_to_headers
deluntil/From/
skip 2
insert -------------------------------------------
next
DEFINE MACRO END
```

In this hypothetical editor, the user defines a macro called *mail_to_headers* by bracketing typical editor statements between a DEFINE MACRO and a DEFINE MACRO END bracket. The statements in this macro indicate to delete everything until the first line with the characters "From," to skip 2 more lines (The "To" line and the "Subject" line in the mail message), to insert a line of underscores, and to go to the line after these new underscores.

Given:

```
From wcs Thu Mar 5 02:49:41 1981
To: nkm
Subject: (un)natural language processing
Cc: wcs

hl nrmn.

ths is a tst of th nw unix* cmnd avd. it mr or ls
blndy strps vwls frm stndd inpt & plcs th rslt
on stndd otpt.
```

```
From avd Fri Mar 6 20:17:16 1981
To: nkm
Subject: Another lost cause
Cc: skf wp

Do you know where the excess fress resource manuals are, or the master
for that matter? Do you know how to copy it off the C-disk so someone
could take a look at it? Where is the source kept these days?
```

```
From skf Fri Mar 6 18:47:14 1981
To: fac grad graphics ugrad
Subject: The ACM Lecture Series: J. Rosebush

On Thu Mar 12 @ 4pm in Pembroke Hall 210, the ACM will be sponsoring a
lecture by Judson Rosebush, president of Digital Effects, a NY-based
company doing commercial computer animation.
will be shown on film/videotape. The talk should be
```

successive invocations of the macro *mail_to_headers* would result in the file being changed to:

Fig. 6. User-defined macros.

From wcs Thu Mar 5 02:49:41 1981
to: nkm
Subject: (un)natural language processing

From avd Fri Mar 6 20:17:16 1981
To: nkm
Subject: Another lost cause

From skf Fri Mar 6 18:47:14 1981
To: fac grad graphics ugrad
Subject: The ACM Lecture Series: J. Rosebush

Fig. 6. (*Continued*)

compilers and interpreters. Since many of these languages were written originally to accept card input, program editors often simulate the structure of a punched card layout and operations. This class of editor frequently has built-in aids for typing in programs—preset tabs for the particular language one is using, upper-case-only character sets, sequence numbering in the last "card" columns, etc. These program editors are often line-oriented, since usually the largest unit of information at which the compiler looks at any given time is the logical line/card image.

Syntax-Directed Editors. Syntax-directed editors offer a radical departure from the typical computer-based text editor. Here, the user is not allowed to type arbitrary sequences of characters, but is restricted to entering pieces of text that exhibit valid syntax in a given (computer) language. Often, the user is given templates of correct syntactical groups and is required (and allowed) only to insert certain pieces of program-dependent text that will cause the template to remain a syntactically valid entity. Thus, not only does the user have the advantage of computer-based editing and revision, but is only allowed to create syntactically correct programs from the beginning.

Text-Oriented Editors. Conventional text-oriented editors allow the user to type information much like one can on a standard typewriter. Line lengths are not limited to 80-column format, text can be entered in upper and lower case, etc. Unit editing natural to free-form (non-program) text, as described above, is usually provided.

Imbedded Formatting Editors. As explained above, text-oriented editors, especially in the word processing field, often have associated with them imbedded formatters. As users type in their texts, they can enter commands that cause their documents to be formatted to their specifications. Type font and size, paragraphing, hyphenation, etc. are some of the more common operations. In many commercial implementations, the simple for-

matting is done with a "what you see is what you get" philosophy; the visual representation of the document maps closely to the hard copy that will result when printing the document.

Structure (Outline) Editors. These editors allow the user to impose some structure on the text. This may be the imposition of hypertext trails, the imposition of an outline scheme, etc. Text may be input with some strict hierarchy that allows the creation, scanning, or revision tasks to be easy. The hierarchy may be an integral part of the document, as in an outline, or may be simply a tool with which to enhance the document, as in hypertext.

Implementations

IBM's CMS Editor. IBM's CMS* editor is a classic example of a language-driven fixed-length line-oriented editor. Assume that the following section of a program, which computes the sum of two matrices, is to be modified to compute the difference of the two matrices.

```
ADD: PROCEDURE;
FOR ROW = 1 TO N DO;
  FOR COLUMN = 1 TO M DO;
    C(ROW,COLUMN) = A(ROW,COLUMN)
                  + B(ROW,COLUMN);
  END;
END;
```

The following sequence of interactions with the editor would provide the necessary changes (the user's requests are in italics and the machine's responses in capital letters).

---

*CMS stands for Conversational Monitor System, the user-level command shell for the IBM VM/370 operating system.

```
find add:
ADD: PROCEDURE;
change / add / subtract
SUBTRACT: PROCEDURE;
next 4
+ B(ROW,COLUMN);
change / + / −
− B(ROW,COLUMN);
top
change / add / subtract / * *
```

The routine ADD: is first located by using the column-dependent *find* command, which without a column parameter searches for the string "ADD:" beginning in the first position of a line. The *current line pointer*, an internal entity that denotes the current window—one line for most editing operations; as many as desired for (delete and move-copy) multiline—now points to the line "ADD: PROCEDURE"; this line is echoed on the screen. The next user command, *change / add / subtract*, affects only the contents of the window: The first occurrence of "ADD" is replaced by "SUBTRACT." Note that the editor does automatic lower to uppercase translation, and that if the maximum line length of 132 characters is exceeded, the line will be truncated (!). The command *next 4* moves the current line pointer (and hence the window) down four lines; the *change* command changes the "+" to a "−." The *top* command moves the current line pointer to the first line of the file. The "* *" operand of the final *change* specifies to change *all* occurrences of "ADD" in *all* lines—this is a global change that will affect the entire file.

The CMS editor provides the ability to set up logical tab stops so that indenting for various applications is facilitated. Certain installation-specific enhancements of the basic CMS editor allow the user to revert commands once they have taken effect, specify scopes by the use of ellipsis so that long scopes need not be typed in their entirety, and do automatic indentation according to language-dependent needs.

Unix ed. The Unix (*q.v.*) text editor, *ed*, is a variable-length line-oriented editor similar to the CMS editor in its interaction syntax. Yet *ed* allows the user to expand the window by prefixing the command with a range of line numbers. Thus, to perform the above change from ADD to SUBTRACT on the first 50 lines of the file, we use the *ed* substitute command:

```
1,50s / add / subtract
                    [substitute is abbreviated to "s"]
```

The special metacharacter "$" indicates the last line of the file. Thus, appending a "1,$" to a command would

cause the window for that command to be the entire file. To move a number of lines, we simply say

```
1,10m / insert after this
                    [move is abbreviated "m"]
```

This will move lines 1 through 10 after the first line in the document that contains the string "insert after this."

To specify scopes, the user is supplied with the metacharacters

```
* $ ^ . [ ] \
```

with which to form regular expressions. Instead of typing out the entirety of the scope, the user can abbreviate by using the compact notation of this type of expression. The "*" is a repetition character. Thus, a character "n" followed by a "*" signals the editor to match the first character string that has zero or more occurrences of "n." The "$" metacharacter in this use matches the end of line, while the " ^ " caret companion matches the beginning of the line. A "." matches any character, while the "\" escape character allows one of the metacharacters to be used as an actual character. Finally, the "[ ]" pair allows the user to specify a range of characters to be matched: [a-l] would match the first string (a single character) containing one of the letters lower case "a" through lower case "l"; [nkm] would match the first string with either an "n" or a "k" or an "m." If you wanted to find the first line that began with a capital letter followed by a vowel in the text of the Ogden Nash poem

> I think that I shall never see
> A billboard lovely as a tree
> Perhaps unless the billboards fall,
> I'll never see a tree at all.

you would specify the search (using / as the find command)

```
/ ^ [A-Z] [aeiou]
```

and would find (and move the current line pointer to)

Perhaps unless the billboards fall,

Rand' NED, Brown's bb. Rand Corporation's NED and Brown's bb editor are quite similar examples of a function-key-oriented screen editor. Text is input on the screen at the position of the cursor; since all typing on the screen is considered text, the commands must be entered either through function keys (see Fig. 7), control characters, or escape sequences, or through the use of a special command line at the bottom of the screen.

escape / shift / **no shift**

f1 LtSlide --- +Pages	f2 RtSlide --- −Pages	f3 VTab --- +Lines	f4 BReturn --- −Lines	f5 Parm --- AddCh	erase Restart Reset LReset	blue +RSrch --- +Srch	red −RSrch --- −Srch	white Indent --- Join

bb input definitions
escape / shift / **no shift**

7 LANG7 PutCh InsCh	8 LANG8 −EOL ↑	9 LANG9 PckCh DelCh
4 LANG4 −Word ←	5 LANG5 BHome Home	6 LANG6 +Word →
1 LANG1 PutLn InsLn	2 LANG2 +EOL ↓	3 LANG3 PckLn DelLn
0 LANG0 --- SetFile	. DoSet --- Do	Enter Mark --- Enter

Control Sequences

↑@	SvPos	↑g	GoTo	↑r	Enter	↑y	*yank*
↑a	Mark	↑k	BTab	↑t	*to*	↑z	Stop
↑b	*back*	↑l	Indent	↑u	Undo	↑\	Knock
↑c	Command	↑n	Join	↑v	InsLn	↑]	InsCh
↑d	Exit	↑o	OpenLn	↑w	−Word	↑^	GoBeg
↑e	GoEnd	↑p	*put*	↑x	*delete*	↑_	Do
↑f	+Word						

Items:

p	Pages	l	Lines	w	Words	c	Chars
e	EOL	b	BlkLn	]	Para	s	Search
t	Tab	h	HfTab	v	VTab		
r	Return	o	Home				

Escape Sequences:

q	DelWrd	w	DelEOL	e	DelBlkLn	r	DelPara
a	PutWrd	s	PutEOL	d	PutBlkLn	f	PutPara
z	PckWrd	x	PckEOL	c	PckBlkLn	v	PckPara
t	DelHfTab	y	+BfSrch	h	+FSrch	n	+RSrch
g	PutHfTab	u	−BfSrch	j	−FSrch	m	−RSrch
b	PckHfTab						
i	+EOL	k	+BlkLn	,	+Para	p	+HfTab
o	−EOL	l	−BlkLn	.	−Para	;	−HfTab
-	VTab	=	BHome	'	BReturn		
'	Help	/	Parm				
1	LtSlide	4	Show	7	MakFile	0	LReset
2	RtSlide	5	BfSave	8	AltFile		
3	Restart	6	BfRstr	9	NxtFile		

Three escapes: Reset

Fig. 7.   The bb system function key layout.

bb provides the user with basic traveling and editing primitives: +/− *pages*, +/− *lines, insert char, tab word*, etc. Some of these may be preceded by a parameter. Thus, + *pages* indicates to scroll forward to the next page, while *3+ pages* indicates a scrolling of three pages.

The window can be moved left and right and two viewports support easy interfile editing. There are three functions—*delete, pick,* and *put*—with four unit modifiers—*character, word, line,* and *paragraph*—that allow natural specifications for deletes, copies, and moves. A marking mode allows the user to cursor-pick two points in the text to define a scope. The deleted text is not discarded, but is put in a buffer. By moving the cursor to the desired point of insertion and specifying the *put* command, the user can insert text that was previously deleted and saved in the buffer. This operation facilitates "cutting and pasting"; to move text, the user "cuts out" a piece of text and "pastes" it elsewhere in the document. The pick command works analogously to the delete command but does not delete the selected text. Pick, then, is the copy feature of the bb editor. In the event of a system crash, automatically created backup files may be run against the keystroke history to recover all but the last operation.

Xerox PARC's Bravo. Xerox PARC's Bravo editing system represents one of the most highly advanced and natural to use text editing environments in existence today, maintaining a "what you see is what you get" philosophy.

Bravo runs on Xerox's Alto series minicomputer, a 16-bit minicomputer with an 808×606 pixel raster graphics display refreshed out of the CPU's memory. Coupled with this screen is a *mouse*, which manipulates a cursor and offers three color-coded buttons to generate interrupts independent of the cursor.

Bravo offers a mix of graphical and keyboard user interfaces. By moving the mouse, the user drags the cursor across the screen. The cursor, which can change shape under program control to provide an iconographic prompt or feedback, addresses characters, special "menu" items, and other *pickable* segments on the screen.

The Bravo screen is divided into several areas. The *system window* contains information concerning what the user has just done and what can presently be done. The *document window* contains the actual text of the document. The *line bar* and *scroll bar* are graphical entities with which the user travels through the document.

The user communicates most of his/her wishes to Bravo through keyboard commands. Most of these are single-letter or CTRL-single-letter sequences. Often, a keyboard command will cause Bravo to prompt the user for some graphical interaction with the mouse.

To travel in Bravo, one moves the double-headed arrow along the scroll bar, a vertical strip at the left side of the document. Pressing the red button on the mouse while the arrow is pointing to a line in the document's viewport causes that line to become the top line in the viewport; pressing the blue button causes the line to become the last line in the viewport. To do more than simply scroll the items currently visible in the viewport, one is supplied with a graphical *thumbnail*, which moves along the scroll bar, and a *bookmark*, which indicates on a linear continuum from "front cover" to "back cover" where in the document one is. To go to a part of the document

before the bookmark, one simply places the thumbnail somewhere before the bookmark and presses the yellow button location; the document will "fall open" at a page relative to the thumb's position between the beginning of the document and the bookmark. By placing the thumbnail after the bookmark, similar traveling occurs through the second half of the document.

Bravo is built upon the concepts of the *selection* and the *command*. A selection is simply the position in the text at which one wants a command to take place—the scope of the command in our previous terms—and the command is what one wants to be done. Selections are made by using the mouse in the following manner.

AREA	Red Button	Yellow Button	Blue Button
Text Area	Select Character	Select Word	Extend
Line Bar	Select Line	Select Para	Extend
Scroll Bar	Scroll up	Thumb	Scroll down

In the text area, then, the RED button would cause the addressed character to be selected as the scope, while the YELLOW button would cause the addressed word to be selected. The line bar takes care of the larger chunks of a document: The RED button here picks a line, while the YELLOW button selects a paragraph. Extending the selection allows the user to specify a scope that lies between two of the entities addressed. Thus, hitting RED in the text area would cause a single character to be selected; hitting BLUE at some other character would cause all the text between (and including) the two selected characters to be picked as the selection. Similarly, a YELLOW BLUE sequence would select all the text between and including two words. In the line bar, a RED BLUE sequence selects all the text between and including two lines; a YELLOW BLUE sequence selects all the text between and including two paragraphs.

Changes on a file operate on the current selection. To delete a word, the user simply selects a word by clicking YELLOW, and then types *D* to execute the delete command. Similarly, to delete all the text between and including two paragraphs, the user would click YELLOW BLUE in the line bar and type *D*. Changes are done analogously. To replace a word, the user clicks YELLOW and types *R*. Bravo deletes the selected word and puts the user into insert mode. Everything the user types until he or she hits an escape key is inserted in place of the old word. The Append and Insert commands allow the user to add information in a similar manner without first deleting a selection.

Like many editors, Bravo has an *undo* command. By simply typing *U*, the user can revert to the state that existed prior to the last command.

The most novel features of Bravo are its interactive formatting facilities. Bravo's unit for specifying the formatting attributes of text is the *look*. Each *character* in the document has associated with it a particular look; the look of any character can be displayed by picking a character and typing *L?*. The looks specify a large assortment of type attributes—font style, font type, point size, subscripting, superscripting, centering, justification, nested indenting, and leading (interline spacing), to name a few that the user can affect by typing *L* followed by a 1 character operand. Other look attributes cannot be changed directly by command; they are the result of previous formatting constraints. As soon as a look command is executed, the document is dynamically reformatted to effect the revision—the document is up to date in both format *and* content at all times.

An important and powerful feature of Bravo is its ability to allow the user to specify multiple (non-overlapping) viewports. These viewports correspond to windows into arbitrary files—one can have multiple windows into the same file or completely independent files. This gives the user the ability to edit one file while examining the content of another, closely simulating the surface of a desk with papers strewn about.

The Xerox Star is a commercial product for office automation based upon the Alto/Bravo hardware and software. Its elegant human interface is even more oriented towards icon menu picking as an alternative interface.

ETUDE. ETUDE (Hammer et al., 1981) is a document production system designed with twin goals: "to *extend* the functionality of conventional word processing systems while *reducing* the complexity of the user interface." To specify all commands, one uses the English-like syntax

action / (optional) *modifier* / *object*

where an *action* might be *move* or *delete*, a modifier might be a number or a word like *start-of* or *next*, and an object might be *paragraph, word, document,* etc.

Like Bravo, ETUDE is a "what you see is what you get" editor. Yet, ETUDE removes the burden of complex formatting from the user to a document database which contains standard formats for a range of documents. For a letter, for example, the ETUDE system will do special formatting for the *returnaddress, address, salutation, body,* and *signature.*

The user interface is designed for various levels of expertise. The user can call a menu to the screen at any time and pick a command with cursor keys (or a pointing device). Alternatively, the user can specify a typed command to perform the same action—or use specialized function keys provided for the most widely used commands.

FRESS. FRESS (File Retrieval and Editing SyStem) (van Dam, 1971) is one of the few existing hypertext editors. Running on an IBM 370 for any terminal from glass teletype (a CRT terminal that acts as if only one line exists and is accessible at any given time) to full-screen display, FRESS is a stream editor that supports embedded formatting codes. FRESS incorporates facilities for completely arbitrary-size string edits, pattern scanning, keyword retrieval, automatic on-line numbering of sections, interfile linking and editing, and protection of files and blocks of text by passwords that can have a mask enabling or disabling each of the hundred-odd commands individually. There is a separate annotation space, a work space for storing currently unused strings, and a structure space that allows easy editing of any hypertext, including outline structures. FRESS has been used as an on-line reading and writing system for teaching purposes; e.g., in a freshman poetry course (Catano, 1979). FRESS has one level of reverts and incrementally backs up each change so that the user loses only the last edit if the system crashes.

NLS/Augment. Augment is the commercial version of NLS, an ongoing project of the Stanford Research Institute since the early 1960s. Augment embodies much more than just a text editor; its aim is to provide a new way of thinking and working by utilizing the power of the computer in all aspects of one's work (Englebart and English, 1968).

> We are concentrating fully upon reaching the point where we can do all of our work on line—placing in computer store all of our specifications, plans, designs, programs, documentation, reports, memos, bibliography and reference notes, etc., and doing all of our scratch work, planning, designing, debugging, etc. and a good deal of our intercommunication, via consoles.

Augment is a hypertext-based system; unlike FRESS, however, a hierarchical outline structure is *always* imposed upon the text. Each node in this structure is a text statement of up to 2,000 characters. Most standard tree manipulations are allowed at a given level in the tree; e.g., locating or deleting the next node or the previous one, locating the first subnode, rearranging neighboring nodes, etc. Note that this hierarchical approach to files, in contrast to the continuous string approach of FRESS, is useful for programs as well as for documents. Also note that the levels of detail in the outline structure can be made invisible; an initial structure is imposed by the system rather than by the user, and is often used for *information hiding*—the selective display or non-display of existing material based on attributes of the text or provided by the user. The user is able, however, to superimpose a network of directed nodes that point to various discrete statements in the outline. Thus, the system-imposed structure gives the user entities to point to, facilitating the creation of a directed graph/hypertext.

Commands in Augment can be executed by using a mouse to pick from a menu on the screen, typing in the keyword on the keyboard, or using the chord (described above) to enter the command with one hand while the mouse is used to pick a location.

Hansen's Structure Editor. Hansen's Emily is one of the earliest syntax-directed editors. Rather than typing in arbitrary text, the user must create and modify text by graphically selecting units of text (templates) that are constructs in a programming language. Text is created with a sequence of selections. The screen appears divided into three areas—text, menu, and message. The text area in the upper two-thirds of the screen displays the text under construction as a string containing the nonterminals (unfinished constructs) of his program, which are highlighted by underlining. One nonterminal is enclosed in a rectangle—this is the current nonterminal. The menu in the lower third of the screen displays a set of possible replacements for the current nonterminal. The user selects a replacement rule and the system makes the substitution, locates a new current nonterminal, and displays a new set of choices. The message area is used for entry of identifiers and also displays status and error messages. Assuming a PL/I type sequence such as the following,

$$<STMT> ::= <VAR> = <EXPR>; \mid$$
$$IF <EXPR> THEN <STMT> \mid$$
$$DO; <STMT*>END;$$
$$<STMT*> ::= <STMT> \mid <STMT>$$
$$<STMT*>$$
$$<EXPR> ::= <EXPR> + <EXPR> \mid$$
$$<VAR>$$
$$<VAR> ::= id$$

where symbols surrounded by "<" and ">" are nonterminals, creation of an IF statement might take place as follows.

```
<STMT>
IF  <EXPR>  THEN  <STMT>
IF  <VAR>   THEN  <STMT>
IF FIRST_TIME THEN  <STMT>
IF FIRST_TIME THEN DO;
    <STMT*>
END;
```

```
IF FIRST_TIME THEN DO;
    FIRST_TIME = FALSE;
    SYMBOLS = NULL;
    END_TIME = DAYMINUTES + 10;
END;
```

The initial current nonterminal was <STMT> and the menu displays the three choices:

```
<VAR> = <EXPR>;
IF <EXPR> THEN <STMT>
DO; <STMT*> END;
```

The user pointed the lightpen at the second of these and the system generated the second line in the above transaction sequence.

As a syntax imposes a hierarchical structure on text, Emily can be used for any hierarchical text structure—an outline being just one example. Each selection from the menu generates a node with space for one pointer for each nonterminal in the replacement string. When a nonterminal is replaced, the corresponding space is filled in with a pointer to the node generated for the replacement. Each nonterminal thus generates a subtree of nodes that is presented on the display, through a tree-walking display routine, as a string of text.

A user can change the view of the text, so that the string generated by any nonterminal is represented by a single identifier. For example, the IF statement above could be displayed with all text generated from the <STMT*> represented by an identifier. In larger programs, this feature means that the user can view the structure of the text without viewing the details. Alternatively, the user can cause the display to descend into the structure and view the details in full.

Text is also modified in terms of its structure. The text represented by any identifier can be deleted, moved, or copied. Modification of the file is made easier by allowing a file to contain any number of arbitrary sized, named text fragments such that text can be moved between them. When text is deleted, it is not destroyed immediately, but is automatically moved to a special system fragment called *DUMP*. If a mistake is discovered before the next text modification is made, the deleted text can be retrieved from this dump.

CPS. CPS, the Cornell Program Synthesizer which runs on the Terak personal computer, operates similarly to Emily for composing programs in PL/CS, the Cornell University student version of PL/I. The user interface, however, is very different. In Emily, the menu supplies the user with all possible expansions of the current nonterminal. In CPS, the user must know the possible expansions of the current nonterminal and must type a command at the keyboard to cause the nonterminal to be expanded.

To start a CPS program editing session, the user types "main <RETURN>" to obtain the template for a PL/CS main program. This template is of the form:

```
/ * comment * /
file-name: PROCEDURE OPTIONS ( MAIN );
   {declaration}
   {statement}
   END file-name;
```

The user can now position the cursor at the word comment and type the text of a comment. Now the user positions the cursor at the nonterminal *declaration*. At this point, we can type •*fx* for a fixed variable, •*fl* for a float variable, •*bt* for a bit variable, •*ch* for a character variable, or •*c* for a comment. For our example, we will choose •*fx*. This expands to the statement:

```
DECLARE ( list-of-variables ) FIXED [ attributes ] ;
```

The cursor is moved to the *list-of-variables* placeholder and the name of the variable is typed. If an illegal variable name had been typed, an error would be generated and running the program would be prohibited. If the attributes are not inserted, as the square brackets indicate, the default values will be used.

CPT. The CPT Disktype 800 is a representative example of a commercial word processing system. It has full (8½ × 11) monospace page display, two floppy disks to store files, and 64K of memory. CPT was the first word-processing system to offer a 8½ × 11″ white screen with black characters, simulating a piece of paper in a typewriter (Seybold, 1979). The display is organized into three areas: The top status line, in which file name, character, and line position, error messages, etc. are displayed. A few lines up from the bottom of the page is the *typing line*. This typing line is meant to simulate the paper bail on the platen of a typewriter. Type-in takes place on the typing line only.

No standard cursor keys exist on the Disktype 8000. Rather, the space bar moves forward on the typing line; the backspace key moves backwards. There is no need for up and down cursor keys, as it is the document that travels up and down past the typing line. Keys exist, therefore, to scroll the document up and down. Margins are set by moving right and left markers on the typing line. Five range keys exist specifying character, word, line, paragraph, and page; these specify the unit that will be acted upon by commands such as *delete, skip, move,* and *insert.*

CPT provides three input modes. *Manual* mode simulates a typewriter; when the user reaches the right margin, a bell rings. *Wraparound* mode provides automatic carriage returns when the right margin is exceeded. *Hyphenation* mode performs automatic hyphenation when a word reaches a system-defined "hot zone" using an algorithm aided by an exceptions dictionary. CPT performs centering by touching a key. Like many word processors, CPT files documents a page at a time on disk. Repagination involves manual work at editing time and is therefore not recommended for large documents, but can be done off line when the document is put through the output formatter.

Future Developments

Evaluation and Benchmarks. Currently, interest in the evaluation of text editors has grown. Card et al. (1976, 1979) and Embley and Nagy (1981) provide good insight into the modeling and measurement of the editing task and into how to allow the design of more user-friendly and more efficient editors.

"What You See is What You Get." Bravo is the first of the sophisticated proportional-space "what you see is what you get" variety of text editors. Here, the guesswork is taken out of text formatting by allowing the user to see the effects immediately. Bravo has the companion drawing tools Markup (Newman, 1978) and Draw (Baudelaire, 1978). Yet these do not let the user combine text and pictures in one step; the user must switch from the text system to the drawing system, each having its own conventions. Several research projects are exploring a user-friendly link between the text and picture production processes that will preserve conventions to present a uniform environment. Much research is being done to refine and enhance these systems (Hammer et al., 1981; Van Wyck, 1980; White, 1981).

Editor in Integrated Programming Environments. Syntax-directed editors increase the productivity of the programmer by removing the time-consuming process of eliminating syntax errors. These editors, however, are hard to build bottom-up—languages such as PL/I have far too many constructs to enable a complete template-oriented editor. Carnegie-Mellon University's Gandalf project has recognized this problem and has designed a programming environment for Ada with a focus on a syntax-directed editor. This editor does not simply recognize the syntax and translate the user's actions into linear text, but instead parses the input into an intermediate form that can be used to generate code. Here, the editor is both a tool for the programmer and a tool for the compiler/interpreter.

Homes, Offices, Classrooms. Text editors in one form or another will become the fundamental tool of modern communication in all walks of life. They will be the key user interface to the personal/home computer, the office workstation, the programming and debugging console, the classroom workstation, the electronic mail terminal, and any other computer-based system in which free-form information is entered, edited, and produced/communicated. They will increasingly be used for do-it-yourself high-quality document production with sophisticated typesetting effects as well as for on-line composition and browsing.

Text Processing Engines. With the decreasing cost of hardware, projects are underway to design and implement a special-purpose text handling processor (Mukhopadhyay, 1980). The instruction set for these processors would contain instructions such as MCHI (match immediate), MCH (match pattern), COUNT (count pattern), TRIM (remove blanks), BREK (break a text string), DEL (delete after match), and LEN (extract a substring). High-level editors, then, will be far easier to implement, as the complex software needed to implement operations such as searching, deleting, and updating will be replaced by hardware.

REFERENCES

1967. Bush, V. "Memex Revisted," in *Science is Not Enough.* New York: William Morrow & Co., pp. 75–101.

1967. Nelson, T. H. "Getting It Out of Our System," in Schector, G. (Ed.), *Information Retrieval: A Critical Review.* Washington, DC: Thompson, pp. 191–210.

1968. Englebart, D. C. and English, W. K. "A Research Center for Augmenting Human Intellect," *Proc. 1968 AFIPS FJCC* **33** *No. 1*: 395–410 (Fall).

1969. Carmody, S., Gross, W., Nelson, T. H., Rice, D. E., and van Dam, A. "A Hypertext Editing System for the /360," in Nievergelt, J. (Ed.), *Pertinent Concepts in Computer Graphics.* Illinois Press, pp. 291–330.

1971. Hansen, W. J. "Creation of Hierarchic Text with a Computer Display," *Report ANL7818.* Argonne National Laboratory (July).

1971. Rice, D. E. and van Dam, A. "On-line Text Editing Systems" in *Advances in Information Systems Science.* New York: Plenum Press.

1971. van Dam, A. and Rice, D. E. "On-Line Text Editing: A Survey," *Computing Surveys* **3**, *No. 3*: 93–114 (September).

1971. van Dam, A. *FRESS (File Retrieval and Editing SyStem).* Barrington, RI: Text Systems, Inc. (July).

1975. Kernighan, B. W. and Cherry, L. L. "A System for Typesetting Mathematics," *Comm. ACM* **18**, *No. 3*: 182–193 (March).

1976. Ossanna, J. "NROFF/TROFF User's Manual," *Technical Report 54.* Murray Hill, NJ: Bell Laboratories.

1976. Lesk, M. E. "TBL—A Program to Format Tables," *Technical Report 49.* Murray Hill, NJ: Bell Laboratories.

1976. Card, S. K., Moran, P., and Newell, A. "The Manuscript Editing Task: A Routine Cognitive Skill," *Report SSL-76-8.* Palo Alto, CA: Xerox Palo Alto Research Center.

1978. Baudelaire, P. C. "Draw," in *Alto User's Handbook.* Palo Alto, CA: Xerox Palo Alto Research Center, pp. 97–128.

1978. Newman, W. M. "Markup," in *Alto User's Handbook.* Palo Alto, CA: Xerox Palo Alto Research Center, pp. 85–96.

1978. Seybold, P. B. "Tymshare's Augment: Heralding a New Era," *The Seybold Report on Word Processing* (October).

1979. Card, S. K., Moran, P., and Newell, A. "The Keystroke-Level Model for User Performance Time with Interactive Systems," *Report SSL-79-1.* Palo Alto, CA: Xerox Palo Alto Research Center.

1979. Catano, J. "Poetry and Computers: Experimenting with the Communal Text," *Computers and the Humanities* **13**: 269–275.

1979. GSPC. "Status Report of the Graphic Standards Planning Committee," *Computer Graphics* **13**, *No. 3* (August).

1979. Goldberg, A. and Robson, D. *A Metaphor for User Interface Design.* Palo Alto, CA: Xerox Palo Alto Research Center.

1979. Knuth, D. E. *TEX and Metafont: New Directions in Typesetting.* Bedford, MA: Digital Press.

1979. Seybold, P. B. "The CPT 8000 & 6000 Word Processing Systems." *The Seybold Report on Word Processing* **2**, *No. 1*: 1–16 (February).

1980. Burkhart, H. and Nievergelt, J. "Structure-Oriented Editors," *Report 38*, Eidgenössische Technische Hochschule Zurich, Institute für Informatik, Zurich, Switzerland (May).

1980. Mukhopadhyay, A. "A Proposal for a Hardware Text Processor," *The Papers of the Fifth Workshop on Computer Architecture for Non-Numeric Processing* (March 11–14).

1980. Reid, B. K. "A High-Level Approach to Computer Document Formatting," *Proc. 7th Annual ACM Symposium on Programming Languages*, pp. 24–30 (January).

1980. VanWyck, C. J. "A Language for Typesetting Graphics," *Report No. STAN-CS-80-803.* Stanford University (June).

1981. Beach, R. J., Beatty, J. C., Booth, K. S., and White, A. R. "Documentation Graphics at the University of Waterloo," *Document Preparation Systems*, pp. 123–125 (February 27–28).

1981. Embley, D. W. and Nagy, G. "Behavioral Aspects of Text Editors," *Computing Surveys* **13**, No. 1: 33–70 (March).

1981. Hammer, M., Ilson, R., Anderson, T., Gilbert, E. J., Good, M., Niamir, B., Rosenstein, L. and Schoicket, S. "Etude: An Integrated Document Processing System," Proceedings of the 1981 Office Automation Conference.

1981. White, A. R. *Pic—A C-Based Illustration Language.* Ontario, Canada: University of Waterloo.

A. VAN DAM AND N. MEYROWITZ

THEOREM PROVING

For articles on related subjects *see* ARTIFICIAL INTELLIGENCE; LOGICS OF PROGRAMS; and PROGRAM VERIFICATION.

The two approaches to automated theorem proving are proof finding and consequence finding. A proof-finding program attempts to find a proof for a certain given theorem. A consequence-finding program is given some axioms and then tries to deduce consequences from the axioms and to select "interesting" consequences.

Some of the purposes of programming a computer to prove theorems concern artificial intelligence (Feigenbaum and Feldman, 1963; Slagle, 1971) and deductions. Artificial intelligence researchers point out that proving a nontrivial theorem is an intellectually difficult problem. Most of the theorem-proving programs we mention in this article use mathematical logic or, to be specific, the *first-order predicate calculus,* which is also called *quantification theory* (Chang and Lee, 1973). In mathematical logic, one can express fairly conveniently almost all kinds of deductive arguments. Writing a theorem-proving program that uses mathematical logic allows the researcher to study deduction in its purest form. Deduction is important because it plays a major role in solving many kinds of problems (not just in mathematics). A program that can prove theorems has what John McCarthy has called *common sense;* i.e., it has the ability to make deductions from given facts. This kind of common sense is an important part of human intelligence. Programs that use mathematical logic to find proofs have been extended to deduce answers to questions.

The other purposes of programming a computer to prove theorems concern mathematics and mathematical logic. Mathematicians point out that a program that could prove new and interesting theorems would be useful in itself. The first new and interesting theorem proved by a program was proved by the program of Guard *et al.* (1969). It would be a tremendous achievement if some program of the future proved or disproved the famous last theorem of Fermat or the Goldbach conjecture. Mathematical logic is well suited to computers, since logicians have striven for decades to make their inference rules "mechanical." It is an attractive idea to write a program based on mathematical logic, since this is a well-formulated and well-studied branch of mathematics. In addition, programming a computer to prove theorems is a way to study mathematical logic. For example, the programmer may develop powerful, natural, intuitive inference rules to which heuristics can be added easily.

We begin the history of automated theorem proving by mentioning some programs that have proved theorems in areas other than the first-order predicate calculus. A 1957 program called the "Logic Theorist," or simply LT, by Allen Newell, J. C. Shaw, and Herbert Simon proves theorems in *propositional calculus* (also called *sentential calculus,* or boolean algebra—*q.v.*). It performs at approximately the level of a fair-to-good college student on the same theorems. A 1959 program mainly due to Herbert Gelernter proves geometry theorems at the level of a good high school student. A program called ADEPT proves theorems in group theory. It performs at approximately the level of an intelligent college student proving the same theorems.

A program of R. Boyer and J. Moore (1979) proved the correctness of one of the fastest string searching algorithms; the correctness of a simple expression parser and the prime factorization theorem; the soundness and completeness of a simple mechanical theorem prover; and the correctness of an arithmetic simplifier. In each of these proofs, the user of the theorem prover must suggest useful intermediate theorems to prove.

P. Gilmore and Hao Wang, as well as Martin Davis and Hilary Putnam were among the first to program a computer to find proofs in the first-order predicate calculus. (Each of these programs substitutes many constant terms for the variables and then checks to see if the theorem has been proved. If not, more constant terms are added and another check is made, etc.) After these programs had been written, J. A. Robinson developed an inference rule, which he called the *resolution principle.* Roughly speaking, the resolution principle draws the most general, possible conclusion from two given statements, where the conclusion and the two statements generally contain variables. The resolution principle is more natural, more intuitive, and easier for people to use than are the inference rules used by the previous predicate calculus programs. Furthermore, it is easier to think of heuristics to add to the resolution principle.

A procedure that uses the resolution principle for proof finding tries to show that the negation of the given theorem to be proved is unsatisfiable (contradictory, inconsistent). The resolution principle is complete for proof finding in the sense of the following theorem, first proved by J. A. Robinson: "If a finite set of clauses [statements] is unsatisfiable, a contradiction can be found in a finite number of applications of the resolution principle." This means that there is, in principle, a computer program which, for any true theorem in first-order predicate calculus, can find a proof using the resolution principle. In practice, however, limitations of computer time and memory space prevent programs from finding proofs for many true theorems. However, various people have written proof-finding programs embodying the resolution principle. These programs are more powerful than the previous predicate calculus programs.

The resolution principle is complete for consequence finding in the sense of the following theorem, first proved by R. Lee: "If a clause C is a consequence of a finite nonempty set of clauses, a clause T can be found in a finite number of applications of the resolution principle such that C is an immediate consequence of T alone." Lee wrote a consequence-finding program based on the resolution principle.

Several researchers have strengthened these completeness theorems by showing that certain restricted forms of the resolution principle are still complete. This is of practical importance to automated theorem proving because theoretical considerations and computer experiments indicate that restricted and complete resolution tends to be more efficient than is unrestricted resolution.

Programs using the resolution principle or its restrictions have proved already known theorems (found proofs and found consequences)—e.g., the first theorems in group theory in abstract algebra. Although quite general, these programs have been so slow that they have proved only a few theorems of any interest. In order to speed up the search for proofs of theorems involving the equality predicate, complete, valid, efficient (in time) inference rules, namely, *paramodulation* and *E-resolution*, were developed for theories with equality. Each of the new rules replaces the equality axioms and is used in addition to the resolution principle. Such a program with paramodulation added (Winker and Wos, 1978) answered some open questions in ternary boolean algebra. Partial ordering (Slagle and Norton, 1973) were built into computer programs, and the experimental results were very favorable. The work of Plotkin (1973) shows ways to build in many equational theories, including theories with commutativity and associativity, which are valuable concepts to build in, since they so frequently occur in important theories—e.g., number theory (plus and times) and set theory (union and intersection).

REFERENCES

1963. Feigenbaum, E. and Feldman, J. (Eds.). *Computers and Thought.* New York: McGraw-Hill.

1969. Guard, J., Oglesby, F., Bennett, J., and Settle, L. "Semi-automated Mathematics," *JACM* **16:** 49–62 (January).

1971. Slagle, J. *Artificial Intelligence: The Heuristic Programming Approach.* New York: McGraw-Hill.

1973. Chang, C. and Lee, R. *Symbolic Logic and Mechanical Theorem Proving.* New York: Academic Press.

1973. Slagle, J. and Norton, L. "Experiments with an Automatic Theorem Prover having Partial Ordering Inference Rules," *Comm. ACM* **16:** 682–688 (November).

1975. Slagle, J. and Norton, L. "Automated Theorem-Proving for the Theories of Partial and Total Ordering," *Computer Journal* **18:** 49–54 (February).

1978. Winker, S. and Wos, L. "Automated Generation of Models and Counter Examples and its Application to Open Questions in Ternary Boolean Algebra," *Proc. of the 8th Int. Symp. on Multiple-Valued Logic.* Rosemont, IL: IEEE.

1979. Boyer, R. and Moore, J. *A Computational Logic.* New York, Academic Press.

J. R. SLAGLE

THRASHING

For articles on related subjects *see* DEADLOCK; MULTIPROGRAMMING; OPERATING SYSTEMS: Principles; OVERHEAD; SCHEDULING ALGORITHM; and TASK.

Thrashing is a collapse of processing efficiency caused by attempted overcommitment of multiprogrammed main memory. If memory is overcommitted, at least one process will not have its working set (*q.v.*) fully present, and so will operate inefficiently. (A working set is the smallest set of instructions and data needed in main memory for efficient processing of a program. It changes as the program executes.) If the memory management policy attempts to satisfy the inefficient process by preempting space from other working sets, they, too, will join in the mode of inefficient operation. When the system is thrashing, most of the processes will be waiting in the swapping queue rather than the CPU ready list.

To avoid thrashing, it is necessary both to have a good estimate of a process' working set, and to control the level of multiprogramming so that the totality of active working sets does not exceed the main store. A working set can be measured accurately by sampling page (or segment) usage bits of a process regularly (Rodriguez, 1973) or by measuring the processing time since the last use of a page (Morris, 1972). Global memory policies (such as the "clock" policy used in VM/370 or Multics) do not distinguish pages by process when measuring usage; these policies tend toward inaccurate working set estimates because the measured utility of pages of one process is confounded by the behavior of all the active processes.

One method of controlling the level of multiprogramming is to defer activating the highest priority waiting process until the pool of unused space is sufficient to contain its working set. This method was used successfully in the CP-67 system (Rodriguez, 1973). Another method, which avoids a pool of unused space, assigns fixed priorities to active processes; if the total of active working sets exceeds memory, space is preempted from the lowest priority active working set. In this way, the k highest priority processes at a given time have their whole working sets in memory (for some k); the remaining process has, at most, a portion of its working set present. With a sufficiently large main memory, the mean value of k will be high enough to maintain high processing efficiency. This control mechanism prevents thrashing by preventing feedback: No process can preempt space held by higher-priority working sets. (See Wilkes, 1975.)

Thrashing can also be mitigated by reducing the access-time ratio between the main store and backing store.

Thrashing has been studied as a natural phenomenon of queueing networks by Courtois (1977). A detailed survey of its causes and prevention has been published by Denning (1980).

REFERENCES

1972. Morris, J. B. "Demand Paging Through the Use of Working Sets on the *MANIAC* II," *Comm. ACM* **15,** *No. 10:* 867–872 (October).

1973. Rodriguez-Rosell, J. and Dupuy, J. P. "The Design, Implementation, and Evaluation of a Working Set Dispatcher," *Comm. ACM* **16**, *No. 4:* 247–253 (April).

1975. Wilkes, M. V. *Time Sharing Computer Systems,* 3rd Ed. New York: Elsevier/MacDonald.

1977. Courtois, P. J. *Decomposability.* New York: Academic Press.

1980. Denning, P. J. "Working Sets Past and Present," *IEEE Trans. Software Engineering* **SE-6** *No. 1:* 64–84 (January).

P. J. Denning and D. E. Denning

THROUGHPUT

For articles on related subjects *see* Job; Performance of Computers; Performance Measurement and Evaluation; Scheduling Algorithm; and Turnaround Time.

The throughput of a computer system during a given interval of time is the average rate at which jobs are completed by the system in that interval. If n jobs are completed in an interval of t seconds, the throughput is taken as n/t jobs per second during that interval.

Throughput is frequently used as a figure of merit for a system: the higher the throughput, the more highly regarded the system. Considered alone, however, throughput can prove to be a most deceptive measure. At least five factors affect throughput: the capacity of the system, the time interval over which throughput is measured, the load on the system, the scheduling method, and the job mix.

The capacity of the system is the maximum rate at which the system can process work. It is usually stated with respect to each job class to which the system caters, a job class being the set of jobs whose resource requirements (processor, memory, devices) fall in specified intervals; for example, all jobs whose processor time requirement is between 30 and 60 sec, main memory requirement is between 5K and 10K words, and which use no I/O devices, might constitute one class.

The precise specifications of job classes in a given system will depend on the objectives of that system. The capacity of a given class is the maximum rate at which the system can complete the jobs in that class. Evidently, the throughput of jobs in a given class cannot exceed the system's capacity in that class; in fact, if the arrival rate of such jobs approaches the capacity of the system to process them, a large backlog will accumulate, making system response time to them unacceptably long. Put another way, whenever throughput is maximized in the sense that it approaches system capacity in each job class, intolerable delays to jobs will be the inevitable result, and throughput in this case clearly gives a deceptive picture of the system's performance.

The time interval over which throughput is measured is the second factor of importance. It is well known that, by giving priority to short jobs (i.e., jobs whose residence time in the system, or whose processing time, is short), the system throughput will be high. However, because little attention is being devoted thereby to the long jobs, a backlog of long jobs may accumulate. Assuming that the system management intends to get all submitted work completed eventually, there will necessarily come a time when the long jobs must be processed and the short ones are left as backlog, but during their processing, the throughput will be low. Thus, over a time interval long enough so that all jobs submitted are processed, the throughput will be proportional to $1/S$, where S is the mean service time over all job classes. However, over an interval during which short jobs are favored, the throughput can be considerably higher than $1/S$, whereas during another interval during which the backlog of long jobs is removed, the throughput can be considerably less than $1/S$. Once again, throughput can give a deceptive picture of system performance.

As suggested in the discussion of the first factor, *the load* on the system is a third factor affecting throughput. For job class i, let F_i denote the fraction of time during which such a job queue for this class is present in the system demanding processing, and let S_i denote the mean time to service each job. Then, the system capacity in class i is proportional to $1/S_i$ (mean output rate if queue is always full), and the throughput in class i is proportional to F_i/S_i. This is illustrated in Fig. 1. Evidently, as the load of class i jobs increases, F_i increases and ap-

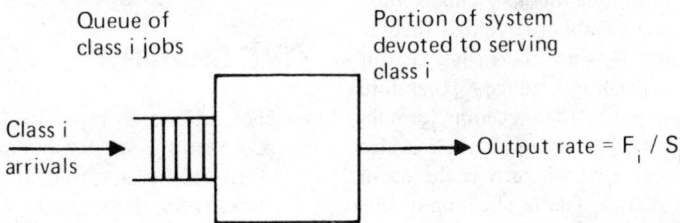

Fig. 1.   Load on the system.

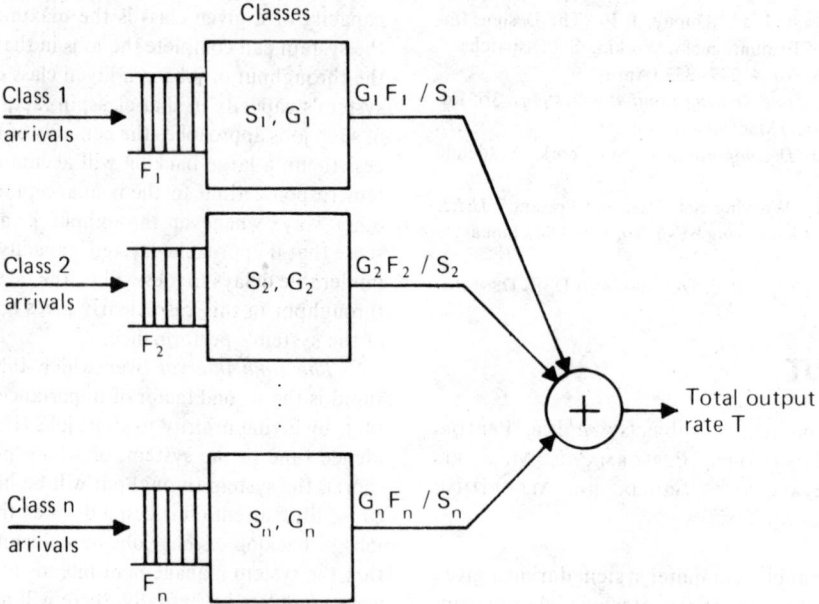

Fig. 2.   Throughput.

proaches unity so that the throughput of class i jobs increases correspondingly. However, even as the load increases, the response time within class i may increase sharply (it is usually proportional to $1/(1 - F_i)$), so that once again judging performance merely by throughput can be deceptive.

The scheduling method is a fourth factor affecting throughput. It was shown above that giving preference to short jobs during an interval will produce high throughput during that interval. In more general terms, suppose the system devotes a fraction G_i of total capacity to class i jobs; the throughput in class i is then proportional to G_iF_i/S_i. Since the values of G_i for each class i are a function of the scheduling method, the throughput in each class depends on the scheduling method, and the total throughput is proportional to T, where

$$T = G_1F_1/S_1 + G_2F_2/S_2 + \ldots + G_nF_n/S_n,$$

will also depend on the scheduling method. This is illustrated in Fig. 2. (The reader should observe that there is interaction between G_i and F_i, since increasing G_i will reduce the backlog in class i and thus reduce F_i; therefore the computation of throughput by the preceding formula cannot be carried out directly.) As noted above, T is also proportional to the constant $1/S$, where S is the mean service time over all job classes. The implication of this is: If the scheduling method increases throughput above $1/S$ for some classes, it will reduce it below $1/S$ for oth-

ers. Once again, the interpretation of the throughput can be deceptive if the scheduling method is unknown.

The final factor affecting throughput is the *job mix,* i.e., the distribution of jobs among the job classes. The effect of this factor should be clear, in light of the preceding discussion.

It is apparent, therefore, that one needs to conduct a thorough analysis of a system with respect to the five factors before a useful or meaningful interpretation can be attached to throughput. It is also apparent that performance of a single system cannot be judged solely by its throughput, nor can two systems be compared simply by comparing their throughputs. Similarly, if one wishes to improve system throughput, consideration must be given to how this can be done while considering the constraints imposed by the five factors. It is not an easy problem.

P. J. DENNING AND D. E. DENNING

TIME SHARING

For articles on related subjects *see* COMPUTER ACCOUNTING AND RESOURCE CONTROL; COMPUTER UTILITY; INTERACTIVE SYSTEMS, USING; MULTIPROGRAMMING; PROCESSING MODES; SCHEDULING ALGORITHM; SWAPPING; TIME SLICE: UNIX TIME-SHARING SYSTEM; and VIRTUAL MEMORY.

Origins. Time sharing is a technique of organizing a computer so that several users can interact with it simultaneously. The term *time sharing* also usually refers to those multi-user systems in which arbitrary general-purpose computation is performed and users operate independently of one another, often at locations remote from the computer itself. Although time sharing was initially perceived by many as a programming convenience for debugging, the perception soon was extended to include the provision of a wide variety of on-line services and the availability of a large central memory shared among the user community.

Time sharing first began to take on its present form in the late 1950s and early 1960s. By then, relatively reliable commercial computers had been available a few years, high-level languages were easing the task of programming applications, and ever larger programs were being constructed. At the same time, the operating staffs of most large computation centers were trying hard to make more efficient use of the still expensive equipment. Typically, programs and data for a batch of jobs would be prerecorded on magnetic tape, and then, under the supervision of a monitor program, the jobs would run serially without interaction until they terminated or, as was too often the case, encountered an error condition. This batch processing mode, which might require 30–90 minutes per batch, while effective in keeping the equipment utilized, made the debugging of programs increasingly difficult. Not only was the time to correct even the most trivial error a matter of a few hours, but the problem was aggravated as one wrote larger and more ambitious programs.

The above state-of-affairs for program debugging was particularly frustrating to users in universities and research laboratories where large programming projects were being attempted, often with computers saturated by near continuous use. Soon, responses to these conditions began to develop. In 1959, Christopher Strachey, then at the National Research Development Corporation in England, presented a paper at a UNESCO Conference describing the possibility of doing program debugging while time-sharing the computer with the normal production computing load; independently, that same year, Professor John McCarthy, in an influential but unpublished internal memorandum at M.I.T., proposed the key hardware modifications to an IBM 709 computer which would allow the possibility of time-shared debugging by multiple users. Indeed, it was McCarthy's early advocacy of time sharing which inspired much of the interest in developing such systems.

In retrospect, it is not surprising that the notion of time sharing emerged, for it was in a sense a rediscovery of earlier, more experimental modes of computer use. Although not widely known, it was in the early 1940s at a mathematics conference that the Stibitz relay computer at the Bell Telephone Laboratories was operated remotely by a single user a few hundred miles away. Also in the early to mid-1950s, there was developed for U.S. Air Defense the massive SAGE System, which at each of several sites had multiple users, each at a terminal interacting independently with information displayed on cathode ray tubes. In addition, in the late 1950s, IBM and American Airlines had begun development of the SABRE System, an on-line airline reservation system with hundreds of terminals distributed geographically. But these early multiterminal systems were dedicated in purpose to their single applications. What was new and striking in the proposals of Strachey and McCarthy was the vision of a computer used independently by different persons for entirely different programs, each of which might still have serious mistakes or "bugs" in them. In short, the notions were planted of a *computer utility* (*q.v.*) where users would view the system as a set of services and conveniences provided to them and the primary goal was the larger one of optimizing the effectiveness of the users and equipment rather than just the equipment alone.

It was also particularly fortunate for the development of time sharing that two key technology improvements occurred when they did. These key changes were the replacement of the vacuum tube by the transistor and the availability of large-capacity rotating disk memories. Without transistors, the higher level of reliability required by on-line systems would have been economically infeasible, and, without the disk memories, the critical central storage for communal programs and data would not have been possible.

By the early 1960s, work on different implementations of the computer utility vision had begun at various places. The Cambridge, MA area was particularly active, largely due to the influence of McCarthy. Some of the first working prototypes were the following: At M.I.T., the Compatible Time Sharing System (CTSS) of F. J. Corbató, initially on an IBM 709 (1961) and, later, the IBM 7090 and 7094 (1963); also at M.I.T., the DEC PDP-1 System of J. B. Dennis; and, at the Bolt Beranek and Newman Company in Cambridge, MA, a DEC PDP-1-based time-sharing system developed by a team consisting of J. McCarthy, S. Boilen, E. Fredkin, and J. C. R. Licklider. Other early influential prototypes were the Dartmouth College Basic System of J. Kemeny and T. Kurtz, initially implemented on a GE 235; the JOSS System implemented at the Rand Corporation by C. Shaw; and, at the System Development Corporation, a time-sharing system developed by J. Schwartz for the AN/FSQ-32 military computer. The emphasis differed in each case. CTSS was oriented toward a general-purpose service offered by a central computing service; this system was to become the initial research vehicle of Project MAC, an M.I.T. research laboratory organized by R. M. Fano to explore the implications of time-sharing and man-machine interactions. The M.I.T. PDP-1 system was organized to allow each user direct control of input/output (I/O) devices in native machine language, but with protection from other users, so that each user was presented with a virtual machine capable of running arbitrary programs. The BBN PDP-1 system was oriented toward an environment for interactive program development which included the use of a high-performance graphical display. The Dartmouth System focused on introducing computing to nonprofessionals with the constrained, but easy to learn, Basic Language; the JOSS system focused on a carefully human engineered computational programming interface; and the developers of the AN/FSQ-32 system were interested in similar objectives to those of CTSS, but in the context of developing and maintaining large programs for military applications.

The above time-sharing systems, while among the earliest and more significant, were not the only ones developed in the 1960s. Rather, they display some of the variety of objectives and directions taken. With hardware obsolescence, none of the systems has survived, except for the Basic system, which, with changes of hardware, continues to evolve as the main computing facility of Dartmouth College. Nevertheless, the early systems have had direct influence on almost all the current time-sharing systems in use, frequently by the students of one system becoming the designers and implementors of the next.

Particularly important to the early growth of time sharing was J. C. R. Licklider, who, after participating in the implementation of the BBN system, joined the Department of Defense Advanced Research Projects Agency (then called ARPA, now DARPA) where he headed the Information Processing Techniques Branch. Licklider was not only an eloquent advocate of the benefits of time-sharing use, but from his ARPA office was also able to support the development of time-sharing systems at several companies and universities active in computer science research.

By the mid 1960s, time-sharing systems, and especially those of M.I.T.'s Project MAC and of Dartmouth College, had attracted considerable attention among computer users, managers, and manufacturers, and the obvious impact of time-sharing systems forced these different groups to reevaluate their roles and the desired modes of computer use. Moreover, development of extensive new time-sharing systems had begun. Among the more notable plans were those for the Multics System, (by M.I.T.'s Project Mac, the Bell Telephone Laboratories, and the General Electric Company), and the TSS System (by IBM for the IBM 360/67), which were especially comprehensive in their goals. Indeed, this very comprehensiveness led to underestimations of the scale of the software engineering required. The Multics System, eventually marketed by Honeywell (which had acquired the GE Computer Department), took several years longer to develop than initially anticipated. The TSS System, implemented by a much larger group, was not as delayed as Multics, but had disappointing performance and human interfaces when first delivered. But despite these warning signs of engineering complexity, by the end of the decade, dozens of time-sharing system implementations were being implemented both by ambitious users and by major manufacturers, and time sharing was well recognized as a significant mode of computer interaction.

How Time Sharing Works. The basic notion of how a time-sharing system works is straightforward. The computer can be considered to have in its main high-speed memory, the programs for each of its users, as well as a master supervisory program (sometimes called an *executive* or *monitor*) under whose control the on-line system runs. The role of the supervisor is to commutate sequentially the central processor through the programs associated with the users, running each for a brief burst of time (often called a *quantum*). One can imagine a simple form of such a system with *n* terminals and up to *n* users, each with a program area in the main computer memory which also contains the supervisor program (see Fig. 1). Of course, any program which is waiting for input from its associated user terminal does not need processor time, nor does a program which completes its immediate computation in less than a quantum need the remainder of the quantum allotted to it. In the simplest or *round robin* case, where all the user programs are cycled through in order, the programs appear to their users to proceed as if they each had the computer all alone, albeit one which appears to operate slower on extensive requests.

To carry out the above scheme effectively requires three hardware features beyond the basic von Neumann computer. The first feature is a program settable "alarm" clock (sometimes called an *interval timer*) which the supervisor can use to interrupt user programs which are not finished after their quantum of time. The second feature is a privileged operation mode for the supervisor, not permitted to the user, which allows only the supervisor to execute the powerful privileged instructions for initiating I/O operations, setting the alarm clock, etc; the effect is that any user program misbehavior, intentional or unintentional, causes program control to revert to the supervisory program. The third feature is a pair of *bounds registers,* set by the supervisor, which can be compared with each memory access attempted by the processor. As with the user mode, any attempt by a user program to reference a location outside of its area in memory, automatically causes program control to revert or *trap* (*q.v.*) into the supervisor program. The important aspect of these

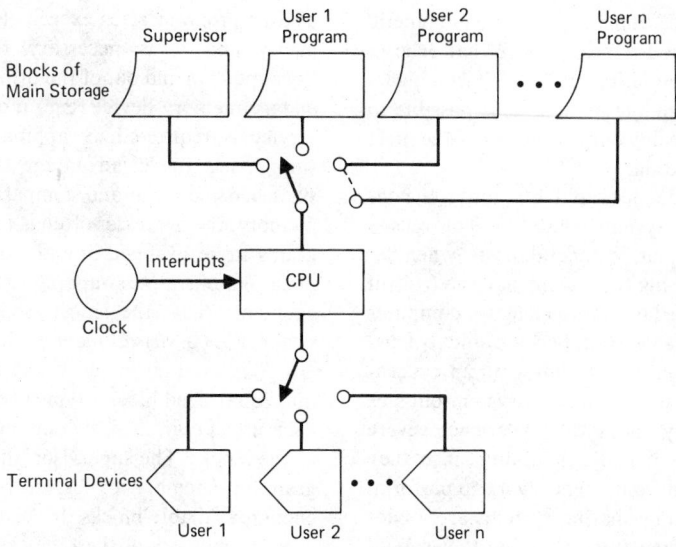

Fig. 1. A highly simplified time-sharing system.

three features is that the supervisory program can never lose control of the computer, no matter how undebugged or misprogrammed a user program might be. Furthermore, one user program can be prevented from interfering with, or even reading, the programs or data of another user.

Consequences. There are several technical and sociological consequences and observations one can observe about the above time-sharing framework. The first is that since users have human response times, the necessary input and output data rates are limited. Because of these limits, telephone lines are usually adequate for user communication, and terminals can be conveniently located remotely. However, this very remoteness introduces anonymity and the need for the supervisor program

to authenticate user identities to prevent improper computer use or program access. Simple password schemes usually suffice to identify users at "login" time for ordinary applications but, when sensitive data is involved, cryptographic techniques and secure communications may be necessary in addition.

A further consequence of users communicating at relatively low data rates with the central computer is that for users to have significant amounts of programs and data available conveniently for processing, it is necessary to store the programs and data centrally on some storage medium, typically a disk memory. But this central storage in turn creates a requirement for great storage reliability so that users feel it is safe to leave the results of many months or years of work inside the system. To ensure such reliability, most time-sharing installations pe-

Fig. 2. The DEC-10 system, the central computer of a widely used time-sharing system.

riodically record "back-up" copies, typically on magnetic tape, of the centrally stored information so that even in the event of a severe system failure or "crash" which garbles the contents of the on-line storage, it is possible to restore operation with possibly only slight loss of the most recently modified information.

Time sharing also demands rapid interactive responsiveness and high overall system reliability. The reason for these requirements is that, in general, users, when devoting their attention to using the system, have no fruitful activity to perform if forced to wait too long for computer responses. Users, if required to wait, become quickly frustrated, much as if they were conversing with an exceedingly slow-speaking person. Similarly, if system outages occur with any frequency, users will experience severe frustration with the system undependability since they will normally not have any contingency work to perform.

Properly managed, time-sharing systems are analogous to electric and telephone utilities in that they should have sufficient processing power, primary memory, and other computing resources to accommodate the peak computing load of the maximum number of users while maintaining good response times for modest requests. One of the potential advantages of time-sharing systems is that the pooling of resources required allows any individual user to have infrequent but large bursts of memory or processing demands. As a consequence, the effective allocation and management of resources is a fundamental requirement of time-sharing supervisor programs. Of course, resource management is also a requirement of any operating system, but because time-sharing systems must be responsive to human users and because allocations and deallocations often occur in fractions of a second, the supervisor program must be particularly well designed and constructed. Moreover, the supervisor, in the case of utility-like operation, should not only be able to keep track of each user's resource usage, but also, for effective administrative control, should be able to prevent a user from exceeding individually preset resource allocations.

Supervisor Techniques. The required supervisor resource allocations extend over many devices, but most critical are those of the processor (or processors in more elaborate systems) and the primary memory. For processor management, the basic alarm or interrupt clock described earlier allows straightforward switching from user to user under the policies of a scheduling algorithm (*q.v.*). However, the case of memory management is more difficult.

The simplest case of memory management occurs in the rare circumstance when the primary memory is larger than the space required by the sum of the user program sizes; then a fixed mapping of user programs to memory suffices. The next level of complication is when the sum of user program sizes exceeds the physical memory capacity and it is necessary that user programs be "swapped" in and out of the primary memory from a secondary memory device (e.g., a disk) whenever processor service is requested. Swapping, although conceptually simple, has the disadvantage that when user program sizes become large and comparable to the size of main memory, the processor often is idle while waiting for programs to be swapped in and out. It is to avoid the complications of simple swapping strategies for memory management that the most sophisticated time-sharing systems use a *virtual memory*.

With virtual memory, the main memory is divided into equal sized blocks, typically 512 or 1,024 words, and each user program is divided into *pages* of the same size as the blocks. The supervisor, then, when bringing a program into memory for service, has only the job of finding enough available blocks. It need not consider location or order in memory of these blocks, since the processor has special page-mapping hardware which allows it to make the program virtual address correspond to the correct physical block. The final refinement of memory management occurs with the strategy of *demand paging*, where the majority of the pages of a user program are not even brought in until the program, while executing, attempts to reference them. In this way, the unnecessary loading of never exercised program sections is avoided.

Supervisor Services. Time-sharing supervisors also need to provide the services of managing secondary storage resources such as magnetic tapes and disk packs. To the extent that storage devices are removable, the supervisor must, of course, mediate a dialogue between an operator at the central facility and a user making a request for mounting or dismounting. However, the most important service the supervisor provides is a *file system* which maps the physical storage resources into a logical framework that users can address in their programs.

File systems at their simplest offer each user a *directory* into which a collection of user named programs or data may be stored, usually without great concern for the physical location of the stored information. In the better-organized systems, users are selectively able to share *segments* of stored information with other users and have detailed control over which users (or user classes) and precisely what kinds of access (e.g., read-only, read-write, append-only) are allowed to each segment.

The most elaborate time-sharing supervisors also provide a large collection of elementary services. One such service, usually supported by special hardware, is a non-recycling calendar clock to provide users with a unique time-stamp for such purposes as branding successive generations of information, preserving event sequences, and facilitating the purging of obsolete files by age or last use. Other services typically include support for a large variety of competitive brands of terminals including both typewriter-like units and cathode ray tube displays.

Interactive Software Services. Time-sharing supervisors are similar to any large operating system in that they offer extensive libraries of subroutines, and often a choice of many programming languages. But, in addition, the interactive environment allows several important new services. One such service is the ability of a user to detach and leave as a batch job an otherwise interactive program along with the anticipated input which the program will need when run automatically at a later time. Thus, in many instances, a time-sharing system combines the virtues of both interactive and batch modes of use.

A second class of service which becomes feasible with time-sharing consists of language and debugging systems that are exclusively designed around interactive use. One of the earliest examples was the Joss system; other examples are the APL, Basic, and Lisp language systems which are in wide use today.

A third service is that of *electronic mail* wherein user A can send a message to user B, directly if B is present and logged in at a terminal, or, if not, indirectly by leaving the message in B's mail box (i.e., a special file in user B's directory). The service resembles a high-speed telegraph system, especially if the time-sharing computer is linked by networking with other such computers geographically distant.

A fourth service follows from the ease of interactive time sharing which encourages the use of computers for natural language text and document preparation. Most systems have one or more *editor* programs, which roughly can be considered sophisticated keyboard machines, and which help a user type and edit a manuscript as it is written and revised. On-line editor programs often have powerful global features (e.g., change all occurrences of "which" to "that" in the entire manuscript) and with the advent of fast communications and flexible display terminals, frequently have intricate interfaces and behavior. Hand-in-hand with the editor programs are the document preparing programs, which, when combined with appropriate output devices, are analogous to phototypesetting machines. Thus, by proper preparation of a manuscript file with suitable embedded instructions for the document preparing program, it is possible to produce output files which can be directly fed into laser-driven xerographic printers or other equally versatile typesetting systems.

The effect of on-line editors and document preparing programs is to transform a user into a combined author, typist, proofreader, editor, layout person, publisher, and printer. Thus, a powerful and sophisticated printing machine of great flexibility is at the user's fingertips. Not surprisingly, the very richness of the available tools presents a user with a new problem of trying to remember the myriad details and literally thousands of commands at the user's disposal. As a consequence of this, and other examples of elaborate application programs, time-sharing systems characteristically also have extensive documentation and "help" files available for on-line perusal. Such files minimize or eliminate the need to reference laboriously in the midst of an interactive session the many volumes of conventional documentation.

Finally, perhaps the most important service provided by a time-sharing system is the most difficult to define, for it is the human engineering of the program and communication conventions. Not only are there many relatively static facets such as the choice of full-duplex or half-duplex terminals (i.e., two-way versus one-way-at-a-time communication), escape conventions (e.g., how you stop what you are doing), whether or not any input character can initiate processor action, command abbreviations, etc., but there are also active features such as the ability to ask for system help information in mid-command or, in some cases, the possibility of "automatic command completion" (i.e., the system completes the command if it is unambiguous from the first few characters typed). Not surprisingly, with so many possible dimensions of design, desirable user interfaces are often the subject of heated debate among time-sharing users.

Future Directions. There were several original motivations for time sharing. They included reducing user costs, allowing interactive program use, and the possibility of users operating as a community and conveniently sharing or exchanging information, data, and programs. Today, as the cost of both computational logic and communications technology decline, new system arrangements are developing where each time-sharing system may be a node in a large network of other computer systems all connected together with high bandwidth packet communications. Furthermore, many of these other computer systems may be time-sharing machines with only one or a few users. (A one user time-sharing system is not as anomalous as it may sound since even one person may have many computing processes proceeding simultaneously, one attached to the terminal, others managing I/O equipment, and some doing background computation.) In the limit, one can imagine a large network connecting nothing but one-person time-sharing systems. With a network of such personal machines in effect, one has both distributed and replicated the functionality of the time-sharing supervisor. Perhaps the greatest advantage of such a structure is that it also partitions the engineering design of the system, allows greater heterogeneity of software and hardware modules, and thereby allows easier system construction and evolution. Nevertheless, such distributed forms of time-sharing systems involving personal computers, if they are to be complete, must include the same user functions and services as a centrally operated time-sharing system, and it is the magnitude of design and engineering effort required to create such systems on modest-sized hardware units which prevents rapid revolutionary changes. Furthermore, there will always remain computational tasks so intensive that, in order to produce useful and timely results, they will require a single large computer system.

Thus, it seems likely that the inner structures of time-sharing systems may continue to evolve as the economics and engineering convenience factors dictate; but it also seems clear that the key advantages which time-sharing systems have—those of convenient interactive service and elaborate software functions—will survive indefinitely.

REFERENCES

1962. McCarthy, J. "Time-Sharing Computer Systems," in Greenberger, Martin (Ed.), *Computers and the World of the Future* (originally published as *Management and the Computer of the Future*). Cambridge: M.I.T. Press.

1970. Watson, Richard W. *Time Sharing System Design Concepts.* New York: McGraw-Hill.

1975. Wilkes, M. V. *Time Sharing Computer Systems,* 3rd Ed. New York: Elsevier.

1979. Dertouzos, Michael L. and Moses, Joel (Eds.). *The Computer Age: A Twenty-Year View.* Cambridge: M.I.T. Press.

F. J. CORBATÓ

TIME SLICE

For articles on related subjects *see* SCHEDULING ALGORITHM; SWAPPING; and TIME SHARING.

In the late 1950s and early 1960s, computer systems were envisioned that could be used simultaneously by several people, each at a typewriterlike terminal, each appearing to have exclusive use of the computer. The computer was to take advantage of the typing time of one user by turning its attention to another. If the computational tasks requested were short enough, then all users could be serviced, and the illusion of a single-user private computer could be maintained. Early systems served less than a dozen people, whereas modern systems service 10 to 100 or more. But what if there were one or more very long computational tasks?

Time slicing provided a part of the answer. At the end of each time slice (or *quantum* of, say, 100 ms), the operating system would interrupt the current user program and turn its attention to other users before returning to the interrupted program for another slice of time. A variety of scheduling algorithms were developed whose general purpose was to maintain high-speed response to terminal requests with reasonable computer efficiency. Multiplexing among compute-bound programs (i.e., ones that require I/O only at relatively long intervals) by time slicing uses the machine less efficiently than serial run-to-completion because a certain amount of time is required to switch from program to program. Also, longer average start-to-finish turnaround times occur: Serially run, two equal jobs finish at time n and $2n$ (for an average turnaround of $3n/2$); with time slicing, both finish in somewhat more than $2n$ for an average of somewhat more than $2n$. But the important characteristics of time sharing and time slicing are high-speed response to many short computational requests and nearly continuous access to the machine; total problem turnaround time is a secondary consideration.

Early systems, which often took care of the low-speed terminal I/O with a separate "front end" computer, were driven exclusively by the time-slice clock and ignored the loss of CPU time incurred by the inability to overlap it with I/O to disk file and tape. The loss became more pronounced as time-sharing system applications became more sophisticated. Explicit interrupt signals from the I/O hardware, together with the later introduction of multiple programs in core storage, combined to give the new operating systems both knowledge of possible overlaps of I/O and CPU execution, and means of making use of these periods of time. Some modern systems can achieve 95% CPU use together with significant concurrent use of swapping and file I/O devices.

The event-driven systems, which required the operating system to make a scheduling decision (not only each time slice, but also for each of many other events such as I/O starts and completes), ran the risk of spending too much time deciding and not enough time doing. To solve this problem, one system, Xerox's UTS and its successor, CP-V, which ran on Sigma 6 and Sigma 9 machines, adopted two control quanta in addition to the primary time-slicing quantum. One of these established a minimum interval between changes from program to program, regardless of the importance of the intervening events; it thus established a lower bound on the system overhead incurred in such changes. The second provided corresponding control and minimums for swapping, allowing a program to execute for a minimum period (if needed) before swapping is permitted.

REFERENCE

1970. Watson, R. W. *Time Sharing System Design Concepts.* New York: McGraw-Hill.

G. EDWARD BRYAN

TOMOGRAPHY, COMPUTED

For articles on related subjects *see* BIOMEDICINE, COMPUTER GRAPHICS IN; COMPUTER GRAPHICS; IMAGE PROCESSING; MEDICAL APPLICATIONS; OPTIMIZATION METHODS; and PATTERN RECOGNITION.

Tomography is defined in Webster as "a diagnostic technique using X-ray photographs in which the shadows of structures before and behind the section under scrutiny do not show." The origin of the word *tomography* is Greek, in which "tomos" means "section." *Computed tomography* (CT) is a relatively recent development in which only the section under scrutiny is irradiated, and a computer (rather than an X-ray film) is used to produce an image of the section. (An alternative abbreviation used for the same process is CAT, for *computer-assisted tomography*.) CT produces images of cross-sections of the human body from measured attenuation of X-rays through the cross-section. Since the appearance of the first commercial CT scanner in 1972 (built by EMI, Ltd.), CT has revolutionized diagnostic radiology. The 1979 Nobel prize in medicine was awarded to Allan M. Cormack and Godfrey N. Hounsfield for their pioneering contributions to the development of CT.

An engineering drawing of a typical CT scanner (one built by the General Electric Company) is shown in Fig. 1. The patient lies on the table, and the table's sliding top moves into the hole of the gantry, which in turn houses the X-ray tube and collimator on one side (the collimator limits the X-ray beam to the section under scrutiny) and the data acquisition/detector unit on the other side. The detector unit contains a large number (typically several hundred) of detectors arranged on an arc of a circle centered at the X-ray source. X-rays travel along straight lines between the source and the detectors. From the strength of the X-ray beam reaching the detector, we can estimate the total X-ray attenuation along the line between the source and the detector. Since tissues and tumors of different types attenuate X-rays differently, such measurements provide us information regarding the cross-section of the body which lies in the plane of the X-ray source and the detectors.

If we keep the X-ray source and detector assembly stationary and slide the patient through the gantry, we can obtain an image similar to images obtained in traditional X-ray film radiography. Such an image is shown at the top left of Fig. 2. Intensities in this image are representative of total X-ray attenuation between source and detector. The image is built up row by row, each row corresponding to a separate incremental position of the patient through the gantry. The intensities in each row correspond to the total X-ray attenuations as measured by the array of detectors. The difficulty with such an output

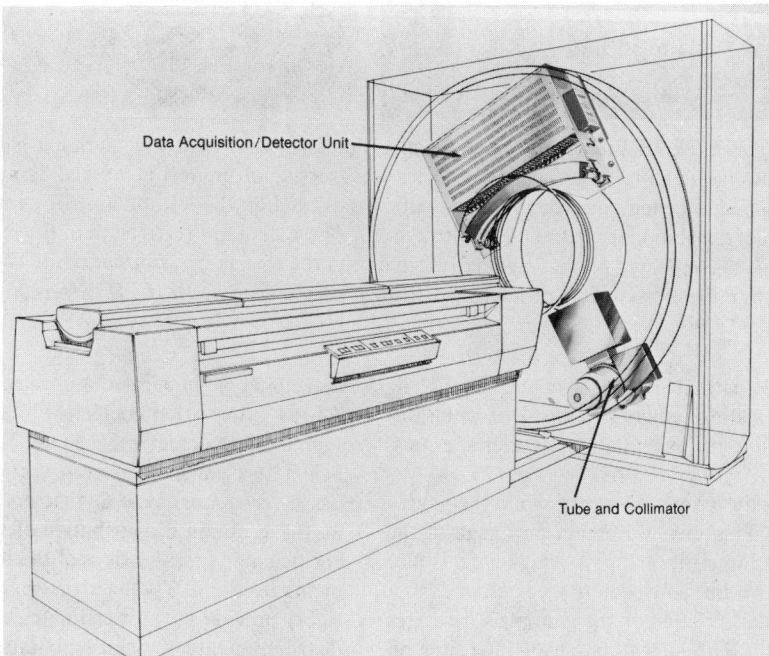

Fig. 1. Engineering drawing of a typical CT scanner. *(Courtesy General Electric Co.)*

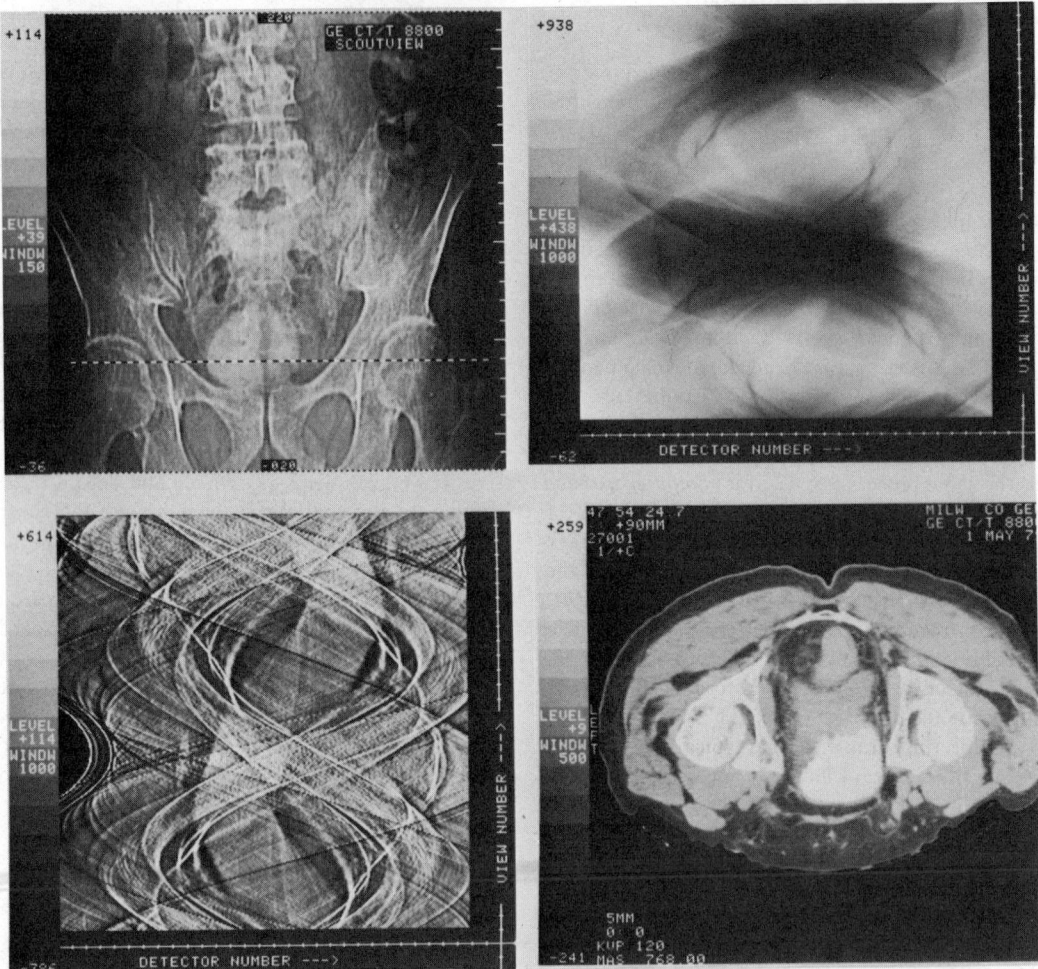

Fig. 2. *Top left:* Scout View (a General Electric Trademark) obtained by sliding a patient through the stationary gantry of a CT scanner. The cross-section of interest is marked by a broken line. *Top right:* Projection data for the cross-section indicated on the left, obtained by rotating the gantry around a stationary patient (see also Fig. 3). These data are referred to in the text as $g_{j,n}$. *Bottom left:* The modified projection data referred to in the text as $g'_{j,n'}$. *Bottom right:* The CT reconstruction of the cross-section of interest. *(Illustration provided by Dr. G. H. Glover.)*

as a diagnostic tool is that images of bones, organs, air spaces, and any existing tumors overlap. It is often impossible to determine the exact nature, or even the presence, of a tumor.

In CT, the body is kept stationary while the gantry rotates around it. This way, we obtain an image of the type shown at the top right of Fig. 2. This image is also built up row by row, but now each row corresponds to a separate incremental position of the gantry as it rotates around the patient. The interpretation of intensities in each row is the same as before.

The total X-ray attenuation between a source and a detector is the integral of a physical parameter called the "X-ray attenuation coefficient" along the line from the source to the detector. Since the X-ray attenuation coefficient at a point in the cross-section is indicative of the tissue (or tumor) type at that point, it is diagnostically useful to obtain a distribution of the X-ray attenuation coefficient in cross-sections of the human body. Measurements by the CT scanner (as represented by Fig. 2 top right) provide us with estimates of the integrals of this distribution along a large number of lines of known location.

A schematic representation of such a situation is

shown in Fig. 3. The distribution of X-ray attenuation coefficients is indicated by a function of two polar variables $f(r,\phi)$. The X-ray source moves in a circle around the origin 0, taking projections at M distinct locations S_1, $\ldots$, S_M. Let $L_{j,n}$ denote the line from S_j to the center of the nth (of an array of $2N + 1$ detectors). Then the measurement for the jth position of the X-ray source at the nth detector is approximately the line integral

$$\int_{L_{j,n}} f(r,\phi) \, ds$$

where ds is the incremental distance from source to detector. Hence, we are faced with the following computational problem: Given estimates of the integrals of an unknown function of two variables along a number of lines of known location, estimate the values of the function at a number of points of given location.

The desired clinical information mandates that we estimate the function at a large number (typically, 10^5–10^6) of closely spaced (typically, less than 1 mm in each direction) points. Accordingly, data is collected for 10^5–10^6 source/detector positions. For such a device to be useful, computational turnaround has to be rapid, and computational costs (which are eventually paid by the patients) have to be kept low. Thus, we are faced with an unusually large computational problem which has to be solved rapidly and inexpensively. Ingenious computational procedures have made the state of the art such that an image of a cross-section (such as shown at the bottom right of Fig. 2) can be produced from the data in a matter of seconds by a minicomputer.

An example of a reconstruction method is the following. Mathematical analysis of the problem leads to three functions, p, q, and w, such that

$$f(r,\phi) \simeq \sum_{j=1}^{M} w(r,\phi,\beta_j) \left[\sum_{n=-N}^{N} q(p(r,\phi,\beta_j),n\sigma) g_{j,n} \right],$$

where the $g_{j,n}$ form the measurement data (approximations to the line integrals defined above) and $f(r,\phi)$ is the distribution to be reconstructed. The functions p, q, and w are chosen independently of data; the important fact is that they can be chosen so that the approximation indicated above is close for the class of functions $f(r,\phi)$ which we desire to reconstruct.

The approximation as shown above implies that a separate double sum has to be calculated for each point (r,ϕ) at which the reconstructed value is to be obtained. Significant speed-up is obtained by the following observation: For a fixed j, the value of the inner sum is the same for all points (r,ϕ) which lie on the same line $L_{j,n'}$. Let, for $1 \leq j \leq M$ and $-N \leq n' \leq N$,

$$g'_{j,n'} = \sum_{\substack{n=-N \\ (r,\phi)\epsilon L_{j,n'}}}^{N} q(p(r,\phi,\beta_j),n\sigma) g_{j,n}.$$

The bottom left of Fig. 2 is a pictorial representation of g' in the same way as the top right of Fig. 2 is a pictorial representation of g. In practice, for each j, the $g'_{j,n'}$ are calculated from the $g_{j,n}$ by the formula given above. Note that this can be done independently for the different js. Special-purpose array processors are usually used for the independent calculations of these sums. The estimation of $f(r,\phi)$ is then done by using interpolation of the $g'_{j,n'}$ to estimate the values of the inner sum for a given j, r, and ϕ. These processes are usually implemented in firmware.

The field of study dedicated to such computer algorithms is referred to as *image reconstruction from projections*. A book devoted to this topic was written by Herman in 1980. The usefulness of image reconstruction goes way beyond CT. Essentially the same computational procedure has been found useful in many other areas of science and medicine, such as radioastronomy, solar physics, nuclear medicine, and physiology (see Herman, 1979).

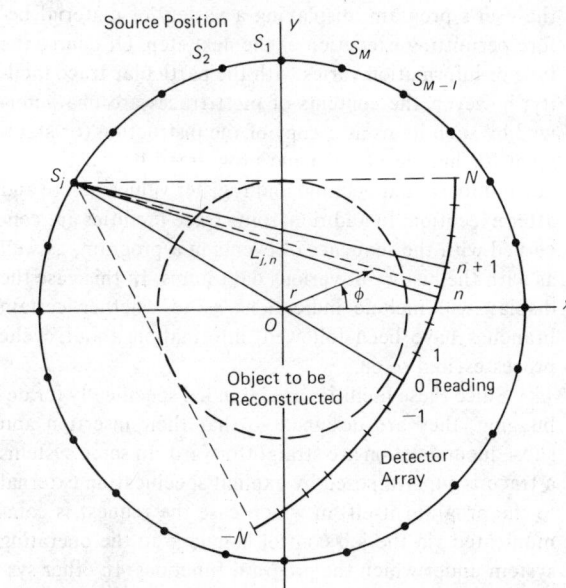

Fig. 3. A schematic drawing showing the lines along which integrals of the X-ray attenuation coefficient distribution in the cross-section are assumed to be collected. (*Reprinted with the permission of G. T. Herman and A. Naparstek, from* "Fast Image Reconstruction Based on a Radon Inversion Formula Appropriate for Rapidly Collected Data," *SIAM J. Appl. Math.* **33**: 511–533, 1977.)

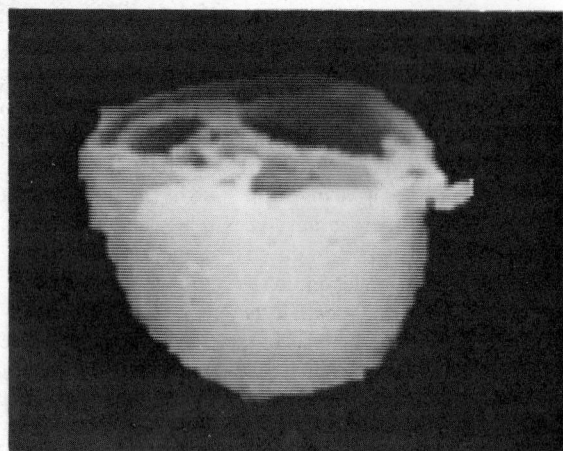

Fig. 4. Three-dimensional computer graphic display of the heart of a dead dog obtained from a series of two-dimensional CT scans. To obtain similar displays for the beating heart of human patients, the data for all cross-sections has to be collected simultaneously. This increases the engineering and computational problems as compared to the presently commercially available scanners discussed in this article. (*Reprinted with the permission of G. T. Herman and H. K. Liu, from* "Display of Three-Dimensional Information in Computed Tomography," *J. Comp. Assist. Tomog.* **1**: 155–160, 1977.)

There are a number of journals which are largely or wholly devoted to CT; two examples are *Computerized Tomography* and the *Journal of Computer Assisted Tomography*.

Current research in CT includes the development of scanners which are fast enough (both physically and computationally) to reconstruct the beating heart inside the intact thorax and to display the appearance of organs, using computer graphics, based on a sequence of computerized tomograms. (See the already cited books for details, and Fig. 4 for an example.) These capabilities justify describing the medical procedures with such machines as *noninvasive vivisection.*

REFERENCES

1979. Herman, G. T. (Ed.). *Image Reconstruction from Projections. Implementation and Applications.* Berlin: Springer-Verlag.

1980. Herman, G. T. *Image Reconstruction from Projections: The Fundamentals of Computerized Tomography.* New York: Academic Press.

1981. Redington, R. W. and Berninger, W. H. "Medical Imaging Systems," *Physics Today* **34**, No. 8: 36–44 (August).

G. T. HERMAN

TRACE

For articles on related subjects *see* DEBUGGING; and PROCEDURE-ORIENTED LANGUAGES, PROGRAMMING IN.

A trace is a debugging aid consisting of a display that chronicles the actions and results of individual steps in a program; the term is sometimes used for a control program that produces this kind of display.

The debugging process precipitates countless problems whose correction may require a detailed stepwise record of a program's execution path. A trace is designed to provide this type of information by taking the user's program and placing it under control of a special routine which monitors the progress of the program. Continuous execution of the user's program is replaced by a process whereby the trace program intercedes between steps of the user's program, displaying a variety of material before permitting execution of the next step. Of course the type of information varies with the particular trace facility; however, the contents of most traces are characterized by such items as a copy of the instruction (or statement for high-level language programs), its location (or line number), and operand and register values before and after execution. In addition, some trace facilities are concerned with the sequence of events in a program, as well as with the history of various data items. In this case the display will include indications as to whether certain branches have been followed, information about cyclic processes, and so on.

Since these facilities are intended specifically for debugging, they are designed so that their insertion and subsequent deletion are straightforward. In some systems a trace is superimposed by explicit specification external to the program itself, in which case the request is communicated via the job control language to the operating system under which the program functions. In other systems, the trace facilities are part of the programming language and can be activated as an intrinsic part of the user's source program. Either form of invocation requires a small amount of highly localized specification that is very easily removed once its purpose has been served.

One such trace facility, provided by the CHECK feature of PL/I, makes it possible to tag selected variable names in a source procedure for automatic tracing. Then, when the program (i.e., its machine language equivalent)

```
R:  PROCEDURE OPTIONS(MAIN):
    PUT LIST ('VALUE OF N','VALUE OF T'); S = 0;
IN: GET LIST(N); IF N = 0 THEN STOP;
       DO K = 1 TO N;     S = S + 1 + SQRT(K);     END;
    T = N**2/S;    PUT SKIP LIST(N,T);     GO TO IN;
    END R;
```

Fig. 1

VALUE OF N	VALUE OF T
3	1.25939E + 00
5	1.21781E + 00
4	5.21600E − 01
6	7.57789E − 01
8	8.91209E − 01
7	5.30934E − 01
9	6.71664E − 01

Fig. 2

executes, each tagged variable name is printed along with its value every time that value changes.

The procedure described below illustrates an aspect of this facility. Its intent is to read successive values of variable N. Each N is printed, accompanied by a value T, which is computed as

$$N^2/\sum_{k=1}^{N} (1 + \sqrt{k}).$$

An N of zero stops the run. (In the PL/I program in Fig. 1, S is used to store the value of the denominator.)

Fig. 2 shows sample output produced by the procedure in Fig. 1. Inspection of the results raises some suspicions: Although the formula for T suggests that its value should increase with increasing N, its behavior apparently contradicts this.

In an effort to shed some light on this anomaly, the variables K and S have been tagged for automatic tracing by specifying them as part of the PROCEDURE statement (Fig. 3). The other statements are unchanged. As a result of this addition, K and S are printed whenever they

VALUE OF N	VALUE OF T

S = 0.00000E + 00;

K =   1;

S = 2.00000E + 00;

K =   2;

S = 4.41421E + 00;

K =   3;

S = 7.14626E + 00;

K =   4;

        3   1.25939E + 00

K =   1;

S = 9.14626E + 00;

K =   2;

S = 1.15604E + 01;

K =   3;

S = 1.42925E + 01;

.
.
.

Fig. 4

change. Examination of this augmented output (Fig. 4) for a repeated run now shows what happened. All is well for the first N. Then, when the second N is read and the summation process is begun again, S keeps right on growing from its previous value, indicating that S is not being reinitialized for each new N.

```
(CHECK(K,S)): R:  PROCEDURE OPTIONS(MAIN);
                  PUT LIST ('VALUE OF N','VALUE OF T'); S = 0
              IN: GET LIST(N); IF N = 0 THEN STOP;
                     DO K = 1 TO N;     S = S + 1 + SQRT(K);     END;
                  T = N**2/S;     PUT SKIP LIST(N,T);     GO TO IN;
                  END R;
```

Fig. 3

Because of its iterations, branches, and calls, the execution of even a modest-sized program may involve thousands of individual steps. Consequently, an unfettered trace routine easily can fill several cubic feet of paper with information, most of which is of no interest. Accordingly, all trace facilities include provisions for damping their zeal. For example, the user may limit the trace to a certain section of the program, allowing the rest of it to execute normally. In addition, one may choose to examine certain variables; if so, the trace output will show only those steps in which the selected variables are affected. Moreover, the user's primary interest may be in the flow of logic, in which case the trace can be restricted to a record of branches, subroutine calls, and other sequence changes.

S. V. POLLACK

TRANSACTION-BASED APPLICATIONS

For articles on related subjects *see* ADMINISTRATIVE APPLICATIONS; BANKING APPLICATIONS; CREDIT SYSTEMS APPLICATIONS; DATABASE MANAGEMENT; DATABASE, ON-LINE; ELECTRONIC FUNDS TRANSFER SYSTEMS; PROCESSING MODES; and TELEPROCESSING SYSTEMS.

A transaction-based application system may be regarded as a specialized type of on-line system where on-line implies that the user of the system is able to interact directly with a computer. The term *transaction-based* means that the user requests and receives application system functions to process a series of individually distinct inputs called transactions.

Successful transaction-based systems for reservations, order processing and inventory control, credit approval, and management information have been in use since the early 1960s. In each case, on-line transaction processing with its delivery of timely information directly to the user offers accurate data, improves control and perhaps a competitive advantage.

Features of Transaction-Based Systems.

A transaction-based business application system is characterized by various features.

While the on-line application system itself operates at a central processing site, access to it may be available concurrently to users at terminals at widely separated locations. The most popular type of terminal is the video display terminal that utilizes a cathode ray tube (CRT) as the image medium and that can display from several hundred to over 3,000 characters of information at once.

A teleprocessing network provides the communication path for the transfer of information between the terminal device and the central computer. Such paths may include special telephone circuits and satellite transmission facilities. Information travels through the network at rates of thousands of characters per second. Typically, all the terminals connected in the network may be in use simultaneously.

Input data enters the system at the point of origin of the data. Output is made available directly at the end-user's location. The system provides, therefore, the potential for optimum information gathering and distribution. Using a remote terminal, information can be supplied where it originates and, typically, by a person who is familiar with the nature of the data. This can eliminate the delay and potential error or confusion of intermediate steps in creating input and passing it to the application. And the results of an on-line application transaction can be returned without delay to the information requestor. Information output can also be sent automatically to other terminals, perhaps at distant locations, keeping other company units informed of actions performed or status changes. At a retail center, for example, customer orders can be taken, stock availability checked, and orders recorded by a salesperson into the on-line application system. Shipping information can be sent to a local or regional distribution point while billing information is sent to the accounting office.

Information is preserved in a database which may be queried or modified by the terminal user. Much of the input information to the on-line application system is recorded at the central computer. This data is organized in a systematic fashion so that the user can subsequently retrieve or modify it.

The application system is designed to respond very rapidly to each user request. In many on-line applications, the information in the database must reflect a rapidly changing "real world." In fact, it is the accuracy and completeness of the response to a query that permits a decision to be made. The utility of an on-line system may depend on its capacity to respond rapidly to a user request to change or report information. Old and/or unreliable information may have no value at all.

The design of the application system provides only limited and discrete functions to the user. As well as referring to the input to be processed, the term "transaction" is used to refer to each such discrete function which may be applied to the input. A simple application system may require the definition of very few transaction functions to satisfy its requirements. A complex application may have a hundred or more unique transaction functions. In a typical on-line order entry application, each of the following functions would be performed by a separate transaction: Create new order; change existing order;

query specific order; query item inventory and backlog; and change client name and address. The scope of functions in a transaction is a key application design factor.

Different functions may be performed concurrently by remote users acting independently. Typically, the user at a remote terminal may perform any authorized transaction whenever necessary. This freedom of action gives rise to the phenomenon of "random arrival." A hypothetical observer at the central processing site, able to watch the inflow of transactions, would be unable to predict precisely when the next transaction will arrive. Nor can it be predicted precisely which transaction function it will be, from which user it will come, and which of all possible segments of the database will need to be accessed. The random nature of events within an on-line system is a key consideration in the design of on-line applications and each transaction program.

Processing Transactions. The objectives, process, and results of a transaction-based on-line application differ materially from those of the traditional "batch processing" solution. Fig. 1 illustrates this contrast.

The design of most on-line systems requires that the use of transactions be carefully controlled. Normally, a user must follow a "sign-on" procedure at the terminal

Typical Batch Job Application System	On-Line Transaction-Based Application System
Unit of work (a batch job) is large to very large.	Unit of work (a transaction) is quite small.
A high volume of data is processed per job.	A low volume of data is processed per transaction.
Multiple functions and processes occur per job.	Specialized and limited functions per transaction.
Most data access is sequential.	Most data is accessed randomly.
Large program modules coded in high-level languages.	Small, often complex program modules coded in assembler or high-level languages.
Data often stored "off-line," requiring manual assistance and scheduling to access.	All data required is normally accessible continuously to the processing system.
Application input conveyed to the processing site on a scheduled basis.	On-line transaction input is transmitted electronically at high speed to the processing site computer as desired.
Input is batched and transcribed into machine-readable form as necessary.	The user at the remote terminal transcribes input data at its origin.
Processing of the application system begins on a scheduled basis.	Processing is "event-driven," and begins when the input data arrives.
	Transaction requests and input may arrive at unpredictable intervals based on the actions and needs of the remote user.
Input data enters the application system, where it is edited and ordered for efficient serial processing. Erroneous input data is rejected or stored to await correction. Correction may not be possible prior to the next scheduled cycle for the application.	Input data is edited as it arrives. Only correct data enters the on-line application system. Erroneous data is identified in the response to the user, so it may be immediately corrected and the transaction attempted again.
Processing is complete in minutes or hours.	Processing is complete in seconds or fractions of a second.
Application system output is staged and prepared for handling and distribution. Results are transported to the users at one or more locations.	Results are electronically returned to one or more user locations in moments.
Results reflect information from minutes to days old.	Information results can be accurate up to the minute.
Interruptions in processing due to application or system failure may not delay the receipt of results by the user.	Failures in the application or interruptions to the on-line service are immediately obvious to the remote user, and may pose costly or critical problems.

Fig. 1. Comparative characteristics.

during which identification is supplied to the on-line system, along with authentication. Unsuccessful or suspicious attempts to access the system are reported to the master operator at the computer.

Next, the user specifies which particular transaction is to be performed. The selection may be made from a "menu" of choices displayed at the terminal. Alternatively, the user will select a transaction by keying in a transaction identifier at the terminal keyboard. Certain items of input data are usually required along with the transaction identification.

The data supplied by the terminal user is transmitted via the teleprocessing network to the computer, where it becomes input to the on-line system. The on-line system evaluates the transaction request, verifying that it is a valid request and that the user who sent it is authorized to perform the function implied. The program needed to process this particular transaction is initiated, first performing syntax and context editing upon the input data received from the terminal. Each item of data is examined for appropriate length, content, and consistency. If an error is found, no further processing takes place. Instead, a message describing the error is immediately transmitted back to the input terminal. The user can correct the erroneous data and quickly re-enter the transaction.

Most transactions involve the retrieval of information stored in the on-line system database. The database is typically recorded on random access disk storage devices from which any specific item of information can be quickly retrieved or modified as needed by the transaction program.

For an "inquiry" transaction (one that only causes information to be retrieved), the transaction program simply creates a formatted display of the desired items from the database and causes this output to be transmitted to the originating terminal. A more complex transaction may require that calculations be performed or data from the database scanned and analyzed. An "update" transaction is one in which the transaction program will modify the database. The modification may be to replace or supplement existing information, or it may require the addition or deletion of whole elements.

The time required for the on-line system to complete the processing of a transaction and return the results to the terminal is called the *response time*. As each transaction is completed, the user may begin another. When there are no transactions to process, the on-line system remains idle, and the resources of the computer are applied to other jobs. A trigger event, the arrival of new transaction input from a remote user terminal, activates the on-line system. For this reason, an on-line system is said to be *event-driven*.

REFERENCES

1965. Martin, James. *Programming Real-Time Computer Systems.* Englewood Cliffs, NJ: Prentice-Hall.

1967. Martin, James. *Design of Real-Time Computer Systems.* Englewood Cliffs, NJ: Prentice-Hall.

1970. Rothstein, Michael. *Guide to the Design of Real-Time Systems.* New York: Wiley.

1972. Yourdon, Edward. *Design of On-Line Computer Systems.* Englewood Cliffs, NJ: Prentice-Hall. (Good overall reference with special emphasis on considerations of business information systems.)

1978. Davis, William S. *Information Processing Systems: An Introduction to Modern Computer-Based Information Systems.* Reading, MA: Addison-Wesley. (An excellent contemporary and comprehensive text for the layperson, well illustrated.)

See also Computing Newsletter, Couger, J. Daniel (Ed.), Colorado Springs, CO Center for Cybernetics Systems Synergism. Publishes annual *Bibliography of Computer-Oriented Books.*

JOHN A. SHANGLER

TRANSLATION, LANGUAGE. *See* LANGUAGE TRANSLATION.

TRAP

For article on related subject *see* INTERRUPT.

When the occurrence of an exceptional event in a processor results in an automatic transfer to a special routine for handling that event, this transfer is called a *trap.*

Some practitioners consider the trap and interrupt as being synonymous, while others use trap in a somewhat narrower context, i.e., the range of exceptional events that occur within the central processor. Whatever the categorization, the point is that when an exceptional condition (such as an attempt to divide by zero) occurs in a processor equipped with trapping facilities, the hardware automatically executes a transfer to a specific storage location that is permanently assigned for that particular contingency. That location is used to store a transfer instruction to the appropriate software handling routine.

Although an exceptional condition may produce circumstances that cannot be remedied by a programmed procedure, there are other conditions from which it is possible to recover. (For example, in some contexts it may be appropriate to set an underflow value to zero without undue harm to the process.) Accordingly, pertinent address information is preserved automatically so that a proper return can be made, once the trapping routine has been completed.

Several such locations might be reserved, depending on the types of conditions the processor is designed to recognize. Typically, separate trapping addresses would be provided for overflow, underflow, illegal address, and illegal operation, in addition to division by zero (sometimes called a *divide check*), already mentioned.

Prior to the introduction of trapping facilities (generally associated with so-called "second generation" computers) the programmer had to include explicit test instructions at each point where some exceptional condition might possibly occur. The need to do this is obviated by the trapping facility, since it operates over the entire program. However, software trapping facilities, such as the ON condition in PL/I, still exist to give programmers additional control over exceptional conditions.

Systems equipped with trapping facilities usually include a machine instruction that allows the user to force one of several kinds of traps, thereby providing the opportunity to simulate a given type of exceptional condition. This capability has been used to considerable advantage in developing a variety of debugging aids and special features in software programs. Certain trapping facilities may also be explicitly turned off (disabled) by the programmer for all or part of a procedure, whereupon the system ignores the precipitating event and refrains from intervention.

S. V. POLLACK AND T. E. STERLING

TREE

For articles on related subjects *see* DATA STRUCTURES; GAMES ON COMPUTERS; and GRAPH THEORY.

A tree is a special form of directed graph with the following properties: (1) either it has no vertices or it has a distinguished vertex called the *root vertex,* which has no predecessors; and (2) every vertex other than the root has a unique predecessor.

Vertices (or *nodes*) of a tree which have successors are called *nonterminal vertices,* while vertices that have no successors are called *terminal vertices* or *leaves*. Fig. 1 illustrates a tree with root vertex *a*; two nonterminal vertices *a, c*; and three leaves *b, d, e*.

Trees in which each nonterminal vertex has at most *n* successors are called *n-ary* trees. Trees in which each nonterminal vertex has at most two successors are called *binary* trees. The tree in Fig. 1 is an example of a binary tree.

Each node of a tree determines a subtree whose root

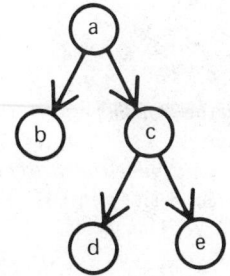

Fig. 1. A tree showing terminal and nonterminal vertices.

is the given node and whose vertices include all descendants of the node. In a binary tree, each nonterminal node has an associated left subtree and right subtree.

A tree is said to be *unordered* if there is no special significance to the order in which the descendants of a given node are listed, and is said to be *ordered* if the order of descendant nodes is significant.

Binary trees are a natural data structure for expressing the operator-operand structure of arithmetic expressions. The expression $x + y * z$ may be represented by the tree structure in Fig. 2, where the operators are represented by nonterminal vertices and the operands of an operator are represented by successor subtrees of the operator vertex. Thus, the operands of $+$ are x and $y * z$, and are represented by successor subtrees of the vertex $+$.

There are three fundamentally different ways to list the nodes of a binary tree. When applied to an expression tree such as that in Fig. 2, each yields a recognizable variation of the original expression.

1. *Preorder traversal.* Visit (print) the root. Traverse the left subtree (if any). Traverse the right subtree (if any). When applied recursively, this

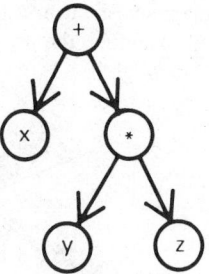

Fig. 2. A tree representing an operator-operand structure.

algorithm yields

$$+ \, X \cdot Y Z,$$

which is the *Polish prefix* form of the original expression.

2. *Inorder (or symmetric) traversal.* Traverse the left subtree. Visit (print) the root. Traverse the right subtree. This yields

$$X + Y \cdot Z,$$

which recaptures the original *infix* form of the expression.

3. *Postorder (or endorder) traversal.* Traverse the left subtree. Traverse the right subtree. Visit the root. This yields

$$X \, Y \, Z \cdot +,$$

which is the *reverse Polish* or *Polish postfix* form of the expression.

Binary trees play an important role in computer science. Of particular importance in various applications are *height-balanced* (also called *AVL*) trees, in which the height (maximum distance from the root to a leaf) of the left subtree of any node differs from that of the right subtree by, at most, one. Now consider the 5-ary tree in Fig. 3. For *n*-ary trees ($n > 2$), inorder traversal has no meaning, but preorder and postorder traversals still do if the subtrees are visited left to right. The preorder traversal of the tree above yields

a b e f g c h i d j k l m n,

which coincides with the ordering obtained by the *depth first search* (*DFS*) algorithm. (An alternative strategy is *breadth-first search* (*BFS*), in which nodes at the same level are listed from left to right, starting at the root. For the above example, BFS yields a b c d e f g h i j k l m n.)

Trees are a natural data structure for any data objects whose components stand in a hierarchical relation to each other. For example, the organization chart of a company may be represented by a tree structure, and family trees are, as their name implies, representable by a tree structure. The biblical family tree in Fig. 4 is taken from Knuth (1973).

Tree structures may be indicated by parentheses, nesting, or indentation, as illustrated in Fig. 5 which shows alternative representations of the tree of Fig. 1.

The representation (A(B) (C(D) (E)) may be viewed as a list structure in which the successor nodes of A are represented by the sublists (B) and (C(D) (E)). This representation is used to represent trees in languages such as Lisp.

Tree structures are convenient for storing sets of lexicographically ordered objects for purposes of alphabetically oriented information retrieval. For example, the five words "dog," "cat," "lion," "fox," "tiger" can be stored in the tree structure shown in Fig. 6. A word in this tree structure can be found by comparing it to successive nodes, starting at the root node and taking the left successor if the word occurs earlier in a dictionary ordering or the right successor if it occurs later. Success is reported if the word matches; failure is reported if there is no successor of the kind required for the next step of search. The failure signal may be used to trigger a procedure for adding the new word to the tree as a new successor at the point of failure.

Example. (1) Assume that we want to determine if the word "fox" is in the tree. The word "fox" is compared with the word "dog," and since it occurs later in the alphabet, the right branch is taken. Then "fox" is compared with "lion," and since it occurs earlier in the alphabet, the left branch is taken. The third comparison results in a match.

(2) Determine whether the word "chicken" is in the tree; if absent, add it to the tree. First compare "chicken" with "dog" and take the left branch. Then compare "chicken" with "cat" and take the right branch. Then report failure because there is no right successor of "cat." Add "chicken" as the new right successor of "cat."

The tree structure representing a given set of sorted words depends on the order in which the words are presented during the construction of the tree. However, the tree representation of the sorted words is convenient, both because of the ease with which new words may be added to the structure and because the number of accesses in general depends on the logarithm of the number of words in the tree.

Trees are often used in the analysis of strategies for games such as chess and checkers. In this case, the vertices of the tree represent positions in the game, and a given vertex has as its successors all vertices that can be reached in one move from the given position. The set of all continuations of a game from a given position can be represented by a tree having the given position as its root

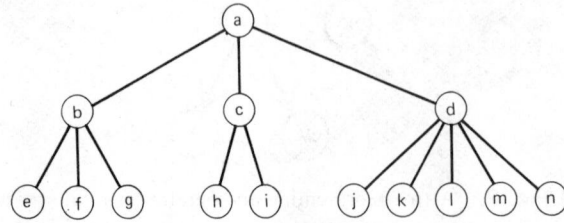

Fig. 3. A 5-ary tree.

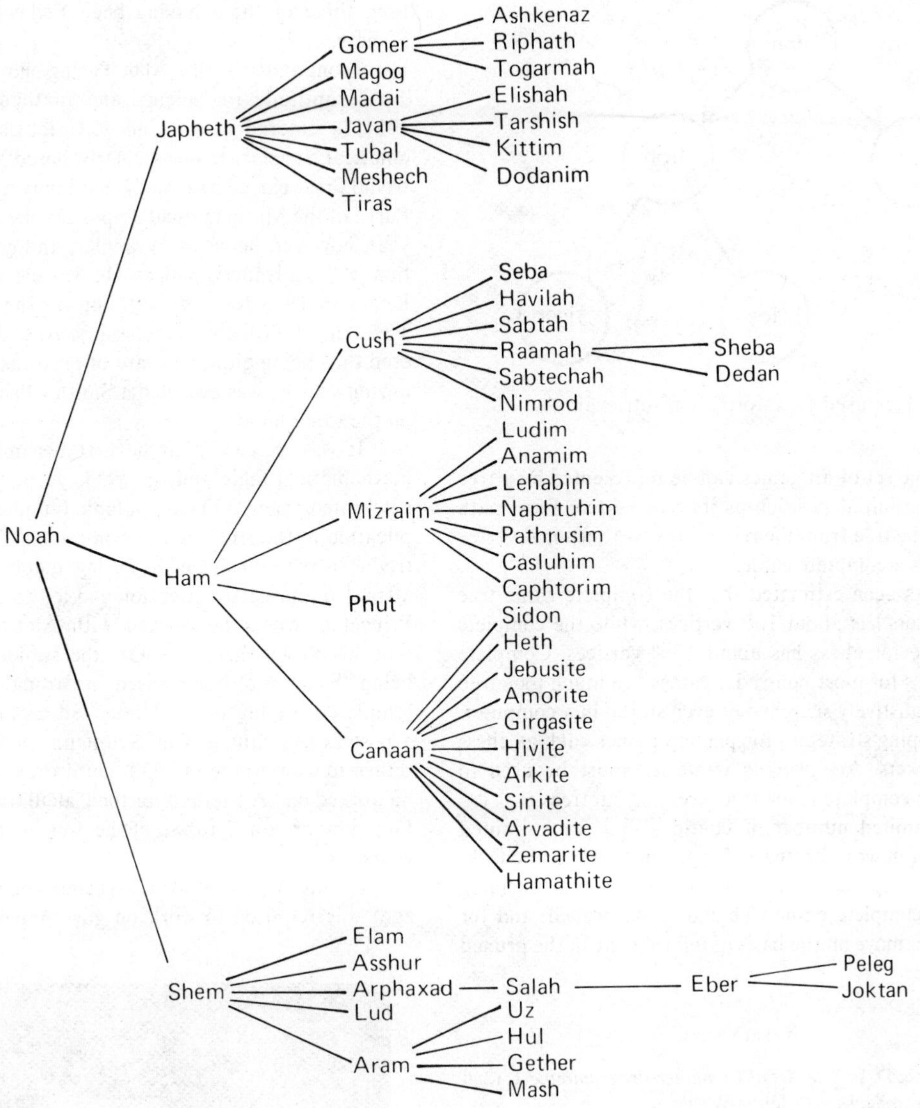

Ashkenaz
Gomer — Riphath
Magog — Togarmah
Madai — Elishah
Japheth — Javan — Tarshish
Tubal — Kittim
Meshech — Dodanim
Tiras

Seba
Havilah
Sabtah
Cush — Raamah — Sheba
Sabtechah — Dedan
Nimrod
Ludim
Anamim
Lehabim
Noah — Ham — Mizraim — Naphtuhim
Pathrusim
Phut — Casluhim
Caphtorim
Sidon
Heth
Jebusite
Amorite
Girgasite
Canaan — Hivite
Arkite
Sinite
Arvadite
Zemarite
Hamathite

Elam
Asshur
Arphaxad — Salah — Eber — Peleg
Shem — Lud — Uz — Joktan
Hul
Aram — Gether
Mash

Fig. 4. Family tree.

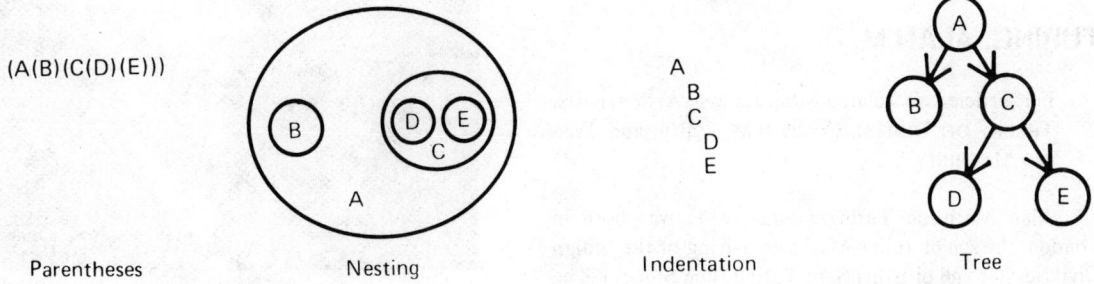

(A(B)(C(D)(E)))

Parentheses   Nesting   Indentation   Tree

Fig. 5. Alternative representations of tree of Fig. 1.

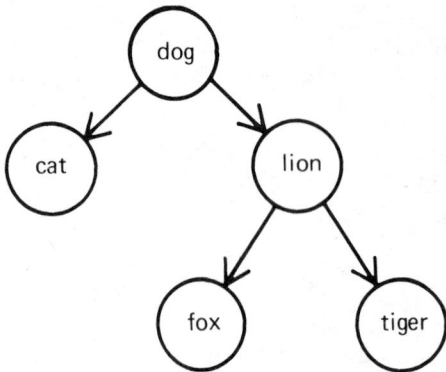

Fig. 6. Tree used for information retrieval.

vertex. The set of all games can be represented by a tree having the initial position as its root vertex. Each path through the tree from the root vertex to a terminal vertex represents a complete game.

It has been estimated that the complete game tree for checkers has about 10^{40} vertices, while the complete game tree for chess has about 10^{120} vertices. Complete game trees for most nontrivial games are much too large to be exhaustively searched or even stored in a computer. In developing strategies for playing games such as chess and checkers, *tree-pruning strategies* must be used to prune the complete game tree, creating subtrees that explore a limited number of continuations for a limited number of moves. Strategies for playing chess and checkers on a computer are effectively strategies for deciding how the complete game tree should be pruned, and for choosing a move on the basis of information in the pruned game tree.

REFERENCES

1973. Knuth, D. E. *The Art of Computer Programming* **1**. (2nd Ed.) Reading, MA: Addison-Wesley.
1978. Gotlieb, C. C. and Gotlieb, L. R. *Data Types and Structures*. Englewood Cliffs, NJ: Prentice Hall.

P. WEGNER

TURING, ALAN M.

For articles on related subjects *see* ALGORITHMS, THEORY OF; DIGITAL COMPUTERS; Early; and TURING MACHINE.

Alan Mathison Turing (1912–1954) was born in London, the son of Julius Mathison Turing of the Indian Civil Service and of Ethel Sara Turing (neé Stoney). The Stoneys were a family of considerable scientific distinc-

tion, three of them having been Fellows of the Royal Society.

From an early age, Alan Turing showed an extraordinary aptitude for science and mathematics, and, in 1931, he entered Kings' College Cambridge as a Mathematical Scholar. He was clearly bored with the rather trivial first-year course, and gained only a second class in Part I of the Mathematical Tripos. At the end of the third year, however, he was a Wrangler, and gained a distinction in the advanced papers. He was elected a Fellow of King's in 1935 for a dissertation on the Central Limit Theorem of Probability. Characteristically he rediscovered this, being quite unaware of previous work. The following year he was awarded a Smith's Prize for his thesis on the same topic.

It was in 1935 that he first became interested in mathematical logic and, in 1937, he published his now celebrated paper "On Computable Numbers with an Application to the Entscheidungsproblem," in which he introduced the concept of a Turing machine. This paper attracted immediate attention and led to an invitation to Princeton, where he worked with Alonzo Church. He took his Ph.D. there in 1938, the subject of his thesis being "Systems of Logic based on Ordinals." Turing contemplated staying in the United States and was offered a post as assistant to von Neumann, but he decided to return to Cambridge in 1938. Until the outbreak of war, he worked on "A Method for the Calculation of the Zeta-Function," a topic to which he was to return in later years.

During World War II, Turing (being of military age) was required to work on government scientific re-

Fig. 1. Alan Mathison Turing.

search. He spent 1939–1945 at the British Foreign Office on work of a highly confidential nature, which has not yet been declassified. For his work he was awarded the Officer Order of the British Empire (OBE). It is certain that in this period he gained a detailed knowledge of pulse techniques, and this was to have a decisive influence on his subsequent career. In 1942, he visited the United States on official business. During this visit he had the opportunity to see the latest work on computers and to renew old contacts at Princeton.

In 1945, he declined an offer of a Fellowship at Kings' in favor of joining the newly formed Mathematics Division at the National Physical Laboratory (NPL). His early work on computability, combined with his wartime experience in electronics, had fired him with an enthusiasm for working on the design of an electronic computer. The machine he designed, which was called the Automatic Computing Engine (ACE) in recognition of Babbage's pioneering work, was characteristically original. Although Turing knew something of the von Neumann proposals for EDVAC, he was not unduly influenced by them. The ACE, as Turing conceived it, was too ambitious a project, considering the current state of electronic techniques. Therefore, he left NPL in 1948, dissatisfied with the rate of progress.

While in the Mathematics Division of NPL, Turing became keenly interested in numerical analysis. His paper, "Rounding-off Errors in Matrix Processes," showed that the acute anxiety about the effect of rounding errors in Gaussian elimination was largely unjustified. This paper has been overshadowed to some extent by the von Neumann and Goldstine paper on matrix inversion, but it is a brilliant piece of work and would have repaid a closer study at the time. After Turing left NPL, it was decided to build a pilot model embodying Turing's ideas (the Pilot ACE), and this was completed in 1950. It was a highly successful computer and some 30 engineered versions of it were subsequently constructed by the English Electric Company under the name DEUCE. The original Pilot ACE is in the Science Museum in Kensington, London.

On leaving NPL, Turing was appointed to a Readership at Manchester University, where he worked in close collaboration with F. C. Williams and T. Kilburn, both pioneers in the electronic computer field. He was elected a Fellow of the Royal Society in 1951. Papers published while he was at Manchester include further work on the Riemann zeta-function, a remarkable discussion on computing machinery and intelligence and the impressive chemical basis of morphogenesis. The latter was his main interest at that time, and he left uncompleted another substantial paper on the same topic.

Turing died tragically in 1954 at the age of 41. His publications, impressive though some of them are, give only the merest hint of his extraordinary originality and versatility. In recognition of his outstanding pioneering work, the ACM has named its most prestigious award, the Turing Award. It is awarded annually for contributions to computer science of a technical nature.

REFERENCES

1955. Newman, M. H. A. *The Biographical Memoirs of Fellows of the Royal Society* **1**. London: The Royal Society, pp. 253–263.
1959. Turing, Sarah. *A. M. Turing.* Cambridge: Heffer & Sons.
1970. Wilkinson, J. H. "Some Comments from a Numerical Analyst" (The 1970 A. M. Turing Lecture), *JACM* **18**, *No. 2:* 137–147.

J. H. WILKINSON

TURING MACHINE

For articles on related subjects *see* ALGORITHMS, THEORY OF; AUTOMATA THEORY; CHOMSKY HIERARCHY; FORMAL LANGUAGES; MARKOV ALGORITHMS; SEQUENTIAL MACHINES; and TURING, ALAN M.

A Turing machine is an abstract computing device invented by Alan M. Turing in 1936. A reprint of his original paper appears in Davis (1965). A Turing machine consists of (1) a *control unit,* which can assume any one of a finite number of possible states; (2) a *tape,* marked off into discrete squares, each of which can store a single symbol, taken from a finite set of possible symbols; and (3) a *read-write head,* which moves along the tape and transmits information to and from the control unit (see Fig. 1).

The Basic Model. A Turing machine computes via a sequence of discrete steps. Its behavior at a given

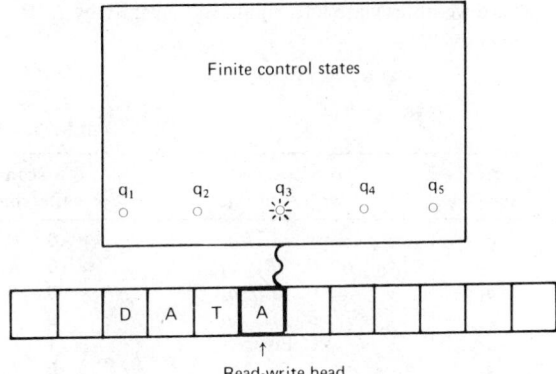

Fig. 1. Architecture of a Turing machine.

time is completely determined by the symbol currently being scanned by the read-write head, and by the internal state of the control unit. On a given step, it will write a symbol on the tape, move along the tape at most one square to the left or right, and enter a new internal state. The new symbol is permitted to be the same as the current symbol; similarly, it is permissible to stay on the same tape square on a given step and/or to reenter the same state. Certain symbol-state situations may cause the machine to halt.

For example, on a single step the machine in Fig. 1 could begin in state q_3, change the A under scan to an E, move left one square and enter state q_5. It would now be scanning a T; its next action would be uniquely determined by the new state q_5 and the fact that it was scanning a T. It would continue indefinitely in this step-by-rr fashion unless it reached a state-symbol combination, causing it to halt.

The tape of a Turing machine is often depicted as infinite, and some persons view this idealization as hopelessly unrealistic. A better approach is to view the tape as finite but indefinitely extendible; i.e., new blank squares can be attached to either end of the tape at will to prevent the machine from running off the tape. Thus, there is no uniform bound on either the time or space used by a Turing machine; both are allowed to grow indefinitely.

The *program* of a Turing machine defines its action for the various state-symbol combinations that are possible. This program can be presented in a number of different ways, e.g., state transition diagrams, assembly-like languages, etc. The two most common ways are a tabular form and representation as a set of quintuples. Each state-symbol combination is represented by either an entry in the table or a single quintuple in the set. In the quintuple convention, the action described above would have been due to the presence of the quintuple

$$\langle q_3, A, E, L, q_5 \rangle$$

where we abbreviate left, right, and no-shift by L, R, N, respectively.

An example of a Turing machine in tabular form is now presented. The state set of this machine M corresponds to rows in Table 1 and the symbol set (alphabet) to columns. The blank symbol is denoted by B. M will compute the function $f(x) = 2^x$ according to the following conventions:

1. x and $f(x)$ are written as binary integers.
2. The tape initially contains x and is blank elsewhere.
3. M begins in state q_1, scanning the leftmost bit of x.
4. When it halts, $f(x)$ will be the only nonblank item on the tape.

The algorithm used is given by the flowchart in Fig. 2. Essentially, each time the string that initially represents x is changed to represent the next smaller integer, a 0 is written on the tape to the right of x. When x has been decreased to 0, a 1 is written to the left of the generated string of x zeros. The zeros to the left of the 1 are then erased, and M halts. As is often the case, the algorithm is best thought of as an exercise in symbol manipulation rather than as arithmetic.

The entries in Table 1 labeled *error* cannot occur in a normal computation. By convention, M would halt if started in such state-symbol situations.

An *instantaneous description* (total machine configuration) of a machine consists of the entire set of machine conditions at a given point in a computation, i.e., the contents of the tape, the position of the read-write head on the tape, and the internal state of the machine. A computation, then, is simply an entire history of instantaneous descriptions beginning with the start configuration and ending with a halt configuration. Table 2 gives the computation of the machine M when started in state q_1 on the input 10 (binary 2). The symbol scanned is set in boldface type. Note that when M halts, its read-write head is not scanning the leftmost digit of the output 100; the reader is invited to add one more state to M and get it to do this.

Table 1.   Program for *M*

Present State	B is scanned write/shift/state	0 is scanned write/shift/state	1 is scanned write/shift/state	Comment
q_1	1, L, q_7	0, R, q_1	1, R, q_2	Is x 0?
q_2	B, R, q_3	0, R, q_2	1, R, q_2	$x \neq 0$
q_3	0, L, q_4	0, R, q_3	Error	Write a new 0
q_4	B, L, q_5	0, L, q_4	Error	Go back to x
q_5	Error	1, L, q_5	0, L, q_6	Decrease x
q_6	B, R, q_1	0, L, q_6	1, L, q_6	Go to starting position
q_7	Halt	B, L, q_7	Error	Clean up

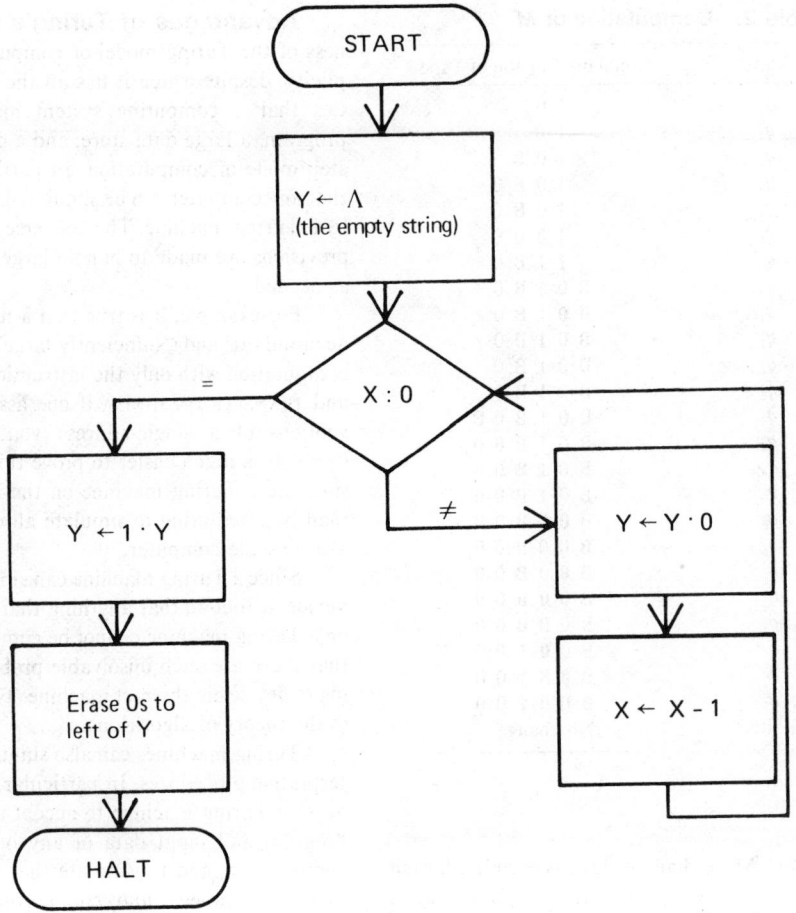

Fig. 2. Flowchart for *M*.

Modified Turing Machines. Turing's original model has been altered in a number of ways by a number of different authors. In each of the cases discussed below, it has been proved that the altered model and the original model can each compute the same class of functions. This is done by showing that for every machine of a given type, there exists a standard Turing machine which can simulate its behavior, and conversely. Turing machines have also been shown capable of defining exactly the same classes of functions definable by the formal systems of Kleene, Church, Rosser, Markov, and others. *Church's Thesis* and *Turing's Thesis* assert that their respective models correctly capture the mathematical notion of *effective computability*, i.e., of explicit algorithmic processes. Since the models are equivalent in the sense given above, the two theses are equivalent.

The following list contains some of the more common variations that do not effect the classes of functions which can be computed (although the efficiency of a computation may change with the model).

1. *Post-Davis*. The machine cannot both change the symbol under scan and move along the tape on the same step (Davis, 1958).
2. *One-ended Tape*. The tape can be extended to the right, but not to the left. Thus, the read-write head could fall off the left end of the tape.
3. *Paper Tape*. A blank square can have a nonblank symbol written on it, but this symbol cannot be changed thereafter.
4. *Two-Symbol*. Only the symbols *B* (blank) and 1 are allowed, although the number of states may be large.
5. *Two-State*. Only two states are permitted, although the number of symbols may be large. The generality of this and the previous case is due to Shannon (1956).

Table 2. Computation of *M*

Time	State	Nonblank Portion of Tape
0	q_1	**1** 0
1	q_2	1 **0**
2	q_2	1 0 **B**
3	q_3	1 0 B **B**
4	q_4	1 0 **B** 0
5	q_5	1 **0** B 0
6	q_5	**1** 1 B 0
7	q_6	**B** 0 1 B 0
8	q_1	B **0** 1 B 0
9	q_1	B 0 **1** B 0
10	q_2	B 0 1 **B** 0
11	q_3	B 0 1 B **0**
12	q_3	B 0 1 B 0 **B**
13	q_4	B 0 1 **B** 0 0
14	q_4	B 0 1 **B** 0 0
15	q_5	B 0 **1** B 0 0
16	q_6	B **0** 0 B 0 0
17	q_6	**B** 0 0 B 0 0
18	q_1	B **0** 0 B 0 0
19	q_1	B 0 **0** B 0 0
20	q_1	B 0 0 **B** 0 0
21	q_7	B 0 **0** 1 0 0
22	q_7	B **0** B 1 0 0
23	q_7	**B** B B 1 0 0
24	Halted	No change

6. *Multitape.* More than one tape is permitted, each tape having its own read-write head. In this case, the action of the machine depends upon the internal state and the symbols scanned by each of the read-write heads; i.e., for a *k*-tape machine, the action depends upon the state and an ordered *k*-tuple of symbols. The tape motions are independent; on a given step some heads could move left, some right, and some could remain in place.

7. *Multihead.* More than one head is allowed per tape. Again, the action of the machine is determined by the state and the ordered set of symbols scanned by the various read-write heads as they crawl around their shared tapes. Usually, the machine is allowed access to information concerning which heads are currently scanning the same tape square.

8. *Multidimensional.* The "tapes" are multidimensional structures. In the two-dimensional case, the plane is marked off into squares and the permissible head motions are north, south, east, west, and no move. For higher dimensions, one uses a coordinate system, and a move changes at most one of the coordinates by ± 1.

Advantages of Turing's Model. The usefulness of the Turing model of computation lies in its simplicity, despite which it has all the fundamental properties that a computing system must possess: a finite program, a large data store, and a deterministic step-by-step mode of computation. In particular, one can show that any computer can be simulated (albeit rather slowly) by a Turing machine. The converse is also true, provided provisions are made to handle larger amounts of storage as needed.

For example, it is true that a minicomputer with an accumulator and "sufficiently large" storage can do any computation with only the instructions SUBTRACT, STORE, and TRANSFER ON MINUS, if one assumes the usual conventions of a single-address von Neumann machine (*q.v.*). It is much easier to prove this by showing how to simulate a Turing machine on the minicomputer rather than by attempting to simulate all of the instructions of a large-scale computer.

Since a Turing machine can simulate any computing device, it follows that anything that cannot be computed on a Turing machine cannot be computed at all. The fact that there are such unsolvable problems motivated Turing to devise his abstract machine. This has also given rise to the theory of algorithms.

Turing machines can also simulate each other by interpretive procedures. In particular, it is possible to program a Turing machine to accept the description of the program and input data of any other Turing machine computation, and to simulate that computation. Such a machine is called a *universal Turing machine*.

Although Turing machines have probably been studied theoretically more than other abstract computing devices, two other models deserve mention. A *random-access machine* looks much like a single-address computer and stores its data in a finite number of cells. The idealization used here is that each cell can store any integer, and hence must have an unbounded number of bits. An *iterative array* consists of a network of finite-state sequential machines. Again, an unbounded memory is needed; this is achieved by allowing the network to be expanded in the middle of a computation, if necessary. Iterative arrays are useful in studying certain kinds of parallel processes.

Time Complexity of Turing Machine Computations. A number of theoretical results have shown that studying the complexity of Turing machine computations can yield insight into the efficiency of computations on real hardware. Within a broad range of conditions, the cost of a computation on a Turing machine (e.g., the number of steps required) is within a polynomial function of the cost of any machine with a finite number of processors. If the real Turing machine has at least two tapes, the relationship to cost on a real machine will often be linear.

On the other hand, Turing machine time studies are insensitive to a constant factor, i.e., computations on a multitape Turing machine can always be sped up by a factor of 2 by increasing the symbol set so as to pack at least two symbols of the original alphabet on a tape square. (Some additional programming is required to make this work in all cases.) Doubling the speed of real machines, on the other hand, cannot be achieved without either a technological breakthrough or increase in the cost of the hardware, and hence the cost per machine hour.

The Post-Davis, one-ended tape, and two-state variants introduced in the preceding section can be made to run as fast as ordinary (one-tape) Turing machines. The two-symbol variant will run within a constant factor of the others, but since the number of symbols is fixed, the speed-up trick may not be employed.

Although the multihead variant appears to be more powerful than the multitape model, P. Fischer, A. Meyer, and A. Rosenberg have shown that the two variants are equivalent in a very strong sense. Any multihead machine can be replaced by an equally fast equivalent multitape machine (but with perhaps a greater total number of heads).

On the other hand, one-tape Turing machines cannot always simulate multitape machines without loss of time. There exist examples for which the time on the one-tape machine must be the square of the multitape machine time. Thus, multitape (and multihead and multidimensional) machines are more efficient than ordinary Turing machines. For this reason, the multitape model is probably the most useful model for efficiency studies, although the one-tape version is better for computability-noncomputability investigations because of its greater simplicity.

The squaring of time to go from a multitape machine to a one-tape machine is never exceeded. In fact, any variant of a Turing machine with a bounded number of processors requiring time t for a computation can be simulated by an ordinary Turing machine in time at most t^2.

When considering multitape Turing machines with different numbers of tapes, some interesting questions remain unsolved. Aanderaa has shown that for any k, certain problems can be solved faster on a k-tape machine than on a $(k - 1)$-tape machine. However, the amount of saving cannot be large, since Hennie and Stearns have shown that any multitape machine requiring time t can be simulated by a two-tape Turing machine in time at most $t(\log_2 t)$. Whether this bound can be improved is still an open question.

REFERENCES

1956. Shannon, C. E., and J. McCarthy (Eds.). *Automata Studies*. Princeton, N.J.: Princeton University Press.
1958. Davis, Martin. *Computability and Unsolvability*. New York: McGraw-Hill.
1963. Trachtenbrot, B. *Algorithms and Automatic Computing Machines*. Boston: D. C. Heath.
1965. Davis, Martin (Ed.). *The Undecidable*. Hewlett: Raven Press.
1978, Hartmanis, J. *Feasible Computations and Provable Complexity Properties*. Philadelphia: Society for Industrial and Applied Mathematics.

P. C. FISCHER

TURNAROUND TIME

For articles on related subjects *see* JOB; TASK; and THROUGHPUT.

Turnaround time is the elapsed time from the time a batch job is submitted to be run on a computer until the results are available. From the point of view of the input/output data control clerk, turnaround extends from the time when the job arrives for processing, to the time when the job deck and report(s) are available to the user. From the machine operator's point of view, it lasts only from the time the job deck is loaded into the card reader until the last line of the report has been printed.

But from the user's point of view, turnaround time is the period that begins when the job is delivered to the point at which it is dispatched to the computing center, and ends when the output is delivered to the point where it can be picked up. These points may be at the computing center itself, in which case the turnaround time for the user is the same as for the data control clerk. But if the user is sufficiently remote from the computing center to require a courier service for pickup and delivery, then the user's turnaround time is longer, perhaps considerably so, than that of the data control clerk. These various differences often give rise to a great deal of lively discussion about computing center performance between users and the staff of the computing center.

In time-sharing systems, the time elapsed between sending a line of input and the computer acceptance of it (when possibly some acknowledgment is returned) is a form of turnaround time called *response time*.

Typical computing center turnaround times vary from a few minutes to a few hours, while response times should be no more than a few seconds (say 5, at most).

From a communications standpoint, turnaround time is the length of time required to reverse a communication line from the send mode to the receive mode. Since messages in some applications are very short (and must be verified through return of some signal), the turn-around time can be as long or longer than the time required to send the message or return the verification. Therefore it becomes an important consideration in investigation of line efficiency.

C. L. MEEK

TURNKEY

For article on related subject *see* SERVICE BUREAUS, DATA PROCESSING.

Turnkey preparation of a facility means that a single contractor acquires and sets up all necessary premises, equipment, supplies, and operating personnel to bring a project to a state of operational readiness. All the customer needs to do is "turn the key" to begin full and effective usage of the new facility. Sometimes the contractor continues to operate the facility for the customer (usually called *facilities management*); in other cases, the customer assumes operational control.

Turnkey facilities are appropriate for customers who are unable to perform (or wish to avoid) their own subcontracting for ordering and testing components acquired from several different vendors. Recruiting, screening, and training a technical staff is also a highly specialized and sensitive task. A turnkey contractor is compensated either through surcharges on each item or service procured for the facility or by a commitment in advance to a fixed price.

D. N. FREEMAN

U

ULTRASONIC MEMORY

For articles on related subjects *see* EDSAC; EDVAC; UNIVAC I; and MEMORY; Main.

Ultrasonic memories played an important role in the early development of digital computers, but are now mainly of historical interest. The report on the EDVAC drafted by von Neumann in June 1945 on behalf of the group at the Moore School of Electrical Engineering, Philadelphia, clearly envisaged this type of memory, although it did not describe the physical principles on which it operated. Of the early machines, the EDSAC, SEAC, Pilot ACE, EDVAC, and UNIVAC all had ultrasonic memories.

The principle is illustrated in Fig. 1. A train of pulses representing the numbers to be stored is modulated onto a carrier and applied to a piezoelectric crystal in contact

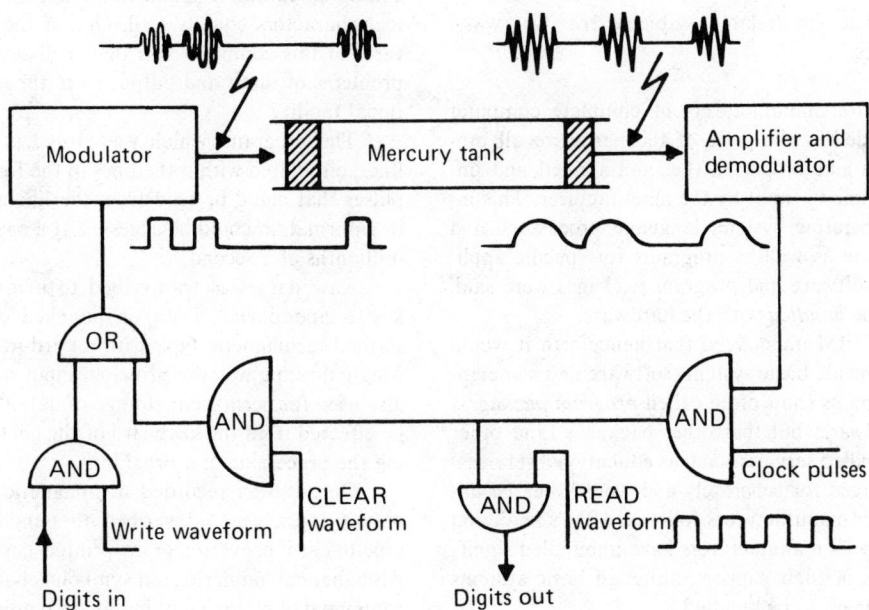

Fig. 1. Ultrasonic memory.

with a column of mercury. The ultrasonic pulses so generated travel along the column until they reach another crystal at the far end. This converts them back into electric signals, which are amplified and rectified. The resulting pulses are applied to a gate together with pulses from a continuously running clock pulse generator. This gating operation serves the twin purposes of regeneration and synchronization. The emerging pulses, which are exact replicas of the original pulses, are reapplied to the modulator and continue to circulate. The operations of reading, clearing, and writing can be performed by applying to the gates shown suitable waveforms accurately synchronized with the clock. A typical main memory consisted of a group of 32 tanks, as the columns were called, each between 0.5 and 1.5 meters long and giving a delay of between one-third and 1 ms.

In the mid-1950s, ultrasonic memories using a fine nickel wire in the form of a coil as the propagation medium appeared in some low-cost computers. The waves were excited by making use of the magnetostrictive properties of the nickel.

REFERENCE

1956. Wilkes, M. V. *Automatic Digital Computers.* New York: Wiley.

M. V. WILKES

UNBUNDLING

For article on related subject *see* SOFTWARE PACKAGES.

Until 1970, manufacturers of complete computer systems included in the price of the hardware all programs written and supported (i.e., maintained and improved from time to time) by the manufacturer. This included the operating system, language processors, and related software as well as programs for specific applications. The software and program packages were said, therefore, to be *bundled* with the hardware.

In 1970, IBM announced that henceforth it would continue to provide basic systems software and some application programs (now often called *program packages*) with the hardware, but that other packages (and other previously bundled services, such as educational services) would be charged for separately and would thus be *unbundled*. Other manufacturers followed IBM's lead, and today virtually all manufacturers have unbundled significant amounts of their support, although basic systems software continues to be bundled.

Types of programs that are typically unbundled are very large applications packages whose cost of development is substantial (e.g., linear programming packages), and language processors that are expected to be used by only a small number of customers.

A. S. DOUGLAS

UNIVAC. *See* COMPUTER INDUSTRY.

UNIVAC I

For articles on related subjects *see* DIGITAL COMPUTERS: Early; ECKERT, J. PRESPER; and MAUCHLY, JOHN W.

UNIVAC I (Universal Automatic Computer) was the world's first commercially available computer. Work on the first system was begun by the Eckert-Mauchly Computer Corporation in 1948 and completed in 1951, when it was delivered to the U.S. Bureau of the Census. During this period, Eckert-Mauchly was acquired by Remington Rand Inc. (subsequently merged with The Sperry Corporation in 1955 to form the Sperry-Rand Corporation).

A total of 46 UNIVAC I computers were delivered to a wide variety of customers during the period 1951–1958. All of them have been subsequently phased out.

The UNIVAC I, a high-speed, general-purpose electronic data processing system, was different from earlier computers in that it handled both numbers and alphabetical characters equally well. One of the innovative features of this computer was that it divorced the complex problems of input and output from the actual computational facility.

The program, which was stored in mercury delay lines, circulated within the lines in the form of acoustical pulses that could be read from the line and written into it. Information could be accessed at a speed of 40 to 400 millionths of a second.

Raw data was transcribed to magnetic tape by a key-to-tape device. Data on punched cards was transcribed to magnetic tape with a card-to-tape converter. Magnetic tape was the principal input medium and was also used for permanent storage of data. Input could also be effected from the keyboard of the control console during the processing of a program.

Output was recorded on magnetic tape. Data on output tapes was transcribed to punched cards by a tape-to-card converter or to printed copy by a printer. Alphabetical, numeric, and symbolic characters were accommodated in any combination in reading, writing, and processing operations.

Buffered storage registers permitted the central computer to continue processing while other data was being read from, or recorded on, magnetic tape. The system featured many automatic self-checking techniques, including duplicate circuits for all computing operations.

The operating characteristics were as follows: circuitry—chiefly serial, 2.25 MHz bit rate; Internal Operating Code—7 bits (four numeric pulses in excess-three notation, two zone pulses, and one parity pulse); word length, 12 characters including sign; block length, 60 words; program code, single address, automatic sequencing; internal storage capacity, 1,000 words or 12,000 characters.

The speed of the basic arithmetic functions were: addition or subtraction, 0.525 ms; multiplication, 2.150 ms; division, 3.890 ms; comparison, 0.365 ms.

M. M. MAYNARD

UNIVAC 1100 SERIES

For articles on related subjects *see* COMPUTER INDUSTRY: United States; and DIGITAL COMPUTERS, HISTORY: Contemporary and Future.

The Sperry Univac 1100 Series is an evolutionary family of medium- to large-scale general-purpose data processing systems (Borgerson, Hanson, and Hartley, 1978). Although some early Sperry Univac systems bore 1100 model numbers (e.g., 1103 and 1105), the evolution of what is now called the 1100 Series started in 1962 with the introduction of the 1107. The only characteristics in common between the early machines and the 1100 Series are one's complement arithmetic and a 36-bit word. Successive models since the 1107 have enhanced the basic

Fig. 1. UNIVAC 1.

architecture while maintaining applications program compatability. A summary of the characteristics of the models of the 1100 Series is given in Table 1.

All models in the 1100 Series since the 1108 have been designed as tightly coupled multiprocessor systems; one to six identical Instruction Processors (IPs) share a common main storage. The IPs are the principal computational units in a system. The number of them in a system is reflected in the nomenclature: An 1100/84 is an 1100/80 system with four IPs. The internal IP design varies throughout the 1100 series. The 1100/40 is pipelined, the 1100/80 uses a cache memory and 1100/60 systems are available with or without a cache. The 1100/60 is implemented using multiple microprocessors (Borgerson, Borne, and Champine, 1979); it is the only 1100 Series IP that is microprogrammed.

In some 1100 Series systems, the transfer of data to and from main memory is controlled by the IPs, but in most systems separate input/output processors (IOPs) do this. The architecture of these differs slightly from model to model; they all share the common main storage with the IPs. All I/O instructions are privileged and the architectural differences in the IOPs are hidden from applications programs by the operating system.

A single operating system, OS1100 (Exec-8), is used on all 1100 systems. Control of a multiprocessor system resides in OS1100 processes that freely migrate among the identical IPs. All IPs execute a single shared copy of OS1100 from the common main storage; each processor schedules itself by examining shared queues of tasks. Synchronization is effected by a test and set instruction and a privileged interprocessor signaling instruction.

The 1100 Series architecture is word-oriented; storage addresses specify 36-bit words and instructions are one word long. Some byte-oriented instructions (e.g., for string editing) exist. Ones-complement arithmetic is used; some models also admit packed decimal data. Single and double precision floating point data are binary normalized with a biased exponent. Many instructions allow parts of words to be expanded and treated as full word arithmetic operands; sixth, quarter, third, and half-word data can be operated upon with this mechanism.

Privileged instructions include those that alter segment relocation and protection data and all I/O instructions. Only OS1100 runs in privileged mode. Model-dependent differences in the privileged instructions are resolved by OS1100 and are invisible to applications programs.

Each IP in a system has its own 128 word general register set (GRS). Forty-four GRS words are used as arithmetic, index, and special-purpose registers for applications programs; another 44 words serve the same purpose for OS1100. The remaining GRS locations have special system functions.

Table 1.   Characteristics of Sperry Univac 1100 Series Systems

	1107	1108	1106	1110	1100/20	1100/40	1100/10	1100/80	1100/60
First delivery	1962	1965	1969	1972	1975	1975	1976	1977	1980
Number of IPs delivered by 1 Aug./80	36	296	338	290	81	173	366	574	193
Maximum number of IPs per system	1	4	2	4	2	6	2	4	2
Integer add time (ns)	4,000	750	1,000[1]	300[7]	875	300[7]	1,125	200[8]	350[8]
FP divide time (ns)	26,700	8,250	11,000[1]	5,200[7]	8,325	5,200[7]	8,625	1,500[8,13]	4,800[8]
Number of IP instructions[14]	117	151	151	206	151	206	151	201[9]	198
Number of segment base registers	0	2[2]	2[2]	4	2[2]	4	2[2]	4	4
Physical storage capacity (words)[3]	64K[4]	256K	256K[5]	256K/1M[6]	512K	512K/1M[6]	512K	16K/8M[10]	8K/2M
Maximum number of IOPs per system[11]	0	2	0	4	0	4	0	4	2[12]
I/O channels per IP	16	16	16	0	16	0	16	0	0
I/O channels per IOP		16		24		24		26	14

[1]Add 500 ns if system has "unitized" storage.

[2]Segment switch instructions are simulated by OS1100 software to achieve 2^{30} word logical address space.

[3]K = 1,024, M = K^2.

[4]Absence of base registers makes logical and physical address spaces identical at 64K.

[5]At initial delivery; field upgradable to 512K.

[6]Main storage is "layered," capacities are primary/secondary." Primary is faster.

[7]Time to execute from "primary" memory.

[8]Time assumes "hit" in cache.

[9]Not including instructions to emulate Sperry Univac 494 system.

[10]Sizes given are "cache/main store."

[11]IOP is a generic name; equivalent devices are designated as IOC, IOAU, IOU, depending on model.

[12]Although functionally distinct, IOPs are physically integrated with IPs on a one-for-one basis.

[13]4800 without Scientific Accelerator Module.

[14]Includes privileged instructions.

Most IP instructions specify both register and main storage operands. Certain storage addresses map to GRS rather than main storage so that register-register operations may be accomplished using the register-storage instruction format. Indirect addressing to arbitrary depth is permitted, and address modification by indexing is independently specifiable at each level. Index registers are auto-incrementable at the programmer's option so that, unlike most computers, loops do not need explicit instructions for index incrementation.

The main storage address space of a process is segmented (Borgerson, Hagerty, and Ryken, 1979). The maximum size of a segment is 256K words (K = 1,024), and all main storage references are relocated by up to four segment base registers. The base registers span an address space of 256K words which can be one large segment or several smaller ones; the boundaries between segments are not fixed positions in the address space. Programmed modification of the base registers allows additional segments to be addressed. The relocation information loaded into the base registers is obtained from hardware protected segment tables maintained by OS1100, thus allowing segments to be positioned anywhere in main storage. Segments are sharable and may be individually read and write protected. Segment swapping allows a program's logical address space to exceed the real storage in a system. The segment tables allow a program to reference up to 4,095 shared and 250 private segments for a total logical address space of 2^{30} words. The real storage capacity of systems is model dependent as shown in Table 1.

A full complement of peripherals (disks, printers, tapes, terminals, etc.) is available, and most peripherals can be used with any 1100 Series system. Device controllers are available that allow access to a given device over two channels; this provides improved system throughput and redundancy.

A number of other components are optionally available on 1100 systems. Switching devices permit the removal of failed units from a system and/or the partitioning of a large system into several smaller ones. Front-end processors to handle communications and (in some cases) paper peripherals are available. These devices typically connect to the host system via an I/O channel. Since all

I/O is handled by OS1100, the existence of these additional devices is hidden from applications.

The Sperry Univac 1100 Series has evolved in a compatible fashion over the nearly 20 years of its existence. New features (e.g., additional base registers and new instructions) have been added as logical extensions of what went before. This compatibility has been possible because the original architecture was sound and because hardware dependencies have always been encapsulated in operating system software.

REFERENCES

1978. Borgerson, B. R., Hanson, M. L., and Hartley, P. A. "The Evolution of the Sperry Univac 1100 Series: A History, Analysis, and Projection," *Comm. ACM* (January), pp. 25–43.

1979. Borgerson, B. R., Godfrey, M. D., Hagerty, P. E., and Ryken, T. R. "The Architecture of the Sperry Univac 1100 Series Systems," *Proceedings of the Sixth Annual International Symposium on Computer Architecture*. Philadelphia (April).

1979. Borgerson, B. R., Borne, L. A., and Champine, G. A. "The Microarchitecture of Univac's 1100/60," *Datamation* (July), pp. 173–178.

P. E. HAGERTY

UNIVAC SCIENTIFIC EXCHANGE. *See* USE.

UNIVERSAL PRODUCT CODE

For articles on related subjects *see* CODES; OPTICAL CHARACTER READER; OPTICAL MARK READERS; PATTERN RECOGNITION; and POINT-OF-SALE TERMINAL.

Symbols such as that shown in Fig. 1 now appear on a wide variety of grocery products in anticipation of eventual widespread use of electronic checkout procedures. The code is designed to be read by an optical scanner, and is obviously non-secret since the numbers used are interpreted at the bottom of the figure. The five leftmost digits identify the manufacturer through a code assigned by the Uniform Grocery Product Code Council. The five rightmost digits are assigned by the manufacturer to identify various individual products; thus, the price itself is not encoded, but instead a product identification number, from which a computer (on-line to the scanner) can obtain the price by table lookup. The digit 0 appearing at the left of the pattern is called the *code symbol;* it will be 0 for grocery products, but some other digit for other

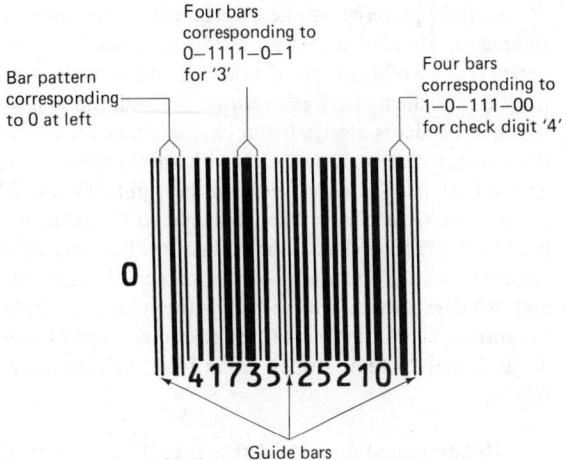

Fig. 1

types of enterprise. Since it will also participate in a *checksum* calculation to be described later, it is incorporated into the bar pattern itself (but not reprinted as an underlying digit).

Disregarding the guide bars at the left and right and the two center bars separating the two five-digit groups, all of which are longer than the bars over the interpreted digits, each digit is encoded by a sequence of four alternating light and dark bars of one of four different thicknesses. Each digit will have a unique sequence of bars, or, more precisely, a pair of such sequences, since the pattern of a digit on the right hand side is the encoded one's complement of the pattern it would have had on the left. This is done so that the program processing the scanner's input can detect whether the product was passed over the reading aperature right-to-left or left-to-right.

Using 0 and 1 to represent the thinnest light and dark stripes, respectively, and 0000 and 1111 the thickest such stripes, the code is as follows.

Digit	Left Representation	Right Representation
0	0001101	1110010
1	0011001	1100110
2	0010011	1101100
3	0111101	1000010
4	0100011	1011100
5	0110001	1001110
6	0101111	1010000
7	0111011	1000100
8	0110111	1001000
9	0001011	1110100

Thus, for example, the code for 4 on the left is, sequentially, the thinnest light bar (0), the thinnest dark bar (1), the next to thickest light bar (000), and the next to thinnest dark bar (11).

Certain patterns can be ascertained in the code assignments. First, note that all left-hand codes have *odd parity* (i.e., an odd number of 1s), so of course their right-hand complements have *even parity*. Second, the first bit of the left codes is always 0 and bit 7 is always 1, so that these code patterns always begin with a light bar and end with a dark one (and *vice versa* on the right). Of the 32 patterns that could have been assigned to the interior 5 bits, 16 (half) have the desired odd parity. But only 10 of these 16—the 10 selected—consist of exactly two light and two dark stripes. This will allow the scanner to make the further check that the pattern read contained exactly 30 dark and 29 light stripes, 59 in total, originating as follows:

10 interpreted digits $\times$ 4 stripes each	= 40
2 uninterpreted digits $\times$ 4 stripes each	= 8
2 dark-light-dark side guides	= 6
1 light-dark-light-dark-light center guide	= 5
Total	59

Since each of the 12 digits has a 7-bit representation and each of the 11 guide stripes a 1-bit representation, these 59 stripes would correspond to a string of 95 bits. The uninterpreted check digit is positioned between the guide bars on the right and the last interpreted digit. For further accuracy, the scanner verifies that the check digit read has a value such that

$3 \times$ [code symbol + 2nd, 4th, 6th, 8th, and 10th printed digit]
+ [1st + 3rd + 5th + 7th + 9th printed digit]
+ check digit

is a multiple of 10. Thus, if the product is a grocery item (code symbol at left = 0) whose identification number is 4173525210 (as in Fig. 1), its check digit must be 4 so that

$3 \times$ [0 + 1 + 3 + 2 + 2 + 0]
+ [4 + 7 + 5 + 5 + 1]
+ 4 (the check digit) = 50, a multiple of 10.

Such bar codes have applications other than for grocery checkout, inventory control being an obvious candidate. Bar encoding is also being tested as an expeditious way to distribute computer software.

REFERENCES

1976. Banks, W. "Samples of Machine Readable Printed Software," *Byte* **1**, *No. 12*: 12.
1977. Mellen, G. E. "Universal Product Code," *The Cryptogram* **42**, *No. 1*: 1–3, 23–24.
1980. Helmers, C. "Bar Codes, Revisited . . . ," *Byte* **5**, *No. 4*: 6–10.

E. D. REILLY, JR.

UNIX TIME-SHARING SYSTEM

For articles on related subjects *see* C; DIGITAL EQUIPMENT CORPORATION PDP SERIES; INTERACTIVE SYSTEMS, USING; OPERATING SYSTEMS; and TIME SHARING.

Introduction. Unix* is a general-purpose time-sharing system developed at Bell Laboratories by Ken Thompson and Dennis Ritchie. The system had its origins in Thompson's experiments with file systems on a PDP-7 in 1969; the first production system was built on a PDP-11/20 in 1971. Since then, Unix systems have spread widely: As of early 1980, there were at least 2,000 throughout the world, on a variety of computers, primarily the PDP-11 and VAX 11/780.

Unix offers:

1. A hierarchical file system incorporating demountable volumes.
2. Compatible file, device, and interprocess I/O.
3. The ability to initiate asynchronous processes.
4. A programmable command language interpreter.
5. A high degree of portability.

In addition, it provides a collection of application programs, particularly for program development and document preparation.

The system kernel (*q.v.*)—the part that does I/O to files and devices, process creation and scheduling, and similar tasks—is quite small, about 8,000 lines of C (*q.v.*) and 800 of assembler. Unix "is simple enough to be comprehended, yet powerful enough to do most of the things its users want. The user interface is clean and relatively surprise-free. It is also terse to the point of being cryptic. It runs on a machine that has become very popular in its own right." (Ritchie, 1978.) Unix is described in the *Bell Sys. Tech. J.* (1978); the programming environment it provides is discussed by Kernighan and Mashey (1979).

Pipes. One notable contribution of Unix is its notation for a "pipeline," a mechanism that facilitates program connection. Usually, programs read from the standard input and write to the standard output streams, both normally attached to the user's terminal. These default

---

*Unix is a Trademark of Bell Laboratories.

assignments may be changed by the command interpreter; for example, either or both may be connected to a file:

prog <infile >outfile

causes *prog* to read from *infile* and write on *outfile*.

In the same way, the standard output of one program can be connected to the standard input of another:

prog1 ¦ prog2.

A hidden temporary file called a "pipe," which obeys a first-in, first-out (FIFO) queue discipline, allows the programs to run concurrently, with the system handling synchronization and the flow of data from one to the next. Thus, *prog2* is activated whenever there is data for it; *prog1* is blocked whenever it has produced too much data for *prog2*.

Since I/O redirection with ¦, <, and > is interpreted by the command interpreter, each program in a pipeline thinks it is reading and writing the terminal.

As a real example of pipes,

list_directory ¦ print_neatly ¦ line_printer_spooler

provides a neatly formatted directory listing on a line printer. (The true names of these commands are more concise.)

The pipeline notation has had a major effect on the programming methodology of its users, because they are encouraged to combine existing programs instead of building new ones. Consider the three programs *who,* which lists the currently logged-on users, one per line; *search,* which searches its input for all occurrences of lines containing a given pattern; and *linecount,* which counts the lines in its input. Individually, each is useful; pipelines permit useful combinations:

who ¦ search joe

tells whether **joe** is presently logged in;

who ¦ linecount

tells how many people are logged in; and

who ¦ search joe ¦ linecount

tells how many times *joe* is logged in.

These examples are small, but the same principles apply to larger tasks. As an example of a production use of program connection, a major application on many Unix systems is document preparation. Three or four sep-

arate programs are normally used to prepare typical documents: *troff,* the basic formatting program that drives a typesetter; *eqn,* a preprocessor for *troff* that deals solely with describing mathematical expressions; *tbl,* a table-formatting program that acts as a preprocessor for both *eqn* and *troff; refer,* a program that converts brief citations to complete ones by searching a database of bibliographic references; and a number of postprocessors for *troff* that produce output on various media other than the typesetter. Placing all of these facilities into one typesetting language and program would create a large and unworkable program. As it is, however, each piece is sufficiently independent that it can be documented and maintained separately. Each is independent of the internal characteristics of the others. Testing and debugging such a sequence of programs is much easier than it would be if they were all one, because the intermediate states are visible and can be materialized in files at any time.

Programmable Command Interpreter. The Unix command interpreter is a user program, not part of the system kernel, so it may be invoked directly. (Different users may select different command interpreters, automatically at login.) Furthermore, its input can be taken from a file by redirection: if commands are placed in a file *cmdfile,* then

cmd_interp <cmdfile

executes them as if they had been typed at a terminal.

The command interpreter is actually a programming language, with variables, control flow, subroutines, and interrupt handling.

If a file of commands is marked executable, it may be invoked by naming it, as in

cmdfile

Thus, a user cannot, by running a program, determine whether it is implemented in the command interpreter language or a conventional compiled language.

Portability. Since Unix is written almost entirely in C, the system and all its applications software can be installed on a new computer with moderate effort, typically two people for six months. About 95% of the system code is identical on the different systems; most applications programs are 100% identical (Johnson and Ritchie, 1978). By early 1980, Unix had been transported to a variety of mainframes, and now runs on at least the DEC PDP-11 and VAX 11/780, the Interdata 7/32 and 8/32, the Amdahl 470, the Univac 1100 series, and several 16-bit microprocessors.

REFERENCES

1978. Ritchie, D. M. "Unix Time-Sharing System: A Retrospective," *Bell Sys. Tech. J.* **57**, *No. 6:* 1947–1969.

1978. "Unix Time-Sharing System," *Bell Sys. Tech. J.* **57**, *No. 6.*

1978. Johnson, S. C. and Ritchie, D. M. "Unix Time-Sharing System: Portability of C Programs and the Unix System," *Bell Sys. Tech. J.* **57**, *No. 6:* 2021–2048.

1979. Kernighan, B. W. and Mashey, John R. "The Unix Programming Environment," *Software Practice and Experience* **9**, *No. 1:* 1–15.

B. W. KERNIGHAN AND D. M. RITCHIE

UPC. *See* UNIVERSAL PRODUCT CODE.

UPDATE

For article on related subject *see* FILES.

To update information is to make it more current by adding, changing, or deleting data in a computer file. Examples are: adding in last week's earnings to bring an earnings record up to date; substituting more recent temperature and wind readings in reporting the latest weather; and keeping a class roster current by deleting the names of students who have resigned from the course.

An update run, or simply an *update,* is a computer run during which information (most commonly in files) is modified (by adding, deleting, or changing it) to make that information more current. Usually, before a tape or disk file is updated, the old file is copied (in the case of tape, transferred from an old reel of tape onto a new one). The copied file is then retained in case an error was made in creating the new one, or in the event the new one might be damaged.

Tables (kept in storage) are also updated by adding, deleting, or changing information. In this case no copy of the old version is typically made; rather it is just altered, and the old version is thereby lost. This means that the superseded table is not reproducible, in contrast to the tape file update, which is reproducible for purposes of auditing or duplication.

C. L. MEEK

USE

For article on related subject *see* COMPUTER USER GROUPS.

In December 1955, four prospective users of UNIVAC 1103A computers and company representatives met in Los Angeles to organize the user's group for large-scale UNIVAC scientific computers, UNIVAC Scientific Exchange, or USE. Over the succeeding three months, policies and objectives were established and three committees were formed: Standards, Programming, and Publications.

These committees soon achieved a number of significant accomplishments. These included development of a language for communications, known as the USE language; the development of standard formats for coding routines and subroutines; and the definition of a minimum USE 1103A.

Probably the most significant undertaking of the group was the production of a compiler known as the USE compiler. This was in fact an assembler with advanced characteristics for the period in which it was produced. It was used successfully for several years.

During the early years of USE, an extensive library of routines and subroutines was distributed to all members and other interested groups.

As the organization expanded, the working committees became the primary structures for determining the activities of the organization and the areas of mutual interest. When a particular interest outgrew the bounds of an existing committee, a new committee was formed to investigate the subject.

As newer computers entered the Sperry UNIVAC product line, USE membership policies were amended to extend invitations to users of the newer computers. In 1964, it was decided to substitute the term "UNIVAC Large-Scale Scientific Computers" rather than refer to specific computer models. In May 1966, the term "Scientific" was removed.

Over the years, USE has cooperated in many activities in the computer field. For example, a USE representative was a member of the United States delegation to the committee that developed Algol. Subsequently, USE members were involved with Codasyl (*q.v.*) in the development of Cobol.

Some members of USE also maintain memberships in the other large UNIVAC users' group, known as AUUA, Inc. (America's UNIVAC Users' Association, formerly UUA), an organization open to the user of any UNIVAC computing system. In 1961, a joint committee was formed, composed of three representatives of USE and UUA, to work out methods of closer cooperation. Several joint conferences were held by USE and UUA between 1965 and 1968. The growth of both organizations led to separate meetings after 1968.

The USE governing body today is a seven-member Board of Governors. It consists of a president and vice-president, each elected for a two-year term; three other members, one elected each year, serving for three years; the past president, who serves for a two-year period; and the executive secretary, who is elected annually by the Board of Directors.

The next level of management within USE is the Technical Program Board, which is composed of the heads of Working Groups and other appointed committees. This board executes technical and program planning functions and is responsible for scheduling and conducting the technical sessions at the semi-annual USE conferences. Its chairman is appointed by the President of USE.

In 1980, USE (which is now officially USE, Inc.) had a membership of about 375 organizations. Two general meetings attended by about 1,000 persons are held each year, one in the spring and the other in the fall. Presidents of USE have been as follows:

Walter F. Bauer, 1955
Randall E. Porter and Jules Mersel, 1956
R. B. Talmadge, 1956–1957
R. P. Rich, 1957–1958
Donn Combelic, 1958
Jules Mersel, 1959
Dorothy P. Armstrong, 1959–1960
J. H. Dietrich, 1960–1961
Ben Mittman, 1961–1962
J. W. Hanson, 1962–1963
R. P. Castanias, 1963
J. W. Hanson and C. D. Card, 1964
Norman Moraff and E. D. P. Gross, 1965
Earl Boone, 1966–1968
Wayne Youtz, 1968–1970
Wayne Fuhrmann, 1970–1972
Bernard Peters, 1972–1974
Robert Lees, 1974–1976
Manly Draper, 1976–1978
O. Ray Pardo, 1978–1980
Dewana Green, 1980–

M. M. Maynard

UTILITY PROGRAM

For articles on related subjects *see* PROGRAM LIBRARIES, NUMERICAL AND STATISTICAL; SORT-MERGE PACKAGES; and UPDATE.

A utility program is one provided by a computing center to its users to perform a task required by many or most of its users. The most common group of utility programs are those that copy information from one medium to another. Characteristically, they have names like *card-to-disk, disk-to-print, tape-to-tape,* etc., and can handle different record lengths, blocking factors, etc. These programs usually do not inspect the information being copied, and therefore they are not used when a selection of records must be made or when records must be altered or deleted. Utility programs are used to streamline an operation. For example, it may be faster to write a file on disk initially (perhaps because the tape drives are tied up) for later copying to tape than to write the file directly onto tape.

Utility programs can be used to great advantage during debugging and testing to assure that the desired information is being written as intended. A programmer will copy a tape file or a disk file to the printer to see what it looks like. Although the output is usually very hard to read (columns will not line up, headings will not be present, and negative numbers may appear as alphabetic characters, all according to the conventions of the machine), it is adequate to check that the file is being written correctly.

Utility programs also include sort-merge programs and certain error-checking programs that locate bad spots on tape or disk, although the latter are more often included with diagnostics or diagnostic programs.

C. L. Meek

V

VARIABLES. *See* CONTROL VARIABLE; and GLOBAL AND LOCAL VARIABLES.

VERIFICATION, PROGRAM. *See* PROGRAM VERIFICATION.

VIDEOTEX. *See* VIEWDATA.

VIENNA DEFINITION LANGUAGE

For articles on related subjects *see* BACKUS-NAUR FORM; METALANGUAGE; PROGRAMMING LINGUISTICS; and SYNTAX, SEMANTICS, AND PRAGMATICS.

The Vienna definition language (VDL) is a language for defining the syntax and semantics of programming languages. It consists of a *syntactic metalanguage* for defining the syntax of program and data structures and a *semantic metalanguage* that specifies programming language semantics "operationally" in terms of the computations to which programs give rise during execution.

Syntactic structures in VDL may be graphically represented by means of unordered trees whose edges are labeled by selectors. For example, the expression $a + b$

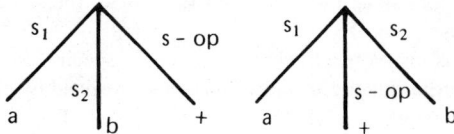

Fig. 1

might be represented in VDL by any one of a set of equivalent unordered trees such as those in Fig. 1.

These tree (t) structures may in turn be represented in linear notation as

$$t = (\langle s_1{:}a \rangle \, \langle s_2{:}b \rangle, \langle s - \mathrm{op}{:}+ \rangle)$$

or

$$t = (\langle s_1{:}a \rangle, \langle s-\mathrm{op}{:}+ \rangle, \langle s_2{:}b \rangle)$$

Selectors in a VDL syntactic structure serve the same role as pointers in a list structure and may be used to select components of the syntactic structure by "applying" the selector to the syntactic structure. In the preceding example, $s_1(t)$, $s_2(t)$, $s-\mathrm{op}(t)$ yield the respective components $a, b, +$.

Syntactic objects may be either *elementary (atomic) objects* with no components (such as the objects $a, b, +$ above) or *composite objects* (such as the tree t above) whose components may be selected by selectors.

The syntactic metalanguage of VDL is illustrated by the following definition of a simple class of arithmetic expressions:

$$\text{expr} = \text{const} \lor \text{var} \lor \text{binary}$$
$$\text{binary} = (\langle s_1{:}\text{expr}\rangle, \langle s_2{:}\text{expr}\rangle, \langle s{-}\text{op: op}\rangle)$$
$$\text{op} = \{+,*\}$$

This definition specifies that an expression can be a *constant* (const), a *variable* (var), or a *binary*, where constants and variables are elementary objects with no components, and a binary is a composite object with two components of the type "expr" selectable by the selectors s_1, s_2, and a third component of the type "op" selectable by $s{-}$op. The expression $a + b * c$ may be represented in terms of the preceding syntax by a tree structure whose edges are labeled by selectors as shown in Fig. 2.

If the tree structure in Fig. 2 is denoted by t, then $s_1(t) = a$, $s_2(t) = b * c$, $s{-}\text{op}(t) = +$, $s_1 \cdot s_2(t) = b$, $s_2 \cdot s_2(t) = c$, and $s{-}\text{op} \cdot s_2(t) = *$.

The example illustrates that syntactic objects in VDL are represented by trees whose edges are labeled by selectors, and that components of a tree-structured syntactic object may be selected by specifying the sequence of selectors along the path from the root to the selected subtree.

It is instructive to contrast syntactic specification in VDL with syntactic specification of a corresponding class of expressions in BNF (Backus-Naur form). The previously given class of arithmetic expressions could be specified in BNF as follows:

$$\langle \text{expr}\rangle ::= \langle \text{const}\rangle \mid \langle \text{var}\rangle \mid \langle \text{binary}\rangle$$
$$\langle \text{binary}\rangle ::= \langle \text{expr}\rangle \langle \text{op}\rangle \langle \text{expr}\rangle$$
$$\langle \text{op}\rangle ::= + \mid *$$

The difference between the BNF and VDL syntactic metalanguages is brought out by comparing the two specifications of binary. In BNF a binary is a string consisting of an expression followed by an operator followed by a second expression. In VDL a binary is a structure with three components selectable by the selectors s_1, s_2 and

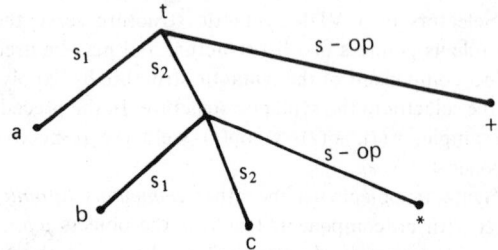

Fig. 2

$s{-}$op. If the representation for expressions were changed from infix to prefix notation, so that $a + b * c$ were written as $+a * bc$, then the BNF specification would have to be modified to reflect this change in order, but the VDL representation could remain the same. Because VDL specifies structure independently of the order in which components appear in a specific representation, a VDL syntactic specification is sometimes referred to as an *abstract syntax*.

The *semantics* of a programming language is defined in VDL in terms of the sequences of information-structure transformations to which programs give rise during execution. Every computation starts with an initial configuration ξ_0, which contains a syntactic representation of both the program structure and the data structure on which the program is to operate. Terminating computations consist of a finite sequence of configurations $\xi_0 \rightarrow \xi_1 \rightarrow \cdots \rightarrow \xi_n$, where ξ_{j+1} is obtained from ξ_j by the execution of an instruction. The configurations ξ_j are referred to as *instantaneous descriptions, snapshots,* or *states.* The instructions form the heart of the semantic specification of a programming language and have the following general form of definition:

$$\text{instruction-name } (x_1, x_2, \ldots, x_n) = p_1 \rightarrow a_1$$
$$p_2 \rightarrow a_2$$
$$\cdots$$
$$p_m \rightarrow a_m$$

where $p_1, p_2, \ldots, p_m$ are a sequence of predicates, $a_1, a_2, \ldots, a_m$ are a sequence of actions to be performed, and $x_1, x_2, \ldots, x_n$ are a sequence of formal parameters that may appear in the predicate specifications p_i and action specifications a_i.

Example

$$\text{abs}(x) = x > 0 \rightarrow x$$
$$x = 0 \rightarrow 0$$
$$x < 0 \rightarrow -x$$

When an instruction of this form is executed with given actual parameters, the current configuration is tested to see whether it satisfies successive predicates p_i for $i = 1, 2, \ldots, n$. The action a_i corresponding to the first true predicate p_i is then executed. Actions a_i specify transformations of the current configuration ξ_j into the next configuration ξ_{j+1}.

The VDL instruction execution cycle differs from that of conventional computers. At any moment of execution there is a tree of executable instructions called a *control tree,* and the next executable instruction may be *any* terminal vertex of the control tree. This leads to a certain amount of nondeterminacy in the instruction execution process, which allows VDL to model nondeterminacy in specifying (for example) the order of execution for certain expressions in PL/I, and also to model nondeterminacy of execution in certain kinds of multitasking.

There are two kinds of instructions in VDL:

1. Self-replacing instructions, which, when they are executed, replace the terminal vertex of the control tree at which they occur by a subtree of instructions.
2. Value-returning instructions, which return a computed value to predecessor vertices of the control tree and delete the executed instruction from the control tree.

A computation in VDL generally starts with a control tree consisting of a single vertex containing an instruction such as interpret-program (t), where t is the syntactic specification of the program to be executed. The first few executed instructions are generally self-replacing instructions that generate successively larger control trees (determined by the abstract syntax of t) until terminal vertices corresponding to value-returning instructions are generated. Execution terminates when an empty control tree is generated.

The Vienna definition language was developed by Peter Lucas, Kurt Walk, and others at the IBM Vienna Laboratory. It has been applied to the definition of PL/I (Lucas and Walk, 1969), Basic (Lee, 1972), and a number of other programming languages. A more detailed introduction to the basic concepts of VDL may be found in Wegner (1972).

REFERENCES

1969. Lucas, P. and Walk, K. "On the Formal Description of PL/I," *Annual Review of Automatic Programming* 6, *No. 9*.
1972. Lee, J. A. N. *Computer Semantics*. New York: Van Nostrand-Reinhold.
1972. Wegner, P. "The Vienna Definition Language," *Computing Surveys* 4: 5–63.

P. WEGNER

VIEWDATA

For articles on related subjects *see* DATA COMMUNICATIONS; MODEMS; PUBLISHING, COMPUTERS IN; TIME SHARING; and WORD PROCESSING.

Viewdata is the generic name for a publicly available information dissemination system developed by the British Post Office (BPO) in the early 1970s and now known by the trade name of *Prestel*. The name *Videotex* is now being used internationally for the same system.

The subscriber's hardware system is a conventional television set, modified by the addition of a modem and some storage and control circuitry, connected via a telephone line to a remote computer which allows access to a database. The database is essentially a tree, although various cross-linkages are allowed. One major design criterion for the system is that the protocol for accessing data should be as simple as possible. On obtaining access to the viewdata computer, the user is presented with the first "routing page," which gives a choice of up to ten options. One is selected by pressing the appropriate digit on the keypad—which also contains # and * for control purposes (see Fig. 1)—and so on until the required information is reached on an "end page." In addition to traversing the tree to obtain the required information, it is possible to obtain pages directly if their numbers are known by the user.

The system is based on an extended ISO7 character set allowing the use of color (red, green, yellow, blue, cyan, magenta, and white) and a relatively simple form of graphics.

The British Post Office undertook a Pilot Trial followed by a restricted Test Service in 1978. The full Public Service started in late 1979 based on a number of GEC 4082 minicomputers. The users access "Retrieval Centers," connected via 2,400 bps leased lines to a single "Update Center." The organizations providing the data (the "Information Providers") edit that information on the Update Center computer, whence it is transmitted to each Retrieval Center within a few minutes. At the beginning of the Public Service, the entire database was replicated in each center, but it is proposed that each center should contain a local database in addition to the national one.

The system can also be used to transmit messages between users, and a facility has already been implemented specifically to allow deaf people to communicate over telephone lines using Viewdata.

Associated with, and compatible with, viewdata (which is an interactive service) are the broadcast *Teletext* services, known commercially as Ceefax and Oracle in Britain. In an ordinary television transmission, there is a period to allow field flyback in receivers, and some of the lines transmitted in this period (which do not appear on the television screen) are already used for such purposes as testing. Teletext uses two such lines for transmitting data, and about 100 separate frames can be transmitted over about a 25-second period. Wideband services are also being developed in which all the lines of the transmission are used for digital data.

The frames in Teletext are transmitted cyclically. Because it is not interactive, it is insensitive to its load

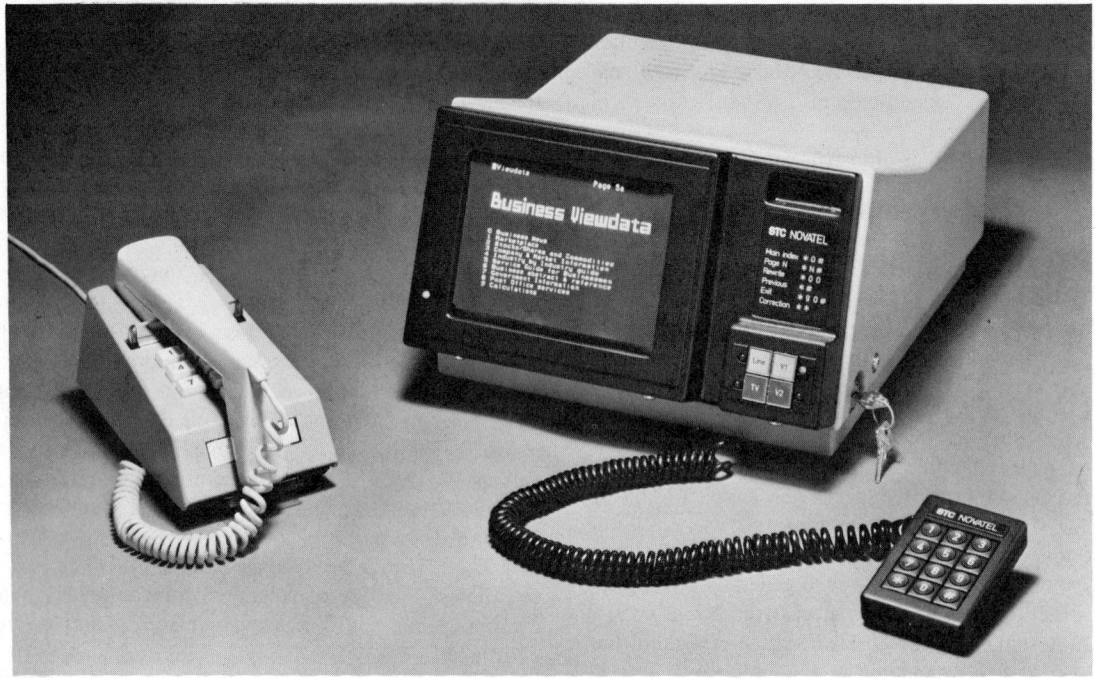

Fig. 1. Terminal and keypad of the Viewdata system.

factor, whereas this can be critical in non-broadcast systems.

Similar systems to Prestel are being developed in other countries—in particular, the Antiope system in France and Telidon in Canada. The latter is of particular interest in that it uses "picture description instructions" which are more analogous to methods used in computer graphics, rather than the Prestel system of transmitting graphics in "alphamosaic" form.

To give an example of the use of Viewdata, consider a user who wishes to know the composition of the House of Commons. The relevant part of the tree (under frame 500) is shown in Fig. 2. The user finds (probably by means of a hard copy index, although it is possible to tra-

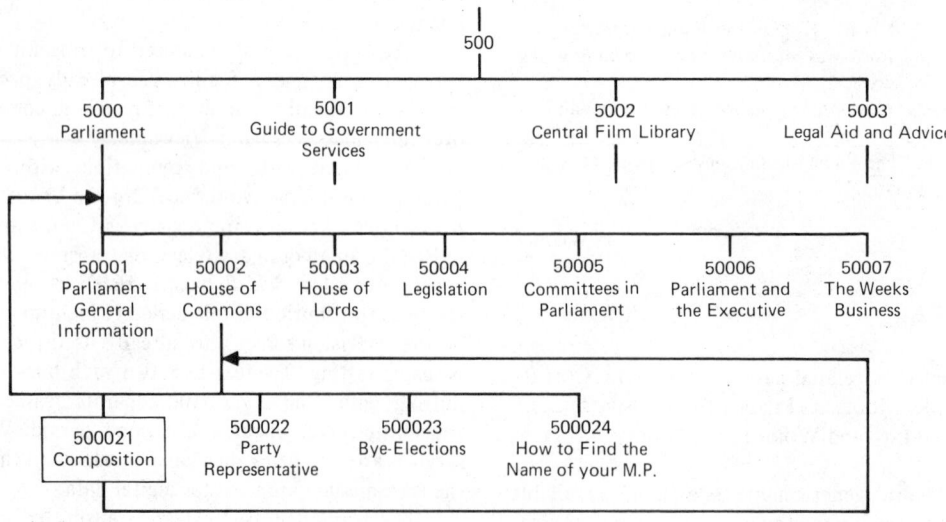

Fig. 2. An example of the Viewdata database.

verse the tree from the root) that frame 500 contains information on government. On keying *500#, a frame is obtained which invites the following key choices.

0. Parliament
1. Guide to Government Services
2. Central Film Library
3. Legal Aid and Advice

The choice is obviously zero and, on keying this, another routing page (5000) is obtained. The user then continues down the tree by keying 2, then 1, and finally obtaining the "end page" 500021, which contains the required information. For an example of a Viewdata frame on another subject, see Fig. 3.

Viewdata is not just an information retrieval database system, but should perhaps best be regarded as a new publishing medium with the significant advantage over conventional media of immediacy of information.

As of 1980, the BPO Prestel system database contained over 150,000 pages of data maintained by more than 200 information providers. The BPO itself operates Prestel as a common carrier abstaining from control over content. Costs to the subscriber, in addition to the modified television set, include those for telephone usage, access to the Prestel system, and whatever charges the information providers make for access to each page of data.

In addition to information and message services, we may expect videotex systems to be used for such things as advertising, entertainment, and retail merchandise ordering.

REFERENCES

1975. Fedida, S. "Viewdata: An Interactive Information Service for the General Public," *Proc. EUROCOMP,* pp. 262–282.
1980. Stokes, A. V. *Viewdata: A Public Information Utility,* 2nd Ed. London: Input Two-Nine Ltd.
1981, Chorafas, D. N. *Interactive Videotex: The Domesticated Computer.* New York: Petrocelli.

ADRIAN V. STOKES

VIM

For articles on related subjects *see* COMPUTER USER GROUPS and CONTROL DATA CORPORATION CYBER SERIES.

VIM began as the "VIM Users Organization for Control Data Corporation (CDC) 6000 Series Computers." The first meeting was held in 1965 and was attended by representatives of ten organizations. The name

Fig. 3.   A Viewdata frame showing the weather forecast in Britain.

"VIM" was suggested by Professor Max Goldstein, New York University, as the pseudo-Roman numeral representation of 6,000. The group incorporated as VIM, Inc. in March 1970. The membership of VIM was expanded in October 1979 to include organizations using any Control Data-manufactured computer systems.

The membership of VIM, Inc. consists (as of 1981) of 430 member organizations located in 36 countries throughout the world. The membership is almost evenly divided among universities, governmental agencies, and corporations.

The principal purposes of VIM are "to foster the development, free exchange and communication of research data pertaining to VIM computers among the users of VIM computers in the best scientific tradition and to provide a means of communication with the manufacturer of VIM computers."

Committees are the primary elements of communication for achieving the purposes of VIM. There are working committees for operating systems, database and business products, languages and processors, applications and graphics products, installation management, data communications, 7000-series development, and user services. The committees interface with manufacturers in the critical review of hardware and software products available for use in conjunction with VIM computers.

General meetings of VIM are held twice a year. The committees meet more frequently and are primarily responsible for providing the technical program at the general meetings.

VIM maintains a library of programs donated by member organizations. Publications of VIM include a catalog of the VIM library and a regular newsletter that contains copies of letters and other documents of interest to its members.

Past presidents of the VIM (or VIM, Inc.) Users Organization, in order of service, are Kent K. Curtis, Ben H. Mount, Thomas R. Parkin, Charles H. Warlick, William L. Evans, F. William Rambo, E. Rex Krueger, Albert L. Siegal, Charles A. Falkner, James A. Brooking, James F. Presti, and Conrad A. Wogrin. The address of VIM is PO Box 1903-HQW09P, Twin Cities Airport Branch, St. Paul, MN 55111.

C. H. WARLICK

VIRTUAL MEMORY

For articles on related subjects *see* ADDRESSING; INTERRUPT; MEMORY: Main; MEMORY PROTECTION; OPERATING SYSTEMS: Principles and Theory; STORAGE ALLOCATION; STORAGE HIERARCHY; and TIME SHARING.

The term *virtual memory* (or *virtual storage*) denotes the memory of a virtual (i.e., simulated) computer. An address (or name) space N of a program is the set of all addresses that can be generated by the processor as it executes the program; if the processor generates a-bit addresses, N contains, at most, 2^a bytes (or words). The name space N is frequently referred to as the *virtual address space* or the *virtual memory* within which the processor operates. The memory space M of the machine is the set of all real location addresses recognized by the main memory hardware; if this hardware recognizes b-bit addresses, M contains 2^b bytes (or words).

As shown in Fig. 1, an address translation mechanism is interposed between the processor and memory. This mechanism uses a mapping table, f, that specifies the correspondence between virtual addresses (in N) and real addresses (in M). If the mapping table entry for a

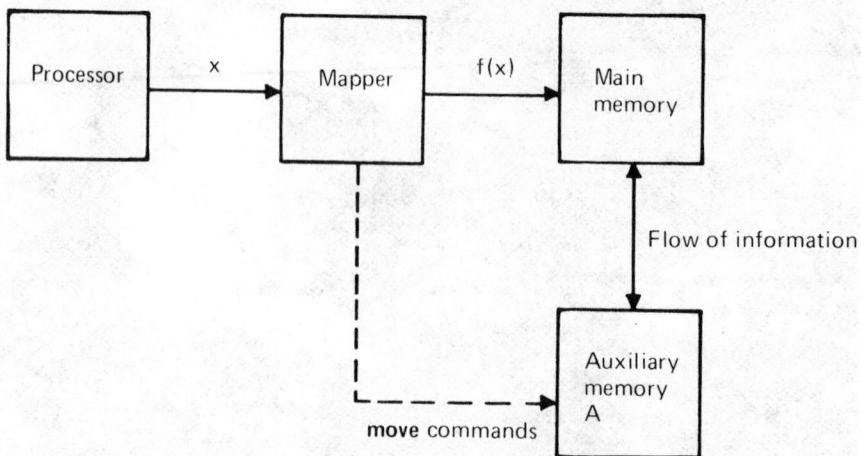

Fig. 1. The mapping function.

given virtual address is marked as "undefined," the mapper will generate an *addressing fault* in case the processor attempts reference to that address. The fault handler will locate the missing information in the auxiliary memory, move it into main memory (perhaps also moving out other information to make room), and update the table f to show the changes. Then, when the interrupted program is resumed, it will find the required table entry defined and can proceed.

An example of the scheme of Fig. 1 is the core/drum configuration, in which M is a core memory and A is a drum. Another example is the cache/core configuration, in which M is a high-speed semiconductor register memory (called a *cache—q.v.*) and A is a core memory or a slow-speed semiconductor memory.

Virtual memory solves the relocation problem because it permits program pieces to be moved around in memory without altering their virtual addresses. It solves the memory protection problem because each program piece can have its own access mode. In case the size of N exceeds the size of M, the virtual memory system also solves the memory management problem by determining which subset of N will reside in M. The CDC Cyber series illustrates that N can be smaller than M, although, in this case, N is not called "virtual memory."

Implementation. The map f is usually a directly indexed table. Its entries correspond to program blocks rather than individual virtual addresses. The blocks are normally used both as units of auxiliary memory storage and as units of transfer. Each block of N is a set of contiguous addresses with a base address and a length. A virtual address x must be represented (or translated to) the form (b, w), where b is a block index and w is an offset (relative address) in block b. The mapping table's entry for block b, denoted $f(b)$, gives the base of the block of M containing b. The translation process consists of three steps:

$$x \rightarrow (b, w) \rightarrow (f(b), w) \rightarrow f(b) + w,$$

as shown in Fig. 2. The translation of x to (b, w) takes time T_1; the translation of (b, w) to $(f(b), w)$ takes time T_2 [the time to look up $f(b)$ in the table]; and the translation of $(f(b), w)$ to $f(b) + w$ takes time T_3.

The translation function would be impractical unless the total translation time $T_1 + T_2 + T_3$ can be made small compared to the main memory reference time. Because the time to add two numbers is small, the efficiency of the translation operation actually depends on $T_1 + T_2$.

The two most common methods of making T_1 negligible or zero are *segmentation* and *paging*. A segmented name space is partitioned into blocks of various sizes (segments), usually corresponding to logical regions. In the Burroughs B5000 and later series, for example, the Algol compiler creates segments corresponding to the block structure of the language and the organization of the data (Organick, 1973). The Honeywell 6180 (which implements a segmented name space under Multics) requires the programmer to define the segments and refer to operands by symbolic two-part addresses of the form (segment-name, offset-name) (Organick, 1972). A paged name space is partitioned into blocks of the same size (pages). Since the page boundaries bear no prior relation to logical boundaries in the name space, the programmer is not generally apprised of the pagination of his or her

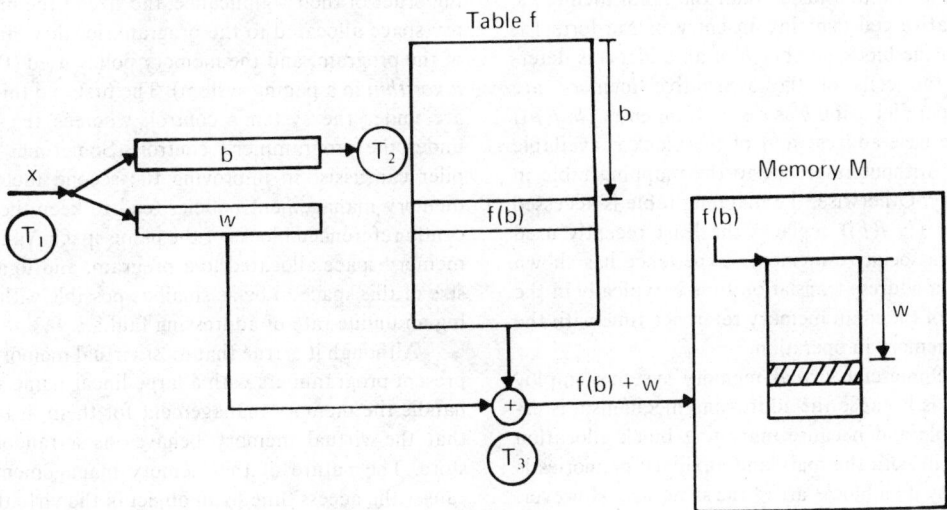

Fig. 2. Block-oriented mapping.

name space; however, the compiler or loader may be designed to reorganize information among pages to improve performance when the cost of such reorganization (which is high) can be justified. Paging's principal attraction has been its simple design.

Under segmentation, the address space is partitioned into regions by the programmer or compiler; each region becomes a block. In this case, all virtual memory references are programmed or compiled in the form of pairs (b, w). Thus, $T_1 = 0$ when segmentation is used.

Under paging, the address space is partitioned into blocks, all of the same size (say, s bytes). All addresses compiled in the program are linear offsets relative to the base of the name space. The computation $x \rightarrow (b, w)$ is specified by

$$(b, w) = (\lfloor x/s \rfloor, x \bmod s),$$

where $\lfloor \ldots \rfloor$ denotes "integer part of," and $x \bmod s$ denotes the remainder in dividing x by s ($0 \leq x \bmod s < s$). If $s = 2^q$ (for some $q \geq 0$) and binary arithmetic is used, this computation is trivial: w is specified by the q low-order bits of the register containing x, and b is specified by the remaining bits. Thus, $T_1 = 0$ when paging is used.

This leaves T_2 as the only time of significance in a paging or segmentation scheme. Most systems do not provide special, high-speed memory for storing the entire mapping table. Accordingly, the time T_2 would seem to be comparable with the main memory reference time, and the objective of making $T_1 + T_2$ small would seem to be unrealizable. An ingenious solution has been found. A small associative memory, typically containing, at most, 16 cells, is included in the mapping mechanism. Its reference time is much faster than the main memory's. Each associative cell contains an entry of the form $(x, f(x))$. When the block number b of an address is determined, all the cells of the associative memory are searched in parallel using b as a key. If an entry $(b, f(b))$ is found, the base address $f(b)$ of the block is available immediately without reference to the mapping table in main memory. Otherwise, the mapping table is accessed and an entry $(b, f(b))$ replaces the least recently used entry in the associative memory. Experience has shown that the mean address translation time is typically in the range 1–3% of the main memory reference time with the associative memory in operation.

Most commercial virtual memory systems employ paging. This is because the addressing mechanism is especially simple and because managing block allocation and transfer in both the main and auxiliary memories is especially easy if all blocks are of the same size. However, the page size must be chosen carefully. Too small a page size will produce large mapping tables and a greater rate of page transfer between main and auxiliary memory. Too large a page size will produce poor storage utilization, since only a portion of the bytes on a page are likely to be referenced during its residence in main memory. Paging alone, even if properly designed, does not alter the linearity of the name space, and thus cannot offer the programmer the significant programming advantages possible in a segmented name space. A compromise using both segmentation and paging can be implemented for this purpose (see Denning, 1970).

Memory protection is easily implemented within a virtual memory mechanism. This is, in fact, one of the main attractions of virtual memory. No program can access any information other than what is in its address space because each and every reference is translated with respect to the mapping table of the currently running program. Also, each entry of the mapping table is actually of the form

$$b: (d, f(b), pc, L),$$

where d is a single bit set to 1 if and only if $f(b)$ is defined, pc is a protection code indicating which types of access are permitted to block b (e.g., read or write), and L is the length of block b (omitted in paging systems). If the offset portion w of the (b, w) address does not satisfy $0 \leq w < L$, or if the type of access being attempted is not authorized by pc, a protection interrupt is generated by the mapping mechanism. (See Wilkes, 1975.)

Performance. The associative memory prevents address translation time from being an important factor in the efficiency of program execution in a virtual memory. The factors that affect performance are, in decreasing order of their significance, the size of the main memory space allocated to the program, locality of reference of the program, and the memory policy used (the *paging algorithm* in a paging system). The first and third factors are under the system's control, whereas the second is under the programmer's control. (Sometimes the compiler can assist in improving the second factor.) Most memory management policies tend to keep the most recently referenced blocks of the name space N in the main memory space allocated to a program, and to adjust the size of this space to be as small as possible without causing an undue rate of addressing faults.

Although it is true that most virtual memory systems present programmers with a large linear name space and handle the memory management for them, it is not true that the virtual memory behaves as a random access store. The nature of the memory management policies causes the access time to an object in the virtual memory to be short when the object or a neighbor has been referenced recently, and long otherwise. The programmer, therefore, can be confident of highly efficient operation of his or her program in a virtual memory only if the algorithm and data have been successfully organized to maximize *locality of reference*. (This means that references are clustered to small groups of objects for extended intervals.)

History and Prospects. Virtual memories have been used to meet one or more of four needs:

1. *Solving the overlay (q.v.) problem* that arises when a program exceeds the size of the main store available to it. Paging on the Atlas machine at the University of Manchester (1959) was the first example.
2. *Storing variable-size program objects* off the runtime stack. The size of local arrays in Algol, for example, may not be known at compile time; storing them in segments elsewhere, with fixed-size descriptors on the stack, permits the compilation of addresses. Segmentation on the Burroughs B5500 (1963) was the first example.
3. *Long-term storage* of files and segments forces the programming of information transfers between the file system and the virtual memory. The Multics virtual memory (1968) eliminated this by merging the two storage systems. Users can declare their own segments and keep them indefinitely in the address space.
4. *Memory protection* requires that references to segments be in range and conform to enabled access modes (read, write, or execute). These constraints are easily checked by the hardware in parallel with the main computation. Several experimental machines have been designed explicitly to study descriptor-based addressing as a means of memory protection and improved software reliability (Myers, 1978).

It is sometimes argued that advancing memory technology will soon permit us to have all the real memory we could possibly want and, hence, we will soon be able to dispense with virtual memory. It has long been a favorite assumption of operating systems prognosticators that resources will by next year be plentiful. Users' ambitions for new ways of using resources have, however, continually defied this assumption. It is unlikely that today's predictions of the passing of the overlay problem will prove to be any more reliable than similar predictions made in 1960, 1965, 1970, and 1975.

What is true is that *paged* virtual stores, which were invented as a simple solution to the overlay problem, will diminish in utility as the last three needs in the list above become critical parts of programming environments. Vir-

tual memories of the future will rely more on segmentation and tagged memory to achieve greater software error tolerance and to narrow the semantic gap between concepts of programming languages and concepts embodied in hardware.

REFERENCES

1970. Denning, P. J. "Virtual Memory," *Computing Surveys* **2**, *No. 3:* 153–189 (September).
1972. Organick, E. I. *The Multics System: An Examination of Its Structure*. Cambridge: M.I.T. Press.
1973. Organick, E. I. *Computer System Organization: The B5700/B6700 System*. New York: Academic Press.
1975. Wilkes, M. V. *Time Sharing Computer Systems,* 3rd Ed. New York: Elsevier/North-Holland.
1976. Denning, P. J. "Fault Tolerant Operating Systems," *Computing Surveys* **8**, *No. 3* (December).
1978. Myers, G. J. *Advances in Computer Architecture*. New York: Wiley.

P. J. DENNING

VLSI. *See* INTEGRATED CIRCUITRY.

VOLUME

For articles on related subjects *see* DATA SET; FILES; and LABEL.

A volume is a physical unit of a storage medium (e.g., tape reel, drum, disk pack) capable of having data recorded on it and subsequently read.

Just as there are single and multivolume books, there are also single and multivolume physical files, or databases. Volumes consist of *extents;* each extent contains one or more *pages* (also called *blocks*). The size of a physical page is generally the function of the physical characteristics of the storage medium, of the computer main store architecture, and of the amount and structure of data.

Corresponding to the title page of a book, the first data element encountered on a volume, called the *data set label,* should—and almost always does—identify the database that (partially or in its entirety) resides on it, the volume number, page size, number of pages, "author," plus whatever additional information (such as read/write authority, available space, etc.) is appropriate to the intelligent perusal of the data contained in the volume.

S. C. BREWER

VON NEUMANN, JOHN

For articles on related subjects *see* DIGITAL COMPUTERS: Early; EDVAC; ENIAC; STORED PROGRAM CONCEPT; and VON NEUMANN MACHINE.

John von Neumann (b. 28 December 1903, Budapest, Hungary; d. 8 February 1957, Washington, D.C.) has become one of the legendary figures of twentieth century mathematics. The stories of his quickness of mind, power of absolute recall, linguistic range, and sense of humor abound in the literature and among his former associates. During his career he made significant contributions to logic, to quantum physics, to the theory of high-speed computing machines, and to economics through the mathematical theory of games and strategy. His work in any one of the fields would have secured him a distinguished position in present-day science.

Von Neumann received his early education at the Lutheran gymnasium in Budapest from 1911 through 1921. Toward the end of this period he was also privately tutored by M. Fekete, later to become another well-known Hungarian mathematician, with whom von Neumann published his first paper before he reached the age of 18.

Fig. 1. John von Neumann (From the Institute for Advanced Study, Princeton, N.J.)

There is a story that von Neumann's father opposed his desire to study mathematics. So, although he enrolled in the University of Budapest, he studied chemistry in Berlin (1921–1923) and Zurich (1923–1925), where he received his diploma in chemical engineering. In 1926, however, he received a Budapest Ph.D. in mathematics with a dissertation concerning the axiomatization of set theory.

During the late 1920s, he was Privatdozent at Berlin and Hamburg. He quickly established a reputation with publications in set theory, algebra, and quantum mechanics in this period. In 1928, he proved the minimax theorem of game theory. This was later elaborated and applied in his work (with Oskar Morganstern), "The Theory of Games and Economic Behavior" (1944).

In 1930 he was invited to be a visiting lecturer at Princeton University. When the Institute for Advanced Study was founded in 1933, he was appointed one of the original six professors of its School of Mathematics. He kept this position for the rest of his life.

Von Neumann's work in the 1930s firmly established his already highly regarded reputation as a mathematician. In 1931, he published a book on the mathematical foundation of quantum mechanics, and in that same decade he formulated and proved the mean ergodic theorem for unitary operators. He published a series of papers (some with F. J. Murray) in the latter half of the 1930s, on what he called "rings of operators" (now known as von Neumann algebras), which led him to work in what he called "continuous" geometry.

World War II was a watershed mark in von Neumann's career. Prior to 1940, his work fell primarily into the area of theoretical mathematics and physics, but for the remainder of his career he appeared as an applied mathematician. The citation on his honorary D.Sc. from Princeton (1947) identified him as a mathematician, but the encomium described him in terms of his impact as a physicist, engineer, and patriot. His papers from 1940 were mainly on statistics, hydrodynamics, ballistics, problems of detonation, meteorology, the applicability of game theory, and the theory and design of computers.

Although von Neumann had the ability to perform incredible mental calculations, his research led him to examine the possibility for machine assistance. His work on the hydrogen bomb in 1944 and the problem of implosion led him to make use of the computational ability of Howard Aiken's Automatic Sequence Control Calculator (Mark I) at Harvard. During the late summer of 1944, a chance encounter with Herman Goldstine made him aware of the world's first electronic computer being built under the direction of John Mauchly and J. Presper Eckert at the Moore School of Electrical Engineering of the University of Pennsylvania. His first visit to the ENIAC project occurred in August of that year, and this marked the beginning of his role in the theory of electronic computers and automata.

Von Neumann's role in the next level of conception and implementation is difficult to assess. There is evidence that Eckert and Mauchly were involved in discussions that included the development of a mercury delay-line memory with the ability to store both numbers and instructions. Shortly before von Neumann's first visit in 1944, the group had already committed itself to the construction of a successor to ENIAC as soon as time permitted. While von Neumann's authorship of the first EDVAC proposal in mid-1945 may not entitle his admirers to claim for him stored program conceptual priority, it is indicative of the great impact of his presence as a consultant to the group, his probing questions, and his ability to synthesize critical ideas. With the EDVAC paper, the modern era of electronic computers took a major stride forward.

By late 1945, von Neumann had decided to build a high-speed, general-purpose electronic computer at the Institute for Advanced Study. His documents of the period clearly articulate his vision on the ability of the proposed computer to " . . . revolutionize the purely mathematical approach to the theory of nonlinear differential equations . . . extend quantum theory to systems of more particles and more degrees of freedom . . . render a computational approach . . . to the phenomenon of turbulence . . . remove many bottlenecks in the computing approach to ordinary and electron optics. . . . Such a machine if intelligently used will completely revolutionize . . . the field of approximation mathematics." (Memorandum on the Program of the High Speed Computer, 8 November 1945.) The impact of the IAS computer and its progeny (such as Illiac, Maniac, Johnniac, etc.) is well known. The whole family is still generally referred to as *von Neumann machines.*

Von Neumann's clarity and precision of thought had a profound impact in many areas from which we will continue to benefit in the decades ahead. He was clearly one of the major scientific figures of this century.

REFERENCES

1958. Bochner, Salomon. "John von Neumann," in National Academy of Sciences *Biographical Memoirs* **32**: 438–457.

1972. Goldstine, Herman H. *The Computer from Pascal to von Neumann.* Princeton: Princeton University Press, pp. 167–183.

1973. Halmos, Paul R. "The Legend of John von Neumann," *American Mathematical Monthly* (April), pp. 382–394.

1980. Heims, Steve J. *John von Neumann and Norbert Wiener: From Mathematics to the Technologies of Life and Death.* Cambridge, MA: MIT Press.

H. S. TROPP

VON NEUMANN MACHINE

For articles on related subjects *see* PROGRAM COUNTER; STORED PROGRAM CONCEPT; and VON NEUMANN, JOHN.

It can be debated at great length as to what person or persons were the first to put forth any given concept, and this holds true in computing as much as it does in aviation, political philosophy, etc. However, probably the most influential paper in the history of computer science, whether or not anyone else expressed similar ideas any earlier, was written in 1946 by John von Neumann, then on the staff of the Institute for Advanced Study at Princeton University, in collaboration with Arthur W. Burks and Herman H. Goldstein. Its title is "Preliminary Discussion of the Logical Design of an Electronic Computing Instrument," and the ideas it contains, collectively known as *the von Neumann machine,* have provided the foundation for essentially all computer system development since that date.

Central to the von Neumann machine is the concept of the stored program—the principle that instructions and data are to be stored together intermixed in a single, uniform storage medium rather than separately, as was previously the case. Not only can computations proceed at electronic speeds, but instructions as well as data can be read and written under program control. From this basic idea it follows that an element in storage has an ambiguous quality with respect to its interpretation; this ambiguity is resolved only temporarily when it is fetched and either executed as an instruction or operated on as data. One exploitation of this ambiguity results in the technique of instruction modification in which a datum, created as the result of some operations in the arithmetic-logic unit of the computer, is placed in storage as would be any other datum but is then fetched and executed as an instruction. Iteration is realized by refetching the instruction as a datum, modifying it by operating on its address field, and then storing it and refetching and reexecuting it as an instruction. Contemporary programming practice, particularly in a multiprogramming environment, precludes the physical modification of instructions in storage. However, the basic idea of logical instruction modification is still central in computer science, but it is supported by more recent developments such as index registers, base registers, and indirect addressing, which provide similar effects but leave instructions unchanged in storage.

Another concept central to the von Neumann machine is the *program counter,* a register that is used to indicate the location of the next instruction to be executed and which is automatically incremented by each instruction fetch. With the rare exception of machines that use rotating memory devices for main storage, essentially all computers use this technique, since it clearly reduces the storage space that would otherwise be necessary if each instruction contained a field to indicate the address of its successor. The idea of branching, which is often very difficult for a beginning machine language programmer to understand, can in this context become obvious in that it is effected merely by the replacement of the contents of the location counter from some other source, often but not always a field in the current instruction.

No short article can do justice to these and the many other ideas expressed so clearly by von Neumann and his colleagues in 1946. Every computer scientist should read the original report, which fortunately can be found in several sources, among them being those below.

REFERENCES

1963. Taub, A. H. (Ed.) *The Collected Works of John von Neumann* **5**. New York: Macmillan, pp. 34–79.
1971. Bell, C. G. and Newell, A. *Computer Structures*. New York: McGraw-Hill, pp. 92–119.

R. F. ROSIN

WATSON, THOMAS J., SR.

For articles on related subjects *see* COMPUTER INDUSTRY; DIGITAL COMPUTERS: Early; and HOLLERITH, HERMAN.

Thomas John Watson was born in East Campbell, Steuben County, New York, on 17 February 1874, of Scots-Irish descent. The son of Thomas and Jane White Watson, he was educated at the Addison Academy and the School of Commerce in Elmira, New York.

He started work in May 1892 as a bookkeeper in Painted Post, New York, at a salary of $6.00 a week. Fol-

Fig. 1. Thomas John Watson.

lowing this first job, he sold sewing machines and musical instruments in the same village before joining the National Cash Register Company in Buffalo, New York, as a salesman. Four years later, National Cash Register promoted him to manager in Rochester. Promotion to special representative followed, and four and a half years later he was appointed the company's general sales manager.

It was at this time that Watson, bent on inspiring a dispirited NCR sales force, introduced the motto "THINK." He is quoted (*THINK,* 1956) as having told a meeting of salesmen that the phrase "I didn't think" had cost the world millions of dollars. Overnight, framed placards with the single word "THINK" sprouted throughout the offices of the company. Later, when he took the helm at IBM, he reintroduced this motto.

Watson resigned from NCR in 1913, a few months after his marriage to Jeannette M. Kittridge, to assume the presidency of the ailing Computing-Tabulating-Recording Company, a 1911 merger of the Computing Scale Company of America, the Tabulating Machine Company, and the International Time Recording Company.

From 1913 until his death 43 years later, Thomas J. Watson built the C-T-R Company, which became the International Business Machines Corporation in 1924, into the leading manufacturer first of automatically operated electromechanical business machines and then of electronic computers and business machines. It became one of the largest, most successful corporations in the world. During this time he always placed heavy emphasis on education, research, and engineering in order to insure the growth of the company. Under his leadership IBM's history was a succession of technical innovations and inventions that included new applications of punched cards to business, government, and education, the introduction of the first commercially successful electric typewriter in 1934, opening the electronic computer era commercially in 1948 with the marketing of the 604 programmable electronic calculator, and the top position in the electronic computing and data processing field in the 1950s.

A great deal of Watson's success was due to his understanding of customer's needs, which resulted in steady improvements in IBM's product lines.

One of Watson's lifelong interests was in education, and he sought to put his business acumen at the service of the universities and their faculties, giving equipment for the Columbia University Statistical Bureau (1928); the Astronomical Computing Bureau at Columbia (1934); designing and building as a gift the first large-scale computer, the IBM Automatic Sequence Controlled Calculator (the Mark I) for Harvard (1944); and dedicating the Selective Sequence Electronic Calculator to "assist the scientist in institutions of higher learning, in government, and in industry to explore the consequences of man's thought to the outermost reaches of time, space, and physical conditions" (1948). In the early 1930s he began serving as a trustee of various universities, including Lafayette College, which always remained a sentimental favorite, partly because it was there that he received the first of over 30 honorary degrees he would accumulate before his death. He also served for many years as a trustee of Columbia University.

A month before he died on 19 June 1956, Watson turned over the post of chief executive officer of IBM to his eldest son, Thomas Watson, Jr., who in 1952 had succeeded his father as president of the corporation.

REFERENCES

1956. Anon. *THINK* (July-August-September), pp. 4–48.
1962. Belden, T. and Belden, M. *The Lengthening Shadow.* Boston: Little, Brown.
1969. Rodgers, W. *THINK— A Biography of the Watsons and IBM.* New York: Stein and Day.

J. C. McPherson

WELL-FORMED FORMULA

For articles on related subjects *see* GRAMMARS; PARSING; PRODUCTION; and PROGRAMMING LINGUISTICS.

A well-formed formula (WFF) over a set G of grammatical or syntactical rules is a finite sequence or string of symbols that is grammatically or syntactically correct; i.e., it belongs to the set of all sequences of symbols that can be constructed or formed by using the rules in G.

For instance, if $G = \{S \rightarrow aSb, S \rightarrow ab\}$ is the set of grammatical rules in a generative grammar, then a string x is well formed if and only if it is of the form $a^n b^n$ for $n \geq 1$. Other examples of well-formed formulas are arithmetic expressions, well-formed parentheses expressions (Dyck sets)—where each left parenthesis has to be properly matched by a right parenthesis—and well-formed formulas in propositional calculus.

Given an arbitrary grammar G, the question whether an arbitrary string is well formed with respect to G is equivalent to the question of whether it belongs to the language generated by G. This question is decidable for many important classes of languages or sets; i.e., there exists an algorithm that determines after finitely many steps whether a given string is well formed. Examples of such languages include WFFs in the propositional calculus, syntactically correct PL/I statements, etc.

P. C. FISCHER AND D. WOTSCHKE

WHIRLWIND I

For article on related subject *see* DIGITAL COMPUTERS: Early.

Project Whirlwind was sponsored at the Massachusetts Institute of Technology by the Special Devices Division of the Office of Research and Inventions, U.S. Navy. It was originally started in 1944 to investigate the solution of aircraft stability and control problems associated with flight simulation by analog methods. By 1946 it had become apparent that the use of an analog computer would lead to excessive complexity, and therefore other computing techniques should be studied. Thus, in 1946, a proposal was made for a 16-bit binary general-purpose computer using electrostatic storage and a 1 MHz pulse rate. Although initially proposed as serial, the requirement for 20,000 multiplications per second led eventually to a parallel machine.

Whirlwind was constructed under the leadership of J. W. Forrester. When first put in service during the third quarter of 1949, the computer had 3,300 tubes and 8,900 crystal diodes (germanium point-contact diodes). By June of 1950, one hour of error-free operation with 256 words of electrostatic storage had been achieved. In March of 1951, it was operational on a routine basis on a 35-hour per week schedule. During 1953 a magnetic tape system and a magnetic drum system were installed and electrostatic storage was replaced by two banks of core memory consisting of 1,024 words of 16 bits each. By December 1954, the computer had grown to 12,500 vacuum tubes and 23,803 crystal diodes.

Whirlwind occupied a two-story building. The CPU, control console, and CRT displays occupied the second floor. One bit of the arithmetic logic unit was a bay of equipment 2 ft wide and 12 ft high. The drum storage system and data communications interface occupied the ground floor. The basement was filled with power supplies, and the roof of the building was covered with air-conditioning equipment to remove the heat generated by a power consumption on the order of 150 KW.

Whirlwind was a 16-bit parallel, single-address, binary computer. Instructions as well as data occupied words of 16 bits in memory. The operation code had 5 bits and the address had 11 bits. Eventually, all 32 possible operation codes were utilized. Multiplication and division were included in the operation codes. The initial program-load problem was solved by the use of a bank of 32 registers of toggle switches. In routine operation, various bootstrap programs were stored in the toggle-switch memory.

Automatic marginal checking was initiated during the fourth quarter of 1949. The computer had the ability to select any section of itself, vary the voltages to that section, and test for failure. By comparing the results from day to day, it was possible to determine if trends toward failure were developing in the components.

Whirlwind used magnetic tape and magnetic drum for auxiliary memory. Input/output equipment included large cathode-ray tubes, photoelectric tape readers, Flexowriters, and, in connection with the Air Force semiautomatic ground-environment air defense system (SAGE), data communication links were established with a number of radar sets and with other computers. One of the cathode-ray tubes had a microfilm camera attached so that large-volume output could be displayed on a CRT and microfilmed. This was a common method of obtaining memory dumps. Prints of the microfilm were available the next morning. With electrostatic storage, the computer was capable of approximately 20,000 operations per second, which increased to 40,000 per second when a magnetic-core memory system was installed.

On the software side, there were pioneering efforts in the development of a symbolic assembler, a comprehensive interpretive system that provided a comprehensive mathematical package including floating-point operations, a batch-operating system, and an off-line printout system that permitted recording the results at high speed on magnetic tape and later printing the results off line without the use of the computer.

Despite its physical size, Whirlwind was, in modern terms, a 16-bit minicomputer. It was, however, a most important project in the development of parallel, binary computers. The Whirlwind project itself and those it spawned (the Memory Test Computer, the TX-0 and TX-2 computers at the Lincoln Laboratory of M.I.T., and the AN/FSQ-7 manufactured by IBM for the SAGE system) led to many hardware and software developments, most notably magnetic-core memories and the first operating systems. Whirlwind influenced the early IBM 700 series computers and the computers developed by the Digital Equipment Corporation, much of whose initial staff came from the Lincoln Laboratory.

Whirlwind operated until 1959. Parts of it are now in the Smithsonian Institution in Washington, DC and the Digital Computer Museum in Marlboro, MA.

REFERENCE

1980. Redmond, K. C. and Smith, T. A. *Project Whirlwind: The History of a Pioneer Computer.* Bedford, MA: Digital Press.

J. N. ACKLEY

WIENER, NORBERT

For articles on related subjects *see* CYBERNETICS; and DIGITAL COMPUTERS: Early.

Norbert Wiener (b. Columbia, Missouri, 26 November 1894; d. Stockholm, Sweden, 18 March 1964) was one of America's most important mathematicians, and a controversial scientist who left a rich heritage of accomplishments, not only through his more than one hundred publications, but also through his personal contacts with scientists throughout the world.

Of his boyhood, Wiener said: "I got my classical education from my father, who was professor of Slavic languages at Harvard. My scientific education I got for myself." (*Current Biography,* 1950.)

Wiener received his A.B. degree from Tufts College in 1909 and his Ph.D. from Harvard in 1913 with a thesis in mathematical logic. The years 1913 to 1915 were significant ones. Traveling under Harvard's Sheldon Fellowship, he worked under Alfred North Whitehead, Bertrand Russell, G. H. Hardy, and J. E. Littlewood in Cambridge, and David Hilbert and Edmund Landau at Göttingen.

After America's entry into World War I, Wiener

Fig. 1. Norbert Wiener.

joined the facility at Aberdeen Proving Ground, where he worked on designing artillery range tables. In 1919, with the help of Harvard Professor W. F. Osgood, he secured an appointment as an instructor at M.I.T., an association he maintained until his retirement in 1960.

He was a Guggenheim Fellow at Copenhagen and Göttingen in 1926, and he was also a visiting lecturer at Cambridge (1931–1932) and at Tsing Hua University in Peiping, China (1935–1936). Many significant influences occurred during this pre-war era. At Cambridge, Bertrand Russell encouraged him to read Rutherford's work on the theory of the electron and the nature of matter. At M.I.T. he formed a close friendship with Harold Hazen, and was early exposed to the theory of feedback and servomechanisms. It was also during this period that he met Arturo Rosenblueth, who was engaged in neurophysiological research.

Wiener's direct contributions to the early development of electronic digital computers are difficult to determine. His wartime work on prediction theory and the research in radar and fire control were all to have a major impact by the end of the 1940s. By then, however, his name was synonomous with cybernetics (Wiener, 1948). In his writings on cybernetics, Wiener laid the foundation for the philosophical relations between mechanistic and mathematical scientific theories. This work may not have directly contributed to the actual machine developments, but it did much to stimulate research in automata and in attempts to stimulate human thought processes. Wiener was also very conscious of the long-range impact of the computer on man and society. In "The Human Use of Human Beings" (Wiener, 1950), he warned of the dangers that could be caused by selfish exploitation of the computer's potential.

Norbert Wiener was active in professional societies both in the United States and abroad. He also received many honors, such as the Bôcher Prize of the American Mathematical Society (1933). His major publications, in addition to the above, include works on the Fourier integral and its application, Brownian motion, time series, relativity and quantum theory, mathematical foundations, postulational theory, vector and differential spaces, and potential theory.

REFERENCES

1948. Wiener, Norbert. *Cybernetics, or Control and Communication in the Animal and Machine.* Cambridge, MA: M.I.T. Press.
1950. Anon. *Current Biography,* pp. 615–617.
1950. Wiener, Norbert. *The Human Use of Human Beings; Cybernetics and Society.* Boston: Houghton Mifflin.
1953. Wiener, Norbert. *Ex-Prodigy.* Cambridge, MA: M.I.T. Press.
1956. Wiener, Norbert. *I Am A Mathematician.* Cambridge, MA: M.I.T. Press.
1980. Heims, Steve J. *John von Neumann and Norbert Wiener: From Mathematics to the Technologies of Life and Death.* Cambridge, MA: MIT Press.

H. TROPP

WILKES, MAURICE V.

For articles on related subjects *see* DIGITAL COMPUTERS: Early; EDSAC; and MICROPROGRAMMING.

Maurice Vincent Wilkes (b. 1913) studied mathematics and physics at Cambridge and conducted research on the ionosphere. He worked on radar during World War II, and then directed the Mathematical Laboratory (now the Computer Laboratory) of the University of Cambridge from 1945 onward throughout the whole development of stored program computers. It was here that the first of these to go into service, the Electronic Delay Storage Automatic Calculator (EDSAC), built by Wilkes and his team, began operating in May 1949. He became a Fellow of the Royal Society in 1956, was the first president of the British Computer Society 1957–1960, and the first United Kingdom member of the Council of IFIP 1960–1963. He was the ACM Turing Lecturer in 1967 and received the Harry Goode Award from

Fig. 1. Maurice Vincent Wilkes.

AFIPS in 1968. In 1974, he was elected a foreign Honorary Member of the American Academy of Arts and Sciences. In 1977, he became a foreign Associate of the U.S. National Academy of Engineering, and in 1980 of the U.S. National Academy of Sciences.

In 1980, he retired from Cambridge as Emeritus Professor of Computer Technology and became Senior Consulting Engineer at Digital Equipment Corporation.

Wilkes led the first practical development of programming for stored program machines, including the first program library. He originated labels (which he called "floating addresses"), an early form of macros (which he called "synthetic orders"), and microprogramming (which was used in the design of the second Cambridge machine, EDSAC II). He later became interested in machine-independent computing, and in this connection developed a simple list-processing language known as Wisp. He was an early advocate of data transmission. He contributed to the development of time sharing systems, both as a visiting member of Project MAC at M.I.T. and through the system developed in his own laboratory during 1965–1970. In particular, he and his colleagues introduced many ideas relating to facilities for filing and editing for the ordinary user.

In addition to numerous papers and articles, he has written the following books: *Oscillations of the Earth's Atmosphere* (1949), *Preparation of Programs for an Electronic Digital Computer* (joint author; 1951, 2d ed. 1958), *Automatic Digital Computers* (1956), *A Short Introduction to Numerical Analysis* (1966), *Time-Sharing Computer Systems* (1966, 2d ed. 1972).

S. GILL

WILLIAMS TUBE MEMORY

For articles on related subjects *see* MEMORY: Main; and ULTRASONIC MEMORY.

The first stored-program computers were based on two kinds of memory—ultrasonic delay lines and a cathode-ray tube (CRT) system named after F. C. Williams of Manchester University. Experimentation with both schemes was being carried on in 1947 in England and in the United States, and by 1949–1950 computers of both types were operational. By 1954 magnetic-core memories had superseded both delay line and Williams' tube memories.

Storage of information at a spot on the inside of the face of the CRT was determined by the relative charge level. The secondary emission ratio for phosphors (and for glass) is greater than 1. Thus, if the face is bombarded with a primary electron beam (1,000–2,000-volt acceleration), then the spot becomes positively charged because more low-energy secondary electrons are emitted by the surface than arrive in the primary electron beam. Equilibrium is reached when the relatively positive charge of the spot attracts enough electrons to balance the flow. If a spot is charged, then the nearby area is "discharged" by the secondary electrons from the primary spot.

Williams used the CRTs in a bit-serial mode. To write information on the tube, the electron beam is deflected along a horizontal line, and at each point where the beam is turned off, a residual positive charge remains (Fig. 1). To read the information from the CRT, an electrode is place on the outside of the face of the CRT (Fig. 2). As the beam again sweeps over a line, the change of potential on the inside face is capacitively picked up by the electrode. Since the spots of positive charge occur just before the turn-off points, the resulting signal occurs in time to again turn off the beam at the same place. (Williams called this an "anticipation" pulse.) As the beam sweeps a horizontal line, the induced potential on the electrode is amplified, and via the gating circuits and the control grid of the CRT (Fig. 2), the beam is turned off in a pattern identical to that of the previous sweep. Thus, the line being read is not destroyed by the reading process. However, since reading a given line tended to discharge the neighboring lines, it was necessary to systematically regenerate the whole array. A typical scheme was to regenerate during odd-word times and to access information during even-word times.

The beam, being on or off at a given position (or clock time), can represent the zeros or ones of a binary number. Alternative storage schemes involved using focus/defocused spots, or dots and dashes, at grid points

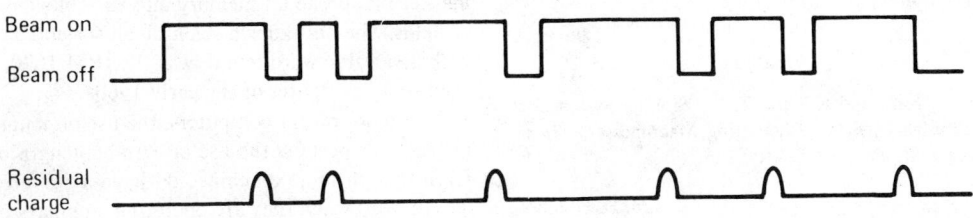

Fig. 1. Williams' charge storage pattern.

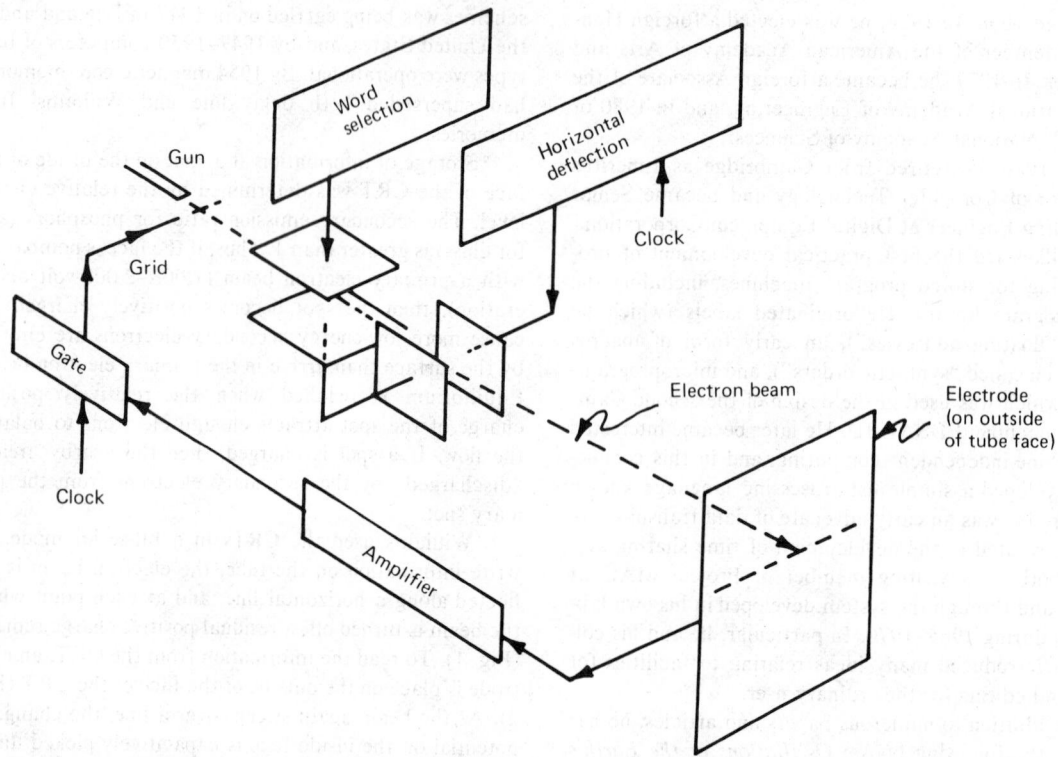

Fig. 2.   Williams' CRT information storage system.

on the face of the cathode-ray tube. By changing the vertical or word deflection (Fig. 2), several different numbers can be stored on one CRT. (Williams stored thirty-two 32-bit numbers.)

The SWAC at the Institute for Numerical Analysis used the Williams tube in a parallel mode with the kth bit of the memory words stored in the kth CRT. Williams tubes in the parallel mode were also used in the computer at the Institute for Advanced Study. Parallel systems stored 256 to 1,024 bits per tube.

Other memory systems (e.g., Whirlwind) used special tubes with a second "flooding gun" to maintain the storage. Rajchman (RCA) designed a special memory tube called the "Selectron," which was originally intended to be used in the computer at the Institute for Advanced Study.

Commercially, Ferranti (England) marketed the Williams serial scheme, and IBM used the parallel mode in its 701 computers (1953).

REFERENCES

1949. Williams, F. C. and Kilburn, T. "A Storage System for Use With Binary Digital Computing Machines," *J. Inst. Elect. Engrs.* **96**, *Part III:* 81–100.

H. D. HUSKEY

WORD LENGTH, VARIABLE

For article on related subject *see* ADDRESSING.

Word length is an important characteristic of most computers. Most minicomputers use 16- or 32-bit words while microprocessors generally have 8- or 16-bit words. The IBM 360/370 series and most systems influenced by the IBM design philosophy use a 32-bit word length. The large Univac and Honeywell machines use 36-bit words; Control Data's Cyber systems are 60-bit word machines, and Burroughs' big systems use 48-bit words.

Computers have been built in which there was no preferred or fixed word length. Most of these were data processing machines that operated on character strings. An example is the IBM 1400 series, in which there was a marker bit (called a *word mark* or *flag*) associated with each character position in memory. The setting of these marker bits broke up memory into variable-length words or fields. The best known scientifically oriented computer with a variable word length was the IBM 1620, a widely used small computer of the early 1960s.

In more recent computers, the use of count fields in instructions permits the use of variable-length operands. Even though most machines do have a preferred fixed-length word when they are operating on binary operands, they can behave as variable-length word machines when they are dealing with operands that consist of strings of coded decimal digits or coded characters.

S. ROSEN

WORD PROCESSING

For articles on related subjects *see* ADMINISTRATIVE APPLICATIONS; NATURAL LANGUAGE PROCESSING; PUBLISHING, COMPUTERS IN; and TEXT EDITING SYSTEMS.

The term *word processing* was invented by the IBM Corporation in 1964 as a way to market a new product, a typewriter which could record words on magnetic tape. This recording capability meant that revisions could be made (on a limited basis) and text could be recycled, permitting unlimited numbers of seemingly hand-typed, personalized letters to be created. IBM initially estimated that the market for such a product was likely to total 5,000 systems. Today, many word processing vendors sell 20,000 systems or more in a single year.

In 16 years, a giant industry has been created. About 10% of the typing positions in business firms now employ some form of word processing equipment. A *word processor* is a device that can create (through a typewriter-like keyboard entry device), store, revise, and output text (see Fig. 1). There are great differences in the prices and capabilities of the word processing systems now on the market. They vary from Electronic Typewriters (for about $1,500), which can create and output text but which can store only very limited amounts (generally one line to several pages) and which can perform only limited manipulations (such as centering text on a line, assisting

1. Author creates text (dictation to stenographer, machine dictation, written in longhand).
2. Word processing operator enters text using keyboard (and optional display) of word processing system.
3. Word processing operator corrects, formats, and prints out text.
4. Text is proofread.
5. Text is returned to author for review.
6. Author makes revisions.
7. Word processing operator enters revisions, reformats, and prints revised copy.
8. Text is proofread (revisions only).
9. Text is returned to author for review.
10. Cycle is repeated until all revisions have been made.
11. Document is distributed.

Fig. 1. The word processing process.

in the production of statistical work, and making error correction easier) to complex, expensive, and very sophisticated systems.

Word processors are designed to let office personnel speedily create, manipulate, and output text; in addition, many word processors also offer extensive formatting capabilities and some limited data processing capability (such as the ability to sort or select records, perform arithmetic calculations, etc.). *Text editing* is a term used to refer to text manipulation, particularly the manipulation that occurs in long documents with extensive revisions, and is now often used interchangeably with word processing.

Most of the word processing systems currently installed are individual (called stand-alone) devices (see Fig. 2). They create, store, manipulate, and output text independently. However, a number of multi-station systems have been developed in the last few years, and this sector of the market is growing significantly. Multi-station systems permit the price of an individual work station to be reduced, through the ability to share storage, processor capability, and peripherals (such as printers, OCR input devices, and photocomposition output devices). Two types of multi-station systems are now in use. *Shared logic systems* (the original design) offer a shared processor attached to "dumb" (non-intelligent) work stations and peripherals. All of the processing power is centrally located (and therefore the entire system is subject to failure if the processor is not operating). The newer *shared resource systems* combine a number of intelligent,

Fig. 2. A typical display word processor (A. M. Jacquard).

independent work stations through the use of a systems integration device. Commonly, this device is a shared, intelligent hard disk for high-capacity, shared storage. Since individual work stations can function independently, some users feel that this kind of system offers enhanced reliability—although it is generally more expensive.

Most microcomputer vendors now offer a form of word processing (from very naive to very sophisticated) on their small systems. This goes with the trend of moving these low-cost devices from their original purpose as personal or "hobby" computers toward a more commercially attractive marketplace as inexpensive computer devices for small businesses or for individual usage. Many microcomputers look remarkably like the word processors distributed through more traditional office equipment channels, but it is well to note that their vendors generally offer a lower level of support and service than word processing vendors, thus requiring users to be more self-reliant.

In 1981, we are in the midst of a structural change in the price of word processing systems, caused by the announcement of the IBM Displaywriter in June of 1980. It is now possible to buy electronic typewriters and obsolete non-display word processors for less than $5,000 (in some cases, as little as $1,500). Classic, display-based word processors with reasonable function, diskette storage, and included printers range in price from about $8,000 to about $14,000. The true cost of a shared system can be expressed in one of two ways: per work station (which ranges, depending on system size, from about $8,000 to about $15,000 per station for dedicated word processing systems) or incremental cost (cost to add an additional work station to an existing system), which is currently $2,000 to $6,000. In all cases, prices for word processing systems are expected to continue to decline; however, the cost of the up-and-coming office automation systems is expected to be less price elastic and substantially more expensive for some time.

Originally, word processing focused only on typing activities. In the early days of word processing, the support staff of entire companies was rearranged to justify more readily the cost of relatively costly word processing systems. Centralized word processing was in its heyday in the mid-1960s to early 1970s and secretaries were divided into word processing or correspondence secretaries (who typed) and administrative support secretaries (who didn't). Centralized word processing permitted the firm to use the smallest number of expensive word processing systems, but it didn't always serve the firm's needs. Often, secretaries couldn't cope with such heterogeneous workloads. Scheduling was difficult. And not every professional or manager was prepared to give up a personal secretary and share part of a correspondence secretary and part of an administrative secretary—neither of whom would be under his/her individual direction and control. So, in the mid-1970s, word processing began to employ a new organizational design, the *work group*. Work groups were built around normal organizational divisions (such as the department) and depended on cooperation and related work. A typical department might trade in its five secretaries for a five-person work group with two correspondence (word processing) secretaries, two administrative assistants, and a "swing" person who did some word processing and some administrative work. Each secretary was familiar with all of the work of the group and could fill in for absent or busy co-workers. It worked! Many firms retain central word processing activities for homogeneous, production-oriented work in high volumes, while converting to work groups for individual department support. Others continue to employ individual secretaries and demand that the vendors offer lower-priced systems that can be cost-justified without rearranging the user organization. And that has begun to happen, too.

Word processing not only offers the ability to enter, revise, and rearrange text with a minimum of rekeyboarding. It also, in many cases, offers sophisticated formatting controls to permit great flexibility in final format with a minimum of operator time and trouble. Some of the commonly offered facilities include changing margins, changing page length, automatically repaginating and renumbering pages (with the system controlling orphans and widows—single lines at the beginning or end of pages), hyphenating through the use of algorithms or dictionaries, and spelling verification through the use of newly "smart" dictionaries that can offer alternative spellings based on phonetic analysis.

Also, word processing has begun to expand in function. Originally concerned only with the speedy, efficient production of text, it has now grown to include many low-level data processing activities as well as such office automation (*q.v.*) activities as electronic mail and data access to internal and external databases. The next step will be to offer word processing-like work stations to non-secretaries and to build new organizational structures in which professionals and secretaries work jointly on the same electronically stored data and text. That is not here yet—but it is likely to occur in significant volume as we reach the end of this century.

REFERENCE

1982. Stultz, R. A. *The Word Processing Handbook.* Englewood Cliffs, NJ: Prentice-Hall.

A. D. WOHL

WORKING SET

For articles on related subjects *see* OPERATING SYSTEMS: Principles and Theory; STORAGE ALLOCATION; THRASHING; and VIRTUAL MEMORY.

Working set, short for "set of working information," is a concept as old as electronic computing. It denotes the smallest subset of a program's address space that can be loaded into the main memory without generating excessive overhead from *overlaying,* the process of replacing old program segments by new ones fetched from the secondary memory. The working set varies in size and content as the program executes.

The working set is a measure of the program's dynamic memory demand—the information that *ought* to be in the main memory. A separate concept is the program's *resident set*—the information *actually* in main memory. A memory policy is a "working set policy" only if its resident set closely approximates (but seldom underestimates) the working set at any given time.

A memory policy that assigns a fixed size resident set to a program is not a working set policy. In some systems, resident sets are called "working sets," while in others (such as IBM's MVS), mean resident set sizes are called "working sets"—even though there is no attempt to determine a program's true dynamic memory demand. These false "working set policies" do not perform as well as true working set policies.

Working sets can be determined from program structure or from measurement. A program's working set on the Burroughs B6700 series is determined by the semantics of Algol; it comprises the current procedure segment, the stack, and all arrays accessible from activated procedures. A program's working set on most paging machines is determined by measurement; it is typically the set of pages or segments whose usage bits are found ON when sampled at regular intervals in the program's *virtual time.* (Virtual time is program execution time with all interruptions removed; it is usually measured by counting memory references.) It is possible to specify precisely the relationships among working set size, processing efficiency, and mean time between references to objects not in the working set (Denning, 1968, 1978).

It is important that working sets be measured separately in each program's virtual time. Many systems lump all active programs together while sampling usage bits; in this case, the working set estimate of one program is confounded by the behavior of all programs. This leads to suboptimal resident sets and can significantly degrade throughput and response time.

The working-set principle of dynamic multiprogramming asserts that a task may be active only if its working set is in main memory. A memory management policy that implements this principle will guarantee each active task a minimal level of processing efficiency, and will usually protect a virtual memory system from *thrashing (q.v.).* When installed on the experimental CP-67, the working set policy significantly improved the system's throughput and response time (Rodriguez, 1973). The available theory and experimental data strongly support the hypothesis that the working set policy is near optimal among nonlookahead policies (Denning, 1980).

Working set policies exploit the property called *locality* (of reference) in program behavior. This is the experimentally observed property that a program's virtual time can be divided into a succession of *phases,* intervals during which the program restricts all its references to a subset of its information. The information referenced during a given phase is called the *locality set* of that phase. The working set estimates the current locality set. When most virtual time is covered by phases long compared to the secondary memory access time (the usual case), the working set is an excellent predictor of memory demand in the immediate future. In paging systems, it is sometimes advantageous to "restructure" a program by assigning small, logical segments to large pages so as to preserve in the page references the locality originally present in the segment references. This technique can reduce a program's space-time product by factors of 3 to 10 as compared to assigning segments to pages in the order of appearance in the program's text. (The space-time product is the integral, over virtual time, of the size of the resident set.)

Because the performance of a virtual memory system depends on program locality, and because locality is a direct result of the way a programmer designs an algorithm and its associated data structure, it is not true (as is often claimed) that virtual memory systems insulate the programmer *completely* from memory management. The performance payoff of virtual memory accrues to those who invest the small effort required to achieve good locality in their programs.

REFERENCES

1968. Denning, P. J. "The Working Set Model for Program Behavior," *Comm. ACM* **11**, *No. 5:* 323–333 (May).

1973. Rodriguez-Rosell, J. and Dupuy, J. P. "The Design, Implementation, and Evaluation of a Working Set Dispatcher," *Comm. ACM* **16**, *No. 4:* 247–253 (April).

1978. Denning, P. J. and Slutz, D. R. "Generalized Working Sets for Segment Reference Strings," *Comm. ACM* **21**, *No. 8:* 750–759 (September).

1980. Denning, P. J. "Working Sets Past and Present," *IEEE Trans. Softw. Engrg.* **SE-6**, *No. 1:* 64–84 (January).

P. J. DENNING AND D. E. DENNING

ZUSE, KONRAD

For article on related subject *see* DIGITAL COMPUTERS: Origins, and Early.

Konrad Zuse (b. 1910 in Berlin) studied construction engineering at the Technische Hochschule Berlin-Charlottenburg and received the degree in Dipl.Ing. in 1935. In 1934, he had already started development work on program-controlled computing machines with electromechanical and mechanical elements. He felt that the tiresome calculations required in this field should be done by a machine. In 1938 he had completed his first model (Z1). In 1941 his first fully working machine (Z3) was operational; it used the binary number system with floating-point arithmetic. Zuse invented a relay adder in which four relays produced the sum of two binary places and which, in an n-place binary adder, yields the n-place sum in one switching step.

During the next four years, Zuse built a number of special machines and the all-purpose relay computer Z4. The Z3 was destroyed by bombs (it was reconstructed in the 1960s), but the Z4 was saved, and in 1949 it was installed at the Eidgenössische Technische Hochschule in Zürich. In 1954, it was transferred to a research institute in St. Louis near Basle, where it was operated for five years. Around 1945, when facilities for circuit development were not available to Zuse, he turned to programming and designing an algorithmic language which he called Plankalkül (Bauer and Wössner, 1972). Its notation was in a kind of matrix form, and it could be used for both numerical and nonnumerical problems (Zuse used it to describe a full chess program).

Fig. 1. Konrad Zuse.

In 1949, Zuse formed his own company ZUSE KG, and went into manufacturing. His first successful product was Z11, a relay computer for geodetical and optical applications. His second product was Z22, a vacuum-tube computer (later replaced by its transistorized version Z23); it had an extremely flexible instruction code, achieved by a set of functional bits, an early form of microprogramming. The Z22 was delivered first in 1958, and more than 50 were made. In 1958, Zuse published one of his ideas that was ahead of his time. This was the field computer, a parallel processor, especially suited for differential equations. In the same year, he designed a computer-controlled plotter called Z64, or Graphomat.

After a number of financial difficulties, Zuse left ZUSE KG, which was absorbed by Siemens AG in 1969. Three years before he had become a professor at the University of Göttingen.

In 1957, Zuse received the honorary degree of Dr.techn. in Berlin; in 1964, he received the Werner von Siemens-Ring; in 1965, the Harry Goode Medal from AFIPS; in 1969, the German Diesel Medal; in the same year, the Austrian Exner Medal; and, in 1975, on his 65th birthday, appointment as an Honorary Citizen of Huenfeld.

The achievements of Dr. Zuse can be properly evaluated only if his isolation is taken into account. His background was construction engineering, and he knew practically nothing about other computer developments (in Germany or abroad, in his time or earlier) until a very late stage. During all his life, Dr. Zuse received too little understanding and support. The German military had no interest in his work, and while the German Research Council after the war did its best to support him, their efforts were not enough to keep his company alive.

REFERENCES

1972. Bauer, F. L. and Wössner, H. "The Plankalkül of Konrad Zuse: A Forerunner of Today's Programming Languages," *Comm. ACM* **15**: 678–685.

1978. *Proceedings of the SEAS Anniversary Meeting in West Berlin: "General Considerations of the Evolution of Computers."*

H. ZEMANEK

Appendix I

ABBREVIATIONS AND ACRONYMS

Computer scientists and technologists love abbreviations and acronyms. The list that follows contains all abbreviations and acronyms related in any way to computer science and technology used in the articles in the Encyclopedia other than those used by authors just for local purposes in their articles. It also contains a few entries in such common use that they serve a reference purpose here. (Programming language acronyms given in the Appendix on Key High-Level Languages are not included in this list.)

More comprehensive listings can be found in:

1981. Wrathall, Claude P. *Computer Acronyms, Abbreviations, Etc.* New York: Petrocelli. (About 10,000 entries.)

1980. Sippl, Charles J. and Sippl, Roger J. *Computer Dictionary and Handbook*. Indianapolis: Howard W. Sams and Co. (About 2000 entries in Appendix M.)

ACC	Accumulator
ACE	Automatic Computing Engine
ACL	Association for Computational Linguistics
ACM	Association for Computing Machinery
ACTRAN	Analog Computer Translator
A/D	Analog-to-Digital
ADAPSO	Association of Data Processing Service Organizations
ADI	American Documentation Institute
ADP	Automatic Data Processing
AED	Automated Engineering Design
AEDS	Association for Educational Data Systems
AESC	American Engineering Standards Committee
AFCET	Association Française pour la Cybernetique Economique et Technique
AFIPS	American Federation of Information Processing Societies
AHPL	A Hardware Programming Language
AI	Artificial Intelligence
AIAA	American Institute of Aeronautics and Astronautics
AIEE	American Institute of Electrical Engineers (now part of IEEE)
AL	Assembly Language
ALU	Arithmetic-Logic Unit
AM	Amplitude Modulation
AMS	American Mathematical Society
ANSI	American National Standards Institute
ANSVIP	American National Standard Vocabulary for Information Processing
APEC	Automated Procedures for Engineering Consultants

APSE	Ada Program Support Environment
ARIES	Automated Reliability Estimation Program
ARPA	Advanced Research Projects Agency
ASA	American Standards Association
ASA	American Statistical Association
ASC	Advanced Scientific Computer
ASCII	American Standard Code for Information Interchange
ASIS	American Society for Information Science
ASL	Available Space List
ASM	Association for Systems Management
ATDM	Asynchronous Time-Division Multiplexing
ATM	Automated Teller Machine
ATS	Administrative Terminal System
ATSU	Association of Time-Sharing Users
AUUA	America's Univac Users Association
AVL	Adel'son-Vel'skii and Landis (trees)
BBN	Bolt Beranek and Newman
BCD	Binary-Coded Decimal
BCPL	Basic Combined Programming Language
BCS	British Computer Society
BDAM	Basic Direct Access Method
BDP	Business Data Processing
BINAC	Binary Northrop Automatic Computer
BISAM	Basic Indexed Sequential Access Method
BMD	Biomedical (Computer Programs)
BMDP	Biomedical (Computer Programs-P Series)
BNF	Backus-Naur Form
BSAM	Basic Sequential Access Method
BSP	Burroughs Scientific Processor
BTAM	Basic Telecommunications Access Method
CACM	Communications of the Association for Computing Machinery
CAD	Computer-Aided Design
CAD/CAM	Computer-Aided Design/Computer-Aided Manufacturing
CAE	Computer-Aided Education
CAI	Computer-Aided Instruction
CAI	Computer-Assisted Instruction
CAL	Computer-Aided Learning
CAM	Computer-Aided Manufacturing
CAN	Computer Architecture News
CARE	Computer-Aided Reliability Estimation
CAT	Computer-Assisted Tomography
CAUSE	College and University System Exchange
CBCT	Customer-Bank Communication Terminal
CBE	Computer-Based Education
CBEMA	Computer and Business Equipment Manufacturers Association
CBI	Charles Babbage Institute
CCD	Charge Coupled Device
CCIIT	Comité Consultatif Internationale Télégraphique et Téléphonique
CDC	Control Data Corporation

CDL	Computer Description Language
CDL	Computer Design Language
CDP	Certificate in Data Processing
CEPA	Civil Engineering Programming Applications
CG	Computer Graphics
CICS	Customer Information Control System
CII	Compagnie Internationale pour Informatique
CIM	Computer Input from Microfilm
CIM	Computer-Integrated Manufacturing
CIPS	Canadian Information Processing Society
CISI	Compagnie Internationale de Services et Informatique
CLSR	Computer Law Service Reporter
CMI	Computer-Managed Instruction
C.mmp	Carnegie Multi-Mini Processor
CMOS	Complementary Metal-Oxide Semiconductor
CMS	Conversational Monitor System
CODASYL	Conference on Data Systems Languages
COM	Computer Output on Microfilm
CONTU	Commission on New Technological Uses of Copyrights
COSATI	Committee on Scientific and Technical Information
COSMIC	Computer Software Management and Information Center
CPC	Card Programmed Calculator
CPM	Critical Path Method
CPU	Central Processing Unit
CRAM	Card Random Access Memory
CRC	Cyclic Redundancy Check
CRT	Cathode Ray Tube
CSE	Computer Science and Engineering
CT	Computed Tomography
CTSS	Compatible Time-Sharing System
CUBE	Cooperating Users of Burroughs Equipment
CUMREC	College and University Machine Record Conference
D/A	Digital-to-Analog
DAA	Data Access Arrangement
DAM	Direct Access Method
DAP	Distributed Array Processor
DARPA	Defense Advanced Research Projects Agency
DAX	Data Acquisition and Control
DBA	Database Administrator
DBM	Database Management
DBMS	Database Management System
DBTG	Database Task Group
DCA	Digital Computer Association
DDL	Data Definition Language
DDP	Distributed Data Processor
DDS	Dataphone Digital Service
DEC	Digital Equipment Corporation
DECUS	Digital Equipment Corporation Users Society
DES	Data Encryption Standard

DETAB	Decision Table (Language)
DFT	Discrete Fourier Transform
DIP	Dual-in-line Pin
DMA	Direct Memory Access
DML	Data Manipulation Language
DOS	Disk Operating System
DPMA	Data Processing Management Association
DRO	Destructive Read-Out
DSS	Decision Support System
DTL	Diode-Transistor Logic
DYANA	Dynamic Analyzer
EAI	Electronic Associates, Inc.
EBCDIC	Extended Binary-Coded Decimal Interchange Code
ECL	Emitter-Coupled Logic
ECMA	European Computer Manufacturers Association
ECR	Electronic Cash Register
ECS	Extended Core Storage
EDP	Electronic Data Processing
EDSAC	Electronic Delay Storage Automatic Calculator
EDUCOM	Educational Communications (name of Interuniversity Communications Council)
EDVAC	Electronic Discrete Variable Automatic Computer
EFTS	Electronic Funds Transfer Systems
EIA	Electronic Industries Association
ELI	Extensible Language I
ENIAC	Electronic Numerical Integrator and Computer
EPROM	Erasable Programmable Read-Only Memory
EPSS	Experimental Packet Switching System
ERA	Engineering Research Associates
FAP	Fortran Assembly Program
FDM	Frequency Division Multiplexing
FET	Field-Effect Transistor
FF	Flip-Flop
FFT	Fast Fourier Transform
FIFO	First-In-First-Out
FIPS	Federal Information Processing Standards
FM	Frequency Modulation
FMS	Fortran Monitor System
FOSDIC	Film Optical Sensing Device for Input to Computers
FPAP	Floating Point Array Processor
FPS	Floating Point Systems
FSM	Finite State Machine
FTMP	Fault Tolerant Multiprocessor System
FTSC	Fault Tolerant Spaceborne Computer
GASP	General Activity Simulation Program
GENESYS	General Engineering System
GIGO	Garbage-In-Garbage-Out
GIPSY	General Information Processing System
GIS	Generalized Information System
GPM	General Purpose Macrogenerator

GRIPHOS	General Retrieval and Information Processing for Humanities-Oriented Studies
GSAM	Generalized Sequential Access Method
GSM	Generalized Sequential Machine
GUIDE	Guidance of Users of Integrated Data Processing Equipment
HASP	Houston Autonomous Spooling Program
HB	Honeywell-Bull
HDAM	Hierarchical Direct Access Method
HDL	Hardware Description Language
HDLC	High-Level Data Link Control
HEP	Heterogeneous Element Processor
HIPAC	Hitachi Parametron Automatic Computer
HIPO	Hierarchy plus Input-Process-Output
HIS	Honeywell Information Systems
HIS	Hospital Information System
HLL	High-Level Language
HOPL	History of Programming Languages
HP	Hewlett-Packard
IAC	International Apple Core
IAG	International Applications Group (of IFIP)
IAL	International Algebraic Language
IAPR	International Association for Pattern Recognition
IASC	International Association for Statistical Computing
IBI	Intergovernmental Bureau for Informatics
IBM	International Business Machines
IC	Instruction Counter
IC	Integrated Circuit
ICC	International Computer Centre
ICCA	International Computer Chess Association
ICL	International Computers Ltd.
ICP	International Computer Programs
ICT	International Computers and Tabulators
IDC	International Data Corporation
IDFT	Inverse Discrete Fourier Transform
IDS	Integrated Data Store
IEEE	Institute of Electrical and Electronic Engineers
IEEE–CS	Institute of Electrical and Electronic Engineers–Computer Society
IFAC	International Federation of Automatic Control
IFIP	International Federation for Information Processing
IFORS	International Federation of Operational Research Societies
ILLIAC	Illinois Automatic Computer
IMACS	International Association for Mathematics and Computing in Simulation
IMIA	International Medical Informatics Association
IMP	Interface Message Processor
IMS	Information Management System
IMSL	International Mathematical and Statistical Libraries
I/O	Input-Output
IOCS	Input-Output Control System
IOP	Input-Output Processor
IP	Instruction Processor

IR	Information Retrieval
IR	Instruction Register
IRE	Institute of Radio Engineers
IRG	Inter-Record Gap
IRIA	Institut de Recherche d'Informatique et d'Automatique
ISA	Instrument Society of America
ISAM	Indexed Sequential Access Method
ISO	International Standards Organization
ISODATA	Iterative Self-Organizing Data Analysis Technique
ISP	Instruction Set Processor
ISPS	Instruction Set Processor Specifications
ISSMB	Information Systems Standards Management Board
JCL	Job Control Language
JOD	Journal of Development
JUG	Joint Users Group
KSR	Keyboard Send-Receive
KWIC	Keyword-In-Context
KWOC	Keyword-Out-of-Context
LALR	Lookahead LR (Left-to-Right, Rightmost)
LARC	Livermore Automatic Research Computer
LBA	Linear Bounded Automaton
LED	Light-Emitting Diode
LIFO	Last-In-First-Out
LINC	Laboratory Instrument Computer
LP	Linear Programming
LRC	Longitudinal Redundancy Check
LRU	Least Recently Used
LS	Least Squares
LSB	Least Significant Bit (or Byte)
LSI	Large-Scale Integration
LSTTL	Low-Power Schottky Transistor-Transistor Logic
LT	Logic Theorist
MAC	Machine-Aided Cognition (or Man and Computer)
MAR	Memory Address Register
MARC	Machine-Readable Cataloging
MBQ	Modified Biquinary Code
MCP	Master Control Program
MDS	Mohawk Data Sciences
MEDLARS	Medical Literature Analysis and Retrieval System
MEDLINE	Medlars On-Line System
MFT	Multiprogramming with a Fixed Number of Tasks
MICR	Magnetic Ink Character Recognition
MIDAC	Michigan Digital Automatic Computer
MIMD	Multiple-Instruction Stream, Multiple Data Stream
MIMR	Magnetic Ink Mark Recognition
MIS	Management Information System
MISD	Multiple-Instruction Stream, Single-Data Stream
MODEM	Modulator-Demodulator
MOS	Metal-Oxide Semiconductor

MOSFET	Metal-Oxide Semiconductor Field Effect Transistor
MPU	Microprocessing Unit
MQ	Multiplier-Quotient
MQR	Multiplier-Quotient Register
MSB	Most Significant Bit (or Byte)
MSI	Medium-Scale Integration
MSS	Mass Storage System
MSUDC	Michigan State University Discrete Computer
MT	Machine Translation
MTBF	Mean Time Between Failures
MTS	Michigan Terminal System
MTTF	Mean Time to Failure
MTTR	Mean Time to Repair
MULTICS	Multiplexed Information and Computer Service
MVS	Multiprogramming with Virtual Storage
MVT	Multiprogramming with a Variable Number of Tasks
NAG	Numerical (formerly Nottingham) Algorithms Group
NAND	Not and
NATS	National Activity to Test Software
NCC	National Computer Conference
NCEFT	National Commission on Electronic Funds Transfers
NCLIS	National Commission on Libraries and Information Science
NCR	National Cash Register
NDRO	Non-Destructive Read-Out
NLP	Nonlinear Programming
NMA	National Micrographics Association
NMOS	Negative Metal-Oxide Semiconductor
NOR	Not or
NORC	Naval Ordnance Research Computer
NP	Nondeterministic Polynomial
OBR	Optical Bar Code
OCR	Optical Character Reading
ODE	Ordinary Differential Equation
OECD	Organization for Economic Cooperation and Development
OEM	Original Equipment Manufacturer
OMR	Optical Mark Reading
ORDVAC	Ordnance Variable Automatic Computer
OS	Operating System
OS/MFT	Operating System/Multiprogramming a Fixed Number of Tasks
OS/MVS	Operating System/Multiprogramming with Virtual Storage
OS/MVT	Operating System/Multiprogramming a Variable Number of Tasks
PCM	Plug Compatible Mainframe
PDE	Partial Differential Equation
PDP	Programmed Data Processor
PERT	Program Evaluation and Review Technique
PIN	Personal Identification Number
PLATO	Programmed Logic for Automatic Teaching Operation
PM	Phase Modulation
PMOS	Positive Metal-Oxide Semiconductor

PMS	Processor-Memory-Switch
POL	Procedure-Oriented Language (or Problem-Oriented Language)
POS	Point-of-Sale
PP	Peripheral Processor
PPL	Polymorphic Programming Language
PROM	Programmable Read-Only Memory
PSA	Pushdown Stack Automaton
PSE	Packet Switching Exchange
PSL/PSA	Problem Statement Language/Problem Specification Analyzer
PSS	Packet Switching Service
PSW	Program Status Word
PTT	Postal-Telephone-Telegraph
PUFFT	Purdue University Fast Fortran Compiler
QISAM	Queued Indexed Sequential Access Method
QSAM	Queued Sequential Access Method
QTAM	Queued Telecommunications Access Method
q.v.	quod vide ("which see")
RAM	Random Access Memory
RAMAC	Random Access Method for Accounting and Control
RJE	Remote Job Entry
RLIN	Research Libraries Information Network
RMM	Read Mostly Memory
ROM	Read-Only Memory
RPG	Report Program Generator
RPS	Rotational Position Sensing
R-S	Reset-Set (Flip-Flop)
RSL	Requirements Specification Language
RT	Register Transfer
RTL	Register-Transistor Logic
RTM	Register Transfer Module
R/W	Read/Write
SAM	Sequential Access Method
SAP	Symbolic Assembly Program
SCI	Simulation Councils, Incorporated
SCS	Society for Computer Simulation
SDI	Selective Dissemination of Information
SDS	Scientific Data Systems
SEAC	Standards Eastern Automatic Computer
SIAM	Society for Industrial and Applied Mathematics
SID	Society for Information Display
SIG	Special Interest Group
SIGARCH	Special Interest Group on Computer Architecture (of ACM)
SIGBDP	Special Interest Group on Business Data Processing (of ACM)
SIGBIO	Special Interest Group on Biomedical Computing (of ACM)
SIGCOSIM	Special Interest Group on Computer Systems Installation Management (of ACM)
SIGCSE	Special Interest Group on Computer Science Education (of ACM)
SIGMICRO	Special Interest Group on Microprogramming (of ACM)
SIGOPS	Special Interest Group on Operating Systems (of ACM)

SIGPLAN	Special Interest Group on Programming Languages (of ACM)
SIGUCC	Special Interest Group on University Computer Centers (of ACM)
SIMD	Single-Instruction Stream, Multiple-Data Stream
SISD	Single-Instruction Stream, Single-Data Stream
SJF	Shortest Job First
SLAM	Simulation Language for Alternative Modeling
SLR	Simple LR (Left-to-Right, Rightmost)
SMIS	Society for Management Information Systems
SNA	System Network Architecture
SOAP	Symbolic Optimizer and Assembly Program
SOR	Successive Overrelaxation
SOS	Share Operating System
SP	Structured Programming
SPA	Systems and Procedures Association
SPARC	Standard Planning and Requirements Committee
SPL	Simple Programming Language
SPOOL	Simultaneous Peripheral Operations On Line
SQUID	Superconducting Quantum Interference Device
S-R	Set-Reset (Flip-Flop)
SRTF	Shortest Remaining Time First
SSEC	Selective Sequence Electronic Calculator
SSI	Small-Scale Integration
SSP	Scientific Subroutine Package
STAR	Self Testing and Repair (Computer)
STDM	Synchronous Time-Division Multiplexing
STRESS	Structural Engineering Systems Solver
STRUDL	Structural Design Language
SWAC	Standards Western Automatic Computer
SWIFT	Society for Worldwide Interbank Financial Telecommunications
TAXIR	Taxonomic Information Retrieval
TBM	Terabit Memory
TDM	Time-Division Multiplexing
TI	Texas Instruments
TICCIT	Time-Shared Interactive Computer-Controlled Informational Television
TIES	Total Integrated Engineering System
TIP	Terminal Interface Message Processor
TMR	Triple Modular Redundancy
TODS	Transactions on Database Systems
TOMS	Transactions on Mathematical Software
TOPLAS	Transactions on Programming Languages and Systems
TSS	Time-Shared System
TTL	Transistor-Transistor Logic
UHF	Ultra-High Frequency
UNIVAC	Universal Automatic Computer
UPC	Universal Product Code
USASCII	USA Standard Code for Information Interchange
USASI	United States of America Standards Institute
USE	Univac Scientific Exchange
UUA	Univac Users Association

VAL	Vicarm Arm Language
VAN	Value-Added Network
VAX	Virtual Address Extension
VC	Virtual Circuit
VDL	Vienna Definition Language
VDU	Video (Visual) Display Unit
VHF	Very High Frequency
VIM	Name of Control Data Corporation 6000 and Cyber series users Organization [Roman 6 (VI) and Roman 1000 (M)]
VLSI	Very Large-Scale Integration
VM	Virtual Memory
VRC	Vertical Redundancy Check
VSAM	Virtual Storage Access Method
VTAM	Virtual Telecommunications Access Method
WATFOR	(University of) Waterloo Fortran
WCS	Writable Control Store
WFF	Well-formed Formula
XOR	Exclusive-or

MATHEMATICAL NOTATION

Symbol	*Meaning*
GENERAL	
Σ	Summation $\left(\sum_{i=1}^{n} a_i = a_1 + a_2 + \ldots + a_n \right)$.
$\int$	Integral
| |	Absolute value ($\|a\| = a$ if $a \geq 0$, $= -a$ if $a < 0$)
$\lfloor \ \rfloor$	Floor function (greatest integer less than or equal to; $\lfloor 2.4 \rfloor = 2$, $\lfloor -2.4 \rfloor = -3$)
$\lceil \ \rceil$	Ceiling function (least integer greater than or equal to $\lceil 2.4 \rceil = 3$, $\lceil -2.4 \rceil = -2$)
[ ]	Closed interval ($[a,b]$ includes all x such that $a \leq x \leq b$)
( )	Open interval $[(a,b)$ includes all x such that $a < x < b]$
[ ), ( ]	Half-open (half-closed) interval $\{[a,b)$ includes all x such that $a \leq x < b\}$
$\approx, \simeq, \cong, \doteq$	Approximately equal
$\sim$	Asymptotic to
$\times$	Set product [$A \times B$ consists of all pairs (a,b) where $a \in A$, $b \in B$]
modulo (or mod)	Remainder (x mod y is remainder when x is divided by y; thus, 8 mod 3 is 2)
$\circ$	Binary operation (i.e., denotes any operation like $+$ which requires two operands)
fl	Floating point ($\mathrm{fl}(x + y)$ denotes the floating-point sum of x and y)
iff	If and only if
LOGIC	
$\vee$	Or
$\wedge$	And
$\sim, \neg$	Not
$\supset$	Implication
$\equiv$	Equivalence
$\not\equiv$	Inequivalence

Notes
1. For a description of the notation used in describing computer language constructs, *see* BACKUS-NAUR FORM.
2. For symbols used in logical circuitry, *see* COMPUTER CIRCUITRY.

UNITS OF MEASURE

This list contains abbreviations of units of measure used in the Encyclopedia; these usually appear in their abbreviated form.

General

K	1,000 or 1024 ($= 2^{10}$); the latter refers mainly to measures of computer storage capacity
M	1,000,000 or 1,048,576 ($= 2^{20}$); the latter refers mainly to measures of computer storage capacity

Time

ms, msec	millisecond (10^{-3} sec)
μs, μsec	microsecond (10^{-6} sec)
ns, nsec	nanosecond (10^{-9} sec)
ps, psec	picosecond (10^{-12} sec)

Speed

Megaflop	Million floating-point operations per second
MIPS	Million instructions processed per second

Electricity

Hz	Hertz (cycles/sec)
KHz	Kilohertz (10^3 cycles/sec)
MHz	Megahertz (10^6 cycles/sec)
Kc	Kilocycle (10^3 cycles)
Mc	Megacycle (10^6 cycles; sometimes, 10^6 cycles/sec = 1 MHz)
μW	Microwatt (10^{-6} watts)
mW	Milliwatt (10^{-3} watts)
KW	Kilowatt (10^3 watts)
mV	Millivolt (10^{-3} volt)
mA	Milliamp (10^{-3} amp)

Storage

Kb	Kilobit (10^3 bits)
Mb	Megabit (10^6 bits)
Gb	Gigabit (10^9 bits)
Tb	Terabit (10^{12} bits)
KB	Kilobyte (10^3 bytes)
MB	Megabyte (10^6 bytes)
GB	Gigabyte (10^9 bytes)
TB	Terabyte (10^{12} bytes)
L(x)	Location of x (in main memory)
C(A)	Contents of location A (in main memory)

I/O

bps	Bits per second
chps	Characters per second
chpi	Characters per inch
cps	Cards per second
cpm	Cards per minute
lpm	Lines per minute
rpm	Revolutions per minute

Miscellaneous

μ	Micron (10^{-6} meter)
mbar	Millibar (10^{-3} bar [cgs unit of pressure])

Appendix II

NUMERICAL TABLES

POWERS OF TWO TABLE

2^n	n	2^{-n}
2	1	0.5
4	2	0.25
8	3	0.125
16	4	0.625 $\times\ 10^{-1}$
32	5	0.312 5 $\times\ 10^{-1}$
64	6	0.156 25 $\times\ 10^{-1}$
128	7	0.781 25 $\times\ 10^{-2}$
256	8	0.390 625 $\times\ 10^{-2}$
512	9	0.195 312 5 $\times\ 10^{-2}$
1 024	10	0.976 562 5 $\times\ 10^{-3}$
2 048	11	0.488 281 25 $\times\ 10^{-3}$
4 096	12	0.244 140 625 $\times\ 10^{-3}$
8 192	13	0.122 070 312 5 $\times\ 10^{-3}$
16 384	14	0.610 351 562 5 $\times\ 10^{-4}$
32 768	15	0.305 175 781 25 $\times\ 10^{-4}$
65 536	16	0.152 587 890 625 $\times\ 10^{-4}$
131 072	17	0.762 939 453 125 $\times\ 10^{-5}$
262 144	18	0.381 469 726 562 5 $\times\ 10^{-5}$
524 288	19	0.190 734 863 281 25 $\times\ 10^{-5}$
1 048 576	20	0.953 674 316 406 25 $\times\ 10^{-6}$
2 097 152	21	0.476 837 158 203 125 $\times\ 10^{-6}$
4 194 304	22	0.238 418 579 101 562 5 $\times\ 10^{-6}$
8 388 608	23	0.119 209 289 550 781 25 $\times\ 10^{-6}$
16 777 216	24	0.596 046 447 753 906 25 $\times\ 10^{-7}$
33 554 432	25	0.298 023 223 876 953 125 $\times\ 10^{-7}$
67 108 864	26	0.149 011 611 938 476 562 5 $\times\ 10^{-7}$
134 217 728	27	0.745 058 059 692 382 812 5 $\times\ 10^{-8}$

POWERS OF TWO TABLE (Continued)

2^n	n	2^{-n}
268 435 456	28	$0.372\ 529\ 029\ 846\ 191\ 406\ 25 \times 10^{-8}$
536 870 912	29	$0.186\ 264\ 514\ 923\ 095\ 703\ 125 \times 10^{-8}$
1 073 741 824	30	$0.931\ 322\ 574\ 615\ 478\ 515\ 625 \times 10^{-9}$
2 147 483 648	31	$0.465\ 661\ 287\ 307\ 739\ 257\ 812\ 5 \times 10^{-9}$
4 294 967 296	32	$0.232\ 830\ 643\ 653\ 869\ 628\ 906\ 25 \times 10^{-9}$
8 589 934 592	33	$0.116\ 415\ 321\ 826\ 934\ 814\ 453\ 125 \times 10^{-9}$
17 179 869 184	34	$0.582\ 076\ 609\ 134\ 674\ 072\ 265\ 625 \times 10^{-10}$
34 359 738 368	35	$0.291\ 038\ 304\ 567\ 337\ 036\ 132\ 812\ 5 \times 10^{-10}$
68 719 476 736	36	$0.145\ 519\ 152\ 283\ 668\ 518\ 066\ 406\ 25 \times 10^{-10}$
137 438 953 472	37	$0.727\ 595\ 761\ 418\ 342\ 590\ 332\ 031\ 25 \times 10^{-11}$
274 877 906 944	38	$0.363\ 797\ 880\ 709\ 171\ 295\ 166\ 015\ 625 \times 10^{-11}$
549 755 813 888	39	$0.181\ 898\ 940\ 354\ 585\ 647\ 583\ 007\ 812\ 5 \times 10^{-11}$
1 099 511 627 776	40	$0.909\ 494\ 701\ 772\ 928\ 237\ 915\ 039\ 062\ 5 \times 10^{-12}$
2 199 023 255 552	41	$0.454\ 747\ 350\ 886\ 464\ 118\ 957\ 519\ 531\ 25 \times 10^{-12}$
4 398 046 511 104	42	$0.227\ 373\ 675\ 443\ 232\ 059\ 478\ 759\ 765\ 625 \times 10^{-12}$
8 796 093 022 208	43	$0.113\ 686\ 837\ 721\ 616\ 029\ 739\ 379\ 882\ 812\ 5 \times 10^{-12}$
17 592 186 044 416	44	$0.568\ 434\ 188\ 608\ 080\ 148\ 696\ 899\ 414\ 062\ 5 \times 10^{-13}$
35 184 372 088 832	45	$0.284\ 217\ 094\ 304\ 040\ 074\ 348\ 449\ 707\ 031\ 25 \times 10^{-13}$
70 368 744 177 664	46	$0.142\ 108\ 547\ 152\ 020\ 037\ 174\ 224\ 853\ 515\ 625 \times 10^{-13}$
140 737 488 355 328	47	$0.710\ 542\ 735\ 760\ 100\ 185\ 871\ 124\ 267\ 578\ 125 \times 10^{-14}$
281 474 976 710 656	48	$0.355\ 271\ 367\ 880\ 050\ 092\ 935\ 562\ 133\ 789\ 062\ 5 \times 10^{-14}$
562 949 953 421 312	49	$0.177\ 635\ 683\ 940\ 025\ 046\ 467\ 781\ 066\ 894\ 531\ 25 \times 10^{-14}$
1 125 899 906 842 624	50	$0.888\ 178\ 419\ 700\ 125\ 232\ 338\ 905\ 334\ 472\ 656\ 25 \times 10^{-15}$
2 251 799 813 685 248	51	$0.444\ 089\ 209\ 850\ 062\ 616\ 169\ 452\ 667\ 236\ 328\ 125 \times 10^{-15}$
4 503 599 627 370 496	52	$0.222\ 044\ 604\ 925\ 031\ 308\ 084\ 726\ 333\ 618\ 164\ 062\ 5 \times 10^{-15}$
9 007 199 254 740 992	53	$0.111\ 022\ 302\ 462\ 515\ 654\ 042\ 363\ 166\ 809\ 082\ 031\ 25 \times 10^{-15}$
18 014 398 509 481 984	54	$0.555\ 111\ 512\ 312\ 578\ 270\ 211\ 815\ 834\ 045\ 410\ 156\ 25 \times 10^{-16}$
36 028 797 018 963 968	55	$0.277\ 555\ 756\ 156\ 289\ 135\ 105\ 907\ 917\ 022\ 705\ 076\ 125 \times 10^{-16}$
72 057 594 037 927 936	56	$0.138\ 777\ 878\ 078\ 144\ 567\ 552\ 953\ 958\ 511\ 352\ 539\ 062\ 5 \times 10^{-16}$
144 115 188 075 855 872	57	$0.693\ 889\ 390\ 390\ 722\ 837\ 764\ 769\ 792\ 556\ 762\ 695\ 312\ 5 \times 10^{-17}$
288 230 376 151 711 744	58	$0.346\ 944\ 695\ 195\ 361\ 418\ 882\ 384\ 896\ 273\ 381\ 347\ 656\ 25 \times 10^{-17}$
576 460 752 303 423 488	59	$0.173\ 472\ 347\ 597\ 680\ 709\ 441\ 192\ 448\ 139\ 190\ 673\ 828\ 125 \times 10^{-17}$

TABLE OF IMPORTANT NUMERICAL CONSTANTS

	Decimal (Rounded)					Hexadecimal (Truncated)				
$\frac{1}{10}$	0.10000	00000	00000	00000	00000	0.1999	9999	9999	9999	9999
$\sqrt{2}$	1.41421	35623	73095	04880	16887	1.6A09	E667	F3BC	C908	B2FB
$\sqrt{3}$	1.73205	08075	68877	29352	74463	1.BB67	AE85	84CA	A73B	2574
$\sqrt{5}$	2.23606	79774	99789	69640	91737	2.3C6E	F372	FE94	F82B	E739
$\sqrt{10}$	3.16227	76601	68379	33199	88935	3.298B	075B	4B6A	5240	9457
$\sqrt[3]{2}$	1.25992	10498	94873	16476	72106	1.428A	2F98	D728	AE22	3DDA
$\ln 2$	0.69314	71805	59945	30941	72321	0.B172	17F7	D1CF	79AB	C9E3
$\ln 10$	2.30258	50929	94045	68401	79915	2.4D76	3776	AAA2	B05B	A95B
$\log_{10} 2$	0.30102	99956	63981	19521	37389	0.4D10	4D42	7DE7	FBCC	47C4
$\log_2 10 = 1/\log_{10} 2$	3.32192	80948	87362	34787	03194	3.5269	E12F	346E	2BF9	24AF
$\log_2 e = 1/\ln 2$	1.44269	50408	88963	40735	99247	1.7154	7652	B82F	E177	7D10
$\log_{10} e = 1/\ln 10$	0.43429	44819	03251	82765	11289	0.6F2D	EC54	9B94	38CA	9AAD
$1° = \pi/180$	0.01745	32925	19943	29576	92369	0.0477	D1A8	94A7	4E45	7076
π	3.14159	26535	89793	23846	26434	3.243F	6A88	85A3	08D3	1319
$1/\pi$	0.31830	98861	83790	67153	77675	0.517C	C1B7	2722	0A94	FE13
π^2	9.86960	44010	89358	61883	44910	9.DE9E	64DF	22EF	2D25	6E26
$\sqrt{\pi}$	1.77245	38509	05516	02729	81675	1.C5BF	891B	4EF6	AA79	C3B0
e	2.71828	18284	59045	23536	02875	2.B7E1	5162	8AED	2A6A	BF71
$1/e$	0.36787	94411	71442	32159	55238	0.5E2D	58D8	B3BC	DF1A	BADE
e^2	7.38905	60989	30650	22723	04275	7.6399	2E35	376B	730C	E8EE
$\sqrt{e}$	1.64872	12707	00128	14684	86508	1.A612	98E1	E069	BC97	2DFE
γ (Euler's constant)	0.57721	56649	01532	86060	65121	0.93C4	67E3	7DB0	C7A4	D1BE
$\phi = \dfrac{1 + \sqrt{5}}{2}$ (Golden Ratio)	1.61803	39887	49894	84820	45868	1.9E37	79B9	7F4A	7C15	F39C

OCTAL-DECIMAL-HEXADECIMAL CONVERSION TABLES

Table A. Decimal Equivalents of Octal Integers from 000 to 377 and Hexadecimal Integers from 00 to FF

Octal:		0	1	2	3	4	5	6	7	10	11	12	13	14	15	16	17
Hex:		0	1	2	3	4	5	6	7	8	9	A	B	C	D	E	F
Octal	*Hex*																
000	00	0	1	2	3	4	5	6	7	8	9	10	11	12	13	14	15
020	10	16	17	18	19	20	21	22	23	24	25	26	27	28	29	30	31
040	20	32	33	34	35	36	37	38	39	40	41	42	43	44	45	46	47
060	30	48	49	50	51	52	53	54	55	56	57	58	59	60	61	62	63
100	40	64	65	66	67	68	69	70	71	72	73	74	75	76	77	78	79
120	50	80	81	82	83	84	85	86	87	88	89	90	91	92	93	94	95
140	60	96	97	98	99	100	101	102	103	104	105	106	107	108	109	110	111
160	70	112	113	114	115	116	117	118	119	120	121	122	123	124	125	126	127
200	80	128	129	130	131	132	133	134	135	136	137	138	139	140	141	142	143
220	90	144	145	146	147	148	149	150	151	152	153	154	155	156	157	158	159
240	A0	160	161	162	163	164	165	166	167	168	169	170	171	172	173	174	175
260	B0	176	177	178	179	180	181	182	183	184	185	186	187	188	189	190	191
300	C0	192	193	194	195	196	197	198	199	200	201	202	203	204	205	206	207
320	D0	208	209	210	211	212	213	214	215	216	217	218	219	220	221	222	223
340	E0	224	225	226	227	228	229	230	231	232	233	234	235	236	237	238	239
360	F0	240	241	242	243	244	245	246	247	248	249	250	251	252	253	254	255

Table B. Decimal Equivalents of Octal Integers 0000, 0400, 1000, . . . , 177400 and Hexadecimal Integers 0000, 0100, 0200, . . . , FF00

Octal:		000	400	1000	1400	2000	2400	3000	3400
Hex:		000	100	200	300	400	500	600	700
Octal	*Hex*								
0000	0000	0	256	512	768	1024	1280	1536	1792
10000	1000	4096	4352	4608	4864	5120	5376	5632	5888
20000	2000	8192	8448	8704	8960	9216	9472	9728	9984
30000	3000	12288	12544	12800	13056	13312	13568	13824	14080
40000	4000	16384	16640	16896	17152	17408	17664	17920	18176
50000	5000	20480	20736	20992	21248	21504	21760	22016	22272
60000	6000	24576	24832	25088	25344	25600	25856	26112	26368
70000	7000	28672	28928	29184	29440	29696	29952	30208	30464
100000	8000	32768	33024	33280	33536	33792	34048	34304	34560
110000	9000	36864	37120	37376	37632	37888	38144	38400	38656
120000	A000	40960	41216	41472	41728	41984	42240	42496	42752
130000	B000	45056	45312	45568	45824	46080	46336	46592	46848
140000	C000	49152	49408	49664	49920	50176	50432	50688	50944
150000	D000	53248	53504	53760	54016	54272	54528	54784	55040
160000	E000	57344	57600	57856	58112	58368	58624	58880	59136
170000	F000	61440	61696	61952	62208	62464	62720	62976	63232

Octal:		4000	4400	5000	5400	6000	6400	7000	7400
Hex:		800	900	A00	B00	C00	D00	E00	F00
Octal	*Hex*								
0000	0000	2048	2304	2560	2816	3072	3328	3584	3840
10000	1000	6144	6400	6656	6912	7168	7424	7680	7936
20000	2000	10240	10496	10752	11008	11264	11520	11776	12032
30000	3000	14336	14592	14848	15104	15360	15616	15872	16128
40000	4000	18432	18688	18944	19200	19456	19712	19968	20224
50000	5000	22528	22784	23040	23296	23552	23808	24064	24320
60000	6000	26624	26880	27136	27392	27648	27904	28160	28416
70000	7000	30720	30976	31232	31488	31744	32000	32256	32512
100000	8000	34816	35072	35328	35584	35840	36096	36352	36608
110000	9000	38912	39168	39424	39680	39936	40192	40448	40704
120000	A000	43008	43264	43520	43776	44032	44288	44544	44800
130000	B000	47104	47360	47616	47872	48128	48384	48640	48896
140000	C000	51200	51456	51712	51968	52224	52480	52736	52992
150000	D000	55296	55552	55808	56064	56320	56576	56832	57088
160000	E000	59392	59648	59904	60160	60416	60672	60928	61184
170000	F000	63488	63744	64000	64256	64512	64768	65024	65280

How to Use These Tables

1. Hexadecimal → Decimal

   Let hex number be *a b c d*

   Find *a*000 on left of Table B, *b*00 on top of Table B and read decimal equivalent at intersection. Do the same for *c*0 and *d* in Table A and add the two decimal equivalents.

   Example: Hex = 4E6A. In Table B use 4000 and E00 to get 19968. Then in Table A use 60 and A to get 106. Add 19968 and 106 to get 20074 decimal (= 4E6A hex).

2. Octal → Decimal

   Let octal number be *a b c d e f*

   a) $d \geq 4$, *e* even

   Find *ab*0000 on left of Table B, *c*400 on top of Table B and read decimal equivalent at intersection. Do same for $(d - 4)e0$ and *f* in Table A and add the two decimal equivalents.

   b) $d \geq 4$, *e* odd

   Same as for (a) except use $(d - 4)(e - 1)0$ and 1*f* in Table A.

   c) $d < 4$, *e* even

   Same as for (a) except use *c*000 on top of Table B and *de*0 on left of Table A.

   d) $d < 4$, *e* odd

   Same as (a) except use *c*000 on top of Table B and $d(e - 1)0$ and 1*f* in Table A.

   Example: Octal = 63732. Since $d \geq 4$ and *e* is odd (note that *a* = 0), use (b). In Table B use 60000 and 3400 to get 26368. Then in Table A use 320 (since $d - 4 = 3$ and $e - 1 = 2$) and 12 to get 218. Add 26368 and 218 to get 26586 decimal (=63732 octal).

3. Decimal → Octal or Hexadecimal

   a) Denote decimal number by *D*. Find largest decimal number smaller than *D* in Table B and read octal or hex equivalent from side and top.

   b) Subtract decimal number found in Table B from *D* and find this number in Table A again reading octal or hex equivalent.

   c) Add the result of (a) to the result of (b).

   Example: D = 53738

   Find 53504 in Table B with hex equivalent D100 (=D000 + 100) and octal equivalent 150400 (=150000 + 0400). Then find 234 (=53738 − 53504) in Table A with hex equivalent EA and octal equivalent 352. Thus

$$53738 \text{ dec} = \text{D1EA hex} = 150752 \text{ octal}$$

Appendix III

COMPUTER SCIENCE AND ENGINEERING RESEARCH JOURNALS

The list of 46 journals which follows includes the major research journals devoted entirely to computer science and engineering as well as a few which publish articles of significant technical interest although they are not necessarily research journals. In addition, we list here four other journals devoted to reviews and abstracts of the computer science and technology literature:

Computing Reviews, published monthly by the Association for Computing Machinery

Computer Abstracts, published monthly by the Technical Information Company in Great Britain

Computer and Control Abstracts, published monthly by Inspec, the Institution of Electrical Engineers

Computer and Information Systems Abstract Journal, published monthly by Cambridge Scientific Abstracts of Riverdale, Maryland and Oxford, England.

The full addresses of all journals listed below can be found periodically in Computing Reviews (e.g., September 1981).

Journal	Publisher	Issues Per Year
ACM Transactions on Database Systems	ACM	4
ACM Transactions on Graphics	ACM	4
ACM Transactions on Mathematical Software	ACM	4
ACM Transactions on Programming Languages & Systems	ACM	4
Acta Informatica	Springer-Verlag	8
Annals of the History of Computing	AFIPS	4
Artificial Intelligence	North Holland	6
Australian Computer Journal	Australian Computer Society	3
Bit (Nordisk Tidskrift for Informationsbehandling)	Swedish Institute for Informationsbehandling	4
Byte	McGraw-Hill	12
Communications of the ACM	ACM	12
Computer	IEEE Computer Society	12
Computer Bulletin	British Computer Society	12
Computer Graphics and Image Processing	Academic Press	12
Computer Journal	British Computer Society	4
Computer Languages	Pergamon Press	4
Computer Networks	North Holland	6
Computers and Graphics	Pergamon Press	4
Computers and the Humanities	North Holland	4
Computers and Mathematics with Applications	Pergamon Press	4
Computing	Springer-Verlag	8
Computing Surveys	ACM	4

Journal	Publisher	Issues Per Year
Creative Computing	Creative Computing, Inc.	12
IBM Systems Journal	IBM	4
IEEE Transactions on Computers	IEEE Computer Society	12
IEEE Transactions on Pattern Analysis and Machine Intelligence	IEEE Computer Society	6
IEEE Transactions on Software Engineering	IEEE Computer Society	6
Information Processing Letters	North Holland	10
Information Sciences	North Holland	9
Information Processing & Management	Pergamon Press	6
International Journal of Computer and Information Sciences	Plenum Press	6
International Journal of Computer Mathematics	Gordon and Breach	4
Journal of the ACM	ACM	4
Journal of Algorithms	Academic Press	4
Journal of the American Society of Information Science	ASIS	6
Journal of Computer and System Sciences	Academic Press	6
Journal of Systems and Software	North Holland	4
Mathematics of Computation	AMS	4
Numerische Mathematik	Springer-Verlag	6
Pattern Recognition	Pergamon Press	6
SIAM Journal on Computing	SIAM	4
SIAM Journal on Numerical Analysis	SIAM	6
Simulation	Society for Computer Simulation	12
Software—Practice and Experience	John Wiley	12
Theoretical Computer Science	North Holland	12
USSR Computational Mathematics and Mathematical Physics	Pergamon Press	6

Appendix IV

UNIVERSITIES OFFERING THE PhD DEGREE IN COMPUTER SCIENCE

The list that follows includes departments at universities in the United States and Canada which offer a PhD in computer science (or in something very similar). Almost all also offer the masters degree and have undergraduate major programs in computer science and/or computer engineering. In addition to the programs listed here some departments of mathematics and electrical engineering also offer doctorates in computer science or with a computer science option. And there are an increasing number of doctoral programs in computer engineering.

University	Name of Department or Program	Telephone No.
University of Alabama in Birmingham	Computer and Information Science	205-934-2213
University of Alberta	Computing Science	403-432-3520
University of Arizona	Computer Science	602-884-3685
University of British Columbia	Computer Science	604-228-3064
Brown University	Computer Science	401-831-5037
California Institute of Technology	Computer Science	213-795-6811
University of California, Berkeley	Electrical Engineering and Computer Science	415-642-0930
University of California, Irvine	Information and Computer Science	714-833-5233
University of California, Los Angeles	Computer Science	213-825-2929
University of California, Santa Barbara	Electrical and Computer Engineering	805-961-3821
University of California, Santa Cruz	Information Science	408-429-2565
Carnegie-Mellon University	Computer Science	412-578-2592
Case Western Reserve University	Computer Engineering and Science	216-368-4076
University of Central Florida	Computer Science	305-275-2341
Colorado State University	Computer Science	303-491-5792
University of Colorado	Computer Science	303-492-7514
Columbia University	Computer Science	212-280-2736
University of Connecticut	Electrical Engineering and Computer Science	203-486-2572
Cornell University	Computer Science	607-256-4052
University of Delaware	Computer and Information Science	302-738-2712
Duke University	Computer Science	919-684-3048
Georgia Institute of Technology	Information and Computer Science	404-894-3152
Harvard University	Research in Computer Technology	617-495-3989
Illinois Institute of Technology	Computer Science	312-567-5150
University of Illinois at Urbana-Champaign	Computer Science	217-333-3426
Indiana University	Computer Science	812-337-6486

1598

University	Name of Department or Program	Telephone No.
Iowa State University	Computer Science	515-294-4377
University of Iowa	Computer Science	319-353-5266
Kansas State University	Computer Science	913-532-6350
University of Kansas	Computer Science	913-864-4482
University of Manitoba	Computer Science	202-474-8313
University of Maryland	Computer Science	301-454-2002
Massachusetts Institute of Technology	Electrical Engineering and Computer Science	617-253-5892
University of Massachusetts	Computer and Information Science	413-545-2742
Michigan State University	Computer Science	517-355-5210
University of Michigan	Computer and Communication Sciences	313-764-8504
University of Michigan	Computer, Information and Control Engineering	313-764-9387
University of Minnesota	Computer Science	612-373-0132
University of Missouri-Rolla	Computer Science	314-341-4491
Universite de Montreal	Information Science	514-343-7090
University of Nebraska-Lincoln	Computer Science	402-472-2402
New Mexico Institute of Mining and Technology	Computer Science	505-835-5126
New Mexico State University	Computer Science	505-646-3723
University of New Mexico	Computer Science	505-277-3113
New York University	Computer Science	212-460-7497
SUNY at Albany	Computer Science	518-457-4602
SUNY at Binghamton	Computer Science	607-798-2793
SUNY at Buffalo	Computer Science	716-831-3061
SUNY at Stony Brook	Computer Science	516-246-7146
University of North Carolina	Computer Science	919-933-2148
Northwestern University	Computer Science and Electrical Engineering	312-492-3641
Ohio State University	Computer and Information Sciences	614-422-5973
University of Oklahoma	Electrical Engineering and Computer Science	405-325-4721
Oklahoma State University	Computing and Information Science	405-624-5668
Oregon State University	Computer Science	503-754-3273
Pennsylvania State University	Computer Science	814-865-9505
University of Pennsylvania	Computer Science	215-243-8540
University of Pittsburgh	Computer Science	412-624-6475
Polytechnic Institute of New York	Electrical Engineering	212-643-4487
Princeton University	Electrical Engineering and Computer Science	609-452-4640
Purdue University	Computer Science	317-749-2356
Rensselaer Polytechnic Institute	Mathematical Sciences	518-270-6414
University of Rochester	Computer Science	716-275-5671
Rutgers University	Computer Science	201-932-3546
University of Southern California	Computer Science	213-741-5501
Southern Methodist University	Computer Science and Engineering	214-692-3083
University of Southwestern Louisiana	Computer Science	318-233-3850
Stanford University	Computer Science	415-497-4079
Syracuse University	Computer Science	315-423-2368

University	Name of Department or Program	Telephone No.
Texas A & M University	Computing Science	713-845-5531
University of Texas	Computer Science	512-471-7316
University of Toronto	Computer Science	416-978-2990
University of Utah	Computer Science	801-581-8224
Vanderbilt University	Computer Science	615-322-2796
University of Virginia	Applied Mathematics and Computer Science	804-924-7201
Virginia Polytechnic Institute and State University	Computer Science	703-951-6931
Washington University (of St. Louis)	Computer Science	314-889-6132
Washington State University	Computer Science	509-335-6636
University of Washington	Computer Science	206-543-1695
University of Waterloo	Computer Science	519-885-1211
Wayne State University	Computer Science	313-577-2477
University of Wisconsin	Computer Science	608-262-1204
Yale University	Computer Science	203-436-8160

Appendix V

KEY HIGH-LEVEL LANGUAGES

Introduction

The following list of languages represents the author's personal view of the (approximately 50) high-level languages which are deemed most significant (in 1981) from among the over 500 high-level implemented languages (not counting dialects) which have been defined since work in computing started. The defined characteristics of a high-level language are given in this author's article on PROGRAMMING LANGUAGES in this encyclopedia. The languages selected had to satisfy (in the author's personal judgment) one or more of these criteria: significant usage, influence on language design, overall impact on the computing environment, novelty (first of its kind), uniqueness, and existing or potential standard.

The languages have been grouped into two major categories: (1) those not really in significant use in 1981 (although perhaps a few hardy souls may continue to use them) and (2) those believed to be in significant use, where "significant" is judged relative to the size of the expected user community for that type of language. Within the second group, the languages have been listed by name under the *primary* application areas for which they are intended. This is because of the author's firm belief that the *most important characteristic* of any programming language is the application area for which it is intended to be used. Of the application areas, the first five (i.e., numerical scientific, business data processing, string and list processing, formula manipulation, and multipurpose) are relatively common or well-known. The remainder are narrow, specialized areas. Following this list, each language is listed in alphabetical order, with the following entries:

> Name
> Meaning of the acronym (when there is one)
> Date of first publication (described below)
> Reference(s) (described below)
> Computers on which the language has been implemented
> The primary application area
> A comment to indicate very briefly something about the language and/or why it is on the list.

For the date of first publication, this means the earliest dissemination of the following (although sometimes labeled "draft" or "preliminary"): published paper, official technical report, language manual, etc. In many cases, the date refers to a much earlier version of the current language. Thus, the 1956 publication on Fortran has little resemblance to the 1978 ANSI standard. Where a question mark is used, it means the author is not certain of the date. In a few cases, a specific date has been omitted entirely because of lack of knowledge.

There are four main sources for finding specific references (and/or more details) on these languages, and they are referred to with the indicated abbreviations in the listings:

Roster: "Roster of Programming Languages for 1976–77," J. E. Sammet, *ACM SIGPLAN Notices* **13**, *No. 11*.
HOPL: *History of Programming Languages*, R. L. Wexelblat (Editor). New York: Academic Press, 1981.

PL: *Programming Languages: History and Fundamentals,* J. E. Sammet. Englewood Cliffs, NJ: Prentice-Hall, 1969.

ANSI: For any language which is an ANSI standard, the number has been included. If standardization is planned but not yet finished, no number is shown.

For any language contained in more than one of the above sources, all relevant references have been given. The reader should note that there may be more current references for some of these languages (including, but not limited to, articles in this encyclopedia). In a very few cases, these have been included.

The computers are described either as a specific family, or as "many" or "most" where there are too many to list. More implementations may exist but are not known to the author.

The list of computers on which the language has been implemented, and, to a lesser extent, the comment and the implicit value judgment in including the language at all, stem primarily from the author's language roster, mentioned above, and some updating of that information. However, time has not permitted a thorough updating of implementation and/or usage details.

J. E. SAMMET

LIST OF LANGUAGES BY APPLICATION AREA

HISTORICALLY IMPORTANT BUT *NOT* IN *SIGNIFICANT* CURRENT USE

Comit [II]
Flow-Matic
IPL-V
IT
Joss
Mad
Neliac

CURRENT USAGE—BROAD APPLICATION AREAS

Numerical Scientific
Algol 60
Basic
Fortran
Speakeasy

Business Data Processing
Cobol

String and List Processing
Lisp
Snobol4
TRAC®

Formula Manipulation
Formac
Macsyma
Reduce

Multipurpose
Ada®
Algol 68
APL
Jovial
Mumps
Pascal
PL/I
Simula 67

Social Science and/or Statistics
OMNITAB II
SPSS

Systems Programming (including debugging aids)
Bliss
C
PL/M

CURRENT LANGUAGES FOR SPECIALIZED APPLICATION AREAS

Computer-Assisted Instruction
Coursewriter III
PILOT
TUTOR

Circuit Design
ECAP II
SCEPTRE

Civil, Mechanical, Structural Engineering
COGO
ICES

Computer Hardware Design (including simulation)
ISPL

Equipment Checkout
ATLAS

Machine Tool Control
APT

Mathematical/Linear Programming
MPSX
PDS/MaGen

Simulation (continuous)
CSMP
CSSL
DYNAMO III

Simulation (discrete)
GPSS
SIMSCRIPT II.5®

DESCRIPTION OF LANGUAGES

Ada®

1979
Reference Manual for the Ada Programming Language,
    U.S. Department of Defense, July 1980. ANSI
    standard under development.
No complete compilers as of late 1981; subsets on sev-
    eral computers.
Multipurpose.
Very powerful language developed over many years
    with much public commentary. Sponsored by U.S.
    Department of Defense but designed by French
    language team. (®Ada is a trademark of the U.S.
    Department of Defense, Ada Joint Program Of-
    fice.)

Algol 60
ALGOrithmic Language 1960
May 1960
Roster, HOPL, PL.
Many computers.
Numerical scientific.
Suitable for problems involving numeric computation
    and/or logical processes. Its predecessor (Algol 58)
    had several significant languages based on it (e.g.,
    Jovial, Mad, Neliac).

Algol 68
ALGOrithmic Language 1968
1968
Roster.
Many computers.
Multipurpose.
Very powerful language but not upward-compatible
    from Algol 60.

APL
A Programming Language
1962
Roster, HOPL, PL, ANSI standard.
Many computers.
Multipurpose.
Has unusual character set and cryptic syntax but has
    very powerful, concise primitive array operations.

APT
Automatically Programmed Tools
1958
Roster, HOPL, PL, ANSI X3.37-1977.
Most computers.
Machine tool control.
Language for programming numerically controlled ma-
    chine tools. Was first language developed for a spe-
    cialized application area.

ATLAS
Abbreviated Test Language for "All" Systems
1968
Roster, ANSI/IEEE Standard 416-1978.
Most computers in differing versions.
Equipment checkout.
For test engineers to control automatic test equipment.

Basic
Beginner's All Purpose Symbolic Instruction Code
1964
Roster, HOPL, PL, ANSI X3.60-1978.
Almost all computers.
Numerical scientific.
Very simple language but with some advanced features.
    Available on many micro and personal computers
    for uses beyond just numerical scientific.

Bliss
*Basic Language for Implementation of System Soft-
    ware*
1970
Roster.
Several computers.
Systems programming.
For writing compilers and operating systems.

C

1975
Roster.
Many computers.
Systems programming.
Used to write the UNIX operating system and most of
its application software.

Cobol
*CO*mmon *B*usiness-*O*riented *L*anguage
1960
Roster, HOPL, PL, ANSI X3.23-1974.
Most computers.
Business data processing.
English-like in style, developed and maintained by com-
mittee of users and manufacturers under Codasyl.
One of the most widely used languages.

COGO
*CO*ordinate *GeO*metry
1963 (?)
Roster, PL.
Several computers.
Civil engineering.
Useful for solving coordinate geometry problems in civil
engineering.

COMIT [II]

1957
Roster, PL.
IBM System/360.
String processing.
First major language for string handling and pattern
matching.

Coursewriter III

1966 (?)
Roster.
IBM System/360.
Computer-assisted instruction.
Simple language for preparing computer-assisted in-
struction courses.

CSMP
*C*ontinuous *S*ystem *M*odeling *P*rogram
1968
Roster.
Several computers.
Simulation (continuous).
General term for two languages (statement- and block-
oriented) used to simulate the dynamics of contin-
uous systems describable by ordinary differential
equations.

CSSL
*C*ontinuous *S*ystems *S*imulation *L*anguage
1967
Roster.
CDC 6400 and XDS Sigma 7.
Simulation (continuous).
Statement-oriented language to simulate dynamics of
continuous systems describable by ordinary differ-
ential equations. Many varying versions with dif-
ferent names are implemented.

DYNAMO III

1959 (?)
Roster.
Most large and medium sized computers.
Simulation (continuous).
Used to construct large models of economic and social
systems.

ECAP II
*E*lectronic *C*ircuit *A*nalysis *P*rogram *II*
1966
Roster.
Several computers.
Circuit design.
Simple language for analyzing electrical networks.

Flow-Matic

1958
PL.
UNIVAC I, II.
Business data processing.
Was first English-like language for business data pro-
cessing and was a major input to design of Cobol.

Formac
*FOR*mula *MA*nipulation *C*ompiler
1964
Roster, PL.
IBM System/360, 370.
Formula manipulation.
First language to be widely used for formal algebraic
manipulation.

Fortran
*FOR*mula *TRAN*slation
1956
Roster, HOPL, PL, ANSI X3.9-1978.
Almost all computers.
Numerical scientific.
First language to be widely used and remains in wide
use.

GPSS
General Purpose Systems Simulator
1961
Roster, HOPL, PL.
Several computers.
Simulation (discrete).
Based on block-diagram approach, with statements used for computer input.

ICES
Integrated Civil Engineering System
1967 (?)
Roster.
Several computers.
Civil engineering.
General system for engineering which has internal languages for subsystem development and includes languages such as COGO and STRUDL.

IPL-V
Information Processing Language V
1957
PL.
Many second-generation computers.
List processing.
Was used heavily in the 1960s for list processing applications. Had close notational resemblance to an assembly language.

ISPL
Instruction Set Processor Language
1971
Roster.
DEC PDP-10.
Computer hardware design.
Used to describe general register transfer systems and digital computer architecture.

IT
Internal Translator
1957
PL.
IBM 650.
Numerical scientific.
First language implemented on small computer; inspired much compiler research.

Joss
JOHNNIAC Open Shop System
1964
Roster, HOPL, PL.
Many computers in different versions.
Numerical scientific.
First language designed for on-line use. Is very simple. Had many dialects under differing names.

Jovial
Jules Own Version of International Algebraic Language
1960
Roster, HOPL, PL.
Many computers in many versions.
Multipurpose.
Based on Algol 58 (originally called International Algebraic Language) and had many versions. Newest version is Jovial J73. Many early Jovial compilers were written in some version of Jovial.

Lisp
LISt Processing
1960
Roster, HOPL, PL.
Many computers.
List processing.
Sophisticated and theoretically oriented with several dialects. Used for much artificial intelligence research.

Macsyma
Project *MAC's SYmbol MAnipulation*
1972
Roster.
DEC PDP-10 and HIS 6180.
Formula manipulation.
Very powerful language for doing formal algebraic manipulation.

Mad
Michigan Algorithm Decoder
1960
Roster, PL.
Several computers.
Systems programming.
Original version was based on Algol 58 and designed for numerical computation. Later version was extended significantly.

MPSX
Mathematical Programming System EXtended
1966
Roster.
IBM System/360, 370.
Mathematical programming.
Controls solution strategy for mathematical programming problems. Other similar languages run on different computers.

Mumps
Massachusetts General Hospital Utility Multi-Programming System

1969
Roster, ANSI X11.1-1977.
Several computers.
Multipurpose.
Fairly general language with emphasis on string handling and complex file handling. Used heavily in medical areas, but also in commercial applications.

Neliac
Navy Electronics Laboratory International Algol Compiler
1960
PL.
Many second-generation computers.
Numerical scientific.
Was based on Algol 58 and was used to write its own compilers.

OMNITAB II

1966
Roster.
Most large computers.
Statistics.
Primarily for non-programmers, using desk-calculator-type operations but also containing powerful mathematical facilities (e.g., regression, matrix inversion).

Pascal

1971
Roster. ANSI standard under development.
Most computers.
Multipurpose.
Small but elegant language with many significant features. Used heavily for teaching programming. Many Pascal compilers are written in Pascal.

PDS/MaGen
Problem Descriptor System
1973 (?)
Roster.
Many computers.
Mathematical programming.
Facilitates generation of matrices and reports for mathematical programming systems.

PILOT

1969 (?)
Roster.
Many computers.
Computer-assisted instruction.

Simple language which has been written in Basic, APL\ 360, Algol, Fortran, and PL/I.

PL/I
(Not an acronym, although often erroneously thought to stand for *Programming Language I*.)
1964
Roster, HOPL, PL, ANSI X3.53-1976.
Several computers.
Multipurpose.
First of the very large, powerful languages, combining many features and concepts from Algol, Cobol, Fortran, and other languages.

PL/M

1974 (?)
Roster.
Intel 8080, Motorola M6800.
Systems programming.
Specifically for use with microprocessors. Varying versions exist for different computers.

Reduce

1967
Roster.
Many computers.
Formula manipulation.
Algol-like language written in itself and using Lisp as an intermediate language.

SCEPTRE

1960s (?)
Roster.
Several computers.
Circuit design.
Used for designing and analyzing circuits.

SIMSCRIPT II.5®

1963 (?)
Roster.
Many computers.
Simulation (discrete).
Advanced language for large discrete simulation problems. Several previous numbered versions exist.
(® Trademark and Service Mark of C.A.C.I., Inc.)

Simula 67
SIMUlation Language, 1967
1967
Roster, HOPL, PL.

Many computers.
Multipurpose.
An extension of Algol 60 and quite distinct from its predecessor (Simula I), which was primarily a simulation language. Introduced the important concept of classes.

Snobol4
StriNg-Oriented SymBOlic Language
1963
Roster, HOPL.
Most large computers.
String processing.
Emphasizes string processing and pattern matching.

Speakeasy

1968
Roster.
Several computers.
Numerical scientific.
Easily learned but powerful array processing language with built-in matrix algebra and powerful library-oriented system.

SPSS
Statistical Programs for the Social Sciences

1975 (?)
Roster.
Most computers.
Statistics.
Is really a language (albeit simple) and is implemented in batch and interactive versions.

TRAC®

1965
Roster, PL.
DEC PDP-10, TI 990.
String processing.
Interactive string manipulation language involving nested functions and macro facilities. (®Trademark and Service Mark of Rockford Research, Inc.)

TUTOR

1971 (?)
Roster.
CDC 6500, Cyber series.
Computer-assisted instruction.
Runs under PLATO.

Appendix VI

GLOSSARY OF MAJOR TERMS IN FIVE LANGUAGES

English	French	German	Spanish	Russian
Access Time	Temps d'Accès	Zugriffszeit	Tiempo de Acceso	Время Выборки, Время Обращения
Accumulator	Accumulateur	Akkumulator	Acumulador	Накопитель
Adder	Additionneur, Addeur	Addierer, Addierwerk	Sumador	Сумматор
Address	Adresse	Adresse	Dirección	Адрес
Algorithm	Algorithme	Algorithmus	Algoritmo	Алгоритм
Alphanumeric	Alphanumérique	Alphanumerisch	Alfanumérico	Алфавитно-Цифровой
Analog Computer	Calculateur Analogique	Analogrechner	Computador Analógico	Аналоговая Вычислительная Машина, Аналоговый Компьютер
Architecture (computer)	Architecture (de système informatique)	Architektur (Rechnerarchitektur)	Arquitectura (De Computadores)	Структура
Argument	Argument	Argument, Parameter, Aktualparameter	Argumento	Переменная, Аргумент
Artificial Intelligence	Intelligence Artificielle	Künstliche Intelligenz	Inteligencia Artificial	Искусственный Разум, Искусственный Интеллект
Assembler	Assembleur	Assemblierer, Assembler	Ensamblador	Ассемблер
Associative Memory	Mémoire Associative	Assoziativspeicher	Memoria Asociativa	Ассоциативная Память
Automation	Automatisation	Automation, Automatisierung	Automatización	Автоматизация
Automaton	Automate	Automat		Автомат
Bandwidth	Largeur de Bande	Bandbreite	Ancho de Banda	Диапазон Частот
Base Register	Registre de Base	Basisregister, Basisaddressregister	Registro Base	Регистр Базы, Базовый Регистр
Benchmark	Banc d'Essai	Benchmark	Banco de Pruebas	Эталон, Начало Отсчета
Binary	Binaire	Binär	Binario	Двойчный
Bit	Bit	Bit	Bit, Dígito Binario	Бит
Block	Bloc	Block, physischer Satz	Bloque	Блок
Branch Instruction	Branchement	Verzweigungsbefehl, Sprungbefehl	Instrucción de Bifurcación	Команда Перехода (Передачи Управления)
Buffer	(Mémoire) Tampon	Puffer, Zwischenspeicher	Memoria Intermedia	Буфер
Bug	Erreur, Défaut, Panne	Fehler, Programmfehler	Error	Ошибка
Bus	Bus	Sammelschiene, Bus, Hauptweg, Hauptverbindungsweg, Übertragungsleitung	Barra, Enlace Común	Шина
Byte	8 Bit Byte = Octet 6 Bit Byte = Sextet	Byte	Octeto	Байт
Cache Memory	Mémoire à Cache	Pufferspeicher, schneller Pufferspeicher	Memoria de Cache	Память
Calling Sequence	Séquence d'Appel	Aufruffolge (eines Unterprogrammes)	Sequencia de Llamada	Вызывающая Последовательность
Card	Carte	Karte, Lochkarte	Tarjeta, Ficha	Карта
Central Processing Unit	Unité Centrale	Zentrale Recheneinheit, Prozessor	Unidad Central de Proceso	Центральный Процессор
Channel	Canal	Kanal	Canal	Канал
Character	Caractère	Zeichen, Schriftzeichen	Carácter	Символ
Compiler	Compilateur	Kompilierer, Compiler, Übersetzer	Compilador	Компилятор
Complement	Complément	Komplement	Complemento	Дополнение
Computability	Calculabilité	Berechenbarkeit	Computabilidad	Вычислимость
Computation	Calcul-Traitement	Berechnung	Computación, Cálculo	Вычисление
Computer	Ordinateur	Rechenanlage, Rechner, Rechenmaschine, Datenverarbeitungsanlage, Computer	Computador	Вычислительная Машина, Компьютер
Computer Science	Informatique	Informatik	Informática, Ciencia de la Computación	Вычислительная Математика и Вычислительная Техника
Concatenation	Concaténation	Verkettung	Concatenación	Сцепление
Constant	Constante	Konstante	Constante	Постоянная, Константа
Control Unit	Unité de Contrôle	Steuereinheit, Steuerwerk, Leitwerk, Kommandowerk	Unidad de Control	Блок (Устройство Управления)
Core Memory	Mémoire à Tores	Kernspeicher	Memoria de Núcleos	Оперативная Память
Cybernetics	Cybernétique	Kybernetik	Cibernética	Кибернетика
Cycle Time	Temps de Base	Zykluszeit	Tiempo de Ciclo	Время Цикла, Время Выборки
Data	Donnée	Daten	Datos	Данные
Data Bank	Banque de Données	Datenbank	Banco de Datos	Банк Данных
Data Communications	Transmission de Données	Datenübermittlung	Comunicación de Datos	Передача Данных

English	French	German	Spanish	Russian
Data Processing	Traitement de l'Information, Informatique	Datenverarbeitung	Proceso de Datos	Обработка Данных
Data Structure	Structure de Données	Datenstruktur	Estructura de Datos	Структура Данных
Database	Base de Données	Datenbasis, Datenbank	Banco de Datos	База Данных
Deadlock	Bloquage	Verklemmung, Systemverklemmung, Deadlock	Punto Muerto, Bloqueo	Стоп, Полная Остановка, Тупиковая Ситуация
Debugging	Mise au Point (d'un programme) Dépannage (d'une machine)	Fehlerbeseitigung, Fehlerkorrektur, Programmdebugging	Depuración, Corrección	Отладка
Delimiter	Borne	Begrenzer, Begrenzungssymbol, Trennzeichen	Delimitar	Ограничитель
Diagnostic	Diagnostique	Diagnoseprogramm	Diagnóstico	Диагностический
Disk Memory	Mémoire à Disque	Plattenspeicher	Memoria de Disco	Дисковая Память
Drum Memory	Mémoire à Tambour	Magnettrommel, Trommelspeicher	Memoria de Tambor	Память на Барабане
Dump	"Dump"–Cliché	Speicherabzug, Speicherauszug	Vaciado de Memoria	Копировать Память на Внешнее Запоминающее Устройство
Exponent	Exposant	Exponent	Exponente	Показатель Степени
Expression	Expression	Ausdruck	Expresión	Выражение
Extensible Language	Langage Extensible	Erweiterbare Sprache	Lenguage Extensible	Свободная Грамматика
Field	Champ (for an instruction field) Domaine (for a field of interest)	Feld	Campo	Поле
File	Fichier	Datei	Archivo	Файл, Массив
Fixed Point	Virgule Fixe	Festpunkt(zahl)	Punto Fijo	Фиксированная Запятая
Flag	Drapeau	Kennzeichen, Marke	Señalador, Indicador	Флаг, Признак
Flip-flop	Flipflop	Flipflop, bistabiles Kippglied	Circuito Biestable, Circuito Basculante	Триггер
Floating Point	Virgule Flottante	Gleitpunkt(zahl)	Punto Flotante	Плавающая Запятая
Flowchart	Organigramme, Ordinogramme	Flussdiagram, Datenflussplan, Programmablaufplan	Carta De Flujo	Блок–Схема
Function	Fonction	Funktion	Función	Функция
Gate	Porte	Gatter, Verknupfungsglied	Puerta	Электронный Переключатель, Логический Элемент
Global Variable	Variable Globale	Globale Variable	Variable Global	Глобальная Переменная
Grammar	Grammaire	Grammatik	Gramática	Грамматика
Graphics	Diagramme, Dessin, Graphique	Graphische Datenverarbeitung	Gráfico	Графики
Hardware	Matériel	Hardware, Maschinenausrüstung, Apparatur	Equipo Físico, Componentes Físicos	Аппаратура
Hashing	Hashing, Hash Code	Hashing (Hash total: Kontrollsumme)		Контрольное Суммирование, Поиск
Heuristic	Heuristique	Heuristisch, Heuristisches Verfahren, Heuristik	Método Heurístico	Эвристический
Hexadecimal	Hexadécimal	Sedezimal, Hexadezimal (coll)	Hexadecimal	Шестнаддатиричный
Hybrid Computer	Calculateur Hybride	Hybridrechner	Computadora Híbrida	Гибридный Компьютер
Identifier	Identification	Identifikator, Identifizierer, Bezeichner, Name	Identificador	Идентификатор
Index Register	Registre d'Index	Indexregister	Registro de Indice	Индексный Регистр
Indirect Address	Adresse Indirecte	Indirekte Adresse	Dirección Indirecta	Косвенный Адрес
Information Processing	Informatique, Traitement de l'Information	Datenverarbeitung, Informationsverarbeitung	Procesamiento de la Información	Обработка Информации
Information Science	Informatique	Informationswissenschaft	Ciencia de la Información	Теория Информации
Input	Entrée	Eingabe, Eingang, eingeben (v), einlesen (v)	Entrada	Ввод, Входные Данные
Instruction	Instruction	Befehl, Instruktion	Instrucción	Команда
Integrated Circuit	Circuit Intégré	Integrierter Schaltkreis, Integrierte Schaltung	Circuito Integrado	Интегральная Схема
Interpreter	Traducteur, Intrepréteur	Interpretierer, Interpretierprogramm, Interpreter	Interpretadora	Интерпретирующая Программа
Interrupt	Interruption	Unterbrechung	Interrupción	Прерывать
Iteration	Itération	Iteration	Iteración	Итерация
Job	Tâche, Travail	Job, Auftrag	Trabajo	Задание
Key	Clé	Schlüssel, Kennbegriff, Taste	Llave	Ключ, Клавиша
Keyboard	Clavier	Tastatur	Teclado	Клавиатура
Label	Etiquette	Marke, Label, Etikett, Kennsatz	Etiqueta	Метка

English	French	German	Spanish	Russian
Language Processor	Compilateur	Sprachprozessor, Sprach-übersetzer, Übersetzer	Procesador de Lenguage, Compilador	Транслятор Языка
Latency	Latence	Wartezeit, Latenzzeit	Latencia	Время Задержки (Часть Времени Выборки)
List Processing	Traitement de Liste	Listenverarbeitung	Procesamiento de Listas	Обработка Списков
Loader	Chargeur	Lader, Ladeprogramm, Programmlader	Cargador	Загрузчик
Loop	Boucle	Schleife	Ciclo Iterativo	Цикл
Machine Language	Langage Machine	Maschinensprache	Lenguage de Máquina	Машинный Язык
Macroinstruction	Macroinstruction	Makroinstruktion, Makro-befehl, Makro (coll)	Macroinstrucción	Макрокоманда
Magnetic Core	Tore Magnétique	Magnetkern	Toroide Magnético, Núcleo Magnético	Магнитная Память
Magnetic Tape	Bande Magnétique	Magnetband	Cinta Magnética	Магнитная Лента
Mantissa	Mantisse	Mantisse	Mantisa	Мантисса
Memory	Mémoire	Speicher, Gedächtnis	Memoria	Память
Memory Protection	Protection de Mémoire	Speicherschutz, Speicher-Schreibsperre	Protección de Memoria	Защита Памяти
Microprocessor	Microprocesseur	Mikroprozessor	Microprocesador	Микропроцессор
Microprogramming	Microprogrammation	Mikroprogrammierung	Microprogrammación	Микропрограммирование
Microcomputer	Micro-Ordinateur	Mikrocomputer, Mikro (coll)	Microcomputador	Микрокомпьютер
Microsecond	Microseconde	Mikrosekunde	Microsegundo	Микросекунда
Millisecond	Milliseconde	Millisekunde	Milisegundo	Миллисекунда
Minicomputer	Mini-Ordinateur	Kleinrechner, Mini-computer, Mini (coll)	Minicomputador	Миникомпьютер
Modem	Modem	Modem, Signalumsetzer	Modulador–Demodulador, Modem	Модем (Модулятор-Демодулятор)
Monitor	Moniteur	Monitor, Überwachungs-programm, überwachen (v)	Monitor	Монитор
Multiplexer	Multiplexeur	Multiplexer (Communica-tions multiplexor: Datenübertragungs-Steuereinheit)	Multiplexor	Мультиплексор
Multiprocessor	Multiprocesseur	Mehrprozessorsystem	Procesador Múltiple	Мультипроцессор
Multiprogramming	Multiprogrammation	Mehrprogrammbetrieb, Multiprogrammierung	Multiprogramación	Мультипрограммиро-вание
Nanosecond	Nanoseconde	Nanosekunde	Nanosegundo	Наносекунда
Network	Réseau	Netzwerk, Rechnernetz	Red (De Computadores)	Сеть
Object Program	Programme Objet	Objektprogramm, Maschinencode — Pro-gramm, Zielprogramm	Programa Objeto	Рабочая Программа (Объектна Про-грамма, Программа на Машинном Языке)
Octal	Octal	Oktal	Octal	Восьмеричный
Operand	Opérande	Operand	Operando	Операнд
Operating System	Système d'Exploitation	Betriebssystem	Sistema Operativo	Операционная Система
Output	Sortie	Ausgabe, ausgeben (v)	Salida	Выход, Выходные Данные, Выдача Результатов
Overflow	Dépassement de Capacité	Überlauf	Sobrecarga, Desborda-miento de Carga	Переполнение
Paper Tape	Bande Perforée	Lochstreifen, Papierstreifen	Cinta de Papel	Перфолента
Parallel Processing	Traitement Parallèle	Parallelverarbeitung, Simultanverarbeitung	Procesamiento en Paralelo	Параллельная Обработка
Parameter	Paramètre	Parameter	Parámetro	Параметр
Parity	Parité	Parität, Parigkeit	Paridad	Четность
Parsing	Analyse Grammaticale	Syntaktische Analyse, Par-sing, Zerteilung	Análisis Gramatical	Анализ Команды
Peripheral	Périphérique	Peripher	Equipo Periférico	Периферический
Plotter	Traceur	Kurvenschreiber, Kurven-zeichner, Plotter, Zeichengerät	Graficador	Графопостроитель
Pointer	Pointeur	Zeiger, Hinweisadresse	Puntero	Указатель
Portability	Portabilité	Übertragbarkeit, Portabilitat	Portabilidad	Портативность
Printer	Imprimante	Drucker	Impresora	Печатающее Устройство
Precision	Précision	Genauigkeit, Stellenzahl	Precisión	Точность
Procedure	Procédure	Prozedur	Procedimiento	Процедура
Processor	Processeur	Prozessor, Zentrale Rechen-einheit, verarbeitende Funktionseinheit in Hard-ware oder Software	Procesador	Процессор

English	French	German	Spanish	Russian
Program	Programme	Programm, programmieren (v)	Programa	Программа
Programmer	Programmeur	Programmierer	Programador	Программист
Queue	File d'Attente	Warteschlange	Cola	Очередь
Random Access	Accès Direct	Direktzugriff, direkter Zugriff, Wahlfreier Zugriff	Acceso Directo	Произвольный Доступ, Прямой Доступ
Random Number	Nombre Aléatoire	Zufallszahl	Número Aleatorio	Случайное Число
Record	Enregistrement	Datensatz, Satz, Aufzeichnung	Registro	Запись
Recursion	Récurrence	Rekursion	Recursión	Рекурсия
Register	Registre	Register	Registro	Регистр
Response Time	Temps de Réponse	Antwortzeit (Ansprechzeit, Anlaufzeit)	Tiempo de Respuesta	Время Ответа
Roundoff Error	Erreur d'Arrondi	Rundungsfehler	Error de Redondeo	Ошибка Округления
Run Time	Temps d'Exploitation	Laufzeit, Durchlaufzeit	Tiempo de Ejecución	Время Выполнения
Scanner	Balayage	Abtaster, Abtastvorrichtung, Scanner	Explorador	Сканирующее Устройство
Scheduler	Régulateur, Planificateur	Scheduler	Regulador, Planificador	Планировщик
Semantics	Sémantique	Semantik	Semántica	Семантика
Shifting	Décalage	Verschieben, Schieben, Stellenversetzen, Schiften (coll)	Desplazamiento	Сдвиг
Side Effect	Effet Secondaire, Effet de Bord	Nebenwirkung, Seiteneffekt	Efecto Secundario	Побочный Эффект
Simulation	Simulation	Simulation, Nachbildung	Simulación	Моделирование
Software	Logiciel	Software, Programmausrüstung	Soporte Lógico, Componentes Lógicos	Программное Обеспечение
Software Engineering	Ingéniérie du Logiciel	Software-Engineering, Software-Technologie	Ingenieria de Software	Разработка Программого Обеспечения
Sorting	Tri	Sortieren, Sortierung	Ordenar, Clasificar	Сортировка
Source Program	Programme Source	Quellprogramm, Quellenprogramm, Primärprogramm, Quelle, Sourceprogramm	Programa Fuente	Исходная Программа
Stack	Pile	Keller, Kellerspeicher, Stapelspeicher	Pila	Набор, Пакет, Буфер
Statement	Déclaration	Anweisung	Sentencia, Instrucción	Команда, Утверждение, Оператор
Storage	Mémoire	Speicher, Speicherung	Almacén	Запоминающее Устройство, Память
String	Chaîne	Zeichenreihe, Zeichenfolge, Kette, Folge, String	Cadena, Serie, Tira	Строка
Structured Programming	Programmation Structurée	Strukturierte Programmierung	Programación Estructurada	Структурное Программирование
Subroutine	Sous-Programme	Unterprogramm, Subroutine	Subrutina	Подпрограмма
Subscript	Indice	Index, indizieren (v)	Subíndice	Индекс
Symbol	Symbole	Symbol	Símbolo	Символ
Symbol Manipulation	Manipulation de Symboles	Symbolverarbeitung, Symbolmanipulation	Manipulación de Símbolos	Обработка Символов
Syntax	Syntaxe	Syntax	Sintaxis	Синтаксис
Systems Analysis	Analyse Fonctionnelle	Systemanalyse	Análisis de Sistemas	Системный Анализ
Systems Programming	Programmation Système	Systemprogrammierung	Programacion de Sistemas	Системное Программирование
Task	Tâche	Task, Aufgabe	Tarea	Задание, Задача
Teleprocessing	Télétraitement	Datenfernverarbeitung	Teleprocesamiento	Телеобработка, Дистанционная Обработка
Terminal	Terminal	Datenstation, Endgerät, Benutzerstation, Terminal, Sichtgerät	Terminal	Терминал, Устройство Ввода/Вывода
Time Sharing	Temps Partagé	Teilnehmerbetrieb, Zeitmultiplexverarbeitung, zeitlich verzahne Verarbeitung	Tiempo Compartido	Система с Разделением Времени
Trace	Trace, Historique	Protokoll, Ablaufprotokoll, Ablaufverfolgung, Ausführungsprotokoll, Trace	Rastreo	След
Tree	Arborescence	Baum	Arbol	Дерево
Variable	Variable	Variable	Variable	Переменная
Virtual Memory	Mémoire Virtuelle	Virtueller Speicher	Memoria Virtual	Виртуальная Память
Word	Mot	Wort	Palabra	Слово

| | P.L. Dreyfus | H. Hünke | E.I. Oviedo | V. Ya. Pan |

Index

PREAMBLE

The *Encyclopedia of Computer Science and Engineering* is a comprehensive reference in which a prodigious number of terms are cited somewhere among its more than 500 articles. Value judgments as to which to index, and in what form, face the compilers of any index. Citation of his or her work in running text usually earned a person an index entry; having one's name on a non-specifically cited reference generally did not. Encyclopedia authors were not necessarily indexed since a comprehensive list of such authors is given elsewhere. Selective exceptions were made to all of these rules in order to include scientists of note whose names appear only as end-of-article references, or, in a few cases, Encyclopedia authors who were too modest to mention that they have made contributions to the subject about which they have written.

A unique feature of this index is its attempt to credit the originators of concepts which bear their name but who are not necessarily mentioned as persons in the text. Who, for example, was the Karnaugh of "Karnaugh map," the Bessel of "Bessel function," or the Seidel of "Gauss-Seidel method"? When known to us, the full names of such persons are given in the index. For particularly historic personages, their dates of birth and death are given in brackets, e.g., [1840–1898].

USE OF THE INDEX

Boldface capitalized entries indicate an article on the subject. The first page reference is to that article; secondary references are then listed in numeric order.

Lower case and non-boldface entries have their page citations listed in numeric order. A leading word or phrase that repeats that of the term above it is suppressed in order to facilitate searching. (See sample excerpt in next paragraph.)

ALPHABETIZATION

All entries are alphabetized under initial letters A to Z without regard to capitalization. This implies that entries which normally start with a digit are listed as spelled-out, e.g., "One's complement" rather than "1's complement". Special symbols, including the blank (space) character, *are* significant; the full *collating sequence (q.v.)* is:

(1) (blank) highest, then
(2) period (.), comma (,), slash (/), hyphen (-), apostrophe ('), and parentheses co-equally, then
(3) letters without regard to upper or lower case.

The precedence of space over comma, in conjunction with indentation, leads to grouping of compound terms into separately alphabetized classes, e.g.:

Code
— generation
— motion
— optimization
Code, access
  , ASCII
  , BCD
  , binary

Each dash (—) preceding a term indicates a repeated word (or hyphenated word), e.g., "—generation" above is read as "Code generation" whereas "— —clerk" under "Data entry" is read as "Data entry clerk".

KEY

A supplementary phrase in normal (rounded) parentheses is an approximate synonym for the indexed term. One or more (or even all) of the references may be to the variant form, e.g.: Rotational delay (latency)

A supplementary phrase in square brackets is given to clarify otherwise ambiguous context, e.g.: Instruction, programmed [education].

Cross references such as "*See* (term)" or "*See also* (other terms)" are to other index entries, but these have been used sparingly since, unless the list of references is long, page citations are repeated to save search time. A small number of entries are marked [n.c.] ("not cited") so as to provide at least a clue as to a missing but important person or concept.

E

N